MACMILLAN
COMPENDIUM

THE 21ST CENTURY

MACMILLAN
COMPENDIUM

THE 21ST CENTURY

SELECTIONS FROM THE TWO-VOLUME

Encyclopedia of the Future

Edited by

George Thomas Kurian

Graham T.T. Molitor

MACMILLAN LIBRARY REFERENCE USA

New York

Interior Design by Kevin Hanek
Cover Design by Judy Kahn

Macmillan Library Reference USA
1633 Broadway, 7th Floor
New York, NY 10019

Manufactured in the United States of America

Printing number
1 2 3 4 5 6 7 8 9 10

Library of Congress Cataloging-in-Publication Data

The 21st century / edited by George Thomas Kurian, Graham T.T.
  Molitor.
        p.   cm. — (Macmillan compendium)
     "Selections from the two-volume Encyclopedia of the future."
     Includes bibliographical references and index.
     ISBN 0-02-864977-X (alk. paper)
     1. Twenty-first century—Forecasts.   2. Social prediction.
  I. Kurian, George Thomas.   II. Molitor, Graham T. T. (Graham Thomas
  Tate)   III. Encyclopedia of the future.   IV. Title: Twenty-first
  century.   V. Series.
  CB161.A114   1999
  303.49—dc21   98-50677
                                                           CIP

This paper meets the requirements of ANSI/NISO Z39.48-1992 (Permanence of Paper).

Contents

Contents

Contents

Preface

Origins

"The future is not a gift; it is an achievement."
Robert Kennedy

The Compendium of the 21st Century distills the thoughts and forecasts of hundreds of the world's leading intellectuals—including Nobel laureates, former heads of government, and distinguished experts in many diverse disciplines. Drawn from the award-winning *Encyclopedia of the Future,* this collection of essays and articles presents a unique perspective on the most critical problems of our times.

The impending millennium provided an added incentive for assembling a convenient reference about the future. Providing prediction and perspective were key goals of this compendium. The dimensions have been articulated by a galaxy of talented writers whose creative thoughts illuminate the changes facing society today and over the next fifty years. Contradictions abound. Some viewpoints are optimistic, others pessimistic. The primary mission of this compendium is to suggest where we seem to be headed and to provide plenty of advance awareness to mend our ways or otherwise capitalize on the moment.

Articles in this compendium provide an often provocative starting point for student term papers, scholarly research, and concerned conversations about the future. Most entries highlight specific issues, problems, and opportunities. Other entries attempt to make some sense of major themes that have dominated the last few decades. A sprinkling of articles deal with forecasting methods. These are designed to familiarize readers with basic techniques and methodologies used in future studies.

Features

To add visual appeal and enhance the usefulness of the volume, the page format was designed to include the following helpful features.

- Call-Out Quotations: These relevant, often provocative quotations are highlighted in order to promote exploration and add visual appeal to the page.

- Cross-References: Appearing at the end of most articles, cross-references will encourage further research.
- Photographs: Chosen to complement the text, the photo program is designed to further engage the reader.
- Chronology of the Future: A provocative chronology of predictions for the next fifty years can be found in the Appendix.

There is also an extensive index at the end of the compendium, which will provide ample opportunities for further exploration.

Acknowledgments

The Compendium of the 21st Century represents dimensions of the future anticipated by a retinue of talented writers whose creative thoughts illuminate the breadth and depth of change altering the landscape of our civilization. As co-editors, we devoted five years to assembling the original two-volume *Encyclopedia of the Future.* Selecting articles for a single-volume version required difficult decisions and compromises. Responding to reader interest, we limited our focus to the most salient and important contemporary topics and events along with their trends and developments. Readers who want to explore the future in depth are encouraged to consult the more comprehensive *Encyclopedia of the Future.*

Jill Lectka deserves special recognition for implementing the concept for this single-volume reference work and for coordinating staff efforts at Macmillan Library Reference. *The Encyclopedia of the Future* represents input from hundreds of people who worked with great dedication, investing their wisdom and scholarship on the project.

This project offered the editors and the contributors alike an exciting challenge and a look at the world of tomorrow. If it does the same for readers, we have succeeded in our task.

George Thomas Kurian
Yorktown Heights, New York

Graham Thomas Tate Molitor
Potomac, Maryland
October 1998

Introduction:
Reflections at the End of an Age

There is no such entity as "the future." This may be an astonishing statement in a concluding introductory essay for an *Encyclopedia of the Future.* Many writers do use the phrase "the future" as if it were a single place in near or distant time, or like a point on the horizon, to be reached by a projectile of words.

"The future" as a phrase by itself (as a philosopher would say) reifies the term, treats it as a "thing," as, somehow, a word with the power to be or to act. But there is no such independent entity. The English language requires us to use such terms as transitive—that is, to establish a following relationship. There can only be "the future *of . . .*" something: the future of the American economy, the future of the American political system, but not the "future of technology," which is too loose. In short, there has to be a boundary condition, of time and place, of a definable entity, to make sense of what we mean.

Can one talk of the "future of society"? Yes, but only if we observe a set of stipulations. A society is not an organism, a biological entity, with a homeostatic regulator (like body temperature in a human being) that seeks to maintain an equilibrium. Nor is society a "system" made up of interlocking variables, so that changes in the magnitudes of the coefficients will affect all the other variables—like an Alexander Calder mobile in motion—and thus move into a different configuration of shapes.

Society is a set of *social arrangements,* of laws and institutions, created by individuals (inherited from a previous time or re-created by agreement), to facilitate and fulfill needs, allocate social and occupational positions, educate the young, guarantee rights, and control impulses. Societies are held together by a normative series of values and authority that is accepted as legitimate by its members—unless they live under coercive and dictatorial rules and thus are not equal as members. The legitimacy of the arrangements implies a sense of justice; authority, the enforcement of such rules, implies legitimate power.

Societies are made up of different realms, each of which operates under different axial principles. The economy—the production and distribution of reciprocal goods and services—is more or less a system because of the interdependence of the economic actors. Change comes from price signals through market transaction. But the polity—the realms of law and authority—is not a system. It is an "order," created by design, a set of rules and norms to regulate the lives of individuals within the polity. In the United States, we live under a constitution, designed by the founding fathers, to establish divided powers, protect liberties, and establish rights under the rules of law. Change occurs by conflict or consensus. The culture—the realm of meanings (religious and philosophical) and of imaginative expressiveness in the arts—is even less of a system. Its meanings are transcendent. The arts are different styles, such as classical, baroque, or modern, established by artists in the exploration of form within a genre, or, as today with postmodernism, amidst the dissolution of all genres.

The point of all this is to emphasize that "societies" are not integrated and do not change by a technological wand, in undivided ways. Nor are there unified periods, radically distinct and cut off from one another by historical time, as is argued, for example, by the Marxian modes of production. If that were the case, how could one explain the persistence of the great historic religions—Buddhism, Hinduism, Confucianism, Shintoism, Judaism, Christianity, Islam—over millennia of time, when economic systems have disappeared and political systems have crumbled. Though these religions have changed in manifold ways, the great cores of belief—the Old Testament in Judaism, the savior figure of Jesus in Christianity, the concepts of karma and nirvana in Buddhism—and their great texts still compel belief today. (It is for this reason that I read with astonishment statements by Alvin Toffler such as this: "We no longer 'feel' life as men did in the past. And this is the ultimate difference, the distinction that separates the truly contemporary man from all others. . . . we have broken irretrievably with the past. We have cut ourselves off from old ways of thinking, of feeling, of adapting. We have set the stage for a completely new society, and are now racing toward it [*Future Shock,*

New York: Random House, 1970, pp. 18, 19]." What, in God's name, does that mean?)

At different times and in different places, one or another of these societal realms has been dominant. Historically, most societies have been organized in empires and monarchies, so the political order has been dominant, subordinating the economy and coexisting with or seeking to vanquish religious authority. In the European Middle Ages and in theocratic Islamic societies today, the religious domain has held sway. In the modern capitalist West, the economic sphere has been primary in the shaping of society.

If societies are not unified, are there some determinate rules of social change? Again, one has to understand the different principles within each realm. Modern Western society saw, for the first time, the relative autonomy of the economic sphere separated from the state. The discovery of "the market," the production of commodities, and the rise of a new class led to the idea of the creation of wealth by private property, rather than the mercantilist state. And modern economics—which itself is only two hundred years old—had formulated the idea of productivity, the notion that, through the use of machines or new organization, one can get a more than proportional return from equal or less effort; and this became codified in the rules of economic change. Thus, if a new invention or innovation is cheaper, or better, or more efficient, then, subject to cost and a better return on investment, it will be used. There is a clear principle of substitution, and change is linear. A second feature of modern economics is that the market—in trade and production—knows no boundaries and oversteps political lines. Thus, in the search for profit, the range of economic activities moves from the regional to the national, to the international, and finally to the fully global (which differs from the international), and becomes a "single" market, for capital and commodities.

Political change—leaving aside the wars between states—has been of two kinds. The most common has been revolution: the overthrow of older privileged classes, freedom from imperial or colonial rule, or, when empires have crumbled, the creation of new states. After World War I, there was the end of the Hohenzollern, Hapsburg, and Romanov empires; after World War II, the end of Western imperialism and the creation of almost one hundred new states; and, in the last decade, the breakup of the communist empire of the Soviet Union and of Yugoslavia. It is a striking historical fact—given the histories of the Roman Empire and subsequent events up to the end of the British and Western European empires—that today, for the first time, there are no major political empires in the world. Whether China will become a new empire in the twenty-first century remains to be seen.

Where one finds stable, democratic societies—and again it is striking how few these are: the United States, the United Kingdom, and the small countries in northwest Europe—political change arises from the inclusion of previously excluded groups (such as women and blacks) into the political order; the checking of corporate economic power, as with the New Deal; the expansion of rights, such as privacy and free sexual choice; the expansion of regulatory power; and, as we have seen increasingly, the reaction to bureaucracy and the centralization of powers in government. One central theme—which was enunciated by Aristotle in his *Politics*—has been the role of inequality in creating political conflict in societies. And the first lines of Tocqueville's *Democracy in America* emphasize the novelty of the search for equality in American life. In the United States, for the past 160 years, we have been sorting out the different kinds of equality, such as the equality of all persons before the law, of civil equality in public accommodations, of voting rights, and equality of opportunity and equality of result.

Changes in culture have many different patterns. In the arts, there is no principle of substitution. Pierre Boulez does not replace J. S. Bach, but widens the esthetic repertoire of mankind. We read *The Iliad* to understand the codes of honor and shame, and the first expression of tragedy in the realization, as in the fates of Patroclus and Hector, of death before its expected time, and even the very idea of death for humans, as against the immortality of the gods. And we read *Antigone* to understand the defiance of Creon by this young woman, in order to provide a decent burial for her brothers, since decent burial, as we had already learned in *The Iliad,* is the mark of respect and of civilized behavior. It was a quest repeated two thousand years later by that extraordinary woman Nadezhda Mandelstam in searching for the body of her husband, the great Russian poet Osip Mandelstam, who had disappeared in the purges, killed by Stalin for the mocking poem he had written about the dictator. Art crosses time and appeals to a common human understanding. Can it be outmoded or rendered obsolete?

In the realm of "meanings," particularly religion, modernity has brought many challenges to established faiths. Most of the Enlightenment thinkers, from Voltaire to Marx, thought that religion would disappear in the twentieth century, for to them religion was superstition, fetishism, and irrational beliefs that would give way to the authority of science and rationalism. Much of this was summed up in the term *secularization,* particularly in the sociology of Max Weber. But the word *secularization,* I believe, is wrong, because it conflates two different processes: changes in *institutions* and changes in *beliefs.* It is quite evident that religion has lost much of its institutional authority, in the sense of providing a commanding set of prohibitions and permissions in many areas of life, particularly private morals. But what we have also witnessed is the multiplication of faiths, the renewal of religions, of new cults and belief systems, as a recurrent feature of life. Beliefs and faith are responses to the existential and nonrational situations—in the facts of death and tragedy and suffering—in the search for meanings beyond the mundane.

These are all multifarious and complicated sets of distinctions, and other social theorists may have different ways of ordering and distinguishing the different facets of social structure and culture. But what cannot be questioned is that any disciplined effort to understand the future configurations of different societies, or of different realms in societies, has to be rooted in history and culture, and the relevant distinctions about the phenomena that are being analyzed. Bombastic phrases, careening about like a Tom-and-Jerry cartoon in overdrive, will not do.

The engine that has driven our world in the past two hundred years has been technology—for what the new technology has given us is the possibility of the mastery and transformation of nature, and only slowly, later, the comprehension as well of the destruction of nature.

The change is marked, by conventional agreement, by the term *industrial revolution.* Yet it is striking to know how belated was the recognition of that change. The phrase, in fact, was first created by Arnold Toynbee, Sr. (the uncle of the famed historian), when in a set of lectures at Oxford, in 1886, he remarked that if we look back a hundred years, we can realize that we have been living through an "industrial revolution." But the unfortunate fact of the single phrase was that it masked two different "revolutions" that had taken place at the time: one in technology, which was the application of controlled energy to machines; the other a "social revolution" in the transformation of work and of the places where people came to live. The failure to distinguish between these two processes has often obscured the different kinds of change in society.

One of the first thinkers to pick up the thread of technology was the writer and renowned historian Henry Adams. For forty-five years, Adams pondered the past, and, as he wrote in his classic *Education* (in the third person), "After ten years of pursuit, he found himself lying in the Gallery of Machines at the Great Exposition in 1900, his historical neck broken by the sudden eruption of forces entirely new."

It was in the great hall of dynamos that this revelation took place. In the energy churning from the dynamo, Adams felt he had a metric to understand the modern world. (In the famous chapter on "The Virgin and the Dynamo," he contrasted the faith of the twelfth century, as exemplified by the cathedrals of Chartres and Mont Saint-Michel, with the power of science in the twentieth century, as exemplified by the dynamo.) In the nineteenth century, Adams wrote, society measured its progress by the output of coal. He suggested that the ratio of increase in the volume of coal power might serve as the "dynamometer of history." Between 1840 and 1900, he pointed out, coal output had doubled every ten years in the form of utilized power, each ton of coal yielding three or four times as much power in 1900 as it had in 1840. The gauge on the dynamometer of history had started out with arithmetical ratios; but new forces emerging around 1900—Adams had in mind the cracking of the world of appearances by X-rays and radium—were creating new "supersensual" forces. What all this showed, he said, was the foundation for a new social physics, for a dynamic law of history, the fundamental secret of social change—the law of acceleration.

Adams, like many writers in the nineteenth century, had been intrigued by the triadic scheme of history proposed by August Comte (who had coined the term sociology) in his *Cours de Positive Philosophie* (1842) involving a theological, a metaphysical, and a positive (or scientific) set of stages of the human mind. Seeking to extend this, Adams had discovered the work of Willard Gibbs, professor of mathematical physics at Yale, who in 1878 had promulgated a "law of phases" which described the transformations of matter (such as water from solid [ice] to liquid [water] to gas [steam]). Adams proposed to apply the "rule of phase to history," by taking Gibbs's mathematical formula of least squares and applying that to Western time.

If one took the year 1600 as a starting point (the work of Galileo was the benchmark), and ended in 1900, this would be the *mechanical* phase, as typified by the views of Isaac Newton and John Dalton. "Supposing the Mechanical Phase to have lasted 300 years from 1600 to 1900, the next or Electric Phase would have a life equal to $\sqrt{300}$, or about seventeen years and a half when—that is, in 1917—it would pass into another Ethereal Phase [i.e., mathematics] which, for half a century, science has been promising, and which would last only $\sqrt{17.5}$ or about four years and bring Thought to the limit of possibilities in the year 1921." Yet, since starting points are difficult to establish, even if one began a hundred years before, "the difference to the last term of the series would be negligible. In that case, the Ethereal Phase would last till about 2025."

Ingenious as this was, Adams's essay only proved that a "social physics" could not be applied to history. Yet the idea of acceleration and exponential growth intrigued scholars, and the most serious effort was made by the Yale historian of science Derek Price, who, in *Science Since Babylon* (1961) and other works, sought to chart the growth of scientific knowledge. Price took the scientific journal and the learned paper as two major indicators of knowledge, and he drew "a law of exponential increase," since the number of new journals and papers had grown exponentially rather than linearly.

Price's work was challenged by other scholars who pointed out that if he had used different starting points, growth rates would have been lower. But the major intellectual problem was the obvious proposition that no increases could continue *ad infinitum*. There had to be some ceiling or boundary conditions. This led to efforts to plot Verhulst or S-shaped sigmoid curves, where the exponential growth of an item (such as population) begins geometrically, until it reaches a "point of inflection," when the rate now reverses itself and tapers off as it reaches the ceiling limit.

The key problem with the use of S-curve analysis is that it works only within some "closed system" based on some fixed resources or physical laws, so that the "ceiling conditions" force the leveling off of the curve. Even efforts to use "piggyback" S-curves for "envelope curve" analysis founder when attempting to find the exact relations between these separate curves. In short, efforts to use such measures for purposes of prediction are very limited.

What is worse is the popular phrase "the pace of change," or, more thumpingly, "the acceleration of the pace of change." The crucial problem is that the terms lack a metric. What is being measured by the words *pace* or *acceleration?* One may run a mile in four minutes: that is a measure. Or with the calculus one can measure how quickly an automobile reaches sixty miles an hour from standstill. But what is being measured simply by the word *change*—change of what?

Even if one talks of technological change, what is being measured? Technological progress may be the better utilization of older organizations of work. It can be the replacement of a man by a machine. It can be a logical analysis in operations research or a mathematical formula such as linear programming. Clearly all these are incommensurate. Even if we were able to take all

these heterogeneous modes and recombine them as homogeneous entities, such as "capital" and "labor" in an economist's production function, the subsequent measures of productivity are rough over-all measures and do not account for the exogenous role of technological innovations. (For a detailed analysis of the problems of measurement and understanding of the idea of the pace of change, see my long chapter "The Dimensions of Knowledge and Technology," pp. 167–212 in my book *The Coming of Post-Industrial Society* [New York: Basic Books, 1973], or the paperback edition with a new introduction [New York: Basic Books, 1976]. The analysis of the work of Derek Price and the examination of S-curves are on pp. 177–187.)

If one generalizes, rashly, to talk of the "pace of societal change," then these have to include political changes, such as the inclusion of minorities into the society; the sociological changes in manners and morals; the cultural changes in the breakup of ordered narrative in fiction or the introduction of abstraction in painting. Clearly there is no simple conceptual way to group all these together and find a common mensuration.

The "pace of change" remains, however, as the leading metaphor to impress people about the radical changes in their lives. But much of this is based on a simple-minded and misleading conception of history, of a once unchanging, traditional society fixed in its ways, as against a modern, fast-paced, changing society. But what periods of history and what peoples have ever lived in that presumably unchanging pattern? What peoples have escaped wars, plagues, famines, exhaustion of soils, migrations, conquests by marauding forces, enslavement, colonial conquest—the sweep of Alexander's armies across Egypt through Persia to India; or the extension of Rome from the Mediterranean to Britain; the Huns and the Mongols and the Turks swooping out of central Asia to Europe; the armies of Napoleon expanding to Egypt and to Moscow; and the imperialism of the European powers who, before World War II, ruled 80 percent of the land mass of the world and 80 percent of the world's peoples?

And if one assesses the changes in Western society since the "industrial revolution," consider this: A person born in 1800 and living to 1860 would have seen the introduction of deep coal-mining (because of steam pumps that allowed mines to be sunk hundreds of feet deep, and hundreds of thousands of men to become coal-miners); of factories with looms close by in the spacing of machines, to conserve the energy of steam, so that hundreds of workers were bunched together in such factories; or railroads, which for the first time allowed individuals to move faster than any animal, and extended the range of travel; of steamships that could bring millions of immigrants across the ocean within a sailing period of a few weeks each.

A person born in 1860 and living to 1920 would have seen electricity, which changes the character of night and day; which allows elevators to go up to fifty or more stories, in new skyscrapers; of oil and petrochemicals which for the first time create materials not found in nature, such as plastics, and which use oil for diesel motors; or the telephone, which allows people to talk to each other readily from a distance (and increases the productivity of doctors, since an individual in a rural area does not have to hitch up a horse and wagon to come to town to summon a doctor, bring him to the farm, and then drive him back, when a telephone call can now make that summons).

Or take an individual born in 1920 and living to 1980, who would have seen automobiles and trucks, propeller planes and jet planes, television and satellite communication, atomic bombs and nuclear energy, laser-guided weapons and intercontinental ballistic missiles.

Were the "future shocks" experienced by individuals living through those six decades any less an upheaval than what may be happening in this generation?

Technology and knowledge have become crucial for the modern world, but we need to be clear what this means. Many people use the term *technology* in relation to machines. But in the past twenty-five years, there has been a crucial change in the character of technology—from a *mechanical* to an *intellectual* technology. Although mechanical technology and machines remain, of course, the newer technologies (i.e., computers and telecommunications, as well as semiautomated production systems) are "driven" by software, programming, computer languages, etc., that are dependent on work in linguistics and mathematics.

The second change is the role of theoretical knowledge, and the codification of theoretical knowledge in the development of innovation. If one looks at the major industries we still have—steel, electricity, telephone, automobile, aviation—they are all nineteenth-century industries (though steel began in the eighteenth century with Darby and the coking process, and aviation in the early twentieth century with the Wright brothers) and their products were created by "talented tinkerers" who worked independently of any comprehensive knowledge of the laws of science. Bessemer, who created the open-hearth furnace for steelmaking, knew little of the work of Sorby on metallurgical properties (Bessemer did his work hoping to win a prize offered by Louis

Napoleon for a new cannon). Thomas Edison, one of the great geniuses as an inventor, having invented, among other things, the electric-light filament, the phonograph, and the motion picture, was indifferent to the work of Maxwell and Faraday on electromagnetism. And Marconi, who invented the wireless, knew little of the work of Hertz on radio waves.

All this changes in the twentieth century, in the transformation of physics following the work of Max Planck and quantum theory. In optics, for example, almost all work leads back to a paper by Albert Einstein, in 1904, on the photoelectric effect (for which he won his only Nobel Prize in 1919). Einstein showed that light was not only a wave, but also a pulse or quanta. Everything from the beams that control elevator doors, to the light meters in cameras, and, in particular, the laser (an acronym for Light Amplification Stimulated by the Emission of Radiation), invented by Charles Townes at Columbia in 1939, derives from theoretical knowledge. All the developments of computers, in particular semiconductors, leading to the transistor and the microprocessor, go back to the early work in solid-state physics and the electron-orbit models of Niels Bohr and Felix Bloch. The revolutionary changes in materials technology, in the "transmutation" of materials, derive from quantum mechanics.

Without an awareness of this change, there is no understanding of the sources of innovation and of the importance of basic science in the modern world. All this makes incomprehensible a statement by Alvin Toffler: "We are creating and using up ideas and images at a faster and faster pace. Knowledge like people, places, things and organizational forms is becoming disposable" (*Future Shock,* p. 145).

There is a further, sociological misunderstanding of the role of technology. This goes back to the phrase "culture lag," created by the sociologist William Fielding Ogburn and used unthinkingly ever since. Ogburn argued that technology had become a leading force for change, but that social institutions and culture had failed to adapt to this, and therefore there was a "culture lag." Ogburn was a "technological determinist," a product of an era in which it was assumed that technology was beneficial and represented progress. But there is the question: Why should we accept or adopt all technological change? Technology (at best) is *instrumental* and not an end in itself. Culture is the realm of values. And for any society it has to be our values that determine whether we accept or reject a technology. The fact that it may now be possible to have an "electronic democracy" does not make it desirable. In fact, the founding fathers of the American constitution would have been horrified at that possibility. This would be a kind of "democracy of the emotions" such as Aristotle had feared. That is why the founders constructed a political order of divided powers, of checks and balances, and of a representative, rather than direct, democracy. One may, or may not, want a more participatory democracy, but it is a decision that must be derived from political theory, not push-button technology.

One of the difficulties with "futurism" as a field, as we can see in its twenty-five-year development, is that it lends itself too easily to "hype"—large claims of innovations that will change society in the twist of a gadget or the doomsday arrival of the apocalypse. Both excite the public. Yet all this discredits the enterprise.

Thirty or so years ago, the technology and popular-science magazines were buzzing about a "revolutionary" new development that would give each person the power that had hitherto been available only in large machines. This was "fractional horsepower," or small motors of one-half or one-fourth horsepower. Revolutionary? With fractional horsepower we now have electric toothbrushes and electric carving knives, as well as power saws and power tools. A convenience for some. And how quickly this has been absorbed into everyday life with nary a thought in anyone's head that it is a development that has transformed their lives.

In 1964, there was great apprehension about automation and the loss of jobs by technological displacement. An "Ad Hoc Committee on the Triple Revolution," headed by the futurist Robert Theobald and the economist Robert Heilbroner, declared that productivity was rising so rapidly that in the near future there would be a cornucopia of goods, so that the link between work and income should be severed and goods distributed freely. President Lyndon B. Johnson set up a National Commission on Technology, Automation, and Economic Progress to assess the issue. After a year of inquiry and fifteen detailed research inquiries, the Commission concluded:

> Our study of the evidence has impressed us with the inadequacy of the basis for any sweeping pronouncements about the speed of scientific and technological progress. . . . Our broad conclusion is that the pace of technological change has increased in recent decades and may increase in the future, but a sharp break in the continuity of technological progress has not occurred, nor is it likely to occur in the next decade.

In fact, much of the increase in productivity at the time occurred in agriculture, which then leveled off, while productivity in the last fifteen years in the United States has been low, about 2 percent a year, or under the historic averages of 3 percent a year. The turn in productivity, particularly in services, has given rise to renewed fears of automation, and these are equally exaggerated.

Often major expectations, much ballyhooed in their time, fail to live up to the promises. In 1948, Denis Gabor invented the hologram, the photographing of three-dimensional images, which many thought would "revolutionize" our modes of imaging, even including the changing at times of the apparent facades of buildings by holographic imaging. After forty years, holograms remain a curiosity or decorative object.

Fifteen years ago, the Japanese announced the "fifth-generation of computers," which would lead to voice recognition and direct language communication with computers. After ten years of work, the project, wildly heralded at the time, was abandoned.

Often innovations are announced as being "far ahead of their time" for many reasons. Facsimile, which is commonplace today, was available more than twenty-five years ago. Indeed, many newspapers assumed that the daily delivery of their paper would be by facsimile through television sets, because of the high cost of transportation and distribution by truck. In Japan, the *Asahi* newspaper, the largest in the world, experimented with a facsimile-delivery system to Hokkaido, in the far north, because of the lack of a tunnel connecting the two large islands of the Japanese archipelago. One can still see in Tokyo the *Asahi* newspaper facsimile as a curio, but the idea was never realized—in large measure because of the slowness and cost of facsimile then. This plan was overtaken by the different innovation of establishing printing plants in different parts of the country and, through satellite, beaming the pages of the paper to those plants for printing there. In this way, the *Wall Street Journal* has a national edition appearing at the same time around the country, as well as Asian and European editions with many of the standard pages.

Even when innovations are made, there are large barriers to their use. Most telecommunication companies in America ten years ago announced the introduction of ISDN—Integrated Services Digital Networks—which would allow for the interchange of voice, text, and image on a common channel. But each company had its own system, and it took ten years to reach a common standard for the compatibility and interconnectedness of the different systems.

Twenty years ago, Jay Forrester and others were announcing the paperless economy and the onset of electronic banking to the home. Twenty years later, major banks are again proposing the onset of electronic banking. And in fanciful fashion, the seer Marshall McLuhan predicted in the 1960s that by the year 2000 the wheel and the highway would become obsolete, giving way to the hovercraft, which would levitate on air—an instance, perhaps, of the medium creating his own medium.

The simple point of all this is not only that technological innovations are uncertain, but that the crucial onset of changes comes with *diffusion,* which is subject to the hazards of cost, old habits, legal barriers, and the like, all of which stretch enormously the time frame of social change.

The credibility of future studies depends on the validity and adequacy of its modes of analysis and the nature of its conceptual schemes. The startling beginning of modern forecasting came with the *Essay on the Principles of Population,* published anonymously by Thomas R. Malthus in 1798, and greatly expanded and altered, in his name, in 1803. Malthus was originally a church curate, and he wrote his essay as a theological-political tract against the "liberationist" views of William Godwin, the political writer and novelist, who was the father of Mary Wollstonecraft Godwin, who herself later married Percy Bysshe Shelley, who in turn endorsed his father-in-law's views. In his *Enquiry Concerning Political Justice* (1793), Godwin said that happiness would incur if one abolished marriage and the family, which constricted human passions. To answer him, Malthus declared that if all restraints on passion were removed, humanity would suffer, for population increases would soon outrun the resources to feed the burgeoning population. Malthus pointed to the New World as providing the optimum conditions of food production and said that while yields would increase arithmetically, populations would increase geometrically, and thus hunger and famine would follow. Charles Darwin said that on reading Malthus on population, he concluded that natural selection was the inevitable result of the rapid increase of all organic beings, for such rapid increase necessarily leads to the struggle for existence.

The population of the world during the time of Malthus was under one billion persons; today it is perhaps five billion. But the long shadow of Malthus reaches over two centuries. Lester Brown, the head of the Worldwatch Institute, and a leading decrier of unrestrained growth, wrote:

> As we make the transition from the third to the final quarter of this century, the world food economy appears to be undergoing a fundamental transformation. Two developments stand out. One, the comfortable reserve of surplus stocks and excess production capacity which the world has enjoyed over the past generation may now be a passing incident in history. Two, the world is becoming overwhelmingly dependent on North America for its food supplies.

This was an article, "The World Food Prospect," in *Science,* December 12, 1975. In 1995, Brown now argues that China's growing demand for grain imports could trigger price shocks, in turn causing starvation for hundreds of millions around the world (*The Economist,* June 10, 1995). In 1968, Gunnar Myrdal, later a Nobel laureate, declared that India would have trouble feeding more than 500 million people. Today, there are close to one billion Indians, and less starvation than twenty-five years ago.

We should not be Pollyannas and assume that all will always be right in the world. But we should be clear as to the reasons for change. In 1975 there was a handful of countries supplying grain to the world—Canada, the United States, Argentina, and Australia. Within twenty years, most parts of the world had become self-sufficient as to stocks of food (though not necessarily in good nutrition), and in Europe, the Common Market has faced repeated crises over the price supports for its agricultural policies and the need to cut back on food production. India, following "the green revolution," is relatively self-sufficient, though distribution remains a problem. Except for a few areas of the world, such as Bangladesh, and the occasional droughts in parts of Africa, food itself is not a worldwide problem.

In fact, the problems are more often *political,* not agricultural or technological. Burma was always a rice-exporting country, feeding large parts of Southeast Asia. But when it was taken over by a xenophobic military dictatorship, rice production collapsed, and Burma (now known as Myanmar) became a rice importer—though its rice-paddy lands remain. Ethiopia has often suffered from droughts, but a small-shopkeeper network provided buffer stocks of food for less extreme periods of famine. However, the Marxist dictatorship of Mengistu smashed the small-shopkeeper system, and Ethiopia starved. In Africa, the Sudan and Somalia fed themselves until ethnic, secessionist, and landlord conflicts devastated those countries. The situation in the former Soviet Union is markedly instructive. The wheat-growing areas of Russia—forming a triangle from Moscow to Rostov to Lake Baikal—are roughly similar to the North American wheat belt from Saskatchewan through North Dakota, though the weather is often more uncertain in Russia. Yet the productivity of North American agriculture has been four to five times that of Russia because the bureaucratic structures of state and collective farms provided few incentives, and these farms often could not obtain machinery from other government firms, so finally Russia had to enter into the world market twenty years ago to obtain sufficient grain. Geography, no; politics, yes.

In assessing modes of analysis, two further, often egregious and misleading modes should be mentioned. One is trend analysis, or "mega-trends." Trend analysis is relatively straightforward. One takes a time-line set of indicators and simply extrapolates these. The assumption is that what was true in the past will continue in the future. Yet this mode in no way identifies "system breaks" or assesses their consequences. Take one fateful trend in American economic—and social—history. From 1900 to 1942 or so, agricultural productivity in the United States averaged about 1 to 2 percent a year. In the 1940s and for more than two decades thereafter, productivity averaged 6 to 8 percent a year. What had happened was the introduction of chemical fertilizers, which increased yields enormously. As a result, from 1950 to 1970 more than twenty million persons left the farms, creating one of the largest internal migrations in American history. A large proportion of them were sharecroppers, mostly black, who were pushed off the farms as unnecessary. Sharecropping, which involved some of the most miserable social problems in the United States before World War II, was largely eliminated. Huge numbers of blacks trekked out of the South, crowding into Watts in Los Angeles, into Bronzeville in Chicago, into Harlem and Detroit. Unemployment figures soared, not because large numbers were suddenly unemployed, but because previously they had been on a farm, and as part of the household economy they were not counted. What was also true is that the runoff of chemical fertilizers from the farms polluted many of the rivers and lakes of America. In an important way, a "system break" such as the trend-line in agriculture became a "strategic site" to trace out social consequences, but such analyses are rarely done, since "futurists" are usually more eager simply to extrapolate trend-lines.

A second example is the "closed system" model. This includes the computer models initiated by Jay Forrester of M.I.T., expanded by his student Dennis Meadows, and given huge publicity in the "Limits of Growth Studies" popularized by the Club of Rome in the 1970s. Such models took a resource that presumably had finite limits—the growth in population and the growth in demand—and by plotting the interaction of these variables showed a ceiling level where the world would exhaust its resources. The Club of Rome achieved worldwide publicity because the release of its claims coincided with the "oil shock" of 1973 and the long lines at the gas stations. The oil shock, however, was not a resource

problem. It was a political club wielded by a cartel, the OPEC nations, which used its then-monopoly position to sharply raise the price of oil.

Actually, the first resource that the Meadows-Club of Rome studies said would be exhausted was copper. Based on identifiable resources and growing demand, the Club of Rome predicted a ceiling on copper. The price of copper did, indeed, begin to rise. A number of oil companies, such as Arco and Sohio (later bought by British Petroleum), bought the Anaconda and Kennicott copper companies as hedges for their oil business, yet each lost several billion dollars. And for twenty years, copper has virtually been a glut on the market, and the commodity price has been constantly low. What happened? For one, the studies never built "price" into their models. With the rising prices, it became profitable to reopen old mines. In the Massai range above Lake Superior, copper, once unprofitable since it yielded only a few pounds in a ton, was extracted. Panama and Zaire began working old mines. Israel reopened mines that had been dormant since King Solomon's time. When new supply came on the market and prices tumbled, a number of these countries sought support from the United Nations, on the ground that they had invested capital to "save" the developed world.

There was still, however, the long-run question of "final" exhaustion. But here a new "surprise" entered into the equation—one that increasingly recurs in the areas of supply—namely, *technological substitution.* In this case, it was the invention of fiber optics that increasingly outmoded the old copper cables in every telecommunication system in the world, and provided cheaper, broader-banded channels for communication.

In fact, with the spread of the "materials revolution," the world need not run out of almost any natural resource—at a cost. Old natural-resource sites are becoming outmoded. More than that, in looking at metals, one does not ask specifically for steel, or zinc, or copper, but for the *properties* wanted—ductility, tensility, conductivity—and these can be supplied in different combinations and composites. In World War II, there was a rubber cartel, a copper cartel, a zinc cartel organized by countries where these natural resources were located. Today, with the exception of oil, no such cartel is possible. And oil—whose cartel is breaking up for political reasons—was possible because oil was so cheap, as against alternatives such as thermal, or shale, or solar, and possibly as against nuclear energy.

Given these cautions, what can one say about identifying social changes? It is necessary, first, to distinguish between *prediction* and *forecasting,* arbitrary as this distinction may be. Prediction is the specification of "point" events—single items or events that may occur in "the future." Yet this is inherently difficult because of the multiple intersection of different variables (as with weather prediction), even if one could plot these in "real time." The other is the limitation of information, particularly in closed arenas. This is what makes political prediction, especially about key decisions, difficult from "the outside." I call this Brzezinski's Law, in honor of my sometime colleague at Columbia who was also a member of the Commission on the Year 2000.

Zbigniew Brzezinski (before going to the White House as national security adviser to President Jimmy Carter) was once being baited on television by a hostile commentator. He asked: Professor Brzezinski, you are a Kremlinologist? Yes, was the reply, if you like that ugly word. You tell the White House what is going on in the Soviet Union? Yes, when they listen. And the interviewer then sprang his trap: Professor Brzezinski, why did you fail to predict the ouster of Nikita Khrushchev? And Brzezinski, who is quick on his feet, replied: Tell me, if Khrushchev could not predict his own ouster, how could you expect me to do so?

The answer is that such timing, when possible, is the product of "intelligence," of knowing the play of political forces and combinations within the arena of a closed circle. Could one have predicted the collapse and breakup of the Soviet Union? One could and did. There were two factors. One was economic, the increasing failure of centralized planning. The Gosplan could not make the literally millions of price decisions necessary for the allocation of resources for production (military and civilian) from a small central office, even with the (theoretical) use of computers to collect and register all the necessary price information (which the Soviet economist Leonid Kantarovich had proposed in his system of dynamic programming). Thus greater and greater inefficiencies and misuse of resources mounted.

The second was moral and political, the evident loss of legitimacy, the end of ideology, and the belief in the future which had first given hope to the adherents of the new faith system. Much of this was evident in Eastern Europe in the Hungarian, Polish, and Czech revolutions, all led by Communists and all crushed by Soviet military forces.

In short, *the process* was clear, though the exact "tipping point" could not, perhaps, have been "predicted." Equally, one cannot predict what is often the decisive role of leadership in historical situations. When the French Army in Algeria, in 1952, threatened to send paratroopers to Paris to seize the government, the continuation of Guy Mollet's weak government might not

have prevented such an act. Yet the recall to power of General Charles de Gaulle with his decisive authority saved the day. One need not subscribe to a "great man" theory of history to acknowledge that the record is full of turning points, by the acts of individuals that were decisive for the fate of nations.

One can forecast when one has an *algorithm,* a decision rule that allows one, with some confidence, to identify future outcomes. Briefly, the following three are worthy of mention:

1. *Institutional stability.* In 1964, when the Commission on the Year 2000 was initiated at the American Academy of Arts and Sciences, I went to John Gardner, then the head of the Carnegie Corporation, to ask for support. The idea is an intriguing one, he said, but give me a "for instance" of serious forecasting. I recalled a remark of Bertrand de Jouvenel (in whose Futuribles project I had been a consultant for the Ford Foundation) and said: This is 1964, and there will be an election for president of the United States. There will be one in 1968, 1972, 1976 . . . 2000. He looked at me and said: That's a damned obvious prediction. And I replied: Yes, but there are now about 120 nations in the world. Of how many nations can one make such claims with confidence?

The degree of institutional stability in the United States and a handful of other democratic nations in the world—where changes of parties in office can take place peacefully through regulated competition, with no resort to force by a loser, and decisions by a Supreme Court to decide contentious issues of interest and morals—is extraordinarily rare in the world. And these conditions of stability, under the rule of law, are a condition for a tolerable life and security.

It is the failure to establish "institutional succession" that often gives rise to crises in regimes when the old leaders die and a struggle for power ensues. This was the case in Yugoslavia after the death of Tito. It was the situation in China after the death of Mao, and it may recur with the death of Deng. In Africa, where the first generation of leaders (e.g., Nkrumah in Ghana) began to weaken, military rule took over. The problem of succession may threaten the stability of countries such as South Africa, Indonesia, and Singapore, with the passing of Mandela, Suharto, and LeeKwan Yew.

2. *Structural changes.* These are changes in the demographic profiles of a society—a bunching of baby-boomers or an increase in longevity, creating a large aging population—all of which create different requirements in an educational system, health expenditures, and the like. And there are sectoral changes, such as

the decline of agriculture or manufacturing, regional changes in the sites of work, and transportation patterns.

It is the awareness of such changes that makes a society flexible and responsive—when there is a political will to make such changes. The transformation of Japan from 1950 to 1990 is a relevant case in point. Japan began its recovery concentrating on textiles and cheap manufactured products based on a low-wage labor force. When Japan became undercut by Hong Kong and other countries, it moved to heavy industry—steel, shipbuilding, and automobiles—then to optics and instruments, and then, because of the oil shock and the rising costs of energy, Japan moved to electronics, computers, and knowledge-based products. There is nothing "automatic" about such progressions, but if a society wishes to make such changes, then a number of "functional requirements" come in their wake. Apart from tribal warfare, for example, Africa today is poorly placed in the world economy for lack of an adequate educational system.

3. *Structural frameworks.* This is an effort to provide a unified and comprehensive social structure based on the *logic* of a set of social principles. I offer, as a case in point, a "picture" of a postindustrial society (see Table 1).

This is *not* a forecast of what will come. It is, rather, as I have stated, "an *as if,* a fiction, a logical construction of what *could be* against which a future social reality can be compared in order to see what intervened to change society in the direction it did take."

There are some methodological stipulations that a disciplined social science inquiry has to observe:

One has to state a *concept,* its *dimensions,* and the *indicators* (statistical, if possible) of those dimensions. Take the concept of the *postindustrial society.* These are its five dimensions:

1. Economic sector: the change from a goods-producing to a service economy.
2. Occupational distribution: the pre-eminence of the professional and technical class.

TABLE 1

FROM INDUSTRIAL TO POSTINDUSTRIAL SOCIETY: GENERAL SCHEMA OF SOCIAL CHANGE

	Preindustrial	Industrial	Postindustrial		
Regions:	Asia Africa Latin America	Western Europe Soviet Union Japan	United States		

Economic sector:	*Primary*
	Extractive:
	  Agriculture
	  Mining
	  Fishing
	  Timber
		Secondary
		Goods producing:
		  Manufacturing
		  Processing
			Tertiary
			Transportation
			Utilities
				Quaternary
				Trade
				Finance
				Insurance
				Real estate
					Quinary
					Health
					Education
					Research
					Government
					Recreation

Occupational slope:	Farmer Miner Fisherman Unskilled worker	Semiskilled worker Engineer	Professional and technical scientists		
Technology:	Raw materials	Energy	Information		
Design:	Game against nature	Game against fabricated nature	Game between persons		
Methodology:	Common sense experience	Empiricism Experimentation	Abstract theory: models, simulation, decision theory, systems analysis		
Time perspective:	Orientation to the past ad hoc responses	Ad hoc adaptiveness Projections	Future orientation Forecasting		
Axial principle:	Traditionalism: Land/resource limitation	Economic growth: State or private control of investment decisions	Centrality of and codification of theoretical knowledge		

From *The Coming of Post-Industrial Society* by Daniel Bell (New York: Basic Books, 1973, p. 117).

3. Axial principle: the centrality of theoretical knowledge as the source of innovation and of policy formulation for the society.
4. Future orientation: the control of technology and technological assessment.
5. Decision-making: the creation of a new "intellectual technology."

The indicators—or the range of effects—would be the changing of numbers of persons in goods production and services, the changes in the numbers of the professional and technical classes, and so on.

There also should be an effort to stipulate an axial principle—in this case, the codification of theoretical knowledge. The change in the character of knowledge is the fulcrum of the change from an industrial to a postindustrial society.

There are two cautions to be noted. The word *society*, again, is somewhat misleading, for I am *not* proposing a *complete* change in the society—considering the disjunctions of realms vis-à-vis the polity and the culture. But one is trapped sometimes by the ubiquitous use of the word, as in *capitalist society* or *bourgeois society*. And this obscures the salient points sketched here, which are the changes in the *techno-economic structure*. These changes do not "determine" other realms of a society, but they do pose management problems, particularly for the political order that has to respond to these changes.

The second point, needless to say, is that this is not the only way one can conceptualize major structural changes in a society. Clearly there could be many others, such as one that makes market transactions, or different emphases of technology, an alternative sketch. Whatever approach is used, it needs to have a disciplined and methodologically self-conscious intellectual structure, if it is to be taken seriously.

Finally, here are three reflections on what an intellectual enterprise dealing with public policy needs to observe:

1. The frequent emphasis of futurism is to look ahead in spectacular and sweeping terms, and to neglect the more difficult, prosaic tasks of seeking to chart the *consequences* of the decisions taken now. I repeat what I wrote on the opening page of *Toward the Year 2000*, almost thirty years ago, because the argument is still relevant:

Time, said St. Augustine, is a three-fold present: the present as we experience it, the past as a present memory, and the future as a present expectation. By that criterion, the world of the year 2000 has already arrived, for in the decisions we make now, in the way we design our environment and thus sketch the lines of

constraints, the future is committed. Just as the grid-iron pattern of city streets in the nineteenth century shaped the linear growth of cities in the twentieth, so the new networks of radial highways, the location of new towns, the reordering of graduate-school curricula, the decision to create or not to create a computer utility as a single system, and the like will frame the tectonics of the twenty-first century. The future is not an overarching leap into the distance; it begins in the present.

2. At the heart of any society is *trust*, the trust of a citizenry in the fairness of the courts, the truth spoken by its leaders, and a belief in the country of which they are part,

Economics, for example, is based on the idea of "stable preferences" in the actions of individuals, so that what may have been true three or four months back will be true three or six months hence. In the econometric models of forecasting, this is called the use of "lagged variables." Yet, as we saw in the rising inflation of the 1970s and '80s, people no longer believed that government policy would bear down steadily on the interest rate, but would relax every four years to obtain votes. So individuals kept on going into debt, believing that the new borrowing would wipe out the debts of the old. It took a more than 20 percent interest rate finally to break the back of inflation. In short, when the "political discount rate," so to speak, is higher than the economic discount rate, policy is in trouble.

And when a government lies to its people (as Nixon did in Watergate and Reagan did in the Iran-Contra affair), it is little wonder that distrust and paranoia spread among a population.

3. Finally, what is crucial to any society is its value system. The virtue of the market is that it coordinates human interdependence in some optimal fashion, in accordance with the expressed preferences of buyers and sellers—within a given distribution of income. Dollars are not like one man, one vote: those who have more can buy more, and can exert a greater influence in shaping the patterns of production and services.

But what ultimately provides direction for the economy is not the signals of the price system, but the value system of the culture in which the economy is embedded. One of the surprises of the past thirty years (though it was anticipated in the Commission on the Year 2000) has been the environmental movement. When swarms of insects were reducing crops, growers rushed quickly to chemical agents such as DDT. Yet as Rachel Carson pointed out in her poignant *Silent Spring* (1962), its effect was also to kill off birds that ingested the chemicals—just as, in later years, large oil spills wiped out sections of marine life. And the value of the environment began to challenge economic efficiency.

The value system of modern Western society has emphasized material growth and the increase of wealth above all other considerations. Yet these have also brought along many social costs. No society can ignore the problem of balance, of leaving the basic decisions either entirely to the market or to bureaucratic rule. These are some of the most difficult problems of political theory. They are value and communal judgments. And technology provides no answers, no matter on what wave it rides.

— DANIEL BELL

A

ABORTION

Historians in the early twenty-first century, looking back at the last quarter of the twentieth century in America, will recognize the abortion issue as one of the period's most divisive, revealing, and costly domestic controversies. They may also be able to see something barely glimpsed in the mid-1990s at the beginning of the end of the abortion wars.

The 1973 U.S. Supreme Court decision in *Roe* v. *Wade* discovered a right to privacy in the Constitution that, in effect, protected a woman's right to request the clinical termination of an unwanted pregnancy. Nearly twenty years later a Supreme Court of a different cast decided that each state could decide its own legal framework, provided that some limited access to abortion remained. Court watchers, noting that President Bill Clinton takes a "permissive" stand at sharp variance with his predecessor (George Bush), believe his Supreme Court appointments may tilt decisions in a "pro-choice" way, favoring readier access to abortion. While the privacy right itself may succumb to challenges, abortion per se is likely to remain court-protected, though increasingly infrequent—this is the major change of the late 1990s.

The antiabortion movement, thoroughly convinced that life begins at conception, and its opponents inhabit irreconcilable moral universes. More use can be expected by the antiabortion movement of research interpretations that view a fetus as a human being, with all attendant rights. As well, the movement is likely to highlight advances in neonatal technology that might enable post-twelve-week fetuses to survive in a hospital incubator. This would alleviate the need for about 12 percent of abortions in the United States, provided that a pregnant woman freely consented to the medical procedures. Overall, however, they probably will have to settle in the 1990s for no more than state-by-state inconveniences, such as parental notification and twenty-four-hour waiting periods. The nation will not permit the recriminalization of abortion.

Throughout the 1990s the culture of advanced industrial nations is likely to place a higher-than-ever value on the well-being of infants. Abortion will be viewed with sympathy when it involves the last resort of a woman unable to provide adequately for a newborn, even though support will probably be forthcoming from both public and private sources to make this choice unnecessary. This is a rare opportunity for collaboration between antiabortion and pro-choice forces that extremists on both sides are likely to thwart.

The Clinton administration is committed to ending the White House-imposed ban on federal funding for abortions requested by women too poor to afford them. To dampen opposition this administration may direct more funds than ever into research directed at improved contraception, including a "pill" for male use.

There are no abortion clinics or participating

hospitals in over 80 percent of America's counties,

largely due to the efforts of abortion opponents

and increasing insurance rates.

Pregnant women were prosecuted in the early 1990s to interrupt and control their use of alcohol and drugs, which harm the fetus. Some were threatened with a court-ordered abortion unless they abstained. Medical insights from prenatal research lent support here, as did the exasperation of the public with childbirths to AIDS carriers, chronic child-abusers, crack addicts, and the like. The Clinton administration, however, is likely to shift emphasis from punishment toward rehabilitation. The Supreme Court, in turn, is likely to ban forced abstention as an unconstitutional violation of an adult woman's personal rights, engendering a more deeply divided public reaction.

Although fewer than 14 percent of 1,400,000 abortions in 1991 were performed on teenagers and only 1 percent on girls under fifteen, the 1990s saw a rapid spread of state laws requiring a teen to tell her parents before obtaining an abortion. Approved in polls by three out of four Americans, these laws, especially when confined to notification rather than consent, were contingent on the ability of a lower court judge to waive the requirement in special cases. A premier example of compromise in the abortion issue, such laws are likely to remain on the books long after their applicability has dwindled or is nil.

Efforts by antiabortion forces to enforce a White House-ordered "gag rule," a ban on the mention of abortion by healthcare professionals in federally funded facilities, were ended early in the Clinton administration. Never popular with the public, opposed by civil libertarians, many physicians, and most ethicists, the "gag rule" will find few mourners aside from its original advocates.

There are no abortion clinics or participating hospitals in over 80 percent of America's counties, largely due to the efforts of abortion opponents and increasing insurance rates. Consequently a small number of illegal abortions are likely to occur throughout the 1990s in the United States. There will be countries, such as Ireland or parts of the Middle East, where contraceptives and all abortions are banned. Although medical advances are likely to reduce the death and/or sterilization toll, illegal abortions will remain a response of desperation.

The waning of the abortion issue can be traced, at least in part, to decidedly pro-choice policies initiated in 1993 by the Clinton administration. Equally significant is the substantial growth expected in the use of

Norplant, the first new contraceptive technology introduced in the United States in over thirty years. A skin implant, Norplant offers up to five years of birth-control protection. Similarly, RU-486, the French abortion pill, once it gets FDA approval, should play a large role in reducing requests for abortion. Finally, the continued threat of AIDS will promote school-based sex education and contraceptive use. These pro-choice policies and improved access could in a decade halve the ratio of abortions to births recorded in 1990 (344:1,000). Should the tide of politics turn conservative again, a flare-up in the abortion issue would probably follow, as new hindrances to birth control invariably have more and more anguished women seeking abortions, the right-to-lifers notwithstanding.

Historians in the twenty-first century who study abortion in post-1973 America will undoubtedly puzzle over the absence of the male from the abortion scene. They will note that the 1973 *Roe* decision required an expectant mother to decide the fate of the fetus. Exactly why the male was treated as irrelevant, was taught noth-

Access to safe and legal abortions is a concern for many people worldwide. In the United States, abortions have become more available, increasing from 18,000 in 1968 to 1,300,000 in 1994, while in India, they are widely available but not always safe. (Janet Wishnetsky/Corbis)

ing about how to provide loving support for his sex partner, and was given no contraceptive advice to help him avoid participating in serial abortions will puzzle twenty-first-century adults. They are likely themselves to see much wisdom in fully involving both women and men in resolving a dilemma posed by their joint behavior. Male involvement in helping pursue pro-choice public policies, and a "techne fix" (Norplant and RU-486), will substantially reduce the need to resort to abortions. Bringing men in from the cold also makes a contribution to tempering the infamous and costly battle of the sexes.

The liberalization of abortion rights is part of the long-term trend of people taking responsibility for themselves and their well-being, and of the growing social and economic equality of women with men.

[See also Family Patterns; Family Planning; Family Values; Sexual Codes of Conduct; Sexual Reproduction.]

BIBLIOGRAPHY

Bonavoglia, Angela. *The Choices We Made: Twenty-Five Women and Men Speak Out about Abortion.* New York: Random House, 1991.

Conduit, Celeste M. *Decoding Abortion Rhetoric: Communicating Social Change.* Chicago: University of Illinois Press, 1990.

Cozic, Charles P., and Stacey L. Tripp, eds. *Abortion: Opposing Viewpoints.* San Diego, CA: Greenhaven Press, 1991.

Faux, Marian. *Crusaders: Voices from the Abortion Front.* New York: Birch Lane Press, 1990.

Rosenblatt, Roger. *Life Itself: Abortion in the American Mind.* New York: Random House, 1992.

Shostak, Arthur B. "Abortion: Ten Cautious Forecasts." *The Futurist* (July–August 1991): 20–24.

Shostak, Arthur B., and McLouth, Gary (with Lynn Seng). *Men and Abortion: Lessons, Losses, and Love.* New York: Praeger, 1984.

Tribe, Lawrence H. *Abortion: The Clash of Absolutes.* New York: W. W. Norton, 1990.

— ARTHUR B. SHOSTAK

ABUSE, CHILD.

See CHILD ABUSE.

ACID RAIN

Acidification of rainfall, and the potential for related damage to forests, inland water bodies, and buildings, originates and mostly occurs in highly industrialized regions. It is caused by air pollution from both stationary and mobile sources. So far, effects are most severe in Europe and the eastern parts of North America, and increasingly in southern China. With increasing industrialization, there is the concomitant potential for problems to emerge in other regions with sensitive soils and surface waters, such as those in northern and eastern parts of Latin America, western equatorial Africa, large parts of the Indian subcontinent, and Southeast Asia. Areas with naturally acidic soils, in prevailing downwind locations from urban and industrial centers, are most at risk.

The acidity of rainfall is measured in pH units, indicating the concentration of hydrogen (H) ions. Rainfall is almost always more acid than pure water with variations from region to region. However, it is generally agreed that a pH less than 5.6 is abnormally acid. Basically, pH 7 is neutral and a reduction of one pH unit represents a tenfold increase in the concentration of H ions.

A variety of pollutants contribute to acidification (Table 1): sulfur dioxide (SO_2) from coal-fired power plants, nitrogen oxides (NO_x) from power plants and automobiles, and volatile organic compounds (VOC) from automobiles and natural sources. In the presence of radiation produced by sunlight, chemical reactions produce sulfuric and nitric acid.

Acid deposition occurs in both wet (acid rain) and dry forms. Acid rain makes up about half of the problem. Dry deposition, either as particulate matter or as undissolved gases, is harder to measure and tends to be deposited closer to the emission source. Because it is deposited directly onto the leaves of plants, dry deposition may be particularly important for heavily vegetated (particularly forested) areas. In addition, there also may be toxicity problems resulting from chemical interactions with soil constituents. For example, the increased solubility of metals at lowered pH levels could create the potential for contamination of drinking water and edible fish.

Evidence of accelerated forest decline during the last thirty years has accumulated in Europe and the United States. The most publicized instance of decline attributed directly or indirectly to manmade pollution occurs in the Harz, Black Forest, and Bavarian Forest in Ger-

TABLE 1

THE CHEMICAL TRANSFORMATION OF AIR POLLUTANTS

Pollutant	Contributing Factors	End Product
NO_x	OH (in air)	HNO_3 (nitric acid)
NO_x + VOC		O_3 (ozone)
VOC	HO_2 (in air)	H_2O_2 (hydrogen peroxide)
SO_2	H_2O_2 and O_3	H_2SO_4 (sulfuric acid)
	OH + O_2 (in air)	
	Oxidants (wet surfaces)	

Source: The National Acid Precipitation Assessment Program. *Interim Assessment, The Causes and Effects of Acidic Deposition, Volume I Executive Summary,* Washington, D.C.: U.S. Government Printing Office, 1987, pp. 1–3.

many. The rapid rate of decline led to public concern about the seriousness of the situation. In the late-1970s silver fir first began to show signs of damage. This was followed by Norway spruce and, in 1982, by hardwoods such as beech and oak. Damage was greatest on west-facing slopes, having the greatest effect on older trees at higher elevations. As many as 50 percent of the trees could be considered in danger. In the case of fir trees, more than 80 percent are affected. However, things may not be as bad as they seem. In recent years, forest surveys have been refined, resulting in more conservative damage estimates. It has also been established that poor forest management is a contributing factor.

In addition to damaging forests, acid rain

is known to reduce crop yields and acidify lakes.

Two major sources of damage were established in Germany: industrial pollution and car exhaust fumes. Car exhaust fumes often damage areas that are not close to industrial sites. Instead, they are concentrated along superhighways. In the United States, forest damage has been more limited. It is concentrated in parts of the Appalachian Mountains and New Hampshire, with smaller affected areas in California.

A large National Acid Precipitation Assessment Program was established by the U.S. Congress in 1980. It took ten years to complete and cost over $500 million. The final report confirms that acid rain harms some lakes and streams, mainly in the northeastern United States. Damage could spread to the southeastern United States.

Damage to forests is complex, because various natural and contributing factors combine to harm trees. It remains difficult to sort out causes and effects. However, it can be said with confidence that acid rain and ozone do contribute to stress on forests. Acid precipitation robs some forest soils of vital nutrients and interferes with the ability of trees to absorb those that are left. This will lead to widespread stunting of some species of trees at high altitudes over the long term. Except for red spruce, there is no convincing evidence that acid precipitation harms trees through direct chemical contact. In the short term, ozone from car exhausts is much more harmful, and has been identified as the cause of damage to southern pine forests and in the San Bernardino Mountains in California. Damage occurs mostly at high altitudes where trees are often bathed in acid mist, clouds, and fogs.

Stunting of growth of trees will result from altered chemistry of mountain forest soil. This damage has two underlying causes: (1) depletion of soil of calcium and magnesium, which are necessary for formation of chlorophyll and wood, and (2) breakdown of soil and release of aluminum. Aluminum, in turn, inhibits the ability of trees to absorb remaining calcium and magnesium. Over a period of up to fifty years this not only may disrupt the physiology of the tree, but in some cases can kill root systems outright.

The true costs of air pollution in general, and acid rain in particular, are hard to determine. In addition to damage to forests, acid rain is known to reduce crop yields and acidify lakes. If the pH of lake water drops below 5, significant death of fish will result, affecting both recreational and commercial fishing. Sulfur dioxide is also a powerful lung irritant and may be the third leading cause of lung disease in the United States. Structural damage to buildings and monuments is well documented, with damage estimates ranging from $15 million to $60 million (Schmandt et al., 1989, p. 112).

Acid rain can be transported across international boundaries, and one country can be bearing the consequences of another's emissions. Scandinavia loudly protested the uncontrolled emissions originating in the United Kingdom and other European countries that were devastating its lakes and forests. Canada became the victim of acid precipitation that originated in the United States. In 1984 Canada, West Germany, and eight other European countries signed a declaration to reduce SO$_2$ emissions by at least 30 percent from 1980 levels within ten years. At that time the United Kingdom and the United States were unwilling to make such a commitment, although the United Kingdom subsequently agreed to the reductions. This left the United States as the only major Western industrialized nation to maintain that there was still insufficient evidence to justify further action, which contributed to deteriorating U.S.-Canadian relations (Regens and Rycroft, 1988, pp. 150–152).

Debate about the need for additional emission controls continued well into the 1980s in the United States. The 1970 Clean Air Act ruled that high levels of air pollution, particularly in urban areas, were unacceptable and needed to be controlled. At the time, sulfur dioxide was known to be a lung irritant and other pollutants, including particulate matter, caused reduced visibility. By concentrating on ambient air quality, the act encouraged the use of tall stacks to dispose of pollution so that local air quality standards could be met. This technique resulted in the dispersion of air pollutants, which travel over long distances and undergo various chemical transformations, including the production of acidic compounds. Thus, reducing local air pollution contributed to long distance acidification.

By 1980 emissions of SO_2 and NO_x in the United States amounted to 25–27 and 21–23 million tons, respectively (Office of Technology Assessment, 1984, p. 149). Stationary sources, particularly electric utilities, were responsible for 80 percent of SO_2 emissions, while mobile sources accounted for almost half of NO_x emissions. Although SO_2 emissions were declining, with the burning of cleaner fuels and emission controls on power plants built after 1978, emissions of NO_x were on the increase (Schmandt et al., 1989, pp. 109–110).

After almost a decade of controversy with Canada, the 1970 Clean Air Act was amended in 1990 to require a 10 million ton reduction in SO_2 emissions and a 2 million ton reduction in NO_x emissions, compared with 1980 levels. Electric utility power plants are the primary focus for SO_2 emission reduction. By January 1, 2000, total emissions of SO_2 by electric utilities will be limited to 8.9 million tons. Old plants will be required to install emission control devices; others will be assigned emission allowances based on actual 1985 emissions. New plants will be required to obtain existing allowances through a system of trading credits administered by the U.S. Environmental Protection Agency.

Debate moved from the specific issue of acid rain to the general issue of transboundary air pollution and efforts to limit greenhouse gas emissions and global warming.

Whether these emission reduction strategies will be effective in reducing the effects of acid rain to acceptable levels is uncertain. In recent years the debate has moved away from the specific issue of acid rain to the more general issue of transboundary air pollution, and international efforts to limit greenhouse gas emissions and global warming. Coal produces the most carbon dioxide per unit of energy. If coal is replaced by other, cleaner burning fuels in an attempt to limit global warming, this will have the added benefit of reducing SO_2 emissions.

[See also Environment; Environmental Behavior; Environmental Ethics; Environmental Indicators; Environmental Policy Changes; Freshwater; Global Environmental Problems; Global Warming; Natural Disasters; Oceans; Ozone Layer Depletion; Sustainability.]

BIBLIOGRAPHY

MacKenzie, J. J., and El-Ashry, M. T. *Ill Winds: Airborne Pollution's Toll on Trees and Crops.* Washington, DC: World Resources Institute, 1988.

Office of Technology Assessment. *Acid Rain and Transported Air Pollutants: Implications for Public Policy.* U.S Congress, OTA-O-204, Washington, DC: Government Printing Office, 1984.

Regens, James L., and Rycroft, Robert W. *The Acid Rain Controversy.* Pittsburgh: University of Pittsburgh Press, 1988.

Schmandt, Jurgen A.; Clarkson, Judith; and Roderick, Hilliard *Acid Rain and Friendly Neighbors: The Policy Dispute between Canada and the United States.* Durham, NC: Duke University Press, 1989.

White, J. C. *Acid Rain: The Relationship Between Sources and Receptors.* New York: Elsevier, 1988.

— JURGEN A. SCHMANDT

ADDITIVES, FOOD.

See FOOD ADDITIVES.

ADULT LEARNING

Most knowledge and skills are learned because adults expect to use them in some practical way. As jobs generally become more complex, they require more learning. As people travel more, try to improve their relationships, take on more do-it-yourself projects, and begin new recreational activities, their learning needs to escalate.

The primary purpose of many adult education institutions is to foster such practical learning. Adults are more willing to pay for practical learning than to pay for satisfying their curiosity, puzzlement, and general learning interests. Practical, useful learning is marketed increasingly by institutions under pressure to be financially self-sufficient or profitable. Liberal arts education and education about world issues, popular well past mid-century, have been deemphasized by many institutions. Some adult educators advocate a renewed sense of social mission, with major or even radical social change as the central purpose, but most of the field shows little sign of heeding this call. Within peace and environmental education for adults, however, and within many grassroots movements, a strong commitment to fundamental social change still is central.

Demand and Populations

Demand for knowledge and skills is very high. Based on statistics for eleven countries, in any given year, 90 percent of adults, for example, engage in at least one major learning effort. They conduct an average of five such projects annually, and spend an average of one hundred hours at each one.

Demand for institutional programs to facilitate this learning is also high. These programs serve at least four target populations: (1) people who need basic skills in reading, communicating, speaking English as a second language, arithmetic, and applying for a job; (2) employed people who need to upgrade their job skills or prepare for new responsibilities as technology and the work world change rapidly; (3) professionals and experts who need to keep up with new knowledge and techniques in their fields; (4) older adults, who are becoming more numerous and more eager to learn. A wide variety of educational enterprises will provide education or training for each of these target groups, sometimes with the cooperation of governments and employers. Adult education is a vast and expanding enterprise, already much larger than elementary or secondary education.

France already requires that businesses employing over 100 workers devote 1.2–3.0 percent of wage costs to training programs. Spending on labor training programs as a percentage of GNP (c. 1991) amounted to 1.79 percent in Sweden, 1.05 percent in Germany, 0.52 percent in Canada, and 0.25 percent in the United States.

Educational Technologies

Computers have assisted instruction for more than twenty years. Using computers to link students and in-

structors is increasingly common in distance education. No matter how far apart they are, computers can send messages to each other instantly; the receiving computer then stores a message until the user requests it at a convenient time. Messages can be sent to one particular person in the class, or to the whole group.

Adult learners are already using teleconferencing, electronic mail, computer bulletin boards, radio and television broadcasts, video cassettes, audio cassettes, laser videodiscs, and CD-ROM reference publications. Access to data and to educational programs, as well as communication among learners, will presumably become faster and easier as technology and media develop further. Voice recognition may even eliminate the need for a keyboard. In addition, artificial intelligence may enable computers to function as sophisticated mentors to the learner, making the instruction much more individualized.

New Roles

Several new roles are likely to develop within adult learning and education during the next few decades. Counseling services may help adults choose their learn-

This black woman graduating as the valedictorian of her class exemplifies the idea that education can be a social leveler. (Annie Griffiths Belt/ Corbis)

ing goals and broad strategy, and improve their individual competence in guiding their own learning. Because worklife now may involve three to five different jobs, each successive career is likely to require specialized training. Information services may provide data about the wide array of available opportunities and resources. Libraries and self-directed learning centers may foster the teaching, learning, and assessment tasks faced during the 70 percent of adult learning that is self-planned. Institutional adult education may provide more help to teachers and workshop leaders who work in the informal sector. Life-planning centers may help men and women cope with a rapidly changing world beset with major problems, and decide how to make their optimum contribution toward a reasonably positive future for humankind.

[See also Higher Education; Human Resources Development; Illiteracy.]

BIBLIOGRAPHY

Brockett, Ralph, ed. *Continuing Education in the Year 2000.* New Directions in Continuing Education, no. 36. San Francisco: Jossey-Bass, 1987.

Ganley, Gladys. *The Exploding Political Power of Personal Media.* Norwood, NJ: Ablex, 1992.

Lewis, Linda H. "New Educational Technologies for the Future." In Sharan Merriam and Phyllis Cunningham, eds., *Handbook of Adult and Continuing Education,* pp. 613–627. San Francisco: Jossey-Bass, 1989.

Rossman, Parker. *The Emerging Worldwide Electronic University.* Westport, CT: Greenwood Press, 1992.

Tough, Allen. "Potential Futures: Implications for Adult Educators." *Lifelong Learning* 11/1 (1987): 10–12.

———. *Crucial Question About the Future.* Lanham, MD: University Press of America, 1991.

– ALLEN TOUGH

ADVERTISING

As the twenty-first century approaches, advertising is undergoing a fundamental realignment in order to accommodate new technologies that "demassify" the media. Advertising agencies realized in the 1990s that they could not grow if they remained focused chiefly on creating campaigns for the mass network television and national magazine audiences. This is because mass media have turned to the new technology to focus more precisely on smaller niche audiences.

Advertisers, imbued for the last few decades with the "global village" ideal, now are moving toward more localized communications. Specific databases open new ways to personalize the ads sent to customers and prospects. The forces behind all this change are altered family relationships and lifestyles, new markets, changing workforce habits and schedules, and a steady flow of new products bursting from high-tech labs. Now available are fiber optics, digitalization, more compact and powerful computers, dazzling software, microwaves, and new broadcast bands to transmit information, entertainment, and advertising messages. Demassification forces television networks to work harder to deliver today's—and tomorrow's—biggest audiences to advertisers. While prime-time TV audiences have declined significantly from their pre-cable 1950–1980 glory years, network TV's viewership numbers remain formidable.

Many ad agencies, by focusing on network TV and mass audience "reach," misjudged the arrival of targeted new media options. One arena in which ad agencies faltered is that of integrated marketing, a database-driven discipline that has advertisers searching for all-encompassing promotional programs inspired by the media. Such programs in theory enable advertisers to choose from among every available promotional venue and media option, whether technologically driven or not. With truly integrated marketing programs, traditional media—print and broadcast—must compete against every other option for a share of the budget.

This is another development forcing agencies to regroup. In creating new tables of organization that bring together people with the technical skills needed to accommodate integrated marketing programs, agencies are in effect setting up "SWAT" teams (multifaceted units). New compensation packages are being designed to reward key members of these media-neutral, flexible units.

Future copywriters and artists will have skills beyond creating TV and radio commercials and writing newspaper and magazine ads. To deal with targeting, their talents will be applied to designing special events; games; data-based coupon, contest, and direct response programs; TV home-shopping programs; "infomercials"; interactive video; virtual-reality formats; "800"- and "900"-like television services; sweepstakes; and premiums.

While advertisers work through this trial-and-error period, the new media elements will show a higher rate of revenue growth than that of traditional broadcast and print media. New media will record revenue gains—much of it local in nature—significantly higher than the 3 to 4 percent associated with older media companies and agencies. Revenue growth will mean tapping into emerging new marketing categories such as computer software and hardware, consumer electronics, entertainment, personal and home security devices, home improvement, new personal-care products, energy-saving devices, grooming and apparel lines, and financial service offerings.

As they move more deeply into developing databases for targeted marketing programs that reach individual customers or prospects, advertisers will grow more interested in experimenting with cable-network channels that cater to special audiences and with "place-based" media that deliver computer-driven programs to offices, schools, colleges, department stores, shopping malls, and other public areas.

Videocassette recorders, rental movies, and video-games contribute to mass media's breakup by making it possible for people to fashion personal viewing schedules. Advertisers can reach them simply by changing the route the sales message takes: telemarketing, catalogues, sponsored information services, commercials on rental tapes, movie theater commercials, sponsored videotapes, and magazines that produce special editions for certain readers and advertisers.

Privately sponsored "information highways" will raise new concerns over issues of privacy, the limits of advertising in terms of free speech, and the dynamics of participatory democracy in a high-tech era.

Ink-jet printing technology leads to personalized editorial sections and ads in magazines, plus split runs based on reader occupation, interests, income, and zip codes. Magazine publishers show increasing interest in creating demographically designed titles and departments to attract readers with common interests—in turn attracting more advertisers. Event marketing—the sponsoring of Olympic teams, sports events, citywide music and arts festivals, special museum exhibitions, and so forth by advertisers—also represents a new challenge for ad agencies.

The hunger of advertisers for new programming that will attract new cable and microwave system subscribers will lead to growing uses of informercials—the sponsored "entertainment" packages that are usually half-hour TV sales messages. Home shopping programs will gain in popularity as they are merged into popular entertainment formats. Such programs also will encourage more manufacturers to develop exclusive product lines for home shoppers.

As privately sponsored "information highways" become a reality, they will attract information suppliers as well as advertisers. Using telephone technology, TV, the full broadcast spectrum, and computers, these "highways" will raise new concerns over such issues as privacy, the limits of advertising in an environment of free speech, the extent to which they exclude people, and the dynamics of participatory democracy in a high-tech era.

Advertisers, capitalizing upon every new gadget and format that enables them to build closer customer relationships, will generate more intrusive advertising and promotional activity. These developments will provide more ammunition for consumer-interest groups, government officials, educators, students, social scientists—the constituency that strives to combat commercialism's inroads into everyday life. The advertising industry will never become immune from attack. While a self-regulatory system monitors the ad claims in national campaigns, this intramural program cannot deter government intervention in marketing. Regulators may agree with the theory that advertising is a form of speech that deserves First Amendment protection, but there are deep differences concerning the degree of protection it deserves. Government will be drawn into the debate as long as there are disagreements over "kidvid," or children-oriented commercials, ads and sales programs, premiums, sales promotion efforts, tobacco advertising, fitness and health claims, advertising by lawyers, doctors, and other professionals, package labeling, advertising content in terms of gender, minority representation, taste, and decency.

The new advertising media add new dimensions to the "free speech" debate. Spawned not as journalistic enterprises grounded in Fourth Estate principles and traditions, the new media often are pure sales-oriented vehicles; they may or may not contain material bordering on borrowed news interest. The program content of such media will largely determine the degree of new friction they cause between advertising and the public.

The question of tobacco companies and their right to advertise a legal product will become less pervasive. Cigarette marketers, their promotional options steadily being narrowed, will continue to focus on ways of addressing smaller niche audiences, and their ads may become more "reminders" than motivational. But as more Americans turn away from cigarettes and tobacco, tax revenues will diminish and government leaders will try to levy new "sin taxes" on other targets: beer, entertainment, distilled liquors, and, yes, even sweets. The advertising community will go on battling against such taxes, even as it argues against proposals to further reduce the tax deductibility levels of advertising costs.

[See also Broadcasting; Communications: Privacy Issues; Media Lab; Telecommunications; Television.]

BIBLIOGRAPHY

Brand, Stewart. *The Media Lab.* New York: Viking, 1987.
Cappo, Joseph. *FutureScope.* Chicago: Longman Financial Services Publishing, 1990.

Mayer, Martin. *Whatever Happened to Madison Avenue?* Boston: Little, Brown, 1991.

Snider, Jim, and Ziporyn, Terra. *Future Shop.* New York: St. Martin's Press, 1992.

– FRED DANZIG

AGENTS OF CHANGE

Twenty years or so ago, futurists would probably have largely agreed when asked about the process of change and how change agents operated. They would have identified a number of people who changed the dynamics of world history. They would have cited experts, scholars, theorists, artists, policy makers and planners, opinion leaders and shapers, popularizers, and the activities of interest groups. They would have broken down these groups into additional categories. For example, they might have classified theorists in terms of visionaries, philosophers, theologians, and utopians, or considered experts in terms of geniuses, leading authorities, researchers, and innovators.

Alternatively, they might have looked at the big names in history. Genghis Khan and Adolf Hitler were change agents. So were Charles Darwin, John Maynard Keynes, William Wilberforce, Harriet Beecher Stowe, Mohandas Gandhi, Martin Luther King, Saint Francis, and Queen Elizabeth I. Change agents are not intrinsically good or bad but belong to this category, because they alter dynamics, not because we either like or despise them.

But who really changes dynamics? Some authorities believe that a few key people drive history, that major figures throughout history have guided the course and direction of events. Others believe that there were particular moments in history when the future was in the balance and that a small event at those critical junctures in time could have altered the world in which we now live.

Still others see the whole process of change as random. Minor incidents clash and combine unpredictably to cause great events. A parallel is drawn with the weather. The latest thinking on this subject is that it never will be possible practically, or even theoretically, to precisely predict the weather more than a few days ahead. This belief is being popularized with an idea derived from a science fiction story—that the flapping of a butterfly's wings on one continent can eventually alter the weather on another.

A new consensus is currently developing about the issue of how change comes about. This approach argues that change today is driven by major forces that are irreversible (or at least highly deterministic), short of massive catastrophe. The technology of production and destruction, ecological constraints, increasing popula-

tion, and movement toward individual freedom are pushing us in new directions. If this view is correct, we shall either adapt, moving from adolescence to adulthood, or we shall perish.

If this new understanding is valid, then today's change agents need to discern the flows of history and work with them. The effective change agent, or leader, "finds the parade" and gets in front of it. Change agents, therefore, help people clarify their real options. They also distinguish between what can and cannot be changed.

The core task of change agents, particularly in today's conditions of rapid change, is to provide people with words, images, and approaches that help grasp the directions needed if they and their children are to survive. This shift in the image of change agents is tied to a major shift in the sciences that started at the beginning of the twentieth century. Scientists such as Werner Heisenburg, Niels Bohr, and Albert Einstein showed Newtonian cause-and-effect thinking as applicable to a small range of cases rather than to all scientific phenomena.

This lesson has been fully understood in the physical sciences only in recent decades. *Chaos* by James Gleick explained this physical science theory as a profoundly new way of understanding the world. We are only just beginning to apply this way of thinking to the social sciences.

There are very practical implications that follow from this new way of looking at the world. First, the idea of strategic planning is losing ground. Nobody knows for certain how to predict events even one year ahead, and there is every reason to believe that the rapids of change will become even more unmanageable. Change agents must be more flexible than ever before.

As the emphasis shifts to a tension between top-down and bottom-up systems, more people see themselves as change agents. They aim to set up systems where opportunities are grasped as they become available and problems are resolved before they become crises. Indeed, many change agents no longer try to bring about change directly but instead work to set up systems in which others can be effective as change agents.

Perceived thus, the job of change agents is to reduce the need for their type of activity in the long run. Of course, they never will be fully successful. However, a commitment to this approach will certainly change lifestyles. Instead of seeing their activities as confined to the elite, they will aim to involve broader segments of the general population. They will be guided by the statement that "at the end of every intellectual journey lies common sense." They will explain what needs to be done in language that can be understood by anybody who cares to make the effort.

Two primary groups of change agents exist today. One group of ideologues tries to change the world so that it conforms to their sense of what is right. We are increasingly discovering that such advocacy is no longer effective. A second group aims to help people cooperate, hoping to ensure very long-term ecological balance accompanied by a higher worldwide quality of life. They also recognize a religious or broadly spiritual commitment as central to their task. The latest vision sees all citizens as players at discovering a viable future. We all have our own roles to play,

[See also Change; Civil Protest; Mind: New Modes of Thinking; Pacesetter Governments; Public Opinion Polls; Record Setting; Social Change: United States.]

BIBLIOGRAPHY

Bateman, Gregory. Steps Toward an Ecology of Mind. New York: Ballantine, 1975.

Greenleaf, Robert K. Servant Leadership. New York: Paulist Press, 1977.

Murray, Charles. In Pursuit of Happiness. New York: Simon & Schuster, 1988.

Theobald, Robert. Turning the Century. Indianapolis: Knowledge Systems, 1993.

— ROBERT THEOBALD

AGING OF THE POPULATION

The aging of the population in the developed industrial countries of North America, Europe, and Japan is a major global trend with implications for future economic, social, and geopolitical developments. Over the next generation, growth of the working age population will slow down significantly in all the advanced industrialized countries relative to growth in other countries.

Growth of the working-age population will slow down significantly in all advanced industrialized countries relative to growth in other countries.

Here, the prospective demographic developments in the United States are examined over the period from 1995 to 2025. These developments and their economic, social, and public finance implications can be assessed with some degree of confidence, though uncertainties are necessarily present. Beyond this time period, the uncertainties are much greater. By the year 2030, the last of the baby boomers will reach age 65; barring unforeseen developments, population trends will then stabilize. This analysis is based on demographic projections that embody the current "middle series" Census Bureau assumptions of birth and survival rates for specific age-race-sex population groups, but assume a higher rate of immigration that would grow in proportion to U.S. population.

The roots of future demographic changes lie deep in the past. The expected changes in the age structure of the population will reflect events as far back as World War I and immigration restrictions of the early 1920s, and especially the effects of the subsequent decline in birthrates during the Depression of the 1930s and World War II, of the "baby boom" of 1946 to 1965, and of the sharp drop in the birthrates during the 1965 to 1972 period. Birthrates and mortality rates are projected to continue to decline in the future.

Dynamics of U.S. Population Aging

The massive "graying of America," which will begin after 2007, will be the result of large numbers of baby boomers growing old while the growth of younger population groups will be much slower owing to the decline of birthrates after 1965. Table 1 summarizes the projected size and growth rates of the young (under 20), the prime working age (20–64), and the elderly (65 and older) population groups. Over the entire period from 1995 to 2025, the growth rates of the young and of the prime working age populations, both averaging 0.7 percent a year, will be much lower than the 2.1 percent annual growth rate projected for the elderly population. The elderly population will almost double, while population under 65 will grow only by 30 percent. This does not mean that the old will outnumber the young. Population under 20 will still be considerably larger than population 65 and older. However, the ratio of old to young will rise from 40 percent in 1995 to 69 percent by 2025.

Growth rates of different population groups will vary significantly over shorter periods. Until 2007, the older population will grow at the same rate as the prime working-age population, because the number of persons reaching 65 during that period will come from the small age cohorts born during the Depression and World War II. After 2007, the growth rate of the elderly population will escalate to 2.8 percent a year, while growth of the young and prime working age populations will slow down considerably.

Over the entire period, 1995–2025, the growth rates of the "younger elderly" group (age 65–74) and the "older elderly" group (age 75 and older) will be the same; but within the latter group, the oldest population will grow more rapidly (see Table 2). However, until 2007, the "younger elderly" population (65–74) will grow only at 0.1 percent a year. Thereafter, its growth will accelerate sharply to 3.5 percent a year from 2007 to 2025. Population of age 75 and over will grow uniformly at 2.1 percent annually. The growth rate of

The number of adults over age 65 in the United States constituted 12.6% of the population in 1995 and will increase to 27% of the population by 2050. (© 1994 Brian Drake/First Image West, Inc)

The ratio of total population to population of prime working age—that is, ages 20–64, will decline from 1.71 in 1995 to 1.69 in 2007. It will then rise to 1.82 in 2025. The projected total support ratio is within the range of the past experience of 1.92 in 1970 and 1.75 in 1980. However, support requirements are shifting progressively from support of children—largely within families—to support of the elderly, largely through government and private money transfer systems. Increased consumption by the elderly will reduce the disposable income and consumption of workers.

The size of the economic burden of support placed on the working population is neither fixed nor determined only by demography. It will also depend on the rate of future economic growth and, in particular, on growth in national productivity and hence in the real earnings of workers. An increase in economic growth will expand the means available in the economy for support of the elderly. For this reason, it will be particularly important to have in effect policies that raise productivity growth. To maintain economic growth during the coming demographic transition, it will be necessary to make changes in tax, expenditure, and regulatory policies before 2007.

Apart from growth policies, two specific approaches have been initiated to limit the cost of support of the elderly population—containing the growth of health care costs and increasing the retirement age. Growth in the real cost of health care (i.e., its growth relative to growth in the general price level) has already been dampened by limits imposed both by government programs and by the private health insurance industry involving payment schedules for specific services and reviews of the choice of services.

Increasing the retirement age is more complicated. It requires changes in incentives, not only for elderly workers to increase the supply of their labor, but also changes in incentives for employers to raise their demand for older workers. Considerable proportions of workers over 40—and especially those workers over 55—who have lost jobs due to plant closings, corporate mergers, and so forth, have not been able to find new jobs and have involuntarily left the labor force. Increases in the age of eligibility for social security retirement benefits, from 65 to 67, have already been legislated and further increases may be added in the future. However, an effective increase in the retirement age will require increasing the labor force participation and employment rates of workers in the younger groups, especially those of age 55 to 64. Partly because of reduced demand by employers for older workers, participation rates of groups age 55 to 65 have been declining. Therefore, in order to assure higher employment rates for workers over 65, it will be necessary to increase employment

population 100 and older will be very rapid, but the number of centenarians will still be small, totaling approximately 0.1 percent of U.S. population in 2025.

Some Possible Problems and Solutions

With increased longevity and larger numbers of elderly, there will be some changes in the lifestyle of many Americans. There will be more families and individuals with both parents and children who require personal attention. The increased numbers of the very old will probably increase the need for personal care to be provided for by relatives, or paid for through the public sector, or from the elderly's own resources. A greater proportion of wealth may be consumed by the elderly rather than being bequeathed to the next generation. This implies an increased need for personal savings by the working population.

By themselves, the demographic changes do not appear to imply big changes in the overall support ratio.

TABLE 1

U.S. POPULATION BY MAJOR AGE GROUP AND THEIR GROWTH RATES, 1995–2025

	Total	0–19	20–64	65+
Total Population (Thousands)				
1995	263,491	75,741	153,815	33,935
2007	295,133	82,425	174,312	38,396
2025	345,459	92,339	189,558	63,562
Annual Growth Rate (Percent per Year)				
1995–2005	0.9	0.7	0.7	2.1
1995–2007	0.9	0.7	1.0	1.0
2007–2025	0.9	0.6	0.5	2.8

Source: NPA Data Services, Inc.

TABLE 2

AGE DETAIL OF THE U.S. ELDERLY POPULATION, 1995–2025

	65–74	75+	75–84	85–99	100+
Population (Thousands)					
1995	18,908	15,027	11,262	3,712	53
2007	19,108	19,288	13,219	5,919	150
2025	35,599	27,963	19,844	7,682	437
Annual Growth Rates (Percent per Year)					
1995–2025	2.1	2.1	1.9	2.5	7.3
1995–2007	0.1	2.1	1.3	4.0	9.1
2007–2025	3.5	2.1	2.3	1.5	6.1

Source: NPA Data Services, Inc.

opportunities for potential workers under 65, because employment continuity is probably the most effective means for raising the age of retirement.

[See also Death and Dying; Demography; Elderly, Living Arrangements; Health Care; Population Growth: United States.]

BIBLIOGRAPHY

Auerbach, James A., and Welsh, Joyce C., eds. *Aging and Competition: Rebuilding the U.S. Workforce.* Washington, DC: National Planning Association, 1994.

Day, Jennifer Cheeseman. *Population Progressions of the United States, by Age, Sex, Race and Hispanic Origin, 1993–2050.* Current Population Reports, No. 1109. Washington, DC: U.S. Bureau of the Census, 1993.

Mannheimer, Ronald J., ed. *Older Americans Almanac: A Reference Work on Seniors in the United States.* Asheville, NC: North Carolina Center for Creative Retirement, University of North Carolina; Detroit: Gale Research, 1994.

Taeuber, Cynthia M. *Sixty-five Plus in America.* Current Population Reports. Washington, DC: U.S. Department of Commerce, Economics and Statistics Administration, Bureau of the Census, 1992.

Terleckyj, Nestor E., and Coleman, Charles D. *U.S. Population Trends, 1995–2025.* National Economic Projections Series, Vol. 94-N-2. Washington, DC: NPA Data Services, 1995.

U.S. Senate Special Committee on Aging. *Aging America: Trends and Projections.* Washington, DC: U.S. Government Printing Office, 1991.

— NESTOR E. TERLECKYJ

AGRICULTURAL TECHNOLOGY

We are moving into an era where knowledge, not labor, raw materials, or capital, is the key resource. This knowledge is giving us the scientific understanding to meet the growing demands of society for a higher quality of life. At the same time, we seek a development process that is sustainable, globally competitive, and market driven.

The opportunities afforded by competencies such as molecular biology, combinatorial chemistry, and smart materials mean that we will have new ways to fulfill the basic needs of food, fiber, and shelter. Yet, the development and commercialization of knowledge-based technologies are becoming increasingly complex as societies and markets try to balance their material needs with other priorities. The sustainability of production systems, the protection of the environment, and the preservation of natural resources are priorities that cannot be forgotten as new technologies are developed.

The balance of the scales is challenged even further by the explosion of science and technology, the escalating cost of achieving and maintaining technical leadership, and the difficulty of protecting technical leadership through intellectual property rights. The value of technological innovation must be captured to ensure continual reinvestment in our future.

How can we achieve balance? It is clear that independent, self-sufficient efforts are unlikely to keep pace with the needs of society and the leading edge of innovation. Change is clearly necessary—our processes must be reinvented so that technology is discovered and developed internationally. Former attorney general Ramsey Clark, the respected American political and social thinker, once described change in this way: "Turbulence is life force. It is opportunity. Let's love turbulence and use it for change."

The underlying turbulence or stress that is currently driving change is fundamentally related to globalization and the transition from an asset to a knowledge-based economy. Within the last five years, we have seen vast political and economic change throughout the world as countries embraced democracy and the free market system. GATT, NAFTA, and the EEC reflect a spirit of global competitiveness and cooperation unlike any we have seen in history.

People on our planet can now share knowledge with one another in an instant. Still and video images can be transmitted cost-effectively. More than forty million people are now linked through Internet, receiving information from more than 100,000 publishing sources. Many of us would not know how to function without electronic mail, faxes, and video conferencing. As business guru Peter Drucker has observed: "There will be no poor countries or industries, only ignorant ones." In other words, knowledge will be the currency of the future.

In summary, we see a world business environment that is undergoing a major transition as local economies regionalize and individual businesses globalize. Tech-

Geometric patterns of contoured farmland signify conservation measures to maximize rainfall and irrigation by limiting runoff and erosion. Erosion could decrease the Earth's surfaces by 40 inches over the next 22,000 years. (Richard Hamilton Smith/Corbis)

nology, capital, and information flow freely across international borders, equalizing some of the previous disparities between countries. Every business is faced with increased competition and increased customer expectation in terms of higher quality, lower prices, a demand for products tailored to individual needs, and a local source of supply. In addition, societal expectations have increased, especially regarding environmental issues and sustainable development.

Knowledge-based technologies, if used wisely and judiciously, can help restore balance (Figure 1). But to be fully effective in the current business environment, these technologies must be researched and developed by a new paradigm.

What does this new paradigm look like? Successful business and technical processes will change from vertical and country-specific to horizontal and international. By reinventing our processes, the fundamental unit of work will be international teams and affiliations tied to a global effort. Alliances will develop that match competencies and compatible goals between partners (Figure 2).

This process is illustrated by changes occurring in agriculture and the technologies being developed in response to these changes. With this level of change, independent, self-sufficient efforts are unlikely to keep pace either with the needs of society or with the leading edge of innovation.

In agriculture, change today manifests itself primarily in four areas: population growth, societal demands, the environment, and the marriage of traditional agriculture with the high-tech world of advanced chemistry, and molecular biology and information technology.

Ninety-seven percent of the world's food supply

is grown on 3 percent of the Earth's surface,

which is unlikely to change to any significant degree.

As we move into the next century, the Earth's population is forecast to double, reaching about eleven billion by the year 2050. It is important to remember that 97 percent of the world's food supply is grown on 3 percent of the Earth's surface, a relationship that is unlikely to change to any significant degree. This means that over the next fifty years or so, we will need to produce more food than in all of history. As this production task unfolds, society will require that it be accomplished while protecting the global environment and preserving natural resources such as land and water.

Over the years, agriculture satisfied these ever-increasing societal needs at an incredible rate of im-

A New Paradigm

⇩

Technology

Explosion Of Science
Technical Leadership
Intellectual Property
Sustainability
Environment
Natural Resources

Figure 1. Restoring balance.

proved efficiency through new crops, better production, better storage, better processing, and better distribution. Agricultural chemicals have been a very significant factor in meeting society's needs—revolutionizing farming practices by reducing labor requirements, increasing crop yields, lowering food costs, and improving food quality. However, as sustainability of the environment becomes a high priority, society is expecting a continuous improvement in the environmental compatibility of these products.

What we have then is a dilemma that has brought us to an important crossroads. On one hand, there is a global ground swell of public concern about the impact of production methods in agriculture. On the other hand, there is increasing concern over the ability of the world's agriculture system to meet future food and fiber demands. The dynamics of global trade will influence the resolution of this dilemma.

What is agriculture's response? Through technology, the potential exists to develop agricultural systems that protect and enhance the global environment. Increasing the intensity of agriculture on highly productive land will reduce the environmental pressure on our forests and wetlands and allow the withdrawal of marginal lands from production. A flexible, sustainable system is being developed that includes reduced chemical input, increased biological input, improved delivery systems, and integrated crop and pest management (see Figure 3).

Although chemicals will remain the principal input, their performance characteristics are changing dramatically. They are being designed to be increasingly effective on target organisms and increasingly safe to the environment and nontarget species. They will possess high biological efficacy to minimize the amount of ma-

A New Paradigm
Horizontal and International Alliances
Matched Competencies
Compatible Goals

Figure 2. A new paradigm.

Figure 3. Sustainable system.

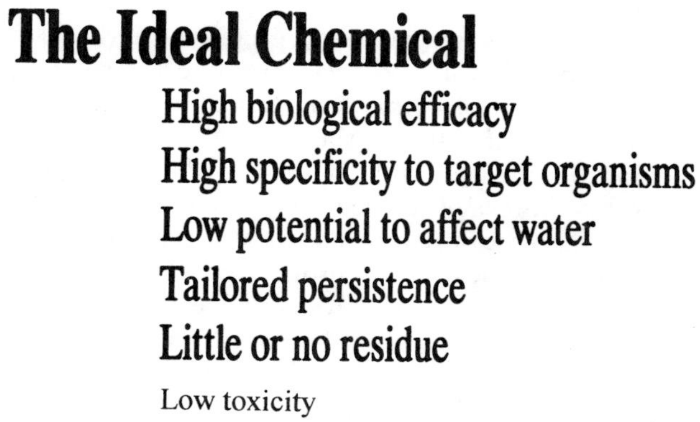

The Ideal Chemical
High biological efficacy
High specificity to target organisms
Low potential to affect water
Tailored persistence
Little or no residue
Low toxicity

Figure 4.

terial introduced into the environment. They will have high specificity to target organisms, but at the same time, softness toward beneficial organisms. There will be low potential to affect surface and ground water and a degree of persistence that can be tailored to match the designed length of pest control, the cropping systems, the soil, and other environmental and food safety considerations. There will be little or no residue on treated crops and low toxicity to man, fish, and other wildlife (see Figure 4).

Quite a challenge, but much progress has already been made. Over the past fifty years, herbicide use rates have been steadily reduced. With the introduction of sulfonyureas, these rates dropped dramatically. Today, a few grams per hectare of a sulfonyurea are as effective as kilograms per hectare of the more conventional herbicides currently in use. This represents a reduction of several hundredfold in the amount of chemicals that are introduced into the environment to achieve the same level of weed control. This knowledge and performance will be prerequisites for product commercialization by the year 2000.

Another important change occurring in agriculture is the marriage of traditional agriculture with advanced chemistry, molecular biology, and information technologies. New synthetic organic techniques combined with molecular biology are increasing the availability of diverse chemistries. Molecular biology also provides an unprecedented level of understanding of key biological processes in plants, fungi, and insects.

We can now produce crops that are resistant to environmentally sound herbicides or have improved disease and insect resistance. Improved microbes for controlling insects, disease, and weeds are also being explored. Although chemicals will remain the major crop-protection technology, improved crops, biological and integrated pest management will become part of a flexible sustainable system.

Diagnostic tests are being developed for early detection of plant disease and work is continuing to better understand multigene traits such as stress, yield, nutritional content, and processing characteristics. More fruits and vegetables will be developed with improved taste, texture, shelf life, and appearance. Edible oils will be tailored with specific nutritional properties such as levels of saturated, unsaturated, and polyunsaturated fatty acids. New uses for plants in areas such as pharmaceuticals, materials, and fuels will spur tremendous opportunities for global production.

The third critical factor concerning the change in agriculture is information technology. Using microcomputers, satellites, soil and crop geographical databases, positioning technologies, decision-support systems, and automatic control of machine functions, farmers can respond to variations in soils such as water content, compaction, and fertility. They can predict leaching and runoff potentials of nutrients and chemicals, as well as identify and measure the density of target weeds, pests, and diseases. Then using sensors, they can measure crop yields, use variable seed rates, and precisely apply fertilizer and chemicals. In other words, farming by the foot. Systems that apply this kind of precision to farming will give us the productivity and sustainability we require in the future.

In summary, there is yet another revolution occurring in farming—a blending of traditional agricultural practices with technology. We are witnessing a marriage where innovations in mechanization, seeds, fertilizer, and crop-protection chemicals are united with advanced chemistry and molecular biology. Information technology provides the interactive link that holds together the system, the facility to share questions and answers.

[See also Biodiversity; Climate and Meteorology; Deforestation; Fisheries; Food and Agriculture; Food and Fiber Production; Food Technologies; Forestry; Genetics: Agricultural Applications; Nutrition; Soil Conditions; Tobacco.]

BIBLIOGRAPHY

Burrus, Dan, and Thomsen, Patti. *Advances in Agriculture: A User Friendly Guide to the Latest Technology.* Milwaukee; WI: International Management, 1994.

Miller, Richard K., and Waller, Terri C. *Robotic, Vision, and AI Applications in Agriculture.* Lilburn, GA: Future Tech Surveys, 1989.

Weir, David S. "Sharing the Vision: The Shape of Things to Come." Keynote lecture, International Symposium on the Frontiers in Chemistry and Chemical Technology, Indian Institute of Chemical Technology, Hyderabad, India, March 1995.

— ASHOK K. DHINGRA
DAVID S. WEIR

AIR TRANSPORT

The direction of development for air transport technology is clear. Speed, safety, noise reduction, energy efficiency, and reliability continue to improve. Materials science contributes to smarter, lighter, and more durable aircraft frames and skins. Information technology will improve aircraft design, pilot performance, air traffic control, navigation, and the interchange among various transportation systems. More specialized aircraft, such as tiltrotors and tiltwings, will be introduced if they become cost-effective.

The schedule of specific advances is less certain than the direction of change. Visions of air transport include birdlike flight and hypersonic entry into orbit. Such visions, technologically possible within the next thirty years, must give way to the practicalities of money, needs, and priorities. Planning, designing, and producing a new commercial aircraft can cost $4 billion.

A hypersonic plane that flies at five times the speed of sound could be developed and commercialized by the 2020s.

Much of aviation for the first decade of the twenty-first century is already in place. Commercial aircraft have a lifespan of thirty to thirty-five years. In 2000, the Boeing 737 and 767 and the Air-bus 310 and 320s will be in their midlife. Subsonic aircraft technology is mature, and most advances will be incremental. The greatest strides will be made in systems integration and information technology. Expert systems will coordinate digital sensors, controls, and onboard and external data, and will increasingly take over control of the flight.

Revolutionary advances are expected for super-sonic transport. Worldwide demand for supersonic aircraft may reach 350 aircraft between 2000 and 2010. Efficiency and noise reduction are expected to improve. A hypersonic plane that flies at Mach 5 (five times the speed of sound) could be developed and commercialized by the 2020s. Hypersonic planes would exit and reenter the atmosphere on trans- and intercontinental flights. Flight times between Europe and the United States would be two hours. The number of passengers per plane could double to 600 or more.

Military procurement and research and development drive air transport technologies and systems because performance is more important than costs. Air transport systems must be effective in battle. Aircraft are designed for acceleration and maneuverability and recently for stealth. Visions of military air power include a hypersonic intercepter, dog-fighting helicopter, and greater use of unmanned, remotely controlled aircraft. Roughly one-third of the U.S. defense budget is devoted to aviation.

Civilian use of military technologies happens only after they become cost-effective. For example, short/vertical takeoff-and-landing (S/VTOL) technology used by the military is too expensive for most civilian use. The divergence of military missions and civilian applications has reduced military-to-civilian technology transfer.

The end of the Cold War has led to military downsizing. The U.S. Air Force will soon have 2,200 fewer aircraft than in the mid-1980s.

Civilian aviation includes passenger travel, air cargo, and general aviation (private and business flying). Between 1980 and 2000, the number of takeoffs and landings in the United States by major and regional air carriers is expected to almost double to 30 million per year. Over the same time, the hours flown by major carriers may increase from 6.5 million to 13.4 million. Air travel accounted for one-fifth of all intercity passenger miles, twice the 1970 rate.

U.S. air travel will grow from 1.4 million passengers per day in 1990 to 4 million or 5 million by 2040. Revenue passenger miles for U.S. major carriers is forecast to increase from 259 billion miles in 1980 to 762 by 2000. People are increasingly financially able to see more of the country and the world. The number of trips abroad by U.S. citizens could reach 27 million by 2025, up from 15 million in 1990. Overseas travelers may take a pill or wear a skin patch to neutralize jet lag. Better

The farming techniques used on Israeli kibbutzes are designed to maximize crop growth within the constraints of a dry, arid climate. Fully applied, existing technologies could increase food production tenfold. (David Rubinger/Corbis)

understanding of chronobiology will allow circadian rhythms to be adjusted by influencing the brain's reaction to light.

World air-passenger miles could quadruple between 1990 and 2025. The strongest growth will likely be in the U.S.-Pacific Basin and Europe-Far East routes. Business globalization and the robust economies of many Asian countries will likely increase the demand for longer, faster commercial travel. Asian air travel is expected to reach up to 22 percent of the global air fleet and 42 percent of air travel by 2010. Transoceanic flights are expected to double between 2000 and 2025.

Competition is increasingly strong and international. Alliances will link airlines around the world. In the United States the large airlines will be supplemented by a growing network of regional airlines.

Air cargo and general aviation will continually grow. Air cargo growth will exceed passenger growth and could reach 5 percent of all commercial aircraft movements by 2010, up from 3 percent in 1990. Modularized container and cargo systems may help move goods from ship to plane to train to warehouse.

By the early twenty-first century, a next-generation supersonic business aircraft could be developed to carry ten business travelers at Mach 2. Personal flight in the next century could be offered by VTOL, but individually owned aircraft replacing a great number of automobiles is virtually impossible.

Aviation forecasting is vulnerable to unforeseen changes in social priorities and economics. New environmental issues could surface. Concern about aircraft noise, for example, was for the most part unforeseen. Telecommunications could reduce travel demand as video-conferencing and other electronic communications increase. Rapidly escalating fuel prices could change technology priorities. Air transport growth could overwhelm the airport and air traffic control infrastructure. Lack of adequate airport runway capacity could be the greatest constraint on growth.

Only three new airports have opened in the U.S. in the past twenty-five years: Dallas-Fort Worth, Southwest Florida Regional, and Denver International. It is unlikely that any other large new airports will be operational before 2000. Thirty-nine U.S. airports could have more than 20,000 hours of flight delays a year in air carrier operations, up from twenty-one airports in 1987. The larger airports could see delays of 50,000 to 100,000 hours annually. The National Airspace System Plan being implemented by the Federal Aviation Administration to reduce delays caused by the air traffic control system will begin to yield benefits only after the year 2000.

An obstacle to airport development or expansion is land. Expansion often is protested by citizen groups concerned about noise. About 20,000 acres of land are required for modern airports including runways, facilities, parking, and sound-buffer zones. Floating airports could be a solution to noise and land scarcity problems for coastal cities.

Information technologies will improve safety and air traffic control. Traffic management works on limited data and is constrained by the ability of air traffic controllers to manage complexity. With the introduction of more computing power and expert systems, a global, comprehensive, integrated airspace system may evolve. The next-generation air traffic control system will include real-time global positioning to a few meters and advanced weather technology. Traffic-management-center computers could use satellite and cellular technology to communicate with computers on board airplanes, as well as with other transportation modes, to improve routing efficiency.

Reducing the potential for human error will improve safety. Better presentation of data on the plane's condition will improve pilot performance. Collision avoidance technologies will improve and become more widespread. Aircraft may be dynamic structures that respond to environmental stresses. Better weather forecasting will come from using supercomputer-based modeling, smart databases, real-time data, and graphic displays. Weather forecasts could be provided in minutes rather than hours.

The adoption of new aviation technology is slow because of exacting safety standards and fear of litigation. Safety-related technology reflects the accident patterns of the preceding few years. Yet air travel remains one the safest modes of transportation available.

Hijackings and other terrorist incidents will always be a threat to aviation. The number and violence of terrorist groups continue to increase. Security systems will need to keep pace with the increasing technological sophistication of terrorists. Biological and chemical weapons are difficult to detect. Terrorists may then turn to other targets that are less protected than airplanes.

[See also Change, Pace of; Macroengineering; Maglev; Railways; Space Flight; Space Travel; Terrorism; Transportation.]

BIBLIOGRAPHY

"Mach 3 Passengers? No Simple Formula." *New York Times,* January 14, 1990.
"The Sky Is Falling." *Christian Science Monitor,* November 20, 1989.
Socher, Eugene. *The Politics of International Aviation.* Iowa City, IA: University of Iowa Press, 1991.
Waters, Somerset R. *Travel Industry World Yearbook: The Big Picture.* Vol. 35. New York: Child & Waters, 1991.

— TOM CONGER

ALCOHOL

Alcoholic beverages have been a part of traditional cuisine and a pleasurable social amenity throughout recorded history. Alcoholic beverages, like many newly introduced consumables, were often prescribed for medical purposes. Sumerian clay tablets dating to 2100 B.C. corroborate such use, as do records of Egyptian physicians during the following millennia, revealing that about 15 percent of "prescriptions" called for alcohol.

Alcohol, once largely the province and privilege of religious orders, also played a role in divination. Priests substituted holy water with alcohol, sometimes insisting it was essential to reaching transcendent states that increased their ability to foretell the fortunes of rulers and prospects for societies.

Consumption

Alcohol used in moderation not only provides recreational diversion, but may be beneficial to health. However, alcohol abuse always has plagued society. Alcohol consumption constitutes the nation's most widespread drug problem. Despite the typical warnings of nausea and dizziness suffered by first-time users, individuals not only learn to tolerate such poisons, but can develop cravings and physical dependence tantamount to addiction.

Heavy drinking became unfashionable during the 1980s, when preventive attitudes surged. Tougher criminal laws, stiffer enforcement of them, and raising the legal drinking age to twenty-one played major roles in this change. The drinking age was raised to a minimum of twenty-one in all states by 1988. Alcohol consumption, as a result, has declined and remained relatively stable over the past fifteen years.

The rate of consumption was highest in 1810 and 1830, when U.S. per capita use amounted to 7.1 gallons of pure alcohol. By 1985, consumption had dropped to 2.58 gallons of absolute alcohol and is likely to decline by only a small amount over the next several decades.

Americans may think that what they drink is healthy, but a look at per capita consumption raises doubts (see Table 1). Consumption of all fluids in 1994 amounted

Beer consumption among Americans in the 1990s ranked second only to soft drinks in amount of beverages consumed per capita. (Paul A. Souders/© Corbis)

TABLE 1

FLUIDS CONSUMED PER CAPITA
IN THE UNITED STATES IN 1994

Type of Liquid	No. Gallons Consumed
Soft Drinks	49.6
Alcoholic Beverages	25.4–36.7
Beer	22.5–32.0
Wine	1.6–2.7
Distilled Spirits	1.3–2.0
Coffee	26.0–28.0
Fluid Milk	19.1–25.0
Bottled Water	11.2
Tea	7.0
Juices	7.0
Powdered Beverages	6.9
Water Content from Solid Foods	34.0–50.0
Total	186.2–221.4

Source: Public Policy Forecasting, 1995: based on USDA, PPFI, and Beverage World data. (Some adjustments exclude or include minors.)

to 186.2–221.4 gallons per capita. Soft drinks, 49.6 gallons of them, far and away constituted the leading beverage. Surprisingly, beer ranks second, at some 22.5–32 gallons per capita. Next comes coffee at 26–28 gallons; and finally, fluid milk, at 19.1–25.0 gallons. Soft drinks, together with bottled water (including flavored varieties), will continue to increase and lead the pack. Coffee, including all its gourmet and upscale varieties, also will experience strong growth. Beer may experience moderate growth. Fast-paced lifestyles and healthier diets will also encourage considerably higher consumption of fruit and vegetable juices.

Consumer Spending

Consumption of alcoholic beverages overall is expected to remain relatively flat, and probably decline somewhat, over the next ten to twenty years; however, expenditures are expected to continue increasing as consumers switch to more costly premium, specialty, imported, flavored, and exotic varieties.

Consumer spending for alcohol reveals a trend favoring moderate products. Consumption of distilled spirits, as a percent of alcoholic beverage sales, fell from 51 percent in 1967 to 31 percent in 1992. Beer's proportion increased from 43 percent to 58 percent. And wine outlays doubled from 6 percent to 12 percent over the same period.

Food stores overtook liquor stores and became the biggest distribution channel in 1986. USDA statistics reveal food stores sold $17.6 billion and liquor stores $17.4 billion during that year. Grocers' marketshare is certain to continue growing. Wine, for example, enjoys

a profit margin of 20–30 percent compared to about 3 percent or so for overall supermarket margins. Beer, wine, and liquor constituted the fourth largest spending category in grocery store sales during 1993—$39 billion of the $423 billion sold through all grocery stores. Soft drinks ranked seventh highest at $21 billion.

Packaged goods accounted for most of 1994 outlays—$49.8 billion—with another $39.4 billion in drinking establishments. Because eating away from home is expected to continue growing, spending for drinks is likely to overtake sales of packaged goods. Eating and drinking places became the largest dollar-volume channel for alcoholic beverages in 1977, when drinks garnered $11.98 billion, liquor stores took in $11.69 billion, and food stores accounted for only $8.04 billion in sales. By 1993 the gulf had further widened: $29.7 billion for eating and drinking places (plus another $4.7 billion in hotels and motels), $21.1 billion in food stores, and $18.6 billion in liquor stores.

Controlling Consumption

During ancient times, as today, excessive drinking came under government regulation. The Code of Hammurabi established by the king of Babylonia by 1770 B.C. responded to excessive intoxication and unruliness among abusing subjects. Not so long ago, almost one-half of all police activity in the United States involved alcohol, one way or another.

Militating against unreasonable consumption of alcoholic beverages are a bevy of powerful forces. Health consequences—early deaths from alcohol-related diseases, accidents, homicides, suicides, alcoholism, birth defects, and a host of other adverse health consequences—pose the strongest imperative for reform. Property damage and added taxpayer burdens also figure prominently. Keener interest in preventive health measures, including sound nutrition, reduction of caloric intake, and the increasing incidence of obesity add to potential widespread interest in curbing and controlling—but not eliminating—alcohol consumption.

Alcohol burdens the economy by as much as $100 billion attributable to health care costs, and lost productivity. There is good reason to impose additional controls and expand educational efforts that seek to modify behavior.

Government Jurisdiction—Revenues or Health Prevention

Taxation has been used to discourage consumption of alcoholic beverages for many years. By the mid-1300s, Germany imposed taxes for this purpose. "Sin taxes," designating revenue raised from alcohol, tobacco, and gambling, gain enormous momentum. Policymakers will strive toward tax levels to offset costs taxpayers otherwise would have to bear. Such taxes are likely to grow enormously. Sweden slaps high prices on alcohol sold in its state-monopoly liquor stores, and boosts prices by the drink to levels that discourage purchase— about twenty-two dollars for a double martini in Swedish restaurants.

For centuries alcoholic beverages were controlled by revenue collectors, because spirits provided a main source of government funds. Today, alcohol revenues constitute a minuscule part of total revenues, and widespread alcohol abuse justifies reassigning jurisdiction to health ministries. Sweden, the bellwether country for undertaking new government policies, transferred jurisdiction to its National Board of Health and Welfare within the Ministry of Health and Social Affairs, a step certain to be emulated.

Drunk Driving

Drunken driver arrests numbered 1.52 million in 1993, down approximately 300,000 from 1990. During 1993, nearly one-fourth of all such arrests (86,570) were for persons under twenty-one. The bad news is that overall, some 42 percent of the 40,655 traffic deaths in the United States during 1994 were alcohol-related. The good news is that alcohol-related deaths dropped from 25,165 (57 percent of traffic deaths) in 1982 to 16,884 (42 percent of traffic fatalities) in 1994, which was about 600 fewer than during 1993. Total costs resulting from alcohol-related motor vehicle accidents in 1993 amounted to an estimated $26.7 billion. Sterner controls are in the offing.

Tougher Penalties

Between 1970 and 1990 literally thousands of new laws were established to deter drunk driving. Recommendations call for reducing culpable blood alcohol concentration (BAC) levels from 0.1 percent to .08 percent, and setting them even lower for repeat offenders and younger drivers. At least five states already had set BAC levels at 0.08 percent by 1993. The trend is toward ever lower tolerance levels.

El Salvador, as of 1979, dealt sternly and finally with drunk drivers whose indiscretion takes another life— death by a firing squad. This response is unlikely to be followed elsewhere.

Some 30–35 percent of all DWD (driving while drunk) drivers are repeat offenders, according to a recent Department of Transportation twelve-state report. Statistics reveal that recidivists are four times more likely than average drivers to be involved in fatal accidents. Getting them off the street is important to the public safety. Four-time offenders in some states are considered

felons and subject to a minimum of two years imprisonment. Plea bargaining also is restricted for such offenses in some jurisdictions. Some states test drunk drivers for alcoholism, and require treatment for persons afflicted as well as for three-time offenders. Stiffer penalties are imposed on DWD drivers with children in the vehicle at the time of arrest.

Withdrawal of driver licenses, including immediate seizing at arrest (which is allowed in thirty-eight states as of 1995), also have been imposed; length of suspension may be pegged to the number of offenses (thirty to ninety days for first offenders, and one year for recidivists). Convicted DWD drivers who continue driving will receive much tougher penalties when caught. Some states confiscate and/or destroy license plates of multiple offenders on the spot if the violations occurred over the past three to ten years. Vehicle impoundment and confiscation have been imposed by other jurisdictions. Courts have held that taking vehicles, plates, or drivers' licenses forecloses any subsequent criminal conviction on grounds of the constitutional bar against double jeopardy (being tried twice for the same crime). Sooner or later, the Supreme Court is likely to validate such "dual" penalties, finding them to be part and parcel of a single transaction.

Consumption of alcoholic beverages is expected to remain relatively flat. However, expenditures are expected to continue increasing as consumers switch to more costly varieties.

One state immobilizes vehicles of multiple offenders with Denver boots. An extreme recommendation involves keeping repeat offenders under intermittent surveillance. Some jurisdictions set up unannounced roadblocks, particularly in nightclub areas, to help keep drunk drivers off the road. Other states require ignition interlocks designed to prevent inebriated drivers from starting up their vehicles (twenty-nine states as of 1995). Another controversial approach involves public humiliation of offenders, such as distinctively designed or colored license plates, license plates beginning with the letter "Z," or bumper stickers warning that the vehicle is operated by a convicted DWD operator or a person driving with a restricted license.

Open containers of alcoholic beverages in vehicles are prohibited in twenty-seven states (as of 1993). At least one state exempts open containers of beer from the prohibition.

Alcohol-Related Deaths

Alcohol, as noted, is a factor in nearly half of all motor vehicle fatalities. Boating deaths attributable to alcohol abuse run about 60 percent. Alcohol also was implicated a contributing factor in approximately 10 percent of all nonvehicular deaths and 5 percent of property damage accidents. Alcohol is a factor in at least 150,000 additional deaths due to homicides, suicides, and accidents of all kinds—some 50 percent of all falls, 50 percent of fire deaths, and 50–68 percent of drownings. Alcohol figures prominently in high percentages of criminal activity in general. The impact of alcohol abuse upon battered spouses, the incidence of divorce, child abuse, and other asocial behavior also are considerations. Over the ten-year period of 1982 to 1992, alcohol-related deaths declined 27 percent.

Alcoholism and Related Diseases

Alcoholism afflicts anywhere from 10–11 to 14–15 million Americans over eighteen years of age. An additional 1.3 million suffer alcohol dependencies. Altogether about 8 percent of adults in the U.S. have serious problems with alcohol. Alcohol abuse or dependence is suffered by about 40 percent of all U.S. family households, according to the National Institute for Alcohol Abuse and Alcoholism. Men are more than three times as likely to be afflicted compared to women.

Retailers in Denmark label the caloric content

of alcoholic beverages, which other calorie-counting

and health-conscious nations will follow.

Federal reports link alcohol abuse to cancer of the mouth, larynx, esophagus, liver, and colon; heart disease; nervous system damage; gastrointestinal tract diseases; depression and suicide; and dangerous drug interactions.

Cirrhosis and Liver Disease

During the "dry" period of 1920 to 1933 imposed by Prohibition, mortality rates for cirrhosis and liver disease plummeted. In 1905 the rate was 14.0 per 100,000 persons, but by 1933 the rate had declined to approximately 7.0 per 100,000. Following repeal of national Prohibition, alcohol use once again began to climb, and the incidence of cirrhosis—an indicator of alcohol abuse—also began an upward climb, with current rates running at about double the level prevailing during the prohibition era (reaching 15.5 per 100,000 persons in 1970, and then declining to 11.7 by 1983).

Fetal Alcohol Syndrome

Perhaps the saddest and most dreadful consequence of alcohol abuse involves fetal injury. Fetal alcohol syndrome has ranked as the third most common cause of birth defects in the United States in recent years. Among the top three birth defects, it is the only one that is preventable. Harms posed by alcoholic beverages during conception are well known, but the severity is underestimated. Chronic heavy drinking during pregnancy can cause microcephaly, prenatal/postnatal growth deficiency, developmental delay and mental retardation, abnormalities of the extremities, and a host of other teratogenic anomalies.

Biblical scriptures warned the mother of Samson, ". . . thou shalt conceive and bear a son. Now therefore beware, I pray thee, and drink not wine nor strong drink. . . ." (Judges 13). Laws of ancient Carthage and Sparta prohibited use of alcohol by newly married couples. Warnings date way back in history, but human behavior stubbornly tends to go on in its carefree and careless manner.

Promotion

Advertising alcoholic beverages traditionally has been controlled by government. A number of precursor countries have banned all advertising of alcohol (for example, Norway). Few jurisdictions are likely to impose total advertising bans, but sharp reductions along the lines of successes established in bellwether countries like Sweden almost certainly will be followed.

Labeling Disclosures

Health-hazard warnings, akin to those required for tobacco products, also are required for alcoholic beverages. Ostensibly to avoid a "strength war" (touting alcoholic strength to attract users), the Supreme Court ruled in 1995 that decisions prohibiting beer labeling disclosing alcoholic content violated freedom of speech rights. This was not a difficult decision, since the Bureau of Alcohol, Tobacco, and Firearms (BATF) rules already required such declarations for wine and spirits. During the 1980s leading retailers in Denmark voluntarily undertook to label the caloric content of alcoholic beverages, a lead that other calorie-counting and health-conscious nations will follow.

Availability

A number of jurisdictions restrict sales of hard liquors to government-run stores, which are purposely limited as to number and hours of operation. Happy hours in bars have been voluntarily eliminated or restricted by statute. Dispensers of alcohol—including commercial operators as well as social hosts—have been held responsible for serving guests too much alcohol and, accordingly, are held jointly responsible for any injuries. Over the long run, availability and access to alcohol will increase, not decrease.

Excusing Behavior

Some social and medical authorities view alcohol abusers as hapless victims and blame alcohol abuse on heredity, bad genes, psychological failing (contending that chronic offenders are mentally ill), physical factors (negating volitional criminal acts by attributing them to symptomology), antisocial personality disorder (ASPD), attention deficit disorder with hyperactivity (ADD-H), addiction, chemical causes, weak tolerance levels, handicapped disablement, and so on. Efforts to explain away and otherwise excuse alcohol abuse aids and abets permissiveness to extremes. In the future, individuals increasingly will be called upon to look to themselves and take responsibility for their own actions.

[See also Drugs, Illicit; Food and Drug Safety, Gambling; Pacesetter Governments; Tobacco.]

BIBLIOGRAPHY

Cahalan, Don. *Understanding America's Drinking Problem: How to Combat the Hazards of Alcohol.* San Francisco, CA: Jossey-Bass, 1987.

Golden, Sandy. *Driving the Drunk Off the Road.* Washington, DC: Acropolis Books, 1983.

Gusfield, Joseph R. *The Culture of Public Problems: Drinking-Driving and the Symbolic Order.* Chicago, IL: University of Chicago Press, 1981.

Klingemann, Harald; Takala, Jukka-Pekka; and Hunt, Geoffrey, eds. *Cure, Care, or Control: Alcoholism Treatment in Sixteen Countries.* New York: New York University Press, 1992.

Lender, Mark Edward, and Martin, James Kirby. *Drinking in America: A History.* Rev. ed. New York: The Free Press, 1987.

Transportation Research Board. *Zero Alcohol and Other Options: Limits for Truck and Bus Drivers.* Washington, DC: National Research Council, 1987.

— GRAHAM T. T. MOLITOR

AMUSEMENT PARKS.

See THEME PARKS AND ORGANIZED ATTRACTIONS.

ANIMAL RIGHTS

The animal rights movement and its central philosophy developed rapidly in the wake of the human rights movement during the 1970s and '80s. It directly challenged conventional, institutionalized, and even religiously sanctioned attitudes toward animals, attitudes that have been responsible for centuries of animal suf-

fering, in the name of custom, pleasure, entertainment, profit, necessity, scientific knowledge, and purported medical progress. The movement raised questions over the ethics and moral costs to society of using animals for testing military weapons and cosmetics; of exploiting them for food and fiber; of killing them for fur and for trophies; of keeping them as pets or in zoos; or using them for students to experiment upon. The movement's radical Animal Liberation Front engaged in frequent acts of civil disobedience, first in the United Kingdom in the 1970s and later spreading to the United States. Various schools of animal rights philosophy evolved in the 1980s. A plethora of books, monographs, symposia, and college courses, indicative of the growing academic and scholarly involvement in the animal rights debate, heralded the birth of a new sensibility toward nonhuman animal life.

The animal rights philosophy contributed to a shift in perception from a chauvinistic, human-centered one to one that embraced a spirit of respect for all life.

It should be recognized that various animals are very different from each other or from the human species. Animal rights are not the same as human rights. All nonhuman animals do, however, have the right to equal and fair consideration.

During the last decade of the twentieth century, the animal rights movement is maturing into a more unified front. Some common ground has been established with other movements, notably those of the environmental, alternative agriculture (organic, sustainable), holistic medicine, and social justice/human rights movements.

The pharmaceutical-medical-industrial complex will continue to face increasing public censure as the health of an economically and ecologically dysfunctional industrial society continues to deteriorate. Opposition toward vivisection (operating on live animals for experimental purposes) continues to intensify as the ethics, scientific validity, and medical relevance of animal experimentation and product testing are being questioned by an increasingly informed public, including physicians, veterinarians, and other professionals not beholden to establishment values.

The petrochemical-based food industry (agribusiness) complex also is facing increasing opposition from the public and from health, environmental, and agricultural experts. The justifications for using pesticides and for the proliferation of cruel factory-like methods of livestock and poultry production cannot be justified.

In response to the burgeoning animal rights movement, counter-organizations and propaganda are being developed by furriers, hunters, trappers, agribusiness, and the biomedical industrial establishment. Such trends are likely to continue.

The interconnection between animal, environmental, and human rights is leading to a convergence of once separate and often opposing movements. This convergence is best exemplified by the theory and practice of alternative, humane sustainable agriculture, which embraces concern for domestic and wild animals, for the land, for all who work the land, and for the consuming public as well.

The Humane Sustainable Agriculture movement was born in the late 1980s, as society began to face a new set of ethical, environmental, and economic questions that a new technology had spawned: genetic engineering biotechnology. The benefits of this technology to society will be dubious, and the costs and risks predict-ably considerable, if it is not linked with preventive, holistic medicine and health maintenance (including family planning)—and with humane sustainable agriculture. It is more likely to intensify rather than alleviate the medical and agricultural nemesis, if the core principle of animal rights philosophy—namely, respect and reverence for all life, including the land—is not incorporated into every component and direction that this new technology takes.

The early 1990s saw a U.S. biotech company develop genetically engineered pigs with human immune systems to serve as organ donors for people in need. It also saw the U.S. government refuse to sign onto an important U.N. treaty to protect biodiversity—wild creatures, plants, and their natural habitats—arguably because the U.S. biotechnology industry saw this treaty as a threat to corporate sovereignty.

In applying biotechnology to propagate endangered species, zoos claimed to be protecting species' right to life. But the animals' right to live in natural conditions, and for zoos to be more actively involved in protecting

Safaris that allow tourists to shoot photographs of animals rather than hunting them are just one example of a growing sensitivity to the rights of animals. (Chris Rainier/Corbis)

wildlife in their natural places of origin, helped unite the animal rights and environmental conservation movements. The need to kill wildlife or use biotechnology to regulate wildlife populations in sanctuaries was another issue that forced animal rights fundamentalists to think ecologically.

In a very profound sense, the animal rights movement and philosophy contributed to a shift in human perception from a chauvinistic, human-centered one to one that embraced the truly compassionate spirit of respect and reverence for all life. This latter world view, like the notion of animal rights, is antithetical to the technocratic, profit-driven motives of corporate industrialism. If the essential unity and interdependence of all life continues to be denied into the next millennium, the destruction of the natural world will be assured.

Increasing opposition to animal rights parallels an increasing disregard for the sanctity of life by those who do not understand the egalitarian philosophy of animal rights, that is, those who continue to adhere to the chauvinistic view that animals were created for humanity's use. If this view prevails, we will be left with a wholly synthetic, bioindustrialized world, with a few scattered wildlife parks and zoological gardens, but no truly natural habitat. Eden, like Paradise, can never be regained, but the restoration and preservation of the remnants of the natural world is still feasible. Acknowledgment that nonhuman animals have rights can help society make the right choice in this direction, if not for its own survival, then for the living memory of our evolutionary history and in recognition of our biological and spiritual kinship with all life in the universe.

[See also Biodiversity, Bioethics; Environmental Behavior; Environmental Ethics; Evolution, Biological; Evolution: Life-Forms in the Universe; Genetic Engineering; Holistic Beliefs; Human Rights; Life Sciences; Pets; Sustainability.]

BIBLIOGRAPHY

Fox, Michael W. *Animals Have Rights, Too.* New York: Continuum, 1991.

Pringle, Lawrence. *Animal Rights Controversy.* San Diego, CA: Harcourt, Brace, Jovanovich, 1989.

Strand, Rod, and Strand, Patti. *The Hijacking of the Humane Movement.* Wilsonville, OR: Doral Publishing, 1992.

— MICHAEL W. FOX

ANTHROPOLOGY.

See SOCIAL SCIENCES.

APOCALYPTIC FUTURE

Apocalypse comes from a Greek word that simply meant "unveiling." But through its association with the New Testament *Book of Revelation* (*Apokalypsis*), it has come to mean a prophecy, fiction, or vision of some final (and usually violent) end.

Speculation about endings is as basic to human nature as the search for ultimate origins. One entire branch of philosophic/religious/mythical studies called *eschatology* deals with "last things."

Ancient depictions of "the End"—the final future—generally involve a cataclysm in which Earth and humans suffer. Ultimately the outcome is considered a blessing, since it marks the final defeat of evil and the triumph of good. Even such bleak visions as the Norse *Ragnarök* (Twilight of the Gods) or the Hindu *Kali Yuga* look beyond the end of this world to a new beginning.

Visions of impending doom,

such as apocalyptic passages in the Old Testament,

emerge during times of social stress.

Visions of impending doom emerge in times of social stress. The best-known apocalyptic passages in the Old Testament (e.g., *Isaiah,* chapters 24–26, and the *Book of Daniel*) were written after Israel had already lost its political independence. A number of noncanonical apocalyptic Jewish writings date from the chaotic periods of revolt against Roman rule in Palestine (A.D. 66–70 and 132–135). Similarly, almost Christian apocalyptics, including the New Testament *Book of Revelation,* date from the late first and second centuries A.D., when the Christian community was widely persecuted.

One particularly influential passage from the *Book of Revelation* (Chapter 20) contains the prediction of a perfected earthly kingdom in which the elect will reign beside the returned Messiah, before the Final Judgment. A thousand-year bridge between normal human history and the divine eternity to follow the "end of the world" is sometimes called the *chiliasm* or *millennium* after the Greek and Latin root words for one thousand. Through the centuries, the desire to realize a chiliastic or millennarian world order has spawned many secular interpretations and parallels: from utopian communities to Adolf Hitler's "thousand-year Reich."

In common usage, an apocalypse is the sudden end of a process or an era. The end in question need not be universal. Decisive battles and natural catastrophes with far-reaching impacts (such as the mass extinctions that closed certain geologic periods) can be termed apocalypses.

At least four "levels" of apocalypse seem relevant to futures research: (1) the end of the universe; (2) the end of Earth; (3) the end of a society or civilization; and (4) individual death.

The end of the universe—whether by implosion ("the Big Crunch") or exhaustion (entropy)—may appear remote in time and beyond the present power of human influence. Even so, fiction writers (e.g., Olaf Stapledon's *Star Maker* [1937]) and physicists offer intriguing material for speculation.

At the other extreme, futurists seem no more willing than others to confront the personal apocalypse: death. While life extension prospects (and their social consequences for population growth and resource scarcity) are sometimes explored, few futurists discuss how to prepare for a future that includes death.

It is the two remaining levels of apocalypse—cultural and planetary endings—that are most often addressed. Visionary warnings of impending doom attract attention, entertain, and on occasion galvanize leaders into action.

St. Augustine and other theologians believed the conversion of the Roman Empire to Christianity marked the start of the thousand-year kingdom of Christ on Earth that would end with the Last Judgment. Later, reformers like Martin Luther were convinced they were living in the era of wars and calamities described in the *Book of Revelation*. Christian sects as varied as the Jehovah's Witnesses and the Branch Davidians continue to expect the imminent coming of a Messiah and the end of the world by divine intervention. Philosophers from Kant and Hegel to Karl Marx came to regard human betterment as the ultimate goal of history, with or without divine guidance. The idea of a cataclysmic End Time was gradually replaced by expectations of inevitable improvement toward perfection—the idea of progress. But in the twentieth century, wars, social injustice, economic chaos, and unsettling scientific discoveries undermined faith in human goodness and universal order, leading many to doubt whether history has any goal at all.

Today, apocalyptic visions abound once more in fiction and popular writing. Specific mechanisms of destruction include: global war; nuclear holocaust plague; collision with a comet or asteroid and a plethora of eco-catastrophes (ozone layer depletion, rapid global warming, mass extinctions of many species, and so forth), generally resulting from human indifference, negligence, or greed.

Secular apocalypses (including works of fiction) often seek to help prevent, mitigate, or ease cataclysmic changes. By contrast, religious apocalyptics tend to believe that the nature and scope of the coming disaster is wholly beyond human control, and urge calm acceptance, or even joy at this final fulfillment of the divine plan. Both secular and religious apocalyptics share a tone of urgency: The future they depict is close at hand—if not already beginning.

The many apocalyptic visions in modern art and literature, and the continuing popular interest in Biblical prophecy, reveal widespread dissatisfaction with present conditions and fears for the future. By helping to focus such fears, apocalyptic writings may promote prudent forethought and stimulate futures research.

[See also Dystopias; Extinction of Species; Human Rights; Nostradamus; Science Fiction; Utopias; Weapons of Mass Destruction; and, in the Appendix, Chronology of the Future.]

BIBLIOGRAPHY

Auden, W. H., and Taylor, Paul B., trans. *The Elder Edda: A Selection.* New York: Random House, 1977.

Barnstone, Willis, ed. *The Other Bible: Jewish Pseudepigrapha, Christian Apocrypha, Gnostic Scriptures, Kabbalah, Dead Sea Scrolls.* San Francisco: Harper, 1984.

Boyer, Paul. *When Time Shall Be No More: Prophecy Belief in Modern American Culture.* Cambridge, MA.: Harvard University Press, 1992.

Davies, Paul. *The Last Three Minutes: Conjectures about the Ultimate Fate of the Universe.* New York: Basic Books, 1994.

Hawking, Stephen W. *A Brief History of Time: From the Big Bang to Black Holes.* New York: Bantam, 1988.

– LANE E. JENNINGS

APPLIANCES, HOUSEHOLD.

See HOUSEHOLD APPLIANCES.

APPROPRIATE TECHNOLOGY

The critical role of technology in economic development, and especially the importance of technology choice, was first brought into focus by the economist E. F. Schumacher, author of *Small Is Beautiful*, in the 1960s. He argued that the conventional technologies of the rich countries—large-scale, capital- and energy-intensive, and laborsaving—were singularly inappropriate for the poor countries of the world. To meet their needs, technologies must be discovered or devised that are relatively small, so as to fit into small, rural markets; they must also be simple, so that they can be operated and maintained by rural men and women; and they must be inexpensive so that they can create workplaces in very large numbers, using local raw materials. Large-scale technologies, he argued, bypass the rural poor and distort the cultures, not only the economies, of poor countries. Technology is not culturally neutral.

This was not a popular argument in the 1960s, when it was widely believed that modern technology and cheap oil guaranteed limitless economic growth for rich and poor countries alike. But by the 1980s, aid and development policies based on these notions had undeniably failed. Escalating rural poverty—more than 1.3 billion men and women could be below the poverty line by early next century—insupportable indebtedness and massive and growing unemployment in developing countries called for a radical change in approach. The central objective now must be to raise the incomes of the rural poor by equipping them with tools and machines that they can own, use, and maintain for themselves.

A wide range of appropriate technologies is now available, along with experience of supporting services such as credit and marketing, thanks to nonprofit bodies such as the Intermediate Technology Group, started by Schumacher in the 1960s and now employing some 200 engineers and other professionals, with offices in Africa, Asia, and Latin America; Appropriate Technology International in the United States; and more than 20 similar groups in Europe, Canada, and developing countries. United Nations agencies such as UNICEF, UNIFEM, UNIDO, and the ILO also are supporting work on appropriate technologies.

Small, efficient, low-cost technologies now exist for agriculture and food processing, water supply, building materials, renewable energy, health, transport, and small industries of many kinds. They enable a new workplace to be created for as little as a few hundred dollars, compared with the ten or twenty thousand dollars it takes

As technology grew by massive leaps, people believed the advantages would quickly spread to all. However, many people in the world remain dependent on the most simple technology. (Hulton-Deutsch Collection/Corbis)

to equip one new workplace in large-scale industry (see Carr [1985] and Smillie [1991]).

Although now widely available, such technologies have not spread rapidly in developing countries because government policies and regulations generally favor big enterprises over small, the rich over the poor, the city over the village. A large firm may borrow, for example, at only 2 or 3 percent interest, whereas the small family firm may have to pay 20 percent or much more. The biggest international lender, the World Bank, still persists with large-scale projects even when small technologies would be cheaper and more efficient and would employ more people. When such biases in favor of capital-intensive industries are removed—and they are increasingly under fire—appropriate technologies will spread rapidly through the market, allowing the poor to work themselves out of their poverty.

By the 1980s it was also becoming evident that conventional capital- and energy-intensive industries had a questionable long-term future, not only in the poor countries of the southern hemisphere but also in the rich industrialized countries of the northern hemisphere. The large-scale, oil-based industry and agriculture of the north are mostly unsustainable because they are on a collision course with the environment, which is being devastated by pollution; with people, because of growing unemployment and pervasive human health hazards; and with the world's resource base, owing to heedless overconsumption. The north's need for appropriate technologies is even more pressing than that of the south: the very existence of life on Earth may now depend upon the north's ability to replace present technologies with sustainable forms of industry and agriculture.

It is no longer enough simply to ask about any new activity, "Does it pay those who undertake it?" Answers must be obtained to three other questions as well:

- What does it do to the environment?
- What does it do to the resource base, renewable and nonrenewable?
- What are its social and political implications?

In all industrial countries, the actions needed to get a more sustainable economy and a more appropriate technological base would include:

- A determined program of energy conservation, and the hastened development of renewable forms of energy, all of which derive from the sun: direct solar power, biomass, wind, water, and geothermal energy. As energy expert Amory Lovins once remarked, solar energy won't run out, explode, or cause cancer. The nuclear lobby argues that nuclear power is also appropriate, but in fact, it may be the least appropriate technology ever created. It is very expensive, highly centralized, and authoritarian,

and it poses serious danger to human life. Because nuclear wastes remain lethally radioactive for up to hundreds of thousands of years, the problem of waste "disposal" may be insoluble. A thoroughgoing policy of energy conservation on both sides of the Atlantic could result in renewables satisfying up to 60 percent of the total energy needs of most industrial countries within the first two decades of the twenty-first century. The progressive introduction of long-lasting products that can be repaired, renewed, and recycled would reduce materials and energy use, and provide work for many people in dispersed small enterprises.

- Transport policies promoting public transport, especially rail, could cut pollution and accidents. Policies favoring local economic development and small enterprises could minimize long-distance hauls of people and goods, and also bring economic activity under the control of local communities.
- Agricultural policies aimed at substituting organic husbandry for the prevalent petrochemical farming, which is bad for people and the environment.

Thus, both in the northern hemisphere and the south, sustainable life-support systems demand appropriate technological means of producing goods and services that are human in scale and respect human needs for useful and satisfying work; that minimize damage to the environment; and that make prudent use of renewable and nonrenewable resources. This is the best way toward an economics of permanence.

[See also Development, Alternative; Energy; Environment; Global Environmental Problems; Resources; Sustainability.]

BIBLIOGRAPHY

Brown, Lester, et al. *State of the World* (annual reports of the Worldwatch Institute). New York: W. W. Norton, 1990–1994.
Carr, Marilyn. *The AT Reader.* London: IT Publications, 1985. (Note: IT Publications books can be obtained from Women Ink, 777 UN Plaza, New York, NY 10017.)
Jazairy, Idriss; Alamgir, Mohiuddin; and Panuccio, Theresa. *The State of the World Rural Poverty.* London: IT Publications, 1992.
Miles, Derek, ed. *A Future That Works.* London: IT Publications, 1983.
Schumacher, E. F. *Small Is Beautiful.* London: Sphere, 1973.
Smillie, Ian. *Mastering the Machine.* London: IT Publications, 1991.
Stewart, Frances; Thomas, Henk; and De Wilde, Ton, eds. *The Other Policy: The Influence of Policy on Technology Choice and Small Enterprise Development.* London: IT Publications, 1990.

— GEORGE MCROBIE

ARCHITECTURAL DESIGN

As the world draws closer to becoming one global market, the practice of architecture will become international. In the future, collaboration between architectural firms in different countries will be common in building better communities and ecologically sound habitation.

New kinds of buildings and more advanced urban networks for the cities of the world will challenge the imagination and technological skills of architects everywhere. Intelligent office buildings that are responsive to workers' needs for personal control of the temperature, light, and fresh air movement in their work spaces and that provide technically advanced communications systems and computer terminals for all types of work will be the norm. Many buildings will provide spaces for living, shopping, recreation, and working within the same structure. In these buildings personal transportation will consist of an elevator instead of an automobile. Clusters of these buildings will form complexes covering areas as large as several city blocks. In such complexes internal gardens and parks, playgrounds, and schools will be accessible to the people who live and work within them without reliance on public or private transportation. Public transportation will connect areas of cities such as airports and urban centers, towns and villages, and countries with rapid means of conveyance connected at transportation nodes.

Many buildings will provide spaces for living,

shopping, recreation, and working

within the same structure. Clusters of these buildings

will cover areas as large as several city blocks.

Architects will design large areas of future cities as well as individual buildings. In addition, new design challenges will stem from increased concern around the world with the preservation of the environment, with the ecologically sound use of materials and methods of building, with historic preservation, and with meeting the special needs of those with disabilities.

The buildings and urban complexes will apply urban planning and land use principles based on intelligent long-term use of our habitats. Urban designers will take maximum advantage of climate variations and changes in the topography of an area, especially in hilly regions and waterfronts.

One of the most significant changes will be in the design tools available to future architects. Advanced computers and ubiquitous information networks using fiber optics and satellite systems will make it possible to link all of the decision makers for a building project. The remainder of this article describes how an architect would work with such advanced technology in designing a university building in the year 2010.

The project would begin with the university planning office searching the architectural database created by scanning architectural magazines for the past twenty years and putting the information into one large graphics database for examples of university buildings with requirements similar to the planned project. When the search produces four or five comparable buildings, the planning office would invite the architects of these buildings to submit credentials over the conference phone now available in most offices.

After one firm has been selected, the university team would travel to the architectural firm's office for a design session. This session will be held in the computer simulation arena within the architect's office, containing a large computer display area, ten feet by fourteen feet in size, in full color. The board-certified master designer from the architect's office will lead the intricate operation of the arena over the next four hours, assisted by a team of specialists, each of whom has gathered critical information needed for the master design.

As the design operation begins, a large topographical plan of the entire building site will be displayed on the arena screen, with climate data, zoning regulations, local building trade practices, and many other variables superimposed in smaller windows around the large display. As design decisions are developed, each of these windows will display an assessment of the design against the particular variable considered in that window. For example, one window will continuously display the energy use characteristics of the proposed building design and show how this use fits energy standards. The master designer can fine-tune changes in the design to bring the energy use in line with standard requirements.

As the master designer begins to plan the building spaces and make materials and equipment selections, additional windows will display three-dimensional views of the interiors and exterior of the building. To one side of the arena a holographic image of the building will show it in three dimensions.

Once the master architect and the university client have agreed on the preliminary design, specialists will ready estimates of building costs based on programmed schematics for local labor, materials, and equipment. This cost estimate will include not only the cost for constructing the building, but the cost of maintaining and updating the building's materials and systems over the next thirty years.

At the end of a session lasting some four hours, the university client will be able to sign a contract to have the building designed and constructed and to keep it up-to-date for thirty years. The building firm in which the master architect is a senior partner will be prepared to sign this contract and guarantee the performance of the new building over that time span. Thus the architectural, construction, and operating team will be assuming the full responsibility on behalf of the university

Preserving historical buildings while meeting the needs of a growing population desiring affordable housing is a challenge for architects and designers. (Kelly-Mooney Photography/Corbis)

for providing and maintaining high-performance educational spaces over a long period of time.

Master architects with the skills and knowledge to work on such design problems will require intensive education in a university followed by many years of experience in each of the specialty areas utilized during the arena operations.

Routine in the new architecture will be involvement in the design by the would-be users and occupants, as well as by others affected by the project. New materials as well as information tools will be crucial to designs, as will the long-term social commitment to recycling of both structures and materials.

[See also Cities; Science Cities; Visual Arts.]

BIBLIOGRAPHY

Davis, Douglas. *Modern Redux: Critical Alternatives for Architecture in the Next Decade.* New York: Grey Art Gallery and Study Center of New York University, 1986.

Papadakis, Andreas. *Modern Pluralism: Just Exactly What Is Going On?* New York: St. Martin's Press, 1992.

Venturi, Robert. *Complexity and Contradiction in Modern Architecture.* New York: Museum of Modern Art, 1977.

Wood, Lebbeus. *The New City.* New York: Simon & Schuster/ Touchstone, 1992.

Wright, Frank Lloyd. *The Future of Architecture.* Reprint. New York: New American Library/Dutton, 1970.

— JOHN P. EBERHARD

ARTIFICIAL INTELLIGENCE

In the last ten years, the field of artificial intelligence (AI) has begun to experience a major paradigm shift. New, sixth-generation computer hardware has begun to permit a brainlike style of computing that was not feasible earlier. This could produce truly brainlike intelligent systems within the next fifty years (or sooner).

Like most new technologies, the developments in AI offer clear benefits, serious hazards, and some consequences that are difficult to evaluate. On the positive side, we will see more efficient controllers, crucial perhaps to the feasibility of gasoline-free cars, airplanes able to reach orbit, and a major reduction in chemical waste. On the negative side, the frightening scenarios depicted in movies like *Terminator 2* or *Colossus: The Forbin Project* are far more realistic than many people appreciate. On the confusing side, intelligent computer personalities can be inserted into the "information utility" or "superhighway" of the future; these systems could help students learn at their own pace, in their own way, but—depending on how they are implemented—they could also interfere with personal freedom and individual initiative. AI technologies also will contribute to the rapid growth of communications and computing, in directions that we already expect—ever-increasing bandwidth, improved graphics and speech recognition, virtual reality, and so on.

In the past, people have argued that humans should learn to understand themselves better before developing such potent technologies. But a deeper, more scientific understanding of intelligence is itself a crucial prerequisite to understanding ourselves better—at the personal level, the social level, and even at the spiritual level. This understanding or awareness will be the most important benefit of AI technology in the long term. Thinking about the future is an essential component of higher-order intelligence. Therefore, new technologies to predict the future are an important component of this field.

Basic Paradigms

AI is a huge field. Researchers in one part of the field generally do not know where the frontiers are in other parts. AI is divided into three major communities:

- First there is the classical or hard-core AI community, based on classical formal logic. Hardcore AI emphasizes symbolic reasoning by computer. It includes expert systems. Classical AI uses left-brain thinking. It builds computer programs that manipulate sentences of propositions. As in Aristotelian logic, all sentences must be true or false—there are no shades of gray. Classical AI is part of computer science, which mainly relies on digital logic.

- Second there is the soft computing community, which uses artificial neural networks (ANNs), fuzzy logic, and genetic algorithms. It even includes embryonic efforts to use chaos or quantum effects in computing. Soft computing has been described as right-brain thinking by computers. Soft computing is a coalition of several different emerging paradigms, thrown together for sociological reasons. These paradigms emphasize continuous variables—the degree of truth, as in fuzzy logic; the strength of a connection, as in ANNs; or the level of performance, as in ANNs or genetic algorithms. Soft computing is mainly practiced by engineers who rely on continuous variables or analog logic.

- Third are the specific-application communities—involving such areas as speech recognition, image processing, and robotics—which mix and match tools from the other communities, from statisticians, and from elsewhere.

Figure 1 illustrates some of the history behind these paradigms.

In the 1960s, when AI was new, it focused on *one* basic question: how could we reproduce "intelligence"—as we see it in the human mind—in computer systems? This leads to the question: What *is* intelligence? There were three different strategies for answering these questions.

One group said, "I can't define 'intelligence,' but I can recognize it when I see it. There are certain difficult problems—like playing a good game of chess or proving hard theorems in logic—that are known to require intelligence. By building systems to solve these specific problems, we will actually learn about intelligence in the general sense." Many early efforts—like Samuels's checker-playing program—did yield important insights. There were three specific applications—speech, image-processing, and robotics—with large commercial markets that did not care about "intelligence" as such; these areas basically split off from classical AI and brought in new techniques from statistics and elsewhere to produce practical results.

A second group argued that intelligence does not lie in specific algorithms to solve specific problems. Rather, it lies in the ability to learn or discover an algorithm, when confronted with a new problem. Algorithms are like clam shells; the life is not in the shell, but in the clam that grows the shell. To understand intelligence, we must develop systems that *learn* to solve "any" new problem—General Problem Solving Systems (GPSS). But how do engineers build a system to "solve all problems"? In practice, the GPSS people mainly focused on two specific problems with general implications: (1) the problem of symbolic reasoning—how to prove the truth or falsity of a proposition, when given a database of initial axioms or assumptions; (2) the problem of "reinforcement learning"—how to maximize some predefined measure of performance, or pleasure, or utility, or profit, over future time, in an unknown environment. Many psychologists believe that the brain is mainly a reinforcement learning machine, which needs large numbers of brain cells to *learn* to do symbolic reasoning.

A third group—the perceptron school—argued that intelligence in the brain results from connecting large numbers of neurons and adapting them over time. They borrowed a simple model of the neuron from the neuroscientists McCulloch and Pitts, and developed ways to train these neurons to recognize simple patterns. Marvin Minsky proved that the perceptron designs of the 1960s were not powerful enough for true intelligence. Nevertheless, progress quietly continued.

In 1968, one researcher combined two existing AI systems to build a flashy display for the Montreal World's Fair: (1) a language-understanding system, to take questions about baseball typed in by human beings; (2) a reasoning system, to use information in the form of axioms about baseball, stored in a database to answer the questions. This was the first expert system. The main applications of classical AI today are expert systems—systems in which the human expert provides the database of facts or assumptions, and the computer answers questions. Important research has focused on machine learning, based on symbolic reasoning, but practical applications are limited.

In 1974, Paul J. Werbos found a solution to Minsky's problems, by combining reinforcement learning and ANN approaches. This solution was based on a generalization of Wiener's concept of "feedback" or of Freud's concept of "psychic energy." After several applications and later papers, the idea took root and was widely popularized in 1986. The ANN field grew rap-

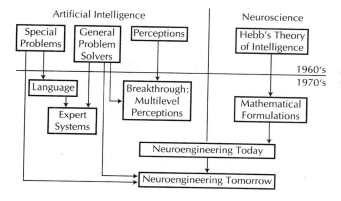

Figure 1. A partial history of artificial intelligence.

idly after that. ANNs are now best known as systems that recognize patterns in data; however, they can also perform prediction, control, reinforcement learning, data clustering, and data compression.

Sixth-generation computer hardware

has begun to permit a brainlike style of computing

that was not feasible earlier.

Fourth-generation computers are like the PC—one central processor or several processors for one computer. *Fifth*-generation computers use many processor chips strung together to achieve "massively parallel processing" (MPP). *Sixth*-generation computers use many very simple processors on a single chip (or in optics) to achieve 1,000 to 1,000,000 more throughput than fifth-generation computers, but they can only run programs designed to run on such machines (the human brain is a sixth-generation machine, which proves that sixth-generation machines can have very general capabilities). The ANN field has developed designs that begin to make good on that promise. New chips have come out that make the high throughput a reality. Brainlike throughput (or many times more) could be developed in ten years.

Application Areas

ANN-based systems already provide humanlike ability to recognize handwritten digits better than earlier methods. Designs for processing sequences of digits and letters will probably be working in ten to twenty years. In speech recognition, ANNs outperform older methods on small-scale tests, but considerable work—(perhaps twenty years of research)—will be needed to integrate this into full-fledged speech recognition.

The most important applications involve control or planning. Classical control theory—the descendant of Norbert Wiener's "cybernetics"—includes some very broad concepts in theory. In practice, the *working* designs of large-scale practical value are all based on the idea of the thermostat—a simple system, forced to stay near a fixed set point; near such a set point, all variations can be understood by the use of linear techniques, used to analyze small perturbations. They are especially useful where *high efficiency* is crucial—reducing weight requirements to permit Earth-orbit capability in an airplane, reducing pollution, and so on.

Symbolic reasoning tasks are far more difficult. For example, there is great interest now in developing "intelligent agents." An intelligent agent might be a smil-ing face that appears on a child's computer screen at school and offers to help the child. For now, classical AI makes it possible to build usable agents even without a true brainlike learning capability. But *hybrids* of AI and ANNs can permit "adaptive interfaces," which *learn* about children over time, so as to improve performance and individualize instruction. Prototypes are being planned for about six years in the future. Some children are excited about the idea of the "happy computer"—a reinforcement learning system the sole objective of which is to make the child "happy" (i.e., to smile or to push a "happy" button on the keyboard). Unfortunately, it is easy to imagine abuses of this technology by the intelligent computer.

Practical applications of fuzzy logic mainly involve control. In fuzzy control, an expert provides a list of simple IF-THEN rules like: "If motor is hot, then turn down fuel valve." Fuzzy logic has proved superior to classical AI in interpreting such rules, which do not require elaborate reasoning to interpret.

The information utility of the future will combine many of these technologies and others. Nippon Telephone and Telegraph (NTT), the world's largest corporation, has prepared a twenty-year plan for the global information utility. In that plan, ANNs and two optical technologies are listed as the two new basic technologies required to implement the rest. Even in the short-term, improved nonlinear control will be a major issue in building such networks. Some analysts have even proposed turning the telephone network itself into a huge neural network, a kind of giant collective happy computer.

[See also Computers: Overview; Digital Communications; Information Society; Information Technology; Interactive Entertainment.]

BIBLIOGRAPHY

The views expressed herein are those of the author, not of the National Science Foundation.
DeBoeck, Guido. *Trading on the Edge: Neural, Genetic and Fuzzy Systems for Chaotic Financial Markets.* New York: Wiley, 1994.
Pribram, Karl, ed. *Origins: the Brain and Self-Organization.* Erlbaum, 1994.
———. *The Roots of Backpropagation: From Ordered Derivatives to Neural Networks and Political Forecasting.* Wiley, 1994.
Werbos, Paul J. "Neural Networks, Consciousness, Ethics and the Soul." In *WCNN94 Proceedings*, Hillsdale, NJ: Erlbaum, 1994.

– PAUL J. WERBOS

ARTIFICIAL LIFE

Can human beings create life? To some the thought is sacreligious; to others, scientifically preposterous. Life as we know it is the result of billions of years of evolution. Its beginnings on Earth are still mysterious, but undeniably impressive: Somehow, protoorganisms managed to metabolize and reproduce, maintaining a delicate molecular balance that distinguished life from anything else. We still argue about the precise definition of life, but know that of all things, life is the least trivial.

However, in the mid-1980s a new science emerged that dared, however tentatively, to presume that a second origin was possible—the creation of an artificial life. Two developments have emboldened scientists to claim that the time is right to begin creating life. First, our knowledge of biology, particularly since the discovery of DNA and its importance, has seemingly turned an important corner. Never before have we understood life so well. Second, we now have the ideal tool for creating life—the computer. Since we now know that information-processing is a critical aspect of life, it makes sense that high-powered computers can model its processes, and perhaps duplicate those processes. At a certain point, those processes may themselves qualify as "alive." Or so goes the unabashedly optimistic logic of artificial life, described by Christopher P. Langton as "the study of man-made systems that exhibit behaviors characteristic of natural living systems."

It was Langton who coined the name (often abbreviated to a-life), but the acknowledged father of artificial life is mathematician John von Neumann. Among his stellar accomplishments was his late-1940s blueprint for a "self-reproducing automaton," a creature literally made of information. It "lived" on an imaginary checkerboard, an infinite grid in mathematical space. Each square, or cell, of the grid was in one of a number of given states; a set of rules dependent on the state of its neighbors determined what state the cell would take in the next step, or generation. After a number of generations, a "daughter" identical to the complex initial pattern would appear, with the ability to reproduce again. The process was remarkably like biological production. In the early 1960s, mathematician John Horton Conway made a much simpler "cellular automaton," calling it "Life." Though Conway's automaton is known mainly for its cult following in computer labs around the world, serious mathematical work was performed with Life. But its most striking aspect was its ability to generate unlimited complexity—even the sort of dazzling complexity associated with biology—from a few simple rules.

In the late-1970s, Christopher Langton, then a student at the University of Arizona, programmed the "Langton Loop," the simplest self-reproducing automaton to date. He did it on an Apple II. Langton became the field's chief proselytizer, and in 1987 he organized the first Artificial Life Conference. Approximately 150 biologists, computer scientists, physicists, and philosophers came to Los Alamos and instantly established the basis of a new multi-disciplinary pursuit. They shared a belief that lifelike behavior in silicon would adhere to the cellular automata methodology of using simple rules to generate complex behavior. One of the a-lifers had a slogan that could apply to artificial life studies in general: "fast, cheap, and out of control."

Since information-processing

is a critical aspect of life, it makes sense

that high-powered computers can model its processes,

and perhaps duplicate those processes.

The most impressive work in artificial life deals in computer-based evolutionary experiments. Usually they involve some variation of the genetic algorithm, a scheme devised by University of Michigan computer scientist John Holland to approximate the mechanics of evolution in a computer program.

As a result, some of the most fascinating work in evolution is now being performed on computers. Particularly notable is Tierra, a computational environment created by Thomas Ray, a University of Delaware ecologist. A single computer-program "organism" in this digital equivalent of primordial soup can reproduce; its offspring mutate, evolve, and turn into a number of identifiable species, co-evolving with each other. Evolutionary battles are waged between hosts and parasites.

Certainly the most visually arresting experiments are those conducted by Karl Sims of Thinking Machines. Using a variation of the genetic algoritithm, Sims "evolves" striking pictures—the artist is not Sims, nor his program, but the mechanics of evolution. Sims has also used similar techniques to "train" computer-based artificial creatures to perform certain tasks, like hitting a virtual ball. Successive generations discover more efficient ways to perform these tasks. Seeing this is like viewing a time-lapse photographic panorama of how movement evolves.

Not all artificial life is conducted inside the computer. Rodney Brooks of the Massachusetts Institute of Technology is one of several roboticists adopting an approach based on the "bottom-up" artificial life approach. Brook's six-legged robots not only look like insects, they behave like them, operating with simple rules that mimic the mechanisms of instinct. Though much less complicated than robots, which operate on the top-down approach associated with artifical intelligence, the faux creatures from Brooks's lab seem more cunning in coping with natural environments.

None of these experiments rival real life. However, the field is young and its practitioners are confident that they or their followers will cook up some indisputably living creatures. If they are successful, the implications will go far beyond science, raising such questions as: Should we regard artificial life with the same respect granted natural life? Can we control our living creations? Ominously, the closest a-life analogue to physical organisms so far are probably computer viruses. Should we even try to? As Doyne Farmer and Alletta d'A. Belin, argue, it is best not to wait until we are on the doorstep of these achievements before considering these questions. "We must take steps now to shape the emergence of artificial organisms," they write. "They have the potential to be either the ugliest terrestrial disaster, or the most beautiful creation of humanity."

[See also Artificial Intelligence; Bioethics; Evolution, Biological; Evolution: Life-Forms in the Universe; Extraterrestrial Life-Forms; Genetics; Genetic Engineering; Genetics: Commercialization; Nanotechnology; Robotics; Sexual Reproduction: Artificial Means.]

BIBLIOGRAPHY

Farmer, Doyne, and Berlin, Alletta d'A. "Artificial Life: The Coming Evolution." In Christopher Langton, et al., ed. *Artificial Life II: Proceedings of the Workshop on Artificial Life Held February 1990 in Santa Fe, New Mexico.* Redwood City, CA: Addison-Wesley, 1992.

Kelly, Kevin. *Out of Control.* Reading, Mass.: Addison Wesley, 1994.

Langton, Christopher. "Artificial Life." In Christopher, Langton, ed. *Artificial Life: The Proceedings of an Interdisciplinary Workshop on the Synthesis and Simulation of Living Systems.* Redwood City, CA: Addison-Wesley, 1989.

Levy, Steven. *Artificial Life: The Quest for a New Creation.* New York: Pantheon, 1992.

— STEVEN LEVY

ARTS

Fourteen years ago this author predicted that much of the future of art would come from two different kinds of developments—first, changes within the society of art and, second, new technological developments. An example of the first is the hypercommercialization of the established art industry. Those few artists who can sell, whether in the retail market of painting or the wholesale markets of book publishing and film, have been able to command far higher prices for themselves while earning far more than ever before for their sponsors. Given both absentee conglomerate ownership and continuing increases in production costs, this hypercommercialization is likely to escalate as well.

Will less profitable art survive, and if so, how? A dozen years ago the growth of small literary presses and alternative art galleries was a positive trend. Conventional wisdom now is that, either in spite of or because of government grants, they have largely missed the opportunity to sponsor the best new work. In art, as in corporate life, not everything survives, and that which dies is not necessarily the worst.

One paradox remains: while the number of those seriously making art in every field has increased substantially through every decade in the postwar period, the number of people becoming cultural celebrities remains remarkably few. Art has always been far more competitive than law, business, or even restaurant proprietorships; with ever more practitioners, it is now yet more competitive. If an ever smaller percentage succeeds, how will such pervasive failure affect the future making of art?

What lends perspective to this present inquiry is recognition of those technological developments that were not expected. Few could have predicted a decade ago that small, silver plastic "donuts" would have replaced larger, more substantial-looking, long-playing records. Fewer would have predicted virtual reality with its capacity to simulate three-dimensional sensory experience. Nor could we have predicted the proliferation of word-processing machines and programs.

This author failed to predict dimensions of the digital revolution in art. Few imagined the developments collectively called desktop publishing, where individuals working largely alone could produce camera-ready paper with the visual and typographic quality of "professionally printed" literature. In 1981 it was possible to compose in an electronic music studio where separate tracks of sound were laid onto multitrack tape, editing and "mixing down" a stereo version composed from many sources. By the late 1980s, most composers were sitting behind cathode ray tubes. The painstaking editing that previously took a week could be replicated on a computer screen, with portions of sounds moved around to taste within a single day.

Equally elusive were the current capabilities of CD-ROM, which can store the art of a whole museum on a single disc, or hypertext literature, whose multipath structures are best read on a computer screen, rather than on printed pages. Composers can pop into a computer a disc that plays an "imaginary orchestra" through amplified speakers. One result of most technological development is the undermining of traditional authorities. Thanks to desktop publishing, an author need not fear the printer's censorship; thanks to electronics, composers can avoid wasting time flattering orchestral conductors and other performing musicians.

Writing at the beginning of the 1980s, one could imagine better paints than the new acrylics, new sculptural materials with "the solidity of steel and the light weight of balsa wood," anthropomorphic machines that could "execute spectacular choreography better than live dancers," electronic instruments that could "imitate the richly varied sounds of a symphony orchestra," a typewriter that could "type out words as they are spoken," a television system that could "reproduce images that are present only in one's head," or computerized retrieval that could give "a writer immediate access to systemized information."

Of these speculations, only the last has been widely realized. A few have access to a computer that can type out spoken words or has the computer moxie to simulate the instruments of a symphony orchestra. The other speculations remain on our collective wish list. Technologies still have a way to go in the arts, which is another way of saying that innovative arts have a future with technologies.

One general esthetic direction is the creation of encompassing worlds. Whereas a church surrounds its visitors with largely static images, more recent environments have been filled with kinetic sources that, like a church, create an immersive sensory experience. These sources can be based upon sound, upon kinetic sculptures, upon moving pictures, or upon effective combinations of such media. Consider Frank Popper's description of an elaborate installation by Wen-ying Tsai, *Desert Spring* (1991):

> A cybernetic sculptural system that focused on the homeostatic relation of art to its environment, . . . it represented a new generation of environmental sculptures based on the concepts of stability and disturbance. The work was endowed with virtual intelligence which enabled it to maintain its internal stablity by coordinating real-time spontaneous and interactive responses that automatically compensate for changes in the environment. When spectactors enter the threshold of this darkened space, this presence is sensed by the sculpture's infra-red and audio antennae; thus, by their movement and sound, the spectators stimulate and destabilize the sculpture from normal relaxed undulation to excited rapid palpitation. It is only when the spectator leaves that the sculpture returns to its usual tranquil undulating state, as if awaiting the next round of confrontation."

Combining new technologies into an innovative integration of different media presages a future for art.

One promise of that new science called robotics is the creation of an immersive physical space in which everything literally can respond to the spectator's presence; so that every move made, from touching to simply shifting weight, triggers a perceptible change in the surroundings. The presence of such a continually responsive artistic environment—the sounds, images, and palpable objects—would become more interesting if the network of computerized responses could be frequently changed; so that the same move producing a certain response now would produce a different one later. Consider in this context the claim of virtual reality to recreate artificially the environmental experience through computer-assisted sensory stimulation.

Surprises are more frequent in art, because it is unencumbered by worldly needs. It does not just progress but literally jumps over fewer resistances.

Emerging technologies will discover content unique to each. The first function of cable television was providing cleaner images of network programs. Only later did cable transmission provide kinds of programming, beginning with locally produced shows, that would never go out on networks. With this principle in mind, consider the artist Manfred Mohr's suggestion that the most appropriate content for computer-generated visual art is not resemblances to familiar images but rules for creating art that are represented on paper through a computer-driven plotter. (One can wager that few people, if any, yet know what the ultimate content of Virtual Reality or CD-ROM might be.)

There will be progress within long-dormant technologies, such as television, beginning with an improved image closer in quality to film on larger screens and probably including dimensionality. Watch as well for developments in under-supported technologies, such as holography, which can represent images at different times in illusory space. One reason why holography has not developed is that holograms are so difficult to make. Video arrived around the same time as holography—in the middle 1960s; now there are millions of video users, nearly all of them amateur, but only a few dozen holographers, nearly all of them professional.

It is striking that new technologies which seem initially destined only for an elite few, such as the videotape camera, are successfully mass-merchandised throughout the world. One result is increasing the sheer amount of artistic experience and esthetic information available to more people around the world. The possibilities available to art a dozen years from now will be as different as those today are from a dozen years ago. Surprises are more frequent in art, because it is unencumbered by worldly needs. It does not just progress but literally jumps over fewer resistances. Even by the time this book appears, it will become apparent that this essay will have missed something important. Whatever that something is, it will probably be a joy to behold.

[See also Interactive Entertainment; Literature; Music; Performing Arts: Dance Theatre; Printed Word.]

BIBLIOGRAPHY

Friedhoff, Richard Mark, and Benzon, William *Visualization: The Second Computer Revolution.* New York: Abrams, 1989.

Kostelanetz, Richard. "The Artistic Explosion (1980)." In *On Innovative Art(ist)s.* Jefferson, NC: McFarland, 1992.

———. *A Dictionary of the Avant-Gardes.* Flemington, NJ: A Capella, 1993.

Mohr, Manfred, "System Esthetics." In Richard Kostelanetz, ed. *Esthetics Contemporary.* 2nd ed. Buffalo, NY: Prometheus, 1989.

Popper, Frank. *Art of the Electronic Age.* New York: Abrams, 1993.

— RICHARD KOSTELANETZ

ARTS, VISUAL.

See VISUAL ARTS.

ASIA

Asia is geographically and demographically the largest continent on Earth. It is characterized by topographic and climatic extremes, differing levels of economic development, diverse systems of governance, and a variety of religions, cultures, and languages. Until the end of World War II, many Asian countries were part of Western colonial empires. Their decolonization was followed by economic development variously based on capitalist or socialist models. During the past fifty years, Asia has witnessed major wars in the Korean Peninsula and in Indochina, the creation of Bangladesh, the fall of an authoritarian regime in the Philippines, and the shift toward democracy and a free-market economy in China.

Asia accounts for 56 percent of the world's population. By the year 2025, its population could equal the present population of the entire world (some 5.6 billion), a 70 percent increase. Of this population, 48 percent (about 2 billion) will inhabit South Asia, 37 percent East Asia, and 15 percent Southeast Asia. Increased longevity and reduced infant mortality are continually changing the shape of the age pyramid. Declining mortality rates have increased the size of the elderly population (65+), which will account for 15 to 25 percent of the overall population by 2025.

Asia is rapidly urbanizing. By the year 2000, around 35 percent of the people will reside in urban areas; the number of Asian cities with one million or greater population will be 101, including 38 in China and 24 in India. Urban growth will continue to diminish agricultural land, creating more slums and squatter settlements and overwhelming city infrastructures. Urbanization seems to be an irreversible process.

Asia accounts for 56 percent of the world's population. By the year 2025, its population could equal the present population of the entire world (some 5.6 billion), a 70 percent increase.

Asia is in the throes of social change. Modernization has touched all spheres of social life. People are mobile—geographically, socially, and psychologically. Local communities are becoming culturally mixed. Exposure to the media has created new areas of awareness and reintroduced people to their own cultural roots. The number of nuclear families is rising with expanding groups of women in their prime reproductive ages. As a result, extended families are breaking into smaller units, through spatial separation; however, such splitting has not affected filial ties. Kinship considerations continue to take priority, even in modern business. The availability of in-laws to look after children facilitates the entry of women into the workforce. Thus families remain lineally linked.

Overconcern with economic development has caused the neglect of the social sphere. The exploding population due to changing fertility and mortality rates is contantly altering demographic patterns. The uneven distribution of the benefits of development is marginalizing populations such as women, tribal and ethnic minorities, and disabled and illiterate people. Unemployment is on the rise among the educated. Large populations live below the poverty line. Social infrastructure, including the provision of basic needs—potable water, essential sanitation, housing and transport, food, and primary education—is still very inadequate. Social discontent occasionally results in violent civil unrest, which often invokes a repressive response from the state. Such a scenario contributes to political instability and hinders economic development. Social policy will have to address these issues.

The region's economic composition is highly diverse. Roughly, it can be categorized into developed economies (Japan); newly industrialized economies (NIEs) such as the Republic of Korea, Taiwan, and Hong Kong; soon-to-be NIEs (Thailand, Malaysia, and Indonesia), developing, least developed, and landlocked economies. GNP per capita ranges from U.S. $27,305 (Japan) to U.S. $100 (Mongolia). Some countries currently exhibit a negative GDP growth. It is, however, widely acknowledged that the world's growth center is shifting to Asia. The Southeast and South Asian subregions have natural and human resources and millions of potential consumers that are attracting world attention as future markets. China, Laos, and Vietnam are moving toward capitalist economies, and new economic powers are emerging in Southeast Asia. The process of industrial restructuring is continuing in all countries. Such progress notwithstanding, there are problems of poverty and unequal distribution of income that affect the region's standard of living.

Asia is rapidly losing its forest cover—5 million hectares were lost in 1991 alone. Continued deforestation has adversely affected biodiversity: over 600 animal species and 5,000 plant species are on the verge of extinc-

tion. Soil erosion, waterlogging, and salinization are causing land degradation, and 860 million hectares are affected by desertification. Over 170 million hectares of wetland have been lost. However, strategies of sustainable development now being devised may help protect the environment from advancing industrialization and prevent the pollution of previously healthy rural areas.

With comparatively limited reserves of oil and gas, Asia depends on its coal reserves. Energy requirements are being met by fuelwood, bagasse (plant residue), and oil—the latter's importation is rising as a result. An increase in fuelwood consumption can accelerate the deforestation process, and the curtailment of its production to save the forests may cause a shortage of fuelwood.

The health situation in Asia has significantly improved in areas such as life expectancy, as reflected in the following statistics: Life expectancy is now 76 years for developed countries, 73 for NIEs, 62 for East and Southeast Asian countries, and 58 for South Asian countries. The average daily calorie intake has increased

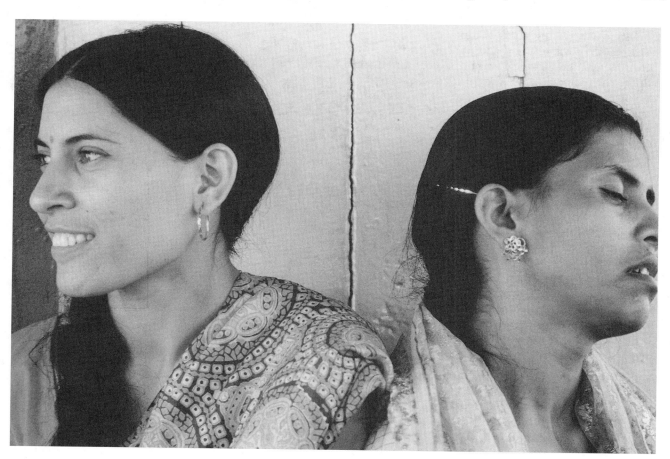

In the 1990s, one out of every seven people on Earth were Indian. India's population will surpass the population of China by the year 2050. (Charles E. Rotkin/© Corbis)

by 18 percent in the last two decades, and more and more children are being immunized against killer diseases. AIDS has become a new health threat. While in 1992 there were less than 5,000 reported AIDS cases, it is projected that by 2000 Asia will have 20 million HIV-infected cases—half of the world figure—and 90 percent of these will be in developing countries.

Education has made impressive advances. Literacy now stands at 70 percent, which still leaves 666 million people, mostly female, who are illiterate. An additional 40 million children do not attend school. Furthermore, advances in science and technology are creating new illiteracies such as "incomputeracy," a lack of basic knowledge of how to use computers. The educational systems throughout Asia need revamping—a process already begun in ex-socialist countries.

Summary

About 4.6 billion people will inhabit Asia by the year 2010, and the age pyramid will show bulges at the apex and base. Although literacy rates will go up, there still will be around 600 million adults, including 25 million adults of school-going age, who will need special programs. The increasing size of the school population will necessitate renovations and additions to existing structures; the changing science and technology profile will require the remodeling of curricula and teaching methodologies. Programs will be needed for new constituencies of illiterates. Growing urbanization will accentuate problems associated with migration, housing, family breakdown, crime, disease, and an increasing pressure on the infrastructure. Demand for higher education will rise. Increasing industrialization will pose problems for the environment. International trade will grow. Cultural identities will continue to remain strong, fostering tradition in the midst of modernity. The population growth rate may stabilize at 1 percent and near-total literacy may be attained by 2010. Sustainable development strategies may halt environmental deterioration. The opening of markets may create further interdependencies between countries and promote internal democratization. Also, remaining socialist regimes may collapse, and supranational groupings like the European Community (EC) may emerge.

Still, the alleviation of poverty may remain a difficult goal. Narrow parochial and ethnic loyalties may continue to surface. If so, Asia will maintain its cultural pluralism in a changing milieu.

[See also China; Development, Alternative; India; Japan.]

BIBLIOGRAPHY

Atal, Yogesh. "Anticipating the Future: Asia-Pacific Region." *Futures Research Quarterly* (Winter 1988): 15–27.

The urbanization of Asia has spawned magnificent architecture, as this view of Singapore shows, as well as a dynamic mix of cultures. Urbanized living will increase from 45.2% of the world population in 1995 to 72.5% in 2025. (Kevin R. Morris/Corbis)

Masini, Eleonora Barbieri, and Atal, Yogesh, eds. *The Futures of Asian Cultures: Perspectives on Asia's Futures*, Vol. 3. Bangkok: UNESCO, 1993.
United Nations Economic and Social Commission for Asia and the Pacific. *State of the Environment in Asia and the Pacific.* Bangkok: UN-ESCAP, 1990.
———. *Towards a Social Development Strategy for the ESCAP Region.* Bangkok: UN-ESCAP, 1992.

– YOGESH ATAL

ASIMOV, ISAAC (1920–1992)

This Russian-born American science fiction writer and popularizer of science was brought to the United States by his parents in 1923. Asimov published his first science fiction story in 1939. He earned a doctorate in chemistry at Columbia University in 1948 and taught at Boston University for several years before becoming a full-time writer. By the time of his death in 1992, he had published well over 400 books, most of them non-fiction. His most influential works of fiction are two series of stories and novels, one recounting the history of a far-future galactic empire in which scientific prediction of the future ("psychohistory") plays a central part, and the other exploring the interaction of human beings and robots. *Foundation* (1951), the first galactic empire novel, and *I, Robot* (1950), a collection of early robot stories, firmly established his reputation. Devoting himself chiefly to science writing and other nonfictional work from 1958 to 1980, Asimov later published a series of novels integrating his visions of galactic empire and robotics, beginning with *Foundation's Edge* (1982). Several of his nonfictional titles deal with speculation about the future, such as *A Choice of Catastrophes* (1979) and (with Frederick Pohl) *Our Angry Earth* (1991). He also edited a volume of essays, *Living in the Future* (1985).

[See also Futurists; Science Fiction.]

BIBLIOGRAPHY

Asimov, Isaac. *In Joy Still Felt*. Garden City, NY: Doubleday, 1980.
———. *In Memory Yet Green*. Garden City, NY: Doubleday, 1979.
Gunn, James E. *Isaac Asimov: The Foundations of Science Fiction*. New York: Oxford University Press, 1982.
Patrouch, Joseph F. *The Science Fiction of Isaac Asimov*. Garden City, NY: Doubleday, 1974.
Touponce, William F. *Isaac Asimov*. Boston: Twayne, 1991.

— W. WARREN WAGAR

ASTRONOMY

The fact that we observe all galaxy clusters to be receding from Earth's own Milky Way galaxy indicates an expanding universe. It also implies that the universe had an origin in time, the "Big Bang" when all matter crowded together at near-infinite density. Determination of the time of the Big Bang, currently set at about 15 billion years ago, depends on accurate measurements of the distances and recession velocities of galaxy clusters hundreds of millions, or even billions, of light years away. The next two decades should allow more accurate dating of the Big Bang to within 500 million years of its occurrence.

Formation and Development of Stars and Planets

The high temperatures within the early universe made it diffuse and unstructured. Significant clumping of matter could begin only after the radiation filling the universe ceased to interact with matter, at a time approximately 300,000 years after the Big Bang. Within the following million years, the clumps of matter that would become galaxies and galaxy clusters must have appeared. Within those clouds, subunits became individual stars. In the Milky Way, a typical giant spiral galaxy, star formation began some 12 billion years ago; and our sun and planets formed 4.6 billion years ago. The initial stages of star formation are poorly understood, although it is clear that once a clump forms that has significantly greater than average density, self-gravitation will squeeze the clump, raising its central temperature and, if the clump is large enough, initiating nuclear fusion at its center. The formation of a planetary system apparently often accompanies the formation of stars. Astronomers have found disks of material surrounding many young stars, thought to be either planets in formation or matter left over from the formation era. They have also discovered planets orbiting pulsars, the remnants of exploded stars; these planets have apparently formed from the debris of the explosion. Observations from space should reveal extra-solar planets around ordinary stars during the first two decades of the next century.

Manmade Evolution of Planets

Although most of a planet's mass lies buried below its surface, it is the surface that interacts with the universe and is most easily altered. Feedback loops present in the atmosphere, oceans, and surface of Earth demonstrate that a small initial effect can produce large consequences in a short time. For example, the addition of carbon dioxide to the atmosphere increases the greenhouse effect. In turn, this warms the planet by trapping infrared radiation from the surface and lower atmosphere. Even a small amount of carbon dioxide produces a noticeable effect. On Venus, a dense atmosphere rich in carbon dioxide keeps the planet's surface 450°C warmer than Earth. The suitable addition of small amounts of such gases into another planet's atmosphere would be relatively easy to accomplish, and could have far-ranging consequences.

Terraforming

Mars is the planet most susceptible to human-induced change. Its thin carbon dioxide atmosphere, if increased with the carbon dioxide now frozen into the Martian polar caps, could trap more heat and allow liquid water to exist (now an impossibility because of the low surface pressure). Such a project, if judged reasonable rather than environmentally unsound, could begin during the second half of the twenty-first century and might yield a planet capable of supporting human colonies.

Black Holes

A black hole is an object with such strong gravitational forces that nothing, not even light, can escape from within a critical distance from its center. Black holes can be detected by their gravitational effects on matter surrounding them that gradually spirals inward, as well as by the effects of gravity on light rays that pass close by them. Several likely black hole candidates have been identified in the Milky Way. Over the next decade several dozen more should be revealed with improved ground- and space-based observations. The Hubble Space Telescope has apparently detected a black hole of two billion solar masses in the core of the galaxy M87.

Pulsars

Pulsars, sources of regularly pulsed radio emission, arise from rapidly rotating neutron stars, the collapsed cores of stars that have exploded as supernovas. The number of known pulsars should reach several thousand by the year 2010, with many pulsars found to have planets in orbit around them.

Asteroids and Meteoroids

Debris left from the formation of the solar system 4.6 billion years ago continues to orbit the sun. Earth often intersects the orbits of small objects, called meteoroids, which produce "shooting stars" or meteors as friction consumes them high in the atmosphere. Larger objects called asteroids typically orbit between Mars and Jupiter, but some have Earth-crossing orbits. A 10-km asteroid's impact apparently caused the extinction of many species, including the dinosauria, 65 million years ago. Such impacts probably occur at 50- to 100-million-year intervals, so we may expect such an impact with 10 percent probability during the next several million years.

The heart of future astronomical observations lies in space, where the Earth's atmosphere neither blurs nor absorbs radiation from celestial objects.

Space-Borne Astronomical Instruments

The heart of future astronomical observations lies in space, where the Earth's atmosphere neither blurs nor

Aided by sophisticated computer-assisted technology, scientists discovered extra-solar planets amidst the 250–400 billion stars in Earth's galaxy. (Dennis di Cicco/Corbis)

absorbs radiation from celestial objects. Since only visible light and radio waves penetrate to the Earth's surface, observation of the universe in the infrared, ultraviolet, X-ray, and gamma-ray portion of the spectrum requires that instruments be sent into orbit above the atmosphere. The Hubble Space Telescope (HST), launched in 1990, has provided important new observations in both visible light and ultraviolet radiation, especially since being fitted with a corrective optical system in 1993. Other satellites now observe the cosmos in types of radiation inaccessible to HST. The most significant new satellite should be the Advanced X-Ray Astrophysics Facility (AXAF), which may be launched by the end of this century. Ground-based telescopes, such as the giant Keck telescope in Hawaii, will remain of crucial importance in following up any discoveries made from space-borne observatories, since only they can provide large amounts of observing time for a particular project.

[See also Natural Disasters; Space Colonization; Space Satellites; Space Travel.]

BIBLIOGRAPHY

Barstusiak, Marcia. *Through a Universe Darkly.* New York: Harper-Collins, 1993.

Beatty, J. Kelly, and Chaikin, Andrew, eds. *The New Solar System,* 3rd ed. Cambridge, MA: Sky Publishing, 1990.

Field, George, and Chaisson, Eric. *The Invisible Universe.* Boston: Birkhäuser Books, 1985.

Goldsmith, Donald W. *The Astronomers.* New York: St. Martin's Press, 1991.

— DONALD W. GOLDSMITH

ATOMIC POWER.

See NUCLEAR POWER; NUCLEAR POWER: CON.

B

BATTERIES

Engineers are waging a worldwide race to improve battery technology used in electric-powered vehicles and consumer products. Advances since the early 1990s offer promise that battery-powered autos will be common before 2000, utility-scale uses of photovoltaic cells could be a reality by 2015, and improved fuel cells will reach the marketplace by 2025. Two movements drive the research: growing environmental concerns and an expanding array of miniaturized electronic devices, from cellular phones and laptop computers to "smart" credit cards. Until the 1990s, only nickel-cadmium batteries (nicads) were rechargeable, presenting an environmental problem because cadmium, a toxic heavy metal, can leach into groundwater when batteries are dumped in landfills. Most disposable batteries are alkaline; new models introduced in 1993 can be recharged 25 times, compared with up to 1,000 recharges for nicads.

Searching to make rechargeables more efficient and environmentally friendly, engineers are testing combinations of plastic-like polymers, carbon materials, and metal alloys. Japanese scientists recently developed two kinds of rechargeable batteries, the nickel metal-hydride and lithium ion, said to be more efficient than nicads. A third design, lithium-polymer batteries, may offer a greater energy output than the Japanese models. In the next decade, lithium polymer, nickel metal-hydride, and lithium ions could replace nickel cadmium in reusable-battery design. Improvements in nickel-zinc batteries, boosting their lifetime from less than 200 recharge cycles to 500 cycles, might make those models viable contenders in the marketplace.

Electric Vehicles

The battery industry's greatest challenge for the 1990s is to develop an efficient, economical battery for electric cars. Stringent clean-air regulations in California require incremental improvements in auto emissions. By 1998, 2 percent of new cars and light trucks that major manufacturers sell in California must emit zero exhaust emissions. The figure rises to 5 percent in 2001 and 10 percent in 2003. Several states have adopted California's air-pollution rules. Given existing technology, only battery-powered vehicles can achieve those standards, but high price tags and limited driving range (typically 80 to 200 miles between eight-hour charges) are major barriers.

Automakers, battery manufacturers, and entrepreneurial engineers around the world hope to develop low-cost batteries with high-energy density and fast recharging capability. Japanese automakers aim to put 200,000 electric vehicles on the road by 2000. Germany's Mercedes-Benz and Volkswagen have formed a joint venture to test sixty different electric prototypes with advanced batteries. Electric Fuel Ltd., based in Jerusalem, Israel, has developed a zinc-air battery that powers a small van 200 miles on a single charge, twice the range of most other batteries. Researchers at Clark University, in Worcester, Mass., are working on a battery with six times as much power per unit of weight as current lead-acid batteries used in experimental electric vehicles. Plans call for the battery to operate at room temperature and to use low-cost materials, sulfur and aluminum. The United States Advanced Battery Consortium, a cooperative program of the nation's Big Three automakers, partly funded by the U.S. Department of Energy, electric utilities, and battery manufacturers, leads U.S. efforts.

Photovoltaic solar-electric cells will power many portable electronic products, from cellular phones to "smart" credit cards with display screens.

Among various designs under consideration, engineers are looking at hybrid vehicle systems that combine features of electric and gasoline power. A hybrid vehicle uses an internal combustion engine to recharge a battery-powered electric drive system. In 1993, General Motors and Ford signed agreements with the Department of Energy to develop a hybrid vehicle within this decade.

Other university and national laboratories, including California's Lawrence Livermore National Laboratory and Tennessee's Oak Ridge National Laboratory have tested the use of flywheel-linked batteries in vehicles. The flywheel principle is based on kinetic energy, the energy of a moving object: When a force sets the heavy rim of a flywheel spinning, the wheel keeps rotating, making it a reservoir of energy. American Flywheel Systems (AFS), a Bellevue, Wash., company believes its patented device will power an electric car 350 miles on one charge and will recharge in 20 minutes. AFS and its technical partner, Honeywell, plan to build prototype batteries by 1995. Whatever their technology, electric vehicles will appear in auto showrooms in the mid to late 1990s and by 2000 could be a familiar sight on U.S. roads.

Fuel Cells

Many engineers believe the real hope for electric cars and other energy users lies in fuel cells. In the early 1990s scientists launched more than a dozen major experiments involving the use of fuel cells in vehicles.

Conventional batteries store energy and take hours to recharge; fuel cells produce energy and recharge in minutes. Like batteries, fuel cells create electricity through a chemical reaction, but they can generate electric current only as long as a stream of fuel and oxygen runs into the cells. Fuel cells do not create nitrogen oxide or sulfuric oxide, major contributors to urban smog. Their biggest drawback is cost: For fuel cells to be price competitive in autos, the cost of a fuel-cell kilowatt must be slashed from almost $10,000 to $50 ($35 per unit of horsepower). Once manufacturers mass-produce fuel cells, the cost should drop dramatically. Some forecasters predict that fuel cells will be a major source of electricity by 2000, with worldwide sales of $6 billion annually.

The public is most aware of fuel cells because of their use by astronauts. An alkaline potassium hydroxide fuel cell generates electricity in space shuttles. However, many scientists believe that phosphoric acid and solid-polymer fuel cells are more versatile. California's South Coast Air Quality Management District uses phosphoric acid fuel cells to generate current. Solid polymer fuel cells are starting to enter mainstream use; their first commercial applications may be in vehicles, in home cogeneration systems, and as substitutes for portable batteries.

Photovoltaic Cells

A battery-related technology, photovoltaic solar-electric cells, will come into wide use in the next decade. The

Current batteries available to power electric vehicles are too expensive and cannot last long enough to offer a viable alternative to most people. The escalation of premium gasoline prices has prompted the search for alternative energy sources. (Joseph Sohm; ChromoSohm Inc./Corbis)

price of these cells has fallen sharply since the 1960s, from $500 a watt to about $4. By the year 2000, they will power many portable electronic products, from cellular phones to "smart" credit cards with display screens. Photovoltaics' source of energy can be the sun or any low-level light. Environmental support is strong, since the cells are virtually pollution free. Because of initially high manufacturing costs, photovoltaic technology has looked mostly to rural customers for large-scale use. For "off-grid" users—homes not served by electric utilities—photovoltaic technology is economically competitive with conventional fuels. Thousands of remote towns around the world, particularly in Mexico, India, and Zimbabwe, rely on solar electrification systems. By 2000, photovoltaic energy could be highly competitive.

[*See also* Energy, Renewable Sources of; Hazardous Wastes; Motor Vehicles; Motor Vehicles, Alternatively Powered.]

BIBLIOGRAPHY

Krause, Reinhardt. "High Energy Batteries." *Popular Science* (February 1993).

McWhirter, William. "Off and Humming." *Time* (April 26, 1993).

Neff, Robert, and Coy, Peter. "The High Voltage Rivalry in Batteries." *Business Week* (February 15, 1993).

Spaid, Elizabeth Levitan. "Energy-Conscious Home Owners Begin to See the Light." *Christian Science Monitor*, October 12, 1993.

Wald, Matthew L. "Going Beyond Batteries to Power Electric Cars." *New York Times*, March 3, 1993.

———. "Imagining the Electric-Car Future." *New York Times*, April 28, 1993.

– JERRY KLINE

BEHAVIOR: SOCIAL CONSTRAINTS

We are at a pivotal juncture in our thinking about how societies guarantee appropriate social behavior. From many directions we are confronted with phenomena that appear to reflect the breakdown of social order—the loss of clear moral codes, growing violence, and deteriorating faith in traditional leadership in almost every sphere, from politics to parenting. Moreover, the customary response to loss of order—increasing the force of traditional controls—turns out to be at best ineffective and often makes matters worse.

Grasping the significance of this apparent impasse is among the most important issues of our time. Making our way in the times ahead will require new, dynamic, and mature ways of understanding and dealing with social order.

Historically, culture imposed social constraint by three means: the state—through laws, royal decrees, and official government acts; the church—through moral codes; and the community—through traditions, social mores, and norms. Throughout this century, the influence and potency of the first and second of these means have been diminishing markedly, and the effectiveness of the third has been severely challenged.

Few people today would describe themselves as having strong bonds in the community or would admit being strongly influenced by community traditions. While the church continues to be a significant force in many people's lives, it exercises considerably less control over the average person. The seven deadly sins—pride, greed, lust, envy, sloth, anger, and gluttony—have now for many been transformed into virtues. We live increasingly in an age of the individual. Individualism carried to extremes inevitably transgresses the rights of others living within the society. Striking a balance between the individual and society in general is not easy. If there is a prevailing moral code in this materialistic country, it is caveat emptor: let the buyer beware.

Of the three traditional means of social constraint, we are left to rely primarily on what is the most institutionalized, and thus best organized, to deal with a social structure defined primarily by the rights of individuals—government and the strong arm of the law. But here we encounter problems as well. A society defined by competition and legalistic rules tends to become more and more litigious and increasingly dependent on police and prisons to keep order. The outcome is governments, courts, police, and prison systems overburdened with issues or people they were not designed to handle. The resulting morass has caused these institutions to be viewed with diminishing respect, thereby impairing their ability to get the job done.

Do these trends reflect a fundamental erosion of our social fabric? This may be, but the evidence suggests that the disorder we witness is more that of transition than of disintegration. If we ignore or run away from the challenges that this disorder represents, destruction is a possible outcome.

The disorder itself may reflect important new possibilities for defining and achieving social coherence. To grasp what is being asked, we might start by looking at several areas where the loss of traditional behavioral codes affects us in particularly poignant ways.

Love is one such area. Not too long ago, we had highly reliable rules of appropriate behavior for love. Society provided us with clear gender roles and codes for how we should behave if we were just friends, dating, engaged, or married. Gender roles are increasingly being challenged and with them established assumptions about the forms that love should appropriately assume.

Many people, appropriately concerned about the breakdown of families, would argue that this is an erosion of social order. But one can argue as well that these new uncertainties reflect first tentative steps toward a new maturity in love, and a new depth and maturity in how we conceive family bonds. Surrendering gender roles moves us beyond the reality of man and woman as two predetermined puzzle parts that come together to find their "better halves" and toward the task of loving as unique, whole people. Succeeding at such a task is not easy; it requires giving up many familiar assumptions. But it offers the possibility of love that more completely embraces all we are capable of being.

Our laws will be effective only to the degree

that they are grounded in a new and deepened sense

of human community.

We can discover a similar dynamic in almost all situations that confront us with new cultural uncertainties. The primary determinant of a healthy future on the international scene will be the degree to which we can move beyond needing the clear rules of a world defined by allies on one side and enemies on the other. One could call this a "messier" world—it certainly gets confusing and complicated if we hold to tactics of the past. But, in fact, the challenge is simply to see other of the world's people more fully for who they are. This is not easy. We must think and respond much more creatively and maturely, see and act from a bigger picture.

Most of the critical emerging social challenges require at least two kinds of social evolution. First, the critical challenges ahead require a willingness to step forward without externally defined, concretely articulated moral, legal, or scientific codes to guide us. This reflects how dynamic and creative—and interesting—reality has become. As Nietzsche said, for the truth of the future, "there is no immaculate perception."

Second, these challenges require that we find a new appreciation for our relatedness—at all levels, from family, to neighborhood, to workplace, to region, and planet. Few of the important challenges ahead are amenable to purely legalistic or institutional solutions. Our laws will be effective only to the degree that they are grounded in a new and deepened sense of human community.

In the past, culture has been like a parent, providing us with well-defined bonds of affiliation and clear codes of right and wrong to guide our actions. The critical questions ahead require a new kind of human maturity. They require that we bring a new consciousness and initiative to our bonds of affiliation, and they ask that we accept new responsibility at all levels in life's deci-

sions—not just in the uncertainties of our personal lives, but as well in the life of our culture. This does not mean playing God, but it does mean accepting that many of the questions ahead have godlike importance and godlike consequences—and appreciating that these awesome decisions are in our hands.

[See also Divorce; Ethics; Evolution, Social; Family Patterns; Family Values; Marriage; Morals; Sexual Behavior; Sexual Codes; Sexual Laws; Social Change: United States; Social Controls; Values; Values Change; Values Formation; Women's Movement.]

BIBLIOGRAPHY

Bellah, Robert. *The Good Society.* New York: Random House, 1992.

Etzioni, Amitai. *The Spirit of Community: Rights, Responsibilities, and the Communitarian Agenda.* New York: Crown, 1993.

Johnston, Charles M. *Necessary Wisdom: Meeting the Challenge of a New Cultural Maturity.* Berkeley, CA: Celestial Arts, 1991.

Kopp, Sheldon. *An End to Innocence.* New York: Bantam, 1978.

Lappé, Frances Moore. *Rediscovering America's Values.* New York: Ballantine, 1989.

– CHARLES M. JOHNSTON

BELL, DANIEL (1919–)

The American sociologist and futurist Daniel Bell is the son of Polish Jewish immigrants. Bell has taught sociology at several major universities, including Chicago, Columbia, and Harvard, and had an early career in journalism and policy analysis. His first major work, *The End of Ideology* (1960), was an examination of the fading of Marxism in American intellectual life and the rise of a new postideological generation for whom the radical passions of the 1930s were no longer relevant. Chairing the Commission on the Year 2000, he edited its celebrated report, *Toward the Year 2000: Work in Progress* (1968). In *The Coming of Post-Industrial Society: A Venture in Social Forecasting* (1973), he anticipated a near-future America in which the great majority of workers find employment in the professions and services. The principal source of wealth, he argues, will be information, grounded in the empirical sciences. Bell has revisited and fine-tuned his prognosis of a "post-industrial" society in his 1987 *Daedalus* article "The World and the United States in 2013." Another book, *The Cultural Contradictions of Capitalism* (1976), follows his study of the disintegration of ideology with a plea for the renewal of religious faith.

[See also Commission on the Year 2000; Futurists.]

BIBLIOGRAPHY

Brick, Howard. *Daniel Bell and the Decline of Intellectual Radicalism.* Madison, WI: University of Wisconsin Press, 1986.

Coates, Joseph F., and Jarrett, Jennifer. *What Futurists Believe*. Mt. Airy, MD: Lomond, 1989, chapter 7.

Liebowitz, Nathan. *Daniel Bell and the Agony of Modern Liberalism*. Westport, CT: Greenwood Press, 1985.

— W. WARREN WAGAR

BICYCLING.

See PERSONAL TRANSPORT.

BIODIVERSITY

Biodiversity is the variety and variability of life—the sum of genes, species, and ecosystems existing in a region. It is extraordinary how little we know about the diversity of life on Earth. Only a decade ago, the best estimate was that about 3 million species coexist on our planet. Since then, an almost unimaginable array of living things has been uncovered. Tropical forests are now thought to be home to millions of undescribed species, and the deep sea floor may host hundreds of thousands, if not millions, more. Even soil samples from around the world are revealing a previously unsuspected variety of life. Estimates of the number of species on Earth now range from 10 million to 100 million, with a mere 1.4 million described and catalogued so far.

Scientists estimate that the Earth's biotic wealth stood at an all-time high when the first human beings appeared. Now it is fast declining, as a result of human activities. Around the world, habitats are being rapidly destroyed. Species are now dying out as fast as at any time since the mass extinction at the end of the Cretaceous period some 65 million years ago.

Tropical forests are home to more than half of the Earth's species, and tropical deforestation is the crucible of today's extinction crisis. About 17 million hectares of tropical forests are cleared annually. Recent estimates of this threat to biodiversity, assuming that deforestation continues at current rates, conclude that at least 5 to 10 percent of tropical forest species will either die out over the next thirty years or be reduced to such small populations that extinction will become a foregone conclusion.

Tropical species are by no means the only ones at risk. Worldwide, the temperate-zone rain forest has shrunk as much as the tropical forest. Other habitats such as wetlands and mangroves, U.S. tall grass prairies, and Central America's dry forests also have been reduced to mere remnants. Some 633 species are listed as being in danger of extinction in the United States alone, and more than 3,000 other species have been proposed for addition to this list. In the past several hundred years, at least 80 species—and possibly as many as 290—have become extinct in the continental United States and Hawaii. Worldwide, more than 700 extinctions of vertebrates, invertebrates, and vascular plants have been recorded since 1600.

Why do these losses matter? The ethical case for preserving biodiversity argues that every form of life is unique and warrants humanity's respect and that people now living have a moral responsibility to future generations to pass on the Earth's store of biotic richness undiminished from that which their forebears inherited. Many of the world's religions teach respect for life's diversity and exhort believers to conserve it. In India, certain societies established spirit sanctuaries—natural areas protected from human disturbance. In the Philippines, farmers still maintain traditional rice varieties for ceremonial occasions. In the United States, ethical, aesthetic, and scientific concerns—not economic considerations—spurred passage of the Endangered Species Act in 1973.

People now living have a moral responsibility to future generations to pass on the Earth's store of biotic richness undiminished.

Biodiversity also is important because it serves as a source of economic benefits and as a reservoir of genetic variety. Humanity derives all its food and many of its medicines and industrial products from both wild and domesticated species. Economic benefits from wild species alone make up an estimated 4.5 percent of the U.S. gross domestic product. Indeed, wild species are dietary mainstays in much of the world. Fisheries, largely composed of wild species, contributed about 100 million tons of food worldwide in 1989. Biotic resources also serve human needs for recreation. Worldwide, nature tourism—a boom that has barely begun—already generates as much as $12 billion in revenues each year.

Formerly, nearly all medicines came from plants and animals, and even today they remain vital. Traditional medicine is the basis of primary health care for about 80 percent of people in developing countries, more than 3 billion people in all. More than 5,100 species are used in Chinese medicine alone, and people in northwestern Amazonia have tapped some 2,000 species for medicinal purposes.

As for modern pharmaceuticals, one fourth of all prescription drugs dispensed in the United States contain active ingredients extracted from plants. Over 3,000 antibiotics—including penicillin and tetracycline—are derived from microorganisms. Cyclosporin, developed from a soil fungus, revolutionized heart and kidney transplant surgery by suppressing the body's immune reaction. Aspirin (acetylsalicylic acid) and many other drugs that now are synthesized in factories were first discovered in nature. Compounds extracted from plants, microbes, and animals were involved in developing all of the twenty bestselling medicines in the United States, drugs whose combined sales approached $6 billion in 1988.

The stock of genetic variations within each species is another vital element of biodiversity—and new technologies are multiplying its value. Genetic engineering made it possible to use genes from wild relatives of domesticated plants and animals to fuel such agricultural advances as modern high-yield crops and livestock. In the United States, plant breeders' use of diverse genes accounted for at least half of the doubling in yields of rice, barley, soybeans, wheat, cotton, and sugarcane between 1930 and 1980—and for tripling tomato yields and quadrupling corn, sorghum, and potato yields. Genetic diversity is needed to maintain crop yields in the face of rapidly evolving pests and diseases. Furthermore, it may prove crucial to maintaining species themselves if the worst global warming forecasts are borne out.

Today, biotechnology is opening another frontier in the exploration of biodiversity. Genetic engineering transforms the world's biota into raw material for the biotech industry. Other new technologies have sparked a resurgence in pharmaceutical companies' screening of wild species as sources of new drugs. Designing drugs from scratch has proved difficult and costly, and cures for diseases such as cancer and AIDS have eluded scientists. Nature provides a veritable storehouse of chemicals with potential medicinal uses. Of the 3,500 new chemical structures discovered worldwide in 1985, some 2,619 were isolated from plants.

It is crucial to preserve the natural wealth upon which so much of human enterprise is built. Even from an economic standpoint alone, there are benefits to maintaining biodiversity. Biodiversity provides an indispensible undergirding for future advances in agriculture, medicine, and industry that far outweigh the short-term monetary benefits obtained from cutting a forest or filling a wetland. We expose ourselves to incalculable risks by threatening the extinction of species whose role in ecosystems is not yet understood, and also future generations are robbed of the benefits that otherwise might be reaped from Earth's biotic storehouse.

For all these reasons, it is auspicious that 156 nations signed the biodiversity treaty at the 1992 Earth Summit in Rio de Janeiro. If nations now begin working together to preserve species, genes, and ecosystems around the world, this decade could mark a turning point in humanity's long history of interaction with Earth's other inhabitants.

[See also Deforestation; Environmental Behavior; Environmental Ethics; Evolution, Biological; Extinction of Species; Forestry; Genetics: Agricultural Applications; Global Warming; Green Revolution; Life Sciences.]

BIBLIOGRAPHY

Noss, Reed F. and Cooperrider, Allen. *Saving Nature's Legacy: Protecting and Restoring Biodiversity.* Washington, DC: Island Press, 1994.

Reid, Walter V., et al. *Biodiversity Prospecting: Using Genetic Resources for Sustainable Development.* Washington, DC: World Resources Institute, 1993.

Szaro, Robert, and Johnston, David W., eds. *Biodiversity in Managed Landscapes.* Oxford, UK: Oxford University Press, 1995.

Wilson, Edward O. *The Diversity of Life.* New York: W. W. Norton, 1993.

World Resources Institute, World Conservation Union (IUCN), United Nations Environment Program. *Global Biodiversity Strategy.* Washington, DC: WRI, IUCN, UNEP, 1992.

– WALTER V. REID
KENTON R. MILLER

BIOETHICS

Although the world abounds with diverse life-forms, people's awareness of the bonds linking humans and other species has been slow to develop. The concept of ecological systems did not gain widespread acceptance until the final decades of the twentieth century. By 1970 the public was aware of environmental deterioration. Danger signs were evident—more and more endangered species disappearing, chemical pollutants poisoning the planet, and new technologies posing ominous risks to living organisms. At last, large numbers of people realized that pioneer ecologist George Perkins Marsh (1801–1882) had been correct when he warned that human efforts directed at "improving" nature's ecosystems possibly might lead instead to the systems' degradation.

Out of this anxiety came *bioethics*—attempts to define modes of responsible human behavior capable of preserving the fragile ecosystems humans share with other species.

Bioethics and the New Genetics

With the advent of molecular genetics in the 1970s, bioethicists were challenged with questions concerning the environmental impact of the new plant and animal genetics. For example: In view of science's emerging capability to transform existing life-forms and also create new ones, is it possible to determine in advance which genetic engineering experiments will lead to beneficial results and which might bring on an environmental catastrophe? How can science justify introducing into the environment novel organisms that might trigger irreversible ecological changes?

Social and economic concerns were voiced as well. Among the questions asked were: Why impose onerous restrictions on biological engineering in agriculture when it can substantially increase the world's food supply? What will be the social costs of high-tech farming systems replacing the family farm and privatized biological research taking the place of public, nonprofit research? And will the Third World be able to progress if farmers there are unable to pay patent holders for the right to raise genetically improved crops and livestock?

Ethical issues of biotechnology are still being debated. Of crucial importance are (1) the maintenance of genetic diversity and (2) science's overall competence: i.e., its ability to foresee and surmount a multitude of problems that will come about as human intervention in the realm of nature becomes more extensive and pervasive. In a world that appears to be undergoing biological transformation, concerned persons are insisting that the agenda of the new genetics should include appraisal of environmental risks and planning to avoid social dislocations.

Patents of Living Organisms

Genetically engineered microorganisms may be patented, the U.S. Supreme Court ruled in the *Diamond v. Chakrababarty* case in 1980. This was a landmark decision, opening the way for patent protection to be extended to genetically altered plants, animals, and various types of living matter, including human and nonhuman cells.

In the years ahead, new biological creations

may take the places of traditional farm animals.

Once the patentability of new organisms had been established, biotechnology firms intensified their development of potentially profitable materials, seeking to maximize returns on each product. This means that seed of a new plant variety—herbicide-resistant corn, for example, or drought-tolerant millet—will be marketed to large numbers of farmers. When one plant variety is grown extensively, the appearance of a new strain of virus or fungus may result in crop failure over huge acreages. Plant diseases are less likely to reach epidemic proportions when farmers grow numerous crop varieties representing a wide range of genetic backgrounds. One of biotechnology's more serious defects may be its tendency to restrict genetic diversity in some situations.

Patenting of animals has been allowed since 1987, when the U.S. Patent Office decided biological inventions merit the same protection as mechanical inventions. In 1988, a patent was issued for the "Harvard Mouse," a genetically altered animal used in cancer research. So-called transgenic animals are useful as disease models and as sources of biologically important drugs and pharmaceuticals. In the years ahead, new biological creations may take the places of traditional farm animals. Animal welfare may become a troublesome issue, since animals are likely to be considered merely units of production on factory farms of the future.

Release of Altered Organisms

In genetic engineering's early years, American researchers were not permitted to release genetically altered organisms into the environment. Possible damage to public health and the environment, it was felt, outweighed the researchers' need for field testing. In 1978, the National Institutes of Health relaxed the rules and permitted field tests under closely regulated conditions. Two tests were conducted of a bacterium that prevents frost damage in field crops. A scheduled third test drew protests from environmentalists, and a court order issued in 1984 halted the test. Subsequently, tests of the "ice-minus" bacterium have been resumed, with no harmful results observed.

Due to intense international competition in the biotechnology industry, restrictions limiting field tests of genetically altered organisms in America and Germany have been opposed by biotech firms in the two countries. Field testing is now taking place in both nations, and restrictions may be eased further in the future. No one can say for certain that field testing will never cause serious health or environmental problems, but the biotech industry's record to date has been excellent.

Biotechnology and the Environment

Commercial-scale introduction of genetically modified organisms could result in environmental nightmares. Super-weeds might come into existence if special genes in herbicide-resistant crops were transmitted to wild species. Unexpectedly, bacteria that are benign and helpful could mutate and endanger the health of animals and humans. Although genetic engineering offers many worthwhile benefits, the possible dangers should not be overlooked. Careful monitoring of the environment will be needed in order to identify problems before they become uncorrectable.

In a positive, clear-eyed approach to biological engineering, possible environmental dangers would be taken into account as policy-makers decided which research and development areas of the new genetics should be given top priority. It would seem desirable to modify plants so that their new characteristics would enrich the environment. Instead of inviting erosion by planting annual crops, we might develop deep-rooted perennial grain crops that could protect the soil from water and wind. If we had crops that grew well on brackish soil, we could reclaim vast areas of wasteland.

Conversely, it does not seem reasonable to "improve" crops in ways that might jeopardize the environment. Genetically altered crops that are highly productive only if sustained by doses of commercial fertilizer, herbicides, and other chemicals may be poorly engineered for a system of agriculture that aspires to be sustainable and responsive to the needs of the environment. How biotechnology shapes the future will be determined by the people who set the early goals for biotechnology's development.

[See also Animal Rights; Artificial Life; Environmental Behavior; Environmental Ethics; Ethics; Genetic Engineering; Genetics; Sexual Reproduction: Artificial Means.]

BIBLIOGRAPHY

Caldwell, Lynton Keith. *Biocracy: Public Policy and the Life Sciences.* Boulder, CO, and London: Westview Press, 1987.

Gendel, Steven M.; Kline, A. David; Warren, D. Michael; and Yates, Faye, eds. *Agricultural Bioethics: Implications of Agricultural Biotechnology.* Ames, IA: Iowa State University Press, 1990.

Lesser, William H., ed. *Animal Patents: The Legal, Economic and Social Issues.* New York: Stockton Press, 1989.

Regan, Tom. *All That Dwell Therein: Animal Rights and Environmental Ethics.* Berkeley, CA: University of California Press, 1982.

Rodd, Rosemary. *Biology, Ethics, and Animals.* New York: Oxford University Press, 1990.

           — CLIFTON E. ANDERSON

BOOKS.

See LITERATURE; PRINTED WORD.

BREAKTHROUGHS, SCIENTIFIC.

See SCIENTIFIC BREAKTHROUGHS.

BROADCASTING

Radio and television broadcasting ushered in the age of electronic information and entertainment beginning in the 1920s. Generations of Americans have grown up with the convenience and familiarity of broadcasting in the twentieth century. Virtually everyone watches television or listens to radio sometime during the week, a pattern that is likely to continue far into the future.

Americans are served by over 1,000 television stations and more than 11,000 radio stations, the highest per capita rate of any major country in the world. There are more households with radio (5.6 sets on average) and television receivers (98 percent penetration with 69 percent having more than one set) than with telephones or running water. The average U.S. household receives 13.3 television stations over the air. This increases to a total 39.4 channels receivable when cable is included. On average, people (two years and older) watch over thirty-five hours of television each week. More than two dozen radio stations are available to the average American, and in bigger markets (or with rooftop antennas) this rises to over eighty radio stations receivable off the air. The average person (twelve years and older) listens to over twenty-three hours of radio programming each week.

Using both wired (telephone or cable) and wireless (spectrum allocations) approaches, new services will allow home viewers to enjoy electronic shopping, information retrieval, interactive games, and computer-based learning.

The first Golden Age of Broadcasting began in mid-century when Americans overwhelmingly adopted radio and television listening and viewing into their lifestyles. The U.S. model of commercially supported, free over-the-air broadcasting is immensely popular and has a sound economic basis. Toward the end of the twentieth century, this model began to be widely imitated around the world with much success. Unlike the United States, much of the rest of the world is dependent upon government sponsored and operated broadcasting, which provides fewer choices and insufficient amounts of popular programming. In many cases, advertising is limited or not allowed, which limits economic growth in many sectors.

From Analog to Digital

In the next Golden Age, we will do more with our radios and television sets than just watch and listen. The radio and television systems we rely on are evolving from analog to computer-based digital electronics that is dramatically changing what broadcasting can do. We will interact, transact, exchange data, personalize, customize, and integrate our media environments. The seeds of the next Golden Age are already being planted. The far-reaching impacts of computer-based digital signal processing and compression techniques are changing assumptions about what is possible in all electronic media. The once comfortable technological policy, and economic barriers keeping industries apart are breaking down and forcing society to change as a result.

Multimedia Convergence

Under the banner of "multimedia convergence" a number of previously distinct industries are banding together in various strategic alliances, partnerships, joint ventures, mergers, and acquisitions. The rush to convergence has blurred the lines between the traditional broadcast, cable, telephone, and consumer electronics industries as each segment considers ways to not only joint venture but also to compete with each other in their traditional product-service marketplaces.

For example, telephone companies are exploring relationships with cable television and programming companies to examine ways to offer audio and video entertainment services. Cable television companies, for their part, are considering what it would take to offer competitive telephony services over their facilities. Broadcasters are exploring new opportunities with digital transmission facilities, including multimedia, interactive, and data broadcasting. Video game and CD-ROM companies are trying new means of distributing their services via broadcast, telephone, and cable systems.

The key elements of the convergence marketplace are *content, distribution,* and *processing.* From the consumers' perspective, any system or combination of systems that improves *control, choice,* and *convenience* is likely to be something they will adopt more readily. For convergence to work in the marketplace, consumers must have confidence that the different systems being offered to them by cable, telephone, broadcast, consumer electronics, and other companies can be hooked up and work together. This connectivity of systems requires standards to guarantee fully compatible interoperability. Technical standards facilitating such integration will have to be set, either by industry or by the government.

What Lies in the Future

TELEVISION. New technology-enabled advances in television permit wider and higher resolution pictures with CD-quality sound, interactivity, multiple services in the same channel, and computer data services. These technologies also provide a platform for television broadcasters to enter the age of digital data systems. All television sets (13 inches or larger) manufactured for sale in the United States since 1993 have the ability to decode closed captioning. Typically, these sets also have the ability to decode and display other kinds of information such as basic programming information (title, length, type of program), and programming guides to better serve viewers.

Interactive broadcast television companies are bringing an entirely new range of services to viewers. Using

Broadcasting via radio and television, such as from this Berlin tower, powerfully shaped the twentieth century and will continue to have a large influence into the next century. (Dave Bartruff/Corbis)

both wired (telephone or cable) and wireless (spectrum allocations) approaches, new services will allow home viewers to enjoy electronic shopping, information retrieval, interactive games, and computer-based learning. Because of more efficient utilization of the available broadcast spectrum, all these services will be offered *in addition* to the conventional television program service to which viewers have become so accustomed.

RADIO. While television often grabs the headlines and consumer attention, broadcast radio services are also undergoing rapid change due to technological advances. From basic improvements to the receivers of both AM and FM broadcast services, to data broadcast and interactive services, radio is rapidly forging its own way into the new multimedia convergence landscape.

For example, by adding a printer interface to a radio, if a listener hears something advertised that is interesting, he or she could simply push a button on the receiver to print out a coupon. Navigational information can be broadcast in part of the radio signal to augment the global positioning satellite (GPS) service many travelers use for orientation. Radio broadcasters are now planning to move from delivering an analog signal to a newer digitally formatted signal with compact disc (CD) quality to listeners. Other radio advances will combine text and graphics with audio for a multimediabased set of services for listeners. As with television advances, these radio advanced services will be in addition to traditional services.

The Next Golden Age

Radio and television broadcasting introduced generations of Americans to electronic media systems with greater success and popularity than any other system to date. As we enter the second century of electronic and computer-based media systems, broadcasters expect to once again be at the forefront of innovation. Broadcasters will be able to flexibly offer multiple and interactive services. This may well be the next Golden Age of Broadcasting.

> [See also Advertising; Communications; Communications: Media Law; Communications: Privacy Issues; Communications Technology; Digital Communications; Electronic Convergence; Electronic Publishing; Information Overload; Information Society; Media Consolidation; Satellite Communications; Telephones; Television.]

BIBLIOGRAPHY

DeSonne, Marcia, ed. *Advanced Broadcast/Media Technologies.* Washington, DC: National Association of Broadcasters, 1992.
———. *Convergence: The Transition to the Electronic Superhighway.* Washington, DC: National Association of Broadcasters, 1994.
Ditingo, Vincent. *The Remaking of Radio.* Boston: Focal Press, 1995.
Doyle, Marc. *The Future of Television.* Lincolnwood, IL: N & C Business Books, 1992.
Giller, George. *Life After Television.* New York: W. W. Norton, 1994.
Jankowski, Gene F., and Fuchs, David C. *Television Today and Tomorrow.* New York: Oxford University Press, 1995.

— EDWARD O. FRITTS

BUSINESS GOVERNANCE

Business grovernance relates to who shall govern a corporation—the owner/share holders, management (directors and senior executives), or other stakeholders—and for what purpose?

In proprietorships and closely held corporations, the owners answer these questions as they wish, so long as they comply with existing law. However, in large publicly held corporations, these questions are complicated by corporate law strictures that separate stock ownership from business management. This arrangement permits a runaway management technocracy in many large publicly held corporations to control director nominations to their boards. Rubber-stamp control enables them to follow their own goals and to escape accountability to individual shareowners, whose holdings are too small to impact on board elections. This situation helped spark the merger and takeover frenzy of the 1980s, when outside investors decided they could manage the corporate assets to better the reward to stockholders.

Since the 1930s, a debate has raged between those who argue that management holds corporate powers in trust for shareholders only and others who hold that these powers are held in trust for society. In more recent times, the terms have changed, but not the concepts: Management holds corporate powers in trust to "maximize shareholder value" (Rappaport, 1986, pp. 1ff.); or, the powers are held in trust to balance or "to optimize the interests of its stakeholders," for example, customers, employees, shareholders, the public. (Ewing, 1987, p. 32).

The question of business governance is further complicated in the industrialized world during the last half of the twentieth century by the concentration of ownership of large corporations in a small number of institutions. The proportion of stock ownership in the United States held by institutional investors grew from 20 percent in 1970 to over 50 percent in the early 1990s. (These institutions, dominated by pension funds, hold about an equal amount of the debt of the largest American corporations.) This concentration of ownership will increase as pension funds grow and individual share ownership decreases. Britain has seen a similar trend.

In Germany, 60 percent of the share capital of large companies is controlled by the three major banks. These holdings are either direct or managed holdings of their customers that the banks vote upon.

In Japan, ownership of large companies is concentrated in the members of a small number of industrial groups, the *keiretsu.* In *keiretsu,* 20 percent to 30 percent of the share capital of member companies is owned by other members, the group's bank and trading company. Estimates of the country-wide concentration of stock ownership of the largest corporations in a small number of *keiretsu* and financial institutions range from 50 percent (Drucker, 1992, p. 236), to 66 percent (Kester, 1991, pp. 57–58).

Japanese and German banks and financial institutions are not only shareholders in their companies but also direct business partners with them. Thus, they are long-term investors in the corporations that they help govern directly through board memberships or indirectly through group affiliations. In these two countries, governance in the long-term interests of owners and society through a loose affiliation with government and labor is not at present a problem. Whether these tight relationships can survive in the world marketplace of the twenty-first century remains to be seen.

Institutional investors in the United States historically have played a passive role in corporate governance, selling their stock when they could no longer vote their proxies in favor of management. However, a more active role in the matter of corporate governance is being assumed.

A move is underway to give the board chairmanship to a full-time outside director and to relegate the senior corporate officer to the position of president and chief executive officer.

Large state and municipal pension funds are becoming active in influencing board member selection, corporate policies, executive compensation, and accountability. Some critics who support corporate governance reform oppose efforts to mandate changes by government. They believe the "marketplace"—the investors—should bring about the changes through existing channels. Others are critical of large pension-fund managers taking a more active role in controlling corporate management. These fund managers can make their decisions without conferring with the individuals who own the stocks held by the funds. Institutional investors respond that they have the resources to consult with the best minds in the country and to find the best business managers in the country, if needed.

Thus, in the 1990s a major shift occurred in business governance as the pendulum began to swing away from the concept that corporate managers hold their powers in trust for the balanced benefit of stakeholders to the concept that the powers are held in trust only to maximize profits. Institutional investors, as they marshall their power to make boards and corporate executives more accountable to shareholders, will benefit individual as well as institutional shareholders. Major pension funds already have forced several corporations to take the power of nominating future directors away from corporate CEOs and place it in the hands of outside (nonemployee) directors.

Although not in place yet, the following changes are possibly—in some cases likely—to be adopted over time as the large pension funds and other institutional investors assert their voting power:

Professional Directors

As institutional investors seek to improve investment performance, they will recruit full-time professional directors, professionals who will be independent of the management but accountable to shareholders. A full-time director might serve on five or more major corporate boards, review strategic plans, debate policies, and monitor management to assure compliance. Full-time directors will be recruited from major accounting firms, business school faculties, successful management consulting firms, mid-career marketing and financial executive ranks, and so forth.

Stakeholder Directors

Many corporations already have outside directors representing minorities, women, and employees. Calls for "public directors" representing local communities, the public in general, and other interests are underway. Calls to elect directors representing the corporate customers surface periodically.

Separation of Chairmanship from CEO Position

A move is underway to reserve the board chairmanship to a full-time outside director and to relegate the senior corporate officer to the position of president and chief executive officer. The chairman's duties would relate to board leadership and strategic management. Allegiance would be to the board and corporate shareholders. The president would report to the entire board, not just to the chairman, and would be responsible for the day-to-day management of the corporation. Under this approach, the board, not the CEO, would prepare all annual reports and control all communications to shareholders. Also, outside directors would nominate and pick new CEOs, with counsel from the retiring CEO.

Restriction of Inside Directors

To strengthen shareholder governance, inside directors would be limited to the president (CEO), the chief operating officer (COO), and the chief financial officer (CFO). Another approach restricts inside directorship to the CEO only, since all other officer expertise is on call at the will of the board.

Management theorist Peter F. Drucker believes that boards and corporate executives hold their powers in trust to "maximize the wealth-producing capacity of the enterprise" (Drucker, 1992, p. 32). He argues that this objective integrates short- and long-term results, business performance and the satisfactions of the stakeholder constituencies. It is possible that current trends in business governance will develop a new social contract between corporations and society as businesses strive to achieve Drucker's objective.

[See also Business Structure: Forms, Impacts; Business Structure: Industrial Policy; Democratic Process; Governance; Social Democracy.]

BIBLIOGRAPHY

Berle, Adolf A., and Means, Gardiner C. *The Modern Corporation and Private Property*, rev. ed. New York: Harcourt, Brace & World, 1968.

Caywood, Clarke L., and Ewing, Raymond P. *The Handbook of Communications in Corporate Restructuring and Takeovers*. Englewood Cliffs, NJ: Prentice Hall, 1992.

Drucker, Peter F. *Managing for the Future: The 1990s and Beyond*. New York: Truman Talley Books/Dutton, 1992.

Ewing, Raymond P. *Managing the New Bottom Line: Issues Management for Senior Executives*. Homewood, IL: Dow Jones-Irwin, 1987.

Kester, W. Carl. *Japanese Takeovers: The Global Contest for Corporate Control*. Boston: Harvard Business School Press, 1991.

Rappaport, Alfred. *Creating Shareholder Value: The New Standard for Business Performance*. New York: Free Press, 1986.

— RAYMOND P. EWING

BUSINESS STRUCTURE: FORMS, IMPACTS

In a democratic society, all institutions exist at the sufferance of the public. As long as they enjoy the consent of the public, they will continue to exist. If that consent were to be withdrawn, no institution could survive. This is the social contract. It is a contract that one party, the public, can decide by itself to continue or discontinue.

It is clear, more so now than ever before, that the institution of business enjoys a high watermark of public consent. Following the virtual collapse of Marxist economics at the end of the 1980s, market-based economics reign supreme. Even in countries with little or no tradition of private enterprise, business is increasingly seen as the means to general prosperity and public well-being.

It would appear, therefore, that what some are calling "the coming golden age" for business may well come about. But keeping in mind the revocable nature of the social contract, consent has to be earned every day. In the context of rising public expectations, a heightened sense of entitlement, and growing competition, this would be a dangerous time for business to become complacent.

There are two broad categories of business structure—one is the legal entity, and the other is the operational form. Examples of the former are the corporation, partnership, sole proprietorship, and so on. The second category is based on how the business organizes itself to perform its functions—what we call the organization chart. This includes the various departments that are set up (e.g., marketing, human resources, and the like) and their positions in the hierarchy.

Both categories are undergoing intense examination as business tries to discover how best to move into the future. The corporate form flowered in the nineteenth century, when businesses grew large and the need for capital exceeded the ability of owning individuals or families to provide. The corporate form, with its limits on individual liability, enabled the twentieth-century shift from owner-run businesses to management-run businesses.

However, that shift, from owners to managers, resulted in what many observers feel is a flaw, particularly in American business: an overwhelming emphasis on short-term profitability rather than long-term viability. In 1992, a private study group, the Council on Competitiveness, chaired by Professor Michael Porter of the Harvard Business School, said that changes intended to encourage a longer-term focus were urgently required if U.S. business was to remain competitive.

In addition, the limits on individual liability are seen as cushioning managers against accountability. As the public increasingly wants to hold leaders of all institutions accountable, this legal protection may not be in the best interests of society. Recent court decisions in the United States that allocate individual responsibility to corporate officers seem to indicate that a fundamental change is occurring in some legal aspects of incorporation.

Unincorporated businesses are those in which the company is, in effect, an extension of the individual owner or owners. Consequently, for most such forms of business there are no limits on liability. The increase in litigiousness means that this individual vulnerability is much greater than it used to be. Law firms, accounting firms, and other personal-service partnerships have become victims of what *The Wall Street Journal* has called "the perils of partnership" (Berton and Lublin, 1992). As a result of lawsuits and often huge liability judgments, many personal-service partnerships are shifting to the corporate form—a change that seems likely to continue as long as the liability and malpractice suit trend prevails. As one leader in the accounting field said, "The partnership may go the way of the dodo." However, critics of the shift say that individual liability is necessary because it enhances client confidence in the integrity of professional service.

The sole proprietorship, the legal form for most small businesses, seems likely to be the one form of business booming in coming years. The restructuring that occurred in large businesses in recent years resulted in the elimination of many managerial positions. Many of the people whose jobs were eliminated went into business for themselves, most often as sole proprietors. In response to this development, governments in many countries are increasingly encouraging the formation of such small businesses.

It is in the second category of business structure, functional structure, that the most profound changes are occurring. These changes will create business organizations vastly different from those we have known in the past.

The restructuring mentioned earlier may prove to be as revolutionary in its results as was the onset of mass production. It represents a shift from structure to function—that is, concern about providing a product or service profitably and effectively supersedes concern about the structure out of which that product or service comes. The past emphasis on structure meant that *efficiency* was the paramount objective. The present and future emphasis on process shifts the focus to *effectiveness*. The difference, as someone once said, is that efficiency means doing things right, while effectiveness means doing the right things.

Two major trends will continue to contribute to and accelerate this development. One is the extraordinary impact of communications and information technologies. American business spent almost $1 trillion on these technologies during the 1980s. In the years ahead, that immense investment will pay off in greatly increased productivity. That increase will come largely from doing more things better, with fewer people—particularly with fewer highly paid people.

One way this will be manifested is in what has been called the "framework organization" (Brown and Weller, 1984). Large companies will operate with a permanent cadre whose skill is in knowing what each particular venture will require and how to meet those requirements. They will know how to get the job done rather than how to do it. They will add people or ally with other organizations to get a particular job done, and they will disengage when that job is done.

The second driving force is competition. In the new world economic order, *competition* is the key word, and competitiveness is the key to national economic well-being. Intensified competition means that businesses have to be both more efficient and more effective to get

and keep customers. One way to do that, obviously, is by keeping labor costs and overhead down.

These trends also contribute to another development that will be a characteristic of business in the future: the nomadic organization. Businesses whose primary assets are intellectual—that is, the minds of their people and the information they have—are not tied down to a place. They can easily (and profitably) move to be closer to their markets and/or cheaper labor or to respond to government pressures or incentives.

What seems increasingly likely is that the new business organization will be flexible rather than rigid, able to respond quickly to change, and pragmatic to the utmost.

[See also Business Governance; Business Structure: Industrial Policy; Capitalism; Global Business: Dominant Organizational Forms.]

BIBLIOGRAPHY

Berton, Lee, and Lublin, Joan S. "Partnership Structure Is Called in Question as Liability Risk Rises." *The Wall Street Journal,* June 10, 1992, pp. A1+.

Brown, Arnold, and Weller, Edith. *Supermanaging.* New York: McGraw-Hill, 1984.

Davis, Bob. "U.S. Capitalism Needs Overhaul to Stay Abreast of Competitors, Report Warns." *The Wall Street Journal,* June 29, 1992, p. A2.

— ARNOLD BROWN

BUSINESS STRUCTURE: INDUSTRIAL POLICY

There are a variety of definitions for "industrial policy," but in its broadest form it can be defined as targeted government programs that redirect resources to maximize national productivity and/or the ability to compete internationally. In its more focused application, industrial policy usually entails a strategy of helping specific industries while at the same time phasing out low-priority industrial segments. More importantly, however, industrial policy supposedly requires *agreement* among government, industry, unions (if applicable), and financial institutions. In addition, in some manifestations, industrial policy consenses will be augmented by including representatives of national media in order to help ensure that the policy is "sold" to a country's citizenry.

While the term *industrial policy* has taken on a negative connotation in the United States during the 1980s, the practice of using government policy to strategically benefit particular industries has always been practiced. Every aspect of government action—taxation, defense spending, the management of currencies and exchange rates, the definition and enforcement of property rights, tariffs, depletion allowances, and so forth—helps or hinders, benefits or harms, one industry or another. Since the time of Ricardo, economic theory has argued that there is no neutral tax, that all forms of taxation distort market behavior in one way or another. The same may be argued for government policy.

What purports to be new in today's debate over industrial policy is the idea of *targeted* government programs. Advocates argue that there is a significant difference between past types of government policy and a formal industrial policy in that the industrial and competitive impacts in the past have generally been haphazard or even indirect consequences, and not a targeted goal. A formal industrial policy, it is argued, should select growth industries and develop programs to support them through direct government incentives.

Advocates of industrial policy favor actions

that will support future growth industries.

This type of industrial policy, in one form or another, is practiced in Germany and Japan and in a number of newly industrializing countries. In Japan, the Ministry of International Trade and Industry (MITI) is the coordinating ministry for industrial policy. MITI selects high-tech industries based on various economic principles. Here, industrial policy is a strategy devised and agreed upon with a goal of facilitating growth or the phasing out of specific industrial segments. Often all that is needed is the publication of the official list of "sunrise" and "sunset" industries to start all sectors of the economy readjusting their priorities and objectives. While Japan tends to have a highly coordinated industry policy focus, other countries have opted to confine their policy to very specific enabling activities such as the U.S. space program.

Market dynamics are altering the world at such a rapid rate that the commanding economic industries of only a decade or two ago have now eroded, or have been totally transformed into almost unrecognizable organizations. In market after market, industrial deconstruction is going on at unprecedented speed. Entirely new industrial forces appear seemingly from nowhere. These changing markets are truly global in scope. Telling an export from an import is virtually meaningless, while the service industries are overwhelming manufactured goods in importance and volume. At the same time, corporations are finding it ever more difficult to calculate the impact and consequences of their own actions and are either operating on ever-shorter planning horizons, or are developing plans that appear robust over a multitude of alternative future scenarios. Their strategic focus has shifted from anticipating future risks and opportunities to developing the ability to take appropriate action whatever it might be, whenever it may be needed.

In today's dynamic competitive environment, the advocates of industrial policy favor actions that will support future growth industries; where these cannot be identified, they favor policies that will foster the emergence and expansion of creative innovation required to produce unspecified future growth industries. Thus, policy focus is shifting to support for the infrastructure of innovation, be it telecommunications, networks, university research programs, or accelerated resolution of industry standards.

The question, then, that needs to be answered is twofold: (1) should countries adopt industrial policies and (2) do industrial policies really work? The answer to the first question is relatively simple: All countries already have industrial policies in one form or another. The differences in how countries apply these policies, however, is not just cosmetic. On the one hand you have policies which "push" certain industries to achieve, for example, by picking winners and losers, as is the case in Japan. On the other hand, you have policies that "pull" new industries into the limelight. Most often this is brought about by government funding or new or improved technologies. Even in cases where governments are not actively funding new technologies, a type of industrial policy may emerge purely within the private sector (such as the Microelectronics and Computer Technology Corporation) where the government's role is the easing of regulations, rather than funding.

The answer to the second question—whether these policies really work—is more complex. For an industrial policy to work, the location, timing, and subject must all coincide. For example, contrast an industrial policy in Japan with one in the United States. In Japan, in recent years, industrial policy seemed to work because they interfaced well with the country's particular culture. MITI decides, based on a rational economic-based life cycle approach, which industries will be "sacrificed" for the good of the overall economy. Japan's approach reflects strong homogeneous social values whereby individual interests are sacrificed for the good of the nation. Conversely, in the United States, where powerful lobbyists represent the interests of specific groups or industries and individualism and entrepreneurial spirit are dominant characteristics, for a national, cohesive industrial policy even to be adopted let alone implemented, is highly problematic.

The issue of timing is also of critical importance. Industrial policies in Japan and Germany emerged after World War II when the rebuilding of entire nations was required. The, economic necessity of rebuilding, coupled with a cultural imperative, allowed for targeting industrial sectors for government support and involvement. And, while this policy has worked well in the past, it remains to be seen if it will serve as well in the future. Careful assessment is complicated by the fact that the global marketplace, along with technology and diffusion rates, is changing so rapidly. In the future it may not seem wise to select a handful of industries based on a set of criteria forged from today's issues and hope that these are the industries that will continue to grow long term.

Finally, and most importantly we have perhaps been asking the wrong question all along. If the definition of an industrial policy is "targeted government programs designed to redirect resources in a way that maximizes national productivity and/or the ability to compete internationally," then the question should not be which industries should be promoted or which technologies should we invest in. Rather, the key question is what are the *fundamental* characteristics which will allow us to maximize national productivity over the long run. When the question is asked this way, there is only one inescapable answer: a highly educated and healthy workforce. It is the investment in these two areas that will distinguish countries with a successful long-term industrial policy.

[See also Business Structure: Forms, Impacts; Global Business: Dominant Organizational Forms; Integrated Performance Systems; International Trade: Regulation; International Trade: Sustaining Growth; Marketplace Economics; Strategic Planning; Workforce Redistribution.]

BIBLIOGRAPHY

Phillips, K. P. "U.S. Industrial Policy: Inevitable and Ineffective." *Harvard Business Review* (July–August 1992): 104–112.
Porter, M. E. *The Competitive Advantage of Nations.* London: Macmillan Press, 1990.
Reich, R. B. *The Work of Nations: Preparing Ourselves for the 21st Century Capitalism.* New York: Alfred Knopf, 1991.
Thurow, L. C. "Who Owns the Twenty-first Century?" *Sloan Management Review* (Spring 1992): 5–17.

— ROBERT H. SMITH

C

CAMPAIGNING, POLITICAL.

See POLITICAL CAMPAIGNING.

CAPITAL FORMATION

The days when banks were the only significant sources of investment capital are long gone. In the future, sources of investment capital are and will be diverse, various, nontraditional, innovative, dynamic, and international.

Industries around the world are constantly and continually restructuring, driven by the need to increase productivity and profitability, and thereby remain competitive. This requires massive capital needs: investment is necessary to fund the invention, discovery, innovation, and creation of new products, processes, designs, and materials (as well as the enhancement of known ones) that will drive future economic growth and wealth creation.

However, banks will still be the main sources of capital funding in the future. They are still the best and biggest reservoirs of capital and determiners of where investment capital is best utilized. In fact, banks are now flush with capital, after suffering a dearth of funds in the early 1990s. According to the Federal Deposit Insurance Corporation (FDIC), U.S. bank lending to industrial and commercial firms is more than $650 billion outstanding. This amount has grown substantially since the early 1990s and can continue to increase significantly without threatening the industry's strong capital/equity ratio.

The drawback is that banks are under enormous pressure from investors to earn a healthy return on their equity. Some observers fear that they will repeat past mistakes in a rush to deploy capital: frenzied lending into boom markets that later go bust (sovereign lending to developing countries in the 1970s, for example, or oil-producing and commercial properties in the 1980s). But with the financial deregulation that has allowed banks to branch into other businesses, interest from loans currently represents a smaller and declining proportion of bank profits. In addition, banks are now cognizant of the need to reduce their exposure to single customers, industries, and regions.

Firms in need of capital have many other options besides banks. Increasingly, large companies are completely bypassing commercial banks and directly tapping into the capital markets, finding individual, corporate, and fund investors who want to make their own investment decisions. There is also a host of new, innovative financial instruments for capital formation. The most famous of these are high-yield securities (also known as "junk bonds" to denote the high risk associated with large potential gain).

In the future, sources of investment capital are diverse, various, nontraditional, innovative, dynamic, and international.

Junk bonds were created in the 1970s, when high inflation and low stock prices together made it extremely difficult to raise funds. (The more favorable tax treatment of debt over equity was also a major contributing factor.) Junk bonds filled an urgent need for financing that the regular capital market was not supplying through normal channels. In this respect they were just one in a long line of such financial innovations (even the first issues of industrial common and preferred shares of stock were considered radical and nearly worthless at the time). Contrary to popular perception, total returns on junk bonds, including all defaults, have been about the same as for higher-grade bonds. In fact, by capitalizing "less than creditworthy" companies, junk bonds made possible an explosion of innovation that propelled entire new technologies and industries (including cable television, cellular telephones, personal computers, software, and scores of others).

Indeed, the entire range of financial innovations introduced during the 1980s, including leveraged buyouts, junk bonds, mergers and acquisitions, etc., have acquired an undeserved bad reputation. Results are now in, and we can see that they were beneficial: lowering costs of capital formation, improving efficiency, and creating wealth. Was all this built on a mountain of debt? The answer is no. Total corporate debt service, at about 16 percent, is approximately the same level that prevailed in the mid-1970s. These and other innovations, which will all be growing sources of financing in the future, include second-tier lenders, sale-leasebacks, partial public offerings, credit-sensitive notes, securitization, and capital recovery.

Another permanent revolution that has come to capital formation is internationalization. As recently as 1984, financial markets remained essentially domestic. Since then, new telecommunications and information technologies—coupled with advances in financial theory, radical innovation in financial products, and a universal process of market deregulation—have transformed financial markets dramatically.

Market capitalization of the world's major stock exchanges grew from $1.7 trillion in 1978 to $10.6 trillion in 1993. Cross-border trading in corporate equities has grown from about $120 billion in 1979 to $1.3 trillion in 1992. The share of U.S. initial public offerings (IPOs) abroad increased from 1.4 percent in 1985 to 19.3 percent in 1992. The market in derivatives—which barely existed before 1980—grew to nearly $9 trillion by 1992, much of that in interest and currency swaps.

Capital formation is the basis for investment, which is the basis for productivity, which is the basis for future economic growth, prosperity, and well-being.

Thus, one in every five transactions in equity markets in the mid-1990s involves cross-border trading. Such investors are estimated to own 10 percent of world equities, a proportion that will rise to 15–20 percent by the end of the decade. Financial transactions with foreigners have grown by a factor of 10 or more for all major industrial economies since the early-1980s. But these developments pale in comparison to the explosion that has characterized foreign exchange markets in recent years. Current estimates cite a daily volume of more than $1.2 trillion, the equivalent of 5 percent of the world's total production of goods and services.

Venture capital has also become an important source of capital formation. After riding an up-and-down roller coaster during the 1980s, venture capital firms are again flush with funds, amassing billions of dollars yearly for investment in newer, smaller, innovative businesses with high growth potential. (Some of the most popular areas in the mid-1990s are biotechnology, computer software, media and communications, and medical devices.)

Today and in the future entrepreneurs will seek loans from private venture-capital partnerships; public venture capital funds; corporate venture capital funds; investment banks; SBICs and SSBICs (privately capitalized venture capital firms regulated by the U.S. Small Business Administration); state development agencies; clients, customers, and vendors; business incubators (private or public/private facilities that provide business development services to start-ups); and "angels," or individuals who invest in new ventures (every year about 250,000 angels pump $10 billion to $15 billion into 30,000 to 40,000 early-stage ventures).

Capital markets will expand and evolve to provide the great capital needs of future decades. New and innovative financial products and mechanisms will be devised. Financing vehicles of the future will be varied and complex, because the demand for capital in the future will be enormous and varied. Capital formation is the basis for investment, which is the basis for productivity, which is the basis for future economic growth, prosperity, and well-being.

[See also Capitalism; Economic Cycles: Models and Simulations; Economics; Entrepreneurship; Estate and Financial Planning; Financial Institutions; Investments; Marketplace Economics; Monetary System; Savings; Wealth.]

BIBLIOGRAPHY

"Coast-to-Coast Angels." *Inc.* (September 1993).
Fisher, Anne B. "Raising Capital for a New Venture." *Fortune* (June 13, 1994).
Frankel, Jeffrey, ed. *The Internationalization of Equity Markets.* Chicago: University of Chicago Press, 1994.
"A Glut of Venture Capital?" *Fortune* (October 31, 1994).
"Seed Corn Is Back in Fashion." *Forbes* (February 27, 1995).
"Time for the Chop?" *The Economist* (February 25, 1995).
Woolley, Suzanne. "The Floodgates Inch Open." *Business Week* (1993 Enterprise Issue): 96–98.

– ROGER SELBERT

CAPITALISM

At the end of the twentieth century, capitalism has evolved into a social system based primarily on individual rights, especially private property rights. Other societies, such as the former Soviet Union, China, and Castro's Cuba, share with capitalist countries the means of production, the industrial plants, the technologies of communications and transportation, and the other physical aspects of the modern industrial state. But what distinguishes a capitalist nation from a socialist, communist, or fascist nation is the extent to which property is privately owned and privately controlled.

There is, of course, a broad continuum from the more capitalistic countries—for example, the United States—to the more collectivist ones—for example, China. At the ends of the continuum the distinction is clear. Few have ever called the United States a communist or socialist society. No one has ever called the former Soviet Union, Castro's Cuba, or China a capitalist society. But in the middle of the continuum the distinctions can blur. Some European countries, while predominantly capitalistic, have major parts of their society under government control and ownership. On the other hand, a socialist country, such as India, can have significant private property rights.

The essence of economic capitalism is private property and private contracts, protected by the rule of law, including a strong criminal justice system. In a capitalist society, the economic role of government is minimized, taxes are kept reasonably low, state regulations are minor, and men and women operate freely in the marketplace. Other key elements of capitalism are a viable stock market, private ownership of the means of production and of the print and electronic media, and voluntary labor unions.

Capitalism is not new. Elements of it were present in ancient civilizations. But it was not until 1776, when Adam Smith in his seminal book *The Wealth of Nations* spelled out in comprehensive detail the theoretical underpinnings of capitalism, that it began to expand in influence. Adam Smith was one of the first to understand and identify what to many is an enduring mystery—how a complex society can and does operate successfully without constant control and regulation by government.

This "spontaneous order" of capitalism is its most powerful strength and its greatest potential weakness. Its strength derives from the natural inclination of men and women to produce and trade voluntarily and the fact that this natural activity often results in a prosperous society. Its weakness is that the complexity underlying this natural economic order is not generally understood, and the natural instinct of people is to attempt to control what they do not understand.

For the last 200 years or so, capitalism has had many competitors, particularly socialism and communism. These political-economic systems promised individual freedom, economic prosperity, a fair distribution of wealth, and personal security. After the Russian Revolution of 1917 competition among these systems largely settled into a two-sided struggle, epitomized on one side by the communist system of the Soviet Union and on the other by the capitalist system of the United States and Western Europe. That struggle metastasized into the Cold War in the late 1940s.

The dramatic internal collapse of the communist government of the Soviet Union in the late 1980s led swiftly to the freeing of Eastern Europe, as country after country discarded the communist model for the capitalist one. What fueled these changes was the clear, convincing evidence in virtually every communist nation that collectivism did not work very well.

In economic terms the contrast between collectivist and capitalist societies is sharp. In standard of living, distribution of income, and the environment, capitalist states are usually far superior to noncapitalist ones.

By no means is capitalism perfect. Whether in the United States, Japan, Britain, or the new Russia, a dynamic free economy sometimes may expand too rapidly, leading to recessions and even depressions. A free economy is oriented toward serving the needs and desires of individual citizens. Where people are free to succeed, they are also free to fail—and they sometimes do.

But the twentieth century has demonstrated, by way of what was perhaps the greatest social experiment in history, that while capitalism may not be the perfect political-economic system, so far it is the most efficacious one.

As the twentieth century closes, we are entering a new era where almost every country in the world has adopted some variant of the capitalist idea. As professor Peter L. Berger noted in his 1986 book *The Capitalist Revolution,* "Capitalism has become a global phenomenon . . . [it] has been one of the most dynamic forces in human history, transforming one society after another, and today it has become established as an international system determining the economic fate of most of mankind and, at least indirectly, its social, political and cultural fate, as well."

The changes in our political and economic thinking have been so profound that it is unlikely that we will see any significant reversals of these changes for decades. In the political and economic world, ideas, for better or worse, shape and drive people's actions. Those ideas are now set in the philosophical mold of capitalism. As these ideas unfold in terms of specific policy actions for different countries, the twenty-first century will most likely host a flowering of many variants of capitalism as nations add private property and the rule of law to their own traditions, customs, and environments.

This new developing capitalism is a powerful idea, but like all ideas, it is not necessarily permanent. Capitalism is an idea that will need constant renewal if its momentum is to continue beyond the early years of the twenty-first century.

[See also Communism; Democracy; Entrepreneurship; Informal Economy; Marketplace Economies; Political Economy; Social Democracy; Socialism.]

BIBLIOGRAPHY

Berger, Peter L. *The Capitalist Revolution: Fifty Propositions about Prosperity, Equality, and Liberty.* New York: Basic Books, 1988.

Friedman, Milton. *Capitalism and Freedom.* Chicago: University of Chicago Press, 1963.

Friedman, Milton, and Friedman, Rose. *Free to Choose.* New York: Harcourt Brace Jovanovich, 1980.

Hayek, Friedrich A. *Capitalism and the Historians.* Chicago: University of Chicago Press, 1963.

———. *Road to Serfdom.* Chicago: University of Chicago Press, 1944, 1956.

Smith, Adam. *Wealth of Nations,* Modern Library edition. New York: Random House, 1993.

Von Mises, Ludwig. *Human Action: A Treatise on Economics,* 3rd ed. Chicago: Contemporary Books, 1966.

— MARTIN ANDERSON

CD-ROM.

See COMPUTERS: SOFTWARE; INTERACTIVE ENTERTAINMENT.

CHANGE

Change was one of the two primary questions considered in the early days of social science. The first question addressed was how society achieved order (social stasis); the second was how that order changed over time (social dynamics). The subject of social change is the number, type, structure, culture, or behavior of people in groups.

Modern society places greater emphasis on change as an intrinsic characteristic. Ancient societies valued traditions and were generally suspicious of change. They viewed change as inconsequential or ephemeral in a world of permanent social arrangements. In contrast, no social or cultural fact is safe from the onslaught of change in modern society. News media chronicle the passage of change daily. Modern society has an ambivalent view of change. On the one hand there is the hope that change will bring a better world, but there is also a longing for the "good old days." Ancient societies had their good old days, or golden ages, but they were shrouded in legend and myth while our perspectives are largely based on the past one or two decades.

One difference between ancient and modern society is the speed of change. Alvin Toffler caught this difference in his book *Future Shock,* observing that everyone in the twentieth century experiences fundamental change in their lifetimes that redefines the basic premises of the world as it is known. With life expectancies double what they were a century ago and major changes happening more frequently, fundamental change often occurs within a generation. People born and socialized into one world-order also live and work in a completely different one before they die.

Forms of Change

Change comes in many forms. The simplest type of change is the discrete or discontinuous change that transforms everything. The Judaeo-Christian view of change includes two such times when God intervened in human history. Modern versions of discontinuous

change involve the New Age beliefs that describe ongoing transformation.

Other forms of change are continuous. Most ancient societies believed decay was the fundamental form of change. They had observed the law of entropy at work positing that disorder in the universe always increases.

Other societies (such as the Hindus of India) see change as long cycles of endless recurrence. Cyclic theories form the basis of grand theories of history, such as those of Arnold Toynbee and Oswald Spengler. More modern cyclic concepts such as long-wave theories of Nicholai Kondratieff, Joseph Schumpeter, and others posit a natural period of fifty to sixty years in economic development. Each cycle is marked by characteristic types of innovation, capital investment, military conflicts, and other social changes. Cyclic theories find recurring patterns in historical data and are used to forecast future change.

Beginning with the Enlightenment, change came to be seen as endless progress toward better states. Francis Bacon was the first champion of science as the key to progress. The writers of the French Enlightenment expanded Bacon's progressive theory of change. Marquis de Condorcet wrote *L'An 2200,* the first utopia set in the future. Herbert Spencer applied evolutionary theory as the mechanism of progressive change.

The modern version of the progressive theories is Alvin Toffler's concept of the information society. Toffler and others pointed out that the technological basis of society has shifted twice in human history—once with the introduction of agriculture and second with the use of machines and fossil fuels. Each change brought a significant increase in the material standard of living and a host of social changes. The third shift based on computers and electronic communication is creating a society in which information replaces material things as the primary economic asset.

Assumptions of Change

Each of these forms of change is produced by an internal or external mechanism or agent. The discrete theories often rely on outside intervention as the primary mechanism of change. Religious theorists believe that supernatural forces create the salvation events that are most significant. Other discrete theories of change see technological breakthroughs, psychological transformations, or emergent paradigms as the primary force of change. Each of these interventions disrupts the continuous flow of human events.

Newer systems theories have focused on internal mechanisms of discrete change, commonly known as self-organizing systems. Ilya Prigogine pointed out how basic chemical systems can achieve a balance or rhythm under certain external conditions. René Thom, a French mathematician, popularized the concept of catastrophe, the sudden change of system behavior under extreme conditions. Sometimes catastrophes are bad, like the death of the system, but they can also be good in moving the system to higher levels. These ideas are now being tested using computer programs.

Pessimists point to the possibility that

the increasing entropy of the physical environment

may someday overwhelm even the most

technologically capable civilization.

The decay theories rely on the force of entropy as their mechanism of change. Derived from the field of thermodynamics, entropy is the process by which ordered states decay to disordered states through a random process. Shuffling cards will probably never re-create the order of the cards as they came out of the box, coins are never as shiny, clothes are never as new, cars never run better than when they are newly made. Entropic theories of social change do not explain the ability of humans to create islands of order in the midst of increasing disorder. So society, a highly improbable arrangement of people and things, is organized amid increasing disorder to the physical environment, beginning with the burning up of the sun but also including the destruction of fossil energy sources, ecosystems and other species. Optimists view the future with unlimited potential for increasing order and sophistication of technology. Pessimists warn of potential limits and point to the possibility that the increasing entropy of the physical environment may someday overwhelm even the most technologically capable civilization. Entropic theories foretell the ultimate collapse of society.

The cyclic theories rely on feedback systems to create their cycles of change. Negative feedback governs a system, keeping its variables within limits. Certain systems dampen all change and eventually reach equilibrium. Other systems oscillate between two states, just as cyclic theories predict. The exact variables depend on the system under investigation. Some theories explain the peaks and troughs of capitalist change as the exploitation and then saturation of major markets. Theories of organizational development explain how some previously very successful companies became locked into old ways of doing business and are reluctant to try out or accept new approaches. Societies which are hardened by adversity and strive for excellence become less capable as affluence makes their lives easier. Each of these forms the basis for a system which repeatedly cycles through various states.

Modern progressive theories have relied on a number of mechanisms for continuous improvement. The first mechanism was rational planning. The Enlightenment theorists had an unbounded belief in the ability of human reason to understand and solve problems. That belief was later shattered by Marx's dialectical view of history and Freud's theories of the subconscious. Rational planning does create much social change, but our belief in its unbounded capability has definitely faded.

Another mechanism of change that appeared during the early industrial period was the dialectical theory of change. First enunciated by Hegel, the process was picked up by Karl Marx to describe the succession of primary social arrangements in human history. Ancient empires were marked by master-slave relations, the feudal periods by lord-serf relations and the industrial period by owner-worker relations. Each relation, although an improvement over its predecessor, also created conditions that led to its destruction. Owners must put workers together in factories to maximize industrial productivity but in doing so they create the conditions for worker organizations and eventually revolutions. Marx's theories of industrial development are in disrepute today, not unrelated to the fall of communist societies, but his mechanism of dialectical change is still a viable theory to account for some social changes.

Biology supplied the guiding principles of other social theories of the nineteenth century. Two such theories emerged. Although both were termed evolutionary, the first set of theories is really developmental. Developmental change proceeds according to a prearranged plan or schedule. For example, humans grow from embryo to infant to adolescent to adult in a genetically programmed sequence. The simplest developmental theory of social change came from Auguste Comte, who posited three stages of human social evolution: the theological (where animistic and supernatural explanations were dominant), the metaphysical (where philosophical arguments reigned), and the positive (where science provided all explanations). The most successful developmental theory was from Herbert Spencer. He believed that societies evolved much like organisms did and that the most advanced societies were more fit for their environments than less advanced societies. Spencer's theories were used to justify all manner of oppression from colonialism to genetic explanations of social class. The developmental theories in general saw a staircase of increasing progress with modern industrial societies at the pinnacle.

Twentieth-century evolutionary theories returned to the purer form of evolution as originally proposed by Darwin. They pointed out that "fitness" was not an absolute standard, as Spencer and others believed, but rather was relative to the environment. Each species (or society) is fit for the environment it finds itself in. Thus the Kalahari bushmen are fit for African savannas just as Japan is fit for the global economy. This new interpretation took the value and directionality out of earlier developmental theories. Societies did evolve, but in no particular direction and for no particular reason. Evolutionists could not discount the tendency toward increasing complexity in modern society, but they insisted that such complexity was not necessarily good. It may just be an episode in the continuous meandering of human civilization. The question of whether human civilization (or any social change) is directed toward some final end state or whether it is a random walk for no particular reason marks the difference between these two fundamentally different interpretations of evolutionary development.

Combinations of assumptions about change are also possible and underlie some of the more modern theories of social change. One of those theories is called interrupted or punctuated equilibrium. This is a modification of traditional evolutionary theory. Darwin's theory of evolution was gradual or incremental. Each generation contributed to the change through minute, indistinguishable mutations. When geologists and biologists finally were able to examine the fossil record, however, they did not see smooth increments between successive generations. Rather they saw many generations that were identical interrupted by sharp points of change. Changed environmental conditions cause species to become extinct, opening the way for the dominance of another. This type of change may occur in social and economic organizations as well as in biological systems.

An emerging field adds another set of assumptions to the theories of social change. Called complexity theory, it is an alternative paradigm of systems behavior. Current systems theory has its roots in cybernetics and feedback as described above. The fundamental unit is the variable (pressure, temperature, population size, and so forth), a quantity that takes on a range of values. A changing variable induces changes in other variables in a domino-like fashion. Ultimately that effect returns to the originating variable, either inducing it to move further in the same direction (positive or reinforcing feedback) or to move in the direction of its initial value (negative or balancing feedback). Systems change

through the effects of positive feedback yet remain stable through the effects of negative feedback.

Rather than being a system of variables, complexity theory conceives the system as a set of actors who behave according to simple rules established in their environment. Actors are independent, but come from cooperative or antagonistic relationships that give rise to mass behavior. The properties studied under traditional systems theory are emergent properties of the actions of these independent entities. In some systems, the conditions change, leading to a change in the behavior of the actors and the emergent properties they spawn. In other systems, the actors themselves learn or evolve to maximize their rewards in the environment. In most real systems, both processes occur simultaneously in a process termed *co-evolution*—the actors and their environment evolving together. Under this theory, change is the result of the mutual, continual adaptation of sets of actors with each other and their environment.

Systems of such actors (termed *cellular automata*) have been created in computer memories that act as laboratories for studying the process of social change. These actors "live" through millions of generations in a short time, evolving to sometimes advanced and complex systems of behavior. These systems demonstrate most of the forms of change described above. They can reach steady states, which may suddenly be transformed into a new system. They progress to higher forms of social organization, decay to lower forms, or endlessly cycle through alternative forms. They evolve but ultimately die.

Current Assumptions

Each of the assumptions of social change is used to form the basis of a major school of thought about the future.

Optimistic views of the future assume that the progress experienced in the industrial age will continue. Optimistic futurists include Herman Kahn, Alvin Toffler, John Naisbitt, and Julian Simon. They point to hundreds of years of continual economic growth and social development. They see no reason that human ingenuity will not continue to push the envelope of technological innovation further to solve Earth's environmental problems, provide food, shelter and employment for the billions of new people on the planet and even begin the serious colonization of outer space. They point to the as-yet unexploited potential of information technology and the biological technologies to increase economic growth and social development to unprecedented levels.

The pessimists nevertheless contend that success is in no way guaranteed. Pessimistic futurists include Lester Brown, Donella Meadows, Paul Ehrlich, and Dennis

Meadows. They point out that progress is always bought with higher levels of entropy somewhere. Pessimists call for a form of society that creates no entropy on the planet itself—a sustainable society that uses land, energy and materials only in proportions that can be easily replaced. Barring that, they forecast an almost inevitable decline in standard of living as one or more critical resources diminish.

Some parts of the social landscape will remain

the same because everything cannot change.

Some continuity must exist.

Cyclic theorists see a continual interplay between the positive and negative forces with neither permanently in place. The good times result from the successful implementation of new, powerful technologies like agriculture, fossil energy, and now telecommunications. Bad times are the transition periods between these eras when the old technology is fully exploited and the new one is not yet in place. Long-wave theorists explain our current economic difficulties as the effect of such a periodic shift. Leaving the energy-rich coal and petroleum economies of the past without having the complete information technologies of the future in place has created transition strains for businesses, workers and consumers alike. Likewise, the shift from agricultural to industrial societies elsewhere in the developing world has created even more massive dislocation, all of which however is temporary. A new information society, including all the countries of the world, will provide a return to prosperity. That prosperity, like all previous ones, is also temporary, however, eventually giving way to the transition preceding a new society, this time probably based on biological technologies.

The transformationalists harbor yet a fourth set of assumptions. They include Willis Harman, Robert Theobald, Marilyn Ferguson, Hazel Henderson, and Amitai Etzioni. They claim we are on the verge of one or more permanent, fundamental shifts in societal organization. These shifts will be the big news of the future. Some look to sustainable technologies of economic development, some to environmental collapse, some to psychological awakening, some to the reemergence of community. Whatever the source, they see another discrete jump to a completely different form of society.

Each of these theories forecasts a much different world of the future. Humans living in groups (families, small groups, organizations and societies) will be af-

fected by such change. Some parts of the social landscape will remain the same because everything cannot change. Some continuity must exist. But those things that do are each foretold, depending on the assumptions one makes about the fundamental shape and mechanisms of change that we are experiencing.

[See also Agents of Change; Change, Cultural; Change, Optimistic and Pessimistic Perspectives; Change, Pace of; Change, Scientific and Technological; Continuity and Discontinuity, Evolution, Social; Global Paradox; Global Turning Points; Information Society; Laws, Evolution of; Public Policy Change; Social Change: United States; Technological Change; Values Change.]

BIBLIOGRAPHY

Ferguson, Marilyn. *The Aquarian Conspiracy.* Los Angeles: Jeremy P. Tarcher, 1987.

Goldstein, Joshua. *Long Cycles: Prosperity and War in the Modern Age.* New Haven, CT. Yale University Press, 1988.

Harman, Willis. *Global Mind Change.* Indianapolis: Knowledge Systems, 1988.

Henderson, Hazel. *Paradigms in Progress: Life Beyond Economics.* Indianapolis: Knowledge Systems, 1991.

Meadows, Donella H., Meadows, Dennis L., and Randers, Jorgen. *Beyond the Limits: Confronting Global Collapse, Envisioning a Sustainable Future.* Post Mills, VT. Chelsea Green Publishing, 1992.

Petersen, John L. *The Road to 2015: Profiles of the Future.* Corte Madera, CA: Waite Group Press, 1995.

Thurow, Lester. *Head to Head: The Coming Economic Battle Among Japan, Europe and America.* New York: Morrow, 1992.

Toffler, Alvin. *The Third Wave.* New York: Morrow, 1980.

— PETER C. BISHOP

CHANGE, CULTURAL

Culture has assumed an exceptionally vital role in shaping the future. According to the cultural historian Christopher Dawson, culture is "an organized way of life which is based on common traditions and conditioned by a common environment."

The classical tradition defines culture as the search for life's highest expressions of truth and beauty. Beauty was said to be an aesthetic analogue for perfection and goodness, while ugliness was an analogue for derangement or evil. Historically, part of the function of culture has been to help the human soul discriminate between good and evil, between what is beautiful and what is ugly. Matthew Arnold described culture as "the study of perfection."

Some of the creative geniuses of culture have clearly supported such a belief. Dante expressed his purpose in writing *The Divine Comedy* as, "Make strong my tongue/That in its words may burn/One spark of all Thy Glory's light/For future generations to discern."

J. S. Bach said his purpose in life was "to write well-ordered music to the glory of God."

Even eighteenth- or nineteenth-century America, while perhaps not manifesting a culture on the level of Dante and Bach, displayed a culture expressing the higher aspects of existence, as in the works of Hawthorne, Whitman, Emerson, Church, Cole, and Innes. Europeans wrote volumes extolling Melville's *Moby Dick* as the American equivalent of Goethe's *Faust*. Nineteenth-century American culture was a culture of process and becoming; it portrayed the hope and promise of the possible.

And today we encounter the likes of *Pulp Fiction*, Serrano, and Mapplethorpe, or Madonna, Ice-T, and Michael Jackson. We see art such as abstract expressionism, which, in the words of Harold Rosenberg, seeks "liberation from value—political, aesthetic, world."

In essence, twentieth-century culture has been accepted as a capricious expression of any human instinct, no matter how base or psychotic, and regardless of its content or effect. It is a culture that acknowledges no hierarchy of values, no social or spiritual tradition; a culture that lives for the moment in a chaos of sensation. Such a culture no longer provides relevant answers to those everlasting questions of meaning and significance that confront all peoples throughout all ages.

Two thoughts may provide a clue to what is happening. First, let us reflect on Dawson's contention that culture is "based on common traditions and conditioned by a common environment."

Common traditions have been in the process of being shredded for the better part of this century. How we spend Sunday is a good example. Most civilizations throughout history have set aside a special time for renewal of the inner spiritual energies of life. In Western Christendom, that time was Sunday. Yet today, for most Americans, while Sunday may give relief from job pressures, it is just another day at the shopping mall, with scant spiritual refurbishment. Tradition has been sundered.

On the Fourth of July, a century ago, people would go to the town park and listen to a distinguished speaker orate for two or three hours on the significance of the Declaration of Independence and the Constitution. Today, the Fourth of July is good for a trip to the beach, and the vast majority of college graduates never read the two most important documents in America's history.

And as global television, computers, the Internet, faxes, cellular phones, and virtual reality increasingly link the world together as part of one intertwining electronic nervous system, tradition will continue to decrease its hold on individual emotions and loyalties, thus further affecting culture.

A second point to consider is the source of culture. Culture, whether sublime or profane, springs from the deepest recesses of the unconscious mind. It is a reflection of what is happening at the intuitive level of the human psyche. It is no use blaming Hollywood for the wasteland of American television and movies. The fact is that what Hollywood produces somehow resonates at some deep level in the American subconscious. If it did not, people would not respond to or pay for it.

What we have been experiencing in the twentieth century is the breakup of inner projections of images of spiritual and psychological wholeness.

Whatever one thought of Bob Dylan singing "How does it feel/to be on your own/with no direction home/like a complete unknown/like a rolling stone?" in 1962, the fact is that Dylan's song reflected the pain, loneliness, and emptiness of a world without metaphysical anchors, a world increasingly inhabited by psychologically alienated Americans. Dylan was only the latest in a long line of twentieth-century artists and writers whose artistic efforts depicted disenchantment and disillusion with the American ideal in particular and with life in general.

If one were to try to pinpoint the starting point in America of such psychological alienation, it might actually have been Herman Melville and *Moby Dick*. *Moby Dick* is generally conceded to be the greatest product of the American literary mind. But when examined from a psychological viewpoint, *Moby Dick* takes on a different hue. Simply by starting the book with "Call me Ishmael," Melville presents us with the biblical figure of the rejected outcast, the alienated man. The opening paragraph of *Moby Dick* strikes the same note as almost all the classic examples of alienation and descent into the underworld, whether Homer's *The Odyssey*, Dante's *Divine Comedy*, or T. S. Eliot's "The Waste Land."

What we have been experiencing in the twentieth century is the breakup of the inner projections of images of spiritual and psychological wholeness. For some 1,800 years, Christianity served as the core spiritual and cultural expression of the inner subjective integrity of the Western world. But with the rise of scientific rationalism in the seventeenth century, and with the increasing emphasis on external, objective reality as opposed to an inner, intuitive reality, the Christian myth lost much of its power as the archetypal image of psychic totality.

With the erosion of the underlying archetype of Western psychological and spiritual integrity, other aspects of the unconscious mind have been activated. These other projections from the unconscious have fashioned most of twentieth-century American culture. Two of those projections are the Apocalypse, as exemplified by any number of horrific depictions of destruction, such as *Natural Born Killers,* and the *Second Coming,* as suggested by the motion picture *E.T.*

Understanding this process is critical to assessing what is happening to our culture. These issues go much deeper than "liberal" or "conservative." The issue is a transformation that is taking place at the deepest level of the unconscious mind, a shift that has been in process for well over two centuries, and expresses itself in a dramatically different style of culture. With the advent of modern means of communication and travel, this shift has gathered substantial momentum in the past nine decades.

If the universal themes of *The Odyssey* or *The Divine Comedy* or Milton's *Paradise Lost* or Eliot's poetry tell us anything, it is that a trip through the spiritual and psychological underworld of life is followed by rebirth and renewal. Thus it is that in the twenty-first century we may see the flowering of a new culture, something beyond anything expressed in America's past—poetry beyond MacLeish, literature beyond Fitzgerald, art beyond Pollack, music beyond anything produced in America in the past two centuries. For as rebirth and renewal come, they will bring with them new forms of culture that express the richest and deepest meanings of a new era of the human odyssey.

[See also Arts; Change; Change, Epochal; Change, Scientific and Technological; Literature; Music; Visual Arts.]

BIBLIOGRAPHY

Barzun, Jacques. *The Culture We Deserve.* Middletown, CT: Wesleyan University Press, 1989.

Gasset, José, Ortega Y. *The Dehumanization of Art.* Princeton, NJ: Princeton University Press, 1968.

Kroeber, A. L. *Configurations of Culture Growth.* Berkeley, CA: University of California Press, 1969.

Malraux, André. *The Voices of Silence.* Princeton, NJ: Princeton University Press, 1978.

Nisbet, Robert. *The Present Age.* New York: Harper & Row, 1988.

Panichas, George A. *The Reverent Discipline.* Knoxville, TN: University of Tennessee Press, 1974.

— WILLIAM VAN DUSEN WISHARD

CHANGE, EPOCHAL

Americans are experiencing an epochal shift in society. Many of us do not even know it, although intuitively we may be aware of it. We feel a pervasive sense that life is out of control and no one is in charge. When the tectonic plates of life shift, everyone feels insecure, whether it's expressed or not. The old meanings about life no longer have the same authority. We are experiencing confusion about everything—about the economy, about education, values, sexual roles, the function of a family, about the source of authority, the role of the state, about the wellsprings of freedom, the existence of God; indeed, about the very meaning of life.

We Americans are in the midst of redefining who we are and what an "American" really is. The consequences of this redefinition go right to the core of life, affecting education, culture, and individual identity. The old perspectives—group identity, structured authority, progress as "more and more," happiness as the constant accumulation of gadgets, freedom as absence of restraint, progress in terms of technology rather than human aspirations—no longer explain life. They no longer work. So we must first find a new perspective, a new way of viewing everything—ourselves, our work, our institutions, our country.

It appears that we have come to the end of roughly a four-hundred-year period where science acted as the primary interpreter of what life is all about. This is causing a disjunction in life.

The technoeconomic realm is driven by the principle of rationality and efficiency. The political realm is theoretically driven by the principle of equality. The cultural realm is driven by unrestrained self-expression. All this leaves us groping for authority and legitimacy in the body politic, and for some transcendental belief in society at large.

For the past three hundred years, the main emphasis of Western development has been on technology and its requirements—power, motion, speed, quantification, precision, uniformity, regularity, control, standardization, and regimentation. This has been accelerated in the twentieth century by the outpouring of new technologies. What we have not realized is that technology does not simply augment existing modes of life. New technologies change the way people perceive reality. They alter our symbolic life. They create new definitions of old terms.

We assume that more technology will solve almost any problem. Clearly, technology is taking us into new realms that enhance and magnify human capabilities. While technology solves old problems, it always creates new ones, and the new ones are usually more complex than the problems solved. Technology, in and of itself, is not an expression of human purpose. It does not create any life-affirming values. It is an extension of means, not a definition of ends.

Today's human needs are overwhelmingly psychological and spiritual, not material or technological, which is why our historic interpretation of progress is largely irrelevant to our present condition. Only a framework of human purpose that gives direction to the use of technology will decide the question in favor of the human race. We must integrate the use of technology with some common affirmation of the underlying meanings that sustain human life and happiness.

The demise of many of the primary intellectual and political themes of the last two centuries has taken place partially because we have effectively reached the end of the Cartesian perspective. The Cartesian approach did more than break down scientific investigation into its discrete parts. It also separated the whole panorama of existence into segments that, by adherence to immutable laws, so it was believed, could be predicted and controlled. The aspects of reality that could not be reduced to mathematical certainty or be seen as the result of the blind operation of material forces were treated as mere subjective impressions of the human mind. Insofar as man himself was viewed as a byproduct of a vast mechanical order, he was denied the link to any possible spiritual significance.

We have come to the end of this reductionist theme as a valid perspective of life. Now we are reintegrating the disparate divisions of life into a larger synthesis. We suddenly see that all things are interconnected—a view held in the West from Heraclitus in sixth-century B.C. Greece up to the time of Descartes. It becomes clear that we can only understand one phenomenon if we look at it in relationship to the totality of which it is a part, and that a complete understanding of reality must include subjective phenomena. This view is well understood in the scientific world, but its application to the social and political realms is only now coming into focus.

Thus we are seeing a shift in our understanding of nature—from solely quantitative relations that are explained by mathematical treatment, to a nature whose essence may be in some realm of reality beyond matter; some expression of reality that flows through the underlying connectivity of all life and events.

Modes of communication have historically determined the structure of cultures, of education, and even of thought and knowledge. So as our modes of communication shift, basic changes will inevitably take place in these other areas as well. The printed word emphasizes logic, sequence, exposition, detachment, and history. For example, television puts its emphasis on imagery, presentness, immediacy, and intimacy. Thus countless studies show that, as the influence of print wanes, the content of politics, religion, education, and anything else that comprises public business must change and be recast in terms that are suitable to television—which is to say that all subject matter must be recast in terms of entertainment and show business.

In education we must ask whether kids are being torn between two differing modes of knowledge transmission—print and electronic knowledge transmission. The 1950s produced the first TV generation, causing our children to be raised in a different context, with wider horizons at earlier ages than any prior generation. This change especially influences children and how they relate to time. For example, historically this has been represented by a circle, whether a sundial or a clock. Now we have the digitized watch, which gives a sense of moment, but not of the larger context in which the moment exists.

Children have always defined themselves by drawing contrasts with animals. Now, brought up with computers and computerized toys, some kids define themselves in relation to the computer. Adolescents are struggling to find their identity, not in relationship to their families or the world around them, but in relation to video games and computers.

The epochal changes raise questions about the basis of our political structure. What is the core of liberty, and how is it sustained? In a society where the primary value source (television) is collective, how does a child develop his or her individual sense of being, yet relate that being to some larger responsibility for the community? In an age of mobility and global television impressions, what can be found to help us realize a sense of roots and our unique position in both time and place? What does a student need to know when there is so much that can be known? How does one gain self-understanding, self-control, and self-direction? What gives life its highest significance, and what saves it from meaninglessness?

Part of the cultural change is a change taking place within you and me. It is a psychological and spiritual change taking place deep within the psyche. It is in the realm of myth and symbol. Our whole understanding of who we are and what the human venture is all about will take a quantum leap forward. There is need for a sense of meaning that enables each of us to know who we are, why we are here, what we are rooted in, and what we are living for. "Know thyself" is more than just a happy aphorism. It is the precondition for the fulfilled personality. Such knowledge is at the very core of any human community—be it a family, a corporation, or a nation.

One of the great tasks of the twenty-first century will be to reconcile the extroverted tendency of the West with the introverted propensity of the East. Basically, we must find a new balance, a dynamic equilibrium between our inner and our outer life. Six thousand years of civilized life have taught us that human health and happiness depend on a certain outward expression of inner psychological wholeness, of a healthy balance between the ego and the larger self. Without such wholeness, however that may be expressed in different cultures, the personality and society disintegrate. Culture must assume again its earlier function—feeding the inner life, and encouraging psychological coherence, which is the foundation of any lasting social order.

One of the great tasks of the twenty-first century will be to reconcile the extroverted tendency of the West with the introverted propensity of the East.

To find such meaning and purpose, we must now give priority to the integrative elements in life—sense, wholeness, intuition, trust, communications, openness, and generosity of spirit. We must reinterpret the "why" of those ethical norms that the experience of civilized life has taught us are essential for psychological and social health and happiness.

We need to understand and develop the subjective side of life, the intuitive. We live in two worlds, the worlds of data and meaning. These two worlds must be linked together by the unity of the objective and the subjective.

Finally, we must learn to make the interconnections between people, between events, and between different categories of life, for interdependence is emerging as a dominant principle of the future.

[See also Agents of Change; Change; Change, Cultural; Change, Pace of; Continuity and Discontinuity; Global Consciousness; Mind: New Modes of Thinking; Modernism and Post-Modernism; Post-Information Age; Religion, Changing Beliefs; Social Change: United States; Social and Political Evolution; Values Change.]

BIBLIOGRAPHY

Capra, Fritjof *The Turning Point.* New York: Simon & Schuster, 1982.

Jung, C. G. *Civilization in Transition.* Vol. 10 of the *Collected Works.* Princeton, NJ: Princeton University Press, 1964.

Sorokin, Pitirim A. *The Crisis of Our Age.* New York: E. P. Dutton, 1941.

Spengler, Oswald. *The Decline of the West.* New York: Alfred A. Knopf, 1932.

Tarnas, Richard. *The Passion of the Western Mind.* New York: Random House, 1991.

Toynbee, Arnold J. *A Study of History.* London: Oxford University Press, 1946.

– WILLIAM VAN DUSEN WISHARD

CHANGE: OPTIMISTIC AND PESSIMISTIC PERSPECTIVES

Human perspectives are tempered by optimism and pessimism. The optimistic outlook welcomes the opportunity to invent the future. It rejects the more pessimistic view of man as a captive of fate.

The Pessimistic Viewpoint

Peddlers of gloom and doom always have been around. Predictions of doomsday persist throughout history. The doomsayers, pessimists, and negativists include influential thinkers such as Jacques Ellul, Lewis Mumford, and Herbert Marcuse. Rousseau, Thoreau, and contemporaries like Paul Ehrlich, Jeremy Rifkin, Ralph Nader, and Barry Commoner hold forth in much the same manner. Doomsayers often play on fears of the uncertain and unknown to stir up angry and emotional responses. They champion their causes and crusades—back-to-nature movements, cultural dropping out, counterculture faddism, anti-establishment activism, and so forth. Premature in many of their conclusions, they often fail to estimate properly the capacity of the human will to alter circumstances and redirect actual outcomes.

Negative attitudes, including alienation, cynicism, disillusionment, helplessness, resignation, despair, passivity, and apathy are among the attitudes that usually creep into policy debates. Pessimism has a dark and foreboding cant to it.

Complaint and criticism seem to dominate our times. Despite the constant carping, the fact is that people live longer, work less, are healthier, have more leisure and recreation as well as better housing, clothes, and food. The list could go on. Virtually everywhere one looks, living conditions and the lot of human beings everywhere are better than they were. In fact, the average person today eats better and enjoys amenities far superior to those restricted to royalty not so long ago. Humans are relentless in their pursuit of something better.

Values, constantly evolving and ascending to new and higher planes, also are at the bottom of any such understanding. They define ideas that unleash the aspirations that eventually become the goals toward which society, as a whole, inevitably strives.

For all its shortcomings, criticism also has a positive side. Criticism tends to bare imperfections and shortcomings. By shedding light they set the stage for optimists to respond.

The Optimistic Viewpoint

The optimistic outlook is a positive one. Optimists are not disillusioned with runaway technologies, excessive economic growth, population explosions, entropy, or any of the other dreary disasters anticipated by doomsayers throughout history. What pessimists see as problems, optimists see as challenges to be overcome by conscious, deliberate, and well-planned effort.

Optimists regard alarms raised by doomsayers, pessimists, and negativists as wake-up calls. They find this discontent useful in alerting society to potential situations or shortcomings requiring attention and resolution.

Optimism is consistent with the rational tradition of Western intellectual history and the scientific method associated with ordering affairs in advanced industrialized nations. This upbeat view considers people in control of their destiny, instead of being its hapless captive. They perceive society as open to intelligent directions and management. Optimists share an abiding belief in the perfectibility of mankind. They view the future neither as inflexible and predetermined nor as unordered and chaotic.

The very size and complexity of activities, coupled with accelerating rates of change, prompt the need for more conscious direction. Impacts from far-reaching decisions have become so broad and pervasive that deliberate effort is required to contain negative effects and accentuate positive benefits.

Through a conscious, comprehensive, and careful scientific understanding of sociopolitical issue genesis and development, wiser alternatives can be selected. Anticipation of unfolding situations affords an opportunity to take steps to minimize, if not avoid, the sometimes protracted, overlapping, and always costly defense of the indefensible. Such an approach enables change—the key concept—to be accommodated with minimal disruption.

Action based on poor understanding of the forces that drive innumerable and unstructured events is likely to be ineffective. Merely muddling through—benevolent neglect, as some have described it—has become too erratic, too costly, and even too dangerous a course. Careful explication of our problems and reasoned analysis are needed now more than ever before. Management of massive modern, subtle, complex, invisible, and qualitative technologies requires much more time and conscious attention. Planning, furthermore, is a necessary tool for getting things done. By anticipating problems, we are able to assess them, assign social priorities, and marshal resources to meet them. Planning provides the opportunity for ushering the desirable future into the present.

Policy makers are beginning to assume a new role as architects of destiny and are no longer willing to remain merely its passive and hapless captives. Many are expressing an interest with respect to a willed, rather than a fated future. No longer are they likely to remain victims of autonomous, directionless change. No longer willing to stand outside the process of change, they are asserting instead a desire to participate in it.

The question is not whether we can change the world, but what kind of a world we want. Fundamental change has come about only in recent times. It is not so much a change in capacity or in events as it is a change in outlook and attitude. There is a growing realization that we can manage change, not merely be managed by it.

[See also Agents of Change; Apocalyptic Future; Change; Change, Cultural; Change, Epochal; Continuity and Discontinuity; Dystopias; Lifestyles, Value-Oriented; Public Policy Change; Religion, Changing Beliefs; Social Change: United States; Social and Political Evolution; Technology and Science; Utopias.]

BIBLIOGRAPHY

Archer, Jules. *The Extremists: Gadflies of American Society.* New York: Hawthorn Books, 1969.

Cerf, Christopher, and Navasky, Victor. *The Experts Speak: The Definitive Compendium of Authoritative Misinformation.* New York: Pantheon Books, 1984.

Cetron, Marvin, and O'Toole, Thomas. *Encounters with the Future: A Forecast of Life into the 21st Century.* New York: McGraw-Hill, 1982.

McCarry, Charles. *Citizen Nader.* London: Jonathan Cape, 1972.

Naisbitt, John. *Megatrends: Ten New Directions Transforming Our Lives.* New York: Warner Books, 1982.

Thomis, Malcolm I. *The Luddites: Machine-Breaking in Regency England.* New York: Schocken Books, 1970.

Toffler, Alvin. *PowerShift: Knowledge, Wealth, and Violence at the Edge of the 21st Century.* New York: Bantam Books, 1990.

– GRAHAM T. T. MOLITOR

CHANGE, PACE OF

The pace of change varies by subject. Astronomically, the creation of the universe probably involves quadrillions of years. The age of the universe, it is generally thought, may be as much as 8–12 billion years, or possibly even as much as 19–20 billion years. Evolution of our sun's planetary system may have involved 4–5 billion years, and scientists predict that our planet will no longer support life as our sun dies out billions of years from now. Evolution of life-forms on Earth dates back at least 3–4 billion years.

The speed of change has increased dramatically over the years. Major change stemming from the discovery, development, and large-scale introduction of new scientific and social technologies has been steadily compressed into ever shorter periods of time. Leads and lags in application of new technologies that used to take thousands of years are accomplished in just a few years.

- 5,000 years elapsed from the time it was noted that the seed of a plant would grow and farming became widespread throughout Europe. (Grain cultivation dates back to 8500 B.C.)
- 3,500 years ago the extraction of iron from ore was discovered, but 1,000 years elapsed before this knowledge spread across the Western world.
- 1,600 years ago the first steam engine toy (aeolipile) was invented by Hero of Alexandria (c. 1000 A.D.), but not until nearly 800 years later, with the invention of Watt's steam engine (1788), did widespread use get underway.
- 112 years lapsed between the discovery of photography in 1727 and its general application by 1839 (although the principle of photography had been noted by Roger Bacon as early as 1267).
- 56 years were required to commercially capitalize on the telephone (1820–1876).
- 35 years were needed to successfully launch radio (1867–1902).
- 6 years were needed to develop the atom bomb (1939–1945).
- 3 years of work were required to introduce the integrated circuit (1958–1961).
- 2 years to launch solar batteries (mid-1960s).

Diffusion from development to commercial mass marketing in specific business sectors reveals three similar rapid-fire patterns. Take diagnostic imaging devices, for example: From the discovery of X-rays by Roentgen in 1895 (a discovery often credited with launching the Second Scientific Revolution), eighteen years lapsed before the first successful commercial application of the principle; five years for computer-aided tomography to be developed; and less than three years for magnetic resonance imaging. No matter where one looks, the pace has picked up.

Even something as apparently basic as the musical pitch of the note A is not immune to change. In fact, the pitch of A has been changed more than twenty times! Currently specified at 440 cycles per second (c.p.s.), historically, the frequency has ranged from 360 to 457 c.p.s. (360 c.p.s. in 1611; 422.5 in 1740; 421.6 in 1780; 431 in 1822; 435 in 1858; 457 in 1880; 440 in 1939). We contend with the relentless pace not only in science-based invention, but also in arbitrary standards established for the convenience of and by the whim of persons involved.

Increased Speed of Human Travel

The speed of human travel on foot remained at 3 miles per hour (m.p.h.) for thousands of years. Horse-drawn carriages and sailing ships averaged about 10 m.p.h. for about one hundred years. Automobiles accelerated the rate of travel to 50–100 m.p.h., and a rocket-powered three-wheel vehicle achieved a record speed of 739.666 m.p.h. (the fastest nonairborne speed to date). Steam-powered locomotives averaged 65 m.p.h. at the height of the age of steam, and steamboats averaged about 36 m.p.h. (The fastest modern rail train, the French TGV, has achieved a record speed of 320.2 m.p.h.).

Leads and lags in application of new technologies that used to take thousands of years are accomplished in just a few years.

Propeller aircraft ushered in a new pace of activity throughout the world—speeding travel up to speeds of 300–500 m.p.h.; with a world speed record of 575 m.p.h. (Mach 0.82—Mach speeds derive from Ernst Mach, an Austrian physicist who calculated the speed of sound at 766.98 m.p.h. at sea level and 15 degrees Centigrade; or about 659 m.p.h. at high altitudes). In earlier times, exceeding the speed of sound was thought to be impossible because the physical barrier, it was thought, could not be exceeded. Jet airliners boosted travel speed to more than 500 m.p.h., with the supersonic Concorde cruising at up to 1,450 m.p.h. (Mach 2.2), and Lockheed's SR-71A or "Blackbird," achieving a world record speed of 2,192.2 m.p.h. (Mach 3). Manned spaceships involve a further new frontier with speeds in excess of 20,000 m.p.h.

At first blush, and by everyday standards, it would seem that such record-shattering travel in excess of the speed of sound is far beyond most everybody's personal experience. Or is it?

Just to prove that all things are relative, consider the following. Asked if they have ever traveled at Mach 1, everyone—except travelers who can afford Concorde ticket prices and pilots of high-performance jet aircraft—will answer "no." The astounding fact is that each and every one of us is now traveling and always has traveled at speeds vastly in excess of Mach I because:

- Earth rotates on its axis at the equator at a speed of more than 1,000 m.p.h. and about 645 m.p.h. at the latitude of Washington, D.C.
- Earth revolves in orbit around our sun at 66,700 m.p.h.
- Earth's galaxy, the Milky Way, orbits around the center of its own galactic group once every 230 million years, traveling at a speed in excess of 492,000 m.p.h.
- Galaxies in a section of the universe measuring at least one billion light years across, which includes the Milky Way and its two satellite Magel-

lanic Clouds, among others, are moving in the same direction at a speed of 1.56 million m.p.h.

And so it is on across the universe, with the most distant galaxies speeding away from us at nearly the speed of light, or 186,283 miles per second (in a vacuum). Although the debate is far from settled, some astronomers—rightly or wrongly—speculate that the "absolute" speed of light may be exceeded under the unique conditions of black holes by as much as sixfold! What's the cosmic rush? Where are we headed? The point made here is that perspective is largely relative.

Most everyone experiences a rapid pace of change every day, often in subjects or areas so mundane that they get scarcely a thought. The rapidity of our lives, for example, can be seen in things as familiar as supermarket shopping. Introduction of new food and household products during 1994 totaled 20,076 (15,006 foods and 5,070 nonfoods). The profusion that confronts grocery shoppers is truly formidable. Active universal-product-coded (UPC) products in grocery channels number 644,782 distinctive items! And an astounding 2,500,000 UPC-coded products are available in the distribution system. The sheer breadth of choice is awesome.

Human ingenuity is boundless, and this pace of change—new product introductions—can be expected to continue increasing. All of this is a far cry from the good old days when all phones were black, bathtubs white, checks green, and Henry Ford sold cars in any color—so long as it was black. Yesterday mustard came in one variety and one-size jar—not the hundreds of blends, variations, forms and colors, sizes and shapes of packages available today. Using the selfsame products, day in and day out, is fine for many. But for the more adventuresome—and that includes almost everybody—there is a cascade of choices and more opportunities for new experiences.

Today, most Americans are in a hurry to get things done and be on their harried way. Lifestyles cater to instant gratification, me-now, self-indulgence, living for the moment, narcissism, and self-centeredness. Instant everything is ingrained in the American experience. Americans insist upon push-button convenience, yet are too busy to be bothered with taking the time to learn how to sequentially program a video recorder.

Our ancestors waited two to three days for stagecoaches that often took weeks or months to reach final destinations. Modern Americans are frustrated if they miss one spin of a revolving door. The pony express has been displaced by airmail, which in turn is being supplanted by overnight mail, electronic mail, and instantaneous facsimile transmissions. We rely on instanta-neous copies from trouble-free and push-button laser printers. Cooking from scratch, kitchen drudgery, and time-consuming household chores have been eased and simplified. The fifteen minutes required to prepare oatmeal in 1922 had been reduced to five minutes by 1939, and to a mere ten seconds during the 1980s in heat-and-serve containers (with no fuss-and-muss cleanup afterward). Motor oil changes that required a long ordeal at local service stations now take less than five minutes. One-hour dry cleaning has been available for years. One-hour photograph processing and prescription eyeglasses are more recent quick fixes.

We have even reduced the time to say or write the words describing things. We have developed a whole new language of short acronyms to speed things up— TV, VCR, CD, PC, MTV, HDTV, FAX, BMW, PCMCIA, and so on. Acronyms, however, do have excesses and limits. Long and windy titles abound in bureaucracies, especially in government and the military, where ADCOMSUBORDCOM-PHIBSPAC stands for Administrative Command: Subordinate Command Amphibious Forces, Pacific Fleet. That one gives some pause for concern. There are others like it.

Politicians have degraded the style and content of political dialogue into a patter of vapid and simple-minded phrases, one-liners, sound bites, parodies, and symbols. Voter lack of attention or interest in what is being said (and by whom) and short attention spans explain this trend. While few voters could give a candidate's position on major foreign or domestic policy questions, they are apt to remember themes that captured recent elections: "Read my lips. No new taxes." Or "Where's the beef?" Or demeaning a candidate by referring to him as "Slick Willie." It's a sad day when political one-liners dominate the simplistic patter of presidential election campaigns, and the voters do not seem to want to take the time to see that the country is headed in the right direction.

[See also Agents of Change; Change; Change, Epochal; Change, Optimistic and Pessimistic Perspectives; Change, Scientific and Technological; Continuity and Discontinuity; Laws, Evolution of; Public Policy Change; Religion: Changing Beliefs; Social Change: United States; Social and Political Evolution; Technological Change; Technology Diffusion; Trend Indicators; Values Change.]

BIBLIOGRAPHY

Grun, Bernard. *The Timetables of History.* New York: Simon & Schuster, 1975.

Kane, Joseph Nathan. *Famous First Facts: A Record of First Happenings, Discoveries and Inventions in the United States.* 3rd ed. Bronx, NY: H. W. Wilson, 1964.

Trager, James. *The People's Chronology: A Year-by-Year Record of Human Events from Prehistory to the Present.* Revised ed. New York: Henry Holt, 1992.

– GRAHAM T. T. MOLITOR

CHANGE, SCIENTIFIC AND TECHNOLOGICAL

Human knowledge has advanced to the point that almost anything that can be conceived can be achieved—at least within the ambit of natural laws as we understand them. In other words, technology is no longer a limiting factor. This new development ushers in a new era.

Science and technology should no longer be allowed to lead us wherever they might take us. Blind trust in technology will no longer suffice. New techniques are needed to anticipate and assess direct and indirect social, economic, and political consequences of technology. Unintended repercussions, sometimes catastrophic in their sweep, need to be avoided or contained.

Just five titanic technologies have transformed the world as we know it—the bomb, contraceptives, the computer, the rocketship, and genetic engineering.

Haphazard technological development with smaller-scale consequences went largely unnoticed in developing countries prior to the Industrial Revolution. As massive new technologies burgeoned, the need for deliberate direction and control emerged. Recognition became more widespread that some technologies could wreak horrendous destruction. Haphazard, unplanned, accidental, and negative impacts of technological and social policy no longer could be tolerated. Constraining second-order consequences and blunting potential adverse impacts before they did much damage became the focal point of these efforts. In short, society now strives toward deliberate direction of technology. Technology is no longer to be just harvested—it will have to be pruned, too.

The mere fact that a particular technology can be developed is not necessarily sufficient justification to proceed because risks of the new technological undertaking may be too great, costs, monetary as well as social, may be too high, ecological imbalances or improper conservation inherent in certain undertakings may prove disastrous, irresponsible development of finite resource may be unwise in the long run, the moral and ethical dilemmas involved with such development

may be potentially catastrophic. Like so many other aspects of modern civilization, technology may be a force for good or for evil. It all depends on how the new capability is applied. Just five titanic technologies have transformed the world as we know it—the bomb, contraceptives, the computer, the rocketship, and genetic engineering.

The Nuclear Bomb

Nightmares of Hiroshima and Nagasaki, amplified by tens of thousands of remaining nuclear weapons, mean that the world still lives just moments on this side of oblivion. But at the same time the introduction of limitless and inexpensive energy from controlled nuclear fusion of hydrogen is a boon.

The Pill

The pill and a range of cheap, simple to use, and effective, birth-control methods have introduced realistic prospects for population stabilization. On the other hand, their adverse side effects cause major grief.

The Computer

Electronic data processing in all its myriad forms, and especially computers, are mainsprings of the ongoing information era. They provide a core resource akin to what steel and electric motors were to the Industrial Revolution. (Symbolic of this change is the $675 worth of steel in 1994 cars, compared with $782 of electronics.)

The Rocketship

Intercontinental ballistic missiles provide a "balance of terror." Space travel, on the other hand, is the ticket to tapping the wonders of the cosmos.

Genetic Engineering

Mapping the human genome portends human control over life itself with bright promise for eradicating disease and dysfunctions. The darker prospect is that of creating a Master Race. William Van Dusen Wishard asserts, "Biotechnology is raising ethical questions that no religious leader could have conceived." He goes on to call for technologies that enhance and assert the primacy of human qualities.

Innovation is the driving force in the economic history of advanced industrialized societies. Joseph Schumpeter noted that bursts of scientific invention occurred in previous historic periods of technological growth and progress, and contended that innovation itself was essentially responsible for the growth that often is attributed to other factors. Boom and bust cycles generated by new technologies destroying and replacing the old—

C

"creative destruction," he termed it—appear to have occurred in a fifty-five-year cycle in recent history. Previous peaks of technology occurred in 1770, 1825, 1880, and 1935. That should place the current peak between 1980 and 2000. If true, this observation signals an explosive period of business growth over the next decade or so.

Where new breakthroughs are expected to occur, at least their general frontiers can be delineated. Only six key frontiers remain to be fully conquered:

The very hot and the very cold. The very hot includes plasma fusion, the fire of the stars, which is expected to be harnessed for commercial energy by 2020. The very cold involves supercool and absolute zero phenomena—cryogenics—which brightens prospects for superconductivity essential for supercomputers and energy conservation.

The very large and the very small. The very large entails fathoming far reaches of the galaxy and universe, searching out the origin of the beginning. The very small involves new capacities to measure parts per quadrillion and to plumb the inner elemental components of subatomic matter with a mind's-eye toward con-

structing perfect and new elements or their allotropes, then building matter onward from there. Biotechnologies and genetic engineering at the molecular level, mapping the human genome, and unravelling the mysteries of DNA also hold exciting promise. (If humans evolved from the Big Bang and possibly originated on Earth as organisms spawned electro-biochemically from the primordial soup millions of years ago, ponder the amazing feat of a mere chemical reaction actually conceiving its own origin!)

The very dense and the very diffuse. Changed states of matter and phenomena under enormous pressure or other variable physical parameters portend untold possibilities, as does unraveling the mystery of Black Holes, whose properties confound the basic natural laws we have constructed to explain reality. The very diffuse involves reaction of matter in super vacuum, including production of new materials in the near-perfect vacuum of outer space, or fully understanding the mysteries of the human psyche.

Throughout history, the expansion of scientific knowledge has always heralded social and cultural change. So, as scientific knowledge increases exponen-

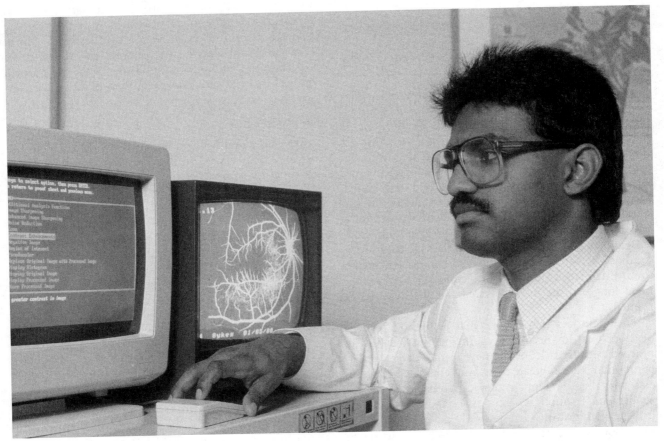

The use of computers has transformed the practice of medicine in a way never dreamed of just decades ago, enhancing diagnosis, prevention, treatment, and education. (James Marshall/Corbis)

tially, we also can expect exponential social and cultural upheaval. Future economic growth will largely be dependent on staying in the forefront of new technologies.

What it all comes down to is this: the excesses that threaten society and environment increasingly need to be curbed. Up to this point, technology has been the determinant of social conditions. We are entering into a new era when just the opposite is likely to happen. Until now, man has been up against nature; from now on, he is likely to be up against his own nature as well.

Technology and its often awesome consequences assure that modern society will require more planning. We cannot wait for crises to bring issues into focus and expect to have all the time needed to respond at the last minute. Responses in such situations may be hasty and ill considered. In short, the future increasingly will be determined by forces that humans can control. Consciously forecasting such long-range impacts will require new responsibilities and keener sophistication on the part of public and private sector leaders.

[See also Change; Political Cycles; Science Issues; Scientific Breakthroughs; Social Change: United States; Technological Change; Technological Innovation; Technology and Science; Technology and Society.]

BIBLIOGRAPHY

Foster, Richard. *Innovation.* New York: Summit Books, 1986.
McHale, John. *The Future of the Future.* New York: George Brazille, 1969.
Nayak, P. Ranganath, and Ketteringham, John M. *Breakthroughs: How the Vision and Drive of Innovators in Sixteen Companies Created Commercial Breakthroughs That Swept the World.* New York: Rawson Associates, 1986.
Rogers, Everett M., and Shoemaker, F. Floyd. *Communication of Inventions: A Cross-Cultural Approach.* 2nd ed. New York: Free Press, 1971.
Vago, Steven. *Social Change.* New York: Holt, Rinehart, and Winston, 1980.

— GRAHAM T. T. MOLITOR

CHEMICALS, FINE

Fine chemicals are high-purity, high-value substances sold on specification with recognized effects in health care (22 percent), agriculture (4 percent), imaging applications (7 percent), electronics (15 percent), nutrition (5 percent), cosmetics (4 percent), and industrial applications (35 percent). Fine chemicals were $60 billion of a total $1 trillion worldwide chemical market in 1992. The fine chemical market is expected to reach $85 billion in 2000, with North America consuming one-third of that total. Fine chemicals are produced by organic and inorganic synthesis, fermentation, and extraction. Frequently, fine chemical manufacturers produce less than 10,000 kg per year of an entity, hold sole

or semiexclusive rights to manufacture the substances, and supply a comparatively small number of customers, with only minimal support required after sales.

Triggers of Change

End-product usage of fine chemicals will increase rapidly, especially in electronics, agriculture, and health care. Increase in the demand for end-use products will be driven by greater automation, the need for more food in developing countries, and improved worldwide health care.

Consumers will demand environmentally safe products with less broad-scale and more tightly targeted effects. Increasingly stringent government regulations are expected in all fields. Claims for efficient environmentally sound products with fewer adverse effects will be the subject of new, more effectively enforced laws.

Technology will be developed to create new methods of manufacture that are more cost-effective, require less capital, and generate fewer undesirable by-products. These environmentally sound processes will involve biotechnology, chirality/stereo-specificity (left- or right-handed molecular configurations that enhance the efficiency of end use), catalysis, and other techniques applied to both the production and refinement of end products.

Technologies will be favored that yield higher purity at lower cost and keener targeted efficacy. Closed-loop extractions, highly automated systems, and in-process, analytical self-adjusting controls will be important. Manufacturing and measurement technique improvements will change production of some specialty chemicals from an imprecise art to a more exact science.

Outcomes

There will be an increase in the cost of product and process research but more cooperation between government, university, and industrial laboratories. A wide variety of products for diverse uses will come from greater investments in tightly focused research. Potential intermediate manufacturers are expected to do less speculative development work than in the past.

The escalating cost of technical development and commercialization will cause increasing concentration in the industry through alliances and acquisitions. The market will also shift geographically to satisfy higher demand in Asia and Eastern Europe.

Sound manufacturing practices will be synchronized worldwide for both end products and intermediates. Larger manufacturers who can handle the required practices will survive and thrive. Highly potent products with keener specificity will require protection against cross-contamination, purity at point and time of use, and vendor certification. More burden will be placed on the producer regarding packaging, handling, and storage. Higher governmental and financial penalties for noncompliance, including legal liabilities and tort claims, are expected.

The use of sophisticated production controls will require increased operator skills. This will be accelerated by the availability of practical information technology. Some specialty chemicals will make the transition from performance requirements to a specifications basis.

Implications

There will be 10 to 20 percent fewer fine-chemical companies than the 10,000 currently existing firms. An increase in alliances between companies is also expected. The market will grow at 6 percent annually through 2005, but there will be high-growth niches with growth rates of 10 to 20 percent.

High expenditures for regulatory requirements will put downward pressure on research and plant expansions. To compensate for costly regulatory compliance, more operations are likely to move offshore, and there will be a tendency to outsource research and manufacturing. Cost-benefit and regulatory pressures will result in fewer new products. Those introduced will be more highly differentiated.

Agriculture, electronics, and medicinals will lead worldwide market growth. Offshore demand will increase at a greater rate in developing countries. Some specialty chemicals will make the transition to become fine chemicals, further increasing the overall size of the fine chemicals market. New investment will be needed to commercialize products made by innovative cost-benefit effective processes. This will also require additional worker training and new skills. In summary, the fine chemical market will remain important and profitable, and it will grow substantially faster than the GNP over the next decade.

[See also Chemistry; Cosmetics and Toiletries; Food Additives; Nutrition; Pharmaceuticals; Photography.]

BIBLIOGRAPHY

Kline Guide to the Chemical Industry. Fairfield, NJ: C. H. Kline, 1990.
Stanford Research Institute. *International Specialty Chemicals.* Menlo Park, CA: Stanford Research Institute, 1993.

— FRED DIMARIA

CHEMISTRY

Chemistry is the branch of natural science that investigates the composition of matter and how its atoms and molecules behave. The most remarkable "composition of matter" is the human being. Thousands of chemical reactions link themselves together within each of the 75 trillion minute cells in the human body: to support life, to digest food, to distribute energy, to produce growth, and to renew the body.

The future of chemistry, and therefore of

the human race and the world,

lies in better understanding of the behavior of

atoms and molecules in different chemical structures.

The future of chemistry, and therefore of the human race and the world, lies in better understanding of the behavior of atoms and molecules in different chemical structures: through controlled experiment and application of knowledge to chemical activity inside, on, and above the surface of our planet.

Anticipating the Future of Chemistry

There are three ways of anticipating the future of chemistry: extension of its basic theory, which leads to new experiments and new knowledge; research into problems that need solutions; and integration of theory, needs, and practice to solve problems.

Three leading trends are emerging: the intermingling of chemistry and physics in the behavior of the smallest units of electrons and nuclei; through examination of the most complex molecules such as DNA; and through understanding the behavior of complex interdependent systems—the environment. These all highlight molecular recognition: how do reacting atoms or molecules "know" which way to react? The simplest model is that of lock-and-key, but modified by the relative size, functionality, and energetics of the atoms involved.

The Experimental Route

The pioneering of a new chemical physics technique, supersonic jet laser beam spectroscopy, enabled new clusters of atoms to be detected, isolated, and described. Using carbon as the feed, a new form appeared, containing 60 carbon atoms arranged symmetrically in hexagons and pentagons to form a molecule resembling a soccer ball. Others have been discovered since. This new class of molecules is called *fullerenes,* or "buckyballs," after Buckminster Fuller and his geodesic domes. $C60$ occurs naturally in candle flames; $C70$ exists; fullerenes containing nitrogen and boron have been made; and fullerenes with water-soluble "tails" have shown activity against the AIDS virus. A new field of chemistry is opening up; much more will follow.

Superconductors that possess very low resistance to the flow of electricity afford another example of unexpected payoff from experimentation. Until recently, superconductors only functioned at temperatures close to absolute zero ($-273°$ C). IBM, working in their Zurich, Switzerland, laboratories in 1986, announced the discovery of ceramic compositions that raised superconductors up to $-118°$ C, and then to $-23°$ C. Soon thereafter French researchers announced similar findings. Though difficult to fabricate, such materials can help reduce electronic transm. ion losses and electronic chip costs.

The rapid development of transistors was based on the ability to etch and build up ever more of them on a single wafer of silicon. It is now also possible to construct patterns by selective removal of atoms from a thin film surface. These new fields of chemistry arose from freshly discovered chemical structures in which specific atoms put in specific places achieve desired results.

The Theoretical Route

The number one killer of men and women is cancer. There is only one way to stop it—early detection. But present detection methods depend on the cancer becoming visible or palpable. Two potentially important new detection approaches are being explored. First, by comparing the infrared spectra of tissue samples with standards, the presence or absence of cancer can be verified much sooner. Second, the samples can be examined under a range of high pressures in a "diamond anvil," which enables changes in the chemical bonds within the cells to be identified. These techniques do two important things: they provide a simple, more accurate cancer test that can be automated for general use; and, by using the pressure tests, the transition from normal to cancerous tissue can be tracked at the molecular level. These could be major gains in what has until recently been a very difficult research field.

The Greatest Chemical Enigma

In the biochemical field the greatest enigma has been the composition of genomes, the key component of the cells of higher living organisms. The first results of the Human Genome Project have just been released as a partial computer listing of this composition, which researchers can access and exploit. This will undoubtedly accelerate research in this and related fields.

The Environment

The environment poses problems on an enormous scale. The present economic system reports only the results of business transactions but not their consequences, such as the accumulation of poisons and wastes in the environment which threaten future generations. Much of the public is aware, but skeptical, of these environmental dangers and of the need to deal

with them: ozone loss; carbon dioxide warming of the Earth; toxic material buildup in the soil, in some atmospheres, in animals, fish, humans, or parts of the Earth.

Paul Hawken contrasts this threatening situation with the three ways that nature has coped over millions of years. Nature recycles waste as food for other species; nature runs on solar energy; nature thrives on diversity and perishes in the imbalance of an unnatural uniformity. Current economic policies are unfortunately directed toward the development of an economically based worldwide uniformity. Chemists will help to challenge this trend toward uniformity by demonstrating that diversity is the soundest future strategy to attain a sustainable Earth. Chemists will also need to make the chemical chains, cycles, and linkages in the environment easier to understand and thus help to reduce present dangers and future crises.

The Industrial Chemical Approach

The chemical industry forms another vital part of the chemical picture. After a successful shift into petrochemicals in the 1960s-1980s, the industry faces major geographical moves, to exploit cheaper natural gas in the Middle East and to meet rising demands in the Asia Pacific zone. But a global vision continues to elude international chemical companies. The obvious fact that Earth runs on the use of chemical energy has to be fully understood. Keener awareness and appreciation that all chemical energy is interlinked, whether it is in the form of ozone, carbon dioxide, gasoline, chloralkali, fertilizers, polyester, plastics, metals, colors, drugs, food, water, or pollution has to be achieved. Either those in the chemical industry today will come to grasp that these are all "one" and begin to act accordingly or, the forecast goes, the industry will be taken over by others who do!

The Pollution Case

The International Institute for Applied Systems Analysis study of the river Rhine in Europe revealed the sources, spread, and deposition of cadmium, lead, zinc, phosphorus, nitrogen, lindane, and polychlorinated biphenyls throughout the Rhine basin and into the North Sea. It showed how closely chemistry links people, agriculture, forestry, electricity, coal, water, industry and air, and what happens when we ignore this. The globe is "chemical," but we still try to treat pollution as something different.

Chemistry and Society

The underrating of the human and social aspects of society in the single-minded pursuit of economic gain is producing serious consequences. These reveal themselves in suspicion, violence, rape, murder, random killing, and ultimate degradation through ethnic and racial "cleansing." Behavior itself has a chemical basis. The primary field is that of neurotransmitters, the chemicals in the brain cells which translate "thought" into action. This field is beginning to be clarified as the separate and combined effects of serotonin, noradrenaline, dopamine, and other neurotransmitters become better understood. Better understanding of how these operate is one way of helping to reveal the causes of violence and of finding ways to dampen and eliminate them.

The greatest problem of all is the expansion

of the human race at a rate faster

than its base of natural resources, food, and energy.

The Sustainability of Planet Earth

The greatest problem of all is the expansion of the human race at a rate faster than its base of natural resources, food, and energy. Much can be done and is being done to improve this situation—for example, in using solar and wind energy. But the conditions for a resilient, sustainable planet will have to be faced if succeeding generations of all living things are to coexist indefinitely into the far future. This is not just an exercise in numeration. It will involve fundamental changes in human, social, business, and political behavior that shift the focus from exploitative to sustainable ways of living. All of these changes will require the development of accurate chemical knowledge. The twenty-first century will be a busy time for chemists, chemical engineers, and chemistry!

Conclusion

Just as chemistry operates at all levels of human and natural behavior, so chemists and chemical engineers of every stripe will contribute to the transition from the discrete ways of the past toward the increasingly integrated ways and cooperation needed to enable the world to continue far into the future.

[See also Chemicals, Fine; Genetics; Global Warming; Nuclear Power; Nuclear Power: Con; Ozone Layer Depletion; Physics; Science Issues; Superconductors; Transuranium Elements.]

BIBLIOGRAPHY

Beardsley, Tim. "A War Not Won." *Scientific American* 270, no. 1 (January 1994): 130–138.

"The Cell: Its Secret Life." *The Economist* 329 (December 25, 1993–January 7, 1994): 109–113.

"Commercial Uses of Fullerenes." *C&EN* (November 22, 1993): 8–18.

Hawken, Paul. *The Ecology of Commerce: A Declaration of Sustainability.* New York: Harper/Collins, 1993.

Restak, Richard. "Brain by Design: An Era of Molecular Engineering." *The Sciences* (September–October 1993): 27–33.

———. *Designer Brain.* New York: Bantam Books, 1994. "Trends in Superconductivity." *Scientific American* 269, no. 12 (December 1993): 118–126.

— W. H. CLIVE SIMMONDS

CHILD ABUSE

The term *child abuse* is defined in various ways depending upon cultural setting. Basically, it involves physical or emotional maltreatment; institutional, educational, or medical neglect; and sexual harassment. At the 1991 World Summit on Children, heads of seventy-one nations committed themselves to improving the well-being of children by the year 2000. One future challenge confronting policy makers and professionals everywhere is the need to broaden public awareness and understanding of child abuse in order to stimulate prevention and treatment of the problem (Daro and McCurdy, 1992, p. 3).

Scope of the Policy Problem

All varieties of serious child abuse, including chronic paddling, spanking, beating, using children for sexual gratification, or depriving them of medical treatment and other basic necessities of life, cannot be tolerated in civilized societies. Protection of children from harm is an ethical imperative.

The U.S. Child Abuse Prevention and Treatment Act of 1974 attempted to establish uniform standards nationwide for the identification and management of child abuse cases. However, it was left to the states to determine investigative procedures and to define maltreatment. Consequently, only limited information on the scope of the child abuse problem was developed. In 1992, the National Committee for the Prevention of Child Abuse (NCPCA) collected data from all fifty states and the District of Columbia, enumerating institutional facilities and reports for the years from 1985 to 1992. NCPCA findings revealed that reported child neglect and abuse increased 50 percent over this seven-year period.

Kinds of Child Abuse and Neglect

Child abuse in the laws of all fifty states is defined broadly to cover harmful behavior impacting on a child's physical, emotional, social, and educational development and well-being. If more effective prevention and treatment services are to be provided, types of maltreatment need to be more carefully and comprehensively examined. In the United States during 1992, 1,261 children—about four children each day—died of neglect or abuse. Types of maltreatment reported in a recent year included physical abuse, 27 percent; sexual abuse, 17 percent; neglect, 45 percent; emotional maltreatment, 7 percent; and others, 8 percent. (The total percentages exceed 100 percent, because they were based on state averages.)

Reports on child abuse continue to increase steadily,

primed by growing economic stress, substance abuse,

and an increased public awareness that fosters

more frequent reporting of maltreatment.

PHYSICAL ABUSE. Physical abuse is most generally defined as the nonaccidental injury of a child. American children today face greater risks because of rapid changes in society, altered family structure, warped values, and inadequate resources needed for nurturing. Corporal punishment is a questionable practice that in extreme forms is forbidden. Striking a child was still permitted in schools in 78 percent of the states as of 1988. Corporal punishment was still legal in some forms in most places in thirty-nine states, but it was outlawed in eleven others (as well as in other individual school districts). Three million times a year, teachers resort to corporal punishment; however, it may not be effective in preserving discipline because it treats symptoms and not underlying causes.

The United States lags behind much of the developed and developing world in prohibiting corporal punishment. Nations already prohibiting corporal punishment include the Netherlands, China, France, Spain, Austria, Denmark, Germany, the United Kingdom, and Russia.

Corporal punishment contradicts national policy dedicated to the elimination of child abuse. Eliminating corporal punishment by federally mandating appropriate disciplinary alternatives that require state and school-district compliance is one possible solution.

NECESSITY DEPRIVATION. Necessity deprivation includes denial of medical treatment because of religious convictions or because of economic inability, and also extends to include the failure to provide nourishment, clothing, shelter, or other essentials (Ingram, 1988, p. 41). In the United States, the care, custody, and nurturing of children are primarily the responsibility of parents. The doctrine of *parens patria*—the sovereign power of the state to protect people under disability,

including children—limits parental autonomy to raise children as they desire. State authorities intervene when parents or other guardians fail to supply necessary medical care or to provide for a child's well-being.

The paramount criterion for state intervention is the best interest of the child. Constitutional protection of religious freedom prohibits states from interfering with religious decisions regarding medical care; nevertheless, numerous child neglect statutes impose criminal liability and provide for the removal of parental custody in life-threatening situations.

SEXUAL MALTREATMENT. The term *sexual abuse* denotes any sexually stimulating act that is inappropriate for a child's age level of development or role within the family (Brant and Tisza, 1977, p. 80). Sexual abuse occurs at all socioeconomic levels, though it is more prevalent among the poor. U.S. Department of Health and Human Services statistics reveal that 80 percent of the children sexually abused are girls. Three types of sexual behavior are identified as (1) noncontact behavior such as "sexy talk" and exposure of intimate body parts to the eyes of the victim by the perpetrator; (2) sexual contact that includes the touching of intimate body parts; (3) sexual exploitation, that is, child prostitution or the use of children in the creation of pornography.

Public awareness of child sexual abuse is increasing because of media attention, community education, and school programs. This increase probably does not reflect so much an increase in incidence as an increase in willingness to report such incidences. A recent NCPCA study sampling sixteen developed countries and fourteen developing countries indicated that 75 percent of the developed countries and 50 percent of the developing countries cited child sexual abuse as the type of maltreatment most time-consuming to professionals.

General population studies in various countries show the problem is widespread (see Table 1).

Evidence of incest can be found in early civilizations. Since the late 1970s, the reluctance to speak out on the

TABLE 1

EPISODES OF SEXUAL ABUSE DURING CHILDHOOD

Country	Females	Males
United States	20.0%	7%
Canada	33.3%	—
Netherlands	33.3%	—
Finland	18.0%	—
Sweden	10.0%	3.3%

Source: *World Perspectives on Child Abuse*, 1992; Ronstrom, 1989, p. 125.

subject has been lifted and the issues slowly have been uncovered, all of which has been featured in the media. Confused values, increased mobility, and society's emphasis on sexuality and performance are contributing factors to the high incidence of incest. Incest, or familial abuse, is now recognized as a national problem that deserves further investigation to devise effective legislation and strategic intervention.

Summary

Reports on child abuse continue to increase steadily, primed by growing economic stress, substance abuse, and an increased public awareness that fosters more frequent reporting of maltreatment. States continue to experience large caseload increases with little or no funding to deal with them. Despite this, states are making headway through innovative programs. Developments include home visiting services; mechanisms addressing the connection between substance abuse and child abuse; and state children's trust funds for prevention. The solution depends on implementing services, providing assistance to individual families, and improving overall living environments. Progress can be made through multifaceted approaches, including:

- A uniform system of common language, definitions, information, and technology worldwide.
- Laws that mandate the link between victim identification and family assistance.
- Increased federal appropriations to prevent and treat child neglect.
- More and better quality recidivism studies to learn more about treatment and punishment alternatives.
- Increased education of the judiciary.
- Comprehension that child abuse cannot be treated as an isolated social problem.
- Improvement of overall living environments.
- The elimination of corporal punishment.

    [See also Abortion; Child Care; Crime Rates; Family Problems; Family Values.]

BIBLIOGRAPHY

Brant, R., and Tisza, V. "The Sexual Misused Child." *American Journal of Orthopsychiatry* (January 1977): 80–90.

Daro, D., and McCurdy, K. *Current Trends in Child Abuse Reporting and Fatalities: The Results of the 1991 Annual Fifty-State Survey.* Chicago: National Committee for Prevention of Child Abuse, 1992.

Ingram, John Dwight. "State Interference with Religiously Motivated Decisions on Medical Treatment." *Dickinson Law Review* (Fall 1988): 41–66.

National Center on Child Abuse Prevention Research, National Committee on the Prevention of Child Abuse. *World Perspectives on Child Abuse: An International Resource Book.* Chicago: National Committee for the Prevention of Child Abuse, 1992.

Ronstrom, Anitha. "Sweden's Children's Ombudsman: A Spokesperson for Children." *Child Welfare* 68 (March–April 1989): 123–128.

Tzeng, Oliver C. S., and Jacobson, Jamia Jasper, eds. *Sourcebook for Child Abuse and Neglect.* Springfield, IL: Charles C. Thomas Publishing, 1988.

— JAN M. GRELL

CHILD CARE

A dramatic increase in mothers' participation in the labor force is currently in progress. In 1965, 25.3 percent of the mothers with children under six years old were in the labor force; in 1990, that figure reached 58 percent. Even more dramatic has been the rise in labor force participation for the mothers of infants and toddlers. In 1965, 21 percent were in the labor force; by 1990 that number had gone up to 54 percent. Likewise, 73 percent of mothers of children five to twelve years old were in the labor force in 1990. These increases have obviously created a greater demand for child care services, which is likely to accelerate further in the future.

Child Care Supply

Not surprisingly, the supply of child care has correspondingly increased. In 1990, there were 80,000 centers in the United States, serving between 4 and 5 million children. Between 1976 and 1990, the number of centers tripled and the number of children in centers quadrupled. Likewise, the number of family child care homes (care for children in the home of the provider) has increased, although the exact increase is difficult to discern because between 82 and 90 percent of family child care homes are not licensed or registered. It is estimated that there are 118,000 regulated homes serving 700,000 children. In addition, there are approximately 685,000 to 1.2 million family child care homes that are not licensed or registered, serving 3.4 million children (Kisker, Hofferth, Phillips, and Farquhar, 1991; Willer, Hofferth, Kisker, Divine-Hawkins, Farquhar, and Glanz, 1991).

There are indications, however, of developing gaps between supply and demand. On average, centers are filled to 88 percent capacity; between two-thirds and three-fourths of centers report having no vacancies. This problem is particularly acute for infants and toddlers (Kisker, Hofferth, Phillips, and Farquhar, 1991). For parents, the issue also seems to be a problem of locating quality care. In a nationally representative study of the U.S. workforce, 58 percent of parents looking for child care report finding no choices. The situation seems likely to exacerbate further in the years ahead.

Usage of Various Child Care Arrangements

Since 1970, the arrangements that families use to care for their children have shifted. Among families with employed mothers and preschool children, there has been a decrease in care by relatives. In 1965, 62 percent of these children under five were cared for by relatives. In 1990, that number dropped to 47 percent. Interestingly, this decrease does not represent less parental care. In 1965, 29 percent of preschool children with employed mothers were cared for by their own parents, while in 1990, that figure was 28 percent. Parents typically care for their own children while employed by working split shifts or taking their children to work. The shift in relative care, therefore, represents a sharp drop in the use of care by relatives other than parents—grandparents, aunts, and uncles. In 1965, 33 percent of the preschool children with employed mothers were cared for by their grandparents, aunts, and uncles, as compared with 19 percent in 1990.

Another notable trend is the increased use of formal child care arrangements, especially among families with children three years and older. In 1990, 14 percent of infants were in center care, 23 percent of toddlers (one-to two-year-olds) were. For children three to four years old, 43 percent were cared for in centers.

Among school-age children with employed mothers, 33 percent are cared for by their parents, 23 percent by other relatives, 3 percent by sitters, 7 percent by family child care providers, 14 percent by centers, 4 percent in self-care, and 15 percent in after-school lessons. This trend is likely to continue.

The Price of Child Care

While the demand and the supply of child care is increasing, the fees that parents pay are remaining virtually flat. Fifty-six percent of families with employed mothers and preschool children pay for child care. In 1975, parents paid $1.40 per hour for center care while in 1990, parents paid $1.67, representing an increase of $0.27 over fifteen years. For parents who used family child care, including licensed, registered, and unlicensed, the fees went from $1.29 an hour in 1975 to $1.35 in 1990, an increase of $0.06 per hour in the same fifteen years.

On average, the yearly 1990 price for all forms of care for preschool children with employed mothers was $3,150. This represents 10 percent of their family in-

As the number of day care centers has risen, interest in the quality of child care has become an important concern for parents and policymakers. (Vince Streano/Corbis)

come. Low-income families, however, pay a much greater share of their family income for child care than higher-income families. Families earning less than $15,000 per year pay 23 percent while families earning $50,000 or more pay 6 percent.

Child Care Quality

There is a growing interest in the quality of child care because it has become apparent that for many children, child care is "education before school" (Galinsky and Friedman, 1993). The first national education goal states that "By the year 2000, all children will enter school ready to learn." If this country is serious about meeting this goal, then the quality of child care settings must be good. Three multisite observational studies of both center care and family child care conducted between 1988 and 1994 reveal a more dismal picture of the quality of child care. These studies indicate that 12–14 percent of the children are in child care arrangements that promote their growth and learning while 12–21 percent are in child care arrangements that are unsafe and harmful to their development. For infants and toddlers, the proportion in unsafe settings is even higher: 35–40 percent (Whitebook, Howes, and Phillips, 1990; Cost, Quality, and Child Outcomes Study Team, 1995).

These studies also uncovered the characteristics associated with higher-quality education and care. They found that children in center-based arrangements fare better emotionally, socially, and cognitively when they are in arrangements that have:

- a sufficient number of adults for each child—that is, high staff-to-child ratios
- smaller group sizes
- higher levels of staff education and specialized training
- low staff turnover and administrative stability
- higher levels of staff compensation.

Studies of center-based arrangements reveal that these characteristics of quality are interrelated. Furthermore, these studies find that quality in child care centers is affected by state regulations: children who live in states with high regulatory standards have higher-quality early care and education than children who live in states with low standards (Cost, Quality, and Child Outcomes Study Team, 1995; Whitebook et al., 1990). Not surprisingly, given the uneven quality of care, there are large variations in standards across the United States.

In family child care, children fare better emotionally and cognitively when their providers:

- are committed to taking care of children and are doing so from a sense that this work is important and it is what they want to be doing.

- seek out opportunities to learn about children's development and child care, have higher levels of education, and participate in family child care training.
- think ahead about what the children are going to do and plan experiences for them.
- seek out the company of others who are providing care and are more involved with other providers.
- are regulated.
- have slightly larger groups (three to six children) and slightly higher numbers of adults per child.
- charge higher rates, and follow standard business and safety practices.

As with center-based arrangements, studies find that these characteristics of quality go together. Providers who have one of these characteristics are likely to have others. In other words, providers who are *intentional* in their approach provide more sensitive and responsive education and care.

There are indications that the quality of care and early education is declining. Although the educational level of staff has improved, ratios and group sizes seem to be growing worse. Furthermore, a number of programs do not meet their own state standards for group size and staff-to-child ratios, especially in programs for infants and toddlers. Moreover, staff turnover is high (Kisker, Hofferth, Phillips, and Farquhar, 1991; Whitebook, Howes, and Phillips, 1990; Whitebook, Phillips, and Howes, 1993).

Recent studies offer some hopeful news about quality. A study of family child care training revealed that the children were more likely to be securely attached to their providers following training, and that the quality of the caregiving environments had improved. In another study where the state had legislated higher staff-to-child ratios and higher educational requirements for staff, the changes in children's development are impressive: they are more securely attached, exhibit better cognitive and social development, are more proficient with language, and have fewer behavior problems (Howes, Smith, and Galinsky, 1994).

[See also Child Abuse; Children, Living Arrangements; Families And Households.]

BIBLIOGRAPHY

Cost, Quality, and Child Outcomes Study Team. *Cost, Quality, and Child Outcomes in Child Care Centers.* Denver: Economics Department, University of Colorado at Denver, 1995.

Galinsky, E., and Friedman, D. E. *Education Before School: Investing in Quality Child Care.* Commissioned by the Committee for Economic Development. New York: Scholastic, 1993.

Howes, C.; Smith, E.; and Galinsky, E. *The Florida Child Care Improvement Study: Interim Report.* New York: Families and Work Institute, 1994.

Kisker, E. E.; Hofferth, S. L.; Phillips, D. A.; and Farquhar, E. *A Profile of Child Care Settings, Early Education, and Care in 1990.* Vol. 1. Princeton, NJ: Mathematica Policy Researh, 1991.

Whitebook, M.; Howes, C.; and Phillips, D. A. *Who Cares? Child Care Teachers and the Quality of Care in America.* Final report of the Child Care Staffing Study. Oakland, CA: Child Care Employee Project, 1990.

Willer, B.; Hofferth, S. L.; Kisker, E. E.; Divine-Hawkins, P.; Farquhar, E.; and Glanz, F. B. *The Demand and Supply of Child Care in 1990.* Washington, DC: National Association for the Education of Young Children; U.S. Department of Health and Human Services, Administration on Children, Youth, and Families; U.S. Department of Education, Office of the Undersecretary, 1991.

– ELLEN GALINSKY

CHILDREN, LIVING ARRANGEMENTS

The living arrangements of the world's children reflect patterns of social change affecting all of us. Patterns displayed by Western nations may or may not be indicative of the world as a whole. Beyond this, available data stress children in families or alternative care. Almost no reliable data exist on the controversial status of abducted children, runaways, or children with homosexual or transracial parents. These childhood situations attract media attention disproportionate to their frequency. Many of the statistics staking out the parameters of these problems are waved about to influence policy or public opinion, and involve wishful thinking, or even outright fabrications.

The most significant of these change patterns are those relating to marriage. Substantial decreases in first marriage rates and increases in the likelihood of divorce have directly affected the nature of families with children. Other factors include falling mortality rates among married individuals and the connected decline in single-parent households plus the growth in the number of families headed by never-married mothers. Finally, the decline of U.S. female fertility rates from 3.7 children on average in 1955 to 2.0 children in 1992 may be considered an indicator of the declining importance of parenthood in modern life. What is clear, at least in Western countries, is that dramatic changes of a much broader nature are under way. Common to social trend foresight, the most reliable guess is that patterns that became evident in the 1980s will continue through to the end of the century. Concise descriptions of some important Western patterns follow.

In the United States fewer people are marrying, they are marrying later, those marrying are having fewer children, and more marriages are ending in divorce. All of these factors affect the living arrangements of children. The United States has the highest divorce rates in the world. It also suffers the most children living in poverty in any Western nation—20 percent (a 21 percent increase since 1970). In justification or explanation of these alarming statistics, it is worth cautioning that the numbers may be erroneous; comparisons may be over-

drawn due to the simple fact that U.S. numbers may be more painstakingly accurate than data collected in other countries.

Children under the age of eighteen are considerably more likely to be living with only one parent today than two decades ago. In 1993, more than one in four children in the United States under eighteen lived with only one parent (27 percent), up from one in eight in 1970. The overwhelming majority of these children—87 percent—lived with their mother. An increasing percentage lived with their father—13 percent, up from 9 percent in 1970. A decade ago, a child in a one-parent family was almost twice as likely to be living with a divorced parent than a never-married parent. However, by 1993 the chances were almost even in the U.S.

In the United States, fewer people are marrying,

they are marrying later, those marrying

are having fewer children,

and more marriages are ending in divorce.

In Great Britain, the change has not been as dramatic. In 1971, single mothers were only 16 percent of single-parent families, while the formerly married comprised 51 percent. By 1991, the single-mother category in Great Britain had doubled to 1 in 3. The formerly married was steady at 52 percent of the total (the drop was in widowed parents, from 21 to 6 percent). In other industrialized countries, the single-mother category is around 20 percent and growing. Only Germany and Italy show averages under 10 percent (and some decline over the past decade).

One important phenomenon is the increase in children living within blended families with combinations of stepparents, step-siblings, and half-siblings. Altogether, this category accounted for 15 percent of all children in the U.S. in 1991.

Arrangements outside of any family connection accounted for 1 percent or less in the United States, and foster or adoptive parents for less than 2 percent. The 1993 U.S. total in foster care alone was only 440,110 out of 67.5 million children under the age of eighteen (0.65 percent). Although these numbers are proportionally small, they do represent a significant policy problem. The trend is what highlights the problem. The number of U.S. children in substitute care almost doubled in the past decade (up from 282,000 in 1982). The number of such children entering into new families through adoption dropped over the same period—from 24,000 annually in 1982 to only 17,000 in 1990. Finally, the ages of children in substitute or foster care have continued to drop, with a 12 percent increase in the number of children under five years of age occurring between 1982 and 1990.

There are clear foster-care differences between racial and ethnic groups. In the U.S., the percentages of white children in foster care dropped from 53 percent of the total in 1982 to 39 percent in 1990, while the percentages of African-American children rose from 34 percent in 1982 to 40 percent in 1990. The highest proportional increase was among Hispanic children— rising from 6 percent in 1982 to 12 percent in 1990— which is likely a reflection of evolving U.S. immigration patterns.

In 1993, one-parent families accounted for 21 percent of white children's situations, 32 percent of Hispanic children, and 57 percent of African-American children under eighteen years of age. In the case of children living with grandparents, the percentages were 4 percent of whites, 6 percent of Hispanics, and 12 percent of all African-American children.

What is becoming clear is that large numbers of children will experience a variety of family types over the course of their lives. However, research in the United Kingdom and the level of disagreement elsewhere indicates no single or straightforward relationship between family disruption, single parenthood, and outcomes for children, either positive or negative. There is no inevitable path down which any one child will travel.

In the United States, an estimated 330,000 children were homeless in 1993. Assumptions concerning associated declines in adequate education, nutrition, and health care are just that—educated assumptions. Certainly much of the homelessness associated with wars and famine throughout the world has negative consequences. According to the UN High Commission on Refugees, the tides of refugees across borders have grown tenfold from the mid-1970s—to a total of 23 million in 1993. As well, internally "displaced persons" within country borders totaled 26 million in 1993.

The challenge is to reach a clearer understanding of the effects these trends impose on the children affected.

Many children will experience a variety of living arrangements over the course of their lifetimes. These children are spending time with their grandmother. (Annie Griffiths Belt/Corbis)

A serious debate has been raging among social scientists concerning the effects. What is the correct definition of a family? Is it bound by sexual ties, blood relation, shared space, shared resources, or all of the above? Is the "family" in decline or is it constructively evolving to meet new social conditions?

The experiences of children

indelibly shape their values and attitudes.

In the clearest possible sense, "children are the future."

Some observers believe the modern family structure now fails to fulfill its traditional roles involving child socialization, economic cooperation, provision of affection and companionship, and the teaching of sexual mores. However, others believe that the trends described above represent movement toward flexibility and away from historically sexist and exploitive structures and situations. It is clear that ideology plays some part in how trends are characterized and how people react to them in a value-laden area such as family patterns.

Changes in Western family structure and the expanding work roles of women have increased the influence of substitute caregivers in modern children's lives. While some luminaries such as Margaret Mead have cogently argued that structured variety in caregiving patterns may in fact be a positive thing, by teaching coping skills and flexibility, it also is clear that the limitations of an inadequate institutional setting can restrain development and self-reliance.

The more interesting question is how much trends in children's living arrangements reflect changes in the underlying relationships between generations, especially as they relate to attitudes and communications. While these factors influence the tone and quality of social structures in the future, they also influence attitudes toward intergenerational commitments such as employee-employer-funded social security programs.

Debates surrounding these issues are compelling and broad-based because children's policy is such a tempting target for foresight-aided policy intervention. Observers point to past intervention failures and to a general shrinking of resources for such ill-defined programs as those aimed at providing for "our children's future." Still others note declining sympathy for children's issues generally in an era of self-absorption and social unrest. In defense of such programs and policies, proponents argue that if we could only understand the changes that families and children are undergoing and fathom their causes, perhaps "ideal" outcomes could be realized through changes in the family policies of nations. This may be part of the thinking behind the 1989 UN Convention of the Rights of the Child, which includes language on the continuity of child-family connections. Children's living arrangements and the causes giving rise to changing conditions are critical issues that demand our attention. The experiences of children indelibly shape their values and attitudes. In the clearest possible sense, "children are the future."

[See also Child Abuse; Child Care; Divorce; Elderly, Living Arrangements; Family Patterns; Family Problems; Family Values; Household Composition; Marriage.]

BIBLIOGRAPHY

Adamson, Peter, ed. *The Progress of Nations: 1994.* New York: UNICEF, 1994.

Behrman, Richard, ed. *The Future of Children: Children and Divorce.* Los Altos, CA: Center of the Future of Children, 1994.

Burghes, Louie. *Lone Parenthood and Family Disruption: The Outcomes for Children.* London: Family Policy Studies Centre, 1994.

Conody, Ann. "Family Index," *Family Policy Bulletin,* May 1994. London: Family Policy Studies Centre, p. 16.

Furukawa, Stacey. *The Diverse Living Arrangements of Children: Summer 1991.* Washington, DC: U.S. Bureau of the Census, 1994.

Hart, Roger, *The Changing City of Childhood: Implications for Play and Learning.* New York: City College Workshop Center, 1986.

Hewlett, Sylvia. *Child Neglect in Rich Nations.* New York: United Nations Children's Fund, 1993.

Kirschten, Dick, "No Refuge," *National Journal* 26/37 (September 10, 1994): 2068.

Popenoe, David, "American Family Decline, 1960–1990: A Review and Appraisal." *Journal of Marriage and the Family* (August 1993): 527.

Saluter, Arlene, *Marital Status and Living Arrangements: March 1993.* Washington, DC: Bureau of Census, 1994.

Tatara, Toshio. *Characteristics of Children in Substitute and Adoptive Care* Washington, DC: American Public Welfare Association, 1993.

– TIMOTHY CRAIG MACK

CHINA

As is true of every nation, China's future is highly indeterminate, including a large number of relevant variables, most of which cannot be quantified. Trend projections are of some use: population statistics, arable land amounts, probable economic growth rates and the like are mostly set for the next decade. Qualitative directions—type of government, ideological orientation, cultural life, and so on—can be assessed with some accuracy for the two-to-three-year future. Moreover, some measures that depend on a mixture of quantitative data and qualitative estimation can also be viewed with a degree of certainty in the period between three and ten years. These include degree of urbanization, social conditions, environmental questions, the energy and natural resource base, and education and health matters.

But the middle of the 1990s already was witnessing fundamental changes that make impossible any reasonably certain forecast of even basic aspects of life and policy in China. The most important was the end of rule, after nearly a half century, of the founding generation of communist rulers. Almost no one shared their ideological outlook yet no one equalled their personal authority. Consequently, China's political and ideological base could change enormously and rapidly in the coming years, with highly uncertain outcomes. Of nearly equal importance were the effects on society and polity of the vast economic changes since 1979.

Huge, annual economic growth rates, the engine of change for the entire post-Maoist period, could not continue. The major issue was whether a "soft landing," in terms of reduced but sustainable growth, acceptable inflation, and reconnecting the infrastructural base with the high-technology/foreign trade/international interdependence superstructure, was still possible. The alternative would be drastic, medium-term economic decline, with the concomitant dangers of mass starvation, ecological disaster, general civil disorder, and possibly even political breakdown.

At the end of the Deng Xiaoping-led decade and a half of economically driven reforms, the polity appeared stable. But that was deceptive. The near-term transition was from totalitarianism to corporate authoritarianism, therefore, with a concomitant distribution of power from center to region and locality and competition for leadership not only among those in the troika of ruling institutions (party, army, and government) but also political newcomers as private entrepreneurs, an urban middle class, and industrial workers. (The peasantry, comprising about 70 percent of the population of 1.2 billion, still lacked serious political representation.) Moreover, the party was no longer a pyramid with all power concentrated at the top, but an umbrella, spreading ever wider and thinner to contain within its bounds the swirl of politics among many organizations and factions that could eventually form the basis of a multiparty, protodemocratic polity. That was years away, however. Meanwhile, China's political options ranged from ragged party-centered authoritarianism to straight military rule (like Poland in the 1980s) to a gradual political coming apart at the seams between central and regional authorities to cautious democratization to full political disintegration.

China's economy was at once its shining light and its danger. Rates of growth for the 1978–1994 period approached 10 percent, despite a strong downturn in the late 1980s and early 1990s. With huge capital inflows (by the mid-1990s, nearly $50 billion per year), high (up to 40 percent) rates of domestic savings, gradual and successful market-directed economic reforms in agriculture, services, and industry, and an opening to the global economy that saw China become within a decade one of the globe's largest trading states ($235 billion of two-way trade in 1994), the economy grew from less than $350 billion to more than $1.5 trillion per annum (on the basis of purchasing-power parity calculations), with a per capita national income of about $1,100 to $1,200.

Within a decade or two, China could be at the cutting edge in practically every area, from aircraft to computers to medicine to satellites.

Coastal and southern areas grew richer much faster than northern and inland provinces, leaving geographic distribution of income highly skewed. But even the latter areas—especially the agriculturally productive countryside—more than doubled their per capita income. The Chinese people, for the first time in their history, had more than enough to eat. Total grain production continued to grow at about 4 percent per annum, to 450 million tons in 1994, and per capita production increased to about 2,700 calories per day (i.e., beyond the approximately 2,200 necessary to keep people alive and productive). Labor mobility was gradually restored, a private internal capital market was gradually created, technological modernization zoomed (although it did not fully make up for the stagnation of the 1958–1976 Maoist past), a legal basis to economic life was laid, and a massive ($500 billion over the next decade) infrastructure construction program was initiated. Most Chinese cities were in the midst of transformation, with high-rise buildings and construction cranes dominating every horizon, and traditional one-story structures rapidly disappearing beneath their shadows or being bulldozed out of existence. The Chinese consumer (now it was possible to speak of such a person) hankered to possess a television, a VCR, a motorcycle, and a washer-dryer, no longer interested in such "lower-order" items as watches, bicycles, and sewing machines.

Other areas closely connected to the economy also prospered greatly. China imported (whether by purchase or purloining) massive amounts of technology, and together with huge domestic efforts, became a technological leader in many areas. With another decade or two (presuming no major setbacks), China would be at the cutting edge in practically every area, from aircraft to computers to medicine to satellites. Chinese scientists, freed generally from ideological constraints and able to communicate with their brethren (especially those of the global Chinese diaspora) in foreign lands, quickly moved to the forefront. Numbers plus official encouragement plus wealth implied a China scientifically rivaling the United States for global primacy within a similar period. China was rapidly progressing through the communications revolution, unifying the nation as never before and bringing China in contact with places and institutions throughout the globe. The transportation system, long anachronistic, much too dependent on the railroad, with a much underdeveloped road net (to say nothing of the absence of the modern superhighway), and an air transport system fully unsuited to rapid economic growth, also began to modernize rapidly. While all these areas would take additional decades of intensive work, it became possible for the first time (at least under ideal circumstances) to move large numbers of people and goods over long distances within reasonable time.

Societal measures were equally encouraging. Average life span by 1994 reached 69 years. Reproduction rates declined swiftly to 2.07. The "life tree" of the Chinese population began to look more like that of the standard developed country, with a constricting base, relatively equal numbers of working age adults, and a growing population of the elderly. Educational attainments were increasingly high: some 100 million Chinese (75 percent of the relevant age group) finished primary school, 30 million (30 percent) finished secondary school, and one million (about 2 percent) attended college. All these figures were significantly higher, year by year and group by group, than the years before the Deng-era reforms began in late 1978 and, of course, represented a sea change from the Cultural Revolution, when schools as a whole were closed for up to a decade. Literacy, at about 85 percent, was at developed-country levels. Literature and the arts, while hardly freed from party control, nonetheless experienced a flowering. Taiwan and Hong Kong served as domesticizing funnels for all kinds of foreign influences. Television, including access to international broadcasting, was available in every village throughout the land. Housing stock grew enormously, and the number of square meters per person in urban areas grew to near 7 (in 1991, up from near 4 in 1978), and above 18 (up from 8 in 1978) in rural areas. That still evidenced very crowded conditions, but was a major improvement from the Maoist quarter century.

Social mobility, in terms of class, wealth, and education, turned from socialist-commanded equality of poverty toward the high degree of differentiation characteristic of most developed societies. There was a re-surgence of interest in religion in China, both in terms of undifferentiated asking of religious questions and of formal religions, especially Christianity and Islam. The movement toward a market economy caused many to think, at least, about the emergence (or reemergence, depending on appraisal of Chinese history) of a civil society in China. In sum, in comparison with the recent past, the quality of life had improved to the point where most people could pursue a variety of private interests relatively unhindered by party control or ideological interference, could concentrate on becoming wealthy if they so chose, and could look forward to a reasonably lengthy life enjoying some of the standard rewards.

But these gains came at very high cost and masked the potential for disaster. The list of ills was very long. Most important was the combination of near-universal corruption and high (in 1994, about 25 percent) inflation. That combination had brought down many a Chinese regime and, if not definitively checked, would by itself spell the end of communist rule and could bring on the chaos that all Chinese feared. But the remainder of the list was also long and equally serious: loosening controls on population growth, the product of declining party authority and inequities in the birth control policy (population totals were already several years ahead even of high-end projections); a massive internal migration problem (the "floating population," estimated at between 50 and 100 million people, moving into the cities without permanent employment); reemergence of economically based class divisions; lack of macro tools of indirect economic control coupled with increasing inability (or unwillingness) to use raw coercion; regional and local centers of economic and political power increasingly autonomous from central control; the center's declining ability to squeeze resources from lower levels; the difficult-to-overcome problem of dissolving the state-run industrial sector and overcoming the attendant "iron rice bowl" syndrome; massive infrastructure bottlenecks, especially in the rail net; power shortages (the country would have to install a new power plant every two weeks just to keep up with demand); rising crime; rural rebellions and urban worker strikes; governmental inability to fulfill grain purchase contracts; lack of a banking system and regulations suitable to a marketizing system; rampant speculation in real estate and stocks; a major capital flight problem (still hidden in 1994 but estimated at up to $40 billion); general decline in education levels and teacher numbers in the primary schools; probable unwillingness of the military to fire upon the people if they demonstrated again in massive numbers; enormous environmental and ecological problems that, if not addressed, would lead to absolute and long-term decline in food production and rise in disease incidence; and a spreading narcotics problem. This list could be lengthened practically at will. When added to the coming political transition and the impossibility of maintaining almost double-digit growth rates, these many troubles could spell disaster for China. To that—hardly a footnote—should be added the very uncertain international situation and the prospect of a much harder military and economic attitude toward the country by its neighbors and other important countries and regions, as China accelerated the process of projecting its power at ever-farther distances from its borders and into situations and disputes with which it previously had had no interest or involvement.

China's medium-long-term future (three to fifteen years) hinges domestically on three alternatives: continuation of economic reforms amid slow political evolution (so-called reformist authoritarian regime); conservative restoration and halting or reversal of economic reforms (a conservative repressive regime); and political decay, loss of economic control, and societal churning (a decaying regime). Internationally, three alternatives also appear: straight-line projection of the ad hoc, laissez-faire post-Cold War international situation; international systemic pulverization characteristic of massive security and economic instability; and international systemic integration on the basis of a great power-led solution to security challenges, reasonably high, all-around economic growth, and a general global movement toward democracy. China's future, a combination of these domestic and international alternatives, seems to consist of nine alternatives.

- A reformist-authoritarian Chinese regime combined with a straight-line projection of the mid-1990s international situation. This would provide China with at least a reasonable chance to develop fully economically and politically, as well as to become a global power.
- A reformist-authoritarian Chinese regime combined with international systemic pulverization would allow China for a while to modernize economically, but hold back democratization, expand its Asian purview to the point of dominating the region, but eventually spell disaster for the country as external markets would dry up, capital and technological flows would cease, and the regime would be gradually overcome by burgeoning domestic ills.
- A reformist-authoritarian China and international systemic integration providing the best chance for successful economic, social, and political modernization at least cost. A secure international atmosphere and a cooperative China would assure the continuation of reforms in all three spheres, high rates of growth, attack against the country's manifold problems, as well as a country threatening no one (except perhaps Taiwan), and acceptable to its neighbors and more distant powers.
- A conservative repressive regime associated with a straight-line projection of the mid-1990s international environment would find the world slowly but steadily becoming more unfriendly and constrictive. Feeling threatened from abroad and increasingly less able to grow economically from internal resources alone, China would enter a vicious circle: more GNP

would go into the military and correspondingly less would be left for economic and social betterment. The regime would be isolated abroad and the party progressively isolated from the populace, and China would lose what chance it might have had to modernize in the full sense of the word and become an accepted, equal partner in global affairs.

- A conservative repressive regime, if emergent along with a pulverized international system, would become an imperialist threat to all of Asia, taking Taiwan at will and making Southeast Asia into an exclusive sphere of influence. Such expansion, while probably successful for a while, would eventually spell the end of the communist regime, for the major powers would finally recover sufficiently to restore the status quo ante and perhaps even conduct highly destructive military operations against China—i.e., wage war. Confronting the need to marshal all resources for a fight for survival and faced with the inevitable internal political and economic decay, the regime would fall, and the country could descend into chaos.
- A conservative repressive regime facing international systemic integration would find life much harder much sooner. An imperialist China would be countered quickly with superior resources. The regime would thus be forced back upon itself after suffering several near-term defeats and squandering enormous resources girding for war. The party would thus confront an angry Chinese populace with nothing to show for their sacrifices. Decay and downfall would soon follow, and China would have to choose between rapid transition to democracy (with all the pitfalls associated with that movement) or, again, chaos, disunion, and possible dismemberment.
- A decaying regime linked with a straight-line extrapolation of the mid-1990s international situation would not be instantly disastrous for the regime, if only because the downward slope would be modulated by useful international economic and political influence. At least such a regime would have a chance to modify its policies in the direction pointed out by China's more successful neighbors. Indeed, it might seize the opportunity to turn around failed economic and political policies and move back to the reformist-authoritarian path, if not onto the road of full marketization and democratization, which is China's only long-term salvation.
- If a decaying regime is matched with international systemic pulverization, however, the danger quotient could rise dramatically. The question is which would decline more rapidly. In China's case, decay could proceed without much worry about international interference. Decay would not necessarily spell collapse; it could eventually lead to transformation through replacement of party rule by some more liberal form of polity, even though that be some version of authoritarianism and not necessarily democracy. But if the rate of downward drift at home were less than that internationally, China might be tempted to project its power abroad faster and farther, through Soviet-like "defensive imperialism." The outcome then would be, in all probability, systemic downfall, collision with the United States, and internal disaster. But comparative rates of decline being inherently difficult to evaluate, miscalculations on all sides would be easy to make and the danger of disaster would be high.
- The final combination would witness the coexistence of a decaying regime with international systemic integration. China would fall into crisis, and perhaps chaos, on its own. But the nation would at least address its internal problems without fear of untoward external involvement, thus providing some support for further marketization and movement toward democracy. Eventually, China—with strong international assistance—would recover sufficiently, become interdependent internationally, and return to the path of full, if postponed, modernization.

Among the nine basic possibilities, some are clearly "better" than others, in the sense of being beneficial for China and its neighbors. The reformist-authoritarian domestic alternative poses the least danger for the country, even when the international environment varies. The conservative repressive regime would be worst for China, over all three international alternatives. A decaying internal Chinese regime would fall somewhere in between. Two conclusions seem apparent. First, China's future is largely in its own hands. That was not the case before the Deng-led reform era began. The probability is that it will succeed in becoming fully modern, although the road will remain tortuous. Second, the outside world will continue to be an important influence over China, for better or worse. In that regard, if other peoples wish the Chinese well, they will take care to arrange their own affairs in such a manner as to maximize the resources available to deal with China, whether necessarily resistant to Chinese interference in their own activities or having at ready the massive level of assistance that might be required to save that country from itself.

An interesting regularity over the past half century shows up—with a massive upheaval occurring about once a decade. The revolution of 1949, the Great Leap, the Cultural Revolution, the initiation of thoroughgoing modernization under Deng, and the Tiananmen Incident all were separated from each other by roughly ten years. The huge upsurge of economic development and the consequent sociopolitical changes of the 1990s actually began shortly after the Tiananmen Incident in 1989. That upsurge will falter after a time, and it is then that China will encounter its next great crisis. If the past pattern is any indication, that crisis could begin in the final year or two of the current millennium.

[See also Asia; Communism.]

BIBLIOGRAPHY

Chu, Godwin C. *The Great Wall in Ruins: Communications and Cultural Change in China.* Albany, NY: State University of New York Press, 1993.

Nagel, Stuart S., and Mills, Miriam K. *Public Policy in China.* Westport, CT: Greenwood Press, 1993.

Overholt, William H. *The Rise of China: How Economic Reform Is Creating a New Superpower.* New York: W. W. Norton, 1993.

— THOMAS W. ROBINSON

CHURCH-STATE AFFAIRS

Emerging patterns of church and state affairs worldwide are primarily affected by the power relationships between nations and the organized churches of Christianity and Judaism in the Western religions, and Islam and others in the Eastern religions. The Western sphere of influence historically has been more sharply focused. However, the future in all regions is likely to see a rising tide of ethnicity intimately tied to religion as an organizing influence shaping state policy and identity.

Moral principles form the basis for the church. Administrative principles based on guiding moral precepts form the basis for government. The reconciliation of these two sets of principles forms a fundamental interaction influencing the governance of society. The heart of the tension lies in the diversity of church influences upon the state. Tensions increase when religious groups attempt to use the state as a conduit of power to shape human conduct. Tensions decrease when the churches maintain an ethical leadership and do not try to manage the political process.

Liberalism and fundamentalism are two trends affecting church-state relations (see Figure 1). They constitute opposing forces. The historic tendency of churches in liberalism's sphere is to influence the state indirectly, while churches in the fundamentalist's sphere attempt to influence the state directly through actions or pronouncements.

Liberalism is a worldwide social trend that grew out of Enlightenment thought of the sixteenth, seventeenth, and eighteenth centuries following a century of religious wars in Europe. Liberalism is characterized by tolerance for opposing ideas. It is adaptive to change. It favors freedom from both traditional moral restraints and the authority of the church. Its rationalism evolved into more revolutionary, idealistic, entrepreneurial individ-

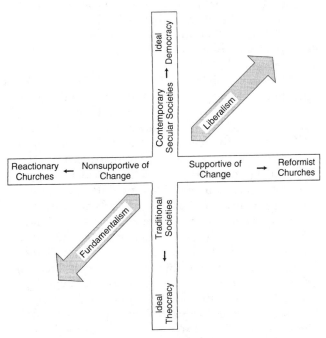

Figure 1. The future of church-state affairs: an axis of trends.

ualism within capitalistic societies benefiting from the "unseen hand" of divine Providence or the free market. Shifting toward individualism during the nonconformist movement of the 1960s, liberalism became an attitudinal trend driven by secularization, modernization, democratization, and pluralism. The recent collapse of communism, however, sparked a renewed emphasis in democracy as a precondition to the successful functioning of a society. In this social context the role of the individual as citizen of the state is to (1) contribute an opinion, (2) respond to the opinions of others, and (3) help solve problems leading to a better future.

Fundamentalism is characterized by suspicion

toward change. It entails a cautious reaction

to rapid change in a world

grown smaller through technologies.

Fundamentalism is a worldwide trend characterized by suspicion toward change. It entails a cautious reaction to rapid change in a world grown smaller through technologies. Fundamentalism uses traditional scripture to justify reversion to the past. From Right-Doctrine Protestantism to Islamic Fundamentalism, this set of attitudes emphasizes idealized traditional values and more homogeneous relationships. Some fundamentalist groups have sought to use the state as a conduit of power in the belief that it is God's will. It is likely that these groups will continue to align and develop strategies that attempt to counterbalance "a secularized society gone awry."

Theocracy is the direct influence of the church upon the state, as seen most clearly in Islamic countries where the "Word of God" reigns as law. Islam's alternative view of institutional structures and goals provides a driving force for scenarios of episodic religious-based revolutions. Rising tides of ethnicity also affect this form of Fundamentalism, which considers religion its sole, authentic source of identity. Both Liberalism and Fundamentalism affect the future of church-state relations. Churches in the liberal sphere tend to influence the state indirectly. In Fundamentalism, the influence is more direct. In a democratic society such as the United States, the crucible of power lies in the people. The First Amendment to the Constitution, which guaranteed religious freedom through the separation of church and state, created a high and impregnable wall between church and state for the first time in history. This demarcation subsequently caught on as a worldwide trend.

Fundamentalism's scenario pushes for uniform laws in the U.S. This mindset often challenges generally accepted notions of privacy and freedom of choice. The general public's weakening allegiances to both political and religious institutions since the 1960s give a stronger political edge to more strident fundamentalist agendas. Passions flare among liberals and fundamentalists at such flash points as school prayer, abortion, and cults. Religion has a profound influence on these issues and is significantly aided by high-visibility fundamentalist television ministries and mass communications.

Liberalism's influence in U.S. church-state relations is more subtle today. Concurrently church-church relations forge new processes that adapt to growing pluralism among world religions. Interfaith and interchurch councils are weaving networks in new, creative structures. These religious councils reject hierarchy, dogma, and exclusivity in favor of the inherent diversity of genuine grass-roots relationships and community building. Religion is forging new ways of resolving social issues like human rights and responsibilities, poverty, and a sustainable civilization. In this the church is teaching the state—a democracy within a democracy reshaping America. Past fractures of allegiance toward the church will mend as these processes wend their way and mature.

As the wounds of history begin to heal, relations between church and state may become intimately tied to making more apparent the Zeitgeist "the spirit of the time." We then can better anticipate the winds of change that will have shifted so unpredictably. The moral and ethical teachings of the church will then be reflected through the individual who simultaneously is a citizen of the state. The world may then become the beneficiary of true communication as the institutions of church and state are both guided by their greatest resource—human thought—which is itself guided by scripture, tradition, experience, and reason in a process of building a civilization that works for everyone.

[See also Religion: Changing Beliefs; Religion: Institutions and Practices; Religion, Spirituality, Morality; Religions, Decline or Rise Of; Religions, Statistical Projections Of.]

BIBLIOGRAPHY

Alley, Robert S. *The Supreme Court on Church and State.* New York: Oxford University Press, 1988.

Cord, Robert L. *Separation of Church and State: Historical Fact and Current Fiction.* Grand Rapids, MI: Baker Books House, 1988.

McCarthy, Martha M. *A Delicate Balance: Church, State, and the Schools.* Bloomington, IN: Phi Delta Kappa Educational Foundation, 1983.

Tierney, Brian. *The Crisis of Church and State.* Toronto: University of Toronto Press, 1988.

— RICHARD J. SPADY, ELLIE BATOR, CECIL H. BELL
WILLIAM B. CATE, WILLIAM D. ELLINGTON, SUSAN JETTE

CIGARETTES, CIGARS.

See TOBACCO.

CITIES

The future of cities is shaped by their history, location, command of technology, quality of human resources, and social institutions. Because they are built environments, cities endure for centuries, but their populations are more fluid and can dramatically change within a few decades. Cities of the future can be rich with innovation and full of individual and institutional vitality.

Alternative Urban Futures

Futurists think about the future in terms of alternatives, usually called scenarios. Arthur Shostak, the noted sociologist, once proposed seven scenarios for Philadelphia. "Conflict city" refers to the intense competition for scarce and shrinking resources awash in an atmosphere of fear and distrust, often expressed along racial and ethnic lines. Private employment decreases or moves elsewhere and the tax base is insufficient to support the public services. Detroit and Newark often are cited as conflict cities.

In the twenty-first century, computers and the now communications systems may decentralize cities.

"Wired city" refers to the emerging Information Age where the Information Superhighway has eliminated much face-to-face communication. In the late nineteenth century, electricity and railroads helped to centralize industrial cities. In the twenty-first century computers and the new communications systems may decentralize cities. *Washington Post* journalist Joel Garreau describes this outcome as an "edge city" scenario. Edge cities already can be seen in shopping malls, electronic office complexes, and new varieties of condohousing in the outskirts of most traditional cities. Edge cities are impersonal and lack a sense of community.

The "neighborhood city" scenario entails a return to a more human scale. The emphasis here is on self-reliance, walking-distance scale, voluntary cooperation, and decentralized leadership. Community schools become a neighborhood meeting place for several generations. Areas of Seattle, Portland, Ore., and Denver resemble this pattern.

The "conservation city" or the eco-village scenario can reflect a technological optimism and a sense of environmental frugality. Urban sprawl accompanied by loss of farmland and recreational spaces are concerns.

Eco-villages feature rooftop gardens, verdant balconies, and apartment waterfalls. Conflict between increased urban densities and the preservation of urban green spaces is resolved through urban planning and managed growth policies. Urban settlements depend heavily upon access to energy and other natural resources. Boulder, Colo., and Berkeley, Calif., are examples.

Different in scale are "international cities" reflecting an emerging world system. Cities now exist serving a global economy and society—a veritable global village where communities are linked together in a world of instantaneous intimacy. Some cities serve as headquarters or key research centers for transnational corporations. Some American industrial cities manifest a global heritage through their immigrant populations. In the twenty-first century the global connectiveness of cities will be an important element of their future. Toronto and Hong Kong represent this emerging international city scenario.

The "regional city" scenario recognizes that core areas and hinterlands also are part of a regional biosystem. Although politics and class differences have contributed to fragmenting urban communities over the last hundred years, political reformers hope to rationalize governance on a regional scale. In the 1990s environmental issues associated with air and water quality, solid waste disposal, and intermodal transportation planning compel local jurisdictions to develop new regional alliances. The regional city scenario involves a more efficient use of its space and ecology. It features cities moving from a concentric-zone model to a multiple-centers model. Cities are becoming multipolar, with a small inner center, and several edge city centers representing new clusters of urban sprawl. This scenario exists in most regions. Creating a regional forum, to devise a common vision, and coordinating infrastructure and transportation needs are major challenges.

"Leisure city" variations include retirement communities clustered around city centers in Sunbelt states, and theme park centers (Disney World and Orlando, Fla.; Williamsburg, Va.; Aspen and Vail, Colo.). As the baby boom population ages, the future of many cities will be determined by their ability to meet retiree needs.

These scenarios represent possible futures. They are not mutually exclusive. They can and already do coexist in some places. These scenarios suggest both technological possibilities and environmental constraints.

The Urban Future

Futures research can be applied to city management, public administration, and urban planning in different ways. City governments responsible for substantial public expenditures can be subjected to rigorous cost-benefit analysis, which forces the political process to rank order capital development projects based upon assessment of economic benefits.

Cities also need to do some environmental scanning concerning the entire range of emerging issues. Emerging social, economic, political, technological, and other trends need to be regularly assessed to determine their consequences for urban life in general and for city issues in particular. Cities must also adapt a more systematic approach to information collection and interdisciplinary analysis.

Effective leadership of a city or a community requires a strong commitment to foresight. Alternative programs—including at least three different discussed scenarios—should be identified and elaborated: (1) a dynamic extension of the status quo; (2) a "better times" projection replete with growth, prosperity, and success; and (3) a "decline and shrinkage" projection where bad things happen in tough times. Current conditions and trends—for the economy, employment, public revenues, and taxes—should be projected by traditional forecasting methods. Good forecasting begins with an accurate assessment of current conditions.

Cities must also develop participatory processes to devise a strategic vision and a consensus from significant leaders, decision makers, and stakeholders in the public and private sectors. Strategic vision should include both hopes and fears. Strategic consensus to back action plans should establish priorities representing the most important concerns for immediate and long-term futures. A city needs to consider at least four major approaches to its future:

The first is a strategic perspective full of dramatic new proposals. It needs to think boldly and aggressively about its potential for the next fifty years.

Second, it needs to have a pragmatic and humane concern for immediate quality-of-life issues. People need safety and efficiency right now, not some time in the future. Quality management carries important implications for the future of a city and its reputation.

A third perspective is the investment in up-to-date technology. Efficient management requires a commitment to technocratic and innovative approaches in everything from recycling to public libraries.

Hong Kong is an "international city." These cities reflect an emerging world system in which cities serve a global economy and society. (Derek M. Allan; Travel Ink/Corbis)

Finally, there must also be utopian proposals and ideas generated by the geniuses of the community. A city must encourage its artists and poets to think beyond the mundane realities of today, go beyond the recurrent budget and election cycle, and conjure up large dreams for the human condition.

When a new global system of cities will come into being, these cities will have larger populations and provide a better quality of life through more efficient and innovative management.

[See also Cities, North American; Land Use Planning; Megacities; Transportation; Urban Transit.]

BIBLIOGRAPHY

Brotchie, John. *The Future of Urban Form: The Impact of New Technology.* Tulsa, OK: GP Publications, 1991.
Fathy, Tarik A. *Telecity: Information Technology and Its Impact on Urban Form.* Westport, CT: Praeger/Greenwood, 1991.
Grappert, Gary, and Knight, Richard V., eds. *Cities in the Twenty-first Century.* Ann Arbor, MI: Books on Demand, 1992.
Hall, Peter. *Cities of Tomorrow.* Cambridge, MA: Blackwell, 1990.

— GARY GAPPERT

CITIES, NORTH AMERICAN

The year 2000, the dawn of the twenty-first century, is less than a decade away. Gone are the more stable days for local governments, when revenues were plentiful and public officials could merely adjust tax rates to balance budgets. The outside environment did not pose many significant challenges, opportunities, or threats. Public programs merely increased in response to citizens' demands for more services.

Traditional local government decision making, previously based on information obtained by projecting past trends into the future and preoccupied with the present, merely reacted to societal change. Nowadays, events and conditions are changing so rapidly that these practices are quickly becoming ineffective and obsolete.

Changes needed include greater government responsiveness, increased ethnic and racial representation, and more comprehensive taxing and spending controls. By proactively adapting to the future, elected and appointed public officials will be able to create a smooth transition to a new reality during the coming decade.

To illustrate the extent of these changing conditions, they are presented in five broad categories. The categories include (1) political trends, (2) major demographic shifts, (3) evolving urban patterns, (4) modern technologies, and (5) contemporary economic factors influencing our local governments.

Political Trends

- More state and federal laws will usurp the home-rule powers of elected officials and serve to limit their discretion in many areas.
- Special interest groups will typically pursue their own narrow goals and will form coalitions around major community issues.
- Limited revenues mean that many political issues will have no clear-cut response.
- Citizens will demand more services, but will not want increased taxation, making it more difficult for public officials to set program priorities and balance their annual budgets.
- Responsibility will continue to shift from the federal and state governments to cities, leaving cities to solve their own problems. Many cities with a low tax-base may have to resort to service reductions.
- More minority group representatives, including women and immigrants, will get involved in the political process, placing greater demands for their representation in the workplace.
- A growing number of senior citizens will become more politically active, because they have more available time.
- Quality-of-life issues, such as those focusing on individual well-being and the state of the environment, will emerge as key areas of public concern.
- The NIMBY ("Not in My Back Yard") movement will continue to grow at neighborhood and community levels. Undesirable public services, such as jails and waste-disposal facilities, will be difficult to locate or relocate.
- Public attention will shift from national to local community issues, such as crime prevention, drug abuse, affordable housing, and shelters for the homeless.
- More coalitions and partnerships involving business, government, education, and the nonprofit sector will emerge to address local social and economic problems.
- The public will demand more "ethics-in-government" mandates to monitor the integrity of their public officials and to ensure that they do not personally gain from their government office.

Major Demographic Shifts

- Senior citizens will demand more specialized public services, such as recreational and other social programs.
- Senior citizens, many of whom are on a fixed income, will seek property tax reductions, forcing others to pay for these programs.
- The number of female heads of households is growing steadily. There will be greater demands for affordable child care and more flexible working hours in the future as this trend continues.
- An increasing number of smaller households will require more high-density residential developments, such as condominiums, townhouses, and apartments, placing greater demands on existing public services.
- There will be a greater number of women in the workforce, and they will become more politically active in the workplace. As a result, such issues as comparable pay and sexual harassment will become increasingly important.
- As the number of minority and immigrant groups increases, new demands for more specialized public services will be created. This will in turn require more bilingual public employees.
- There will be more minority and ethnic groups participating in the political process, creating growing demands for district elections and greater minority and ethnic representation in the political arena.
- Existing public officials will feel the increasing political influence of these special interest groups (for example, seniors, women, immigrants).

- Any new federal grants will be limited to those programs that help achieve national goals (such as affordable housing, lower unemployment, and shelters for the homeless).

Evolving Urban Patterns

- Urban sprawl will increase, primarily along major vehicle transportation corridors and public mass-transit routes.
- Cities will witness greater "in-fill" development in already urbanized areas. Land areas that once were marginal will be purchased and upgraded for new development.
- Older land uses, such as outdated industrial plants and commercial centers, will be upgraded and/or retrofitted with new amenities to make them more marketable and appealing to consumers.
- In central city areas, continuing high land values will lead to increased gentrification, further exacerbating the need for more affordable housing for low- to moderate-income citizens.
- Immigrant and refugee groups will relocate primarily to the city centers of large metropolitan areas.
- New "ethnic centers" will evolve in metropolitan areas. These "new" immigrants will stress the maintenance of the cultural traditions, values, and customs of their respective homelands.

New "ethnic centers" will evolve in metropolitan areas. These "new" immigrants will stress the maintenance of cultural traditions, values, and customs of their respective homelands.

- Higher energy costs and greater traffic congestion will create more political pressure for public mass-transit systems. Emphasis will be placed on multimodal systems that offer greater transportation options to the public.
- Public services will increasingly be tailored to better represent these growing minority and ethnic population centers.
- The population explosion in the suburban areas will lead to greater pressures for additional public infrastructure, with limited funds to finance these much-needed improvements.
- As the urban population shifts to suburban areas of cities, housing starts will not keep pace with this population movement, creating housing shortages in these areas.
- The shifting population, from urban to suburban areas, will create an erosion of the corporate tax base in these locations, forcing service reductions and/or tax increases.

Modern Technologies

- There will be an increased use of microcomputers in the workplace, brought about by more sophisticated systems, lower costs, and more user-friendly software.
- Policies will emerge to ensure the compatibility of computer hardware and software, which will require uniformity among applications, facilitate training, and minimize system downtime.

- Expensive standalone computer systems will disappear, due to enhanced and inexpensive networking techniques and the use of more sophisticated microcomputers.
- Information management will become necessary as computers make more information networks and databases available. The emphasis will switch from receiving "more" information to receiving "quality" information.
- Management by computer systems will become a common technique to monitor and limit energy consumption in public buildings and grounds.
- More public meetings will be aired on local public-access cable television stations. These stations will also be used to educate citizens on available services and key issues facing their community.
- Greater energy costs will continue to shape our lifestyles and technologies (for example, smaller cars, less spacious offices, new energy-saving devices, and more sophisticated building techniques).
- Advanced telecommunication systems, such as those with conference-calling and facsimile-transmission capabilities, will reduce the number of business meetings and related personnel and travel costs.
- Increased public pressure for mass transit, and greater construction costs, will lead to shorter routes in more densely populated high-traffic areas. Light-rail systems will replace the expensive underground subways of the past.
- More labor-saving devices of all types will be used, out of necessity, in order to hold down personnel costs (the largest component of any government's budget).

Economic Factors

- Ever-increasing energy costs will require the greater use of energy-conservation techniques (see above).
- Citizens will increasingly demand higher standards and accountability for air and water quality, especially in densely populated urban areas.
- Public officials will stress economic development as a vehicle to raise revenues without increasing taxes. Highly urbanized cities will have to resort to redevelopment for their financial survival.
- Since nearly every community provides the "hard" services (police, fire, and public works), there will be an increasing demand for the so-called "soft" services (recreation, museums, libraries, and cultural programs).
- Federal subsidies for mass transit in urban areas will decrease, forcing fare increases to operate these systems and to make them cost-covering.
- The public's aversion to new taxes, and higher user fees and charges, will severely limit the growth of government services.
- Taxpayers increasingly will acknowledge that it is the legitimate role of government to provide "safety net" services to citizens (that is, essential services to the truly needy).
- Limited new revenues will be earmarked for those public services and programs with the highest payoff—from both a political and productivity standpoint.
- The availability of federally funded grant programs will be limited, and greater competition will exist among cities for these funds. They will be earmarked for those cities with large low-income populations and related social and housing problems.
- The public will continue to advocate the "controlled growth" of government by opposing increased taxation and the growth of user fees and charges. They will also demand greater accountability and productivity for existing services.
- Due to more double-income families, employers will offer "cafeteria style" fringe-benefit options. Employees will also be asked to bear an increasing share of these benefit costs.

• Severe national budget deficits will continue to limit federal involvement in social programs, forcing state and local governments to pay for these services.

• Privatization trends will continue, making the private sector a provider of public services. Greater public accountability will be demanded of these "private" providers.

Change Is Essential

New models of governance are essential in times of fewer grant programs, complex and interrelated issues, fragmented and piecemeal local policies, rising citizen expectations regarding public services, skepticism of government in general, and the public's aversion to increased taxation.

Planning for change, a common practice in the private sector over the past few decades, needs to be extended to the public sector to enable government officials to adapt successfully to changing conditions. New political models must encompass multiple community issues, be nonhierarchical in nature, and help achieve a public consensus on the major issues and problems facing a municipality.

The Future

It is imperative that public officials provide comprehensive and consensus-based solutions to complex public policies. At the same time they also need to provide a collective vision for their community and its municipal organization. A shared understanding of the issues, problems, and goals facing a community not only provides a unified vision of the future, but it also helps to mobilize all available resources to effectively manage change.

It is only through the process of politically adapting our local governments to the electorate's expectations that public confidence in local government institutions can be restored.

[See also Cities; Civil Protest, Institutions, Confidence in; Land Use Planning; Megacities; Transportation; Urban Transit.]

BIBLIOGRAPHY

Kemp, Roger L. *America's Cities: Strategic Planning for the Future.* Danville, IL: Interstate Press, 1988.

———. *Economic Development in Local Government: A Handbook for Public Officials and Citizens.* Jefferson, NC: McFarland, 1995.

———. *Privatization: The Provision of Public Services by the Private Sector.* Jefferson, NC: McFarland, 1991.

———. *Strategic Planning for Local Governments: A Handbook for Officials and Citizens.* Jefferson, NC: McFarland, 1993.

— ROGER L. KEMP

CIVIL LIBERTIES.

See COMMUNICATIONS: PRIVACY ISSUES; COMPUTERS: PRIVACY ISSUES; HUMAN RIGHTS.

CIVIL PROTEST

Among the varieties of civil protest are (1) violence; (2) nonviolent direct action, as practiced by the civil rights and peace movements; and (3) conventional collective action, including public demonstrations, boycotts, lobbying, and litigation. Such repertories span the spectrum of collective action from single-issue protests to rebellion seeking governmental overthrow.

Periods of Conflict

Conflict is pervasive. Worldwide, 5,400 political demonstrations occurring between 1948 and 1967 were documented by one study. Another identified 2,200 episodes of conflict in eighty-seven of the world's largest nations from 1961 through 1970. During the 1960s, over 500 race riots took place in the United States.

Excluding the Revolutionary War in the United States, there have been three periods of conflict: (1) the Civil War and Reconstruction Era (1850s–1876); (2) industrial and labor conflict coinciding with the era of immigration, industrial growth, and urbanization (1880s–1920s); and (3) contemporary social movements and political reaction (mid-1950s and 1960s).

Fields of Literature

Collective action and protest are the focus of three different literary fields of study: social movements, political interest groups, and violence. Three disciplines—sociology, political science, and history—are principal contributors.

Variations in Conflict

Political institutions and economic development levels affect conflict. Peaceful reformist demands are more frequent in democratic and wealthier societies. Violent revolutionary demands are more common in autocratic or elitist states, and in less developed nations (Gurr, 1989).

Grievances in developed democracies are channeled into legitimate avenues of political expression. Among the 6 million Americans who participated in the 1960s' civil protests, 80 percent did so in peaceful and legal demonstrations.

Violence used as a tool of protest carries a high degree of risk. Violence polarizes political forces, discredits its sponsors, alienates the public, invites repression, and reduces leverage by removing the uncertainty of escalation to violence others strive to avoid.

Explanations for Conflict

Breakdown theories of the 1960s concluded that urbanization and social disorganization led to urban riots.

The McCone Commission (formed after the 1965 Watts riots) propounded a "riffraff" theory, contending that the rioters were a tiny faction of hoodlums, not supported by most blacks. The Kerner Commission (formed after the 1967 riots) concluded that the riots were spontaneous and unorganized voices of protest in the ghetto, reflecting the breakdown theory.

Three theories currently explain civil protest:

1. *Relative deprivation theory* maintains that protest ensues when social conditions give rise to grievances and to expectations that political systems cannot meet. Such conflict has not occurred along class lines but along ethnic, religious, and national cleavages in the United States. Civil rights and peace movement participants cut across class lines of income and occupation. This approach also fails to explain the student and peace movements of the 1960s, which were products of affluence.

2. *Resource mobilization theory* has been the dominant explanation of collective action since 1980. Its essential assumptions are listed here:
   a. Deprivation or grievances do not automatically translate into social movement activity.
   b. Movements form on the basis of rational calculations of costs and benefits.
   c. Mobilization of resources may occur from within an aggrieved group or from external resources.
   d. The costs of participating in a movement can be raised or lowered by state support or repression.
   e. Movement outcomes are problematic; success does not automatically follow from movement activity.
   f. People do not join movements just for marginal utility but to gain solidarity or to advance a cause.
   g. Movements are of no certain size.
   h. A movement is a mediated, informal set of relationships among organizations, coalitions of organizations, and their members.
   "Movement entrepreneurs" mobilize resources and participants from social networks and capitalize upon mobilizing structures, such as lecture tours, prayer meetings, and e-mail networks. Critics contend that much protest occurs spontaneously, without the benefit of organizations, and point out that formal organizations tend to inhibit more militant protest. Relative deprivation theory may be a better explanation of American protest, and resource mobilization theory may apply more to Europe.

3. *Political opportunity* theory provides the newest explanation (Tarrow, 1994). While deprivation and organizational capacity might partially explain *why* and *how* protest occurs, political opportunity theory best explains *when* protest might occur. Four elements prompt political opportunity structures: (a) increasing access to power opens up (e.g., through electoral opportunities); (b) shifts in ruling alignments occur (e.g., when conservative Southerners left the Democratic party during the civil rights era); (c) influential allies become available (e.g., when urban liberals supported farmworker organizing and boycotts in the late 1960s); and (d) ruling elites are divided among themselves (such as during the Vietnam War era).

Arguably, if the Democratic party realigns into a more centrist party, its disaffected constituents and their allies could bolt the party and launch a wave of reformist protest. That has been a recurring pattern in American politics, just as conservative activism emerges when the Republican party moves toward the center.

Cycles of Protest

When one movement achieves gains through protest, other groups often emulate—the feminist and ecology movements followed in the wake of the 1960s' civil rights and antiwar movements.

Activism has a long-term effect on the political socialization of its participants,

who often move on to other social movements

and organizations to continue their activism.

Initiatives by one movement may generate countermovements. Gay rights activism has mobilized conservative religious groups, and right-to-life and pro-choice groups on the abortion issue proliferate.

Impacts of Protest

Political response to social protest and allied movements entails repression and/or reform, or cooptation. Activism of any form has a long-term effect on the political socialization of its participants, and they often move on to other social movements and organizations to continue their activism. Success rates are highest among occupational groups, followed by reform groups. Socialist groups, right wing, and nativist groups have most often collapsed far short of success. Some movements, such as the women's movement, have had a long-term impact on social, political, cultural, and economic institutions.

Rebellion

Richard Rubenstein, an authority on conflict resolution, suggests four preconditions for rebellion: (1) slowing of immigration, giving identity groups the opportunity to integrate existing immigrants; (2) decline in local rates of economic growth; (3) failure of local political leaders to improve a group's status; and (4) intensified outside pressure on the aggrieved factions; e.g., through a war on crime. Open rebellion is unlikely in the United States.

Global Outlook

Sidney Tarrow also suggests the possibility that the United States has evolved into a "movement society." Single-issue groups are regularly at the forefront of civil protests. In an age of global communications and a wide array of sophisticated political tactics, genuinely transnational movements have emerged on such issues as the environment. Beyond this, global ideological and religious movements have made all nations prospective targets of terrorist activities. Recent low levels of movement violence may be giving way to more violence. Murders by fundamentalist pro-life followers may be indication of this shift. Finally, not only governments have been the targets of activism and protest. Individual companies and entire industries have been the focus of a wide range of citizen activism; this will increase with the spread of free markets.

[See also Class and Underclass; Ethnic and Cultural Separatism; Human Rights; Institutions, Confidence in; International Tensions; Race, Caste, and Ethnic Diversity.]

BIBLIOGRAPHY

Gamson, William. *The Strategy of Social Protest*, 2nd ed. Belmont, CA: Wadsworth, 1990.
Gurr, Ted Robert, ed. *Violence in America: Protest, Rebellion, Reform*, Vol. 2. Newbury Park, CA: SAGE, 1989.
Morris, Aldon D., and Mueller, Carol McClung, eds. *Frontiers in Social Movement Theory*. New Haven, CT: Yale University Press, 1992.
Tarrow, Sidney. *Power in Movement: Social Movements, Collective Action and Politics*. New York: Cambridge University Press, 1994.
Zald, Mayer N., and McCarthy, John D., eds. *Social Movements in an Organizational Society*. New Brunswick, NJ: Transaction Books, 1987.

— JOHN M. HOLCOMB

CLARKE, ARTHUR CHARLES (1917–)

Born in Minehead, U.K., science fiction writer and prophet of space flight Arthur C. Clarke has been domiciled since 1956 in Sri Lanka, serving there as chancellor of the University of Moratuwa. Clarke's article "Extra-Terrestrial Relays" (1945) is believed to have been the inspiration for communications satellites. Clarke joined the fledgling British Interplanetary Society at age seventeen, becoming its chairman while completing his studies at King's College in London during the late 1940s. *The Exploration of Space* (1951) was the first of many books that made him a prophet of the new space age. His forays into science fiction earned him an international audience on the same scale as Isaac Asimov, Ray Bradbury, and Robert A. Heinlein. Clarke's novels include *Childhood's End* (1953), *The City and the Stars* (1956), *A Fall of Moondust* (1961), *Rendezvous with Rama* (1973), and *The Songs of Distant Earth* (1986). With Stanley Kubrick, he wrote the movie script for *2001: A Space Odyssey* (based in part on an earlier Clarke short story, "The Sentinel").

Clarke's visions of the future sometimes involve a rational "hard science" approach (e.g., *A Fall of Moondust*) and sometimes verge on a kind of New Age mysticism (e.g., *The City and the Stars*). His futurist works include *Profiles of the Future: An Inquiry into the Limits of the Possible* (1962), *The Worlds of Tomorrow* (1972), and *Life in the 21st Century* (1986). In 1980 he hosted *The Mysterious World of Arthur C. Clarke*, a television program.

[See also Isaac Asimov; Communications Technology, Global Consciousness; Satellite Communications; Science Fiction; Space Satellites.]

BIBLIOGRAPHY

Olander, Joseph D., and Greenberg, Martin H., eds. *Arthur C. Clarke*. Writers of the Twenty-first Century Series. New York: Taplinger, 1976.

— GEORGE THOMAS KURIAN

CLASS AND UNDERCLASS

Events of the final years of the twentieth century accent the continued relevance of social class to an understanding of human affairs. The collapse of the Soviet Union marked the end of a long quest for a classless utopia. Much political rhetoric in the United States is about social class. Presidents and would-be presidents pledge support for policies beneficial to a "forgotten middle class." Liberals attack conservatives for advocating tax laws favoring a monied upper class. Both vow an end to programs that foster a problem-laden underclass.

The underclass has received special attention in recent years. This is a population caught in a web of problems and destructive behaviors, such as high rates of illegitimate births, female-headed households, substance abuse, and withdrawal from the labor market. The underclass population is heavily dependent on public-sector spending to survive and imposes burdens upon public spending for special-education programs, the judicial system, and prisons.

Attention to the normal and abnormal classes is not surprising; the idea of class is fundamental to any description of societal structure. It is also central to the concept of social stratification, the placement of individuals and groups in higher- and lower-status categories. Class hierarchies reflect values and characteristics that a society considers important.

Class has been long studied. Karl Marx and his followers held that historic developments were conditioned by the economic system and its property relationships. A class order, ultimately consisting of only two elements—capitalists and workers—they prophesied, would result from the dynamics of exploitation inherent in prevailing modes of production. They maintained that, until the order is overthrown, there will be biases and inequities throughout the system.

Max Weber, and those who built upon his theoretical insights, found the world to be more complex. Social stratification involved an economic-based class component, but also status and power components. In modern, developed societies, social class status is apportioned in terms of an individual's contributions to the division of labor. The apportioned status allocates economic, social, and power positions in such a way as to assure the effective and efficient conduct of societal affairs.

Five broad classes are typically cited by researchers. The five classes and examples of sources of wealth and income include: *upper class*—inherited family wealth, investment income, corporate control; *upper middle class*—leading professions, major business ownership, executive/management positions in private and public bureaucracies; *lower middle class*—lesser professions, sales, skilled crafts; *working class*—industrial production, construction, clerical, personal service; *lower class*—unemployment or irregular employment in low-skill jobs. Daniel Rossides estimated the size of the respective classes in the mid-1990s as a percent of total U.S. population at 1–3 percent, 10–15 percent, 30–35 percent, 40–45 percent, and 20–25 percent. This distribution roughly resembles a diamond with its thicker portion below the middle.

Elements of social stratification are correlated; those ranking high in one tend to rank high in the other two. Education and hard work, for example, are prerequisites to economic success as a professional, entrepreneur, or corporate executive. The affluence of economic success allows for a lifestyle and good works that lead to high status in the local community and beyond. Prestige occupations, wealth, and high status tend to facilitate political participation. The upper and upper-middle classes are the "natural" recruitment pool for political office, and the more prestigious the office, the higher the implicit entry-level class requirement. Obviously, a reverse pattern could be traced; those ranking low in one of the social stratification elements tend to also rank low in the other two.

In the American context, evidence of a class identity and consciousness is weak. Lack of a feudal tradition inhibited the emergence of a well-defined class structure. Commentators have long pointed to the absence of a viable socialist tradition or successful working-class political party. And American culture emphasizes individualism. The lone man or woman overcoming extraordinary obstacles through hard work on the way to success continues to be a familiar theme in American literature and mythology. Where success and failure are individually based, class consciousness will not flourish.

For the future society, any upsurge in class consciousness is unlikely. Rank will be determined, as in the past, by the combined effects of achieved class and the ascribed characteristics of ethnicity, religion, race, and gender. The interaction of class and ascribed characteristics often produces a homogeneous cultural environment so that the primary agents of socialization—family, school, peers, and religion—convey a consistent message with future consequences. As Charles Murray (1984) indicates, "Young people—not just poor young people, but all young people—try to make sense of the world around them. They behave in ways that reflect what they observe." In the homogeneous environment, children, young adults, and elders receive and give cues on matters as basic as orientation to the future, work, proper behavior, admirable qualities in parents, spouses, and citizens.

Rank will be determined, as in the past,

by the combination of class, ethnicity,

religion, race, and gender.

The most significant developments affecting future class conditions will be economic. Transformations in a global economy have already eroded the competitive advantage of American workers. The stability of the lower-middle and working classes after World War II owed much to jobs in manufacturing. Over the course of a work life, the ambitious moved from low-skill to high-skill factory jobs. Strong unions gained good wages and extensive benefits, including medical and retirement benefits.

Future employment growth in the postindustrial economy will be bifurcated, most pronounced at the extremes on an employment-income continuum. At one end will be rewarding positions in innovative fields based on new technologies, creative development strategies, and exotic sciences. Entry-level requirements will demand extensive education, theoretical sophistication, and communication skills.

At the other end will be jobs in services and routine production. Few skills will be called for. New workers need only demonstrate promptness, an ability to deal with the public in service roles, and a capacity to cope with boredom in repetitive tasks. Most of the jobs will be part-time, at low wages, with few benefits.

If the class structure of the past resembled a diamond, that of the future will resemble an hourglass with the top part considerably smaller than the bottom. As members of the lower-middle and working classes fall into the bottom half of the hourglass, economic insecurity coupled with racial attitudes will likely further suppress working-class solidarity. For the past quarter century, racial attitudes of the white working class have been shaped by negative experiences and perceptions of breakdowns in traditional values and prominority and antiwhite working-class biases of major institutions. This has resulted in conflict over public policy for education, welfare, and affirmative action. These controversies have contributed a profound instability in American politics, evidenced in the elections of 1992 and 1994.

Developments working against the lower-middle and working classes will strengthen class consciousness in the upper and upper-middle classes. Wealth has become increasingly concentrated; by 1989 the wealthiest 1 percent of households controlled 10.9 percent of total income and 37.1 percent of total net worth.

Suburbanization has segregated populations by housing values, income, and social class. Those in affluent jurisdictions are aware of the importance of strategic thinking about life and careers. Community resources are committed to quality education, and family resources are invested in children from preschool through the best graduate and professional schools. Peers, work associates, and marriage partners come from like upper- and upper-middle-class, if not ethnic or religious, backgrounds. In the twenty-first century, the gulf between the upper and lower classes in income, lifestyle, and culture will be wider than in the past.

Of greatest concern for future elites should be the growth of the underclass. Though there is no agreement on basic causes or feasible policy solutions, underclass conditions in many central city neighborhoods are like those of a war zone: life is brutish, the young kill each other, and the old are preyed upon by their progeny. If the conditions remain unabated, the potential long-term costs are incalculable. Like their counterparts in earlier regimes, those in the upper and upper-middle classes need to be advocates for those beneath them if the order upon which their elite status rests is to be maintained.

[See also Disabled Persons' Rights; Ethnic and Cultural Separatism; Families and Households; Household Composition; Human Rights; Migration, International; Minorities; Poverty, Feminization of; Public Assistance Programs; Race, Caste, and Ethnic Diversity; Racial and Ethnic Conflict; Refugees; Social Welfare Philosophies; Unemployment; Wealth; Workforce Diversity.]

BIBLIOGRAPHY

Dionne, E. J. *Why Americans Hate Politics.* New York: Simon and Schuster, 1991.

Ehrenreich, Barbara. *Fear of Falling: The Inner Life of the Middle Class.* New York: Harper Perennial, 1990.

Murray, Charles. *Losing Ground: American Social Policy, 1950–1980.* New York: Basic Books, 1984.

Reich, Robert. *The Work of Nations.* New York: Vintage Books, 1992.

Sowell, Thomas. *Ethnic America.* New York: Basic Books, 1981.

Strobel, Frederick. *Upward Dreams, Downward Mobility.* Lanham, MD: Rowman and Littlefield, 1993.

Vanneman, Reeve, and Cannon, Lynn Weber. *The American Perception of Class.* Philadelphia: Temple University Press, 1987.

Wilson, William Julius. *The Truly Disadvantaged: The Inner City, the Underclass, and Public Policy.* Chicago: University of Chicago Press, 1987.

– JOHN J. GARGAN

CLIMATE AND METEOROLOGY

By the year 2100, the current scientific consensus anticipates that the mean global surface air temperature will be 3° C (5.4° F) warmer (range 2–5° C [3.6–9° F] warmer) than it is today. Unless deliberate steps are taken to reduce emissions of greenhouse gases, the warming will continue well beyond 2100. If 3° C doesn't sound like much of a warming, one should recall that the mean global temperature at the time of maximum glaciation 18,000 years ago was only 5° C cooler than today. More important than the absolute rise in temperature may be the *rate* of the warming projected over the next century and beyond. The rate seems likely to be 20 to 100 times more rapid than the rate associated with the retreat of glaciers between 12,000 and 8,000 years ago. These and other long-range climatological forecasts are based on computer modeling whose reliability is steadily improving.

The warming is projected on the basis of two scientifically established facts. The first is the existence of the greenhouse effect—the heat-trapping capacity of gases in the atmosphere. The effect is natural; it is responsible for the Earth's being 33°C (59.4° F) warmer at present than it would be in the absence of the greenhouse effect. Without this natural effect, life would not exist on the planet. The second recognized fact is the increasing atmospheric concentrations of the gases responsible for the greenhouse effect. Increasing concentrations of carbon dioxide, methane, nitrous oxide, and chlorofluorocarbons (CFCs) are largely the result of industrial activity, with a smaller contribution (about 20 percent) from conversion of forests to agricultural lands. The greenhouse gas responsible for the greatest warming is water vapor. Water vapor is not directly affected by human activity, but a warming itself will increase the concentration of water vapor in the atmosphere. Thus, a human-induced warming can be expected to amplify itself through natural processes.

Under future scenarios in which current growth rates of greenhouse gas emissions are assumed to continue, the mean global temperature is predicted to increase by about 0.3°C (0.54° F) per decade over the next century. The range of uncertainty includes 0.2 to 0.5°C (0.36 to 0.9° F) per decade. The average warming will be about 1° C (1.8° F) by 2025 and 3° C (5.4° F) by 2100. Under the same scenarios, sea level is predicted to rise about 6 cm (2.34 in) per decade (range 3 to 10 cm [1.17 to 3.1 in] per decade) over the next century. The rise will amount to about 65 cm (25.35 in) by 2100.

Under different scenarios with increasing levels of controls on emissions of greenhouse gases, the predicted increase in global mean temperature is 0.1 to 0.2° C (.18 to .36° F) per decade, and the predicted rise in sea level is also reduced.

These global averages will not be observed in individual regions. Mid-latitude regions are expected to warm more than tropical latitudes. Different models of climate give a range of results. Furthermore, predictions of regional changes in precipitation and soil moisture, probably more important than temperature for most of the tropics, are even less-consistently predicted by the models. Thus, the specific changes in climate for a particular region are very uncertain.

Predictions to the year 2100 are thus not very disturbing or compelling except for low-lying coastal communities. But the fact that scientists cannot yet make specific predictions should not be confused with the possibility that the changes will be large. The possible effects include massive disturbance of climate, with associated disruption of agricultural production and political systems. The specific effects may be uncertain, but the effects upon regions already close to the edge of survival are not difficult to imagine. The world's population is expected to double in the next thirty to forty years. Is there enough arable land to provide twice the food now produced? The answer could be yes if new lands brought into agriculture were managed sustainably, but the increasing area of degraded lands in the tropics shows this not to be the case. Will new strains of crops help double production? Will the effects of the warming together with increased levels of atmospheric carbon dioxide actually increase agricultural production? Perhaps, but for how long? Add to the growing world population a changing climate with year-to-year variation in rainfall, frosts, droughts, storms, and other unpredictable events, and the picture is not reassuring.

Although not quantitative, the following aspects of climatic change are cause for concern:

- The warming is likely to be *rapid* unless major steps are taken now to reduce emissions of greenhouse gasses. The rate of the warming is ex-

pected to be more rapid than ever experienced in human history. Rapid change is difficult to foresee and prepare for, and difficult to adjust to.

- The warming will be *continuous*. Any policy of dealing with climatic change that is based on adaptation or coping will find itself several steps behind the existing climate. Rapid and continuous change together mean that adjustments to change will face continuously changing conditions. There will be no new climate to adjust to; adjustments must be to change itself.

- The changes will be irreversible within a single human generation, and probably within several generations. If the change turns out to be unacceptable, there will be no way to undo its harmful effects for decades. If all releases of greenhouse gases were stopped tomorrow, for example, the earth would continue to warm approximately 0.5°C (0.9° F) or more. The longer greenhouse gases are emitted to the atmosphere, the larger will be this commitment to a further warming. The commitment is to an additional warming that *follows* what has already been realized. Warming continues because of the long atmospheric lifetime of most of the greenhouse gases, and because of the slow heat-absorbing capacity of the oceans. Policies proposed to reduce climatic change will affect future *emissions* of greenhouse gases. Nothing but time will be able to reduce *concentrations* of the gases that have already been released to the atmosphere.

- Finally, the change is almost *open-ended*. Carbon dioxide concentrations will not stop at a doubling, as experiments with global climate models tend to imply, unless deliberate policies are enacted to reduce further emissions. There is enough fossil fuel in recoverable reserves to raise the atmospheric concentrations of carbon dioxide by a factor of five to ten above preindustrial levels. There is enough carbon in the trees and soils of Earth to double or triple atmospheric concentrations.

These statements, although qualitative, suggest that climatic change will be difficult for most nations of the world.

[See also Acid Rain; Deforestation; Global Warming; Oceans; Ozone Layer Depletion.]

BIBLIOGRAPHY

Houghton, R. A. "The Role of the World's Forests in Global Warming." In: K. Ramakrishna and G. M. Woodwell, eds. *World Forests for the Future. Their Use and Conservation.* New Haven, CT: Yale University Press, 1993.

Houghton, J. T.; Jenkins, G. J., and Ephraums, J. J., eds. *Climate Change: The IPCC Scientific Assessment.* Cambridge, U.K.: Cambridge University Press, 1990.

Schneider, S. H. "The Greenhouse Effect: Science and Policy." *Science* 243 (1989): 771–781.

Woodwell, G. M., and Mackenzie, F. T., eds. *Biotic Feedbacks in the Global Climatic System: Will the Warming Feed the Warming?* New York: Oxford University Press, 1995.

– R. A. HOUGHTON

CLOTHING

In 1946, James Laver in *A Letter to a Girl on the Future of Clothes* wrote, "I must perforce try to deduce the shape of your clothes by what I think is likely to be the state of the world . . ." Laver argued that clothing reflected the political conditions so sensitively that clothing transformations were in tandem with political fact and discourse. While technology and other aesthetic disciplines play a role, fashion is chiefly determined by social conditions. Standards of beauty and fashion have changed over time—from the life-affirming volume of voluptuous Rubenesque beauty in times of plague and physical peril in Europe as if to assert corpulence as the presence of the body, to modern sleek gym-toned bodies in the 1980s as a reflection of physical and aesthetic control as well as hard, lean self-control. Appearance serves as both self-image and social discourse: fashion's future is indivisibly linked to the technological and social forces patterning the future. Clothing, like society, promises to be more conformist and less expressive. In some respects, everyone comes into intimate, self-defining contact with the future first in apparel, and self-image constitutes the first social shape.

Future clothing, like society, promises to be

more conformist and less expressive.

Clothing is a fixed human need arising from utility and a convention of modesty; fashion is a modern phenomenon of change. In the West, fashion arrived along with democracy at the close of the eighteenth century, when dissemination of fashion plates and massive textile production allowed the bourgeoisie to simulate court clothing. Fashion became dominant a century later as department stores, ready-to-wear clothing, and women's periodicals spread out from such fashion centers as Paris, London, and New York, and commerce inevitably replaced the court as fashion's arbiter and index. The commerce in clothing answers, however, to many other issues as well. Changing perceptions of modesty are morally induced and enforced. The first bikinis of the 1940s seemed, in their time, shocking in exposure: today, the same garments would appear demure. American beaches allowed men to go topless only gradually in the 1930s. Sexuality is conventionally associated with dress: fashion finds focus in shifting erogenous zones, probably not first determined by fashion, but by social propriety and preference. Western dress has become more or less universal, both assimilating aspects of African, Middle Eastern, and Asian apparel, and in offering solutions to clothing utility along with convenience in mass production.

Appearance may also include cosmetics and fragrance as elements of fashion. Cosmetics temporarily alter physical appearance, especially of the face. Once relentless in the pursuit of standardized beauty, cosmetics are increasingly under criticism for artificiality and deleterious personal-health and environmental effects. Moreover, some cosmetic effects are more permanently achieved through plastic surgery rather than applications of cosmetic materials. Sight and touch are essential to effective apparel, but so is scent. Fragrance has primarily been associated with the body, though by the 1990s, fragrance was also transmitted through controlled environments.

While clothing began with natural materials and thence to natural fibers, the twentieth century has seen the domination of synthetic textiles extending the potentially limited resources in natural materials. In this century, the preference has invariably (with a notable exception of some Japanese designers of the 1980s) been for natural fibers in high-end markets and synthetics for cheaper prices and markets. Furs, for example, were effectively simulated in man-made materials, but the first synthetic fur coats were thought inferior to the true furs until sentiment about animals finally reversed the aversion to the synthetic. In the 1990s, ethical value was attached to garments that were ecologically sensitive. Arguably, some synthetics were prematurely launched (polyester, for example) and failed in consumer tests of comfort. In the future, increasingly percentages of apparel materials will be man-made and will meet a standard of comfort, both resembling and feeling like natural fibers. Textile technology is producing garments that feel like silk, knitted cotton, or other natural materials and offer superior shaping, durability, and comfort. Any textile production also reaches the consumer with expectations for limited care: standard washing-machine or drycleaning care must be sufficient for textile maintenance. Hand-ironing is already recognized as too labor-intensive in pants that require no ironing and other wrinkle-resistant textiles. Alternatively, we will develop an aesthetic rationale for wrinkled clothes, because it is clear that we are not returning to a society of ironing.

Dress codes once prevailed socially and for business. For the man, the business suit was *de rigueur* almost through the twentieth century. Swelled leisure, indistinct separations of home and office, communications technology, and casual preferences are leading to the extinction of traditional business dress for both men and women. The market for tailored (suits and jackets) clothing for men is decreasing by roughly 10 percent a year in the United States, reflecting more casual lifestyles. Without specific dress codes, superfluous and uncomfortable clothing will be discarded. Hats, gloves, and accessories exist even today almost solely for utility, not for aesthetics of dress alone. Separate wardrobes of business attire and sports clothing will no longer be sustained. While special-event clothing will be retained for celebrations, there will not be the kind of clothing changes by occasion and time of day once practiced. One outfit for the entire day will suffice. Cross-training footwear and sports apparel is increasingly in evidence and gives the sign of clothing adaptable for different purposes: clothing is increasingly multi-purpose, with active sports a notable exception. Social, business, and sports occasions may be pursued in the same shoes, whereas a few decades ago footwear was distinctive to discrete activities.

Wearing apparel as a consumer-driven industry also follows demographics. An enlarged population of the aging and an enlarged population of the enlarged means fashion sizing and styling for the elderly and large sizes. Of course, older people used to wear black or otherwise discrete clothing from the population majority; by the 1970s, fashion for the elderly was no different in style from the most comfortable clothing for the general population. Clothing requires more and more convenience, e.g., Velcro fastening replacing the age-old button and the fifty-year-old zipper. The 1980s street-savvy oversized recreational clothing also recognizes the ampler, older audience as prime buyers of clothing. Conformity also means easier purchasing: sizes S, M, L, and XL allow for mail-order and computerized shopping.

Clothing technologies are seldom generated in laboratories or clinical circumstance. In the same way in which style is the elegant wearer's comportment, so clothing technology is generally tested by use. Everyday clothing is often derived from aviation, fire-fighting and other practical uniforms, and military gear rendered first in utility and thereafter for an extended, already proven, use. In addition, there is always the patina of glamour whether the trenchcoat that survived war or the astronaut outfit that sets spirits soaring.

Clothing followed in the Garden of Eden immediately upon gender differentiation and has always been a signifier of gender. To be sure, men learn from women and women from men (the former less than the latter, due to prejudice) in all fields, including fashion. The bifurcated trousers so successful for men have now been accommodated to much women's apparel. But the woman's jacket still buttons opposite to the man's. Symbolically, clothing will always express gender difference. Practically, there will be more and more uniformity, but not the arcadian unisex anticipated in the 1960s. Clothing's symbolic gender differentiation will be maintained as long as sexuality inheres to the body (and mind).

Traditionally, fashion had been thought to be determined first by the *haute couture*. Then, fashion was determined by the young. In the future, fashion will be increasingly set by the middle-aged middle class as de-

termined by the market. Not only do the demographics indicate this change, but the erosion of home-sewing capability and the increasing mass production of fashion represent a decline in self-expression and nonconformist options. Conformity to templates of size, style, and fashion are required and—given that fashion seeks to persuade the consumer—desired.

Clothing has always been a way of altering and ameliorating appearance, humankind's most abiding mode of self-imaging. Other than the first decorations of scarification and anatomical distortion, all adorning beauty of the body was vested in clothing. By the late twentieth century, cosmetic surgery offered a significant option to alter the body, even without the stigmatic, apparent elements of body deformity in other cultures and first culture. Now, we can hope for the medical idealism that shifts the burden back to the body and away from clothing's glamorization and/or distortion. Significantly, body sculpting and alteration is likely to become the body ideal and clothing will be assumed for more practical reasons and purposes. Both self-esteem and sexual allure may seem to be enhanced in this new way. That apparel might be supplanted as the first technique of physical expression and social presentation by body refinement is not unexpected. Anthropologically, decoration began with body adornment. But clothing is not, even with plastic surgery, without its utility of temperature control, modesty, social identification, and other purposes that have been sustained from fig leaf to animal skin to kimono to denim to Lycra. If the ideal configuration of the human body is otherwise achieved in the mirror's reflection, clothing still has its important place of allowing interaction and of styling the human discourse. In *Penguin Island*, Anatole France imagined a world without clothing that was then made ludicrous by the imposition of clothes. Rather, we will need clothes, even aside from decoration and apart from variable modesty, to serve practical needs.

[See also Cosmetics and Toiletries; Fragrances.]

BIBLIOGRAPHY

Davis, Fred. *Fashion, Culture, and Identity.* Chicago: University of Chicago Press, 1992.
Hoffman, Kurt, and Rush, Howard. *Micro-Electronics and Clothing: The Impact of Technological Change on a Global Industry.* New York: Praeger, 1988.

                                                    — RICHARD MARTIN

COAL

Coal is the paramount source of electric power in the United States and the primary domestic energy in both production and reserves. Comprising nine-tenths of available fuel reserves, its recoverable energy content is approximately four times the energy content of the oil reserves of Saudi Arabia. The United States is a foremost producer, user, and exporter, and the leading developer of advanced power-generation technology. Coal also supplies 44 percent of the world's electricity. United States and global reliance on coal will grow as this century closes and the next century begins.

World Energy Use—Long- and Shorter-Term Forecasts

One projection for 2050 sees overall demand rising by a factor of 4.5, with coal supplying 45 percent of all energy, its use exceeding that of oil by 2.5 times. Forecasts, each founded on different economic assumptions, vary widely. The range of most sees overall energy use as doubling or tripling through 2030. Governing actual demand will be a projected population growth of three billion in the developing nations, their economic development, economic cycles, technological advances, and the availability of a given energy. Greatest demand growth will occur in developing nations, many of which are energy-poor.

Mid-range, shorter-term forecasts see faster growth in coal than overall demand: 22 percent through 1996; 28 percent through 2000; and 45 percent through 2010. High-range projections see an end-term increase of 70 percent.

Developments of the last two decades drive the trends of the next two and set the stage for the next century. From the 1970s through the early 1990s, a series of shocks and surprises caused worldwide reappraisal and revision of plans and practices. First the Arab embargo and the Islamic revolution in Iran caused oil-related dislocations of the global economy; then the accident at Chernobyl intensified efforts to raise questions about nuclear power's safety; and, finally, the Persian Gulf War underscored the instabilities of the dominant oil-producing region. Energy security became a stronger influence—supply questions of availability, stability, and diversity assumed a vital significance. Demand for coal has grown faster in the last quarter of this century than for any other type of energy (see Figure 1).

Forces driving coal demand include: (1) world reserves and the need for secure energy; (2) rapidly rising requirements for electric power; (3) advanced power-generation technology that resolves environmental concerns; and (4) the performance of the U.S. coal industry at home and in the world market.

RESERVES AND PRODUCTION—ENERGY SECURITY. World reserves are quite extensive. By all estimates, the amount of presently recoverable coal exceeds one trillion tons, and total reserves may approach 15

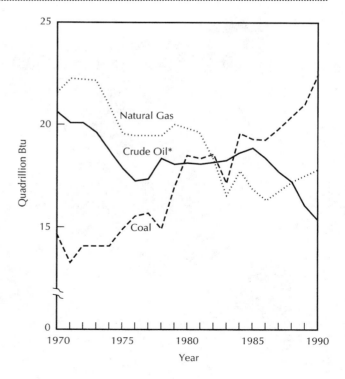

Figure 1. *U.S. energy production by major source, 1970–1990.*

trillion tons. Recoverable reserves include all coal judged mineable with current technology at current prices; and advances in either technology or market prices can raise estimates. The worldwide recovery rate is about 50 percent. The U.S. rate is 75 percent, a result of recent modernization.

America's recoverable coal may exceed 290 billion tons, the energy equivalent of the proved world oil reserve. Oil reserves and production concentrate around the Persian Gulf. Fifty nations produce coal, the most widely distributed resource. Other major holders are the Commonwealth of Independent States (the former Soviet Union), 270 billion tons; and the People's Republic of China, 109 billion tons. Lesser holders include Australia, Canada, Germany, India, Poland, South Africa, and the United Kingdom.

Richest also in energy content, U.S. deposits are in the Appalachian Basin (from Pennsylvania to Alabama); the interior (Illinois to Texas); and the West (North Dakota to Arizona). Thirty-eight states hold reserves. Foremost are Montana, Illinois, Wyoming, West Virginia, Kentucky, Pennsylvania, Ohio, Colorado, Texas, and Indiana (see Figure 2).

World coal production increased to 5 billion tons—by 63 percent overall and 71 percent in the United States—from 1970 through 1990. Coal displaced oil and natural gas in and by power generation. The largest

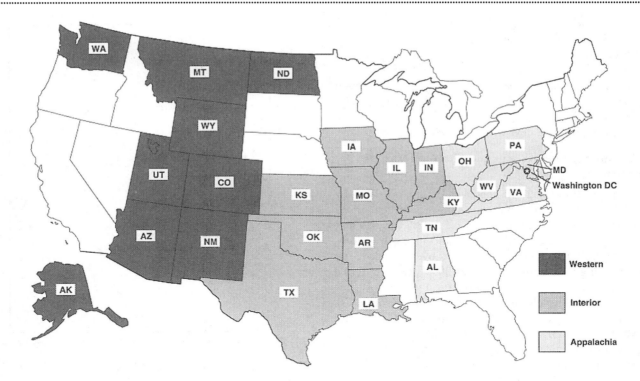

Figure 2. U.S. coal-producing regions. (Energy Information Administration, Office of Coal, Nuclear, Electric and Alternate Fuels)

producers are the United States and China, both with about one billion tons, and the Commonwealth of Independent States (CIS) with 694 billion tons. Others include Australia, Canada, Germany, India, Poland, Turkey, the Czech Republic, and Slovakia.

American coal production rose from 603 million tons to one billion, including coal for export. About 60 percent of this is mined east of the Mississippi River, and more than 60 percent is from surface mines. Twenty-seven states produce coal. The top ten coal producers are Wyoming, West Virginia, Kentucky, Pennsylvania, Illinois, Texas, Virginia, Montana, Indiana, and Ohio.

At recent production levels, the world has at least

a 230-year supply of coal, 44 years of oil,

and 56 years of natural gas.

At recent production levels the world has at least a 230-year supply of coal, 44 years of oil, and 56 years of natural gas. Demand will rise as other reserves diminish and prices increase. Low and stable long-term costs are significant considerations in electric power.

ELECTRIC-POWER DEMAND—WORLD AND UNITED STATES. Electric power accounts for most new energy demand, globally and in the United States. Electricity is the most efficient, economic, versatile, and cleanest end-use energy. Additions to the world generating capacity should exceed 1.4-million megawatts through 2010. One hundred developing nations account for 45 percent; the CIS and Eastern Europe, 17 percent; other industrialized nations, 19 percent; and the United States, almost 20 percent.

More power generation leads to projected world use of at least 6.2 billion tons by 1995; 6.6 billion by 2000; and 7.4 billion in 2010. Most demand will be in energy-poor developing nations and reserve-holding nations—in particular, China, the CIS, India, and the United States.

In the United States, electricity filled 24 percent of all energy demand in 1970; by 1990 it was 36 percent; and by 2010 it should be 41 percent. Coal generated more power in 1990 than all energy sources combined in 1970 (see Figure 3). Utility use increased 142 percent, from 320 million tons to 774 million. Forecasters see power production rising 30 percent to 60 percent.

The United States will require up to 233,000 megawatts of new capacity for baseload, or around-the-clock,

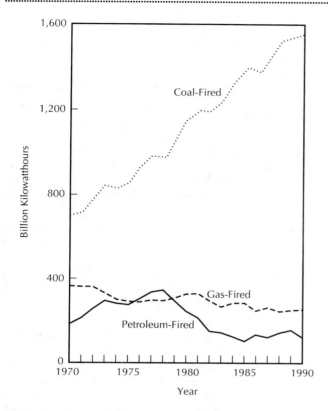

Figure 3. Electric utility fossil-fired steam generation by fuel type, 1970–1990. (Energy Information Administration, Annual Energy Review, *1991)*

use by 2010; the need will be in addition to gains in conservation and end-use efficiency. Forecasts say that coal will fuel at least half due to long-term fuel costs. Present capacity of all kinds is about 700,000 megawatts.

U.S. coal-burn projections are: 1.0 billion tons by 2000, 1.3 billion by 2010, and 1.6 billion by 2030. However, these estimates are based on the assumption that government policy will revive nuclear power; failing this, electric generation may call for 2 billion tons in the closing year.

Relative share of domestic power in 1990 was: 55.6 percent, coal; 20.5 percent, nuclear generation; 9.9 percent, hydroelectric; 8.7 percent, natural gas; and 4 percent, oil. Coal share will range from 50 percent to 59 percent through 2010, although a weak or failed nuclear revival could put it at 75 percent by 2030.

ADVANCED POWER-GENERATING TECHNOLOGIES. The United States leads in research, development, and demonstration. Recent government policy emphasized the Clean Coal Technology (CCT) and Coal Research programs. Goals of these programs include

higher thermal efficiencies, lower capital costs, and emissions at one-tenth of current standards. First-generation technologies, in demonstration, should enter commercial use after 1995; and a second generation, in research, after 2010.

First-generation demonstrations are in the CCT program, a $5 billion joint venture with participant industries paying 60 percent. Most promising to repower old plants and for new capacity are pressurized-fluidized-bed combustion (PFBC) and integrated-gasification-combined-cycle generation (IGCC); both use the energy of combustion twice. In PFBC, steam from a boiler drives one generating turbine, and pressurized exhaust gases another; combustion is on a bed of limestone to absorb pollutants. In IGCC, gas produced from coal is burned in a generating turbine, and the hot exhaust raises steam to turn a second. The former eliminates at least 90 percent of sulfur emissions and the latter 99 percent. The first IGGC demonstration, in California, used most ranks of high- and low-sulfur coal, and bettered standards of the world's strictest emissions permit. Conventional thermal efficiency averages 33 percent; PFBC achieves 40 percent, and IGCC 42 percent.

Second-generation efficiencies range from 42 to 60 percent; applications include advanced state-of-the-art conventional generation, advanced PFBC and IGCC, fuel cells, and magnetohydrodynamics.

The efficiencies of conventional coal generation improved by a factor of eight in the twentieth century; without this gain the United States might have eight times the present power costs and eight times the pollutant emissions of current concern: sulfur and carbon dioxide. With the new technologies, the cumulative gains rise to a full order of magnitude; they raise power output at still lower costs and fuel input; they reduce carbon dioxide output by up to 20 percent per unit of power in the first generation and 40 percent in the second. They deliver the ability to increase power production while answering concerns about environmental and climatic changes.

Other research goals include the production of liquid fuel, chemicals, and other products at costs equivalent to feedstock oil at $30 a barrel.

THE U.S. INDUSTRY—DOMESTIC AND WORLD MARKETS. The U.S. industry is the world's most modern and productive. Increased demand led to capital investment, and productivity rose 126 percent in the twelve years ending in 1990. Investment transformed the mines and the market. Forces driving modernization, and others put in motion by it, will influence demand, domestic and foreign, into the twenty-first century.

In the mines: underground, investment improved continuous miner production, and deployed 90 to 100 longwall mining systems that each can deliver more than 2,000 tons a shift; and it opened rich, new fields and new surface mines while allowing the introduction of larger equipment. Investment and productivity gains are expected to continue. Meanwhile, coal mining fatalities declined from 266 in 1970 to 66 in 1990, safety was emphasized, and coal now ranks below twenty industries in injury-incidence rate; underground mines operate at average dust levels below those scientifically determined to preclude new cases of black lung; and reclamation quickly returns all surface mines to original contour and productive use; examples of how former surface-mine sites have been put to productive use include tree farms, pasturage, cropland, and wildlife refuges.

In the domestic market, competition lowered coal prices in constant (1982) dollars in every year of the

Coal remains the paramount source of electric power in the United States, and worldwide reliance on coal is expected to grow. (Galen Rowell/Corbis)

1980s; average price was one-half that of oil, two-thirds of natural gas, even when those prices fell; and variable power-plant costs were lower than for oil, gas, or nuclear generation. Coal became the power-fuel of economic choice. As a growing economy demanded more electricity, coal units were put in service earlier and kept longer. In Ohio a contested nuclear plant was converted to coal in mid-construction. In 1993 the largest fifty planned additions to capacity were coal-fired. Meanwhile, as twenty-year use more than doubled, sulfur emissions declined; the causes of these improvements included precombustion preparation, blending, and flue-gas desulfurization.

In world production, the coal industry outdistanced others. Each American miner produces 7,800 tons of coal a year. The best available figures offer these comparisons: miners in Poland produced 432 tons; in Germany, 729 tons; in the United Kingdom, 1,400 tons; and in Australia, 5,400 tons.

The United States led in remaking the world market. Once dominated by steelmakers' needs for metallurgical coal, it now is predominantly an energy market competing with other fuels. America's ready response to sudden demand in the 1980s fostered this change; its productivity underwrites permanence and price competitiveness, answers to the security questions of availability and stability. Geographic and geopolitical distribution ensure diversity of supply. Unlike oil exporters, the principal traders are committed to free markets and competition, and reserves are not concentrated.

World trade could more than double to 900 million tons by 2020, primarily due to power in developing nations. A strong, but shorter-term, influence will be the end of production subsidies in Europe. Leading exporters are Australia, the United States, South Africa, and Canada. Others include Colombia, Venezuela, Indonesia, Poland, the CIS, and China.

Annual U.S. exports are expected to increase to 136 million tons by 2000; to 199 million by 2005; to 250–282 million by 2010; and to possibly as much as 300 million by 2020. The United States is expected to again be the number one exporter early in the period. The only net export in energy, annual coal shipments in excess of 100 million tons now add $4.5 billion to the plus side of the trade balance. Other exports will be tied to growth: precombustion preparation, and new generating technologies. Capacity additions outside the United States will be a $3 trillion market for equipment and services through 2010.

Almost nine-tenths of production goes to power generation and export. Other important domestic use includes: conversion to coke for basic steel-making; as a source of heat or steam in the manufacture of cement, chemicals, and paper and paperboard; and for the same purposes in general industrial activity. In addition, the Dakota Gasification Company economically produces pipeline-quality synthetic natural gas from North Dakota lignite, a low-rank coal; and the Tennessee Eastman Company gasifies coal to produce raw material for Kodak film and other products.

The Future

All forecasts begin with assumptions that may meet, fail, or exceed expectations as unforseeable developments of passing years prove them right or wrong. U.S. coal production passed one billion tons five years ahead of predictions made only in the mid-1980s, the result of power demand and industry performance.

Coal will be a mainstay of the United States and the world in balancing and solving the problems of the twenty-first century.

Increased—or decreased—performance also may change other projections—year by year, decade by decade. Continued poverty in the developing world points to unabated population growth and global political unrest; but economic development could bring stability and lower birthrates toward the replacement-only levels of industrialized nations. Success in developing a competitive electric automobile would raise power demand above all forecasts, and also eliminate most anthropogenic carbon dioxide. Energy and advanced technology are critical in dealing with concerns, real or postulated.

The power in coal is a versatile factor in the important equations of the future. No longer the "King Coal" of 1900, nor the obsolescent resource of 1950, coal will nevertheless be a mainstay of the United States and the world in balancing and solving the problems of the twenty-first century; indeed, they may be insoluble without it.

[See also Electric Power; Energy; Energy, Renewable Sources Of; Energy Conservation; Minerals; Natural Gas; Natural Resources: Use Of; Nuclear Power: Con; Petroleum; Pipelines; Soil Conditions; Transuranium Elements.]

BIBLIOGRAPHY

Annual Energy Outlook 1991. Washington, DC: Energy Information Administration, U.S. Department of Energy, 1991.

Annual Energy Outlook 1993. Washington, DC: Energy Information Administration, U.S. Department of Energy, 1993.

Annual Energy Review 1991. Washington, DC: Energy Information Administration, U.S. Department of Energy, 1991.

BP Statistical Review of World Energy. London: British Petroleum Company, 1990.

Coal Data: A Reference. Washington, DC: U.S. Department of Energy; 1992.

"Coal Quietly Regains a Dominant Chunk of Generating Market." *Wall Street Journal,* August 20, 1992, p. 1.

International Energy Outlook 1990. Washington, DC: Energy Information Administration, U.S. Department of Energy, 1990.

— RICHARD L. LAWSON

COMIC BOOKS

Story telling by means of illustrations has come a long way since cartoons were crudely scratched on the walls of caves by prehistoric man. It was in the 1930s that comic strips were first collected from newspapers and printed in magazine form. That was when they gained the name "comic books." More than one-quarter billion American comic books are sold annually, with the number growing all the time.

One trend that shows no sign of abating is the amazing increase in the age of readers. Where such magazines were once read primarily by children under the age of ten, ever since the 1960s the median age has been growing until it is now in the middle teens, with young adults now equaling the number of children who qualify as regular readers. As the subject matter of many comic books grows more and more sophisticated, and as the comics industry's so-called "graphic novels" are printed in ever more expensive, coffee-table editions, the time will come when comic books are no longer thought of as merely entertainment for children. Indeed, in France, Italy, and Japan, the comic book format has for many years been considered literature for adults.

The growing acceptance of comic books is something of a self-fulfilling prophecy. As their sales increase, the publishers are able to pay higher rates to their artists and writers. As these rates increase, more and better talents are drawn to the field. As the quality of the stories and artwork increases, ever more discerning readers join the legion of fans.

A spectacular new development has been a growing recognition of the value of comic book artwork. Prestigious organizations such as Sotheby's have held auctions of comic book covers and illustrated pages in which the bidding has reached into the high thousands for both illustrations and collectible comics from the last few decades. In the future, comic books will be bought, sold, and traded by investors and collectors much in the same manner as postage stamps, lithographs, and baseball trading cards are.

The coming decade will bring us more and more comic books being sold in the large, prestigious book chains. Concurrently, there will be newspaper columns that critique the latest comic book releases in the same way that columnists review motion pictures, books, and television shows. Inevitably it will follow that an Academy of Comic Book Arts will be established, along the lines of the motion picture and television academies, to give awards to the most creative and imaginative work produced by the writers, artists, inkers, letterers, and colorists, as well as the editors and art directors within the comic book industry.

In the future, comic books will be bought, sold,

and traded by investors and collectors

much in the same manner as postage stamps

and baseball trading cards are.

Comic books will soon be taking their place on the cultural totem pole alongside of popular novels, motion pictures, and television.

What was once considered merely a product for young, naive children is increasingly becoming one of the standard literary and art forms of our time, an art form that will help to usher us into the twenty-first century.

[See also Free Time; Intellectual Property; Leisure Time; Literature; Newspapers; Printed Word; Science Fiction.]

BIBLIOGRAPHY

Daniels, Les. *MARVEL: Five Fabulous Decades of the World's Greatest Comics.* New York: Harry N. Abrams, 1993.

Horn, Maurice, ed. *The World Encyclopedia of Cartoons.* 6 vols. New York: Chelsea House, 1982.

Jacobs, Will, and Jones, Gerald. *The Comicbook Heroes.* New York: Crown, 1986.

— STAN LEE

COMMISSION ON THE YEAR 2000

The Commission on the Year 2000 was the first serious effort in the United States to identify future problems confronting the society in the next thirty years. Initiated in 1965, it was chaired by Daniel Bell and comprised thirty-eight individuals from universities, government, and research organizations who occupied leading positions in these institutions.

Among the members (and their present or later positions) were William O. Baker, the head of Bell Labs; Harvey Brooks, Harvard, who headed the National Science Foundation committee that proposed the Office of Technology Assessment; Zbigniew Brzezinski, na-

tional security adviser to President Carter; Hedley Donovan, editor-in-chief, Time, Inc.; Erik Erikson, psychoanalyst; Robert Fano, director of the Laboratory of Computer Science, M.I.T.; Stanley Hoffmann, Harvard; Samuel P. Huntington, Harvard; Fred G. Iklé, Under-Secretary of Defense in the Reagan administration; Herman Kahn, a theorist on nuclear war; Wassily Leontief, Nobel laureate in economics; Ernst Mayr, biologist, Harvard; Matthew Meselson, biologist, Harvard; Daniel P. Moynihan, senator from New York; Emanuel R. Piore, chief scientist, IBM; Roger Revelle, oceanographer; David Riesman, Harvard; Eugene Rostow, dean, Yale Law School and Under-Secretary of State in the Carter administration; Krister Stendhal, dean of the Divinity School, Harvard; Robert C. Wood, Secretary of Housing and Urban Development, Johnson administration.

The commission's members felt that American society was ill-prepared to deal with social issues, because there was no mechanism to anticipate them. The commission did not believe in "sky-writing" about "the future." As Daniel Bell wrote in the first working paper: "The future is not an overarching leap in the distance; it begins in the present . . . for in the decisions we make now, in the way we design our environment and thus sketch the lines of constraints, the future is committed."

The first efforts of the commission—working papers, transcripts of several meetings, and thirty-seven essays by members—were published in full in mimeographed form, and three thousand sets of these volumes went to individuals in universities, government, and business. A selection from these volumes was published in the September 1967 issue of *Daedalus,* the journal of the American Academy of Arts and Sciences, under the title of "Toward the Year 2000: Work in Progress," and more than 100,000 copies were sold. A hardcover edition was published by Houghton Mifflin; and a paperback edition, later, by the Beacon Press. In addition, materials from volumes II and IIa of the working papers were revised and published independently by its authors, Herman Kahn and Anthony J. Wiener, under the title *The Year 2000.*

In laying out its agenda (I paraphrase and quote here from pp. 3–7 of the "Toward the Year 2000" report), the commission stated that the basic framework of day-to-day life has been shaped by the ways the automobile, the airplane, the telephone, and television have brought people together and increased the networks and interactions among them. The major technological changes would be in the development of computers and biomedical engineering. "We will probably see a national information-computer-utility system with tens of thousands of terminals in homes and offices . . . providing library and information services, retailing, ordering, and billing services, and the like." Biomedical work with organic transplant, genetic modification, and control of disease would produce an aging population.

In respect to structural changes the commission noted that "the centralization of the American political system has marked an extraordinary transformation of American life." A postindustrial system is reducing the role of employment in manufacturing. The older bureaucratic patterns of hierarchy may force institutions to reorganize. Individuals will face the need for renewed education. The family as a source of primordial attachment may become less important. The culture will become more hedonistic, expressive, and distrustful of authority. Further, as a result of the greater public focus on visible issues, social and political conflict may become more marked.

Thirty-one papers exploring these issues were printed in the volume. Eight further working groups were set up—one on the structure of government, chaired by Harvey Perloff; another on values and rights, chaired by Fred G. Iklé; intellectual institutions, by Stephen Graubard; the life cycle, by Kai Erikson; the international system, by Stanlev Hoffmann; the social impact of the computer, by Robert Fano; science and society, by Franklin Long and Robert S. Morison; business institutions, by Martin Shubik. In all more than two hundred individuals participated in the work of these groups. A major project, *The Future of the U.S. Government*, edited by Harvey Perloff (with papers by Rexford Tugwell, John Brademas and Henry, Reuss, as well as Richard P. Nathan, George C. Lodge, and others) was published in 1971. In pointing to the patchwork system of governmental units and the need for decentralization, the volume stated: "The major problem in the years ahead will be to define the effective size and scope of the appropriate social units for coping with the different levels of problems: what should be decided and performed on the neighborhood, city, metropolitan and federal levels."

In reviewing the work of the commission, thirty years later, what is most striking is the "freshness" of its observations, if only because of the persistence of the issues it identified, amidst all the flurry of words about the shock of change.

BIBLIOGRAPHY

Bell, Daniel, ed. "Toward the Year 2000: Work in Progress." *Daedalus* 96/3 (Summer 1967).
Kahn, Herman, and Wiener, Anthony J. *The Year 2000*. New York: Macmillan, 1967.

Perloff, Harvey, ed. *The Future of the U.S. Government*. New York: George Braziller, 1971.

– DANIEL BELL

COMMUNICATIONS

Communications will mold the structure and essence of twenty-first-century communities, wherever they exist and whatever purposes they fulfill. Indeed, the common root of these words ties them to the concept of sharing—the exchange of ideas, information, money, goods, entertainment, and most everything else of which society is comprised. In this sense, we have always lived in an information society, but now the sharing will leave no one untouched and will interconnect everybody and everything to a much greater degree.

The U.S. Postal Service will decline. E-mail and facsimiles are completing the elimination of first-class mail begun by the telephone and electronic funds transfer.

Major advances in communication—e.g., the appearance of oral language in tribal communities, pictographic languages such as hieroglyphics in Egypt or cuneiform in Mesopotamia, and the alphabet in Europe and Asia—have brought about dramatic changes in societies since the first spoken word. Paper preserved and spread ideas and images throughout the global community, and the printing press greatly expanded the sharing of knowledge.

Small uses were found for electrons in communications over the last century with the invention of the telegraph and telephone. Photons, hundreds of times more powerful in communication, will support the next societal revolution.

The technology of and for optical communications will connect the twenty-first-century citizen to the ideas, knowledge, and happenings of an immensely varied set of communities. The twentieth-century mind cannot yet conceive how it will cope with—or even survive the infoglut or overload inherent in so much sharing.

The term *information society* arose because information technology advances have often heralded or even brought about major societal changes. In such a society, the exchange of information is not only a decisive factor, but is overwhelmingly dominant in all facets and activities of the community.

Information exchange will consume more of our time and resources, and information systems will control an increasingly larger part of physical activities such as transportation, manufacturing, and distribution.

What now exist as numbers and words for "throughput" in the communication systems will be converted into more useful forms. First will come transformation into useful data. Next will come algorithms to process the data into information. Expert systems will translate information into intelligence. Neural systems embedded in the communications network may ultimately even impart a degree of learning to users.

Perhaps the earliest example of such systems will involve language. Of all the features defining community, a shared language is the most important. Computers capable of real-time translation will accelerate the move toward a worldwide community. Imagine a conversation by phone with anyone, anywhere, with both speakers speaking and hearing in their native languages.

Will the present generation be the last to use the printed word? In the long battle of attrition between hard copy and electronic media, the armies of print and film continue to lose both people and territory. This conflict, begun in 1837 with the telegraph, may have reached the end of the beginning in 1937 with television, and we are almost certainly near the beginning of the end today. Many battles yet remain, but the retreat by Gutenberg's legions should end this 200-year war by 2037 or there-about. In each domain where paper and type have held advantages over electronics, continued improvements in the newer technology have eventually eliminated those advantages. The still-developing, electronic network will be a faster, more accurate, more efficient, and more satisfying creator and servant of communities than ink and paper could ever be.

Newspapers may continue to be major purveyors of "news" during the near-term future. As of now, they are the principal source of expository news for both local and larger communities in contrast to the "sound bytes," "talking heads," and occasionally graphic images of television. The future presents a dilemma. Will the market for real news decline as a result of cultural change, or will the visual media find a way to deliver news with substantial content? Given the ongoing

Optic fiber cables will replace the copper cables currently in use for communications transmission. Optical transmission rates will increase from 80 gigabits/second in 1997 to 100 gigabits/second in 2011. (James L. Amos/Corbis)

multimedia experiments and increasing capabilities of video communications, the latter seems most likely to end the newspaper dominions.

Advertising is not only a form of communication in its own right, but it also often subsidizes other communications. What mechanism would support newspapers and magazines in the absence of advertising? Home shopping will not only compete for advertising revenues, but will also reduce the economic base that purchases ads. The encroachment by electronic media upon print media will continue to be reflected in the shift of advertising revenues, a problem that will no longer be masked by overall growth in the economy.

Libraries will become less and less the storers and providers of books. As dispensers of information, they will survive if they incorporate newer methods for storage and distribution of information. However, the threat to local institutions again comes from the exponentially expanding ability of electronic media to accomplish these functions.

Continued sniping at the U.S. Postal Service will hasten its inevitable decline. E-mail and facsimiles are completing the elimination of first-class mail begun by the telephone and electronic funds transfer. In every other postal sphere concerned with the transport of communication, such as magazines, catalogues, and advertising, the transformation of these physical forms into electronically equivalent services will reduce postal carriage.

The past decade of revolutionary change in the U.S. telephone system is only a prelude to the changes of the next twenty years. Dissolution of the AT&T monolith, thought to presage the end of the world's best telephone operation, instead unleashed a torrent of advance that would have been unlikely under the old monopoly. By the year 2013 or thereabouts, every element of today's telephone system will have been completely replaced by newer technologies. Optical fiber and cellular radio will have virtually supplanted the last vestiges of the copper network. All analog elements will have long since been replaced by digital systems. Digital radio networks, including low-orbit earth satellites, will enable personal communication connections any time, anywhere, with anyone.

Two-way interactive video communications will be the new transport vehicle for many of the forms of sharing and exchange which now require the movement of people. For shopping, your fingers and eyes will do the walking and driving.

Advances in financial transaction methods will be among the most important features of the Information Society. These advances will include the ability for anyone to transfer funds anywhere, at any time. The effectiveness of media for the exchange of money will be a major influence in stabilizing world society.

Satellites, as both generators and transporters of information, will continue these functions, unseen and unappreciated. Although connections between earth and low-altitude satellites are limited to radio frequencies, laser beams between the satellites could provide worldwide broadband trunking circuits. The twenty-first century will commence with massive competition and cooperation among fiber optics, cellular radio, and satellites in meeting communication and transportation needs.

Just as Gutenberg kicked off a world revolution with movable type, and Giotto's geometry led to new concepts in visual presentation, so too photography and electronic imaging affected every aspect of society. In the future, how will the competition between film and electronics play out? Video cameras have driven out motion picture filming from all except the highest-definition recording. The realm of still photography is similarly vulnerable. A similar situation faces all recording. Can delivery from central sources, on demand, be provided at lower cost than music or video record purchase or rental?

Most, if not all, of the advances in communication technology have advanced freedom and democracy. Developments such as facsimiles, copy machines, electronic mail, home videos, and cellular phones facilitate the rapid uncontrolled distribution of information essential to informed deliberation.

Whatever the future holds for communication, it will hold for all the world communities. Even when we can do no more than define the direction that communications developments are taking, we can be sure that society will ultimately benefit, as it always has.

[See also Advertising; Broadcasting; Communications: Media Law; Communications: Privacy Issues; Communication Technology; Digital Communications; Electronic Convergence; Newspapers; On-Line Services; Postal Services; Printed Word; Telecommunications; Telephones; Television.]

BIBLIOGRAPHY

Davis, Stan, and Davidson, Bill. *2020 Vision.* New York: Simon & Schuster, 1991.

Grant, A. *Communication Update,* 3rd ed. Stoneham, MA: Focal Press, 1994.

Lenz, Ralph C. "Crossroads En Route to the Information Highway." *New Telecom Quarterly* (October—December 1993).

Vanston, Lawrence K. "Technological Substitution in Telecom Equipment." *New Telecom Quarterly* (January—March 1994).

– RALPH C. LENZ
LAWRENCE K. VANSTON

COMMUNICATIONS: DIGITAL.
See DIGITAL COMMUNICATIONS.

COMMUNICATIONS: MEDIA LAW

Social and technological advances are usually followed by legislative responses aimed at restraints that moderate social change. Legislators, torn between the public interest and special interests, usually favor the special interests. Attempts to modify the Communications Act of 1937 and coordinate it with the requirements of emerging technologies have made little progress. Distribution of limited-frequency and channel spaces overwhelmed by the increased use of interactive multimedia communications should force an overhaul of communications law by the turn of the century.

Attempts to prevent the distribution, publication, and transmission of "controversial" written materials are doomed to failure. No moral restraint on the arts has ever succeeded in controlling creative expression.

Information-based technologies, advancing at an accelerating rate, are providing more knowledge to more people than ever before in history. Mass information technologies, over the short term, tend to be concentrated in fewer hands. This trend is likely to be slowly reversed over the next decade. Antitrust laws, administered by the Federal Trade Commission, the Federal Communications Commission, and the U.S. Department of Justice, may have to be strengthened.

New services such as the Internet accelerate a trend toward ever-more information—for better or worse. Access to such services increases the availability and diversity of fact and opinion and decreases dependence on any one provider. Attempts to control and suppress the dissemination of the diverse materials will increasingly be attempted. New laws may decentralize controls over all forms of communications.

Censorship

The fear of change has always been a primary cause of censorship. Throughout history, ruling elites have used their moral attitudes and legal authority to control many information sources.

The U.S. Supreme Court has protected and expanded free expression over the past two centuries. As rights of expression expand, increased responsibility over expression must expand commensurately. The regulatory authority of the Federal Communications Commission is increasingly inadequate to resolve the abuses of socially irresponsible communication.

Books and Publications

Increasingly we may read reports of attempts by small, vocal minorities to censor what is read or taught. At times, some legislators may be foolish enough to act, but ultimately attempts to prevent the distribution, publication, and transmission of "controversial" written materials are doomed to failure.

Works of Art

No moral restraint on the arts has ever succeeded in controlling creative expression. Definitions of what art is evolve. Social, moral, and intellectual attempts to inhibit the expansion of human consciousness by imposing artificial values will continue. Top-down attempts at censorship will continue to conflict with expanding constitutional guarantees of socially responsible expression.

Teachers

Almost always, attempts to increase knowledge or information arouse cultural opposition. Increased intellectual independence inherently involves decreased reliance on and obedience of arbitrary authority. The manipulation of educational systems to advance narrowly based political agendas are underway now. Efforts by conservative religious groups to privatize schools also entail curricula control that may involve a hidden agenda to undermine the educational processes through censorship and budgetary control.

While there is an increased movement toward uniform educational standards, on-line services such as the Internet promote diversity. Public policies that encourage the proliferation of such technology-based services are being developed. As communication technologies become easier to use, broad-based public participation in education will eventually spawn a diverse, nonhierarchical, fully participatory, and truly democratic system.

Libel and Slander

Intellectual enlightenment is threatened by egalitarian tendencies to devolve to the lowest common denominator. Media pandering to the emotions, fantasies, gossip, and misinformation debase and demean a society already wallowing in superficialities. Improved ethical standards, voluntarily assumed by the media and sometimes enforced by government agencies, will help assure a more responsible media.

The U.S. Supreme Court ruled that commercial speech is not protected by the First Amendment of the

Constitution if it involves the dissemination of false and misleading advertising. An increased need to broaden that rule is emerging. Viable legal standards to prevent the dissemination of libel, slander, misinformation, and fiction disguised as fact will be devised without impairing freedom of speech.

Court rulings limit the ability of public figures to obtain full legal recourse and damages for slander and libel. Mass media tend to emphasize hearsay and innuendo while shielded by defense of the public's need to know.

In an electronically interconnected society, the right of privacy will be protected. The right of the media or any agent of government to invade the privacy of any individual and disseminate personal information in the absence of a clear and present danger to the public is excessive. Allegations by public authorities affecting public policy should require corroboration. The absence of malice is less and less of a defense.

Simultaneously, the right of free expression must be protected. Attempts to suppress commentary through the courts may be mitigated by requiring the moving party to pay the defendant's court costs, legal fees, and ancillary expenses in the absence of a finding on the part of the plaintiff.

Media Complaints

Media complaints usually emanate from pressure groups pursuing self-promotion and preservation. As media outlets increase and audiences fragment, an increasing number of such groups will attempt to impose controls on the media. Over the long term, these same increases in information sources and diverse opinion should produce an enlightenment causing such problems to self-correct.

Claims of media bias will increase. Increased diversity of opinion prompts increased disagreement. There will never be complete agreement on any issue, nor should there be. Problems occur when attempts are undertaken to suppress valid, informed opinions.

Attempts to increase media holdings will increase over the short term. However, such consolidation could seriously threaten access to information and entertainment. Although attempts to control the content of what is available in such circumstances are more likely to be motivated by profit rather than ideology, the net effect could be the same as with ideological censorship: a restriction of the diversity of viewpoints accessible to the public.

Antitrust authority over media consolidations is vested in the Federal Trade Commission, the Federal Communications Commission, and the Department of Justice. Reduced competition is occurring between promoters of various transmission technologies. Market forces that might have increased diversity and reduced costs through competition have not been set into motion. Statutory limitations based on total market share and percentage of broadcast band access may have to be enacted to protect the public interest.

Consumer Fraud

Exposure to temptation in America's consumer-oriented society, which increased during the previous decade, will continue to increase. The consumer's ability to order something on impulse by telephone increases unabated. New temptation through multimedia and computer-based shopping escalates this trend. Informed decisions based upon brief and usually incomplete representations by telemarketing spokespersons is limited; comparison shopping is all but nonexistent. Full, clear, and conspicuous disclosure of the quality, price, terms of sale, and other relevant criteria to compare goods and services will have to be provided.

Protection also may be established for consumers by requiring a mandatory three-day cooling-off period following receipt of contracts for all purchases (excluding perishable items). Advertising misrepresentations concurrently dealt with by state and local authorities will be strengthened to protect private rights of action by consumers. Federal preemption is no longer viable.

Civil actions are increasingly inadequate. State and local injunctive relief and restitution orders, which have no force or effect beyond jurisdictional lines, are increasingly ignored in a highly mobile society. The capacity of mobile merchants to evade the snare of state and local laws will be countered by increasing civil and criminal jurisdiction and penalties involving fraud in interstate commerce. The act of fraud will be redefined to include any misrepresentation of goods or services, or the failure to provide goods or services under the merchant's direct control. Mere proof of the act of fraud itself, not proof of *intent* to defraud, will be sufficient to enhance criminal prosecutions and protect consumers under this new definition.

Computers

Telephone lines and modems that allow anyone to communicate with anyone else via computer also allow them to interfere with other computers. The extent of unauthorized, unwarranted, and improper incursions into business and government databases increased during the past decade. There is little doubt that such incursions will continue to increase.

Unauthorized access to a database without owner authorization violates existing federal law. Prosecutions and convictions under this law have been few and far between. Perpetrators, often students thoughtlessly acting out immature rebellions, are usually treated leniently. As technologies improve, however, the number of "white-collar criminals" may increase.

Law enforcement tends to focus on crimes of violence, all but ignoring economic crimes. Wire fraud involving improper electronic fund transfers, banking frauds, and massive telemarketing schemes get less attention. What the public and Congress have not yet meaningfully addressed is that economic crimes impose costs substantially larger than crimes involving violence.

As the methods of access to bank accounts through computers and other electronic means increase, losses increase. Most economic crimes continue to be treated as civil rather than criminal violations and may not be included in crime statistics; as a consequence, they are not dealt with in a manner that discourages their spread. Laws defining and imposing penalties for communications fraud are in the offing and will be under the concurrent jurisdiction of state and federal agencies.

Different parts of the world currently have different communication standards and interfaces involving television, computers, and virtually all other commercial factors. The development of high-definition television (HDTV) provides an example of the pushing and pulling in attempting to develop a worldwide state-of-the-art standard. Worldwide intergovernmental cooperation in conjunction with the private sector is essential to achieve uniform interfaces and standards. How soon such standards are adopted will depend on the willingness of the various elements within the private sector to share technologies and share the costs of research and development.

[See also Advertising; Communications; Communications: Privacy Issues; Computers: Privacy Laws; Consumer Protection/Regulation; Intellectual Property; Marketing; Telecommunications.]

BIBLIOGRAPHY

Bagdikian, Ben H. *The Media Monopoly*, 4th ed. Boston: Beacon Press, 1992.

Burris, Daniel, with Roger Gittenes. *Technotrends: How to Use Technology to Go Beyond Your Competition.* New York: Harper Collins, 1993.

Combs, James E., and Nimmo, Dan D. *The New Propaganda: The Dictatorship of Palaver in Contemporary Politics.* New York: Longman, 1993.

Dublin, Max. *Futurehype: The Tyranny of Prophecy.* New York: Dutton, 1989.

Glastonbury, Bryan, and Lamendola, Walter. *The Integrity of Intelligence: A Bill of Rights for the Information Age.* New York: St. Martin's, 1992.

Yankelovich, Daniel. *Coming to Public Judgment: Making Democracy Work in a Complex World.* Syracuse, NY. Syracuse University Press, 1991.

Zaller, John R. *The Nature and Origins of Mass Opinion.* New York: Cambridge University Press, 1992.

— ABRAHAM MOSES GENEN

COMMUNICATIONS: PRIVACY ISSUES

Modern society is in the midst of a technological upheaval comparable to the advent of the steam engine and electricity. By the end of the next decade, almost every U.S. business, government agency, library, school, and home will be plugged into a high-speed, interactive communications network. In this new "infostructure," a single, fiber-optic terminal will transmit words, images, music, medical information, and industrial charts. With everyone connected electronically, there will be greatly reduced need for such familiar services as mail delivery or newspapers as we know them today. People will receive personalized magazines and newspapers customized to fit their own interests. Students will communicate with teachers from home terminals and design their own individualized home-based learning programs. With tele-medicine, people will get medical advice from electronic medical databanks rather than doctors.

Communications advances will lead to increased use of electronic money, and currency may be abandoned entirely.

Signal compression techniques will enable cable television companies to devote a channel for an individual customer's use, allowing personalized programming. In the next century, people from all over the world will have computer access to the 500 miles of shelved books in the Library of Congress. We will be able to order a copy of any Library of Congress holding, any painting that hangs in the Louvre, or any movie from the comfort of our living room. Electronic robots will do our research for us by scanning the contents of distant libraries without human intervention. Virtual reality systems open up opportunities for interaction with computer-modeled environments, allowing a variety of activities to be experienced without ever leaving home. Communications advances will lead to increased use of electronic money, and currency may be abandoned entirely.

These wonders of technology will bring with them increased concern for personal privacy. Unless current trends change, computers will be used to track customers' shopping, banking, and leisure habits to an even greater extent than today. Cable companies, advertisers, direct marketers, and investigative firms will seek such data, much as they do today. This information will be stored and readily available, thereby representing an ever-increasing threat to personal privacy.

Tiny, hand-held devices will allow instant communications with anyone else in the world. People will never be out of touch, and calls will be placed to individuals instead of to places as they are today. The tendency toward constant communication will lead to a communications network that will be able to locate every individual's whereabouts.

British Telecommunications PLC is spending more than $1 billion over the next several years to develop a multimedia voice, data, and video digital-transmission network called Cyclone that will encompass many of these features. After initial outlays, the cost of establishing personal communications networks will be much lower than the cost of traditional wire-based connections. Therefore, these services will be affordable for average consumers.

Meanwhile, new methods of communicating are replacing more traditional forms. Although 60–90 percent of all nonspoken communications are now paper-based, this is rapidly changing. There are already an estimated 32,000 electronic bulletin boards in North America and 45,000 worldwide. The most notable of these, the Internet, links millions of users around the world.

Taken one step further, it will soon become as easy to transmit data through the air as it is today through wires. The new wireless telephone technology will allow salespeople to carry laptop computers connected directly to their home base by radio. Airlines already enable passengers to link up with their office computers, sending and receiving e-mail messages and faxes while in the air. Future office workers will not be typing at keyboards; they will be talking to computers that will have the ability to recognize human speech.

With more of the nation's business conducted over wireless networks, computer encoding is expected to grow rapidly by having devices such as clipper chips installed to protect privacy. Clipper chips are microcircuits that scramble telecommunications by using an algorithm.

Privacy also will continue to be a fundamental workplace issue. Managers will increasingly use new surveillance technology to monitor worker behavior. While management will attempt to enhance their control over the workplace, workers will devise new methods to protect their rights.

The revolution in technology development is being stimulated by the use of fiber-optic cables—a transmitting medium with enormous capacity. Fiber-optic cable is made up of hair-thin strands of glass so pure that it is theoretically possible to "see through" about 60 miles of fiber. It is the most powerful carrier of information ever invented and currently can transmit up to a billion bits of information per second. In a few years, a bundle of fiber-optic cable just half an inch thick will carry up to 32 million conversations.

Fiber-optic advances will be accompanied by continuing advances in computer technology. Future computers may be controlled directly by human thoughts. Fujitsu, Japan's largest computer company, is developing a computer controlled by a person's thoughts and body motions. At the Nippon Telegraph and Telephone Corporation, researchers have been able to communicate brain waves to control joystick movement, and a similar project is underway at Graz University in Austria.

Researchers at the New York State Department of Health have already produced a system that allows control of a computer screen cursor by mental action alone, and University of Illinois psychologists are working on a project that allows people to type characters by spelling out words in their minds.

AT&T's new hand-held computers and notepads, such as Apple's Newton, take commands written with an electronic pen and function both as computer and communications device. By the turn of the century, we shall be able to give computers commands using voice and hand gestures, as the interface between people and machines becomes more user-friendly. People already dial telephone numbers by speaking the names of the persons they wish to call. Shoppers will browse through the contents of an entire shopping mall without ever leaving their chairs.

New developments in communications and information technology no longer take place in a linear fashion, separated by decades, with enough time in between for their implications to be sorted out. A wide range of converging technologies force us to make immediate choices, leaving considerably less time for decision-making.

In the information age, data does not move from one private space to another, but travels along networks. These networks create a connectedness that reduces individual isolation and zones of privacy.

When communication was by hieroglyphics written on stone, knowledge was extremely limited. As it progressed to communicating with pencil and paper, knowledge and its diffusion were significantly increased. Printing dramatically quickened the pace. Now, we have a quantum leap into electronic communication. How a person communicates essentially molds how one thinks, the pace at which one thinks, what one thinks, and the amount and complexity of knowledge one is able to develop. The new communication technologies will profoundly change the way we live our lives.

[See also Communications; Communications: Media Law; Computers: Privacy; Information Society; Intellectual Property; Media Consolidation; Telecommunications.]

BIBLIOGRAPHY

Flaherty, David H. *Protecting Privacy in Surveillance Societies.* Chapel Hill, NC: University of North Carolina Press, 1989.

Linowes, David F. *Personal Privacy in an Information Society.* Report of the Privacy Protection Commission. Washington, DC: U.S. Government Printing Office, 1977.

———. *Privacy in America: Is Your Private Life in the Public Eye?* Champaign, IL: University of Illinois Press, 1989.

Peck, Robert S., ed. *To Govern a Changing Society: Constitutionalism and the Challenge of New Technology.* Washington and London: Smithsonian Institution Press, 1990.

— DAVID F. LINOWES

COMMUNICATIONS TECHNOLOGY

Communications has been essential to the evolution of human society since civilization began. As communications technologies change, so does the structure of society. However, the past century has seen extraordinary advances in the technology of communications, and none more critical than a change in the speed of transmission and the scope of coverage.

Before the advent of electrical and electronic communications, the speed of communications and transportation were equivalent. Prior to the nineteenth century, information was moved at the same rate as goods and services, which limited the potential structural options for society. If a government wanted to send out a decree, that information traveled by messenger. If a person wanted to write a friend, or a merchant wanted to conclude a trade arrangement, the same limitations prevailed for those activities as well.

Thus, the ability of human beings to collaborate and work together depended upon their ability to come together in the same place at the same time. Technological advances beginning in the mid-nineteenth century, and continuing ever since, have transformed this relationship, so that it has become possible for people to do increasingly more without being in the same physical space.

Telegraphy led the way as the first of these innovations. This technology invented by Samuel Morse in the 1850s, allowed people to send messages by code (Morse Code) over transmission wires strung across the United States. It provided an instantaneity of communication that was revolutionary at the time but allowed for very little information to be passed from one person to another, and there was little or no interactivity in the communication. It was a low *volume/low interactivity* technology.

Since the invention of the telegraph, the trend in communications has been toward *high volume/high interactivity.* The telephone followed the telegraph and offered a higher level of interactivity, but initially only between two people at a time. Television, in its initial broadcast format, offered high-volume but very low interactivity.

A New Era

The advent of communications satellites has ushered in a new era of opportunity in the communications field. It was first noted in the late 1940s by British scientist and author Arthur C. Clarke that a satellite placed in geosynchronous orbit (22,500 miles from the surface) over the Earth would be essentially stationary in relationship to the planet. Such a technology could therefore be used to relay signals from one point on Earth to another.

It was in the 1960s that the first communications satellite was in fact placed in orbit. This meant that all kinds of communications, whether low volume/low interactivity or high volume/high interactivity, could be transmitted instantaneously from one person to another, almost as if time and space were irrelevant.

The revolution caused by communications satellites and global wiring of telephones and computers has created the "global village" prophesied by media philosopher Marshall McLuhan.

The revolution caused by communications satellites and global wiring of telephones and computers has created the "global village" prophesied by media philosopher Marshall McLuhan, who also wrote and lectured extensively in the 1960s. While the planet itself has not changed in size, the communications process has changed significantly, so that we interact with one another like villagers in an earlier time. The latest developments in communications technology include a convergence of all kinds of media into one so-called "electronic superhighway."

The electronic superhighway, or National Information Infrastructure (NII), is envisioned as a fiber-optic interconnection of homes, schools, and businesses, initially nationwide in the United States and eventually worldwide, capable of carrying voice, images, data, and other forms of information. After a century of communications developing separately, many will converge into one integrated system. Computers and television sets are likely to merge as well, creating the smart television at home and in the office.

Other developments are beginning to transform not only human perceptions of space and time, but of reality itself. Interconnected communications systems, such as the Internet and the World Wide Web, are called "cyberspace" by their users and represent a new frontier for human exploration and settlement. *Virtual reality* is an extension of the cyberspace concept.

Virtual reality uses communications technology to create a digital universe that humans can "enter," pseudo-physically as well as mentally. The virtual reality concept opens up the possibility of virtual communities that are disconnected in physical time and space.

Other developments in the combined technologies of computing and communications promise the use of computer "agents," or pieces of software that would roam the worldwide communications networks in search of relevant information for human users. Intelligent agents can, and probably will, begin to replace certain human functions, such as repetitive writing activities.

The specific long-term future of communications technology essentially is beyond prediction, because of the speed with which changes are taking place. For example, automatic language translators, long a goal of computer developers, now seem to be within reach. We may also witness marriages between the technologies of computers, communications, and biotechnology to produce enhanced human beings who will be able to have information communicated directly to the brain without going through the computer, television, or other media.

In general, we can see an entirely new kind of system being created on Earth, consisting of a natural system (the Earth itself), a human system (humanity), and a technosystem (the worldwide network of computer and communications technologies). This "planetary overview system" is radically unique in the history of the planet and of humanity itself.

Issues and Concerns

The evolution of communications technology brings with it many challenges. For example, will people who are attracted to the virtual reality environment become addicted to it, preferring that state to so-called "normal reality?" The individual's rights to privacy are already being called into question, as increasingly detailed personal information is put on-line in computer networks. The kinds of crime that occur in normal reality have begun to occur in cyberspace as well, and law-enforcement agencies are just beginning to understand how to cope with criminal activity in the electronic world.

Other central questions include these: As information becomes more of a commodity, broadly available around the world, how will producers of information be compensated and how will copyright be protected? What is the role of universities and other learning institutions in circumstances where much of the planet's knowledge and many of its leading thinkers are available electronically? With human population growing and with more people spending more time communicating in more ways, are we really *communicating* better—or are we apt to drown in an ever-growing load of information?

As humans have evolved over the millennia, we have been forced to confront similarly challenging dilemmas, and so far the responses to these issues have supported our evolution as a species. It is an open question, however, whether our response to the explosion in information/communication technology will have the same effect.

[See also Communications; Digital Communications; Electronic Convergence; Electronic Publishing; Information Overload; Information Society; Information Technology; On-line Services; Satellite Communications; Telecommunications; Telephones; Television.]

BIBLIOGRAPHY

McLuhan, Marshall. *Understanding Media: The Extensions of Man.* New York: McGraw-Hill, 1964.
White, Frank. *The Overview Effect: Space Exploration and Human Evolution.* Boston: Houghton Mifflin, 1987.

— FRANK WHITE

COMMUNISM

Communism has been defined as a society or social system in which there is no private property, no differentiation among social classes, and no money, with all goods being distributed according to need. It has also been identified as the doctrine for creating such a society. The following historical summary will look at the roots of communism and attempt to show why it is a failed doctrine that appears at this point in time to have no future.

The earliest roots of communist doctrine can be found in various utopian writings by Plato, Thomas More, Tommasso Campanella, Abbé de Mably, and others. However, it was not until the second half of the nineteenth century that what we know today as communism was first formulated, chiefly by the German political philosophers Karl Marx and Friedrich Engels. After the 1917 revolution in Russia, the Marxism of Marx and Engels became the Marxism-Leninism of Vladimir Lenin. According to this doctrine, "socialism"—a term which has been used to describe an enormous variety of disparate socio + political systems—was considered to be the first stage of communism, a necessary transition between capitalism and communism.

As it was practiced and promulgated, Marxism-Leninism took on a quasi-religious character with its own canon of "holy books"—the works of Marx, Engels, Lenin, and others. Despite its dogmatic character, Marxism claimed to be the result of a scientific analysis of society and branded traditional religions as the opiate of the people. "Scientific" communism has its own philosophy of nature (dialectical materialism), philosophy of history (historical materialism), and a collection of demagogic postulates on "labor as the first vital need," "no difference between town and village," "mental and manual labor," "no state government, self-government only," and so on. But many of these postulates are empty phrases, attractive to credulous people at times, but with little or no claim to scientific validity. Slogans aside, the real essence of communist doctrine consists of the three following postulates: (1) the destratification of society to eliminate social classes; (2) the demarketization of the economy (replacing private ownership of property and a free market with state ownership of property and central planning of production and consumption); and (3) the demonetarization of finances (i.e., "soft currency," or nonconvertible bank notes that can be printed in any needed quantities irrespective of available goods, instead of the "hard currency" of a market economy). These three principles were supposed to be achieved through a "socialist revolution" and a "dictatorship of the proletariat," which in practice was tantamount to the dictatorship of a Communist party controlled by an individual dictator like Lenin or Stalin or Mao Ze Dong.

The first attempt to realize this doctrine was made by radical extremists among the social democrats of Europe at the end of World War I, in 1917 and 1918. In some countries (Germany, Hungary, and Finland), there were attempts to foment a communist revolution that failed. Only in Russia did communists actually manage to seize power. In spite of the communist victory in the 1918–1922 civil war that followed the overthrow of the czar, it soon became apparent that implementation of true communism was not viable. Renamed the Union of Soviet Socialist Republics, or U.S.S.R., Russia was thrown into a state of dictatorship, ruled by a group of zealots who undermined industry and trade, and who destroyed and robbed the peasantry, causing the total collapse of the economy. Soon thereafter most of the peasantry, constituting 85 percent of the population, rebelled against the ideologues in the Kremlin; there were workers' strikes in Moscow, Petrograd, and elsewhere, and there was mutiny in the military.

Lenin responded by declaring the New Economic Policy (1921–1929), which restored private property and entrepreneurship, hard currency, and some degree of a market economy. Nevertheless, the new ruling class, or *nomenklatura,* remained in power, and in 1929 a new dictator, Joseph Stalin, undertook a second wave of reforms. As a result, for more than sixty years, until August 1991, there existed in the U.S.S.R. a totalitarian regime with mass repressions, hard labor, compulsory Marxist-Leninist ideology, and quasi-military social relations—like those in any army barracks where any officer could bully his subordinates. During this era, 60 million people were shot or perished in prisons or in exile—nearly one out of every three Soviet citizens. Those who evaded forced labor or doubted Marxist tenets shared the same fate: imprisonment.

Those who evaded forced labor or doubted

Marxist tenets shared the same fate: imprisonment.

There was evidence from the beginning of the inability of Marxism to compete with market-based economies. But sweeping events tended to mask some of these failures. During the 1930s, when the country was preparing for the war against Germany and Japan, as well as during the war itself and the painful period of reconstruction afterward, noneconomic forces worked to preserve and prolong the status quo. However, in the mid-1950s it finally became clear to the ruling clique that economic and eventually political catastrophe was inevitable unless drastic measures were undertaken. As a result there were successive waves of attempts to revitalize socialism and make it competitive with the free-market West: the reforms of 1956–1964, 1966–1971, 1979, 1983, and 1985–1991. All of these attempts failed.

Simultaneously efforts were made to find a way out of permanent crisis by military means. After Russia's victory in World War II, won with the help of Great Britain and the United States, pro-communist totalitarian regimes were established in many countries of the world, comprising nearly one-third of the globe's population. In addition, certain alternative varieties of nineteenth-century socialism and communism began to proliferate in the form of various kinds of anarchism, guild-socialism, and Christian, Islamic, Buddhist, and African socialism. Non-Marxist totalitarianism, loosely or not at all dependent on the U.S.S.R., triumphed in Libya, Iraq, Syria, Myanmar, Iran, Ethiopia, Angola, Mozambique, and some other countries of the Third World. Numerous attempts were undertaken to expand the sphere of the "world socialist system" and satellite totalitarian regimes: the blockade of West Berlin, military adventures in Greece, Iran, Korea, Angola, an attempt to seize control of Bosphorus and the Dardanelles, the deployment of Soviet nuclear weapons in Cuba in order to blackmail the United States, and so on. In the long run, none of these attempts were successful.

By the early 1970s it became clear to the Soviet ruling clique that the arms race with NATO, which was four times more powerful economically and incomparably more powerful technologically, had been irreversibly lost. The Soviet leadership tried to counter this trend through negotiations (especially dangerous to the U.S.S.R. was the American Strategic Defense Initiative in space, which the U.S.S.R. had no means to counteract). However, the inertia of the long-lasting duel between the two superpowers continued to propel Soviet leaders toward further military adventurism, culminating with the invasion of Afghanistan, which involved the U.S.S.R. in a long, frustrating, demoralizing, and exhausting war, similar to the American experience in Vietnam.

It is important to emphasize that one of the main impulses for the last attempt to find a way out of the crisis, Gorbachev's *perestroika* (1985–1991), was an open admission of defeat in the Cold War and a last-ditch effort to save the "world socialist system" by bringing the arms race to a halt.

As is well known, totalitarianism can only flourish in an atmosphere of fear and mass repression. When fear and repression are lessened, totalitarianism inevitably collapses. The successive rebellions in Eastern Europe—East Germany in 1953, Hungary in 1956, Czechoslovakia in 1968, Poland in the late 1970s—point to the gathering momentum of the anticommunist movement in that region from year to year. There was also a steadily increasing flow of refugees to Western countries. In the second half of the 1980s, their numbers were so significant that the Soviet government was confronted with a dilemma: either to step up the occupation of Eastern Europe to 1945 levels (and face the prospect of a world war they could not hope to win) or to capitulate. The struggle within the inner circles of leadership intensified, and the latter course was chosen. As a result, the Soviet socialist empire collapsed in 1989 followed by the disintegration of the U.S.S.R. itself in 1991 and by the virtually total rejection of the idea of communism by public opinion worldwide.

It is important to emphasize that communism is not merely an abstract idea but has constituted a global tragedy that brought grief to millions of victims throughout the world. By 1992 the world socialist empire had al-

most totally collapsed. Only a few separate countries retained Marxism as their official ideology—China, North Korea, Cuba, Vietnam—and they no longer constitute a united front, some of them being inimical to each other. Very close to these countries in the political, social, economic, and ideological sense are such totalitarian countries as Libya, Iran, Iraq, Syria, some of the former Soviet republics of Central Asia, and others. But these are mainly a remnant, and it is only a question of time before they return from social pathology to social norm.

Communist parties, which until recently existed in more than 120 countries, have been discredited almost everywhere that communists are not still in power, and many of them have dissolved, no longer able to turn to Moscow for subsidy of their activities. Even so, communist ideas are still rather popular among certain social and intellectual groups in the former U.S.S.R. and other countries of the world. The diehards include some members of the older generation who are used to living under totalitarianism and find it difficult to alter their mind-sets, as well as some younger people who resent the national humiliation caused by the downfall of the socialist empire. There has also been some reaction against the new varieties of corruption that have been manifest in the transition from totalitarianism to democracy. Even among those who reject communism there are those who hold the opinion that communists are not state criminals on a par with Hitler's Nazis. It will take perhaps two generations for people to adjust to the new democratic order and become real citizens of a real democracy. It will not be easy and many uncertainties remain.

[See also China; International Tensions; Political Economy; Russia; Social Democracy; Socialism.]

BIBLIOGRAPHY

Brzezinski, Zbigniew. *The Grand Failure: The Birth and Death of Communism in the 20th Century.* New York: Macmillan, 1990.
Ederstadt, Nick. *The Poverty of Communism.* New Brunswick, NJ: Transaction Books, 1989.
Pryer, Peter. *The New Communism.* New York: State Mutual, 1988.
Westoby, Adam. *Evolution of Communism.* New York: Free Press, 1989.

– IGOR BESTUZHEV-LADA

COMMUNITARIANISM

The communitarian movement seeks to shore up the moral, social, and political foundations of society. It builds on the elementary social science observation that people are born without any moral or social values. If they are to become civil, they must acquire values. Later, they may rebel against these values or seek to modify them, but they first must have some.

Historically, the family was the societal entity entrusted with laying the foundation for moral education. Schools were the second line of defense. Community bonds—whether clustered around religious institutions, schools, town meetings, or other establishments—served to reinforce values previously acquired. These social institutions have been the seedbeds of virtue, in which values are planted and cultivated.

In contemporary society, to a significant extent, these seedbeds have been allowed to wither. We should not be surprised, then, that the young ignore our entreaties to "just say no" to the numerous temptations society puts in their way, or when children kill children without showing remorse.

We need to restore the seedbeds of virtue

if society is to regain civility.

Such restoration does not entail a simple return

to the traditional past.

We need to restore the seedbeds of virtue if society is to regain civility. Such restoration does not entail a simple return to the traditional past, a past that had its own defects—a society that did discriminate against women and minorities and that was at least a bit authoritarian. Specifically, we need first of all to expect that both mothers and fathers be more dedicated to their children and that as a community we again value children. We must enable parents to be parents by allowing more flex time, work at home, and paid leave when children are born (as is the case throughout Europe), and by reducing the marriage penalty in the tax code.

Schools must put character education at the top of their agenda and not allow academic pressures to crowd out their civilizing agenda. Everything that happens in schools generates experiences and sends messages to the students. Are the corridors, parking areas, and cafeterias disorderly danger zones or places where people learn to respect one another? Is sport used to teach that winning is the only thing or that playing by the rules is essential? Are grades handed out on the basis of hard work—or some other social criteria? Schools need to engage in self-evaluation and line up the experiences they generate so that they will reinforce rather than undermine the educational message that they are supposed to carry.

Communities happen to a large extent in public spaces. When our parks, sidewalks, squares, and other public spaces are threatened by crime, communities are thwarted. Community policing, neighborhood crime watches, drug checkpoints, and domestic disarmament are among the new devices that may help communities recapture those spaces. Above all, we need to increase the certitude that those who commit a crime will be punished, and it may not be enough to merely increase the size of their penalty. Needless to say, if families and schools will do a better job in transmitting values, the communities' public safety burden will grow lighter.

Finally, civility requires that the vigilant protection of rights not be turned into extremism in which new rights are manufactured at will. There are reasonable limits to behavior, and the unlimited "right" to rent a car or for women to use the men's room may exceed the limits of civility. There are limitations to individual rights, and if each right is treated as an absolute, the rights of other persons inevitably are diminished.

The Constitution opens by directing the federal government to insure the general welfare, the common good. The courts have long balanced individual rights with social responsibilities. They authorized drug testing for those who have the lives of others directly in their hands, sobriety checkpoints, and screening gates at airports. A civil society requires careful nurturing of both rights and responsibilities—not the dominance of one at the expense of the other.

Communitarian ideas have long been with us. They are found in writings of the ancient Greek philosophers and the Old and New Testaments. The contemporary communitarian movement in the United States was established in 1990. Its first formal expression was the only communitarian quarterly in the world, *The Responsive Community.* In 1991 a communitarian platform was issued and was endorsed by 100 leading Americans. In 1993 a membership organization, The Communitarian Network was established and headquartered in Washington, D.C. A book explicating its philosophy was issued: *The Spirit of Community, Rights, Responsibilities, and the Communitarian Agenda* in 1993.

[See also Change, Cultural; Ethics; Modernism and Postmodernism; Morals; Political Cycles; Political Parties; Political Party Realignment; Values; Values Change; Values Formation.]

BIBLIOGRAPHY

Etzioni, Amitai. *The Spirit of Community: Rights, Responsibilities and the Communitarian Agenda.* New York: Crown Publishing, 1993.
Hughes, Robert. *Culture or Complaint: The Fraying of America.* New York: Oxford University Press, 1993.

Magnet, Myron. *The Dream and the Nightmare: The Sixties' Legacy to the Underclass.* New York: William Morrow, 1993.

— AMITAI ETZIONI

COMPETITIVE SPORTS AND GAMES.

See SPORTS AND GAMES, COMPETITIVE.

COMPUTER GAMES.

See INTERACTIVE ENTERTAINMENT.

COMPUTER HARDWARE

Gordon Moore, cofounder of chipmaker Intel Corporation, predicted in the early 1970s that the speed of the microprocessor chip would double every eighteen months. His prediction, known as "Moore's Law," has been correct so far. Many forecasters expect Moore's Law to remain valid or nearly so well into the twenty-first century. Ironically, though, Moore himself raised doubts in 1993. If the law does hold, the computer chip—which has dramatically changed our daily lives—will continue to shape society for several decades to come.

To the consumer, the increasing speed of the computer chip is most obvious in the form of gadgets, small appliances, and personal computers. Inexpensive watches now contain functions that would have been inconceivable at any price in the mechanical-watch era. Single-lens reflex cameras, once the bulky and expensive tools of skilled photographers, now weigh a few ounces, cost about $100, and are nearly foolproof.

Electronic games far more complex than those once played on multimillion-dollar mainframes now fit in a pocket. Also pocket-sized and affordable are navigation devices that motorists, hikers, and sailors can use to locate any point on Earth within 300 feet. These devices receive data from the global positioning system, a satellite network installed for military navigation.

During the 1960s, telephone companies rationed mobile phones and typically reserved them for physicians. The electronics occupied a big box in the trunk of a sedan. Now hand-held mobile phones are so popular that telephone companies are scrambling to keep

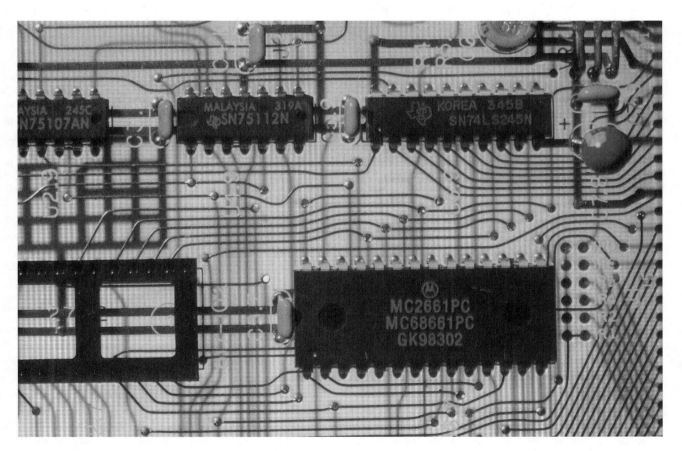

The decreasing size and faster speed of computer hardware is key to the computer revolution. Intel's first integrated circuit contained 2,300 transistors, and 3-D chips, a cubic centimeter in size with a billion bit capacity, are currently on drawing boards. (Ed Eckstein/Corbis)

up with the demand for additional telephone numbers, exchanges, and area codes.

In the kitchen, even children can program multiple-step cooking instructions into a microwave oven. In the home or workplace, the power of yesterday's supercomputer resides in a $2,000 desktop computer. These are the obvious and everyday points at which individuals are aware of the effect of Moore's Law. Equally significant are the behind-the-scenes effects and startling implications for the future.

Inexpensive computers and reliable satellite communication have made the home office —located in an urban area or a country town— an economical powerhouse.

Behind the scenes, speedier computer chips have enabled a worldwide revolution in manufacturing efficiency. The same technology that puts microchips into cameras and desktop computers has made the supercomputer, the mainframe, and the minicomputer so affordable and so reliable that few manufacturers still rely on a manager's pad and pencil for calculations or plans of any type. As a result, the prices of many manufactured products—from motor vehicles to ballpoint pens—have remained affordable or even fallen. It is probable that the deflationary impact of computerized manufacturing will continue far into the twenty-first century. Increasing affordability of computers enhances prospects for the rapid economic development of less developed countries.

The cost of telecommunication services will continue to fall, as they have throughout the twentieth century. The computer chip is a key reason: It provides the rapid switching that can pack more signals into existing circuits—not only in the highly promising fiber-optic and satellite circuits but also in the copper wire that the telephone companies have been installing since the late nineteenth century.

The convergence of computing, telecommunications, and entertainment is occurring. Because we can safely assume that chips will become even faster and that the bandwidth (signal-carrying capacity) of communication circuits will continue to increase rapidly, software will become the industry of the future. In a convergent world, we think of software not in the traditional narrow definition of programs for business computers, but in a broader definition that includes communications, motion pictures, musical recordings,

sequencers and other music programs, games, virtual reality systems, desktop video, and electronic storage of the contents of entire public libraries.

Defined in this way, software already is the most significant export of the United States. Giant corporations—including Microsoft, Viacom, and the regional Bell operating companies—may battle for position in a highly visible way, but the future may be even brighter for a worldwide cottage industry in software. Because software is not necessarily a capital-intensive business, it holds great promise for entrepreneurs and workers in smaller and developing countries. It is already happening: Software developers are writing and exporting products from countries such as Guatemala, and the continuing robustness of the worldwide telecommunication infrastructure overcomes the transportation problems that hinder other forms of manufacturing in many countries, such as those in central Africa. It is plausible that, within the next few decades, anyone could use a converged device (whatever it may be called) to download and store almost any motion picture ever made, to correspond with friends anywhere in the world, or to look up information in a distant library—and get a passable translation done in seconds, if necessary. What we now call personal digital assistants could become mighty computers, storage devices, and telecommunications tools. For example, a person could store his or her financial records, correspondence, family photos, favorite music, and entire medical history in such a portable device.

Perhaps the most interesting societal effect of Moore's Law is its impact on large private and public organizations. So far, the computer chip has tended to empower individuals in their private lives and in the workplace, and to flatten organizations. In the private sector, for example, networks of cheaper computers enabled the massive restructuring of U.S. corporations during the 1980s and '90s. As corporations began to use desktop computers and data communication to share work-related information more widely, they needed fewer layers of middle managers, whose main job was the manual processing and distribution of information. The old organizational model was a hierarchy, in which communication was primarily vertical: managers handed down the orders and assignments, and workers handed up the feedback and results. The new organization is becoming flatter with fewer layers of management, and is using more horizontal communication. Teamwork is replacing the hierarchical, command-and-control model of the past. Bosses are learning to act more like coaches.

This horizontal trend is unlikely to reverse soon. In fact, it's highly probable that companies will outsource even more of their work to vendors—including home-based workers. Inexpensive computers and reliable satellite communication have made the home office—located in an urban area or a country town—an economical powerhouse that would have been unthinkable as recently as the early 1980s. The same horizontal trend is at work in the public sector. Computer power on the citizen's desktop—and the telecommunication services to link to other desktops worldwide—may change a citizen's relationship to government. For example, approximately twenty million people now use the Internet, an informal worldwide network made up of private and public networks. The Internet operates mostly outside the control of any government. Many observers interpret the U.S. government's interest in network-building as a defensive measure, designed to get free-market networks under government control before they become larger. Governments see worldwide private-sector networks as a threat to their power to govern.

But the network is only half of the threat to government power; the other half is electronic encryption. Personal computers have become so powerful that they can create encryption codes that even supercomputers cannot crack. As more and more citizens use encrypted electronic messages, they could hide financial transactions from the tax collector. Governments would find it difficult or impossible to collect some income taxes. Some people speculate that the end of the income tax could lead to the end of the welfare system, and that could drive some former recipients to crime and even lead to civil war. The Federal Bureau of Investigation and the National Security Agency want computer and telecommunication companies to use encryption methods that would give a key to the U.S. government. So far, the companies have not welcomed the idea; individuals, meanwhile, already are using encryption software available on the market. However the private-public conflict may be resolved, it is clear that the computer chip will be an engine for the empowerment of individuals—from budding software entrepreneurs to billions of consumers who simply want more goods and services at less cost.

[See also Communications; Computers: Overview; Computers: Software; Interactive Entertainment; Telecommunications.]

BIBLIOGRAPHY

"Auctioning the Airways." *Forbes: ASAP* (April 11, 1994).
Davidson, James Dale, and Rees-Mogg, Lord William. *The Great Reckoning.* New York, Simon & Schuster, 1993.
"Hollywired." *The Wall Street Journal,* March 21, 1994.
"No More Moore's Law: Moore." *Electronic Engineering Times,* May 17, 1993.

— JEAN L. FARINELLI
JOSEPH R. ROY

COMPUTER LINKAGE

From a user perspective, we can expect Local Area Networks (LANs) to disappear. Instead of an environment that offers geographically limited access to a well-defined group of machines, users will interact with a particular "server"—irrespective of where they happen to be. And this server, in turn, will present the user with a location-independent image of the rest of the world.

Thanks to the Asynchronous Transfer Mode (ATM) transmission and switching standard (which should become the medium of choice by the mid-1990s), so-called *local* and *wide*-area networks will hand off traffic to one another with minimal notice of boundaries. At the same time, ubiquitous use of the uniform-size, limited-header, ATM cell format will support voice and video calls over virtual circuits, as well as traditional datagram traffic—thereby blurring the distinction between LANs and PBXs as well.

Low-cost, large-vocabulary speech recognition

in the late 1990s will allow users

to dictate messages and see the resulting text

appear in real time on screens in front of them.

Finally, a steadily growing shift toward wireless access will create demand for a uniform environment—available worldwide—from users who wish to carry their "terminals" in their pockets wherever they travel. In this scenario, the server located at a user's home base in Massachusetts would, for example, arrange to have paper copies of its client's messages delivered by a laser printer in a Paris airport. When this becomes commonplace, "local" will mean "anywhere on the planet."

Electronic Mail

While most future e-mail users will continue to *receive* a large portion of their messages as typed text, much of that material will originate from other modalities. In particular, the likely emergence of low-cost, large-vocabulary speech recognition in the late 1990s will allow users to dictate messages and see the resulting text appear in real time on the screens in front of them. Furthermore, since pen-based tablets, natural-sounding text-to-speech, scanners, and recognizers will become commonplace in that same time frame, the distinction between electronic mail and other forms of communication will surely blur as time goes on. A scanned-in image sent as part of an e-mail message would turn the combination into an annotated fax, for example, but how would one characterize it with a video insert added? Tomorrow's multimedia will make such distinctions obsolete.

Since tomorrow's personal workstations must travel with their owners worldwide, they will feature built-in modems and encryption circuitry, assuring reliable connectivity from out-of-the-way places not yet served by broadband networks. Each machine's owner will obtain robust access safeguards via a combination of voice and visual recognition, together with unobtrusive conversational interrogation based on the user's profile. Conversely, that same profile will restrict access in the other direction, via customized screening of incoming messages. Indeed, the conventional (paper mail) postal service's inability to provide sensitive automatic screening may well prove a decisive handicap in the struggle to maintain economic viability vis-à-vis electronic alternatives.

National and International Networks

Given the multiplicity of networking options and user needs, it seems likely that an interoperating group of specialized networks will prevail in the coming decades. While government-supported networks will address some needs, just as Internet does today, private-sector network providers will compete with one another in providing guaranteed levels of performance, facilities management, rapid rearrangement, and other features, to an increasingly demanding body of worldwide users.

Technology of Computer Networks

Looking forward, we can expect a continued mix of optical fibers for most land-line applications, and radio for individual mobility, together with a mixture of other technologies—such as metallic cables, and through-the-air optics—for special applications. If optoelectronic device yields and packaging technologies improve markedly, costs should drop to a level that will make hundreds of megabits per second available at the desktop, along with one-hundred-times-greater bandwidths in links between network servers. Moreover, the use of so-called *soliton* pulses in lightwave systems will permit even higher speeds, by circumventing lightguide nonlinearities that would otherwise limit transmission capacity.

Digital Data

While data networks will continue to support datagram service, a connection-oriented ATM network (based on virtual circuit technology) will actually provide the underlying connectivity—thereby providing better security and consistent performance. At the same time, many applications can be expected to make direct use of the virtual circuit's separation of data and control information in its messaging format.

Data Compression

While the size of some data files in the coming decades may seem huge by today's standards, we can expect even larger traffic volume from high-resolution images in a true multimedia environment. As a result, the need to cram data as tightly as possible into undersized pipes will lose much of its urgency. In its place, the main focus of compression technology will shift toward the realistic rendition of complex three-dimensional environments, especially as virtual reality and telepresence become commonplace networking features.

[See also Communications: Technology; Computers: Overview; Data Storage; Digital Communications; Electronic Publishing; Interactive Entertainment; Networking; On-Line Services; Satellite Communications; Superconductors; Telecommunications; Telephones; Television.]

BIBLIOGRAPHY

Gilster, Paul. *The Internet Navigator.* New York: John Wiley, 1993.
Jussawalla, Meheroo, ed. *Global Telecommunications Policies: The Challenge of Change.* Westport, CT: Greenwood Press, 1993.
Rheingold, Howard. *The Virtual Community: Homesteading on the Electronic Frontier.* Reading, MA: Addison-Wesley, 1993.
Rushkoff, Douglas. *Cyberia: Life in the Trenches of Hyperspace.* San Francisco: HarperCollins, 1994.

— ARNO PENZIAS
BONNIE PENZIAS

COMPUTERS: OVERVIEW

Computers have made fundamental and accelerating changes in human society since the first programmable calculators were introduced in the nineteenth century. Computers enabled the emergence of the information sector as the dominant component of the U.S. economy in the mid-1950s. In 1998, about three of every five people employed in developed countries were information workers, people whose livelihoods depended on the creation, manipulation, transformation, or dissemination of information, or operation of information machines—computers. Although not all information workers regularly used computers in 1994, by the year 2000 most will. And, at least 60 percent of economic activity will be computer-dependent.

The root of all this transformation since the 1950s is solid-state physics, particularly semiconductor technology. First transistors, then integrated circuits, the first microprocessors, memory chips, lasers, magnetic and optical storage media, and display devices—all joined a diversifying array of components and systems that proved to be irresistible to people who wanted tools to accomplish their information work. A fundamental rule of thumb in this technological explosion is Moore's law, which states: the number of components on a state-of-the-art microchip doubles every other year. What Moore's law doesn't state, but what appears to be true in practice, is that the cost of the latest chip doesn't change much. In terms of cost per unit of information processing power Figure 1 tells the story. So far, each time that there seemed to be a technological limit to the number of components per chip, there has been a breakthrough that extended Moore's law for an additional few years. However, around 2010 we may find that continuation of the bottom curve of Figure 1 may not be possible.

A similar rule holds for related technologies such as magnetic and optical storage devices. Hard discs, once considered capacious if they held ten megabytes of information, are now capable of multibillion-byte capacity—in a module 3.5 inches wide. High-density magnetic tape storage is competing with removable magneto-optical discs that begin to rival hard discs in speed and exceed them in capacity.

The central effect of these trends is that information processing power that was once reserved for very large organizations is now available on desktops, in briefcases and pockets, automobiles, washing machines, microwave ovens, and telephones. Computers have spawned subindustries that were not even imagined at the beginning of the twentieth century.

The hierarchy of computers generally runs in decreasing order of size or processing power:

- Supercomputers
- Mainframes
- Minicomputers
- Engineering workstations
- Personal computers (PCs) and other microcomputers
- Personal digital assistants (PDAs)
- Organizers and calculators
- Embedded computers and smart devices.

In 1975, personal computers and PDAs didn't exist, the mainframe was considered to be the king of computers, and the dominant manufacturer was IBM. Supercomputers, such as the Cray series, were used pri-

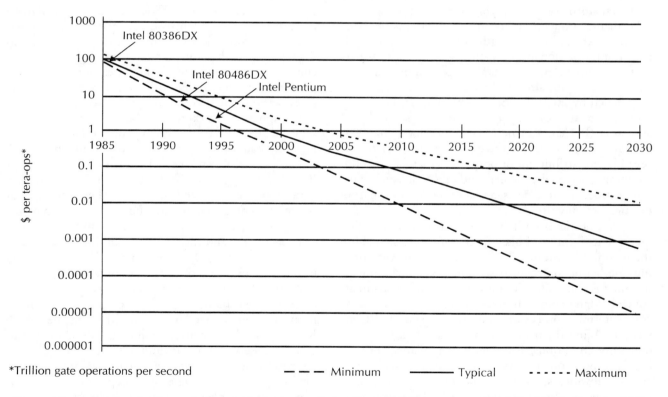

*Trillion gate operations per second   ----- Minimum   ——— Typical   ····· Maximum

Figure 1. Past and projected performance ranges for the Intel series of microchips; a similiar pattern was also exhibited by the Motorola 68000 series of microchips and will likely also be exhibited by successive generations of RISC-based or other processors in the years ahead, with an evenual slowing of the pace of change.

marily by the military or research organizations that required huge amounts of calculation, such as for detailed modeling of the weather. Even then, the growing power of minicomputers, led by machines produced by Digital Equipment Corporation and Data General, were eroding the market for mainframes. Workstations—microminicomputers—by Sun Microsystems and Hewlett-Packard, for example, became the powerful tools of engineers and scientists engaged in complex design projects.

By 1998, personal computers were taking market share away from workstations, minicomputers, and mainframes. The term *downsizing* applied not only to the trend of large corporations to slough off excess staff, but to the movement from mainframes to minis to workstations to PCs, and from central to local control of the organization's information activities.

Even at the supercomputer level, the effects of Moore's law are being felt. Once composed of a single, very-high-speed central processor surrounded by closely spaced memory banks (to minimize cable lengths; every foot of wire introduces a nanosecond of delay), new supercomputers are being built of large arrays of interconnected microprocessors operating in parallel. The same transformation is applying to mainframes. On the other hand, minicomputers and workstations may disappear as a class by 2000, either merging upward with mainframes or downward with high-end PCs. Whatever the nomenclature, general purpose computers will be associated with almost every office desk and laboratory bench by 2000. Personal computers are becoming more personal with the appearance of personal digital assistants (PDAs). At an introductory level in 1994, they are likely to become the equivalent, in variety and breadth of distribution, of pocket calculators by 2000, containing personal, financial, and health data, telecommunications interconnects, and a variety of information utilities for daily use.

At another level entirely, microprocessors are being incorporated into a huge variety of devices, making them "smart." Automobiles have a significant and growing number of computer-based functions, including ignition, fuel, air-conditioning, brakes, and instrument control. Many common household devices already incorporate microprocessors and "fuzzy logic" soft/firmware, enabling them to sense and react to a variety of operating conditions. Rudimentary appliance controllers have been on the market for several years, but as communications standards—and the size of the market—develop, "smart" buildings will also become increasingly common. These homes and offices will incorporate intercommunicating environmental and security devices that will run under their own programs,

possibly with a central computer controller, and will also be accessible remotely via the telephone system. The new generation of digital high-definition television (HDTV) requires computer memory arrays and processing in the set to provide theater-quality viewing and sound.

The equivalent of Moore's law also is in operation for telecommunications technology. While computers, particularly personal computers, have been largely "stand-alone" machines much of the time, they are increasingly becoming interconnected via telecommunications. This fact—the jointly increasing power per dollar spent of both computers and telecommunications—has far-reaching implications.

Telecommunications using copper wires are being replaced by higher-capacity, speedier optical fibers. Huge mechanical switches for telephone interconnection have been replaced by much smaller computers. At the level of a single organization, computers interconnected by local area networks (LANs) are a large part of the trend toward elimination of mainframes. They also permit more effective operation of work groups through such means as electronic mail and joint editing of documents, spreadsheets, graphics, and other forms of analysis and documentation. Wide area networks (WANs) extend this reach to continental or global scales. Wireless data communications, first through analog, then digital cellular telephones, and next through cellular satellite transmission, extend the interconnective computer reach both to mobile offices and to rural or remote areas without wired communications access.

Computer networking in the early 1990s closely resembled the early days of the telephone industry: each network had its own set of standards and protocols, often incompatible with other networks. But as interest in networking grew, so did systems and standards for communication between computers. The technique of packet switching gave rise to a new revolution in global communication, as typified by several commercial computer networks and the Internet—an informal organization of individual computer networks that included more than two million host computers covering the globe by 1993. As this form of networking expands and evolves, it will be possible for a computer to communicate with another computer anywhere in the world. Key steps in this expansion will be the development of globally observed directory and interface protocols, and encryption techniques indecipherable by interlopers for message protection. These latter steps are necessary for effective commercial acceptance of networking.

At the first level of impact, computers alone and telecommunications-connected computers are used primarily to increase the efficiency of existing operations.

After a period varying from a few months to years, new applications and configurations arise that use the improved technologies. One of the most significant of these is telework: the substitution of information technology for work-related travel—transporting the work instead of the worker. Because of these technological changes, teleworking will be a viable option for at least one-half the workforce of developed countries by 2000.

Telework is the substitution of information technology for work-related travel. Teleworking will be a viable option for at least one-half the workforce of developed countries by 2000.

Teleworking and its major component telecommuting have a number of positive consequences for employers, employees, and the communities in which the employees live. For employers, the primary benefits include increases in worker effectiveness and teamwork, and decreases in operating costs, office space, and turnover rates. For employees, the benefits include reduced stress from commuting, increases in—and greater control over—discretionary time, access to education via interactive distance learning programs, and better family life in properly managed telework situations, without negative effects on their careers. For urban communities, reduced traffic congestion and air pollution as well as reduced crime rates are the payoff. For rural communities, these technologies bring economic revitalization and development as both work and new educational opportunities become independent of the location of the worker or student. All of these consequences have been demonstrated in the past two decades, and the growth of telecommuting applications is accelerating.

The fundamental attribute of teleworking is independence of location. Because of information technology, many work functions can be performed anywhere. This gives rise to new structure and forms of organizations. Within an organization, for example, teams can be formed that include members who may be scattered around the globe.

Traditionally, such teamwork always required a large amount of face-to-face interaction. Simple telephone communications were considered poor substitutes. Now, digital videoconferencing and other multimedia communications are becoming economically practical for general use and approximate face-to-face interaction. Network and evanescent organizations are developing globally, coalescing for particular projects, then reforming in new combinations as new opportunities arise. The objectives of these organizations can be business, government, public interest, education, or some combination.

Increased computer use causes some forms of structural unemployment. That is, some jobs disappear or are distinctly downgraded because computers take over some or all of the job's functions. For example, the traditional job functions of a secretary, once primarily involving telephone answering and text processing services, are being supplanted by computer-enabled voice mail or answering machines and PC-based text processing software operated by the originator of the message—not the secretary. One outcome of this process is for the job of secretary to disappear. Another is for the job to be upgraded or enriched: secretaries become administrative assistants, handle spreadsheets and database searches, act as personnel coordinators, or otherwise diversify. Although some jobs clearly become extinct because of computers, new jobs arise. For example, the professions of computer programmer, database search expert, CAD/CAM engineer, or computer graphics artist didn't exist in 1950. The central question is: Will the new jobs be more numerous and better—in terms of economic rewards and personal satisfaction—than the vanished ones? The evidence so far is that they will.

Whatever the details, everyone's life will be moderated by computers in the years to come.

[See also Artificial Intelligence; Communications; Computer Hardware; Computers: Software; Data Storage; Digital Communications; Electronic Publishing; Information Society; Information Technology; Telecommunications.]

BIBLIOGRAPHY

Drexler, K. Eric. Nanosystems: Molecular Machinery, Manufacturing, and Computation. New York: John Wiley and Sons, 1992.
The Internet Unleashed. Indianapolis, IN: Sams Publishing, 1994.
Nilles, Jack M. *Making Telecommuting Happen: A Guide for Telemanagers and Telecommuters.* New York: Van Nostrand Reinhold, 1994.
Nilles, Jack M., et al. *A Technology Assessment of Personal Computers,* 3 Vols. Los Angeles: University of Southern California, Center for Futures Research, 1980.
Porat, Marc U. *The Information Economy: Definition and Measurement.* Washington: U.S. Department of Commerce, Office of Telecommunications, 1977.
Toffler, Alvin. *The Third Wave.* New York: William Morrow, 1980.

– JACK M. NILLES

COMPUTERS: PRIVACY LAWS

Today we live in the earliest stages of a new era in which information itself is considered by many the most valuable commodity of all. This view is rooted in the technological power of the computer, and its growing role in every aspect of modern life. Less noticed, but no less significant in contributing to the growing impact of the computer, is the ongoing revolution in the communications networks of today.

Evolution of the Era

An understanding of the problems that stem from such technology begins with an understanding of the evolution of this new era, the speed with which it has emerged, and the uses that are only now beginning to be understood.

In 1950, there was no such thing as the computer business. But, one year later, the first real-time computer called the Whirlwind became operational at MIT. Two years later, IBM shipped its first stored-program computer, the 701.

The rapid deployment of the computer over the thirty years from 1960 to 1990 was unimaginable. In 1960, 1,790 mainframe computers were being shipped domestically at a value approaching $600 million. Fifteen years later in 1975, the value of all computers and related peripheral equipment shipped into the U.S. market had risen to roughly $7.5 billion. But the nature and magnitude of computing power being shipped had changed dramatically. Mainframe shipments had grown to 6,790 units, but so-called minicomputers and microcomputers were also being shipped at the annual rate of 26,990 and 10,500, respectively. By 1997, the value of shipments approached $84 billion and included more than 8 million units. Thus, from 1975 to 1990, the economic value of computer shipments climbed by a factor of 7.4, while the raw number of units shipped jumped by a factor of more than 165! That trend has continued to the present so that by 1998, the U.S. computer industry was shipping more than 28 million computers a year, or roughly one computer for every 9 people. By the year 2000 forecasters estimate that one billion computers and smart-card computers will be in use in the United States.

To service this new industry, America's educational institutions began training men and women at an equally impressive rate. The first Ph.D. in the field of computer science was granted by the University of Pennsylvania in 1965. By 1996, 3 percent of all bachelor's degrees and more than 3 percent of all doctorates awarded annually in American universities were in the field of computer science.

For all of the impressive growth figures in the computer industry though, no single technical invention has been considered more important to the quality of life than the telephone. For years, the guiding U.S. policy for telecommunications was universal service. (In much of the developing world, that still is a goal.) To achieve that end, U.S. policy controlled telephone companies almost completely and used long distance rates to subsidize local phone service. The policy was so effective that in the 40 years between 1930 and 1970 phone service grew from a service for a very few privileged households into a standard convenience that was installed in 87 percent of all homes. Today, in the United States and most developed nations, that goal has been essentially realized. For example, telephone service now reaches more than 93 percent of all occupied houses in the United States.

A latecomer to the communications revolution, cable television now boasts penetration rates in excess of 60 percent of all households in the United States. (In 1970, only 6.7 percent of households had cable TV.)

By almost any measure, the "wiring of the modern world" has proceeded at an awesome pace.

Converging Industries

The telecommunications infrastructure is now truly global in reach. More than 280,000 miles of fiber-optic cable with virtually infinite bandwidth span the globe. This capability is augmented by wireless technologies from satellites, microwaves, and in the forseeable future, lasers. The result of this is that today there is truly no place on Earth where the telecommunications network is not available in some form.

The technological basis of communications and computers is merging. Computers were designed on a binary basis and therefore utilized digital transmission from the beginning. The public switched telephone network (PSTN) was designed as an analog transmission system to carry voice. Technically and economically, there were sound reasons for this disparate development. But, recent advances in digitalization and more powerful microprocessors have led to superior quality in digital transmission. Historically, computers had to transmit information through the PSTN by converting from digital to analog and then reconverting back to digital form at the receiving end. Clearly, the process of conversion was inefficient. With both systems using digital technology, the need for this inefficiency vanishes. Moreover, the technical base of the two industries is converging so that the sharp distinction that historically existed between telecommunications and computers as an industry is not sustainable.

The Chip Culture

Add to these facts another facet. Linked by miles of cable or wireless transmission to every conceivable type of equipment and each other, computers monitor, control, and record millions of routine events and actions every day.

Computers, in the form of microchips, have been widely integrated into almost everything that we buy or use from automobiles to refrigerators. They control the engines in the cars we drive, enhance our vision from space, monitor and direct factories, enable physicians to perform microsurgery, allow us to program VCRs, control the utilities in a house or commercial building, and more.

The Capacity for Good Versus the Potential for Evil

The technological capacity we now possess to acquire, store, retrieve, and process information opens the door to major improvements in the quality of life, but misused, it also confronts society with completely new challenges. The fact is that the current ethical, policy, and legal structure that oversees this data-intensive age is, in some key aspects, critically deficient. In order to understand this reality, policy makers, ethicists, managers, citizens, and lawmakers must now struggle with understanding the nature of the deficiencies and what to do to redress them.

Nowhere are these deficiencies more pressing than in the right to personal privacy. By all indications, most people consider personal privacy to be a fundamental right. Even the courts have recognized a right to privacy. Privacy is essential to a reasonable quality of life. Yet the precise definition of what the right to privacy covers is far from clear. The advent of the information society is posing questions about that right that have never been considered before. How we draw the line between the free use and exchange of information on the one hand, and the right to privacy on the other, will fundamentally shape our lives in the future.

Living with the Information Age

An examination of daily life reveals the collection of an ominously long and growing list of details and information about the life of the average individual: records of bill payment, medical histories, books purchased at the local store or checked out at the local library, programs watched on cable television and/or the videos rented for home viewing, courses taken in various schools attended and the grades received, employment evaluations, personal productivity statistics, items purchased at the grocery store (including products for personal use), any records related to law enforcement, tax records, driver's licenses, applications for credit, credit history, insurance policies, travel records, and so on. All of these data and more are stored somewhere in the electronic information superstructure of the modern world.

The presence of such an overwhelming amount of information and the increasingly ubiquitous nature of the telecommunications system raise three distinct threats to personal privacy.

The current ethical, policy, and legal structure that oversees this data-intensive age is, in some key aspects, critically deficient.

The first is the illicit interception of personal messages and conversations by unintended parties. "Wiretapping" of course was always technically possible, but the sophistication required to do it and the legal procedures established to prevent its abuse were generally sufficient to protect privacy. As recent history has shown, however, wireless telephones open a whole new set of possibilities to would-be eavesdroppers. Likewise, e-mail systems and phone-mail systems are subject to penetration and "eavesdropping" by unintended parties.

The second, and more difficult, threat is the use or misuse of the information that can now be readily assembled about groups of people or individuals. Information has always been available, but historically the time and effort required to gather large amounts of it have provided a natural defense. Now, however, it can be assembled in relatively short periods of time. Moreover, because the incremental cost is minimal, more detailed information is routinely kept and available in hundreds of disconnected databases. That poses society with some new problems when it comes to privacy.

Consider the following examples: State governments have always maintained complete records of drivers' licenses and car tags matched to the people who own them. Such records were necessary to administer the licensing of vehicles. Historically, such records have been considered public information and hence available for public inspection on government premises. But, since it is public information, why not make it available in an easier-to-use form? At least one state now provides a complete listing of motor vehicle license plates and their owners on magnetic media for a nominal service fee. Now, a list that would have required thousands of man-hours to assemble can be acquired in virtually no time at minimal cost. An automobile dealer might acquire and use such a list to send direct mailings to all the Pontiac owners in his or her service area. Does this constitute an invasion of privacy?

On another front, one of the most popular phenomena of our time has been the rapid growth of stores that rent movies to customers. The computerized check-out systems used by most video stores provide complete and detailed rental histories for every customer. Because such information is available, political candidates, for instance, have found themselves pressed to release the history of their VCR movie rentals to the public. Is such information, privately held, a legitimate target of public political inquiry or not?

If an insurance company were to decide to use a list of subscribers to a gay magazine as a prescreening device for insurance applicants who might have AIDS, would that constitute an invasion of privacy, or illegitimate treatment of some type?

Many institutions, from hospitals to churches, keep computer records. With how much security should they be required to maintain these records? In an electronic age, unethical employees, service technicians, or others could copy and pass on detailed personal records without ever being detected. Security countermeasures exist, but as with all security systems, the costs in terms of user-friendliness and expense have to be weighed by the information provider or holder. The information holder may not always value security as much as the people on whom information is held.

The third and most potentially troubling use of information technology is to monitor the actions of others. At the extreme end, many states are experimenting with programs that place minor criminals under house arrest and monitor their whereabouts by electronic means. This is a cheaper, and in many ways better, alternative to prison. But on another more controversial front, an estimated 26 million Americans now have their work monitored by computers, and the number is climbing. These systems can be designed to keep track of productivity (keystrokes per minute or number of phone calls handled per hour) and even advise when it is time to take a break. But they also offer employers the opportunity to monitor phone conversations, track how much time employees spend in the bathroom, or enable supervisors to periodically monitor the work of subordinates while remaining undetected themselves.

Troubling Questions

Several questions arise as one considers these matters. Should the definition of "public information" change or should access somehow be limited? How safe are the security systems used now and how safe do they need to be? Should different systems be required by law to conform to certain levels of security? Are records contained in business files, like those of the video rental store, public or private? What happens when employees or others with access to data not generally available to the public make it available to other people or the press?

Should businesses have the right to sell their own customer lists and information about those customers to other parties who may want them? If so, are there any limits on how the information can be sold? Who guarantees the accuracy of information in all these sources? Who is liable for intentional or accidental harm resulting to individuals damaged by erroneous information? For example, if a hospital incorrectly identifies a person as having contracted HIV or if an erroneous credit record causes someone to be denied credit, housing, or even employment, who has legal liability? What constitutes fair or unfair use of information? How does society police the illicit sale of information? What kind of enforcement can and should governments provide for whatever body of laws emerge in this area? Does employer monitoring of work produce undue stress, and if so, are employers liable for some type of stress-related damage caused to an employee?

How safe are the security systems used now

and how safe do they need to be?

Are records contained in business files

public or private?

The list of troubling considerations is almost without limit. Some of the issues are not new, but the potential magnitude of the problem has fundamentally changed the calculus that will be applied in the legal and political system.

An Evolving Future

One of the certainties in modern life is the fact that governments at all levels will have to grapple with these issues. Tough, pragmatic standards that ensure fairness, economic affordability, enforceability, and the continued free flow of information will have to be developed. Law enforcement procedures, standards of accountability, and professional ethics all will have to evolve in the near future as public and private parties struggle with the still unwritten rules.

The bodies that will write these rules have yet to clearly assert themselves. Political bodies will certainly play a major role, but unless private industry professionals move to the foreground of the debate fairly quickly, the courts will probably assume the dominant role.

Unfortunately, that will take time. Indeed, the nature of legal systems is to proceed slowly until considered reason and case history support a well-established body of precedents. In the meantime, there are almost certain to be cases of grievous personal harm. How we deal with those cases as a society will do much to define the legitimate and illegitimate uses of information and guarantee the safeguarding of "personal" information.

[See also Communications: Privacy Issues; Computers: Overview.]

BIBLIOGRAPHY

BloomBecker, Jay, ed. *Computer Crime, Computer Security, Computer Ethics.* Santa Cruz, CA: National Center for Computer Crime, 1986.

Hoffman, Lance J. *Security and Privacy in Computer Systems.* Ann Arbor, MI: Books-on-Demand, 1993.

Security and Privacy, Research In. Symposium. Los Alamitos, CA: IEEE Computer Society, 1991.

— WES WILLIAMS

COMPUTERS: SAFETY

The basic technology of the video display terminal (VDT), or computer monitor, was developed for television reception early in the twentieth century. Inside the VDT is a cathode-ray tube (CRT) similar to the picture tube in a television receiver. In a CRT, the cathode (an electrode in the end of the tube closer to the back of the television set or VDT) emits a beam of electrons aimed at the center of the screen. Electromagnetic deflection coils or electrostatic plates surround the neck of the tube and control the direction of the beam. At the point where it strikes the screen, the beam triggers illumination in the chemicals that coat the inside surface of the screen. The beam sweeps across the screen line by line to create an image. The image is updated a number of times per second. This "refresh rate" varies in different computer monitors, but sixty times per second is typical. The lower the refresh rate, the more the screen appears to flicker and the more fatiguing, many researchers say, the work becomes.

Researchers have estimated that more than fifty million people in the United States use VDTs every day in their work.

Historically, as more workers began to use VDTs, some workers began to complain of eye strain, headaches, and other ailments. Gradually, from the 1960s through the early 1990s, the number and variety of complaints kept rising. So did the variety of the medical diagnoses and the number of private-sector and public-sector studies of various VDT hazards. Researchers are concerned primarily about the electromagnetic fields (EMFs) generated within the VDT. During the 1970s, two landmark VDT-hazard incidents occurred in Sweden and the United States. In 1975, Swedish scientists reported that VDT operators were complaining of

blurred vision and inability to focus their eyes. In 1976, two young copy editors at the *New York Times* developed opacities in both eyes—a precursor of cataracts, which rarely occur in young people. There have been many studies since, some of them in conflict. The list of ailments attributed to VDTs has grown, especially injuries to the unborn. Unions in many countries have pushed for regulatory safeguards. The regulatory leaders have been Sweden, Germany, France, the United Kingdom, and Japan. In addition, many state and local jurisdictions in the United States established regulations.

However, a clear scientific consensus still has not emerged. Some manufacturers continue to deny that VDT hazards exist; others have redesigned their products to meet the strict Swedish standards. Proper CRT design and effective shielding of electromagnetic field radiation are the key precautions. For their part, many

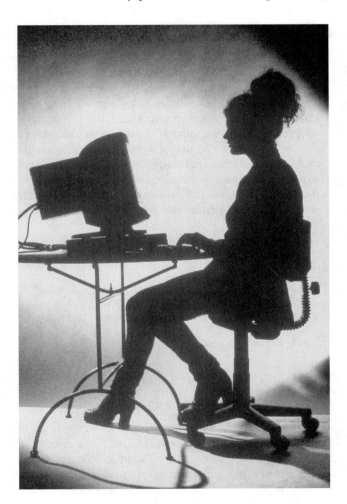

As over 50 million Americans use computer screens in their work each day, concern has grown about the physical stresses placed on the body from sitting for such long periods, staring at a screen, repetitive motion, and electromagnetic radiation. (Niall MacLeod/Corbis)

employers are concerned for the safety of their VDT users. Some have adopted remedies, such as installing glare screens, repositioning equipment to minimize exposure, encouraging frequent breaks, and advising pregnant women on the possible dangers to unborn children. Researchers who agree that CRTs impose hazards are also concerned about larger television screens, which will become increasingly popular and affordable, and about the future widespread adoption of high-definition television (HDTV). In the United States, preschoolers watch television more than twenty hours per week on average; millions of adults watch between thirty and forty hours per week.

While this controversy may continue, it is possible that alternative technologies gradually will replace CRTs. The technologies include liquid crystal, gas plasma, and semiconductor-based displays. Unlike CRTs, these technologies do not involve significant EMF emanations. However, the widespread adoption of these technologies may be slow. They are more expensive or they lack the clarity and fast response of the better-established CRT technology. If the history of most technologies is any guide, the wider adoption of CRT alternatives may well lead to design improvements and lower costs, which in turn could accelerate their adoption. Another approach would be to reduce VDT use by increasing the use of other input technologies, such as optical character recognition scanning and voice recognition. Both technologies are burgeoning and show great promise for the future, and both offer efficiency gains aside from any relief they may offer from VDT hazards.

[See also Computers: Overview; Computers: Privacy Laws.]

BIBLIOGRAPHY

"The Big Question: Is the PC Environment a Safe Place to Work?" *PC Magazine* (December 12, 1989).
"Terminal Damage." *The Jerusalem Post*, November 16, 1989.
"VDT Safety Debate Is Still Plugged In." *The Business Journal-Sacramento*, October 22, 1990.

— JEAN L. FARINELLI
JOSEPH R. ROY

COMPUTERS: SOFTWARE

The connotations of the word *software* range from the mundane to the metaphysical. The most commonly employed usage refers quite pragmatically to a commodity bought in retail stores to enable computers to perform particular functions, such as figuring taxes or amusing children. At the opposite end of this scale, philosophers (e.g., Daniel Dennett, Hillary Putnam, John Searle) have fiercely debated whether the relationship between mind and brain is equivalent to the relationship between software and hardware in computers.

Debates about mind as software are not without real-world significance. They have a bearing on what kind of machine, if any at all, can emulate human intelligence. In the reverse direction, such debates have influenced how psychologists think about the human mind. They are also related to a more general intellectual perspective with widespread implications for public policy and economic development: the concept of software reflects a previously unthinkable separation between the physical properties of a machine and the function that it performs. In its most abstract sense this insight can be credited to Alan Turing, who had already formulated in the 1930s the concept of a universal computing machine (known in his honor as a "Turing Machine") that could (in a certain formal sense) act like any other computing machine; in modern jargon functional differences between physically identical machines would lie in the software. The practical sweep of this idea has been enormously extended as the development of digital technologies brings more and more functionality under the rubric of "computing machine."

A simple example that will illustrate the general point is a profound shift in views (see Nicholas Negroponte, *Being Digital*) about "standards" for communication industries. Today most television sets used in the United States would not work in France, because the way signals are turned into pictures is determined by the hardware. Soon the insides of a television set will be a "universal computing machine" whose software will enable it to accept signals in whatever digital form they come. This shift will transcend not only boundaries between nations but also between such media as television, telephones, print, and personal computers.

The liberation of television from such standards as picture shape and resolution is part of a deeper evolution of the stuff of which artifacts are made. Pictures painted by stone-age artists on the walls of caves or by Picasso on canvas are all composed of atoms. What can be done with them is limited by the properties of matter. When I place a picture on my computer screen, I may see it through the mediation of a material screen, but the entity I bring (or "down-load" from a site on the Internet) is made of a different kind of stuff. It is not a physical entity but a software entity. It is not composed of atoms but of bits; and because bits are not restrained by physical laws, software entities can be transformed, transmitted, and reproduced in so nearly arbitrary ways that nobody yet has more than a glimmer of any limiting laws that may exist.

Software is seen in the largest historical perspective by recalling how early stages in human industry, indeed in civilization itself, are conventionally marked by turning points in the stuff of artifacts: the Stone Age, the Bronze Age, and the Iron Ages opened new vistas for our ancestors on the variety and complexity of life. For many millennia industry was about transforming and transporting matter. It is only in the past century that a new stuff became prominent: we moved into a period in which large fortunes were made, and world politics shaped, by dealing in energy. It appears to be a safe prediction that in the twenty-first century the third stuff in the sequence—matter, energy, software—will become dominant as measured by the numbers of people engaged and most especially as measured by the importance in shaping society.

The shift to software objects and to software tools for working with them is ubiquitous and far-reaching in its consequences. Shifting from quill pens to fountain pens to ball-point pens changed the ease but not the nature of making financial records and projections. Shifting from figures made of ink to figures made of software radically changes what can be done and who can do it. Financial deals of unprecedented complexity can be developed with a rapidity that was unprecedented even for all but the simplest transactions in the past. Moreover, such a plan can be developed by an executive with minimal arithmetical and bookkeeping skills.

One of the most strikingly novel features of the pattern of appropriation is the presence of children in the population of users. Here too it is instructive to contrast the nature of previous shifts in toys (e.g., from wooden trucks and cloth dolls to plastic forms of each) with the shift from material toys to software toys. On the economic level the importance of children as consumers of software is seen in the fact that multibillion-dollar companies in this area (e.g., Nintendo) have grown as dramatically as their counterparts (e.g., Microsoft) in business software. But the greater potential importance of the presence of software in the lives of children comes through its impact on the learning environment.

A full appreciation of the trends in software requires one to discount a phenomenon that happens to be well illustrated in the development of software for children. The uses to which software is put follow a pattern that is shared by the process of social appropriation of any new technology. The first application almost always consists of using it to achieve improvement in something that had been done before—for example, making movies by acting in front of the camera just as if it were in a theater. It took many years for anything resembling what we now call "cinema" to emerge, with all the paraphernalia of Hollywood, of stardom, of techniques such as closeups and editing that make it very different from stage acting.

An analog to photographing the stage is making software to teach children the number skills that are made unnecessary by the presence of computers. Most computer games can be seen in the same spirit, as children engaging in new action games that differ from the old simply in speed and glitter. The seeds of something more essentially different are present when children begin to take control of the computer to roam the globe on the Internet. But in the context of thinking about the development of software, the most poignant example of a new direction must be recognizing the need to create software to provide children with activities that are as natural as making drawings, making sandcastles, and making up stories. This beginning trend (see Papert, *The Children's Machine*) is significant not only because making software is new but also because it offers children the possibility for the first time of creatively appropriating a cutting-edge technology and of sharing with the business, scientific, and engineering worlds the opportunity to carry out projects of unprecedented complexity.

[See also Computer Hardware; Computers: Overview; Computers: Privacy Laws; Electronic Convergence; Interactive Entertainment; Media Lab; On-Line Services; Telecommunications.]

BIBLIOGRAPHY

Negroponte, Nicholas. *Being Digital.* New York: Bowker, 1995.
Papert, Seymour. *The Children's Machine: Bringing the Computer Revolution to Our Schools.* New York: Basic Books, 1993.

— SEYMOUR PAPERT

CONFLICT, ETHNIC AND RACIAL.
See ETHNIC AND CULTURAL SEPARATISM.

CONSCIOUS EVOLUTION

Conscious evolution is a new world view that has emerged in the latter half of the twentieth century. Through the development of scientific, technological,

---

Through the development of scientific, technological,

and social capabilities, we have gained the power

to affect our own evolution and that of life on Earth.

---

and social capabilities we have gained the power to affect our own evolution and that of life on Earth, for better or for worse. *Conscious* evolution is the effort to learn how to be responsible for guiding evolution on a planetary scale and eventually a solar system scale.

As Dr. Jonas Salk wrote in his *Anatomy of Reality,* human beings now play an active and critical role not only in the process of their own evolution but in the survival and evolution of all living beings. *Awareness of this places upon human beings a responsibility for their participation in and contribution to the process of evolution.* If humankind would accept and acknowledge this responsibility and become creatively engaged in the process of metabiological evolution consciously as well as unconsciously, a new reality would emerge, and a new age could be born.

The roots of conscious evolution go back to the dawn of human awareness that this current stage of life is not ultimate, that something new is being born out of the human struggle. It has been nourished by visionaries and scientists of the human race who sensed the possibility of a quantum jump in capacity and consciousness and foresaw the possibility of the regeneration or transformation of the human race. But only now, in our lifetime, do we have the actual power to destroy or transform our world. Only now has the responsibility for conscious evolution become a pragmatic necessity for our survival and fulfillment. It is a new field, brought into focus by three radically new conditions called the "Three C's"—the new cosmology, crises, and capacities.

The New Cosmology

Conscious evolution arises from cosmogenesis, the discovery that the universe had a beginning, has been evolving for billions of years, and is evolving through us now. This awareness gives us a new identity, capability, and responsibility to be conscious coevolvers, participants in the process of creation. From the perspective of the new cosmology our future is envisioned as a continuum in the process of continuous transformation—open-ended, immeasurable, radically new, and filled with hope. This future is seen, however, as a contingency, not an inevitability. It depends on what we do. Conscious evolution makes us potentialists, not optimists. We seek to understand what is potential, good and desirable in the whole system, and how to manifest it in our lives.

The New Crises

The complex set of environmental/economic and social crises presents an unprecedented threat to our species. Never before in human history have we been required to change our behavior or suffer the destruction of our life support system within a very short time frame. This generation is called upon to manage a planetary ecology, to provide sustenance for humans throughout the world without further damage to the environment, to control population growth, to handle our own wastes, to shift from nonrenewable to renewable resources, to liberate

human potential everywhere. Conscious evolution is the context for the development of these new capabilities.

The New Capacities

Advanced technologies such as microbiology, nuclear power, cybernetics, astronautics, nanotechnology, barely a generation old, give us vast new powers over the material world. We are already intervening in evolution directly. We can create new life-forms and new worlds. If we combine the *science of matter* with the *science of mind* (our potential for spiritual evolution), we see the possibility of a quantum leap from one phase of evolution to the next. Yet we are collectively without a positive vision of our future commensurate with our new powers. To envision such a future is a major emphasis for conscious evolution. In the effort to participate in the process of transformation, conscious evolution synthesizes three ways of knowing.

Conscious evolution is experienced *spiritually* as the subjective apprehension of a designing universal intelligence, a pan*en*theism, transcendent yet immanent, which is manifesting at all levels of being from the atomic to the galactic. It is experienced as our individual desire to align with the process of creation and to express that intention, or "implicate order," in our own lives as participants in the evolution of the larger community.

It is manifested *socially* in our growing efforts to design new social systems—in health, environmental protection, governance, education, business—to enhance creativity, cooperation, and sustainability.

It is discovered *experimentally* through science and technology as we learn how nature works by exploring the invisible technologies of creation, such as the gene, the atom, and the brain, so that we can coevolve with nature.

Conscious evolution can serve as a meta-discipline,

a new framework to offer coherence, direction,

and purpose to various aspects of human endeavor.

Conscious evolution can serve as a meta-discipline, a new framework to offer coherence, direction, and purpose to various aspects of human endeavor. Education becomes the process of learning cosmic, personal, social, and vocational evolution, so each of us can give our creative gift to the evolution of our world. It offers to religion a new ground of the whole in which each faith can contribute its unique gift to the evolution of humanity. It provides for science a "telos" that offers the understanding and the technologies to meet an evolutionary agenda aimed at bringing about a universal future for humanity, one that is sustainable, open, and full of a wide range of choices. It gives futurism a new context and values to envision, plan, and guide us toward the next stage of our evolution.

[See also Evolution, Social; Global Consciousness; High Technology; Mind: New Modes of Thinking; Nanotechnology.]

BIBLIOGRAPHY

Grosso, Michael. *The Millennium Myth.* Wheaton, IL: Quest Books, 1995.

Hubbard, Barbara Marx. *The Evolutionary Journey.* Miami, FL: Evolutionary Press, 1982.

Murphy, Michael. *The Future of the Body: Explorations into the Further Evolution of Human Nature.* Los Angeles, CA: Tarcher, 1992.

Roszak, Theodore. *The Voice of the Earth.* New York: Simon and Schuster, 1992.

Russell, Peter. *The Global Brain Awakens: Our Next Evolutionary Leap.* Global Brain, 1995.

Salk, Jonas. *The Anatomy of Reality.* New York: Columbia University Press, 1983.

Savage, Marshall T. *The Millennial Project: Colonizing the Galaxy in Eight Easy Steps.* Little, Brown, 1992.

Stock, Gregory. *Metaman: The Merging of Human and Machines into a Global Superorganism.* New York: Simon and Schuster, 1993.

— BARBARA MARX HUBBARD

CONSERVATISM, POLITICAL

A discussion of the future of conservatism requires attending to the elusive concept of conservatism per se. The difficulty in defining conservatism derives primarily from its frequent use as a defense of the status quo or the status quo ante. Thus, conservatism in the Kremlin embraced those who wished to return to Stalinist practices. Conservatism has also been associated with the nineteenth-century social and economic standpattism of the British. On the other hand, in some parts of the world (e.g., Latin America), the word has had no ideological overtones. And as the status quo shifts in the years ahead, the connotations of the word may well undergo corresponding transformations.

Nevertheless, it was in the United States during the New Deal years (1933–1945) that political conservatism crystallized with a new meaning that overtook competing meanings. Conservatives rallied in reaction against the centralizing tendencies of what in America came to be known as "liberalism." Up until World War I, liberalism was generally used to designate the doctrine that expanded individual liberty; and liberty was generally understood to describe protections from the oppressors of the individual. Thus, we find Woodrow Wilson pronouncing that "the history of liberty is a history of resistance . . . of the limitation of governmental power, not the increase of it."

New Deal liberals tended to approach problems on a grand scale as fit subjects for government reform. Thus, in comprehensive ways, "liberal" government undertook to mobilize the state to combat virtually all social problems—unemployment, agricultural distress, a shortage of electricity, illiteracy, malnutrition, among others.

Conservatives sought to abide by what is widely known as the rule of "subsidiarity." This principle asserts that a social problem that can be handled by the private sector should not be taken over by the public sector; and that a problem that can be handled by a lesser unit of the public sector must not be given to a more central unit. Thus, e.g., the care of children of working mothers should be a private responsibility, to be handled where possible by churches or other private associations; only if this is not possible should the responsibility be taken by the state—and last of all, by the federal government.

Since the vision of conservatism is not eschatological—i.e., it does not conceive of redemptive ends implicit in its conventions—the conservative approach to the future has tended toward the cautionary rather than the utopian. True to the concept of utopia as imagined by Samuel Butler in *Erewhon,* for conservatives an earthly utopia *is* nowhere. It does not exist at present, did not exist in an idyllic, idealized past, and will not exist in the future, especially not as a consequence of humanity being uplifted by the benign (or malevolent) authority of big government to a new plateau of enforced egalitarian tranquility.

Most conservatives are men and women who have a religious faith, and they reserve their vision of ultimates for extraterrestrial phenomena. It is for this reason that conservatism has been marked mostly by negative importunities against human inclinations, as is the case with the Ten Commandments and the Constitution, both of which emphasize that which ought *not* to be done.

The conservative believes that the threat of the omnipotent state is endemic and historically insistent, and that as a state acquires power, so the individual loses it. For that reason, it is presumptively against state action, but always allowing for the rebuttability of presumption, which is a logical rule. Conservatism believes also that in free circumstances, the social sector will mobilize to satisfy felt economic needs. During the twentieth century, conservatism addressed its Achilles' heel, unemployment, with special emphasis, developing knowledge and insights that dispelled any probability of unemployment on the scale in which it was suffered during the 1930s. Conservatism was especially alert during the years of the Cold War to urge that the protection of national sovereignty, and within it of individual liberty, justified enormous corporate sacrifices, and also justified a nuclear deterrent. It is likely to remain alert to whatever needs for similar sacrifice that may arise in times to come.

Conservatism is firmly rooted in a concept of human equality that is narrowly defined. This doctrine acknowledges the binding kinship of all men and women, and for this reason the law must not distinguish in its treatment of any human being. But within the bounds of equal protection under the law, conservatism remains obliged to respect vast differences in individual abilities, and to resist any arbitrary regulatory quagmires, such as affirmative action, that give special consideration to special minorities, or confiscatory taxation that seeks to level for the sake of levelling.

Unlike Marxism and socialism, conservatism does not attempt to solve problems it cannot solve. It presupposes limitations in human nature readily understandable to Christians who believe in original sin, otherwise deduceable by non-Christian conservatives who study the history of humanity. They know that the propensity to self-indulgence must be denied. And correspondingly, the state must be denied such powers as are necessary for authoritative action, while denying it such powers as encourage authoritarian action. Believing, then, that most problems derive from a deficiency in human nature, conservatism comes to terms, or seeks to do so, with the limitations of politics: problems are seldom "solved"; they can only be ameliorated. Someone somewhere expressed this principle by noting, "You cannot eliminate Skid Row."

Conservatives recognize that the fundamental issues are likely to remain the same, though specific contexts will certainly alter in barely imaginable ways, in response to new technologies, shifts in the dynamics of international relations in the post-Cold War era, the exacerbation or amelioration of existing social problems, or the appearance of new ones. Conservatives face the future, ever aware of the dangers of the swollen state, deriving as they do from the weaknesses of the citizens in a state, whose calling is always to struggle lest they become the subjects of the state.

[See also Communitarianism; Liberalism, Political; Political Cycles; Political Parties; Political Party Realignment; Third Political Parties.]

BIBLIOGRAPHY

Buckley, William F., Jr., and Kesler, Charles R., eds. *Modern American Conservative Thought.* New York: HarperCollins, 1988.

Ferguson, Thomas, and Rogers, Joel. *The Decline of the Democrats and the Future of American Politics.* New York: Hill and Wang, 1986.

Kirk, Russell. *Prospects for Conservatives,* rev. ed. Washington, DC: Regnery-Gateway, 1989.

— WILLIAM F. BUCKLEY, JR.

CONSUMER PROTECTION/REGULATION

"Consumption," wrote Adam Smith in *The Wealth of Nations,* "is the sole end and purpose of all production; and the interest of the producer ought to be attended to, only in so far as it may be necessary for promoting that of the consumer."

This statement, the economic corollary of Thomas Jefferson's nearly simultaneous 1776 political assertion that all governments derive "their just powers from the consent of the governed," underpins the operation of the American economy. Smith and Jefferson forged what Max Lerner called the new doctrine of "economic liberalism and freedom from governmental interference"—the driving force of the most powerful economy in history.

In the 1790s, when most Americans lived on farms or ran small businesses, Jefferson recommended a set of weights and measures standards, kicking off American consumer protection.

Economic dependence destroys political freedom according to Jefferson. Liberty rested on economically independent small businesses and farms. Weights and measures rules protect the weaker from the more powerful buyers and sellers.

Between 1800 and the end of the Civil War in 1865, America developed an industrial corporate sector, which was beset by boom and bust economic cycles, robber baron excesses, and political corruption. In 1887 Congress passed the Interstate Commerce Act, with consumer protection rhetoric, launching the thirty-year Progressive Era.

Government protection of railroad consumers—farmers, miners, businesses owners—from exploitative rates seemed an antidote to corporate abuse, but the bill passed only when railroaders saw that it helped *them.*

Legislative success with railroads led Progressives to try other regulation. These efforts led to the creation of the Federal Reserve, Food and Drug Administration, Federal Trade Commission, meat inspection, and antitrust laws, among others. Between 1887 and 1916, Congress passed fifty-six consumer laws. Still, corporations accumulated more economic power while Americans remained agrarian (60 percent lived on farms in 1900).

World War I diverted America from its regulatory binge. But in the twenty-two years following World

War I, including Franklin Delano Roosevelt's New Deal, the nation again turned to consumer protection laws, passing seventy-three new ones or 3.3 a year, as compared to 1.9 yearly by the Progressives.

New Dealer Gardner Means called Franklin Roosevelt's consumer programs "the peculiar American answer to the economic forces driving the rest of the world to choose between Communism and Fascism." Then World War II briefly led the nation away from its regulatory impulse.

After World War II (1951 to 1980) regulatory legislation got back on track with 227 new consumer laws passed—a 7.6 per year average. In the meantime, Sweden's consumer protection government (1930s to '80s) developed the world's highest standard of living.

In 1962, in a Jeffersonian vein, President John F. Kennedy announced a Consumer Bill of Rights to Congress. He also ordered expanded use of the federal weights and measures program to assure, in particular, the integrity of packaged goods, and to protect consumer rights nationwide. This Kennedy message highlighted modern consumerism. Fewer than 6 percent of postwar Americans worked on farms. Most of the rest worked for wages, many in large corporations or government. Americans expressed their economic stake primarily as consumers.

Alvin Toffler writes that "The Second Wave [industrialism], drove a giant invisible wedge into our economy, our psyches, and even our sexual selves . . . [splitting apart] production and consumption . . . that had always, until then, been one."

Industrial workers and managers struggled, obscuring the deeper conflict between producer (worker and manager) demands for higher wages, profits, and benefits and the counterdemands of consumers (the same people) for lower prices.

Industrialism advanced individuals economically by raising income. Postwar consumerism built individual economic power by improving outgo. It tried modestly to narrow the price/quality and production/consumption gaps created by industrialism.

This history establishes the framework for an even more vigorous consumer protection future. Cyclical projection and precursor jurisdiction methodology developed by Graham Molitor forecast 350 to 450 new consumer laws for debate and passage between 1989 and 2018.

Early 1990s' food label, organic farming, and cable TV rules suggest the soundness of this projection and a future consumerism looking much like its past. Consumer redress, choice, safety, and information create the competition that disciplines markets. During the next twenty-five years, 350 to 450 new consumer laws and rules would regulate the Internet, finance (S&L's), trade, safety, quality and price information, privacy, and speech.

However, the current context—a global economy; the information revolution; an aging, low-birthrate population—underlines Toffler's observation that increasingly knowledge, not force or wealth, defines power and magnifies the power of consumers.

Consumers are to economics what voters are to politics. Using powerful new information tools, consumers increasingly influence markets.

Focus on government's role, an important secondary topic, may obscure a deeper power shift from organizations toward persons that increases individual empowerment. However, certification, registration, and local regulation all increase rules while ostensibly lessening overt government control. Devolution to something other than strong federal laws, to more subtle administrative rules and decentralized decision making, shift the focus and onus of new consumer protection.

Consumers are to economics what voters are to politics. Using powerful new information tools, consumers increasingly influence markets. Consumer protection rules play a key role managing this power from knowledge. Consumer regulation faces a robust future.

[See also Communications: Privacy Issues; Counterfeiting; Food Additives; Food and Drug Safety; Food Laws; Pharmaceuticals.]

BIBLIOGRAPHY

Kolko, Gabriel. *Railroads and Regulation*, 1877–1916. Westport, CT: Greenwood Press, 1970.

Molitor, Graham T. T., and Plumb, James. "Reading the Cycles of Consumerism." *Mobius* (Fall 1989).

Smith, Adam. *The Wealth of Nations.* New York: Random House/Modern Library, 1937, p. 625.

"TechnoMania: The Future Isn't What You Think." *Newsweek* (February 27, 1995): 43.

Toffler, Alvin. *Power Shift: Knowledge, Wealth, and Violence at the Edge of the 21st Century.* New York: Bantam Books, 1990.

———. *The Third Wave.* New York: Bantam Books, 1984.

Turner, James S. *The Chemical Feast.* New York: Grossman Publishers, 1970.

— JAMES S. TURNER

CONTAGIOUS DISEASES.

See EPIDEMICS; PUBLIC HEALTH.

CONTINUING EDUCATION.

See ADULT LEARNING.

CONTINUITY AND DISCONTINUITY

Continuity, slow evolution, and strong inertial drift are the general guiding principles of virtually all sociopolitical change. Human nature itself exhibits a natural reluctance to embrace change. These limiting influences minimize upheaval, ameliorate dislocation of established large-scale investments, limit dislocation, and minimize individual disorientation. Rapid and drastic shifts in established institutions, procedures, and other trappings of an established society disrupt social equilibrium. To temper disruptive influences a variety of conscious and unconscious social counterforces are interposed.

The rapidity, depth, breadth, and complexity of change are constantly transforming society. Change is incremental and evolutionary, and lodged upon us case-by-case and crisis-by-crisis. Pieces of the puzzle describing societies never seem to quite fit because the picture is constantly changing. When we attempt to assess the salient features of society, so much is happening in so many areas that we lose perspective and have difficulty fathoming the meaning of our times. The old moorings and familiar landmarks no longer provide the same sense of conventional reference.

Continuity

To an extent greater than most would surmise, the future already is shaped by past events. Historical momentum so strongly grips the present that many forecasters look to the past to gain a sense of the future. Confucius concurred in this approach, putting it this way: "Coming events cast their shadows before them." Auguste Comte also underscored the importance of the past by proclaiming, "No conception can be understood except through history." Leibnitz stated, "The past is pregnant with the future," and Winston Churchill asserted, "The further backward you can look, the further forward you can see."

Many other prominent thinkers have acknowledged the role the past chain of events, ideas, and leaders plays in determining the future. Isaac Newton said, "if I have seen further (than others), it is by standing on the shoulders of giants." Victor Hugo underscored the importance of ideas by asserting, "No army can stop an idea whose time has come." Progress is the triumphant convergence of many factors.

The past chain of events, though it exerts a powerful influence in shaping future developments, is not a fa-

talistic force. Human willpower, properly directed, can alter the course of almost anything. As William James put it, "Man alone, of all the creatures of Earth, can change his own pattern. Man is the architect of his destiny." The future is not undiscernible or unknowable. It is an evolutionary state toward which we are ever tending.

Man-made systems, logically, are subject to greater human control than most natural systems. What humans have created, they essentially are capable of tearing asunder and refashioning according to need. Not that all man-made systems are easily manipulated. Things were easier in simpler times but are more difficult in today's complex environment.

There are few limits to what the human race

can achieve given imagination, understanding,

and commitment to realize our goals.

Natural occurrences, subject to nature's whim and caprice, tend to be less predictable than manmade phenomena. Continuing advancements in knowledge, however, strip away uncertainty and enhance understanding, which advances the predictability of many natural phenomena. Satellite surveillance and massive computer surveys greatly enhance predicting weather and agricultural crop yields. Tectonic plate theories as well as sophisticated computer analysis and simulation make earthquake prediction reasonably certain.

Change is a constant and ceaseless phenomenon of societies. Society is dynamic, not static. The social systems in which we live are constantly changing, always churning, consistently in a state of flux.

Semantic gradations describe rates of change. Evolution usually connotes slow-paced change. *Revolution* is among the terms used to describe a pace of change at cataclysmic or rapid rates. Revolutionary change may characterize a single phenomenon or a considerable range of coterminous changes that radically transform. In the overall scheme of things, change occurs at an increasing tempo, covers an ever broader and more comprehensive range.

Our inspirational moments are driven by a desire to refine, extend, elaborate, and better what has gone before. The search for something better, new, or novel is constant. New high-water marks become points of departure to be surmounted. New vantage points sharpen the vision of additional peaks to be conquered. There are few limits to what the human race can achieve given imagination, understanding, and commitment to realize our goals.

The ceaseless search for perfection, improvement, doing something better gives rise to constant unrest. Events being at rest or at status quo give rise to a new unrest, and an ensuing quest for experimentation and novelty follows. New experimentation becomes the harbinger of another wave of change. This helical process usually is forward moving, ever expanding, and upward tending. As something new is mastered and widely accepted, it becomes routinized, standardized, institutionalized, normalized, and gets taken for granted. Rising expectations drive us toward higher levels. Everyone yearns for a new and better tomorrow. Eventually new heights become a mere floor, not a ceiling.

Human inquisitiveness never seems to be quite satisfied. Constantly restless, it searches for the next step forward. So ultimates often are merely temporary way stations.

Humans constantly strive for perfection. This constant upgrading assumes imperfection. Human activity almost always is fraught with faults and foibles, shortcomings and defects. Humans are destined to strive perpetually toward, but never actually to reach perfection. No matter how long and how hard the attempts to close gaps, the job never is fully or finally concluded. Even if a balanced state could be achieved, it never could be maintained. Perpetual pursuit of goals always just beyond reach indicates that the nature of change is destined to be eternal. Perfection is an ideal state or condition, an abstraction not attainable on Earth. It remains eternally elusive. The ceaseless search may be viewed as one of the greatest cosmic mysteries, or as the driving force toward human greatness.

Discontinuity

Discontinuity denotes breaks with the past involving gaps, interruptions, or even cessation. Careful examination of sociopolitical change processes, however, reveals another perspective that dispels notions of discontinuity. What are popularly perceived as discontinuities often are misleadingly based on insufficient data or incomplete analysis. Changes in human affairs involve extraordinarily long time frames. Meticulous analysis reveals patterns of constant incremental development leading to changes that dispel any notion of discontinuity.

Rarely, if ever, are there sharp and total breaks or discontinuities with the past. There are many early warnings that signal impending change. Change rarely is thrust on established systems by a single grand stroke. Instead, there are many ministeps by which the new is incorporated into the existing system. Very little that is built up over time is discarded by single bold strokes or by one fell swoop. Past traditions and established institutions are given up reluctantly. Sharp breaks with past events seldom occur. Perspective depends on how carefully one looks at the forces of change.

Few persons can afford the time or have the resources to assess societal drift fully. Demands of everyday living are so overwhelming that usually most of us see only a dizzying blur of events, not the overall pattern. This shortcoming may explain the tendency to embrace discontinuity uncritically.

What may be truly remarkable about these times is the pace and breadth of change. When so many things change so fast, there is little time to get acclimatized. Prior historical periods, changing at a slower pace and far simpler in complexity, had the benefit of thousands or hundreds of years to accommodate transformation. Contemporary society responds in periods measured by mere decades. Thus, there is ample reason for many to feel insecure, uncertain of where things are headed. Dealing with continuity is much easier than dealing with change, especially deep and pervasive change.

The future speaks to us with hundreds of signals. Society or human affairs need not drift haplessly and blindly toward tomorrow. We are not mere victims of a thousand random events. Change originates in dissatisfaction, is focused by vision, implemented by practical first steps, then confirmed and fine-tuned by implementation. The key to tracking the future is deeply and firmly embedded in the past. Continuity is a reliable guide.

The essential understanding in coping with change is to realize that there is no fixed destination—only a continuing series of way stations. Societies are dynamic, constantly changing, never the same at any two points in time. Human beings face a perpetual process of changing to and readapting to new circumstances. History entails a progressive adjustment to change, a continuous abandonment of the status quo.

[See also Change; Change, Epochal; Change, Optimistic and Pessimistic Perspectives; Change, Pace of; Global Turning Points.]

BIBLIOGRAPHY

Aubert, Wilhelm, ed. *Sociology of Law.* Baltimore: Penguin Books, 1969.

Drucker, Peter F. *The Age of Discontinuity: Guidelines to Our Changing Society.* New York: Harper & Row, 1968.

Horowitz Harold W., and Karst, Kenneth L. *Law, Lawyers, and Social Change: Cases and Materials on the Abolition of Slavery, Racial Segregation, and Inequality of Educational Opportunity.* Indianapolis, IN: Bobbs-Merrill, 1969.

Kahn, Herman A., and Briggs, B. Bruce. *Things to Come: Thinking About the '70s and '80s.* New York: Macmillan, 1972.

Kairys, David, ed. *The Politics of Law: A Progressive Critique.* New York: Pantheon Books, 1990.

Schur, Edwin M. *Law and Society: A Sociological View.* New York: Random House, 1968.

— GRAHAM T. T. MOLITOR

CORNISH, EDWARD S. (1927–)

Born in New York City, Edward Cornish is president of the World Future Society and editor of *The Futurist* (since 1966). After attending the University of Paris and Harvard University, he entered journalism as a copyboy for the *Washington Star.* In 1951 he joined the United Press Association (later known as UPI) and served in the agency's bureaus in Richmond, Va.; Raleigh, N.C.; London; Paris; and Rome. In 1957 he joined the National Geographic Society as a staff writer. There his interest turned to the new technologies and their potential impact on human life, an interest that led him to publish (irregularly) a six-page newsletter entitled *The Futurist.* Positive response to the newsletter prompted the formation of the World Future Society (WFS) on October 18, 1966, with Cornish as director; in 1967 *The Futurist* was expanded to journal size, with a more regular publication schedule. As the only president the WFS has ever had, Cornish has presided over its growth from 3,000 members in 1969 to 30,000 in 1994. Cornish brings a rare objectivity to the field and presents a balanced view of short-term futures. Cornish's many books include *The Study of the Future* (1986), *Communications Tomorrow: The Coming of the Information Society* (1982), *Careers Tomorrow: The Outlook for Work in a Changing World* (1983), *The Great Transformation: Alternative Futures for Global Society* (1983), *Global Solutions: Innovative Approaches for World Problems* (1984), *The Computerized Society: Living and Working in an Electronic Age* (1985), and *The 1990s and Beyond* (1990).

[See also Futurists.]

— GEORGE THOMAS KURIAN

COSMETICS AND TOILETRIES

Cosmetics and toiletries in the twenty-first century, reflecting scientific strides forward, will function by reacting chemically and physiologically with skin and hair. Products will be available to increase or decrease the amount of sebum secreted from the sebaceous glands, for persons with dry or oily skin respectively. With aging the microcirculation in the skin atrophies and the skin cells are undernourished, resulting in a sallow complexion. Products will be available that will enhance the microcirculation when applied topically, resulting in a healthier skin with a rosy complexion.

The stratum corneum—the outermost dead layer of skin cells that acts as a barrier to body-moisture loss and penetration of extraneous poisons into the body—is continually being shed and new stratum corneum forms as living cells from the basal layer move upward through the epidermis. This cell "turnover time" is normally about three weeks. With aging, the cell turnover time increases and the skin becomes drier and loses its healthy glow. Products will be available that will control the skin turnover time at any safe rate desired.

Wrinkles form on aging because the collagen and elastin in the dermis become cross-linked—due to the action of free radicals—and lose their ability to act as a cushion and provide turgor to the skin. New materials will be available that when applied topically will penetrate and activate the fibroblast cells in the dermis to produce fresh new collagen and elastin. Thus it will be possible to retard wrinkle formation early on.

Dry skin is caused by overcleaning the skin with soaps and detergent products. These cleansers remove from the skin the naturally occurring humectants and barrier lipids that are required to maintain the proper amount of moisture in the stratum corneum. Today's skin moisturizers all contain water-soluble humectants and several types of oleaginous materials to enhance the skin's moisture level. In the next century products for alleviating dry skin will contain hydrogels that are capable of holding hundreds of times their weight in water and yet not be water soluble. Such materials will lay down a film on the skin that is not easily removed and will continually bathe the skin in a film of water. Dietary polyunsaturated fatty acids are required for the skin to manufacture ceramides and glycosphingolipids having the correct chemical structure and spatial configuration to provide a good moisture-loss barrier. Barrier lipids, such as ceramides and glycosphingolipids, are currently available, but the cost is exorbitant. These materials will be manufactured by genetic engineering and will become more affordable so that skin-moisturizing products will contain effective concentrations to maintain appropriate moisture levels in the stratum corneum.

Cleansing products for the hair and skin will be based on mild biodegradable surfactants that will be completely nonirritating to the skin and not defat the skin or impair the barrier layer—thus alleviating the major cause for dry skin condition. The consumer also will come to understand that an abundance of lather is not necessary to obtain good cleaning. Shampoos will be

Concern over the effects of ultraviolet light from the sun's rays has spawned general use of chemical aids to prevention of skin damage. (Christine Osborne/Corbis)

available that will clean and condition the hair without drying out the scalp. Specialty shampoos will also be available that will wave, set, or color the hair as desired.

Hair waving and hair removal will no longer depend on the use of smelly mercaptans. These functions will be accomplished by using appropriate enzymic systems that will break and remake disulfide linkages in the hair as desired or will further split the keratin protein into simple water-soluble polypeptides and amino acids.

Exposure to ultraviolet light (UV) in several discrete bandwidths is known to be the major cause for premature skin aging; excessive exposure can lead to skin cancer. Today's sunscreens, while effective screens for UVB rays (290–320 nanometers), are not very effective in screening out UVA (320–400 nm) and are completely ineffective for UVC (rays below 290 nm). While at one time UVA rays were thought of as the "tanning

rays" and as not harming the skin, recent studies have shown that UVA rays penetrate more deeply than those in the UVB and that daily exposure to these can also cause premature skin wrinkles. UVC rays are normally screened out by the ozone layer in the stratosphere, but increasing damage to this protective layer will allow ever-increasing amounts of UVC to penetrate to Earth and lead to an increased incidence of skin cancer. The products of the next century will contain highly effective screens to filter out harmful UV rays in the 200 to 400 nm range of the spectrum. In addition, effective antioxidants will be present to allay the formation of free radicals—the major cause of skin aging.

Many Caucasians prefer to have a tanned look and yet do not want to expose themselves to UV sunlight without wearing a high sunscreen protective factor (SPF) preparation. This can be accomplished by using sunless self-tanning creams and lotions containing dihydroxyacetone, which reacts with several amino acids in the skin to develop a jaundiced yellow color. Products of the twenty-first century will be vastly improved and will impart a longer lasting rich bronze color to the skin, utilizing compounds that will develop substantive pigments resembling melanin—the naturally occurring pigmenting agent.

The market for nail lacquers is huge, although most nail lacquers do not wear well. The next century will bring to the consumer nail lacquers that will last for several weeks without cracking or peeling, and nail lacquer removers will be available that will not harm or weaken the nails. Today's nail strengtheners are based primarily on the use of formaldehyde, which is a potent skin-sensitizing agent and possible carcinogen. Nail strengtheners will be available based on agents that will cross-link the keratin protein of the nail without irritation or sensitization reactions.

Use of fluorides in water supplies and in dentifrices in this century resulted in a major reduction in the formation of cavities. In the next century there will be a vast improvement in the type of agents used to reduce or eliminate plaque formation, which if uncontrolled results in gingivitis and eventually periodontal disease and tooth loss. Thus, the mouthwash of the future will not only provide sustained-release control for pleasant breath but be formulated to help eliminate gingivitis and periodontal disease.

[See also Dentistry; Fragrances; Ozone Layer Depletion.]

BIBLIOGRAPHY

Estrin, Norman, and Jungermann, Eric, eds. *The Cosmetics Industry: Scientific and Regulatory Foundations.* New York: Marcel Dekker, 1984.

Romm, R. *The Changing Face of Beauty*. St. Louis, MO: Mosby Year Book, 1990.

Umbach, Wilfried. *Cosmetics and Toiletries*. Englewood Cliffs, NJ: Prentice-Hall, 1991.

— CHARLES FOX

COUNTERFEITING

Counterfeiting has become one of the world's fastest-growing methods for committing fraud. It has grown at a record pace over the past decade and will continue to flourish well into the next century.

Counterfeiting has become one of the world's fastest-growing methods for committing fraud and will continue to flourish well into the next century.

In addition to greed, there are two primary forces that will drive growth in counterfeiting. First, people in emerging and developing nations rely on U.S. currency for security more than at any other time in history. Second, modern technology—particularly accessible low-cost items such as personal computers, imaging software, scanners, color copiers, and laser printers—make counterfeiting relatively easy. The days of the stereotypical engraver laboring in a basement to etch a perfect set of plates on behalf of an organized crime kingpin are gone. As Doug McClellan of the *Albuquerque Journal* stated, "counterfeiting has gone mainstream." Counterfeiting has become and will continue to grow as a cottage industry.

The range of products being counterfeited extends from T-shirts to auto parts and from sophisticated computer systems to telephone calling cards. In the future, growth in product copying will occur most rapidly in Asia and Eastern Europe, with the large volume of counterfeited products being exported throughout the world with relatively low risk.

Phone cards, computer software, credit cards, prescription forms, checks, securities and a myriad of other documents, as well as technology, will be targeted by counterfeiters in the United States and Western Europe. Worldwide, currency will remain the counterfeiter's staple.

Over a two-year period, the U.S. banking industry alone reported a 43 percent increase in fraud, with over 1 million reported cases and total losses in excess of $800 million. The U.S. Secret Service estimates that computer-aided forgery of bank notes may exceed $2 billion by the turn of the century. The National Research Council (National Academy of Sciences) iden-

tified counterfeiting using desktop technology as the biggest future threat to U.S. currency.

Methods of counterfeiting are being developed and refined much faster than preventive and enforcement measures can be put into place. Counterfeiting will increase rapidly in Eastern European countries, China, and other nations in which people save U.S. currency, rather than that of their own nation, as a means protecting their future. Counterfeiting U.S. dollars is a huge growth industry in emerging and developing nations, particularly those that have yet to embrace checks, credit cards, and computerized transactions as common tools of trade. In the two years from 1992 to 1993, the amount of counterfeit U.S. currency seized overseas rose from $30 million to $120 million.

Counterfeiting is and will continue to be an international problem. Mafia-like crime organizations have led counterfeiting in Eastern Europe, freely crossing national borders. But because so much of the counterfeit market is in U.S. dollars, the burden and cost for prevention and enforcement primarily falls on the U.S. government.

Methods of counterfeit prevention will continue to go high-tech. Experiments are underway to use an individual's DNA as a means for authenticating his or her identification.

Based on small computer chips, smart cards (prepaid cards containing stored values to be used at retailers) will be used with greater frequency. With smart cards, retailers receive money from the system providers, who receive money in advance from their customers. Secured data representing the value is exchanged rather than currency.

Public key cryptology and digital signatures will replace today's credit and automated teller cards as well as other means for conducting transactions. A financial institution or corporation maintains a public encryption key, while the private key is known only to the owner. What the private key encrypts, the public key decrypts and vice versa.

The United States and other nations will continue to experiment with new ways to protect their currency. New dollar designs, water marks, special inks, holographic images, polyester fibers that mar images when copied, and special fibers embedded in strategic locations on bills are some of the methods that will be used more frequently.

In the United States, the Bureau of Engraving will design and issue new currency for the first time in over sixty years, with an aim toward reducing counterfeiting. The National Academy of Sciences established the Committee on Next-Generation Currency Design that will share its findings with the Bureau of Engraving.

The U.S. Treasury Department has begun using security threads, visible by bright light but difficult to reproduce, and microprinting, a process for printing words so small that they cannot be duplicated easily and appear as a straight line to the naked eye. The U.S. State Department is applying the same principles to passports, and the Immigration and Naturalization Service is seeking new ways to secure cards and forms related to an individual's immigration status. In Australia, currency has been redesigned and is being printed on polymer (plastic) stock designed to make copying difficult. Other countries are making comparable changes in their currency.

Unless the computer industry undertakes more comprehensive self-regulation, there will be greater regulatory controls placed on the distribution of computer chips, in part to stem their use in product counterfeiting.

[See also Consumer Protection/Regulation.]

BIBLIOGRAPHY

Bloom, Murray T. *Money of Their Own.* Clinton, OH: BNR Press, 1983.

Rochette, E. C. *Making Money.* Frederick, CO: Renaissance House, 1986.

Rowell, Roland. *Counterfeiting and Forgery.* Stoneham, MA: Butterworth, 1986.

— SHELDON F. GREENBERG

COURTS.

See CRIMINAL JUSTICE; JUDICIAL REFORM; LAWMAKING, JUDICIAL; LAWYERS AND LEGAL PROFESSION.

CREATIVITY

Creativity should be a top priority in preparations for the future because it is critical for forecasts and possible futures and for the construction of preferable futures. Forecasts must recognize a range of possibilities, some of which are entirely hypothetical. To be considered, they must be defined. Creative thought can produce, manipulate, and evaluate hypothetical outcomes. Since the 1950s, influenced by seminal work by J. P. Guilford at the University of Southern California, creative thinking has been viewed as a divergence of thought that allows original insight and the exploration of the hypothetical.

If all relevant information is available, prediction is a matter of calculation. All trends can be used as indicators of what is to come. But the future will be significantly influenced by events about which we have virtually no clues. There are many possible futures, some of which may be largely unrelated to present trends.

They are, however, anticipatable with informed and creative forecasts.

Creativity involves more than the ability

to produce alternatives. It is often expressed

as a kind of adaptive thinking.

Creativity involves more than the ability to produce alternatives. It is often expressed as a kind of adaptive thinking. It is not synonymous with divergent thinking, and not just something that leads to originality. It also involves good judgment and an appreciation of useful and fresh possibilities. This adaptive facet is what makes creativity critical for studies of the future. What could be more important for the future than adaptability? As Jerome Bruner, the Harvard psychologist, suggested, we cannot predict the details of the future, so we must prepare ourselves—and our children—for the unforeseeable. Creativity is an adaptive skill that will allow individuals or organizations to cope with such unforeseeable futures.

One current research program defines creative thought as the ability to integrate and synthesize. Creative thought often uses seemingly discrepant information, such as when a physicist recognizes that light has features of both a wave and a particle. Albert Rothenberg described creative integrations as "janusian," after Janus, the Roman god who kept a simultaneous watch in two opposite directions. Others have noted the ability of creative thought to synthesize the opposites. The point is that this manifestation of creativity may be important for predicting and coping with the future, especially in the midst of the current information explosion. How can we make sense of it all? How can trends be identified? If we think of the diversification of the human population as generating a multitude of perspectives, the question becomes one of integrating diverse opinions, needs, and values. Here again, creativity can help us.

Much of the above implies educational need. The students of the last decade of the twentieth century, and those of the first years of the twenty-first, will need to be more creative than ever before. Fortunately, most educators and parents see the value of creativity. It is not always easy to appreciate or encourage the specific traits that allow creativity, such as nonconformity and independence. It may help educators to know that creativity is a reflection of psychological health. Creativity allows adaptability. Healthy individuals, organizations, and societies will undoubtedly adapt.

One of the most pertinent lines of educational research was initiated by E. Paul Torrance of the University of Georgia. His program, *Future Problem Solving*, focuses on realistic problems, with original and flexible thinking modeled and encouraged. The realistic nature of the tasks distinguishes his work, since many other creativity programs use artificial assignments. This feature also suggests that future problem solving may produce generalizable effects that are useful in the natural environment.

Most educational efforts, including Torrance's, consider creativity to be a special kind of problem solving. Here again we must be careful, for creativity is broader than problem solving; it is also problem finding and problem definition, and certainly is not always reactive. Proactive creativity can be distinguished from passive reactive problem solving. The former is particularly relevant for the construction and selection of preferable futures. Reactive creativity may be useful when dealing with problems as they arise or after the fact. Proactive creativity, on the other hand, can be used to avoid problems, or to adjust and accommodate to them.

Proactive creativity might also operate in the moral domain. Here the need to construct preferable futures is especially clear. Perhaps for this reason, this is an area of recent creativity research. Howard Gruber and Doris Wallace edited a collection of papers on this topic, with a number of contributors noting how creativity can be used to adapt, to solve problems, and to determine directions for effort. Creativity in the moral domain might involve some problem solving, but also involves what Gruber called decisions about what ought to be done to shape the future. The alternatives may be many, if we are creative.

[See also Mind: New Modes of Thinking; Surprises; Visionary Thinking; Wildcards.]

BIBLIOGRAPHY

Gruber, H. E., and Wallace, D., eds. "Creativity in the Moral Domain" special issue. *Creativity Research Journal 6* (1993): 1–200.
Bruner, J. "The Growth of Mind." *American Psychologist* 20 (1965): 1007–1017.
Runco, M. A., ed. *Problem finding, problem solving, and creativity.* Norwood, NJ: Ablex Publishing, 1994.
Shaw, M. P., and Runco, M. A., eds. *Creativity and Affect.* Norwood, NJ: Ablex Publishing, 1994.

— MARK A. RUNCO

CREDIT, DEBT, AND BORROWING

Worldwide there has been an explosion of debt. Governments in the developed world have dramatically increased their debt (see Figure 1), though none as dramatically as the United States (Figure 2). Federal debt in 1993 stood in excess of $4.8 trillion. In the United States, the cost of servicing this debt has exploded (Figure 3), and now represents one of the largest items in the federal budget ($292 billion in 1992 and projected to reach $407 billion by 1998). Corporate debt in 1992 stood at $2.9 trillion, which represents an increasing burden to corporate earnings. American households increased their debt (home mortgages and consumer debt) almost threefold during the 1980s—from $1.3 trillion in 1980 to $3.4 trillion in 1990 and $4.2 trillion in 1993. The average U.S. household owed $35,000 by 1991, and paid interest of $3,500 per year (approximately 18 percent of its disposable income). Many Americans are going into debt to maintain their standard of living. A myriad of credit devices encourage and facilitate the accumulation of debt: credit unions, credit cards, smart cards, super-smart cards, and now debit-loaded cards.

Total debt in the U.S. is rising faster than the GNP. U.S. government debt is rising faster than the U.S. GNP, corporate debt has increased faster than earnings, and consumer debt during the 1980s grew 50 percent faster than consumer income. Total U.S. debt by 1992 stood at approximately $16 trillion.

Furthermore, that figure, however gargantuan, does not include unfunded liabilities—i.e., military and federal civil service pensions and unfunded social security, and the unfunded cost of dealing with the disposal of nuclear wastes. These considerable obligations lock into future spending and represent a "stealth budget" that does not appear in usual government estimates of the debt. However, it does represent an obligation to be paid off by future taxpayers.

Additionally there are large contingent liabilities that the government may or may not be called upon to cover. These contingent obligations include federal deposit insurance, the Federal Pension Benefit Guarantee Fund, crop insurance, flood insurance, and the list goes on and on. Since this category is a contingent liability, it is impossible to estimate a total figure of governmental debt—but some estimates put government debt alone at $16 trillion in 1993, with total governmental and private debt considerably higher.

Business failures are on the upswing (see Figure 4). Commercial bank failures also have grown. Federal bailout of failed banks could add up to as much as $200–400 billion. Luckily, low interest rates have kept disasters to a minimum.

The question that must be asked is how long debt can go on compounding faster than income. Credit cycles inevitably end when the society runs out of creditworthy borrowers and when creditors recognize from the size of the total debt guarantees that much of it must

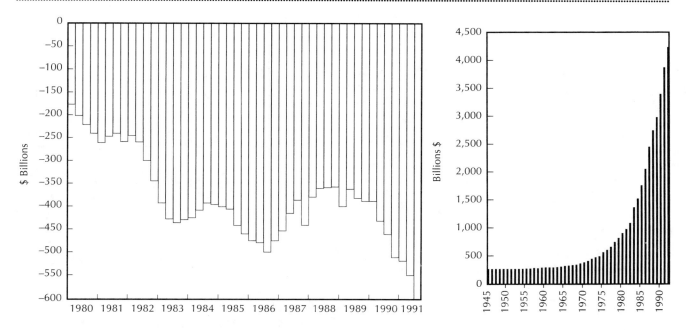

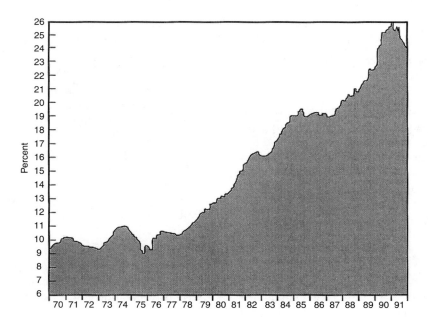

Figure 1. Total quarterly budget deficit for ten representative countries between 1980 and the third quarter of 1991 (the latest quarter for which complete data were available). The countries included (with their percentage of the total for the third quarter of 1991 listed in parentheses) are as follows: United States (44.8%), Italy (22.3%), Japan (16.3%), Germany (5.7%), Canada (4.1%), France (2.9%), Spain (1.9%), United Kingdom (1.5%), Switzerland (0.3%), Australia (0.2%). (International Monetary Fund)

Figure 2. Annual gross federal debt in the United States, 1945–1992 (in billions of dollars).

Figure 3. Federal government interest expense plus outlays for the Resolution Trust Corporation as a percentage of total government budget expenditures. (U.S. Treasury monthly statements.)

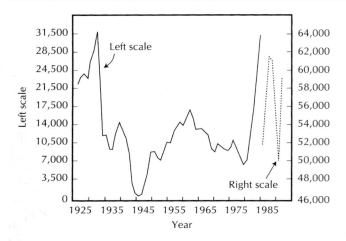

Figure 4. *Business failures in the United States, 1925–1992. Left scale: 1925–1982; right scale: 1985–1992. (Dun & Bradstreet)*

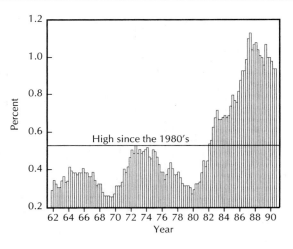

Figure 6. *U.S. mortgage foreclosure rate, 1960–1991. (Mortgage Bankers Association of America)*

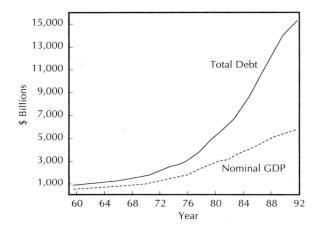

Figure 5. *Divergence of: U.S. debt and ability to serve that debt, 1960–1993. (Department of Commerce, Federal Reserve Flow of Funds)*

keep the accumulated debt from deflating the economy—or if the U.S. will experience an asset liquidation and deflation. Excess is usually followed by contraction.

[*See also* Deficits, Governmental; Economic Cycles: Models and Simulations; Public Finance; Savings; Taxes; Wealth.]

BIBLIOGRAPHY

Davidson, James Dale, and Rees-Mogg, Lord William. *The Great Reckoning.* New York: Summit Books, 1991.
Friedman, Benjamin M. *Day of Reckoning.* New York: Random House, 1988.
Grant, James. *Money of the Mind.* New York: Farrar Straus Giroux, 1992.

— RICHARD D. LAMM

be defaulted. Some believe we are in the terminal phase of a long credit expansion that has far outstripped our ability to service, let alone repay, the debt (see Figure 5). Mortgage foreclosures approached record highs as we entered the 1990s (see Figure 6).

Debt fueled the economy since the end of World War II, a trend which was greatly exacerbated in the 1980s. One author calls it the "democratization of lending and the socialization of risk" where credit is increasingly extended to less credit-worthy people and more and more debt is guaranteed by the federal government. This system allows the maximization of credit, but runs the risk of imploding. Government has already guaranteed far more debt than it could practically pay off without causing an economic disaster.

The question for the future is whether the federal government, by its use of monetary and fiscal tools, can

CRIME, NONVIOLENT

Nonviolent crime, victimless crime, has been defined as "an illegal act in which no one is harmed, or if harm occurs it is negated due to the informed consent of the participants." This definition is predicated on the assumptions that those who provide consent are adults and that harm is caused to the person's body or psyche, property, society, or to personal freedom. Gambling, illegal drug use, pornography, and prostitution are generally classified as victimless crimes.

Types of Victimless Crime

GAMBLING. There has been a spectacular expansion of legal gaming. Industry revenues from lotteries, bingo, casino games, and horse race betting almost tripled in the 1980s to some $300 billion annually. It is forecast that spending on gambling will double by the year 2000. The FBI estimates that far more is still wagered illegally than legally.

The experience of Atlantic City and Las Vegas indicates that development of casinos in urban areas causes a change in community character, including an increase in crime and other undesirable activities such as loan-sharking, pickpocketing, and prostitution. It appears that there is no such thing as "painless prosperity." The cost to society is increased violent and nonviolent crime, a threat of organized crime's participation, and potential corruption of government officials.

PROSTITUTION AND PORNOGRAPHY. Emphasis on the rights of the individual and the liberation of sexual behavior beginning in the 1960s will continue to conflict with certain community attitudes about undesirable sexual conduct. The criminal justice system will continue to struggle with the enforcement of restrictive sexual conduct statutes. Sexual acts that involve violence, incest, and acts against children will be the targets of enforcement action.

"Victimless" sexual conduct, such as prostitution and soft pornography, are considered to present less of a threat to the society. Tenderloin crimes of street prostitution, "skin flick" theaters, and adult book stores will receive little attention in "controlled" districts for two reasons: too few police resources and victimless crime by consenting adults. Senator Daniel Moynihan recently noted this as a degradation of social mores and pointed to society's "redefining deviance so as to exempt much conduct previously stigmatized."

Technological advancements in the distribution of pornography will present many problems for law enforcement. The emerging information technology will reorganize people's recreation as drastically as it has their work environment. Sexually explicit fiction and digitized photographs of naked people are common on the nation's rapidly growing computer networks, as are forums for discussing sexual fantasies.

Because of the international nature of the Internet, creators of sexually explicit material can quickly set up operations overseas or transfer their material to foreign computer networks. Enforcement officers will have to gain additional expertise in collecting evidence that can be presented in court and countering arguments about individual freedom.

Some "cybersex" advocates view virtual reality computer technology as an opportunity. One author says that ". . . ultimately consumers will have virtual reality home-entertainment centers, consisting of three-dimensional stereoscopic displays and control mechanisms, coupled with CD-ROM and some 'sexy' robust software."

Public Disobedience

Public disobedience is related to the amount of social tension in the society. The United States has been undergoing a period of declining trust in government and its ability to provide a quality of life seen by prior generations. Many young people believe that their future standard of living will be lower than that of their parents. Add the increasing legal and illegal immigration (bringing with it differing social, moral, and political views) to the widening economic chasm between rich and poor—and the social crucible will be ripe for increased public disorder. There will be increased potential for ethnic conflicts and domination by single-issue politics.

Society has been experiencing a growing disparity between the haves and the have-nots—in education, economic status, skills, and access to the political arena. As the underclass continues to struggle with the shortage of skills and education necessary to compete in the information job market, homelessness will increase. Those communities with growing shares of lower and welfare class populations and deteriorating economies will face severe budget shortages and have less ability to reverse these conditions.

The number of people in the nation without housing and jobs will result in increased visible panhandling, squatting in abandoned buildings, vagrancy in the form of wandering from place to place in search of subsistence-level existence, and increased levels of disorderly conduct, as the business community tries to have police impose some form of control.

Homelessness is a growing problem in society, and its impact will become more profound in the future as a significant law enforcement issue. Homeless children and families may become a particular concern. Many runaway youths will continue to engage in prostitution—trading sex for survival.

The recognition that a tremendous amount of money is being spent on the enforcement of drugs may force additional legalization of narcotic possession and use. States are no longer able to continue to fill jails with drug law violators while reducing sentences for violent criminals due to lack of jail space. Many leading figures call for legalization to remove the profit from the drug trade and slash drug-related crime, arguing that government efforts to eradicate drug use through punishment have only aggravated the problem. Some advocate the legalization of heroin, marijuana, and cocaine. Legalization advocates propose high taxes on legalized drugs so that the drug consumers will pay for the networks of regulation, education programs, administration, and rehabilitation efforts for those who want to escape their dependence.

Opponents say that the legalization of drugs would only create more drug users and turn casual users into addicts. Two questions will have to be addressed. First is the problem of how the new legal drugs would be controlled and distributed, and at what level of government such a system would operate. Second, as the scientific search continues for more understanding of how the brain works, some criminals will learn to alter the chemistry of moods and sexual desire.

Homelessness is a growing problem in society,

and its impact will become more profound

in the future as a significant law enforcement issue.

During the 1990s, the advance of elementary genetic engineering may make it possible for the commercial production of Beta-endorphins, replacing morphine and cocaine as a local anesthetic. By the turn of the century, understanding of the body's own mood-monitoring system may progress to the point where it will be possible to reset the "chemostat" regulating the body's own production of mood-altering hormones. Scientific advances in chemical methods of altering individual mood have been adopted by the illegal drug manufacturers. The drugs may be produced so easily and changed so rapidly that society may not be able to regulate their production and use.

Crimes Against Property

Computer-related crime is one of the most challenging problems facing law enforcement today and in the future. Most people are aware of hackers: those who surreptitiously enter computer systems to destroy or steal data, intentionally and maliciously. However, of more concern are the insiders who have the confidence of management and then betray that confidence with fraud, embezzlement, larceny, and sometimes even sabotage.

The growing popularity of computers has provided the latest opportunity resource for criminal misuse. This is largely because computers are being frequently employed to provide direct access to cash or merchandise. The proliferation of smaller, more powerful computers combined with the changing nature of American business will contribute greatly to an increasing rate of computer crime. The computer literacy of the nation is rising rapidly as "user-friendly" computer hardware and software make them easier to use. The result is more savvy computer users, with access to more computers and their data, offering innumerable possibilities for data manipulation, vandalism, and theft.

The ability of local jurisdictions to comprehend, identify, investigate, and prosecute high-tech, electronic crimes—involving illegal access and transfers of mon-

ies, information altering, or sabotage—will be sorely tested.

Computer crimes fall into four main categories: internal computer disruptions such as the planting of viruses or logic bombs; telecommunicating crimes like "phone phreaking" (hacking or misusing the telephone system); computer manipulation crimes such as embezzlement or frauds; activities in support of criminal enterprises, like money laundering or selling of criminal information to criminal syndicates; and hardware/software piracy.

High-technology crimes will have a significant impact on police budgets because of the complexity of the cases. Estimates range from four months to a year for thorough investigations. Computer crimes may extend into several jurisdictions and even into other states or countries. Law enforcement strategies must include better on-site investigative ability; better ability to store properly the computer hardware and software seized in investigations; understanding between law enforcement and corporate businesses of each others' capabilities and clarification of each others' roles regarding computer-related crime; establishment of regional task forces to investigate computer crime; and ability to have contractual services for computer-related crimes in need of such expertise.

Tax Evasion

In the United States, the underground economy is estimated at between 10 and 28 percent of the gross national product. Internal Revenue Service (IRS) researchers suggest that almost all hidden labor is paid in currency and that the balance of underground activity is perhaps 50 percent cash. As the economy remains stagnant and a larger portion of the underclass struggles with reduced resources, there will be more barter for services. The exchange of services for other services siphons tax revenue from governmental entities. Law enforcement may be called upon to enforce tax collection on barter-type activity.

[See also Alcohol; Behavior: Social Constraints; Child Abuse; Civil Protest; Counterfeiting; Crime Rates; Drugs, Illicit; Espionage and Counterintelligence; Gambling; Sexual Codes; Sexual Laws; Social Controls; Taxes.]

BIBLIOGRAPHY

Albanese, Jay S., and Pursley, Robert D. *Crime in America: Some Existing and Emerging Issues.* Englewood Cliff, NJ: Regents/Prentice Hall, 1993.
"New Puzzle: High-Tech Pedophilia." *Los Angeles Times,* March 5, 1993.
"Pot, Heroin Unlock New Areas for Neuroscience." *Science* (December 18, 1992).

Roberts, Sam. *Who We Are: A Portrait of America Based on the Latest U.S. Census.* New York: Random House/Times Books, 1993.
"Tomorrow's Thieves." *Futurist* (September-October 1988).
"Trends in Crime, Punishment, Race, and Drugs: The Connections Emerge." *Future Scan* (May 17, 1993).

— RUSSELL KINDERMAN

CRIME, ORGANIZED

Organized crime is structured, goal-directed criminal activity organized as a profit-making enterprise. The relationships and hierarchy in any organized-crime group are based largely on personalities, power, influence, success, and loyalty. Although organized-crime groups often operate somewhat like businesses, their structure is usually more unconventional. Organized crime is *profit-motivated,* attempting to earn money through unlawful means. Violence is not its goal—it is a tool used to obtain and maintain compliance in order for the organization to flourish. While the focus of this essay is on North America, organized crime exists worldwide.

The most common vision of organized crime is the "traditional" Cosa Nostra, or the Mafia, with roots in Italian and Sicilian "families." The reference to families is twofold: the first is a family of persons related by blood or marriage. The second refers to a strong kinship of trust and respect among a group of people with common (in this case, criminal) goals, values, and beliefs.

La Cosa Nostra is noteworthy because of its prominence and rapid expansion during Prohibition, when sales of liquor provided vast profits for expansion of the organization into gambling and prostitution while permitting it to maintain its interests in theft, black marketing, and loan sharking. Lucrative profits from illegitimate activities also permitted investments in legitimate businesses, blurring the distinction between lawful and unlawful activities.

The Mafia did not start during Prohibition; it simply grew during that time. It has not been eliminated—or even seriously thwarted—as a result of the convictions of high-level members in recent years. Like most large organizations, Cosa Nostra is readily able to replace its leaders with new ones from within its ranks. Recent assessments of the Mafia find that it is becoming more sophisticated in its operating practices and uses of technology. The organization grows increasingly complex as new layers of corporate entities are added, further integration with legitimate businesses proceeds, and alliances are formed with other organized-crime groups. These trends will not only continue, but are likely to grow over the next decade as social, political, and economic conditions change.

Despite the traditional view of organized crime as synonymous with La Cosa Nostra, there are other organized-crime groups, some of which have been growing rapidly recently. Among these, some but not all are ethnically based.

Latin America and the Caribbean

The organized-crime groups best known in this region are the Colombian Medellín and Cali cartels, which concentrate on the vastly profitable cocaine trafficking and money laundering. The profits from drug trafficking have been invested in legitimate businesses, stocks, and U.S. real estate. Power in these cartels is concentrated, and it is delegated to a much lesser degree than in La Cosa Nostra. Nevertheless, the Colombian groups are extensive, with regional drug distribution networks throughout North America, and possibly expanding into Western Europe via agreements with La Cosa Nostra. Beyond the Colombian cartels, there also are smaller Peruvian and Bolivian cartels involved in cocaine trafficking.

Also well known are the Jamaican "posses" which have been surprisingly evident throughout the United States, often involving Jamaican residents. These posses are involved in drug trafficking and often deal with "competitors" through violent acts including maiming and disfigurement. While the presence of Jamaican posses has diminished somewhat, they remain active in the drug trade, predominantly in large cities.

Eastern Europe and Central Asia

Ethnically based organized-crime groups in Eastern Europe and Central Asia are perhaps among the fastest growing, resulting from the breakup of the Soviet Union, the movement of Eastern European countries toward market-based economies, reduced government controls and surveillance, and changes in Western Europe associated with the European Community. European Community developments facilitating criminal activity include the virtual elimination of border controls, new laws that make international business transactions easier, and relaxed transnational monetary regulations. Organized crime may be taking more rapid advantage of these factors than legal businesses. Impact of such expansion already has touched North America and will likely increase significantly.

European organized crime has focused largely on consumer goods. Shipments of products are stolen and sold on the black market. If there is a demand for a product, it is a potential target. In one case, organized crime groups were found to have stolen radioactive material with the intent to sell it to the highest bidder. These groups also have been involved in counterfeiting various consumer goods (jeans, tennis shoes, watches, videotapes, and other consumer items), and even in the theft of counterfeit items produced by other organized-crime groups. Given the changing world economic market to one of free enterprise and consumerism, it is likely this activity will continue to expand.

Central Asian organized-crime groups, largely in the southeastern republics of the former Soviet Union, also are involved in black marketing. They tend, however, to be more actively involved in drug trafficking, terrorism, and political insurgency. Preliminary indicators suggest that the economic successes of organized crime activity may be more rewarding than any political accomplishments. Growth and expansion in these criminal enterprises can be expected.

Pacific Rim

The presence of organized-crime groups from the Pacific Rim clearly exists in North America. Hong Kong Chinese, ethnic Chinese, Taiwanese, and Thai elements exist in the United States and Canada. To a large extent their role provides "supply and support" for other organized-crime groups in Asia and the Pacific. More prevalent and better established in North America are Japanese, Vietnamese, and Korean crime groups. Their involvement in drug trafficking (mostly in heroin) has grown substantially, but they are also involved in loan sharking, black marketing, and, to a lesser degree, "protection" rackets.

Most notorious of the Pacific Rim organized-crime groups are the Japanese Triads—highly organized crime cartels characterized by loyalty, rigid structure, and aggressive ruthlessness. The focal leadership of the Triads remains in Japan; however, their presence is pervasive throughout North America. Although extremely difficult to penetrate, the Triads seem not only to have investments in legitimate businesses, both in North America and Japan, but also government ties in Japan. The sociocultural characteristics with which Japanese industry has been so successful are magnified in the Triads. As a result, they may emerge as a "world crime cartel" in the not too distant future.

Gangs

Traditionally viewed simply as groups of local, frequently violent juvenile delinquents interested in protecting their "turf," gangs are in transition. Gangs increasingly are involved in drug trafficking, theft, extortion, and other crimes at the local, regional, and national levels. It is difficult to make any meaningful generalizations about gangs as a form of organized crime, simply because they vary so much. Gangs tend to be neither very sophisticated nor well organized (e.g., the "Crips" and "Bloods" of Los Angeles). They are formed largely along racial or ethnic lines and tend to cooperate predominantly with similar ethnic groups.

Alliances are generally short-term and informal. Despite these factors, a growing number of these gangs are taking on characteristics of organized crime. If these trends continue, gangs are likely to become a more dominant force, particularly at the local level.

Diverse organized-crime groups will continue to flourish for two reasons: they are profitable and are difficult to prosecute successfully.

Summary

Diverse organized-crime groups will continue to flourish for two reasons: they are profitable and are difficult to prosecute successfully. Given the diversity of the groups, increased competition for their respective "markets" is likely. While violence will always be a part of organized crime, it does not appear that the future competition will be as bloody as that between the Cosa Nostra groups in the 1920s. Rather, competition is more likely to involve aggressive marketing tactics. Organized-crime leaders of today are more sophisticated and future-oriented than their predecessors were. They recognize that violence will attract law enforcement and public attention, both of which are "bad for business." Over the years, organized-crime groups have shown creativity and resourcefulness. Intellectual property, information crimes, and high technology all appear to be areas that organized crime will pursue with vigor.

[See also Crime, Nonviolent: Crime, Violent; Crime Rates; Drugs, Illicit; Terrorism.]

BIBLIOGRAPHY

Abadinsky, Howard. *Organized Crime,* 2nd ed. Chicago, Ill.: Nelson-Hall Publishers, 1988.
Booth, Martin. *The Triads.* London: Grafton Books, 1990.
Fox, Stephen. *Blood and Power: Organized Crime in Twentieth Century America.* New York: Penguin Books, 1989.
President's Commission on Organized Crime. *The Impact: Organized Crime Today.* Washington, DC: U.S. Government Printing Office, 1986.

– DAVID L. CARTER

CRIME, VIOLENT

Violence is a complex social problem occurring under a wide variety of circumstances and conditions produced by the interaction of many factors. Levels of violence have increased worldwide, becoming so pervasive in America, that the U.S. Center for Disease Control now characterizes violence as a public health problem.

Indeed, the leading cause of death among young black men is homicide.

Crime

Violent crime results from such varied forms of behavior and circumstances that it cannot be solved by any blanket remedy. Each type of violence must be combated through a response tailored to the special nature of the act (such as domestic violence, rape, drive-by shootings, robberies, and so forth). Violent behavior is heterogeneous, and heterogeneous approaches are needed to deal with it.

The number of assaults, homicides, robberies, and criminal sexual assaults continues to rise disproportionately to population increases. In cities such as Detroit and St. Louis, the number of violent crimes continues to rise, even though the population is decreasing.

A violent crime that emerged in the early 1990s is "car jacking." This is a robbery wherein a driver is confronted by a menacing or armed thief who steals the car. In a number of incidents victims have been assaulted or even killed. The crime attracted such notoriety that a federal law was passed prohibiting it.

Weapons

The frequency and intensity of violence is related to the availability of weapons, although weapons availability alone is not "the cause" of violence. The availability of firearms and the increased capacity of firepower, particularly in semiautomatic weapons, contributes to the seriousness of violent acts. While not as pervasive, there also has been an increase in the use of nonlethal weapons, such as knives, tear gas, and stun guns. Underscoring the awareness of growing violence, criminals have protected themselves with body armor similar to that worn by police officers.

Drug Trade

There can be no doubt that violence is escalated by drug trafficking. Violence and drugs interact in several ways, notably in the cities. National Institute of Justice Drug Use Forecasting (DUF) findings show that a high proportion of persons commit crimes while under the influence of drugs. Twenty of twenty-four cities testing arrestees for the presence of drugs found that over 50 percent of them tested positive for at least one drug. In Manhattan, DUF data showed that 79 percent of those arrested tested positive for some drug. Research further shows that a number of criminals use drugs in order to "build up their courage" to commit a crime. Criminals under the influence of drugs are likely to respond violently if confronted by a citizen or police officer.

Competing drug trafficking organizations, when attempting to dominate drug markets and to gain control of a geographic area, also resort to violence. Drive-by shootings used by competing groups to discourage competition are particularly noteworthy. While drive-by shootings are also used for other motives, they are most common in drug dealing. The Jamaican "posses" earned a notorious reputation by shooting indiscriminately at a group of people in order to be certain that their target was killed.

Human Interaction

To understand violent behavior, it is necessary to understand how people interact. Trends in violence over the past decade indicate growing tolerance for and reliance on violent behavior and aggression rather than negotiation to resolve conflict. In other words, when people engage in conflict, there is a greater tendency to resolve it through aggressive behavior rather than through negotiation. In increasing numbers, this aggression might be described as "mindless or motiveless violence." People have been killed over trivial arguments related to cooking food, possession of clothing, and spilled beer. Similarly, ramming cars, dropping objects on vehicles from expressway overpasses, and motorists shooting at each other became so commonplace that the California Highway Patrol began keeping statistics on "freeway violence."

Media portrayals of violence may contribute to aggressive behavior. Consistent exposure to violent acts in media portrayals "teach" violence as a response to conflict and people essentially "learn" aggression through sustained exposure to these actions.

Schools

Violence and aggression in the nation's schools has reached unprecedented levels. Contrary to popular belief, these problems are not limited to inner-city schools, but also encompass rural and suburban areas. Nor is the problem just in the high schools—middle and elementary schools also have experienced increases in violent behavior.

Violent acts can be characterized as "student-on-student" and "student-on-teacher" aggression. Both types have increased. The presence of guns and knives has risen significantly. One estimate from the Center for Handgun Violence is that on any given day 100,000 students go to school with a gun. The number of schools that employed security guards, established their own police force, or installed metal detectors to screen persons entering the school are further indicators of this escalating problem.

Surprisingly, drugs and violence in schools do not seem to be strongly correlated. In fact, violence and aggression appear to be more pervasive in schools than are drug and alcohol abuse. This is particularly evident when examined across all grade levels. Still, drugs and alcohol do contribute to a general atmosphere of disorder which, in turn, creates an environment conducive to violence. Other contributing factors include an increased number of children who have experienced fetal alcohol syndrome (which entails consequential behavioral problems); increasing numbers of students with attention deficit disorder; significant court and/or administrative restrictions on school disciplinary policies; reduced parental involvement in both the educational process and discipline; and changing values and lifestyles among youth. These are long-term, endemic problems which require aggressive and sustained intervention. Consequently, levels of violence, aggression, and disorder in the schools will likely continue to increase into the foreseeable future.

Levels of violence have increased worldwide, becoming so pervasive in America that the U.S. Center for Disease Control now characterizes violence as a public health problem.

Terrorism

Until the carefully planned and coordinated attack on the World Trade Center in February 1994, there had been relatively few international terrorist attacks in North America, due to our comparative geographic isolation, effective intelligence operations, prevention initiatives, and limited numbers of sympathizers to the ideologies of Middle Eastern or other terrorist groups. These groups had found that terrorist targets in the United States were simply too difficult and expensive to attack. Heightened security measures in the aftermath of the World Trade Center tragedy may reinstate that opinion, but the feeling that the United States is somehow immune to terrorism has been at the very least greatly reduced, if not eliminated.

The Irish Republican Army (IRA) generally has had no desire to stage terrorism in the United States because it receives contributions and support from some members of the Irish-American community that the IRA does not want to offend. Abroad, terrorism remains an on-going problem. U.S. targets—embassies, military bases, and U.S. citizens—remain more vulnerable, but attacks are still relatively rare. Given the changes in world politics, only carefully orchestrated attacks against U.S. targets are likely to come about.

Domestic terrorism is different but still relatively rare. This encompasses violent behavior by groups in the United States who oppose American laws, policies, and sociopolitical trends. In the 1960s, extreme political leftist groups—e.g., the Weathermen and Students for a Democratic Society (SDS)—were responsible for various terrorist acts. While these groups are largely gone, they have been replaced by political ideologues, predominantly of the extreme right. Groups such as the Aryan Nations, the Order, the Covenant, Sword, and Arm of the Lord, and neo-Nazis seek a white, Protestant America with limited governmental controls. They particularly support violent acts against minorities, Jews, homosexuals, and people who support these groups. Right-wing groups are well-armed ideologues who possess the potential for increased terrorist violence, at least in geographic pockets.

Riots

Mounting evidence suggests that riots may again emerge in the United States. While the 1960s riots were focused on institutional change related to the civil rights movement and the Vietnam War, the impetus for riots in the future will be different. Deteriorating economic conditions, growing chasms between white America and people of color, decaying urban America, and the growing political power of the affluent at the expense of the shrinking middle class and the poor will ignite future riots. Moreover, according to FBI agent and futurist William Tafoya, the riots of the future will surpass those of the 1960s in duration, intensity, and violence. In the past four years there have been civil disorders in Miami, Shreveport, New York, Virginia Beach, and Los Angeles. The signs of stress are emerging on our campuses and in our cities. The future holds a strong potential for violent unrest unless actions are taken to temper the social, economic, and political strains currently emerging.

Summary

Violence is a learned phenomenon which becomes part of the behavioral pathology of a culture. It has been molded by a series of complex, interactive patterns over a generation which cannot be changed in the short term. As a result, it is unlikely that levels of violence will decrease over the next few years. Violent acts will probably increase, albeit at a slower rate, in the coming years until institutional change reshapes the behavioral patterns of the next generation.

[See also Child Abuse; Crime, Nonviolent; Crime, Organized; Crime Rates; Drugs, Illicit; Law Enforcement; Lethal Weapons; Terrorism.]

BIBLIOGRAPHY

Bastian, Lisa, and Taylor, Bruce. *School Crime.* Washington, DC: Bureau of Justice Statistics, 1991.

Caught in the Crossfire: A Report on Gun Violence in the Nation's Schools. Washington, DC: Center to Prevent Handgun Violence, 1991.

Cromwell, Paul, et al. *Breaking and Entering: An Ethnographic Analysis of Burglary.* Newbury Park, CA: Sage Publishing Company, 1991.

National Institute of Justice. *Drug Use Forecasting—Second Quarter 1992.* Washington, DC: U.S. Department of Justice, 1992.

Rohr, Janelle. *Violence in America: Opposing Viewpoints.* San Diego, CA: Greenhaven Press, 1990.

Tafoya, William L. "Rioting in the Streets: Déjà Vu?" *CJ the Americas* 2:6 (1990):1, 19–23.

— DAVID L. CARTER
JOHN H. CAMPBELL

CRIME RATES

Soaring crime erodes America's social fabric. Rampant crime is associated with declining morals, breakdown of traditional values, liberalized codes that define criminal conduct more permissively, individual rights delinked from social responsibilities, pursuit of self-expression without self-control, tolerant attitudes toward criminal behavior, weak law enforcement and crime detection methods, overemphasis on criminal rights to the virtual exclusion of victim rights, and softening of penalties that detract from deterrence of criminal behavior. Further aggravating this pervasive social malaise are public indifference and tolerance for the turmoil, havoc, despair, and even death.

Rules that govern "acceptable" social behavior have been eroded. Forms of misbehavior once forbidden by criminal codes are now excused. These radical reversals in basic principles of criminal law, which reflect what society will and will not tolerate, occurred in just a few decades. The spiral downward has been swift and pervasive. The following cursory review reveals how ethics and morals that once anchored social order have been reversed.

Mugging has become so commonplace, and chances of tracking down culprits so slim, that no follow-up is likely and most of these crimes go unreported. This is a bonanza for strongarm hoodlums who shy away from burglary because mugging provides quick cash with no fencing of stolen goods, and no sting operations to get trapped by.

Unruly civil disturbances previously constituted a breach of the public peace and were repressed. All too often perpetrators are allowed to wreak destruction, take property, and otherwise threaten or endanger others. Demagogic politicians frequently encourage civil disobedience—in overly zealous pursuit of civil rights that occasionally escalate into full-scale riot and rebellion.

On a communitywide scale, looting Los Angeles-style carries personal property crimes to new heights. Offenders may be let free to run their course. Full force

of repression, the kind of police response that used to be fielded to protect citizens and to cut short and deter further uprisings of a violent nature, now is downplayed, and rioters on a spree are given license to "do their thing." A hands-off attitude encourages mob frenzy. When things get out of hand and authorities no longer are able to provide protection, government lets the public absorb the brunt of the unruly mob. Rights of the mob are allowed to prevail over individual rights. Because police shy from using whatever may be required to protect life and limb or private property, some victims in these powder kegs organize armed vigilantes. For their efforts, they sometimes wind up themselves being prosecuted for illegal conduct.

Union hooliganism far too often resorts to vandalism, sabotage, beatings, bullying, and belligerent threats. Strikebreakers often fear for their personal safety. Unions, initially intended to redress power disparities between workers and management, sometimes are intentionally used to force capitulation, even if it means forcing a business into bankruptcy or out of business. Such an abuse of power seems to be "too hot a potato" for politicians to address.

Environmental extremists seem to be given wide latitude, even when they pursue harmful tactics. Monkey-wrenching—spiking trees or sabotaging equipment, for example—sometimes causes lumberjack or sawmill worker deaths. Extremist acts in defense of admirable objectives never should be tolerated.

Parking tickets, a bane and a bother to drivers (but a boon to nearby merchants), are allowed to pile up. Scofflaws may get hailed into court when the number of tickets mount. In Tokyo, where parking tickets can draw fines of $2,000 each, a different incentive applies.

Communities into which parolees are released are forbidden from notifying neighborhoods of potential threats, even from dangerous repeat offenders. Unleashing risky repeat offenders upon an unwary community respects criminals' rights over those of the community upon whom they prey. Criminals used to go to jail—and stay there. Now, early release from prison, weekend passes, and other humanitarian-inspired methods seek to reintegrate ex-convicts into society. All too often these well-intentioned efforts go awry. In a recent presidential election, the Willie Horton incident (involving a felon parolee who committed another grievous crime following early release from prison) became a major campaign issue. At least nine states have taken steps to abolish early release from prison terms.

Vagrants and loiterers—who used to be characterized as bums, hobos, drifters, and so on—once were tossed into jail or run out of town. Now they are housed, clothed, fed, and cared for by government. Street people are permitted to construct shantytowns or hovels on public grounds in a manner that effectively runs the general public out. A long-suffering public is expected to endure these depredations. Panhandlers and beggars, once confined to skid rows, the Bowery, or similar areas, have spread communitywide. Panhandling locations even are approved by government, the only restriction being to mooch in nonthreatening ways.

Shoplifting and pilferage have reached epidemic proportions. Thieves, especially juveniles, all too often are let off scot-free or with a mere slap on the wrist. Making up losses from pilferage adds about 10 percent to retail prices. In addition, store security systems and guards, electronic or explosive-dye security tags, hidden surveillance cameras, parking lot patrols, and so on add incrementally to costs.

Usury once was the domain of loan sharks and unscrupulous predators. Pawnshops that used to extort interest on pledged goods effectively amounting to 20 percent to 25 percent or higher were largely driven out of business. At least for the present time, it has become permissible for credit card firms, banks, and other credit givers to charge exorbitant rates hovering close to 20 percent, a rate previously held to be usurious.

Debtor prisons have given way to revolving-door bankruptcy. Profligacy is rewarded by wiping the slate clean and letting perpetrators take another round at bilking honest businesses and citizens.

Automatic guns, assault rifles, machine pistols, guns with unprecedented firepower, clips that carry hundreds of rounds, and ever larger bores—all once strictly prohibited—can be openly or clandestinely purchased virtually anywhere. Kids tote deadly weapons to school. Schools respond with metal detectors, surveillance, frisking, and locker searches. Civil rights advocates wince. Worse, the number of young Americans killed by guns was up twofold, rising from 1,059 in 1970 to 2,162 in 1990. Kids accidentally shooting kids sometimes results in parents being charged with reckless endangerment. To deter such mishaps, laws require trigger guards and other locks or tamper-resistant features.

Drive-by shootings have become rites of passage for some youth gang members. "Mushrooms" or accidental victims caught in crossfire, many of them babies and children, have become all too frequent. Gun control efforts falter. More than 20,000 gun laws already on the law books in 1988 apparently have done little to stem the tide of gun violence that wracks society. Twice the number of Americans were killed by firearms at home as were killed in Vietnam (84,633 versus 46,752). In a pitiful show of political courage, politicians have zeroed in on geyserlike squirt guns and proposed legislation banning their sale. So-called super-soakers are little more than bothersome and certainly not lethal. Legis-

lators also seek to minimize realistic mock guns and children's toy guns in committing real crimes. Because "toys" involve no deadly force potential, perpetrators can get off on reduced charges not involving real guns. Turning the tables on victims, some criminals have been able to sue police or citizens who respond to the confrontation with toy guns by shooting perpetrators. To distinguish such toys and replicas, red-tipped muzzles or other identifying marks have been proposed.

Crime profits in 1994 worldwide amounted to

an estimated $1 trillion, half of it from drugs.

America's most valuable crop

was marijuana in the mid-1990s.

Drug abuse contributes to escalating crime. Addicts who pursue a life of crime to support drug habits have spawned the worst crime wave in U.S. history. Crime profits in 1994 worldwide amounted to an estimated $1 trillion, half of it in drugs. Illegal drugs generated an estimated $500 billion worldwide in 1954. America's most valuable crop is marijuana, with a value exceeding $32 billion in the mid-1990s. The value of the nation's most important food crops—corn at $14 billion, and soybeans at $11 billion—pale by comparison.

Some states imposed tax stamps on illegal drugs to help facilitate prosecution and seizure of untaxed drugs. Stamp collectors responded by scooping them up. Against this sordid backdrop of illicit drugs, the Presidential Commission on Marijuana and Drug Abuse Decriminalization, under President Carter, advocated decriminalization in 1977. The Netherlands tried lax enforcement, open drug areas, and clean-needle exchange between 1978 and 1995; results are unclear. A few jurisdictions tolerate or actually legalize drugs—Christiana, Denmark; North Rhine-Westphalia, Germany; and Amsterdam among them. U.S. litigation permits marijuana for medicinal purposes. As of January 1991, several dozen persons have been authorized to rely upon such therapy.

Alcohol abuse is abetted by government-run stores in some jurisdictions. At least one jurisdiction offers private government brands for exclusive sale in government-owned and -run shops (Montgomery County, Maryland). Sales of alcoholic beverages were formerly restricted to a few licensed outlets with rigidly controlled hours of operation intended to limit sales. Now alcoholic beverages are increasingly available from almost any retailer. The pain and suffering linked to alcohol abuse impose costly burdens. One of every thirteen American adults is an alcoholic. Fetal alcohol syndrome ranks as the third most common cause of birth defects, afflicting, 4,000 to 12,000 victims annually.

Sobriety checkpoints attempt to stem alcohol-related motorcar mayhem. Yet, one-third of the states outlaw these checkpoints as an infringement on free movement and an invasion of privacy. Some jurisdictions make providers of excess alcohol liable for ensuing acts of their drunken guests. Taking such incidental liability one step farther, persons who fail to stop obviously inebriated individuals who come across their path (such as gas station attendants who might have an opportunity to intervene) have been held liable for ensuing damages caused by persons they failed to detain. Sweden pursues an economic route (among others) to discourage alcohol consumption. To dissuade public drinking, Swedish restaurants charge about $22 for a double martini.

Sobriety measurement devices at bars sometimes encourage "good ole boys" to vie with bar buddies to see who can consume enough alcohol to blow the meters off the scale. Unobtrusive breath analyzers built into police flashlights are assailed as an invasion of privacy or illegal search. Ignition interlocks making it difficult for inebriates to start cars may be required for drivers repeatedly convicted for driving under the influence.

Gambling, once forbidden by government, has become a government monopoly. Numbers and lotteries have been taken over by the government. Adding insult to injury, governments wantonly encourage gambling through mass advertising campaigns. All other manner of gaming, from casinos and riverboats to slots, roulette, cards, and off-track betting, is being authorized on an unprecedented scale. Legal gambling mushroomed into a $300 billion enterprise in 1992, plus another estimated $40 billion in illegal gaming. In European Union nations, gambling ranked as the twelfth-largest industry in 1989.

Government corruption, bribes, and kickbacks also have reached all-time highs. The morality of elected officials from presidents to mayors is being questioned. But despite their personal shortcomings, voters elect them.

Health insurance fraud burgeons. A few years ago an estimated $60 billion, or 10 percent of health-care costs, were siphoned off in this manner. An estimated 20 percent of all automobile insurance payments are diverted to bogus claims. Citizen attitudes toward "deep pocket" providers have waned.

White-collar crime accounts for as much as ten times the amount stolen in street crime. Yet only one of ten perpetrators receives a sentence.

Embezzlement and fraud took four times more money stealthily out of banks than robbers took out the front door during the early 1990s. And the stakes are enormous. Charles Keating's failed Lincoln Savings & Loan may have cost taxpayers up to $2 billion.

Champerty and barratry—ambulance-chasing—encourage litigation. Fomenting spurious litigation—including mass media inducements—encourages feigned injuries and frivolous lawsuits.

Enforcement of truancy laws, previously strictly enforced, has become lax. Today, when major enforcement is undertaken, it's a news event. Spanking, once used to drive home moral lessons, has been outlawed in some jurisdictions. In the name of child abuse, parents and guardians are forbidden to use physical reprimands.

Juvenile crime is largely hidden from public view. Mollycoddling may be a misguided effort intended to protect youth from notoriety that could adversely affect the rest of their lives. Because kids cannot be prosecuted as adults, callous drug dealers use them as "mules" to shield drug pushers from being charged with physical possession of illegal drugs. Only occasionally are hardened, repeat offenders, or those charged with especially horrendous crimes, tried as adults.

Law enforcement officers used to respond to violence with armed force. Now trained riot troops are armed with rubber bullets, water cannons, electronic prods, disabling "sticky-goo," and tear gas. Even regular tear gas has been judged too dangerous, and pepper compounds have been substituted. Police uniforms used to be sufficient to deter harm being directed their way. Now police wear protective vests, helmets, shields, and so on. Everyday policing involves a retreat from excessive or deadly force. "Speak first and hold fire" has become the rule, increasing chances of police officers being shot. The number of police officers shot dead in the line of duty doubled between 1961 and 1989, increasing from 73 to 146 deaths.

"Cop killer" bullets—ammunition with Teflon coatings or hollow points—are permitted. At least one jurisdiction, frustrated at an inability to directly ban guns, attempted to limit gun use by outlawing the sale of ammunition. Like so many other well-intentioned efforts, this approach has been overturned.

Historically the death penalty has had a checkered use. Between 1968 and 1976, nobody sentenced for a capital crime in the United States was executed. Since then, many states have reinstated the death penalty. In 1992, thirty-one persons were executed.

Retreat from hot pursuit is another limitation on law enforcement. High-speed chases that might expose innocent civilians to danger must be terminated. Thugs, as a result, sometimes resort to chase evasion in the sanctuary of crowded neighborhoods. Another hobbling influence involves search and seizure. Evidence gleaned is subject to severely restricting strictures.

Sophisticated crime detection methods—including DNA type matching—undergo severe impediments. Meticulous procedures and burdensome costs discourage effective use. Fingerprint use and blood sample matching have undergone similar introductory ordeals.

Myriad restraints impede policing. A "subway vigilante" (Bernhard Goetz), after being mugged several times with impunity, took things into his own hands and shot the next group of hoodlums that attempted to rob him. He was tried and convicted on a variety of charges for his "misdeed." In like manner, in the midst of the Los Angeles riots, Korean shopkeepers, upon recognizing the absence of effective police protection, organized their own armed vigilante groups.

Self-expression is no excuse for lack of self-control.

The operative principle of moral codes is restraint.

Regular citizens have become prisoners in their own homes. They retreat into walled communities, or erect antitheft barricades and alarms to protect themselves. Organized crime and gangs rule certain neighborhoods or areas. Freedom of association protects such groups. Criminal rights prevail over the broader community interest. An overly tolerant attitude prevails in society today. Indiscriminate acceptance of any and every idea, of every act of individual expression, is, quite simply, wrong. Permissiveness—doing your own thing with impunity and total disregard for the rights of others— cannot be allowed to infringe obtrusively on and compromise or ruin the rights of others. Self-expression is no excuse for lack of self-control. The operative principle of moral codes is restraint. The fact is that toleration has its limits. Liberty is not license. Codes of acceptable behavior that have been reversed a full 180 degrees to accommodate individual rights may be swinging back to broader social obligations.

Criminals these days seem to have more going for them than their victims do. In the interest of preserving individual freedom and minimizing the potential heavy-handedness of a repressive police state, attitudes toward those accused of criminal conduct have been softened. Thus criminal codes have given way to the rights of accused (perpetrators). Bending over too far in pursuit of protecting individual freedom impairs civil liberties communitywide and threatens the lives of everybody else.

This review highlights where these changes have taken us. Criminal codes must increasingly be scrutinized as to focus. Social or community interests will have to be reasserted to make streets safe once again. Political leaders in the years ahead will be compelled to take stock and to rethink whether current trends and directions in criminal law are appropriate to the times.

[See also Behavior: Social Constraints; Child Abuse; Civil Protest; Counterfeiting; Crime, Nonviolent; Crime, Organized; Crime, Violent; Criminal Justice; Criminal Punishment; Drugs, Illicit; Law Enforcement; Lethal Weapons; Prisons; Sexual Codes; Sexual Laws; Social Controls; Terrorism.]

BIBLIOGRAPHY

Bouza, Anthony V. *The Police Mystique: An Insider's Look at Cops, Crime, and the Criminal Justice System.* New York: Plenum Press, 1990.

Currie, Elliott. *Confronting Crime: An American Challenge.* New York: Pantheon Books, 1985.

DiIolio, John J., Jr. *No Escape: The Future of American Corrections.* New York: Basic Books, 1991.

Gordon, Diana R. *The Justice Juggernaut: Fighting Street Crime, Controlling Citizens.* New Brunswick, NJ: Rutgers University Press, 1990.

Lurigio, Arthur J., et al., eds. *Victims of Crime: Problems, Policies, and Programs.* Newbury Park, CA: Sage Publications, 1990.

U.S. Bureau of the Census. *Statistical Abstract of the United States, 1994.* Washington, DC: U.S. Government Printing Office, 1994.

— GRAHAM T. T. MOLITOR

CRIMINAL JUSTICE

Technology and politics, two separate but interrelated forces, are likely to be the primary forces driving future developments in the criminal justice field. In the short run, rationality, democratic values, and compassion are likely to give way to fear, rejection of the principle of proportionality, and repression.

Fear, rationally based or not, has reinforced a social conditioning that is receptive to a variety of approaches to the crime problem. In poll after poll, "crime" has consistently ranked as the most serious or one of the most serious social problems confronting the nation. Unemployment, job security, homelessness, AIDS, and international security issues seldom evoke the same intensity of citizen concern.

Therefore, it has been the rare public official, elected or appointed, who would risk public wrath by speaking in a moderating voice or questioning public "mandates" to manage crime and delinquency concerns. Political officials responded accordingly often by simplistically trying to outdo others in being tough on crime.

Bush and Clinton crime bills created the most massive expansion of the federal role over crime control in

U.S. history. This included the "invention" of more than fifty new federal capital offenses. Traditional exponents of states rights were silent on this expansion of the federal role, as were those representatives and senators traditionally opposed to the death penalty.

Conceding the many limitations of various measurement tools, there is a gap between subjective-based fear and the objective reality of crime. Nearly all the data reveals that the amount of crime actually decreased or plateaued during the 1990s. Politicians fixated on the erroneous impression of escalating crime perpetuate this myth, ignoring reality.

Explanation for this misplaced emphasis can be attributed to the increased reporting by television of spectacular and violent crimes. Body bags and SWAT teams have replaced balanced reporting of local news. Youthful violence also adds a new and terrifying element. Just as television coverage of mass starvation spurred reluctant political leaders into action in Somalia, Ruwanda, and Haiti, so, too, television images of death and violence spurred them into action in attempts to control crime.

There is no reason to believe that the social impact of television will decrease in the near future. Indeed, just the opposite can be expected with improvements in image resolution and the combination of television and computers into a new generation of user-friendly multimedia control centers, which will be common in perhaps one-third of U.S. homes and almost certainly in nearly every school. The political response to new imagery control is likely to be driven by images created by the powerful new media and enhanced by a keener texture of information.

There are related communication spin-offs in the presentation of evidence to juries and other fact finders. Simulations of crime scenes and the construction of computer-based alternative scenarios of crime reenactments have assisted juries in their decision-making role. The development of Automated Fingerprint Identification Systems (AFIS) have increased the number of identifications of suspects in murder cases, some of them inactive for many years.

Technology, of course, encompasses more than computer-based communications. DNA-testing has revolutionized the process of eliminating or including potential suspects in a variety of types of cases. In the mid-1990s, the investigation and prosecution of O. J. Simpson focused the attention of the public and the legal profession on both the value and the limitations of DNA as an investigatory and probative tool.

The deluge of communications vehicles and equipment relaying the Simpson trial proceedings to the public raised public consciousness of the value of forensic evidence. Implicitly and explicitly, this information raised questions about the scientific objectivity as well as the competence of laboratory personnel. It also highlighted discrepancies between the forensic resources available to the state (prosecution) and the defendant. This was the trial of a wealthy defendant rather than an indigent defendant. Whereas the prosecutor has access to a costly array of forensic services and the gratis testimony of experts, the defense may be limited to services costing less than $500 for an entire case! In the Simpson case, however, it was suggested that the resources of one rich defendant might actually exceed those available to the entire County of Los Angeles!

The most expensive and longest prosecution in U.S. history—the McMartin school child-abuse case (also in Los Angeles County) caused a rethinking of prosecutorial decision making. How many prosecutions can the state afford, even in aggravated cases? In its early stages, the expense of the O. J. Simpson prosecution was estimated to be in excess of $20 million.

In the early 1990s, there were a series of prosecutions of police officers and laboratory personnel—in widely dispersed parts of the nation—for tampering with, altering, or fabricating evidence in criminal trials. Although not widely publicized outside the immediate environs of the cases, the public at large has begun to understand that government investigators may not always be the objective pursuers of fact envisioned by professional standards. The public may be ready to accept the notion that some police/investigatory personnel can just as easily become "advocates," selecting and construing the evidence in a manner pursuant to their own bias of the case.

The number of private-security personnel assigned to both residential and commercial areas was estimated in the mid-1990s to be greater than the total number of public police.

Finally, the impact of economic considerations on the criminal-justice process is largely unknown. Fiscal realities in the mid-1980s resulted in some rethinking of governmental organization and delivery of a range of criminal-justice services. This has caused some diminution in the nation's nearly 29,000 police agencies as contracts, merging or pooling of operations, consolidations of staff services, privatizations, and so on took hold.

In the 1970s fiscal as well as operational realities led a number of jurisdictions to adopt management information systems to assist in assigning priorities to both criminal investigation and prosecution. Finite resources could no longer be automatically devoted to every deserving case.

In one sense, policing/order maintenance efforts have seen a greater degree of privatization than other aspects of the criminal-justice process. The number of private-security personnel assigned duties in both residential and commercial areas was in the mid-1990s estimated to be greater than the total number of public police, which totaled approximately 600,000 nationwide.

Privatization has been tried in all other aspects of criminal justice, including prosecution and the courts in various diversion and conflict-resolution programs. Private entrepreneurs have also entered some portions of the correctional field, both in administering institutions and various probation and parole endeavors. Due-process considerations will figure prominently in whether these efforts are allowed to stand by various courts.

[See also Alcohol; Child Abuse; Crime, Nonviolent; Crime, Organized; Crime Rates; Criminal Punishment; Drugs, Illicit; Law Enforcement; Laws, Evolution of; Prisons; Sexual Codes; Sexual Laws; Tobacco.]

BIBLIOGRAPHY

The Criminal Justice System and the Future. Claremont, CA: Claremont Graduate School/National Conference of Christians and Jews, June 1983.
"The Global Crime Wave." *Futurist* (July–August 1994).
Stephens, Gene. *The Future of Criminal Justice.* Cincinnatti: Anderson Publishing, 1992.
"Trends in Crime and Criminal Justice." *Future Scan* (February 27, 1989).

– GORDON MISNER

CRIMINAL PUNISHMENT

Jails and prisons will remain the principal correctional institutions in the twenty-first century, but they will be more attractive architecturally than the traditional fortresses of the nineteenth and twentieth centuries, though still with slit or barred windows and tangles of concertina wire. More, perhaps eventually most, of the newer facilities will be privately owned and operated as the privatization phenomenon accelerates, but under close and strict governmental supervision. Inside, there will be activities very much like those of today, many of them rehabilitative, but they will be voluntary rather than mandatory. The spirit of such facilities will be more punitive, because of changing philosophical principles; the style, however, will be more humane, because of changing administrative practices.

A smaller portion of the general population will be housed in such facilities than now, but a larger portion

of the population will be subject to lesser constraints and to supervision, some in newly developed circumstances. In other words (but expressed in today's numbers), fewer than 1,000,000 will be incarcerated but more than 3,000,000 will be under supervision or some other constraint. This may be the most salient characteristic of corrections in the early twenty-first century. Relatively fewer inmates will occupy celled space of the sort one finds in today's maximum and medium security prisons, though more of those, who would otherwise have been there, will instead be in somewhat lower security (even camplike) facilities. Many more will be placed in what amounts to traditional probation or parole but under more intensive supervision. What will be different for some portion of those under constraint will be facilities with electronically secured perimeters (cross the line and you die) confining inmates to grounds on which they will live in barracks, dormitories, cottages, even tents, and move about relatively freely. What will not be new for many of the supervised, except in terms of magnitude, will be the numbers placed in electronically monitored "house arrest." These two technologically based developments will greatly reduce the portion of the convict population that would otherwise be under loose or no supervision. They will experience the "net-widening" effect of the expanded capacity of additional facilities.

More convicts will be in some degree of correctional constraint under judicial or executive jurisdiction because of a growing acceptance of the idea of alternative or intermediate sanctions for many convicted criminals. This will owe partly to the availability of fail-safe electronic monitoring devices and partly to a desire to see more prisoners treated humanely. Much of this will take the form of "community service orders," often in combination with limited periods of constraint (e.g., evenings, weekends). These shifts reflect a philosophy of engaging more persons earlier in their criminal "careers" with lower levels of sanctions and measures that do not call for costly institutionalization. These shifts will also represent a blurring of the formal-informal, public-private, and central-local distinctions that have characterized governmental arrangements generally. There will be many experiments with contractual arrangements among correctional agencies and those institutions with some contribution to make to the correctional functions, such as schools, welfare organizations, and private corporations. The arm of the law, so to speak, will be longer, though the weight of its hand will be lighter for many.

Correctional philosophy as well as technological development and cost-cutting experiments will account for this. Two principles of punishment will have come to be more acceptable: (1) retribution requires the pain of liberty lost; and (2) incapacitation is cost-effective. A third may be acknowledged as well: (3) the lessons of constraint, of liberty lost, are learned by those who become aware of it by personal experience or by word of it "on the street." This means that some inmates will be behind bars or under constraint because they deserve to be, whatever the cost may be—and the public will increasingly insist on this. Others will be confined because it will be accepted that a few people, who can be identified with increasing accuracy, commit a disproportionate amount of crime, which costs victims and communities more than their incapacitation. These principles will reflect the values of the middle-aging portion of the general population, which will increase in number and no longer feel quite so outnumbered, surrounded, and daunted by the younger generation as their counterparts did in the late 1960s and '70s.

The number of persons who will be subjected to correctional constraints is all but impossible to forecast beyond three to five years.

This is consistent with the movement to legislatively restrict the sentencing decision—more recently, to relax it somewhat. The trend toward increasing judicial discretion was reversed after the 1970s, when legislatures imposed mandatory sentences and/or guided discretion in sentencing (as in sentencing guidelines). The sentencing decision probably will continue to be constrained for more serious offenses, but as the level of seriousness declines, legislatures will tend to back off, in effect, to allow judges more discretion in fashioning correctional measures tailored to each individual offender.

There is a prospect, however, for movement toward even more restricted decision making. The capacity of computers to store vast amounts and kinds of information and to retrieve it instantly will make it attractive—in spite of resistance to invasions of privacy—to "assist" decisions with dossiers that provide the basis for projected penalties with much greater refinement. This, in principle, is what sentencing guidelines do with the convict's record; the practice would be merely(!) an extension of the sophistication.

The number of persons who will be subjected to correctional constraints, institutional and otherwise, is all but impossible to forecast beyond the three to five years that is the outside limit of traditional forecasting in the corrections field. In a simple world, one would project the general population for each year, noting the changing demographics as baby booms and busts mature and

the prison-prone years follow the crime-prone years (15–24) by some seven or eight years. But prison population also depends on crime rates, which depend, in turn, on a complex set of factors criminologists have yet to figure out fully. However, even if demographic and crime rate projections were dependable, it would be difficult to project what has been called "the scale of imprisonment." Complicating factors include public opinion, economic conditions, and policy decisions. An example is the "war" on drugs (with mandatory penalties) that has swelled prisons with drug offenders and the more recent "truce" that has reduced prison admissions.

Changes less subtle, though also less far-reaching, can be anticipated. Technological capabilities, as ever before, will be all but irresistible. The ability to inflict pain without lasting physical effects will make corporal punishment an attractive alternative to the "pains of imprisonment" behind bars—for the convict as well as for the authorities. Capital punishment, which will continue to be important symbolically though not instrumentally, will have nearly disappeared in the United States, as in other industrialized nations. But its decline will not be so much a matter of outright abolishment, even though a constitutional peg may have been found from which to hang a decision to abolish it. Instead, it will be the continuing political ambivalence of the people, who both want and do not want the death penalty. Citizens want capital punishment on the books as a deterrent or retribution. But when it comes down to the reality of executions, they do not favor it in practice.

Rehabilitation, which fell from favor for reasons both philosophical and fiscal in the 1970s and '80s, will not make a comeback by the early decades of the twenty-first century. Should there be some major discoveries by then of why criminal conduct occurs at all, and what can be done to change the disposition to murder, rape, and rob, rehabilitative efforts would advance. But this seems unlikely in general, though some programs, such as drug treatment regimens, may prove effective.

Major discoveries with correctional implications can be anticipated in one area of crime-causation: in the biological, chemical, electrical workings of the brain. These will make it possible, hence irresistibly attractive, to treat a small number of offenders whose behavior is known to have been produced by brain malfunction. The efficacy of surgical and especially of pharmacological intervention in such cases will often overwhelm what might be called the "ethicacy" of such measures, by which we would otherwise have resisted them in the interest of the "patient's" psychological autonomy and physical integrity.

Thus, decades into the twenty-first century, the look of corrections will be very much like it is becoming as we approach the end of this century. Prisons and jails will continue to be very important, but alternatives will reduce relatively the number in such institutions. The alternatives will be attractive enough (to the authorities, not the offenders) to greatly increase the number sentenced to them rather than left in loosely supervised probation or unattended altogether. There will possibly be some high-tech corporal punishment and probably even less capital punishment than now, of any "tech" whatsoever. Rehabilitation, by and large, will be limited, at least in any therapeutic sense, and will be largely voluntary to the extent that it is practiced. In short, for corrections there will be more of the same for the most part, but with some interesting differences—much as its future has always been.

[See also Crime Rates; Criminal Justice; Law Enforcement; Prisons.]

BIBLIOGRAPHY

Dilulio, John J., Jr. *No Escape: The Future of American Corrections.* New York: Basic Books, 1991.

Durham, Alexis M., III. *Crisis and Reform: Current Issues in American Punishment.* Boston: Little, Brown, 1994.

Garland, David. *Punishment and Modern Society.* Oxford: Oxford University Press, 1990.

Morris, Norval, and Tonry, Michael. *Between Prison and Probation: Intermediate Punishments in a Rational Sentencing System.* New York: Oxford University Press, 1990.

Zimring, Franklin E., and Hawkins, Gordon. *The Scale of Imprisonment.* Chicago: University of Chicago Press, 1991.

— LAURIN A. WOLLAN, JR.

D

DATA STORAGE

Data storage is the fastest-growing segment of the computer hardware industry. Already it is estimated to approach $100 billion a year in sales. It is estimated that as of the mid-1990s, however, less than 5 percent of information is stored electronically. As of the mid-1990s the cost of electronically storing information is comparable to the cost of storing information on paper. However, the cost of electronic storage is decreasing rapidly, and it is expected that before the turn of the century, the cost will be significantly less than on paper. As the cost of electronic storage becomes less than that of paper, one can expect the growth of the electronic data storage industry to accelerate even further.

Since 1960, electronic data storage has predominantly been by magnetic recording, either on disks or tapes, and it is likely that this will remain the main data storage technology until at least the year 2015. Since 1957 the areal storage density on magnetic disk has increased by about 500,000 times, so that it is possible to store about 50,000 pages of text on one square inch of magnetic recording medium. In spite of this amazing increase in storage density, the physical limits to storage density on magnetic media are still orders of magnitude higher than we can achieve today. In a laboratory demonstration, workers from AT&T Bell Laboratories and Carnegie Mellon University demonstrated a storage density sufficient to store more than 2 million pages of text on a square inch of a magnetic thin film (Betzig et al., 1992).

A schematic diagram of a magnetic recording head and medium is shown in Figure 1. To record information in the medium, electric current is passed through the windings on the recording head, causing it to be magnetized. Due to the gap in the recording head, the magnetic field produced by the current emanates from the head and penetrates the medium. The medium, which is a magnetic coating on either a flexible tape or floppy disk or a rigid aluminum alloy (rigid disk), is magnetized either to the right or left, depending on the direction of current in the windings around the head. The coincidence of a transition in magnetization direction with a clock pulse can be used to represent a "1," while the absence of a transition represents a "0" in a binary encoding of information. To read the stored information, the medium is moved past the head. Magnetic flux produced by the transition in the magnetization direction in the medium is picked up by the head and transformed into a voltage pulse across the windings around the head.

It is now possible to store about 50,000 pages of text on one square inch of magnetic recording medium.

To achieve higher storage densities, it is necessary to make the gap in the recording head narrower, to make the medium thinner, to move the head closer to the medium, to raise the coercive force (field required to reverse the magnetization of the medium), and to increase the magnetization of the recording head. Technology in the mid-1990s is far from the fundamental limits in any of these areas. The fundamental limit to recording density is believed to be determined by the smallest magnetized region that will remain stable against thermal demagnetization. This limit is estimated to be about 10^{12} bits/in^2 or about 50 million pages per square inch.

It is expected that by the turn of the century the storage density on a magnetic disk will reach 5 billion bits per square inch (about 250,000 pages per square inch) (Grachowski and Thompson, 1994). Such a storage density would make possible 750-megabyte disk drives that use 1-inch disks and are put into packages scarcely larger than a microprocessor. These miniaturized drives would no longer be thought of as computer peripherals, but would be components plugged onto a board just like semiconductor chips. It is likely that several such small drives will be put onto a printed circuit board. This will make possible not only larger total storage capacities but also faster access to data, higher data rates, and improved reliability. Work with arrays of disks has shown that it is possible to organize the data in the array so that with a small amount (perhaps 20 percent) of extra storage capacity, it is possible to have one drive in the array fail and still lose no data.

Another data storage technology that is earning a growing share of the data storage market is optical recording. Optical recording uses a variety of different types of media and can be of the write-once, read-many-times variety, or the erasable variety. As of the mid-1990s, erasable optical recording uses magneto-optical

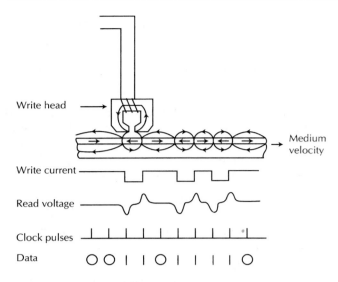

Figure 1. Magnetic recording system.

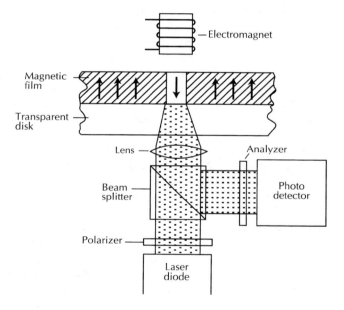

Figure 2. A magneto-optic recording system.

net, and the laser diode is pulsed. Although the medium requires a very large field at room temperature to cause it to change magnetization direction, at the high temperatures to which the focused laser beam heats it, the magnetization is easily switched. Thus, in the small region heated by the laser beam, the magnetization direction can be controlled by the applied magnetic field. In the medium, upward-pointing magnetization represents a "1" and downward-pointing magnetization represents a "0" in a binary encoding of information. To read out the information, the laser beam is used, but at reduced power, so there is insufficient heating to cause a change in magnetization direction. The laser beam is plane-polarized by a polarizer, and when it reflects from the magnetic medium, the plane of polarization is rotated either clockwise or counterclockwise, depending on whether the magnetization is directed upward or downward. This change in polarization is converted to a change in light intensity by passing the reflected beam through a second polarizer (the analyzer) and then is detected by a photodetector. Since the magnetization may be switched repeatedly by applying the magnetic field in alternating directions and pulsing the diode laser, the medium is erasable and rewritable.

The areal storage density on magneto-optical disks is, as of the mid-1990s, about the same as on a magnetic hard disk. As for the hard disks, it can be expected that the density will greatly increase to about the year 2015. Through use of shorter-wavelength lasers, improved optics, more sophisticated coding, and signal processing electronics, it is projected that at least a 32X improvement in storage density is possible.

Magneto-optical disk drives have lower data storage rates and longer access times than magnetic disk drives; however, a magneto-optical disk may be removed from the drive, much like a flexible magnetic disk can. In comparison to a flexible disk, however, a magneto-optical disk offers about 100 times more storage capacity. Thus future computer systems using large databases and images will likely use magneto-optical disk drives in place of flexible disk drives. As of the mid-1990s, the price of a magneto-optical drive is too high (about $700) for magneto-optical drives to replace flexible disk drives in low-cost systems, but magneto-optical drives are comparable in complexity to magnetic hard disk drives. Hence, as the volume of sales increases and the economies of large-volume manufacturing are realized, magneto-optical drive prices should decline to less than $500, at which point they will become much more widely used.

Other technologies, not discussed here, such as holographic storage, ferroelectric storage, and flash memory, may find application in certain market segments,

storage media and is the fastest-growing segment of the optical recording market.

A schematic diagram of an apparatus for magneto-optical recording is shown in Figure 2. A laser diode provides a beam of light to write and read information in the medium. The medium is a magnetic thin film that can be magnetized either up or down, relative to the film plane. To write information into the medium, a magnetic field is applied to the medium in either the upward or the downward direction by an electromag-

but are not considered likely to displace magnetic recording as the main data storage technology until about the year 2005. The market size and investment in magnetic recording technology, its prospects for future progress, and the fact that it is actually accelerating its rate of progress, all suggest it will remain the dominant storage technology for the foreseeable future.

[See also Artificial Intelligence; Change, Pace of; Communications: Technology; Computer Hardware; Computers: Overview; Digital Communications; Electronic Convergence; Information Overload; Information Technology; Media Lab; Superconductivity; Technology Diffusion.]

BIBLIOGRAPHY

Betzig, R. E.; Trautman, J. K.; Wolfe, R.; Gyorgy, E. M.; Finn, P. L.; Kryder, M. H.; and Chang, C. H. "Near-Field Magneto-Optics and High-Density Data Storage." *Applied Physics Letters* 61 (1992):142–144.

Grachowski, E. and Thompson, D. "Outlook for Maintaining Areal Density Growth Rule in Magnetic Recording." *IEEE Transactions on Magnetics* 30 (1994):3797–3800.

— MARK H. KRYDER

DEATH AND DYING

Attitudes Toward Death

Attitudes toward death change in different eras and among different cultures. These attitudes, in turn, affect moral judgments about how to die with dignity and to what extent others may help us. Traditionally, physicians have considered their professional role to preserve life. This ethic led them to resist efforts to permit persons to withdraw life support in order to die. More important, preserving life and the cultural rule against killing are central values in the debate about euthanasia.

Changes in attitudes are largely caused by new technologies. Technology today has created many more opportunities for choices about how to die. The physician's duty to preserve life is not as clear-cut. Further, the patients' rights movement succeeded in placing many of these choices in the hands of patients, their families, or their surrogates. Thus, how we die is no longer a medical judgment. As it was in ancient times, it has again become personal, familial, and social.

Mortality

A major change in our time is how people die. In the past, death came to most persons rather suddenly, either from an incurable disease or accident. Because of the many possible medical interventions in the mid-1990s, about 80 percent of most people in technologically advanced countries die long, lingering deaths. This fact increases the stages of dying during which persons may make choices about their care and try to enlist their doctors and others in those decisions.

If trends continue, in the future there will be greater and greater longevity, with emphasis on improved quality of life during that period. When one's quality of life diminishes to an intolerable level, greater demand for a "decent way out" will occur. We already can detect that demand in the current debate about euthanasia.

Euthanasia

Euthanasia is the controversial practice of painlessly ending the lives of people who have incurable, terminal diseases or painful, distressing, irreversible handicaps. The term comes from the Greek words for "good" and "death." There are different kinds of euthanasia.

The first is called *active* or *direct* euthanasia. This occurs when terminally ill persons ask their doctor, or in some cases, friends or relatives, to put them to death to avoid further pain and suffering. In this action, the cause of death is the direct and intentional action of the one helping the patient to die. Mercy killing takes place under similar circumstances, except that the patient is incapable of asking for a good death, for example, a severely defective newborn, or a severely demented, elderly person. Active euthanasia is by consent; mercy killing is euthanasia without consent.

Active euthanasia is illegal throughout the world, although it is tolerated in the Netherlands under strict guidelines. If physicians follow those guidelines, they are not prosecuted after the case is reported to and reviewed by the authorities. Mercy killing is always illegal. Yet when physicians, nurses, or family members are prosecuted for mercy killing, the jury often refuses to indict or convict them because of the human tragedy involved. Euthanasia and mercy killing are often compared to the atrocities of the Nazis. Some Nazi programs were mercy killing, but most were outright killing without consent. No one can support such programs.

A third form of euthanasia is called *passive* or *indirect*. This is because the intention is not to take the life of the person directly, but to withdraw an intervention that is delaying the dying process. Withholding and withdrawing treatments are not controversial when they are done through advance directives or the current wishes of the patient. The United States Supreme Court ruled in 1990 that competent persons have a right to refuse treatment at any time, even if the treatment might prolong their lives.

Withdrawal of care becomes ethically controversial when it is discussed without clear evidence of the patient's wishes. In such cases, physicians and families rely on previously expressed values or on a value history of the patient. This is combined with a poor prognosis, a calculus of risks and benefits, and of medical futility. Thus surrogates help decide when to withdraw or withhold treatment and allow the person to die.

Another method of obtaining a painless death is by self-induced euthanasia, or suicide. To avoid the possibility of pain and suffering during a suicide attempt, or the possibility of its failure, physicians have sometimes helped patients by providing the drugs or other means necessary to take their own lives. This is called physician-assisted suicide. In some cultures taking one's own life is considered a noble act. Some people think that suicide can be a decent "way out" of life today to avoid a lingering death. Except in Oregon, which has legalized physician-assisted suicide, it is illegal elsewhere. Yet a majority of the population supports the concept. A minority argues that doctors should never kill, because their training and public profession is to preserve life. However, Dr. Jack Kevorkian, a Michigan pathologist, has helped selected people suffering terminal illness to commit suicide in an effort to focus public attention on what doctors do privately and to help legalize assisted suicide in every state.

Death with Dignity

Some people think that everyone ought to have an unqualified right to die. Others limit this right to the withholding and withdrawing of care. Still others consider all forms of euthanasia to be unethical. The moral questions involved in all these actions are whether they violate the rule against killing and whether there is any valid distinction between killing and allowing someone to die. Once the understanding exists that death is a good for the patient, do the means by which this is brought about make any moral difference?

Most everyone agrees that physicians

should help people die with dignity,

but the moral consequences of that assistance

must be discussed with each patient.

Yet persons in each group might agree that fundamental dignity is lost in contemporary modes of dying, in which people are tethered to machines. Death with dignity is hard to define because "dignity," like its companion concept, "quality of life," means different things to different people. For one person, it may mean stoically accepting one's pain and suffering; for another it may mean fighting the indignities of the disease at every step and not giving up; for another it may mean ac-

cepting one's mortality and determining ahead of time which treatments will be acceptable; for still another it may mean maintaining control throughout the dying process, even to the point of setting the time that one will die through direct euthanasia or assisted suicide. Most everyone agrees, therefore, that physicians should help people die with dignity, but the moral consequences of that assistance must be discussed with each patient.

Advance Directives

The principal way of ensuring death with dignity is through advance directives. Advance directives is a catchall term that encompasses all forms of establishing one's preferences about medical care in advance. These are not limited to the dying process, because in the United States and in other countries individuals have a right to determine their own medical care and can refuse it even if it means that they will die without it. Any discussion of preferences with one's family, friends, or doctor is a form of advance directive and should be honored.

When disputes arise or to avoid disputes altogether, one can execute a durable power of attorney for health care. This document spells out one's wishes in a legal format and designates a surrogate decision maker who will make decisions when an individual becomes incompetent. It is limited to medical decisions only, and is in force only while the patient cannot competently express his or her wishes. Some states, like Illinois, have established a set of surrogates in the law in case an incompetent patient is incapable of designating a surrogate.

A living will is a form of advance directive that covers the dying situation exclusively. It is a legal document written in advance, by which the patient determines which treatments he or she will accept or reject during the final stages of the dying process. It applies only if a person is irreversibly, terminally ill and in the final stages of dying.

In the United States, hospitals, home health institutions, and nursing homes are all legally required (in order to receive federal funds) through the Patient Self-Determination Act to notify patients prior to admission of their right to execute advance directives. Many patients decide not to do so because they either believe their family can make decisions for them or they do not want to tie the hands of their doctors. When they become incompetent, it is not always clear to the family or doctor what their wishes might be. This is a cause for confusion and anxiety at the bedside.

Hospice

An alternative to difficult hospital stays during the dying process is to choose hospice care. A hospice is a community of volunteers and professionals who help a dying patient, the family, and friends to accept death in a peaceful and dignified way. This is done by support other than most medical interventions. Comfort care, pain control, discussions of fears, assistance with unfinished business, preparation of one's will, saying goodbye, and many other compassionate actions are provided at home or in specially designated institutions.

Hospice care in the mid-1990s receives federal funding and is increasingly provided by home health-care companies, thus losing some of its former voluntary status. It is increasingly popular because it is both less expensive than hospital care and it allows loved ones to be cared for in a home environment with ready access to family and friends during the last six months of life.

Autopsies and Burial

The special circumstances of death in almost every culture call for rituals for the living. Autopsies of the dead person are done to advance the scientific understanding of disease or, in sudden deaths, to determine the cause of death or the possibility of a criminal act. Some religions oppose autopsies and embalming because these practices are thought to violate the sacredness of the body and affront the Creator.

Most often burial rites include stories about the deceased, a reminder of the journey of life (and the afterlife in some cases), and comfort or prayers for the living. The rituals are designed to show the community's support of those who must grieve. The power of grief itself demonstrates the importance of surrounding the dying with the best possible procedures of respect, support, and comfort for all.

[See also Aging of the Population; Bioethics; Demography; Genetic Technologies; Health Care: Moral Issues; Health Care: Technological Developments; Longevity.]

BIBLIOGRAPHY

Baird, R. M., and Rosenbaum, S. E., eds. *Euthanasia: The Moral Issues*. Buffalo, NY: Prometheus Press, 1989.
de Veber, L. L.; Henry, F.; Nadeau, R.; Cassidy, E., Gentles, I.; and Bierling, G. *Public Policy, Private Voices: The Euthanasia Debate*. Toronto: Human Life Research Institute, 1992.
Gaylin W.; Kass L.; Pellegrino, E. D.; and Siegler, M. "Doctors Must Not Kill." *Journal of the American Medical Association* 259 (April 8, 1988): 2139–2140.
Gomez, C. F. *Regulating Death: Euthanasia and the Case of the Netherlands*. New York: The Free Press, 1991.
Gula R. "Moral Principles Shaping Public Policy on Euthanasia." *Second Opinion* 14 (July 1990): 73–83.
Hackler, C.; Moseley, R.; and Yawter, D. E., eds. *Advance Directives in Medicine*. New York: Praeger, 1989.
Hamel, R. ed. *Active Euthanasia, Religion, and the Public Debate*. Chicago, IL: Park Ridge Center, 1991.
Humphrey, D., and Wickett, A., eds. *The Right to Die: Understanding Euthanasia*. London: The Bodley Head, 1986.
Kilner, J. *Life on the Line: Ethics, Aging, Ending Patients' Lives and Allocating Vital Resources*. Grand Rapids, MI: W. B. Eerdmans, 1992.
Kohl, M., ed. *Beneficent Euthanasia*. Buffalo, NY: Prometheus Books, 1975.
Lynn, J., ed. *By No Extraordinary Means: The Choice to Forgo Life Sustaining Food and Water*. Bloomington, IN: Indiana University Press, 1989.
Meisel, A. *The Right to Die*. New York: John Wiley, 1989.
Rachels, J. *The End of Life: Euthanasia and Morality*. New York: Oxford University Press, 1986.
Ramsey, P. *Ethics at the Edges of Life*. New Haven, Conn.: Yale University Press, 1978.
Thomasma, D., and Graber, G. C. *Euthanasia: Towards an Ethical Social Policy*. New York: Continuum Books, 1990.

– DAVID C. THOMASMA

DEBT.

See CREDIT, DEBT, AND BORROWING.

DEFICITS, GOVERNMENTAL

The federal government budget and net export deficits, the so-called twin deficits, have loomed large over U.S. economic and political policies for several decades. Their significance has long been overrated.

The first is simply the excess of federal government outlays for goods and services, subsidies, welfare, and interest over revenues, mainly from taxes, social security contributions, fines, and fees during a fiscal or calendar year. A deficit means that the government is adding more to the nation's income and expenditure than it removes, which provides a net stimulus to total spending or gross domestic product (GDP). Growth of the deficit enhances the stimulus, while a decrease contracts it. These effects create the possibility of countercyclical fiscal policies to offset increases in unemployment or inflation. A deficit is an instrument of policy, and it is either useful or detrimental, depending upon the expected state of the economy.

Despite the utility of the instrumental aspects of deficits, governments tend to seek a balanced budget as a goal rather than as a means, at least during periods of full employment and stable prices. The absolute size of deficits decreased from about $50 billion during the last three years of World War II to smallish sums averaging three to four billion dollars during the 1950s and '60s, including five years of surpluses of similar size. In the late 1970s they rose above previous highs, burgeoned to over $200 billion in the mid-1980s, and surged to $300 billion in fiscal year 1992. The 1993 deficit was $255 billion.

More meaningfully, the size of the deficit relative to the gross domestic product has ranged from a 30 percent high in World War II to a small surplus of almost 5 percent in 1948. Since 1969, when deficits came to stay, their proportions have fluctuated mostly between 3 and 6 percent. In the first three years of the 1990s, they averaged 4.5 percent, with an estimated 4 percent for fiscal 1993. They are not large by historical standards, nor are they growing relatively.

Often deficits are overstated in an important sense. In the United States, all federal outlays are treated as "current," with no distinction between those that would be constituted "capital" in business and those that would be amortized over some future period. Many other governments distinguish between current and capital expenditures and calculate deficits or surpluses accordingly. Because of its unusual accounting practice, the entire U.S. deficit is construed as *dissaving* and is subtracted from private national saving.

Besides their relatively small size, likely overstatement, and utility in offsetting recessions, deficits do not cause inflation, cannot lead to national bankruptcy, and do not shift burdens to future generations, as is so often alleged. They do add to the national debt, but since this is owned overwhelmingly by U.S. residents, firms, and government entities, the interest and principal payments represent mainly an internal transfer from U.S. taxpayers to U.S. bondholders. Excessive concerns about the deficit arise largely from false analogies with business losses, a feeling that the recent deficits are "out of control" and are somehow immoral, profligate, and evidence of failure. Nonetheless, deficits have obviously become inconvenient. There will be therefore persistent attempts to reduce and keep them as close to zero or balance as possible.

Future of the Budget Deficit

Future trends in the deficit depend upon the growth rates of receipts and outlays. On the receipts side, there is a strong correlation between the growth of nominal GDP (defined as the sum of real GDP) and inflation growth rates.

Real GDP growth averaged about 2.5 percent per year between 1973 and 1993, two decades aptly characterized as the "silent depression" or "high level creeping stagnation." But there is impressive evidence that the long decline in U.S. productivity is over and that both manufacturing and service sectors are once more highly competitive in world markets. Therefore, future real growth should easily average about 3.5–4 percent per year over the next two decades, which is less than the average for the 1950s and '60s.

Inflation will doubtless be better contained in the next two decades below levels prevailing between 1970 and 1990, when they hovered at over 6 percent per year. Thus far in the 1990s annual inflation is in the 3–4

percent range per year and falling. A reasonable long-run scenario envisages U.S. annual inflation rates of 3.5–4.5 percent per year.

Thus nominal GDP growth, to which federal revenues are closely tied, should center around 8 percent. Federal revenues may average even more than 8 percent growth with the higher tax rates established during 1993, especially if the composition of expenditures inclines toward more investment-type outlays for infrastructure and human capital, as now envisaged.

Excessive concerns about the deficit arise largely from false analogies with business losses, a feeling that the recent deficits are "out of control" and are somehow immoral, profligate, and evidence of failure.

It will be more difficult to constrain the growth of federal spending much below 8 percent per year. Over three-quarters of expenditures are contractual, military, or in the form of entitlements. Further military cutbacks are less likely. Urgent initiatives in education, health, crime, environment, and so on require costly federal support.

However, the past decade has seen nominal federal outlays held to an average of less than 6 percent per year. Though painful to many programs, this rate seems sustainable for another decade or so. Thus if federal receipts and outlays grow at 8 percent and 6 percent respectively, the deficit would shrink from $255 billion in fiscal 1993 to zero in ten years. If the spread between the growth rates rises to 3 percent, a balanced budget can be achieved before the year 2001. The ratio of the deficit to GDP will fall to 2 percent or less within three to five years if the spread is 3 percent or 2 percent respectively. Beyond that time it is likely that the federal deficit can be maintained close to balance on average.

The Foreign Trade Deficit

U.S. exports of goods and services exceeded imports every year between 1946 and 1982. Net exports have been negative ever since, reaching record levels of well over $100 billion from 1984 through 1988. During this period the United States was alleged to have shifted from the world's biggest creditor to the biggest debtor, although such statements are exaggerations. Since 1988 the absolute and relative size of the net export deficit has dropped to less dramatic levels.

The share of exports plus imports to GDP more than doubled over the past two decades as more industries sought overseas markets. Future exports depend upon rates of economic growth and import accessibility among U.S. trade partners. The United States, especially if it grows as rapidly as forecast, remains a powerful magnet for imports. This implies the need for strong export growth to offset and balance trade accounts. The prospects of this occurring are favorable. The adoption of NAFTA (North American Free Trade Agreement) and GATT (General Agreement of Tariffs and Trade) and the expansion of freer trade opens up foreign markets.

The future of both deficits ultimately depends upon the growth of the U.S. economy, itself increasingly integrated with global development and growth.

There are powerful reasons for expecting the twin deficits to move toward balance. First, they are interrelated and partially interdependent. Second, there is strong public pressure for their reduction in ways that contribute to sustainable long-run growth rather than protectionism, subsidies, or increased regulation. Third, market and democratic forces unleashed since the fall of communism will add additional and compelling pressures toward balance.

The challenges to economic growth will no longer be as circumscribed as in the past. The problems of wisely "investing" a growing economic surplus and reducing rising inequality are not determined by any inherent scarcity of natural resources nor by any neo-Malthusian drive to excess procreation. They are political. The enemy is "us," as the cartoon character Pogo put it. Certainly the real enemy never was either of the twin deficits now launched upon a path toward balance.

[See also Credit, Debt, and Borrowing; Economic Cycles: Model and Simulations; Public Finance; Savings; Taxes; Wealth.]

BIBLIOGRAPHY

Eisner, Robert. *How Real Is the Federal Deficit?* New York: The Free Press, 1986.
Heilbroner, Robert, and Bernstein, Peter. *The Debt and the Deficit.* New York: W. W. Norton, 1989.
Kotlikoff, Laurence J. "Deficit Delusion." *The Public Interest* (Summer 1986): 53–65.
Wilson, George W. "Deficits: Another Look." *Business Horizons* 31 (1988): 2–13.

— GEORGE W. WILSON

DEFORESTATION

Deforestation and degradation of the world's forests show little sign of abating.

Tropical forest loss is likely to continue into the next century, at an annual rate of 15–20 million hectares, equivalent to an area about the size of the state of Georgia in the United States. Trees in the temperate zone are dying a slower death, afflicted by air pollution, which already has led to a 20–25 percent defoliation in Europe. Deforestation contributes to global warming, species extinction, loss of livelihoods and of human shelter. There are also many indirect costs. When forests are cleared, soil is no longer held by tree roots and washes away. Streams and rivers become more shallow and flood more easily. Reservoirs behind dams fill up with soil, decreasing their water-holding capacity. Forest dwellers migrate to cities. Prices increase for forest resources such as tropical timber.

Over the coming half century the last great forest countries of the world will suffer a vicious assault as timber prices rise and aggressive commercial enterprises seek to maintain timber flows. These remaining major forests are found in Brazil, Suriname, Guyana, South America, Laos, Cambodia, mainland Southeast Asia, the Russian Far East, and Zaire.

Agricultural land use will continue to expand and feed a human population that is not only growing but also seeking ever more protein and fat-rich foodstuffs. Recent studies suggest that global demand for food may triple by the year 2050. Ominously, production growth rates have declined. Forest lands, therefore, will continue to be a very tempting target for conversion to agricultural purposes.

Logging and agriculture will continue to be the major proximate causes of deforestation. The "root causes" or "drivers" of forest loss will be government policies and institutional arrangements that encourage forest clearance. These signals include enormous subsidies for agriculture. There is no comparable assistance to entrepreneurs interested in "sustainable" forest management, even though careful forest management can produce a continuous stream of timber, fruits, fiber, and medicines and also provide "environmental services."

International efforts to slow forest loss show no sign of substantial success in the near future. Some local and national efforts, however, do look promising. New logging technologies, currently seen only on the drawing board, could soon be employed in tropical forests. These might include use of lighter than air balloons to pluck trees from forests without roads and tractors that impose severe impacts and open the forests to subsequent colonization.

As indigenous peoples and other forest-land dwellers acquire greater control of the forests they inhabit, they may help to lead the way to more careful use of the resource. They will team up with businesses to capitalize upon their unparalleled knowledge of forests, and to market new foods and medicines. Genes from some forest plants might, in turn, help to increase agricultural production yields and reduce pressure for further encroachment on forest lands.

Governments will become more concerned about forest loss and implement reforms to reduce the pressure to convert forests to other land uses. Perhaps the most interesting policy options will be those that increase a forest's economic value. This is done, for example, by increasing the taxes on timber extraction so as to make wood more valuable. This stimulates conservation and promotes more careful extraction. A more far-reaching option would be to charge a fee to utility companies that rely upon forests to control the flow of water into hydroelectric dams so as to cover the "environmental service" provided by the forest. The fees, in turn, might be used to develop alternatives for small farmers who are living in the region and who might otherwise be motivated to convert the forest to agricultural uses.

Tropical forest loss is likely to continue into the next century, at an annual rate of 15 to 20 million hectares, equivalent to an area about the size of the state of Georgia in the United States.

Governments may also agree to a global limit on forest loss and embody those objectives in a Global Forests Convention. Such an agreement already is being debated. Developing countries that view logging forests and converting them to agriculture as good ways to finance their own national development are reluctant to agree. Such an agreement might become more attractive as developed countries, pressured by their citizens, offer funds to support forest reduction elsewhere. Thus, a multibillion dollar "Global Forests Fund" might come into being.

Much will be lost unless governments, industry, and citizens join forces to seek agreement on how to save forest resources. As many as half a billion people worldwide are directly dependent on forests for food, income, and shelter. Furthermore, tropical forests are the richest natural source of biological diversity. Disappearing at current rates, as many as 10–15 percent of the world's species may be doomed to extinction over the next twenty years. This represents an annual loss of from 8,000 to 28,000 species (the wide range reflecting uncertainty over total species numbers). While we cannot predict what *will* be done, it will become clearer to a growing number of decision makers that something *must* be done.

[*See also* Biodiversity; Bioethics; Environment; Environmental Behavior; Environmental Ethics; Environmental Indicators; Environmental Policy Changes; Forestry; Global Warming; Natural Disasters; Natural Resources: Use Of; Resources; Soil Conditions.*]

BIBLIOGRAPHY

Anderson, Anthony B., ed. *Alternatives to Deforestation: Steps Toward Sustainable Use of the Amazon Rain Forest.* New York: Columbia University Press, 1992.

Gillis, Malcolm, and Repetto, Robert. *Deforestation and Government Policy.* San Francisco: ICS Press, 1988.

Pitt, D. C., ed. *Deforestation: Social Dynamics in Watersheds and Mountain Ecosystems.* New York: Routledge, 1988.

World Bank. *The Forest Sector.* Washington, DC: World Bank, 1991.

— NIGEL SIZER

DELPHI METHOD.

See FORECASTING METHODS.

DEMOCRACY

Democracy was devised by the Greeks over 2,000 years ago, in Athens, but the democratic regimes of the ancient world disappeared with the demise of the Roman empire. Democracy was embraced in Western societies only after the disappearance of feudalism, and its reappearance was brought about by the enfranchisement of the masses. Equally important was the willingness of Europe's emergent merchant classes to embrace public aspirations toward self-government. They came to see this as a means of establishing a civic order that would evoke broadly based public support for the kind of institutional infrastructure—such as effective transportation, nationwide monetary systems (including banks), and general education—that would sustain the market economies through which they expected to prosper.

It is often said that the reappearance of democratic government in Europe anticipated the onset of the Industrial Revolution and with it the establishment of the modern nation-state. Out of the turmoil of these times, democracy emerged, sometimes haltingly, as the dominant form of government in Western societies—not because of an intrinsic moral value or its coupling with capitalistic economies, but because it proved to be a useful vehicle for promoting egalitarian forms of societal development where "rising waters lift every ship."

Joseph Schumpeter, among others, would argue that the inconsistencies inherent in our conceptions of democracy are so intractable that it cannot be translated into a stable framework for an enduring system of government. While democracy's supporters claim it is superior to other forms of government because it encourages socially responsible political activity, political scientists focus on its utility as a means of bringing elected members of legislative bodies to defuse social conflict by fashioning compromises and building public consensus on basic political values from which government ultimately derives its legitimacy. Although the decision-making processes of authoritarian systems are more orderly and more fully rational in comparison with the often jumbled, sometimes haphazard, processes of a democratic assembly, the openness and permeability of representative bodies appear to be more conducive to promoting adaptive forms of social change. In a world where the quest for progress has driven rates of social change to previously unknown heights, democracy has been embraced as the preferred means of dealing with this challenge.

Nowhere is this potential more easily seen than in the American Revolution, which, de Tocqueville said, gave rebirth to democracy as a way of adapting operations of government to serve the "needs of a diverse people." Interestingly, Americans tend to view the historic thrust of this process as an effort to translate the blueprint contained in their Constitution into a fully elaborated, stable system of government.

Paradoxically, the outcome of two centuries of seeking to perfect the promise of the document produced by the Constitutional Convention of 1787 suggests that de Tocqueville may have been overly optimistic. Nor is there any doubt about the need to strengthen the governments of the rest of the Western democracies. The *pivotal issue* that preoccupies all of those concerned with the viability of this fragile institution is which among the hodgepodge of changes that have been put forward are most likely over time *to compensate for the inherent instability of participatory government.*

Basic Characteristics

Because institutional change should strengthen the mechanisms through which self-government is carried on, it would be helpful to consider first the basic elements of a democratic government. Figure 1 summarizes these components, which come to focus around universal suffrage. As this diagram indicates, there are (1) a number of characteristic structural components of democratic government that (2) have been fused into a more or less functioning whole in Western democracies, and which (3) taken together are meant to assure that the basic needs of a preponderance of the members of a society are adequately provided for (4) in a manner that is fair and just as possible.

But the hallmarks of democratic government are the manifold *political processes* that move forward within this framework; Figure 2 summarizes these.

If democracy is to serve as the means through which the competing interests that energize participatory government find ways to fuse around a familiar mix of public programs, linked together so as to sustain a rewarding way of life, the character of the politics through which this takes place becomes critically important. The first and ultimate prerequisite of a viable democracy is that its political processes generate continuing, enduring public support for self-government. Ideally this is accomplished not by pandering to public tastes, but by promoting wide-ranging public dialogue through which majority support is generated for a relevant agenda of pertinent issues dealing with real rather than apparent needs. This in turn requires setting aside ("putting on the shelf") enough equally appealing issues to avoid overwhelming the system's limited decision-making capacity. More specifically, it is the potential (not always realized) for promulgating agendas that balance the *need for change* with the equally imperative *need for institutional continuity* that has led mass publics in the Western democracies to support participatory government.

Democracy's Pivotal Dilemma

During those uncomfortable moments in history when controversy cannot be resolved by seeking compromises between those interests holding with existing arrangements and those demanding change, decision-makers may be driven to consider another, more rudimentary dilemma—one that runs like an earthquake faultline through the framework of democratic government. On

---

As massive social change sweeps nations toward the future, social adaptivity becomes the key to the viability of government.

---

the one hand, there are the essential needs of individuals seeking to sustain a civilized and secure way of life for themselves, including the need for food, housing, and employment. On the other, there are equally essential collective needs which, though different in character from those of individuals, are just as essential, including public safety, education, and economic growth. As societal development moves forward, *the numbers of both of these types of needs increase,* sometimes at an exponential rate. This leaves government facing not just the burden of more ponderous agendas, but the sometimes foreboding prospect of making choices about sensitive issues that exceed the public's readiness for change even though existing policies are seen as untenable.

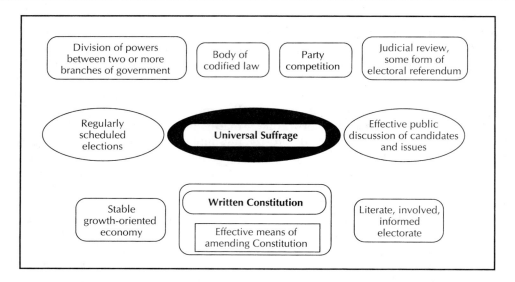

Figure 1. Elements of universal suffrage.

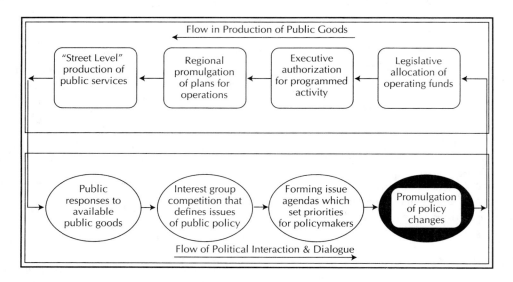

Figure 2. The decision-making cycle: core process in democratic government.

At this point, familiar elements such as widespread participation in elections, an electorate that is motivated to become sufficiently well informed to cast meaningful votes, and a capacity for compromise become the means through which tradeoffs that are binding on everyone are expected to be formed. But the transcendent challenge to participatory government is more subtle and at the same time more demanding.

- On what basis can the atomistic needs of individuals be equated with the collective needs that define the general welfare of all of the members of society?
- If elected officials and their constituents are to "keep faith" with one another, how shall the use of raw political power—which too often displaces trust-based relationships—be constrained so as to allow those who are ruled to make truly propitious choices about who shall serve as their rulers?

Questions such as these have been of concern to both political philosophers and practitioners of politics from antiquity to the present. Even after several centuries, attempts to fashion a coherent response have failed to produce a generally accepted rationale for self-government. Instead, two contending, and in some respects incompatible, conceptions have emerged, introducing ambiguity into the very foundations of democracy.

TABLE 1

TYPES OF DEMOCRACY

	Liberal	Social Democratic
Key Imperative	Achieve the greatest good for the greatest number, sometimes at the expense of the general welfare	Promote the general welfare of the members of society as a whole, sometimes at the expense of individuals
Central Focus	Individuals—especially their felt needs and their preferences	Collectives—especially arrangements that enhance quality of the civic order
Core Values	Liberty and opportunity	Equality and justice
Clashing Conceptions	Commonly shared ends, so pivotal to social democrats, are seen as highly symbolic and ephemeral, hence not a reliable means of identifying ways of promoting well-being	Self-interest of individuals, and especially their vaunted "preferences", are seen as insubstantial, transient, and anchored in circumstances rather than enduring social values
Critical Assumption Regarding Human Nature	Each individual has the right and the capacity to delineate and pursue their own best interests	The civic order as a buffer against the "unkind blows of fate" in which everyone has an equal and common stake

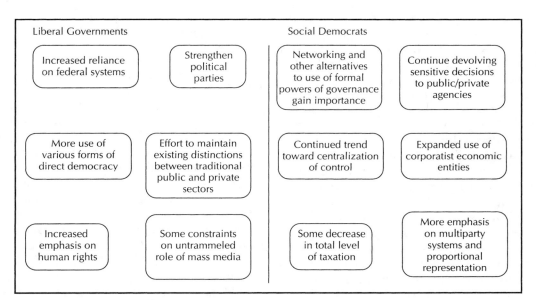

Figure 3. Characteristics of liberal governments (e.g., United States, Canada, and Australia) and social democracies (e.g., Sweden, Norway, and Denmark.

Liberal Versus Social Democracy Perspectives

In the spirit of the dictum that "what you see depends upon where you stand," it is useful to note that these contending perspectives toward participatory government are anchored in the disjuncture between individual and collective needs. Broadly, liberals hold that public agenda should be gauged, and public programs judged, by the degree to which they meet the basic needs of the greatest number of citizens while social democrats want government programs to foster social justice and serve the long-term collective interests of society.

In Table 1, several of the more specific contradictions setting off the liberal and social democratic conceptions of democracy are paired as a way of emphasizing the fractured nature of our understanding of self-government.

As massive social change sweeps nations toward a future where the only certainty is that familiar ways of carrying out the ordinary tasks of life can be disrupted or even displaced, social adaptivity becomes the key to the viability of government. As uncertainty builds and change carries us toward a new world order, the central challenge facing public leaders will be sorting through issues and sifting through alternative ways of maintaining a meaningful balance between the past and the future.

Given the nature of the changes that democratic leaders will confront, it is inevitable that some of the public policy issues will raise questions about the adequacy of the form and functioning of their governments. While democracy is the accepted basis for government in the West, the responses of societies where liberal democracy is ascendant (as is the case in the United States) can be expected to differ from those where social democracy is the basis for the organization of government (as is the case in several Scandinavian countries).

More specifically, given the fractured nature of our conceptions of democracy, it is to be expected that governments will adapt to the shifting international situation by reviewing their historical attachment to the liberal versus the social democratic versions of self-government. Figure 3 summarizes some of the lines of response they may adopt, taking into account their divergent perspectives:

In the largest sense, democracy has yet to be perfected; perhaps de Tocqueville should be faulted for insisting that this was possible. Yet the experiment with which he was so taken has demonstrated the enduring place of democracy in Western civilization, even if it has fallen short of a single, coherent framework for democratic government. History may show that Schumpeter was correct in pointing out democracy's flawed conception but erred in suggesting that this was a fatal flaw. In one sense the coexistence of two distinguishable forms of democracy in Western society, where each moves toward or away from the other as circumstances and convictions dictate, may be a living testimony to the consummate resilience of self-government.

[See also Capitalism; Democratic Process; Political Cycles; Social Democracy; Social and Political Evolution; Voting.]

BIBLIOGRAPHY

Dahl, Robert A. *Dilemmas of Pluralistic Democracy.* New Haven: Yale University Press, 1982.

Hamilton, Alexander, et al. *The Federalist Papers.* Baltimore: Johns Hopkins University Press, 1981.

Plamenatz, John. *Democracy and Illusion.* London: Longmans, 1973.

Riker, William. *Liberalism Against Populism.* San Francisco: W. H. Freeman & Co., 1982.

Schumpeter, Joseph. *Capitalism, Socialism, and Democracy.* New York: Harper and Brothers, 1942.

Tocqueville, Alexis de, ed. Phillips Bradley, *Democracy in America.* New York: Alfred Knopf, 1945.

— WILLIAM J. GORE

DEMOCRATIC PROCESS

Nations can be overwhelmed by external threats and internal vulnerabilities. If not adequately addressed, problems of security, cohesion, order, and leadership can destroy or transform any political system.

Despite trends to embrace democracy and market-oriented economies at the end of the Cold War, democratic and market-oriented outcomes are not inevitable. Other periods in history have displayed trends toward democratic governance, only to be succeeded by dictatorships and totalitarianism. Belief in the ideas of and trust in the institutions of democracy can decline if democratic political systems fail to provide an adequate level of security, order, and well-being.

One can imagine alternate scenarios for democracy in the United States and abroad, each with a different probability, impact, desirability, and feasibility. Each scenario is based on trends in, and interactions among, the various parts of the political and economic system; on trends and impacts of technology; upon internal and external threats; and upon the varying success of policies to address them:

An optimistic scenario for democracy in the United States could involve the successful resolution of domestic problems and the continued perfection of self-government and freedom under law domestically, combined with the expansion and strengthening of democracy internationally, thereby reducing the probability of war and the oppression of people by their own governments. Failures of representative democracy, rising expectations, and higher levels of education and income could lead to a greater emphasis on direct democracy under which citizens voting for specific policies would be conducted by a referendum, a process that is increasingly enabled by technology.

Possible pessimistic scenarios involve trends that could damage the old and new democracies. The end of the Cold War and a declining external threat may be followed by increased disunity within the United States. At the same time, intensification and spread of pre-existing overseas conflicts based on nationality, kinship, locality, race, ethnicity, and religion might be exacerbated by the extreme application of self-determination and on the continuation of antidemocratic ideological trends.

Observers have noted a range of inadequately addressed problems that could lead, through a vicious circle of interacting causes and effects, to the erosion of democracy. Substantive problems include crime, drugs, and an urban underclass; environment-population stresses; the strains between freedom and order; rifts between the ideal of political equality and the glaring reality of extreme social inequality; and creating and maintaining unity out of diversity in the absence of a clear external threat to good response.

Defects in the process and conditions for democracy can be found in its constitution and laws, institutions, political culture, and the character of its citizens. Specific issues include declines in the effectiveness of political institutions, as well as in their legitimacy, authority, and trust; weakening of social groups intermediate between the individual and government (family, neighborhood, and voluntary associations); the depredation of citizenship, self-government, and political participation; and shortcomings of an inadequately expressed will of the citizenry, low voter turnout, weak political parties, strong lobbies, and powerful media.

Failures of representative democracy could lead to a greater emphasis on direct democracy under which citizens voting for specific policies would be conducted by a referendum.

Political gridlock, or the incapacity to act expeditiously and effectively may occur because of the weakness of political parties or the fact that different parties control Congress and the executive branch. Presidential democracies, in contrast to a parliamentary democracy, run an increased risk of gridlock that can provoke a constitutional crisis. The expense of elections and the skewed system for financing them create unequal access to the political process, undermine the loyalty or integrity of officeholders, and bestow undue influence upon large contributors.

The political culture (shared beliefs, attitudes, and values) may be too weak to enable the nation to strengthen the democratic process or address its substantive problems effectively. The character and political virtue of citizens and leaders may be inadequate, thereby eroding the conditions for and competency of democracy. Inadequate transmission to new citizens (native as well as foreign born) of the political beliefs, attitudes, values, skills, and character traits may jeopardize sustaining a healthy democracy. Ill-designed for the problems they purport to address, policies may be fragmented, short-range, and lacking in adequate understanding, consensus, continuity, and coordination.

A strategy for democracy could include the following elements, each of which may exist today to some degree, but in a weak and loosely integrated state:

1. Internationally, increase the spread of democracies and cooperation among them in order to strengthen democratic processes and more effectively address shared concerns.

2. Domestically, stimulate national dialogue concerning the viability and effectiveness of democracy (through periodic congressional hearings, for example) to increase understanding and agreement needed to develop strategies for strengthening democracy.

3. Report periodically on problems, indicators, and trends in democratic political systems, including options for change and improvement.

4. Synthesize and disseminate what is known about democracy (the state of the art), what additional knowledge is needed (an agenda of necessary research and experimentation), and what resources are required for implementation.

5. Analyze, evaluate, and communicate lessons learned from various attempts to improve the policy process, including efforts to enhance the institutions, social process, intellectual tools, and technologies for improved self-government, citizen education, dialogue, and deliberation.

6. Map and display policy debates (their history, status, arguments, and change agents) to improve public understanding, policy dialogue, and, it is hoped, policy outcome.

7. Create museums to inform the public about the history of self-government, freedom, and democracy, as well as about the options, arguments, and trade-offs involved in a range of public policy issues, but without becoming advocates and propagandists for any one option.

8. Support and strengthen the network of individuals and organizations working to improve democracy.

Developing strategies for survival and success of democracy is an unmet need. Within the range of possible futures, many pessimistic possibilities could be realized in the absence of adequate strategies to prevent their occurrence. The future health and survival of democratic political systems depend, in part, not only on how well substantive problems are addressed, but also on actions undertaken to protect and promote democracy itself. It is, therefore, important that we design and implement strategies at home and abroad to increase democracy's margin of safety, effectiveness, and success.

[See also Conservatism, Political; Liberalism, Political; Political Campaigning; Political Cycles; Political Parties; Political Party Realignment; Public Opinion Polls; Social Democracy; Social and Political Evolution; Third Political Parties; Voting.]

BIBLIOGRAPHY

Beedham, Brian. "What Next for Democracy?" In "The Future: An Anniversary Supplement." *The Economist* 328/7228 (September 11, 1993): 5–8.

Broder, David S. "Gridlock Begins at Home: How We Build Political Failure into the System." *Washington Post*, January 23, 1994, pp. C1–2.

Karatnycky, Adrian. "Freedom in Retreat." *Freedom Review* 25 (1994): 4–9.

Lamson, Robert W. "Improving Democratic Participation." *National Civic Review* 82 (1993): 186–189.

Porter, Bruce D. "Can American Democracy Survive?" *Commentary* 96 (1993): 37–40.

– ROBERT W. LAMSON

DEMOGRAPHY

Demography is about people—how many people, what kind of people, where do they live? Demography is a necessary complement to the social sciences as they attempt to better understand our economy and society.

Demography emphasizes the study of (1) the size, composition, and distribution of the population in a given area; (2) changes in population size, composition, and distribution; (3) the components of these changes; (4) the factors that affect these components; and (5) the consequences of changes in population size, composition, and distribution or in the components themselves.

Demography deals with numbers. It requires some knowledge of basic mathematics. However, demography is not dull. It is also amazingly simple. All population size and compositional change can come only from shifts in the three demographic variables: fertility, migration, and mortality.

People decide whether or not to have children and how many to have. People move once, twice, often or not at all. Sometimes people cross an international border in the process. We all die once. Yet to a considerable extent the age at which we die is dependent on social as well as biological factors. All of us, past, present, and future, are population actors and our acts determine what our society looks like—today as well as tomorrow. That in a word is what demography is all about.

If demographic behavior shifts, an area may gain or lose people. That behavior determines what kind of people live in that area—young or old, rich or poor, black or white, and so on. This is what makes demography exciting. We, as population actors, are shaping the kind of society we live in, now and in the future.

Demographic Behavior

Fertility is the major demographic act. It is a two-generational phenomenon. Potential parents, who themselves are the products of the acts of their parents, decide whether to have children and how many.

Shifts in fertility have occurred often in American history. During the 1950s and early 1960s, American women were averaging between three and four children. This was the "baby boom" era. Beginning in 1972, women averaged less than two children. Then in 1989, fertility began to rise once again and is now approaching 2.1 births per woman. Thus American women have altered their fertility behavior dramatically in a relatively brief period.

How is fertility measured? On the macro level, crude birth rates indicate how many births occur per 1,000 people in a specific year and place. In the United States,

for example, the crude birth in 1992 was 16.2. There were 16.2 births per 1,000 people.

The total fertility rate (TFR), a micro measure, is more informative. The TFR takes the age-specific rates of a given year and assumes that women will follow that rate through their reproductive period. In the United States, the TFR is 2.04. If women acted according to the age-specific rates of 1992, they would have on average, just over two live births.

Even a slight change in the TFR can yield vast differences a few decades later. A Census Bureau projection illustrates this point. Assuming that mortality and migration don't change, a variation of 0.4 births per woman would result in a difference of 20 million people by 2020!

As people throughout the world move more and more, migration as a demographic variable is becoming almost as important as fertility.

As a population act, mortality contributes to a decline in the number of people. While it is not voluntary as fertility is, many people do something that may lengthen, or shorten, their lives. Some change their health habits. Many have given up smoking, reduced their alcohol intake, exercise more frequently, and pay more attention to what they eat. The result is increased longevity. The opposite is often true. Some of us turn to violence whether on the streets or between nations. That contributes to reductions in life expectancy. Other factors contribute to variations in longevity. On the whole, women live longer than men, married people live longer than single people, and whites live longer than blacks.

The crude death rate indicates the number of deaths per 1,000 population. Here the term *crude* is particularly advisable. Everything else being equal, a population with many old people will have a higher crude death rate than one with many young people.

Life expectancy, usually at birth, is a more reliable measure of longevity. It resembles the total fertility rate in that it relies on the age-specific death rates of one year and assumes that individuals live their lives according to those rates. In the United States, life expectancy is about seventy-five years. A child born in 1992 can expect to live that many years, on average, according to the age-specific death rates of 1992.

We sometimes neglect mortality when discussing population change. It is an important variable. Again, citing from Census Bureau projections, a difference of six years in life expectancy results in a difference of eight million people within thirty years.

As a population act, migration adds one person to the place of destination and subtracts one from the place of origin. As people throughout the world move more and more, migration as a demographic variable is becoming almost as important as fertility.

The size of the United States is not determined solely by the population acts of Americans. Many people from other countries move here, either legally or illegally. Increasingly, people are coming from Latin America and Asia rather than from Europe as was the case earlier in this century. This population act affects those individuals and all Americans as well.

Holding fertility and mortality constant, a difference of 300,000 per year in immigration results in a difference of 13 million in the nation's population in 2020.

Measuring migration is not as clear-cut as fertility and mortality. Whereas births and deaths are registered in vital statistics, such is not the case with migration. Americans are free to move anywhere in the nation. Legal immigration records are maintained by the Immigration and Naturalization Service (INS) but no records are kept of people leaving the country. Finally, it is next to impossible to determine how many enter the country illegally and how many remain.

Despite these statistical difficulties, estimates are made of the extent of migration and immigration. Americans are movers. On average, Americans move thirteen times in their lives. Certain places are selected more than others. Cities are abandoned while suburbs grow; southern and western states grow as northern and eastern states decline. Even these patterns are subject to radical and quick changes as personal tastes and economic conditions vary.

In recent years, immigration has risen considerably, and today perhaps over 1 million enter the country with the intention of remaining. Together these moves—domestic and international—contribute to population growth in many parts of the country.

In sum, the size of the nation's or any region's population is determined by this complex web of population acts performed by millions of individuals. Their decisions regarding fertility and migration and their ability to postpone death all contribute to the fact that in 1990 the Census Bureau enumerated 249 million Americans.

Age Composition

Knowing about population size is important, but equally important is knowing about age composition. This characteristic is related to each of the demographic variables. Changes in the demographic variables affect a nation's age composition and, in turn, changes in age composition affect the demographic variables.

Demographically, nations can be "young" or "old." A nation is old if it has a large proportion of elderly persons in its population; it is young if it contains a large share of youths. Population pyramids are a convenient way of presenting the age-distribution profile. The shape of a pyramid yields clues concerning past levels of demographic behavior as well as information concerning current composition and possible future trends.

A close examination of the 1990 United States population pyramid shows how the baby boom period of high fertility is affecting the nation's composition. The baby boomers are now between twenty-five and forty. The baby bust period followed the boom era. Finally, there is what demographers call the baby boom echo in the ages below ten. These are the babies of the baby boom mothers. Although their fertility has remained low, their sheer numbers resulted in an increase in the *number* of births—a phenomenon called "population momentum." Even if the fertility rate is low, when there are many women of reproductive age, from the earlier generation, the number of births will increase.

It is commonly believed that reductions in mortality cause the aging of a society. Such reductions increase the average age at death and increase the number of old people. Is it reasonable to conclude that reductions in mortality cause the population to "age"? The answer is no. Indeed, reduced mortality has increased the number of young persons more than it has increased the number of older persons because typical improvements in health and medicine reduce mortality more among the young than among the old. Thus, reductions in mortality often produce a younger population. Low fertility is the principal ingredient of aging. With fewer children being born, the proportion of older persons increases.

Migration also influences age composition. Immigrants are usually disproportionately young adults, and this contributes to a younger age distribution. Internal migration plays an important role in determining the age composition of certain regions. St. Petersburg, Fla., for example, has an old population because of massive in-migration of older Americans. The demographic variables all contribute to changes in age composition. In turn age composition affects fertility and mortality.

One of the factors explaining the baby boom was the greater-than-normal proportion of women in the childbearing years as a result of high fertility in the 1920s. Fertility has climbed recently in part because of the baby boomers reaching their reproductive years. If there are many women in that stage of life, an increase in births can be expected.

Differences in age composition help explain unexpected differences in death rates. We have the strange anomaly of an advanced country like Sweden having a crude death rate of 11 while a less developed country like Mexico has a rate of 6 per 1,000. Mexico has a young population while Sweden has a much older population. Only 20 percent of Sweden's population is under fifteen and 15 percent is over sixty-five. By contrast, 46 percent of Mexico's population is fourteen or younger and only 4 percent is sixty-five or older.

There is a constant interplay between the demographic variables and the age distribution of a population. Shifts in one affect the other, and this goes on indefinitely.

Causes of Shifts in the Demographic Variables

We have discussed some of the causes of mortality shifts. Since we all die eventually, little can be done except to postpone this inevitability for as long as possible. But fertility and migration are both voluntary. We do not have to conceive children; we do not have to move.

Many factors help explain why fertility is high or low. First and foremost is marital status. While pregnancy outside of marriage is increasingly common, most births still occur within marriage. In the United States, age at marriage has risen in recent decades. On average, women marry at 23.9, men at 26.1, quite a difference from just thirty years ago, when the respective ages were 20.3 and 22.8. Women are having their children later in life and this contributes to smaller families.

Divorce rates have also climbed in recent decades and this too contributes to small families. In 1990, the divorce rate was 4.7 per 1,000 compared to only 2.2 in 1960. There are 142 divorced persons per 1,000 married persons with spouse present. In 1960, there were 35.

Together the postponement of marriage and the rapid increase in divorce contribute to the decline in fertility. Other factors are also present. Generally, the higher the education of the woman, the lower the fertility; being employed and, especially, being employed in white-collar jobs results in lower fertility. Usually, the rich have fewer children than the poor.

Moving is a voluntary decision. People usually move to better their lot in life. This often means getting a job or getting a better job. Older people are apt to move for retirement reasons. There has long been a stream of elderly migrants out of the north into the south and southwest.

International migrants also move for economic reasons. The situation in the mother country may be so bad that crossing the border may be the only solution. Sometimes, the lure of the United States suffices to entice a foreigner to immigrate. Here again, the generalization holds—people move to better their lot in life.

The Future

What does the current demographic behavior and the age-sex composition of the nation portend for the future? We will continue to grow; we will age; and we will become more ethnically diverse.

With fertility at just over 2 births per woman and with immigration at the highest levels in history, the population of the United States could reach 400 million by the middle of the next century. As the baby boomers move into retirement soon after the turn of the century, the share of the population who are elderly could rise from 11 percent today to almost 20 percent.

With immigration so high and with immigrants coming overwhelmingly from Latin America and Asia, the proportion of the society who are immigrants or their children will grow. By 2060 there may be no ethnic majority in the United States. Together low fertility among residents and high immigration will result in an ever more heterogeneous nation.

As we enter the twenty-first century, we need to be aware of the shifts already in progress because of our past and present demographic behavior. In this way we as a nation can better prepare ourselves to face the challenges that are bound to follow from such a massive restructuring of the population—all the results of countless individual population acts.

[See also Aging of the Population; Children, Living Arrangements; Crime Rates; Divorce; Economics; Elderly, Living Arrangements; Evolution, Social; Household Composition; Housing, Demographic and Lifestyle Impacts of; Internal Migration, United States; Longevity; Migration, International; Population Growth: United States; Population Growth: Worldwide; Social Change: United States; Social and Political Evolution; Workforce Redistribution.]

BIBLIOGRAPHY

Abernathy, Virginia D., ed. Population Policies: The Choices That Shape Our Future. New York: Insight Books, 1993.
Bouvier, Leon F. and Grant, Lindsey. How Many Americans? Population, Immigration, and the Environment. San Francisco, CA: Sierra Club Books, 1994.
Haub, Carl and Yanagishita, Machiko. 1995 World Population Data Sheet. Washington, DC: Population Reference Bureau, 1995.
Russell, Cheryl. The Master Trend: How the Baby Boom Generation Is Remaking America. New York: Plenum Press, 1993.

— LEON BOUVIER

DENTISTRY

Dentistry became a profession in 1728 when a French surgeon, Pierre Fauchard, published a monumental work that encompassed all of the dental knowledge up to that time. Theretofore, dental treatment had been provided by a variety of practitioners, from barber-surgeons to roving charlatans and mountebanks. Treatment consisted mainly of extraction; cavities were filled with a variety of worthless substances, including mouse dung, cobwebs, and tree rosins.

From the 1700s onward, dentistry moved on apace. In 1839, the first dental school in the world was founded in Baltimore. Subsequently hundreds of schools were established worldwide. Today, dental schools are affiliated with universities and require a minimum of four years of study. The eleven recognized specialties require advanced, postdoctoral study of from two to three years.

The understanding of the causes and repair of tooth decay grew in the 1900s and will likely lead to a cure in the next century. (Richard T. Nowitz/Corbis)

From the latter part of the nineteenth century, dentistry made very great advances. Greene Vardiman Black put its practice on a sound scientific basis. W. D. Miller promulgated the theory of the bacterio-parasitic origin of dental caries, which laid the groundwork for all further studies in the prevention of dental decay. Remarkable advances in instrumentation and materials took place, starting in the latter part of the century. The discovery of anesthesia in 1844 by the Connecticut dentist Horace Wells permitted dreaded dental procedures to be performed without pain. The introduction of vulcanized rubber, in 1851, made dentures available to the masses at a low cost. Wholesale extraction of teeth followed, and their replacement with prosthetic appliances became the most common treatment offered by dentists.

The invention of precision casting in 1907, however, stimulated a leap forward in restorative dentistry, using gold inlays, bridges, and crowns. Improvements in root-canal therapy saved countless teeth. The introduction of porcelain into restorative dentistry gave impetus to the drive for greater esthetics.

Major Advances in the Twentieth Century

The first half of this century saw the improvement of techniques and the introduction of new and better materials. Acrylic resins supplanted rubber in dentures; composite resins provided a filling material both long-lasting and tooth colored; chromium-cobalt-molybdenum alloys replaced gold in partial dentures; even amalgam was improved upon. A major breakthrough was the veneering of porcelain onto metal crowns. The most significant instrument advance was the air-driven turbine drill, introduced in 1957, with speeds of over 350,000 rpm. With vibrationless cutting, exceptionally fine tasks could be performed with a minimum of discomfort.

One of the greatest public health measures of all time, begun in the early 1950s, was the fluoridation of public water supplies. By adding sodium fluoride, in the amount of one part per million, to public water supplies, children's decay rate in those cities was cut 60 percent. The benefit of fluoride was extended by painting it onto the teeth and by adding it to toothpaste and mouthwash.

Important Recent Advances Point to the Future

Important new diagnostic techniques just coming onto the market allow earlier detection of abnormalities. An electronic cavity detector measures the density of tooth surfaces, pinpointing those that show incipient decay, since even minutely demineralized areas allow greater passage of electric current. New panoramic X-ray machines take sharper and more diagnostic radiographs with a shorter exposure, subjecting the patient to far less radiation.

Because of the reduction in tooth decay to less than half of what it had been several decades earlier, emphasis shifted to improvement of the health of the tissues investing the teeth—the bone and gums. Research identified plaque—the sticky film secreted by bacteria—as the cause of periodontal disease, and the germ *Streptococcus mutans* as the causative organism of caries. Great advances in periodontic techniques have been made in the last several decades, including an improved method of grafting bone into areas where it had been lost.

An exciting new development is the implant. Pioneered about thirty-five years ago, the technique consists of inserting into the jawbone screws, or other variously shaped devices, to which either single teeth, or multiple-tooth bridges, can be affixed. New design of the implants, and new materials, encourage osseo-integration, where bone becomes tightly bound to the implant.

Since the causative agent of caries is known,

this will lead to the development of a vaccine.

Other new developments are based on the use of the computer, coupled with fiber-optic imaging. A penlike camera is run around the patient's mouth, and the data "seen" by the probe is transferred to the computer, which can then do a variety of things: It can print out a chart of the mouth; it can display the current oral status on the monitor screen; and it can allow the dentist to manipulate the picture on the screen so that the patient can see exactly what the present condition is and what it will be following dental treatment. Another innovation is the use of this probe to scan a tooth that has been prepared by the dentist for a crown. This information is fed to a machine that mills a perfectly fitting crown out of a block of ceramic in about thirty minutes, allowing restorations to be completed in one sitting.

What of the Future?

Several areas of research offer the most promise for the future. Although caries has declined, it still must be treated. New filling materials will have fluoride in them, which will be continuously released. Since the causative agent of caries is known, this will lead to the development of a vaccine. Increased public education about diet and oral hygiene will dramatically alter the caries rate.

The laser, already used in periodontal surgery, will be used for caries removal and tooth reduction. This, coupled with decay-dissolving liquids applied by the dentist, will do away with the need for drilling.

In the field of periodontics, new products for removal of plaque by the patient at home, will bring about a great reduction of periodontal disease. It is also likely that antiplaque agents will be incorporated into foodstuffs and chewing gum, and vaccines will also be introduced to combat the bacteria that secrete plaque. Regarding treatment, a new technique that is only now being developed will be greatly expanded. This consists of draping a tiny synthetic mesh over the root of a bone-denuded tooth; the mesh encourages growth of new bone without allowing soft-tissue encroachment into the surgical area.

The current emphasis on esthetics will lead to advances in bonding techniques. Fractured or malformed teeth will be improved by painting a tooth colored material directly on the tooth, without the need for grinding or drilling. Today, these bonding agents must be cured under a special light; bonding agents of the future will be self-hardening. Root-canal treatment will become less laborious; new methods of cleansing the canal of debris and filling it with a liquid sealer, which will harden in the canal, will mean that the number of visits for the procedure will be greatly reduced.

Orthodontic treatment, which has seen great strides, will see even more. Wires and bands, which at present are more esthetically acceptable than they had been for decades, will be improved by using almost invisible plastic bands that will be "spot-welded" onto the tooth with a laser. Miniaturization, which has brought such remarkable changes in the field of electronics, will be adapted to orthodontic treatment. Microminiature motors, powered by tiny batteries, will be placed in the mouth and will serve to apply tiny forces to move teeth more predictably and with less discomfort.

In the field of anesthesia, new techniques bode well for the future. Electric current as a pain suppressant, which has tantalized dentists for years, seems about to become a reality. Low-voltage but high-frequency current will be applied in such a way that the body's natural pain blockers, endorphins, will be released in greater numbers. Local anesthesia, which has been, for almost a century, the dentist's principal pain fighter, will be greatly improved. Intraligamentary anesthesia will become standard. With this method, a needle, almost as fine as a hair, is inserted into the exact area to be deadened, obviating the uncomfortable long-lasting numbness over a large area.

Dentistry a hundred years from now will be as unlike today's as that of the 1890s is to what is practiced now.

[See also Medical Care Providers.]

BIBLIOGRAPHY

Conley, Jack F. "Dentistry in the 21st Century." *Journal of the California Dental Association.* 22/1 (January 1994).

Demirjian, Arto. "Teaching Dentistry in the 21st Century." *The Compendium of Continuing Education in Dentistry.* 15/1 (January 1994).

Ring, Malvin E. *Dentistry: An Illustrated History.* New York: Harry N. Abrams, 1985.

– MALVIN E. RING

DETERMINISM.

See FORECASTING, DETERMINISTIC.

DEVELOPMENT, ALTERNATIVE

The goal of development in the Second and Third Worlds since World War II has been to create independent social institutions and to establish strong nonfeudal economies. Through massive aid and loans, it was hoped that all nations could rapidly industrialize as the West had done. Ignored, however, were the impacts of colonialism (the extraction of wealth and the creation of a collective inferiority complex), and the cultural and spiritual contradictions embedded in the Western industrial model. Development alternatives were nation-state-oriented, narrowly defined by the discipline of economics and focused on bureaucrats, capitalists, and technocrats as agents of change. Economic development merely created a new elite and further impoverished the poor.

Recent efforts to rethink development have attempted to deconstruct the power relations embedded in the idea of development itself, particularly to free development from its Social Darwinian views of past and future. Emerging models focus on the contribution of factors that have been the traditional basic materials of development: rural labor, women and children, as well as the environment.

Shifting from national, technocratic, and bureaucratic orientation—with the multinational corporation as the exemplar—alternative development approaches now focus on local peoples' organizations and international nongovernmental organizations as agents of transformation.

In contrast to the capitalist notion of development, which emphasizes freedom for capital, individual mobility, and labor mobility within nations, local models of development stress identity and survival. They focus on policies that do not degrade the environment or increase inequality among classes. These models are often nonlinear in their assumptions—that is, they are not based on the belief that there is an end stage of modernity to reach; rather they believe that all polities, individuals, and economies follow a cyclical rise and fall, expansion and contraction. Within this framework, development is not based on the extraneous values of those presently wealthy, but rather on the notion that all regions can shape their own model of the ideal society.

Local models, however, have not been able to solve the problem of globalization, or to meet the desire for Westernization among local communities. Local models, while giving communities a sense of history and pride, have failed at providing plentiful consumer goods.

The previous alternative to capitalist development, the communist model—which focused not on the idea of individual freedom leading to growth but state power ideally leading to justice—has been discarded. Communist systems at best met only survival needs, fell short of advancing well-being, and faltered in advancing economic growth.

In contrast, the new Japanese-Confucian model has attempted to perfect the traditional development paradigm without pitting the state against business and labor against management. Based on education and long-term planning cycles, the state and the corporation provide collective unity as well as hierarchical discipline. Economic growth takes precedence over identity and social freedom. However, as economic well-being has increased, the problem of individual identity has re-emerged, as have spiritual needs previously relegated to history by the glitter of modernity.

Successful future development models must meet many needs: freedom, mobility, identity (above and beyond nation and ethnicity), survival, and well-being. These models must be able to provide for economic growth (supported by savings, a hard-work ethic, and an efficient distribution system), development without exploitation of people or the environment, and distributive justice. Emerging models must be eclectic, including ideas from capitalist, collective, welfare, and diverse cultural traditions. They must also include gender fairness and environmental sustainability. Decisions must include women's categories of knowledge and their important contribution to the informal home and formal exchange economy. Finally, empirical indicators of new models must include the contribution of these factors: women, community, and the environment, in such a manner as to show the imbalances caused by each model.

An emerging global alternative development model is the Progressive Utilization Theory of the Indian philosopher Prabhat Ranjan Sarkar. This model has the necessary dimensions for both strong economic growth (through the development of material, intellectual, and spiritual potentials) and for distributive justice (through economic democracy). Cooperatives make up its prime economic organization. Identity is based on spiritual, not national, character. The spiritual state is manifested by conditions of *prama,* or balance. There must be balance among and between many realms: the material and spiritual, the physical (economic balance between regions), intellectual (an eclectic or multiple view of reality), and the spiritual (in the form of individual trans-formation).

This model would encourage free trade, but under conditions of equality between nations. Until these criteria are met, regions should withhold and not export their raw materials.

The overarching goal is a world

in which development is not based on

the exploitation of the many for the few,

nor measured in linear or materialistic terms.

Manufacturing, ideally, should be established away from populated cities in decentralized areas. Ideally, economic activity should be based on bioregions. With increased communication and trade, regions could evolve into confederations, until a true world economy emerges. The overarching goal is a world in which development is not based on the exploitation of the many for the few, nor measured in linear or materialistic terms. The past few centuries have been characterized by great imbalance. Alternative development models aim not only to restore the ancient cyclical balance but to create systems based on a dynamic view of order and disorder, of chaos and complexity.

[See also Asia; Development: Western Perspective; India.]

BIBLIOGRAPHY

Carley, Michael and Ian Christie. *Managing Sustainable Development.* London: Earthscan, 1992.

Daly, Herman E., and Cobb, John E. Jr. *For the Common Good: Redirecting the Economy Towards the Community, the Environment and a Sustainable Future.* Boston: Beacon Press, 1990.

de la Court, Thijs. *Beyond Brundtland: Development in the Nineties.* London, Zed Books, 1990.

Harrison, Paul. *The Third Revolution: Environment, Population and a Sustainable World.* New York: Tauris, 1992.

Pearce, David; Barbier, Edward; and Markandaya, Anil. *Sustainable Development: Economics and Environment in the Third World.* London: Earthscan: 1991.

Redclift, Michael. *Sustainable Development: Exploring the Contradictions.* New York: Methuen, 1987.

Schneider, Bertrand. *The Barefoot Revolution: A Report to the Club of Rome.* London: Intermediate Technology Publications, 1989.

World Commission on Environment and Development. *Our Common Future.* New York: Oxford University Press, 1987.

— SOHAIL INAYATULLAH

DEVELOPMENT: WESTERN PERSPECTIVE

Nine out of every ten persons under the age of fifteen are Third World citizens. The vast majority of Earth's resources also are in the developing world. How these regions and people develop will shape the twenty-first century.

The purpose of development is enlightened growth within a social setting of peace and plenty. Western development philosophy assumes that transferring the "things of development," such as schools, hospitals, machines, computers, and highways, to poorer regions inevitably leads to development. This approach has brought about some improvements. According to the United Nations Development Program's *Human Development Report* (1993), there has been some significant progress. Safe water access rose from 10 percent of population to 60 percent over the last two decades. Life expectancy increased 33 percent during the last three decades. Economic growth averaged 7 percent during the 1980s in South and East Asia, which has 66 percent of the Third World's population. Fifty countries meet their daily caloric requirements, up from 25 percent of that total in 1965. High school enrollment grew from 25 percent to 40 percent in two decades, and world military spending has begun to decline.

This "Western form of development" led to mammoth private and public debts as these countries struggled to pay for teachers, doctors, machine repairs, and road maintenance. Richer countries tax business for public revenue, but there was little business in the developing world to tax. Without a major effort to strengthen and expand the smaller economic activities and the foresight to manage the technological change, the policy of duplicating the "things of development" was doomed to failure.

Massive migration and famine in Africa; environmental time bombs inherent in rapid industrialization in China; ethnic wars in sixty countries; jobless economic growth; continued financial debt; one billion illiterate people; political instability; and the population growth rates across the Third World—all these factors will increasingly affect the richer countries. By involving themselves in efforts to solve or ameliorate these conditions through enlightened self-interest, the affluent countries will benefit themselves and the international support system.

It took the developed world one hundred years to double its per capita income, but just thirty years for

TABLE 1

A SIMPLIFIED VIEW OF WESTERN DEVELOPMENT

Age (Major Activity)	Product	Wealth	Power	Location
Agricultural	Food	Land	Religion	Farm
Industrial	Machinery	Capital	State	Factory
Information	Service/Info	Access	Corporation	Office
Conscious Technology	Linkage	Being	Individual	Motion

some developing nations. Korea's GDP per capita was the same as Ghana's at independence. Ghana is poorer today, while Korea is a rich, dynamic country; Korea embraced technology, free market incentives, and long-term planning—and Ghana did not. About 700 American corporations have invested $4 billion in Singapore, because it has a free economy, a hard-work ethic, and enthusiastic people. Still, economic growth without increased employment should be expected to continue as the technology of automation is transferred to the less developed regions. Hence, the current unemployment rates of over 20 percent will increase until new kinds of economic activity are created.

Futurists such as R. Buckminster Fuller, Herman Kahn, and Arthur C. Clarke have suggested that poorer regions of the world will be able to catch up with the West by "leap-frogging" past the industrial era, jumping from the agricultural to the information age. Table 1 highlights these key stages in the Western view on development.

People are "underdeveloped" both because of wrong consciousness and technology, whether in Haiti or America. Where people tend to be fatalistic, development will not happen until the grip of fatalism and dependency is broken. As long as people define the solution to their problems as outside their control, they are dependent and will remain underdeveloped. Too often poorer nations see the solutions to their problems as beyond their ability. More developed groups define a problem in such a way that it is within their ability to solve it or at least to take the first step on the road to solution.

The poorer regions of the world inherit technology and concepts from the more developed and richer regions. Those that decided to define their future and to invent their long-range strategy—for example, Japan, Mauritius, and Korea—have done well. Such long-range thinking is becoming more acceptable in development. One of the first examples of this shift in development philosophy is the UNDP's African Futures program to assist every country in Africa to develop its long-term strategy.

Meanwhile during the 1980s, the Western approach to development began shifting from bilateral aid for large-scale public-sector projects to create the "things of development" toward smaller-scale private-sector development. With this focus on private-sector growth and the new interest in long-term strategic thinking, unique market niches that are international as well as local can be anticipated. The Third World could take the initiative to form partnerships with the most advanced technological conceptual initiators to invent their future together.

[See also Change, Epochal; Development, Alternative; Information Society; Religion: Changing Beliefs; Workforce Redistribution.]

BIBLIOGRAPHY

Bowers, C. A. *Education, Cultural Myths, and the Ecological Crisis: Toward Deep Changes.* Albany, NY: State University of New York Press, 1993.

Glenn, Jerome C. "Economic Development in the Third World." In *Future Mind: Merging the Mystical and the Technological in the 21st Century.* Washington, DC: Acropolis Books, 1989.

Global Outlook 2000: An Economic, Social, and Environmental Perspective. New York: UN Publications, 1993.

Human Development Report: United Nations Development Program, 1990–1993. New York: UN Publications, 1993.

Kennedy, Paul. *Preparing for the Twenty-first Century.* New York: Random House, 1993.

Pirages, C. Dennis, and Sylvester, Christine. *Transformation in the Global Political Economy.* New York: St. Martin's Press, 1990.

— JEROME C. GLENN

DIET.

See NUTRITION.

DIGITAL COMMUNICATIONS

Throughout the 1930s, '40s, and '50s, communications blossomed in both the wireless and wireline worlds of radio and telephone, and later television. The predominant technologies were based upon various analog modulation/demodulation techniques as voice, data, and video signals were superimposed on high-frequency carriers and multiplexed together to be transported from here to there to everywhere. As high-wattage radio antennas were established on high-rise towers to broadcast radio frequencies long distances, the telephone took the wireline route, as telephone poles were established down country lanes, while urban cable vaults blossomed as they terminated hundreds of thousands of copper pairs, bringing analog voice conversations to large central switching offices. (In time, past the middle of the century, after Sputnik, satellites were universally deployed commercially to distribute wireless television signals to remote locations.)

Unfortunately with regard to wireline, there was considerable expense in dedicating each conversation to a single wire pair and considerable maintenance time required to hook up and hand-wire each new request for service within the cable distribution plant and main distribution frames of the central office. Here, stored program controlled (SPC) switching and service systems helped speed up the customer service changes enabling numbering changes, number translations, and new routing table updates, as well as the enhanced capability, to provide new features more easily in a timely manner. But there was still a serious need to reduce the cost of the distribution plant, improve the quality of service, and reduce the proliferation of new central switching offices requiring new blocks of the dwindling resources of seven-digit local codes.

To address these needs, especially for long distance carrier transport, AT&T introduced digital communications in the early 1970s, based upon pulse code modulation techniques developed in the 1930s by an earlier pioneer, ITT Laboratories. Here, AT&T's T1 carrier systems, operating at 1.544 million bits per second (Mb/s), were able to transport 24 voice conversations over a pair of copper wires, where each voice conversation was sampled 8,000 times per second with each sample level coded in blocks of 8 ones and zeros (bits). Hence, 8 times 8,000 or 64,000 digital bits were sent each second to represent a single-voice conversation. Thus, 24 times 64,000 bits were sent together with specialized synchronization (bits) information to formulate the T1 1.544 Mb/s transport system. Later, capabilities were expanded to T2 (6.31 Mb/s) and eventually T3 (45 Mb/s) capabilities.

It was soon noted in the mid-1970s by GTE engineers that their central offices in remote rural towns could "home in" on a single large office located usually at the county seat. Hence, they extended the digital long distance transport to the local community, as remote switching units were deployed in remote locations to "home" on centrally based units, thereby establishing digital clusters of 15 or so small towns and villages with the county seat. Thus were born integrated digital networks (IDN).

Though there were administrative economies of scale and number group savings in deploying digital to the voice world in this manner, much, much more could

be achieved by integrating digital voice with the world of data. This was the purpose and charge of integrated services digital networks (ISDN). Their initial task was to enable the customer to send and receive voice or data from their location over the copper pair, and to provide the capability to take immediate advantage of shared digital transport and switching facilities. In this, the user was provided a 2B + D interface, with the B channel having the capability of sending/receiving 64,000 bits per second and the D channel enabling 16,000 bits per second of signalling and control information. Thus, the user is able to send a digital voice in one B channel, as well as simultaneous digital data in the other B channel, or have two separate voice conversations in the two B channels or digital data in both B channels at a total rate of 128,000 bits per second, while having 16,000 bits of out-of-band signalling and control information in the D channel. This D channel is also able to send data in a packet form (with information packaged in a variable or fixed number of 8 bit bytes, having a header and a tail to differentiate the beginning and end of the message; here, the D channel's transport rate for packet data was 9,600 bits per second).

Customers will be able to use high-definition

video channels, paving the way for

high-definition videophone and high-speed

computer-to-computer data traffic.

Hence, this 2B + D interface was called the basic rate interface (BRI), enabling voice or data to be mixed together, or allowing two voice conversations or two data conversations to be transported. These narrowband capabilities were then augmented by a higher-speed (wideband) ISDN primary rate interface (PRI), enabling 23 B channels of 64 Kb/s and one D channel having 64 Kb/s of signalling and control information, equating to the T1 transport rate of 1.544 Mb/s.

In time, broadband capabilities will be available enabling the user network interface (UNI) to deliver 155 million bits per second (Mb/s) and 622 Mb/s to the customer over fiber-optic local loops. These optical carrier rates are multiples of OC-1 (51.8 Mb/s). It should be noted that American and European systems will be in step at the internationally agreed standard of OC-3 or 155 Mb/s, with Americans evolving from the T1 rate of 1.544 Mb/s and Europeans from the El rate of 2.048 Mb/s.

Here, information will be digitally transported, using the synchronous optical network (SONET) transport capabilities, enabling voice, data, text, image, and video to be dynamically modulated and multiplexed over gigabit facilities. This then will be switched utilizing asynchronous transfer mode (ATM) fast packet-switching technologies, as well as synchronous transfer mode (STM) circuit-switching capabilities. These techniques will later be complemented and extended by photonic multiple-frequency (colors) optical-electrical switching transport systems, handling terabits of information.

Using these capabilities, as fiber is delivered first to the office (FTTO), then to the residential curb (FTTC), and later to the home (FTTH), customers will be able to see four or so high-definition video channels and communicate to the world at the 155 Mb/s rate, thereby paving the way for high-definition videophone, high-speed computer-to-computer data traffic, and the ability to dial up high-quality musical and sporting events, etc. In this manner, narrowband and broadband ISDN digital communications will establish the communications infrastructure for a new society—the information society in the twenty-first century.

[See also Broadcasting; Communications; Computer Linkage; Computers: Overview; Data Storage; Electronic Convergence; Information Technology; Libraries: Electronic Formats; Media Lab; Networking; On-Line Services; Postal Services; Satellite Communications; Space Satellites; Telecommunications; Telephones; Television.]

BIBLIOGRAPHY

Bradley, Stephen B, Hausman, Jerry A., Nolan, Richard L., eds. *Globalization, Technology, and Competition: The Fusion of Computers and Telecommunications in the 1990s.* Boston: Harvard Business School Press, 1993.

Connors, Michael. *The Race to the Intelligent State: Towards the Global Information Economy of 2005.* Oxford, U.K. and Cambridge, MA: Blackwell Business, 1993.

Harasim, Linda M. *Global Networks: Computers and International Communication.* Cambridge, MA: MIT Press, 1993.

Jussawalla, Meheroo, ed. *Global Telecommunications Policies: The Challenge of Change.* Westport, CT. Greenwood Press, 1993.

Nordenstreng, Kaarle, and Schiller, Herbert I., eds. *Beyond National Sovereignty: International Communication in the 1990s.* Norwood, NJ: Ablex Publishing Corp., 1993.

Parker, Edwin B.; Hudson, Heather; et al., eds. *Electronic Byways: State Policies for Rural Development Through Telecommunications.* Boulder, CO: Westview Press, 1992.

– ROBERT K. HELDMAN

DISABLED PERSONS' RIGHTS

Problems of stigma and discrimination have long been associated with physical and mental impairments. Because of negative attitudes and their manifestation in architectural design and societal norms, individuals with disabilities who have been able to work and otherwise participate in public life have often been denied the opportunity to do so. For example, in a 1986 survey of working age persons with disabilities, 47 percent of the respondents stated that employers' negative attitudes about their work potential resulted in them working part-time or not at all, and 25 percent of those working reported experiencing discrimination.

The first significant laws prohibiting discrimination in access to public accommodations were the white cane and guide dog laws enacted by a few states in the 1930s and in most jurisdictions by the early 1960s. These laws prohibited restrictions on blind people using canes or guide dogs in public buildings and on streets. However, individuals with disabilities other than blindness, and blind people who did not use canes or guide dogs were not affected.

Rulings that provided equal access to public education regardless of disabling condition established by several federal court decisions during the early 1970s were broader in scope (*Pennsylvania Association for Retarded Citizens* v. *Commonwealth of Pennsylvania* and *Mills* v. *Board of Education*). Subsequently, public policies acknowledged that unfair stereotypes and discrimination were as great a problem for many people with disabilities as were their impairments.

The first two major federal laws protecting the rights of people with disabilities were passed in the early 1970s. The Rehabilitation Act of 1973 prohibited discrimination on the basis of disability by recipients of federal assistance (such as state and local governments, schools and colleges, hospitals, and public transit systems), and by federal contractors. This statute required that federally supported services be accessible and that they practice nondiscrimination in providing service and in employment practices.

The Education for All Handicapped Children Act of 1974 required equal access to public education and related services for all children regardless of their handicaps. This program led to the inclusion in regular school programs of many disabled children who had previously been segregated into special education classes or refused services altogether.

Antidiscrimination laws and rulings were the result of demands for legal protection by people with disabilities and their advocates. At least three major groups were involved. The first included concerned family members and other non-disabled advocates for people with disabilities often unable to advocate for themselves, such as children and people with severe cognitive or emotional impairments.

The second group championing disabled rights included organizations of people with disabilities who were active in lobbying on their own behalf for equal access to public life. This group of advocates, sometimes known as the disability rights movement, included groups organized around specific impairments such as blindness, deafness, or paraplegia, and coalitions including a wide range of disabling conditions. Such organizations were particularly concerned about the enactment and enforcement of prohibitions of discrimination in public accommodation, public transportation, employment, housing, and communication systems.

> *Although people with disabilities have gained the legal right to participate in the mainstream of American society, rights in themselves are no guarantee of social change.*

The third major group of advocates established the independent living movement. This movement included local self-help and advocacy groups that set up independent living centers. The centers were organized in communities around the country during the 1960s following the founding of the first such enterprise in Berkeley, California. Independent living centers seek to assist people who might otherwise be forced to live in institutional settings and are typically led by individuals who themselves have disabilities. The independent living movement has been active in promoting self-sufficiency by shifting service provision from institutional to community settings, promoting accessible housing, transportation, and employment, and giving people with disabilities more control over services they receive and those who provide them.

After the legislative gains of the 1970s, the legal status of people with disabilities as a protected minority group was tested in the courts and debated as part of the attack on government regulation during the 1980s. Overall, the case for guaranteeing people with disabilities access to public life came to be accepted across the political spectrum. Several issues were hotly contested, the most visible of which in the 1980s was the demand by disability rights groups that urban mass transit systems be made accessible through mandating wheelchair access to bus, rail, and subway systems. While the cost of transition to fully accessible systems was high and the demand uncertain, disability advocates viewed accessibility as a measure of legal equality. Critics of full accessibility argued for the alternative of separate "paratransit" systems utilizing vans and taxis, although the service provided by many such systems was often unreliable and subject to limitations on the time and purpose of travel. The debate over accessible mainstream transit versus segregated paratransit was largely resolved by the 1990s in favor of accessibility.

The landmark statute guaranteeing the rights of people with disabilities is the Americans with Disabilities Act of 1990 (ADA), which prohibits discrimination on the basis of disability in employment, public accommodation, public transportation, and telecommunications. It parallels the prohibition on racial discrimination of the Civil Rights Act of 1964. Some of the major provisions of this law include the requirement that private employers with more than fifteen workers practice nondiscrimination in hiring and make facilities and services accessible to qualified disabled employees, that all new vehicles purchased or leased by public transit agencies be accessible, that public and private providers of public accommodations practice non-discrimination and remove architectural barriers, and that telecommunications relay services for speech and hearing impaired individuals be established under the supervision of the Federal Communications Commission.

With the enactment of ADA, persons with disabilities have gained the legal right to participate in the mainstream of American society on the basis of their abilities. Rights in themselves are no guarantee of social change. Issues of participation, social integration, and independent living will continue to pose challenges for disabled individuals.

[See also Health Care: Moral Issues; Public Assistance Programs: Social Security; Social Welfare Philosophies; Unemployment Insurance, Workers' Compensation.]

BIBLIOGRAPHY

DeJong, G., and Lifchez, R. "Physical Disability and Public Policy." *Scientific American* 248 (1983): 40–49.

Percy, Stephen L. *Disability, Civil Rights, and Public Policy: The Politics of Implementation.* Tuscaloosa, AL: University of Alabama Press, 1989.

Scotch, Richard K. *From Good Will to Civil Rights: Transforming Federal Disability Policy.* Philadelphia: Temple University Press, 1984.

West, Jane, ed. *The Americans With Disabilities Act: From Policy to Practice.* New York: Milbank Memorial Fund, 1991.

— RICHARD K. SCOTCH

DISASTERS, PLANNING FOR

Following the devastating earthquake in Kobe, Japan, on January 24, 1995, which registered a 7.2 magnitude on the Richter scale, the city council of New York City decided that all new construction in the city will be required to have greater resistance to earthquakes. New York City does not have the tectonic activity of a truly major fault (as do California and Japan) because it is in the middle of a geologic plate. But New York City is built on geologic faults, so earthquakes do occur— about once a century. Hence the possibility cannot be ruled out of a New York City quake with an intensity measuring 5.0 on the logarithmic Richter scale (i.e., more than 100 times weaker than the Kobe quake). Its likelihood can be said to approach "zero," and yet the potential economic damage from such an occurrence was estimated at $25 billion.

To guard in this way against a peril we hope will never occur is accepted as a part of the cost of promoting public safety. Doing so is expensive, however, and it becomes a policy dilemma when such calamities are infrequent and their frequency is thought to approach zero. Fundamental questions involving risk/benefit assessment are at stake here.

The Zero-Infinity Dilemma

Rare occurrences like the Kobe earthquake force us to alter our planning for the future. It may appear that there is close to zero chance that a given hypothetical event might occur; nevertheless, when such an event does occur, the disruption it causes may be so great, conceptually, that it may seem to approach infinity—hence the concept of the "zero-infinity dilemma."

How Much Protection—and How Much Risk?

How much should society spend to protect itself now against such potentially disastrous but probably unlikely future events? In thinking about this it is helpful to examine other examples of the zero-infinity dilemma.

During World War II, scientists of the U.S. Manhattan Project thought it entirely possible—but unlikely—that exploding an atomic bomb might ignite the Earth's atmosphere and burn up all its oxygen, ending life. There are extremely important questions about whether any nation or group ever should presume to take such a risk for everyone else and for all time. But they took that risk, and their worst fears did not happen. And this fact reminds us vividly that the unlikely catastrophic event does *not* always happen.

Again, in the 1970s when natural gas began to be liquefied for transport and sale worldwide, special tankers were built to bring the liquefied natural gas (LNG) to transfer points on distant shores. One such transfer station was to be built in Everett, a working-class community adjacent to the busy Boston harbor and downtown Boston. There was speculation in some circles at the Massachusetts Institute of Technology in nearby Cambridge about what might happen if one of the LNG tankers ever were involved in a collision with another ship in Boston harbor. It was known that when a small amount of LNG was dropped into water, it exploded; also that LNG, when released from being pressurized, turned to vapor and became a dense and very combustible fog (if it did not immediately explode) which would quickly fill the harbor and downtown Boston, smothering all in its path; and finally the vapor,

like all natural gas, could easily be ignited by a single spark in a great conflagration. It is characteristic of the zero-infinity dilemma that no laboratory tests, scale model tests, or even pilot plant tests can show us in advance what the full-scale event will entail. Just as no one knew in advance the consequences of the Exxon Valdez oil tanker accident off Alaska, which involved releasing a large amount of oil into the waters and fisheries of Fitzwilliam Sound, so too the consequences of a sudden large LNG release into water has still unknown consequences. The LNG terminal in busy Boston harbor has been in safe operation for the past twenty years without an LNG tanker collision.

Bad Things Do Happen

Big technology often involves big unknowns. Standard behavior of such technologies is familiar and safe, but occasionally a malfunction or accident sets in motion unprecedented and unfamiliar behaviors. Recent examples are the nuclear meltdown at the Chernobyl power plant in the Soviet Union (April 26, 1986); the Exxon Valdez oil spill (March 24, 1989); and the failure of the northeastern U.S. power-generating and distribution network on November 9, 1965. In the last instance, in 2.7 seconds more than 30 million people over 80,000 square miles were cast into darkness, and 800,000 people were trapped in New York City's subways.

Rare occurrences such as the earthquake in Kobe, Japan, on January 24, 1995, force us to alter our planning for the future.

It is fortunate that such events are rare. But they can and do occur. One of our most challenging responsibilities for the future is identifying such zero-infinity possibilities and then deciding how to protect society from potentially enormous disruptions and hazards, if they should ever occur.

When Those Put at Risk Are Not Those Getting Benefits

Further complicating our assessments in such matters is the frequent separation between *those who will benefit* from putting everyone at such great (but probably unlikely) risk, and all *those who will be hurt* should that worst eventuality happen. At Chernobyl, the power generated was used within the Soviet Union. But after the nuclear meltdown, the radiation that spilled into the atmosphere was transported by wind currents to points throughout Eastern and Central Europe and as far west as France and north throughout Scandinavia.

Again, the benefits are often for *those living now,* and the potential catastrophic costs or damage (if the event occurs) will be borne by *those who will live in the future.* So the intergenerational questions of the zero-infinity dilemma focus on how risks and benefits should be distributed among different generations. Earlier generations often decide these questions before subsequent generations are even born. In doing so they face difficult policy dilemmas. Do we go for the benefit now? And how concerned are we about potential downside risks that could impose great consequences on future generations? The question remains the same: How well do we guard ourselves and others against low-likelihood but very big disasters?

[See also Natural Disasters; Surprises; Wildcards.]

BIBLIOGRAPHY

Bertell, Rosalie. *No Immediate Danger. Prognosis for a Radioactive Earth.* Summertown, TN: Book Publishing Co., 1985.
Commoner, Barry. *The Closing Circle: Nature, Man and Technology.* New York: Alfred Knopf, 1971.
Winner, Langdon. *Autonomous Technology: Technics-out-of-Control as a Theme in Political Thought.* Cambridge, MA.: MIT Press, 1977.

– DAVID DODSON GRAY

DIVORCE

When looking at trends relating to divorce, it is immediately clear that married couples around the world now divorce and remarry in numbers that would have been beyond comprehension thirty years ago. Over the past two decades, more women raised children without marriage and many couples married later than previously. In the future, it is safe to assume that a large segment of the adult population will flow into and out of several marital categories during their lives, and the proportion of children in a traditional nuclear family will continue to decline as family patterns grow more complex.

It is very likely that marriage at later ages, no marriage, and no remarriage will continue to increase. Divorce is not expected to exceed 60 percent and in fact is likely to decline. At least one forecast holds out 40 percent divorce rates and 65 percent remarriage rates as world maximums for the year 2000, and cohabitation among younger couples and the elderly will continue to serve as a factor in keeping official divorce rates down.

Although projecting future trends directly from past events is a complex endeavor in a time of change (especially when social trends are involved), in the case of divorce trends around the world, a look at the past may be helpful. Some dramatic changes have already occurred, and we seem to be entering a period of relative stability. Over the past several decades, we have seen major alterations, especially in the United States, of marriage patterns, childbearing, women's employment, parenting, and attitudes toward marriage. Both pro-family and anti-family forces have been at work affecting rates of divorce worldwide. These include later first marriages, delayed childbearing, and increased education and work experience among women.

Between the late 1960s and 1980, the divorce rate in the United States, for example, doubled—to the point where one out of two marriages could be expected to end in divorce. This rate of change reflects an accelerating curve, from a seven percent divorce rate in 1860 to twenty-five percent in 1945. The rate plateaued for about fifteen years, then climbed again, then plateaued again. The interesting question is whether 1995 will mark the start of another steep climb.

There continues to be an inverse relationship between age and the likelihood of divorce, and an inverse relationship between divorce and the attainment of formal educational degrees, no matter what the level of overall education. As well, premarital conception or birth of children seems to be directly related to divorce rates.

A complicating factor in forecasting social change is the interactive nature of these dynamics. For example, higher divorce rates create a larger pool of eligibles for remarriage. In 1991, more than four out of ten American marriages were second marriages or above, but the rate of remarriage after divorce has declined over the past fifteen years—while the overall divorce rate remained constant. Like many social phenomena, divorce and its counterpart, marriage, are individual decisions, resulting from individual factors, such as age, education, pregnancy, etc. Whether or not societies function as systems with discernible internal dynamics continues to be a matter of debate. It is just as arguable that the regularities of collective behavior represent responses to common stimuli.

The differences in marriage and divorce laws among countries present challenges for international comparability of data, as does the accuracy of polling surveys. Divorced people often represent themselves as single, married, or widowed, for a variety of personal reasons. While increases in divorce rate have occurred in both developed countries other than the U.S. and undeveloped countries, the relative rates are always lower, as American divorce rates are the highest in the world (and U.S. data on divorce are the most detailed). Divorce rates in the United States are twice those in Europe, except for the countries of the former Soviet Union, which nearly match those of their former enemy. However, the marriage rates of Western and Northern Europe are about half that of the United States, producing many fewer couples to divorce. In Asia, rates range from one-fourth to one-tenth those of the United States, and are also holding steady. Data from South America show levels and patterns similar to those of Asia.

> *In the future, a large segment of the adult*
>
> *population will flow into and out of*
>
> *several marital categories during their lives.*

There is little information on divorce in the African countries, with only 12 percent of the nearly sixty countries in Africa providing data to the United Nations. In African countries, divorce is not a universal right for men, much less for women, and there was not the substantial increase in divorce rates during the 1970s that occurred elsewhere. In Muslim countries, women have no right of divorce whatsoever. These data highlight the differences among countries—i.e., how cultural norms strongly influence social trends like marriage and divorce. What is clear across all countries, however, is that the impacts of divorce are strikingly different between men and women, especially women with children.

In addition, it is not very accurate to speak of divorce rates or any other social trends as if a given society was wholly homogeneous, exhibiting change uniformly throughout. One area of distinctions within countries or societies in the past has been among racial or ethnic groups. This is most clearly shown in the United States, where the most detailed data exist. In all cases, changes in divorce rates have been strongly tied to rates of marriage. In 1975, there was only a 7 percent variance between the rates of black versus white women who had ever married. By 1990, only 75 percent of black women in their late thirties had ever married, compared with 91 percent of white women in the same age group—Hispanic rates were similar to those of whites. It is useful to contrast this with racial or ethnic group attitudes toward marriage. Life-long marriage continues to be the ideal among those polled on the subject, in all but about 12 percent of the population. The one exception to this was black men, where the rate of those who rejected marriage as a lifetime goal increased to 23 percent. Again, white and Hispanic rates were very similar in this area.

As important as the raw numerical data are the implications of these trends in terms of the human condition. One impact of divorce is the one-parent family, which also shows variation among racial or ethnic groups. Blacks, for example, now have the highest single-parent rates of any racial group in the U.S., with 55 percent of all American black children living with only one parent in 1990 (versus 27 percent of Hispanic and 19 percent of white families). The impact also varied by gender. Six percent of these one-parent black children lived with a father rather than a mother, as opposed to 10 percent of Hispanic one-parent families and 15 percent of whites. Estimates are that nearly half of those children alive today will spend time in a one-parent family. In Europe and elsewhere in the world, the growth of single-parent families has been much less than in the United States, with most births occurring to couples (whether married or unmarried) followed by lower rates of divorce or separation. The developed regions have the highest number of single-parent households, with Latin America and the Caribbean next, Africa third, and Asia lowest, with under 10 percent overall.

Another area of substantial change is in the growth of cohabitation, especially among older adults. This was especially true in the developed regions, Latin America, and the Caribbean. These unions remain poorly defined and largely under-reflected in public data, as they are without official beginning or end. Some estimate that as much as half of the population will experience a period of cohabitation by their mid-thirties over the next decade. When measured by such factors as births to unmarried couples, the rates are clearly rising. For example, the percentage of married births in France declined from 60 percent of the total in 1970 to 40 percent by 1980. Across regions, Africa, the Caribbean, and Europe all showed rates of over 40 percent unmarried births, in 1985, while Japan had only 1 percent of its births outside marriage. In the United States, less than 15 percent of American adults polled recently disapprove of cohabitation under any circumstances. With a growing acceptance of alternatives, the data on divorce may have less policy impact, as living arrangements and parenting decisions come to depend less on marital status.

[See also Change; Child Care; Children, Living Arrangements; Families and Households; Family Patterns; Family Problems; Family Values; Household Composition; Marriage; Social Change: United States; Values; Values Change; Values Formation; Women and Work; Women's Movement.]

BIBLIOGRAPHY

Bumpers, Larry L., "What's Happening to the Family? Interactions Between Demographic and Institutional Change." *Demography* 27 (1990): 483–498.

Norton, Arthur J., and Miller, Louisa F. *Marriage Divorce and Remarriage in the 1990s.* Washington, DC: Bureau of the Census, 1992.

Seager, Joni, and Olson, Ann. *Women in the World.* London, U.K.: Pluto Press, 1986.

South, Scott. "Racial Ethnic Differences in the Desire to Marry." *Journal of Marriage and the Family* 55 (1993): 357–370.

The World's Women, 1970–1990: Trends and Statistics, New York: United Nations, 1992.

Women's Indicators and Statistical Spreadsheet Database. New York, United Nations, 1992.

– TIMOTHY CRAIG MACK

DRUGS, ILLICIT

As the twenty-first century begins, the detrimental effects of illicit drugs will touch every segment of society. There is no class, race, ethnic or age group, or geographic region immune from the human suffering, crime, violence, and devastation of illicit drugs. The impact of illicit drugs is immeasurable, with some estimates putting the cost at over $67 billion per year. Over the past decade, federal funds spent on law enforcement interdiction efforts increased 27 percent; state and local funds spent on drug control 1,000 percent; funds allocated to drug treatment 1,700 percent; and funds spent on drug treatment 400 percent.

The United States has seen a decline in the number of illicit drug users since 1979, when it peaked at 24 million, with a slight resurgence in the mid-1990s but uncertainty as to its continuation. Debate will also continue about the so-called "war on drugs" and whether a combat-like approach, with emphasis on enforcement, is more effective than a health and prevention approach.

The change toward more conservative politics in the United States will shift emphasis in dealing with illicit drugs to enforcement and incarceration from rehabilitation, harm reduction, and other alternatives to traditional approaches.

Among the most dramatic trends that will continue into the next century is the aging of current users. In the fifteen years from 1979 to 1993, rates of current illicit drug use declined among people twelve to thirty-four years of age. By contrast, use increased among people aged thirty-five and older (10 percent in 1979 to 28 percent in 1993), due in part to heavy drug use by this population in the 1960s and '70s. The decline among younger people is attributed to education, prevention, and fear of the drug-related sexually transmitted disease HIV.

While international cooperation has increased along with federal resources allocated to drug enforcement, primary responsibility for enforcement of street-level illicit drug use continues to rest with local police departments. Drug sweeps and crackdowns to reduce open-air drug markets in neighborhoods, problem-solving programs as a component of community policing, and prevention programs such as D.A.R.E. will continue to be implemented by city and county police agencies, supported by federal agencies and/or grants. The lack of resources, combined with a fragmented criminal justice system, places future odds in favor of drug merchants, according to some authorities.

The Anti-Drug Abuse Act of 1986 provided $230 million for enhanced drug enforcement by state and local law enforcement agencies. No study or other measure of effectiveness has authenticated that this infusion of funds had any significant effect on the illicit drug trade at the street (retail), wholesale, dealer, manufacturer, or kingpin level. One of the primary areas of need in coming years will be to assess the cost-effectiveness of antidrug enforcement efforts.

Some successes in reducing illicit drugs—such as international cooperation, more efficient use of interagency task forces, multilateral action against money laundering, and more stringent control of essential and precursor chemicals needed to manufacture illicit drugs—will continue into the twenty-first century. The failures will also continue.

Illicit drugs, including crops needed to produce them (coca, opium), will continue to be a financial boon to drug lords and corrupt officials in the developing nations. Hundreds of tons of cocaine and heroin will be transported into the United States, Europe, and Central Asia. Consumption of illicit drugs will increase in Latin America. Drug trafficking will expand dramatically in Eastern Europe, particularly in former Soviet states. Infusion of large amounts of money, primarily from the United States, will be the mainstay for the limited interdiction and reduction activities that occur in these countries.

Cocaine and its highly addictive derivative, crack, will remain a major high-use, high-demand product in the United States and Europe. Cocaine will remain a staple of illicit drug users, but recent decline in use among young people should continue.

Crack is a relatively new drug, first appearing on the market in the late 1980s. It is and will remain one of the fastest growing drugs in the United States. Crack is cheap. It gives a "high" that only lasts five to twenty minutes, meaning that addicts require frequent hits and will commit crimes necessary as needed to get the money they need to make a purchase. Crack usually produces a powerful chemical dependency within two weeks. A byproduct of the crack trade requiring attention well into the future is the birth of so-called "crack babies," a new population born with a dependency and other ill effects. Crack babies will require significant medical, educational, and other human service resources.

Approximately 1.3 million people—0.6 percent of the United States population—are cocaine users. Of this group, about 500,000 are considered frequent cocaine users, which means they have used it at least weekly for a period of one or more years. While the number of users remains stable, overall use of cocaine has declined steadily since 1985. This trend will continue.

Over half of the people in local jails in

the United States committed the offense

for which they were incarcerated while under

the influence of drugs, alcohol, or both.

Cocaine will continue to affect people of all races, ethnic groups, and socioeconomic classes. Fifty-nine percent of cocaine users are white, 23 percent are black, and 16 percent are Hispanic. A higher percentage of high school-educated people (1.3 percent) use cocaine than those with some college (0.7 percent) or a college degree (0.8 percent). These trends will continue.

To stem the volume of cocaine and other illicit drugs, increased emphasis will be placed on reducing cultivation. By 1990, every state in the United States participated in the cannabis-eradication program sponsored by the Drug Enforcement Agency, eliminating 29,000 cannabis plots and 7.3 million cultivated plants.

With most of the world's supply of coca limited to three countries (Peru, Colombia, and Bolivia), crop suppression is and will remain a potentially viable method for eradication. However, its success will continue to be hampered by political influence and corruption fostered by the drug cartels, and changing political and enforcement priorities. Due to ineffective enforcement by the government and a growing crop, Peru will remain the world's primary producer of coca well into the twenty-first century.

In past decades, most of the heroin used in the United States came from Southeast and Southwest Asia (Myanmar, Laos, Afghanistan) and Mexico. But the supply market is beginning to shift. Southeast and Southwest Asia produce white refined heroin while Mexico produces "black tar." Both of these sources will continue.

In the years ahead, an increasing volume of heroin will come from Colombia. Opium cultivation will increase in countries such as Pakistan (the fifth largest producer in the world) and Afghanistan (the second largest producer) due to limited eradication and prosecution efforts and banking regulations that allow money laundering to occur without restraint. Three-fourths of the world's opium supply is produced in an area known as the Golden Triangle (Thailand, Myanmar, Laos). Due to corruption in the government and military and direct ties between the military and growers, Myanmar will continue to grow opiates at increased rates with few, if any, constraints.

The number of heroin users in the United States is conservatively estimated at almost 2.5 million people, a fluctuating but continually growing number. Growth in the number of heroin users should continue at a steady rate well into the future, with increased reliance on smokable varieties rather than those taken through injection. Regardless of the variety, heroin will receive increased attention as its use and the subsequent number of heroin-related deaths grows.

The most common illicit drug is marijuana, used by three-fourths (77 percent) of all drug users. However, its use is in decline. Researchers debate whether the decline will continue. In 1993, 4.3 percent of the American population (approximately 9 million people) was using marijuana or hashish. This is a steady drop in use from 1985 when 9.3 percent of the population (approximately 17.8 million people) used marijuana or hashish. Despite the debate, stabilization or a small decline in the use of marijuana is expected to continue in the years ahead, with the exception of the school-age population, as new medical findings point to it being more dangerous.

There was a decline in the nonmedical use of psychotherapeutic drugs from 1985 to 1991. By 1992, the decline ceased and nonmedical use of sedatives, stimulants, and analgesics stabilized. Since then, there has been a slow increase in the illicit use of these drugs. The nonmedical use of tranquilizers has continued to decline. These trends are expected to change along with the demographics of the population.

As the population of the United States ages and the baby boomers experience some of the ailments associated with aging, illicit use and abuse of prescription medication will grow. Self-medication using legally obtained prescriptions will become more prevalent as will sharing and reselling of legally obtained medications. The market for illegally obtained prescription medications will also expand. Counterfeiting prescriptions will become a growing problem for both law enforcement and health organizations.

According to the National Household Survey on Drug Abuse, there have been no noteworthy changes in the use of hallucinogens (LSD, amphetamine variants, mescaline and peyote, and phencyclidine [PCP]) or inhalants (glue, paint, petroleum products) in recent years. As new hallucinogens and derivatives of known hallucinogens are found, there may be a wave of increased use. While the extent of use has changed little, the potency and dangers of the hallucinogens being used have increased. Health officials have estimated the potency of some forms of LSD to be ten times greater than the drug used in the late 1960s. Law enforcement has been mildly effective in supporting legislation to control ingredients used to manufacture some chemically based hallucinogens and will continue to pursue this avenue for prevention.

The correlation between illicit drugs (trafficking and use) and violence will continue into the next century. Studies of street use of illicit drugs by criminals now serving time in prison for both violent and nonviolent offenses support this. Among the approximately 400,000 men and women in local jails in the United States, 23 percent are incarcerated for drug-related offenses, representing an increase of 9 percent over a six year period.

Over half of the people incarcerated in local jails in the United States admitted to committing the offense for which they were incarcerated while under the influence of drugs, alcohol, or both. One in four convicted inmates admitted to using major drugs—heroin, cocaine, crack, LSD, or PCP—in the period prior to committing their crime.

Approximately 29 percent of jail inmates committed their crime while under the sole influence of alcohol, 15 percent under the influence of drugs, and 12 percent under the influence of both alcohol and drugs. There is no indication that the number of criminals who use drugs or the number of crimes committed by people while under the influence of drugs will decline.

Violence will continue to stem from disputes among rival street-level distributors, conflicts between buyers and sellers, domestic arguments in which one or both parties are influenced by drugs or alcohol, and confrontations between police and those involved in the drug trade. Third party injuries—including deaths to bystanders and other innocent people—will continue as low-level "franchise" dealers who deal their merchandise in neighborhoods rely on violence to resolve disputes.

As street gangs and pseudo gangs (youth modeling gang behavior) continue to emerge, there will be more franchising of the illicit drug trade. It will take its form in highly structured street markets and informal get-rich-quick schemes. Young people will assume a greater role in dealing drugs in neighborhoods, paying a percent of their profits to the person who gave them the franchise to deal. In turn, they may franchise part of their small operation to others.

This street-level franchising of the drug trade will perpetuate both wanton and planned violence. Street-level dealers will be well armed and willing to kill or maim anyone over a small amount of money or to protect his or her franchise. They will plague law enforcement agencies and their communities. In response, law enforcement agencies will expand the concept of drug market analysis to anticipate where and how the drug trade and its franchisees move, support tighter gun laws, and pursue mandatory sentences without parole for drug dealers who use weapons.

Estimates place annual spending on enforcement of the drug laws at $2–4.4 billion. The number of full-time law enforcement officers assigned to drug enforcement is small and will remain so. There are two primary reasons that more police resources will not be not assigned to address illicit drugs: declining local and federal government funds and the movement toward community policing.

As of 1990, over 3,200 law enforcement agencies in the United States operated special drug units, including 29 state police organizations. Approximately 6,000 local police officers, 3,500 sheriffs deputies, and 2,000 state police officers are assigned to drug units.

Local police will continue to focus the majority of drug enforcement efforts on street-level activities. Covert police operations designed to infiltrate cartels and large-scale drug operations drain resources, consume a great deal of time, and therefore will remain few in number.

Limited law enforcement resources combined with increased citizen fear about illicit drugs will cause an increased number of communities to turn to private or contractual security forces to provide basic protective services.

Asset forfeiture laws allow the government to seize cash, vehicles, houses, and other goods gained as a result of trading in illicit drugs. State and local laws dictate how seized assets may be used.

There has been significant debate about whether funds resulting from seized assets should be reallocated to police service or returned to the government's general fund to serve a multitude of uses. In recent years, the trend has been to allocate all or a larger portion of seized assets to law enforcement agencies, and this will continue.

A concern for the future is that the potential to seize assets may dictate how and where law enforcement agencies channel drug investigations and resources. This is of particular concern in jurisdictions in which police departments are in need of equipment and other items not available through their operating budget. Strict controls over allocation of investigative resources will be required to prevent emphasis on seizing assets as a primary thrust in conducting investigations into illicit drugs.

Drug losses in the workplace are measured in billions of dollars annually. On-the-job injuries, losses due to excessive sick leave (16 times higher than average for someone who is drug or alcohol dependent), violence, and other byproducts of drug use in the work place will continue. However, drug testing prior to and as part of employment has begun to have a positive effect. Employers will continue to screen out at-risk employees. Ultimately, drug testing of all candidates and random, select, or total testing of work forces will become commonplace.

There is a resurgence in the call for legalization and decriminalization of drugs and this will continue. The last significant movement toward legalization occurred in the late 1960s and early '70s. Current proponents discuss legalization as part of "harm reduction," the concept of supporting addicts so that they can function within the society; legalization of some drugs is required. Proponents of this approach cite less reliance on illegal drugs, more effective monitoring of addicts, reduced profits for illegal drug dealers, and less strain on the criminal justice system as benefits. The legalization and harm reduction movement will continue to gain respectability.

While theories have been put forward there has been little research to show that legalization and decriminalization of hard drugs will reduce deaths, injuries, and other crimes related to drug abuse. In Amsterdam, the Netherlands, legalization of marijuana has reduced some crimes and stabilized the number of hard drug users. According to polls, the majority of the public and elected officials in the United States do not favor legalization of drugs.

People often confuse calls for increased treatment, reduced incarceration, and rehabilitation with legalization. As traditional methods of enforcement and treatment fail to provide solutions to the problems caused by illicit drugs, additional funds will be channeled to research on legalization.

[See also Alcohol; Crime, Nonviolent; Tobacco.]

BIBLIOGRAPHY

Chaiken, Marcia R. Street Level Drug Enforcement: Examining the Issues. Washington, DC: National Institute of Justice, U.S. Department of Justice, 1988.

International Narcotics Control Strategy Report. Washington, DC: Bureau of International Narcotics Measures, U.S. Department of State, 1993.

Drugs, Crime, and the Justice System. Washington, DC: Bureau of Justice Statistics, U.S. Department of Justice, 1992.

— SHELDON F. GREENBERG

DYING.

See DEATH AND DYING.

DYSTOPIAS

The concept of *dystopia* was apparently first used by English philosopher John Stuart Mill in the mid-nineteenth century. The word is formed by using the Greek root *dys-*, "with the notion of hard, bad, unlucky, etc.," to replace the first syllable in *utopia*. A synonym (also coined by Mill) is *cacotopia*. Since cacophony or dissonance are the opposites of euphony (good sound), so dystopia and cacotopia are the opposites of utopia (really *eu*-topia) meaning "good place."

Strictly defined, a dystopia is "a place or condition in which everything is as bad as possible." Thus a dystopian vision of the future emphasizes the serious problems that may result from deliberate policies, indecision and indifference, or simply bad luck in humanity's attempts to manage its affairs.

The secret to being a futurist lies in taking a critical view of both dystopian and utopian visions— balancing the need to prepare for the worst with a desire to achieve the best.

In fiction, dystopian visions have most often taken the form of antiutopias—satirical or prophetic warnings against the proposed "improvement" of society by some political faction, class interest, technology, or other artifact. Perhaps the best known and most relentlessly bleak examples of political dystopias in fiction are Eugene Zamiatin's novel *We* (1924), and George Orwell's *Nineteen Eighty-Four* (1949).

But in the late twentieth century, dystopian visions in fiction have grown more complex, embracing such diverse ingredients as: nuclear war (Nevil Shute's *On the Beach*, 1957); overpopulation (John Brunner's *Stand on Zanzibar*, 1968); pollution (Philip Wylie's *The End of the Dream*, 1972), or cultural breakdown and subversion (Anthony Burgess's *A Clockwork Orange*, 1962).

Dystopian visions have dominated movies set in the future from the early silent classic *Metropolis* (1926) to contemporary adventure films like *Road Warrior* (1981), *Blade Runner* (1982), *The Terminator* (1984), or *Total Recall* (1990). Whether the hero triumphs or barely squeaks by, most future films leave viewers feeling that tomorrow's world is likely to be crowded, regimented, crumbling, and extremely violent. Even such relatively upbeat films as *2001: A Space Odyssey* (1968), or the fairytale-like *Star Wars* trilogy (1977–1983) dwell on the trials and dangers of a perilous existence.

On television, too, attempts to depict future society have generally emphasized dystopian visions. About the only "*eu*-topian" futures presented in the mass media have come from the television series *Star Trek* (1966–1969) and *Star Trek: The Next Generation* (1987–1994). But even here the belief in progress does not imply that perfection will ever be achieved.

The prevalence of dystopian future visions in fiction is not surprising. Conflict is the heart of fiction, and conflict in a perfect society is hard to find. Utopia may be a wonderful place to live in, but it often is dull to hear about or view secondhand.

Dystopian visions outside fiction presumably do not arise from any desire to entertain. True, bad news often sells better than good. But to be successful, a prophet needs to offer some hope. From the Old Testament Book of Jonah to the Club of Rome Report, *The Limits to Growth* (1972) and its 1992 sequel, *Beyond the Limits,* the point of issuing a serious warning has been to inspire timely counteraction and thereby to prevent, if possible, a dystopian vision from becoming reality. However pessimistic their predictions, most scientists and scholars who warn of impending disaster are really acting from antidystopian motives. If they did not believe there was some chance to avert disaster or shape a better future, they would not warn us.

In contrast to the numerous attempts made to establish utopian communities, there has probably never been a self-acknowledged dystopia in practice. Even most prison systems claim improvement as their goal. Just how bad must a society be to qualify as a dystopia? Also, who is to judge what is good and bad?

Aldous Huxley's novel *Brave New World* (1932) is often called a technological dystopia, but the society it describes holds more attractions for readers today (particularly young ones) than its author intended. The question arises: can dystopia and utopia exist simultaneously, depending on one's point of view?

The ancient city-state of Athens under Pericles may have seemed a near utopia to its wealthy and well-educated citizens, but the powerless and ignorant slaves whose labor made Athenian society possible experienced life very differently in that same time and place.

The value of fictional dystopias and of pessimistic warnings by scientists and scholars is to counteract the optimistic bias in human nature—the tendency to deny unwelcome truths that psychologists Margaret Matlin and David Stang identify in their book *The Pollyanna Principle* (1978). Whatever goals we set ourselves, careful planning and hard work are often needed to turn dreams into reality. Unless we face our fears, we risk becoming prematurely complacent and may fail to follow through on difficult or complex projects.

But the dystopian vision is also limiting and contains a special danger: it can poison our outlook on the present, or even prompt us to give up trying to do better. Anyone who sets out to create a believable utopia must be prepared to answer skeptics with reasoned arguments and facts. Yet we can build powerful dystopian visions in our own minds by piling up isolated pieces of bad news without ever questioning their source or relative importance in a global context.

Natural disasters, accidents, crime, war, disease, social injustice—all these and many other insults assault us daily through alarming headlines and "sound bites." Taken together, to some they convey a picture of a world where nothing works—in short, dystopia now. If we accept this image uncritically, it can make all future planning and risk-taking seem pointless.

Perhaps the secret to being a futurist lies in taking a critical view of both dystopian and utopian visions—balancing the need to prepare for the worst with a desire to achieve the best.

[See also Apocalyptic Future; Change, Optimistic and Pessimistic Perspectives; Science Fiction; Utopias.]

BIBLIOGRAPHY

Amis, Kingsley. *New Maps of Hell. A Survey of Science Fiction.* New York: Harcourt, Brace, 1960.

Clarke, I. F. *The Tale of the Future,* 3rd ed. London: The Library Association, 1979.

———. *Voices Prophesying War. Future Wars 1763–3749.* 2nd ed. New York: Oxford University Press, 1992. (See esp. pp. 149–153, and Chapter 6, "From the Flame Deluge to the Bad Time," pp. 165–217.)

Stableford, Brian M. "Dystopias." In John Clute and Peter Nicholls, eds. *The Encyclopedia of Science Fiction.* 2nd ed. New York: St. Martin's Press, 1993, pp. 360–362.

— LANE E. JENNINGS

E

ECONOMIC CYCLES: MODELS AND SIMULATIONS

Unfavorable forces have been exerting growing pressures on the U.S. economy for decades. Government and private sector policies since 1960 have caused severe economic imbalances that may take years to correct. These imbalances include excess manufacturing capacity, rising corporate and personal debt, large trade imbalances, and chronic budget deficits.

Is such an array of forces merely a streak of bad luck or are they only multiple coincidences? Or are they connected below the surface to powerful forces of change? The best explanation may be found in a mode of behavior called the economic long-wave, popularly known as the Kondratieff Cycle, after the Russian economist, Nikolai Kondratieff.

The economic long-wave is controversial, both as to its cause and even as to its existence. Those who believe in its existence see it as a great rise and fall of economic activity, with peaks and valleys some forty-five to sixty years apart. It is considered to be the cause of the great depressions of the 1830s, 1890s, and 1930s. The nature of the economic long-wave remains unclear in the absence of a theory on how it is generated. Instead, depressions have been attributed to accidents or mismanagement. For example, the Great Depression of the 1930s has been blamed on the mistaken policies of the Federal Reserve. Most economic theory is based on equilibrium, or steady-state, conditions that leave little room for long-term fluctuations between booms and depressions. However, at least one comprehensive and coherent theory is able to explain the economic long-wave. It is the Systems Dynamics National Model developed at the Sloan School of Management at MIT. The National Model is a computer-simulation model based on the policies followed in banks, industries, markets, and governments. The model is self-contained and operates without external inputs controlling its behavior. It generates short-term business cycles with peaks some three to ten years apart and economic long-waves with a major rise and fall in economic activity having peaks some fifty years apart.

A computer-simulation model is a theory of the behavior it creates. The structure of the model and the decision-making policies within it cause the resulting behavior. The model can be used to understand how production, investment, savings, construction, and credit can interact to produce, over many decades, great waves of excessive economic expansion and contraction.

Powerful computer simulation models are available that can help governments and corporations manage complex economic and social problems.

The National Model provides a unique perspective from which to interpret the economy and understand real-world economic behavior. It sheds new light on the meaning of many puzzling and controversial things. For example, real interest rates (bank interest minus inflation) drop to low or negative values before a long-wave peak, as they did in the 1970s, and then quickly rise to high values after the peak, as they did in the early 1930s. Such interest behavior seems little affected by government policies but is deeply embedded in private sector borrowing and investment. Prices and wages rise to a maximum shortly after the peak of long-wave activity and fall during deflation after the peak, as they did sixty years ago. In the early part of a long-wave expansion money is borrowed to build factories; after the peak, depreciation cash flows and new borrowing are used for speculation in land, for corporate acquisitions, and for bidding up prices in the equities markets beyond the underlying business realities. Just before a long-wave peaks, waves of speculation move through the economy, with the run-up in agricultural land prices coming early, speculative peaks and collapses moving through other physical assets, and ending in the peak and fall of urban land prices and the Wall Street stock market.

The central long-wave driving force is overinvestment in physical capital. Construction of physical facilities increases employment and personal income, which, in turn, support more purchasing and the apparent need for still more production facilities. As the economy moves toward a peak and the need for more physical investment diminishes, government makes credit more freely available and introduces investment tax credits to sustain the boom, leading to still more excess physical investment. When prices begin to rise steeply during the late stages of an expansion, the inflation in price of physical assets encourages additional

193

construction as a hedge against prices rising still higher. The demand for more physical capital requires expansion of the capital-producing sectors of the economy for which they also need more capital plant. This "self-ordering" process adds still more to pressures for expansion. The net result is to encourage continuation of construction well beyond actual need.

The long-wave affects the magnitude of business cycles. During long-wave expansion, a shortage of both physical plant and labor limits the overbuilding of inventories of goods and restrains excesses at top business cycles. Also, during the long-wave expansion there is an excess of consumer demand, which keeps the economy from sinking into a recession. However, conditions change after the expansion phase of the long-wave. During a long-wave peak and downturn, the short-term business cycle grows in both its up and down swings. On the up side, excess physical capacity and labor allow overexpansion of business-cycle recoveries, while on the down side, demand is no longer strong enough to avert deeper recessions.

The economic long-wave is a worldwide phenomenon. Trade and money flows lock the world economies together into about the same timing of long-wave rise and fall. There is excess production internationally. Every country is trying to solve its domestic economic weakness by exporting more than it imports, which is not possible. The total must balance.

Long-wave peaks and downturns are times of great international danger. World War I occurred at the peak of a long-wave and World War II in its valley. As internal economic and social conditions worsen, governments tend to divert the attention of their people by engaging in military adventures. A small fraction of the resources devoted to the military would help us to understand and counter the debilitating effects of business cycles. Powerful computer simulation models are available that can help governments and corporations manage complex economic and social problems.

[See also Change; Economics; Forecasting Methods; Macroeconomics; Trend Indicators.]

BIBLIOGRAPHY

Dewey, Edward R., and Dakin, Edwin F. *Cycles: The Science of Prediction.* New York: Henry Holt, 1949.

Forrester, Jay W. *Collected Papers of Jay Forrester.* Cambridge, MA: Wright-Allen Press, 1975.

————. *Urban Dynamics.* Cambridge, MA: The MIT Press, 1960.

————. *World Dynamics.* Cambridge, MA: Wright-Allen Press, 1971.

Frumkin, Norman. *Guide to Economic Indicators.* Armonk, NY: M. E. Sharpe, 1990.

Goldstein, Joshua S. *Long Cycles: Prosperity and War in the Modern Age.* New Haven, CT: Yale University Press, 1988.

Moore, Geoffrey H. *Leading Indicators for the 1990s.* Homewood, IL: Dow Jones-Irwin, 1990.

Ross, Myron H. *A Gale of Creative Destruction: The Coming Economic Boom, 1992–2020.* New York: Praeger; Westport, CT: Greenwood Press, 1989.

Rostow, W. W. *The Stages of Economic Growth.* Cambridge, MA: MIT Press, 1965.

Schlesinger, Arthur M., Jr. *The Cycles of American History.* Boston: Houghton Mifflin, 1986.

Shuman, James B., and Rosenau, David. *The Kondratieff Wave: The Future of America Until 1984 and Beyond.* New York: World Publishing/Times Mirror, 1972.

— JAY W. FORRESTER

ECONOMICS

The early decades of the twenty-first century and the years leading up to it are likely to exhibit a new economic pattern. While retaining important features of the past, they will add new elements to produce historical uniqueness: long-term economic recovery and global growth, along with globalization, market orientation, more widespread economic development, altered industrial structures, and new cyclic manifestations

---

Long-term cyclic forces,

particularly in technology, will play a major role

in the global economic upswing.

Despite serious difficulties, in many ways this is an age of achievement. The promise awakened with the breakdown of the Berlin Wall will haltingly, gradually, but largely be fulfilled. European integration will continue to evolve and to encompass a growing number of countries and arrangements. The United States will further revitalize its economy and dramatically improve its international trade position. The world trading and finance systems will modernize with passage of the GATT agreements, expansion of IMF and World Bank activities, the North American Free Trade Agreement, and the evolution of other specialized and regional institutions.

Economic Development

Economic development will continue to spread to less developed countries, with growth increasingly rapid in large countries. The Latin American economies will undergo a broad resurgence after their long period of stagnation. The true emergence of a "Pacific century" will dawn with the rapid growth of China (see Figure 1) and the appearance of many new Asian tigers.

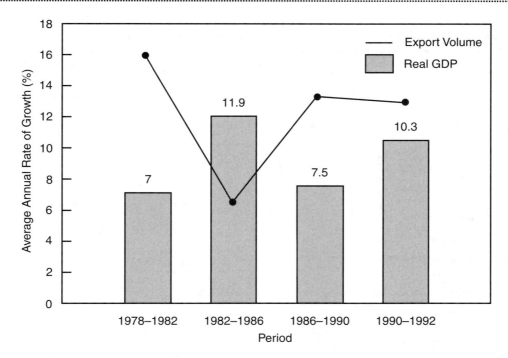

Figure 1. China's gross domestic product (GDP). (International Monetary Fund. World Economic Outlook, *May 1993, p. 53)*

The United States will come out of its period of stagnation. Japan painfully will work off its speculative bubble. Europe will be forced to come to grips with rising global competition. Russia will primarily rely on markets despite traditions and nationalism that can slow or reverse progress.

Consumers and businesses, enlightened by vast information resources, will continue to grow in sophistication. Even as some advanced nations expand the role of government, reliance on markets will increase, especially in countries that depended on them least.

Helping to propel advances (Table 1) will be the spread of economic development around the world and the resurgence of formerly communist nations. Long-term cyclic forces (i.e., upswings in cycles that last fifty to sixty years), particularly in technology, will play a major role in the global economic upswing. The Third World will be a rapidly growing source of demand for goods and capital.

Difficulties will come from heightened nationalism in many countries and regions. Local wars and revolutions, some of great international concern, will punctuate the economic landscape. More countries will break apart. Inflation may be rekindled, and protectionism will increase. Environmental actions, both beneficial and excessive, will dampen growth. Overall, however, progress will continue at a significantly more rapid pace than in the two decades following the 1973 oil shock. The United States will find that it is no longer alone at the top, but must share economic and political power with a growing number of countries and regions.

Long Economic Cycles Suggest Upswing

Herman Kahn (1979), the noted futurist, identified four major periods of the twentieth century in terms of global economic performance. The years of 1886–1913, which he called the First Good Era, were a time of rapid growth and social upheaval. The period of 1914–1947, the Bad Era, encompassed the Great Depression and two world wars. From 1948 to 1973, the world experienced a Second Good Era, a quarter century of growth more rapid than in the 1886–1913 period. The Second Good Era was the first time that sustained economic growth reached beyond a set of no more than twenty countries. World economic development was on its way. Progress, however, came to an abrupt end with the oil shock and worldwide recession of 1973–1975, ushering in a new Era of Malaise, characterized by extensive economic readjustment on a global scale that Kahn felt was likely to extend until the year 2000. Kahn's analysis is consistent with the view that U.S. and world economic cycles tend to last for decades; however, it does not depend on any particular mechanism or insist that such cycles are necessarily automatically self-repeating.

TABLE 1

PROJECTED WORLD RATES OF GROWTH OF REAL GROSS DOMESTIC PRODUCT

| | 1975–1984 | 1985–1994 | 1995–2014 | Subperiod Projections | |
				1995–2004	2005–2014
World	3.3%	2.9%	3.6%	3.7%	3.6%
Industrial Countries	2.5	2.5	2.8	2.9	2.7
United States	2.5	2.5	2.8	2.9	2.8
Canada	3.2	2.5	3.0	3.1	2.9
Japan	4.0	3.3	2.8	2.8	2.8
European Community	2.0	2.3	2.5	2.7	2.4
Developing Countries*	4.5	5.1	5.6	5.8	5.5
Asia**	6.3	7.4	7.0	7.2	6.7
Western Hemisphere	3.2	2.7	4.2	4.3	4.1
Countries in Transition***	3.9	−3.3	6.0	7.0	5.5

* Includes developing countries of Europe, the Middle East and Africa.
** Includes China.
*** Former Soviet Union and Eastern Europe.
Source: Leveson Consulting projections; historical data from Council of Economic Advisors based on OECD.

Nicolai Kondratieff (1935) found cycles in prices and other phenomena, amplified by wars, and lasting an average of about fifty-four years. There have been many other long-cycle interpretations dealing with production (Kuznets, 1965), population and associated investment (Easterlin, 1968), capital investment, technology (Schumpeter, 1939; Freeman et al., 1982), natural resources, war, and debt (Eichengreen and Lindert, 1989).

Long-economic-cycle interpretations differ widely, but they put the latest cycle trough somewhere in the Era of Malaise, with an upswing gradually to follow.

Complexities and Challenges of Change

Europe in the early 1990s was mired in a persistent recession. Many countries, most notably Germany, experienced serious declines in competitiveness from many years of rapid wage increases, despite improvements in export sector productivity. Japan, too, faced high costs without the chance for immigration or better utilization of its female labor force to dampen wage gains, but some economic opening had begun.

The shift to capitalism in formerly communist countries came in response to: (1) decades of communism, socialism, bureaucracy, and central planning failing to cope with rapid change, (2) stultifying effects of centralized control on the human spirit, and (3) an information revolution that promoted interaction and global opportunities and advances that could be attained. Following GNP declines of as much as 50 percent, the nations of the former Soviet Union and Eastern Europe are positioned to grow by 6 percent per year or faster for at least a decade, provided they are more open to basic tenets of capitalism, including property rights and the rule of law.

The United States struggles with huge government budget deficits that are dangerous over the long run. Efforts to deal effectively with reducing them would slow the economy for years. High debt levels continue among companies and households, and the overhang of real estate and financial problems will moderate only gradually. Ideas for dramatically raising investment and savings rates largely go unheeded.

The massive problem of rising health care costs, while particularly virulent in the United States, increasingly will be a worldwide problem as technology and expectations spread. The health care cost issue threatens to disrupt government and personal finances for generations. Containing medical costs threatens to slow national economic growth, impede innovation, and constrict job creation.

Job growth in the U.S. will be far slower than that of the period 1962–1989, when fifty million jobs were created amid a rapid influx of women and youth into the labor force. Cost-consciousness of business, advances in automation, global production shifts, increased employee benefits, and government regulation in health and other areas weaken job growth for the foreseeable future.

Wage rates in the middle of the income distribution were promoted by regulation and unionization in the 1950s and 1960s, and then eroded by large labor supplies and heightened international competition. The new emphasis on government policies toward equalizing the distribution of income can impose disincentives that work against income and job growth.

The New Social Cycle

Since 1988 the United States has shown increasing signs of going through an upswing in a social cycle described by Arthur Schlesinger, Jr. (1986, chapter 2) and others who discern thirty-year swings between liberalism and conservatism.

The new social cycle interacts with the long economic cycle. It is tempered by economic and budget limitations which deny the economic basis for costly programs. Stymied on the one front, reformers turn to issues such as insurance reform, health, abortion, employer mandates, political correctness, and the populism expressed in the 1994 congressional and local elections. There are some indications that this social cycle is becoming global in scope.

History Repeats Itself

The economic situation in the United States bears striking resemblance to conditions a hundred years ago. The depression of the 1870s was followed by two decades in which increases in output depended on rapid growth in the factors of production accompanied by little national productivity growth. There was a long period of deflation. Technology was rapidly creating new production processes and opening up markets, and exports grew rapidly. By the 1890s there was an acceleration of productivity growth. The first *Belle Epoque* also was a time of severe business cycles and great social change.

With time a new progress, the *Age of Achievement*, can emerge strongly in the 1990s and early years of the twenty-first century. During this era, developed countries will benefit significantly from progress in the developing world.

Monetary Policy Will Again Dominate Business Cycles

Inflationary pressures with strong world growth and increased vulnerability to debt and energy price shocks threaten economic stability. Business cycles are once again becoming dominated by periodic efforts to check the rise in inflation, with swings between monetary tightening and subsequent easing.

We normally would expect business cycles to be shorter and less sharp during a period of rapid economic growth and as we get farther into the upswing of a long economic cycle. However, high debt makes economies more sensitive to interest rates. Thus, the shape of what has been thought of as a four-year business cycle, while affected, may not change that much.

Corporate Restructuring

Shifts in interest rates, financial innovation, exchange rates, and the policy prompted widespread corporate restructuring. More fundamental stimuli to restructuring have been intensified international competition, slow growth and disinflation, rapid technological change, and the end of the Cold War. Major changes in the business mix have come along with mergers and acquisitions, strategic alliances, divestitures, and downsizing, both for firms and entire economic sectors.

Retirement costs will impose huge, long-lasting, and negative effects on the economy after 2015, even if individuals, companies, and governments save enough money.

Companies have gone back to basics, concentrating on businesses they best understand, and divesting peripheral subsidiaries and affiliates. Many start-up firms responded to new business conditions and technologies. Consequently, major consolidations occurred as firms moved from local and regional to national and international status, and as surviving winners in new industries emerged.

The Growth of Services, the Information Revolution, and the Superindustrial Society

The growth of services reflects shifting demands as societies develop. Growth of the service industries' share of output and employment has been dramatic (Fuchs, 1968). The United States has become a superindustrial society in which services are increasingly automated and efficient. The superindustrial society is an extension of the industrial revolution to the formerly lagging service sector combined with the integration of the information revolution into the entire economic and social fabric (Leveson, 1991). The superindustrial society paradigm describes a growing number of advanced nations.

Revitalization has been even more intense in manufacturing (e.g., Klier, 1993). Large improvements in productivity and growth contradict ideas about deindustrialization and decline. The expansion of service industries, the growth and role of information-based activities, and the presence of an informal economy are making it increasingly difficult to measure economic growth. Some have suggested that growth in the United States may be greater than officially reported.

Founding the Future

Prospect for two decades of higher growth in the United States and the world opens up exciting opportunities. Additional resources can be used to build future growth.

However, even greater challenges lie beyond the next two decades. Their resolution also depends on the actions taken today.

Changes in the age distribution in the United States have been a spur to economic growth, but they can be expected to work in reverse when the baby boom generation retires (Social Security and Medicare Boards of Trustees, 1993). Retirement costs will impose huge, long-lasting, and negative effects on the economy after 2015, even if individuals, companies, and governments save enough. However, we do not save nearly enough. There is a high risk of a severe and extremely long-lasting depression when demographic realities clash with retirement and health care costs. Nations will be tested not only in terms of how well they do in the new global and technological environment, but also in terms of how well they prepare for the next generation. Discussions about deficits and responsibilities of generations are only a first step.

[See also Capital Formation; Change, Scientific and Technological; Economic Cycles: Models and Simulations; International Trade: Sustaining Growth; Investments; Macroeconomics; Political Cycles; Technological Determinism; Workforce Redistribution.]

BIBLIOGRAPHY

Drucker, Peter. Managing for the Future: The 1990s and Beyond. New York: Penguin Books, 1992.

Eichengreen, Barry, and Lindert, Peter H., eds. The International Debt Crisis in Historical Perspective. Cambridge, MA.: MIT Press, 1989.

Freeman, Christopher; Clark, John; and Soete, Luc. Unemployment and Technical Innovation. Westport, CT: Greenwood Press, 1982.

Fuchs, Victor R. The Service Economy. New York: National Bureau of Economic Research, 1968.

Kahn, Herman. World Economic Development. Boulder, CO: Westview Press, 1979.

Klier, Thomas H. "Lean Manufacturing: Understanding a New Manufacturing System." Chicago Federal Letter 67 (March 1993): 1–3.

Kondratieff, Nicolai D. "The Long Waves in Economic Life." Review of Economics and Statistics (November 1935): 105–115.

Kuznets, Simon. Modern Economic Growth: Rate, Structure, and Spread. New Haven: Yale University Press, 1965.

Leveson, Irving. American Challenges: Business and Government in the World of the 1990s. New York: Praeger Publishers, 1991.

Porter, Michael E. The Competitive Advantage of Nations. New York: The Free Press, 1990.

Reich, Robert. Tales of a New America. New York: Times Books, 1987.

Schlesinger, Arthur, Jr. The Cycles of History. Boston: Houghton Mifflin, 1986.

Schumpeter, Joseph A. Business Cycles. New York: McGraw-Hill, 1939.

Social Security and Medicare Boards of Trustees. Status of the Social Security and Medicare Programs. Washington, DC: Boards of Trustees, 1993.

World Bank. World Development Report. Washington, DC, annual.

— IRVING LEVESON

ECONOMY, INFORMAL.

See INFORMAL ECONOMY.

EDUCATIONAL TECHNOLOGIES

Of all society's institutions, schooling is among the least affected by advances in technology since the Industrial Revolution. If transported forward in time from 1850 to the present, a farmer or a banker, a factory worker or a business proprietor would find many technology-driven changes in his or her work role. In contrast, an instructor from more than a century ago would see little different in today's teaching methods. During the next several decades, however, advances in information technology could transform education as thoroughly as they have altered civilization's other human services.

Information technologies have the potential to transform classrooms into reality amplifiers, in which students can synthesize knowledge from a mixture of real and simulated experiences.

Several trends in the evolution of information technology are driving its emerging impact on teaching, learning, and instructional management. Increases in the power of computers coupled with decreases in their size and cost are creating a world of "intelligent objects" with embedded microprocessors. Just as motors shrank in size and effectively "disappeared" during the Industrial Revolution, so computers are vanishing into our everyday context, supplementing physical reality with a virtual overlay of data.

Simultaneously, broad-band, wide-area telecommunications webs are interconnecting knowledge sources to create a universal information infrastructure that bridges people across time and distance. This twenty-first-century equivalent of the industrial economy's highways and railroads is emerging as a nervous system for global civilization. What do these technological trends mean for today's schools and universities?

For thousands of years, education has centered around two types of knowledge sources: the teacher lecturing and the library acting as an information extender, informing learners of experiences and ideas beyond those available firsthand. For the first time in history, information technologies have the potential to transform classrooms into reality amplifiers, in which students can synthesize knowledge from a mixture of real and simulated experiences. In such a setting, the role of the instructor shifts to that of guide and facilitator, helping students to find patterns of knowledge in a deluge of information, teaching learners how to avoid drowning in a surfeit of data.

Such an environment for learning is not a new concept in education. Learning by doing, individualized tutoring, mastering authentic skills in contexts similar to real-world settings, collaborative learning, interdisciplinary instruction, and tailoring teaching to multiple learning styles are pedagogical strategies that long predate educational devices. Sophisticated information technologies add richness, motivation, and magic to these kinds of learning experiences, as well as making them sustainable by providing extensive managerial scaffolding for teachers and administrators.

For example, today's educational television is in the process of transforming to multimedia that combine video, audio, text, images, and animations to represent knowledge in multiple ways. Over the next two decades, multimedia will in turn evolve into virtual reality, using computer-actuated clothing to help immerse the learner's senses in elaborate simulated environments. Because virtual reality devices have numerous applications in business and entertainment, the demand for equipment generated by these large markets will drive prices down to a level affordable by schools and students.

As an illustration of what this might mean for education, imagine a biology student entering an immersive virtual laboratory environment that includes simulated molecules. The learner can pick up two molecules and attempt to fit them together, exploring docking sites. In addition to the interactive three-dimensional images in the head-mounted display, the gesture gloves on his hands press back to provide feedback to his sense of touch. Alternatively, the student can expand a molecule to the size of a large building and visually fly around inside it, examining the internal structure.

Another intriguing educational possibility is to create physical shapes and forms for intangible things, such as frameworks of information. The instructor could literally give a student a "piece of her mind," enabling the learner to examine patterns of interrelationships among ideas in a manner analogous to tracing bonds within a molecule. Data visualization techniques that enable mapping information from symbolic representations to geometric entities are empowering this type of simulated environment. Simultaneously, a new, nonlinear medium called "hypertext" is making the construction of rich knowledge webs much easier.

The intelligent objects mentioned earlier may appear in classrooms as smart manipulatives, providing individualized coaching for learners. As one illustration, imagine a child stacking blocks in order of size from biggest to smallest to form a tower. When he picks up a block whose size is out of sequence, it could say, "Not me," while the correct block lights up and says, "My turn."

More sophisticated "knowbots" (machine-based intelligent agents) can enhance education by making learners' information processing activities more efficient. For example, a knowbot can scan arriving electronic information for topics of particular interest to the student, selecting and filing material for future reading. Smart badges broadcasting the wearer's identity can link to smart bulletin boards that, when approached, alter their content to match that person's interests. Smart materials can unobtrusively notify a teacher when a learner seems to be unproductively floundering and appears to need help. Knowbots can even populate virtual environments with simulated personalities, allowing students to learn interpersonal skills through structured interactions with machine-based participants that model real-world situations involving teamwork.

What could block this vision from occurring? Some of the limits that may prevent this technology-intensive paradigm of teaching/learning from becoming society's dominant model for schooling are technical and economic. However, these constraints are steadily receding with price/performance improvements in information technology. The more profound barriers are psychological and political, reflecting people's unwillingness to change from familiar, if less effective, educational approaches.

Instruction based on collaborative, interdisciplinary learning about real world tasks necessitates major shifts in current schooling practices. Successful transformation to this model of teaching will require not only the widespread dissemination of sophisticated educational technologies, but also interdependent innovations in evaluation criteria and methods, class scheduling, staff development, authority structures, personnel incentives, student/teacher ratios, and the roles of parents and communities.

Technology can empower many of these shifts and can provide the managerial knowhow to make the new approach sustainable. However, the collective will to accomplish such an unprecedented change must come from a broad-based commitment to redesign education to match the requirements of the postindustrial, knowledge-based workplace. Whether this affirmation to transform will materialize over the next several decades is uncertain, but there is reason to be cautiously optimistic. If it does not, information technology will remain an ornament for the conventional classroom rather than a driving force for educational reform.

[See also Artificial Intelligence; Interactive Entertainment; Libraries; Libraries: Electronic Formats.]

BIBLIOGRAPHY

Dede, Christopher J. "The Future of Multimedia: Bridging to Virtual Worlds." *Educational Technology* 31 (May 1992): 54–60.
———. "Education in the Twenty-first Century." *Annals of the American Academy for Political and Social Science* 522 (July 1992): 104–115.
Dede, Christopher J., and Palumbo, David. "Implications of Hypermedia for Cognition and Communication." *Impact Assessment Bulletin* 9 (Summer 1991): 15–28.
Weiser, Mark. "The Computer for the Twenty-first Century." *Scientific American* 265/3 (September 1991): 94–105.

— CHRISTOPHER J. DEDE

These women make craft items in a retirement community that offers a broad range of services for elderly people. The per person annual cost of nursing home care will probably be $55,000 by 2018. (© 1990 Tim W. Fuller)

ELDERLY, LIVING ARRANGEMENTS

It will be increasingly common for people to live into their eighties or even to become centenarians. As people plan for a longer senior period in their lives, new living arrangements will become essential.

Elderly people, a heterogeneous group, vary in needs, attitudes, and expectations about aging. Census surveys reveal that most older people prefer to retain the living arrangements established in young adulthood or middle age—owned or rented homes, often near children and relatives. Eighty percent of older persons have living children, and two-thirds live within a half hour of a child. Many will move from individual housing to alternatives that permit them to maintain their independence for as long as possible and that, when and if needed, offer graded levels of assisted living.

Demographics

The United States, long thought of as a youthful country, now has a larger proportion of middle-aged and older persons than ever in its history. Since 1980, older Americans increased by 22 percent compared with an increase of 8 percent in the under-sixty-five population. When the postwar baby-boom generation reaches age sixty-five between 2010 and 2030, the older population will experience its most rapid increase. The U.S. Census Bureau projects that by 2030, there will be sixty-six million persons older than sixty-five, or two-and-one-half times their number in 1980. Persons over sixty-five will constitute 13 percent of the population in the year 2000, and 22 percent by 2030.

The most senior segment of the older population is showing the largest change in absolute numbers. The over-eighty-five group was twenty-four times greater in 1990 than in 1900, and is projected to grow even more.

Although the data presented here are for the United States, virtually all other parts of the world are experiencing increases in the numbers of persons who live longer. In the more developed nations, the proportion of older persons is increasing faster than the birth rate.

Because men on average die at a younger age than women, older men in 1990 were about twice as likely to be married as older women (77 percent versus 42 percent), and half of older women were widows. In the same year, 5 percent of older persons had never married, and 5 percent were divorced. A pattern of survivors finding new partners to live with (if not always to marry) is likely.

Living Arrangements

Among persons over sixty-five, about 5 percent live in nursing homes. Nursing home residents include only 1 percent of sixty-five- to seventy-four-year-olds but 25 percent of persons over eighty-five. Of those in 1990 who are not institutionalized, the majority live in a family setting. Thirty-one percent live alone, and the vast preponderance of these are women.

Sandwich Generation Households

The fact that people are living longer and living in their own residences or with their adult children has spun a new phrase—"the sandwich generation"—to describe the living situation of adults who are caring for both their children and their parents simultaneously. In some families the oldest generation cares for the youngest, but in others both the children and oldest adults use day-care services.

Elder Care

Because most older persons live by themselves or with family and prefer to remain in such living arrangements, it will be socially and economically desirable when assistance is needed to provide it through day care offered either within or outside of the home. Whereas in the past two decades, child care has been viewed as a pressing social-economic need, there will be a demand in the future for elder care to an extent similar to the past demand for child day care. Regular elder day care and respite care will especially be needed by multi-career households. Its very availability is likely to foster intergenerational arrangements, especially if it is offered at the same site as child care by the same provider. Even now, workplace-based elder care is becoming available and is likely to be preferable to more conventional church-based or community-based care for the same reasons that workplace-based child care is chosen, i.e., convenience, increased time with family, option of visiting with custodial person during the workday if necessary, and minimized transportation stress. It could be economically viable as an employment benefit or as a shared cost among employees.

Health-care suites—modular living units designed to fit inside an existing garage—have been proposed by Stephen Menke. They respect the preferences of the older person to remain with his or her family, allow access for the older person and caregiver, maintain privacy for older persons and the caregiver family, allow maintenance of social interactions, and are more economical than nursing-home placement.

Retirement Communities

During the past quarter century, retirement communities restricted to persons over age fifty or fifty-five, have sprung up throughout the Sun Belt and to a lesser extent in other regions. These communities provide security surveillance, houses or apartments designed for older persons, social centers, continuing-education programs, recreational facilities, and opportunities to become involved in governance.

Communities populated by persons who were in their fifties when they arrived could become depressed when large numbers of them become ill and die in their eighties. The future-oriented view aims at reserving amenities that appeal to older people and designing intergenerational and socioeconomic mixing to minimize overly homogeneous social clustering.

Communities designed for residential purposes often have restrictive zoning that precludes inclusion of elder-oriented commercial and social-support activities and services. It is imperative to have mixed zoning and tax and other economic advantages for businesses and services that locate in such communities so as to encourage commercial zones as well as age and socioeconomic integration.

Campus-Style Communities

Communities with individual and low-rise living units around green space and with some facilities for common use are patterned after school campuses and resort communities. Experience with campus-style communities is that access becomes increasingly difficult as people progress from being young-old to the oldest-old. Management and caregivers contend that campus-style communities are more costly and inefficient to service than compact high-rise or garden apartment designs that feature transport over smaller distances to get to central community social, dining, health, or commercial establishments.

Restricted Mobility Units

Many people remain mentally alert throughout their lives. Others maintain physical functioning in later years yet suffer from impaired cognitive functioning brought about by Alzheimer's disease and other dementias. Such people often are restless and may become irritable when confined. For these individuals, residential arrangements must provide for a more active lifestyle than is possible in traditional nursing-home settings. Technological devices that monitor an individual's whereabouts by telemetry can provide subjective freedom for such individuals and minimize endangerment from wandering off or failing to remember to eat or to check in with caregivers. Closed-circuit-television monitoring provides a more intrusive alternative.

Group Units

Group homes are being used increasingly to provide more homelike rather than institutional environments that still manage to meet the needs of those who require some surveillance or assistance. Group living allows members to do what they are able or prefer to do with the entire group and to benefit from what others are able to do for themselves and the others. For example, in a group situation, one member might manage household finances, another might do laundry, while another might cook or tend to each member's medications, appointments, or health routines.

Personal experience with group living in college and during one's single years may help make such arrangements more acceptable to older persons in the future. If so, they could go a long way toward providing economically feasible living arrangements, supplemented with home health care or other services as needed. They could also provide the social stimulation and companionship so often lacking among isolated elderly persons and, in the process, reduce some of the depression that accompanies a feeling of abandonment.

There will be a demand in the future

for elder care to an extent similar

to the past demand for child day care.

Progressive Care

Progressive or continuing-care communities represent an extension of retirement communities that acknowledge needs for increasingly intensive levels of assistance as persons become less independent. Continuing-care communities are able to provide the familiarity and continuity of social environment and caregiver services that enhance the quality of care and quality of life. Despite the extension of life that we have been observing, all people eventually die. Therefore, a full range of levels of caregiving services will become the norm in residential communities that are intentionally designed to serve older people. Hospices provide another option for persons who elect to die at home or in a homelike setting surrounded by family and friends.

Design Accommodation

The Americans for Disability Act of 1992 and a generation of socially conscious persons who are committed to access for persons with disabilities will result in increasing availability of living units designed to be "friendly" to the physically challenged. Design standards may change so that accessible housing will become the norm rather than the exception. Those without special needs will accommodate to altered dimensions in order to foster physical mobility for persons with special needs. Examples include wider door openings, adjustable cabinet heights and work-surface, and altered location of switches and knobs or handles that can be manipulated by people with problems in motor coordination or who are wheelchair-bound.

The simple reality that nursing-home care costs four to five times as much as home-based care, coupled with strong preferences for home-based care, will stimulate planners and designers as well as market forces to in-

crease choices of types of living arrangements available to the diverse populations of older people.

[See also Aging of the Population; Disabled Persons' Rights; Families and Households; Household Composition; Housing: Demographic and Lifestyle Impacts On; Longevity; Public Assistance Programs: Social Security.]

BIBLIOGRAPHY

Fowles, Donald G., ed. *A Profile of Older Americans: 1991.* Washington, DC: U.S. Department of Health and Human Services/American Association of Retired Persons and the Administration on Aging, 1992.

Taeuber, Cynthia M., ed. *Sixty-Five Plus in America.* Washington, DC: U.S. Government Printing Office, 1992.

U.S. Senate Special Committee on Aging, the American Association of Retired Persons, the Federal Council on the Aging, and the U.S. Administration on Aging. *Aging American: Trends and Projections, 1991.* DHHS Publication No. (FCoA) 91-28001. Washington, DC: U.S. Department of Health and Human Services, 1991.

– MIRIAM FRIEDMAN KELTY

ELECTRIC POWER

During the 1980s, U.S. electric utilities began changing from the vertically integrated monopolies that characterized the industry during the century since Thomas Edison established the first central generating station in New York City to a new era of competition with other energy suppliers. Companies that controlled the electric power market from generation through distribution to end users were forced to fight to retain existing customers and to win new markets.

Two federal laws passed by the Congress in 1978 were instrumental in moving electric utilities from protected markets and virtually guaranteed returns to the new world of free competition and increased efficiency, while continuing some regulation.

The Public Utility Regulatory Policies Act (PURPA) and the Powerplant and Industrial Fuel Use Act (FUA) provided the ground rules for entry of new players into the previously closed group of utilities, and set the stage for dramatic changes in electric generation sources.

PURPA encouraged the development of an entirely new class of electric power facilities: independent power projects (IPPs) and cogenerators, which utilize otherwise wasted heat or energy from industrial processes to generate power. These plants, usually smaller and able to be built more quickly than large centralized power plants, are often owned by nonutility companies. They mostly used natural gas rather than the coal and nuclear energy that still account for a majority of utility-owned power generation.

FUA provisions that discouraged use of natural gas for electric power generation were eliminated by amendment, and environmental priorities simultaneously increased demands for the use of natural gas, the cleanest fossil fuel. As a result, gas has become the fuel of choice for most new small and mid-sized generating units built, by utilities and independent firms.

For the larger generating units needed to service areas with extraordinary power needs, however, coal remains the most economical generating fuel.

Annual increases in electricity demand, which reached the 7 percent level in the early 1970s, declined to near zero in the aftermath of the 1973 Arab oil embargo. By the mid 1990s, yearly increases in power demand rebounded to the 5 percent range, and the surplus generating capacity prevalent for nearly two decades largely disappeared. Demand for electricity in traditional and new applications is likely to grow throughout the remainder of the 1990s and into the twenty-first century.

As needs for new generating capacity grow, utilities are turning toward two types of capacity enhancement that offer shorter lead times for construction and lower capital costs: purchases of power from nonutility generators, and construction of smaller generating units. The latter are usually natural gas-fired combustion turbines or combined-cycle units pairing a combustion turbine with a steam generator powered by the turbine's waste heat.

Utilities have also developed numerous "demand side management" techniques to encourage more efficient use of power. Time-of-day and seasonal pricing are designed to discourage power use at peak demand periods and to encourage customers to switch electricity use to times when overall demand is lower. This has the advantage of leveling demand peaks and valleys, making use of existing generating units more efficient, and reducing the total generating capacity needed.

Other programs pursued by some utilities offer subsidies to large users who install more energy-efficient equipment or reduce peak consumption. At the residential level, many utilities now offer rebates and other inducements for installation of peak-load controls on water heaters and other energy-intensive appliances. Other demand management programs include direct payments and offers of reduced rates to large electricity users for load-balancing actions. These incentives vary widely from state to state, as utility pricing policies are controlled by separate regulatory commissions in each state.

Construction of new power plants is now a last resort for many utilities. The high cost of new plants, the uncertainty of regulatory approval for recovery of construction costs, the resistance of citizens to the location of new facilities in their vicinity (which has become

known as the "Not In My Back Yard," or NIMBY problem), and increasingly stringent environmental regulations make demand controls and increased efficiency preferable to capacity enhancement.

Responding to environmental concerns, electric utilities moved toward burning cleaner fuels, such as natural gas, and sought acceptable ways to use conventional fuels, such as coal and oil. Coal gasification, fluidized bed combustion of coal, methods to clean coal before combustion, and "co-firing" of natural gas with coal have permitted utilities to continue using coal while observing pollutant emission limits imposed by the Clean Air Act.

Some potential environmental problems remain unresolved for electric utilities. Several methods are under development for disposal of spent fuel from nuclear reactors, but no single satisfactory method has been proven. Until the federal government decides how and where to store or dispose of radioactive waste products, nuclear utilities will continue to store spent fuel at reactor sites in protective containers.

Controversy continues over whether electromagnetic fields (EMFs) found close to electric transmission lines are harmful to the public. Scientific and academic studies have indicated that the effects of EMFs are minimal, but some environmentalists have suggested that any EMF impact is unacceptable. This question is unlikely to be resolved before the late 1990s.

Congress considered in 1993 imposing new taxes on all energy consumption, based on the British thermal unit (Btu) content of fuels and equivalent measurements for nuclear energy. The Btu-based tax, which would have significantly increased electric power costs, was voted down in favor of a levy on transportation fuels only. However, it may well resurface later in the decade for reconsideration. The United States has traditionally imposed lower taxes on energy than most other countries, and efforts to exploit this revenue source are likely to continue.

If global warming continues to be a significant environmental concern, moves toward taxation of utilities on the basis of carbon emissions, already debated during 1993 energy tax revisions, are likely to recur.

Several emerging trends will influence the electric utility industry during the latter part of the 1990s and the early years of the twenty-first century. One benchmark indicator is the extent to which a growing number of mergers can reduce inefficiencies in the national electric power supply system while avoiding antitrust objections.

Another looming question is whether the proliferation of IPPs and cogenerators during the late 1980s and early 1990s ultimately will be proven economical sources of generating capacity as reliable as utility-owned facilities. Major bond-rating agencies have questioned whether nonutility generators offer financial stability comparable to generating facilities constructed and operated by utilities. Bonds of some major utilities have been "downrated" as a result of increasing dependence on independent generators. In isolated instances, nonutility generators have been forced into bankruptcy. In such cases, utility customers of the failed generator usually have taken over the independent firm's operations, often at bargain prices compared to new construction by the utility.

If global warming continues to be a significant

concern, moves toward taxation of utilities

on the basis of carbon emissions are likely to recur.

Another challenge for electric utilities involves fostering the development of new "electrotechnologies" and other new uses for electric power. These innovative new uses may be offset by declines in power demand made possible by conservation efforts and the increased efficiency of electric appliances and equipment.

The single most promising area for expanded electrification is the transportation sector. State regulations pioneered in California mandating "zero-emission" vehicles impose requirements that only electric motors can meet. Already electric utilities have undertaken pilot programs to electrify commercial and industrial fleet vehicles in areas subject to intense air pollution, such as airports and densely populated urban areas. The same air quality concerns will enhance the attractiveness of electrified urban mass transit systems, including subways, light rail, and electric buses.

Business activity in the twenty-first century will inevitably depend ever more heavily on electronic data storage and retrieval, new forms of high-speed communications, and efficient manufacturing processes, all of which are dependent either largely or exclusively on electric power.

Utilities will meet these needs with a mix of traditional generating technologies and a variety of new methods now in the development and testing stages. Among those are fuel cells, which convert fuels directly into electricity without using a generating turbine; solar energy, which converts sunlight directly into electric current; wind power, which harnesses natural air currents; and geothermal energy, tapping underground heat to drive conventional turbines. None has yet proven economically viable on a commercial basis in large-scale applications, but all have proven technically feasible, and further technological advances and economies of scale are likely to make some widely available in the next century.

[*See also Coal; Energy; Energy, Renewable Sources of; Natural Gas; Nuclear Power; Nuclear Power: Con; Petroleum.*]

BIBLIOGRAPHY

Chase, Milton. *Electric Power: An Industry at the Crossroads.* Westport, CT: Greenwood/Praeger, 1988.
Electric Power Today: Problems and Potential. New York: American Society of Civil Engineers, 1979.
Hill, Phillip G. *Power Generation: Resources, Hazards, Technology, and Costs.* Cambridge, MA: MIT Press, 1977.

– PAUL M. FEINE

ELECTRONIC CONVERGENCE

Convergence describes a number of phenomena relating to electronic technologies. It is used in the dictionary sense of "to come together," or "to unite in common interest or focus." There will be a continuing convergence of electronic components, manufactured products, the uses to which they are put, the form in which media are stored and transmitted, and the firms that manufacture the products or offer the services.

For most of the nineteenth and twentieth centuries, there were clear distinctions between vacuum tubes, wire, resistors, capacitors, relays, and switches. As tubes are replaced by transistors, and transistors by microprocessor chips, there will be a continuing convergence of these components into single printed circuit boards and chips, and even organically grown devices.

In the early twentieth century there was a clear distinction between telegraph messages and telephonic voice messages, between print and radio, silent motion pictures and phonograph recordings. With the transformation of all media from distinct analog form into interchangeable digital bits and bytes, all messages, information, and entertainment converge into the same basic components that can be stored and transmitted, with perfect accuracy, through any medium.

By the time that television and computers came to be more widely available, in the mid-twentieth century, they were seen as two totally distinct technologies, manufactured by different firms, and serving different functions for the user. The same would be said for the telephone and cable television—the former providing voice communication between two persons, and the latter providing one-way delivery of entertainment program.

In the twenty-first century, television and computers will converge. The telephone, computer, and cable television networks will converge.

As computer screen technology improves, computer memory size and speed continue to increase, and networks have more broadband capacity, multimedia computers will become more common. They will be able to utilize both the evolving CD-ROM technology (and its successors) and wired and wireless network connections to receive the massive amounts of information necessary to create the images that were earlier called television—as well as graphics, audio only, and text files.

At the same time, increasing computational capacity will be built into television sets. Already used as a screen for the computers called video games, interactive television will involve computer-like control devices for selecting programming, making purchases, engaging in home banking, or sending other kinds of messages to and from what was earlier called a television screen.

Indeed, once telephones have screens, computers have telephones networked by the cable television companies, television sets are hooked up to the phone company, and computer networks are delivering music and video programming, these converged technologies will be virtually indistinguishable in function.

Transmission technologies will also be converging. The coaxial cable, or optic fiber, used by cable television companies—once it is designed as two-way, with some switching capability—will be able to provide voice telephone and data services. The optic fiber of the telephone company, and even its earlier twisted pair of copper wires (with compression technology), will be able to provide a video dial-tone service to carry entertainment television programming to screens normally connected to a computer, telephone, or television set—or provide a video image of the person on the other end of what was formerly a voice communication. Communications satellite technology will, as well, deliver to ever-smaller dishes the digital bits that will sort themselves out on the receiving end into voice conversations, entertainment television, faxes, printed newspapers, and data files.

Convergence will also be quite obvious and dramatic in mobile or personal wireless communications. As computers decrease in size (from mainframes, to mini, to micro, to desktop, to lugable, to laptop, to notebook, to palmtop, to wristwatch-size), they will became truly portable communications devices not only for voice, data, and faxes, but audio and video material as well. What is now thought of as a pager, notifying the owner of a received voice-phone call at another location, will add screens of sufficient size to receive text messages (not just buzz or provide a phone number or brief voice message). What began as mobile radios and mobile telephones, and subsequently evolved into voice cellular phones (actually radios) with more channels and range, will acquire screens and incorporate the ability to send and receive video and audio as well as voice, computer messages, and faxes. Personal data assistants will combine all of these functions into a single device. But all will have converged into alternatives with common features that (with low orbit and conventional, communications satellites) include global reach to personalized and global numbers (addresses).

In the broadest sense, there will also be a convergence of function between entertainment and education, or education and training. The functions of employees will converge with those of customers and suppliers (such as the bank teller's function being performed by the ATM [automated teller] machine user).

At the same time that there will be a convergence of technology, form, function, and utility, there will also be a convergence of the firms involved in providing these goods and services. Paging services will provide cellular and personal-data-assistant networks. Cellular phone companies will provide data and fax services. Computer software companies will incorporate the capacity for computers to send messages to pagers; and entertainment television, music, computer and video games, and telephone firms will enter each other's businesses.

Convergence of firms will occur in two other ways as well. There will be a growing merger movement that will produce fewer and fewer multimedia global conglomerates with ever-increasing market power and control. Such firms will combine ownership of the creative talent and intellectual property, the media manufacturing (books, newspapers, movies, videotape, computer games, and software), and distribution (over-the-air broadcasting, cable television, telephone, videotape rental) systems. In addition to this merger movement (in the sense of 100 percent ownership of subsidiaries providing vertical and horizontal integration), there will also be a growing tendency of such firms to acquire minority stakeholder investments in a wide variety of firms engaged in these converging businesses. Such investments will be both a hedge in an uncertain and rapidly changing economic environment and also an additional driving force toward corporate convergence.

Notwithstanding the movement to convergence, the mid-twentieth-century predictions of a single home computer, providing all computational functions, did not come about. With the rapidly decreasing cost and size of microprocessors they—like the electric motor technology before them—will continue to be designed, not for a single home device, but for very specific functions and implanted in a wide array of home products, from microwave ovens, furnace thermostats, videotape recorders, refrigerators, and washing machines to automobiles and other personal products used outside the home. Thus, the early twenty-first century will see,

---

There will be a growing merger movement

that will produce fewer and fewer multimedia

global conglomerates with ever-increasing

market power and control.

---

simultaneously, both the trend to convergence and the growing specialization and diversity in the use of computer and other electronic technologies.

[See also Broadcasting; Communications; Communications: Technology; Computer Linkage; Digital Communications; Electronic Publishing; Information Society; Interactive Entertainment; Media Lab; Networking; Newspapers; On-line Services; Photography; Satellite Communications; Telecommunications; Telephones; Television.]

BIBLIOGRAPHY

Bagdikian, Ben H. *The Media Monopoly.* Boston, MA: Beacon Press, 1992.
Harasim, Linda M. *Global Networks: Computers and International Communication.* Cambridge, MA: MIT Press, 1993.

— NICHOLAS JOHNSON

ELECTRONIC PUBLISHING

So dramatically has the computer revolutionized publishing that words such as *magazine, newspaper,* and *book* are edging toward obsolescence. Tomorrow's publishers, with a few exceptions, will be purveyors of information. Unconstrained by any single delivery mode, a broad variety of text, music, and video will be merged into databases, accessible whenever and wherever the user chooses—an always open, universal-access "information library."

Production tools such as pasteboards, glue, and scissors have all but disappeared, replaced by software that fosters unprecedented experimentation, precision, and speed. The plunging prices of computers and their rapid proliferation have democratized publishing, giving millions of individuals and small businesses the means to create professional-quality newsletters, brochures, and advertisements.

In the years ahead, electronic publishing's focus will shift from the production of printed materials to the wireless and paperless dissemination of information. Using computers of all sizes and capacity—on the desk-

top or dashboard, in the pocket or backpack, even worn like a watch or a ring—people everywhere will have instant access to a vast array of information. What they do with that data—download, print, annotate, respond to, or transmit to colleagues in a dozen other countries—will be up to them. All information will be portable, pliable, and interactive.

The Multimedia News

In the early 1980s, the print media began experimenting with electronic distribution, prompted by surging competition, shrinking advertising revenues, and rising newsprint costs. Videotex, fax, and the floppy disk, for the most part, initially failed to attract subscribers. More user-friendly—and viable—were commercial on-line services and CD-ROM (compact disc, read-only memory). By the late 1990s, PC (personal computer) makers will equip most new personal computer models with built-in CD-ROM drives. By the dawn of the twenty-first century, all major newspaper and magazine publishers will offer interactive editions, integrating text, sound, still video, and animation. Added value will be the linchpin to electronic systems' financial success. Far more than digital displays of the printed page, the emerging media will provide an immediacy, vividness, and emotional impact unattainable in print.

Consumers tomorrow will be able to scan summaries or delve deeper into a topic, calling up a historical overview, video footage, text of a speech, charts and graphs, or related stories. By tapping a few keys, touching an icon, or speaking a command, users will respond to classified ads, buy stocks, book reservations, correspond with editors, or join electronic discussion groups. Prospective buyers can shop for advertised items, hear snippets of compact discs, or view homes.

The media will become increasingly customized—a coping response to the threat of information overload. A "personal index" will ferret out preferred topics. Formats will be as familiar (modeled on the *New York Times,* for instance) or as unique as the user wishes. For those too busy to read the news, the digitized voice of their choice will read it to them. Users will arrange news feeds for specified times of the day, such as financial data after the stock market closes.

Research and Education

Digital technologies bestow order on conducting research. The twentieth century will be the last in which students, taxpayers, engineers, reporters, or anyone else must plow through reams of paper, pore over tiny print, or even drive miles to the library—only to find that a reference is unavailable, outdated, stored away, or incomplete.

Enormous stores of information will exist in the form of portable multimedia libraries. In 1993, a CD-ROM could store 680 megabytes of data—the equivalent of 20 four-drawer file cabinets—on a single half-ounce disk. With the click of a button, users could watch an old newsreel, navigate any street in America, hear symphonic music, research a business, decipher a tax code, locate a Supreme Court decision, find an antidote, or "tour" the human anatomy.

In the years ahead, these options and many more will be available through centrally located electronic databases. Users will be able to print or download all or part of a text, image, recording, or video onto their own system. Downloading copyrighted material will require permission, licensing, or royalty payment.

Interactive multimedia will become a leading educational tool. Sound, animation, cross-referencing, and user-controlled pacing provide an engaging "flight simulator" approach to learning. Digital lessons in everything from ancient history to molecular physics will complement, and eventually replace, unwieldy, one-dimensional textbooks. Publishers of do-it-yourself books and manufacturers of toy-model kits will supplant paper instructions with multimedia "toolkits."

Arts and Leisure

Emerging technologies will add new dimensions to the pursuit of pleasure. Books will become multi-media experiences enhanced with sideline "excursions"—supplementary music, narrative, video, related readings, or historical annotations. Readers will be able to modify text, edit photo spreads, and download passages. They will also alter contents and outcomes—solving mysteries alongside fictional detectives, for instance.

Armchair travelers will embark on electronic tours to hundreds of destinations. Publishers and travel agencies will team up to form on-line reservation and itinerary-planning services.

Marketing and Advertising

Electronic publishing will give marketers unprecedented reach, precision, and creativity—at lower expense than high-overhead stores or costly mailings. The growth of CD-ROM and completion of the data superhighway will prompt thousands of retailers to list their merchandise in "electronic catalogs." Compact, comprehensive, and easy to update, these will gain early favor among suppliers of high-volume products such as auto and appliance parts.

Multimedia marketing will tailor sales pitches to special-interest groups and even individuals. Consumers will be able to browse among products that interest them. They'll "try on" items in clothing catalogs by programming their computers with data such as height and weight. Software, music, book, and video catalogs will be encrypted so users can "sample" slivers of each item; to buy, they'll inexpensively download the items onto their systems.

Eventually, through virtual reality, shoppers will be able to simulate a product's taste, smell, or feel—such as a car's ride on a bumpy road, on a hot day.

Challenges

As new options proliferate, the major technological obstacle will be the development and implementation of industry-wide standards that let all formats and devices communicate with one another. Industry-government coalitions are working toward this goal.

The greatest challenge, of course, is consumer acceptance. Paper—user-friendly, portable, and generally serviceable—remains for most people the best way to deliver ideas and store information. Most likely, paper will never disappear, but will become just another media option, used for applications most suited to it. Its popularity will erode over time, however, as computers become more pervasive and portable, electronic data services become faster and easier to use, and the flood of paper creates a need for compressed storage.

[See also Communications: Media Law; Computer Linkage; Computers: Overview; Computers: Privacy Laws; Computers: Software; Information Technology; Intellectual Property; Interactive Entertainment; Libraries; Libraries: Electronic Formats; Literature; Media Lab; Newspapers; Printed Word.]

BIBLIOGRAPHY

"CD-ROM 101." *Forbes FYI,* Fall 1993.

"The Digital Press." *Forbes* (September 27, 1993).

"For Magazines, a Multimedia Wonderland." *The New York Times,* October 11, 1993.

Goodrum, Charles A., and Dalrymple, Helen. "The Computer and the Book." In *Books in Our Future,* ed. John Y. Cole. Washington, DC: Library of Congress, 1987.

"Publishers Deliver Reams of Data on CDs." *The Wall Street Journal,* February 22, 1993.

"The Tools of a New Art Form." *The New York Times,* September 19, 1993.

– LEAH THAYER

ELEMENTARY AND SECONDARY EDUCATION

Public K-12 education costs too much and delivers too little. Educational achievement is down but spending is up. Over the past several decades education outlays have doubled or tripled—even while the number of students has shrunk—yet academic performance has declined. Spending increasing amounts of money ostensibly to improve education, only to have it grow worse, is a shortcoming that will pervade the politics of the late 1990s and beyond.

Education is one of the few endeavors where the solution for poor performance is to throw more money at it. There is no other major institution where consistent shortcoming—failure—is a perpetual excuse to increase funding. Rewarding failure sends the wrong message.

Education never has been so important. Complexity, an integral part of scientific progress that hallmarks the information era enterprise, demands more and better schooling. Knowledge, information, and education are the central resources of these times.

Less than optimal intellectual development squanders human resources and relegates the nation to second-rate accomplishment. Education provides the passport to personal advancement, increased earning ability, and is determinative of domestic well-being and international competitiveness. America may be losing the global economic race as much in the classroom as in factories and offices.

Total expenditures for public elementary and secondary schools have increased by leaps and bounds: $71.2 billion in 1960; to $144.2 billion in 1970; to $241.9 billion in 1993. Bluntly put, are we getting 3.4 times more?

A fairer evaluation expresses K-12 public education expenditures in constant 1990–1991 dollars: $201.3 billion in 1970, to $334.6 billion in 1991. On this basis, are we getting 1.7 times more?

Putting these changes in perspective, spending per pupil increased from $1,500 in 1955 to $4,500 in 1986. Are taxpayers getting 3.0 times as much for their money? Compared to other nations, spending during the early 1980s for public and private primary and secondary schools per pupil amounted to $3,843 in the United States; $2,470 in Germany; $2,438 in the United Kingdom; and $1,978 in Japan.

The baby boom echo and the influx of immigrants are expected to increase public K-12 school enrollment from 45 million in 1995 to 49.3 million by 2003. Adding further to overall education costs is the fact that kindergarten and preschooling begin at ever younger ages. By 1992, 55.7 percent of three- to five-year-old Americans attended preparatory schools (6.4 million of 11.5 million in that age group). Currently a privately financed choice, the trend in precursor countries in Scandinavia and Europe has been to provide it universally (free—or mostly so). In addition, growing numbers of American students are staying in school longer, pursuing postgraduate degrees. Starting school earlier and staying longer prolongs matriculation and increases public education costs.

General fund appropriations among the states for fiscal year 1994 averaged 41.9 percent for education (29.9 percent for grades K-12, 12 percent for higher education). When spending for a program category dominates all other government obligations, attention inevitably will be drawn to it. States provided 46.8 percent, local governments 46.3 percent, and the federal government 6.9 percent of all revenues for public K-12 school costs in 1993. Taxpayers, hard pressed by escalating costs of government, will demand a better accounting.

Illiteracy

The extent of illiteracy provides one measurement of the educational system. Literacy in the U.S. ranks a dismal forty-ninth among the 158 UN-member states! A 1993 Department of Education report estimated that 23 percent (40–44 million) Americans were illiterate (25 percent of them immigrants), and another 25.8 percent (50 million) were considered functionally illiterate. Augmented by increasing immigration, functional illiteracy in the United States is expected to grow from 60 million in 1990 to 90 million by 2000.

High School Dropouts

Another way to judge K-12 compulsory education is the number of pupils completing the curriculum. High school completion during the early 1990s was 82 percent for whites, 70 percent for African Americans, and 53 percent for Hispanics. In Japan, the number of dropouts, 12 percent, is less than half the U.S. rate of 25 percent. This poor showing is a goad to continuing improvement.

SAT Score Decline

SAT scores have dropped substantially and are not rebounding well from their low point. Verbal scores plunged from a postwar high of 479 in 1956 to 422 in 1991, and rose to 423 in 1994. Scores for mathematics dropped from a postwar high of 502 in 1963 to a low point of 466 in 1980, and then slowly rose to 479 in 1994. Until these performance levels improve, angered parents will keep the pressure on for education reform.

Intelligence Quotients

IQ scores among Asian and European youth also exceed those of U.S. counterparts. Japanese students score ten to fifteen points higher than do Americans. Asian immigrant students in the United States also outperform all other peers. In the 1988 International Assessment of Educational Programs testing science skills, American students scored last among nations that were tested. The U.S. student mean score of 474 was about one hundred points lower than the 568 score among Korean students. Part of this increase is attributed to strong will, determination, and dedication to a serious work ethic.

Other factors contributing to flagging education performance and intellectual accomplishment include more broken homes, more teenage mothers, more neglected or abused children, more abject poverty, and a deterioration of nurturing family environments. Some argue that a generation of Dr. Benjamin Spock-inspired permissiveness has contributed to the decline.

Spending increasing amounts of money

to improve education, only to have it grow worse,

is a shortcoming that will pervade the politics

of the late 1990s and beyond.

It also can be argued that overly zealous pursuit of egalitarianism contributed to educational decline. Providing the same thing for all comers—even though they are radically different and have vastly different needs—may not be wise. Mainlining dysfunctional students is counterproductive when it intrudes upon the rights of the many. A few violent, constantly noisy, interminably demanding underachievers who excessively intrude upon and impede regular class functioning shortchange the many.

Remedial Training

Remedial training provides another indication of schooling shortfall. Disgraceful numbers of entering college freshmen are required to take remedial ("bonehead") courses to bring them up to acceptable college standards. By the late 1980s, college remedial training was offered by 80 percent of all higher education institutions, and the percentage of entering freshmen taking remedial courses in 1984 was 25 percent in math, 21 percent in writing, and 16 percent in reading.

The workplace provides one final indicator of preparatory education shortcomings. Employers, finding workers ill-prepared to assume even rudimentary tasks, have increased on-the-job training. Spending levels, according to some estimates, rival public education costs. During 1990–1991, $221.6 billion went for public elementary/secondary education. A few years earlier (1989), it was estimated that business spent the equivalent of $328 billion for formal and on-the-job training.

Social Costs of Under-Education

One 1988 report estimated that an uneducated populace cost America at least $224 billion in crime, prison costs, welfare payments, incompetent job performance,

and lost tax revenues. Today that economic cost might easily be doubled.

Classroom Time

Attendance in the classroom varies greatly from nation to nation. To begin with, the length of the school day of seven to eight hours in Japan compares to only six hours per day in the United States. The number of school days in attendance also differs drastically (1991): 243 days in Japan; 210 days in Germany; 192 days in the United Kingdom; and only 180 days in the United States. Summer vacations in the United States amount to twelve weeks, compared to seven weeks in Germany, and six weeks in Japan and the United Kingdom. Overall, the number of *years* of compulsory schooling completed provide an important perspective on educational achievement (1989): eleven years in the United States, ten years in Germany, and nine years in Japan. Despite the smaller number of classroom days that U.S. students receive, spending on American students was almost double that in Japan in 1985: $3,310 versus $1,805.

Teacher/Pupil Ratio

The educational establishment insisted over the years that the key to enhancing public education was a smaller teacher-pupil ratio. So the ratio was reduced. In 1960 the ratio stood at 25.8 to 1; it stood at 17.2 in 1991 and is projected to drop to 16.9 by 2004.

Questioning the teacher/pupil contention is the fact that Japan gets superior results with a much bigger classroom size. In Japan the number of students per teacher has been increasing, not decreasing. Despite the fact that Japanese classrooms are three to four times larger than in the United States, student achievement in Japan betters the United States. In 1987 there were forty-nine Japanese students for each teacher; by 1989 the ratio had been upped to sixty to one.

Core Curriculum

Shunning "basics" also contributes to lackluster educational performance. Students in other advanced postindustrial nations spend as much as twice the number of hours on basic core subjects compared to U.S. students. The situation is worsened, bit by bit, as single-issue zealots goad governments to impose ever-growing numbers of well-intentioned but nonessential courses on K-12 curricula, thereby displacing more fundamental courses. The highly regarded 1983 report *A Nation At Risk* urged a core curriculum for high schools consisting of four years of English; three years each of social studies, science, and math; two years of a foreign language, and one-half year of computer science. In 1982, only 2 percent of students satisfied this curriculum, but only 17 percent in 1990. The trend, hopefully, will continue.

Education Reform

For all the money that goes into it, American public K-12 education needs drastic reform. Something must be wrong somewhere. Instead of just running students "through the mill," much more attention must be focused on results.

Until the late 1980s, debate surrounding educational quality focused on inputs—spending levels, teacher/pupil ratios, teacher salaries, educational attainment of teachers, and so forth. Now the focus is on outcome, end results. Flagging SAT scores, comparatively lower IQ scores, and mounting illiteracy have been important catalysts. Suggestions that teachers assume an increasing responsibility for student outcomes—such as merit pay incentives—draw vitriolic response from educator unions.

Educational Bureaucracy

The proportion of nonteaching bureaucrats rose from about one-third of all full-time hires in 1960 to one-half in 1991. Public education, grades K-12, allocated full-time staff as follows:

Year	Classroom Teachers	Nonteaching Staff
1960	64.8%	35.2%
1992	55.2	44.8

A few years back one writer pointed out the disparity of overhead staff between public and private schools in New York City, where Catholic schools were administered by thirty-five bureaucrats and public schools by 20,000 nonclassroom bureaucrats. The writer pointed out that New York City education bureaucrats were more numerous than education administrators for the entire nation of France! The conclusion would seem to call for fewer frills and featherbedding, and more basics and teachers in the classroom.

High and increasing levels of education spending coupled with lesser levels of educational achievement, deplorable illiteracy/functional illiteracy rates, and lackluster SAT test scores will drive education reforms. Over the long term, the emphasis will be less upon inputs/quantitative indicators and more upon outcomes/qualitative results. All told, education spending increasingly will have to prove itself. Results will count. Excellence in education is imperative to national survival.

[See also Adult Learning; Educational Technologies; Higher Education.]

BIBLIOGRAPHY

Forbes, Malcolm S., Jr. "Quality Time." *Forbes* (September 12, 1994).

Kelly, Dennis. "Core Curriculum Toughening Up U.S. Students." *USA Today*, June 21, 1994.

Peterson, John E. "Why Schools Are Tumbling Down: The Fiscal Story." *Governing* (April 1994).

Samuelson, Robert J. "Merchants of Mediocrity: The College Board Nationalizes Grade Inflation." *Newsweek* (August 1, 1994).

Shanker, A. "Where We Stand on the Rush to Inclusion." *Vital Speeches of the Day* (March 1, 1994).

– GRAHAM T. T. MOLITOR

END OF THE WORLD.

See APOCALYPTIC FUTURE.

ENERGY

The modern energy economy was created virtually out of whole cloth in the short period between 1890 and 1910, transforming many American and European cities. On the streets, horses were replaced by automobiles, while candles and gaslights were supplanted by electric lights. Such transitions are usually driven by an array of social and economic forces, coupled with the availability of technologies that can be applied in new ways.

If these are the conditions needed for rapid change, then the final decade of the twentieth century and the first decade of the next may be as revolutionary as those of one hundred years ago. Indeed, rapid change of many kinds is already taking place, though to see it, one has to delve beneath the broad energy statistics that preoccupy most analytical efforts.

As we consider the future of the energy economy, we may learn more by studying the electronic revolution of the late twentieth century than by applying the geopolitical and geophysical framework of conventional energy analysis. Rapidly evolving technologies, many of them incorporating the latest electronics as a way of raising efficiencies and lowering costs, are now on the verge of commercializations. A variety of stronger, lighter, more versatile synthetic materials will also be applied to everything from wind turbine blades to car frames.

Such technologies are leading to a new generation of relatively small energy-conversion devices that can be mass-produced in factories—a stark contrast to the huge oil refineries and power plants that dominate the energy economy of the late twentieth century. The economies of mass manufacturing will quickly bring down the cost of the new technologies, and ongoing innovations will be rapidly incorporated in new products, in much the way that today's consumer electronics industry operates.

Efficient use of energy is the cornerstone of a more sustainable energy system. Several studies show that it should be possible to double the current level of global energy productivity—the amount of energy needed to produce a dollar of gross world product—over the next four to five decades. From light bulbs to refrigerators, many new energy-using technologies are at least 75 percent more efficient than the current standard. Even in the power industry, which has sought to improve the efficiency of its equipment for a century, the power plants that opened in the early 1990s are 50 percent more efficient than a decade earlier.

By 2025, renewables could displace oil

as the world's second-largest energy source,

providing more than half the world's primary energy,

with the share rising as high as 90 percent by 2100.

Natural gas is the second key to a sustainable world energy system. Gas is far more abundant than oil and much less polluting as well. Natural gas also lends itself to efficient applications, including potentially widespread cogeneration of electricity and heat in factories and buildings. Natural gas resources appear adequate to permit a tripling in global production by 2025. Although such estimates are somewhat speculative, our relatively conservative figures suggest that world gas consumption would peak by about 2030, fall sharply after 2050, and be largely phased out by the end of the twenty-first century.

The third step to a sustainable future is the development of carbon-free ambient energy sources such as wind and solar power. Technologies for harnessing these energy sources are advancing rapidly, and together they can provide three times as much primary energy in 2025 as nuclear power now does.

Some 20,000 wind turbines are already spread across the mountain passes of California and the northern plains of Europe, and the market is expanding at a rate of 20 percent annually. The most extensive wind development in the mid-1990s is occurring in Germany and India. The new generation wind turbines are made of high-tech synthetic materials and incorporate the latest in variable electric drives and electronic controls. As a result, wind power costs have declined by a factor of four since the early 1980s, reaching as low as four to five cents per kilowatt hour for some commercial projects in the United States—which is less than the cost of many coal-fired projects.

The cost of photovoltaic solar cells has fallen even faster—from $20 per watt in 1980 (in 1994 dollars) to $4 per watt in 1994. This has made solar electricity economical in many areas where conventional electric lines are not present. By the end of 1994, some 250,000 Third World households were using solar power. India alone accounted for 12 percent of the world market in solar cells. Even bigger projects are coming. In early 1995, Enron Corporation announced plans for several hundred megawatts of grid-connected solar power plants in India, Pakistan, and China—deals which, by themselves, could easily triple the world production of solar cells.

Solar and wind energy are far more abundant than any of the fossil energy resources in use today, and declining costs are expected to make them fully competitive in the near future. Three states alone—the Dakotas and Texas—have enough wind to provide all U.S. electricity, while a tiny fraction of the southwestern deserts could supply all the country's transportation fuel needs via solar-derived hydrogen. By 2025, renewables could displace oil as the world's second-largest energy source, providing more than half the world's primary energy, with the share rising as high as 90 percent by 2100.

The 1990s are marked by another unanticipated technological development: viable alternatives to the gasoline-powered internal-combustion engine. Lightweight hybrid-electric vehicles made of synthetic materials and run on devices such as gas turbines, fuel cells, and flywheels are about to emerge from engineering labs around the world. With fuel economies that are three to four times the current average and emissions of air pollutants that may be a mere 5 percent of currently permitted levels, these revolutionary new cars, trucks, and buses appear likely to enter the commercial market by the end of this decade, ushering in an era when automobiles can be refueled at home from the local electric or gas system.

Although an energy system this different may be hard to envision, there are no foreseen technical or economic barriers to such a transition. The projected annual growth in new renewable-energy technologies—as high as 20 to 30 percent—is actually slower than the growth rates of nuclear power in the 1960s and '70s, or of personal computers in the 1980s. By 2025, the renewable-energy industry could have annual revenues as high as $200 billion (in 1993 dollars)—twice the 1993 revenues of Exxon, the world's largest oil company.

As natural gas supplies level off or are voluntarily kept in the ground to reduce carbon emissions, a substitute will be needed in the decades ahead. The fuel most likely to fill this niche is hydrogen, the simplest of the chemical fuels—in essence a hydrocarbon without the carbon. Hydrogen is the lightest of the elements as well as the most abundant. When combined with oxygen to produce heat or electricity, the main emission product is water. Although hydrogen has a reputation as a dangerous fuel, this is largely a myth. If properly handled, hydrogen will probably be safer than the major fuels in use today.

Electricity can be used to split water molecules through electrolysis, a century-old technology already used commercially. Although it is relatively expensive today, costs would come down as the technology is scaled up. As far as water is concerned, the requirements are relatively modest. In fact, all current U.S. energy needs could be derived from just 1 percent of today's U.S. water supply. Even in most arid regions, water requirements will not be a major constraint on hydrogen production. The water needed by a photovoltaic power plant producing hydrogen is equivalent to just 2.7 centimeters of rain annually over an area the size of the plant. And in the long run, hydrogen may be derived from seawater.

As large wind farms and solar ranches appear in sunny and windy reaches of the world, they can generate electricity that is fed into the grid when power demand is high and be used to produce hydrogen when it is not. Additional hydrogen could be produced in individual homes and commercial buildings using rooftop solar cells. Hydrogen can either be stored in a basement tank or piped into a local hydrogen-distribution system.

Hydrogen could gradually fill the niches occupied by oil and natural gas today—including home and water heating, cooking, industrial heat, and transportation. Hydrogen-powered cars have already been developed by several companies, with the main future challenges being an improved storage tank and an inexpensive fuel cell engine. In addition, a new technology called a fuel cell—first used widely in the U.S. space program—can convert hydrogen to electricity via an electrochemical process, at an efficiency as high as 60–80 percent. Fuel cells could be used to provide electricity in buildings and also to power hybrid-electric cars. Several companies are already developing commercial fuel cells.

Wind power turns these turbines in California, where nearly all U.S. capacity is located. World wind energy capacity increased from ten megawatts in 1980 to 7,630 megawatts in 1997. (© W. Borges, 1991/Stock Montage)

Eventually much of the world's hydrogen is likely to be carried to where it is needed through pipelines similar to those now used to carry natural gas. This is more efficient than the oil or electricity distribution systems in place today. In the early stages of the transition to hydrogen, the new energy gas can be added to natural gas pipelines in concentrations up to 15 percent—a clean-burning mixture known as hythane. Hydrogen could also be produced from natural gas, either in central facilities or gas stations. Later, engineers believe that it will not be too difficult to modify today's natural gas pipelines so that they will be able to transport hydrogen.

Over time, solar- and wind-derived hydrogen could become the foundation of a new global energy economy. All major population centers are within reach of sunny and wind-rich areas. The Great Plains of North America, for instance, could supply much of Canada and the United States with both electricity or hydrogen fuel. The pipelines that now link the gas fields of Texas and Oklahoma with the Midwest and Northeast could carry hydrogen to these industrial regions. Although renewable energy sources are more abundant in some areas than others, they are far less concentrated than oil, with two-thirds of proven world petroleum reserves being in the Persian Gulf.

For Europe, solar power plants could be built in southern Spain or North Africa. From the latter, hydrogen could be transported into Europe along existing gas pipeline routes. To the east, Kazakhstan and other semiarid Asian republics could supply energy to Russia and central Europe. For India, the sun-drenched Thar Desert is within easy range of the rest of the country. For the more than 1 billion people of China, hydrogen could be produced in the country's vast central and northwestern regions and shipped to the population centers on the coast.

How quickly might the transition unfold? When oil prices first soared in the 1970s, energy markets responded slowly at first, but then quickened. Government responses were initially misguided, but gradually the more foolish projects were abandoned, and better policies emerged. The strongest pressure to move away from fossil fuels is environmental—particularly the greenhouse effect of warming that is occurring as a result of fossil-fuel combustion. In order to stabilize concentrations of carbon dioxide in the atmosphere, we will have to move away from fossil fuels and toward the array of available, new energy technologies. The world has been laying the policy and technical groundwork for such a system for two decades; with sufficient political pressure, it could accelerate the process dramatically.

History suggests that major energy transitions—from wood to coal or coal to oil—take time to gather momentum. But once economic and political resistance is overcome and the new technologies prove themselves, things can unfold rapidly. If the past is any guide, unexpected events, new scientific developments, and technologies not yet on the drawing board could push the pace of change even faster.

All current energy needs of the United States could be derived from just 1 percent of its water supply.

This is how today's energy systems emerged at the end of the nineteenth century, and it may be the way a sustainable energy economy begins to emerge at the end of the twentieth century. If so, the coming energy revolution will have profound effects on the way all of us work and live, as well as on the health of the global environment on which we depend.

[See also Coal; Electric Power; Energy Conservation; Energy, Renewable Sources of; Natural Gas; Nuclear Power; Nuclear Power: Con; Petroleum.]

BIBLIOGRAPHY

Flavin, Christopher, and Lenssen, Nicholas. *Power Surge: Guide to the Energy Revolution.* New York: Norton, 1994.
Hoffmann, Peter. *The Forever Fuel. The Story of Hydrogen.* Boulder, CO: Westview Press, 1981.
Ogden, Joan M., and Williams, Robert H. *Solar Hydrogen: Moving Beyond Fossil Fuels.* Washington, DC: World Resources Institute, 1989.
World Energy Council. *Energy for Tomorrow's World.* New York: St. Martin's Press, 1993.

— CHRISTOPHER FLAVIN

ENERGY, RENEWABLE SOURCES OF

"Renewable" energy sources are those sources that are not running out or limited by their total quantity, as with the remaining reserves of petroleum, coal, or natural gas. Renewable sources of energy are limited rather by the rate at which they are available or can be exploited. For example, the total amount of sunlight that shines on any given surface is limited, but it does not deplete or is not reduced in any meaningful sense through its use or "consumption." The sun is expected to keep shining for another nine to ten billion years—eight orders of magnitude longer than petroleum's expected life span.

Among the renewable energy sources are all forms of solar power, plus power derived from the wind, rivers, heat from the Earth (geothermal), waves, tides, and biomass that is either burned or turned into fuels such as ethanol. Hydrogen, the most common element in the universe, can also be used as a renewable fuel. In addition, one of the largest sources of energy today, con-

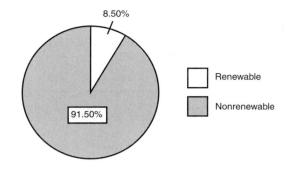

Figure 1. World energy production.

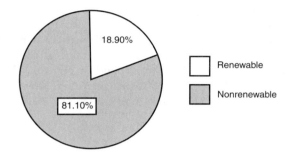

Figure 2. World electricity production.

servation or increasing the efficiency of our current uses of energy, does not involve tapping any one source of energy but rather utilizes new technological advances. In many places in the industrial world, but especially the United States, this is the least costly and the largest energy source.

Renewable energy sources play an important role in meeting the world's energy demands, although they are not in as widespread commercial use throughout the world as the nonrenewable (depleting) energy sources. In the early 1990s, renewable energy sources supplied 8.5 percent of the world's total *commercial* energy needs. The total contribution of renewable energy to meeting the world's energy needs is much larger but much renewable energy is not bought and sold in the global marketplace. For example, most firewood that is consumed in the developing world is gathered and used by families, and it never enters the market. In today's market, the renewable energy sources are often perceived as more expensive than the main commercial energy sources. Part of the reason for this is that renewable energy sources have traditionally not been subsidized by government research, tax breaks, insurance, and other means to the extent of the nonrenewable energy sources.

That renewable energy is not commercially bought and sold as much or as often as the more "traditional" energy sources of coal, oil, and natural gas does not

mean that these energy sources do not play a large role in the global economy or in the everyday lives of billions of people on this planet. Actually, solar energy supplies over 99 percent of all the energy used in the world—it just doesn't get counted in our economic accounting system. When we turn on our furnaces in the winter, we think we are heating our homes with oil or natural gas. In fact, we would be heating our homes from a −240° centigrade temperature if solar energy were not heating our planet to begin with.

Because the primary energy sources that society relies on are depleting, the price for these energy sources will increase. Eventually, with a growing world economy, the depleting energy sources will become so expensive that the conversion to renewable energy sources will become a natural process. As economic competitors seek the least-cost way of producing quality products in a global economy, the lower-cost renewable energy sources of today will become the mainstream energy sources of tomorrow. Some analysts point out that this conversion to renewable energy could happen even sooner as technological progress in this area is advancing much faster than in the nonrenewable area.

For example, electricity produced from wind energy is already competitive in many parts of the world with coal, oil, natural gas, and nuclear powered electrical plants. Solar power is also in use throughout the world as the least-cost option for producing heat and hot water. In remote regions away from the electric grid, solar-powered photovoltaic cells are also the least-cost option for producing electricity.

Hydro, or river, power has been in use for millennia, providing transportation and the power to mill grain, cut lumber, and more recently to produce electricity. The most developed of the renewable energy sources, hydroelectric power provides 18.6 percent of the world's total electric power cleanly and efficiently. Hydro power does not produce carbon to add to the Earth's warming nor does it produce any other air pollutants. However, hydro power does cause changes in ecological cycles and loss of land. The total global hydro power potential from large hydro sites is about equal to the world's current consumption of energy in all forms. Small-scale hydro power is a proven technology and can add significantly to meeting the world's need for clean energy without damaging the surrounding ecosystems.

Biomass is solar energy that has been captured and stored by nature through photosynthesis. It currently provides a significant portion of the world's energy supply: 5.7 percent of the world's total commercial energy use, primarily in the developing world. Biomass is used for energy in the form of wood, dung, crop residues, and crops that are turned into fuel alcohol, ethanol, or methane.

Geothermal energy is the heat from inside the Earth trapped at shallow depths as dry steam, wet steam, brine, hot dry rock, pressurized liquid, or magma. It has been in use since the early 1900s producing electricity. Geothermal energy currently supplies less than 1 percent of the world's electricity needs. Tapping just the molten rock in the Earth's upper ten kilometers could provide a virtually unlimited energy source capable of powering the entire world. Like other renewable energy sources, the technology that would make this an affordable option has not been fully developed.

One of the most promising renewable energy sources is hydrogen. Made from water, it could supply clean, abundant fuel for automobiles, trains, airplanes, industry, heating, and even electricity in the form of hydrogen-powered fuel cells. When "consumed," or used, hydrogen produces water (H_2O) and heat. As such, it is the cleanest of all fuels and could play a significant role in lessening the impact of global warming. It is also an ideal medium for storing other renewable energy sources such as solar and wind power; first, the

solar or wind energy is converted into electricity, and then through electrolysis hydrogen is produced from water. Hydrogen has a few other advantages: Many existing energy converters can readily switch to using hydrogen fuel, and it has the greatest energy per unit mass of any chemical fuel (two and a half times the energy per unit weight of gasoline). Its major disadvantages are that it is still too expensive to produce to compete effectively with conventional fuels, and it is so light that it is not concentrated enough to store easily.

[See also Electric Power; Energy; Energy Conservation; Motor Vehicles, Alternatively Powered; Nuclear Power.]

BIBLIOGRAPHY

Energy Statistical Yearbook. New York: United Nations, 1991.
Johannson, Thomas D., et al. Renewable Energy: Sources for Fuel and Electricity. Washington, DC: Island Press, 1993.

— MEDARD GABEL

ENERGY CONSERVATION

People do not want energy for its own sake. Rather they want the "end-uses," the services, that energy provides:

Solar power will be a source of energy for at least another five billion years until the Earth's sun turns into a supernova and extinguishes life in this solar system. (Chinch Gryniewicz; Ecoscene/Corbis)

hot showers and cold beer, visibility and mobility, baked bread and smelted alumina. *End-use efficiency* is defined as how much service is delivered per unit of delivered energy used. Raising that efficiency is the most important, easiest, fastest, cleanest, cheapest, and most profitable way to provide more and better energy services. With the possible exception of new doubled-efficiency electric generators, it is also by far the greatest opportunity to wring more work out of each unit of primary energy such as coal, natural gas, or crude oil.

End-use efficiency does more with less, providing unchanged or improved services with less energy and more brains. (One-third of Americans think *energy conservation* means doing less, worse, or without—privation, discomfort, and curtailment—so we avoid that ambiguous term.) During 1979 to 1986, Americans' energy savings delivered seven times as much new energy as all net increases in energy supply, just over half of which were renewable. By 1994, the United States was saving about $160 billion per year compared with the energy it would have had to buy if it were still as inefficient as in 1973. Billions of tiny choices by tens of millions of individuals—insulation, caulk guns, duct tape, plugged steam leaks, and slightly more efficient cars—were providing a new national energy "source" two-fifths bigger than the domestic oil industry.

Almost all of these savings came not from making power plants and refineries more efficient, or from reducing distribution losses in pipelines, tankers, and power lines, but from more efficient end-use. Perhaps the most spectacular example was in cars and light trucks. From 1973 to 1986, government standards were largely or wholly responsible for doubling new cars' average efficiency to twenty-nine miles per gallon (mpg). Largely in consequence, oil imports fell from 46 percent of U.S. consumption in 1977 to 28 percent five years later. By 1985, oil imports from the Persian Gulf were only one-tenth of their 1979 peak.

End-use efficiency requires consistent effort if its benefits are not to be swallowed up by growing population and affluence. Thus after 1985, oil imports rebounded as car efficiency stagnated: more than half of the mpg improvements went into making cars accelerate faster. Such choices have consequences. President Reagan's 1986 rollback of light-vehicle efficiency standards promptly doubled Gulf imports and wasted more oil than the Bush administration and the 1995 Congress hoped to find under the Arctic National Wildlife Refuge. In 1990 to 1991, many young Americans went to the Persian Gulf in 0.56-mpg tanks and seventeen-feet-per-gallon aircraft carriers, because we had not all been driving thirty-two-mpg cars. That would have

been enough, had we done nothing else to eliminate the need for oil imports from the Persian Gulf. If Americans had continued to save oil as rapidly after 1985 as they did for the previous nine years, no oil from the Gulf would have been needed from then on. Not doing so increased oil-import bills and balance-of-trade deficits by $23 billion in 1993 alone. It costs roughly $50 billion every year for the peacetime readiness costs of forces earmarked for intervention in the Gulf.

How much better could we do? In the mid-1980s, about a dozen automakers demonstrated internal-combustion-engine family cars achieving 67 to 138 mpg via better aerodynamics and lighter metals such as aluminum and magnesium. At least two of these concept cars reportedly would have cost no more to make; several offered equivalent or better comfort and safety. None entered mass production. In 1993, however, a vastly larger potential emerged, properly combining the best available technologies could yield: safe, spacious, affordable, high-performance family cars that could drive coast to coast on one tank of any convenient fuel. Full worldwide use of such cars, and of analogous heavier vehicles, will ultimately save as much oil as OPEC (the Organization of Petroleum Exporting Countries) now extracts.

Such "hypercars" artfully combine two main elements. First, they replace heavy steel with extremely light but strong polymer composites, such as the carbon fiber familiar in sporting goods, to make the car lighter and cut friction with sleeker shapes and better tires. Such "ultralight" cars are twice as efficient, as General Motors demonstrated in 1991. Second, hypercars add "hybrid-electric drive": the wheels are driven by special electric motors, but the electricity, instead of coming from heavy batteries recharged from the utility grid, is made onboard from fuel as needed. Since fuel has about a hundred times as much energy per pound as batteries, this saves weight and cost. A small battery or other storage device temporarily stores braking energy, recovered when the wheel motors convert unwanted motion back into useful electricity for reuse in hill climbing and acceleration.

Adding hybrid-electric drive to an ultralight car can boost its efficiency by about 400 to 1,000 percent. The car becomes radically simpler and cheaper to build, more than compensating for its costlier materials. Its product cycle time, tooling cost, parts count, assembly labor, and space requirement are roughly one-tenth of today's cars. Starting in 1994, these potentially decisive competitive advantages led many current and potential automakers to launch major development efforts. During 1994–1995, several prototypes three to five times as efficient as production cars emerged. By the late 1990s, hypercars may well trigger the biggest shift in industrial structure since the microchip.

Light vehicles use about 37 percent of America's oil (roughly half imported at a cost of about $50 billion a year). The rest goes to heavy road vehicles, aircraft, ships, industrial heat, and feedstocks, as well as space and water heating in buildings. But even in 1988, straightforward technological improvements could have saved most of that oil very cheaply. Even before hypercars were invented, fully using mid-1980s' technologies could have saved four-fifths of U.S. oil use at an average cost of a few dollars per barrel—cheaper than drilling for more. (Today the savings would be even bigger and cheaper.) Widespread use of "superwindows"—which have heat-reflecting thin films and insulating heavy gas fillings that insulate as well as up to twelve sheets of glass—could save twice as much oil and gas as Americans obtain from Alaska.

Better yet is the recent discovery that *big energy savings can be cheaper than small ones.* For example, superwindows don't just save energy. They also provide numerous other benefits, such as efficient motors, and dimmable electronic ballasts to control fluorescent lamps; but these devices are often more than paid for by just one or two of their benefits, making their energy savings better than free. In the early 1990s, this surprise showed up in big and small buildings, hot and cold climates, motor and lighting systems, hot-water and computer systems, and even car design. It is starting to revolutionize the way we think about the economics of end-use efficiency.

For example, a house built in Davis, California, in 1993 needed only one-fifth the energy allowed by the strictest U.S. energy code for all its major uses. Yet because it provided superior comfort with no furnace or air-conditioner, even at 113° F (45° C), it would cost, if widely imitated, about $1,800 *less* than average to build and $1,600 less than average to maintain. Rocky Mountain Institute's superinsulated, superwindowed headquarters showed this a decade earlier in a cold climate (down to −47° F, or −44° C), eliminating the furnace while *reducing* total construction cost.

Careful timing can also make big savings cheaper than small ones. More than 100,000 big all-glass office buildings need reglazing because the window seals fail after about twenty years. In one such building near Chicago, replacing the dark-bronze glass with superwindows could allow less unwanted heat but six times as much daylight (bounceable deep inside), insulate four times as well, yet cost nearly the same. The lighting and office equipment could also be made to work the same

or better, look better, and use 80 percent less energy. These combined actions would reduce cooling requirements by nearly fourfold. It would then cost $200,000 less to replace the cooling system with a far smaller one nearly four times as efficient than to renovate the old one. The money saved would pay for the better lights and windows. The building's total energy use would fall by about 75 percent, repaying its investment in less than a year.

Combining the best available technologies

could yield safe, affordable, high-performance cars

that could drive coast to coast

on one tank of any convenient fuel.

Cost-effective, state-of-the-art designs can save about 75 percent of the energy in most existing buildings. In new buildings, the savings are often even larger, and the construction cost typically goes *down.* Savings are often about 50 percent in big motor systems, rising to as much as 90 percent if the driven equipment (such as fans and ducts or pumps and pipes) can also be improved. Such savings often pay for themselves in a few years as a retrofit, and cost less than average in new construction. Office air-conditioning savings can run as high as 97 percent. Around 75 percent of all U.S. electricity can be saved at a cost several times lower than that of just *operating* a typical coal-fired power plant. Because it is cheaper to save the coal than to burn it, the resulting global warming and acid rain are abated not at a cost, but at a profit—and, being profitable, this can be done in the marketplace.

In practice, however, this huge technical potential is being achieved far too slowly because of pervasive market failures. Most states reward utilities for selling more energy, not saving it. Architects and engineers are paid for what they spend, not what they save; all two dozen parties in the real-estate process are systematically rewarded for inefficiency and penalized for efficiency. Most designers use obsolete rules of thumb, not real whole-system optimization. People buying energy efficiency typically want their money back ten times as fast as energy companies recover their investment in increased supply—equivalent to a tenfold price bias against end-use efficiency. Subsidies and asymmetrical tax rules increase that bias. Incentives are split between landlords and tenants, builders and buyers, equipment manufacturers and users. Most people have poor information about what the best buys are, where to get them, and how to shop for them. Overcoming such persistent obstacles will be a key to achieving a prosperous economy, a just society, and a secure, sustainable world.

[See also Energy; Energy, Renewable Sources of; Natural Gas.]

BIBLIOGRAPHY

Fickett, Arnold P.; Gellings, Clark W.; and Lovins, Amory B. "Efficient Use of Electricity." *Scientific American* (September 1990): 65–74.

Heede, H. Richard, et al. *Homemade Money: How to Save Energy and Dollars in Your Home.* Snowmass, CO: Rocky Mountain Institute; Amherst, NH: Brick House, 1995.

Lovins, Amory B. "The Negawatt Revolution." *Across the Board* (September 1990): 18–23.

Lovins, Amory B., and Hunter, L. "Least-Cost Climatic Stabilization." *Annual Review of Energy and the Environment* 16 (1991): 433–531.

———. "Reinventing the Wheels." *Atlantic Monthly* (January 1995): 75–86.

Lovins, Amory B., and Browning, William D. "Negawatts for Buildings." *Urban Land* (July 1992): 26–29.

– AMORY B. LOVINS

ENGINEERING

Engineering is involved in the extension of our biological capabilities through the design, production, and operation of artifacts, from bridges to airplanes to artificial organs. As engineering continues to carry out its historic function in the future, a number of trends will be increasingly important:

New Physical Frontiers

There will be continued expansion of the human reach into new physical frontiers—space and the oceans— way beyond what we have been able to achieve thus far. The next century will see, through engineering and intelligent management, a greater ability to utilize the oceans as sources of food and other important materials; the design of long-term human habitats in space; possibly the establishment of industries on the planets and asteroids; more ambitious explorations of the galaxy through unmanned probes; the enhanced use of space for telecommunications through satellites; and greater utilization of all the electromagnetic spectrum frequencies.

Concern with Society

Engineering has addressed societal problems throughout its history, but the complexity of the problems of the cities, poverty, health care, transportation, and employment, as well as the ambiguous attitude of society toward technology, will require new engineering skills and a clearer sense of how technology can realize its

beneficial potential while minimizing negative social side effects. Crucial concerns will include the role of engineering in (1) achieving on a global scale a civilized sustainable living standard, while preserving ecology and environment; (2) addressing the structural unemployment created by increasing technological efficiencies in all sectors of employment; and (3) establishing a reasonable balance between traditional aspects of sovereignty, economics, and politics, and the profound changes created in these domains by telecommunications and information technology. The appropriateness of specific engineering projects—whether, what, how, and when to build—will be increasingly scrutinized. Also, engineers will seek a larger role in the governance of society.

A big area of future engineering development is biotechnology and its transformation from a laboratory operation to widely used and large-scale industrial applications.

Concern with Environment

Engineering increasingly will be called upon to prevent or remedy the environmental problems—such as waste, noise, air and water pollution—created by industrialization and continuing population increases. A particularly enduring set of issues is how to treat toxic waste, especially from nuclear materials.

Convergence of Engineering and Science

This is already beginning to occur. Scientists are creating tools and artifacts—in genetic engineering or in new synthetic molecules, for example—while engineers endeavor to use their techniques to understand physical and biological systems. The convergence will extend to the behavioral and social sciences, such as psychology, or to economics.

Interdisciplinary Integration

This general trend will show itself in new kinds of engineering designs, from sensors combining biological and electronic elements or concepts to a closer integration of structures and electronics in ship or aircraft design. The picture, in jest, of an airplane as a microchip with peripherals makes the point. The integration of design and flexible manufacturing will make it practical to mass-produce, individually, different parts and systems. A fundamental challenge will be how to integrate vast decentralized entities, be they computer networks, factories, or suburbs.

Blending of Biology and Engineering

Clearly manifest at the end of this century is the application of engineering to the solution of biomedical problems, from instrumentation to physiological simulations, to artificial organs and better mechanisms for the delivery of medication. The reverse direction—transfer of knowledge gleaned from biology to the design of engineering systems—will become increasingly common because of the imaginative solutions that have emerged through biological evolution, including ways to sense, to create and shape materials, to integrate systems, and to transform energy in environmentally benign ways. A big area of future engineering development is biotechnology and its transformation from a laboratory operation to widely used and large-scale industrial applications.

Intelligent Capabilities in Ever Wider Classes of Artifacts

The ability to provide flexible responses to inputs, maintain the memory of past events, and perform log-

This engineer displays a group of energy-saving devices created in response to environmental concerns. The United States, with less than 5% of the world population, accounted for 25% of global oil use in 1997. (Roger Ressmeyer/© Corbis)

ical decisions will be increasingly embodied in new computing devices, in new materials, and in many other engineering systems. It will lead to myriad applications, including intelligent telecommunications networks and sophisticated and flexible robots capable of responding to a variety of human needs, e.g., as house-helpers.

Enhanced Value-Added Through Multifunctionality

Many engineered artifacts will have more than one capability, such as self-diagnosis of malfunctions and self-repair, or inherent decision making. This broad new frontier will be one of the most significant generators of new kinds of engineering design and industrial opportunities.

Relentless Pursuit of Cost Reduction

Material, manufacturing, operating, and disposal costs—a constant concern of engineers—will be reduced through simplicity of design, "just in time" techniques, modularity, new ways of enhancing maintainability and repairability, and recycling the products of design, and through a ubiquitous drive toward total quality.

Greater and Smaller Dimensions, Speed, and Power

These traditional engineering goals will lead to hypersonic commercial planes, faster land and sea vehicles, more powerful nonnuclear explosives, planes for a thousand or more passengers, transcontinental highways (e.g., in Asia) and other macroengineering projects, ever-longer bridge spans or tunnels, and faster construction and excavation methods. The traditional goals are leading to molecular composites with properties varying at the molecular scale and assembled molecule by molecule, and to molecular engines composed of a few molecules. Such developments are the extension of the submicron focus at the core of today's semiconductor industry. Defense will continue to be a major engineering arena, with an increasing shift toward smart weapons, electronic warfare, more effective navigation systems, and stronger protection for tanks. From all of this, technologies capable of both military and civilian use will emerge.

New Areas for Engineering Endeavors

Engineers will be increasingly involved in the area of services ranging from financial services (in operations and in the mathematical modeling of financial variables) to the area of security (from the design of overall security systems to that of better systems for identification and encryption of confidential data). The management of natural and human-made catastrophes and of the associated risks will be of mounting engineering concern. The complexity of today's technology, and the expansion of dense human habitats increase people's exposure to potential disasters. Other new domains are exemplified by engineering and law, including issues of intellectual property and of forensic engineering. Sports engineering, an increasingly indispensable tool for competitiveness accomplished with wind tunnel tests of shapes, skiing configurations, and trajectories, will also flourish.

Globalization and Reorganization of the Engineering Process

Advances in telecommunications and information processing will transform engineering into a global process with teams working concurrently on the same design or project across the globe. This will force a rethinking of the engineering profession, from the issue of standards to the preparation of managers of global real-time engineering teams. There will be ubiquitous expert systems, much closer ties of design to production, and interpenetration of the design teams of suppliers and main project contractors.

Rethinking Engineering Education and the Role of Engineering Schools

There will be an ever greater trend toward inter-disciplinarity, increasing efforts to reverse the decline of interest of American students in engineering, and efforts to remedy the underrepresentation of minorities. The number of women engineering students will equal that of men, changing the attitude of society toward engineering—and vice versa. Engineering schools will continue to seek a balance between expanding demands on the curriculum and the need to produce engineers in a reasonable number of years. They also will struggle with the conflicting needs to assert the differences between the engineering and the scientific process, while at the same time bringing engineers in closer contact with a broader range of scientific subjects. Engineering schools will develop closer ties with industry and the community and will be seen increasingly as a resource for economic and social development.

[See also Air Transport; Appropriate Technology; Factories and Manufacturing; Macroengineering; Pipelines; Railways.]

BIBLIOGRAPHY

Bugliarello, George. "Technology and the Environment." In D. B. Botkin, M. F. Caswell, J. E. Estes, and A. A. Orio, eds. *Changing the Global Environment.* New York: Academic Press, 1989.

Drexler, Eric K. *Engineers of Creation: The Coming Era of Nanotechnology.* New York: Doubleday/Anchor Books, 1987.

Negroponte, Nicholas. *Being Digital.* New York: Bowker, 1995.

Sladovich, Hedi E. *Engineering As a Social Enterprise.* Washington, DC: National Academy Press, 1991.

– GEORGE BUGLIARELLO

ENTITLEMENT PROGRAMS

In the words of Dietrich Bonhoeffer, "The ultimate test of a moral society is the kind of world it leaves to its children." Every generation of Americans has struggled to realize progress. And to date, every generation has succeeded in making America, if not the world, a better place. Yet America's current generation of leaders may be failing to meet Bonhoeffer's mandate. Many now question the future of the American dream—and the steady productivity increases on which that dream depends. Most policy analysts agree that some necessary investments in the future are today being crowded out by unnecessary and excessive government spending and borrowing.

> *"The ultimate test of a moral society is the kind of world it leaves to its children."*

Over the last thirty years, the federal government has racked up enormous deficits. Currently, the national debt is approximately $4.8 trillion dollars, or $18,460 for every man, woman, and child in the United States. In order to pay for annual deficits, the government borrows from the nation's pool of savings, leaving less money for private investment. Lower private investment in new equipment, technology, and worker training—that is, less investment in the future—means American industries are not as competitive as they used to be. As America's competitive edge slips away, the nation earns less money. As a result, wages go down, standards of living stagnate, and jobs become worse and harder to find, especially for young people just entering the work force.

The Problem

The responsibility for America's national debt rests on the shoulders of all Americans. As citizens, Americans have demanded the best of both worlds: lots of funding for many public programs, without the pain caused by higher taxes. Ironically, the lion's share of federal spending has not gone to discretionary programs—education, infrastructure, crime prevention, the environment, or even national defense. Rather, the majority of federal funds today go to interest on the national debt and to "entitlement" programs (see Figure 1).

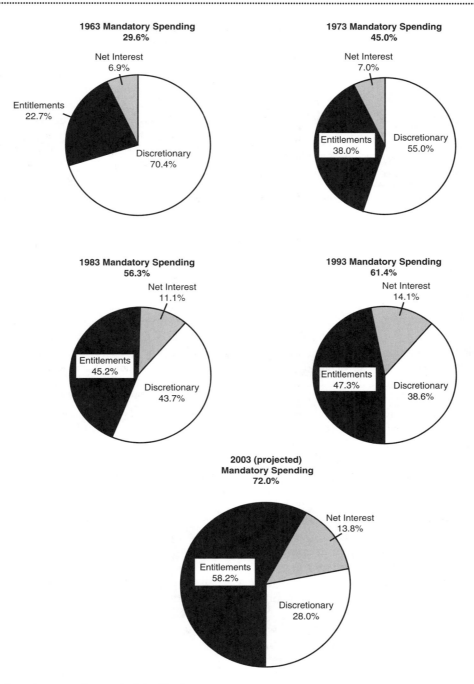

Figure 1. Growth of mandatory spending in the federal budget.

Entitlements are the federal government's promises to deliver benefits to anyone who meets certain eligibility criteria. Popular entitlement programs include Medicare, Medicaid, veterans benefits, Social Security, farm subsidies, and a host of other programs. Unlike "discretionary" programs (education, transportation, and so on) entitlements are funded automatically and without annual Congressional review. Entitlements have served as important sources of support for many Americans. Yet the facts regarding entitlement spending are sobering. If present spending trends continue, the United States government will simply not have enough money to deliver on its current promises very far into the next century.

- Entitlement spending and interest on the national debt together consume more than 60 percent of federal outlays today, double the percentage of just twenty-five years ago, and they are projected to exceed 70 percent of total federal outlays by 2003.
- More than three-quarters of all entitlement spending goes to just four programs: Social Security, Medicare, Medicaid, and federal pensions.
- The Public Trustees of Medicare have concluded that the Medicare Health Insurance program will run out of money by 2002 in the absence of new funding.
- By 2013, according to the Public Trustees of Social Security, Social Security will be in the red, with benefit payments exceeding the tax revenues dedicated to the program. By 2029, unless appropriate changes are made in the interim, Social Security is projected to be bankrupt.
- By 2030, projected spending for Medicare, Medicaid, Social Security, and federal employee retirement programs alone will consume all tax revenues collected by the federal government.

Many people understandably blame the national debt and deficit on "waste, fraud, and abuse" in discretionary programs. While waste, fraud, and abuse are serious problems, they are not the source of our long-term financial problems. Even if the federal government eliminates all discretionary spending—closes down Congress, the White House, and the Pentagon, stops spending on education, job training, and NASA—it would barely have enough money by 2012 to meet mandatory entitlement payments and interest on the national debt.

What this means is that just as the students of the 1990s reach the height of their careers, political leaders of the future will have to raise taxes dramatically, or there will be no money available for any discretionary program. Fifty years ago America was able to fight a world war, build an interstate highway system, and provide a just level of benefits. But if the United States continues down its current fiscal path, today's twenty-something generation will inherit dysfunctional entitlement programs, a deteriorating American economy, and the potential for skyrocketing taxes.

Many entitlement programs are growing at only a moderate rate. It is America's federal retirement and health costs that have exploded in recent years. Social Security was established in 1935 as a pay-as-you-go system in which each generation of workers pays, through payroll taxes during their working years, for the retirement benefits of the generation before it. Medicare has a similar design, except that a large portion of Medicare comes from general revenues. The systems were enormous successes because each generation of workers had

enough children to fund its own retirement. That held true until the baby boom ended in the 1960s.

When Congress enacted Social Security there were over ten workers to support each retiree. However, in 2008 the baby boom generation will begin to retire, and in a single decade the ratio of working Americans to retired Americans will be cut by 40 percent (from a ratio of 5:1 to 3:1). In addition, thanks to the fantastic medical advances of the last 20 years, Americans are living longer, healthier lives, and as a result are collecting far more lifetime Social Security and Medicare benefits. Although most retirees believe they are simply getting back what they put into the system, the facts contradict that belief. Within a decade, a typical middle-income couple retiring in the early 1980s had already received back, with interest, the total value of their lifetime Social Security and Medicare taxes *and* the total value of their lifetime federal income taxes.

Under these demographic forces, America's federal retirement programs will be severely strained. Unless America acts soon to account for its changing demographics, the nation will face a choice between dramatic tax hikes or draconian benefit cuts.

Treading on Sacred Ground

Most national politicians treat Social Security and Medicare as the most politically unassailable federal programs. Indeed, the programs have done a tremendous amount of good and deserve respect. In 1935, the elderly, as a group, were America's poorest people. Today, they are among the nation's wealthiest. But the success of Social Security and Medicare must not mask the problems future generations face if the programs go untouched. The federal government spends nearly ten times more on every person over sixty-five than it spends on those under age eighteen. Moreover, the overall poverty rate among Americans under age six is nearly three times the rate of poverty among Americans over sixty-five.

Furthermore, Social Security and Medicare are now on a collision course with bankruptcy. The facts are backed by experts from the Congressional Budget Office, the Federal Reserve, and the Social Security Administration. Politicians are not doing these programs any favors by ignoring the experts and avoiding the programs' shortfalls. Those who promise to leave Social Security and Medicare "off the table" from government cuts are denying the overwhelming forces of arithmetic and demographics. Further, they are saddling America's future with dysfunctional programs. The longer America waits to change course, the more drastic the reforms will have to be. Postponing reform is a moral and economic assault on future generations.

The Solutions

Reducing the deficit and getting a handle on entitlement programs will not be easy. The nation's leaders cannot do it just by attacking "waste, fraud, and abuse." Nor will a slight tax increase solve the problem. Raising taxes on some groups might be justified, but if the federal government relied only on tax increases to solve long-term entitlement problems, every federal tax would have to double in order to meet spending obligations. To address America's addiction to entitlement spending and changing American demographics, American citizens will have to make some difficult choices about raising the retirement age, scaling back benefits for wealthier segments of society, and even eliminating programs that do not work. The good news is that if the nation acts quickly, it can take moderate, incremental steps to plan for a promising future.

However, if the nation fails to act quickly, the youth of the 1990s will inherit a world of crumbling entitlement programs, a burgeoning national debt, decreased national savings, and an increasing number of retirees who have unrealistic expectations. As a generation, today's young Americans cannot face that tremendous fiscal burden and still lead this nation into greatness.

[See also Class and Underclass; Deficits, Governmental; Health Care Costs; Health Care: Moral Issues; Health Care: Technological Developments; Human Rights; Public Assistance Programs; Public Assistance Programs: Social Security.]

BIBLIOGRAPHY

The Bipartisan Commission on Entitlement and Tax Reform. *Final Report to the President.* Washington, DC: U.S. Government Printing Office, January 1995.

———. *Interim Report to the President.* Washington, DC: U.S. Government Printing Office, August 1994.

Kotlikoff, Laurence J. *Generational Accounting.* New York: Free Press, 1992.

Longman, Phillip. *Born to Pay.* Boston: Houghton Mifflin, 1987.

Penny, Timothy J. *Common Cents.* Boston: Little, Brown, 1995.

Peterson, Peter G. *Facing Up: How to Rescue the Economy from Crushing Debt and Restore the American Dream.* New York: Simon & Schuster, 1993.

— ROBERT M. MCCORD
HEATHER LAMM

ENTREPRENEURSHIP

Entrepreneurship is about individuals taking risks in business to develop and deliver innovative products and services. In doing so, entrepreneurs change people's lives and even large societies.

In the future, the entrepreneurial role will expand. The complexity of a global economy, shifting financial resources, the demand for more devices, the emergence of competitive Third World economies, and the continuing disintegration of Cold War-based policies entail new problems that will demand the kind of creative solutions that entrepreneurs can provide. However, the future entrepreneur will look different from today's typical practitioner, because the relationship between emerging enterprises and established corporate organizations will change and women and minorities will play greater roles.

Philosophically, entrepreneurs are

the cowboys of the commercial world,

driven by a passionate desire for autonomy.

Philosophically, entrepreneurs are the cowboys of the commercial world. They are driven more by a passionate desire for autonomy and belief in their product and less by profits or shareholder interests. In classic cases, they take higher than average financial risks to deliver new, innovative products and services to new, never-before-tested consumer groups. Size is a key component. Generally, entrepreneurs run small, fast, flexible organizations. In recent years, restructuring has forced some people into becoming entrepreneurs.

Entrepreneurial power in the marketplace has been documented. Between 1972 and 1982, over three million new entrepreneurial businesses were formed throughout the world, including countries with controlled economies. During that same period, a study by the U.S. Commerce Department shows that small businesses responded more quickly to market opportunities, creating more than their proportionate share of new jobs. By the year 2000, 85 percent of the U.S. labor force will work in firms employing fewer than 200 people.

In terms of innovation, a National Science Foundation study reports small firms perform better. They produced approximately four times as many innovations per research-and-development dollar as medium-sized firms and twenty-four times as many as large firms.

Today, the method, manner, and content of production is changing dramatically. Globalization is expanding the marketplace. Financial investment is shifting from developed to emerging countries. Disposable income is in the hands of more diverse and demanding consumers who seek immediate gratification. In this environment, success depends on how fast companies respond to the varied needs of new customers.

Entrepreneurs, unlike large corporations, are better equipped to move quickly to meet these demands. Big enterprises, even those with entrepreneurial founding fathers, usually are not structured for flexibility and speed. Traditional manufacturing companies are hierarchically organized for control. Even those that have flattened their organizations by eliminating management levels and introducing quality circles and teams are still encumbered and impeded by the problems of size.

While many entrepreneurs' main clients are corporations, in general these two groups operate separately in different, parallel commercial worlds. There is little cross-activity between them. Over time, successful entrepreneurial activities evolve into larger, more organized organizations that eventually "mature" and become part of the established commercial world.

In the future, this relationship will be different. The gulf between small and large corporate entities will expand. Megacorporations without national boundaries will organize to serve the demands of a global-driven marketplace for basic goods and services. Medium-sized companies without the capital to compete will merge or be forced out. However, small companies will flourish focusing on niche sectors and local needs and becoming, in the process, the hothouses for tomorrow's entrepreneurial activities.

Large companies will actively seek out these smaller businesses to form partnerships, buy intellectual properties, or simply acquire them. International entrepreneurial product brokers will represent small companies. Research and development will become less prominent in the corporate structure. The corporation will float grants, seed money, or resources to entrepreneurial groups outside its structure (or sometimes within its own ranks) to entrepreneurs who are supported by the host company and allowed to "sink or swim."

The large involvement of women and minorities in this arena is another significant development. Because of the free-form nature of the entrepreneurial process, more women and minorities are finding rewarding opportunities as they become a predominant part of this world. Today, women are starting businesses at over twice the rate of men and could own over 50 percent of U.S. small businesses by 2000.

Entrepreneurs are recognized as a dynamic factor in the marketplace—breaking norms, creating and delivering new products, and changing societies. Because of their flexibility and innovative approaches, their role will expand as opportunities to solve future problems grow in an increasingly complex global economy.

[*See also Business Structure: Industrial Policy; Capital Formation; Creativity; Investments; Research and Development; Science Cities; Scientific Breakthroughs; Technological Change; Technological Innovation.*]

BIBLIOGRAPHY

Brown, Jonathan, and Rose, Mary B., eds. *Entrepreneurship, Networks, and Modern Business.* Manchester: Manchester University Press, 1993.

Drucker, Peter T. *Managing for the Future: The 1990s and Beyond.* New York: Penguin Books, 1992.

Kuratko, Donald F., and Hodgetts, Richard M. *Entrepreneurship: A Contemporary Approach.* 2nd ed. Fort Worth, TX: Dryden Press, 1992.

– LAUREN HUDDLESTON

ENVIRONMENT

Millions of people around the world gasped with wonder in 1969 as a man set foot on the dusty gray surface of the Moon. Later, they thrilled to see a televised view of their own planet from outer space—round and gleaming, awesomely finite and deceptively simple from 240,000 miles away. It was an exhilarating and sobering picture of Spaceship Earth, a depiction in which national boundaries could not be discerned. Nor could distinctions be made between the gleaming office towers and manicured lawns of the modern industrialized parts of the globe and the teeming cities, depleted forests, and degraded farmlands of the developing regions. And while that glistening orb—our Earth and our home—appeared serene, it also looked disturbingly small and fragile.

These dramatic new glimpses of Earth heightened a nascent awareness that all humankind was in the same boat—that whatever threatened a part of the planet menaced the world's inhabitants as a single community.

If Earth were photographed from the Moon today, it would look much the same. One could not see the disappearance of more than forty species of animal life or the net increase of the Earth's human population from nearly four billion to almost six billion. But it is those two trends—and the political, economic, social, and environmental stresses and tensions associated with them—that have made our world ever more fragile and vulnerable as humankind approaches the twenty-first century.

The advance of industrial civilization and the burgeoning of population in the developing countries have produced imbalances that now threaten the future of us all. The most ominous are the concentration of economic growth in the industrialized countries and population increases in the developing nations. Nearly three-quarters of the population increase of the quarter-century since 1969 occurred in the developing countries. During the same period, the gross global product rose to $20 trillion, more than 70 percent of it in the industrialized countries.

The benefits of these dramatic changes accrued largely to the minority of the world's people who live in the highly industrialized countries. The majority of the population, living in the less developed areas, received few, if any, of the benefits; yet they share disproportionately in the costs and risks. These people remain at an early stage of economic development, and many live in a state of dire and debilitating poverty in which the day-to-day imperatives of survival drive them to exploitative practices that destroy the resource base on which their future depends.

The advance of industrial civilization and the burgeoning of population in the developing countries have produced imbalances that now threaten the future of us all.

Three years after the remarkable space achievement of 1969, the international community focused more closely on Earth and its problems. The United Nations Conference on the Human Environment held in Stockholm during 1972 was the first attempt to bring a global perspective to—and obtain worldwide agreement on—the fact that humankind was on a course that could lead to ruin. A major achievement of that conference was the endorsement by 113 nations of a declaration that all humans bear "a solemn responsibility to protect and improve the environment for present and future generations."

This custodial notion was elaborated by the United Nations World Commission on Environment and Development (UNCED), headed by Norwegian Prime Minister Gro Harlem Brundtland. Its report in 1987, *Our Common Future,* calls for a full integration of the environmental dimension into all areas of political, economic, social, and industrial policy, and decision making. The result of this radical process eventually would come to be called "sustainable development." But the degradation of the Earth continued, despite the earnest declarations of the Stockholm Conference, the Brundtland Commission's reassurance that environmental responsibility and economic growth were not incompatible, and a growing public awareness of the complex and interrelated environmental issues.

Against this background the United Nations General Assembly convened a global conference on environment and development during 1992 in Brazil. Following two and one-half years of intensive preparations, the conference brought together in Rio de Janeiro leaders of virtually all the nations of the world, including more heads of state and government than had ever before come together. The 1992 UN Conference on Environment and Development was the world's first true "Earth Summit." World leaders were joined at the conference and at the accompanying "People's Summit" by unprecedented numbers of people representing a broad spectrum of nongovernmental organizations and citizen groups, and by more than twice the number of media representatives than had ever before covered a world conference. People throughout the world were attuned to the conference and its importance.

This "people-pressure" helped to move governments to agree on a declaration of principles, the Declaration of Rio, and on Agenda 21, a comprehensive program of action to give effect to these principles. Despite some compromises to achieve consensus, Agenda 21 constituted the most comprehensive and far-reaching program of action of its kind ever agreed to by the nations of the world. And the fact that this agreement was reached at the highest political level lent its pronouncements a unique authority. It presented detailed policy and action recommendations on a broad range of issues central to prospects for survival and well-being. And it did this within an integrated framework that enables our response to these issues to be guided by an understanding of the systemic linkages and interactions among them.

What all of these issues of environment and development have in common is that they must be managed on an integrated, cooperative basis, if the risks to which they give rise are to be averted or contained within tolerable limits. This will require a vast strengthening and reorientation of institutional mechanisms and capacities at every level, and an incorporation of the objectives of Agenda 21 into international agreements and arrangements involving trade, investment, and finance.

This will require the development of an effective and enforceable international legal system which will further extend into the international arena the rule of law, which is the solid basis for the effective and equitable functioning of nations. Success will require the integration of ecological disciplines into our educational system, and the additional development of the understanding and skills required to manage these issues. The values on which implementation of Agenda 21 will depend require integration into cultural and social systems. To be effective, each sector of society—business and industry, trade unions, scientists, farmers, educators, religious leaders, communicators, indigenous people, women, children, and youth—must become fully committed to and engaged in the implementation of Agenda 21.

All of the environmental deterioration we have witnessed to date has resulted from levels of population and human activity which, while unprecedentedly high, are still a great deal less than they will be in the period ahead. One of the traditional outlets for the pressures generated by population growth, conflict and economic difficulties has been migration. But today, as pressures for migration escalate, the national borders of the world are closing. Scarcely had the tearing down of the Berlin Wall in 1989 been celebrated than new barriers were being erected in Europe against the entry of the poor, the homeless, and the dispossessed from the eastern and southern parts of Europe.

A new world order must include full and fair participation by the majority of the people of the world who currently inhabit the developing countries. They must have equitable opportunities to share the benefits of technological civilization, just as they share the risks. And surely the highest priority should be accorded to eradication of the poverty that condemns so many people to suffering and hunger and is an affront to the moral basis of civilization.

As we moved through the last decade of the twentieth century, there were few signs that governments were giving priority to implementing the agreements reached in Rio. To some degree this was understandable. The changes called for at Rio were fundamental in nature and will not come quickly or easily. In addition, political leaders were preoccupied with a vast array of more immediate and compelling pressures, both domestic and international. All these factors, however, are much less important to the future of their societies than the issues addressed at Rio.

There have been some positive developments. The United Nations Commission on Sustainable Development was established as the forum for continuing consultation and cooperation and for following up and implementing the agreements reached in 1992 at UNCED. The United States in 1993 reasserted and reestablished its leadership in respect of the issues ad-

Humans have become conscious that we share a planet on which the actions of one person or nation affect that of another, no matter how distant they may seem. (David Samuel Robbins/Corbis)

dressed at Rio by signing the Biological Diversity Convention and by setting up a new Presidential Commission on Sustainable Development. A number of countries, including China, are developing their own national "Agenda 21" in response to the global agenda. Japan, which has made great environmental strides domestically, is poised also to take on an international leadership role.

The most exciting and promising developments, however, are occurring outside of government. Since the Rio conference, there has been a virtual explosion of activities on the part of grass-roots organizations, citizen groups, and key sectors of society—including business, scientists, architects, engineers, educators, and religious leaders. Representatives of these groups returned from Rio determined to translate basic environmental themes into their own responses to Agenda 21. The Business Council for Sustainable Development comprise some sixty chief executive officers of leading transnational corporations. In its 1992 report, "Changing Course," this influential group made an important contribution to the Earth Summit, and it has been subsequently reconstituted with a commitment to bringing about the changed course it called for at Rio.

The proliferation of private initiatives and grass-roots activity has promise of infusing new energies into the political process and ensuring that the issues of Rio will be moved back into prominence in the political agenda. The pressures for follow-up and implementation of the results of the Earth Summit will increase as the necessity becomes ever more evident.

Necessity always has driven change. Throughout history, nations have demonstrated their willingness to devote the resources, establish the alliances, and make the sacrifices required to confront risks to their security. Today, as never before, the people and nations of the world are joined in facing the greatest threat ever to their common security—the threat to the capacity of our planet to sustain life as we know it. Only by forging a new global alliance, embracing North, South, East, West, rich and poor, can this challenge be met effectively. The agreements reached at the Earth Summit—the Declaration of Rio and Agenda 21—provide the foundations for the construction of this new alliance. Our common future depends on it.

[See Jan Tinbergen on Socialism for further discussion of the disparity between developed and developing countries.]

[See also Acid Rain; Development, Alternative; Development: Western Perspective; Environmental Behavior; Environmental Ethics; Environmental Indicators; Environmental Policy Changes; Global Environmental Problems; Global Warming; Hazardous Wastes.]

BIBLIOGRAPHY

Brundtland, Gro Harlem. *Our Common Future: Report of the World Commission on Environment and Development.* New York: Oxford University Press, 1987.

Commission on Global Governance. *Our Global Neighbourhood: The Report of the Commission on Global Governance.* New York: Oxford University Press, 1995.

Myers, Norman. *Ultimate Security: The Environmental Basis of Political Stability.* New York: Norton, 1993.

Schmidheiny, Stephan. *Changing Course: A Global Business Perspective on Development and the Environment.* Cambridge, MA: MIT Press, 1992.

Shabecoff, Philip. *A Fierce Green Fire: The American Environmental Movement.* New York: Hill and Wang, 1993.

Ward, Barbara, and Dubos, Rene J. *Only One Earth: The Care and Maintenance of a Small Planet.* New York: W. W. Norton, 1972.

– MAURICE STRONG

ENVIRONMENTAL BEHAVIOR

Environmental ethics (and the behavior it engenders) involves a major shift in the frame of reference within which traditional ethics is contemplated. Ethics in Western thought has been an aspect of philosophy and theology, and it has shared their focus upon the individual and the human, describing desirable human goals, ideals, moral character, and behavior. Various theologians or philosophers have differed about important details, but always nature (or "God's Creation") was the stage or backdrop. So the focus of moral attention remained upon humans (or upon humans and God).

This traditional view has been challenged by the scientific perception that individuals (and the entire human species) participate fully in the physical and biological processes that create, sustain, and change life. We are totally within those processes, not somehow apart from or above or beneath them.

Ecology entails the systematic integration of biology, chemistry, and physics to account for the creation and stability of living communities (ecosystems) made up of many species interacting with one another and their environment. Environmental ethics no longer sees humans as separate from the rest of life around us and no longer in mastery over it all.

The biblical environmental ethic was one of "dominion." Responsible "stewardship" has been proposed as an improved biblical ethic. But stewardship still assumes that humans know enough about complex natural systems to be able to be "good stewards." Elizabeth Dodson Gray has proposed as an alternative an environmental ethic of "attunement," based upon "ecological reconnaissance," with humans aiming to attune and fit in with ecosystems, particularly those deemed unique or fragile.

We humans are making major changes to the present and future environments of the globe and its regions. A major example is certainly the rapid increase in the total human population from 2 billion (1930) to 5.3 billion (1995). Humans of a particular localized ecosystem can degrade and decrease its life-sustaining potential (or "carrying capacity"). We have done this to major worldwide systems (such as oceans, fisheries, soils, and the ozone layer in the upper atmosphere).

Spaceship ethics sees all on the planet

as in the same boat, a single spaceship,

and the needed response is conserving and sharing.

A major controversy within environmental ethics has been between a global and a regional focus: "spaceship ethics" is different from "lifeboat ethics." Spaceship ethics sees all on the planet as in the same boat (a single spaceship), and the needed response is conserving and sharing. Lifeboat ethics sees many boats on the sea of life (many regions, continents, ecosystems). Garrett Hardin (1976) criticizes Kenneth Boulding (1966) and R. Buckminster Fuller (1969) for not taking sufficient account of human mismanagement of shared resources. The conserving and sharing assumed by spaceship ethics, says Hardin, often works out badly in practice when a common resource (such as air, water, fisheries) is unstructured and so left to a first-come-first-served process in which human greed and desire for profit can often dominate the more noble sentiments of planetary sharing.

Hardin's lifeboat ethics is based upon a biologist's understanding of carrying capacity. Hardin proposes that spaceship Earth is akin to a naval ship. Such ships are built to be divided in emergencies into watertight compartments (regions or ecosystems) so as to not endanger the entire ship (or planet) when there is severe damage to one or more compartments.

In lifeboat ethics, each boat has the opportunity and responsibility for its own survival. It must stay within its own national or regional carrying capacity. Exporting surplus populations, Hardin says, should not in the future be a permitted solution for nations (lifeboats) that allow their populations to continue to grow. Such out-migration mattered less in the recent past when human numbers were far fewer. But as all boats approach (or pass) their various carrying capacities, each boat must take responsibility for its own people and its own viability. Not to do that would make all equally irresponsible and similarly miserable.

The assumed "care horizon" for human actions and accountability in traditional ethics was measured in one or perhaps two human lifetimes. Environmental ethicists are now reckoning with present-day responsibilities for safe long-term storage of highly toxic nuclear wastes (plutonium, for example, has a radioactive half-life of nearly 25,000 years, or three to four times longer than all of previous human civilization). So ethics now asks, what are the rights of those who are currently voiceless because they are not yet born? And again, should other species, who also have no voice in human affairs, have any say about human actions affecting the shared environment and so affecting them?

The scope of environmental ethics is so radically enlarged because both the scale and the duration of our human impacts are now so much bigger. Human actions are still important to environmental ethics. But humans are no longer assumed to be the only point of ethical concern. Human life is now seen as completely rooted in and depending upon viable ecosystems and a viable planet, so environmental ethics moves moral thinking about human actions into this wider context. Then, in that wider context, it asks the traditional sorts of ethical questions about proper human goals, ideals, moral character, and responsible behavior.

[See also Environment; Environmental Ethics; Environmental Policy Changes; Green Revolution; Natural Resources, Use of.]

BIBLIOGRAPHY

Boulding, Kenneth E. *Human Values on the Spaceship Earth.* New York: Council Press, 1966.
Fuller, R. Buckminster. *Operating Manual for Spaceship Earth.* Mattituck, NY: Amereon, 1969.
Gray, Elizabeth Dodson. "Come Inside the Circle of Creation: The Ethic of Attunement." In Frederick Ferré and Peter Hartel, eds. *Ethics and Environmental Policy: Theory Meets Practice.* Athens, GA: University of Georgia Press, 1994.
Lucas, George R., and Ogletree, Thomas W. *Lifeboat Ethics.* New York: Harper & Row, 1976.

— DAVID DODSON GRAY

ENVIRONMENTAL ETHICS

In response to widespread human destruction of the environment, thinkers such as Baird Callicott, Aldo Leopold, Holmes Rolston (1988), and Paul Taylor (1986) have called for a new environmental ethic: one that is *biocentric.* They point out that all beings on the Earth are interdependent and that because of this interdependence, individualistic, *anthropocentric* (human-centered) ethics are not appropriate.

Traditional ethics or moral philosophy, especially in the West, have been anthropocentric. They teach that nonhuman beings have only instrumental value, as means to human ends, such as food. Only humans, according to anthropocentric ethics, have inherent value, or value in themselves, apart from their worth to humanity.

Proponents of biocentric ethics, on the other hand, argue for a holistic approach that recognizes the inherent value of the entire planet. They criticize the human chauvinism, speciesism, and arrogance that many humans exhibit toward nature.

Responding to the biocentric arguments, philosophers such as William Frankena and Kristin Shrader-Frechette (1991a, 1991b) claim that a genuine environmental ethic can be anthropocentric. They contend that even anthropocentric ethics condemn the greed, arrogance, and insensitivity that cause environmental destruction. Moreover, they maintain that although all environmental degradation must stop, it is not possible to give all beings on the planet equal "rights" because not all beings are equal. Tom Regan argues that if we follow biocentric ethics and claim that human rights are equal to those of all other beings, then we would become victims of "environmental fascism" (Regan, 1983, p. 262). That is, we would make all human rights to life, liberty, and dignity subject to the welfare of the environment. For example, taken to an extreme, we could kill humans to save snail darters.

Apart from whether they are anthropocentric or biocentric, most environmental ethics focus on the question of whether duties to the environment—or to other human beings—take primacy. Arguing for "lifeboat ethics," Garrett Hardin says that the planet may be thought of as a sea on which there are lifeboats. The poor of the world are falling out of their crowded lifeboats and trying to swim to the uncrowded, rich lifeboats of the developed nations. Hardin contends that genuine environmental ethics require that persons on the rich boats not help those on the poor lifeboats, because doing so would cause the rich boats to capsize as they exceeded the carrying capacity of their crafts.

Buckminster Fuller, Kenneth Boulding, and others, however, reject lifeboat ethics as unjust and argue for "spaceship ethics." They propose thinking of Earth as a finite, closed spacecraft on which we must conserve and share resources equitably if the entire craft is to survive. For proponents of spaceship ethics, planetary sisterhood and brotherhood are necessary to environmental ethics.

In addition to different general theories—anthropocentric versus biocentric, spaceship versus lifeboat—governing norms for human behavior, proponents of environmental ethics also address a number of more specific issues. Among them is the question of whether animals and/or natural objects have rights, whether there are duties to members of future generations, and whether use of technologies such as commercial nuclear power and long-lived chemical pesticides are unethical. Relentless pursuit of a balanced perspective will continue on into the future.

[See also Environment; Environmental Behavior; Environmental Policy Changes; Green Revolution; Natural Resources: Use of.]

BIBLIOGRAPHY

Attfield, Robin. *The Ethics of Environmental Concern.* New York: Columbia University Press, 1983.

Hargrove, Eugene. *Foundations of Environmental Ethics.* Englewood Cliffs, NJ: Prentice-Hall, 1989.

Regan, Tom. *The Case for Animal Rights.* Berkeley, CA: University of California Press, 1983.

Rolston, Holmes. *Environmental Ethics.* Philadelphia, PA: Temple University Press, 1988.

Scherer, Donald, and Attig, Thomas, eds. *Ethics and the Environment.* Englewood Cliffs, NJ: Prentice-Hall, 1983.

Shrader-Frechette, Kristin. *Environmental Ethics.* Pacific Grove, CA: Boxwood Press, 1991.

———. "Ethics and the Environmental." *World Health Forum* 12 (1991b): 311–321.

Taylor, Paul. *Respect for Nature.* Princeton, NJ: Princeton University Press, 1986.

— KRISTIN S. SHRADER-FRECHETTE

ENVIRONMENTAL INDICATORS

Accounts placing monetary evaluations or otherwise measuring and quantifying the value of natural resources and environmental factors shed new light on the costs of ecological depredations. Prior to this, little effort had been made to value clean air and water, other than estimating damage to buildings caused by particulates and other contaminants or health costs of these to living beings. Economists refer to such costs as "externalities" (i.e., costs of production externalized from company balance sheets, not added into prices but passed on to taxpayers and future generations). Cost calculations vary because quantifying environmental amenities, let alone the value of human life, is speculative.

The United Nations

The United Nations has promoted social indicators at least since 1954, and its latest, most comprehensive work is the UN Development Program's *Human Development Report* of 1990–1992, which introduces the new Human Development Index, a measure that specifically includes environmental indicators. Economists who deal with environmental, natural resource, or ecological matters, as well as statisticians from other disciplines, tend to resist translating pollution and resource-depletion data into monetary coefficients. Some question whether any index combining comprehensive aspects of "quality of life"—such as the UN's Human Development Index or the World Bank's Index of Sustainable Economic Welfare—can be any more meaningful than GNP. The economic approach focuses on single indices using money equivalents and weighting priorities in economic terms, for example, as between urban clean air, public health, preserving rain forests, preventing global warming, or ozone depletion on the one hand and per capita income increases on the other hand. Of course, some kind of environmental capital consumption deflator would be better than the GNP/GDP-based current accounting, which ignores environmental resources altogether.

Green taxes could become so large a revenue source

that eventually they may replace income taxes.

Some scientists believe that environmental pollution and resource depletion are best left specific and "unbundled"—expressed as parts per million of pollutants in the air or water and hectares of land lost to desertification and deforestation, for example—rather than buried in some new single-index version of GNP. A broader, unbundled quality-of-life indicator that parallels but does not replace GNP is termed the Country Futures Indicators (CFI), as shown in Table 1 (see also Henderson, 1991).

OECD Environmental Indicators

Long involved in developing quantitative and qualitative measures of human conditions, the Organization for Economic Cooperation and Development also publishes its own environmental indicators. OECD has also prepared several working papers featuring environmental measurements in specific countries such as Norway (1992).

The OECD promulgated in the early 1970s the so-called polluter pays principle, which helped legitimize and implement the collection of pollution cost data. This led to the introduction of pollution levies on polluters. Eighty-five different so-called green taxes in effect during 1992 fall into four categories: (1) emissions of pollutants such as carbon dioxide, nitrogen oxides, or toxic waste; (2) the depletion of natural resources, for example, mining; (3) generation of waste, for example, overpackaging; and (4) planned obsolescence, for example, throw-away lighters, one-time cameras, and so on. Green taxes could become so large a revenue source that eventually they may replace income taxes.

National Experience

Exemplary of future environmental accounting is *A Report on Canada's Progress toward a National Set of Environmental Indicators* (1991). Forty-three specific indicators in eighteen issue areas, including air and water quality, solid wastes, and contamination in species of bird and fish are represented.

New Zealand reformulated national accounts by adding to GNP/GDP accounts a capital-asset account that represents the value of infrastructure (public buildings, railroads, highways, dams, ports, bridges, etc.). Most nations do not carry such assets on the balance sheet (as do corporations) in order to arrive at a country's "net" worth. This omission led to poor maintenance, short-term thinking, and under-investment in public sector goods and services. Possibly, this concept will be broadened to include environmental assets, such as forests. The Netherlands is overhauling its GNP/GDP accounts, along with over twenty other countries, including Germany, France, Denmark, Canada, Venezuela, India, and Indonesia. Japan deducts social and environmental costs of urban congestion in calculating its GNP/GDP.

Natural Resource Accounting

Progress in natural resource accounting has accelerated since 1990, mainly in valuing forest resources. Institutions now studying and producing natural resource accounting models include the following:

- UN-ECOSOC (New York)
- United Nations Environment Program (New York and Nairobi, Kenya)
- The World Bank (Washington, D.C.)
- World Resources Institute (Washington, D.C.)
- Organization for Economic Cooperation and Development (Paris and Washington, D.C.)
- World Wildlife Fund International (Gland, Switzerland)
- European Association for Bioeconomic Studies (Milan, Italy)
- International Society for Ecological Economics (Solomons, Maryland)
- Worldwatch Institute (Washington, D.C.)
- Environment Canada (Ottawa)
- ECOTROPIC (Rio de Janeiro)
- Wuppertal Institute for Climate, Environment, and Energy (Germany)
- New Economics Foundation (London)
- International Academy of Environment (Conches, Switzerland)

Life Cycle Accounting

Another tool in the growing array of environmental indicators is life cycle accounting. This method fully accounts for natural resources and their conservation spread over the useful life of products and services. This approach accurately balances the often high initial costs of resource-conserving technologies with the net savings

TABLE 1

COUNTRY FUTURES INDICATORS

Beyond money-denominated, per-capita averaged growth of GNP

Reformulated GNP to Correct Errors and Provide More Information	Complementary Indicators of Progress Toward Society's Goals
• *Purchasing power parity (PPP).* Corrects for currency fluctuations. • *Income distribution.* Is the poverty gap widening or narrowing? • *Community-based accounting.* Complements current enterprise-basis. • *Informal, household-sector production.* Measures all hours worked (paid and unpaid). • *Deduct social and environmental costs.* A "net" accounting avoids double counting. • *Account for depletion of nonrenewable resources.* Analogous to a capital-consumption deflator. • *Energy input/GDP ratio.* Measures energy efficiency, recycling. • *Military/civilian budget ratio.* Measures effectiveness of governments. • *Capital asset account for built infrastructure and public resources.* Many economists agreed this is needed; some include environment as a resource.	• *Population.* Birthrates, crowding, age distribution. • *Education.* Literacy levels, school dropout and repetition rates. • *Health.* Infant mortality, low birth weight and weight/height/age correlations. • *Nutrition.* Calories per day, protein/carbohydrates ratio, etc. • *Basic services.* Access to clean water, etc. • *Shelter.* Housing availability/quality, homelessness, etc. • *Public safety.* Crime. • *Child development.* World Health Organization, UNESCO, etc. • *Political participation and democratic process.* Amnesty International data, money-influence in elections, electoral participation rates, etc. • *Status of minority and ethnic populations and women.* Human rights data. • *Air and water quality and environmental pollutions levels.* Air pollution in urban areas. • *Environmental resource depletion.* Hectares of land, forests lost annually. • *Biodiversity and species loss.* Canada's environmental indicators. • *Culture, recreational resources.* Jacksonville, Fla., etc.

From Paradigms in Progress: Life Beyond Economics by Hazel Henderson (1991). Table copyright © 1989 Hazel Henderson, used with permission.

they produce over their period of use. For example, a house built to rely on solar energy may be less expensive than a conventional house when savings in energy bills are costed out over the life of the structure, even though the initial cost of such a house would be high.

Unit-Waste Pricing

Unit-waste pricing, also known as full-cost pricing, refers to prices of products that fully account for and include social and environmental costs. Calculating longer-term costs or costs displaced to other regions (transborder pollution or depredation of the global commons, for example) is exceedingly difficult.

Green Indices

Green indices appeared during the 1990s. *The Green Index, 1991–1992* is a state-by-state guide to environmental health in the United States, published by the Institute for Southern Studies in Durham, N.C., and the Island Press in Washington, D.C. Canada's green indicators have been mentioned previously, and there is also the *Green Budget* from the British Green Party and Merlin Press of London.

> *[See also Environment; Forestry; Green Revolution; Natural Resources, Use of; Social Indicators.]*

BIBLIOGRAPHY

Anderson, Victor. *Alternative Economic Indicators.* London: Routledge, 1991.

Cairncross, Frances. *Costing the Earth.* Boston: Harvard Business Review Press, 1992.

Daly, Herman, and Cobb, John. *For the Common Good.* Boston: Beacon Press, 1990.

Ekins, Paul, Hillman, Mayer, and Hutchison, Robert. *The Gaia Atlas of Green Economics.* New York: Anchor Books, 1992.

Henderson, Hazel. *Paradigms in Progress.* Indianapolis, IN: Knowledge Systems, 1991, chapters 6 and 7.

"Statistical Needs for a Changing Economy." Background Paper, September 1989. Washington, DC: U.S. Office of Technology Assessment.

— HAZEL HENDERSON

ENVIRONMENTAL POLICY CHANGES

Environmental policy evolves as we learn more about how the world works, as new technologies are developed, as we uncover problems, as efforts at solution create new problems, as we assign new responsibilities to government, as we develop deeper understanding of quality in living, and as we look further into the future. Contemporary policy making is restrained by old ways of thinking and by existing structures of government that do not fit newly discovered realities. In nearly every country except China the people are ahead of the government in perceiving environmental problems and urging corrective action. Wariness about health threats has been foremost in eliciting concern and demanding action. Victims of dangerous actions by others have often turned into environmentalists. The visibility of some forms of pollution and their detrimental side effects may be the reason why many people define environmental problems as pollution.

The Basic Underlying Learning Curve

A century ago those concerned with the preservation of beautiful natural places called themselves *conservationists*. Concern about increasing industrial pollution in the 1950s and '60s led to a sister movement of persons who called themselves *environmentalists*. Both movements, in those early days, accepted the premise that while modern society was basically sound, nature would have to be protected by better technology as well as by better and more vigorously enforced laws. Current public discourse about environmental problems is still based on that premise, which is accepted by most governments as well.

Future-oriented environmentalists see environmental problems differently. They point out that the world has a population of 6 billion. This could double to 12 billion by 2035 (and could double again to 24 billion by 2075). Economic throughput (the speed with which we take things from the earth, process them, use them, and discard them as waste) grows even faster than population. Meanwhile, mineral stocks are being used up; deforestation is spreading; species extinction is accelerating; deserts are expanding; soils are depleting swiftly; fish stocks are diminishing; wildlife habitat is disappearing; toxic poisons are circulating from air to water to soil to food and bioaccumulating up the food chain; the protective ozone shield is thinning rapidly; and greenhouse gases are threatening to alter climatic systems—perhaps sending them into chaos. Without intending to, just by doing better and better that which people had always done, humans are changing the way the planet's life support systems work. At the very time when increasing numbers of people need sustenance, we are crippling the ability of life systems to provide it.

It became clear to these environmentalists that better laws and better technology are unlikely to reverse the accelerating negative trends; that continued environmental exploitation and ruin is rooted in the fundamental beliefs and values of modern society—that society itself must be transformed. But how should we characterize the new society they seek?

In the later half of the 1970s the phrase "sustainable society" began to be used and soon became widely accepted. The phrase implies that our present trajectory was not sustainable, that growth in population and economic throughput has to be limited. No one argued against the desirability of sustainability, but there was considerable disagreement about what it would require in everyday practice. Even so, people of many persuasions felt comfortable under this umbrella. The perceived need to address urgently the whole set of interconnected global environmental problems drew the conservation and environmental movements together so that they are now close partners and nearly indistinguishable.

"Sustainable development is development

that meets the needs of the present

without compromising the ability

of future generations to meet their own needs."

The United Nations General Assembly established in 1983 a World Commission on Environment and Development (WCED). In its report, *Our Common Future* (1987), it called for "sustainable development." The phrase caught on, becoming the topic of hundreds of books and thousands of conferences and discussions. It became the central focus of the United Nations Conference on Environment and Development held in Rio de Janeiro in June 1992. This first planet-wide summit of national leaders was soon dubbed the "Earth Summit" and firmly established environmental concerns and the sustainability of society and its ecosystems at the top of the world's agenda. Today nearly everyone recognizes that there are severe environmental problems on planet Earth; but are they fixable by better laws and better technology or must our whole society be transformed? Let us call the two camps transformationalists and fixers.

A much quoted definition of sustainable development in *Our Common Future* reads: "Sustainable development is development that meets the needs of the present without compromising the ability of future generations to meet their own needs" (p. 43). The fixers interpret that statement as endorsing economic growth as desirable and sustainable. Transformationalists caution, however, that sustainable growth is an oxymoron; the two terms are contradictory. We must distinguish growth from development. Development implies improvement and has no inherent limit but continuous growth is physically impossible. Tragically, population growth is such a sensitive issue that the WCED did not forthrightly confront it; the topic was even excluded from discussion at the Earth Summit. The United Nations did hold a separate conference on population in Cairo in September 1994. That conference achieved agreement that population growth must be limited and that emancipation of women would be the most effective strategy for doing so. Currently, fixers control nearly every government and economic growth is urgently being encouraged around the planet. Even though humankind continues to desire unlimited growth, that desire will not change the physical reality that growth in population and economic throughput must cease.

Learning a New Way of Thinking

The "let's fix it" mentality dominated early thinking about environmental policy. We sought specific solutions to specific problems: national parks to preserve beautiful places; filtration plants to cleanse dirty water; tall smokestacks to disperse air pollutants; treatments for cancer caused by polluted environments; and so forth. Early efforts to solve discrete problems were assigned to different governmental departments. Even when these disparate efforts were reassigned to newly established environmental ministries to upgrade their effectiveness and improve coordination, the old divisions (air, water, land, etc.) were retained. The U.S. Environmental Protection Agency (EPA) concluded from an internal policy review in the 1980s that this piecemeal approach merely moved problems from one place to another without really eliminating them; but the U.S. Congress still has not seen fit to change the EPA's structure.

Recent studies show that most people, all around the planet, are aware of and highly concerned about environmental problems. They want government and industry to correct these problems, although they have little confidence that they will. Other studies show that most people and their leaders are ignorant of the basic dynamic principles of the planet's life support systems and the interaction of those systems with socioeconomic-political systems. For example, every school child should be taught that matter and energy can neither be created nor destroyed, they can only be transformed (the first law of thermodynamics). Environmentalists derive four maxims for everyday living from that basic law of nature: *everything has to go somewhere, we can never do merely one thing, everything is connected to everything else,* and *we should always ask "And then what?"* This new way of thinking can be characterized

as holistic, systemic (seeing the world as a system of systems), integrative, and future oriented.

Not only is environmental education absent from the curriculum of most schools, the educational establishment in most places resists adding this new subject. Most young people pick up what little they know from television, which is effective in arousing concern but not very effective in teaching people how to think about the environment.

The effects of ignorance became painfully visible in the 1960s and 1970s as unsophisticated policy makers, who had not yet learned to ask "And then what?", committed new errors with their solutions: tall smokestacks increased acid rain; waste incinerators increased air and water pollution; landfilling toxic wastes polluted groundwater; sludge from sewage treatment plants polluted land; and closing air leaks from buildings to save energy increased indoor air pollution. The "And then what?" question also should have been applied to new technologies but almost never was: widespread use of chlorofluorocarbons dangerously thinned the protective ozone layer; pesticides caused cancer and other diseases in humans and other creatures; widespread use of trucks increased energy consumption; and the invention of new chemicals (4,000 to 5,000 each year) overwhelmed the regulatory capability of the EPA.

More mistakes were made by allowing each level of government to establish its own environmental regulations, thereby introducing competition between cities, states, and nations to lower environmental standards in order to attract industries that pollute. The persistent effort to lower trade barriers between nations has another unintended consequence as footloose transnational corporations will be able to demand greater weakening of environmental standards in nations hoping to attract and retain industry.

Policy makers must learn how policy sectors are interconnected. Policy for transportation, agriculture, energy, commerce, labor, health, foreign affairs, defense, even justice, also impinge on environmental policy. The preservation of life systems on our planet will require transformation in all those sectors.

The Future?

Human civilization is threatening life systems. How much time do we have? Only a few decades. How fast can we learn? That depends. History shows us that social learning is agonizingly slow. Sometimes, however, it is astonishingly swift. As we persist in damaging life systems, nature will be our most powerful teacher. Will we look ahead and learn? Or will we wait for nature to use death to convince?

[See also Environment; Environmental Ethics; Extinction of Species; Global Environmental Problems; Global Warming; Megacities; Ozone Layer Depletion; Public Policy Change.]

BIBLIOGRAPHY

Daly, Herman E. and Cobb, John B. Jr., *For the Common Good: Redirecting the Economy Toward Community, the Environment, and a Sustainable Future.* Boston: Beacon Press, 1989.

Gore, Al. *Earth in the Balance: Ecology and the Human Spirit.* Boston: Houghton Mifflin, 1992.

Milbrath, Lester. *Envisioning a Sustainable Society: Learning Our Way Out.* Albany, NY: SUNY Press, 1989.

———. *Learning to Think Environmentally.* Albany, NY: SUNY Press, 1995.

— LESTER W. MILBRATH

EPIDEMICS

Large-scale, even global epidemics of infectious disease, of which the current pandemic of human immunodeficiency virus (HIV) infection is a powerful example, are likely to become increasingly common in the future. The extraordinary increases in movements of people, goods, and ideas which characterize the modern world provide the critical ingredient for such worldwide epidemics.

The world contains many microbiological threats to health which currently have a limited geographical scope. In addition, new disease-causing agents have been recently discovered, including the agents of Legionnaire's disease, hepatitis C virus, Lassa fever virus, the Hantavirus recently identified in the southwestern United States, and HIV itself. It is generally assumed that these pathogens have existed for a long time.

The recognition of "new diseases" may result from several, often interacting factors. For example, Legionnaire's disease required a cluster of infections at a major urban convention for its discovery. Also while the disease caused by the newly recognized Hantavirus in the United States undoubtedly existed in the past, a specific cluster of infections was required for its identification (as with Lassa fever).

In addition, some "new diseases" may result from changes in human behavior or in related ecologic factors. For example, human exposure to Legionnaire's disease appears related to specific technologies involving water use (i.e., cooling towers which provided the mode for propagation). Human actions, such as inadequate sterilization of medical or other skin-piercing equipment, contribute to the spread of the Ebola virus as well as HIV. Environmental changes, including large-scale problems of global warming, may produce conditions which favor the spread of infectious agents, such as cholera.

Yet the movements of people, goods, and ideas represent the most important underlying stimuli for new global epidemics of infectious disease. Since about 1950, the number of international tourists has increased nearly twenty-fold; travel and tourism is now considered to be the largest industry in the world. In addition to tourists, business travelers, migrants, and refugees contribute to the movements of people within and between countries.

Global economic interdependence is well established, based on the increasingly unconstrained movements of capital, labor, and goods. Goods may carry or help transmit infectious agents directly, as when mosquitoes infected with the dengue virus were carried from Asia to Latin America in used automobile tires. In addition, adverse global economic conditions contribute to or even create the vulnerability of populations to infectious diseases by depressing living standards and diminishing access to health services.

The movement of ideas is also vital. Global communications create and convey powerful images of modernity and sophistication to people around the world. In turn, these images influence individual behaviors in ways that can increase health risks (i.e., sexual behavior, cigarette smoking, and violence).

The combination of social forces described above virtually ensures that new microbial threats to health will emerge on a global scale in the future. The HIV pandemic not only illustrates the speed and intensity of the global spread of an infectious agent, but also demonstrates the high level of global vulnerability to new epidemics.

While the origin of HIV is obscure and may never be known with certainty, the worldwide spread of the virus appears to have started in the mid-1970s. By 1980, an estimated 100,000 people had become infected with HIV; during the 1980s, this number increased about 100-fold, to about 10 million. According to some recent estimates, a cumulative total of between 40 and 110 million people may have been HIV infected by the year 2000. Although first recognized in the United States, HIV infections clearly had occurred in other parts of the world, including Africa and Haiti, prior to its recognition and discovery. By early 1993, not only had virtually every country been affected by HIV, but Asia, a region little affected in the mid-1980s, experienced explosive epidemics of the HIV infection. The future of this dynamic and volatile pandemic will be determined by the scope, intensity, and capacity of the human response to it, which includes both societal and scientific dimensions.

There is a major lesson from the HIV experience beyond the recognition of our modern vulnerability to the spread of infectious agents. The great likelihood that new pandemic threats will emerge, and given the ways in which a new health problem in any country may rapidly become a multinational or even global problem, it is essential to develop a global monitoring, detection, and rapid response capacity. Currently, no such system exists in any meaningful way. For example, the discovery of AIDS in 1981 was highly fortuitous, requiring: (a) the recent scientific advances allowing identification of human retroviruses; (b) the occurrence of AIDS in an industrialized country with excellent diagnostic capacity and a national surveillance system; (c) the appearance of highly unusual infections and cancers which facilitated awareness and recognition of a new health problem; and (d) the involvement of a self-aware and distinct community (homosexual men) which also helped stimulate concern and awareness. Had AIDS involved only developing countries, or caused an increase in "normal" illnesses, or been widely spread throughout society, it would have taken longer to recognize and identify.

A truly global system of disease surveillance is the appropriate response to the changes in global society and ecology which will continue to make the modern world highly vulnerable.

A truly global system of disease surveillance and response is the appropriate response to the changes in global society and ecology which will continue to make the modern world highly vulnerable to epidemic disease. Rather than considering infectious diseases as stories of the past (plague, cholera, tuberculosis), the world faces perhaps more danger from epidemic disease than ever before. Still, the conditions of global communication which underlie the threat also offer the potential for scientific and societal collaboration, at a global level, which can make all the difference.

[See also Bioethics; Environment; Environmental Refugees; Genetic Technologies; Public Health.]

BIBLIOGRAPHY

Centers for Disease Control. "Addressing Emerging Infectious Disease Threats. A Prevention Strategy for the United States." *Morbidity and Mortality Weekly Report.* No. RR-5 (1994): 43.

Garrett, Laurie. *The Coming Plague.* New York: Farrar, Strauss, and Giroux, 1994.

Levins, R.; Awerbuch, T.; Brinkmann, U., et al. "The Emergence of New Diseases." *American Scientist* 82 (1994): 52–60.

Mann, Jonathan M.; Tarantola, D.; and Netter, T., eds. *AIDS in the World.* Cambridge, MA: Harvard University Press, 1992.

— JONATHAN M. MANN

ESCHATOLOGY.

See APOCALYPTIC FUTURE.

ESPIONAGE AND COUNTERINTELLIGENCE

Intelligence, as it has been understood since the end of World War II, is a dying business. The end of the Cold War brought with it the destruction of a world where each intelligence agency had clear targets, broadly understood the nature of the threat, and had a clear role and the technical means to combat it.

The overwhelming amount of work carried out by the main intelligence agencies in the NATO and Warsaw Pact countries was in support of the Cold War. It was aimed either at gathering intelligence about the enemy or trying to prevent the enemy's spies from gathering information. Despite the end of the Cold War, it is clear that every country needs an intelligence service that can play a part in guaranteeing national security. In those countries of the former communist bloc where new agencies are emerging from the old, they are doing so with the help of their former enemies in the West. Being born with all the safeguards of a modern Western intelligence agency might ensure that they do not become political tools, but are used only for the collection and analysis of information vital to the security of the state (as opposed to individual governments of whatever political complexion).

The end of the Cold War also brought with it calls for cutbacks in both the military and intelligence communities. As a result, every intelligence agency suffered budget cuts—but some less than others. In 1993, for example, Britain's Secret Intelligence Service reduced its staff by only 50 out of around 1,900, while the Security Service maintained its existing staff. The American and Russian intelligence agencies were not so fortunate.

The KGB has been destroyed, its old directorates broken up, and its power cut. Staff abroad has been reduced by 50 percent, and some thirty stations have been closed. As the KGB fell apart after the second Russian revolution, so a new era began that divided the old monolith into a number of different parts, all of which are subject to a form of parliamentary oversight. The old First Chief Directorate, which was responsible for foreign spying, became the SVR but with altered responsibilities. According to Yevgeni Primakov, the head of the SVR, in the future there will be no spying for political rather than national security purposes. Attempts to subvert foreign governments through covert support of terrorist organizations, opposition groups, or even agents in place will not be tolerated. This new pragmatism is driven in part by changing political circumstances, but also because the SVR simply does not have the cash to pay for such extravagance. Greater sharing of intelligence on such matters as drugs, organized crime, and proliferation is being established.

Military threats to the state, proliferation,

counter-espionage, drugs, terrorism,

industrial espionage, and international

financial crime are the new priorities

for intelligence agencies around the world.

There has been little reduction in the activities of the intelligence arm of the Russian military. They continue to try and steal western scientific and technological secrets to help the struggling Russian industrial base. They are also active in trying to recruit spies in the major industrial countries.

Public protestations aside, many of the old KGB have simply donned new uniforms and overnight become staunch democrats. It is difficult to believe that all these thousands of men and women are genuine converts, and there is ample evidence that at many levels in the current Russian political system the levers are still being pulled by the old KGB operators. At the wish of their political masters, most Western spy agencies, such as those in America, Germany, and France, have been forced publicly to embrace the new KGB, exchanging delegations and declaring their chief spies in each other's capitals.

Aside from Russia, the end of the Cold War has had the most dramatic effect in Britain. In the space of four years, the secrecy that surrounded the three principal intelligence organizations—the SIS (Secret Intelligence Service), the Security Service, and the GCHQ (Government Communications Headquarters)—has ended. Two new acts of Parliament have brought the agencies out into the light, complete with a visible Parliamentary oversight system. For a country like Britain, where the overwhelming majority of the population are tolerant of a secret society in a way that would be both illegal and unacceptable in America, these changes have been little short of revolutionary. In America, Congress cut the budget of the American intelligence community by

about 25 percent and a budget of $28 billion was authorized for 1994. The CIA has changed its priorities and has become a more open intelligence service, although the basic structure of American intelligence remains in place.

Military threats to the state, proliferation, counter-espionage, drugs, terrorism, industrial espionage, and international financial crime are the new priorities for intelligence agencies around the world. The new world order is so unstable that each of these areas requires additional resources if the challenges are to be met effectively.

The end of the Cold War and the collapse of authoritarian communist states released ethnic tensions that go back hundreds of years and are only now finding expression. In the early part of this century, many of these ethnic tensions were limited in their influence because of a lack of technology or weaponry. Now modern conventional and unconventional weapons are readily available. It is certain that there will be a proliferation of small wars in the future.

Terrorism, arms control, and drugs pose unique challenges to the intelligence community. By the end of this century, a number of Middle Eastern countries are likely to have ballistic missiles that can carry, chemical or nuclear warheads and will have the range to reach most of Western Europe. As the intelligence failures in Iraq demonstrated, there must be a determined effort to gather the information and act upon it before it is too late.

Both drugs and terrorism are more insidious, but their impact can be enormous. The cost of fighting the drug war in America is currently over $13 billion a year and rising, without a commensurate reduction either in the amount of drug use or the profits being generated for the drug barons. New patterns of trafficking emerging out of the former communist countries suggest that there will be new sources of supply and an increased number of illegal drugs in the future.

In terrorism, too, the nature of the problem is escalating rapidly, in part through the rise of Islamic fundamentalism, which has produced a new brand of terror. There is no grand conspiracy to replace the illusion of a grand conspiracy of the Marxist-Leninist terrorists of the 1970s. Then it was convenient to think of Moscow as the architect of the bombings and the killings, the single hand controlling the explosion of revolutionary fervor that erupted almost simultaneously all over the world.

There needs to be a greater emphasis on human sources. To a large extent, only personnel on the ground can bring back intelligence on terrorists, underground arms networks, or the release of nuclear materials onto the black market. The illegal operators, be they terrorists or arms dealers, now understand the capabilities of the various technical means of gathering intelligence, and have developed effective methods of combatting them. The terrorists no longer talk on the telephone (unless they are amateurs like those who bombed the World Trade Center in New York), and drug dealers do not communicate by fax or arms merchants through a single front-company via telex. Such communications are easily intercepted. Intelligence increasingly will become a high-tech game.

[See also International Tensions; National Security; Terrorism.]

BIBLIOGRAPHY

Bathurst, Robert B. *Intelligence and the Mirror: On Creating an Enemy.* Newbury Park, CA: Sage Publications, 1993.
Jordan, Amos A. *American National Security: Policy and Protest.* 4th ed. Baltimore, MD: Johns Hopkins University Press, 1993.
Toffler, Alvin, and Toffler, Heidi. *War and Anti-War: Survival at the Dawn of the 21st Century.* Boston: Little, Brown, 1993.

— JAMES ADAMS

ESTATE AND FINANCIAL PLANNING

Several trends that have affected estate and financial planning in the latter part of the twentieth century will continue, even accelerate, in the years to come. The role played by financial planners and estate-planning specialists in the wealth transmission process will remain an important one.

The first trend, what might be called the "democratization" of estate planning, has been the most significant one. Until the late 1960s, estate planning—the utilization of trusts and other arrangements to reduce the tax cost of transferring wealth to the next generation—was a concern only to the ultra wealthy. Since World War II, unprecedented wealth has been accumulated by a broad segment of the populace, most notably through the growth of closely held businesses and investments in securities, mutual funds, life insurance, and pension plans, and through increases in the value of homes and real estate. Over the next two decades, all of this wealth—estimates have been as high as $8 trillion—will pass through the owners' estates to the next generation or to charity. Many persons whose parents made do with simple wills (if they had wills at all) will find it essential to employ far more sophisticated arrangements if they do not want the taxing authorities to be major beneficiaries of their estates.

For many years, a $60,000 exemption from the estate tax kept the vast majority of Americans off the transfer tax rolls. By the mid-1970s, the $60,000 figure had become unrealistically low, and in 1976 Congress re-

placed it with an exemption (actually an "exemption equivalent" tied to a tax credit) of $175,625, to be phased in gradually. In 1981, this figure was increased to $600,000 (again, to be phased in gradually). As wealth continues to accumulate and the value of the dollar declines, Congress is likely to reconsider again the appropriate amount of an exemption from transfer taxes.

A second trend has been the incessant reexamination of our transfer tax laws by Congress. For many years, the tax laws affecting wealth transmission were relatively constant. From the enactment of the Internal Revenue Code of 1954 until 1976, the only major change was a 1969 statute dealing with "charitable remainder" trusts. In this environment, clients could rely on an established and predictable tax system in formulating estate plans for themselves and their families. Persons did not have to review or revise their wills unless their economic circumstances or family situations changed.

Beginning with the Tax Reform Act of 1976, fundamental changes in the transfer tax laws have been made on almost an annual basis. The Revenue Reconciliation Act of 1993 was the tenth major amendment to our tax laws since 1976, not to mention several technical corrections acts in between. Each of these new laws affected existing estate plans, often in major ways. Income-shifting and estate-planning techniques that could be employed in the early 1980s no longer exist and have been replaced with new ones. Authors have despaired of publishing hardcover books, concerned that the printed materials may soon become obsolete or even dangerously wrong. Some of the most intrusive laws, enacted with uncommon haste, proved to be unworkable and were later repealed or replaced. One of the most notable, a "carryover basis" rule enacted in 1976, was repealed in 1979. The notorious "antifreeze" statute enacted in 1987, overhauled by amendments in 1988 and 1989, was repealed in 1990. A generation-skipping transfer tax enacted in 1976 was repealed retroactively in 1986, only to be replaced with a more draconian measure that taxes offending generation-skipping transfers at a 55 percent rate. In response to these changes, many persons have found it necessary to revise their estate plans in light of a significant new tax law, only to see the law modified, repealed, or replaced a few years later.

Although the estate and gift taxes raise relatively little revenue in the federal scheme, it is likely that the transfer laws will undergo periodic review and revision in the coming decades impelled largely by the federal deficit. Staying abreast of any changes will continue to be important to all persons with accumulated wealth, and to the professionals who advise them.

A third trend has been the increased importance of "nonprobate" assets in the planning decisions of many clients. (Nonprobate assets are interests in property that pass at death other than by will or intestate succession and which are not subject to administration in the probate courts.) Two of the most significant forms of wealth that many individuals have involve such nonprobate assets: life insurance and deferred compensation benefits prominent among them. For an increasing number of individuals, a last will and testament will be the least important document relating to the disposition of wealth—often far less important, in terms of the dollars involved, than life insurance, pension plan, or individual retirement account (IRA) beneficiary designations.

Since World War II, the dollar value of life-insurance coverage has greatly increased, not only for the traditional purpose of providing economic protection for surviving family members, but also to fund buy-sell agreements and other business arrangements and to address liquidity problems that an estate may face. The Treasury Department can be expected to continue to challenge techniques whereby life insurance proceeds escape transfer taxes on the insured's death. In response, taxpayers' counselors will continue to devise new planning strategies.

A 1980 U.S. Department of Labor report projected that by 1995, the holdings in private pension plans would exceed $900 billion. In fact, figures reported several years later showed that by 1980 there already were assets valued at $642 billion in 480,000 private pension plans. In 1988, 730,000 private pension plans (146,000 defined benefit plans and 584,000 defined contribution plans) held assets worth $1.94 trillion, and by 1992 the value had grown to $3.3 trillion. Adding in the $988 billion in funded state and local government pension plans, $304 billion in the funded federal civil-service and railroad retirement programs, and $647 billion in IRAs, the value of assets in private and public pension plans in 1992 totalled $5.25 trillion (1993 Statistical Abstract of the United States 526 [1994]). All indications are that this form of wealth will continue to grow, not only from continuing contributions by workers and their employers, but because the tax-deferred buildup of investment income make such plans so attractive.

A complex scheme of "minimum distribution rules" reflects a congressional policy that the benefits of qualified pension plans and IRAs are to be used to provide funds for the plan participant's retirement and not for the tax-free buildup of an inheritance for the participant's heirs. Under current law, distributions from a qualified plan or IRA must commence no later than April 1 following the year in which the participant reaches age 70 1/2. Despite this requirement, substantial funds will pass to designated beneficiaries on the participant's death, when the funds are subject to both income tax and estate tax. Without planning, combined taxes on these benefits can reach confiscatory levels. Planning decisions will continue to be challenging, as the rules governing distribution and taxation of plan benefits are dismayingly complex even by Internal Revenue Code standards.

Although all qualified plan benefits ultimately must pass through the income tax mill, the assurance that tax revenues will be received in the future tends not to assuage the appetite of any current administration. In recent years, Congress has limited the amounts that can be contributed to a qualified plan and has enacted a supplemental tax on excess accumulations and excess distributions from a plan or IRA. The phenomenal growth and tempting size of such funds make it likely that additional limits and taxes on plan benefits will be proposed.

Prolonging life will lead to

an increased use and refinement of health care

powers of attorney and "living wills."

Another trend affecting estate planning has been the increase in life expectancies brought about by advances in medical science and technology. The financial and medical problems faced by an aging population will continue to have a profound effect on the estate planning practice. Until very recently, lawyers and other professionals in the estate practice dealt almost exclusively with the property consequences of death. Lawyers drafted wills to govern the disposition of property and then, after the client died, supervised the estate's administration. The lawyer's client was never around to participate in, or obtain directly the benefits of, the estate planning that he or she had paid for. In contrast, estate planning professionals are increasingly involved with events that take place during the client's lifetime and in providing advice and services that benefit the client as well as his or her successors.

With increased longevity have come increased concerns as to the management of property in the event of a temporary or permanent incapacity as well as concerns about who will make health care decisions if the client loses the ability to make them. While guardianship and conservatorship laws have been reformed, in most states these are still seen as the least effective means of handling the property of a disabled person and as the refuge of those who do not plan in advance. Revocable trusts, almost unheard of until the late 1960s, are now staples in estate planning, in many cases supplanting the need for a will. Greater use will be made of revocable trusts, durable powers of attorney, and other property management arrangements in handling the property of incapacitated persons. On another front, heightened awareness of the economic and emotional costs of prolonging life will lead to an increased use and refinement of health care powers of attorney and "living wills."

Finally, the changing structure of American families has made planning decisions more complicated for many couples. The dramatic rise in the divorce rate, with divorce often followed by remarriage, has increased the instances in which one or both spouses have children by an earlier marriage. In this setting, devising an estate plan that will be seen as satisfactory by all surviving family members is no easy task. While the level of will contests may remain relatively constant, fiduciary litigation over the administration of estates and trusts is likely to increase, making one's appointment as executor or trustee a more hazardous undertaking than in the past.

[See also Aging of the Population; Home Ownership; Insurance; Investments; Longevity; Public Assistance Programs: Social Security.]

BIBLIOGRAPHY

Christensen, Donald. *Surviving the Coming Mutual Fund Crisis.* Boston: Little, Brown, 1994.
Clark, Gordon L. *Pensions and Corporate Restructuring in American Industry: A Crisis of Regulation.* Baltimore: Johns Hopkins University Press, 1993.
Rappaport, Anna M., ed. *Demography and Retirement: The Twenty-First Century.* Westport, CT. Praeger, 1993.

— STANLEY JOHANSON

ETHICS

Contemporary emphasis on autonomy has led us to think of the individual as an isolated being, complete in his or her own self. From this view, the community is frequently seen as an obstacle—if not an outright barrier—preventing the individual from achieving his or her desires or goals.

The most basic reason for this state of affairs is that the society we experience today is the consequence of decades of the determined and single-minded practice of autonomy. Society has reached an impasse. It has arrived at the point of being unable even to suggest a criticism of individual action, regardless of what that act is or what consequences it might have. It means that no one can suggest what might be good or helpful for an individual, whether in the area of individual matur-

ity, design or school curricula, or appropriate health practices.

The consequence of this recent dominance of autonomy, occurring in an arena of rapidly increasing technology, has been the total isolation of the individual from the family and community. The upshot is that autonomy, though an important and critical value in our society, is simply inadequate to help us resolve critical social issues. In particular, what our over-reliance on autonomy has done is seduce us into thinking that all difficulties or dilemmas are individual problems that can be resolved on a purely individual level. That someone makes an autonomous decision does not mean that all impacts on others or on the community should not be taken into account.

Healthcare Ethical Dilemmas

One such impact involves the runaway cost of health care on the community. We are beginning to realize that individual, autonomous choices have social effects that are of profound significance. Medical ethics provides a case study of this phenomenon and its consequences for religion, spirituality, and morality.

Medical ethics has been characterized by two dominant, interrelated realities, one technical and one ethical in nature. We are faced with the continuing pace and implementation of technological and medical developments. Progress in imaging technologies has given us a detailed new look at the human interior. Developments in artificial reproduction have allowed individuals with all manner of reproductive difficulties to conceive and bear children. Increasing success in mapping the human genome has led to success in locating specific genes responsible for various diseases. In turn, this has led to the development of genetic therapies. On the ethical front, it also poses ominous questions involving the ethics of selective genetic engineering.

Increasingly we are recognizing that the cumulative costs of all the autonomous choices in medical care are staggering. We are now recognizing that not everyone receives—or is even able to receive—the same medical therapy, even though everyone's needs may be similar. The shortage of organs for transplantation, for example, continually brings this problem to public awareness.

Another area of concern is the increasingly strident debate over euthanasia, whether done as an individual act or with the assistance of a physician. In addition, given that health insurance in America is largely private and contingent on one's employment, we find autonomy confronting a rather insurmountable corporate barrier.

The second consideration involves the almost exclusive reliance on the autonomy of the individual as the defining and normative ethical concept in decisionmaking, whether on the individual or social level.

Parallel to technological developments has been an increasing focus on the rights of patients. This was the logical consequence of court cases in the early 1940s and '50s that focused on informed consent and the right to know what was going to be done to a patient before a procedure was initiated. Up to that time medicine was paternalistic, and many physicians were reluctant to tell patients much of anything, especially if the diagnosis was problematic. This tendency has been almost totally reversed, with the obtaining of informed consent for any medical procedure having become an elaborate process accompanied by legal strictures and advice.

The rights of the individual (or the autonomous choices of the individual) are essentially "trumps" that the patient can use either to demand therapy (even when the value of such therapy may be marginal or nonexistent) or to reject any therapy (even when there may be demonstrably positive outcomes from the therapy). The autonomous individual thus stands in final and total judgment of all that affects him or her. The immediate shortcoming of this approach becomes clear and most problematic when the patient is unable to speak on his or her own behalf—that is, if a patient is comatose, unconscious, or in some other way incompetent.

Current attempts to resolve this dilemma are based on the perception that incompetence is not a disqualification for the exercise of autonomy. We are beginning to recognize that some requests or demands made by an autonomous individual can be problematic. The fact that someone chooses a therapy does not automatically qualify that person for that therapy. Furthermore, if one chooses a therapy, it does not mean that the therapy will be successful. Likewise, the fact that one rejects a therapy does not mean that such a decision is an appropriate one.

Community Vision and Standards

All things considered, the most urgent ethical task of the future lies not in resolving particular problems or providing specific social (or medical) programs—though to be sure these are on the substantive agenda to be resolved. The most urgent problem of the present—and therefore of the future—is to develop an understanding of the individual in relation to the community, or to develop a model of the community in which its needs also have standing. A notion of the common good of society or, minimally, of goods we hold in common must be developed.

As things stand, we as a society lack the philosophical basis either to critique individual action or to offer a compelling vision of goods or services incumbent on all which would benefit the community. Already we experience the cost of the lack of such a vision: social isolation, the abandonment of individuals to their own devices or lack thereof, and the indifference to social entities larger than the individual or perhaps that individual's nuclear family. We know that our society cannot bear much more of the same, for these experiences are beginning to overwhelm us.

Just as the seeds of autonomy are present in the traditions of our American culture, so are the seeds of community. Our most serious ethical task is to construct a vision of the community, presenting a compelling social good to which all will aspire and seek to achieve, and creating an ethic that takes seriously the rights of *both* the individual and the community. These seeds now need planting and careful cultivation. For if we do not care for the whole of the harvest, perhaps there may not be a harvest for anyone.

[See also Communitarianism; Death and Dying; Health Care: Moral Issues; Religion, Spirituality, Morality; Values.]

BIBLIOGRAPHY

Bellah, Robert; Madsen, Richard; Sullivan, William M.; Swidler, and Tipton, Steven M. *Habits of the Heart: Individualism and Commitment in American Life.* Berkeley, CA: University of California Press, 1985.

———. *The Good Society.* Berkeley, CA: University of California Press, 1991.

Himes, Michael J., and Himes, Kenneth R., O.F.M. *Fullness of Faith: The Public Significance of Theology.* Mahwah, NJ: Paulist Press, 1993.

Sullivan, William M. *Reconstructing Public Philosophy.* Berkeley, CA: University of California Press, 1986.

— THOMAS A. SHANNON

ETHICS, MEDICAL.

See BIOETHICS; HEALTH CARE: MORAL ISSUES.

ETHNIC AND CULTURAL SEPARATISM

Since the rise of the nation-state, people have lived within their own ethnic, national, and cultural boundaries. Sometimes those boundaries were between nations, sometimes such boundaries were formed by enclaves within nations. Living within a cultural boundary, gave people a distinct sense of identity, of belonging to a clearly defined social unit. Myths and traditions interpreted the meanings of that culture and reinforced the sense of belonging.

Today, through global television, proliferating communications technologies, and jet travel, historic boundaries are falling, and they no longer constitute the outer limits of a people's identity. We have come to the end of several thousand years of different civilizations living side by side without having significant cross-cultural effect on each other. From now on, integration and cross-fertilization will shape cultural, economic, and educational developments. A new uniformity of human experiences is in the making, with more people coming to share similar impressions and experiences more rapidly. Thus the fabric of tradition in countless nations is being shredded, and a new fabric must be woven. In an age of mobility and global impressions, we must foster a sense of rootedness in time and place.

The basic referent is no longer my tribe, my nation, or even my civilization. For the first time in human history, we are forging an awareness of our existence that embraces humanity as a species.

Cultural and national groupings obviously still exist, but they no longer form a relevant psychological boundary. So painful questions face each of us: With whom do I identify? Who is my group? Indeed, do I have a group any longer? As a separate, isolated, psychologically closed unit, all the groups we have known in the past have now been merged with one larger human family. What each person is facing is the painful necessity to adjust to this new reality.

The basic referent is no longer my tribe, my nation, or even my civilization. We have moved from the era of nation-states to the age of a world community as the defining political and economic framework. In this new era, we are incorporating the planetary dimensions of life into the fabric of our economics, politics, international relations, and culture. For the first time in human history, we are forging an awareness of our existence that embraces humanity as a species.

This collapse of boundaries is one of the primary consequences of space exploration. Seeing Earth from the Moon in the 1960s was a seminal event in human history, both scientifically and psychologically. When we saw a picture of Earth from space, our view of who we are and to what cultural group we belong was forever changed. All of a sudden, everyone saw themselves as part of one human community without all the national, cultural, or religious distinctions by which we had defined ourselves for centuries.

We have entered a period when life needs to be seen whole to be understood. For the first time in history we see that Earth whole, and we need a new understanding that is based on wholeness rather than on reductionism.

None of the major issues we face can be resolved within a national context—not the environment, not economic growth, not Third World debt, not even illegal drugs or AIDS.

The collapse of boundaries is bringing with it a redefinition of nationhood. It is happening everywhere—Russia, South Africa, Germany, even the United States. Nationalism—in the nineteenth-century sense of constituting the outer limits of a people's political awareness—is on the wane. What surfaces in places such as Bosnia, Georgia, or Turkmenistan is not historic nationalism but an old ethnicity that cries out for a new expression.

Demography is a major force shaping destiny. Statistical projections precisely laying out population numbers, distribution, patterns, and trends span the next seventy to eighty years with a very high degree of assurance. People already born today fulfill those projections. Because we know human proclivities and can assess the risks, there is a high degree of certainty concerning outcomes. Population trends provide a powerful trajectory into the future.

Barring some unforeseen use of birth control, world population will double from 5.6 billion in 1994 to 12.6 billion by the year 2100. Millions of years were required for population to reach the first billion mark, in 1800. The second billion mark was reached in 130 years. Thirty years later we hit the third billion mark. Fourteen years after that we reached the fourth billion mark. The fifth billion was hit in twelve years, and the sixth billion increment will have been reached in an eleven-year span (by 1997). To put this in perspective, 18 percent of all the people who ever lived since the birth of Christ are alive today.

Hard as it may be to appreciate fully, these population projections mean that globally, the equivalent of an entire second Earth stands in the offing, bringing along with it all the attendant needs of housing, feeding, and jobs. The United States, the third most populous nation in 1994, will drop to eighth by 2050. Nigeria, Pakistan, Indonesia, and Brazil will all pass us by. These are vast nations already struggling to provide the good life for their teeming residents. And India's population is projected finally to overtake and exceed that of currently top-ranked China by the year 2050.

Globally, the political trend is toward separatism. By World War II, 50 independent nations could be counted. That number exceeded 190 by 1993 and could reach 300 by the year 2000. The former Soviet Union—now 15 nations—may fragment into as many as 60 to 70 independent nations. China also could break up into numerous subdivisions.

The breakup of existing nations and the assertion of new rights by separatist groups will punctuate the twenty-first century with a flurry of wars, ethnic and religious violence, coups d'état, border disputes, civil upheavals, and terrorist attacks. These developments have multiplied world dynamics on an enormous scale, and their repercussions reach to the very core of American life.

In the United States, demographic trends indicate that Hispanics will surpass African Americans as America's largest minority by 2020. Ethnic minorities, furthermore, may account for 30 percent of the U.S. population by 2033. And European Americans are projected to become a minority group by 2060.

A key question is whether America's melting pot tradition still will continue and newcomers will be assimilated into a united nation. Or will a mosaic society emerge, marked by separatism and multiculturalism?

The fragmentation of America is representative of a deeper global force at work. The new view is one of a multicultural perspective where ethnic, sexual, and cultural differences are emphasized. Group and ethnic interests are emerging as preeminent, and the very idea of a common culture is under assault.

How does a pluralist society, comprised of diverse cultures and traditions, and daily bombarded by modern communications, divergent themes, and conflicting philosophies cohere and rise above intense parochial interests to forge the larger common interest? Can we successfully come to grips with these changes and evolve some moral consensus and plan that can make a pluralistic world creative rather than destructive? That is a legitimate question, but it is almost impossible to answer. Scenarios could be developed where America becomes so choked by multiculturalism that consensus on how to deal with common problems becomes impossible. In such a case, America could stagnate and lose any sense of common purpose and identity.

In a complete reversal of the historic idea of America, the degree of common ground could be shrinking. "If separatist tendencies go unchecked," writes Arthur Schlesinger, Jr., one of America's most prominent historians, "the result can only be the fragmentation, re-segregation, and tribalization of American life."

A nation dwelling primarily on its differences cannot survive. Nationhood grows out of what a people have in common. Multiculturalism must become a means of melding parochial interests with national interests, of enabling diverse views to contribute to a multifaceted political pattern.

[See also Global Culture; Lifestyle; Nationalism; Pluralism.]

BIBLIOGRAPHY

Hacker, Andrew. *Two Nations: Black and White, Separate, Hostile, Unequal.* New York: Scribner, 1992.

Hughes, Robert. *Culture of Complaint.* New York: Warner Books, 1993.

Kennedy, Paul. *Preparing for the Twenty-First Century.* New York: Vintage Books, 1993.

Lasch, Christopher. *The True and Only Heaven.* New York: W. W. Norton, 1991.

McCarthy, Eugene. *A Colony of the World: The United States Today.* New York: Hippocrene Books, 1992.

Schein, Edgar H. *Organizational Culture and Leadership.* 2nd ed. San Francisco, CA: Jossey-Bass Publishers, 1992.

Shaffer, Carolyn R., and Anundsen, Kristin. *Creating Community Anywhere: Finding Support and Connection in a Fragmented World.* Los Angeles, CA: J. P. Tarcher, 1993.

Stewart, Edward C., and Bennett, Milton J. *American Cultural Patterns: A Cross-Cultural Perspective.* Rev. ed. Yarmouth, ME: Intercultural Press, 1991.

– GRAHAM T. T. MOLITOR
WILLIAM VAN DUSEN WISHARD

ETHNIC DIVERSITY.

See RACE, CASTE, AND ETHNIC DIVERSITY.

EUTHANASIA.

See DEATH AND DYING.

EVOLUTION, BIOLOGICAL

With the major developments of the space age, our interest in the question of life's origins has rocketed to new heights. A question which has been asked mainly in the field of metaphysics has emerged in the domain of chemistry and physics. Along with the problem of the origin of the universe and the origin of intelligence, it may be considered to be among the most fundamental questions of all science.

The idea of life arising from nonlife, or the theory of spontaneous generation, had been accepted for centuries. One had only to observe the evidence of the senses, thought the ancients: worms seemed to emerge from mud, maggots from decaying meat, and mice from old linen.

The Darwinian theory of evolution subsequently postulated the unity of the Earth's entire biosphere. According to Darwin, the higher forms of life evolved from the lower over a very extended period in the life of this planet. Alexander Ivanovich Oparin gave us the idea of the continuity of the universe from the inorganic to the organic, from the elements to the small molecules. The concept of cosmic evolution, then, comes to us from his early writings. One could say that what

Darwin is to biological evolution, Oparin is to chemical evolution. Oparin spoke of the general origins of life—not as a special event, but as a phenomenon that could commonly take place.

If we go back all the way to the earliest times on Earth, we know that the Earth had been formed from the dust cloud out of which all the planets of the solar system emerged about 4.5 billion years ago. The most recent evidence for the oldest life on Earth from the studies of the Greenland rocks date back 3.8 billion years. Life on Earth must have begun between these two points in time. There was, therefore, a time when no life existed on Earth.

The great impetus, however, to the experimental study of the origin of life began with Oparin pointing out, "that there was no fundamental difference between a living organism and brute matter. The complex combination of manifestations and properties so characteristic of life must have arisen in the process of the evolution of matter." According to Oparin:

> at first there were the simple solutions of organic substances whose behavior was governed by the properties of their component atoms and the arrangement of these atoms in the molecular structure. But gradually, as a result of growth. and increasing complexity of the molecules, new properties have come into being and a new colloidal chemical order was imposed on the more simple organic chemical relations. These newer properties were determined by the spatial arrangement and mutual relationship of the molecules. In this process biological orderliness already comes into prominence.

From a scientific point of view, possibly the greatest contribution Oparin made to the study of the origins of life was his careful analysis of the nature of the primitive atmosphere. He suggested that the carbides in the crust of the Earth may have given rise to hydrocarbons. Indeed, the carbides may have come from meteorites. Here, then, was a source of the reduced carbon necessary for the organic molecule. Oparin also argued that in the amino acids the carbon and nitrogen are in the reduced form and that, therefore, the starting materials for life may have been in that form.

Independently of Oparin, Haldane in 1928, had speculated on the early conditions suitable for the emergence of terrestrial life:

> When ultraviolet light acts on a mixture of water, carbon dioxide and ammonia, a variety of organic substances are made, including sugars and apparently some of the materials from which proteins are built up. Be-

fore the origin of life they must have accumulated until the primitive oceans reached the constituency of a hot dilute soup.

Experiments in the laboratory have simulated conditions in prebiotic times. The building blocks of life have been synthesized under such conditions. The processes are simple and the pathways are chemically elegant. Amino acids, carbohydrates, and the genetic bases are all sequentially made by such processes such as an electric discharge, simulating lightning, striking a primitive atmosphere of methane, nitrogen, and water. Several attempts also have been made to string these components together to give rise to polymers resembling proteins and nucleic acids. A certain measure of success has also been achieved here and the prerequisite for such processes to take place have been clearly demonstrated.

Alexander Ivanovich Oparin gave us the idea of the continuity of the universe from the inorganic to the organic, from the elements to the small molecules.

The energies available for the synthesis of organic compounds under primitive Earth conditions are ultraviolet light from the sun, electric discharges, ionizing radiation, and heat. It is evident that sunlight was the principal source of energy. Photochemical reactions would have taken place in the upper atmosphere and the products transferred by convection. Next in importance as a source of energy are electric discharges such as lightning and corona discharges from pointed objects. These occur close to the Earth's surface, and hence, would more efficiently deposit the reaction products in the primitive oceans. A certain amount of energy was also available from the disintegration of uranium, thorium, and potassium 40. While some of this energy may have been expended on solid material such as rocks, a certain proportion of it was available in the oceans and the atmosphere. Heat from volcanoes may also have been effective in primordial organic synthesis. In comparison to the energy from the sun and electric discharges, this was perhaps not too widely distributed and its effect may have been only local—on the sides of volcanoes, for example. Most of these forms of energy have been used in the laboratory for the synthesis of organic molecules. Simulation experiments have been devised to study the effect of ionizing radiation, electric discharges, heat and ultraviolet light on the assumed early atmosphere of Earth. The analysis of the end products has often yielded, very surprisingly, the very compounds that we consider today as important for living systems.

In the experiments in our own laboratory, we have adopted the simple working hypothesis that the molecules that are fundamental now were fundamental at the time of the origin of life. We are analyzing "the primordial soup" described by Haldane. The various forms of energy that are thought to have been present in the primitive Earth have been used by us in a series of experiments. In the experiments with methane, ammonia, and water, electron irradiation was used as a convenient source of ionizing radiation simulating the potassium on the primitive Earth. The results of this investigation clearly establish adenine (one of the basic chemical components of the genetic code) as a product of the irradiation of methane, ammonia, and water. It is the single largest nonvolatile compound produced. The apparent preference for adenine synthesis may be related to adenine's multiple roles in biological systems. Not only is it a constituent of both the nucleic acids DNA and RNA, but it is also a unit of many important cofactors. In these and other experiments, most of the molecules necessary for life have been synthesized.

Chemical evolution may be considered to have taken place in three stages: from inorganic chemistry to organic chemistry, and from organic chemistry to biological chemistry. The first stage of chemical evolution perhaps began with the very origin of matter. In a series of cataclysmic reactions during the birth of a star, the elements of the periodic table must have been formed. Almost 15 billion years later, when the solar system was being formed, the highly reactive elements that occur in living organisms, probably existed in combination with hydrogen—carbon as methane, nitrogen as ammonia, and oxygen as water. Four-and-a-half billion years ago, when the planet Earth was arising from the primitive dust cloud, the rudimentary molecules, which were the forerunners of the complex biological polymers of today, were perhaps already in existence. Within this framework, life appears to be a special property of matter, a property that arose at a particular period in the existence of our planet and resulted from its orderly development.

The consideration of biological evolution thus leads us logically to another form of evolution, namely, chemical evolution. Recent biochemical discoveries have underlined the remarkable unity of living matter. In all living organisms, from the smallest microbe to the largest mammal, there are two basic molecules. Their interaction appears to result in that unique property of matter that is generally described by the word *life*. These two molecules are the nucleic acids and protein. While each one of these molecules is complex in form, the units comprising them are few in number. The nucleic acid molecule consists of nucleotides strung together like beads along a chain. The nucleotides in turn are made up of a purine or pyrimidine base, a sugar, and a phosphate. In the protein molecule, twenty amino acids link up with one another to give the macromolecule. A study of the composition of living matter thus leads us to the inescapable conclusion that all living organisms must have had some common chemical ancestry. A form of evolution purely chemical in nature must of necessity have preceded biological evolution.

Chemical evolution may be considered

to have taken place in three stages:

from inorganic chemistry to organic chemistry,

and from organic chemistry to biological chemistry.

A few years ago *Alvin,* the robotic unmanned submarine that went down to the bottom of the ocean, brought back to us samples from the hydrothermal vents. For almost forty years we had worked in our laboratories on the assumption that the conditions suitable for the origins of life had disappeared. But here we find them anew. Therefore, we must rationally accept the likelihood that life is arising there now. This is perhaps one of the great discoveries of modern biology: that it is possible for life to exist under those conditions. We have worked in the laboratory in the assumption that the conditions that prevailed 4 billion years ago have disappeared from the face of Earth. But we find them now right at the bottom of the ocean. So here we have an opportunity to examine what Oparin described as the general origins of life, that it is not something confined to one place or one time on Earth, but perhaps to the end of the universe. Is it possible that the life is arising right now? Neo-abiogenesis may be a reality.

The sequence from atoms to small molecules to large molecules to life thus appears to be natural. Laboratory experiments have clearly demonstrated that the molecules necessary for life can be synthesized under simulated planetary environments. There is no reason to doubt that we shall rediscover, one by one, the precise processes of physical and chemical evolution. We may even reproduce the intermediate steps in the laboratory. Looking back upon the biochemical understanding gained during the span of one human generation, we have the right to be quite optimistic.

[See also Biodiversity; Evolution: Life-Forms in the Universe; Evolution, Social; Extinction of Species; Genetic Engineering; Genetics; Genetics Commercialization; Genetic Technologies; Sexual Reproduction: Artificial Means.]

BIBLIOGRAPHY

Anfinsen, Christian B. *The Molecular Basis of Evolution.* New York: John Wiley, 1959.

Oparin, A. I. *The Origin of Life on Earth.* 3rd ed. New York: Academic Press, 1957.

Ponnamperuma, Cyril, and Chela-Flores, Julian, eds. *Chemical Evolution: Origin of Life.* Hampton, VA: A. Deepak Publishing, 1993.

Young, J. Z., and Margerison, Tom, eds. *From Molecule to Man.* New York: Crown, 1969.

— CYRIL PONNAMPERUMA

EVOLUTION, SOCIAL

Evolution is rather obvious in a broad sense, because even children understand that life emerged billions of years ago and that beings like ourselves then slowly evolved. Yet this grand process is fraught with controversy, raising such perennial questions as, Does social progress really improve human welfare? For example, the Information Age promises to unify the globe, yet it is also helping to spark wars between ethnic groups, as in the former Yugoslavia, fostering violent youths in the United States and other nations, and swamping people in a morass of data overload.

By analyzing evolution using general systems theory, we can achieve a better understanding of this complex process, and gain insights into the stages lying ahead. From a systems view, the history of change seems to form a great pattern that comprises a life cycle for the planet. This "life cycle of evolution" (LCE) is similar to the life cycle of ordinary organisms, such as humans, but vastly larger in scope and duration. Like any life cycle, life on Earth has evolved from a rudimentary biological level to advanced social, intellectual, and spiritual phases.

The key to understanding evolution is to see that today's changes are cultural equivalents of biological evolution, as shown in Table 1. Biological evolution comprises the first stages in this process, while the remaining six stages involve cultural evolution. A brief outline characterizing how life evolves through these stages shows the commonality that unites this entire process.

Life on Earth began some four billion years ago and eventually flowered into a rich array of species, including primitive humans. Roughly three million years ago, people formed tribal societies that used stone tools to hunt and gather food. Agrarian civilization emerged about 7000 B.C., when farming permitted settled communities and cities. About 1850 A.D., the Industrial Revolution automated farming, thereby forcing most people to work in factories; today less than 3 percent of the U.S. labor force works on farms.

The next transition in 1950 introduced a service economy consisting predominantly of white-collar jobs in restaurants, hotels, banks, media, government, and the like. Only 20 percent of American workers do blue-

TABLE 1

STAGES OF EVOLUTION

Main Characteristics	1 Biological Era	2 Tribal Era	3 Agrarian Era	4 Industrial Era	5 Service Era	6 Knowledge Era	7 Existential Era
Technical Base	genetics	primitive tools	agriculture	manufacturing	social structure and interaction	computerized information processing	mental/spiritual technology
Beginning of Era	4 billion B.C.	3 million B.C.	7000 B.C.	1850 A.D.	1950 A.D.	2000 A.D.*	2100 A.D.†
Initiating Step	appearance of life	development of humans	agricultural revolution	industrial revolution	postindustrial revolution	global information systems	steady-state physical world
Energy Source	biomass	human labor	animals	machines	attitudes and emotions	data and knowledge	symbols, beliefs, and values
Form of Organization	organisms	nomadic tribes	feudal estates	factories and distribution systems	complex organizations	information networks	global community leading to a space age

* This estimate is based on various studies (per #2); margin of error about ± 5 years.
† Based on extrapolating the LCE; probable margin of error about ± 50 years.

collar work now, and that number should fall to 10 percent or less in a decade or two. As the information revolution automates service jobs (ATM machines in banking, and so forth), a Knowledge Society should appear about the year 2000 that focuses on using information to solve difficult problems in education, science, the environment, and so on.

Thinking about the next stage beyond the Information Age is obviously speculative, but many believe it will focus on that vast realm of emotion, awareness, power, choice, wisdom, idealism, and other concerns that transcend knowledge to comprise the human spirit. This poorly understood domain of the spirit does not consist merely of blissful experiences, but a more existential state of being in which people struggle to guide more complex matters. Life at advanced levels of evolution seems to be more *intense;* it requires the careful use of sophisticated capabilities to choose among greater

options in order to carry out grave new responsibilities. A good example is the power to control life itself now being conferred by biotechnology.

This systems perspective illustrates the fundamental process that underlies the entire LCE. All forms of evolution experiment with tentative advances, leaving the best adapted inventions to survive. In biological evolution, a struggle takes place among various species, while in cultural evolution it is a competition between machines, information systems, and other cultural artifacts. Passage through these stages is driven by necessity. Each stage presents new problems as well as new gains, disposing civilization to evolve continually toward higher stages of development. For instance, the industrial age produced historic gains in physical comfort, but at the cost of war, pollution, and other drawbacks that require the powers of a knowledge society to resolve. Thus, evolution is neither "good" nor

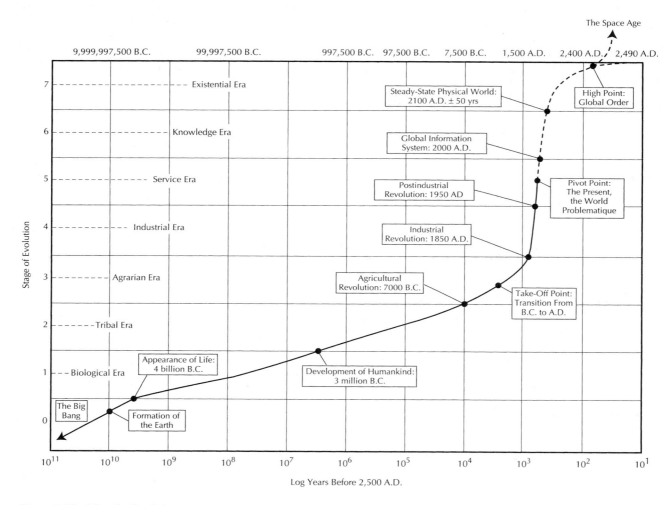

Figure 1. The life cycle of evolution.

"bad"; it simply heightens the existential challenge of life.

The LCE can also be plotted, as shown in Figure 1, to put this historic process in perspective. The times when each stage occurred are shown on a logarithmic scale in order to compress the enormous differences of early stages and spread out the later stages into a comprehensible figure. Figure 1 illustrates how the planet has evolved through its development along the same S-curve that characterizes all life cycles: a culture of bacteria, a human being, or the overall evolution of life on this planet. A few special points of interest are also highlighted by this S-curve.

The "take-off point" when the LCE begins to rise upward through the industrial, service, and knowledge eras seems to coincide with the end of the Middle Ages. Since then, change has accelerated over time by almost any measure: world population, the speed of travel, and countless other factors all bend sharply upward during the past few centuries. This striking pattern is apparent by noting that the times between stages are shorter by orders of magnitude: four *billion* years of biological evolution were needed to develop humans; three *million* years passed before the onset of an agrarian age; nine *thousand* years later the Industrial Revolution occurred; one *hundred* years after that the service era began, and it required only five *decades* to reach the knowledge age.

This acceleration of evolution reaches its peak at the "pivot point"—the contemporary decades that seem so hectic with chaotic change. The pivot point represents that unique inflection point when physical growth slows down to reach toward an equilibrium. This juncture provokes controversial issues that comprise the "world problematique"—a constellation of interrelated crises involving the environment, population growth, a global economy, and other challenges that require a fundamentally different worldview.

Recently, the arrival of an environmental ethic, the collapse of communism, the onset of the information revolution, and other unprecedented changes suggest that this transformation is likely to be resolved in time, leading to a global maturing into a stable physical system sometime during the twenty-first century. While this may represent the "high point" of our planet, the serious colonization of outer space is expected to become a reality at about that same time, which may then initiate another, even higher life cycle of evolution as the space age launches life into the universe.

> [See also Change; Change, Cultural; Change, Pace of; Change, Scientific and Technological; Evolution, Biological; Laws, Evolution of; Public Policy Change; Record Setting; Social Inventions; Social and Political Evolution; Technological Change.]

BIBLIOGRAPHY

Halal, William E. "The Life Cycle of Evolution." *ICIS Forum* (January 1990).
———. "World 2000." *Futures* (January/February 1993).
Harman, Willis. *Global Mind Change* (Indianapolis, IN: Knowledge Systems, 1991).
Marien, Michael. *Societal Directions and Alternatives.* Lafayette, NY: Information for Policy Design, 1976.
Sperry, Roger. "Psychology's Mentalist Paradigm." *American Psychologist* (August 1988).

– WILLIAM E. HALAL

EVOLUTION: LIFE-FORMS IN THE UNIVERSE

We are awed by the mystery of the universe around us. The question looms larger than ever: "Are we alone in the universe?"

Over 500 years ago, Copernicus showed that the Earth was one of the many planets revolving round the sun. A hundred years ago Darwin pointed out that there was a continuity in the biosphere from the microbe to man. Not since Darwin, and before him Copernicus, has science had an opportunity for so great an understanding of man. The scientific question at stake in exobiology is the most challenging and most profound issue not only of this century but of the entire naturalistic movement that has characterized Western thoughts for over three hundred years and Asian thought for thousands of years.

In our search for the existence of extraterrestrial life three possible approaches present themselves. First, the landing of instruments or man somewhere in the universe. With our present knowledge, this attempt would undoubtedly be restricted to our own planetary system. A second method is via radio contact with civilizations in outer space. This presupposes the existence of intelligent beings in space with a technology as advanced as or even greater than our own. Thirdly, we have the experimental attack on the problem. Here life is considered an inevitable consequence of the evolution of matter. Since the laws of chemistry and physics are universal laws, the retracing, in the laboratory, of the path by which life appeared on Earth would give strong support to our belief in its existence elsewhere in the universe.

Alexander Ivanovich Oparin's reflections on the origins of life led him to examine the possibility of life beyond the Earth. He postulated that the conditions suitable for the origins of life had existed on the primitive Earth, but that the primitive Earth was only one of many suitable locations in the universe. Modern astronomy tells us that there are billions and billions of sites in the universe where life is possible. An estimate of the distribution of intelligent life in the universe, made by Carl Sagan of Cornell University, puts the figure at a million in our own galaxy.

There are billions of sites in the universe

where life is possible. An estimate puts the figure

at a million in our own galaxy.

On the basis of our sampling of galaxy populations to the limit attainable by present-day telescopes, we can readily compute that there are more than 10^{23} stars in the universe. Each one of these can maintain the photochemical reactions that are the basis of plant and animal life. Let us impose a number of restrictions in considering the stars that can support life. Suppose that because of doubling, clustering, and secondary collisions, only one star in a thousand has a planetary system. Suppose that only one out of a thousand of those stars with planetary systems has a planet at the right distance from a star to provide the water and the warmth that life requires. In our own planetary system we have two such planets. Further, let us suppose that only one out of a thousand of those stars with planets at the right distance has a planet large enough to hold an atmosphere. In our planetary system at least seven of the nine can do that. Suppose a further restriction is made, and we suggest that the right chemical composition for life to arise occurs only once in a thousand times. Assuming all these four restrictions, we come to the conclusion that there are at least 100 million possibilities for the existence of life. This is a conservative estimate made by Harlow Shapley.

More recent studies, taking into account the time scales of stellar, planetary, and biological evolution, reveal to us that at least 1 percent of all stars in the universe must have conditions around them suitable for life. We are still talking about a colossal number: 10^{21} possibilities. Planets are plentiful in the universe.

A starting point for any experimental consideration of the origin of life turns on the question of the cosmic distribution of elements. Astronomical spectroscopy reveals that with surprising uniformity the most abundant elements in our galaxy are, in the order of rank: hydrogen, helium, oxygen, nitrogen, and carbon. Hydrogen, oxygen, nitrogen, and carbon are indeed the basic constituents of living systems. In the presence of hydrogen, carbon will be in the form of methane, oxygen as water, and nitrogen as ammonia. It is this atmosphere of water vapor, containing C, H, N, and O, which is considered in this discussion as the primitive atmosphere of Earth.

Within our own planetary system we have explored the surface of Mars, the atmospheres of the giant planets Jupiter and Saturn, and the surface of many of their satellites. The soil of Earth's moon was brought back, and we have analyzed it in the laboratory. We looked for evidence of organic matter, but there was no evidence of any molecules related to life, and the total amount of carbon was about two thousand parts per million. This was easily understood because the surface of the moon had been exposed to large amounts of ultraviolet radiation and, in the high vacuum, carbon bonds could not survive on the surface. It was inhospitable; life could not have come into being there.

However, like a gift from heaven, we have received on Earth meteorites containing organic molecules. Careful analysis has indicated that several of them contain carbonaceous materials and are therefore described as carbonaceous chondrites. Amino acids of extraterrestrial origin have been found in them. Beginning with the Murchison meteorite, which fell to Earth in 1969 in Australia, the presence of organic molecules have been observed in several carbonaceous chondrites. Expeditions to the Antarctic during the last few years have brought back several thousand samples, many containing organic compounds. They are pristine in not being contaminated by terrestrial organic debris. However, the evidence was clear that they were prebiological. The fact that they were formed so easily suggests that life must be a common process in the universe.

Observations of Halley's Comet reveal the presence of various hydrocarbons, hydrogen cyanide, and so forth. We are moving, then, from the idea of the primitive atmosphere of the Earth to the primitive atmospheres of other planets to the general presence of organic matter under interstellar conditions. If this is indeed the case, surely life would have evolved to the point where intelligent life is present elsewhere.

Moving from the asteroid belt to the giant planets, the Voyager satellite has indicated large-scale processes in the atmosphere of both Jupiter and Saturn and infrared spectroscopy has provided evidence of organic matter. Organic molecules, which are the basis of life, appear to be common in these atmospheres. The satellites of the giant planets have also given us evidence of organic matter. Titan has an atmosphere and there is possible evidence of a very exciting organic chemistry. But, alas, it is too cold for life to begin and evolve. One possibility may be the satellite Iapetus, which has an area covered with dark material, and if there is a heat source inside and the ice is melting there may be possibility for life.

Our effort to land an instrument or eventually a scientist astronaut on a neighboring planet has been primarily directed to the planet Mars. The possibility of life on Mars has often been raised. The canal-like structures on Mars and the seasonal wave of darkening across the planet have led many to believe that there must be some form of life on Mars. Some have suggested the existence of highly intelligent beings that have saved for themselves the depleting water supply on the planet by incredible feats of engineering—that is, the construction of mammoth canals crisscrossing the planet. All these speculations have fired the imagination of planetary scientists and made them determined to find out the answer to the question, "Is there life on Mars?"

A very sketchy survey of the physical parameters of Mars indicate to us that, although the conditions are rigorous as compared to the Earth, they are within the range in which microorganisms can survive. Indeed, laboratory, experiments in which these conditions have been simulated have shown that some Earth microorganisms can survive and even multiply under such conditions. Furthermore, if we consider planetary evolution in the context of the smallness of the planet Mars, the processes of chemical evolution may have proceeded very rapidly. Life may have evolved and disappeared. Visitors to Mars may be greeted by relics or fossils of a once-thriving biosphere.

Several experiments of interest to the life scientists were performed on the surface of Mars. A handful of soil was analyzed for organic matter. The surprising result was that less than five parts per billion of carbon was detected. This was a figure that was least expected, considering that the moon gave us 200 parts per million. There was less carbon on Mars than on the moon. In the absence of carbon would there be life? It is most unlikely. The Viking missions to Mars provided no evidence of the presence of life on the red planet. Further missions to Mars may explore the ancient history of the planet and give us some information about the early history of life there if it really did exist.

Our studies of the solar system by man and instrumental exploration has not provided any convincing evidence of the presence of life outside the Earth. We have therefore to go beyond our solar system and at the moment this cannot be done except by the use of radio or optical telescopes.

Looking beyond our own solar system, astronomers have discovered a vast array of organic molecules. The latest count gives fifty-three of them. Many of these are intermediates in prebiotic synthesis, such as hydrogen cyanide and formaldehyde. The marriage of chemistry and astronomy gives us the emerging picture of a universe where chemistry related to prebiotic processes is cosmic in nature. God himself must be an organic chemist. The universe appears to be striving to make

life. Life itself must be commonplace in the universe. Today our studies of the cosmos are giving us a more profound view of the universe indicating that, indeed, life itself is an integral component of the universe, and that our brothers and sisters may be dwelling in distant planets around far-off stars.

[See also Evolution, Biological; Extraterrestrial Life-Forms; Genetics; Space Travel.]

BIBLIOGRAPHY

Crowe, Michael J. *The Extraterrestrial Life Debate: 1750–1900.* Cambridge: Cambridge University Press, 1992.
Sagan, Carl, with Agel, Jerome. *The Cosmic Connection: An Extraterrestrial Perspective.* Garden City, NY: Anchor/Doubleday, 1973.
Shklovskii, I. S., and Sagan, Carl. *Intelligent Life in the Universe.* New York: Delta/Dell, 1966.

— CYRIL PONNAMPERUMA

EXECUTIVE BRANCH

The U.S. Constitution assigns to the executive branch the execution of the laws and the administration of the national government other than Congress and the courts. It charges the President with five principal responsibilities:

1. Participating in the creation of laws by assenting to, or vetoing, bills approved by Congress.
2. Commanding the armed forces.
3. Conducting foreign relations.
4. Appointing judges, ambassadors, and subordinate officials.
5. Administering the executive branch.

During the terms of the first thirty-one Presidents, the president largely confined himself to these functions. With the administration of Franklin D. Roosevelt (1933–1945), the role and function of the executive branch increased radically. After five years of rapid, Depression-induced government growth, the Brownlow Committee on Administrative Management recommended, and Roosevelt initiated, a major expansion and reorganization of what is now known as the executive office of the president.

In the postwar years the executive branch mushroomed until (in 1994) it dispensed annual outlays of more than $1.4 trillion, employed 3,000,000 civilians, and maintained more than 1,500,000 in the armed forces. Not since 1969 has the federal government balanced its annual budget; deficits in the 1990s consistently exceeded $200 billion, and by 1995 the gross federal debt is projected to surpass $5 trillion.

The tasks of the presidency have expanded far beyond those envisioned in the Constitution. The President must now be a leader in proposing and managing domestic as well as foreign policy, shaping economic policy, managing crises, building effective political coalitions, and advancing the fortunes of his political party. He must persuade the people to trust him and support his goals, and he must try to implement his policies through the vast and often unwieldy machinery of the branch he heads.

A "Council of State" composed of respected senior men and women could periodically assess for the President the status of the presidency, the condition of the nation, and the concerns of the people.

In carrying out these responsibilities, the President is in constant tension with, and often faces outright opposition from, various Nayers in national policy making. He must:

- Constantly resolve disagreements among his own cabinet and executive office appointees and persuade them to stay in line with his policies instead of yielding to the appeals of powerful members of Congress and special-interest groups.
- Struggle to persuade the vast and often lethargic civil service bureaucracy to carry out his policies, but without the ability to fire those who are obstructionist or nonproductive.
- Find some way to work with a Congress that may be dominated by special-interest advocates and controlled by opponents seeking to tie his hands (as with the War Powers Act or the Budget and Impoundment Act) or even bring him down.
- Seek a working arrangement with governors of the states, thwart the aims of political rivals, and withstand or temper the pleadings of organizations representing business, labor, women, veterans, minorities, environmental concerns, and many other special interests.
- Avoid confrontations with the judicial branch and take care to avoid interference with the process of justice.
- Interact constructively with the news media, the principal means for transmitting his message and his performance to the electorate.
- Seek some way to stay in touch with new ideas and the sentiments of the American people, while remaining virtually isolated in the White House.

Numerous proposals have been advanced for re-shaping the presidency and the executive. One, debated for more than two hundred years, would require a further limitation of presidential service, most commonly one six-year term instead of a maximum of two four-year terms. Another would give the president new budget management tools, notably: "enhanced rescission power (the line-item veto, including authority to reduce or eliminate appropriations unless overridden by Con-

gress), a federal budget redesigned for sound management, financial controls, reporting, and audits, and a balanced-budget constitutional amendment (not a mere statutory provision that could be ignored at congressional whim). Another proposal would create an executive branch "First Secretary" to free the President from the pressure of managerial duties.

A more sweeping set of proposals aims at diminishing the size of the national government itself, through abandoning functions altogether (such as transportation regulation and farm price supports), redelegating functions to state governments, sometimes with either the funds (Nixon) or the tax sources (Reagan) to pay program costs (welfare, highways, airports, etc.); privatizing government programs (selling off government-owned land and power corporations, competitive contracting for facilities management, shifting grants to public-housing bureaucracies to vouchers for housing consumers); and introducing more market-oriented flexibility in government agencies.

Another type of proposal aims at generating important feedback to the presidency. One proposes the use of interactive video and satellite technology to allow the President and his top officials to converse with ordinary citizens at "town meetings." Another, typical of parliamentary systems, would bring those officials onto the floor of Congress for an open "question period." Another would create a "Council of State" composed of respected senior men and women no longer active in public life to periodically assess for the President the status of the presidency, the condition of the nation, and the concerns of the people.

Finally, there are long-standing proposals for converting to a parliamentary system such as is found in most other Western democracies, notably the United Kingdom and Canada. In such a system the executive branch is managed by the leaders of the legislative branch, selected by the party holding a majority in the popularly elected house of Parliament. The party leader becomes the prime minister and head of government. If the party loses its majority in Parliament, through defections or special elections, it is obliged to call a general election to reestablish a popular mandate to govern.

In authoritarian systems, such as North Korea, Cuba, and many nations in Asia, Africa, and in parts of the former Soviet Union, there is no independent legislative or judicial branch. Instead of a constitutional balance of powers, such nations are ruled by the groups that seize power and maintain control through an army, national police force, and mass party or religious organizations. Fortunately, these models are diminishing in significance.

[See also Executive Branch: The Presidency; Judicial Reform; Leadership; Legislative and Parliamentary Systems.]

BIBLIOGRAPHY

Cronin, Thomas E. *Inventing the American Presidency.* Boston: Little, Brown & Co., 1989.
———— *The State of the Presidency.* Boston: Little, Brown & Co., 1980.
Hart, John. *The Presidential Branch.* Elmsford, NY: Pergamon Press, 1987.
Hess, Stephen. *Organizing the Presidency.* Washington, D.C.: Brookings Institution, 1988.
Neustadt, Richard E. *Presidential Power and Modern Presidents.* New York: Macmillan, 1990.
Rossiter, Clinton. *The American Presidency.* New York: New American Library, 1960.
Schlesinger Jr., Arthur M. *The Imperial Presidency.* Boston: Houghton Mifflin, 1973.

— JOHN MCCLAUGHRY

EXECUTIVE BRANCH: THE PRESIDENCY

After several decades in which governmental power had increasingly been centralized, and in which government had taken prime responsibility for many major societal functions, the United States, like other countries, began in the 1990s a decentralization of governmental power, a devolution to other levels of government and the private sector, and a relaxing of constraints and regulations that were hampering national competitiveness in the world economy.

These changes were taking place in part because of the end of the Cold War and the centralized defense and industrial policies fostered by it. But they also were triggered by the need of the United States and other countries to reduce the burdens of the welfare state, cut government spending as a percent of GDP, and allocate resources more effectively in an increasingly global financial and economic framework.

The American presidency and executive branch, no longer able to mobilize public and congressional opinion behind national security imperatives, had by the mid-1990s lost much of the authority necessary to generate consensus behind anything other than least-common-denominator policies.

Barring an unforeseen international military, financial, or economic crisis—forcing dramatic, unifying actions by the federal government and American people—this diffusion of power is likely to continue into the twenty-first century.

The *international security function* will, of course, remain lodged principally with the president and executive branch. But the use of American military forces, or even the application of major diplomacy, increasingly will require prior congressional and public consensus.

The paradigm will be that of World War II rather than that of the Korean or Vietnam wars. Responsibility for *economic growth and job creation* increasingly will be returned to the private sector and financial markets as the federal government loosens regulation and constraints that hamper the United States in international competition.

The *social safety net,* including such programs as Social Security, Medicare, Medicaid, and public welfare, will remain a high national priority. But rather than being funded and administered wholly through federal agencies, they will in some cases be provided through lower levels of government, through contracting with the private sector, or through provision of vouchers to individual recipients so that they can make individual choices.

Responsibility for economic growth and job creation increasingly will be returned to the private sector and financial markets.

Federal *regulation* will continue to be enforced over areas where health and safety must be protected. But those areas, in turn, will be more narrowly defined. And economic regulation, not necessarily affecting health and safety, will be diminished as attempts are made to reduce public spending and to remove constraints from institutions whose principal competitors will be offshore. *Competition policy,* relatedly, will be administered by the Justice Department and federal regulatory agencies with international, rather than domestic, criteria in mind.

With the national-crisis mentality fostered over sixty years by challenges of the Depression, world war, and Cold War having been removed, the United States presidency and executive branch will in fact return to the more traditional position they have held within the American system. That is, they will be held accountable for providing for the common defense, in consultation with the Congress, but they will play a more catalytic and less central role in providing for the general welfare.

The imperatives imposed by external economic competition, requiring flexibility and responsiveness, will be fortified by the worldwide trend toward localization (in its more negative forms, "balkanization"), in which states, regions, localities, and particular groups of people seek autonomy within a larger political unit.

In its more positive aspects, this new era will relieve the president and federal government from the performance of functions for which they are not best suited.

But there will be a negative side as well. Accustomed to following national leadership only occasionally and in a limited number of areas, the American people will not necessarily respond to their president and the executive branch when difficult and urgent actions are required. The well-told stories of President Abraham Lincoln's attempt to save the Union and avert civil war, of President Woodrow Wilson's inability to gain support for League of Nations membership, of President Franklin Roosevelt's difficulties in mobilizing opposition to Nazi aggression, or even of President Bill Clinton's attempt to mount continuing support for Mexico through its economic and financial crisis will be repeated on many fronts in coming years. In some cases these challenges will be transcended by extraordinary presidential leadership. But the country will not always be able to count on inspiring presidential leaders with an ability to overcome public resistance and galvanize national opinion. More often, the presidency will as in the past continue to be filled by a series of persons who will alternatively be brilliant, inadequate, or simply ordinary.

The national political process that spawns presidents and presidential candidates also will continue its path since the 1960s toward diffusion and decentralization. Therefore, presidents will continue to come from the cadre of officeholders and ambitious politicians who will be able to mobilize money, media attention, and organizational support without regard for the formal structures of the major political parties. They will emerge not because of respect by their peers, or because their parties judge them qualified for the presidency, but because their skills at campaigning can bring them through a Darwinian selection process in which skills at governance may carry little weight.

The presidency and executive branch of the future, except in times of crisis requiring national unity and uniquely presidential leadership, thus will be less powerful central institutions than those that most living Americans have known. Rather, they are more likely to resemble those of the late nineteenth and early twentieth century in which other institutions were of equal or greater importance. The initial impulse of the country's original settlers—that is, to escape centralized and sometimes oppressive government power—will, as it always has, reassert itself.

At the heart so the unique and unmistakable American character is the notion that free men and women, except in extraordinary circumstances, should be left alone to do as they please and only at their periodic pleasure should invite government to assert itself. Part of that character is illusory. But much of it is authentic. It will be more clearly evident in the years ahead.

[See also Executive Branch.]

BIBLIOGRAPHY

Caplan, Richard, and Feffer, John. *State of the Union 1994: The Clinton Administration and the Nation in Profile.* Boulder, CO: Westview Press, 1994.

Light, Paul C. *The President's Agenda: Domestic Policy Choice from Kennedy to Reagan.* Rev. ed. Baltimore: Johns Hopkins University Press, 1991.

Wildavsky, Aaron. *The Beleagured Presidency.* New Brunswick, NJ: Transaction Publishers, 1991.

– TED VAN DYK

EXERCISE AND FITNESS

The writing is on the arterial wall. The American Heart Association recently moved physical inactivity from its list of "contributing factors" for heart and blood-vessel diseases and stroke to the status of "risk factor." This puts the slothful lifestyle on a par with high blood cholesterol, high blood pressure, and cigarette smoking as a deadly killer.

More and more research continues to link regular exercise to lower risk for osteoporosis, heart disease, Parkinson's disease, arthritis, high blood pressure, and diabetes. Without exercise or some kind of leisurely activity, weight-gain develops, which is key in boosting the risk for many of these illnesses.

The popular press has not ignored this information, although much of the American public has. A recent study, for example, found that children weigh an average of 11.4 pounds more now than they did in 1973, while eating the same amount of calories and less dietary fat and without measurable change in height. No longer are kids turning into couch potatoes. They are turning into couches—soft, puffy, and immobile.

No one would argue that exercise and fitness are unhealthy. Being unfit causes a lot of problems that being fit cures. That first step—realizing the necessity of exercise—is easy.

The second step—getting an inactive society active, thus saving thousands of lives and billions of dollars in escalating health care costs—is much tougher. Government cannot force people to exercise and eat bran muffins. Unless we are to become a sweat-suited version of *1984,* with Big P.E. Teacher replacing Big Brother, no one can force people to do things they do not want to do. A democratic society allows each of us the freedom to kill ourselves slowly—with a couch, a remote control, and a bag of fat-laden, calorie-rich, salty, or sugary snacks.

That is why the future of fitness and leisure lies not in new sports, games, or equipment—but in encouragement and incentives. Instead of introducing new gadgets and gizmos to the same group of fitness elites who always buy them, fitness as a general prescription must be introduced to the rest of America. The key is to integrate physical activity into everyday living for everyday people. Call it "fitness populism."

Who Will Take the Lead?

The best way to get people moving toward healthier lifestyles via fitness will be through imaginative, experimental efforts by the private sector—principally our employers and the health club industry. With escalating health care costs burdening all businesses, employers have a huge stake in maintaining the health of their workers. Health clubs and gyms are already realizing that reaching a wider audience through a pro-active approach will help to make them more profitable.

The Workplace Workout

Research already suggests that being in good shape reduces absenteeism on the job. In one study, workers deemed poorly fit had two and one-half times the rate of absenteeism of those who were in excellent shape. Since employers can expect fewer sick days from fit people, they may try to hire more fit people. This trend should encourage more people to keep fit to enhance chances of getting hired. Employers also will encourage employees to get and stay in shape, knowing that over time this will increase productivity and save money.

Companies can experiment with financial incentives to get their employees fit. Bluntly put:

- They can require employees to take part in an exercise regimen to be eligible for health benefits.
- Insurance premiums can be linked to an employee's physical fitness.
- Employees may have to furnish proof of exercise by signing in at their company gym or local YMCA. They can fill out training logs to document the amount of time spent exercising on their own.

Health clubs and gyms will continue to be an important element in the maintenance of people's health and physical fitness. Insufficient exercise and improper diet are linked to six of ten fatal diseases. (© 1995 Melanie Carr/First Image West, Inc)

- Some companies will experiment with gentler approaches to urge their employees to get healthier, making incentive programs optional instead of mandatory.
- People who fill out activity forms and show improvement through on-site exercise testing may lower their premiums or get rebates—just as a good driver can lower his or her car insurance with a clean record.
- Employees can win awards for reaching new fitness goals. Being able to jog thirty minutes continuously may earn someone a company t-shirt or a free lunch. Bicycling to work once a week might earn a gift certificate at a sporting goods store at the end of the year.
- Employers can make physical fitness infectious, by offering rewards for employees who get *other* employees involved in exercise.
- Incentive programs can reach beyond exercise into other areas of health improvement. Boosting one's use of seat belts or cutting out fried foods are examples that might earn special bonuses or rewards.
- Programs also will offer screening of major disease risk factors. More employers will experiment with weight-loss and quit-smoking clinics, stress management, mammography, blood pressure monitoring and cholesterol-lowering clinics. If you bring your cholesterol out of the danger zone, for example, you may get a reduced insurance premium or a cash prize.

For this culture of fitness to grow, worksite fitness is key. Gyms and clubs will become as ubiquitous at the jobsite as the in-house cafeteria, only healthier in content.

The worksite club will not simply feature a wide range of fitness machines and weights to improve and maintain workforce fitness. The club will become the focal point for all health-promoting behaviors—the place to get blood pressure checked, have a mammogram done, or sign up for the organization's marathon.

Onsite exercise need not be limited to the predictable. Ballroom dancing, walking vigorously, playing tennis, or rollerblading will serve just as fine as calisthenics. The emphasis will be on activity, regardless of what kind.

The Health Club of the Future

The idea of the gym as an arsenal of iron will soon fade.

- To encourage more people to buy memberships, health clubs will offer more options—from beginning weightlifting classes and ballroom dancing lessons to weight-loss clinics and yoga/relaxation workshops.
- Gyms and clubs will go beyond the needs of the baby boomers—and go after their youngsters. Some gyms have already instituted programs designed for children. This approach helps to improve the club image and also brings in cash from a previously untapped source. This trend may also boost the exercise equipment industry—who else would produce the special child-sized equipment needed?
- Competition for the club market will come from an unlikely place—academia. Colleges already have hi-tech gyms—but these state-of-the-art fitness centers will now begin to pull business away from private clubs. Members can be enlisted from students, faculty, staff, alumni, and their families.

- The sexual revolution will reach the gym as women-only health clubs become more popular and widespread. Co-ed gyms will remain alive and well, preserving healthy terrain for people with more social motives than fitness goals in mind.
- Clubs will soon respond to the needs of the older segment of the fitness market for a place to exercise where they would feel less self-conscious and more comfortable. Fifty-plus gyms will start up, while other clubs may make certain times of the day off-limits to anyone born after 1935. Senior-citizen discounts—prevalent in movie theaters and restaurants—will become commonplace at health clubs.

Profit from Prevention

In the future, the private sector will take the lead in encouraging better health through exercise and fitness. The allure of fitness makes money, and being fit saves money. Preventive health through exercise means profit—and that is all the private industry needs to know to make it work.

[See also Food Consumption; Free Time; Leisure Time; Nutrition; Outdoor Recreation and Leisure Pursuits; Performing Arts: Dance and Theater; Personal Transport; Sports and Games, Competitive.]

BIBLIOGRAPHY

"Breaking the Age Barrier." *Prevention* (August 1992).
"Building a Healthy Child." *Prevention* (October 1992).
"Flex Rx." *Prevention* (February 1992).
"The New Club." *Club Industry* (December 1992).
"Worksite Health Promotion: Enhancing Human Resource Capital." *American Journal of Health Promotion* (January–February 1993).

— GREG GUTFELD

EXTINCTION OF SPECIES

With the development of artificial life, new knowledge in genetics and the postmodern paradigm of complex dynamics, the concept of extinction has lost its crisp definition. As species evolve, the underlying genetic information that defines unique character has changed. At what point in the transition is a species extinct and when does one have a new species? Biologists are not even in total agreement when they try to construct family trees for plants or animals. With experiments in genetic engineering and artificial life systems on computers, questions of what is alive become more than philosophical rhetoric; and the issues of life, death, creation, and extinction are far from trivial.

Some evolutionary models allow for catastrophic changes, calling into question the concept of a continuous evolution which had created the need to locate or identify a lot of missing links in the evolutionary chain. This does not deny the demise of certain living entities; but it does raise the issue of how and when one species may or may not evolve or become extinct. The apparent differences may lead to false organizational perceptions in an evolutionary hierarchy, further confusing extinction and evolution.

Additionally, computer models coupled with work on the human genome project give indications that genetic codes for creation or recreation can be defined, and potentially assembled at will. Even though certain genetic patterns may be "lost," it is understood that such permutations and combinations can be restored given time, even when such efforts are random or semi-random. Thus, if the building blocks are available, but the physical form is no longer extant, is a species extinct?

The importance or interest in extinction rests not with the study of a single species. Rather it lies with the changes in time and space that either lead to such an extinction or the potential impacts that such an extinction may cause or foreshadow. While ostensibly this questions the survival of life on planet Earth, pragmatically the ultimate issue is the survival of human life. Ironically it is possible that humans may become the first species to create its own evolutionary successors.

Will this imply the extinction of the human species or the development of parallel life-forms?

Numerous species have become extinct within the historic period. Human intervention has played a significant role in many of these extinctions. The consequences of such actions are not yet fully understood within a larger time/space domain.

The underlying assumption here is that humans are already in their most highly evolved form and that any activity which could significantly alter the larger ecosystem could yield consequences that could only be described as resulting in the extinction of the human race. A potential transformation that significantly altered the genetic materials or the physical appearance would be perceived, in the current environment, as equivalent to extinction.

Extinction is not a value-neutral term. Under certain circumstances it might be considered to be universally beneficial, such as the eradication of smallpox. Yet we realize that such actions have a variety of consequences that might be mixed blessings in the long term. For example, weed elimination may have costs and benefits.

The Bengal Tiger of Asia is under threat of extinction due to encroachment on its habitat by humans. Endangered animal species, numbering 1,386 worldwide in 1997, will continue to increase in the 21st century. (David A. Northcott/Corbis)

Thus, today, concerns have been raised that the loss of even one species may mean the loss of some significant genetic pool with potential benefits as yet to be determined.

With the development of artificial life, new knowledge in genetics, and the postmodern paradigm of complex dynamics, the concept of extinction has lost its crisp definition.

This concern operates at two levels. The first is manifest in the potential loss of plant materials, particularly in tropical areas such as the Amazon Basin or Africa. Here the issue is primarily pragmatic. Natural products have potential in the area of medicines that could be beneficial, in the near term, to human life.

The second level comes from a systems perspective and the realization that the biota of the planet are integrated in a poorly understood matrix. There is concern that the extinction of one or more species in, for example, the Amazon may potentially be felt in China (the so called "butterfly effect" of modern "chaos" theory). Additionally, there is uncertainty as to how much of the web can be allowed to become extinct before the system collapses or undergoes significant reorganization.

The question of extinction raises further the relationship between humans and nature, particularly when the dimension of time is taken into consideration. Desertification in the African Sahel has been attributed to mismanagement by humans. Yet, Earth satellite data seem to indicate that the natural ebb and flow of the desert, dancing with the vegetative edge, is significantly larger than any manifestation caused by humans. Similarly, major volcanic eruptions release greater destructive forces and nature recovers more quickly than that expected by any current understanding of modern science. Additionally, models of ocean fisheries show that current management techniques, even in conservative terms, do not stop shifts in relationships between marine populations. Standard equilibrium models do not work in dynamic, open, systems.

Thus, regardless of the problems created by humans and the clearly identifiable destructive forces unleashed by humans, nature in both short and long time cycles creates greater evolutionary changes. Thus, the issue of human intervention in the biosphere may, ultimately, prove to be trivial except where its own survival is concerned.

One of the fears is that humans, with their consciousness and ego, may be driven to try to prove that they can both create life and cause extinctions *pare passu* with nature. Several authors have raised the point that when Mother Nature created humans, she took a chance. Intelligence may not be a survival characteristic.

[See also Astronomy; Biodiversity; Evolution, Biological; Evolution, Life-Forms in the Universe; Genetic Engineering; Genetics; Genetics: Agricultural Applications; Genetics: Commercialization; Genetic Technologies; Green Revolution; Natural Disasters.]

BIBLIOGRAPHY

Ainsworth-Land, George. *Grow or Die,* New York: John Wiley, 1986.

Casti, John, *Complexification,* New York: HarperCollins, 1994.

Hayles, N. Katherine. *The Cosmic Web.* Ithaca, NY: Cornell University Press, 1984.

Kellert, Stephen. *In the Wake of Chaos.* Chicago: University of Chicago Press, 1993.

Laszlo, Erwin, ed. *The New Evolutionary Paradigm.* New York: Gordon Breach, 1991.

Stein, Wilfred, and Varela, Francisco. *Thinking About Biology.* Reading, MA: Addison-Wesley, 1993.

— TOM ABELES

EXTRATERRESTRIAL LIFE-FORMS

Since the dawn of consciousness, human beings have speculated on the possibility that intelligent beings might inhabit other worlds. Since the eighteenth century, science has sought answers to the question "Are we alone?"

Scientists are divided on this issue. In one camp stand those who believe that the laws of the universe are similar everywhere, and what we see in our solar system is likely to have been repeated elsewhere many times. If this assumption holds, then the universe is probably filled with life and intelligence. Our sun is an average star, and there are an estimated 200 to 400 billion stars in our galaxy alone, the Milky Way, with an estimated 100 billion galaxies in the universe. Thus, there are trillions of potential sites where life and intelligence might emerge and evolve.

The numbers dwindle when we ask, "How many stars are like our sun, how many have planets, and how many of those can support life? Once life starts, how often does it evolve into intelligence, and how often does that intelligence attempt to communicate?"

The issues to be considered in determining the likely number of advanced technological communicating civilizations were summarized by Frank Drake in a mathematical statement known as the Drake Equation:

N = R(s) [Rate of Star Formation] · F(p) [Fraction of Stars with Planets] · N(e) [Number of planets ecologically suitable for life] · F(l) [Fraction of planets suitable for life where life has evolved] · F(i) [Fraction of "life-starts" where intelligence has appeared] · F(c) [Fraction of intelligent species who have created technical civilizations] · F(L) [Estimated lifetime of technical civilizations]

The Drake Equation shows that we can derive an estimate of millions of worlds harboring intelligent life, or only one, depending on our assumptions about several variable factors. However, most of these factors can only be estimated, which means that the equation cannot prove anything.

In fact, not all scientists believe that intelligence is common in the universe. They point out that of the nine planets and many more moons in our solar system, only one, Earth, is known to support life and intelligence. How do we know that other solar systems are constructed in the same way, with even one life-supporting planet? Perhaps it would take an entire galaxy to produce the necessary conditions for intelligence to appear on just one planet—or even an entire universe.

The probability that extraterrestrial life-forms—intelligent or otherwise—exist or would want to contact us is unknown. Advanced life-forms, evolving on planets dramatically different from Earth, might never develop our kind of technology and might advance so far beyond human society that they would have no interest in contacting us. It is because of these uncertainties that scientists tend to agree only that experiments should be conducted to determine whether we are living in a universe that is sparsely populated or filled with life.

Types of Contact

Contact between humans and extraterrestrials might occur in a variety of ways. For example, extraterrestrials could send a robot probe from their own solar system to explore nearby systems.

Crews of extraterrestrials in spacecraft might also arrive in our solar system and make direct contact with us. Many people believe that UFOs (unidentified flying objects) are spacecraft and that not only have humans been contacted by the occupants of these vessels but they have even been abducted by them and used for various experiments. So far, we have no confirmation that UFOs are extraterrestrial in origin, or even that they exist, so we cannot yet say that contact with extraterrestrial life-forms has taken place.

Another approach to contact, known as SETI (Search for Extra-Terrestrial Intelligence) refers to the search for artificially created electronic signals emanating from other star systems. SETI commenced in 1959 with a paper by physicists Philip Morrison and Giuseppe Cocconi, who argued that the time might be right for beginning a serious search for extraterrestrial intelligence.

Perhaps it would take an entire galaxy to produce the necessary conditions for intelligence to appear on just one planet—or even an entire universe.

Within a year, Frank Drake, an important SETI pioneer, implemented this suggestion with project Ozma. Using a radiotelescope in Green Bank, West Virginia, he looked for signals from Epsilon Eridani and Tau Ceti, two Sun-like stars situated ten to twelve light-years from Earth.

Until 1992, the most ambitious search ever undertaken was Project Meta, sponsored by the Planetary Society and conducted by Harvard professor Paul Horowitz. Project Meta initiated its searches at a site outside Boston in 1983. On Columbus Day, 1992, NASA began a "targeted search" of some one thousand Sun-like stars and a survey of the entire night sky visible from the northern hemisphere. However, this ambitious project lost its funding when Congress voted to terminate it after about a year of operation.

SETI scientists have yet to find any signals that are undeniably of extraterrestrial origin. Intriguing anomalies were turned up by Project Meta—signals have been detected that seemed to be of unnatural origin. However, the signals do not repeat, and researchers have withheld judgment as to what they are.

The Impact of Contact

What would happen if we made open, unambiguous contact with extraterrestrials? The impact on Earth's society would most likely be significant, but it would depend on several factors:

DISTANCE. Impact will be greater if the signal comes from a star system close to Earth. If the Earth receives a signal from a civilization 100,000 light-years away, it will have been en route for 100,000 years, and any response will take 100,000 years—a round-trip of 200,000 years. If the signal is only a brief "hello," impact will be limited to the knowledge that we are not alone.

On the other hand, if the signal comes from a nearby star system, such as Alpha Centauri, only 4.3 light-years away, an active dialogue would be possible, since round-trip discussions would take only eight years.

PARITY. Impact will vary also according to the differences in development between our society and the contacting civilization. If the contacting civilization is at the same stage of development as ourselves, we may teach as much as we learn. However, if the other civilization is even a few hundred years ahead of us, it may be very challenging for terrestrial society.

Rather than being contacted by a single planet, we may be signaled by an advanced galactic federation consisting of many worlds. After being the most advanced species on Earth for thousands of years, humans may find themselves in a "galactic kindergarten."

VOLUME. Finally, impact will depend upon the volume of information transmitted. If the contacting civilization is far away, but sends us the equivalent of the *Encyclopedia Galactica,* all of its knowledge of the universe, then the impact clearly will be enormous.

These and other variables have been used by this author to develop a "contact impact model," which has several levels of complexity. However, in its simplest form, the model can be expressed in a single expression, known as the White equation:

I (Impact) = Pd (parity difference in years at time of transmission) − D (Distance in light years) · Vi (fraction of extraterrestrial knowledge base transmitted per year)

This equation assumes that the level of impact will depend primarily upon how much new knowledge is transmitted in a given period of time. In terms of getting ready for SETI, the equation shows that we have limited control over the impact of contact, since we cannot predetermine who will contact us, nor how much of their knowledge they will share.

Preparations for contact are already underway. For example, a group of SETI researchers created a set of "detection protocols," including suggested guidelines for what should be done in the event that a signal is found. These activities prepare a worldwide cadre to help our planet respond intelligently to detection of extraterrestrial intelligence.

Summary

The search for extraterrestrial intelligence has long captured the imagination of the human species. By trying to understand the nature of extraterrestrials, we are simultaneously searching for self-knowledge, because we can only define ourselves in relationship to others. For this reason, if for no other, the search will continue.

[See also Evolution, Biological; Evolution: Life-Forms in the Universe; Genetics; Space Travel.]

BIBLIOGRAPHY

Barrow, John D., and Tipler, Frank J. *The Anthropic Cosmological Principle.* Oxford: Oxford University Press, 1988.

Cocconi, Giuseppe, and Morrison, Philip. "Searching for Interstellar Communications." *Nature* 184 (1959): 844.

Crowe, Michael J. *The Extraterrestrial Life Debate: 1750–1900.* "The Idea of a Plurality of Worlds, from Kant to Lowell." Cambridge: Cambridge University Press, 1986.

Drake, Frank, and Sobel, Dava. *Is Anyone Out There?: The Scientific Search for Extraterrestrial Intelligence.* New York: Delacorte Press, 1992.

Easterbrook, Gregg. "Are We Alone?" *Atlantic Monthly* (August 1988).

Shklovskii, I. S., and Sagan, Carl. *Intelligent Life in the Universe.* New York: Delta Books/Dell Publishing, 1966.

White, Frank. *The SETI Factor: How the Search for Extraterrestrial Intelligence Is Transforming Our View of the Universe and Ourselves.* New York: Walker, 1990.

— FRANK WHITE

F

FACTORIES AND MANUFACTURING

Themes likely to dominate manufacturing through the first decade of the twenty-first century include a continued emphasis on quality, concurrent approaches to *everything* (especially design, processing, and distribution), and globalization (especially marketing, distribution, and customer support). Quality will continue to be a major driver, including statistical process control (SPC), quality function deployment (QFD), design of experiments (DoE), "re-engineering" of operating processes, and other quality improvement efforts.

Concurrent engineering will grow and become the standard for development of new products and processes. New products will be configured in a manner that is most "producible" based on existing or planned manufacturing processes, a significant departure from today's standard approach, which involves designing the product and worrying later about how to build it.

Actual factory size is likely to diminish generally as equipment becomes more compact, materials become more adaptable to final fabricated shapes, and efficiency improves.

Globalization will be a major change agent over the next two or three decades. Led by globalization in markets and distribution activity, mainstream manufacturers from all major industrialized countries will find themselves drawn into multinational status. This will dramatically affect management training and skills, as well as the cultural make-up of multinational manufacturing work forces, particularly in management and technical areas.

Locations for production operations are selected today based on such criteria as the availability of skilled labor, adequate distribution modes, tax breaks, and other political-economic incentives. Over the next ten to twenty years, domestic production facilities will shift from the Midwest to the Sun Belt states and especially to second-tier cities and large-city suburbs. Internationally, fabrication in general (particularly low-tech fabrication operations—metal bending, sewing, etc.) will move from industrialized countries to less developed, industrializing countries. This will allow companies to take advantage of lower labor rates, looser environmental and other regulations, and trade offsets.

Actual factory size is likely to diminish generally as equipment becomes more compact, materials become more adaptable to final fabricated shapes, and efficiency improves, and also as large manufacturers move away from vertical integration. Average factories by the year 2000 will employ half the number of a decade earlier.

Human resources, the most critical aspect of any company's operations, will face new challenges as a result of two primary, factors. First, the work force will not have all the education, skills, and training required to operate the increasingly complex manufacturing and information-processing equipment. Educational levels, both in the United States and in most other industrialized nations, are woefully inadequate and may not improve quickly enough to keep pace with future workplace demands. The shortages may be acute in engineering, product and process research, physical sciences, and computer sciences. Secondly, the values of tomorrows' workers will be quite different. People entering the manufacturing work force are less eager for overtime pay and for job stability at any cost, and likely to be more interested in free time and personal fulfillment. As a result, the most talented people will be far less responsive to the deadlines and other regimens imposed regularly in today's manufacturing settings. This will mean rapid expansion of temporary workers contracted for specific assignments, free-lance management specialists and technical people, and telecommuting from distant locations in job categories not requiring face-to-face dealings.

Automation levels through 2010 will grow exponentially. Rather than earlier images of an army of humanoid robots moving up and down aisles and assembling manufactured goods in the place of people, the robotics applications in factories will stem from initial successes in redundant operations, hazardous processes (such as welding and spray painting), in areas requiring precision and high levels of accurate repeatability (such as data entry and mixing of chemical compounds), and in areas where human strength is inadequate (such as the continuous lifting of heavy loads).

2010–2030

Themes that will dominate the manufacturing world between 2010 and 2030 are likely to include knowl-

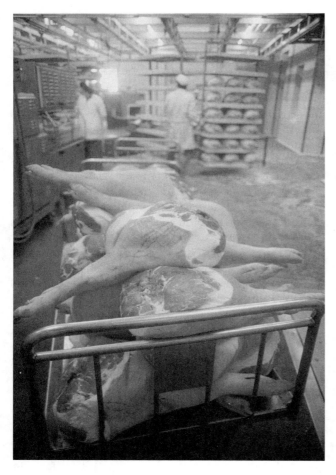

Work now done by people in factories, such as these men processing hams, will be increasingly automated through the use of robotics. (Owen Franken/Corbis)

edge-based systems development and deployment, the development of product and service infrastructures, and the integration of technologies into "seamless" process development activities.

Knowledge-based systems will be used to determine optimum product configurations and availability; to allow materials management professionals to calculate optimum inventory investment levels and procurement timing; to enable finance departments to take maximum advantage of lending rates, tax laws, and other financial opportunities; to allow transportation/distribution professionals to identify the lowest-fare carriers and shortest-time distribution channels; and to let production departments schedule optimum production flow rates so as to maximize direct labor efficiency. These systems will grow out of the converging technologies of expert systems, natural language processors, telecommunications, and computers.

Infrastructure building will likely be recognized as critical for success. Infrastructures, environmental factors, and systems required for support include sales and distribution networks, legislation, and even cultural factors that influence product "demand."

Technology integration will be a distinguishing characteristic as lines blur between materials sciences and manufacturing engineering, between sales and distribution, and between design and production. Cross-training will enhance the breadth of individual expertise levels. Single work-stations operated by one or two individuals may be able to take the "design" process from concept through (simulated) testing, (simulated) marketing, production process development and scheduling, packaging development, and distribution channel selection.

Factory locations are expected to follow patterns exhibited in the previous decade. The size of the factories is likely to continue to shrink as personnel are cross-trained, knowledge-based systems provide technical "expertise" as needed, and new materials technologies reduce floor space requirements.

Human resources will continue to be a critical aspect, as more heavily cross-trained and broadly skilled and educated personnel are required. Strategic alliances between manufacturers and trade schools, universities, and community colleges are likely to proliferate.

Automation will continue to grow as a percentage of the value-adding component of manufacturing. Interchangeable "plug-and-play" process component equipment should be available for most standard manufacturing processes during this period, assuming that we have dealt with these interface communications issues.

2030–2050

The period from 2030 through the 2050s in manufacturing will likely be typified by the developments of microfabrication, virtual marketing and testing, and biocomputing. Microfabrication will be the most exciting development for manufacturing since the advent of the computer. It will allow the fabrication of materials and parts at the molecular level, building them with the features we desire (strength, weight, flexibility, and so forth). Left behind will be the era of excavating ore from the ground, refining it, and beating it into the forms we want. Common materials such as sand (silica) will require minor modification to configure them into extremely property-rich materials.

Virtual marketing will move to the forefront of marketing, sales, and distribution activity. Based on enormous volumes of information available through accessible on-line services and data bases, "virtual" markets may be accurately evaluated without major cost.

Biocomputers promise staggering computational power and memory capabilities. Combined with nanotechnology, prodigious information processing capability will easily support "virtual marketing."

Location will begin to wane in importance as micro-fabrication becomes possible and the possibility of "portable manufacturing" emerges.

Location will begin to wane in importance as microfabrication becomes possible, and the possibility of "portable manufacturing" emerges. Since face-to-face labor requirements will be virtually eliminated, and "pollution" or other environmental side effects will be effectively eliminated, there will be very little restriction as to appropriateness of such "factory" sites.

Factory size will at this point become a function of manufacturing equipment size, which will gradually become smaller just as computers did. Automation will be at the heart of most microfabrication operations, since handling molecules and monitoring molecular construction are not activities for which humans are well suited.

Beyond 2050

Themes likely to dominate include the balance of nanotechnology operations (namely microassembly, disassembly, replication, and altered replication), and the return to space exploration.

Nanotechnology will continue to supplant traditional manufacturing processes, replacing not only fabrication but assembly processes as well. Disassemblers may be constructed that allow virtually any substance to be broken down into its molecular components. We may be able to disassemble just about anything, and reconstruct it molecule by molecule, replicating it over and over again, even with alterations. Manufacturing will most closely resemble today's pharmaceutical industry, with vats and pipes and mixing slurries of chemicals.

As nanotechnology opens new vistas of economy and power for manufacturing, the lure of space exploration will likely become irresistible. New industries supporting space exploration will spring up to expand Earth's domain without ruining our existing habitat. This will also perhaps enable us to do space-based manufacturing of substances that can only be readily generated in gravity-free environments.

In the years ahead, factory size will be gradually reduced as manufacturing processes become encoded in

robotic microfabricators and microassemblers. Eventually, as they are catalogued and made available "over the counter," an entire "factory" may well be comprised of a handful of individuals dedicated primarily to conceiving of, developing, and selling products.

[See also Appropriate Technology; Business Structure: Forms, Impacts; Global Business: Dominant Organizational Forms; Management; Materials: Research and Development; Nanotechnology; Robotics; Science Cities; Work, Quality of; Work Ethic; Workforce Redistribution; Working Conditions.]

BIBLIOGRAPHY

Boyett, Joseph, and Conn, Henry. *Workplace 2000.* New York: Dutton, 1991.
Cetron, Marvin, and Davies, Owen. *American Renaissance.* New York: St. Martin's Press, 1989.
Drexler, K. Eric, et al. *Unbounding the Future.* New York: Morrow, 1991.
Duncan, William L. *Manufacturing 2000.* New York: AMACOM, 1994.

– WILLIAM L. DUNCAN

FAMILIES AND HOUSEHOLDS

Many prognostications about the future devote considerable attention to the potential impact of technological change on various institutions such as the family. This is neither surprising nor inappropriate. Technology is almost always a major force—indeed, at times, the major force driving social and economic change. The Industrial Revolution exerted a profound and far-reaching impact on family life in American society, affecting everything from where families lived to how they organized and carried out their social and economic responsibilities.

Nevertheless, it is a mistaken emphasis, at this juncture in U.S. history, for an examination of the future of family life in American society to focus primarily on the effects of technology. Fascinating though it may be to consider whether twenty-first-century Americans will be flying around in space-mobiles like George and Jane Jetson, the future of the family in American society will be determined far less by technological change than by the outcome of raging conflicts over values. At the heart of this cultural battle is a sizeable and growing gap between traditional standards and actual behavior, between how we want our families to be and how they actually are.

Most Americans want to be happy at home. In survey after survey, Americans consistently identify marital happiness and a strong family unit among their top goals in life. Amidst all of the cultural turbulence in recent years, baby boomers are expressing a growing concern about and interest in family life.

Not only do surveys consistently show a high appreciation for family life, but they consistently produce results that affirm many of the time-honored principles providing a firm foundation for achieving a strong family. According to survey data, Americans believe it is best for marriages to last until the death of one spouse, for married couples to be faithful to one another, for children to be born in wedlock, for children to grow up in a two-parent household, for parents to organize their work-and-family responsibilities in a manner that minimizes time away from their children.

Yet, the reality of family life in American society often falls short of these aspirations:

- America, for better or worse, has the highest divorce rate in the world, with half of all marriages ending in divorce. More than half of all divorces involve children; disrupted family life often results in severe emotional scars, especially for young children.
- Children born out of wedlock constituted 30 percent of all births in 1991 (up from 5 percent in 1960, and projected to reach 40 percent by 2000; among blacks the percent soared from 23 to 68 percent between 1960 and 1991). Illegitimate children incur higher infant mortality, suffer lower birth weights, and are relegated to growing up poor (with increased risks of not completing school or becoming involved in crime).
- Almost 90 percent of all single-parent households in 1991 were fatherless; half of all divorced fathers seldom see their offspring, and most do not provide child support. By the mid-1990s, the number of fatherless households resulting from unwed childbearing is projected to exceed the number created by divorce.
- Among children born in 1980, only 6 percent of blacks and 30 percent of whites will live with their parents through age eighteen. Recent reports indicate that children raised in single-parent households are two to three times more likely to suffer emotional/behavioral problems as children from two-parent families are; also, they are more likely to become high school dropouts, pregnant teenagers, or drug abusers, and to engage in criminal behavior.

No one seriously argues that we are living in an era marked by family strength. Faced with the gap between traditional standards and actual behavior, one side in this cultural conflict calls for lowering or doing away with traditional guidelines governing human behavior and family life. It maintains that eliminating standards will enable people to live any lifestyle they want, to redefine the family in any way they so choose.

Others urge behavioral changes to conform with time-honored guidelines, since such standards have proved throughout history to limit human suffering and promote human happiness. Indeed, they argue that the fall of every great civilization was preceded by a retreat from time-honored principles governing human behavior and family relationships.

Should the proponents of family redefinition prevail, then the families of the future may bear less resemblance to the family pattern to which most Americans today aspire. Instead, the twenty-first century may see more adultery, divorce, and illegitimacy than that found today. Child abuse, neglect, and abandonment also may rise, as children and childrearing become less and less valued. Schools, day care centers, corporations, and governments may be called upon to assume more and more traditional family functions. Ultimately, a system of year-round, all-day, cradle-to-college programs may evolve.

Divorced from the commitments of marriage,

sex may become increasingly

a mechanical recreational activity,

just another pleasurable experience.

Divorced from the commitments of marriage, sex may become increasingly a mechanical recreational activity, just another pleasurable experience. Traditional taboos against behaviors such as incest and man-boy sex may wane, as practitioners seek "tolerance" from those who do not share their sexual preferences. Advanced contraceptive technologies such as Norplant will be used to lessen the need for responsible decision making about sex among teenagers. RU-486 and other abortion pills will be used to terminate unwanted pregnancies.

Euthanasia may become widely available, particularly when baby boomers reach retirement age and demand old-age entitlement benefits. Genetic engineering could be utilized to provide prospective parents with designer babies, screened to eliminate undesirable genetic hazards (for example, hereditary disposition to cancer). Carried to the extreme, parents may be able to change desired genetically determined traits.

Youth gangs will proliferate by offering youngsters who have been deprived of strong families a group identity and sense of belonging they never had. Violent crime, particularly crimes against women, also may rise. All of the above trends portend disaster. In the wake of their cumulative swathe, social chaos and anarchy will cast dark shadows.

Conversely, if the defenders of time-honored standards prevail, we are apt to see a cultural revamping in which Americans commit or recommit themselves to living up to the ideals of marital fidelity and marital childbearing. In this climate, fewer children would be growing up in homes where parents had divorced or both parents worked. Family incomes would then be reduced to one income rather than two.

Information Era communication technologies also exert important influences on family life. For example, some family-oriented workers will be able to find work that allows them to earn their income by working at home using personal computers, faxes, modems, and interactive television. In addition, parents will make increasing use of these new technologies in educating their children. They also will rely upon these technologies to educate themselves as society relies less upon formal classroom education and moves toward "lifelong learning" that is integrated into economic pursuits. Families will be linked to vast electronic networks of businesses, financial institutions, government agencies, schools, universities, libraries, and museums. All this may vastly expand a family's access to the wider world. These information and entertainment networks change what is possible for American families and change the family itself.

Americans consistently identify a strong family as a goal, but the idealized family unit is not the one that is statistically prominent. Single-parent families rose from 12% of the American population in 1970 to 28% in 1996. (© 1993 Melanie Carr/First Image West, Inc)

In many ways, the postindustrial family of the twenty-first century may bear some resemblance to the preindustrial farm or small-town family of the eighteenth and nineteenth centuries. The home, once again, may become more of a place for pursuing economic livelihoods as well as the focus of education and training.

By taking advantage of home-based employment opportunities, fathers and mothers may be able to stay at home and divide their attention between work and family demands. They would be more accessible to nurture their children during the day. In addition, families will find it easier to build and to retain home-based kin networks as more and more jobs in the information-based economy change to brainpower rather than "brawnpower" work. Such change would enhance family responsibilities over a worker's life cycle by lessening the workload when children are young, and would open up opportunities for extending careers well into the worker's sixties and seventies once children have left the home.

Obviously, such transformations will not take place overnight. It is possible that we will continue to see some countervailing trends occurring simultaneously. What happens to families is very responsive to economic and tax policies of the government as well as government regulation of the use of homes as workplaces. Laws were enacted in earlier decades to protect women and children from home-based sweatshop working conditions and to limit child labor for output sold outside the home.

It is unlikely that the turbulent redefinition of "values" will last forever. One side or the other will gain consensus and cultural dominance. A likely key to gaining dominance will be based on framing the issues to one's advantage.

Many of the polarizing issues that lie at the heart of the clash over appropriate values—abortion, illegitimacy, pornography, divorce, TV violence, homosexuality, and day care—involve issues that pit adult liberty against child well-being. Family priorities, choices, and the quality of family life are shaped differently depending upon what is important to a family and to a society. One viewpoint prizes freedom and choice and entrepreneurial liberty. Another perspective reveres an often religiously based tradition, continuity, and conventional standards such as "the sanctity of the family." Such conflicts between "moral relativists" and "religious and cultural traditionalists" are not easily reconciled.

Many issues at the heart of the controversy do not easily lend themselves to compromise. However the current conflict is resolved, the outcome is likely to have a more dramatic effect on the future of the family than will any technological change.

[See also Abortion; Child Care; Children, Living Arrangements; Divorce; Elderly, Living Arrangements; Family Patterns; Family Planning; Family Problems; Family Values; Household Composition; Housing, Demographic and Lifestyle Impacts on; Lifestyles, Alternative; Marriage; Sexual Laws; Social Controls.]

BIBLIOGRAPHY

Beuttler, William. *Family: The Future.* Chicago: Libra, 1990.
Fletcher, Ronald. *The Abolitionists: The Family and Marriage Under Attack.* New York: Routledge, 1988.
Hutter, Mark. *The Changing Family: Comparative Perspectives.* New York: Macmillan, 1988.
Kirkendall, Lester A., and Gravatt, Arthur E. *Marriage and the Family in the Year 2020.* Buffalo, NY: Prometheus, 1989.
Levitan, Sar A. *What's Happening to the American Family? Tensions, Hopes, Realities.* Baltimore: Johns Hopkins University Press, 1988.
Moynihan, Daniel Patrick. *Family and Nation.* New York: Harcourt Brace Jovanovich, 1987.

— GARY L. BAUER

FAMILY PATTERNS

Nostalgic discussion of the "old-fashioned" American family and "family values" idealizes the husband-father as breadwinner, wife-mother as housekeeper, and children who are seen but not heard. These sentiments memorialize patriarchal values, legal restrictions hobbling women's economic independence, and divorce as a seldom-used alternative.

Even in the past there was no one American family, traditional or otherwise. Because families were more economically interdependent, they were more stable. But we do not know how many couples stayed together for lack of acceptable alternatives and how many for love. Wives in black families, in immigrant families, and in working-class families always had to share the breadwinning role with their husbands. The size, the composition, the structure, and the living arrangements of families in the United States and Western Europe have undergone changes so profound as to raise the question, is the family as we have known it becoming outmoded and obsolete?

Cultural experience indicates that children benefit from having two parents who share a stable relationship. Separation and divorce are obvious stressors for children. The long-term outcome depends on the circumstances of the custodial parent after the separation, and on the quality of the children's relationship with each parent. Even after income and ethnicity are taken into account, children from single-parent families simply fare worse.

In 1900, when a woman's life expectancy was about forty-eight years, she spent almost all her adult life bearing and rearing children. Today, with an expectancy of eighty years, women have a long postreproductive life. For most women, that longer life includes years of separation, divorce, or widowhood.

As the result of changes in types and venues of work, in vocational characteristics, in the economics of family life, and in custom and law, the stability of the family has declined sharply in Western Europe and America. Most women today work because they have to and because the economy needs them in the workforce. With paid employment, wives have become less dependent on their husbands. Divorce, once a luxury restricted to the wealthy who could afford to buy it, is now a recourse more common among the working class.

Europe and the United States differ greatly in the percentage of births that take place out of wedlock. In 1992 the percentage for Greece was 2.6, well below that for any other country in the European Union (compare: Italy 5.8, Ireland 11.7, and France 26.3 percent). The figure for the United States is now 27 percent, 2.5 times greater than it was two decades ago. The rate for Sweden is twice again as high; *half the births* take place out of wedlock. Yet there is little public alarm in Sweden but widespread consternation in the United States about an "epidemic of teenage pregnancy." Why the difference?

Out-of-wedlock births occur under entirely different social circumstances in the two countries. Births to unwed teenagers have been increasing in the United States at the same time that they have been decreasing in Sweden. Infants born out of wedlock in Sweden enter a family of two parents most likely living in a consensual union. Such infants in the United States most often have only a mother to care for them—a mother living in poverty, to boot.

Among industrialized nations, the United States has the highest teenage pregnancy rate and the highest teenage childbirth rate. This is *despite* the United States, having the highest teenage abortion rate. All this is *not* because we have the highest rates of nonmarital adolescent cohabitation; the rate for Sweden is actually higher. In Sweden, public school education about human sexuality and access to contraception have been systematically provided to adolescents for many years; in contrast, both education and access have been restricted in the United States for fear of "encouraging promiscuity."

When the data are disaggregated by ethnic group, profound differences become apparent. Overall, 29.5 percent of all 1991 births were to unmarried women; the rate for blacks was 67.9 percent, for whites 21.8 percent, and for Hispanics 38 percent.

Even when they work full time, most single mothers in America remain near or below the poverty line because their wages are so low. They are vulnerable to frequent layoffs; high expenses for child care deplete their meager earnings; they lose Medicaid if they work. In Sweden, the support system is more favorable. Single parents benefit from an extensive social support system—housing subsidies, child support, day care, and medical care—that cushions the mother and her children against adversity.

Why These Social Changes?

What accounts for the increase in consensual unions, the decline in marriage, and the increase in divorce during successive decades in this century? There is no simple or completely satisfactory explanation. The striking differences among countries demonstrate the importance of local variations in custom, in history, in the influence of religion, and in economics. Divorce rates regularly increase with industrialization in the West, yet remain low in Japan.

Decisions about whether to marry, to stay married,

and to have children are influenced by

job availability, tax structure, housing markets,

rules governing social welfare benefits,

and other economic considerations.

In earlier centuries, husbands and wives were tightly bound to each other. A traditional family economy enforced mutual dependence. There were simply no viable alternatives for a place to live, for subsistence, and for security. When divorce was difficult or impossible to obtain, abandonment was common. But as women earned wages, they gained independence and it became possible for women to choose to leave.

Decisions about whether to marry, to stay married, and to have children are influenced by job availability, tax structure, housing markets, rules governing social welfare benefits, and other economic considerations. The disappearance of blue-collar jobs has shut low-income and minority youth out of the workforce. For a young woman to marry a man with no prospects for employment is to take responsibility for him as well as the infant.

Does the expansion of welfare benefits account for single motherhood? Both welfare benefits and single parenthood *did* increase in parallel in the 1960s and

'70s. During the past twenty years, however, benefits have *declined* in real dollar value by 26 percent, whereas single parenthood has continued to increase.

Looking to the Future

Moral exhortation for premarital chastity and an end to divorce is unlikely to succeed in reconstituting family stability in the future any more than it has in the past. National employment policies in the future may recast work patterns designed to enhance family life. This might include flexible schedules, alternative work locations, and part-time work.

The federal government also may consider implementing a full-employment policy to assure young adults who enter the labor market incomes sufficient to support families. Increasing the minimum wage is merely one step. There is no safety net for poor two-parent families. A comprehensive family assistance policy might embrace a decent basic living standard, cover unemployed two-parent as well as single-parent families, subsidize low-income housing, assure access to health care, and provide work training to enhance adult skills.

Eighteen months (recently scaled back to twelve months) of paid leave after childbirth or adoption, already the case in Sweden, might be made available in the United States for either parent with guaranteed job protection. Paid parental leave permits infant care in the home. Payments to single mothers might include a decent standard of living guarantee, including subsidized housing.

Access to good-quality infant and child day care for all families is also on the agenda. Both parents assume responsibility for children. Nonresident fathers who are employed are expected to share their income with their children; child support awards require vigorous enforcement. Security for mothers and children could be assured by a guaranteed minimum child support benefit paid directly by the government and recouped from the father, so far as possible.

Success in marriage requires shared values, reasonable expectations, willingness to compromise, and moral commitment. These are the family values that make for stability, durability, and fairness in family relationships today and in the future.

Will these policies bring about a golden age of the family? Clearly not. But they will cushion children against neglect and misfortune.

[See also Child Care; Divorce; Families and Households; Family Planning; Family Problems; Family Values; Household Composition; Marriage; Sexual Behavior; Sexual Codes; Sexual Laws; Social Change: United States; Values; Values Change; Women and Work; Women's Movement; Women's Rights.]

BIBLIOGRAPHY

Dawson, D. A. "Family Structure and Children's Health and Well-Being: Data from the 1988 National Health Interview Survey on Child Health." *Journal of Marriage and the Family* 53 (1991): 573–584.

Gibbs, J. T. "The Social Context of Teenage Pregnancy and Parenting in the Black Community." In M. K. Rosenheim and F. F. Testa, eds. *Early Parenthood and Coming of Age in the 1990s.* New Brunswick, NJ: Rutgers University Press, 1992, pp. 71–88.

Hoem, B., and Hoem, J. M. "The Swedish Family: Aspects of Contemporary Developments." *Journal of Family Issues* 9 (1988): 397–424.

Massey, D. S., and Denton, N. A. "Hypersegregation in U.S. Metropolitan Areas: Black and Hispanic Segregation Along Five Dimensions." *Demography* 26 (1989): 373–391.

McLanahan, S. S., and Sandefur, G. *Growing Up with a Single Parent.* Cambridge, MA: Harvard University Press, 1994.

Wilson, W. J. *The Truly Disadvantaged: The Inner City, the Underclass, and Public Policy.* Chicago, IL: University of Chicago Press, 1987.

– LEON EISENBERG

FAMILY PLANNING

Family planning means, to most people, limiting the number of children born. But it can mean timing births, spacing births, or meeting a large family-size target.

People delay and limit births or voluntarily remain childless for many reasons. Having a child often means doing without something else because childrearing costs time and money. Couples may delay a first birth from a sense of economic insecurity, in order to save, afford more living space or other goods, or retain personal flexibility. Some couples limit family size or avoid childbearing altogether out of concern for the burden that growing populations put on the environment.

Strategies for limiting family size run the gamut from individual to cultural, from benign to brutal. A continuum of strategies and lifestyles worldwide that affect family size can be arrayed approximately from the most to the least acceptable to Western religious and other cultural values. These approaches include abstinence, delayed marriage, premarital virginity, breastfeeding, modern contraception, coitus interruptus, long postpartum-sex taboos, abortion, polygyny (multiple wives, who may be sisters), polyandry (multiple husbands, who are always brothers), arranged marriage combined with discrimination against young widows, subincision (splitting the underside of the penis so that most semen is lost during coitus), infibulation (cutting and joining the labia in order to nearly fuse the vaginal orifice), female infanticide, and the abuse and sexual exploitation or even murder of young women or widows.

Many cultural practices work indirectly and synergistically. For example, a long postpartum-sex taboo is easier to observe when a man has access to more than one sexual partner, as in polygynous marriages. Polyandry limits the total fertility rate because, where one woman weds several men, other women necessarily remain unmarried. Many behaviors are rationalized by values other than limiting family size (e.g., subincised men are supposedly more attractive to women). Others (such as child abandonment or infanticide and bride murder) are illicit or illegal, although, in some societies, rarely prosecuted.

Intentional family-size limitation and cultural patterns that support it keep population size in balance with resources. Societies lacking self-regulating mechanisms will grow beyond the carrying capacity of their environment and finally disperse or die off.

The great virtue of modern contraception is to offer a humane alternative to such practices. Its shortcoming is that only women or couples who expressly intend to limit childbearing are likely to use it. Total and easy

People who are able to regulate the size of their families often benefit financially and have adequate resources to live well. Raising a child to age 17 cost between $130,000 and $260,000 in 1995. (© Melanie Carr/First Image West, Inc)

access to modern contraception would probably reduce childbearing by only one-third of the amount needed to bring Third World fertility to a level where parents just replace themselves in the population.

Population policies promulgated by governments, whether pro- or antinatalist, have been somewhat ineffective in gaining public compliance. For example, the later Roman emperors as well as the recent dictator of Romania, Nikolae Ceausescu, pursued aggressively pronatalist policies; but people two thousand years apart in time reacted similarly to their deteriorating economies by avoiding family responsibilities. Likewise, government-sponsored family planning programs fail without incentives which reinforce a desire for small family size.

People want more children when they perceive expanding economic opportunity. Conversely, a sense of limited resources is an incentive for marital and reproductive caution. Government encouragement of small family size is often undermined by the simultaneous subsidy of consumer goods and social services.

AIDS and other endemic diseases can slow population growth. Even in high-fertility countries in Africa, AIDS is expected to stop population growth by the year 2020. Rwanda, Sudan, and other countries experiencing economic downturns since about 1980 have seen fertility rates decline as much as 25 percent in the decade. In Asia, Myanmar has had a similar experience. In Myanmar and Sudan, where less than 10 percent of couples use modern contraception, the decline is attributed to delaying marriage.

[See also Abortion; Artificial Life; Demography; Divorce; Families and Households; Family Patterns; Family Problems; Family Values; Population Growth: United States; Population Growth: Worldwide; Sexual Behavior; Sexual Codes; Sexual Reproduction; Sexual Reproduction: Artificial Means.]

BIBLIOGRAPHY

Abernethy, Virginia Deane. *Population Politics: The Choices That Shape Our Future.* New York: Plenum Press (Insight Books), 1993.
Demeny, Paul. "Social Science and Population Policy." *Population and Development Review* 14 (1988): 451–480.
Nag, Moni. *Factors Affecting Human Fertility in Nonindustrial Societies: A Cross Cultural Study.* New Haven: Human Relations Area Files, 1968.

— VIRGINIA DEANE ABERNETHY

FAMILY PROBLEMS

The future social problems of American families already are on the horizon. Families will become further divided between haves and have-nots. Women with children will be increasingly estranged from the men who fathered those children, and this will deepen the eco-

nomic and social divisions between the sexes. However, even families that have two parents will struggle to integrate two jobs in a rigid work environment while attempting, simultaneously, to care for children.

Haves and Have-Nots: Homeless Families and Childhood Hunger

There has been an increasing polarization of the rich and the poor, resulting in wide discrepancies between the classes' standards of living. For the poor, this has resulted in the creation of seemingly inescapable conditions of social inequity. Homelessness increased fourfold during the 1980s. Families make up almost 40 percent of the estimated half-million homeless population. These families suffer higher infant mortality rates and their children have a harder time in school.

Struggles to make ends meet are not, however, limited to the homeless. Half of all food stamp recipients are children. In Massachusetts, for example, one in four children under the age of twelve is affected by hunger. Large numbers of the working poor are having difficulty feeding their families. Furthermore, parental unemployment, coupled with cuts in state and local aid, have contributed to childhood hunger. The percentage of children living in poverty will continue to rise unless there is some mechanism for further economic redistribution.

Female Heads of Household: Teen Mothers and Divorced Women

It is increasingly the norm for children to spend a portion of their lives with only one parent—usually their mothers. This development is driven by growth in the size of two groups: teen mothers who may eventually (though not necessarily) marry the fathers of their children; and divorced women who may remarry some other men. Men are increasingly absent or transient members of these households.

Poverty among teen mothers is the major reason why childbearing among this age group has become a social problem. The alternatives have recently been framed as continuing support for welfare versus placing the children of these mothers in orphanages in order to break the cycle of teen pregnancy (and intergenerational poverty). However, pregnancy does not cause poverty. These teens were already poor when they became pregnant. Teenage pregnancy has soared, particularly for African-American teens, but it is also increasingly common among white teens. The social stigma of being an "unwed mother" no longer exists or is waning. In addition, the foster care system commonly used by teen mothers is strained, and in some cities the system is unable to handle the large numbers of children in it.

Children pay the price—emotionally and socially—of constantly living in limbo between biological mothers and foster care or between foster care placements.

Policy makers view teen mothers as both victims and creators of their own fate. Some scholars and politicians have argued that the problems of inner-city teens could be solved by providing meaningful jobs for the men. The assumption is that if men had employment that paid a decent wage, they would marry, thus returning the family to a nuclear form of a breadwinner husband and stay-at-home mother. Perhaps this would happen. It remains unclear, however, why men would share their wages with women. What is needed are jobs for women, in order for women to be able to support themselves and their children. Returning women to dependence on men for economic survival is not likely to happen among this welfare group unless the men are given jobs that pay a family wage, something that was long ago eroded. Fatherless homes have higher crime rates, lower educational attainment, and more women and children on welfare—leading to more and more children in the United States living in poverty.

In virtually half of all first marriages and among the divorced, most men abandon the responsibilities of parenthood and fail to pay child support. As a result, women and their children are rapidly becoming segregated economically from their former husbands, particularly among the middle class. Regardless of how they became single mothers, women and children—of all races—are more likely to live in poverty when men are not present. Fathers who do pay child support may spend more time visiting with children, and they often are involved in decisions about their children's lives. However, there is no national policy to enforce child support payments even though social pressure to do so does exist. Efforts are underway to see to it that as a last resort fathers are made to pay up, have their wages attached and garnished, or are arrested for failure to pay.

When men remarry, they remain biological parents to children they do not live with and become social parents to the children of the women whom they remarry. Such families become networks and chains of relations, which are built more upon social ties than upon biological ones. The legal system has yet to formalize these social ties or to give step-family parents legal rights or (economic) responsibilities for these children.

Dual Earner Couples: Asymmetry in Gender Relations

Among married couples today, there is a strain to find adequate jobs, to care for children, and still find time for one another, an increasing but largely unacknowl-

edged social problem. An ideology of equality in marriage is what most newlyweds want, but they find it far from easy to achieve. Women remain the primary childcare providers and continue to do more housework than men. Partly, this is due to the economic reality that women, overall, are paid less than men for doing the same or comparable work. Only a very small percentage of women in the United States—those at opposite ends of the economic continuum—equal or exceed their spouse's earnings. Men are still considered the primary breadwinners, even though women's incomes have become essential to the family's remaining in the middle class. As a result, this pattern of women's employment being of "lesser value," coupled with their continued responsibility for the home and children, makes marriage far from an equal institution.

The social stigma of being an "unwed mother"

no longer exists or is waning.

Among those couples who are economically positioned to choose, women have a broader range of options. They can choose full-time or part-time motherhood. Or they can choose full-time or part-time employment, coupled with some type of day-care. Men's choices are much more constrained: house husbands remain rare. As more men embrace the nurturing of children as an important part of their fathering, they may broaden their view of themselves as caring for their family through their economic contributions and may assume a fuller range of possibilities. In that case women will no longer be the sole socio-emotional conduits of family life. In order for this symmetry in gender relations to occur two related arenas must change: (1) The care of children and household tasks must be equally shared by women and men. (2) Women must be viewed as essential and permanent labor force participants if the sexual division of labor and the devaluation of women's work is to change. The linchpins of dual-earner couples' abilities to integrate their family lives with employment will be employment policies that are family-friendly as well as changes in childcare provisions.

Day Care and Afterschool Programs: The Raising of the Next Generation of Children

Day care remains a leading social problem that families face, regardless of whether the family has two employed parents or is comprised of only one parent—mother or father—living with children. Parents are left to solve this problem by taking personal responsibility for and finding suitable solutions. The responsibility might be passed along to other providers. Since there is no comprehensive national family policy, couples are left to piece together suitable ways to cover child care while trying to meet the requirements set by their employers. In order for parents to give their utmost to their jobs, they need to feel that their children are cared for in safe and loving environments. One of the critical problems in this country is the lack of sufficient child care facilities or arrangements and the failure to regulate such child care. Unlike the day care offered in other industrialized nations, the care that does exist in the United States is not subsidized by the government, nor is parental leave sufficient to cover infant and toddler care. Workplaces are coming around to acknowledging that their employees are parents by becoming more family-friendly. For example, some already provide adequate parental leaves to cover the early years and arrange on-site day care facilities or vouchers for community day care; some also accommodate elder care arrangements and sick leaves. Public policy debates, at bottom, strive to delineate institutional roles—or those of employers, employees, and government itself. Without changes in an inflexible workplace, parents will be caught between their obligations to family and the demands of employers.

The educational system in the United States also may become increasingly involved in caring for children. At the present there is a lack of before-school and after-school programs. In addition, the school calendar leaves parents without child care for about three months a year. The problem society faces is who will provide all the various child care activities, and how are we going to raise the next generation of children? What kind of care arrangements are best for young children with employed parents? The private and often piecemeal ways that families try to care for their children, and the nature and scope of new arrangements, will be a matter of continuing public debate until those issues are satisfactorily resolved.

[See also Child Care; Children, Living Arrangements; Family Values; Women and Work.]

BIBLIOGRAPHY

Arendell, Terry. *Mothers and Divorce: Legal, Economic, and Social Dilemmas.* Berkeley, CA, and London: University of California Press, 1986.

Hertz, Rosanna. *More Equal Than Others: Women and Men in Dual-Career Marriages.* Berkeley, CA, and London: University of California Press, 1986.

Kozol, Jonathan. *Rachel and Her Children: Homeless Families in America.* New York: Fawcett Columbine, 1988.

Williams, Constance Willard. *Black Teenage Mothers: Pregnancy and Childrearing from Their Perspective.* Lexington, MA: Lexington Books, 1991.

— ROSANNA HERTZ

FAMILY VALUES

The family values debate in America began with a bang in 1965 when a young assistant secretary of labor in the administration of President Lyndon B. Johnson called attention to the growing number of black children being born into fatherless families. The so-called Moynihan Report, named for author Daniel Patrick Moynihan, who would later be elected to the U.S. Senate, issued a prophetic warning: "A community that allows a large number of young men to grow up in broken families, dominated by women, never acquiring any stable relationship to male authority, never acquiring any set of rational expectations about the future, that community asks for and gets chaos."

That early warning went unheeded. The Moynihan report provoked such a firestorm of protest—with critics unfairly accusing the author of racism—that for more than a quarter of a century the subject of family breakdown became a taboo topic for public discussion. By the early 1990s, when public attention again focused on the problem of fatherless children, the situation had worsened dramatically. Official data showed a soaring number of births to unmarried women of all races and in every social class. By 1991, nearly 30 percent of all births in the United States were to unmarried mothers—about five times what the rate had been only thirty years earlier. Over the same period, the divorce rate almost tripled as well.

The combination of these two trends has produced a social revolution unprecedented in American history. Some experts estimate that fewer than 40 percent of the children born in the decade of the 1990s will have both a mother and a father at home throughout the first eighteen years of their lives.

The widespread breakdown of the traditional family has grim consequences, both for the children who are denied the support and guidance of two parents and for the broader society in which they live. While a small but influential group of elites has attempted to defend the single-parent family as an alternative lifestyle, or as a progressive experiment in nontraditional family forms, a mountain of evidence has accumulated to show that children in single-parent homes have the deck stacked against them.

Fatherless children are disproportionately likely to live in poverty and to lead disordered lives, including as violent criminals. Consider just a few figures: Almost half of all fatherless families receive some form of financial assistance from government. The comparable figure for families with two parents is under 10 percent. Girls who grow up in households without a father are roughly 50 percent more likely to become pregnant out of wedlock than girls who do have a father at home. Nearly two-thirds of the juveniles convicted of rape and three-quarters of those convicted of murder come from fatherless homes. Indeed, more than 70 percent of juvenile criminals who have been imprisoned or institutionalized come from single-parent families.

Fatherless children are disproportionately likely to live in poverty and to lead disordered lives, including as violent criminals.

All of these figures, it should be emphasized, are probabilities or averages. There have always been, and always will be exceptions—children who grow up without both parents certainly can succeed in life. Many always have and many will continue to do so. It should also be emphasized that the millions of women who are struggling, often heroically, to raise their children alone are not necessarily bad parents. They are not the ones who have abandoned their children, shirked their duties, and refused to shoulder the obligations of parenthood.

The urgent question as we look ahead to the twenty-first century is how to reverse these destructive trends. This is a pressing issue not just in the United States but in many industrialized nations, where the illegitimacy rates, while lower than in the U.S., are also rising rapidly.

A combination of private and public efforts will clearly be required. While the rise of the modern welfare state has accompanied the breakdown of the family—and has probably contributed to the problem by cushioning the extreme hardship that once was the common fate of fatherless families—scholars disagree about the precise cause and effect. And even those who attribute a large part of the responsibility for family breakdown to government programs that provide financial support to single-parent households are uncertain whether the ethic of self-sacrifice and obligation that once held families together "for the sake of the children" can be revived even by radical reforms of the welfare system.

The decision to bear children responsibly and to sacrifice for their well-being is fundamentally a matter of personal character and morality. Individuals ultimately must resolve to do the right thing; government, however, can reasonably be expected to encourage those who make the right choices and to discourage those whose irresponsibility profoundly harms the prospects of their children and the health of the larger society. Deliberations over public policy in the years ahead will be increasingly devoted to the question of how precisely government can meet this challenge.

Since the collapse of the Soviet empire at the end of the 1980s, the American people have focused increasingly on this domestic challenge. Their confidence in the future, as expressed in numerous public opinion polls, has been shaken by their recognition that the epidemic rates of illegitimacy and family breakdown have created a society adrift in uncharted waters.

Yet there is reason to believe that Americans will rise to meet this challenge, as they have met other challenges in the past—with sustained personal and community efforts, inspired by their traditional belief in a better future. A heartening number of private, voluntary organizations have already arisen, aiming in different ways to encourage parental responsibility. Some emphasize moral obligations; others aim to provide job training and counseling to unemployed, unmarried young fathers. Still others focus on instilling virtue in young people through traditional religious teachings, encouraging them to marry before having children. These private efforts may hold the best long-term hope for reweaving a social fabric in which two-parent families are the norm.

Twenty years from now—fully a half century since the Moynihan report—America will still be facing the consequences of family breakdown. Daniel Patrick Moynihan's original warning, however, will no longer be controversial. It is customary to think of the future in terms of the novelties it will bring—new technologies, or things that are bigger, better, faster, or simply different than what we are accustomed to. When it comes to the family, however, the America of tomorrow will be a place that has restored the primacy of an institution as old as mankind itself: the tried and true model of the mother and father raising children. The family of the future will look a lot like the family of the past.

[See also Abortion; Child Abuse; Divorce; Families and Households; Family Planning; Family Problems; Marriage; Sexual Behavior; Sexual Codes; Sexual Laws; Social Change: United States; Women's Movement.]

BIBLIOGRAPHY

Blankenhorn, David. *Fatherless America: Confronting Our Most Urgent Social Problem.* New York: Basic Books, 1995.
Himmelfarb, Gertrude. *The De-Moralization of Society: From Victorian Virtues to Modern Values.* New York: Alfred A. Knopf, 1995.

Moynihan, Daniel Patrick. *The Negro Family: The Case for National Action.* Washington, DC: U.S. Department of Labor, 1965.

Whitehead, Barbara Dafoc. "Dan Quayle Was Right." *Atlantic Monthly* (April 1993).

– DAN QUAYLE

FARM POLICY

Farm policy is, generally speaking, the course of action taken by the federal government with respect to farmers and farming, particularly to maintain farm income. Ever since the days when George Washington advocated the establishment of an agency devoted to the welfare of farmers, the government has adopted policies favoring farmers. However, as the twenty-first century approaches there has been a change in attitudes. Perhaps this shift occurred because when Washington was president over 90 percent of Americans made their living from agriculture, while two centuries later less than 2 percent of workers are engaged in farming.

Major policies respecting agriculture have for the most part been adopted during two periods in American history, first in the year 1862 and second in the decade of the 1930s. Although modified in many respects, the legislation passed during these two periods remains the basis of American farm policy. However, in the near future, in part because of the declining numbers of farmers and, indeed, of the success of the past programs, there will be substantial modifications in the farm subsidy programs and pressure for elimination of the Department of Agriculture.

In 1862, President Abraham Lincoln signed three laws primarily devoted to the welfare of family farmers. The first provided for a Department of Agriculture; the second granted 160 acres of unclaimed federal lands to any person who would settle on and farm them; and the third granted federal lands to the states for the purpose of establishing colleges to teach agriculture, mechanical engineering, and the military arts.

The second series of laws was passed during the New Deal of the 1930s. The Agricultural Adjustment Act, signed by President Franklin D. Roosevelt on May 12, 1933, offered farmers specific prices, called parity or fair prices, for compliance with production controls. Invalidated by the Supreme Court, this act was replaced by acts in 1936, 1938, and 1949. The acts of 1938 and 1949, with modifications, are still in effect almost fifty years later.

Most agricultural subsidy programs in the 1990s and beyond will be of an indirect nature, such as the assistance offered farmers by county agents and the increased demand for farm products resulting from the school lunch and food stamp programs, although the county agent program will be substantially reduced or even eliminated by the turn of the century. Some programs, such as the Reclamation Act of 1903, which provided many farmers with irrigated lands, have a long-term impact and are also indirect in nature.

Price support, also known as commodity stabilization, and soil conservation programs are the most direct in nature. Commodity stabilization is sought through commodity loans, purchases, and payments to eligible producers. Basically, if prices in the marketplace do not reach a particular level, farmers who have allotments from a past history of producing the commodity receive direct payments to make up the difference between what they receive in the marketplace and what they should receive by law. Only crops specified by law are supported. While the list has varied over the years, few animal products have been supported since World War II.

The Soil Conservation Service is concerned with preserving the soil and water of the nation. Its local agents work directly with farm groups and with individual farmers to develop programs for soil preservation and water conservation. As the century nears its end, the service and farmers are urged by groups concerned with natural resource preservation to cut back on intensive cultivation, the use of fertilizer, and other production stimulants in order to conserve the soil and other resources.

The federal government maintains many programs, including research, regulation, and education, to assist farmers. For example, the Farm Credit Administration, an independent agency, supervises institutions operating under government sponsorship to make credit available to farmers and their credit cooperatives.

Government policy over the years encouraged agricultural exports and protected American farmers from unfair foreign competition. Most of the effort has gone into promoting exports since, except for a few commodities such as seasonal fruits and vegetables and wool, American farm products are competitive in a free market. However, many nations control their imports of farm products. The world prices of those not controlled are sometimes maintained at levels that American farmers cannot compete against.

The Foreign Agricultural Service of the Department of Agriculture and the Agency for International Development are both concerned with exports of agricultural products, the Foreign Agricultural Service mainly from a commercial viewpoint and the Agency for International Development mainly from an humanitarian viewpoint. Both have responsibilities under the Agricultural Trade and Development Act of 1954, known as Public Law 480, passed primarily to help rid the government of surplus commodities. The law authorized the government to make agreements for the sale of farm products for foreign currency, to make shipments for emergency relief and other aid, and to barter farm products for needed materials. P.L. 480 proved so valuable that, in a modified form, it has been extended into the 1990s and doubtless will be further extended, but it has been far from a complete answer to the surplus problem. However, the emergency relief and similar programs have saved and improved the lives of many people around the world.

U.S. farm policies will undergo major changes

by the turn of the century, possibly including

the elimination of direct subsidy payments.

The Foreign Agricultural Service collects and makes available information on agricultural production in other countries, advises commercial exporters, makes subsidies available to producers or exporters who are suffering from unfair trade practices abroad, and, in general, aids in the export of American farm products. Farm products made up some 20 percent of America's total exports in 1980, but the figure fell to 10 percent in 1992. Farm organizations usually look with favor on international agreements promoting free trade but are wary of the importation of commodities subsidized by other nations.

The GATT Uruguay Round trade agreement proposed the countries mutually dismantle agricultural subsidy programs that artificially skew international commerce. The Blair House accord called for subsidized agricultural exports to be cut by 21 percent in volume (measured against the 1986–1990 base period), and by 36 percent in value; in addition, domestic subsidies were to be cut by 20 percent over six years. Changes are in prospect.

How much farm support programs cost varies from year to year. Direct agricultural support payments averaged about $10 billion a year during the early 1990s. Global cost estimates incurred by the industrial nations of the world mounted to $150 billion.

U.S. farm policies, a patchwork whole made up of literally hundreds of programs and policies, will undergo major changes by the turn of the century, possibly including the elimination of direct subsidy payments. Cost considerations are likely to impose substantial changes, even though the policies and programs result in lower food costs to the consumer. At the same time, future farm policies will keep farmers a small minority of the population and will continue to replace a dis-

tinctly rural system with the values of industrial capitalism.

[See also Alcohol; Animal Rights; Fisheries; Food and Agriculture; Food and Drug Safety; Food Laws; Food Technologies; Food and Fiber Production; Forestry; Genetics: Agricultural Applications; Nutrition; Tobacco.]

BIBLIOGRAPHY

Baker, Gladys L.; Rasmussen, Wayne D.; Wiser, Vivian; and Porter, Jane M. *Century of Service: The First 100 Years of the United States Department of Agriculture.* Washington, DC: U.S. Department of Agriculture, 1963.
Cochrane, Willard W. *The Development of American Agriculture: A Historical Analysis,* 2nd ed. Minneapolis: University of Minnesota Press, 1993.
Hallam, Arne, ed. *Size, Structure, and the Changing Face of American Agriculture.* Boulder, CO: Westview Press, 1993.
Rasmussen, Wayne D. *American Agriculture: A Documentary History.* 4 vols. New York: Random House, 1975.
———. *Taking the University to The People; Seventy-five Years of Cooperative Extension.* Ames, IA: Iowa State University Press, 1989.

— WAYNE D. RASMUSSEN

FEMINIZATION OF POVERTY.

See POVERTY, FEMINIZATION OF.

FINANCIAL INSTITUTIONS

Financial services solve business problems, fuel economic growth, and help bring the world closer together. They also can contribute to inflation and instability. As a result, they operate under a highly regulated structure that, in the United States in particular, separates the functions of traditional types of organizations. In the 1980s the separation of powers began to weaken. Dramatic changes occurred in the United Kingdom and Canada, moving them closer in structure to the universal banking systems of continental Europe. The U.S. banking structure has responded slowly to international competition, technology, and a climate in which market forces generally are allowed to have greater reign. Nevertheless, the United States is leading in the extensive financial innovation that this climate engenders.

Financial Innovations

Financial innovations are making it easier to reduce the risks associated with doing business internationally, to make assets more liquid, to economize on capital, and to overcome distance and time. Securitization of assets, which allows financial institutions to sell assets so they can relend the same money, has become commonplace in the United States and has started to become important in Europe and elsewhere. Derivatives and related risk management products (such as options, futures, and interest rate and currency swaps) enable the parties to a transaction to insulate themselves to a degree from fluctuations in interest rates, exchange rates, and securities prices while locking in desired patterns of cash flow. Investment pools have grown to facilitate markets for products from high-grade investment paper to below investment-grade securities and to create vehicles through which institutional investors such as pensions and life insurance companies can easily place funds.

In the future, accepted financial solutions will be more widely used. Impending innovations will allow financing for longer periods of time, provide greater protection against inflation, provide guarantees for funds invested in engineering construction megaprojects, and create much larger risk pools to allow diversification of risky investments—particularly in formerly socialist countries, new industries, and emerging nations.

Technology is at the heart of the revolution in financial services. Powerful and low-cost computers and communications have led to the growth of computer screen-based trading; regional, national and international credit card systems; ATM (automated teller) machines; and electronic data exchange for ordering, shipping, and bill-paying.

The rise of the Internet and the spread of the personal computer, along with developments in software for financial analysis and database management, will enable a new level of electronic banking and merchandising for individuals and businesses. Increasingly sophisticated consumers will do more for themselves, and more of what they do will be done electronically. The United States will remain the leader in creating and promoting new financial instruments and arrangements and increasingly will export its techniques and services to the rest of the world.

U.S. Banks

Financial sectors are subject to their own special pressures and trends. The business of banking has changed dramatically with the advent of money funds, the growth of mutual funds, and the expansion of 401-K plans and other defined contribution pension arrangements. Despite the lifting of interest rate ceilings on deposit interest rates and the creation of certificates of deposit, the banking industry's share of consumer financial assets has declined, particularly for savings and loan associations and savings banks. Higher capital requirements after earlier misadventures with real estate and other loans have raised costs and hampered the competitiveness of banks and S&Ls as holders of assets. No longer as able to profit from intermediating low-cost deposits into loans, and faced with slower mortgage lending as baby boomers passed homebuying age, banks

have expanded fee-income. They have increased the charges for many services to offset the need to pay market interest rates. And they have restructured to make more effective use of assets and provide additional fee-based services.

Banks have created securities pools for fees and sold them to lend again. Larger banks have become more involved in offering risk management services. They have taken on more consumer risk through the expansion of credit cards, which also are an important source of fee-income. Some have provided transaction and other technology-based services, often to other banks.

At times banks have taken on more risk, lending mortgages long term while sources of funds were relatively short term, lending large sums to Third World nations at low margins, lending heavily to real estate developers, lending for mergers and acquisitions, and trading for their own accounts. Banks and S&Ls have gotten into major trouble periodically. As they become more sophisticated and large enough to average some risks internally, it is to be hoped they will not pose new threats for the financial system—but new temptations and unknowns tend to foster history repeating itself.

Banks will continue to consolidate, to move interstate by acquisition under new legislation, and, as permitted, will pursue de novo branching. They will expand further in providing fee-based services to companies, and will provide a growing array of products to consumers through securities subsidiaries. Annuities will be a source of particular growth. Banks will continue to automate and provide enhanced automated analysis and advice, transaction services, and investing. Holding companies will be allowed to operate full-service securities firms and investment banks in subsidiaries, and eventually they will have a growing role in insurance sales and possibly in underwriting. However, it is unlikely that commercial and industrial firms will be allowed to own banks.

U.S. Securities Firms

Securities firms make their money from a combination of selling securities, underwriting, trading for their own account, and doing deals such as mergers. The industry is composed of firms that specialize in one or more of these functions and large, multiline firms. Since trading commissions were deregulated in 1975, discount brokers have taken market share from other financial houses. The largest discounters have emerged as major offerers of their own mutual funds. There also has been pressure on commissions for underwriting and trading as electronics and global markets have advanced.

Many securities firms have sought additional income in the market for corporate restructuring. Some, especially boutiques such as Kohlberg, Kravis and Roberts, have taken increasingly large equity and "junk bond" positions in commercial and industrial companies, which they hold for some time and later try to sell. This model is more akin to traditional European investment banking and to banking in the United States before the Glass Steagall Act of 1933 separated securities and bank powers. Securities firms also have become quite active in the international arena, including emerging markets. They and mutual fund companies have created numerous investment pools that allow investors to diversify among investments and take advantage of their expertise.

Ownership of unrelated businesses and internationalization will shape the securities industry in the years ahead. So will the acquisition by banks as banking powers are revised. Many of the largest securities firms already are owned by life insurance or other financial firms. The extent of conglomeration will largely depend on whether holding companies that own banks are allowed to own insurance companies.

U.S. Insurance Companies

Insurance companies are adjusting to their heavy real estate losses of the 1980s and a climate of slow growth in life insurance. They are making the transition from selling insurance to cover family needs after death to preparing people for the prospect of long life. An increase of twenty years in the average remaining life expectancy for persons at age sixty-five, together with an average retirement age of sixty-three, have produced a greater need for retirement savings. It has also become more important to have an orderly system of pension withdrawals through annuities, either built into a pension or sold separately, that guarantee payment no matter how long one lives. Life insurance products continue to benefit from important tax advantages: Death benefits are not taxable, and the buildup of investment income in an annuity is only taxed when the funds are withdrawn. The rules may change somewhat, but there are likely to be important continuing tax benefits.

The property/casualty side of the insurance business has had difficulty from increased consumer-oriented regulation and large disasters. However, there are signs that the cycles (as distinct from the supplies) the industry experiences may be moderating, at least for a while. Also new risk coverage needs are evolving. It is likely that in the next generation we will find the amount of insurance business related to computers and communications will become as large as the motor vehicle-related market, which traditionally accounted for 40 to 50 percent of the sector business.

Insurance companies also are taking on a new role in the health field. The traditional claims-based profit center is being supplanted by managed care, with large insurers not only underwriting risks and investing premiums but also operating managed care health delivery systems tied to their insurance plans. Insurers could find some of their role taken over by the government, but it is more likely the government will turn to the industry to handle the system, as it did with Medicare; this time both (1) to enroll and pay and (2) to manage and operate managed care networks that serve the public.

International Financial Services and Capital Flows

European integration has spurred cross-industry and cross-national alliances and mergers in financial services. Universal banking that combines banking, insurance, and brokerage has spread. The United States and Japan have been laggards but are likely to follow. U.S. banks are puny in size compared to those of Europe and Japan—only a half dozen have assets of $100 billion or more compared to banks with $400 billion or more in Europe and Japan. The United States will create many large conglomerates to compete internationally and the efforts of U.S. financial firms will turn more international. Internationalization will mean the expansion of financial firms across regions and between the developed and the developing world. New financial centers will continue to emerge alongside New York, London, and Tokyo in continental Europe, Singapore and other parts of Asia, Latin America, and Africa. Electronic financial services increasingly will be cross-border for households as well as businesses.

Insurance companies are making the transition from selling insurance to cover family needs after death to preparing people for the prospect of long life.

Capital flows will rise rapidly with long-term world recovery. Net capital flows tended to occur almost entirely among developed countries in 1980s. The coming decades will see a great rise in capital flows to and from the developing world and among its members with the spread of regional arrangements. There may be global capital shortages from time to time as demands of world growth put pressure on available savings. The financial markets will continue to innovate to solve problems such as managing the risks and needs inherent in international markets and in long-term global economic development.

[See also Capital Formation; Credit, Debt, and Borrowing; Economics; Informal Economy; Insurance; International Governance and Regional Authorities; Investments; Public Finance.]

BIBLIOGRAPHY

Federal Reserve Bank of New York. *International Competitiveness of U.S. Financial Firms.* New York: Federal Reserve Bank of New York, 1992.
International Capital Markets. Washington, DC: International Monetary Fund (annual).
Market 2000: An Examination of Current Equity Market Developments. Washington, DC: U.S. Securities and Exchange Commission, 1994.
World Bank. *Financial Systems and Development, World Development Report, 1989,* Washington, DC: The World Bank, 1989.

— IRVING LEVESON

FISHERIES

About 8 percent of the animal proteins consumed in the United States are fish and shellfish. The U.S. industry produced a record 11 billion pounds in 1993, doubling volume during a steady growth period that began in 1977 after establishment of a 200-mile Exclusive Economic Zone encompassing all coastal waters. Globally, fish production grew steadily from the 1950s to the late 1980s, plateauing at about one hundred million metric tons.

Despite the growth, troubling signs have appeared in many fishery resources. The once rich, traditional cod, haddock, and flounder resources off New England have slipped badly. Major stocks in the Chesapeake have dwindled, and salmon runs in California, Oregon, and Washington have declined, some to the point of endangerment.

The declines occurred despite a fisheries management system that sets quotas and other limits on the harvest. The system has been very successful in some fisheries but a failure in others as overly optimistic quotas, unanticipated environmental conditions, and habitat destruction have taken a toll. Faltering catches are generating new approaches to fisheries management, technology, and practice internationally and domestically.

Overfishing, Overcapacity

The world's fishing fleets, including those in the United States, are grossly overcapitalized, with far more capacity than is needed. The U.S. marine fisheries traditionally have been open to all citizens; anyone with a boat can try to make a living by catching fish. Conservation and management controls are in the form of industry-wide quotas, with seasonal and gear-type restrictions.

Since difficulties in maintaining fish stocks at maximum yield levels are attributed in part to the overcapacity resulting from open access policies, limited access schemes such as Individual Transferable Quotas (ITQ) are being established. Vessel owners are given rights to a certain percentage of the allowable harvest. These rights, in turn, may be sold or leased. The evolution of open access to individual quotas will inevitably lead to fees from the fishermen to the government to pay for costs associated with managing the fishery, and perhaps lead also to the collection of an economic rent. Even in those fisheries where limited access is not feasible, resource management agencies will implement more restrictive conservation measures.

A precautionary approach is being built into management plans to provide greater assurance against resource depletion. The precautionary approach to resource utilization is finding its way into international fisheries as well. The United Nations is continuously working on multilateral agreements to control fishing in international waters. Some of these will give coastal nations more controls beyond the 200-mile lines.

International concerns over resource depletion and the need for more production to feed growing populations are creating pressure for more selectivity in fishing. As much as 27 percent of fish caught in nets are discarded at sea because they are undesirable species, too small, or restricted by law. Discards become part of the food chain, avoiding biological waste. Yet the pressure for more conservation is intensifying research on more-selective fishing technology. Devices are being developed for insertion in nets to allow non-target fish to escape.

Aquaculture

Even with more effective fisheries management and selectivity, catches from the oceans will not keep pace with fish consumption needs, spurring greatly increased aquaculture production. U.S. aquaculture operations in 1994 produced an estimated one billion pounds of such species as catfish, trout, salmon, shrimp, and striped bass. Throughout the world, aquaculture grew at a compounded rate of 9 percent a year in the 1980s, reaching 16 percent of overall fish production by 1993.

Continued aquaculture growth is dependent on extensive capital investment, primarily in tropical and subtropical areas. Health authority approval of therapeutants necessary to control disease in intensive culture environments will enhance production. Fish-dependent nations will invest more in stock enhancement programs whereby fish are raised in hatcheries to their juvenile life stage and then released to the oceans, protecting the fish during the early life stage when they are most vulnerable to predation.

Whales and Other Marine Mammals

Once a major target species of many fishing nations, whales have been given special protection. Only small harvests are allowed for aboriginal peoples. The conservation has resulted in healthier whale stocks generally, with some species in great abundance.

Eventually commercial harvest on a limited basis will be resumed by nations with a whaling tradition. Unchecked growth of protected seal herds will create renewed pressure to control the populations of animals whose predation has a major impact on fish populations needed for human food.

[See also Acid Rain; Animal Rights; Biodiversity; Food and Fiber Production; Freshwater; Global Environmental Problems; Hazardous Wastes; Oceans; Ozone Layer Depletion; Resources; Sustainability.]

BIBLIOGRAPHY

Aquaculture Situation and Outlook. Washington, DC: U.S. Department of Agriculture, 1994.
Fisheries of the United States. Washington, DC: U.S. Department of Commerce, 1994.
The State of World Fisheries and Aquaculture. Rome: Food and Agriculture Organization of the United Nations, 1994.

— LEE J. WEDDIG

FITNESS.

See EXERCISE AND FITNESS.

FOOD ADDITIVES

From almost the beginning, the human species has been involved in a constant struggle to ensure a safe and abundant food supply. Described often as a war, the conflict results from the fact that humans have no natural right to the bounties of nature, but have to compete with rats, mice, locusts, molds, viruses, and bacteria. Among the successful weapons that human society have developed are various chemical additives. Fermentation, salting, and smoking are only a few of the ways in which early societies used chemicals to preserve food. Moreover, these additives not only protect the food, but also improve its nutritive value and palatability. Food is not food until someone eats it. Taste, flavor, texture, and odor are all essential components influencing the acceptability of food. In their concern over the chemicals in food, the public often forgets these aspects of food additives. It is clear that to efficiently supply an increasingly urbanized society with adequate food, many new food formulations will have to be devised: to be nutri-

tionally adequate, to present a variety of organoleptic characteristics, and at the same time to ensure their safety.

Modern biology is spectacularly increasing the possibility of modifying traditional foods and developing new food sources and ingredients to meet newly defined health needs.

Modern biology is spectacularly increasing the possibility of modifying traditional foods and developing new food sources and ingredients to meet newly defined health needs. For the first time the scientific community has the opportunity to design and construct foods having specially desired characteristics based on a more refined definition of human health and nutrition requirements. In other words, new food sources not only meet these newly defined, precise health needs, but are also optimal for the particular environment in which the consumer is living and in which the food is to be grown. The essence of good diet is the consumption of a variety of foods, not food components. The target needs to be to change the nature of foods, rather than to simply add individual nutrients.

It is possible to divide these new foods and additives into several broad categories:

1. Foods that traditionally are not widely used as food, such as foods derived from yeast.
2. Products constructed from food materials that have rarely been used as foods, such as certain fungi.
3. Formulations constructed largely of the products of chemical synthesis or the physical modifications of traditional foods such as artificial sweeteners and fat substitutes.
4. Products constructed from or consisting of organisms resulting from genetic manipulations. These will include such things as food enzymes having greater stability or better control and new plant cultivars having special characteristics such as better shipping qualities. They may provide better flavor or better profiles or allow many new environments in which the plant could flourish.
5. New packaging materials that offer better protection of the food from the environment. At the same time, these new products will themselves be environmentally friendly. These new packaging materials will permit the movement of gases in and out of the food package in a controlled manner, thus ensuring the quality of the food. Moreover, such packages will contain indicators to demonstrate when the integrity of the package has been broken or when the food has become contaminated with pathogenic organisms. It is also possible that these packages can be designed to combine with new, unique processing methods to produce room-temperature shelf-stable food, thus reducing the number of products requiring refrigeration or freezer storage.

A comment must be made about the safety of these new materials. The public is concerned about modification of their food supply. The same science that will develop these new products will also provide the basis for more accurate and predictable tests for food safety. Not only will it ensure better control over microbial contamination of foods (the greatest threat to human health), but also it will provide the means to better predict the potential toxicity of chemical substances added to food or the safety of new plant and animal varieties.

Over the past two hundred years it has become increasingly evident that diet plays a significant role in human health. Modern food science with its ability to modify existing plant and animal species and to construct new food materials based upon more precise knowledge of human metabolism and needs will bring human society something it has only dreamed of: a supply of high-quality food that will not only nourish but also improve the health of the public.

[See also Chemicals, Fine; Food and Drug Safety; Food Laws; Food Technologies; Genetics: Commercialization; New Consumer Products; Nutrition; Soil Conditions; Tobacco.]

BIBLIOGRAPHY

Goodman, David, and Redclift, Michael. *Refashioning Nature*. New York: Routledge, 1992.
Lewis, Richard J. *Food Additives Handbook*. New York: Van Nostrand Reinhold, 1989.
Saulson, Donald S., and Saulson, Elizabeth M. *A Pocket Guide to Food Additives*. Huntington Beach, CA: VPS Publishing, 1991.

— SANFORD A. MILLER

FOOD AND AGRICULTURE

Food and agriculture will continue to be the world's largest productive industry in the twenty-first century, representing over 50 percent of the total activity in individual regions. It will continue to employ more people, develop more technology, and link providers and consumers with more new products and services. It will continue to improve as agriculture moves from the "green revolution" to the "gene revolution" worldwide.

Agriculture operates a highly productive system that provides food, fiber, and timber for basic world sustenance and survival. This system will continue to improve in both industrial and developing countries. But agriculture is shifting its problem-solving talent to the more pressing issues of producing renewable feedstock inputs for basic industries, providing affordable personal health, managing productive ecosystems, and developing thriving communities. In the twenty-first century, agriculture will add four new product services:

1. Fuels, plastics, biochemicals from renewable crop cycles
2. Preventive health, nutrients, vitamins from quality foods
3. Sound productive ecosystems from sustainable conservation
4. Robust rural communities from regional design/development

The 200-Year Agricultural Development Recipe

This can be summarized by the following equation:

$$\text{Agriculture} = \text{Population} + \text{Technology} + \text{Institutions} + \text{Environment}$$

The world's agrifood system is not uniform or monolithic. Each region has its own recipe for development. It depends on the makeup of the population, the availability of technology, the incentive climate of rulemaking institutions, and the natural resource base.

During the past two hundred years agriculture has developed the capacity to supply almost 6 billion cus-

Each region of the world has its own recipe for agricultural development, depending on domestic needs and natural resources. (Tom Bean/Corbis)

tomers. This was a remarkable accomplishment that is now taken for granted. Two hundred years ago, feeding a world of one billion people was a controversial topic. T. R. Malthus and William Godwin debated whether man and science together could manage the Earth without catastrophe. In the 1990s, this same debate continues, but with a different focus. The agrifood system has demonstrated that it can feed a sixfold increase in world population, and now it is developing new technologies to tackle other problems.

"Freedom from want" was the clarion call that has empowered and will empower agriculture from 1800 to 2000. "Sustainable human development" will be the theme for the next century. The evolution of the agriculture industry into the ecoculture industry of the next century will be a bridge between the resource-using, person-replacing technologies of the economic growth era and the resource-renewing, person-enhancing technologies of the sustainable human development era.

The combination of computer and recombinant DNA technology will drive the next generation of agriculture technology.

Quality products and services from the gene revolution will replace the quantity products from the green revolution. The worldwide extension of computers, telecommunications, and biotechnology will provide the operating basis for managing human ecosystems rather than farms.

Agriculture and Renewable Industrial Feedstocks

Genetically engineering new crops and new products is becoming possible with increased computer capacity to process the massive genetic maps of humans, plants, animals, and ecosystems. The combination of computer and recombinant DNA technology will drive the next generation of agriculture technology. This twenty-first-century technology will move agriculture from improved production to improved quality cycles of food, fiber, and timber, as well as new fuels, lubricants, biochemicals, and plastics. This technological shift to bioengineered products will result from the development of a new agro-industrial process relying on renewable crops. The process is already beginning, and laboratory experiments now are exploring a variety of genetic engineering products, such as using tobacco to produce hepatitis B vaccine, the cultivation of milkweed for fuel, and the extraction of renewable chemicals, plastics, inks, and lubricants from oil seeds.

Agriculture and Preventive Health

Access to enough good quality food is basic to providing robust health. Agriculture's green revolution has provided the basis for producing enough food to improve health and longevity. Movement to the gene revolution will continue the ability to produce enough food, but it will also provide the ability to design foods and diets for personal health enhancement. Food processing companies already are designing foods to give athletes peak physical performance, to encourage healthy infant growth, and to provide the vitamins, medicines, and nutrients to improve the health of the sick and the elderly. Mapping the human genome (chromosome structure) by the year 2000 will provide a more complete understanding of the human biosystem. This, together with maps of animal and plant genomes, will provide food-health scientists with the tools to design foods for individual health. A step in this direction is the development of a detailed food specification database at the U.S. Department of Agriculture, which allows any consumer to identify the precise characteristics of any food.

Agriculture and Sustainable Ecosystem Management

Some 80 percent of the world's arable land and water is directly linked to the food-fiber-fishery-forestry system. Conservation of these natural resources is an investment in long-term productivity. But the conservation technology of the past century is now evolving into a total ecosystem technology to deal with cycles that sustain not only soil and water but the entire biotic and human development cycle. New DNA technology and computer science provide the tools that make ecosystem demographics and design possible for the next century. Some experiments are beginning to demonstrate what this new technology can accomplish. Some cities are using aquatic plants and farmland together with municipal effluent and compost to define a new bioindustrial cycle. The utilization of specific crops to remove toxic materials and radioactive waste from contaminated soil demonstrates the use of agricultural processes to deal with manmade waste cycles. With sufficient investment in research, ecosystem technology will turn wastes from one process into inputs to other processes in a closed-loop sustained human development cycle.

Agriculture and Regional Community Development

More than any other industry, agrifood enterprises link families, communities, commerce, and natural resources in a renewable system. This process of using technology to produce a variety of useful products from the biosphere not only creates jobs and businesses, but also supports basic human needs and links families and their communities into regional socioeconomic systems. The entire cycle creates, sustains, and enhances human interplay. It promotes life, growth, development, and security.

[See also Food Additives; Food Consumption; Food Distribution; Food and Drug Safety; Food and Fiber Production; Food Laws; Food Services; Food Technologies; Genetics: Agricultural Applications; Nutrition.]

BIBLIOGRAPHY

Avery, Dennis T. *Global Food Progress.* Indianapolis: Hudson Institute, 1991.

Brown, Lester R., et al. *Vital Signs: The Trends That Are Shaping Our Future.* New York: Norton, 1992.

Food and Agriculture Organization of the United Nations. *1991: The State of Food and Agriculture.* Rome: FAO, 1991.

Office of Technology Assessment, Congress of the United States. *A New Technological Era for American Agriculture.* Publication No. F-474. Washington, DC: OTA, 1992.

Vosti, Stephan A.; Reardon, Thomas; and von Urff, Winfried, eds. *Agricultural Sustainability, Growth, and Poverty Alleviation: Issues and Policies.* Washington, DC: International Food Policy Research Institute; Feldafing, Germany: German Foundation for International Development, 1991.

— WILLIAM E. GAHR

FOOD CONSUMPTION

Food preferences are deeply ingrained, but dietary patterns do change over time. It is reasonable to predict that as new food technologies are perfected and as biomedical science uncovers the benefits and risks to human health of various components of food, people will gradually add new foods and drop others from their meals and snacks.

What people choose, and choose not, to eat is also influenced by:

- Broader economic trends such as the widening gap between affluent people and households with very limited food dollars as well as homeless people and those living in poverty
- The relative importance for various population segments of the health benefits versus taste, convenience, and other attributes of food
- Whether people believe food marketing promises and trust health promotion messages
- Changing values regarding the social role of food in family and interpersonal relationships

Dietary surveys are an effective way of documenting current food intake of consumers, and, to a certain degree, of predicting changes in food consumption patterns. Another less quantitative, but very useful, technique for anticipating future consumer preferences is to analyze what people are reading in the popular press about diet/health relationships, food safety, and other topics that influence eating choices. The database for this review includes approximately 250 food and health-related articles per month from 50 U.S. and Canadian monthly consumer magazines from 1989 to 1994.

Nutrition and Dieting

The consumer food press has strongly communicated the dietary recommendations of major health policy documents, especially the advice that people should reduce total dietary fat intake. The advice to reduce saturated fat and cholesterol is given less emphasis. Journalists are writing less frequently now about whether monounsaturated fatty acids are healthier than polyunsaturated fats, but interest in trans-fatty acids is growing.

Magazine editors seem so convinced that dietary fat is dangerous to their readers that they have given much less attention to potential problems caused by fat substitutes than they did with the introduction of sweetener substitutes. However, journalists often point out the lack of controlled studies to document the value of such ingredients for losing weight. A few writers encourage readers to learn how to eat healthily, without relying on "processed" foods that contain fat substitutes; but, in general, the consumer press is promoting consumer acceptance of these products. The availability of fat substitutes could theoretically have a significant effect on total dietary fat consumption, but quantitation of actual change is difficult to predict until taste-related technologies are improved and prices of reduced-fat products become competitive with their traditional counterparts in certain food categories.

Journalists' advice to increase dietary fiber intake declined in the early 1990s. This message was replaced by the more general recommendation in nutrition policy documents to eat more fruits, vegetables, and grain products. The consumer press is giving heavy coverage to this change in advice, especially as biomedical and epidemiological research reveals better understanding of the benefits, and potential risks of antioxidants (such as beta-carotene and vitamin E) supplements versus foods that contain these and other nutrients. Consumption of foods of plant (rather than animal) origin will probably increase, but the evolving consumer interest in moderate, rather than drastic, dietary changes suggests that this transition will probably not be as extreme as is currently recommended by health professionals.

Dieting continues to be a popular topic in the consumer press. Articles on this subject appear frequently in health-oriented magazines for men, as well as mainstream publications for women. The evolving trend that will probably affect future consumer eating patterns most is the advice to lose weight without "dieting," as it has been defined in the past. "Don't diet" articles, which are becoming more common, are based on research relating the dangers of "yo-yo dieting." This change is also being driven by evidence that exercise produces health benefits beyond weight reduction. According to journalists, another reason to avoid strict diets is that the psychological value of liking yourself outweighs the harm that results from being a little overweight.

Combined, these influences suggest that consumers of the future will place more emphasis on exercising rather than on eating significantly more reduced-calorie or low-calorie products. Food choices will probably be based more on fat content than on the calorie value of foods.

A major variable that will affect future food patterns is whether increased Food and Drug Administration control of the truthfulness and consistency of food package information will overcome consumer skepticism regarding health-benefit promises which were used in food marketing prior to 1994. Consumer magazines are emphasizing the reliability of information on food labels, but this focus will probably call attention to the lack of parallel regulation of advertising messages until such changes are made by the Federal Trade Commission.

Looking and Feeling Younger

Another editorial message that will affect future dietary patterns is that the health reward of wise food choices extends beyond simply reducing the risk of heart disease and cancer. The consumer press in the early 1990s had not fully accepted the food technologists' term, "nutraceuticals," but magazines do discuss certain foods that might enable people to live longer, or at least postpone the processes that make their bodies look and feel old.

Part of this trend blends with the emphasis on fruits and vegetables, but magazines are also communicating the potential health benefits of garlic, peppers, and other herbs and spices in the context of articles about the recently funded research program of the Office of Alternative Medicine within the National Institutes of Health. Antiaging articles usually begin with research reports regarding anti-oxidants and their effects on immune functions, such as infection resistance and protection from environmental pollution. Journalists then exercise their editorial prerogative and weave in themes, such as herbology, Asian and African medicine, and holistic healing, treatments that are not widely endorsed by the traditional biomedical community.

The feel-younger, live-longer message will shape future food patterns. More consumers will select diets based on concepts that have not yet been scientifically documented. Self-medication in the grocery store may partially replace reliance on advice from health professionals. Furthermore, as global barriers to food export and import recede, culturally associated ideas about single foods with special healing powers will also cross international borders.

Bioengineered and Irradiated Foods

Although food scientists envision major usage of these technologies in the future of foods, consumers are still evaluating their benefits and risks. The public's concerns are directed not only at the safety of such foods per se, but also at the perceived danger that these processes will unleash unknown, and therefore potentially more frightening, consequences. For example, biotechnology conjures up consumer images of "tinkering with" nature and the possibility that what scientists do intentionally for the benefit of society might lead to other events that are harmful, either through negligence or malicious purpose. Irradiation brings to mind nuclear power plant accidents that not only resulted in immediate, confirmed damage, but also raised the haunting possibility of future harm, perhaps even to children yet unborn.

Biotechnology and irradiation offer many potential benefits: feeding hungry people, reducing post-harvest waste, and improving quality attributes of foods. The marketplace acceptance of such foods will probably be determined by the safety records of bioengineering research laboratories and nuclear energy plants. Consumer attitudes will also be influenced by how honestly industry representatives and government officials explain unavoidable risks, regardless of how small, associated with these technologies.

Environmental Influences

Since Earth Day in April 1990, environmental sensitivity has escalated. In the future, protecting the health of the planet may influence food choices more than protecting individual health.

Several comparisons suggest that environmental concerns may shape future eating patterns more than nutrition:

- The benefits of protecting the Earth endure for generations, whereas nutrition benefits last, at most, a lifetime.
- Protecting the Earth helps people everywhere; healthy eating improves only your own life.
- Environmentalists can rally around the "fight the money-hungry industry" flag, whereas opposing food companies has less "David-versus-Goliath" appeal.

The environmental movement, regardless of whether it *competes* with nutrition, will have other effects on food choices of the future. Opposition to excess packaging might drive consumers toward less processed foods. Also, unless the world economy improves, even nonvegetarians will consume fewer meat products. The sustainable agriculture movement will no doubt further affect how and where food is grown.

[*See also Agricultural Technology; Food Additives; Food and Agriculture; Food Distribution; Food and Drug Safety; Food and Fiber Production; Food Services; Food Technologies; Heath Care: Alternative Therapies; New Consumer Products; Nutrition.*]

BIBLIOGRAPHY

Duckham, A. N. *Food Production and Consumption.* New York: Elsevier, 1987.

National Research Council Assembly of Life Sciences. *Assessing Changing Food Consumption Patterns.* Washington, DC: National Academy Press, 1981.

Review of Food Consumption Survey. *Household Food Consumption by Economic Groups.* Rome: FAO, 1983.

Worman, Sterling, and Cummings, Jr., Ralph W. *To Feed the World: The Challenge and the Strategy.* Baltimore: Johns Hopkins University Press, 1978.

— KRISTEN MCNUTT

FOOD DISTRIBUTION

Americans allocated about 11.7 percent of disposable personal income to food in 1992. Approximately 30 percent of this went to purchase the raw agricultural products used in the food supply while the other 70 percent, over $500 billion, paid for the processing, transporting, sorting, distributing, retailing, and servicing of the raw food supply. This intricate and interacting network of institutions that transform the food supply between the farm gate and the consumer is the food marketing system.

The food marketing system includes an estimated 400,000 companies—16,000 food processors, 135,000 retailers, and 200,000 restaurateurs—with a total of well over 1 million places of business. They distribute the output of nearly 3 million farmers to the nation's 256 million consumers. About 12 million Americans are directly or indirectly employed in distributing this food.

The U.S. food distribution system going into the twenty-first century is considerably changed in size, structure, competitive conduct, and performance from the 1950s. It is considerably more globalized, moving toward larger firms producing more differentiated products, serving a market that is becoming older and more ethnically diverse, yet accounting for a smaller share of the consumer's total budget. The same trends can be expected to continue in the next century.

Declining Growth Rate of Food Marketing

The U.S. food marketing system is the largest aggregate marketing institution in the American economy, but it is growing more slowly than the nonfood sector. This trend will likely continue. In 1972, American food marketers accounted for 15.5 percent of the value added to the nation's Gross Domestic Product; by 1992 this contribution had fallen to 10.5 percent, as fewer and fewer of the nation's resources—land, labor, capital, and management—were devoted to distributing the nation's food supply. It will likely fall to 9 percent in 2010 (see Figure 1). This decline will be caused by two factors: continued efficiency in U.S. food distribution and continued growth in income.

The efficiency of the U.S. food system is reflected by its output growth. About 1,400 pounds of food per person left farms in 1992, a number almost unchanged since 1952. In 1952, food processors employed 1.8 million workers to feed 150 million Americans. By 1992, fewer workers (1.2 million) were employed to feed more Americans (256 million), and they provided a higher degree of processing in doing so. The farmers' share of domestically provided farm foods fell from 42 percent to 22 percent of the food dollar over the same period while the retailing, wholesaling, and food service share of marketing costs increased because of more service provided by these sectors. Although the food marketing system generated 15 percent of the nation's employment in 1970, this figure had fallen to 11.4 percent in 1990, and will likely drop to 10 percent by 2010 (see Figure 2). As an economy prospers, more of its income is allocated to nonbasic or luxury items. Hence, the share of income directly spent for food declined from nearly 21 percent in 1950 to 11.7 percent in 1992, and will likely decline to 10.5 percent in 2010 (see Figure

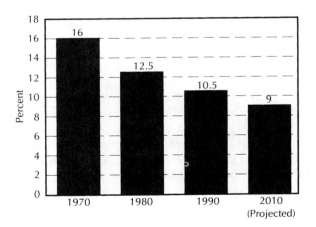

Figure 1. Share of Gross National Product generated by the U.S. food marketing system. (Gallo, 1992)

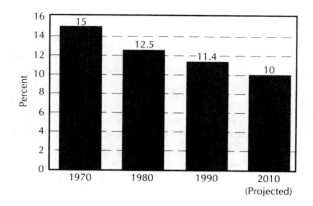

Figure 2. Share of employment generated by the U.S. food marketing system. (Gallo, 1992)

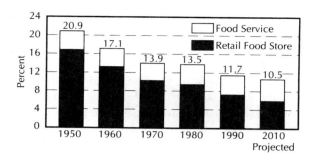

Figure 3. Food marketing system's share of disposable personal income, excluding alcohol and nonfood groceries. (Gallo, 1992)

3). The slow-growing demand of the U.S. food market will continue to have implications for U.S. food manufacturers, retailers, and wholesalers throughout the twenty-first century. First, there will be continued competition by fewer and larger firms within the domestic market to acquire or maintain market share. Second, food processors will continue responding to changing U.S. market demographics. Third, the food system will continue expanding into world markets through globalization via foreign investment and exports.

Competition Among Giants

The number of food processors declined from over 32,000 in 1963 to 16,000 in 1987, while the number of foodstores fell by about one-third (Table 1). Within this domestic market, each of the four major food marketing industries has experienced higher market concentration, where a larger share of total output is controlled by fewer and fewer firms in either local or national markets. Consequently, fewer firms are controlling a larger share of a slow-growth market, and this concentration will likely continue to rise in the twenty-first century (Table 2). The battle of giant firms for market share will continue well into the twenty-first century. Nonprice competition in the food system throughout the latter part of the twentieth century has been reflected in more product differentiation through new product introductions and advertising. Nearly 17,000 new grocery products were introduced in 1992; about 100,000 have been introduced between 1983 and 1993. Nearly $12 billion was spent on consumer advertising. Food will continue its role as the overwhelming leader among all industries in advertising and new product introductions in the twenty-first century.

Some of the competition will continue to be reflected in the struggle between the at-home and away-from-home food markets. Food service sales accounted for about one-fourth of all retail food sales in 1952; this had increased to 45 percent by 1992. Inroads by restaurants into the at-home food market have stabilized in recent slow-growth years. That stability is likely to persist into the twenty-first century as the saturation point may have already been reached.

Responding to Changing Demographics

Changing demographics dominated changes in the type of food processed and sold in the last half of the twentieth century. Household and family sizes have declined; the proportion of families with more than one wage owner has increased. The nonwhite proportion of the population has increased. More income, less time for food shopping, and interest in convenience and health have resulted in food marketers responding to a changing consumer climate. Changing lifestyles and demographics will mean shifting consumption patterns. As the link between farmer and consumer, the food marketing system will continue to respond to consumer preferences. For example, over the past fifty years, less milk, eggs, pork, and beef and more chicken, fish, fats and oils, and vegetables have been consumed. The degree of processing has changed drastically from less processed to more processed food. And, consumers make the bulk of their purchases in large supermarkets. Fast food restaurants have come to dominate the food service market.

Table 3 contains the projected changes in per capita consumption between 1990 and 2010 due to projected changes in demographic characteristics and to assumed income growth.

Changes in age distribution are likely to have the biggest impact on per person demand. Age distribution changes are projected to increase per capita food expenditures by 1.0 percent over the twenty-year period. Regional population distribution changes are expected to have a slight positive effect on total food expenditures,

TABLE 1

NUMBER OF FOOD MARKETING COMPANIES

| Year | Processing | Wholesaling | | Food Service[1] | Retailing | | Total |
		Grocery	Liquor		Food-Stores[1]	Liquor Stores	
				Number			
1963	32,617	35,666	7,598	175,117	162,273	28,624	441,895
1967	26,549	33,848	6,246	170,851	131,926	20,200	389,620
1972	22,171	32,053	5,792	179,578	122,592	28,378	390,564
1977	20,616	31,670	5,518	186,625	120,107	29,741	394,277
1982	16,800	31,290	5,158	198,088	109,567	28,977	389,880
1987	15,692	34,155	5,835	191,798	108,439	25,163	381,082
2010	13,000	34,000	5,000	109,000	407,000		

[1] Firms with paid employees.
Source: Gallo (1992).

TABLE 2

AGGREGATE CONCENTRATION IN FOOD MARKETING

| | Share of Market Controlled by Top Firms | | | |
Year	Top 50 Processing Firms	Top 50 Wholesaling Firms	Top 20 Retailing Firms	Top 50 Foodservice Firms
		Percent		
1967	35.0	NA	34.4	NA
1972	38.0	48.0	34.8	13.3
1977	40.0	57.0	34.5	17.8
1982	43.0	64.0	34.9	20.2
1987	47.0[1]	71.4	36.5	22.3
2010	52.0	78.0	39.0	30.0

NA = not available
[1] Estimated.
Source: Gallo (1992).

TABLE 3

ESTIMATED PERCENTAGE CHANGE IN PER CAPITA FOOD EXPENDITURES, 1990–2010

Food Group	Age Distribution	Regional Distribution	Race	Income	Total[1]
All food	1.0	0.1	−0.2	14.9	16.1
Beef	3.7	0.1	0.1	3.5	7.5
Pork	4.1	−0.3	0.3	1.3	6.2
Poultry	2.7	0.1	0.7	5.3	9.6
Cereals and baked goods	2.6	0.0	−0.2	4.7	7.3
Dairy products	1.5	0.1	−0.4	4.7	6.0
Fruits	3.7	0.1	−0.1	10.5	14.8
Vegetables	4.3	0.5	−0.1	6.1	11.1
Sugars and sweeteners	2.4	0.3	−0.1	6.2	8.8
Fats and oils	4.2	0.2	−0.2	4.6	8.9

[1] Net adjustment after accounting for projected changes in all variables.
Source: Blisard (1993).

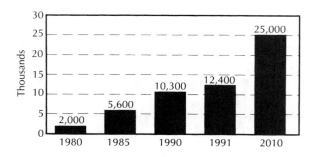

Figure 4. New food product introductions. (Gallo, 1992)

TABLE 4

WORLD TRADE IN MANUFACTURED FOODS AND BEVERAGES, 1962–1990

Year	Nominal Value	Value in 1987 Dollars[1]
	Dollars (in millions)	
1962	16,219.9	49,749.7
1967	21,973.3	62,496.5
1972	38,033.8	88,801.3
1977	89,084.7	133,083.6
1982	129,838.7	132,318.4
1987	167,916.1	167,916.1
1990	205,955.6	181,298.9

[1] Based on the Producer Price Index for Finished Consumer Foods.
Source: Handy and Henderson (1992).

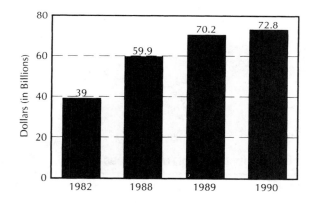

Figure 5. U.S. investment abroad in food processing: value of shipments by U.S.-owned affiliates. (Gallo, 1992)

and changing racial mix will have a slight negative impact.

Competition for Shelf Space

Changing consumption patterns and a slowly growing market will mean continued competition for retail shelfspace. New product introductions have burgeoned from 1,000 in 1964 to over 17,000 in 1992. At the

TABLE 5

U.S. EXPORTS OF MANUFACTURED FOODS AND BEVERAGES, 1962–1991

Year	Nominal Value	Value in 1987 Dollars[1]
	Dollars (in millions)	
1962	1,206.8	3,701.9
1972	2,787.1	6,507.2
1982	11,088.4	12,136.2
1990	17,490.4	15,396.5
1991	20,084.4	17,726.2

[1] Based on the Producer Price Index for Finished Consumer Foods.
Source: Handy and Henderson (1992).

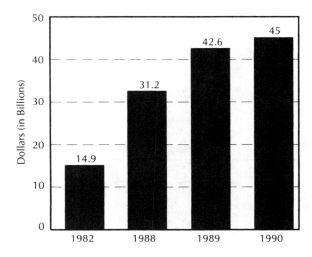

Figure 6. Foreign investment in American food processing: value of shipments by U.S. affiliates of foreign firms. (Gallo, 1992)

recent rate of increase, about 25,000 could be introduced in the year 2010 (see Figure 4). Although the discontinuance rate on these items is in the 95–99 percent range, they will pose a problem of shelfspace allocation. The average market currently has space for 30,000 items. Superstores carry 40,000 items. The total number of different labeled packaged foods available in the marketplace exceeds 257,000 items. What items will be stocked on shelves? Will small firms be deterred from entering the market?

Global Expansion

The U.S. food distribution system will continue looking to expansion in foreign markets, either through exports or investment. World trade in processed foods rose from $16 billion in 1962 to $206 billion in 1990 (Table 4). In 1990, sales of foreign subsidiaries of U.S. food firms reached $75 billion, up from $39 billion in 1982 (Figure 5). Exports amounted to $20 billion in 1992 (see Table 5). Foreign investment in the United States was reflected in a sales rise from $15 billion in 1982 to $45 billion in 1991. The United States accounted for 8.5 percent of the $206 billion (Table 5) world trade in food and beverages, ranking behind France and the Netherlands (Figure 6).

[See also Farm Policy; Fisheries; Food Additives; Food and Agriculture; Food and Fiber Production; Food Laws; Food Services; Food Technologies; New Consumer Products; Nutrition.]

BIBLIOGRAPHY

Blisard, Noel. *Food Expenditure Projections, 1990–2010.* Outlook Conference, November 1993. Washington, DC: U.S. Dept. of Agriculture, n.d.

Gallo, Anthony E., et al. *Food Marketing Review* (annual), 1992 edition. Washington, DC: U.S. Dept. of Agriculture, 1993.

Manchester, Alden G. *Rearranging the Economic Landscape: The Food Marketing Revolution, 1950–1991.* Washington, DC: U.S. Dept. of Agriculture, Economic Research Service, 1992.

— ANTHONY E. GALLO

FOOD AND DRUG SAFETY

The United States has long been a leader in the establishment of food safety standards. The Delaney Clause, prohibiting the addition of any human or animal carcinogens to food, was adopted as an amendment to the Food, Drug, and Cosmetic Act in 1958. No other country has adopted such a zero-tolerance requirement. Increasingly, however, scientific evidence has provided a basis for modifying this draconian approach to regulation. Indeed, the European Union issued a directive on July 20, 1993, for assessing the risks of chemical hazards embodying the principle that a tolerance can be established for nongenotoxic carcinogens; and any toxic substances, including carcinogens, would be subject to regulation on a case-by-case basis. Differences in national approaches to the regulation of carcinogens can be expected to become issues before the World Trade Organization as it proceeds to carry out its charter in administering the new General Agreement on Tariffs and Trade (GATT).

In a related area, the U.S. Food and Drug Administration (FDA) pioneered the use of quantitative risk assessment methods for evaluating the carcinogenic risks in foods from the residues of veterinary drugs used in the production of food animals and from the residues of agricultural pesticides and other unavoidable food contaminants. These methods have undergone considerable development in the past twenty years, as the United States and other countries have invested considerable regulatory and scientific efforts to rationalize their use.

Notwithstanding these efforts, quantitative risk assessment has not been uniformly adopted by scientific and regulatory organizations around the world. Further, there are marked differences in the ways in which different organizations approach the testing and evaluation of potential carcinogens.

The Codex Alimentarius Commission has established maximum residue levels (MRL) for pesticide residues that may safely exist in foods as a result of agricultural production methods. The MRLs serve as the basis for acceptance and rejection of commodities in international trade. These MRLs are developed without formal risk assessments, but do take into account the "mechanism of action" as a means of evaluating potential carcinogens. Understandably, the Codex MRL standards differ in a number of instances from those established for pesticides by the U.S. Environmental Protection Agency (EPA). The EPA uses the Delaney Clause as well as its own methods of doing risk assessments and conducting tests to evaluate carcinogenic potential.

There is now an organized effort being planned by the Organization for Economic Cooperation and Development (OECD) to achieve international standards for risk assessment. Without a harmonized approach to risk-assessment criteria and methods, the ability of the GATT agreement to reduce trade barriers will be seriously compromised. Reaching agreements on uniform risk assessment approaches will be difficult and will require changes in regulatory standards by all involved.

Biotechnology

The benefits of genetic manipulation in food production have just now begun to be realized. Tomatoes, cheese enzymes, and milk promoters in cows have been the first products to be commercially introduced, not without considerable controversy. Other food products, including squash and oilseeds, are under development and may soon be introduced.

The regulatory approach to such products varies considerably from country to country, and is far from settled. In the United States, regulatory requirements are based on existing laws and regulations, supplemented by policy guidance from the FDA regarding the scientific resolution of safety issues. This approach is intended to assure safety while providing developers of new food products with flexibility, but is opposed by some consumer organizations and anti-biotechnology activists. Under consideration by the FDA is a new regulation that would require premarketing notification for foods produced or manufactured by genetic manipulation. Labeling of such foods is being approached for the present on a case-by-case basis.

Other countries or political bodies, notably the European Union (EU) and Canada, take a substantially different approach. The concept of "novel foods" has been introduced, which includes foods produced by genetic manipulation and foods produced by nontraditional methods. Both products and processes would be subject to premarketing approval. The inclusion of new production processes would dramatically extend the scope of food regulation. Premarketing approval could significantly impede the introduction of new products and processes, as well as alter the conduct of food research. Researchers and entrepreneurs would seek out those countries that offer the greatest flexibility and opportunity to conduct their activities.

International standards or guidelines for the use of genetically modified foods and conduct of research have not been developed. The OECD has published a description of concepts and principles for evaluating foods produced by modern biotechnology, but these have not been incorporated into the EU and Canadian approaches. Again, the lack of consensus among the largest international trading partners indicates that national regulatory policies will be unsettled and under revision for some time to come, with concomitant disruption in business and agricultural research.

Regulatory Processes

With shrinking resources, governments around the world will find it necessary to reduce certain activities or raise additional revenue sources, including those for regulatory agencies. This is certainly true in the United States, where the president's budget has included user fees to help cover the costs of regulatory agency operations, including the FDA and the U.S. Department of Agriculture (USDA). Such fees also have been imposed in some countries in Europe and elsewhere, where food manufacturers are required to fund the costs of plant inspections. In the United States, user fees have already been adopted to enhance the resources needed for the safety and effectiveness review of new drug applications. The continued pressure to reduce government spending

The United States is a leader in food safety, having come a long way since markets of the early century displayed their food unprotected. (© Stock Montage Inc)

may see an expansion of user fees to other areas of product safety.

The user fee concept, however, can be implemented in ways other than by simply employing additional government scientists for reviewing new product applications, whether they are for food additives, drugs, or medical devices. The EU, for example, contemplates the use of nongovernment experts for safety evaluations of food additives and foods from biotechnology. Preliminary explorations of the use of outside experts for food additive safety evaluations have begun in the United States.

> *Certification and inspection will become increasingly important with the growth of international trade in food to assure the safety of both domestic and imported foods.*

The use of outside experts can be helpful in providing needed expertise and reducing time for safety evaluations by focusing efforts. Such an approach is likely to raise other fundamental questions, for example, whether the recommendations and findings of outside bodies should have regulatory decision status, and whether government agencies should be required to adopt their findings as a default position to reduce the duplication of efforts and to enhance the productivity of both public and private resources. Changes in law would be necessary to accomplish this.

Food Inspection Standards

Resource constraints coupled with interests in tighter regulatory control over microbiological hazards have prompted the FDA and USDA to adopt the use of hazard analysis and critical control point (HACCP) systems as the basis for food plant inspection. Other regulatory agencies are also adopting such regulations, and the Codex Alimentarius Commission is developing HACCP standards for hygiene and for the certification and inspection of imported foods. Although there appears to be consensus on the technical standards for HACCP, there is not yet agreement on how to certify imported foods: The key issues involve how to ensure the competency of certifying organizations and how to judge the acceptability of nongovernment (private sector) groups as certifying bodies. Certification and inspection will become increasingly important with the growth of international trade in food and the inability of resource-limited regulatory agencies to meet the workload cre-

ated in assuring the safety of both domestic and imported foods.

Conclusion

Food safety regulations will be the subject of change during the next several years resulting from changes in science and the desire of international trading partners to reduce conflicts—or at least to resolve trade issues. National approaches will have to accommodate international standards, and each interested nation can be expected to work to protect its approach.

[See also Chemicals, Fine; Food Additives; Food Laws; Food Technologies; Genetics, Commercialization; Hazardous Wastes; New Consumer Products; Nutrition; Soil Conditions.]

BIBLIOGRAPHY

Gardner, Sherwin. "Food Safety: An Overview of International Regulatory Programs." *Regulatory Affairs Professionals Society Journal* (Spring 1995).
General Agreement on Tariffs and Trade. *Agreement on the Application of Sanitary and Phytosanitary Measures*, 1994.
Lister, C. *Regulation of Food Products by the European Community.* London: Butterworths, 1992.
Organization for Economic Cooperation and Development. *Safety Evaluation of Foods Derived by Modern Biotechnology.* Paris: OECD, 1993.

— SHERWIN GARDNER

FOOD AND FIBER PRODUCTION

Food is our most important renewable resource, and agriculture is America's and the world's number one industry. Nearly half of the world's population is engaged in food and fiber production. Nearly 30 percent of the land surface is used for agriculture, 10 percent for raising crops, and nearly 20 percent for grazing livestock. Of the arable land used for crops, the 17 percent that is irrigated contributes one third of the total production.

Plants provide, directly or indirectly, most of the world's food supply. Globally, twenty-one crops stand between people and starvation. In order of importance, they are rice, wheat, corn, potato, barley, sweet potato, cassava, soybean, oat, sorghum, millet, sugar cane, sugar beet, rye, peanut, field bean, chick pea, pigeon pea, cowpea, banana, and coconut. The global importance of these basic crops will continue, with the possible exception of the sugar crops. Sucrose is being replaced by other sweeteners.

Food animals are literally protein factories that convert vegetation and grains into milk, meat, and eggs. Livestock supply one-third of all dietary protein. Milk production provides one-fourth of this, with India and Russia consuming the most in liquid form, and the

Nearly half of the world's population works with food or fiber production. This large combine can harvest a cotton field in a fraction of the time it could be done by hand. Just 2% of the U.S. workforce provide 60%–86% of the output for certain crops. (Richard Hamilton Smith/Corbis)

world's human population enjoys adequate nutrition than ever before. This trend will continue.

World food demand will skyrocket. Farm output increases are already winning the race with a population growth of 1.5 percent annually, rice by 3.5 percent, and oilseeds by nearly 5 percent. Globally, there have been path-breaking developments in plant breeding, the hybrid rice of China, Poland's triticale, Brazil's acid-soil corn, Nigeria's soybeans and polyploid cassava, a new grain sorghum from the Sudan, and the Indonesian dryland sugarcane.

In the future, farm capacities will expand. Land and water resources are sufficient to sustain needed growth into the twenty-first century. In the United States, 25 to 30 million acres of cropland are diverted annually from production, and another 35 million are under the long-term Conservation Reserve. Argentina has 80 million acres of pasture land that could be readily planted with food crops, if there were a market. Even in China, there are an estimated 25 million acres that could yet be converted into food production. For technological inputs, we now have a confluence of major achievements in biotechnology, microbiological transformations, crop and livestock production, controlled environments, and intensive crop and livestock management. These achievements will increase productivity and overall output. Poultry production in the United States has been industrialized and hog production soon will be. With a sustainability of natural resource inputs and no major threats to the environment, a degree of world food security may be realized.

How can all this come about? What are the new developments and changes that will shape food and fiber production for the future? Three general types of food production technologies may be described. All have some common elements that at times overlap and are not always easily distinguishable.

The first entails mechanization involving extensive use of land, water, and energy resources and the moderate use of biotechnologies. This approach is characterized by the United States system. One farmer in the United States now produces enough food for 124 people, enough to feed 94 in the United States and 34 abroad.

The second pattern is labor-intensive, small in size, more biologically based and scientifically oriented, but sparing of land, water, and energy resources. New inventions surmount the land resource constraint; Japan represents this approach with the highest yields of rice of any nation.

A third wave of the future, with elements of the previous two, is the alternative or sustainable approach, defined as the successful management of resources for agriculture to satisfy changing human needs, while

United States consuming the most as butter and cheese. In addition to 1.3 billion dairy and beef cattle, there are nearly 1 billion pigs, 2 billion sheep and goats, and over 10 billion chickens. China, with its 1.20 billion people, leads the world in both pigs and chickens. Consumption of poultry meat now exceeds that of beef, in both the United States and most of the rest of the world.

Hunger is the world's oldest enemy, but it has been overcome in the developed world of the twentieth century, and portions of the yet developing world during the past two decades. A golden age of agricultural technology is at hand to ensure sustainability and food security. Expansion of the world's food supply will depend, in the future, less on natural resources (climate, land, water, or energy) than on the power of human knowledge and initiative. A larger proportion of the

maintaining or enhancing the natural resource base and minimizing environmental depredation. The model for this approach is China, where food and fiber are provided for 22 percent of the world's people on only 7 percent of the arable land.

The main adjustable components are fertilizers, pesticides, and cultivations (tillage). Others include rotation, innovative cultural technologies, machinery inputs, organic matter, and crop breeding. There is the challenge to assemble and characterize the plant and animal genetic resources of the world to transform the now conventional biological technology of the twentieth century to a biotechnology-based agriculture for the twenty-first century. Plants, other than the conventional annual grain crops which now contribute over half the world's food and feed, may be developed.

Specifically, we can look forward to the following: The power of technology will expand the resource base, which will change with time and technology. This is true of all the resource inputs (land, water, climate, genetic, and human) into crop and livestock production. Water will become the most critical input. Greater efficiency in crop irrigation will become a high priority. The positive direct effects of a rising level of atmospheric carbon dioxide on increased photosynthetic and water use efficiency in crops will more than offset any adverse affects of climate change or global warming.

The first biotechnological breakthrough during the next decade will be the Bovine Somatotropine (BST) and the Porcine Somatotropine (PST). A 15 to 20 percent increase in milk production for dairy cattle and 10 to 15 percent more lean meat, with 30 percent less body fat, and a 25 percent reduction in feed are projected for hogs and beef cattle. Either the growth hormone will be used directly, or transgenic animals will manufacture their own. An ultra-high-yielding rice, which will produce 20 to 30 percent more (raising yield from 9 to 13 tons per hectare) and be harvestable in 100 to 130 days, may be developed within five to eight years. New processing technologies for cotton, the world's leading fiber crop, will enhance competition with synthetic nonwoven fabrics. Integrated pest management will become an arsenal of tactics favorable to the environment, human health, food safety, economics, food ecology, and sustainability. Crops, including cotton, wheat, soybean, and corn, with genetically built-in protection against pests (bio-pesticides), will reduce chemical pesticide use by 75 percent.

Another breakthrough appears imminent in the controlled ripening of tomatoes and other fruit. Consumer demand for vine-ripened produce is increasing. Tomatoes and many other fruits ripened on the vine are flavorful, aromatic, juicy, and soft, but they quickly rot. Control of the ripening process and ethylene biogenesis now appears possible, through the use of transgenic plants biotechnologically manipulated to control the plant's ethylene output. The first such tomatoes were introduced in 1992 to be followed by other soft and perishable fruits, including raspberries and tropical products.

"Food ecology," the relationship between

food products and the environment,

will heavily influence consumer choice.

Dramatic changes are taking place in dietary habits. People are on a health blitz. Fresh fruits and vegetables, along with whole-grain cereal products, fish, and poultry will become increasingly important. Green (environmental, ecological) consumerism will become manifest in America's $280 billion food industry. "Food ecology," the relationship between food products and the environment, will heavily influence consumer choice. The organic movement, food products labeled "natural," the Reform (health food) Stores of Western Europe, and health food stores in the United States will gain in prominence. Nutritional policies will powerfully influence food policies.

Agricultural knowledge is becoming internationalized. Discoveries made in one country will be quickly available in others through literature, computer accessing, FAX transmissions, and personnel exchange. Contributions will be selective, adaptive, and chosen, rather than prescribed. It is easier to adopt than to wholly create the new. Science for the future of agriculturally developing nations will be a mixture of the borrowed and created. Research activities of the thirteen international agricultural research centers will be expanded to include forestry, agroforestry, fisheries, vegetables, bananas, and irrigation management. The cornucopia of the future is an overflowing one.

[See also Alcohol; Farm Policy; Fisheries; Food and Agriculture; Food Consumption; Food Distribution; Food and Drug Safety; Food Technologies; Forestry; Genetics: Agricultural Applications; Green Revolution; New Consumer Products; Soil Conditions; Tobacco.]

BIBLIOGRAPHY

Avery, Dennis E. *Global Food Progress 1991.* A Report from Hudson Institute Center for Global Food Issues. Indianapolis: Hudson Institute, 1991.

Board on Agriculture/National Research Council. *Alternative Agriculture.* Washington, DC: National Academy Press, 1989.

Gibbs, Martin, and Carlson, Carla, eds. *Crop Productivity—Research Imperatives Revisited.* East Lansing, MI: Michigan State University, 1985.

Mayer, Andre, and Mayer, Jean. "Agriculture, the Island Empire." *Daedalus* 103/3 (1974): 83.

Paarlberg, Don. *Toward a Well-Fed World.* Ames, IA: Iowa State University Press, 1988.

Wittwer, Sylvan H. "Food Ecology and Choices." *Food and Nutrition News* 64/3 (1992).

Wittwer, Sylvan H., Yu Youtai, Sun Han, and Wang Lianzheng. *Feeding a Billion: Frontiers of Chinese Agriculture.* East Lansing, MI: Michigan State University Press, 1987.

World Bank. *Agricultural Biotechnology, The Next "Green Revolution."* Washington, DC: World Bank, 1991.

— SYLVAN H. WITTWER

FOOD LAWS

Since the earliest recorded civilizations, one of the essential functions of government has been to assure the safety, quality, and proper labeling of the food supply. As our scientific base has developed, our regulatory mechanisms have correspondingly increased (see Table 1).

Labeling

When Congress enacted our first national food law, the Food and Drugs Act of 1906, it included no mandatory food labeling. When the 1906 act was replaced by the Federal Food, Drug, and Cosmetic Act (FD&C Act) of 1938, however, Congress included four mandatory elements of food labeling: the name of the food, the statement of ingredients, the name and address of the

TABLE 1

FOOD REGULATION THROUGH THE CENTURIES

Ancient Sumeria	Net weight controls
Biblical era	Dietary restrictions
Roman empire	Food labeling Food standards
Medieval England	Prohibition of corrupt or unwholesome food
Nineteenth century	Prohibition of adulterated or misbranded food
1950–2000	Premarket approval of functional food ingredients Anticancer provisions Labeling of nutrient content Control of disease prevention claims
Twenty-first century	Regulation of genetically altered food Improved sanitation controls Emphasis on diet and health

manufacturer or distributor, and the net quantity of contents.

From 1938 until the early 1970s, food labeling closely followed the requirements of the FD&C Act and thus was relatively simple. In the early 1970s, the Food and Drug Administration (FDA) promulgated a series of regulations that transformed food labeling. Names of foods were required to be more descriptive and informative. Full nutrition labeling was required for any food for which a nutrition claim was made or to which a nutrient was added. The FDA began to define nutrient descriptor terms, such as "reduced" and "low" calorie. Mandatory information was required to appear on a single information panel in a minimum or greater type size. In the mid-1980s, the FDA also began to regulate specific disease prevention claims for food, such as the claim that a food product "helps reduce the risk of cancer."

Congress codified and extended these reforms in the Nutrition Labeling and Education Act of 1990. First, nutrition labeling was made mandatory for all food. Second, the FDA was required to complete the job of defining nutrient descriptors. Third, the FDA was also required to complete the job of regulating disease prevention claims.

As scientific information increases, the food label can be expected to change in the future in two respects. First, the FDA will refine its definitions for nutrient descriptors to be more precise with respect to the levels that represent a low, moderate, or high level of individual nutrients. Second, labeling statements about the relationship of individual nutrients to health and disease will become more focused and precise.

Food Identity and Quality

Since ancient times, attempts have repeatedly been made to describe, and to set standards of identity for, individual food products. Initially these efforts were directed at assuring the basic quality of the food by preventing unintended or purposeful adulteration. Later, these standards of identity were designed to protect the safety and nutritional quality of the food as well.

With increased knowledge about the relationship of dietary components to health and disease, food manufacturers will engineer traditional products to make them more nutritious and less likely to contribute to disease. This will be done in three ways. First, macronutrients and other components that contribute to the potential for disease will be reduced or eliminated through traditional methods of food technology—for example, substituting water for fat. Second, entirely new functional food ingredients will be developed and (after FDA review of safety) used for the same functional purposes as the less desirable macronutrients. Third, raw agricultural commodities will themselves be changed by genetic engineering, to reduce or eliminate undesirable constituents and to increase desirable constituents.

The Nutrient Content of Food

Discrete micronutrients (vitamins and minerals) were first added to the food supply in the 1930s. Modification of the macronutrient content of food began with the invention of saccharin in the late 1800s, but has remained stalled for many years because of the lack of truly adequate substitutes for such important macronutrients as sodium and fat. In the future, based on new technology, the nutrient content of any food will be fine-tuned to meet virtually any nutritional requirement.

Dietary Supplements

Ever since the inception of cod liver oil containing vitamins in the 1920s, the FDA has fought a tireless campaign against dietary supplements of vitamins, minerals, and other dietary substances. For decades, the FDA has preached that, with rare exceptions, people who eat an adequate diet simply do not need nutrient supplementation.

When the FDA has sought to implement this policy, however, it has been brought to a halt both in the courts and by Congress. The FDA retains authority to establish safe limits for any nutrient, but its authority to establish controls for perceived economic or nutritional reasons has been severely limited.

The FDA is unlikely to give up its vendetta against dietary supplement products. Manufacturers and consumers, on the other hand, will continue to argue that these products are safe and provide an important insurance for those who do not consume an adequate or balanced diet. As more detailed scientific information emerges about the biochemistry and nutritional importance of specific nutrients in the daily diet and their relation to health and disease, the arguments in favor of dietary supplements are likely to gain strength and ultimately to overwhelm the FDA objections.

Food Sanitation

From ancient times to the present, contagion and communicable disease have been spread through the food supply. Our modern food supply is unquestionably the safest in history. Nonetheless, such pathogenic organisms as salmonella and listeria continue to elude control.

In the future, new technology will offer the possibility of even more effective antimicrobial agents to reduce the likelihood of food contamination. As public accep-

tance of irradiation increases, this technique will assume a much larger role in combatting pathogenic organisms. Use of recombinant DNA technology to build antimicrobial capacity directly into raw agricultural commodities themselves is also at hand.

The Safety of Food Constituents

Under the 1906 F&D Act and the FD&C Act of 1938, it has been illegal to add any poisonous or deleterious substance to the food supply. In the Food Additives Amendment of 1958, Congress required that all food additives—food substances not generally recognized as safe—must first be the subject of extensive testing by the food manufacturer and then approval for safety by the FDA before they can be used in the food supply.

With increased knowledge about the relationship

of diet to health, food manufacturers

will engineer products to make them

less likely to contribute to disease.

Since 1958, the American food industry and FDA have cooperated on a massive review of the safety of functional food ingredients—flavors, colors, emulsifiers, nonnutritive sweeteners, nutrients, and other substances used to achieve a specific intended purpose in the food supply. Raw agricultural commodities, in contrast, have undergone no such review. We continue to eat the same basic food products as our ancestors, without the same assurance of safety that we have imposed on functional food ingredients. As more scientific information becomes available about the relationship of our diet to health and disease, the safety of our natural food products is likely to come into greater question.

The rapid increase in the availability of genetically altered raw agricultural commodities will force even greater scrutiny of the safety of very familiar but significantly changed food items. Completely new approaches to the evaluation of food safety will become essential once the full impact of biotechnology is reflected in the food supply.

Conclusion

Laws and regulations governing the food supply have not changed dramatically in more than one hundred years. What has changed is our knowledge about the safety, quality, sanitation, and nutrient value of the food we eat. Accordingly, it is the progress of science, not the development of laws and regulations, that will determine the course of government regulation of the food supply in the future.

[See also Consumer Protection/Regulation; Farm Policy; Food Additives; Food and Agriculture; Food and Drug Safety; Genetics: Agricultural Applications; Nutrition.]

BIBLIOGRAPHY

Hutt, Peter Barton, and Merrill, Richard A. *Food and Drug Law: Cases and Materials,* 2nd ed. Westbury, NY: Foundation Press, 1991.

— PETER BARTON HUTT

FOOD SERVICES

Food service is the serving of prepared meals and snacks for immediate consumption away from home. Away-from-home eating has grown faster than at-home eating since the Great Depression. Food service accounted for 45 percent of all food dollars in 1992, compared with 40 percent a decade ago, and 25 percent in 1954 (see Figure 1).

The food-service industry is made up of more than 732,000 establishments comprised of individual market segments commonly divided into two major sectors: commercial and noncommercial. Commercial food service is the largest sector of the food-service industry, accounting for 76 percent of the total $250.5 billion spent in 1992 (Table 1). The commercial segment includes for-profit establishments, such as full-service restaurants and lunchrooms, fast-food/limited-service outlets, cafeterias and social caterers, as well as lodging places, retail hosts, recreation and entertainment facilities, and separate drinking places. The food may be consumed on the premises or eaten elsewhere. Fast-food outlets and restaurants and lunchrooms dominate commercial food-service sales.

The primary purpose of noncommercial food-service operations is to render a service rather than to make a profit. Noncommercial food service provides food in establishments such as nursing homes, child day-care centers, university or school cafeterias, and hospitals.

Fast-Food Outlets

Fast-food outlets are those establishments where food is ordered and picked up from a counter. The menu is limited and seating or stand-up facilities are located elsewhere in the establishment. Other services, such as drive-thru, carryout, and/or delivery may also be offered. Some outlets have only drive-through or carryout service.

Fast-food is the largest segment in the food-service industry with 1992 sales of $83.6 billion—exceeding sales of $72.7 billion at full-service restaurants and lunchrooms. Fast-food began in the 1950s and, because of its speed and convenience, grew rapidly. Fast-food captured an increasing share of separate eating-place sales during the past decade—from 46 percent in 1982 to 52 percent in 1992 (see Table 1).

Domestic market saturation by fast-food outlets led to expansion into other countries in the 1970s. By 1992 there were over 14,000 fast-food outlets of U.S. companies in other countries, compared to 980 in 1971. Canada, Japan, the United Kingdom, and Australia are popular foreign locations.

Restaurants and Lunchrooms

Restaurants and lunchrooms, the more traditional eating places, now make up the second largest segment of

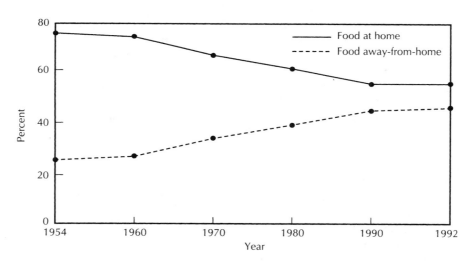

Figure 1. Food eaten away from home captures an increasing share of the food dollar. (U.S. Food Expenditures, USDA/ERS)

TABLE 1

SALES OF MEALS AND SNACKS BY FOODSERVICE INDUSTRY, 1982–1992*

Industry Segment and Type of Establishment	1982	1992	Percent Change
		Billion dollars	
Commercial			
Separate eating places:			
Fast-food outlets	36.5	83.6	129
Restaurants and lunchrooms	40.9	72.7	78
Cafeterias	2.7	3.9	45
Social caterers	—	1.6	—
Total	80.1	161.8	102
Lodging places	6.2	12.4	100
Retail hosts	3.9	8.9	129
Recreation and entertainment	2.8	6.0	115
Separate drinking places	1.1	1.6	46
Commercial feeding total	94.1	190.7	103
Noncommercial			
Institutional:			
Elementary and secondary schools	7.4	10.5	42
Colleges and universities	3.7	9.3	152
Plants and office buildings	5.9	5.3	−11
Hospitals	5.6	3.8	−33
Extended care facilities	4.8	9.3	94
Vending	3.2	6.7	110
Transportation	1.7	4.8	183
Associations	1.4	1.8	29
Correctional facilities	1.0	2.5	150
Child day-care centers	0.6	1.6	167
Elderly feeding programs	0.6	0.2	−67
Other	0.2	2.5	1150
Total	36.1	58.3	62
Military services:			
Troop feeding	1.6	1.0	−38
Clubs and exchanges	0.5	0.5	0
Total	2.2	1.5	−32
Noncommercial feeding total	38.3	59.8	57
GRAND TOTAL	132.4	250.5	90

* Excludes sales taxes and tips.

Source: *Food Marketing Review*, selected issues.

commercial eating places. While fast-foods' share of separate eating place sales increased over the last decade, restaurants and lunchrooms' share decreased from 51 percent in 1982 to 45 percent in 1992. Casual restaurants lead this sector of separate eating places, followed by family dining, and fine-dining restaurants. Cafeterias and caterers accounted for sales of $5.5 billion or 4 percent of eating place sales. In contrast to the commercial sector, noncommercial sales are spread broadly among different kinds of institutional feeders.

Institutions

Over the last decade, institutional food-service sales grew 62 percent from $36.1 billion in 1982 to $58.3 billion in 1992. The transportation segment accounts for the largest percentage increase, followed by colleges and universities, and child day-care centers (see Table 1).

Future Growth

The away-from-home eating market has a bright future. Rising incomes and changing lifestyles have been primary reasons for success in this market. Incomes will continue to rise due to (1) the proportion of women in the labor force continuing to increase (now at an all-time high of 57.8 percent); (2) a high birthrate in the years ahead (Technomic, a research consulting firm, predicts a 10.8 percent increase in the school-age population between 1990 and the year 2000); and (3) an increasing elderly population with more time and money to spend on leisure activities such as travel and dining out. Food-service sales are projected to reach $300 billion by 1995 and $400 billion by the year 2000.

Technology, such as touch screens

and other forms of electronic interactive ordering,

will likely replace spoken communication

at the counter and perhaps even the table.

Domestically, fast-food firms will continue to focus more on alternative or nontraditional ways to expand the market and increase sales. Much fast-food is already reaching nontraditional locations such as hospitals, gas stations, department stores, schools, supermarkets, shopping malls, theme parks, stadiums, airports, bus terminals, and practically anywhere else hungry people are found. Though fast-food outlets led the move into nontraditional markets, more casual restaurants going beyond the traditional markets are likely. Foreign countries, particularly in Europe, and also China and Russia, offer opportunities for outlets in the next decade.

As food-service establishments cater to consumers' interest in fitness and nutrition, we will likely see more healthful, low-fat foods on the menu, such as salads and salad dressings, broiled and baked chicken items, steamed rice versus fried rice, and low-fat dairy products. Advancing technology, such as touch screens and other forms of electronic interactive ordering, will likely replace spoken communication at the counter, the drive-through, and perhaps even the table in the next few years. Both concepts are already being tested in some stores.

[See also Food and Agriculture; Food Consumption; Food Technologies.]

BIBLIOGRAPHY

Bartlett, Michael, and Bertaagnoli, Lisa. "R&I Forecast 93." *Restaurants and Institutions* (January 1993).

Price, Charlene C. "Fast Food Chains Penetrate New Markets." *Food Review* 16/1 (January–April 1993).

———. "Foodservice." In *Food Marketing Review, 1992–93.* Washington, DC: U.S. Department of Agriculture, Economic Research Service, Publication No. AER-678.

Wallace, Jane. "$400 Billion by 2000." *Restaurants and Institutions* (January 1993).

— CHARLENE C. PRICE

FOOD TECHNOLOGIES

Prediction of the future of technology is always hazardous. Extrapolating from scientific knowledge results largely in the extension of what already is rather than of what might be. The development of new technology demands new scientific insights. The results of contemporary research will impact on food processing in ways that we do not yet understand.

Nevertheless, ongoing developments in food science and technology permit an attempt at predicting the near future. The three areas of investigation most likely to have their greatest impact on food processing are computer science, genetic modification, and materials science. New computer software and hardware have already had an enormous effect on the practices of the food industry. Not only is modern analytical technology dependent on computers, but process control and automated manufacturing is expanding rapidly with the development of new hardware and software. The availability of software programs to maintain inventory control and the development of automated warehousing technologies will assure consumers that the product they receive will be fresh and of high quality. Totally automated processing, storage, and distribution systems will provide a seamless system from farm to market.

Increasing capability in genetic modification will continue to result in the ability to produce from microbes the specific enzymes used in food processing. Rennin, for example, normally is obtained from higher organisms. This capacity will increase the availability of important processing aids or food components at a much reduced price.

Materials science will provide the foundation for the development of "engineered" foods. Today we see the increasing appearance of reformed meats, diet drinks with alternative sweeteners, and the development of fat substitutes. Not only will these engineered foods deliver a desired characteristic, for example, sweetness, a fat-like mouthfeel or a particular texture, but will also provide enhanced nutritional characteristics. Among the technologies that appear ready to be utilized in the near future is super-critical fluid extraction, which results in the removal of cholesterol from butter and eggs and similar products while maintaining acceptable taste and flavor.

The use of ionizing radiation to ensure the microbial safety of foods will increase. There are few other food processes that permit the same level of assurance of safety from microbial contamination. It is likely that radiation will not be used by itself, but rather in combination with other food-processing methods such as heat treatment, refrigeration, and freezing. This will, in turn, permit the use of lower doses of radiation to ac-

also resulted in technologists looking for ways to modify foods to allow preparation with microwave finishing and yet result in the same product that is obtained from preparation by other processes such as heating.

The potential exists for the development of food polymers and lipids that may be engineered to carry functional groups that can signal the presence of pathogenic bacteria or to carry a specific taste or flavor or texture. While we have not yet actually duplicated all the flavors in nature, we are beginning to understand better how the human organism detects and distinguishes among various flavors. If we know how these substances interact with the sensors in the nose or the mouth and how that signal is translated, a revolution in flavor engineering can take place that will permit the design of specific molecules to provide specific tastes. This most important area of food and flavor engineering will be derived from research in the brain and central nervous system. Increasingly we are beginning to understand how to control appetite, where sensory input pathways are located, and how to control these systems. With this information, food technologists will be able to design products that will both provide taste and flavor and, at the same time, control appetite.

This Italian man is overseeing the extraction of olive oil from olives, a centuries-old method. Food manufacturing, refined over thousands of years, is among the most technologically advanced industries. (Vittoriano Rastelli/Corbis)

A revolution in flavor engineering can take place that will permit the design of specific molecules to provide specific tastes.

complish desired preservation tasks. Moreover, it is likely that the use of machine-produced electrons will replace isotope irradiators, reducing significantly the possible risks associated with such facilities.

Membrane processes are common in the food industry today, but new combinations will have the potential to produce novel products such as low-fat, low-sodium cheese. A variety of approaches have been proposed, including reverse osmosis, electrode dialysis, and dialysis.

From the point of view of the consumer, the most obvious changes will occur in the area of engineered foods. The engineering of foods offers major advantages in terms of their flexibility. A processor can vary the source of protein, vary the sweetener, vary the fat source—or any combination of these—and yet end up with basically the same product. The development of other technologies such as microwave processing has

It is important to understand that humanity has been modifying and engineering foods from the earliest of times. The development of fermentation technologies such as brewing of beer and the baking of bread are perfect examples of engineered products. Bread, in particular, is an excellent example. It has built into it a range of specific properties such as a certain number of air cells, a crust, a crumb, a caloric content, and a retinue of nutritional values. When combined with advances in the creation of foods and food additives, new technologies will provide an entirely new approach to foods and assure the public that the food they eat not only tastes good, but also fulfills the needs for health and nutrition.

[See also Chemicals, Fine; Food Additives; Food Distribution; Food and Drug Safety; Food and Fiber Production; Food Laws; Food Services; Genetics, Commercialization; Genetic Technologies; Genetics: Agricultural Applications; Green Revolution; New Consumer Products; Nutrition.]

BIBLIOGRAPHY

Busch, Lawrence; Lacy, William B.; and Lacy, Laura R. *Plants, Power, and Profit: Social, Economic, and Ethical Consequences of the New Biotechnologies.* Cambridge, MA: Basil Blackwell, 1991.

Gasser, Charles S. "Transgenic Crops." *Scientific American* 266/6 (June 1992).

Hobbelink, Henk. *Biotechnology and the Future of World Agriculture: The Fourth Resource.* London and Atlantic Highlands, NJ: Zed Books, 1991.

Molnar, Joseph J., and Kinnucan, Henry. *Biotechnology and the New Agricultural Revolution.* Boulder, CO: Westview Press, 1989.

Office of Technology Assessment. *A New Technological Era for American Agriculture.* Washington, DC: U.S. Government Printing Office, 1992.

Palmer, Sushma. "Food and Nutrition Policy: Challenges for the 1990s." *Health Affairs* 9/2 (Summer 1990).

Rosenblum, John W., *Agriculture in the Twenty-first Century.* New York: John Wiley, 1983.

— SANFORD A. MILLER

FORECASTING, DETERMINISTIC

In this generation, the world is passing through the greatest evolutionary jump in human history. The immense technological developments since about 1940 have changed human powers, human interactions, and human perceptions, more than any changes before:

- The biotechnology revolution has given us the power to reduce birthrates, control disease, transform farming, manipulate genes, and alter species. This is happening with a speed and on a scale unmatched in evolutionary history.

- Nuclear energy, fission (and, someday, fusion), for power as well as bombs, and cheaper solar-electric power with photovoltaic cells will far surpass our limited supplies of fossil coal, oil, and gas. It is the greatest change in supplies of energy since the development of photosynthesis two billion years ago.

- Our venture into space, with men walking on the moon and unmanned planetary probes, is the greatest jump into a new habitat since the land animals first came ashore.

- Jet planes are the most dramatic advances in travel and global accessibility since the development of seaborne ships five thousand years ago.

- The development of long-range nuclear rockets and of automated factories and automatic feedback-control systems since about 1940 is a new quantum jump.

- The greatest recent development may be in the field of electronics. First, in electromagnetic transmission and communications, public and private, from radar maps to television, FAX, and e-mail, with pictures and data exchanged around the world at the speed of light, by fiber-optic networks or satellite relays 40,000 kilometers up. We spend half our leisure time with television, and today over half the human race can watch a sports event or a catastrophe simultaneously. Even speech and language, writing and printing, pale in comparison to the scale and immediacy of broadcast vision. And now videocassettes and recorders, with their stored vision, make further worlds available at everyone's fingertips.

- In addition, electronic data processing, transmission, and storage can solve scientific and technical problems at speeds millions of times faster than ever before. Advanced technology has transformed daily life, from the electronic kitchen and living room to electronic schools and offices, from social records to global credit cards, from home camcorders to satellite surveillance.

Possibilities and Uncertainties of Prediction

The coming together of so many factors spreading all over the world in our time is a far more powerful force than the technical changes that produced the Industrial Revolution two hundred years ago. But some of them are already pressing the limits of what is physically possible in several fields, so that their limits can be predicted, if not their speeds of advance or interaction. Thus, there are limits to orbital speeds, atmospheric sinks, food production, and human information capacity. Likewise, there are self-maintaining social patterns or limit-states whose continuity is predictable in sustainable societies, like traffic rules and rules of parliamentary order. Today, the only useful historical comparisons are not with times of constancy but with times of immensely rapid change. Nevertheless, certain aspects of the coming decades may be easier to predict just because of the determinism underneath the changes.

How could we make such predictions? How many of the present developments could have been, or were, predicted? The answer is that it is not as impossible as usually supposed. Throughout his lifetime, for example, H. G. Wells used his realistic scientific imagination to make many successful forecasts, not just the apparent "fantasies" of space missiles, but wars and their timing and technology, and atomic energy, decades ahead. In *Anticipations* in 1902, he tried to predict for the whole twentieth century, and actually foresaw, for example, many of the social consequences of the horseless carriage in war and peace. But the speed of advances outran even Wells. Just one year before Kitty Hawk, he thought that the airplane was far off and would be unimportant; his century-predictions were fulfilled within twenty-five years and were surpassed by many developments in areas he missed.

Of course, anyone can make fairly reliable predictions of trends and social consequences in certain areas. Barring global catastrophes, we can predict population within a few percentage points one or two decades ahead, because most of that population is already living today. Even a great change in birthrates or death rates would not change the total very fast. The population forecasts, in turn, determine fairly accurately the pressures on food and resources, pollution, and urban growth, for the near term.

Conversely, the prediction of wild and improbable events that change everything—a message from space, or a catastrophic asteroid impact—is obviously impossible. This is also true of really new discoveries or inventions. Heavier-than-air flight had been hoped for and worked on ever since Daedalus, but success was not certain until the Wright brothers solved the problems of power and control. And the dramatic new powers of lasers and recombinant DNA were not anticipated by scientists even three years ahead.

Yet there are constancies even here. Evolutionists like Waddington and others have compared these "evolutionary jumps" to traveling over an unknown landscape and finding a hidden valley. There is a combination of surprise and inevitability, as many paths lead downward to the same pattern at the bottom. While flight was not certain for animals or humans, many ways were finally found to achieve it, from insects to birds to bats to airplanes of many types. And they all look surprisingly alike, because they satisfy the same physical requirements.

Nuclear weapons and electronics

seem to have stopped certain kinds of great wars

and changed the scale of others.

Evidently, to make good forecasts, we must look for constancies of these types. Technological constancies are much more predictable than the accidents of fashion or leadership or wars, and technosocial change often rides over this accidental "noise." Nuclear weapons and electronics, for example, seem to have stopped certain kinds of great wars and changed the scale of others. And television and public feedback have changed the responsiveness of presidents and the nature of politics and international interactions.

There is therefore a "technological determinism" that occurs when we are rushing into an evolutionary valley, when technosocial inventions are feasible and desired by all. In an open and diverse society equipped to produce them, such developments become "self-propagating" everywhere, almost invariant to accidents of history or national differences. All want health and longer life; less farm labor and higher yields; cars, television, and cassettes if they can get them. Change feeds on itself. The young rush to it. It crosses borders, sold or smuggled, and undermines old ways and opposition and authority. Television makes addicts, yes, but also inspires instant outrage, stimulates instant imitation, and creates instant demands. Why else the same movements in every country, after it arrived?

Determinisms of this kind can evidently be used, within limits, to make social and global forecasts for the next few decades that will be relatively invariant to the turbulence of events. We find such invariances in three different stages of the technosocial sequence: (1) ongoing consequences of present technology; (2) probable consequences of new self-propagating technologies; and (3) long-range limits of technology and self-maintaining patterns in a sustainable society.

Predictable Invariances from Present Technology

CONVERGENT GLOBAL CHANGES, 1960–1990. First we can look for the ongoing social consequences of present technologies, where parallel effects in different countries already show that there must be common deterministic causal patterns. In the last thirty years, we have seen:

- The end of centuries of colonialism; new nations and their troubles; independence movements. Why? Changes in farm and factory, education, television, national and international awareness.
- The longest period of peace between the European powers in history, with expected economic and political unification, the end of the Cold War, and arms reductions. Why? Nuclear rockets, satellite surveillance, television, tourism, and trade.
- The rise of a multipolar world. Global linkage, trade and business and tourism, with multinational corporations, high-tech banking, and mobility. No country any longer controls its own economy or stock market or exports. One terrorist act may cost billions, showing how intense the positive connection is.
- Global and satellite television, penetrating all borders. Electronics changing all family, society, government patterns.
- The information society. The transformation of agriculture by the Green Revolution, of industry by automation, and of business and government by computers. As labor changes from farming and construction to information handling and services, farms empty and cities explode. Work is light; education is long; retirement can be early; and television, entertainment, sports, and travel can fill the days. It is the greatest revolution in work and time since the invention of agriculture.
- Mass protest movements everywhere, for rights and other causes. Hundreds of thousands mobilize in the streets as never before. When television makes problems vivid to millions, they become intolerable—a war, injustice, the deaths of seabirds. So television becomes to a surprising degree a conscience machine, a sympathy and tolerance machine, forcing corrections.
- The increase of refugees and migrants and guest-workers, legal and illegal, in all countries and cities. Uprooted by revolution or famine, or seeking jobs, they force cultural diversity and a new underclass on many surprised societies.
- The increase of health and longevity resulting from the conquest of diseases. In the United States, life expectancy has increased by about ten years in the last thirty years. This stretches out the stages of life; childhoods are long and dependent; families age, migrate, and divorce; seniors multiply. And populations explode wherever there is death control without birth control.
- The increase of education, especially higher education, in all countries, with lighter labor and more need for literacy and technical training. The world education budget has exceeded the world military budget in several

recent years, surely for the first time in human history. Universities multiply everywhere.

- The decline of mainline Western religions, whose dogmas seem quaint to the liberal world of television and living room immediacy. The rise of dynamic and intolerant fundamentalism simultaneously in Islam, Judaism, and Christianity is a reaction against these modern forces that are threatening tradition.

We could add a hundred other great jumps in this generation: new architecture; electronic social records and global credit networks; the high-tech sciences; universal television and its marketing effects and mental effects, good and bad; and so on and on. All together, this remarkable set of rapid social changes since 1960 or so has no explanation other than the astonishing technical developments of the previous two decades. The surprising thing is that it has been such a great revolution in our minds and in the inner connections of society with so little violence in the streets. With a few awful exceptions—amplified by television—it has not been a blood revolution but an information revolution, a "velvet revolution." Officials often were not fired or hanged, but simply turned their politics around—sometimes within twenty-four hours. This new feedback flexibility is itself a revolution in social organization.

ONGOING CONSEQUENCES 1990–2020. A continuation of these social consequences into the next generation will be almost equally inevitable. For example:

- We may be seeing the end of five thousand years of large-scale armies and wars. Nuclear war seems less likely, with only one dominant power left; and the Persian Gulf War, with its one-sided, high-tech outcome, might be the last war of the great powers. They might now actually unite to stop arms sales and curb the fierce new wars between liberated minorities.

- In the next ten years, millions of species of plants and animals—perhaps 10 percent of those on Earth—will probably be wiped out. Their extinction will be primarily from human destruction of their habitats, from population growth and deforestation and pollution. By great effort a few hundred species may be saved. Zoos may concentrate on rare breeding, and great wild parks of hundreds of square miles, especially in the tropics, will be set up to save a few ecological systems. But it will be only a breath against the juggernaut, perhaps the greatest loss of species since the extinction of the dinosaurs 65 million years ago. Nevertheless the losses will not touch most people, and the biggest effects may be indirect, a permanent heightening of environmental concern and far tighter conservation and controls.

- Other environmental changes and catastrophes are feared by many, such as waste disposal problems, ocean pollution, and atmospheric problems of smog, ozone, and global warming. Television heightens awareness of the damage, but also our sense of the need of uniting to protect nature and our beautiful earth. As a result, within ten years or so, the international environmental movement, growing in all countries, may become the very strongest force for global integration and management for the long-range future.

- Within ten years, the world's dependence on oil may level off or decrease, partly because of these environmental pressures. The watchwords are conservation and improved efficiency; replacement by natural gas or even liquid hydrogen; cleaner nuclear power; and solar power with photovoltaic cells, which may decentralize our living patterns.

- Entertainment and tourism will go on to become our biggest industries. The young and the old, the literate and the illiterate, the well-fed and the hungry, demand television, video entertainment, and computer games. Tourism, whetted by inescapable advertising, with easy travel and credit cards, has become the main income of many cities and countries, with tourists outnumbering the inhabitants. As old cultures are lost or blended together, the strangeness disappears; the world becomes a common ground.

- The man-in-space projects may slow down for several years, along with the attempt to militarize space and other macroengineering projects, because of the costs and difficulties and the low payoffs, in a time of retrenchment and other priorities. But unmanned space projects, for communications, surveillance, navigation, and environmental studies, have value for every country and may continue expanding rapidly.

New Self-Propagating Technologies

Similar consequences may follow from some new technologies just ahead:

- The world's population may begin to level off or drop in the late 1990s, because of several new and more efficient contraceptives or abortifacients such as the French "morning-after pill," RU486. It costs far less and has much smaller side effects than any present contraceptive methods; so it may reduce births much faster and more widely even than the birth control methods of the 1950s, which brought birthrates below replacement levels in one-third of the world in less than twenty years. Because it can replace millions of surgical abortions, it will be pushed for birth control by large countries, such as China, and India. A population peaking below 8 billion by 2005 is now possible.

- New ranges of crime and terrorism will be made easier by mobility and anonymity, automatic weapons, and rich networks of support. The old villages were safe because some Granny Smith was watching, knowing who came and went. In the global village, the answer to modern mobility and anonymity may be modern watching, electronic surveillance and identification. It will surely grow for the poor and the outs, as it has already become universal for the rich and the ins, who need it for their credit cards and computers. Democracies will have to find out how to combine surveillance with safeguards, to reestablish safety and openness for all.

- Direct satellite-to-home television, along with fiber optics and interactive-learning disks, will decentralize and multiply the personal options for entertainment, business, and study. With public or private specialties, and an informational feast, it cannot help but change education, creativity, culture, politics, and global networks of participation.

- Together these massive global changes and dangers in the next ten years or so add up to mounting pressure for global reorganization and integration. The rapid organizing of the European common market and reduction of barriers will be a pattern for many other parts of the world. But the problems of nuclear and other arms control, environmental protection and control, monetary management, rescue for collapsing countries, and other global problems, are too large for any nation or any regional agreements, and they demand new global institutions. These institutions will have to operate by consent and with checks and balances to prevent dictatorial behavior and ensure responsive and competent operation, but they will require some surrender of independent national sovereignties in these areas, just like the European Community.

Such institutions may be set up piecemeal, sector by sector, just as global monetary links and credit and trade and tourism have been set up in the last thirty years. They may be in effective operation long before there are such things as global elections or an individually elected global parliament. As a result, the world may become more and more like an integrated biological organism, with its various feedback loops—the circulatory system, the nervous system, and so on—all stabilizing themselves with responsive connections to each other, without confrontational elections or a parliament. Eventually, a world democracy sensitive to the needs of all its citizens may be more like this pattern than we have supposed; if so, we are surprisingly close to it already.

Long-Range Limits and Self-Maintaining Patterns

Since the globe is finite, we can predict that in the long run, regardless of details, the growth of any technology will reach certain limits on this Earth, such as those we can see already with pollution and extinctions. Three kinds of limits are particularly important:

- *Limits to growth for a sustainable society.* The Club of Rome's hundred-year analysis of *The Limits to Growth*, by Meadows et al. in 1972, is still broadly valid. To keep a high-interaction society from running away to exponential booms and crashes will require hands-on management of population, pollution, resource use, and investment, as well as weapons—with strong agencies for monitoring and anticipatory corrections. We see them coming already, and they will be major parts of global reorganization by 2010 or so. Cleanup and recycling of everything, as in any closed system, will be a major feature.

  The adjustment to sustainable patterns will not happen instantly. It takes time for the effects of new technology to be fully understood, and it always requires "working through," with second-stage and third-stage technology, such as pollution controls, to correct unforeseen dangers or side effects. It is Ashby's Law of Requisite Variety: there must be at least as many controls as there are problems to be solved. The limits to growth will finally be maintained by many social controls.

- *Self-stabilizing patterns in complex systems.* With feedback communication, the subsystems will always develop a working balance, not optimizing but "satisficing," moment by moment. In the future global society, with television and fast communication of complaints and demands, the balancing of interests will require something like John Rawls's idea of "justice as fairness." In his system, any inequalities in shares and privileges can be justified and defended only as long as the lot of the least fortunate improves as much as possible. Probably no other pattern of distribution will be stable in the long run. This means guaranteed entitlements, insurance and transfer payments; ombudsmen in all organizations; and Marshall-type plans for Third World rescue.

Stabilization will also require real "checks and balances" feedbacks, like those in the U.S. Constitution, so that the governed can control their governments and their economic systems. High-information management elites will always tend to expand and exploit their knowledge and will have to be curbed. Strong autonomous subsystems with their own information networks will be needed, like the organs of a healthy organism.

- *Blocks to technology.* A very different kind of limits would be imposed if science and technology were someday banned, as they were in Islam in the 1100s by a religious hierarchy, and in China in the 1400s by a fearful bureaucracy—which is why both cultures "lost out" to the then-primitive West. Today, some major high-tech catastrophe might likewise unite the antitech fears and the fundamentalists to stop growth around the world, perhaps under a charismatic television revivalist using electronic technology to stop all the rest.

But as Joel Mokyr has convincingly shown in *The Lever of Riches,* the West's explosion of science and technological growth was due to its diversity. New ideas that were blocked by guilds or governments could always find other channels and markets. With world society now moving toward still more diversity—with more individualist and small-group technologies!—there will always be channels of change, and no real blocks to technological determinism seem likely for a long time to come. Even with disasters, risky but useful technologies will be debated and corrected, rather than abandoned.

What we are passing through is a unique metamorphosis in the whole history of the human race—like that of a caterpillar into a butterfly.

In the other direction, a great expansion of limits will come if and when *self-supporting space habitats* can be developed outside the Earth, with shielding and artificial gravity for long-run living. With recycling and abundant energy and asteroidal and lunar materials for expansion, different groups could find new evolutionary niches and possibilities. It would complete the evolutionary jump into the new medium of space. Is this possible? Will it happen? As with flying, in the centuries before the Wright brothers, we cannot know ahead of time. But technological determinism—which is another name for intelligence that meets the wants of humanity—says that if it is feasible, it will be done.

Whether this happens or not, with this level of control and communication and mutual interaction, the human race, if it survives, cannot help but become something like an *integrated global organism*. It will not be a dictatorship. People will fight to shape their own tastes and lives, so there will be enormous local autonomy. The world may have more patches than a calico cat; but on the overall problems of survival of ourselves and of our Earth, we will still move together—simply because we have to.

After this great shock wave has passed, we might go on for generations or centuries in the new world with nothing like this rate of change and reorganization again. What we are passing through is a unique metamorphosis in the whole history of the human race—like that of a caterpillar into a butterfly, like the birth of a baby—and this is what it looks like from inside. But the necessary end is so surely visible that many aspects of this remarkable new world of our children and grandchildren can already be broadly predicted.

[See also Change, Scientific and Technological; Forecasting Methods; Forecasting, Mistakes in; Scientific Breakthroughs; Technology Forecasting and Assessment; Wells, H. G.]

BIBLIOGRAPHY

Asimov, Isaac, and White, Frank. *The March of the Millennia: A Key to Looking at History.* New York: Walker and Company, 1991.

Deutsch, K. W.; Markovitz, A. S.; and Platt, J. *Advances in the Social Sciences, 1900–1980: What, Who, Where, How?* Cambridge, MA: Abt Books, 1986.

Feather, Frank. *G-Forces: Reinventing the World. The Thirty-five Global Forces Restructuring Our Future.* Toronto: Summerhill Press, 1989.

Goodman, Allan E. *A Brief History of the Future: The United States in a Changing World Order.* Boulder, CO: Westview Press, 1993.

Laszlo, Ervin, and Masulli, Ignazio, eds. *The Evolution of Cognitive Maps: New Paradigms for the Twenty-first Century.* Langhorne, PA: Gordon and Breach, 1993.

Linstone, Harold A., and Mitroff, Ian I. *The Challenge of the Twenty-first Century: Managing Technology and Ourselves in a Shrinking World.* Albany, NY: State University of New York Press, 1994.

Wagar, W. Warren. *A History of the Future.* Chicago: IL: University of Chicago Press, 1989.

———. *The Next Three Futures: Paradigms of Things to Come.* Westport, CT. Greenwood Press, 1991.

– JOHN PLATT

FORECASTING, MISTAKES IN

Could forecasters have accurately predicted the extent to which the social problems engulfing America would worsen between 1960 and 1993? During that period, total crimes have gone up 300 percent, violent crimes by 550 percent. Illegitimate births have increased by 400 percent overall, with illegitimacies by teenagers up 200 percent. Teen suicides have gone up more than 300 percent. Divorce has risen more than 200 percent. Although elementary and secondary education outlays are up by 200 percent, scholastic aptitude test (SAT) scores have plummeted an average of 73 points.

Political forecasts and prognostications may be even riskier. Half a century after the women's suffrage movement had begun and had gained much public support, Grover Cleveland, America's twenty-second and twenty-fourth president, contended in 1905 that "Sensible and responsible women do not want to vote." Following Barry Goldwater's rout by President Lyndon Johnson in 1964, serious commentators wondered whether the Republican party would survive or would ever again attain the presidency; but Republicans won five of the next seven presidential elections. East German leaders boasted in early 1989 that the Berlin Wall would stand for another hundred years; but several months later it was torn down and the communist tide had turned.

Even moguls of industry go awry in forecasting their might. Thomas Watson, IBM's founder, speculated, "I think there is a world market for about five computers." The president of the Dean Telephone Company made a similar error, prognosticating in 1907, "You could put in this [office] all the radiotelephone apparatus that the country will ever need." Western Union, in another classic miscalculation in 1876, refused to buy Alexander Graham Bell's telephone invention for $100,000; after all, telegraph was "king." At the turn of the century, Britain's Chief Engineer of the Post Office proclaimed, "The Americans have need of the telephone but we do not ... we have plenty of messenger boys." Harry Warner of Warner Brothers asserted in 1927: "Who the hell wants to hear actors talk?" Introduction of television at the 1939 World's Fair prompted the *New York Times* to report: "The problem with television is that people must sit and keep their eyes glued to the screen; the average American family hasn't time for it." The average daily television viewing per household amounted to 7:04 hours in 1992, by far the greatest leisure time pursuit. The list of errors in calculation could go on endlessly.

At the height of the Information Age, these prescriptions for wrongly estimating communications technologies and social response suggest the need to take matters more seriously. Predicting future developments and trends requires soberly imaginative professional futurists skilled in detecting, interpreting, and anticipating patterns of change.

[See also Change, Pace of; Forecasting Methods; Planning; Scanning; Scenarios; Surprises; Wildcards.]

BIBLIOGRAPHY

Cerf, Christopher, and Navasty, Victor. *The Experts Speak: The Definitive Compendium of Authoritative Misinformation.* New York: Random House/Pantheon Books, 1984.

Goldberg, M. Hirsch. *The Blunder Book.* New York: William Morrow, 1984.

— WILLIAM L. RENFRO

FORECASTING METHODS

There is no one best forecasting technique. The methods used must be tailored to the particular problem and the resources available to complete the forecast. The huge expenditures involved in constructing the dynamic models employed by the Club of Rome would not be appropriate for the entrepreneur wanting to predict short fluctuations in the commodities market. Tremendous efforts to collect detailed energy-sector data for state input/output tables proved "untimely" when, a few years later, the results were available. Senior state officials needed to make broad policy/investment decisions in a period of world energy shortages, not of surpluses. Often a combination of methods produces the best results—perhaps a Delphi approach to frame the problem via expert opinion followed by more quantitative modeling techniques.

There are hundreds of forecasting techniques or approaches from which to choose, as the following list only begins to suggest:

1. Forecasting via surveys
   a. Delphi methods
   b. Panels
   c. Public opinion polls
   d. Surveys of activities, events, units, intentions, attitudes, priorities, hopes, and fears
2. Barometric or indicator forecasting
   a. Economic and social indicators
   b. Precursor events
   c. Signals of change
   d. Technological audits
   e. Analysis of limits and barriers
   f. Prediction of changeover points
3. Forecasting via trends
   a. Trend extrapolation
   b. Exponential smoothing
   c. Time-series data

To begin the selection process, the planner should have the answers to the following questions: What is it you are looking for? What are you going to get when all is said and done? How do you do it? What do you need? A sample write-up for a cross-impact analysis is shown here:

1. What is it?
   - *Name:* Cross-impact analysis.

- *Definition/description:* Comparison of individual forecasts, on a pairwise basis, to determine whether there are interactions or to provide a systematic method for examining the interactions among several forecasts.
- *History/degree of provenness/promise:* Devised by Theodore Gordon and O. Helmer in the late 1960s. Numerous applications—it works. High degree of promise.
2. What are you going to get?
   - *Uses and limitations:* Comparisons of forecasts and testing policies. Provides greater clarification of issues and better definitions of the risk and uncertainties in the subject being forecast, as well as a more complete and consistent picture of some future time period.
   - *Limitations:* Number of forecasts that can be made and possible methodological inflexibility.
   - *Forms of output:* A matrix of events in rows and columns depicting the interaction between events.
   - *Level of detail:* While extensive detail is possible (more than twenty-five events), the procedure becomes tedious and evaluation complex when too many events are involved.
   - *Level of confidence:* Judgmental, but use of experts and probabilities provides for extensive feedback and review.
   - *Span of forecast:* Flexible (long- or short-term) and determined by the nature of events.
3. How do you do it?
   - *Procedures:* Very systematic. Events are suggested with probabilities and year of occurrence. Events are then arranged in columns and rows. The interaction between events is shown in terms of mode (i.e., whether one event enhances, enables, or prevents another), strength (10–100 percent), and time lag (from immediate to x years).
4. What do you need?
   - *Data requirements and availability:* Forecasts—the results of these often is from Delphi methods or panels, but can be from any source.
   - *People, including organizational backup:* Need "experts" to determine events, probability, and time of occurrence. Also, must evaluate the interaction among events.
   - *Time:* One day to one year, depending upon complexity, with a median required duration of one month.
   - *Money:* Cost for such analysis can range from modest to high, depending upon the complexity of events being analyzed, type of "experts" required to take part, and whether a computer is utilized.

To assist the planner in identifying the most appropriate methods, the types of methods discussed in this article are compared with various areas of analysis, resource conditions, and special situations as respectively shown in Tables 1 and 2.

Forecasting Techniques Using Time Series and Projections

These methods may involve pattern identification, trend extrapolation, and probabilistic forecasting. Series of historical data are subjected to various kinds of statistical analysis to generate forecasts of the future. Although the mathematics used is sometimes quite ad-

TABLE 1

AREAS OF ANALYSIS

Focus of Forecast	Time Series and Projections			Models and Simulations					Qualitative and Holistic			
	Trend Extrapolation	Pattern Identification	Probabilistic Forecasting	Dynamic Models	Cross-Impact Analysis	KSIM	Input-Output Analysis	Policy Capture	Scenarios and Related Methods	Expert-Opinion Methods	Alternative Futures	Values Forecasting
Economic	X	X	X	X			X		X	X	X	
Technological	X	X	X				X		X	X	X	
Social	X	X	X	X	X	X		X	X	X	X	X
Environmental	X	X	X	X	X	X		X	X	X	X	X
Values		X			X	X		X	X	X	X	X
Institutional					X	X		X	X	X	X	X

TABLE 2

RESOURCES NEEDED TO USE THE TECHNIQUES

Type of Resource	Time Series and Projections			Models and Simulations					Qualitative and Holistic			
	Trend Extrapolation	Pattern Identification	Probabilistic Forecasting	Dynamic Models	Cross-Impact Analysis	KSIM	Input-Output Analysis	Policy Capture	Scenarios and Related Methods	Expert-Opinion Methods	Alternative Futures	Values Forecasting
Data												
Historical	X	X	X	X	X	X	X					X
Public opinion								X				X
Expert opinion				X	X	X		X		X	X	X
Imagination/ speculation					X	X		X	X	X	X	X
Personnel												
Generalists				X	X	X		X	X		X	X
Methodologists				X	X	X	X			X		X
Subject experts		X		X	X	X	X	X	X	X	X	X
Mathematicians/ statisticians	X	X	X	X			X	X				
Writers/ communicators									X		X	
Literature searchers									X		X	X
Computer programmers		X	X	X	X	X	X					
Questionnaire and survey experts										X		X
Physical												
Computers	X	X	X	X	X	X	X					
Programmable hand calculators	X							X				
Existing computer programs	X		X	X	X	X	X					
Statistical packages	X	X	X				X	X				
Data banks	X		X				X					

vanced and the concepts may be quite subtle, this type of analysis, on the whole, is the easiest to use and understand of all forecasting approaches. These methods are quite flexible in terms of the kinds of problems that can be treated and in terms of the level of detail in the results. Although time series and projection forecasting can be used alone to generate forecasts on specific subjects, they can also be used in conjunction with other methods, such as those based on models or those that are derived from more wholistic, non-quantitative kinds of forecasting.

Trend extrapolation refers to a number of different mathematically based kinds of forecasting. All trend extrapolation seeks to determine the future values for a single variable through some process of identifying a relationship valid for the past values of the variables and determining a solution for future values. This single variable may be highly complex in that it may reflect or be the re-suit of numerous trends. The greatest limitation of trend extrapolation is that it is unable to deal with unanticipated changes in the historical pattern of the data. It does not take into account such wild card phenomena as sudden shifts or breakthroughs. Valid trend extrapolation may include such methods as "eyeballing," moving averages, exponential smoothing, substitution and growth curves, envelope curves, and simple and multiple regression.

Forecasting methods based on *pattern identification* seek to recognize a developmental pattern in historical data and to use it as the basis of forecasting future events. This method is useful both for time-series data, for which more direct extrapolating methods do not work, and for interpreting numerous social trends. The Box-Jenkins method is an example of the former; Normex forecasting and analysis of precursor events are examples of the latter. However, pattern identification methods sometimes suffer from a poor database, varied interpretations, and hence questionable reliability.

Many phenomena for which forecasts are needed appear to change randomly, albeit within recognizable limits. *Probabilistic forecasting* methods use mathematical models of such phenomena. Numerical odds are assigned to every possible outcome or combination of outcomes. On the basis of such assigned odds, predictive statements are made about the future behavior of the phenomenon. Probabilistic forecasts are helpful in discovering where, how, and when a phenomenon may best be anticipated in the future, and where nonpredictable occurrences must be accepted. Such methods should not be used in cases where adequate mathematical models cannot be developed, or when the results must be understood and accepted by decision makers untrained in these specialized techniques.

Forecasting Techniques Using Models and Simulations

These techniques include dynamic models, cross-impact analysis and KSIM, input-output analysis, and policy capture. This group of techniques demonstrates the interactions of the separate elements of a system or problem, as well as their combined overall effect. Such models are helpful in attaining a broad perspective and a better grasp of the totality of a problem and in foreseeing effects that might otherwise be overlooked. These models can range in complexity and difficulty from an easily accomplished graphic display to a comprehensive, formal dynamic model that deals with quantitative relationships over time and requires special skills and computerization.

Dynamic models of complex, nonlinear systems are extremely useful for forecasting futures resulting from interacting events. The simulation model, which is usually numeric, reveals the evolution of systems through time under specified conditions of feedback. By changing equations or adding interacting trends, a large number of possible futures can be explored in computer runs. Dynamic models are also helpful in gaining qualitative insight into the interactions of system elements. Dynamic models require extensive time, resources, and skills on the part of the developers.

Cross-impact analysis strives to identify interactions among events or developments by specifying how one event will influence the likelihood, timing, and mode of impact of another event in a different but associated field. Cross-impact analysis is used not only to probe primary and secondary effects of a specified event, but to improve forecasts and to generate single forecasts from multiple forecasts. *KSIM* is a tool that utilizes a small group of people to complete a cross-impact table and evaluate the changes over time in a few significant variables produced by simple dynamic model. Cross-impact analysis is a basic forecasting tool helpful to most forecasters dealing with interacting trends.

Input-output (IO) analysis is a means of interrelating industry inputs and outputs in a single model, showing the consequences to all other sectors of a specified change in one. Different models deal with the nation, with regions, with specific industries, and so on. IO analyses are of great value in quantifying changes in a region's or subregion's commodity flows and likely industrialization patterns resulting from specific projects—such as improved navigational facilities or a new recreational site. Principal problems to its use include lack of detail on coverage in IO matrices, out-of-date data, and the high cost of developing specialty IO tables.

Policy capture involves building a model that, given the same information the individual has, will accurately reproduce his or her judgments and hence policies. The goal is not simply to predict or reproduce judgments accurately; rather, policy capture seeks to generate descriptions of the judgmental behavior that are helpful in identifying characteristic differences between individuals. It is believed that the judgmental process can be described mathematically with a reasonable amount of success.

Qualitative and Holistic Forecasting Techniques

This type of forecasting may involve scenario building and related methods, expert-opinion methods, and values forecasting. These techniques are aimed at portraying the system as a whole. The forecaster typically starts with an intuitive sense of the totality instead of with a specific component of the whole. With the total context in mind, the planner next identifies the elements, how they fit together to make the whole, the driving forces of change, and so forth. Then, such methods as trend extrapolation and modeling come into play, but they are used in the service of explaining the whole. This kind of forecasting thus tends to be more global, more qualitative, and "softer" than more conventional approaches.

Scenarios, alternative futures, modes and mechanisms of change, authority forecasting, and surprise-free futures all depend upon logical, plausible, and imaginative conjectures that are most properly regarded as descriptions of potential futures rather than probabilistic forecasts of actual futures. Such methods are most often used in conjecturing about complex, little-understood social phenomena, for which more rigorous quantitative forecasting methods do not exist.

Expert-opinion methods, including the use of panels, surveys of intentions and attitudes, and Delphi polls, may be used either for actual forecasting or to make conjectural explorations of potential futures. Identifying, qualifying, and making pertinent experts credible is a central issue with these methods. While the findings of expert-opinion studies are usually easy to communicate, it is often difficult to convey the specialized information and the reasoning on which findings are based.

People's values (priorities, opinions, attitudes, and so on) are of crucial importance in judging what public actions and policies they will support. *Values forecasting* usually involves clustering values into topology and forecasting changes in values on the basis of demographic shifts or broad societal scenarios. Values forecasting is essential for the purpose of reflecting soft human factors in long-term planning and policy analysis. Values studies are extremely helpful when used in conjunction with other forecasting methods, but are of limited reliability or detail when used alone.

Conclusion

The methods presented here can be employed for a wide variety of purposes. Forecasting can focus on predicting the future course of events. It can also focus more broadly on identifying a range of *probable* outcomes. At other times it may seek to determine the physical plausibility of achieving some set of results. It can also be an instrument to bring about a specific moral agenda by beginning with a notion of what the future *ought* to be like and then proceeding to map out the actions that are needed to bring about such a future. All of these approaches are characteristic of forecasting, broadly defined.

Forecasting can be short-term, mid-term, long-range, comprehensive, farseeing, logical, deliberate, rational, definite, intricate, elaborate, complicated, detailed, simple, clear-cut, solid, daring, or subtle. It can also be

---

Values forecasting is essential for the purpose

of reflecting soft human factors in

long-term planning and policy analysis.

---

accurate, sophisticated, makeshift, tentative, grandiose, linear, nonlinear, unproductive, frantic, weird, unbelievable. . . . The horizons are limitless.

[See also Forecasting, Deterministic; Forecasting, Mistakes in; Scenarios; Social Indicators; Surprises; Technology Forecasting and Assessment; Trend Indicators; Wildcards.]

BIBLIOGRAPHY

Abraham, Bovas, and Ledolter, Johannes. *Statistical Methods for Forecasting.* New York: John Wiley, 1983.

Armstrong, J. Scott. *Long-Range Forecasting: From Crystal Ball to Computer.* New York: John Wiley, 1985.

Casti, John. *Searching for Certainty: How Scientists Predict the Future.* New York: William Morrow, 1991.

Levenbach, Hans, and Cleary, James. *The Beginning Forecaster: The Forecasting Process Through Data Analysis.* New York: Van Nostrand Reinhold, 1981.

— PAMELA G. KRUZIC

FOREIGN AID/ASSISTANCE

Foreign aid or assistance refers to the flow of resources in the form of money or "in kind" from more wealthy developed countries to poorer developing countries. Two basic kinds of assistance can be distinguished: (1) military assistance provided primarily in pursuit of the defense objectives of the donor, and (2) economic assistance provided primarily in support of the long-term economic development of the recipient. Arms transfers from the developed countries, including the former Soviet Union plus China (a low-income developing country), amounted to $24.7 billion in 1991, the latest year for which data are available. By comparison, the total amount of economic assistance provided in 1993 was $74.8 billion. The end of the Cold War is likely to reduce military shipments. The emphasis now, and even more in the future, will be on economic assistance.

Most of the economic assistance, amounting to $68.5 billion in 1993, consisted of official development finance (ODF) provided by governments (bilateral aid) and by multilateral organizations (multilateral aid) such as the World Bank and regional development banks (e.g., the Inter-American and Asian Development

Banks) that have been established to support the economic development efforts of poor countries. A small amount, $6.3 billion, was provided by private voluntary organizations such as CARE and OXFAM. These totals exclude credits provided by the International Monetary Fund (IMF), Official Export Credit agencies, and private banks. The IMF provides credits to all countries, wealthy or poor, to help them cope with temporary balance-of-payments problems, while export credit agencies such as the U.S. Export-Import Bank and private commercial banks provide credits in pursuit of private gain.

The terms on which ODF is provided vary. Some development finance is in the form of grants which the recipient does not have to repay. Most are loans at interest rates and maturities (interval to final repayment) more advantageous to the recipient than loans offered by commercial banks. The largest category of aid is entitled Official Development Assistance (ODA). This involves grants or loans provided by governments or multilateral organizations for economic development purposes at interest rates less than 5 percent and maturities longer than ten years. Such aid amounted to $55.2 billion in 1993. The bulk of ODA (which is also called "concessional" assistance) is directed to developing countries with per capita income of less than $765 in 1991. Budgetary constraints in all major donors are likely to limit future ODA levels and reduce its share of development finance.

Some economic assistance is in the form of technical aid to finance the costs of training or the salaries of foreign experts providing technical advice to developing countries. Some of this is in the form of credits to finance the costs of a particular project (e.g., the building of a highway or an irrigation system); some is in kind (e.g., the shipment of food to a country facing famine); and some is in the form of general financing of imports in support of a broad program of development reforms. Doubts about the effectiveness of aid in support of general import financing is likely to reduce its role in future aid programs.

Japan and the United States are the two largest providers of bilateral ODA with net disbursements (i.e., after repayment of the principal on previous loans) of $11.3 and $9.7 billion respectively, in 1993. The World Bank is the largest provider of multilateral assistance, with total gross disbursements of about $18.1 billion in 1993. Of this total, the World Bank provided $4.9 billion in very long-term credits (ODA) to low-income countries and about $13.2 billion in development finance to other countries.

The World Bank finances flows of assistance in two ways. It uses contributions by the developed countries to finance flows of ODA and it borrows in the private capital market and then lends the proceeds to developing countries. Because of its strong credit rating in international capital markets, the World Bank is able to borrow at attractive terms and offer credits to developing countries on terms and maturities more advantageous than what they themselves could secure by borrowing in the capital markets directly. Most World Bank lending finances discrete projects, especially in infrastructure, energy, the environment, agriculture, health, and education. About 20 to 25 percent of gross disbursements, however, involves credits in support of programs of structural and sectoral policy reform undertaken by aid recipients. This so-called "policy-based" lending, which involves the provision of foreign exchange that can be used for the purchase of imports needed for the overall development effort of the recipient, is conditioned on explicit undertakings by the recipient to put in place specific policies conducive to longer term development. In the future, multilateral programs such as those of the World Bank which are based on capital market borrowing, are likely to continue to be a major source of development finance. But concessional programs are likely to face problems in getting funded.

In 1993 the four largest recipients of ODA worldwide were China ($3.3 billion), Egypt ($2.3 billion), Indonesia ($2.0 billion), and India ($1.5 billion). Most of these large, populous countries received low amounts relative to the size of their economies. The highest aid recipients relative to their gross national product (GNP) are in Africa, where in 1991–1992 Tanzania received ODA amounting to 96 percent of its GNP, Uganda 43 percent, and Ethiopia 15 percent. By contrast, ODA received by China and India was only 0.4 percent and 0.8 percent of their GNP, respectively. Since 1991, a number of countries in Eastern Europe and the former Soviet Union have also received economic assistance. The share of development finance going to these countries is likely to rise in the future, while that going to countries of East Asia which have developed good access to international capital markets, is bound to diminish.

Over the years, many questions have been raised regarding the effectiveness of foreign assistance in promoting development. Critics have argued that assistance has gone to corrupt governments with ineffective policies, which have wasted it, and that assistance tends to substitute rather than augment domestic resource mobilization for development. Experience has shown that while, as with all government programs, some aid resources have been wasted or badly utilized, foreign assistance can make a significant contribution to economic development, if certain conditions are met: First, that the recipient government is committed to a program of effective development policies; second, that the recipient institutions are sound, or can be strengthened, so as to absorb foreign aid efficiently; and finally, that donors provide assistance with the sole objective of promoting the recipient's economic development rather than their own foreign policy or commercial objectives.

Over the years, many questions have been raised

regarding the effectiveness of foreign assistance

in promoting development.

Because donor governments find it difficult to obtain public support for their assistance, unless they use it in the pursuit of foreign policy or commercial objectives, assistance from multilateral organizations, which are not affected by such considerations to a significant degree, has tended to provide more effective support for development.

[See also Development, Alternative; Global Business: Dominant Organizational Forms; International Governance and Regional Authorities; International Trade: Sustaining Growth.]

BIBLIOGRAPHY

Cassen, Robert, et al. *Does Aid Work?* Oxford: Clarendon Press, 1986.
Development Co-operation. Paris: Organization for Economic Co-operation and Development, 1994.
Krueger, Anne O.; Michalopoulos, Constantine; and Ruttan, Vernon W. *Aid and Development.* Baltimore: Johns Hopkins University Press, 1989.

— CONSTANTINE MICHALOPOULOS

FOREIGN RELATIONS.

See INTERNATIONAL DIPLOMACY; INTERNATIONAL TENSIONS.

FORESTRY

Urban and community forests mitigate environmental impacts by moderating climate, conserving energy, removing carbon dioxide, storing water, improving air quality, controlling rainfall runoff, minimizing flooding, lowering noise levels, harboring wildlife, and enhancing the attractiveness of cities. Benefits may be partially offset by problems caused by vegetation, including pollen discharges, hydrocarbon emissions, green waste disposal, water consumption, and the displacement of native species by exotic ones (i.e., species that did not evolve there but were imported by humans).

Forestlands

The total forest area of 4.2 billion hectares covers 32 percent of the total land area of 13.1 billion hectares. Another 675 million hectares are classified as shrub land and 406 million hectares are categorized as forest fallow—lands that have been cleared for shifting cultivation in the past twenty years. The world's coniferous forests cover 1.1 billion hectares, with 83 percent of these situated in North America and the former U.S.S.R. Nonconiferous forests cover 1.7 billion hectares with large areas in Africa, South America, and Asia. Tropical forests cover nearly 3 billion hectares worldwide.

Temperate forest areas in Europe, Asia, and Oceania have grown slightly over the last three decades as reforestation and reversion of cropland to forestland more than offset losses to urbanization, roads, and other uses. Between the 1950s and the 1980s, forest area in Central America declined 38 percent and 23 percent in Africa. Deforestation results from slash-and-burn agriculture, which can lead to land degradation, logging, and demand for fuelwood, fodder, and other forest products.

Forest Management

Most of the world's forests are not consciously managed for sustained production. Most of the managed forest throughout the world is natural forest. If forests are not managed for sustainable harvests, overcutting can result in thinner stands.

Catastrophic wildfires occasionally occur, but prevention, detection, and suppression activities have done much to alleviate fire damage. Nevertheless, millions of hectares are burned each year, with associated damages in the hundreds of millions of dollars.

Forest Pests

Outbreaks of forest insects and diseases commonly occur when forests become stressed because of drought or other environmental factors. Some insects and diseases are endemic to forests. Outbreaks may be widespread, such as the gypsy moth in North America, or more localized. The damage may lead to tree mortality or slow tree growth. Annual mortality from all causes is probably in the hundreds of millions of cubic meters. Wildlife can become a pest by damaging regeneration or by overgrazing.

Watershed Use

The watershed values of forests have long been recognized. For example, the legislation that created the U.S. National Forest System in 1897 stated that the purposes of national forests were to include securing favorable water-flow conditions. Unmanaged harvest of forests in watersheds can aggregate flooding and decrease water quality.

Trees and Forest Products

Trees are converted into fuelwood, lumber, panels, various pulp and paper products, and other miscellaneous products. In 1990, a total of 3.3 billion cubic meters of roundwood was produced worldwide. Some 54 percent of total roundwood production was used for fuelwood, and the remainder is described as industrial roundwood used for the manufacture of products. About 30 percent of the total roundwood production was used as sawlogs and veneer logs, and 13 percent was processed as pulpwood. Chips and byproducts from the manufacture of lumber and panels are also used in the manufacture of pulp.

About 45 percent of the world's roundwood is produced in developed countries and 55 percent in developing countries. Some 87 percent of the fuel-wood is produced in developing countries, but only 24 percent of the industrial roundwood. Worldwide, only 0.2 percent of fuelwood and charcoal and 7 percent of industrial wood is exported. About 40 percent of the world's industrial wood exports are shipped to Japan.

The possibility of global warming has heightened interest in the role that forest biomass plays as a carbon sink. Forests act as carbon sinks by absorbing carbon dioxide. Agriculture and burning of tropical forests contribute to global warming, but to a much lesser degree than the combustion of fossil fuels and industrial activities in the developed world.

Logging

Logging practices vary around the world and depend in large measure on forest management practices. Harvest of ancient forests occurs in portions of North America, Russia (the CIS), and the tropical rainforests. Temperate hardwoods tend to regenerate naturally. Logging operations necessitate the development of a transportation infrastructure that, if not well designed, can contribute to soil erosion and water pollution. In the tropics, this infrastructure also provides access for people who develop land for agriculture.

In some countries, development of plantations of quick-growth species has been the choice over management of naturally occurring forests. There has been special interest in the development of these plantations in the tropics, where growth rates can be high. The total area of plantations in tropical areas amounts to some 25 to 35 million hectares. These plantations account for a small portion of the total forest area in the tropics. Worldwide, there are some 130 million hectares of plantations, situated mainly in Brazil, Chile, New Zealand, and the American South.

End Products

The use of end products from timber processing varies with climate, customs, and income. For example, in Japan, the Scandinavian countries, the United States, and Canada, wood is used extensively in framing for home construction. In Mexico, China, and many European countries, wood is used mainly for forming concrete, and in window and door frame applications. Developed countries account for 77 percent of the production of sawnwood and sleepers (railway ties)—486 million cubic meters—and they account for 87 percent of world imports of these products that total 94.6 million cubic meters.

Developed countries account for about two-thirds of the plywood production of 49.7 million cubic meters. Much of the remainder is produced in the Far East; Indonesia is an especially important source of plywood made from tropical species. Developed countries account for about 65 percent of world plywood imports of 14.3 million cubic meters.

About two-thirds of the material used in paper and paperboard production is wood pulp. The other major source of fiber is waste paper. Most wood pulp is made by heating wood chips in a mixture of chemicals that leave the cellulose fibers for further processing into pulp. Recycling of paper and paperboard is increasing rapidly in developed countries and is expected to become a more important source of fiber in the future for the United States and other countries.

The possibility of global warming has heightened interest in the role that forest biomass plays as a carbon sink. Forests act as carbon sinks by absorbing carbon dioxide.

Developed countries account for 93 percent of world production of 154.4 million metric tons of wood pulp and 83 percent of world imports of 25.6 million tons. Much of the production in developing countries is in Latin America, especially Brazil.

End products from forests, such as nuts, contribute to the food supply. Forests have long been a source for pharmaceuticals. For example, Andean Indians employed cinchona bark from *Cinchona ledgeriana* trees to fight malaria long before the time of European discovery. Many people claim there are further discoveries to be made. Recently, taxol from the Pacific yew was found to be useful in treating cancer.

Forest preservation looms as an increasingly important issue in the years ahead. Products ranging from food and pharmaceuticals to paper and a profusion of wood products require sound forest management. Touted paperless-office forecasts fade as paper use soars. Vital roles in global climate, preserving biodiversity, contributing to water availability and quality—all these things, and much more, demand nurturing forestlands, one of the world's few sustainable resources.

[See also Biodiversity; Environmental Behavior; Environmental Ethics; Genetics: Agricultural Applications; Green Revolution; Parks and Wilderness.]

BIBLIOGRAPHY

Food and Agriculture Organization of the United Nations. *FAO Yearbook: Forest Products, 1990.* Forestry Series, 25. Rome: FAO, 1992.
Oldfield, Margery L. *The Value of Conserving Genetic Resources.* Washington, DC: U.S. Department of Interior, National Park Service, 1984.
World Resources Institute. *World Resources 1987.* New York: Basic Books, 1987.

— DAVID R. DARR

FORRESTER, JAY W. (1918–)

Born in Climax, Nebraska, Jay Forrester received engineering degrees from the University of Nebraska and Massachusetts Institute of Technology (MIT). From 1946 to 1951 he was director of the MIT Digital Computer Laboratory, responsible for the design and construction of Whirlwind I, one of the first high-speed computers. He also invented random-access coincident-current magnetic storage, which was for many years the standard memory device for digital computers. He headed the Digital Computer Division of MIT's Lincoln Laboratory from 1952 to 1956, where he guided the development of the Air Force SAGE (Semiautomatic Ground Environment) System. In 1956 Forrester became professor of management at the MIT Sloan School of Management, where he applied his background in computer sciences and engineering to the development of a social science field known as system dynamics, based on simulation and modeling. His first book in this field was *Indusrial Dynamics* (1961), followed by *Principles of Systems* (1968), *Urban Dynamics* (1969), and *World Dynamics* (1971). Forrester's work brought him seven honorary doctorates and numerous awards, including the National Medal of Technology (1989), the Computer Pioneer Award from the Institute of Electrical and Electronics Engineers (IEEE) Computer Society (1982), the IEEE Medal of Honor (1972), and the Valdemar Poulsen Gold Medal from the Danish Academy of Technical Sciences (1969). He was inducted into the National Inventors Hall of Fame in 1979. Thomas J. Watson, Jr., endowed the Jay W. Forrester Chair of Computer Studies at MIT in 1986. Forrester's principal contribution to futurism is his development of system dynamics as a tool to study the future of institutions and organizations.

[See also Economic Cycles: Models and Simulations.]

BIBLIOGRAPHY

Forrester, Jay W. *From the Ranch to System Dynamics: An Autobiography.* New Haven, CT: Jai Press, 1991.

— GEORGE THOMAS KURIAN

FORTUNETELLERS.

See PSEUDO-FUTURISTS.

FRAGRANCES

Fragrance in the 1990s is at the center of an olfactory revolution. Its use as a personal adornment continues unabated, but at the same time fragrance has become the focus of scientific study, as olfactory researchers and sensory psychologists search for clues to the human response to odors. Much of this research is being conducted by the nonprofit Olfactory Research Fund, the only charitable organization in the world dedicated to the study of the sense of smell and the psychological benefits of fragrance. The fund studies the effects of scent on human behavior, including such areas as sleep, stress, alertness, and social interaction.

Never have there been so many fragrance choices: over 800 scents are available in America alone. Women's fragrances are available in a broad variety, but the basics are perfume (the strongest, longest-lasting), eau de parfum, or toilet water (the next longest-lasting), and cologne (the lightest form). For men, the most concentrated scent is cologne, followed by body splash and aftershave.

In recent years, an ever-wider variety of soaps, body lotions, creams, shampoos, and gels have become increasingly popular. They offer well-known scents, as well as specially blended fragrances that have been formulated expressly to soothe or stimulate.

Our Unique Sense of Smell

Each person has his or her own individual, unique odor identity, determined by genes, skin type (dry/oily), hair color, diet (high or low fat), mental and physical health, anxiety, fear, happiness, and environmental conditions. The sense of smell is keenest between the ages of twenty and forty. It helps determine our food preferences, warns of danger, helps us make decisions about products, places and people, and enhances our well-being.

Women in general have a keener sense of smell than men, but much of this ability is learned. Women in our society are typically encouraged to use their noses more often than men are through their traditional interest in cooking, flower arrangements, interior environments, and the early use of fragrances. The fluctuations in a woman's sense of smell during a twenty-four hour period is systematically greater than a man's, due in part to female hormones.

Fragrance and Our Environment

Japan led the way in redefining the multifaceted roles of fragrance during the latter part of the twentieth century. The Shimuzu Construction Company of Tokyo developed the first computerized delivery system to circulate fragrance within closed environments (e.g., homes, office buildings, hotels, hospitals), utilizing different fragrances appropriate for each environment.

Shimuzu's studies reveal that subliminally perceived aromas have positive psychophysiological effects. Piped into convention centers, offices, or hotels, lavender, jasmine, and lemon increase the efficiency of meetings and decrease keypunch errors. Scents of seasonal flowers and ocean breezes eliminate anxiety. Lavender and peppermint help lessen mental fatigue and reduce the urge to smoke. Lemon, proven to have a stimulating effect, can energize visitors in morning conferences or inspire a mood of festivity in the banquet rooms in the evening. Jasmine works to soothe weary guests. The scent of Japanese cypress has a relaxing effect. Cinnamon piped into lounges "induces calmness." Used in an athletic facility, scents activate the circulatory system.

The problem of interior air pollution is known as "sick-building syndrome," a result of the 1973 energy crisis, which led to tighter sealing of the building envelope to conserve fuel. The Shimuzu system is designed to avoid the health hazards of the syndrome. Initially, it filters and purifies recirculated air and conditions new air, which is then fragranced as it circulates. Japan is also leading with sophisticated car deodorants, fragrance alarm clocks, fragrant games for children, and scented containers to attach to telephone mouth-pieces.

Looking to the Future

In the twenty-first century, fragrance will be more than a glamorous fashion accessory or statement of personal style. It may be routinely used to promote relaxation and reduce stress; improve work performance; elevate mood and reduce depression; modify sleep and dreams; enhance self-image; retrieve memories; enhance sexuality; and improve social relationships.

Our new comprehension of the psychological and physiological effects of fragrance will result in scientific and medical applications as well:

- Doctors will use fragrance to reduce anxiety during medical testing.
- Doctors and sensory psychologists may be able to cure functional anosmia (the inability to smell) when it is not due to nerve damage.
- People on weight-loss diets may use flavor enhancers and sprays (of food odors) to satisfy their food craving.
- Our aging population, with diminished sense of taste and smell due to the aging process, may be able to restimulate these functions with fragrance and olfactory exercises.
- Women going through menopause may use fragrances to alleviate related depressions and mood swings.
- An infant's early ability to recognize and respond to smells may be used to diagnose potential learning disabilities later in life.

As virtual reality systems mature, they may be developed to allow a person not only to see, hear, and touch, but also to smell the simulated world and the adventures within it. Fragrances will increasingly play a prominent, positive role in enhancing and expanding our sensory experiences and our daily lives.

[See also Cosmetics and Toiletries.]

BIBLIOGRAPHY

Ackerman, Diane. *Natural History of the Senses.* New York: Random House, 1990.
Jellinek, J. Stephan. "Aroma-chology: A Status Review." *Perfumer and Flavorist* 19 (September-October 1994): 25–49.
"Living Well with Your Sense of Smell." New York: Olfactory Research Fund, 1992.

— ANNETTE GREEN

FREE TIME

Free time is usually thought of as a prime indicator of the quality of life in society, because free time activities provide individuals with optimum opportunity for choice, involvement, and enjoyment. Shorter workweeks advance the quality of life in Western countries because they increase free time. However, the last half-century has produced remarkably little change in the estimated length of the American workweek. In contrast to a decline of 2.7 hours per decade in the workweek between 1850 and 1940, the per-decade decline has been less than 1 hour per week since 1940, with virtually no decrease since 1950.

These aggregate work data, however, conceal many important changes within the world of work:

- The proportion of men working has declined, particularly in the fifty-five to sixty-four age bracket (from 83 percent in 1970 to 67 percent in 1988). The average workweek for those older men who do work has declined as well.
- At the same time, there has been virtually no increase in the proportion of women aged fifty-five to sixty-four in the labor force.
- With advanced education, most individuals enter the labor force later in their lives.
- More people past age sixty-five have retired from work.
- More vacation days and holidays are available.

All these factors undoubtedly have led to less overall time spent working per lifetime for those who live to sixty-five or beyond, and likewise have reduced significantly the ratio of people presently at work to the total population. These discrepancies between official work-week figures and the "actual" time that people spend working over their lifetime indicate that the role of working time and its impact on contemporary life have been given undue prominence.

Such considerations led to the first calculation of figures for the total years spent in one's work life by the Bureau of Labor Statistics in 1985, estimated at 55 percent (38.8 years) for men and 38 percent (29.4 years) for women. No trend figures have been compiled since then, but there is good reason to expect that they are on the decline.

Data from national time-diary studies suggest that these work estimate figures do not tell the whole story about free time. The time diary is a survey instrument that attempts to account for all the ways that people spend time. Respondents are instructed to begin at midnight on a designated diary day and to report all their activities in the order in which they occurred across that entire twenty-four-hour day. In this way the diary utilizes time as a measuring tool and monitors the tradeoffs in time spent on various activities.

Because of its ability to capture all activity with minimal reporting burden, memory loss, and embarrassment to the respondent, time-diary data are now regularly collected by several government agencies in European societies. In time-diary studies free time is defined as what is left over after subtracting the time people spend working and commuting, taking care of families, doing housework, shopping, sleeping, eating, and going about other personal care activities. Stated positively, free time includes the time adults spend going to school; participating in clubs and other organizational activities; taking part in sports, recreational activities, and hobbies; or watching television, reading,

and visiting with friends and relatives—as well as all related travel time.

The Americans' Use of Time Project data in Table 1 suggest that Americans of working age have five hours *more* free time now than in the 1960s. In 1985 men had forty-one hours of free time a week, and women had forty hours of free time. Both time and demographic factors underlie this shift.

Free time is usually thought of

as a prime indicator of quality of life,

because free-time activities provide optimum

opportunity for choice, involvement, and enjoyment.

Two activity-related reasons help to account for this increase in free time: (1) Women are doing much less housework than they did several decades ago, (2) The diary workweek is shorter today than it was in 1965—not the "official" hours of work Americans report, but the work hours they record in their single-day diaries. While official workweek figures have remained fairly constant over the past few decades, the number of work hours people actually record in their diaries has fallen significantly for both men and women between 1965 and 1985 (Robinson and Bostrom, 1994).

The diary evidence is not the only data to suggest that Americans' free time should be expanding. Two demographic trends also indicate this: (1) Fewer households have children. (2) Americans are also spending more of their adult lives unmarried. At the same time, most Americans have more free time today than they did in 1965, regardless of their living arrangements. The ages of such people in the sample need to be taken into account, because people aged from fifty-one to sixty-four have gained the most free time since 1965 due to shorter workweeks.

Today's forty-hour workweek is balanced by a forty-hour play week. Like all averages, the diary data hide much individual variation and the diary data of working parents give evidence of severe time pressure. On balance, however, more people are gaining free time than losing it.

Besides showing the upward trends in the amount of free time since 1965, Table 1 also shows the domination of television in the way free time is spent, and the relatively small difference between men and women in uses of free time. Free time is not likely to decrease unless work hours increase, more adults become married, or more people decide to have children. Data on TV time

TABLE 1

HOW FREE TIME IS DISTRIBUTED ACROSS ACTIVITIES, BY YEAR AND GENDER (HOURS PER WEEK)

	Total			Men			Women	
	1985	1975	1965	1985	1975	1965	1985	1975
Total	40.1	38.3	34.5	41.1	38.6	35.6	39.6	38.3
TV	15.1	15.2	10.5	15.7	16.2	11.9	14.5	14.1
Visiting	4.9	5.5	6.6	5.0	5.1	5.9	4.8	5.7
Talking	4.3	2.2	2.6	3.5	1.9	1.8	5.1	2.7
Traveling	3.1	2.6	2.7	3.4	2.8	3.2	3.0	2.4
Reading	2.8	3.1	3.7	2.7	3.0	4.3	2.9	3.3
Sports/Outdoors	2.2	1.5	0.9	2.9	2.3	1.5	1.5	0.8
Hobbies	2.2	2.3	2.1	1.9	1.6	1.5	2.6	3.0
Adult Education	1.9	1.6	1.3	2.2	2.1	1.7	1.6	1.3
Thinking/Relaxing	1.0	1.1	0.5	1.2	1.0	0.2	0.9	1.2
Religion	0.8	1.0	0.9	0.6	0.8	0.8	1.0	1.3
Cultural Events	0.8	0.5	1.1	0.8	0.3	1.3	0.8	0.6
Clubs/Organizations	0.7	1.2	1.0	0.8	0.9	0.8	0.6	1.5
Radio/Recordings	0.3	0.5	0.6	0.4	0.6	0.7	0.3	0.4

* 1965 data not available for women.

Source: Americans' Use of Time Project.

and free time from other research organizations suggest no decrease in free time since 1985.

Television consumes about 40 percent of free time, and closer to 50 percent of viewing if a secondary activity is included. Reading time has declined, but only because of the decline in newspaper reading; book and magazine reading have increased somewhat. Other ways of spending free time have remained fairly steady across time, although attending social life—the second most popular way of spending free time—has declined somewhat.

Two additional non-diary studies provide a more detailed glimpse into trends on two important free-time activities since the 1980s, namely arts participation and fitness. Arts participation stayed relatively steady between 1982 and 1992, despite difficult conditions for the arts. The increased attendance at arts museums was offset by declines in musical theater and historic parks. Use of radio for classical music and jazz showed a notable increase, although the reading of literature showed some decline.

In the area of fitness participation, the increases found in diary studies between 1965 and 1985 have not held up since then: instead there has been a roughly 10 percent decline in overall fitness participation between 1985 and 1991. Most importantly, the declines were greater among the youngest adults (aged eighteen to twenty-five), the group that could be the trendsetters for the future. Much the same decline in arts participation is found in this group, perhaps sig-

naling the arrival of a more passive adult population in the future.

One more hopeful sign in the Table 1 data diary is that the distinctions in free time activities between men and women have decreased since 1965. That does not mean equality has been achieved, only that the trends mainly move in that direction. At the same time, other studies show that young women's fitness activity between 1985 and 1991 declined more than any other group, perhaps signaling a return to less active lifestyles of women.

In summary, Americans in general have more free time than twenty or thirty years ago. This comes both from increased life spans and its consequent increased years in retirement and from more free time for the younger (preretirement) work force. Signs are that this unofficial decrease in work time is also increasing. The lengthening life span will only accentuate that trend.

Unless more adults have children or stay married longer, or need to work longer hours to keep up their standard of living, it is doubtful the American population will experience any significant decrease in free time in the near future. Nor is there any evidence of a decrease in the dominance of TV in free time.

[See also Arts; Broadcasting; Change, Pace of; Exercise and Fitness; Gambling; Interactive Entertainment; Leisure Time; Longevity; Mass Culture and Arts; Motion Pictures; Museums; Music; Outdoor Recreation and Leisure Pursuits; Sports and Activities, Spectator; Sports and Games, Competitive; Television; Theme Parks and Organized Attractions; Tourism; Visual Arts.]

BIBLIOGRAPHY

DeGrazia, Sebastian. *Of Time, Work, and Leisure.* New York: Free Press, 1962.

Robinson, John P. *How Americans Use Time.* New York: Praeger, 1977.

———. *The Demographics of Time.* Ithaca, NY. American Demographics, 1994.

Robinson, John P., and Bostrom, Ann. "The Overestimated Workweek: What Time-Diary Studies Suggest." Monthly Labor Review (August 1994).

Robinson, John P., and Gershuny, Jonathan. "Measuring Hours of Paid Work: Time-Diary vs. Estimate Questions." *Bulletin of Labor Statistics* (January 1994).

— JOHN P. ROBINSON

FREE TRADE

Free trade or, more aptly, freer trade, has been a recent hallmark of democratic societies. Unfettered commerce creates wealth by promoting efficient use of resources and provides consumer access to lower prices and greater choice. Even though most agree that free trade has positive results in the long run, its benefits are spread unevenly among nations and groups within nations. This leads threatened groups to seek protection from their governments and leads nations to shape policies that at least attempt to create advantages for themselves in the competition between nations.

Trading blocs will dominate world trade

through the first half of the twenty-first century.

Governments intervene in trade and will increasingly do so in the future. By the twenty-first century, national governments will increasingly direct trade in their own self-interest while trying to enlarge the benefits of free trade. This give-and-take will be carried out by trading blocs that will dominate world trade through the first half of the twenty-first century.

The most likely result is a new triad of geopolitical power: one regional trade bloc in North America, another in Europe, and the third in the Pacific Rim. The reason that regionalism in trade is the likely next step in global economic evolution is that jumping from national economies to the world economy is simply too big a leap. Economist Lester Thurow has suggested that it is necessary to take smaller intermediate steps first. Regional trading blocs characterized by free trade combined with managed trade between blocs may be such a necessary step.

Why Free Trade

In 1776 Adam Smith, an early exponent of free trade, wrote in his *Wealth of Nations* that nations benefit when their citizens can buy and sell free of barriers. The low-cost producer of a commodity, Smith argues, has an advantage, because he is able to export to wider markets, while consumers benefit from being able to buy goods at low cost.

In the early 1800s, David Ricardo strengthened the free trade argument with the idea of "comparative advantage." This process leads producers in each nation or area to specialize in industries where their costs are lower. Each nation then imports goods that are relatively costlier for it to produce. Producers follow their comparative advantage, which leads to maximum worldwide production, and consumers have access to the largest possible supply of goods at lower cost.

A Cycle of Winners and Losers—Past and Future

However, there is a pattern of winners and losers in free trade. Nations that are low-cost producers favor free trade (even if they desire to protect their home markets). Their markets are greatly expanded by removing foreign barriers to trade. Nations that run a trade deficit often look to protectionism, as they see their trade position worsen.

That Adam Smith first argued for free trade at the beginning of the British Industrial Revolution is no accident. Britain needed access to large foreign markets to maximize the advantage of its increasing productive capacity. The standard of living of consumers elsewhere was enhanced through access to inexpensive British commodities, but the leaders of those nations often found British trade a disadvantage to their national well-being and attempted to close their borders.

This pattern of a small trading nation needing access to large, relatively wealthy markets recurs. The pattern repeated in the relationship between Japan and the United States. New producers need access to large foreign markets to fuel growth and favor free trade to gain such access. This has limited ill effect on the large nation unless it runs a trade deficit. Trade deficits often lead to limiting imports to create a more favorable trade balance and to shelter the domestic workforce.

Workers in displaced sectors see themselves as losers in a free trade environment and seek government protection. Even if long-term benefits from free trade are admitted, the short-term dislocation in the economy produces problems that can't be ignored.

Contemporary events in the United States show this same pattern of winners and losers. Some economists, such as Paul Krugman, advocate a "strategic trade policy." This approach calls for government protection and incentives for U.S. industries that may not be low-cost producers but are deemed important because of national interests or jobs.

Other economists, such as Robert Kuttner, argue that other countries, primarily Japan, already manage trade in their national interest; therefore, we should too. When Japan or Europe furthers its self-interest with trade policy, it frustrates the reciprocity needed for free trade to work. For example, the effort in Europe to produce a new passenger jet aircraft gave Europe an advantage over the U.S. aircraft industry. This development demonstrates the vulnerability of a strategic export industry to managed trade from other countries.

Strategic trade policy and other protectionist ideas cast a pall on free trade into the next century. Offsetting this trend, a new combination of trading arrangements is coming into being that will maximize many of the benefits of free trade and minimize adverse influences of protectionism. These new arrangements will be established by the end of the 1990s and are likely to persist well into the next century.

A Regional Trading Approach

Three great trading regions are forming. The creation of an expanded European Union (EU) has made greater Europe the leading new trading region. The EU will enlarge its present membership to include Scandinavia, the remaining countries of Central Europe, and most of Eastern Europe. The EU already comprises the world's largest single economy, which will grow as countries are added. It is likely the EU will expand in phases, so that new national economies can be most easily assimilated.

Free trade will come to dominate commerce between member countries. There will be labor mobility and specialization based on the low-cost producers within the trading bloc. They will manage trade with the rest of the world to protect their own strategic industries.

The North American trade bloc had its beginning with the approval of the U.S.-Canada Free Trade Agreement in 1988, capped by the North American Free Trade Agreement in 1993. These agreements bring Canada, Mexico, and the United States into closer trading cooperation. At the turn of the century this union will be strengthened by the addition of the Caribbean nations. Eventually, the rest of the Americas may be included in this trade bloc. Over the short term, however, Latin American economies add little to the North American economies.

The third trading bloc among economies of the Pacific Rim is likely to be centered on Japan and other nations of the Far East. The area could be formed into a regional free trade area, but there are difficulties for the Japanese to open their system enough to admit others. The economies of South Korea, Taiwan, Hong Kong, and Singapore are unlikely to welcome a closer association with Japan and may look toward alliance with China. Any trade bloc formed in this area is likely to be centered on the vast Chinese market. The Japanese may choose to forestall this development by creating what would better be characterized as a Japanese co-prosperity sphere, rather than a European- or North-American-style trading region.

Each of these three mega-regions will attempt to protect their own interests and manage trade accordingly with the rest of the world. International tensions may grow if regional protectionism leads to competition for an extended period. This competition, along with cultural differences could lead to what it has led to in the past, namely, open conflict. A more optimistic scenario features a phased integration of the large trading blocs later in the twenty-first century. What that integrated system would look like depends on which region emerges as the leader of the new economic system.

Future Regional Competitive Advantage

One of the three regions, Europe, North America, or the Pacific Rim, will assume world leadership in the twenty-first century. Momentum is on the side of a Japan-centered Pacific Rim. To continue this momentum, Japan would have to redefine its cultural solidarity, which has been one of its great strengths, to include others. Currently this appears difficult for Japan to do; but it will be a key to any future leadership role the country may have.

The United States, and with it the rest of North America, has great flexibility and an unmatched ability to organize when directly challenged. It starts out with more wealth and power than any other region. The disadvantage for North America in continuing its leadership role is its legacy of military and social commitments that currently exceed its ability to fund. Also working in its disfavor is its current leadership position. If the United States, redefined to include all of North America, assumes leadership of the next century, it will be the first time that the leader of a former system makes the transition to also lead the new.

The strategic advantage is with the Europeans. The EU has no choice but to include Middle and Eastern Europe in what Lester Thurow calls the "House of Europe." If they follow strategic considerations, they will become the leaders of the new economic system. History suggests it will be far easier for the Japanese and the Americans to put off doing what they need to do to win. Future historians may well record that the twenty-first century belonged to the House of Europe.

[See also Global Business: Dominant Organizational Forms; International Trade: Regional Trade Agreements; International Trade: Regulation; International Trade: Sustaining Growth.]

BIBLIOGRAPHY

Cleveland, Harlan. *Birth of a New World: An Open Moment for International Leadership.* San Francisco: Jossey-Bass, 1993.

Kennedy, Paul. *Preparing for the Twenty-First Century.* New York: Random House, 1993.

Krugman, Paul. *The Age of Diminished Expectations: U.S. Economic Policy in the 1990s.* Cambridge, MA: MIT Press, 1994.

Porter, Michael E. *The Competitive Advantage of Nations.* New York: Free Press, 1990.

Roberts, Russell D. *The Choice: A Fable of Free Trade and Protectionism.* Englewood Cliffs, NJ: Prentice Hall, 1994.

Smith, Adam. *An Inquiry into the Nature and Causes of the Wealth of Nations,* 1776. Reprint. New York: The Modern Library, 1937.

Thurow, Lester. *Head to Head: The Coming Economic Battle Among Japan, Europe, and America.* New York: Warner Books, 1993.

— SCOTT W. ERICKSON

FRESHWATER

Viewed from space, Earth is a strikingly blue planet. The total volume of water, some 1,360,000,000 cu km, would cover the globe to a height of 2.7 km if spread evenly over its surface. But more than 97 percent is seawater, 2 percent is locked in icecaps and glaciers, and a large portion of the remaining 1 percent lies too far underground to exploit.

Fortunately, a tiny fraction of the planet's water is renewed and made fresh by nature's solar-powered water cycle. Each year, evaporation fueled by the sun's energy lifts some 500,000 cubic kilometers of moisture into the atmosphere—86 percent from the oceans and 14 percent from the land. An equal amount falls back to the surface as rain, sleet, or snow, but it is distributed in different proportions; whereas the continents lose about 70,000 cu km through evaporation, they gain 110,000 through precipitation.

As a result, roughly 40,000 cubic kilometers are transferred from the sea to the land each year. This constitutes the world's renewable freshwater supply—what can be counted on year after year. With today's population size, it amounts to an annual average of about 7,400 cubic meters per person, several times what is needed to support a moderate standard of living. But not all this water can be used by humans as it makes its way back to the sea. Two-thirds runs off in floods, leaving about 14,000 cubic kilometers as a relatively stable source of supply. And even this stable supply is distributed very unevenly and is not always available when and where it is needed.

In each major area of water use—agriculture, industry, and cities—demands have increased rapidly. Global water use has tripled since 1950 and now stands at an estimated 4,340 cubic kilometers per year—eight times the annual flow of the Mississippi River. This total, which includes only what is removed from rivers, lakes, and ground-water, amounts to 30 percent of the world's stable renewable supply. But we actually rely on a far larger share since water bodies dilute pollution, generate electricity, and support fisheries and wildlife. And because of improved living standards, world water demand has been growing faster than population: at 800 cubic meters, per capita use today is nearly 50 percent higher than it was in 1950, and in most of the world it continues to climb.

Global water use has tripled since 1950 and now stands at an estimated 4,340 cubic kilometers per year— eight times the annual flow of the Mississippi River.

For decades, planners have met this rising demand by turning to ever more and larger "water development" projects, particularly dams and river diversions, to deliver water when and where it is wanted. Engineers have built more than 36,000 large dams around the world to control floods and to provide hydroelectric power, irrigation, industrial supplies, and drinking water to an expanding global population and economy. Rare is the river that now runs freely toward the sea, and many that still do are slated to come under control soon.

But limits to this ever expanding supply are swiftly coming to light. Engineers naturally first selected the easiest and least costly sites for water development. Over time, water projects have become increasingly complex, expensive to build, and damaging to the environment. Fewer dams and diversion projects are making it off the drawing boards, and most of those that do will deliver water at a far higher price than in the past. Worldwide, the rate of dam construction during the last decade has averaged only half that of the preceding 25 years—170 dams annually, compared with some 360 per year from 1951 to 1977. In Australia, North America, and Western Europe, few affordable and acceptable sites remain for damming and diverting more river water.

Desalination of seawater, in a sense the "ultimate" solution to the world's water problems, remains among the most expensive water supply options. At one to two dollars per cubic meter, turning ocean water into drinking water is four to eight times more expensive than the average cost of urban water supplies today, and at least ten to twenty times the prices that farmers pay currently, which are often heavily subsidized. More than 7,500 desalting plants of various kinds and sizes now operate worldwide, collectively producing 0.1 percent of the world's total water use. Desalination will be an expensive lifesaver to a growing number of coastal cities and towns bumping up against supply limits, but it will not solve the bulk of the world's water problems for the foreseeable future.

Meeting human needs while facing up to water's limits—economic, ecological, and political—entails developing a wholly new relationship to water systems. Historically we have managed water with a frontier philosophy, manipulating natural systems to whatever degree engineering know-how would permit. Modern society has come to view water only as a resource that is there for the taking, rather than as a living system that drives the workings of a natural world we depend on. Now, instead of continuously reaching out for more, we must begin to look within our regions, communities, homes, and even ourselves for ways to meet our needs while respecting water's life-sustaining functions.

Conservation, once viewed as just an emergency response to drought, has been transformed in recent years into a sophisticated package of measures that offers a cost-effective and environmentally sound way of balancing water budgets. By using water more efficiently, in effect, we create a new source of supply. Each liter conserved can help meet new water demands without damming another stretch of river or depleting more ground-water. Reducing irrigation needs by one-tenth, for instance, would free up enough water to roughly double domestic water use worldwide.

With technologies and methods available today, many farmers could cut their water needs by 10 to 50 percent, industries by 40 to 90 percent, and cities by one-third, with no sacrifice of economic output or quality of life. Besides being more ecologically sound, most investments in water efficiency, recycling, reuse, and conservation yield more usable water per dollar than do investments in conventional water supply projects. Putting in place the policies, laws, and institutions that

Only a small, precious fraction of the Earth's total water volume is freshwater that we can use. (Danny Lehman/© Corbis)

encourage the spread of water-saving measures is an urgent challenge in building a society that is sustainable in all respects.

[See also Acid Rain; Deforestation; Environment; Fisheries; Oceans; Resources.]

BIBLIOGRAPHY

Gleick, Peter H., ed. *Water in Crisis: A Guide to the World's Fresh Water Resources.* New York: Oxford University Press, 1993.

Moore, Deborah, and Willey, Zach. "Water in the American West: Institutional Evolution and Environmental Restoration in the Twenty-first Century." *Colorado Law Review* 62/4 (1991): 775–825.

Postel, Sandra L. *Last Oasis: Facing Water Scarcity.* New York: W. W. Norton, 1992.

Shiklomanov, I. A. "Global Water Resources." *Nature and Resources* 26/3 (1990): 34–43.

Van der Leeden, Frits; Troise, Fred L.; and Todd, David Keith, eds. *The Water Encyclopedia.* Chelsea, MI: Lewis Publishers, 1990.

— SANDRA L. POSTEL

FULLER, RICHARD BUCKMINSTER (1895–1983)

Born in Milton, Massachusetts, R. Buckminster Fuller was a maverick American inventor, philosopher, and author who steadfastly remained a generalist in an era of specialization. He achieved universal recognition for his contributions to architecture, yet he was not an architect in the strict sense, but an engineer of huge structures. The best-known of these structures are the geodesic domes based on three-dimensional principles that he developed to achieve maximum spans with a minimum of materials. The most spectacular one was built for the Montreal Exposition of 1967. Fuller produced his most important design, the Dymaxion (the name derived from "dynamic plus maximum efficiency") in 1927. He was fascinated with simple, lightweight structures. "How much does the building weigh?" was his favorite question. What set Fuller apart from other architects and engineers was his invincible optimism and his belief in technology as the driver of social change. A rugged individualist, he filled his writings with the spirit of a scientific frontiersman: *Ideas and Integrities: A Spontaneous Autobiographical Disclosure* (1963), *I Seem to Be a Verb* (1970), and *Critical Path* (1983). The word *livingry* (meaning "tools for living," modeled on *weaponry*) was one of his contributions to the English language.

BIBLIOGRAPHY

Edmondson, Amy C. *A Fuller Explanation: The Synergistic Geometry of R. Buckminster Fuller.* Boston: Birkhauser, 1986.

Seiden, L. S. *Buckminster Fuller's Universe.* New York: Plenum Press, 1989.

— GEORGE THOMAS KURIAN

FUTURE: NEAR-, MID-, AND LONG-TERM

What is the future?

The future is all that is not yet. The future comprises all that could be but is not now. The future is all possible tomorrows taken together. If the present is "now," then the future is all the potential or possible "nows."

What we mean by the present may be as thin a slice of time as the present instant or tick of the clock—or it may be a much looser term, referring to "nowadays," as contrasted with "olden times."

The past also is an imprecise term. Sometimes it means what just happened and everything that preceded it. But at other times we mean by the past everything that happened "before my lifetime" or "before the present era."

What we mean by the future is similarly elastic. On the one hand, the future is what will happen tomorrow, next year, and after we are dead and gone. But the future in considerable measure is also the result of what is being done (or not done) today and was done in the past by people like ourselves.

Not Entirely of Our Doing

The future, like the present and the past, is made possible by all the biological and physical (geological, chemical, meteorological, gravitational, magnetic) processes of planet Earth. The physical energy that drives these processes, and makes life and the future possible, comes to the Earth from Earth's star, our sun. So, like the past and the present, the future is not entirely of our human doing.

The physical energy that makes the future possible is channeled through the succession of present moments like a river. This energy cascades not only through the biological and physical processes of our bodies and the body of planet Earth; it is also directed by our human activities so that it passes through the technologies and institutions and social orders that have been and are being invented by human minds and then fashioned into the human-created worlds of yesterday, today, and tomorrow.

So the making of the future is a very natural thing that happens apart from us. And at the same time it is also a very human process that we all participate in, even if it is not entirely of our doing.

Starting to Map the Future

Maps usually refer to towns and to terrain and geography. But maps also can refer to what is not yet, what we are trying to understand or give shape. For example, before a skyscraper or a new type of airplane is built, there are extensive working drawings or blueprints as well as budgets. All of these are kinds of maps. Such maps of the future help us think through our planning processes. Later, they help guide us in creating the physical embodiments of what we are inventing.

The future is a natural thing that happens

apart from us. At the same time, it is also

a human process that we all participate in,

even if it is not entirely of our doing.

So maps are mental models of a present or future reality (or even of a past reality). Sometimes the maps are detailed and precise; sometimes they are very broad and general. A map of your neighborhood can be very detailed, while a map of a continent necessarily has to be very general and leaves out everything but the most general outlines.

In mapping the future it is helpful to distinguish among several kinds of future maps. One kind of future map lays out what is "in the cards" and nearly certain to happen. For example, if we drop a glass marble out of a window, it is nearly certain to hit the ground. Of course, someone might be passing by and catch it, and then it would not hit the ground. But apart from that sort of major interference, we expect that in the next instant of time a marble we drop will hit the ground.

In a similar way, demographers who study changes in the size of our human numbers can tell us with nearly as great certainty the number of women of childbearing age there will be twenty years from now. The reason for their near-certainty is that these future women are today's young girls.

So in some respects the near and also the more distant future have built-in momentum to them. They are in those respects going to be the consequences of forces and processes that have been (or are just now being) set in motion. So these aspects of the future can already be observed today.

When we can see a future consequence that has this sort of relative clarity, it is part of what it is useful to think of as "the near future." The near future refers to your marble hitting the ground in the next instant as well as to the number of women of childbearing age twenty years from now. Likewise, atmospheric scientists know with reasonable certainty that it will take nearly a century for the upper atmosphere to neutralize the chlorofluorocarbons that are causing the ozone hole there. So the near future that we can see with relative clarity can include events even a century hence.

It is useful also to speak of "the distant future," meaning all the things about future tomorrows that we cannot yet know. This is the portion of the future that is still unforeseeable and is truly a mystery to us.

The person who tonight wins the lottery (or is hit by a car) is experiencing an event that for him or her (and for us) is still in the distant future. These events are in what we are calling the distant future, because they are still over the horizon of the future, beyond our present field of vision and anticipation.

So the term *the distant future* can refer to events as soon as the next instant and also as distant as a very long time hence. The essential thing about the distant future is that it is still unknowable.

Attempting to Explore "The Middle Future"

Then there is another part of the future we can call "the middle future." This is the part of the future we can glimpse in some of its outlines today but that is still very much subject to being reshaped by our human activities and actions and inactions.

By the middle future we mean those parts of the future we can still do something about, to help or to hinder, to accelerate or to slow, to bring about or to prevent totally. The middle future is for many people the most interesting part of the future. Various techniques have been developed to explore the middle future and to study what is becoming more clear to us as within the range of our potential futures.

After one of those possible futures has happened, it becomes the present, and then the past. Then it will appear always to have been inevitable. But as long as it is still in the future, it is uncertain and competing with many other similar (and dissimilar) alternative futures that also might come to be.

Think about it this way: The world we live in today was not inevitable. It very well could have turned out differently.

In a similar way, the rest of the future is not just going to occur. Futures are actively chosen and made *to happen* by individuals, by organizations, by technologies, by entire cultures. We make these choices of our future by what we do—and also by what we ignore or forget or neglect or simply are unwilling to do.

Techniques for exploring the middle future are important tools for helping us imagine, or "see," what we might be doing, or what we might be choosing. These techniques function for us the way headlights do for someone who is driving an automobile at night. They help us see where we will soon be going, so we can choose where to steer, to go faster or slower, or to stop and go by some better way.

Forecasting is a way of extending what has been happening into the future, to see where the present path will take us if nothing intervenes. *Scenarios* of the future usually start with a desired objective or goal and then attempt to find a path from now to that desired future. Scenarios are like a spotlight into a night sky, in that what is illuminated is a portion (often called "an envelope") of the possible future. Forecasting tells us where we are likely to go, based on the past; scenarios tell us where we might go, if we choose to.

None of these methods prescribes a definite future or completely predicts a future. But like driving a car at night with the headlights turned on, they are better than no light at all.

Computer specialist Douglas Roberts says: "Your future won't announce itself with great fanfare. It is simply the continuous melding of today with tomorrow. It will occur over and over again. Its brightness is a matter of how much of what you do today is usable tomorrow." On a different note, Mostafa K. Tolba says: "The problems that overwhelm us today are precisely those we failed to solve decades ago."

[See also *Apocalyptic Future; Change, Cultural; Change, Epochal; Change, Pace of; Continuity and Discontinuity; Dystopias; Economic Cycles: Models and Simulations; Forecasting Methods; Futures Concepts; Futurism; Laws, Evolution of; Multifold Trend; Surveys.*]

BIBLIOGRAPHY

Jouvenel, Bertrand de. *The Art of Conjecture.* New York: Basic Books, 1967.
Martel, Leon. *Mastering Change: The Key to Business Success.* New York: Simon & Schuster, 1986.
Merriam, John E., and Makower, Joel. *Trend Watching: How the Media Create Trends and How to Be the First to Uncover Them.* New York: AMACON/Tilden Press, 1988.
United Nations. *Global Outlook 2000: An Economic, Social, and Environmental Perspective.* New York: United Nations, 1990.

— DAVID DODSON GRAY

FUTURES CONCEPTS

Futures concepts are among the primary "building blocks" of the futures field. They enhance the capacity to engage in futures work and to create structures of increasing sophistication such as theories, methodologies, and literature. In short, they provide a basis for futures discourse.

Futures concepts can be explored through a core knowledge base. Components of this core knowledge include:

- Language, concepts, and metaphors
- Theories, ideas, and images
- Literature and practitioners
- Organizations, institutions, and networks
- Methodologies, tools, and practices
- Social movements and innovations

Stereotyped accounts of the futures field throw these core elements out of focus and fail to portray the substantive work of practicing futurists. For example, "the future" has been intellectually miscast as an "empty space" rather than as a dynamic field of potentials interacting richly with the present. It also has been overly identified with prediction, forecasting, think tanks, and Western corporate, positivistic "futurology."

Much visually compelling but often spurious, pseudo-futuristic imagery from film, television, and science fiction tends to be diversionary or ambiguous.

Pop futurists, such as John Naisbitt and Alvin and Heidi Toffler, achieved widespread attention with concepts such as "megatrends" and "future shock." Futures scholars, however, tend to be critical of the pop futurist perspective, arguing that it takes existing social relations as a given constant, is ideologically naive, provides unconscious support for the status quo, and places undue emphasis on the superficial aspects of technology and science. Much visually compelling but often spurious, pseudo-futuristic imagery from film, television, and science fiction tends to be diversionary or ambiguous. Mass culture material of this sort can stimulate useful questions. On the whole, however, it fails to explore real alternatives or to describe more substantive matters.

Futures studies possesses a developing substantive knowledge base. It can be accessed, in part, through periodicals. Two of the leading journals are *Futures* (U.K.) and *Technological Forecasting and Social Change* (U.S.). These are complemented by *Futures Research Quarterly, Future Survey, The Futurist* (published by the World Future Society), and *21C* (Australia). Others include the *Future Generations Journal* (Malta) and *Social Inventions* (London).

Many publications are put out by futures organizations such as the World Future Society (WFS) based in Washington, and the World Futures Studies Federation (WFSF) with its secretariat located in Brisbane, Australia. The former is the largest such organization in the world. It hosts some fine, well-attended conferences, but it tends to be popular, noncritical, and corporatist in outlook. The much smaller WFSF with about 500 members, is more facilitative, culturally critical, and genuinely international in outlook.

A range of institutions and organizations cluster around the core. They include the Institute for Futures Studies (Stockholm), the Club of Rome (Italy), the Network on Responsibilities to Future Generations (Malta), the Secretariat for Futures Studies (Germany), the Institute for Social Inventions (London), the Robert Jungk Futures Library (Salzburg), and Australia's Commission for the Future (Melbourne). There are a hundred or more of these organizations worldwide. Some are underfunded and understaffed. By pioneering "institutions of foresight" they provide a valuable seedbed for innovation. Overlapping these near-core units is a diverse range of futures-related organizations including private consultancies and other nongovernmental organizations, government bodies, and other international groups. Together these institutions constitute a powerful force for innovation, constructive change, and a means of responding to the challenges of the future.

At the core of applied futures work is methodology. Theodore J. Gordon's summary of forecasting methods is shown in Table 1.

Martha J. Garret (1993) describes the elements and methods of futures study in terms of a number of categories, or steps: limiting the scope of a particular study;

TABLE 1

AN OUTLINE OF FORECASTING METHODS

	Normative	Explanatory
Quantiative	Scenarios	Scenarios
	Technology	Time series
	sequence analysis	Regression analysis
		Multiple-equation
		models
		Probabilistic
		models
		• Trend impact
		• Cross impact
		• Interax
		Nonlinear models
Qualitative	Scenarios	Scenarios
	Delphi	Delphi
	In-depth interviews	In-depth interviews
	Expert groups	Expert groups
	Genius	Genius
	Science fiction	

Source: Gordon, 1992.

gathering information; determining key variables; examining the past and the present; identifying the actors; choosing the assumptions; constructing scenarios; evaluating choices; and selecting strategies and tactics. Other practitioners have developed a variety of sequenced steps or methodologies that incorporate these and other elements—for example, Michel Godet's *Prospective,* Joseph Coates's *Issues and Management,* and the quest technique pioneered by Burt Nanus and Selwyn Enzer. Overall, there are at least three distinct futures traditions: (1) the empirical/analytic tradition, as exemplified by the writings of Herman Kahn and Julian Simon, which is positivist, corporate in nature, and primarily North American in origin and orientation; (2) the critical-interpretative tradition, exemplified by Bertrand de Jouvenel and Robert Jungk, which can be characterized as comparative, critical, and unaligned, and is primarily European in origin; and (3) the activist-visionary tradition, exemplified by Elise Boulding and Joanna Macy, which is characterized as applied, facilitative, and universal. Although these traditions are quite distinct, they are not completely separate.

In addition, differences of method and approach can be clarified by recognizing distinct levels of futures work: pop futurism, problem-focused futures study, critical futures study, and epistemological futures study.

Pop futurism identifies problems and seeks to explore solutions at an empirical or taken-for-granted level. It overlooks the central role of world-view assumptions and cultural editing. Prime examples include *The Limits to Growth* (Dennis Meadows et al., 1972) and *Engines of Creation* (Eric Drexler, 1986).

Critical futures study involves the comparative analysis of assumptions, presuppositions, and paradigms. It actively considers the influence of different cultural orientations and traditions of enquiry—for example, *Paradigms in Progress* (Hazel Henderson, 1991) and *Global Mind Change* (Willis Harman, 1988).

Epistemological futures study locates and describes sources of "problems" in worldviews and ways of knowing; it sees "solutions" as arising from deep-seated and unpredictable shifts at this level and reveals the deepest sources of cultural innovation and adaptability—for example, *The Reenchantment of the World* (Morris Berman, 1981) and *Eye to Eye: The Quest for the New Paradigm* (Ken Wilber, 1990).

Progression though this tier escalates in sophistication as problems and methods become increasingly challenging. At the same time the ability to grasp and understand deeply embedded cultural and futures concerns is progressively enhanced by increasingly elaborate methods. From this it may be surmised that the "best" futures work and the most productive futures concepts are structurally simple, yet both are capable of substantial elaboration and deepening, according to capacity and need. Most futures studies are likely to draw on more than one level of futures methodology.

[See also Future Studies; Futures Education; Futurism; Futurists; de Jouvenel, Bertrand; Kahn, Herman; Naisbitt, John; Scenarios; Science Fiction; Toffler, Alvin and Heidi.]

BIBLIOGRAPHY

Coates, Joseph F. *Issues Management.* Washington, DC: Lomond, 1986.

Garrett, Martha J. "A Way Through the Maze: What Futurists Do and How They Do It." *Futures* 25/3 (1993): 254–274.

Godet, Michel. *From Anticipation to Action.* Paris: UNESCO, 1993.

Gordon, Theodore J. "The Methods of Futures Research." *Annals* (AAPSS) 522 (1992): 25–35.

Henderson, Hazel. "Social Innovation and Citizen Movements." *Futures* 25/3 (1993): 339–347.

Nanus, Burt. "QUEST—Quick Environmental Scanning Technique." *Long-Range Planning* 15/2 (1982): 39–45.

Slaughter, Richard A. *Futures Concepts and Powerful Ideas.* Melbourne: Futures Study Centre, 1991. Revised and expanded, 1995.

— RICHARD A. SLAUGHTER

FUTURES EDUCATION

The fundamental objective of "futures studies" or "future-oriented education" is to gain an awareness of probable and possible future perils, problems, and promises resulting from scientific and technological innovations and their myriad effects upon the global environment, life in general, and humanity. Such studies serve not only to enlighten but also to stimulate timely action to meet the challenges or opportunities that confront humanity.

Futures studies by their nature are interdisciplinary in that they often transcend traditional academic boundaries and avoid narrow specializations. Instead, they concentrate on complex, interrelated phenomena affecting the natural environment, demography, society, economy, politics, and religion.

Futures studies are especially important today as the environmental toll of the worldwide spread of industrial civilization is coming due. The Industrial Revolution improved the living conditions of vast numbers of people, but by the mid-twentieth century it became increasingly clear that a high—but heretofore overlooked—price was being paid for material progress. All too frequently that price was not recognized or regarded with sufficient seriousness. This shortsightedness stemmed more from ignorance or difficulties of calculation than from malice.

High-tech civilization is characterized by ever more ingenious innovations, expanding new fields of scientific exploration, and achievement with expectations of more marvels to come. In the aftermath of these advances there is a growing apprehension about the planet's ecological future.

At present, the power in human hands is awesome and truly unique. The ability to cause widespread or permanent destruction is now being coupled with the capacity to play the role of gods in creating or refashioning life on this planet through biotechnology and genetic engineering. Such unprecedented developments suggest the genuine need for and the wisdom of developing a serious, sustained interest in the future.

The advent of the twenty-first century is being marked by worldwide attempts to conceptualize the likely positive and negative effects of scientific and technological trends and developments. In this context, futures studies can perform a vital role by providing early warning of serious problems ahead and casting new light on today's problems. Other useful functions involve technological forecasting and the creation of imaginative scenarios depicting alternative futures. These studies serve yet another valuable function in providing "self-negating forecasts." These forecasts have considerable social utility in that they elicit positive action to thwart the forecast made and thereby invalidate it.

Growing numbers of educators in the highly developed as well as developing nations recognize the important role such studies play in preparing people for their own future, that of their country, and that of future generations. This situation has given rise to the growth of future-oriented courses and programs worldwide, especially in the Western world, on the Indian subcontinent, and in East Asia.

Following numerous national, regional, and global futurist meetings over several years, the need for improving currently offered courses in futures studies was discussed, and guidance in the development of new courses and programs was sought. In late 1990, following the initial efforts of Michael Marien, editor of *Future Survey,* and Allen Tough, professor of futures studies at the Ontario Institute for Studies in Education, the Prep 21 Project was inaugurated to encourage future-oriented studies in universities and colleges, as well as in secondary schools, worldwide. A core curriculum of courses, it was felt, could help educators to prepare for the challenges and opportunities ahead.

Worldwide examples of futurist courses of study have been gathered together and presented in the *Prep 21 Course/Program Guide.* This selection of future-oriented programs, many of them oriented to higher education, could be modified for use at the secondary level. The Future Problem Solving Program may not constitute futures studies as conceived by many futurists, but it possesses features that most futurists may wish to emulate. An estimated 200,000 students nationally and internationally use the program materials, which cover students from kindergarden through twelfth grade.

A descriptive brochure provides an overview of the educational program:

> The Future Problem Solving Program is a year-long program in which teams of four students use a six-step problem solving process to deal with complex scientific and social problems of the future. At regular intervals throughout the year, the teams mail their work to evaluators, who review it and return it with their suggestions for improvement. As the year progresses, the teams become increasingly more proficient in problem solving. The Future Problem Solving Program takes students beyond memorization. The program challenges students to apply information they have learned to some of the most complex issues facing society. They are asked to *think,* to make decisions, and, in some instances, to carry out their solutions.

Though the challenges before humanity are complex, difficult, and all too frequently may appear daunting, there is cause for tempered optimism. If we are able to enlist the creative imagination, energy, and dedication of the world's students, we have every reason to face the future with confidence. An education which incorporates future-oriented studies may facilitate the achievement of this end.

[See also Future Studies; Futurism.]

BIBLIOGRAPHY

Cornish, Edward. *The Study of the Future: An Introduction to the Art and Science of Understanding and Shaping Tomorrow's World.* Washington, DC: World Future Society, 1977.

Didsbury, Jr., Howard F. *Prep 21 Course/Program Guide. A Selection of Future-Oriented Courses/Programs.* Bethesda, MD: World Future Society, 1994.

Jennings, Lane, ed. *The Futures Research Directory: Organizations and Periodicals, 1993–1994.* Bethesda, MD: World Future Society, 1993.

Klare, Michael T., ed. *Peace and World Security Studies: A Curriculum Guide,* 6th ed. Boulder, CO: n.p., 1994.

World Future Society Project Staff. *The Futures Research Directory: Individuals, 1991–1992.* Bethesda, MD: World Future Society, 1991.

– HOWARD F. DIDSBURY, JR.

FUTURE STUDIES

Future studies lacks a shared understanding of what it is and a shared vision of what it ought to be. The collective study of the future also is known as "futures studies," to emphasize alternative futures. Some term the enterprise futurology. The terms *futurology* or *futurologist,* which suggest some sort of rigorous science, may be overreaching. Future studies has little to do with science fiction, and science fiction authors have made only modest contributions to nonfictional futures thinking. Future studies, at its best, draws from the natural and social sciences.

In time, future studies may develop into something resembling an academic field of study or a discipline.

Some contend that future studies is a field of study or even a discipline. Little evidence is given to support this wishful assertion. In time, the embryonic enterprise of future studies may develop into something resembling an academic field of study or a discipline.

Futures studies may be conceived as a very fuzzy "multifield," or the key integrative core that enables a broad and long-term approach to human understanding. The fuzzy core entity approach derives from looking at the people involved, the topics considered, and the methods used. *Future Survey* (1979–1994) lists 13,000 abstracts of futures-relevant books, reports, and articles; and the two volumes of the *Futures Research Directory* assemble information on 1,172 individuals, 187 organizations, and 124 periodicals. Both the abstracts and the directories identify something less than half of only the English language part of future studies worldwide.

Who Is a Futurist?

There are no set qualifications for someone to be a "futurist." Some call themselves forecasters, trend-watchers, planners, policy analysts, social critics, environmentalists, and so on. Others call themselves futurists, but as a secondary identity thereby retaining their primary identity as a sociologist, consultant, or other professional practitioner. In a 1993 survey only 25 percent identified themselves primarily as futurists, with another 43 percent calling themselves secondarily futurists. The most popular primary identity, indicated by 34 percent of respondents, was as "planners."

Very roughly, about one-quarter of the literature cited in *Future Survey* was written by people who call themselves futurists, primarily or secondarily. Another quarter of the literature—writing that is equally broad and long-term—is published by non-avowed futurists.

Roughly half of the literature is written by obvious specialists, albeit "futurized specialists" who are experts in thinking somewhat broadly about the future of their field.

What Does a Futurist Think About?

Statements about what a futurist ought to think about often suggest an informed generalist who can wisely prognosticate about a wide variety of matters. A few futurists approach this ideal, but the vast majority of necessity specialize in one or a few sectors.

Richard Slaughter has recently proposed twenty key concepts (such as sustainability, the metaproblem, choices, and so forth) that *ideally* should be shared by practitioners in the "futures field." A 1989 study by Joseph F. Coates and Jennifer Jarratt covering seventeen aging male futurists (all but one of them American) revealed a surprising diversity of views.

The index in this encyclopedia or the table of contents in *Future Survey Annual* indicates the diversity of "future studies." The fourteen major FS categories include: World Futures, the Global Economy, World Regions and Nations, Defense and Disarmament, Sustainability (added in 1993), Environmental Issues, Food and Agriculture, Society and Politics (including Crime, previously a separate category), the Economy and Cities (including Work, previously separate), Health, Education, Communications, Science and Technology, and Methods to Shape the Future.

Futurists think broadly about global issues (or the global aspects of domestic issues), acknowledge the imperatives of sustainability, think about new technologies, consider alternative futures (both possible and preferable), and stress the complexity of a dynamic world.

Four distinct "cultures" of futures studies have emerged in recent years: Science and Technology Futurists (including those who focus on the emerging information society), holding a long-term and optimistic view; Business Futurists (including people in business, consultants, and business school professors), with a short-term and optimistic view; Social Issue Futurists (including those who specialize in education, health, families, cities, or work), with a short-term and pessimistic view; and Green Futurists (including environmentalists and those who advocate a sustainable world, who often hold a long-term and pessimistic view.

How Does a Futurist Think?

Popular myths about futurists associate them with crystal balls, and predictions of what will happen. Futurists think and write in a variety of styles, ranging from lightly popular to impenetrable academic language.

Many futurists believe that the primary activity of future studies is forecasting, or thinking about the most probable future, involving computers and quantifying methods, such as Delphi, cross-impact matrices, and complex models. The Delphi technique, presumably a key method of future studies, is expensive to employ and subject to much abuse. Moreover, there is no batting average for futurists in anticipating various developments.

In an increasingly uncertain world that nevertheless needs some forward-thinking as guidance, there is a movement away from forecasting the most probable future to sketching scenarios of possible futures (e.g., the best possible, best probable, worst probable, and worst possible). In an increasingly complex world, the emphasis shifts from long-term futures to short-term futures and trying to make sense of present trends. With the growing concern for ethics, there is a trend away from passive forecasting of probable and possible futures to advocating preferable futures—what we should do.

Sound thinking about the future involves three obvious "P's": studying the probable, the possible, and the preferable; and, there are three less obvious "P's": studying the present (including recent changes and new ways to think about our condition), studying the past (especially our historical anticipations and how they turned out), and encouraging the panoramic (promoting integration, overviews, systems thinking, and wide-angled views).

Futurists do not predict so much as they portray what is probable, possible, and preferable. Furthermore, when well executed, the present, the past, and the panoramic are properly addressed. Developing such perspectives is a demanding task. There are many imperfect efforts.

Recent Trends and Possible Futures

People everywhere will always think about the future, in one way or another. As suggested in the introduction to this encyclopedia by Alvin and Heidi Toffler, everyone is a futurist.

There is no common background for professional futurists. Only a handful of academic courses and programs in the field of future studies per se are currently available. There are, however, many courses and programs in related subject areas, such as environmental studies, peace studies, science and technology studies, and so on.

Since the early 1980s, there has been a proliferation of futures-relevant magazines, journals, and especially newsletters. The number of new futures-relevant books has remained about the same in recent times.

Currently, the need is greater than ever for some sort of specialty in broad and long-term thinking about human affairs—for "horizontal" thinkers who can integrate the many ideas of the more conventional "vertical" thinkers who are constrained by the boundaries of their traditional disciplines and professions.

There have been several futurist movements throughout American history, and perhaps elsewhere in the world. Edward Bellamy's "nationalist movement" in the 1890s was widely acclaimed. Another future studies movement may well arise, perhaps precipitated by the magic of the millennial year 2000. On the other hand, it may already be under way, building on the widespread interest in sustainability.

[See also Futures Concepts; Futures Education; Futurism; Futurists; Toffler, Alvin and Heidi.]

BIBLIOGRAPHY

Coates, Joseph F., and Jarratt, Jennifer. *What Futurists Believe.* Mt. Airy, MD: Lomond Publications; Bethesda, MD: World Future Society, 1989.

Kerr, Clark. *Higher Education Cannot Escape History: Issues for the Twenty-first Century.* Albany, NY: State University of New York Press, 1994.

Marien, Michael, ed. *Future Survey Annual, 1995.* Bethesda, MD: World Future Society, 1995.

Masini, Eleonora Barbieri. *Why Futures Studies?* London: Grey Seal Books, 1993.

Slaughter, Richard, ed. "The Knowledge Base of Futures Studies." *Futures* 25/3 (1993). 227–274.

— MICHAEL MARIEN

FUTURISM

In common parlance, the term *futurism* refers either to a belief that human life will be fulfilled in some future epoch or to a movement in the fine arts that repudiates the heritage of the past. In recent decades, it has also become more or less synonymous with the study of possible, preferable, and probable futures. A *futurist,* by the same token, is defined as a practitioner of futures inquiry.

Men and women have tried to foresee the future throughout history. In premodern times, their principal method was divination—the interpretation by priests or oracles of portents in nature, from the movements of the stars (astrology) to the entrails of sacrificial animals (haruspication). In the Jewish tradition, the role of the diviner was played by the divinely inspired prophet, and in the Christian tradition, by the apostles and fathers of the early church. Several books of the Jewish Bible, such as *Jeremiah* and *Daniel,* and the last book of the Christian New Testament, *The Revelation of St. John,* are explicitly futurist texts. Together with a few seminal works by churchmen, notably St. Augustine's *City of God,* these texts shaped serious thought about the future throughout medieval and early modern times.

As a general rule, what minds can conceive almost always can be created, given the necessary resources and time.

In the late eighteenth century, a purely secular vision of the future arose, based in good measure on readings of the advancement of mathematics and the natural sciences. Thinkers such as the Marquis de Condorcet argued that the progress of the human mind in the modern era would usher in a golden age of world peace, prosperity, and equality. In the nineteenth century, belief in the general, virtually inevitable progress of humankind became a dogma of social science, as illustrated by the influential treatises of the founders of sociology, Auguste Comte in France and Herbert Spencer in Great Britain. Karl Marx anticipated the future worldwide triumph of socialism on the basis of a reputedly scientific analysis of socioeconomic history. By the second half of the nineteenth century, science had largely replaced magic and divine revelation as the way to fathom the future.

Futurism in the twentieth century continues to be dominated by the conviction that methodologies borrowed from mathematics and the natural and social sciences can yield knowledge of future times. Few practitioners, however, still believe that the future—and in particular the long-term future—can be "predicted" with deadly accuracy. As Edward Cornish has written, "The study of the future is, strictly speaking, the study of ideas about the future." No one can predict the future, because to some indefinable extent, it is a time that living men and women will shape by their free decisions in the here and now. In effect, futurist inquiry has become the study of possibilities that are plausible in terms of present-day knowledge and theory.

The genesis of contemporary futurism can be traced to the beginning of the twentieth century, when many social scientists and others tried to imagine what life would be like in the new century. The most durable of these efforts was *Anticipations of the Reaction of Mechanical and Scientific Progress upon Human Life and*

Thought, written in 1901 and published as a book the following year by the English novelist and social philosopher H. G. Wells. In 1902 Wells also delivered a lecture, "The Discovery of the Future," in which he called for the founding of a systematic science of the future.

Over the next forty-four years, until his death in 1946, Wells published dozens of prophetic books that made skillful application of his talents as a science writer, historian, and sociologist. The author of *The Time Machine, The War of the Worlds,* and *The First Men in the Moon,* he was also one of the founders of modern science fiction, which has made a significant contribution to futurist speculation in this century. As a general rule, what minds can conceive almost always can be created, given the necessary resources and time. In 1914, in his novel *The World Set Free,* Wells foresaw in remarkably prescient detail the coming of the nuclear power industry and the invention and use in warfare of the atomic bomb.

Wells's appeal to establish a science of the future was not answered during his lifetime. But he helped keep futurism alive, as did various thinkers and writers in the generation that followed his. Systematic efforts to probe the future were made during the early and middle decades of the century by several renowned thinkers, including the historians Oswald Spengler and Arnold J. Toynbee, who utilized a cyclical theory of comparative world history to forecast the decline and fall of Western civilization, and the Jesuit anthropologist and philosopher Pierre Teilhard de Chardin, who combined insights from science and religion to outline the future societal and spiritual evolution of humankind.

Futures studies as a self-conscious movement of thought and research did not crystallize, however, until the 1960s. A confluence of trends made this possible. These included the urgent need of ever-expanding government departments and multinational corporations for long-range planning, advances in economic and technological forecasting, progress in the policy sciences, and the erosion of disciplinary boundaries in academic life, making it increasingly possible for social and natural scientists and even humanists to work together on common tasks. Associations of futurists such as the World Future Society (founded in 1966 in Washington), the Association Internationale Futuribles (founded in 1967 in Paris), and the Club of Rome (founded in 1968), gave wide publicity to the futures movement.

Soon, hundreds of researchers in various fields who had known little or nothing of one another's work began to interact. Two defining moments in the rise of contemporary futurism were the publication of *Future Shock* by Alvin Toffler in 1970 and of *The Limits to Growth* by Donella H. Meadows and associates under the sponsorship of the Club of Rome in 1972. Both books became bestsellers, helping to make the study of the future a matter of broad public as well as scholarly interest. At about the same time, many colleges and universities started to offer courses and interdisciplinary programs in futures studies, especially in the United States. The 1970s were a particularly rich decade for futurism, as major books appeared from such luminaries as Daniel Bell, Herman Kahn, and E. F. Schumacher. Modest growth continued in the 1980s and '90s, in Asia, Africa, and Latin America as well as in North America and Europe.

The methods used by futurists today range from the abstruse, highly technical procedures of econometric forecasters to intuitive speculation by specialists in the psychospiritual future. At least five methodologies are especially popular: trend extrapolation, mathematical modeling, the Delphi technique for pooling expert opinion, scenario building (which may include the more serious sorts of science fiction), and "probabilistic" techniques (e.g., trend-impact and cross-impact analysis). Some futurists outside the mainstream also continue to show interest in the insights of Marxian analysis. Others find stimulus in holistic philosophies grounded in ecological thought and contemporary revivals of traditional religious belief.

The challenge for futurists in the twenty-first century is to develop an integrative methodology that can fuse some or many of these approaches and create what H. G. Wells hoped for in his path-breaking, 1902 lecture—an authentic science of futures inquiry.

[See also Bell, Daniel; Cornish, Edward S.; Dystopias; Forecasting Methods; Future Studies; Futures Concepts; Futures Education; Futurists; Kahn, Herman; Pseudo-Futurists; Scenarios; Science Fiction; Spengler, Oswald; Toffler, Alvin and Heidi; Utopias; Wells, H. G.]

BIBLIOGRAPHY

Clarke, I. F. *The Pattern of Expectation, 1644–2001.* New York: Basic Books, 1979.

Gordon, Theodore J. "The Methods of Futures Research." *The Annals of the American Academy of Political and Social Science* 522 (1992): 25–35.

Helmer, Olaf. *Looking Forward: A Guide to Futures Research.* Beverly Hills, CA: Sage Publications, 1983.

Hughes, Barry B. *World Futures: A Critical Analysis of Alternatives.* Baltimore: Johns Hopkins University Press, 1985.

Polak, Frederik L. *The Image of the Future.* New York: Oceana Publications, 1961.

Wagar, W. Warren. *The Next Three Futures: Paradigms of Things to Come.* Westport, CT: Greenwood Press, 1991.

— W. WARREN WAGAR

FUTURISTS

Futurists are people who have a special interest in what may happen in the years ahead and think seriously about what lies beyond the short-term perspective. However, they generally pay little attention to possible developments more than fifty years ahead, which may lie largely beyond the realm of plausible speculation.

Futurists are especially concerned about the impact on the future of what is done in the present. Typically, they focus on the next five to twenty-five years, which are clearly being shaped by current trends in society and technology.

A main point in thinking about the future is to change it—to make it better than it would be without deliberate choices and actions.

Futurists use rational or scientific methods to understand alternative futures. They do not use the mystical or supernatural means employed by fortunetellers, seers, palmists, astrologers, and clairvoyants, who claim to foretell future events. A main point in thinking about the future is to change it—to make it better than it would be without deliberate choices and actions. Futurists believe that people shape their own futures by what they choose to do. The futurists' view is that the future is shaped by man, rather than ordained by fate.

The idea that societies change began to be considered seriously in the early seventeenth century, when Francis Bacon argued that advancing knowledge could and should be used to improve the human condition. Bacon's disciples became outspoken prophets for this idea of social progress. Scholars, such as the Marquis de Condorcet, began to think seriously about what the future would be like as a result of continuing progress. Condorcet's book *A Sketch for a Historical Portrait of the Progress of the Human Mind* offered remarkably accurate forecasts, such as the end of slavery, the political independence of the European colonies in America, and the spread of birth control.

Belief in progress became the conventional wisdom of the nineteenth century. The steady appearance of exciting inventions like railroads and electric lights seemed to prove that the future would bring worldwide abundance and happiness. Social change seemed so positive and continuous that H. G. Wells proposed, in 1902, the establishment of a "science of the future," so that people could know in advance about the good things to come.

Optimistic confidence in the future fell victim to the horrors of World War I. Progress, it seemed, was not inevitable; on the contrary, the future now seemed nightmarish. Even when progress appeared benign, it held hidden dangers: faster transportation destroyed local communities; the increased production of goods threw people out of their jobs.

After World War II, with its death camps and atomic bombs, pessimism about the future replaced the optimism of the pre-World War I period. The French experience as an occupied nation during World War II produced a powerful philosophical movement, existentialism, which emphasized deliberate human choice as the prime force determining the future. The future is undetermined, argued Jean-Paul Sartre, and therefore must be invented. And if individuals choose their future, so must nations: the new French regime embarked on a series of national plans to shape the nation's destiny. The planners immediately wanted to know what assumptions could be made about the future as a basis for their plans, so they called upon the nation's intellectuals. One who responded to the call was the economist-philosopher Bertrand de Jouvenel. With Ford Foundation support, his Futuribles group published an influential series of books and papers dealing with the future of France and the world. The most important book, *The Art of Conjecture* (1964), laid down basic principles for intelligently thinking about the future.

U.S. military planners had also been seeking ways to meet the many contingencies posed by the nuclear era. The Air Force created the Rand Corporation, where scholars were paid to think and write about future possibilities, such as new technologies that might be developed and alternative strategies for dealing with foreign nations.

The Rand scholars often found themselves relying on nothing more than people's opinions, an unorthodox methodology that raised eyebrows among many scientists. In justification, Rand mathematician Olaf Helmer and philosopher Nicholas Rescher wrote an influential 1959 paper, "The Epistemology of the Inexact Sciences," which argued that in fields that have not developed to the point of having scientific laws, the testimony of experts provided a useful guide. The paper provided a general rationale for a science of forecasting and specific support for the Delphi method, a technique of getting expert opinions and combining them in ways that avoided follow-the-leader and other tendencies that distort group decision making.

Helmer left Rand in 1968 to head the new Institute for the Future, which has produced numerous papers, reports, and books applying Delphi and other techniques to the study of future possibilities. In 1971, Theodore J. Gordon, a technology-oriented analyst, departed with two colleagues to found the Futures Group, a profit-making research organization emphasizing proprietary research.

Meanwhile, the Hudson Institute, founded by another Rand researcher, physicist Herman Kahn, had become a major center of future-oriented research. Kahn gained notoriety as the author of *On Thermonuclear War* (1961), which described how thermonuclear wars could be fought and even won. In 1967, he and Hudson colleague Anthony J. Wiener published *The Year 2000: A Framework for Speculation on the Next Thirty-three Years* (1967), a book that impressed scholars with its many charts, graphs, and tables.

These new future-oriented institutions and scholarly studies convinced many knowledgeable people that it is possible to think rationally and intelligently about the future. When the World Future Society was founded in 1966, as an association for futurists, it soon enlisted thousands of members, many of whom were well-known and respected scientists, scholars, and public leaders.

Since the 1960s, future-oriented governmental agencies have appeared in many nations and at many levels of government. Typically, such agencies prepare a series of reports and disband, having fulfilled their mandate. Permanent bodies also have been established such as the U.S. Office of Technology Assessment, which became operational in 1974. Sweden's Secretariat for Future Studies, established in 1974, was the first high-level governmental office of its kind (it has since closed down).

Business corporations regularly hire futurists to advise them on possible future developments, and numerous colleges and universities offer courses on the future. The University of Houston at Clear Lake City, for example, has developed a future-studies program leading to a master's degree, and many of its graduates have gone on to find employment as consultants in business and government.

Futurists are still popularly thought of as trying to predict the future—and are sometimes scorned for failing to do so. However, futurists have gained increasing respect in recent decades. Top business and government leaders often speak at meetings of the World Future Society. President Ronald Reagan honored futurists with a special luncheon in the White House in 1985. Senator Albert Gore, a committed futurist and regular participant in World Future Society conferences, was elected as vice president of the United States in 1992. Newt Gingrich, another long-time futurist, became speaker of the U.S. House of Representatives in 1995, and many of its graduates have gone on to find employment as consultants in business and government.

[See also Future Studies; Futures Concepts; Futures Education; Futurism; de Jouvenel, Bertrand; Pseudo-Futurists; Wells, H. G.]

BIBLIOGRAPHY

Coates, Joseph, and Jarrat, Jennifer. *What Futurists Believe.* Bethesda, MD, 1989.

Cornish, Edward J. *The Study of the Future: An Introduction to the Art and Science of Understanding and Shaping Tomorrow's World.* Bethesda, MD: World Future Society, 1977.

De Jouvenel, Bertrand. *The Art of Conjecture.* New York: Basic Books, 1967.

Kahn, Herman, and Wiener, Anthony J. *The Year 2000: A Framework for Speculation on the Next Thirty-three Years.* New York: Macmillan, 1967.

Nanus, Burt. *Visionary Leadership.* San Francisco: Jossey-Bass, 1992.

— EDWARD S. CORNISH

G

GAMBLING

The United States is experiencing an unprecedented boom in commercial gambling. The casino business is the fastest growing segment of the entertainment industry. There are compelling reasons to expect that casinos, and to a lesser extent lotteries, will continue to proliferate well into the twenty-first century. Psychological, social, and political forces suggest why commercial gambling will thrive in the next two decades.

Games of chance offering prizes have been part of human culture for over 4,000 years, and part of American culture since colonial times. Early settlers in Jamestown sold lottery tickets to pay for their passages from Europe. The Continental Congress in 1776 funded the revolutionary army from the sale of lottery tickets—George Washington purchased the first ticket. Nineteenth-century frontier gambling saloons and riverboat gambling halls are legendary in American history.

In the United States, the growth of casino gaming

will far outpace growth in lotteries

and pari-mutuel betting.

In 1993, Americans wagered more than $394 billion on legal gambling enterprises; casinos, lotteries, and pari-mutuel wagering accounted for about 90 percent of the total. Some believe that gambling meets a human need to choose and control one's exposure to risk, while others say gambling is an escape from a humdrum daily existence. Still others assert that people gamble only to win prizes.

The stigma that until recently surrounded gambling behavior has faded. Gambling is now less frequently viewed as a sin or vice, and more frequently as legitimate adult recreation and entertainment activity. A 1994 national survey showed that acceptance of casino gambling—"casino gaming," in today's nomenclature—in the United States now stands at 92 percent, with 59 percent declaring gaming perfectly acceptable for anyone, and 33 percent saying it is acceptable for others, but not themselves.

Casino Gaming

In the United States, the growth of casino gaming will far outpace growth in lotteries and pari-mutuel betting. The number of states permitting casino gaming grew from only two—Nevada and New Jersey—in 1988 to 24 in 1994. There are four kinds of casinos:

- Traditional land-based casinos, like the unlimited stakes casinos in Nevada and New Jersey
- Limited stakes casinos, like those in historic towns in South Dakota and Colorado
- Riverboat and dockside casinos, like those in Illinois and Mississippi
- Tribal casinos owned by American Indian tribes in more than a dozen states, operated under federal law and agreements with state governments

Casino gaming will proliferate during the next decade because

- casinos create jobs and increase tax revenues. Recession and voter resistance to new taxes have stretched thin the budgets of state and local governments, while taxes on casino revenue continue to be more palatable politically than other taxes.
- casinos satisfy the recreational needs of a broad segment of the public. Research shows why people enjoy casinos: First, they provide social environments, where customers share laughter and companionship with other customers and the casino staff. Second, they provide a participatory entertainment experience, whose pace is customer-controlled. And third, they provide competition and a chance to win.
- new casino jurisdictions will demonstrate that the old myths about casino gaming are untrue. Casino gaming neither preys upon the poor nor brings crime, vice, or moral decay. Tomorrow's casino industry will continue to be among the most tightly regulated businesses in America.

Technological advances, some predict, will soon render casinos obsolete. Why visit a casino when you can adopt the persona of, say, Mark Twain and link via the electronic highway to a "virtual" casino filled with similarly colorful characters? Game manufacturers have already taken some first steps: a multiplayer blackjack game with a video-based "dealer" is now available. The technical prowess of future computer wizards, however, cannot displace the personal and social aspects of the casino experience: games of bluff and counter-bluff between stoic "poker-faced" customers; squeals of unbridled delight from the successful slot machine player; and the sympathetic smiles and subtle compassion of dealers whose loyal customers have lost a few hands in a row. The social interactions and the total casino en-

TABLE 1

NUMBER OF STATES WHERE CASINOS ARE/MAY BE LEGAL

Casino Type	1994	1998 (estimates)	2003 (estimates)
Riverboat Casinos	6	13	18
Limited Stakes Casinos	2	2	6
Indian Casinos	20	26	27
Traditional Land-Based Casinos	3	8	14

tertainment are among the primary draws to many casino patrons.

Table 1, summarizes the future of the casino industry in the United States. Rapid growth in riverboat and tribal casino jurisdiction is likely, especially during the mid-1990s. Legalization of full land-based casinos will accelerate after mid-decade. By 2002, more than two-thirds of the nation's population will live in states with some form of legalized casino gaming. Casinos will be just another choice for adults planning an afternoon or evening's entertainment, and no more expensive than attending a professional football game or a theatrical performance.

Pari-Mutuel Wagering

Legal pari-mutuel wagering—in which bettors wager against each other, as opposed to against "the house"—on races involving horses and dogs took place in thirty-seven states during 1993. Inter-track wagering, off-track wagering, and home-based wagering will expand the distribution of betting locations, but the total amount wagered on pari-mutuel events (horse racing, harness racing, and the like) will continue a slide that began in the 1970s. Pari-mutuel wagering lacks the broad appeal of casino entertainment, spectator sports, and feature films. Adults seeking entertainment are likely to perceive racetracks as places where nothing happens in the long gaps between races.

Casino gambling will continue to grow because casinos create jobs and a great number of people enjoy the casino environment. Gambling revenue will increase from $515 billion in 1996 to $1.5 trillion in 2005. (© 1993 Kevin Syms/First Image West, Inc)

Off-track and home-based betting could consolidate the pari-mutuel industry, such that ultimately ten to fifteen major tracks would feed a nationwide network of off-track betting parlors and interactive television systems. This scenario is especially likely if smaller tracks find it more economical to stop live racing and become off-track betting facilities.

Another scenario features land-based casinos at pari-mutuel facilities, with some revenues from casino gaming distributed to live race purses. This could increase interest in betting on live races. It is unclear whether this development would be a temporary prop for the pari-mutuel industry or a key to its long-term viability. If they are to reverse their slump, they must attract a new generation of customers.

State Lotteries

State lotteries in 1994 operated in thirty-six states and may expand to forty-four states by 2003. Except in new lottery states, lottery revenue of late has been flat or declining. This trend will continue, with temporary jumps in overall lottery play when new states legalize, and stabilization as lotteries mature. About 90 percent of the American public now has access to lottery play. Combined with their inherently low entertainment value, the existing wide access means that overall levels of lottery play will not significantly increase even if lotteries proliferate.

State lotteries have recently begun operation of casino-like games. Video lotteries, which are essentially networks of electronic casino games (poker, blackjack, etc.) linked to a central computer, operate in six states. Video lottery machines are typically found in bars, lounges, and racetracks. Several states also offer keno-like games (keno is a fast-paced variation of lotto). Because video lotteries and keno share the fast action and high entertainment value of casino games, they have the potential for rapid growth.

Gambling and Society

Some people have difficulty controlling how much they gamble. Most of the casino industry and some lotteries now recognize compulsive gambling as a problem for a small percentage of customers and as a detriment to the industry's growth. Socially responsible casino companies are addressing problem gaming: providing funds for treatment and counseling and training employees to identify potential pathological gamblers and steer them to treatment. Socially responsible casino companies are also addressing the problem of underage gambling. How casinos and lotteries respond to the potential social implications of their proliferation will—and should—influence public acceptance of gambling as a

form of entertainment and a source of economic growth and tax revenue during the twenty-first century.

In addition to legalized and regulated gambling, there will also likely be a continuation of illegal gambling, mainly involving betting on sports events. In the long term, casino gaming may be only one entertainment option in recreational complexes that will include virtual reality games/rides and other emerging forms of entertainment.

[See also Crime Rates; Interactive Entertainment; Social Controls; Sports and Activities, Spectator.]

BIBLIOGRAPHY

Abt, Vicki; Smith, James F.; and Christiansen, Eugene M. *The Business of Risk: Commercial Gambling in Mainstream America.* Lawrence: University of Kansas Press, 1985.

Clotfelter, Charles, and Cook, Phillip. *Selling Hope: State Lotteries in America.* Cambridge, MA: Harvard University Press, 1989.

Eadington, William R., and Cornelius, Judy A., eds. *Gambling and Commercial Gaming: Essays in Business, Economics, Philosophy and Science.* Reno, NV: Institute for the Study of Gambling and Commercial Gaming, 1992.

Helm, Michael. *A Breed Apart: The Horses and the Players.* New York: Henry Holt, 1991.

— PHILIP G. SATRE

GAMES.

See INTERACTIVE ENTERTAINMENT; SPORTS AND GAMES, COMPETITIVE.

GAS.

See INDUSTRIAL GASES; NATURAL GAS.

GENETIC ENGINEERING

The term *genetic engineering* refers to a body of techniques used to manipulate DNA (deoxyribonucleic acid) and its products, RNA (ribonucleic acid), and protein. By means of genetic engineering, genes can be isolated, purified, reproduced, and moved from one organism into another. This technique not only contributes to basic scientific research, it also provides procedures for changing the properties of microorganisms, plants, and animals. This ability to transfer genes, and with them specific characteristics, has raised a host of issues—ethical, social, legal, even philosophical. Can the genetic engineering of crops and livestock solve the economic problems of developing countries? Are there hidden dangers that require strict controls? Should experimental procedures be regulated? Should any limits be placed on how far scientists go in investigating the mechanisms of life? Should researchers be allowed to patent cloned genes? What are the ethics of applying these techniques to human beings?

Comprehension of genetic engineering depends on an understanding of DNA, RNA, protein, and the fundamental cell processes of replication and protein synthesis. The basic ideas follow:

- DNA consists of two parallel chains of molecules, called nucleotides or bases, linked together, like beads on a string. There are four nucleotides, A, G, C, and T, which stand respectively for adenine, guanine, cytosine, and thymine. A given sequence on one strand of DNA determines the opposite sequence on the other strand, by the mechanism of base-pairing. That is, A can only pair with T, and G can only pair with C. Thus, the two strands contain the same information. When a cell divides, the two strands separate, and each one then is a template for the formation of a new double helix identical to the original. This is the famous "double helix" model of DNA (see Figure 1).
- DNA is found in the chromosomes of every cell of every organism. Genes—the hereditary units—consist of sequences of nucleotides within these chromosomes. The order of these nucleotides is a "code" which contains the genetic information.
- The primary product of each gene is a protein. One gene is said to code for one protein, and when a gene is translated by the cellular machinery into a protein, it is said to be "expressed." This process is carried out or mediated through molecules of *messenger RNA*, short-lived copies of the

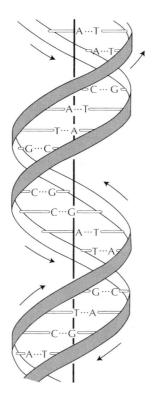

Figure 1. Schematic drawing of the DNA double helix. The sugar-phosphate backbones run at the periphery of the helix in antiparallel orientation. Base-pairs (A—T and G—C) drawn symbolically as bars between chains are stacked along the center of the helix.

genes that act as templates for the assembly of the amino acids that make up the protein.

The ability to transfer genes, and with them specific characteristics, has raised a host of issues— ethical, social, legal, even philosophical.

The tools to move genes from one organism to another are referred to as *recombinant DNA technology*. The arts of animal husbandry and plant horticulture have for centuries manipulated the genetic material of organisms indirectly, by means of selection of visible traits. Recombinant DNA technology manipulates the genetic material directly. Theoretically, any gene from any organism may be moved into the genome—i.e., the set of genes—of any other organism. Thus, human genes have been moved into bacteria. Genes from insects have been spliced into the genome of tomatoes and have conferred upon tomatoes the ability to produce natural insecticides. Bacterial genes have been moved into plants. Human genes related to the onset of cancer have been successfully incorporated into yeast, thus providing a simplified biological system in which to study their function.

It is thought that genes control the characteristics of an organism, but this link is clear only in the simplest cases. For example, certain diseases are known to be caused by a defect in a single gene (sickle cell anemia, Tay-Sachs disease, Lesch-Nyhan syndrome). The immediate product of a gene is a protein—and to understand the function of this protein is often very difficult.

The first published example of genetic engineering was reported in a 1973 paper by Boyer, Cohen, Chang, and Helling. Since then, there have been countless other examples. The basic technique of artificial recombination is a patented procedure, licensed by Stanford University.

We now turn to some of the applications which are currently possible, keeping in mind that new ones are being designed literally every day.

Mass Production of Proteins

A common procedure is to turn bacteria into "factories" for a useful protein that is produced in nature only in very small amounts. For example, by isolating the gene for human insulin and inducing its expression in billions of bacteria, this protein, insulin, can be economically mass produced in the lab. The same technique is used to produce proteins of use to medicine, industry, or basic research, including growth hormones, somatostatin (a growth inhibitor), and interferon (a protein produced by the immune system).

Agriculture—Crop Improvement

Tomatoes have been genetically engineered to stay riper longer and to produce their own insecticide. Efforts are focused on producing plants that grow faster, have greater resistance to pests, are cheaper to grow, or are less dependent on water (and thus better able to resist drought). This can be accomplished by incorporating genes from a microorganism or an insect into a plant. Progress in these areas may be crucial to meeting the world's growing demand for food. The first genetically engineered vegetable became commercially available in 1994.

More Productive Livestock

Genetic engineering of the pituitary growth hormone has already produced "giant" mice, and the same technique may be applied to cattle. Researchers are developing methods for transferring genes to commercially capitalize upon important traits, such as milk yield. This is technically difficult because most of these traits

are the result of several genes. Another area of exploration involves the creation of new vaccines to protect farm animals from disease.

Waste Management and Mining

Microbes are being designed to break down the waste products of various industries, including the livestock industry and the paper industry; to gobble up oil spills; and to extract minerals from the earth.

Transgenosis

Transgenic animals have been created and patented. These are animals that contain genes from other species. Moreover, these genes have been inserted at a very early stage of development and therefore are also in the sex cells of the animal. Thus, these genes are passed on to their offspring. In the future transgenic animals may be important sources of food and may serve as potent tools for medical and biological research.

Genetic Therapy

Some of the most exciting applications of DNA technology are in the diagnosis and treatment of genetic

Scientists studying the structure of DNA will continue to learn how it works and how to manipulate its structure. Biotechnologies will dominate world economic activity by 2200. (Richard T. Nowitz/Corbis)

diseases. Prenatal diagnoses of certain hereditary diseases, using genetic probes extracted from a gene library, are available and becoming more common. Some of these diseases are hemophilia, growth hormone deficiency, and various blood diseases. Genetic therapy is still in a speculative stage, but the idea holds promise. If a disease can be localized to a single gene—and many devastating diseases can—then, if a healthy copy of that gene can be incorporated into the affected cells, the disease could be cured. Now there are viruses—called retroviruses—which stitch themselves into the genome of their host. If such a virus could be stripped of all the "bad" DNA and replaced with the gene of interest, then this gene could be carried into the appropriate target tissues of the patient. Although there are several technical difficulties, such procedures are beginning to be worked out for people who are gravely ill and have no other recourse. It is too soon to know if there are any success stories, but this field is likely to develop very fast.

Genetic research is outpacing society's ability to comprehend, integrate, and control its discoveries.

Even if an individual could be thus cured, his or her children would still be susceptible to the disease. This problem suggests a logical extension of these ideas to the concept of *germ-line therapy*. This would involve the creation of "transgenic" humans—in which the germ line itself had been modified, thus making the change heritable—essentially a change to the species itself. This is very controversial, because any hidden, secondary effects would affect all future generations. At this point, there are no plans to attempt this kind of procedure.

The initial reaction of some scientists to the news that it was possible to move genes among or between organisms was one of alarm. In February 1975, a group of molecular biologists organized a now famous conference in Asilomar, Calif., at which recombination experiments were classified according to risks, containment procedures were recommended, and it was urged that certain experiments be indefinitely deferred. Although some scientists now believe that the Asilomar conference was unnecessary, the episode shows that it is natural even for professionals to react with a certain amount of awe to the development of techniques that allow for the creation of forms of life that could not have been reproduced by nature.

Along with great hopes, these powerful new techniques for experimenting with life-forms have generated fears of three basic types:

1. A dangerous new virus or bacterium might be created and released into the environment. For instance, when researchers splice a known cancer-causing gene into *Escherichia coli,* a bacterial strain commonly found in the human digestive system, might this not lead to dire consequences? At present the threat of such an accident does not appear likely, since laboratory strains of bacteria do not survive in the wild.

2. Genetic engineering of crops and livestock may reduce the diversity in the biosphere and diminish the robustness of our ecology.

3. The technologies can be applied toward questionable, even evil ends. The example of the Nazi eugenics programs is often cited. Furthermore, the connection with various reproductive technologies is a source of deep ethical debates. To cite one example, a couple at risk of conceiving a child with a genetic disease could produce several embryos by means of in vitro fertilization (fertilization outside the womb). These embryos could then be screened for the disease, and a healthy one selected for reimplantation into the womb of the mother. The others would be disposed of, or perhaps used for fetal research, which itself raises hackles. On the one hand, this seems to guarantee the parents a child free from a particular disease. On the other hand, this sort of procedure is viewed by some as a precursor to people no longer being ends in themselves, but commodities serving the ends of other people.

4. Finally, the development of biotechnologies may well have profound geoeconomic and geopolitical consequences, as do all new technologies. As François Gros puts it in *The Gene Civilization,* "We must not be afraid to acknowledge that the face of the Earth may be changed as a result of these new technologies." An important issue is how Third World countries will be affected. If, for example, a strain of coffee bean were developed to grow in cold weather, the economy of Brazil could be disrupted. in turn, this would reduce the buying power of an important market and compound the serious debt problem that already exists in that country.

Genetic engineering makes us the first species with the potential power to shape its own evolution. Surely in the next century there will be planned and unplanned actions directed at human enhancement and species improvement.

Conclusion

The industrial use of organisms bred for advantageous and profitable properties is not new. What is new is the ability to directly alter the genotype. Whereas traditional breeding relies on the selection of visible characteristics (phenotype) without fully understanding the underlying changes in the genotype, genetic engineering reverses this pattern by relying on manipulation of the genes without fully understanding all the effects on phenotype. This is a real revolution, and it is reasonable to be amazed as well as concerned. Genetic research is outpacing society's ability to comprehend, integrate, and control its discoveries. The techniques of genetic engineering and their implications are likely to be at the forefront of human concerns for the foreseeable future.

[See also Bioethics; Genetics; Genetics: Agricultural Applications; Genetics: Commercialization; Genetic Technologies; Life Sciences; Scientific Breakthroughs.]

BIBLIOGRAPHY

Emery, Alan E. H. *An Introduction to Recombinant DNA.* New York: John Wiley, 1984.

Gros, François, *The Gene Civilization.* New York: McGraw-Hill, 1989.

Nossal, Gustav, J. V. *Reshaping Life.* New York: Cambridge University Press, 1985.

Watson, J. D., and Tooze, J. *The DNA Story.* New York: W. H. Freeman, 1981.

– MICHAEL COOK

GENETICS

Genetics, as the science of heredity and variation, has undergone the most rapid development of any biological science in the twentieth century. Genetics in the latter half of the twentieth century has increased our understanding of how life on Earth has evolved and how life processes operate, and has provided the potential for the control or alteration of the hereditary material that contributes to the development and expression of traits in all living organisms. The science of modern genetics has spawned a number of new fields of science and technology, including molecular biology, genetic engineering, molecular diagnostics, molecular medicine, gene therapy, and computational molecular biology.

Mendelian Genetics

Mendelian classical genetics up to the 1940s can be summarized as follows:

1. It postulated the existence of a gene as a replicating unit and as the basis for all living activity and the transmission of hereditary information.
2. It proposed that genes are arranged in a pattern or system on a structure, the chromosomes, contained in all cells and transmitted to its progeny.
3. Changes (mutations) in the gene can occur either spontaneously or in response to certain physical (ionizing radiation) or chemical environmental influences.
4. The mutations are the basis for evolutionary changes in species and populations of living organisms.
5. Genes control metabolic processes and the development of organisms.

New Genetics

In the late 1930s and early 1940s a series of experiments were carried out that have transformed genetics.

- Genes have been found to contain deoxyribonucleic acid (DNA).
- Researchers have purified and crystallized DNA so that it can be subjected to the analytical process of X-ray diffraction, the patterns of which give important clues about the relative location of molecular groups.
- In 1953 James D. Watson and Francis H. C. Crick of Cambridge University, U.K., proposed a double-helical structure for DNA. This structure was said to consist of two strands of linearly arrayed nucleotides consisting of two purines, adenine (A) and guanine (G), and two pyrimidines, thymine (T) and cytosine (C), in the form of a double helix. The

strands are joined so that a purine is always paired with a pyrimidine and form a strong bond that holds the strands together with the sugar phosphate (ribose) on the outside forming the backbone of the molecule. This structure suggests a mechanism for the storage of information (in the sequence of ATGC) and replication of the information. As the double helix unwinds during cell division, each strand acts as a template for the assembly of identical strands.

Subsequent work confirmed the accuracy of the Watson-Crick proposal. Genes consisting of DNA express their message through another nucleic acid, ribose nucleic acid (mRNA), and the transcription of this message is eventually translated into a protein through certain cellular structures (polysomes) located in the cystoplasm. This has been summarized as the central dogma of molecular genetics:

$$DNA \rightarrow mRNA \rightarrow Protein$$

How DNA replicates and transcribes a message that is subsequently translated into a protein product is the basis of the new molecular biology.

Genes

Genes consist of stretches of DNA that may contain from a few thousand to a million nucleotides and are located in a linear arrangement on the long strands of DNA. Each human consists of more than a trillion cells and each cell contains over six feet of DNA. The strands of the DNA double helix are coiled around cores of protein that together form the structures known as chromosomes. Departures from a normal genetic condition have to be determined by an analysis of the sequence of purines and pyrimidines (the nucleotides) that make up the gene.

The total genetic information contained in the DNA nucleotide sequence is the genome. It is anticipated that by the year 2005 the complete sequence of the three billion pairs of nucleotides that make up the human genome will be known. The Human Genome Project, initiated in 1987 by the U.S. Department of Energy, now involves other U.S. agencies, including the National Institutes of Health. On the basis of techniques currently in use, it will be possible to excise, delete, or insert parts or whole genes in order to correct genetic deficiencies (gene therapy). In 1994, over seventy trials in humans testing the safety and efficacy of gene therapy were under way.

In addition to the development of new methodologies, the various genome projects that are studying humans and a variety of plants and animals of economic and scientific importance are primarily aimed at identifying and physically mapping all the genes on the chromosomes. The tasks of gene identification and determining the gene's physical location on the chromosome will clearly continue well into the twenty-first century and provide the basis for a great deal of exciting and important research.

The number of human genes was originally estimated to be in the range of 50,000 to 100,000. It now appears that there might well be substantially more than 100,000 human genes. In 1994, only a few thousand genes have been identified, and many of these remain to be mapped, sequenced, and their functions determined.

Although many genes consist of an uninterrupted sequence of nucleotides, it is now clear that many other genes are made up of various fragments of DNA that must be assembled (spliced) during the process of transcription and translation to construct a protein coding gene. This phenomenon has been particularly elucidated in the studies on how genes control the production of antibodies (immunoglobulins) that are created in response to the challenges of multiple infectious agents. In the late 1970s it became apparent that many mammalian genes exist in the genome as a discontinuous series of coding (Exons) and non-coding (Introns) regions. The process of excising the noncoding regions and splicing the coding regions into a contiguous gene is under active research. The situation is further complicated by evidence that a mechanism of "proofreading" corrects mistakes in the mRNA and, further, some protein products are "edited" posttranslationally.

The Genetic Code

After the discovery that the hereditary information was somehow encoded in the DNA and in the linear se-

These five brothers are not identical, but genetic similarities are evident in their facial features. Genetically engineered "designer babies" may create new forms of discrimination. (Philip Gould/Corbis)

TABLE 1

THE GENETIC CODE

First Position (5′ end)	Second Position				Third Position (3′ end)
	U	C	A	G	
U	PHE	SER	TYR	CYS	U
	PHE	SER	TYR	CYS	C
	LEU	SER	Stop	Stop	A
	LEU	SER	Stop	TRP	G
C	LEU	PRO	HIS	ARG	U
	LEU	PRO	HIS	ARG	C
	LEU	PRO	GLN	ARG	A
	LEU	PRO	GLN	ARG	G
A	ILE	THR	ASN	SER	U
	ILE	THR	ASN	SER	C
	ILE	THR	LYS	ARG	A
	MET	THR	LYS	ARG	G
G	VAL	ALA	ASP	GLY	U
	VAL	ALA	ASP	GLY	C
	VAL	ALA	GLU	GLY	A
	VAL	ALA	GLU	GLY	G

Note: Given the position of the bases in a codon, it is possible to find the corresponding amino acid. For example, the codon (5′)AUG(3′) on mRNA specifies methionine, whereas CAU specifies histidine. UAA, UAG, and UGA are termination signals. AUG is part of the initiation signal, and it codes for internal methionines as well. (After J. D. Watson, J. Tooze, and D. Kurtz, *Recombinant DNA: A Short Course* [1983], p. 38.)

quences of the four nucleotides ATGC, the unraveling of the genetic code became a major challenge. The code was deciphered in the early 1960s.

As previously indicated, the central dogma of molecular genetics, proven by many experiments, is that DNA replicates itself and also acts as a template for the formation of mRNA. The message encoded in mRNA is translated into protein in the cytoplasm of a cell. Proteins are made from amino acids (AA), of which there are twenty different basic types. The assembly of a specific protein requires the selection and joining together of the correct sequence of amino acids from the pool that exists in the cytoplasm. As a result of the correct sequence of AAs to form a polypeptide, the molecule will fold itself into a three-dimensional structure.

Early on, it was concluded that with an alphabet of four nucleotides (ATGC) it requires a minimum of three bases to code (codon) for a single amino acid. Since the number of coding possibilities is 64, it more than meets the need for protein assembly from a pool of 20 amino acids. Indeed, of the 64 coding possibilities, 61 are used to designate specific amino acids, three codons signal to stop translation of the DNA information, and one codon signals to start. It soon became

apparent that some of the different codons designate identical AAs—e.g., ACC, ACA, ACG, ACU all code for the AA threonine (see Table 1).

Understanding the mechanisms that are involved in decoding the genetic message and translating the message faithfully into a protein product will provide challenges for researchers for many years.

With the deciphering of the genetic code, it became theoretically feasible to predict from the nucleotide sequence the approximate nature of the protein product. Understanding the mechanisms that are involved in decoding the genetic message and translating the message faithfully into a protein product will provide challenges for researchers for many years.

DNA/RNA

As described above, the information contained in the DNA is transcribed and translated through the agencies of ribose nucleic acids (RNAs). RNA differs from DNA in its sugar component and in the use of the pyrimidine nucleotide uracil (U), instead of thymidine (T), in its base sequence. At least three different RNA molecules are involved in decoding and translating the DNA:

- *mRNA:* Messenger RNA is transcribed on a template of the DNA during gene activation.
- *tRNA:* Transfer RNA recognizes and transfers specific AAs to an anticodon recognition site in the sequence determined by mRNA.
- *rRNA:* Ribosomal RNA constitutes cytoplasmic particles that provide an environment for the assembly of protein.

In the 1980s, it was discovered that certain RNA molecules could act as enzymes (ribozymes) in the absence of protein. The ribozymes have been used to catalyze many chemical reactions, including self-replication. It has been suggested that the first molecules capable of replication in the organic evolution of Earth probably were RNAs.

Cell Biology

The basic unit of life is the cell. In the case of acellular viruses that consist primarily of DNA or RNA, it is necessary to invade a cell to use the host's mechanisms for replication. Bacterial cells (prokaryotes) and more complex animal and plant cells (eukaryotes) have the same basic subcellular components. The majority of early molecular genetics experiments were carried out with viruses that used bacteria as host cells. Eventually it was learned that the basic principles of gene replication, transcription, and translation applied equally to prokaryotic and eukaryotic cells and organisms.

The progress in techniques to cultivate tissues and cells in test tubes (in vitro) facilitated studies that were previously difficult or impossible to do. In vitro tissue culture systems enabled scientists to explore means of excising and inserting genetic material and to learn how genes express their message. Application of these in vitro manipulations has enabled scientists to correct a defect in children born with a genetically transmitted immunodeficiency disease.

Genetic Engineering: Evolutionary Concerns

The techniques that have emerged from the development of the science of molecular genetics have created the power for scientists to do some remarkable things. While much remains to be done to perfect the techniques, the following represent some future prospects:

1. It is increasingly possible to predict future health concerns by genomic analysis. Genetic markers for a number of specific diseases have been identified (cystic fibrosis, Huntington's, Tay Sachs, and others). Markers for heart disease, cancer, and mental health are being sought.

2. Through the methods being perfected for the application of gene therapy, diseases and afflictions such as hemophilia, sickle anemia, diabetes, and others may be cured by a single procedure designed to correct the genetic defect.

3. By using genetic engineering techniques for excising, inserting, splicing, and cloning genetic messages, it has become possible to modify many animals and plants. Tomatoes, corn, soybeans, and farm animals are prime targets for such research. Some plants (tobacco) and animals (goats) are being engineered to produce human proteins including antibodies for clinical therapeutic applications.

4. Substances previously not available in adequate amounts are being produced through genetic engineering. Insulin, erythropoietin, granulocytic colony factor, and the interleukins are just a few of the hormones and cell regulator substances becoming commercially available.

Powerful new technologies resulting from molecular genetics have increased the accountability of humans over Earth's evolution. Thousands of years of domesticating plants and animals have sharply reduced genetic diversity and the number of species. Through increasingly efficient hunting and fishing techniques, humans have eliminated or brought to the brink of extinction many thousands of species. Unrestrained population growth, doubling about every twenty-five to thirty years, may overwhelm demands for energy, food and fiber. Already the polluting effects of human activity have stressed and destroyed many ecosystems. Such aspects of human activity can be exacerbated or ameliorated by genetic engineering. Humanity will need all the wisdom it can muster in the way it uses these pow-

erful technologies. Informed laypersons, philosophers, ethicists, ecologists, scientists, and political leaders will need to cooperate in determining appropriate social policies and priorities. This will require a level of commitment and collaboration characteristic of wartime activity. Circumstances justify a similar level of societal response to the opportunities and dangers in the use or misuse of these powerful genetic engineering methodologies.

[See also Artificial Life; Bioethics; Evolution, Biological; Food Technologies; Genetic Engineering; Genetics: Agricultural Applications; Genetics: Commercialization; Genetic Technologies; Life Sciences.]

BIBLIOGRAPHY

Anderson, Walter Truett. *To Govern Evolution.* Boston: Harcourt Brace Jovanovich, 1987.

Singer, Maxine, and Berg, Paul. *Genes and Genomes.* Mill Valley, CA: University Science Books, 1991.

Watson, James D.; Tooze, John; and Kurtz, David T. *Recombinant DNA: A Short Course.* New York: W. H. Freeman, 1983.

— PAUL H. SILVERMAN

GENETICS: AGRICULTURAL APPLICATIONS

Since antiquity mankind has domesticated animals and crop plants to produce food and fiber. In ancient times farmers could only save seed from plants that demonstrated desirable properties. The breeding of animals was often accomplished by trial and error. Gregor Mendel's discovery of the rudiments of genetics in the mid-1800s provided the scientific basis for modern plant and animal breeding. The development of hybrid corn in the 1920s initiated a revolution in plant breeding, increasing the yield of this key crop tenfold.

Developments in molecular genetics or biotechnology over the past forty years give plant and animal breeders new biotechnology tools to feed the ever-expanding world population. It is critical that we use genetic sources wisely to conserve crop diversity and improve the productivity of our farm land. One key aspect of biotechnology that will help in this endeavor is recombinant DNA (r-DNA) technology or genetic engineering.

Twenty years ago, scientists learned how to use special restriction enzymes to cut genetic information out of one organism and splice it into another. At first a laboratory curiosity, r-DNA technology formed the underpinning of the emerging biotechnology industry that formed in the late 1970s and early '80s. While many of the significant advances to date have occurred in health care, the same techniques that allow us to produce human insulin in bacteria can improve agricultural production. Agricultural biotechnology is poised to deliver significant new advances to both farmers and consumers throughout the remainder of this decade. The same techniques that allow us to produce human insulin in bacteria can improve agricultural production.

Plant scientists can add discrete, well-characterized genes to plants to improve their quality, nutrition, and other characteristics. Using new biotechnology approaches, a useful trait found in wheat conferring pest resistance can be transferred to corn. In this manner, plant scientists can harness nature's proteins to improve nutritional factors such as amino acid composition, the degree of unsaturated oils in various seed crops, and increase the use of natural resistance to insects and disease.

Among the major food crops that have been genetically modified are tomato, potato, corn, and soybean. Important traits such as viral resistance, insect resistance, herbicide tolerance, and processing quality have been added. Farmers will benefit from a greater number of pest-management options using environmentally preferable crop protection products and management programs.

The consumer will benefit directly from fruits and vegetables that are tastier and have improved quality and shelf life. Oils that are lower in saturated and higher in unsaturated fat content and grain crops with more balanced protein carry the potential for major health benefits.

The use of microbial pesticides has been increasing in recent years as farmers and foresters have been exploring nonchemical approaches to pest control. *Bacillus thuringiensis* is frequently used to control gypsy moth infestations in forestry settings. New microorganisms are being studied for pesticidal activity. Recently a microorganism has been identified that controls Colorado potato beetles, a key agricultural pest.

Many of these biopesticides produce a toxin with a limited target range. However, the toxin's limited persistence in the environment necessitates frequent spraying. Genetic engineering is being used to improve the field performance of these natural pesticides, making them more appealing for commercial farmers. Over half the pesticides approved by the Environmental Protection Agency during the past three years have been microbial pesticides.

Over 700 million animals (poultry, swine, cattle, and sheep) are raised annually by American farmers. Improving production in this agricultural sector is just as important as it is for the major crops. Protein growth hormones (also called somatotropins) are now being produced in bulk through biotechnology. These natural compounds promote the growth of animals by improving feed efficiency. This shortens the time to market, improving the farmer's profits and assuring a stable meat supply. The use of porcine somatotropin leads to pigs with leaner meat, an important feature for today's nutritionally conscious consumers.

Of all the agricultural biotechnology products, bovine somatotropin (BST) is the most controversial. BST enhances milk production in lactating cows. Questions have been raised about the safety of milk from cows given BST, as well as whether there is a need for the product when we currently produce more dairy products than are consumed.

BST has been the most widely studied animal drug in history. It has been administered to thousands of cows in test herds. The nutritional quality of the milk is unchanged and the Food and Drug Administration (FDA) has approved the sale and use of dairy products from cows given BST. In fact, BST is a natural component of milk and present in every glass we drink.

The issue of dairy surpluses is largely political and is complicated by marketing orders and the price support system. There is no question that BST can improve the efficiency of our nation's dairy farmers. A well-managed dairy farm using BST can reduce the size of the herd without a decrease in milk production. This will reduce the amount of farm labor needed and may be most important for small farmers whose labor costs form the most significant part of the operation.

By the end of this decade, several important pharmaceuticals may be produced more efficiently in animals than through conventional processes.

r-DNA can be used to insert new genetic material into animals to cause them to grow faster, produce valuable pharmaceutical proteins, or improve their resistance to certain diseases. "Transgenic" fish containing genes for growth hormones grow faster and are the subject of research interest because of the shifting dietary preferences of American consumers. Goats and swine have been genetically modified to produce important blood proteins such as human hemoglobin. By the end of this decade, several important pharmaceuticals may be produced more efficiently in animals than through conventional processes.

Enzymes are important to the food processing industry. These proteins catalyze or speed up chemical reactions and are used in the production of a number of key food ingredients. High-fructose corn syrup, commonly used as a sweetener in beverages and baked goods, is one such product. Enzymes are used to degrade the corn starch down to individual sugar units, known as glucose. An enzyme called an isomerase is then used to convert the glucose, which is not sweet, to fructose, which is very sweet.

The production of food enzymes can be enhanced through biotechnology. The enzyme chymosin is used to clot milk, the first step in cheese making. The traditional source of this enzyme has been an extract from the stomachs of unweaned calves. Recently r-DNA has been used to move the calf gene for the enzyme into a microorganism. Chymosin can be produced by microbial fermentation in a cost effective manner. Since this form of the enzyme is identical to that found in the calf's stomach, cheese manufacturers have a reliable supply of the enzyme. Moreover, its cheese-making properties are unchanged.

The current U.S. food safety evaluation system, comprised of plant breeders and food processors, has assured the safest food supply in the world. The developers of these new agricultural biotechnology products regularly consult with federal agencies such as the Food and Drug Administration to assure their safe introduction into the marketplace.

[See also Biodiversity, Food and Agriculture; Food Technologies; Genetic Engineering, Genetics; Genetics: Commercialization; Nutrition.]

BIBLIOGRAPHY

"Biotechnology and the American Agriculture Industry." *Journal of the American Medical Association* (March 20, 1991).
"Improving Plant Disease Resistance." *Science* (July 24, 1992).
Kessler, David A.; Taylor, Michael R.; Maryanski, James H.; Flamm, Eric L.; and Kahl, Linda S. "The Safety of Foods Developed by Biotechnology." *Science* (June 26, 1992).
U.S. Congress, Office of Technology Assessment. "A New Technological Era for American Agriculture." OTA-F-474. Washington, DC: U.S. Government Printing Office, 1992.

— ALAN GOLDHAMMER

GENETICS: COMMERCIALIZATION

Genetic engineering is the altering of plants, animals, and organisms at the molecular level to make or modify products, improve plants or animals, or develop microorganisms. It is a result of the discovery of the double-helix structure of human deoxyribonucleic acid, or DNA, by Francis Crick and James D. Watson in the early 1950s. Since the first cloning of a gene (recombinant DNA) in 1973, scientific research has discovered processes and products of potential social and economic value; these findings have also challenged existing legal and regulatory doctrine.

The genetic revolution has the potential for altering the social, economic, and legal bases of agriculture, medicine, and manufacturing. Potential applications in agriculture are increased crop productivity through the design of transgenic plants and animals with "built-in" disease and herbicide resistance, tolerance to frost or heat, and low-fat and low-cholesterol meat. Potential applications in medicine include better diagnostic procedures through genetic screening, treatment of some diseases with gene therapy, production of medicines based on limited enzymes and hormones, and better preventive medicine due to genetic identification of disease. Potential applications in manufacturing include biosensors to more accurately detect minute traces of various substances and bioremediation, which uses specially designed organisms to break down oil deposits and other hazardous products.

Emerging Commercial Applications

In 1992, there were more than 1,200 companies in some aspect of research, development, or production of genetically engineered products affecting health care, agriculture, energy, or environmental improvement. This fledgling industry employed more than 79,000 persons in 1992, and it is expected to employ more than 200,000 by the turn of the century. Because this is a new and knowledge-intensive industry, firms have high capital needs to sustain large research and development budgets and to long (seven- to ten-year) product approval periods.

Since Genentech, the first U.S. genetic engineering firm, was founded in 1976, the commercialization of genetic engineering has developed on a number of application and regulatory fronts. In 1981, the Food and Drug Administration (FDA) first approved monoconal antibody diagnostic kits, followed the next year by the first approval of a genetically engineered pharmaceutical product (human insulin). Another early medical application of genetic engineering was TPA (tissue plasminogen activator) used to reduce blood clotting and, thus, the probability of heart attacks. In 1990, the FDA approved the first genetically engineered food additive, recombinant renin, an enzyme used to produce cheese. In 1993, the FDA approved the "Flavr Savr" tomato, a genetically engineered vegetable resistant to spoilage that can be ripened on the vine, thus increasing its commercial appeal.

FDA approval of bovine somatotropin (BST), in late 1993, culminated a decade-long controversy about the safety of genetically engineered food products. A naturally occurring hormone, BST increases milk production in dairy cows; it was available only in limited supplies until biotechnological processes to reproduce it were developed.

Current Government Regulation

The Supreme Court decision in *Diamond* v. *Chakrabarty* (1980) that extended patent rights to genetically engineered organisms paved the way for the development of the industry. Prior to this decision, only plants were subject to patent protection under the Townsend Purnell Plant Act and the Plant Variety Protection Act. In 1988, the first U.S. patent on an animal was issued to Harvard University for a mouse genetically engineered to contain a cancer-causing gene.

The genetic revolution has the potential

for altering the social, economic, and legal bases

of agriculture, medicine, and manufacturing.

The Coordinated Framework for Regulation of Biotechnology was established by the U.S. Office of Science and Technology Policy in 1986 to coordinate five federal agencies (Environmental Protection Agency, Food and Drug Administration, Department of Agriculture, Occupational Safety and Health Administration, and the National Institutes of Health) to regulate biotechnology. The Coordinated Framework depends on existing agencies that, under present law, have concurrent jurisdiction. For example, a food product produced using a genetically altered microorganism might be viewed as a "chemical substance" and regulated by the Toxic Substance Control Act administered by the Environmental Protection Agency, or it could be viewed as a food additive normally regulated by the Food and Drug Administration according to the Food, Drug, and Cosmetic Act. And, because of its responsibility to inspect meat and poultry products, the Department of Agriculture has a claim to jurisdiction. While the effectiveness of this regulatory approach has been subject to debate by both proponents and opponents of genetic engineering, its adoption extended the doctrine that chemicals and organisms are usually regulated in the United States according to their intended use and not by their method of production.

The National Institutes of Health, the National Science Foundation, and the Department of Agriculture have funded genetic-engineering-related research programs with animal, plant, and human applications. One highly visible federal policy decision was the $3 billion authorization of the Human Genome Project, which

began on October 1, 1990. This project, expected to take fifteen years, is a worldwide research effort to map and define the sequence of all the 50,000 to 100,000 genes in humans.

Public-Policy Concerns

Recent surveys of American public opinion find that while about nine out of ten Americans approve of genetic research and gene therapy, and more than three-quarters would take genetic tests, about seven out of ten support greater governmental regulation of gene therapy and the use of genetic information. Concerns about the more effective genetic testing that will be practical as the Human Genome Project progresses relate to issues of workplace discrimination, legal rights of confidentiality, uncertain effects on life and health insurance, and the effects of more genetic information on reproduction decisions. Two specific problems faced by genetic screening clinics are requests to perform prenatal tests for sex selection, and the generation of "unwanted information." An instance of such information might be learning that one tests positive for a genetic abnormality like cystic fibrosis or Huntington's disease without the ability to correct it, and then facing potential adverse reactions from employers or health-insurance companies. To date, genetic counselors have few public-policy directives to assist them in making such decisions.

There are environmental and consumer concerns about genetic engineering as well. Environmental concerns include the risk of release of genetically engineered organisms into the environment, and the threat of increased pesticide use due to the ability of pesticide-tolerant crops to withstand the previously harmful effects of excessive exposure. Consumer issues involving product labeling and the safety of biotechnology products still surface when new applications of genetic engineering to produce food are announced.

Prospects for Future Developments

Despite an impressive record of scientific advancement, the future of the biotechnology industry is unclear. Like other high-tech industries, the biotechnology industry has large capital requirements, and its ability to attract investments depends on the economic and regulatory climate. Both the direction and pace of applications of genetic engineering in the United States depend on public-policy decisions affecting the legal, economic, and governmental support for further research, development, and, ultimately, applications. There appears to be a public consensus that U.S. international economic competitiveness depends on technological advancement, and biotechnology is widely viewed as one of the nation's most promising advanced technologies. However, harnessing that potential requires that, in addition to continual scientific advancement, intellectual-property rights be modified to protect genetically engineered products and that consumer confidence be maintained through adequate, competent environmental and consumer regulation.

In summary, genetics, particularly the developments in molecular biology and the understanding of the human genome, will for the first time give us direct control over our own evolution. Most visible to us will be the effects on body, brain, and behavior. As the genetic base of those three elements of our lives becomes clearer, there will be many successful positive interventions. Genetics will also bring separate waves of benefits to humankind in agriculture and industrial processes.

[See also Biodiversity; Food and Agriculture; Food Technologies; Genetic Engineering; Genetics; Genetics: Agricultural Applications; Genetic Technologies; Life Sciences.]

BIBLIOGRAPHY

Bishop, Jerry E., and Waldholz, Michael. *Genome: The Story of the Most Astonishing Scientific Adventure of Our Time—the Attempt To Map All the Genes in the Human Body.* New York: Simon & Schuster, 1990.

Davis, Bernard D., ed. *The Genetic Revolution: Scientific Prospects and Public Perceptions.* Baltimore, MD: Johns Hopkins, 1991.

U.S. Congress, Office of Technology Assessment. *Biotechnology in a Global Economy.* Washington, DC: U.S. Government Printing Office, 1991.

— DAVID J. WEBBER

GENETIC TECHNOLOGIES

In the second half of the twentieth century, a cascading series of new discoveries in genetics launched a "biological revolution" that soon began to transform medicine, agriculture, and several other fields of human activity. The pace of new discoveries and new applications is certain to increase rapidly in the decades ahead. Biology will become the "master science" of the twenty-first century—as physics was the master science of the twentieth—and biotechnology will replace or perhaps merge with electronics at the cutting edge of technological innovation.

Among the genetic technologies currently in use are the following:

- *Recombinant DNA.* For example, when a gene from one organism is "spliced" into the DNA of another, the host organism can then produce a new protein. In this way, bacteria are used to manufacture products such as human insulin.
- *Protein engineering.* "Conventional" recombinant DNA produces a familiar protein manufactured by a different organism; further genetic

modifications can produce entirely new proteins with different characteristics—such as the ability to metabolize at different temperatures.

- Antisense technology. When an exact but sequence-reversed segment of synthetic DNA is inserted into a cell, it binds with the complementary segment of messenger RNA and prevents the expression of that gene. The first commercial application of this technology controlled the gene that causes softening in tomatoes.
- *Biosensors.* When an organic element is integrated with an electronic system, it makes possible instant detection of the presence or quantity of certain chemicals.
- *Cell and tissue culture.* Although not an entirely new technology, culture has made dramatic advances in the genetic age, enabling cultivation of animal cells—human skin tissue, for example—and plant cells.
- *Monoclonal antibodies.* Antibodies for use in research and therapy were rare and expensive until genetic technology developed a procedure for mass producing them through a new form of cell culture in which a type of cancer cell is fused with the antibody-producing "B" cell.

Applications of the New Genetic Technologies:

The revolutionary impact of the new technologies was felt first in medicine, then in agriculture—two traditionally biologically-based fields of human endeavor. In future the revolution will transform other fields that were not previously biologically based, such as energy production, various kinds of manufacturing, and possibly even computer electronics.

Monoclonal antibodies are a useful tool for medical diagnosis, since they quickly and accurately identify various diseases such as malaria, schistosomiasis, and some types of cancer.

MEDICAL APPLICATIONS. *Diagnosis.* Monoclonal antibodies are a useful tool for medical diagnosis, since they quickly and accurately identify various diseases such as malaria, schistosomiasis, and some types of cancer. They also are used in kits for detecting pregnancy. Another tool, the DNA probe—a specific piece of selected or synthesized DNA that recognizes the DNA of an infectious organism—is an effective diagnostic method that replaces tedious and expensive laboratory analysis. Likely future development: instant and precise diagnosis of most diseases.

Gene Therapy. Many serious diseases are caused by the malfunctioning of a single gene. When healthy genes are inserted into defective cells, they enable the cell to function properly. This approach is called "somatic" gene therapy because it treats only the cells of the patient; its effects are not inherited. A more controversial but highly probable future development, germline therapy, would correct genes in the germline (reproductive) cells, and the effects would be inherited. Antisense technology opens up yet another approach to genetic therapy: It can block the activity of an infectious organism such as a malaria parasite or an AIDS virus, or stop the proliferation of artery-hardening cells on the inner walls of blood vessels. Ultimately, such genetic therapies could make drugs obsolete.

Immunology. When people learned that deliberate infection with the relatively mild cowpox could produce resistance to smallpox, immunology began. Later, vaccines against viral diseases such as polio generally employed a weakened form of the virus. In either case, the general idea was to trick the body into producing enough antigen to confer immunity. New genetic technologies perform this same operation with greater precision and less danger. The future of immunology includes protection against an increasing number of diseases, including malaria caused by parasites, and new ways of getting the vaccine into the body (e.g., by pills or nasal spray).

AGRICULTURAL APPLICATIONS. As new knowledge about human genetics leads to fundamentally new kinds of medicine, so does new understanding of plant and animal genetics lead to new kinds of agriculture—it begins to redefine completely what agriculture is. We will soon see traditional food and fiber products coming out of factories rather than farms. At the same time, many more farms will be used to grow products other than food and fiber.

Modified Crop Plants. Through recombinant DNA and other methods (generally in combination with traditional methods of plant breeding), crop plants with a host of new characteristics—such as self-fertilization, pest resistance, and new flavor and nutrition qualities—are being developed.

Pharming. "Pharming" is the name given to a new kind of agriculture, in which pharmaceutical proteins can be produced in the milk of genetically modified domestic animals. Scientists also see a good possibility of modifying tobacco plants to produce medically useful chemicals, so that tobacco farming can become a socially beneficial form of agriculture.

Food Without Farms. In 1991 a California bio-technology company took out a patent on a process to manufacture "real" vanilla extract through tissue culture. The resultant product has much richer flavor than the synthetic vanilla extract used in most commercial products and is also far lower in cost than the extract produced from beans handpicked from the vanilla orchid, which grows in a few tropical regions such as Madagascar. This approach will be used to produce many kinds of food products such as "real" fruit juices, fibers

such as cotton, and plant-derived medicines such as the cancer treatment taxol, which comes from the bark of yew trees.

INDUSTRIAL APPLICATIONS. Chemicals for various industrial purposes can be produced from organic materials through biotechnology, making it possible to replace petrochemicals for manufacturing or fuel with similar chemicals produced from farm crops. This is already being done in a limited way, but more effective ways of biologically processing common substances such as lignocellulose (present in wood chips, straw, corncobs) will greatly increase the economic independence of developing countries. Biotechnology can also yield entirely new industrial products. Some scientists propose, for example, that a spider's genetic code might be used to make a polymer that would be five to ten times stronger than steel and could be pulled out by 20 percent of its length without breaking.

Environmental Cleanup. Bacteria already are being used to clean up oil spills and other forms of environmental pollution. With genetic modification, they promise to become capable of biodegrading a wide range of toxic substances.

Biotechnologies of the Future

Bioelectronics began in the 1980s with the first use of biosensors. A possible future development will be protein-engineered "biochips" that usher in a new generation of computer technology.

Nanotechnology is the term for a predicted next generation of engineering as people learn how to manufacture machines of microscopic dimensions—small enough to travel through capillaries and operate within living cells. Such devices might then be able to cure diseases, reverse aging, and give the body new strengths and abilities.

[See also Bioethics; Genetic Engineering; Genetics; Genetics: Agricultural and Forestry Applications; Genetics: Commercialization; Life Sciences; Nanotechnology, Scientific Breakthroughs.]

BIBLIOGRAPHY

Anderson, Walter Truett. "Food Without Farms: The Biotech Revolution in Agriculture." *Futurist* 24 (1990): 16–21.

———. *To Govern Evolution: Further Adventures of the Political Animal.* Boston: Harcourt Brace Jovanovich, 1987.

Drexler, K. Eric. *Engines of Creation: The Coming Era of Nanotechnology.* Garden City, NY: Doubleday, 1986.

Fisher, Jeffrey A. *Rx 2000: Breakthroughs in Health, Medicine, and Longevity by the Year 2000 and Beyond.* New York: Simon and Schuster, 1992.

Office of Technology Assessment, U.S. Congress. *Commercial Biotechnology: An International Analysis.* Washington, DC: U.S. Government Printing Office, 1984.

Zimmerman, Burke. *Biofuture: Confronting the Genetic Era.* New York: Plenum, 1984.

— WALTER TRUETT ANDERSON

GERIATRICS.

See AGING OF THE POPULATION; ELDERLY, LIVING ARRANGEMENTS.

GERMANY

Tomorrow's Federal Republic of Germany will be very different from the country that existed in the four decades following World War II for reasons that go considerably beyond the impact of unification. Among the large, industrialized countries, Germany is unique in the pressures it faces to redefine its social contract and its external relationships simultaneously.

Pressures Within and Without

On the economic side, Germany must respond to three challenges at the same time. First, it must complete the economic unification of the country, a process of rebuilding that will extend well into the twenty-first century. Massive infrastructure projects will be continued for at least the next two decades in the fields of energy, environmental cleanup, housing, transportation, and telecommunications. Private investment and entrepreneurial initiatives are needed to create jobs for the almost three million unemployed eastern German workers.

Second, Germany must halt and, it is to be hoped, reverse a startling decline in its global economic competitiveness. The development of technology in Germany is held back by intense regulation, the difficulty of financing risky ventures, a bureaucratized research-and-development (R&D) culture, and a widespread pessimism about the effects of new technology on social life and the environment. Germany's widely heralded status as a major exporter masks the fact that its global share of the high-technology export market is significantly smaller than its overall market share in manufactured goods (15 percent as opposed to 20 percent in 1992). That condition does not bode well for the future, since it is primarily in the most advanced sectors that German firms will be able to hold off low-wage competitors. Labor costs in Germany are the highest in the world, and German labor-market regulations are highly rigid, discouraging part-time and short-term employment, shift work, and the employment of pensioners and students. German workers—who enjoy six- to eight-week vacations and more than a dozen annual holidays—put in 15 to 20 percent fewer hours on the job each year than their Asian and North American coun-

terparts. Not surprisingly, the Federal Republic's attractiveness to investment is in decline.

The third element in this mix of economic challenges is a major actuarial problem. Germany stands at what might be called the limits of the welfare state and must discover a means to balance its entitlements accounts and/or reduce the expectations of its citizens drastically. It is common for university students to reach the age of thirty before entering the workforce, even as the average retirement age in Germany creeps down to fifty-nine and life expectancies increase. Meanwhile, the range of benefits promised to the German population surpasses what might be called a safety net and now constitutes a cradle-to-grave cushion against every conceivable setback. For many large firms operating in Germany, contributions to mandated entitlement and insurance programs account for more than eighty-five pfennig on top of every deutsche mark that is paid in wages.

The future of Germany will be shaped as well by the demands of its new place on the world stage. For the foreseeable future, Russia's behavior toward Central and Eastern Europe probably will be an uncomfortable mixture of disinterest and intimidation. While Russia offers little that might ease the economic difficulties and political tensions of the region, its powerful militarists will remain jealously opposed to the incorporation of the Soviet Union's former satellite countries into the North Atlantic Treaty Organization (NATO) and other Western security organizations. At the same time, the European Union (EU) maintains trade barriers to eastern goods and offers no time tables for eventual Central and Eastern European membership in a united Europe. The net effect is the virtual isolation of the entire region astride Germany's eastern border.

If countries such as the Czech Republic, Hungary, Poland, and Slovakia fail to achieve sustained economic growth, political stability, and external security in the 1990s, they may instead be a source of large refugee flows into Germany. Military violence within and between the Central European countries cannot be ruled out. Such developments would destroy German hopes for expanded trade and investment opportunities in the region and further diminish Germany's competitive position worldwide.

A New Social Contract

In the twenty-first century, Germany will move in the direction of the market and away from social security. That is not to say that Germany will dismantle its social welfare system. The Federal Republic will be a more competitive society, one in which more is expected of individuals and private firms while less is expected of governments.

Job creation in the Federal Republic seems likely to override the traditional resistance of policymakers and unions to a more flexible labor market. Some firms may preserve jobs during difficult periods by combining shorter work weeks and reduced wages, and others may experiment with pail-time and shift work. Forty-hour work weeks may once again become the norm. Labor mobility almost certainly will increase. German firms will seek strategic alliances worldwide in an effort to improve their technological capacities, while both public and private R&D places more emphasis on industrial applications and less on basic research.

In the effort to accommodate foreign workers,

enlightened Germans will accept more

liberal immigration and citizenship laws.

The creation of new jobs in Germany will do much to balance the country's social-welfare accounts, but not enough. To sustain its social safety net and vast retired population in the twenty-first century, the country will need to address its demographic problems. Subreplacement birthrates persist in the Federal Republic, which means that Germany's closed-door policy on immigration is not sustainable. In the effort to accommodate foreign workers, enlightened Germans will accept more liberal immigration and citizenship laws. Many other Germans will resist such changes, heightening social tensions in Germany for the foreseeable future and leading to occasional violent outbursts against foreigners.

Income disparities seem likely to increase. Violent strikes and other forms of economic protest (such as traffic blockades) may become relatively common features of German life. Extremist political groups almost certainly will seek to incite or take advantage of such developments. While Germany's 5 percent threshold for parliamentary representation will keep most of those groups away from the halls of power, some will be successful—and mainstream political parties will be tempted to pander to their constituencies. Germany's firm moorings in liberal democracy are not in doubt, but the long periods of stable coalition government to which the Federal Republic is accustomed could give way to more frequent transitions and unlikely political bedfellows.

If it can create jobs by reducing the excesses of the welfare state, foster technological development, and accept foreigners as an asset rather than a liability, twenty-first century Germany will be more humane, more competitive, and ultimately more powerful than ever before.

An Assertive Foreign Policy

West German governments spent forty years telling the rest of the world, in effect, that Germany had no national interests—that it was tied inextricably to the Atlantic Alliance and that what was good for Western Europe as a whole was good for Germany. There was no deliberate deception in that message. National interests were sublimated in the effort to rehabilitate Germany from its aggressive, criminal reputation in World War II.

German unification and the collapse of the Soviet Union marked the beginning of the end of that Federal Republic. Gone are the ultimate carrot (the prospect of unity), and the ultimate stick (the prospect of Soviet invasion) that kept Germany from deviating too far from plans laid out in the meeting rooms of the EU and NATO. The new Germany will not revert to aggression. But Germany also will not remain forever enthralled by what are now quite vague understandings of Europe's greater good. Germany's current leaders still are afraid to speak and act forcefully in the name of their country's own interests. Their successors, however, will not hesitate to do so.

Germany almost certainly will try to turn the EU eastward at the expense (at least for the foreseeable future) of grandiose plans for a common currency and political federation in Europe. Germany will find many reasons—including access to much-needed markets, political stability on its borders, and the creation of a buffer against an unpredictable Russia—for expanding the EU's membership and its trade to Central and Eastern Europe. If the EU does not follow Germany eastward, then Germany will go alone—spreading aid and investment and thereby gaining political influence.

Similarly, Germany will convince NATO to take responsibility for the security of Central and Eastern Europe or it will try to do the job itself. *Der Osten* (the East) has been an obsession of German leaders throughout their nation's history and it will remain so. Germany's future policy in the region, if NATO holds back, will be some combination of several elements: diplomatic understandings with Russia, a defensive military buildup, more visible military exercises with its neighbors, preferential trade deals, and/or the creation of a separate Central European trading sphere under German tutelage.

Gradually putting aside its reputation for pacifism during the Cold War and resolving its constitutional conundrum on the use of military force, Germany in the 1990s and beyond will play an occasional military role in safeguarding its economic interests and contributing to crisis management outside of Europe. So long as the U.S. continues to respond to the most egregious threats against global resource and trade flows, however, Germany will find few reasons to make independent investments in power-projection capabilities.

Summary

Germany will change quite dramatically by the early twenty-first century—emphasizing market mechanisms over government intervention, striving to accommodate ethnic diversity, enduring greater political and social volatility, articulating new or rediscovered national interests, and shedding its geopolitical reticence. At the same time, however, the Federal Republic seems likely to retain many familiar reference points: the guarantee of basic social welfare, the belief in universal economic opportunity, a preference for multinational over independent actions, and a primary focus on Europe rather than the global political arena. Observers will recognize the Federal Republic of Germany, even as it moves well beyond its one-time economic miracle, its division, and the constraints of the Cold War.

[*See also Development: Western Perspective.*]

BIBLIOGRAPHY

Bergner, Jeffrey T. *The New Superpowers.* New York: St. Martin's Press, 1991.

Geipel, Gary L., ed. *Germany in a New Era.* Indianapolis: Hudson Institute, 1993.

Huelshoff, Michael G., Markovits, Andrei S., and Reich, Simon, eds. *From Bundesrepublik to Deutschland: German Politics After Unification.* Ann Arbor, MI: University of Michigan Press, 1993.

Mattox, Gale A., and Shingleton, A. Bradley, eds. *Germany at the Crossroads.* Boulder, CO: Westview Press, 1992.

Smyser, W. R. *The Economy of United Germany.* New York: St. Martin's Press, 1992.

Stares, Paul B., ed. *The New Germany and the New Europe.* Washington, DC: Brookings, 1992.

— GARY L. GEIPEL

GLOBAL BUSINESS: DOMINANT ORGANIZATIONAL FORMS

The global corporation has not yet arrived; it has long been predicted but will arrive only when all countries are open economically. Its size and shape will differ from that envisioned by many, for it will not be monolithic either in size or construct. Rather, it will develop in response to the emerging patterns of international economic integration, as determined by governments and influenced by markets around the world.

The evolution of global business began with the joint ventures across national boundaries prior to the advent of the Industrial Revolution and capitalism. These early units were essentially trading or financial ventures. A distinguishing feature of the nineteenth- and early twentieth-century organizational forms in Europe and the United States was the rise of investment in manufacturing operations abroad. These international corporations largely served local national markets ("market-seekers") or brought resources back to the parent company ("resource-seekers"). Organizationally, this corporate form was often separate from operations in the home country, being legally incorporated as a separate entity.

Following World War II, international business became characterized by foreign affiliates established to develop the most effective organization for production among several locations to serve multiple national markets at least cost ("efficiency seekers"). Known as the "multinational enterprise" (MNE), or the "transnational corporation," this form became the basis for closer international integration of economies through mobility of capital, technology transfers, exchange of management, greater access to resources, and dispersion of corporate cultures.

It now became evident that international economic integration, formerly presumed to occur through trade, was more effectively accomplished through foreign direct investment (FDI). Trade, after all, could be terminated much more readily than direct investment, and the presence of an organization in a country built ties that became permanent. By the 1930s, international businesses conducted over half of international trade in manufactures within their corporate structures—i.e., as intra-company trade. Furthermore, if trade with non-affiliates was included, such global trade accounted for an overwhelming majority of total international industrial trade. Government efforts to alter the trade balance of a country, therefore, had to take fully into account the nature of trade among these major worldwide corporations.

Reception by Governments

There was considerable opposition initially to each of the three forms of international business because they were regarded as an extension of colonialism. By the 1990s, no significant country continued to oppose internal FDI. To the contrary, virtually all countries were seeking to attract MNEs as a key means of stimulating economic growth and increasing higher-skilled employment. Even former communist countries have now become eager to join the world economy through ties with MNEs. Many developing countries still preferred or required joint ventures (JVs), especially in key sectors, with local investors to reduce the "presence" of or control by foreigners.

Experience with JVs has not always been favorable in the view of Western international corporations, who preferred 100 percent ownership for its neat lines of authority and the absence of extraneous interests. However, JVs were formed when necessary because of a partner's strength in the local market, access to needed capital, unique management skills within a foreign culture, technology position and strength, or insistence by host governments.

Diverse Forms

Different corporate organizational forms arose in Europe and Asia. European enterprises, formed similarly to those in the United States, combine forces by integrating operations more closely through a variety of cartel arrangements. Similar arrangements, illegal in the United States, are permitted under European laws as long as their power is not abusive. In some instances,

as with the OPEC arrangements among Arab countries, cartel activity was mandated by the governments.

The Japanese *keiretsu* and the Korean *coebol* (types of holding companies) are the major forms for large corporations in these respective countries. Structural ties link dozens and even hundreds of companies together in mutual shareholding, cross-directorates, and close supplier-vendor relationships. This organizational form permitted ready international expansion of several companies simultaneously and promoted collaboration and inter-company trade as suppliers or vendors. Such ties and collaboration, regarded as "anticompetitive" in the eyes of many observers, are not opposed openly in Europe, but they are considered a significant threat to competition.

Future Integration

The structure of international business began to change in the late twentieth century as economies became more open and more closely integrated. As a consequence,

The truly global corporation has yet to materialize, but a customer at this tea shop in India can choose a soft drink from a major American company. (Earl Kowall/Corbis)

the markets that could be served became larger and also more diverse in the styles and qualities of products demanded. Size and diversity opened up "niche" markets that fostered multiple ties or "strategic alliances" among major corporations to build competitive strength in particular functions or product lines. Within and among countries, alliances were formed in marketing, in production, and in research and development. The new arrangements led to reliance on "comparative advantage" among enterprises rather than among countries. These developments reflected the opening of economies worldwide and the reduction of governmental intervention in the flow of FDI.

The opening of global markets

will give further impetus to the grouping of nations

into regional economic associations.

The opening of global markets will give further impetus to the grouping of nations into regional economic associations. Within these regional trade alliances or blocs, markets will be virtually wholly open. Sectoral agreements within these blocs will set the rules for FDI in specific industries, such as autos, pharmaceuticals, chemicals, and electronics. These agreements are likely to provide a perceived *equity* in the distribution of the benefits of economic growth among participating nations through the allocation of investment, thereby creating employment, promoting new skills, and offering additional choices for consumers.

Regulation

Government regulation of trade, technology, transfer, investment, and ownership has controlled and curtailed the development of international business, but this is likely to change. Efforts at intergovernmental regulation through the United Nations will continue to be largely ineffective, since it will not be perceived as needed. With the eagerness of all governments to attract these engines of growth, intervening rules will become fewer.

National governments are likely to have less to say about where investment takes place. Municipalities and state governments eager to attract FDI, to establish ties with local industry, to promote local R&D activities, and to enhance employment opportunities within their jurisdiction will have more of a say. The regulations will be few and the incentives large. However, the competitive use of incentives will be costly to the hosts of global corporations.

Given the competition to attract FDI, the creation of social responsibility within the global corporation may not be demanded by the local government. However, these companies will be influenced by consumer and community attitudes and will move toward self-regulation because of public awareness of the impacts of what they are doing.

The future structure of the global corporation will permit a high degree of mobility. Thus, governments, local as well as national, will be induced to learn more about the activities of the companies and to work with them to increase both the volume and quality of the benefits to each.

Benefits

The development of the global corporation awaits a fully global economy, which is not yet in sight. Its rise will be favorable in that it will spread the benefits of employment, trade, and technology (providing higher skills and opportunities for creativity) among more countries. And it will achieve long-term objectives of *efficiency, equity,* and *participation* by more peoples and countries, as corporations are drawn to address the social as well as economic objectives of their hosts. Further, the opening of more opportunities will permit small companies to become global also, reducing the dominance of large corporations.

The remaining challenge to these corporations is to adopt policies attuned to the cultures and socio-political interests of host countries so that they are seen less as "foreign" and more as locally oriented.

[See also Business Structure: Forms, Impacts; Global Culture; International Trade: Regulation; International Trade: Sustaining Growth; Management; Participative Management.]

BIBLIOGRAPHY

Behrman, Jack N. *Industrial Policies: International Restructuring and Transnationals.* Lexington, MA: Lexington Books, 1984.
Behrman, Jack N., and Grosse, Robert E. *International Business and Governments: Issues and Institutions,* Columbia, SC: University of South Carolina Press, 1990.
Dunning, John H., and Usiu, Mikoto, eds. *Structural Change, Economic Interdependence and World Development.* London: Macmillan, 1987.
Moran, Theodore H., ed. *Multinational Corporations: The Political Economy of Foreign Direct Investment.* Lexington, MA: Lexington Books, 1985.
Robinson, Richard D. *Direct Foreign Investments: Costs and Benefits.* New York: Praeger, 1987.

– JACK N. BEHRMAN

GLOBAL CONSCIOUSNESS

The central evolutionary trap in human history can be described as follows: When one species attains a position of dominance over all the other species in the ecology of its planet, if it is both egocentrically greedy and has a powerful set of technologies through which to amplify the expression of that greed, unless that dominant species can find a way to limit or to transform its egocentric greediness into something more wholesome, it will foul its planetary nest as surely as the night follows the day . . . perhaps even to its own extinction. This is an accurate synopsis of the writings of Olaf Stapledon and Gregory Bateson.

Olaf Stapledon (1886–1950) is an author whose visionary contributions to the futures community are perhaps underrecognized. Of Stapledon's many multifaceted themes, perhaps the most provocative is what nowadays is useful to call *global consciousness*—a phrase meaning at least two kinds of things:

- Improved awareness of our planetary ecology as a whole system of physical and nonphysical interactions across time.
- The expansion of consciousness beyond the confines of an egocentric sense of self to include transpersonal experiences and/or transcendent self-identity as well.

At issue is whether or not the widespread attainment of global consciousness could provide a necessary (and sufficient) set of conditions for preventing the ecological carrying capacity of the planet from being overshot by runaway growth in "ecological load"—precisely what is currently destabilizing the essential life-support systems of Spaceship Earth. (See Figure 1.)

Stapledon's two main books for futurists are: *Last and First Men* (1931) and *Starmaker* (1937). Together, they stand out as key classics in the field, each being something of a visionary "Encyclopedia of Alternative Futures"—both for humankind as a species unto itself and as depictions of the various ways in which humankind might co-evolve with other intelligent life-systems within and beyond this universe.

Last and First Men

Last and First Men (1931) is an extended scenario in which "Last Men" contact "First Men" (us) in order to communicate a better understanding of the future, which they believe critically important for us to grasp. The book traces a plausible, alternative future history spanning some eighteen separate species of humankind across some 22 billion years between "First and Last Men" and the facing of ultimate physical limits such as the universe entropically "winding-down" as implied by the Second Law of Thermodynamics. Each chapter spans an order of magnitude of ten times more time than the preceding one—a task that, when realized, has much in common with the fugue form perfected by J. S.

Bach (but along many more dimensions and exploring many more types of cyclic alternatives). It has even more in common with the system dynamics modeling approach pioneered by Jay Forrester and his colleagues at M.I.T.

Evidence of Stapledon's capacity as a true visionary is the fact that the book, although written in 1930, contains highly accurate descriptions of such technological innovations as nuclear fission and global mainframe computers (at that time undreamt of) as well as a genetically engineered species of humankind ("Fifth Men"). It is also shown by the fact that he wrote his manuscript in much the same way as Mozart composed music: He wrote the first draft cleanly and straightforwardly, and made only relatively minor, cosmetic changes in the second and published version. *Last and First Men* is a veritable handbook of alternative-future scenario possibilities and has been used as such by science fiction writers—e.g., Arthur C. Clarke—for decades. It could similarly be used to great advantage by scenario writers and futurists who wish to expand their personal repertories of alternative future possibilities.

Starmaker

Stapledon's masterwork *Starmaker* (1937) is a high-water mark in the science fiction literature dealing with global consciousness. Using the concept of *mindedness,* Stapledon explores various ways in which capacity for global consciousness in a species can give it the resources it needs to resolve, transform, and transcend the "Evolutionary Trap" summarized in the opening statement of this article. By *mindedness* is meant "a state/process of global consciousness involving the integration of individual minds in such a way that each is a sentiently knowing part of each other and of the whole." And Stapledon explores the possible ramifications of the phenomenon of mindedness in a way parallel to that used in the earlier book. (Where each chapter of *Last and First Men* covers an order-of-magnitude greater span of *time*, each chapter of *Starmaker* covers ten times greater *space*, while at the same time expanding the time dimension even further.)

Species Death and the Nature of Source Causality

Stapledon treated two additional themes having great relevance for the human species as it confronts the "Central Evolutionary Trap" noted above. How future generations of humankind might respond to the threat of species death is a theme explored in both *Last and First Men* and *Starmaker*. In both, Stapledon provides a range of plausible and highly relevant alternative conjectures, all described with the highly sensory concreteness that is desired in a good scenario.

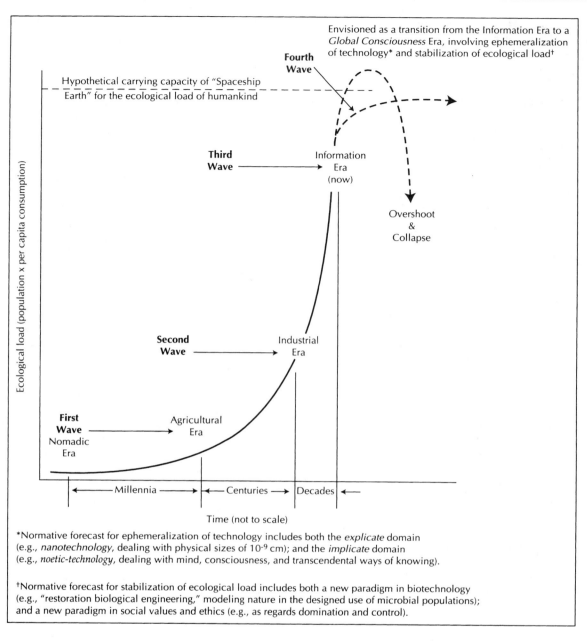

*Normative forecast for ephemeralization of technology includes both the *explicate* domain (e.g., *nanotechnology*, dealing with physical sizes of 10^{-9} cm); and the *implicate* domain (e.g., *noetic-technology*, dealing with mind, consciousness, and transcendental ways of knowing).

†Normative forecast for stabilization of ecological load includes both a new paradigm in biotechnology (e.g., "restoration biological engineering," modeling nature in the designed use of microbial populations); and a new paradigm in social values and ethics (e.g., as regards domination and control).

Figure 1. Two alternative outcomes to the central evolutionary trap of human history.

The nature of ultimate source causality—a theme left virtually untreated in the modern futures literature—was an important theme for Stapledon, and the way he treated it could be important for the integration of currently competing paradigms. Stapledon's conception of God (the Starmaker) integrates essential elements of *both* the "Creationist" and "Evolutionary" paradigms of thought about source causality. As such, Stapledon's vision of the divine has an as yet unrealized potential for helping to generate a new paradigm of understand-

ing in Judeo-Christian-Islamic cultures—one that could integrate the religious and the secular in a way that is inclusive, rather than exclusive.

Related Writings of Importance for Futurists

The global consciousness thread that flows through Stapledon's writings can also be found in other works of considerable relevance for futurists. The Stapledonian vision of global consciousness is undoubtedly carried forth in its purest form in Peter Russell's *The Global*

Brain (1983) and The *Global Brain Awakens* (1995). By way of exploring Stapledon's concept of mindedness at a planetary level, Russell accurately anticipated the synthesis of computer-based systems and human consciousness that is emerging in the mid-1990s with the development of artificial intelligence, virtual reality, and Information Era arts, sciences, and technologies.

A Fourth Wave transition from

the Information Era to a new era,

called the Era of Global Consciousness,

became organized around the "ephemeralization

of technology" and "stabilization of ecological load."

From within this viewpoint it is straightforward to envision how a transition from the "runaway ecological load" to "sustainable, humane culture" might be possible and even feasible. Just as the Third Wave is thought to be bringing a transition from the Industrial Era to the Information Era, at some reasonably close distance in the future there could be a further transition: a Fourth Wave transition from the Information Era to a new era, called the Era of Global Consciousness, organized around the "ephemeralization of technology" and "stabilization of ecological load," rather than "overshoot and collapse"—the other alternative future possibility. (See Figure 1.)

Russell's exploration *The White Hole in Time* (1992) further expands on this theme by exploring the evolutionary significance of light and time—especially the significance of *now*.

Other complementary, Western writings of relevance for futurists include:

- *The Image of the Future* (1954; trans. 1961), the epic treatise of the Dutch social philosopher Fred Polak, who feared the demise of Western culture due to a dearth of adequate "guiding images" for the future.
- *The Phenomenon of Man* (1959), the classic work of the late French Jesuit paleontologist Pierre Teilhard de Chardin, who foresaw the rise of global consciousness in his concepts of *Noosphere*, and *Omega Point*.
- The writings of Willis Harman and his colleagues, which deal with noetic arts, sciences, and technology (defined as dealing with mind, consciousness, and transcendental ways of knowing), including *Old Wine in New Wineskins* (Harman, 1967), *The Emergence of Paraphysics* (O'Regan, 1974), *Changing Images of Man* (Markley and Harman, 1974/1982), *Voluntary Simplicity* (Elgin, 1981/1993), *Global Mind Change* (Harman, 1988), *Hero with a Thousand Faces* (Campbell, 1949/1990), *With the Tongues of Men and Angels* (Hastings, 1991), *Awakening Earth* (Elgin, 1993); and *Using Depth Intuition Methods for Creative Problem Solving and Strategic Innovation* (Markley, 1988/1992).

A Potential Breakthrough in Theory

One of the major barriers to a satisfactory theory of consciousness (ego-centered *or* global) lies in the difficulty of explaining the causal relationship between what the late physicist David Bohm termed the *implicate* and the *explicate* domains of reality (e.g., how is it that free will and determinism interact, as when one decides to bend one's elbow?). A recent article in *The Sciences* offers a concise, nonmathematical, and easy-to-read introduction of a new mathematical-physics theory of "Zero-Point Energy"—a type of energy that may in the near future be shown to be the *source* of the explicate domain—and may also be a direct expression of the source of the implicate domain. (The energy density of the Zero-Point Field is theoretically derived to be proportional to the cube of the frequency: if you double the frequency, you get eight times more energy density!) This theory potentially may form a key part of the technical underpinnings supporting the emergence of a transphysical theory of global consciousness. The article is: "Beyond E = mc²" (Haisch, Rueda, and Puthoff, 1994).

[See also Apocalyptic Future; Conscious Evolution; Evolution, Life-Forms in the Universe; Global Culture; Holistic Beliefs; Mind: New Modes of Thinking; Science Fiction.]

BIBLIOGRAPHY

Bateson, Gregory. *Mind and Nature: A Necessary Unity.* New York: Bantam Books, 1988.

Campbell, Joseph. *Hero with a Thousand Faces,* rev. ed. Princeton, NJ: Princeton University Press, 1990.

Elgin, Duane. *Awakening Earth: Exploring the Evolution of Human Culture and Consciousness.* New York: William Morrow, 1993.

———. *Voluntary Simplicity: Toward a Way of Life That Is Outwardly Simple, Inwardly Rich,* rev. ed. New York: William Morrow, 1993.

Haisch, Bernhard; Rueda, Alfonso; and Puthoff, H. E. "Beyond E = mc²." *The Sciences* (November–December 1994): 26–31.

Harman, Willis. *Global Mind Change: The New Age Revolution in the Way We Think.* New York: Warner, 1988.

———. "Old Wine in New Wineskins," Chapter 33 in J. F. T. Bugental, ed. *Challenges of Humanistic Psychology.* New York: McGraw-Hill, 1967.

Markley, O. W. "Using Depth Intuition Methods for Creative Problem Solving and Strategic Innovation." *Journal of Creative Behavior* 22/2 (1988): 85–100.

Markley, O. W., and Harman, Willis W. *Changing Images of Man.* New York: Pergamon Press, 1982.

Moskowitz, Sam. *Far Future Calling: Uncollected Science Fiction and Fantasies of Olaf Stapledon, with an Authorized Biography.* Philadelphia: Oswald Train, 1979.

O'Regan, Brendan. "The Emergence of Paraphysics: Theoretical Foundations." In E. Mitchell, ed. *Psychic Explorations: A Challenge for Science.* New York: G. P. Putnam, 1974.

Russell, Peter. *The Global Brain Awakens.* Palo Alto, CA: Atrium, 1995.

———. *The White Hole in Time: Our Future Evolution and the Meaning of Now.* San Francisco: Harper San Francisco, 1992.

Stapledon, Olaf. *Last and First Men* (1931), bound together with *Starmaker* (1937). New York: Dover, 1968.

Teilhard de Chardin, Pierre. *The Phenomenon of Man.* New York, Harper & Row, 1959.

— OLIVER W. MARKLEY

GLOBAL CULTURE

Global civilization is here, yet its era has scarcely begun. Although this civilization has been slowly developing for centuries, its emergence in these times has been hastened by the end of the Cold War and also by rapid increases in human mobility and communications. In coming decades, globalization will proceed at a rapid, even dizzying, pace.

The present global culture includes a global economy, a rudimentary system of global governance, and a rapidly growing common storehouse of ideas, symbols, values, and beliefs.

The most visible part of this—so conspicuous that one might easily take it to be the whole thing—is a global *popular* culture linked to the mass entertainment media. Global pop culture was dominated at first by products from the West, particularly the United States: rock music, television shows, Hollywood movies. Now it is becoming truly international as other entertainments—such as Asian martial-arts films and Latin American soap operas—find widespread mass followings. In the future, popular culture will become even more international—with constant fads and many combinations of the cultures of different times and places. There are already Japanese salsa bands and Polish rap singers. As globalization proceeds, all cultural styles and symbols become part of a common storehouse. Clearly there is much more to global culture than popular entertainments. All the things we associate with tribal and national cultures—including stories, myths, rituals, structures of thought, and social institutions—now have their global counterparts.

Coming Together, Spinning Apart

Like all great historical processes, cultural globalization produces its own reactions. As the world becomes more unified it also becomes, in many ways, more divided.

To many people, the pervasive encroachment of global culture is a highly undesirable development. Their greatest fear is that it will bring universal standardization and homogenization, the loss of all differences. This fear has produced a variety of counter-globalization movements. Patriots struggle to protect the classical cultures of the nation-states. Other activists lament the loss of tribal cultures with their rich heritages of language, art, and ritual. Religious fundamentalists of various persuasions see global culture as a vehicle of permissiveness and materialism; they struggle—sometimes violently—against its corrupting influences.

Yet at the same time that globalization brings trivialities and troubles, it also brings new freedom, political maturity, and a sense of responsibility for the biosphere. The last years of the twentieth century achieved a rapid, sometimes turbulent, spread of democracy as countries with no history of it leaped into free elections and constitution writing. Theorists who studied "political culture" as a phenomenon of specific bounded societies are now discovering that a global political culture—with common ideas about human rights—is rapidly taking form. Just as artists and performers borrow from around the world, national leaders borrow freely from the world's common pool of political ideas and methods of governance.

There is a polarization between those who seek to hasten the development of a global civilization and those who yearn to return to more familiar forms of life.

Among the forces that have contributed to this globalization of political culture are the consciousness aroused by the women's movement and concern about the global environment. The women's movement is an international one, with common goals that transcend boundaries. Global environmental awareness comes with an image of the world as a whole and of transboundary threats such as ozone depletion. These globalizing forces are empowering for certain people and groups, but also strongly threatening to many established cultural and political orders.

So globalization itself becomes a global political issue as people take sides for and against it. The world becomes accustomed to a new kind of polarization: conflict between those who seek to hasten the development of a global civilization and those who yearn to return to simpler and more familiar forms of life. And, as the game is played out, the shape of the playing field keeps changing.

Postmodernism: New Creations, New Diversities

Global civilization is a postmodern civilization in which people everywhere recognize that the forms of culture are socially constructed. They cannot avoid developing such a postmodern consciousness: Life in pluralistic societies, with constant exposure to the news and entertainments of the mass media, generates many daily encounters with deeply different ways of being. The stressful experience called "culture shock" becomes commonplace in everyday life, and people regard turning from one cultural form to another as similar to the transience of buildings and works of art: They are regarded as things that people create and can modify as they choose. Postmodernity nurtures eclecticism, choice, and improvisation—and continual cultural change. All of this change can be unsettling.

Where will it go from here? Three scenarios can illuminate possible change in the twenty-first century:

1. Back to Basics

The world separates into a number of distinct social entities. Different regions become bastions of fundamentalist Christianity, fundamentalist Islam, Marxism, or clearly defined ethnic groups such as Basques, American Indian tribes, Palestinians—each group maintaining its traditions and lifestyles with minimal change or outside interference. (This scenario is popular with cultural preservationists and enthusiasts for the currently fashionable agenda of "devolving" global society into smaller social and political units.)

2. Tomorrow the World

Global civilization comes together under one belief system. Peace and stability are achieved as all learn to understand reality according to the same teachings. (Although most of us would regard this scenario as highly unlikely, many people still hope to unite the world as one great Christian, Islamic, Marxist, or otherwise monolithic society. New Age fundamentalists have their own agendas for cultural unification, different in kind but similar in intent.)

3. A Plurality of Pluralisms

All regions of the world become pluralistic, with people of different races, religions, worldviews, and traditions living in close contact with one another and exposed to global events. There are not only many beliefs, but many beliefs about belief. People inhabit cultures in different ways, improvise, create new forms. "Culture war" (conflict between traditionalists and innovators) becomes a familiar part of social and political life everywhere.

[See also Change, Cultural; Change, Epochal; Human Rights; Lifestyles, Ethnic; Lifestyles, Value-Oriented; Mass Culture and Arts; Multifold Trend; Values Change; Values Formation.]

BIBLIOGRAPHY

Anderson, Walter Truett. *Reality Isn't What It Used to Be.* San Francisco: HarperCollins, 1990, 1991.

Cleveland, Harlan. *Birth of a New World.* San Francisco: Jossey-Bass, 1993.

Dayan, Daniel, and Katz, Elihu. *Media Events: The Live Broadcasting of History.* Cambridge, MA: Harvard University Press, 1992.

Gergen, Kenneth J. *The Saturated Self.* New York: Basic Books, 1991.

Hunter, James Davison. *Culture Wars.* New York: Basic Books, 1991.

Rosenau, James N. *Turbulence in World Politics.* Princeton, NJ: Princeton University Press, 1990.

– WALTER TRUETT ANDERSON

GLOBAL ENVIRONMENTAL PROBLEMS

What are the long-term options for growth that are still available to humanity? What are the physical dimensions of growth that are still possible in population, food production, pollution, industrial production, and our use of energy and resources?

The Limits to Growth, a 1972 study for the Club of Rome, examined the long-term causes and consequences of physical growth on the planet. Twenty years later, *Beyond the Limits* updated the data and conducted new computer-simulation studies.

The genius of Aurelio Peccei, who founded the Club of Rome, was that he was several decades ahead of his audience. Many of the world's leaders today have finally achieved an understanding of global problems akin to what Peccei set forth almost a quarter-century ago in his 1969 book *The Chasm Ahead.* National leaders today are joining the struggle to find an appropriate response. Peccei wrote in his last book, *Before It Is Too Late,* published after his death in 1984, about the preconditions for a sustainable society. Despite world leaders' perception of the threat of emerging environmental problems, they still do not understand the profound changes required to deal fundamentally with problems of growth. So what we have experienced is a quarter century of delay, without significant corrective actions being taken. This delay has allowed the problems to intensify, and it has diminished the physical resources available for their solution.

Beyond the Limits reaffirmed the urgent importance of bringing coordination among the family of nations in an effort to reduce drastically humanity's assault on the environment and to pursue deliberately the preconditions for a sustainable world.

Transition to a Stable World Future

The Limits to Growth (1972) warned that if the present growth trends "continue unchanged, the limits to growth on this planet will be reached sometime within the next one hundred years. The most probable result will be a rather sudden and uncontrollable decline in both population and industrial capacity." In 1995 global systems are already above sustainable levels.

Because the systems responsible for population growth and economic output have a momentum that keeps their growth going, delays in making appropriate adaptations to the new conditions are almost certain. These delays will make the final changes harder and more abrupt. But within the next fifty years humanity, in order to survive, will finally be forced to reduce its numbers and to economize drastically its use of energy, raw materials, and environmental resources.

There are three different ways in which this transition can occur. The first, and most probable, is that we will overshoot some important global thresholds such as global climate change, the hole in the ozone layer, or massive radiation releases.

Such an overshooting is inevitable because it takes considerable time for political, technological, and ecological systems to respond *after* something drastic happens. The full knowledge of the consequences of such an overshoot usually comes considerably later. It is later still that those consequences become obvious to everyone. It takes even longer before appropriate alternative responses are discovered or invented. These ecological, technological, and political alternatives must then be tested—and only then are appropriate political and economic decisions made and acted upon. If climate patterns shift drastically or ultraviolet radiation increases rapidly not just at the North and South poles but in the lower latitudes, then the reductions in populations and material economies would occur everywhere around the globe.

The second possibility is that, probably through sheer luck, we manage not to trespass beyond important global thresholds. For example, we might stave off ozone depletion, avert climate change, avoid further nuclear disasters like Chernobyl and Three Mile Island. Then the rich countries might continue to grow for at most another fifty years. But the poorer nations would pay the environmental costs of providing ever more raw materials and energy to the richer countries, and stockpile for the richer countries ever more toxic wastes and pollutants.

The third possibility is that humanity understands what it is up against and takes universal corrective measures. Population would decline, not because of famine and epidemics but because people decide that they want to have smaller families. Energy use and resource use would diminish, not because of scarcities but through universal gains in the desire as well as the capability to do more with less. In this scenario, societies worldwide would work deliberately to achieve dramatic economies in their use of energy and resources. Major initiatives in environmental protection would be undertaken ev-

erywhere. And people everywhere would work for a more equitable distribution of the goods and services and technologies required for a humane existence.

Living Held Within the Web of Life

Whatever the path we take, the final result will be the same: Human numbers and human consumption will decline until they reach an equilibrium, or balance, within the resource limits and the ecological limits of the globe.

A sustainable society is one that is farseeing enough, flexible enough, and wise enough not to undermine either its physical or its social systems of support.

Humanity cannot avoid making some choice among these three options. To ignore the issue is merely to opt for the first or second possibility, with chance determining the final outcome. Human life always exists in the interrelated web of pressures that the environment exerts on any physically expanding system which has grown large enough to encroach on planetary limits.

But it is clear that the three paths would entail radically different implications for what life would be like after the transition. There would be major differences in each path for our morality, environment, political and military institutions, and the quality of political and economic life after the transition.

The fundamental question with which we are left is this: How do we harmonize human systems and the life-supporting systems of our planet?

The Sustainable Society

Beyond the Limits outlined not only our present predicament but also what it will take for society to be sustainable over the long haul, for generations. A sustainable society is one that is farseeing enough, flexible enough, and wise enough not to undermine either its physical or its social systems of support. In the words of the World Commission on Environment and Development, it is a society that "meets the needs of the present without compromising the ability of future generations to meet their own needs."

The current global economy is so wasteful, inefficient, and inequitable that, in a perverse way, it also has tremendous potential for reducing both what it requires from the planet and also what it then spews back into natural systems as pollution and wastes. So in these circumstances it is still possible greatly to reduce total throughput while at the same time raising the quality of life for everyone.

A sustainable society is not necessarily a "zero growth" society, a society in continual economic recession or depression. Rather, in a sustainable society the population and the leaders would ask what growth is for; who would benefit; what it would cost; how long it would last; and whether it can be accommodated by the Earth's storehouse of raw materials and its capacities to recycle, store, or dispose of resultant pollutants and wastes. The difference between the transition to a sustainable society and a present-day economic recession can be likened to the difference between stopping an automobile using its own brakes or by crashing it into a brick wall. A deliberate transition to sustainability would take place slowly enough and carefully enough so that people and businesses could find their proper place in the new society.

There is no reason why a sustainable society has to be either technically or culturally primitive. Nor would a sustainable world have to be a rigid one, or a centrally controlled one. Like every human culture, a sustainable society needs its own rules, laws, standards, boundaries, and social agreements. Rules for sustainability, like every workable social rule, would be put into place not to remove freedoms but to create them and to protect them against their enemies. Such rules could permit many more freedoms than would ever be possible in a world that continues to crowd against its limits.

Diversity is both a cause and a result of sustainability in nature, and therefore a sustainable human society would be diverse in both nature and culture.

A sustainable society could and should be democratic, evolutionary, technically advanced, and challenging. It would have plenty of problems to solve and plenty of ways for people to prove themselves, to serve each other, to realize their abilities, and to live good lives—perhaps more satisfying lives than any available today.

[See also Acid Rain; Apocalyptic Future; Change, Optimistic and Pessimistic Perspectives; Climate and Meteorology; Continuity and Discontinuity; Deforestation; Demography; Development, Alternative; Environment; Environmental Policy Changes; Extinction of Species; Global Warming; Hazardous Wastes; Ozone Layer Depletion; Resources; Sustainability; Trend Indicators.]

BIBLIOGRAPHY

Meadows, Donella H., et al. *The Limits to Growth.* New York: Universe Books, 1972.
Meadows, Donella H.; Meadows, Dennis L.; and Randers, Jorgen. *Beyond the Limits.* Post Mills, VT: Chelsea Green Publishing, 1992.
Peccei, Aurelio. *The Chasm Ahead.* New York: Macmillan, 1969.
Peccei, Aurelio, and Ikeda, Daisaku. *Before It Is Too Late.* Tokyo: Kodansha International, 1984.

– DENNIS L. MEADOWS

GLOBAL PARADOX

A bigger and more open world economy will be dominated by smaller and middle-sized companies, compounding entrenched expectations. Fortune 500 companies now account for only 10 percent of the U.S. economy, down from 20 percent in 1970. This is news to most Americans because the U.S. business media are passionately devoted to covering the Fortune 500 companies almost exclusively, even though small- and medium-sized companies account for 90 percent of the economy. Individual entrepreneurs are creating the new U.S. economy, and entrepreneurs everywhere are recasting the global economy.

Big companies today are trying to act like small companies in order to survive. Jack Welch, the CEO of General Electric, says: "What we are trying relentlessly to do is get that small-company soul—and small-company speed—inside our big company body." In today's competitive world, quality can be replicated anywhere. The competitive edge is marketing innovation and swiftness. Small, agile companies will beat big bureaucracies every time. It is not that small is beautiful. Small is powerful.

The most decentralized of the large companies is Asea Brown Boveri, the world's largest power engineering company with annual revenues exceeding $30 billion from 1,200 companies. Each company averages 200 people. CEO Percy Barnevik says, "We are not a global business. We are a collection of local businesses with intense global coordination."

The global paradox is being powered by the revolution in telecommunications.

In the center of Europe sits European Telecom, a Belgian phone company that helps Europeans save money by routing their international calls through American carriers in California. This arrangement saves customers one-third against the costly European rates. European Telecom has only three employees and only $50,000 worth of equipment.

The almost perfect metaphor for the movement from bureaucracies of every kind to small, autonomous units is the shift from the mainframe to network PCs. What is unfolding is a global paradox. The bigger the world economy, the more powerful its smallest players: countries, companies, right down to the individual.

As the world integrates economically, the component parts are becoming smaller and more numerous and more important. At once, the global economy is growing while its parts are shrinking. The bigger the system, the more efficient its parts must be. The great negative example is the former Soviet Union, whose inefficient parts brought about its collapse. Business units must become smaller in order to more efficiently globalize the world economy.

All over the world, people are agreeing to trade

more freely with each other, but at the same time

are asserting their independence, sovereignty,

and distinctiveness.

The paradox continues: The huge economy is generating smaller and smaller market niches. A Mexican company saw a market niche for small refrigerators for hotel rooms, dormitory rooms, and offices. Today that company sells more refrigerators to the United States than any other company in the world. Thus, the more the world's economies integrate, the more they will differentiate. Differentiation is now a powerful driver of change.

The more democratic the world, the greater the number of countries. In Barcelona in the 1992 Summer Olympics, there were teams representing 172 countries. Well over 200 countries will participate in the 1996 Olympics in Atlanta and as many as 300 countries in the 2000 Olympics in Sydney.

This spread of self-rule will characterize the decade ahead of us. As 200 countries become 300 countries, heading toward a world of 1,000 countries, along the way it will become overwhelmingly apparent that the idea of countries and borders is less and less relevant. Boundaries may be important symbolically and culturally, but not too relevant in a single world economy dominated by person-to-person communications.

The global paradox is being powered by the revolution in telecommunications. Enhanced communication is the driving force that simultaneously is creating the huge global economy and making its parts smaller and more powerful.

We are moving toward a world where everyone will be hooked up with everyone else in the world, able to communicate with anyone in the world by voice, data, and image, all by wireless transmission. It will take a long time to get there, but that is where we are going.

Today a person's business card might list a phone number for office and home, a fax number, an E-mail number, an Internet number, and car phone number. But in the not too distant future, each of us will be assigned a lifelong number. Personal computer assistants (carried by persons) will sort out what messages go where. Individuals will phone others wherever they are in the world—without knowing their actual location. Until now we have always called a place and asked for a person. In the new world, we will call a person's unique number and the computer in the sky will ring him or her.

The new telecommunications revolution, zeroing in on the individual, will give new and powerful meaning to the global paradox. The bigger the world economy, the more powerful its smallest players.

Another major paradox that helps us sort out what is going on in the world is, the more universal we become, the more tribal we act.

The tension between the tribal and the universal has always been with us. Now democracy and the revolution in telecommunications (which spreads the word about democracy and gives it urgency) have brought a need for balance between tribal and universal to a new level.

As we globalize the world's economies, many more things will become universal. Yet at the same time, what remains tribal will become more important and powerful. Take language. Even as English becomes the language of the world, non-English languages are gaining in importance within their national boundaries.

The tribal/universal paradox accounts for the ambiguity being experienced throughout Europe. All over the world, people are agreeing to trade more freely with each other, but at the same time are asserting their independence, sovereignty, and distinctiveness. The economic interdependence of the European Union has led people in its member nations to otherwise want to hold on to their identity, their language, their culture, their history.

The riddle of the 1990s is: What will become universal? What will remain tribal?

With the new emphasis on what is tribal in a world increasingly global, the New Age mantra, "Think globally, act locally," is turned on its head. It is now, "Think locally, act globally."

We have witnessed the end of communism, the decline of the nation-state, the emergence of a single-market world economy, the spread of democracy throughout the world, and the new revolution in tele-communications. What we do not yet understand is that these changes set the stage for extraordinary new opportunities for entrepreneurs and small companies. The global paradox tells us that the opportunities for each of us as individuals are far greater than at any time in human history.

[See also Change, Cultural; Economics; Global Business: Dominant Organizational Forms; Global Culture; Multifold Trend.]

BIBLIOGRAPHY

Aburdene, Patricia, and Naisbitt, John. *Megatrends for Women.* New York: Villard Books/Random House, 1992.

Naisbitt, John. *Global Paradox: The Bigger the World Economy, the More Powerful Its Smallest Players.* New York: William Morrow, 1994.

————. *Megatrends: Ten New Directions Transforming Our Lives.* New York: Warner Books, 1982.

Naisbitt, John, and Aburdene, Patricia. *Megatrends 2000: Ten New Directions for the 1990's.* New York: William Morrow, 1990.

————. *Reinventing the Corporation: Transforming Your Job and Your Company for the New Information Society.* New York: Warner Books, 1985.

— JOHN NAISBITT

GLOBAL STATISTICS

Detailed statistical projections estimating the size of major categories for future years are an essential component of any long-term global program. From the founding of the United Nations in 1945, that organization has spearheaded this task by compiling and regularly publishing every two years global statistics including future projections.

Table 1, "Global Statistics of the Future," describes the global situation in past, present, and future covering twenty-three major subject spheres.

The base demographic statistics come from two United Nations publications. The first is *World Population Prospects: The 1992 Revision* (New York: United Nations, 1993). Its future projections to 2025 are given under four alternate scenarios. These are labeled Medium-Variant, High-Variant, Low-Variant, and Constant Fertility Variant projections.

The United Nations has also published *Long-Range World Population Projections: Two Centuries of Population Growth, 1950–2150* (New York, 1992). Statistics are provided for seven alternate scenarios: a Medium-Fertility, High-Fertility, Medium/High-Fertility, Low-Fertility, Medium/Low-Fertility, Constant-Fertility, and Instant-Replacement-Fertility extensions. This table utilizes the most likely of the seven, namely the Medium-Variant and Medium-Fertility extensions.

Comprehensive demographics for the year 1900 were collected in national population censuses by all countries of the world at that time. These have been compiled in the *World Christian Encyclopedia* (Oxford University Press, 1982 and subsequently).

Past and present figures for a vast number of non-demographic categories are given in B. R. Mitchell, *International Historical Statistics, 1750–1988* (Macmillan/UK, 1990, three volumes). Future figures shown here for the years 2025 and 2200 have been published, in the *AD 2000 Global Monitor,* issues numbers 23–27 (September 1992-January 1993). Other topics come from a handbook of global statistics entitled *Our Globe and How to Reach It* (1990). Some data sets are repeated under a second heading to improve comprehensiveness.

Detailed statistical projections

estimating the size of major categories

for future years are an essential component

of any long-term global program.

The two columns for the years 2025 and 2200 should not be considered as concrete predictions. They give only the figures considered most likely in the present investigation or by authorities in their fields.

There are numerous appearances of *0* (zero) in the first column, for over thirty categories. These simply mean that in the year 1900 they did not exist or had not yet started. Radio and television, for instance, had not yet been invented. The AIDS epidemic had not begun.

Another surprising aspect is the string of forty-six zeroes in the last column representing the most likely situation in 2200. Zeroes are not due to naive utopianism. Many represent a realistic assessment of what would appear very probable after 250 years of determined, informed, aggressive, democratic activism. Many futurists see various diseases or social disorders as certain to be eliminated once and for all by advances in medical expertise. Also, total electronic monitoring may well eliminate crime, fraud, and an extensive array of other antisocial behavior patterns.

A number of other categories that have declined dramatically in numbers do so for similar reasons. It means that the world's activists are dealing successfully with the intolerable situation of earlier years.

— DAVID B. BARRETT

TABLE 1

GLOBAL STATISTICS OF THE FUTURE, 1900–2200

	Year			
	1900	**1995**	**2025**	**2200**
GLOBAL POPULATION				
World	1,620 million	5,759 million	8,472 million	11,600 million
Males	818 million	2,900 million	4,256 million	5,810 million
Females	802 million	2,859 million	4,217 million	5,790 million
Ratio males to females	1.020	1.014	1.009	1.003
Population density, per sq. km.	12	42	62	85
Age distribution, as % of world:				
Infants, ages 0–4	12.0	11.5	8.4	5.0
Children, ages 5–14	18.0	20.4	16.5	12.7
Children under 15	30.0	31.9	24.9	17.7
Youths, ages 15–24	25.0	17.9	15.9	13.0
Seniors, ages 60 or over	2.5	9.5	14.1	30.0
Elderly, ages 65 or over	1.3	6.5	9.7	24.6
Aged, ages 80 or over	0.2	1.0	1.6	10.6
School-age children (6–11)	10.0	12.4	9.9	6.0
School-age children (12–14)	4.0	5.8	4.9	3.0
School-age children (15–17)	5.0	5.4	4.9	3.0
Student-age youths (18–23)	13.0	10.8	9.5	7.0
Median age, years	15.0	25.1	31.0	42.7
VITAL STATISTICS				
Population increase p.a.	14.6 million	93.3 million	84.5 million	2.3 million
Births p.a.	58.3 million	144.8 million	147.9 million	141.5 million
Deaths p.a.	43.7 million	51.5 million	63.4 million	139.2 million
Natural increase, % p.a.	0.90	1.63	1.02	0.02
Birth rate % p.a.	3.60	2.51	1.79	1.22
Death rate % p.a.	2.70	0.89	0.77	1.20
Life expectancy, years	36.2	65.4	72.5	84.9
Males	34.0	63.4	70.2	82.5
Females	39.0	67.5	75.0	87.5
CITIES WORLDWIDE				
Metropolises (over 100,000 population)	300	3,780	6,800	65,000
Megacities (over 1 million population)	20	380	650	3,050
Urbanites (urban dwellers)	233 million	2,603 million	5,185 million	10,440 million
Ruralites (rural dwellers)	1,387 million	3,156 million	3,287 million	1,160 million
Urbanites, % of world	14.4	45.2	61.2	90.0
Ruralites, % of world	85.6	54.8	38.8	10.0
Urban poor	100 million	1,640 million	3,050 million	100 million
Urban slum dwellers	20 million	810 million	2,100 million	50 million[1]
GEOPOLITICAL WORLDS				
Group I (UN terminology)	*501 million*	*1,126 million*	*1,288 million*	*1,182 million*
Europe	287 million	516 million	542 million	420 million
Northern America	82 million	292 million	361 million	306 million
Oceania	6 million	29 million	41 million	41 million
Eurasia (former U.S.S.R.)	126 million	289 million	344 million	415 million
Group II	*1,119 million*	*4,633 million*	*7,185 million*	*10,418 million*
Africa	108 million	744 million	1,582 million	3,130 million
Latin America	65 million	482 million	702 million	1,125 million
China	472 million	1,238 million	1,540 million	1,383 million
India	230 million	931 million	1,394 million	1,955 million
Other Asia	244 million	1,238 million	1,967 million	2,825 million[2]
GLOBE	*1,620 million*	*5,759 million*	*8,472 million*	*11,600 million*

TABLE 1

GLOBAL STATISTICS OF THE FUTURE, 1900–2200 (CONTINUED)

	Year			
	1900	**1995**	**2025**	**2200**
STATUS OF WOMEN				
Global female population	802 million	2,859 million	4,217 million	5,790 million
% literates among women	15	56	70	85
Female life expectancy, years	39.0	67.5	75.0	87.5
Women denied full rights or equality	750 million	2,500 million	1,800 million	100 million[3]
% world income received by women	1	10	20	40
% world property owned by women	0	1	3	20
Women as % of all poor	80	70	60	55
Women as % of all illiterates	80	66	55	52
Women as % of all refugees	65	80	70	60
Women as % of all ill/sick	60	75	57	52
Female urban poor	20 million	700 million	1,400 million	80 million
Female urban slum dwellers	2 million	320 million	980 million	40 million
MOTHERHOOD				
Women of childbearing age (15–49)	389 million	1,341 million	2,041 million	2,320 million
Ditto, % of world population	24.0	25.3	24.7	20.0
Fertility rate (births per woman)	4.0	3.17	2.36	2.06
Gross reproduction rate, per woman	2.0	1.55	1.15	0.7
Net reproduction rate, per woman	1.8	1.36	1.08	0.6
Contraceptive prevalence rate, %	5	56	75	95
Birth rate, % p.a. (males, females)	3.60	2.51	1.79	1.22
Births p.a. (males, females)	58.3 million	144.8 million	147.9 million	141.5 million
Induced abortions, p.a.	5 million	60 million	130 million	500 million
Maternal mortality, p.a., total	550,000	500,000	400,000	80,000[4]
Ditto due to abortion	210,000	200,000	150,000	30,000
FAMILIES				
Families/homes/households	324 million	1,339 million	2,118 million	3,135 million
Household size, persons	5.0	4.3	4.0	3.7
Households headed by women, %	3	33	55	70
New families each year	12 million	34 million	38 million	39 million
% women 15–19 already married	15	23	25	35
Dependency ratio, %	70.0	62.6	52.1	45.0
Marriage rate per 1000 population p.a.	3	4	5	6
Divorce rate per 1000 population p.a.	0.05	0.4	1	3
Battered women	95 million	200 million	500 million	100 million[5]
Women raped p.a.	10 million	15 million	25 million	5 million[6]
Child-abuse incidents p.a.	15 million	90 million	70 million	30 million[7]
CHILDREN				
Infants (0–4 years)	194 million	662 million	712 million	580 million
Children (5–14)	292 million	1,175 million	1,398 million	1,473 million
School-age children (6–14)	227 million	1,048 million	1,254 million	1,044 million
Babies born malnourished, p.a.	8 million	10 million	25 million	1 million[8]
Sick/ill children	300 million	600 million	1,000 million	200 million[9]
Exploited child labor	30 million	50 million	200 million	20 million[10]
Orphans	150 million	450 million	1,000 million	1,500 million
Abandoned children and infants	140 million	60 million	260 million	500 million
Homeless/familyless children	250 million	300 million	700 million	1,000 million
Magacity street children	1 million	100 million	300 million	800 million
Infant mortality (under 1), % p.a.	9.0	5.9	3.1	0.5
Toddler mortality (1–4 years), % p.a.	3.0	1.0	0.7	0.1
EDUCATION				
Primary schools	300,000	3.2 million	4 million	5 million
Pupils in school	35 million	980 million	1.5 billion	1.3 billion

TABLE 1

GLOBAL STATISTICS OF THE FUTURE, 1900–2200 *(CONTINUED)*

	Year			
	1900	1995	2025	2200
EDUCATION *(continued)*				
Adults, primary-educated	100 million	1.2 billion	3.3 billion	7.5 billion
Adults without primary education	926 million	2.7 billion	3.1 billion	2.0 billion
School teachers	2 million	39 million	50 million	100 million
University campuses	500	20,000	30,000	100,000
College students	2 million	65 million	120 million	500 million
Foreign students	20,000	3 million	15 million	100 million
ILLNESS AND DISEASE				
Sufferers from disease or illness	420 million	1,152 million	1,395 million	15 million[11]
Sufferers experiencing chronic pain	350 million	900 million	1,400 million	14 million[12]
Nonsighted (totally blind)	9 million	28 million	35 million	50 million
Hearing-impaired (deaf)	90 million	320 million	500 million	700 million
Leprosy sufferers (lepers)	5 million	13 million	1 million	0[13]
New malaria cases p.a.	100 million	400 million	30 million	0
Psychotics	10 million	51 million	10 million	0
Schizophrenics	2 million	10 million	0	0
Psychoneurotics	150 million	950 million	1.1 billion	1.5 billion
Suicides per year	300,000	410,000	500,000	1 million
Disabled (handicapped)	400 million	1.6 billion	1.8 billion	2 billion
Handicapped children	100 million	340 million	500 million	700 million
Severely mentally-retarded	40 million	130 million	50 million	0
Arthritics	80 million	300 million	50 million	0
Persons not immunized	1.4 billion	4 billion	100 million	0
Diarrheal deaths of under-5-year olds, p.a.	2 million	5 million	700,000	0
AIDS carriers	0	70 million	400 million	0
AIDS-related deaths p.a.	0	500,000	10 million	0
Tobacco smokers	42 million	650 million	20 million	0
Tobacco-related deaths p.a.	150,000	2.6 million	5 million	0
Drug addicts (illicit drug users)	1 million	65 million	100 million	0
HEALTH CARE				
Persons in good health	300 million	1.1 billion	2.4 billion	7 billion
Physicians	1 million	5.2 million	7.9 million	13 million
Nurses and midwives	2 million	7.7 million	10.5 million	16 million
Dentists	100,000	500,000	800,000	1,400,000
Pharmacists	50,000	520,000	1 billion	1.6 billion
World pharmaceutical market, $ p.a.	200 million	130 billion	400 billion	2 trillion
Hospitals	60,000	240,000	300,000	500,000
Hospital beds	4 million	18.2 million	23 million	35 million
Mental institutions	20,000	150,000	200,000	1,000[14]
Health care costs, $ p.a.	10 billion	2,500 billion	4 trillion	10 trillion
Population per doctor	9,500	3,780	2,500	500
HUMAN RIGHTS AND ABUSES				
The poor (living in poverty)	1.2 billion	2.4 billion	3.3 billion	100 million
Absolutely poor (in absolute poverty)	900 million	960 million	700 million	0[15]
Undernourished	1.2 billion	1.8 billion	500 million	0
Hungry	700 million	950 million	400 million	0
Severely malnourished	500 million	550 million	300 million	0
On verge of starvation	200 million	400 million	200 million	0
Starvation-related deaths p.a.	20 million	20 million	10 million	0
Without safe drinking water	1.4 billion	1.3 billion	1 billion	0
With unsafe water and bad sanitation	1.5 billion	3.0 billion	1 billion	30 million
Killed by dirty water, per day	20,000	25,000	10,000	0
With no access to electricity, %	86	41	30	0
With no access to radio or TV, %	100	67	20	0

TABLE 1

GLOBAL STATISTICS OF THE FUTURE, 1900–2200 *(CONTINUED)*

	Year			
	1900	**1995**	**2025**	**2200**
HUMAN RIGHTS AND ABUSES *(continued)*				
Without adequate shelter	200 million	1.1 billion	700 million	10 million
With no shelter whatsoever	50 million	100 million	30 million	0
No access to schools	1.2 billion	1 billion	500 million	0
Without money to buy food	500 million	1.1 billion	700 million	0
With no access to medical care	1.1 billion	1.5 billion	700 million	0
Cave-dwellers	200 million	50 million	10 million	0
Stateless (with no nationality)	1 million	10 million	5 million	0
Prisoners	5 million	100 million	50 million	10 million
Prisoners being tortured	500,000	100,000	0	0
Disenfranchised (no control by vote)	1.2 billion	2.1 billion	100 million	0
Non-readers (orate, illiterate adults)	739 million	1,392 million	1,171 million	382 million
Permanently unsettled refugees	50 million	14 million	10 million	0
Persons abused in childhood	400 million	300 million	350 million	0
Persons with human rights violated	1.4 billion	2,590 million	1.7 billion	30 million
COMMUNICATION				
Languages	11,600	9,500	8,000	2,000
Trade languages	200	700	800	2,000
Official state languages	25	95	150	500
Countries with own radio services	0	270	300	100
Countries with own TV services	0	150	250	100
Radio sets in use	0	1.8 billion	5 billion	9 billion
Radio hours broadcast p.a.	0	24 million	60 million	1 billion
Television sets	0	850 million	5 billion	10 billion
TV hours broadcast	0	21 million	70 million	1 billion
Ham radio operators	0	1.2 million	2 million	30 million
Daily newspapers	750	8,300	7,000	20,000
Newspaper circulation	70 million	590 million	1 billion	3 billion
Newsprint per global inhabitant, pounds p.a.	0.1	12	10	10
Mail, pieces p.a.	1 billion	280 billion	450 billion	2 trillion
Electronic mail messages p.a.	0	6 billion	50 billion	1 trillion
Telephones	3 million	750 million	1.1 billion	4 billion
Direct-dial telephones	0	710 million	1.1 billion	4 billion
Telephone calls made, p.a.	150 million	120 billion	300 billion	1 trillion
Fax machines	0	35 million	350 million	10 billion
Videocassette recorders (VCRs)	0	500 million	2 billion	10 billion
Cinemas	100	250,000	400,000	2 billion
Cinema seats	5,000	75 million	200 million	1 billion
Cinema attenders p.a.	200,000	15 billion	30 billion	1 trillion
General-purpose computers	0	150 million	850 million	700 billion
Computer sales p.a.	0	35 million	80 million	1 billion
Computer power, MIPS (world total)	0	29 million	500 million	25 trillion
Electronic bulletin boards	0	100,000	1 million	100 million
Internet computer users	0	18 million	80 million	2 billion
TRANSPORTATION				
Roads, length in miles	1 million	17 million	25 million	40 million
Bicycles	10,000	850 million	1.7 billion	2 billion
Commercial vehicles	0	120 million	250 million	300 million
Passenger cars	30,000	410 million	500 million	700 million
Cars produced p.a.	3,000	45 million	40 million	50 million
Railway track, length in miles	454,730	880,000	1.5 million	5 million
Rail passenger-miles p.a.	10 billion	1,100 billion	2 trillion	3 trillion
Air traffic, passenger-miles p.a.	0	950 billion	3 trillion	10 trillion
Airport and airfields	0	67,000	100,000	500,000
Sea traffic: merchant ships	2,000	75,300	100,000	300,000

TABLE 1

GLOBAL STATISTICS OF THE FUTURE, 1900–2200 *(CONTINUED)*

	Year			
	1900	**1995**	**2025**	**2200**
TRANSPORTATION *(continued)*				
Sea freight, tons p.a.	10 million	3.6 billion	10 billion	100 billion
Seamen (merchant seafarers)	300,000	10 million	15 million	10 million
AGRICULTURE AND LIVESTOCK				
Agricultural land, sq. km.	15 million	46.5 million	55 million	70 million
Agricultural land as % all land	11	34	40	51
Forest land, sq. km.	100 million	40.1 million	20 million	5 million
Harvested land as % all arable land	15	77	90	98
Global agricultural research, $ p.a.	3 million	9 billion	20 billion	50 billion
Tractors in use	0	22 million	40 million	200 million
Fish catches, metric tons p.a.	1 million	91 million	100 million	150 million
Cattle	80 million	1.3 billion	1.0 billion	300 million[16]
Sheep	200 million	1.1 billion	800 million	100 million
Chickens	600 million	9.0 billion	5 billion	1 billion
Horses, mules, asses	20 million	120 million	150 million	300 million
Rats	500 million	20 billion	10 billion	1 billion[17]
Food/property destroyed by rats, $ p.a.	5 billion	350 billion	100 billion	500 million
Domestic pets	5 million	1 billion	1.5 billion	100 million
Nomads and pastoralists	40 million	220 million	100 million	10 million
INDUSTRIALIZATION				
Economically active persons	300 million	2.4 billion	3 billion	5 billion
Labor force, persons	100 million	1.9 billion	2.5 billion	4 billion
Unemployed	10 million	100 million	200 million	500 million
Underemployed	30 million	600 million	1 billion	2 billion
Beggars	10 million	80 million	150 million	300 million
Scientists and engineers	1 million	38 million	60 million	100 million
Pure scientists	10,000	1 million	1.3 million	2 million
Scientific research, $ p.a.	100 million	125 billion	200 billion	400 billion
Industrial robots	0	14 million	25 million	100 million
Known chemicals	5,000	7 million	10 million	20 million
New chemicals created p.a.	200	10,000	50,000	60,000
Police officers	400,000	5.1 million	6 million	7 million
Professional firefighters	100,000	2 million	2.5 million	3 million
Lawyers	300,000	6 million	8 million	9 million
Labor migrants	2 million	150 million	300 million	500 million
ENERGY PRODUCTION				
Primary energy, quads BTU p.a.	10 billion	3.2 quadrillion	9 quadrillion	10 quintillion
Coal, known reserves, metric tons	50 billion	7,600 billion	8 trillion	4 trillion
Coal, kg mined per capita p.a.	1,000	1,870	2,000	2,500
Electricity, kilowatt hours p.a.	100 million	9.7 trillion	100 trillion	1 quadrillion
Petroleum, known reserves, metric tons	0	91 billion	100 billion	1 billion[18]
Oil, total recoverable reserves, barrels	1 billion	1,635 billion	2 trillion	0
Oil, output in barrels p.a.	1 million	19.8 billion	30 billion	1 billion
Nuclear power produced, kilowatt hours p.a.	0	630 billion	1 trillion	100 trillion
Natural gas, known reserves, cubic meters	100 billion	86 trillion	100 trillion	200 trillion
TOURISM				
Foreign tourists p.a.	1 million	350 million	600 million	2 billion
Domestic tourists p.a.	5 million	3.7 billion	4.5 billion	5 billion
Registered hotel beds	500,000	15.0 million	30 million	100 million
Religious pilgrims p.a.	2 million	350 million	800 million	1.5 billion

TABLE 1

GLOBAL STATISTICS OF THE FUTURE, 1900–2200 *(CONTINUED)*

	Year			
	1900	1995	2025	2200
FINANCE AND TRADE				
Gross world product, $ p.a.	200 billion	18 trillion	30 trillion	300 trillion
World imports, $ p.a.	30 billion	2,200 billion	4 trillion	25 trillion
World exports, $ p.a.	25 billion	2,100 billion	3 trillion	20 trillion
Balance of trade, $	5 billion	100 billion	1 trillion	5 trillion
Gold reserves, kg	2 million	32 million	50 million	1 billion
Foreign economic aid, $ p.a.	50 million	60 billion	200 billion	2 trillion
Average income per person, $ p.a.	125	3,120	3,540	25,860
Average family income, $ p.a.	625	13,440	14,160	95,700
Transnationals (TNCs, multinationals)	400	10,800	20,000	300,000
Nongovernmental organizations (NGOs)	50	3,500	10,000	100,000
Millionaires (each worth over $1 million)	20,000	2.5 million	6 million	300 million
Billionaires (each worth over $1 billion)	10	400	600	10,000
Cost of advertising, $ p.a.	300 million	120 billion	300 billion	2 trillion
Betting and gambling, $ p.a.	1 billion	700 billion	1,500 billion	3 trillion
Business failures (bankruptcies) p.a.	5,000	250,000	300,000	100,000
MILITARIZATION				
Military expenditures, $ p.a.	500 million	950 billion	100 billion	20 billion[19]
Troops in regular armed forces	5 million	25 million	15 million	2 million
Paramilitary troops	2 million	280 million	5 million	1 million
Military supply personnel	200,000	52 million	20 million	30 million
Combat aircraft	0	60,000	20,000	2,000
Nuclear warheads	0	65,000	1,000	0[20]
Submarine-borne SLBMs	0	9,200	500	0
Chemical weapons, tons	1,000	300,000	10,000	0
International arms trade, $ p.a.	5 million	42 billion	20 billion	0
Handguns (personal firearms)	1 million	600 million	100 million	0
CRIME				
Crimes (registered) p.a.	5 million	500 million	400 million	10 million[21]
Property crimes p.a.	2 million	100 million	50 million	1 million
Violent crimes p.a.	2 million	27 million	30 million	1 million
Criminals	4 million	550 million	350 million	15 million
Murders p.a.	500,000	950,000	800,000	10,000
Terrorist incidents p.a.	100	4,000	2,000	200
Cost of all varieties of crime, $ p.a.	750 million	3,300 billion	2 trillion	10 billion
White-collar crime, $ p.a.	200 million	1,000 billion	500 billion	1 billion
Financial fraud, $ p.a.	150 million	900 billion	400 billion	1 billion
Organized crime, $ p.a.	100 million	600 billion	1 trillion	2 billion
Credit card fraud, $ p.a.	0	550 million	200 billion	1 billion
Alcohol/liquor expenditures, $ p.a.	50 million	380 billion	50 billion	0[22]
World purchases of cigarettes, $ p.a.	30 million	290 billion	10 billion	0
Illegal drug traffic, $ p.a.	20 million	150 billion	10 billion	0
Shoplifting, $ p.a.	20 million	95 billion	5 billion	0[23]
Computer crime, $ p.a.	0	60 billion	10 billion	1 billion
Major art thefts, $ p.a.	100 million	25 billion	1 billion	0
Pornography, $ p.a.	20 million	20 billion	1 billion	0
Automobile thefts, $ p.a.	0	20 billion	1 billion	0
RELIGION				
Christians	558,056,000	1,923,812,000	3,022,623,000	4,397,929,000
Muslims	200,102,000	1,047,616,000	1,716,091,000	2,624,567,000
Nonreligious	2,923,000	931,409,000	1,279,525,000	1,626,497,000
Hindus	203,033,000	772,896,000	1,113,103,000	1,398,329,000
Buddhists	127,159,000	336,742,000	484,432,000	607,601,000
Atheists	226,000	231,150,000	237,257,000	249,000,000

TABLE 1

GLOBAL STATISTICS OF THE FUTURE, 1900–2200 *(CONTINUED)*

	Year			
	1900	**1995**	**2025**	**2200**
RELIGION *(continued)*				
Chinese folk-religionists	380,404,000	195,156,000	233,813,000	253,162,000
New-religionists	5,910,000	151,209,000	217,314,000	272,280,000
Tribal religionists	106,340,000	99,460,000	77,026,000	15,416,000
Sikhs	2,961,000	19,811,000	28,370,000	35,434,000
Jews	12,270,000	16,986,000	21,468,000	24,697,000
Shamanists	11,341,000	11,057,000	15,849,000	19,859,000
Confucians	640,000	6,357,000	9,142,000	11,459,000
Baha'is	9,000	5,892,000	9,544,000	14,559,000
Jains	1,323,000	4,003,000	5,795,000	7,351,000
Shintoists	6,720,000	3,399,000	4,892,000	6,138,00
Other religionists	470,000	19,541,000	27,978,000	36,273,000
LITERATURE				
Adult population (over 15)	1,026 million	3,937 million	6,421 million	9,547 million
Literates	287 million	2,545 million	5,250 million	9,165 million
Nonliterates	739 million	1,392 million	1,171 million	382 million
Literates, % of adults	27.9	54.7	81.8	96.0
Nonliterates, % of adults	72.1	45.3	18.2	4.0
New book titles yearly	40,000	880,000	950,000	3 million
Books printed yearly	900 million	30 billion	50 billion	100 million
Scientific journals	15,000	350,000	450,000	2 million
Scientific articles published yearly	60,000	2 million	3 million	10 million
Periodicals	9,000	130,000	180,000	500,000
Magazines	40,000	500,000	700,000	3 million
Encyclopedias	100	500	1,000	3,000
General encyclopedias	20	70	200	500
Subject encyclopedias	80	430	800	2,500
Bookshops	65,000	600,000	1 million	10 million
Public libraries	30,000	270,000	500,000	2 million
Library volumes (books)	70 million	3.7 billion	10 billion	100 billion

Notes: p.a. = per annum (per year); all sums of money are given in U.S. dollars ($).

Notes for 2200 (end column):

[1] Likely to decrease drastically as urban planning tackles the problem.

[2] Countries are specified, and Groups I and II defined, in the UN's *Long-Range World Population Projections* (1992).

[3] Falling dramatically over 200 years as women's full rights are established.

[4] Falling with enforced universal medical coverage.

[5] Falling as the practice becomes fully exposed and unacceptable.

[6] Dropping due to public awareness and universal protection.

[7] Falling with massive public determination and safeguards.

[8] Dramatic reduction due to strict medical requirements.

[9] Falling with fuller medical programs.

[10] No longer acceptable, legal, or in most countries even possible by 2200.

[11] Drastic decline as universal health care spreads.

[12] Controlled then virtually eliminated by medical advances.

[13] Leprosy and the other diseases or disabilities enumerated in the 13 lines with zeros in this section are likely to have been eradicated medically by 2200.

[14] Disappearing as medical science conquers all mental illnesses as anticipated.

[15] All lines in this section reaching zero by 2200 reflect successful worldwide campaigns to completely eradicate unacceptable aspects of poverty and other human rights abuses as politically and ethically intolerable.

[16] Declining in numbers as the global beef industry yields to varieties of vegetarianism for a number of reasons (likewise with the next two lines).

[17] Expected to be finally eradicated within two centuries, with scientific solutions.

[18] Petroleum and oil reserves (next two lines) are likely to be fully used up within 200 years.

[19] Expected to fall drastically from their untenable high point in 1995.

[20] Nuclear weapons may well be totally eliminated within 20–200 years, likewise (next four lines) other mass-destruction weapons. The arms trade could be liquidated through political action, and handgun epidemics through bans on manufacture and through rigid electronic monitoring.

[21] Virtually eliminated in many categories through strict electronic monitoring.

[22] Likely to follow tobacco and other drugs as harmful, hence undesirable.

[23] Full eliminated through rigid electronic monitoring and policies.

GLOBAL TURNING POINTS

How are we to understand the turbulence of our times? Is there a frame of reference within which we can make sense of the American experience as the twentieth century draws to a close? A look at the past may offer us a clue.

Many historians divide Western history into clearly defined periods, shaped by unique characteristics. This demarcation is never neat or tidy. The characteristics that shape a particular period also influence the succeeding phase of history. The shift from one age to the next has always produced a time of dissolution of old patterns or paradigms of life, of turbulence as old forms lose their force, and of creativity as new patterns of life and organization evolve. Such major changes in perspective have sometimes been described as *paradigm shifts*.

The American story encompasses what is generally referred to as the modern age, which began around 1500. Characteristics defining the modern age include geographical exploration, the expansion of Europe, and the creation of colonial empires; the rise of the nation-state; the Newtonian view of the universe and of physical reality; the printing press with the subsequent diffusion of knowledge that followed its invention in 1453; the introduction of gunpowder; the predominance of sea power; progress defined as the expansion of the scientific and material realms; the triumph of reason over faith as the perceived foundation of reality; and an enlarged understanding of liberty.

The twentieth century marks the end of the modern age and the beginning of a new epoch of history. The forces that shaped the last five hundred years are giving way to a new set of defining impulses. Thus, we live in a century characterized by the massive dissolution of authority, the decline of established institutions, and fundamental shifts in the patterns of life. It is, as well, a time of unprecedented creation of new understandings and possibilities. This shift has shaped the twentieth century. It has been the seedbed of two world wars, of the rise and fall of communism, and of great economic/material growth and political independence.

What are some of the characteristics shaping the future?

- We are moving from the era of nation-states to the age of a world community as the defining political and economic framework. All of the major issues confronting America—economic growth, energy resources, finance capital, AIDS, protection of the environment, immigration, drugs, institutional stability—are global issues.
- Electronics is challenging print as the main medium of visual communication. Any change in the primary mode of communication in a society has significant consequences for other aspects of life such as culture, education, and the family.
- Interdependence is becoming the dominant requirement for future progress. In biology and the natural world, the progression of life goes from dependence to independence, to interdependence. The same is true of the social/political realm. We are moving into a phase where we are adapting to the imperatives of interdependence just as we adapted to the evolution of independence two hundred years ago.
- We are the first generation to seek an empirical/scientific comprehension of the origin of the universe. We have come to see ourselves as part of an unfolding story, and we are trying to understand the human relationship to the beginnings of time and matter. This alters our view of who we are and where we come from.
- We have the potential to become partners with nature in defining what constitutes a human being. With genetic engineering, we can determine some characteristics of unborn children— in effect, create *designer children*. It may be possible to transfer genetic traits between species, thus blurring the distinction between species—hopefully with more positive results than imagined by H. G. WELLS in *The Island of Doctor Moreau*.
- Whereas the masculine impulse was predominant in the modern age, the feminine instinct, as expressed in both men and women, is becoming more pronounced in shaping the future. We see this in the collapse of hierarchical structures and the emergence of more cooperative modes of organization, in a new emphasis on intuition, in an effort to reintegrate ourselves with Earth and the natural order from whence we tore ourselves during the industrial revolution and subsequent urbanization, and in an increased emphasis on *being* rather than *having*.
- The assumptions underlying almost five hundred years of Western science are yielding to new assumptions. The scientific enterprise was built on the belief that there is an objective universe that can be explored by methods of scientific inquiry (the objectivist assumption); that what is scientifically real must take as its basic datum only that which is physically observable (the positivist assumption); and that scientific description consists in explaining complex phenomena in terms of more elemental events (the reductionist assumption). The new assumptions for the science of the future are likely to be an emphatic departure from many of these past assumptions. For example, quantum mechanics is beginning to suggest that consciousness may not be the end-product of material evolution; rather, that consciousness was here first. Consciousness may be causal.

Such trends bring us to one of the major watersheds of history. André Malraux, a noted French cultural authority, suggested that the historical shift the world is experiencing "has but one precedent; the discovery of fire." Czech writer and political leader Václav Havel warned that some of the tasks we face "might be as extended and complex a process as the creation of a Christian Europe" in the centuries following the bifurcation and collapse of Roman Empire.

What is the core challenge as we move deeper into a new historical era? It is to evolve a legitimizing vision of life that expresses the spiritual essence of the human journey with such force and resonance as to define world purposes and standards of conduct for a new epoch of history. For each one of us, it means thinking through who we are, what we believe, and what we are living for.

No generation was ever offered a challenge of greater magnitude, possibility, and hope.

[See also Change, Epochal; Evolution, Biological; Evolution, Social; Genetic Engineering; Global Consciousness; Global Culture; Literature; Mind: New Modes of Thinking; Printed Word.]

BIBLIOGRAPHY

Attali, Jacques. *Millennium.* New York: Random House, Inc., 1991.
Drucker, Peter F. *The New Realities.* New York: Harper & Row, 1989.
Halberstam, David. *The Next Century.* New York: William Morrow, 1991.
Harman, Willis. *Global Mind Change.* Indianapolis, IN: Knowledge Systems, 1988.
Havel, Václav. *Disturbing the Peace.* New York: Knopf, 1990.
Lukacs, John. *The End of the Twentieth Century and of the Modern Age.* New York: Ticknor & Fields, 1993.
May, Rollo. *The Cry for Myth.* New York: Norton, 1991.
Postman, Neil. *Technopoly.* New York: Knopf, 1992.
Swimme, Brian, and Berry, Thomas. *The Universe Story.* New York: HarperCollins, 1992.

— WILLIAM VAN DUSEN WISHARD

GLOBAL WARMING

During the 2-million-year-long great, or Pleistocene, Ice Age which ended about 10,000 years ago, several intensely cold periods known as *glacials* alternated with much warmer periods called *interglacials.* These warming and cooling trends were caused by natural climatic factors—complex interactions of the sun, Earth, atmosphere, and ocean. In more recent times, warming and cooling trends have continued, but on a much smaller time scale. For example, the "Medieval Warm" extended from about 700 AD to about 1150 AD, while the "Little Ice Age" began about 1180 AD and ended only a century ago.

The Little Ice Age was characterized by glacial advances in both North America and Europe. Moveover, alpine glaciers in New Zealand and the Andes moved further downslope than at any time in the previous 8,000 years. By the late 1400s, the sea ice had completely blocked the shipping lanes between Iceland and Greenland and elsewhere. It was so cold that farmers could no longer raise grain in Iceland. Eventually, however, the glacial shrinking of the late nineteenth century signaled that the Little Ice Age had come to an end.

For hundreds of years, astronomers have tried to link the twenty-two-year sunspot cycle with temperature changes on Earth. Sunspots are caused by turbulence in the sun's magnetic field. During one phase of the cycle, the spots are most numerous in the northern hemisphere, while in the southern hemisphere there is a simultaneous minimum. A few years later, the pattern is reversed. With the aid of satellite imagery, astronomers have succeeded in measuring solar energy production throughout a given cycle. They noticed that solar energy generation declines somewhat when the sunspots disappear. Most climatologists have concluded, however, that the change in energy production has very little influence on the actual temperature of the Earth.

Many climatologists predict that if CO_2 levels continue to increase at the current rate, the average global temperature could rise 5° F (3° C) by 2035.

The oceans, which cover over 70 percent of the Earth's surface, are active components of the global climatic system. They can influence long-term variations in the temperature of our planet. The oceans' most important feature, in this regard, is their ability to absorb, recirculate, and release heat. The surface temperature of the ocean varies from 28° F ($-2°$ C) near the North and South poles to a maximum of 86° F (30° C) near the equator. The ocean currents, in particular, are dynamic forces in the transfer of warmth from one region of the Earth to another. Two of the most important currents in this regard are the Gulf Stream and El Niño.

The Gulf Stream has its origin in the western Caribbean, where it is warmed up by the equatorial sun. It then flows through the Gulf of Mexico, around the tip of Florida, and then northward along the Atlantic coast of the United States to North Carolina. From there it passes northeastward across the Atlantic. While off coastal North Carolina, the Gulf Stream is about 15° F (6° C) warmer than the water around it, and during winter, it is actually warmer than the overlying atmosphere. As a result, the winds that blow toward Europe are warmed considerably as they move eastward over the Gulf Stream. This results in unusually mild winters for Great Britain and Norway.

El Niño is another major ocean current that may have a warming influence on certain regions of the Earth. With the aid of satellites and computers, scientists have recently learned a great deal about it. El Niño has its origin in the eastward shift of a pool of warm water that usually is confined to the equatorial Pacific, just northeast of Australia. This shift occurs at intervals of three to seven years, the last two occurring in 1986 to 1987 and 1991 to 1992. The tropical heat that is released into the atmosphere from El Niño displaces eastwardly, blowing jet streams high in the atmosphere to new positions over North and South America, generally resulting in highly unusual weather conditions. For example, El Niño in 1991 to 1992 brought torrential rainfall along the Gulf Coast and shirtsleeve weather to the region around Fargo, North Dakota. After reaching the Pacific Coast of North America, El Niño flows southward and warms up the weather in Ecuador and Peru.

The Earth's atmospheric temperature would be considerably higher were it not for the heat "sink" function performed by the global oceans. These vast bodies of water, up to six miles deep, absorb a considerable amount of atmospheric heat. Then, over a period of years, this heat is slowly released back into the atmosphere. Scientists are still not exactly sure of the role played by the oceans in shaping the world's climate. There is no doubt, however, that major ocean currents like the Gulf Stream and El Niño and the ocean's func-

Global warming appears to have caused the Earth's water level to rise by about 1 foot in the past century due to melting glaciers, snow fields, and polar icecaps. (Joel W. Rogers/Corbis)

tion as a thermal sink must have a major influence on the warming phenomenon, highly publicized in recent years, known as the *greenhouse effect.*

Have you ever parked your car on a sunny summer day with the windows closed? When you reentered your car some time later, it felt like an oven. Why? Because of the greenhouse effect. The solar (short-wave) radiation freely passed through your car's glass windows. These short waves were then converted into long-wave heat (infrared) radiation, much of which could not pass back through the glass to the outside. As a result, the car warmed up because of the greenhouse effect.

Carbon dioxide operates very much like the windows of your car, or like greenhouse glass, in trapping heat and preventing it from passing out of the atmosphere. However, since the dawn of the Industrial Revolution in the mid-nineteenth century, large quantities of carbon dioxide generated by human activities have been released into the atmosphere from factories, coal-fired power plants, gasoline-powered motor vehicles, and the consumption of fossil fuels for the purpose of warming homes, stores, and industries. In addition to carbon dioxide, however, modern society has also been releasing ever-increasing amounts of other greenhouse gases, such as methane, nitrous oxide, and ozone.

Atmospheric levels of carbon dioxide, the most important greenhouse gas, remained at about 270 parts per million for thousands of years. Then, with the beginning of the industrial age and the accelerated consumption of fossil fuels (coal, oil, and natural gas), the carbon dioxide levels rose substantially, from 270 ppm to 350 ppm by 1990—an increase of almost 30 percent.

As of 1990, the burning of fossil fuels worldwide has been causing the release of five billion metric tons of carbon dioxide into the air every year—almost one ton for each person on Earth, and about 53 times the rate back in 1860. The burning of tropical forests to clear areas for cattle ranching and farming causes the annual release of still another 1.6 billion tons. Many climatologists predict that if CO_2 levels continue to increase at the current rate, the average global temperature could rise 5° F (3° C) by 2035. However, the increase at the poles would be considerably greater—about 13° to 18° F (7° to 10° C).

This artificially induced global warming is reinforced by a natural phenomenon known as the *albedo effect*—the reflection of light (and hence heat) back into the atmosphere from rocks, soil, water, homes, factories, highways, plants, animals, and all other entities on the surface of this planet. Darker materials, like rocks, soil, and trees, have relatively little albedo effect. On the other hand, materials like snow and ice reflect light more intensely. One major effect of the man-induced greenhouse effect will be the melting of glaciers, snow fields, and icecaps in the polar regions. The eventual result will be the exposure of increasingly large areas of rocks, soil, and water—all materials with much lower albedo values. The net effect would be a warming of the planet due to the increased absorption of sunlight.

Many experts agree that the global warming that has already resulted because of the artificially induced greenhouse effect caused ocean levels to rise 1 foot (0.3 meters) in the past century due to the melting of glaciers, ice fields, and polar icecaps. The U.S. Environmental Protection Agency predicts that the oceans could rise another 3.3 feet (1 meter) by 2035. This would be catastrophic for millions of people occupying lowland areas bordering the sea. Among the most vulnerable (and highly populated) regions would be Indonesia, Pakistan, Thailand, the Ganges Delta of Bangladesh, and the Nile Delta in Egypt. Of course, the inundation not only would displace large numbers of people but, especially in the case of the fertile lowlands along the Nile and Ganges, would permanently submerge extremely fertile farmlands, upon which considerable segments of humanity depend for food.

What about the situation in the United States? There is no doubt that a 3.3-foot (1-meter) rise in ocean levels by 2035 would cause a dramatic re-shaping of our Atlantic and Gulf shorelines. The seas would move an average of about one hundred feet (30 meters) inland. Extensive low-lying areas in coastal Louisiana and Florida would become part of the ocean floor. "Environmental evacuees" from the flooded seaboards would number in the millions. Multibillion-dollar devastation would be caused by the massive flooding of highways, railroads, homes, schools, stores, and factories. It is estimated that the rising seas would wreak $650 million in damage in Charleston, S.C., alone. Even greater destruction would be experienced by Boston, New York City, Philadelphia, Norfolk, Miami, New Orleans, and Houston. Human anxiety, emotional stress, severe discomfort, as well as serious financial setbacks would be commonplace.

Although the human-caused greenhouse phenomenon will certainly be highly destructive, it will have some redeeming features. One beneficial effect would be lengthened growing seasons in northern latitudes. A predicted warmup of 5° F (3.5° C) or more by 2035 would be a boon to residents of Canada and northern Europe. For one thing, the cost of heating homes, shops, and factories during winter would be sharply reduced. Moreover, the longer growing seasons in these regions would boost agricultural production. For ex-

ample, the relatively brief 110-day growing season in Canada's wheat belt would be extended to 160 days—an increase of more than 45 percent, thus permitting more diverse crop production. As Robert Stewart, an agricultural climatologist with the Canadian government, remarked, "The greenhouse effect will not be gloom and doom for Canada in any sense."

[See also Acid Rain; Climate and Meteorology; Deforestation; Disasters, Planning For; Ozone Layer Depletion; Resources.]

BIBLIOGRAPHY

Beardsley, Tim. "Add Ozone to the Global Warming Equation." *Scientific American* (March 1992).

Benedick, Richard Elliott. "Essay: A Case of Déjà Vu." *Scientific American* (April 1992).

Kerr, Richard. "A Successful Forecast of an El Niño Winter." *Science* 255 (1992): 402.

Monistersky, Richard. "Do Clouds Provide a Greenhouse Thermostat?" *Science News* 141 (1992): 69.

Owen, Oliver S. "The Heat Is On: The Greenhouse Effect and the Earth's Future." *Futurist* (September— October 1989).

———. *Natural Resource Conservation: An Ecological Approach.* New York: Macmillan, 1990.

– OLIVER S. OWEN

GOVERNANCE

Governance, in all its forms, must undergo radical transformation to meet the needs of the future: Increasingly powerful instruments at the disposal of humanity make failure rates too costly; globalization of problems and processes (such as climate changes and financial markets) can no longer be handled by national governments or by existing supranational authorities; changing values require novel political expressions; the growing power of non-Western cultures makes present Western-based political ideologies increasingly obsolete; and so on. In short, a high-technology, multicultural, increasingly integrated world of 10 to 15 billion people cannot be managed by present governance slightly reformed. Needed instead are radically novel forms of governance.

Future governance will be pluralistic and based on different values, conditions, and traditions. But to meet emerging challenges, all undertakings will have to meet requisites not satisfied by present governance. Seven requisites illustrate future requirements that are becoming increasingly pressing. The contradictions between some of them exposes the tensions that will characterize governance debates.

Requisites of Future Governance

BASED ON CONSENT. Governance that does not enjoy broad consent will not work and will not be acceptable valuewise. Democratic elections will provide a main consent procedure, as will electronic direct democracy based on emerging technologies. Other forms of consent, such as those based on religious beliefs, also will characterize future governance.

Generating intelligent public opinion will become

an increasingly necessary government task.

But being "intelligent" does not necessarily mean

being "enlightened."

INTELLIGENT PUBLIC OPINION. For governance to handle complex issues on the basis of consent, public opinion in turn must be based on better understanding. Generating intelligent public opinion will become an increasingly necessary government task. But being "intelligent" does not necessarily mean being "enlightened." Fundamentalist worldviews, for example, may well go together with intelligent public opinion, producing high-quality governance on very different lines than Western democratic ones.

SOME DETACHMENT FROM SHIFTING PUBLIC OPINION. Based on intelligent consent, governance will also require detachment from shifting public opinion, in order to accommodate the needs of future generations, to cope with issues too complex for general understanding, and to generate more intelligent public opinion. This means that there may be limits on direct or popular democracy; intervals between elections may have to be increased; nondemocratic institutions, such as central banks, special project agencies, and "councils of state" may be left in charge of important functions; and that professional elites will be allowed to fulfill major roles in governance. In democracies, all governing institutions will be subject to override by majority rule.

BETTER INTEGRATION OF KNOWLEDGE INTO POWER. Governance will be based on full utilization of all available knowledge requiring novel forms of integrating knowledge with power. This might include new types of professional senior civil services, extensive training, and the conferring of autonomous knowledge-bodies such as "think tanks," with statutory powers.

UPGRADING POLITICIANS. Hand in hand with consent and better-informed publics, governance will become elitist. Approaches will differ between countries and cultural areas, but in all of them political elites will be of crucial importance. Deliberate efforts to upgrade the quality of politicians will become essential, however

taboo such measures may seem according to present political myths.

Interdependent steps in this direction include

- elimination of corruption, by reducing the dependence of politicians on money, providing politicians with adequate remuneration, and punishing corruption harshly
- changing the rules of democratic elections by requiring full disclosure of personal histories and subjecting candidates to intensive public interrogations—to break through "television masks" so the public will be better informed
- integrating systematic learning opportunities and incentives into the career of politicians, such as by paid study leaves and establishing policy colleges for politicians
- imposing strictly enforced codes of ethics for politicians, including accountability for all aspects of their private behavior that might adversely affect their public functions

NEW BALANCE BETWEEN LEVELS OF GOVERNANCE. To handle human problems well, local governance will become more important. To handle economic and social issues, multistate governance will also become more important, along the lines of the European Union. But to handle the problems of humanity as a whole, global government will become much stronger and be equipped with effective enforcement powers and instruments. As a consequence, the importance of states in their present formats will diminish.

TOWARD A NEW POLITICAL PHILOSOPHY. Governance is grounded in political philosophies. However, available political philosophies are grossly inadequate, especially concerning increasingly crucial issues such as "global equity," public control of biotechnology and of mass media, and space travel. New political philosophies will emerge, driven by the inadequacies of present ones.

There is no strong reason to presume that these new political philosophies will be based on what we at present regard as "obvious." If and when radically new political philosophies emerge, governance will undergo transformations. To perform effectively, it will have to satisfy many of the requirements postulated above.

Future-shaping issues of globalization, population growth, economic and social disparities, climate change, space travel, uses and misuses of new technologies, ideological conflicts, and many more will prove increasingly unmanageable by market processes and civil societies. Therefore, politics and governance will rise again as master architects of social life on a global scale, for better or worse.

The basic choice between good and evil governance will continue to vex humanity, becoming more important than ever. Optimistic assumptions on a benign "end of history" have no basis, either in human experience or in what we know of human nature. Conscious efforts to move toward good governance, subject to changes in what constitutes "good" governance, are imperative. The outcome is not preordained, but depends on our ideas and deeds.

The more we engage in deliberative governance redesign to better fit the future in moral ways, the higher are the chances that governance will operate for the better. But if we leave unavoidable shifts in governance to chance and shock effects, the future of governance may be dismal indeed.

Adequate action depends on ideas. Present thinking on the future of governance is quite inadequate, suffering inter alia from fixation on western experiences and reliance on overoptimistic assumptions. Creative thinking on the future of governance is, therefore, urgently needed.

[See also Executive Branch; Executive Branch: The Presidency; Global Business: Dominant Organizational Forms; International Governance and Regional Authorities; Leadership.]

BIBLIOGRAPHY

Dror, Yehezkel. *The Capacity to Govern: A Report to the Club of Rome.* English version in publication.
———. *Public Policymaking Reexamined.* Scranton, PA: Chandler Publishing, 1968.
Page, William, ed. *The Future of Politics.* London: Frances Pinter, 1983.
The Report of the Commission on Global Governance. *Our Global Neighborhood.* Oxford, UK: Oxford University Press, 1995.

— YEHEZKEL DROR

GOVERNMENT ORGANIZATION

The most remarkable political development in the closing decade of the twentieth century was the rise of liberal democracy as the chosen form of government for most of the world's nations. This dramatic shift raises a profound question for governance: will this represent the "end of history"—or a new beginning? Francis Fukuyama, in a provocative book entitled *The End of History and the Last Man,* argues that history has progressed to liberal democracy and capitalism, and that while changes and refinements will be made and are needed, no other forms of human political and economic organization will replace liberal democracy and capitalism. Forces in place give credence to the accuracy of Fukuyama's prediction, but there are some trouble spots.

The biggest source of trouble is nationalism. Given license, old hatreds and rivalries have been reignited and magnified in ways that challenge the new world order and threaten the stability and promise of liberal de-

mocracy. Various regions of the former Soviet Union, the countries of Eastern Europe, India, Pakistan, Bangladesh, Lebanon, Sri Lanka, and Nigeria are among those countries dangerously divided along ethnic lines in a manner that calls into question their capability to secure and maintain liberal democracy. Can Russians who live in Georgia or Serbs who live in Croatia ever be reconciled to the political boundaries that existed at the time of the breakup of the Soviet bloc?

While changes and refinements will be made, it is possible that no other forms of human political and economic organization will replace liberal democracy and capitalism.

The essential challenge is whether nations can modify the liberal democratic form in ways that reconcile unity and diversity to deal with ethnic rivalries and nationality tensions. Some form of federalism is seemingly vital for the survival of liberal democracy.

Federalism

Federalism requires recognition of and respect for individual rights, a democratic form, and a substantial political, financial, and programmatic role for regional governments that are the arbiters of the local units of which they are composed. Prior to the U.S. Constitution, the idea of federalism referred to a league that formed a club of states. Each state was a member of a central body. The U.S. founding fathers, in James Madison's words, invented a "new composition" that is "neither wholly *federal* nor wholly *national.*" In this new federal form, citizens acquired dual citizenship of both the national and the state government, and secured rights to participate in the affairs of both. Conceptual boundaries of this federal-state relationship were deliberately blurred to accommodate shifts in the way responsibilities, functions, and finances were divided between the national government and the states.

American federalism when diagrammed shows a steady accretion of central powers, but with a wavy upward line reflecting cyclical variations in the relative strength in different periods of the role of state governments vis-à-vis the central government. The 1980s and early 1990s brought about increasing reliance on the states under Reagan and the Republicans, as contrasted to the accretion of national governmental power in domestic affairs over the period from Franklin Roosevelt's New Deal through the late 1970s. Other periods in

U.S. history—the 1880s and 1920s—also were characterized by the rising role of the states. Despite advancing and retreating state power, the trend, overall, has been toward centralization. Similar centralization trends are found in other federal nations, including Germany, Australia, and Canada.

The best way to understand modern federal systems is to compare the relative role of the states, which are called by different names in different federal countries—provinces in Canada, *Länder* in Germany, and cantons in Switzerland. A continuum of "federalness" showing relative roles would place Switzerland at one end as the most decentralized federal country. It would place Brazil, India, and Australia at the opposite end as the least decentralized federal countries in terms of the power of regional governments in relation to the central government.

Federalism as defined so far is described in terms of structure. Left out is something very important—a spirit of community. The regions in federal nations are rooted in tradition and history with which citizens identify, often in very strong ways. In the early history of the United States, citizens might have described themselves as Vermonters, New Yorkers, or Virginians, but not as Americans. Among modern federal countries, Switzerland is the most clearly divided between different nationality groups, with Germans, French, and Italians concentrated in different cantons. In this respect, the Swiss brand of federalism offers the best model of a country that has successfully dealt with geographically differentiated nationality groups.

Governance Issues

Beyond the idea of federalism as a way to reconcile unity and diversity, and the way it relates to the current challenge of ethnic and national divisiveness, are important questions of form and function in the United States.

INTERGOVERNMENTAL FINANCE. In the United States, federal grants-in-aid are made to state governments, and also to localities, in some cases. They can be: broad, like revenue sharing; focused on functional areas, like education, health, the environment, and so forth; open-ended, like welfare grants; closed-ended; conceived for narrow or for broad purposes; based on a formula or a project basis; or targeted at capital, operating, or income-transfer purposes. Needed for the future are new intergovernmental fiscal mechanisms much more selective than past grants. States differ greatly in their governmental and managerial capacity. A new form of what might be termed "functional-flexibility" grants is needed to take these state differences into account. Conditional grants conferring upon states wide discretion in the absence of failure to conform with acceptable standards might also specify a national government takeover or close federal supervision when activities funded under that grant failed to conform.

MANAGERIAL EFFICIENCY. Liberal democracy needs constant refinement. In an increasingly interconnected global economy, the managerial efficiency of democracy requires a delicate balancing of time-consuming open decision processes, and the ability to make and execute policies on a timely basis. Vibrant political pluralism enables the nation to deal with stalemates between political leaders and the public who want to make changes, against other powerful stakeholders whose interest is to prevent change. Institutional arrangements are needed in these confrontational situations (health policy is a good example) to permit specially created bodies to develop and advance plans for systemic change. The legislative and executive branches might be given the power to reject these plans, but not to modify them. This would provide a way to break stalemates while preserving political legitimacy. Military base closing commission recommendations that could be voted up or down, but not modified by carving out politically inspired base-saving exceptions, set a poignant precedent.

METROPOLITAN GOVERNMENT. The fragmentation of local government in the United States also presents a governance challenge that in many regions requires new instruments. Regional government is usually not the answer, but the establishment of regional service compacts in major functional areas often is. This solution reflects the "public choice" theory that says, in effect, that the geographic service area for different functions should vary, but that common matters may be dealt with collectively, often with considerable savings.

ROLE OF COMMUNITY-BASED ORGANIZATIONS. In the United States, the biggest recent structural change in urban policy has not been "privatization," but the *nonprofitization* of social services. Many government-funded social services that are operated by nonprofit community-based groups now perform in a competitive marketplace where urban services are rewarded for efficiency, managerial talent, and entrepreneurial skills. This trend towards "nonprofitization" will continue; however, refinement of the basic organizational model is needed.

All over the world, liberal democracy as a governmental form is on the march. Its future seems bright. But problems of ethnic and nationality rivalries and institutional rigidities challenge liberal democratic governments to be inventive in the twenty-first century. Federalism has great potential as a formula for stabilizing and buttressing the liberal democracies of the future.

[See also Capitalism; Communism; Conservatism, Political; Democracy; Democratic Process; International Governance and Regional Authorities; Liberalism, Political; Political Cycles; Political Party Realignment; Social Democracy; Socialism.]

BIBLIOGRAPHY

Hamilton, Alexander; Madison, James; and Jay, John. *The Federalist Papers*. New York: New American Library, 1961.
Fukuyama, Francis. *The End of History and the Last Man*. New York: Free Press, 1992.
Nathan, Richard P. "Federalism—the Great Composition," In Anthony King, ed. *The New American Political System*. Washington, DC: American Enterprise Institute Press, 1990.

— RICHARD P. NATHAN

GREEN REVOLUTION

As long as there is hunger in developing nations, the "green revolution" will pit scientists, farmers, agricultural researchers, and health activists against the forces of nature and industry. By 2050 or so, when the world's population peaks at ten to twelve billion, the winner—either sustainable, self-sufficient agricultural systems or a perpetual cycle of poverty and famine in some lands—will be apparent.

The green revolution (GR) began in the mid-1960s, launched by agricultural researchers concerned about sustaining life on an increasingly crowded planet. Their goal was to maximize harvest yields and to end hunger. GR technologies departed from conventional farming methods in three ways: planting high-yield grain varieties, expanding irrigation, and increasing the use of chemical pesticides and fertilizers.

In its first thirty years, the revolution boosted land productivity and crop yields in many developing countries, where agriculture not only is a primary food source but also generates up to sixty percent of the Gross Domestic Product (GDP). By the early 1990s, the International Food Policy Research Institute reported that GR investments exceeded expectations: crop yields in many developing countries showed significant gains with no sign of slowing down.

Challenges

Despite impressive achievements, the green revolution is far from complete. More than half a billion people

The green revolution maximized crop yields by expanding irrigation and increasing the use of pesticides and fertilizers. Genetic applications will dramatically increase yields while reducing chemical inputs. (Ted Streshinsky/Corbis)

worldwide live in a constant state of hunger, according to the 1992 annual report of the Bread for the World Institute on Hunger and Development. In addition, another one billion people cannot afford an adequate diet to sustain an active worklife.

Several obstacles keep GR proponents from reaching their ultimate goal. One is that GR methodologies have not reached many regions. Until they do, and until these areas' infrastructures can accommodate greater use, population growth will continue to exceed food production growth. Another is the environmental impact. Deforestation and overgrazing accelerate soil erosion and degrade land. The loss of natural ecosystems threatens genetic raw materials critical to agriculture. Similarly, the expansion of cultivated land—a key GR strategy—is nearing its physical limits. Future growth must come not from increased acreage, but from yet higher yields.

Other factors are beyond science's control. Most hungry people starve not because of a global food shortage, but because of political instability or lack of money. More ominous is global climate change. The greenhouse effect on temperature and rainfall patterns could reduce agricultural output by fifteen to twenty-five percent over the next fifty to one hundred years.

Theories

Because there is no single cause for hunger, no one strategy can end it forever. Immediate, short-term "cures" such as emergency food shipments are no panacea: food aid has never freed a country from famine. Instead, to become famine-free long term, a developing country must have a sustainable agricultural system.

GR proponents agree that strong infrastructures and agricultural research systems are essential for achieving sustainability. Equally important are elements such as stable and open international markets, broad participation achieved by expanding education to rural areas, and decentralized, competitive domestic markets to encourage small farmers to adopt new technologies. China, for instance, became the world's biggest food producer in the 1980s by adopting reforms linking farmers' rewards to output.

Pierre Crosson, a senior fellow at Resources for the Future, argues that a system's success hinges upon its ability to mobilize "social capital," or energy, land, irrigation water, plant genetic material, climate, and knowledge.

The Bread for the World Institute offers concrete suggestions. They include establishing policies that merge new agricultural techniques with support for small rural enterprises, and integrating ecological and development concerns such as environmentally sound tourism. It also recommends nonagrarian tactics, including food stockpiling.

David Norse, a research associate for the Overseas Development Institute, advocates grass-roots empowerment. He calls for local level husbandry and development through organizations such as grazing associations and water user groups.

The single most important element of a sustainable agricultural system is knowledge—individual, technological, and institutional. Knowledge imbues developing countries with self-reliance. It is also subject to few physical constraints.

Efforts to build managerial and analytical skills in developing countries have been successful and relatively inexpensive. Given the necessary training, poor farmers are quick to adopt new technologies when it's in their interest to do so.

The best hope in the years ahead may come from foreign donors. Developed nations will boost their funding of, and provide more expertise for, schools and research centers, and will enable more students from developing countries to study agriculture abroad.

Strategies for the Future

Little new land is available for cultivation, but the global food supply must increase threefold by 2030 to sustain population growth. The best hope for meeting this need lies in science, especially in bioengineered crops—genetically altered to produce higher, hardier yields that defy drought, resist disease and spoilage, withstand pests, and require no fertilization. By the early 1990s, biotechnology brought tremendous gains to Asian countries such as China and Thailand, but found few takers in other developing nations. Biotechnology not only is environmentally benign, but also is a cheaper and more effective way to manage weeds and pests than conventional herbicides and pesticides.

A movement to revive ancient food sources is another approach to help resolve the challenges ahead. Just 150 of 4,000 or so edible plant species are widely cultivated. In 1993, the Food and Agriculture Organization launched an effort to identify and protect the other 3,850 or so, as well as animals with livestock potential. Among early successes were the maram bean, which resists drought, tastes good, and has more protein than peanuts, and the min pig, which is low in fat, tolerates extreme temperatures, is highly fertile, and survives well on poor feed.

Similarly innovative is the "perennial polyculture" or "domestic prairie" theory, which turns modern science—and the green revolution—on its head. The Land Institute, in Sierra, Kansas, answers the sustainability question by crossing a wheat field with a prairie—planting three or four perennial crops, adding no chemicals, and leaving the field untilled for years at a stretch. As a result, roots survive, while creating more soil and finding their own moisture and sustenance. The domestic prairie yields prolifically, requires little labor, and does not pollute. Its main detractor, however, is time: in an era of rapid change and instant results, a program that could take one hundred years to reach fruition wins little attention.

The greenhouse effect on temperature and rainfall

patterns could reduce agricultural output

by 15 to 25 percent over the next 50 to 100 years.

Numerous other initiatives will add fuel to the fire of the green revolution in the twenty-first century. Some, such as tree-planting schemes to regenerate woodlands or to protect pastures and fields from wind and sun, are not new. More laborious efforts—controlling runoff, erosion, and damage to rivers from siltation, for instance—may be improved with technol-

ogy. Other strategies include using fast-growing trees and grasses as "biofuels" to reduce reliance on fossil fuels, curb carbon emissions, and revitalize rural economies.

[See also Food and Agriculture; Food and Fiber Production; Food Technologies; Genetics: Agricultural Applications; Genetics: Commercialization; Global Warming; New Consumer Products; Soil Conditions.]

BIBLIOGRAPHY

Borlaug, Norman E., and Dowswell, Christopher R. "World Revolution in Agriculture." In *Encyclopaedia Britannica 1988 Book of the Year.* Chicago: Encyclopaedia Britannica, 1988.
Norse, David. "Feeding a Crowded Planet." *Environment* 34/5 (1992): 6–11, 32–39.
Crosson, Pierre. "Sustainable Agriculture: A Global Perspective." *Choices* (Second Quarter 1993): 38–42.
Mellor, John W., and Riely, Frank Z. "Expanding the Green Revolution." *Issues in Science and Technology* (Fall 1989): 66–74.

— LEAH THAYER
JERRY KLINE

GUNS.

See LETHAL WEAPONS.

H

HANDICAPPED, RIGHTS OF.
See DISABLED PERSONS' RIGHTS.

HARASSMENT, SEXUAL.
See SEXUAL HARASSMENT.

HARDWARE, COMPUTER.
See COMPUTER HARDWARE.

HAZARDOUS WASTES

Human activities create "wastes"—the by-products of daily life that were not there the day before. Wastes appear and then accumulate, and have no apparent use or desirability to whomever leaves them behind. Households generate literally mountains of trash annually. Riding to work leaves rubber on the road, exhaust fumes in the air, and brake lining dust on the ground. On the farm, spoiled hay, rusty tools, and runoff (including fertilizer and pesticides) abound. In strip-mine country, acidic tailings; in foundries, broken castings. In outer space, old satellites and rocket parts. In the ocean below, radioactive wastes and sewage sludge.

About 10 percent to 15 percent of all wastes generated in the United States are hazardous.

The United States alone creates more than 6 billion tons of waste of all kinds annually, nearly 50,000 pounds per person (NRC, 1991, p. 1). Some of these wastes are innocuous and others are mostly harmless, except that the principles of ecology recognize that all wastes must eventually go somewhere.

Some wastes are harmful, even deadly, or can become so under certain circumstances. About 10 percent to 15 percent of all wastes generated in the United States are hazardous (Wentz, 1989, p. 13).

The documented history of human and environmental health toxicology is fascinating. One classic account is W. Eugene and Aileen M. Smith's *Minamata* (1975). Their description and pictures portrayed the crippling spread of mercury poisoning among Japanese coastal families during the 1950s and '60s. The culprit was methyl mercury waste from the manufacture of acetaldehyde and vinyl chloride discharged into Japan's Minimata Bay. By 1959, mercury concentration in the bay's bottom mud exceeded 2,000 parts per million. The mercury entered the bay's food chain, passing from smaller life-forms to fish and eventually to human consumers of fish. By sharing a common bay, the people and the poisons were on a collision course. The adverse health effects, known as "Minamata disease," ranged from debilitating to deadly. Subsequently the disease was eventually found in communities throughout the Shiranui Sea in southern Japan. Over one hundred Japanese died from mercury poisoning between 1953 and 1965, and the problem persisted for more than twenty years (Smith and Smith, 1975).

Social and Economic Contexts of Hazardous Wastes

It appears to be getting more difficult to stay one jump ahead of disaster. In time, Minamata disease was found outside of Japan. Then, poisonings from other hazardous wastes were discovered—pesticides, lead, and asbestos, among them. Minamata signaled the beginning of the Toxics Era, not a surprising development for several reasons: the crushing increase in world population, the burgeoning demand for material goods, the growth of organic chemistry based on cheap petroleum, the related increase in synthetics production, the attendant wastes, and the release of toxins into the environment.

Society's ability to detect danger or act on warnings tends to lag behind the inclination to pursue profits, power, or special interests, no matter what the cost to the environment or human communities. The damage created "by the few on the many" spawns suspicion, polarization, and conflict within and among societies.

Finding, controlling, and removing hazardous waste creates major economic crises. It is estimated that there are 300,000–400,000 or more toxic sites in the United States alone (NRC, 1991, p. 9). The bill for hazardous-waste management and cleanup easily exceeds $6 billion annually (Mucci, 1987, p. 8). These outlays compete with society's other basic funding priorities: education, old-age security, health, conservation, agriculture, transportation, community improvement, and international peacemaking. Further, the labor requirement is immense and will continue to be; it will divert the talents of millions of workers who might otherwise be involved in more productive livelihoods.

Dimensions of Hazardous Wastes Exposure

Many believe that there is far more hazard in our lives than need be. How has this occurred? First, we have altered or countermanded nature by dividing and then valuing higher the parts most immediately used or demanded ("the products"), while valuing lower what we leave behind ("the wastes"). These priorities virtually ensure that resources will be used inefficiently and wastes will accumulate. Second, we pursue lifestyles that have seemingly insatiable, material demands, coupled with a consumer ethic based on the "freedom to waste." Economies consequently take great risks in acquiring, producing, and delivering goods. Third, we have poorly defined and underestimated the significance and volume of the wastes generated—their monetary, social, and environmental costs, now and for future generations.

Hazardous waste troubles have been experienced in all the basic sectors of our society, including energy, petrochemicals, fertilizers, metals, communication, transportation, and military defense. In the chemicals industry, 80,000 chemicals are in commercial use today and about 1,000 more are introduced each year (Gerrard, 1994, p. 7). Annual chemical production exceeds 300 billion pounds (Epstein, 1982, p. ix). Only a few hundred chemicals are regulated under hazardous-waste laws, and only a small fraction of the rest have been thoroughly tested for toxicity (Gerrard, 1994, p. 7). There are serious questions about which of these untested chemicals are, indeed, innocuous. For example, of approximately 1,200 "inert" ingredients in pesticides, the U.S. Environmental Protection Agency claims that about 50 are of significant toxicological concern and an additional 60 are considered potentially toxic (NRC, 1991, p. 110). Even silicone, originally promoted as inert and user-friendly, is now suspected to be chemically reactive within the human body.

Wastes have the tendency to degrade or transform over time. However, they do not always become less toxic. The anaerobic microbial transformation of inorganic mercury into methyl mercury is an example of the secondary compound being much more troublesome than the first.

When toxic wastes are loose in the environment, both the routes and the intensity of exposure may drastically change. For example, workers' exposure to certain volatile dry-cleaning solvents, some of which are known cancer-causing agents, is typically by inhalation or absorption. Waste solvents also may find a way down a drain, onto the ground, or into a landfill, exposing unsuspecting people to groundwater and drinking water pollution. Each year, thousands of wells are closed because of hazardous-waste contamination (NRC, 1991, p. 5).

The human body's capacity to detoxify chemicals is definitely limited. At first, there may be no symptoms, but with prolonged exposure, a variety of symptoms can appear. Adverse health consequences may include modified or irregular behavior, central-nervous-system disorientation, impairment of body functions, allergic reactions, skin and eye irritation or damage, respiratory, distress and cardiac collapse, pulmonary edema, or less obvious delayed reactions that may take years before producing carcinogenic, mutagenic, or teratogenic effects in essential organs (Fawcett, 1988, p. 84). Pregnant women and nursing mothers, babies, children, the elderly, and others in poor health or recovering from surgery or other medical treatment are especially vulnerable.

The "Catalog" of Hazardous Wastes

One taxonomy of waste problems consists of five categories: (1) parent materials or derivatives; (2) reactions and transformations over time and under various conditions; (3) interactions with other substances, including other wastes; (4) range and severity of effects on life-forms; and (5) relative difficulty in locating, identifying, isolating, and assimilating or disposing of wastes. To address the hazardous waste problem, it is essential to understand how each waste fits these categories, how it got there, and how to remove it without causing yet another waste problem.

Hazardous wastes come from both natural materials and synthetic compounds. Some 90 percent are generated by manufacturing. More than 99 percent are produced by large-quantity generators—that is, sources accounting for more than 1,000 kg per month. Just 1 percent of all generators create 97 percent of all hazardous wastes in the United States, and three plants—operated by DuPont, Dow Chemical, and Eastman Kodak—generate 57 percent of all hazardous wastes nationwide (Gerrard, 1994, p. 8). It has been estimated that the chemical and petroleum industries account for approximately 70 percent to above 88 percent of hazardous wastes, and the metal-related industries for 22 percent (Mucci, 1987, p. 10; Wentz, 1989, p. 2).

The U.S. military is a significant hazardous-waste generator, accounting for approximately 700,000 tons of hazardous wastes annually, including paint thinner, spilled solvents, hydraulic fuel, aviation fuel, fuel tank and sewage sludges, and herbicides. A total of 1,877 installations have been targeted for cleanup, with an estimated total cost of $24.5 billion (Gerrard, 1994, p. 15). Extensive soil contamination has occurred at hundreds of air bases and elsewhere, and upwards of 100

Hazardous-waste cleanup has become a profitable industry that employs on-site investigators, engineers, technologists, and laboratory personnel. The worldwide revenue from pollution control and environmental enterprise will increase from $292 billion to $572 billion, 1992–2001. (UPI/Corbis-Bettmann)

million tons of military ordnance require disposal. There is also an estimated 10 million tons per year of waste munitions and more than 1 million tons per year of naval paint and plating wastes (Dawson, 1986, p. 120). No matter where one looks, it is obvious that the dimensions of the problem are immense.

Many people believe that this generation

of high-level wastes has been totally immoral,

amounting to an undeclared war

on future generations.

Radioactive wastes, mostly from atomic weapons manufacture and nuclear power plants, are classified as high-level or low-level. Included are wastes that will be dangerous for thousands of years. Many people believe that this generation of high-level wastes has been totally immoral, amounting to an undeclared war on future generations. Highly radioactive wastes from plutonium warhead production are stored at government installations in Washington state and South Carolina. Most of the approximately 10,000 cubic meters of radioactive spent-fuel rods from more than 100 nuclear power plants are being stored on site. About 1,900 tons of spent fuel are generated each year (Gerrard, 1994, pp. 29–30). There are almost 3 million cubic meters of low-level wastes from nuclear weapons manufacture in Washington State, South Carolina, and Tennessee, mostly buried in shallow trenches; prior to 1970 the U.S. military practiced ocean dumping (Gerrard, 1994, p. 33). Most civilian wastes have been stored at six sites, all of which will be closed before the end of the century, leaving it up to individual states to establish their own disposal sites. Siting has become a very controversial issue. Finally, there are more than a dozen extremely contaminated sites (collectively known as the Nuclear Weapons Complex), where atomic weapons were made. Cleaning up these sites will cost more than $200 billion and will take at least twenty to thirty years (Gerrard, 1994, p. 36).

The Citizen Factor

Since the beginning of the Toxics Era, from the mid-1960s through the '70s, concerned citizens have been in an intelligent debate with scientists, engineers, politicians, and others to (1) find, study, and rank the hazards of wastes as a guide to assessing the threats to health, aesthetics, and the environment; (2) try to arrive at "acceptable limits" of environmental concentrations and personal exposure for various compounds; (3) di-

rect the investment of public and private funds and technology development to minimize or eliminate the damage caused; (4) prevent the worldwide proliferation of wastes and waste-causing activities; and (5) explore pathways to a world where no wastes would be hazardous.

Little initiative and follow-up has come from government and industry; the U.S. National Research Council concluded, ". . . The intent of Congress in creating Superfund (the Comprehensive Environmental Response, Compensation, and Liability Act of 1980) has not been realized, in that the public health consequences of exposures to substances from hazardous-waste sites have not been adequately assessed. Moreover, there is little reason to believe that current procedures identify the most important abandoned hazardous-waste sites, from the point of view of public health" (NRC, 1991, p. 6).

Too often, citizens have had to hire lawyers to sue their own governments—first, to hold hearings on hazardous wastes; then to propose and enact legislation; and then to force slow, indifferent, or even belligerent agencies to release information on waste generators and disposal sites and to implement the authorized programs. Although much has been attempted in the way of mediation and conflict resolution, the adversarial relationship, backed by the threat of litigation, is still the prime mover. This situation has persisted regardless of changes in political administrations.

The continuing suspicion and animosity are fueled by the media's vivid reporting of new toxic-waste catastrophes. Among these are: oil spills, truck and rail accidents, community evacuations, toxic building fires, medical wastes washing up on beaches, garbage barges wandering the oceans, leukemia and cancer clusters near toxic sites. Public opinion surveys consistently rank hazardous-waste sites among the most serious environmental risks, and the environment as an issue of great public concern (NRC, 1991, p. 5).

Tens of thousands of recognized toxic sites and more than 16,000 active landfills in the United States (NRC, 1991, p. 112)—a large portion of them designated as federal "Superfund" sites—has prompted ad hoc voluntary organizations of impacted or frightened residents. Other organizations and union research committees have formed at industrial plants, mining sites, and military installations. A recent U.S. Environmental Protection Agency survey found that more than 40 million people live within four miles and about 4 million within one mile of a Superfund site (NRC, 1991, p. 2). Group leaders are often those who believe they are the most immediately or severely affected: people with unexplained cancers, metabolic diseases, sick children.

Worldwide, hazardous-waste sites probably number in the millions. They may be small, concealed, and dispersed "nonpoint" sources of gasoline-soaked subsoil or leaking underground storage tanks. In the United States alone, the latter are estimated to be a third of the 2.4 million to 4.8 million tanks holding kerosene, heating oil, cleaning solvents, and other dangerous fluids (Mucci, 1987, p. 22; NRC, 1991, p. 112). Or they may be "point sources," large enough to be visible from space, such as Chernobyl's 30-kilometer-radius intensely radioactive "dead zone."

The Hazardous-Wastes Industry

The public's concern about hazardous wastes has stimulated tremendous growth in technology to deal mostly with the wastes already generated. The major focus has been on learning how to handle wastes at contaminated sites. Remote sensing and sophisticated subsurface investigation try to track and predict the movement of toxic plumes. Highly selective, large-capacity filtration systems have been designed to intercept advancing wastes. A variety of on-site air strippers and combusters, and experimental in situ waste treatment—solidifiers, vitrifiers, and broths of microorganisms, for example— are beginning to fill the catalog of available equipment and methods.

In the United States and other industrialized countries, hazardous-waste cleanup and disposal have become a profitable industry of major proportions, supporting engineers, on-site investigators, waste detection technologists, instrumentation specialists, laboratory personnel, and research and education centers. The entire national cleanup program, known as Superfund, is under fire for spending billions of dollars on what might be termed glorified landscaping and pork barrel projects for engineers and contractors without actually cleaning up the sites.

Looking Forward

Remember that the hazardous-waste crisis is made by people. Thus, even before speculating on its outcome, we must ask, "Who wants what to happen when?" The "who" is basically three categories of actors, although they sometimes overlap: concerned citizens, government, and business.

The agenda for the future of hazardous wastes is being hammered out publicly and privately, from small towns to international conferences. It is being punctuated and pushed along in the media whenever, for example, a tank truck jackknifes on a highway, or a new microbe is discovered with an appetite for leachate.

In 1992, thousands of representatives from around the world addressed hazardous wastes at the United Nations' Earth Summit in Rio de Janeiro. Chapter 20 in the summit's culminating *Agenda 21* acknowledges that "human health and environmental quality are un-

dergoing continuous degradation by the increasing amount of hazardous wastes being produced. There are increasing direct and indirect costs to society and to individual citizens in connection with the generation, handling, and disposal of such wastes. It is therefore crucial to enhance knowledge and information on the economics of prevention and management of hazardous wastes. . . . One of the first priorities in hazardous waste management is minimization, as part of a broader approach to changing industrial processes and consumer patterns through pollution prevention and cleaner production strategies. Among the most important factors in these strategies is the recovery of hazardous wastes and their transformation into useful material. . . ." (United Nations, 1992).

Major citizen efforts are already under way to reject certain products, processes, and classes of compounds whose waste products are hazardous. The antichlorine movement, for example, changed circuit-board and computer manufacturing in fewer than five years: Once the pressure was applied, closed-loop and water-based methods for cleaning high-tech components replaced chlorinated solvents.

The most significant trend has been the emergence of "pollution prevention" as part of the environmental ethic. The U.S. Environmental Protection Agency and many states now subscribe to pollution prevention as the preferred way to meet current and future environmental goals. Front-end prevention is generally less expensive and hazardous than rear-end control.

"NIMBY"

"Not in my backyard!" the people shout. Since the 1970s, this cry has been a shield for millions of citizens all over the world in defense against the twin plagues of pollution and life-threatening wastes that have been spread over the land; injected into the soil, water, and air; and passed through virtually every corner of the planet, often while no one was looking.

It is not by coincidence that the tone of defiance in "Not in my backyard!" echoes Benjamin Franklin's famous "Don't tread on me!," which landed hard on the chin of the British monarchy and unified the American colonies into a groundswell for complete independence two hundred years ago. "Not in my backyard!" and its global extension, "Not in anyone's backyard!," bring this revolutionary challenge up to date. They invoke the moral obligation to reject any conditions where pollution and disaster endanger the well-being of communities. Two hundred years ago, the battle was political; today, for many, it is clearly environmental.

[See also Acid Rain; Deforestation; Disasters, Planning for; Factories and Manufacturing; Freshwater; Nuclear Power: Con; Oceans; Soil Conditions; Solid Waste.]

BIBLIOGRAPHY

Dawson, Gaynor W., and Mercer, Basil W. *Hazardous Waste Management.* New York: John Wiley & Sons, 1986.

Epstein, Samuel S.; Brown, Lester O.; and Pope, Carl. *Hazardous Waste in America.* San Francisco: Sierra Club Books, 1982.

Fawcett, Howard H. *Hazardous and Toxic Materials: Safe Handling and Disposal.* New York: John Wiley & Sons, 1988.

Gerrard, Michael B. *Whose Backyard, Whose Risk: Fear and Fairness in Toxics and Nuclear Waste Siting.* Cambridge, MA: MIT Press, 1994.

Mucci, Nick. *Hazardous Waste Industry: Overview.* Braintree, MA: Clean Harbors, 1987.

National Research Council [NRC], Committee on Environmental Epidemiology. *Environmental Epidemiology: Public Health and Hazardous Wastes.* Washington, DC: National Academy Press, 1991.

Smith, W. Eugene, and Smith, Aileen M. *Minamata.* New York: Holt, Rinehart, & Winston, 1975.

United Nations. *Agenda 21.* New York: U.N. Department of Public Information, 1992.

Wentz, Charles A. *Hazardous Waste Management.* New York: McGraw-Hill, 1989.

– STUART M. LEIDERMAN

HEALTH CARE

Health care—the management of the resources of healing—is one of the most complex and difficult enterprises on the planet, and in the mid-1990s it is changing with great speed and turbulence. This turbulence is likely to continue for some time into the future, for a combination of reasons both within health care and outside it.

Where We Are Now

In the mid-1990s, relatively few nations are satisfied with their health-care systems. In the United States, health care costs have ballooned to $1 trillion, accounting for nearly 15 percent of the U.S. economy. Yet the

---

More than half of the world's 5.6 billion people lack access to the most essential drugs, and more than one-third of the world's children are malnourished.

United States consistently falls behind many other industrialized nations in infant mortality, longevity, and other benchmarks, and some 40 million Americans lack health insurance. Despite these facts, the chance for significant health care reform seems to have come and gone after the defeat of President Bill Clinton's plan and all of its rivals in late 1994.

Other developed nations, though their per capita costs are far lower, also face tough political struggles over rising costs and constricted resources. At the other end of the scale, the World Health Organization (WHO) estimates that more than half of the world's 5.6 billion people lack access to the most essential drugs—vaccines, antibiotics, and painkillers—and more than one-third of the world's children are malnourished. Many Third World governments spend less than 1 percent of gross domestic product on health care.

Factors in the Future of Health Care

A number of outside factors will affect health care in the future. A less predictable climate worldwide means an increase in natural disasters such as floods, droughts, famines, and typhoons. The absence of the constraints of the Cold War, the continued devolution of the former Soviet countries, the increase in effectiveness and the lower cost of many weapons (especially conventional small arms), growing atomization along ethnic and nationalist lines, and the growing scarcity and depletion of natural resources, point to the likelihood of increased chaos and war. For health care this means an increase in trauma, in malnutrition (as the chaos disrupts food supplies), of infectious disease, and stress-induced illness, as well as a diversion of resources away from health-care toward arms and reconstruction.

Other trends point toward continued and locally increased industrial pollution, which affects people's health over wide areas. Continued population growth will stretch all resources thinner. Increasing industrialization and urbanization around the world tend to break up the family, clan, and village support systems that have traditionally supported health. The increasing power and size of global corporations, less stable global finances, the increasing influence of donor nations, of central finance agencies such as the World Bank and the International Monetary Fund, and of the central government banks and finance ministries of wealthy countries, may mean even more constraint on resources for health care in many Third World countries.

Finally, certain medical changes endanger health care around the world. In the ongoing war between pathogens and antibiotics, overused antibiotics seem to be losing their effectiveness against the rapidly evolving pathogens. And the rapid increase in cheap international travel allows new epidemics to rapidly become global. The spread of human immunodeficiency virus (HIV) has gone essentially unchecked in much of the world. As of 1994, HIV was infecting 13 million adults a year. The WHO expects that 5 million children worldwide will become infected with HIV between 1995 and 2000. Southern Asia and sub-Saharan Africa are expected to bear the brunt of this epidemic.

All these changes will tend to push national health systems increasingly into crisis and chaos. The effect will be most marked at the ends of the economic spectrum, in the bloated U.S. health care industry, and in the highly strained economies of the Third World. It will be least marked in the other industrialized nations and in the robust "tiger" economies of East and Southeast Asia.

China, with the world's largest population (1.17 billion), presents an enigmatic future. Since the 1949 revolution, China has built a health care infrastructure that has been widely admired for its comprehensiveness, wide social base, preventive focus, and efficient use of the country's scant economic resources. China's economy is growing rapidly, and it is expected within a decade or so to become an economic powerhouse, a middle-income country, which always bodes well for health care. But early signs warn of an increasing gap between classes, urban and rural areas, and coastal and inland areas. There are also signs of increasing social strain, such as the open reemergence of infanticide,

baby-selling, and prostitution, and a rise in the death rates of children under five. Some observers, as well, express concern over China's long-term political stability. The most hopeful signs for the future of health in China are: (1) the government's strong, widespread family planning programs, (2) its focus on strengthening the corps of low-cost primary health professionals in the neighborhoods and villages, and (3) its focus on educating girls and the relatively high literacy rate of its women (68 percent). Studies by the World Bank and the WHO have shown the education of females to be the most effective method of improving the health of populations.

Technical Advances

We cannot expect technical developments with anything like the life-changing power that the inventions of antibiotics, antisepsis, painkillers, and X-rays brought to the early decades of this century. And some technical advances, such as distance surgery, may be spectacular but are unlikely to have a large effect on the health of

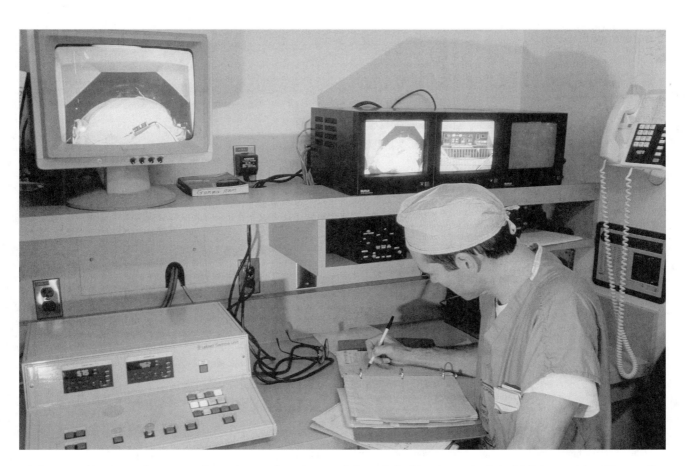

A doctor watching surgery from a control room is part of a major type of change in health care, a technological shift in caregiving. The cost of U.S. health care will likely increase from $1.15 trillion in 1998 to $2.1 trillion in 2007. (Jim Sugar Photography/Corbis)

most people. The areas that show the most promise for actually improving people's health include:

- the Human Genome Project, which may isolate the genetic roots of many human diseases—including many that are not generally considered genetic.
- the use of genetic markers to screen mass populations and prevent (through diet, gene substitution, or other special therapies) the specific diseases that individuals are likely to develop.
- nanotechnology, the newly developed craft of building molecular-scale machines, which holds the promise of completely new types of drugs: tiny machines with the tools and intelligence to perform specific tasks, kill certain viruses, repair certain cells, and manufacture certain necessary proteins or enzymes.
- new modes of pharmaceutical research that go far beyond the old, blind trial-and-error techniques to actually building the molecules (or evolving the bacteria) that can carry out specific tasks, lock onto specific receptor sites in the body, or defeat specific pathogens.

In fact, the most important effect of technical advances will not come through the invention of new medical techniques, but in the more effective use of the techniques that already exist.

Shifts in Direction

We can expect to see four major types of change in health care around the world in the coming decades, and two others that will be most pronounced in the United States.

- *Computers, Telecommunications, Databasing.* Advances in health-oriented telecommunications, medical imaging, massive databasing, memory miniaturization, satellite technology, and other information systems lay the groundwork for fundamental changes in the organization of health care. These new technologies will allow doctors to communicate far more easily and quickly and will allow health-care managers to drive their systems in real time. At the same time that they push consumer awareness about health to an entirely new level through the use of interactive cable systems, on-line forums, and personal health-information systems in a wide variety of formats.
- *Outcomes Management and Expert Systems.* Outcomes measurement uses massive databases scanning millions of cases to determine what therapies actually work best in particular circumstances. Its use as a management tool tends to make the practice of medicine more of a science and less of a craft, decreasing costs and increasing quality at the same time. Broadly applied, it will also open the gates to a number of highly effective and inexpensive nonmedical methods that are considered "alternative" or "complementary" in the Western countries. The ability to measure all interventions by outcome and cost will push all therapies toward greater unity, bring a wider range of therapies into official payment systems, and allow true comparison of intervention and prevention strategies. Outcomes management is spreading rapidly in the United States, but has only begun to penetrate other countries. Medical knowledge is expanding faster than any human can learn it. Computer programs called "expert systems" help physicians and other health practitioners move much more rapidly and effectively through the decisions of diagnosis and therapy,

isolating rare diseases, differentiating among similar syndromes, and discovering the latest research on the most effective therapies. Their widespread use is likely to significantly change the role of a doctor away from knowing facts and toward the more human elements of the craft, such as making difficult decisions and helping patients change their behavior.

- *Going "upstream."* The focus of health care will move increasingly out of the acute-care hospital to clinics, doctors' offices, and even into schools, workplaces, and the home. The focus will change as well, away from intervening in the acute phase of the disease toward early screening, detection, treatment, and even toward preventing the disease in the first place. This will happen because it is not only more effective to diagnose diseases early, it is far cheaper.
- *Population health.* According to the National Institutes of Health, about half of all health problems are caused by behavior such as smoking, excess drinking, and poor diet. Many of the rest are caused by problems in the environment, such as pollution and unsafe working conditions. All of these are preventable. A growing number of health care professionals around the world view changing the behavior of populations (as Americans changed their smoking habits) and cleaning up the environment as a highly effective use of health care funds. One expression of this is the rapid growth of the WHO's "Healthy Cities" movement.

U.S. Trends

Within the United States, two trends stand out:

- *Restructuring.* As health care moves "upstream," acute health care will continue to shrink drastically. In 1982, for every 1,000 U.S. citizens, American hospitals logged 1,132 nights in a hospital bed—more than one night per citizen. By 1992, that had dropped to 607. By 1995, some states were as low as 225, with some specific markets (such as San Diego County in California) as low as 160. Health futurist Jeff Goldsmith estimates that within a decade, most markets will log only seventy or eighty nights in a hospital per year for every 1,000 citizens. One-third to one-half or more of all hospitals will close. The rest will shrink and become much more intensive. Almost all will join one of the many different large-scale organizations that are bringing together hospitals, doctors, payment structures, and many other services under single ownership.
- *Reform.* Congress is not likely to enact significant health care reform anytime soon. But we will see a wide array of experiments at the local and state level. Business will become more heavily involved in health care negotiations, but in an increasingly sophisticated way, moving from simply bargaining for cheaper rates, to working with the doctors and hospitals to keep quality up and costs down, and finally to working with people from government, health care, education, and other sectors to make the whole community healthier.

[See also Health Care: Alternative Therapies; Health Care Costs; Health Care Financing; Health Care: Moral Issues; Health Care: Technological Developments; Medical Care Providers; Mental Health; Nursing; Psychiatry; Public Health.]

BIBLIOGRAPHY

Annis, Edward R. *The Future of Health Policy.* Cambridge, MA: Harvard University Press, 1993.

Graig, Laurene A. *Health of Nations: An International Perspective on U.S. Health Care Reform.* 2nd ed. Washington, DC: Congressional Quarterly, 1993.

Fuchs, Victor F. *The Future of Health Policy.* Cambridge, MA: Harvard University Press, 1993.

Hammerle, Nancy. *Private Choices, Social Costs, and Public Policy: An Economic Analysis of Public Health Issues.* Westport, CT: Praeger/Greenwood, 1992.

Lathrop, J. Philip. *Restructuring Health Care: The Patient-Focused Paradigm.* San Francisco: Jossey-Bass, 1993.

Schechter, Malvin. *Beyond Medicare: Achieving Long-Term Care Security.* San Francisco: Jossey-Bass, 1993.

— JOSEPH FLOWER

HEALTH CARE: ALTERNATIVE THERAPIES

Alternative therapies have grown into a multibillion-dollar-a-year industry. As the new century approaches, people are determined to find what to them constitutes acceptable total health care. Among the more acceptable remedies are the following:

Folk Remedies

These treatments have long been regarded as little more than superstition or witchcraft. In all parts of the inhabited world, recipes, ingredients, and remedies have been handed down from one generation to another. Many treatments and alleged cures have passed the test of centuries and now merit serious scrutiny for their valuable contribution to medicine. In Native American societies a medicine man could read the mysteries of nature. He knew the curative properties of roots, leaves, seeds, blossoms, tubers, berries, and fruit of almost every plant, shrub, or tree. Every old woman in a community gathered her own medicine, and medical doctors were called only in extreme circumstances.

Now medical science wants to know the secrets of the medicine man and the old woman. Was it more than belief in the magical power of the healer that brought about the wonderful cures?

Folk remedies from the past that continue to be used include: white willow for pain, catnip for colic, ginger for digestion, and purgatives such as castor oil, rhubarb, or calomel.

Herbal Healing

"A weed is a plant whose virtues we do not yet know," said Emerson. Pliny the Elder (c. 79 A.D.), a Roman naturalist who wrote the book *Natural History,* held a similar view. He stated that every plant had a special medicinal value if only we could discover it, and that for every disease there was a plant that would cure it.

Herbs grow everywhere: in fields or forest, along roadsides, mountains, backyards, nurseries, or on a windowsill.

For common ailments the home medicine shelf may stock arnica for bruises and pain, echincea for immune building, golden seal as an antiseptic/bacteriostatic agent, valerian for calming and insomnia.

Even in the high-technology world of drug design the search continues for the fountain of youth in a jar or the secret of longevity and rejuvenation harvested from botanical sources.

Acupuncture

The use of acupuncture as a healing technique is over four thousand years old. It is practiced not only in the Orient but generally worldwide. The oriental explanation of its mode of function is that in addition to the flow of blood, lymph, and nervous impulse there is also a flow of energy in the body that is called Chi. Chi flows along pathways called meridians. Whenever the flow of energy is obstructed, the potential for disease is present. The acupuncturist is able to diagnose the obstruction and to release normal energy flow by inserting needles to stimulate the appropriate meridian at specific points. In the days of the *Yellow Emperor's Classic of*

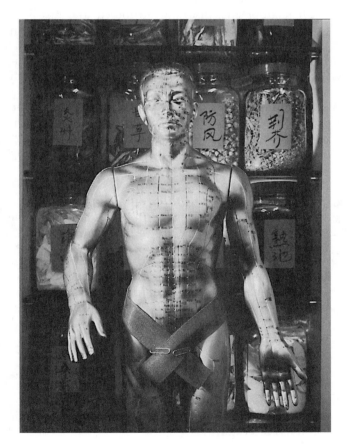

Acupuncture is a 4,000-year-old healing technique that continues to gain popularity in this century. This model charts the body's energy lines as used by acupuncturists. (© Charles Walker Collection/Stock Montage, Inc.)

381

Internal Medicine, stone needles were used; then iron needles progressed to silver or gold. Today stainless-steel needles of very fine caliber are used.

Mind power is a recognized factor in health:

it can influence illness or wellness.

The general requirements in basic training that are essential for the safe and competent practice of acupuncture are a knowledge of anatomy, physiology, pathology, medicine, pharmacology as well as diagnostic skills. Acupuncture is a unique system for pain relief. Supporters claim it can cure many ailments and maintain health.

Chiropractic

Ever since chiropractic was founded in 1895, it has focused on the nervous system and its lifeline, the spinal column, as the integrator of all body functions.

In chiropractic, disease is attributed to a misalignment of individual vertebrae that creates pressure on nerve tissue and interferes with nerve impulses. Although the traditional treatment focuses mainly on spinal manipulation, many chiropractors also work with nutrition and physiotherapy.

Rigorous studies have shown manipulations of the spine to be effective in relieving lower-back pain. Claims are that chiropractic outdistances drugs for long-term management of headaches. As a holistic healing art it is considered whole-person therapy.

Faith Healing

Although one can be helped without expressing faith, it is the healer who must have real faith in the power to heal. Human beings, like all other living systems, possess great powers of spontaneous recovery, and often a healer can effectively trigger such an occurrence.

Studies have been made of the effectiveness of so-called places of miracles such as Lourdes, sacred shrines, holy water, holy objects, the touch of a priest, and blessed amulets or talismans.

Spiritual Fate

The motive of the practitioner is of prime concern. Those who believe in karma or cause and effect do not take lightly their capacity to influence profoundly on all levels of health.

Criminal Liability

As an adjunct to medicine, faith healing is subject to the same creed, "Do good if you can, but do no harm," observing the Hippocratic oath. Sometimes failure to resort to conventional medical intervention based on beliefs denying outside intercession can be surmounted and help in grave situations mandated by public authorities.

Natural Healing

Self-care and the people's responsibility for their own health can no longer be ignored. Every doctor and patient can work out guidelines for maintaining optimal health.

The body will often heal itself without any intervention. The revolution in health practices reveals the requirements for optimal health and the way to avoid debilitating diseases. Longevity and good health are synonymous with the way we think about the future in medicine.

Natural healing is assisted by balanced nutrition including herbs to prevent illness, exercise, vitamins, and a collection of easy, safe home remedies for common ailments, The media offer free advice on avoiding major illnesses such as heart attacks, cancer, and strokes. Mind power is a recognized factor in health: It can influence illness or wellness. Breath is the basic life energy, and together with mind power it can be a transformative tool for healing. Natural healing is the new medicine for the year 2000 and beyond.

Holistic Health Care

Holistic is the term used to describe alternative healing therapies from acupuncture to Zen macrobiotics. The treatment views the patient as a whole: body, mind, attitude, and emotions. It is considered drugless because it concentrates on diet, exercise, meditation, and natural medications. The healers include not only medical physicians but lay practitioners skilled in the art and science of healing to expand the spectrum of holistic treatment.

The cornerstone of holistic philosophy is the sharing of responsibility equally by physician and patient. The physician assumes the greater role as health educator. As adviser the holistic doctor may ask questions instead of giving answers to help redefine the problem. Holistic prescriptions are more likely to be books, workshops, health spas, support groups, and nutrition counseling. Symptoms are analyzed to determine what changes in lifestyle might prevent recurrences and would inspire them to take responsibility for their own health.

Yoga

Yoga systems include raja, kundalini, hatha and tantra, inherited from the five-thousand-year-old tradition of the Himalayan sages. These teachings promise to develop a physical, mental, and spiritual life leading to total well-being. Karma yoga also teaches how to apply the principle of cause and effect to enhance daily living.

The practice of yoga is organized around meditation to bring harmony to body, mind, and spirit. The stillness of body and mind is achieved by rest, breath, sound, rhythm, simplicity, and wholeness. Various postures for balancing the body are designed to improve health in general or to correct specific spinal problems such as lumbar lordosis or misalignments.

Homeopathic Medicine

Homeopathy is a complete system of healing discovered two hundred years ago by a German physician, Dr. Samuel Hahnemann. The basic belief is: "Like cures like." In conventional medicine, the suppression of disease is considered the cure. Homeopathy sees the symptoms as evidence that the body is working in a healthy way to overcome the condition by stimulating the body's own self-healing power.

There is increased interest in homeopathy because of growing concern about toxic side effects used in mainstream medicine. Homeopathy has been the focus of scientific research. The medicines are prepared from fresh plant, animal, or mineral sources. One part of the original substance is mixed with nine parts of an inert substance or liquid. Potencies are then formulated for a wide variety of ailments. Homeopathy can be used without harm by following recommended dosages exactly.

Allopathic Medicine

Medical practice that seeks to cure disease by producing a condition incompatible or antagonistic to the condition to be cured is termed *allopathic medicine.*

Almost all conventionally trained physicians are specialists. Whether they are general internists, pediatricians, or family physicians (the major primary-care specialties), they are board-certified and go through a residency after medical school.

Hippocrates, the father of medicine, was the first to examine the sick carefully and record the signs and symptoms of disease. His accumulation of facts is among the first organized and systematic knowledge on which modern medicine rests.

The sophisticated scope of future medicine will enable the physician to control and stimulate healing at will. Science fiction healing increasingly becomes reality.

Rehabilitative Therapies

Illness that requires rehabilitation involves psychological as well as physiological trauma. Therapy centers report that treatment must take into account mind, body, and emotions. Stressful emotions resulting from traumatic injuries, fear, anger, frustration, and depression all stimulate the body to produce excess adrenaline and cortisone that upset the balance of body functions.

Rehabilitation requires specialized training with more communication, more interaction between therapist and patient.

Among therapies used are the following examples: guided imagery and hypnosis for pain control, massage for muscular disease, exercise, and nutrition to build immunity.

Empowerment is a potent medicine that gives freedom in decision making and responsibility for each individual's recovery and health.

[See also Health Care; Health Care: Moral Issues; Health Care: Technological Developments; Nutrition; Sexual Reproduction: Artificial Means.]

BIBLIOGRAPHY

Huard, Pierre, and Wong, Ming. *Chinese Medicine.* New York: McGraw-Hill, 1968.
Meyer, Joseph E. *The Herbalist.* Chicago: Rand-McNally, 1960.
Vithoulkas, George. *Homeopathy: Medicine for the New Man.* New York: Arco, 1979.
Weil, Andrew. *Natural Health, Natural Medicine.* Boston: Houghton Mifflin, 1990.

– ETEL E. DE LOACH

HEALTH CARE COSTS

In the mid-1990s, the United States was spending more than a trillion dollars a year on health care, 15 percent of the nation's gross domestic product. Americans were paying $4,000 a year for the health care of each man, woman, and child. Hospitals, doctors, pharmaceutical companies, medical equipment manufacturers, insurers, and nursing homes were billing the country $3 billion a day, an amount equal to more than the daily production of goods and services of half the states in the country.

Experts believe the United States could eliminate one-quarter of all surgical and medical procedures without any impact on health.

Every president since Harry S. Truman has tried to restructure America's health care system in an effort to assure every citizen access to quality care at reasonable cost. While progress was made, the cost of the system continued to grow and the number of citizens who lacked health insurance increased to 40 million. Driven by the sober realization that the nation could no longer afford the rising costs of care or tolerate the social injustice of gaps in health coverage, the president, the Congress, and the country's leading employers reconsidered the foundations and operation of a system providing the most technologically advanced care in the world.

Health care reform involves the training of doctors and paramedicals, the regulation of research, the role and funding of hospitals, the financing mechanisms of insurers and health maintenance organizations (HMOs), the pricing of pharmaceuticals and medical devices, the provision of nursing home care for the expanding elderly population, and the lifestyle of individual patients with regard to diet, exercise, stress, sex, and substance abuse (including legal and illegal drugs, nicotine, and alcohol).

Further complicating the task, the health industry contributes millions of dollars to presidential candidates and members of Congress to protect the industry's financial interests in the details of health legislation. The same individuals who on the one hand believe the nation must control its health care spending and that doctors charge too much, insist on the other hand that no care is too expensive for their sick parents, spouse, and children, and that their own doctors' fees are reasonable.

In 1965, when President Lyndon B. Johnson persuaded Congress to enact Medicare, which provides insurance for the elderly, and Medicaid, which provides insurance for poor Americans, the health system accounted for less than 6 percent of the domestic economy. In the mid-1990s, advocates of reform believed that without radical reform the health industry would absorb $2 trillion annually and account for close to 20 percent of the economy by the year 2000.

By the mid 1990s, health was America's biggest business. It employed almost 11 million people, more than the number working in transportation and construction combined. The nation spent on health twice what it spent on defense or education. Gaining control of health spending, the fastest-growing component of the federal budget, was essential in efforts to close the budget deficit, which threatened to reach $500 billion by the year 2000. At the state level, only the rate of increase in prison costs comes close to the rise in health care spending.

The United States spends more on health care per person than its international peers. In 1993, the U.S. paid $3,300 per capita, compared to $1,900 in Germany and $1,500 in Japan. But Americans have a shorter life expectancy than Germans or Japanese.

The American health care system has produced miraculous achievements in the quest to solve the riddles of the human body and mind. The nation's medical centers are the envy of the world for their advanced technology and innovative treatment, attracting patients from around the globe. In 1993, the federal government spent $12 billion on health research and development, with the bulk supporting basic research. The private sector spent another $16.8 billion, with most supporting applied research.

Yet the rising price of advanced technology pushed the highest-quality care above what many insurance policies cover and beyond the reach of many Americans. At the same time, waste, fraud, and abuse consumed at least $250 billion—a quarter of all health spending in 1994, and despite its spectacular technological abilities, the country ranks below most developed countries in its ability to prevent infant deaths. A quarter of all pregnant women do not get early prenatal care, an important factor in preventing infant mortality.

The United States also has one of the lowest rates in the Western Hemisphere for preschool immunizations against diseases such as measles, mumps, and polio. From 1989 to 1991, a decade after the country was on the verge of eradicating measles within its borders, 55,000 Americans contracted measles and 130 of them died. Only about half of all urban preschoolers are fully immunized.

Measuring the quality of health care has always been a difficult task. The American system intensively uses high technology and innovative drugs. These expenses may be sensible if they prevent ill health, pain, and suffering, as many do. But striking variations in the level of care across the country have raised the question of whether the nation's health care dollars are buying unnecessary or inappropriate care.

Research has found, for example, that if you are a man who retires in Florida rather than in Maine, you are four times as likely to have your prostate surgically removed. If you are a woman with localized breast cancer, your chances of a radical mastectomy are a third higher if you live in Iowa rather than Seattle, Washington. Much of the variation reflects uncertainty among doctors about what works in treating illness, but in some cases it reflects inappropriate care. Some experts believe the country could eliminate one-quarter of all surgical and medical procedures without any impact on health.

Beginning in the 1980s, variations in practice combined with rapidly increasing costs prompted many employers and insurers to question the autonomy of the nation's 600,000 active doctors. The special expertise of physicians had generally shielded them from scrutiny outside their professional domain. But they suddenly found themselves answering questions from a host of nonphysician reviewers, who created a mound of paperwork for America's health care providers. Today the proportion of health spending devoted to administrative expenses in the American system is extraordinarily high—roughly twice the share of administrative costs in the Canadian system.

The elderly account for a heavy share of the nation's health care budget, using almost four times as much health care per capita as people under age sixty-five.

Furthermore, the growing distrust of doctors, combined with the litigious American legal system, sparked an explosion in malpractice suits, costing $10 billion a year in the early 1990s. In turn this prompted roughly $10 billion in unnecessary tests and procedures that doctors ordered to protect themselves from potential litigants. Such "defensive medicine" contributes precious little to health outcome. All of these forces have demoralized many doctors; some are retiring early or going into other fields.

The increasing number of elderly citizens also adds to the challenge of providing quality care for every American. Not only is the elderly population growing in size, but more of its members are living longer and using the health care system frequently. The number of people age sixty-five in the U.S. increases by nearly 6,000 every day. Many of them can now expect to live past age eighty. By 2010, the elderly will total 40 million. By 2030, the group will number 70 million as baby boomers enter their golden years.

The elderly already account for a heavy share of the nation's health care budget and its high-technology miracles. They use almost four times as much health care per capita as people under age sixty-five. Medicare, the primary source of insurance for the elderly's hospital and doctor bills, covered 37 million Americans, most sixty-five or older, at a cost of $160 billion in 1994.

The growing elderly population has caused expansion of the nursing home industry as well. Back in 1985, the country spent $34 billion on long-term care. The bill doubled in eight years, and will double again by the year 2000. Nearly a third of the Medicaid budget, which reached $150 billion in 1994, pays nursing home bills for the elderly. In 1993, Medicaid spent $9,595 for the average elderly patient, compared to only $1,444 for each poor child and $2,419 for each poor adult.

The nation's 6,500 hospitals, which house 1.2 million beds, account for 40 percent of every health care dollar. Since the middle of the twentieth century, hos-

pitals have largely enjoyed full reimbursement from government and private insurers for the services and new technologies they offered. Hospitals competed for the best doctors and the most patients by offering the latest technological advances and procedures, regardless of cost.

Beginning in the 1980s, government and private insurers pushed hospitals to reduce expensive hospital stays. In 1983, the federal government introduced Diagnosis Related Groups (DRGs), a prospective payment system affecting hospitals receiving Medicare. By notifying hospitals how much payment they would receive for a certain patient or therapy, DRGs prevented hospitals from providing unlimited care with the expectation that Medicare would pay the bill. In response, hospitals ratcheted up their patients to the highest intensity care possible, cut their costs, or shifted them to privately insured patients whose health plans lacked such limits.

Pressured by public and private insurers to eliminate unnecessary admissions, hospitals also cut the number of patients hospitalized from 36 million in 1982 to 31 million in 1992. Hospitals eliminated 182,000 beds. Hundreds of hospitals closed their doors. At the same time, patient stays in hospitals grew shorter, especially among the elderly. The average length of stay among seniors fell 18 percent from 10.1 days in 1982 to 8.3 in 1992. After leaving the hospital, many received care at home or in hospices.

Even with these changes, higher costs related in part to the use of expensive technology more than doubled the price of hospital stays from 1982 to 1992. Meanwhile, the number of outpatient visits grew by 40 percent, providing a surge of income for hospitals. Both developments helped ease the pressure to eliminate empty beds. On a typical day, only two-thirds of all beds are occupied. Hospitals have at least 250,000 more beds than the nation needs, costing more than 8 billion dollars a year to maintain.

How doctors receive payment for their services has become another focus of reform. The nation's doctors consume 20 percent of every health care dollar, but their decisions affect about 75 percent of all spending. Traditionally, doctors collected fees for the services they provided, giving them a financial incentive to provide more care than absolutely necessary. Well-insured patients, who usually paid little or none of their medical bills, had no incentive to minimize their use of the health system and little ability to second-guess their doctor's decisions.

Beginning in the 1980s, many doctors responded to concerns about costs by moving to a payment system in which they collected an annual salary, rather than individual fees for each procedure they performed. This migration was part of the shift to "managed care" in which HMOs encouraged doctors to consider costs when treating their patients, and insurance companies hired reviewers to look over the shoulders of doctors to weed out unnecessary care.

Employers, who pay more than a quarter of the nation's personal health expenditures, have nurtured many of the financing and delivery innovations that continue to redraw the face of health care in the U.S. Many employers encourage workers to use "preferred providers" who offer care at reduced prices. They push employees to negotiate doctor bills just as they would question the sticker price on a new car. They give workers incentives to use HMOs, forcing them to pay higher prices for care outside the HMO of the company's choice.

Employers also have restrained their health spending by shifting costs to employees in the form of lower wages. Many companies shed the burden of health benefits by moving cafeteria workers, janitors, and entry-level staff from full-time status to contract status without benefits, or by discontinuing coverage for full-time employees. Others increased deductibles, copayments, and employee contributions to premiums.

While these tactics have produced savings, fundamental problems—such as substance abuse and addiction, poverty, violence, and individual behaviors that adversely affect health—continue to fuel the demand for health care. In the early 1990s, legal and illegal drugs, alcohol, and tobacco were responsible for some $200 billion in health care costs annually. Half of the nation's hospital beds held victims of violence, auto and home accidents, cancer, heart disease, AIDS, tuberculosis, liver, kidney, and respiratory illnesses, all caused or exacerbated by the abuse of tobacco, alcohol, and drugs.

Much of the effort to restructure the health system has focused on the challenge of assuring universal access to care. As the twenty-first century begins, public and private leaders alike will also face the tasks of reducing waste, fraud, and abuse, emphasizing health promotion and disease prevention, providing care for the elderly that enables them to live their final years independently and in dignity, and freeing every American from the dehumanizing grip of substance abuse and addiction. An agenda of this urgency and complexity will keep health care at the center of the nation's radar screen well into the twenty-first century.

[See also Death and Dying; Entitlement Programs; Health Care; Health Care: Moral Issues; Health Care: Technological Developments; Medical Care Providers; Public Health; Social Welfare Philosophies.]

BIBLIOGRAPHY

Aaron, Henry J., and Schwartz, William B. *The Painful Prescription.* Washington, D.C.: The Brookings Institution, 1984.

Bovbjerg, Randall R.; Griffin, Charles C.; and Carroll, Caitlin E. "U.S. Health Care Coverage and Costs: Historical Development and Choices for the 1990s." *The Journal of Law, Medicine and Ethics* 21 (Summer 1993): 141–162.

Burner, Sally T.; Waldo, Daniel R.; and McKusick, David R. "National Health Expenditures Projections Through 2030." *Health Care Financing Review* 14 (Fall 1992): 1–29.

Califano, Joseph A. *Radical Surgery: What's Next for America's Health Care.* New York: Times Books, 1994.

Congressional Budget Office. *Economic Implications of Rising Health Care Costs.* Washington, DC: C.B.O., October 1992.

National Center for Health Statistics. *Health, United States, 1991.* Hyattsville, MD: Public Health Service, 1992.

Schroeder, Steven A. "A Comparison of Western European and U.S. University Hospitals; A Case Report from Leuven, West Berlin, Leiden, London, and San Francisco." *Journal of the American Medical Association* 252 (July 13, 1984): 240–246.

Starr, Paul. *The Social Transformation of American Medicine.* New York: Basic Books, 1982.

Woolhandler, Steffie, and Himmelstein, David. "The Deteriorating Efficiency of the U.S. Health Care System." *The New England Journal of Medicine* 324 (May 2, 1991): 1253–1258.

— JOSEPH A. CALIFANO

HEALTH CARE FINANCING

Public policy in health care financing has to answer three basic questions:

- Who is covered?
- What is covered?
- How is it paid for?

The U.S. federal government, and virtually every state, is working to reform health care delivery and financing systems and to establish some form of universal care covering all citizens, with a standard package of at least basic benefits. Assuming the continued goal of universal coverage, policy makers face three financing options:

1. Separating health care coverage from employment and financing it by general taxation. This option can be made much more progressive and avoids forcing employers to trade off health care benefits against job creation.

2. A totally private system that will shift financing to the individual by mandating that every citizen have health insurance. Upon examination, simply ordering people to have health insurance is an impractical alternative. The government must do more than mandate individual action because, among other reasons, many people cannot afford or will not buy health insurance privately.

3. A public/private partnership system, which is essentially the model that the United States now follows, however inadequately. Public policy makers have to decide what is covered by the public system and what

is covered by the private system. While the delivery systems vary considerably, the financing under this alternative generally provides public funding for the medically indigent, the blind, and the elderly, while the employers continue to finance employees (who usually also are required to contribute). These latter systems subsidize small employers, or allow a phase-in period.

Those who argue for health care market reform usually also limit the amount that employers can deduct for providing health insurance to the cost of a basic benefit package (thereby creating an incentive for employers to select an efficient plan), and requiring the cost of any plan more expensive than a basic benefit package to be included in the employee's income (creating an incentive for the employee to select an efficient plan). Many proposals also include a small copayment for most medical services to make patients think twice before accessing the system.

What Does the Future Hold?

Reforming one-seventh of the national economy is a gargantuan task filled with a myriad of special interest pitfalls. Many congresspersons and legislators never had to deal with the health issue and are loathe to interject themselves into a subject that has so many conflicting interests. Members of Congress who have studied the issue are split between those who want a single payor (Canadian-type) system and those who want to reform the health care market. It is hard to see these two deeply held, but inconsistent, philosophies reconciled—but it will and must happen because health care costs are growing at two and one-half times the rate of inflation and unduly interfering with other important public and private needs.

The most likely scenario will be for a national bill that will encourage a number of states to reform their systems in the interim until a more comprehensive national legislation can be instituted in 1996. The most probable form that legislation will take will be for employer mandate with a phase-in for small employers. A Canadian-type system would require shifting over $300 billion (1992 dollars) in premiums now paid by employers to new taxes. This seems unlikely, however powerful the arguments supporting it are. The least political resistance will be to build on the existing system, and the fact that over three-quarters of U.S. employers now voluntarily cover their employees (and dependents) will furnish a model that requires the least amount of new taxes and generates the least amount of political opposition. Evolution is always more likely than revolution in a democracy.

Government will cover those who are not connected to the workplace, most likely out of "sin" taxes and general revenues. Medicaid will be folded into the new system, but Medicare will initially be maintained separately because of the power of the elderly lobby. Eventually, Medicare will be eliminated and its beneficiaries will be added to the new plan.

Health care reform will not be a one-time event,

but an incremental and evolutionary process

that will likely last at least a decade.

Health care reform will not be a one-time event, but an incremental and evolutionary process which will likely last at least a decade. If employer mandate proves inefficient or does not generate the expected stability of health care costs, new reforms will be initiated. No nation can tolerate health care doubling its share of the GDP every twenty years. If market reform does not produce a high level of health care at affordable prices, government will redeploy much more blunt instruments to achieve this goal.

[See also Death and Dying; Entitlement Programs; Health Care: Moral Issues; Health Care: Technological Developments.]

BIBLIOGRAPHY

Aaron, Henry J. *Serious and Unstable Condition: Financing America's Health Care.* Washington, DC: Brookings Institute, 1991.

Califano, Joseph A., Jr. *America's Health Care Revolution.* New York: Touchstone Books, 1986.

Fuchs, Victor R. *The Health Economy.* Cambridge, MA: Harvard University Press, 1986.

— RICHARD D. LAMM

HEALTH CARE: MORAL ISSUES

Who lives, who dies, and how much public money should be spent determining the answers to these questions are moral issues that will continue to challenge our society in the twenty-first century. New knowledge will reframe these issues and confront old beliefs. Knowledge of genetics and complex systems will lead people to rethink moral choices. This new knowledge can help society distinguish practices that are based upon carelessness from those resting on deeply held beliefs.

Careless allocation of health care resources creates one of the future moral issues likely to be reshaped by new knowledge. Early in the twenty-first century, the map of the human genome will be largely filled in and many genes will be fully sequenced. Geneticists will provide far better predictions about the potential for long life, early sickness, or susceptibility to specific environmental exposures. These predictions will both illuminate and trouble the decisions of individuals and organized health care providers who determine the allocation of health care dollars. It is hard to stop trying to save a life, even when realistically the effort holds little help. Although genetic information will be incomplete and probabilistic, it is still likely to be used to ration such care. Rationing of care in the mid-1990s is less informed and will likely be seen to be morally repugnant. Enormous expenditures are made on futile, heroic measures to stave off death for short periods during which people are incapacitated. The ability to more accurately predict probable deaths through molecular genetics will help society confront the moral question about who receives expensive treatments and who does not.

Social values are visible in both cases where health care dollars are spent and where they are not. As we create better models, using concepts from the growing field of evolutionary systems (sometimes called complexity, dynamic systems, or chaos theory) and supercomputers to perform massive computations, the economics of the health care system will be better understood. More people will see what society buys with its health care dollars and what it fails to buy. Fewer allocation decisions in the future will profit from the ignorance of true costs and social benefits than is the case in today's world.

The money spent on children, for example, exemplifies the high value placed on technological intervention and the low value placed on community health. Neonatal intensive care units (NICUs) have grown capable of saving premature babies who would die without the use of expensive technology. Months after these low-birthweight babies leave the NICUs, however, studies show a high proportion are plagued with problems that lead to early death or severe impairments. Many may go to homes or institutions to suffer horrible childhoods with little community support. Knowledge of long-term (more than a year) outcomes of saving premature infants at the edge of viability is incomplete. Our fragmented information system fails to keep track of most health care results over time.

Answers dealing with these vexing problems will likely not resolve fully the questions raised. Compelling studies do show, however, that dollars spent to foster healthy communities can create higher-quality life, particularly for children in poverty. Looked at from a systems perspective, health care allocations show a kind of carelessness about children, a fact that is mirrored by society's poverty rates for children, educational failures, and divorces. The allocation of health care resources tends to go to the extremes—the end of life and the beginning of life—which has been described as "the zone of medical futility." If those resources were spent to create healthy environments that support the maximum capacity of individuals within a community, health care would be very different. Expenditures would go to prevent problems that are currently treated, and children, in particular, would receive more care.

Hopeful forecasts anticipate that values will shift in our society as idealistic baby boomers mature into a generation that makes the care of children more important. Already the first baby-boom president and his wife represent a hope for rekindled commitment to America's children. They began the health-care reform debate with childhood vaccination. While this debate appears to be stalled, or even failed, it is likely to be simply the beginning of another reform era that will reflect the ascending leadership of the baby-boom generation. As the debate moves to the Medicare program, which represents the many dollars spent on the burden of illness borne by the elderly, the hope remains that a new selflessness might arise in our society.

When health care reform is marked by selflessness instead of selfishness, the debate can move from illness to health. When institutions and individuals throughout the nation answer the call to idealism, the commitment shifts to creating healthy people in healthy communities. Then the use of resources changes. Children who have a hope for a better life will receive more care. Those likely to die may receive more humane care that does not sap dollars that can be better used to support health. These resource issues are ultimately moral issues. The first century will see a healthy society and a caring society only if the moral issues are embraced during the era of reform that lies ahead.

[See also Abortion; Bioethics; Death and Dying; Disabled Persons' Rights; Epidemics; Family Planning; Genetic Technologies; Health Care; Health Care: Technological Developments; Sexual Reproduction: Artificial Means.]

BIBLIOGRAPHY

Biemesderfer, Susan C. *Healthy Babies: State Initiatives for Pregnant Women at Risk.* Denver, CO: National Conference of State Legislators, 1993.

Hurowitz, James C. "Toward a Social Policy for Health." *New England Journal of Medicine* 329/2 (July 8, 1993): 130–133.

Kimbrell, Andrew. *The Human Body Shop: The Engineering and Marketing of Life.* San Francisco, CA: Harper Collins, 1993.

"Your Final 30 Days—Free: Let's Ban Doctor and Hospital Bills for Futile Care of the Dying." *Washington Post,* May 2, 1993.

– JONATHAN PECK

HEALTH CARE PROVIDERS.

See DENTISTRY; MEDICAL CARE PROVIDERS; MENTAL HEALTH; NURSING; PSYCHIATRY.

HEALTH CARE: TECHNOLOGICAL DEVELOPMENTS

Human health services stand at the threshold of a new revolution. The process of creating health care breakthroughs is accelerating and producing revolutionary consequences for medicine in the next century.

Early in the century the primary cause of death and disability was disease organisms. Due to advances in medicine and public health (including waste disposal and sanitation systems), many infectious diseases have been eliminated or reduced. But new ones have been added, such as AIDS and environmental risks posed by toxic substances. One by one, disfiguring and disabling

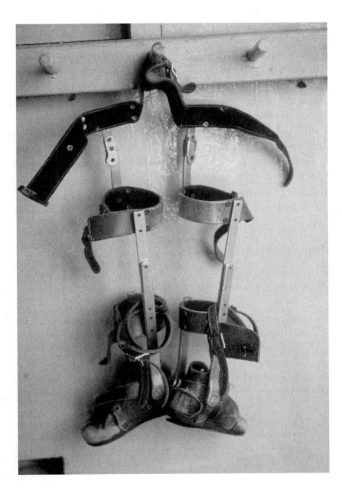

These leg braces at an orphanage for polio victims attest to a major medical triumph of the 1990s: the eradication of the polio virus through vaccination. (Steve Raymer/Corbis)

childhood diseases have succumbed to breakthroughs in medical science. Rubella, mumps, and measles have been almost relegated to history books in the aftermath of vaccinations. Next, medical advances could eliminate cancer and heart disease as the main killers and bring vaccines for other diseases—genital herpes, flu, AIDS, and so forth.

Now the health issues have been redefined to include those matters once considered social problems: drunkenness, smoking, chemical dependency, environmental concerns, workplace management matters, and so on. In developed countries today worries about the drunken driver have replaced worries about Typhoid Mary. Concerns about the outpouring of noxious vapors from automobiles and factories have replaced concerns about microbes in drinking water (which, before sanitation systems, killed millions yearly). Tobacco smoke now is the major destroyer of our lungs, not tuberculosis. Up to age forty in the U.S., auto accidents are the major killer. After age forty, the biggest health problem and killer of humans is attributable to smoking. Auto accidents kill about 40,000 Americans per year, whereas smoking has been traced to cause over 300,000 deaths per year. Our own actions or inactions relative to our lifestyle decisions have become the chief causes of disability and death. High-tech medical R&D is beginning to attack such "health" problems.

Lengthening Life

Developing trends create forces-of-change that weave the fabric of the future—this is especially true in the medical field as it relates to the elderly. Because we are learning more about how to initiate and implement change, we are beginning to realize that the future is coming more under our control. Certainly, death is predictable from the viewpoint of the knowledge that all of us will die sometime, as we have in the past. So far we can only predict the event but not the date—will it always be thus?

Throughout human history, life expectancy has been increasing. Back in the Stone Age, the average life expectancy was about eighteen years. By the year 1900 Americans had an average life expectancy of slightly over forty years of age. Today, in the U.S., the average life expectancy is approaching age eighty. Will this trend continue? Recent research indicates that our life span can be significantly increased.

The next question for each of us is, can we expect to live to be more than one hundred years old? Or, when can we expect to live two hundred years or more? Obviously, living longer is desirable only if we can live more years of calendar time to reach a physical age of considerably fewer years—for example, to take 150 years of calendar time to reach a physical age of sixty. With recent advances in our knowledge of why and how we age, resulting from genetic and computer studies, many scientists are now optimistic that such agendas for the future are now opening to the human race.

Now, with the new high technology of computers and recombinant-DNA genetics, scientists see pathways into the future for moving the end-point of death farther out. This process is known as lifespan-extending. Thus, scientists and futurists, finding life expectancy too difficult to predict, invent ways to prolong life and thus bypass the need to predict death!

The process of creating health care breakthroughs is accelerating and producing revolutionary consequences for medicine in the next century.

Living longer shifts major diseases and health concerns from youth to the elderly. Average life expectancy at the turn of the century in the U.S. was somewhat over four decades; now it is nearly eight decades. Research points toward another doubling in the next century with humans living to 150 years of age. Beyond this, farther advances are not possible without genetic intervention. Knowledge gained from genetic mapping suggests that there is no genetically programmed upper limit to life! Of course, longer life spans equate to a growth of trips to hospitals—ever more, the older we get.

Gene Technology

The genetic revolution portends a bigger breakthrough than any previous one in human history. New knowledge of the human gene, advances in genetic engineering will drive health care advances and preempt trial-and-error evolution by nature.

Modifying defective genes by replacing or augmenting them with nucleotide sequences of predeterminable specificity and design stand in the offing. The power to intervene genetically, to edit and redesign humans, is awesome.

Prenatal life is already open to genetic scrutiny. Prognostic genetic screening of adults, children, and embryos is becoming ever more routine and prevalent. Gene therapies for correcting congenital disorders, proven in animal models, is poised for application soon in humans—even to grow new limbs and other organs. We are already modifying germ lines of livestock and plants—soon such procedures could become commonplace even for humans. Soon we will be re-engineering

immune systems. It is inevitable that somatic cell gene therapy will be eventually adapted to the treatment of diseases and enhancements of the central nervous system—the last frontier or the beginning of a new frontier, depending on one's point of view of molecular genetics.

DNA/RNA intervention technology has augmented the power of medical diagnostics several orders of magnitude, especially through monoclonal antibody re-engineering. This same technology has made somatic gene therapy a reality. In the future it may be possible to piggyback specific genetic materials aboard "tame" viruses that could be sprayed over large areas to eliminate an oncoming flu outbreak or to "cure" plant disease.

Molecular medicine raises ethical issues and challenges for coping with inherited disorders, programs for genetic screening, genetic counseling, radical modification of humans, and power to enhance (accelerate) human evolution. These awesome new powers require societal and political guidance.

Computers, previously used for paperwork, administration, patient record keeping and accounting, and intensive care monitoring, are moving into the diagnostic arena and toward doctor/nurse/patient cognitive skill amplifiers. Artificial intelligence (AI) or applied intelligence amasses expert knowledge for syndication by others. Imagine a future in which all health care knowledge is available to everyone, in an understandable and usable form, in the real-time of need and continually updated as new knowledge is developed! This will first be used by health professionals to amplify their practice, and may be mandated by law to assure use of the best available skills.

Hospitals of the Future

Computers will further automate the hospital and health care. Some trends and issues involved are:

- Intelligent (AI [Artificial Intelligence] expert knowledge-based) health machines—X-rays, CAT and NMR scanners, intensive care units, beds, patient/doctor/nurse/lab technician amplifiers.
- Computer-automated operations and the OR (operating room).
- Self-cleaning/deodorizing rooms, ORs, labs, floors, clothes, and so on.
- Super-cleaning and perpetually sterile instruments—e.g., using a new form of Teflon so slick that even bacteria cannot adhere to it.
- Soft systems (machines, walls, floors) with computerized sensors/detectors and actuators/controllers to prevent hard falls, slips, and damage to limitedly ambulatory patients.
- Totally automated record keeping—without clerks.
- A move away from "pill hill hospitals," toward preventive-medicine practice—e.g., computerized collision-avoidance equipment in automobiles to prevent auto accidents and thus largely eliminate the need for hospitals to patch up people after accidents. A paradigm change is forecast for the

medical field and hospital research toward the microminiaturization of hospitals via computer technology, which may prevent or lessen the need to go to the hospital.

- Hospitals becoming more like networks, regional specialists, consortia; health centers with distributed and remote health-delivery nodes, and the like—i.e., a new form of high-tech hospital.

Computers in Medicine

New health/medical opportunities are resulting from the continued speedup of computer technology advances:

- Speech recognition and reply—talk, listen, and dialogue-producing medical hardware and systems—resulting in next-generation, "user-friendly" systems.
- Intelligent expert-knowledge-based systems—medical tools and instruments that permit health professionals to have access to the total knowledge of their special area to apply for personal, professional, embedded amplification in the real-time of their need.

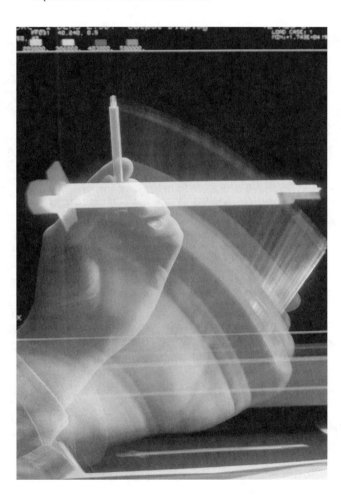

Technicians using computer imaging to design a syringe accelerate patient benefits. Medical record preparation will become more efficient with spoken word data entry. (Bob Krist/Corbis)

- Computers and AI (Artificial Intelligence) embedded in all manner of medical equipment—"smart" and "intelligent" medical high-tech devices.
- Health computers—eventually worn as part of one's attire.
- Sense environment and take-initiative health systems—health-wellness sensors and controllers.
- Health high-tech microsensors—future "source-date collection automation" devices for automating the sensing and recording of health data.
- Convivial and congenial computers—smart and intelligent health machines that are nice, friendly, easy to use, aware, and so on.

Health Professionals/Practitioners Impacts

- High-tech capabilities that "de-skill" the medical professions—impacting on doctors, nurses, and other health professionals, resulting from future, deeper penetration of PCs (personal computers) and AI (Artificial Intelligence).
- Doctors and other health professionals turning more toward research rather than being a prime factor in the delivery of health services
- Reduction of hospital, nurses, and health-services paperwork.
- Upturn of emergency medicine/doctors—as other areas are "de-skilled" and/or automated.
- Expertise of doctors contained in knowledge-based expert systems, allowing growth of the vocation of health technicians—and eventually allowing the average person/patient to perform health care functions at the same level of expertise, or above, of today's doctor or medical practitioner.

Patient Impacts

The real winner in the accelerating advances of computers and medical technology is the future patient, who would benefit from developments such as these:

- Patient becomes more of a health consumer and/or client.
- New patient rights achieved.
- Patient as a habitual seeker of second and third opinions—often using computers or knowledge-based expert systems.
- Patient shopping around to get "best" (cost and expertise) health deal—often via computer—without a reduction in the level of care.
- Patient being better informed to the "expert" level, allowing for self-help scenarios and getting away from being administered to by a health professional/practitioner.
- On-line health utility services remotely available and deliverable to patient—via high-tech medical/health information utility services or computer networks.
- Longer life with a higher quality of health.

The roles of doctors and nurses also are in transition. The nature of the doctor-patient interaction is changing from the family general practitioner toward clinical settings. Doctors are better trained and more specialized. Hospitals and doctors have more high-tech instruments for diagnosis, the operating room, intensive care, and health care/medical administration. Currently, the medical field is under siege, beset with paperwork, requirements for tests to avoid malpractice claims, and a public and politicians screaming for lower costs. Physicians are delivering more cognitive services and fewer procedural services, which increasingly are being performed by nurses and technicians. Machines are becoming more automated, making the health technician's job easier, but also more cognitive. One possible future is a "post-physician" or computer-delivered health care era wherein health technicians, paraprofessionals, and "health care robots" deliver health services while doctors work more to advance the medical state-of-the-art.

Genetic engineering spawns

new forms of medical diagnostics,

new roles for health care professionals and hospitals,

new "cures," and now, new life-forms.

Information technology has recently entered a new era of end-user computing, user-friendly systems, networked personal computing, information centers/utilities, office automation, expert systems, health management systems, and much more. Trends allow medical practitioners to more easily apply advanced technology to amplify what they can do. As a result, a new medical computer technology revolution definitely seems to be in the making that will greatly reduce the paperwork of health professionals (especially supervising nurses), allowing them more time to deal with each patient's health/medical problem.

Nanotechnology

Breakthroughs portending even greater impact on health care and society than molecular cell biology or AI involve nanotechnology. Nanotechnology can use the same DNA/RNA mechanisms in living systems to grow all manner of biological, chemical, and physical things. In this future, which has already begun, the production of things is replaced by the means to grow them—including everything from body parts to new species. Nanotechnology, in the eyes of many researchers and futurists, may become the biggest breakthrough in history.

Feats of genetic engineering spawn new forms of medical diagnostics, new therapies, new roles for health care professionals and hospitals, new "cures," and now, new life-forms—and new futures. It is hardly deniable that the fruits of scientific discovery color our perception of the world and increase our odds for a healthier life.

Health Care Costs

To reiterate, as we learn more about how to keep people healthier, younger, and living longer, it obviously should cost more to do so. That is, as we continue to evolve a better medical and health science, the percentage of GNP spent on health care must go up. This truism is perhaps the hardest trend challenge for the future that politicians will increasingly need to deal with and resolve. The current push to lower the costs of health care will speed high technology into the health care field to raise the productivity of hospitals, professionals/people, energy, and so on, and to:

- Expand the role of health centers and HMOs.
- Advance computer technology for microminiaturizing expensive health care machinery and to reduce the cost of such machinery in the future.
- Develop medical technology to raise the productivity of the health care industry—e.g., using NMR and CAT scanners to eliminate the need for exploratory operations.
- Encourage more cooperative sharing between hospitals linked via computer networks, especially initial costly medical high technology.

Medical/health care technology, rather than a villain, is a lifesaver as well as a long-term cost reducer. Noninvasive imaging technology, for example, often eliminates the need for more expensive exploratory operations. Computers reduce paperwork and administrative costs. Technology used for early diagnoses and prevention radically reduces mortality and medical costs. Computers will be used to lower the cost of health care services, thereby increasing availability, especially for persons of limited means.

Demanding health as an entitlement means that more medical technology will be required. Society in the future will not opt for lesser health care than made possible by the health knowledge available to it, at least not for long.

With an accelerating growth of knowledge about human health and the means for improving it, high medical advances, especially with future molecular genetics, nanotechnology, computers, and AI (Artificial Intelligence), there should be little doubt of the future direction of health care and health delivery. For each of us, it means a higher health-quality-of-life.

[See also Aging of the Population; Artificial Life; Bioethics; Death and Dying; Genetic Engineering; Genetic Technologies; Health Care; Health Care: Alternative Therapies; Health Care Costs; Health Care: Moral Issues; High Technology; Longevity; Medical Care Providers; Nanotechnology; Nutrition; Pharmaceuticals; Sexual Reproduction: Artificial Means.]

BIBLIOGRAPHY

Bunton, Robin, and Macdonald, Gordon, eds. *Health Promotion: Disciplines and Diversity.* London and New York: Routledge, 1992.

Emmeche, Claus. *The Garden in the Machine: The Emerging Science of Artificial Life*. Princeton, NJ: Princeton University Press, 1994.

Foote, Susan B. *Managing the Medical Arms Race: Public Policy and Medical Devices*. Berkeley, CA: University of California Press, 1992.

Fuchs, Victor R. *The Future of Health Policy*. Cambridge, MA: Harvard University Press, 1993.

Hubbard, Ruth and Wald, Elijah. *Exploding the Gene Myth: How Genetic Information Is Produced and Manipulated by Scientists, Insurance Companies, Educators and Law Enforcers*. Boston, MA: Beacon Press, 1993.

Kimbrell, Andrew. *The Human Body Shop: The Engineering and Marketing of Life*. San Francisco, CA: Harper San Francisco, 1993.

Lafaille, Robert, and Fulder, Stephen, eds. *Towards a New Science of Health*. London and New York: Routledge, 1993.

Larue, Gerald A. and Bayly, Rich. *Long-Term Care in an Aging Society: Choices and Challenges for the '90s*. Buffalo, NY. Prometheus Books, 1992.

— EARL C. JOSEPH

HIGHER EDUCATION

The evolution of higher education has seen several major periods of development. As American higher education is poised for a similar major readjustment, elements of past periods are still evidenced in its basic values structure and will play a part in how higher education evolves to about the year 2015. Originally, higher education was a personal relationship between teachers and students. The students studied with only a few scholars and paid for their education after the class was over, according to their feeling of the worth of the class. If the scholars felt mistreated by the town, they would move to another town, taking their students with them. Colleges were gradually formed as an administrative conveyance primarily to provide better facilities. In the Middle Ages, the primary source of an advanced education was provided through the most educated profession: the clergy. Because of the near monopoly that the church had on education, there developed the concept of separation and isolation of higher education from the secular and political world. The college as an intellectual sanctuary comes directly from the role that churches played as a spiritual sanctuary.

The Evolution of Higher Education in America

The first college in America was Harvard, founded in 1636. For the first two hundred years the American college was modeled after the English college, where faculty and students lived and learned together. The primary goal was to form the "whole" student based on a classical and spiritual education. In the mid-1800s the German university concept, with its emphasis on graduate research and intellectual and spiritual separation between faculty and students, appeared at the same time

that there was a general discontent with the English/classical model. This discontent resulted in the passage of the Morrill Act of 1862, which established the land-grant, state-supported universities that were charged to focus on agriculture, mechanical subjects, and the applied arts. In the 1950s there was an increased demand for postsecondary education training that was less than the traditional four-year college. This lead to the development of the comprehensive two-year community college. The creation of the land-grant public college system and the community college led to the establishment of a fundamental value that all citizens who are intellectually qualified for college should be able to attend regardless of income.

Thus the characteristics and values of the independent faculty entrepreneur, intellectually separate from the community; religious and sectarian control; private and public support; and classical and applied education could be found throughout American higher education. Each institution was distinctively different from the other. However, prior to the 1960s, what was common to all was that they were small in size because the majority of Americans did not feel that higher education was very important to their success. In the 1930s fewer than 5 percent of Americans had any post-high school education. In the 1990s more than 50 percent of the population have had some post-high school education, and nearly 25 percent of the population have a baccalaureate degree. Although higher education has grown from fewer than one million students in the 1930s to more than twelve million students in the 1990s, the basic academic values and governance structure have remained essentially the same.

Why higher education is poised for a major change to the year 2015 is due to three converging forces of increased accountability. The first force is the realization that higher education is too important to the economy and social structure of our society to allow it to remain basically unaccountable for the quality of its outputs (i.e., the educational quality of its students, the relevance of the research being performed by its faculty, and the amount of public service provided to society). The second force for greater accountability is due to a decrease in the amount of available funds from all sectors—personal, corporate, and public—to support higher education. Having citizens graduate from college is no longer enough; how well they are educated is also important. The third force comes from an evolution in the management of businesses. Starting in Japan after World War II and spreading in the 1970s and '80s to the United States and Europe, the concept of managing through carefully defining results, relating accomplishment of these results to refining the systems or interrelations within the organization, and giving decision-making authority to the people at the lowest possible level became the dominate management paradigm. Thus the future of American higher education will be shaped by these three external changes: a public's unwillingness to allow higher education institutions total autonomy because they have become too important to the individual and society; restricting resources that demand greater efficiencies; and new management concepts that will allow for responsible academic independence while providing for accountability to the various publics.

Demographics

Until the year 2005 there will be an increase of 20 percent in the traditional group—eighteen to twenty-four years old—that attends college. This increase in potential college students will be reflected in the enrollments shown in Table 1.

The expenditure for higher education over this same period of time will increase from $171.1 billion (1993–1994) to $229.4 billion (2004–2005). This projection represents an average annual increase of 3.4 percent. At the same time, support from state and federal sources are projected to remain stable at best, and some projections indicate dramatic decreases. As of the mid 1990s the cost of going to a public institution is approximately 15 percent of the disposable income for middle-income families; for a private education this figure is closer to 35 percent. If current trends continue, the differences in cost between public and private institutions will become even greater, resulting in more students applying to public institutions.

Pressures for Change

Keeping the expenditures and cost of college in mind, the changing enrollment figures indicate several sources of conflict for higher education. During the 1980s, when the number of traditional college-age students was decreasing, institutions developed new but more costly programs that attracted older students, minorities, and

TABLE 1

HIGHER EDUCATION (NUMBERS IN THOUSANDS)

Enrollments	1982–1983	1993–1994 (estimate)	2004–2005 (projected)	Percent Change 1982–1983 to 1993–1994	Percent Change 1993–1994 to 2004–2005
Total	12,426	14,762	15,976	19	8
Control of institution					
Public	9,696	11,569	12,529	19	8
Private	2,730	3,193	3,447	17	8
Type of institution					
4-year	7,654	9,073	9,818	19	8
2-year	4,772	5,689	6,158	19	8
Sex of student					
Women	6,394	8,119	8,745	27	9
Men	6,031	6,643	7,231	10	8
Age					
19 yrs. and under	2,959	2,861	3,501	−3	22
20–21 yrs. old	2,539	2,762	3,108	9	13
22–24 yrs. old	2,081	2,596	2,798	25	8
25–29 yrs. old	1,995	2,091	1,915	5	−8
30–34 yrs. old	1,263	1,538	1,406	22	−9
35 yrs. or over	1,589	2,915	3,248	83	11
Attendance Status					
Full-time	7,221	8,220	9,053	14	10
Part-time	5,205	6,542	6,923	26	6
Level					
Undergraduate	10,825	12,686	13,969	17	10
Graduate	1,322	1,774	1,810	34	2
First professional	278	302	295	34	−2
Full-time equivalent	9,092	10,579	11,548	16	9

Source: National Center for Educational Statistics, *Projections of Education Statistics to 2005*. Washington, DC: U.S. Department of Education, 1995.

students with learning or physical disabilities. With an increase in enrollment of the more traditional students, colleges will feel pressure to lower costs by eliminating these more costly programs that are serving people with disadvantages.

The pressure for demonstrating greater education outcomes will come from the increasing number of students who are thirty-five years or over. A majority of these students will not be entering college for the first time but will be returning to college through employer-assisted tuition programs to develop additional job skills. Both the students and the employers will be insisting that colleges demonstrate that the education offered is relevant to their needs.

Changing Accountability—Changing Learning—Changing Management

The changing demographic and continued financial pressures will foster a demand for greater accountability for higher education institutions to demonstrate that what they are doing is worth the investment of time and resources. The adversarial tension that these demands for accountability generated in the 1980s and early '90s will change to a greater sense of partnership. This change will first be promoted by a need for institutions to gain financial support from the business and foundation sectors to supplement loss of support from the public sector.

A second reason will be the rapid expansion of knowledge that will occur in many fields, especially in areas such as computers, genetics, and health. This expansion of knowledge will be faster than most colleges can keep up with under traditional ways of educating faculty and having them keep abreast of their field by taking sabbaticals every seven years. Instead, there will be a need for greater sharing of technology, equipment, and experiences. The process to do this will be developed through cooperative agreements with business and industry.

A third pressure for better assessment of the teaching-learning process will come from within the institutions, with faculty and administrative leaders developing a link between the values of education and the usefulness of using purpose or outcome-driven teaching and management problem-solving techniques. Learning these techniques will be encouraged through grant programs sponsored by corporations using the same techniques, state and federal quality award programs, and college reputational ranking surveys that will begin to assess institutions by how well they can document their educational practices.

The end result will be an integration of all parties that play a role and receive a benefit from higher education. This integration will take the form of establish-ing outcome expectations for the education process, greater awareness of the teaching-learning process, and a more continuous flow of faculty in and out of non-collegiate settings.

Curriculum

For the curriculum the changes will be significant. Historically the primary teaching method has been lecturing. At first this style was used to transfer basic knowledge because of the scarcity of books; later this style was used to integrate knowledge from a variety of sources. However, with the development of the electronic transfer of information, such as computer networks, CD-ROM discs, and videotapes, much of which has been combined into one source, the lecture style no longer will be acceptable. A second pressure to move away from the passive lecture style to a more active faculty-to-student and student-to-student style of learning involve the findings of education research that have developed considerable evidence on the effectiveness of other teaching styles as well as the necessity to accommodate different individual learning styles.

With the development of the electronic transfer of information, such as computer networks, CD-ROM discs, and videotapes, the lecture style no longer will be acceptable.

The pressure for changing teaching styles will be heightened by both the development of new knowledge bases and areas of study and rapid changes in the delivery of education through electronic transfer of data. Specialty academic programs never conceived of in the 1960s will emerge at the turn of the century. Courses dealing with new health fields involving genetics, new technology systems, or new areas of study such as dealing with social discontent, will emerge. Advances in computer, video, and audio technology will allow for greater distant interaction between the professor and the student. CD-ROM and holographic projections will allow an interconnectivity that will make education available regardless of geography and time.

Since the publication of *Scholarship Reconsidered: Priorities of the Professoriate* (Boyer, 1991) there has been a debate concerning what activities should be considered appropriate scholarship for faculty. For most of the twentieth century, original research, published in refereed journals and presented at national conferences, was considered the only legitimate form of scholarship. This was a process approach to scholarship. As an outcome approach—creating, discovering, or combining knowledge that expands the knowledge base—becomes more acceptable, then different forms of scholarship will become more recognized. This new scholarship would include the creation of new computer programs, excelling in the performing arts, or teaching. One of the discoveries concerning the judging of scholarship is the recognition that what is considered scholarship is partly a product of a process: The product is often the result of collaborative efforts, the end product is documented well enough so it can be replicated by others, it appears in a form than can be observed and judged, two or more colleagues make a judgment on its contribution to the knowledge base, and others build on it to create new knowledge. These elements of collaboration, visibility, and documentation will be taken into other areas of higher education, especially teaching, to create a more open, valued, and respected part of higher education.

Class Society Based on Levels of Education

Increasingly there is concern over the possibility of the United States developing a class society based on levels of education. One of the consequences of evolving into a postindustrial society with an information and service industry base is the elimination of many middle management positions. This will create a bimodal job force of lower-paid service workers and a much smaller number in a highly educated professional, technical, and managerial class. With a decrease in the availability of student aid, which will provide both access to a higher education and the ability to select the best possible institution, regardless of cost, there will be an increasing gap of haves and have-nots based on education.

During times of prosperity this gap will not be noticeable, but by the year 2005, as the number of workers decreases in relation to nonworkers (primarily retired individuals), the economy will begin to feel the strain. In the 1990s the unemployment rate for a person with a college degree was 2.9 per-cent, while for a person without a high school diploma the unemployment rate was 13.5 percent. Combining this aspect with the decline or lower levels of participation of male African Americans and Hispanics in higher education, the likelihood of increased social discontent based on the availability of a higher education is very high. As this becomes more apparent, both government and industry will take steps to build a more equitable system that minimizes financial barriers to attend college and accepts the reality that in a nation of great diversity, the educational system must also be diverse at all levels to provide opportunities for all.

As outcome-driven decisions become the common method of problem-solving, only the quality of the final education outcome will be important; all other parts of higher education will be subject to being questioned and changed. This will be the true revolution of higher education.

[See also Adult Learning; Education Technologies; Elementary and Secondary Education.]

BIBLIOGRAPHY

Boyer, E. L. *Scholarship Reconsidered: Priorities of the Professoriate.* Princeton, NJ: Princeton University Press, 1991.

Caffee, Ellen Earle, and Sherr, Lawrence A. *Quality: Transforming Postsecondary Education.* Washington, DC: George Washington University Graduate School of Education and Human Development, 1992.

National Center for Educational Statistics. *Projections of Education Statistics to 2005.* Washington, DC: U.S. Department of Education, 1995.

Sims, Ronald R.; and Sims, Serbrenia J., eds. *Managing Institutions of Higher Education into the 21st Century: Issues and Implications.* Westport, CT: Greenwood Press, 1991.

— JONATHAN D. FIFE

HIGH TECHNOLOGY

Technology is moving so fast today that it carries its own warning: keep up, retrain, or drop out. Technology is changing not only the rules but the game itself. As change accelerates, it is not impossible that the bulk of all the goods and services that humans will be interacting with by the start of the third millennium have not yet been developed. This acceleration will make many things obsolete within the next decade. Traditional approaches will be left in the dust.

The turn of the millennium could be termed the end of the age of credentialism. The prime requisites for the employment of tomorrow are going to be attitude and aptitude. People with the right attitude and aptitude can be trained for anything—and rapidly. Many conventional paths to learning will no longer exist or will become unrecognizable in the future. Those who expect to survive on past talents and beliefs will fare badly.

New opportunities will continue to open in fields now unknown or only vaguely seen. Technology is no longer limited to the manipulation of the inorganic. Organic fields beckon. Biotechnology will allow the creation of new life-forms that in time may more than replace the species disappearing due to a changing planetary environment.

Biohackers—young, probably undisciplined minds who, for various reasons, do not find a suitable mode to enter exciting fields of science and technology—will create their own laboratories. They will use equipment and techniques not unlike those used by young, 1970s computer geeks who created in a garage what highly trained and conformist computer scientists were unable to accomplish in multimillion-dollar institutions. The origin of the Apple Computer Company is one such example.

The spectrum of life-forms that can be created

with biogenetics may be totally open-ended.

Many such new life-forms will be chimeras—living organisms containing tissues of varied genetic structure. Previously forbidden boundaries already have been crossed with transmission into a tobacco plant of the gene that causes the glow in a firefly. Such experiments suggest that many unthinkable things are possible. The spectrum of life-forms that can be created with biogenetics may be totally open-ended and have no end.

Totally new forms of entertainment, created especially for the home, will appear quickly and dramatically. Virtual reality (VR), the result of a computer designing a real world or other worlds that could not exist under natural laws yet which viewers can enter, will change humans more than the automobile has. VR will become the preferred mode of training for most fields. It will, for example, enable an eighty-five-year-old bedridden grandmother to get together with her grandson and go skydiving or scuba diving. VR will provide emotional as well as visual and aural experiences. People will become participants, not passive spectators. VR will revolutionize show business as we know it.

Coupled with ground-linked, global fiber-optic networks, satellite transmissions—a concept introduced to the world by visionary author and scientist Arthur C. Clarke in 1945 before anyone but astronomers thought a satellite was anything but our moon—will radically transform our lives. They will bring unlimited knowledge to anyone with the right attitude and aptitude. The continuing technological advance of relatively inexpensive equipment for use in the home will pave the way for previously unimaginable New Age breakthroughs.

Medical technology, which has doubled lifespans in technologically advanced societies since the agricultural age, will make astounding forward strides. Such advances will ultimately allow some humans to "grow" themselves back to health.

Technology that can convert once harmful pollution into viable and valuable new compounds or easily detoxify hazardous ones will shortly spring forth from Japan and other locations. Developments could make former sterile lands productive and reduce toxic substances in the atmosphere. Conversion of seawater into potable water is already possible, though at prices somewhat above present usual water costs, in some arid areas. At the same time, and possibly built into desalination plants, converters will produce hydrogen for powering the nonpolluting vehicles of tomorrow.

The development of efficient modes of transportation on land, sea, and in the air may be accomplished in months compared with what required years previously. The development and application of super and paralleled computers will vastly accelerate and bring forth vehicles previously unimaginable. Newly developed transport systems should perform flawlessly during their first demonstrations. They will have been repeatedly tested and improved and tested again on computers before being introduced to the public.

Technology will invade home and workplace as ceramics, new materials, and innovative techniques penetrate and replace traditional building construction. "Smart" materials that can transform the shape of airplane wings or ship hulls as they respond to changing conditions will spread to buildings and bridges, making them more malleable and responsive to forces acting on them.

Such developments will come from the five billion minds now on the planet. Working more and more with emerging computer technologies, enhanced by optical and crystal storage units such as SERODS (Surface Enhanced Optical Data Storage) capable of storing on one twelve-inch disc all the information contained in an entire large university library. Information will be accessible from anywhere in the world at costs lower than what you now put in a parking meter in front of present libraries. The possibilities are limitless.

[See also Change, Pace of; Clarke, Arthur Charles; Genetic Technologies; Interactive Entertainment; Medica Lab; Satellite Communications; Space Satellites; Technological Change.]

BIBLIOGRAPHY

Brand, Stewart. *The Media Lab: Inventing the Future at M.I.T.* New York: Penguin, 1988.
Coghlan, Andy. "Smart Ways to Treat Materials." *New Scientist* (July 4, 1992).
Ogden, Frank. *Dr. Tomorrow's Lessons from the Future.* Bellingham, WA: 21st Century Media Communications, 1992.
Rheingold, Howard. *Virtual Reality.* New York: Summit Books/Simon and Schuster, 1992.

— FRANK OGDEN

HOLISTIC BELIEFS

From 1970 on there have been many indications of a shift toward a more holistic view in health, ecology, education, management, the feminist movement, and so on. Among the factors promoting such a shift were dissatisfactions with conventional medicine, consequences of the fragmentation of knowledge, perceived failures of education based on such a fragmentary view, reaction of feminists to the nonholistic features of patriarchal society, environmental mishaps resulting from the failure to take a holistic view of ecological systems, and a rising appreciation of the holistic worldview of the world's indigenous peoples.

Such a shift in worldview has the most profound implications for prevailing values in a society. Values can be thought of as particular kinds of beliefs—namely, beliefs about the desirability of something. Viewed in that way, a person's values are part of the total belief structure, some parts of which are relatively superficial and easily changed, while other parts are partly or largely unconsciously held and relatively resistant to change. For example, some value changes are matters of fluctuating fashion or taste; others may be variations in the way a deeper-level value or belief is expressed (as, for instance, in the shift from emphasis on outer to inner indicators for validating one's feeling of self-esteem). The most powerful values are derived from the deepest, core beliefs—about individual identity, the nature of the universe, the role of the self in the total environment, and a sense of what is most important. For example, values in modern society with regard to nature, other living creatures, and the land are very different from those in Native American culture with a more holistic worldview.

Thus, although changes in value emphases are taking place in society all the time, and superficial value changes may be influenced by fashion, education, or advertising, major and persistent shifts tend to be associated with changes in the collectively held worldview.

As the findings of modern science made increasing impact on society, the power of the religious foundations of values decreased, with the result that by mid-century little value consensus remained. This general confusion about values was a consequence of the fact that modern society was attempting to operate from two different and contradictory worldviews—one scientific-economic, the other humanistic-spiritual. The tension brought about by this situation resulted in continued attempts to reconcile science and spirituality. These only began to appear successful in the 1990s, due to two important developments.

One of these developments was in comparative religion. Essentially, it was the discovery that diverse as the exoteric or public forms of the world's religious traditions may be, their esoteric, inner-circle forms—which typically are more experiential, involving some kind of meditative discipline—are quite compatible with one another. This common core of the world's

spiritual traditions has been termed the "perennial wisdom."

The other development, reassessment of the suitability of positivistic, reductionistic science to provide a complete and adequate societal worldview, has been gaining strength since the 1960s. One form of the reassessment, which we shall examine below, challenges the fitness of the metaphysical foundations of modern science.

Basic to the contemplative traditions

is the proposition that human beings

have a higher spiritual nature;

each is part of, and in touch with, the Whole.

The Western industrial, "modern" paradigm amounted to a shift from the more holistic medieval paradigm to one more characterized by separateness. This is exemplified in politics by the emphasis on individual rights; in economics by emphasis on competition; in science by the ontological assumption that ultimate reality is "fundamental particles." By the early 1990s there were multifold indications of a shift away from the reductionistic, positivistic paradigm of mid-twentieth-century science, toward a more holistic paradigm, with more attention to subjective experience as allowable data, and with a more participatory methodology.

In reassessing the consequences of the ontological assumption of separateness, it appears in retrospect that practically all of present science remains in place if a different assumption is made—namely the assumption that *everything in human experience, mental as well as physical, is part of a unity, an intercommunicating oneness.* This implies that the positivistic epistemological assumption, that the only way we contact reality is through the physical senses, is replaced by an assumption that we contact reality in not one, but *two* ways. One is through the physical senses; the other is (since we are each ineluctably part of the oneness) through deep intuition. Reductionistic science is then seen as a special case, valid in its realm but not suited to be elevated to the position of a worldview by which we live our lives and guide society. For science to merit that position, it would have to be restructured on the basis of an ontological assumption of wholeness, and an epistemological assumption that subjective experience is potentially a valid source of knowledge of the whole.

Such an "extended" science is potentially compatible with the "perennial wisdom" of the world's contemplative traditions, and hence a complete reconciliation of C. P. Snow's "two cultures." It is also in accord with cultural shifts that are perhaps most obviously manifested in transpersonal psychology and the so-called "New Thought" churches.

Basic to the contemplative traditions is the proposition (or, rather, the experiential *knowing*) that human beings have a higher spiritual nature; that in that nature each is part of, and in touch with, the Whole; and that basic to that state of being is a natural compassion and love for other humans, and indeed for all of nature and all aspects of the Whole. Contemplative traditions generally concur that in our usual state we are estranged from our higher nature by our attachments, in particular to our own belief structures—we are estranged by our beliefs in separateness.

If we are correct in our premise that the future prevailing worldview will be something like this reconciliation of an "extended" science with the understandings of the contemplative traditions, then the prevailing value emphases can be anticipated to be those which follow from that worldview. It is not accidental that those values are essentially those of the contemporary, eco-feminist movement.

These arguments would forecast very strong emphasis on the value of human growth and development, to the point that this represents the lodestar of society's "central project." The economy and technological advance will be seen, properly, as *means,* rather than mistakenly perceived as ends in themselves (the present position). Cultural diversity will be valued, not only because it makes for a more resilient global society, but because it adds to the richness of the experience of all.

The essence of their worldview was once described by one Native American as (a) *everything* in the universe is *alive;* and (b) we are *all relatives!* The future worldview we are describing will have something of this flavor, and will cherish all creatures and everything in nature. Thus preserving biodiversity will be a strong value, and not because plants with as yet undiscovered properties will be valuable to the pharmaceutical industry.

Creative altruism—altruism guided by an intuitive sense of what will be in the real interest of the other—will be a widespread human trait. Because it is recognized as a natural trait, society will be dedicated to removal of the obstacles that inhibit its expression. This will be characteristic of education and indeed of all social institutions.

Society will value freedom—the freedom to discover and be oneself. This involves valuing the inner life, being in touch with the deep Center. But it also values finding one's purposeful work in the work—work which not only contributes to the whole, but also, through accomplishments and failures, provides feedback from the universe to help bring one back to being "on purpose." Society will value balance—between contemplation and action, masculine and feminine.

Most of these value emphases are not new. They will be in a new context, however—not authoritarian or inflexible religious tradition, but vibrant, living, transcendent spirituality.

Because people will be in varying states of clarity and self-understanding, even if the above value emphases predominate there will be need for political institutions such as the rule of law, disciplinary strictures, and a balance of powers. People will not be morally perfect, but the society-wide commitment to, and realization of, the highest values may well in the long run be greater than at any previous time in human history.

[See also Global Turning Points; Green Revolution; Lifestyles, Alternative; Mind: New Modes of Thinking; Sustainability.]

BIBLIOGRAPHY

Berman, Morris. *The Reenchantment of the World.* Ithaca, NY: Cornell University Press, 1981.
Bberry, Thomas. *The Dream of the Earth.* San Francisco: Sierra Club Books, 1988.
Bohm, David, and Peat, F. David. *Science, Order, and Creativity.* New York: Bantam Books, 1987.
Griffin, David, ed. *The Reenchantment of Science.* Albany, NY: State University of New York Press, 1988.
Harman, Willis W. *Creative Work.* Indianapolis: Knowledge Systems, 1991.
Hayward, Jeremy W. *Shifting Worlds, Changing Minds: Where the Sciences and Buddhism Meet.* Boston: New Science Library, 1987.
Henderson, Hazel. *Paradigms in Progress: Life Beyond Economics.* Indianapolis: Knowledge Systems, *1992.*
Smith, Huston. *Forgotten Truth: The Primordial Tradition.* New York: Harper and Row, 1977.

— WILLIS W. HARMAN

HOME OWNERSHIP

Home ownership seems likely to continue to be the preferred form of housing for most Americans. The proportion of Americans owning their homes will rise slowly throughout the next half century as incomes increase and families and individuals seek privacy, security, and an investment for the future.

Determinants of Home Ownership

As in the past, demand for home ownership will depend on demographics, economics and tax policy. The demographic trends important to home ownership are population growth and household formations and to a lesser extent the social acceptance of different living arrangements. The economic trends affecting home ownership are incomes, housing costs, including taxes. Deviations from the trend will occur as interest rates rise and fall, as the general economy grows or diminishes, and as different regions fare better or worse than others.

The primary determinant of how many households there will be is the rate at which the adult population forms and maintains separate households. The level of household formations is driven by the age distribution of the population and by social trends in living arrangements and family formations. Most new household formations occur when people are between twenty and thirty-four years old. Home ownership occurs later, when the household head is in his or her late twenties or thirties. Social and individual acceptance of living arrangements further influence the amount of home ownership by permissive (or nonpermissive) attitudes toward singles living alone, unmarried couples living together, and single parents staying single.

The single largest determinant of whether households will be owners or renters is household income. For instance, the rate of ownership is 25 percent greater for households with incomes around $50,000 than it is for households with incomes around $25,000.

Similarly, housing prices determine the amount of home ownership, although there is a dual effect that sometimes obscures the relationship. Higher house prices mean that households must devote a greater share of their income to a home purchase and that fewer households are willing to purchase. In addition, because most households borrow to purchase a home, the credit criteria of mortgage lenders limit the proportion of income that can be devoted to mortgage obligations.

Home ownership offers three benefits not available to renters. First, an owned home allows the household to provide the members with exactly the type, condition, and appearance of shelter that they want. Their home can be adapted (within the local zoning and use restrictions) to suit their needs without permission from an outside owner. Their length of stay and most of their costs are determined by their use rather than by a landlord or property owner. Second, an owned home is also a source of wealth, allowing families and individuals to put money into an asset that presumably will grow in value and yield a return that has historically risen at a rate greater than the general rate of inflation. The third benefit is subsidization in the form of tax relief.

Because an owned home serves as an asset as well as providing shelter, higher home prices have a dual effect on the number of households that choose home ownership. Higher prices deter some from owning because they require of buyers a greater down payment and more of their income than they are willing or financially qualified to spend. But rising prices are often seen as precursors of future rising prices. In addition, capital gains can offset the increased monthly costs.

Production Levels

Housing production for home ownership will increase as the population and numbers of households increases. However, slow growth and a decline during the early twenty-first century in the population group of ages twenty-five to thirty-nine will slow production, which could mean some declines in the annual output of new homes.

The production level of homes intended for ownership exceeded 1.5 million homes per year in the late 1970s, averaged 1.1 million homes in the 1980s, and dropped to 1.0 million homes per year in the early 1990s. The late 1990s will see an average annual production of 1.2 million homes intended for ownership. The early 2000s will see declines, as the people born in the low-birthrate years of the late 1960s and '70s reach home-buying age.

Although the number of new homes produced each year could dip in the first two decades of the twenty-first century, the value of the construction should continue to increase as homes become larger and more amenities are installed. New homes are more likely to be purchased by households that already have a home or are selling it and therefore have sufficient equity to purchase a larger, more elaborate home. The median sales price of new homes has increased 2 percentage points above inflation rates since 1970. The increase in prices is expected to continue as present home owners use their earned equity in their present home to trade up to a larger home with more amenities.

Type of Home

Eighty-six percent of the owned homes in 1991 were single-family homes, either freestanding, detached, or attached in a row as townhouses. Another 8 percent were manufactured housing, produced in a factory and shipped to the location. Most of these were in rural areas, and half were in the South. The remaining 6 percent were in buildings with more than one housing unit (multifamily housing). Ninety-two percent of the multifamily, owner-occupied homes were in urban areas.

The median size of all owner-occupied homes was 1,775 square feet, the median number of rooms was 6.1, the median number of bedrooms was 2.9, and the median number of bathrooms was one. Half of the owner-occupied homes were built in the previous twenty-five years.

Over 90 percent of the single-family homes built in the early 1990s were single-family detached. Owned multifamily homes account for about one in every five new multifamily units and about 5 percent of the homes built for an owner-occupant.

New single-family detached homes are larger than the existing stock of single-family homes. The median size (in square feet) of a new home increased slightly more than 1 percent per year in the 1970s and about 2 percent per year in the 1980s. By the early 1990s, the median square footage of new single family homes was just over 1,900 square feet. The space increases occurred in the family areas of the home: the family room, den, kitchen, entry foyer, and halls. Bedroom and bathroom sizes have not increased significantly.

Special-use rooms will be more prevalent,

like exercise rooms, home office space,

and hobby or workshop areas.

The size of new single family homes will continue to increase in the range of 1 to 2 percent per year. Average size will increase because fewer new homes will be sold to first-time buyers, thereby leaving more of the market to trade-up buyers who prefer larger homes. Amplifying the trend, the trade-up buyers will want even larger, more elaborate homes than previous trade-up buyers because they will have more housing equity to roll over into a new home.

Space allocations in the new homes built in the late 1990s and early twenty-first century will increase in the informal areas of the home such as family rooms and will decline in the formal areas such as dining rooms and formal living rooms. Bedroom space will expand, especially for the master bedroom. Special-use rooms will also be more prevalent, like exercise rooms, home office space, and hobby or workshop areas.

Single-family detached homes will remain the preferred style of home for most home owners. However, the size of the lot upon which the home is built will not increase as much as the home. Lot sizes for single-family homes increased 1 percent per year in the 1980s, but that trend will be more difficult to maintain as concerns about growth, environmental impact, traffic congestion, and the need for more local services increases. Lower residential density requires more roads, greater amounts of infrastructure, and public utility investment. Even if new home buyers are willing to bear their private costs for the lower densities, local governmental bodies will apply restrictions that address the social costs of development.

[See also Elderly, Living Arrangements; Household Composition; Housing, Affordable; Housing, Cost and Availability of; Housing, Demographic and Lifestyle Impacts on.]

BIBLIOGRAPHY

Apgar, William C., Jr., et al. *The Housing Outlook 1980–1990.* Westport, CT: Greenwood/Praeger, 1985.

Drakakis-Smith, David. *Urbanization, Housing, and the Development Process.* New York: St. Martin's Press, 1980.

Galster, George C. *Homeowners and Neighborhood Reinvestment.* Durham, NC: Duke University Press, 1986.

Ransom, P. *Healthy Housing: A Practical Guide.* New York: Van Nostrand Reinhold, 1991.

Turner, John F. *Housing by People: Towards Autonomy in Building Environments.* 2nd ed. New York: Marion Boyars, 1990.

– DAVID CROWE

HOMOSEXUALITY.

See SEXUAL BEHAVIOR; SEXUAL LAWS.

HOSPITALITY INDUSTRY: LODGINGS AND ACCOMMODATIONS

The astonishing events at the close of the twentieth century, including the fall of the Berlin Wall and the lifting of the Iron Curtain, signalled the end of the Cold War and the beginnings of freedom of movement for hundreds of millions of people. In fact, one of the first rights demanded by Eastern Europeans as they regained control of their governments was the right to travel.

Paralleling these events has been a rapid globalization of economic enterprise, lowering of trade barriers, transition to free-market economies, and in general a global trend toward democratization leading to higher standards of living. The continual expansion of world trade is generating growth in international business travel.

The confluence of these trends, coupled with the emergence of global communication technology, has made Marshall McLuhan's notion of the "Global Village" a reality. There is now a general awareness of people of other nations, their cultures, landscapes, and cityscapes, creating a strong desire among more and more people to want to experience these destinations firsthand.

Economic Significance of Tourism

Travel and tourism became the world's largest industry in the 1990s and the largest generator of jobs. The World Travel and Tourism Council (WTTC) estimates that the travel and tourism industry worldwide will generate a gross output of U.S. $3.4 trillion in 1995 when expenditures for both business and consumer travel, plus capital investment and government expenditures for tourism are included. By 2005, the figure is projected to double to U.S. $7.2 trillion (hereafter all dollar amounts are in U.S. dollars).

If all the people whose jobs are generated by the world travel and tourism industry lived in one country, that country would rank fourth in population (after the United States) with 212 million people. The gross domestic product (GDP) of that country would be $3.4 trillion, second only to the United States. And that country, according to WTTC statistics, would account for 10.9 percent of the world's GDP and 11.4 percent of the world's capital investment (see Table 1).

While Western Europe and North America are currently the dominant markets for the industry, major gains will be made over the next ten years in Latin America, Central and Eastern Europe, and the Asia Pacific Region. China is expected to be both a major generator of tourists, as well as a major destination market early in the twenty-first century.

Tourism's Contribution to Emerging Economies

Tourism offers excellent potential for sustained economic development of emerging economies. In 1991, tourism earned developing countries $312 billion in foreign currency, second only to oil revenues. Table 2 demonstrates the impressive growth of tourism over a ten-year period to selected countries.

TABLE 1

TRAVEL AND TOURISM, WORLD ESTIMATES

	1995	2005
Jobs	212 million	338 million
Output	$3.4 trillion	$7.2 trillion
GDP	10.9%	11.4%
Investment	11.4%	11.8%
Taxes	$655 billion	$1.4 trillion
Real Growth	5.5% p.a.	n.a.

Source: World Travel & Tourism Council.

TABLE 2

GROWTH OF TOURISM TO SELECTED DESTINATIONS

	Tourist arrivals (thousands)		Tourism receipts (US $ millions)	
	1981	1990	1981	1990
Belize	93	222	8	91
Costa Rica	333	435	94	275
Ecuador	245	332	131	193
Dominica	16	45	2	25
Kenya	373	801	175	443
Botswana	227	844	22	65
Madagascar	12	53	5	43
Maldives	60	195	15	85

Source: World Tourism Organization.

Tourism in the Caribbean for example, is the major industry of each of the thirty states in the region, contributing an estimated 25 percent of the regional economy. Tourism has been the only industry in the Caribbean has demonstrated steady growth over the past twenty years. The travel and tourism industry has provided the thirty diverse states of the region—states with different languages (French, English, Dutch, Spanish) and cultures a reason to come together to collaborate in the common purpose of marketing tourism on a regional basis. More recently they have been collaborating in meeting other challenges faced by this industry, such as environmental protection.

Protecting Environment and Heritage

Beyond its potential as an engine for economic development, the travel and tourism industry can make a major contribution to protecting both environment and heritage. Approximately 650 million people visit the national parks and protected areas in Kenya each year, spending some $350 million. A World Bank study has estimated that an average elephant herd generates $610,050 per year in income, or an individual elephant approximately $900,000 over the course of its sixty-year life span.

Tourism provides both the audience and economic engine for museums, the performing and visual arts, and the preservation of heritage. Singapore, for example, has recently set aside $1 billion to preserve the city's architectural heritage and culture.

Indigenous people, as well, are increasingly responding to the opportunities provided by tourism to preserve unique aspects of their heritage in the form of dance, music, and artifacts.

Global Leadership—The Green Globe Program

"Nature tourism," or ecotourism, is the most rapidly growing segment of the travel and tourism industry. Much of the potential for ecotourism is in the rich, biodiverse areas of developing countries. Revenues generated from ecotourism have provided an economic rationale for setting aside vast tracts of land as parks and wilderness areas in countries around the world. Visitors to these areas experience the beauty and majesty of the world's finest natural features and come away with a heightened appreciation of environmental values.

Leaders within the travel and tourism industry have recognized that the environment is its basic product. It is one of the first industries to respond to the challenge of the UN Conference on Environment and Development (UNCED), held in Rio de Janeiro in 1992 by introducing a "Green Globe" program. Green Globe has been developed by the World Travel and Tourism

Council as a worldwide environmental management and awareness program. The program is designed to encourage all companies in the Travel and Tourism Industry to commit to environmentally compatible development and sound environmental-management techniques based on environmental guidelines and international best practices.

Tourism—The World's Peace Industry

With the end of the Cold War came an end to a world divided by two opposing ideological camps. A wave of democratization and economic liberalism soon followed. Ironically, the end of the Cold War also heightened the incidence of ethnic violence in certain regions of the world. The United Nations declared 1995 as the International Year of Tolerance in recognition of the need for promoting greater tolerance within the global family.

Through travel, people are discovering one another

and the beauty of nature.

In the process, they are discovering themselves.

The challenge facing the travel and tourism industry is to take a leadership role in promoting greater tolerance, to help bring about greater understanding and respect among members of the global family in a spirit of joy and appreciation of the diversity which illuminates and strengthens us as a global family. Through travel, people are finding friends in every corner of the Earth, establishing common bonds with other members of the global family, and spreading messages of hope for a peaceful world. Through travel, people are discovering one another and the beauty of nature. In the process they are discovering themselves.

By creatively nurturing and facilitating this act of discovery, the tourism industry has the potential to become the world's peace industry, an industry that recognizes, promotes, and supports the belief that every traveler is potentially an ambassador for peace within the global family and with nature.

[See also Air Transport; Free Time; Global Culture; Interactive Entertainment; Leisure Time; Mass Culture and Arts; Outdoor Recreation and Leisure Pursuits; Space Travel; Tourism; Workforce Redistribution.]

BIBLIOGRAPHY

Poon, Auliana. *Tourism, Technology and Competitive Strategies.* Wallingford, Oxon, U.K.: C.A.B. International, 1993.

Ritchie, J. R. Brent, and Hawkins, Donald E., eds. *World Travel and Tourism Review: Indicators, Trends, and Issues.* Vol. 3. Wallingford, Oxon, U.K.: C.A.B. International, 1993.
Robinson, James D., III. *Travel and Tourism: The World's Largest Industry.* Brussels: The World Travel and Tourism Council, 1992.
Waters, Somerset R. *Travel Industry World Yearbook: The Big Picture, 1993–94.* Rye, NY: Child and Wages, 1993.

– LOUIS J. D'AMORE

HOUSEHOLD APPLIANCES

Technology and the miniaturization and falling prices of microprocessors will transform everyday objects and appliances into high-tech appliances. For example, "smart" electrochromic windows that automatically vary their transparency at specified optical wavelengths will save energy by reflecting sunlight in hot weather and letting the sun shine in during cold weather.

Japan's NTT Company has already introduced a tankless, microprocessor-controlled toilet that flushes by pushbutton and has a heated seat. A warm water spray function followed by an air dry cycle is supposed to make toilet tissue unnecessary. The toilet has a built-in urine analyzer that measures levels of sugar, protein, red and white blood cells, and ketones. The user can stick a finger into a specially defined armrest to measure blood pressure, pulse, and body temperature. This diagnostic information can be displayed to the toilet user on a small screen informational display or relayed by modem to a doctor.

In addition to technology, home appliance design in the future will be shaped largely by three other factors: shrinking living space, easier-to-use controls, and growing environmental regulation.

Shrinking Living Space

Much of the impetus for smaller-scale living space comes from Japan, where living quarters already are very small by North American standards. While it may be a while before America living space shrinks to Japanese dimensions, this trend will have major effects on both the functionality and styling of tomorrow's appliances.

FUNCTIONAL INTEGRATION. The design of future appliances will be altered to save space (particularly floor space) and there will be a trend toward combining related appliances into multifunction units:

- Consumer electronics: Audio and video equipment will be increasingly combined into all-in-one entertainment modules, reversing the component trend of the middle-to-late twentieth century.
- Television: The exception to this trend will be television sets. These will remain separate as they grow to become ubiquitous. High-resolution, flat screens will transform the television from a box to a wall hanging with integral high-fidelity speakers. Every room in the house will have a screen, which will function as a video intercom system, house controller, and

access point for on-line services. When not being used for communications or control, televisions will function as an art gallery or "virtual interior design." Homeowners will be able to select paintings or even complete audio/video environments with a touch of a button, from a library of images stored on interactive CD-ROM.

- Telecommunications: The telephone, computer/house controller, and fax machine will merge into an electronic voice and data transfer system. For example, when a fax is sent to the home, it will automatically print out on the laser printer. The home controller will respond to voice commands phoned in from a remote location.
- Laundry: Clothes washers and dryers will be combined into a single unit that washes and dries clothes all in one operation. A combination of much higher washer spin speeds and microwave clothes drying (which operates at lower temperatures than hot-air drying) will conserve energy, extend clothing life, and reduce dryer exhaust problems.
- Cooking: Combination microwave/conventional ovens will both optimize use of kitchen space and provide larger oven cavities for microwaving food.
- Water heating: Small point-of-use instantaneous water heaters mounted beneath sinks will replace large forty- to fifty-gallon storage tank water heaters. These small local water heaters will be combined with electronically controlled faucets that provide one-touch temperature control and adjust automatically to maintain a steady water temperature. Clothes washers will have integral "booster" water heaters as dishwashers do today.

APPLIANCE STYLING. Shrinking living space will mean that reducing visual "clutter" due to appliances and other consumer products will be more than just an aesthetic concept. It will become more psychologically important as dozens of differently styled products, in the same small space, compete for visual attention and jar the senses.

The need to reduce visual clutter and save floor space will lead appliance styling in two contradictory directions:

1. Blending: The inconspicuous blend-in look is the wave of the future. Those home appliances with which consumers have a merely functional relationship (laundry, area heating, ventilating, air conditioning, water heating) will be chameleonlike products that blend with any decor (their surroundings).
2. Furniture: Those appliances with which consumers have a more personal relationship (cooking, audio/video, telecom) will be designed more as art objects that express an individual vision and substitute as furniture.

COOKING TECHNOLOGY. Microwaving will become the dominant food preparation mode due to its speed, convenience, and improvements in cooking ability. Increasingly, foods will go from freezer to ready-to-eat in a single operation, nearly untouched by human hands.

Various "niche" cooking technologies will gain in popularity. Induction cooking using magnetic energy to heat food in ferrous pans, without creating a touch or fire hazard, for example. Induction units built into dining tables will gently heat ferrous inserts in dinnerware to keep food warm.

Easier-to-Use Controls

Controls on every type of appliance will become simpler, more "intelligent and adaptive," and easier for homeowners to use. Just as high-end audio appliances are using fewer controls today, so in the future will all appliances.

Ideally, appliance controls will become so intuitive that user manuals would be unnecessary. But the drive toward higher levels of features inevitably adds complexity.

Improvements in speech recognition

will replace remote controls with speech commands,

at least for controlling basic functions.

Greater use of graphic displays on appliances will help solve this problem. Touch screens will simplify the user interface by storing control and on-screen "help" features in software. The ubiquitous wall-screen television will become the control interface for major house systems. A screen showing the layout of your house will let homeowners control the HVAC system with an easy-to-use universal remote control.

Intelligent adaptive controls will "learn" homeowner patterns [routines] of behavior so that the home and its appliances function in various "default" modes that the user can interrupt and change as desired.

Improvements in speech recognition will replace remote controls with speech commands, at least for controlling basic functions.

Growing Environmental Regulation

While there is little evidence that North American consumers will pay extra for "green" appliances, government regulation is driving appliances in the direction of increasing environmental friendliness. Three major trends for the future:

1. Ozone-safe cooling appliances: Increasing government regulation will eliminate the use of refrigerant chemicals with ozone-depleting potential or global-warming potential. Future household cooling appliances will use hydrocarbon chemicals such as cyclopentane and isobutane. Because these replacement chemicals are less energy-efficient than the CFCs and HFCs they replace, refrigerators will be built with improved insulation such as vacuum panels to replace the polyurethane insulation used today. Many of these changes will be invisible to consumers.

2. Design for recycling: Future appliances will be constructed of fewer materials and constructed so that they can be disassembled more easily, to facilitate recycling. Home appliances will be manufactured to a greater extent from recycled materials.

3. Water conservation: Laundry appliances and plumbing fixtures will use less water and energy. Government regulation will eliminate garbage disposers and trash compactors as methods of disposing of kitchen waste. Some observers see waterless toilets that use microwave energy to reduce human wastes to powder, and microwave home incinerators for kitchen waste.

[See also Clothing; Environment; Household Composition; Interactive Entertainment; Telecommunications.]

BIBLIOGRAPHY

Babyak, Richard J. "Designing the Future." *Appliance Manufacturer* 41/7 (July 1993): 31–39.

"Domotechnica: The World's Fair of Appliances." *Appliance Manufacturer* 41/4 (April 1993): 28–40.

Kesselring, John. "Microwave Clothes Dryers." *EPRI Journal* 24/6 (June 1992): 15–17.

Norman, Donald A. *The Psychology of Everyday Things.* New York, NY: Basic Books, 1988.

Stauffer, H. Brooke. *Smart House Wiring.* Albany, NY: Delmar Publishers, 1993.

— H. BROOKE STAUFFER

HOUSEHOLD COMPOSITION

The gigantic demographic tsunami called the Baby Boom can be easily tracked from its origin between 1946 and 1964. We can watch it rush past us into the future all the way to 2047 when the first of these "baby boomers" become centenarians. The effect of the Baby Boom upon household composition is already visible to us.

The U.S. Bureau of the Census defines a household as "all the persons who occupy a housing unit. These persons may be related, unrelated, or living alone." The Census Bureau then goes on to define "a family household" as one consisting of "the householder, and at least one additional person related to the householder through marriage, birth, or adoption" (U.S. Bureau of the Census Report. *Households, Families, and Children: A 30-Year Perspective*, P23–181, pp. 14, 15. Washington, DC, November 1992).

A "housing unit" may consist of a single-family home, duplex, multifamily dwelling, or mobile home (home to 6.75 percent of all Americans). Not to be discussed here are what the Census Bureau calls "group quarters," where all those individuals not living in households, live in schools, hospitals, mental hospitals, treatment centers, nursing homes, orphanages, as well as in correctional facilities (prisons, jails, military stockades), college dormitories, military barracks, and various kinds of shelters.

Diversity—it becomes glaringly evident—is the word which best describes the dramatic changes that have taken place in where we live, and especially within households during the first fifty years of the Baby Boom. Let us look first at changes in one type of household, the family household.

Changes in the Family Household

During the 1930s, 1940s, and 1950s the predominant model of the idealized family consisted of two parents and two or more children. The father was the breadwinner and the mother the homemaker. This is still held by many as an ideal. But as early as 1980 one survey showed that this type of family household represented only 7 percent of the U.S. population.

By 1991 one in eight households was headed by a single parent, with 25 percent of all children living with only one parent. Children who were living with grandparents had increased from 3 percent in 1970 to 5 percent in 1991. Among African-Americans, 12 percent of children live with grandparents; 6 percent of Hispanic children live with their grandparents.

More than half of those ages eighteen–twenty-five in 1991 lived with their parents in 1991. The median age for getting married and starting a new household was twenty-four for women and twenty-six for men. With the increase in the divorce rate, the expectation of remaining married was about 50 percent.

Waning disapproval of divorce and increasing ease of remarriage have been partially responsible for a cycle of marry-divorce-remarry-divorce-remarry, which has been reflected in household composition. Children often have multiple parents and siblings, stepmothers, stepfathers, stepsisters, and stepbrothers. One divorced couple, to provide the continuity and emotional stability and security of a family household for their twelve-year-old son, set up a separate apartment for him, with the mother spending one week with him, the father the next. Clearly, diversity and often ingenuity characterize family household composition in the 1990s.

There are also often important surrogate members of households. Sometimes these are live-in companions or nursing aides for the elderly. Sometimes these are close friends who are perceived as "belonging" to the family group.

The television set has introduced important new relationships to households, marked by new electronic surrogate-family members (98.2 percent of all households have an average of 2.1 TV sets according to Arbitron). The most immediate and important emotional attachments, especially among the elderly living alone (the center of their sense of companionship and the focus of their day-to-day concern), is sometimes with the lives and roles portrayed by actors in the dramas of daytime "soaps" and everyday primetime "reruns." The emotional depths of immediacy and caring evoked by these relationships with figures in television dramas often surpasses those with members of one's own often distant family.

The networks of telecommunications embedded

in cellular phones, pagers, faxes,

and laptop computers, are transforming

many cars and homes into mini-offices.

In 1990 54.8 million households also shared their living space with a companion animal ("pet"), according to the American Veterinary Medical Association. For many years dogs, cats, and numerous other animals have served as emotionally important participating members of families and households. The value of animals has been proven in assisting the blind, and there is growing appreciation of the benefit of pets for the elderly. An aging population coupled with increased longevity means that housing needs to accommodate age-related limitations will have to be met. Special household arrangements will include nursing homes, retirement settlements, and hospices. Similarly, needs will be posed by disabled and handicapped individuals who want to live independently.

Changes in Nonfamily Households

Nonfamily households are made up of (1) single men or women living alone (widowed, divorced, never-married), or (2) unrelated persons living together in groups. With the growing acceptance of divorce, childlessness, and singleness, single occupancy households have risen from one in eight of all households in 1960 to one out of every four in 1992. In 1991, one quarter of these occupants of nonfamily households are under the age of thirty-five, one quarter between thirty-five and fifty-five, and half older than fifty-five. These singles constitute nine-tenths of all nonfamily households. Women living alone (13.9 million) are the largest group after married couples with or without children (52.3 million). Nine million men live alone.

In 1992 there were 4.3 million households made up of "unrelated persons living together." These include boarders and apartment sharers in high-rent areas, older unmarried couples sharing social security benefits, people of the opposite sex sharing living quarters, gay and lesbian couples, college students not living in dormi-

tories or with their parents, and unrelated refugees and ethnic groups sharing housing. Unmarried couple households will continue to raise many legal issues related to inheritance and other rights of such "partners."

New Utilization Patterns of Households

How many hours or days are "homes" used during a given period—day, week, month, year? With parent(s) working during the day and children in nursery school, day care, school, or with baby sitters, many living units are completely unoccupied more and more during certain time periods.

But there is also a movement to reclaim this "empty" time for homes and use it in new ways. The networks of telecommunications embedded in cellular phones, pagers, faxes, notebook and lap-top computers, are transforming many cars and homes into minioffices. Many workers are being encouraged by their companies to substitute their own living space for some or all of their working time, and in response they are creating "work centers" within their homes. These trends, combined with the increase of home businesses, are changing the function of households at a time when their composition has already been changing rapidly.

[See also Demography; Divorce; Families and Households; Family Patterns; Family Values; Housing, Demographic and Lifestyle Impacts on; Marriage; Pets; Social Change: United States.]

BIBLIOGRAPHY

Ahlburg, Dennis A., and Carol J. DeVita. *New Realities of the American Family. Population Bulletin* 47/2 (1992).
Dychtwald, Ken, and Plower, Joe. *Age Wave.* Los Angeles: Jeremy P. Tarcher, 1989.
Hughes, James W., and Zimmerman, Todd. "The Dream Is Alive." *American Demographics* (August 1993): 32–37.
Russell, Cheryl, *The Master Trend.* New York: Plenum Press, 1993.
Toffler, Alvin. *The Third Wave.* New York: William Morrow, 1980.
———. *War and Antiwar.* New York: Little, Brown, 1993, chapters 10–11.
U.S. Bureau of the Census, and Lugalla, Terry. *Households, Families, and Children: A 30-Year Perspective.* Washington, DC: Current Population Reports P23–181, 1992.
———, and Saluter, Arlene P. *Marital Status and Living Arrangements.* Washington, DC: Current Population Reports P20–468, 1992.

– ROBERT E. MASTON

HOUSING, AFFORDABLE

One of the fundamental needs of modern life among people of all classes is for a place to live that is affordable. Though what may be affordable to a bricklayer in Glasgow is something quite different than what is affordable to an investment banker in New York City or a civil service official in Lagos, Nigeria, the common denominator of affordable housing functions as a cornerstone for how well or poorly people live together.

Regardless of contemporary densities, all nations will be challenged in the twenty-first century to construct sustainable living conditions that enable the majority of their citizens to live decently and affordably by their own country's standards. This will be achieved not through technological advances in materials or methods. And it will not be materially achieved through alterations in the structure of housing finance.

Rather, achievements in constructing sustainable living conditions in the United States, Russia, or elsewhere, will be made for three principal reasons: (1) Alterations in land-use development patterns must effectively curb low-density development. (2) Land-use patterns must begin to reflect a reliance on mass transit-oriented development rather than freeway-oriented (auto) development. (3) Each country facing housing affordability crises in the first decades of the twenty-first century will need to accept and cope with the interrelationship between air quality, housing affordability, and surface transportation.

As the twentieth century draws to a close, the concept of housing is defined quite differently around the world. In Port-au-Prince, basic shelter remains a distant goal for large numbers of Haitians living in a country atrophied by despotism and civil unrest. In Tokyo, an 800-square-foot apartment can rent for 10,000 times as much as the annual per capita income for a Palestinian in Gaza. And in San Francisco, a well-educated teacher with advanced degrees earning only 30 percent of the area median income will find the goal of home ownership utterly unattainable without significant public subsidy.

For better or worse, public subsidy, in one form or another, has thus become the essential ingredient in making housing widely affordable, whether in the United States, Australia, or Mexico. Since sustainable urban living is related to air quality, housing affordability, and surface transportation, the major issue facing governments will be what form their housing subsidies take, and to whom those subsidies flow.

If housing affordability for the vast majority of people is thus a reality that is going to be made possible only with public participation, it raises the issue of the relationship between the individual and society.

Countries that achieve a sustainable balance between the rights and privileges of individual citizens and the country as a whole will reap the rewards of a preserved civic realm. Continued public participation whose effect is to increase affordability without sacrificing the quality of the civic realm is the seed corn for sustainable high-density living.

But because high-density living inevitably suggests mixed-class living, there will be considerable resistance to public efforts either to mandate outright or passively to permit such arrangements. It will always be more politically remunerative in the short run for jurisdictions to gobble up land and to separate citizens according to wealth. But the intersection of global economic interdependency and land scarcity at precisely this moment in history suggests that such actions will prove costly in the long run.

The cauldron of low-wage workers from all countries being necessarily mixed together in the modern era means that for the foreseeable future, industrial countries will see an ever widening gap between what housing costs and what low-skilled workers can afford. When juxtaposed alongside of low-density development patterns fostered by public land-use and tax policies, the distance between the haves and the have-nots will be nowhere more evident than in housing disparity.

It will be inevitable that this disparity, in Canada, Australia, or Israel, will be momentarily closed by concomitant subsidies for highways that enable low-wage workers to live in one place and work in another. But the resulting reductions in air quality are not long supportable, especially since such arrangements only serve to perpetuate harmful land-development tendencies.

In the end, failure to reckon with the absolute necessity for people of differing classes to live in closer proximity to one another will only prove calamitous. In such instances there will be increased tendencies to look to technology and housing finance for remedies. But only in altered outlooks on the relationship of individual and society, the pluses and minuses of dense urban living, the preservation of agricultural space and ecosystems made possible by the elimination of low-density sprawl, and an enhanced belief in the importance of the civic realm, will housing affordability be achieved in any meaningful way.

[See also Entitlement Programs; Home Ownership; Housing, Cost and Availability of; Housing, Demographic and Lifestyle Impacts on; Land Use Planning.]

BIBLIOGRAPHY

Jencks, Christopher. *The Homeless.* Cambridge, MA: Harvard University Press, 1994.
Nathan, Richard P. *The New Agenda for Cities.* Washington, DC: National League of Cities, 1992.

– CHARLES BUKI

HOUSING, COST AND AVAILABILITY OF

The market is positive for owner-occupied housing over the next ten years or so. The pace of housing construction activity and housing price appreciation will probably fall short of that experienced during the 1970s, but ought to exceed the rate that occurred through most of the 1980s. The reasons underlying these opinions and a brief review of the performance of the housing market during the past three decades follow.

Review of Recent Housing Market Activity

Volatility in the U.S. housing market has been particularly apparent during the past thirty years or so. The numerous causes include: severe ebbs and flows of funds into financial institutions that specialize in housing finance (as in the mid-1960s to late 1970s); the demand surge caused by the "baby boom" generation coming of age during the late 1970s to late '80s; a high and unstable interest rate environment (in the 1970s and '80s); and substantial income growth and decline among many local housing markets—e.g., the Texas oil boom and bust. Few local housing markets have been immune from the unexpected surges and declines in the price of housing associated with these volatile factors.

Time series of owner-occupied housing costs are compared with an index of the purchase price of a constant-quality new house in Figure 1. The cost of owner-occupied housing represents the sum of the mortgage payment, the interest that could be earned on the household's housing equity, property taxes, and miscellaneous expenses, less income tax benefits and capital gains. Both series are smoothed using a four-quarter moving average and are expressed in real terms (1964 dollars). The two series demonstrate the volatility in housing prices during the past twenty-five years. Note especially the surge in housing prices in the late 1970s,

which was largely fueled by the entry of the baby boom population into the market for owner-occupied housing. Prices in real terms were lower at the end of the 1980s than at the beginning. A high and volatile interest rate environment combined with a reduction in capital gains expectations triggered this decline.

Volatility in the housing market is especially noticeable in the construction statistics presented in Figure 2. The two series are smoothed using a four-quarter moving average of the housing start data. The construction of housing experienced wide swings in the 1960s as a result of fluctuations in the supply of funds available to financial institutions. A record number of houses were built in two major housing booms during the beginning and end of the 1970s. The 1980s began with a sudden reversal of this trend. Interest rates rose dramatically, the national economy experienced a recession, and some regions of the country such as Texas suffered a severe depression. Although the late 1980s witnessed improvements in the economy and housing, the final scorecard showed a decline in home ownership, a rise in the cost of owner-occupied housing, and a slowdown in household expectations and realizations of capital gains.

The rental housing market also experienced its ups and downs. Multifamily housing construction (housing structures with five or more housing units) boomed in the early 1970s, due in part to large government rental-housing programs. Tax legislation enacted in the early 1980s and excessive investment in all forms of commercial real estate associated with the savings and loan (S&L) debacle were major causes behind the increase in the construction of multifamily housing in the early and mid-1980s. The Tax Reform Act of 1986 and res-

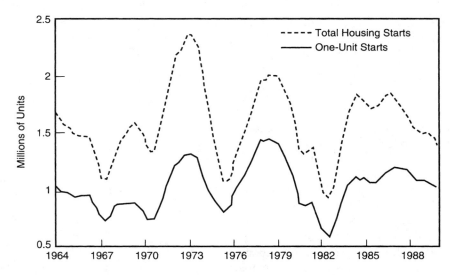

Figure 1. Housing starts, 1964–1989.

Figure 2. Home owner cost versus purchase price (in 1964 dollars).

olution of the savings-and-loan crisis brought this rental housing boom to a sharp and sudden conclusion.

Forecasts of Future Housing Market Directions

The primary basis for optimism regarding owner-occupied housing is posited on the population of potential home buyers that will continue to grow during the 1990s. Total population growth will probably be around 7 to 8 percent during the 1990s, representing about 15 to 20 million people. If income growth is modest (1.5 percent real growth per year) and interest rates remain in the 7 to 8 percent range, the number of owner-occupied households can be expected to increase from about 60 million to well over 65 million.

The percentage growth in the number of renter households will probably exceed that of homeowners. Population growth also will stimulate the demand for rental housing. Growth among the elderly, especially those above seventy years of age, and among persons in the age group from twenty-five to thirty-four years will be especially important in prompting this increased demand. Rental housing also will benefit from the slow growth and even decline in real wages among segments of the population; those without a college education and those adversely affected by declining job prospects in manufacturing will be most susceptible to real wage declines.

The housing construction industry has a strong history of responding adequately to demand. As a consequence, housing prices for the most part follow trends in the overall price level. Price "bubbles," like the one experienced during the late-1970s tend to be short-lived and concentrated in rapidly growing urban areas. There is good reason to remain confident in the ability of the housing construction industry. As a consequence, hous-

ing prices will probably not appreciate much beyond the average rate of inflation for the entire economy in most parts of the country during the 1990s.

This forecast comes with one important caveat: Growth management strategies may lead to sizeable increases in housing prices in some fast-growing areas. Society has yet to settle upon appropriate strategies with which to manage the impact of population growth on local housing markets. Many current growth management policies—e.g., zoning and large development-fees—tend to drive up the cost of housing in ways that help those already in the select neighborhoods and hurt those who wish to enter them. Until more equitable and efficient strategies can be developed, the cost of housing will exceed the cost of construction in the areas in which growth controls are most prevalent.

Many other government policies also will affect the housing market, such as "affordable" housing programs designed to assist low- and middle-income households to switch to home ownership. The federal government will likely continue to pressure Fannie Mae, Freddie Mac, and other financial institutions to offer low down-payment programs with flexible underwriting criteria in order to improve access to mortgage credit and home ownership for low- and middle-income households. Some of these efforts are worthy; however, these programs will be unable to offset the deeper economic problems faced by many young people who enter the labor market with inadequate job training and education. For many of these would-be homeowners, the primary obstacle to home ownership is an inadequate and unstable income, not a poorly performing housing or mortgage housing market.

Will the 1990s be a good time to buy a house? Homebuyers ought to be more selective in the 1990s than in the past ten to fifteen years. They cannot count on substantial capital gains to offset the high cost of entering home ownership, although some lucky households will reap such rewards. The tax advantage of owning versus renting remains, but its absolute size has declined for many in the middle class. Regardless, home ownership remains a good economic decision for most middle-income households who expect stable employment and to remain in their houses for several years.

Growth management strategies

may lead to sizeable increases in housing prices

in some fast-growing areas.

Home ownership will also be attractive to those fortunate ones able to participate in affordable housing initiatives. For those with less secure employment prospects and lower incomes, rental housing is likely to be the preferred form of housing tenure.

[See also Elderly, Living Arrangements; Families and Households; Home Ownership; Household Composition; Housing, Affordable; Housing, Demographic and Lifestyle Impacts on.]

BIBLIOGRAPHY

Follain, James R. "The Outlook for Owner-Occupied Housing in the Year 2000." In Frank Bonnello and Tom Swartz, eds. *Upheaval in Urban Housing Markets.* Sage Press, 1993.
Follain, James R., Patric H. Hendershott, and David C. Ling. "Real Estate Markets Since 1980: What Role Have the Tax Changes Played?" *National Tax Journal* (September 1992): 253–266.

— JAMES R. FOLLAIN

HOUSING, DEMOGRAPHIC AND LIFESTYLE IMPACTS ON

Demographic change and social adaptation have produced dramatic shifts in housing patterns in the past, and can be expected to do so in the future. In Europe, the character of most old cities and towns, with their dense honeycombs of houses and courtyards, is the direct result of seventeenth- and eighteenth-century property owners' practice of building homes for their relatives or employees on back-garden plots. The overcrowded tenements of early industrial Europe and America were largely the consequences of extended families' occupying living quarters that factory owners originally had designed to house working couples and their children.

In modern times, the bleak economic conditions of the 1930s caused a one-third drop in marriage rates. As a result, the proportion of single Americans nearly doubled, from 15 percent in 1930 to 29 percent in 1940. Depression-era singles often rented modest but genteel quarters from the managerial-professional class, many of whom were unemployed and impoverished following the 1929 financial collapse and converted their large, formal homes into boarding and rooming houses. When prosperity returned after World War II, marriage rates soared and the U.S. middle class expanded. The rebound was so great that builders and developers had to mass-produce millions of "tract houses," standardized on the statistically dominant nuclear family: one married couple and their offspring. By 1950, only 3.2 percent of Americans lived alone.

While industrial era economists from Adam Smith (1723–1790) to 1992 Nobel Laureate Gary Becker have detailed the benefits of monogamous marriage, both to its participants and to society as a whole, it is not clear that the nuclear family will remain the dominant household form. By the 1980s, many social scientists had become comfortable with the idea that the nuclear family's predominance in Western industrial nations was a temporary, circumstantial phenomenon. Currently, nearly 12 percent of American adults live alone. Steadily increasing longevity, and high divorce rates suggest that marriage may become a temporary stage of adulthood—for parenthood—before and after which most people will live alone or in small, intentional groups. Meanwhile sequential marriages are creating extended and blended "co-families" or network households. Above all, economic restructuring in the United States has curtailed the growth of prosperity during the past twenty-five years, fostering greater intergenerational interdependence, including more extended, multigenerational households.

From 1990 to 2010, new household formation rates will be at a seventy-five-year low, due largely to the low birthrates of the 1970s and '80s. The housing industry during this period will largely be involved with: (1) responding to government and community mandates for more "affordable" housing, and (2) adapting existing housing stock to the changing needs of an aging population. Current U.S. housing, built almost entirely for nuclear families, will have to accommodate a growing diversity of living arrangements, including singles; unrelated roommates ("mingles"); childless couples, including gay and lesbian partners; and groups of three or more unrelated adults, especially young adults and self-sufficient seniors living together as a family (in congregate or group housing). Simultaneously, there will be an ongoing construction boom in additions to existing housing, to accommodate mother-in-law wings and granny-flats, as greater longevity and the high cost of housing and health care promote the increase of three- and four-generation households.

The rise of home-based self-employment and salaried work-at-home ("flex-place") also will reshape U.S. housing arrangements in the future. Because the great productivity achieved by labor-intensive mass-market economies requires large-scale physical facilities such as factories, offices, schools, or service facilities, most high-value jobs in such economies are necessarily located away from employees' homes. Because electronics make it much cheaper and faster to move information than to move people, enormous efficiencies will be achieved in the information-intensive economies of the future by bringing office work to the employees rather than vice versa. The movement of gainful employment back into the home, the locus for most employment in agrarian and mercantile economies, will strengthen the family both economically and culturally. Substantial rearrangement of metropolitan traffic and energy flows will fundamentally alter the nature of residential neighborhoods and suburban communities.

Demographic and lifestyle changes shape housing patterns on a national scale, as well as at the neighborhood and community levels. Cities grew from the Civil War until 1950, as the industrial share of U.S. jobs grew. Millions of rural Americans, their jobs eliminated by agricultural mechanization, migrated to cities in search of employment. From the 1950s on, however, most older central cities in *all* mature industrial countries began to lose population. First the exodus was to the suburbs, and after 1970, to exurban and rural areas. As technology reduces the amount of direct labor needed for manufacturing, some producers relocated to rural communities where business operating costs are characteristically 15 to 20 percent lower than in cities and suburbs. Simultaneously, a substantial portion of current rural population growth is due to in-migration of people, including many information workers and retirees, whose income is not geographically dependent.

Demographic changes influence housing patterns and styles. This housing development in Scottsdale, Arizona, exemplifies the growth of Sun Belt areas. (© Robert Dawson/First Image West, Inc)

411

In the United States, fully one-third of seniors who relocate when they retire now move to rural communities near where they lived for most of their lives, rather than moving to areas such as the Sun Belt.

So long as the costs of urban life and work continue to rise and the quality of urban life and work continue to decline, the dispersion of population and

---

Enormous efficiencies will be achieved in the

information-intensive economies of the future

by bringing office work to the employees

rather than vice versa.

---

production to rural areas and the exurban fringes of metropolitan regions will grow. This shift will accelerate if less developed areas retain fewer statutory restrictions upon innovative land use, residential living arrangements, and working arrangements. Urban and suburban jurisdictions that accommodate innovative lifestyles—such as congregate living, greater residential-commercial integration, and flexible cohousing—will compete more effectively for productive populations than those communities that adhere to restrictive twentieth-century zoning, building, and land-use codes intended to protect existing property values.

[See also Demography; Families and Households; Home Ownership; Household Composition; Housing, Cost and Availability of; Lifestyles.]

BIBLIOGRAPHY

Becker, Gary E. *A Treatise on the Family.* Cambridge, MA: Harvard University Press, 1981.

Girouard, Mark. *Cities and People.* New Haven, CT: Yale University Press, 1985.

Morrison, Peter A., *Demographic Factors Shaping The U.S. Market For New Housing.* Santa Monica, CA: The Rand Corp. Population Research Center, 1988. Monograph.

Snyder, David Pearce. "The Corporate Family: A Look at a Proposed Social Invention." *The Futurist* (December 1976): 323–335.

———. The Family in Post-Industrial America. Boulder, CO: Westview Press, 1979.

— DAVID PEARCE SNYDER

HUMAN RESOURCES DEVELOPMENT

Human resources development will change dramatically as the twentieth century draws to a close. The work force will be older, more stable, and more diverse. Compensation costs will increase as workers try to regain ground lost in the 1980s.

The American Work Force Is on the Move

The U.S. Bureau of Labor Statistics (BLS) estimates that nearly one in five workers changes jobs in a given year. Half or more of these changes involve occupational changes as well.

Job mobility may decline over the next few decades. The post-World War II baby boom generation, which now accounts for more than half of the work force, will reach its mid-thirties to mid-fifties at the turn of the century. Older workers change jobs less frequently than younger workers do.

The impending bulge in experienced workers could benefit firms trying to boost efficiency and competitiveness. The changing work force is also changing human resource management practices. A larger number of seasoned workers competing for fewer senior positions, portends that a promotion increasingly means a change, rather than an increase, in responsibilities. Likewise, frequent job changes by a worker now indicate broadened experience, not instability.

Some companies are responding to changing work force dynamics by investing more in their workers to keep them challenged, productive, and committed. New investments include additional benefits such as child care centers, sabbaticals to pursue professional or personal interests, and worker retraining.

The Challenge of Diversity

The workforce is becoming more diverse. In 1970, nearly 62 percent of the workforce was male and nearly 90 percent was white. In 1991, men accounted for 55 percent of the workforce and whites for 86 percent.

Government, the courts, and employees themselves expect employers to accommodate diversity. Numerous court decisions have found that employers are responsible for ensuring that the workplace is not just physically safe, but also psychologically safe. As a result, increasing attention will be directed at harassment, prejudice, and discrimination.

The Americans with Disabilities Act of 1990 (ADA), one of the most important pieces of civil rights legislation in a generation, imposes special responsibilities on employers. The law prohibits employers from discriminating against a current or prospective employee with certain handicaps, so long as the employee can perform the essential functions of the position with reasonable accommodation on the part of the employer. Among the protected groups of employees and applicants are those with HIV/AIDS, alcoholics. AIDS has already become the most litigated disease in history. Pursuant to statutory protection of the ADA, other conditions may be not far behind.

The farsighted employer will inventory its employees' skills and responsibilities and implement performance evaluations that accurately reflect the responsibilities of each position. Finally, the employer will state its personnel policies clearly and apply them equitably. For example, prohibitions against drinking on the job may not be enforced against alcoholics if violations by occasional drinkers who are not alcoholics are routinely ignored.

Americans Are Working Harder

The decline or death of the American work ethic has been exaggerated. More Americans are working than ever before, and they are working longer hours.

In 1970, 60 percent of the population aged sixteen and older was either working or looking for work. By 1991, this share had risen to over 66 percent, higher than that in all developed, industrialized countries other than Sweden and Canada.

In 1970, 70 percent of those at work worked full-time (at least thirty-five hours weekly). By 1991, this share was up to 81 percent. Over the last two decades, the proportion of workers holding more than one job rose from just over 5 percent to just over 6 percent.

Money Matters

While American workers are working harder, they are losing purchasing power. Between 1981 and 1990, inflation averaged just under 5 percent annually and labor productivity grew nearly 1 percent annually. Average hourly earnings, over the same period, grew just over 3 percent per year. Wages thus fell behind over 2 percent each year. Workers will expect to catch up over the next decade.

The relative position of women workers has improved. In 1991, women working full-time earned seventy-four cents for every dollar earned by men, up from sixty-two cents a decade ago. Much of this increase reflects women's expanded opportunities. Women working full-time are now as likely to be employed in high-paying professional, technical, and managerial jobs as men are.

Women, however, still earn less than men in similar industries or occupations or with similar characteristics. The male-female earnings gap has narrowed, in part because women's earnings have improved and in part because men's earnings have declined after adjusting for inflation.

White workers earn more than African-American workers, but the earnings differential by race is not as large as that by gender. Full-time African-American workers earn seventy-eight cents for every dollar earned by white workers. However, this figure is down from eighty-one cents a decade ago.

Employee Benefits

In 1990, employers spent $375 billion on employee benefits other than Social Security. Contributions to retirement plans accounted for 34 percent of the total, while health benefits accounted for 47 percent. As recently as 1980, these proportions were reversed; retirement benefits accounted for 48 percent of employer spending, while health benefits took up only 31 percent.

The increased importance of health care benefits reflects their growing cost. General inflation reached historic lows during the 1980s and early '90s, but employers' health care costs continue to rise at 10 to 20 percent yearly.

This growth reflects several factors. Sixteen percent of the U.S. population under age sixty-five lacks health care coverage from any source. Physicians and hospitals often raise charges to those with coverage to reflect uncompensated or under-compensated care. Providers who fear malpractice litigation may add to overall costs by overtreating or overtesting patients. Medical advances add treatment options, but often raise costs as well.

Most ominously, more than ten cents of every dollar paid out in health care claims pays for mental health care, substance abuse treatment, or both, and these costs are among the fastest-growing health care costs. Employers can no longer consider drug abuse a law enforcement problem; it is now an employee compensation issue.

Employers are responding to growing health care costs in many ways. Flexible benefit plans have allowed employers and employees to get more for their money, particularly in health care spending. In these plans, also called cafeteria plans, employees choosing less-generous health care plans "earn" credits that can be applied to other benefits. According to the BLS, about one in four employees in firms with one hundred or more employees is now eligible to participate in some type of flexible benefit plan. Forty percent of employees in these firms also participate in retirement plans offering a choice between current cash and deferred compensation.

Runaway health care costs have also prompted interest in comprehensive health care reform. Just as retirement benefit security was the major compensation question of the 1960s and early '70s, health care reform will be the major compensation question of the late twentieth and, perhaps, early twenty-first centuries. In the 1990s, policy makers will have to find a way to expand health care coverage while containing the growth of health care costs, maintaining U.S. competitiveness, and reversing the erosion of real wages and living standards.

[See also Disabled Persons' Rights; Insurance; Unemployment; Unemployment Insurance; Work; Work Ethic; Work, Quality of; Working Conditions.]

BIBLIOGRAPHY

Executive Office of the President. *Economic Report of the President.* Washington, DC: U.S. Government Printing Office, 1992.

Piacentini, Joseph S., and Foley, Jill D. *EBRI Databook on Employee Benefits.* Washington, DC: Employee Benefit Research Institute, 1992.

U.S. Department of Commerce, Bureau of the Census. *Statistical Abstract of the United States 1991.* Washington, DC: U.S. Government Printing Office, 1991.

U.S. Department of Labor, Bureau of Labor Statistics. *Employee Benefits in Medium and Large Firms, 1989.* Washington, DC: U.S. Government Printing Office, 1990.

— KENNETH E. FELTMAN

HUMAN RIGHTS

After World War II, "human rights" began to refer to claims (or demands) to be legitimated in the future for all human beings. It also was used to prohibit certain forms of barbarism and to protect specified groups of people who might otherwise suffer from oppression, deprivation, or discrimination. Commitment to future fulfillment was intended to help the weak enjoy rights already available for the strong.

Actually, the basic substance of many ethical ideals now called human rights began with the first human beings. Anthropologists report that early kinship groups were knit together by tacit standards specifying what people had no right to do—such as committing incest. Other social norms established hunting, fishing, or grazing rights in territories regarded as their collective, often "God given," property. They also imposed responsibilities not only for the division of labor but also for nurturing infants, sharing food, honoring elders, and favoring kinsfolk. These responsibilities conferred implicit rights on the beneficiaries. To this day, the notion of interweaving rights and responsibilities (or duties), together with some action to attain these ideals and contend with transgressions, drives most serious human rights efforts.

Long before recorded history the strongest people proved that they could suppress many rights of weaker people. With the help of superior weaponry, numbers, and force, they secured widespread acceptance for slavery: "might makes right." They established patriarchal subordination of women: "male makes right." For themselves, they won various privileges, immunities, and entitlements. These included the power to make war, seize the property and women of others, build empires, settle disputes, and levy taxes. They also were able to control coinage and accumulate wealth: "money makes right."

With the development of writing came codification of evolving standards. The code of Hammurabi (ca. 1750 B.C.) set forth the rights of rulers, fathers, mothers, and children, together with penalties for wrongdoing. The Hindu Code of the Manus listed hundreds of written rights, duties, and penalties; these were amplified in the *Bhagavad-gita* and *Ramayana.* The many authors of the Hebrew scriptures went far beyond the basic ten commandments and compiled 613 rules, over 400 of which were about what people have no right to do. Generations of commentators went still further. The Christian scriptures and the sacred texts of Islam, Buddhism, Shintoism, and Taoism developed similar traditions. All of these codes included some standards that transcended particular religions by expressing shared human values that protect weaker or poorer people. These codes stood alongside other religious doctrines that justified the right of one group to dominate another, or even to wage "just" wars.

Supported by priests, many rulers were deified. As "gods," these humans enjoyed the right to make law and to stand above it. Aristocrats did not always accept this situation. They often banded together to overthrow rulers. English barons and bishops staged a rebellion in 1215 against King John, forcing him to promulgate a "Magna Carta." This Great Charter denied the monarchy's right to ignore law, gave aristocrats rights to be consulted, and conferred a few rights on lesser folk. Gradually, elected assemblies became forums for consultation with nobles, ecclesiastics, city people, merchants, and other mercantile capitalists. The members of these parliaments gradually established stronger rights of consultation and rights to override a monarch's decree and actually to enact law. The 1689 English Bill of Rights limited the monarchy and established many civil and religious rights.

Expanding wealth and sea power allowed the English the unwritten right to build a huge empire. Later, English power was temporarily checked by the rebellion of its North American colonies. The 1776 Declaration of Independence, the 1789 U.S. Constitution (ratified the same year as the French Declaration of the Rights of Man and the Citizen), and the 1791 U.S. Bill of Rights helped shape the new country's character in the capitalist-industrial era. In the United States and England, as in Western Europe generally, profit-seeking corporations became "fictitious persons" enjoying many of the rights accorded individual males. Backed by armed might and bolstered by dedication to a "civilizing mission" ideology, industrialized nation-states competed with each other in exercising their "sovereign rights and responsibilities" to control lives, governments, and cultures in Africa, Asia, Latin America, and Oceania. After the mid-nineteenth century abolition of slavery, the United States entered this fray with a "Manifest Destiny" to dominate the whole North American continent. This ideology put armed power behind the concept that "white (or lighter-skinned) makes right."

After taking over the former Tsarist empire in 1917, the Russian communists built a regime immensely destructive of human rights. Yet they attained international prestige by guaranteeing some minimal economic rights (particularly paid employment), supporting anti-colonial movements, opposing South African apartheid, and helping defeat the fascist Axis powers in World War II. In many countries during the early twentieth century women won the right to vote and labor unions won rights to organize and bargain collectively.

After World War II, the victors established the United Nations. This institution created a Security Council with the right to use military force, as a last resort, for keeping or making peace. Its charter gave each permanent member of the Security Council (originally the Republic of China, France, the United Kingdom, the United States, and the Soviet Union) a veto right over Security Council actions. After abstractly encouraging member states to respect "human rights and fundamental freedoms," the United Nations created a human rights commission to prepare an international bill of rights treaty. Since support could not be obtained for any treaty that might conflict with prevailing elite interests, the "nonbinding" 1948 Universal Declaration of Human Rights (UDHR) was adopted by the General Assembly as "a common standard of achievement for all peoples and all nations." This 1948 resolution combined economic, social, and cultural rights (including property rights) with civil and political rights.

The UDHR has since been endorsed in many national constitutions and international agreements and is widely regarded as part of humankind's "common law." But efforts to expand its generalities into the specifics of a single treaty were blocked by those who opposed giving equal weight to economic rights, then widely regarded as socialist inventions. The outcome was two treaties: a weak UN Covenant on Economic, Social, and Cultural Rights (with property rights omitted), and a stronger UN Covenant on Civil and Political Rights. The right to self-determination was added to both. An optional protocol gave persons the right to appeal to the UN over the head of their own government concerning alleged violations of civil and political rights. These four documents were temporarily labeled the "International Bill of Human Rights." They were soon followed by other UN treaties dealing with genocide, torture, racism, discrimination against women, employee and employer rights of association, war crimes refugees, and children. New treaty ideas deal with the disabled, sustainable development, and peace. Regional human rights charters or conventions have been established in Western Europe, Africa, and the Western hemisphere.

In the world of events rather than ideals,

the greatest human rights triumph

has been the end of the Cold War.

Of the treaties already formally proposed, many remain unratified by many countries. In the name of "sovereignty rights," most governments have refused to endorse the Optional Protocol. The United States has been pondering ratification of the Covenant on Economic, Social and Cultural Rights and the Convention on the Rights of the Child. Ratification, once it occurs, is often a stealth process, with neither governments nor media informing people about treaty-protected rights or governments' responsibilities toward them. Officials may then more readily ignore violations, evade responsibilities, and deny remedies.

In the world of events rather than ideals, the greatest human rights triumph has been the end of the Cold War. Human rights activists played notable (although not exclusive) roles in the collapse of the Berlin wall, the Solidarity victories in Poland, the Charter 77 success in Czechoslovakia, and the breakup of the Soviet Union. They also were crucial in displacing authoritarian regimes in Greece, Spain, Portugal, the Philippines, Argentina, Chile, and Brazil. They demonstrated their power in the conversion from apartheid to constitutional democracy in South Africa. In many other countries, partial triumphs have been won concerning the rights of women, ethnic or religious minorities, homosexuals and bisexuals, children, older people, criminals, crime victims, prisoners, students, teachers, tenants, consumers, and the disabled.

Some people shirk the language of rights on the ground that hypocritical rhetoric may render overly abstract rights meaningless. Commitment to a well-defined right provides explicit responsibilities, remedies, and resources nurturing expectations that fine words really may be followed by specific actions. Those whose perceived interests could be even slightly compromised may find rights (such as the right to earn a living at decent wages) too meaningful a threat. In response, they may try to delegitimate that right, remove it from the agenda of accepted policy discussion, or weaken it by restrictive reservations, understandings, and declarations.

In balancing conflicts among human rights and responsibilities, power is usually decisive. Much more than physical force is entailed. Power (or influence) may be understood as the ability to have some effect on some part of the world. Religion, love, beauty, philosophy, and law, as well as organization, leadership, and nonviolent activism, all may be sources of power. The legitimacy of such power (actual or potential) depends on the depth and breadth of acceptance through silent, grudging, or active consent. To the extent that it is dispersed widely and deeply, the relative power of males, money or the light-skinned might decline. Through the spirit and machinery of democracy, might (widely dispersed) might make right.

For human rights ideals to be realized,

action is needed

to strengthen private and public structures

—local, national, regional, and global—

of rights, responsibilities, action, and resources.

Whether it does so depends on millions of people resisting the barbarous enemies of human rights: poverty, hunger, disease, environmental depredation, ignorance, sexism, homophobia, ageism, repression, corruption, nationalist extremism, dehumanizing technologies, violence of all sorts, and war. For human rights ideals to be realized, action is needed to strengthen private and public structures—local, national, regional, and global—of rights, responsibilities, action, and resources. Human rights advocates would have to recognize the importance of labor and management rights. Civil liberties specialists would have to recognize the importance of international law. International human rights law might thus become a stronger global force as an evolving bill of human rights and responsibilities. In a world suffering from hopelessness and chaos, leadership along those lines could help build foundations for "human rights democracies." More and more people—particularly women and children—might thus enjoy economic, social, cultural, civil, and political rights, signaling the emergence, however slow, of a more civilized world society.

[See also Behavior: Social Constraints; Bioethics; Child Abuse; Civil Protest; Communications: Privacy Issues; Communitarianism; Criminal Justice; Criminal Punishment; Death and Dying; Disabled Persons' Rights; Entitlement Programs; Ethnic and Cultural Separatism; Laws, Evolution of; Media Consolidation; Refugees; Religion: Changing Beliefs; Social Controls; Social Welfare Philosophies; Women's Rights.]

BIBLIOGRAPHY

Adler, Mortimer J., "From Political to Economic Rights." In Mortimer J. Adler, *We Hold These Truths: Understanding the Ideas and Ideals of the Constitution.* New York: Collier Books, 1987.

Alderman, Ellen, and Kennedy, Caroline. *In Our Defense: The Bill of Rights in Action.* New York: Morrow, 1991.

Burns, McGregor James, and Burns, Stuart. *A People's Charter: The History of Human Rights in America.* New York: Knopf, 1991.

Dorsen, Norman, ed. *Our Endangered Rights.* New York: Pantheon, 1984

Drinan, Robert F. *Cry of the Oppressed: The History and Hope of the Human Rights Revolution.* New York: Harper & Row, 1987.

Glendon, Mary Ann. *Rights Talk: The Impoverishment of Political Discourse.* Free Press, 1991.

Henkin, Louis. *The Age of Rights.* New York: Columbia University Press, 1990.

Laqueur, Walter, and Rubin, Barry, eds. *The Human Rights Reader.* Rev. ed. New American Library, Penguin, 1990.

Nickel, James. *Making Sense of Human Rights.* Berkeley, CA: University of California Press, 1987.

Siegel, Richard Lewis. *Employment and Human Rights: The International Dimension.* Philadelphia: University of Pennsylvania Press, 1994.

Williams, Patricia J. *The Alchemy of Race and Rights.* Cambridge, MA: Harvard University Press, 1991.

– BERTRAM GROSS

HYDROELECTRIC POWER.

See ELECTRIC POWER.

I

ILLITERACY

Global literacy is a goal of the United Nations and a specific undertaking of the United States for its people by the year 2000. In the United States, state governors have set a goal of 100 percent literacy by the year 2000. The United States has the largest number of functional illiterates of any industrialized nation—an estimated 60 million adults in 1990, and the number may reach 90 million by 2000. UN surveys rank the United States forty-ninth among 158 member states—not an impressive record. Remedial efforts will have to continue until well into the next century.

As the twentieth century closes, no universal definition of literacy has been settled upon, and strategies to overcome illiteracy are varied. Controversy about the nature of the problem and disagreement concerning which skills and functional levels of performance will be adequate to meet living and working needs beyond the year 2000 are mostly unsettled.

In the past, literacy meant the ability to read and write one's name, together with some degree of reading skill. Later, literacy was defined as the attainment of a fourth-grade level of ability, essentially restricted to "the three R's"—reading, writing, and arithmetic. World War II, however, fundamentally changed the nature of literacy. Soldiers were given paper-and-pencil tests, and the results were used to sort out intelligence and literacy levels. Intelligence required the ability to read questions and select or write answers. Levels of schooling defined literacy.

By standards applied a few decades ago, today's young adult population (ages twenty-one to twenty-five) would be 95 percent literate. This standard, based on a fourth-grade level of reading and writing, was established fifty years ago. By the 1960s, the War on Poverty standards were based on young adults meeting or exceeding eighth-grade levels of literacy performance.

These earlier definitions of literacy have become inadequate. These times require information manipulation and application as a part of our work or social world. As we attempt to define new standards and prepare ourselves for literacy demands of the twenty-first century, we must realize that 80 percent of the workforce in the year 2000 is already at work today. Therefore, to reduce illiteracy, programs will have to be applied in the workplace and include lifelong learning.

Literacy training can never again be viewed solely as a school-based problem.

Other challenges in eliminating illiteracy involve skill level change and new criteria to meet the new requirements of the Information Era. Already, demands of information age technology and the skills required of new job opportunities not dreamed of a decade ago have drastically changed the old definitions.

The United States has the largest number of functional illiterates of any industrialized nation, with a number that may reach 90 million by 2000.

Literate high school graduates in the year 2007 must be ready for livelihoods that did not exist when a majority of the new workers started school in 1994. Furthermore, students preparing to be "literate" in science, mathematics, computer use, or in any discipline, can expect that preparation to be outmoded in a short time. Constant upgrading of skills is becoming imperative. Accelerating change illustrates the obvious: old concepts of literacy, of life and job preparation, and of schooling, must continue to change and keep pace with the times.

The dictionary defines *literate* as "educated: especially able to read and write" and "having or showing extensive knowledge, experience, or culture." This description does not suggest the flexibility required for lifelong learning or for undergoing rapid changes essential for survival in the future.

Literacy surveys by the U.S. Department of Labor of the twenty million people engaged in DOL programs concluded that 40–50 percent need literacy training to qualify for new jobs. An estimated 22 percent of U.S. adults are considered illiterate, and an additional 23 percent are functionally illiterate.

An Office of Technology Assessment study concluded: ". . . we as a nation must respond to the literacy challenge, not only to preserve our economic vitality, but also to ensure that every individual has a full range of opportunities for personal fulfillment and participation in society." (U.S. Congress, 1993).

Literacy rates vary worldwide from 99 percent in Sweden and Korea to 14 percent in Mozambique. However, comparisons can be misleading due to widely differing definitions. The Educational Testing Service has defined literacy as "... using printed and written information to function in society, to achieve one's goals, and to develop one's knowledge and potential" (Campbell et al., 1992). Definitions of this type may be helpful in developing measuring instruments, but in societies in which citizens get most of their information by viewing television screens (video or computer), we must move beyond reading and writing. Literacy in the future will have to be defined in terms of the media in which it is practiced. Future trends indicate that functional, practiced literacy includes the ability to:

1. Read about, observe, and listen to information and be able to communicate and demonstrate understanding.
2. Possess lifelong learning skills that enable self-directed, necessary changes in work and lifestyle.
3. Have the necessary skills to function in society and to pursue self-directed achievements.

Future prospects for reaching toward universal, global literacy are positive. New technologies are about to unleash better tools with which to teach and learn. The new literacy for the twenty-first century must not ignore the 98 percent of the world's illiterates who live in developing countries. Dignity and respect for a diversity of cultures and pluralistic ideologies must not be glossed over; nor should singular and unified efforts be allowed to homogenize differences. There is strength in diversity, and proper recognition of that elemental truth must not be allowed to wither and wane.

[See also Adult Learning; Development, Alternative; Educational Technologies; Elementary and Secondary Education; Higher Education; Literature.]

BIBLIOGRAPHY

Applebee, Arthur N.; Langer, Judith A. M.; Jenkins, Lynn B.; Mullin, Ina V. S.; and Foertsch, Mary A. *Learning to Work in Our Nation's Schools*. Princeton, NJ: Educational Testing Service, 1990.

Bhola, H. S. *Evaluating "Literacy for Development" Projects, Programs and Campaigns*. Quebec: UNESCO Institute for Education and German Foundation for International Development, 1990.

Hautecouer, Jean-Paul. *ALPHA 92 Current Research in Literacy: Literacy Strategies in the Community Movement*. Quebec: UNESCO Institute of Education, 1992.

Kirsch, Irwin S., and Jungeblut, Ann. *Literacy: Profiles of America's Young Adults*. Princeton, NJ: Educational Testing Service, 1986.

Kirsch, Irwin S.; Jungeblut, Ann; and Campbell, Ann. *Beyond the School Doors: The Literacy Needs of Job Seekers Served by the U.S. Department of Labor*. Princeton, NJ: Educational Testing Service, 1992.

Kirsch, Irwin S.; Jungeblut, Ann; Jenkins, Lynn; and Kolstad, Andrew. *Adult Literacy in America*. Princeton, NJ: Educational Testing Service, 1993.

Langer, Judith A.; Aplebee, Arthur N.; Mullis, Ina V. S.; Foertsch, Mary A. *Learning to Read in Our Nation's Schools*. Princeton, NJ: Educational Testing Service, 1990.

Lib, Barbara, and Stacey, Nevzer, Cochairs, et al. Office of Educational Research and Improvement (ORE), *Reaching the Goals: Adult Literacy and Lifelong Learning*. Washington, DC: U.S. Government Printing Office, 1993.

U.S. Congress, Office of Technology Assessment. *Adult Literacy and New Technologies: Tools for a Lifetime*, O.T.A.-SET-550. Washington, DC: U.S. Government Printing Office, 1993.

– LE ROY OWENS

IMMIGRATION.

See MIGRATION, INTERNATIONAL.

INDIA

Like the rest of the world, India is undergoing such rapid change that predictions of future scenarios are tentative at best. Above all, the industrial structure and socioeconomic framework of recent decades are falling apart. Money and power seem to be losing their importance. The growing feeling among Indians is a sense of helplessness and uncertainty coupled with a tenacious resolution to look for and implement alternatives.

Politics and Governance

Since India gained freedom from British rule in 1947, the major party in power has been the Congress party, with brief interruptions since 1976. However, a significant continuing trend is the declining trust and support of the Indian people for their government, which is widely viewed as becoming too large, too complex, and too distant from the common citizenry (Drucker, 1992). A crucial factor is the loss of the faith that problems can be solved by government.

Every seventh person in the world is Indian.

With 880 million people, India ranks second only

to China, and is the world's largest democracy.

Internationally, India's policy has been one of nonalignment. However, with the collapse of communism the dynamics of international diplomacy are changing dramatically worldwide. Moreover, the Indian government's fascination with large-scale industrial and economic projects will increasingly require outside financial support. Meanwhile, the industrialized countries will continue to get deeper into economic messes themselves, consequently losing their former glamor and role-model appeal for other countries. India, like other

Asian and African nations, will therefore pay increasing attention to its internal affairs.

Sources of Potential Conflict

In India poverty and unemployment loom large as the major source of internal conflicts. Even when these conflicts appear to be social (such as those arising from job discrimination against socially "backward" classes) or linguistic (such as those arising from the formation of states on the basis of language or dialect), the underlying element is economic—i.e., the effect of such policies on the growth of income and jobs.

Population and Demographics

India's population is huge. Every seventh person in the world is Indian. With 880 million people, India ranks second only to China, and is in fact the world's largest democracy. The size and growth rate of the Indian population are shown in Figure 1.

Population control policies have, therefore, assumed a top priority. Some crucial reasons for the explosive increase in population, particularly among low-income groups, can be traced to their economic predicament.

Physical labor is the major source of livelihood for the poor. In old age, therefore, the poor must rely on their children. Just as a large bank balance or insurance policy is a hedge against old age for the rich, so is an abundance of children for the poor. Children are their only asset in cases of emergency, disability, and old age. Another reason for the high birthrate among the poor is the high mortality rate in families due to malnutrition and other scarcities. In the future it will become im-

perative to create alternative sources of livelihood and better standards of living to solve the population explosion problem.

Urbanization

In recent decades, all village-based occupations, beginning with cloth production, have been destroyed by the massively aggressive industrialization of cities. There are literally no jobs and no industries in the smaller villages. This has forced large rural populations to migrate to cities in search of livelihood (*India 1992*, p. 66). Contrary to western economic theories, in India urbanization has led not to economic growth but to massive, crowded, filthy slums, which have become breeding grounds for crime and disease.

In coming years, however, the failure of industrialization will revive rural industries, rendering them economically more viable and profitable, and populations will shift back from cities to villages.

Social Conditions

For thousands of years, Indian society and its central units, the family, were peaceful, rural, and flourishing. But the industrial revolution, which spread worldwide through international trade during the last two centuries, tore apart this smooth and colorful social fabric.

Economic production in India had been cottage-based, involving all family members. But with industrialization, husbands left home to work in urban factories and wives became unemployed and dependent on them. In the future, when industries return to villages, Indian society will regain its social and economic well-being.

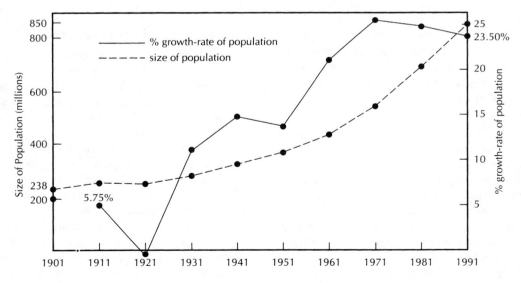

Figure 1. Size and growth-rate of the Indian population, 1901–1991. (India 1992, p. 54.)

TABLE 1

TRENDS OF URBANIZATION

Year	Population (Millions)		% of Total Population	
	Rural	Urban	Rural	Urban
1901	213	25	89	11
1971	439	109	80	20
1981	525	160	77	23
1991	627	217	74	26

TABLE 2

GROWTH OF PRODUCTION OF SELECTED INDUSTRIES

Industry	Unit (Millions)	1987–88	1990–91
Petroleum	Metric tons	30	33
Steel castings	Metric tons	0.170	0.256
Machine tools	Rupees	3,900	7,650
Automobiles	Rupees		366
Paper and boards	Metric tons	1.6	2
Cement	Metric tons	40	49
Sugar	Metric tons	9	12
Cotton cloth	Square meters	12,626	13,400
Power transformers	KVA	25	37
Electricity generated	Billion kwh	202	265

Quality of Life

Measured in terms of a wide variety of indicators, the quality of life of Indians has rapidly deteriorated in recent years. For example, in India divorce was unheard of, or at least stigmatized, only a few decades ago. Now marital separations are commonplace. Drinking and drug addiction are spreading among all age groups. Reverence, consideration, and care, not only for fellow citizens but for family members and friends, have become concepts of the past. Violent crimes, arson, and terrorism are rampant.

Economic Scenario

Modern industries must survive in international markets. In the future, a lack of international competitiveness will become a major hurdle to the progress of Indian industry.

Nevertheless, some Indian industries have shown remarkable growth recently, as indicated in Table 2.

In 1992, reports of major Indian companies show a decline in production, sales, and profits, causing deep concern, if not alarm. In the future, a crucial advantage India holds is its own local markets, which it can acquire by revitalizing village industries and, in turn, Indian agriculture. Agricultural workers in India are mostly landless and work only during the farming seasons. The shift of industries to villages will provide work and livelihood to these people year-round and will substantially strengthen agriculture.

International Trade

International trade has been the harbinger of economic growth only in the Western industrialized countries. For India—as for a few other countries of Asia, Africa, and Latin America—international trade has brought colonialism, the destruction of villages, unemployment, and poverty. Instead of reducing scarcities, it has led to the concentration of incomes in a few pockets in other, often distant countries.

India's share of world exports amounted to only 0.5 percent in 1988, and even that consisted of primary materials like tea, spices, iron ore, leather, precious stones, and cloth. India's trade balance (exports f.o.b.– imports c.i.f.) declined from Rs.-93 billion in 1987 and 1988 to Rs.-124 billion in 1989 and 1990 (*India: 1992,* p. 162).

It would be nearly impossible for India to raise the standard of living of its huge population through international trade, as it would entail earning unrealistically large profits abroad. Moreover, India should not even wish to raise the living standards of its people through international trade, because the latter often creates prosperity in one country at the expense of other countries. Instead, by relying on rural industrialization, India can bring itself prosperity in both a sustainable and humane way.

Transportation and Communication

Scientists in industrialized countries have labeled the present as "the Information Age." Such a description is meaningless for most of the world community living in Asia, Africa, and Latin America, as a few statistics about transportation and communication facilities in India attest.

Although India has intensively planned for modern technology since 1951, according to Indian government data, approximately 400,000 villages out of a total of 600,000—comprising 75 percent of the country's population—do not have an access road in the monsoon season. Out of these, about 200,000 villages do not have an access road for the rest of the year either. About 450,000 villages do not have a post office, and 540,000 do not have telephone service. Still, the initial hope is being nurtured that an industrial-information revolution will be advanced with the use of even more advanced technology.

Education and Health Care

On the educational and health fronts, facilities have improved in recent years but still remain scanty, considering the size of the total population, as shown in Table 3.

Alternative Futures and Sustainable Development (2000 and Beyond)

India's economic future lies in changing to the new system of local-production-for-local-markets by revitalizing village industries, beginning with cloth-production using the spinning wheel and then exchanging cloth with other commodities by gradually reestablishing local, cottage-based production.

Times are changing so rapidly that projections for the year 2000 and beyond cannot be made simply by extending the statistical trends mentioned above. Widespread unemployment, escalating inflation, rising crime rates, and increasing scarcity of food supplies are among the many factors which will bring fundamental changes. Forces are already on the move to launch a new rural industrial revolution in India. The new local-production-for-local-market will eliminate the present huge overhead and thus curb inflation.

By virtue of the spinning wheel's widespread availability, the weaker sections of society will produce cloth, the pivotal commodity. This will enable all the rest to be productive, using simple tools, local materials, and other commodities and services to barter local cloth with one another, leading to full employment and self-sustaining growth.

The new system of rural industrialization will eliminate most poverty and unemployment, inflation and

sluggishness in effective demand, energy prices and costs of high-tech machinery, bureaucratic red tape and the burden of middlemen chains, environmental damages and ecological imbalances, pressures due to urbanization and loss of contact with nature, subordination of women and mistreatment of minorities, destructive use of scientific knowledge and the lack of relevance of the educational system, increasing crime rates, and escalating arms production.

[See also Asia; Development, Alternative.]

BIBLIOGRAPHY

Drucker, Peter F. *Managing for the Future: The 1990s and Beyond.* New York: New American Library/Dutton, 1992.
Galbraith, John Kenneth. *The Nature of Mass Poverty.* Cambridge, MA: Harvard University Press, 1979.
Gandhi, Mohandas K. *Constructive Programme.* Ahmedabad, India: Navjivan, 1945.
India 1992. New Delhi: Observer Research Foundation, 1992.
Joshi, Nandini. *Development Without Destruction: Economics of the Spinning Wheel.* Ahmedabad, India: Navjivan, 1992.

– NANDINI JOSHI

INDUSTRIAL DESIGN

Industrial design and the industrial designer are at the center of the transformation of mass production manufacturing and the globalization of culture. Industrial design is emerging as a major strategic tool in international economic competition. Industrial designers are an inseparable part of product development groups, working with engineers, marketing staff, accountants, and strategic planners from concept to market, bringing better products to market faster. The role of the industrial designer and the designer's relationship to the consumer are being transformed as consumers increasingly demand that products meet their specific needs, possess utility, and delight their individual sensibilities.

The industrial designer is moving out of the studio and away from the drafting table to the computer console. Computer technology has allowed more people, from engineers and planners to marketers and consumers, to input more data into the design process. Up-to-the-minute consumer data and wider access to critical decision points has increased the possibility that consumers are offered products they need, want, and will buy.

Computer chips and circuit boards having led to the miniaturization of many products for the office and home, human scale is often the only reason for mass and size. Components inside the product are very tiny. The size of the product need not be determined by the size of its internal components, but by the size, dexterity, and comfort level of the user.

TABLE 3

EDUCATION AND HEALTH CARE IN INDIA

	1980–81	1987–88
Primary school enrollment (millions)	69	93
Middle school enrollment (millions)	18	30
Secondary school enrollment (millions)	9	18
Hospitals and dispensaries (thousands)	23	38
Beds per million population	8.3	9.1
Medical practitioners per million population	3.9	4.2

Source: *India 1992*, pp. 252–253.

Aesthetics in design are changing. A transcultural, global aesthetic is emerging as technology links people and cultures worldwide. Technology has made it possible for the same product designed and manufactured by different manufacturers to have the same basic functions. The design's competitive edge goes beyond utility to delight the user aesthetically or to perform additional, desired functions beyond the basic ones. User delight is value added.

Industrial design and the industrial designer are at the center of the transformation of mass production manufacturing and the globalization of culture.

Technology has brought the consumer right to the heart of the design process. Manufacturers are increasingly attentive to the needs and concerns of consumers. As global competition has forced more manufacturers to compete for the same consumer, manufacturers have begun to ask consumers what they want and need, and then use this data in product planning and design. Nowhere is this more evident than in the international automotive industry. The success of Japanese manufacturers was largely based on creating products that were excellent in quality, economical, and aesthetically pleasing. The Japanese were also the first to shorten drastically the time in getting products to market; they were able to provide products when they were needed. North American and European manufacturers, as they adopt similar consumer-centered practices, are closing the competitive gap and surpassing their rivals.

The development of "expert" software systems makes it possible for the consumer to custom-design products. Soon, the consumer will meet with a designer-facilitator and work at a design kiosk using computer technology to assemble a product to meet that consumer's individual needs, wants, and aesthetic sensibilities. Virtual reality technology also should allow the consumer-designer to "try on" the product and make changes, before the product is manufactured. There will be no warehouse or inventory as the product is built and delivered direct to the consumer. The industrial designer has two key roles in this process: first by developing the "expert" software systems that provide the design components for the consumer to manipulate, next by helping the consumer make design decisions during the consumer-centered design process.

Second only to computer technology in significance, environmental concerns are transforming design and manufacturing. The need to eliminate materials that are toxic or cannot be recycled, as well as concerns involving the depletion of global resources, have drawn new, "green" design solutions from industrial designers. Increasingly, as manufacturers are being held accountable by consumers and by government, they are taking responsibility for recycling or disposing of toxic and waste components in their products. It will become commonplace for manufacturers to retain ownership of selected products, lease them to consumers, then take them back for recycling or environmentally safe disposal.

As technology and green design push back the limits of design possibilities, industrial designers are being challenged to solve design problems wherever they occur. A laptop computer with a modem can take the design process to the problem site. Designers in the remotest areas can draw on "expert" systems software and databases around the globe to create customized, indigenous solutions. As designers work on-site rather than remotely, local traditional design and aesthetics will influence specific design solutions. Perhaps more significantly, the global exposure of the industrial designer together with the transglobal popularization of aesthetics are shaping global design. Industrial designers are responding to the increasing value placed on hand-made, ethnic, one-of-a-kind products by the globally conscious consumer. Most industrial designers will work in multidisciplinary product development teams much of the time. Individual designers will also take "time out" to work in fluid, changing coalitions with other designers, enabling them to practice as "artisan designers," creating custom, one-of-a-kind products.

Historically, the industrial designer became involved near the end of the product development process to make the product look attractive. The engineer was typically at the center of the process, the product being "engineered" rather than "designed." By training, engineers push a process or product to its capacity, to see how far it can go; industrial designers are trained to begin with the consumer. Manufacturers have discovered that complexity, incorporating all the functions possible in the product, creates serious problems for the consumer. Consumer complaints and returns often are based on complexity, which often perplexes them, rather than on quality problems. Many manufacturers have redesigned their products, substituting utility for complexity. Utility means: Does it work? Is it useful? Can I operate it? As the consumer becomes central to product development, industrial design will become a coordinating, synthesizing discipline. Industrial designers should become the multiskilled project synthesizers who integrate input from all of the disciplines in the product development group, keeping the consumer central to the process.

The transformation of industrial design poses serious implications for the training of industrial designers. All industrial design curricula will place increasing emphasis on developing designers' skills in three key areas: (1) Industrial designers will learn how to make maximum use of state-of-the-art computer-aided design hardware and software. (2) They will be trained to push designs beyond utility to delight, stressing the value-added qualities of aesthetics. (3) A new emphasis will be placed on team building and team work skills, as well as human factors and psychology.

Industrial design is emerging as both a tactical and a strategic tool in world competition. Design is no longer an afterthought, but is emerging as the core of the product development process. Intrinsic factors, aesthetics, and human factors provide the competitive edge. As the project design group takes hold and becomes the normative approach to product development, industrial designers will become project integrators and multiskilled synthesizers.

Industrial design is emerging as both a tactical and a strategic tool in world competition. Design is no longer an afterthought, but is emerging as the core of product development. At the extrinsic level, involving such factors as technology and engineering, competitors are on essentially equal footing. Intrinsic factors, such as aesthetics and human factors, provide the source of any competitive edge. As the product-design-group approach takes hold and becomes the typical approach to product development, industrial designers will become project integrators and multiskilled synthesizers.

[See also Architectural Design; Computers: Software; Creativity; Marketing Breakthroughs; Nanotechnology; Visual Arts.]

BIBLIOGRAPHY

Caplan, Ralph. "Designers and Engineers: Strange but Essential Bedfellows." *Technology Review* (February–March 1983).

Hawken, Paul. "The Ecology of Commerce." *INC.* (April 1992).

Hawken, Paul, and McDonough, William. "Seven Steps to Doing Good Business." *INC.* (November 1993).

Sedgewick, John. "The Complexity Problem." *Atlantic Monthly* (March 1993).

Smith, P. G., and Reinertsen, D. G. *Developing Products in Half the Time.* New York: Van Nostrand Reinhold, 1991.

– JOSEPHINE KELSEY

INDUSTRIAL GASES

Industrial gases are an important, growing component of our economy. Industrial gases are commonly categorized in terms of the containers in which they are stored or shipped. The most common container is the relatively compact cylinder, followed by the larger tank or tanker and then the pipeline. Such gases are respectively referred to as "cylinder," "bulk," or "pipeline" gases. The atmospheric gases oxygen, nitrogen, and argon are the most commonly used and bring in the most revenue. Other commonly used gases are hydrogen, helium, carbon dioxide, and acetylene. Industrial gases are used in a wide variety of industrial applications, ranging from basic metals to chemicals, food processing, and medicine.

New applications are bringing gases closer to the customer in uses never before contemplated. Some applications require a greater degree of purity and extremes of temperature in the cryogenic (super-cooled) range. Probably the most opportune use for industrial gases in the future is in cleaning up our environment. Applications of gases, primarily oxygen, for environmental cleanup extend from actual remediation of contaminated land and water to reducing pollution in various manufacturing processes. Hydrogen can be mixed with other fuels to increase reactivity, which also reduces the level of pollution.

At the same time that we are discovering new applications for gases, we also are discovering new, more efficient methods of separating the atmospheric gases. These new methods of air separation are noncryogenic (i.e., they do not require very low temperatures to take place). Two commonly used noncryogenic air-separation methods are pressure-swing absorption and membrane filters. While noncryogenic gases are cheaper to produce, they have a more limited degree of applicability. Noncryogenic gases are generally not as pure as those produced by the cryogenic process, and since they are not liquid, they cannot be used for applications requiring extremes of cold. However, the noncryogenic gases can be produced by a relatively small "black box" installed at a manufacturing site, eliminating the need for cylinders or bulk gas transport and pipelines. As gases are used more broadly, the noncryogenic processes are likely to become more refined and competitive so that by the turn of the century, a significant amount of the new growth in atmospheric gases could be satisfied by noncryogenic gas processes.

Even though noncryogenic gases will enjoy significant growth, cryogenic gases will always fill an important need. Cryogenic liquid gases are much more efficient to transport (700 times more compact as a liquid than as a gas), and liquefied gases represent the only way to achieve the cold temperature essential for superconductivity. Present commercial applications of superconductivity require liquid helium ($-452°$ F). The principal use of liquid helium for superconductivity is in magnetic resonance imaging (MRI) technology for noninvasive medical diagnostic applications.

Recent discoveries of higher-temperature superconducting materials have increased the enthusiasm for superconducting. This has meant more use of liquid helium, both for commercial and research applications. As higher temperature superconductivity materials are discovered, other higher temperature cryogenic liquids are likely to be used, such as liquid nitrogen ($-346°$ F). Since nitrogen is far more plentiful than helium, and requires less energy to liquefy, the cost of superconducting systems will be more affordable and therefore more commercially viable.

High-temperature superconductivity (HTS) will have major applications for the generation, transmission, and use of electric power. HTS will revolutionize our use of power and help solve our need for cleaner, less-polluting transportation.

Hydrogen also holds great potential for our transportation needs in the future. Hydrogen is very clean-burning, producing only heat and water. Currently, hydrogen is supplied for many essential uses including aerospace, chemicals, food, electronics, glass, metals, nuclear power, petroleum, and pharmaceuticals.

Demand for cleaner air has created a need for transitional low-emission motor vehicles (TLEV), low-emission vehicles (LEV), ultra-low-emission vehicles (ULEV) and zero-emission vehicles (ZEV). California already has an emission-reduction plan in place; other states will follow. Hydrogen is likely to be a key component in satisfying emission-reduction plans. In addition to battery-driven electric vehicles, only hydrogen with a fuel-cell/electric-motor drive can meet the zero-emission vehicle requirements. With the advent of the 1990 Clean Air Act amendments, refineries are required to produce cleaner-burning fuels. This is most effectively accomplished through hydrogen processing to significantly reduce the sulfur, olefins, and aromatics content in the transportation fuels a refinery produces. Clean-burning hydrogen, or blends of hydrogen and natural gas in internal combustion engines are candidates to meet less-stringent, but still challenging, ultra-low-emission vehicle standards.

Gases can themselves be pollutants. Carbon dioxide has many beneficial uses, but is a product of combustion. The level of carbon dioxide in our environment is increasing, due largely to the burning of fossil fuels and deforestation. At the beginning of the Industrial Revolution, there were about 280 parts per million (ppm) of CO_2 in the atmosphere. Today, there are about 360 ppm, a 30 percent rise. The annual increase is 2 ppm and rising. If present trends continue, the concentration of CO_2 in the atmosphere will double to about 700 ppm in the latter half of the twenty-first century. This increase would not be a direct threat to human life, but it does pose an indirect threat due to the greenhouse effect. Man-made change of such magnitude requires careful consideration to understand the consequences. Scientists have developed models to show the effect of the global warming caused by the rise of CO_2 and other so-called greenhouse gases. The debate rages on with other scientists refuting the global warming hypothesis. Nevertheless, we are now changing the composition of our atmosphere. We are in effect conducting a global environmental experiment without knowing the result. While some of the change that higher levels of CO_2 in our atmosphere will bring about may raise concerns, it is also important to stress the beneficial aspects of higher CO_2 concentrations for some food crops, trees, and plants.

Probably the most opportune use for industrial gases in the future is in cleaning up our environment.

While there is significant disagreement about the global warming phenomenon, there is agreement that rising concentrations of CO_2 in the atmosphere will increase the growth of plant life. A doubling of CO_2 concentrations will cause plants to grow larger and faster, with increases in leaf size and thickness, stem height, branching, and seed production. Fruits and flowers will also increase in size and number.

Industrial gases will also be a factor in sewage conditioning and garbage disposal. In areas of high geothermal activity, deep shafts can be drilled into areas of high temperature. Sewage can be injected with oxygen and pumped down the shaft where the oxygen and high temperature work on the sewage making it into an easily manageable and safe compost suitable for gardening.

Everywhere we look, industrial gases play an important part in the way we live: in processing and serving food, steel production, making semiconductors, treating the sick, carbonating beverages, and providing fuels, to cite but a few examples. Industrial gases will continue to be used in commerce as well as on the leading edge of technology. Gases will also be important in finding ways to satisfy our growing need for energy and to help clean up our environment. Industrial gases will continue to be an essential part of our economy while enhancing our quality of life.

[See also Acid Rain; Batteries; Chemicals, Fine; Chemistry; Global Warming; Maglev; Motor Vehicles, Alternatively Powered; Natural Gas; Ozone Layer Depletion; Space Travel; Superconductors.]

BIBLIOGRAPHY

Carbon Dioxide. Publication No. CGA C-6. Arlington, VA: Compressed Gas Association, 1993.

Handbook of Compressed Gases. Arlington, VA: Compressed Gas Association, 1990.

Proposed Regulations for Low Emission Vehicles and Clean Fuels. Sacramento, CA: California Air Resources Board, 1990.

Safe Handling of Cryogenic Liquids. Publication No. CGA P-12. Arlington, VA: Compressed Gas Association, 1993.

Wittwer, Sylvan H. "In Praise of Carbon Dioxide." *Policy Review* (Heritage Foundation) (Fall 1992).

– CARL T. JOHNSON

INDUSTRIAL POLICY.

See BUSINESS STRUCTURE: INDUSTRIAL POLICY.

INFORMAL ECONOMY

The informal economy consists of all productive but unpaid work, including household maintenance, do-it-yourself repairs, and home building; food growing for personal use; child care; looking after the sick, elderly, and disabled; and volunteer work. These vast informal sectors are generally ignored by economists and do not show up in their money-dominated, macroeconomic statistics such as gross national product (GNP), gross domestic product (GDP), savings investment rates, and so forth.

The enormous contribution to national wealth made by these informal sectors led to reappraisal during the 1980s. Figure 1, "Total Productive System of an Industrial Society," shows both the paid and unpaid sectors. This four-layer cake shows the GNP, money-denominated sectors as the two top layers that correspond to the more familiar economists' pie charts: the private and public sectors, as well as the underground economy of cash-based drugs, off-the-books work, money laundering, and other illegal activities. Below the middle line are the unpaid or unaccounted productive activities of the informal, unpaid "love economy." The bottom layer of the cake diagram consists of nature's productivity.

A very important subdefinition for all activities of the informal economy differentiates between (1) the love economy: altruistic, largely local activities such as volunteering, family and community care, mutual aid, subsistence work, and local skills (sharing, bartering), and (2) the underground economy: activities that are criminal, quasi-criminal, tax-avoiding in nature, involving gray and black markets and unreported trade, and often national and international in scope.

Bartering

Bartering is ubiquitous in all human societies, from ancient times to the present, and is found across all societies in both legal and criminal activity. Countries experiencing shortages of foreign exchange—for example, Russia and China—often resort to barter. Such bartering is usually facilitated by intermediaries and referred to as countertrade. Some of this countertrade is undertaken to avoid taxes, or to take advantage of loopholes that allow global intracompany trading to escape or minimize host-country taxes. Global bartering is thought to encompass almost one-quarter of all world trade.

Within a love economy, bartering is very different, embracing cooperative and altruistic undertakings and activities of simpler village life so as to optimize community resources in societies where little money is used. Barter such as this escapes statistical report or review.

Barter often resurges in economies hit by hard times and also in more isolated communities. Forms of such barter include exchange clubs for used clothing and appliances, baby-sitter co-ops, community workshops where tools can be shared, mutual aid networks, and even local "currencies" (such as the "local exchange trading systems" invented by Michael Linton in Vancouver, Canada).

Black Markets

Black markets occur in situations where there are shortages of needed goods and services. Transactions usually involve hoarders, speculators, and middlemen who try to corner the market on scarce goods. Objects of such trade include legal commodities such as food and housing, or illegal ones such as narcotics, and may be widely practiced where political controls are weak.

Causes

Informal economies are, and have been throughout history, at the base of all human societies. In a very real sense, informal economies are statistical artifacts born of excessively narrow economic theories, models, and statistics that defined such activities as "uneconomic" and outside the scope of GNP/GDP national accounts. Economic theory holds that most caring, cooperative, unpaid, and volunteer work, such as is characteristic of the love economy, is "irrational." Persons operating in the underground economy, on the other hand, work surreptitiously and hide their activities to avoid persecution for tax avoidance or other crimes.

During the 1970s and '80s, GNP/GDP and national statistical accounts began to be readdressed by documenting some sectors of the informal economy such as unpaid work, unreported international trade, and barter transactions. Governments, however, have often avoided documenting large areas of informal activities, notably global and domestic drug trade.

Another problem highlighted by studies of informal economies involved methods used to compile labor statistics, such as unemployment. Until the late 1970s, textbooks defined an economy as fully employed when only approximately one-half of the adult population was working in a paid job. That half of the population consisted primarily of heads of households. This household model assumed there was a breadwinner (usually male) with a dependent wife and children.

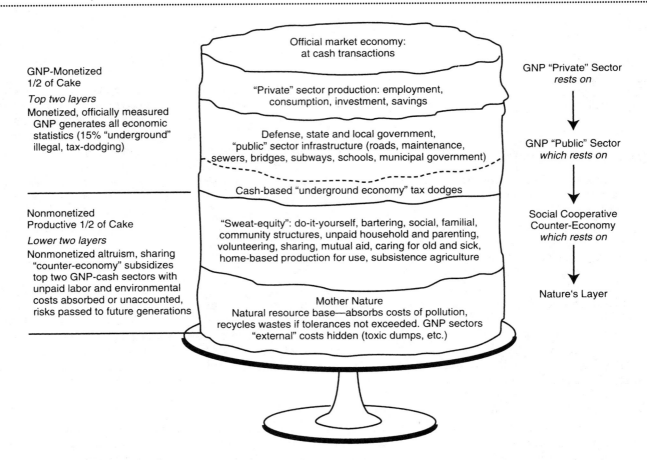

GNP-Monetized
1/2 of Cake

Top two layers
Monetized, officially measured
GNP generates all economic
statistics (15% "underground"
illegal, tax-dodging)

Nonmonetized
Productive 1/2 of Cake

Lower two layers
Nonmonetized altruism, sharing
"counter-economy" subsidizes
top two GNP-cash sectors with
unpaid labor and environmental
costs absorbed or unaccounted,
risks passed to future generations

Official market economy:
at cash transactions

"Private" sector production: employment,
consumption, investment, savings

Defense, state and local government,
"public" sector infrastructure (roads, maintenance,
sewers, bridges, subways, schools, municipal government)

Cash-based "underground economy" tax dodges

"Sweat-equity": do-it-yourself, bartering, social, familial,
community structures, unpaid household and parenting,
volunteering, sharing, mutual aid, caring for old and sick,
home-based production for use, subsistence agriculture

Mother Nature
Natural resource base—absorbs costs of pollution,
recycles wastes if tolerances not exceeded. GNP sectors
"external" costs hidden (toxic dumps, etc.)

GNP "Private" Sector
rests on

↓

GNP "Public" Sector
which rests on

↓

Social Cooperative
Counter-Economy
which rests on

↓

Nature's Layer

Figure 1. Total productive system of an industrial society (three-layer cake with icing metaphor).

Surprisingly, even among the world's twenty-four major industrial countries that are members of the Organization for Economic Cooperation and Development (OECD), such unpaid activities account for approximately half of all productive hours worked. In the United States, unpaid work accounted for an estimated 60 percent of GNP (according to Burns, 1977). In the U.S. "love economy" some 94.2 million Americans performed 20.5 billion hours of volunteer work in 1991, valued at $176 billion. In developing countries, where approximately three-quarters of the world's population live, unpaid work accounts for three-quarters of all productive hours worked. This reflects the persistence in these countries of large subsistence sectors and traditional communities that still function outside of the money-based economy, or that only use cash for items that cannot be produced or bartered locally.

Information quantifying these informal economies is collected by the United Nations. For example, household work is usually reported in terms of the unpaid hours. No OECD country includes this data in GNP/GDP figures, but some (Canada, Denmark, and Finland) have officially worked up the statistics. Denmark

values household work the highest (at 50 percent of GNP), with Norway at 41 percent and Finland at 31 percent. A 1929 report estimated that household work was valued at 25 percent of GNP in the United States, but since then only a few privately commissioned studies have been made.

Data is very sparse in developing countries. Venezuela's Central Bank estimated household work at 22 percent of GNP in 1982. In the same year, the National Committee on the Role of Filipino Women estimated the value of household work at only 11 percent of GNP. The collection of such data is affected not only by the economic biases mentioned but also by cultural values such as male dominance.

During the 1980s, household incomes in the United States eroded. Not only were women obliged to enter the paid work force, but male household heads often held down two jobs to make ends meet. Full-time jobs shrank while enormous numbers of 20-hour-a-week jobs were created.

Today, some 30 percent of U.S. workers shed from company payrolls have become "contingency" workers, while part-time jobs have also burgeoned. During the

1990s, with fewer at-home unpaid spouses doing household, parenting, and community duties, new businesses providing such services have boomed. They include: fast foods, day care, home helpers, visiting nursing and rehabilitation services, child minders, self-help seminars, and preschools.

Unpaid activities account for approximately half

of all productive hours worked.

In the United States, unpaid work accounted for

an estimated 60 percent of GNP.

Informal economies will likely remain unmeasured as long as nations have crime and other illicit activities, and as long as some types of work, particularly that performed within homes and communities, go unrecognized and financially unrewarded. However, there are signs that some of this activity is being acknowledged as societies modernize and women enter the work force. Illicit aspects of the underground economy are likely to remain unless laws prohibiting "immoral" behavior, such as drug use, are dropped and these activities become accepted as economic undertakings.

[See also Drugs, Illicit; Women and Work; Work; Work, Quality of; Workforce Diversity.]

BIBLIOGRAPHY

Henderson, Hazel. *Paradigms in Progress,* Chapters 4 and 6. Indianapolis: Knowledge Systems, 1991.

Nicholls, William M., and Dyson, William A. *The Informal Economy.* Montreal: VIS Publication Renouf, 1983.

Schumacher, E. F. *Small Is Beautiful.* New York: Harper & Row, 1973.

Shankland, Graeme. *Wonted Work, A Guide to the Informal Economy.* New York: Bootstrap Press, 1988.

Ul Haq, Mabub, ed. *Human Development Report.* New York: United Nations Development Program, 1990, 1991, 1992.

Waring, Marilyn. *If Women Counted.* San Francisco: Harper & Row, 1989.

— HAZEL HENDERSON

INFORMATION OVERLOAD

It is well known that the primary force driving the world economy and most other aspects of society is the flood of new information and knowledge. General information doubling time occurs about every 2.5 years (each 900 days).

As of the mid-1990s, 90 percent of all the scientists who ever lived are still alive. Scientific information doubles about every 12 years (1994). The number of scientific articles, as such, doubled every 5.5 years during the early 1980s. The number of scholarly scientific journals rose from 70,000 in 1970 to 108,590 in 1990. One million papers published in mathematics found their way into the literature between 1984 and 1994. Scientific knowledge itself doubles every decade or so. More scientific knowledge has been produced since 1960 than was produced in all history prior to 1960. This is generating a torrent of information and fostering a trend toward specialization.

Since the mid-1950s, science has learned more about how the world and universe work than had been learned in the previous 5,000 years. By the year 2000, the base of scientific knowledge is likely to grow by 200 percent. In 1945 we could identify two galaxies. Today we can identify 2 billion galaxies. We even seem to have made contact with radiation left over from what some scientists consider to be the Big Bang, which took place perhaps fifteen billion years ago. Thus it appears that we may have established a direct link with the beginnings of time and space.

Earth's galaxy, the Milky Way as we call it, is comprised of 250 billion to 400 billion stars. It is only a single galaxy of 100 billion galaxies within our universe. There may be 10,000 to 100,000 advanced civilizations in this galaxy alone! Carl Sagan estimates that up to one million technical civilizations may exist in Earth's galaxy alone. If we are alone—and we may know the answer within the next twenty-five to fifty years—that poses an enormous responsibility. If we are only one of millions, that, too, is equally mind-boggling. One thing for certain is that a little humility as well as awe are in order. Whatever the outcome, the immensity of, the sheer magnitude of knowledge throughout an expanding universe is awesome to contemplate.

The number of printed articles soars. More than 12,000 magazines were published in America in 1990. Over the same period, 350,000 new books were published worldwide. The number of books in our leading libraries doubles every fourteen years. Literature overall doubles every ten to fifteen years.

This torrent of new knowledge means that most technology is obsolete within five to seven years. In certain areas, particularly computers and electronics, technology becomes obsolete usually within two to three years.

The pace of technological catch-up is so fast that a company has to recover its production costs in three to six months on a new electronic product, for example. After that, rivals will have produced a competitive look-alike for the market. As product life cycles are getting shorter (half of what they were a decade ago), corporations are seeking greater flexibility. Technology is changing so quickly that companies do not necessarily want to tie themselves down to making a particular product. Joint ventures and other alliances offer far more flexibility in a fast-changing environment.

Accelerating growth of knowledge looked at in another manner means that by the time a child born today finishes college, knowledge may have increased fourfold. By the time that person reaches fifty years of age, accumulated knowledge may have grown thirty-two fold. It means that 97 percent of all knowledge will have been acquired since that person was born.

Increased Speed of Communication

Long-distance transmission of data has accelerated from two bits per second by smoke signals to unbelievable new speeds. Beams of light, for example, may transmit a mind-boggling one million times more information in a given unit of time than present radio wave technology. Electromagnetic fields conceptualized as beams of light change polarity approximately one trillion times per second. The ability to transmit bits of data on light waves at rates of one trillion bits per second means that someone could transmit 200,000 average-size books in one second! The Library of Congress's entire 1991 collection of books, amounting to 25 terabits, could be transmitted in just over five minutes (312.5 seconds). A gigabyte (one billionth of a second) is to one second what one second is to 31.7 years. Just as we are becoming familiar with "megabytes" in mere thousandths, technology is ushering in terabytes—rates of data handling equivalent to 1 trillion bits per second.

The first edition of the *Encyclopaedia Britannica,* published in 1771, ran only three volumes in length, with 2,659 pages. The thirty-two volume *Encyclopaedia Britannica,* published in 1993, included 44 million words (300 megabytes) and 23,000 illustrations (600–700 megabytes)—in electrical data processing terms, 1 gigabyte total.

New fiber-optic cables developed during the mid-1990s by AT&T advance transmission capability over today's standard by at least sixteen-fold. By substantially reducing interference between wavelengths (colors), the new cables can transmit 80 gigabytes per second. Thus the entire contents of the *Encyclopaedia Britannica* (1 terabit) could be transmitted in about one-eightieth of a second!

Information Overload

The profusion of scientific information has generated a Niagara of information. This cascade of information inundates the American mind daily. A person reading the entire Sunday edition of the *New York Times* would be exposed to more information in that one reading than was absorbed in a lifetime by the average American living in Thomas Jefferson's day. (On November 13, 1987, the *New York Times* published an edition that was 1,612 pages long and contained more than 12 million words.)

By one estimate the amount of information an individual uses in a lifetime is equivalent to 20 billion bits of data. That amount of data can be transmitted in the parsing of a second. In other words, everything one will ever think or say in an entire lifetime can be flicked around the globe in a millisecond.

The ability to transmit bits of data on light waves

at rates of one trillion bits per second

means that someone could transmit

200,000 average-size books in one second!

This onrush of information has brought us to a point where we have more information than we can possibly use. We may have reached the point of what's called "negative information"—so much information that the quality of decision is actually decreased. No longer does the assumption that says more information produces better solutions hold. Too much information creates a sense of numbness and discouragement. What is needed is an understanding of the contexts and cultures in which all this information is embedded. In a negative information environment, the very concept of civil society loses focus and form. The civil society is, in part, an outgrowth of human relationships, and the avalanche of information swamping us every day means that we tend to develop "contacts" rather than human relationships, the latter of which are of a deeper quality and character and can only grow over time.

The positive results of all this information are obvious. People's lives have been enriched in countless ways. But we have yet to find a way of compensating for other, less obvious consequences. For example, psychologists tell us that information overload is now a significant cause of mental illness.

In the past, the transmission of information, ideas, and images took place slowly, sometimes taking centuries to move around the world. This gave people time to adjust psychologically to a new information environment. But today, children who use computers in classrooms represent a generation that grows impatient with teachers and parents whose explanations are drawn out or too wordy. Impatience and expectation of perfection from spouse or child is increasing as an attitude of those whose work involves extensive use of computers. Computer operators internalize the computer's standards for speed, accuracy, perfection, and yes or no answers. They show little patience for nuance or ambiguity, and none for error. In an age where students have access to all knowledge by the mere press of a button, how does education develop the judgment and wisdom an individual needs to use that knowledge to best advantage?

The sheer volume of the data confronting us daily—information overload—virtually forces a reduction in our span of focus on events. No human brain can begin to comprehend the sum total of the mass-produced data we generate. Thus we lose context and perspective, and with them, a clear sense of the meaning of the information we amass; the tie between information and human purpose is severed.

Compare this endless stream of data with the elegant simplicity of our basic communication symbols:

- A mere twenty-six letters comprise the English alphabet. Despite the tiny number of symbols, the language derived from them is limitless.
- A scant ten Arabic symbols comprise our number system, yet calculations and manipulation of these numbers into combinations is circumscribed only by time.
- Just twelve notes make up our basic chromatic scale for music, yet infinite combinations are possible.
- From the basic ten commandments, basic tenets of those principles have been recast into well over three million laws, with more coming every day.

The whole of our civilized life has rested on these few communication symbols. This should remind us that human affairs are infinite, not finite; limitless, not limited.

Exponential Rate of Change

Trillions of calculations per second usher in a rate of speed that divorces time from any human comprehension. We solve problems now in seconds that, in bygone ages, would have taken armies of people, working their entire lifetimes, to solve. In a world of super speeds, the human reaction time of 1.5 seconds to push a button is far too slow. Combat jets rely, to a large extent, on machines performing with split-second timing.

The marriage of information and communication technologies has created a new force—telepower—which is the driving force of global change. Computers, telephones, television, faxes, and robots—connected by wire or satellites—constitute the largest technical machine in the world. In terms of technology, the telecommunications industry is going to see more change in the next six years than it has seen in the past ninety-four years.

Building the next phase of the American Experiment requires a new form of leadership. And that's because instant information has virtually eliminated the knowledge gap between the leaders and the led.

One thing has become clear: The more information we amass, the more important context and meaning become. We live in two worlds—the world of data and the world of meaning. Knowledge does not exist in a vacuum. It always moves forward and demands the application of meaning.

Meaning requires reflection and time-consuming thought. In this respect, Harvard Business School, AT&T, Pepsi, Aetna, and numerous other companies are training managers in the exercise of reflection, in various forms of inner awareness. This is based on the belief that the key trait of a good leader is having an inward center of reflection from which to make considered decisions. While information agents such as "wildfire" may help filter out overload, such an inward center can only emanate from an internal search in life that has noting to do with technology.

As life becomes more information-driven, it becomes more essential for each manager to know how to provide his or her personnel with the requisite meaning and context.

[See also Communication: Technology; Information Society; Information Technology; Libraries; Libraries: Electronic Formats; Telecommunications.]

BIBLIOGRAPHY

Bathurst, Diana, and Bathurst, Robin. *The Telling Image: The Changing Balance Between Pictures and Words in a Technological Age.* Oxford, UK: Oxford University Press, 1990.

Glastonbury, Bryan, and Lemendela, Walter. *The Integrity of Intelligence: A Bill of Rights for the Information Age.* New York: St. Martin's Press, 1992.

McLuhan, Marshall, with introduction by Lewis H. Lapham. *Understanding Media: The Extensions of Man.* Reprint. Cambridge, MA: MIT Press, 1994.

Postman, Neil. *Technopoly.* New York: Alfred A. Knopf, 1992.

Sakaiya, Neil. *The Knowledge-Value Revolution.* New York: Kodansha America, 1991.

Wurman, Richard Saul. *Information Anxiety.* New York: Bantam Books, 1989.

– GRAHAM T. T. MOLITOR
WILLIAM VAN DUSEN WISHARD

INFORMATION SOCIETY

Information society, service society, postindustrial society, technological society, computer society, knowledge society—all of these terms are labels that attempt to make sense of the profound transformation wracking industrial societies since the mid-1950s. Regardless of which label is used, the central assertion is that industrial societies are evolving into a new form of society.

While the term *postindustrial* first appeared in print in 1917, the term *information society* was not used until 1968. *Service society,* describing a slightly different economic base, was the preferred term in the 1970s. Peter Drucker referred to our *knowledge society* in 1969. The earliest substantial book on a knowledge-based society is Daniel Bell's 1973 *The Coming of Postindustrial Society*, although nowhere therein does he actually refer to the phrase *information society*. The Organization for Economic Cooperation and Development published a report entitled *The Information Society* in 1975, and by the early 1980s the term *information society* started to come into common use, prompting John Naisbitt to declare in 1982 that "it is now clear that the postindustrial society is the information society" (Naisbitt, 1982, p. 4).

In the 1970s and '80s, people talked about

"mass production" of information,

the "information explosion," and

the possibility of informational overload or

"infoglut."

Even today there is no widely accepted formal definition of either the industrial or the information stages of socioeconomic development. However, the following features are commonly used to distinguish between them:

- *Industrial societies* are dominated by blue-collar workers who labor in large organizations under close supervision, using industrial technologies to process physical materials in order to mass-produce physical goods. Few of these goods require high levels of information or information technologies to design, manufacture, sell, or maintain.
- *Information societies* are dominated by team-based knowledge workers who add value by strategically utilizing high-quality information in the creation of goods, services, and relationships. All of these undertakings require high levels of information and information technologies to create, market, and maintain.

Two major developments—one technological, the other human—dominate information society discussions: The first is the emergence of powerful, computer-based information technologies that for the first time in history make the sharing of information, regardless of its form or content, cheap, easy, and distance-independent. The second is the corollary requirement that, in order to sustain success, individuals, organizations, and societies must develop an ability to routinely utilize high-quality information and to do so strategically.

These are startling developments when seen against the taken-for-granted world of the mid-twentieth century. Then, communications and travel over long distances were occasions for excitement; personal long-distance phone calls, always operator-dialed, often meant very special circumstances such as births, deaths, or a year-end holiday. Boundaryless networks of self-managed work teams did not exist and were in fact virtually unimaginable.

Diverse developments heralded the demise of the industrial order:

- In 1954 only twenty computers were shipped to customers in the United States. In Europe, in 1958, only 160 computers were in use. In contrast, by the early 1990s, 140 million personal computers were in use worldwide, and over 400 million microprocessors were embedded in autos, telephones, televisions, and a variety of appliances. By 1994, the Internet had over 30 million users worldwide.
- In the mid-1950s, 80 percent of the cost of a new car represented materials and wages. The cost of services and information—design, marketing, engineering, management, and health care—accounted for the rest. By the mid-1980s, these ratios had reversed.
- In 1956, for the first time, white-collar workers outnumbered blue-collar workers in the United States. This date, well before the advent of the microprocessor, is customarily used to mark the arrival of the information society in the United States.
- By the early 1990s, national politics, professional sports, entertainment, and evangelism had all developed a significant dependence on their electronic audiences. Live performances still brought in substantial sums, but proportionally much less than previously.
- By the early 1990s, every form of information—data, text, pictures, sound, art—could be fully digitized and therefore integrated. The familiar distinctions among media delivery systems—computers, telephones, cable, radio, CDs, wireless, publishing, movies, and databases—were becoming increasingly blurred.
- By 1991 computer hardware and software exports from the United States were almost $48 billion—more than double the value of exported autos and auto parts ($22 billion).
- In 1993, Americans spent $341 billion on entertainment and recreation, almost ten cents of every nonmedical consumer dollar. This was more than the worldwide value of computer hardware and software sales ($300 billion). The amount of information available continues to double roughly every five years.

Such far-reaching developments herald the end of the industrialized world as we have known it. The significance of such events began to be apparent by the 1970s. Reports were commissioned by governments: e.g., the 1972 Computer-Communications Task Force report of the government of Canada. National policy conferences were organized—e.g., the annual Telecommunications Policy Review Conference, first held in 1973. Journals were established such as *The Information Society*, which appeared in 1981. Consultants developed management information systems (MIS). Database libraries were created—e.g., Dialog and Lockheed in the late 1960s. Computer-conferencing systems were developed: Internet in the 1970s.

In the 1970s and '80s, many people welcomed the information age, whether or not they really understood its significance. Others, however, worried about the negative effects of the emerging informational order. The sheer volume of information that could be created, stored, and accessed, many people felt, would prove to be unmanageable. There was much talk about the "mass production" of information, the "information explosion," and the possibility of informational overload or "infoglut." People were also concerned about the number of blue-collar and clerical jobs that would be lost because of the widespread use of information technologies. (Interestingly, though, the decimation of middle management, now a reality, was seldom foreseen.) There was fear, too, that privacy might be severely threatened, that individuals would be depersonalized, and that a centralized surveillance society might develop. As if confirming this, there was bold talk about the need for public bodies to exert control over these new technologies and determine who would benefit from their use. The "new world-information order" discussed by developing nations at the United Nations was but one example. Few persons then understood that in an information society such control by governments or others would become increasingly difficult.

In the twenty-first century, similar discussions may be dominated by considerations such as the following:

- Because knowledge is inherently a personal, social, and cultural creation, an information society is ultimately more, not less, personal than an industrial society. This means that an information society requires new epistemological foundations—a new understanding of what knowledge is, how it is created, and how it is validated. Knowledge can no longer be seen merely as complex information. Rather, knowledge is information that has been internalized and made useful by users.
- Knowledge-in-use, not merely the possession of information, is the key to sustained success in every area of life. The new challenge—for individuals, families, organizations, or societies—is not merely to possess quality information but to digest it and put it to use.
- Attention is increasingly focused on the creation, testing, and use of knowledge and not merely on the technologies by which we possess and transmit information. This human dimension is revealed in the growing preoccupation with the formation of subcultures—within families, organizations, or societies—that are able to sustain self-critical learning and self-monitored performance.

When Diana, the Princess of Wales, died tragically in 1997, people around the world watched her funeral on television. To some, the massive coverage of her death seemed to be a case of information overload. Information doubles every 2–2.5 years. (Liba Taylor/Corbis)

- The most profound question facing the information society is this: When many citizens are well educated, widely traveled, and linked to quality sources of information, how can sound and binding judgments and consensus be developed? Increasingly, it is apparent that this can no longer be achieved by the assertion of one's authority—technical or structural—or by the use of majority votes. Unconvinced minorities now undercut virtually every majority decision. Yet a community will disintegrate and become ungovernable without the capacity to create and act upon knowledge which is commonly accepted. Survival as free persons and societies requires a much greater capacity than is now possessed by any industrial society to democratically deliberate, to cocreate, and to achieve consensus.

The ultimate challenge facing us in our transition to an information society, therefore, is to mature into a truly responsible, deeply thoughtful democracy.

[See also Communications; Communication: Technology; Computers: Overview; Evolution, Social; Global Paradox; Illiteracy; Information Overload; Information Technology; Intellectual Property; Languages; Literature; Multifold Trend; Naisbitt, John; Telecommunications; Workforce Diversity.]

BIBLIOGRAPHY

Bell, Daniel. *The Coming of Post-Industrial Society: A Venture in Social Forecasting.* New York: Basic Books, 1973.

Cleveland, Harlan. *The Knowledge Executive.* New York: E. P. Dutton, 1985.

Drucker, Peter F. *The New Realities.* New York: Harper & Row, 1989.

Naisbitt, John. *Megatrends: Ten New Directions Transforming Our Lives.* New York: Warner Books, 1984.

Rosell, Steven A., ed. *Governing in an Information Society.* Montreal: Institute for Research on Public Policy, 1992.

Zuboff, Shoshana. *In the Age of the Smart Machine: The Future of Work and Power.* New York: Basic Books, 1988.

— RUBEN F. W. NELSON

INFORMATION TECHNOLOGY

Information technology will shape the future, because information is central to the organization and coordination of social activities. Technology that supports and extends the ability to generate, use, transmit, and store information will grow in importance as social institutions continue to become more complex, powerful, and global. The term *information technology* spans the inventions of writing, the printing press, nineteenth-century telegraphy and telephony, and now includes computers, telecommunications, and dependent technologies such as software, computerized databases, numerically controlled machines, and robots.

Driving Forces

Rapid development of information technology since 1950 has been driven by the burgeoning services sector of the economies in postindustrial nations. Most services, beyond those of simple personal or domestic labor, involve the generation, processing, dissemination, or transmission of information.

"Technology push"—the imperative to develop new areas of technology long before useful applications are identified—drove the early years of information technology. "Market pull," or response to corporate and consumer demand, drives present and future developments. The development of global markets and transnational enterprise further reinforces the demand for information technology. Most large corporations have national or even global telecommunications and computer networks.

Long-Range Technological Trends

Four phases of computer development have occurred: large central mainframes for scientific research and then for institutional data management; personal computers and decentralized data processing; networking of personal computers within organizations; and the convergence of computing and communicating technology and the creation of farflung networks. Consistently information technology is becoming more powerful, faster, and cheaper. Other dominant trends include development of packaged easy-to-use software so that users need less training; increasing compatibility of systems enabling interconnecting components from many sources; and increasing mobility enhanced by the development of portable computers, cellular telephones, and similar devices.

Distinctions between computing and communicating technologies have become progressively blurred: telephone switches are really computers; data flow from computer to computer over cables also may carry voice, graphics, and video signals; information is switched from satellite to microwave to cable channels by computer controllers and routers; the household telephone touch-tone pad serves as a computer input device. Information technology has become both more versatile (a single workstation may function as computer, telephone, fax, printer, and copier) and more specialized (computer chips embedded in household appliances or a plastic "smart card"). Enormous interconnected computerized databases have become a striking characteristic of modern society.

Other technological trends that will shape the future of the technology are the digitization of data and their "capture at the source," the evolution of artificial intelligence, and the search for new interfaces between people and information machines. Increasingly, useful information—whether in the form of text, numerics, sound, images, or pictures—is "digitized" or converted to binary signals that can be manipulated, stored, transmitted, and reconverted using information technologies. This common machine language enables data to pass from computer to computer through telecommunications networks without human handling. Data are increasingly captured at the source by electronic scanners, bar code readers, or consumer input (e.g., at automated teller machines, voting machines, and the like). Among the third-order effects are reduced demand for clerical labor (so-called technological unemployment) and the creation of interconnected data banks that contribute greatly to scientific research, corporate productivity, and government efficiency. One disturbing threat posed involves the invasion of individual privacy.

Artificial intelligence, or the emulation of human mental functions by computers, has progressed to the point that knowledge and decision-rules gleaned from experts are available to nonspecialists through interactive software packages. Work continues to equip computers and robots, physically active forms of information technology, with sensors and effectors allowing them to perform many routine human tasks.

Outlook for Information Technology

New advances are likely in person-machine interfaces, artificial intelligence, advanced processing, and miniaturization. So that information technology can be thoroughly integrated into nearly all kinds of human activity, the present cumbersome and restricting channels of interaction between people and technology—keyboards, mouses, number pads, artificial languages, and stationary display screens—will be eliminated. Computer voice recognition and generation, long promised advances, are on the verge of major breakthroughs. Optical character recognition (computer scanning of printed material) also should improve. "Virtual reality" is being developed to combine computer capabilities and human sensibilities in a three-dimensional interface that uses goggles, gloves, and other appliances to allow people to interact with computer-manipulated perceived environments.

We can expect greater ability to store, manipulate, and transmit both two-dimensional and three-dimensional (holographic) images; high definition imaging systems for medical and other important applications as well as for television are already close at hand. Near-term advances can be expected in parallel and neural net processing. In order to escape what now look like ultimate limits on speed and size-reduction, scientists are developing ways to build molecule-scale computers (nanotechnology) and photonic computers, which will use light rays rather than electrons.

Information technology will become more pervasive in two ways. As passive technology, computer chips will increasingly make familiar objects and surroundings (from kitchen tools to automobiles) more responsive to users' needs. Actively manipulated computers, no longer tied to a desk and requiring no more specialized knowledge than is necessary for telephoning or driving an automobile, will increasingly be used in a wide range of household, sports, consumer, and educational activities. Computer systems will become, like traffic lights and public telephone booths, part of the social infrastructure serving the community as a whole.

Impacts on Employment, Industry, and Government

Growing demand for information in developing nations and slow-to-modernize industries (such as mining, education, and aids for the disabled) should create many future jobs. Some experts argue that increasing productivity and encouragement of innovation through information technology will benefit most production and services sectors, reducing the costs of consumer goods and stimulating economic growth. Others, pointing out that demand for information may not be indefinitely insatiable, expect eventual reductions in white-collar employment. This would result from elimination of much clerical work associated with keyboarding, a reduced need for middle-level managers, and computer support or substitution for professional tasks such as diagnosis, research, auditing, and drafting.

Future society may be the privileged domain of "technocrats" whose power is based on information rather than birth, property, or armed force.

Many industries face restructuring as technological change introduces new competitive rivalries. For example, banks now operate electronic networks, telecommunications operators offer financial services in competition with banks, cable television providers may be allowed to transmit telephone messages, and television companies may offer a wide range of videotext and other information services.

Consequences for People and Institutions

Both electronic databases and remote sensors (another type of information technology) pose intrusions on individual privacy and otherwise increase the potential for the misuse of personal information. Safeguarding "intellectual property" (the unique representation of artistic, scientific, or intellectual work, traditionally protected by copyrights or patents) has been compromised by the new capability to copy or change such work, even with inexpensive home equipment. Decision-support technology, such as models, decision systems, and expert systems, can be misused to the harm of individuals or groups—for example, models for predicting criminal recidivism that use race or ethnic origin as indicators. Such Information Era issues may become increasingly troublesome in the future.

Information technology is inherently democratizing because it makes state monopoly of information difficult to maintain. At the same time, it could foster economic elitism if important information, once widely shared in simpler societies, is increasingly digitized, commercialized, and accessible only through technology that may not be universally available. Zbigniew Brzezinski and George Orwell have anticipated that future society may be the privileged domain of "technocrats" whose power is based on information rather than birth, property, or armed force. Daniel Bell pictured these experts somewhat less threateningly as a "meritocratic elite." Nevertheless, these and many more recent thinkers agree that we have entered an age of information, and the way that we organize and manage information technology will determine how good or bad that future will be.

[See also Artificial Intelligence; Bell, Daniel; Communications; Computers: Overview; Digital Communications; Information Overload; Information Society; Multifold Trend; Nanotechnology; Orwell, George; Technological Change; Technological Innovation; Technology Diffusion; Telecommunications.]

BIBLIOGRAPHY

Bell, Daniel. *The Coming of Post-Industrial Society: A Venture in Social Forecasting.* New York: Basic Books, 1973.
Brzezinski, Zbigniew. *Between Two Ages: America's Role in the Technetronic Age.* New York: Viking Press, 1968.
Leebaert, Derek, ed. *Technology 2001: The Future of Computing and Communications.* Cambridge, MA: The MIT Press, 1991.
Sola Pool, Ithiel de. *Technologies of Freedom.* Boston: Harvard University Press, 1983.

(The views expressed in this article are solely the responsibility of the author and not those of the Office of Technology Assessment or its governing board.)

— VARY T. COATES

INSTITUTIONS, CONFIDENCE IN

Business, government, education, and other social institutions can be thought of as the major organs of the body politic, and public support of them is essential. Surveys are conducted periodically to assess the confidence people place in those institutions. Despite differences among various institutions and nations, decline has swept across most institutions over the past two decades. Confidence fell by more than half during this period, declining a combined average of 48 percent in 1966 to 22 percent in 1992. While nearly a majority of Americans once felt confident toward key institutions, currently only a small minority express confidence in government, major companies, educational, and other major institutions.

Social disorders of the 1960s

marked the onset of a postindustrial society

in which a new economic order was based on

powerful new information technologies.

The meaning of this decline is open to controversy because it involves many diverse causes. Historically it reflects the passing of a simpler "Industrial Age" which prevailed at least through the 1950s when approval of institutions was high because they served the needs of the time. Social disorders of the 1960s marked the onset of a postindustrial society or an information age, which introduced a new economic order based, among other things, on television, global communications, computer networks, and other powerful new information technologies.

As a result of this historic shift, people have become better educated and ever more critical just when these old industrial-based structures are unable to cope with the emerging, knowledge-based global economy. Changes wrought by this shift are so pervasive that they also were responsible for the collapse of authoritarian governments in the Communist bloc. Lech Walesa contended that the underlying force that powered the revolutionary reforms in Poland were the result of computers, communication satellites, and television.

Trust in the U.S. government has eroded steadily since the Reagan Revolution, reaching a new low in 1992, when Congress and the President proved unable to control federal spending to reduce the budget deficit, revitalize the economy, or resolve other key issues. Business confidence decline may be ascribed to eroding global dominance of companies like GM and IBM, heightened competition, and overconcern with short-term profits that often places them at odds with environmental protection, employee welfare, and other long-term public interests. Education also has been widely criticized for failing to train young people for a modern world. A recent study ranked American student achievement at the bottom of the list of industrialized nations. Other institutions suffer from similar problems. Military services may be an exception, owing to public approval of the military's performance in the Gulf War.

Public discontent manifested by these declines also exerts pressure for innovative reforms. A mere 33 percent of voters bothered to vote in the midterm 1990 congressional elections. Roughly forty states are resorting to a more entrepreneurial form of government in order to rejuvenate economic progress and, hopefully, more effectively serve public needs. Corporate structural changes introduced since the 1980s include decentralization of large bureaucratic companies like IBM into flexible systems composed of small internal enterprises. "Quasi-democratic" business forms in which managers collaborate with their employees, customers, suppliers, and government have been introduced in firms like the Saturn division of GM. Education also is on the verge of historic change. Some communities are permitting students a choice of schools in order to replace the former bureaucracy with market accountability, and a new concept of local control is emerging in which teachers, parents, and educators work together on policies to mange schools.

Three scenarios seem most likely as these conflicting forces of declining confidence grapple with change. Perpetuating the status quo of low confidence in a slowly declining society, it is possible that many institutions will remain unaffected by these innovations. There is also the possibility that the situation will deteriorate to such an extent that all public confidence will collapse and a state of crisis may come into being. A third possibility is that there will be a progressive swing in national opinion that will stimulate a major restructuring of institutions, thereby producing a broader social renaissance of sorts.

Environmental scanning suggests the likelihood of some type of major transition in American institutions during the 1990s, as is summarized in the following list:

- *Liberal phase in the political cycle.* Historian Arthur Schlesinger, Jr., has described a twelve- to thirty-year cycle in American politics alternating between liberalism and conservatism, between public purpose and private interest, with a new phase of progressive change likely to occur in the mid- to late 1990s.
- *Move to social values.* Author Tom Wolfe, who predicted the "me-decade" of the 1970s and the "money madness" of the 1980s, now sees a swing toward social values. "There will be a lot of discussion in the '90s about morality," he said recently, "and it has already begun."
- *Revival of political activism.* Robert Teeter, chief opinion analyst for President George Bush, thinks the nation is heading toward a revival of political activism akin to the disorders of the 1960s.
- *Rise of economic populism.* Kevin Phillips, a political analyst who invented the successful Republican "southern strategy," counsels that a "political counterreaction" is coming, "a resurgence of economic populism based on a concern over the decline of the U.S. economy, and maldistribution of income among the super-rich.
- *Shift in power structures.* Futurist Alvin Toffler anticipates a coming "powershift" to a decentralized, participatory social order driven by today's revolution in information technology. This agrees with the views of Frank Doyle, a senior GE executive who claims that "the power of the nineties will be people power."

- *Transition to a new paradigm.* Futurists Herman Kahn and Willis Harman began stressing that a paradigm shift was underway during the 1970s. *Time* magazine noted, "The 1990s has become a transforming boundary between one age and another, between a scheme of things that has disintegrated and another taking shape." The industrial paradigm—a rational, technocratic, linear, quantitative, materialistic, utilitarian, male-centered model—is being replaced by another model based on collaboration, common good, global concern, pluralism, and critical dialogue.
- *Institutional changes.* Studies show that widespread institutional changes are underway. Surveys of scholars and executives in the United States, Europe, and Japan concur that a more entrepreneurial, participative "New Capitalism" is emerging and should enter the mainstream during the next five to ten years.

According to this viewpoint, the United States appears to be heading toward a major turning point as increasing dissatisfaction strengthens the resolve of liberals to confront the conservative policies that have dominated over the past two decades.

Environmental scanning also indicates a growing consensus in favor of a "powershift" involving decentralized, democratic institutional forms suitable for a new era and roughly similar to the "Renaissance" scenario. The transformation of the former Soviet Union into a modern society, despite all the uncertainty ahead, illustrates the enormous power of historic change when the time has arrived.

Today's movement of communist states to free markets and democracy, the imminent unification of Europe, and the emergence of a global economy are an essential part of this historic transition, which is causing wrenching institutional changes all around the world. The Industrial Revolution introduced similar transitions, so this process in not unprecedented. Current trends indicate that the early phase of this societal restructuring is underway. Barring unforeseen events, the forecasts summarized here suggest that institutions are reforming in ways that may restore public confidence over the next decade or so.

[See also Change; Change, Cultural; Change, Optimistic and Pessimistic Perspectives; Civil Protest; Continuity and Discontinuity; Global Culture; Global Turning Points; Information Overload; Institutions and Organizations; Kahn, Herman; Media Consolidation; Public Opinion Polls; Social Change: United States; Toffler, Alvin and Heidi.]

BIBLIOGRAPHY

Bell, Daniel. *The Coming of Post-Industrial Society.* New York: Basic Books, 1973.
Cetron, Marvin, and Davies, Owen. *American Renaissance: Life at the Turn of the 21st Century.* New York: St. Martin's Press, 1989.
Doyle, Denis. "America 2000." *Phi Delta Kappan* 73/33 (November 1991): 185–191.
Halal, William E. *The New Capitalism.* New York: John Wiley, 1986.

———. "The New Management: Business and Social Institutions for an Information Age." *Business in the Contemporary World* (Winter 1990).

Lipset, Seymour Martin, and Schneider, William. *The Confidence Gap: Business, Labor, and Government in the Public Mind.* New York: Free Press, 1983.

Osborne, David, and Gaebler, Ted. *Reinventing Government.* Reading, MA: Addison-Wesley, 1992.

Schlesinger, Arthur M., Jr. *The Cycles of American History.* Boston: Houghton-Mifflin, 1986.

Toffler, Alvin. *Powershift.* New York: Bantam, 1990.

Vickers, Geoffrey. *Making Institutions Work.* New York: John Wiley, 1973.

Yankelovich, Daniel. *The New Morality: A Profile of American Youth in the '70s.* New York: McGraw-Hill, 1974.

— WILLIAM E. HALAL

INSTITUTIONS AND ORGANIZATIONS

People create organizations and negotiate rules, rights, and responsibilities to govern their activities. Organizations allow people to combine their knowledge, skills, and resources and to allocate tasks among the participants, who benefit from greater accomplishment than they could achieve individually. They also share in the profits and losses, acclaims, and defeats resulting from their collective actions. Thus organizations are built on collaborative relationships established by agreement to carry out recurring specified transactions. Groups of organizations that perform similar social and economic functions are called institutions, such as churches and religion, or banks and banking.

Spanning Traditional Boundaries to Create Networked Institutions for the Future

In earlier eras, most relationships and transactions occurred within a local marketplace, with only a few national institutions. In the twentieth century, relationships and markets expanded to a national scale, with hierarchical industrial organizations such as automobile companies dominating. People migrated from communities to cities where the factories and jobs were located.

In the past few decades, the technological capacity to quickly move ideas, information, financial resources, and products and services across global boundaries has encouraged the formation of new types of relationships and transactions. Thinking and acting internationally, as well as nationally and locally, is now possible and often necessary.

The transformation of long-distance travel and communications illustrates forces prompting these changes. Industrial era society was dependent upon railroads, highways, airlines, and telephones organized with rigid structures and dominated by a few huge companies.

Our modern society is shifting to a wide array of services for moving people, information, and materials while providing individuals and business the means to design their own routes and timing relative to needs and budgets. Meeting basic mobility needs is now the end purpose of numerous organizations working in networked relationships to provide continuous worldwide service, including transportation reservation systems; airport and airline operating systems; and hotels, rental cars, food service, telecommunications, police and protection services, and local transportation services.

Central to the change in organizations from hierarchies to networks is the shift of the "middle manager" from controller to boundary spanner. In rigidly hierarchical relationships, the middle levels control the processes, which are highly structured and routinized. Relationships are defined by the design and rules of the process—a manufacturing task or the processing of an item of information. Beyond the designers of such systems most people's knowledge is limited to the domain of the specific tasks they perform. There is no need to know about the entire process or the overarching social purpose of the organization. Contact with people in other parts of the organization and other organizations is minimal. This approach makes optimal use of physical plants and equipment, which is the bedrock infrastructure of industrial organizations. Rigorous control to reduce the risk of deviation from norms requires close supervision performed by layers of middle managers. Large inventories and available, unemployed people provide backup to reduce the risk of running out of resources or production capability to meet changing demand. People are a resource in the industrial processes. This industrial model for institutions continues to dominate today, in part because many people prefer the perceived security of such long-standing, bureaucratic organizations.

The new era of networked relationships will require the spanning of boundaries across organizations, disciplines, cultures, and time. In a commercial setting, the connections among diverse groups must be managed—each with the capability of providing only part of the products and services required to seamlessly meet customers needs. Networks and boundary spanning require that all participants have a general understanding of essential needs and of the integrated capacity of the network, so they can contribute most effectively and efficiently. Networked organizations are driving the creation of "hyphenated disciplines" such as bioengineering, the growth of multidisciplinary fields such as ecology, and the search for new leadership capabilities for integrating and guiding—but not controlling—the networks across new frontiers with clear and shared visions of just what is possible.

Networks are built upon mutual respect, and the sharing of information, ideas, and trust. Creating or joining a global networked organization means respecting both emerging international norms and diverse cultures with their varying foundation of rights and responsibilities. This does *not* mean imposing U.S. norms on other cultures. The U.S. government, businesses, and American interest groups are working with representatives of other countries to adopt common international rules for trade and investment that will allow unrestricted flows of goods, services, and investments among nations. Similar international work is addressing ways to strengthen mutual security, to achieve basic human rights for everyone, and to protect the environment while developing at sustainable levels. At the same time, the United States is changing its rules and practices to conform to the new international standards and is working with individual countries to seek compliance and resolve disputes. Multinational institutions such as the World Trade Organization provide a means to achieve a consensus on rules for international relationships and transactions and to resolve disputes that cannot be settled directly.

"Real time" is a central concept for this new era. Long lead and lag times are inherent in industrial processes, which are by nature slow to change and lack mobility. Today, information about changing conditions is broadcast worldwide continuously, reaching everyone at the same time. The challenge is to be able to respond quickly to new opportunities, while avoiding or minimizing new threats. Networks have substantial capabilities for meeting these types of challenges. Because participants share information and ideas, their collective knowledge base can be used for anticipating changes and considering alternative actions, as well as acting quickly when changes do occur. Similarly, commercial networks are better able to meet changes in customers' needs quickly by altering priorities and reconfiguring flows rather than waiting for the activation of excess capacity (unemployed people and unused plants). Operating in real time requires flexible, dynamic, and trusting relationships.

Peter Drucker's idea of the "network society" (summarized in *The Wall Street Journal*, March 29, 1995) emphasizes these changes. He argues that increasingly, people will not be employees of organizations, but contractors, part-timers, and temporary workers. Among businesses, alliances and consortia are among the techniques that will be used increasingly to build partnership rather than ownership connections. Drucker says that "in a partnership one cannot command. One can only gain trust."

Institutional Change in the Future

Organizations engaged in change throughout the world use terms such as *restructuring, reinventing, reengineering, outsourcing, rightsizing, privatizing, deregulation,* and *liberalization.* What is involved is disintegrating obsolete institutions and integrating new ones, although most change has been in the direction of disintegration. Businesses are cutting layers of middle managers, outsourcing functions that others can perform better, selling units that are incompatible with core businesses, reengineering processes to make them more efficient, and changing policies to set the stage for integration of the remaining functions into networks. Similarly, governments are deregulating; privatizing functions that can be performed by businesses; and restructuring policies and programs to shift greater responsibility to individuals and business. For example, after the collapse of the Soviet Union, the former communist countries are restructuring their policies, institutions, and organizations to comply with international norms and become more fully integrated into global institutions and markets.

Political institutions are the battleground

of special interests, where consensus is developed

or where barriers to change are played out.

Creating networked organizations that have global capabilities requires expanding the foundation of rights, responsibilities, and rule of law upon which they are built. This is being done through changes in national laws, development of new legal systems in the nations in transition from communism, and through international treaty institutions. Changing the rules of the game is the work of political institutions. Throughout the world, they are under pressure to overhaul policies and programs as well as to provide relief and assistance to the people and organizations affected by changing conditions. Political institutions are always the battleground of special interests. They are the places where consensus is developed or where gridlock and barriers to change are played out. In transformational processes, political institutions normally are better able to adapt policy to fit a redefined world based on a clear demonstration of what that world might look like. Thus, pioneering organizations are those that are able to overcome barriers and invent new institutions of value that meet people's basic needs and provide a benchmark for changing the rules of the game. Businesses and governmental institutions are now in the midst of such transformational processes, and this process is likely to dominate legislative bodies and international treaty institutions for another decade or more.

Education and training for working effectively in these new networked institutions are at the core of transition-support services. This in turn will require the restructuring of education and training institutions to become institutional change leaders and focal points for transition-support services. The critical resources of organizations—their infrastructure—are their human knowledge, boundary-spanning skills, and trust-building capabilities. Acquiring the ability to learn and work collaboratively is critical to the success of individuals and organizations.

Other Futures Are Possible

The changes described here are based on fuller use of existing technologies, primarily the integrated use of computer, communications, and management technologies. Breakthroughs in biotechnology, energy capabilities, and materials could reinforce or shift the direction of development. Similarly, failure to control the proliferation of weapons of mass destruction, to contain ethnic conflicts and terrorist actions, and to continue the process of liberalizing international trading and investment practices while integrating the countries in transition into the global economy could undermine progress in human development and alter the opportunities available to individuals and organizations. Without doubt, we are living in interesting, uncertain, and challenging times.

[See also Business Governance; Business Structure: Forms, Impacts; Global Business: Dominant Organizational Forms; Institutions, Confidence in.]

BIBLIOGRAPHY

Cowhey, Peter F., and Aronson, Jonathan D. *Managing the World Economy: The Consequences of Corporate Alliances.* New York: Council on Foreign Relations Press, 1993.

Dicken, Peter. *Global Shift: The Internationalization of Economic Activity.* New York: The Guildford Press, 1992.

Drucker, Peter. "The Network Society." *Wall Street Journal,* March 29, 1995.

Dunning, John H. *The Globalization of Business: The Challenge of the 1990s.* New York: Routledge, 1993.

– KENNETH W. HUNTER

INSURANCE

Insurance is a social device for managing the financial consequences of risk. The future of insurance depends on the risks faced by individuals and organizations in the future and on the decisions made about the use of alternative devices for managing risks and allocating the costs of uncertain events.

Risks are created by the environment. Although death may be certain, its time and financial consequences are uncertain. In addition, financial losses due to illness, accidents, fires, storms, earthquakes, and economic fluctuations are inevitable, but their size and timing are uncertain.

Society creates incentives for individuals and organizations to adopt safety and loss-prevention measures. Beyond that, systems are adopted for allocating the costs of risk events that persist despite efforts to reduce their frequency and severity. These costs can fall on individuals, families, businesses, governments, or on special-purpose financial security (insurance) organizations created to pool the costs. The allocation system selected usually depends on the degree of economic development of the society and its political organization. For example, the replacement of earned income because of premature death might be borne by the family in an agricultural society, by a life insurance company in an industrial market economy, or by government in a socialist state. Similarly, health care costs can be allocated through the tax structure, individual payments to health care providers, insurance premiums, or reduced wages.

Trends

Insurance is shaped by the same forces that form other aspects of a society:

MORTALITY. Mortality has declined in Europe and North America for more than five hundred years. In the past century, the rate of decline has been especially significant. In the first seventy years of the century, the decline was largely among the young because of improved sanitation, nutrition, and medical advances against infectious diseases. In the last twenty-five years, the improvement has been in the middle and older ages and is attributable primarily to success against cardiovascular diseases.

HEALTH COSTS. The allocation of income to purchase health care increased in developed nations over the past fifty years. In the United States, approximately 14 percent of gross domestic product went for health care in 1993. Productivity gains in manufacturing and agriculture facilitated this reallocation.

AGING. The combination of reduced mortality and fertility increased the portion of older persons in most developed countries. The rate at which the proportion of the population over age eighty-five is increasing in a given country depends primarily on when the post-

World War II boom in the fertility rate peaked. In the United States the peak occurred in approximately 1960.

TECHNOLOGY. The development of medical technology influenced the cost of health care, and the associated reduction in mortality rates contributed to the aging of the population. New technology also created hazardous wastes and associated disposal costs that must be allocated. Other technical developments now permit the identification and measurement of particular risks, such as radiation, that previously were not readily discernible or were assumed to be a part of general background hazard.

In the future, there will be a search

for a cost allocation system

that builds expected environmental cleanup costs

into the prices of the goods creating the hazards.

ECONOMIC DEVELOPMENT. The transition from an agricultural to an industrial economy also drove the development of insurance. The costs of risk no longer are borne by families but are absorbed by insurance organizations. Economic development also concentrated risks and increased the severity of losses. Industrial and residential development in coastal areas subject to tropical storms provide examples.

INTERNATIONALIZATION. The growth of global trade is intertwined with economic development and the growth of technology. The internationalization of commerce has increased the demand for insurance to facilitate trade. This was historically the first application of insurance. Internationalization permitted the pooling of losses over the world through reinsurance contracts. It also created a host of regulatory issues when insurance transactions bridge traditional national regulation.

CONSERVATISM. The dominant political trend of the past decade has been toward conservatism and a more individualistic ethic. The collapse of the U.S.S.R., shifts in the political organization of Eastern Europe and election results in the United States and Western Europe affirm this trend. The consequences for the allocation of the costs of risks is a trend away from distribution through the tax structure.

NEW IDEAS. During the past fifty years new ideas in the theory of finance rapidly developed. These developments involved creating models for pricing and managing uncertain future cash flows. This set of new ideas was applied almost immediately in existing financial markets and helped to create new markets such as those for futures and options. It is not known how these ideas will influence insurance management or how insurance markets will be absorbed into general markets for future uncertain cash flows.

Insurance Implications

The study of insurance has traditionally been organized by the nature of the risk insured.

LIFE INSURANCE. The life insurance industry grew in importance both for its role in pooling the costs of premature death and in marshalling savings. These savings have been intended primarily for use in financing old-age income. The relative emphasis in the function of bearing mortality risk and managing savings shifted toward the savings function in recent years. The shift had important implications on managing a life insurance company. The decline in mortality and the prevalence of multiple family members in the work force providing income security retard the growth of the risk-pooling aspect of life insurance. The aging of the population and the decline in the reliance on government and corporate old-age income systems will also give impetus to the role of life insurance companies in marshalling, investing, and dispersing old-age income funds.

OLD-AGE INCOME. In response to the aging of the population, old-age income systems that are funded on a current-cost basis must dramatically increase required contributions. This includes the U.S. Social Security system. To moderate higher contribution rates, increases in the age of normal retirement are expected. Funded old-age income systems can escape increases in required contributions to maintain level real-benefits only if, in the aggregate, their investments succeed in significantly increasing the per capita productivity of the working population.

PROPERTY. Competitive forces work toward an efficient insurance market. In a technically efficient insurance market, premiums are based on expected losses. These market forces tend to provide cost incentives to inhibit building in high-risk areas such as flood plains, earthquake zones, high-crime districts, and coastal areas subject to storms. Regional political pressure that attempts to force insurance prices that are not based on expected losses will continue.

ENVIRONMENTAL RISKS. The costs of environmental degradation have been borne directly or allocated through the tort liability system (see below). In the future there will be a search for a cost allocation system that builds expected environmental cleanup costs into the prices of the goods creating the hazards. Long-term financial security systems will have to be developed because frequently there is a delay between the manufacture of a good and its ultimate cleanup.

LIABILITY. Tort liability is a judicial process for allocating the costs of some unforeseen events by using the concept of fault. Liability insurance was designed to spread damage-award costs, imposed by the judicial system, to a broad group of insureds. The control issue in the tort system involves prudently balancing its incentives with the relative high cost of the judicial process and the pooling of these costs through insurance. Early in the twentieth century, a political decision was made to create a separate system—workers' compensation—for allocating the cost of industrial accidents. The same sort of decision may have to be made regarding the cost/benefits of the tort liability system for other ubiquitous risks.

HEALTH CARE. Health care costs have been a perplexing problem. For individuals, part of health care costs are not unexpected, others are candidates for insurance pooling. The scope of health care and its cost has been influenced by technology, which has vastly expanded the scope and induced an upgraded demand for health care. Competitive forces tend to push premiums in an open insurance market as a function of expected costs; those individuals with high expected health costs pay high premiums in such a market. These high premiums may be viewed as socially unacceptable. As of 1994, the United States was using the political process to make basic decisions about providing incentives for efficiency in health care and for allocating the costs.

[See also Conservatism, Political; Entitlement Programs; Financial Institutions; Global Culture; Hazardous Wastes; Health Care Costs; Social Welfare Philosophies.]

BIBLIOGRAPHY

Froot, Kenneth A.; Scharfstein, David S.; and Stein, Jeremy C. "A Framework for Risk Management." *Harvard Business Review* 72/6 (November-December 1994).

Huber, Peter. "Environmental Hazards and Liability Law." *Liability: Perspectives and Policy.* In Robert E. Litan and Clifford Winston, eds., Washington, DC: Brookings Institute, 1988.

World Bank Research Report. *Averting the Old Age Crisis: Policies to Protect the Old and Promote Growth.* New York: Oxford University Press, 1994.

— JAMES C. HICKMAN

INTEGRATED PERFORMANCE SYSTEMS

Whether you are running a small business or a global corporation, the customary job is to gather the components which you then have to assemble to serve some need. In the construction business, for instance, the installation of energy-using systems in buildings includes buying steam boilers and air-conditioners, oil/gas/electricity and pipes/wiring to run them and conduits to distribute their output; hiring skilled workers to assemble them all into a workable system; and buying light fittings and more electricity for illumination.

Such aggregations and combinations of components lead to systems that are wasteful of energy, people, resources, and capital. Energy use in buildings, for instance, could now be cut by one-third, if all cost-effective, energy-efficient technologies were used. But incentives to make such innovative investments are stymied by the jerry-built characteristics of the system itself.

The integrated performance system concept (IPS) denotes that, in the future, organizations will contract to provide performance of a total—integrated—system to serve the functional needs of society. Thus, the business of the future will supply functions, not hardware or people. The hardware and people will be the organization's means to an end.

IPS can go a long way toward achieving desired goals (e.g., energy conservation in our example) while opening up exciting new commercial opportunities. IPS holds the greatest appeal for the principal stakeholders of the enterprise. In the case of energy efficiency in buildings, these are the public utilities now supplying electric power and gas, as well as the companies now supplying heating oil.

- What if these organizations—for example, under the leadership of the electric power company—were to take the initiative in forming a consortium of business entities that comprise all the complementary resources—technical, human, and financial—to put in place complete systems to perform all the energy-performing functions in buildings?
- What if this consortium were thereby able to offer arrangements for supplying building occupants with all the energy-consuming amenities (heating, cooling, lighting, and so on) using the consortium's *own*, state-of-the-art equipment and systems?
- What if this selling of performance were cost-effective—i.e., competitive—with the customary cost of products and their operation (e.g., heating and air-conditioning equipment) that building occupants must now own, operate, maintain, upgrade, and finally dispose of themselves?

This significant institutional innovation—IPS—will quite possibly be seen as the means of satisfying market demands for efficiency, quality, service, and socioeconomic well-being: in short, as a means for propelling American business and industry into the forefront of twenty-first-century competition.

Energy efficiency in buildings is but one example to introduce the concept of IPS. This concept has limitless applications. IPS calls for no basic change from our profit-motivated, market-driven system. This system can be strengthened and the corporation's competitive edge can be sharpened when business focuses its strategy on performance rather than on particular products or services.

In every key function—health, shelter, food, education, energy, transportation, communication—society needs systems offering competing performance of these functions. IPS is a package of complementary technologies—hardware, software—operated by an umbrella organization so that its customers can buy as much of the system's performance as they need, with a minimum of transaction costs and wasted resources. The umbrella organization would most often be a consortium of companies whose complementary resources and capabilities are needed for the research-and-development, production, operation, maintenance, and continued upgrading of the integrated performance system.

Inherent advantages of the IPS approach include the following:

For business:

- Business practices are formulated that are more capable of higher risk taking by virtue of managing all the elements that make for systems efficiency and innovation.
- There is an increased perception of, and demand for, continuous technical and institutional innovation—i.e., "market-pull for the better."
- Acting is more often in anticipation of needs rather than in reaction to crisis. Fear of product obsolescence is abated.
- Functional performance-oriented enterprises can better gain international competitiveness through greater pull for and better management of advanced technology. Their enhanced power to absorb and employ technologies will accelerate the commercialization of new ideas, increase productivity, reduce costs of industrial production, and increase consumer satisfaction.
- It is easier to implement a closer approach to quality, service, and reliability in all aspects of the business, particularly in meeting customer needs.
- There is greater facilitation of access to foreign markets by providing a unique competitive edge.
- There is an increased demand for higher skills in management, engineering, and labor: employment opportunities are upgraded.

For the nation:

- There is increased productivity, leading to better allocation of resources as the key to achieving multiple national goals simultaneously.
- There is improvement in the quality of human life through *humane* technology, inasmuch as the advent of new technologies can be significantly influenced by consideration of societal good through an IPS enterprise's pursuit of total system cost-effectiveness.

For the consumer:

- Advantageous new market choices are possible: there is a new-found ability to buy performance of functional needs, realizing that the technical and institutional means reflect the best available at a competitive price, without any concomitant burden of product ownership. For those who prefer to continue owning products, better ones will be available as a result of the advances made by IPS enterprises and their equipment suppliers.

IPS goes far beyond vertical or horizontal integration and alliances, or the usual approaches to efficiency, quality, service, and reliability. Integrated performance systems are the business of the the future.

[See also Business Structure: Forms, Impacts; Business Structure: Industrial Policy; Energy Conservation; Factories and Manufacturing; Productivity, Robotics; Visionary Thinking.]

BIBLIOGRAPHY

Band, William A. *Touchstones: Ten New Ideas for Revolutionizing Business.* New York: John Wiley, 1994.

Campbell, Andrew, and Nash, Laura L. *A Sense of Mission: Defining Direction for the Large Corporation.* Reading, MA: Addison-Wesley, 1993.

Hammer, Michael, and Champy, James. *Reengineering the Corporation: A Manifesto for Business Revolution.* New York: HarperBusiness/Harper Collins, 1993.

Hayes, Robert H., Wheelwright, Steven C., and Clark, Kim B. *Dynamic Manufacturing; Creating the Learning Organization.* New York: Free Press, 1988.

Quinn, Robert E., and Cameron, Kim S. *Paradox and Transformation: Toward a Theory of Change in Organization and Management.* Cambridge, MA: Ballinger, 1988.

Shetty, Y. K., and Buehler, Vernon B., eds. *Competing Through Productivity and Quality.* Cambridge, MA and Norwalk, CT: Productivity Press, 1988.

Tomasko, Robert M. *Rethinking the Corporation: The Architecture of Change.* New York: AMACOM, 1993.

— MICHAEL MICHAELIS

INTELLECTUAL PROPERTY

The notion of private property—distinguishing private ownership of land and goods from other forms of rights to use—has been central to economic thought for centuries. Marxists opposed private ownership of "the means of production," but this argument would have

---

Patents are the most important form of intellectual property from an economic perspective.

---

been meaningless before private ownership had become established as a concept. Until recent centuries, the idea of property was largely limited to land or tangible goods. The first major extension was to include debt instruments (e.g., mortgages) or shares in joint stock companies, as a form of property. Much more recently, the notion of products of the human mind as a form of wealth—and therefore, of property—has begun to take legal form. The generic term is *intellectual property.* Such works have commercial value to the extent that they can be protected.

There are many types of intellectual property but only four methods of protection, the choice depending on circumstances. The first approach, applicable to inventions (and possibly to computer programs and synthetic bio-molecules) is to rely on patents. These are published descriptions of operating principles, specific designs, formulas, processes, or end uses. The second alternative is the secret process or formula: a plan or process, tool, mechanism, or compound known only to its owners or other confidants. The famous "secret formula" of Coca-Cola is an example. The third possibility is the trademark, a unique name, symbol, mark, motto, device, emblem, or distinctive logo that identifies the commercial products of a particular manufacturer or other organization. Trademark protection can be indefinite. The fourth and last protection is the copyright. This applies to written material, including artwork, music, and computer programs.

Patents

Patents are the most important form of intellectual property from an economic perspective. A patent is a form of publication that contains a detailed description of the invention, as well as a list of related prior inventions. In theory, the award of a limited monopoly (protection against competition) for a limited time is provided simply as an inducement to publish new ideas, thus benefitting society as a whole. Considerable debate rages among economists as to the optimum degree of protection from the societal perspective.

Worldwide approximately one million patent applications are filed yearly; 166,000 applications were filed in the United States in 1989 and 102,712 were granted. There is a growing trend toward internationalization of U.S. patent applications. In 1967 only 20 percent of the patent grants in the United States went to foreigners as compared to 47 percent in 1989. The United States in that year, granted 21,090 patents to Japanese, 8,560 to West Germans, 3,299 to the French, and 3,281 to citizens of the United Kingdom.

Any invention can be patented provided (1) that it is novel and resulted from an act of invention (i.e., it cannot be derived by a practitioner in a clear-cut way from the state-of-the-art in that field) and (2) that it has a practical application. In principle a patent grants an exploitation monopoly on the invention to the patent holder for a period of years (seventeen in the United States) and within a specific country. A patent (backed up ultimately by know-how) is an incorporeal or intangible good that can be sold or licensed either exclusively or not in exchange for money or reciprocal licenses. A

very few important patents in the past have brought fortunes to their inventors. In most such cases the inventor secured "blanket" patents that covered all of the likely alternatives, associated process technologies, and end-use applications. In addition, such innovators were commercially oriented enough to build a successful manufacturing business based on the technology. George Eastman of Kodak and Edwin Land of Polaroid are familiar examples. However, some of the more valuable inventions, such as the telephone, the vacuum tube, FM radio, and the computer, resulted in expensive litigation that took many years to resolve and often left the inventors with very little at the end.

In practice, the protection provided by a patent registered in the United States or elsewhere is minimal. Foreign patents are not effectively enforced against domestic infringers by many governments. Many Asian and Latin American governments make it difficult for foreign firms to obtain patent protection; some, including Brazil, Taiwan, and South Korea, go further and actively encourage national firms to evade or infringe on patents held by foreign firms. Deficiencies in international patent protection were a major topic of the 1993 "Uruguay Round" negotiations of the General Agreement for Tariffs and Trade (GATT).

Trade Secrets

Chemical processes, as well as processes for the manufacture of specialized food products (e.g., food additives and sauces), perfumes, liqueurs, and cosmetics, are sometimes kept as trade secrets because of the relatively short life and often ineffective protection offered by patents. Trade secrets have been held for considerable periods, an example being the secret "Chatham process" discovered in the 1940s for manufacturing synthetic gem-quality emeralds, rubies, and sapphires sold in jewelry shops. Some trade secrets have been held for a century or more.

The economic value of trade secrets is problematic because they are difficult to buy and sell. A usual prerequisite to the sale of secret technology is the release of a certain minimum amount of technical and commercial data. Theoretically, this is protected by a "nondisclosure agreement." Civil codes of most industrialized countries provide penalties for violating such agreements. However, legal proof of a violation is very difficult to establish.

Trademarks

Trademarks, brand names, logos, and other symbolic devices are means of identifying a product or service (and its producer/supplier) as it is presented in the marketplace. A distinctive label constitutes an almost indispensable support in developing a market and an advertising campaign. For example, "Bibendum" has contributed to global product-recognition for Michelin tires. In the United States in 1989, 63,100 certificates were issued in 1989, of which 7,800 were renewals. The total number in force is around 500,000. An international classification system of thirty-four product and eight service categories has been established under which trademarks can be officially registered. Protection is renewable and lasts for ten years. This protection, such as it is, can be acquired in many countries.

Copyrights

Copyrights are applicable to written documents, computer software (which also may be patentable), sound recordings, and works of the visual arts (including movies). When these materials can be shown to be original and the personal work of their creator, they can be protected by a copyright under international agreements. This prohibits the reproduction (including photocopying) without authorization from the originator. In 1989, 618,300 copyrights were issued in the United States, of which 38,600 were renewals. Written materials (categorized as monographs and serials) accounted for 187,000 of the total, while musical works accounted for 197,200. It is of interest that 1,200 copyrights were issued for semiconductor chip products. (Software is included under "monographs.")

Infringements, Clones, and Counterfeits

Imitation may be the sincerest form of flattery, but it can also be very damaging to inventors and innovators. New products, even when protected by patents, trademarks, copyrights, and model registration, have always been a target for fraudulent and illicit reproduction. The Museum of Patent Infringement in Paris displays some particularly spectacular examples. When a company is a market leader, its products are relentlessly imitated. This process is sometimes beneficial to the consumer, at least in the short run, since it minimizes monopoly profits and (possibly) encourages even more rapid technological improvement by the market leader in its effort to stay ahead of the pack.

On the other hand, unrestrained imitation deprives innovators of the needed return on research and development (R&D) costs, not to mention entrepreneurial risk-taking. If expensive R&D is not rewarded, there is little if any economic incentive to undertake it. This would have a harmful effect on the main source of economic growth. The biotechnology and pharmaceutical industries provide clear examples. Research needed to develop new drugs can be exceedingly costly. Most biotechnology companies have yet to reap any significant return on capital invested; most of the costs went for investments in R&D and clinical testing. Even so, drugs can be fairly easy to manufacture. There are a number of firms (many in Italy) that specialize in generic versions of proprietary drugs, which can sell at prices far below those set by the original manufacturers. Italy is unique in that it does not allow patents for pharmaceuticals. Carried to a logical extreme, such practices could destroy the economic incentive for pursuing drug-related research.

If protection for intellectual property is not significantly strengthened by international agreement, it is likely that R&D investment in design-based products will decline.

Another form of industrial piracy is the unauthorized use of trademarks to sell cheap copies of expensive, premium-quality consumer goods such as Rolex watches, Parker pens, Gucci luggage, videocassette recordings, and so on. Both the customer and the manufacturer whose trademark has been violated are victimized by this practice. Gullible customers do not get the "bargain" they think they are getting, and the reputation of the name-brand is smirched. Nevertheless, this sort of theft is tolerated, or even actively encouraged, by a number of unsympathetic or unscrupulous governments, especially in Asia.

Unfortunately, piracy seems to be a growth industry, as modern communications and "reverse engineering" technology (the ability to disassemble and dissect a product with intent to replicate it) have made it possible for design-based products (especially computer software and hardware) to be copied and reproduced in weeks if not hours. This reduces the inherent advantage of the innovator and helps the imitator.

If protection for intellectual property is not significantly strengthened by international agreement in the next few years, it is likely that R&D investment in design-based products will decline, with more investment going to process technologies (which are more difficult to copy). The economic value of patents is also likely to decline, as businesses seek other means of protecting themselves.

[See also Artificial Life; Counterfeiting; Creativity; Marketing Breakthroughs; Research and Development; Technological Change; Technological Innovation; Technology Diffusion.]

BIBLIOGRAPHY

Dimanescu, Dan, and Botkin, James. *The New Alliance: America's R&D Consortia.* Cambridge: MA: Ballinger, 1986.

Hippel, Eric von. *The Sources of Innovation.* New York: Oxford University Press, 1988.

"In the Realm of Technology, Japan Looms Ever Larger." *New York Times,* May 28, 1991, p. c-1.

National Science Board. *Science and Engineering Indicators.* 10th ed. Washington, DC: U.S. Government Printing Office, 1991.

Samuels, Jeffrey M., ed. *Patent, Trademark, and Copyright Law.* Washington, DC: Bureau of National Affairs, 1985.

Servi, Italo S. *New Product Development and Marketing: A Practical Guide.* New York, Praeger, 1990.

— ROBERT U. AYRES

INTERACTIVE ENTERTAINMENT

Interactivity has attracted considerable press attention lately, and most major entertainment/media companies are becoming involved in or are seriously exploring the interactive entertainment market. Interactive entertainment is part of the natural evolution of media/entertainment, a rapidly changing market in which new products/services are introduced only to become obsolete within a matter of a few years. The term "interactive" has been applied to so many disparate products, services, and programs that its exact meaning has become elusive. It is broadly defined here as any entertainment in which the user can participate. There are many different levels of interactivity, ranging from simply selecting programming of interest and watching it at one's convenience to substantially shaping, manipulating, or exercising control over a particular program/experience.

An array of key factors has created a hospitable environment for interactive entertainment: (1) the growing desire of consumers to control their entertainment habits, as shown by the success of video games and the strong market penetration of VCRs; (2) the growing familiarity of consumers, especially young people, with computers and other interactive devices; (3) the increasing fusion of education and entertainment; (4) the growing convergence of computers and video and of computers and telecommunications; (5) the trend toward experiential entertainment (realistic simulations and fantasies); (6) the increasing drive of entertainment/media companies to generate new sources of revenue and open up new markets; (7) the rise of narrowcasting; (8) the increasing popularity of new forms of programming that could lend themselves well to interactivity, such as hybrid programming (i.e., docudramas) and segmented programming, especially magazine-style programming; (9) the rise of special interest programming and special interest publications; (10) the increasing desire and need for enhanced social communication, especially among people with special interests; (11) the arrival of more advanced, economical, and convenient technologies; (12) the integration of interactive technologies with other new technologies, such as high-definition television, in new home entertainment systems; (13) the strong impact of direct marketing and the growing effort of advertisers/ad agencies to devise more effective and targeted ways of reaching consumers; and (14) increased competitiveness in the highly crowded media/entertainment industry.

Forms of Interactive Entertainment

VIDEO GAMES. These consist of electronic game cartridges with audio and animation played on special consoles. There are a variety of video game systems, including hand-held systems and systems that display images on full-size consoles and television sets. Coin-operated video games are typically found in video arcades, family amusement centers, bars, and other public places. Joysticks or more elaborate game pads are typically used to control game action on regular-size video games.

COMPUTER SOFTWARE. This category includes entertainment, educational, and other types of software. Typically computer games offer a higher level of interactivity and greater audiovisual capability than video games. Keyboards, joysticks, and mice are used to access material on computers. Computer software can offer graphics, text, animation, audio, still video, and limited full-motion video with the help of video compression techniques.

VIDEOTEXT/ONLINE SERVICES. Interactive services can be accessed by modem-equipped personal computers or by "dedicated" videotext terminals hooked up by phone or cable, or by other link with a central computer. These services, which include informational (news), entertainment (games), and transactional (home shopping) services, provide text and graphics. A few computer games allow play-by-modem provided that all participants have computers, input devices, monitors, and copies of the game software.

AUDIOTEXT. Audio programs and services of an informational or entertainment nature can be accessed over the telephone for free or for a (sometimes substantial) charge, as in the case of 900 phone numbers. Audiotext programs vary in their degree of interactivity.

INTERACTIVE TELEVISION. A range of interactive television services permit viewers to interact with their televisions. These services include: (1) video-on-demand, which allows users to view programs of their choice at a time of their choosing (at present most such services require a short waiting period before users can watch the program of their choice); (2) play-along systems, which allow viewers to play along with programs on the air (i.e., responding to a trivia question on a game show), typically using some kind of console device, without actually affecting the program content; (3) audiotext-based interactive television services, which allow viewers to either play along with programming on the air or to exercise some influence or control over program content using the phone; and (4) branching/video manipulation systems, which allow viewers to manipulate/influence/control the program content in some way, typically using a console or other device (these systems vary considerably in the degree of video manipulation they afford, with fiber optic systems offering a much higher degree of control). Play-along and branching systems can be one-way or two-way interactive. Interactive television services are delivered over a variety of media, including cable television, satellite television, broadcast television, and fiber optics.

Interactive Multimedia

This term refers to interactive optical disk technologies that offer a combination of visuals, sound, and text on optical disks, primarily compact discs. These technologies include:

INTERACTIVE VIDEODISCS. Offering full-motion video, graphics, animation, still video, audio, and text, these 8″ and 12″ interactive (analog) optical disks have different levels of interactivity—generally they become more truly interactive when hooked up with computers.

CD-ROM. An interactive compact disc technology offering audio, text, graphics, animation, and still video on a 5″ compact disc, CD-ROM players are attached to personal computers. CD-ROM players (and other interactive CD players) have a large storage capacity. Limited full-motion video can be offered on CD-ROM using video compression techniques, such as Quick Time and MPEG, though the quality of that video was initially mediocre. Full-motion video chips and modules are being added to several CD-based platforms and feature-length movies with laser-disc quality video are expected to become widely available in the very near future. All interactive CD systems play regular compact (audio) discs, and there is a smaller degree of cross-platform software compatibility between certain types of CD-ROM devices and software.

CD STAND-ALONES. Interactive compact disc stand-alone systems that hook up with the television and/or monitor and the stereo also offer audio, graphics, animation, still video, and text on a 5″ compact disc. There

A child in a museum plays with an interactive television game. Television, telephony, radio, and computers have transformed information delivery. (Raymond Gehman/Corbis)

are also some dedicated CD-based game systems that hook up to existing video game systems from those systems' manufacturers, and a few CD stand-alone devices can even be upgraded into computers with add-on keyboards, disk drives, and the like. At present some of these CD stand-alones are hampered by extremely limited save-game capacities, overall program storage capacity notwithstanding.

Social interaction will also be a key element in interactive entertainment of the future, especially given the rising popularity of computer chat rooms and bulletin boards.

KARAOKE. First developed by the Japanese, these audio/video systems permit the user to "sing along" with recorded music using a microphone. (The original vocal tracks are deleted, while the backing music is retained.) These systems use a number of different technologies, including regular CDs, videotape, laser-discs, and interactive CDs.

INTERACTIVE LIVE THEATER. The level of participation varies widely in these live plays. Audience participation ranges from simply voting on the identity of the culprit in murder-mystery plays to actually playing a role in the drama itself (as in *Tony 'N' Tina's Wedding*).

INTERACTIVE FILMS. In these movies, which are shown in movie theaters, museums, amusement parks, and other public places, the audience can make plot choices at particular points, and influence the action on the screen by pressing buttons near their seats or through some other means. Such interactive technologies as laser-discs are used for interactive films in theaters and other public places. These interactive films are not to be confused with "interactive movies" on computer software, interactive compact discs, and other media in the home.

VIRTUAL REALITY. The term *virtual reality* has many different connotations. Sometimes it is merely empty media hype, but generally speaking, it refers to computerized systems that place the users in a simulated 3D graphic environment: (1) immersive systems that seemingly plunge the user directly into a particular environment, typically using head-mounted displays and data gloves; or (2) nonimmersive systems, which project the user into an environment and allow him or her to interact directly with that environment without the use of such external devices as head-mounted displays.

Current Market Analysis and Future Prospects

The largest segment of the interactive entertainment industry by far is video games, with home video games generating currently about $5 billion in revenues. Despite all the hype about multimedia and other new advanced interactive products, the most successful forms of interactive entertainment to date have been fairly simple, easy to use, lower-level interactive, more convenient, and less expensive. These forms include video games, audiotext, interactive live theater, and karaoke. The most promising interactive products in the short-term future are likely to be similar in nature. As consumers become more acclimated to interactivity, a higher level of interactive sophistication is likely to emerge. Interactive CD products are not likely to have a significant impact until the late 1990s, when player prices will be more affordable. At that time there will be a greater supply of higher quality software and full-motion video products, dominant standards will emerge, consumers will be better acclimated to interactivity, and young people raised on video games will reach a purchasing age and be prime consumers of multimedia products. When reasonably priced recordable-and-erasable CDs and CD players appear on the home market, the new home entertainment center will begin to take shape and become more firmly established.

There has been much talk about electronic databases and special interest interactive programming, but up to now entertainment (especially games) has been the driving force behind interactive media. Broad-appeal entertainment programming, such as movies, science fiction, games, and music, is likely to dominate the interactive market initially. Children's programming may also fare well initially, but special-interest interactive programming is not likely to sell well early on. The electronic database design model may work in education and other institutional/industrial markets, but it has little appeal with most consumers, as indicated by the poor early performance of videotext. Consumers need to have a clear idea of precisely what these devices are to be used for before they will be willing to buy them. In order to succeed in the broader consumer market, interactive entertainment programs will need to offer strong dynamics, storylines, and characterizations—not merely dazzling graphics but meaningful opportunity for user involvement—elements that consumers have come to expect from mainstream linear entertainment. Social interaction will also be a key element in interactive entertainment of the future, especially given the rising popularity of chat/bulletin board services.

Interactive entertainment in video arcades, amusement parks, museums, movie theaters, and other public places will play a central role in educating consumers about interactivity by allowing them to try out new interactive products/experiences at little or no risk. These places provide an ideal testing ground for new interactive products/experiences. Such interactive products/experiences as interactive lasers, interactive CDs, videotext, virtual reality, interactive rides/interactive simulators, and teleconferencing are likely to figure more prominently in amusement parks and other public places of the future.

Interactive entertainment is likely to develop into a broader, more substantial market over the next ten years and will have a strong impact on media/entertainment in general. Although the technical aspects of the media are rapidly changing, the actual growth of the market will be a slower, more evolutionary process.

[See also Communications; Computers: Software; Telecommunications; Theme Parks and Organized Attractions.]

BIBLIOGRAPHY

Morrison, Mike and Sandie, C. *The Magic of Interactive Entertainment.* Indianapolis: SAMS Publishing, 1994.
Morrow, Cindy, ed. *Cyberlife.* Indianapolis: SAMS Publishing, 1994.
Rheingold, Howard. *Virtual Reality.* New York: Touchstone Books, 1991.

— MICHAEL MASCIONI

INTERNAL MIGRATION, UNITED STATES

In common parlance, *internal migration* refers to the geographic relocation of persons within a given country. *International migration* relates to geographic relocation across national boundaries. In official U.S. statistics, *internal migration* is defined more narrowly as the movement of persons from one usual residence to another that involves crossing a county line and is intended to be for an indefinite period. As a rule, the volume of residential movement within counties exceeds that of such movement between counties. In the following discussion, we adopt the first-cited, broader concept of internal migration but make distinctions among types of mobility and migration where relevant.

Migration combines with fertility and mortality of an area to determine its relative population change. The smaller the geographic area, the greater likelihood that migration will be the critical component of population change. Because migration rates typically vary from area to area more than do fertility and mortality rates, migration contributes substantially to population redistribution within the country.

Not all people are equally likely to move. In the recent history of the United States between 15 and 20 percent of the population moved each year. At least one-third of persons in their twenties, but less than 10 percent of those forty-five and over, move in any one year. These age differences hold despite the distance of the move. Hispanics and blacks are more likely than whites to move locally but less apt to move across county or state lines. Education makes little difference with regard to local mobility, but the better-educated are likely to move longer distances. The unemployed are more likely to migrate than those who work or are out of the labor market. Among the regions of the United States, the West exhibits the greatest degree of within-county mobility, and the South has the highest rate of between-county migration.

Migratory patterns are fairly stable over short periods, but are apt to vary over longer intervals. This makes estimation of future migration difficult. Three factors that most influence the level and variation in mobility and migration patterns are the vibrancy of the economy, especially job availability; the changing size and composition of households; and the condition of residential areas. Business closures lead to net out-migration. Economic development causes in-migration. Lower fertility, longer life expectancy, and population aging increase the number of smaller households, alter housing demand, and stimulate mobility. Decaying urban neighborhoods can result in structural renewal projects that displace people en masse.

Migration contributes substantially to population redistribution within the United States. In recent U.S. history, between 15 and 20 percent of the population moved each year.

The most widely consulted source of information about future migration and redistribution of population within the United States is probably the Census Bureau's recurrent series of population projections for states. The most recent of these, by Campbell (1994), is the first to have been prepared after completion of the 1990 census. It contains more detailed race/ethnicity information than was in predecessor studies. Scenarios based on the latest census data do not suggest any dramatic break from trends of the recent past with respect either to favored destinations of migrants or to differences in migration behaviors among demographic groups. The Census Bureau figures suggest a continued pattern of movement away from the Northeast and Midwest toward the South. In the 1990s, the census forecast a net out-migration of 3.3 million persons from the Northeast and the same magnitude of net in-migration to the South. The census study suggests that while the volume of internal migration is likely to diminish, the Northeast and increasingly the Midwest should lose population from internal migration directed almost exclusively to the South. In every five-year period between 1990–1995 and 2020–2025, the state of Florida is projected to gain about 600,000 persons from net internal migration, more than twice the levels anticipated for the second through fourth states on this list (North Carolina, Washington, and Georgia).

A principal reason for the expected decline in internal migration is the aging of our population. While migration will vary according to other demographic variables, the relationship between chronological age and the limited tendency for migration is well known and consistent over both time and place (Rogers and Castro, 1984). Applying the most recent figures (for 1991–1992) showing the proportion of each group that moves during a year to the current population reveals that 16.8 percent of all Americans aged one and over would live in a different *house* from the one they had lived in at the beginning of the year, and that 6.0 percent would live in a different *county*. Taking the same set of movement rates, but using the population as projected to the year 2020, we find that 15.4 percent of all Americans aged one and over will live in a different *house* from the one they lived in at the beginning of the year, and that 5.6 percent will live in a different *county*. Even though the number of persons moving and migrating will grow with the population, the changes in age distribution should reduce the fraction of the population moving and migrating.

Zelinsky (1971) proposed that societies go through mobility transition stages much as they go through mortality and fertility transition stages. Based on what he saw as logical extension of earlier mobility stages, he projected these probable trends:

- A decline in the level of residential migration
- Most migration occurring between cities
- Acceleration in circulatory mobility, as people identify with multiple residences
- Stricter political controls on internal migration

Whether or not Zelinsky's conjectures are correct, mobility and migration patterns of the recent past in the United States will continue in the near future, barring cataclysmic events. Modifications of those patterns may take place in later years as the country's social institutions are reshaped by economic, social, and environmental changes.

[See also Demography; Land Use Planning; Lifestyles, Regional; Megacities; Migration, International; Multifold Trend; Population Growth: United States; Population Growth: Worldwide; Refugees.]

BIBLIOGRAPHY

Campbell, Paul R. "Population Projections for States, by Age, Sex, Race, and Hispanic Origin: 1994 to 2020." *Current Population Reports.* Series P-25, No. 1111. Washington, DC: U.S. Bureau of the Census, 1994.

Hansen, Kristin A. "Geographical Mobility: March 1991 to March 1992." *Current Population Reports.* Series P-20, No. 473. Washington, DC: U.S. Bureau of the Census, 1993.

Rogers, Andrei, and Castro, Luis B. "Model Migration Schedules." In A. Rogers, ed. *Migration, Urbanization and Spatial Population Dynamics.* Boulder, CO: Westview Press, 1984.

Zelinsky, Wilbur. "The Hypothesis of the Mobility Transition." *Geographical Review* 61 (1971): 219–249.

– CHARLES B. NAM
WILLIAM J. SEROW

INTERNATIONAL DIPLOMACY

The end of the Cold War between communism led by the Soviet Union and the West led by the United States revealed a world, part of which was different than anything that had gone before. The security of almost all of the greatest powers came less from their military forces and alliances than from the fact that their neighbors were all democracies—and no one thought that any of the modern democracies would attack another.

At the turn of the new millennium, the great powers of the world are the United States, Japan, Germany, France, Great Britain, Italy, and China. Russia, despite its nuclear weapons, is too internally divided and unstable to be a great power except defensively. India, as the second most populous country in the world, expected to become nearly China's equal, also has special importance and may soon become a great power.

Because all of the great powers except China are modern democracies, they do not fear attack from one another, and because all of them except China are among the most productive in the world, their actual and potential power frees them from fear of attack by other countries. Therefore the areas where only these and other democracies are located are "zones of peace and democracy."

Some traditional questions about the relation between power and law in international affairs have become obsolete for the great powers, because for the first time in history these countries are not divided into competing military-political power blocs whose balance determines the security of all nations. During the twenty-first century a new diplomacy of "geoeconomics" will develop for the relationships among powers in the zones of peace, to replace traditional diplomacy based on concerns about alliance needed to provide fundamental safety.

During the next century or two the rest of the world will go through the process that the countries of the zones of peace went through during the last two centuries. Most countries will move from poor to wealthy, from authoritarian to democratic, and from a diplomacy dominated by the need to protect against military conquest or domination, to a diplomacy concerned with less vital national interests and concern for the quality of the international order.

The worldwide passage from a poor and natural world to a world of wealth, democracy, and peace, will be the central feature of the history of the next two centuries; it will be the environment that shapes international diplomacy. This passage began as recently as the end of the eighteenth century. By the end of the twentieth century one-seventh of the world had completed it—and most of the rest of the world was already greatly changed by beginning to move through it. Before the passage there were no wealthy countries in the world—measuring by absolute standards.

The twenty-first century will see the countries with more than half of the world's expanding population cross the threshold of absolute wealth that was crossed for the first time by the United States early in the twentieth century. As a result, by the end of the twenty-first century about three-quarters of the world's eight to twelve billion people will live in countries where life expectancy is well over seventy, where almost all children get a high school education, where most people work indoors with their minds and their fingers—rather than working with their backs and muscles while exposed to the elements—and where most people have at least potential access to the whole world and to many choices.

The twenty-first century will also see a change in the role of and threat from nuclear weapons. In 1989 the United States and the Soviet Union had nearly 50,000 nuclear weapons, all or most essentially aimed at each other. Nuclear deterrence was the centerpiece of national security policy. Nuclear weapons posed a danger of killing hundreds of millions of people in a week. With the end of the Cold War these dangers have largely disappeared, and the number of nuclear weapons has begun to come down.

In the twenty-first century the threat from nuclear weapons will change to be primarily a threat from weak countries (or subnational groups) and probably mostly

a threat to cities rather than nations—except for Israel, the most likely target, which is so small that it could be destroyed by a relatively small number of nuclear weapons, and which is confronted by enemies whose goal is its destruction.

By the end of the twenty-first or twenty-second century, the great majority of the world's population will live in zones of peace and democracy.

The twenty-first century will also see the world choose between two possible nuclear paths: the first involves the further spread of nuclear weapons to twenty or forty or more countries and groups, or, alternatively, a path which reverses direction and leads to a smaller number of nuclear powers, and possibly to the practical removal of nuclear weapons from the field of diplomacy. If this second path is chosen, it will not be based on a new global idealism, but on a sophisticated understanding of the realities of power and of national interest.

The fundamental features of the nation-state system will continue through the twenty-first century—although there will be a substantial evolution in its character. The basic security and identity of countries will continue to be organized by sovereign nations; no world government will supersede national governments or gain the power to protect against strong nations. But the end of military dangers to the integrity of states will gradually lead to the division of many states into smaller units for most political activities and ordinary economic management. Some of these smaller units will be separate states, but most of them will continue as units of larger national governments which continue to provide the primary identity of their citizens.

Simultaneously with the devolution of governmental power to smaller units, other governmental functions will be delegated by nations to international organizations—either regional, like the European Union, or functional, like the World Postal Union and other specialized agencies.

The United Nations will continue through the twenty-first century as the institutional forum for considering worldwide issues—the only organization in which virtually all peoples are represented. However, it will continue to be based on the equal dignity—and voting power—of all sovereign states, from tiny island nations with less than 100,000 population to continental-wide nations with 1,000,000,000 or more people, from democracies whose governments legitimately speak for their citizens to absolute tyrannies where the government speaks for no one except a dictator who rules by fear and force. The threat of war will be reduced, not neatly by the establishment of a super authority, but gradually by fallible human measures by which nation after nation becomes part of zones of peace and democracy where live those countries who have painfully learned the lessons of peaceful self-government.

The most important result of international diplomatic development will be that by the end of the twenty-first or twenty-second century the great majority of the world's population will live in zones of peace and democracy, and the fear of war between great powers will seem to be a thing of the past.

[See also Communism; Democracy; Espionage and Counterintelligence; Global Culture; Nationalism; Peacekeeping; Weapons of Mass Destruction.]

BIBLIOGRAPHY

Singer, Max. *Passage to A Human World.* New Brunswick, NJ: Transaction Publishers, 1989.
Singer, Max, and Wildasky, Aaron. *The REAL World Order. Zones of Peace/Zones of Turmoil.* Chatham, NJ: Chatham House Publishers, 1993.

— MAX SINGER

INTERNATIONAL GOVERNANCE AND REGIONAL AUTHORITIES

For the last fifty years, global politics and economics have been largely divided along ideological and development lines: communism versus market economies, totalitarianism versus democracy, developed versus developing nation. Institutions and alliances developed to support the divisions, among them the North Atlantic Treaty Organization (NATO), the Organization for Economic Cooperation and Development (OECD), the Council for Mutual Economic Assistance (COMECON), and the UN Conference on Trade and Development (UNCTAD).

The relative stability of these divisions has been ruptured in recent years by the collapse of Soviet-style communism, the rise of Islamic fundamentalism, the eruption of ethnic hostilities, and the spread of nuclear weapons that created new potential threats and alliances. At the same time, economic development differences shifted the center of economic activity away from the United States–Western Europe and COMECON axes toward Asia. Differences in economic development among developing countries and intractable differences between developed countries on certain fundamental economic issues have rendered the "north/south" or

"developed/developing" divisions less important in international economics and politics.

In such a setting it is hardly surprising that international and regional organizations face an uncertain future. Current security structures, especially the United Nations and NATO, are struggling to better define their purpose in an era in which threats to international security are not marked by a superpower struggle. China, a second military superpower, albeit weakened, continues to exist and could potentially become a third superpower through complex issues such as ethnic conflict and nuclear proliferation. At the same time, regional economic organizations are proliferating, both to facilitate international competitiveness and to secure access to important or fast-growing markets.

In terms of economic integration, the most comprehensive effort to date has been accomplished by the European Union (EU) through the establishment of the Common Market and political institutions including the European Parliament and Commission. The EU has political and economic goals, seeking both to institutionalize the balance of power needed to minimize the recurrence of military conflicts on the Continent and to promote greater economic growth through regional integration. However, efforts toward deeper integration, such as the introduction of a common European currency, will continue to present challenges to the EU, as will efforts toward broader integration through eastward expansion.

To initiate the expansion effort, the EU has signed agreements with Poland, Hungary, the Czech and Slovak republics, Bulgaria, and Romania to expand trade relations and provide trade preferences. The expense of extending EU benefits to Eastern European countries will, however, cause enormous debate within the EU member states as public opinion may not support the large expenditures needed. Further, this issue has caused tension between the EU leading members, as Germany's interest in promoting expansion is not matched by other members who believe eastward expansion will allow for German domination of the group. Competing interests of European nation-states will likely limit the speed and degree of integration in coming years.

Other regional political and economic organizations, such as Mercosur in Latin America, ASEAN in Asia, or ECOWAS, UDEAC, PTA, and SADCC in Africa allow for regional dialogue on political and economic issues, but there is presently no real effort toward integration in terms of establishing common institutions or policies on the scale accomplished in Europe.

The leading trend toward increased economic integration has been accomplished through trade arrangements. The highlight of multilateralism in trade was realized through the successful conclusion of the Uruguay Round and the establishment of the World Trade Organization. Simultaneous to those developments was a proliferation of regional trade arrangements. In the Western Hemisphere, this included the United States–Canada Free Trade Agreement, followed by the North American Free Trade Agreement (NAFTA). The Summit of the Americas in December 1994 formally initiated the effort to expand NAFTA to include Chile. In addition to NAFTA expansion, the summit also produced an initiative to create free trade in the hemisphere early in the next century.

As the world approaches the next millennium,

one is likely to see increasing economic integration

for much of the Americas and Europe.

The existence of other regional trade blocs such as Mercosur and that of the Andean countries is creating an interrelated web of trade preferences for much of the hemisphere. Among the reasons for this move toward regional trade blocs in the hemisphere has been the desire to offset the European-centered trade focus of the European Union. One result of the NAFTA and Summit of the Americas efforts has been to prompt negotiations between the European Union and the Mercosur countries for a possible free trade agreement.

In Asia, APEC has evolved institutionally in recent years and now includes numerous committees and working groups that promote regional cooperation on issues as divergent as customs, investment, transportation, and education. APEC has received most attention for its initiative to achieve regional free trade for member countries on both sides of the Pacific—by 2010 for developed countries and 2020 for developing nations. Activities of the working groups and committees indicate further integration beyond trade relations. Evolving political alliances and dramatic existing differences in level of development and economic philosophy caution that the road to economic integration in the Pacific area will be difficult to achieve.

While not indicative of increased economic integration, international financial institutions such as the World Bank and the International Monetary Fund (IMF) play an important role in economic development. The IMF is also relied upon in economic crises, as was demonstrated recently by the joint IMF-US effort to bolster the Mexican peso. Competing interests and priorities currently plaguing member states of international security institutions could reduce support for multilateral economic cooperation. These institutions will be hard pressed to meet the substantially expanded needs of both countries in transition and other developing countries.

On another front, there is growing uncertainty and confusion regarding the purpose of multilateral and regional security organizations. NATO and the United Nations have lost prestige due to their inability to resolve regional conflicts, particularly in Bosnia. These organizations are currently in a stage of disengagement regarding the ethnic conflicts that have escalated and proliferated in recent years.

Declining international support for the United Nations will likely lead to funding reductions, especially for international peacekeeping activities. It is likely that the UN will seek to limit operations to more clearly defined and supported objectives, such as humanitarian aid and disaster relief.

The leading regional security organization, NATO, is also struggling to redefine its purpose in the aftermath of the Cold War. The potential for further balkanization of Europe could require NATO to rapidly redefine how it will approach conflicts on the Continent. NATO's principal response to redefining regional security has been to focus on expanding the organization by including states in Central and Eastern Europe. NATO is likely to focus more on issues outside of Europe as they emerge as potential threats to international security.

In the future, security threats will also increasingly emerge from Asia and the Persian Gulf region, especially as states in these regions seek nuclear capability, as already demonstrated by North Korea, Iran, and Iraq. There are also increasing concerns in Asia regarding the prospects of an aggressive China that might launch a military campaign toward Taiwan or attempt to resolve regional territorial claims by force. Regional security organizations, such as the Gulf Cooperation Council (GCC), originally established in response to the Iranian revolution, or the ASEAN Regional Forum (ARF), which held the first ever regional security forum for the Asia-Pacific region in 1994, will play an increasingly important role in security matters.

Thus, as the world approaches the next millennium, one is likely to see increasing economic integration for much of the Americas and Europe and possibly Eastern Asia. Such regional economic integration will also benefit multilateralism in trade and investment. More uncertain will be the evolution of alliances to deal with the political crises flowing from some of the remaining isolated (or partially isolated) countries—China, North Korea, Iran, Iraq—and from the traditional sources of international conflict. The perceived recent ineffectiveness of international organizations—principally the

UN and NATO—in resolving conflicts successfully or cost-effectively is likely to result in reduced multilateral funding of these institutions. In turn this may increase local conflicts, which are unchecked by international groups and which foster the reemergence of armed conflicts with local or regional defenders.

[See also Free Trade; Global Culture; Global Environmental Problems; Governance; Hazardous Wastes; Holistic Beliefs; Human Rights; International Diplomacy; International Trade: Regional Trade Agreements; International Tensions; Laws, Evolution of; Multifold Trend; Pacesetter Governments; Peacekeeping.]

BIBLIOGRAPHY

Cameron, David M. *Regionalism and Supranationalism.* Brookfield, VT: Gower, 1981.

Feld, Werner J., and Jordan, Robert S. *International Organizations: A Comparative Approach.* Westport, CT: Greenwood Press, 1988.

Mitrany, David. *The Progress of International Government.* Northford, CT: Elliot Books, 1983.

— TERENCE STEWART

INTERNATIONAL TENSIONS

International tensions in political, military, economic, technological, and sociocultural relationships are the main sources of international conflict. International conflicts created by international tensions range from nonviolent but vigorous competition, through heavily armed, potentially violent "cold war," to escalating degrees of local conventional warfare, all the way to the threat of global war employing atomic, biological, and chemical weapons of mass destruction.

International tensions can be both creative and destructive, but most are seen as destructive and leading to costly diversions of national resources to military forces for containing or fighting wars if deterrence fails. Creative international tensions include peaceful positive-sum competitions in the arts and sciences, business, commerce, education, sports, and trade that benefit all participants but some more than others. Examples abound in the sciences and arts, where international competition and cooperation stimulate and support mutual achievement.

Recent major international political tensions include those between *politically* different forms of national government, such as those between democratic and authoritarian governments. At their most intense, these political tensions are strongest between countries actually at full-scale war with each other, or that regard each other as enemies or potential aggressors. Current examples of warring nations include countries in each of the four major continents and the Middle East: in North America, Mexico and its southernmost state as well as Guatemala and the Mayan Indians; in South America, Ecuador and Peru; in Europe, Bosnia and Serbia, Russia and Chechnya, and Russia and Moldova; in Asia, South and North Korea, Afghanistan, Kashmir, Sri Lanka, and Timor; in Africa, Burundi; in the Middle East, Israel and Lebanon, Syria, Gaza, and the West Bank, and in Turkey and Iraq with the Kurds.

The miniaturization and diffusion

of easy-to-manufacture biological, chemical,

or nuclear weapons of mass destruction

may serve to exacerbate social, political,

and economic conflicts into military engagements.

Countries not engaged in major shooting wars with each other, but engaging in limited violence through terrorism and counterterrorism, include Iran, Iraq, and Libya vis-à-vis the United States; in Europe, the United Kingdom and Ireland, Croatia and Serbia, and others. In all of these cases, political tensions—some associated with cultural and religious tensions, as in Bosnia between Eastern Orthodox and Muslims—have resulted in violent conflict and warfare.

In the next century these international political tensions are likely to persist as a major cause of militarization—war preparations and arms races—and actual shooting wars and their subsequent recovery and rehabilitation efforts (which, in wars involving weapons of mass destruction, may exceed war preparation and war fighting costs and duration). New international political tensions that threaten to increase military costs and increase war risks are likely to intensify between new global military-economic powers such as China, and large neighboring and competing countries such as Russia, Japan, South Korea, Taiwan, Vietnam, Malaysia, India, the United States, the Philippines, and Indonesia. The first eight of these ten countries have experienced war with China in this century. To the extent that China increases international tensions in the ongoing dispute over the ownership of the Spratly Islands oil fields, the risk of arms buildups and war between China and several of these countries will increase.

The internal tensions of the great power coalitions of the Cold War have fragmented some and stressed others. In the decade after World War II the world went through a fragmentation of old colonial empires as former colonies became independent nations. At the same time the Soviet empire extinguished the independence of most of the Eastern European nations. That same Soviet empire of the Soviet Union and its satellite states ended in 1991, and the union of Yugoslavia ended shortly thereafter, both breaking up into smaller, independent states—some parting peacefully, others with violence and civil war. In the former Yugoslavia and the Caucasus, the overriding powers relaxed their superordinate, political-military suppression of ethnic, religious, and economic/ideological conflicts among these smaller, independent nation-states.

Currently the major international tension of the nuclear and conventional stalemate between the old Communist Bloc/Warsaw Pact and the U.S.-led Western alliances of NATO, CENTO, and SEATO has abated into international cooperative threat reduction and conversion of surplus militarized resources to cooperative and technically assisted economic development. What lies ahead in international tensions is the proliferation of democratized communications and the technologies of freedom, apace with the proliferation of the technologies of war and oppression. The most socially advanced, wealthiest, and industrialized nations such as the United States, Japan, the United Kingdom, France, Germany, and Italy, as well as economies in transition, such as Russia and China, are suffering from varying but generally increasing degrees of domestic violence and disorder, from drug abuse and family breakdown to increases in violent crime resulting from the growth of organized crime, local vigilantism, and mass terrorism. It is not clear yet if democratic institutions of the rule of law, civil liberties, and freedom of expression will be able to provide sufficient physical security to law-abiding citizens to withstand these assaults.

The inexorable diffusion of the weapons technologies of mass destruction—nuclear, biological, and chemical—together with cheap and pervasive communications, computing, and sensor systems for targeting and intelligence, threaten the domestic peace of all countries. Where the international arms trade—in which the major nuclear powers are the market leaders—together with domestic internal conflicts supported by nationally sponsored international-terrorist and other violent, criminal organizations interact, we have a rapidly growing source of international tensions. The major powers cannot totally defend themselves from smaller-state-sponsored terrorism, whether conventional or nuclear, without ultimately threatening massive retaliation and destruction of the terrorist-sponsoring government. Whether internal pacification of such national sponsors

of international terrorism is feasible without recourse to war by the larger countries remains to be seen. In any case this development will be one of the most ominous sources of international tensions in the next century.

Major current sources of international tensions are likely to continue to grow or evolve in the next century, involving a variety of forces or factors, as outlined here:

- Cultural: Judeo-Christian versus Islamic or Confucian/Buddhist.
- Economic: Rich versus poor; capitalist versus socialist systems.
- Military: Nuclear versus conventional warfare; strong, global nuclear powers versus weaker, local, or regional ones.
- Political: Democracy versus authoritarianism.
- Technological: Advanced technologies, versus those trying to catch up, versus backward ones, who may have piecemeal access to some elements of advanced technology.

In particular, the miniaturization and diffusion of cheap, easy-to-manufacture biological, chemical, or nuclear weapons of mass destruction may serve to exacerbate these growing social, political, and economic conflicts into violent military engagements.

[See also Apocalyptic Future; Espionage and Counterintelligence; Ethnic and Cultural Separatism; Global Statistics; Human Rights; International Trade: Sustaining Growth; Migration, International; Nationalism; Peacekeeping; Population Growth: Worldwide; Terrorism; Weapons of Mass Destruction; World: Prologue and Epilogue.]

BIBLIOGRAPHY

Banks, Michael. *Conflict in World Society: A New Perspective on International Relations.* New York: St. Martin's Press, 1984.

Bartlett, C. J. *Global Conflict: International Rivalry of the Great Powers.* White Plains, NY: Longman, 1984.

Bloomfield, Lincoln P. *Management of Global Disorder.* Lanham, MD: University Press of America, 1988.

Brecher, Michael, and Wilkenfeld, Jonathan. *Crisis, Conflict and Instability.* Elmsford, NY: Pergamon, 1989.

Holsti, Kalevi J. *Peace and War: Armed Conflict in International Order.* New York: Cambridge University Press, 1991.

Klare, Michael T., and Thomas, Daniel C. *World Security: Trends and Changes at Century's End.* New York: St. Martin's Press, 1991.

Mandel, Robert. *Irrationality in International Confrontation.* Westport, CT: Greenwood Press, 1989.

Matthews, Robert O. *International Conflict and Conflict Management.* New York: Prentice-Hall, 1994.

Ordeshook, Peter C. *The Balance of Power Stability and Instability in International Systems.* New York: Cambridge University Press, 1989.

Stillman, Edmund O., and Pfaff, William. *The Politics of Hysteria: The Sources of Twentieth Century Conflict.* Westport, CT: Greenwood Press, 1981.

— CLARK C. ABT

INTERNATIONAL TRADE: REGIONAL TRADE AGREEMENTS

Regional trade agreements (RTAS) have proliferated since World War II, and more than eighty have now been notified to the General Agreement on Tariffs and Trade (GATT). This survey only considers the most active groups (see Table 1). The two most common variants of RTAs are Customs Unions (CUs), which impose a common external tariff (CET) on nonmembers, and Free Trade Areas (FTAs), in which individual members maintain their separate tariff schedules for nonmembers. The motivations for RTAs are both political (to alleviate political tensions between neighboring countries) and economic (to gain the benefits of mutual trade liberalization). In principle, multilateral liberalization on a global scale could confer greater economic benefits, but RTAs are often justified as a quicker means for achieving deeper liberalization within a smaller group of countries. Countries outside the trade "blocs" fear that they will lose export markets to countries within the group; GATT rules minimize these adverse impacts.

Europe

The European Economic Community (EEC), also known as the European Common Market, was launched in 1957 with the passage of the Treaty of Rome specifying "four freedoms"—free movement of goods, services, capital, and people. A classic customs union, the group adopted the name European Community and then changed it to European Union (EU) in 1993. The initial membership of six grew to twelve countries by 1986 (see Table 1). Austria, Finland, Norway, and Sweden are scheduled to join in 1995, and the group may be enlarged to include Eastern European countries within another ten years. The "Europe 1992" program, launched in 1985, sought to eliminate all residual barriers to achievement of the four freedoms before January 1993. The Maastricht Treaty of 1991 set out to create a single currency and the same degree of economic cohesion as in the United States. Though unification is far from complete, the EU already has achieved more integration than any other regional group.

The European Free Trade Association (EFTA) was created in 1960 as a free trade area. Membership dwindled with the departure of the United Kingdom, Ireland, and Denmark in 1973, and three of the six remaining EFTA members are seeking to join the EU.

North America

The North American Free Trade Agreement (NAFTA) augments the U.S.–Canada Free Trade Agreement of 1988 by the addition of Mexico. Basically, the NAFTA provides for free trade in goods and services, and the free movement of capital after a phase-in period of about ten years.

Pacific Rim

In the Asia-Pacific region, formal economic cooperation originated in 1967 with the creation of the Association of Southeast Asian Nations (ASEAN). The inspiration for ASEAN was political (as a regional security body), not economic. Only with the 1991 agreement to create an ASEAN Free Trade Area (AFTA) did the nations seriously turn to economic integration. AFTA's progress is still hampered by nonbinding liberalization schedules, lengthy transition periods, and an unwillingness to commit to free trade in sensitive products.

The Australia-New Zealand Closer Economic Relations Trade Agreement (ANZCERTA or CER) entails strong economic cooperation between two countries that have long been political allies. Since its creation in 1983, ANZCERTA has removed all merchandise trade barriers between Australia and New Zealand, and has instituted precedent-setting rules on trade in services, harmonization of commercial codes, and competition policies.

The newest regional umbrella organization, the Asia Pacific Economic Cooperation (APEC), contains eighteen members (Table 1). APEC was created in late 1989 to provide a consultative forum in which the members can discuss economic policy issues, somewhat similar to the OECD (Organization for Economic Cooperation and Development). Since 1992, APEC has begun strengthening its institutional structure, by creating a permanent secretariat in Singapore, an Eminent Persons Group to lay out a vision for the organization, and a Committee on Trade and Investment. At the 1994 summit in Bogor, APEC leaders resolved to achieve free trade and investment in the region by 2020 (2010 for industrialized countries).

Lastly, a number of subregional economic zones (SREZs) have been created in Southeast Asia in recent years. SREZs usually include parts of neighboring countries, rather than the entire countries themselves. Examples include the SIJORI growth triangle, covering Singapore, Malaysia's Johor province, and Indonesia's Riau province; the Greater South China Economic Zone, covering coastal South China, Taiwan, and Hong Kong; and the Yellow Sea Economic Zone, covering Northern China, Japan, and South Korea.

Latin America

Economic integration in Latin America originated in the early 1960s, inspired by the political doctrines of

TABLE 1

SUMMARY OF REGIONAL TRADE AGREEMENTS

Name and Year Signed	Membership (Year signed, if not original member)
Europe	
European Union (EU, 1957)	Belgium, Denmark (1973), France, Germany, Greece (1981), Ireland (1973), Italy, Luxembourg, the Netherlands, Portugal (1986), Spain (1986), and the United Kingdom (1973).
European Free Trade Association (EFTA, 1960)	Austria, Finland (1961), Iceland (1970), Liechtenstein (1991), Norway, Sweden, and Switzerland.
North America	
North American Free Trade Agreement (NAFTA, 1993)	Canada, Mexico, and the United States.
Pacific Rim	
Association of Southeast Asian Nations (ASEAN, 1967)	Brunei (1988), Indonesia, Malaysia, the Philippines, Singapore, and Thailand.
Asia Pacific Economic Cooperation (APEC, 1989)	Australia, Brunei, Canada, Chile (1994), China (1991), Chinese Taipei (Taiwan, 1991), Hong Kong (1991), Indonesia, Japan, Korea, Malaysia, Mexico (1993), New Zealand, Papua New Guinea (1993), the Philippines, Singapore, Thailand, and the United States.
Australia–New Zealand Closer Economic Relations Trade Agreement (ANZCERTA, 1983)	Australia and New Zealand.
Latin America	
Latin American Free Trade Association (LAFTA, 1960), renamed Latin American Integration Association (LAIA, 1980)	Mexico and all the South American countries except Guyana, French Guiana, and Suriname.
Central American Common Market (CACM, 1960)	Costa Rica (1962), El Salvador, Guatemala, Honduras, and Nicaragua.
Caribbean Community (CARICOM, 1973)	Antigua and Barbuda, the Bahamas (1983), Barbados, Belize (1974), Dominica (1974), Grenada (1974), Guyana, Jamaica, Montserrat (1974), St. Kitts and Nevis, St. Lucia (1974), St. Vincent and the Grenadines (1974), and Trinidad and Tobago.
Andean Pact (1969)	Bolivia, Colombia, Ecuador, Peru, and Venezuela (Chile withdrew in 1976).
Mercado Común del Sur (MERCOSUR, 1991)	Argentina, Brazil, Paraguay, and Uruguay.
Africa	
South African Customs Union (SACU, 1910)	Botswana, Lesotho, Namibia, South Africa, and Swaziland.
South African Development Coordination Conference (SADCC, 1980)	Angola, Botswana, Mozambique, Tanzania, Zambia, and Zimbabwe.
Economic Community of West African States (ECOWAS, 1975)	Benin, Burkina Faso, Cape Verde, Côte d'Ivoire, The Gambia, Ghana, Guinea, Guinea-Bissau, Liberia, Mali, Mauritania, Niger, Nigeria, Sénégal, Sierra Leone, and Togo.
Communauté Economique de l'Afrique de l'Ouest (CEAO, 1973)	Benin (1984), Burkina Faso, Côte d'Ivoire, Mali, Mauritania, Niger, and Sénégal.
Mano River Union (MRU, 1973)	Guinea (1980), Liberia, and Sierra Leone.
Customs and Economic Union of Central Africa (UDEAC, 1964)	Cameroon, Central African Republic, Congo, Gabon, Chad, and Equatorial Guinea.
Preferential Trade Area for Eastern and Southern African States (PTA, 1981)	Angola, Burundi, Comoros, Djibouti, Ethiopia, Kenya, Lesotho, Malawi, Mauritius, Mozambique, Namibia (1991), Rwanda, Somalia, Sudan, Swaziland, Tanzania, Uganda, Zambia, and Zimbabwe.

Sources: International Monetary Fund, *World Economic Outlook.* (May 1993): 107–108; De Melo and Panagariya. *New Dimensions in Regional Integration.* Cambridge, U.K.: Cambridge University Press.

import substitution and self-sufficiency. The hope was to expand exports and overcome foreign exchange shortages through greater trade within the region, but little integration was achieved until the mid-1980s, when regional pacts were rejuvenated on the basis of market-oriented principles. At the Miami Summit of the Americas in December 1994, Western Hemisphere leaders agreed to integrate existing subregional agreements into one encompassing "Free Trade Area of the Americas."

The proliferation of regional trade agreements raises the question whether they create commercial tensions between regions or whether they presage global economic integration.

The Latin American Free-Trade Association (LAFTA)—replaced by Latin American Integration Association (LAIA) in 1980—and the Central American Common Market (CACM) were created in 1960. LAIA has remained a talk-shop organization, which ambitiously encompasses all of South America and Mexico. Because of political turmoil in Central America, CACM accomplished little until the late 1980s. Since then, the CACM members have agreed to drop internal duties on agricultural trade, impose a CET by 1995, and establish a free trade area with Mexico by 1997.

The Andean Pact was created in 1969. Encouraged by market-oriented reforms of the mid-1980s, its members agreed in 1990 to achieve regional free trade by 1992; Bolivia, Colombia, and Venezuela eliminated tariffs on schedule, while Ecuador has fallen behind and Peru has withdrawn from the group.

The Caribbean Community (CARICOM) evolved from the Caribbean Free Trade Area (CARIFTA) in 1973. The group, with a membership of thirteen Caribbean nations, became active in the late 1980s, but has repeatedly postponed deadlines for establishing a CET, while trade liberalization among members has progressed at different rates.

The Mercado Común del Sur (MERCOSUR) is the youngest of Latin America's regional trading blocs. Created in 1991, MERCOSUR's schedule calls for free internal trade and a CET by 1995. This schedule is proceeding as planned, although macroeconomic instability in Brazil has created severe strains.

Africa

African regional integration attempts have been mostly unsuccessful, with the exception of South African Cus-

toms Union (SACU) and South African Development Coordination Conference (SADCC). SACU, created in 1910 by South Africa, Botswana, Lesotho, and Swaziland (Namibia joined in 1990), has a CET and a centralized monetary policy. SADCC was created by the other southern African states to reduce their dependence on South Africa during the apartheid era.

Other "paper" groups include the Economic Community of West African States (ECOWAS); Communauté Economique de l'Afrique de l'Ouest (CEAO); Mano River Union (MRU); the Customs and Economic Union of Central Africa (UDEAC); and the Preferential Trade Area for Eastern and Southern African States (PTA). None of these groups has achieved meaningful trade liberalization or established a CET.

Do Regional Trade Agreements Presage Global Integration?

The proliferation of regional trade agreements raises the question whether RTAs create commercial tensions between regions, or whether they presage global economic integration. The GATT requires that participants in RTAs eliminate barriers on "substantially all" trade; that average external duties in a customs union should not "on the whole be higher or more restrictive" than the duties previously imposed by the member countries; and that interim agreements should lead to CUs or FTAs "within a reasonable amount of time." All of these conditions are criticized as too vague, permitting too much discrimination against nonmembers. Meanwhile, it is an open question whether, over the next decade, RTAs will inspire or impede the newly created World Trade Organization.

Trade Patterns

Intraregional exports as a percentage of total regional exports are depicted in Table 2, which shows that intraregional trade has increased over the last two decades for the larger groups (especially EU and NAFTA). This relative growth in intraregional trade can be interpreted in two ways. It could come at the expense of trade with nonmembers ("trade diversion"); or it could result from an overall increase in trade due to liberalization ("trade creation"). Research suggests that trade creation is generally more important; but countries that are not members of a particular group are especially sensitive to trade diversion.

[See also Free Trade; Global Business; International Trade: Regulation; International Trade: Sustaining Growth.]

BIBLIOGRAPHY

Anderson, Kym, and Blackhurst, Richard. *Regional Integration and the Global Trading System.* New York: St. Martin's Press, 1993.

TABLE 2

INTRAREGIONAL EXPORTS AS A SHARE OF TOTAL REGIONAL EXPORTS

Regional Trade Agreement	1970	1975	1980	1985	1990
EU	51.0	50.0	54.0	54.4	60.4
EFTA	28.0	35.2	32.6	31.2	28.2
NAFTA	36.3	35.0	33.6	39.7	41.5
ASEAN	20.7	15.9	16.9	18.4	18.4
ANZCERTA	6.1	6.2	6.4	7.0	7.6
LAFTA/LAIA	9.9	13.6	13.7	8.3	10.6
CACM	25.7	23.3	24.1	14.7	14.8
ANDEAN PACT	2.0	3.7	3.8	3.4	4.6
SADCC	2.6	3.7	2.1	3.9	4.8
ECOWAS	2.9	4.0	3.5	5.3	5.7
CEAO	6.3	12.7	8.9	8.7	10.5
MRU	0.2	0.4	0.5	0.4	0.1
UDEAC	4.8	2.7	1.6	1.9	3.0
PTA	8.0	9.3	7.6	5.5	5.9

Sources: De Melo and Panagariya. *New Dimensions in Regional Integration.* Cambridge, UK: Cambridge University Press, 1993: 247–248; International Monetary Fund. *World Economic Outlook* (May 1993): 112.

De Melo, Jaime, and Panagariya, Arvind. *New Dimensions in Regional Integration.* Cambridge, U.K.: Cambridge University Press, 1993.

Garnaut, Ross, and Drysdale, Peter. *Asia Pacific Regionalism: Readings in International Economic Relations.* Pymble, Australia: HarperEducational, 1994.

Henning, C. Randall; Hochreiter, Eduard; and Hufbauer, Gary C. *Reviving the European Union.* Washington, DC: Institute for International Economics, 1994.

Hufbauer, Gary C., and Schott, Jeffrey J. *NAFTA: An Assessment.* Washington, DC: Institute for International Economics, 1993.

Hufbauer, Gary C., and Schott, Jeffrey J. *Western Hemisphere Economic Integration.* Washington, DC: Institute for International Economics, 1994.

(The author would like to acknowledge the invaluable assistance of Gautam Jaggi in the preparation of this article.)

— GARY HUFBAUER

INTERNATIONAL TRADE: REGULATION

From a strictly economic perspective, there are only two valid reasons for international trade: to expand markets (and demand) for domestic capacity and to acquire something of value not comparably available from domestic sources. However, actual trade involves a more complex rationale flowing from a diverse network of geopolitical and social purposes. This forecast delves into trends and changes affecting international trade between 1955 and 2020, chiefly from a U.S. perspective.

Historic Perspectives

Two methods of calculating U.S. trade trends in quantitative terms—the five-year moving average and the exponential fit—make it dramatically apparent that the United States cannot remain either a major world power or a leading world economy if ongoing trends are projected ahead twenty-five years. Therefore, U.S. trade policies will have to change if a major, more favorable shift in these trends is to occur. More careful forecasts require an understanding of the policy dynamics that underlie these numbers.

An analysis of socioeconomic history and a cursory review of the trade agreements, policies, and programs of the United States summarizes the sweep of history. This pattern of U.S. trade history is consistent with the global patterns.

From this historical perspective, significant changes in philosophy or policy features determine each "new" historic era. This "historic era" concept is an important construct or tool in any forecast. If the forecasting horizon does not involve a transition into a "new era," one can more confidently assume a "strategic stability" in the underlying driving forces. Impending transition into a new era supports (selectively) more reliance upon projections. At the same time, when an "era transition" is in progress, projections are more likely to yield inaccurate results.

On the basis of these few foundations, a new era is probably emerging today. The following forecasts are based upon this premise. This estimate is based upon the unacceptability of projected trends, the dynamics associated with emerging technologies, and institutional changes within the emerging global economy.

Forecasts

The emergence of global telecommunications, manufacturing technologies, the weaponry of sabotage, global finance, the emergence of the global market, and the emerging dominance of the transnational corporation (replacing the international and multinational-type companies) are the principal forces driving the future of international trade.

Given the geographic redistribution of manufacturing and value-added roles associated with the evolving transnational corporations, the volume of world exports is expected to grow rapidly. The U.S. effort to capture 20 percent of world exports will require a major expansion of exports. As the value-added functions of trade shift from national concentrations of commercial enterprise toward global optimization based on global markets and global manufacturing/services, wherever they might be located, imports will steadily rise. Imports will continue to be carefully controlled, but the onus of regulation will gradually shift from treaties, compacts, and trade agreements toward voluntary controls involving new accountability standards related to processing quality and production costs.

Global telecommunications, manufacturing technologies, the weaponry of sabotage, global finance, emergence of the global market, and the emerging dominance of the transnational corporation are the principal forces driving the future of international trade.

The U.S. economy will remain a major import market, but the comparative attractions will erode considerably. This shift will lower U.S. trade negotiation leverage. However, efforts will be undertaken to offset this eroding influence in other ways.

International trade will become much more a function of marginal economic advantage. Subsidies intended to spur economic development or bestow political reward (i.e., the awarding of most-favored-nation status and the like) will wane.

Policy Goals

U.S. policy goals can be summarized as follows:

- To remain a "dominant" world power, with the military capability to back up that role.
- To sustain democracy as the predominant political system of choice.
- To maintain market-driven capitalism as the economic system of choice.
- To retain effective sovereignty of the nation-state by selectively delegating sovereignty to world trade regulatory bodies, though limiting this sovereignty to specified circumstances.
- To redefine national security so that it includes many aspects of economic and sociopolitical value protection. This will lead to a world power-based economy capable of supporting with minimal dependency the military capability required to support the world role and the protection of U.S. freedoms and living standards.
- To implement import controls that will prevent imports from eroding the strategic power of the U.S. economy.
- To sustain national competitiveness within the global economy.
- To attain for the United States at least 20 percent of the world's exports, with two or more U.S.-based transnational companies among the top-ten global firms within each major industry or economic sector. (A result of this strategy will be the development of new kinds of partnerships between the U.S. government and various transnational firms.)
- To achieve a strategic equilibrium of trade and monetary exchange balances.

- To establish global production and trade standards that assure certain quality and "comparability" in labor rates and environmental standards.
- To achieve regulatory control of the transnational "corporate state."
- To foster developmental economics that will shift the focus from the nation-state to identifiable population subsets within nation-states.

Ultimate Sovereignty

The most significant judgment to be made is the estimate of where the ultimate sovereignty will reside—i.e., in the political configuration (whether nation-states, regional federations, or a global government) or the corporate state (i.e., the network of emerging global corporations). The assessment must go beyond rhetorical structures to an estimate of where the effective operational power to define and control policy lies.

Continued erosion of the relative power and effective sovereignty of the nation-states will occur over the next five to ten years. Some sovereignty will be relegated to regional coordinating bodies (e.g., the European Economic Community) and ultimately to their political counterparts (e.g., the United States of Europe).

Regional entities (economic and geopolitical) will reflect matrices of geographically contiguous areas (Europe, the Americas, Asia/Pacific) and political alliances (the Muslim states). Culturally based concepts such as "Western civilization" will gradually be eroded as the amalgamation of cultures progresses within nations. (Only states clearly defining cultural values as a heritage to be protected and propagated will involve themselves in transregional/transnational alliances.)

Regional entities will contend for increased power via delegated sovereignty from constituent nation-states. Accelerating concentration of global economic wealth and power in the top transnational corporations will occur in the near term. Before the end of the first decade of the next century, the concept of the corporate state as a geopolitical power will be well defined. Many current U.S. philosophies and goals will be at serious risk unless "national interests" are reinstated as the primary criteria governing international policies and relations. (At this point there will be a major drive to rebuild the nation-state(s) as the primary sovereign entity.) The ultimate outcome will depend upon the network of nations, and their related philosophies, goals, and economic resources. The United States will adjust its policy structure and evolve a coherent industrial policy of the type required to remain a major factor in this block of world power nations.

Controlling Transnational Corporations

If current trends continue through the forecasting period, the corporate state, composed of fewer than 400 transnational corporations, will represent a power base that will erode and eventually dominate the policy structures within which trade is conducted. National interests will increasingly be defined by economic determinism based upon "optimization" of the corporate economy.

New controls over transnational corporate communities will evolve. One major mechanism for this regulatory control will be new process quality standards and audit systems. (Whatever the ultimate form, the corporate state will remain subject to the collective authority of nation-states.)

There should be no underestimation of the influence that the corporate state can bring to bear on the network of national and regional policies. It is not likely that a renewal of isolationism will materialize. There may be some degree of nationalistic "protectionism" on a selective basis, but this phenomenon is not likely to become widespread. Similarly, total subservience of the corporate state to any particular nation-states will not occur.

These tensions will exert a dominant influence over the dynamics of international trade for the next twenty-five years.

Cross-National Equity in Process Quality and Costs

The current drive in the EEC for "uniformity" in product reliability as a function of specific process and quality standards will become a global model. Process standard concepts will be extended to services such as stock market operations, banking, and other major economic undertakings. Process standards and audits will become major mechanisms for equalizing such factors as environmental quality and labor costs. Ultimately, all goods and services entering global markets will compete, with the competitive edge determined by productivity, innovation, and other legitimate differentiating factors.

These developments will shift much of the trade regulatory function onto individual company behavior, with less emphasis upon nations or entire industries. Compliance with process and quality standards will require certification by independent audits, much like today's independent auditor certifications of financial statements.

Legally Regulated Transactions

Regulated transactions will be expanded to encompass financial services and, ultimately, capital investment. A coherent U.S. industrial policy will evolve that sustains industrial capabilities associated with national security on a minimum dependence basis. Provision also may be made to protect selected key employment centers required to sustain continued growth of the U.S. national markets so that they remain attractive to imports

and investments, protect overall U.S. standards of living, and sustain ecological standards, intellectual property rights, and so forth.

Illegal Transactions

Banned imports or exports will expand to include the following:

- Items or goods that pose public health risks (e.g., certain drugs and adulterated or contaminated foods or beverages).
- Items or goods found to be in noncompliance with process and quality standards or that have not been audited or tested to see if they are in compliance.
- Items or transactions that pose a threat to national security or sovereignty.

Barter Exchanges

Trade regulatory systems will require companies engaging in global trade to report transactions on a value-added basis. Data acquired will be used to monitor the financial dealings of each nation and company. Black market bartering among transnational companies intended to circumvent regulations standing in the way of the company goals will increase, driven by economic motives. Tensions between accountable barter and black market barter will become a major problem in international trade during the next century.

[See also Free Trade; International Governance and Regional Authorities; International Trade: Regional Trade Agreements; International Trade: Sustaining Growth.]

BIBLIOGRAPHY

Adelman, Carol C., ed. *International Regulation: New Rules in a Changing World Order.* San Francisco, CA: Lehrman Institute/Institute for Contemporary Studies Press, 1988.

Brown, Michael B. *Fair Trade: Reform and Realities in the International Trading System.* Atlantic Highlands, NJ: Zed Books, 1993.

Howell, T. R.; Wolff, A. W.; Bartlett, B. L.; and Gadbaw, R. M., eds. *Conflict Among Nations: Trade Policies in the 1990s.* Boulder, CO: Westview Press, 1992.

Ohmae, Kenichi. *The Borderless World: Power and Strategy in the Interlinked Economy.* New York: Harper-Collins, 1990.

Runnalls, David, and Cosby, Aaron. *Trade and Sustainable Development: A Survey of the Issues and a New Research Agenda.* Winnipeg, Manitoba: International Institute for Sustainable Development, 1992.

Starr, Martin K. *Global Competitiveness: Getting the U.S. Back on Track.* New York: W. W. Norton, 1988.

Vernon, Raymond, and Spar, Debora. *Beyond Globalism: Remaking American Foreign Economic Policy.* New York: Free Press, 1989.

– CHARLES W. WILLIAMS
WESLEY H. WILLIAMS

INTERNATIONAL TRADE: SUSTAINING GROWTH

The United States has been promoting a multilateral open trade policy since the end of World War II. This policy is expected to continue for the remainder of this century. U.S. economic policy analysts expect that international exports will become a major factor in sustaining U.S. economic growth and living standards during this time. This entry looks at historic data regarding the growth of world trade and the U.S. economy, particularly as it pertains to these expectations.

World merchandise trade (in current dollars) has more than doubled over the past decade. In the process, however, persistent bilateral trade imbalances emerged. Advocates of multilateral open trade minimize the significance of these bilateral imbalances, claiming that multilateral balance will be achieved over time. Even so, the persistence of the imbalances of the United States and Japan, not just with each other but with the world, suggests that multilateral balance may be a long time in coming.

Another problem associated with imbalances is how they transmit recessions among trading partners. For example, in the 1990–1991 period, while the U.S. economy was in recession, U.S. imports declined slightly but recovered vigorously shortly thereafter. In contrast, the Japanese recession, which also began in 1990, has persisted through 1994 and is not expected to end before the end of 1995. Not only do American exporters suffer from the shrinking export market, but attempts to bring the national trade accounts into balance will invariably fail, along with the political friendships that inevitably develop between trading partners.

Over the past few decades, the United States has gone from being the world's largest creditor to the world's largest debtor, with Japan becoming the world's largest creditor. This does not augur well for claims about multilateral accounts balancing over the long term.

U.S. budget deficits are commanding an enormous amount of political attention today. As devastating as the overall budget deficit is to the U.S. economy, it pales in importance with persistent current account deficits. The cumulative current account imbalances indicate that the United States ran up deficits totaling about $1.2 trillion over the past decade. This debt is somewhat offset by U.S. holdings of international assets, but a growing portion of U.S. debt is held by foreigners—in 1992, about 15 percent of the national debt was held by foreigners.

The reasons foreigners hold U.S. dollars, or invest in dollar-denominated assets, are quite different than they are for Americans. Foreigners hold U.S. dollars to facilitate trade (since most international trade is denominated in dollars) and as an investment. As foreign dollar holdings increase, the investment value becomes more important. If the return on dollar investments erodes or if the creditors need domestic currency (e.g., if the Japanese need more yen), they will become sellers of their

dollar holdings. This would in turn cause a decline in the value of the dollar and reduce the return on dollar-denominated assets—a vicious cycle. Recent experiences with Mexico provide a good example of how this phenomenon works. While there are vast differences between the United States and Mexico, the United States may not be far behind with regard to currency crises. Clearly, the U.S. ability to regulate the dollar or intervene in international economic crises has been strongly eroded by foreign dollar holdings.

The international economy is organizing itself

into three major trading blocs.

Collectively these three blocs account

for more than 80 percent of world trade.

With regard to the U.S. living standards, current account deficits have both positive and negative aspects. On the positive side, they allow the United States to consume more than it produces. On the negative side, they create a dependence on foreign goods. And since these goods are bought on credit, they produce a debt that will have to be serviced until it is repaid. However, the debt will never be repaid until the United States runs a current account surplus. In addition, transferring wealth to international creditors makes it more difficult for the Federal Reserve to control the domestic economy and erodes the strength of the U.S. economy in general.

U.S. trade deficits over the past decade are the result of a three-pronged U.S. policy: (1) to reduce inflation; (2) to increase military spending (during the Cold War); and (3) to promote multilateral open trade by unilaterally offering itself as an example of the benefits that accrue to an open-trader (especially one with a sound currency and high interest rates). In many ways, the policy has been successful. U.S. inflation rates have been held in check despite a horrendous rise in budget deficits. The Soviet Union actually collapsed—exceeding the most optimistic expectations of its supporters, and, because of America's willingness to accept imports, the United States was able to get others to support U.S. living standards by exporting goods to the country on credit. Unfortunately, this policy had many side effects, which are now extremely difficult to correct.

In addition to the transfer of economic power discussed previously, the world has come to rely on U.S. markets and trade deficits. But, perhaps more important, the United States has become dependent on exporters for a wide variety of industrial and consumer products. These conditions make it very difficult for the United States to deal firmly with trading partners who deny American companies access to the markets that their own companies enjoy in the United States. Therefore, notwithstanding the fact that the United States is currently among the most highly productive nations in the world, it is virtually unable to increase its exports or even gain access to many of its trading partners' markets or to protect its intellectual property rights, the old (but real and important) unleveled playing field argument.

Some economists expect that services trade will be the means by which the United States reverses its trade deficits. The country currently runs a surplus of about $50 billion in its service trade, but this will be difficult to increase. The U.S. services trade is less than 25 percent of its merchandise trade, and most services trade is for tourism, shipping, and royalties. Potentially expandable services trade (e.g., financial services) is tied to capital, and because of America's international indebtedness, it has little capital to support these opportunities should they materialize. Japan is far better positioned to take advantage of such opportunities. The only real hope for an increase in U.S. services trade surpluses is from open and protected markets for intellectual property. It will take more than reluctantly signed trade agreements to secure meaningful protection of intellectual property.

Japan's merchandise trade picture stands in dramatic contrast. Japan runs a trade surplus with all of its trading partners except for raw materials exporters (e.g., oil, copper, steel ore). While the Japanese consumer may be paying more than Americans for many consumer products, even for those produced in Japan, this may be offset by greater economic stability.

The difficulty America has had in negotiating a greater access to the Japanese marketplace is not going to change without increased American pressure. Furthermore, America's ability to apply such pressure weakens steadily as America's international debt continues to rise, as the dollar weakens, and as the world military threat declines.

Statistically the European Community (EC) is the world's largest trade group. However, most EC trade is conducted with the other member states under economic agreements that make their behavior resemble a single nation. The EC's external trade provides a somewhat more accurate picture of their international trade. However, the pending expansion of the EC is not reflected in these data.

The EC merchandise trade picture is changing dramatically as a result of new European countries joining the EC and an internal restructuring of the rules moving them toward greater economic unification. None-

theless, EC trade is more balanced than that of either the United States or Japan.

The EC is still in a recession. However, with the end of the recession expected by 1996 and with the opening of the East European economies imminent, the EC economic outlook is bright.

In spite of an orchestrated effort to create an open multilateral trade system, and without any formal constituency to promote it, the international economy is organizing itself into three major trading blocs. Collectively these three blocs account for more than 80 percent of world trade, more than half of which is intrabloc trade.

A glaring distinction between these blocs is that the Asia/Pacific-10 has been in surplus for more than a decade, and (barring any major shifts in the international economy) this is expected to continue for many years to come. The question is whether or not the other blocs or the international financial markets will permit these trade surpluses to continue.

Also, the internal trade of the West European bloc is more than double its external trade. The trend toward greater concentration of bloc trade is likely to increase as internal economic consolidation continues.

Many global companies recognize this tripolar trend and are positioning their divisions to locate in each of these three blocs in ways that make them appear as if they were "naturalized citizens" of the regions in which they operate.

U.S. macroeconomic trends are as follows: (1) U.S. total trade (merchandise and services exports plus imports) and (2) individual income taxes and social insurance payments have been increasing far more rapidly than (3) U.S. GDP, and all three have been expanding more rapidly than (4) median U.S. family incomes.

These measures clearly show that U.S. family incomes have been lagging behind both trade and GDP trends. Furthermore, the net income has been declining even further since taxes have also been increasing more rapidly than incomes and because more family members had to work to maintain the low levels of growth in family incomes shown here.

Many argue that these conditions are not a result of international trade or global competition, but a consequence of technological progress that has eliminated many highly paid jobs while creating primarily low-paying jobs. Others consider the primary cause to be a result of U.S. companies out-sourcing high-paid, labor-intensive jobs that have been made more easily transferable by technological progress. Clearly both technology and the globalization of business have contributed to the trends.

Regardless of the degree to which trade or technology has contributed to the present trends, if they continue,

461

American attitudes toward multilateral open trade will turn increasingly protectionist. But it is not likely that American support for technology will decrease. Americans will continue to have faith in technology and in their ability to develop technology. They will be firm in their belief that if they use the technology they develop wisely (i.e., do not give it away), American living standards will improve. However, if the United States continues to pursue policies directed toward promoting a global multilateral open trade system, and if American living standards do not improve, the political backlash against these trade policies will be severe, at least at the ballot box.

While no one would seriously argue that this is strictly a result of America's pursuit of multilateral open trade policies, it can certainly be argued that globalization of business has put highly paid American workers in direct competition with low-paid foreign workers, and that the American worker is the loser in the process. In an attempt to offset the erosion of income, more women in general, and wives in particular, entered the labor force despite the tax consequences, the fact that they were underpaid (relative to men), and the job-related expenses incurred.

In order to change these trends, the United States must break the deficit mentality that is built into U.S. economic policies. Instead, there must be a focus on measures that will bring production and consumption into balance. Even before the recent decline in the dollar, the United States was among the most productive nations in the world. Nevertheless, the United States cannot sell sufficient product on the domestic and export markets combined to equal its consumption. Hence the country runs trade and current account deficits—deficits that are major factors in the U.S. inability to bring the overall budget into balance. When the United States runs a current account deficit in excess of $150 billion, as it did in 1994, it further debases the dollar as the world's reserve currency.

To change this, Americans will have to muster all of the country's technological and innovative skills to increase the competitiveness of American companies and to support this effort with appropriate economic policies—especially leveling the playing field and keeping it level.

The importance of the level playing field is not because of the export opportunities it will present to U.S. businesses, but because leveling the playing field abroad will also level it at home. Anyone who has traveled to Japan knows that one can usually buy Japanese products at lower prices in the United States than one can in Japan. This procedure, whereby an exporter earns excess profits from domestic sales and uses the surplus to offset lower profits (or even losses) from exports, is often referred to as cross-subsidization.

An American business in a domestic market where a foreign competitor employs cross-subsidization can be at an impossible disadvantage. Furthermore, it is almost impossible to design regulations to prevent cross-subsidization. For example, it is impossible to distinguish between selling at a loss during a "clearance sale" and cross-subsidization. The only effective way to prevent cross-subsidization is to level the playing field so that an exporter's domestic market is not protected, and therefore cannot be used for cross-subsidization. In short, leveling the playing field not only opens foreign markets to U.S. products, it levels the competition at home as well.

One way to accomplish this that would be supported by most Americans is to demand bilateral reciprocity. If the United States were to seek reciprocity via the kind of trade negotiations recently witnessed, it would be negotiating forever, or so it seems. Bilateral reciprocity will have to be unilaterally imposed prior to the usual hearings from the opposition as to issues of unfairness. And since the only trade regulations that the United States controls are U.S. regulations, unilateral change means that the United States will only limit its trading partners to the same privileges American businesses enjoy in other countries.

The details of how to implement this policy will be very contentious, but the specifics are less important than the commitment to changing the rules and U.S. economic policies to make it possible for U.S. businesses to once again produce an amount at least equal to America's consumption. There will surely be many complaints from U.S. companies who depend on foreign production sources and technology, and from those trading partners whose competitiveness would be threatened by such a policy. This should not prevent the United States from following this course. It may be the only way to (1) balance domestic accounts; (2) save the dollar; and (3) prevent the international economy from complete collapse.

[See also Free Trade; Global Business: Dominant Organizational Forms; Global Culture; Intellectual Property; International Trade: Regional Trade Agreements; International Trade: Regulation; Tourism.]

BIBLIOGRAPHY

Batra, Ravi. *The Myth of Free Trade: A Plan for America's Revival.* New York: Charles Scribner, 1993.

Brown, Michael B. *Fair Trade: Reform and Realities in the International Trading System.* London and Atlantic Highlands, NJ: Zed Books, 1993.

Howell, Thomas R., and Wolff, Brent L. *Conflict Among Nations: Trade Policy in the 1990s.* Boulder, CO: Westview Press, 1992.
– SELWYN ENZER

INVESTMENTS

The importance of investments in any assessment of the future cannot be overestimated. Following the dramatic collapse of communism in 1989–1991, and the subsequent rise of democratic free enterprise worldwide, investments of all types are taking on vital significance as the *sine qua non* of world economic development and prosperity. The United States has been the global leader for democracy and free enterprise for the community of nations. One of the reasons for the political/economic ascendance of the United States was the rapid development of its capital markets, especially in the period following the Civil War.

A brief survey of different investment terms follows.

Debt Instruments

A "debt security" is evidence of borrowing that must be repaid, stating the amount, maturity date (or dates), and a specific rate of interest (or discount). Debt securities can be traded among investors before they mature. A corporate bond is a certificate of indebtedness extended over a period of from several years to a century. It is issued by a company which also has common stock. Bonds are considered a senior security in the capital structure of the corporation and have first call on revenues of the corporation to pay their interest and also preference over the assets of the company to insure the return of money lent when the bonds were issued. Bonds are rated based on the outlook for the corporation's business and other factors, with "Triple A" being the highest bond rating. The federal government also issues debt securities ranging from short-term Treasury bills, maturing in a year or less, to the well-known thirty-year Treasury bond. Since Washington is assumed to be able always to raise taxes to pay interest, the quality of the $4 trillion federal debt is considered to be the highest. There is varied tax treatment of different types of debt securities. Municipal bonds, issued by local governments, for example, pay interest that is not taxed by the federal government. The dollar value of trading in the bond market surpasses that of the stock market.

Stocks

Stocks or equities represent ownership in companies. Common stock is issued to shareholders when a company first "goes public" in a "primary offering." The company then uses the money from the offering to develop a business providing a product or service. After the initial stock sale to investors, shares of stock are traded in "secondary markets"—i.e., on the major exchanges (such as the New York Stock Exchange or the American Stock Exchange) or through the over-the-counter dealer network. Stockholders, as owners of a company, benefit when the company earns profits and suffer when it is unprofitable because stock prices and dividends rise and fall, in each respective situation.

The number of publicly traded companies in America totals approximately 8,000.

The "dividend yield" on a stock is a function of its dividend and price per share. A "cash dividend" is a cash payment to a company's stockholders made from current earnings or accumulated profits. Investors can also benefit from "dividend reinvestment" plans—i.e., purchasing more shares of a company with its cash dividend payments. Some companies have automatic reinvestment programs for their dividends. In contrast to dividend income, "capital gains" on stocks result when share prices appreciate and are defined as the selling price minus the cost basis. The tax rate on long-term capital gains is currently a 28 percent maximum, contrasted to a much higher maximum marginal rate of 39.6 percent for ordinary income.

"Options" are contracts giving the right to buy (a *call* option) or to sell (a *put* option) a stock, commodity, or financial instrument at a predetermined price and within a preset time period. In the context of a specific company, employee options usually refer to the right to purchase shares of the company, usually below their value in the secondary market, as an incentive for superior performance by employees.

Investors can purchase stocks directly from some major companies without transaction costs, or through discount brokers that charge low commissions or at full-service brokerage firms. It is also possible to purchase shares of companies that are listed on foreign stock exchanges by buying American Depository Receipts for those stocks on our exchanges.

Stock investment strategies range widely from simple value investing, which focuses on share prices selling at low multiples of earnings, to exotic "arbitrage," the practice of buying and selling two different but related securities to profit from a temporary divergence in their values.

Stock Market

The stock market is composed of a large number of individual stocks. There are approximately 2,200 common stocks listed on the New York Stock Exchange and several times that number are traded on the American Stock Exchange and in the NASDAQ market. The number of publicly traded companies in America totals approximately 8,000.

The long-term return for the stock market, which may be thought of as an "investment yield," is approximately 9 percent per year. This return includes both price appreciation and dividends. During the 1980s, when the Dow Jones Industrial Average of thirty well-known stocks rose from 1,000 to nearly 3,000, the return was twice the long-term norm.

While an individual stock can rise and fall substantially based on company developments, the entire stock market is usually less volatile and reflects not only the diverse movements of many common stocks, but also broad factors like economic recoveries and recessions that influence the overall level of corporate profits and interest rates. Also, political developments, such as changes in taxes, and monetary policies implemented by the independent Federal Reserve Board can affect the stock market. There are brief periods when influences on the entire stock market can overshadow all company-level factors. The 1987 stock market crash is an example where the widely watched Dow Jones Industrial Average plunged approximately 1,000 points in only a few weeks, with one giant drop of over 500 points occurring on October 19, 1987. Economic events that may have been responsible for the initial part of the decline included an increase in interest rates by the Federal Reserve. Importantly, another relatively new instrument in U.S. financial markets, termed a "derivative," was responsible for the extreme nature of decline.

A "derivative" product is a contract that has its price determined by an underlying asset such as a stock index, a currency, or a commodity. In the 1987 case, the derivative in question was stock index futures. While the intended use of derivatives by large institutional investors was to reduce risk, the result was just the opposite. A tactic called "portfolio insurance" resulted in the selling of stock index futures as the market began to decline. When the value of these futures dropped below the value of the underlying stock market index, interaction with another derivative tactic termed program trading resulted in a "meltdown." The aforesaid sounds confusing because it is, and the message is that today's financial markets are increasingly complex and subject to forces well beyond fundamental developments in individual companies and normal economic trends. Precautions have, of course, been taken by the exchanges and regulatory authorities to prevent a repeat of the fall of 1987.

Another risk factor in the stock market is related to the purchase of stocks on "margin"—i.e., with borrowed money. While this enhances gains during rising markets, when sudden declines in a common stock, or worse in the entire market, occur, the declining value of stocks held on margin requires that they be sold if new money is not deposited. In most cases, including the fall of 1987, the stocks held on margin are sold, adding to the downward pressure on prices. A long-term investor holding stocks that were fully paid, however, could ride through the 1987 crash without being forced to sell.

Commodities

The original definition of "commodities," bulk goods such as metals or foodstuffs, has been expanded to include financial instruments. Commodity prices are determined by competitive bids and offers, similar to the pricing of stocks. Trading in commodities is usually confined to the futures markets. "Futures" are exchange-standardized contracts for the purchase or sale of a commodity at a future date. Gold is one well-known futures contract, as is the thirty-year Treasury bond. Options can be purchased on commodity futures contracts, just as with stocks. Commodity contracts usually involve high risk.

Mutual Funds

An increasingly popular investment medium in recent years is the "mutual fund," an investment company offering its fund shares for purchase by the public and investing on behalf of its shareholders who may also sell their shares at will, usually at net asset value in the case of open-end funds. Mutual funds can invest in stocks, debt instruments, and even commodities. Specialized funds invest in sectors of the equity market, such as environmental stocks. Over two thousand funds now offer professional management and diversification to investors, but superior performance is not assured.

Future Investment Trends

What might be termed "future shock" certainly characterizes the investment world today—i.e., an increasingly rapid pace of change involving new capital markets, new financial instruments, and new investment strategies. With the collapse of the Berlin Wall, new stock exchanges are opening all around the globe. If one thinks Hong Kong is a frontier stock exchange, what about Mongolia? In Poland, market for the exchange of stock shares began its trading in a building formerly used to store Marxist papers? By the twenty-first century there may well be over one hundred active stock exchanges around the world, many increasingly linked by instant telecommunications and around-the-clock trading. Such growing capital markets will foster the spread of democratic free enterprise.

By the twenty-first century

there may well be over one hundred

active stock exchanges around the world.

New financial instruments will continue to offer opportunities, but not without risks. Possibly financial futures will emerge on the gross domestic products of leading industrial countries so that investors can actually buy and sell proxies for the major global economies for both speculative and hedging purposes. On the regulatory front, government policymakers are expected to index capital gains for inflation so taxes will not be paid on phantom gains.

Innovative investment strategies will also characterize the twenty-first century. Asset allocation among various stock markets around the globe will certainly become increasingly popular and rewarding. Possibly one of the most exciting investment philosophies of the future—one that is now crystallizing—is democratic capitalism. This philosophy for managing portfolios seeks to invest in companies where workers at all levels own shares in the enterprise that employs them. If the worker is also an owner and decision maker, there is a growing body of evidence that the company is more productive and profitable. The shares of productive and profitable companies rise faster and higher than the average stock, and both investors and employee/owners benefit accordingly. Significantly, democratic capitalism is not just an investment phenomenon, but a tangible reality that will make all economies where it is practiced more prosperous.

Despite periodic crashes and other shocks that will always occur, stock markets around the globe offer the most exciting investment opportunities for the twenty-first century as an increasing number of the world's more than six billion inhabitants become sufficiently affluent to invest in their own future. In America, a Dow level of 10,000 will probably be one of the first investment milestones of the new century.

[See also Capitalism; Capital Formation; Credit, Debt, and Borrowing; Financial Institutions; Monetary System; Savings; Taxes; Wealth.]

BIBLIOGRAPHY

Alexander, Gordon J., and Sharpe, William F. *Fundamentals of Investment.* New York: Prentice-Hall, 1989.

Delaco, Enrico, and Hornell, Erik. *Technology and Investment: Crucial Issues for the 1990s.* New York: St. Martin's Press, 1991.

Wood, John H., and Wood, Norma L. *Financial Markets.* Fort Worth: Dryden Press, 1990.

— DAVID B. BOSTIAN

J

JAPAN

The maturing of the Japanese economy is producing long-run changes, not only in economic life, but also in politics and society. Accumulated social changes are beginning to affect politics, with consequences for the economy. Political choices will determine whether Japan's maturity will be vigorous or stagnant. Many policies and behavior linked to Japan's post-World War II economic success could endanger transformation into a successful twenty-first-century society if left unchanged.

The Japanese economic miracle peaked in the early 1970s. From a 10 percent real annual per capita growth rate of gross national product between 1955 and 1970, Japan's economy slowed to 3 percent growth in the following fifteen years. The 1990s and beyond are likely to witness further declines because the sources of earlier growth—investment, increases in labor supply, and productivity growth—are slowing. Higher productivity is key because it allows greater outputs from the same inputs, higher personal income, superior products, more convenience, and additional leisure. Higher productivity also makes business more competitive by reducing costs and improving products.

Economists have long recognized the possibility of economic stagnation as the returns to investment decline with the increasing capital intensity of production. Japan's economic growth, in particular, is susceptible to that prospect since it was driven by high rates of business investment. In the 1960s, for example, more than one out of every five yen of output was plowed back into equipment investment. As the capital intensity of Japanese production overtook levels in the United States and other advanced industrial economies, the nation's industries earned ever-lower returns on their investments. Economists estimated that the 1990 marginal returns to capital in Japan were about one-third less than in the United States.

Prior to the 1980s, high domestic savings channeled to favored industries through regulated financial institutions provided a below-market cost of funds to many Japanese manufacturing firms. Now, however, Japanese companies pay competitive global rates because of financial market globalization and liberalization. In contrast to the time when companies could rely on large profits or low interest rates, they will now have to make investment decisions balancing real financial costs against declining investment returns. This changing financial reality will require shifting focus from growth to profits. Investment, therefore, is likely to decline.

Demographic shifts in Japan will cause the labor force to decline during the late 1990s. As wages rise due to the falling supply, more older people and women will be drawn into the labor force, which will somewhat mitigate the shortage. Nevertheless, higher wages could raise the cost of output in Japan and erode the share of income going to profits, which in turn would further reduce the internal company funds available for investment.

According to Japanese government estimates, approximately 40 percent of the economy is subject to explicit regulation. Regulatory constraints are retarding Japanese innovation in several of the most dynamic new industries.

Investment in education, which complements investments in physical capital, plateaued in the 1970s with almost 100 percent literacy and a large proportion of the population completing secondary education. The average level of formal education barely has changed since then. The gains from further extensions of educational attainment will have to come primarily from increasing the share of people with university degrees, which in 1995 is almost 30 percent below the American level for twenty-two-year-olds. Impending labor shortages and a shift to electronics technologies in manufacturing and services could increase the demand for more educated employees to help offset higher real wages and to operate the more complex technology. A similar shift in the demand for educated workers has occurred in the United States since the 1970s.

Productivity growth and investment are related because new equipment and technology typically include the most advanced capabilities. As investment falls, productivity growth from this source is likely to follow. Another retarding factor is that countries gain an extra boost from their investment when they are technological laggards. Japan's manufacturing productivity seemed to have stopped benefiting from the laggard effect in the 1970s when its capital stock was the youngest of the industrial countries.

Productivity gains among mature economies, however, need not go to zero. Over the twenty-year period from 1969 to 1989, the so-called total factor productivity (which accounts for the contributions of all inputs) of the ten industrial countries with the highest per capita incomes increased at an annual rate of 1 to 2 percent. Although explanations for this growth and its variations are not fully satisfactory, international openness and competition, research and development (R&D), especially basic research, and the adaptability of the economy seem to be the key factors for success of the mature economy. Japan's prospects in these areas are mixed.

Several indicators place Japan's R&D efforts ahead of the United States; for example, Japan's ratio of research scientists and engineers to the labor force was 17 percent higher than in the United States in 1989. In absolute terms, however, American R&D was approximately twice as great. Moreover, Japan is relatively weak in basic research, which seems to have several times more impact on productivity than either physical investment or applied research. On another front, American authors turned out more than 35 percent of the world's scientific and research literature in 1991 versus 8.5 percent for Japanese scientists; this difference is twice as large as would be expected on the basis of expenditures.

Cross-country studies of productivity conclude that variations in the intensity of competition faced by managers and their exposure to producers on the leading edge are the factors most closely linked to productivity leadership. Illustrating these findings is the Japanese productivity in motor vehicles, automotive parts, steel, consumer electronics, and machine and precision tools, which were all above American levels in 1990. These industries faced high levels of domestic or international competition and were challenged to come up with better ways of making things while adopting the best practices of others. One of the outstanding innovations of the twentieth century, the Toyota production system, came out of this experience.

Japanese manufacturing productivity averages only 80 percent of the American level. The partially regulated food processing business, for example, was two-thirds below American levels in 1990. Japanese economywide productivity was even lower. Gross domestic product per employee in the market sector, which accounted for 81 percent of GDP and 87 percent of employment in 1990, was only 61 percent of the American

value and also fell below the levels of France, Germany, and the United Kingdom.

Slower economic and productivity growth and significant lags in productivity levels combine with other forces to increase the pressure for change. The principal reason for lagging productivity is overt regulation or other forms of noncompetitive behavior condoned and sanctioned by the government. According to Japanese government estimates, approximately 40 percent of the economy is subject to explicit regulation. Regulatory constraints are retarding Japanese innovation in several of the most dynamic new industries such as multimedia, which combines telecommunications, computing, and the broadcast media. Without significant deregulation, Japanese participation in these emerging industries will be thwarted.

The Japanese are more likely in the future than in the past to question policies that have favored the narrow interests of producers and the special interests of politically favored groups over those of individuals. The pressure for change arises in part from demographic and economic changes. Relatively fewer people work in the formerly favored sectors. Manufacturing employment fell from a 1970s high of almost 30 percent of all workers to 24 percent in 1991. Heavy industries such as steel and petroleum products lost more than one-third of their employees. Services (including transport, communications, wholesale and retail trade, finance, insurance, real estate, government, and others) rose from 40 percent to 60 percent of the labor force between 1960 and 1991. Over these same years, agricultural employment fell by more than 10 million—from 30 percent of the labor force to 6 percent. From 1966 to 1991, the number of small retail shops fell by 22 percent and employed 430,000 fewer people while the economy as a whole grew by 400 percent. The inhabitants of smaller towns and villages fell from 36 percent to 23 percent of total population. All of these trends are continuing.

Despite these substantial shifts, politics remained straitjacketed. Incomplete adjustment of legislative districts left rural areas overrepresented in the national parliament by more than three to one over urban districts. The political alignments that brought the Liberal-Democratic party to power in 1955 managed to hold the reins of government until 1993. In the meantime, producers (especially heavy industry), agriculture, small shopkeepers, and small-town and rural interests continued to be favored by government policy.

Negative side effects of regulations intended to protect the public or support industrial growth became more apparent as economic growth slowed and as millions of Japanese who traveled abroad each year could see directly that other policies were both feasible and desirable. Additional pressures for change come from the internationally competitive business sector whose efficiency is dragged down by their inefficient domestic suppliers. The international community is also urging Japan to continue the deregulation and market-opening process initiated in the late 1970s. Foreign companies that believe they could be profitable in more open and less regulated Japanese markets are pressuring their governments to negotiate market-opening arrangements.

Change will be profoundly political. Many benefit from the status quo and will fight deregulation and pro-competition policies. Inefficient firms, workers facing job loss, cities and regions confronting decline, and government ministries giving up their authority all face real losses. Other political forces, though, push in the opposite direction. Political reforms passed in 1994 under the first non-Liberal-Democratic administration in thirty-eight years should go a long way to begin shifting the balance of legislative influence in favor of urban and consumer interests and away from the old power structure.

In the meantime, slower economic growth is transforming customary relations. Lifetime employment patterns, which made sense when growth was rapid, have declined since the 1970s slowdown; its erosion will accelerate in the coming decade. High levels of corporate cross-shareholding, an effective tool against takeovers when profits seemed to be perpetually rocketing upward, is a costly practice when capital is less available and profits grow more slowly. Similarly, the deep pockets of *keiretsu*—the large vertical or horizontal groupings of companies either in the same business or affiliated with a corporate family bank—that could sustain unprofitable diversifications and ward off acquisitions and mergers will not be as deep or effective as they once were. Therefore, we are likely to see more unfriendly business acquisitions—both domestic and foreign.

Labor market shortages could have significant consequences for the role of women in society. Women are the great underused resource in Japan's economic life. Slow progress has been made by women in penetrating the upper levels of management and technical jobs. Higher labor costs and the gradual decay of the rigid lifetime employment system will aid in prying open opportunities for women. Already more women are attending four-year universities than previously, although their proportion is lower than that of men, which is the reverse of American experience. Also, women's age of marriage is on the rise as they take more time to try their hands at careers. However, sociologists suggest that changes in the attitudes of men and women toward work and family roles will probably be the slowest to occur. Substantial change is only likely as new groups of both men and women move through gradually shifting work and home patterns. Economic forces could take a long time to alter traditional Japanese gender roles, although the direction of change is toward fuller participation by women in the work of the nation.

[*See also Asia; Free Trade; International Trade: Sustaining Growth.*]

BIBLIOGRAPHY

Alexander, Arthur J. "Japan as Number Three: Long-Term Productivity and Growth Problems in the Economy." *JEI Report* 17A (1994): 1–15.

Brinton, Mary C. *Women and the Economic Miracle: Gender and Work in Postwar Japan.* Berkeley, CA: University of California Press, 1993.

Ito, Takatoshi. *The Japanese Economy.* Cambridge, MA: MIT Press, 1992.

Japan, Statistics Bureau, Management and Coordination Agency. *Japan Statistical Yearbook: 1993.* Tokyo, 1993.

World Bank. *The East Asian Miracle: Economic Growth and Public Policy.* New York: Oxford University Press, 1993.

— ARTHUR J. ALEXANDER

JOB SECURITY.

See *UNEMPLOYMENT INSURANCE, WORKMEN'S COMPENSATION, JOB SECURITY.*

JOHN THE DIVINE (C. 50–100 A.D.)

According to Christian tradition, John—also known as John the Evangelist, John the Apostle, or Saint John—was a disciple of Jesus and the author of the fourth

The book of Revelation

is generally regarded as the most influential text

in the history of Western futurism.

gospel of the New Testament, three epistles, and Revelation. He is thought to have died c. A.D. 100. Modern biblical scholars doubt that all five books are the work of the same man. Purportedly written by John while in exile on the Aegean island of Patmos, Revelation may have been assembled from the writings of several visionaries who date from near the end of the first century. Whatever its authorship, Revelation is generally regarded as the most influential text in the history of Western futurism. It foretells a time of calamities inflicted on sinful humankind by God, a terrible war between the forces of Satan and the forces of God, and the return of Christ to earth at the head of a victorious army of martyrs. Christ will rule for a thousand years—the Millennium—after which Satan will be loosed, defeated once more, and cast into a lake of fire. The damned will join him in the lake, and a bejewelled city will descend from Heaven where the faithful will spend eternity in glory and honor.

[See also Apocalyptic Future.]

BIBLIOGRAPHY

Bullinger, E. W. *Commentary on Revelation.* Grand Rapids, MI: Kregel Publishers, 1984.

Ellul, Jacques. *L'Apocalypse: architecture en mouvement,* 1975. Translated by George W. Schreiner as *Apocalypse: The Book of Revelation.* New York: Seabury Press, 1977.

Ford, J. Massyngberde. *Revelation.* Anchor Bible annotated text and commentary. Garden City, NY: Doubleday, 1975.

Thomas, W. H. *The Apostle John: Studies in His Life and Writings.* Grand Rapids, MI: Eerdmans, 1946.

— W. WARREN WAGAR

JOUVENEL, BERTRAND DE (1903–1987)

The son of a prominent diplomat, the French economist, political philosopher, and futurist Bertrand de Jouvenel wrote extensively on politics and foreign affairs for the French press between the two World Wars. His first book, *L'Economie dirigée* (1928), was a discussion of state economic planning. In mid-life he published an important series of theoretical works, including *Du Pouvoir* (1945; in English, *On Power,* 1949); *De la Souveraineté* (1955; in English, *Sovereignty,* 1957); and *De la Politique pure* (1963; in English, *The Pure Theory of Politics,* 1963). At the same time he became a leading world figure in the burgeoning futurist movement. The activities of the international study group that he organized in 1960, known as Futuribles (a word of his own coinage), led eventually to the founding of the leading French futures journal *Futuribles: Analyse, Prévision, Prospective.* He made his greatest theoretical contribution to futures research in *L'Art de la conjecture* (1964; in English, *The Art of Conjecture,* 1967), a sophisticated analysis of the limits and possibilities of forecasting in human affairs. In this work he defined futuribles as states of affairs in the future whose "mode of production from the present state of affairs is plausible and imaginable."

[See also Futurists.]

BIBLIOGRAPHY

Cornish, Edward, et al. *The Study of the Future.* Washington: World Future Society, 1977, Chapter 9.

Slevin, Carl. "Social Change and Human Values: A Study of the Thought of Bertrand de Jouvenel." *Political Studies* 19 (March 1971): 49–62.

Jouvenel, Bertrand de. "Introduction." In Dennis Hale and Marc Landy, eds., *The Nature of Politics: Selected Essays of Bertrand de Jouvenel.* New York: Schocken Books, 1987.

— W. WARREN WAGAR

JUDICIAL REFORM

Seven judicial problem areas can be identified where reform is needed in the near future, involving criminal and/or civil cases: (1) problems involving pretrial release and bail procedures; (2) difficulties in finding and providing adequate legal counsel for the poor in criminal and civil proceedings; (3) delays in criminal and civil cases resulting from overcrowded dockets or other factors; (4) problems with media coverage of pending cases and cases in progress; (5) judicial selection; (6) jury shortcomings; and (7) judicial nullification of legislative and administrative laws.

Pretrial Release and Bail Reform

Releasing or not releasing suspects prior to trial depends on (1) whether they can deposit sufficient money to assure that a suspect on trial will return for the trial (the traditional bail bond system) or (2) whether personal circumstances are such that return for trial is a near certainty (release on one's own recognizance, often referred to as the ROR system). Bail has been the dominant method, because individuals were economically motivated and partly because it favored the middle-class interests that dominate legal rulemaking. Reform is likely to occur in the direction of a more objective and scientific variant on the ROR system.

Studies by the Vera Institute in New York City show that screening to separate suspects into good- and bad-risk groups (largely based on community roots and affected by the seriousness of the crime) can be equally as effective in assuring court appearance as the traditional money-deposit system. Trial-day mail or phone reminders also help assure appearances. Studies show that the screening and notification system enables more arrested suspects to be released from jail pending trial than is allowed under the money-deposit system. Released suspects can (1) continue their jobs, (2) better prepare their cases and prove their innocence, (3) save taxpayers money by not being jailed and (4) be less embittered than if time were spent in jail and they were then acquitted. The money-deposit system so inherently discriminates against the poor that the Supreme Court may declare that it violates the equal-protection constitutional guarantee.

One objection to the ROR system is that it may sometimes release arrested suspects who will commit additional crimes while awaiting trial. One response to this objection is to require that dangerous persons be detained regardless of their ability to post a large bail or bail bond. It may be, however, that pretrial crimes are more often due to long delays prior to trial than to poor screening or the lack of a bail bond.

Legal Counsel for the Poor

Since 1962, criminal defendants who cannot afford an attorney have been entitled to be provided one by the government, at least for crimes with penalties involving more than six months imprisonment. The big problem now is how, not whether, to provide counsel. Alternatives include: (1) using unpaid or paid volunteer attorneys, (2) using court-assigned attorneys, or (3) hiring full-time public defenders salaried by the government.

A "judicare" system would provide civil legal aid enabling poor clients to hire attorneys of their choice, for which the government would pay, as in Medicare.

The unpaid volunteer system too often attracts young attorneys seeking experience to the detriment of clients whose liberty might be jeopardized. The paid volunteer system works well if only well-qualified attorneys are allowed and if they are fairly compensated for their services. Where assigned counsel is used, clients are frequently represented by reluctant attorneys or by attorneys with little or no criminal case experience. The full-time public defender system is being increasingly used, although many such offices are underfinanced and understaffed.

Although the Supreme Court has not yet required free counsel for the poor in housing eviction, motor vehicle repossession, or other civil cases, the federal Office of Economic Opportunity (OEO) and most local communities have sought to provide it. These efforts promote respect for the law, protect the innocent, promote orderly law reform, and educate the poor concerning their legal rights and obligations. Civil legal aid alternatives are similar to those for criminal legal aid. The traditional system has involved volunteer attorneys whose availability is generally limited. The OEO has provided many cities with full-time civil legal services programs similar to public defender offices in recent

years. A "judicare" system would provide civil legal aid enabling poor clients to hire attorneys of their choice, for which the government would pay, as in Medicare.

Legal insurance and plans designating attorneys for unions or other organizations to represent individual members also have been developed. Bar associations object that organization attorneys will lack a close attorney-client relationship, and they oppose the economic competition posed to traditional lawyers. Certain of these organizational schemes, already declared by the Supreme Court to be protected by the freedom of assembly clause of the Constitution, may flourish.

Court Delays

Increased industrialization and urbanization have contributed to undesirable delays in civil as well as criminal cases. Automobile accidents are mainly at fault in causing the long delays in civil cases. Urbanization and concomitant increased crime add to criminal court docket congestion.

When personal injury cases are delayed, the injured party may be unable to collect because of the forgetfulness or unavailability of witnesses and may be unduly pressured to settle for quicker (though reduced) damage payments. Although criminal case delays tend to be shorter, they become objectionable if the arrested suspect must wait in jail pending trial, and all the more objectionable when an acquittal or a sentence shorter than the time already spent in jail results.

Civil case reforms designed to encourage out-of-court settlements provide for impartial medical experts, pretrial settlement conferences, and pretrial proceedings to enable the parties to know where they stand with regard to each other's evidence and to impose interest charges beginning with the day of the accident. Other reforms remove personal injury cases from the courts by shifting them to less formal administrative agencies for speedier disposition or by requiring injured parties to automatically collect from their own insurance company, regardless of their negligence (as with fire insurance).

Protracted jury trials can be reduced by imposing high jury fees, providing quicker trials for nonjury cases, randomly picking twelve jurors (thereby avoiding lengthy selection), and by separating the liability and damage issues (so there is no need to discuss damages if the defendant is found nonliable, and settlement can be facilitated if liability is established). Reformers also have recommended that delay be reduced by having more judges, and more work days and/or work hours per day, shifting judges from low-volume to high-volume courts, and conserving judges' time to resolve situations such as those involving the simultaneous scheduling of the same attorney in two different courts, for example.

Reforms to reduce criminal case delays include: better screening of complaints; more encouragement of guilty pleas, if merited; more criminal court personnel; less use of grand jury indictments; more pretrial proceedings to narrow the issues; random jury selection; and release of the defendant within a specified period of time if not tried.

Media Reporting

Mass media reporting on pending criminal cases involves conflict between two civil liberties: freedom of speech and freedom of the press, which includes the right to report on pending cases; and the constitutional right to a fair trial unprejudiced by distorted reporting, by reporting evidence inadmissible in court, or by sensational coverage.

The Supreme Court favors holding sensational trials away from the community where the crime was committed; reprimanding attorneys for gossiping to reporters; keeping jurors and sometimes witnesses from seeing newspapers; holding in contempt reporters who print gossip while a trial is still in process; and limiting the number of reporters allowed in the courtroom.

Many newspaper and newspaper association rules establish voluntary press restraints. American Bar Association rules restrain attorneys in criminal cases from communicating prejudicial information to the press. Reformers favor the British system holding newspapers in contempt of court for publishing almost anything other than the barest facts about criminal trials until the trial is completed.

Judicial Selection

Judges are chosen by two basic methods: (1) they may be appointed by the president, governor, or mayor—with or without the approval of a bipartisan nominating commission or the legislature; or (2) they may be elected by the general public under partisan or nonpartisan election procedures. Originally, nearly all United States judges were appointed. Federal judges have always been appointed as specified in the Constitution. During the period of Jacksonian democracy, however, a shift toward electing state and local judges began. In the last few decades, there has been a shift back to gubernatorial appointment of state and local judges.

Those favoring elected judges point out that judicial decision making frequently involves subjective value judgments that should reflect public opinion. Electoral advocates also point out that elected judges will come closer in their backgrounds to the general public than

appointed judges, especially if the nominating commission tends to be dominated by the state bar association.

Those favoring appointed judges contend that appointed judges are less partisan in their judicial voting behavior. This outcome may be due more to the bipartisan approval needed for appointment, to appointment across party lines by some governors, or to the differences in how appointed judges view their roles, rather than being directly related to the selection process. Appointment advocates also argue that appointed judges are technically more competent because they tend to come from better law schools and colleges than elected judges do, a conclusion not supported by empirical evidence.

The most controversial aspect of appellate and trial court decision making is the court's power to nullify legislative laws and administrative regulations.

Judicial reformers usually advocate both appointive selection and longer judicial terms. Longer terms give a judge more independence from political pressures. Such terms, however, are likely to make judges less responsive to public opinion, although possibly more sensitive to minority rights.

Some jurisdictions provide for regular elections to fill vacant judgeships (with provision for opposition candidates), to be followed periodically by retention elections (whereby each sitting judge runs against his record with the voters being able to vote only yes or no on his retention). Such compromises will probably become increasingly prevalent.

Jury Shortcomings

Jurors in medieval England were originally persons from the community who had actually witnessed the facts in dispute. Eventually, the jury evolved into a group of community representatives who resolved factual disputes in cases, while the judge determined the applicable law. Traditionally the jury has consisted of twelve people chosen by both sides from a list of voters charged to determine guilt in criminal cases and liability in civil cases by unanimous decision. The idea of having juries to supplement the work of judges has come under attack in recent years.

Critics contend that jury trials consume too much time, suggesting that jurors often lack competence and sometimes ignore the legal instructions given them.

Defenders point out that a jury trial is more likely to free the innocent than a bench trial, because all jury members must agree to convict and because jurors tend to be more like defendants than judges are. Judges and juries agree approximately 83 percent of the time in criminal cases, but when they disagree, the jury is nearly always pro-defendant and the judge pro-prosecutor. They also argue that juries, by providing public participation, encourage respect for the law. Before-and-after tests show that serving as a juror does improve one's attitude toward the legal system. Public participation of jurors also resolves ambiguities in the facts or law in accord with public opinion.

The trends point toward juries smaller than twelve persons who decide by less than a unanimous vote. This trend has been especially evident in civil cases, and recently was extended by the Supreme Court to criminal cases.

Judicial Nullification of Legislative and Administrative Laws

The most controversial aspect of appellate and trial court decision making is the court's power to nullify legislative laws and administrative regulations. Congress, it is argued, cannot be trusted to police itself since it has a vested interest in its own legislative edicts. Another strong point is that unpopular minority viewpoints need the courts to protect them. It is also said that constitutional interpretation requires technical legal training, which the courts have, and that the courts have less political bias than legislatures do.

Arguments against judicial review emphasize that Congress is more responsive to public opinion. Past attacks stressed the conservatism of the courts, particularly with regard to economic regulation. It is further noted that the lack of preciseness in the Constitution makes it more a political than a legal document.

Between the positions of complete judicial review over all types of statutes and no judicial review at all, there are many intermediate ways to restrict judicial review: (1) by requiring more than a simple majority of judicial votes; (2) by providing for congressional override or veto; (3) by limiting judicial review to legislation relating to matters involving special protective interests, state legislation (to preserve American federalism), or civil liberties (to protect ideological, ethnic, or other minority interests). The trend is toward a civil-liberties-oriented judicial review. Other ways to make the Supreme Court more responsive include: (1) requiring that the Court be composed of representatives of all three branches of government, as in some Western Eu-

ropean systems; (2) giving justices an elected or fixed-term tenure; or (3) providing for representation on an expanded court from all fifty states (proposed in a constitutional amendment already passed by some states).

A Changing Environment

The fact that reform is needed does not necessarily indicate that the American system of justice has been inefficient or discriminatory. It is indicative of organizational changes affecting efficiency and reflecting a keener sensitivity to discriminatory injustices. Encouraging as it is that courts and other policy-making bodies have recently instituted innovations in an attempt to cope with the problems raised by pretrial release, legal aid, court delay, pretrial reporting, judicial selection, the jury system, and judicial review, much more remains to be done.

[See also Crime, Nonviolent; Crime, Violent; Crime Rates; Criminal Punishment; Lawmaking, Judicial; Laws, Evolution of; Lawyers and the Legal Profession.]

BIBLIOGRAPHY

Aron, Nan. *Liberty and Justice for All. Public Interest Law in the 1980s and Beyond.* Boulder, CO: Westview, 1989.

Dean, H. *Judicial Review and Democracy.* New York: Random House, 1966.

Dubois, Philip. *The Analysis of Judicial Reform.* Lexington, MA: Lexington-Heath, 1982.

Freed, D., and Wald, P. *Bail in the United States.* Washington, DC: U.S. Government Printing Office, 1964.

Goldfarb, R. *Ransom: A Critique of the American Bail System.* New York: Harper & Row, 1965.

Handler, Joel. *Social Movements and the Legal System: A Theory of Law Reform and Social Change.* New York: Academic Press, 1978.

Joiner, C. *Civic Justice and the Jury.* Englewood Cliffs, NJ: Prentice-Hall, 1962.

Jones, H. *The Courts, the Public, and the Laws Explosion.* Englewood Cliffs, NJ: Prentice-Hall, 1965.

Kalven, H., and Zeisel, H. *The American Jury.* Boston: Little, Brown, 1966.

Sigler, Jay, and Beede, Benjamin. *The Legal Sources of Public Policy.* Lexington, MA: Lexington-Heath, 1977.

Silverstein, L. *Defense of the Poor.* Boston: Little, Brown, 1966.

Skoonick, J. *Justice Without Trial: Law Enforcement in a Democratic Society.* New York: John Wiley, 1967.

Watson, R., and Downing, R. *The Politics of the Bench and the Bar: Judicial Selection Under the Missouri Nonpartisan Court Plan.* New York: John Wiley, 1969.

Wilson, James Q., ed. *Crime and Public Policy.* New Brunswick, NJ: Transaction, 1983.

Zeisel, H.; Kalven, Hans; and Buchholz, B. *Delay in the Court.* Boston: Little, Brown, 1959.

— STUART S. NAGEL

K

KAHN, HERMAN (1922–1983)

A native of Bayonne, N.J., American defense analyst and futurist Herman Kahn became a staff physicist for the Rand Corporation in 1948 and went on to build a formidable reputation as one of the world's preeminent students of nuclear war strategy. His books, *On Thermonuclear War* (1960) and *Thinking About the Unthinkable* (1962), made the case that nuclear war is not only probable at some time in the future but can also, at certain levels of intensity and with adequate civil defense precautions, be survived. In 1961 in collaboration with Max Singer, Kahn founded the Hudson Institute. Under Kahn's leadership, the institute won many civilian as well as defense-related research contracts. He spent most of his later years in nonmilitary areas of futures inquiry. *The Year 2000* (1967), written with Anthony Wiener and others, is one of the most influential futures books of the century. Other books include *The Next 200 Years* (1976, with William Brown and Leon Martel), and *The Coming Boom: Economic, Political and Social* (1982). *Thinking About the Unthinkable in the 1980s* (1984), a revisiting of his earlier studies of nuclear war strategy, was published posthumously. Despite his reputation as a prophet of nuclear war, Kahn was always an optimist, displaying a reasoned faith in the power of science, technology, and capitalism to solve the pressing problems of modern civilization.

[See also Futurists.]

BIBLIOGRAPHY

Cornish, Edward, et al. *The Study of the Future.* Washington, DC: World Future Society, 1977, Chapter 9.
Clarke, I. F. "Obituary." *Futures* 15 (December 1983): 540–544.

— W. WARREN WAGAR

L

LABOR UNIONS.

See UNIONISM.

LAND USE PLANNING

Land use planning is both as old as civilization and as new as bioengineering. It is practiced routinely, to varying degrees, by both governments and private organizations. It has become an established occupation and profession for individual practitioners. Many people believe it is now essential to preserving life on Earth. But it remains a highly controversial field of endeavor.

Narrowly defined, land use planning is the preparation and adoption of plans to govern the spatial pattern produced by human activities within a designated geographical area. Loosely construed, the term is used often to include, not only the plans themselves, but also the implementation of the plans over time and sometimes also the broader social purposes that the plans are intended to promote.

Land use plans typically consist of a map with text and illustrations, which together describe how each of the different subareas within the total planning area are to be "used" by human beings. The descriptive technique usually includes listing either the kind of uses encouraged or permitted in each subarea or the kind discouraged or prohibited. Sometimes the uses are described in operational or functional terms, and sometimes in terms of the physical shape to which the structures housing the uses must conform.

Land use plans may be simple or complex. They may cover a parcel, a municipality, a region, or a nation. Most typical are plans for areas that coincide with the jurisdictions of particular governments. In the United States, the constitutional authority to make and implement comprehensive land use plans resides at the state level, but it has been generally delegated to the level of local government. Consequently, most land use plans are made by town, city, and county governments.

The general social purpose behind land use planning is to promote the safety, health, and welfare of the community as a whole. Beneath this commonly cited "umbrella" goal, communities often choose to emphasize certain subgoals, such as economic development, affordable housing, transportation accessibility, environmental amenity, social equity, or resource protection. Usually this choice of social goals, as well as their level of aspiration, is tempered by an assessment of how difficult or how costly it may be to achieve them.

The implementation phase of land use planning typically involves the use of two major instruments of governmental power: the police power, to regulate the activities of private citizens and corporations, and the purse power, to collect taxes to pay for the construction and operation of public works and services. When land use planning is undertaken by private corporations, a variant of these same instruments is used, involving legal covenants to govern the use of land by purchasers or tenants and commitments to repay money borrowed for construction and operational expenses.

The general social purpose behind land use planning is to promote the safety, health, and welfare of the community as a whole.

The most controversial aspect of land use planning revolves around which of these two powers of government should be relied on more to implement the plan—the police power or the purse power. The U.S. Constitution protects private property, including land, from unwarranted intrusion or expropriation by the government without the due process of law and just compensation. Land use plans typically involve limiting the range of uses permissible on private property in certain areas to preserve public amenity and natural/cultural resources. Hence, in the United States, land use planning gives rise to a continual stream of litigation that is referred to and resolved by the judicial system.

As an occupation or profession, land use planning comprises one of a number of specializations within a broader discipline called by such various names as city, urban, or regional planning. Dating as a separate profession from the early twentieth century, this field has developed a theoretical base that combines elements from architecture, landscape architecture, civil engineering, public health, public administration, political science, and other related disciplines. Because urban planning, like medicine, involves prescription as well as description, its theoretical base is constantly evolving in response to new challenges for solutions to problems in the real world.

Largely in response to economic and civil rights problems, urban planning since 1960 has sought to expand its understanding of the "use" element (the social practices and structures of the community), while still retaining the "land" element (their geographical or physical manifestations) as a defining characteristic of the field. Today the growing awareness of the global and regional fragility of the natural environment is tending to return attention to the "land" element, as pollution, congestion, and the fragility of entire ecosystems increasingly press themselves onto the political agenda. Thus, the challenge to integrate the functional with the physical within land use planning is increasing.

A concentration on the functional/operational aspect of planning, as contrasted with its physical/spatial aspect, is not unique to urban planning. It is true to an even greater extent for most other types of group planning activities, such as business planning, strategic planning, and policy planning. Beneath the differences, however, all these fields of planning employ a common procedural method. It involves four sequential steps: survey, analysis, choice, and implementation. Successful application of these four steps requires in most cases, an approach that combines both science and art.

For example, in land use planning, the survey and analysis steps rely heavily on scientific methods that include such sophisticated mathematical tools as geographic information systems, computer simulation models, and statistically extrapolated opinion polls. Ecological "reconnaissance" of ecosystems and populations that are to be impacted by future uses is also needed. But, in the choice of a particular plan and the sequence of actions to implement it, large measures of social intuition and political craftsmanship are necessary. Without them, plans usually fail to be accepted or implemented.

Humanity faces unprecedented changes on a global scale as it approaches the twenty-first century. The 1992 United Nations Conference on Environment and Development showed how important it is for the international community to come to grips with the effects of industry on nature. At this conference, the term *sustainable development* was adopted by the major nations of the world, to set a new goal for all future efforts to manage the built environment. Whether history will catalog this vision as the cloud castle of a Quixote or the El Dorado of a Columbus will depend greatly on how much skill the land use and urban planning profession can muster in the years ahead.

[See also Appropriate Technology; Cities; Cities, North American; Megacities; Planning.]

BIBLIOGRAPHY

Chapin, F. Stuart, Jr., and Kaiser, Edward J. *Urban Land Use Planning,* 2nd ed. Chicago: University of Illinois Press, 1994.

Leung, Hok Lin. *Land Use Planning Made Plain.* Kingston, Ontario: P. Frye and Company, 1989.

So, Frank S., and Getzels, Judith. *The Practice of Local Government Planning.* Washington, DC: International City Managers' Association, 1988.

So, Frank S., et al. *The Practice of State and Regional Planning.* Chicago: American Planning Association Planners Press, 1985.

Kent, T. J., Jr. *The Urban General Plan.* Reprint. Chicago: American Planning Association Planners Press, 1990.

– RICHARD E. TUSTIAN

LANGUAGES

The spoken languages of humanity have always formed part of a single system of communication around the globe, the *logosphere,* the opposite ends of which were joined across the Atlantic five centuries ago. Just as the subsequent development of languages was affected by the printing revolution, so the future of languages will be increasingly determined by the electronics and telecommunications revolution.

Instant worldwide communication has helped the spoken word to regain its primacy over the printed word. Whereas the logosphere has consisted until now of sequences of links among individual spoken languages papered over by written languages, it now functions as a worldwide vehicle of human expression. In this situation, the development and wider use of English and a few other languages will be favored over that of others internationally.

English

The accelerating bandwagon of English as the unrivalled, worldwide vehicle for science and security, trade and travel, will be unstoppable. Compromise between American and British models of pronunciation and usage will lead to the increasing cultivation of a "mid-Atlantic" standard of mainstream English. There also are indications that the spread of this prestige variety will be paralleled by the worldwide spread of counter-stream English, an international "youth" English associated with video-clips and teenage culture, a nonstandard English that will draw together popular elements and linguistic innovations from sources as diverse as New York, Jamaica, London, and Sydney. The increasing use of English by nonnative speakers will lead in any case to a greater tolerance of variations in English between these two extremes.

Bilingualism

Although there will be a vast increase in bilingualism throughout the non-English-speaking world, involving English as a second language, this is unlikely to be matched by a corresponding degree of bilingualism in the English-speaking world. This will be disadvantageous to native English speakers in two ways. Many of

---

There will be a vast increase in bilingualism throughout the non-English-speaking world, involving English as a second language.

---

their children will miss the educational, cultural, and intellectual benefits of studying another language and culture. In many non-English parts of the world there will be hostility toward the perceived "arrogance" of monolingual English speakers.

Other Major Languages

French, although lagging far behind, is likely to remain the only language competing with English. Widespread antipathy to the idea of a linguistic monopoly in world affairs will make it easier for French to maintain its "number two" status. With a narrow base of native speakers (not more than 70 million), the international future of French will depend on its continuing as an official or auxiliary future of French will depend on its continuing as an official or auxiliary language in almost forty countries—in Africa, Europe, the Americas, and Oceania.

Certain continental or subcontinental languages will enjoy a more secure place in their coverage of specific parts of the globe: modern standard Arabic, Chinese (Mandarin and Cantonese), German, Hindi-Urdu, Japanese, Russian, Spanish-Portuguese. Their regional roles will be strengthened by their use in state-run television networks.

More Localized Languages

As English and other major languages are spread by global media, many more localized languages will also benefit from permanent recording and diffusion by audiocassettes, video, and television. Their role as vehicles of in group communication and cultural identity will often be strengthened. As the audiovisual screen lessens the impact of the printed page, speakers of one language will tend to acquire passive understanding of other closely related languages, since the spoken word permits more variation than the written.

If very closely related languages are considered together in clusters, then fewer than 10 percent of the world's total of over two thousand language-clusters are likely to fall into complete disuse during the twenty-first century. Even where this does occur, audiovisual archiving will preserve individual languages and prevent them from being totally lost.

Some languages may die for nonlinguistic reasons, if ethnic groups are exterminated on a large scale by environmental disaster, disease, famine, war, or genocide. Still, languages may survive in their spoken form even if the number of speakers is small, if those speakers struggle consciously to preserve them.

Language Policy

Thanks to international communications, nation-states will have less control over the development of languages and education. Increasingly it will be recognized that the right to one's own language is a fundamental human right. Countries with more democratic systems will give increasing recognition to minority languages, including regional forms of their official languages. Conventions on the usage and spelling of some international languages may be agreed to at the world or regional level, but there will be generally less emphasis on written standardization, except in such fields as science, law, or public health and safety.

Language Translation Machines

There will be a breakthrough in the perfection of translation machines, especially from and into English, or between closely related languages. Translation programs among non-English languages will often use English-based programs as a "go-between." Pocket translation machines will be widely available at modest cost by the early twenty-first century.

Subtitling will be an important industry, with eventual new techniques for automatic written translation from a spoken text. Computerized voice recognition will progressively be extended to the recognition of individual spoken languages, not only of major international languages and their varieties, but also of more localized languages and dialects.

[See also Communications; Global Culture; Telecommunications.]

BIBLIOGRAPHY

Bauerle, Rainer, et al., eds. *Meaning, Use, and Interpretation of Languages.* Hawthorn, NY. De Gruyter, 1983.

Bleich, David. *The Double Perspective: Language, Literacy, and Social Relations.* New York: Oxford University Press, 1988.

Lieberman, Philip. *The Biology and Evolution of Language.* Cambridge, MA: Harvard University Press, 1984.

Wright, Will. *Wild Knowledge: Science, Language, and Social Life in a Fragile Environment.* Minneapolis: University of Minnesota Press, 1992.

— DAVID DALBY

LAW ENFORCEMENT

High-tech crime, from computer-assisted theft to illegal biotech adaptations to human organ trade, will dominate the early twenty-first century. As electronic banking replaces cash and checks, muggings and armed robberies will fade, replaced by computer hackers breaking into electronic banking files and diverting funds for their own purposes. Computer terrorism, threatening to destroy vital records unless ransom is paid, can be expected along with other innovative computer fraud. As virtual reality progresses, computer fraud will take on new meaning, as illusionary worlds become "real" and elaborate ruses are perpetrated upon the unwary.

With the completion of the Human Genome Project mapping human genes, the ability to manipulate genes for profit will be performed legally and illegally. Legitimate enterprises will create new life-forms to serve humankind, microbes that eat chemical waste or viruses that attack cancer cells. Illegitimate ones will develop deadly germs that could kill massive numbers of humans if placed in water or food supplies, or oxygen-destroying organisms that could render a home or business unsuitable for human habitation and thus easy prey for pressurized-suit-wearing thieves. As human and mammal/fish/bird/plant genes are intermingled via genetic engineering, even more bizarre crimes will emerge and "genetic predisposition" may be used as a defense in the courts.

The early twenty-first century will be plagued by a severe shortage of body parts needed for transplanting. As the world population ages and human life expectancy increases through biotech advances, the demand for replacement parts will escalate rapidly. The illegal theft of body parts, a phenomenon first recognized in the 1990s, will increase if organized crime invades this lucrative field. In some cases the poor and desperate will be coerced to "sell" their body organs, though such practices are presently illegal. In other cases, donors will disappear, and their kidneys and livers will show up on the international "transplants available" black market.

Other crimes expected to escalate include land fraud as space becomes limited; environmental crimes from polluting to "speciescide"; energy crimes such as power theft by a homeowner tapping into a neighbor's sources; patent/copyright infringement, as copying machines and computer mail networks are merged; and health care quackery as desperate victims are duped into believing cures are available for exotic and deadly new illnesses.

Meanwhile, the public safety system will see massive improvements in its arsenal to control crime. The emphasis will be on prevention and behavior modification, a shift focusing on how to prevent crime rather than on how to catch criminals.

The most difficult crimes to control will be "white collar" ones, as universal access to computers and networks facilitates electronic theft and fraud.

The most effective of these new approaches will be "community-oriented." As police change from crime fighters to crime preventers, the rest of the system, courts and corrections, will follow in the same direction.

Public service officers (formerly called police) will seek to identify crime-breeding situations such as homelessness, joblessness, mental illness, and truancy. They will take proactive steps to match at-risk or needy citizens with appropriate social and medical services to head off crime.

Mediation and arbitration will largely replace adversarial proceedings to settle criminal disputes. Courts will recognize a more heterogeneous society brought on by immigration and differential ethnic birth rates that result in a mosaic of races and cultures. Lifestyles and cultural differences will be reassessed and handled equitably rather than criminally. All litigants will be viewed as having rights/claims in conflict rather than designated as either victim or defendant.

Corrections will focus on the reconciliation of the offenders, assisting victims via restitution/restoration, and reclamation of the violator when appropriate and necessary. The benefits will mean both less street crime and, more significantly, less fear of crime and criminals. Corrections will also focus on reintegrating law violators into the community. It will strive to help offenders to acquire the new skills, ranging from vocational to emotional, that may be needed to help individuals live within the law and in harmony with others.

Here, too, a plethora of technologies will be available. Public service officers will be able to keep suspects, or even entire citizenry under constant surveillance via cameras and listening devices that see and hear from far away, and later from bionic eyes and ears obtained as replacement body parts. Life-to-death dossiers of "all" activities for each citizen will be available via electronic recordkeeping and networking computerized files of all government/business enterprises. Officers may "fly" patrols with jetpacks on their backs, and will never be "out of service" as their universal, instantaneous "Dick Tracy" communicators will be strapped on their wrists or possibly implanted in their larynx.

Community orientation will lower crime and fear of crime. "Smart" houses and vehicles also will protect the potential victims. Houses and motor vehicles will be equipped to deny access and even to take defensive action against unauthorized intruders, by calling the police, and releasing knockout gas into the home or vehicle.

Serious offenders will be kept under control not by costly imprisonment, but by "walking prisons,"—an "electronic bug" implanted in or affixed to their bodies so they can be kept under constant surveillance. In addition, biochemical implants that monitor emotions and aggression levels and can release soothing chemicals into the bloodstream to keep at-risk persons calm, cool, and nonthreatening. Subliminal messages intoning, "be honest, do not hurt others, do the right thing," may be used to constantly bombard and subdue the brains of the more dangerous violators.

The publicly funded criminal justice system will be supplemented by privately funded groups such as community security officers, neighborhood mediation centers, and storefront treatment programs. These phenomena accelerated in the early 1990s, when there were twice as many private police as public police in the United States. Citizens will become involved as "controllers" of the system, not just volunteers or privately paid supplements. Law and enforcement policies will be tailored to meet the needs at the individual neighborhood levels. Citizen groups, in consultation with public service departments, will set the agenda and priorities to bring order and peace to their communities.

Philosophically, it will be recognized that the key to crime control will be the scope of criminal behavior, not reducing the supply of criminals and potential criminals. Since nearly all citizens commit occasional violations of the law and thus all are potential criminals, the supply-reduction approach would mean eventually convicting and correcting everyone. More cost-effective and less intrusive into citizens' lives will be alleviation of the problems that lead citizens to desire to commit crime—from unnecessary "meddling" laws (e.g., gambling prohibitions) to greed, poverty, homelessness, truancy, fear, ignorance, mental illness, and a full range of other shortcomings. As whole communities become involved in the process, citizens in need of assistance to alleviate these problems will become easier to identify and help.

The key here is the change from seeking retribution to seeking reconciliation as the desired outcome of the process.

The most difficult crime problems to bring under control in the twenty-first century will be in the "white collar" area, as the universal access to computers and networks facilitates electronic theft and fraud. If the twentieth-century attitudes toward business-related crimes—"it's just the way business operates, no real harm is done"—prevail, it will be difficult to control such offenses. But as the business community moves from the highly competitive industrial era into the heavily networked, cooperative information age, there is hope that the interdependence of individuals necessary to succeed in the twenty-first-century business world will bring recognition that such theft and fraud hurts everyone, including the violator. The world economy will be one in which everyone's self-interest is enhanced by a functioning, secure international information network that everyone can confidently use to pursue his/her own agenda for fun and profit.

Thus the twenty-first century can be a morass of greed and suppression, or it can be virtually crime-free. It depends on how policymakers progress with the reforms begun in the late twentieth century. The emerging technology is "amoral." Policy and practice will give it morality or immorality and determine whether it is used to enslave humankind or to free it.

[See also Crime, Nonviolent; Crime, Organized; Crime, Violent; Crime Rates; Criminal Justice; Criminal Punishment; High Technology; Prisons.]

BIBLIOGRAPHY

Bennett, G. *Crimewarps.* Garden City, NY: Anchor/Doubleday, 1987.
Bequai, A. *Technocrimes.* Lexington, MA: Lexington Books, 1987.
Schmalleger, F., ed. *Computers in criminal justice.* Bristol, IN: Wyndham Hall Press, 1990.
Stephens, G. "Crime and the Biotech Revolution." *The Futurist* (November–December 1992): 38–42.
——. "Drugs and Crime in the Twenty-first Century." *The Futurist* (May–June 1992): 19–22.

— GENE STEPHENS

LAW OF THE LAND

In 1927 the U.S. Supreme Court had to decide whether tapping a telephone line constituted a "search and seizure" within the meaning of the Fourth Amendment. Telephones, of course, did not exist when the founding fathers drafted the Bill of Rights. They are "objects of which the Fathers could not have dreamed," as Justice Brandeis wrote at the time. (*Olmstead* v. *United States*, 1928, p. 472). What would the founders have done if confronted with the telephone? Chief Justice (and former president) Taft wrote for the Court that the Fourth Amendment protected only the searching of physical things. It would be another forty years before the Court overruled this case and concluded that a search warrant was required for tapping a telephone line—a protection of liberty many people now take for granted.

Like other systems, the law experiences relatively long periods of stability that are interrupted by periods of rapid change or transformation.

The law, like other areas of society, faces profound challenges from the changing social, political, economic, and technological environments in which it operates. Throughout history, changing social conditions and new technologies have forced changes within the legal system. The end of the feudal system revolutionized the law of property and contract. Industrialization of the nineteenth century caused fundamental changes in personal injury law (called tort law) and gave rise to widespread workers' compensation legislation. The economic turmoil of the 1930s gave rise to new administrative agencies and increased economic regulation.

Today various forces, including new technology, computers, communications technology, biotechnology, the women's movement, multiculturalism, environmentalism—to name a few—are forcing changes in the law. Legal questions that were unimaginable twenty or thirty years ago now confront courts, legislatures, and voters. Is there a constitutional right to die? What happens to frozen embryos if the parents divorce? Is a computer network, such as the Internet, more like a newspaper and so responsible for what is "published" on its bulletin boards, or is it more like a telephone company and so not responsible for any defamatory communications? Who owns genetic information? Can international environmental issues—like the depletion of the ozone layer or the greenhouse effect—be controlled by treaties?

While these questions are new, the legal system has always had to adapt to changed circumstances. Looking at how it has responded in the past provides a basis for predicting, or at least imagining, what the future might bring.

American law consists of the U.S. Constitution, which was adopted by the original thirteen states and has been amended twenty-six times since; statutes, which are passed by the U.S. Congress and by state legislatures and local elected bodies (such as town councils); regulations, which are written by the executive branch of the government, based on the authority delegated to them by the legislature; common law, which is judge-made law; and treaties, which are negotiated by the president of the United States and ratified by the U.S. Senate. Each of these sources of law is changing in subtle and not so subtle ways.

Like other systems, the law experiences relatively long periods of stability that are interrupted by periods of rapid change or transformation, something futurists have come to call paradigm shifts. Not surprisingly, these shifts in the law parallel social transformations. For example, the social "revolution" of the 1960s brought with it many changes in the legal system, including legislation prohibiting discrimination on the basis of race or sex, environmental legislation, and greater constitutional protection for criminal defendants. And as social and technological change has accelerated, so has change in the law.

Scholars have identified three important periods of transformation in the history of U.S. law: the American Revolution and the creation of our basic system of government; the American Civil War; and the Great Depression. (It is perhaps too early to assess the importance of the transformations begun in the 1960s.) Each of these periods transformed our laws and legal systems in fundamental ways. Today's technological revolutions may be ushering in another such paradigm shift.

Despite these discontinuities, some trends have been quite steady in the development of American law. One is increasing protection for individual liberties. Another is the rising importance of the political branches of government—the legislative and the executive branches—in the creation of law. A third is expansion of the franchise: giving more people the right to vote, and to vote directly on a wider array of issues. A fourth trend, federalization, may have reached its peak as the political branches are returning programs to the states; the Supreme Court, for the first time in sixty years, invalidated a federal law regulating private activity as exceeding the powers granted to the federal government by the Constitution.

All these changes in our legal system occur within the framework of the U.S. Constitution. That this is the world's oldest written constitution speaks both to its stability and to its flexibility. While the Constitution, by definition, must consist of fixed principles, such principles must be adaptable to respond to new societal and technological developments that the founders could not have imagined. As society advances, different parts of the Constitution may take on new importance, even new meaning. As Woodrow Wilson wrote almost ninety years ago, constitutional government "does not remain fixed in any unchanging form, but grows with the growth and is altered with the change of the nation's needs and purposes." (Horwitz, 1993, pp. 51–52).

The U.S. Constitution has always stood for limited government of specified powers, but the contours of these limits and the freedoms they protect have changed during its two-hundred-year history and will continue to change in the years ahead. Imagining what the next paradigm shift might look like and how general trends may continue to operate requires a review of history.

Protection of Individual Rights

As originally conceived, the Constitution was less concerned with protecting individuals from government incursion—the focus of much Constitutional theory today—than with protecting states from the powers of the federal government. The Bill of Rights limited only the federal government from restricting speech, affecting the establishment of religion, taking of property without just compensation, and from restricting the many other rights protected by the Constitution; states, however, could pass laws affecting any of these rights, unless their own constitutions prohibited them.

This basic structure changed with the Civil War amendments to the Constitution, most importantly, the Fourteenth Amendment. The Fourteenth Amendment applies to the states and restricts the power of the states to encroach on basic liberties. However, determining which liberties are so "basic" as to be protected within the Fourteenth Amendment is a complicated endeavor and one that the Court has approached with varying methods and viewpoints over the years. It is also an area that will certainly see further changes in the future.

As the nation became increasingly industrialized toward the end of the nineteenth century, people began to see the need to regulate business and the relationship between employers and employees. Such problems had not occurred before, when more people were self-employed and did not have to rely so much on large-scale businesses for their livelihoods. In response, various labor laws were passed regulating wages and the number of hours that could be worked.

These laws were consistently struck down by the Supreme Court as unconstitutionally impinging on "liberty of contract." Using the Civil War amendments, the Supreme Court had constitutionalized common law "liberty" rights, principally liberty of property and liberty of contract. Thus state and federal governments alike could not enact laws that the Court felt would limit these freedoms—for example, minimum wage laws or maximum hours laws that the Court felt encroached on these liberties. At the same time, more and more people felt that there was no genuine liberty of contract at stake because of the unequal bargaining power between workers and industry.

With the social disruption of the Great Depression, however, the Court's view changed, and such laws were found not to violate the due process clause of the Fourteenth Amendment. The transformation engendered by the Great Depression changed many areas of society, including the law, and the change in the view of liberty of contract is just part of the changes in the legal system engendered by the Depression. The 1930s also saw the creation of large federal administrative agencies, which combined legislative, adjudicatory, and enforcement powers under one roof, and displaced much state law.

Property rights have also shifted as the ways in which people use land has changed. When the nation was founded, property rights could be closer to "absolute"—one had greater freedom to do what one wanted with his or her property. Of course, one also had much less ability to substantially alter his or her land, because the technologies either did not exist or were expensive and inefficient to build a skyscraper or drain a swamp, for example. With fewer people, large areas of undeveloped land, and limited knowledge of environmental consequences of development, most people could do as they pleased with their land and cause little inconvenience to their neighbors. But as more people lived in closer quarters, and scientists and medical doctors began to understand environmental and public health consequences of building decisions, zoning, building codes and environmental regulations were put in place to deal with these problems. The Supreme Court recognized this in a famous case about zoning almost seventy years ago, in which it noted that when "urban life was comparatively simple," intrusive zoning laws might be unconstitutional, and that "while the meaning of constitutional guaranties never varies, the scope of their application must expand or contract to meet the new and different conditions which are constantly coming within the field of their operation." (*Euclid* v. *Ambler Realty*, 1926, pp. 386–387).

While once liberty of property and contract was nearly absolute, freedom of speech barely existed. Yet in the past seventy-five years or so, freedom of speech has become a virtually absolute liberty. Perhaps free speech doctrine developed in response to a deemphasis on liberty of property and contract, as lawyers and judges sought other principles with which to protect the individual from government, or perhaps these changes were each separate responses to a changing society. Regardless, both have changed profoundly during this century and are now at the center of activity and debate again.

Some scholars predict that free speech doctrine may go through a Great Depression-type watershed—a "New Deal for speech." On this view, increasing concern about unequal distribution of "speech resources" (money to buy television time, for example) may come to justify regulations to redistribute these speech resources or to protect people from the harmful effects of speech. For example, legislatures have made attempts to equalize speech regardless of whether one is rich or poor by placing certain restrictions on financing election campaigns. Scholars and activists have sought to pass laws that would hold purveyors of pornography responsible for any harms that could linked to the pornography—such as a rapist imitating something he sees in a pornographic film. Some laws have sought to criminalize certain expressive activity if the expression is calculated to outrage the recipient. Each of these legislative efforts runs into the First Amendment. While the current Court remains committed to maximum protection for speech—a laissez-faire doctrine for the marketplace of ideas—ongoing concerns about the harmful effects of speech and the influence of money in elections are likely to bring about some changes in free speech doctrine in the next few decades.

Going in the other direction, toward greater protection of individual liberty and greater restriction on governmental authority (i.e., the right of the majority to control the minority) is a resurgence of interest in property rights. This resurgence comes both from the legislature and the courts. The Supreme Court has taken a stronger view of the takings clause of the Fifth Amendment, which forbids the taking of private property for public use without just compensation, limiting the ability of the government to regulate the use of property without compensating owners. At the same time, Congress is considering laws to require payments to landowners if the land's value is reduced by environmental regulations.

The Rising Importance of Politics in Making Law

In addition to substantive changes in the law, the process by which law is created is also changing. Historically, most law was made by judges rather than legislatures. Known as "common law," this judge-made law was derived from precedent and analogy—that is, by looking at what judges had done in similar situations in the past and trying to discern how the meaning of their prior actions should apply to the new case. But over the years the trend has been to shift policy-making authority in one subject after another from judges to legislatures. Before the Civil War, state and federal legislatures did relatively little. Judges, by default, made most law. Only after the Civil War, did the well-known "rule" that courts do not make law, they only interpret the law as it currently exists, come into existence. Legislatures then began to pass more and more laws, either to codify common law rules or to change them.

Similarly, the legislature has delegated more and more lawmaking to the executive branch, by creating regulatory agencies. The Supreme Court has granted executive agencies still more power by deferring to their interpretations of the law unless "clearly erroneous."

Finally, there is a strong trend toward "direct democracy." Seven of the sixteen amendments to the Constitution since the Bill of Rights concern expanding the franchise (the right to vote), or enhancing democracy. More and more state constitutions provide for referenda for a wide range of issues, including amending the state constitution. And public opinion polls are increasingly important in decision making by elected officials.

In recent years some of the most hard-fought elections have not been votes for candidates but votes directly on new laws, such as the California proposition to restrict public services for illegal aliens and the Colorado proposition that prohibits antidiscrimination laws from protecting homosexuals. While such direct democracy is useful in giving people a direct voice in government, it presents new challenges as well. Many people may vote on a measure about which they know very little. Such referenda may be as vulnerable or even more vulnerable to special-interest money than legislative decisions, as effective media campaigns are very expensive. Nonetheless, the trend toward direct democracy is likely to continue in the near term.

Conclusion

Stability and predictability are essential elements to a legal system; otherwise people would be unable to make sensible decisions. Thus, most changes in the law should occur relatively slowly in the years ahead. However, crises and new problems will continue to confront the legal system, and changes as dramatic as those surrounding the Civil War and the Great Depression will occur again.

[See also Change, Pace of; Communications: Media Law; Communications: Privacy Issues; Global Turning Points; Judicial Reform; Lawmaking, Judicial; Laws, Evolution of; Lawyers and the Legal Profession.]

BIBLIOGRAPHY

Ackerman, Bruce. "Constitutional Politics/Constitutional Law." *Yale Law Journal* 99 (1989): 453–547.

Calabresi, Guido. "Foreward: Antidiscrimination and Constitutional Accountability (What the Bork-Brennan Debate Ignores)." *Harvard Law Review* 105 (1990): 80–151.

"Constitutional Scholars Assess Impact of Supreme Court's 1993–94 Term." *United States Law Week* 63 (1994): 2229–2243.

Horwitz, Morton J.. "Foreward: The Constitution of Change: Legal Fundamentality without Fundamentalism." *Harvard Law Review* 107 (1993): 30–117.

Gilmore, Grant. *The Ages of American Law.* New Haven: Yale University Press, 1977.

Gunther, Gerald. *Constitutional Law.* Westbury, N.Y: Foundation Press, 1991.

Harrell, Mary Ann, and Anderson, Burnett. *Equal Justice Under Law: The Supreme Court in American Life.* Washington, DC: Supreme Court Historical Society, 1988.

Linowitz, Sol M. *The Betrayed Profession: Lawyering at the End of the Twentieth Century.* New York: Scribner, 1994.

Pope, James Gray. "Republican Moments: The Role of Direct Popular Power in the American Constitutional Order." *University of Pennsylvania Law Review* 139 (1990): 287–368.

Sullivan, Kathleen M. "Foreward: The Justices of Rules and Standards." *Harvard Law Review* 106 (1992): 24–123.

— BLAKE M. CORNISH

LAWMAKING, JUDICIAL

Most people would probably maintain that the U.S. federal government has become, over the years, significantly more powerful than any state or the states as a whole. Most people would probably also say that the powers of the American president (and many state governors) have grown at the expense of the U.S. Congress (or the state legislatures). Virtually no one would argue that the U.S. judiciary or the state judiciaries are more powerful than one or both of the other two branches, the executive and the legislative branches. Nevertheless, the importance of the state courts should not be overlooked or underestimated.

First, most U.S. citizens are more likely to come into direct and repeated contact with a state (or local) officer than a federal officer (except perhaps someone in the U.S. postal service). And that state officer is more likely to be an administrative officer of the judiciary (a police officer, prosecuting attorney, or public defender) or a member of the judiciary (a clerk or judge) than a governor, some other administrative officer, or legislative aide.

Second, because of the doctrine of judicial review, first enunciated by Chief Justice John Marshall of the U.S. Supreme Court in the case of *Marbury* v. *Madison* in 1803, all courts, federal and state, have the power to declare the law of any legislature, and actions carried out by any federal or state officer, to be contrary to the Constitution (i.e., to be unconstitutional) and thus null and void. Hence, in a very important sense, in the United States and each state, "law is what the judges say it is."

Third, for a variety of structural and political reasons, legislators and executives at both levels of government in the United States have increasingly left the most difficult policy decisions up to the courts, so that in controversial matters, public policy is made by judges, not by state legislatures or the U.S. Congress, or by presidential or gubernatorial decree. This is often decried by political commentators as inappropriate "judicial activism," and frequently denied by judges who hide behind a cloak of conservatism and legal precedence. However, it does seem to be the case that judges as a whole exercise a rather impressive degree of leadership on substantive issues within the American system.

Matters once left to individual discretion or private resolution have been criminalized or otherwise made justiciable.

Finally, more and more matters once left to individual discretion or private resolution have been criminalized or otherwise made justiciable. The caseloads of almost all courts have risen enormously—far faster than the number of courts and judges available to promptly resolve the conflicts fully and equitably. Allegedly in the interest of achieving fairness and decisional predictability and conformity, Congress and most legislatures also recently reduced the discretion of judges. They now require judges to hear cases that might otherwise be dismissed, and to reach specified decisions (often with specified sentences) even if a judge might prefer a different outcome in a specific case. This has been especially true of drug-related cases since the 1980s. Many criminal courts are severely backlogged as a consequence. Similarly, the increase of civil litigation means that civil courts (which deal with noncriminal conflicts between individuals or corporations) are ever more seriously backlogged.

At the same time, new technologies have emerged that are changing the way business, commerce, entertainment, religion, and all other facets of daily life are conducted. With varying degrees of enthusiasm and funding, most courts also are using new technologies in all aspects of judicial administration and decision making.

As the percentage of minorities increases in the United States and elsewhere, and as these minorities begin to insist that judicial procedures and principles follow their traditions rather than those of the historically dominant culture, choice and diversity might become more typical of the judiciary of the future than it ever was in the courts of the states. This possibility is even greater given the rising claims of the indigenous peoples of the American states.

The judicial overload and decreased relative or real funding on the one hand and the growth of new technologies and the movement for alternative dispute resolution techniques on the other is altering the judicial system. The combined effect of these developments led almost all state judiciaries during the 1980s and '90s to engage in a series of future-oriented activities aimed at more or less completely "reinventing justice" in the United States.

Taking into account the continuation of past and present trends and challenges, and the active attempts by judiciaries and members of the public generally to design new (or reinstate old) systems of conflict resolution, one can anticipate several possible future courses of development for state courts in the United States. Four of these alternatives follow:

1. *Generic justice.* The antigovernment political climate continues, even as the demand for judicial services continues to increase along with the crime rate. At the same time, the public continues to criticize all branches of government, including the courts, and refuses to pay sufficient taxes for the services it demands. Thus, traditional guarantees of due process of law diminish (especially for the poor), and most decisions are reached in a cookie-cutter, assembly-line fashion.

2. *Judicial leadership.* The incorporation of humane, consumer-sensitive, integrated, and future-oriented methods and procedures into the administration of justice enables the formal system to regain the confidence of the public, and to settle all issues brought before it in a timely and fair manner.

3. *The multidoor dispute-resolution facility.* The formal judiciary acknowledges and/or embraces many different forms of dispute resolution, with the present monopolistic system being but one choice contestants can make in order to settle their disputes.

4. *The global virtual courthouse.* Modern and emerging communications technologies break down the barriers of time and space so that people no longer need to meet at a specific day, hour, and place to settle their disputes. Moreover, local, state, and national judiciaries give way to global dispute-resolution procedures necessary for the global world of tomorrow.

Any one of these four alternatives is not likely to encompass the totality of the future American state judiciary. Parts of each will combine with problems, opportunities, and visions as yet unforeseen to form the likely components of the American state courts of the future.

[See also Criminal Justice; Judicial Reform; Law of the Land; Lawyers and the Legal Profession.]

BIBLIOGRAPHY

Dator, James A. "The Dancing Judicial Zen Masters." *Technological Forecasting and Social Change* 46/1 (May 1994): 59–70.

Dator, James A., and Rodgers, Sharon. *Alternative Futures for the State Courts of 2020.* Chicago: State Justice Institute and the American Judicature Society, 1991.

Inayatullah, Sohail, ed. "The Futures of State Courts." Two entire issues of *Futures Research Quarterly* 9/4 (Winter 1993); 10/1 (Spring 1994).

Katsh, M. Ethan. *Electronic Media and the Transformation of Law.* New York: Oxford University Press, 1989.

———. *Law in a Digital World.* New York: Oxford University Press, 1995.

Schultz, Wendy, et al. *Reinventing Courts for the Twenty-first Century: Designing a Vision Process.* Williamsburg, VA: National Center for State Courts, 1993.

— JAMES A. DATOR

LAWS, EVOLUTION OF

Change is relentless and never stops. Society is constantly evolving and changing so that final fashioning of laws is simply not possible. Change assumes a ceaseless tinkering, an all-encompassing discontent with things as they are. The underlying assumption is that humans will always attempt to perfect their affairs incrementally. These assumptions entail a perpetual process of change and adaptation to evolving new circumstances.

Each new social milieu prompts new policies or revisions of previous ones. Finding the optimum balance in response to a dynamic environment requires constant adjustment and readjustment. Regulatory developments of all kinds are never-ending.

Great movements championing change alternate with periods of relative decline and quiescence. Even as basic a quest as equality comes to the fore only intermittently as injustices gather and the number of concerned persons increases. Equality is the driving force behind many ongoing quests to secure realization of the ideal society. Egalitarian quests of all kinds are always with us—movements for women's rights, minority rights, and the like will never disappear until the disparities are totally rectified and balanced. The stark reality is that humans never will fully or finally achieve perfectly balanced equality. Equality is an abstract and idealistic goal at odds with practical human experience. Furthermore, humans are destined to achieve different levels of attainment. There always will be superachievers and underachievers, haves and have-nots, geniuses and idiots, beautiful as well as ugly persons, and so on ad infinitum. Given the elusive nature of absolutes, these issues are perpetually destined to confront and confound society.

The episodic periodicity with which issues recur manifests itself in lawmaking. Laws are little more than institutional propositions that continuously are expanded to cope with life's myriad problems as they become bigger, more complicated, more technical, and so on. The larger and more complicated society becomes, there is inevitably more opportunity for variant forms of human interaction and conflict. Laws are devised to redress and minimize these conflicts.

Laws are a means for containing and institutionalizing public policy confrontations and a mechanism for implementing orderly transitions. A well-ordered and predictable society depends on rules of law as a buffer against capricious acts. Lawmaking has an evolutionary character based on its ability to respond to changing circumstances. Such responses are predictable and consequently enable us to predict stages of legal development.

Laws are institutional propositions that continuously

are expanded to cope with life's myriad problems,

as they become bigger, more complicated,

and more technical.

Environmental protection, for example, is no recent phenomenon. It evolved over a very long period of time. Fundamental philosophical and ideological concepts such as the "conservation ethic" have persisted over thousands of years. Such concerns throughout all of recorded history, up to and including contemporary times, become the subject of legislative tinkering.

Finally, we must recognize that there are no permanent solutions to society's problems. The process of change and adaptation to new circumstances is neverending. Therefore, from this perspective we need to recognize that humanity's work is never finished. Public policy, correspondingly, is in a constant state of flux as it continually responds to altered social circumstances.

Evolutionary and devolutionary trends, such as the emergence and demise (life cycle) of social phenomena, provide a useful framework to gauge the future. These dynamics are useful in plotting the trend and direction of impending change. The process involves a kind of "staging." The staging advances in a manner similar to an unfolding set of stairs. The law establishes norms intended to constrain the excesses of human behavior that emerge from time to time. Eventually, however, the law is overtaken by events. Ingenious humans always find a way around the law. Or, structural changes introduced by new technologies give rise to a series of problems that prompt an updated response to the old circumstance. The solutions, usually in the form of a new law or regulation (although it may come about by voluntary act, custom, or some other less formal mechanism), involves the next step upward. Often remaining

at a plateau for some time, there usually appears a jolt upward to the next step as the new rule of law is imposed.

Public policy issues, as they are taken up, often are considered as if they are new. Nothing could be further from the truth. There is a certain timelessness about issues. They recur again and again.

The fact is that great issues in history—such as economic equality, justice, environmental improvement, indeed, all progress, have persisted since time immemorial. Ideal philosophical concepts governing social behavior never are fully or finally realized. Detailed refinements, extensions, exceptions, and improvements of all other types continue to emerge. In relentless procession the "filigree" of an issue is fully fashioned. Basic issues tend to receive sporadic bursts of attention.

Philosophical roots of many contemporary issues can be traced all the way back to the very beginnings of recorded history. Certain age-old aspirations of humanity illuminate basic, underlying currents in ongoing public policy change. Following is a random list of sociopolitical issues, policies, and programs that date back as long as 4,000 years. Actual rhetoric surrounding debate on these issues and the statements of intended results had a familiar ring then as they have now. This tabulation strives to corroborate the conclusion that most every contemporary problem one can imagine has been and probably always will be around. They are, therefore, timeless issues.

- Taxes first imposed in Sumer, c. 3000 B.C.
- Price regulation dating back to Hittite Kingdom, c. 1300 B.C.
- Strikes used as an economic weapon to achieve concessions, Rome, 494 B.C.
- Virtually parroting today's key policy concerns, Marcus Cicero, Roman statesman and writer (106–43 B.C.), stated: "The . . . budget must be balanced. The . . . treasury should be filled. Government indebtedness must be reduced. The arrogance of the authorities must be moderated and controlled. The people should learn to work again, instead of living off the public dole."
- Titus Livius (Livy), Roman historian (c. 59 B.C.–A.D. 17), objected to greedy self-indulgence, moral rot, failure to save income, and slipping standards of conduct.
- Free food for the poor first provided by P. Claudius, Rome, 58 B.C.
- Poor aid provided by compulsory use of tithes, King Ethelred, England, A.D. 1014.
- Poor law promulgated by English Parliament, A.D. 1388.
- Law to repress begging, English Parliament, A.D. 1536.
- Socrates (500–450 B.C.), Athenian philosopher, assailed earlier generations for destroying the forests and landscape.
- Graffiti adorned town walls in Pompeii prior to eruption of Mount Vesuvius in A.D. 79.
- Julius Caesar (45 B.C.), frustrated with traffic congestion, dust, and noise, banned all wheeled vehicles from Rome during daylight hours.
- Rebelling against willy-nilly town streets in Mohenjo-Daro, the area was laid out gridiron fashion, c. 2513 B.C.

- Sesotris II (1887–1849 B.C.), Egypt, was criticized for constructing mass transportation links (canals along the Nile).
- Building extensive parks under the rule of Hammurabi, king of Babylonia, was both praised and condemned, c. 1758 B.C.
- Corrupting youth of Athens was the charge leading to Socrates' death, c. 399 B.C.
- Aristotle (384–322 B.C.) criticized young people as thoughtless, unmindful of parents, and unruly in school.
- Tuition fees for students established, Sumer, 2500 B.C.
- State control of education established, Athens, 500 B.C.
- State-supported schools inaugurated by Julius Caesar, Rome, 46 B.C.
- Teachers licensed by Emperor Julian, Rome, A.D. 362.
- State-supported university established by Emperor Theodosius, Constantinople, A.D. 410.
- Written code of law established, Sumer, 2100 B.C.
- Compensation for bodily injuries written into legal texts by Ur-Namnu, king of Ur (Mesopotamia), c. 2100 B.C.
- Code of law (282 paragraphs long) published by Hammurabi, king of Babylonia, c. 1758 B.C.
- Xenophon (c. 430–354 B.C.), Greek historian, complained of litigiousness clogging the courts.
- Systematizing civil service by ordering into nine ranks undertaken, China, c. 221 B.C.
- Fed up with nepotism, court intrigue, and incompetence, competitive written civil-service exams were inaugurated, China, c. 200 B.C.
- Weights and measures standards established, Sumer, 3000 B.C.
- Racial equality (including intermarriage among Greeks, Macedonians, and Persians) decreed by Alexander the Great, 325–323 B.C.
- Divorce law, Babylon, Code of Hammurabi, 1800 B.C.
- Women's right to divorce (including recoupment of her property) accorded in Minoan Code, c. 1500 B.C.
- Adoption of children begun, Sumer, 1800 B.C.
- Prostitution regulated, Sumer, 1950 B.C.

This list, even though a bit wearying, has been gleaned from among great and small issues. The distinguished philosopher George Santayana (1863–1952) gave us good reason to heed previous trials and tribulations by noting: "Those who do not learn from history are condemned to repeat it." The Bible put it another way: "There is no new thing under the sun." (Ecclesiastes 1:9).

> [See also Continuity and Discontinuity; Ethics; Food Laws; Law of the Land; Public Policy Change; Social Inventions; Social and Political Evolution.]

BIBLIOGRAPHY

Asimov, Isaac. *Asimov's Chronology of the World: The History of the World From the Big Bang to Modern Times.* New York: HarperCollins, 1991.

Carruth, Gorton. *The Encyclopedia of American Facts and Dates,* 8th ed. New York: Harper & Row, 1987.

Goldberg, M. Hirsch. *The Blunder Book: Colossal Errors, Minor Mistakes, and Surprising Slipups That Have Changed the Course of History.* New York: Quill/William Morrow, 1984.

Robertson, Patrick. *The Book of Firsts.* New York: Bramhall House, 1982.

Urdand, Laurence, ed. *The Timetables of American History.* New York: Simon & Schuster, 1981.

— GRAHAM T. T. MOLITOR

LAWYERS AND THE LEGAL PROFESSION

The law—the agreed-upon framework for acceptable human and organizational relations—will continue to evolve in scope and complexity at a dizzying speed during the next thirty to fifty years. Lawyers as counselors, advocates, and judges will be the ones to interpret, apply, and test the forces governing those fast-evolving relationships. Further, to a significant extent, it will be lawyers themselves as legislators who shape the driving forces.

By the year 2005 there will be no more debate over whether the United States has too many lawyers (especially as compared with Asian countries). The future will show that the United States was merely setting the trend for handling complex relationships. Other countries will follow, as homogeneous populations become more multicultural and international transactions increase. Thus, "lawyering" will continue to be a growth profession throughout the next century.

The Present

The number of lawyers in the United States has been increasing for more than forty years, in both constant numbers and as a ratio of lawyers to the entire population. The American Bar Association and its associated American Bar Foundation report the statistics and projections: shown in Table 1.

In the federal trial courts, civil case filings increased 1,424 percent between 1904 and 1994, with most of that growth after 1960; criminal cases increased only 157 percent during that period, but they became much more difficult to prosecute and defend; hence, they occupy a considerably higher proportion of court time.

TABLE 1

NUMBERS AND RATIOS OF LAWYERS IN THE UNITED STATES

Year	No. of Lawyers	People per Lawyer
1951	221,605	695/1
1960	285,933	627/1
1971	355,242	418/1
1980	542,205	403/1
1985	655,191	360/1
1988	723,189	340/1
1991	805,872	313/1
1995	896,172	290/1
1999	984,843	271/1
2000	1,005,842	267/1

As of 1992, for example, most federal trial courts devoted more than 50 percent of their trial dockets to criminal cases. By 1994, drug offenses accounted for 40 percent of the criminal filings. The Judicial Conference of the United States reports historical data and projections for U.S. District Courts, which are the federal trial courts of general jurisdiction (and do not include bankruptcy and other specialized courts) as shown in Table 2.

The most remarkable growth has occurred in the federal courts of appeals, which have experienced enormous increases generally and in appeals by prisoners seeking to reopen their cases as shown in Table 3.

The number of federal judges in District Courts and courts of general appeal have continued to increase over the years, but less so than their case loads, as the Judicial Conference data in Table 4 demonstrate.

TABLE 2

CASES BEGUN IN U.S. DISTRICT COURTS

(12-Month Periods Ending June 30)

Year	Criminal Cases	Civil Cases
1940	33,401	34,734
1950	36,383	54,622
1960	28,137	59,284
1970	38,102	87,321
1980	27,968	168,789
1990	46,530	217,879
1994	44,919	235,996
2000	51,600	334,600
2010	66,000	576,500
2020	89,400	1,019,900

TABLE 3

ACTUAL AND PROJECTED APPEALS FILED IN U.S. COURTS OF APPEALS

(12-Month Periods Ending June 30)

Year	Total Appeals	Criminal Appeals	Prisoner Petitions	Other Appeals
1940	3,505	260	65	3,180
1950	2,830	308	286	2,236
1960	3,899	623	290	2,986
1970	11,662	2,660	2,440	6,562
1980	23,200	4,405	3,675	15,120
1990	40,898	9,493	9,941	21,464
1994	48,815	11,052	12,772	24,991
2000	84,800	11,600	35,500	37,700
2010	171,600	16,000	81,900	73,700
2020	325,100	22,300	155,900	146,900

The Future

Congress will soon realize that it cannot allow the federal court system to continue to grow at the current (and projected) rate. Alone the appointment and confirmation process for thousands of judges would be unworkable. By the year 2000, Congress will have begun in earnest the difficult task of dismantling the federal court battleships and converting them to sleek missile carriers with highly defined missions. This will require state courts and private dispute resolution systems to make up the difference in criminal and civil cases.

By 2010 Congress will have virtually eliminated so-called general diversity jurisdiction, under which a citizen of one state may sue a citizen of another in federal court for violation of state law. Also by that time, the federal trial courts no longer will be swamped by drug "busts" and other local crime prosecutions. These courts primarily will be venues for adjudicating matters of clear national interest. The state and local courts will have to absorb the rest of the criminal activity, perhaps with federal monetary assistance.

The current trend toward resolving disputes outside the courts will continue at a rapid pace in federal and state jurisdictions. By 2010, virtually all courts will require that certain types of civil cases undergo pre-trial alternative dispute resolution (ADR) efforts before experienced "neutrals," who will try to facilitate settlement through mediation.

By 2010, ADR will be the rule and litigation in court the exception for civil cases. Competitive corporations will set up private judicial systems, with their own professional judges and juries who will adjudicate, on a confidential basis, controversies between competitors. ADR in the form of private, confidential arbitration will

TABLE 4

FEDERAL APPELLATE AND DISTRICT COURT JUDGESHIPS

(Excluding the Specialized Federal Circuit Court of Appeals)

Year	Appeals Court Judges	District (Trial) Judges
1940	57	191
1950	65	224
1960	68	245
1970	97	401
1980	132	516
1990	156	575
1994	167	649
2000	430	940
2010	840	1,510
2020	1,580	2,530

be the only form of individual relief for many disputes between employees and employers and buyers and sellers. There will be virtually no way to appeal such decisions to any court.

By 2020, the trial of cases before federal, state,

or local government judges

will in large part be "pre-packaged."

By 2020, the trial of cases before federal, state, or local government judges will in large part be "pre-packaged." The process will be similar to the "video trials" used in some midwestern courts today, but the recording medium and presentations will be much more advanced than the relatively crude video tape presentations now made in these courts. In video trials the entire trial will be finished and edited before the jury is selected and seated. The jury will view the trial as it would an instructional film and then try to reach a verdict.

A trial judge need not be present while video cases are being presented to a jury, but he or she could be available for unusual situations. Once the judge or jury has seen the trial and is in the process of trying to reach a decision or verdict, the video record, which would include readable versions of all written exhibits, will be made available to the factfinder(s). The video record will be accessible randomly and quickly, since it will contain its own self-made index. Thus, a jury could call up a particular document and re-read it, see and listen to a particular witness again, or accumulate and review all evidence on a particular point.

By 2020, most exhibits and records at all levels of adjudication will be submitted on data discs or cells, instead of bulky paper. The new media will allow lawyers and decision makers instant access to information when they need it. Texts of legal authorities will be implanted in the cyberbriefs and cybermemoranda submitted to decision makers to allow them to create a computer window, call up, and review a cited court decision or statute at any point.

By 2020, most three-dimensional evidence will be accessible as well through video discs or cells and be capable of presentation through holographic- and virtual-reality-like presentations. Thus, a jury could be invited to "walk through" the scene of the crime or accident, rather than merely look at a photograph. Indeed, there will be computer animations and recreations designed to allow jurors to view and experience (to a degree) what happened.

[See also Criminal Justice; Judicial Reform; Law of the Land; Lawmaking, Judicial; Laws, Evolution of.]

BIBLIOGRAPHY

Benson, Bruce L. *The Enterprise of Law: Justice Without the State.* San Francisco, CA: Pacific Research Institute for Public Policy, 1990.

Huber, Peter W. *The Legal Revolution and Its Consequences.* New York: Basic Books, 1988.

Kairys, David, ed. *The Politics of Law: A Progressive Critique.* New York: Pantheon Books, 1990.

Lamm, Richard D. "Lawyers and Lawyering: The Legal System and Its Cost to American Society." *Vital Speeches of the Day* 55/7 (January 15, 1989).

– RICHARD J. LEIGHTON

LEADERSHIP

There is not much written about leadership in the future. Out of a thousand books on leadership, only a dozen project leadership thought and practice into the future. Eight of them are discussed here.

James MacGregor Burns (1978) initiated the idea that the old models of leadership may be inadequate for the future, and he developed a theory of transformational leadership that required "leaders and followers raise one another to higher levels of motivation and morality" (p. 20). Burns also insisted that leadership produce "real, intended change" (p. 461) through a collective, dissensual process that develops mutual goals. Burns's work is viewed by many as the beginning of a new theory of leadership.

James M. Kouzes and Barry Z. Posner followed up their previous work on leadership with a book on leadership and credibility (1993). Defining leadership as "a reciprocal relationship between those who choose to lead and those who decide to follow" (p. 1), the authors argued that credibility will be the most crucial ingredient in leadership relationships in the future. Their credibility model includes six practices: (1) discovering your self, (2) appreciating constituents, (3) affirming shared values, (4) developing capacity, (5) serving a purpose, and (6) sustaining hope (p. 51). Kouzes and Posner believe that closing the credibility gap is the key to building and sustaining effective leadership relationships in the organizations of the future.

Feminist writers often call for a new paradigm of leadership for the future, an overarching view of leadership that is fundamentally different from the male models of leadership that dominated the twentieth century. Helen S. Astin and Carole Leland's work (1990) is perhaps the best example of a feminist perspective on leadership in the future. "Leadership is a process by which members of a group are empowered to work together synergistically toward a common goal or vision that will create change, transform institutions, and thus improve the quality of life" (p. 8). Throughout the book, the authors viewed leadership as a process of social change to improve the human condition. Theirs is a constructionist perspective with a generous portion of adult development to make the needed connections between research and practice.

Burt Nanus, the futurist turned leadership expert, wrote two books after his successful collaboration with Bennis in 1985. *The Leader's Edge* (1989) develops the notion of the futures-creative leader, who must develop seven megaskills, "competencies [that] are needed to exercise effective leadership in the new age" (p. 8). In his 1992 book *Visionary Leadership,* Nanus argued that twenty-first-century organizations require visionary leaders, and the book gives detailed steps for vision making.

The political mindset has made inroads into a futurist understanding of leadership. Heifetz's (1994) prescriptive understanding of leadership is the mobilizing of people and communities to do adaptive work, that is, to tackle the tough problems that must be solved in a society. While Heifetz's view of leadership has been influenced by psychology, his concept of leadership is primarily about the politics of authority and influence among people who want to solve difficult problems in a democratic society.

Joseph C. Rost (1991) constructed a prescriptive definition of leadership, one that embodies a postindustrial paradigm of leadership for the twenty-first century. "Leadership is an influence relationship among leaders and followers who intend real changes that reflect their mutual purposes" (p. 102).

Feminist writers often call for a new paradigm of leadership for the future, an overarching view of leadership that is fundamentally different from the male models of leadership.

Robert E. Kelley (1992) critiqued the myth of leadership for concentrating only on the leader. His book on followership looks to the future where exemplary followers will be seen as vital to the leadership process as leaders. Kelley details the skills and styles of followers and calls upon scholars and practitioners to balance the myth of leadership with the reality of followership.

In summary, there are a few scholars who are agitating for a new understanding of leadership more in tune with a postindustrial world view, but these voices have not yet become the majority view.

[See also Agents of Change; Artificial Intelligence; Business Governance; Civil Protest; Conscious Evolution; Governance; Pacesetter Governments; Participative Management; Pluralism; Political Parties; Public Opinion Polls; Record Setting; Strategic Planning.]

BIBLIOGRAPHY

Astin, Helen S., and Leland, Carole. *Women of Influence, Women of Vision.* San Francisco: Jossey-Bass, 1991.

Burns, James MacGregor. *Leadership.* New York: Harper & Row, 1978.

Heifetz, Ronald A. *Leadership without Easy Answers.* Cambridge, MA: Harvard University Press, 1994.

Kelley, Robert E. *The Power of Followership.* New York: Doubleday, 1992.

Kouzes, James M., and Posner, Barry Z. *Credibility.* San Francisco: Jossey-Bass, 1993.

Nanus, Burt. *The Leader's Edge.* Chicago: Contemporary Books, 1989.

———. *Visionary Leadership.* San Francisco: Jossey-Bass, 1992.

Rost, Joseph C. *Leadership for the Twenty-First Century.* New York: Praeger, 1991.

— JOSEPH C. ROST

LEGAL PROFESSION

See LAWYERS AND LEGAL PROFESSION.

LEGISLATIVE AND PARLIAMENTARY SYSTEMS

Let us begin by imagining what a session of the U.S. House of Representatives might be like in decades to come. The Speaker of the House enters and takes the chair. He leads the Pledge of Allegiance. There is no chaplain present and no opening prayer. "In God We Trust" has been removed from above the rostrum.

The Speaker announces the consideration of the first bill: the federal government will give every newborn child a computer. It will be paid for by a new voluntary tax on the number of cable channels received in each home. An immediate vote is declared. There is no debate. The members of the House have already studied the issue using the vast resources of a worldwide database. The Library of Congress has compiled a list of pros and cons on the bill, complete with environmental and economic impact studies.

The members have digested these reports off their computer screens at home. In fact, there are few members even present in the chamber. Most are at home connected by a secure fiber-optic network. There are no staffers around either. The advocates of reducing staffs have succeeded beyond their wildest dreams. All committees and subcommittees are gone. The Library of Congress does all the research work and the government agencies solve all the constituent problems. The General Accounting Office and the Office of Technology Assessment have been discontinued.

No one has lobbied members on the issue. All lobbyists have been abolished. And all the members are freshmen—the term-limit advocates have won out.

The Speaker types his security code on his key pad to activate the voting machine. Members sitting at home push a button to record their votes. The Speaker asks the computer for the results. A voice-activated machine replies in a seemingly human voice: "The bill passes 435 to 0." The House adjourns.

Is this too far-fetched a scenario?

First, there is the matter of the chaplain and the opening prayer. For decades, this practice has been under attack. Those who want God out of every public ceremony have tried to abolish it. After the Supreme Court eliminated prayer in schools, the then-speaker, John McCormack, retaliated. There was a row of decorative brass stars above the rostrum. McCormack had the center ones replaced with the words "In God We Trust," declaring "This is one place where God will be present."

Congressional staff size became an issue in the 1970s when the Democrats, having lost the White House, found themselves literally outmanned by an administration that tried to preempt even the legislative process. Divided government did not mean surrender to the executive branch, congressional Democrats argued. Weren't the separate branches of government coequal? And, if they were, how many computers did the executive branch have and how many did Congress have. In an effort to level the playing field, staff and computer capacity multiplied, and the Congress felt justified. The rapid growth presented an easy target for critics of Congress, particularly by the Republicans and particularly by advocates of a strong executive.

What does the future hold? With an increasingly complex society and the federal government becoming more involved in its citizens' lives, an increase in staff for Congress is more likely than a decrease. Although there are fewer federal dollars to be spent, Congress nonetheless takes its oversight responsibility seriously and requires staff to do it.

Lobbyists are another growth occupation. As government swelled and the subjects it addressed became more intricate, experts—outside as well as inside—proliferated. Congressmen and their staff sought information about companies and their products that were changing the lives of Americans.

Industry was convinced, too, that representation in Washington was important because new federal regulations could be affected, and contracts could be won. Perhaps most important to the growth in the ranks of lobbyists, a company could help itself in Congress as well as with the administration. Divided government had emboldened the legislative branch to become a player in an area previously ceded to the executive.

Efforts to reduce the lobbying ranks took the form of limiting the activity of government workers, congressional and executive branch alike. The so-called revolving door provision prohibited lobbying one's colleagues for a specified time after moving to the private sector.

Looking to the future, lobbyists argue that they have the same constitutional right to petition the government as is granted to any citizen or group of citizens. Some further narrowing of their right is probable, but the basic right will be preserved.

Aside from formal lobbying, the United States has seen the perfection of another form of influencing the government—single-issue lobbying. A group of like-minded citizens forms around one issue. They organize, pressure their elected officials to agree with them, and threaten defeat to those who do not comply. The elected officials who do not acquiesce then try to deflect the attention from the issue by stressing other parts of their record and hoping for the best.

These single-issue groups have already become an important part of the electoral process and will likely become more so. Television lends itself to coverage of those groups that devise attention-getting gimmicks and tactics. More television in the future means more opportunity for these groups to make an impact on policy making.

If there has been any change in the Congress, it has been in the area of ethics. The future holds even more opportunity, and inevitability.

Former Speaker of the House "Tip" O'Neill preached in the 1980s that "the ethics of politics has changed." By this he meant that the closer media scrutiny of the private lives of politicians and other public figures had indelibly changed the basic machinery of governance. It was no longer possible to practice "business as usual." Increased press scrutiny and the drawing of contrasting moral values more sharply contributed to the change.

Many politicians did not understand what was happening—and they were defeated. Others changed with the times and survived. This trend is likely to continue. Lessons are being learned at the ballot box, and overall the system seems to be improving.

The big question for the Congress in the future is whether it can survive such "purification" and still perform its function of serving the people. Retention of the two-year term in the House of Representatives would ensure this. The Founding Fathers created the shortest term of any elected office in the United States to keep the representatives accountable to the people. They were not trying to fashion the most efficient form of government, only the freest. The future Congress will be measured by that standard.

[See also Democratic Process; Executive Branch; Executive Branch: The Presidency; Governance; Government Organization; Judicial Reform; Lawmaking, Judicial; Law of the Land; Laws, Evolution of.]

BIBLIOGRAPHY

Aydelotte, William O. History of Parliamentary Behavior. Princeton, NJ: Princeton University Press, 1977.

Callahan, Daniel, et al. Congress and the Media: The Ethical Connection. Briarcliff Manor, NY. Hastings Center, 1985.

Gross, Bertram, and Schneier, Edward V. Congress Today. New York: St. Martin's Press, 1993.

Hayes, Michael T. Lobbyists and Legislators: A Theory of Political Markets. New Brunswick, NJ: Rutgers University Press, 1984.

Norton, Philip, ed. Legislatures. New York: Oxford University Press, 1990.

Truman, David B., ed. Congress and America's Future. New York: American Assembly/Columbia University, 1973.

— GARY HYMEL

LEISURE TIME

Since the 1962 publication of Sebastian de Grazia's Of Time, Work, and Leisure, leisure and free time are generally regarded as quite separable and different. Free time is that residual of time not required by work, maintenance of one's person and property, or compelled by some external force or need. Free time is a quantitative commodity we measure with clocks and calendars. Leisure has philosophical and spiritual dimensions clocks cannot measure. Since nearly all conversational and mass-media references to leisure relate to free time, it seems appropriate to address that first.

For the past several decades there has been a widespread belief that free time has been increasing steadily due to efficiency, productivity, laborsaving devices, and unprecedented increases in affluence and general welfare. However, that has not gone undisputed. The reduction in working hours per week from about seventy in 1850 to about forty in 1950 was, and is, de Grazia argued, largely illusory. In 1971, Swedish economist Staffan Linder argued in The Harried Leisure Class that increases in productivity and material wealth resulted

in time becoming increasingly scarce. More recently, Harvard economist Juliet Schor's The Overworked American: The Unexpected Decline of Leisure (1991) became a bestseller. It reinforced both the perception people repeatedly voice of never having enough time and opinion poll reports that the workweek was increasing. Results of time-diary studies do not, however, confirm reports of a lengthened workweek during the past decade or so. Yet if the workweek is not longer than two decades ago, it is widely perceived as being so.

There is widespread agreement that reduced hours in the workweek and work year do not necessarily translate into more free time.

On other matters there is at least general agreement. Over the past 150 years, much free time has been gained via later entry into the labor force, life-expectancy increases resulting in ten to fifteen years of retirement, a shorter workweek, more holidays, and longer vacations. There is also widespread agreement that reduced hours in the workweek and work year do not necessarily translate into more free time. No one defines free time as the hours spent commuting or keeping up with increasingly rapid technological, organizational, and social change. Even "working out" is considered obligatory by many, and thus regarded as work.

The pace of work has also changed; thus, there is more stress than was the case historically. Further, the growth in labor force participation by women might lead one to conclude that there is much more work than ever before.

There is also general agreement that the workweek has not changed much since the 1950s; it has hovered between forty and forty-five hours per week. But averages may mask as much as they reveal. Hours of work per week and per year vary extensively by occupations and individuals, hours seldom reflect preferences, and quantitative measures equate migrant workers picking crops for an hour with millionaires attending a one-hour board meeting. Quite remarkable differences do not appear in our calculations. One such difference is that the potential for free time within working hours is completely masked by quantitative measures.

Despite our recent history, there are *a priori* grounds for projecting there will be more free time in the future. Whether that is chosen or imposed, and therefore realized as leisure or idleness, is at the center of our hopes and fears about the future. Authors of utopian literature have been consistent in often describing a workweek of twenty hours. Juliet Schor (1991) observed that had we been content with the standard of living of 1948, we would have a workweek of twenty hours, or six months' vacation per year, or every other year off, with pay. J. M. Keynes, in an essay published in 1930, proposed the workweek in 2030 could be fifteen hours per week, which would include a few hours we work on behalf of others.

As work becomes further deskilled, increasing numbers of workers, concluding that their jobs are not their lives, seek rewards less exclusively in work and more inclusively in all areas of life. As both Adam Smith and Karl Marx argued, the full realization of one's humanity, civility, and talent will most likely occur outside of work in time freed from work by increased productivity. "The Society for the Reduction of Human Labor" may be less quixotic than superficial appraisals suggest.

More and more people, pollsters find, would prefer to work fewer hours, even if it meant giving up some or all of the income proportionate to the reduced hours.

More people identify themselves by their avocations: increasing numbers are intentionally downwardly mobile, trading off more material goods for more free time. Thus, there are a number of indicators that free time will, for that reason, increase. This portends free time realized as leisure engagements chosen because they are pleasing, intrinsically rewarding, and intuitively worthwhile. Those finding little real value in their work will continue to look for it in free time.

Alternatively, imposed idleness, unemployment and insufficient means for modest but dignified living, is a specter that haunts us when economies, increasingly global in nature, falter. The unemployed in what is now a global labor force number nearly 800 million people (Barnet, 1993). The depressing effect on wages of those in mature economies has been evident and acknowledged. The effect on rates and hours of employment is increasingly evident as well. About twice as many people work for Manpower, Inc., a temporary service agency, as for General Motors. From that and other, similar data spring our concern about the loss of "real" jobs.

Increasing numbers of people seek rewarding experiences outside of their work. This woman chooses to raft down the Colorado River in the Grand Canyon. Leisure will constitute 50% of lifetime activity by the year 2010. (© First Image West, Inc.)

The information age and the global economy are not producing jobs, at least not in the United States, Canada, and other mature, Western economies (Barnet, 1993). Japan, whose workers have the world's longest workweek and year among the developed countries, is trying diligently to reduce work hours. Political parties of both the left and right in Germany and France have recently touted the four-day, thirty- to thirty-two-hour workweek as a solution to intransigent unemployment.

Television and its elaborations in multiple forms are likely to continue absorbing the lion's share of people's free time. They are comparatively inexpensive measured on a per hour basis, are convenient, and make few demands. Virtual reality and a virtually endless variety of content and interaction make them increasingly seductive, even if, as many observe, also escapist and debilitating.

Further growth in high-risk, or at least high-thrill and high-adventure activities, can also be expected. Some of this may be attributed to boredom due to unchallenging work, some to the quest for identity, some to the saturation of those slightly tamer places and activities of yesterday's adventurers.

There is a growing appreciation of leisure as intrinsically rewarding and intuitively worthwhile, which offers a source of meaning, purpose, and belongingness at all levels. Such leisure activity—including the arts, sports, hobbies, and volunteer services—is characterized by love and absorption so complete as to transcend the spatial and temporal bounds of here and now. Surgeons, chess players, dancers, journalists all experience what has been labeled "flow," otherwise described as peak or optimal experience. "Serious leisure" engaged in by dedicated amateurs will continue to grow rapidly.

Thus far, there is more hope than evidence that the individualism of recent decades has run its course and increasing amounts of free time will be devoted to reconstituting those convivial institutions of family, neighborhood, and community. Interesting evidence is mounting that peak or optimal experiences, which produce "flow," and voluntary-service activities, which produce a sense of contributing and making a difference, are healthy. Work that is stressful, unchallenging, or devoid of intrinsic worth, is unhealthy. And television, we know, is linked not only to obesity and lethargy but also to asocial, violent activity.

In short, new conditions and strong forces are imposing free time in the form of unemployment and underemployment. Much of our use of that time will remain passive and routine, but we are learning that leisure can be found in more ways and places than heretofore realized. Those who find too little meaning in work will choose leisure when they can. Imposed free time used in largely escapist fashion will remain the rule, but choosing leisure for meaning and intrinsic worth will become less the exception. Education and the distribution of jobs and income will determine how much idleness or leisure emerge. The political and economic dimensions of the amount and distribution of free time are becoming more apparent. This trend will continue in the years to come.

[See also Free Time; Gambling; Interactive Entertainment; Outdoor Recreation and Leisure Pursuits; Sports and Activities, Spectator; Sports and Games, Competitive; Theme Parks and Organized Attractions; Tourism.]

BIBLIOGRAPHY

Barnet, Richard J. "The End of Jobs." Harper's 287 (September 1993): 47–52.
De Grazia, Sebastian. Of Time, Work, and Leisure. New York: Twentieth Century Fund, 1962.
Godbey, Geoffrey C. The Future of Leisure Services. State College, PA: Venture Publishing, 1989.
———. "Leisure in the 1990s." The World and I (January 1990): 95–105.
Hunnicutt, Benjamin K. Work Without End. Philadelphia: Temple University Press, 1988.
Reich, Robert. The Work of Nations. New York: Alfred A. Knopf, 1991.
Schor, Juliet. The Overworked American: The Unexpected Decline of Leisure. New York: Basic Books, 1991.

– TOM GOODALE

LETHAL WEAPONS

The production of firearms will continue to proliferate in the years ahead. More and more powerful weapons will become available to the general public. Approximately 4 million firearms were produced in the United States during 1989. Of these, 62,900 were revolvers and 1.4 million were pistols. During the twentieth century over 250 million firearms (excluding military weapons) were manufactured or imported into the United States. Sales of firearms are likely to greatly increase in both legitimate retail outlets and in the black market.

Illegal ownership will remain relatively stable because the powerful firearms manufacturers and their lobbies will eliminate many local laws presently making the possession of firearms illegal. Thus, there will be many more guns, but fewer of them will be owned illegally. As of 1990, an estimated 180–200 million firearms were in circulation. As many as 50 percent of American households own one or more guns. Only a fourth of the 200 million or so firearms in circulation during 1990 were legitimately owned according to the letter of the laws. Firearms availability and use for deadly purposes increases despite the fact that over 20,000 gun laws were on the books by the end of the 1980s.

Ownership Restrictions

Licensing, registration, mandatory waiting periods, proof of fitness to possess firearms, and marksmanship qualifications have repeatedly been prevented from enactment by powerful political lobbies. However, effective control measures of this sort seem to work well in other nations, especially in Sweden. In Japan and the United Kingdom, handguns are banned, excepting gun club members and collectors. American public opinion favors tougher controls. Gallup Poll data reveals that some 80 percent of persons polled favor stricter controls, and 95 percent support federal legislation requiring a seven-day waiting period for handgun purchases.

As of 1990, an estimated 180–200 million firearms were in circulation. As many as 50 percent of American households own one or more guns.

Laws will attempt to distinguish between automatic and semiautomatic firearms and curb the availability of guns with high firepower rates. Following the killing of five children and the wounding of thirty others by an individual wielding a semiautomatic AK-47 rifle in Stockton, California, within months fifty bills regulating the sale or possession of semiautomatic weapons had been introduced in seventeen states. Few effective laws passed. Laws regulating machine guns, assault weapons, "Saturday night specials," zip guns, and hand guns will continue to be undermined by legal challenges on definition. From 650,000 to 2 million weapons, including smuggled and stolen automatic and semiautomatic firearms, are thought to be in the hands of criminals. Firearms manufacturers and their lobbies will probably continue to be successful, at least in the United States, in getting various local jurisdictions to pass laws giving absolute liberty to possess firearms and in incrementally removing reasonable limitations.

Use Restrictions

The storage of firearm components in separate locations will be encouraged in public health and education campaigns, but they will not be legally required. Similarly, trigger locks and other safety devices will be marketed but not required. Only a very small number of firearm owners will actually acquire such devices and fewer still are likely to actually employ them. Visual tagging of firearm replicas to distinguish them from real firearms will increase, since this is not an area of concern for the firearms lobby. Laws against celebration shooting, such as on New Year's Eve or the Fourth of July, will increase, since the firearms lobby's principal interest is in selling weapons and generally not in challenging laws prohibiting their illegal use in public. There will be no increase in laws requiring weapons training and qualification, since these are successfully opposed by the firearms lobby, which fights any measures leading potential firearms purchasers to think about, or hesitate in, buying new weapons.

Ammunition

Laws regulating the possession and use of "cop-killer" bullets—teflon-coated bullets, spent uranium rounds, hollow point bullets, contact-exploding rounds, and modified slugs—will generally continue in place and perhaps increase in use. As the number of firearms, the rates of fire, and the lethal nature of bullets escalate, more police officers and more citizens will be killed by them.

The number of police officers killed in the line of duty rose from 73 in 1961 to 146 in 1989. Murders committed by handguns numbered 8,915 in the United States during 1989. In stark contrast there were only 7 murders by handguns in the United Kingdom, 8 in Canada, and 19 in Sweden during the same year. There is one final shocking statistic that may increase public clamor for tougher firearms controls: Handguns increasingly claim the lives of children, with an average of one child under fourteen years of age killed by a handgun every day. Law enforcement officers have successfully challenged the firearms lobby on these issues. Furthermore, individual states are not as economically important to the firearms manufacturers and their lobbies.

Self-Defense Paraphernalia

Bulletproof clothing, and other bullet-resistant shields will become more common as the number of firearms and shootings increases. For example, the use of metal detectors at schools and in other public buildings is rapidly increasing. Bullet-resistant civilian clothing has even been developed for children! Terrorist attacks, kidnappings, and random thrill shooting all contribute to the development of protective gear to safeguard against shootings. Bullet-proof and even bomb-proof motor vehicles, briefcase shields, and Kevlar-jacketed, bullet-deflecting bibles are on the market.

Paraphernalia such as mace, incapacitating stun-guns, and disabling high-intensity lamps will not proliferate because potential buyers will realize that many more criminals will be armed with firearms, against which mace and other merely incapacitating devices are no match.

Explosives

Dynamite, plastic, detonators, triggering devices, and bombs will continue to be heavily regulated because manufacturers have not developed effective propaganda campaigns as in the firearms industry. Consequently, control of such substances or devices arouses little public or political opposition. Ingenious microtaggants identifying sources of supply have been developed to facilitate criminal investigations. These microscopic markers survive explosions and enable investigators to track down possible users.

Other Lethal Weapons

Crossbows, bows and arrows, martial arts equipment, and killer pets will be subject to increased legal controls. Organized pro-gun lobbies do not oppose such legislation and at times support it. Representative laws go so far as to ban dart guns, pea shooters, and slingshots. By 1985 twelve states banned the sales of martial arts weapons.

Weapons controls are nothing new. Pope Innocent II, expressing fear that the newly created cross-bow might wipe out Western civilization, issued a decree forbidding its use by any state against another. As new weapons are developed and come into use, efforts to prevent their illegal use and accidental deaths and injuries will continue.

[See also Crime, Violent; Crime Rates; Criminal Punishment; Weapons of Mass Destruction.]

BIBLIOGRAPHY

Davidson, Osha Gray. *Under Fire: The NRA and the Battle for Gun Control.* New York: Henry Holt, 1993.
Larson, Erik. *Lethal Passage.* New York: Crown, 1994.
Silberman, Charles. *Criminal Violence, Criminal Justice.* New York: Random House, 1978.
Wintemute, Garen. "Firearms as a Cause of Death in the United States." *Journal of Trauma* 27 (May 1987): 5.

— JOSEPH D. MCNAMARA

LIBERALISM, POLITICAL

From the beginning, America has been endowed with two enduring political traditions—conservatism and liberalism. Led by Secretary of State Thomas Jefferson and Secretary of the Treasury Alexander Hamilton in the opening administration of President George Washington, these rival systems of political thought competed for the nation's political soul. The creative, corrective, and balancing tension between liberalism and conservatism has been the genius of American democracy with its two-party system.

Part of the greatness of Washington, who is rightly known as "the father of his country," is that he successfully balanced the claims of Hamiltonian conservatism and Jeffersonian liberalism. The country's political balance and the health of its democracy are endangered when either of our central traditions—conservatism or liberalism—is denigrated and left undefended, as now seems to be the fate of liberalism.

It is not always easy to draw the distinction between these rival traditions, because most Americans, including our greatest leaders, have borrowed from both conservatism and liberalism. There is also an ongoing process of political realignment as historical circumstances change.

At the beginning, Hamilton—long admired as the apostle of conservatism—championed the causes of business, commerce, and the national bank, believing that the best way to serve those interests was through a strong national government. Jefferson, the apostle of liberalism, was the champion of small landholders, artisans, tradesmen, and—above all—individual liberty, believing that those concerns were best served by a limited national government with greater power in state and local hands.

With the passage of time, Andrew Jackson and other Democrats came to believe that the interests of the "common man" were better served by a stronger national government. In a sense they sought Jeffersonian ends by Hamiltonian means—the interests of the common man were advanced by a positive national governing authority.

Conservative and liberal principles were again mingled when Abraham Lincoln, the father of the Republican party, asserted that preserving the unity and the authority of the federal government was more important than states' rights. Lincoln's Republican views were so anathema to the slave-holding South that the southern states tried to withdraw from the federal union. They were prevented from doing so by Lincoln and the Union armies, but only after an incredible slaughter of Americans by Americans and the physical destruction of the South. The "solid South" remained fiercely Democratic for nearly the next century.

The Democrats found their strongest defining twentieth-century leaders in Woodrow Wilson, who shaped the progressivism and internationalism of the World War I era, and in Franklin Roosevelt, who launched the New Deal economic reforms of the 1930s and reasserted Wilsonian internationalism in the 1940s.

The liberalism and internationalism of Wilson and Roosevelt have remained the hallmarks of the Democratic party in much of the twentieth century to the present day. Although some Republicans have embraced New Deal liberalism and internationalism, most Republicans have preferred a more business-oriented, free enterprise, conservative approach. Their heroes have been McKinley, Hoover, Eisenhower, Taft, Nixon, and Reagan.

A new political alignment finds the Republican Party

growing stronger among constituencies once

considered safely Democratic.

In more recent years, the composition of both the generally liberal Democratic party and the generally conservative Republican party have been changing. The civil rights movement, championed largely by northern Democrats in the last four decades, alienated much of the southern Democratic establishment and sent the once solid Democratic South into the Republican party, except for the black voters.

Other issues, such as the Vietnam War, gun control, feminism, gay rights, abortion, arms control, and affirmative action, have further convinced many Southerners as well as some northern blue-collar workers, middle Americans, and religious fundamentalists that the Republican party was a more appropriate home. Some of these concerns, along with traditional "rugged individualism," also resonated in the American West.

Thus a new political alignment finds the Republican party growing stronger among constituencies once considered safely Democratic. It is now exceedingly difficult for a Democratic liberal-internationalist to win a national election, as witness the defeats of Adlai Stevenson, Hubert Humphrey, Walter Mondale, Michael Dukakis, and the author of this article. Even more conservative southern Democratic contenders such as Jimmy Carter and Bill Clinton are said to be too liberal for what appears to be an increasingly conservative electorate. The surest applause lines these days are those that assail the federal government. Washington, D.C., is now regarded as the Sodom and Gomorrah of America. The current Speaker of the House has gone so far as to declare that the occupants of the Clinton White House are not "normal people"—that, indeed, the president and first lady are "counter-culture McGoverniks."

What constitutes liberalism and conservatism in America today? Is the now beleaguered liberal heritage of the Democratic party worth reviving, or should we give up on the old-fashioned Democratic values and become "New Democrats" of some kind or another?

Perhaps I can best define conservatism through the eyes of my father—a Wesleyan Methodist clergyman and lifelong South Dakota Republican. He believed in a limited government of laws guided by the Constitution, which he placed second only to the Bible. He was opposed to deficit financing and to any extravagance in personal or public expenditures. He and my mother were living examples of self-reliance and personal responsibility. I always think of them when I think of conservatism at its best.

Liberalism is the philosophy I generally favor—although I have frequently borrowed from the insights of my parents and the conservative tradition. Liberalism combines much of the philosophies of Jefferson, Lincoln, Wilson, and Roosevelt—my four political heroes. Liberalism holds that there is a positive role for government in American life in such activities as ending slavery, opening up the West for settlement and development, conservation, pure food and drugs, child labor protection, Social Security, Medicare, public safety, civil rights, rural electrification, collective bargaining rights, student loans, and the environment.

In recent decades, liberalism has become identified also with new controversial political and social issues that have sometimes alienated Americans of both liberal and conservative leanings: court-ordered school busing, quotas and affirmative action, gun control, abortion, feminism, gay rights—and massive protests against the Vietnam War. The emergence of these issues is associated in the public mind with the sexual revolution and youthful lifestyles that seem to be marked by permissiveness, relaxed moral standards, risqué television and movie scripts, and the decline of family stability. The proliferation of government regulations, the litigation explosion, and high tax rates are further sources of tension and conflict for which liberals are frequently blamed.

Indeed, the argument has been widely advanced in recent elections and by new, right-wing talk show hosts that since liberals have been running the country for the past half-century, liberalism is responsible for the current troubled state of the nation. In fact, if liberalism is a threat to America, the nation should have been relatively safe these past four decades, because the long list of liberal presidential contenders mentioned earlier were all defeated. The White House since the Truman administration has been in Republican hands for twenty-eight years and in Democratic hands for fourteen years.

As for Congress, since 1938 a coalition of Republicans and equally conservative southern Democrats has been running that institution. The one exception to this was in 1964 and 1965, when President Lyndon Johnson's Great Society carried the day until it was overrun by the Vietnam War, which then dominated the nation and claimed its moral, political, and economic resources for a decade marked by rancorous and divisive internal conflict.

So where do we go from here? We should first recognize that America needs to nurture and maintain both of its historic political traditions—conservatism and liberalism. Each of these political value systems has contributed so much to our way of life that every American would be threatened if our nation were to fall under the grip of a single ideology unchallenged by a competing system of thought.

Would not both Democratic liberalism and Republican conservatism be enriched today by genuine debate between contrasting views of government and rival agendas rather than by simply arguing over how much of the Republican Contract with America should be swallowed by Democrats?

[See also Communitarianism; Conservatism, Political; Political Campaigning; Political Cycles; Political Parties; Political Party Realignment; Public Opinion Polls; Surveys; Third Political Parties; Voting.]

BIBLIOGRAPHY

Green, Mark, ed. *Changing America: Blueprints for the New Administration.* New York: Newmarket Press, 1992.

Griffin, David R., and Falk, Richard. *Postmodern Politics for a Planet in Crises: Policy, Process, and Presidential Vision.* Albany, NY: State University of New York Press, 1993.

Theobald, Robert. *Turning the Century: Personal and Organizational Strategies for Your Changed World.* Indianapolis, IN: Knowledge Systems, 1992.

Wishard, William Van Dusen. *The American Future (What Would George and Tom Do Now?).* Washington, DC: The Congressional Institute, 1992.

— GEORGE MCGOVERN

LIBERATION, WOMEN'S.

See WOMEN'S MOVEMENT.

LIBRARIES

Libraries historically have been places where information is stored for use. In the future, the library will be significantly changed by the technologies used to store, retrieve, and present information. Its basic purpose, however, will continue to fill humanity's basic need to find answers to questions.

In the past 6,000 years, information storage has come a long way. From clay tablets that could store about one character or symbol per cubic inch we have advanced to digital storage systems capable of billions of characters per cubic inch. Along the way there was papyrus and then paper, accommodating up to five hundred characters per cubic inch. Microfilm approached the density of modern electronic storage, but it was never widely accepted by library users as a convenient means of retrieval and display. In each of these cases, the purpose of placing symbols on some medium was to preserve and communicate information—the traditional purpose of libraries.

Some of the oldest libraries known to exist were in Mesopotamia and Egypt. They were filled with material collected by various methods, including conquest and persuasion. Access to their information was often restricted to an elite population of scholars, clergy, or other intelligentsia (lack of reading skills was a major barrier to access as well). Despite the role of these ancient libraries in preserving knowledge, very little of their collections has been preserved through the ages. While fire was blamed as the culprit in the destruction of the library of Alexandria, it is unlikely that the collection was destroyed in this way because parchment does not burn. The destruction of this vast collection, and many others, most likely was due to neglect, the ravages of war, lack of political and public support, and slow deterioration of the materials.

No era typifies the traditional problem of library material deterioration more than the early twentieth century, when paper for books was made from wood pulp rather than linen or rags. This wood-pulp, high-acid paper destroys itself over time in what has been referred to as a "slow fire." Historically, libraries have not played a significant role in the long-term survival of books, which was assured by the reprinting of great works by publishers. In this century, however, major efforts have been made by libraries to stop the "slow fires" of paper deterioration and to preserve material not likely to be reprinted.

The challenge of the library of today and tomorrow is to preserve and provide access to all forms of information.

The preservation issues of interest to libraries concerned with paper deterioration, however, are paled by a new "fire" rapidly consuming other forms of library-related material. As electronic information products evolve, the mechanisms for producing, storing, and retrieving this material evolve as well. Information stored digitally on a medium that was state-of-the-art twenty years ago is virtually unreadable today (e.g., round-hole punch cards or magnetic tape in proprietary formats from companies no longer in business). These technologically induced fires consume information at a far faster rate than the deterioration of paper ever did. The challenge of the library of today and tomorrow, then, is to preserve and provide access to all forms of information.

Just as technology is challenging libraries in their preservation role, so is it challenging them in their communication role. In the past, access was assured by physical possession of the material, and libraries measured their worth by the size of their collections. With the rapidly emerging technology of high-speed telecommunications, computing, and networking, it is no longer necessary to have material on site to have it accessible. This change in factors determining accessibility is shifting the distribution of materials from hard copy

Electronic networks make more information available all the time, creating the prospect of individuals accessing many libraries' worth of information from home. Public libraries worldwide will increase from 210,000 in 1995 to 500,000 in 2025. (Michael Dunne; Elizabeth Whiting & Associate/Corbis)

to electronic form (with the associated preservation problems mentioned above). While most material will continue to be available in print in paper form, access increasingly is in electronic form as well. Libraries must use scarce resources to assure access in traditional as well as emerging forms and formats, as long as information is published in a variety of media formats.

Librarians are struggling with maintaining three library functions or formats.

- The library of the past, focused on building collections and providing direct physical access to printed materials.
- The library of the present, with extraordinary added costs of inflation, automation, and, for many, the preservation of decaying material.
- The library of the future for which they must plan, which includes not only the development of new ideas, but the implementation of new prototypes for publishing, acquiring, storing, and providing access to information through new technology and new attitudes about such fundamental things as ownership and access.

As a result of emerging electronic information networks as well as traditional publishing expansion into new markets and interest areas, more information is available than at any time previously—so much that it would be well nigh impossible for any one person to absorb or grasp more than a fraction of what is out there. Many humans are capable of processing only a few hundred symbols per minute at best. At the same time, tools with prodigious instantaneous output focus on producing rather than absorbing and condensing information. For the librarian, the dilemma is significant: Will the profession continue to serve as an intermediary between users and information? Or will it create tools and methods to allow users to become self-sufficient?

If librarians are to build and maintain the information systems of tomorrow, they will have to collaborate with technical and business enterprises to design information delivery systems. The approach taken must be oriented to self-sufficient users capable of gleaning the information they need from the large stores of potentially relevant material. The technologies that will be applied in the library of the future may be beyond our imagination today, but not the purpose to which they will be put. They will enable citizens to be independent problem solvers, using information to address the challenges that are important to them.

[See also Communications; Information Overload; Information Society; Information Technology; Libraries: Electronic Format; Literature; Networking; On-Line Services; Printed Word.]

BIBLIOGRAPHY

Buckland, Michael. *Redesigning Library Services.* Chicago: American Library Association, 1992.

Frye, Billy E. "The University Context and the Research Library." *Library Hi Tech* 40 (1992): 27–37.

Gore, Daniel, ed. *Farewell to Alexandria.* Westport, CT: Greenwood Press, 1976.

Penniman, W. David. "The Library of Tomorrow." *Library Hi Tech* 40 (1992): 23–26.

– W. DAVID PENNIMAN

LIBRARIES: ELECTRONIC FORMAT

Forecasts relating to future capabilities of libraries date back at least to 1907 when John Cotton Dana described, probably facetiously, a "Who, What, and Why Machine" capable of dealing automatically with the questions for which answers are most frequently sought by library users. A decade ago, Lancaster (1982) identified several forecasts characterizing the future of libraries. These ranged from the conservative—the future library looks only cosmetically different from that of today—to the radical extreme—libraries as we now know them essentially disappear. Since these various forecasts were categorized and summarized, enough changes have occurred in library and information services to make the revolutionary scenarios increasingly credible.

Systems maintain electronic records of library materials from when they are ordered to when they are discarded. Automated circulation systems yield valuable management data on how the collection is used, as well as providing the more obvious records on who has borrowed what. Card and printed catalogs of library holdings have virtually disappeared, being replaced by online catalogs that can be consulted by users in the library or remote locations in the office, home, or elsewhere. These catalogs have been expanded allowing users access to other libraries' holdings on a regional, state, national, and even international basis. Not only can users find which library owns particular items, but they can determine whether these items are immediately available, and they may even be able to use the terminal to "charge" the items and request delivery to their offices. Moreover, the terminal or workstation that gives access to the library's catalog may also provide access to other electronic resources, such as indexes to the periodical literature or even to other resources, perhaps compiled by the library itself. Examples, in the case of a public library, include calendars of local events or car-pooling information. Indeed, what was once the catalog of the collection of a single library is now becoming essentially a window to a universe of information resources.

Traditionally, libraries have been judged by the size of their collections, a criterion perpetuated by agencies of accreditation and by the compilers of library statistics. It is now widely recognized that this is no longer meaningful for a variety of reasons: the continued rapid growth and diversity of the published and semipublished literature; the obsolescence of much material (collections are continuously "weeded" in some libraries); the decline of library budgets in purchasing power; and, perhaps most important, the sharing of resources among libraries facilitated by computer and telecommunications technologies—allowing access to a universe of information resources that is rapidly increasing in size and variety.

Between 1976 and 1982, Lancaster (1978, 1982), produced several scenarios that predicted the gradual "disembodiment" of the library: publications in print-on-paper form would gradually be replaced by publications in electronic form, many accessible through various networks. Carried to its logical conclusion, this would eventually result in a "library without walls" or, put somewhat differently, a situation in which every library would essentially "have" the same collection—the universe of information resources that is network-accessible.

At the time, these ideas were not widely accepted by librarians. Today, however, "access rather than ownership" has become virtually the motto of the profession.

Of course, what happens to the library in the future to a very large extent will depend on developments in related sectors, most obviously the publishing industry. The proportion of the world's publications issued in electronic form will presumably increase; thus, the proportion issued as print on paper will decline. What is less clear is the form that electronic publishing will take. How much will consist of resources that can only be accessed through networks and how much will actually be distributed, for purchase or lease, as CD-ROM, videotape, videodisk, electronic book (e.g., the Sony Data Discman), or formats yet to be devised?

While electronic resources that are distributed as physical artifacts (such as CD-ROM) can continue to be collected, those that exist only in network-accessible form present libraries with a completely different problem. Libraries have traditionally been builders of collections, but what does *collection building* really mean in an electronic world? Jutta Reed-Scott believes that "building collections will move from a static process of acquiring library resources to a more fluid position of providing access to information."

As the Internet expands into the much-publicized information superhighway, it seems reasonable to assume that present trends will continue—that electronic publishing will grow at the expense of printing on paper and that much of this output will be network-accessible rather than distributed. In such an environment, what happens to the library and what happens to the librarian?

Views on the future of the library as a physical facility range from one extreme to another. For example, the future public library might be electronically connected to all homes in the community and able to transmit recreational and informational services into these homes. Academic libraries could become mere study halls, because access to information resources would be provided directly by the various academic departments.

The future public library might be electronically connected to all homes in the community and able to transmit recreational and informational services into these homes.

Some see the library as becoming a kind of switching center, possibly also having such value-added responsibilities as user education. For example, William Britten has said that "libraries should not think primarily in terms of collecting information stored on networks, but should instead pursue strategies for teaching users how to locate and retrieve this information."

This agrees with the ideas of several prominent librarians, who see the library of the future as primarily a node in a vast information network. Frederick Kilgour, for example, believes that a major function of such a node will be to build local indexes to aid users in accessing remote sources.

Other librarians disagree with the view that the library should be a mere switching center. Ross Atkinson cautions that such a role can be performed by a computer center (e.g., on campus). A library must be much more if it is to survive. Atkinson urges that libraries must go beyond the role of interface to remote resources by taking on additional functions: downloading to local storage those resources most likely to be of value to the library's constituency; building new electronic information composites for users by drawing text and illustrations from various parts of the network; and possibly acting as electronic publisher (e.g., a university library might assume the role of publisher of the institution's own research output). If the continued growth of networked electronic publishing does in fact imply the decline or demise of the library as a physical facility, does it also imply the decline or demise of the librarian?

Unfortunately for the profession, the librarian is still viewed as primarily a custodian by a large part of the general public. But the librarian of today is, or should be, primarily an information or reading consultant, diagnosing the information or reading (or viewing or listening) needs of a library user and prescribing a solution. It is in this role that the real professional expertise lies.

If librarians are seen as consultants of this type rather than managers of physical facilities, they could have very important roles to play in even a networked "virtual" information environment. In fact, their value could actually increase. This view is espoused by Mark Eagle, Karen Drabenstott, Vicki Anders, Colleen Cook, and Roberta Pitts, among others. Drabenstott states:

A few reference staff will be physically present in the library building to assist users in person in collection navigation. Most reference staff will be posted on the network where they will respond to user calls for assistance by monitoring a user's ongoing search. Such calls could come from users who are navigating digital libraries from workstations in their home, dormitory rooms, or offices. . . . Staff could work out of their homes because they would use the capabilities of the information network to interact with users. . . . Public library environments would feature itinerant reference staff whose duties resemble today's information brokers.

Anders put it this way:

When everyone is plugged in, the librarian becomes the "gateway." . . . Presently, there are so many gateways that one needs a gateway to the gateways. This is the librarian's job—to interpret the means of access. . . . The gateway librarian who advises on the best route to information and interprets the language of access will have job security for years to come.

Other writers see the librarian transformed into a kind of "knowledge engineer," engaged in a variety of rather sophisticated information processing activities. Ray DeBuse claims that "some librarians will become hypertext engineers. . . . They will provide intellectual connections between the works of different authors or convert linear publications to hypermedia publications."

Some librarians are already working with the technologies of artificial intelligence and expert systems in an attempt to develop programs that will perform some of the tasks now performed by skilled librarians, such as cataloging, indexing, the selection of databases, the searching of databases, and the answering of factual-type questions. Many believe that this work must continue. Others caution that it is extremely difficult to replace the true human expert and that a danger exists that such systems will emulate the mediocre librarian rather than the expert.

Even if the library as physical facility does decline in importance, there is some agreement in the profession that the librarian could continue to play an important role as information intermediary.

[See also Communications; Information Overload; Information Society; Information Technology; Libraries; Literature; Networking; On-Line Services; Printed Word.]

BIBLIOGRAPHY

Anders, Vicki; Cook, Colleen; and Pitts, Roberta. "A Glimpse Into a Crystal Ball: Academic Libraries in the Year 2000." *Wilson Library Bulletin* 67 (October 1992): 36–40.

Atkinson, Ross. "Text Mutability and Collection Administration." *Library Acquisitions: Practice and Theory* 14 (1990): 355–358.

Birdsall, William F. *The Myth of the Electronic Library: Librarianship and Social Change in America.* Westport, CT: Greenwood Press, 1994.

Dougherty, Richard M., and Hughes, Carol. *Preferred Futures for Libraries.* Mountain View, CA, Research Libraries Group, 1991.

Kilgour, Frederick G. "The Metamorphosis of Libraries during the Foreseeable Future." In *Libraries and the Future: Essays on the Library in the Twenty-first Century,* ed., F. Wilfrid Lancaster. Binghamton, NY: Haworth Press, 1993.

Lancaster, F. Wilfrid. *Libraries and Librarians in an Age of Electronics.* Arlington, VA: Information Resources Press, 1982.

———. *Toward Paperless Information Systems.* New York: Academic Press, 1978.

Martyn, John; Vickers, Peter; and Feeney, Mary, eds. *Information UK 2000.* London: Bowker-Saur, 1990.

Reed-Scott, Jutta. "Information Technologies and Collection Development." *Collection Building* 9/3–4, (1989): 47–51.

Riggs, Donald E., and Sabine, Gordon A. *Libraries in the '90s: What the Leaders Expect.* Phoenix, AZ: Oryx, 1988.

Von Wahlde, Barbara, and Schiller, Nancy. "Creating the Virtual Library: Strategic Issues." In Laverna M. Saunders, ed. *The Virtual Library: Visions and Realities.* Westport, CT: Meckler, 1993.

— F. WILFRID LANCASTER

LIFE ON OTHER PLANETS.

See EVOLUTION: LIFE-FORMS IN THE UNIVERSE; EXTRATERRESTRIAL LIFE-FORMS.

LIFE SCIENCES

The past fifty years since the discovery of DNA have seen sweeping changes in life sciences, and the future promises more. Modern biology has been changed by the availability of close-up images of cell structure, called ultrastructure, produced by electron microscopes. Molecular biology has provided evidence for what were once considered fanciful ideas, turning theory into truths.

Outdated encyclopedias and old textbooks divide all life into either animals, the object of study of zoology, and plants, the object of study of botany. When the Dutchman Anton van Leeuwenhoek used an early version of the microscope to peer at microorganisms for the first time, he described them as minute animals. Such animals came to be known as *protozoa,* from Greek words meaning "first animals." Protozoa is a term whose use has only now begun to fade. All moving organisms, even the smallest, were classified as a form of animal—unless they were green, or not sufficiently rapid, in which case they were considered primitive plants.

Like the chimera, a mythical creature of antiquity combining lion, goat, and snake, all plants and animals are highly organized bacterial monsters.

Ernst Haeckel (1834–1919), questioning the plant/animal dichotomy, recognized a vast array of diversity in the microscopic world, especially in plankton. Considering microbes more primitive than plants and animals and assigning them their own kingdom (the *monera*), Haeckel asserted that microbes were the ancestors of all larger organisms. Enigmas such as *Euglena gracilis,* a photosynthetic swimmer that seemed to combine the traits of both plants and animals, and yet as a single cell was really neither, were accommodated in the Haeckelian kingdom of the very small.

Haeckel's three-kingdom system, never broadly adopted, has given way to the five-kingdom system, which recognizes the importance of the *bacteria,* the oldest kingdom, some of whose members combined to give rise to the other four kingdoms. Bacteria lack nuclei in their cells; they include about 15,000 described types, including 500 estimated genera of the distinctive archaebacteria. The second kingdom of organisms to appear in the fossil record of evolution, the *protoctists,* includes all organisms composed of cells with nuclei and not accommodated in the three kingdoms of larger organisms: plants, animals, and fungi.

The ancient division between plants and animals has been entirely replaced with the recognition that the biggest difference distinguishing life forms is whether their cells lack nuclei (bacteria) or not (all other organisms). If an organism is composed of cells with nuclei—either one cell with one nucleus, like an amoeba, or many cells with many nuclei, like mushrooms, rose bushes, and human beings—the organism is considered *eukaryotic.* The term *eukaryotic* comes from Greek words meaning "true" (*eu*) and "seeded" (*karyon*). Cells that do not have nuclei are called prokaryotic, from *pro,* meaning "before" in ancient Greek, and *karyon.* Prokaryotes, cells without nuclei, is another name for bacteria. The essential structural and chemical differences between bacteria (prokaryotes) and all other life-forms on Earth, eukaryotes, have been confirmed by microscopic, biochemical, and genetic studies.

Modern biology has revealed something even more startling than the essential similarities between plants and animals. We now know that all plants, animals, fungi, and protoctists—the four kingdoms of eukaryotic organisms—evolved from bacteria. Cells with nuclei also have an area around the nucleus inside the cell. This egg white-like area is called the *cytoplasm.* Inside the cytoplasm of most protoctists and all plants, animals, and fungi are structures known as *mitochondria.* The mitochondria of complex, nucleated cells respire oxygen in a chemical reaction that provides cells with the energy they need to function. Although the bacterial ancestry of mitochondria was suspected in the late nineteenth century, the last two decades have revealed beyond a reasonable doubt that mitochondria are the living remnants of bacteria that invaded, or were eaten by, larger cells. In addition to mitochondria, all plants and algae (all the photosynthetic protoctists) have *plastids* in their cells. When green (they can also be red, yellow, and brown), plastids are called *chloroplasts.* Plastids of any color carry out the essential "plantlike" process of photosynthesis, in which, using the energy of the sun, carbon from carbon dioxide in the air reacts with hydrogen from water molecules. Photosynthesis assembles the carbon-hydrogen compounds forming the active chemistry of cells, simultaneously releasing the oxygen from water. Plastids, like mitochondria, are remains of captive bacteria that, trapped inside the cytoplasm of larger cells, continued to function. Molecular biology, which analyzes and compares the sequences of base pairs in DNA, has confirmed that all cells with nuclei are the result of living mergers between distinct kinds of bacteria. Like the chimera, a mythical creature of antiquity combining lion, goat, and snake, all plants and animals are highly organized bacterial monsters.

As we look to the future, lessons can be drawn from the processes of life's past. Darwin's theory once represented evolution as a bloody struggle in which each being battles others and only the strong survive. The actual scientific record of life, however, suggests just as strongly that long-term interaction, including the close physical association known as symbiosis, is required for survival. *Symbiosis,* from the Greek words meaning "to live together," is the biological term for the process in which distinct life forms are in protracted close association. *Endosymbiosis* refers to cells or animals, perhaps initially hostile, that come to dwell inside each other. Some photosynthetic algae, for example, have merged with microbes called ciliates; still others have insinuated themselves into the hair follicles of polar bears, giving the white animals a greenish tint.

As life-forms, thought to have first evolved some four billion years ago, grow into each other and the surface mineral environment of Earth, the necessity to live with other beings becomes ever more intense. As human beings trying to ensure a long-term future on this planet, we may learn from organisms such as the latter-day bacteria that still dwell as mitochondria in each of our cells: the most successful life-forms have not been isolated from the rest of life on Earth, nor have they been mere stewards magnanimously helping other life-forms. Rather, the most abundant life-forms are those that have literally embedded themselves in a living landscape and joined their destiny to the lives of beings greater than they. If we substitute ourselves for mitochondria, and the living Earth for the larger bacterial cells that the ancestors of mitochondria originally entered, we will find the lesson that our own future success may depend upon our learning to live and recycle our material waste in settings still rich in the estimated 3–30 million non-human life-forms with which we share this planet's surface.

[See also Biodiversity; Evolution, Biological; Extinction of Species.]

BIBLIOGRAPHY

Margulis, Lynn, and Sagan, Dorion. *Microcosmos: Four Billion Years of Microbial Evolution.* New York: Touchstone Books, 1991.
———. *What Is Life?* New York: Simon & Schuster, 1995.
Sagan, Dorion. *Biospheres: Reproducing Planet Earth.* New York: Bantam, 1990.
Wilson, Edward O. *The Diversity of Life.* Cambridge, MA: Harvard University Press, 1992.

– DORION SAGAN
LYNN MARGULIS

LIFESTYLES, ALTERNATIVE

Powerful trends are changing the way we live and work. Three driving trends illustrate our predicament. Within a generation, world reserves of easily accessible oil are expected to be depleted, there will be another 3 billion persons on the planet, and the world's climate is expected to heat up as a result of the greenhouse effect. Without cheap petroleum to provide the pesticides and fertilizers for high-yield agriculture, and with the real prospect of droughts due to climate changes, the likelihood of massive famines seems very high. When ozone depletion, rainforest destruction, soil erosion, acid rain, and species extinction, are factored in, it becomes all the more obvious that we face an unprecedented and intertwined pattern of challenges. Dramatic adjustments in our manner of living are indicated.

We have two options—we can adapt, either by choice or necessity. If we adapt by choice, we can mobilize our creativity and commitment to build a sustainable and satisfying future. If we ignore the trends converging around us and are forced to adapt by necessity, our future is likely to be insecure, divisive, and mean-spirited.

We face a crisis in the interconnected global system, and changes at every level are needed. At a personal level, citizens of developed nations need to adopt simple lifestyles. At a neighborhood level, we need to build new types of communities designed for sustainable living. At a national level, we need to adopt new policies with regard to energy, environment, education, and media. At a global level, economically developed nations need to forge a new partnership with developing nations. Envisioning and implementing this broad range of changes is the new global challenge.

As individuals, we need to undertake a conscious social experiment in developing simpler or more ecological ways of living. Although there is no cookbook for ecological living, certain common themes often characterize this approach to life: developing the full spectrum of one's potentials: physical, emotional, intellectual, and spiritual; reducing undue clutter by giving away or selling seldom-used things that would be useful to others; buying products that are nonpolluting, energy-efficient, and easy to repair; recycling metal, glass, and paper, and cutting back on things that use nonrenewable resources; eating foods lower on the food chain—less meat, sugar, and highly processed foods; cultivating the ability to do one thing at a time, with full attention and appreciation; and pursuing a livelihood or work that contributes to the well-being of the world.

A simpler life should not be equated with a return to the past or turning away from technological progress. The problems of the modern era require us not to move backwards but to move ahead so that we are no longer an enemy of nature but a part of it. Nor should simpler living be equated with moving to a rural area and living on a farm; to the contrary, our cities are one of the most important places for developing ecological approaches to living. An ecological way of life is not a retreat from progress; in fact, it is essential to the advance of our civilization.

To limit the damaging impact of our consumption of natural resources, persons in developed nations will have to do more than cut back at the margins. They will need to restructure their lives and design more sustainable neighborhoods or "ecovillages." For example, a city block or suburban block could be transformed from isolated houses into an organic cluster of housing types, gardens, shops, and areas for living and working. Each microcommunity could specialize in specific areas of interest to provide satisfying work for many of its inhabitants (for example, crafts, health care, child care, gardening, art, education, and so on). Each ecovillage could have a community garden for local food production, a system of recycling, a telecommuting center, and perhaps a solar energy system. If each microcommunity were designed to reflect the values and interests of different groups of people, it would foster an exciting diversity of designs for living. These ecocommunities could have the feeling and cohesiveness of a small town and would provide a strong foundation for building a sustainable future.

We also need new policies at the national level that support changes at the personal and neighborhood level. We need to develop renewable sources of energy—solar, wind, geothermal, and biomass—and make the transition away from nonrenewable energy. We need to invest in fiber-optic communications networks so people have the "information highways" essential for living and working productively in the next century. We need to invest in the education of our children and the continuing education of adults. Furthermore, we need vigorous environmental policies that protect Earth's air, land, and water.

In a sustainable economy, work will be far more purposeful—emphasizing activities that are essential to the well-being of people. Such an economy offers the intangible but immensely important benefit of generating a wide range of satisfying jobs: building renewable energy systems, retrofitting and rebuilding our neighborhoods, providing life-long education in practical skills, redesigning and rebuilding our waste recycling systems, and rebuilding our transportation systems to be as energy-efficient as possible. No one should lack a meaningful job in an economy oriented toward sustainability.

Currently, television is being programmed primarily for commercial success, and as a result, our civilizational consciousness is being programmed for ecological failure. We need a new social ethic that holds the mass media accountable for how it programs our society's consciousness. Such an approach can help to break through the cultural hypnosis of consumerism and augment it with programming that fosters a sustainability consciousness. We need to use the mass media in ways that help awaken a new understanding and caring for the planet and the future. The point is not to condemn television; rather, it is to acknowledge our great need for balance and perspective in our diet of images and information so we can take a healthy approach to consumption.

At a global level, we need a new partnership with and commitment to developing nations, where more than a billion persons live at the very edge of existence in absolute poverty. Just to survive, people must often take actions in the short run that result in greater environmental destruction in the longer run. More compassionate and less wasteful living by affluent nations is vital to serve the well-being of all. With simplicity, an increasing increment of national wealth can be used to provide food, housing, health care, and education to those who are homeless and otherwise in desperate need. With basic necessities assured, the whole human family can work together to restore the environment.

More compassionate and less wasteful living by affluent nations is vital to the well-being of all.

There are hopeful visions of a workable and meaningful future. We have but a few crucial decades in which to make essential changes, voluntarily—the blink of an eye in the lifespan of civilizations. We need leadership that calls forth a new global dream of ecological lifestyles, steady efforts to rebuild our communities at the local scale, good jobs that are satisfying and contributory, new energy policies, mature uses of the mass media, and so on. Overall, we need a "politics of sustainability" that recognizes the dramatic changes occurring in the world and the need to respond in a coherent and determined way at every level of life.

We also need a new level of citizenship. Few politicians will be willing to advocate the sweeping changes required to achieve sustainability until they are assured that their constituencies will support them. When citizens can tell their leaders with conviction where they want to go and how fast they want to get there, then leaders can do their job. Before our leaders can act with confidence, citizens need to revitalize the conversation of democracy by engaging in an entirely new level of dialogue that builds a working consensus for the future. Regular "electronic town meetings" held over television that consider a key issue in detail and then obtain feedback from a scientific sample of citizens, offer a powerful way for citizens to discover their common views and to communicate with their representatives in government.

We can prosper, live purposeful lives, advance our civilizations, enrich our cultures, and serve the well-being of the world. With an engaged citizenry, strong leadership, and ecological approaches to living, we can rise to the new global challenge of building a sustainable and satisfying future.

[See also Animal Rights; Deforestation; Energy, Renewable Sources of; Global Environmental Problems; Green Revolution; Lifestyles, Value-Oriented; Natural Resources, Use of; Sustainability.]

BIBLIOGRAPHY

Gutknecht, Douglas B., and Butler, Edgar W. *Family, Self and Society: Emerging Issues, Alternatives and Interventions.* Lanham, MD: University Press of America, 1986.

Harland, John. *Brave New World: A Different Projection.* Rochester, WA: Sovereign Press, 1984.

Partridge, William L. *The Hippie Ghetto: The Natural History of a Subculture.* Prospect Heights, IL: Waveland Press, 1985.

— DUANE S. ELGIN

LIFESYTLES, ETHNIC

The second half of the twentieth century has been characterized by political, social, and cultural movements toward localized, regionalistic, and isolationistic heterogeneity. After the end of World War II, many new, independent nations were freed from colonial subjugation. In the 1960s, two types of movements held sway in the United States: ethnic minority groups asserting their own cultures and civil rights in the form of black power, brown power, red power, and yellow power; and hippies turning inward individually or forming secluded groups with slogans such as "Drop out!" or "Tune in!" or "Turn on!" or "Grow your own potatoes!" The first movement was an assertion and revival of suppressed ethnic cultures. The second was a withdrawal. Similar withdrawal occurred in Germany during the 1950s in the form of *ohne mich*-ism ("without me-ism"), in which freedom was interpreted as freedom *from* social and political involvement. By the 1970s, the minority group movements expanded to include gray power, gay power, and women power. Then, in the early 1990s, we witnessed another surge of movements toward independence: this time within countries such as the former Soviet Union, Yugoslavia, and Czechoslovakia. All this prompted worry about the segmentation of society.

Trends in the opposite direction became gradually noticeable in the 1980s, however. The formation of the European common market was intended to increase economic interaction and mutual benefit without destroying the cultures and languages in Europe. Less publicized was the massive migration of people in Europe; first from south to north, then from east to west. The first migrations from Turkey, Yugoslavia, and other Southern European countries to Germany and Sweden continued for several decades and were a demand-pull phenomenon: factories in Germany and Sweden needed factory workers. The number of migrants was considerable, but not threatening to the cultures of the host countries. By contrast, the post-*perestroika* migration from Eastern Europe to the West is a different phenomenon. There simply are no jobs, housing, schools, or medical facilities to accommodate even a fraction of these new immigrants. Drastic social and legal changes are inevitable. There is a new anxiety rampant in Europe, caused by these massive westward migrations, coming as they do on top of continuing migrations from the south. This time it is not the oppression of powerful governments, but poor, powerless foreign individuals that are the source of the anxiety. The xenophobic reactions sometimes take on neo-Fascist dimensions, or are reflected in the revival of the Ku Klux Klan and other racist activities in the United States fostered by rising unemployment—itself a result of the loss of international competitiveness by American business firms.

Japan, after some time lag, is now encountering similar problems. There was a shortage of engineers and factory workers in Japan, and many migrants from China, Taiwan, Iran, and Southeast Asia filled these needs, often illegally. Labor shortages still exist in some categories of work, and the Japanese immigration law has undergone successive modifications to legalize foreign workers. The number of Brazilians, Peruvians and Argentines, in particular, has increased in Japan. Yet, workers of unwanted categories arrive in large numbers, either with tourist visas (after which they stay over illegally), or in boats as fake political refugees. Japanese schools, health-care facilities, and housing cannot accommodate these legal and illegal foreigners. Some illegal foreigners behave well and cause no problems. For example, when recently, Iranians who could not find or afford living accommodations, congregated and slept in Japanese parks, they did no harm to the community. But the illegal workers are not eligible for medical insurance, and in the past, hospitals have had to absorb the costs of their care. The Japanese social system has not adjusted to such new situations.

Whatever the circumstances, one trend is unmistakable: all industrialized countries are becoming multiethnic and multicultural. The "original" inhabitants of these countries—for example, native Swedes or native Japanese—in contrast to foreigners, are individually heterogenizing themselves, choosing and taking up aspects of various foreign cultures. Even though some still believe that international contacts will lead to homogenization, the reverse is occurring, imperceptibly at first, but more and more visibly as we move toward the twenty-first century.

Fallacious Assumptions Held in the Twentieth Century

Some of the assumptions commonly held in the social sciences and psychology are incorrect. Examples are: (1) each culture is perfect and should never be changed; (2) all "normal" individuals in a given culture are acculturated and are epistemologically and psychologically homogeneous; (3) babies are born with a blank mind, to be filled with culture; (4) a culture is a mentally healthy environment for all its "normal" members; (5) rapid social change is traumatic to all persons; (6) cross-cultural or cross-national migration increases anxiety; (7) contact with many cultures will make the individual lose his/her identity.

These fallacious assumptions stem from epistemological errors made in the twentieth century. Incorrect epistemologies (i.e., knowledge theories or frameworks) were also sources of various political and social phenomena such as the colonialism that began in the sixteenth century; the isolationism, separatism, and regionalism of the twentieth century; and the seclusionistic aspects of the hippy movement in the 1960s. The interactive and interwoven cultural and individual heterogeneity of the twenty-first century will require a new epistemological framework.

Coming Decades

Massive cross-national migrations and cross-national career advancement in international business firms, and other professional and private movements of people across national boundaries are making each society more multiethnic and multicultural. The world is moving toward interwoven and interactive heterogeneity instead of localized, regionalized, and isolationistic homogeneity.

At the same time, the accessibility to information, entertainment, and lifestyles from many cultures is increasingly available to each individual, providing more opportunities for self-heterogenization and the creation of individually unique combinations for ego identity. Self-heterogenization comes from the increased accessibility to different cultures, lifestyles, entertainments, foods, and languages. One can choose from an array of foreign books, videocassettes, and other commodities, can as it were turn them on and off and assemble one's own eclectic combinations. As a result, one is an active pattern-maker, not a passive victim of one radio station or a single newspaper as occurred at the beginning of mass-media technology. Today, there are many television channels to choose from, including programs from foreign countries.

Exposure to heterogeneity does not mean a loss of identity for individuals. It means a more unique individual identity. The same can be said of each nation. Increased immigration does not mean the loss of national identity. Rather, it provides an opportunity for making the nation more unique in redesigning its educational system, welfare system, community planning, and other systems.

Still, it requires hard work. The problems of unemployment, housing shortages, and meeting basic needs are enormous. Yet they should not be regarded as an unwelcome evil. They are a necessary step toward a new stage of our social evolution—toward an interwoven and interactive heterogeneity.

[See also Ethnic and Cultural Separatism; Global Culture; Global Statistics; Internal Migration, United States; Lifestyles, Alternative; Lifestyles, Regional; Lifestyles, Value-Oriented; Migration, International.]

BIBLIOGRAPHY

Maruyama, Magoroh. "Human Futuristics and Urban Planning." *Journal of American Institute of Planners* 29 (1973): 346–357.
———. "Interwoven and Interactive Heterogeneity in the Twenty-first Century." *Technological Forecasting and Social Change* 45 (1994): 93–102.
———. "Mindscapes and Science Theories." *Current Anthropology* 21 (1980): 589–599.
———. "The New Logic of Japan's Young Generations." *Technological Forecasting and Social Change* 28 (1985): 351–364.

— MAGOROH MARUYAMA

LIFESTYLES, REGIONAL

Without fanfare, the Congressional Office of Technological Assessment in 1987 estimated that only 50,000 farms would produce 75 percent of America's food by 2000. Nothing was said about the other predictable effects of fewer farms and farm-based small towns: family breakdown, crime, failing schools, homelessness, or social polarization, all of which are likely to worsen. Societies that become too urbanized and cut off from their rural roots begin to drift toward biological and cultural extinction.

In the America of the future, regions with more farms and small towns—for example, New England and the Midwest—will stay culturally healthy longer. If farms continue to go under, farm-based small towns will either face extinction or become inhabited by culturally urbanized commuters to a city.

Lifestyles and culture are not the same thing. A culture is a ready-made design for living, with behavior and views on family, religion, work, and morality handed down from generation to generation. For example, some Jewish cultural traits go back about 160 generations to Abraham's departure from Ur. In villages the world over, race and religion aside, there is a common universal culture. Villages are made up of people who farm land. Naturally, they put prime value on property (land) and family (the work unit). Consequently, property and family are the basic rural social institutions, along with a work ethic and agricultural moral code ("You help me with my harvest, and I'll help you with yours").

California led the shift from inherited culture to freely chosen lifestyles, followed by the South. The late twentieth century saw a great shift of farms away from the South (52 percent of the American total in 1950, half that in the 1990s) to the Midwest (32 percent to 51 percent over the same period). But California's problem is complicated—some might say alleviated—by millions of immigrants, mostly from Mexico and Latin America, but also from Asia, who do possess strong rural-based cultural traits, including high birthrates.

As in highly urbanized Russia and Europe, the birthrate among the white population of the United States declined below the replacement rate in 1972. (This is also related to farms: Over long spans of history, city dwellers fail to reproduce themselves at replacement rates while rural people fail to limit births.) In California, if existing rates of birth and migration are maintained, Americans of European descent will soon become a minority class. If Spanish-speaking immigrants keep their language and culture, California will soon be more Latino than Yankee, with a predominantly Asian professional elite.

California's biological and cultural dilemma is also complicated by the emergence of *lifestyles,* a word coined to fit a new late twentieth-century reality. Per capita GNP of $10,000–$30,000 over much of North America and Europe and the more urbanized parts of East Asia allow people to do something totally new in human society: namely, to live freely according to individual choice. Lifestyles are freely chosen; like fashions, they can be tried, kept, or discarded, something American commercial pop culture has been quick to exploit. American television and films penetrated to the world's remotest villages in the 1980s. Most people on Earth now see America as a splendid land of star treks, star wars, and stardust, where Superman swoops among skyscrapers, Batman and Dick Tracy keep the peace, and Jane Wyman fights for her vineyards and water rights.

The instant gratification and a refusal to subordinate a personal impulse to any larger social purpose or solidarity, which are implicit in lifestyles of what has been called "yuppie" behavior, help to polarize society and make cultural reproduction that much harder. As biological knowledge and computer technology explode, and galaxies and molecules are charted as never before, those in computers, semiconductors, telecommunications, robotics, electronics, politics, and the media prosper, but others do poorly.

A culture does not reproduce itself automatically from generation to generation. Families pass it on, helped by schools and churches. The experience of African Americans is illustrative. In the early 1940s, 75 percent of African Americans lived in the mainly rural South. As agriculture mechanized, 95 percent of all black-operated tenant farms—about 350,000—went under from 1950 to 1970. At the same time, white tenant farms dropped by 70 percent in the South, a decline involving about 1 million units. In 1988, 33,250 black-owned farms were left, but those families were expected to virtually disappear by 2000.

A culture does not reproduce itself automatically from generation to generation. Families pass it on, helped by schools and churches.

Where have they been going? To the cities of the North and West. Between 1940 and 1980 Chicago went from 8 percent to 40 percent black, Detroit from 9 percent to 63 percent, Washington, D.C. from 28 percent to 70 percent. A good many, perhaps half, made it into the middle class and accept its values. Those left behind are isolated in the ugliest, loneliest, most alienated and rootless, most crime-ridden, and most poorly educated slums in America. Many children are brought up by semiliterate teenage mothers on welfare in crowded public housing. America's 31 million African Americans in 1992, 12 percent of its people, learned less, earned less, lived worse, and died younger than anybody else. Homicide was the leading cause of death among young people. One young black man in four was either in prison, on parole, or on probation. Median black family income was 56 percent of whites, and blacks were twice as likely to be jobless. Nearly a third of all blacks, versus 10 percent of whites, lived below the poverty level, among them 45 percent of all black children.

African Americans show what could happen wherever people lose the natural apprenticeship to adult life that rural families used to give their children. In a city, the family is no longer the work unit, work itself is monetarized, teaching has shifted from parents to schools and to the mass media and to other youths, who educate peers according to their own antisocial norms. In inner-city neighborhoods, African Americans, Asians, Hispanics, and whites are caught in the same cultural trap, a subculture that produces youngsters unfit for anything but crime.

One way to solve this crisis of cultural reproduction is through a reruralization of America. This means a return to farms and small towns, to the family as the unit of both home and work to solve the problem of nurture and cultural transmission. No half-steps, like the essentially failed experiment of suburbia, which lacks a farm-based economy, can culturally work. (See

India for another perspective on the matter of reruralization.)

Without this reruralization, cultural contradictions will continue to come together, clash, ignite, and explode—as has already happened in Los Angeles.

[See also Change; Change, Cultural; Change, Epochal; Cities, North American; Ethnic and Cultural Separatism; Families and Households; India; Lifestyles, Alternative; Lifestyles, Ethnic; Lifestyles, Value-Oriented; Religion: Changing Beliefs; Social Controls; Values Change.]

BIBLIOGRAPHY

Critchfield, Richard P. *Villagers: Changed Values, Altered Lives: The Closing of the Urban-Rural Gap.* New York: Doubleday, 1994.

— RICHARD P. CRITCHFIELD

LIFESTYLES, VALUE-ORIENTED

Individual and social values are both products of their times and shaped by them. The values of the baby-boom generation, for example, stemmed largely from the increasing levels of education, affluence, and technology available in the 1950s and '60s. Those baby-boom values in turn gave shape not only to individual lifestyles but also to the social movements of those times: to the women's, minorities', consumer, and environmental movements that have endured and grown; and to the counterculture and me-generation attitudes that have largely faded.

Values and lifestyles of the future will reflect the influence of forces shaping the 1990s:

- Economic and financial concerns will play a much greater role in most Americans' daily lives as industries struggle to adapt to global competition and national economic restructuring affects employment levels.

- Demographic trends point to an aging population and increasing ethnic diversity.
- The baby-boom generation will reach middle age, pass through their own midlife crises, and emerge to assume leadership positions in business and politics.
- Women in increasing numbers will continue to assume new economic and political roles, but may opt for more flexible ways to combine their work and home lives.
- Environmentalism will spread, focusing more on local or indoor threats to human health and on planetwide concerns such as acid rain, ozone depletion, and the greenhouse effect.
- "Cocooning," a tendency to center one's life on one's home, will increase as technologies expand potentials to work and play at home and as people seek a retreat from the strains of public life.
- Time pressures, or at least individuals' perceptions of them, will intensify as the pace of change quickens and complexity increases in every facet of life.

There is no certainty as to how exactly these forces will play out, let alone what their effects on lifestyles will actually turn out to be. Speculation about the future is better focused on a range of alternative outcomes—"scenarios"—so that the full spectrum of possibilities comes to light. A framework for such speculation can be derived from the interplay of two critical dimensions of uncertainty—economic restructuring and the sociocultural environment. These uncertainties raise two key questions:

1. Will U.S. (and global) economic restructuring proceed successfully and relatively smoothly? Or will it be volatile and have only partial success?
2. Will private (personal) agendas converge with or diverge from public (social and political) agendas? Such a shift is akin to Arthur Schlesinger's theme of alternating cycles between "private interest" and "public purpose."

Clearly, there will be major differences in the patterns of lifestyles, depending on which scenario develops.

TABLE 1

SHIFTS IN U.S. CONSUMER LIFESTYLE GROUPS, 1988–2000 (PERCENT OF ADULT POPULATION)*

Group	1988	Year 2000 Scenarios			
		Freewheeling Consumption	Neoconsumerism	Stagnation and Conflict	Return of Commonweal
Actualizers	8	13	12	8	9
Fulfilleds	11	15	15	14	15
Believers	16	15	15	13	16
Achievers	13	11	12	12	12
Strivers	13	13	15	14	15
Experiencers	12	11	8	6	9
Makers	12	10	11	15	10
Strugglers	14	14	14	18	16

*Totals may not add to 100 because of rounding.

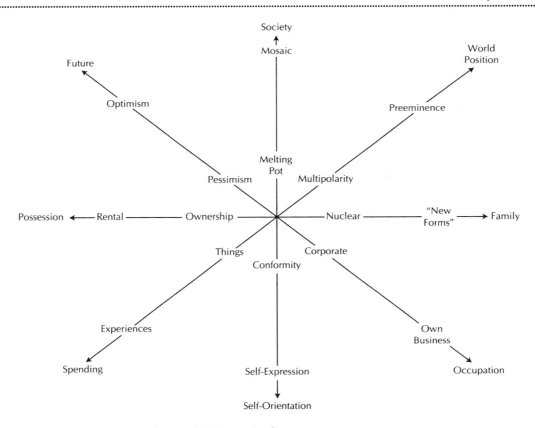

Figure 1. The American Dream: axes or a reshaping. (SRI International)

Stanford Research Institute's (SRI's) Values and Lifestyles typology (see Table 1) portrays the following shifts among U.S. consumers: Generally, all four scenarios provide a favorable social environment for Actualizers and especially for Fulfilleds. In large part, this development reflects the aging of the baby-boom generation and that large cohort's increasing access to substantially greater resources. It also reflects a warming of sociocultural concerns in America. On the other hand, the numbers of Experiencers and, to a lesser extent, Makers will most likely decline, in part because both groups represent entry points into the system for new adults; and the overall shift toward an older, more mature population will move the social focus away from the youthful experiences that have dominated the past two or three decades. Finally, the Strivers and, even more, the Strugglers will probably increase as a percentage of the adult population, reflecting the nation's struggle to deal with the problems of economic restructuring (particularly in the "Stagnation" and "Commonweal" scenarios).

Another perspective on future lifestyles can be discerned in the reshaping of the "American Dream" by these same formative forces. The post—World War II version of "the Dream" was summarized by Robert Settle and Pamela Alreck in the March 1988 issue of *Marketing Communication:*

> Knowing that they had saved the world, Americans were thoroughly immersed in optimism and conformity. The good job with a large company, marriage and family, the new suburban tract home, and the station wagon and car coat to go with it. Dad worked, but Mom usually didn't. He had the job. She had the kids. It was all pretty nice. And for those baby-boom kids, it was going to be even nicer when they grew up. They firmly believed it and expected it.

We can anticipate that these forces will reshape the values and lifestyles associated with this Dream along eight axes or dimensions:

1. *Revisioning society*—from the centralizing, homogeneous tendencies of the "melting pot" to the decentralizing, diversifying "mosaic society" of the future.

2. *Reassessing U.S. world position*—from the unquestioned world dominance of the late 1940s, through confrontation with the former com-

511

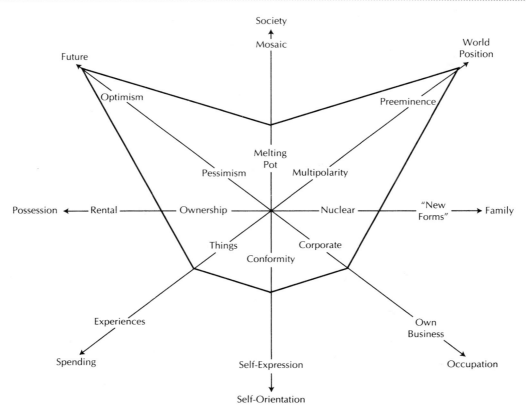

Figure 2. The Old Dream. (SRI International)

munist bloc, to the uncertainties of a multipolar world (as the sole remaining superpower).

3. *Redefining family*—from the Norman Rockwell nuclear family of the 1950s to the many new definitions of "family" in the 1990s.

4. *Realigning occupation*—from the aspiration of stable corporate employment to the reality of uncertain job restructuring and the pursuit of multiple careers in a lifetime.

5. *Reorienting self*—from outer-directed conformity to inner-directed self-actualization (if economic circumstances permit).

6. *Revaluing spending*—"from the acquisition of products with utility to the enjoyment of experiences with intensity," as futurist Jay Ogilvy has phrased it.

7. *Rethinking ownership*—from the pride (and status) of ownership to the growing convenience of leasing and renting.

8. *Reappraising the future*—from the boundless optimism of the postwar era to caution about an uncertain future and, in some cases, a lowering of consumer expectations.

The nature and extent of this "reshaping" can be illustrated graphically by means of three charts. This representation should not be taken too literally, but it does suggest a deeper and more serious truth: the United States is no longer the nation it was even forty years ago—in many important ways, Americans think differently, behave differently, and dream differently than we did. And these differences can only expand in the future.

SRI's Typology of Lifestyles

SRI International's Values and Lifestyles (VALS 2); program groups consumers into eight segments within a conceptual framework of "self-orientation" and "resources available." Self-orientation distinguishes between those who make decisions with a "principle-orientation" (e.g., using criteria such as quality, integrity, tradition) and those who are either "status-oriented" or "action-oriented." The eight types are as follows:

- *Actualizers* have sufficient resources to have a unique orientation—a mixture of the active and the reflective. As consumers, they are adventurous, quality-conscious, and exhibit cultivated taste for "the finer things in life."

- *Fulfilleds* turn their principle-orientation and high level of resources into a mature, self-confident outlook. As consumers, they are conservative and practical, but open to new products and services.

- *Believers,* with their principle-orientation and moderate resources, have a traditional, comfortable outlook based on family, community, and moral precepts. They are loyal and predictable consumers, not easily persuaded to change their buying patterns.

- *Achievers,* with a status orientation and high level of resources, define their goals and valued activities in terms of their relationships with social, professional, and family groups. As consumers, they prefer established brands, and they respond to products and services that they feel will enhance their position in the eyes of their peers.

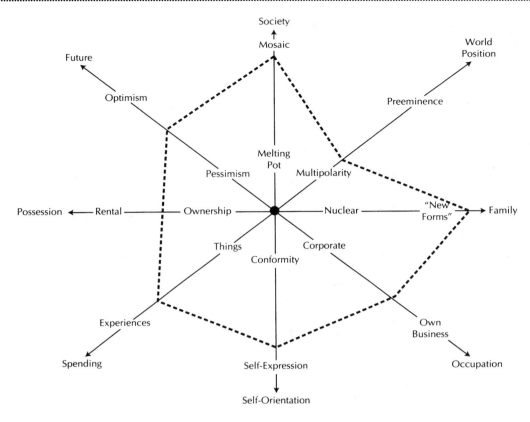

Figure 3. The New Dream. (SRI International)

- *Strivers* are status-oriented, but their modest resources make them unsure of themselves and concerned with the opinions of others. As consumers, they follow fashions and fads and often desire products that are financially beyond their reach.
- *Experiencers* combine an action-orientation with a high level of resources, and savor the new, the offbeat, the risky. As consumers, they buy on impulse and are effectively persuaded by promises of action, variety, and adventure.
- *Makers* express their action-orientation and moderate level of resources in constructive activity, working on or building from the things that surround them. As consumers, they seek products with a practical purpose and make decisions based on considerations like comfort, durability, and utility.
- *Strugglers* have a low level of resources and little clear self-orientation. Experiencing the world as pressing and difficult, they are satisfied just to meet immediate demands. As consumers, they are extremely price-sensitive and constitute a "low-yield" market.

    [See also Behavior: Social Constraints; Holistic Beliefs; Population Growth: United States; Social Change: United States; Values.]

BIBLIOGRAPHY

Piscatella, Joseph. *Choices for a Healthy Heart.* New York: Workman Publishing, 1987.
Settle, Robert, and Alreck, Pamela. "Reshaping the American Dream." *Marketing Communication* (March 1988).
White, John. *Lifestyle Priorities.* Wheaton, IL: Harold Shaw Publications, 1990.

– IAN H. WILSON

LITERACY.

See ILLITERACY.

LITERATURE

The art of writing was invented some 5,000 years ago, and the things called books came along not many centuries after. Originally, rolls of papyrus or vellum were called *biblia* (hence the Bible) from the name of the material, while folded pages stitched together were *codices, codex* in the singular. The Jews chose the roll form for their sacred texts (and still do); Christians chose the codex form. It was not long before codices also began to be termed *books,* which they are to this day.

What is a book? Is it the physical object in your hand? Or is it the contents, the thoughts or story in your head but also in the book? The question is important for the future of books. When codices became popular, around 500 A.D., they did so because they were more convenient than rolls, which had to be rolled out—a cumbersome process with a lengthy text—in order to be read. Flipping pages was easier, especially after paper replaced parchment around 1450. Paper could also be printed on with movable type presses—Gutenberg's great invention, which ensured the triumph of that other great invention, the book itself, for the next five centuries.

In fifty years, most people will live and die without ever seeing a physical book except in a museum or in churches, which both tend to be conservative.

Technology is ruthless; what is more convenient always wins. Today, physical volumes are becoming comparatively less easy to use than they were. Their competitors, CD-ROMs or online services, will be much preferable in the not-distant future. Parchment rolls endured for centuries after codices replaced them for most uses, and physical books are likely to endure in the future as curiosities, as lovely collector's items, and because for some purposes they remain useful. Would a CD stop a bullet as well as a Bible in your pocket? Could you fold faded flowers in an online service for a lover to come upon some day? Such trivialities apart, books will not be around much longer. In fifty years most people will live and die without ever seeing a physical book except in a museum or in churches, which both tend to be conservative.

That part is easy. It is harder to predict the effect of this change on books in the other sense of the term: on literature. The Greeks invented most of the literary forms we have today: poems, long and short; dramas, tragic and comic; novels and stories; histories; mathematical and scientific treatises; philosophy, both practical (including economics) and theoretical (including psychology). All these types of subject matter survived from rolls to codices, from codices to printed books. They will also probably survive when electronic "books" replace physical ones.

Nevertheless, there were subtle changes. Codices were read by many more people than rolls; their subject matter therefore became more popular. Cheap printed books could be used to promote new ideas and ideologies; every man, and then every woman, could be an authority if he or she published a book. Even so, there were still obstacles to communication: linguistic, economic, censorial, and others. An industry grew up, and publishers insisted that a book have an identifiable audience before they would invest in it; the bottom line was king. But it was just that sort of information monopoly Gutenberg had dreamed of overcoming. At least

Luther dreamed of it, and saw in the new books the promise of a better, freer age.

Today, things (are they spiritual or material beings?) like Internet hold out a similar promise. A boy (or girl) in Des Moines can reach out to children of similar interests in Vitebsk; a girl (or boy) from Lillehammer can reach out to children in San Francisco. All the walls are coming down, and anyone will be able to publish, to say nothing of writing, his or her own book. "Writing" may not be the right word. Many of the new "books" will be spoken, felt, visualized, or dreamed, not written down. Will they be truer or less true? Perhaps truth itself will change. Will they be better or worse? Most will be worthless, like most books today: vapid, jejeune, or offensive. A few will be better than anything that has ever been, in ways it is utterly impossible to predict.

The first printed books were more private than the codices they replaced; the new technology made that possible. The new books of the near future will be intensely personal, the outpourings of lonely, naked souls seeking to touch someone, somewhere, to find a home in another human breast. We see it happening already, where authors seem to conceal nothing from readers, revealing their deepest hopes, fears, prejudices. But is this merely a new kind of concealment when such books have to be published, publicized, and sold, their authors interviewed and displayed? The publishing business demands this from its professionals. The rest of us are amateurs, and we all have one great story to tell, which we compose ceaselessly as long as we live; it is the story of our own life. Without it, we are not sane, perhaps not even human. Future authors, ourselves, will be truly private persons, awaking in the night to share our thoughts, to tell our stories to just anybody, anywhere. What of forms? There will be none, or new forms will come into being, also unpredictable. A new, great, different literature will come into existence, and everything before it will seem stodgy and old.

As one side effect, writing, invented 5,000 years ago and for five millennia the key to power, wealth, and fame, will cease to have any importance whatsoever. Since this is inevitable, whether or not it is to be wept over is also of no importance whatsoever.

[See also Arts; Electronic Publishing; Libraries; Printed Word.]

BIBLIOGRAPHY

Jaynes, Julian. *The Origin of Consciousness in the Breakdown of the Bicameral Mind,* 2nd ed. Boston: Houghton Mifflin, 1989.

Ong, Walter J. *Orality and Literacy: The Technologizing of the World.* Bradford, MA: Routledge, Chapman, & Hall, 1982.

Postman, Neil. *Technopoly: The Surrender of Culture to Technology.* New York: Alfred Knopf, 1992.

Van Doren, Charles. *A History of Knowledge*. New York: Carol Publishing Group, 1991.

— CHARLES VAN DOREN

LONGEVITY

How long on average can a child born today expect to live? Are there fixed limits on how long people can live? What are the prospects for human life extension through advances in biology and medical technology? As people become increasingly concerned with the ways in which diet, exercise, and lifestyle affect their health, can modifications in behavior result in longer, healthier lives?

Tales of extraordinarily long lives, such as the biblical Methuselah, who allegedly died at the age of 969, or the eighteenth-century British farmer Thomas Parr, who supposedly died shortly before his 153rd birthday, reflect the belief that remarkably long life may be possible.

Life Expectancy

Life expectancy refers to the average number of years a person or group of people born at a specific time can expect to live. When Julius Caesar was born, some 2,000 years ago, average life expectancy at birth was only about eighteen to twenty-two years. By 1900 life expectancy at birth was forty-nine years. In contrast, an American infant born in 1990 can expect to live an average of 75.4 years. The striking increase in life expectancy at birth during the twentieth century is primarily attributable to public-health advances that have controlled the spread of contagious diseases. Today, death before age sixty-five is way down in the United States; about seven in ten deaths occur to people age sixty-five or older.

Life expectancy of infants is affected by birth defects and infectious disease, the life expectancy of young men by war, and that of women by the number of pregnancies experienced. Life expectancy for all ages may be changed by famine and malnutrition, civil unrest, epi-

The average life expectancy was 65.4 years in 1995 but it ranged from 25 to 120 years, being highest in developed nations. Individual longevity, such as that of this Indian man, is a combination of many factors. (Richard Bickel/Corbis)

demics, sanitation, and the quality of medical care available.

Today females can expect to live longer than males in industrialized societies. In the United States in 1990, for example, male life expectancy at birth had increased from forty-six years in 1900 to about seventy-two years. During the same period, life expectancy for females went from forty-eight to seventy-nine years. Men who reached age sixty-five in 1990 had an average remaining life of about fifteen years, women nearly nineteen years.

African Americans and Native Americans of both sexes today have shorter life expectancies at birth than whites, reflecting their persistently lower family income. African-American males have an average life expectancy at birth of about sixty-five years; and females, seventy-four. For each racial or ethnic group, the higher the level of family income, the longer the life expectancy at birth.

In nations where the majority of the population is poor, life expectancy is much shorter. Even in a wealthy country such as the United States, in a very poor state such as Louisiana, life expectancy is several years less than for the nation as a whole.

Life Span

Although life expectancy has changed dramatically throughout industrialized nations, many scientists believe that all living beings may have a biologically fixed life span, a maximum number of years that it is theoretically possible to live. Remarkably long lives reported in the past reflect a mix of different ways of counting years, lack of accurate records, deliberate falsification of records, and wishful thinking. The longest authenticated life span is 120 years (Shigechizo Izumi, Japan). The growth in absolute numbers of old people in industrialized nations such as the United States thus reflects not changes in lifespan but changes in average life expectancy. In 1900 only 42 percent of Americans could expect to live until their sixty-fifth birthday; three-fourths will do so today.

Why do all living organisms age? Scientists have proposed various hypotheses. Two common categories are (1) damage or "wear-and-tear" theories, and (2) program theories. Wear-and-tear theories argue that cells or organs of the body are unable to repair themselves asthey age due to inability of the immune system to resist disease. Program theories suggest that longevity is genetically controlled: a "biological clock" programs the body. The existence of a "death hormone" has also been proposed by some biologists.

Actuarial Estimates

Several nations have higher life expectancies than that of the United States. Japan has the world's highest life expectancy at birth (eighty-two for females and seventy-

six for males) and at age sixty-five (eighty-five for females and eighty-one for males). Other nations with greater life expectancies at birth than that of the United States include Sweden, Iceland, the Netherlands, Australia, Canada, Norway, Spain, the United Kingdom, Italy, Switzerland, Hong Kong, Andorra, and some twenty others. Life-expectancy estimates usually rely on the premise that all current age-specific death rates will continue in force for everyone in the population throughout their lives. If health conditions of the population continue to improve, some scientists argue that this assumption underestimates actual life expectancy. If we assume that a lowering of the death rate at each age continues at the same pace as it did during the 1980s, life expectancy at birth for a child born in 1990 may increase by ten years, with the result that children born in 2015 could expect to live into their nineties.

Life Extension

TRENDS. Some scientists also argue that there is no biological limit to life itself, but only age-related physiological deterioration for which intervention may be possible in the future. Recent laboratory research on fruit flies indicates that when several inbred strains of flies are placed in different environments, some strains do not age. Such research has raised two important questions: (1) Are there biologically fixed and species-specific limits to the life span? (2) Do environmental risk factors influence longevity?

Some scientists argue that there is no biological limit to life itself, only age-related physiological deterioration for which intervention may be possible in the future.

Prevention programs that reduce risk factors—lack of exercise, smoking, high-cholesterol diets implicated in heart disease, postmenopausal use of estrogen (implicated in certain types of cancer)—and adoption of a healthy lifestyle may result only in a one- or two-year increase in life expectancy.

How would life expectancy and life span be affected if all causes of death due to disease and accidents were eliminated? According to some scientists, if people were allowed to live out their lives free from heart disease, cancer, other diseases, and accidents, the average life span might be extended to about age one hundred. An opposing view offered by University of Chicago and Argonne National Laboratory scientists suggests that such gains are unrealistic, because science and medicine have pushed human life expectancy to its natural biological limit of about eighty-five years.

Closely allied to the issue of life extension is the question: What is normal aging? A promising area for investigation lies in genetics. Biologists studying simpler organisms have begun to develop frameworks to distinguish various types of genes interacting both with each other and with external factors.

A second promising area of research is the effect of dietary restriction. In the 1930s, scientists recognized that the lives of rats could be extended if their intake of calories was reduced, a finding replicated in numerous species. Caloric restriction not only prolongs life but is associated with later appearance and lower incidence of most spontaneous diseases among relatively simple species. Studies at the National Institutes of Health and elsewhere are evaluating whether restricted, nutritionally adequate diets slow aging among more complex species, such as nonhuman primates. Whether caloric restriction among human beings reduces aging, however, remains controversial.

TECHNOLOGIES. Breakthroughs in modern health care and medicine, such as antibiotics and organ transplants, have permitted more people to reach old age. If life expectancies continue to increase, issues arise about the quality of life for older people: the number of years of active life expectancy versus the number of years of chronic illness or incapacity. Merely expanding life expectancy without eradicating chronic disabilities would swell the proportion of people who are likely to suffer from dementia, arthritis, diabetes, and so forth.

Advances in biotechnology, detection methods, and ways to modify disease processes hold enormous promise. Studies in molecular biology and immunology indicate that certain molecules on cancer cells might be able to eradicate cancer cells by triggering the body's immune system. Studies in human genetics now enable discovery of many genetic disorders before their onset. By 1992, gene mapping of the DNA in cells had identified twenty-three of the twenty-four types of human chromosomes. Many diseases result from defects in specific genes. Because chromosome 21 is associated with some forms of dementia and other disorders, a clearer understanding of its genetic content is expected to have great medical relevance.

As techniques become available to repair genetic defects or replace defective genes, such diseases can be treated at their source. Searches for specific drugs that supplant the loss of genetic function and directly or indirectly regulate the rate of age-related diseases and perhaps aging itself, are underway. Research on a human growth hormone, for example, indicates that six months of injections of a genetically engineered version of the body's natural growth hormone reversed many age-related changes in the body by as much as twenty years.

If the genetic program for aging can be stopped or slowed, human life expectancy can be strikingly extended. Gene therapy, however, raises controversial social-policy issues associated with eugenics or selective breeding. Genetic engineering and gene therapy hold promise for bringing about radical changes in the physical and psychological attributes of human beings. Who should decide what normal human functioning is? If indeed the human life span can be extended so that there are no natural limits, how many years should people live? What changes in our social institutions would be required if life expectancy increases dramatically, or if there is no limit to the life span? These are challenges for the future.

[See also Aging of the Population; Death and Dying; Elderly, Living Arrangements; Genetic Engineering; Genetics.]

BIBLIOGRAPHY

Angier, Natalie. "Human Growth Hormone Reverses Effects of Age." New York Times, July 5, 1990.
Boon, Thierry. "Teaching the Immune System to Fight Cancer." Scientific American (March 1993): 83–89.
Kolata, Gina. "Study Challenges Longevity Theory." New York Times, October 21, 1992.
Lewis, Paul. "Japanese Live Longer, the U.N. Finds." New York Times, April 26, 1992.
Olshansky, S. Jay. "Estimating the Upper Limits to Human Longevity." Population Today 20/1 (1992): 6–8.
Tauber, Cynthia M. "Sixty-five Plus in America." In Current Population Reports. Washington, DC: U.S. Department of Commerce, Bureau of the Census, 1993.

— ELIZABETH W. MARKSON

LOTTERIES.

See CRIME RATES; GAMBLING.

M

MACROECONOMICS

Macroeconomists study the complex "whole" of an economy, exploring how relationships among such factors as levels of taxes, savings, investment, and employment determine the total economic output of a nation. The goal of economists has long been to turn their field into a science, a "values-free" discipline in which the interplay of factors such as those mentioned above could be forecast as reliably as astronomers plot the motion of planets. By mid-century—thanks to computers and advanced mathematical modeling—this dream appeared realizable. To some, however, the goal remained an idealistic pipedream.

This divergence of opinion arises because economics is both a science and an ideology, concerned both with measuring what is and advocating what should be. As philosopher David Hume stated two centuries ago, it is nearly impossible to distinguish the line between descriptions of fact and prescriptions of what ought to be. The U.S. government has been caught in that muddle of confusion from the day in 1791 when Secretary of the Treasury Alexander Hamilton first attempted to macromanage the national economy. Hamilton believed that the United States would be a stronger and richer nation if it rejected Thomas Jefferson's dream of an agrarian society composed of "virtuous" farmers living in decentralized communities and, instead, embraced wholeheartedly the urban English model of industrialization. Significantly, Hamilton did not make his case in terms of a personal vision; instead, he argued against Jefferson on "scientific" grounds, purporting to show that there was greater potential for gains in productivity in manufacturing than in agriculture. To achieve those higher levels of economic growth, Hamilton advocated a national industrial policy in which emerging industries manifesting the greatest potential for growth would be identified—and their domestic development incentivized—by means of government subsidies, tariff protection, and provision of such enabling "infrastructure" as roads, canals, and ports. He even called for the creation of a national ministry to promote the technological state of the art in the emerging industries. According to Hamilton, it was necessary to make government the partner of domestic industry because American industry needed the same kind of support that the French, Dutch, and particularly the British were giving their prime exporters.

In making this argument, Hamilton found himself directly at odds with the new economic philosophy of laissez-faire, articulated in 1776 by Adam Smith in *The Wealth of Nations*. In that influential work, Smith argued that the economy of a country would grow faster and more efficiently without governmental intervention. Thus, a debate was joined that persists to this day between economists, like Hamilton, who believe it necessary for government to take remedial and proactive measures to make economies produce at a peak level and economists, like Smith, who believe that "the invisible hand" that regulates free markets will produce the greatest overall good for society. Smith's Law of Supply and Demand, for much of American history, was the ruling principle for national economic policy, violated only as an exception—and seldom avowedly.

The close of the 1980s marked the end of the Keynesian era of expanding government that had begun fifty years earlier in the New Deal.

The Hamiltonian school achieved its moment of ascendancy during the Great Depression. John Maynard Keynes argued successfully that when levels of aggregate demand were insufficient to tap the nation's full capacity to produce goods and services, it was prudent—and probably necessary—for government to spur demand by increasing public expenditures. Keynes argued that, left to its own devices, the market was not self-regulating as Smith had claimed; rather, government must intervene when private savings and investment were insufficient to produce full employment. Thus, by manipulating the nation's fiscal (spending) policy, the Keynesian descendants of Hamilton believed government could produce a more desirable outcome than would be derived from the workings of the market alone.

In this century, the Smithian school reasserted itself in the post-World War II era, particularly in the writings of Milton Friedman and his fellow free-market economists. This school argued that the economy could be macromanaged more effectively through the manipulation of the quantity of money in circulation than through the more interventionist fiscal route. During the presidency of Ronald Reagan, these "monetarists" reached their peak of influence, advocating a minimalist role for government.

The somewhat arcane differences between those who advocate the fiscal and the monetary approaches become concrete in the matter of taxation. At times, Keynesian methods require significant tax increases, while monetarist methods usually have less impact on taxpayers' purses. To achieve what are felt to be higher-order goals—for instance, fuller employment, greater social opportunity—the Keynesians are more willing than the Smithians to spend public funds and thus either to raise taxes or to incur public debt. For their part, the followers of Smith are more willing to accept whatever social and economic outcomes—good or ill—emerge as consequences of the free play of market forces. Differences between the two philosophies are self-evident. The latter believe that the market naturally rewards the virtuous; therefore, nothing effective can be done to alter the existing order of society. The former believe that because social outcomes derive from arrangements that were designed by humans, they do not represent a natural order; therefore, the existing order effectively can be changed by intervening.

However, among most economists, the controversy between these two schools of thought typically rages *not* over their underlying ideological differences but over what they call empirical matters: specifically, over the extent to which levels of taxation affect national economic growth. For example, the disciples of Keynes argue that, by judicious use of government spending on social welfare, underemployed humans can become more fully productive; thus, in the long run, the overall economy will grow. In contrast, the disciples of Smith argue that the economy will grow faster if money is left in the hands of those who earned it, because they will invest it more efficiently than will government officials. Both sides attempt to marshall data to buttress their respective cases. Unfortunately, it is devilishly hard to trace objective causal relationships between a nation's level of taxation and its gross domestic product (GDP)—let alone to establish a meaningful correlation between taxation and the more difficult to measure "standard of living" or "quality of life." The subjectivity of this purportedly empirical issue is illustrated by the exhibits that follow.

Who can conclude from this data what the optimal level of taxation ought to be in order to maximize the overall wealth of a nation? As evidenced, some rich nations tax heavily, as do some poor ones; and some rich nations tax lightly, as do some poor ones. It is not simply that rates of taxation do not correlate well with

TABLE 1

PER CAPITA GDP OF SELECTED NATIONS

Richest Countries (rank order based on GDP per capita)		Most Heavily Taxed (rank order based on total tax revenue for 1992 as percent of GDP)
1. Switzerland	$33,085	20
2. Finland	27,527	14
3. Sweden	26,652	1
4. Denmark	25,150	2
5. Norway	24,924	4
6. Japan	23,801	22
7. West Germany	23,536	10
8. Iceland	22,907	19
9. Luxembourg	22,895	3
10. United States	21,449	23
11. Canada	21,418	15
12. France	21,105	7
13. Austria	20,391	8
14. Belgium	19,303	6
15. Italy	18,921	9
16. Holland	18,676	5
17. Australia	17,215	24
18. U.K.	16,985	18
19. New Zealand	13,020	16
20. Spain	12,609	17
21. Ireland	12,131	12
22. Greece	6,505	11
23. Portugal	6,085	13
24. Turkey	1,896	21

Source: OECD. GDP figures, 1990. Tax figures, 1992.

per capita GDP (or with other standard economic measures, such as productivity). More to the point, among the developed nations the least-taxed people (namely, Americans) have for the last several decades been the most vociferous in proclaiming themselves "overtaxed." If nothing else, this illustrates Hume's observation about the essential confusion between what is and what ought to be.

The American feeling of being overtaxed led to a series of taxpayer revolts, the most recent beginning in the 1970s. The close of the 1980s marked the end of the Keynesian era of expanding government that had begun fifty years earlier in the New Deal. As the rate of growth in taxation slowed, there was also an increase in the growth of deficit spending. The relationship between these two factors became itself a matter of considerable controversy, with one side arguing that the deficit was caused by "taxing and spending" and the other by "borrowing and spending." What is now clearer to both sides is that the economy seldom behaves in practice as it is supposed to in theory. For example,

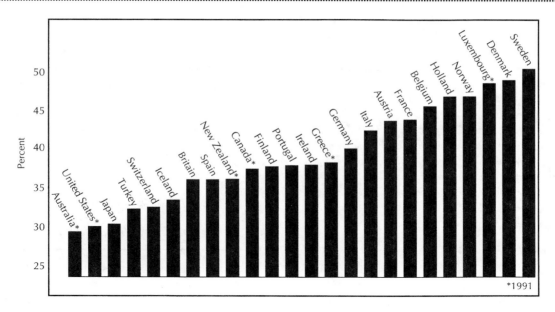

Figure 1. Total tax revenue as a percentage of GDP. (OECD)

the 1980s experiment with "supply-side" economics produced almost exactly the opposite of the intended effect: drastically lowering taxes produced more debt and dampened productive activity.

One constant throughout these controversies has been the self-confidence of economists that there is a "technological fix" to the problem of macromanagement. There has been nearly unlimited faith that—along with the manifest increase in the sophistication of their mathematical modeling—inevitably they will find the answer to such questions as "how much taxation will produce the optimal rate of economic growth?" Indeed, many prominent futurists share the belief that an increase in scientific knowledge will result in the ability to successfully plan for full employment. The "input-output" models of the economy pioneered by Jan Tinbergen, Wassily Leontief, Lawrence Klein, and others are often cited as an indication that economic policymaking might become a purely technical matter free of ideology. The most recent models involve hundreds of simultaneous equations describing the dynamic interactions of dozens of variables, including prices, wage, interest, tax, and investment rates, and a myriad of other factors that influence the overall wealth of a nation. Not only have these models begun to explain the causes of domestic business cycles, but they are being expanded to show the interrelationships among all the nations in the evolving world economy. These models promise not only sound scientific guidance on the best policies for domestic economies, but they also hold

promise for knowledgeably addressing the more pressing problems of global economic development.

Will these promises be realized? The answers to that question are ultimately predicated on whether one believes that economics is, in the final analysis, a true science. If it is, then economies will one day be modeled successfully, and the ideology that now dominates policy debates may well disappear. But if economics proves to be the study of human behavior—infinitely varied, complex, and value-laden—then it probably will remain forever unmodelable. As a consequence, the politics of economics will continue to be as it has been: a great debate over choice among alternative visions of the good society.

The "input-output" models of the economy

are often cited as an indication

that economic policymaking might become

a purely technical matter free of ideology.

Doubtless, there is a part of economics—perhaps the largest part—that is measurable and, thus, susceptible to the kind of development in terms of models and instruments of measurement found in the hard sciences. There is no question that the increased application of such tools is necessary for social progress. The complexity of history, however, lends credence to the belief that the measurement of what "is" may be the easiest part. The centuries-old debate over what "ought" to be is not only more difficult, it is the most marvelously human element in one of the most quintessentially human of all activities: the production and distribution of the fruits of society.

[See also Conservatism, Political; Credit, Debt, and Borrowing; Deficits, Governmental; Economic Cycles: Models and Simulations; Economics; Free Trade; Global Business: Dominant Organizational Forms; Investments; Liberalism, Political; Marketplace Economics; Productivity; Savings; Taxes; Unemployment.]

BIBLIOGRAPHY

Bach, George L. *Macroeconomics: Analysis, Decisionmaking and Policy.* Englewood Cliffs, NJ: Prentice-Hall, 1987.

Bober, Stanley. *Modern Microeconomics: A Post-Keynesian Perspective.* London: Croom Helm, 1987.

Buiter, Willem H. *International Macroeconomics.* New York: Oxford University Press, 1990.

Dernberg, Thomas F. *Global Macroeconomics.* New York: Harper-Collins, 1988.

Froyen, Richard T. *Macroeconomics: Theories and Policies.* New York: Macmillan, 1990.

Perkins, J. O. *General Approach to Macroeconomic Theory.* New York: St. Martin's Press, 1990.

Pratten, C. F. *Applied Macroeconomics.* New York: Oxford University Press, 1990.

Wonnacott, Paul. *Macroeconomics.* New York: John Wiley, 1990.

— JAMES O'TOOLE

MACROENGINEERING

As population pressures increase, we must seek to use the vast ocean spaces to relieve congestion and meet other global needs. The future will bring many large-scale projects that utilize sites above and beneath oceans and along newly created shorelines. Such projects will be developed first by nations such as Japan, which have very high population densities, a shortage of land sites for new construction, and the available money to spend for the development of structures floating on the surface.

Floating Structures

A Japanese engineering firm has designed "an all-embracing plan for the utilization of marine space" in the form of a floating station that includes a fish farm, a marina, a convention center, shops, and restaurants. The Mediterranean principality Monaco is studying the possibility of building floating island clusters within a protective seawall to gain more development sites. This project could be completed early in the twenty-first century. Another offshore floating city, proposed for Sa-

gami Bay, Japan, would connect the Tsukuba science city and Narita airport via a subsurface line.

Planners have long sought to create airports at midocean locations via various types of floating rafts and even icebergs. Because of environmental problems and costs, building new airports near large cities is becoming prohibitive. Consequently, interest in developing floating airports serving coastal cities has been renewed.

New technology makes it possible to fulfill the centuries-old dreams of connecting the world's land masses.

There is also growing interest in floating hotels, power-generating stations, water treatment plants, offices, and other industrial facilities. Floating hotels can move from one site to another with the seasons or provide overflow accommodations for major events. A large pulp mill has been towed from Japan and sited on the Amazon River. Floating power plants serve at numerous locations around the world. A Norwegian firm has built a floating resort condominium. A proposed 220-meter ship providing 120 floating offices renting at one-tenth of the usual Tokyo rates could also offer recreational cruises on weekends.

Off-Shore Construction

While floating facilities are suited for deep water, there is actually more activity and planning involving shallow-water site development of structures that can be built on man-made islands or moored to the sea floor. The new Kansai airport being built in Osaka Bay, Japan, features a man-made island large enough for jet runways. Built by moving a small mountain from the nearby shore via barges, the island is linked to the shore by a bridge-causeway. This project may provide the precedent and guidelines for other offshore airports in Japan, including those already planned for Nagoya and Fukuoka and under discussion for Tokyo Bay.

In Macao, on the coast of China, a new airport is being built on a site in the Pearl River near Taipa Island. The site has been filled and pilings have been sunk more than 61 meters deep to support the runway. A development group has proposed a new airport for the Toronto area, situated in the Georgian Bay about sixteen kilometers offshore.

More ambitious is the proposed island city for Tokyo Bay, which would provide a site of 30,000 hectares in size and could support a population of 5 million. Another Japanese proposal involves diking 800 kilometers of river frontage in the Tokyo-Osaka area. This frontage would be up to 200–300 meters wide and would provide sites for housing, roads, parks, and infrastructure. The project would add 650,000 housing units by the year 2020. Singapore, another crowded nation, has added substantial areas via the reclamation of sites in shallow waters. Most noteworthy has been the huge long-term program of reclaiming land from the sea in the Netherlands, which has effectively doubled the land area of the nation!

An interesting possibility for the future involves growing new atolls by stimulating coral growth with electric currents. Development of this technology would make it possible to create many new sites where none exist today.

Undersea Habitation

Scuba diving has led to an explosive growth in tourism in many locations where the diving environment is particularly attractive. To serve this fast-growing market, entrepreneurs have developed dive centers, including underwater observation or rest facilities in tropical waters. The next step will be to develop underwater hotels and resorts. Improving technology for underwater work and travel ultimately may lead to the construction of new communities and cities under water. This technology may open a vast new world of sites twice as large as our present land areas.

Continental Links

New technology makes it possible to fulfill the centuries-old dreams of connecting the world's land masses. In 1988 Japan celebrated the connection of two main islands, Honshu and Hokkaido, via the new fifty-five-kilometer Seikan tunnel, the world's longest tunnel. More than 200 years after Napoleon proposed it, the tunnel between France and the United Kingdom nears completion. Consisting of two parallel railroad tunnels and a service tunnel, the trio of fifty-kilometer tubes extends from Calais to Folkestone. This new channel tunnel or "chunnel" will enable high-speed rail service from London to Paris. Motorists will be able to drive onto rail cars at one end and be carried quickly to interconnecting super highways on the opposite end. A long-sought link between Europe and Africa at Gibraltar, urged by the United Nations, involves a tunnel or combined tunnel-bridge-causeway. Under construction is Scanlink, which will connect Scandinavia and Europe via three interrelated projects: the Oresund Bridge between Sweden and Denmark, the Danish Great Belt tunnel-causeway among several islands, and the Fehmarn bridge/tunnel between Denmark and Germany.

Such projects are pale compared to proposals for a transatlantic tube for supersonic trains. Furthermore, Dr. Yutaka Mochida, one of the world's leading tunnel experts, proposes a global transportation system that involves tunnels under the Pacific.

Canals and Locks

Not to be overlooked among new global links are a number of canal projects. The just completed link between the Rhine and Danube rivers provides a connection between Rotterdam and the Black Sea. First undertaken by Holy Roman Emperor Charlemagne in the seventh century, this project was completed with the construction of a canal in southwestern Germany in 1992. Now, planners are talking about an even more ambitious project to link Vienna with Hamburg via a Danube-Oder-Elbe canal system.

In the Pacific Rim region a planned 102-kilometer canal across Thailand's Isthmus of Kra would shorten ocean routes by more than 1,000 kilometers for tankers moving from the Persian Gulf past Singapore to Japan. Discussions of a second Central American canal have been revived recently by a group of investors who might operate it for profit. One possible route crosses Nicaragua.

Global super projects published in *Site World* in 1992 tallied 1,334 projects, of which approximately one-third were under construction, another one-third were in the design stage, and the balance were in early planning. More and more, macroengineering is not constrained by what minds can conjure.

[See also Development, Alternative; Engineering; Global Environmental Problems; High Technology; Land Use Planning; Nuclear Power; Science Cities; Space Colonization; Space Flight; Transportation.]

BIBLIOGRAPHY

Conway, McKinley. *Airport Cities 21*. Atlanta: Conway Data, 1993.
———. *Geo-Economics: The New Science, or The Gospel of Development According to Chairman Mac*. Atlanta: Conway Data, 1993.
———. *A Glimpse of the Future*. Atlanta: Conway Data, 1992.

— MCKINLEY CONWAY

MAGAZINES.

See PRINTED WORD.

MAGLEV

Maglev is a new mode of transport in which passenger and freight vehicles are magnetically levitated above a guideway. The elimination of mechanical contact and the reduction of atmospheric friction enables vehicles to travel at high speeds, limited only by aerodynamic drag and route straightness. Speeds of 300 miles (500 kilometers) per hour are practical for vehicles traveling in the atmosphere; speeds of thousands of miles per hour are possible in low-pressure evacuated tunnels and tubes.

The idea of magnetically levitated transport was first described in the early 1900s by Goddard and others. Bachelet (1912) proposed levitating vehicles using the repulsive magnetic force between AC (alternating current) coils and induced currents in an aluminum sheet guideway, while Graemiger (1911) proposed using the attractive magnetic force between a vehicle's electromagnets and a guideway with iron rails.

Figure 1 illustrates the basic principles of the two types of magnetic suspensions. Repulsive force suspensions are inherently stable—if the vehicle moves toward the guideway, the magnetic force continuously increases. The vehicle then automatically levitates and stabilizes itself without external control at a distance where the upward magnetic force equals its weight. In contrast, attractive force suspensions are inherently unstable. If the vehicle starts to move closer to the guideway, the continuously increasing magnetic force pulls it upward till contact occurs.

The early Maglev concepts were not practical. The repulsive force AC coil suspension required too much electrical power, while the attractive force electromagnetic suspension could not be stabilized. The first practical Maglev system was invented by Powell and Danby in 1966. They proposed placing an alternating sequence of powerful superconducting (SC) magnets on a vehicle. The magnets induce opposing currents in the aluminum loop guideway underneath the vehicle, which magnetically levitate and stabilize it several meters above the guideway. The guideway is designed also to stabilize the vehicle horizontally, as well as in the pitch, yaw, and roll directions. Vehicles move freely along the guideway, but cannot touch it, even when strong external forces, such as high wind gusts, act on them.

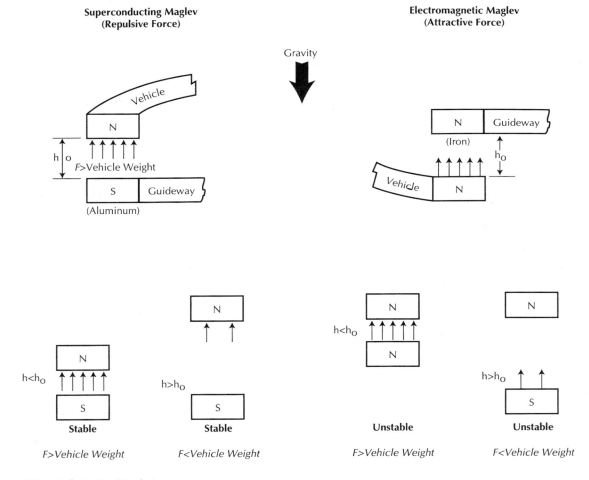

Figure 1. Magnetic levitation (Maglev).

To propel the Maglev vehicles, Powell and Danby also proposed (1971) using AC current windings in the guideway. When energized by a power line, a small current in the windings magnetically interacts with the strong superconducting magnets on the vehicles, pushing it forward at a constant speed determined only by the AC frequency. This concept, called the Linear Synchronous Motor (LSM), makes all vehicles on the guideway move at the same speed, regardless of individual variations in drag force that occur due to local head or tail winds, up or down grades, and so on. Thus vehicles cannot change their relative spacing. This allows a large number of high-speed vehicles to operate safely on the same guideway.

Besides being extremely safe, the LSM is very efficient. Almost all of the input power to the guideway propels the vehicles, with only a small amount lost to I^2R heating in the windings. Not all of the guideway is continuously energized; drive power is only switched into the guideway blocks—typically, about one mile in length—that actually have vehicles. As a vehicle leaves one block, power is then switched into the next block.

Japan and Germany have both demonstrated full-scale Maglev prototypes, and are proceeding with first-generation commercial systems. Japan has developed the superconducting Maglev system originally proposed by Powell and Danby, while Germany has developed a modern version of the electromagnetic Maglev concept proposed by Graemiger. Although electromagnetic suspensions are inherently unstable, it is possible to use them for high-speed vehicles if the current in the conventional (room temperature) magnets is continuously controlled and adjusted by a rapid response servo system. When the vehicle magnet moves upwards to the rail from its normal position, current is reduced; conversely, when it drops below its nominal position, current is increased. The servo control system acts very quickly, in milliseconds, to keep the vehicle safely levitated.

In superconducting Maglev systems, the gap between vehicles and the guideway is large, typically six inches; in electromagnetic Maglev, the gap must be much smaller, typically one-third of an inch, in order that the magnet input power is reasonable. As a result, its guideway must be built to much tighter tolerances than those for superconducting Maglev, increasing cost.

Prototypes of a Japanese superconducting Maglev vehicle on a test track in Miyazaki (Kyotani, 1975) have operated at over 300 miles per hour. A 300-mile-long route between Tokyo and Osaka is planned for operation shortly after 2000 A.D. The first thirty-mile section of the route is now under construction in Yamanishi Prefective north of Mount Fuji.

A German Transrapid electromagnetic Maglev vehicle (Miller, 1987), on its test track in Emsland has achieved speeds over 250 miles per hour. Germany plans a Hamburg-Berlin Maglev route.

Maglev may well be a major mode of transport in the twenty-first century because of its excellent energy efficiency and mobility, absence of pollution, independence from oil fuel, and low cost.

Maglev vehicles traveling in the atmosphere at 300 miles per hour use only half of the primary energy per passenger mile that is used by 60 m.p.h. automobiles, and a quarter of that used by 500 m.p.h. jet airliners. Here, primary energy refers to the thermal energy into the electric power plant that propels the Maglev vehicles, or the thermal energy in the petroleum-based fuel used by the auto or the airplane. In fact, the electricity used by Maglev could come from solar, nuclear, hydroelectric, or any nonpolluting energy source.

Maglev vehicles operating in low-pressure tunnels or tubes will be virtually frictionless, even though they travel at hypersonic speeds. One could go from New York to California in an hour, with an energy usage equivalent to less than one gallon of gasoline per passenger.

Figure 2 shows a possible national Maglev network for the United States that could be constructed along sections of the existing Interstate Highway System. This network would carry passengers and truck-type freight at 300 m.p.h. using vehicles traveling in the atmosphere. Approximately two-thirds of the U.S. population would live within 15 miles of a Maglev station, and 95 percent within the states served.

The projected costs—energy, vehicle amortization, and system personnel—are much lower for Maglev than for other modes of transport. At 300 m.p.h., Maglev will cost approximately 3 cents per passenger mile and 7 cents per ton mile for freight, compared to 15 cents per passenger mile for auto and air travel and 30 cents per ton mile for truck freight.

The development of lightweight beam-type prefabricated guideways will allow rapid construction of routes along existing rights of way such as highways, railroads, and power line corridors. A 20,000 mile U.S. network could be constructed in ten to twenty years at a total cost of about $200 billion. The savings in operating costs resulting from the Maglev system could pay back its capital cost in as little as three years.

A two-way Maglev guideway can easily carry over 100,000 passengers per day, plus thousands of freight containers. It will be virtually impossible to saturate the traffic capacity of a Maglev route—unlike air travel, Maglev scheduling can be very precise, with virtually no delays due to congestion or bad weather.

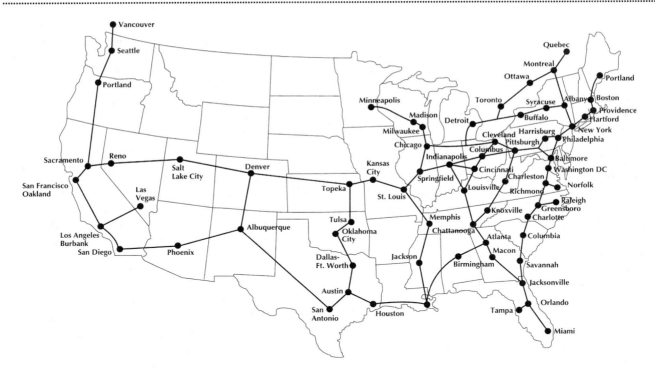

Figure 2. A proposed national Maglev system.

By the middle of the twenty-first century, Maglev systems could carry a large fraction of the world's passenger and freight traffic. The resultant economic and energy savings, enhanced mobility, and reduced pollution, would contribute significantly to a cleaner world and a higher standard of living for its inhabitants.

[See also Air Transport; Motor Vehicles; Motor Vehicles, Alternatively Powered; Railways; Transportation; Urban Transit.]

BIBLIOGRAPHY

Bachelet, E. "Foucault and Eddy Currents Put to Service." *Engineer* 114 (1912): 420.

Miller, L. "Transrapid 06 II—Performance and Characteristics." *Proceedings of the International Conference on Maglev and Linear Drives.* Institute of Electrical and Electronic Engineers Report 87CH2443-0, 1987, p. 129.

Powell, James R., and Danby, Gordon T. *Cryogenics* 11 (1971): 171.

———. "High Speed Transport by Magnetically Suspended Trains." *Mechanical Engineering* 89 (1967): 30.

— JAMES R. POWELL
GORDON T. DANBY

MANAGEMENT, PARTICIPATIVE.

See PARTICIPATIVE MANAGEMENT.

MARKETING

Businesses look to marketing and marketers to solve a small number of important problems that they face.

The shorter-run problems are: which products (and services) should the business provide, what distribution channels should it choose to get them into the hands of customers, what prices should it set, and how should it communicate (by means of advertising, sales force, or sales promotion) with its customers and its distributors? The longer-run problems are: which groups of customers should it seek; and how should it adapt its products, prices, communications, and channels of distribution to likely changes in how customers buy and what they think? This article discusses likely changes in demographics and the four elements of the marketing mix—product, price, communications, and distribution.

Customer Differences

Forces altering competition continue and are likely to continue in the future: increasing international competition, accelerating technological change, the maturing or stagnating of certain markets, and continuing cycles of regulation and deregulation.

It is an inescapable truism that people differ. Marketers prefer to say, instead, that market segments differ. For most of the twentieth century, marketers directed their attention to the mass consumer. In doing so they ignored, or overlooked, differences between market segments. The singular arrogance of Henry Ford's declaration regarding color choice for his Model T, "You can have any color as long as it's black," marks the epitome of this perspective. Demographic and lifestyle changes as well as education and information have long since interceded to weaken mass marketing and erode brand loyalty. In the future, computers, scanners, and changes in payment technology will allow businesses to adapt more closely to market differences and cater to their every whim, be it ever so slight. Increasing market fragmentation will make this necessary. Hence, each business will have to learn about the specific things that make its market segments unique. "What the consumer wants, is what the consumer will get," has never been truer.

There will be more emphasis on what we now call minorities, as blacks, Hispanics, women, and the elderly assume larger roles in the economy. The elderly, in particular, have become an attractive marketing target; their relative financial well-being and access to large financial resources is accompanied by few of the obligations that attend raising a family.

Elements of the Marketing Mix

PRODUCT. Most components of product marketing strategy—presale service, after-sale service, technical marketing research, and product testing—will assume greater importance in the future. As products adapt to niche marketing, a proliferation of product offerings may increase competition to the point that the risks and costs of product failure escalate dramatically. In turn, this outcome may dampen the enthusiasm for businesses to develop new products.

Time needed to develop new products has decreased over the past few decades. It is unlikely to fall much more. Confounding this shortened product development cycle is the lengthened time requirement interposed by government regulators. Pharmaceutical products and food additives, in particular, require protracted regulatory approval periods.

PRICE. There will be increased emphasis on cost-plus pricing and pricing that conforms to government regulations. Government purchasing power constitutes the largest buyer segment for many products. Purchasing specifications, including prices, exert a powerful pressure by lowest-cost pricing.

Niche marketing is likely to bring relatively high prices and high margins, because the competition forces are weakened. Even specialty marketing is likely to give

Dropping barriers to international trade allows developing countries to reach new markets with their products. Rapid world trade growth, up 4.4% in 1997, will continue through the next century. (Macduff Everton/© Corbis)

ground to the huge onslaught of deep-discount retailers; sooner or later immense mass marketers (like Wal-Mart) will make inroads on niche merchandising. Beyond domestic skirmishing, the expansion of international competition in commodities and general classes of goods will have an influence on moderating price increases in the United States and elsewhere.

MARKETING COMMUNICATIONS. The length and size of advertisements will decrease. Fifteen-second advertisements will probably become the standard on television. Thus, one will see more advertisements in a given amount of time. New electronic media will continue to emerge, and one can expect advertisements on such media as electronic bulletin boards, computer networks, home-shopping cable-TV channels, CD-ROM disks, and lengthy infomercials. There will probably be a continued increase in public skepticism toward advertising and resistance to its messages.

Fifteen-second advertisements will probably become the standard on television. Thus, one will see more advertisements in a given amount of time.

New systems for delivering coupons will allow marketers to focus on specific customer segments. For example, it will be possible to deliver coupons for one brand only to buyers of a competing brand (including house brands at point of purchase), and coupons for related brands of one manufacturer only to buyers of other brands of the same manufacturer.

DISTRIBUTION. Lower barriers to international trade and economic growth in developing countries will stimulate the demand for franchise services. It is likely that franchising's share will increase from one-third of all retail sales (in 1990) to one-half by 2010. The increases will be predominantly in what are called packaged franchises, those where the franchiser seeks to have franchisees reproduce in their local communities an entire business concept—products, trademarks, uniforms, and methods of operation.

Other factors likely to influence distribution strategy include: increased direct selling costs that many industries face; prominence of computerized links among manufacturers, customers, and distributors; the appearance of new channels that perform a variety of value-added services beyond those performed by traditional distributors; the growing power of the retail trade versus that of the manufacturers in consumer brand goods; and increasing concentration within channels of distribution that were long fragmented.

[See also Advertising; Marketing Breakthroughs; Marketplace Economics.]

BIBLIOGRAPHY

Dychtwald, Ken, and Gable, Greg. "Portrait of a Changing Consumer." *Business Horizons* (January/February 1990): 62–73.

Lazer, William; LaBarbera, Priscilla; MacLachlan, James M.; and Smith, Allen E., eds. *Marketing 2000 and Beyond.* Chicago: American Marketing Association, 1990.

Smith, Allen E.; MacLachlan, James M.; Lazer, William; and LaBarbera, Priscilla. *Marketing 2000: Future Perspectives on Marketing.* Chicago: American Marketing Association, 1990.

– DAVID L. RADOS

MARKETING BREAKTHROUGHS

A breakthrough is an idea that is so different it cannot be compared to any existing practices or perceptions. Employing new technology and creating new markets, breakthroughs are conceptual shifts that make history. Incremental innovation may arise through the application of new technology to an existing product, process, or system; or through the introduction of existing technology into a new market; or, sometimes merely through identifying customers' needs more effectively. Breakthroughs tend to work in all these dimensions at once.

Recognizing a marketing breakthrough is not hard: Nautilus exercise equipment, Club Med vacations, fax machines, Post-It note pads, personal copiers, compact discs, and cellular telephones readily come to mind. Successful creators of these and other breakthroughs tend to be very good at bringing about an interaction between the world of problems (situations faced by customers) and the world of solutions (technology).

A good example of this is the microwave oven, a breakthrough that began when Raytheon workers assembling radar units during World War II noticed that they could warm their hands in front of microwave-emitting magnetron tubes. In 1955, using Raytheon's magnetrons, Tappan introduced the first microwave oven for the home. These new ovens—the size of refrigerators and costing more than some new cars—did not meet the needs of customers, and not many were sold.

Across the Pacific, the Japanese quickly saw the potential of microwave cooking, but realized that the magnetron used in radar was not the appropriate one for heating soup. Several companies tried to make smaller, cheaper magnetrons, but the New Japan Radio Company (NJRC) was the only one to succeed. In 1961, Raytheon bought one-third of NJRC and thus gained access to these smaller magnetrons, but still had trouble getting the product into kitchens.

In 1965, Raytheon turned to Amana, a company with vast expertise in home appliances. The combination of Raytheon's technology, NJRC's improved magnetrons, and Amana's marketing produced a countertop microwave oven for less than $500. The solution side of the equation was now ready.

The next challenge was convincing consumers and educating wholesalers and retailers about the full range of the new product's capabilities. One of the participants recalled the role of popcorn in this process. "[Customers] would watch the molecular disturbance and the bursting of the popcorn," he said. "They would smell and hear it popping. Finally, we'd give them some, and then they'd stand around and say, 'This thing really does work!'" The microwave oven landed squarely between customers' needs and technology, and millions of them now occupy prominent places in kitchens.

Because people have long regarded such breakthroughs as the road to wealth and recognition, the creative process has been intensely analyzed. Bell Laboratories once tried to quantify the attributes of the "creative type." They found only two clearly common characteristics: an exceptional tolerance for messy work environments and a well-developed sense of humor. A wider examination of many breakthroughs, however, reveals three important elements:

The Individual

While it certainly does not hurt to have genius, the adjective more likely to describe a breakthrough originator is *obsessive*. Such a person will work on a problem twenty-four hours a day—not just from nine to five. People who bring about breakthroughs also tend to be good at what Arthur Koestler, in *The Act of Creation*, calls "bisociative" skills—the ability to connect ideas that no one has connected before. Archimedes did this when ordered to determine whether a king's crown was pure gold without melting it. The displacement solution to this early example of nondestructive testing finally came to this obsessed individual while he was taking a bath. A modern example of an obsessive inventor is Arthur Jones, the creator of Nautilus exercise equipment. Working for years at all hours of the day and night, he built and tested models until he perfected the kind of machines now found in fitness centers around the world.

Special Environment

Breakthroughs have come out of every imaginable workplace: basement workshops, small companies, and multinational corporations. The best environments, however, possess an aspect that can be called a sword and a shield. Inventors need someone acting as a sword to cut through red tape, change standard procedures, and thus allow something different to emerge. Akio Morita, then chairman of Sony, early on recognized the possibilities of the Walkman and wielded the sword of his position to bring it to the market. Similarly, a shield is required to protect a fledgling product from overzealous managers who do not want to waste money on something that shows little immediate reward. The 3M Company's Post-It note pads would never have become ubiquitous in modern offices if someone had not shielded their inventor from devotees of the bottom line. Another aspect of the best environments is that they place technologists in the world of customers, thereby facilitating bisociation.

Consider the Market

Problem-solvers who think like customers are more likely to please those customers, as the development of the videocassette recorder (VCR) demonstrates. Sony hit the market first with Betamax, a technologically stunning product. However, the electronic giant did not understand that potential purchasers wanted to record shows that were two hours long. JVC did, and their VHS VCRs left Betamax in the dust.

Finally, there is one further step. Assuming an individual working in a special environment can listen to customers and come up with a breakthrough, he or she must at some point let others make their contributions to the project. Sir Godfrey Hounsfield of the United Kingdom's EMI invented the CAT scanner, yet it was John Powell's management of its marketing and manufacturing that got the device into every hospital that could afford one.

What is the best way to bring about a breakthrough? Getting customers who have needs together with people who know how to fulfill them is a start. Once an idea is hatched, companies should carefully nurture it. To produce a breakthrough, it takes many people saying "yes" to transform an idea to a success; often one "no" can kill it. The right people in the right environment—combined with a little luck—can make it happen.

[See also Change, Pace of; Continuity and Discontinuity; Creativity; Marketing; Materials: Research and Development; New Consumer Products; Scientific Breakthroughs; Surprises; Technological Change; Wild Cards.]

BIBLIOGRAPHY

Foster, Richard. *Innovation: The Attacker's Advantage.* New York: Summit, 1986.
McKenna, Regis. *The Regis Touch: Million-Dollar Advice from America's Top Marketing Consultant.* Reading, MA: Addison-Wesley, 1985.
Miller, Jule A. *From Ideas to Profit.* New York: Van Nostrand-Reinhold, 1986.

Nayak, P. Ranganath, and Ketteringham, John M. *Breakthroughs!* New York: Rawson, 1986.

Porter, Michael E. *Competitive Strategy—Techniques for Analyzing Industries and Competitors.* New York: Free Press, 1980.

Servi, Italo S. *New Product Development and Marketing.* New York: Praeger, 1990.

Souder, William E. *Managing New Product Innovations.* Lexington, MA: D. C. Heath, 1987.

— P. RANGANATH NAYAK

MARKETPLACE ECONOMICS

In the next several decades, fundamental changes likely will be occurring in the nature of private business enterprises as they respond to the developing threats and opportunities of the global marketplace. The most domestic-oriented firm will be increasing its geographic reach because its suppliers and customers, with increasing frequency, will be located on a variety of continents.

As the intensity of global competition increases, companies will be forced to reevaluate their roles in the world economy. For some, this will entail strengthening their domestic position against competing foreign products. Others will expand their operations into foreign markets. For many, collaborative agreements with other businesses will be an effective alternative to the more traditional approaches.

The modern enterprise will increasingly develop multinational networks composed of alliances, partially owned subsidiaries, associated firms, affiliates, licensees, and other cooperative arrangements. On a rising scale, mergers and acquisitions will involve crossing national boundaries—and dealing with several national governments, as well as with a variety of state, provincial, and local authorities.

Large enterprises that had once been content to concentrate their production, research, and exports in their home economies will be forging international ties. Often the same companies will engage in joint ventures to develop new products, coproduce existing products, serve as sources of supply for each other, share output, and compete with each other. No universal pattern will emerge. The specific ways in which companies establish their presence in overseas markets will be strongly influenced by the obstacles and incentives established by the host country and occasionally by the home country.

Companies increasingly will assume some of the functions formerly vested primarily in national governments. This will reflect the growing belief that the business firm can conduct activities more efficiently than government.

Business Responses

Many firms will take on characteristics of an open and interactive network, selectively sharing control, technology, and markets with organizations beyond their formal structure. As a result of rapid changes in technology and markets, the traditional boundaries between formal enterprises and more informal business relationships will gradually blur. For knowledge-intensive production, the distinction between maker and user is neither clear-cut nor invariant.

Many firms will take on characteristics of an open and interactive network, selectively sharing control, technology, and markets with organizations beyond their formal structure.

Many innovative forms will be utilized. In some high-technology areas, the business firm of the future will consist primarily of a central coordination center and several semiindependent internal organizations. Business activity will consequently operate on the basis of fluid ties with the internal organizations of other companies.

The predominant type of corporation will be one in which individual staff members take upon themselves the task of solving problems and revamping operations—but hopefully within an overall harmony that causes these individual efforts to converge toward the realization of the company's strategic goals. In contrast, the traditional bureaucratic organization, with its somewhat rigid hierarchies and singleminded emphasis on efficiency, was easier to manage. Yet that structure is not likely to provide the necessary decentralized autonomy, intellectual stimulation, or motivation to those engaged in creative work.

The traditional hierarchical form of business organization will not be totally abandoned. It will be appropriate for stable, slow-growth, low-tech, natural resource-based industries like metal production, oil, paper, and forest products. In contrast, the standard model is becoming obsolete in rapidly changing, high-tech markets such as computers, telecommunications, and aerospace.

The key will be to develop a subtle compromise—to allow individual employees to develop plans and programs on their own initiative while using a cooperative relationship to focus these individual efforts toward the realization of the company's goals and objectives. Fundamental to this process will be the development of a clear-cut corporate identity generated by leadership with a well-articulated vision of where the company should go. In the multinational firm of the future, the formal linkages that bind the vast corporate network will be technology, common values, and shared resources.

Government and Business

Technological progress makes possible, and economically feasible, a variety of business innovations to overcome governmental obstacles to global commerce. These barriers will continue to take many forms, ranging from tariffs and quotas on trade to restrictions on foreign ownership of domestic businesses—but the global enterprise increasingly will learn how to overcome them, albeit at a price.

In a passive mode, exporters will absorb the added costs imposed by governmental barriers to international commerce—at least to some extent. In the case of quotas imposed by the importing nations, companies can shift to higher-priced items on which unit profits are also greater. When faced with more onerous obstacles, businesses will draw on a variety of alternatives to direct exporting.

Businesses can set up new manufacturing facilities in the host nation or they can respond by acquiring existing local companies. Other alternatives that business firms will increasingly rely upon to develop positions in the markets of other nations include subcontracting production, purchasing locally, and developing products jointly with local firms.

Joint ventures, particularly those involving manufacturing operations, will often be necessary to overcome trade restrictions. On other occasions, firms will be facing sharp limits to foreign ownership of local enterprises. Barriers can include formal restrictions on investment, or less formal but often equally powerful tax and regulatory advantages limited to local companies. National antitrust laws—and their enforcement—will be geared to the global nature of the marketplace. Thus, two or three giant firms—such as the automotive industry in the United States—will be seen to be a competitive portion of a larger worldwide market for cars and trucks.

When governments restrict repatriation of earnings or foreign businesses fear future expropriation of their assets, global enterprises will frequently set up affiliate or correspondent relationships with local firms. This approach will minimize risk and liability—and also profit potentials. When other barriers are imposed by governments in the more advanced economies, licensing arrangements can be made with domestic firms in exchange for market entry. These governmental obstacles may include local political or industrial pressures and local distribution systems strongly favoring home-produced products. Enterprises in advanced economies thus will be able to respond to attractive overseas markets without directly penetrating them.

With the increasing globalization of the international economy, companies experiencing difficulty introducing products in their home country due to government requirements will license their products to firms in other countries in an effort to introduce them into markets more quickly.

It will be especially helpful under rapidly changing political circumstances to do business in several countries. When faced with rising government burdens in one nation, a firm can shift its high value-added activities to other nations in which it operates, specifically those with lower taxes and less burdensome regulation.

[See also Business Structure: Forms, Impacts; Economics; Entrepreneurship; Global Business: Dominant Organizational Forms; Political Economy.]

BIBLIOGRAPHY

James, Jr., Harvey S., and Weidenbaum, Murray. *When Businesses Cross International Borders: Strategic Alliances and Their Alternatives.* Westport, CT: Praeger Publishers, 1993.

Weidenbaum, Murray. *Business and Government in the Global Marketplace,* 5th ed. Englewood Cliffs, NJ: Prentice Hall, 1995.

———. "The Emerging Transnational Enterprise." *Business and the Contemporary World* 5/1 (Winter 1993).

— MURRAY L. WEIDENBAUM

MARRIAGE

The debate over family values makes it clear that the concept of family will continue to be important to society, to undergo change (as it always has), and to generate a great deal of controversy. The following definitions are but a sampling of the changing ways in which people are coming to view the "family":

- Webster's Ninth Collegiate Dictionary defines *family* as "the basic unit in society having as its nucleus two or more adults living together and cooperating in the care and rearing of their own or adopted children."
- A family is an institution found in many forms that provides children with legal guardianship within the larger society and with the physical and emotional nurturance that will enable them to develop into fully functioning members of society.
- The U.S. Census Bureau defines family as a group of two or more persons related by birth, marriage, or adoption and residing together.
- The New York Court of Appeals says the family can be defined by examining several factors, including "exclusivity and longevity" and the "level of emotional and financial commitment of a relationship." "It is the totality of the relationship as evidenced by the dedication, caring and self-sacrifice of the partners."

When one speaks of family, it must be remembered that families will have many common characteristics as well as many unique characteristics. Table 1 examines

TABLE 1

SOME DEMOGRAPHIC VARIABLES FOR FOUR FAMILY GROUPS

Variable	Asian-American[†]	African-American	Hispanic	Caucasian
Percent of population*	3% (7.5 million)	12.3% (30.31 million)	9% (23 million)	75.6% (188 million)
Percent of married-couple families	80%	47%	56%	83%
Birthrates per 1,000 women, ages 15–44	58%	85%	93%	67%
Birthrates per 1,000 population	18%	22%	27%	15%
Percent of women childless, ages 35–44	40%	13%	12%	18%
Out-of-wedlock births	6%	50%	25%	12%
Percent of one-parent families	14%	57%	32%	21%
Children under 18 living with:				
2 parents	84%	36%	65%	80%
1 parent	14%	57%	32%	21%
Mother only	10%	53%	28%	18%
Father only	2%	3%	4%	3%
Percent of divorced persons	2.1% (men)	8.4% (men)	6.1% (men)	7.1% (men)
	5.7% (women)	11.5% (women)	8.6% (women)	8.9% (women)
Percent high school graduates	82%	68%	53%	80%
Median family income	$42,250	$21,550	$23,912	$38,909
Median income of married couples	high	$34,196	$28,513	$42,738
Percent of persons below poverty level	12.2%	30%	29.5%	11%
Percent of children below poverty level	8%	44%	40%	15%

* The population of the United States was approximately 254 million January 1, 1992.

† Some figures for the Asian-American population are estimates.

some of the characteristics of families in four different ethnic groups. The table represents group averages and does not necessarily represent individual families.

The marriage rate (marriages per 1000 population) varies over time. It was 9.1 in 1994, the lowest since 1965. This should not be taken to mean that fewer Americans in the future will want to enter into long-term intimate relationships. Well over 90 percent of Americans marry in their lifetime, and this is the highest percentage of any industrialized country. Marriage will likely remain a goal for most Americans.

The current low marriage rate results from several trends. First marriage is being postponed by young people. In 1994 the median age of first marriage was 26.8 years for men and 23.8 years for women. This is the highest median age for both sexes since 1890. Postponement of marriage partially results from women's growing interest in career work, and this interest will continue to grow in the future.

Cohabitation among unmarried couples is increasing, and is partially taking the place of marriage. When cohabitation statistics are added to marriage statistics, it would appear that the forming of intimate long-term relationships by Americans is as popular as ever, and it seems likely to continue in the future.

Research evidence about the relationship between cohabitation and future marriage stability is mixed. For never-married couples, cohabitation prior to marriage appears to reduce slightly the chances of future marital success. For previously married couples, cohabitation appears to increase the chances of future marital success. Impacts of these observations upon future marriage trends are self-evident.

Postponement of first marriage, educational advancement, and the growth of economic opportunities for women in the labor market are combining to reduce birth rates and also shift the timing of childbearing toward older ages. Birth rates declined rapidly during the 1960s and early 1970s, reaching an historical low of 1.74 births per woman in 1976. Since that time, fertility rates have leveled off at about 2.1 births per woman, which is approximately the population replacement rate. As women become more career oriented, they tend to postpone parenthood. More than in the past, women claim when young that they will not have children. But the childlessness rate for the first decade of baby boomers 35–44 years old is only running about 17 percent. Most women are opting to have fewer children rather than remaining childless.

Divorce rates are high. The rate (4.7 per 1,000 population) has dropped slightly and leveled off for the past several years from the all-time high (5.3 divorces per 1,000 population), which occurred in 1981. This high divorce rate does not mean that Americans are giving

Percent of total households

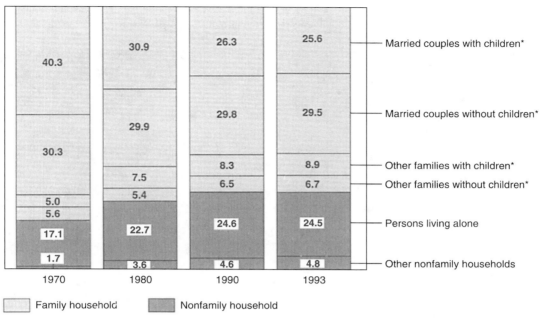

*Own children under 18.

Figure 1. Household composition: 1970–1993.

up on marriage. A high remarriage rate among divorced persons indicates that people are divorcing their spouses, not rejecting the idea of marriage itself. For several centuries, serial marriage has been a proper description of American pattern of marriage, divorce, and remarriage. Americans believe in monogamy, one spouse at a time, but often have more than one spouse over a lifetime.

> *Well over 90 percent of Americans*
>
> *marry in their lifetime,*
>
> *and this is the highest percentage*
>
> *of any industrialized country.*

Such trends mean that future marriages will more and more be between persons, one or both of whom have been married before. At this time, almost half of all marriages involve one or more previously married persons. This will create increasing numbers of "blended" families, which may have his, hers, and their children living in the family home. Partners in a blended family may have economic obligations (such as child support payments) to prior family members. Part-

ners may have to assume stepparent roles to the children of their previously married spouse. They may have to endure separation from their own biological children. What for a family that has remained together is a simple question (where shall we have Christmas or Thanksgiving?) becomes a logistical problem in the blended family.

These trends are reflected in the changing composition of the American family, as shown in Figures 1 and 2. The number of married couples living together with their children has diminished, while the number of men and women living alone and/or with their children is increasing.

The proportion of children living with only one parent has doubled in the past two decades, from 12 percent to 25 percent. The overwhelming majority of children in one-parent families live with their mothers (87 percent). Many of these families live below the poverty level. For many single-parent families, however, the situation is transitional, lasting only until the single-parent marries again.

Projections

It is likely that in the years ahead the creation of long-lasting intimate relationships will remain a goal for most Americans. Most Americans will fulfill this goal by marrying, although an increasing number will cohabit at

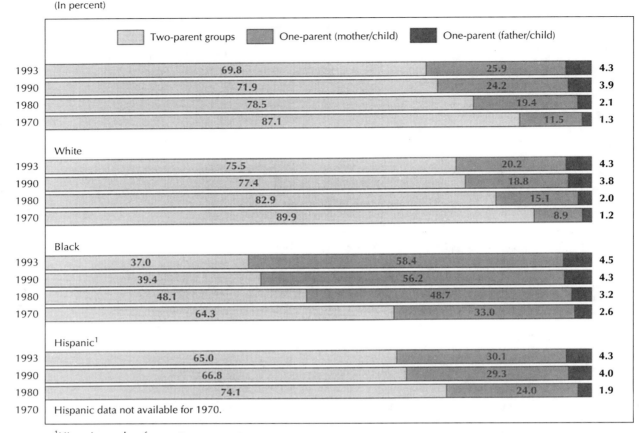

(In percent)

	Two-parent groups	One-parent (mother/child)	One-parent (father/child)

1993	69.8	25.9	4.3
1990	71.9	24.2	3.9
1980	78.5	19.4	2.1
1970	87.1	11.5	1.3
White			
1993	75.5	20.2	4.3
1990	77.4	18.8	3.8
1980	82.9	15.1	2.0
1970	89.9	8.9	1.2
Black			
1993	37.0	58.4	4.5
1990	39.4	56.2	4.3
1980	48.1	48.7	3.2
1970	64.3	33.0	2.6
Hispanic[1]			
1993	65.0	30.1	4.3
1990	66.8	29.3	4.0
1980	74.1	24.0	1.9
1970	Hispanic data not available for 1970.		

[1]Hispanic may be of any race.

Figure 2. Composition of family groups with children by race and Hispanic origin: 1970–1993 (in percent).

least temporarily prior to marriage. As more and more women find satisfaction in the world of career work, marriage and parenthood will continue to be postponed. The increase in single-parent families will probably level off as the divorce rate levels off and remarriage remains popular. The number of blended families in which one or both of the partners have been previously married will continue to increase. Monogamy will remain as a goal and become even more important as society becomes increasingly familiar with and concerned to limit personal exposure to sexually transmitted diseases such as AIDS.

[See also Demographics; Divorce; Families and Households; Family Planning; Family Problems; Family Values; Sexual Codes; Sexual Reproduction.]

BIBLIOGRAPHY

U.S. Bureau of the Census. "The Asian and Pacific Islander Population in the United States: March 1991 and 1990." *Current Population Reports.* P20-459. Washington, DC: U.S. Government Printing Office, 1992.

———. "The Black Population in the United States: March 1992." *Current Population Reports.* P20-471. Washington, DC: U.S. Government Printing Office, 1994.

———. "Fertility of American Women: June 1992." *Current Population Reports.* P20-470. Washington, DC: U.S. Government Printing Office, 1993.

———. "The Hispanic Population in the United States: March 1993." *Current Population Reports.* P20-475. Washington, DC: U.S. Government Printing Office, 1994.

———. "Marital Status and Living Arrangements: March 1993." *Current Population Reports.* P20-478. Washington, DC: U.S. Government Printing Office, 1994.

———. "Money Income of Households, Families, and Persons in the United States: 1992." *Current Population Reports.* P-60-184. Washington, DC: U.S. Government Printing Office, 1993.

———. *Statistical Abstract of the United States: 1994.* Washington, DC: U.S. Government Printing Office, 1994.

— FRANK D. COX

MASS CULTURE AND ARTS

The future of art and mass culture should take into account the many ways in which we define *art* and *culture.* We generally assume broad agreement on such definitions. In fact, they are almost as varied as the modes of expression in the arts, and as diverse as individual experiences of culture. Even the relationship of art *to* culture, though, much explored, remains an open issue embracing many different and conflicting theories.

The world we now live in with its particular qualities of rapid change, physical and psychic mobility, and multiple channels of swift communications and diffusion has few historical precedents as a cultural context. Even the term *mass,* in relation to its prevailing cultural forms, may require qualification in view of the variety and heterogeneity of both its products and its participants.

The Past

The major points regarding the emergence of mass culture, and attitudes toward its growth, tend to focus for various reasons on Western culture, and to suggest that in primitive societies, the arts and culture were coextensive with the society itself, permeating all individual and social activities. As societies and civilizations developed, in complexity and functional specialization, art became more autonomous as an activity. It diverged from its linkage to religion and its direct relationship to the crafts.

The judgmental canons for high culture tended to reflect the societal beliefs and prevailing dogma within which they were created. Conceiving of such work as enduring through time, and as universally applicable expressions of the human condition, of "beauty," "truth," and so forth, these canons also carried with them ideas of permanence, uniqueness, and accessibility according to taste. They also tended to associate aesthetic pleasure with concepts and conditions of moral judgment.

The French and the Industrial Revolutions of the late eighteenth and early nineteenth century contributed significantly to a change in attitudes and focus—the former through its egalitarian principles and elevation of "mass" sentiments and taste; the latter through the

Mass media in the 20th century has had unprecedented influence on culture. New cultural media will be broadcast to a world audience in a lavish diversity of simultaneous modes. (Owen Franken/Corbis)

mass production of vast quantities of economically cheap goods and cultural products via machine manufacture.

Views to the Future

Many recent critical assessments of the future of art and mass culture are focusing more broadly on a crisis in the relationship of culture to society, or within the concept of culture itself.

We need to broaden our definition of culture. A key proposition, therefore, in considering the future of art and mass culture is that development of the mass cultural media involves changes in the very culture itself. As Marshall McLuhan underlined, the medium is the message. This means, in terms of the electronic age, that a totally new cultural environment has been created (McLuhan, 1964). Another commentator (Alloway, 1969) suggests in more pragmatic terms:

> Acceptance of the mass media entails a shift in our notion of what culture is. Instead of reserving the word for the highest artifacts and the noblest thoughts of history's top ten, it needs to be used more widely as the description of "what a society does." Then, unique oil paintings and highly personal poems as well as mass-distributed films and group-aimed magazines can be placed in a continuum rather than frozen in layers in a pyramid.

We have, then, few historical precedents to gauge the future directions of mass culture. Many of the physical instrumentalities that render it possible have not previously existed, and the broad social changes accompanying their developments pose larger and more fundamental questions than we can address in the present discussion.

While cultural messages have traveled in the past slowly along restricted routes to equally restricted audiences, the new cultural media are broadcast to a world audience in a lavish diversity of simultaneous modes. The earlier vertical-oriented elite presenting and directing cultural preferences became simply one of a plurality of elites or "taste groups" that overlap horizontally and are as diverse as their audiences and ingroups. The apex of the taste pyramid became only one node in a mesh of interrelated cultural networks.

> . . . the high scale societies of the Western world are becoming increasingly heterogeneous, comprising thousands of minority groups, *each* joined around common interest, common value systems and shared stylistic preferences that differ from those of other groups. As the sheer value of information and knowledge increases, as technological developments farther expand the range options, and as awareness of the liberty to deviate and differentiate spreads, more variations are *possible*. Rising affluence or, even more, growing desire for at least subcultural identity induces groups to exploit these options and to invent new ones. We might almost say irregular cultural permutations are becoming the rule. (Rittel and Webber, 1973)

The increase of options and choices also entails an increase in the range of responses and value preferences. This weakens individual identification with any fixed cultural community in favor of an increasingly "privatized," temporal, and shifting range of cultural allegiances. We note one aspect of this in the increased differentiation of the individual life cycle where each age group begins to be its own subculture. The problem may, of course, not reach extreme forms due to the paradoxical quality of human proclivities. Just at the point when the increasing rapid diffusion of ideas and artifacts is creating a planetary culture, we have the parallel phenomena of increased interest in, and revival of, local cultural forms—languages, folk styles, and so on.

Art is no longer solely in "the frame"

or in the sculptured form.

In many cases, it moves toward continuous formats.

This *inclusive* tendency also marks the future trends in cultural values that can no longer be judged in "either/or" terms within some implicitly vertical scale. A specific characteristic of future cultural creation and participation may be its "both/and" quality. In order to create, appreciate, and participate in one form, you need not forego a whole range of others. There is no inherent value contradiction in enjoying both a comic book and a symphony.

Interesting consequences for the future of cultural products may have to be mostly questions. What is the status of an "original" work—when it may be replicated by the million or when, as an original or "masterwork," it has no unique form other than as a spool of reproducible film, magnetic tape, or a diskette?

Art Futures

Art is no longer solely in "the frame" or in the sculptured form. In many cases, it moves toward continuous formats, as in the Rauschenberg type of "combine," juxtaposing still image, live radio, and video in the same piece that characteristically spills out into the environment. Or, as in the "happening," the "event," or the conceptual artwork, what is presented *is* the experience or is a communication through which the experience may be reconstructed. The "event" is one of temporal immersion in a flow of communicated experiences, in which the technical means or media are increasingly less obtrusive or constraining. Though much has been made of the antiart quality of these latter manifestations, they probably are less "anti" than some examples of the past tradition. Instead, they are more concerned with a transformation of the idea of art in itself.

> Rather than mocking the idea of the past, artistic practitioners today don't give a damn about it. The art of the past has no more to do with them than past medicine, past theology, and past plumbing . . . "art for art's sake" is no longer being discussed. Life for art's sake also seems Victorian . . . Life for life's sake, or more life for more life's sake is an aesthetic summation of current artistic expression. (Steele, 1971)

The future of art, therefore, seems not to lie so much with the creation of enduring masterworks, but, in part, with the exploration and definition of alternative social and cultural directions. It is not the isolated work that may be important but the overall context, or lifestyle and attitude, within which it is produced. An illustrative example: the late Andy Warhol, the artist, and the Rolling Stones, as a rock group, where the lifestyle of the artist or the group also becomes part of the artwork. The entire persona is presented and becomes an attitudinal model or "ikon" for its audience.

"Life styling" in itself may be viewed, in some senses, as one of the personalized artworks of the future. Such a metamorphosis of lifestyle into cultural expression and creative art is more than a mere change of external forms. It emerges from, and expresses, changes in the values of, and modes of evaluating, the core institutions of society.

The ongoing revolution in information and communications technologies and their ancillary software and interaction are creating what is virtually a new information environment. It is that new environment that is reshaping the cultural content and perception of society itself.

We may speculate, therefore, that where past societies have tended to be dominated exclusively by one measure or calculus for social or cultural worth, such measures could become more diversified in the future. Where previously, for example, the military and more recently the economic calculus were dominant measures for evaluating individual or collective activities, we may emerge into societal forms in which the aesthetic calculus becomes a dominant measure. Ancient China selected its most prestigious officials on the basis of their performance as poets or calligraphers. We may, in the future, consider the poet or painter as no less qualified for public office than the lawyer or businessman—should such fixed occupational roles still exist.

The future of art and mass culture, though treated here as a single theme, needs to be considered as only one aspect of the transformative changes through which we are passing on our way to the future. In order to understand the fundamental bases for change in our conceptions of art and culture "we must begin with a sense of change potential in the most critical of all variables—human beings themselves," (Simon, 1973) rather than with some ultimate fixed human nature through which the expressions of art and culture are governed.

Underlying our conjectures regarding the future of art and mass culture, there are the more central questions of the ways in which personal choices and collective responses must be more consciously oriented toward broadening the imaginative reach and cultural repertory of human possibilities. Art and culture, mass or otherwise, are merely aspects of the larger challenge and long exploratory voyage which faces us—that of learning to be human.

[See also Arts; Literature; Music; Performing Arts: Dance and Theatre; Visual Arts.]

BIBLIOGRAPHY

Alloway, Lawrence. "The Long Front of Culture." In John Russell and Suzi Gablik, eds. *Pop Art Redefined.* New York: Praeger, 1969.

McLuhan, Marshall. *Understanding Media.* New York: McGraw-Hill, 1964.

Rittel, Horst W. T., and Webber, Melvin M. "Dilemmas in a General Theory of Planning." *Policy Sciences* 4/2 (June 1973).

Simon, William. "Future Relationships Between Man and Society." Paper presented at the Rome Special World Conference on Futures Research, September 1973.

Steele, Robert. "Art, Youth Culture, and the Movies." In Bernard Rosenberg and David Manning, eds. *Mass Culture Revisited.* New York: Van Nostrand-Reinhold, 1971.

— JOHN MCHALE
MAGDA MCHALE

MATERIALS: RESEARCH AND DEVELOPMENT

The history of human development can be told through changes in the use and manipulation of materials. The progress of humankind and its technological sophistication has been determined by the materials of construction available at the time. The stone age began when primitive man learned to shape stones into tools. With the dawn of the bronze age, humans learned to smelt metals and make copper and bronze tools to aid in food gathering and preparation. The development of iron technology allowed increases in the span of structures as well as decreases in their bulk. More complicated design allowed materials to be used much more efficiently. For example, truss structures made from cast iron were used by railroads to span rivers and canyons. The industrial revolution would not have been possible without the development of tough, high-strength steels. Steel expanded the scope of material designs from the truss to the cantilever beam. Lightweight metals such as aluminum, magnesium, and titanium permitted designers to build practical aircraft and aerospace structures, meeting the needs of the emerging space age in the 1950s.

Polymeric Materials

Polymeric materials have evolved to replace metals in many applications because of performance, availability, and reduced systems cost. In the early twentieth century, chemistry played a key role in the evolution of polymeric materials. Synthetic polymers were first explored in Europe in the early twentieth century. In the 1930s, the fundamental research of Wallace Carothers and his associates led to better understanding of polymeric structures and the development of neoprene synthetic rubber and nylon fibers. From that time on, progress has been swift as synthetic polymeric materials have rapidly evolved to replace older products, i.e., synthetic rubber for natural rubber, synthetic fibers for natural fibers, plastic containers and plastic bottles for metals and glass bottles, engineering plastic for die cast metals.

Synthetic polymeric materials offer several advantages over metals, among them excellent strength for equivalent weight, improved corrosion resistance, design flexibility, and easy fabrication. Polymeric materials have significantly better properties than aluminum and steel for engineering applications. Another factor important today because of limited energy resources is the energy required to produce materials (energy content). This energy is significantly higher for metals.

The world's polymer industry has undergone a remarkable period of sustained growth beginning with World War II and lasting about twenty-five years to the beginning of the 1970s. This growth was fueled by an explosion of new knowledge in macromolecular chemistry, polymerization technology, structure property relationships, and mechanical shaping technology. New monomers and new methods of polymerization were investigated, seeking new materials and properties. This

led to remarkable improvements in the basic properties of polymeric materials.

Metal Replacement

The first wave of metals replacement by engineering plastics began in secondary, noncritical application with the commercialization of nylon resin in 1950. DuPont and Celanese introduced polyacetal resin in 1959 followed by polycarbonate from General Electric in 1964. In 1965, General Electric commercialized one of the first polymeric alloys, a modified phenylene oxide. Polymeric alloys became even more evident as blending, reinforcement, and toughening technology opened up hundreds of new applications. Additional generic molding resins such as PBT polyesters from Celanese, PET polyesters from DuPont, and their alloys were introduced in the 1970s. The early 1980s saw the introduction of supertough nylon and acetals and stiffened PET polyesters. Although plastic resins cost more than steel on a pound-for-pound basis, assembled and finished plastic parts often offer a total system cost savings because of lower density, lower tooling and fabrication costs, design flexibility, parts consolidation, and fewer assembly steps. The growth of engineering polymers has primarily been in metal substitution or replacement, particularly for die-cast metals and hot rolled steel.

The history of human development can be told through changes in the use and manipulation of materials.

The volume of synthetic polymers grew from 15 million in 1923 to over 60 billion pounds in 1990, representing a compound annual growth rate of 15 percent for over sixty years. DuPont in particular derived the majority of its revenue and earnings during this period by replacing traditional materials (wood, metal, cotton, wool) with synthetic polymeric materials made from petroleum. Leading this great wave of replacement was the substitution of noncellulosic fibers for cellulosic fibers.

Generically, new polymers such as Lycra® spandex, Nomex®, and Kevlar® aramids and nonwoven sheet structures such as Tyvek® fueled the substitution. A large part of the entire textile system (texturing, weaving, dyeing, permanent press washing cycles, etc.) was transformed in order to accommodate the new polymeric fibers.

The second great wave of polymeric materials substitution is the replacement of metals by engineering and reinforced plastics in critical primary structural applications. This wave of metal replacement began with the development of superstrong, superstiff, lightweight fibers such as carbon, graphite, aramid, and silicon carbide. Advanced polymeric materials based on high-performance carbon and aramid fibers have begun to replace the two primary metals aluminum and steel in demanding structural applications. The projection is mathematically calculated according to technological substitution theory. We used a volume basis in calculating this curve because in many cases it is the volume of a material that is performing a task, not its weight. This S-curve shows dramatically that the rapid takeover phase of engineering and reinforced plastics for metals is about to begin. By the year 2015, these sophisticated materials should have gained about half the market. We are now perched at the cusp of a growth surge to come. In the middle of the next century when this S-curve is coming to an end, we (or our descendants) should see the end of rust as a problem and a largely polymeric personal vehicle in every garage. The consumption of steel and aluminum is mature and declining. Metal replacement represents an enormous market potential—over 30 billion pounds in the United States and about 200 billion pounds worldwide.

Systems Thinking and the Specific Solution

What will it take to fulfill the promise of this growth curve? Many people think we should concentrate on two areas: systems thinking and specific solutions. This process is more challenging than the simple materials substitution we saw in the fibers case. As the substitution for metals continues, new, integrated engineering concepts and specifically designed polymeric composite systems will be needed. We will not simply replace metals: we will put together these materials in new ways, designing their properties to our own specifications. It will be a substitution of new, tailor-made, anisotropic, synthetic material systems for traditional isotropic materials.

Earlier ages were eras of specific solutions. Primitives built a stone ax to meet their own specific needs. Of course, it was primitive, but they knew what they wanted. The industrial revolution changed all that. As new materials and manufacturing technologies were developed, the era of the general solution was born and was exemplified by automobile manufacturer Henry Ford. He had a famous slogan during the 1920s: "Any color you want as long as it's black." This slogan symbolized mass production. Massive quantities of generic materials (steel, glass) were assembled repeatedly in the same way and huge cost savings resulted. You could not buy exactly what you wanted—it was too expensive—but you could at least get something close. Now, and especially in the future, you can have it both ways. People will demand a specific solution to meet their needs and they will get it because it will be technically feasible at a reasonable cost.

It is the new computer technology, in the broadest sense, that makes it possible to pursue specific solutions again through flexible, intelligent manufacturing and distribution systems. In addition, some cost savings are inherent to specific solutions because only the materials needed for that specific task will be used.

In theory, everything we buy will be tailor-made to meet our specific needs. It is already happening. In medicine, we can go from broad-spectrum antibiotics to disease-specific diagnosis and treatment. In agriculture, from general fertilizers and herbicides to the ability to feed and protect crops in specific soils and climates and also to design those crops for specific food industry needs. The world of structural materials is not immune to this phenomenon; what once was only isotropic steel and commodity polymer is now moving toward more use of anisotropic material systems where a particular arrangement of components solves a specific problem.

Revolutionary Material Developments

Dramatic advances in material systems will come when some level of intelligence is embedded into the system itself. Smartness in systems is entering our everyday lives today. It consists of three elements: sensing, analysis, and feedback control or response. More and more automobiles today can adjust their own brakes and carburetor fuel mixtures. Some cars give their drivers a continuous analysis of the state of their systems and recommend preventive maintenance. The continuously self-tuning internal combustion engine is being developed. Today, the smart house, where utilities are automatically monitored and adjusted to meet the needs of its residents, is almost a reality.

Embedding intelligence in material systems will help overcome current limitations holding back their pervasive substitution for metals. This materials revolution will proceed in four distinct but overlapping phases.

The first phase is already in progress; replacement occurs on a one-for-one basis, usually a polymer composite for a metal. The design of the system does not change. In the second phase, the system design is changed to take advantage of the multifunctional properties of the new materials. In both of these first two phases, the composite systems are passive, i.e., made up of basic material components in specific ways that do more than the simple sum of their parts, but that generate no useful information. The most dramatic advances will come in the third and fourth phases when material systems are developed that will be able to "sense" their environment *and* respond to such an environment by either adapting themselves (i.e., their properties) to be more productive and/or by actually changing their environment. It is during this third phase that the rapid substitution of active for passive material systems will occur. These active material systems that are responsive and adaptive are truly smart systems.

Dramatic advances in material systems

will come when some level of intelligence

is embedded into the system itself.

In the future, we will learn from nature and biological polymers in our design of polymeric material systems. Biological polymers have an architecture that is precisely matched to the stresses they experience. We are aware today that natural material synthesis is carried out in a very specific and precise fashion against chemical templates. These templates can be DNA itself or the chemical catalyst enzymes specified by DNA. What is perhaps less well known is that these natural materials, once synthesized, are internally programmed to self-order themselves into higher-level structures or material systems. A good example is the tendon tissue. The tendon has six distinct levels of organization starting with molecules of collagen in fibrous form assembled into a triple helix and finishing with a crimped bundle of fiber assemblages called fascicles. No synthetic material known has the strength and long-lasting three-dimensional flexibility of tendon tissue. But then, no synthetic material is assembled into such a highly ordered and complex material system—we simply do not know enough to do it. But nature does, and we must learn creatively from nature.

Our challenge is to learn how to make more efficient material systems using these natural, highly ordered systems as models. Sensors, controllers, and actuators small enough to be incorporated into composites without significantly limiting their integrity are within sight. Intelligent material systems will be a reality in the first quarter of the twenty-first century.

In conclusion, most of the new knowledge that will drive wealth-creation well into the next century is centered in three areas: advanced materials, bioscience, and information science. How we apply this knowledge to solve increasingly more difficult and important problems will determine how well we replace metals with polymeric materials. Success in the twenty-first century

will demand continuously learning organizations that evolve toward multifunctional, multidisciplined technical networks to develop new technologies.

[*See also* Batteries; Clothing; Engineering; Genetic Technologies; Hazardous Wastes; Industrial Design; Minerals; Motor Vehicles; Petroleum; Scientific Breakthroughs; Solid Waste; Technology Diffusion.]

BIBLIOGRAPHY

Business Week, (February 9, 1987).

Dhingra, A. K. "Metals Replacement by Composites." *Journal of Metals* (March 1986): 17.

Dhingra, A. K.; Cunning, J. D.; Doherty, T. P.; and Pletcher, T. C. "Future Systems Integration for Development of Advanced Fibers and Composite Materials. Advanced Materials for Future Industries: Needs and Seeds." In *Proceedings of the Second Japan International SAMPE Symposium and Exhibition.* Chiba, Japan, December 11–14, 1991.

Dhingra, A. K., and Doherty, T. P. "Future Trends in Advanced Fibers and Composite Materials Technology." In T. Chandra and A. K. Dhingra, eds. *Advanced Composites '93.* Minerals, Metals & Materials (TMS) Society, 1993.

Miller, J. A. "Polymers in the 21st Century." Keynote lecture at Polymers '94 Symposium, Indian Petrochemicals Corporation Ltd, Vadodara, India, February 8–10, 1994.

Morgan, R. J.; Baer, E.; and Hiltner, A. "Advanced Structural Multiperformance Materials for the Next Century." *SAMPE Journal,* 29/2 (March/April 1993).

Tanner, D.; Dhingra, A. K.; Cooper, J. L.; and Pigliacampi, J. "Future of Aramid Fiber Composites as a General Engineering Material." *Nippon Fukugo Zairyo Gakkaishi* 2/5 (1985).

– J. A. MILLER

A. J. DAHL

ASHOK K. DHINGRA

MEDIA CONSOLIDATION

The media and cultural industries are joining, if not leading, the globalization of corporate enterprise. Paralleling the rapid expansion since World War II of American corporate production sites around the world, newspaper, television, film, publishing, recording, and advertising companies increasingly have been selling their product in scores of national markets.

Massive corporate conglomerates of cultural production, based in a few metropolitan centers, now produce and sell the bulk of the world's entertainment and informational (news and data) fare. Time-Warner, Disney, Murdoch's News Corporation, Bertelsmann, Sony, Matsushita, El Globo, Hachette, Viacom, and a few other similar combines preside over what the global audience sees, hears, and reads.

Facilitating the growth of these international combines has been a continuing explosion of new information technologies—television, satellite communications, cable TV, computerization, fiber optics, and so on. These technologies provide instantaneous global (and national) transmission and reception of messages and images with economies of scale that reduce costs and allow the global media products to overwhelm local outputs.

Other large corporate enterprises engaged in producing, collecting, organizing, and disseminating information also have emerged alongside the pop culture combines. These include financial and business service companies and electronic database producers who assemble vast stockpiles of information that can be accessed electronically, worldwide, wherever terminals exist, *at a price.* Accordingly, Reuters, Dow-Jones, McGraw-Hill, Reed-Elsevier, Knight-Ridder, and a handful of similar firms have become the producers and custodians of a good chunk of the world's information, and to a certain extent, the global memory. They make this available to users—governmental, corporate, and individual—who can afford to pay-for it.

This institutional arrangement almost inevitably ensures a growing gap between those who can purchase information and those who cannot. No less consequential, *what* will be collected and made available in the commercial informational stockpile is largely governed by the needs of the most influential and well-off users.

There are other effects as well—not the least of which is the threat to the survival of diverse opinion and free expression.

First, the large-scale corporate entertainment and information enterprises, by their command of enormous resources, marginalize and often eliminate the smaller, less well-financed alternative sources. Secondly, the willingness of the large, heavily concentrated cultural combines to allow a full range of opinion and creative effort in their offerings is governed by financial and ideological considerations.

High production costs of programming make corporate media managers reluctant to go outside tried and tested formulaic material. Excluded almost automatically at the outset are formats and ideas that challenge routine patterns in any serious way. Reinforcing this cautiousness is an equally strong managerial suspicion of thematic material that is critical of established, dominant values and institutions.

There is a third, and perhaps the most important, structural element in the limitation of speech: the primacy of corporate sponsorship. Dependent on advertising revenue, television in the United States is essentially a conduit for the sales messages of big corporate goods-and-services providers. Their sales messages create the commercial atmosphere that pervades American TV. Since a commercial's objective is usually to encourage the consumption of this or that good or service,

the omnipresence of commercials overwhelms and often trivializes whatever programming material that precedes or follows it.

The national sponsors, who are the main supporters of TV (and a good part of the other media as well), are also exceedingly sensitive to any views that they consider potentially injurious to their economic interests. All the same, open censorship in the American media is infrequent. Much more significant, though less easy to comprehend, *censorship is embedded in the institutional structures of the media.* It is implemented daily, even hourly, by decisions made by media broadcasters, journalists, editors, scriptwriters, and others, who have internalized, knowingly or not, the values of their corporate employers. Most media hands are well aware of what is expected of them. If not, they are quickly informed.

In the 1990s, many observers acknowledge the decline of U.S. power internationally. Yet, however true this may be with regard to industrial activity, it is, at least to date, totally inapplicable to American worldwide information-cultural power. In fact, this power has never been stronger. U.S. exports of movies, TV programs, books and magazines, tapes and recordings, even theme parks, information from electronic databases, and *language itself* (the world increasingly speaks English) confirm the dominant position of the United States in the global cultural-media sphere.

In the 1970s, scores of nations objected to the one-way flow of American media product—from Hollywood or New York to everywhere else. These countries expressed their hope in numerous meetings and resolutions for a new international information order (NIIO). This hope has not been realized. The strength of U.S. media products in the world market—compared to that of the rest of the world—is greater than ever. The "free flow of information"—the code expression for the unrestricted global movement of the products and services of Western media conglomerates—has gained, and maintained, a global advantage for American cultural material.

United States dominance of the information realm now extends to newer information forms such as electronic databases. In 1990, the United States produced 70 percent of the world's databases. Whoever accesses these electronic data repositories, especially those holding social data, not only pays for this service, but also receives subtle but not inconsequential social perspectives that guided the compiler's selection and organization of the data.

It is difficult to predict precisely at this time how far into the future American primacy in information, entertainment, and pop culture will endure. Indeed, how long can it flourish if the economic underpinning continues to erode? Also, it is hardly likely that the widespread demand for information equality and cultural sovereignty will disappear. If anything, it is going to grow stronger. This suggests that in the cultural and information realms in the years ahead, a deepening struggle will develop, domestically and internationally, for freedom of personal and creative expression. The times are bound to be conflictive, exciting, and hopeful.

[See also Communications; Communications: Privacy Issues; Communications Technology; Computer Linkage; Electronic Convergence; Global Culture; Information Society; Media Lab; Printed Word; Satellite Communications; Telecommunications; Television.]

BIBLIOGRAPHY

Bagdikian, Ben. Media Monopoly. Boston: Beacon Press, 1992.
Bennett, James R. Control of the Media in the United States: An Annotated Bibliography. New York: Garland, 1992.
Dennis, Everett, and Merrill, John C. Media Debates: Issues in Mass Communication. White Plains, NY: Longman, 1991.
Herman, Edward S., and Chomsky, Noam. Manufacturing Consent. New York: Pantheon, 1988.
Schiller, Herbert. Culture Inc.: The Corporate Takeover of Public Expression. New York: Oxford University Press, 1989.

— HERBERT I. SCHILLER

MEDIA OF EXCHANGE

Media of exchange (MOE) will continue to evolve—from barter to commodity money such as cattle or tobacco, to precious metals, to paper currencies backed by precious metals, to currencies backed by governments and good faith—by becoming increasingly electronic over the next generation. Cash and currency will still be with us, but they will be augmented and increasingly replaced by electronic MOE, with countertrade—in which goods are exchanged without cash changing hands—the most prominent alternative. Indeed, electronics may enable us to arrive at a global currency.

Forces Shaping the Future Media of Exchange

The technological infrastructure supporting electronic MOE is growing rapidly. The information infrastructure is flowering as the fiber-optic backbone and wireless ancillaries are put in place. Computers are becoming ubiquitous at the office and school, on the road, and in the home. On the social side, increasing time pressures in business, such as the move to just-in-time delivery, and the rise of dual-income households are impelling the move toward faster and more convenient electronic transactions.

Banks are moving to electronic service delivery. There were about 96,000 ATMs (automatic teller machines) and 200,000 POS (point of sale) terminals in 1993, according to Bank Network News. Perhaps 40 percent of the country's 100,000 bank branches will be closed by the year 2000, replaced by ATMS and videoconferencing, according to Joel Friedman of Andersen Consulting. Credit and debit cards are used for a growing share of purchases—about 12.3 million households use a debit card and 66.5 million a major credit card, according to Payment Systems Incorporated.

A global economy is steadily emerging as indicated by the growing percentage of national GNPs derived from international trade. Businesses searching for new markets will require new tools for dealing with developing nations, which are often financially strapped. Increased international trade will encourage nations to harmonize disparate currencies.

Three Primary Conclusions About the Future Media of Exchange

The forces described above will lead to three significant changes in future MOE. First, money will become increasingly electronic. Today's alphabet soup of electronic money—ATM (automatic teller machines, owned both by banks and nonbanks), POS (point-of-sale), EFT (electronic funds transfer)—is an integral element moving us toward reliance on electronic MOE. Big institutional money already is electronic. Electronic wire transfers from Fedwire, the Clearinghouse International Payment System (CHIPS), and retail transactions account for a daily flow of electronic money equal to over one-third of the annual U.S. GNP (Solomon, 1993, pp. 69–70).

The progression will be as follows: first, from ATM to POS terminals at checkouts using debit and credit cards; next, to wireless, portable checkout, as used today by car rental firms, including Hertz; finally, to smart "digicash" cards. These machines or their equivalents will be readily available in public domains (kiosks in malls) and in businesses, as well as in the home. The transactions performed electronically will become increasingly sophisticated—for example, Citibank will eventually allow its customers to trade money-market and mutual fund shares at ATMs.

Cash for small transactions will be the last to go electronic. New schemes for digital cash address and strive to resolve privacy concerns and transaction costs that marred previous attempts. Companies would sell e-money refills, similar to traveler's checks, that are anonymous and untraceable using security-protected digital signatures. For example, a digicash card used to pay for a steak would allow both the merchant and the bank to record the transaction but not to link those transactions to a specific person. Other possibilities include attaching electronic money to e-mail or automatically sending the bill for renting a video as it is played (Kelly, 1993, pp. 56–57).

Secondly, a global capital market and global currency will more fully emerge. Global capital markets will enable borrowers to traverse the globe in search of the best terms. The time and space barriers that have kept financial markets and MOE local and national will be surmounted by information technology and financial networks. Global currency will gain increasing support and momentum as nations and businesses seek protection from wildly fluctuating exchange rates. Regional currency is already emerging in the EC (European Community), even as individual nations maintain their own medium of exchange.

Perhaps 40 percent of the country's 100,000 bank branches will be closed by the year 2000, replaced by ATMs and videoconferencing.

The obstacles to global currency include national politics and the absence of a common monetary policy or credible international mechanisms for determining that policy. Economist Gary Hufbauer points out that "a common currency is the last state of a lot of other integration that takes place first."

Thirdly, countertrade will be an increasingly important mechanism for doing business in developing nations.

A key challenge for the global economy is to close the gap between rich and poor nations. Businesses in developed nations will also be searching for new markets in developing nations with growing populations and economies. In business terms, a key question is how to do business with a cash-poor or bankrupt customer.

Countertrade is accelerating as an MOE, enabling developed and developing nations to trade, as well as enhancing trade among developing nations. Such transactions account for an estimated 10–20 percent of world trade today, according to the United Nations Commission on Trade and Development (UNCTAD). Almost two-thirds of the Fortune 500 companies have used it or are using it now.

Countertrade consists mainly of barter and counterpurchase transactions that commit the exporter to buy goods from the importer. A cash value is fixed for accounting, taxation, and insurance purposes.

In summary, future MOE will be increasingly electronic and global, alongside persisting traditional mechanisms, including cash and counter-trade or barter.

[See also Capital Formation; Communications; Communications: Privacy Issues; Investments; Monetary System; Telecommunications.]

BIBLIOGRAPHY

Kelly, Kevin. "Cyberpunks, E-Money, and the Technologies of Disconnection." *Whole Earth Catalog* (Summer 1993).
Kurtzman, Joel. *The Death of Money.* New York: Simon & Schuster, 1993.
Solomon, Elinor Harris. "Electronic Funds Transfer: Challenges for the Computer Age." *Bankers Magazine* (January–February 1993): 69–70.

– ANDY HINES

MEDIA LAB

The Media Lab at the Massachusetts Institute of Technology is the brainchild of Nicholas Negroponte, its founder, director, and chief visionary. In 1985, Negroponte, now the Wiesner Professor of Media Technology, united a group of diverse MIT research groups and gave them a common purpose: to devise new ways for people to interact with information. He was driven, in large measure, by the inadequacy and user-unfriendliness of computers and other information technologies. Personal computers, he maintained, are anything but personal. Under Negroponte's guidance, the Media Lab began to create a new world of machines that see, hear, and talk and computers that can produce a custom blend of information based on personal interests of the reader. The guiding vision was to create personalized technologies that know and serve their human masters in the manner of an English butler. Examples are refrigerators that will order milk before the carton is empty and telephones that will tell callers to try later.

Within ten years of its founding, the Media Lab has grown into a $20 million/year research and teaching organization with twenty-three faculty members and more than one hundred graduate students. Approximately 70 percent of the contract research funding comes from industrial sponsors and the balance from various agencies of the federal government. Sponsor companies range from telecommunications to advertising, from publishing to finance. Of the sponsors, 25 percent are Japanese and another 25 percent European.

One of the main areas of Media Lab research is speech recognition by machines. It is trying to build machines that could turn out whole spoken conversation into a printout and has already produced a "Dataglove" that translates hand motion into electronic instructions for a computer. It is working on ways to pump video signals down a 1.2-megabit-per-second communications channel. This would permit transmission of movies to homes using existing telephone wires, with a picture quality better than that from VHS videocassettes. It has also been instrumental in furthering the development of the graphical user interface found in home computers today and in helping to foster the ongoing evolution of the blend of text, graphics, sound manipulation, and image processing that is known as multimedia computing.

The Media Lab is engaged in a number of projects that will change the computer environment of the future and break engineering deadlocks.

- Matthew Brand is working on visual intelligence with the goal of producing robots that are visually fluent and can cooperate with humans in the design, assembly, and repair of objects.
- Justin Cassell is designing a system that integrates gesture, intonation, and facial expressions into multimodal human figure animation.
- Kenneth Haase is creating memory-based representational systems for comprehending, filtering, and summarizing news stories. Memory-based representation uses analogies between descriptions to identify semantic roles and categories. This would lead to natural-sounding computer-synthesized speech combining semantic and contextual information such as pause, intonation, rhythm, and inflection.
- Haase and Gloriana Davenport are working on storyteller systems that can produce customized stories adapted to the listener's background, preferences, and interests. Such systems transform the nature of publication; rather than producing epistles, they produce emissaries.
- Henry Lieberman is combining representation and learning techniques from artificial intelligence with interactive graphical editors to create programming by example.
- Pattie Moses has created ALIVE (Artificial Life Interactive Video Entertainment), a novel system that allows wireless full-body interaction between a human participant and a rich graphical world inhabited by autonomous agents. This is achieved through the use of interface agents or digital assistants. Interface agents may be used to select news articles, videos, music, and television shows; they also serve as personal critics and editors to recommend books, software, and videos.
- Michael Resnick, Seymour Papert, and Fred Martin have built programmable LEGO bricks that enable children to create robots and sensory rooms.
- Richard Bolt and Ronald MacNeil are building DataWall, an ultra-high-definition, seamlessly tiled, wall-sized display with which human beings can interact using natural language and gestures.
- Alex Pentland, Michael Hawley, Rosalind Picard, and Thad Starner are working on compact computers that can be "worn" like eyeglasses or clothing. With heads-up displays, unobtrusive input devices, and a host of other sensing and communication tools, wearable computers can serve as intelligent assistants. A related project is the BodyNet, a local wireless network that will integrate all the information appliances on a person—cameras, watches, calculators, notebooks, date books, checkbooks, and credit cards—connected to advanced displays, radios, and other communication systems.
- Christopher Schmandt is working on a hand-held, audio note-taker, with a speech-recognition interface, as well as an interactive radio with programs compiled from a number of sources presented on demand over the telephone or on a computer workstation.
- Barry Vercoe has built a computer-driven piano to show that computers can exhibit real-time musical behavior similar to that of skilled human performers.

- Walter Bender has devised Data-Hiding or Steganography, the process of embedding data into image and audio signals. This technique is being evaluated in the light of three applications: copyright-protection, tamper-proofing, and augmentation-data embedding.
- Michael Klug has created a holographic laser printer that allows hardcopy holograms to be generated in minutes rather than hours, automatically and without wet processing.
- V. Michael Bove has built eight systems of Cheops, including a data-flow television receiver, a compact imaging system and modular platform for acquisition, real-time processing, display of digital video sequences, and model-based representations of moving scenes.
- Michael Hawley's Media Fab is a 254-thread-per-inch multicolor printer that outputs to garments instead of photocopy paper.
- Andrew Lippman's Media Bank is a distributed web of processors that contains audio and video bits, snippets, and movies. The system is designed to synthesize programs on demand and assemble movies from multiple depositories. A Mosaic-based browser navigates through the migratory and evolving data, and an automatic page-generator depicts the current content and object location.
- The Visible Language Workshop is a seamless, sophisticated, graphical, dynamic, and interactive testbed for use in prototyping tools, editors, and scenarios.

The Media Lab is pushing the envelope in many promising directions with the goal of making technology more user-friendly and intuitive. In the world of frontier information technology it is serving as the advance guard working with ideas that will drive the future.

[See also Communications: Technology; Computers: Overview; Computers: Software; Interactive Entertainment.]

BIBLIOGRAPHY

Brand, Stewart. *Media Lab: Inventing the Future at MIT.* New York: Viking-Penguin, 1988.

— GEORGE THOMAS KURIAN

MEDIA LAW.

See COMMUNICATIONS: MEDIA LAW.

MEDICAL CARE PROVIDERS

In the years ahead, health professionals will be able to enhance or restore health far better than at present. However, the future boundaries, responsibilities, and reimbursement mechanisms for health care professionals are unclear. The future of the various health professions will be shaped by a variety of developments in each profession, as well as by more general trends in health care and society. Generally, the capacity of a specific health-care professional to be a healer will increase, as will the ability of consumers to handle more sophisticated self-care at home. Expert systems and advancing biological knowledge will mean a decline in the demand for some providers. The most effective health care professionals will be rewarded accordingly. As a result, providers with poor performance may not be allowed to practice. Even where certifying or licensing groups do not remove them, they may find it more difficult to get patients or jobs.

Major Trends

THE PREDICT-AND-MANAGE APPROACH. Health care, benefiting from advances in the knowledge of disease processes, aging, and genetic influences, will shift its focus from treating health conditions after they arise to preventing them or at least minimizing their impact. This predict-and-manage approach will hasten new consumer-oriented use of technologies, as well as decentralizing expert medical knowledge to primary-care providers (both doctors and nurses) and consumers.

HEALTH INFORMATION SYSTEMS. Four related developments in information systems will profoundly shape health professions. First, computer-based medical records will store all patient information including problems, test results, orders submitted, treatment plans, X rays, and other data. Over time, new types of information on genetic and biochemical proclivities to disease will be incorporated. Second, consumers will have greater access to health information through interactive learning and communication technologies, including detailed information about their own health conditions as well as information about disease prevention and health promotion. Third, expert systems will assist physicians, other health-care providers, and consumers in making therapeutic decisions. Fourth, inexpensive, non-invasive, or minimally invasive body-function monitoring devices (such as health-monitoring wristwatches) will be integral to prevention and treatment efforts.

THE BIOLOGICAL REVOLUTION. By the year 2010, the human genome will be completely sequenced, heightening the understanding of genetic influences on health and disease. Coupled with a clearer understanding of our current health, mental health, and disease states—culled from more effective medical information management—health care will use this new knowledge to develop more biochemically unique care, more refined biological markers, and better targeted therapeutics.

HEALTH OUTCOMES MEASUREMENTS. Major efforts are under way in Europe and the United States to develop and apply measures of health outcome. The implementation of electronic medical records facilitates gathering and analyzing large amounts of patient data. Better patient data will allow comparisons of individual health provider results and different therapies. Health outcome measurements will play a growing role in exposing inappropriate medical practices and enhancing therapeutic selection. Locally, consumer groups will de-

velop comparative success statistics for physicians, nurses, and other health care providers.

THE HEALTH PROMOTION MOVEMENT. Sickness care still dominates: 96 percent of medical expenditures are related to treatment, less than 4 percent to prevention. Growing understanding that the leading causes of death and disability are greatly influenced by behavior will change this. Cost constraints will encourage health promotion as the best strategy for reducing costs in the long run, while markedly improving health.

The capacity of a specific health-care professional to be a healer will increase, as will the ability of consumers to handle more sophisticated self-care at home.

DEMOGRAPHICS. As the baby boomer generation ages, a larger proportion of the population also will become older. This translates not only into a greater demand for elder care, but for more sophisticated prevention and better treatment services prompted by rising expectations and entitlements

LICENSURE. Health care professionals, particularly physicians, must be "licensed" to practice. Licensure of physicians was originally established as a public policy measure to protect consumers from fraudulent providers. However, licensure grants physicians a monopoly over the right to practice medicine. Other licensed health care providers (dentists, pharmacists, nurses, and less tightly regulated providers such as homeopaths and other alternative care providers) offer physicians relatively little direct competition at present. In the near future, increasing dissatisfaction with physicians, the anticipated growth of nurse practitioners, competition from alternative providers, increased access to health information through decentralizing technology, and health-outcome measures showing that some health care providers (especially nurses) are more cost-effective will elicit cries for changing medical licensure. Nurses and allied health professionals will push to gain professional status and equality through revised controls over practice. Licensure will move toward outcome-based judgments of quality, limiting the ability of physicians to limit the scope of activity of other licensed professionals.

MALPRACTICE. Direct medical liability costs (insurance premiums) were conservatively estimated in the late 1980s to represent less than 1 percent of the nation's total health care expenditures. Defensive medical procedures cost around $15 billion in 1989, for a whopping $23 billion in total costs annually, by AMA estimates. Most malpractice claims are directed at physicians. Tort laws may be modified to limit the amount of malpractice awards, which could bring about a drop in insurance premiums and unnecessary testing. Specific ways to accomplish this may include: a monetary cap on "pain and suffering" damages that a jury can award; a sliding-scale limit on attorney contingency fees; and/or a provision to allow damages over a specific amount to be paid in installments.

The Health Professions

PHYSICIANS. In the last two decades, physicians have gravitated toward specialty practices, where remuneration is high and results are immediate and clear-cut. The number of primary care physicians in the United States declined dramatically in the last decade, falling 19 percent between 1986 and 1992. Strong pressure will be applied to increase the proportion of active primary care physicians. The number of active physicians is projected to rise from around 600,000 in 1992 to 720,000 by the year 2000.

At the same time, nurses and other health practitioners will assume more responsibility for primary care. As health promotion becomes dominant, health care providers will increasingly assume the role of "health coaches."

As expert systems decentralize knowledge, there will be fewer specialty physicians needed in fields that deal largely with information rather than physical procedures (e.g., surgery). Many physical procedures may be automated and become accessible to primary care providers. Overall there will be a shift to primary care, with keener competition among types of providers and therapies. Providing favorable outcomes in cost-competitive ways will become hallmarks of success.

NURSES. Changing technology and the increased role for "healers" could dramatically alter the nurse's role. Nurses already handle many aspects of primary care more cost-effectively than physicians, and this trend will continue as demands for care increase. Recent attempts to raise academic and licensure requirements to practice nursing emphasize this expanding role. Nurses will need to demonstrate their effectiveness, measured through outcomes data, to foster these changes. Even so, a decline in the demand for nurses will come as hospital inpatient care declines.

DENTISTS. Better oral hygiene dramatically cut the demand for dentists, leading the dental profession to voluntarily limit student enrollment in dental schools. By 2000, only 3,200 dental students may graduate from dental schools, down from a peak of 5,756 in 1983. Dentists, in the past, delegated many tasks to their den-

tal hygienists. If demand falls, dentists may seek to reclaim some of these tasks, lowering demand for dental hygienists' services. Adult orthodontics and treatment for gum disease will provide some degree of business, but professional teeth-cleaning services will continue to be dentistry's economic mainstay. However, if dental licensing changes, oral hygienists could offer these services independently.

PHARMACISTS. Pharmacy professionals created a valuable position for themselves in hospitals when they established their role as clinical pharmacists, significantly aiding the improvement of hospital drug therapy. While pharmacists will continue to be needed in hospitals and in managed-care settings such as HMOs, overall, the hospital pharmacy business will decline as the size and number of hospitals decline. Demand for consulting pharmacists in nursing homes will grow.

As the dispensing aspects of their job become increasingly automated, community pharmacies will need to become more involved in counseling customers about drug use and related health issues.

As the dispensing aspects of their job become increasingly automated, community pharmacists will need to become more involved in counseling customers about drug use and related health issues. If community pharmacists—especially smaller retail pharmacists—do not reinvent their role, they will see a decline in demand for their services, left behind by technological advancement and economies of scale. With the rise of expert systems and the decentralization of health information, pharmacists will have tougher competition, particularly from mail-order firms. Also, pharmaceutical products and allied product lines will become more complex. Some pharmacies will use "designer gene machines" to develop medications uniquely suited to specific customers.

ALLIED HEALTH. Other allied health professions can be divided into those related to physical touching or personal coaching (such as physical therapy and occupational therapy) and those built around specific medical technologies.

Therapies that involve physical touch draw the greatest demand, a trend that will continue unabated into the next century; these health professions will be the last to be automated. Likewise, jobs that force allied health professionals to successfully coach their patients will also grow in demand.

While "aides" in some fields are declining, this trend could reverse. Cost-effectiveness in health care, the inability of physicians to limit the competitive roles of other providers, and the capacity for expert systems to decentralize expertise may mean that low-level, low-paying entry-level positions will remain or reappear. Workers in these positions will be dramatically assisted by expert systems and technology.

Conclusion

As society and health care undergo these transformations, persons currently exploring career opportunities might get a fatalistic feeling that nothing can be done to change the course of a particular health profession. To some degree this is true. Technology, for example, will progress regardless of how willing health professionals are to accept it. Health professions will prosper or falter depending on roles they stake out and how well they deal with change.

[See also Dentistry; Health Care; Health Care: Alternative Therapies; Health Care Costs; Health Care Financing; Health Care: Moral Issues; Health Care: Technological Developments; Mental Health; Nursing; Psychiatry; Public Health.]

BIBLIOGRAPHY

Bezold, Clement. "The Future of Health Care: Implications for the Allied Health Professions." *Journal of Allied Health* 18/5 (Fall 1989).

Bezold, Clement, et al. *The Future of Work and Health.* Dover, MA: Auburn House, 1986.

———. *Pharmacy in the 21st Century.* Bethesda, MD: United States Pharmacopeial Convention, 1985.

Levinsky, Norman G. "Recruiting for Primary Care." *New England Journal of Medicine* (March 4, 1993): 656–660.

— CLEMENT BEZOLD

MEGACITIES

For millennia, cities have been the centers of culture and crucibles of civilization. Until recently, the vast majority of the population lived in tiny settlements, villages, and small towns, whereas only 3 percent lived in urban areas. By the year 2000, however, over 50 percent will live in cities. It is projected that twenty-three of these cities will be megacities with more than 10 million people each. Fifty years ago there was only one. Reflecting another fundamental transformation, eighteen of these megacities will be in the developing countries. By the year 2000, the urban population of developing countries will be almost twice that of developed nations; and, by the year 2025, almost four times as large.

Every city has a unique history, culture, and style. Yet in spite of differences and contrasts in demographic makeup, level of economic development, and political structure, megacities have much in common. Size alone presents a situation for which we lack collective experience. No precedent exists for feeding, sheltering, or transporting so many people in so dense an area, nor for removing their waste products or providing clean drinking water. Urban systems based on human settlements of 50,000 or 250,000 may accommodate urban populations of one million but break down at 4 million and become unworkable at 11 million. The infrastructural and managerial systems developed in the nineteenth century have become outmoded to handle the scale and complexity of today's cities.

Exacerbating the problem, megacities are experiencing critical environmental degradation, pushing to the limit their ability to sustain a viable quality of life. While all urbanites are affected, the urban poor are the most vulnerable, since squatter settlements are often located in the most undesirable areas of cities, such as floodplains or steep hillsides, or are adjacent to dangerous industries. Environmental degradation now represents one of the most formidable constraints on productivity for the urban poor by threatening their physical security and possessions and by increasing the incidence of diseases.

Radically new approaches are needed. They face powerful obstacles. The fragmented and overlapping structures of city agencies, departments, and divisions and the isolation of the government from both the private sector and the community are reinforced by incentive systems that discourage risk-taking by policy makers. Administrative systems' resistance to change is compounded by the persistence of outmoded assumptions among policymakers about urban development and by a paralyzing sense of hopelessness and despair about problem scale.

Megacities in developing countries bear added burdens. Although it is estimated that, by the end of the 1990s, half of the poor will be concentrated in urban areas, the international donor community has been slow to respond. Most aid agencies and development banks allocate less than 15 percent of their funds to basic needs projects in urban areas, and less than 20 percent to all other urban development projects. While there are signs of change, the focus of development assistance continues to be on the rural peasant and agricultural policy rather than on the city squatter and urban policy.

A consensus is emerging that improved resource allocation, ecological sustainability, and the acceleration of innovation processes must be policy priorities at both the international and urban levels.

1. *Improved resource allocation.* Efforts to stem cityward migration are based on a mistaken premise that urban growth is detrimental to national productivity. In

fact, according to World Bank estimates, in 1989 60 percent of gross domestic product in most developing countries was generated in cities and about 80 percent of GDP growth is expected to occur in these cities. Large cities create economies of scale in public infrastructure and an investment climate that reduces capital costs, service delivery costs, maintenance costs and therefore per-unit expenditures.

In most Third World cities the informal labor market absorbs nearly one-third of the economically active urban labor force. Many workers deliberately choose informal sector jobs for their flexibility, freedom, lifestyle, and higher earnings. Because informal economies are inseparable from the formal economy, the provision of credit, training, and technical assistance to micro-enterprises and self-help efforts in low-income communities can help not only the urban poor but the entire urban and even national economy.

2. *Ecological sustainability.* Public awareness of the fragility of the planet's ecological balance has resulted in calls for limits on city size. However, experts are beginning to recognize that as the world's population increases, dense agglomerations are more efficient than space-consuming suburban style developments. Concentration in cities can save open space and natural habitats to increase food production.

3. *Accelerating innovation.* There is a desperate need to shorten the usual twenty-to-twenty-five-year lag between new ideas and their implementation. An ongoing forum that treats megacities as a global laboratory would permit this accelerated problem solving. The concept is based on mounting evidence that the most innovative urban solutions have often come not from government or academia but from the grassroots. The task is to make these innovations available to cities around the world—with the awareness that innovation transfers can flow from developing nations to advanced industrialized ones as well as the reverse.

Within cities, strategies for facilitating innovation include decentralizing some urban management functions; creating new "six sector" partnerships made up of public and private sectors, nongovernmental organizations, grassroots groups, academia, and the media; and developing mechanisms to reward innovators and disseminate local successes.

Underlying these and other strategies for improved resource allocation, ecological sustainability and accelerated innovation processes is the beginning of a powerful and profound new vision of urban life. Our ability to act on that vision will be critical in ensuring the well-being of the 322.56 million people who will live in megacities in the year 2000.

[*See also Cities; Cities, North American; Environment; Land Use Planning; Science Cities; Urban Transit.*]

BIBLIOGRAPHY

Conway, McKinley. "Tomorrow's Supercities: For Land, Sea, and Air." *Futurist* 27/3 (May–June 1993).

Downs, Anthony. *New Visions for Metropolitan America.* Washington, DC: Brookings Institution, 1994.

Girardet, Herbert. *The Gaia of Cities: New Directions for Sustainable Urban Living.* New York: Anchor/Doubleday, 1993.

Katz, Peter. *The New Urbanism: Toward an Architecture of Community.* New York: McGraw-Hill, 1994.

Peirce, Neal R. *Citystates: How Urban America Can Prosper in a Competitive World.* Washington, DC: Seven Locks Press, 1993.

Simonds, John O. *Garden Cities 21: Creating a Livable Urban Environment.* New York: McGraw-Hill, 1994.

— JANICE E. PERLMAN

MENTAL HEALTH

Of all types of human illness, mental illness is the least understood. This is especially tragic because mental illness impairs precisely those capacities that distinguish our human species, such as the faculties for abstract thought, complex language, and sophisticated social relationships. Although clinicians can already effectively treat most mental illnesses, research in mental health holds much promise to dramatically improve the quality of human life over the next fifty years.

Fifty percent of Americans suffer at least one bout with mental illness during their lifetime. Sufferers, whether or not they fully meet the formal definition of mental illness, fail to thrive because emotional conflicts block their capacity to adapt.

Mental health researchers seek both to treat illness and to improve the adaptation of humans to their environment. Investigators increasingly find the roots of mental illness in atypical biology. Those studying adaptation, on the other hand, trace most influences to experience, particularly during infancy and childhood. While biological advances in diagnosing and treating mental illness promise to transform the lives of the patients afflicted, enhancing human adaptation might help to make society itself more peaceful and productive.

Researchers studying the brain have progressed slowly, because the brain is by far the most complex organ in the body and because its physical function is difficult to measure. Scientists can study such organs as the lung or heart by observing their movements. Others, including the kidney and adrenal gland, affect easily measurable substances in the blood. The brain, in contrast, is essentially immobile, and thus far neuroscientists have been unable to find any substance that is a useful marker of its activity.

In part because of difficulty in developing a biologic understanding of mental illness, professionals heretofore have focused on the role of other factors. The currently dominant "bio-psychosocial" model, as its name suggests, seeks to balance the effect of several forces in causing mental illness. This model presumes that all human brains have some biological vulnerability to particular types of stress, but that in most cases, only those that undergo stress to which they are vulnerable develop mental illness.

Most models of psychological stress still rest on variants of the conceptual foundation laid by Sigmund Freud, who proposed that unconscious conflicts between inborn impulses and learned prohibitions lead to psychological distress. According to this view, the distress is difficult to relieve, because the conflicts are outside awareness. Freud always considered this an interim model, eventually to be supplemented or supplanted by a more biological approach.

Many contemporary psychological therapies still rest on the original Freudian model. These approaches attempt to relieve distress by making conflicts conscious so that with this "insight" the patient can actively resolve them. Other kinds of psychotherapies, such as supportive, cognitive, and behavioral, focus on helping patients to solve practical problems. These therapies usually proceed without the patient developing an understanding of any unconscious meaning.

Although the various effective types of psychotherapies differ greatly in approach, they all affect the underlying biology of the brain. Recently researchers have detected changes in brain metabolism following successful behavioral psychotherapy for obsessive-compulsive disorder. It is virtually certain that similar biological changes occur with successful psychotherapy for other psychiatric conditions.

Conversely, brain biology shapes individual experience. For example, a patient with a biological depression may inaccurately perceive people as unfriendly and work as onerous, but these distortions disappear when the depression fades. As research continues to clarify the complex interactions between experience and biology, increasingly therapists will need expertise in both psychotherapy and in biology; or they will have to work in concert with professionals possessing complementary skills.

Social stress takes many forms, but at its core is a fear of the loss of the physical and emotional supports the individual needs to survive. Social support programs attempt to provide food, shelter, and clothing, as well as companionship. In selected cases patients may be hospitalized to provide a highly supportive, albeit temporary, social setting. Improved treatments and rising costs are reducing both the frequency and duration of hospitalization for mental illness, increasing the importance of outpatient programs. This trend, which began in the 1960s, is likely to continue.

Fifty percent of Americans suffer at least one bout with mental illness during their lifetime.

Over the past several decades researchers have developed increasingly reliable psychological tests that have helped to standardize diagnosis. Several new techniques still under development measure the brain's physical function, providing information that may eventually replace psychological tests as the standard for diagnosis. New noninvasive "imaging" techniques that produce accurate picture-like representations of living tissue give researchers and clinicians their first view of a working human brain. Several of the methods, such as computer-assisted tomography (CAT) and magnetic resonance imaging (MRI), provide images that depict detailed brain structure. More important for the future, however, are a host of new technologies that detect brain activity. Already scientists have used these methods in identifying characteristic activity that accompanies such diverse operations as performing mathematical calculations and listening to classical music. These emerging technologies include "functional" MRI, single positron emission computed tomography (SPECT), and positron emission tomography (PET).

Such advanced methods promise to reveal distinctive patterns of mental disease. Researchers have found suggestions of unique patterns, in some cases of Alzheimer's dementia, panic disorder, obsessive-compulsive disorder, and certain types of mood disorders. With such tools scientists may be able to identify activity patterns that cause anxiety or depression, or even feelings of love or security. Further, physicians treating at least some mental illnesses will base diagnoses on images of brain activity, much as X-ray images are used to diagnose a fractured bone today.

In the coming decade, brain-imaging techniques will allow exact measurements of medicines in the brain. This approach will likely replace blood tests as the preferred technique for determining proper drug dose. Such methods may also transform psychotherapy. In the future the clinician may be able to obtain objective information that correlates with the patient's thoughts and feelings. The patient and the therapist then could use this data to help them change maladaptive behaviors to more effective ones.

Although the underlying cause

of most mental illnesses is currently unknown,

it appears likely that genetics will be seen

as playing an important role in most of them.

Another developing technology that promises to transform the field of mental health derives from molecular genetics. Research on identical twins and family genealogies indicates that many mental illnesses formerly attributed to childhood experiences, including schizophrenia and manic-depressive disorder, are substantially inherited. Although the underlying cause of most mental illnesses is currently unknown, it appears likely that genetics will play an important role in most of them.

It is probable that scientists will link at least some types of mental illness to specific genetic defects in the next decade and that genetic tests for susceptibility to these diseases will follow. Gene therapy, in which physicians repair genetic defects, holds the promise of dramatic and precise treatment by the middle of the next century, at least for those mental illnesses with genetic roots. Some may wish to use these gene alterations, not only to repair damage, but to improve on normal performance, just as some currently use anabolic steroids to build muscles beyond normal size or strength. If this happens, money may serve not only to buy happiness, but also intelligence, wit, and a magnetic personality. Unchecked, this process could lead to a widening gap between classes, as for the first time money could directly buy an increase in ability. Society will need to create regulations to ensure fairness in the availability of genetic enhancement as well as to protect consumers from possible biological side effects.

There are other opportunities—and complexities—as well. With the power to determine in childhood which children are by constitution vulnerable to specific stresses, one could develop specific child-rearing methods for minimizing the risk that these children would develop mental illness. It seems probable that a number of mental illnesses result from more than one gene, and so potential parents may be able to cross-check their genomes to assure the health of their offspring. Thoughtful approaches, including legislation, however, will be needed to prevent this information from being used in harmful ways. For example, employers might wish to screen applicants for jobs, or, in an Orwellian future, authorities might try to control the right to reproduce. Mental illness may sometimes be linked to desirable mental traits. Many of the greatest minds in history may have suffered mental illness, including Isaac Newton, Abraham Lincoln, and Vincent van Gogh. It is vital that we as a society not meddle in the natural selection of genes affecting the development of the brain until we have a much deeper knowledge of the consequences.

One might hope that in the future, studies on mental health may influence the shaping of social policy. Untreated mental illness exacts a great cost from society. In the United States 70 to 80 percent of crimes are committed by persons intoxicated with alcohol or illegal drugs, conditions considered by the American Psychiatric Association to be types of mental illness.

Mental health issues may affect society in more subtle and profound ways as well. For example, research in transcultural anthropology suggests that the social goals are primarily learned. These goals can have a marked effect on the functioning of an individual in a society, as well as on the harmony of the society as a whole. There is evidence, for example, that children raised in conflict-ridden homes, particularly those who were emotionally or physically abused, are in turn likely to be emotionally and physically abusive as adults. Children whom adults consistently love and nurture, however, generally develop into emotionally secure, cooperative, and peaceable adults themselves. As a society, we might choose to shape our educational and legal practices so as to foster more beneficent child rearing.

Biological methods for treating mental illness and techniques designed to aid adaptation hold greatest promise if harnessed together. Most "biological" mental illnesses are responsive to social stress, and their incidence will diminish if society becomes more harmonious. Untreated or undertreated mental illnesses in turn damage society. Crime and violence are the most obvious costs, but there are others: lost job productivity, alienated communities, and broken families. Repairing society and aiding the mentally ill are both vital goals. Pursuit of both is the best approach to achieve either.

[See also Change, Pace of; Conscious Evolution; Creativity; Holistic Beliefs; Information Overload; Mind: New Modes of Thinking; Psychiatry; Psychology.]

BIBLIOGRAPHY

Freeman, Hugh L. *Mental Health and the Environment.* New York: Churchill, 1985.

Martin, Alfred. *Mental Health: Psychotherapy of Tomorrow.* Quincy, IL: Franciscan Press, 1980.

Warr, Peter. *Work, Unemployment, and Mental Health.* New York: Oxford University Press, 1987.

– JOSHUA FRIEDMAN
RODERIC GORNEY

METEOROLOGY.

See CLIMATE AND METEOROLOGY.

MICROMINIATURIZATION.

See NANOTECHNOLOGY.

MIGRATION, INTERNATIONAL

International migration—ranging from the relatively permanent movement of people across national boundaries to temporary flows involving students, business travelers, and seasonal workers—is likely to increase in the future. Migration's root causes include the push of war, ethnic repression, and economic hardship, and the pull of political freedom, better jobs, and beckoning family members. Worldwide population growth, especially in less developed countries, provides a growing pool of would-be emigrants. Since young workers migrate most, population growth today will influence international labor flows well into the first decades of the twenty-first century.

The decision to migrate is ultimately personal, but decisions are influenced by families, communities, and nations. Would-be movers weigh real and imagined job opportunities, wage scales, and personal networks in their country of origin and in potential destinations.

Future international migration depends on different types of movers and factors affecting each type. Migrants differ by length of stay (permanent versus temporary moves), distance traveled (adjacent versus intercontinental moves), reasons for moving (economic, political, or personal), and their legal status in the receiving country (documented versus undocumented). These distinctions, however, will blur. Temporary migrants often become permanent. Adjacent countries often are stepping-stones to more distant destinations. Economic migrants, once settled, often send for their families. Some legal temporary movers will overstay their visas, becoming illegal migrants. Distinctions between political asylees and economic refugees will meld for migrants whose native land provides neither freedom nor livelihood.

Cheaper communication and transportation will reduce real and perceived distances. As the world shrinks, distance as a barrier to movement declines. The global diffusion of information and cultural symbols—from the daily news to the daily reminders of popular images—plants the seeds of future immigration.

Positive as well as negative factors in countries of origin affect international migration. Severe environmental degradation and the depletion of soil, water, and forest resources can cause out-migration. About 10 percent of the world's population (500 million people) live in agricultural areas affected by natural disasters like periodic flooding, drought, and severe soil erosion. Others simply have no access to food or food-producing resources. These factors, coupled with continued rural population growth will produce a steady stream of migrants to major urban areas. Rural economic development, however, tends to increase productivity, reducing the need for farm labor and prompting the need for fewer workers in farming and an increase in rural-to-urban migration.

By 2000, developing countries will contain sixteen of the world's twenty largest cities—the megacities which are here defined as exceeding twelve million people. Vast areas of Mexico City, São Paulo, Shanghai, Calcutta, and Bombay are already economic and environmental catastrophes. International migration will flow between the megacities and the developed world in an increasingly integrated global economy. Migrants will come from professional, technical, and business classes as well as from less advantaged groups.

Economic gaps will widen between richer and poorer nations, creating a growing potential for international migration from developing to developed countries.

Economic gaps will widen between richer and poorer nations. Nearly all of the growth in per capita income from 1950 to 1990 occurred in the developed countries of Europe, Asia, and North America, but 85 percent of the world's population growth occurred in developing countries. This imbalance points to a growing potential for international migration from developing to developed countries, both within and among the major regions of the world.

Regional economic blocs (EC in Europe, NAFTA in North America, and AFTA in Asia) are likely to increase international migration in at least three ways: from less developed to more developed countries within each region; between developed countries within each region; and from developed countries in one region to developed countries in other regions. Europe (primarily the

EC nations), the Far East (primarily Japan, Hong Kong, the Republic of Korea, and Singapore), and North America (primarily the United States and Canada) are likely to remain global economic development centers. As these three regions consolidate economically, they will attract international migrants: to Europe from Eastern Europe, the Middle East, and North Africa; to Japan, the Republic of Korea, and Singapore from surrounding Asian countries; to Canada and the United States from Latin America and the Caribbean.

Intercontinental migration streams are already evident and will probably grow: from China, Hong Kong, Japan, the Republic of Korea, the Philippines, and Southeast Asia, as well as from Europe to the United States and Canada; from Latin America to Spain, Portugal, and Italy; from the Caribbean and South Asia to the United Kingdom; from North Africa, the Caribbean, and the Pacific to France; and from India, Pakistan, the Republic of Korea, and the Philippines to the oil-producing Arab states. Some of these streams reflect cultural, colonial, and linguistic ties; others represent the long reach of labor demand.

Compared to world population growth and differential development in a global economy, receiving-country politics and policies exert a minor influence in the migration equation. Immigration policies are more regulatory than restrictive. Experts note, for example, that major changes in U.S. immigration legislation during 1986 and 1990 did little to decrease long-term immigration and may ultimately increase it. As of 1993, U.S. Census Bureau projections assume more, not less, immigration. The bureau's middle-series population projection indicates the year 2000 U.S. population will be 8.8 million larger than in 1991 because of permanent net increases from international migration of all types, legal and illegal. By 2050 the U.S. population will be 82 million larger than in 1991 (21 percent of the total population) due to the compound effects of net immigrants and their descendants.

Of course, politics will shape the future immigration policies. Arguments for and against immigration cross political lines. The right, in general, is split between anti-immigration and pro-growth positions. Slow growth or population decline in industrialized countries will lead to labor shortages and slow growth of consumer markets. Some economists and business leaders, therefore, argue for more immigration. Others, especially in areas of heavy immigration, argue that the cost of the cultural adaptation and public services outweigh the benefits. The left is split between those who believe that poverty and emigration result from worker exploitation, not rapid population growth, and those who be-

lieve that rapid population growth increases poverty directly. The latter promote access to health care and family planning in order to increase family welfare and decrease poverty. These fissures are not likely to subside. They will color future debates regarding population and development policies worldwide.

The collapse of communism in Eastern Europe and the former Soviet Union, as well as the adoption of market policies in China, will boost future international migration to and from those areas. The opening of borders in those states will provide for the emigration of political and economic refugees, as well as the movement of religious and ethnic groups. Redrawing a national map may change citizenship without international migration, but events in Eastern Europe suggest that shifting political boundaries often stimulates emigration and immigration.

Because characteristics of immigrants and emigrants may differ by such factors as language and skill level, two countries may experience similar net migration but experience widely differing cultural or economic effects. An equal net effect can result from large or small gross flows.

Long-term trends in international migration will depend on the success of development policies and the course of future population growth. Near-term economic development will stimulate international migration among business and professional classes as well as among the poor. But only slower population growth and sustainable, national development in the major sending regions of Asia, Africa, and Latin America will reduce the irregular, illegal, and unpredictable flows of individuals and families who would risk their lives to cross an international boundary.

In some countries today, including France, Germany, and the United States, there is a growing fear of the cultural and economic threat posed by large numbers of immigrants. Consequently, many countries may more rigorously enforce border controls to further regulate and restrict the migrant flow. Some may even enact laws restricting the citizenship of children born to guest workers in the receiving countries.

[See also Change, Cultural; Ethnic and Cultural Separatism; Global Culture; Internal Migration: United States; Minorities; Population Growth: Worldwide; Race, Caste, and Ethnic Diversity; Refugees; Space Colonization; Tourism.]

BIBLIOGRAPHY

Appleyard, Reginald. *International Migration: Challenge for the 1990s*. Geneva: International Organization for Migration, 1991.

OECD Continuing Reporting System on Migration (SOPEMI). *Trends in International Migration*. Paris: OECD, 1992.

Russell, Sharon Stanton, and Teitlebaum, Michael. *International Migration and International Trade,* World Bank Discussion Papers, 160. Washington, DC: World Bank, 1992.

Sadik, Nafis. *The State of World Population, 1993.* New York: UNFPA/United Nations Fund for Population, 1993.

— THOMAS G. EXTER

MILITARY TECHNOLOGIES

With the end of the massive military confrontation between the United States and what was the U.S.S.R., the nature of potential conflicts has changed significantly. Future wars are likely to be much smaller in scale, and this will be a major determinant of the course of future military technological development.

The most important new military technologies are: long-range and real-time surveillance and target identification systems—sensor and guidance systems for ultrasmart autonomous "fire-and-forget" missiles that are able to detect, identify, and effectively attack armored vehicles, combat aircraft and warships, as well as hardened, fixed targets like command-and-control centers,

The military can use such advanced surveillance equipment as this portable radar unit to detect enemies deep in their territory. (Robin Adshead; The Military Picture Library/Corbis)

in all types of weather and battlefield conditions; very powerful conventional warheads; and computerized command, control, communications, and intelligence systems.

With the new surveillance and target identification technologies the military can now detect and track, in real time, enemy forces deep in their territory. Sensors on board satellites, manned aircraft, and remotely piloted vehicles (RPVs) give advance warning of preparations for attack. Rapid advances are being made in a broad range of sensors—photographic and return beam vidicon television cameras, multispectral scanners, visible and infrared radiometers and microwave synthetic aperture radars, charged couple devices, sensors sensitive to gamma rays, X-rays and electronic signals, and communications-monitoring devices.

Long-range reconnaissance equipment will be increasingly carried by remotely piloted vehicles rather than manned aircraft, because the former are less vulnerable to air defense systems. Much cheaper than manned aircraft, they can be used in relatively large numbers. They will eventually be given more battlefield roles, such as ground attack and even air combat.

Modern weapons can be guided to their targets with great accuracy by real-time, midcourse guidance and, more importantly, by terminal guidance. Accuracy is, or soon will be, virtually independent of range. Terminally guided missiles use radar or a laser system to search the area around the target, compare it with a map preprogrammed in the warhead's computer, and then guide the warhead precisely onto it.

Terminally guided submunitions—small bombs (bomblets) and mines—are being developed that can distinguish between different types of moving vehicles and attack them at their weakest point (such as the turret of a tank).

An example of a new powerful conventional warhead is the fuel air explosive. The weapon produces an aerosol cloud of a substance like propylene oxide vapor. When mixed with air, the substance is very explosive, and the aerosol cloud, ignited when at its optimum size, produces a powerful explosion. The explosion is five to ten times as effective, weight for weight, as a conventional high explosive. Fuel air explosives can be made as powerful as low-yield nuclear weapons.

Cluster bombs and fragmentation munitions are another example. Exploding fragmentation bomblets scatter small, jagged chunks of metal over a large area. The fragments have razor-sharp edges, are very hot, and travel at high speeds.

Weapon systems based on antitank, antiaircraft, and antiship missiles are particularly benefiting from the new technologies. New antitank missiles, for example, are rapidly making the main battle tank obsolete, particularly when used on helicopters.

The United States is investigating three different technologies for an advanced, light, multipurpose antitank missile. One uses a laser beam-riding guidance system. The warhead is fused to detonate at the optimum time to do maximum damage to the tank, attacking the turret from above. The second uses fiber-optics guidance and an infrared imager to acquire the target. Fiber-optics guidance is a powerful technique, useful for very long-range (tens of kilometers) missiles. The third technology is based on an autonomous missile that is locked on to the target before launch. A focal-plane infrared seeker acquires the target. Once the seeker is locked on and the missile is launched, it guides itself automatically to the target so that the operator can engage another target.

Today's helicopters have top speeds of approximately 400 kilometers per hour. Using technologies such as the Advancing Blade Concept (with two contra-rotating ro-

tors), Tilt Rotor (in which the rotors tilt through a right angle to provide lift or thrust, or a combination of both), and the X-wing, even supersonic speeds will become possible.

Recent technological advances have considerably increased the accuracy of nuclear warhead delivery. Accuracy normally is measured by its circular error probability (CEP), defined as the radius of the circle centered on the target within which a half of a large number of warheads of the same type fired at the target will fall. For example, the CEP of a Minuteman II intercontinental ballistic missile warhead is about 370 meters; the new MX missile has a CEP of about 100 meters.

Similar developments are taking place in submarine-launched ballistic missiles. The new American Trident D-5 submarine-launched ballistic missile, for example, has a CEP of about 120 meters, whereas the CEP of the older Trident C-4 is 450 meters. Strategic missiles may eventually be fitted with terminal guidance that will reduce their CEPs to about 40 meters.

Military technologies, such as this global positioning system used by soldiers to track their location, often lead to civilian applications. Civilian uses include aircraft navigation as well as satellite tracking of elephant herds and stolen vehicles. (Leif Skoogfors/Corbis)

The Pentagon is planning the Phase One Strategic Defense System, known as Global Protection Against Limited Strikes (GPALS), designed to defend against a ballistic missile attack of up to 200 nuclear warheads. GPALS is a defense against an accidental attack involving one or a small number of missiles, a limited attack launched by a mad military commander, or an attack by a third world country involving a few long-range missiles.

In the space-based layer, Brilliant Pebbles missiles, now under development, are designed to destroy enemy ballistic missiles in their boost phase, before they release their warheads and decoys. Each Brilliant Pebble carries sensors to pick up radiations from rocket exhaust upon launch from their silos, to calculate speed and trajectory, and to program the missile onto an interception course, relying on the kinetic energy of impact to destroy targets. Current plans call for deploying 1,000 or so satellites orbiting at altitudes of about 960 kilometers. Each missile is about 1 meter long, 0.3 meters wide, and weighs about 45 kilograms.

During the next phase, the ground-based interceptor missiles, the High-Altitude Endoatmospheric Defense Interceptor (HEDI), will attack enemy warheads that survive the Brilliant Pebbles, shortly after they reenter Earth's atmosphere. Deployment of between 750 and 1,000 HEDI antiballistic missiles is called for.

The Boost Surveillance and Tracking System will detect enemy missile launches, track the boosters, and assess the number of missiles destroyed. The Space Surveillance and Tracking System will acquire and track postboost vehicles and reentry vehicles, satellites, and antisatellite weapons, and assess the destruction of enemy warheads. The Airborne Optical Adjunct, an infrared radiation sensor system carried on a Boeing 767 aircraft to track warheads in their midcourse and terminal stages, is in an advanced state of development. The Ground-Based Surveillance and Tracking System will discriminate between reentry warheads and decoys, track reentry vehicles and decoys, and assess the destruction of enemy warheads. The command center will link all these systems and control the space battle.

Theater antiballistic missiles are being developed to defend against attacks by tactical ballistic missiles. Current U.S. research and development programs include improvements for the existing Patriot surface-to-air system; the Extended Range Interceptor; the Arrow missile, a joint U.S.—Israel program to develop a high-altitude interceptor; and the Theater High Altitude Area Defense system.

[See also Weapons of Mass Destruction.]

BIBLIOGRAPHY

Munro, Neil. *Electronic Combat and Modern Warfare.* London: Macmillan, 1991.
Schulsky, Abram N. *Silent Warfare—Understanding the World of Intelligence.* London: Brassey's, 1991.
Smith, Graham. *Weapons of the Gulf War.* London: Salamander Books, 1991.
Thompson, Julian. *The Lifeblood of War—Logistics in Armed Conflict.* London: Brassey's, 1991.
Watson, Bruce W., ed. *Military Lessons of the Gulf War.* Novato, CA: Presidio Press, 1991.

— FRANK BARNABY

MIND: NEW MODES OF THINKING

The human intellect evolved through the selection, among one branch of primates, of larger and larger brains, whose adaptiveness resides in those functional capabilities we label as "mind." The mind's most critical attribute is memory: the ability to store and recall past events, to perceive patterns, and hence to *predict* future events, such as the coming seasons. Along with detailed memory, the mind evolved a second critical ability that enormously enhanced its usefulness, namely metaphoric, or symbolic communication. At first, gestures were used to signify ideas. Then, about 200,000 years ago, symbolic vocalizations became possible, giving rise to language.

About 200,000 years ago, symbolic vocalizations became possible, giving rise to language.

The mind, then, consists of an enlarged memory that can be recalled and shared symbolically with others. It is thus a social phenomenon, allowing the transmission of accumulated knowledge orally (and today in writing, on electronic tapes, or via films) within and between generations, greatly increasing the potential for survival-enhancing, adaptive behavior. "Learning" and "knowledge" for humans are no longer restricted to single individuals, as is largely the case with other social animals. Besides "knowledge" of the external world, the human mind is also capable of creating imagined worlds, and hence of making behavioral choices.

Factual knowledge, however, is not all that the mind encompasses. It also stores values and attitudes regarding what concerns are "important" and what actions are "right." Furthermore, it involves feelings or emotions, including not only desires for physiological needs (food, water, warmth, sex) but also powerful desires to belong to a social group (bonding) and a strong need for a sense of purpose in life (sacred meaning). Without the satisfaction of these latter needs, humans may become depressed and ill, or angry and violent.

"Mind" is never acquired outside a social context. The knowledge framework, the values, the affective behaviors needed for acceptance, and the meaning of life are all taught. Each child undergoes, through immersion in his or her culture, an apprenticeship in thinking. The world view or shared "mind" of one's culture helps one "see" and participate in its particular vision of reality, signaling what to notice and what to ignore, how to interpret, and how to behave. Shared values and meaning are thus implicit in shaping the inner mental reality that forms the map by which one is able to act effectively. Not surprisingly, we feel a strong attachment to our world view; beliefs and values and our social identity are as important to us as food and water.

Because reality—the totality of possible external information that our sensory system is actually exposed to—is far too complex, all cultures, perforce, must choose what to notice, and filter out the rest. Thus, two cultures existing side-by-side can hold dissimilar world views, based on diverse values and meanings. Each uses a different filter system. Of course, individuals within a culture can hold disparate values, too, but usually not to the same degree. Indeed, the more cohesive a culture, the more its members share values and traditions; larger, less personal societies, being less cohesive, often require complex legal systems to "govern" their divergent values and behaviors. This diversity gives rise to "politics," which is often highly emotional.

Learning, or changing the way we think, occurs at two levels. One is personal learning, by which individuals hone their understanding of their surroundings, usually in order to fit better into their own social milieu. This is the sort of learning that mostly goes on in schools and colleges. The individual adapts to the society, modifying her or his personal ways of thinking.

The other level of learning occurs when a whole society changes its way of thinking. By replacing an old way of seeing and valuing the world with a new one, it is presumably adapting to changed circumstances. It is this sort of *active search* for "new modes of thinking" that many believe is essential for humans to survive in the decades ahead.

This is historically a new activity. In the past, changes in world views have been slow, often unconscious adaptations to changing circumstances, as with the origins of agriculture. Intentional changes in world view have been rare. The Golden Age of Greece (500–400 B.C.) and the Renaissance/Enlightenment (1500–1800 A.D.) are two exceptional examples from Western history. World view changes imposed from outside a society are almost always violently opposed, often being resented

for generations. Rapid, nonviolent changes in fundamental ways of thinking are historical anomalies, and most world views have not included changes in their underlying assumptions as one of their internal values. Indeed, modern Western beliefs in "progress" and "change" relate only to technical change, and presume that the underlying values of individualism, efficiency, competition, and materialism will remain intact.

Three major barriers block social change. First is our psychic attachment to the familiar map imparted to us by our own cultural world view. Even a clearly dysfunctional set of values, just like an abusive parent, is hard to disown. Second, those who hold power are usually those benefiting most from the status quo, and therefore the most difficult to persuade of the need to change. Third, changing our social thinking often means changing not only our patterns of social interaction, but also much of our physical infrastructure as well. Both bring heavy costs to a society attempting rapid change.

Change, however, appears unavoidable. Today, crises are overtaking many once stable societies whose members are being forced to abandon old assumptions and values without having had the social dialogue necessary to envision and fully develop new ones. Without a widely shared world view, a society disintegrates. The future of humankind depends on societies learning how to deliberately "change their minds" rapidly enough to adapt to crises already created and avoid creating further ones. Examples of people already doing this (e.g., the Indian state of Kerala, the Mondragon cooperatives in Spain, Grameen Bank in Bangladesh) offer visions to other societies facing the difficult process of social change. Humanity's ultimate survival may well depend on multiple world views, coexisting and adapting side-by-side, cross-fertilizing each other.

[See also Creativity; Values, Nonwestern; Visionary Thinking.]

BIBLIOGRAPHY

Boulding, Kenneth E. "What Do We Know About Knowledge?" *Issues in Integrative Studies* 9 (1991): 75–89.
Clark, Mary E. *Ariadne's Thread: The Search for New Modes of Thinking.* New York: St. Martin's, 1989.
———. "Meaningful Social Bonding as a Universal Human Need." In John W. Burton, ed. *Conflict: Human Needs Theory.* New York: St. Martin's, 1990.
Donald, Merlin. *The Origins of the Modern Mind.* Cambridge, MA: Harvard University Press, 1991.
Rogoff, Barbara. *Apprenticeship in Thinking.* New York: Oxford University Press, 1990.

– MARY E. CLARK

MINERALS

Mineral resources—both metallic and nonmetallic—are inorganic substances taken from the earth for potential use by humans. Their diversity is remarkable. Metallic minerals are the raw materials upon which many important materials and technologies are based. Metal use is concentrated in four economic sectors: construction; transportation equipment (e.g., automobiles, airplanes, ships); capital equipment (e.g., factory machinery); and consumer durables (e.g., bicycles and refrigerators). Metals can be grouped in three broad categories: first, there are *major metals,* used in large quantities throughout the economy—e.g., iron and steel in bridges, buildings, motor vehicles, and kitchenware; aluminum in beverage containers, foil, and aircraft; copper in wiring, electronics, and plumbing; lead in batteries of all types; and zinc as a corrosion-resistant coating on various types of steel. Second, there are the so-called *minor metals* used in smaller quantities for specialized applications, including beryllium in electronic components; chromium and cobalt as alloying elements in steel; various rare-earth elements in petroleum-refining equipment and pollution-control catalysts; and zirconium as a refractory material in the process of producing metal and glass products. Third, there are *pre-cious metals*—such as gold and silver—used primarily in jewelry and art objects.

Nonmetallic minerals make up the second large class of mineral resources. They are even more diverse than metallic minerals. At one extreme are the bulk building materials with low value per unit of weight, such as cement (made up of lime and clay), sand, and gravel. At the other extreme are gems with high unit values, such as diamonds, emeralds, and amethysts. In between are fertilizer minerals, such as phosphate rock and potash, ceramic minerals such as feldspar and clays, abrasive minerals such as sandstone and industrial diamonds, and pigments and fillers such as diatomite and barite.

Despite their diverse uses, both metallic and non-metallic mineral resources share similarities in production, which typically takes place in the following four stages:

The first stage is *exploration,* in which mineral deposits are discovered and their technical and economic viability demonstrated. The second stage is *development,* in which mineral deposits are prepared for production;

As the world's population grows, so too will its demand for minerals. How will that demand be met without depleting the Earth's mineral resources? (© 1993 Tom Campbell/First Image West, Inc)

e.g., the mine and associated facilities are designed and constructed. The third stage is *extraction,* or *mining,* in which mineral-bearing rock is taken out of the ground from either underground or surface mines. Typically only a fraction of the mined rock is valuable, and thus the fourth stage, *processing,* is dedicated to upgrading the material extracted from the mine. For metallic minerals, processing usually begins with crushing, grinding, and washing of rock to facilitate separation of unwanted material from valuable rock known as ore. Ore, in turn, is upgraded or purified through a series of metallurgical processes that vary from metal to metal. Some processes use heat to upgrade the metallic ore (pyrometallurgy); others use electricity (electrometallurgy); still others use solutions (hydrometallurgy). For nonmetallic minerals, upgrading and purification also take place, but processing typically is less complicated technologically than that of metals.

An important, underappreciated source of metals is recycling. Recycled metal from scrapped batteries produces more than half of the lead used each year in the United States. For other metals, although recycling is relatively less important, it still is significant. For iron and steel, scrap metal from obsolete and discarded products probably represents one-quarter of the iron and steel used in new products each year; for copper also perhaps one-quarter; and for aluminum and zinc one-tenth to one-fifth.

As human population and the demand for minerals continue to rise, the question arises: What are the prospects for mineral availability? Are we in danger of running out of essential mineral resources? Alarming statistics allegedly show that mineral reserves—i.e., minerals known to exist and capable of being produced at a profit under current conditions—will be depleted in several decades at current rates of use. These statistical claims are misleading. Known reserves represent only a small portion of the ultimate amount of mineral resource in Earth's crust. Responding to the depletion of known deposits, exploration geologists are continuing to discover previously unknown deposits. Mining companies are moving to higher-cost mineral deposits that are deeper below Earth's surface, located in more remote places, or contain less valuable mineral content per unit of mined rock. Engineers are discovering new ways of finding, extracting, and processing minerals that lower mineral production costs.

Society is likewise responding to the depletion of known deposits by reducing the demand for specific minerals in two ways. First, more abundant materials are being used instead of less abundant ones (material substitution). Second, engineers are reducing the material needed for specific applications (resource-saving technological change). Recent examples are thinner aluminum walls in beverage containers and thinner steel door panels in automobiles that nevertheless are designed to be more crashworthy than their thicker predecessors.

The net effect is that most mineral resources are becoming less costly to produce and less expensive for consumers to purchase. This trend has been in motion for the last century or so. Scarcity, to be sure, varies considerably from mineral to mineral. But in general, mineral resources are becoming less, rather than more, scarce in this economic sense.

Seabeds, as well as the Moon

and other extraterrestrial bodies,

represent important untapped sources.

The critical long-run issue for the future, therefore, is the extent to which society will be able to continue to be ingenious in its response to the depletion of known mineral deposits. To what extent will cost-reducing technologic advances in exploration, mining, and processing offset the cost-increasing effects of the depletion of known deposits and of pollution? To what extent will advances in the use of minerals allow more abundant materials to replace less abundant ones? These questions are largely unanswerable. Human ingenuity to date, combined with ongoing technologic developments, arguably allow us to be optimistic. Scientists and engineers are making great progress in commercializing new techniques of remote sensing, solution mining (including bioextraction techniques using micro-organisms to extract metal from rock), and methods of extraction permitting profitable recovery of minerals from past mining wastes. Seabeds, as well as the Moon and other extraterrestrial bodies, represent important untapped sources. Materials scientists are making great progress in designing and commercializing advanced materials—newly engineered materials using metals, ceramics, polymers, and composites of two or more of these material types. Advanced materials provide enhanced properties, such as strength, electrical conductivity, and corrosion resistance, compared to traditional materials (e.g., metals, plastics, cardboard).

For the coming decade or so, three short-run, specific issues will be key determinants of the demand for and supply of minerals. First, how fast will the developing economies grow, including most importantly those of the former Soviet Union, China, and India? The level of economic activity is perhaps the most important of the many determinants of mineral demand. These three countries arguably have the largest potential for economic growth. Second, how will mineral production evolve in the former Soviet Union and China as these countries move toward market economies and perhaps even democratic political institutions? The former Soviet Union and China have significant geologic potential, but it is unclear whether their mineral output will rise or fall in a market economy. Third, how will society's demand for a cleaner environment affect the costs of mineral production? Mining and mineral processing inevitably disturb the environment—mining requires that large amounts of earth and rock be moved, and mineral processing by its nature involves separating valuable minerals from unwanted associated material. Environmental consequences can be mitigated if we are willing to pay more for the minerals we use. Over time, however, human ingenuity and technological innovation hold forth the promise of improving the way we find, extract, and process minerals *and* of reducing the environmental damages of mineral production.

[See also Chemicals, Fine; Chemistry; Coal; Hazardous Wastes; Materials: Research and Development; Resources.]

BIBLIOGRAPHY

Eggert, Roderick G., ed. *Mining and the Environment: International Perspectives on Public Policy.* Washington, DC: Resources for the Future, 1994.

Tilton, John E. *World Metal Demand: Trends and Prospects.* Washington, DC: Resources for the Future, 1990.

U.S. Department of the Interior, Bureau of Mines. *Minerals Yearbook.* Washington, DC: U.S. Government Printing Office, published annually.

U.S. Department of the Interior, Bureau of Mines. *The New Materials Society: Challenges and Opportunities.* Washington, DC: U.S. Government Printing Office, Vols. 1 and 2, 1990; Vol. 3, 1991.

Vogeley, William A., ed. *Economics of the Mineral Industries.* New York: American Institute of Mining, Metallurgical, and Petroleum Engineers, 1985.

— RODERICK G. EGGERT

MINORITIES

By the middle of the next century, no single racial group will comprise majority status, given current United States demographic trends (see Table 1). This situation will have important economic and political consequences for the country. This article examines future population and employment trends for the four largest minority groups: blacks; Hispanics; Native Americans (including Eskimos and Aleutian Islanders); and Asians (including Pacific islanders) recognized by the United States Bureau of the Census.

Blacks

Blacks constitute the slowest-growing minority group in the United States and, while currently the second largest racial group, by 2020 blacks will drop to third

TABLE 1

PERCENT DISTRIBUTION OF THE U.S. POPULATION, BY RACE AND ETHNICITY, 1990 AND PREDICTED 2050

Race or Ethnic Group	Percentage of Total Population in 1990	Percentage of Total Population Predicted in 2050
Total, United States	100.0	100.0
White, non-Hispanic	75.7	72.8
Black	12.8	15.7
Native American	0.8	1.1
Asian	3.0	10.3
Hispanic (of any race)	9.0	22.5

Source: U.S. Bureau of the Census, Population Projections of the United States, by Age, Sex, Race, and Hispanic Origin: 1993 to 2050, November 1993.

behind whites and Hispanics. Nevertheless, by the middle of the twenty-first century, this population is expected to double from 30.6 million in 1991 to 61.6 million in 2050, according to data from the United States Bureau of the Census. Blacks also will represent a larger share of the labor force in the next century but most likely will be overtaken by Hispanics by 2020, if current United States Bureau of Labor Statistics projections hold.

The projected annual growth rate in employment for blacks is 1.9 percent for the 1990–2005 period, or slightly below the rate for the 1975–1990 period. Currently, blacks are more likely to be employed in occupations that will grow more slowly or actually decline in the future. Only in a few of the fast-growing service areas does the black share of jobs equal or exceed its share of the total population. The fastest-growing jobs are those that require at least some higher education, and currently blacks are underrepresented among college graduates.

Hispanics

Hispanics constitute the most rapidly growing minority group. Projected increases are expected to raise the Hispanic share of the total United States population from 9 percent in 1990 to 22.5 percent by 2050. The rapid growth of this population will fuel the increase in the total population, accounting for 44 percent on average of overall population growth. Hispanics are predicted to increase nearly fourfold by 2050. Much of this growth will be the result of more births. By 2050, one in three births will be Hispanic. In addition, Hispanic immigration is predicted to add 322,000 new people annually between 1990 and 2050.

In 1990, Hispanics were nearly 8 percent of the United States labor force. During the 1975–1990 period, they entered the United States workforce at an annual rate of 5.9 percent. This rate of increase is predicted to slow slightly to 3.8 percent annually by 2005. By that year, 11.1 percent of the work-force will be Hispanic. Hispanics, however, are currently underrepresented in all of the fast-growing parts of the economy, and overrepresented in the slow-growing or declining parts. This condition results from their currently low levels of education. For example, in 1990, 41 percent of Hispanic workers had not completed high school.

For many Hispanics, whether immigrants or native to the United States, Spanish is the primary language spoken in the home and English is learned outside. This creates specific educational problems related to bilingual education, which is hotly debated by educators and policy planners. Most public education in the United States (and nearly all advanced technical education) is entirely in English. In addition, most Hispanic immigrants to the United States have not received extensive formal education even in their native countries, leaving them poorly equipped to undertake both the linguistic training and technical education required for increasingly technical occupations within the information economy. Thus, our rapidly increasing Hispanic population may find itself at an occupational disadvantage not simply because of language differences but also because of a lack of previous institutional empowerment and acculturation in their homelands. Unlike some other immigrants to the United States, who come with technical educations in place, Hispanic immigrants are not technically proficient.

Asians

Asians are the fastest-growing minority group, predicted to grow more than fivefold from 7.6 million people in 1990 to 41 million in 2050. As a share of the total United States population, Asians will go from 3 percent in 1990 to 10 percent in 2050. Much of the growth in the Asian population is predicted to be fueled by net immigration, not domestic births. The Census Bureau predicts that more Asians will immigrate to the United States than will be born here during the 1990–2050 period. The Asian (and other) share of the labor force is also expected to grow at an annual rate of 3.8 percent. (This group includes Asians, Pacific islanders, Native Americans, and natives of Alaska.) A higher percentage of Asians are predicted to fill positions in the fast-growing sectors of the economy than either blacks or Hispanics because of their generally higher levels of education.

Although Asian immigrants also encounter second-language problems when coming to the United States, two factors tend to mitigate their experience in this regard. First, many immigrants come with a strong background in formal education, especially in technical areas. Second, those seeking enfranchisement in technical communities find that their ethnic, linguistic, and cultural heritage is already well represented in such communities. In both academe and industry, Asian-Americans tend to occupy a sizable portion of the positions that demand advanced training in science and technology.

Asians are the fastest-growing minority group in America, predicted to grow more than fivefold from 7.6 million people in 1990 to 41 million in 2050.

Native Americans

Currently, the Native American, or American Indian, population comprises less than 1 percent of the total United States population with 2.1 million people. It is predicted to grow steadily so that by 2050, the number of Native Americans is predicted to total 4.3 million or slightly more than 1 percent of the United States population. Estimates of Native American participation in the future workforce are difficult to obtain because the Department of Labor includes them in the "Asians and others" category. Currently, however, Native American educational attainment is low, and they are underrepresented in the fastest-growing jobs.

Consequences for Politics and Economy

As a result of their rates of growth, and the relative decline of the non-Hispanic white population, minority political power will probably increase. In the largest states with the most political clout—New York, California, Texas, and Florida—each minority group is getting larger. Hispanics are particularly likely to benefit politically. Combined with and undermining this likely expansion of political power, however, is the likelihood that blacks and Hispanics will be increasingly closed out of well-paying, high-status jobs in the information economy because of their currently low levels of educational attainment. One of the critical political and social issues over the next fifty years, therefore, is raising the education levels of blacks, Hispanics, and Native Americans. No society can fully participate in the Information Age if a large percentage of its population and more than half its youth lack adequate access to and understanding of information technology.

[See also Change, Cultural; Class and Underclass; Demography; Ethnic and Cultural Separatism; Global Culture; Race, Caste, and Ethnic Diversity; Refugees.]

BIBLIOGRAPHY

Ong, Walter J., S.J., *Orality and Literacy: the Technologizing of the Word.* New York: Routledge, 1993.

U.S. Bureau of the Census, *Current Population Report: Population Projections of the United States, by Age, Sex, Race, and Hispanic Origin: 1993 to 2050.* Washington, DC: U.S. Bureau of the Census, 1993.

U.S. Bureau of Labor Statistics, *BLS Bulletin 2402: Outlook 1990– 2005.* Washington, DC: U.S. Bureau of Labor Statistics, 1992.

— ROBERT A. CROPF
VINCENT CASAREGOLA

MODERNISM AND POSTMODERNISM

Future historians may say that the primary story of the twentieth century is that it marks the end of the Modern Age and the beginning of a new epoch of the human journey. The impulses that have shaped the last five hundred years are yielding to a new set of impulses. Thus we live in a century of massive dissolution of authority, of established institutions, and of patterns of life.

This shift is the essence of the turbulence that shakes America and the world. We are not simply going through a rough patch, after which life will revert to something we like to think of as normal. The old normalcy is gone. We are passing through a shift from one order of life to another.

Radical changes involving the basic principles of human life generally have happened only once in about five hundred years. Such turning points include the decline of antiquity, the surge of monasticism in the sixth century, the emergence of new intellectual currents in the Church in the eleventh century, and the arrival of the scientific outlook in the sixteenth century.

Ages of great change in world view, which can also be described as psychological reorientation, have generally displayed similar characteristics. Some of these include: a rise in general warfare; increase in internal discontent and uprisings; economic instability; a shift of emphasis in the fine arts, which lose any sense of unity; institutional exhaustion; weakening of the moral ethos and religious bonds; rise in crime; and an increase in psychological stress and in suicide.

Such characteristics have shown themselves in every major shift of world view that has taken place, from eighth century B.C. Greece to twentieth century America.

A shift of this consequence creates what Jacques Barzun termed "dissolving times." Throughout history, Barzun noted, dissolving times have manifested certain characteristics, which are once again in evidence:

- The tendency to blur distinctions of purpose, function, and form.
- A desire to simplify, to return to the innocent beginnings of things.
- The decay of public hope and common purpose.
- The fragmenting of authority, with all its consequences in terms of self-government and social order.
- In some quarters, a hatred and repudiation of the past.
- The proliferation of experimental ideas and cultural modes.
- A sense of loss, of decline.
- Institutional collapse as the cohesive force diminishes.
- The rise in general uncertainty about life.

One of the clearest signs of the end of the Modern Era is the confusion as to what to call the period we have entered. Names abound: the postindustrial, postmodern, or global age; the Pacific century; the information age; the quantum age; the post-scientific era; the era of the Earth; the age of Aquarius; and on and on.

It is certainly clear that we are in a postcapitalist (Drucker), postsocialist, postnationalist, postindustrial era. And as far as our culture goes, we are even in the postbelief era, because no sustaining belief now informs our culture.

Such a postbelief cultural phase has been unfolding for the past 150 years. The modernist influence held sway in Western culture from roughly 1850 to 1950, and it was followed in the 1960s by the postmodernist period.

Modernism was the cultural expression of the belief that life had lost its mystery, that men, not gods, rule the world, that tradition must yield to experimentation in every aspect of life, and that at the core of life there is nothing, just the void of nihilism.

The thrust of modernism was to substitute an aesthetic justification of life for the prevailing moral and spiritual order. Modernism, wrote Irving Howe, was "an unyielding rage against the existing order." The emphasis of modernism was a repudiation of the past with the belief that only the present has authority.

The aesthetic expression of this view demanded liberation from all inner restraints, as well as the destruction of all prevailing forms. It held that experience is the touchstone of life, that tradition is to be negated, that art must pursue the infinite along all paths, including eroticism, cruelty, and terror.

The failure of modernism was that it never understood the function of tradition. Tradition is not the sentimental attachment to the past. Tradition presupposes the timeless reality of what endures through all ages. Tradition is the carrying forward of those attitudes and forms that human experience has taught us are the highest the human spirit can attain.

Modernism waged relentless war against tradition, and consequently against the transcendent impulses that tradition manifests.

In the 1960s, the powerful current of post-modernism developed, which carried the logic of modernism to its farthermost reaches. Against the aesthetic justification of life, postmodernism substituted the instinctual. For the postmodernist, impulse and pleasure alone were real and life affirming; all else was neurosis and death. Postmodernism tore down the boundaries between art and life and insisted that acting out, instead of making distinctions, was the path to knowledge.

The thrust of modernism was to substitute

an aesthetic justification of life

for the prevailing moral and spiritual order.

Despite the vitality and energy that have produced modernist and postmodernist works of art, when these two strains of expression are carried to their ultimate conclusion the result is a culture that fastens on disintegration, rage, and madness—themes that characterize so much of twentieth-century art, literature, and entertainment.

The effects of modernism and postmodernism have been so great that the "avant-garde" has disappeared, for only a minority in the culture is any longer on the side of order and tradition. Few people believe that there is any tradition left to trade for the future. Thus today we are reaping the results of a culture detached from any ethical standard or spiritual moorings.

The collapse of modernism and postmodernism has been accompanied by the exhaustion of the intellectual themes that have occupied the West for well over two centuries.

Few people any longer believe in reason as an ultimate authority in ordering life. Faith in the perfectibility of man—a cornerstone of the Enlightenment—fell victim to the wholesale slaughter of two world wars. Belief in utopias has vanished. Liberalism, having won historic gains, now languishes in exhaustion.

Socialism is discredited. Marxism has collapsed. Communism has been buried. Fascism enlists no loyalties.

Nationalism—in the nineteenth-century sense of constituting the outer limits of a people's political

awareness—is on the wane. What surfaces in places such as Bosnia, Georgia, and Tajikistan is not historic nationalism, but an old ethnicity that cries out for new expression.

Even confidence in progress has substantially waned. Indeed, most of the social agenda that constituted the faith in progress has now been enacted into law. Progress has achieved its earlier goals and now needs redefinition.

While the concept of Liberty still occupies the public mind, we must ask whether such freedom is more a matter of the absence of restraint than it is the expression of some creative inner mode of being emanating from deep within the human soul. For it may well be that the idea of independence, while still obviously valid, is no longer at the cutting edge of political necessity. It has been replaced by the greater necessity of *inter*dependence.

Great motifs of life carried Western civilization through two of the most progressive—if destabilizing—centuries in history. But the end of the Modern Age and the opening up of a global era now require broader themes to encompass this fresh period of human development.

The great task now is to save progress from merely a technological interpretation, and to redefine it in terms of a new historical era, of expanding human capabilities and aspirations. We need a cultural climate that portrays the wonder and magnificence of life in all its forms; a cultural climate that helps people find deeper meanings to life, even as they struggle to make a living.

[See also Change; Change, Cultural; Change, Epochal; Change, Optimistic and Pessimistic Perspectives; Continuity and Discontinuity; Global Consciousness; Global Turning Points.]

BIBLIOGRAPHY

Barraclough, Geoffrey. *Turning Points in World History.* London: Thames and Hudson, 1979.
Bell, Daniel. *The Winding Passage.* New York: Basic Books, 1980.
Drucker, Peter F. *Landmarks of Tomorrow.* New York: Harper & Row, 1957.
Toynbee, Arnold J. *A Study of History.* London: Oxford University Press, 1946.
Roberts, J. M. *The Triumph of the West.* Boston: Little, Brown, 1985.
Smith, Houston. *Beyond the Post-Modern Mind.* New York: Crossroads, 1989.

— WILLIAM VAN DUSEN WISHARD

MONETARY SYSTEM

The international monetary system in the foreseeable future will evolve out of the present system. It is highly improbable that any wholly new system, which a few experts are sometimes advocating, will be introduced.

Building on the present means starting from a system in which exchange rates for the major currencies—the U.S. dollar, the Canadian dollar, the Japanese yen, and other currencies—are determined in exchange markets around the world and in which European countries try to keep their own exchange rates fixed, within limits, vis-à-vis each other through an exchange rate mechanism (ERM), which is part of the European Monetary System (EMS). This "floating rate system" has existed since March 1973.

Contrary to earlier expectations, the floating rate system has been plagued by instability. Large day-to-day and week-to-week fluctuations in exchange rates occur, as well as large longer-term swings. These changes in exchange rates usually result from sudden, massive movements of short-term capital and generally have little to do with the economic fundamentals of countries' economies or their trade and balance-of-payments positions. With the continual introduction of innovative financial instruments (most recently "derivatives"), the growth of emerging stock and bond markets in developing countries, the expansion of mutual funds in industrial countries in which even small investors put money abroad, and the increase in the use of computers and other electronic devices, money now crosses international boundaries instantaneously. It is exchanged through a variety of financial instruments offered by banks, mutual funds, and brokerage houses, in magnitudes that have grown exponentially in the last five years, reaching $1 trillion a day.

This growth and internationalization of private capital markets has made the international monetary system more vulnerable than ever to differences in the overall economic performance of both industrial and developing countries, and even to expectations of their economic performance. Since 1993, for example, sudden capital movements have exerted overwhelming pressures on the pound sterling, the Italian lira, the French franc, the Spanish peseta, the Portuguese escudo, the U.S. dollar, and the Mexican peso. The United Kingdom and Italy have had to withdraw from the ERM. Because France was unable to stay within the agreed limits, the previously narrow bands of the mechanism have been widened considerably.

To help limit exchange rate instability and uncertainty about future exchange rates, which are damaging to trade and international investment and upsetting to countries' economies and economic policy, authorities of the main industrial countries are likely to continue, and possibly enlarge and make more frequent, their interventions in exchange markets, attempting to make such interventions more effective than in the past. Central banks will hold larger reserves than they might otherwise desire of currencies under pressure and to diversify their reserves; they will increasingly supplement the dollar as a reserve currency by use of other currencies, notably the Deutschemark and the Japanese yen.

Stronger, more concerted efforts to enhance exchange rate stability and foster a more stable international monetary system, as well as to induce a more rapidly growing world economy also can be expected. It is highly unlikely, however, that any system of fixed rates—even rates that allow some fluctuation within a narrow band, such as target rates that are being advocated by several former financial officials and other experts—will be introduced anytime soon. Such rates require that national economic policies and differences in the macroeconomic performance—their rates of growth and inflation—be minimal.

For any system with relatively fixed exchange rates to work, the economies in the arrangement generally have to converge. Such convergence depends on the willingness of monetary authorities to pursue policies that are in harmony with those of the other participating countries. Given the differences in the present and likely rates of growth and inflation in the main industrial countries, monetary authorities have been extremely reluctant to surrender independence over monetary policy. Monetary policy is the prime instrument through which authorities influence the performance of their domestic economies. With the prevalence of burgeoning budget deficits, alternative instruments such as fiscal policy have been delimited. In fact, it was the desire of authorities for independence of monetary policy that brought the floating rate system into effect in the first place.

Nor is it likely that any system resembling the classical gold standard will be introduced, despite its devotees. Its requirements are very much stricter, authorities are all too familiar with its potentially deflationary consequences, and many countries, especially developing countries, have no gold. On another bleak note, it is unlikely that any common currency, even that of the ECU in Europe, will be accepted.

Despite their unwillingness to agree to fixed rates, authorities of the industrial nations are also likely to intensify efforts at policy coordination, especially through the Group of Seven—Canada, France, Germany, Italy, Japan, the United Kingdom, and the United States. The G-7 may be enlarged to include Russia and some developing countries, possibly India and China, especially if developing countries continue to be dynamos of world economic growth.

The International Monetary Fund (IMF) will have an enlarged role in the policy coordination process, working more closely with the G-7 and with more clout. To prevent further financial crises like the one that hit Mexico in late 1994 and 1995, the IMF will probably initiate several measures. It may create a last-resort financial safety net for the world that is some facility for financing capital flight situations. It may develop the role of special drawing rights (SDR), the reserve asset that the IMF issues, to supplement reserves in national currencies. The IMF will reform the arrangement by which it lends money to help low-income countries, to make it better suited to these countries, by making money available for a longer time than in the past. These measures will require enlargement of the IMF's capital base. These intensified efforts by monetary authorities and the IMF will all occur simultaneously.

[See also Capital Formation; Credit, Debt, and Borrowing; Economics; Financial Institutions; Global Statistics; International Trade: Sustaining Growth; Macroeconomics; Media of Exchange; Savings; Wealth.]

BIBLIOGRAPHY

Bretton Woods: Looking to the Future. Washington, DC: Bretton Woods Commission, 1994.

Deane, Marjorie, and Pringle, Robert. The Central Banks. London: Hamish Hamilton, 1994.

De Vries, Margaret Garritsen. The IMF in a Changing World. Washington, DC: The International Monetary Fund, 1986.

Friedman, Irving S. Toward World Prosperity: Reshaping the Global Money System. Lexington, MA: D. C. Health/Lexington Books, 1987.

Kenen, Peter B. Managing Exchange Rates. London: Royal Institute of International Affairs, 1988.

————. Managing the World Economy, Fifty Years After Bretton Woods. Washington, DC: Institute for International Economics, 1994.

Williamson, John, and Miller, Marcus H. Targets and Indicators: A Blueprint for the International Coordination of Economic Policies. Washington, DC: Institute for International Economics, 1987.

— MARGARET DE VRIES

MORALS

The fundamental questions of morals concern the standards of good character and social interaction: Are they merely variable cultural elements, or do they have an invariant core based in our common human nature? Are they rationally defensible? Is their focus on which specific actions we perform and their effects on others, or on the kinds of persons we become as reflected in our likes and aspirations?

Beyond Moral Skepticism

The first decades of the twenty-first century should solidify the abandonment of the skeptical conceptions of the nature of morality that predominated among twentieth-century intellectuals. Cultural relativism, non-

cognitivism, and both Freudian and Marxist reductionism all lost favor toward the century's turn.

Cultural relativism—the view that morality, like etiquette or civil law, is a creature of local custom—appears insufficiently to ground criticism of cultural forms as intellectuals strive to expunge nationalism, genocide, racism, and sexism from Western social orders while recognizing the near universality of these and comparable social phenomena.

The first decades of the twenty-first century should solidify the abandonment of the skeptical conceptions of the nature of morality that predominated among twentieth-century intellectuals.

Noncognitivism—the view that moral judgments are not factual claims but more akin to cries of social or personal pleasure and revulsion—is unlikely to prove itself capable of accounting for the subtlety and intricacy of moral discourse and its grammatical transformations.

Freud's system conceptualizes morality as the "super-ego's" internalization of the feared parent's commands to children. It stands little chance of recovering from feminist critics who fault it for sexism, for downplaying child abuse, and for psychologically manipulating analysands. Philosophers of science criticize the Freudian theory for its unfalsifiability and lack of predictive power. The spread of free markets and the collapse of Marxist political systems in Russia and Eastern Europe cast doubt on Marxist economic analyses and predictions at the same time that social theorists found alternative explanations for Marxist sociological hypotheses. It is unlikely that Marx's view of morality—as part of an elaborate ideological "superstructure," which functions merely to rationalize and facilitate capitalism's oppression of workers—will survive these challenges to the rest of the theory.

Postmodernist Morality

The new millennium begins with postmodernist trends within moral thought. These emphasize diversity of ethnicity, culture, and gender, and are skeptical about the efforts to ground morality on conceptions of universal human nature and universal reason that characterized the premodern and modern epochs respectively. It is unlikely that many of these trends will prove lasting. Anglo-American philosophy has resisted the over-attention to race, gender, and ethnicity found elsewhere in the humanities, but some moral theorists have proposed that ethnicity and, especially, gender yield special and important moral perspectives. These views face probably insurmountable problems: the growing recognition of the unscientific character of many racial classifications, the near-universality of mixed "race," and the fact that individuals manifest diversity in themselves ("microdiversity"). All of these factors undermine this line of thought. Moral perspectives do not come one to a group. Moreover, it is unclear which of the several strands of feminism that emerged near the turn of the century is most promising. Carol Gilligan claims that women's moral thinking tends toward a "care-perspective," which downplays concern over rights and instead emphasizes feelings, special connections, and maintaining relationships. However, such a view runs the risk of perpetuating gender stereotypes ("maternal thinking"). Furthermore, reducing these emphases merely to aspects of one gender's thinking may hinder our ability to see their universal centrality within ethics and the injustice of their neglect by moral philosophers.

A different strain of feminism stresses and extends political egalitarianism, as expressed in the slogan "the personal is political." This movement is useful for legitimating and facilitating cross-cultural moral critique and its opposition to gender-relativism. However, its dangers include hyper-individualism, which can undermine the givenness of role obligations (such as that of father or mother), exaggeration of the very limited utility of such political concepts as justice in intimate relationships, and a tendency to replicate and even magnify the social atomism for which communitarians fault liberal individualism.

The multiculturalist movement is useful because it sensitizes us to the way overhasty universalization can misdescribe one culture's peculiarities as universal human features. Unfortunately, it threatens to degenerate into a cultural relativism that merely ratifies the status quo. In addition, any moral view that thus stresses individuals' social role and status confronts them with the choice between complacent and oppositional responses to their "station." Rationally choosing a mode of response requires appeal to something beyond culture, presumably a return either to reason or human nature. Even Hegel, regarded as a patron saint by the multiculturalists, recognized this. His insistence on judging any social context by its place in the history of progress separates him from his multiculturalist followers, to the latter's disadvantage.

As the use of new technologies becomes more widespread, and as modern thinkers continue to demand release from the eroded values of traditional religions—especially to legitimize sexual behaviors once commonly dismissed as "deviant"—society will require more thoughtful and deeper moral inquiry. We can expect the cultural relativism that lurks behind multiculturalism to prove untenable and unappealing because multicultural society makes implausible the relativist's implicit claim that real moral disputes are few, shallow, and small.

Emerging Trends in Moral Thinking

Renewed interest in the moral virtues will grow, but ultimately will need to ground virtues either in culture or in human nature. The next few decades should see a resurgence of interest and work both in theories of human nature and in moral theories closely tied to them.

Some directions these researchers might take are indicated by sociobiology and by the rehabilitation and empirically based reconception of "moral sense" approaches from seventeenth- and eighteenth-century Britain. It seems likely that dissatisfaction with modernism's instrumentalist rationality will grow, and the absurdity of abandoning rationality (as some radical postmodernists recommend) will become manifest. Sympathetic reconsideration of premodern approaches to rationality and human nature then appears unavoidable. This should spark renewed attention to religious ethics. One important example of this revitalization near the turn of the century is the reformulation of the bases of Christian morals in the voluminous codifications, catechisms, and other documents issued from the Catholic church during the influential papacy of John Paul II, especially in his 1992 encyclical letter *Veritatis Splendor*.

A question asked by Alasdair MacIntyre will focus the debate among these rival approaches: Can any one of them (or combination of them) establish its rational superiority to the others by standards accepted within those other approaches?

[See also Behavior: Social Constraints; Bio-ethics; Death and Dying; Ethics; Human Rights; Sexual Codes; Sexual Laws; Social Controls; Women's Movement.]

BIBLIOGRAPHY

Cortese, Anthony. *Ethnic Ethics: The Restructuring of Moral Theory.* Albany, NY. State University of New York Press, 1990.
Crews, Frederick. *Out of My System: Psychoanalysis, Ideology, and Critical Method.* New York: Oxford University Press, 1986.
Elster, Jon. *Making Sense of Marx.* New York: Cambridge University Press, 1985.
Gilligan, Carol. *In a Different Voice: Psychological Theory and Women's Development.* Cambridge, MA: Harvard University Press, 1982.
MacIntyre, Alasdair. *After Virtue: A Study in Moral Theory,* 2d ed. Notre Dame, IN: University of Notre Dame Press, 1984.
Okin, Susan Miller. *Gender, Justice, and the Family.* New York: Basic Books, 1989.
Ruddick, Sara. *Maternal Thinking: Towards a Politics of Peace.* Boston: Beacon, 1989.

Singer, Peter. *The Expanding Circle: Ethics and Sociobiology.* New York: Farrar, Straus & Giroux, 1989.

Wilson, Edward O. *Sociobiology: The New Synthesis.* Cambridge, MA: Harvard University Press, 1975.

Wilson, James Q. *The Moral Sense.* New York: Free Press, 1993.

— J. L. A. GARCIA

MORE, SAINT THOMAS (1477–1535)

English humanist and statesman. A native of London, More entered the legal profession in 1501 and soon gained recognition as a distinguished barrister, scholar, and diplomat. Under Henry VIII, he served in various high posts, including that of Lord Chancellor. In 1535 he was beheaded for his refusal to take an oath of assent to the act that established a Protestant succession. Pope Pius XI canonized him in 1935. More wrote many volumes of theology, history, and classical scholarship, but the work by which he is principally known today is his *Utopia* (1516), the tale of a visit to an imaginary ideal commonwealth. More took the name Utopia from two Greek words meaning "no place." In Utopia, the system of government is representative democracy and the economy is communist. Clergy may marry, several forms of religious belief are tolerated, and euthanasia is available for the incurably ill. *Utopia* has been interpreted in many ways. It can be read as a monkish denunciation of the materialism of the Renaissance, a learned satire poking fun at human frailty, or a blueprint for a democratic socialist future. Whatever More had in mind, his book has become the model for all subsequent utopian speculation and a classic of world literature.

[See also Utopias.]

BIBLIOGRAPHY

Baker-Smith, Dominic. *More's Utopia.* London: Harper Collins, 1991.

Hexter, Jack H. *More's Utopia: The Biography of an Idea.* Princeton, NJ: Princeton University Press, 1952.

Logan, George M. *The Meaning of More's "Utopia".* Princeton, NJ: Princeton University Press, 1983.

Marius, Richard. *Thomas More: A Biography.* New York: Alfred Knopf, 1984.

Reynolds, E. E. *The Field Is Won: The Life and Death of Saint Thomas More.* Milwaukee: Bruce, 1968.

— W. WARREN WAGAR

MOTION PICTURES

The movies, the dominant art form of the twentieth century, evince both maturity and stability as the medium celebrates its centennial and the century comes to a close. That is the good news and the bad. For the first seventy-five years of film history, the medium was characterized by constant and repeated waves of innovation, as filmmakers in the United States, Europe, and elsewhere excitedly explored the new art, testing its limits and expanding its horizons. Constantly challenged by advances in technology, film artists devised the dramatic feature and perfected slapstick comedy in the 1910s; integrated the techniques and concerns of painters, musicians, and novelists in the 1920s, and reveled in dialogue in the 1930s, as they took on much of the artistic responsibility of modern drama. The 1940s and 1950s saw the cinema establish itself as the medium of choice for many of the major artists of the modern period: a separate art with its own newly founded traditions finally operating independent of the older pictorial and narrative arts.

By the late fifties and early 1960s, the filmmakers of the New Wave (Godard and Truffaut in particular) began to reflect the rapidly expanding legacy of movie history, integrating the work of their predecessors, and commenting on the art's past. For the first time, it became necessary for a filmgoer to have an education in the medium in order to fully appreciate new work. By the early 1970s, Hollywood had imported the New Wave's reflexive attitude. As the American sixties generation (Coppola, Lucas, Spielberg, Scorsese) established themselves in positions of power, the lengthy youth of the movies came to a close. The art had matured. While there have been occasional blooms of new talent in one national cinema or another (China in the late 1980s, Finland in the early 1990s), the genres and techniques of movies at the close of the century—in the United States, Europe, and elsewhere—are more or less what they were twenty-five years ago. The level of product is very high, and movies still hold pride of place in our culture, but the excitement of discovery and change that characterized the first seventy-five years of their history is gone. In this, film is no different from the other arts—music, painting, the novel, drama—all of which reached a point of post-modern stasis in the early seventies. As Alain Tanner put it with great prescience in *Au Milieu du Monde* (1972): "We live in a time of normalization, when exchange is permitted, but nothing changes." The idea of an avant-garde in art is now a historical curiosity.

Yet, while the esthetics of the medium haven't changed perceptibly, the technology has been preparing for the profound revolution of digitization that is now occurring, preparing us for a very different world of film in the twenty-first century. With hindsight we can see that the chemical and mechanical art of celluloid film, born of the nineteenth century, was a transitional phase. Since the 1980s, television has been the main popular dramatic medium, freeing "cinema" to evolve into an elite art. Very quickly in the 1980s, the development of videotape technology drastically changed the way most people experience movies, moving the economic locus of the art from the theater to the living room.

At the end of the 1970s, people saw movies in theaters, listened to music on records, watched one of the four national television networks (actually getting up out of their chairs to change channels on occasion), used telephones with wires tethering them to the wall, and, if they were so inclined, corresponded with each other using pens, pencils, typewriters, paper, and the U.S. Postal Service. They had been doing things this way since the turn of the century.

By the early 1990s, these same folks saw movies mainly at home on videotape, listened to digital music on compact discs (more often walking in the street than sitting at home), had their choice of forty or more cable channels from which to choose (and channel-surfed without leaving their chairs), made telephone calls in their cars or walking around, and, if they were so inclined, corresponded with each other via fax or electronic mail.

They could also, if they so chose, buy a camcorder that would let them shoot videotape of near-professional quality. They could install a home theater with a screen almost as large as the ones at the local sixplex (and with a sound system that was markedly better). They could watch videodiscs, skipping, browsing, freezing, and skimming as they might with a book; install their very own satellite dish; or buy a computer for the kids to play with that had the power of a 1980s IBM mainframe.

The continuing microcomputer revolution has prepared the ground for a further shift: from the living room to the laptop. As digital techniques are perfected, movies become individual experiences on personal screens, as easily manipulated as books, and increasingly integrated with text in a new medium called (rather unimaginatively) "multimedia." Of course, film itself was the first multi-medium, combining most of the techniques (and all of the concerns) of previous media. But digitization completes the journey the Lumière brothers and Georges Méliès began more than a hundred years ago. In the context of multimedia, film for

Movies are one of the world's most popular and affordable forms of entertainment. This theater is in India, which has one of the world's most prolific motion picture industries. (Sheldan Collins/Corbis)

the first time is truly a personal medium, both for the producer and the consumer.

Just as television did not replace theatrical film, neither will multimedia. We can expect the mature art and business of films shown in theaters to continue throughout the next century. But the artistic innovation in the general medium and, perhaps more important, the economy of the business will shift rapidly to multimedia: cinematic/textual products privately experienced and personally controlled by individual users.

Videotape technology drastically changed the way most people experience movies, moving the economic locus of the art from the theater to the living room.

This is not necessarily good news for cinéastes. The control that multimedia gives to the user is antithetical to the rhythmic mysteries of traditional film composition. And then, too, as part of multi-media, cinema plays a necessarily subordinate role. Perhaps most important, because it is infinitely adjustable, a fully digital film sequence loses all touch with reality. We can no longer trust it as a representation of the real world: the exciting tension between film and its object disappears: Méliès, champion of pure fantasy, has won; the Lumières, proponents of verisimilitude, have lost.

Digital techniques make film a tool of pure imagination. Filmmakers are now thoroughly liberated from any dependence on reality as their subject. That is the good news for the twenty-first century—and the bad. At worst, the basic genre of the medium will become the music video. But at best, the next generation of filmmakers will discover new truths in these new techniques that will reinvent the relevance, vitality, and passion of this past century's central art.

However, in the context of not just a new century, but a new millennium, perhaps the idea of progress that visions of the future imply is itself outmoded. The challenge of the next epoch will be the achievement of a steady state, in film and culture as well as in economics and ecology. This new cultural equilibrium, paradoxically, will bring new strength to the art of the past just as the new technology will increase our intimacy with its history. Thus, to a remarkable extent the future of film is also its past.

[See also Broadcasting; Communications; Electronic Convergence; Interactive Entertainment; Media Lab; Photography; Recording Industry; Television.]

BIBLIOGRAPHY

Ebert, Roger, and Siskel, Gene. *The Future of the Movies.* Chicago: Andrews and McMeel, 1991.

Hollander, Anne. *Moving Pictures.* Cambridge, MA: Harvard University Press, 1991.

Miller, Mark C. *Seeing Through Movies.* New York: Pantheon, 1990.

Monaco, James. *How to Read a Film.* New York: Oxford University Press, 1995.

— JAMES MONACO

MOTOR VEHICLES

In the year 2020, a Californian may order a battery-powered car on a refurbished chassis, built a decade earlier from a plant co-owned by General Motors and Toyota, directly from a personal computer. In Texas, a rancher may select a four-wheel-drive, dual fuel pickup truck fitted out with computers that calculate tailpipe emissions and gasoline usage to allow the driver to switch instantly to natural gas when pollution and gasoline consumption exceed predetermined standards. In New York, a harried executive may opt for a vehicle as fully equipped as a business office and with an onboard guidance system that lays out the routines to and from home, business, and points in between with the least amount of traffic congestion and distance control devices that prevent collisions.

Choices may differ in other parts of the world. Germans may prefer cars designed and manufactured for disassembly for mandatory recycling, while Estonians may purchase relatively inexpensive compact cars with minimal exhaust pollution. Japanese and Koreans may seek fuel-efficient vehicles to reduce oil imports, while the Chinese and Indians may purchase all-purpose vehicles for transportation that double as tractors or as a power source for irrigating farmlands. Different national needs will induce production differentiation particularly as demand for vehicles increases among developing nations. The car of the future will hardly be a single, uniform prototype, but a variety of models with different power sources, engine designs, materials, and other features and options.

As industrializing markets continue to develop, demand for automobiles will increase in direct proportion, as has occurred, for example, in Korea, Brazil, and Mexico. Estimates of future vehicle demand worldwide up to the year 2020 appear in Table 1.

While demand for automobiles will expand in both industrialized and industrializing countries, the patterns of demand are likely to differ from market to market, depending on consumer preferences, government regulations, and local manufacturing requirements. As a consequence, the 2020 model-year vehicle in Pakistan

TABLE 1

FUTURE MOTOR VEHICLE PRODUCTION

	Industrialized Countries			Developing Countries				
	United States	Germany	Japan	Korea	China	India	Mexico	Total
	Average Growth Rate							
1970–1990	3%	2%	3%	25%	12%	8%	9%	4%
1985–1990	2%	3%	2%	35%	16%	14%	14%	4%
Est. Growth rate	2%	2%	2%	10%	12%	10%	9%	3%
	Future Production							
1990	9,782,997	4,976,552	13,486,796	1,321,630	509,242	364,181	820,558	31,261,956
1994	10,180,226	5,386,780	14,598,542	1,934,998	801,302	533,197	1,158,285	34,593,330
2000	10,806,515	6,066,389	16,440,329	3,427,968	1,581,628	944,592	1,942,559	41,209,980
2010	11,937,116	7,394,894	20,040,669	8,891,266	4,912,298	2,450,028	4,598,744	60,225,014
2020	13,186,002	9,014,335	24,429,464	23,061,654	15,256,851	6,354,741	10,886,900	102,189,946

Sources: World Automotive Market Report 1994–1995, Auto & Truck International; World Motor Vehicle Data 1992 Edition, Motor Vehicle Manufacturers Association of the United States, Inc.

Note: The total growth rates are calculated by weighting with production of 1990.

may exhibit much different features from the same model-year vehicle in Ecuador.

In industrializing nations today, one does see vehicles typically targeted for the United States and Europe. To accommodate different market and regulatory requirements, automobile companies have achieved the capability of adapting vehicles with minor technical changes for export to both industrialized and developing markets. For example, Mercedes-Benz installs exhaust systems that satisfy U.S. environmental regulations for exports to North America while retaining conventional exhaust systems for Europe. Honda's United States plant affixes right-hand steering-wheel mechanisms for exports to the United Kingdom, Japan, and other markets with similar driving conventions.

Instead of evolving toward the uniformity of a prototype car of the future, diversity among vehicles seems to be proliferating. Even since the 1980s, automobile companies have been introducing a variety of models and styles for particular market niches. In 1994, a survey of automobile manufacturers revealed sixty different models of sport utility vehicles alone with various options. The diversity stems from changes in the traditional styling and performance characteristics—bigger or smaller engines for power or fuel efficiency, wider bodies and cargo space, larger or more compact bodies, or improvements in braking, suspension, handling, and safety. Future changes are likely to embody changes in societal preferences and needs.

The extent of product diversity will surely widen. By the year 2020, industrialized markets with high per capita incomes will continue to demand variety in vehicles with costly electronic equipment, innovative materials, and differing power sources such as batteries or natural gas. The industrializing nations will seek basic transportation at affordable prices. Unless consumers in the United States and other industrialized nations are willing to freeze the level of technology in their vehicles while developing nations attain parity, the possibility of a universal world-model vehicle, even one with some adaptability and variation, seems remote.

In the year 2020, cars will still look and drive much as they do today. Some cars will appear sleeker or fatter than they did in 1995. It may even seem that the styles leap backward a few decades to hot rods of the 1950s or to the Corvettes and Thunderbirds of the 1960s, while the appearance of others may seem to bypass a decade or two with lines and angles akin to a Stealth fighter. Some may accelerate faster or slower. Some may streak along the Autobahn, while others putter around city streets and culs-de-sac of suburban neighborhoods or unpaved roads in Peru or Bombay. All vehicles will brake and ride on suspension systems much improved from today and weighing between 10 and 25 percent less.

Except for cosmetic changes in body styling and modifications in performance as measured by acceleration, speed, handling, and feel of the ride, the car of the future will still look like a direct descendant of the car of today. Most people can envision these incremental improvements or engineered adaptations of existing technologies refined to reflect consumer preferences. The revolutionary changes that would radically transform the mobility for the automobile are still undergoing futuristic planning on designers' worktables or computer-aided design systems. Certainly, such chimera as steering by remote controls and videos or vehicles hovering magically over highways are not practical possibilities for the year 2020.

Instead of evolving toward the uniformity

of a prototype car of the future,

diversity among vehicles seems to be proliferating.

Overriding changes in the car of the future will pass undetected by the eye, at least at first appearance. A few vehicles, though not many, will harness batteries for electric propulsion instead of the gasoline engine. A few others will install canisters for compressed or liquefied natural gas. Most will still fill up with gasoline or diesel fuel, although these fuels may be treated with ethanol, methanol, or other chemicals that improve combustion and thus lower the expulsion of pollutants.

The significant changes will come from a set of consumer priorities emphasizing unique materials, highly efficient engine designs, and extremely crash-resistant structures and apparatus to protect driver and passengers.

The Automobile as a Symbol of Society

The automobile symbolizes the society that produces it. The Volkswagen became the car of the people; the Ferrari, the essence of Italian styling; the Chevy, Ford, and Chrysler, the manifestations of the American dream. The automobile in the United States and other countries represents the icon of society—its values, clashes, conflicts, and contradictions. People wait in traffic jams for hours rather than riding a train or subway; the internal-combustion engine pollutes the air, yet drivers putter around streets carefree. Drivers cherish safety and the sanctity of life, yet they refuse to wear seat belts and often oppose laws requiring motorists to do so.

As a symbol of society, the automobile will conform to societal values as they change. Three factors are reorganizing the social values of the United States and other countries: (1) the environment and management and resource conservation; (2) traffic congestion; and (3) the outpouring of technical innovations, particularly

materials and electronics such as computers and telecommunications. While each of these factors has influenced the design, manufacture, and use of the automobile, primarily through government regulation, only in recent years have companies begun to incorporate these factors into their strategies for product development. As these factors grow in influence, they will shape consumer preferences, the economics, and the politics involved in the automobile.

Environment and Resource Conservation

For years consumers recognized the damage to the environment and depletion of natural resources inflicted by the automobile. Various regulations have attempted to curb the automobile's excesses. The U.S. government and other governments have imposed corporate average fuel efficiency (CAFE) or comparable regulations for cars to reduce the amount of energy utilized and pollutants emitted. The oil crises in 1973 and 1979 alerted consumers to the authentic concerns of resource depletion, although with lowering oil prices and additional surplus, the trend has been shifting to vehicles with increasing fuel usage. Nonetheless, the price of oil, a finite resource, will escalate, which will inevitably reduce the demand for excessive gas-guzzling engines.

Regulations, in seeking to sustain the environment, are transforming ecology into a highly prized commodity in the market. Recently the United States, Sweden, and other European countries have enacted regulations for reformulated fuel to reduce tailpipe emissions. The laws and regulations in nearly every nation imposing restraints have scheduled increasingly stringent requirements to be phased in over the next decade. In Germany, environmental concerns spawned laws about recycling the automobile.

Overall, the welling importance of the environment has become irreversible. In the worst case, environmental regulations may stall at present levels. Yet, a wholesale relaxation of environmental controls to the level of the 1950s and '60s remains improbable. Consumer awareness of environmental and resource management is evident in several pockets of demand such as vehicles that are fuel efficient, enhanced with front and side air bags, and even the nonpolluting exhaust of the electric car, which, unfortunately, may only transfer the source of pollution from individual vehicles to power-generating plants.

Congestion

Few cities in the world are exempt from traffic jams: New York; Frankfurt, Germany; Milan, Italy; Los Angeles; Tokyo; and other cities in industrialized countries all are experiencing a growing concern with traffic congestion. However, even in the developing countries, congestion is a major problem—as, for example, in such cities as São Paulo and Rio de Janeiro in Brazil, Mexico City, and Seoul, Korea. Congestion around the world will contribute to a rethinking of the entire issue of mobility. There are many implications to the congestion problem. One is the effect on the environment and on resource conservation. Waiting in traffic jams exhausts vast supplies of oil while contributing to the decline in the quality of air. Equally important is the decline in productivity of drivers and passengers. In many large cities, passengers may compensate by utilizing mobile telephones for communications or hand-held dictating machines. If the automobile can be turned into a mobile office, the productivity loss would decline. Similarly, revamping cars to consume less or

This electrically powered bus is being recharged. These vehicles have yet to reach their full potential as alternative transportation. (Nick Hawkes; Ecoscene/Corbis)

perhaps no fossil fuel blunts some of the impact. Yet congestion exacts a price with delays and frustration on motorists.

Technological Advancement

By some estimates, the car of the 1990s contains more computing than the first landing craft on the moon. During the past three decades, an avalanche of technical innovation has occurred, particularly in computers, telecommunications, electronics, and materials. Samsung estimates that in the next twenty years approximately half the weight of the car will be in electronic components instead of metal body parts and engines. These present multiple benefits. Materials such as polymers, plastics, and composites contribute to lowering the weight of the car, which reduces fuel use and air pollution. Other technologies, such as fiber optics, are already in use in some cars, further lightening the weight of the automobile and reducing pollution and gas consumption without sacrificing safety.

Automobile companies as well as other technology-based companies with computers and telecommunications are investigating the intelligent vehicle highway system (IVHS), which allows drivers to determine their location and optimum routes. Such technologies may indeed allow the automobile to become a mobile office with guidance systems and mechanisms for piloting the automobile without the full attention of the driver. The electronic car may ease the congestion by circumnavigating through alternate routes. Other electronics may aid in stabilizing and braking the automobile while others correct for driver error by monitoring the distance between vehicles and automatically stopping the car to avoid a collision.

Social Choices: Preferences, Economics, and Politics

Over the next twenty-five years, it seems likely that consumer attitudes and preferences will vary over each of these social concerns as they have over other social values. These preferences will swing depending on perception of environmental damage, seriousness of resource mishandling, choices for mobility, and acceptance of new technologies. Without addressing either the economics or the politics of each of these issues, consumer preferences are likely to remain mixed. Nuclear power is an example. Many oppose nuclear power regardless of its costs; they would oppose it even if it were free. Similar controversies arise with genetic engineering, biotechnology, and even the environment itself. As technology accelerates, creating more questions than answers, consumer preferences are likely to splinter about the relative importance of these various issues.

Foreseeing the car of the future inevitably drags in economics as the yardstick of social preferences. For the most part, the issues attach themselves more to economics than to technology. Many of the technologies that may be commercialized in the future are feasible today. Examples are the electric car and IVHS. Consumers could acquire these technologies; however, they may shy away from paying the price of an electric car, including the inconvenience of recharging the battery and limited range and speed. IVHS technology exists; yet it requires a major infrastructure change to implement. Neither politicians nor consumers appear willing to invest the sums necessary for these technologies to achieve commercial application. Clearly, some technologies in the early stages of development cost more than they will after the innovations are accepted into the market and economies of scale in manufacturing kick in. Nonetheless, if consumers are willing to buy electric cars for some multiple of the price for a comparable gasoline-powered vehicle, they can do so.

The electric car may only transfer the source of pollution from individual vehicles to power-generating plants.

Similarly, economics influences social decisions about the environment, congestion, and technology. While most people would agree that clean air is important they often balk when asked to pay for the clean environment through higher-priced fuel or increased inspections on automobiles. Other's are willing to pay a higher price for the fuel, while still others want no change at all despite the preference for clean air. The same applies to congestion and technology. While many commuters may prefer to drive to work, at some point, the price of the automobile will induce those commuters to seek alternative means such as commuter rail or buses. As a consequence, economics winnows the possibilities for the car of the future.

Politics further limits the car of the future. Market failures, typified by environmental degradation and traffic congestion, invite political intervention to correct the problems. While some motorists may selflessly volunteer to drive less to save fuel and to shield the environment from further degradation, most will not without government incentive or enforcement. The political process may incorporate regulations or requirements of the automobile that reflect preferences for some as well as higher costs and specification of particular technologies and materials.

Politics affects the car of the future in other ways besides regulating characteristics and requirements for specific automobiles. Almost every government in the world seeks to attract investments in the national automobile industry. The reasoning is apparent. As the automobile often symbolizes the improvement in society for both industrialized and developing nations, the automobile industry produces thousands of jobs directly in the plant, with suppliers, and with the retail sector. Countries such as those in the EU that are trying to reject investment by Japanese auto plants in their countries may limit themselves to domestic technologies and types of cars while rejecting the innovations of the Japanese firms. Similarly, some countries attract investment, but the companies themselves may prefer to transfer vehicle models that fit the needs of the country rather than use the latest technologies.

The Company of the Future

The most significant change in the future will occur not with the automobile itself but with the companies that manufacture them. With the proliferation of models and technologies, the automobile industry will undergo a transformation of its structure. In many ways it will resemble the automobile industry before Henry Ford introduced the assembly line in Highland Park, Michigan.

In the industry's formative years, the vehicles themselves took on many different characteristics. Essentially there was no uniformity in automobile design and characteristics. Some models installed steam or electricity for power systems; others located the gasoline engines in the front, rear, or center of the chassis. Some experimented with hand brakes and throttles and an assortment of steering mechanisms. Customized for individual owners, each vehicle was distinctive and unique. No two were identical.

By 1908, a dominant design for the automobile was emerging. This design represented a consensus among consumers about the preferred features and characteristics in an automobile. Consumer experimentation with various designs and models converged into a relatively standardized, uniform automobile with rubber tires, gasoline engines, foot pedals for the throttle, brake, and the clutch, and front-end-mounted engine. Only after the design of the automobile stabilized could Henry Ford begin the assembly line to produce identical cars.

A similar fragmentation is likely to occur in the automobile industry with change in social values toward the environment, resource conservation, mobility, and new technologies. Experimentation is ongoing with battery-powered cars, natural gas combustion engines,

reformulated fuels, new materials, and novel electronic and navigational technologies. Society is still pondering and debating the social value of the environment, resource management, mobility, and the direction of various technologies without having yet reached a consensus. This debate could persist for decades before being resolved. Meanwhile, the discovery of new technologies and the refinement of existing, but as yet unmarketed, technologies will influence social choices, demand patterns, and production processes, particularly as commercialization of technical alternatives affects their production costs, the environment, and the risks of society.

The technical diversity of automobiles of the future implies the necessity for equally diverse business practices for manufacturers. The rate of technological change has been accelerating so rapidly that hardly any one company holds a mastery of all the technology required for its vehicles. The pace will continue. If automobile companies do try to develop technologies solely by themselves rather than relying on specialist companies, such as suppliers or other automobile companies, these go-it-alone companies will tend to incur higher costs than they would otherwise.

Despite some adaptability in product diversity, many companies currently encounter difficulties in gaining flexibility for extensive model changes for a number of reasons—technical rigidity in the production process, organizational inertia to adapt flexible methods, unyielding labor responsiveness on the assembly line, and unmanageable sources of supply. To accomplish the technological goals, automobile companies will be engaging in joint ventures with other companies.

Some joint ventures will link horizontally, such as the present one between General Motors (GM) and Toyota in the New United Motor Manufacturing, Inc. (NUMMI). Each of the two firms are exploiting the other's competitive advantage lacking in their respective organizations. Such collaborations may include product design, marketing, manufacturing, or a set of skills such as the lean production technique that Toyota had honed, but GM lacked in the United States.

Other types of joint ventures are likely to develop vertically. Some will reach backward to suppliers. With the increasing cost of development, automobile companies are finding that suppliers' special knowledge and skills can design modular components such as suspension or braking systems at less cost and in a shorter time to meet market demands. Others will move forward to distributors and sales organizations, which themselves will employ unique marketing technologies such as computer ordering from home and virtual reality test drives of various vehicles.

[See also Motor Vehicles, Alternatively Powered; Personal Transport; Transportation; Urban Transit.]

BIBLIOGRAPHY

Arnesen, Peter J., ed. *The Auto Industry Ahead: Who's Driving?* Ann Arbor, MI: University of Michigan Center for Japanese Studies, 1989.

Automobiles and the Future: Competition, Cooperation, and Change. Warrendale, PA: Society of Automotive Engineers, 1989.

Cole, Robert E., ed. *The American Automobile Industry: Rebirth or Requiem?* Ann Arbor, MI: University of Michigan Center for Japanese Studies, 1984.

Law, Christopher M., ed. *Restructuring the Global Automobile Industry: Global, National, and Regional Impacts.* New York: Routledge, 1991.

— FRANK C. SCHULLER

MOTOR VEHICLES, ALTERNATIVELY POWERED

Petroleum fuels have powered virtually all motor vehicles since the early years of this century. That is likely to change. The leading contenders are ethanol, methanol, natural gas, hydrogen, and electricity. The use of these alternative fuels would reduce petroleum consumption and provide at least some environmental advantage relative to gasoline and diesel fuel. Their relative attractiveness will depend upon the perceived importance of energy and environmental goals, the cost of producing and delivering fuels, and the cost and performance of vehicles that consume those fuels. In general, those energy options with the greatest environmental advantages face the largest start-up barriers, and those with the smallest environmental advantages face the smallest start-up barriers.

Alcohol fuels (ethanol and methanol) require the least change in vehicle design and the least investment in new infrastructure. They also provide the smallest air pollution benefits and provide few or no greenhouse gas benefits when made from natural gas, grains, and sugar crops.

Pure ethanol made from sugar cane has been used to power vehicles in Brazil since 1980. At its peak in the mid-1980s, over 90 percent of the country's new cars and light trucks were designed to burn ethanol. Ethanol's share of the new car market slowly eroded thereafter to about half the new car market by the mid-1990s. In the United States, ethanol is made mostly from corn and only used as an additive. It is mixed with petroleum in small proportions to produce a "cleaner burning" gasoline. In that form, it has accounted for about 5 to 8 percent of U.S. gasoline consumption since the early 1980s.

When made from corn, ethanol's environmental and energy advantages are virtually nonexistent. Ethanol combustion in vehicles emits somewhat fewer and less-reactive air pollutants than gasoline combustion, but large amounts of fossil fuel are used in growing, harvesting, and processing the corn. The net result is that ethanol made from corn in the United States has about the same greenhouse gas emissions as gasoline. It is also much more expensive. Ethanol is used in the United States because of generous subsidies from the federal government and various corn-growing mid-western states.

Methanol made from natural gas is widely used for a variety of industrial purposes. It is less expensive than ethanol on an energy-equivalent basis but up to 30 percent more costly in monetary terms than gasoline. It received considerable attention through the 1980s, largely because of its potential to reduce air pollution. In the early 1990s, several thousand methanol vehicles were sold in the United States by major automakers. These so-called flexible-fuel vehicles (FFVS) require minimal modification, and cost and perform about the same as gasoline vehicles. While the vehicles can operate on any mixture of gasoline and methanol, in practice the methanol fuel was sold as an 85/15 mixture with gasoline. The 15 percent gasoline was blended in for safety to assure that the fuel would burn with a visible flame, and for performance to facilitate starting in cold weather. These methanol/gasoline blends tend to have a small positive effect on vehicle emissions and little or no net effect on greenhouse gas emissions. If used as 100 percent methanol, the air quality benefits would be much greater, but the fuel would be less safe and not start well in cold weather.

Alternatively, methanol and ethanol could be made from cellulosic biomass—that is, from trees and grasses. The U.S. Department of Energy has provided substantial R&D support for this option since the 1970s. The first attraction of these biomass fuels is potentially lower cost. The second is greatly reduced greenhouse gas emissions (because cultivation is less energy intensive. (The biomass can be burned to power the processing plants, and carbon dioxide emissions resulting from combustion can be recycled through photosynthesis.) The disadvantages are large land requirements, increased soil erosion, and possible reductions in biodiversity.

Oil refiners have responded to the alcohol fuel challenge by reformulating gasoline to reduce vehicular emissions. Since first introduced in Los Angeles in 1989 by ARCO, oil refiners have made steady progress. Costing less and providing almost as much air quality benefit, reformulated gasoline has undermined interest in methanol and ethanol.

Perhaps the leading alternative fuel for internal combustion engines is natural gas. Rather than conversion to methanol, natural gas instead can be burned directly, just like gasoline and alcohol fuels. Over half a million vehicles operate on natural gas worldwide. In almost all vehicles, natural gas is stored inboard in pressurized tanks and almost all have bi-fuel capability, allowing the driver to change from natural gas to gasoline by simply flipping a switch inside the vehicle. Because they are simpler and can be optimized for a single fuel, dedicated natural gas vehicles are superior to bi-fuel vehicles in terms of cost, emissions, performance, and energy efficiency. But unless natural gas is available at many fuel stations, consumers will not buy the vehicles and manufacturers will not build or sell them. Dedicated natural gas vehicles have greater potential to reduce emissions than methanol and ethanol, would have lower life cycle costs under most conditions (the extra $1,000 for storage tanks being roughly offset by lower fuel costs), and somewhat lower greenhouse gas emissions.

The use of alternative fuels

would reduce petroleum consumption

and provide at least some environmental advantage

relative to gasoline and diesel fuel.

Hydrogen is an attractive transportation fuel because it can be produced from a large number of renewable feedstocks and has great potential to drastically reduce all regulated automobile emissions. However, high production costs and low energy density will prevent hydrogen from being a plausible transportation fuel for many years. The first application of hydrogen fuel will probably be in electric vehicles (EVs) using fuel cells rather than direct combustion in dedicated hydrogen vehicles. Fuel cells convert hydrogen, methanol, and other fuels into electricity that can then be used to power vehicles. Fuel cells have a much higher ratio of power output to weight than batteries, but their bulkiness and high costs have so far precluded their use in automobiles. Rapid strides have been made during the 1990s in reducing the cost and size of fuel cells.

Electric vehicle research has focused on battery development for inboard electricity storage. The major international automobile manufacturers have prototype electric vehicles that can travel at freeway speeds and are capable of eighty or more miles of travel per charge. A number of smaller companies are also developing battery-powered EVs.

EV success does not hinge on battery technology advances alone. Advances being made in drivetrain effi-

ciencies, lightweight materials, and recharging rates could make EVs a viable option for many households and business fleets within the next decade. These improvements may even make it possible to downsize EV batteries, which in turn would decrease the vehicle purchase cost (batteries are the largest cost component of an EV).

In addition to battery-powered EVs, research is also progressing on hybrid electric vehicles. These combine a small internal combustion engine (gas turbine, diesel, or spark ignition) with an electric motor and electricity storage device (probably a battery). The small combustion engine provides a longer range but with much fewer emissions and petroleum use than a gasoline vehicle.

Electric vehicles are a tantalizing prospect because of their unsurpassed potential to reduce drastically automobile emissions, greenhouse gases, and petroleum use. In most situations, even with today's relatively inefficient fossil-fuel power plants, the use of an electric vehicle would nearly eliminate hydrocarbon and carbon monoxide emissions and petroleum use, reduce nitrogen oxides by over 50 percent, and moderately reduce greenhouse gases. With fuel cells, the advantages would be even greater.

Although it will take some years, perhaps decades, for alternative fuels to replace petroleum on a large scale, their role in transportation will be determined by decisions made today. An immediate transition to marginally cleaner fuels may be the path of least resistance, but it could come at the expensive of forestalling alternatives that offer far more substantial benefits. In any case, government intervention will play a vital role in the development of alternative fuel markets because neither energy security nor environmental issues are fully accounted for in the marketplace. No alternative fuel is a clear winner or loser (except perhaps ethanol made from corn). The fuels used to power automobiles of the future will depend on political convictions, technological advances, and the tenacity with which the petroleum industry protects the status quo.

[See also Electric Power; Energy, Renewable Sources of; Motor Vehicles; Personal Transport; Petroleum.]

BIBLIOGRAPHY

Ayres, Robert U., and McKenna, Richard P. *Alternatives to the Internal Combustion Engine: Impacts on Environmental Quality.* Baltimore: Johns Hopkins University Press, 1972.

Recent Advances in Electric Vehicle Technology. Warrendale, PA: Society of Automotive Engineers, 1989.

Seiffert, Ulrich, and Walzer, Peter. *Automobile Technology of the Future.* Warrendale, PA: Society of Automotive Engineers, 1991.

— DANIEL SPERLING
KEVIN NESBITT

MULTIFOLD TREND

Herman Kahn was one of the great futurist thinkers of the twentieth century. Although many people disagreed with him—especially in the period just before his untimely death in 1983, when he openly supported the policies of the Reagan administration—no one ever questioned his awesome intellect or his well-informed, broad-ranging, and provocative ideas.

The idea of a multifold trend of interacting elements

was seen as an important organizational concept.

Perhaps the most important concept that Kahn fashioned, one that could well benefit futures thinkers of today and tomorrow, is his "basic, long-term multifold trend."

The idea of a multifold trend of interacting elements was seen as an important organizational concept—a "long-term base line which may include within it certain short-term fluctuations." It was assumed that "in most countries of the world it looks as if this Multifold Trend is going to continue, but with important differences in detail in various areas." Nor does the trend suggest beneficial progress: "This is just the way the world seems to be going in the long run, like it or not."

According to Kahn, the multifold trend "goes back about a thousand years and is one of the most basic and enduring tendencies of Western culture." It is best seen as a single entity, where every aspect is to some degree both a cause and an effect. Despite leading and lagging sectors, it goes in one direction—at least on the average and over a long period of time. But it should not be thought of as a fixed, straight railroad track: "We should allow for some curves, some switching back and forth, and even occasional changes in railroad lines."

At least three largely similar versions of the multifold trend concept were published—in 1967, 1972, and 1979. The 1979 version is presented below, slightly abbreviated:

1. *Increasingly sensate culture*—empirical, this-worldly, secular, humanistic, pragmatic, manipulative, rational, hedonistic, recently exhibiting an almost complete decline of the sacred.
2. *Accumulation of scientific and technological knowledge.*
3. *Institutionalization of technological change,* especially research, development, innovation, and diffusion.
4. *Increasing role of bourgeois, bureaucratic, "meritocratic" elites,* increasing literacy and education for everyone.
5. *Increasing military capability of Western cultures*—recently, issues of mass destruction, terrorism, and the diffusion of advanced military technologies (both nuclear and conventional) to non-Western cultures.

6. *Increasing area of world dominated or greatly influenced by Western culture,* but recent emphasis on synthesis with indigenous cultures and various "ethnic" revivals.
7. *Increasing affluence,* recently with more stress on egalitarianism.
8. *Increasing rate of world population growth,* until recently—this rate has probably passed its zenith or soon will.
9. *Urbanization*—and, recently, suburbanization and "urban sprawl"; soon the growth of megalopoli, "sun belts," and rural areas with urban infrastructure and amenities.
10. *Increasing recent attention to macroenvironmental issues*—e.g., constraints set by finiteness of Earth and limited capacity of various local and global reservoirs to accept pollution.
11. *Decreasing importance of primary and recently secondary occupations*—soon a similar decline in tertiary occupations and increasing emphasis on advanced, honorific, or desirable quaternary occupations and activities (quaternary occupations are defined by Kahn as those that render services to tertiary occupations or to each other).
12. *Emphasis on "progress" and future-oriented thinking, discussion, and planning*—recently, some retrogression in the technical quality of such activities.
13. *Increasing universality of the multifold trend.*
14. *Increasing tempo of change* in all the above areas, though this may soon peak in many areas.

Sixteen years later (1995), how does the multi-fold trend concept hold up?

Clearly, many of the elements still ring quite true, especially item 2, the accumulation of knowledge; item 3, technological change; item 5, weapons proliferation; item 6, the peaking of rate of world population growth, (although the actual numbers added per year will continue at top levels for perhaps another decade); item 9, urbanization; item 10, macroenvironmental issues; item 13, the universality of the multifold trend; and item 14, the growing tempo of change.

Two of these trends deserve special comment. Technological change (item 3) as envisioned in 1967 was clearly overstated. Many of Kahn's list of "one hundred technical innovations very likely in the last third of the twentieth century" have not come about, or are not yet nearly as widespread as envisioned. In contrast, the focus on macroenvironmental issues (item 10), which was absent in the 1967 and 1972 versions of the multifold trend, may well be understated. As several authors have noted, the twenty-first century is likely to be "the Century of the Environment," in which issues of sustainability are the major driving forces of human action, and necessary actions reverse certain tendencies of industrialism and modernity.

Two of the fourteen elements have reversed direction over the past decade or so, and seem likely to continue at least in the near future: item 1, the trend to sensate culture and item 7, the increasing affluence and egalitarianism. Contrary to the widespread expectations of social science that the role of the spiritual would continue to wane—a process that Kahn thought "may be the single most important aspect of the long-term Multifold Trend"—religion has taken on new forms (fundamentalism, Pentacostalism, New Age spirituality) and is doing quite well, despite the decline of mainline Protestant denominations. If anything, it is social science that has faltered. As for the expected trend toward greater affluence, growth in real income has been stable or declining for most people over the last decade or so, and gaps between the rich and poor (both within and between countries) have been growing.

Three other elements of Kahn's multifold trend are ambiguous at best: item 4, increasing literacy and education; and item 11, the shift to "quaternary" occupations, and item 12, futures thinking and planning. Absolute progress in literacy and education for all is problematic; indeed, in view of rising standards and more-or-less constant (if not declining) levels of achievement, it could well be said that we are falling behind. A "knowledge industry" has emerged, but it does not account for much employment, nor is it in an overall robust condition at present. There has been an ongoing decline of primary (agricultural) and secondary (manufacturing) occupations, and a decline in tertiary (service) occupations is underway, reflected in downsizing of many public and private organizations. But this is not resulting in great numbers of desirable quaternary occupations; rather, new jobs in all sectors are characterized as part-time, contingent, and generally poorly paid. Progress in "future-oriented thinking, discussion, and planning" is stagnant at best.

In sum, nine of the fourteen elements of the multifold trend still hold true, although one of these was notably overstated, and one was understated. Two of the elements have clearly reversed and three others have probably reversed. Kahn warned of "curves, switching back and forth, and occasional changes in railroad lines." The key question deserving intense ongoing debate is whether changes in the elements of the multifold trend represent temporary "switching back and forth" (perhaps over a matter of decades), or whether we have switched tracks and railroad lines, moving in a substantially new direction toward some vision of a sustainable world. Most observers would argue for the latter interpretation.

Despite falling well short of perfection, is Kahn's batting average of hits versus misses a respectable one? No judgment is possible, because futurists, unlike baseball players, have not been rated on their successes. We can say that, unlike many others, Kahn swung for the fences in pronouncing on most if not all of the big issues.

Whatever the flaws of the older versions, the multifold trend is still a key idea. If Herman Kahn were still around, he surely would have provided the needed updating.

[See also Change; Change, Pace of; Global Culture; Kahn, Herman; Sustainability; Technology Diffusion.]

BIBLIOGRAPHY

Kahn, Herman, and Wiener, Anthony J. *The Year 2000: A Framework for Speculation on the Next Thirty-Three Years.* New York: Macmillan, 1967.

Kahn, Herman, and Bruce-Briggs, B. *Things to Come: Thinking About the Seventies and Eighties.* New York: Macmillan, 1972.

Kahn, Herman. *World Economic Development: Projections from 1978 to the Year 2000.* Boulder, CO: Westview Press, 1979. Brief adaptation in the *Futurist* 13:3 (June 1979): 202–222.

McKenzie-Mohr, Doug, and Marien, Michael, eds. "Visions of Sustainability." *Futures* 26:2 (March 1994): 115–256.

— MICHAEL MARIEN

MUSEUMS

Museums are at once conservative and innovative institutions. They are conservative in their traditional functions of collecting and preserving material culture and natural history. They are innovative in their many efforts to interpret and exhibit this heritage to the public. In the future, they are likely to experience increasing tension as they attempt to fulfill long-standing missions and expand programs for public service in the face of

Forces shaping museums include the broad desire to touch, handle, and experience, not merely to see or listen.

straitened financial circumstances. How they respond will test their abilities to innovate.

While most European museums began as princely collections in search of a public purpose, American museums began as public-spirited ideas in the minds of civic leaders. The signal contribution of United States museums has been democratization.

The great institutions founded in the nineteenth century were committed to advancing and diffusing knowledge. Historical societies, art collections, natural history museums, and zoos justified their existence in terms of public service. Newer types of museums, including art centers, children's museums, nature centers, and science and technology centers, are even more clearly dedicated to education. Many of them do not own collections but borrow them for display. Others use reproductions and hands-on exhibits to promote understanding of art, nature, or technology and scientific principles. These new types of museums testify to the responsiveness of the museum as an institution to trends in scholarship and public demand for education.

Museums respond to the cultural diversity in the United States and to pressing public policy issues. Although ethnic museums are not new—the American Swedish Historical Foundation and Museum in Philadelphia, for example, was founded in 1926—specifically African-American museums are new. While black schools and colleges long collected art and artifacts, most black museums were founded in the wake of the civil rights movement. With their emphasis on contemporary problems and community service, they have pushed the museum to a further democratization. There are more than one hundred African-American museums in the United States, and the Smithsonian Institution is committed to developing an African-American museum on the National Mall.

The Smithsonian recently established the National Museum of the American Indian. Now tribal councils throughout the country are calling for museums to rethink the way they have displayed native cultures and to return human remains and sacred objects. Across the street from the Smithsonian complex in Washington is the new United States Holocaust Memorial Museum. It testifies to the sensitivity of the museum as an institution to cultural consciousness and to new exhibit techniques.

Museums of all types are increasingly responsive to social issues. Art museums with exhibits on ecology, history museums with exhibits on endangered species, university museums with exhibits on sexual abuse, or natural history museums with exhibits on garbage or waste amply demonstrate that conventional museums are engaging in public policy debates in an attempt to move visitors to action rather than mere contemplation.

Attendance is generally on the increase. In 1988 American museums had more than half a billion visits. On average, Americans visit a museum or participate in a museum program three times a year. However, financial support is not on the increase. To help cover expenses, more than half of all museums now charge admission, and many have established development offices, fund-raising programs, and endowments. Re-

Using a computer to gather data at an archeological site can help a museum keep its exhibits current. (Vittoriano Rastelli/Corbis)

cent trends indicate that private support for museums is increasing, while the percentage of museum income from government allocations and from earned income (including admission fees) is declining.

Other forces shaping museums include the broad desire to touch, handle, and experience, not merely to see or listen. Museums are forming alliances and branches to make better use of their holdings. Most important of all will be the effects of information technology. Computers and information networks will serve to open museums to the wider world, providing endless depths of information on any artifact or work of art for the real or virtual visitor.

In the future, museums will use a variety of imaginative strategies to educate and to secure the financial support required. They will defend their traditional roles as the collectors and preservers of natural and human history at the same time that they broaden their audiences and their base of public support. They will find it financially difficult to compete in the art market for new acquisitions and will be constrained by the need to comply with legal restrictions regarding cultural materials and natural specimens.

[See also Arts; Clothing; Interactive Entertainment; Mass Culture and Arts; Visual Arts.]

BIBLIOGRAPHY

Coates, Joseph F. "The Future of Museums." *The Futurist* (August 1984): 40–45.

Excellence and Equity: Education and the Public Dimension of Museums. Washington, DC: American Association of Museums, 1992.

Museums Count. Washington, DC: American Association of Museums, 1994.

Museums for a New Century: A Report of the Commission on Museums for a New Century. Washington, DC: American Association of Museums, 1984.

— ANN HOFSTRA GROGG

MUSIC

Music has always played a role in both shaping society and reflecting its verve. Before the widespread advent of the printed word, wandering minstrels helped communicate stories of the times. Soul singers and blues balladeers, folksingers, and rappers have sometimes exerted powerful influence over social and political change. That which artists play and sing emotes pathos, pinpoints problems, and gives meaning to people's hopes and aspirations—the very grist of social change.

Music fulfills many roles. National anthems help to unify countries. Theatrical productions like *Hair* or *Oh Calcutta!* are both a response to changing sexual mores and a stimulus for such changes. Classical music, because of the considerable expense involved in its per-

formance (especially when larger performing forces are required), has generally been more beholden to official channels for dissemination. Even so, classical music composition today seems to be moving out of its ghetto of governmentally and corporately subsidized elitism. Contemporary works are being created in an enormous variety of styles, with a slowly growing degree of popular support. More broadly, the emergence of a global community is also serving to blur the distinctions between different types of music and to foster a true multicultural awareness, the likes of which have perhaps never been seen before.

The internationalized range of musical elements available to musicians now is further enhanced by the infinite possibilities afforded by electronic and computer technology.

Rock music is as good an explanation as any for the fall of the Berlin Wall. The relationship between rock music and former East German youth poignantly illustrates the complex roles of music within the overall social context. The production of music is influenced by the ongoing impact of technological change. Musical styles today are being shaped by seemingly opposite trends of increased globalization and a renewal of indigenization. The interrelated development of music and technology points toward our social future.

When the Soviet Union took over the eastern part of Germany during the late 1940s, it decided that the imposition of Soviet culture could not stamp out Nazi values. Instead, East Germans were encouraged to return to traditional German culture, including German classical music, and from those roots to forge a new East German society distinct from that of West Germany. However, unlike citizens of other authoritarian regimes such as Albania and North Korea, East Germans could not be isolated from the rest of the world. In particular, residents of East Berlin could see and hear television and radio broadcasts from West Germany and from the Western occupying forces.

Coincidentally, just as the Berlin Wall went up, rock music became a world music, and the Wall could not keep it out. The East German government, in acknowledgment of the power of this invading cultural form, encouraged its musicians to make their own rock music. At first, these musicians merely copied Western rock, but in a few years they began to incorporate elements from their own musical tradition, elements better able to accommodate the German language and sensibility, and, finally, to make uniquely East German rock with politically charged lyrics.

Bypassing state sponsorship and a state owned recording company, some peripheral East German musicians succeeded in self-producing and distributing their own inexpensive cassette tapes, as did their Soviet counterparts and other musicians around the world. Primarily in the United States and Western Europe, but also in such far-flung and impoverished places as Jamaica and Nigeria, musicians are self-producing professional-quality tapes, vinyl recordings, and, more recently, compact disks. Although distribution of these recordings in many cases remains localized, some well-known musicians distribute self-produced, high-quality material worldwide, and some types of inexpensive homemade tapes are heard throughout large regions. For example, highly politicized, self-produced tapes appear everywhere in South and Central America.

Another manifestation of the ability of musicians to work outside the recording industry and to profit directly from their own work lies in the proliferation of live music around the world as more musicians form local groups and perform for local audiences. These groups, although often culturally and politically opposed to the values of the established recording industry, are a source of innovation and raw talent for core production, a facet of the tension between increasing globalization and strengthening indigenization of cultural products.

The West has sent music, classical and popular, to the rest of the world for centuries. This music has influenced, but has not obliterated, indigenous cultural creativity. Western rock music is itself a combination of West African and European musical elements as combined by slaves, sailors, soldiers, and ministers as well as, in more recent times, direct and recorded contact among professional musicians. With the advent of recording technology and jet travel, the pace of musical experimentation has accelerated tremendously. The internationalized range of musical elements available to musicians now is further enhanced by the infinite possibilities afforded by electronic and computer technology.

Recording technology allows a Louis Armstrong fan to listen to an authentic reproduction of his 1920s band in high-quality digital sound. Recently developed nano-CDs, the size of a penny, hold 800 times the capacity of the current compact disk. (© Stock Montage)

Electronic technology also has separated performance of live music and production of recorded music into two distinct art forms. For decades now, recording experts have lamented their inability to reproduce accurately the ambience of live music, a gap that is rapidly closing with the development of virtual sound and digital signal processing whereby sounds can be adjusted electronically and accurately to various types of listening environments. At the same time, recording technology has made possible musical experiences that cannot be repeated on stage.

The fall of the Berlin Wall symbolizes emerging global harmony at the same time that ethnic divisions in the former Yugoslavia and Somalia indicate a desire for more localized cultural identification and control over everyday situations. Current production of music presents the same contradictory picture of the new global order where more collaborative decisions are made on an international level while, at the same time, people everywhere assume responsibility for their own affairs.

[See also Arts; Literature; Mass Culture and Arts; Performing Arts: Dance and Theatre; Visual Arts.]

BIBLIOGRAPHY

Attali, Jacques. *Noise: The Political Economy of Music.* Minneapolis: University of Minnesota Press, 1985.

Jones, Steve. *Rock Formation: Technology, Music and Mass Communication.* Newbury Park, CA: Sage Publications, 1992.

Nettl, Bruno. *The Western Impact on World Music: Change, Adaptation, and Survival.* New York: Schirmer, 1985.

Robinson, Deanna Campbell; Buck, Elizabeth R.; Cuthbert, Marlene; and the International Communication and Youth Culture Consortium. *Music at the Margins: Popular Music and Global Cultural Diversity.* Newbury Park, CA: Sage Publications, 1991.

Wallis, Roger, and Malm, Kristen. *Big Sounds from Small Peoples: The Music Industry in Small Countries.* London: Constable, 1984.

— DEANNA CAMPBELL ROBINSON

N

NAISBITT, JOHN (1929–)

One of the world's leading trends forecasters and analysts, John Naisbitt is also a bestselling author whose books have sold in the millions. Born in 1929 in Salt Lake City, he dropped out of school in the tenth grade, and joined the Marine Corps two years later. In 1948, he enrolled in the University of Utah, graduating with academic honors in 1952. During the next fifteen years, he served in a number of corporate and government positions, notably as Assistant Commissioner of Education under President Kennedy. He formed his own company, Urban Research Corporation (later known as the Naisbitt Group), in 1967 and has been an entrepreneur ever since. Naisbitt's career as an author began in 1982 with the publication of *Megatrends*. The book presaged the coming shift from industrial to information societies, from national economies to a global economy, and from hierarchical organizations to networking organizations. Published in forty-four countries, the book has sold over 9 million copies. Almost a decade later, *Megatrends 2000* (coauthored with his wife, Patricia Aburdene) updated many of his forecasts for the 1990s and beyond. His sixth book, *Global Paradox* (1994), offers glimpses of paradoxical changes in the global village, displaying once again an ability to weave together disparate trends into simple, yet visionary future-scapes. Naisbitt is also a much sought-after public speaker and consultant to governments and corporations.

[See Naisbitt's article Global Paradox in this volume.]
– GEORGE THOMAS KURIAN

NANOTECHNOLOGY

Nanotechnology is an embryonic, multidisciplinary field with the ambitious goal of manipulating matter at the atomic and molecular level. It is a speculative field, with no working models so far. Its commercial impacts, if any, are most likely a generation away.

Nanotechnology involves technology and materials at nanometer scale—one-billionth of a meter or about ten atoms long. Current technology is at the micrometer scale (one-millionth of a meter), where many experts believe it is reaching physical limits. Advocates propose nanotechnology as a new approach to reaching the nanometer scale, with the benefits of using fewer materials and less energy, and creating less waste.

Nobel Prize-winning physicist Richard Feynman anticipated the field in a 1959 speech when he asked, "What would happen if we could arrange atoms, one by one, the way we needed?" The concept became known as nanotechnology and gained popularity in the 1980s largely due to a single individual, K. Eric Drexler. The essence of Drexler's vision is that molecular machines will assemble other molecular machines and team up to do useful work, which ranges from the practical—faster computing—to the exotic—building advanced spacesuits and arresting aging processes.

Three paths are most likely for commercialization. They will be concurrent and overlapping, rather than exclusive.

- *Molecular engineering:* The human body is a living example of a nanotechnology. Nature builds self-assembling nanodevices and systems routinely, using information stored in genes to transcribe proteins for carrying out the body's functions. Biotechnology is unraveling more of nature's secrets daily. Drexler, on the other hand, takes a purely nanotechnological stance in *Unbounding the Future* (1991, pp. 19–20), stating that "nanotechnology won't be biotechnology because it won't rely on altering life. . . . Molecular nanotechnology will use molecular machinery, but unlike biotechnology, it will not rely on genetic meddling. It will be not an extension of biotechnology, but an alternative or a replacement."

- *Miniaturization of electromechanical systems:* The current approach to miniaturization is to make big things smaller—for example, by breaking down materials into their constituent parts. Micromachines, which are etched out of silicon, can operate at the micro scale. The goal is to fit them with valves, gears, and motors to carry out their tasks, perhaps as sensors in vehicles, gauges, and medical tools. Nanotechnology reverses this approach to miniaturization by seeking to make small things bigger—assembling atoms into molecules. Drexler envisions a molecular assembler, a device resembling a microscopic industrial robot arm built from rigid molecular parts, driven by motors, controlled by computers, and able to grasp and apply molecular-scale tools. Assemblers would build molecular machines and other assemblers to perform work at the nanometer scale.

- *Molecular computing:* Current semiconductor technology may be approaching its physical limits, which would mean that the doubling of computer power that has been taking place every eighteen months would slow and eventually stop. This possibility is driving interest in alternative approaches, such as molecular computing. It has been demonstrated that a bacteria molecule (bacteriodhopsin) can be used as a switch or signal transmitting device for optical computing, which uses photons (light) rather than electrons to transmit information more rapidly. Molecules are also being investigated for data storage and as materials for flat screen displays.

Improved tools will cross the three commercialization paths. The scanning tunneling microscope (STM) can locate and arrange atoms, as IBM demonstrated when it spelled out its logo with thirty-five xenon atoms in 1990. But it is a big step from there to useful products. While manipulating individual atoms like this means that it is theoretically possible to store all human publications ever written in a credit-card-sized device, it would take billions of years using current STM technology.

Manipulating individual atoms means that it is theoretically possible to store all human publications ever written in a credit-card-sized device.

The atomic force microscope adds the capability of working in open air and probing biological samples, where the STM works only in a vacuum and on conducting surfaces, such as metals. Scanning probe microscopes can create three-dimensional images of atomic structures by physically sensing surfaces instead of magnifying them. Computer simulations are increasingly useful, and as virtual reality technology improves, it should lend a boost to the field.

The most significant brakes on development are likely to be the unanticipated effects or properties of manipulating matter at the atomic scale. For example, quantum effects, in which matter at the atomic scale alternates between wave and particle form, may prove more difficult to deal with than expected. Another important consideration is what to do in the event of self-assembling nanodevices evading human control—that is, continuing to assemble despite instructions to cease.

Nanotechnology is highly multidisciplinary. It includes computer scientists and engineers, chemists, physicists, materials scientists, biotechnologists, and biophysicists. Work is going on in university and corporate research labs around the world, such as the Jet Propulsion Lab, the Naval Research Lab, and IBM. Cornell University has established a nanotechnology research institute and Japan's Ministry of International Trade and Industry is in the middle of a ten-year, $200-million Atom Technology Project.

The earliest applications of nanotechnology are likely to be in electronics and computing. Research-and-development labs are exploring the use of molecular electronic devices, in which single molecules function as computing devices. Possibilities include using atoms to represent bits of information to pack billions of electronic devices onto a single square centimeter chip or linking them to resemble neurons in the brain to form neural network computers. Other possibilities being explored take advantage of molecular magnetic properties to boost optical-disk storage by orders of magnitude. A longer-term possibility, biochips (biological computer chips), would integrate biological capabilities onto computer chips, possibly for tactile pattern recognition. Or, entering the realm of science fiction, biochips might be directly inserted into the brain.

Nanotechnology may supplement, team with, or replace biotechnology in current health areas such as diagnostics, pharmaceutical delivery, biosensors, or genetic therapies. Farther off is Drexler's oft-cited vision of millions and even billions of nanoscale devices floating through the human bloodstream to monitor and maintain health.

Nanotechnology has the potential to transform materials and manufacturing if the molecular self-assembly concept proves practical. Current research includes testing self-assembling materials as coatings to modify surfaces, such as for making a gold-surface coating uniform. The long-term vision is for structures from desks to buildings to aircraft to be built through the combination of billions of self-assembling nanodevices.

Other applications could include energy, in which nanodevices could be catalysts for producing fuel from hydrogen and carbon monoxide. In waste disposal, nanomachines could be set upon solid or hazardous waste sites to break down toxins, perhaps converting them into useful chemical or energy feedstocks.

Because the vision has arrived before the capability, nanotechnology offers society the unique opportunity to consider its potential effects and guide its development before it is in use. It has the potential to transform society, along the line of predecessors such as the steam engine, electricity, and the computer. At the same time, its prospects for being a dead end, or being subsumed into other disciplines, are perhaps equally likely within a time frame of the year 2020. The concept is sound—nature provides a working example of nanotechnology—but the challenge may take decades to meet. This potential, however, merits careful monitoring.

[See also Computers: Overview; Genetic Technologies; Health Care: Technological Developments; Robotics; Scientific Breakthroughs; Technological Change.]

BIBLIOGRAPHY

Drexler, K. Eric. *Nanosystems: Molecular Machinery, Manufacturing, and Computation.* New York: John Wiley, 1992.

Drexler, K. Eric, and Peterson, Chris, with Gayle Perganit. *Unbounding the Future: The Nanotechnology Revolution.* New York: William Morrow, 1991.

Langreth, Robert. "Why Scientists Are Thinking Small." *Popular Science* (May 1993).

– ANDY HINES

NATIONALISM

Despite many challenges throughout this century, nationalism remains a potent force at the end of the millennium. Both Marxist internationalism (metanationalism) and liberal democratic universalism had cast aspersions on the regressive (capitalistic) and aggressive (antidemocratic) characteristics of nationalism. Nevertheless, since the decline of the Soviet-dominated, communist satellite states in Eastern Europe in the 1980s and the collapse of the Soviet Union in 1991, nationalism in its new guise—ethnonationalism—has reemerged with extraordinary vitality and ferocity—so much so that it is safe to predict that ethnonationalism will become even more of a global issue than it already is.

In large measure, ethnonationalism is both a continuation of nineteenth-century European *völkisch* nationalism (such as the unification of Italy and Germany), as well as a reaction to the oppression endured by ethnic majorities and minorities in communist countries, in which each cultural group was exposed to intense assimilationist policies, some of them bordering on outright genocide (such as Stalin's wholesale deportation toward the end of World War II of a half dozen ethnic groups).

Independent of these forms of ethnonationalism, there has been a growing thread of separatist ethnonationalism throughout the postcolonial world (such as the mid-1960s secessionist drive by the Ibos in Nigeria and the ongoing struggles of the East Timorese against Indonesia). Worldwide, interethnic conflict, from Canada (Francophones versus Anglophones) to Sri Lanka (Hindu Tamils versus Buddhist Sinhalese) and from Northern Ireland (pro-English Anglicans versus pro-Irish Catholics) to Burundi and Rwanda (Hutus versus Tutsis), is continually threatening the present international order with a fundamental revision of international borders.

Whereas the racist monoethnicity of Nazi Germany (which culminated in the genocide of European Jewry) was long perceived as an exception, half a century later, Hitlerian German nationalism looks more like a prologue. In the light of the phenomenon of brutal, uncompromising ethnic cleansing witnessed during the recent disintegration of Yugoslavia, the genocidal danger inherent in latter-day ethnonationalist politics suggests the ferocity with which secessionist ethnic conflicts may be resolved in the future, unless the means (creative diplomacy and effective intervention) can be developed to diffuse the controversy and separate contestants. So far, however, international organizations, such as the United Nations, the North Atlantic Treaty Organization, or the European Union, and the waning superpower diplomacy of the United States, have failed to stem the rising tide of separatist ethnonationalism.

In essence, ethnonationalism calls for sovereignty—namely, the power to promote the cultural welfare of an identifiable ethnic group, or *ethnos*. That means winning a favorable climate in which to encourage its language, religion, history, customs, and so on; more often than not that means the exclusion of other minorities, which are encouraged either to assimilate or emigrate. Thus, most postcommunist and post-Soviet states are presently engaged in a chronic duel between the dominant *ethnos* and other minorities, resulting in a number of related developments: (a) *ethnoseparatism,* such as the Abkhazian secession from the former Soviet Georgia; (b) *ethnoseparatism and merger,* such as Nagorno-Karabakh, the Armenian district in Azerbaijan seeking to join with Armenia; and (c) *ethnounification,* such as the Serbian striving for a "Greater Serbia."

All three types of mono-ethnonationalism can be detected as actual or potential developments throughout the world, some of them likely to be violent. In group (a) one can include Tibet (from China), Quebec (from Canada), Wales (from Great Britain), Chechnya (from Russia), and Catalonia (from Spain); in group (b) belong the Albanians in Kosovo (Serbia), the non-Han Muslims (China), and the North and South Ossetians (Georgia and Russia, respectively); and in group (c) one can include the Kurds (in Iran, Iraq, Syria, and Turkey), the Hungarians (in Slovakia, Serbia, and Romania), the Basques (Spain and France), the Albanians (Macedonia), and the Maya Indians (Mexico and Guatemala).

At the same time one has to take note of the several, large multinational states that are most susceptible to interethnic strife and, therefore, to ethnoseparatism. Both Nigeria and India are prime targets for fragmentation along ethnoregional lines. The signs are already visible in both countries as ethnic fault lines begin to move, pressured by a combination of economic disparity, social tension, language rivalry, and religious hatred. There is little reason to believe these heavily populated countries will remain intact once the centrifugal forces of numerous ethnoseparatist nationalisms have been unleashed.

As in the past, ethnonationalism will be challenged by other modern forms of human organization. Multinational corporations, international banking institutions, electronic technology, all are meta-ethnic in their appeal and may help overcome or discourage the tendency toward ethnofragmentation. Then again, the computer is an ideal tool for a small, ethno-based body politic. Thus, as usual, the future is unclear and unpredictable; nevertheless, what remains certain is that ethnonationalism will play a prominent role in it.

Above all, ethnonationalism—which places the interests of the group over those of the individual—will remain a serious threat to societies based on liberal democratic values, in which individual rights rank first, above collective communal priorities.

To what extent, if at all, the monoethnic state can accommodate liberal principles has yet to be determined. Whether or not a bona fide, liberal (open) civil society can coexist inside a monoethnic state that grants ethnic minorities less than equality will depend upon the cultural heritage of each ethnos and a great deal on the enlightenment of its political leadership. The tensions from this conflict will affect both the internal stability of each state and also its behavior in the international arena. As is envisioned from today's perspective, international peace will be much more difficult to maintain in an era of unfettered ethnonationalism.

[See also Ethnic and Cultural Separatism; Global Culture; International Tensions; World: Prologue and Epilogue.]

BIBLIOGRAPHY

Alter, Peter. *Nationalism.* New York: Routledge, Chapman, and Hall, 1989.

Birch, Anthony H. *Nationalism and National Integration.* Boston: Unwin Hyman, 1989.

Breuilly, John. *Nationalism and the State.* New York: St. Martin's Press, 1982.

Featherstone, Mike. *Global Culture: Nationalism, Globalization, and Modernity.* Newbury Park, CA: Sage, 1990.

Gellner, Ernest. *Nations and Nationalism.* Ithaca, NY: Cornell University Press, 1983.

Josey, Charles C. *Philosophy of Nationalism.* McLean, VA: Cliveden Press, 1984.

Kohn, Hans. *Nationalism: Its Meaning and History.* Melbourne, FL: Krieger, 1982.

Seton-Watson, Hugh. *Nations and States: An Inquiry into the Origins of Nations and the Politics of Nationalism.* Boulder, CO: Westview, 1977.

Smith, Anthony D. *Nationalism in the Twentieth Century.* New York: New York University Press, 1979.

Snyder, Louis. *Encyclopedia of Nationalism.* New York: Paragon House, 1990.

— HENRY R. HUTTENBACH

NATIONAL PARKS.

See FORESTRY; PARKS AND WILDERNESS.

NATIONAL SECURITY

For the first time in centuries, the very concept of national security is changing. During this historic period,

fundamental forces will converge to produce new threats to the well-being of nations. National security is about protecting resources—resources that produce wealth, quality of life, and opportunity for a nation's citizens. Since the mid-seventeenth century, wealth and power have been defined primarily in terms of money, which enabled the acquisition of armed forces to project one's will. Countries went to war over economic interests: natural resources, land, boundaries, labor forces, and markets. There was an assumption that a nation could control what passed through its borders, so all national security efforts were based, in some way, on the integrity of those borders. In general, national security was understood to be about defending against threats to one's own resources and dependencies from outside of one's borders. In the future, variations of those problems will persist. However, even though the era of large, Napoleonic wars may well be over, local, ethnic and religious conflict—quite a different problem—is expanding to take its place.

Powerful new forces that include shifts in technology, science, the natural environment, and the world's population are combining with other trends to change the definitions of wealth and power—and consequently national security, particularly in the developed world. The exponential increases in the capability and ubiquity of information technology assure that future wealth and power will be derived primarily from the access to information and knowledge, rather than money. Increasingly, the ability to manipulate systems—economic, political, scientific, and military—is based on information. Information as the capital commodity of the developed world is fundamentally changing the wealth-production equation. Unlike any of the earlier resources that were central to security, information, which is difficult to control, easily crosses borders, and even when given to someone else, is still retained by the giver. Historical policies and philosophies built upon controlling limited, tangible resources are quickly beginning to erode.

The ability to easily acquire information empowers individuals at the expense of larger institutions like governments. A single person can access, through computer networks, more information faster than government can effectively control it . . . and can as well loose a computer virus that may seriously damage governments or militaries. Thus, this driving force of information technology also threatens the present forms of government. Other technologies, like molecular nanotechnology and zero-point energy, have the potential of making obsolete, within the next two decades, most manufacturing and energy production processes. If they evolve as their proponents have envisioned, the geopolitical and economic structure that supports the current notion of security will be further weakened.

Science and the practical implications of quantum mechanics are changing fundamentally the understanding of physical reality, suggesting that the human mind has a causal relationship to matter. These principles will lend credibility to many "paranormal" phenomena that have been discounted and discredited in the past. The militaries of some nations have been working in this area for some time now. Within the next two decades, these principles will shake modern civilization, and give them a new perspective of reality as much, or more so, than the discoveries of Copernicus and Galileo did in their times. The common understanding of what *contributes* to security will be turned on its end.

Because the exponential growth of world population is mostly in poor areas, it is producing major concerns about the migration of large numbers of poor people from their homes to wealthier countries.

In both global and U.S. domestic terms, there is a clear broadening of the disparity between rich and poor. Because the exponential growth of world population is mostly in poor areas, it is producing major concerns about the migration of large numbers of poor people from their homes to wealthier countries. A number of major nations see this trend as a significant security issue that threatens the stability of their economies. Across the world, the poor are moving to large urban areas, producing local dysfunctional environments that are ridden with crime, which increasingly threatens the well-being of the larger metropolitan area. In 1993, Washington, D.C., perhaps anticipating similar considerations by other American cities, debated whether to call up the National Guard to deal with its crime problem.

The waste and pollution produced by this demographic explosion is beginning to threaten some social and physical support systems at local, regional, and global levels. Inadequate drinking water is a growing problem in many poor countries as well as in China, Russia, Israel, Saudi Arabia, and the United States. Some scientists believe the continued thinning of the ozone layer could, within the next decade, begin to kill off the ocean phytoplankton, generating in turn, a massive failure of ocean aquatic life and also eliminating the source of an estimated forty percent of the planet's oxygen-producing capability.

In addition to these fundamental shifts, exotic weapons (nuclear, chemical, biological, and radiological) and their delivery systems are proliferating dangerously in the hands of both renegade nations, and sub- and transnational terrorist groups that are not controlled by legitimate governments. As the poor get poorer, they will have no reason to avoid threatening the stability of large wealthy societies. Increasingly armed with these weapons, they will have the ability to effectively carry out these threats. There are a number of wild cards, such as changing global weather patterns, increases in natural disasters, and other unanticipated events that could also radically restructure attitudes toward security.

The future security of developed countries will not be won without a significant investment of effort and funds on both the external and internal fronts. In each area, new threats as well as old ones will need to be addressed. Global and transnational issues like atmospheric pollution will need to be balanced with the need for something to be done about deteriorating inner cities, faltering or inadequate education systems, and rampant migration. National security will become much less related to borders, and be both broader and narrower in scope, addressing global as well as domestic issues.

[See also Communism; Espionage and Counterintelligence; International Diplomacy; International Tensions; Military Technologies; Peacekeeping; Terrorism; Weapons of Mass Destruction.]

BIBLIOGRAPHY

Petersen, John L. "New Roles for the U.S. Military." *Sloan Management Review* 34/2 (Winter 1993): 93–98.

———. *The Road to 2015: Profiles of the Future.* Corte Madera, CA: Waite Group Press, 1994.

———. "Will the Military Miss the Market?" *Whole Earth Review* (Fall 1992): 62–70.

Toffler, Alvin. *Power Shift: Knowledge, Wealth, and Violence at the End of the Twenty-first Century.* New York: Bantam, 1990.

Toffler, Alvin, and Toffler, Heidi. *War and Antiwar: Survival at the Dawn of the Twenty-first Century.* Boston: Little, Brown, 1993.

— JOHN L. PETERSEN

NATURAL DISASTERS

Human awareness of and responses to natural hazards (see Table 1 for a breakdown by physical process) are *not* dependent solely upon geophysical conditions, but are contingent upon the concerns, pressures, goals, and risks of society, not the least being the effectiveness of measures to reduce calamity (Hewitt, 1983). Better understanding of society, including those processes that affect the choices of society's members, is the key to defining natural hazards and determining future hazard vulnerability (Blaikie et al., 1994).

TABLE 1

NATURAL HAZARDS CLASSIFIED BY PHYSICAL PROCESS

Meteorological	Geological	Hydrological	Extraterrestrial
Hurricanes	Earthquakes	Floods	Asteroids
Thunderstorms	Volcanoes	Droughts	Meteorites
Tornadoes	Landslides	Wildfire	
Lightning	Subsidence		
Hailstorms	Mudflows		
Windstorms	Sinkholes		
Ice storms	Tidal waves		
Snowstorms			
Blizzards			
Cold waves			
Heat waves			
Avalanches			
Fog			
Frost			

Squatters and slum dwellers, who number millions around the world, have little or no choice in their location and few options in responding to hazards. In fact, such marginalized groups often are too poor to move elsewhere. Disasters compound the difficulties for these unfortunate people and further exacerbate the poverty trap in which they exist. Crisis management, relief aid, restoration policies, and reconstruction invariably set out to re-create "normal" conditions (Hewitt, 1983).

Natural hazards constitute a complex web of physical and environmental factors interacting with the social, economic, and political realities of society.

A simple focus on the physical world that emphasizes geophysical processes leads to an incomplete understanding of natural hazards. The human element is important, not only because humans are the victims, but also because by their exposure they define the very dimensions of natural hazards. Natural hazards constitute a complex web of physical and environmental factors interacting with the social, economic, and political realities of society.

Risk and Vulnerability

Natural hazards by definition constitute a risk to society because humans and/or their activities are constantly exposed to these extreme forces. For instance, by locating property on floodplains, by undertaking agriculture on the slopes of active volcanoes, and by developing housing in hurricane-prone coastal zones, humans are wittingly exposed to hazard risk. Given the ubiquitous nature of natural hazards, all communities face an element of risk, but not all are equally vulnerable. Some communities have adopted stringent regulations and constructed major projects to protect themselves from disasters. In this way, the vulnerability of the community has been reduced. For example, the construction of earthquake-proof structures can significantly reduce the vulnerability of a community to earthquake losses. Similarly, zoning land for low-density uses can minimize the impacts of flooding, hurricanes, and tidal waves (tsunamis).

This is not to assume that all human activities reduce the hazard risk. Indeed, there are many land-use and societal decisions that exacerbate problems and increase vulnerability. For instance, the expansion of urban areas onto floodplains, wetlands, and steep slopes has heightened the hazard risk.

Trends in Death and Damage

Every year natural hazards place a heavy toll on society, killing large numbers of people, destroying homes, and damaging property throughout the world. Assessing the number of deaths and totaling damages is no easy task, especially during the immediate post-hazard impact phase, when emergency relief and rehabilitation are priorities and general confusion prevails. Data on natural hazards can be sketchy and is frequently exaggerated, especially during the early hours of the event. It is not unusual to find initial unofficial estimates of deaths and damages to be considerably higher than final figures (Alexander, 1993). On other occasions, deaths are significantly underestimated, as in the Kobe (Japan) earthquake of 1995, when early reports put deaths below 50

man (1992), utilizing information from more than twenty European and U.S. data sources, nevertheless underrepresents the impacts. Excluded from their analysis were pervasive hazards such as droughts, and events that did not lead to 25 deaths or more, even if they had been economically devastating. They found that, between 1945 and 1986, there were 1,267 global natural disasters that caused 2,343,000 deaths, for an average of 56,000 deaths per year. A closer examination of these statistics shows that 3 events accounted for a substantial number of deaths. Two earthquakes, one in the former Soviet Union (1948) and one in China (1976), killed 110,000 and 700,000 people respectively, and a tropical cyclone in Bangladesh (1970) killed 500,000 people. If these major catastrophes are removed from the data set, then the number of deaths per year falls to 25,000 and the average per disaster to 837.

It is also true that large-magnitude events account for the greatest number of deaths from natural hazards. Keith Smith (1992), for instance, found that there were 17 major disasters since 1949, defined as those that have killed more than 10,000. Using the Glickman et al. data, only 29 disasters (2.3 percent) met this criterion of 10,000 deaths; yet, they accounted for 1.9 million deaths (81.2 percent).

Temporal Trends

The hazard data on disasters and deaths show distinct trends over time (see Table 3). The number of disasters per 7-year period has gradually risen from 107 between 1945 and 1951, to 303 between 1980 and 1986, while the number of deaths shows a similar pattern, at least until the last period. Global economic losses have also increased dramatically. For instance, losses per decade from weather-related natural disasters have risen from $400 billion in the 1950s to ninety times that value in the 1980s.

Spatial Trends

The spatial pattern of disaster deaths and damages is even more telling. Ninety-five percent of all disaster-related deaths occur among the 67 percent of the population that lives in the world's poorer nations, whereas 75 percent of the economic losses accrues to those in the wealthy nations. Data show that East Asia and the Pacific region, Southern Asia, Latin America, and the Caribbean have experienced the most deaths and disasters during the 42-year period. Controlling for size of resident populations, the Middle East and North Africa also join Latin America and the Caribbean as the worst-hit areas (see Table 4). When these data are broken down by country different pattern emerge. Between

Technology provides increasingly sensitive monitoring and timely warning about natural disasters. This satellite view is of a Hawaiian volcano site. (NASA/Corbis)

but the final death toll actually exceeded 5,000 people. Similarly, estimates of economic losses are also vague and notoriously inaccurate. Despite these limitations, the data provide an indication of the impacts associated with hazard losses (see Table 2).

An important review of disaster trends by Theodore S. Glickman, Dominic Golding, and Emily D. Silver-

TABLE 2

SELECTED NATURAL DISASTERS WORLDWIDE, 1900–1995

Hurricanes/Typhoons/Tropical Cyclones*			Earthquakes, Tsunamis, and Associated Events		
Year	Location	Deaths	Year	Location	Deaths
1900	United States	6,000	1906	Taiwan	6,000
1906	Hong Kong	10,000	1906	United States	1,500
1928	United States	2,000	1908	Italy	75,000
1938	United States	600	1915	Italy	30,000
1959	Japan	4,600	1920	China	200,000
1961	Hong Kong	400	1923	Japan	143,000
1963	Bangladesh	22,000	1932	China	70,000
1965	Bangladesh	17,000	1933	Japan	3,000
1965	Bangladesh	30,000	1935	India	60,000
1965	Bangladesh	10,000	1939	Chile	30,000
1970	Bangladesh	300,000	1948	USSR	100,000
1971	India	25,000	1949	USSR	20,000
1977	India	20,000	1960	Morocco	12,000
1985	Bangladesh	10,000	1962	Iran	12,000
1988	Caribbean	25,000	1968	Iran	12,000
1989	Caribbean/U.S.	56	1970	Peru	70,000
			1972	Nicaragua	6,000
			1976	China	250,000
Volcanic Activities			1976	Guatemala	24,000
			1976	Italy	900
Year	Location	Deaths	1978	Iran	25,000
			1980	Italy	1,300
1902	Martinique	29,000	1985	Mexico	1,700
1902	Guatemala	6,000	1988	Armenia	10,000
1911	Philippines	1,300	1990	Iran	25,000
1919	Indonesia	5,200	1995	Japan	5,200
1930	Indonesia	1,400			
1951	Papua New Guinea	2,900	**Floods**		
1963	Indonesia	1,200			
1980	United States	70	Year	Location	Deaths
1982	Mexico	1,700			
1985	Colombia	22,000	1945	Japan	1,200
			1949	China	57,000
			1953	North Sea coast	1,800
			1954	China	40,000
			1993	United States	50

* The name for large tropical storms of 75 m.p.h. or greater wind intensity is hurricane in the Atlantic-Caribbean and the eastern Pacific, typhoon in the western Pacific, tropical cyclone in the Indian Ocean, and various other names in other regions.

Source: Office of Foreign Disaster Assistance (1988) and Eric Noji (1991).

1900 and 1988, India suffered most disasters, while the U.S.S.R. experienced most disaster-related deaths, but Italy the most economic loss (see Table 5) (OFDA, 1988). (Note that the United States was omitted from these statistics.)

These statistics, however, fail to reflect the significance of economic loss in the different countries. Greater affluence means that more property is at risk; hence, losses are often high whenever disaster strikes a wealthy community. But the loss sustained by poorer nations is actually greater in real terms than that in wealthy nations. A family in Bangladesh may lose all its possessions in a tropical cyclone and still only accrue tens of dollars in damage. In contrast, when an automobile is crushed by falling debris in a Californian earthquake, the economic loss is high but the personal costs may be low. Disaster losses as a percentage of the GNP can be much higher in poorer nations than in wealthy ones. For example, the growth of the gross domestic product (GDP) in five Central American countries was reduced by 2.3 percent annually between 1960 and 1974 as a consequence of natural disasters. Smith

TABLE 3

TEMPORAL TRENDS IN NATURAL DISASTERS, 1945–1986

Period	Number of Disasters	Thousands of Deaths	Deaths per Disaster	Deaths per Year
1945–1951	107 (106)	252 (142)	2,351 (1,336)	36,000 (20,286)
1952–1958	172	92	534	13,143
1959–1965	197	239	1,212	34,143
1966–1972	244 (243)	706 (206)	2,892 (847)	100,857 (29,428)
1973–1979	244 (243)	921 (221)	3,777 (912)	131,571 (31,571)
1980–1986	303	134	441	19,143
Total	1,267	2,343	1,849	55,786

Note: Data in parentheses exclude three worst disasters for the period.
Source: Glickman, Golding, and Silverman (1992).

TABLE 4

SPATIAL PATTERNS OF NATURAL DISASTERS, 1945–1986

Region	Number of Disasters	Thousands of Deaths	Deaths per Disaster	Deaths per Million People
East Asia/Pacific	401 (400)	977 (277)	2,435 (691)	5
Latin America/Caribbean	239	239	999	21
Southern Asia	234 (233)	808 (308)	3,452 (1,321)	10
North America	149	15	104	2
Europe/U.S.S.R.	127 (126)	166 (56)	1,308 (444)	2
Middle East/North Africa	86	129	1,505	24
Sub-Saharan Africa	45	9	201	1
Total	1,267	2,343	1,849	

Note: Data in parentheses exclude three worst disasters for the period.
Source: Glickman, Golding, and Silverman (1992).

(1992) pointed out that hurricane losses in the Dominican Republic (1979), Haiti, St. Lucia, and St. Vincent (1980) rose to 15 percent of the gross national product (GNP). The scale of these losses means that the potential for development for many of these countries is undermined by the recurring disasters and the efforts and finance needed for recovery.

Geophysical Patterns

If these hazard data are broken down by geophysical event, then distinct patterns emerge (see Table 6). First, floods are clearly the most common natural hazard during the post-World War II period, accounting for over 30 percent of all disasters. Hurricanes and tropical cyclones make up about 20 percent; earthquakes between 15 percent and 17 percent; and tornadoes approximately 12 percent of natural hazards (Glickman et al., 1992).

In terms of deaths, the pattern is different. The Glickman, Golding, and Silverman (1992) study indicated that earthquakes and hurricanes/tropical cyclones

killed more people than any other hazard, with floods dropping to third. Even when the three largest events are removed from the data, earthquakes and tropical cyclones still account for more deaths than other hazards.

Conclusions

Various hypotheses have been put forward to explain these spatial and temporal trends in hazards data. First, it is conceivable that the frequency of extreme geophysical events has increased over the last twenty or thirty years, thus accounting for the rise in number of hazards and the jump in number of deaths. Studies of geophysical processes do not support this contention, although it is possible that certain natural hazards have increased because of human activities. Drainage of wetlands, urbanization, and deforestation have all modified the storm hydrograph, resulting in more incidents of small-scale flooding. On the other hand, it is unlikely that humans have had any significant impact on the frequency of volcanic activity, earthquakes, or tropical

TABLE 5

DISASTERS, DEATHS, AND DAMAGE BY COUNTRY

Disasters		Disaster Deaths per Event		Disaster Damage per Event (Thousands of U.S. $)	
India	199	U.S.S.R.	284,334	Italy	611,694
Philippines	134	China	80,812	Spain	374,686
Indonesia	110	India	4,379	Chile	121,505
Bangladesh	109	Bangladesh	26,981	U.S.S.R.	90,645
Japan	91	Ethiopia	16,138	Argentina	84,758
China	89	Niger	7,826	Mexico	80,563
Brazil	68	Mozambique	7,262	Colombia	51,969
Mexico	60	Italy	949	Pakistan	39,370
Peru	55	Pakistan	2,061	China	39,296
Iran	53	Japan	2,005	Peru	32,498
Turkey	43	Peru	1,355	India	31,940
Colombia	39	Chile	1,107	Sri Lanka	31,734
Italy	39	Iran	1,103	Japan	30,416
Korea	38	Turkey	1,027	Bangladesh	26,831
Chile	37	Colombia	705	Korea	25,116
Myanmar	36	Haiti	429	Philippines	13,393
Pakistan	33	Vietnam	412	Haita	10,460
Vietnam	32	Sri Lanka	317	Mozambique	9,588
U.S.S.R.	31	Mexico	287	Ecuador	8,830
Ecuador	30	Ecuador	261	Brazil	6,964
Argentina	29	Indonesia	225	Indonesia	6,838
Sri Lanka	29	Philippines	222	Niger	4,322
Niger	27	Argentina	202	Myanmar	4,280
Haiti	26	Myanmar	176	Ethiopia	3,129
Ethiopia	25	Korea	107	Vietnam	2,296
Mozambique	25	Spain	106	Iran	1,415
South Africa	25	Brazil	99	South Africa	40
Spain	25	South Africa	73		

Source: Office of Foreign Disaster Assistance (1988) and Smith (1992).

TABLE 6

LOSS OF LIFE BY SELECTED GEOPHYSICAL EVENT, 1945–1986

Disaster Type	Number of Disasters	Thousands of Deaths	Deaths per Disaster
Floods	395	244	618
Hurricanes/Tropical Cyclones	272 (271)	791 (291)	2,907 (1,072)
Other Storms	212	28	131
Heat Waves	23	5	223
Cold Waves	15	4	275
Earthquakes	191 (189)	1,198 (388)	6,272 (2,053)
Volcanic Eruptions	27	40	1,494
Tsunamis	7	3	271
Landslides	85	25	295
Fires	40	6	157
Total	1,267 (1,264)	2,343 (1,033)	1,849 (837)

cyclones. Nevertheless, we can expect to see increasing impacts from human activities, at least at the local levels, for many years to come.

A second explanation for these trends might be the tremendous increase in population, rapid urbanization, and continuing development of squatter settlements in hazard-prone areas. In addition, the movement to large urban agglomerations has exacerbated the hazard problem by increasing the density of people living in certain high-risk areas. Finally, the growth of squatter settlements has also exacerbated hazards. These patterns will continue as poverty, population pressures, and other social constraints force people into these unsafe and unsavory conditions.

A third argument suggests that the spatial and temporal patterns are a product of better data collection and reporting. Certainly data collection has improved over the years as global connections have shrunk with new technological advances. Thus, pictures of famines and floods in "remote" parts of the world can be flashed instantaneously onto television screens, heightening our awareness.

Problems are no longer viewed as purely physical in nature but comprised of political, social, and economic forces, as well as natural processes. This changing focus has greatly enhanced our understanding of hazards and improved our ability to mitigate disaster losses. National governments are increasingly looking at disaster policies and how best to serve their populations. At the international level, the United Nations Disaster Relief Office, the Red Cross, and Red Crescent societies have been active in alleviating suffering. The 1990s was designated the International Decade for Natural Disaster Reduction by the United Nations, to encourage implementation of comprehensive disaster plans.

In spite of all this activity, natural hazards will continue virtually unabated. The number of deaths accruing from hazards will increase, and economic losses will jump significantly in the next fifty years. Without careful planning and major adjustments in policies, these consequences are unavoidable. There are vast numbers of people living in highly vulnerable locations, many of whom will die and others of whom will lose everything they own. Research reveals the root causes of natural hazards, but there is little evidence of political commitment or social will to change behavior that can alleviate future suffering.

[See also Apocalyptic Future; Astronomy; Biodiversity; Disasters, Planning for; Epidemics; Evolution, Biological; Extinction of Species; Global Environmental Problems; Global Warming.]

BIBLIOGRAPHY

Alexander, David. *Natural Hazards.* New York: Chapman and Hall, 1993.
Blaikie, Piers; Cannon, Terry; Davis, Ian; and Wisner, Ben. *At Risk: Natural Hazards, People's Vulnerability, and Disasters.* London and New York: Routledge, 1994.
Glickman, Theodore S.; Golding, Dominic; and Silverman, Emily D. *Acts of God and Acts of Man: Recent Trends in Natural Disasters and Major Industrial Accidents.* Washington, DC: Center for Risk Management, Discussion Paper 92–02. Resources for the Future, 1992.
Hewitt, Kenneth. "The Idea of Calamity in a Technocratic Age." In *The Interpretations of Calamity,* ed. K. Hewitt. Winchester, MA: Allen and Unwin, 1983.
Smith, Keith. *Environmental Hazards: Assessing Risk and Reducing Disaster.* London and New York: Routledge, 1992.
Taylor, Anthony J. W. *Disasters and Disaster Stress.* Stress in Modern Society, 10. New York: AMS Press, 1989.
White, Gilbert F. *Choice of Adjustments to Floods.* Department of Geography Research Paper, 93. Chicago: University of Chicago Press, 1964.
———. *Human Adjustments to Floods.* Department of Geography Research Paper, 29. Chicago: University of Chicago Press, 1945.
White, Gilbert F., ed. *Papers on Flood Problems.* Department of Geography Research Paper No. 70. Chicago: University of Chicago Press, 1961.

— GRAHAM A. TOBIN

NATURAL GAS

Methane, or natural gas as it is commonly known, has increased in importance as a fuel throughout the twentieth century. Today methane provides nearly a quarter of all of the world's primary energy, and this contribution is likely to grow even larger in the future. Although gas utilization expanded most rapidly in the industrialized countries since 1950, dramatic shifts toward increased methane usage occurred in many less developed nations over the past twenty years. Rising world oil

Many gas deposits that were not economically attractive for production twenty years ago are now being routinely developed.

prices in the 1970s triggered this trend. These price signals motivated nations to develop indigenous fuel resources. In many nations this indigenous fuel was methane.

Methane Reserves

One measure of the amount of methane available is the quantity of proved reserves, that is, the amount of methane that: (1) is known to exist with reasonable certainty and (2) is producible under current economic and operating conditions. A more comprehensive category of methane is the total quantity of methane estimated to comprise the potential resource base, that is, the quantity of methane thought to be economically recoverable in the foreseeable future. To illustrate the difference in these statistics, the United States has 170 quads (a quad represents a quantity of energy equal to 10^{15} British Thermal Units) of proved reserves of methane and well over 1,000 quads of recoverable resources of methane.

Each year a part of these gas resources is converted into proved reserves, and some of the proved reserves are produced and used as fuels.

Producers find and make available the production from proved reserves to satisfy the demand for gas. They do this by drilling wells that penetrate geological formations beneath Earth's crust. These wells provide the gas to the pipeline systems that transport the gas to the burner or other end-use equipment.

This entire process of natural gas discovery, production, and transmission, is technically challenging. Since 1980 the technology to find and produce gas advanced very rapidly. As a result, methane production is now more efficient and many gas deposits that were not economically attractive for production twenty years ago are now being routinely developed. One consequence of this rapidly increasing efficiency is that more and more methane deposits are now being judged to be economically producible. In other words, new technology caused both the methane resource base and reserves to increase.

THE ORIGINS OF METHANE. Traditional petroleum geology postulates that most of the hydrocarbons, such as oil, methane, coal, and so on, are the transformed remains of plants and animals that lived millions of years ago. These biological remains, compressed and heated deep within rock formations, became oil, gas, or coal over time. This interpretation has physical support from the organisms found in the rocks; further, this hypothesis is the basis for most of the hydrocarbon exploration and production to date.

A more recent and still controversial theory cites the existence of methane throughout our solar system, especially in the four gas-giant planets. This theory postulates that methane is a basic building block of nature and holds that Earth's formation trapped large quantities of methane deep in the earth. The theory further stipulates that methane found today identifies a path of migration from deep methane deposits to Earth's surface. Massive quantities of methane are found in any rock formations on the migrational path that could hold the gas. One popular advocate of this theory is Thomas Gold, an astrophysicist, whose name has been used to label this hypothesis as the Gold Theory.

Despite the major differences between the traditional interpretations and the Gold Theory there are some im-

Huge pipelines such as this one in British Columbia bring clean, relatively safe, natural gas to thousands of homes. (Gunter Marx/Corbis)

portant points that are not in dispute. Almost everyone agrees that some methane is a result of biological processes of decay. In our everyday experience we observe that methane is generated from biological decay in swamps, animal digestive tracts, and in rice paddies. Also, most scholars agree that some methane is abiogenic, that is, not of animal or plant origin. The theories differ about which is the dominant source of methane—abiogenic or biological. Additional evidence continues to be collected and analyzed from volcanoes, deep wells in nonproducing regions of the world, and in methane deposits in ice-like formations on the ocean floor. As usual in science, each newly discovered answer raises new questions.

Scientists have not been able to determine the true origin of most methane. Yet while the scholars pursue these fundamental questions, more and more people use methane as a primary fuel to heat or cool the world around them.

[See also Coal; Energy; Energy, Renewable Sources of; Minerals; Natural Resources, Use of; Nuclear Power; Nuclear Power: Con; Petroleum; Pipelines; Resources.]

BIBLIOGRAPHY

Oppenheimer, Ernest J. *U.S. Energy Independence.* New York: Pen and Podium Productions, 1980.
Special Energy Report Supplement. *National Geographic* 159 (February 1981): 560.
Stobaugh, Robert, and Yergin, Daniel, eds. *Energy Future.* New York: Ballantine Books, 1980.
Weaver, Jacqueline. *The Case for Natural Gas, Publication No. 91–11.* Houston: Center for Public Policy, University of Houston, 1991.

— NELSON HAY
ROBERT KALISCH

NATURAL RESOURCES, USE OF

In a 1968 article in *Science* magazine, biologist Garrett Hardin identified an important type of future problem in our use and management of the Earth's natural resources. He pointed out that overusing a resource usually is constrained because it is someone's property, and there is an inherent self-interest in taking good care of it and safeguarding its use. But, Hardin asked, what about resources that no one owns and all use in common? What about shared-use resources, such as the air we breathe or the oceans that make up more than half our planet's surface? Who or what protects shared-use resources from overuse when all of us can use these resources?

Hardin cited the experience of the common pasture in preindustrial times. Everyone got milk from their own cow, which each household kept on "the commons." It was in each household's self-interest to get still more milk by adding for themselves another cow to the commons. Furthermore, any family's restraint would not stop others from making additional demands upon the commons, until the commons was degraded or destroyed.

Individual Powerlessness and Shared Destruction

What Hardin termed "the tragedy of the commons" is akin to what nonsmokers long experienced in restaurants where others were smoking: the nonsmoker was powerless to protect the air everyone breathes by restraining the behavior of smokers. The only solution Hardin saw was "mutual coercion mutually agreed upon." During the late 1980s the rise of the "Smoke-Free Movement" resulted in many public spaces becoming legally smoke-free through voluntary or government-mandated action.

The present dilemma is how to protect shared-use resources, used by all in common but owned by none.

Carrying this concept to an extreme, the legal scholar Christopher D. Stone has proposed also that natural objects in general should be granted legal standing in our courts, just as ships and corporations are. His intent was to provide a basis for broad and sweeping environmental protection whereby lawsuits could be brought to protect an endangered stand of trees—or a lake or stream or fishery. Currently natural objects have virtually no standing of their own and are protected only as someone's property.

Now, a generation later, the degradation of resources used in common has become a major public policy dilemma. We are facing a future in which our present actions (or inactions) are shaping the fate of basic resources. For example, the great fisheries of Georges Bank in the North Atlantic off New England and Nova Scotia were suddenly in the late 1980s overfished and out of stock, with annual fish-catches plummeting. The fishing practices of the industry were threatening the ability of a common resource to recharge or regenerate itself. Despite the declining stock, fishermen intensified their activities in order to sustain profitability. How, short of closing them down, could fisheries be protected from such overuse by all those who depend upon them for a livelihood?

Similarly, in the 1980s scientists discovered that chlorofluorocarbons (CFCs) from spray cans, air conditioning, refrigeration, and industrial solvents were being dissipated into the Earth's upper atmosphere, depleting the ozone layer, thinning out the protective sunscreen in the Northern mid-latitudes, and creating over the entire South Pole a seasonal "ozone hole" the size of all of North America. The natural sunscreen effect of the atmosphere has been degraded to such an extent that even if there is widespread restraint in the use of CFCs, the problem will persist for some time. Only a sustained effort worldwide is likely to alleviate present conditions.

On another front, rivers and lakes and oceans have been convenient dumping grounds for millennia, receiving sewage and industrial wastes and bilge wastes from ships all around the world. The present dilemma is how to protect all such shared-use resources, used by all in common but owned by none.

"The Public Interest" as a Shared Resource in Politics

In the politics of governance, the public interest is a similar kind of shared-use resource. We strive to fulfill the Kantian ideal of the greatest good for the greatest number. The long and short of it is that national well-being and the political processes of government are used by all but owned by none. Akin to exploitive and selfish use of resources, in politics and government each interest group's selfishness is driven by a stubbornly rational pattern of political and economic behavior in which the benefits it seeks are captured for itself and the costs incurred are spread diffusely to all others. From one viewpoint, the long-run advantage of every group might benefit if all groups surrendered just enough of their own self-interest to achieve a greater common good. But it makes no sense for any beneficiary to surrender unilaterally. Like fishing boat captains, the political special interests are driven by selfish—perhaps innate—behavior.

Treaties among nations to regulate CFC use and governmental regulations regarding auto emissions, clean air standards, and clean water standards have not yet succeeded in adequately diverting us from degrading these shared-use resources. Hardin's prophetic call to resolve the tragedy of the commons remains an ongoing challenge. His "mutual coercion mutually agreed upon" is repeatedly resisted. Until the larger self-interest in

Each individual's efforts to protect our natural resources by using clean energy sources, such as solar power, benefits everyone. (Jim Sugar Photography/Corbis)

596

everyone's common future is widely perceived and becomes the operative principle, there will be little relief for "the tragedy of the commons."

[See also Acid Rain; Agents of Change; Civil Protest; Climate and Meteorology; Deforestation; Environmental Behavior; Environmental Ethics; Environmental Policy Changes; Fisheries; Freshwater; Global Environmental Problems; Global Warming; Green Revolution; Hazardous Wastes; Ozone Layer Depletion; Solid Waste; Sustainability.]

BIBLIOGRAPHY

Hardin, Garrett. "Second Thoughts on 'The Tragedy of the Commons.'" In *Economics, Ecology, Ethics,* ed., Herman E. Daly. San Francisco: W. H. Freeman, 1980.

——. "The Tragedy of the Commons." *Science* 162 (December 13, 1968): 1243–1248. Reprinted in his *Exploring New Ethics of Survival.* New York: Viking, 1972.

Hardin, Garrett, and Baden, John, eds. *Managing the Commons.* San Francisco: W. H. Freeman, 1977.

Stone, Christopher D. *Should Trees Have Standing?: Toward Legal Rights for Natural Objects.* Los Altos, CA: W. H. Freeman, 1974.

— DAVID DODSON GRAY

NETWORKING

The last frontier of exploration will not be space or the sea; it will be the silicon chip and the bits that make up computers. In this frontier, nothing is constant except change. The rate of technological change has accelerated so greatly that growth is virtually exponential. As a result, we can hardly envision clearly the networking industry in 2010. However, there are likely scenarios of how networking will affect the way we work and live in the early part of the twenty-first century.

Entertainment

The information super highway (ISH) is primarily an entertainment network for mass-produced and inexpensive entertainment. It is estimated that it will contain more than 500 entertainment channels. With the gigabit-per-second national backbone, bandwidth is not an issue, and access will be inexpensive. ISH applications will include:

- Movies on demand produced by telecable companies.
- Personal home videos made with digital cameras and built-in optical disks (videophones will grow less popular because they intrude on privacy).
- Video shopping in which people will interact directly with video catalogs, checking availability and pricing with the store's database and even trying on clothing in electronic "dressing rooms."
- Interactive games will be popular with the MTV generation.
- Education—people everywhere will have access to electronic classrooms and research materials. All large libraries, including the Library of Congress, will be fully digitized, and navigation software will make it easier to locate and download information.

- Information publishing—in interactive publishing, the information faucet can be controlled to provide customized news mixing text, photos, sound, and video in the right amount and at the right time.

The ISH will become the underpinning for business-to-business communication, particularly document transfer and videoconferencing. However, leading-edge companies will not use the ISH because of privacy and security concerns. They will use ATM2. The ATM superhighway with its ISDN on-ramps is owned by bit-pushers like Sony, Time-Warner, R. J. Reynolds/IBM/Dow Jones (RID), or by telecable companies. Nearly all businesses will have fiber connections to the ISH. In homes, television sets will have fiber-optic connections, optical disks, and digital cameras, all linked to the phone. Programming will be selected by remote PDAs (personal digital assistants) and drag-and-drop interfaces of Microsoft/Intel selectors or audiotext provided by telecable. All telephones will have integrated data-fax modems. The danger of the ISH is that people will be so bombarded with MTV-type information that they will become desensitized to substantive information.

Private Networks

The ISH as a vehicle to deliver business information will be a failure, because in a competitive world, corporations need ownership of their own dedicated networks. Large companies will bypass the ISH to build their own highly functional networks to be used not only for internal communications but also for business-to-business communications. With such networks, companies will be free to disperse their employees. Most companies will lease their wide-area bandwidth (usually ATM or clear-channel T-4) from WAN service providers. Most desktop computers will have 128-bit operating systems, such as Microsoft's RNT/4 with its integrated file/mail/print/fax services. AT&T/Novell Netware will be the main remote operating system. Desktop computers will have 155-Mbps interfaces to the internal networks. Directory services (updated on a subscription basis) will help users locate services available on their networks. The biggest advance will be application integration. People will have to buy a certain operating system, such as UNIX, but they will be able to point, click, drag, and drop, and speak from one application to another. Most simple commands will be by voice.

Portable Consumer Computing Devices

To appreciate the free-floating computers of 2010, it is necessary to look at the shortcomings of its ancestor, the PC. The PC was an uninspired machine, a square, stale heap of hardware, strapped by wires, and trapped to the desk by an overweight and clunky CPU, not to mention the keyboard and the mouse. As a result, in 1995 a mere 3 percent of the world's population used computers. By 1995, consumer electronics companies began building computers for computer-illiterates, using sophisticated electronics with no-brainer user interfaces. As a result, computers became more like television sets, available in the same price range. By 2010, companies like Sony and Sharp, rather than IBM or Apple, will be producing the most popular computers, and they will be selling portable consumer computing devices (CCDs) with a wide variety of network options and in designer colors. These devices will use the pen rather than the mouse or keyboard. These portables will be small, lightweight, and energy-efficient, running off a watch battery. Network protocols for local and remote access will be embedded into the personal operating system with infrared transmission for the short trek and spread-spectrum radio for long-distance access to public and private networks. Each CCD will be compatible with other CCDs, making it easy to exchange information and also connect peer-to-peer networks over slow ethernet. Voice annotation will be standard as well as a variety of personal security guards, such as fingerprint locks. While CCD-based consumer networks proliferate, business users will use integrated machines, such as AT&T's Personal Electronic Organizer Node (PEON) with its built-in fax, copier, scanner, phone, and printer. Pagers will have pull-down menus in which users can scan multiple incoming phone numbers.

The Work Environment

Microsoft will remain the largest player in the industry, although it will be forced to break up into a number of "Baby Bills." The trend to build up gigantic consolidated databases will bring back the IBM mainframe to its linchpin role. Whereas 100 MHz was considered fast in 1995, most computers will need 1 GHz to process the vast amounts of data coming across airwaves or the wire. Voice-driven systems will become universal. While screen radiation and carpal tunnel syndrome become less serious hazards, most users in 2010 will complain of dry throats as a result of talking to their computers all day. The real winners in 2010 will be otolaryngologists and voice trainers. Fax machines will have become extinct. People will not have as many computers because there will be less need to own separate desktop and portable machines. All the off-shelf software will be downloaded automatically on-line using automatic license meters. Virtual-reality glasses will be worn like eyeglasses. These eyeglasses will take their orders wirelessly from wrist-mounted personal communicators.

Network-Driven Divisions

The rise of networks will hasten the polarization of the world into technological haves and have-nots. Even in developed societies, computer illiterates will become the new underclass. The same will be true of corporations, as information-rich companies outsmart the information-poor. Information will replace capital as the key wealth builder. As the world becomes more networked, network managers will become the new elite. Geographically, networks will reinforce the trend toward a border-less world. Inexpensive, high-speed wide-area communications will disperse databases.

[See also Communications; Communications Technology; Computer Linkage; Computers: Overview; Electronic Convergence; Electronic Publishing; High Technology; Information Overload; Information Society; Information Technology; Interactive Entertainment; Media Lab; On-Line Services; Telecommunications.]

BIBLIOGRAPHY

Krol, Ed. *Whole Internet User Guide,* 2d ed. Petaluma, CA: O'Reilly & Associates, 1994.
McMullen, Melanie. *Networks 2000.* San Francisco: Miller Freeman, 1994.
Schnaidt, Patricia. *LAN Tutorial,* 3rd ed., San Francisco: Miller Freeman, 1994.

– MELANIE MCMULLEN
THE EDITORS OF LAN MAGAZINE

NEW CONSUMER PRODUCTS

In 1994, 20,076 new supermarket and drugstore products were introduced to United States consumers—at a rate of 55 per day. (See Figure 1.) Back in 1964, the total number of new products introduced was only 1,281. New food and drug products arriving on the store shelves increased approximately 1,609 percent in the past thirty years!

New product introductions have increased virtually every year for the past three decades, with annual increases averaging 5.3 percent. This growth pattern has been due to major technological developments in the manufacture of foods and non-foods, as well as significant lifestyle changes in American society. With important food science refinements on the immediate horizon, and with consumer attitudes toward and usage of foods and nonfoods remaining in flux, there are ample reasons to predict continuing growth of new product activity. In addition, the resurgence of private labels will compel food and drug manufacturers to resist this challenge with an increasing flow of imaginative new products. Food and drug marketers live by the axiom "innovate or die." There is nothing to suggest that, in a market share-based economic system, any company can afford to reduce its new product development efforts in the coming years. (See Figure 2.)

The palate of today's food shopper is increasingly more sophisticated. Americans currently travel more, read gourmet publications, and eat in a wide variety of ethnic restaurants. The emergence of "foodies" in the mass market has prompted an explosion of ethnic food products in supermarkets. While this category is still dominated by foods derived from Asian, Italian, and

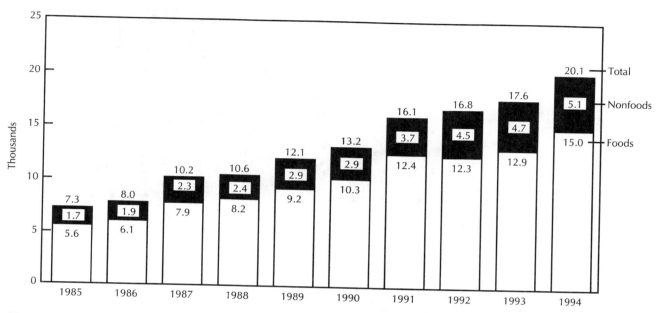

Figure 1. Increases in new food/nonfood consumer product introductions, 1985–1994. Source: U.S. Dept. of Agriculture (New Product News, January 8, 1995).

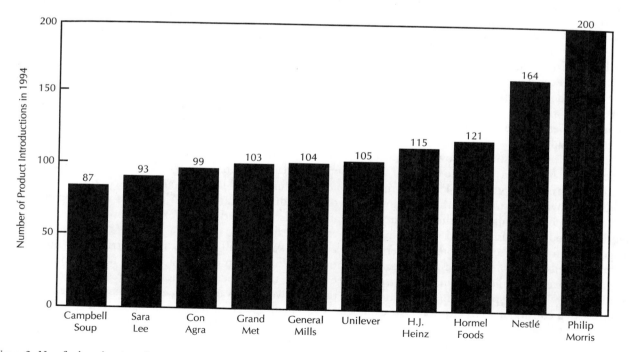

Figure 2. New food product introductions, 1994. Source: U.S. Dept. of Agriculture (New Product News, January 8, 1995).

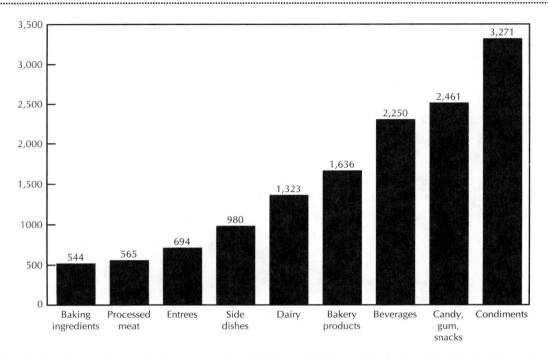

*Figure 3. New food product introductions, leading categories in 1994. Source: U.S. Dept. of Agriculture (*New Product News, *January 8, 1995).*

Mexican cuisines, other ethnic cuisines—Thai, Vietnamese, Caribbean, East Indian, and Cajun—will become more prominent in the future. (Note that all these fares are very spicy.) Also, there will be an upgrading of traditional ethnic offerings. Thirty years ago, Mexican food meant chili and beans. Now, consumers can find more exotic varieties, such as chimichangas, quesadillas, and black bean salsa. What appears on an Italian, Chinese, or Mexican restaurant menu today will be available as branded supermarket selections in the coming years. Daily response to menu changes preferred by restaurant-goers define desires that become tomorrow's packaged products.

Along with the consumer's move to more adventuresome ethnic foods has been the constant quality upgrading of basic food products. This "gourmetizing" of foods, to provide consumers with more diverse flavors and recipes, not only influences the manufacture of conventional foods, but also has led to a dramatic growth in gourmet foods. Specialty store shoppers can select from hundreds of flavored coffees, teas, preserves, mustards, or cheeses, while supermarkets also have expanded their limited specialty food selections. As the sophisticated consumer seeks out new taste experiences, it can be expected that domestic and import suppliers will continue to market new specialty food options. What today is an exotic gourmet food, tomorrow will be standard supermarket fare.

Perhaps the most dramatic impetus in new product development in the past ten years has been the growth of nutritionally oriented foods. While so-called "health foods" have been available for decades, only in the late 1980s and early '90s has the consumer interest in the enhancement of foods through the addition of useful ingredients or the subtraction of harmful ingredients produced so many new food categories. Consumers and health experts have asked for, and received, new foods that are sodium-reduced, fiber-added, calcium-fortified, cholesterol-decreased, calorie-controlled, sugar-substituted, nitrate-eliminated, or additive-excised. In 1995, the nutritional emphasis is on fat annihilation, with products such as Nabisco's fat-free, fat-reduced SnackWell becoming the best-selling cookie in the country. As long as cardiologists continue to urge fat reduction, fat-reduced products will flood the market. Also, vegetarian and organic foods will expand in the near future.

What will be the next nutritional "hot button"? Whatever emerges as a harmful food or food ingredient in the medical and popular press will be quickly followed by a variety of new products that reduce or eliminate the latest nutritional hazard. In addition, food industry researchers are working on products with far greater health implications. Words or phrases such as functional foods, nutraceuticals, pharmfoods, and designer foods now are part of a food technologist's vocabulary. While the specific definition may vary somewhat, these terms all refer to future foods containing properties believed either to help prevent diseases or heal them, or to enhance human performance. While functional foods (isotonic sports beverages, sleep-aid teas, calcium-fortified orange juice, etc.) are proliferating in Europe and Japan, they have made only limited and discreet inroads in the United States. However, as scientific progress accelerates and U.S. regulatory testing produces efficacy evidence, the impact of functional foods will be influential on overall U.S. food marketing.

Domestic and import suppliers will continue

to market new specialty food options.

What today is an exotic gourmet food,

tomorrow will be standard supermarket fare.

There has been great progress in the development of bio-engineered foods. In 1994, the government approved Calgene's Flavr Savr tomato, the first genetically manipulated food to be sold on a mass market basis. Calgene scientists slowed the ripening gene in the ordinary tomato, allowing it to stay on the vine longer before being picked. Some other genetically engineered foods we may see in stores some day include: snack cakes that provide total daily nutritional needs; potatoes with a chicken gene to better resist spoilage; instant meals that expand in the stomach, creating a sense of fullness; and canned or bottled drinks that make major nutritional claims (these are already major successes in Japan). Phytochemicals, which naturally appear in fruits and vegetables, and which may help prevent cancer and heart disease, already appear in newly marketed vitamins.

While food manufacturers have made great strides in delivering enhanced taste and improved nutrition to their products, their prediction of greater convenience in food preparation has been disappointed. Although the majority of homes have a microwave oven, only 30 percent use it for anything other than reheating food. The most common use for microwave ovens is making popcorn. However, a major technological breakthrough in microwave cooking, such as quick browning, could renew microwaves' promise.

Minor marketing moves have increased food preparation convenience somewhat. New "speed scratch" meal kits combine various ingredients so that cooks must only add fresh meat to produce a dinner entree. Specialty appliances permit easier home bread-baking, pasta preparation, and espresso coffee brewing. Other convenience products that aid meal preparers pressed for time are cooking sauces, stuffing mixes, prepackaged fresh salads, pasta, and refrigerated entrees and lunches. There will be significant increases in take-out and home delivery of food.

Although over 20,000 new food and drug products were introduced in 1994, this total includes many local, regional, and test market products, as well as many items sold only in gourmet shops, health food stores, and drugstores. The 20,000-plus total is a national conglomeration. (See Figure 3.) No retailer or consumer in the United States was exposed to all 20,000 items. It should also be noted that from 80 to 90 percent of new food and drug products can be described as line extensions—including new flavors, colors, or varieties. Few so-called "new" products are true breakthroughs—totally new to the world. Any changes in U.S. consumption of foods or drugs will be evolutionary rather than revolutionary, since humans are conservative about what they put in or on their bodies. Nevertheless, important changes in how we produce, distribute, prepare, and eat foods will occur in the future. Dynamic marketplace, scientific, medical, and behavioral influences will not permit any status-quo outlook.

[See also Alcohol; Batteries; Chemicals, Fine; Clothing; Comic Books; Food Additives; Food Consumption; Food Distribution; Food Technologies; Fragrances; Genetics, Commercialization; Nutrition; Pharmaceuticals; Recording Industry; Tobacco.]

BIBLIOGRAPHY

Abrams, Malcolm, and Bernstein, Harriet. *Future Stuff*. New York: Viking-Penguin, 1989.
———. *More Future Stuff*. New York: Viking-Penguin, 1991.
Apple, L. Eugene, and Hustad, Thomas P., eds. *Product Development: Prospering in a Rapidly Changing World*. Indianapolis: Product Development Management Association, 1990.
Salder, William E. *Managing New Product Innovations*. New York: Free Press, 1986.

— MARTIN FRIEDMAN

NEWSPAPERS

Newspapers as we know them today may not even exist in the future. The general circulation newspaper of general interest, published daily, is threatened with obsolescence, as people find other methods of keeping informed.

Most people now have radios, televisions, and telephones. Many have personal computers as well. In the future, all these information technologies will be combined in integrated systems. An investor could find out how the stock market is doing and send instructions to her broker. A sports fan could read about the big game

Newspapers remain a primary source of information and news for many people in the world, but U.S. daily newspaper circulation has trended downward over the past twenty-five years. (Steve Raymer/ Corbis)

try—although in the future, these readers may be reading on-line rather than a printed copy delivered by a carrier.

Local newspapers may also find themselves in a better position. People care about what is happening in their community. They want to know where the neighborhood break-ins have occurred and which restaurants have been shut down for health-code violations. After all, you might not find your local classified ads or police-beat entries on the Internet. Newspapers that tailor themselves to a specific, small area could become more financially secure than the giants who attempt to grab every reader all over the country.

For similar reasons, specialty newsletters may flourish. With a few key strokes, the reader could find up-to-the-minute information on whatever is of special interest. With the whole world as a potential market, even the most obscure publications could find an audience.

Ironically, the new technology could get us back to our American journalistic roots: the pamphleteer. Anyone with a computer can become a publisher and put out the information he considers to be important. And anyone with a computer could receive it.

Specialized reading will also require specialized reporting. The job of the newspaper reporter is also likely to be quite different in the future. Instead of being a generalist knowing a little bit about a lot of topics, the reporter of the future may be an expert in a narrow field. This trend is already becoming well established.

The mechanics of reporting also will evolve. The computer has changed the way reporters do their job. Most reporters now file their stories electronically, sending their stories to their editors via a computer. Through portable computers and cellular phones, or even satellite phones, reporters can stay in touch with the office even while covering events in a remote area. This ability can only expand in the future.

Many more reporters will use the computer as a resource tool to find information on a particular issue or to find experts to quote on a particular topic. Need a political scientist to comment on declining voter turnout? Put out the message on the Internet and political scientists from around the world will respond, with no need for the reporter to work the phones. This method can only increase as more people get on-line. Reporters could find themselves covering their beat in front of a computer screen as often as not.

Also the need actually to cover that school board meeting or zoning commission hearing in person may decline as more people get access to the event itself. Citizens who are interested will be able to call up the transcript or a video record of the proceeding. Interested citizens likewise will be able to instantly register their opinion of how public officials are doing. One could

and watch a tape of the deciding play. A consumer can find out what is on sale at the local supermarket and place an electronic order for delivery.

Many of the needs now met by newspapers thus will be met with more options by the home media center. Newspapers that want to survive will be on-line and compatible with the other technologies. Nor will readers be satisfied with seeing what some editor thinks is the news. Instant access to information worldwide will enable readers to pick and choose—and to find stories on almost any subject.

Similarly, some papers have found their niche and are likely to remain there—for example, the *New York Times,* the *Wall Street Journal,* and the *Washington Post.* These and other major daily newspapers have branched out beyond their original markets and have developed a loyal readership among readers elsewhere in the coun-

read the debate, watch the vote, and then send off a message of praise or protest.

But won't we always need "real" newspapers—printed matter that can be stuffed in a briefcase and perused on the way to work? After all, you cannot take a computer on the bus. Well, maybe someday everyone can own a computer that is light enough and portable enough to access information anywhere.

Anyone with a computer can become a publisher and put out the information he or she considers to be important.

Perhaps newspaper racks will give way to computerized outlets offering passers-by a selection of reading materials, sort of like public, coin-operated copy machines of the kind that are now available everywhere, from libraries to convenience stores. Readers who like the feel of paper can simply print out whatever interests them, in whatever order they like. In effect, people will be able to construct their own newspapers, lifting a column from one source, a cartoon from another.

Regrettably, there is a growing number of people who do not find newspapers important to their lives. They catch televised news once in a while and gossip with fellow office workers. They do not see current events as relevant to their lives. Furthermore, they distrust the ability or willingness of newspapers, television, and magazines to give them the true story. Perhaps if "readers" have more discretion in what they can get access to, they will be less distrustful of the messengers. If newspapers are to survive, they will have to keep up with the technology and the changing needs of readers.

[See also Communications; Electronic Convergence; On-Line Services; Printed Word; Telecommunications.]

BIBLIOGRAPHY

Toffler, Alvin. *Power Shift.* New York: Bantam Books, 1990.
Straussman, Paul A. *Information Pay-off.* New York: Free Press, 1985.
Underwood, Doug. *When MBAs Rule the Newsroom.* New York: Columbia University Press, 1993.

— NORA RAUM

NONGOVERNMENTAL ORGANIZATIONS

Nongovernmental Organizations (NGOs) are nonprofit associations that address public issues, social concerns, or more limited interests, but are not a part of government. In addition to providing social services, many of these organizations seek to influence governmental decisions through expert testimony, public in-formation campaigns, and professional research. They operate at local, national, and international levels. Some NGOs, such as hospitals and universities, attempt to work for the public good with minimum government intrusion, especially in the United States. Sometimes this involvement may only be limited to registration with the government and possibly with the attainment of a tax-exempt status. In some societies, NGOs may be quasi-governmental entities.

Approximately eighty million adults work as volunteers for nonprofit organizations in the United States, such as the Girl Scouts, United Way, the Salvation Army, and others (Drucker, 1992, p. 203). From 1962 until 1993 charitable contributions to NGOs in the United States grew, in constant dollars, from $61 billion to $124 billion. This contribution level is 2.1 percent of the economy, and 88 percent of the donations came from individuals, with foundations and corporations making up the rest. NGOs have become increasingly influential to assist the more than 83,000 total governmental units in the United States, which employ fifteen million civil servants, of which three million are working for the national government (Gaebler, et al., 1992, p. xxi). In comparison, there are approximately 7.5 million people employed by NGOs in the United States.

The past four American presidents have strongly emphasized the need to streamline government bureaucracy at all levels and to privatize many government services. President Bill Clinton referred to "reinventing government," while President George H. Bush spoke of NGOs as a "thousand points of light." It seems there is a growing, nonpartisan recognition of citizen responsibility as an untapped asset that could be more effectively used in improving communities and individual lives. The number of tax-exempt, nonprofit organizations in the United States has roughly doubled in the past ten years, while the number of supporting charitable foundations has nearly quadrupled to approximately 34,000. Only about 10 percent of these have assets greater than $5 million, and they account for 75 percent of the total amount of foundation grant money.

The advantages of NGOs, as opposed to government, often include flexible and creative response to human problems as well as the ability to channel the enthusiasm of volunteers and concerned citizens. For instance, Robert Macauley founded Americares in the 1980s to provide rapid airlift anywhere a major disaster occurred. By 1991 it had carried more than $100 million of food and medicine on short notice to seventy-five countries. Often governments require time-consuming authorizations, studies, and procedures that are ill-suited for rapidly or effectively meeting human needs. NGOs are not bound by these restrictions. Management guru Peter Drucker has praised many NGOs for their ability to define their missions and to develop cost-effective strategies in accomplishing them. Many of them are "working out policies and practices that business will have to learn tomorrow." (Drucker, 1992, p. 203)

The growth of NGOs is likely to continue

well into the future because of their demonstrated

efficiency and effectiveness at problem solving.

Because NGOs often are largely dependent on charitable contributions, there are problems. First, funding may be unreliable. Further, some NGOs are not candid in regard to how they spend their money. Their descriptive literature sometimes bears little resemblance to reality. In some cases, annual reports, if available, obscure true financial status. The Better Business Bureau often keeps track of problems with such organizations. Furthermore, most reputable charitable organizations will be audited each year by an outside accounting firm, which prepares a detailed financial statement. While most NGOs undoubtedly operate at high levels of integrity, those that do not may encourage increased future government scrutiny and regulation.

In addition to charitable service organizations, NGOs also can refer to advocacy groups that tout such causes as the environment, a strong national defense, or human life. Furthermore, some NGOs may represent the interests and concerns of professions, such as attorneys, scientists, accountants, or even nonprofit association executives. The past twenty years has seen a proliferation of more than 1,000 nonprofit research organizations, or think tanks, which are a newer addition to the world of NGOs.

Think tanks often combine professional research with advocacy related to government or social policy. With the growth and increasing complexity of government, especially after World War II, there has arisen a new group of specialists who continually research and test ideas for changes in public policies.

Some think tanks are "big concept" in focus with a high level of imagination and speculation, while others are more technical in nature and focus on methods of implementing public policy. Perhaps the most visible pioneer of think tanks was Herman Kahn, who worked for the Rand Corporation after World War II and who then founded the Hudson Institute in the early 1960s. Best known for his ideas on nuclear war, Kahn also studied a wide variety of economic and social problems.

In evaluating think tank research, the prudent consumer would do well to know about funding sources, since the source of funding may influence the type of research gathered and conclusions drawn. Support can come from combinations of government, business, interest groups, foundations, or individuals, and each of these sources may have beliefs or interests they wish to advance.

The growth of NGOs in recent years is likely to continue well into the future because of their demonstrated efficiency and effectiveness at problem solving. Nonetheless, with all this growth there may also occur the threat of or need for increased government regulation.

[See also Institutions and Organizations; Organizational Complexity.]

BIBLIOGRAPHY

Drucker, Peter F. *Managing for the Future: The 1990s and Beyond.* New York: Truman Talley Books/Dutton, 1992.

Gallup, Jr., George. *Forecast 2000.* New York: William Morrow, 1984.

Gaebler, Ted, and Osborne, David. *Reinventing Government: How the Entrepreneurial Spirit is Transforming the Public Sector from Schoolhouse to Statehouse, City Hall to the Pentagon.* Reading, MA: Addison-Wesley, 1992.

Smith, James A. *The Idea Brokers: Think Tanks and the Rise of the New Policy Elite.* New York: Free Press, 1991.

Templeton, John Marks, ed. *Looking Forward: The Next Forty Years.* New York: K. S. Giniger Co., 1993.

— MICHAEL Y. WARDER

NOSTRADAMUS (MICHEL DE NOSTREDAME, 1503–1566)

French physician and astrologer Nostradamus is the best remembered of the many diviners of the future who practiced their art during the Renaissance. He began his professional career as a physician, rising to the rank of court physician to Charles IX of France. Blending biblical, astrological, and literary lore, he wrote a long series of cryptic verses, including nearly 1,000 rhymed quatrains grouped in "centuries" (sets of 100 quatrains) as well as a smaller number of sextains. The first edition of his *Centuries* appeared in 1555. In a prefatory letter addressed to his newborn son, Nostradamus explained that he had deliberately cast his predictions "in nebulous rather than plainly prophetic form." The apparent success of some of his forecasts gained him widespread celebrity during his lifetime. His fame continued to grow long after his death. His works were formally condemned by the Catholic Church in 1781. In the twentieth century, they have been studied exhaustively by latter-day disciples, who claim that he foresaw many of the tribulations of our time. But his ambiguous verses can be interpreted to mean almost anything; few professional futurists take them seriously.

[See also Apocalyptic Future; Futurism; Futurists.]

BIBLIOGRAPHY

Cheetham, Erika, ed. and tr. *The Prophecies of Nostradamus.* London: Neville Spearman, 1974.

Fontbrune, Jean-Charles de. *Nostradamus: Countdown to Apocalypse.* London: Hutchinson, 1983. Translation by Alexis Lykiard of *Nostradamus: historien et prophète: les prophéties de 1555 a l'an 2000,* 1980.

— W. WARREN WAGAR

NUCLEAR POWER

Some time fairly early in the next century, nuclear power is likely to become the predominant source of energy throughout much of the world. The supply of fossil fuels is diminishing rapidly and alternative sources of energy are unlikely to suffice for the widespread, varying applications that will be needed in the near and short term.

Uranium Supplies and Reserves

The rich uranium deposits (i.e., concentrations of greater than 0.1 percent) utilized at present are believed to be quite limited, perhaps only enough to last for 50–100 years. There are supplies of lower grade ores (concentrations of about 0.005 percent) that could last for several centuries. Since the cost of raw uranium now represents only about 1 percent of that of nuclear electricity, the use of these lower grade ores would tend to raise the cost of electricity by perhaps 20 percent.

For the longer term, the problem can best be solved by using breeder reactors that derive 100 times as much energy from each pound of uranium. This means that it is economically feasible to use uranium costing a hundred times its current price. In turn this makes extraction of uranium from seawater an economically attractive alternative. The uranium now found in seawater could provide the world's electricity needs for a few million years. Rivers are constantly dissolving uranium out of rock and carrying it into the seas. Taking this process into account, seawater could provide all the world's ura-

In spite of general worry about the safety of nuclear power, these plants have continued to be built and used. They will predominate as a source of power in the next century. Commercial fusion, expected by the year 2025, will provide virtually limitless energy. (Yann Arthus-Bertrand/Corbis)

nium needs for several billion years, which is as long as Earth will be habitable.

Cold Fusion

There has been a great deal of publicity about "cold fusion," thermonuclear reactions at room temperature mediated by the absorption of hydrogen isotopes in the metallic element palladium. However, a large majority of the scientific community is convinced that there is no credible evidence that the reported effects are real. Even if such reactions were real, no one has suggested a practical method for generating large quantities of useful energy from them.

Standard Approaches

Research on the two standard approaches to thermonuclear fusion—magnetic confinement and inertial confinement—has continued, and there is a high degree of confidence that "scientific feasibility" will be demonstrated within the next several years. The significance of this is that the energy generated by thermonuclear reactions will be larger than the electrical energy input to operate the system. This condition will persist for perhaps one second and will be repeatable only about once an hour.

The ground is full of natural radioactivity,

and adding radioactive waste from nuclear energy

production adds very little to the total.

The next step, technical feasibility, will be a difficult and expensive one, extending over thirty years or more. The repetition rate must be greatly increased. Efficient capture of the released energy and its conversion into electricity must be developed. The technology also must breed tritium fuel to replace the fuel consumed. Maintenance problems of unprecedented severity will have to be worked out. Problems of economic feasibility in continuing these activities must be faced, and a great deal of optimism is required to believe that the outcome will be favorable. Many proponents of fusion research now concede that its application to large-scale electricity generation will not be economically feasible. Interest in pursuing these efforts is largely motivated by other potential applications.

Safety

The science of probabilistic risk analysis (PRA) for studying the safety of nuclear reactors has recently de-

veloped to the point that it is widely accepted in the technical and regulatory communities. For the present generation of 1,000-MWe (megawatt electrical output) light water reactors, the PRA indicate that we may expect one severe accident per 20,000 reactor years of operation, with an average of 400 deaths per accident, or 0.02 deaths per 1000 MWe-year. This is less than 0.1 percent of the number of deaths estimated from coal burning, and substantially less than the estimated number from any competitive technology.

However, safety can be further improved by reducing the size to 600 MWe. At this lower power level, active systems with pumps, now required to cool the reactor fuel and protect the containment structure from overpressure under accident conditions, can be replaced by passive systems with water flow driven by gravity. This approach eliminates the problem of electric power loss (including back-up diesel generators) and pump failures, which are the most prominent causes of accidents in 1,000-MWe reactors. Other simplifications allowed by the lower power reduce the cost-per-MWe, compensating for most of the economies of scale in the larger reactors. Simplicity also inherently improves safety.

In the United States, with its numerous small utilities, there are also institutional problems favoring the smaller units. The 600-MWe reactors are targeted at that market. Large national utilities like those in Britain, France, and Japan still favor plants of greater than 1,000-MWe size.

Disposal of Radioactive Waste

The technical side of radioactive waste disposal is very simple—convert it into a "rock-like" material, and bury it in the natural habitat of rocks, deep underground. There is abundant evidence on the behavior of average rock materials, and if this is applied to the radioactive waste buried at random locations, it is easy to show that health impacts will be about 0.02 eventual deaths per gigawatt electrical output-year or GWe-year (1 GWe-year = 1,000 MWe-years). This is less than 0.1 percent of the consequences of air pollution and wastes resulting from fossil fuel burning. It is also less than 0.1 percent of the deaths per GWe-year attributed to chemical carcinogens released into the ground in coal burning, or from the eventual radon emissions from uranium dispersed by coal burning. With careful siting and use of engineered safeguards, such as enclosing wastes in leach-resistant casings, the release of buried waste should be much less probable than that of materials in average rock.

The ground is full of natural radioactivity, and adding radioactive waste from nuclear energy production adds very little to the total. The fact that the waste will be concentrated in a small area does not increase its potential danger to human health.

Politics of Nuclear Energy

In the last quarter of the twentieth century, nuclear power development was adversely impacted upon and even halted by political opposition. Environmental groups attacked nuclear power, although coal burning, according to all scientific evidence, is far more harmful. Media attacks swayed public opinion to the point that politicians found opposition to be hard to resist. Approximately 1,000 extra people are condemned to a premature death each time a coal-burning plant is built instead of a nuclear plant. This is true even if we accept the risks of nuclear accidents proposed by the principal antinuclear activist organization—the Union of Concerned Scientists. Their estimates are one hundred times those given by PRAs.

It is difficult to predict how long this irrational situation will persist, but there are powerful forces at work that hopefully will overcome it. France, Japan, and other countries are maintaining strong nuclear power programs with advantages that in time will become evident. Concern over the greenhouse effect, acid rain, and air pollution will drive up the cost of coal burning and force it into a difficult competitive position. The public must eventually come to realize that solar electricity can never compete economically with nuclear power at night and in winter, and that the latter is environmentally preferable in any case.

The political problems and opposition facing nuclear power should fade away, and it will become dominant sometime in the twenty-first century. Ultimately, the dominance of nuclear power seems all but certain, since within a few hundred years available fossil fuels will become scarce and expensive. Nuclear power may well be the dominant energy source one thousand years from now, one million years from now, and even a billion years from now—for as long as intelligent beings inhabit Earth.

For a different, cautionary look at nuclear power, *see NUCLEAR POWER: CON.*

[See also Energy; Hazardous Wastes; Terrorism; Transuranium Elements; Weapons of Mass Destruction.]

BIBLIOGRAPHY

Cohen, Bernard L. *The Nuclear Energy Option.* New York: Plenum, 1990.
———. "Risk Analysis of Buried Waste from Electricity Generation." *American Journal of Physics* 54 (1986): 38.
"The New Reactors." *Nuclear News* (September 1992): 65–90.
"Severe Accident Risks." Washington, DC: U.S. Nuclear Regulatory Commission, Document NUREG-1150, 1989.

– BERNARD L. COHEN

NUCLEAR POWER: CON

Approximately 112 nuclear power plants operating in the United States generate about 20 percent of the country's electricity. Globally, nuclear power accounts for about 10 percent of the electricity generated. At its inception during the 1950s and early '60s, commercial nuclear power promised much. Nuclear power was to generate clean, safe, and cheap electricity. Today, with social and political attention focused on threats to the global environment posed by fossil fuels, nuclear power's future would seem bright. An energy source that did not contribute to acid rain or ozone depletion would seem to have a secure place in the world's energy future. Curiously, such is not the case. In the United States, no new nuclear power plants have been ordered since 1978 and those ordered since 1974 have been cancelled. Internationally, the picture is mixed. Countries such as Japan, France, and Germany rely on nuclear power. Elsewhere, opposition has halted nuclear power in Australia, New Zealand, Denmark, and Sweden.

Six key reasons for the lack of enthusiasm for nuclear power can be reduced to a simple proposition: Nuclear power may play a significant part in the energy future if the public perceives the cost of nuclear power to be cheaper than that of electricity from fossil fuels.

There are three variables in that last statement—*public perception, costs,* and *fossil fuels*—which must be explained. Public perception encompasses questions about the perceptions of risk and the cost of paying for nuclear-generated electricity. Cost, in turn, encompasses both the direct and indirect economic costs, as well as social costs attendant on this controversial energy source. Finally, nuclear power must be cheaper than generating electricity from fossil fuels—coal, oil, and natural gas—that are primarily responsible for global environmental damages.

Six Arguments Against Nuclear Power

THE DIRECT AND INDIRECT COST OF NUCLEAR POWER. Nuclear power plants, expensive to construct, were expected to be cheap to operate relative to the cost of fuel. Unfortunately, construction costs were grossly underestimated. The decade of the 1970s was financially disastrous to the industry as increasing inflation, higher labor and construction costs, longer lead times, more regulatory burdens, and changing public attitude raised construction costs several factors. It was not unusual to project a cost of $800 million for a plant and then have that cost escalate to over $2 billion as it took eight to twelve years to complete.

Operating costs are another matter. At one time it was believed that a plant would last forty or fifty years, but that figure has been revised downward to twenty-five years or less. Construction cost overruns, inattention to the back end of the fuel cycle—for example, waste disposal and plant decommission—and increasing regulatory requirements have contributed to make nuclear-generated electricity more expensive than coal-generated electricity as nuclear power plants fail to achieve hoped-for economies of scale.

While construction and operating costs are considered direct economic costs, social or external costs include such matters as the health and environmental costs of routine and nonroutine radiation emission, and property and personal damages caused by routine emissions and nuclear accidents. Admittedly, these costs are difficult to quantify and quantification relies more on modeling than empirical data. Moreover, discussion and analysis of such environmental costs are highly politicized.

NUCLEAR SAFETY. The accidents at Three Mile Island (TMI) and Chernobyl and plant cancellations, such as the Shoreham fiasco, destroyed the confidence of the public in the safety of nuclear power and became symbolic of questions of safety and risks. Even though risks from nuclear power are not statistically inordinate, nuclear power presents serious problems of perception. Even the small risk of a core meltdown creates the real possibility of nuclear catastrophe. An early, and disputed, study noted that even though the chance of a serious accident was only one in 200 million reactor years, the cost of such an accident would be 3,000 to 4,000 lives and over $14 billion of property damage. In other words, while the probability of accidents is small, the costs are enormous, and these costs have captured public attention.

WASTE DISPOSAL. The nuclear industry produces radioactive waste from mining, processing, and burning the fuel. Nuclear power plants produce two forms of radioactive waste—high-level waste from spent fuel and low-level waste from reactor cooling water. Little in the United States was done to provide for the disposal of nuclear plant waste until the passage of the Nuclear Waste Policy Act in 1982 and the Low-Level Radioactive Waste Policy Act of 1980. Both acts establish complex mechanisms for the siting of nuclear waste disposal facilities; however, as of the date of this writing, no permanent storage for spent fuel has been established. To further aggravate this problem, the stockpiling of

commercial nuclear waste on site as well as environmental harm caused at nuclear weapons facilities, such as Fernald in Ohio and Rocky Flats in Colorado, have made the public more suspicious of radioactive waste storage. To exacerbate matters further, the transportation of nuclear waste, both domestically and internationally, has raised further public concern.

DECOMMISSIONING. The back end of the fuel cycle not only entails the temporary storage of waste on site and the permanent storage of nuclear waste in a facility, it also involves the decommissioning of nuclear power plants. The two basic forms of decommissioning are the dismantling and long-term storage of a plant and the entombment of a plant in concrete. Decommissioning takes years, is extremely expensive, can amount to the cost of building a new plant, and presents transportation problems as well.

In some instances, decommissioning may be more expensive than building and operating a nuclear plant. A Japanese utility has estimated that decommissioning costs for a unit will be $1.2 billion, and Three Mile Island decommissioning and clean-up costs are projected at $3.2 billion.

GOVERNMENT REGULATION. Government regulation of any industry necessarily entails costs to that industry. Measures to reduce the cost of federal regulation in the nuclear field would include streamlining licensing, standardizing plants (including their safety designs), and further centralizing decision making in the federal government as opposed to the states. Some of these regulatory reform measures are part of the National Energy Security Act of 1992. Internationally, regulatory problems increase exponentially as one considers: the transboundary effects of routine and accidental radiation from plants; the need for international codes, practices, and agreements; the consequences of the international movement of wastes; and international protection for waste repositories, site selection, and decontamination and dismantling.

PUBLIC ACCEPTANCE. Over the last twenty years or more, nuclear power plants have been a cause célèbre among environmental activists. Threats of catastrophic accident, radiation effects of plant operation, and waste disposal efforts as well as transportation of nuclear fuel have caused concern among nuclear critics. While it is difficult to turn around public perception regarding the risks of radioactivity, until that perception is reversed, nuclear power prospects will be bleak. If the public perceives fossil fuel plants to be more dangerous to the global environment than nuclear power, this trend could possibly be reversed. If it becomes both technologically and economically feasible to harness the power of nuclear fusion, rather than fission, nuclear power could gain a new prominence, but this does not appear at all likely in the near term.

THE FUTURE. Although a nuclear resurgence in the near term is unlikely, the key variables for a nuclear future are clear. Direct, external, and regulatory costs must all decrease to the point that nuclear power is a more attractive energy alternative than fossil fuels, especially coal. Public attitude must adjust to the point that personal, property, and environmental risks of nuclear power are less than the risks from other energy sources.

See the essay nuclear power preceding this one for a more favorable viewpoint on this form of energy.

[See also Energy; Environmental Refugees; Hazardous Wastes; Nuclear Power; Terrorism; Transuranium Elements; Weapons of Mass Destruction.]

BIBLIOGRAPHY

Carter, Luther J. *Nuclear Imperatives and Public Trust: Dealing with Radioactive Waste.* Washington, DC: Resources for the Future, 1987.

International Energy Agency. *Global Energy: The Changing Outlook.* Paris: Organization for Economic Cooperation and Development, 1992.

Tester, Jefferson W.; Wood, David O.; and Ferrari, Nancy A., eds. *Energy and the Environment in the Twenty-first Century.* Cambridge, MA: MIT Press, 1991.

Tomain, Joseph P. *Nuclear Power Transportation.* Bloomington, IN: Indiana University Press, 1987.

Union of Concerned Scientists. *Safety Second: The NRC and America's Nuclear Power Plants.* Bloomington, IN: Indiana University Press, 1987.

– JOSEPH R. TOMAIN

NURSING

Registered nurses (RNs) are independent health care practitioners who are officially recognized through licensure and registration by the individual states in which they practice. The nursing profession acknowledges an individual's competency at a specific level through the certification process. Nurses are therefore identified both officially and professionally. Nurses often collaborate with or practice in conjunction with a variety of other individuals from other disciplines, including but not limited to physicians, respiratory and physical therapists, social workers, pharmacists, and dieticians.

"Nursing is the diagnosis and treatment of human responses to actual or potential health problems" (American Nurses' Association, 1980, p. 9). One of the fundamental roles of a nurse has been to provide care to those who would ordinarily be able to care for themselves, if they had the ability to do so. Nurses are most commonly recognized for their delivery of direct "hands-on" care to individual patients, typically in hospital settings. But nurses have historically provided care everywhere people are—in the home, community, school, street, workplace, hospital, hospice, or health center. Nurses also deliver a variety of other types of therapeutic, supportive, and palliative care. Nursing's future will continue to build upon its strengths: the diversity of the profession's constituents and of the populations cared for, an ongoing flexibility in approaches to patient care, and a continuing ability to adapt to changes in diverse areas.

Patients will be cared for increasingly in the home, with services such as nursing being brought in.

The nursing profession has historically been predominantly female. However, a growing number of men are entering the profession. This trend is expected to continue into the next century. The nursing profession can be expected to draw members from all segments of the population.

Nurses have always cared for those in need—whoever and wherever they are. The profession's heterogeneity has added to its ability to care for those from all walks of life and will continue to do so. The flexibility in the delivery of care is reflected through the classic nursing process—assessing a patient's condition, diagnosing the problem or need, formulating a plan of care, implementing the plan, and then evaluating it. This approach allows care to be custom-tailored to each individual situation. The consideration of each patient's unique strengths, weaknesses, support systems, and resources increases the possibility for successful intervention—whether smoking cessation or postcardiac surgery rehabilitation is involved. This holistic approach to care will help perpetuate nursing's human service ideology.

The nursing profession will be influenced by and will influence social, financial, environmental, educational, governmental, and professional forces. Any change in the demographics of the population will precipitate a concomitant change in the delivery of nursing care. As a larger segment of the population moves into the over-sixty-five category, nurses will adapt to meet the special needs of this group. This adaptation and specialization will become increasingly evident through the growing prominence of such nursing roles as the gerontological nurse practitioner.

A shift in the focus of care from the acute, tertiary care to primary, preventative care will result in a related shift in job opportunities. Nurses will continue to build the primary care foundation in the community. Acute care hospitals will continue to become places where only the most intense care is delivered. Patients will be cared for increasingly in the home, with services such as nursing being brought in. In-patient hospital nursing opportunities will shift from the general medical/surgical units to intensive care environments. Reimbursement for specific nursing interventions and intensity of care is foreseen at the service-provider level. Nursing opportunities will increase in the community and home care areas.

Technological advances will drive the need for specialization of nursing skills in some areas. The specialization will require supplemental education and will provide additional employment opportunities.

Nursing will confront the diverse preparatory routes that lead to entry into practice. Preparation at the baccalaureate level is anticipated to increase. Additional preparation at the postgraduate or master's level for advanced practice providers, such as certified nurse midwives (CNMs), clinical nurse specialists (CNSs), and nurse practitioners (NPs), is expected to sharply escalate and increase in importance.

A dramatic increase in the number of CNMs, CNSs, and NPs is anticipated to continue for several years and then level off. The scope of skills and autonomy of these advanced nurse clinicians is expected to grow. Predicted changes include direct reimbursement by patients or health-insurance plans for services at the individual-practitioner level for advanced nurse clinicians, and a new authority for such clinicians to issue medical prescriptions for specific classes of pharmacologic agents. There will be a growth in the amount of research devoted to confirming the efficacy, efficiency, and cost-effectiveness of nursing interventions. Professional certification is expected to increase in the areas of specialization. National centralization of registration and licensure is also predicted.

Health care reform on the national, state, regional, and community levels is envisioned. Nursing will be at the forefront of these reform efforts. Nursing will continue to remain at the pivotal core of the future health care system by continuing to increase its political activity and visibility. It will also continue to build upon its traditional strengths by providing an increasing majority of direct patient care—wherever, whenever, or for whomever it is needed—and by providing continual, comprehensive, coordinated care throughout each patient's life span.

By continuing to anticipate change, the profession will be able to adapt to new conditions on an "as needed" basis. This adaptability will serve to further the primary care foundation in the community-at-large. It will also give rise to an increase in the scope of advanced-practice nursing clinicians, such as certified nurse midwives, clinical nurse specialists, and nurse practitioners.

[See also Health Care; Health Care: Alternative Therapies; Health Care Costs; Health Care Financing; Health Care: Moral Issues In; Health Care: Technological Developments; Medical Care Providers.]

BIBLIOGRAPHY

American Nurses' Association. *Nursing: A Social Policy Statement.* Kansas City, MO: American Nurses' Association, 1980.
———. *Standards of Practice for the Primary Health Care Nurse Practitioner.* Kansas City, MO: American Nurses' Association, 1987.
Lee, Philip R., and Estes, Carroll L., eds. *The Nation's Health.* Boston: Jones and Bartlett, 1994.
U.S. Department of Health and Human Services. *Health Personnel in the United States: Eighth Report to Congress, 1991—Nursing.* Washington, DC: U.S. Government Printing Office, 1991.

– JOSEPH J. NAPOLITANO

NUTRITION

As we move into an increasingly health-conscious era, we need to foster an awareness that an optimum diet consists of a variety of foods that provide (1) sufficient energy (calories) to satisfy energy needs without causing undesirable weight gain, (2) levels of essential nutrients (protein, vitamins, and minerals) to meet body needs and maintain body reserves, and (3) moderate amounts of components associated with chronic diseases (i.e., fat, saturated fat, cholesterol, sodium, and alcohol). Dietary guidelines have been devised that encourage Americans to:

- Eat a variety of foods
- Maintain a healthy body weight
- Choose a diet low in fat, saturated fat, and cholesterol
- Select a diet with plenty of vegetables, fruit, and grain products
- Consume sugars only in moderation
- Use only moderate amounts of salt and sodium
- Drink alcoholic beverages in moderation, if at all

These guidelines are based on scientific literature showing the relationship of diet to health and disease.

Macronutrition

Dietary guidelines specify that humans should consume 30 percent or less of calories as fat, less than 10 percent of calories as saturated fat, and 300 or fewer milligrams of cholesterol per day to minimize risk for certain types of cancer and heart disease. For a diet of 2,000 calories per day, this would amount to about 65 or fewer grams of fat, and 20 or fewer grams of saturated fat. One can maintain a diet low in fat by eating primarily grain products, vegetables, and fruits; using fats and oils sparingly in cooking and at the table; selecting lean cuts of meat, poultry, and fish; and using nonfat or low-fat dairy products. The use of polyunsaturated vegetable oils (e.g., safflower, sunflower, and corn oils) in place of more saturated fats (e.g., butter or shortening) helps maintain a low intake of saturated fat. Moderate intake of animal products (especially egg yolk) helps to maintain a low intake of cholesterol.

Vegetables, fruits, and grain products are good sources of complex carbohydrates (starches), and dietary fiber, as well as various vitamins and minerals. Carbohydrates should provide at least 55 percent of the daily calories (about 275 grams for a daily intake of 2,000 calories). Adults should eat at least three servings of vegetables, two servings of fruits, and six servings of grain products (breads, cereals, pasta, and rice—with an emphasis on whole grains) per day. Dietary fiber is important for proper bowel function and can reduce symptoms of chronic constipation, diverticular disease, and hemorrhoids. People with diets low in dietary fiber

and complex carbohydrates and high in fat, tend to have more heart disease, obesity, and some types of cancer. Foods high in sugars (simple carbohydrates) should be consumed in moderation because they tend to be low in essential nutrients and may contribute to tooth decay.

Adequate protein is essential for growth and maintenance of body tissues. Daily intakes for women and men of 50 and 63 grams, respectively, are recommended. Moderate protein intake is recommended because there are no known benefits, and possibly some risks, in consuming diets with a high animal protein content. A strict vegetarian (vegan) diet can meet protein needs with a balance of legumes and grains.

Alcoholic beverages are not recommended because they provide calories but few nutrients, can be addictive, are linked to many health problems, and are a contributing factor in many accidents. Adults who consume alcoholic beverages should drink moderately: no more than 1 drink per day for women, and no more than 2 per day for men (1 drink is equivalent to 12 ounces of regular beer, 5 ounces of wine, or 1.5 ounces of distilled spirits). Some people should not drink alcoholic bev-

For many people in the world, meeting minimum daily calorie requirements involves a majority of their efforts. Undernutrition afflicts 800 million people worldwide. (Barnabas Bosshart/Corbis)

TABLE 1

VITAMINS AND MINERALS REQUIRED BY HUMANS

Vitamins	Minerals (atomic symbols)
Vitamin A	Sodium (Na)
Thiamin (Vitamin B₁)	Potassium (K)
Riboflavin (Vitamin B₂)	Calcium (Ca)
Niacin	Phosphorus (P)
Vitamin B₆	Magnesium (Mg)
Folic Acid	Iron (Fe)
Vitamin B₁₂	Zinc (Zn)
Biotin	Copper (Cu)
Pantothenic Acid	Manganese (Mn)
Vitamin C (Ascorbic Acid)	Iodine (I)
Vitamin D	Selenium (Se)
Vitamin E	Molybdenum (Mo)
Vitamin K	Chromium (Cr)
	Fluoride (F)

erages, including children and adolescents, women who are pregnant or trying to conceive, individuals who engage in activities that require attention or skill, individuals using medicines, and individuals addicted to alcohol.

Improved eating habits (e.g., lower fat intake) and increased exercise are the best ways to achieve a desirable weight. Excessive amounts of body fat are associated with high blood pressure, heart disease, stroke, diabetes, and certain types of cancer. Extreme approaches to losing weight, such as induced vomiting or the use of laxatives, amphetamines, and diuretics, can be dangerous and should be avoided.

Micronutrition

An adequate intake of fruits, vegetables, grain products, dairy products, and meats supply the micronutrients (vitamins and minerals) needed for normal body functioning (see Table 1). Two minerals of special concern in U.S. diets are calcium and iron. Inadequate intake of calcium is associated with osteoporosis along with other factors including genetics, hormone levels (estrogen), and physical activity. Adults require two or more servings of dairy products per day to meet calcium requirements; children need four or more servings per

Sedentary individuals in post-industrial nations jeopardize health by consuming an overabundance of food. A majority of Americans are overweight or obese. (James L. Amos/Corbis)

day. Iron deficiency is a problem for teenage girls and women of childbearing age because of iron losses during menstruation, and the increased requirements during pregnancy. Pregnant and lactating women can help to meet their increased nutrient requirements with supplements of vitamins and minerals.

Dietary sodium intake is related to blood pressure in some individuals. Reduced sodium intake for these individuals helps to lower blood pressure. Sodium is reduced by avoiding the use of salt and sodium-containing flavoring agents (e.g., soy sauce) during cooking and at the table. Intake of processed foods to which salt has been added (e.g., potato chips, corned beef, cheeses, luncheon meats, canned foods, and crackers) also should be reduced. Grain products may be high in sodium if made with baking powder or baking soda. Commercial products identified as low-sodium or reduced-sodium provide alternatives to higher-sodium counterparts.

Enteral and Parenteral Nutrition

Enteral (tube) formulas provide nutrients in liquid form and are used in hospitals for patients who, for various reasons, cannot retain food (vomiting or obstruction), or who cannot or will not eat. Enteral formulas, which are digested and absorbed through the gastrointestinal tract, usually contain protein (or protein hydrolysates or free amino acids), fats, carbohydrates, vitamins, electrolytes, and trace minerals, and may contain dietary fiber. The tube usually extends from the nose to the esophagus, stomach, or upper small intestine. Tubes also may be surgically placed into the pharynx, esophagus, duodenum, stomach, or jejunum.

Parenteral nutrition refers to nutrients that are provided intravenously. For patients whose nutritional needs can be partially met by mouth or tube, supplementary parenteral nutrition may be a useful adjunct. Parenteral solutions usually contain water, glucose, lipid emulsions, amino acids, vitamins, electrolytes, and trace elements.

A formula selected for enteral or parenteral use should meet the specific caloric and nutrient requirements of a patient. For patients recovering from surgery, shock, trauma, burns, or other massive injuries, it is essential that the formulas meet the increased nutrient requirements needed to repair and build new tissue.

Nutrition for Animals

Nutritional requirements vary among animal species; more highly evolved creatures (i.e., primates) have more complex nutrient requirements. For example, vitamin C is required by humans, but most other animals synthesize it from glucose and do not require an exogenous source. Commercial livestock feeds and pet foods are generally designed to meet the specific requirements of each species for calories, protein, and various vitamins and minerals. One nutritional problem of domestic dogs and cats is their tendency to gain weight. A relatively new market is opening up for dog and cat foods for different life stages, with the caloric content generally decreasing for the older animals.

Public awareness of the vitamins, minerals,

and nutrients considered essential to health

will hopefully continue to expand in the future.

Public awareness of the vitamins, minerals, and nutrients considered essential to health will hopefully continue to expand in the future. Precise levels of need are continually being fine-tuned as experience with traditional foods, nutritional supplements, enteral and parenteral administration, and requirements for commercial livestock, pets, and animals of all kinds grows.

[See also Alcohol; Fisheries; Food Additives; Food Consumption; Food and Drug Safety; Food Laws; Food Technologies; Health Care: Techonological Developments.]

BIBLIOGRAPHY

Committee on Diet and Health, Food and Nutrition Board, Commission on Life Sciences, National Research Council. *Diet and Health: Implications for Reducing Chronic Disease Risk.* Washington, DC: National Academy Press, 1989.

U.S. Department of Agriculture and U.S. Department of Health and Human Services. *Nutrition and Your Health: Dietary Guidelines for Americans,* 3rd ed. Washington, DC: U.S. Government Printing Office, 1990.

U.S. Department of Health and Human Services. *The Surgeon General's Report on Nutrition and Health.* DHHS (PHS) Publication, 88–50211. Washington, DC: U.S. Government Printing Office, 1988.

– JEAN PENNINGTON

OCEANS

The world ocean is frequently referred to as humankind's last frontier. It may not be the last, but certainly it is a frontier space that we are discovering, exploiting, and endangering.

The scientific exploration of ocean space is an exciting adventure, involving a large number of disciplines and countries. We have discovered that oceans are born and grow, as new ocean floor wells up from Earth's mantle through the volcanic activities of the huge mountain chains (mid-oceanic ridges) that traverse the world's oceans. Seafloor spreading forces continents apart. Oceans shrink and "die" when more seafloor is swallowed, disappearing in volcanic trenches along "active" coastlines, than is produced at the mid-oceanic ridges. The lifetime of an ocean may be on the order of 800 million years. The hydrology of the whole system, covering two-thirds of the surface of our planet, and the interaction between ocean surface and atmosphere have a decisive influence on the world's climate. This interaction is as yet poorly understood. Global warming would entail the melting of polar ice masses, with a consequent sea level rise and the flooding of coastal areas and cities such as Boston, as well as the disappearance of low-lying islands such as the Maldives. This, however, is a hypothesis that has to be dealt with in the light of uncertainty.

In our age, we are witnessing the penetration of this frontier space by the industrial revolution. All traditional sea uses—fishing, shipping, tourism, waste disposal, military uses—have been drastically transformed by modern high technology. And new uses have been generated, such as seabed mining and the production of energy from tides, waves, currents, biomass, and temperature and salinity differentials. Artificial islands, whether for waste disposal or human habitation, are appearing offshore to relieve overcrowded coastal areas. Floating cities, made of new materials and organized in "modules," are conceived to eliminate the woes besetting our overgrown, decaying metropolises: crowding, traffic jams, air pollution, and unsustainable energy consumption. These ocean cities rise upward and descend below the water surface. They are still on the drawing boards of futuristic architects, in the United States, Japan, Italy, France, and the United Kingdom. They may become realities in the next century.

The wealth of the oceans is awesome and could make a far more important contribution to sustainable development in the future than it has in the past.

Fishing may have reached or passed its limits. Many stocks are overfished, and many species are endangered by unselective and destructive gear, pollution, and the destruction of habitat. About 60 percent of the world's population lives within sixty miles of the world ocean's coasts. Poor coastal management, entailing beach erosion and silting, together with poorly controlled agricultural, domestic, and industrial wastes, are a serious threat to coastal waters and enclosed and semienclosed seas; this in turn is a threat to the ocean's fauna and flora and to human health.

The wealth of the oceans could make a far more important contribution to sustainable development in the future than it has in the past.

The end of an old and exhausted system may give way to the emergence of a new one. Fishing from the wild is coming to an end, but we are witnessing its transformation into a new system of husbanding aquatic animals and cultivating aquatic plants. Aquaculture and mariculture are already producing about 15 percent of the global fish and algae production, and this new industry is growing at a rate of about 6 percent a year. The emergence of aquaculture, making the transition from "hunting" to "culture" in the oceans, is by itself a revolutionary event comparable to the emergence of "agriculture" from the hunting and gathering that preceded it ten thousand years or so ago. What we are witnessing today, however, is a revolution within this evolution: the penetration of aquaculture by genetic engineering and bioindustrial processes. Aquaculture will be radically altered by the biotechnology revolution. This development could alleviate the hunger problem. It also opens new horizons for a number of other industries, including the pharmaceutical and chemical industries, the extraction of metals and minerals from ores or water bodies, whether for combatting pollution or processing minerals.

There are other new uses of the oceans made possible by contemporary technology. The extraction of energy, in various forms, directly from seawater, will be a key component of the diversified, renewable, and nonpolluting energy systems of the future. Desalinization and the extraction of fresh water from the oceans will play a major role in solving the world's acute and growing water problems. Ocean mineral mining will become an important industry early in the twenty-first century.

Trillions of potato-shaped manganese nodules litter the deep seabed, at depths of about 5,000 meters. They contain nickel, copper, cobalt, and manganese. Technologies exist to lift them and to process their useful metals. The United Nations Convention on the Law of the Sea (1982) has declared that these resources, along with any other mineral resources on or under the deep seabed beyond the limits of national jurisdiction, to be a "common heritage of mankind." This important new concept in international law is fundamental to the economics of "sustainable development." Resources that are the common heritage of humankind cannot be appropriated by anybody; they must be managed for the benefit of humankind as a whole, with particular regard for the needs of poor countries; they must be managed with due regard for the conservation of the environment and reserved for exclusively peaceful purposes.

The United Nations Convention on the Law of the Sea has been called "a constitution for the Oceans." It has radically redistributed ocean space. One-third of the world ocean now falls under coastal-state jurisdiction, in the form of extended territorial seas, exclusive economic zones, and continental shelves. Tiny island states and archipelagos now enjoy sovereign rights over huge ocean spaces and their resources. This may cause boundary conflicts in a number of cases, but the convention also provides for mandatory, binding, and peaceful settlement of all disputes. It has established a new International Tribunal for the Law of the Sea, with its seat in Hamburg, Germany, to deal with these disputes.

The convention also has established an International Seabed Authority, based in Jamaica, to manage the mineral wealth of the oceans for the benefit of humankind as a whole, based on the principle of the common heritage.

The convention covers all major uses of the seas and oceans; enhances both sustainable economic development and the protection of the environment; and fosters peace, international cooperation, development of human resources, and the advancement of the marine sciences and technologies.

[See also Acid Rain; Fisheries; Freshwater; Genetics; Global Warming.]

BIBLIOGRAPHY

Borgese, Elisabeth Mann. *The Future of the Oceans.* Montreal: Harvest House, 1986.
Borgese, Elisabeth Mann; Ginsburg, Norton; and Morgan, Joseph, eds. *Ocean Yearbook,* Vols. 1–11. Chicago: University of Chicago Press, 1980–present.
Sanger, Clyde. *Ordering the Oceans: The Making of the Law of the Sea.* London: Zed Books Ltd., 1986.

— ELISABETH MANN BORGESE

OGBURN, WILLIAM FIELDING (1886–1959)

American sociologist William Ogburn was born in Georgia and took his doctorate at Columbia University in 1912. From 1919 until his retirement in 1951, he taught sociology at Columbia, Barnard College, and later the University of Chicago. During the Hoover administration, he served as research director of the President's Research Committee on Social Trends, an early example of state-sponsored futurism in the United States. Later, he chaired the Subcommittee on Technology of the National Resources Committee and took a leading part in the preparation of its 1937 report, *Technological Trends and National Policy.* His pioneering interest in technology assessment was carried further in *The Social Effects of Aviation* (1946), coauthored with Jean L. Adams and S. G. Gilfillan. Ogburn's most influential book is *Social Change, With Respect to Culture and Original Nature* (1922; revised, 1950). In this and other writings he expressed confidence in the predictive powers of sociological analysis, believing that many trends could safely be extrapolated into the near future and even beyond. He is best remembered for his theory of "cultural lag," the tendency of cultures to adapt slowly and reluctantly to technological innovation and socioeconomic change.

BIBLIOGRAPHY

Jaffe, A. J. "William Fielding Ogburn." *International Encyclopedia of the Social Sciences.* New York: Macmillan, 1968.
Martindale, Don. *The Nature and Types of Sociological Theory.* Boston: Houghton Mifflin, 1960.

— W. WARREN WAGAR

OIL.

See PETROLEUM.

ON-LINE SERVICES

Communication over distance by means of on-line services, though beginning in the 1970s, has cultural roots as distant as the earliest smoke signals and drumbeats. Then and now communication has been governed by access and technology. Communication around the world on self-designed schedules signals a new means of communicating and changes how and with whom we communicate. For most of the last twenty-five years, the number of users of these services has been small. In the 1990s, the number jumped into the millions, with projections of continued rapid growth.

With entire communities turning into

"electronic villages," all sectors of society

will begin the twenty-first century

with rich opportunities and share information.

The on-line services user base grows in size and composition as the very nature of the services and access to technology change. What has been service for a few is rapidly becoming widespread for business, education, and individuals. On-line services are a new means to communicate for most that will transform how they communicate and that promise to be as monumental in impact as the printed word, which changed communication from acoustical interaction to more restrictive print. Print is now only part of how we communicate. Gesture, sound, and image as well as text are the tools to shape the way people communicate and the services they use. The mid-1990s is at the threshold of on-line video, images, audio and virtual reality. The advanced computers that make this possible in the 1990s will gradually be replaced by low-cost devices in the next century.

Experience with computers in the 1980s strengthened the perception that "a picture is worth a thousand words." By the 1990s, applications required not only images but video, audio, as well as text. On-line services are evolving to fully mature on-line services capable of delivering different types of information (video, images, audio, and text.) By the mid-1990s improvement in transmission speeds, better software, and a greater desire to use multimedia had begun a three- to five-year process of testing and delivering a variety of fully mature on-line services.

The pace of implementation varies from one country to another. In countries such as France, on-line services are being introduced and sustained earlier than in a more market-oriented economy such as the United States. Since the pace of innovation varies from one country to another, the emphasis is focused on the United States, where there is a freer interplay of technology, access, and market acceptance.

Computer conferencing, one of the earliest kinds of on-line service, became popular in the 1970s. Predating the existence of personal computers, it depended on using "dumb" terminals connected to mainframe computers. The slow communication speeds and limited graphics capabilities restricted most of these services to text. However, a few professional services such as economic analysis provided black-and-white vector graphics.

The desire to upgrade services to include color images was central to the development of consumer videotex services delivered in the television signal or over telephone lines. Large companies such as Knight-Ridder in Miami and Bell Canada in Canada experimented in delivering and building market acceptance of videotex services with graphics in the early to mid-1980s. These experiments proved premature despite large investments of money, though they did provide experience in constructing applications, market testing, and delivering a variety of services to consumers and businesses that provided information in the 1990s for interactive television experiments.

After the demise of videotex services with graphics, videotex survived in the form of on-line services such as the Source. By the end of the 1980s, a number of on-line services were available—some already providing users with graphic access screens.

From 1985 to the early 1990s, the rapid expansion of computers, low-cost communications software, and modems served an ever larger number of sophisticated users who could access on-line services directly from their home or business. Services were designed to work with these devices and allow for the downloading of files (text and graphics). Many services such as those provided by America Online provided a user-friendly graphics interface on the user's computer for point-and-click access. Additional graphics were downloaded when users logged on. By the mid-1990s, the most successful on-line services provided graphic access screens to make their services easier to use.

By the mid-1990s, development and acceptance of better compression techniques for video, images, and audio as well as small, inexpensive processors set the scene for the development of on-line services with video, audio, and images. The success of these technical developments and the lure of large consumer markets prompted a number of large international companies to also announce trial interactive television services. The trade-offs of speed, cost, resolution, and content—much as those of videotex a decade earlier—were again put to the test.

In 1994 and 1995, new experimentation began with a heavy emphasis on interactive video delivered to the television set. The interactive television trials continued the ongoing process of experimentation and market testing that has persistently moved industrial countries closer to the time when fully mature on-line services will be available. Service providers again needed to provide the device, now called a set-top box, for these new services. Existing personal computers did not meet the video requirements.

On-line services are usually one-on-one communications over a variety of communications transport media such as cable, fiber, twisted-pair, telephone lines, as well as a number of wireless transmission technologies. Though this early development and use of on-line services will continue, the emerging technology increasingly will grow to accommodate more group-to-group communications. Video and voice transmissions are equally well suited to group communication, as is the case in video conferencing.

Group chat sessions are common on private on-line services such as CompuServe, Prodigy, GEnie, and America Online. The Internet began in the mid-1990s to provide real-time services with most of its use reserved for the exchange of text messages. With the advent of the World Wide Web, users had Internet access to images, audio, and video. Underlying software programs are providing Web sites with productivity tools to search increasingly large multimedia databases. Once information is found, the Web services provide users with the option to download image, text, and video files.

While the technologies are more advanced, the decision that video is key to any new on-line consumer service has raised the technological threshold. The adoption of more advanced video compression standards such as the Motion Picture Experimental Group (MPEG), faster networks, and more capable set-top boxes are untested in the mid-1990s marketplace. The quest for a "killer application" eludes industry giants, but projected demand for more technology solutions for education, consumer information, and business, and the increased cost-effectiveness of computing and communications technology suggest, finally, the often heralded convergence of the necessary market conditions. Tests during the 1995–1998 period will measure whether the perceived value of on-line services is enough to encourage and economically sustain a sizable market.

On-line services are sometimes combined with devices that play compact discs. In these instances, the soon-to-be larger capacity compact discs (projected over the next three years to be able to hold more than 3.5 gigabytes of visual and audio information) will enhance these services beginning in 1997. These services will combine the benefits of large, low-cost storage and reduced transmission requirements to provide up-to-date information to users. The on-line services provide up-to-date information to complement the compact discs and can facilitate access to specific subjects.

With entire communities turning into "electronic villages," all sectors of society will begin the twenty-first century with rich opportunities to communicate and share information. The emphasis will shift from whether it can be accomplished technically to whether the content is adequately customized to meet the individual and group needs of homes and in businesses. The pace, number of users, and types of use will depend on whether access is determined on economic terms or subsidized by government and other organizations to meet specific social and political needs.

[See also Communications; Communications Technology; Computer Linkage; Computers: Overview; Electronic Convergence; Electronic Publishing; High Technology; Information Overload; Information Society; Information Technology; Interactive Entertainment; Media Lab; Networking; Telecommunications.]

BIBLIOGRAPHY

Ciampa, John A. *Communication: The Living End.* New York: Philosophical Library, 1989.
Gilster, Paul. *The Internet Navigator.* New York: John Wiley, 1993.
McLuhan, Marshall. *Counterblast.* New York: Harcourt, Brace, & World, 1969.
Rushkoff, Douglas. *Cyberia: Life in the Trenches of Hyperspace.* San Francisco: HarperCollins, 1994.

— RICHARD G. MAYNARD

OPINION POLLS.

See PUBLIC OPINION POLLS; SURVEYS.

ORGANIZATIONAL COMPLEXITY

Predicting the future may be controversial, but one thing almost everyone can agree on is that it will be far more complex than the past. The exponential rise of information technology (IT), increasing competition in a global economy, a mounting environmental crisis, and other revolutionary trends make it clear that the world is entering a turbulent epoch of constant change, exploding diversity, and unmanageable complexity.

For instance, automation is eliminating jobs and leaving roughly half of all workers floating in a "contingency status" between temporary positions. Entire industries are being transformed. Convergence of the computer, communication, and entertainment fields is an example. Large organizations, such as AT&T and IBM, are being disaggregated at the very time they are forming alliances with other organizations.

This shift to a complex world is so striking that a new field of science has emerged devoted to the study of complexity and chaos. Institutions are in crisis because they were designed on simple, hierarchical principles. The unpleasant fact is that most organizations today share the same problem that brought about the collapse of communism: an authoritarian, centrally coordinated hierarchy that is simply too cumbersome to manage the complexity of the information age. Large corporations such as General Motors have suffered such massive financial losses that their former CEOs have been replaced. Bureaucratic governments are running unsustainable deficits and many are collapsing; communism was simply the most extreme case because it had the most rigid hierarchy. Furthermore, almost all Americans acknowledge that health care and education are badly in need of reform.

The type of organization evolving now is fundamentally different because there is a growing recognition of the shortcomings in controlling complex behavior from the top down. Emerging is an "organic" theoretical perspective. This approach creates loosely structured organizations with each unit possessing sufficient autonomy and intelligence to manage its own actions at the grass roots. This system is then guided (rather than controlled) by response to market forces and information systems. The result is a self-organizing system of small, self-managed units, enjoying wide participation, with decisions originating from the bottom up.

The principles needed to produce this organic behavior are extensions of Western ideals of free enterprise and democracy. These powerful concepts have not been applied within institutions generally, but recently the information revolution has been driving an organizational transformation toward a new system of management and economics called the "New Management" and the "New Capitalism."

The most crucial aspect of this organizational revolution focuses on the application of free market concepts. Today, many trends are under way to bring free market mechanisms *inside* organizations, resulting in the reduction or elimination of middle-management levels, the breakup of big companies like IBM into autonomous units, a new kind of company-internal entrepreneurship, and so on. Even governments are becoming entrepreneurial and are privatizing some undertakings.

Each unit in such an organization (including line and staff units, manufacturing facilities, research and development, and other functions) is being defined as a self-managed "internal enterprise." Funds are allocated in proportion to performance, and units are allowed the freedom to manage their operations as they think best.

Executives focus their efforts on designing and regulating this organizational economy and providing collaborative leadership, just as government manages a national economy.

By accepting the loss of control over details and allowing people greater freedom as well as accountability, a different form of sophisticated, creative control is likely to be achieved.

Some of the most dynamic corporations increasingly are designed along these lines. MCI, the young upstart that successfully challenged the AT&T monopoly, credits its success to a unique culture that embraces entrepreneurship and initiative. Hewlett-Packard avoided the recent difficulties of IBM, DEC, Commodore, and other computer makers by keeping each division a small, independent unit free of bureaucratic controls. Johnson & Johnson has thrived for decades using a decentralized system of 168 independent divisions. Asea Brown Boveri's 1,200 companies and 5,000 intersecting profit centers have become a model for other global corporations.

Market concepts are also spreading into government. Roughly forty states have been moving in this direction for years, and even the federal government is struggling to become entrepreneurial. The Department of Defense, the Federal Aviation Agency, and other departments are creating "information utilities" in which internal units pay for services. The trend is convincingly clear in education, where the concept of "choice" is introducing competition among schools. New York City's worst school districts have been turned around by decentralizing large schools into small, self-managed units and allowing students greater freedom in selecting the curriculum they prefer. Mexico City converted a central licensing bureau into competing offices with great improvement in service.

This transitional change poses major challenges for managers and employees. Organizations may gain accountability for performance, entrepreneurial freedom, creative solutions, rapid response time, improved quality and services, and other advantages of free enterprise—at the cost of tolerating the messy disorder that is also characteristic of markets. People can find these new work roles more financially rewarding, liberating, and satisfying—if they show the initiative that is required and are prepared to take on the risks that are unavoidable.

This should prove an unusually demanding challenge because a very different management logic is involved. Many will resist it. Most large institutions are likely to be forced in this direction, however, out of the necessity to manage an increasingly turbulent world. By accepting the loss of control over details and allowing people greater freedom as well as accountability, a different form of sophisticated, creative control is likely to be achieved. Educated people may then pursue their needs through market-based, democratic institutions, producing a more organic society better able to manage the enormous complexity that lies ahead.

[See also Business Governance; Business Structure: Forms, Impacts; Governance; Government Organization; Institutions and Organizations.]

BIBLIOGRAPHY

Freedman, David. "Is Management Still a Science?" *Harvard Business Review* (November–December 1992).

Halal, William E.; Geranmayeh, Ali; and Pourdehnad, John. *Internal Markets: Bringing the Power of Free Enterprise Inside Your Organization.* New York: John Wiley, 1993.

Kelly, Kevin. *Out of Control: The Rise of Neo-Biological Civilization.* Reading, MA: Addison-Wesley, 1994.

Osborne, David, and Gaebler, Ted. *Reinventing Government.* Reading, MA: Addison-Wesley, 1992.

Waldrop, Mitchell. *Complexity: The Emerging Science at the Edge of Order and Chaos.* New York: Simon and Schuster, 1992.

— WILLIAM E. HALAL

ORWELL, GEORGE (1903–1950)

"George Orwell" is the pseudonym of the writer Eric Arthur Blair, who was born in Motihari, Bengal, India. He was educated at Eton (where he claimed to have learned nothing) and later joined the Burmese police force. A socialist at heart, like many of his generation, he contended by 1927 that British imperialism was "largely a racket." This conviction, plus his ill health and a desire to write, led him to return to Europe. Adopting the pen name of George Orwell, he wrote *Burmese Days* in 1934. It brought him enough income to devote himself to writing full-time. In 1928 he published his most admired book, *Homage to Catalonia,* based on his experiences as a member of the Republican Army in the Spanish Civil War. Although Orwell claimed that he was not really a novelist, he is best remembered for his two novels *Animal Farm* (1945) and *Nineteen Eighty-Four* (1949). The former was a bitter anti-Stalinist satire that shook the Socialist establishment. Orwell's main contribution to futurism was *Nineteen Eighty-Four,* a grimly dystopian warning predicting the spread of Stalinist-type tyranny throughout much of the world. Ironically, none of Orwell's predictions came true; there is more freedom half a century after his death than at any time in human history. He died in London on January 1, 1950, still committed to his own highly idiosyncratic form of Marxist socialism, which because of his own intense intellectual honesty was in no sense doctrinaire.

[See also Dystopias.]

BIBLIOGRAPHY

Buitenhuis, Peter, and Nadel, Ira B. *George Orwell: A Reassessment.* New York: St. Martin's Press, 1988.

Fishman, Robert L. *Nineteen Eighty-Four in Nineteen Eighty-Four: Orwell as Prophecy.* Trenton, NJ: New Jersey State Museum, 1986.

Hunter, Lynette. *George Orwell: The Search for a Voice.* London: Open University Press, 1984.

Rai, Alok. *Orwell and the Politics of Despair.* New York: Cambridge University Press, 1990.

Williams, Raymond. *George Orwell.* New York: Columbia University Press, 1981.

— GEORGE THOMAS KURIAN

OUTDOOR RECREATION AND LEISURE PURSUITS

Participation in outdoor recreation increased tremendously in the past generation. The most noteworthy trend was the great popularity of physically demanding activities, especially canoeing, swimming, boating, walking, bicycling, and snow-skiing. The number of canoeists grew fivefold in one twenty-year span; the number of bicyclists, almost four-fold.

This growth is expected to continue, although not at such fast rates. The U.S. Forest Service projects that between the years 2000 and 2040, canoeing will grow by 70 percent and bicycling by 120 percent.

Some of the factors contributing to this growth include the increased concern with health and physical fitness, greater accessibility of recreation areas, and equipment advances that make activities safer, more comfortable, and within the abilities of more people.

Demographics

The aging of the population will be as important to the future of outdoor recreation as to other areas of life. Participation increased in thrill-seeking sports, such as rock climbing, bungee jumping, and river running, partly because equipment that improved safety raised the level of risk that people seem willing to accept. Equipment advances may continue to pull younger people in this direction.

People continue to do many of the outdoor activities they adopted before age forty, but are less able to do

People have sought out increased challenges in their recreational pursuits. Rock climbing ranks among one of the most dangerous of the "extreme sports" but attracts increasing numbers of people. (© 1997 Jim Marshall/First Image West, Inc.)

ample, pollution has cut visibility by one-third to one-half in Western parks, and by more in the East.

At flagship national parks such as Yosemite and Yellowstone, reservations are necessary to obtain campsites. Overuse has forced the closure of some areas, and closures are likely to increase because of concerns such as harm to endangered species. This pressure could lead to the preservation of more land in the public domain and the development of more land for recreation—especially closer to population centers.

More remote areas will undoubtedly see more use as people travel farther to get away from each other. For example, the land overseen by the Bureau of Land Management, an area nearly one-eighth the size of the United States, has been largely overlooked, because it was thought of as undesirable desert. But its many beautiful areas are now being developed and marketed as alternatives to more famous destinations.

One reason that recreation supporters will win many resource conflicts is the increasing recognition of recreation's economic importance. In Colorado, tourism income outweighs the economic contributions of traditional industries, such as mining and logging; and tourists come to the Rockies for outdoor activities, such as skiing. Georgia's Chattahoochee National Forest is expected to produce $108 million from timber and $637 million from recreation over the next fifty years.

But some kinds of outdoor recreation will run into environmental conflicts of their own: Snow-skiing's popularity has led to a demand for more facilities, which may not be a problem in some parts of the country. But places like the Northeast, which is dependent on snowmaking, water availability, and quality issues, as well as land availability, could limit future developments.

some of the most strenuous activities. Consequently, activities like backpacking are down 50 percent from the 1970s, a change that coincided with baby-boomers having children of their own.

A complementary trend toward seeking activities closer to home is expected to continue, and more facilities will be developed to meet this need. The conversion of multipurpose trails from abandoned railroad lines reflects this trend.

Quality of the Experience

More conflicts over resource use are likely in the years ahead. The quality of many outdoor-recreation activities depends upon the quality of the environment in which they are enjoyed, and that quality has eroded with population and development pressures. For ex-

Technology

Technical developments have fostered an endless number of new sports: from the introduction of ski lifts and equipment that differentiated downhill from Nordic skiing, to lightweight materials that made backpacking accessible to the average participant, to radio collars for dogs that have changed hunting, to reliable mountain-climbing equipment, to mountain bicycles allowing riders to pedal places once thought impossible, to snowboards, off-road vehicles, snowmobiles, jet skis, hang gliders, ultralight aircraft, and bungee jumping. Options have exploded in recent years and will continue to do so, in such diverse directions as fantasy baseball camps, where one can actually play the game with professional athletes, and guided trips to almost anywhere.

Of course, technical advances mean more competition for leisure time, as VCRs and cable television have demonstrated in the past decade. And who can predict the next invention—will virtual reality enable a person to experience the thrill of climbing Mount Everest without ever leaving the living room?

Global positioning system units could become

so inexpensive that people would never get lost.

Some looming developments could be all-terrain skateboards and in-line skates with brakes or go-anywhere cellular phones to call for help. Global positioning system units could become so inexpensive that people would never get lost.

Some Trends

- Equipment will undoubtedly continue to evolve and become more specialized. A typical enthusiast's closet already contains a dozen shoes with particular abilities, from running to rock climbing. Inventions such as the breathable polyester fabrics that revolutionized clothing are certain to find their way to market. Materials continue to grow lighter, stronger, and more versatile.

- The line between the natural and artificial worlds will continue to blur. Climbers build walls indoors and on freeway overpass supports; kayakers practice and compete on artificial white-water runs. Year-round skiing on the snow equivalent of Astroturf and surfing on waves generated in amusement parks are possibilities. Such developments mesh well with the increased desire for recreation closer to home.

- Trends increasing inequality in income may also be felt: Permits to climb Mount Everest are limited, expensive, and increasingly go to rich people being led by guides instead of pioneering climbers. The availability of places to hunt has decreased with suburban and exurban sprawl and the disappearance of much farmland. The decrease in opportunities could lead to an increase in the importance of hunting reserves and clubs, including exclusive ones that raise animals, then release them for patrons to shoot or fish. The majority who cannot afford those clubs may have to crowd onto public areas.

- Campgrounds and other developments in parks and forests may tend less toward the primitive and contain more amenities in keeping with the desires of older users.

- Some things remain constant through time: Despite the inroads of new sports and technology, the most low-tech activity imaginable—walking—continues to be the most popular form of outdoor recreation among Americans and shows no signs of relinquishing its primacy.

On the other hand, we may ration the unusual recreation site—those in excess demand—not by cost but by qualifications. Access to many areas may depend upon the certified ability to use that site effectively.

[See also Exercise and Fitness; Free Time; Leisure Time; Parks and Wilderness; Sports and Activities, Spectator; Sports and Games, Competitive; Theme Parks and Organized Attractions.]

BIBLIOGRAPHY

Abrams, Malcolm, and Bernstein, Harriett. *More Future Stuff: Over 250 Inventions That Will Change Your Life by 2001.* New York: Penguin Books, 1991.

Future Vision: The 189 Most Important Trends of the 1990s. Compiled by the editors of *Research Alert.* Naperville, IL: Sourcebooks, 1991.

Report of the President's Commission on Americans Outdoors. *Americans Outdoors: The Legacy, The Challenge.* Washington, DC: Island Press, 1987.

U.S. Forest Service. *An Analysis of the Outdoor Recreation and Wilderness Situation in the U.S., 1989–2040.* Washington, DC: U.S. Department of Agriculture, 1989.

— ERIC SEABORG

OZONE LAYER DEPLETION

A thin layer of ozone molecules in the stratosphere, twice as high as jet planes fly, shields the Earth's surface from the full force of the sun's hazardous ultraviolet rays. The depletion of this ozone layer is widely recognized as the first truly *global* environmental crisis. Fortunately, ozone is a "renewable resource" in the sense that it is continuously created by ultraviolet radiation striking the upper atmosphere. The ozone layer will slowly mend itself if we act quickly to halt ozone depletion.

First Evidence and Response

In 1974 two scientific papers, published independently, first suggested a threat to the ozone layer. The first study described how chlorine atoms that reach the ozone layer could act as powerful ozone destroyers. The second study reported that chemical compounds called chlorofluorocarbons (CFCs) were reaching the stratosphere, were breaking up, and were releasing chlorine atoms. Taken together, these studies suggested that harmless-seeming CFCs being widely used for propellants in aerosol cans, coolants in refrigerators and air conditioners, industrial cleaning solvents, and for many other purposes might be producing a massive depletion of stratospheric ozone.

This was alarming news because the ozone layer prevents most of a dangerous ultraviolet wavelength of the sun's light, called UV-B, from searing the Earth's surface. UV-B radiation breaks down organic molecules. If the amount of UV-B that reaches the top of the atmosphere were to penetrate to ground level, Earth would become virtually uninhabitable.

In response to this scientific alarm, environmental and consumer groups targeted aerosol spray cans, creating a symbolic ozone villain to sway public opinion. Sales of these products plunged by over 60 percent, placing heavy pressure on legislators to respond. In

1978, the United States criminalized and otherwise discouraged the use of CFCs as aerosol propellants. Unfortunately, the use of CFCs in spray cans in other countries as well as in other applications drove worldwide CFC use back to its 1975 peak use level by the mid-1980s.

The Ozone Hole

In 1984, a shocking event catapulted ozone depletion into the international limelight. Scientists of the British Antarctic Survey reported a 40 percent decrease in ozone in the stratosphere over their survey site. Initially, many scientists were skeptical. Computer models based on knowledge of atmospheric chemistry at the time could not explain such a large drop. Measurements of atmospheric ozone taken routinely since 1978 by the National Aeronautics and Space Administration's (NASA) Nimbus-7 satellite had never shown Antarctic ozone depletion.

Within a year, however, evidence for the existence of what was termed an "ozone hole" in the southern hemisphere became overwhelming. Other measuring stations in Antarctica confirmed the British findings. Checking Nimbus-7 readings, NASA scientists found that their computers had been programmed to reject very low ozone readings as instrument error. The rejected Nimbus-7 data showed that ozone levels had been dropping over the South Pole ever since the satellite measurements began, creating an ozone hole as large as the continental United States.

Scientists around the world raced to understand why the ozone hole was forming and why it was positioned over Antarctica. Dramatic evidence linking CFCs to the ozone hole was gathered in September 1987, when scientists flew a high-altitude research aircraft from Punta Arenas, Chile, toward the South Pole. As the plane entered the ozone hole, its instruments registered a jump in chlorine monoxide molecules to about 500 times normal levels, while the ozone concentration plummeted. These measurements, shown in Figure 1, are often referred to as the "smoking gun" that convinced even CFC manufacturers that CFCs were the culprit.

Further research showed that ozone depletion is especially pronounced in the Antarctic because the continent's extremely cold, dry air is full of ice crystals that provide surfaces on which chlorine and ozone can alight and react with each other. Also, each winter the prevailing wind pattern—a circumpolar vortex—keeps Antarctic air from blending with the rest of the atmosphere, concentrating the CFCs there.

The Montreal Protocol and London Agreements

The discovery of the Antarctic ozone hole had a galvanizing impact on international discussions that were

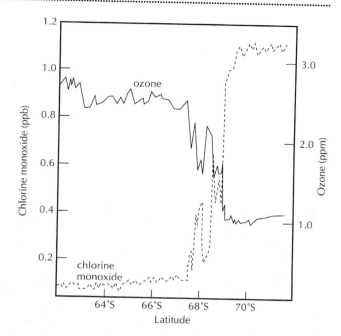

Figure 1. As chlorine increases, Antarctic ozone decreases.

already underway to limit CFC production. The United Nations Environmental Program (UNEP) also played an important role by assembling the scientific evidence and providing a neutral forum for discussion and resolution. Responding to pressures from all sides—scientists, environmentalists, journalists, and UNEP—thirty-six nations signed the historic 1987 Montreal Protocol on Substances that Deplete the Ozone Layer. The Montreal Protocol stipulated that world production of the five most common CFCs should initially be frozen at 1986 levels, then reduced 20 percent by 1993, and cut an additional 30 percent by 1998.

When the "smoking gun" evidence (Figure 1) was published several months after the Montreal Protocol was signed, many scientists concluded that an even faster CFC phase-out was necessary. At that point, Dupont, the world's largest CFC producer, announced that it would completely phase out its CFC manufacturing. Dupont's environmental leadership brought around many of the remaining doubters in the chemical industry. After further negotiations, again led by UNEP, ninety-two countries signed the "London Agreement," which phases out all CFC production (as well as several other ozone-destroying chemicals) by the year 2000. An international fund also was created to help developing countries shift to CFC alternatives.

Alternative Ozone Futures

Figure 2 shows three different scenarios of the future concentration of ozone-destroying chlorine in the stratosphere. Scenario A shows how chlorine would build up in the stratosphere in a "no controls" situation, in which CFC emissions continue at the 1986 rate. Scenario B projects the CFC production cuts agreed to in the Montreal Protocol, which still allows a doubling of stratospheric chlorine concentrations by 2100. Scenario C projects the CFC phase-out agreed to in the London Agreement. In Scenario C, ozone depletion peaks around the year 2000 and then the ozone layer slowly starts becoming thicker. Even in Scenario C, it takes at least a century for the ozone layer to return to its normal thickness, with chlorine completely eliminated from the stratosphere. The world is on a path that is clearly much closer to Scenario C than to Scenario A. Some uncertainty remains, however, about whether our actual situation is quite as optimistic as Scenario C.

Continuing Uncertainty

One major source of uncertainty is the level of compliance with the London Agreement. Some of the signa-

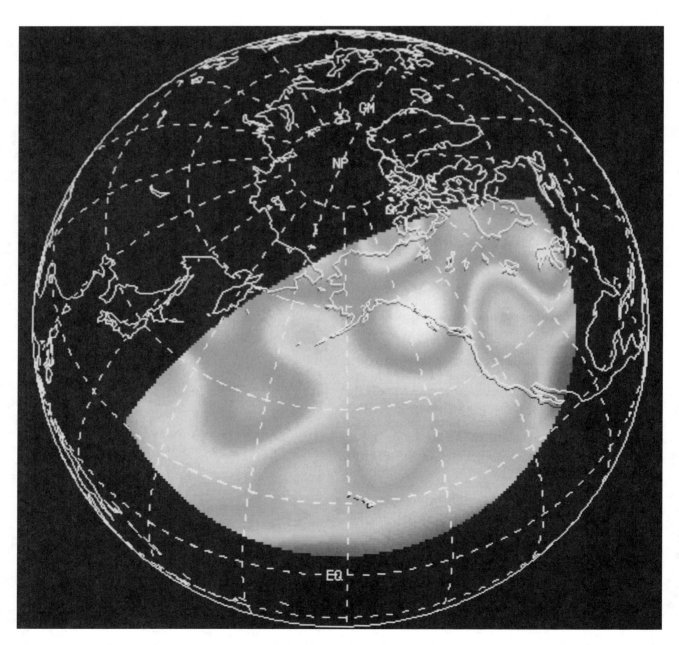

A computer image diagrams the ozone concentration in the Earth's atmosphere. Changes in the ozone layer can be caused by pollutants, seasonal temperature changes, shifting winds, changing ocean currents, latitude, and solar flare-ups. (NASA/Corbis)

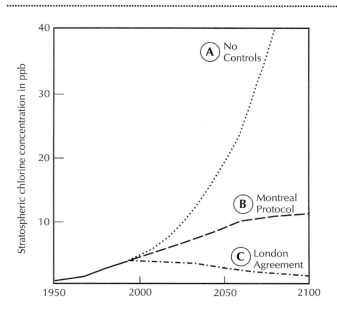

Figure 2. Alternative scenarios of stratospheric chlorine concentrations due to chlorofluorocarbon emissions.

tory nations, such as the nations of the former Soviet Union, may fail to meet the agreement's phase-out schedule, pleading economic difficulties. And many of the developing nations of the southern hemisphere and elsewhere have not yet signed the agreement or may find it difficult to comply. Actions by developing countries will be critical for the ozone future. China and India, for example, are just now trying to equip most households with their first refrigerators, which will produce enormous new demands for Freon unless CFC substitutes are utilized.

The other major source of uncertainty is our imperfect understanding of atmospheric physics and chemistry. In 1991, for example, NASA announced that new satellite measurements show that ozone depletion over populated areas in North America, Europe, and Central Asia is occurring twice as fast as previously predicted. Even more surprisingly, middle latitude ozone depletion in both the northern and southern hemispheres is extending, for the first time, into spring and summer months when radiation damage to people, crops, and other living things is likely to be greatest.

In 1993 NASA reported a startling decrease in the average amount of ozone over the planet as a whole. Over some parts of the temperate zone, ozone loss during the winter of 1992 was as severe as 14 percent. NASA researchers attributed this sudden change to the eruption of Mount Pinatubo in 1991, which injected large quantities of particulates into the stratosphere, thereby altering stratospheric wind and temperature

patterns. The researchers' computer models failed to predict the scale of Mount Pinatubo's effects on the ozone layer. As long as such large uncertainties and knowledge gaps remain, it is too soon to become complacent about having put the ozone crisis behind us.

Potential Impacts of Increased UV-B

Better instrumentation and longer periods of data collection are needed to assess how much UV radiation is actually reaching the ground as the ozone layer thins. If UV levels are increasing, they potentially pose serious health hazards for humans and other animals. The United Nations Environmental Programme predicts a 26 percent rise in the incidence of melanoma skin cancers worldwide if overall ozone levels drop 10 percent. Increased UV radiation may also suppress immune systems, reducing the body's ability to fight cancers and making people more susceptible to a wide range of infectious diseases. UV-B can also damage the retina and produce cataracts in the eye's lens, which can lead to blindness if untreated.

A growing body of evidence suggests that these potential hazards should be taken seriously. In Australia, for example, health officials report that skin cancers have tripled over the past decade. In Patagonia, at the tip of South America, there are reports of hunters finding blind rabbits and anglers catching blind fish. For many scientists, however, this kind of evidence is not yet convincing. Skin cancer rates have been climbing in many countries through most of this century, probably due to lifestyle changes such as wearing skimpier clothing in summer. As a result, it is extremely difficult to assess how much skin cancer is attributable to ozone depletion. Efforts to link the Patagonian fish and rabbit claims to ozone depletion also have failed. As the long-running debates over cigarette smoking show, it is not easy to demonstrate irrefutable links between potential health hazards and actual health impacts.

Despite the uncertainties, some governments are beginning to base policies on the assumption that actual health impacts are occurring. School children in New Zealand are urged to wear hats to school and play and eat their lunches in the shade of trees. In Australia, the government issues alerts when especially high UV levels are expected. Public service ads warn of the dangers of sunbathing, much as U.S. ads warn of the health hazards of smoking.

Just as worrisome is the threat to the world's food supply. When fifty crop varieties were exposed to a 50 percent increase in UV levels (much higher than scientists anticipate will actually occur), about two-thirds of the varieties displayed reduced yields. The most sensitive soybean varieties, for example, lost over 25 percent of their yield. UV-B can also kill phytoplankton and krill, which are at the base of most ocean food chains. Therefore large increases in UV-B could be expected to affect many populations of ocean life, possibly even causing maritime food shortages.

It is extremely difficult to assess how much skin cancer is attributable to ozone depletion.

As in the area of health hazards, it is not clear how serious these potential threats to the food supply are in practice. The most credible claim of an effect on food systems that has already occurred comes from studies showing a 6 to 12 percent decline in planktonic organisms in the ocean surrounding Antarctica where the ozone hole is open. Some Australian scientists believe that their crops of wheat, sorghum, and peas have already been affected, but this claim remains controversial.

Fortunately, organisms are not helpless against UV radiation. Both ocean algae (eaten by planktonic animals) and land plants produce a natural "sunscreen" molecules when exposed to increased UV. Nature's ingenious self-defense strategies will protect organisms up to a point, but no one knows just what that point is.

Lessons from the Ozone Problem

Because the ozone problem is relatively uncomplicated, with one major cause (CFCs) and one major effect (ozone depletion), it is relatively easy to draw lessons from it that may apply to other global environmental problems. One lesson is that where knowledge is incomplete, good research and constant monitoring of the actual state of the environment are critical. Agreements were possible on the ozone problem largely because reliable measurements and credible research findings influenced the views of the parties involved.

Another lesson is the importance of responsible action by all major actors. In the ozone controversy, environmentalists sometimes exaggerated, but on the whole, they based their case on research findings and played a critical role alerting the public and putting pressure on governments and corporations. Chemical companies at first acted as foot-draggers, but as the evidence for the role of CFCs in ozone depletion grew more convincing, some companies displayed extraordinary responsibility and environmental leadership. International organizations, such as UNEP, while limited in power, showed they can be very effective in prodding national governments to action and helping them negotiate. Scientists from many fields shifted their research priorities to focus on the ozone problem, and many took it upon themselves to communicate directly with the media and policy makers. Today, technologists and corporations are playing an indispensable role developing and marketing CFC alternatives that will be both profitable and good for the environment.

The most important lesson is simply that global environmental problems can be solved, despite vested interests, political conflicts, underdeveloped global institutions, and imperfect scientific understanding. Response to the ozone problem holds out the promise that it is possible to create a successful, sustainable society in harmony with the Earth.

[See also Acid Rain; Chemistry; Deforestation; Environment; Environmental Behavior; Environmental Ethics; Forestry; Global Environmental Problems; Global Warming; Oceans; Sustainability.]

BIBLIOGRAPHY

Benedick, Richard E. *Ozone Diplomacy.* Cambridge, MA: Harvard University Press, 1991.

Gleason, J. F., et al. "Record Low Global Ozone in 1992." *Science* 260 (1993): 523–526.

Leaf, Alexander. "Potential Health Effects of Global Climatic and Environmental Changes." *The New England Journal of Medicine* 321 (1989): 1577–1583.

Mathews, Jessica Tuchman, ed. *Preserving the Global Environment: The Challenge of Shared Leadership.* The American Assembly and World Resources Institute. New York: W. W. Norton, 1990.

Molina, Mario J., and Rowland, Sherwood F. "Stratospheric Sink for Chlorofluoromethanes: Chlorine Atomic Catalyzed Destruction of Ozone." *Nature 249* (1974):810.

Toon, Owen B., and Turco, Richard P. "Polar Stratospheric Clouds and Ozone Depletion." *Scientific American* (June 1991): 68–74.

— ROBERT L. OLSON

P

PACESETTER GOVERNMENTS

Governments that consistently pioneer public policy innovations at international, state, and local government levels are known as pacesetters, bellwethers, telltales, precursors, or just leading jurisdictions. During a given period of time, an identifiable vanguard of governments consistently attains prominence as the most adventuresome, experimental, and progressive. In short, there are a few identifiable governments that consistently tend to be the first to try the new.

Shifting Concepts from Theory to Practice

Implementation of public policy transforms proposals from concept to practice, from mere discussion to actual realization. Trial-and-error experimentation tests the merit of new concepts and their capacity to resolve problems. Unsound approaches become glaringly evident and the best concepts survive. Usually it is only a matter of time until proven approaches are copied elsewhere.

Telltale Diffusion Pattern

Diffusion—lead-lag relationships among public policy leaders, followers, and laggards—varies by jurisdictional level, time, and issue. Timelines graphically displaying past and present public policy responses on specific issues indicate the likelihood of further action among the remaining non-responding jurisdictions.

Implementation of public policy

transforms proposals from concept to practice,

from mere discussion to actual realization.

Timelines demonstrating the implementation of a specific law year by year typically show an S-curve pattern. This is so because lawmaking on any issue virtually never occurs everywhere at the same time. The sequence starts slowly with a few initial innovators, followed by a somewhat larger group of early adopters. Next comes a surge of followers during mid-sequence, and the timeline ends with a slow response or outright rejection by a relatively small group of laggards. One move is followed by another, an action-response pattern akin to a row of falling dominoes. A very few diehard holdouts may not respond at all.

State-level lawmaking by all or nearly all U.S. states typically requires a minimum of five to ten years, but the usual response period is from eleven to twenty-six years. The primary diffusion time for the surge of laws updating air pollution controls among the fifty U.S. states spanned a period of twenty-three years, for example, and the process is not entirely complete today.

Bellwether jurisdictions are not always the first to adopt every new law. Nevertheless, a pattern of early response to many issues over a long period of time is so consistent that ascertaining action taken on an issue in just a few key jurisdictions reliably indicates coming change elsewhere.

State Pacesetters

The leading wedge of early-adopter states include California, New York, and Massachusetts. Additional early adopters sometimes include Pennsylvania, Illinois, and New Jersey. During colonial times, Massachusetts typically was the usual first innovator. Over time, New York moved to the forefront. Following westward expansion, California became the pacesetter and it retains that leadership role today.

In addition to the usual early adopters, a number of other bellwethers for one or more issue-specific topics can be identified. Oregon, Washington, Minnesota, and Maine, for example, are pacesetters for environmental issues. Wisconsin has been a noted leader in the area of social welfare since the Progressive party era. Maryland has become a precursor for privacy issues. State leaders on other specific topics have been identified. Laggard state and local U.S. jurisdictions include Mississippi, Alabama, Arkansas, South Dakota, and Louisiana.

Local Bellwethers

City and county bellwethers in the United States include New York, Boston, and Berkeley, California.

Outside the United States, notable local-government pacesetters include Stockholm, Oslo, Copenhagen, Amsterdam, The Hague, Bonn, London, Brussels, Zürich, Basel, Bern, and Tokyo. Internationally, state or provincial bellwethers have included North Rhine–Westphalia in Germany, Saskatchewan in Canada, New South Wales in Australia, and St. Gallen in Switzerland.

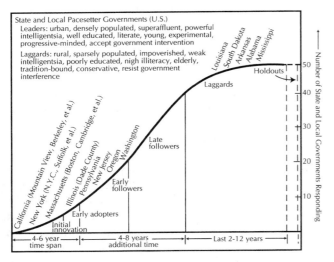

Figure 1. Molitor's multiple-timeline model of change—1. (Graham T. T. Molitor, Public Policy Forecasting, Inc.)

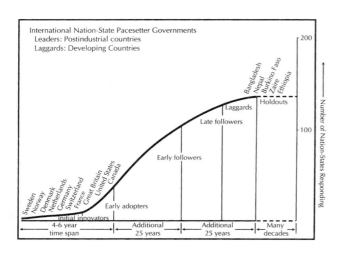

Figure 2. Molitor's multiple-timeline model of change—2. (Graham T. T. Molitor, Public Policy Forecasting, Inc.)

International Pacesetters

Response by nation-states also occurs in predictable patterns. Listed by region, pacesetter countries currently include Scandinavia (Sweden, Norway, Denmark); Western Europe (the Netherlands, Germany, Switzerland, France, Great Britain); North America (the United States, Canada). Developing nations in Asia (Bangladesh, Nepal, etc.) and Africa (Burkina Faso, Zaire, Ethiopia, etc.) and elsewhere are consistently among the laggards. Rank-ordered adoption of public policy frequently follows this very sequence. Principles proven effective by one nation often spread to other countries.

Additional countries occasionally among the early adopters include Australia, New Zealand, Japan, and Iceland. Eastern European nations (Poland, the Czech Republic, and the former U.S.S.R.) also have at times been leaders (at least in terms of their enactment of written laws) for some issues, such as certain environmental problems (pesticide pollution, the harmful effects of synthetic food colors, or electromagnetic field hazards).

Two Leading Bellwethers

Sweden and California are almost always in the forefront of change. By studying the responses of just these two jurisdictions, forecasters can anticipate similar developments likely to be undertaken elsewhere at a later date. Since the end of World War II, Sweden has consistently led all other jurisdictions in pioneering pacesetting public policy responses to most problems: social welfare programs, tax policies, environmental controls, consumer programs, video display tube safety, automotive safety, and prison reform. If not always first, Sweden has invariably been an early adopter. California, partly because it is a heterogeneous macrocosm for the nation as a whole, has served as the proving grounds for new policies in the United States.

Corroboration of Forecasts

Diffusion patterns among pacesetter jurisdictions pertain not only to legislation and regulation. Judicial decisions, quasi-legislative responses, self-government measures, voluntary accommodation patterns, contractual arrangements, and informal customs are among the social controls that follow similar patterns. The composite timelines of all such public policy responses among state and local, national and international jurisdictions provide an interesting study of the evolution of public policy. Change originates in creative minds, is focused by vision, advanced by deliberation, and confirmed by practical application, commencing with pacesetter jurisdictions.

[See also Agents of Change; Change; Environmental Policy Changes; Forecasting, Deterministic; Forecasting Methods; Laws, Evolution of; Public Policy Change.]

BIBLIOGRAPHY

Coates, Joseph F., et al. *Issues Management: How You Can Plan, Organize, and Manage for the Future.* Mt. Airy, MD: Lomond Publications, 1986.

Crawford, Charles, and Molitor, Graham T. T. *The Evolution of Electro-magnetic Fields as a Public Policy Issue: Analysis and Response Options.* Washington, DC: Hill and Knowlton, 1991.

Molitor, Graham T. T. "Look Out: Here Comes Consumerism Again!" *Mobius* 8/4 (Fall 1989): 7–11.

———. "Plotting Patterns of Change." *Enterprise* 8/2 (March 1984): 4–9.

———. "Swedish Benefits Today: U.S. Benefits Tomorrow?" *Innovations* (March 1990): 6–18.

— GRAHAM T. T. MOLITOR

PARADIGM SHIFT.

See GLOBAL TURNING POINTS; MULTIFOLD TREND.

PARASENSORY PHENOMENA

Parasensory, "paranormal," or "psi" phenomena are phenomena that *appear to be* in some sense beyond the senses. The study of such phenomena is variously termed "parasensory investigation," "parapsychology," or "psi research."

The range of such phenomena is vast, and the boundary between "normal" and "paranormal" is somewhat indistinct. There are usually considered to be three main categories of (purported) paranormal phenomena:

1. *Entrasensory perception:* Apparent perception "beyond the senses." Examples include telepathic communication, clairvoyant remote viewing, remote diagnosis, precognition, retrocognition, and verisimilar memories of another life.
2. *Psychokinesis:* Apparent influence of the physical environment by mental states. Examples include remote actuation, poltergeist, teleportation, levitation (of one's own body), psychic surgery, and psychic healing, "thought photography."
3. *Evidence of disembodied self:* Examples include spirit possession, hauntings, spirit communication, some poltergeists, apparitions of the dead.

Parapsychology is typically assumed to be concerned with only the first two categories.

Much of the history of research in this area can be characterized as follows:

- The phenomena are considered paranormal, which in effect means that the phenomena do not appear to be explicable in known or imaginable scientific causal terms, and they tend to be sporadic in occurrence.
- Research has tended to focus on one of two types of situations—either those where a "star performer" seems to be able to produce "spectacular" phenomena more or less at will, or where low-level phenomena seemingly produced by persons not specially endowed can be studied statistically.
- Both kinds of research result tend to be unconvincing to the "tough-minded" scientist, for different reasons—the first because of nonreproducibility and the second because of methodological questions.
- The chief factor behind the unfriendly reception to research in psi phenomena by the scientific and medical communities has been the fact that the meaning and significance people tended to attach to these experiences seemed to clash so directly with prevailing assumptions about the nature of scientific reality.

The possibility of a change in this situation seems now on the horizon. W. V. O. Quine, a major figure in the recent philosophy of science, has given us an important clue regarding what to do about these anomalous phenomena. He argued that the scientific explanation for any phenomenon is embedded in a theoretical network that involves multitudinous assumptions, including:

- assumptions involved in observation of the phenomenon
- hypotheses about the context of the phenomenon
- underlying theoretical hypotheses
- "basic laws" of the pertinent area of science
- the accepted nature of scientific methodology
- epistemological assumptions underlying scientific inquiry
- ontological assumptions about the basic nature of reality

When there is an "anomaly," or a failure of observations to conform to scientific expectations, it means that *somewhere* in that network there is a falsity. There is no way to tell just where in the theoretical network the falsity lies. Thus in the face of an anomaly we must consider revising any or all elements of the network. There is ultimately no such thing as a "crucial experiment" to "prove" a scientific hypothesis; the best that can be said is that a hypothesis is not challenged by any known anomalies. A consequence of Quine's view is that even our epistemological convictions about how we acquire knowledge, and about the nature of explanation, justification, and confirmation, are subject to revision and correction.

It is precisely to that point that we are brought by the impressive amount of empirical and anecdotal data regarding psi phenomena. For an assortment of reasons, Western science by the eighteenth century had adopted *an ontological assumption of separateness:* the separability of observer from observed; of humankind from nature; of mind from matter; of science from religion; the separateness of "fundamental particles" from one another; the separability of the parts of a system or organism with the assumption that one can understand the whole through understanding the parts; the separateness of scientific disciplines; the separateness of investigators competing over who was the first discoverer.

The assumption of separateness leads to the myth of the "objective observer" and to the search for reductionist explanations. It implies the locality of causes; that is, it precludes "action at a distance," either in space or time. It implies the *epistemological assumption* that our sole empirical basis for constructing a science is the data from our physical senses (positivism). These assumptions taken together have been termed the position of *logical empiricism.* By the middle of this century there was almost complete consensus that these are the proper foundation assumptions for science.

Scientists typically take these ontological and epistemological premises to be inviolate, to be an inherent and ineluctable part of the definition of science, rather than the optional assumptions which in fact they are. These underlying assumptions (which have been somewhat modified with the advent of quantum physics) are put in question by the data of psi research. More importantly, the worldview based on these assumptions seems to deny the validity of much of our everyday experience, including the sense of conscious awareness, of volition or "free will," of discoverable meaning and purpose in life, of apparently teleological influences in nature. Few have dared to suggest a reassessment of these most basic underlying ontological and epistemological assumptions, yet that is where we now must seek the resolution of the puzzle posed by psi phenomena.

Heretofore science has started with a limiting set of assumptions and then found it necessary to deny the possibility of a host of reported phenomena that do not fit within those limits.

The above arguments suggest the need for an "extended" science based upon (a) an *ontological assumption of oneness, wholeness,* the interconnectedness of everything, and (b) an *epistemological assumption that we contact reality in not one but two ways*—one of these being through physical sense data (forming the basis of normal science); the other through being ourselves part of the oneness, that is, through a deep intuitive "inner knowing." This "wholeness-based" science would regard present science as useful but having limited application.

Imagine, in accordance with this proposition, starting from the holistic assumption that everything—not only physical things but all things experienced, including sensations, emotions, feelings, motivations, thoughts—is really part of a single unity. Everything is interconnected in a *ground of being* (not really harder to imagine than everything being connected by an all-pervasive gravitational field). It is a bit like your experience of your own mind, wherein different parts of the mind may be relatively isolated from one another, each doing its own thing, and yet in the end your mind, conscious and unconscious, is experienced as a single, connected unity. One part of your mind hides things from another part of your mind (repression); different parts may be

relatively autonomous with respect to one another (multiple personality syndrome being an extreme example); one part of your mind may communicate falsehood to another part—yet there is no doubt it is one mind.

Thus in a "wholeness-based" science apparent telepathic communication between two individuals does not appear as "anomalous"; rather, the puzzle is why one's mind is not perpetually cluttered by information coming in from other minds. Psychokinesis—mind affecting a remote part of the environment—is no more anomalous than volition—mind affecting the muscles in my arm and hand. Similarly, with the "oneness" assumption, one does not find other states of consciousness, teleological influences, "meaningful coincidences" (see Beloff, 1977), and so on, to be "anomalous." If volition or purpose or meaning exist in myself, then *ipso facto* they exist in the universe; there is nothing to be "explained," only explored.

If you try to imagine that the universe might be something like this, the first thing you notice is that it *feels* right. Every one of us has had trouble trying to feel at home in the universe that science pictured to us. We just never could feel as though consciousness and volition were simply illusions; as though our deeply felt values and purposes are simply made up; as though we humans exist in a meaningless universe having evolved through random mechanical processes; as though love, truth, beauty, and goodness have no more foundation than our hunger pains and sexual urges. How much more true it feels to imagine being at home in the universe, part of a meaningful whole. (Why "meaningful"? Because if I find meaning in myself, then by the basic unitive assumption, meaning exists in the universe.)

The significance of psi phenomena in the context of science has been that they seemed to challenge a view of science that some saw as inadequate. A "wholeness-based" science resolves that difficulty. Certain aspects of the unity that is the whole will continue to be quite profitably studied by means of "separateness-based science"; however, that kind of science—as only part of a more extended science—would no longer have the authority to insist that we are here, solely through random causes, in a meaningless universe. Likewise it would no longer be able to assert that our consciousness is "merely" the chemical and physical processes of the brain or to suggest that claimed psi phenomena could not have occurred "because they violate scientific laws."

Heretofore science has started with a limiting set of assumptions and has then found it necessary to deny the validity and even the possibility of a host of reported phenomena that do not fit within those limits. A tremendous amount of effort has gone on within science defending the barricades against, or explaining away, these outcasts—a category containing paranormal events like "miraculous" healings and "psi phenomena," but also including more ordinary experiences such as volition, selective attention, and the hunger for meaning.

Rather than having to defend against the anomalous, "wholeness-based science" would incorporate the assumption that any class of inner experiences that have been reported, or of phenomena that have been observed, down through the ages and across cultures, apparently in some sense exist, and have a *face validity* that cannot be denied.

[See also Conscious Evolution; Global Turning Points; Holistic Beliefs; Mind: New Modes of Thinking; Values; Values, Nonwestern.]

BIBLIOGRAPHY

Beloff, John. "Psi Phenomena: Causal versus Acausal Interpretation." *Journal of the Society for Psychical Research* 49/773 (September 1977).

Eisenbud, Jule. *Parapsychology and the Unconscious.* Berkeley, CA: North Atlantic Books, 1983.

Guiley, Rosemary E. *Harper's Encyclopedia of Mystical and Paranormal Experience.* San Francisco: Harper-Collins, 1991.

Jahn, Robert, and Dunne, Brenda. *Margins of Reality: The Role of Consciousness in the Physical World.* New York: Harcourt Brace Jovanovich, 1987.

Leshan, Lawrence. *The Science of the Paranormal.* London: Thorsons, 1987.

Mitchell, Edgar D., ed. *Psychic Exploration: A Challenge for Science.* New York: G. P. Putnam's Sons, 1974.

Peat, F. David. *Synchronicity: The Bridge Between Matter and Mind.* New York: Bantam, 1987.

— WILLIS W. HARMAN

PARKS AND WILDERNESS

The United States gave the world a model when it made Yellowstone Park the first national park in 1872. Since then, nations around the globe also have protected areas of outstanding natural beauty or scientific uniqueness. Earlier actions by monarchs had designated lands for their personal pleasure or for state purposes, but national parks were different in that they were established for the benefit of the people.

Overall, Americans enjoy a rich mosaic of public and private lands that provide scenery, open space, recreation, and nature protection. Congress broadened the concept of national parks over the years. Now there are national monuments, recreation areas, historical sites (or historical parks), seashores, lakeshores, trails, and wild and scenic rivers, among others. In 1964 Congress established the National Wilderness Preservation System, intended to maintain tracts of federal land in un-

spoiled condition. Much of this expansion was driven by the 1962 recommendations of the Outdoor Recreation Resources Review Commission (ORRRC), established by law in 1958 to make studies and recommendations that would help ensure that accessible high-quality outdoor recreation resources are available.

State and local governments also contribute many outdoor recreational resources: parks, forests, beaches, playgrounds, ball fields, and wilderness camping areas. Following ORRC recommendations, many states created river and trail systems paralleling those of the federal government.

Vast federal acreage dedicated to agricultural commodity production, forestry, or wildlife protection supplement these park and recreation lands. The national forests, wildlife refuges, and public domain lands serve both commodity and conservation roles, as well as serving the demands for outdoor recreational activities. Many designated wilderness areas, trails, or wild and scenic rivers are found on these lands managed by the U.S. departments of Agriculture and the Interior.

The private sector also contributes importantly to the variety of outdoor recreation lands. Private owners develop facilities—such as golf courses—that the federal government does not consider appropriate in national parks or recreation areas, or that local governments may find too expensive to build and maintain. Similarly, more elaborate facilities are often found at commercial campgrounds and resorts than at public areas.

Some nongovernmental organizations, such as the Nature Conservancy, Conservation Fund, and Audubon Society, also protect natural areas. These organizations, using funds from members or donors, buy lands to protect their natural resources. Some public access to these lands is allowed if it does not threaten plants, wildlife, or other fragile resources.

These private lands help fill a gap in outdoor opportunities. In the United States most federal lands are situated in the West, relatively removed from centers of population, leaving the rest of the country with generally smaller federal land units, primarily national forests and state or local parks. Private lands thus meet open space needs nearer to population concentrations.

The political process largely drives the supply and use of public land. During the 1960s and 1970s, advocates got Congress to designate significant acreages of federal land as protected; millions of acres of public-domain and national forest lands were thus converted to national parks, recreation areas, and wilderness. Congress also funded the purchase of private lands to add to the national recreation estate at federal, state, and local levels. Environmental groups supported legislation that emphasized resource protection over general recreational use of federal lands. Budget constraints and differing priorities during the Reagan administration limited federal funds available for land acquisition at all government levels.

Just as the supply and diversity of park lands has increased over time, so have the demands people place on these resources. Technology, social trends, and demographics drive these new uses; these factors are likely to cause even more changes in the future.

The growth of dual-income households has eroded the time available for recreational activities.

Technological changes include the development of new materials or applications that make outdoor recreation more convenient: lightweight tents and packs, freeze-dried foods, comfortable but protective clothing, and high-performance sporting equipment.

Crossover technology from military applications plays an important role in changing outdoor recreation. The first, perhaps, was the conversion of World War II life rafts to recreational use on white-water rivers, now a major recreational activity for all ages. Other transfers include snowmobiles and four-wheel-drive vehicles. More recently, new night vision gear and global-positioning satellite equipment to maintain precise tabs on one's location in the wilderness or anywhere have begun to open up new areas for nocturnal recreational activity.

Social trends include a concern for protection of the environment, maintenance of health and fitness, and a perceived decline in the amount of leisure time. These trends impose differing demands pressures on park resources and their management. A major need is for more and better park and outdoor recreational opportunities closer to where people live. These demands may influence building and development patterns in the future to ensure that parks are part of any successful new real estate project.

The aging and cultural diversification of the population are dominant demographic trends affecting the use of recreation lands. In the past, an aging population made fewer demands for outdoor recreation opportunities. Now, however, health and fitness concerns are keeping individuals involved in many activities later in life. When visiting parks far from home, these older users may prefer comfortable lodge-type accommodations or facilities for recreational vehicles, amenities disliked by preservation groups. People of different ethnic and cultural backgrounds may have different expecta-

tions of parks. At the very least, there is a need for park managers to learn these expectations and communicate with these new clients.

Changes in family composition and the issue of economic disparity are other important demographic and financial considerations in assessing the demand for park and recreational resources in the next century. The growth of dual-income households has eroded the time available for recreational activities. Single-parent households often suffer from both loss of time and money; this can doubly constrain the ability to participate in many recreational activities. Increased supervised recreational activity may be an emerging response to these trends, although local budget problems may limit this amenity.

It was a political process inspired by a vision for the future that provided our heritage of federal, state, and local parks. Can that process continue to adequately provide for tomorrow's park and recreation needs?

[See also Aging of the Population; Deforestation; Forestry; Green Revolution; Natural Resources, Use of; Outdoor Recreation and Leisure Pursuits; Resources; Theme Parks and Organized Attractions.]

BIBLIOGRAPHY

Endicott, Eve, ed. *Land Conservation through Public/Private Partnerships.* Washington, DC: Island Press, 1993.
Frome, Michael. *Regreening the National Parks.* Tucson, AZ: University of Arizona Press, 1992.
McNeely, Jeffrey A. "The Future of National Parks." *Environment* (January–February 1990): 16–20.

                                                    – GEORGE H. SIEHL

PARTICIPATIVE MANAGEMENT

The concept of participation in decision making, or PDM, was popularized in North America as a result of experiments with school children conducted by psychologist Kurt Lewin and his colleagues in the late 1930s. These studies claimed to show the superiority of groups that were democratically led over those autocratically led, especially when the leader was absent. The PDM idea was reinforced by a widely publicized study conducted in 1948 in a pajama factory by Coch and French, which claimed to show that PDM reduced resistance to change among employees. Although both claims were later disputed, these studies were widely influential.

After World War II, the idea of democratic leadership spread to Western Europe, mainly in the form of official, often legally mandated, worker representation systems, that guaranteed direct or indirect employee-representation on boards of directors or other decision-making bodies in business. These systems differ from country to country and are known by various names (e.g., codetermination, joint consultation, works councils). PDM has also been used in non-European countries. In Israel PDM was advocated mainly by the Kibbutz, as well as the labor or Histadrut sector, which owns and manages many companies. In Japan, PDM is fostered by an intensive, multidirectional communication system, although this takes place within a strongly hierarchical and status-focused organizational structure.

In Canada and the United States, the PDM movement spread informally through training managers in participative leadership methods; the use of management by objectives (MBO), with objectives being set jointly by superior and subordinate; the adoption of productivity-sharing plans such as the Scanlon Plan, which include mechanisms for increasing employee involvement; the quality movement; and employee ownership plans (e.g., ESOP's). American unions, however, were very reluctant participants in the PDM movement, fearing that it would coopt their members and undermine the unions' traditional adversarial role.

PDM Research

In the United States there now are, roughly speaking, two schools of thought about PDM. One school views it as a "moral imperative" and thus eschews any need to study the phenomenon empirically. The other school views PDM as one of many management tools and seeks to understand the actual conditions under which PDM will be most effective.

Those who favor the empirical approach find that PDM is much less effective in raising morale and productivity than has been assumed by people in academia and industry. Many PDM studies, including the early ones done in the United States and noted earlier, were widely criticized on methodological grounds. Even ignoring these criticisms, the average productivity increase resulting from PDM programs in organizational settings is only about 0.5 percent. Studies of participation in setting goals found that PDM results in no greater commitment to goals than simply telling people what goals to achieve accompanied by a rationale. PDM, however, sometimes leads to higher goals being set, thus stimulating higher productivity.

More recent studies suggest, however, that the benefits of PDM may be more cognitive than motivational—that is, PDM may foster better performance not so much by raising commitment (which can be achieved through other means such as visionary leadership and incentives) as by facilitating the exchange of information between supervisor and subordinate, leading in turn to better decision making.

This finding has an important caveat. Information exchange will be most beneficial when subordinates possess knowledge not possessed by supervisors. This contingency does not limit the effective use of PDM as much as one might think, however, because subordinates often know a lot more about many aspects of their own, specific jobs than do their bosses. It is widely believed (not without cause) that many managers underestimate the knowledge and capability of their subordinates. On the other hand, it would obviously not be very beneficial to practice PDM in cases where subordinates clearly lack relevant knowledge.

PDM Today

PDM is evolving in North America, and to an extent in other countries, toward delegation of responsibility to self-managing teams and work groups. Such groups make decisions on their own about their own jobs (e.g., scheduling, assignment of tasks) and the coordination of their work with that of other teams. After appropriate training, such groups may also discover ways to improve work processes and to improve work quality. They may also have direct contact with customers and responsibility for customer service. In addition, individual training in self-management has been used to overcome such seemingly intractable problems as absenteeism.

More business decisions will be made by small, autonomous work teams which will be connected to the organization through high technology information and communication systems.

The trend toward self-management has coincided with the trend in organizational design toward flatter, leaner structures. Due to rapid changes in technology and increased global competition, modern organizations need to be closer to the customer, faster moving, and more flexible than in the past. Autonomous work teams, bound together by a common vision and careful measurement of work performance accompanied by clear standards, help to fulfill these needs. Thus far, the results look very promising.

The main obstacle to this trend is the reluctance of some managers to give up their traditional power, either because they like the power or because they do not trust workers to be either responsible or knowledgeable.

Strong organizational leadership is needed to overcome such reluctance.

PDM in the Future

The workplace trend toward empowerment at every level is likely to continue. Not only is this virtually necessitated by the realities of modern, global business, but workers are becoming more educated and well-trained. The labor force is becoming increasingly dominated by skilled knowledge workers who need to engage routinely in creative problem-solving in order to be effective. It is reasonable to forecast that more and more business decisions will be made by small, autonomous work teams which will be connected to other parts of the organization and customers through high technology information and communication systems and held accountable for their results by means of performance standards. Of course, not everyone likes to work continuously in teams, not everyone wants responsibility, and not everyone in authority wants to give it. Thus, we should continue to see variety in organizational forms and perhaps even a backlash against too much "groupism" due to its sometimes pernicious effects on independent thinking and healthy conflict.

The irony of these changes is that PDM itself increasingly will become an inadequate concept for describing the new business realities. PDM refers to joint-decision making, but autonomous work teams are actually delegated full responsibility for their work processes and typically have no supervisors at all. Furthermore, performance standards will probably be imposed by top management based on competitive necessity (as is common now) and not set jointly. Finally, the concept of continuous communication in all directions will replace the idea of participation between supervisor and subordinate.

[See also Business Governance; Democratic Process; Governance; Social Democracy.]

BIBLIOGRAPHY

Lathan, G.; Winters, D.; and Locke, E. "Cognitive and Motivational Effects of Participation: A Mediator Study." *Journal of Organizational Behavior* 15 (1994): 49–63.

Locke, E. and Latham, G. *A Theory of Goal Setting and Task Performance.* Englewood Cliffs, NJ: Prentice Hall, 1990.

Locke, E., and Schweiger, D. "Participation in Decision Making: One More Look." In B. Staw, ed. *Research in Organizational Behavior*, vol. 1. Greenwich, CT: JAI Press, 1979.

Manz, C., and Sims, H. *Business Without Bosses: How Self-Managed Teams Are Producing High Performance Companies.* New York: Wiley, 1993.

— EDWIN A. LOCKE

GARY P. LATHAN

PEACEKEEPING

The term *peacekeeping* has at least five different interpretations, each one depending on a particular concept of peace, as illustrated in Figure 1.

Peacekeeping as War Prevention

If peace is seen as the absence of war, then peacekeeping requires the use, or threat of use, of military power. During the Cold War, both the United States and the Soviet Union adopted the theory of nuclear deterrence to keep the peace. They believed this standoff was the only strategy that would prevent the other from attacking. Many analysts argued that the common policy of Mutually Assured Destruction (MAD), a policy based on the enormous destructive capability of the 50,000 nuclear warheads that were then in existence, prevented a war between the two sides. The motto of the U.S. Strategic Air Command, "Peace is our profession," enshrines this view of peacekeeping between states.

With the end of the Cold War, the world has seen a dramatic increase in internal conflicts or civil wars within states. For example, in 1992, thirty-nine of the forty armed conflicts fought in the world were internal conflicts. In states such as Somalia, Russia, Mexico, and the former Yugoslavia, military force has been used in internal conflicts, either as a deterrent, or in peacekeeping operations.

Peacekeeping and the International System

This view of peacekeeping arose in the 1960s as a result of U.N. military interventions to help maintain cease-fires, assist in troop withdrawals, or provide a buffer between opposing forces. Here peace-keeping uses armed personnel, such as the U.N. "blue helmets," but does not provide an overwhelming military force. They carry light arms and are allowed to use minimum force only in self-defense; their effectiveness depends on the moral authority of the United Nations and the expressed concern of the international system. This approach assumes peace requires a balance of military, political, economic, and social forces operating across a range of levels from the local community to the international system.

There has been a dramatic increase in U.N. peacekeeping operations since the end of the Cold War. From 1948 to May 1993, more than 600,000 soldiers and civilians have served in twenty-eight U.N. peacekeeping operations. Fifteen of these have been established since 1988, and the number of personnel involved has increased from a maximum of about 20,000 in any one year prior to 1990 to more than 80,000 in May 1993.

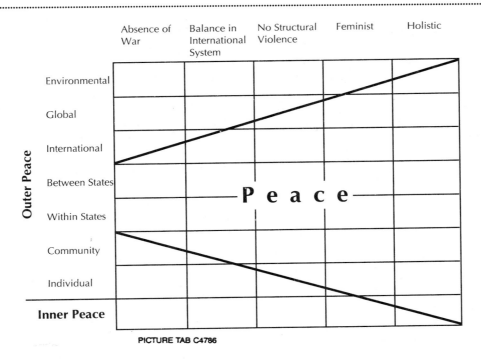

Figure 1. Elements of peace.

Peacekeeping and Structural Violence

There has also been a steady shift away from the primarily military goals of keeping the warring parties apart toward a concern with combating "structural violence"—the social, political, and economic structures that contribute to poverty, starvation, and diminished life expectancy. U.N. policy endorses this approach: "Complicated military tasks must be complemented by measures to strengthen institutions, encourage political participation, protect human rights, organize elections and promote economic and social development" (United Nations, 1993, p. 8).

With the emergence of truly global actors—such as transnational corporations, whose economic interests transcend those of any nation or state, and international nongovernmental organizations (INGOs), whose members act as world citizens—peacekeeping operations have broadened their mandate to include a concern for both physical and structural violence. This has meant that peacekeeping operations increasingly "require peacekeeping troops to work closely with civilian police, elected officials, human rights observers, refugee specialists and many others from a variety of nations" (Smith, 1993, p. ix).

Peacekeeping in the latter 1990s requires the participation of many different groups to both deal with immediate crises, such as humanitarian aid, and longer-term problems, such as creating conditions for peace and stability in the country concerned. It also involves international cooperation to combat terrorism.

Peacekeeping in a Feminist Framework

Feminist definitions of peace include the abolition of violence against women and children in the home and on the streets, as well as doing away with patriarchal economic, political, and social structures—structural violence—that directly affect people at the individual level. Peacekeeping in this sense includes a broad range of "conflict resolution" and counseling procedures that are designed to control, or prevent, physical violence against individual women, men, and children, as well as encourage the evolution of new customs and mores that change traditional gender roles.

Peacekeeping thus involves the police force, the courts, schools, and other community agencies that are working to stop wife beating, gang violence, and other forms of local violence that directly affect individuals. Feminist definitions also include a concern with all of the other levels of analysis, from community to global, and with all forms of violence against and between people.

Holistic Peacekeeping

Holistic interpretations can be expanded to apply the peacekeeping concept still further to include peace with the environment. This means that peacekeeping would be carried out in an environmentally sound fashion. Holistic peacekeeping would also be based on a more balanced peace concept that includes both outer and inner peace. While outer peace focuses on events in the material world, such as war, starvation, or pollution, inner peace is a spiritual state of oneness that can be developed through various spiritual practices, such as meditation or prayer.

If peace is seen as both inner and outer,

balanced in harmony, then peacekeeping

will require both action in the outer material world

and exploration of the inner spiritual one.

If peace is seen as both inner and outer, balanced in harmony, then peacekeeping will require both action in the outer material world and exploration of the inner spiritual one. The relationship between inner peace and outer peace is of fundamental importance for holistic peacekeeping, as illustrated by Gandhi's approach to nonviolent action, which involved a period of inner searching and purification prior to action in the outer world.

Conclusion

Peacekeeping seems to be evolving from the mainly military interpretation associated with peace as the absence of war, to the broader structural-violence interpretation that emerged in the 1990s. In the future, the term may expand further and be based on feminist definitions of peace, in which the abolition of all forms of violence against people is required, and holistic interpretations that balance the demands of both outer and inner notions of peace.

[See also International Governance and Regional Authorities; International Tensions.]

BIBLIOGRAPHY

Childers, Erskine, and Urquhart, Brian. *Renewing the United Nations System.* Uppsala: Dag Hammarskjöld Foundation, 1994.
Durch, William J. *The Evolution of UN Peacekeeping: Case Studies and Comparative Analysis.* New York: St. Martin's Press, 1993.
Smith, Hugh, ed. *Peacekeeping: Challenges for the Future.* Canberra: Australian Defence Studies Centre, 1993.
United Nations Department of Public Information. *The Blue Helmets: A Review of United Nations Peace-keeping.* New York: United Nations Publications, 1985.
———. *United Nations Peacekeeping.* New York: United Nations Publications, 1993.

— PAUL SMOKER

PEDIATRICS.

See CHILD CARE.

PERFORMING ARTS: DANCE AND THEATER

The performing arts mirror trends in society. Recessions, new technologies, political conservatism, an aging society, rapid social change, multiculturalism, and even a new understanding of nature all have challenged the arts and offer creative opportunities.

In *Megatrends 2000,* futurists John Naisbitt and Patricia Aburdene predicted that the 1990s would see a renaissance in the arts and that "the arts will gradually replace sports as society's primary leisure activity." Trends supporting this prediction include the increased education and economic influence of women and older people, who tend to prefer cultural activities over sports and the recognition among corporations and communities of the economic benefits of the arts, including more jobs, tax revenues, urban renewal, and tourism income.

Despite record receipts at the box office—attributable more to skyrocketing ticket prices than to increases in attendance or in numbers of new productions—the recession of the early 1990s struck fear into the hearts of arts' producers. New musicals were especially hard hit by the recession. Veteran Broadway director/producer Harold Prince has suggested that one reason musicals have suffered is that Hollywood films and television have been siphoning off the best creative talents for the past thirty years. Enormous investments are required for presenting musicals, and so there is no room for failure—and no second chances for composers, lyricists, and playwrights to learn from their mistakes. Thus, Broadway is rapidly becoming a repository for safe, familiar material, especially revivals and "musicalized" versions of such popular movies as *Sunset Boulevard* and *Kiss of the Spider Woman.*

Future creativity and growth of new audiences will come from outside Broadway, in the more than 200 professional theaters around the United States. But these smaller companies, too, face several challenges. Where will the new plays come from when all the best writers are in Hollywood? What will happen to acting when skills such as projecting the voice are being lost in the age of microphones? Where are the new audiences going to come from if parents don't take their children to the theater? Where will the leadership come from when people must devote years of life to a small theater and still have to struggle to make ends meet? And where will the money come from? Public and private support for the arts has dwindled. Another challenge is where tomorrow's actors, dancers, playwrights, choreographers, and directors will come from when so many of the most able young talents are succumbing to AIDS.

Addressing these challenges will require creativity—which is of course the lifeblood of performing artists. For instance, the challenge of AIDS has led to a burst of creativity in new plays about the disease, and the challenge of finding jobs in the theater has led to a resurgence of one-person plays.

The future of the performing arts will rely on nurturing tomorrow's artists and audiences. Many theater and dance groups work with children. For instance, former dancer Jacques d'Amboise's National Dance Institute has taught dancing to more than 100,000 schoolchildren, primarily in inner-city schools. And the 1994 Goals 2000 education program promises to sharply increase the role of the arts in U.S. school curricula.

The Future of Theater

Theater will continue to stretch its boundaries, incorporating not only dance and music but the visual and electronic arts. Advances in virtual reality will make some forms of theater interactive, allowing audiences to participate in or create an individual theatrical experience. New scenarios for plays could be written, based on psychological and behavioral databases for individual characters, and the audience could vote on Hamlet's fate: "Press 'one' for 'To Be'; press 'two' for 'Not to Be.'"

Experimental theater has challenged the formalism of the Aristotelian aesthetic for at least a century, offering a nonlinear drama of existence that more closely "imitates" what we perceive as reality. Aristotle's emphasis on plot led to the structure used in much of Western drama up to the twentieth century—that is, an action culminating in a single climactic moment. However, modern theater gives equal weight to isolated moments and keeps the audience in the present. This new "aesthetic of the event" is more in tune with the information age. Audiences raised on *Sesame Street* and MTV, where everything seems to happen at once, are becoming increasingly "omniattentive," capable of perceiving many things at once and discontinuously.

As theater moves more toward an aesthetic of experience, the text of a play, considered a work of art or literature on its own in the Aristotelian aesthetic, will increasingly be used only as a starting point. Some performances may not even begin with a script—*A Chorus Line,* for instance, was developed in workshops after an all-night discussion among some eighteen dancers. Acting styles for stage work now develop from improvisa-

tional techniques (responding to experiences as they occur) rather than Method acting (a naturalistic style more appropriate to film).

Still, the Aristotelian structure of the well-made play will not disappear, and the plays of Shakespeare will live for centuries to come, though adapted to future tastes and preferences. The text may make a comeback as tomorrow's audiences become suspicious of the image—which can be infinitely manipulated by technology—and long for great words spoken by resonant, well-trained voices.

The Future of Dance

Dance, as one top arts administrator noted, "arguably is the least popular of the art forms in terms of ticket-buying public." The challenge of bringing in audiences has led to dramatic changes in philosophy, and notable ballet companies have commissioned works by rock musicians to give dance a wider and more youthful appeal.

Audiences are becoming increasingly "omniattentive," capable of perceiving many things at once and discontinuously.

Like theater, dance is exploring a new aesthetic based on contemporary values. Young choreographers frequently reject gender stereotyping; the corps de ballet in Mark Morris's *The Hard Nut*—a reinterpretation of *The Nutcracker*—is an equal opportunity employer for male "snowflakes."

Choreographers have also rejected the linear progression of the Aristotelian aesthetic, using chance methods of construction and stringing disparate elements together. Merce Cunningham's *Breakers* is danced to an electronic score that the audience *and* the dancers heard for the first time on opening night, defying a clear relationship between dance, dancers, and music.

Cunningham is among those using the computer software LifeForms to store, retrieve, and manipulate movement passages. Computer and video technology will allow both the preservation of classic choreography and the creation of new works. Classically trained dancers such as Mikhail Baryshnikov have created a bridge between the old and the new. Baryshnikov, founder of the White Oak Dance Project, draws much of the troupe's repertoire from modern-dance choreographers, using his fame to widen the younger creators' circle of admirers and establish them for the future.

[See also Arts; Creativity; Mass Culture and Arts; Music; Public Assistance Programs; Visual Arts.]

BIBLIOGRAPHY

Larijani, L. Casey. *The Virtual Reality Primer.* New York: McGraw-Hill, 1994.

Naisbitt, John, and Aburdene, Patricia. "Renaissance in the Arts." In *Megatrends 2000: Ten New Directions for the 1990s.* New York: Morrow, 1990.

Prince, Harold. "The Good New Days." *American Theatre* (January 1993).

Schmitt, Natalie Crohn. *Actors and Onlookers: Theater and Twentieth-Century Scientific Views of Nature.* Evanston, IL: Northwestern University Press, 1990.

— CYNTHIA G. WAGNER

PERFUMES.

See FRAGRANCES.

PERSONAL TRANSPORT

To many people, the phrase *personal vehicle* is synonymous with *automobile.* Yet a look at the global transportation picture reveals that far more of humanity relies not on engine power, but on human power—in the form of bicycles, cycle rickshas, and similar two- and three-wheelers. Bicycles in Asia alone outnumber the world's 460 million automobiles. This gap is sure to widen in the future, since annual car production worldwide is barely one-third that of bicycles.

The bicycle's fate has been intertwined with the automobile's ever since they were both invented in the late nineteenth century. By demanding that the government build a road network, U.S. bicyclists in the 1880s literally paved the way for the motorcar, which in subsequent decades would supersede pedal power. Today in the United States, as in most countries, the extent of bicycle use is closely tied to automobile ownership. With nearly one bicycle for every two people, the country has one of the world's largest bicycle fleets. But since even more Americans own cars, few rely on cycling for everyday transport.

Pedal power is most important in Asia, where bicycles provide personal transport in much the same manner as private cars do in the United States, rickshas provide taxi service, and heavy-duty tricycles do the work of light trucks. In many cities, nonmotorized vehicles account for up to 60 percent of total trips. Much of the goods transport in China and India is by human-powered three-wheelers—which can haul loads of up to half a ton. In Bangladesh, these vehicles transport a greater total of tonnage than motor vehicles do.

Elsewhere in the developing world, bicycles are at once indispensable and undervalued. Governments in Africa and Latin America have long ignored non-motorized vehicles in transport policy, adopting the motorized bias of aid-donor countries and international lending banks. Still, the scarcity of other options has led to heavy reliance on bicycles in many areas for commuting to work, reaching remote rural communities, and hauling vegetables to market. Parts of Zimbabwe, Ghana, and other African countries have considerable bicycle use.

Japan and several European countries are notable for their relatively widespread use of bicycles despite high rates of auto ownership. In the Netherlands and Denmark, bicycling makes up 20 to 30 percent of all urban trips—up to half in some cities. Railway passengers in Japan and Europe rely on bicycles as a convenient, affordable way to reach train stations. On a typical weekday, nearly 3 million bicycles are parked at rail stations throughout Japan. In Denmark, 25–30 percent of commuter rail passengers set out from home on two wheels.

Bicycles are experiencing something of a comeback in North America and Australia, where car driving had all but replaced cycling in the decades after World War II. Environmental concerns and a new interest in personal fitness have helped revive these countries' interest in pedal power since the 1970s. The number of Americans who regularly commute to work by bicycle has roughly tripled since the early 1980s, to an estimated 3 million riders.

Future prospects for pedal power are bright. World bicycle production is currently about 110 million bicycles annually and continues to climb. The popularity of new, sturdier models is quickly expanding the use of bicycles for urban commuting and riding on rugged, off-road terrain. Some governments that formerly pursued strictly car-oriented policies are now promoting cycling to reduce air pollution, traffic congestion, and transport infrastructure spending. Even in the United States, local governments today have the flexibility to provide bicycle lanes and paths with much of the federal funding previously reserved for highways.

Incongruously, officials in major cities in China—where there are 250 bicycles for every automobile—have threatened to ban bicycles from selected thoroughfares in order to make way for cars and trucks. Intense public outcries so far have fended off such prohibitions. Meanwhile, the World Bank and other development institutions have supported a handful of small but highly successful nonmotorized transport projects. Several cities in Africa and Latin America are building bicycle lanes and educating people about the advantages of bicycling.

Transport planners recognize that certain conditions are necessary for pedal power to fulfill its potential role in personal transportation. A formidable obstacle in cities worldwide is the danger posed by fast-moving motorized traffic and drivers who are not trained to share the road with cyclists. Until governments treat nonmotorized vehicles as an important transport mode and invest in the provision of bicycle facilities, safety fears will continue to deter many would-be cyclists, and those who do choose to pedal will remain at risk. Making adequate provision for bicycle transportation will continue to include well-designed bicycle paths, secure parking, and ample space to accommodate bicycles on regular roads.

[See also Motor Vehicles; Motor Vehicles, Alternatively Powered; Transportation; Urban Transit.]

BIBLIOGRAPHY

Forester, John. *Bicycle Transportation: A Handbook.* Cambridge, MA: MIT Press, 1994.

Leccese, Michael, and Plevin, Arlene. *The Bicyclist's Sourcebook.* Rockville, MD: Woodbine House, 1991.

Lowe, Marcia D. "Bicycle Production Rises Again." In Lester R. Brown et al., *Vital Signs 1994: The Trends That Are Shaping Our Future.* New York: W. W. Norton, 1994.

————. *The Bicycle: Vehicle for a Small Planet.* World-watch Papers, 90. Washington, DC: Worldwatch Institute, September 1989.

McGurn, James. *On Your Bicycle: An Illustrated History of Cycling.* London: John Murray, 1987.

Strebeigh, Fred. "Wheels Freedom." *Bicycling* (April 1991).

— MARCIA D. LOWE

PETROLEUM

Oil has long been one of the most important energy sources. In 1930 it provided one-fourth of total U.S. energy demand; by 1991 oil supplied 40 percent of U.S. energy (DeGolyer and MacNaughton, 1992). For most of the twentieth century, oil has played a central role in world economic development, as well as in military conflicts.

Natural gas also is an important energy source. Together, oil and natural gas account for 65 percent of U.S. primary energy supply.

As the twentieth century draws to a close, world supplies of oil are adequate to meet expected demand for at least several more decades. Oil consumption will not grow as rapidly as in the past and its share of the energy market will decline. There will be continued pressure to reduce oil consumption for environmental reasons. In the United States, oil imports increasingly pose security and trade deficit concerns. Despite these changes, oil will continue to be the primary energy source well into the next century.

Petroleum Product Demand

Demand for all types of energy will grow at a slower pace in the 1990s and beyond in industrialized coun-

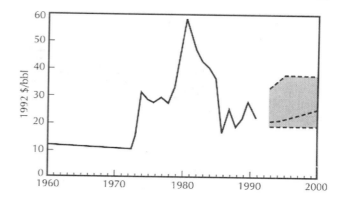

Figure 1. *Projected petroleum prices. (Conoco, Oil & Gas Journal, June 22, 1992. Used with permission.)*

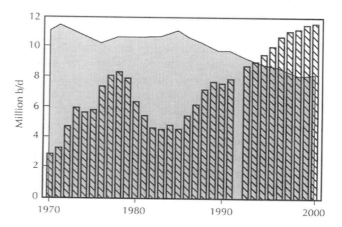

Figure 2. *Supply sources of petroleum in the United States. (Conoco, Oil & Gas Journal, June 22, 1992. Used with permission.)*

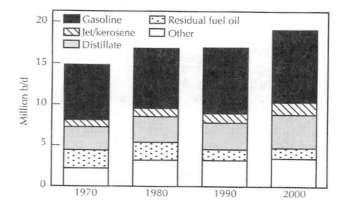

Figure 3. *Demand in the United States by petroleum product. (Conoco, Oil & Gas Journal, June 22, 1992. Used with permission.)*

tries. Economic growth will be more modest as compared with the 1980s, and energy efficiency will continue to improve. In less developed countries, however, energy demand will grow more rapidly.

639

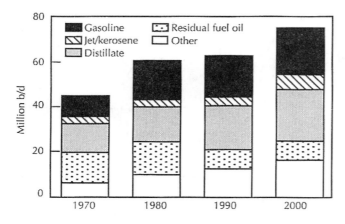

Figure 4. Demand worldwide by petroleum product. (Source: Conoco, Oil & Gas Journal, June 22, 1992. Used with permission.)

Total energy demand will increase faster than demand for oil products because environmental pressures on oil consumption will increase, and the efficiency with which petroleum is used will continue to improve. World oil demand will grow at an average rate of 1.5–1.8 percent per year through the 1990s. U.S. petroleum demand will increase at slightly more than 1 percent per year, according to most estimates. In Asia demand will grow at 4–6 percent per year.

Refineries convert crude oil into consumer oil products. On January 1, 1995, U.S. refining capacity stood at 15.3 million barrels per day, and world refining capacity totaled 74.2 million barrels per day (Rhodes, 1994).

Consumption of one of the most important petroleum products in the U.S.—gasoline—reached 7.6 million barrels per day in 1994. U.S. gasoline demand peaked earlier at 7.41 million barrels per day in 1978 (Beck, 1995). Higher prices and federal automobile mileage standards drove gasoline consumption down to 6.6 million barrels per day in 1982. When oil prices fell again in the mid-1980s, gasoline consumption began a steady increase.

Gasoline demand will grow slowly in the United States in the years ahead. Higher taxes, more use of natural gas and electricity-powered vehicles, and steady improvement in fleet fuel efficiency will combine to limit gasoline use.

U.S. consumption of other petroleum products in 1992 included 3.2 million barrels per day of distillate for home heating, truck and railroad fuel, and industry; and 1.5 million barrels per day of jet fuel (Beck, 1995).

In the early 1980s refinery shutdowns reduced excess capacity dramatically, and by 1993 U.S. refineries were operating at about 90 percent of capacity. A further reduction in U.S. refining capacity is likely in the 1990s. As a result, imports of gasoline and other petroleum products will increase.

Some smaller U.S. refineries, unable to make the large investments needed to meet the requirements of the 1990 amendments to the Clean Air Act, will be shut down, reducing capacity. Environmental restrictions make it almost impossible to build a new refinery or expand an existing plant.

Supply Fundamentals

There are two measures of crude oil supply. Reserves indicate the long-term supply, and productive capacity determines short-term availability.

Proved reserves are those that have been defined by drilling and other methods; potential reserves have not been proved. Only about one-third of the oil that has been found can be produced with today's technology and at today's prices.

Proven world reserves of crude oil stood at almost 1 trillion barrels at the beginning of 1995, enough to last 45 years at current production rates (*Oil & Gas Journal,* 1994).

Members of the Organization of Petroleum Exporting Countries (OPEC) own more than three-fourths of the world's proven oil reserves. Saudi Arabia alone has 25 percent of the world's reserves.

Much of the world's productive capacity also exists in the Middle East. Saudi Arabia's productive capacity of more than 8.5 million barrels per day will be expanded by the mid-1990s. Other OPEC producers also have plans to expand capacity.

Members of the Organization of

Petroleum Exporting Countries (OPEC)

own more than three-fourths

of the world's proven oil reserves.

U.S. production has declined steadily since 1985 due to reduced exploration and drilling activity. In 1995, U.S. crude oil production was expected to be 6.5 million barrels per day, the lowest level in thirty-five years. Further declines in U.S. output are expected.

Exploration

The search for new oil and gas reserves in the U.S. reached record low levels in the early 1990s. Environmental restrictions limited access to promising areas;

low prices and tax disincentives limited producers' cash flow and capital.

Many parts of the U.S. outer continental shelf (OCS) are potentially rich in oil and gas, and Alaska is likely to contain large oil reserves in areas where exploration has not yet been permitted. The lower forty-eight states also contain significant undiscovered and undeveloped reserves according to geologists.

Although more than 70 percent of U.S. offshore production is natural gas, there is still public fear that offshore development will harm the environment. As long as that fear exists, not many new areas will be opened for development.

About 12 percent of U.S. proven oil reserves of 26 billion barrels is located offshore (DeGolyer and MacNaughton, 1992).

Wells have been drilled in more than 6,000 feet of water. And production operations and drilling in several hundred feet of water are routine in offshore regions around the world.

Dependence on Foreign Supplies

As U.S. oil production declines and demand for petroleum products increases, the gap between supply and demand must be filled by importing foreign oil. In 1994, U.S. imports of crude oil and products reached 8.9 million barrels per day, or 50.4 percent of domestic demand (Beck, 1995). Imports reached their previous highest share, 48 percent of demand, in 1977. OPEC producers supplied 50 percent of U.S. imported crude in 1994; the largest contributor was Saudi Arabia.

Imports could increase further during the rest of the 1990s. But higher taxes on oil and oil products, and greater use of natural gas will slow—or even reverse—the growth in oil demand.

The United States will never be self-sufficient in oil. But the security risk associated with high import levels has lessened in recent years.

The U.S. Strategic Petroleum Reserve (SPR), for example, now contains about 600 million barrels. Foreign sources of U.S. crude are also more diverse now, low-

The Alaskan Pipeline remains a major accomplishment of transportation of petroleum from its source to production facilities. (Vince Streano/Corbis)

ering the risk of a critical supply interruption. In addition, crude oil markets are much more efficient at allocating available supplies than during the interruptions of the 1970s. Also, Middle East producers have integrated into refining and marketing, giving them a greater interest in market stability.

Market Control

Early in the twentieth century, the Standard Oil Trust controlled oil markets. After it was broken up, the large integrated, multinational oil companies influenced supply and therefore, prices.

Oil companies began to lose control of world oil markets when OPEC was established. Now with twelve members, OPEC exerted growing influence on the market through the 1970s and 1980s. OPEC now controls most of the world's excess producing capacity and can manipulate the price of oil by restricting or increasing production.

There are signs, however, that OPEC is interested in stabilizing the market to ensure a long-term demand for its members' oil. There is some agreement that a benchmark price of about $20 per barrel is low enough to allow demand to grow yet high enough to provide OPEC members with needed revenue.

OPEC—Saudi Arabia in particular—will continue to hold the oil market balance of power. Even as demand rises, planned capacity expansions by OPEC members will maintain an excess supply well into the future. Non-OPEC production will decline.

There will be price fluctuations and political crises affecting supply. But the average cost of crude oil, in constant dollars, is likely to increase only at the rate of inflation.

Social Costs

Concern for the environment has brought many changes in oil production, processing, and consumption. The 1990 amendments to the U.S. Clean Air Act called for new transportation fuels and much stricter emissions standards. The *Valdez* tanker spill offshore Alaska in 1989 resulted in new laws concerning oil spill preparedness, tanker design, and shipper liability.

Strict environmental regulations governing offshore drilling and producing operations have dramatically lowered the risk of offshore pollution incidents. Beyond this, the Marine Spill Response Corporation in the U.S. is prepared to help industry and coastal areas deal with accidents.

Safety in refineries and in other facilities, along with attention to air and water quality, have become the top priorities of petroleum companies everywhere in the world. Typically U.S.-based companies follow U.S.

standards when operating in other countries, even though local regulations may be less strict.

Environmental issues will increasingly affect oil consumption, too. Efforts to reduce the use of oil—and other fossil fuels—will continue. Higher taxes on oil and oil products, or on the carbon content of fuels, will be used to reduce the consumption of gasoline and other oil products.

[See also Coal; Electric Power; Energy; Energy, Renewable Sources of; Hazardous Wastes; Motor Vehicles, Alternatively Powered; Natural Gas; Nuclear Power; Nuclear Power: Con; Resources; Transuranium Elements.]

BIBLIOGRAPHY

Beck, Robert J. "Economic Growth, Low Prices to Lift U.S. Oil and Gas Demand in 1995." *Oil & Gas Journal* (January 30, 1995).

Rhodes, Anne K. "World Crude Capacity, Conversion Capability Inch Upward." *Oil & Gas Journal* (December 19, 1994).

"Worldwide Oil Flow Up, Reserves Steady in '94." *Oil & Gas Journal* (December 26, 1994).

— JOHN L. KENNEDY

PETS

In the 1980s, the cat finally surpassed the dog as our most popular companion animal. The latest statistics from the American Veterinary Medical Association show that Americans have 57 million cats and 52.5 million dogs.

There are many reasons for the cat boom. Urban and suburban areas mushroomed and floor space decreased, but because felines can live comfortably without great amounts of room, they fit well into an increasingly congested world. Also, due to a dramatic rise in the number of two-income families, leisure time declined. The more self-sufficient cat—needing no outdoor exercise and less attention than a dog—became the ideal pet for busy people.

As the world becomes more crowded and regulated, will be rethinking many of our views on cat care. Roaming cats are becoming less acceptable to society, and a growing number of people are keeping their cats safely indoors. In the next few decades, cat laws will more closely mimic existing dog laws. For example, cats will not be allowed outside unless they are confined or controlled. Because indoor cats are happier with playmates, we will see a marked rise in multicat households. And as people share closer quarters with their pets, they will be tapping into an ever-widening network of resources—for example, animal behavior information—to resolve pet problems such as cats scratching furniture.

A 1990 Gallup survey demonstrated that nine out of ten Americans with pets think of their animals as family members. Hefty percentages of interviewees reported giving their pets Christmas gifts and keeping pictures of pets in their wallets. Over the last twenty years, there has been a notable trend toward treating pets as surrogate children. Statistics demonstrate that many people are marrying later and bearing fewer children: pets often wind up occupying center stage. Already, a number of businesses cater to working, pet-owning "parents." Such services, including summer camps, play-groups, and day care for dogs, are evidence of a growing demand for services similar to child care.

As people who have animal companions continue to gain clout, it could become unacceptable or maybe even illegal to summarily bar pets from rental housing. People may be allowed to list their pets as dependents to gain tax deductions. Just as some companies offer day care for children, it could become widely acceptable for employees to bring their pets to work. Pets might also be covered with health insurance through a national program as part of an employee benefits package.

In short, as cats and dogs become truly valued members of our society, their hierarchical status in the world will increase. Dogs completing obedience courses might receive access rights, much like today's guide dogs, to restaurants, hotels, and motels. With a heightened sensitivity to the invaluable gift of an animal's companionship, people will no longer think of pets as property and will replace the term *pet owner* with *animal companion*.

Studies show that pets are good for our mental and even physical well-being. Statistics document that we are living longer, and as the baby-boom generation ages, we will be faced with an enormous population of older people. Animals can help to prevent these elderly citizens from feeling depressed and isolated, and we could see an upsurge of resident pets in hospitals and nursing homes. Today, people over sixty are often reluctant to adopt pets that could outlive them. In the future, people in their seventies, eighties, and nineties will be able to rely on readoption programs or lifetime pet homes to safeguard their animals should they pass away before their pets.

As a group, people with pets can afford to give their animals the best of care. A survey commissioned by the American Veterinary Medical Association showed that

Many Americans treat their pets as family members, doting on them with gourmet food, air-conditioned dog houses, and summer camps. (Tom Nebbia/Corbis)

people who have pets have higher than average incomes and are more likely to own their homes. A desire to pamper pets has created a market for gourmet pet foods and treats. The growth in cat popularity and the move toward keeping cats safely indoors ushered in fleets of innovative products, including the feline version of MTV: videos of lively birds. Pets in the future may keep themselves happily occupied indoors with high-tech interactive video games that have symbols they can push to produce different sounds, smells (such as aromatic food smells), or visuals.

In the 1980s, the cat finally surpassed the dog

as our most popular companion animal.

As society continues to become more industrialized, products like commercial pet food (rather than food scraps) should gain an international market. Increased knowledge of medical care, nutrition, and animal behavior—everything from state-of-the-art surgery to more nutritious pet foods—will continue to better pets' lives.

Unfortunately, despite the bright outlook for most of our companion animals, inappropriate pets remain a problem. Although the enforcement of existing regulations and the enactment of new laws has helped to put a dent in the exotic pet trade, a demand for exotic pets (both legal and illegal) continues to devastate wildlife populations. However, humane education is the hope of the future. Already, many airlines are refusing to transport wild birds for ethical reasons. As people become more aware of the issues surrounding exotic pets, one hopes the demand for these animals will decline.

Education must also play a key role in another animal welfare problem: vicious pet dogs. In the mid 1980s and early '90s, fatal attacks on humans by pit bull terriers made international headlines. Public awareness about illegal dog fighting and aggressive, uncontrollable pet dogs (a macho status symbol) was raised, but the ensuing media frenzy obscured the fact that irresponsible people were at the root of the problem.

Laws that target human behavior, such as stiffer sentences for those who train and keep aggressive animals, have already proved far more effective deterrents than banning specific dog breeds. As such laws are strengthened, future generations should hold humans—and not abused animals—responsible for dangerous dogs.

[See also Animal Rights; Housing: Demographic and Lifestyle Impacts on; Leisure Time.]

BIBLIOGRAPHY

"Crazy Over Cats." *Time* (December 7, 1981).
"Furry and Feathery Therapists." *Time* (March 30, 1987).
"Warriors in the Parrot Game." *International Wildlife* (September–October 1990).
"The Year of the Cat." *Shelter Sense* (December 1992–January 1993).

— RICHARD AVANZINO

PHARMACEUTICALS

By 2020, pharmaceuticals will have played an important role in curing and preventing major diseases. Pharmaceuticals will be an integrated component of health care customized for each of us as biochemically unique individuals. Pharmaceutical tools that operate at the molecular level will both effectively treat disease and play a role in health promotion. Pharmaceuticals will have evolved to include biosensors and biocontrollers that circulate in the body, monitoring conditions, manufacturing the relevant therapeutic agent in the body, and delivering it directly to the diseased cells. Responding to and anticipating scientific breakthroughs, the pharmaceutical industry will have undergone significant changes.

Prospect of Definitive Cures

According to the late Lewis Thomas, author of *Lives of a Cell,* diseases are biological puzzles that we are on the verge of solving, thus heralding a relatively disease-free society. While research has promised breakthroughs for decades, the next twenty-five years (from 1995 to 2020) are likely to see definitive control of heart disease, cancer, and some neurologic diseases. Research focusing on the molecular level is likely to uncover the role genetics plays in instigating or making us more susceptible to disease.

There are several promising approaches now on the horizon. Disarmed viruses will be used to attack diseased cells, carrying information that reprograms the diseased cells' DNA. The recognition that the cells and molecules of our immune, cardiovascular, neural, and digestive systems are valuable information centers useful in disease prevention and treatment will lead to new and profitable scientific approaches. Another promising technology is "anti-sense." This technology blocks the molecular information necessary for the disease to flourish. Messenger RNA is essential to the successful replication of cells. Antisense devices string together nucleic acids that define the RNA so as to be complementary or opposite to the original RNA sequence. The antisense sequence binds to the original sequence, preventing the original sequence from conveying its information, thus disabling the cellular reproduction mechanisms. This will give an accuracy for treatment far higher than in the late twentieth century. According to Stuart Davidson, director of the Center for Technology Assessment, in 1995 anti-sense compounds were being developed for use against Alzheimer's disease, many cancers, autoimmune disorders including rheumatoid arthritis, viral diseases, and coronary artery disease. Whether through molecular or other approaches, research will be successful in controlling major diseases in the first quarter of the twenty-first century. However, these molecular approaches are only part of the story of the future of pharmaceuticals.

Customization of Health Care with a Broader Focus

Health care will approach and treat each of us as biochemically unique individuals by 2020. The human genome will be mapped and largely understood, making "DNA fingerprints" part of a person's medical record. Health care will also recognize our unique personal and psychological characteristics and will move to take full advantage of these to enhance our health. Keep in mind that the U.S. Surgeon General's Office has argued that 50 percent of the variance in our illness over our life course is related to our behavior, 20 percent to our environment, 20 percent to our genes, and 10 percent to medical care—including pharmaceuticals as we have thought about them historically. Pharmaceuticals will be integrated into very effective preventive and therapeutic protocols that include diet, exercise, stress, and personal growth factors. These therapeutic and preventive protocols will be available in our homes, often given to us by our health care providers in whatever state-of-the-art electronic form that is available at the time. The pharmaceutical component of these protocols will include nonprescription medications; among these will be a broader range of what in the late twentieth century were considered alternative remedies, such as homeopathy. Further into the twenty-first century we will have "pharmaceuticals" in the form of small devices ingested or implanted in the body to monitor continuously our condition and to manufacture and deliver the appropriate medication as diseases begin to appear.

The pharmaceutical industry will undergo the type of consolidation the transportation sector experienced in the early part of the twentieth century. The transportation sector went from dozens of car makers to a handful worldwide. The pharmaceutical industry has begun this consolidation process. Simultaneously, the economics of pharmaceutical development will be changed. The regulatory framework that governs new drug development was put in place in the middle of the twentieth century (particularly the 1962 amendments to the U.S. Food, Drug, and Cosmetic Act). Installed at the height of the industrial era, this legislation seeks to ensure uniform standards of safety and efficacy. These will likely change in response to the shift in health care to customized medicine. Pharmaceuticals will be focused on individuals who, because of their genetic makeup or other factors, are particularly likely to respond to the drug. In the twentieth century, many "me too" drugs were not successful because they benefited only 10, 20, or 30 percent of the people with that particular condition. In the twenty-first century, health care will target such individuals and seek out cost-effective versions of those new compounds. This will accelerate the changes already in place in pharmaceutical selection toward using pharmacoeconomics in deciding which new drug candidates to pursue.

Health care providers will take a more active part in targeting research. The development of electronic medical record keeping, consumer health approaches, personal biomonitoring, and more active consumer involvement will mean that health care providers, particularly large managed-care groups, will be able to do clinical trials at virtually no additional costs to their ongoing medical care for their customers. Health care providers will partner in clinical trials, and the cost of pharmaceutical development will plummet. As the information revolution grows, it is also possible that the prospects for drug discovery by individuals and small companies will become relatively easier. Thus, while the pharmaceutical industry will consolidate, the number of sources for new pharmaceutical discovery may remain high.

Pharmaceutical development will help redefine the meaning of health care in the twenty-first century, as pharmaceutical "tools" are used to enhance and promote health at the individual and societal level. A broader understanding of health care will blur the boundaries between markets and institutions, spawning sustained innovation and creating a "healthier" future.

[See also Health Care; Health Care, Alternative Therapies; Health Care, Technological Developments; Health Care Costs; Medical Care Providers.]

BIBLIOGRAPHY

Bezold, Clement; Halpern, Jerome A.; and Eng, Jacqueline L., eds. *2020 Visions: Health Care Information, Standards, and Technologies.* Rockville, MD: United States Pharmacopeial Convention, 1993.

Bezold, Clement, and Knabner, Klaus, eds. *Health Care 2010: Health Care Delivery, Therapies, and the Pharmaceutical Industry.* Berlin and New York: Springer Verlag, 1994.

Davidson, Stuart. "Therapeutics for Tomorrow." *Health-care Forum Journal* (January–February 1995): 55.

— CLEMENT BEZOLD

PHILANTHROPY

As the twenty-first century approaches, it seems clear that the accelerating pace of change in society will create new challenges and unexpected opportunities for organized philanthropy. The models of organized philanthropy that have developed over the last hundred years or so—foundations and corporate giving programs—evolved as the American private sector's response to certain social and economic conditions.

The beginning of this century was a watershed moment in the transition from the age of the individual to the age of the organization. "Charity," which had been primarily individual, affective, and largely ad hoc for many of the leading families, was transformed into organized philanthropy, which was more systematic, cognitive, and strategic. The models of philanthropy pioneered by wealthy families and bankers like Frederick Goff, who formed the first community foundation in 1914, have withstood the test of time, but new models are emerging that at the beginning of the century could not have been anticipated. Who would have imagined just a few years ago, for example, that one of the largest donors in Minnesota would be the Native American Gaming Commission?

The Changing Context of Philanthropy

The first set of challenges and opportunities facing foundations and corporate givers in the coming era has to do with those changes in the social, economic, and political environment that increase the opportunity to promote the growth and protect the interest of philanthropy. Much is said and written about the intergenerational transfer of wealth, the expectation that within the next two decades as much as 8 trillion dollars may be passed down from Americans now over age fifty to their children and grandchildren. Many groups, both profit and nonprofit, are considering what needs to be done to encourage, activate, or cultivate the charitable impulse so that the intergenerational transfer of wealth includes a transfer of the charitable commitment as well.

There have been a number of recent legislative changes that could spur a major growth of interest in organized philanthropy in its varied forms, such as:

- Higher marginal tax rates. (The Revenue Act of 1993 raised the highest marginal tax rates to 39.6 percent from 31 percent.)
- Fewer available deductions. (The 1986 Tax reform Act greatly reduced the number of deductions available to higher income tax payers.)
- The increase in maximum estate and gift tax rates. (When federal and state estate taxes are combined, donors may be looking at combined tax rates for their estates nearing 70 percent.)
- Relief from the alternative minimum tax rate (ATM).

A third major change that could influence the growth of philanthropy is the changing profile of the potential donor. As the demographic makeup of the country, and the world, changes, so will the donor pool. Many of the potential donors in the next few years will be very different from the donors we know today, not only in values, lifestyles, and attitudes, but in racial and ethnic composition as well. Much of the emphasis on diversity in philanthropy has been on the "demand" side (recipients), but there will be increasing opportunity for diversity on the "supply" side (donors). Very little attention has been given to the growth in the buying power of people of color, which is projected to reach $640 billion by the year 2000. (Present purchasing power of African Americans is $211 billion, $141 billion for Hispanics, and $120 billion for Asians.) There has been considerable growth in the development of foundations and charitable funds among minorities, but as more people of color are exposed to the many options for organized giving, that growth is expected to accelerate.

Within the next two decades,

as much as 8 trillion dollars may be passed down

from Americans now over age fifty

to their children and grandchildren.

The trend in foundation formation among all Americans is also favorable. More than 2,000 foundations were formed in 1994. Foundation formation peaked in the 1980s with the establishment of more than 9,000 new foundations, almost doubling the number created in the 1950s, the largest previous decade of growth. Three thousand of these were large enough for inclusion in the Foundation Center's *Foundation Directory* by qualifying with endowments of at least $1 million in assets or in charitable expenditures of at least $100,000 each year.

Two other changes in the environment can be foreseen, both representing new opportunities for collaboration. The last two decades have seen the growth and strengthening of the infrastructure supporting organized giving, particularly through nonprofit associations that promote and protect philanthropy. The next decade will likely see the growth and strengthening of profit-making alternatives, as entrepreneurs of all sorts turn their attention to this field. Many will have values and objectives widely different from the Council on Foundations and regional associations of grant-makers.

Attitudes and approaches to collaboration are also changing. The last two decades have seen a significant increase in the willingness of foundations to collaborate with each other and with the giving programs of business corporations. More recently, there has also been significant increase in the number of foundations wanting to collaborate with government or work in some other way to shape an informed public opinion. The next major growth area for collaboration is with organized religion. Many grantmakers have discovered since the Los Angeles disruptions that ethnic churches are not only the most stable organization in minority communities, but that they make good partners in implementation. A recent conference in Washington on "Religion, Philanthropy and Civil Society" focused on "models of hope," collaborative ventures between foundations and churches that were providing help and hope to those trapped in central cities.

The next major change is the increasing pluralism of the philanthropic sector. Ever since the Hudson Institute published *Workforce 2000* in 1987, the public and private sectors have been preparing for the massive demographic shifts that were predicted and that to some extent have already occurred. When the Council on Foundations issued a statement about inclusiveness in its principles and practices more than a dozen years ago, many people believed that diversity was just another euphemism for affirmative action, setting goals to recruit, retain, and promote people of color based on their representation in the labor force. What many organizations have come to realize is that simply changing the mix without changing the organizational culture is sometimes counterproductive. Diversity does not of itself create community.

Groups representing minority and women grantmakers are seeking a greater commitment to diversity on the part of foundations, but this is not unique to the field. Every major association, along with nonprofit agencies and many corporations, is seeking effective ways to promote diversity and inclusiveness. When Elizabeth Dole announced a new inclusiveness initiative at the American Red Cross, she also announced the allocation of a million dollars to provide for leadership development scholarships, a minority internship program, staff exchange programs, executive forums and a president's fund to develop additional initiatives.

While many foundations and corporate giving programs have led the way in emphasizing and practicing inclusiveness, there nevertheless is a growing frustration among minority staff in the field, about hiring practices, opportunities for professional growth and mobility, organizational culture, and openness and accessibility. Recent studies have found that the nonprofit sector lags behind business and government in the hiring of minority employees. Inclusiveness is a concern that is likely to be on the front burner of issues in the field for a while.

Another change that will have an impact on philanthropy is the increasing internationalization of society and our sector. The changing boundaries of society are changing the boundaries of philanthropy. Not only has the nation-state declined as the primary custodian of the civic culture, but an international perspective is no longer simply the concern of international foundations making what used to be called foreign or overseas grants. Community foundations are finding that they can no longer effectively address local issues or solve local problems by remaining within the limits of the old geographical boundaries. Corporate giving programs are looking beyond their headquarters communities to plant and facility communities around the world, and even small family foundations are making grants that seek to advance international understanding and cooperation.

In Eastern Europe, Central and Latin America, and South Africa, many efforts are underway not simply to develop foundations, but to preserve an intermediate space between government and business where private energy can be mobilized and deployed for the public good. The increasing globalization of philanthropy, however, should not be seen exclusively as an opportunity to promote civic values that empower people elsewhere to solve local problems locally, but as an opportunity to learn from other cultures as well.

The Changing Craft of Philanthropy

The increasing concern with public accountability has gone beyond public access and public reporting to include management and governance as well. There has been much public attention directed toward the compensation practices of foundations and other nonprofits. Yet, a primary issue for the nonprofit sector continues to be how best to attract and retain the best minds and the best managers for the sector. This will require competitive levels of compensation and other incentives, but the public must be convinced that standards of pay are closely tied to job requirements and standards of performance. Managing the multimillion dollar foundation requires managers as competent as those who run multimillion dollar businesses. It makes no sense to pretend that foundations with millions of dollars of assets have the same management requirement as the small, neighborhood organization.

Council on Foundations surveys continue to find grantmaking foundations to be among the most prudent organizations in the nonprofit sector in setting staff compensation. In reviewing what is appropriate and reasonable, many trustees ask three important questions: What functions are required and actually performed by staff? What levels of skills and experience are necessary in order to perform those functions? What is the market in which the foundation chooses to compete for the professional skills required? The questions are somewhat different for corporate giving programs where the comparison is more likely to be with other officers in the corporation.

The changing boundaries of society

are changing the boundaries of philanthropy.

Another area of concern is communications, including a reconsideration of what kind of public information is useful and how best to provide it. The 990 forms that nonprofit organizations submit annually to the Internal Revenue Service were developed by regulators for regulators, but they are used increasingly as a source of public information as well. Many foundations still do not publish an annual report, so perhaps the 990 could be revised, changing the kind of data required to information useful and helpful to a public that wants to know more about what drives nonprofits—how they make decisions and what shapes their priorities.

So far, much of the response to the changing public climate has focused on such external factors as myths and misinformation in the media, the increased attention to compensation practices, and the need to better educate the public on how public charities differ from the other twenty-four categories of tax-exempt organizations.

The Changing Concept of Philanthropy

Finally, as philanthropy becomes more pluralistic, public expectations of how these tax-exempt funds should be used may become even more varied. Nowhere is this likely to be more evident than in the increased public debate about how best to cultivate the moral virtues essential to good character. The concern with values has become a national obsession, creating what a national magazine recently called a new kind of politics and a new class of "virtuecrats." No organization sanctioned by the public to serve public purposes is likely to escape the scrutiny of the 76 percent of the American public who regard the erosion of values as one of the really critical issues of our time.

The problem is that the public discourse about values has become politicized. Those who talk most about good values are often those who want simply to argue

that someone else has bad values. But if anyone is likely to be able to depoliticize the discussion, it is likely to be organizations with an image of neutrality and nonpartisanship.

The historian Arthur M. Schlesinger, Jr., wrote a few years ago that American society is never fixed nor final. Like every other aspect of our society, philanthropy too is changing. If foundations and corporate giving programs—the institutions of organized philanthropy that have developed over the course of this century—are to have proportionately the same impact on American life in the next century, they must commit themselves to the idea that the fear of difference is fear of the future. If they want to form a more perfect union, they must begin within themselves, striving to include all who have a stake in their endeavors. They must cultivate a passion for responsibility as well as effectiveness, and for civility as well as civic engagement.

[See also Investments; Nongovernmental Organizations; Public Assistance Programs; Values; Wealth.]

BIBLIOGRAPHY

CIBA Foundation. *Future of Philanthropic Foundations.* Ann Arbor: Books on Demand, 1977.
Freeman, David. *Handbook on Private Foundations.* Washington, DC: Council on Foundations, 1991.
Joseph, James A. *Remaking America: How the Benevolent Traditions of Many Cultures Are Transforming Our National Life.* San Francisco: Jossey-Bass, 1995.
Pifer, Alan. *Philanthropy in an Age of Transition.* New York: Foundation Center, 1984.

— JAMES A. JOSEPH

PHOTOGRAPHY

Since its introduction in 1839, silver-based photography has been the principal process for capturing, recording, and preserving images in all fields of human activity. The ever-growing demand for such images has spawned an international photographic industry, centered in the United States, Western Europe, and Japan. In 1994, the worldwide sales of imaging materials and associated special equipment and services totaled about $55 billion in U.S. dollars.

The major photography industry sectors in terms of product volume and value are (1) amateur, (2) professional, (3) medical diagnostic imaging, (4) motion picture, and (5) graphic arts. Although each sector requires somewhat different imaging materials, all have the same basic structure—they are laminates, consisting of a surface-treated support and bonded gelatin layers. The support can be transparent or translucent (cellulose triacetate or polyester film) or white opaque (mostly resin-coated paper). The gelatin layers serve one of two purposes: image formation or control of chemical reactions and/or physical characteristics. Imaging layers (called emulsions) contain millions of silver halide crystals, as well as dye formers in the case of modern color films and color papers.

The creation of an image with silver halide-type products usually involves two basic steps: (1) exposure to a pattern of light or other actinic radiation to produce a latent image; and (2) wet chemical processing that transforms the latent into a visible black-and-white silver image or a three-color dye image, and renders the image permanent.

Amateur Photography

Today, amateurs overwhelmingly take pictures with 35-mm cameras and color negative film, because they want color prints, and this is the best means to that end. Statistics for worldwide amateur photography in 1950 and 1994 attest to the remarkable growth and popularity of this system: In 1950 there were 1.65 billion pictures taken, 9 percent of them in color, whereas in 1994 there were some 60 billion pictures taken, 92 percent in color.

A yearly 4 to 6 percent increase in the use of color negative film and color paper can be expected during the period 1995 to 2005 for the following reasons:

- Color negative images have unsurpassed information content—20,000,000 pixels per 35-mm frame compared with 350,000 to 600,000 with current sensors in amateur electronic still cameras. Also, color paper prints have excellent image quality and stability and can be mass-produced at low cost.
- Further improvements in color film performance and processing technology are in the offing.
- The system has been introduced in several of the most populous countries, including China and India. This is bound to foster increasing use.
- A new "advanced photo system" will be introduced in 1996. It includes new cameras and films with magnetic strips for encoding camera exposure data, image format selection, photofinishing instructions, and text to be recorded on the print image. These novel features are designed to stimulate picture taking and increase the demand for prints.

To date, magnetic tape recordings made with camcorders have replaced 8-mm. home movies, because videotapes do not require expensive wet processing and offer the convenience of viewing on home television sets. However, electronic still cameras for amateurs have been unsuccessful so far, mainly because of inferior image quality and higher prices. These disadvantages will be reduced, but not eliminated for many years. Meanwhile, the application of hybrid systems, such as the Kodak Photo CD, will provide amateurs with many new options for manipulating, displaying, reproducing, and transmitting images captured on color film. Also,

digital color printing systems will grow in importance, especially in the United States. In summary, electronic imaging systems are likely to play an increasingly important role, but continuing dominance of silver-based products well into the twenty-first century seems assured.

Professional Photography

Professional photography has two main segments: portraiture and commercial. Aggregate turnover generated in these two U.S. market sectors during 1994 was about $9 billion, or about 35 percent of the estimated world total.

Silver halide-type films and papers are the principal imaging materials in professional photography, but black-and-white and color reversal films account for more than 55 percent of total film consumption and black-and-white paper for about 25 percent. Electronic still cameras have gained acceptance in press, industrial, and military operations when rapid access and transmission of images have high priority and where the high price of 1.5 to 4 million pixel cameras is not a major deterrent. Hybrid systems are used increasingly in professional processing laboratories, including film scanners and digital workstations. The digitized images can be modified, enhanced, and combined with other images and/or text and recorded on magnetic tape or disc, or optical disc. They can then be viewed on a monitor screen prior to outputting on photographic film, or on photographic, thermal dyetransfer, ink-jet, or electrophotographic paper.

George Fisher, chairman and CEO of the Eastman Kodak Company, acknowledges that the breakneck evolution of communication technology is transforming imaging. With the remarkable drop in the cost of computing power over the past decade, "labs and photographers now have affordable access to potent image-manipulation 'horsepower' on the desktop. In addition, the huge expansion of the bandwidth accommodates photographic-quality images, which are so information-rich that they use up huge chunks of bandwidth.

Medical Diagnostic Imaging

Most medical diagnostic images are radiographs made with duplitized X-ray films (emulsion on both sides), exposed in cassettes with light emitted by fluorescent screens. Single-coated X-ray films and special cassettes and screens are used for mammography. Dental and industrial radiographs are made by direct X-ray exposure of silver-rich films. New imaging systems introduced since 1950 are displayed on blue or green fluorescing CRT screens or black-and-white video monitors that can be photographed with special single-coated films. More recently, infrared and helium-neon laser printers have been introduced for recording digitally based images on high-resolution films.

In the future, alternate systems employing optical disc technology will find more widespread acceptance. Such systems are available already. One of them can capture images from computed radiography and film radiographs and provide instant image transmission to several viewing stations within a hospital, as well as to off-site facilities via a network of fiber-optic or coaxial cables, or by infrared and microwaves, or satellite. "Jukeboxes" can be used for storage and retrieval of discs holding millions of images. Video display options include banks of monitors for primary diagnosis, for consultation and review, and display on personal computers. Film images can be generated from the optical discs with laser printers.

The main obstacles to the acquisition and use of such systems have been and will be the cost of the equipment and networking, the unaccustomed viewing mode, and the stress induced by prolonged viewing of screen images. Therefore, silver halide films will continue to be the main image capture and recording material for at least ten years. Thereafter, all-electronic imaging systems are likely to predominate in large health care facilities in wealthy countries, but universal replacement of silver halide-based systems will not occur for the foreseeable future.

Motion Pictures

Predictions of the demise of motion picture theaters in the United States seemed a sure bet when television started to invade American homes in the early 1950s. Less than ten years later, the same fate was forecast for motion picture film—that it would soon be replaced by magnetic videotape. Actually, an initial restructuring and contraction of the industry was soon followed by renewed growth of Hollywood studio operations, as they added film production for television shows to their traditional program. Movie attendance also recovered steadily, as the public rediscovered the pleasure of uninterrupted, large-screen presentations. As a result, the number of theater screens increased from 17,590 in 1980 to 26,586 in 1994, the number of admissions from about 1 billion to 1.3 billion, and ticket revenues from $2.75 billion to $5.4 billion. Also, about 80 percent of all prime-time television shows are still recorded on 35-mm motion picture film before being transferred to videotape or laser discs for broadcasting.

The main reasons for this staying power of the photographic system have been the superior image quality and stability of color film images, the substantial ad-

vantages in light output and image sharpness of optical over digital projectors, and the large investment in photographic cameras, printers, processors, and projectors. These advantages are not about to disappear, especially since continuing progress in color emulsion technology will bring further improvements in imaging efficiency and quality. Also, hybrid systems have already been developed that allow key-coding of film images during camera exposure and include film readers for scanning of the images and digital workstations for editing, production of special effects, titling, and other operations involved in converting the camera images into final print images.

Graphic Arts

Photographic films and papers are used in pre-press operations—i.e., the preparation and assembly of images and/or text for imposition onto printing plates. Different products having different photographic and processing characteristics are supplied to match the requirements of the four major printing processes—letterpress, lithography, gravure, and stencil. In 1994, graphic arts films accounted for about 25 percent of worldwide film production and graphic arts papers for about 12 percent.

During the past twenty years, hybrid systems (phototypesetters, scanners, and image setters) have been used increasingly to streamline prepress operations through the reduction or elimination of multiple operations involving separate reproduction of text on photographic paper and of pictures on film, followed by manual assembly into complete page layouts. Still, the demand for photographic films has increased steadily and will continue to increase by about 4 percent per year during the next decade, due to growth in worldwide demand for printed material and a shift to color printing that requires four films instead of the one needed for black-and-white images. However, the use of photographic paper has declined substantially and will continue on a downward trend.

[See also Chemicals, Fine; Communications: Technology; Data Storage; Digital Communications; Electronic Convergence; Electronic Publishing; Interactive Entertainment; Media Lab; Motion Pictures; On-Line Services; Television; Visual Arts.]

BIBLIOGRAPHY

Collins, D. *The Story of Kodak.* New York: Harry N. Abrams, 1990.
Coote, J. H. *The Illustrated History of Color Photography.* Surbiton, Surrey, U.K.: Fountain Press, 1993.
James, T. H. *The Theory of the Photographic Process,* 4th ed. New York: Macmillan, 1977.
Rosenblum, N. *A World History of Photography.* New York: Abbeville Press, 1984.

Sturge, J.; Walworth, V.; and Shepp, A. *Imaging Processes and Materials: Neblette's Eighth Edition.* New York: Van Nostrand Reinhold, 1989.

— TOM DUFFICY

PHYSICS

In the twenty-first century the most important development in physics will be the maturity of our knowledge of reality. One hundred years from now we will know all there is to know—except for some details—about the basic structure of matter and the nature of the universe.

One hundred years from now

we will know all there is to know

—except for some details—

about the basic structure of matter

and the nature of the universe.

A glance back at the enormous increase of knowledge during the past century gives convincing evidence that the above prediction is not fantasy. As recently as 1890 most scientists doubted that matter consisted of atoms, for no direct evidence of their existence had been found. The atomic age started in 1897 with the discovery of the electron. During the next fifty years many particles believed to be fundamental had been discovered: electrons, protons and neutrons within the atom, plus many mesons (generated in high energy particle accelerators) whose status was unclear. However, as evidence continued to accumulate, it gradually became evident that most of these particles were not really fundamental, but were made of other particles named *quarks.* Starting in the 1960s a detailed model of matter emerged. This model, called *The Standard Model of Particle Physics,* is able to explain almost every phenomenon observed in particle, nuclear, and atomic physics.

In the Standard Model, matter is made up of a relatively small number of fundamental particles: six kinds of heavy particles (the quarks), and six kinds of light particles, (the electron, the muon, the tau particle, the electron neutrino, the muon neutrino, and the tau neutrino). These twelve particles and their associated antiparticles are divided into three families.

Experimental evidence accumulated during the early 1990s at the Stanford Linear Accelerator and the Large Electron-Positron Collider in Switzerland proves that the three families of particles described above include all the existing particles of matter. The Standard Model became complete when the Tevatron at the Fermi National Accelerator Laboratory in Batavia, Illinois, discovered the top quark in 1994.

Future accelerators that can reach higher energies are expected to solve a second mystery of particle physics. At the heart of the Standard Model is the idea that all the events in the universe are governed by only four different forces: gravitational, electromagnetic, nuclear, and weak. When two particles feel a force of attraction or repulsion between them, it is because these particles exchange other "messenger" particles. For example, the electromagnetic force between two electric charges is caused by an exchange of photons. The Standard Model considers the electromagnetic force and the weak force to be two aspects of a single force: the *electroweak force.* The mathematical theory of the Standard Model predicts that the electroweak force is associated with the hypothetical Higgs particle. The Higgs particle is important because in theory it causes other particles to have mass.

With this background, we can make the following predictions for the next century of particle physics:

- New machines will be built that accelerate particles to energies greater than one teravolt. One of these is the Large Hadron Collider at CERN, the European Laboratory for Particle Physics, on the border between France and Switzerland. While there has been considerable political opposition to the proposed Superconducting Supercollider, mainly because of its great cost—over $8 billion—it is likely to be completed within a few decades.

- The Higgs particle will be generated in these machines and its properties will be measured. These measurements will complete the verification of the Standard Model of Particle Physics.

- By the end of the twenty-first century particle physics will be essentially complete. We will understand all the properties of all the possible particles, and we will understand the nature of all the fundamental interactions. Furthermore, we will learn that the four forces are merely four aspects of one fundamental force. The merging of gravitation with the theory of quantum mechanics will be accomplished. The Grand Unified Theory, or an equivalent theory, will be verified.

Quantum mechanics is a mathematical system of describing particles using wave equations. There are some basic questions in quantum theory that are not understood at the present time, even though as a whole the theory is extremely successful in describing the behavior of matter and energy. One peculiar phenomenon is observed when an atom emits two photons simultaneously. If these photons travel in opposite directions and are detected by instruments located far from each other, each detector seems to know instantaneously what kind of photon is observed by the distant detector. How this happens is not understood.

The outstanding puzzles of quantum mechanics will be solved during the twenty-first century. However, the paradoxical behavior of quanta will not provide methods of sending messages faster than the speed of light, as some authors claim, and will not be found to facilitate extrasensory perception and other paranormal effects, as other authors claim.

The phenomenon of superconductivity has been known since 1911. Superconductivity occurs when certain metals and alloys are cooled to extremely low temperatures. At a certain temperature, called the critical temperature, the material loses all resistance to the flow of electricity. This property makes possible the construction of electromagnets that require no power to operate once the electric current generating the magnetic field is started. The first superconductors required cooling the wires down to the temperature of liquid helium—minus 269° Celsius, which is only four degrees above absolute zero (4° K).

High-temperature superconductivity was discovered during the 1980s. Certain compounds become superconducting when cooled to the temperature of liquid nitrogen (77° K). The advantage of this is that liquid nitrogen is much cheaper than liquid helium. The disadvantage is that most of the high-temperature superconductors investigated to date lose their superconductivity when subject to high magnetic fields. This, of course, nullifies the most important uses of superconductors. Recent progress allows us to make some predictions:

- Materials will be found within the next few decades that permit the manufacture of super-conductors capable of generating intense magnetic fields at liquid nitrogen temperatures. These superconductors will be used in the construction of high energy particle accelerators and trains levitated by magnetic fields.
- A more precarious prediction is this: Materials will ultimately be found that become superconductors at ordinary room temperatures. This will allow the construction of strong magnets without the use of any cooling at all. No one knows how this will be done, but there are no laws of nature that say this development is impossible.

Physicists use computers to model molecules, atoms, and subatomic particles in ways that they may not be able to envision otherwise. (Bob Krist/ Corbis)

Superconductivity is just one area of research in solid state physics or the physics of condensed matter. In 1948, solid state physics led to the invention of the transistor, which made possible the packing of more and more electronics into smaller spaces—the miniaturization of electronics. Progress continues as we learn to make electronic components smaller and smaller.

The further miniaturization of electronics

will make possible computers

that can think essentially like human beings,

giving rise to robots that behave in human ways.

The further miniaturization of electronics will make possible the commercialization of hand-held computers with the power of present super-computers. This will result in computers that can think essentially like human beings, giving rise to robots that behave in human ways. In this area the predictions of science fiction will come true, for we do not know enough to set limits on the possibilities of the computer.

Plasma physics is a specialty that did not exist fifty years ago. A plasma is a gas existing at such a high temperature that some or all of the electrons are stripped from the atoms that make up the gas. The study of plasma physics is important for two reasons. First, most of the matter in the universe is in the plasma state, so that astrophysics is largely about plasma physics. Second, the search for a new form of nuclear energy by the process of thermonuclear fusion requires heating a volume of deuterium gas, or deuterium plus tritium, to such a high temperature that it is rendered to the plasma state. If it can be confined by a magnetic field, or otherwise, long enough for energy-releasing reactions to take place among the deuterium nuclei, then the goal of fusion energy is reached. Devices to create fusion energy are extremely large, complex, and expensive. However, the development of a practical fusion generator would be one of the most important events in science history, since it would provide the world with an almost inexhaustible source of useful energy, without most of the drawbacks of conventional nuclear power which depends upon fission energy. During the past few decades, gradual progress has brought the promise of fusion energy close to feasibility.

- In the near future the feasibility of fusion energy will be demonstrated in a device that generates more energy than is required to run it.

- During the first half of the twenty-first century a practical fusion generating plant will be built. This will provide a source of concentrated electrical power without the pollution of coal, oil, and uranium fission, but will not be "cheap."
- Cold fusion will prove to be an unachievable dream.

Predictions are hazardous. All of the above predictions are based on developments already in the pipeline, and they represent only a fraction of what the future holds. Not mentioned for obvious reasons are unsuspected discoveries that might be made. On the other hand, predictions that violate fundamental principles are *not* going to happen. Examples of these impossibilities are: a faster-than-light spaceship or message transmitter; an antigravity machine; a perpetual motion machine; a time machine; or a satellite that hovers over one spot on Earth's surface while tethered to it with a long cable. These predictions exist only in science fiction, not in reality.

[See also Astronomy; Batteries; Chemistry; Digital Communications; Media Lab; Scientific Breakthroughs; Semiconductors; Superconductors.]

BIBLIOGRAPHY

Besançon, Robert M., ed. *The Encyclopedia of Physics.* New York: Van Nostrand Reinhold, 1985.
Cava, Robert J. "Superconductors beyond 1-2-3." *Scientific American* 263 (1990): 42–49.
Davies, Paul, ed. *The New Physics.* Cambridge: Cambridge University Press, 1989.
Huth, John. "The Search for the Top Quark." *American Scientist* 80 (1992): 430–443.
Quigg, Chris. "Elementary Particles and Forces." *Scientific American* 252 (1985): 84–95.
Rothman, Milton. *The Science Gap: Dispelling the Myths and Understanding the Reality of Science.* Buffalo, NY: Prometheus Books, 1992.
Weinberg, Stephen. "Unified Theories of Elementary Particle Interaction." *Scientific American* 231 (1974): 50–59.

– MILTON ROTHMAN

PIPELINES

Pipelines transport liquids, gases, and slurries of liquids and solids. Pipeline transport is the safest form of transportation, invisible to consumers (being mostly underground) and economical for many products.

Pipelines for Energy Transportation

Pipelines deliver essentially 100 percent of the natural gas used in the United States. Nearly 300,000 miles of high-pressure, long-distance transmission pipelines and over 800,000 miles of local distribution mains were in the ground in 1990. Total throughput in 1991 amounted to about 20 trillion cubic feet of gas, or about

23 percent of U.S. energy consumption. Worldwide, over 500,000 miles of gas transmission lines have been constructed.

In the United States, pipelines are also the primary mode for transporting crude oil to refineries and refined products to consumers. Over 150,000 miles of liquid-carrying pipelines have been constructed in the United States and nearly 400,000 miles worldwide. In 1989 U.S. pipelines moved 53.4 percent of liquids, ships and barges moved 42.6 percent, and trucks and railroads transported the remaining 4 percent. These pipelines delivered 6.6 billion barrels (Bbbl) of crude oil and 4.8 Bbbl of refined products in 1990.

Hydrogen generated from solar energy or nuclear electric energy may begin to replace natural gas by the middle of the next century.

Pipelines are also in limited use for the transport of coal. Coal must first be pulverized, then mixed with water to form a slurry that is pumped through a pipeline. About 400 miles of U.S. pipelines annually carry over 8 million tons of coal from mines to electric power plants.

Other Uses

About 1 million miles of pipelines and aqueducts deliver over 300 billion gallons of water per day in the United States. Pipelines also transport mineral products from mines to product refineries, operating in the same manner as the coal slurry lines described above. Products transported include limestone, copper, iron, phosphate, zinc phosphate, gilsonite, and kaolin, as well as mine tailings for disposal. About 2,000 miles of such pipelines exist worldwide. A number of pipelines transport gases such as carbon dioxide, hydrogen, and helium.

Pipeline Economics

Construction of a high-pressure transmission pipeline is costly. However, once constructed and operating, a pipeline represents a very economical means of transport. Construction costs depend on the size and pressure of the pipeline, the terrain to be crossed, and the population density. Large-diameter (30–36 inches), high-pressure pipelines cost an average of about $800,000 per mile to construct. Smaller pipelines (8–16 inches) cost about $100,000 to $300,000 per mile.

Construction costs have remained generally constant over the past ten years. Rising labor, material, right-of-

way, and permitting costs have been largely offset by improvements in construction technology.

Compressor stations, consisting of large gas turbine or reciprocating engines that drive gas compressors, are necessary to pump gas through the pipeline. Compressor stations range in size from 1,000 to 100,000 horsepower (hp), with installation costs averaging $1,200 per hp. Other pipeline system components include flow-control valves and metering stations to measure gas flow and energy content.

In 1989 pipeline operating expenses amounted to $2.6 billion. These expenses add less than fifteen cents per thousand cubic feet to the gas price, amounting to about two cents per gallon of gasoline.

Pipeline Technology Trends

The technology for pipeline construction, operation, and maintenance has evolved dramatically over the past forty years. High-strength, crack-resistant steels, advanced welding technology, corrosion protection and control, high-efficiency compressor engines, and compressor automation have had major impacts.

Hydrocarbon transport in pipelines must increase in the future to achieve the energy goals of the United States and other countries. Increased use of natural gas is a key strategy in numerous countries that are currently dependent on petroleum and coal, such as Japan, Russia, and the countries of Central Europe. In the United States the Energy Policy Act of 1992 calls for greater use of natural gas because of its relative abundance and because natural gas is the cleanest burning of the fossil fuels. Expanded uses will require new pipelines for delivery.

CONSTRUCTION AND MATERIALS. For the next decade the material of choice for pipelines will continue to be high-strength steel. The average natural gas transmission line has 132 girth welds per mile. Continued improvements in pipeline metallurgy and welding will ensure pipeline integrity.

Looking to the future, composite pipeline materials (e.g., steel reinforced by a glass-fiber/resin composite) and entirely new, overwrapped joining techniques will become commonplace. These new materials will virtually eliminate external corrosion and stress corrosion cracking. New internal coatings or ribbed surfaces may reduce the drag in the pipe, cut pressure losses and thereby lower compressor fuel use. Planning future pipeline rights-of-way will be done using advanced geographic information systems. Satellite-based systems will optimize routing and construction that minimize environmental impact and construction cost.

OPERATIONS. Federal regulations that govern pipeline operation have increased competition among pipeline operators. Liquid pipelines have already been essentially deregulated and gas pipelines are becoming partially deregulated.

Supervisory Control and Data Acquisition (SCADA) computerized systems provide operators with vital data on compressor conditions and gas-flow information, such as pressure, flow rate, and valve position. SCADA systems, electronic flow measurement, compressor station automation, diagnostic systems, and real-time pipeline computer models allow optimum operation of a pipeline system.

MAINTENANCE. As the existing U.S. pipeline system ages (about 50 percent of the system will be greater than twenty-five years old by the year 2000), inspection and maintenance will assume greater importance. The pipeline transportation system is one of the safest modes of transportation. To maintain this record, operators will employ advanced pipeline inspection techniques, corrosion prevention technologies, and pipeline monitoring systems, as well as improved repair technologies.

Future pipeline inspection will be accomplished using so-called smart pigs. These are mechanical devices

Figure 1. Part of a gas pipeline compressor station.

Figure 2. A "smart pig" being inserted into a pipeline to inspect for defects in the pipe wall.

that travel through a pipeline and inspect the pipe wall, looking for cracks and areas where wall thickness has been reduced by a gouge or corrosion damage.

THE PROBABLE FUTURE. Many changes can be expected in the next century, both in energy sources and uses and in transportation systems. While supplies of fossil fuels, especially coal and natural gas, will be sufficient over this period, their costs will continue to rise in comparison to alternative, renewable sources. Hydrogen generated from solar energy or nuclear electric energy may begin to replace natural gas by the middle of the next century. The gas pipeline system can be used to transport hydrogen. Of course, upgraded materials or internal coatings may be necessary since hydrogen causes cracks to form in most steels.

Coal is still the most abundant energy form in the United States. However, its use creates the most pollutant emissions of the fossil fuels, including the highest level of carbon dioxide emissions, and emissions contribute to the "greenhouse" effect. Carbon dioxide emissions are likely to be restricted in the next century. But pipeline technology may play a role in allowing continued use of coal. For example, transporting coal in a slurry pipeline using a new solvent or refining chemical instead of water could actually refine the coal in the pipe to upgrade coal quality. Carbon dioxide pipelines could transport carbon dioxide captured at an electric utility generating plant from the plant to a disposal, storage, or use site.

Finally, the rising cost and environmental impact of rail and over-the-road freight shipment may stimulate entirely new applications for pipelines. It may become economically efficient to transport grains, minerals, or other products primarily by pipeline.

In conclusion, pipelines are a critical element of the world's energy transportation system. Continued advances in construction, operations, and maintenance technology will keep pipeline transport in the forefront through the next century as new concepts for energy and transportation evolve.

[See also Coal; Energy; Engineering; Materials: Research and Development; Natural Gas; Petroleum.]

BIBLIOGRAPHY

Clark, Judy R. "1992—A Year with a View." Pipeline Digest (January 1992).
Hiratsoo, J. N. H., ed. World Pipelines and International Directory, 1st ed. Beaconsfield, U.K.: Pipes & Pipelines International, 1983.
Quarles, William R. "Pipe Line Companies to Install 19,512 Miles of Lines in 1992." Pipe Line Industry (January 1992).
Robinson, Ronald C. "Computerized Monitoring Enhances Corrosion Detection." Pipe Line Industry (March 1992).
Vincent-Genod, Jacques. Fundamentals of Pipeline Engineering. Houston: Gulf Publishing, 1984.

Watts, Jim. "Dimensions of the 500 Leading U.S. Energy Pipeline Companies." *Pipeline & Gas Journal* (September 1991).

— WILLIAM M. BURNETT

PLANNING

A major task of organizations involved in advancing planning and forecasting, such as the Strategic Leadership Forum, is to ensure that future directions become apparent in time to adjust social and business institutions to the desired course of action. Leaders responsible for setting direction in their organizations need access to four basic kinds of support:

1. Access to important new ideas while they are still a faint "blip" on the radar screen;
2. Access to real-world cases of practitioners at the leading edge of an applicable discipline;
3. Knowledge received just in time to be applied to unique problems;
4. A network of experts and successful peers.

The future is not anticipated through the perfect plan as much as through a powerful, evolving process that keeps leaders exposed to and aware of change.

Strategy Implementation

Successful authors of books on managing change and the future suggest various approaches to planning. William C. Finnie (1994), for example, outlines a four-cycle approach that has been successfully used in more than a hundred corporations. The first cycle creates links among concepts about shareholder value, planning, implementation, and customer- and competitor-driven strategies. The second cycle employs strategic thinking concepts. The third promotes shared goals. The fourth keeps plans fresh and action-oriented.

Margaret Wheatley (1992) connects strategic thinking with the revolutionary discoveries being made in quantum physics, chaos theory, and evolutionary biology, conceptual breakthroughs that are changing our fundamental understanding of the universe. She proposes how to find order in a chaotic world and distinguishes order from control.

C. Davis Fogg (1994) brings us back to earth with dozens of hands-on tools that help as team-based strategy evolves, including models to forecast five-year results, keys to plotting the ongoing processes, guides for facilitators, and miscellaneous troubleshooting advice.

William A. Band (1994) reviews ten touchstones for the year 2000 and beyond: delivering superior value, revamping business processes, thriving on rapid change, developing a highly motivated workforce, building supplier and customer alliances, aligning work with strategy, creating a learning organization, building change leadership, and leveraging technologies.

Finally, Peter Senge and coauthors (1994) move from the theory of learning organizations to practical applications with an incisive workbook. The case histories in the workbook show that companies, businesses, schools, agencies, and even communities can undo their "learning disabilities" and achieve greater performance.

Tools and Techniques

Over the past decade, executives have witnessed an explosion of management tools and techniques such as reengineering, total quality management, and benchmarking, each offering to help organizations adjust to the future. Keeping up with these and deciding which ones to use have become essential parts of an executive's responsibilities.

Key findings of the Strategic Leadership Forum annual survey appraising success with strategy tools reveal that tool usage is growing but that there is no correlation between the number of tools used and the satisfactoriness of the results. Greatest satisfaction occurs when strategy tools are used to uncover new opportunities to serve customers, help build distinctive organization capabilities, and help exploit competitor vulnerabilities.

Human Potential

A crystal ball would reveal people becoming intensely individualistic due to the influence of technology, while continually evolving in their knowledge and becoming more flexible in their associations. Clearly, people will also require some stability—and an opportunity to touch and feel what they experience in a wired world.

Technology is increasingly permitting an individual's aspirations and needs to be addressed directly; yet, paradoxically, this only intensifies the individual's need for association.

With posthumous apologies to John Donne for tinkering with and perhaps contradicting his famous quote, the future holds the distinct prospect that "every man *is* an island." As it continues to evolve, technology is increasingly permitting an individual's aspirations and needs to be addressed directly; yet, paradoxically, this only intensifies the individual's need for association. As public companies give way to private enterprise and as public services shrink in their role of serving an ill-defined public good, the need heightens for voluntary associations of complementary interests.

As highly structured formal business and social institutions shrink in the future, the static concept of a career will change to a dynamic, evolutionary process of learning. So, too, the static concept of an institution containing the sum of all knowledge on a subject changes to a dynamic process of people coming together, to participate in a common task and associate the work of their team with other teams, forming flexible, vital organisms.

A Fundamentally Different World

Increasingly, labor, capital, technology, knowledge, and physical assets will transcend national boundaries. No matter where pooled, resources will be available to all through global market mechanisms. Increasingly, global business and organizational cultures will trade in knowledge and will form alliances far more than they will engage in competition and resource control. Global knowledge, experiences, and mobility will cut across boundaries of language, political geography, and property. Customers will be found everywhere and grouped around expectations that will be identified globally. Global identity may be more powerful than local identity.

Organizational Renaissance

No perfect plan or strategy is recognized, but definite progress on anticipating the future is being made. Planning and the future are not an oxymoron provided that planning is free of extensive prediction and avoids proposing highly structured solutions. Perhaps the greatest progress in understanding the future has been to avoid looking through the distorting filter of our present attempts at solutions.

At bottom it is imperative to recognize that we face a fundamentally different world, one for which we can never fully or finally prepare. Therefore, we must keep our sights set on maximal exposure to change. We also must reconnect with the fact that organizations are simply human constructs, and accord greater freedom for the coming together and breaking apart of work groups.

The complex and rapid change we face is still susceptible to management. The tools and techniques used to allow organizations to adjust to change may need constant reevaluation to produce desired results. Even as tools become obsolete or unresponsive, new authors and new ideas crop up and provide new ways to get back on track with exciting concepts to meet the challenges of a changing global society. Human creativity knows no bounds—the future is an open-ended quest.

[See also Change, Optimistic and Pessimistic Perspectives; Continuity and Discontinuity; Forecasting Methods; Strategic Planning; Surveys.]

BIBLIOGRAPHY

Band, William A. *Touchstones—Ten New Ideas Revolutionizing Business.* New York: John Wiley, 1994.

Finnie, William C. *Hands on Strategy—The Guide to Crafting Your Company's Future.* New York: John Wiley, 1994.

Fogg, C. Davis. *Team-Based Strategic Planning—A Complete Guide to Structuring, Facilitating, and Implementing the Process.* New York: American Management Association, 1994.

Senge, Peter, et al. *The Fifth Discipline Fieldbook.* New York: Doubleday, 1994.

Wheatley, Margaret J. *Leadership and the New Science—Learning About Organization from an Orderly Universe.* San Francisco: Berrett-Koehler, 1992.

– A. BRUCE WILSON

PLURALISM

The term *pluralism* has roots in philosophy, where it is contrasted with *monism*. In the social sciences, its primary use has been in political science and political philosophy, where it refers to both the analytical view that there are many sources of power in a society, state, or community, and to the normative view that this is a desirable state of affairs, which should be encouraged through the devolution of central state power to other actors—governmental and nongovernmental. The alternative viewpoints would be that empirically the power to make key decisions flows from a single ruling elite, or closely linked ruling elites, both within and outside government, and normatively that the dispersion of power that pluralists prefer is inefficient and ineffective in fulfilling the aims of government or in serving the national or community interests.

In American political science, there has been an extended debate on the nature of power in American society and government between pluralists and their opponents. Some of its leading participants have been C. Wright Mills (1956), Floyd Hunter, Robert Dahl (1961), Nelson Polsby, and Seymour Martin Lipset (1960). The variety of groups that pluralists believe actually participate in or should participate in power and decision making have included business associations, trade unions, community organizations, religious groups, the various levels of government, and indeed the whole range of associations into which men and women enter.

In the 1980s and '90s, racial and ethnic groups have become more prominent as candidates for the proper devolution of power and influence in a plural society. This has led to a debate in the United States over "multiculturalism"—that is, over the degree to which racial and ethnic groups should be recognized as distinct in their interests and culture, possessing some degree of stability and permanence, and legitimately entitled to have their distinctive interests and points of view expressed in education, the media, public ceremonies, and government. In opposition to multiculturalism is the position that racial and ethnic groups in the United States have in the past assimilated to a common American culture; that this culture is derived from England primarily, but from Europe in general; and that these groups have thus become "Americanized," and should continue to do so.

Multiculturalism was in earlier decades called *cultural pluralism,* a term coined by philosopher Horace M. Kallen during World War I, in opposition to heightened demands then made on new European immigrant groups that they become assimilated and Americanized. Kallen, along with the social critic Randolph Bourne, asserted that the United States was and should remain a society in which each group maintained its identity and contributed its distinctive strain to the common culture.

Cultural pluralism had little influence until the civil rights movement of the 1960s. Until then American Negroes, the largest minority in the United States, had fought and hoped for assimilation into American society. While this objective was not abandoned in respect to participation in the economy and government, in the course of the 1970s and '80s Negroes, whose preferred name rapidly changed first to *blacks* and then to *African Americans,* increasingly emphasized their distinctive culture and demanded that it be recognized in schools, colleges, universities, and public life. This demand became the moving force in a new cultural pluralism, labeled *multiculturalism* in the 1990s.

Black demands were echoed by other groups, in particular Mexican Americans, whose numbers expanded in the 1970s and later decades through increased immigration. Some elements among Asian-American groups, greatly expanded in numbers by immigration, also raised multicultural demands. The older European ethnic groups, whose distinctiveness had been defended by Kallen and Bourne, do not participate in the multicultural movement. Indeed, some intellectuals whose forebears came from these older European ethnic immigrant groups are among the leading critics of multiculturalism. Few from European ethnic groups protest against their cultural assimilation into American life. Seventy years after the end of mass European immigration to the United States, the identity and distinctiveness of these groups have been much altered by assimilatory forces and high rates of intermarriage.

The greatest success of multiculturalism has been in colleges and universities, where distinctive academic programs on black literature, culture, and history have been created in the hundreds, along with fewer, but still quite numerous, programs dealing with Hispanic and Asian-American culture and history; and in the elementary and high schools, where curricula in literature, history, and social science have been sharply modified to take account of multicultural demands. Multiculturalism has been strongly attacked by Arthur M. Schlesinger, Jr. (1991), and Richard Bernstein (1994), among others. It has not been defended by prominent intellectuals, but it is nevertheless solidly rooted in the educational system, higher and lower, and treated with deference in the mass media.

One success of multiculturalism has been in gaining recognition in state laws and in court decisions of the right of children speaking a foreign language to be educated for a few years in that language. The educational basis for such "bilingual" programs is educational effectiveness, on the grounds that children must have a few years to learn English before attending classes in which all teaching is in that language. But multicultural proponents would also like to see home languages maintained through school programs and to have group and homeland culture also taught, along with language. In some states those who would prefer a more rapid transition to English have tried to lessen state bilingual requirements. The great majority of those enrolled in bilingual programs are Spanish-speaking—from Mexico, Cuba, Puerto Rico, and other Spanish-speaking Latin American countries. Thus in many cities the conflict over the extent and duration of bilingual programs is drawn between Hispanic activists and community leaders and the non-Spanish-speaking majority.

The term *multiculturalism* has been broadened to cover controversies that have little to do with culture; for example, the conflict over affirmative action—preference in employment, or in bidding for government contracts, or in admission to selective college and professional schools on the basis of race, ethnicity, and sex—and the conflict over special efforts to fashion black-majority voting districts so that the number of elected black representatives can be increased. These issues and similar ones have led to important U.S. Supreme Court cases and will continue to do so.

While the controversies over pluralism and multiculturalism have received the most attention in the United States, almost identical issues have emerged in other major countries of immigration, such as Australia and Canada. Even formerly homogeneous European nations such as France, Germany, the Netherlands, and others must deal with issues of pluralism and multiculturalism because large numbers of people from different cultures have immigrated and permanently settled there. In a world in which migration, despite efforts to control it, is a permanent feature, and migrants are drawn from increasingly distant and various countries and cultures, more and more countries are dealing with the issues that have emerged so sharply in the United States, as it moves from the demand for full assimilation to some variant of multiculturalism.

[See also "China;" Class and Underclass; Democracy; Democratic Process; Ethnic and Cultural Separatism; Global Culture; Human Rights; Lifestyles, Ethnic; Lifestyles, Value-Oriented; Mass Culture and Arts; Minorities; Political Party Realignment; Race, Caste, and Ethnic Diversity; Values; Workforce Diversity.]

BIBLIOGRAPHY

Bernstein, Richard. *Dictatorship of Virtue: Multiculturalism and the Battle for America's Future.* New York: Alfred A. Knopf, 1994.

Dahl, Robert. *Who Governs? Democracy and Power in an American City.* New Haven, CT. Yale University Press, 1961.

Glazer, Nathan. *Ethnic Dilemmas, 1954–1982.* Cambridge, MA: Harvard University Press, 1983.

———. "Is Assimilation Dead?" *The Annals* 530 (November 1993): 122–136.

Higham, John. "Multiculturalism and Universalism: A History and Critique." *American Quarterly* 45 (1993): 195–256.

Kallen, Horace M. "Democracy *Versus* the Melting Pot." *The Nation* (February 18 and 25, 1916): 190–192 and 217–220. Reprinted in Kallen, Horace M. *Culture and Democracy in the United States.* New York: Boni and Liveright, 1924.

Kariel, Henry S. "Pluralism." In *International Encyclopedia of the Social Sciences.* Vol. 12. New York: Macmillan, 1968.

Lipset, Seymour Martin. *Political Man: The Social Bases of Politics.* Garden City, NY: Doubleday, 1960.

Mills, C. Wright. *The Power Elite.* New York: Oxford University Press, 1956.

Schlesinger, Arthur M., Jr. *The Disuniting of America: Reflections on a Multicultural Society.* New York: Norton, 1991.

— NATHAN GLAZER

POLICY CHANGES.

See PUBLIC POLICY CHANGE.

POLITICAL CAMPAIGNING

Political campaigning in developed democratic nations in the twenty-first century will be affected by significant changes in the ways citizens register to vote, select candidates, cast ballots, receive both information and propaganda, and function as partisans in the election process.

Over the next fifty years, as more households become linked by national interactive computer-video-telephone-fax network grids, the process, not just of political communication but of active participation, will become increasingly home based. Voters will be able to register, mark and record ballots, interview office seekers, attend and address campaign strategy meetings, work precincts, use credit cards to make financial con-

tributions, and circulate literature—all from their homes.

Computer retrieval of information available in hundreds of independent data banks, as well as the material sanctioned by campaign headquarters, will permit public scrutiny of the finances, personal affairs, business involvements, and membership associations of office seekers in such detail as regularly to reopen the historic debates about appropriate privacy.

By the year 2050, people of color will exceed Caucasians in number for the first time; whites will be the slowest-growing population component and may even be in decline.

Conversely, and perhaps more important, the volumes of market research information that candidates can obtain about voters from computer research and constant interactive surveying will combine with advanced information processing to revolutionize statistical analysis in political campaigns. Pivotal voting blocs will be identified, and within these groups voters with shared, or even subliminally shared, special interests will be isolated and appealed to with tailored messages quite apart from the general campaign rhetoric.

Electronic bulletin boards and E-mail will permit quick and controlled distribution of messages to targeted groups. Closed circuit television and televised telephone conference facilities will allow candidates to speak at length to regional and national rallies of voters with specific special interests. Those in the audience who participate in these rallies will be no less responsive, and no less militant, even though they may be home alone. In fifty years a major skill of professional campaign managers will be the ability, using computer data, survey testing, and intuition, to identify and address those inconspicuous elements of shared anxiety or enthusiasm among voters who are otherwise markedly different in experience, intellect, economic position, and personal history.

The public theater that characterizes national elections will remain. Political platforms will continue to reflect common-denominator themes. But increasingly, the most productive work of a campaign in terms of winning over and galvanizing the uncommitted will be done by candidates from a single communication center. Hour after hour they will dial into and present their views to one prearranged special interest rally after the next. Comparatively silent and invisible, extremely expensive, and potentially very effective, this method of

A certain amount of theatrics will continue to characterize political campaigns, just as they did in this 1952 Republican convention parade. Unfortunately, voter participation seems to be waning, reaching an all-time low of 17.4% in the 1998 primaries. (UPI/Corbis-Bettmann)

political campaigning will employ to the fullest the developing technologies in high-speed research, processing, distribution and communication.

Population dynamics will also impact on the strategy, the organization, and the cost of campaigning in the next century. Not only will populations increase, but a significantly higher percentage of citizens will register to vote and actually vote because both can be done at home. New power concentrations will emerge. In the United States, Asian Americans will continue to be the fastest-growing population group, increasing by more than 350 percent to forty-one million by mid-century. At that time African Americans will number sixty-two million, up 94 percent. Hispanics will total eighty-one million, reflecting a 24 percent increase. By the year 2050, people of color will exceed Caucasians in number for the first time; whites will be by far the slowest-growing population component and may even be in decline.

Older Americans of all races and nationalities will constitute the country's largest, most powerful, and most demanding voter bloc. By mid-twenty-first century 20 percent of the population will be sixty-five years of age or older. One of the dominant political tensions in the United States and other advanced democracies—an issue which will have to be dealt with by every political candidate in every election—will result from the demand for better and more widely distributed medical care: An increasingly older, retired citizenry with clout at the polls will need support from a steadily shrinking base of younger taxpayers.

Political debate will focus as well on institutions made obsolescent by scientific development and social change. High on this list will be the election process itself, bringing changes which will affect campaigns. Modernization in the United States will include efforts to eliminate the Electoral College; to discontinue tabulation of votes by states in presidential elections; to end the requirement of printed ballots so that all votes can be cast electronically; to permit votes to be cast at home as well as at neighborhood polling stations. There will be initiatives to set a single day for a nationwide presidential primary in each party; to reduce by half the length of all state and national election campaigns; to arrange for weekend voting with all ballots cast from East to West over precisely the same forty-eight-hour period; to stimulate voter participation by authorizing official announcement of election results, minute by minute, as they are received and recorded at electronic counting centers.

Campaigns for public office, as they will evolve in the twenty-first century, will require massive initial outlays for equipment and systems development and major year-round funding for program maintenance. This need for expensive continuing operations will produce a resurgence in political parties. It will also exacerbate the threat to democratic processes posed by wealthy special-interest organizations able to invest in the mechanics of political persuasion. Wealthy candidates will benefit disproportionately from campaigns which employ high-tech home-based electronics. Even with the greater ease by which citizens will register and vote, this electronic infrastructure will have a conservative influence on future elections and may also contribute to an electoral elite in modern democracies. These and other subtle, secondary consequences of change must not be ignored. We were not always successful in the twentieth century in providing equal opportunity for voters, guaranteeing majority rule, protecting minority voices, and avoiding fraud. The challenge will be no less great in the twenty-first century.

[See also Communitarianism; Conservatism, Political; Liberalism, Political; Political Cycles; Political Parties; Political Party Realignment; Third Political Parties; Voting.]

BIBLIOGRAPHY

"The Aging of the Human Species." *Scientific American* (April 1993).
"Electronic Town Halls?" *National Journal* (June 6, 1992).
"The New Computer Revolution." *Fortune* (June 14, 1993).
"Techno-Politics Is Coming of Age." *Boston Globe,* June 1, 1992.
"The Tekkie on the Ticket." *Washington Post,* October 18, 1992.
Wiesendanger, Betsy. "Electronic Delivery and Feedback Systems Come of Age." *Public Relations Journal* (January 1993).

— RICHARD H. BLADES

POLITICAL CYCLES

Ebbs and flows in politics are shaped by two types of cyclical behavior. The first is the cyclical rhythm of government involvement in public and private affairs, which follows changes in generations occurring about every thirty years. The second type of political cycle is the change in world leadership among nations based on uneven growth rates between economies as well as technological innovations that bring greater advantage to one society over the others.

The American Political Cycle

American politics alternates between what Emerson in 1841 called conservatism and innovation. Many observed this cycle, but descriptions and definitions vary. Henry Adams described an oscillation between diffusion and centralization of national purpose. Arthur M. Schlesinger, Sr., defined the cycle as a swing between conservatism and liberalism. Each of these descriptions is accurate in its own way, but these well-used terms are subject to varying definitions.

Economist Albert O. Hirschman helped to clarify this problem by characterizing the cycle as a shift in focus between the conflicting goals of private and public happiness. Arthur M. Schlesinger, Jr., further summarized the cycle as a continuing shift in national involvement between public purpose and private interest.

Periods of government action devoted to public purpose began in 1900, 1932, 1960, and 1992. Periods in this thirty-year cycle that focus on private interest followed in 1920, 1952, and 1980, with the next forecast to arrive at the end of the first decade in the next century.

Each phase in the cycle breeds contradictions. During times of public purpose, reform comes in bursts. Public action piles up change and disappointment as well. A nation is worn out by constant summons to battle and becomes weary of ceaseless political activity that produces mixed results. Individuals then turn to private action to solve problems.

The current age of television, plastic, and oil is being supplemented by a new age of information based on computers, silicon, and fiber optics.

Concentration on private affairs produces contradictions as well because some segments of the population do not share in the common good. Examples of excessive private acquisitiveness remind people of their public obligations and people consequently seek meaning in life beyond themselves.

Shifts in thinking between the generations is the mainspring of the political cycle. John Stuart Mill, in 1843, held that major changes in history required the appearance of a new generation open to new ideas. Ortega y Gasset, in 1961, reaffirmed the role played by successive generations and identified a thirty-year recurring pattern. It consists of a period of coming of political age challenging incumbents, followed by a period of control before the next generation takes over. As each generation attains power, it tends to repudiate the work of those it displaces and to follow the ideals of its own formative days thirty years before. This phenomenon produces a thirty-year rhythm that swings between public purpose and private interest.

The Next Cycle of Public Purpose: 1992–2000

Politics in the United States, beginning in 1992, entered a period of change dominated by public purpose. Bellwether government initiatives provide a forecast of what is likely to happen during this political cycle. Several governments in Europe—especially Sweden, as well as key state and city governments in the United States—have experimented with reforms likely to be on the United States federal government's agenda during the balance of this cycle. Among the many possibilities for change are these:

- *Employee benefits.* Longer vacations; time off; inconvenient and uncomfortable working hour pay supplements.
- *Health care.* National, universal, comprehensive, compulsory coverage; catastrophic care; right to die laws; meshing public/private benefits; health insurance courts; cooperative hospitals; environmental injury benefits; death benefits in advance of death; artificial part replacements; genetic intervention coverage.
- *Job security.* Lifetime job guarantee; industrial democratization; worker board of director membership; permanent, portable pensions; shorter pension vesting period; taxation of nonwage benefits.
- *Retirement.* Life expectancy escalators; later retirement; voluntary retirement; consolidation of government retirement programs.
- *Women.* Family leaves; universal, free, public preschooling; childcare and aging parents time-off benefits; mandatory flextime and job-sharing.

Some of these trend-setting initiatives worked well, others did not; but they point to areas where reform will be introduced in the United States during this next part of the cycle. Concurrent with the U.S. political cycle that ushered in an era of public purpose is another cyclic phenomenon driven by long waves of recurring change in the world economy.

The Long Wave

The long wave is a forty-five- to sixty-year cycle of economic growth and decline that was identified in the 1920s by a Russian economist, Nicolai Kondratieff. He presented statistical evidence of a cycle of prosperity, recession, depression, and recovery in the economies of France, Great Britain, Germany, and the United States. Closely studied since then, the cycle has completed an ebb and flow in economic development four times since the Industrial Revolution began late in the eighteenth century.

In the 1990s we will complete a transition to the next long wave. This wave, like the four previous ones, is being defined by a set of technological breakthroughs and organizational innovations that eventually will bring advantage to societies that successfully initiate and utilize them.

This will happen because downturns between each wave prompt innovation. Successful innovations become extremely profitable and form leading-edge industrial sectors that characterize the following forty-five- to sixty-year period. Prospects for increasing prosperity lead to building productive capacity beyond market need that in turn produces economic downturn until the stage has been cleared for yet another era of building.

Expansions at the start of each long wave grow around an integrated and mutually supporting combination of technologies. German economist Gerhard Mensch identified clusters of innovations that helped launch each long wave. Innovation peaked at the beginning of the Industrial Revolution in the 1770s–1780s and in the transition between long waves in the 1830s–1840s, the 1880s–1890s, and the 1930s–1940s. Once a set of innovations is established, they define the new system, and incompatible technologies are rejected as impractical. This is why innovations that define a long wave era are grouped into a ten- to fifteen-year window during the transition between long wave eras. The world is in the midst of another such transition now.

Each long wave era is fueled by an innovative industry and supporting technologies that comes to define each age. In each long wave, the nation that best capitalizes on innovation leads economic growth and through its economic power dominates world events. See Table 1.

The transition between the fourth and fifth long wave will last for the remainder of this century. It will continue to be a time of innovation. As in former transitions, new industries will build on the dominant industries of the previous era. The current age of television, plastic, and oil is being supplemented by a new age of information based on computers, silicon, and fiber optics.

New economic powers that emerge at the beginning of each wave are drawn into the power vacuum created by the relative decline of the previous wave's hegemonic power. This decline occurs because at the end of each wave the dominant power overextends itself. Attempts to fulfill commitments to foreign and domestic programs deplete resources, and the wherewithal to mount new ventures, accordingly, is diminished.

The French attempt at hegemony during the first long wave, opposed by the rising economic might of Great Britain, ended in defeat at Waterloo. Britain, in turn, found itself replaced as the world's leading industrial economy by both Germany and the United States as the second wave drew to a close at the end of the nineteenth century. Germany's attempt at domination in the third wave was crushed in 1918 and 1945. The fourth wave's hegemonic power has been the United States, which until recently was constantly challenged by the old Soviet Union. The United States may surrender economic and political leadership at the end of this century as we make the transition from the fourth to the fifth long wave. In fact, part of the transition has already occurred. The nations of the European Community (EC) have constituted the world's largest economy since 1990, and Japan has become the financial capital of the world.

The United States is still the world's most open society, and that provides fertile ground for further innovation and growth. But to maintain its leadership role as the next long wave gathers speed, the United States must overcome history; the leader of the old system has rarely been the leader of the new.

Conclusion

The United States has entered a cycle dominated by public purpose, where much needs to be done to solve problems, but limited funds are available to spend for such purposes. At the same time, global political leadership is in transition, as economic power, the cornerstone of military and political influence, is shifting. The United States is the hegemonic power from the old era, weighted down with commitments that were part of its previous success, but that cannot easily be paid for in the future. Whether the United States plays the leading role in the future will be determined by how quickly it can discard the baggage of the past and embrace the future.

[See also Change; Communitarianism; Conservatism, Political; Liberalism, Political; Pacesetter Governments; Political Parties; Political Party Realignment; Public Policy Change; Technological Change.]

BIBLIOGRAPHY

Erickson, Scott W. "The Transition Between Eras: The Long Wave Cycle," *Futurist* 19/4 (1985): 40–44.

Forrester, Jay W. "Economic Conditions Ahead: Understanding the Kondratieff Wave," *Futurist* 19/3 (1985): 16–20.

TABLE 1

DOMINANT TECHNOLOGICAL FORCES CHARACTERIZING ECONOMIC LONG WAVES

	First Wave	Second Wave	Third Wave	Fourth Wave	Fifth Wave
Industry	Textile	Railroad	Automobile	Television	Computer
Material	Cotton	Iron	Steel	Plastic	Silicon
Energy	Water	Wood	Coal	Oil	Solar
Communication	Semaphore	Telegraph	Telephone	Electronic	Fiberoptic
Nation	France	United Kingdom	Germany	United States	European Community

Goldstein, Joshua S. *Long Cycles: Prosperity and War in the Modern Age.* New Haven: Yale University Press, 1988.

Kennedy, Paul. *The Rise and Fall of the Great Powers: Economic Change and Military Conflict from 1500 to 2000.* New York: Random House, 1987.

Kondratieff, Nikolai. *The Long Wave Cycle.* Trans. Guy Daniels. New York: Richardson & Snyder, 1984.

Molitor, Graham T. T. "Swedish Benefits Today—U.S. Benefits Tomorrow?" *Innovations* (Fall 1993): 6–18.

Schlesinger, Arthur M., Jr. *The Cycles of American History.* Boston: Houghton Mifflin, 1986.

Strauss, William, and Howe, Neil. *Generations: The History of America's Future 1584 to 2069.* New York: Quill/Morrow, 1991.

— SCOTT W. ERICKSON

POLITICAL ECONOMY

Economics and its nineteenth-century predecessor, political economy, may become academic curiosities unless their ancient meaning can be adapted to a postmodern world view in renewed systems of governance. The conditions under which they can be effective and beneficial are disappearing.

Economy is derived from a Greek compound word for household administration (a small business operation). It exemplified what Aristotle called *practical* reason, by which he meant making decisions on *what should be done,* given that there is rarely enough time, resources, or freedom to do everything. This dilemma—limited means and unlimited wants—is the essential core of economic reasoning. It implies that interpersonal conflict is inevitable and therefore raises moral issues, which Aristotle treated as topics in his *Ethics* and *Politics.*

Moral and political philosophers were the custodians of economic thought for many centuries. In the late Middle Ages, they were concerned about the *justness* of prices at a time when the rapid expansion of commerce was upsetting centuries of social-class stability. The rise of the bourgeoisie shifted the locus of political power from the allegiance of heavily armored men on horseback to an ability to pay cash for the upkeep of armies. Kings and lords were forced to collaborate with wealthy burgesses, whose assets were in coin rather than land. Moralists condemned the practice of taking interest, believing with Aristotle that the accumulation of money is an unnatural form of wealth. Profound change was imminent.

Renaissance philosophers replaced God with humankind as the *final cause,* the focus of creation. No longer inhibited by the belief that natural processes are sacrosanct, humanists began to view nature as something to be used. The new view also eroded belief in social structures as an immutable natural order. Thomas More's *Utopia* (1516) was the most systematic of their proposals for government as an instrument to promote material security, individual contentment, and civic virtue. More was original in postulating economic growth as an instrument of national policy. The belief that nature could be manipulated by technology and the presumption of a bounded nation-state were also fundamental in systems conceived by political philosophers such as Bodin, Hobbes, Bacon, Locke, and Montesquieu.

The nation-state required accounting procedures to cope with bills of exchange, deferred payments, banking, insurance, and other instruments invented by its commercial partners. This *political arithmetic* cemented the familiar but unfortunate association of economics with money. (Money appears in many *manifestations* of the economic problem, but is not of the essence.) The original meaning of economy was later applied to the nation-state in the term *political economy,* and described as the art of kings.

Enthusiastic philosophers in the eighteenth century (e.g., Godwin, Condorcet) believed that reason would assure material and social progress. Skeptical economists, however, discounted these expectations by pointing not only to the limited capacity of nature but also to human nature as self-defeating. The Malthusian theorem on population growth became a principle of classical political economy, earning it the label of *dismal science.* To counter this negative image, economists devised political structures to encourage human creative energy. At one extreme these formulas focused on freedom of action (market capitalism in the tradition of Adam Smith) and at the other on rational control by government (scientific socialism, following Karl Marx). Both sought an appropriate balance between increased production and distributive justice.

Nineteenth-century economists postulated an economic *system* that can be investigated by methods similar to those of physics, with the results used to engineer better system performance. They changed the name of their discipline to *economics* in the twentieth century and described it as a *challenge* to scarcity. So long as the focus of analysis was local, the issue of global or ultimate limits (entropic and ecological) could be ignored, and usually was. The growth-by-technology solution (use of *speculative* and *productive* reason in Aristotle's tripartite classification) is a clear departure from the original meaning of economy as part of the classical Greek quest for the "Golden Mean."

Government support for economics research has encouraged the technological focus, for material abundance is politically popular and puts off the time when uncomfortable choices are inescapable. Hence, economic studies of the kind that acknowledge limits and address the choice implications have been progressively avoided in roughly inverse proportion to the accumulating knowledge of global imbalance between population and resources. Engineers, sociologists, statisticians, computer scientists, financial analysts, management specialists, historians, and political scientists have all contributed to techniques and empirical knowledge that are useful in economics work—but without the focus on the collective choice dilemma, they are *not* economics or political economy. The confusion of money, finance, business enterprise, or decision-making technique with economics and political economy impairs the resolution of very serious problems of interpersonal, international, and human-environment relationships. Greater profits for some individuals or groups do not automatically increase the collective welfare, invocations of Adam Smith to the contrary notwithstanding.

The nation-state is weakening

relative to transnational corporations,

which consume collective resources relentlessly,

destroying the powers of nature in the process.

Political economy can be useful only if its postulates hold, and they are showing signs of exhaustion today. The nation-state is weakening relative to transnational corporations, which consume collective resources relentlessly, destroying the powers of nature in the process. Access to the means for earning a living is evaporating in a new, multinational version of the sixteenth-century enclosure movement. An effective market system requires institutions of law, justice, and morality—hence governments, boundaries, and wide consensus on the purpose and nature of rules. Without these conditions, macroeconomic policy instruments are ineffective, and redistributive programs become impossible to justify or administer.

A political economy that has meaning for the future must be based in an ecological worldview and in political structures that assure that the classic concept of economy as a best possible *human* adjustment to limits is applied to means-ends decisions. In the absence of global government, a global economy will reenact the lawless frontier of nineteenth-century America in combination with massive numbers of underemployed, displaced people. Individuals and families will solve their personal economic problems in any way they can. These may involve cooperative local solutions, tribal connections, and group solidarity among geographically dispersed people held together by shared religious commitment. But even though they may have procedures, policies, and techniques for production, distribution, and exchange, these cannot by definition constitute a form of political economy.

[See also Business Structure: Industrial Policy; Capital Formation; Capitalism; Economic Cycles: Models and Simulations; Economics; Entrepreneurship; Ethics; Evolution, Social; Free Trade; Global Culture; Governance; Information Society; International Trade: Regional Trade Agreements; Investments; Marketplace Economics; Morals; Multifold Trend; Political Cycles; Post-Information Age; Race, Caste, and Ethnic Diversity; Social and Political Evolution; Technological Change; Utopias; Workforce Redistribution.]

BIBLIOGRAPHY

Bonar, James. *Philosophy and Political Economy.* New Brunswick, NJ: Transaction Publishers, 1991.
Daley, Herman E., and Cobb, John B., Jr. *For the Common Good.* Boston: Beacon Press, 1991.
Tinder, Glen. "Can We Be Good Without God?" *Atlantic Monthly* (December 1989).

– KEITH D. WILDE

POLITICAL PARTIES

The best way to examine the future of American political parties is to look at trends in the past. The history of political parties in America is filled with paradoxes. Parties are not mentioned at all in the Constitution; the framers never considered them as an essential or even as particularly desirable. But parties developed immediately as a basic organizing medium for the varying political approaches and philosophies that characterized politics in the late eighteenth century. The parties of the early Congresses faded and were replaced by others, but a party system, essentially based on two major parties vying for control of state and national governmental institutions and for the allegiance of voters, has existed continuously since the beginning of the republic.

If parties have a long history, their venerability is not widely appreciated in the mid-1990s. Few people outside the parties themselves have good words to say about the parties and the party system. Fewer voters identify with either of the two major parties than at any time in the past several decades, and those who do tend to have weaker allegiances than they did several years ago. The trend toward independence among voters has been growing for more than a decade and was underscored in November 1992 by the 19 percent voter support for the independent presidential candidacy of H. Ross Perot.

Voters in focus groups talk about voting for the man (or woman) and not for the party, and decry the partisanship that has characterized policy-making in Congress. But voters also like, by a two-to-one margin, divided government, which accentuates partisan differences, and their collective judgment in November 1994 further polarized the political parties in Congress on left/right and partisan lines. The 1994 election, if a vote against divisive partisanship, also had striking partisan dimensions; while Democrats suffered serious losses for the first time in modern American history not a single Republican incumbent member of the House or Senate, or among the governors, was defeated for reelection.

What do these realities portend for the future of political parties in America? First, parties and the two-party system will not wither away. They will still be with us, in a dominant way, for some time, at least as an organizing principle in Washington and state capitals around the country. But the role of the Democratic and Republican parties will be quite fluid; the opportunity for some kind of third force, if not an organized political party, to play a major role, will be greater; and the parties will remain diffuse and decentralized entities, even if they show occasional surprising unity and strength in individual institutions, such as occurred in the House of Representatives in 1995.

Parties and the Public

Social scientists have been measuring public opinion toward the parties systematically for more than fifty years, looking particularly at partisan affiliation or party identification. For much of that time—at least from the early 1950s through the late '70s—party identification was very stable. Roughly three-fourths of Americans identified clearly with one or the other of the two parties; only one-tenth of Americans were characterized as independents or were without any identification at all with a party. Through most of that time, the Democratic party had a clear edge over the Republicans, typically running roughly 47 to 37 percent or so.

As we moved to the early 1980s, the Reagan era, Republicans moved to a stronger position, but the stability in party identification declined, as did the strength and durability of party identification generally.

In the mid-1990s, the parties moved to a position of near equity in party identification, but with both parties weaker in terms of numbers and intensity than they had been in decades past. In the summer of 1994, a major national survey found that more than one-third of Americans (35 percent) called themselves independents, while 33 percent identified as Democrats and 29 percent as Republicans. By December 1994, after the stunning 1994 election, 35 percent identified as Republicans and only 30 percent as Democrats. The turnaround in the parties' fortunes is likely to be more a

demonstration of the lack of stability in partisanship than a permanent shift in party positions.

What about the future? A look at party identification trends by age group gives us clues about the future of the parties. Start with the young. The Republican party squandered an advantage it held among young voters at the beginning of George Bush's presidency in 1989. Democrats, in turn, failed to win over the young people attracted as a consequence to Bill Clinton in 1992. As of mid-1994, neither party showed any advantage among Americans under thirty, or even among those aged thirty to forty-nine.

Older voters, those over fifty, show a strong preference for the Democrats based on their generational affinity with the New Deal and John F. Kennedy. It is possible, of course, that young voters will find events or political figures in the late 1990s or the early part of the twenty-first century that will solidify their own partisan feelings. Perhaps Newt Gingrich or another Republican figure, or Al Gore or some future Democratic leader, will capture the imaginations of young voters the way FDR or JFK did. But the lack of such enduring impact by Ronald Reagan would suggest it is more likely that neither party will establish a clear growth pattern or enduring advantage in the near future—and that independence will be at least on a par with partisanship. As the older generation dies out, however, Democrats will lose a major part of their partisan base and, in a fluid atmosphere, will be at a general competitive disadvantage vis-à-vis the GOP.

Looking at other groups in the electorate does show some more significant trends that have strong political implications in the future. Racial and gender differences in partisanship are clear. Blacks overwhelmingly identify as Democrats, while Republicans have a slight lead among whites (although more whites are independents than identifiers with either party). There are some signs of a slight movement among young black voters toward the GOP, but little that would suggest a real competition between the parties for allegiance of the African-American electorate. Republicans have an advantage among men, while Democrats have an edge among women, leaving about a 10 percentage-point "gender gap" between the parties that seems quite stable looking to the future.

Republicans have made significant gains in the past decade among several significant subgroups of voters—particularly among white Southerners, white evangelicals, and white non-Hispanic Catholics. These gains clearly made some difference in the ability of the GOP to win congressional seats in 1994 and to create serious problems for Democrats in finding a winning presidential electoral coalition into at least the early part of the twenty-first century. Even so, it would take striking political developments in the next several years for these GOP advantages to develop into a long-term Republican partisan majority in the country.

Parties in Government

If parties are weaker in the electorate, they are stronger in Congress. However, they are not stronger as national forces binding a presidential party together with a congressional party. In Congress, parties are stronger largely in the House of Representatives, not in the more individualized U.S. Senate.

Parties in the mid-1990s continued to be

the major paradox in American politics,

simultaneously strong and weak,

important and insignificant.

In Congress, the 1994 elections ushered in the first Republican-majority House of Representatives in forty years, joining a Republican-majority Senate to make the first entirely Republican-majority Congress to face a Democratic president since 1947–48. The election of a Republican House was made possible in part by extraordinary party unity by the minority Republicans in the 103rd Congress in 1993–94. The Republicans seized on their opportunity to provide more formal powers to their new Speaker, Newt Gingrich, than any Speaker since Joseph Cannon, who served as Speaker from 1903 to 1911.

Democrats had more difficulty reaching the same levels of unity, but still showed stronger solidarity than in the past several decades, brought about more by greater philosophical coherence across regions than by formal rules or procedures. The party cohesion, more generally, meant a greater number of partisan divisions on key votes than were seen in the 1960s and '70s. The Democratic party in Congress has gradually become more liberal, as conservative Southern Democrats were replaced by moderates and liberals (including some blacks) and in many cases by Republicans. The Republican party in Congress has become more conservative, as it has built a new base in the South and West, while losing its old dominance in the Northeast. These trends, toward a more liberal Democratic party, based more in the East, Midwest, and Far West, and a more conservative Republican party anchored in the South, Midwest, and Rocky Mountain region, should solidify in the next decade or so. But, to reiterate, the growing

ideological and partisan gulf inside Congress does not fit any comparable set of trends in the public arena. And despite the growth in independence in the electorate, only a single independent or third party representative has been elected to Congress in nearly two decades—one Socialist from Vermont serves in the House—leaving party as the sole organizing element of the legislature for the foreseeable future, as it has been throughout the past.

Parties in Campaigns and Elections

The partisan unity in Congress is in a small way a reflection of more activity by national political parties to attract, recruit, and nominate candidates for the House and Senate. But most of the candidates who run for Congress are self-starters, who win nominations in primaries without the approval of local, state, or national parties, raise most of their money on their own, win on their own, and enter elective office as individual go-getters. That fact alone makes any strong degree of partisan unity in Congress quite striking. No reforms realistically on the horizon, from campaign finance changes to party reforms, are likely to change that situation more than marginally. Parties are likely, at the level of campaigns and elections, to remain organizationally weak. The structure of the election process and the continuing high level of voter identification with the two parties make it very difficult, despite the parties' structural weaknesses, for a third party or an independent movement to develop, take root, and succeed at the state or congressional level.

However, the situation may develop differently at the gubernatorial and even presidential level. Independent candidates for governor have had some success, winning in the early 1990s in Connecticut, Alaska, and Maine, and reaching respectable vote totals in many other states. H. Ross Perot's 19 percent of the popular vote for president in 1992 was the strongest showing nationwide for an independent in eight decades, and polls showed continuing strong support for individual, independent candidacies for president, reaching in some cases over one-third of the electorate for a popular and attractive possibility such as Colin Powell.

Conclusions

Parties in the mid-1990s continued to be the major paradox in American politics, simultaneously strong and weak, important and insignificant. Their fundamental position and roles had changed only marginally in the post–World War II era, and most evidence suggested that would continue to be the case into the early part of the twenty-first century. But the marginal changes, and dramatic elections in the post–Cold War era, suggest the possibility of more signal changes in the future. If the odds remained long, even so—more than at any time in modern American history—political, social, and economic conditions created a greater opening for an independent candidacy for president to succeed. If that were to happen, it clearly would have repercussions on parties in Congress and candidacies to Congress, and would make possible the institutionalization of a new party or at least an enduring independent movement. That is perhaps the most important trend to watch in the next decade and more.

[See also Communitarianism; Conservatism, Political; Liberalism, Political; Pluralism; Political Campaigning; Political Cycles; Political Party Realignment; Social and Political Evolution; Third Political Parties; Voting.]

BIBLIOGRAPHY

Baumgartner, Frank R., and Jones, Bryan D. Agendas and Instability in American Politics. Chicago and London: University of Chicago Press, 1993.
Brown, Peter. Restoring the Public Trust: A Fresh Vision for Progressive Government in America. Boston: Beacon Press, 1994.
Craig, Stephen C. The Malevolent Leaders: Popular Discontent in America. Boulder, CO: Westview Press, 1993.
Lynch, William M. The Nationalization of American Politics. Berkeley, CA: University of California Press, 1987.

— NORMAN J. ORNSTEIN

POLITICAL PARTY REALIGNMENT

We have reached one of those great epochal divides when new ideological distinctions reflecting the new values and a new paradigm are being defined. On the political plane, this requires rethinking fundamental assumptions about individuals, institutions, policies, and programs. What exactly do political parties stand for?

This search involves examining the underlying paradigm shift, staking out political claims on new ideologies, and setting new political landmarks to guide popular thinking. It requires a rethinking of the major issues that reflect the tempo of the times and that resonate with the majority. Voter loyalties have reached a point requiring them to be forged anew under a program that entails essential changes in direction.

Some looming themes of political-party realignment address the depressing social cacophony that casts a pall over the country. The despair of these times is linked to rotten urban cores, disadvantaged youth, a growing underclass, deterioration of family values, and a pervading moral malaise. It is undergirded by age-old cyclical themes: big government versus little government; centralization versus decentralization; financial and fiscal profligacy versus restraint; and an end to tax burdens

on a weary public. The philosophical principle that permeates this restructuring involves changing values and lifestyles, and balancing rights and responsibilities. At the core of this reform and rebalancing are a host of viewpoints that interminably oscillate between support for the well-to-do and support for the down-and-out, and the overall swing between the liberal and conservative perspectives.

Arthur Schlesinger, Sr., noted swings that averaged 16.5 years between increasing democracy and containing or restricting it, between shifting emphasis from the rights of a few to concerns for the wrongs of the many. Arthur Schlesinger, Jr., noted changes in U.S. political cycles averaging thirty years' duration, and asserted that political party realignment occurred at intervals of forty years.

Carrying policies too far in one direction invites a counterforce. History is characterized by an ebb and flow between extremes of all kinds. The United States is in the midst of a long sweep of the political pendulum shifting from central control to restoring state and local government responsibilities. Too heavy a hand imposing regulatory burdens invites new efforts to minimize them. Trends in the next political cycle of leadership involve shifts from:

- Big government to limited government
- Centralization to decentralization
- Control to freedom of action
- Direct to indirect control
- Oppression to liberty
- Planning to laissez-faire
- Top-down to bottom-up
- Compulsion to voluntarism
- Universality to diversity
- Dependence to independence
- Security to venturesomeness/risk taking
- Paternalism to self-help
- Individualism to communitarianism
- Protectionism to freer trade
- Egalitarian leveling to extolling excellence
- Profligate to penurious spending
- Tax increases/complexity to tax reductions/simplification

The Molitor cyclic modeling of great issues reveals that different categories of issues move at different speeds and that over the past several centuries these ebbs and flows have greatly accelerated. Molitor's cyclic models based on year-by-year counts of federal laws covering an issue category reveal bursts of new developments in laws occurring in twenty- to twenty-six-year cycles in the United States. The Molitor model places commencement of the postindustrial-era political realignment in 1980, with a serious gathering of momentum in 1988, culminating in sharp cleavage between contesting major U.S. political parties by 2000, and then tapering off between 2010 and 2018 as a new cycle gets under way.

This process of political change and adaptation generally is expressed by two points of view: (1) conservative or tradition-bound; and (2) liberal or progressive. That is one way of looking at it. Recent political history involves a continual abandonment of the status quo, a constant process of adjustment to change, and—hopefully—a steadily advancing or progressive trend. Political policy perspectives respond to change, moving along over time in a progressive mode.

U.S. history reveals an incremental progression and eventual nearly universal acceptance of liberal causes. Slowly, the nation has inched forward. Liberalism's main defining point or difference with conservatives since the New Deal has been essentially its emphasis on the welfare state. Now that liberalism has attained most of its coveted objectives, and they have become so familiar a part of the contemporary social fabric, there is little dispute over their merit. Relatively indistinguishable and undistinguished tweedledee and tweedledum positions on New Deal programs have become ingrained and no longer generate fierce debate as they once did. No longer do voters cast ballots on pro or con viewpoints involving the welfare state. Attention has shifted to other less familiar and more controversial areas.

Until the recent and resounding defeat of full-fledged socialized medicine, conservatives by and large had gone along (albeit grudgingly) with most of these paternalistic programs. But a new mood is stirring. Even the incumbent Democrat president favors reform of "welfare as we know it"—whatever that might mean. Conservatives have their own and, doubtless, more drastic version of welfare reform and advocate returning responsibility for the pottage of welfare programs back to the states. Overindulging the needy—even though sparked by a humanitarian compassion—cannot completely ignore human nature. When recipients become overly dependent and give up on helping themselves, they are more in need of a hand up than a handout. New battle lines are being drawn.

Demographically, as the elderly cohort swells, so does its political power. Political survival requires addressing health care delivery questions. When 34 to 37 percent of the public are uninsured, the issue can hardly be ignored.

Society undergoes recurring pendulumlike swings from one extreme to the other but seldom reverts to the old status quo (regression contra-distinguished from progression). A good metaphor characterizing this change is that of a spiral or, better yet, a helix. The pattern is ever onward, a lifting or raising and advance.

Political policy-making in the United States is essentially confined to the two major political parties. Discernible ideological division between them has become muddled. Both political parties are searching for principles defining what they stand for and offering voters clear-cut and decisively different choices. To attract and retain voters, political parties rise and fall based on the policies and programs with which they are identified.

Both political parties scramble to hold the middle ground and try to do all things for all persons. Pandering to the amorphous middle ground lessens voter attachment to either party.

Meantime, both political parties scramble to hold the middle ground and try to do all things for all persons. Pandering to the amorphous middle ground lessens voter attachment to either party. When both parties stand for and occupy the common middle ground, distinctions congeal and get lost. As a result, voting hinges more on superficial aspects of the political process—personalities, campaign styles, and political "spin."

For almost a half century, U.S. government power has been divided, with Congress controlled by one party and the executive branch by the other. This state of affairs led to a virtual stalemate in a patchquilt of consensus politics that blurred distinctions between the parties. This expedient pattern, at least until the 1994 elections, stymied bold departures in ideology. Gridlocked government, with neither party able to take bold and aggressive action or reform, hobbled sweeping policy changes. Compromise—the essence of recent federal decision making—has added to voter apathy. A steady drumbeat of federal scandals, rampant porkbarrel politics, and the sophistry of national politicians have created a wave of cynicism that has dragged down voter turnout to all-time lows.

Third political parties, splinter parties, and political opportunists chime in. Their good ideas invariably get taken over by a major party. In this sense they serve a vital purpose in helping to shape, but not dominate, the new political agenda.

Confounding political change is the growing ethnicity and diversity of the population. Coupled with the growth of superzealotry—religious, ethnic, single-purpose interest groups, and so on—the discordant sway of proliferating special-interest groups has the cauldron seething. When so many diverse groups fight for individual or group advantage and their "piece of the action," the commonweal suffers. By selfishly seeking their own aims and transgressing the broader social interest, these special interests add new urgency to political agenda setting. This restatement of principles requires moderating self-interest and deferring to the broader social interest.

Central to political party realignment is the age-old question involving the best balance between individual rights and social responsibilities. These touchstones are at one of those great historic divides. In the spirit of pursuing freedom to buttress a truly democratic society, things currently have gotten out of hand. Overly zealous pursuit of individual rights is bound to interfere with somebody else's rights. Total wanton and self-centered freedom creates anarchy. Freedom left to run its full course—untrammeled freedom, extremist individualism, liberty carried to ultimate limits—can lead to tyranny. Liberty does not include unlimited license. Self-restraint is essential. Individual extremism is well suited to a single person like Robinson Crusoe living alone on a deserted island. Living in society requires accommodating and acceding to the rights of others as well. Utilitarianism—the greatest good for the greatest number—is the mediating principle. Rights must include responsibilities in a well-ordered society.

At this juncture, a swing back toward communitarian values—more identified with Republicans at this point—seems to be in prospect. Willpower, self-determination, individual responsibility, self-control, social restraint, a sense of community duty, and taking responsibility for one's acts are the touchstones that grip this ongoing debate. This approach will redress the balance by emphasizing old-fashioned self-discipline and insisting on individuals taking responsibility for their own volitional acts and not seeking refuge in some excuse.

Laws are made by legislators and may be changed by them. Slavery, once the law of the land, has long since been outlawed. Dueling, once the accepted way of resolving personal disputes, has been outlawed. One of the most difficult and contentious aspects of political party reform involves rhetoric that casts privileges into rights and rights into "untouchable" entitlements. Taking without giving entails a certain self-centered, egoistic, and self-indulgent cant. Privileges must be earned. It is wrong to make demands on but not contributions to the commonweal. Society has obligations to its citizens, just as citizens have obligations to society. It is a two-way street. Providing excuses for less fortunate persons tends to eliminate incentives to step up and seek improvement. Providing aid that enables the poor to stay where they are and fatalistically resign themselves to the "hand that has been dealt them" is wrong. The time may have arrived to encourage those on welfare to do more to help themselves. The ultimate truth may be that we must expect—or even demand—from everyone the same standards of behavior we expect from one another.

The new political agenda requires a fresh vision to guide the nation along innovative paths of development. We need a better fix on where we are headed—and why. In short, we need an agenda spelling out specific goals infused with a renewed sense of national purpose and direction. Sociopolitical change, however obscure its overall design may appear to be, is neither random nor aimless. Although precise details cannot be discerned, the basic shape of things to come looms on the horizon. You cannot navigate the ship of state by staring at the wake behind the ship. We need to muster the courage and invoke the foresight of a lookout. We need to look ahead and gather information to steer us forward.

Our comprehension of domestic political trends, however imperfect it may be, must be improved. Surmising the future by mere intuition, impulse, or opinion is insufficient. Convincing proof in the form of systematic, comprehensive, accurate, and timely forecasts of public policy goals is needed. Political parties, in this sense, carry a vital, yet unfilled function. New policy directions more accurately reflecting the changed tempo of the times and the pervasive influence of the information era offer an inchoate and essentially unfulfilled opportunity.

[See also Agents of Change; Communitarianism; Conservatism, Political; Crime Rates; Entitlement Programs; Health Care Costs; Institutions, Confidence in; Liberalism, Political; Multifold Trend; Pluralism; Political Cycles; Political Parties; Public Policy Change; Social and Political Evolution; Third Political Parties; Voting.]

BIBLIOGRAPHY

Bennett, William J. *The Index of Leading Cultural Indicators: Facts and Figures on the State of American Society.* New York: Simon & Schuster/Touchstone, 1994.

Etzioni, Amitai. *The Spirit of Community: Rights, Responsibilities, and the Communitarian Agenda.* New York: Crown, 1993.

Gingrich, Newt, with David Drake and Marianne Gingrich. *Window of Opportunity: A Blueprint for the Future.* New York: Tom Doherty Associates/Baen Enterprises, 1984.

Hughes, Robert. *Culture of Complaint: The Fraying of America.* New York: Oxford University Press, 1993.

Mead, Lawrence M. *Beyond Entitlement: The Social Obligations of Citizenship.* New York: Free Press, 1986.
Phillips, Kevin. *Boiling Point: Democrats, Republicans, and the Decline of Middle-Class Prosperity.* New York: Harper Perennial, 1993.

— GRAHAM T. T. MOLITOR

POLLS, OPINION.

See PUBLIC OPINION POLLS; SURVEYS.

POPULARIZED FUTURES

Fascination with the future is one of the defining characteristics of the human race. It is a fascination that is born of a mixture of curiosity and dread. The urge to step beyond the thin, moving line that divides the present from the future and to part the curtains that divide the known from the unknown is inescapable.

Martin Heidegger is not generally acknowledged as a futurist, but his *Sein und Zeit* was a seminal work that explored the roots of the human concern with the future. *Dasein,* the existence into which humans are "thrown," as objects are thrown into a river, is not a state but a flow. It is a condition characterized by anxiety about and awareness of the future, as containing both the necessity and the choice of death.

Time is an arrow, and human existence is conditioned by the fact that the arrow is unidirectional and irreversible. The opposite of the future is not the past. The anguish of becoming, the dread of the disorderliness and chaos of change, makes the future a subject of interest not merely to the specialist and the intellectual, but to everyone alive.

The earliest popularized futures were religious or quasi-religious. The mantic, or prophetic, arts, which combined religion, magic, and the quest for the future, included divination, astrology, and palmistry. Roget records some sixty-nine forms of divination, including cartomancy (playing cards), pyromancy (fire), sortilege (lots), oneiromancy (dreams), lithomancy (stones), onychomancy (fingernails), geomancy (earth), hydromancy (water), and necromancy (dead bodies). In China, the I Ching was developed along with tarot cards and other esoteric means of appraising the future. Augury was the art of scanning the future by interpreting omens, especially through the study of the flight of birds, the appearance of the internal organs of sacrificed animals, and the occasion of thunder and lightning. Haruspicy involved the study of the liver for the same purpose. (The haruspices, an order of minor priests charged with this function in ancient Rome, may be considered the first group of professional futurists.) Astrology is the oldest art of predicting the future; it originated in Mesopotamia in 3000 B.C. It is also the most widespread,

being found in every culture; even today it is consulted by over one billion people worldwide. Astrology is based on the belief that the stars, as Shakespeare said, govern our destinies (*King Lear,* IV, iii, 34).

The vatic (divination) arts were practiced by oracles, sibyls, and prophets. In Greece, the pythoness, a priestess of Apollo at Delphi, commonly known as the Delphic Oracle, was a national institution. Other major Greek oracles were those of Zeus at Dodona in Epirus and of Trophonius in Boeotia. The principal Egyptian oracles were at Apis and Memphis. There were also seers, such as Tiresias the blind Theban, familiar to readers of T. S. Eliot. In Hebrew culture, the tradition of prophet (literally "foreteller") was highly developed. As oracles of God, prophets enjoyed a standing almost equal to that of kings. Isaiah, the greatest of the Hebrew prophets, combined fulminations and prophecies in cadenced prose. The tradition of prophecy was preserved in the Christian church. In the stark majesty of its language, the Apocalypse of John, known also as Revelation, has no peer. Its influence is attested by the fact that over 7,000 commentaries have been written on it in more than 50 languages. One of them, *The Late Great Planet Earth* by Hal Lindsey, is the best-selling futures book in the twentieth century.

The tradition of prophecy was preserved in the Christian church. In the stark majesty of its language, the Apocalypse of John, known also as Revelation, has no peer.

In the Middle Ages, the mantic arts and the vatic arts went underground, but one late mediaeval name stands out, that of Nostradamus. A physician by profession, and perhaps a charlatan to boot, Nostradamus has become a synonym for a forecaster. His fame rests on his book *The Centuries,* a collection of rhymed quatrains published in 1555. Many of his supposed predictions are almost Delphic in their obscurity and could be interpreted to mean almost anything.

It was only in the late twentieth century that interest in a scientific or rational—as distinguished from a personal—future became widespread. H. G. Wells, whom W. Warren Wagar calls the father of futurism, is said to have founded the field in 1902 with his book *The Discovery of the Future,* followed in 1933 by *The Shape of Things to Come.* The future was viewed as a foreign country, an unknown timescape, that needed a few explorers to map its terrain.

A new wave of trail-blazing futurists emerged after World War II. They were responsible for shaping futurism as a profession and as an intellectual niche. (The words *futurism* and *futurist* are used here for want of a better word. There are many, like Michael Marien, who insist with good reason that futurism is neither an *-ism*, nor a science.) Futurism may be said to have come of age in the 1960s with the founding of organizations like the Club of Rome (1968), the World Future Society (1966), and Futuribles International (1960). As happens to all vigorous movements, futurism began to undergo a process known as twigging: first the trunk, then the branches, and then the twigs. One branch, led by intellectuals, like Daniel Bell, concentrated on the task of laying down the philosophical groundwork while exploring the frontiers. A second group, mostly business-oriented futurists, like Herman Kahn and Joseph Coates, wrote massive reports in seamless futurese. Another group turned to writing and publishing, still others to policy studies and computer modelling. "Macfuturists" also emerged by the score, popularizing a Chinese-cookie style of forecasting. They are adept at producing small nuggets of wisdom that at first seem unassailable but on closer examination prove to be of the maybe/maybe-not variety.

Popularized futures form only a twig, a small but vital part of the whole body of futurism. Pop future books are the stuff of bestsellers, the proof being John Naisbitt's *Megatrends* (1990); Alvin and Heidi Toffler's many books, including *Future Shock* (1970), *The Third Wave* (1980), and *Powershift* (1990); Frank Feather's *G Forces: Reinventing the World* (1989); Richard Carlson and Bruce Goldman's *20/20 Vision: Long View of a Changing World* (1990, 1994); Norman Myers's *The Gaia Atlas of a Changing World* (1990); and Marvin Cetron's *Crystal Globe* (1991).

Also popular are descriptions of the future, a genre in which I. F. Clarke's *Tales of the Future* lists 3,300 titles published between 1644 and 1976. The most notable among them are W. Warren Wagar's *A Short History of the Future* (1989); Alberto Villoldo's *Millennium: Glimpses into the 21st Century* (1981); Norman Macrae's *The 2025 Report: A Concise History of the Future* (1984); Brian M. Stableford and David Langford's *The Third Millennium: A History of the World, 2000–3000* (1985); Arthur C. Clarke's *July 20, 2019: Life in the 21st Century* (1986); and Adrian Berry's *The Next 10,000 Years* (1974).

New Age futurism is represented by Marilyn Ferguson's *The Aquarian Conspiracy* (1980); Willis Harman's *The Global Mind Change* (1988); Fritjof Capra's *The*

Turning Point (1982); and Mary E. Clarke's *Ariadne's Thread: The Search for New Modes of Thinking* (1989).

Panoptic futurism or global surveys abound. The best are the annual Worldwatch *State of the World Report;* the UN's *Global Outlook 2000* (1990); *Our Common Future* by the World Commission on Environment and Development (1987); and UNESCO'S *World by the Year 2000.*

Panglossian futurism is exemplified by Herman Kahn's writings; Gerard K. O'Neill's *A Hopeful View of the Human Future* (1981); and Julian Simon's *The Resourceful Earth* (1983). The opposite, Cassandra futurism, has an even broader audience. In his *Terminal Visions: The Literature of Last Things* (1982), W. Warren Wagar lists 300 titles on doom, none more frightening than Jerome Deshusses' *The Eighth Night of Creation* (1982). Gee-whiz futurism, in which only technology matters, is represented by Morris Abrams and Harriet Bernstein's *Future Stuff* (1991), and eco-futurism by Al Gore's *Earth in the Balance: Ecology and the Human Spirit* (1992).

[See also Bell, Daniel; Forecasting Methods; Future Studies; Futures Concepts; Futurism; Futurists; Kahn, Herman; Nostradamus; Science Fiction; Wells, H. G.]

BIBLIOGRAPHY

Howe, Leo, and Wain, Alan. *Predicting the Future.* New York: Cambridge University Press, 1993.

Wagar, W. Warren. *A Short History of the Future.* Chicago: University of Chicago Press, 1989.

— GEORGE THOMAS KURIAN

POPULAR MUSIC.

See MUSIC.

POPULATION GROWTH: UNITED STATES

Demographers define the "baby-boom generation" as Americans born from 1946 through 1964. During those nineteen years, 76 million people were born. Given the family-size norms of the time, this was about 17 million more people than demographers expected.

In the years immediately following World War II, births in the United States rose sharply because many Americans delayed marrying and having children until the end of the war. When the soldiers came home, marriage rates rose. Soon after, maternity wards began to fill with babies. Technically, the first baby boomers were born in June 1946, about nine months after soldiers began to return from Europe. For convenience, however, demographers include anyone born during 1946 in the "official" definition of the baby-boom generation.

By the end of 1946, American women were having 100,000 more babies each month than during the same month one year earlier. Overall, 3.4 million babies were born in 1946. In 1947, 3.8 million babies were born, fully 1 million more than in 1945.

Much to the surprise of demographers, the baby boom did not stop there. For the next seventeen years, births remained at record levels, peaking in the late 1950s. More than 4 million babies were born each year from 1954 through 1964. The birth boom lasted for nearly two decades because the young women of the 1950s chose to have larger families than their mothers did, an average of three or four children each. They gave birth to the largest generation in American history.

The rapid expansion of the number of people in their forties has already moved middle-aged concerns to the top of the national agenda.

During the nearly two decades of record-level births, demographers began to predict that the birth boom would never end. They contended that larger families were the new American lifestyle. But the baby boom did come to an end nineteen years after it began. In 1965, births plummeted, women joined the workforce, and the baby-boom generation was complete.

The smaller generation that followed the baby boom, born from 1965 through 1976, is sometimes called the "baby-bust generation" because of the sharp drop in births during those years. In the 1960s and '70s, the fertility of American women fell dramatically, to an average of only 1.7 children per woman.

This decline in fertility to negative replacement rates surprised many. Demographers had been predicting another birth boom as the enormous baby-boom generation had children. Instead, baby-boom women went to college and embarked on careers, delaying marriage and childbearing.

In the late 1970s, the annual number of births slowly began to rise as the long-awaited "echo boom" finally appeared. Birth edged up from a low of 3.1 million in 1973 to 3.6 million in 1980. By the late 1980s, births were reaching levels not seen since the early 1960s and fertility rates were rising as well. The average number of children per woman rose to 2.1, reaching replacement level. Because of this surge in fertility, coupled with a large influx of immigrants during the 1980s, the Census Bureau projects that the American population will grow substantially during the next fifty years. The bureau's "most likely" scenario shows the total population climbing by more than 100 million over the next five decades, from 260 million in 1994 to 392 million in 2050.

Today, the baby-boom generation is a huge bulge in the American population. There are now 77 million baby boomers in the United States. This number is slightly greater than the 76 million born during the baby-boom years because immigrants of baby-boom age have arrived in the United States and raised the numbers. Baby boomers account for 29 percent of all Americans and for 42 percent of Americans aged eighteen or older. Because so many Americans crowd a nineteen-year age span, popular culture reflects and magnifies their experiences. Today the baby boom is a powerful economic and political force. It will remain so over the next thirty years.

Because baby boomers dominate the demographic landscape, they are a prime target for businesses and a mass audience for the entertainment industry. Consequently, American culture responds to their needs. When baby boomers needed schools, their communities built schools. More elementary schools were built in 1957 than in any other year before or since. Ten years later, in 1967, more colleges opened than in any year before or since. Consequently, baby boomers had the best access to education of any generation in American history. More than one-half have some college experience and one-fourth earned college degrees. When baby boomers needed cars, businesses built or imported small and inexpensive cars just for them. When baby boomers needed houses in the 1970s, housing starts rose to record levels. When baby boomers needed jobs, jobs were created by the millions.

The consequences of population growth are profound. As baby boomers joined the workforce and earned a paycheck in the 1970s, businesses saw opportunity in the numbers. There were profits to be made in giving millions of young people what they wanted. In the competition for this huge market, businesses offered baby boomers a growing variety of products and services. With so much choice available to them, baby boomers became increasingly diverse and individualistic. As baby boomers came of age, individualism became the dominant social and economic force in American society. The individualistic nature of the baby-boom generation has been transforming the United States for the past thirty years. Sociologists define individualism as the tendency to withdraw from social institutions and groups—including families, local communities, political parties, churches, and the nation. Individualists put their personal needs ahead of community needs. They make commitments for personal gain rather than for moral reasons. As individualistic baby boomers came of age over the past thirty years, voting rates fell, a rising proportion of Americans withdrew from organized religion, divorce became acceptable, materialism gained importance, and leisure was preferred to work.

The rise of individualism is the "master trend" of our time. This master trend drives a myriad of smaller trends. Individualism is behind the rise in divorce and in violent crime. It is one reason behind soaring health care costs, political gridlock, and racial tensions. It is eroding the loyalty of workers toward their employers. It is driving the accelerating pace of daily life. Individualism shapes the worldview of baby boomers and younger generations of Americans. The perspectives of these generations will shape the future of the United States.

By 2004 all baby boomers will be middle-aged. The number of people in mid-life, stretching roughly from ages thirty-five to fifty-four, will grow four times faster than the population as a whole during the 1990s. The rapid expansion of the number of people in their forties has already moved middle-aged concerns to the top of the national agenda. These concerns include family issues, health care, tax rates, crime prevention, and education. These issues will command the attention of voters and politicians well into the next century.

Middle-aged baby boomers are prominent now in politics. The first baby boomer was elected president in 1992. Baby boomers are likely to control the White House for most of the next thirty years. The baby-boom generation is becoming an important force in Congress. In the business world, few baby boomers head the nation's largest corporations today. But in ten years, most of the CEOs of the largest companies will be members of the baby-boom generation.

Baby boomers are also gaining economic power. People aged thirty-five to fifty-four spend more money than any other age group. With the baby boom increasing the number of thirty-five- to fifty-four-year-olds during the next few decades, the middle-aged will account for well over one-half of all consumer spending. They will dominate markets for nearly every category of goods and services, from shoes to insurance.

Not until boomers begin to fade from the demographic landscape, in about thirty years, will their influence begin to wane. But because younger generations (the children of the baby boom) are even more individualistic than boomers themselves, the social transformations caused by the baby-boom generation represent only the beginning of a new way of life. The individualistic perspectives of the baby-boom and younger generations of Americans are transforming the slow-moving and bureaucratic industrial economy of the mid-twentieth century into the fast-paced and diverse personalized economy of the twenty-first century.

The world of the baby-boom echo will be different. The baby boomers were born into families with large numbers of children where the mother was a homemaker. The echo babies are small numbers of children born to large numbers of families where the mother most likely works and where both parents are older, better off economically, and more mature. These changes will create a different echo generation as it matures.

Population growth also comes about from declining death rates and from immigration. Death rates are remarkably stable or slowly falling. Immigration is the big indeterminate factor in the nation's growth, in spite of the census bureau forecast.

[See also Aging of the Population; Longevity; Migration, International; Population Growth: Worldwide; United States.]

BIBLIOGRAPHY

Russell, Cheryl. The Master Trend: How the Baby Boom Generation Is Remaking America. New York: Plenum, 1993.

— CHERYL RUSSELL

POPULATION GROWTH: WORLDWIDE

During the 1990s, world population will grow to a greater extent than at any previous time in history. Although the growth rate declined somewhat from the late 1960s peak (from 2.0 percent per year to 1.7 percent in the early 1990s), the number of people added has risen. This is due to the much larger base population, 5.5 billion, compared to 1965's 3.3 billion.

Nearly all of the future world population growth will occur in the developing countries, which already account for three-fourths of the world total.

Long-range population projections from both the United Nations (UN) and the World Bank suggest a future world population about twice the present size. These projections assume, however, that birthrate declines occurring in many developing countries will continue. If this does not happen, total world population would not stop at the "medium" projection of about 12 billion. It could easily rise to 20 or 30 billion, or even more. It is important to note that nearly all of the future world population growth will occur in the developing countries, which already account for three-fourths of the world total.

The past fifteen years have seen rapid growth in world demographic information. Nearly every country has taken a census and the data from most are usable.

Notable exceptions are Chad, Nigeria, and Saudi Arabia. Additional invaluable sources include many fertility surveys taken in Third World countries since the World Fertility Survey program began in the mid-1970s. This program, which continues today as the Demographic and Health Survey, provided a first look at actual birth-rate trends in developing countries that lack vital statistics.

The most recent (1992) UN long-range projections anticipate a world population approaching 11.5 billion by the end of the next century. These projections will result in a constant world population size at some point in the future. This occurs because it is assumed that women will average two children each, meaning that each generation just replaces itself.

But projections are subject to a great deal of variation, depending on just how good the assumptions underlying them prove to be. For example, if women worldwide average not 2 but 2.5 children, world population would grow to 28 billion—not 11.5 as in the projection noted previously. This is a huge difference. Likewise, if women averaged fewer than two children each—say, 1.7—world population would be decreasing at the end of the next century, to a point less than today's total.

In the industrialized countries, birthrates have dropped so low that many of these nations—without augmenting growth by other means, such as immigration—face the prospect of population decline. A key indicator here is the total fertility rate (TFR), or the average number of children women bear during their lifetimes. If this average drops below 2.0 over a protracted period, population decrease is inevitable.

In Europe, women average only about 1.6 children each. Surprisingly, Italy's birthrate is now the world's lowest. At only 1.26 children per woman on average, it is also the lowest ever recorded. Population projections issued by many European countries now routinely forecast population decline. The importance of the birthrate is also somewhat magnified since few European countries accept, much less welcome, many immigrants.

In the United States, fertility near the "two-child" level and continued significant immigration will, in all likelihood, result in relatively brisk population growth well into the next century. The United States gains nearly one million new legal residents a year by immigration, the highest number in the world. The most recent U.S. Census Bureau projections show that, at present levels of fertility and immigration, the population will rise from 260 million in 1994 to more than 380 million by 2050.

The greatest potential for population growth, of course, is in the developing countries. Since World War II, advances in health care have led to longer life ex-

Asian streets such as this one in Ho Chi Minh City, Vietnam, teem with life and energy. (Kevin R. Morris/Corbis)

pectancy and, as a result, lower death rates. Many developing countries found themselves with growth rates rising to 3 or 4 percent per year. Growth rates of that magnitude will double a population in only twenty years. Recognition of this record-setting growth fostered expressions such as the "population explosion."

Concern about the effects of rapid population growth led to considerable concern that the world's ability to provide sufficient food would be overburdened and Earth's ecological systems overwhelmed. Those concerns remain, but in the early 1990s, it should be noted that the spread of family planning in the Third World is making a real difference.

Family planning programs got under way in the 1960s and accelerated in the 1970s, although the number of countries involved was not large at first. There were notable success stories—Thailand, Indonesia, Taiwan, Colombia, Mexico, and Costa Rica among them. In most countries of the Third World, women averaged five or six children each during their lifetimes. Throughout Africa and the Middle East, families often average six or more children.

In many developing countries the desire for large numbers of children was, and often still is, steeped in social tradition as well as in the perceived need for security in old age that large families can provide. Higher birthrates are nearly always associated with the proportion of the population living in rural areas and engaged in agriculture. Birthrates often decrease as societies become more and more urban. But in areas such as sub-Saharan Africa, 80 percent of the population lives in the rural regions.

During the 1970s, the governments of many developing countries resisted the idea of promoting family planning. This resistance crystallized at the 1974 World Population Conference in Bucharest, Romania. Saying that "development is the best contraceptive," Third World leaders argued that birthrates would come down as a natural result of economic development, not because contraception was forced upon an often uninterested populace. Ten years later, at a similar conference in Mexico City, the situation had changed dramatically. By that time, most developing countries had adopted official policies contending with birthrates that were too high.

In Asia, the one-child policy promulgated in China often captured headlines. With over one billion people, China's numbers weigh heavily in world totals. The Chinese government recognized that the finite limits of China's arable land and other resources dictated that the country's population not be allowed to rise into the many billions. China's policy has been fraught with controversy; the rather strict programs of incentives and disincentives would probably not be appropriate or possible elsewhere. But most of the program's goals were achieved. By the early 1990s, Chinese women were averaging only about 2.2 children each, down from 5 in the 1960s.

Eastern Asia provides the most dramatic examples of sharply decreased birthrates. Innovative family planning programs have caused fertility to tumble to low levels in Thailand. Economic progress, augmented by well-organized family planning programs, are often credited with similar outcomes in Taiwan and South Korea. In South Korea, the total fertility rate is an astoundingly low 1.6 children per woman, exactly the same as Europe. In Japan, Asia's only "developed" country by the UN's classification, very low fertility is causing concern. A recent Japanese newspaper headlined "1.57 Shock" to draw attention to a story on Japan's total fertility rate dropping to that level. In Japan, the very low birthrate, it is feared, will lead to labor force shortages, already a reality, and a country topheavy with the aged. In ad-

dition, an aging labor force is expensive in Japan, since salary rates are directly tied to seniority.

In South Asia, change has come more slowly. India's population program experienced some early success, but ran into political difficulties in the late 1970s, when some aspects of it were considered overzealous. As a result, India's TFR has been about 4.0 for over a decade. In Bangladesh, a long period of high fertility that has resisted family planning efforts came to an end in the late 1980s. Although still relatively high at a TFR of about 4.9 children per woman, this represents quite a drop from 7 children per woman in the past. Unfortunately, it is likely that simple overcrowding and the lack of additional land that forced many to seek opportunities in the city partially motivated the decrease.

In other areas of Asia, there are as many stories as there are countries. In Pakistan, with a population numbering about 125 million, there has been no sign of any decrease at all. In the Philippines, the momentum has gone out of the family planning program, in part due to lack of interest by President Corazon Aquino and her successor Fidel Ramos. In Vietnam, the world's thirteenth most densely populated country, a vigorous government policy seems to be working to bring down birthrates, at least for now.

Latin America has no truly dramatic example such as China or South Korea, but birthrates are surprisingly low nonetheless. Latin America's overall TFR of 3.4 is lower than that of Asia (excluding China). Religious considerations often discourage official government policies, leaving much of the management of family planning programs to private organizations.

In Brazil, Latin America's largest country in population at 151 million, the TFR has now dropped to about 3.1. In the region, only two countries have TFRs of 5.0 or higher, Guatemala and Nicaragua. Mexico enthusiastically adopted a population program in 1974 after earlier equating population growth with prosperity. The Mexican program has featured a wide variety of novel approaches such as soap operas featuring family planning and pop songs that appeal to young adults and adolescents.

It is in Africa that the least progress has been made. Today, in sub-Saharan Africa, it is typical for women to average six or seven children. In addition, life expectancy is still quite low. As a consequence, there is great potential for very high rates of growth if death rates fall but birthrates do not.

Family planning is a new idea in many parts of Africa. There are no success stories on that continent as yet. Still, the 1980s witnessed a virtual explosion of interest. While family planning use rates are low or nonexistent in most countries of Africa, in countries such as Botswana, Zimbabwe, and Kenya, rising usage rates show that real potential does exist.

Success in lowering birthrates often leads to concerns about an aging labor force, a stagnant domestic market, the expense of old-age health care, and strains on retirement systems.

For the most part, countries rarely adopt official "pronatalist" attitudes, despite concerns that may be raised unofficially or in the press about the consequences of population decline. Still, Sweden has recently attracted attention with a striking increase in its TFR to 2.1 in 1990, up from a low of 1.6. Many feel that Sweden's generous salary support for new mothers has played a significant role. In Asia, South Korea, with very low fertility, now feels that direct support of family planning is no longer needed. Singapore also toned down its policy when fertility sank to 1.8 children per woman. Even in China, it is thought that concerns about a rapidly aging population may have caused a mid-1980s relaxation of the pressure to have only one child.

Today, we can only speculate on the world's demographic future: eleven billion? six billion? thirty billion? Any of these futures is possible. Such a wide variation in possibilities causes obvious concern for food production, the environment, and all other supportive resources, which could suffer greatly if growth occurred too quickly to be accommodated. We know that the 1990s will be the most expansive decade for world population growth in recorded history. What we cannot know is whether it will prove to be the fastest of all time.

The ultimate question is whether population growth will stop before we exceed the ability to feed, house, and cloth everyone. If it does not stop, disease, war, and natural disasters will settle the matter, resulting in a monstrously rapid population decline.

[See also Change, Optimistic and Pessimistic Perspectives; Demography; Family Planning; Global Consciousness; Global Environmental Problems; Lifestyles, Alternative; Migration, International; Population Growth: United States; Refugees; Sexual Reproduction; Sexual Reproduction: Artificial Means; Surprises; Sustainability; Wild Cards.]

BIBLIOGRAPHY

Bulatao, Rudolfo A. *World Population Projections: Short- and Long-Term Estimates.* Baltimore: Johns Hopkins University Press, 1990.

Davis, Kingsley, and Bernstein, Mikhail S. *Resources, Environment, and Population: Present Knowledge and Future Options.* New York: Oxford University Press, 1991.

Ehrlich, Paul R., and Ehrlich, Anne H. *The Population Explosion.* Simon & Schuster, 1990.

Keyfitz, Nathan, and Flieger, Wilhelm. *World Population Growth and Aging: Demographic Trends in the Late 20th Century.* Chicago: University of Chicago Press, 1991.

Lappe, Frances Moore, and Schurman, Rachel. *Taking Population Seriously: The Missing Piece in the Population Puzzle.* London: Earthscan, 1989.

Marden, Parker G. *Population in the Global Arena: Actors, Values, Policies, and Futures.* Durham, NC: Duke University Press, 1982.

Marks, Eli S. *Population Growth Estimation: A Handbook of Vital Statistics Measurement.* Washington, DC: Population Council, 1974.

Newman, James L. and Matzke, Gorden E. *Population Patterns, Dynamics, and Prospects.* New York: Prentice-Hall, 1984.

Salvatore, Dominick. *World Population Trends and their Impact on Economic Development.* Westport, CT: Greenwood Press, 1988.

United Nations Population Fund. *State of the World's Population.* New York: United Nations, 1994.

Ville, Claude A., Jr. *Fallout from the Population Explosion.* New York: Paragon House, 1986.

– CARL HAUB
STEVEN GURLEY

POSTAL SERVICES

By the year 2000, the U.S. Postal Service (USPS) will be delivering over 200 billion pieces of mail, about 750 pieces per person. Approximately half will be first-class letters and cards, and another 40 percent will be third-class bulk mail consisting largely of advertising and nonprofit solicitations. The remainder will be a mix of express mail, second-class publications, fourth-class parcels, and international mail.

Privately written messages can now be sent

cheaply and quickly by fax, e-mail,

and electronic data interchange.

Since 1900, the total volume of mail has grown more rapidly than the nation's real GNP and much more rapidly than its population. This persistent growth tendency is the most conspicuous long-term feature of volume trends (see Figure 1). However, mail volumes are also affected by business conditions, service offerings, competition, demographic trends, the quality of postal services, and postal rates including discounts.

The mail stream is primarily generated by the requirements of commerce. Only 7.5 percent of first-class mail is correspondence between households. Almost everything else involves a nonhousehold, either as a sender or recipient. For example, most of third-class bulk rate regular mail is direct mail advertising from businesses to households. Expenditures for direct mail are an increasing share of total advertising expenditures.

Recent studies have shown that most types of mail are relatively insensitive to increases in rates. A 1 percent increase in the rate for most mail will decrease the volume by much less than 1 percent. For example, a 1 percent increase in the rate for first-class letters will cause that volume to decrease by only about 0.2 percent.

Today's large volume of mail is the result of a sustained period of growth beginning around 1977. Total mail volume approximately doubled between 1977 and 1994, from about 85 billion annually to 178 billion. Some of this growth can be attributed to the social shift that increased the proportion of women in the workforce and stimulated shopping by mail. Also, during this period the USPS introduced and enlarged discounts for work sharing. At the same time, data processing technology improved in ways that enhanced the effectiveness of direct mail. It reduced the costs of preparing mailings and made work sharing economically attractive to most bulk mailers.

Work sharing occurs when mailers perform for themselves tasks such as sorting, bar-coding, transporting, and other preparation, which reduces the Postal Service's work. Most of the growth in volume since 1977 has been in categories that receive discounts for work sharing. Ordinary nonpresorted first-class mail has grown very little, from about 50 billion to 55 billion annually. Work sharing and automation will be prominent features of the postal system in the twenty-first century. By the year 2000, mail sorting will be fully automated, and mailers will be encouraged by discounts to presort their mail, to apply bar codes and to facilitate automated processing in other ways.

Although the overall volume of transmitted messages has grown rapidly in recent years, the Postal Service's share has decreased. Today, the USPS faces a large, varied, and growing array of competitors, many of whom are not subject to regulation. Telephone, telegraph, telex, and messenger services have always been imperfect competitors with the mail, but now, privately written messages can be sent cheaply and quickly by fax, e-mail, and electronic data interchange. Electronic funds transfers may soon become an easy substitute for the mailed check. Most newspapers are delivered directly to

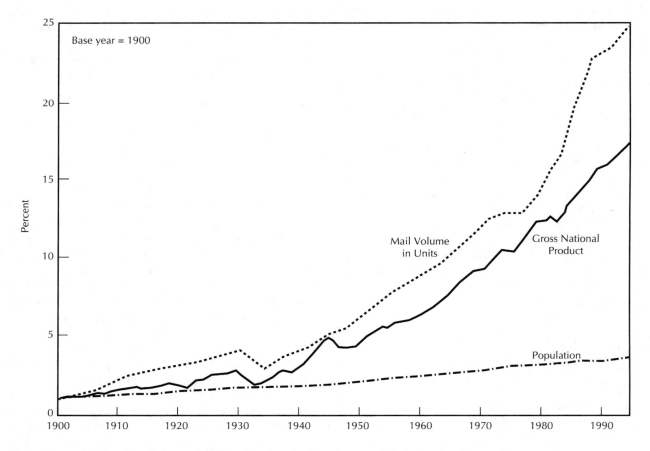

Figure 1. Growth index of population, real GNP, and total mail volume (in 1982 dollars). (DRI/McGraw-Hill.)

Postal delivery, the essential task of a modern mailperson, differs little from the 1880s when this man rode from farm to farm on horseback. (© Stock Montage, Inc.)

subscribers, and many include advertising supplements that compete directly with third-class bulk mail. The USPS's express mail, priority mail, parcel post, and money order services also have big, direct, and aggressive private competitors.

In the future, the USPS's share of the communications market will remain vulnerable to alternative services offering new and improved communications technologies. The rate of growth of both first-class mail and third-class mail has slowed in recent years. Not long after the year 2000 many observers expect the volume of first-class mail to level off, with third-class volume continuing to increase but at a slower rate.

[See also Communications; On-Line Services; Telecommunications.]

BIBLIOGRAPHY

Crew, Michael A., ed. *Competition and Innovation in Postal Services.* Norwell, MA: Kluwer, 1991.

Fleischman, Joel L. *The Future of the Postal Service.* Westport, CT: Greenwood Press, 1983.

— ROBERT H. COHEN, EDWARD S. PEARSALL
SPYROS S. XENAKIS, HEE SUN KIM

POST-INFORMATION AGE

Futurists are inclined to divide history into agricultural, industrial, and information ages. They see each age and culture as defined by its primary economic activity. These ages and cultures also tend to have their own concurrent source of social power, wealth, place of work, and sense of time. Today, advanced nations are completing the transition from the industrial to the information age. The early signs of the post-information age are barely visible, but do point to the emergence of a new age and civilization that can be anticipated.

Technological trends in microminiaturization, communications, voice recognition and synthesis, artificial intelligence, human interactivity with software, biotechnology, genetic engineering, bionics, and manufactured objects with built-in intelligence should continue and become increasingly and mutually reinforcing. The social trends in public participation, globalization, democracy, lifelong learning, and the rate of scientific inquiry and curiosity should also continue and become increasingly and mutually reinforcing. The interaction of these social and technological trends over the next century will create the *post-information age.*

In the post-information age, we will be as integrated with technology as technology is integrated with us. Distinctions between humans and machines will begin to blur. Humanity and intelligent technology will become an interrelated whole. The built environment will seem to become alive with artificial intelligence, communications, and voice recognition and synthesis. Our bodies will be augmented with technology and interconnected with global civilization. The post-information age will seem to become a "conscious technology," a continuum of human consciousness and technology.

The whole thrust of cyborg advances is to take the best of our external technology, miniaturize it, and then make it part of our bodies. We have already seen miniature pancreaslike pumps, heart pacemakers, microelectronically driven limbs, intraocular eye lenses, plastic skin, and artificial kidneys, hearts, ears, blood vessels, and bones. A cyborg is a living person who is dependent on technology for some vital function. All astronauts and scuba divers are temporary cyborgs. They use technological skins and organs to enhance abilities to move underwater and in outer space. The miniaturization of technology for both remedial purposes and the amplification of human capacity represents a strong trend toward the "cyborganization" of humanity.

Simultaneously, the whole thrust of advances in software is to take the best of our consciousness, simulate it in computer programs, and make it part of our environment. We can already talk to computers that recognize tens of thousands of words, giving us the eerie feeling that they are aware. Even buildings have sensors that make them seem alive, like the computer HAL in the movie *2001: A Space Odyssey.* This will make inanimate objects immediately responsive to our thoughts. With advancing computer power, microminiaturization, and simulated human communication, we can tell many inanimate objects what to do, and they can tell us what to do. Our whole environment will seem to change from dumb matter to one of conscious partnership as we tell our telephones to phone home, our lights to turn off, and our music to turn on.

Humanity is becoming a technologically interconnected, self-conscious whole. When the majority's awareness and technology are so interconnected, we will have left the information age and entered the conscious-technology age.

Concurrent with the built environment becoming intelligent and humans becoming cyborgs will be the rapid growth of knowledge and the number of globally aware individuals. The time from curiosity to response is shrinking, while the scope of inquiry is expanding. Humanity is becoming a technologically interconnected, self-conscious whole. When the majority's awareness and technology are so interconnected, we will have left the information age and entered the conscious-technology age.

The primary economic activity of this new age will be the linkage of human to technology and technology to human. Just as marriage brokers connected boys and girls for marriage, and travel agents connected tourists to vacation destinations for new experiences, post-information age workers will connect themselves and others via complex technologies to invent new culture and realities.

In such a post-information age, individuals become extraordinarily powerful. They can create themselves in many physical forms with technological augmentation and in even more forms in cyberspace. They grant or block access to themselves through software intelligence agents that communicate for them. This power will be like the power nations have today to grant visas. Unfortunately, like nations, others may wish to invade and manipulate others' perception without permission. The power of corporate marketing to influence behavior in the mid-1990s will seem slight compared with individuals' ability to influence human sensory systems and media upon which one bases metaphysical certainty. Information warfare and perceptual manipulation could become dominant forms of conflict waged by nations, corporations, interest groups, and individuals.

Individual power also is increased by creating barter transactions worldwide, as if each person were coining his or her own money. The exchange of virtual reality experiences will become as common as e-mail is today. Individuals will switch loyalties among corporations more easily than corporations switch capital among nations. They will invent their own nations, corporate holding companies, and religions, composed of networks of virtual realities in cyberspace, complete with software intelligence agents interacting with our technologically augmented bodies and environments.

Wealth in the post-information age becomes the quality of one's experiences, life, and being. An individual with vast expanses of land, capital, and access, but who is boring and unhappy, will be seen as less wealthy than another individual whose daily life is filled with a vastly richer set of intensely personal yet global experiences, even though the second individual might own less land, capital, and access. By agricultural age standards of wealth—land per capita—today's Japanese would be considered poor. By industrial age standards—capital per capita—today's Japanese are considered wealthy. By information age standards—access per capita—they are just beginning to get wealthy. By conscious-technology age standards—uniqueness of experience per capita—they would be poor.

In such a conscious-technology world, one will conduct his or her livelihood anywhere, with anyone, at

TABLE 1

OVERVIEW OF TRANSITION TO THE POST-INFORMATION AGE

Age	Product	Power	Wealth	Place	Time
Agricultural	Food	Religion	Land	Farm	Cyclical
Industrial	Machine	State	Capital	Factory	Linear
Information	Info/Service	Corporation	Access	Office	Relativistic
Conscious-Tech	Linkage	Individual	Being	Motion	Invented

any time. They will be viewed by others as constantly in motion. One can travel through three-dimensional space via many earthly and orbital transportation systems to reach anywhere in less than a day. One can also travel anywhere in the cyber-dimensional space almost instantaneously.

Since we will have more control over our daily reality, we can control the sequence and pace of events. This will change our sense of time. In the agricultural age, the perception of time tended to be cyclical, due to the importance of seasonal cycles so vital to agriculture. In the industrial age it tended to be more linear, with concepts of progress and increasing production efficiencies. In the information age, the perception of time has become more relativistic. As we enter the next age of increasing personal power to invent reality, time itself will seem an invention.

Table 1 summarizes some distinguishing characteristics of the post-information age compared with previous ages and cultures:

[See also Artificial Intelligence; Change, Cultural; Change, Epochal; Change, Pace of; Change, Scientific and Technological; Communications; Continuity and Discontinuity; Genetic Engineering; Genetic Technologies; Global Culture; Information Overload; Information Society; Information Technology; Interactive Entertainment; Lifestyles, Value-Oriented; Mass Culture and Arts; Technological Determinism; Values; Workforce Redistribution.]

BIBLIOGRAPHY

Bell, Daniel. *The Coming of Post-Industrial Society.* New York: Basic Books, 1973.

Connors, Michael. *The Race to the Intelligent State: Towards the Global Information Economy of 2005.* Cambridge: MA: Blackwell Business, 1993.

Dordick, Herbert S., and Wang, Georgette. *The Information Society: A Retrospective View.* Newbury Park, CA: Sage Publications, 1993.

Weinberg, Nathan. *Computers in the Information Society.* Boulder, CO: Westview Press, 1990.

— JEROME C. GLENN

POSTMODERNISM.

See MODERNISM AND POSTMODERNISM.

POVERTY, FEMINIZATION OF

Between 1960 and 1990, the most significant change to take place in American society was the stark realization that single women and their children constituted the majority of all victims of poverty. In 1960 female-headed households accounted for only 23.7 percent of all poor families in America. Their percentage of all

poor families grew to 37.1 percent in 1970, 47.8 percent in 1980, and 54.0 percent in 1991. As female-headed households became the dominant family type among the poor, women and children became an ever larger percentage of all the impoverished. In 1960 about 27 percent of all the poor lived in female-headed households. This percentage nearly doubled to 50 percent by 1976 and has remained at about 50 percent ever since.

Female-headed households are poor at a rate almost six times greater than the rate for intact married-couple families. In 1991 only 6.0 percent of all married couple families lived in poverty, compared to 35.6 percent of all female-headed families. Yet, female-headed families are the fastest growing household type in the nation. Between 1959 and 1991 the number of female-headed households with children tripled to 23 percent of all families with children. This included 17.5 percent of white families, 27 percent of Hispanic, and 54 percent of all black families with children. Over half of all children living in these households lived in poverty, with particularly high rates for minority children.

The poverty of so many female-headed families is the primary reason why poverty among American children has increased dramatically over the last fifteen years. More than 20 percent of American children are poor. Young single mothers form the poorest of all age groups in America.

Why are female-headed households in such jeopardy in America? There are many reasons, including the fact that females on average earn only about 71 percent of their male counterparts. The most important reason is that America's social welfare programs have not been redesigned to reflect this fact. Immense and fundamental alterations in the family structure have taken place in America over the last thirty years. Women head more households and are more often employed.

America lags behind most Western industrial nations in developing family support policies and welfare programs designed to move the poor out of poverty. A recent study showed that, using the same definition of poverty, postwelfare poverty in America averages 3.8 to 2.4 times the rates of the Western European nations. The United States is the only advanced nation with a double-digit rate of poverty. This is true despite the fact that the American poor are more likely to be employed, and that prewelfare poverty in Western Europe is actually higher. Thus, the European nations start with a higher rate of poverty, but do a much better job of reducing it through effective welfare programs. European nations spend more on welfare, target it better, and design their programs to promote economic independence.

In no small measure, the answers for dealing effectively with poverty and family supports are to be found in the laws of other advanced nations. For well over one hundred years, U.S. social policies and programs have consistently emulated those established elsewhere at earlier points in time. We can expect more of the same in the years to come.

[See also Families and Households; Family Patterns; Family Values; Public Assistance Programs; Public Assistance Programs: Social Security; Social Welfare Philosophies; Unemployment; Women and Work.]

BIBLIOGRAPHY

Cottingham, P. H., and Ellwood, D. T., eds. *Welfare Policies for the 1990s.* Cambridge, MA: Harvard University Press, 1989.

Ellwood, D. T. *Poor Support: Poverty in the American Family.* New York: Basic Books, 1988.

McLanahan, S., and Booth, K. "Mother-Only Families: Problems, Prospects, and Politics." *Journal of Marriage and Family* 51 (August 1989): 557–580.

Rodgers, Harrell R. *Poor Women, Poor Families: The Economic Plight of America's Female-Headed Families.* Armonk, NY. M. E. Sharpe, 1990.

Rodgers, Harrell R., ed. *Beyond Welfare: New Approaches to the Problem of Poverty in America.* Armonk NY. M. E. Sharpe, 1988.

— HARRELL R. RODGERS

PRESCHOOL EDUCATION

The number of American children receiving education before age six has risen sharply in the last 25 years and will probably continue to rise in the years ahead. In 1991, 6.3 million children ages three to five were enrolled in preprimary programs, up 54 percent from 1970 when only 4.1 million were enrolled. Enrollment in kindergarten also climbed from 3.0 million in 1970 to 3.5 million in 1991, a 17 percent increase. This surge in preprimary education is all the more remarkable given that overall elementary school enrollment actually dropped slightly (.001 percent) between 1970 and 1991.

Although some day-care centers for infants and toddlers pursue no educational objectives, many do. Consequently, large numbers of the more than 1.5 million infants and toddlers in day-care centers now receive preschool instruction. Meanwhile, through government-sponsored Parents as Teachers (PAT) programs, a growing number of parents are also receiving training in how to foster the intellectual development of their children in their own homes.

Alongside the mainstream preschool programs, increasingly ambitious and sophisticated projects have emerged to meet the needs of impoverished and disadvantaged children. Designed as a preschool program to foster education receptivity and achievement among disadvantaged children, Head Start enrolled almost 714,000 children from poor households in 1993, compared to only 477,400 in 1970. However, because poverty among children has surged in recent decades, the percentage of poor preschool children enrolled in Head Start has actually dipped slightly, from 13 percent in 1970 to 12 percent in 1994. Originally launched in 1965 as part of President Lyndon Johnson's War on Poverty, Head Start has attracted strong support from both political parties as a means of helping disadvantaged children—specially minorities—break out of the cycle of poverty. In 1993, Head Start received $2.6 billion in federal money, and many child development experts feel it deserves significant increases in the years ahead.

Supporters of Head Start point to the remarkable outcomes documented for the Perry Pre-School Project (later known as High/Scope). Among young adults who were enrolled as young children in this experimental preschool project, researchers found significantly higher educational and economic attainments, and significantly lower crime rates compared to peers who were not enrolled. One analysis concluded that every dollar invested in the High/Scope program returned at least $7 (adjusted for inflation) to society by reducing the costs of remedial education, juvenile delinquency, and welfare. In light of such findings, Head Start is likely to grow in the decades ahead.

However, the growth of preschool education has not been without controversy. One such controversy concerns the longevity of positive effects from preschool. Defenders of Head Start have had to overcome American and British studies concluding that the benefits of preschool interventions largely disappear by the time students reach the third grade. Recent investigations reassure that preschool intervention benefits are long-lived, at least for the most seriously disadvantaged students. Nonetheless, the debate continues.

The hottest debates, though, have raged over the placement of infants in day-care centers. Some researchers—most prominently, psychologist Jay Belsky—have reported evidence that placement of infants below the age of one in day-care centers weakens bonding to their mothers. Evidence further indicates that infants receive less affectionate and responsive treatment in day care than at home. Although defenders of infant day care have challenged the methodologies and findings of some cautionary studies, concerns about very early placement in day-care centers also are widespread among child psychologists, many of whom recommend that one or both parents arrange for at least six months' leave of absence from their employers following the birth of a child.

Day care for preschoolers beyond infancy has been linked in some studies to heightened aggression and noncompliance. Some research indicates that the day care most likely to foster aggressive behavior—hitting, kicking, pushing, threatening, swearing, teasing, and arguing—may actually be the more "cognitively oriented" or educationally ambitious programs! On the other hand, psychologist Tiffany Field reports that "stable high-quality day care" will *reduce* subsequent aggressive behavior and improve academic performance among those enrolled.

Many Americans hope for a national

day-care system based on the Scandinavian model,

in which governments provide high-quality

day care for infants and preschoolers.

Many Americans hope for the creation of a national day-care system based on the Scandinavian model, in which governments provide high-quality, educationally oriented day care for infants and preschoolers, free of charge. Scandinavian children coming out of these systems score high in cognitive and socio-emotional competence. Yet, the director of Denmark's highly lauded day-care system, Jacob Vedel-Petersen, laments that, in his country, "one can observe an eagerness to appropriate or monopolize the children's spare time. Childhood is about to become a phase of life thoroughly programmed from morning to night." In American day-care centers and preschools, pediatric researcher David Elkind sees a kind of "miseducation" based on the false premise that "earlier is better." Premature education may "put young children at risk for short-term stress and long-term personality problems," warns Elkind. He fears that many parents are now receptive to a dubious "conception of infantile competence," primarily because of new adult lifestyles based on dual-career marriages, not because of new research on children's educational needs.

The most intractable disputes over preschool education are, indeed, those defined by divergent attitudes toward family life. Many who view traditional family life as narrow and constraining see modern families evolving in exciting new ways. They generally regard day care and preschool as parts of a liberating formula opening new possibilities for women and new lifestyles for everyone. But others see in the increasing reliance upon day care and preschool a symptom of a broader retreat from family life. They do not see evolution in modern family life but decay—evident in high rates for divorce, cohabitation, and illegitimacy and low rates for marriage and childbearing. Exponents of this viewpoint draw upon the views of Harvard sociologist Pitirim Sorokin, who interpreted ever earlier separation of children from parents as evidence of profound cultural malaise. Some also worry that freedom from the traditional moral restraints of family life is illusory in that such freedom requires a growing number of government surrogates for the family (such as government-funded day-care centers and government-employed PAT social workers), which reduces family autonomy and increases tax burdens.

Statistical trends portend a future in which the great majority of American children will receive preprimary education. Universal publicly financed programs already abound in other advanced nations. Many Americans remain confident that similar educational pathways will help pave the way to social and technological progress. Others fear that the multiplication of preschools will not mean progress if such multiplication entails further retreat from family life.

[See also Child Care; Elementary and Secondary Education; Families and Households; Family Problems.]

BIBLIOGRAPHY

Administration on Children, Youth, and Families. "Project Head Start Statistical Fact Sheet." Washington, DC: U.S. Department of Health and Human Services, 1994.

Andersson, Bengt-Erik. "Effects of Day-Care on Cognitive and Socioemotional Competence of Thirteen-Year-Old Swedish Schoolchildren." *Child Development* 63 (1992): 20–36.

Belsky, Jay. "Infant Day Care and Socioemotional Development: The United States." *Journal of Child Psychology and Psychiatry* 29 (1988): 397–406.

Elkind, David. "Miseducation: Young Children at Risk." *Pediatrics* 83 (1989): 119–121.

Field, Tiffany. "Quality Infant Day-Care and Grade School Behavior and Performance." *Child Development* 62 (1991): 863–870.

Haskins, Ron. "Public School Aggression among Children with Varying Day Care Experience." *Child Development* 56 (1985): 694–703.

Melhuish, E. C., et al. "Type of Childcare at Eighteen Months—I. Differences in Interactional Experience." *Journal of Child Psychology and Psychiatry* 31 (1990): 849–857.

Sorokin, Pitirim. *Social and Cultural Dynamics: A Study of Change in Major Systems of Art, Truth, Ethics, Law, and Social Relationships*, revised and abridged ed., 1957. Reprint. New Brunswick, NJ: Transaction, 1985, pp. 700–707.

Sylva, Kathy. "School Influences on Children's Development." *Journal of Child Psychology and Psychiatry* 35 (1994): 135–170.

Towers, James T. "Attitudes Toward the All-Day, Everyday Kindergarten." *Children Today* (January–February 1991): 25–27.

U.S. Bureau of the Census. *Statistical Abstract of the United States,
1993*. Washington, DC: U.S. Government Printing Office,
1993.

Vedel-Petersen, Jacob. "Children in Denmark: Day Care Issues."
Child Welfare 68 (1989): 261–264.

— BRYCE L. CHRISTENSEN

PREVENTIVE HEALTH CARE.

See HEALTH CARE.

PRINTED WORD

One thousand years from now, our descendants will look at written records of our time and ponder how much, or perhaps how little, humans have changed. What will not have changed is the use of visual representations of sounds to signify words that express the world we perceive and our thoughts about it. The human eye is a scanner for that most convenient "computer," the human brain. Its richest data input today is the printed word. Elsewhere you will read how words will increasingly be generated electronically and be available instantaneously worldwide via computer networks. But the printed word as we know it and the process of publishing that has grown up around it will be with us for a long, long time.

In the United States alone,

some 50,000 new titles are published each year,

with no sign of diminishing.

Publishers in the beginning were essentially printers, manufacturers of books who owned presses to impart print images to paper. These printers subsequently became more and more involved with the authors of the works they printed and with the distribution of the finished product. Eventually, as publishers, they became in effect the bankers of the knowledge enterprise. Today their role is to select the work to be published, perfect its form, make known its appearance, provide for its availability over an extended period, and maintain the property rights of the author. These functions will continue to be essential to publishing, whether the printed word is read on a piece of paper or on a video screen, and whether the agency is called a publisher or something new like a "knowledge manager." In the academic world there is talk of a campus department that might unite a faculty author, the library, and the computer center. In this configuration, it is supposed that the author's work would be more immediately available, but by computer retrieval from a data bank rather than from a library book.

In the meantime, a seemingly endless cycle of birth, growth, and consolidation continues in conventional "trade" publishing, which produces the books we buy in stores. Many companies whose names were household words have disappeared from the publishing scene or lost their independence as media giants and foreign publishers have gobbled them up. This has been thought by some to narrow avenues of communication for unconventional writers. At the same time, however, creative entrepreneurs have continued to start up small publishing enterprises, often in some area of specialization personally close to their hearts, and some university presses have shown more interest in the experimental and the intellectually avant-garde. The cost of entry in the publishing business has always been low; basically it comprises the salaries of the staff. With the advent of computer technologies for production and distribution, the future is likely to see a vast proliferation of low-overhead publishers catering to every new intellectual and consumer interest.

Magazines and journals have always been a print avenue for very special interests, especially series in the fields of science and technology; and in recent years a far higher proportion of library budgets has been spent on these so-called "serials" than heretofore. Unfortunately, larger and larger expenditures for serials have not led to a comparable increase in the number of serials acquired; rather, serial prices have been inflated. One anticipated result will be the publication of "electronic journals," which will be more closely controlled by their intellectual sources and more readily available simply by logging onto a journal sponsors's "file server."

Often overlooked is that literary works of art and entertainment have never, as a category, been a dependable financial investment. Probably such publishing is inherently unprofitable—as with serious theater, music, and dance. Whether disseminated conventionally or electronically, artistic and scholarly compositions of the printed word will have to be subsidized by the revenues from more mundane subject matters of mass media information and instruction.

The emerging electronic transmission systems themselves may not be available to the unprofitable arts—or to education, for that matter—if government does not pay the bill as it already does in other countries. There is, however, great danger in a knowledge-transmission system dependent on the good will of a bureaucracy! What if authorities in the future decide to censor the computer network? What if funding is cut back or withdrawn? It has been much harder to shut down all the printing presses and burn all the books.

Although more books are published today than ever before, television and other distractions lead some to conclude that books and reading are losing importance. One reported result is a rise in the study of "book history" based on the premise that the book is already taking its place along with household servants and railroad trains as a quaint relic. Until recently largely taken for granted, reading itself is studied by researchers for clues to past human behavior. The influence of what we would now call "newsletters" on the French Revolution is well understood. What will be the seditious effect of e-mail? Dante's lovers were seduced by a book, but will future sweethearts kiss as they behold their computer display?

The prospect of computer-generated multimedia experiences that combine the written word with illustrations and sounds, weaving text with supplementary interactive data banks, makes the printed word alone seem tame to some. But more exciting to book devotees is the emergence of new ways to keep the printed word alive and available to readers. Xerox is pioneering a promising technology for the production of books, now called the "Docutech," which combines a scanning capability with a high-speed printing and collating function. Binding is still handled separately, but one day the process may be fully integrated. The output of this system is a short run of copies "on demand" as a means of keeping in print forever titles that heretofore could not be reprinted economically in small quantities. The system also may facilitate the publication of short runs of specialized books that could not be manufactured economically by conventional means in the first place. Similar methods may ease the production of large-type books for readers with visual impairment and even lead to new Braille technologies.

A possible loss feared by bibliophiles is the perfected aesthetic form. Originally dictated by the folding and assembly of larger sheets of printed pages, the typical six-inch-by-nine-inch object we hold in our hands, carry about, and display in our libraries has become a highly stylized art form, with its own aesthetics of proportion, typographic display, illustration, and mate-

Tibetan Buddhists left these hand engraved stones in the Himalayan Mountains which present a stark contrast to today's silicon-chip etchings that pack billions of characters into one square inch. (David Samuel Robbins/Corbis)

rial—even feel and smell. Fortunately the champions of new print technologies promise that these qualities, too, can be reproduced in due course—and that in any case we will eventually learn to delight in the appearance of our computer monitors.

Whether the printed word appears in a conventional book, a desktop computer printout, a Docutech edition, or transitorally on the screen, the author's manuscript ("hand-writing") will increasingly be created on a computer disk that will generate a variety of computer outputs. The revision and copyediting of the work will take place "on screen" as succeeding generations of authors, computer-literate from the primary grades, will no longer have patience with old-fashioned interlineation and crossing out. A most unfortunate loss in this process will be the draft record of the creative changes leading to the published version that tell us so much about a work's meaning and about the mind of the author.

For all the understandable excitement generated by futuristic prospects for the printed word, a monumental 500-year investment remains in the book as we know it. In the United States alone, some 50,000 new titles are published each year, with no sign of diminishing. A universally understood method of communication, an exceedingly efficient medium, infinitely refined production processes, countless libraries, enormous investments in distribution mechanisms and an integrated process of education worldwide will be substantially transformed only after many generations that will still turn to the printed word, though in new forms of displays.

Still, one may ask why our technologically accomplished progeny would not do away entirely with printed records in favor of electronic signals. The reason is that as long as the species has eyes to see and a voice to speak, the printed word will be easily accessible. Even the most technologically adept creature in the year 3000 will not want to make the effort to arrange to display a 1995 CD, even if it should survive with its data intact by enhancement, if instead she could consult a microfilm much as we today consult the Dead Sea Scrolls. We must think of the interests of these descendants as well as our immediate convenience because their day is closer than we can comprehend.

[See also Advertising; Arts; Digital Communications; Electronic Publishing; Information Overload; Information Society; Intellectual Property; Libraries; Libraries: Electronic Formats; Literature; Newspapers; Photography; Postal Services.]

BIBLIOGRAPHY

Alston, A. C., and Fellner, H., eds. *Publishing, the Booktrade, and the Diffusion of Knowledge.* Cambridge, U.K.: Chadwyck-Healy, 1992.

Cummings, G., et al. *University Libraries and Scholarly Communication.* Washington, DC: Association of Research Libraries, 1992.
Olmert, Michael. *The Smithsonian Book of Books.* Washington, DC: Smithsonian Books, 1992.
Smith, Datus C., Jr. *A Guide to Book Publishing,* rev. ed. Seattle: University of Washington Press, 1989.

– PETER C. GRENQUIST

PRISONS

By the mid-twenty-first century the only prison bars will be in the minds of public offenders. Expensive cell blocks will be replaced by more intrusive mind control methods that are both cheaper and more effective in dealing with criminal behavior.

On the way to this new day in biotech behavioral control, some very old methods will be tried again and eventually discarded. When the Quakers arrived in the American colonies in the early eighteenth century, they developed a method of incarcerating offenders to give

The high cost of incarcerating prisoners, approximately $30,000 per year for each federal inmate, has motivated social service policymakers to seek better options. (UPI/Corbis-Bettmann)

them time to repent (penitentiaries) and reform (reformatories). The idea caught on worldwide, but in no place was it more popular than in the United States. By the mid-1990s more than one million inmates were in American prisons on any given day. By the turn of the twenty-first century this number is expected to double and possibly even triple.

The idea of the reformation/rehabilitation of offenders was replaced in the latter part of the twentieth century by a focus on an even older idea—retribution and revenge. Prisons became "spartan warehouses," so prisoners would feel the pain of crime and never want to return. It was generally believed that offenders could be deterred from further crime by harsh punishment, despite empirical evidence to the contrary.

Early in the twenty-first century, the crippling cost of indiscriminate incarceration of law violators will force change in the "corrections" system. When costs of imprisonment exceed costs of education, policy will shift to accommodate the greater need. The most violent, hardened, and undeterrable offenders will still be incarcerated, but other violators will be handled in new ways.

For the minority who still must be incarcerated, undersea and space prisons will become the new method—again reviving an age-old idea of "transporting" or sending criminals somewhere else (as England transported its public offenders first to the American colonies and later to Australia). Colonies deep under the ocean will be self-supporting prisons, as inmates grow food via aquaculture. Mining asteroids may make space prisons self-sustaining as well. Both types will be easy to secure and will make escape highly unlikely.

For the moderately dangerous and incorrigible offenders, late-twentieth-century technology—electronic monitoring—will be improved and increasingly used. Using geo-based tracking systems, monitored offenders will be followed around the clock wherever they go. Eventually monitors will be implanted inside the offender's body—though only by court order—and for the most dangerous, electrodes will be attached to shock the offenders if they leave their territory. Only when a violator returns to home, work, or an approved site will the electroshock cease.

Minor offenders will be diverted from the correctional system into more productive alternatives. Community-service work will become increasingly popular, as it both forces offenders to labor and pay for their crimes and provides public services—from litter control to government building and grounds maintenance and construction—all at a savings to the taxpayer.

For offenders who are not dangerous but have no funds, homes, or skills to live on their own, old alternatives will continue to be used early in the twenty-first century. Halfway houses and group homes, along with residential drug-treatment, education, and job-training programs will be found to be cheaper and more effective than prisons.

In the early part of the twenty-first century, capital punishment will still be used for a few extreme cases—terrorists' acts causing multiple deaths, serial murders, and other isolated atrocities. Lethal injection will become the method of choice in almost all jurisdictions. New methods may emerge—such as instant death by laser ray or dematerialization by ultrasound—before capital punishment is eventually abolished as unnecessary to protect society.

Community-service work will become increasingly popular, as it both forces offenders to labor and pay for their crimes and provides public services.

Second-quarter twenty-first-century technology will make available the means to put the "bars in the minds" of offenders, as most citizens will have computer implants in their brains to increase their capacity to store and recall massive amounts of information and provide numerous types of leisure activities, from virtual reality games to soothing subliminal messages ("you are doing well"; "life is good"; "things are getting better and better"; etc.). Thus it will be a minor step further to order law violators to be "programmed" to obey—forcing compliance by eliminating alternatives. The computer inside simply will not allow the individual to disobey the law—chemical reactions will cause nausea while subliminal messages will bombard the subconscious ("obey the law"; "do the right things"; and so on).

Still, the future is one of choice. The methods described above do not have to occur, but may be reserved for a few extreme cases.

A major alternative to this high-tech scenario is a "humanized approach"—changing the basic belief about crime and justice from combating criminals on the "mean streets" to creating and maintaining "peaceful communities." Instead of reacting to crime by emphasizing "capturing criminals," the focus will change to proactively seeking to prevent crime by early identification of crime-breeding problems followed by action to remedy the situations. The bases for this approach were established in the early 1990s and will escalate in the twenty-first century. If successful, community-oriented policing combined with community-oriented justice via replacing adversarial proceedings with mediation and arbitration will mean fewer criminals and thus less need for prisons and other draconian actions. Community crime prevention will only work, however, if citizens are willing to give up their "war" mentality and adopt a "peace" approach that substitutes pragmatic restitution, restoration, and reconciliation for vindictive retribution, revenge, and retaliation. Above all else, communal attention to tender, loving care of all children ("It takes a whole village to raise a child") could ultimately eliminate the need for prisons altogether.

[See also Crime, Nonviolent; Crime, Organized; Crime, Violent; Crime Rates; Criminal Justice; Criminal Punishment; Drugs, Illicit; Law Enforcement; Lethal Weapons.]

BIBLIOGRAPHY

Montgomery, R. H., and MacDougall, E. C. "Curing Criminals: The High-Tech Prisons of Tomorrow." *The Futurist* (January–February 1986): 36–37.

Stephens, Gene. "Drugs and Crime in the Twenty-first Century." *The Futurist* (May–June 1992): 19–22.

———. "Impact of Emerging Police and Corrections Technology on Constitutional Rights." In F. Schmallenger, ed. *Computers in Criminal Justice: Issues and Applications,* Bristol, IN: Wyndham Hall Press, 1990.

— GENE STEPHENS

PRIVACY LAWS.

See COMMUNICATIONS: PRIVACY ISSUES; COMPUTERS: PRIVACY LAWS.

PRODUCTIVITY

Productivity is usually defined as the ratio of output to any or all associated inputs in real (physical volume) terms. "Total factor productivity" (TFP) is the ratio of real gross product, whether of a nation or an industry, to total real, tangible factor inputs of labor and capital (man-made and natural). Its increase over time reflects savings in real costs per unit of output due to improvements in the quality and efficiency of the factors of production. In the long run, productivity gains result from innovations in the technology and organization of production, and from human investments, especially in education and training. In modern times innovations are increasingly the result of investments in research and development (R&D).

The familiar "labor productivity" ratio (output per worker or per hour worked) reflects not only technological progress, but also increases in tangible capital goods per worker. Noninvestment forces affecting productivity generally include economies of scale, fluctuations in output, exogenous variables such as governmental fiscal and regulatory policies, and changes in social values and institutions.

The United States Record

The progress of productivity has been uneven. In the United States, as shown in Table 1, the growth rate of TFP averaged only 0.3 percent a year in the period of 1800 to 1890 before accelerating to 2.2 percent for the 1919 to 1973 period. The low growth prior to 1890 is not surprising since back-casting the twentieth-century rate would result in zero production in colonial days. The acceleration beginning in the 1890s reflected especially the beginning of research and development (R&D) as a specialized function in larger firms; the development of the field of management science and the

TABLE 1

REAL GROSS PRODUCT, POPULATION, REAL PRODUCT PER CAPITA, FACTOR INPUTS, AND PRODUCTIVITY RATIOS

U.S. Domestic Business Economy, Selected Periods 1800–1993 (average annual percentage rates of change)

	1800–1855	1855–1890	1890–1919	1919–1948	1948–1973	1973–1993
Real gross product	4.2	4.0	3.9	3.0	4.0	2.6
Population	3.1	2.4	1.8	1.2	1.5	1.7
Real product per capita	1.1	1.6	2.1	1.8	2.5	0.9
Tangible factor inputs: total	3.9	3.6	2.2	0.8	1.8	2.2
Labor	3.7	2.8	1.8	0.6	0.9	1.7
Capital	4.3	4.6	3.1	1.2	3.9	3.5
Factor productivity ratios: total	0.3	0.3	1.7	2.2	2.2	0.3
Labor	0.5	1.1	2.0	2.4	3.4	1.3
Capital	−0.1	−0.6	0.7	1.6	0.1	−0.9

Sources: For 1800–1890: M. Abramovitz and P. David, "Economic Growth in America: Historical Parables and Realities," Stanford University, Center for Research in Economic Growth, Reprint No. 105, 1973. For 1890–1948: J. W. Kendrick, *Productivity Trends in the United States.* New York: National Bureau of Economic Research, 1961. For 1973–1993: Bureau of Labor Statistics, U.S. Department of Labor.

Productivity gains result from innovations in the technology and organization of production and from human investments, especially in education and training. (Vittoriano Rastelli/Corbis)

establishment of collegiate schools of business beginning with Wharton in 1887; and increases in the average education and training of the workforce.

The productivity slowdown after 1973 is a bit of a puzzle but reflects a decline in the rate of growth of intangible investments (in education, R&D, etc.) per unit of tangible input following major increases before then. Rates of return on the stocks of intangible capital designed to increase the quality and efficiency of inputs were also declining. Increasing outlays for antipollution and other social objectives likewise retarded growth, at least in the short run. Finally, the "oil shock" of 1973 ignited accelerating inflation in the later 1970s, followed by a painful disinflation.

Looking ahead, it is encouraging that the 1990 to 1994 rate of growth in TFP moved up to 1 percent a year while inflation remained low. This suggests that performance should be at least as good for the rest of the decade. Indeed, TFP growth might well accelerate further to the average 1948 to 1994 rate of 1.4 percent. It seems unlikely, however, that this country will again experience the 2.2 percent rate of 1948 to 1973 that

reflected the backlogs of demand and potential innovations accumulated during the Great Depression and World War II.

Going beyond the year 2000, relatively high rates of TFP growth between 1.4 and 2 percent could be realized if strong intangible capital formation continues, and if the socioeconomic environment is favorable to entrepreneurial activity. But slowdowns such as occurred in the 1970s could happen again, moderating long-term growth rates.

There is considerable dispersion in rates of productivity change among industries. Between 1950 and 1990 average annual rates of change in real gross product per labor hour in the United States ranged from 4.8 percent in communications and 4.0 percent in agriculture down to 0.8 percent in services and a slight negative in contract construction. Manufacturing at 2.6 percent was a bit above the average of 2.1 percent for all private industry. It is generally believed that there is some downward bias in the real product and productivity trends, especially in the finance and services sectors, and in construction, because of inadequate price deflators. Real product in almost half of these sectors is assumed to move with employment, without allowance for productivity increases.

REST OF THE WORLD. Since the reconstruction following World War II, there has been impressive convergence in labor productivity levels between the United States and other industrialized nations. Between 1960 and 1992, thirteen other OECD countries increased real GDP per person at an average annual rate of 3 percent compared with 1.2 percent for the United States. Growth rates ranged from around 5 percent for South Korea and Japan, and 3.5 percent for Italy, down to 2 percent for Sweden and the United Kingdom. As a result, the average productivity level of the thirteen increased from 46.5 percent of that of the United States in 1960 to 76.6 percent in 1992. The productivity gap narrowed for two main reasons: (1) higher rates of saving and capital formation abroad and (2) technological catch-up with the United States.

As other countries come close to U.S. productivity levels, their growth rates slow down. This is already occurring since borrowing advanced technology is much cheaper than creating it through R&D. Thus, growth rates of other industrial nations will tend to converge with that of the United States, whose rate may be enhanced somewhat by increasing opportunities to borrow technology from others. But even a 1.5 percent growth rate means a doubling in less than fifty years. A major question is whether national resource and environmental constraints will slow economic progress in the new century.

There is as yet no general convergence of productivity rates and levels among the less developed countries (LDCs). Some are doing very well—for example, China since 1979. Others, such as India, are making slow progress, while the transitional economies of the former Soviet Union and Eastern Europe have had at least temporary setbacks. Fortunately, countries that seem to be mired in low-level stagnation, as are some in Southeast Asia and Central Africa, comprise only about 5 percent of world population.

In the future, an increasing proportion of LDCs should be taking off into stronger economic growth given increasing aid and investment from industrial nations, including direct investments by multinational corporations and from international organizations such as the World Bank. Public investments in infrastructure and human resources are important prerequisites to productivity growth, as are gradual increases in domestic saving and investment to supplement that from foreign sources. Development is a slow process, but it is possible that during the twenty-first century increases in planes of living made possible by productivity growth could virtually eliminate poverty in most parts of the world.

[See also Capital Formation; Entrepreneurship; Investments; Savings; Work; Work, Quality of.]

BIBLIOGRAPHY

Baumol, William J.; Nelson, Richard R.; and Wolff, Edward M. *Convergence of Productivity: Cross-National Studies and Historical Evidence.* Oxford, U.K.: Oxford University Press, 1994.
Kendrick, John W. *Productivity Trends in the United States.* Princeton, NJ: Princeton University Press for the National Bureau of Economic Research, 1961.
Kendrick, John W., and Grossman, Elliot. *Productivity in the United States: Trends and Cycles.* Baltimore, MD: Johns Hopkins University Press, 1980.

– JOHN W. KENDRICK

PROTEST.

See CIVIL PROTEST.

PSYCHIATRY

The psychiatry of the future will be shaped by rapid advances in biological, psychological, and social sciences, by radical shifts in health care financing and treatment practices, and by innovations in computer technology and communication.

Scientific Advances

Advances in brain imaging using positron emission tomography (PET), magnetic resonance imaging (MRI), single photon emission tomography (SPEC), and specialized quantitative electroencephalography (QEEG) will continue providing remarkable, increasingly on-line images of the structure and physiology of the living brain. These developments will yield important information about the biological bases of the major mental disorders, particularly Alzheimer's disease, schizophrenia, manic-depressive disorder, serious depressions, anxiety and panic disorders, alcohol and drug abuse, obsessive-compulsive disorders, personality disorders, and others. As the details of the entire human genome are uncovered in the next decade, we will be able to better clarify how harmful genes, family, and social environments contribute to psychiatric disorders. Techniques of molecular genetics, neurochemistry, and neurophysiology will also unravel the nature of psychiatric symptoms, identifying involved brain pathways and chemical processes, and leading to improved laboratory testing and diagnosis. Many new psychiatric treatments can be expected, including entirely new classes of "designer" medications that may offer prevention as well as treatment with far fewer side effects.

Studies in human behavioral genetics show that many aspects of personality, such as shyness, and various features of intelligence result as much from genetic as from environmental influences. New personality theories will emerge from these findings and will examine how inborn tendencies complement and/or conflict with one another. These theories should help explain how and why certain parenting patterns, early traumas, and adverse life events affect some children much more than others and even predict specific personality and interpersonal problems that someone is likely to develop. Medications to treat some personality disorders and to enhance memory and other intellectual functions can be expected. Improved strategies for psychotherapies, social interventions, and preventing psychiatric problems should also result.

New theories of the healthy and diseased mind will also stem from advances in computational neurobiology. Computer models of evolving neural networks, related to "complexity theory," will increasingly mimic human mental phenomena.

Psychiatric Services

As in other fields of medicine, most patients will receive psychiatric care through large, highly regulated, organized systems of "managed" care, financed by employers or public funds. Clinicians working for these systems will increasingly use treatments that have been objectively demonstrated to be efficient, effective, cost-effective, and satisfying to the patients, clients, and families. Health insurance benefits for psychiatric problems are likely to be limited to serious psychiatric disorders, with more services than at present available for biologically based psychiatric disorders such as schizophrenia and manic-depressive disease, in part due to political action by advocacy groups composed of patients and their families. Research will help show which combinations and lengths of treatment are necessary to reverse acute conditions and prevent recurrences. Much more psychotherapy in the future will be based on educationally oriented, interpersonally focused, skill and coping-style enhancing, short-term psychotherapies explicitly described in workbooks used by clinicians and patients. These therapies will emphasize ways to resolve symptoms and problems through specifically prescribed changes in thinking and behavior. Biological and psychological treatments shown through research to be ineffective will be eliminated. Officially sanctioned *practice guidelines* will be increasingly used by health care organizations to guide, if not prescribe, the types of biological treatments, psychotherapies, hospital-based, and outpatient treatments to be offered for specific sorts of problems. Studies comparing the costs and results of care for various problems as provided by psychiatrists, primary care physicians, nurses, psychologists, social workers, and other therapists, working individually or in teams, will determine what sorts of professionals will

be asked to provide various aspects of care—for example, prescribing medications and/or conducting psychotherapy. In some geographic regions, psychiatric nurses and possibly psychologists with special training and licensing may be allowed to prescribe some medications independently of psychiatrists or other physicians. Because they are inexpensive to run yet relatively effective for certain problems such as alcoholism and addictions, special attention will be given to examining the cost-effectiveness of twelve-step programs based on Alcoholics Anonymous and other treatments offered by nonprofessionals. Traditional fee-for-service therapists in solo practice will still be available for those willing and able to pay out of pocket.

Computer Technology

Much more sophisticated and extensive computer-assisted psychiatric assessments and psychotherapies, based on expert systems, will provide individually tailored "virtual therapists." Virtual reality programming will be used increasingly to expose patients to provocative stimuli in the treatment of phobias, addictions, interpersonal conflicts, and other problems. Clinicians will increasingly access on-line information, ranging

---

Virtual reality programming will be used increasingly to expose patients to provocative stimuli in the treatment of phobias, addictions, interpersonal conflicts, and other problems.

---

from past medical records to literature searches on any psychological or medical topic. At the same time, patients and their families will have access to increasing amounts of on-line information about their providers and treatments, including credentials and any malpractice histories. Patient education will be greatly facilitated by easily available interactive media. Consultations and therapies provided at a distance, teleconsultation, and teletherapy will be increasingly available due to the widespread availability of videophones.

[See also Genetics; Health Care; Medical Care Providers; Mental Health; Psychology.]

BIBLIOGRAPHY

Moore-Ede, Martin. *The Twenty-Four Hour Society: Understanding Human Limits to a World That Never Stops.* Reading, MA: Addison-Wesley, 1993.

U.S. Congress, Office of Technology Assessment. *The Biology of Mental Disorder.* Washington, DC: U.S. Government Printing Office, 1992.

Yager, Joel. *The Future of Psychiatry.* Washington, DC: American Psychiatric Press, 1989.

— JOEL YAGER

PSYCHOLOGY

During the past thirty years, as its base of knowledge has matured and deepened, psychology has branched into a wide array of subfields. These subfields include artificial intelligence; behavioral medicine; cognitive science; development over the life span; educational psychology; public health and wellness promotion; learning; language processing; mental health treatment and research; neuropsychology; industrial psychology and organizational behavior; perception; rehabilitation; chronic pain management; and research and treatment of sleep/wake disorders. While not a comprehensive list, these subfields are representative of the many areas in which psychology collaborates with scientists in other disciplines and about which it has generated substantial bodies of knowledge. These advances will continue to improve our understanding of human behavior. Scientific understanding of normal, abnormal, and optimal human functioning will benefit individuals who suffer from impaired functioning and will extend the benefits of normal and optimal functioning to individuals, communities, and organizations.

Two of the most significant advances in psychology that will shape the future of the discipline are (1) the demolition of the duality of cause and effect and (2) the rejection of either/or questions like those spawned by the mind/body problem. Psychologists no longer pose such questions as "What is the cause of X?" or "Which exercises the greatest influence over behavior, the body or the mind?" Such formulations are too simplistic and lead to research that can only yield incomplete answers. Psychologists recognize that the interactions that occur between physical and mental processes, or those between people and their environments, are too complex to sort into "cause" and "effect." The various factors involved influence one another. Research is now aimed at understanding the degree of influence the various factors exercise and how they affect one another. Future research in psychology will continue to investigate complex interactions. Researchers will formulate questions such as "How many and what are the factors that produced this outcome?" and "How did the factors interact with each other to produce the outcome?"

A third development that will influence the course of psychology in the future is a revolution in the method of scientific inquiry. Along with other disciplines, psychology will continue to contribute to the development of a scientific method that (1) can accommodate the study of interactions; (2) is more responsive to the needs of society rather than rigorously separated from it; and (3) is cognizant of the reciprocal relationships between the knower and the known. The adjustments necessitated by accommodation to the postmodern constructivist perspective in science will become ever more apparent in the future of psychology.

Scales for measuring good mental health will become more sophisticated, as will the means of preventing illness and promoting psychological wellbeing.

Recent advances in the behavioral sciences, along with the fruits of decades of research, explain the origins of mental disorders; how people think, reason, and make decisions; the role of emotions in behavior and health; the subtle ways in which parents and children influence one another; and how schools shape self-concept and self-esteem. Research on cultural differences in attitudes, social status, social bonds, and attitudes and beliefs will continue to improve our understanding of the role of society in the life of the individual and may in time explain why social prejudices and stereotypes are so long lasting. It is hoped that this knowledge will lead to techniques that will result in improved human relations.

Social problems and moral development will remain targets of psychological research aimed at improving the welfare of society. Occupational and industrial psychology will continue to be concerned with the effects of the dramatic changes in the world marketplace, in global competition, information technology, and the disappearance of certain types of jobs—with the effects of all these changes not only upon workers at home and in the workplace but upon the way business is conducted.

Techniques for assessing and diagnosing brain damage, autism, and mental disorders will continue to improve, as will methods of assessing academic, cognitive, and other types of human functioning. Individual differences in brain functions at the neuromolecular, neuropsychological, and neurochemical levels will be measured accurately. Differences in how individuals receive, store, and process information will also be measured with greater specificity than they can be today.

Scales for measuring good mental health will become more sophisticated, as will the means of preventing illness and promoting psychological wellbeing. Studies of the brain will continue to illuminate what is already known about how immune functions are influenced by the central nervous system, which is in turn affected by psychological states.

Behavioral genetics, which explores the complex interactions between constitutional factors, genetic inheritance, and the environment, will continue to yield insights into the development of schizophrenia and other mental disorders, leading to more effective treatment. The diathesis-stress model of mental illness will continue to point to the direction for future research on mental illness. A full understanding of mental health and illness will require the inclusion of genetic, biochemical, neurological, interpersonal, and cultural factors.

Research with animals will remain important in psychology. According to a distinguished panel of forty behavioral scientists who advise the National Institute of Mental Health (NIMH), "Behavioral studies with animals have provided many important insights into learning and the processes affecting motivation, including hunger, thirst, sleep, and sex. Studies with animals in the future will continue to permit researchers to examine fundamental behavioral processes apart from the impact of human cultures and institutions." Social influences on biological processes and interactions—such as those between nutrition and environment or those between aggressive behavior and biochemistry—will continue to emanate from research with animals.

Psychology will continue to broaden its scope in the future. Research on the long-term development of species will increase our understanding of the influence of evolution upon behavior. Advances in evolutionary theory and new discoveries about how humans have evolved will add to our understanding of why humans behave as they do. "Cross-cultural studies will yield knowledge of which aspects of human functioning represent biological imperatives and which represent cultural options" (NIMH report). Psychological study of conflicts among groups, social issues, moral exclusion, and conflict resolution will contribute to the improvement of relations between different cultures and nations. The practice of psychology and its applications to education, social issues, and the workplace will be disseminated internationally. Global dissemination will enable more people to have the most effective treatments for mental disorders and to enjoy the benefits of better techniques for education, and will encourage the application of human factors research to a wide array of environments. Research findings that are germane to public policy, the natural environment, and systems of law and adjudication will permit societies to formulate objectives and implement policies that promote well-being. Psychology will continue to participate in and contribute to the development of a scientific method that can accommodate all the facets of humans and their environments.

[See also Mental Health; Psychiatry; Public Health; Social Sciences.]

BIBLIOGRAPHY

Buss, D. M. "Evolutionary Psychology: A New Paradigm for Psychological Science." *Psychological Inquiry* 6 (1995):1–30.
Cacioppo, J. T., and Bernston, G. G. "Social Psychological Contributions to the Decade of the Brain: Doctrine of Multilevel Analysis." *American Psychologist* 47/8 (1992): 1019–1028.
Cole, J. D., et al. "The Science of Prevention: A Conceptual Framework and Some Directions for a National Research Program." *American Psychologist* 48/10 (1993): 1013–1022.
Deutsch, M. A. "Educating for a Peaceful World." *American Psychologist* 48/5 (1993): 510–517.
Maier, S. F.; Watkins, L. R.; and Fleshner, M. "Psychoneuroimmunology: The Interface between Behavior, Brain, and Immunity." *American Psychologist* 49/12 (1994): 1004–1017.
Matarazzo, J. D. "Psychological Testing and Assessment in the Twenty-First Century." *American Psychologist* 47/8 (1992): 1007–1018.
National Institute of Mental Health. *Basic Behavioral Science for Mental Health: A National Investment.* Washington, DC: U.S. Government Printing Office, 1995.
Stokols, D. "Establishing and Maintaining and Healthy Environments: Toward a Social Ecology of Health Promotion." *American Psychologist* 47/1 (1992): 6–22.

— MELISSA G. WARREN

PUBLIC ASSISTANCE PROGRAMS

As the twentieth century draws to a close, the social landscape is shifting. In the United States and many other developed Western nations, we witness disturbing increases in economic inequality, single parenthood, homeless and ill-housed families, detached and disaffected youths, drug use, violent crime, and distrust among the races. Following "the American Century" of economic and political triumphs, we find ourselves in a state of social disarray with misgivings about the future.

At the same time, welfare state policies seem out of touch with today's and tomorrow's social issues. Public assistance or "welfare" does little except maintain poor people in their poverty, and spending for entitlements, which go mostly to the middle class, is out of control, threatening fiscal crisis in the years ahead.

Questions must be raised about the very assumptions underlying public assistance and the welfare state. During coming decades it is all but inevitable that domestic policy will undergo a fundamental transformation. While the ultimate outcome of this transformation is impossible to predict, it is likely that a new emphasis on *development* will replace the traditional welfare state emphasis on maintenance.

Public Assistance and Other Welfare State Spending

In financial terms, social spending has been the chief function of the modern state. Social spending (i.e., government payments to individuals for income security, medical care, nutrition, housing, social services, and so forth) makes up over half of federal expenditures in the United States and even more in Western Europe. This spending comes in three basic forms: public assistance, tax expenditures (or "tax benefits"), and social insurance.

PUBLIC ASSISTANCE. Public assistance or "welfare" is financial aid, food, housing, health care, or other assistance that is provided by "means test," i.e., it is targeted to people who are thought to have insufficient means to survive on their own. Although the general public seems to think of "welfare" as a huge expenditure, in fact it makes up only 16 percent of all social spending at the federal level.

By far the largest part of public assistance spending goes to the elderly and the disabled. They are the major recipients of income support through Supplemental Security Income (SSI) and the major recipients of medical

TABLE 1

FEDERAL SPENDING FOR MEANS-TESTED PUBLIC ASSISTANCE PROGRAMS IN BILLIONS OF DOLLARS, 1992*

	Amount	Percent
Total Means-Tested Public Assistance	*178.6*	*100.0*
Income Support	32.3	18.1
Aid to Families with Dependent Children	13.6	
Supplemental Security Income	18.7	
Medical Care	75.6	42.3
Medicaid	67.8	
Medical Care for Veterans	7.8	
Food and Nutrition	30.8	17.2
Food Stamps	23.5	
School Lunch and Other	7.3	
Housing	17.3	9.7
Section 8 Rental Assistance	12.3	
Low-Rent Public Housing	5.0	
Education and Training	17.8	10.0
College Grants and Loans	11.1	
All Other	6.7	
Social Services	4.8	2.7

* Source: Ross, Jane L. *Means-Tested Programs: An Overview, Problems, and Issues.* GAO Report T-HEHS-95-76. Washington, DC: U.S. General Accounting Office (citing Congressional Research Service), 1995.

care through Medicaid (see Table 1). In contrast, Aid to Families with Dependent Children (AFDC), which has been the target of heated "welfare reform" debates during the 1990s, is a comparatively modest expenditure. Also noteworthy are the small expenditures for education and training, and the even smaller expenditures for child care and other social services.

Spending trends in public assistance can be summarized succinctly: Medicaid is rising rapidly, and everything else is staying about the same. With an aging population, the rise in Medicaid is likely to continue. Because states cosponsor Medicaid, it is a growing budgetary problem in virtually all states.

At this writing, the Republican congressional majority, in its "Contract with America," is attacking public assistance for the poor. They seek to limit spending and reorganize public assistance programs into "block grants" under state control. But the proposals do not include Medicaid, which is the major budgetary problem. "Managed care" and other administrative controls will become more common in Medicaid, but these will not alter the underlying trend.

TAX EXPENDITURES. The second, often overlooked leg of the welfare state is tax expenditures. In 1995, tax expenditures to individuals are estimated at $392 billion, much of this amount in housing, health care, and retirement security (see Table 2). These are hidden welfare benefits to the middle class—"hidden" because most of the public does not view them as the welfare transfers that they are. Several points about tax expenditures are important to bear in mind. First, by far the most tax expenditures go to individuals rather than to corporations. Second, almost none of the tax expenditures go to the poor. Third, tax expenditures to individuals far exceed in size all public assistance programs to the poor combined. Fourth, tax expenditures to individuals go largely into asset accumulation (mostly in homes and retirement accounts), while most other welfare state spending (in public assistance and social insurance) is oriented toward consumption. Indeed, public assistance programs for the poor do not permit asset accumulation (a very misguided policy), while tax benefits programs for the middle class promote asset accumulation.

Trends in tax expenditures are uncertain. At this writing, Republican congressional leaders and President Bill Clinton are proposing more tax cuts. The wisdom of large tax cuts when federal spending is producing chronic deficits is much in doubt.

Also gaining momentum are proposals to replace the progressive income tax and most accompanying tax deductions with a flat tax and/or a consumption tax. If these tax reform initiatives are accompanied by (1) exclusion of tax liability for low-income households and (2) elimination of tax deductions and credits across the board (two very big ifs), tax reform would be desirable.

SOCIAL INSURANCE. By far the largest social expenditures are for social insurance or "entitlements," represented primarily by Social Security, Medicare, and federal pensions. It is important to make a few summary observations. First, at more than $600 billion in 1995, entitlement spending is about three times greater than public assistance spending. Second, this spending is not means-tested; most of it goes not to the poor but to the middle class. Third, a huge proportion of entitlement spending is for the elderly (an even bigger proportion than in public assistance spending). Fourth, up to the present, recipients of retirement and old-age medical benefits have received much more than they have put into the system (this will not be possible in the near future). Fifth, entitlement spending is rising rapidly; by 2003, mandatory entitlements are projected to make up 58.2 percent of all federal spending. Sixth, the tax collections ("insurance premiums") for these programs will not be enough to meet obligations in the near future: Medicare expenditures already exceed revenues, and Social Security retirement benefits will exceed revenues around 2012 (see Figures 1 and 2). Although "trust funds" have theoretically been accumulated for these programs that would carry Medicare until 2001 and Social Security until 2029, in fact this money exists only on paper. (As a population, we have voted entitlement benefits for ourselves but also voted to spend the trust fund money in other ways, all the while telling ourselves that the trust fund money is sacrosanct. In the long run, the hypocrisy of these actions cannot be painted over by self-delusion or political posturing.)

A fiscal crisis is on the horizon. Revenue short-falls will be severe by 2012, and under current projections, entitlement spending would exceed *all* federal revenues by the year 2030. The entitlements simply cannot be

TABLE 2

ESTIMATED FEDERAL TAX EXPENDITURES TO INDIVIDUALS AND CORPORATIONS IN BILLIONS OF DOLLARS, 1995 AND 1999*

	Amount	Percent
Tax Expenditures to Individuals	*392.0*	*504.6*
Housing		
Mortgage Interest Tax Deduction	53.5	67.8
Other Home-Ownership Tax Benefits	33.4	39.8
Health Care		
Exclusion of Medical Insurance Premiums	45.8	62.6
Exclusion of Untaxed Medicare Benefits	13.1	25.2
Retirement Security		
Exclusion of Pension Contributions/Earnings	80.9	102.0
Exclusion of Untaxed Social Security and Railroad Retirement Benefits	23.1	27.1
Exclusion of Income on Life Insurance and Annuities	10.3	14.3
Capital Gains and Other Income/ Property Benefits		
Exclusion of Capital Gains at Death	12.7	18.3
Maximum 28% Tax Rate on Capital Gains	9.1	13.9
Exclusion of State and Local Income and Personal Property Taxes	24.7	31.0
All Other Tax Expenditures to Individuals	85.4	102.9
Tax Expenditures to Corporations	*58.7*	*59.9*
Total Tax Expenditures	*450.7*	*564.5*

* Source: Calculated from U.S. Congress, Joint Committee on Taxation. *Estimates of Federal Tax Expenditures for Fiscal Years 1995–1999.* Washington, DC: U.S. Government Printing Office, 1994.

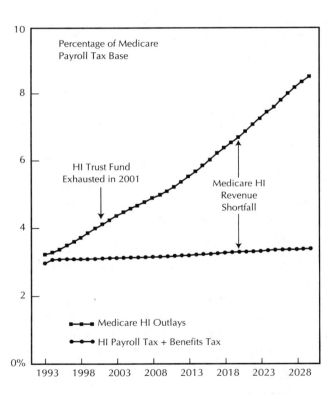

Figure 1. Projections for Medicare revenues and expenses. (Bipartisan Commission on Entitlement and Tax Reform. Interim Report to the President. *Washington, DC: U.S. Government Printing Office, 1994.)*

695

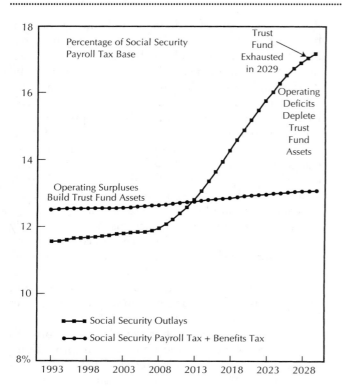

Figure 2. Projections for Social Security revenues and expenses. (Bipartisan Commission on Entitlement and Tax Reform. Interim Report to the President. Washington, DC: U.S. Government Printing Office, 1994.)

paid for in their current form without grave injustice to future generations and serious harm to the U.S. economy (see Peterson, 1993). Every policy analyst and politician of substance knows this to be the case. Yet, at present, few politicians dare speak the truth lest they not be reelected. The longer this moratorium on truth prevails, the more difficult the adjustments will be when they finally arrive. Public denial may last until 2010 or 2015, when change will take place in a crisis atmosphere.

Maintenance: The Welfare State of the Twentieth Century

Overall, the welfare state of the twentieth century can be characterized as oriented toward maintenance with five distinguishing characteristics: transfer of income, passive support for the unemployed, preoccupation with problems, focus on individuals, and bureaucratic organization.

TRANSFER OF INCOME. Foremost, the welfare state is characterized by the transfer of income to support consumption. Social insurance and means-tested transfers make up most social spending. In this social policy

scheme, an individual's "welfare" (well-being) is defined by his or her level of income, and it is assumed that this income supports a certain level of consumption. This perspective rests on flawed intellectual foundations in neoclassical economics, in which well-being derives only from consumption. But as any accountant or financial planner knows, consumption by itself does not constitute well-being. Savings and investment—asset building—must be taken into consideration as well.

PASSIVE SUPPORT FOR THE UNEMPLOYED. The origins of the welfare state were in a system of industrial capitalism wherein most employees worked productively with little education and training. Consistent with these conditions, welfare state provisions such as Social Security benefits, workers' compensation, and unemployment insurance were designed to support people off the job, but not to prepare people for new jobs. Since those days, the world of work has changed dramatically, but U.S. social policy has not. In a post-industrial era, ever more skills—and more flexible skills—will be required to succeed in the labor market. Policies designed solely to support the unemployed and nonemployed are tragically out of date.

PREOCCUPATION WITH PROBLEMS. On the services side, the welfare state has been dominated by modern-day social work and other professions with an orientation toward problem solving. The basic idea has been to identify an individual or family "problem," and then "intervene" in an attempt to solve that problem. With this narrow focus, social workers often overlook opportunities for success.

FOCUS ON INDIVIDUALS. Despite community-oriented rhetoric, most social policies address individual issues—rental subsidies for the unhoused, food stamps for the unfed, criminal justice for the unruly, and psychotherapy for the unhinged. The vast majority of today's social workers ply their trade with individuals, in agencies and offices quite removed from community settings. The welfare state is, in reality, highly individualistic. Both income support and services have been aimed almost exclusively at individuals. Occasionally the policy focuses on families, but seldom on neighborhoods and communities. In sharp juxtaposition to this individual focus, it is apparent that the most vexing social issues of our time—alienated youth, crime, drug abuse, AIDS, homelessness, violence within families—stem from social and economic institutions, such as loss of employment, racial discrimination, weakening of community organizations, changes in family structure, and failing schools.

BUREAUCRATIC ORGANIZATION. The welfare state has been organized primarily as a public-sector, top-down, bureaucratic, and largely disconnected set of activities. To be sure, we have enacted lofty and well-intentioned policies, but we have paid too little attention to what those policies actually do when they "reach the ground" in communities and households. Programs and services are often not what they were intended to be. They are fragmented and unresponsive to genuine needs.

The welfare state had been organized primarily

as a public-sector, top-down, bureaucratic,

and largely disconnected set of activities.

These five characteristics together constitute the maintenance orientation of the welfare state of the twentieth century. This emphasis on maintenance has alleviated suffering, but it has done little to build capacities that would enable people and communities to become self-sufficient. As the century draws to a close, it is clear that maintenance by itself is an inadequate foundation for constructing social policy.

Development: Domestic Policy in the Twenty-first Century

Because the fiscal problems are overwhelming, and because maintenance strategies are not responding to the most pressing social issues of our time, it is very likely that domestic policy will undergo a major transformation in the decades ahead. The nature of this transformation is impossible to predict, but it would be desirable to shift from maintenance toward development.

In contrast to the five maintenance characteristics described above, a development policy would emphasize the opposites: building assets instead of providing income for consumption, developing human capital instead of aimless support for the unemployed, enhancing capacities instead of problem-centered treatment, building communities instead of isolating individuals, and creating responsive human service organizations instead of bureaucracies.

BUILDING ASSETS. A development policy would promote asset accumulation. This policy would recognize that individuals, families, and the nation as a whole must counterbalance income-and-consumption with savings-and-investment. Moreover, asset building would become a foundation of social policy, so that many social and economic goals—especially higher education, home ownership, small business development, retirement security, and even health care—are achieved to a significant extent through programs of asset accumulation, even for the poorest families. Work

in this area has been pioneered by Sherraden (1991), who proposes a new domestic policy based on Individual Development Accounts (IDAs). This thinking has generated widespread discussion and policy initiatives (Edwards and Sherraden, 1995).

INVESTING IN PEOPLE. As the nations of East Asia are demonstrating, social policy cannot be separated from economic policy. Social policy should promote education, job skills, and labor market participation. In the United States we now realize that more attention must be paid to developing a labor force capable of competing in the international arena (Hornbeck and Salamon, 1990). We have more discussion of the importance of primary and secondary education, and effective transitions from school to work. Also, there is increasing attention to means-tested transfers as a possible deterrent to labor market participation. Little attention has yet been paid, however, to transformation of the largest social policy provisions—particularly Social Security benefits, unemployment insurance, and workers' compensation—so that they can contribute to enhancement of skills, participation, and productivity.

FOCUSING ON PERSONAL, INTERPERSONAL, AND FAMILY POTENTIAL. Instead of a narrow focus on personal problems (deviance, deficiency, abnormality), a development policy would affirm ordinary life events and opportunities. (To those who are therapy-minded, this approach may sound peculiar. Perhaps it can be understood by analogy: Peter Drucker, the management guru, has identified a common managerial error that he calls "feeding problems and starving solutions." According to Drucker, what one gets by "problem-solving" is damage containment. Only opportunities produce growth. Drucker suggests that a manager first draw up a list of opportunities facing the organization and make sure that each is adequately staffed. Only then should the manager draw up a list of problems.) The logic of development is that the best uses of energy and resources are in building social skills and strong families, promoting resilience, and striving for success. The helping professions had these traditions prior to the creation of the welfare state. Much work remains to be done in revitalizing these traditions for the twenty-first century.

PROMOTING CITIZENSHIP, MUTUALITY, AND INTERRACIAL UNDERSTANDING. However great a society's commitment to individuality and freedom, it requires a countervailing commitment to community and civic participation. Voluntary association has been a hallmark of American democracy, and mutual ties have served as an essential counterbalance to America's economic individualism. This was recognized from the outset of the republic by Jefferson, later noted by de Tocqueville, and has reappeared in calls for greater social responsibility and a stronger sense of community in work by Etzioni (1993) and others.

Although an emphasis on community is not by itself a solution (one is reminded of rather naive community action efforts during the 1960s), it is an essential starting point. Fortunately, extreme individualism in social policy and practice may be changing. Nonmilitary national service has joined military service, albeit in a small way, as a national policy (Eberly and Sherraden, 1990). In the social work profession, there is a call for a return to community-based services rather than office-based psychotherapies. Recent successes of community development corporations (CDCs) are noteworthy. Community-based youth development is being emphasized anew (Sherraden, 1992). These community-building efforts also forge ties across racial groups. In the years ahead, community-building is likely to become a stronger feature of social policy and practice in the United States.

CREATING RESPONSIVE AND EFFECTIVE HUMAN SERVICE ORGANIZATIONS. Dramatic change is needed in the administration of social policy, including fewer layers in the organizational structure, fewer forms to fill out, more integrated delivery systems, more incentives for outstanding performance, more control by those who are in the front lines, greater responsiveness to individual needs and circumstances, more emphasis on outcomes, and measurement of returns on public investment. State and local governments have been in the forefront in "reinventing" policy, organizations, programs, and services that deliver domestic policy. This thinking is beginning to emerge at the federal level. Recent innovations in areas such as public/private partnerships, collaboration across different service areas, devolution of authority to local control, client "empowerment" strategies, "one-stop shopping" for services, use of telecommunications to reduce paperwork and office visits, and return on investment accounting are all encouraging developments. But welfare-state bureaucracies are deeply entrenched. A great deal remains to be done, particularly in linking new organizational forms to family and community development.

[See also Entitlement Programs; Health Care Financing; Public Assistance Programs: Social Security; Social Welfare Philosophies; Unemployment; Unemployment Insurance, Workmen's Compensation.]

BIBLIOGRAPHY

Eberly, Donald, and Sherraden, Michael, eds. *The Moral Equivalent of War? A Study of Non-Military Service in Nine Nations.* Westport, CT. Greenwood Press, 1990.

Edwards, Karen, and Sherraden, Michael. *Individual Development Accounts: Asset-Based Policy Innovation.* St. Louis: Center for Social Development, Washington University, 1995.

Etzioni, Amitai. *The Spirit of Community: Rights, Responsibilities, and the Communitarian Agenda.* New York: Crown Publishers, 1993.

Hornbeck, David W., and Salamon, Lester M., eds. *Human Capital and America's Future.* Baltimore, MD: Johns Hopkins University Press, 1990.

Peterson, Peter G. *Facing Up: How to Rescue the Economy from Crushing Debt and Restore the American Dream.* New York: Simon & Schuster, 1993.

Ross, Jane L. *Means-Tested Programs: An Overview, Problems, and Issues.* GAO Report T-HEHS-95–76. Washington, DC: U.S. General Accounting Office, 1995.

Sherraden, Michael. *Assets and the Poor: A New American Welfare Policy.* Armonk, NY. M. E. Sharpe, 1991.

———. *Community-Based Youth Services in International Perspective.* Washington, DC: Carnegie Council on Adolescent Development and W. T. Grant Foundation Commission on Youth and America's Future, 1992.

— MICHAEL SHERRADEN

PUBLIC ASSISTANCE PROGRAMS: SOCIAL SECURITY

Social Security programs in the United States raise funds from payroll taxes to provide income support to retired or disabled workers and their dependents, as well as Medicare Hospital Insurance (HI) for those over sixty-five or suffering long-term disabilities. In addition, Medicare Supplementary Insurance (SMI) covers doctors' fees and outpatient services for this portion of the population, mainly financed through general revenues (one-fourth is paid for by premiums from those who enroll).

Operating as a chain of promises through time, Social Security is the one federal program most inescapably concerned with the future. By paying for benefits earlier promised to yesterday's workers (today's retirees), today's workers earn "entitlements" they can expect to redeem as tomorrow's beneficiaries. Since as workers they will be paying those future bills, today's children are directly involved in this chain of promises we are making for them.

Since the basic demographic patterns are already in place, there is relatively little uncertainty about the future size of the beneficiary population and the workforce that will be available to support it. Changes in fertility, immigration, and death rates can alter this picture only gradually and in the very long term. The postwar baby boomers will begin pressing on Social Security funds around 2010. Likewise, lower birthrates after the mid-1960s will produce relatively fewer workers in the early part of the next century. These established facts, along with a gradual growth of life expectancy in old age, will produce an overall aging of American society and strains on Social Security finances. The number of workers for each Social Security beneficiary will have gone from 16 in 1950 to 3.7 in 1970; 3.3 in 1990; and 1.7–2.2 workers by 2030 (depending on different assumptions).

At the other extreme of uncertainty are inherently unforeseeable developments: technological breakthroughs, pandemics, wars, culture shifts, and the like. No one can say if these will occur to produce discontinuities in demographic trends or different social understandings of dependency, aging, and obligations. At an intermediate level of uncertainty are projections in standard economic variables, such as employment, wages, and GNP growth. Greater affluence and productivity per worker can offset some of the consequences of fewer workers. Such projections give modest guidance for weighing the future, even if we have no way of finally settling on optimistic or pessimistic projections or any point in between.

Operating as a chain of promises through time,

Social Security is the one federal program

most inescapably concerned with the future.

Most people think about Social Security in terms of financial outlook—"Will it be there for me and my family?" In a very basic sense, the answer will be what it has always been: Social Security will be there five or fifty years from now, depending on the will of the voters and the willingness of the working population to pay the taxes that make good on promised benefit entitlements. The more complex issue thus becomes one of estimating how financially burdensome it may be to keep the chain of promises intact.

Major reforms in 1983 sought to ease the future financial burden in three ways. First, the retirement age for earning full benefits will gradually rise from 65 in 2003 to 67 in 2025. Second, beneficiaries with gross incomes over certain limits ($25,000 for single persons, $32,000 for married couples) have up to half their benefits subject to income taxation. Finally, payroll taxes were increased (from 9.35 percent in 1983 to 15.3 percent in 1990 and all years thereafter) to provide a growing surplus in the Social Security Trust Fund. The fund holdings—IOUs in the form of treasury bonds and the interest they earn—will be drawn down to help cover the gap as projected payroll tax receipts begin lagging behind spending on the growing ranks of retired baby boomers, sometime around 2016. By 2025, all of the baby boomers will have retired, the annual tax-to-

spending shortfall will be $60 billion, and depletion of the fund surplus will accelerate until it is exhausted in 2036. One should note that if spending promises are to be kept, the treasury bonds redeemed from the fund from 2016 to 2036 will have to be paid for with higher taxes or further borrowing on financial markets. Once the fund is insolvent in 2036, the choices will be to cut benefits, sharply increase payroll taxes, continue funding Social Security from general revenues, or some combination of these options.

The financial outlook worsens and need for higher taxes grows when we consider the health insurance side of Social Security. Government forecasts show Medicare's HI producing a deficit of spending to payroll tax revenues in the mid-1990s and the HI Trust Fund becoming insolvent in 2002. Medicare insurance for physician services had no comparable trust fund and official projections are not made beyond 2000. But many of the same forces drive both HI and SMI spending, and forecasts are that both together will equal or exceed Social Security spending on retirement and disability by the year 2020. Yet even these projections assume that medical costs, while rising faster than general inflation, will grow substantially slower than they did in the 1970s and 1980s. Whether reform of the health system in the 1990s will produce such a slowdown in the growth of health care costs remains to be seen.

Considering Social Security and HI together, projected income should be enough to cover projected spending for perhaps the next 10 to 15 years. After about 2010, a large deficit will begin accumulating. While the future payroll tax rate is set by law at 15.3 percent of earnings (divided equally between worker and employer), projected spending will be 20 percent of payroll earnings by 2020. If the SMI portion of Medicare obligations is projected in the same way as hospital insurance, the figure grows to 26 percent in 2020, implying payroll taxes two-thirds higher than those today. This large gap between income and outgo will eventually have to be closed by enacting substantially higher taxes, lower benefits, or some combination of the two. The total of the actuarial deficit that lies ahead over the next seventy-five years is estimated at $13.2 trillion. (Actuarial deficit is defined as the amount by which projected future expenditures for benefits and administration exceed the projected income and value of the trust funds.) These projections are based on what Social Security program trustees term "intermediate" assumptions about the future. However, evidence from prevailing historical trends in birth, mortality, and productivity rates is more in line with what are conventionally labeled as the trustees' "pessimistic" alternative assumptions. If those are used, the projected deficits and need for more tax revenue would begin toward the end of the 1990s, with a total actuarial deficit estimated at $22.8 trillion. (For perspective, spending $1 million a day, it would take about 2,700 years to spend $1 trillion.)

Social Security has become institutionalized both in public beliefs about the value of the program as well as in individual and employer planning for retirement. However, there is very little public understanding of the program, the chain of promises it represents, or the immense future commitments that exist. At the same time, politicians will no doubt continue to avoid saying or doing anything controversial that could improve understanding of the program and its future commitments.

Improved health and living conditions for many older persons will help undermine beliefs about the elderly as a homogenous and needy group.

Despite the popularity of Social Security today, surveys generally show 60 percent or more of non-retired adults have little confidence that funds will be available to pay their retirement benefits. There is a good possibility that public support for the system may slowly erode in the years ahead. First, the very high ratio of benefits received to contributions paid by those participating in the early decades of the Social Security program has now come to an end and will no longer be available to build popular support. Second, improving health, increasing wealth, and better living conditions for many older persons will help undermine once prevalent beliefs about the elderly as a homogeneous and inherently needy group. Third, the gradually emerging but huge actuarial deficit will strain the tolerance of working-age persons for ever higher payroll taxes. Fourth, economic inequality, which is greater among the elderly than among the working aged, will persist and probably grow, given prevailing inequalities in education, home ownership, occupational structure, and private employer benefits. This will increase resistance to transferring resources to elderly persons regardless of need. Finally, greater income testing of Social Security benefits will erode program support from higher income groups, whose benefits are proportionately less in relation to contributions than is the case for lower income groups. Currently, only 6 percent of workers are above the earnings ceiling at which Social Security taxes cease ($57,300 in 1993), and since this limit is indexed to constantly adjust upward with average wage in-

creases, not many are ever likely to get beyond the tax ceiling. On the other hand, the income ceiling at which people have to start paying income tax on their Social Security benefits is unindexed; hence the current 22 percent of beneficiaries who find their entitlements subject to taxation will find their ranks constantly growing.

While Social Security will certainly provide most Americans with a minimum level of income support for many years to come, new ways of thinking about the issues are likely to be sought. Pressures will grow to use the Trust Fund surplus (projected to peak at $5.6 trillion in 2024) in more constructive ways than the current accumulation of treasury IOUs that help finance current deficit spending in the federal budget. If more active use of the surplus for public and private investment were to raise economic growth over what it would have been, future taxes to honor Social Security promises would be relatively less burdensome at the resulting higher levels of national income. Efforts will probably be made to allow individuals to apply a portion of their Social Security taxes to individual accounts for investment and future returns.

Further increases in the official retirement age are likely. Moreover, the very concept of retirement may be questioned and reformulated. It is a concept created by public policy from an earlier era of industrial factory life. Rather than compartmentalizing education, work, and leisure into sequential age categories, a postindustrial society may see these fundamental human activities as attributes of a person's security and welfare throughout a lifetime. Some form of personal account to draw upon and pay into may well be developed to allow individuals greater choice in arranging their own combinations of work, study, and leisure throughout the life cycle.

In light of existing commitments to those in and nearing old age, any such changes undoubtedly will have to be phased in gradually, as is the currently mandated increase in the retirement age after 2003. But for the 178 million Americans now under age 45, with time to adjust their retirement plans, and for the post-Cold War generation now being born, it is highly prudent and appropriate to rethink these issues.

[See also Health Care Financing; Public Assistance Programs; Unemployment Insurance, Workmen's Compensation.]

BIBLIOGRAPHY

Aaron, Henry J.; Bosworth, Barry P.; and Burtless, Gary. *Can Americans Afford to Grow Old?* Washington, DC: Brookings Institution, 1989.

Cook, Fay Lomax, and Barrett, Edith J. "Public Support for Social Security." *Journal of Aging Studies* 2/4 (1988): 339–356.

Koitz, David. "The Financial Outlook for Social Security and Medicare." In *CRS Report for Congress*. CRS Publication, 92–608 EPW, July 31, 1992. Washington, DC: Congressional Research Service, 1992.

Kotlikoff, Laurence J. *Generational Accounting*. New York: Free Press, 1992.

Organization for Economic Cooperation and Development. *Aging Populations*. Paris: OECD, 1988.

— HUGH HECLO

PUBLIC FINANCE

The information revolution will continue to force dramatic changes in public finance. Still, it is not yet clear whether a powerful trend toward limited government will soon prevail over welfare state programs that are headed for fiscal disaster.

The information age has unleashed unprecedented economic competition but also cooperation between governments—cooperation because trade barriers are falling. Lower tariffs in one region of the world lead to pressures in other regions to reduce restraints on trade.

In the past, governments could charge monopolistic prices because citizens had little choice but to pay. Thanks to computer and communications technological advances, many economic transactions can now be performed anywhere in the world. This will force governments to compete by becoming more efficient by lowering taxes. Such pressures may lead to the adoption by the United States of a greatly simplified flat-rate income tax. Countries that maintain high tax rates will see capital and highly skilled entrepreneurs flee to more friendly areas.

The 1980s brought a significant decline in marginal tax rates—the tax rate paid on the last dollar earned. The cut in tax rates during President Ronald Reagan's first term was followed by the 1986 Tax Reform Act, which slashed the top tax rate to almost one-half the 70 percent rate last seen in 1980. These U.S. tax rate reductions led to tax rate cuts in many states and countries. Future elections may usher in sweeping tax reforms, such as the replacement of the current income tax with a flat-rate income tax or sales tax.

The future will also bring passage of additional constitutional limits on federal and state government taxes, spending, and debt. The Balanced Budget Amendment passed the House of Representatives for the first time ever in 1995, only to fail by one vote in the Senate. An additional attempt to pass it is likely in the near future.

The House of Representatives is expected to vote by April 1996 for the first time ever on a proposed tax limitation constitutional amendment. While the two-thirds vote necessary to approve such an amendment is unlikely, proponents may obtain over 250 of the 435 votes cast on the measure.

This tax limitation amendment would require a three-fifths vote of each house of Congress in order to pass a tax increase bill. It is similar to measures that have grown increasingly common in state constitutions, although most state limits require a two-thirds vote.

Twenty years ago, tax limits on state governments were rare. By 1995, twenty-eight states have adopted various tax or expenditure limits, and several states have adopted multiple limits. Since 1978 five states have added tax increase "supermajority" vote requirements.

Not only is the information age likely to lead to further limits on government taxes and spending, it will also shape the design of the limits. As access to information improves, voters will want to exercise more direct control over government. Since 1992, voters in five states have endorsed requirements for voter approval before certain higher taxes can become law. Several similar measures were narrowly rejected in the 1994 election, but will likely pass in future elections.

Even though there is a strong trend toward limits on government spending and taxes, the welfare state will not shrink easily. Unless current laws are changed soon, an aging population will cause spending on so-called entitlements to explode early in the next century. These entitlement programs cause government benefit checks to be written to people who meet certain criteria for age, income, or wealth.

Spending on entitlement programs, along with interest on the national debt, is projected to equal all federal taxes by the year 2012. That would leave no funds for any of the other functions of government such as defense, highways, courts, education, or law enforcement.

The two largest entitlement programs are Social Security and Medicare. The current tax rate for these two programs is 15.2 percent. Official government projections estimate that the tax rate would have to rise to between 38 and 62 percent by 2040 to pay for benefits promised under current laws. Such tax rates would crush the nation's economy and these programs are widely acknowledged to be unsustainable in their current form.

Unfunded benefit liabilities for these two programs plus federal worker pensions totaled over $14.4 trillion in 1991, or more than triple the U.S. government's debt. By the year 2025, Social Security and Medicare programs are projected to run an annual deficit of over $750 billion under current policies.

The average age of Americans is increasing, leaving fewer workers to pay the taxes that fund these old-age benefits. In 1985, there were more than five workers for each retiree. In 2030, there will be fewer than three. People are also collecting old-age benefits for a longer period of time. When Social Security began in 1935, the average life expectancy was sixty-one years. Today it is seventy-six.

Despite these ominous demographic trends, current laws promise even higher benefits. For example, if a family's wages equal $24,000, a retiree in the year 2000 will receive Social Security benefits of $11,380. With the same wages (adjusted for inflation to 1994 dollars), a retiree will collect $13,020 in 2030, and $14,630 in 2060.

Although changes are considered politically impossible now, that may soon change. A recent public opinion poll showed that more workers under thirty-five believed in UFOs than in the future of Social Security. Younger citizens would welcome political candor on this issue so they can properly plan for their retirement future.

Some countries have privatized their Social Security system. Chile did so in the early 1980s, and the typical Chilean worker's net worth may soon surpass that of the average American worker. When that happens, the fact will be broadly noted in the United States, further weakening public support for Social Security in its current form.

[See also Credit, Debt, and Borrowing; Deficits, Governmental; Economic Cycles: Models amd Simulations; Entitlement Programs; Health Care Financing; Monetary System; Public Assistance Programs; Social Welfare Philosophies; Taxes.]

BIBLIOGRAPHY

Bartley, Robert L. *The Seven Fat Years and How to Do It Again*. New York: Free Press, 1992.
Bipartisan Commission on Entitlement and Tax Reform: Final Report. Washington, DC: U.S. Government, Superintendent of Documents, 1995.
"The Case for Killing Social Security." *Time* (March 20, 1995).
Davidson, James Dale, and Rees-Mogg, Lord William. *The Great Reckoning*. New York: Summit Books, 1991.
Hall, Robert E., and Rabushka, Alvin. *The Flat Tax*. Stanford, CA: Hoover Institution Press, 1995.
Lindsey, Lawrence. *The Growth Experiment: How the New Tax Policy Is Transforming the U.S. Economy*. New York: Basic Books, 1990.
Payne, James L. *Costly Returns: The Burdens of the U.S. Tax System*. San Francisco: Institute for Contemporary Studies Press, 1993.
"The Pension Time Bomb." *Washington Monthly* (January–February 1995).

— DAVID KEATING

PUBLIC HEALTH

Medical care has been a minor determinant of improved health over the past 150 years. Improved health has resulted primarily from better economic, environmental, and social conditions. McKeown (1979) states that improvement in health in the past was due to reduced family size, improved nutrition, hygiene, sanitation, and latterly by vaccines and antibiotics. Recent declines in deaths from heart disease in North America and Europe

By the year 2000, for the first time, half of the world's population will live in urban areas, some inhabited by tens of millions.

are ascribed mainly to lifestyle changes (quitting smoking, lower-fat diets, more exercise), and simple medical measures (control of high blood pressure) rather than to high-tech interventions such as bypass surgery and transplants. Health status will also be determined mainly by our future environmental, social, and economic situation, and by our lifestyles. Future technological and organizational developments in the delivery of medical care may play a relatively small role.

Level of Economic Development, Wealth, and Equity

Health status will vary enormously from country to country—and within countries—depending on the degree of industrialization and development. Health problems in the least developed countries will continue, at least for several decades, to include high infant mortality rates and infectious diseases. In the industrialized countries, poor health and disability (primarily among the aged) associated with chronic diseases such as heart disease, cancer, and arthritis will constitute the major health problems.

Wealth is closely associated with the level of industrialization and health. As countries industrialize, they will likely experience improved health, except among the poor as they move from rural villages to urban slums.

Overall health status in societies committed to social and economic equity is greater than in countries with a lesser degree of equity. Poverty and powerlessness are associated with poor health. Measures to alleviate poverty and ensure that everyone has access to basic prerequisites of health such as food, shelter, clean water, education, a clean, safe environment, and more control over their lives, will remain fundamental to achieving better health for all in the twenty-first century.

Global Environmental Crisis, Population Growth, and Material Expectations

Regardless of their level of economic development, all countries are likely to face a similar set of health threats in the twenty-first century, rooted in major global environmental change; only their capacity to manage these challenges will differ. Such changes are rooted in a combination of population growth, economic growth, and rising material expectations, which are having three major health-threatening impacts: global atmospheric change, resource depletion, and increasing toxification of the ecosystem.

Ozone depletion and a resultant increase in ultraviolet radiation threatens increased rates of skin cancer, cataracts, and possible interference in immune system functioning. Acid rain is associated with respiratory disease. Global warming could disrupt agricultural production, resulting in malnutrition and famine, the spread of tropical infectious diseases transmitted by insects (e.g., malaria, yellow fever); inundate heavily populated, low-lying areas (such as Bangladesh, Florida, or the Nile Delta) as a result of rising ocean levels that also could cause major population shifts aggravating the health and social problems of "eco-refugees."

Another global environmental danger arises from the impact of toxic pollution on ecosystems and the food chain (ecotoxicity). Subtle genetic, hormonal, immunological, and psychological effects of these chemicals

may impose an increasing toll on health. In addition, we can expect increasing conflict within and between nations over diminishing natural resources that will result in death and disease for the civilian populations caught in the middle, many of whom will be forced to become refugees.

Population growth in the least developed countries also is of concern. Coping strategies include improving the education of women, increasing their participation in the workforce, reducing infant mortality, and ensuring economic development. These steps, together with a shift toward a more environmentally sustainable form of economic development, may be among the most important strategies for achieving health for all in the twenty-first century.

Urbanization

By the year 2000, for the first time, half the world's population will live in urban areas, some inhabited by tens of millions. Urbanization poses threats as well as opportunities. Threats arise from poor environmental conditions that increase potentials for epidemic diseases

As countries industrialize and grow wealthier, their people will likely experience improved health, except among the poor who move from rural areas to city slums. (Jack Fields/Corbis)

and introduce the potential for social disintegration and violence. Opportunities arise from the potential to meet the human needs of large populations efficiently by harnessing the human creativity and energy. The World Health Organization's "Healthy Cities" project, developed in the 1980s, may play a vital role in igniting a new urban public health movement in the twenty-first century.

Lifestyle Changes

Lifestyles, while to some extent a matter of choice, also are significantly influenced by environmental, cultural, social, and economic circumstances. What we eat, whether we smoke or drink or use drugs, how much and how fast we drive, how much we exercise, how stressful our home and work life are—all of these and many other lifestyle behaviors affect our health.

The World Health Organization reported in 1993 that tobacco-related deaths globally rose from one million to three million annually between the 1960s and the '90s and indicated that the toll would rise to seven million annually in the Third World alone within the next two or three decades. We also can expect rising death and disability in the Third World from diseases related to alcohol use, high-fat and low-fiber diets and sedentary lifestyle associated with advanced industrialization. On the other hand, recent progress in reducing lifestyle-related death and disease in Western Europe and North America will likely continue, and in time may well diffuse to industrializing countries.

New and Old Diseases

We can be reasonably certain that we will be confronted with new diseases in the twenty-first century. Some of these will be old diseases in new places (because of the impacts of globalization and health infrastructure breakdowns), or old diseases in new forms as pathogens mutate or our immunological resistance changes. Others will be truly new diseases, either infectious like AIDS, or noninfectious, due perhaps to the impact of cumulative ecotoxicity. Nevertheless, it is likely that the broad pattern of diseases will remain much the same over the next few decades, with increasing numbers of countries undergoing the epidemiological transition to industrial patterns of disease.

Role of Health Care System and Health Technology

One of the significant developments in the 1980s was the realization that the health care system is not the major determinant of our health. Health care systems will most likely evolve into more community-based and -managed arrangements, with emphasis on primary care using fewer physicians and more nurses and other allied health professionals. Technological innovations in telematics, biotechnology, and materials technology will doubtless continue at a rapid pace, but the proportionate impact of these developments on the health status of populations will remain problematic. Moreover, as life expectancy increases, the focus of the system may well shift from cure to care, ensuring a higher quality of life—and death—for an aging population.

There is growing evidence of the effect the psyche can have on the body's hormonal and immunological systems and thus on disease processes.

Mental States

One final potential development that could have an impact on health involves harnessing the power of the mind. There is growing evidence of the effect the psyche can have on the body's hormonal and immunological systems and thus on disease processes. The negative side involves the effect of stress and powerlessness on physical health; the reverse aspect entails learning how to design environments, social structures, work settings, and living conditions—even hospitals—in ways that not only reduce stress but actively promote healing and maintain health. Perhaps individuals will learn to intentionally trigger the positive effects of this psychoneuroimmune system, with potential influence on immunologically related disorders such as cancer, autoimmune diseases, allergies, and infections.

Conclusion

Optimists point to the steadily rising level of health in virtually every country over the past fifty years (with the notable exception of Eastern Europe, where health status declined in the 1970s and '80s), and to a variety of positive factors that suggest this rising level of health may continue. Pessimists point to environmental challenges and to the increasing demands of our growing populations which suggest that these gains are at risk.

[See also Acid Rain; Epidemics; Food Additives; Food and Drug Safety; Freshwater; Global Warming; Nutrition; Ozone Layer Depletion; Population Growth: United States; Population Growth: Worldwide.]

BIBLIOGRAPHY

Ashton, John, ed. *Healthy Cities.* Milton Keynes, UK: Open University Press, 1992.
Canadian Public Health Association. *Human and Ecosystem Health.* Ottawa: CPHA, 1992.

Evans, R.; Barer, M.; and Marmore, T. *Why Are Some People Healthy and Others Not?* New York: A. de Gruyter, 1994.

Homer-Dixon, Thomas; Boutwell, Jeffrey; and Rathiens, George. "Environmental Change and Violent Conflict." *Scientific American* 268/2 (1993): 38–45.

Karasek, Robert, and Theorell, Thores. *Healthy Work.* New York: Basic Books, 1989.

McKeown, T. *The Role of Medicine: Dream, Mirage, or Nemesis.* Oxford, U.K.: Basil Blackwell, 1979.

— TREVOR HANCOCK

PUBLIC OPINION POLLS

Until general elections became common during the second half of the nineteenth century, there was essentially no linkage between what the public desired or thought and *either* political campaigning *or* political ideology. Since there were few public election campaigns (outside the United States), formal political thinking remained largely the provenance of scholars and philosophers who were principally concerned with describing a rational system of principles for explaining sociopolitical realities in the manner of the scientific enlightenment (Hobbes, Locke, the Mills and Bentham, and so forth).

The term *ideology* (*idéologie* in French) was coined around 1801 by a French philosopher, Destutt de Tracy, to describe an objective "science of ideas" that he had developed to reveal to people the sources of their biases and erroneous beliefs. But contemporary observers, including Napoleon I, dismissed de Tracy's new "science" as an artful contrivance of simplistic observations that masked dangerously "republican" underlying motives. (Napoleon himself is credited with coining the term "ideologue" to describe all those who promote simple theories for curing social and economic ills.)

The twin connotations of naïveté and hidden intentions have been associated with "ideology" since that time. The term achieved historic currency in the middle of the nineteenth century, when Marx and Engels first characterized formalized history as ideology ("a pack of lies agreed upon by the winners") and argued that all such ideologies serve to justify or rationalize a specific set of interests.

Public Opinion and Political Ideology: Separate but Equal Developments

Throughout the nineteenth century, with the exception of Marx and Engels, there continued to be a remarkable disconnection between actual public opinion and political ideology. In 1848, when the members of the Paris Revolutionary Commune had completed its Declaration of Workers' Rights, the assembly of lawyers, artists, professors, and students had to send a delegation to search the city to find at least one genuine working man

to sign the document. In Britain, the first genuinely popular statement of public political desires, *The People's Charter* (drafted by the London Working Men's Association in 1838), called for voting by secret ballot, universal male suffrage, and the elimination of property qualifications for political office holders. In spite of mass demonstrations involving hundreds of thousands of protesters, all formal political parties rejected the charter repeatedly over a ten-year period.

In fact, a principal concern of most political philosophers from the seventeenth to nineteenth centuries was to devise ways that the interests of the working classes could be served without actually involving them in the governing processes. The ruling classes—the aristocracy, the entrepreneurs, the property holders, and the intellectual elite—commonly held that working class desires were driven entirely by selfish, short-term interests rather than by a coherent understanding of large-scale economic or social realities. Political philosophers, including most of America's "Founding Fathers," feared that direct involvement of the general public in governance would lead to demagoguery, mob rule, and anarchy. As a consequence, it was not until the second half of the nineteenth century, when the writings of Marx and Engels gave rise to *socialist ideology* and provided the labor movement with a formal doctrine, that general public opinion claimed a legitimate voice on such issues as foreign or economic policy.

Given the small scale of democratic processes in nineteenth-century Europe (less than 10 percent of the adult population was eligible to vote in the larger nations), it should not be surprising that the first political public opinion surveys appeared in the United States, where newspapers began conducting "show polls" or "straw votes" of their readers as early as 1824 (Harrisburg, Pa., and Raleigh, N.C.; they picked Andrew Jackson to beat John Quincy Adams, but Adams won). The increasingly frequent voter polls mounted by U.S. magazines and newspapers during the 1800s simply asked readers for their candidate of choice or party preference, *not* for their positions on specific issues. Thus, the European disconnect between public opinion and political ideology was maintained in the United States.

Post-World War I: Documenting Doctrine

A 1916 reader's survey by the *Literary Digest* on whether the United States should enter the Great War appears to have been the world's first national public opinion poll on a political issue. A majority of responses said, "Stay out," which augured well for President Woodrow Wilson's reelection under the slogan, "He kept us out of war!" But thirty days after his second inaugural, Wilson broke off diplomatic relations with Germany and asked Congress to declare war. In spite of such occasional forays into political issues, especially during the late 1930s, most opinion polls continued to solicit input *only* on party and candidate preference until after World War II.

From the mid-1950s on, the broadcast networks joined newspapers and magazines in conducting public opinion polls. These soundings increasingly solicited voter input on political issues, first on foreign policy (1950s to early 1960s); later they expanded to include domestic issues (mid-1960s to the present). National opinion polls during the late 1960s and '70s consistently showed that the great majority of Americans supported civil rights, peace in Vietnam, environmental and privacy protection, worker and consumer protection, access to information, and a wide variety of progressive agendas. This gave the impression of a de facto consensus about American ideology that made the adoption of progressive legislation in these areas not merely expedient, but a dutiful obligation for both major parties.

During the 1970s and '80s, advances in information technology made increasingly sophisticated analytical tools available to market researchers. These advances enabled manufacturers and retailers to target products and sales promotions for specific clientele with ever-greater pinpoint accuracy and effectiveness. Initially refined for the marketing of goods and services, in the early 1980s these techniques were adopted by political practitioners at all levels to package candidates and causes both for fund-raising and mobilizing constituents. In this context, opinion polls are increasingly being used not so much by political candidates to learn about the public's wishes or judgments as by interest groups to demonstrate to politicians, voters, and political contributors the extent of the electorate's support for each group's specific cause. Survey results, in other words, are being used less to *shape* political ideology and more to *promote* political ideology.

The Future

Through the mid-1990s, the increasing power of "info-com" technology has led to dramatic reductions in the costs of gathering and packaging information. The evolution of diverse new electronic distribution capabilities (e.g., cable, cellular, satellite) has made it possible for ever-smaller operators to produce and distribute high-quality packages of information—talk shows, news, entertainment, etc.—for ever-smaller ideological niches. An extrapolation of the trends of the past ten to fifteen years would suggest the impending emergence of a marketplace for ideologic information segmented by the

major political parties, plus dozens of continually changing special-interest groups—e.g., gays, retirees, welfare recipients, and welfare reformers. Each of these groups will use the electronic infostructure to create and sustain their ideologically based niche markets, continually polling their constituents and using psycho-demographic measures to design promotions and alliances to help increase their share of the electorate and to enhance their power to influence the larger system.

Once all Americans are connected to the information highway, legislators will be able to continually poll their constituents to find out exactly how they feel about each issue.

Clearly, the electronic infostructure will be exploited to mobilize new interest groups and ideologies. It also has been suggested that once all Americans are connected to the information highway, legislators will be able to continually poll their constituents to find out exactly how they feel about each issue. A principal problem with voter issues polls is certain to be the ambiguity of their results. Contextual and semantic conditionalities obscure the meaning of *both* their questions *and* their outputs. To date, public issues surveys have proved to be volatile tools, both in campaigns and in drafting party platforms and policy papers.

Researchers have found that through successive interactions, it is possible for pollsters and the public to communicate genuine understanding of complex problems and to identify ranges of acceptable actions. Already, members of the U.S. Congress are connected to the information highway, as are about half of all state legislatures. The more successful legislators of the electronic age will be those who are most adept at correctly identifying their constituents' ideologic parameters and crafting actions that will satisfy those parameters. These developments could largely eliminate the need for intermediate agents, such as political parties or pollsters.

Multiple complex issues—and issues-related information—confronting the twenty-first century will create a boom in simulation models, expert systems, and information agents by which decision makers—and voters—can optimize use of all input. It is reasonable to assume that, during the first quarter of the twenty-first century, successful elected officials will be those who master these tools. In achieving this, politicians will transcend traditional ideologies, although, no doubt, new ideologies will arise through continuing discourse in the electronic marketplace of ideas and information.

[See also Change, Optimistic and Pessimistic Perspectives; Democratic Process; Electronic Publising; Holistic Beliefs; On-Line Services; Political Campaigning; Political Parties; Public Policy Change; Social Controls; Surveys; Voting.]

BIBLIOGRAPHY

Bullock, Alan, and Stallybrass, Oliver. *The Harper Dictionary of Modern Thought*. New York: Harper and Row, 1977.
Kay, Alan; Greenberg, Stanley; Steeper, Frederick; and Henderson, Hazel. *Americans Talk Issues*. St. Augustine, FL: Americans Talk Issues Foundation, 1993.
Thompson, David. *Europe Since Napoleon*. New York: Alfred A. Knopf, 1959.

— DAVID PEARCE SNYDER

PUBLIC POLICY CHANGE

Public policy change rarely comes about abruptly and typically progresses through twenty to thirty distinctive steps over a period of twenty to a hundred years. (See Figure 1.) Timelines depicting each step are hallmarked by distinctive sequences. These steps and sequences constitute the "signatures of change." The characteristic sequences within each evolutionary step coalesce and reinforce each other, and the prospects for impending change may be gauged from their growth rates.

Momentum Behind Trend Extension

Forces of change steadily build over long periods and acquire a powerful momentum, like an avalanche on a mountain slope. Abrupt breaks or discontinuities in ongoing change patterns seldom occur. The cumulative force of the combined trends determines eventual outcomes. When a number of benchmark developments begin to occur and to peak simultaneously, a "critical mass" is achieved. At such "take-off points" outcomes become deterministic but not wholly fatalistic, in as much as that human will, properly and punctually directed, can alter almost any outcome.

Understanding these phenomena and their characteristic development paths provides a way to forecast public policy change with a great degree of accuracy. Public policies generally move from conception to conclusion in relatively broad time spans—twenty to a hundred years, or sometimes even longer. Such an extended time frame provides ample opportunity to grapple with public policy issues.

Public policy issues evolve through three generic phases as shown by the Multiple-Timeline Change Model (Figure 1). The three phases may be summarized as follows:

- *Framing issues.* Intellectual development of ideas gives rise to innovations that cause events from which issues emerge.
- *Advancing issue consideration.* Institutions provide a framework for publicizing and promoting issues, thereby shaping public opinion. The clamor for change may sometimes be influenced by catastrophe or cyclic phenomena.
- *Resolving issues.* An array of informal and formal means to contend with or resolve issues and to accommodate change.

Framing the Issues

Timelines associated with initiating change include five basic steps. Public policy commences with ideas, the wellspring of change. Ideas give rise to *innovation* (both technological *and* social, as well as practical) by which theoretical concepts are transformed into useful application. In turn, widespread implementation of new inventions introduces *events*. Disruptive effects brought on by innovative undertakings prompt the issues.

Ability to interpret steps in this process is greatly augmented by knowledge of the *external environment* in which they arise. Situational contexts provide an important frame of reference to assess evolutionary patterns in specific locales. Factors that influence the climate for change include: natural resources, human resources, educational status, social setting, economic systems, political climate, technological capabilities, and institutional infrastructure.

Advancing Issue Consideration

There are seven additional timelines during the second phase, which is characterized by on-going change. Occasionally, unusual phenomena (i.e., catastrophes) intervene to speed up the process. Change agents—ranging from victims who emote wrongs, intellectual elites who interpret developments, and crusaders who popularize them—flesh out commentary.

Responding to controversy, communications of all sorts pick up the issues, firm up findings, chronicle debate, and create widespread awareness. Communications, covering issues from development to disposition, span a minimum of twenty to thirty years, but more often forty to eighty years. Scientific and professional literature coverage typically precedes popular press coverage by many decades. When specialized journals or television specials exclusively devoted to covering or tracking an issue emerge, and books that summarize decades of wearying developments hit the marketplace, public policy response is imminent.

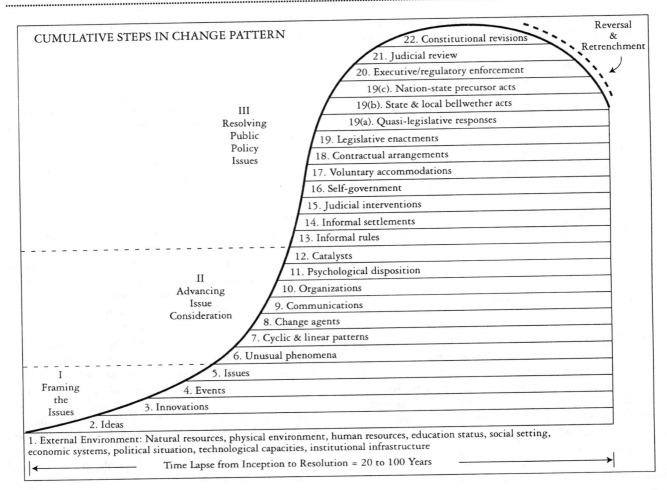

Figure 1. Molitor's multiple-timeline model of change, showing cumulative steps in change pattern. (Graham T. T. Molitor, Public Policy Forecasting, Inc.)

New organizations form, or established ones take up causes, address and sustain deliberation. Institutional frameworks provide continuity in the pursuit of change.

Public opinion polls mirror the psychological disposition of moods toward change. By piercing the veil of apathy and creating understanding, they unleash pressures for change. Catalysts, such as a major industrial accident (Bhopal or Chernobyl, for example), sometimes shock the public and provoke swift public policy response.

Cyclic and linear patterns, analogous to those in economics, may propel trends along. Social-political reform cycles, since the late 1800s, averaged twenty to twenty-six years' duration in the United States. The postindustrial political realignment cycle, underway since 1989, is projected to persist until 2010–2018 and may herald a new era of wrenching reforms akin to the previous Progressive, New Deal, and New Frontier/New Politics cycles.

The onslaught of individual actions, organizational undertakings, institutional activities, widespread communication of views, and resulting public opinion mount the drumbeat for change. The subsequent clamor escalates pressure for response.

Resolving Issues

Ten timelines, resolving confrontations during the third and final tier of steps, conclude the overall pattern of change. Informal rules—unwritten codes of behavior, values, beliefs, customs, traditions, and so forth—sometimes suffice to unofficially resolve issues. Regardless of their specific, direct effect, they nearly always influence outcomes by exerting indirect moral-ethical strictures. Case-by-case litigation also can resolve individual (or class) grievances. Sometimes self-government responses, principally by the initiative and referendum, address issues not moving fast enough through traditional channels.

Voluntary accommodation—self-policing by affected interests, for example—may be interposed to stave off formal regulatory controls. Informal settlements, including conciliation, mediation, arbitration, and other resolution approaches, mostly fall outside of official government channels, though they may be enforceable by government.

Contractual arrangements, enforceable through legal channels, provide another layer of self-help remedies. Common sense impels persons (individuals as well as other legal entities) to secure specific rights. Insurers, mortgagers, and lenders, for example, are swift to specify contract provisos that safeguard them. Labor unions secure collective bargaining contracts locking in protections for their members.

Quasi-legislative forums regulating specialized problems are likely to be in the forefront for matters under their purview. Worker compensation boards are typically the first to deal with toxic torts, and labor relations forums are the first to grapple with employee grievances.

Legislative response, wending through twenty-five to forty steps in a two-house legislature, is a time-consuming but predictable process. Legislative action almost always originates in a few bellwether jurisdictions. Initial innovators are soon followed by early adopters; then come the followers; and the laggards bring up the rear.

Lawmaking responses usually emerge first in state and local precursor jurisdictions. Implementation tests the mettle and effectiveness of specific solutions. Response by international precursor jurisdictions usually is contemporaneous with—and often ahead of—domestic precursors.

Following enactment, new laws move to implementation through executive-regulatory enforcement bureaucracies. Protracted procedural delays to fill in regulatory details or secure compliance often are interposed to extend the process.

Possible challenges posed by judicial review of laws and regulations involve last-ditch efforts to defeat, modify, or validate legislative regulatory handiwork. Court challenges, exhausting three or more levels of review, further postpone final determinations. In extreme instances, constitutional revision may be undertaken to reverse or otherwise alter fundamental principles and change outcomes. Judicial review or constitutional change efforts may bring pursuit of public policy to an

end—or, the outcome may start the public policy change process anew.

[See also Agents of Change; Change; Civil Protest; Continuity and Discontinuity; Economic Cycles: Models and Simulations; Laws, Evolution of; Pacesetter Governments; Political Cycles; Public Opinion Polls; Record Setting; Social Controls; Technological Change; Technology Forecasting and Assessment; Trend Indicators; Values; Values Change.]

BIBLIOGRAPHY

Lawless, Edward W. *Technology and Social Shock.* New Brunswick, NJ: Rutgers University Press, 1977.

Martel, Leon. *Mastering Change: The Key to Business Success.* New York: Simon & Schuster, 1986.

Molitor, Graham T. T. *Evaluation of Causal Forces Related to Why Issues Emerge.* Palo Alto, CA: Electric Power Research Institue, 1989.

Schlesinger, Arthur M., Jr. *The Cycles of American History.* Boston: Houghton Mifflin, 1986.

Vago, Steven. *Social Change.* New York: Holt, Rinehart and Winston, 1980.

– GRAHAM T. T. MOLITOR

PUBLIC RELATIONS

In the Western world, organizations and individuals carry out their activities only within the context of public acceptance. Influencing that public acceptance will be the increasingly difficult responsibility of the public relations practitioner as we move to the twenty-first century.

Edward Bernays, the "father" of public relations, established a definition for public relations practitioners that has held up for decades: "an applied social scientist who advises clients or employers on the social attitudes or actions to take to win support of the publics upon which survival of the client depends."

In his introduction to *The Engineering of Consent* (1955), one of the basic references on the theory and practice of public relations, Bernays foresaw "new instruments of transportation and mass communication, airplane, radio, movies, television [that would] accelerate the spread of ideas. People who previously had little access to them are exposed to attitudes, ideas and courses of action."

Over the following forty years, the acceleration of ideas through instantaneous global communications has transformed the world to a degree almost unimaginable in 1955: powerful minicomputers, the Internet, cable and satellite television, pocket-sized video cameras, cellular phones, and fax machines.

When Bernays edited *The Engineering of Consent,* the term *public relations* was virtually synonymous with *press relations.* It attracted many former journalists who had left that field to become "press agents." College public relations courses were mostly thought of as pathetic by both faculty and students.

Today, several hundred degree-granting colleges offer a public relations major. In many of these institutions, the public relations sequence is the largest within the journalism or communications school. But the future demands on those graduates may be quite different from what they are being taught to expect.

The challenge of public relations professionals

of the future will be to break through the clutter

of message noise assaulting every human being

to get their message heard, understood, and accepted.

The practice of public relations is roughly divided into two parts: active and reactive. In *active* public relations programs, the objective is to maintain or improve the climate of acceptance within which a company, organization, agency, or individual operates. *Reactive* public relations programs attempt to influence public policy or attitudes (almost always established by someone else), or to control the damage done by an incident, and replenish the reservoir of public goodwill that any organization requires to operate effectively or profitably.

In *The Engineering of Consent,* Bernays wrote that "public relations is the attempt, by information, persuasion and adjustment, to engineer public support for an activity, cause, movement or institution."

Today, "consent engineering" is the responsibility of everyone involved with the organization. Because, in reality, the public relations profile of any company, government agency, organization, or individual is really the sum of the actions, past and present, of that organization in relation to its interaction with various groups of people or publics.

Whether that profile can be "engineered" by a public relations professional today is debatable. What that practitioner attempts to do is help shape the profile (or help reconstruct it following some kind of public disaster) by providing information geared to the interests of those groups whose knowledge and attitude can help or hurt the organization or individual the most.

Some recent examples of corporate disasters illustrate the point, such as the 1984 tragedy at a Union Carbide facility at Bhopal, India, where 3,800 died and 11,000 were injured. According to Jackson B. Browning, then a Union Carbide vice president, "the first report of the disaster reached Union Carbide executives in the United States more than twelve hours after the incident." (Two years later, it was discovered that the incident had been caused by sabotage.)

Were the Bhopal tragedy to occur today, the entire episode would be played out live to the world through television. Corporate executives, as well as the media and the public, would be immediately involved in their own offices and living rooms everywhere in the world on a minute-by-minute basis.

In this case, as in many others, including the Johnson & Johnson Tylenol poisoning scare and the Exxon *Valdez* oil-spill incident, the degree to which corporations were damaged was based on four factors, only two of which involve public relations: (1) the perception of the company by those public groups important to its success (stockholders, employees, customers, government regulators) before the incident and (2) efforts by communicators to restore the levels of understanding and support. The other two factors—the degree of corporate culpability in the incident itself and the company's willingness to try to prevent future occurrences—were corporate decisions that had nothing to do with public relations.

Clearly, the practice of public relations is much too important to be left up to former newspaper reporters or rosy-cheeked college graduates clutching a degree and ready to take on the world. It is not something that will be left to a corporate department, any more than obeying the law is a responsibility of only the legal department.

In *Managing Public Relations,* a textbook written the same year as the Bhopal incident, the case is made for a theoretical model that authors James Grunig and Todd Hunt describe as "two-way symmetrical," in which the public relations practitioner serves "as a mediator between organizations and their publics." According to their model, the authors argue that persuasion—the purpose of most of today's public relations programs—moves two ways: (1) from the organization or individual out to the publics and (2) from the members of the various publics back to the organization or individual with the purpose of modifying programs or actions.

We are currently living in a world where the capacity of the conduits carrying information often and usually exceeds the amount of important information there is to communicate. The conduits are likely to continue to expand while the information will probably stay relatively stable.

The result will be even more far-ranging communications, ultimately surrounding each citizen of the global village with so much information at any given time that there is a very real danger of overloading the circuits.

The challenge of public relations professionals of the future will be to break through the clutter of message noise assaulting every human being on Earth to get their message even heard, much less understood and accepted. This will take a much greater understanding of how and why opinions are formed and how they can be changed. Edward Bernays's description of a public relations practitioner as a "social scientist" will be truer than it was decades ago.

[See also Advertising; Communications; Global Culture; Telecommunications.]

BIBLIOGRAPHY

Bernays, Edward L., ed. *The Engineering of Consent.* Norman: University of Oklahoma Press, 1955.

Gottschalk, Jack A. *Crisis Response.* Visible Ink Press, 1993.

Grunig, James E., and Hunt, Todd. *Managing Public Relations.* New York: Holt, Rinehart, Winston, 1984.

— JAMES W. PLUMB

R

RACE, CASTE, AND ETHNIC DIVERSITY

Evolution, having clearly differentiated the human species from every other manifestation of life, went on to create a dazzling array of racial and ethnic groups. The human species then proceeded to diversify itself along national and class lines. The gender factor, the basic divide that unifies and enriches virtually every species of life, added an additional level of complexity to overall human diversity.

Viewed positively, these multiple identifying characteristics are a highly valuable facet of the human family. They testify to the essential oneness of this family, while simultaneously expanding its vistas and its creative possibilities. Over the centuries, the varying racial and ethnic groups, in developing their particular means of self-expression and achievement, have inadvertently enriched the lives of other groups with whom they have had contact. In turn, each has been enriched by the other.

At the same time, however, the very existence of these racial and ethnic differences has been a divisive factor, facilitating if not encouraging the separation of peoples along racial lines. These distinctions provide an obvious opportunity for political, economic, and social manipulation, pitting groups against one another for individual or collective aggrandizement. Indeed, the history of the human species is permeated by accounts of minor and major eruptions of animosity among various racial, ethnic, and national groups. By the same token, history is replete with accounts of personal slights, real or imagined, inflicted by and on persons of another group, often motivated by racial or ethnic hostility.

Biological science has not yet provided us the last word on whether racial and ethnic animosity has a genetic basis. Its stubborn persistence throughout human history, however, suggests that a biological basis is possible.

The social sciences have had a great deal to say about racial and ethnic friction. Economists, in particular, have provided readily understandable analyses for the observed exploitation of one racial or ethnic group by another. This has usually been achieved by technological superiority, either in weaponry or science, or by numerical superiority or treachery—and sometimes by some combination of all of the foregoing.

Paradoxically, coincident with such acts of political and economic subjugation of one group by another, the daily relations between individual members of these presumably antagonistic groups sometimes remain free of all hostility and are characterized by intermarriage and other racially and ethnically neutral behavior. This paradox suggests that the impetus for the racial and ethnic exploitation may be found in benefits that accrue to those who have the power to institute the exploitation, rather than with the general membership of the exploiting racial/ethnic group. On the other hand, the fact that the members of the group allow themselves to become passionate participants in these intergroup hostilities suggests that noneconomic factors also are involved.

Biological science has not yet provided us the last word on whether racial and ethnic animosity has a genetic basis.

In addition to *inter*group hostilities, human history is studded with a variety of *intra*group animosities and discriminatory practices. Most prominent among these is discrimination based on caste and gender. Caste or class discrimination is clearly a type of economic behavior, for the very concepts of caste and class arise from the economic stratification of society. Although historically these concepts were not universally perceived as pejorative, largely because political and intellectual leadership has traditionally come from the upper class, their affront to human dignity has become apparent as democratic values become more widely accepted as the norm.

In India, where the caste system reached its apogee, the system was outlawed four decades ago, but it continues to survive with diminished force in much of the subcontinent. Less formalized manifestations of class antagonism continue to thrive virtually everywhere, conferring economic benefits on those in the dominant group at the expense of those who are not so favored. In the industrialized countries class antagonism may be diminishing as a social and political force as the portion of the population that perceives itself as "middle class" expands along with the ever-expanding ownership of consumer products.

713

Gender discrimination is even more widespread than caste/class discrimination. Almost universally, the female gender has been exploited. Here too, economics is a strong explanatory factor. In all likelihood, gender discrimination is far more complex in its origins than other types of discrimination.

In recent years the United States and some other countries have introduced affirmative action programs of various types to correct some of the more overt discriminatory practices and to help rebalance or compensate for deficiencies still borne by the victims of discrimination. Such programs have enjoyed considerable success, but are encountering increasing opposition in the United States owing to the persistent economic stagnation and declining horizons of opportunity that the general populace has been experiencing for several years.

The concepts of race and ethnic diversity have a unique history and significance in the United States. It is a country peopled overwhelmingly by immigrants from all corners of Earth who usurped a land occupied by Native Americans and simultaneously enslaved a significant portion of Africa's population in order to develop it. Centuries later, Native American and slave descendants (African Americans) remain the most economically deprived racial groups in the United States. Collectively, there is an undercurrent that condemns or disdains such groups; those attitudes are shared by a significant but diminishing portion of the population. In recent years a realization has begun to emerge that these and other marginalized racial and ethnic groups, in fact, enrich the general society in myriad ways.

As a result, diversity is currently being consciously sought, most prominently in cultural aspects. Not surprisingly, the concept of diversity as a positive societal good has both powerful detractors as well as passionate supporters. Consequently, given the recentness of its popular acceptance, it is unclear whether it should be viewed as a permanent aspect of American society.

Modern transportation and communications technology have effectively shrunk the globe, reducing all of mankind to a degree of neighborly intimacy unprecedented in human history. Racial isolation and ethnic purity are no longer possible, and encounters with the diversity of the human species are now a commonplace element of daily life for most people. Racial and ethnic diversity shares the current spotlight of heightened awareness with global ecology and human interdependence. Against this backdrop, the decision of whether the increasing proximity of human diversity is to be embraced with enthusiasm or resisted with hostility will be a powerful determinant in shaping the future.

[See also Class and Underclass; Ethnic and Cultural Separatism; Lifestyles, Alternative; Lifestyles, Ethnic; Lifestyles, Regional; Racial and Ethnic Conflict; Workforce Diversity.]

These Balinese people celebrate a family wedding in a style that is unique to their own culture yet quite universal in many ways. (Jack Fields/Corbis)

BIBLIOGRAPHY

Aburdene, Patricia, and Naisbitt, John. *Megatrends for Women.* New York: Villard Books/Random House, 1992.

Davidson, Art. *Endangered Peoples.* San Francisco, CA: Sierra Club Books, 1993.

Deng, Francis M. *Protecting the Dispossessed: A Challenge for the International Community.* Washington, DC: The Brookings Institution, 1993.

Franklin, John H. *The Color Line: Legacy for the Twenty-First Century.* Columbia, MO: University of Missouri Press, 1993.

Held, Virginia. *Feminist Morality: Transforming Culture.* Chicago: University of Chicago Press, 1993.

Magnet, Myron. *The Dream and the Nightmare: The Sixties' Legacy to the Underclass.* New York: William Morrow, 1993.

Massey, Douglas S., and Denton, Nancy A. *American Apartheid: Segregation and the Making of the Underclass.* Cambridge, MA: Harvard University Press, 1993.

Peterson, V. Spike, and Runyan, Asses S. *Global Gender Issues.* Boulder, CO: Westview Press, 1993.

Schafer, D. Paul. "Cultures and Economics: Irresistible Forces Encounter Immovable Objects." *Futures* 26/8 (October 1994).

Taylor, Jared. *Paved with Good Intentions: The Failure of Race Relations in Contemporary America.* New York: Carroll & Graf, 1992.

West, Cornel. *Beyond Eurocentrism and Multiculturalism.* 2 vols. Monroe, ME: Common Courage Press, 1993.

– ROBERT S. BROWNE

RACIAL AND ETHNIC CONFLICT

Race is an anthropological reference emphasizing physical features, such as skin color, hair texture, and facial features, in the three great racial groupings of Negro, Mongol, and Caucasian races. *Ethnicity* is a reference to culture, including language, religion, family organization, social institutions, history, and heritage.

Racial and ethnic conflict will continue to be as tenacious a threat to human cooperation and development in the twenty-first century as it has been in the twentieth century.

Racial and ethnic conflict will continue to be as tenacious a threat to human cooperation and development in the twenty-first century as it has been in the twentieth century. It can be defined in economic, cultural, social, and political terms of confrontation and non-cooperation, both between groups who identify themselves as distinct from their competitors and combatants *and* within groups who may be culturally homogeneous but differ on strategies of interaction with dissimilar groups. Racial and ethnic conflict is both a global phenomena with pervasive local impacts and a local phenomena capable of profound global consequences.

This essay briefly addresses demographic, historical, institutional, and economic dimensions of racial and ethnic conflict. All of these dimensions pour into the strategic actions and aspirations of racial and ethnic groups. Ted Robert Gurr argues that the Bosnians, the Kurds, the Shi'is of Iraq, and black South Africans are among the most visible of more than two hundred ethnic and religious minorities and subordinate majorities throughout the world who are contesting the terms of their incorporation into the world order. Their status in the twenty-first century largely depends upon the utilization of these dimensions to press their objectives.

The Demographic Dimension

Malappropriated demography continues to contribute to racial and ethnic conflict. The continuing trend of global economic integration is enhanced by more efficient and cheaper transportation and communication technologies and by increasing resort to large trading blocks. These trends confront 75 percent of the world's labor force, largely residing in Africa, Asia, Latin America, and islands of the Pacific, Indian, and Atlantic oceans. In the populations of nations situated in these areas the working age is younger, less experienced, and less well educated than in most "developed" nations. The developing country share of the world labor force will increase to 83 percent by 2025. Similar macro-level differences at the global level are also reflected in micro-level conflicts within "developed nations"—African and Hispanic Americans in the United States, Quebecois in Canada, African and colored populations in South Africa, and *gastarbeiters* (guest workers of color) in Holland and Germany. Lower socioeconomic status among these populations continues to stimulate conflicts and confrontations with policy-making authorities in those nations, and also divides the racial or ethnic group on issues of strategy.

The Historical Dimension

Contemporary and future demographic trends reflect the vast and complex history of racial and ethnic conflict. The legacy of the African slave trade in the sixteenth through nineteenth centuries, the colonialization of Africa, Asia, the Caribbean, and Latin America, and continuing struggles between "the North" and "South" persist. They have given way in the twenty-first century to racial and ethnic conflicts within both formerly colonized and formerly colonizing nations, and to the phenomenon of North, South, and Far East conflicts due to transitions from military to economic conflict.

However, three consequences of the historic dimension include the continuing diasporas of racial, ethnic, and language groups beyond their motherland borders, the use of historical symbols and images of oppression and exploitation as tools of conflict, and the use of history as a frame of reference for future images of racial and ethnic identity.

The Institutional Dimension

Closely connected to the historical dimension of racial and ethnic conflict is its institutional dimension. Historical patterns of racial and ethnic subordination and oppression continue to reflect their legacies in future patterns of racial and ethnic relationships. Although apartheid and segregation have been officially eliminated by the legal systems of South Africa and the United States, many institutions have yet to fully integrate. Beyond integration, the institutional policies, symbols, and practices of many racial and ethnic groups continue to alienate other groups.

Institutions based on the Sikh, Hindu, or Muslim religion or on language or cultural differences between Tamils and other Indians enflame and perpetuate racial and ethnic conflict in India. Failure of the nation-state as an institution to appropriately incorporate Bosnians, Serbs, and Croats eliminated the Yugoslav nation and led to the creation of separate Czech and Slovak nations. Often, the inability of disaffected groups to find a national home exacerbates conflict. The Zulus of South Africa, the Indians of Chiappas, Mexico, and the Sikhs and Kashmiris of India offer lurid examples of conflicts suspended between national incorporation and the creation of new, racially or ethnically homogenous nations.

Without significant reorientation of many global, regional, and national institutions, the sheer force of institutional patterns, reflexes, instincts, and symbols hurl themselves forcefully into twenty-first-century racial and ethnic relations.

The Economic Dimension

Clearly, racial and ethnic conflict will continue to be driven by scarce financial, human, technological, and infrastructural resources. Continued differences in economic status persist between African Americans and others in the United States, the Chinese minority in Indonesia, the Arab minority in Israel, and the Kurdish populations in Turkey and Iraq. The lack of educational or wage-labor job opportunities, entrepreneurial development, collective bargaining on the terms and conditions of employment, exploitation of natural resources, and quality-of-life differentials provide clear and convincing evidence to some racial and ethnic groups that they are involved in a long-term struggle for economic equity and opportunity. The revision of affirmative action policies in the United States and the insistence of the World Bank on structural adjustment of the debt, civil service, private sector, and center-periphery relations in developing nations will further exacerbate conflict as the public sector role in racial and ethnic conflict resolution continues to diminish.

A Final Word

Global economic integration, the inculcation of positive values of racial and ethnic diversity, the economic uplifting of more disadvantaged racial and ethnic groups, and the restructuring of the global, regional, national, and local labor force contribute to the emergence of a vibrant racial and ethnic middle class. This middle class is a key variable in twenty-first-century racial and ethnic conflicts. It can facilitate or catalyze integrative, cooperative tendencies or provoke more insular, conflict tendencies. The subdivision of the world into economic trading blocs, the burgeoning telecommunications and information systems technology, and the perennial tension of global commercial and social values with localized traditional religious and humanistic values are key instruments of various racial and ethnic groups, and their constituent economic classes. These factors surely will play key roles for either conflict-resolving or conflict-exacerbating strategies in the twenty-first century.

[See also Class and Underclass; Ethnic and Cultural Separatism; Race, Caste, and Ethnic Diversity.]

BIBLIOGRAPHY

Bloom, David E., and Brender, Adi. *Labor and the Emerging World Economy.* Washington, DC: Population Reference Bureau, 1993.

Gurr, Ted Roberts. *Minorities at Risk: A Global View of Ethnopolitical Conflicts.* Washington, DC: United States Institute of Peace, 1993.

Harris, Joseph E., ed. *Global Dimensions of the African Diaspora,* 2nd ed. Washington, DC: Howard University Press, 1993.

Henderson, Lenneal J. "Africans in Search of Work." *The Urban League Review* (September 1983): 56–71.

— LENNEAL J. HENDERSON

RADIO.

See BROADCASTING; ELECTRONIC CONVERGENCE.

RAILWAYS

Forecasters may be wrong, but they never are in doubt. For instance, the March 1825 issue of England's *Quarterly Review* asserted: "What could be more palpably absurd than the prospect held out of locomotives travelling twice as fast as stagecoaches." London's first public railway, which began operating in 1803, used horses to haul passengers and freight at a speed of about five miles per hour, hardly a match for stagecoaches. Horse-drawn coaches could attain top speeds of about ten miles per hour (m.p.h.). But technological advances quickly altered the existing state of affairs. Richard Trevithick invented a high-pressure steam engine in 1800, used it to power a road carriage in 1801, a locomotive in 1804, and a rail-mounted locomotive in 1804. By 1830, the first successful steam railroad providing public service was inaugurated in England. The mode and speed of travel was about to be transformed. Steam engines, largely because of their roles in powering railways, ships, motorcars, and providing energy for the machines of modern industrial production were poised to play a major role in ushering in the Industrial Revolution.

Even as these events were transforming the way people traveled, Professor Dionysus Lardner of London's University College asserted: "Rail travel at high speed is not possible because passengers, unable to breathe, would die of asphyxia." Not until 1938 was the record speed for a steam locomotive—125 miles per hour (m.p.h.)—achieved. Today the world's fastest railway (the French TGV) set a record speed of 320.2 m.p.h. in 1990. Going far beyond these accomplishments, an unmanned railed rocket sled achieved a speed of 6,121 m.p.h. in 1982, and railguns capable of accelerating projectiles to speeds sufficient to escape Earth's gravity

---

Railguns capable of accelerating projectiles

to speeds sufficient to escape Earth's gravity

are under development.

(about 20,000 m.p.h.) are under development. This a far cry from the beginning of rail systems, termed "wagonways" (essentially wagons run on wooden tracks serving mines that carried freight and miners), that date back as early as the fifteenth century. Considering the threshold presented by these new technological advances, rail systems may be poised for greater things.

Diesel

Approximately 99 percent of all locomotive horsepower within the United States today is diesel-electric. In this process, a diesel-powered prime mover turns a generator or alternator to produce electrical power for traction. The horsepower generated by such an arrangement can vary, with modern mainline locomotives producing up to 4,400-horsepower each, and 6,000-horsepower models planned for release by the end of 1995.

Traditionally, this electrical native power has been at 600 volts DC, but recent technology makes the use of AC power preferable. Amtrak made use of such locomotives beginning in the early 1990s. The Burlington Northern was the first U.S. freight railroad to order large numbers of the AC-powered engines, and they began receiving AC-powered freight locomotives in 1994. Currently, both of the major U.S. manufacturers of diesel locomotives, General Electric and EMD, include such locomotives in their production plans.

Electrified

The straight electric locomotive draws its power directly from an overhead wire or a third rail immediately adjacent to the track. This type of locomotive is limited to an area where a system has been constructed for such power distribution. This system is expensive to build and requires heavy use to be economically justified. Electrification is common in much of Europe, in the

northeast part of the United States, and on heavily traveled lines in Russia and China. Electrified rail generally has a longer life span and is more economically and environmentally sensitive once built.

Magnetically Levitated

Magnetic levitation, or Maglev, is a technology first proposed in the 1950s whereby a vehicle is magnetically propelled and levitated along a fixed guideway. The magnetic field used for such a system is produced electrically, which has sparked great interest and research into a superconducting material. Reduced military requirements have redirected some government research efforts to develop a U.S. maglev system for civilian use.

Germany and Japan have tested such systems; however, critics of Maglev point out that both countries ultimately built only traditional high-speed rail systems, and stress that Maglev is not compatible with existing transportation systems. Environmental issues stemming from Maglev involve right-of-way, material needs, and health concerns supposedly associated with exposure to high-power electromagnetic fields.

Superfast (200–380 m.p.h.)

Considered by many to be the future of medium-distance transportation, high-speed rail (HSR) is currently operating at speeds approaching 200 m.p.h. on dedicated routes. Japan, Germany, and France are the leaders in the field with extensive operating systems. However, a number of other countries have such systems under development. Test runs in Germany already have exceeded 252 m.p.h., and 321 m.p.h. has been reached in Japan.

One concern of HSR has been keeping trains on the track and its level of safety in the event that a derailment might occur. On December 21, 1993, the first major test of the safety aspects of an HSR operation occurred when an in-service French TGV train derailed at its maximum normal operating speed of 185 m.p.h. Although such a train takes more than a mile to stop under normal conditions, the entire train remained together and upright after the derailment, primarily due to the design of the car-coupling system. No serious injuries were reported to either the crew or passengers.

Monorail

The monorail is a rail transportation system generally used as a theme park ride. Despite practical attributes, these systems have found limited use. The major advantages of a monorail are the reduction in the number of needed rails for the guideway, and the elimination of the need to level and gauge the parallel guideway rails. Disadvantages include the lack of static stability, the loss

TABLE 1

STATISTICS FOR RAILROADS AROUND THE WORLD

Country	Data Year	Locomotives			Freight Cars	Passenger Coaches	KM of Line
		Diesel	Steam	Electric			
Argentina	1991	986	0	6	32,823	1,702	34,059
Australia	1990	771	0	0	13,167	240	14,288
Brazil	1991	1,780	27	179	53,646	1,176	26,944
Canada	1990	2,672	0	14	106,334	565	54,771
China	1991	6,111	5,986	1,809	370,000	27,612	53,416
Czechoslovakia	1991	2,562	14	1,586	134,074	6,250	13,116
France	1991	3,297	0	2,244	141,800	9,647	33,446
India	1991	3,905	2,492	1,871	346,394	29,501	62,458
Italy	1991	1,167	26	1,976	97,323	1,701	16,066
Japan	1991	664	8	1,018	30,231	2,169	20,252
Mexico	1991	1,700	0	0	44,003	1,263	20,324
Poland	1992	3,928	12	2,406	140,885	7,690	23,399
Romania	1991	2,278	989	1,061	142,222	6,520	11,365
South Africa	1992	1,442	181	2,321	153,396	3,776	21,635
Soviet Union (Former)	1991	20,767	0	13,399	1,657,400	56,287	147,500
Spain	1991	666	0	593	36,073	1,878	12,570
Sweden	1991	373	0	591	24,993	1,183	10,970
United Kingdom	1991	2,243	56	263	30,888	2,722	16,584
United States	1992	18,004	0*	59*	1,173,136	4,045	227,113
West Germany	1991	3,359	0	2,535	244,287	11,636	27,079

* Class I railroads only.
Source: World Bank Railway Database, Association of American Railroads.

of carrying capacity when base supported, the complex arrangements needed to switch from one route to another and to provide carrying support when suspended.

Roadrailer

The Roadrailer is one of several techniques used by railroads to compete with intermodal freight carriers. Essentially, the Roadrailer is a truck trailer that can be placed on a railroad track and hauled behind a locomotive without the use of a flatcar or other carrying device. Two types are currently in use. The older style has its own railroad wheels permanently attached, which reduces the carrying capacity of the trailer on the highway. The newer trailer design has wheels attached at the rail site. Currently, the use of Roadrailers is limited to the eastern half of the United States. However, rail carriers in other parts of the world are looking at the technology.

Regulatory Environment

PRIVATIZATION. Most of the world's railroads are owned and operated by national governments. The United States and several other Western countries are the major exceptions to this rule. However, recent movements toward railroad privatization have occurred

in New Zealand, the United Kingdom, and a number of countries in South America and continental Europe.

SAFETY. U.S. rail regulation changed from one of economic regulation to safety regulation pursuant to the Staggers Rail Act of 1980 and other deregulation statutes passed at that time. These acts greatly reduced the Interstate Commerce Commission's role to provide oversight to the transportation industry. Antitrust legislation also plays a role in preventing discriminatory practices within the industry. Additionally, the Federal Railroad Administration (FRA) plays a major role in safety enforcement. Similar regulatory frameworks are in place worldwide.

Safety is a major advantage for railroads. Compared to motor carriers, railroads are more than four times safer based upon ton/miles. Vehicles at grade crossings and pedestrian trespassers account for the vast majority of accidents involving U.S. railroads. To combat this problem, Operation Lifesaver has been formed to provide public education. The success of this and other measures is resulting in a declining accident rate even as total train miles operated continue to increase.

ABANDONMENTS. Within the United States, deregulation made it easier for a railroad to abandon trackage. At the same time, economic changes resulting from deregulation also made it easier for small, specialized carriers to operate many of these lines, resulting in an increase in the number of Class III, or shortline, carriers. Worldwide, track abandonment has been a concern in developed countries, especially when government subsidy reductions or privatization has been proposed.

RIGHTS-OF-WAY. The obtainment of a railroad right-of-way can be through purchase, lease, or easement. Each provides a linear route which is ideal for joint use with communication and pipeline systems.

ENVIRONMENTAL PROBLEMS. Railroads are considered to be more environmentally friendly than other modes of transportation due to their better fuel efficiency, greater carrying capacity, and ability to be fully electrified. An additional improvement has been the introduction of locomotives which use cleaner-burning natural gas.

[See also Air Transport; Energy Conservation; Environment; Maglev; Motor Vehicles; Motor Vehicles, Alternatively Powered; Personal Transport; Petroleum; Pipelines; Transporation; Urban Transit.]

BIBLIOGRAPHY

Gomez-Ibáñez, José A., and Meyer, John R. *Going Private: The International Experience with Transport Privatization.* Washington, DC: Brookings Institution, 1993.
Lowe, Marcia. *Back on Track: The Global Rail Revival.* Washington, DC: Worldwatch Institute, 1994.

Research assistance provided by Barton Jennings, University of Tennessee.

— ROSALYN A. WILSON

RECORDING INDUSTRY

Three trends will affect all recording technologies in the future: miniaturization, increasing power and capability, and declining cost. These trends apply to both the professional recording industry as well as the consumer audio and video technology. At the same time, digital recording and playback equipment will be the preeminent audio and video technology by the late 1990s and into the twenty-first century.

Digital recording is a computer-based technology. Like other such computer technologies, it involves the capture and storage of data onto various types of magnetic hard or floppy computer discs, cartridges, tapes, or perhaps eventually integrated circuits themselves. Unlike earlier (and still widely used) recording technology, optical information is encoded directly onto the storage medium—a master disc or, for consumer use, a compact disc (CD) for music and other sound recordings, or a laser disc for audiovisual images. Both formats are played on a system that uses a laser for scanning and decoding the audio or visual information encoded on the disc.

As is usually the case with new technology, audio compact disc technology was initially prohibitively expensive for most consumers—both for playback equipment and for the CDs themselves. However, prices for CD players had plummeted by the end of the 1980s, and the cost of CDs fell somewhat as well. At the same time, CD players and professional recording equipment shrank in size, leading to portable units, and grew in capability, leading to such innovations as programmable CD players and multi-CD units. As the prices fell and the capabilities expanded, sales of both CD players and CDs grew considerably.

The second half of the 1980s saw a rapid and dramatic move away from the use of the phonograph record toward digital technology in the form of the CD. While the professional recording industry has been using digital technology in the studio for nearly two decades, the full effect of its clarity and depth was usually lost on vinyl phonograph records. The sound reproduction capability of phonograph records degrades by repeated playing. CDs, on the other hand, provide a near-optimum means of reproducing digital recordings, and are far more durable than phonograph records. Sophisticated LP turntables and accessories were developed, but they were never as user-friendly as CD players, requiring fine-tuning and nimble fingers to ensure optimal performance. By the mid-1990s, the vast majority of recordings were available only on CD or on magnetic audio cassette tape.

Cassette tapes provide reasonably high quality sound reproduction. Moreover, they are recordable—even editable—by consumers, something not possible with LPs or CDs (although blank CDs and CD players with once-only recording capabilities have been developed and sold, and may become available at reasonable prices within a few years). However, the sound-reproducing quality of cassette tapes is inferior to CDs. Cassette tapes are also very slow to rewind, and they lack the rapid access to specific points typical of CDs. Moreover, cassette tapes are far more fragile than CDs or even LPs, and will degrade with time or be ruined if exposed to magnetic fields. While magnetic audio cassette tapes likely will remain a popular, convenient format throughout the 1990s, they will continue to lose ground to the increasingly affordable CD.

Digital audio taping (DAT) is a hybrid between magnetic audio cassette tapes and digital technology. DAT encodes digital information onto a smaller cassette than the standard audio cassette and, like the CD, is played on a laser scanning and playback system. Unlike the CD, DAT tapes are recordable and editable. DAT tapes have superior sound reproduction capabilities, less distortion, rewind more quickly, and are more durable than magnetic audio cassettes.

DAT, already popular in Japan and Europe, has been obstructed from entering the U.S. market through the efforts of the professional recording industry. The recording industry fears widespread problems with piracy, resulting in a loss of royalties to both artists and recording companies. DAT players are also significantly more expensive on average than either magnetic audio cassette or CD players. Nonetheless, the growth of DAT will continue worldwide throughout the 1990s. DAT, or some other, similar format likely will replace traditional magnetic audio cassette tapes eventually, as costs fall and availability grows.

Digital technology will transform video recording

in the same manner that it has transformed

the consumer audio industry.

Digital technology will transform video recording in the same manner that it has transformed the consumer audio industry. Consumer home video recording and playback, like the compact disc, experienced explosive growth in the 1980s. Videotape rental stores, unknown in 1980, were a feature of every shopping center by 1990. However, this thriving industry stands at a crossroads, as it moves inexorably from magnetic videotape to optical discs that can utilize digital technology.

Magnetic videotape, like magnetic audiotape, presents problems with the quality of visual and sound reproduction, and it degrades with use. Optical discs, on the other hand, offer superior audio and visual reproduction and are far more durable than magnetic videotapes. Equally important, they are far smaller than magnetic videotapes, meaning that both cameras and playback units are smaller as well. As sales and rentals of such discs continue to grow rapidly, a growing number of video rental outlets also rent optical laser discs.

On-line video communications also may threaten the now booming video rental business. The growth of fiber optic communications in the United States, Europe, and Asia will make possible the transmission of visual as well as audio information via telephone lines. New signal compression techniques that enormously increase the carrying capacity of both wired (fiber optical, copper, or coaxial) and broadcast transmissions hasten this shift. This means that consumers could "rent" videos by dialing a number and having the video transmitted electronically to their playback unit. Federal regulators already have authorized phone companies to provide a "video dial tone." Using special receivers, an entire feature-length movie could be "burst-loaded" to a home in less than ten seconds for viewing at the consumer's pleasure. It would eliminate the need to pick up or return a videocassette, and it would solve such problems as tapes jamming or poor image/sound quality due to overuse by renters.

The large investment already made by businesses in the form of videotapes and rental outlets and by consumers in the form of videotape cameras and players creates something of a dilemma. Optical discs are clearly superior to magnetic videotapes in terms of sound and visual reproduction capability, durability, and even size. Furthermore, the on-line transmission of audio and visual information offers many advantages over video rental. But the transition to optical disc technology would be very costly in terms of replacing current consumer videotape equipment, and a move to on-line video communications and rentals has the potential to put an entire industry—videotape sales and rentals—out of business.

For these reasons, videotapes and the surrounding industry are likely to be with us for the next decade or more. Nonetheless, digital recording technology—for both audio and visual applications—will continue to grow throughout the 1990s and, in the early twenty-first century, is very likely to be the predominant professional and consumer recording and playback technology.

[See also Communications; Communications: Technology; Digital Communications; Electronic Convergence; Interactive Entertainment; Telecommunications; Television.]

BIBLIOGRAPHY

Brand, Stewart. *The Media Lab: Inventing the Future at MIT.* New York: Viking, 1987.

Freese, Robert P. "Optical Disks Become Erasable." *IEEE Spectrum* 26:2, February 1988.

Hakanen, Ernest A. "Digital Audio Broadcasting: Promises and Policy Issues in the USA." *Telecommunications Policy* 15:6, December 1991.

Latamore, G. Berton. "Smart Cards Get Smarter." *Technology Business* 7:9, September 1987.

Levy, Mark R. *The VCR Age: Home Video and Mass Communication.* Newbury Park, CA: Sage Publications, 1989.

Miles, Ian. *Home Informatics: Information Technology and the Transformation of Everyday Life.* London: Pinter Publishers (distributed in U.S. by Columbia University Press), 1988.

Provenzo, Eugene F. *Video Kids: Making Sense of Nintendo.* Cambridge, MA: Harvard University Press, 1991.

Robinson, Deanna C. and Buck, Elizabeth B. *Music at the Margins: Popular Music and Global Cultural Diversity.* Newbury Park, CA: Sage Publications, 1991.

Twitchell, James B. *Carnival Culture: The Trashing of Taste in America.* New York: Columbia University Press, 1992.

— TIMOTHY WILLARD

RECORD SETTING

Almost any aspect of society, at any given moment, seems to have reached an apparent end, the "brickwall" finality of an absolute. History reveals, however, that these apparent limits, time and time again, have been surpassed. Each step along the way tends to be hailed as an "ultimate" achievement. In other words, there are few, if any, absolutes.

Constant upgrading is easily explained. No matter what subject one looks at, close and careful scrutiny invariably bares shortcomings of one sort or another. Nothing is ever good enough. Humans never seem fully or finally satisfied with contemporary accomplishments, but pursue new standards of excellence. There is always room for improvement. Something better can always be achieved. Human inspiration is driven by an all-consuming desire not only to better but to refine, elaborate, and extend that which has gone before.

Human affairs incessantly are being constructed only to be redesigned, then rebuilt anew. Human endeavors and the social order are open-ended, not closed. Most accomplishments, no matter how impressive they may seem at the time, represent only a continuing succession of interim advancements, a part of the overall progression and evolution of society itself.

In almost every field of human endeavor and experience there is an eternal effort under way to achieve still higher levels of perfection. Perfection, as an absolute, may eternally be just out of our grasp. Nonetheless, there is always someone out there somewhere who will strive to better the previous mark.

Pace-setting records are established only to be broken. Record setting provides a convenient benchmark for measuring the limits of earthly experiences and human capabilities. Records do represent pinnacles of achievement, at least for the moment. Invariably they turn out to be jumping-off points for going one step farther, a target to shoot at and surmount.

Field-and-track events demonstrate that nearly any human endeavor constantly is being improved upon. The world record for the mile at the turn of the century was just under five minutes. An arbitrary limit—the "impossible" four-minute mile—was taken for granted for many years. Athletes, however, never gave up the quest. Marks of any one record setter simply set the next person's aspirations that much higher. In 1954 Roger Bannister surpassed that benchmark by running the mile in a pace-setting 3:59.4. Those following him relentlessly and single-mindedly strove to better the mark. Now the world record holder has shaved nearly fifteen seconds off the "impossible" four-minute mile. The world's fastest miler and current record holder, Steven Cram (U.K.), has run the distance in 3:46.832.

In the pole vault, the pattern is much the same. When bamboo and aluminum poles were supplanted by fiberglass and boron-reinforced composites, the additional whipsaw helped catapult vaulters to add nearly two feet to previous world records. Sometimes collateral changes in materials "chime in" to push records higher yet. The current all-time record holder, Sergei Bubka (U.S.S.R.), cleared the bar at 20'1/2" in 1992.

Here is one final example in the sports field. High jumpers had never cleared over seven feet until 1956. Shortly thereafter, the "Fosburg Flop" was introduced at the 1968 Olympic Games. Instead of the classic scissor or forward-roll that always had been the style, Fosburg arched his back over the bar and soared 7'4.25". So the process or procedure accompanying endeavors can augment the capacity to shatter previous records. Since 1989, Javier Sotomayur (U.S.) cleared the eight-foot mark. The long and the short of it is that "the best never rest."

History is replete with examples of triumphs

over the seemingly impossible.

Record setting sometimes verges on the unbelievable. All-time world fuel economy records for passenger-carrying motor vehicles stagger the imagination. The world's record, set in Switzerland at the 1979 International Fuel Saving Competition for cars and special vehicles, a three-wheel diesel driven by Franz Maier (Germany), was an impressive 3,020.28 miles per gallon (mpg)! By 1994 a 50 percent increase in that astounding record was accomplished when Canada's Challenge X, constructed by University of Saskatchewan engineering students, achieved a mind-shattering 4,738 mpg. For commercial vehicles, one Japanese diesel compact automobile, a regular production model in the early 1980s, was getting 68 mpg. German automakers agreed in 1995 to raise fuel economy standards for passenger automobiles, set in 1990 at 31.4 mpg, to 39.9 mpg by 2005. In the United States, domestic new car fuel efficiency topped out at 27.4 mpg in 1991, then dropped to 26.9 mpg in 1992. American automobile manufacturers obviously have a long way to go. These impressive records indicate how far we can go. Thus, they provide solid evidence and a stimulus for improving everyday efficiencies.

Examples of impressive records abound in almost any other field of interest. Average U.S. corn production of 28.9 bushels per acre in 1940–1941 had risen to 131 bushels by 1992. Hens running in the wild might annually lay one or more clutches of eggs for a total of six to ten eggs. The current record-holder hen laid 361 eggs in 364 days. The green revolution has worked miracles, agricultural chemistry adds further enhancement, and genetic engineering promises to push records higher still.

Life expectancy itself has dramatically increased, rising from an average of eighteen years back in 1 B.C. to more than seventy-five years in modern times. Scientific advances, augmented by genetic engineering, portend substantial and accelerating increases in life expectancies to 125, or perhaps even 160 years, according to some forecasters. On the basis of this steady evolutionary increase and projected further increases, we can surmise that human longevity, while it has come a long way, has a much longer way to go.

Similar achievements and advancements could go on interminably. The phenomena described here apply, in principle, to virtually every other human endeavor. History is replete with examples of triumphs over the seemingly impossible. Society is open-ended, encouraging, if not necessitating, a dynamic system in which the event and levels of accomplishment will be ever-changing. Forecasting social and cultural change assumes a ceaseless tinkering and a benign dissatisfaction with things as they are. It assumes that humans will always attempt to upgrade and perfect their affairs. Human beings just cannot be complacent. The sky is the limit.

[See also Change, Pace of; Change, Scientific and Technological; Continuity and Discontinuity; Information Overload; Longevity; Scientific Breakthroughs.]

BIBLIOGRAPHY

Ash, Russell. *The Top 10 of Everything.* New York: Dorling Kindersley, 1994.

Harvey, Edmund H., Jr., ed. *The Reader's Digest Book of Facts.* Pleasantville, NY: The Reader's Digest Association, 1987.

Krantz, Les, ed. *The Best and Worst of Everything.* New York: Prentice Hall, 1991.

Lee, Stan. *The Best of the World's Worst: World Class Blunders: Screw-Ups, Oddballs, Misfits, and Rotten Ideas.* Los Angeles, General Publishing, 1994.

Matthews, Peter, ed. *The Guiness Book of Records 1995.* New York: Bantam Books, 1995.

— GRAHAM T. T. MOLITOR

RECREATION, OUTDOOR.

See OUTDOOR RECREATION AND LEISURE PURSUITS.

REFUGEES

As long as human conflict occurs, refugees will flee their homelands, leaving behind most everything they hold dear. But the post-Cold War world will respond to them in different, and not always better, ways than in recent decades.

Millions of people leave their home countries each year for many reasons. Refugees do not want to leave, but do so because of persecution and/or violence, often perpetrated by their own government. By seeking asylum in another country, refugees qualify for important protections under international law. Only limited protection exists for internally displaced people, those who are uprooted by violence but who remain in their home country. People whose flight is caused by poverty, natural disaster, or environmental degradation—key determinative factors in future migrations—also do not benefit from the international system of refugee protection.

Most refugees who need protection and assistance are in the developing world, often seeking safety in some of the world's poorest countries, such as Malawi, Pakistan, and Bangladesh. Of the seventeen million refugees in such need in 1992, less than one million were in Europe and North America. Most of the world's more than twenty million internally displaced people are also located in the developing world—in Mozambique, Rwanda, Sudan, Myanmar, and other impoverished, war-torn countries.

Undoubtedly, this picture of refugee demographics will remain true in coming years. The poorest of people and nations will continue to suffer the most from upheaval and displacement. Whether the developed world will continue to assist them, now that their strategic value has diminished, is the larger question for the 1990s and beyond.

Despite the relatively small numbers seeking asylum in Western developed nations, recent trends show a fortress mentality. Europe, especially, is shutting the doors on asylum seekers. Germany, in particular, encountered a violent reaction by political extremists to all foreigners, including asylum seekers. Many countries in Europe refused in the early 1990s to accept refugees from genocidal violence in the former Yugoslavia. This trend runs against the letter and spirit of the international protocols signed by those nations after World War II intended to prevent just such reactions.

The United States has a history different from Europe. Because of that history, the United States will remain far more open to refugees and asylum seekers than Europe. However, the changing demographics of American society will raise the priority of debates on immigration generally, including questions involving refugee resettlement and asylum.

Since 1951, the office of the UN High Commissioner for Refugees (UNHCR) has been at the center of the international refugee protection system. It is charged with protecting refugees and assisting them until there is a solution to their homelessness. Those solutions include refugees returning voluntarily to their home country, integrating into the country that has given them asylum, or resettling in a third country, usually in the developed world. The majority of refugees wish only to return home when it is safe to do so. Resettlement outside their region is a last resort for UNHCR, for governments, and for most refugees.

For the great majority of refugees, however, the last several decades produced no solutions. Instead, refugees endured years of forced exile, often in large, dehumanizing, and often dangerous camps or settlements with minimal services and opportunities. Refugee children often had no formal education, refugee women endured brutal mistreatment, and refugee men were unable to fulfill traditional family roles.

How will these conditions change with the demise of the Cold War? As many of the long proxy wars that created these refugees inch toward resolution, millions of refugees are finally daring to dream of going home. In most cases, however, their homelands are entirely devastated. A sudden, ill-planned, underfunded repatriation may result in desperate refugees moving home spontaneously, only to compete with internally displaced people for meager resources. The fragile peace accords of Afghanistan, Cambodia, Angola, Mozambique, and other major refugee-producing conflicts can quickly shatter under such strain. One critical prerequisite for lasting repatriation is sufficient international support and planning. The superpowers invested billions of dollars in the wars that uprooted these civilians. Will the world community have the wisdom to invest in their healing during the coming years?

Conversely, the demise of the Cold War has accelerated the disintegration of old states and the creation of new ones. Fundamental change of this nature will almost always involve violence. The raging nationalism obvious in the debris of the former Soviet Union and

Most refugees flee areas afflicted by poverty, war, and environmental depredation. This Somali woman is a refugee living in London. Refugees receiving U.N. assistance rose from 1.4 million in 1961 to 22.7 million in 1997. (Howard Davies/Corbis)

Yugoslavia, also highly visible in Africa and elsewhere, is likely to continue to flare for some years. One obvious result will be an increase in the number of sovereign states. However, this trend can also be expected to produce large numbers of refugees and internally displaced people. This result can be contained if the United Nations is allowed to become an effective force in peace-making and peacekeeping.

One important trend within the international community is a willingness for international bodies to intervene in conflicts where massive numbers of civilians are at risk.

One important, clearly visible trend, within the international community generally and the UN specifically, is a willingness for international bodies to intervene, militarily or otherwise, in conflicts where massive numbers of civilians are at risk, or in instances of massive human rights abuse where a recognized government is itself the abuser, or where there is no recognized government. The early 1990s saw international military intervention to protect Kurdish civilians in Iraq, and to halt mass starvation in Somalia. This controversial trend is exacerbated in part because the UN structure is dominated by the five permanent members of the Security Council. It is likely that superpower accommodation will be reached on this. It is also likely that regional intergovernmental bodies such as the Organization of African Unity will move in a similar direction. This is important because it will help clarify international responsibility for internally displaced people and help establish the principle that sovereign governments not only have rights but also responsibilities toward all their citizens.

The international community will be compelled by events to confront continuing large-scale populations of uprooted people. How the world community responds to refugee flows in the future will depend on whether or not it perceives refugees as the problem or understands that they are the victims of problems, such as persecution or violence.

The refugee situation may worsen worldwide if two trends continue. First, violent conflict is likely to increase over the next decade or so in balkanizing and irredentist struggles as well as from civil wars, border conflicts, and rebellions. ("Balkanization" is a process of political fragmentation along narrowly religious or ethnic lines; "irredentism" refers to the tendency of one group to exercise political power in an area over another group that has deep social and cultural roots in that area.) These conflicts, primarily in the developing world, will create tens of millions of refugees. Second, with general population growth stressing the resources of many economies, there will be vigorous rejection of masses of refugees from adjacent countries.

[See also Ethnic and Cultural Separatism; Human Rights; Migration, International.]

BIBLIOGRAPHY

Deng, Frances M. *Protecting the Dispossessed: A Challenge for the International Community.* Washington, DC: Brookings Institution, 1993.
Loescher, Gil. *Beyond Charity: International Cooperation and the Global Refugee Crises.* New York: Oxford University Press, 1993.

— ROGER P. WINTER

REGIONAL TRADE AGREEMENTS.

See INTERNATIONAL TRADE: REGIONAL TRADE AGREEMENTS.

RELIGION: CHANGING BELIEFS

Historians note that the great world religions are experiencing a diminution of their primary role as the cohesive, culture-shaping force in society. Resurgent fundamentalism notwithstanding, the church, mosque, and temple seem less able to provide the eternal certainties that once gave people an anchor in life and that bound people together in a clear sense of their place in the universal order.

Psychologically, religions can be understood as projections of the unconscious mind, as containers of eternal images of the soul that ascribe an order to life. Such symbols express the deepest of unarticulated meaning. Our historic spiritual disciplines are systems for psychic healing and wholeness. Their evident practical function has been to maintain the inner balance of the individual and to provide coherence and anchorage to human lives.

The emergence of the religious mind may have been part of a seminal shift of history—the appearance of consciousness as we now experience it.

We tend to view the past in terms of the present, to project backward what we are like today. But there was a time when consciousness, as we experience it, did not exist. Humans did not always have the same capacity for subjectivity, reflection, introspection, assimilation, and the capacity for willing, as we have today. Rather, "thoughts" were the result of some inner revelation; they simply *appeared*. People heard internal voices that said, "Do this, do that." Parts of the Old Testament reflect this type of mind, as does the *Iliad,* where you do not get reasoned thought, but rather gods giving commands on the field of battle.

But there came a period when the capacity for reflection, for willing, and for purposive thinking began to evolve. As Aeschylus had Prometheus say, "I gave them understanding." In biblical terms, man ate the fruit of the tree of knowledge. A major psychological reorientation took place.

Thus many of the Greek myths and Biblical texts can be interpreted as the emergence of consciousness as we now experience it. It was at this point that man changed from being merely an object of creation, and, in a sense, became a co-creator with the Divine.

With the emergence of consciousness came the recognition of good and evil as distinct choices in life, choices that either advance or retard the quality of the human condition. This evolution of good and evil as conscious choice can be seen as the birth of freedom. In this sense, consciousness, good, evil, and freedom are inextricably bound together.

During different phases of this period, the great religions of the world were born, save for Islam, which emerged in the seventh century. The great religions of the world became metaphors by which humankind could experience the transcendent mystery of life. Religions became the symbol/systems of psychic wholeness that emanate from the collective unconscious. At this same time came the concept of human-hearted caring and compassion as the desirable bonding force of social cohesion.

But in the past two centuries, and especially in the twentieth century, our awareness of the natural order has vastly expanded. So have our powers of technology. As this has happened, our defining reality has become the awareness of the human community as a single entity. The basic referent is no longer "my tribe," "my nation," or even "my civilization."

In this new era, we are incorporating the planetary dimensions of life into the fabric of our economics, politics, international relations, and culture. For the first time in human history, we are forging an awareness of our existence that embraces humanity as a whole. We may now have a unifying language out of which we can begin to organize ourselves on the level of a specie. What is emerging is a new context for all discussion of value, meaning, purpose, or ultimacy of any sort.

In light of a change on this scale, the ability of the historic world religions to carry living meaning has weakened over the past two centuries. As a container of divine significance, the soul seems to have become enfeebled. A similar process took place at the time of the Roman Caesars, when the gods lost their living force.

As the historical spiritual images of wholeness have been withdrawn as living projections, the archetypal contents of the unconscious have been activated and projected as contemporary images in our culture. As the eminent cultural historian Christopher Dawson wrote, "When the prophets are silent and society no longer possesses the channel of communication with the divine world, the way to the lower world is still open, and man's frustrated spiritual powers will find their outlet in the unlimited will to power and destruction." These other images have given rise to the psychic content of twentieth-century culture, with its portrayal of the American dream gone awry as in *The Great Gatsby,* or the negation of any life-affirming impulse as in the film *Pulp Fiction.*

We tend to take such cultural images as ominous forebodings of doom. But it is a psychological fact that every increase in consciousness derives from a creative encounter with darkness. As chaos prevails, the law of compensating opposites is engaged and eventually new projections of light and life emanate from the psyche.

We see this process expressed in literature in Odysseus' trip to the Underworld before he was able to return home to Ithaca and Penelope. In like manner, Dante's descent into the Inferno was but the prelude to Paradise. In this sense, the wasteland—the Underworld—of contemporary American culture can be seen as a prelude to a rebirth, a fresh spiritual advance to be experienced in the coming century.

It is against this background that the metaphors by which we experience transcendent reality, by which we express the deepest unknown mysteries of life, must be reinterpreted to accommodate a new stage of human development. This does not necessarily imply rejection of the spiritual metaphors and disciplines that have served us thus far. But the life of the spirit is dynamic, not static. It must be eternally renewed, and never frozen in time or form.

What we are engaged in is the soul's search for a greater expression of life. We seek a legitimizing vision of life that expresses the spiritual essence of the human journey with such force and resonance so as to define world purposes and standards of conduct for a new epoch of human development. Only by the unyielding pursuit of its inner creativeness and the texture of its truth can the human soul advance. This is, in fact, the divine process of continuous creation and recreation through human maturation.

It is impossible to predict how this spiritual search will ultimately manifest itself. We are not engaged in a rational, objective process. Nor is this a search that has to do with any particular religion. It involves all of us as individuals, and it is the most hopeful portent of the future.

While we tend to focus on the collapse of old forms, in point of fact, we are beginning to see the emergence of new expressions of eternal images of spiritual wholeness that will enable consciousness to be reborn on a higher level.

[See also Global Consciousness; Mind: New Modes of Thinking; Religion, Spirituality, Morality; Religions, Decline or Rise of.]

BIBLIOGRAPHY

Armstrong, Karen. *The History of God.* New York: Ballantine Books, 1993.
Campbell, Joseph. *The Inner Reaches of Outer Space.* New York: Harper & Row, 1986.
Edinger, Edward F. *Ego and Archetype.* Boston: Shambhala, 1972.
Davies, Paul. *The Mind of God.* New York: Simon & Schuster, 1992.
Jung, C. G. *Psychology and Religion: West and East.* Vol. 11 of *Collected Works.* Princeton, NJ: Princeton University Press, 1969.
Swimme, Brian, and Berry, Thomas. *The Universe Story.* New York: HarperCollins, 1992.

— WILLIAM VAN DUSEN WISHARD

RELIGION: INSTITUTIONS AND PRACTICES

Until recently, most social scientists would have agreed with the eminent anthropologist Anthony F. C. Wallace, when he said:

> The evolutionary future of religion is extinction. Belief in supernatural beings and in supernatural forces that affect nature without obeying nature's laws will erode and become only an interesting historical memory. To be sure, this event is not likely to occur in the next generation; the process will very likely take several hundred years, and there will always remain individuals, or even occasional small cult groups, who respond to hallucination, trance, and obsession with a supernatural interpretation. But as a cultural trait, belief in supernatural powers is doomed to die out, all over the world, as a result of the increasing adequacy and diffusion of scientific knowledge (Wallace, 1966, p. 264).

Since Wallace wrote, however, the continued vigor of American churches, coupled with the proliferation of new religious movements around the world, has brought this secularization thesis into grave doubt. As outlined by sociologists Rodney Stark, William Sims Bainbridge, and Roger Finke, the dominant current model of secularization notes that the most liberal denominations in all periods of history tend to lose their faith and thus their adherents. The close connection these denominations enjoy with secular powers is a chief reason for their loss of faith, but it also gives them some capacity to suppress competing sects. Eventually, revival movements arise within the dominant religious tradition, often in the form of sects that erupt from the denominations through disruptive schisms.

In time, the most successful of these sects will develop connections with the secular elites, transform into moderate denominations, and set the stage for a new generation of schismatic sects. Over the very long haul, an entire religious tradition can become secularized, but this only clears the social landscape for entirely new traditions that emerge in the form of radical cults.

Entirely new religious traditions succeed only when standard traditions have been discredited and social chaos drives people to seek radical solutions to life's problems.

In the United States, from 1971 to 1990, the Episcopal church lost 19 percent of its membership and the United Church of Christ (Congregationalists) lost 12 percent even as the general population was growing. At the same time that these liberal denominations were shrinking, the conservative Mormons gained 66 percent, and the Seventh-Day Adventists, 68 percent. Projected into the future, these trends predict decline for the liberal denominations, more than balanced by growth in evangelical ones. However, the growing religious movements will probably moderate, and the net result may be overall stability for decades to come.

Since colonial times, the United States has been home to many innovative cults, and a few, such as Christian Science and Scientology, have claimed to be especially well designed for the modern era. However, Pitirim Sorokin was probably right when he argued that entirely new religious traditions succeed only when standard traditions have been discredited, and widespread social chaos drives multitudes of people to seek radical solutions to life's problems. These conditions currently exist in China and the former Soviet Union— a basis for some speculative thinking.

In Russia, three generations have grown up under a repressive regime that was resolutely atheistic. It is perhaps too much to hope that their newfound freedoms will continue indefinitely, but for the present they suddenly are able to create any kind of religion they wish. Because Marxism broke the power of the Orthodox church, and few citizens have been securely socialized into any particular faith, we can expect to see the wildest possible experimentation with radical sects and cults. New dictatorships may arise upon the ashes of the old, and their orientation to religion is highly unpredictable. In the 1930s and '40s the Nazis indulged deeply in Wagnerian cultism and attempted the eradication of Jews; conceivably Russia will become a religious battleground, with Baptists the victims and pseudo-Orthodox Rasputins the villains. Alternatively, like Judea two thousand years earlier, Russia may give birth to an entirely new benevolent world religion, perhaps healing the wounds of ethnic and national wars from the Caucasus to Capetown.

The secrets of success for a new religion are relatively simple, although most cults go out of existence when the founder loses his or her grip, or the first generation of members die off. To instill faith, a religion must first inspire hope. This means it must compellingly promise to solve the major life problems faced by potential recruits, but it must not claim to deliver the desired rewards immediately in the material world, because such claims are too easy to disprove. Faith is strengthened when religious activities offer considerable experiential rewards, such as fellowship and ecstasy.

A cult or sect grows through development and activation of social bonds linking members to nonmembers, and much of its strength comes from emotional attachments linking members with each other. A person is easier to recruit if weak in social relationships. In such a circumstance, sect members can more readily form friendships with these persons and draw them into the group. In addition, such persons lack countervailing friendships with nonmembers that might seek to pull them away. However, a new recruit who possesses friendships with nonmembers can be used as a bridge to recruit them as well. This means that the most successful religious movements recruit socially connected people and spread outward through their friendship and family networks. Thus, they become locked in fierce competition with other movements that are doing the same thing, and they must be exceedingly well organized to win.

Ecstasy is both a blessing and a curse. It inspires members with great commitment, but it also places a few of them in control of powerful emotional resources that may be used to challenge the leadership. Frequently this leads to fragmentation of the group. Partly in consequence, most cults are remarkably dull and uncreative. A sectlike cult that innovates only moderately, combining much of the traditional religion of the society with carefully chosen new elements, has the advantage of exploiting existing faith and can plausibly claim to be an improved version. American examples include Mormonism, Adventism, and Christian Science. Christianity itself was originally a Jewish cult, as Buddhism was a Hindu one.

Given the preeminence of science in the modern world, wholly new religious traditions may draw upon scientific metaphors, especially if science succeeds in discrediting older religious traditions and then slumps into a malaise of its own as fresh scientific discoveries become ever more expensive and remote from the everyday world of human existence. Thus, the future of religion depends to some extent upon the future of science.

The essential question is not whether religion will continue to be a potent force in human affairs, for it will. Instead, the question is how long the currently popular religions will hold dominance until being replaced by radically different religious visions that today can hardly be imagined.

[See also Church-State Affairs; Religion, Changing Beliefs; Religion, Spirituality, Morality; Religions, Decline or Rise of; Religions, Statistical Projections of.]

BIBLIOGRAPHY

Finke, Roger, and Stark, Rodney. *The Churching of America: 1776–1990.* New Brunswick, NJ: Rutgers University Press, 1992.

Sorokin, Pitirim A. *Social and Cultural Dynamics.* New York: American Book Company, 1937.

Stark, Rodney, and Bainbridge, William Sims. *The Future of Religion.* Berkeley, CA: University of California Press, 1985.

Wallace, Anthony F. C. *Religion: An Anthropological View.* New York: Random House, 1966.

— WILLIAM SIMS BAINBRIDGE

RELIGION, SPIRITUALITY, MORALITY

Protestant theologian Paul Tillich (1886–1965) contended that every human being has a religion, at least of a kind, for each of us has an "ultimate concern." Religions can be classified in various ways. Distinction can be drawn between revealed religions, which claim that God has revealed divinity and divine purposes to us in ways that can be understood, and religions based on human inquiry, philosophical speculation, and mystical experience.

The major revealed religions are Judaism, Christianity, and Islam. These three are related historically. Christianity accepts the validity of Jewish revelation, the Hebrew Scriptures; Islam accepts at least some elements of both Judaism and Christianity. Revealed religions typically propound doctrines (statements regarded as objectively true that adherents are expected to believe) and commandments (a way of life based on rules considered binding on all members or, in some cases, on people in general).

The development of religion, spirituality, and morality depends on whether the revealed religions will be able to defend their distinctive doctrines and ways of life in an increasingly multicultural world or will have to yield to nondogmatic kinds of spirituality. If so, they will survive and grow; if not, they will decline and the others will grow.

Prospects for the revealed religions indicate that many adherents will make a concerted stand in defense of their beliefs and associated ways of life. Such people are called "orthodox," "traditionalists," or sometimes "fundamentalists." Also included are many more people than those in the groups and sects within Judaism, Christianity, and Islam who are also commonly called "fundamentalists." Other people will move in the direction of mysticism or nondogmatic spirituality, or may drop out of organized religion altogether. Adherents of the revealed religions will defend their doctrines energetically. They will demand of themselves, and sometimes of others, adherence to the rules of conduct that grow out of those doctrines. This probably will lead to an intensification of the conflict that James Davison Hunter calls "culture wars" in his 1991 book of that title, namely, to a conflict that pits traditional ways and believers on one side against "liberal" ways and believers and nonbelievers on the other.

For those who emphasize tradition, faith and conduct are interdependent. Especially for traditional Christians, it is on the doctrines they hold to be true that they see the commandments prescribing moral conduct. Thus, the first of the Ten Commandments reads: "I am the LORD thy God, that brought thee up out of the land of Egypt. . . . Thou shalt have none other gods before me" (Exodus 20:2).

Traditional believers cannot give up their doctrines, on which both their pattern of conduct in this world and their hope of salvation hereafter are based. They feel themselves threatened by both scientific and pseudo-scientific views that question the factual basis of their revelation, as well as by widely practiced behaviors that they find immoral. One example is the theory of evolution when it is interpreted to deny the existence of God as well as of any divine design or purpose. Another example is the kind of psychology which asserts that behavior urged or prohibited by religion is psychologically or genetically determined and not subject to human moral control—for example, behavior involving sex (especially homosexuality) and violence. These doctrines imply that some people, or even people in general, simply cannot be expected to behave as the traditional revealed religions demand.

In reaction, we can expect traditionalists to continue to set up rival institutions of science and learning to defend their positions, and to make an effort to see their moral convictions made a part of the civil law. Conservative Christians already have attempted this in the United States. In Israel, orthodox Judaism makes similar efforts to make Israeli law conform to religious law, and Muslims frequently establish *Sharia* (Islamic law) in societies where they are dominant.

Morality for religious adherents is tied to religion. The culture can be viewed as the fulfillment of God's intentions and embraced, or the religious adherents can separate more and more from the rest of society to the extent that they view society as secular, pluralistic, and permissive—which, in the eyes of those adherents, means immoral. Ernst Troeltsch and later H. Richard Niebuhr made the study of this variety of relationships between "Christ and culture" their life work.

Much revealed religion is characterized by apocalypticism, which claims to have revelation that accurately predicts the impending end of the world and divine judgment. Orthodox Christianity believes in the return of Christ and the Last Judgment, but does not claim to know the day and hour of these events. Apocalyptic movements, claiming to know when all this will happen, arise and gain a following in times of social, political, and economic troubles. These movements suddenly flourish and usually fade even more suddenly when the dates set by their predictions pass without incident. The popular fundamentalist Christian author Hal Lindsey's record-breaking bestseller *The Late Great Planet Earth* (1971) is a contemporary example of this phenomenon. Such apocalyptic phenomena will probably increase, especially as the twentieth century draws to a close.

Traditionalism and orthodoxy, with their doctrines that have to be believed and rules that must be obeyed, will appeal only to a minority of people. Religious feminists also will continue to put pressure on Judaism, Christianity, and Islam, criticizing them as "male-dominated" and patriarchal. In fact, the status of women in late antiquity, in the first three centuries after Christ, was far higher in Judaism and especially in Christianity than it was in the surrounding religions of that time.

Most human beings seem to be unable to live entirely without religion. Where the traditional religions of the West decline, the great world religions based on philosophy and mysticism, notably Hinduism and Buddhism, will continue to gain adherents in the West, including former Christians, Jews, and people who grew up with no religion. However, these religions from Asia frequently entail codes of conduct and spiritual disciplines that are very demanding. Consequently, they do not appeal to people increasingly eager for instant gratification and in pursuit of unbridled individualism.

Some movements claim to be resurrecting

ancient beliefs, for example, the worship of Gaia,

meaning the Earth personified as a goddess,

and Wicca, a modern form of witchcraft

claiming ancient origins.

Hinduism and Buddhism will be less attractive than what the late Francis A. Schaeffer (1912–1984) called "contentless mysticism," an expression to be seen as descriptive rather than pejorative. Instead of claiming roots in objectively true divine revelation, or in the intensely demanding spiritual disciplines of religious giants such as the Buddha, many varieties of New Age spirituality, rather like the early Christian heresy called gnosticism, present an elaborate structure of concepts and teachings but do not base them on biblical, historical, or scientific evidence. They appeal to a group that sees itself as a kind of spiritual elite.

Feminist concepts and female leaders are prominent in this New Age movement, dating back to Helena Blavatsky (1831–1891), and Annie Besant (1847–1933). Although both Hinduism and Buddhism arose in highly patriarchal cultures, their modern offshoots, grouped under the heading New Age, are characterized by feminist activism, often by goddess worship, and sometimes by great sexual freedom, which their critics call licentiousness and degeneracy. Some New Age and related movements claim to be resurrecting ancient beliefs, for example, the worship of Gaia, meaning the Earth personified as a goddess, and Wicca, a modern form of witchcraft claiming very ancient origins. Traditional Hindu and Buddhist concepts, such as reincarnation, will continue to gain popularity, especially when they are presented in a nondemanding kind of "pop" religion without the moral and spiritual requirements of the Asian religions.

In conclusion, human beings are and will remain religious by nature. Even worldviews that are supposedly based on objective science have a strong "belief" component, one that cannot be documented scientifically but must be taken by faith. See, for example, the world-

view presented by Cornell University astronomer Carl Sagan in his book *Cosmos* (1980). The traditional revealed religions demand loyalty and impose standards of belief and/or conduct to which adherents of New Age and other movements, as well as nonreligious people, will object.

Unless the future brings a great spiritual renewal across whole societies, or a great "falling away" from faith—both of which are mentioned in biblical prophecy—we can expect continuing "culture wars." This conflict will rage on between traditionalist believers and moralists in Judaism, Christianity, and Islam on the one hand, the secularizing Western culture of technology, New Agers, and moral relativists on the other.

[See also Apocalyptic Future; Evolution, Biological; Holistic Beliefs; Religion: Institutions and Practices; Religions, Decline or Rise of; Religions, Statistical Projections of; Women and Religion.]

BIBLIOGRAPHY

Ellul, Jacques. *The Technological Bluff.* Grand Rapids, MI: Eerdmans, 1990.

Grenz, Stanley. *The Millennial Maze: Sorting Out Evangelical Options.* Downers Grove, IL, and Grand Rapids, MI: Inter-Varsity Press, 1992.

Martin, Ralph. *The Catholic Church at the End of an Age.* San Francisco: Ignatius, 1994.

Sagan, Carl. *Cosmos.* New York: Random House, 1980.

Schwarz, Hans. *The Way to the Future.* Minneapolis: Augsburg, 1972.

Suchocki, Marjorie. *The End of Evil: Process Eschatology in the Light of Current Trends in Religion.* Albany, NY: State University of New York Press, 1988.

Toffler, Alvin. *Powershift: Knowledge, Wealth and Violence at the Edge of the 21st Century.* New York: Bantam, 1990.

– HAROLD O. J. BROWN

RELIGIONS, DECLINE OR RISE OF

Writing about the future of religion has always been a hazardous business. Those brave enough to venture into this realm are drawn inexorably to two visions of the religious future of mankind— from fanciful predictions of religious utopia (such as Bellamy, *Looking Backward, 2000–1887,* a long-term future scenario of utopia as the result of mankind's obedience to Christian principles) on the one side, to predictions of inexorable decline and collapse (such as Lorie and Murray-Clark, *History of the Future: a Chronology,* which predicts the collapse of organized religion beginning in 2006—the Age of Aquarius) on the other. Perhaps this is due to the strong opinions of the authors—either as devout religionists or as those opposed to organized religion.

"Religion—it's hard to kill" sums up the feeling of many futurists (*What Futurists Believe,* Coates and Jarratt, 1989). In this book, the two authors demonstrate that most futurists do not take religion seriously or are interested in only its aberrations or extremes (e.g., fanaticism, fundamentalism). Stark and Bainbridge begin their book *The Future of Religion* with the following observation: "The most illustrious figures in sociology, anthropology, and psychology have unanimously expressed confidence that their children, or surely their grandchildren, would live to see the dawn of a new era in which, to paraphrase Freud, the infantile illusions of religion would be outgrown" (Stark and Bainbridge, 1985, p. 1). The fourth major trend in social scientist Burnham Beckwith's *The Next 500 Years* is "the decline of religion and superstition." Beckwith includes this in a list of thirty-one major trends he believes will shape the next few centuries. Sociologist Brian M. Stableford and weapons physicist David Langford also see religion on the decline. In their masterful *The Third Millennium: a History of the World, AD 2000–3000,* by the middle of the twenty-first century, the last great "religion," Marxism, is on the decline (Stableford and Langford, 1985, p. 24). The world's old faiths have all but disappeared.

Equally prolific are the writers expounding a future where religion is central to the destiny of mankind. This ranges from pseudo-humanistic utopias (still based on religion) to Christian, Muslim, or Buddhist eschatological visions to New Age "cosmic consciousness" sans organized religion. It should be noted that the best-selling futurist work in the 1970s was Hal Lindsey's *Late Great Planet Earth* (Lindsey and Carlson, 1976) with 25 million copies in print and still selling strong in the 1990s. The most widely read futurist work of any kind in history is *The Revelation of John* (c. A.D. 90), which has been translated into over 1,000 languages. It is also important to note a new attitude among Muslims about their future. "At the beginning of the 20th century, Islam—colonized, defeated, stagnant—could easily have been written off from history and the future. At the dawn of the 21st century, Islam—resurgent, confident, 'militant,' 'fundamentalist,' very much alive—is poised to become a global force" (Sardar, 1991, p. 223).

Futurist H. Gerjouy in "The Most Significant Events of the Next Thousand Years" (Gerjouy, 1992, p. 6) counters pessimistic views of the future by stating that "there will be a radiation and proliferation of religions, and new important religions will spring up that will attract many adherents."

Hiley H. Ward set out a scenario of religion in the twenty-second century in his 1975 work *Religion 2102 A.D.* Ward suggests that "Christianity is likely to be around for a long time to come in some form." He then surveys the current literature on futurism, drawing out its implications for religion in the future with such interesting applications as telepathic sermons, God as supermachine, and pluralistic Christianity.

L. E. Browne, writing in the *International Review of Missions* in 1949, ventured his opinion under the title "The Religion of the World in AD 3000." Browne predicts the extinction of not only polytheism (including Hinduism) but also of all major religions except Christianity. He goes on to say that the only competitor to Christianity will be materialism, which is essentially a belief that man does not need God or ethics.

The reader of literature on the future of religion is confronted with a dizzying range of opinions.

Perhaps the Christian theologian to write most seriously on the future is the German Catholic Hans Küng. His major treatise *Theology for the Third Millennium* deals with a paradigm shift that represents a narrowing of the perceived chasm between the various Christian traditions (particularly Catholicism, Orthodoxy, and Protestantism). Christianity in the future need not be polarized, as differences in theology are often artificially accentuated by the political and structural context. The new paradigm is an ecumenical one, but without sacrificing distinctions of faith and tradition. He extends this to include solidarity with all of the world's religious traditions—always searching for a common ground in solving mankind's problems.

In conclusion, the reader of literature on the future of religion is confronted with a dizzying range of opinions. Writing from a wide range of disciplines and personal perspectives, scholars, economists, environmentalists, and science fiction writers paint a future for religion ranging from its extinction to its central role for human survival. Perhaps Futurist Warren Wagar put it best: "As futurists, we are really out of our depth in trying to chart the far future of religion" (1991:140).

[See also Religion: Institutions and Practices; Religion, Spirituality, Morality; Religions, Statistical Projections of.]

BIBLIOGRAPHY

Beckwith, Burnham. *The Next 500 Years.* New York: Harper & Row, 1967.

Bellamy, Edward. *Looking Backward, 2000–1887.* Boston: Houghton Mifflin Company, 1887.

Browne, L. E. "The Religion of the World in AD 3000." *International Review of Missions* 38/104 (1949): 463–468.

Coates, Joseph F., and Jarratt, Jennifer. *What Futurists Believe.* Mt. Airy, MD: Lomond, 1989.

Gerjouy, Herbert G. "The Most Significant Events of the Next Thousand Years." *Futures Research Quarterly.* 8/3 (Fall 1992): 5–21.

Küng, Hans. *Theology for the Third Millennium: An Ecumenical View.* New York: Doubleday, 1988.

Lindsey, Hal, and Carlson, C. C. *The Late Great Planet Earth.* Grand Rapids, MI: Zondervan, 1976.

Lorie, Peter, and Murray-Clark, Sidd. *History of the Future: a Chronology.* New York: Doubleday, 1989.

Sardar, Ziauddin, ed. Special issue. "Islam and the Future." *Futures* 23/3 (April 1991): 223–332.

Stableford, Brian M., and Langford, David. *The Third Millennium: A History of the World: AD 2000–3000.* London: Sidgwick & Jackson, 1985.

Stark, Rodney, and Bainbridge, William Sims. *The Future of Religion: Secularization, Revival, and Cult Formation.* Berkeley, CA: University of California Press, 1985.

Wagar, W. Warren. *The Next Three Futures: Paradigms of Things to Come.* New York: Praeger, 1991.

Ward, Hiley H. *Religion 2101 A.D.* Garden City, NY: Doubleday, 1975.

– TODD M. JOHNSON

RELIGIONS, STATISTICAL PROJECTIONS OF

The opportunity to project the future of religious affiliation has presented itself for the first time with the recent availability of four publications and two databases. Foundational demographic data for every country in the world are available for the years 1950–2025 through the United Nations Demographic Database (see United Nations, 1994). Data on religions and Christianity for every country are available through the World Evangelization Database (see *World Christian Encyclopedia* [1982] and *Our Globe and How to Reach It* [1990]). Data beyond 2025 for the world's nine major continental areas are available for the first time in the UN's publication *Long-Range World Population Projections: Two Centuries of Population Growth, 1950–2150* (1992).

The intersection of these data form the starting point for a quantitative analysis of the future of religion. The demographic projections of the United Nations provide a foundation on which religious data can be compared. This can be described as a five-stage process.

Stage One

Christian data are more complete globally than data on other religions. A detailed analysis can be performed by matching data on Christianity with the population projections for every country of the world. If none of the 1990 percentages are adjusted but assumed to remain static, the demographic effects on Christian affiliation can be analyzed on both regional and global levels. This reveals the differential growth of adherents to Christianity depending on population growth where they live. This is the first stage of demographic analysis by country.

Stage Two

A more realistic application is to use current trends to make adjustments to the Christian data. Thus, if evidence exists that the Christian church is in decline in a particular country, then the percentage to be matched to that country at a future date will be lowered to an appropriate level. With adjustments made to Christian populations in each country a second stage of analysis is added. Now one can view the effects of not only demographic change but change in religious adherence.

But these first two stages of analysis have two important limitations. First, they only analyze the Christian situation. Without reference to other religions and nonreligions, it is easy to miss the overall context of religious change either by country, region, or globally. Second, they only take us to the year 2025. Our next stages will, therefore, have to overcome both of these limitations.

Stage Three

The most detailed table of religions by United Nations regions is published yearly by *Encyclopaedia Britannica* in its *Britannica Book of the Year.* This table includes all religions by major region and is thus suited perfectly for demographic manipulation. It overcomes the first limitation of the first two stages—all major religions are included. The second limitation is overcome in that regional projections have been published by the United Nations for the years 2025–2200.

Analysis of the *Britannica* tables begins by using the 1990 table as a base from which to project all future tables (to 2200) using only demographic tools. Thus, the regional totals reflect United Nations projections while all religious percentages within a region remain unchanged. This allows us to examine how demographic growth or decline alone within a particular region affects the global total. This yields remarkable insights into what we can expect from the most consistent source of growth and decline of religious and nonreligious adherence—births and deaths. This amounts to our third stage of analysis of the future of religion.

Stage Four

The fourth stage allows us to use results from our country-by-country analysis to update the *Britannica* tables to 2025. From this base, more reasonable demographic future projections can be made. In addition, for the first

TABLE 1

SCENARIOS FOR ADHERENTS OF WORLD RELIGIONS, 1900–2200

	1900	%	1950	%	1990	%	2000	%	2020	%
Christians	558,056,000	34.5%	849,352,000	33.8%	1,757,206,000	33.2%	2,090,417,000	33.4%	3,022,623,000	35.5%
Muslims	200,102,000	12.4%	379,295,000	15.1%	935,331,000	17.7%	1,159,901,000	18.5%	1,716,091,000	20.2%
Nonreligious	2,923,000	0.2%	332,170,000	13.2%	857,708,000	16.2%	1,005,109,000	16.1%	1,279,525,000	15.0%
Hindus	203,033,000	12.5%	326,269,000	13.0%	705,000,000	13.3%	840,792,000	13.4%	1,113,103,000	13.1%
Buddhists	127,159,000	7.8%	171,118,000	6.8%	307,219,000	5.8%	366,265,000	5.9%	484,432,000	5.7%
Atheists	226,000	0.0%	100,658,000	4.0%	229,000,000	4.3%	233,301,000	3.7%	237,257,000	2.8%
Chinese folk-religionists	380,404,000	23.5%	208,865,000	8.3%	180,000,000	3.4%	210,313,000	3.4%	233,813,000	2.7%
New-Religionists	5,910,000	0.4%	27,379,000	1.1%	138,000,000	2.6%	164,418,000	2.6%	217,314,000	2.6%
Tribal religionists	106,340,000	6.6%	83,729,000	3.3%	102,242,000	1.9%	96,677,000	1.5%	77,026,000	0.9%
Sikhs	2,961,000	0.2%	6,515,000	0.3%	18,100,000	0.3%	21,522,000	0.3%	28,370,000	0.3%
Jews	12,270,000	0.8%	11,641,000	0.5%	16,500,000	0.3%	17,473,000	0.3%	21,468,000	0.3%
Shamanists	11,341,000	0.7%	8,558,000	0.3%	10,100,000	0.2%	12,015,000	0.2%	15,849,000	0.2%
Confucians	640,000	0.0%	1,752,000	0.1%	5,800,000	0.1%	6,913,000	0.1%	9,142,000	0.1%
Baha'is	9,000	0.0%	251,000	0.0%	5,300,000	0.1%	6,485,000	0.1%	9,544,000	0.1%
Jains	1,323,000	0.1%	1,871,000	0.1%	3,650,000	0.1%	4,357,000	0.1%	5,795,000	0.1%
Shintoists	6,720,000	0.4%	3,519,000	0.1%	3,100,000	0.1%	3,698,000	0.1%	4,892,000	0.1%
Other religionists	470,000	0.0%	2,861,000	0.1%	17,938,000	0.3%	21,144,000	0.3%	27,978,000	0.3%
Total population	1,619,887,000	100.0%	2,516,443,000	100.0%	5,292,194,000	100.0%	6,260,800,000	100.0%	8,504,222,000	100.0%

	Demographic from 1990		Demographic from 2025		Most likely		Muslim revival		Nonreligious	
	2200	%	2200	%	2200	%	2200	%	2200	%
Christians	3,779,997,000	32.6%	4,257,919,000	36.7%	4,397,929,000	37.9%	4,291,467,000	37.0%	4,397,929,000	37.9%
Muslims	2,582,642,000	22.3%	2,607,061,000	22.5%	2,624,567,000	22.6%	2,730,478,000	23.5%	2,485,513,320	21.4%
Nonreligious	1,609,929,000	13.9%	1,580,647,000	13.6%	1,626,497,000	14.0%	1,626,497,000	14.0%	1,764,999,680	15.2%
Hindus	1,398,329,000	12.1%	1,398,329,000	12.1%	1,398,329,000	12.1%	1,398,329,000	12.1%	1,398,329,000	12.1%
Buddhists	607,601,000	5.2%	607,601,000	5.2%	607,601,000	5.2%	607,601,000	5.2%	607,601,000	5.2%
Atheists	409,408,000	3.5%	291,083,000	2.5%	249,000,000	2.1%	249,000,000	2.1%	249,000,000	2.1%
Chinese folk-religionists	356,278,000	3.1%	293,297,000	2.5%	253,162,000	2.2%	253,162,000	2.2%	253,162,000	2.2%
New-Religionists	272,280,000	2.3%	272,280,000	2.3%	272,280,000	2.3%	272,280,000	2.3%	272,280,000	2.3%
Tribal religionists	426,416,000	3.7%	136,010,000	1.2%	15,416,000	0.1%	15,416,000	0.1%	15,416,000	0.1%
Sikhs	35,434,000	0.3%	35,434,000	0.3%	35,434,000	0.3%	35,434,000	0.3%	35,434,000	0.3%
Jews	26,035,000	0.2%	24,697,000	0.2%	24,697,000	0.2%	24,697,000	0.2%	24,697,000	0.2%
Shamanists	19,859,000	0.2%	19,859,000	0.2%	19,859,000	0.2%	19,859,000	0.2%	19,859,000	0.2%
Confucians	11,459,000	0.1%	11,459,000	0.1%	11,459,000	0.1%	11,459,000	0.1%	11,459,000	0.1%
Baha'is	14,559,000	0.1%	14,559,000	0.1%	14,559,000	0.1%	14,559,000	0.1%	14,559,000	0.1%
Jains	7,351,000	0.1%	7,351,000	0.1%	7,351,000	0.1%	7,351,000	0.1%	7,351,000	0.1%
Shintoists	6,138,000	0.1%	6,138,000	0.1%	6,138,000	0.1%	6,138,000	0.1%	6,138,000	0.1%
Other religionists	36,273,000	0.3%	36,273,000	0.3%	36,273,000	0.3%	36,273,000	0.3%	36,273,000	0.3%
Total population	11,600,000,000	100.0%	11,600,000,000	100.0%	11,600,000,000	100.0%	11,600,000,000	100.0%	11,600,000,000	100.0%

Source: *World Christian Encyclopedia*; future figures projected and adjusted.

time we can see our Christian projections in the context of the world's religions and nonreligions.

Stage Five

The fifth stage of analysis completes our methodology by making adjustments to the end of our study period, A.D. 2200, based on conservative assumptions about religious change. The adjustments yield what could be considered our most likely scenario.

Conclusions

The results from the fifth stage are presented in Table 1, "Scenarios for Adherents of World Religions, 1900–2200." This table shows Christianity increasing from 33.2 percent in 1990 to 37.9 percent by 2200 while Islam also increases from 17.7 percent in 1990 to 22.6 percent in 2200. Nonreligious persons and atheists, on the other hand, grew rapidly over the period 1900–1990, then decrease from a combined percentage of 19.6 percent in 1990 to 16.1 percent by A.D. 2200.

These results could be revised simply by modifying either the assumptions or the actual figures used to calculate religious change. For illustrative purposes, two additional scenarios have been added to Table 1. First, a plausible future is one in which Islam makes unprecedented inroads into the Western world. (See columns labeled "Muslim revival"). The assumption is made that 1 percent of the Christians in Europe, North America, and Oceania defect to Islam every twenty-five years. In this scenario Christians lose 0.9 percent of the world's population (dropping from 37.9 to 37.0 percent while Muslims gain from 22.6 to 23.5 percent) over the 175-year period 2025–2200.

A second alternative scenario is constructed by assuming that Muslims in Asia are hard hit by secularization, losing 0.5 percent every twenty-five years from 2025 to 2200. The result, presented under "Nonreligious" in Table 1, is that Muslims lose 1.2 percent of the world's population over the 175-year period.

A secondary side effect of this study is the evidence it provides for the quantitative resiliency of religion over the next two hundred years. Purely demographic changes do not show a massive decline in religious adherence. The onus would be on the person putting forth such a statement to prove that massive defections from religious adherence represent a plausible assumption.

[See also Religion: Institutions and Practices; Religion, Spirituality, Morality; Religions, Decline or Rise of.]

BIBLIOGRAPHY

Barrett, David B. *World Christian Encyclopedia: a Comparative Survey of Churches and Religions in the Modern World, AD 1900–2000.* New York: Oxford University Press, 1982.

———. "World Religious Statistics" (annual compilation). In *Britannica Book of the Year.* Chicago: Encyclopaedia Britannica, 1994.

Barrett, David B., and Johnson, Todd M. *Our Globe and How to Reach It: Seeing the World Evangelized by AD 2000 and Beyond.* Birmingham, AL: New Hope, 1990.

United Nations. *Long-Range World Population Projections: Two Centuries of Population Growth, 1950–2150.* New York: United Nations, 1992.

———. *World Population Prospects 1992.* New York: United Nations, 1994.

– TODD M. JOHNSON

RESEARCH AND DEVELOPMENT

There is a clear link between technological progress and economic growth. This link, long recognized by economists, accounts for the strong interest of many governments in promoting the creation of new technology, primarily by investing in research and development (R&D). Neither invention nor innovation absolutely requires R&D. Some important historical inventions and a larger number of new applications of old ideas have resulted from pure inspiration. Others, mostly in the past, undoubtedly occurred almost by accident. Archaeologists speculate, for example, that the uses of fire for cooking meat and making pottery may have evolved in this way, thousands of years ago. However, inspiration and lucky accidents occur too seldom to be reliable sources of new discoveries or inventions. In the modern world it is necessary to search both intensively and systematically. The search process may be quite informal, in some cases, but when it is carried out by trained engineers and scientists, it is called R&D.

Most firms do not invest in fundamental research because of the long delay in capturing a significant portion of the benefits.

It has been shown quite conclusively that industrial R&D yields very high returns compared to other types of investments. Studies have shown that there is a very close statistical correlation between R&D per employee, sales per employee, and profit margins when firms in the same type of business are compared. To be sure, R&D could well be a consequence of high profit margins and sales. Yet the weight of evidence suggests strongly that applied R&D on average yields high returns.

The case for fundamental research is less easy to document statistically. Yet it is fundamental scientific research that pays some of the biggest dividends for society as a whole, even though the immediate sponsors may not gain any direct or immediate economic benefit. For this reason, fundamental research tends to be carried out primarily in universities, where the primary justification is educational.

Most firms do not invest in fundamental research because of the long lags before commercial payoff and the difficulty in capturing a significant portion of the benefits. There have been a few exceptions. Bell Telephone Labs, GE, and IBM have supported a modest amount of fundamental research of Nobel Prize caliber in their own corporate laboratories, especially in solid-state physics.

R&D at the National Level

Since World War II, governments have increasingly realized the importance of technology as the basis of economic power without which there is no military power. In recent decades R&D expenditures at the national level as well as public financing, for civilian and military purposes, have become increasingly important. The greatest proportion of basic research is financed by national governments. Governments also finance both a major part of applications-oriented research and development in areas that have a public character. In most countries these include defense, public safety, energy, transportation, communication, health—all areas that have a major political component. In the United States, however, the federal government has concentrated its R&D overwhelmingly on defense, health, and space.

Overall, between 1978 and 1988, the United States, the United Kingdom, France, Japan, and West Germany devoted roughly the same percentage of their GDP to R&D—around 2.5 percent. In the United States and the United Kingdom the total has traditionally been slightly higher, but "defense" accounted for a large portion of the total. In Japan and West Germany, by contrast, the civilian portion was by far the larger. (See Table 1.)

The distribution of R&D expenditures among the various sectors in major OECD countries in 1987 is shown in Figure 1. It is notable that the first two sectors, defense and civilian space, represented 40 percent of the total. They benefitted, to be sure, by receiving the lion's share of government aid. This situation is not confined to France. However, industrial participation in the financing of R&D in these two sectors was a great deal more important in Japan (around 65 percent), and West Germany (around 60 percent), than in the United States (around 50 percent).

The lower level of defense-oriented R&D in Germany and Japan has released engineers and scientists for other purposes. This job concentration provides a plausible explanation of the competitive strength of Japan and Germany, particularly in the manufacture of sophisticated capital goods.

In Japan, most R&D is application-oriented and is carried out either in industrial laboratories or in universities with direct industrial support. Even the universities do not yet do much fundamental research, although this is gradually changing. An important government function in Japan, performed mainly by the Ministry of International Trade and Industry (MITI), is to organize consortia of private firms to carry out major R&D tasks, using relatively small amounts of "seed money" from the government to leverage much larger amounts of corporate money.

States and provinces play a significant role in supporting R&D in several countries. In Germany, states (*Länder*) provide approximately half the public funding for all applied R&D, much of it through the Frauenhofer Institutes. The individual German states provide

TABLE 1

R&D EXPENDITURE IN OECD COUNTRIES

Country	Percentage share of gross output		Percentage share of value added		Percentage share of fixed investment in manufacturing sector	
	1981	1985	1981	1985	1981	1985
Denmark	1.0	1.2	2.5	2.9	28.2	25.5
Finland	0.8	1.1	2.2	3.2	13.2	19.9
FRG	2.0	2.3	4.3	5.2	47.8	55.8
Japan	1.5	2.1	4.3	5.6	43.0	51.5
Norway	0.7	1.0	2.6	3.7	12.3	22.2
Sweden	2.2	3.1	5.3	7.6	41.5	56.7
UK	2.0	2.0	4.9	5.0	58.1	50.6
USA	2.5	3.3	6.0	7.6	63.2	91.0

Source: OECD.

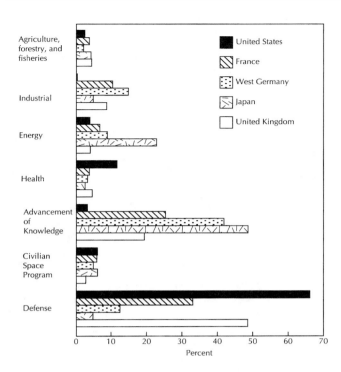

Figure 1. The distribution of R&D expenditures among the various sectors in major OECD countries, as of 1987.

a lesser, but still significant portion of the support for basic research, through the various universities (state supported) and through the Max Planck Institutes for research.

In the United States many of the larger universities are state supported, especially in the Midwest and Western states, where so-called land-grant agricultural and mechanical (A&M) colleges were created in the nineteenth century to train agronomists and engineers. Some state universities, such as the universities of California (Berkeley), Illinois, Michigan, Minnesota, and Wisconsin, have reached world-class status as research centers. Most agricultural research in the United States is still carried out through these and similar institutions.

R&D at the Business Level

Nations, taken as a whole, typically spend 2–3 percent of gross output and 5–7.5 percent of value added on R&D. Firms in mature commodity and service industries tend to spend less (often 0.5–1 percent of gross output). Firms in newer technologies and more dynamic activities—such as microelectronics, information technology, robotics, specialty chemicals, biotechnology, and pharmaceuticals—typically devote a greater percentage of their total budget to R&D. For instance, in the data-processing (computer) field for the year

1986, 55 (of 64) U.S. firms spent $28.5 billion on R&D (7.1 percent of revenues), 13 (of 15) Japanese firms spent $9.6 billion on R&D (5.8 percent of revenues), while 2 (of 4) German firms spent $2.7 billion on R&D, which was 11.3 percent of revenues. For other high-tech firms, especially genetic engineering and software firms, R&D expenditures are even higher. For instance, the first and largest of the genetic engineering firms, Genentech, was spending 38 percent of total revenues on R&D as recently as 1989.

Total industrial R&D financed by U.S.-based firms reached $65 billion (1989 dollars) in 1989, up 10 percent from the previous year. This was roughly equal to the total of industrial R&D expenditures for the rest of the OECD countries. Japanese firms spent $26.3 billion on R&D. The leaders (excluding Toyota, for which figures were not available) were Hitachi ($2.9 billion), Matsushita ($2.4 billion), Fujitsu, Toshiba, NTT, NEC, and Honda. German firms spent $11.4 billion, led by Siemens ($3.7 billion), and the three chemical giants (Bayer, Hoechst, and BASF) with a total of $3.8 billion among them. Other countries' firms contributed as follows: the United Kingdom ($5.7 billion); France ($4.9 billion, excluding Peugeot, for which data were not available); the Netherlands ($3.5 billion, of which Phillips alone accounted for $2.2 billion); Switzerland ($3 billion); Sweden ($2.9 billion); Italy ($2.9 billion); and Canada ($2 billion).

Most international firms do not perform all of their R&D in their own countries. (The Japanese are the exception in this respect.) A business, even a large multinational firm, must consult in a regular and timely fashion with technical centers, universities, and other outside sources in order to keep up with the increasing complexity and variety of areas encountered in a program of R&D. Industry contributions to university R&D increased nearly fivefold (to $900 million) from 1979 to 1989. Joint ventures now account for as much as 25 percent of total R&D. The rapid growth of international R&D joint-venturing is largely due to the fact that nowadays even the very largest firms can no longer afford to be fully aware—still less, on the frontier—of every technology that affects them. A business must thus provide financing not only for direct R&D expenditures in its own laboratories, but also indirect R&D expenditures through other organizations.

R&D at the Supranational Level

In Western Europe, a coordinating function similar to that performed by MITI in Japan, is performed by the supranational European Union (EU), headquartered in Brussels. It is possible for a European-based business in association with one or more other businesses from other countries, to obtain financing from the EU to cover the cost of "pre-competitive" R&D programs in a core set of well-defined areas. The EU's research budget accounts for only 4 percent of total civilian R&D in the European Union however.

The European Strategic Program for R&D in Information Technology (ESPRIT) program was launched in 1984. It was designed as a ten-year program with three major objectives: (1) to develop industrial technologies in the information technology area, (2) to promote European industrial cooperation, and (3) to promote the development of international standards for information technology. It is focused mainly on microelectronics, information processing systems, and applications such as computer-integrated manufacturing (CIM). In the first phase (1984–1989), more than 200 projects were initiated. As of mid-1992, ESPRIT claimed to have generated 700 information technology prototypes, tools, or standards, including some commercial successes.

In addition to the EU programs there are a number of broader cooperative programs in both science and technology, encompassing nineteen Western European countries. These include "big science" efforts such as the European Center for Nuclear Research (CERN) in Geneva, the European Organization for Astronomical Research in the Southern Hemisphere, the European Space Agency, the European Science Foundation, and the European Molecular Biology Laboratory.

The most ambitious supranational program is EUREKA, which began in 1985 as a response to the U.S. Strategic Defense Initiative. It represents 19 countries plus the Commission of the EU. The approved budget (1989) for 297 EUREKA-sponsored projects was $6.5 billion, of which 25 percent to 50 percent represented public funding. Annual spending (1989) was about $1 billion. No money crossed national borders.

The general patterns shown above will continue. More newly industrialized countries will commit to R&D. In all countries the focus of private and public research will be more consciously directed at practical uses and competitive advantage. In the United States, defense budgets will decline to the advantage of civil sector research.

[See also Appropriate Technology; Change, Scientific and Technological; Health Care: Technological Developments; Intellectual Property; Record Setting; Science Cities; Scientific Breakthroughs; Technological Change; Technological Innovation.]

BIBLIOGRAPHY

Ayres, Robert U. *Technological Forecasting and Long-Range Planning.* New York: McGraw-Hill, 1969.

Botkin, James, and Dimanescu, Dan. *The New Alliance: America's R & D Consortia.* Cambridge, MA: Ballinger, 1986.

Roman, Daniel D. *Research and Development Management: The Economics and Administration of Technology.* New York: Appleton-Century-Crofts, 1968.

Souder, William E. *Managing New Product Innovations.* Lexington, MA: Lexington Books/D. C. Heath, 1987.

— ROBERT U. AYRES

RESOURCES

Global industrialization has been resource-intensive. Quite naturally, concerns about the adequacy of the world's resource base to support future industrialization have been raised. The contemporary controversy received a strong impetus from the publication of *The Limits to Growth* in 1972 (updated in 1992 as *Beyond the Limits;* see bibliography). Publication of the book was soon followed by the OAPEC (Organization of Arab Petroleum Exporting Countries) oil embargo, which triggered rapid increases in the prices of fuels and many other basic commodities. These developments fostered the perception that the world would soon run out of the resources required for future industrialization. Over the two decades that followed, perceptions of scarcity varied along with estimates of the strength of global economic growth.

Natural resources are defined as anything required by a population to facilitate growth. Thus, commodities such as coal, oil, minerals, water, and food have been the focus of concern in debates over the future of industrial growth. More recently, the worldwide circulation of water and air through the hydrosphere and atmosphere have been recognized as providing not unlimited environmental waste dispersal services, and thus are also recognized as scarce resources.

Concern over resource limits to growth has focused on energy, particularly world reserves of oil, because energy can be used to overcome other resource shortages. For example, an abundant supply of energy would permit arid Middle Eastern countries to desalinate sea water and overcome freshwater limitations. Oil is particularly critical since so much of world production enters into international trade.

Patterns of world resource consumption are currently undergoing an important transformation. At present, the world's industrialized countries consume the vast majority of resources. It is estimated, for example, that each person living in the industrialized countries consumes between ten and twenty times as much commercial energy as his or her counterparts living elsewhere. To meet these demands, resources generally flow from the less to the more industrialized parts of the world. However, a structural transformation of the industrialized countries from the production of goods to provision of services, combined with materials conservation and recycling, is reducing the resource intensity of economic growth. Still, continued industrialization of the world's less wealthy countries will account for the biggest increases in future resource consumption.

Largely because of slower economic growth and the structural transformation of the industrial countries, worldwide commercial energy consumption has been growing very slowly in recent years. According to the World Resources Institute, consumption grew only 18 percent from 1979 to 1989. On a per capita basis this represented a 1 percent decline in energy usage. Worldwide commercial production of solid fuels, which accounted for 31 percent of all energy produced, was up 26 percent in the 1979–1989 period. Natural gas production accounted for 22 percent of energy produced and was up 33 percent during the period. However, worldwide production of oil and other liquid fuels, ac-

counting for 42 percent of commercial energy production, actually fell by 4 percent. The rest of the world's energy production is split almost equally between renewables and nuclear that accounts for only 5 percent of the total. A substantial increase in energy prices would give a significant boost to supplies of fossil fuels, and would also make renewable energy sources more attractive. In the early 1990s, energy production and consumption growth continued to slow and was nearly flat by 1994.

Anxieties about the adequacy of world energy and nonfuel mineral reserves have recently given way to concern over future market stability. Proven world petroleum reserves have grown steadily to nearly one trillion barrels in recent years, which represents about forty-six years of consumption at current rates. Add to this a considerable surplus of petroleum in storage as well as much excess production capacity around the world and a potential for discovering more reserves. The World Resources Institute reports a 200-year supply of alu-

Natural resources, including water and air, are required for survival. A rapidly expanding world population, expected to double by the year 2100, will undoubtedly deplete Earth's reserves of natural resources. (Raymond Gehman/Corbis)

minum in current reserves, a 175-year reserve of iron ore, and a 36-year supply of copper (all at present production rates).

Each person living in the industrialized countries consumes between ten and twenty times as much commercial energy as his or her counterparts living elsewhere.

These reserve figures may well understate the magnitude of future supplies since they are based on reserves that are known and economically recoverable at current prices. If a larger "reserve base" is used, composed of what is known to exist but not economically recoverable at today's prices, the depletion horizons are much extended. These perspectives should not be cause for complacency, however, because recent consumption figures have been gathered during years of economic stagnation. Should the global economy suddenly surge forward, resource consumption could quickly rise and depletion horizons would shorten dramatically.

World food production over the last two decades has kept slightly ahead of population growth. Production increases in many less industrialized countries, however, have not kept up with population. Expanded agricultural production in the industrial countries created large surpluses. Even as technology increases yields and more crops are grown on marginal lands, the specter of future global warming threatens possible major dislocations in world agricultural productivity.

Freshwater is likely to be the resource that most limits future food production. While the world has a tremendous supply of water, only 3 percent of it is fresh, the rest being saltwater in the world's oceans and inland seas. Of the small amount of freshwater available, 87 percent is locked in polar ice caps, glaciers, or other unreachable places. While there is still enough water to meet human needs on a global scale, local shortages are already apparent. The North China plain, which includes Beijing, could face a shortage of 6 percent of demand in only a few years. The Sahel region of West Africa has repeatedly suffered from severe drought and related famine, and the Middle East is a tinderbox of disputes over scarce water. The western part of the United States faces significant problems as the growing population presses up against available water supplies.

One future partial solution to freshwater scarcity is desalinization, but water gained from such processes currently can cost up to four times the price of water from other sources. Still, the World Resources Institute reports a doubling of desalinization plants, from 3,527 at the beginning of 1987 to 7,536 at the beginning of 1990.

The original pessimism about running out of raw materials, expressed in *The Limits to Growth,* now has been replaced by more sophisticated understanding of the problems of basic commodity markets. The major future resource threat to global economic security is maintaining a reliable and sustainable flow of natural resources from producing to consuming countries. If producing countries interrupt the flow of important basic commodities, particularly oil, prices would rise dramatically and destabilize the importing countries' economies. But if the importers cut back substantially on resource consumption, the less industrialized producers would be devastated.

The recent demise of the former Soviet Union has been a major destabilizing factor in resource markets. The tremendous decline in the economies of the former Soviet republics has lessened domestic resource requirements and spurred foreign sales. Thus, the Russian aluminum industry has been exporting into a glutted world market well below the costs of production among established Western manufacturers, thus creating a crisis in the aluminum market.

The current apparent abundance of fuels, food, and minerals should not give rise to complacency about the future. An upturn in the global economy, a major war, or a revolution in the Middle East could quickly destabilize resource markets. But even successfully meeting the industrialization goals to produce jobs for the growing populations of poorer countries would substantially alter future resource requirements and severely strain environmental services. Imagine, for example, the global resource impact of a future China elevated to just half the United States level of living.

Concern continues to mount over the ability of the atmosphere and hydrosphere, important "environmental sinks," to sustain future industrial growth. The build-up of carbon dioxide in the atmosphere, closely related to burning fossil fuels, threatens to increase global temperatures by one to three degrees Celsius over the next century. This could lead to major dislocations in world agriculture as well as a rise in sea level due largely to polar thawing.

Projected global warming, water shortages, and other natural resource problems have raised concern over the sustainability of the model of industrial progress that is now being emulated, more or less successfully, by many of the world's less industrialized countries. Questions about the long-term sustainability of the industrial way of life in a more densely populated world began to grow in the mid-1970s, and received official acknowledgement in the Bruntland Commission Report of 1987. The commission officially sanctioned a debate over the nature of sustainable development, defined as that which "meets the needs of the present without compromising the ability of future generations to meet their own needs." Some consider sustainable development a contradiction in terms. Others appropriated the term to their own causes, making sustainability an umbrella sheltering many different points of view.

Sustainability dialogue will occupy scholars and politicians well into the next century. The dialogue grows from a concern that future development take place within the long-term constraints of nature, and that the welfare of future generations be enhanced by current patterns of economic growth. The focus is on environmentally benign growth which uses fewer nonrenewable resources, shifts to renewables where possible, and stresses recycling as a way of easing environmental burdens. A transformation of values is also implicit in sustainable development, since meeting human needs while limiting human wants is part of the future agenda.

The 1992 United Nations Conference on the Environment and Development (UNCED) sharpened the dialogue between the industrially developed countries of the North and the less industrialized countries of the South. The debate over sustainable development now centers on the course of future industrial development in the South, the transfer of environmentally benign technologies from North to South, and proposed transfers of wealth to compensate the less industrialized countries that forego future development opportunities.

[See also Energy; Energy Conservation; Energy, Renewable Sources of; Freshwater; Global Warming.]

BIBLIOGRAPHY

Brown, Lester R., et al. *State of the World 1993*. New York: W. W. Norton, 1993.

Meadows, Donella H., et al. *Beyond the Limits*. Post Mills, VT: Chelsea Green, 1992.

Repetto, Robert C., ed. *The Global Possible: Resources, Development, and the New Century*. New Haven: Yale University Press, 1985.

World Commission on Environment and Development. *Our Common Future*. New York: Oxford University Press, 1987.

World Resources Institute. *World Resources 1994–95*. New York: Oxford University Press, 1994.

— DENNIS PIRAGES

RIGHT TO LIFE.

See ABORTION; FAMILY PLANNING.

ROBOTICS

Oscar Wilde contended that humankind required slavery. Indeed, Greek philosophers claimed that without someone to do the slow and boring work, in order to release the rest of humankind to dream and create, civilization would come to a standstill. Since the slavery of sentient beings is considered evil, immoral, and demoralizing, the advance of civilization depends upon the slavery of machines! Karel Čapek gave these machines a name. He called them *robota*, Czech for "obligatory work" or "servitude."

There were 500,000 robots in the world in 1992 compared to 16,000 in 1980; 400,000 of these were in Japan with only 40,000 in the United States. The growth of the service economy, the increased competition in the industrial economy and downsizing of corporations will increase the robot population as they replace humans. In the industrial area alone current trends indicate a worldwide work force of 1.2 to 1.5 million robots by 2001. This will result in a loss of 3 to 4 million jobs as robots continue to replace humans in the boring repetitive activities like assembly, welding, and painting, among others; and hazardous jobs such as, environmental cleanup, bomb disposal, oil rig maintenance, and so forth. It is estimated that robots will virtually replace humans in the manufacturing sector early in the twenty-first century.

Robots markedly increase productivity

because they do not take personal or sick leave,

require much less energy, do not quit,

and can work twenty-four hours a day.

There is a simple reason for this: Robots markedly increase productivity because they do not take personal or sick leave, require much less energy, do not quit, and can work twenty-four hours a day. Several automated factories in Japan already operate "lights out" with only a few humans present to monitor and maintain the computers and robots. New factories being built in the United States require much fewer workers than in the past as well. In addition, as U.S. manufacturers upgrade, they are replacing outmoded machinery, with flexible manufacturing systems (FMS) that employ robots to operate, service, and maintain high-tolerance advanced machine tools, and to assemble and package the finished products.

Processes such as computer-aided design and computer-aided manufacturing (CAD/CAM) are incorporating robots when planning the manufacturing process. Computer-integrated manufacturing (CIM) is bringing the factory under direct control of management through desktop manufacturing, and under indirect control of the customer through feedback. These advancements enable U.S. factories to produce customized products at lower costs than manufacturing with cheap labor in developing countries. Robots are making inroads in the service industry. They will eventually perform most janitorial activities. Robots will largely replace humans in the food service industry too, as increasing wages force owners to automate. MacDonalds will be replaced by MacRobot and will become a robotic automat. Banking also is being transformed; automated teller machines (ATMs)—robot tellers are everywhere.

Meanwhile, robots (under human tutelage) are building robots, *and* robots are building the robots that build robots. Feedback systems enable the robot-building robots to improve on the design; hence robots are evolving. Ongoing research and development (R&D) efforts are investigating the creation of self-replicating robots and factories. These self-replicating devices can be deposited in remote areas to literally grow a manufacturing facility and make specific products, using local raw materials, while getting power directly from the sun.

None of this bodes well for the unskilled worker; however, there are solutions to the worker displacement problem. Specifically by educating workers to design, develop, manufacture, supervise, and maintain the automation systems and robots that replaced them. These replacement jobs will be superior in quality to the assembly line jobs that are lost. In general, schools will prepare people for the service industry and other jobs created for the age of automation, information and knowledge. A unique process for coping with automation is presented in James Albus's book *People's Capitalism,* in which he outlines a program to replace people with robots slowly and with the least disruption through

This Mars rover was able to explore areas that humans could not reach. Robots can perform dangerous tasks that eliminate risk of human injury. (Roger Ressmeyer/© Corbis)

reeducation, government involvement, changes in monetary policy, changes in tax policies, and new approaches for people to obtain income.

Robots are encroaching on skilled jobs as well. Several chores in health care will be performed by robots. These include patient rehabilitation, assistance, and entertainment, as well as routine functions now performed by nurses and orderlies. Robots will assist doctors in performing delicate operations like eye surgery, brain surgery, and parts replacement. Eventually micro-robots (microbots) will be injected into a vein. These microbots will scurry through our bodies, keeping them clean and functioning as they probe for signs of deterioration and affect repairs. Other microbots will be programmed to seek out specific sites in the body, like the brain, the heart, the liver, or individual cells, and implant themselves. They will then monitor the functions or products of that site, and transmit this information to the outside world.

Eventually robots will be inexpensive enough to be used in the home. These robots will not be humanoid, using tools designed for humans; rather, they will be designed to perform particular tasks. Robots in general will not resemble the popular picture presented by movies and television; instead, they will be formed to fulfill a function: janitor robots may resemble large vacuum cleaners, robots that haul things will look like wagons, space robots will look like space ships, and so on. An outdoor robot could be a snow blower, a hedge trimmer, or a fertilizer spreader depending on the attachment installed. An indoor robot will vacuum, clean rugs, or polish floors, and with a little ingenuity maybe even wash windows. There will not be a kitchen robot per se, rather the kitchen *will be* a robot that will plan and prepare meals, and clean up afterward. Once they become affordable and useful, robots will multiply exponentially, like the telephone and the personal computer. Within ten years of introduction there could be 20 to 25 million robots in U.S. homes.

Other skilled tasks performed by robots will include: flying airplanes, with pilots acting as flight supervisors; driving trucks, with dispatchers controlling them from their home; or operating farm machinery (with a little positional information from satellites to ensure they are in the right field), under the management of the farmer sitting in her/his living room. In schools robots will be teaching assistants with the teachers being facilitators. The secretary or receptionist will be a virtual robot residing in an information system. A virtual traveler may use robots to tour distant lands.

Robots are already venturing into space. Early in the twenty-first century the self-replicating robots will build colonies and manufacturing facilities on the Moon, then mine asteroids and deliver raw materials to these colonies. Someday robots may terraform Mars and make it habitable for humans. Meanwhile, back on Earth, robots will be diving and trudging around on the ocean floors to retrieve the large nuggets of pure minerals that have formed there. Robots will build and maintain underwater colonies and assist humans in these colonies to monitor and operate underwater farms.

Robots of the future will have the power of vision, touch, speech, and speech recognition. They will ingest, digest, and incorporate information from these senses using signal processing, pattern recognition, inference machines, and learning attributes to make decisions and take action. Researchers are experimenting with neural network processing techniques that will provide the robot with learning and memory capabilities similar to humans. Further, these senses will enable robots to communicate easily with human beings. Robots will replace the seeing eye dog; they will talk for the mute; they will be able to feel and judge objects, weights; and textures with enough precision to lift a brick or an egg. Advanced medical techniques will permit a human to become a cyborg (a being part human and part machine), either by necessity or by choice. Using nanotechnology scientists will create devices that can be used to replace human parts: eyes, ears, internal organs, and skin—to name a few. Implanted math chips, language chips, telecommunications chips, and on-board expert systems chips will enhance the powers of the human brain. Exoskeletons will provide strength for those who need it: an arm, a leg, and even a whole body.

During the next century nanotechnology may produce the first android (a programmable robot biologically or chemically grown), either through the manipulation of molecules or the programming of DNA. Imagine creating a special-purpose android, equipped with gills and a functional tail for mobility, to work underwater. Including features such as eyes, ears, and arms will allow this android to farm and mine the ocean for human masters. Will these androids be human? Will they have feelings, emotions, desires? Will they rise in revolt and overthrow their masters? Will they replace the human race? All of these things are possible. All of them have been the stuff of science fiction for decades.

The robots around today are a small hint of the things to come. The robots of the future will truly become servants of human beings. They will provide the manual labor to provide all of the material things humans require and additional brain power to assist humans in things of the mind. They will finally release humans from the drudgeries of life and give them the freedom to do as they please, to exist in harmony, to create, to enjoy, to explore the universe.

[See also Factories and Manufacturing; Genetic Engineering; Genetics; Nanotechnology; Productivity; Science Fiction; Space Travel.]

BIBLIOGRAPHY

Albus, James S. *People's Capitalism: Economics of the Robot Revolution.* College Park, MD: New World Books, 1976.
————. *Brains, Behavior, and Robotics.* Peterborough, NH: BYTE Books, 1981.
Asimov, Isaac, and Frenkel, Karen A. *Robots: Machines in Man's Image.* New York: Harmony Books, 1985.
Connel, Jonathan H., and Mahadavan, Sridhar, eds. *Robot Learning.* Boston: Kluwer Academic Publishers, 1993.
Kosko, Bart. *Fuzzy Thinking: The New Science of Fuzzy Logic.* New York: Hyperion, 1993.
Safford, Edward L., Jr. *The Complete Handbook of Robotics.* Blue Ridge Summit, PA: TAB Books, 1980.
Tzafestas, Spyros G., ed. *Intelligent Robotic Systems.* New York: Marcel Dekker, 1991.

— BRIAN K. TOREN

ROCKETRY.

See SPACE FLIGHT.

RUSSIA

The political future of Russia is vitally important but difficult to predict. The forces of nationalism which disintegrated the Soviet Union also threaten the Russian Federation. Russians constitute 82 percent of the population, but there are over 100 other ethnic groups and 20 areas with ethnic populations sufficiently large to constitute autonomous republics. In addition to Chechnya, where there has been bloody fighting, secessionist movements also exist in Tatarstan, Dagestan, the Tuva Republics, and Northern Ingushetia. Besides ethnic separatism, the desire for independence is sometimes fueled by the desire to fully control rich natural resources, such as the oil in Tatarstan or the diamonds, natural gas, timber, and other natural resources of Siberia.

These forces for independence, however, are countered by long associations with Moscow, strong economic interdependence with the rest of Russia, the cost and weakness of a small state providing for its own national security, and the frequent absence of clear ethnic boundaries. Moscow's role in regional affairs will continue to decrease, allowing local cultures to prevail and administration of public sector activities to improve, but few if any splinter states are likely to emerge because of the forces mentioned above and Russian determination to hold key areas. Over time, economic progress will reduce ethnic tensions and secessionist tendencies.

These same centripetal forces will probably bring closer ties between Russia and other republics of the former Soviet Union. The relationship which emerges between Russia and Ukraine will be particularly important to both republics. Many sources of tension exist, including a predominantly Russian population in the Crimean portion of Ukraine, but economic interdependence, particularly Ukraine's need for Russian oil, will encourage increasing cooperation.

Extreme Russian nationalists and unreformed Communists might conceivably reestablish an authoritarian government if economic hardships and rampant crime continue or separatism grows stronger. However, there also are signs favorable to democracy. The August 1991 coup attempt had little popular support. A large, well-educated middle class has been exposed to Western ideas, and younger Russians are less inclined than their elders to accept state authority. Independent media and democratic elections have taken hold.

Despite Soviet military disarray after the U.S.S.R. breakup, Russia is likely to remain a major military power. Lengthy borders, uncertain relations with neighbors, a large, well-trained officer corps, advanced equipment, and a long military tradition point to continuing prominence. Nuclear forces, though reduced to a fraction of Cold War levels, will be retained as a deterrent.

Its seat on the UN Security Council and powerful military forces will keep Russia a major player in international relations. Because economic and political interests go hand-in-hand, Russia will seek to maintain good relations with the United States, Europe (particularly Germany), Japan, China, Korea, and the Middle East.

Fertility rates for ethnic Russians are likely to remain at or below the replacement rate; the non-Russian population has had higher fertility rates, but these are decreasing and probably will continue to do so. Some increase in the present population of just under 150 million will probably result from inward migration by some of the 26 million Russians in the other former Soviet republics. This migration could reach millions if economic hardship in neighboring republics or discrimination against Russians living there worsens. In twenty years the population may reach 160 million—with the percentage of Russians remaining about the same. Political turbulence, however, could also spur large-scale migration to the West.

Urbanization will continue, following the worldwide pattern for developed countries. As agriculture becomes more productive and the infrastructure improves, the large gap in living conditions between urban and rural areas will decrease.

The Russian economy is as difficult to predict as the political future. Privatization appears irreversible, but questions remain about the level of government regulation, the pace of macroeconomic reform, and how to soften the impact of change.

The Russian economy is as difficult to predict

as the political future.

Privatization appears irreversible,

but questions remain

about the level of government regulation.

In the past, Russia needed to import large amounts of food. The high ratio of arable land to people provides the potential for Russia to become an agricultural net exporter—as it was before World War I. Privatization will increase motivation; technical assistance from the West can increase yields and, coupled with infrastructure improvements, decrease spoilage losses.

The outlook for manufacturing is not so good. Few factories are capable of competing in global markets. To build a modern industrial base will require investing hundreds of billions of dollars.

The future of the Russian economy will be determined by how well the Russian government creates a climate attractive to foreign investment and how well it encourages savings and investment over consumption as the economy grows. Aided by its enormous natural resources—oil, natural gas, coal, forests, and mineral deposits—the Russian economy could approach Western European performance levels within twenty-five years.

A very pessimistic economic scenario also is possible. To date, Russia has attracted little foreign investment—and the technology and know-how which come with it—because of uncertainties over ownership of assets, shifting regulations and laws (including taxes), and overlapping jurisdiction among levels of government. Xenophobia, lack of understanding of the value of capital, and the absence of a developed banking system also impede foreign investment. In a country where unemployment has been virtually unknown, creating efficient enterprises will require tolerating levels of unemployment, which could lead to labor unrest and work stop-

pages. Another problem that could get worse is the occurrence of production shutdowns due to a lack of raw materials or components previously supplied by other republics.

The well-educated Russian workforce favors economic growth. Under communism no attention was paid to productivity, cost reduction, or quality. Privatization and foreign investment will change this—and experience has shown that young Russian workers perform very well when given proper training and incentives. New programs will teach managerial skills and nurture the work ethic necessary in a market economy.

Women in Russia traditionally have been relegated to lower-paid jobs, and their ability to compete with men has been crippled by the time required for shopping and household chores. As managers, pressured by competition, pay more attention to who performs best, opportunities for women will improve. While women will continue to do most household chores, these will become less time-consuming as shopping becomes more efficient, convenience foods become available, and household appliances become better and more reliable.

The large network of scientific and research institutes will undergo major changes in the next few years because of less government funding. Part of the expected downsizing will result from emigration of scientists, part from attrition. In the past, members of these institutes did little teaching or nonmilitary research; in the future, most will work part-time or full-time in higher education or industrial research. Despite transitional problems, Russian science will remain world-class in areas like theoretical physics, mathematics, nuclear science, and astronomy.

Major environmental policy changes will take place. In the past, little attention was paid in the U.S.S.R. to the environmental consequences of the single-minded pursuit of economic growth. Chernobyl is the most infamous environmental disaster, but there have been many others. Huge investments must be made to prevent further damage, and the cost of cleanups to improve health conditions will be very large.

Environmental neglect has created a strong environmental movement, which not only prevented construction of new facilities that would cause environmental problems (e.g., a plant to destroy chemical weapons), but has shut down existing polluting facilities. Past environmental disasters may make Russia insistent on balancing economic development with long-range environmental needs—in much the same way that Hiroshima made Japan so opposed to nuclear weapons.

One safe prediction is that health care will improve. Even special clinics previously reserved for elites lack equipment routinely available in the West, and most Russians cannot get medicines available to the poorest Western patients. The abysmal state of health care has become widely recognized in Russia; while it will be many years before the care available to ordinary citizens will approach that in the West, widespread public knowledge of this need and the enormous market for improved health care products should result in improvements within a relatively short time.

In many areas what happens in Russia will largely parallel what happens in the rest of the world. A global culture (in the broadest sense) is emerging as a result of mass media, and over 90 percent of Russian homes have television sets connecting them to the outside world.

BIBLIOGRAPHY

Conquest, Robert, ed. *The Last Empire: Nationality and the Soviet Future.* Stanford, CA: Hoover Institution Press, 1986.

Feshbach, Murray, and Friendly, Alfred Jr. *Ecocide in the U.S.S.R.* New York: Basic Books, 1992.

Hecht, James L., ed. *Rubles and Dollars.* New York: Harper Business, 1991.

Hosking, Geoffrey. *The Awakening of the Soviet Union.* Cambridge, MA: Harvard University Press, 1990.

Hough, Jerry. *Russia and the West.* New York: Simon & Schuster, 1988.

Smith, Hedrick. *The New Russians.* New York: Random House, 1990.

Yergin, Daniel, and Gustafson, Thane. *Russia 2010 and What It Means for the World.* New York: Random House, 1993.

(The views expressed in this article are the opinions of the authors and do not necessarily represent the opinions or positions of the U.S. government or of any of its agencies.)

— JAMES L. HECHT
LAWRENCE E. MODISETT

S

SAFETY, FOOD AND DRUG.

See FOOD AND DRUG SAFETY; FOOD LAWS.

SATELLITE COMMUNICATIONS

Most communications satellites are placed in a geostationary orbit 22,300 miles (36,000 kilometers) above the equator, a concept first envisioned by Arthur C. Clarke in 1945. At this altitude the geostationary satellite takes twenty-four hours to travel around Earth, appearing to remain stationary as Earth rotates on its axis. Signals are transmitted from Earth stations to the satellite and back to one or more receiving stations. Typically, the satellite simply receives and amplifies the signal, changes its frequency, and retransmits it to Earth. More intelligent satellites have "on-board processing" in which the signal may be switched to a specific site or data may be stored. Future satellites will relay the signal from one satellite to another, avoiding the delay required when a signal must "double-hop" through two satellites or from a small station to a master station and again through the satellite to another small station to reach its destination.

Some satellites, known as "LEOs" (low Earth-orbiting satellites), operate in much lower orbits, appearing to pass overhead several times per day. An example of a simple LEO is the Oscar satellite used by radio amateurs. Small, inexpensive terminals transmit data to the satellite when it passes overhead. The satellite then reads the address of the message, stores the data, and forwards the message to the receiving terminal. Several companies have proposed to operate multiple-satellite LEO systems that would be accessible by small, handheld receivers from virtually anywhere on Earth.

Since the first commercial satellite transmissions in the early 1960s, communications satellites have come to be taken for granted. Live global television coverage of the Olympics and the World Cup, as well as of natural disasters and political upheavals, reaches hundreds of millions of viewers. Nightly television news programs carry stories from around the world. Less obvious are the many satellite networks that carry information about orders, sales transactions, and inventory levels from thousands of retailers to their headquarters or command centers. Satellites also have extended the range of education: Students in rural schools can take high school science and foreign language courses via satellite; professionals can watch televised lectures delivered via satellite to study for advanced degrees without leaving their workplace.

Satellites are used for a wide range of applications that can be divided into point-to-point and point-to-multipoint or broadcasting communications. Point-to-point applications include: transmitting telephone traffic from one location to another (for example, to link

---

Satellites are particularly important to developing countries, where they can bring telephone and broadcasting services to villages far from urban centers.

---

villages in remote areas, and to link developing countries where terrestrial networks are very limited); transmitting data (such as financial transactions for banks, airline reservations, and credit card verifications); and transmitting video signals from one place to another (such as for a video teleconference or for a video feed from a remote location to a television station). Broadcasting applications include: distribution of television programs to numerous television stations or cable television head-ends, and transmission of data such as stock market reports and weather forecasts to multiple receiving sites. Transmission of television programs directly to households equipped with small receiving antennas is called direct broadcasting via satellite (DBS). DBS systems are now used in Western Europe and Japan, and are on the verge of being introduced in North America.

Satellites are particularly important to developing countries, where they can bring telephone and broadcasting services to villages far from urban centers. Some developing countries and regions such as the Arab states, Brazil, India, Indonesia, and Mexico have their own domestic satellites; other countries and regions in Africa, Latin America, Southeast Asia, and the South Pacific are planning to get satellites of their own. These satellites will help to overcome the isolation of millions of people by providing them with reliable communications for the first time.

Satellite Earth stations vary in diameter from nearly 100 feet for large INTELSAT stations that carry thousands of channels of voice or data traffic between countries or continents to very small-aperture terminals (VSATs) as small as two feet in diameter. VSATs may be installed on rooftops or even in windowsills to pick up television or data signals. Some VSATs are used for interactive data communications, such as transmitting point-of-sale data from department stores and gas stations. Somewhat larger Earth stations approximately ten feet in diameter have been installed in backyards and on hotels in North America to pick up television signals from satellites in areas where there are no cable systems, or to pick up specialized programming, or for videoconferencing. In some locations, zoning restrictions may make it difficult to install such antennas; however, the smallest VSATs are very unobtrusive and unlikely to be aesthetically objectionable.

As terrestrial optical-fiber-based networks become more widespread, some people wonder whether satellites will become obsolete. It is more likely, however, that they will become increasingly specialized and used for several growing applications:

- basic telecommunications to remote locations, particularly in the developing world, where terrestrial facilities are cost-prohibitive and not available

- broadcasting of video or data to multiple locations through pay television channels to millions of homes and through news service information to thousands of offices

- interactive, low-volume data communications from multiple sites or remote locations, such as point-of-sale and inventory data from hundreds of stores, and monitoring data from remote pipelines and oil rigs

- mobile and eventually personal communications from small transceivers mounted on vehicles or carried in a briefcase, or even in one's purse or pocket

- transmission of very-high-quality broadcast signals such as digital audio for direct reception by small radio receivers, and reception of high-definition television (HDTV), including digitized video that will have very high resolution

Communications satellites will continue to be important for services that take advantage of their assets

An Eskimo uses a global positioning system (GPS) to find his way on a hunting trip. One private company plans to use 280 satellites in order to provide less expensive GPS service. (Caroline Penn/Corbis)

that include cost insensitivity to distance; wide coverage of countries, continents, or oceans; and flexibility in the location of facilities without the need for terrestrial links. As Arthur C. Clarke has forecast, every call will be "local" and long-distance charges will be eliminated.

[See also Clarke, Arthur Charles; Communications; Communications: Technology; Computer Linkage; Digital Communications; Electronic Convergence; Media Consolidation; Space Satellites; Telecommunications; Telephones.]

BIBLIOGRAPHY

Baylin, Frank. *Satellites Today: The Guide to Satellite Television.* Indianapolis, IN: Howard A. Sams, 1986.

Codding, George A., Jr. *The Future of Satellite Communications.* Boulder, CO: Westview, 1990.

Hudson, Heather E. *Communication Satellites: Their Development and Impact.* New York: Free Press, 1990.

Rees, David W. *Satellite Communications: The First Quarter Century of Service.* New York: John Wiley & Sons, 1990.

— HEATHER E. HUDSON

SAVINGS

Economists have been warning for years that the rate of savings in the United States may be too low to sustain the level of investment and economic growth needed to produce a desirable future. Net domestic investment is currently about 3.8 percent of gross domestic product, about half the level of the 1960s. Household saving as a percentage of disposable income is about 4.6 percent, down from 9.1 percent in 1981 and far below that of other OECD countries (for example, 14.6 percent in Japan, 12.1 percent in Germany).

Why is saving so low in the United States? One reason is the method of measurement: under current practices, different forms of saving, like business investment, consumer durables, education, research and development, are not counted as such. Another reason is simply the fact that the United States is such a wealthy country: a high ratio of capital to labor means a lower rate of return on capital (and therefore on saving). A third reason lies in the tax code: through high marginal tax rates on corporate dividends, capital gains, estates, profits, retirement, investment and interest income, the government double-taxes, and even triple-taxes, saving.

On the other hand, maybe it is mostly a matter of demographics. According to the life cycle hypothesis of saving, people save more as they age, and the American population *is* aging. By the year 2020, one out of every six Americans will be sixty-five or over; by 2050, one in every five. Indeed, according to a recent McKinsey & Company analysis, the United States and most of the rest of the developed world is about to experience an incredible saving surge, due to aging populations and an integrating global capital market (which places real limits on government indebtedness and inflationary inclinations).

In the United States the baby-boom cohort—those Americans born between 1946 and 1964—are entering the period in their life cycle when they will save at higher rates. This means that they will enter their peak years for financial asset accumulation over the next two decades. In fact, high-savers as a percentage of the total workforce will peak at 55 percent in the year 2010.

What will these savings add up to? McKinsey projected that the supply of net household financial assets in the developed world will increase by nearly $12 trillion in real terms over a ten-year period. And because the global capital market is increasingly acting as one single market operating under the law of one price, it seems likely that these savings will be well invested.

In other words, the discipline that a unified global market brings to bear on investors means that money will flow to where it has the best prospects for healthy returns at comparatively lower risk. This will induce developing nations to grow and modernize faster to attract and retain investment, and it will induce *all* governments to limit indebtedness that either funds consumption or creates inflation.

McKinsey concluded that the returns from these investments may be sufficient to provide the baby-boom generation with comfortable retirements while at the same time stimulating worldwide economic growth. Indeed, they view this "best case" scenario as the most likely outcome.

An analysis by economists at the New York Federal Reserve Bank is not so sanguine. They examine the demographic argument—that baby boomers will start to save more as they age through the life cycle's saving stages—and find it inadequate. They argue that any rise in baby-boomer saving rates will be offset by a continued high rate of early retirement and an increasing share of households headed by people over sixty-five and under thirty-five—those who usually save little.

In 1990, when boomers were twenty-five to forty-four, they headed 41 million households, about 44 percent of the total. By 2010, when baby boomers will be between forty-five and sixty-four, they will head about 46 million households, or only 39 percent of the total. This relative decline will diminish baby boomers' potential impact on the aggregate savings rate, according to New York Fed economists.

But perhaps they are too pessimistic. A recent survey for the Employee Benefit Research Institute found that 61 percent of today's workers are saving for retirement, and started saving at an average age of thirty. By comparison, only 55 percent of today's retirees saved for retirement, and those savers did not start saving until they were thirty-eight.

According to the U.S. Department of Labor, more than 25 million workers have 401(k) income deferment accounts, up from only 2.7 million ten years ago. There is about $500 billion invested in 401(k) plans, with about $50 billion a year in new money pouring in. The higher the age and wage, the more likely the participation. But it is not just older, better-paid workers who are stashing it away: at companies offering 401(k) plans, nearly 70 percent of workers of ages thirty-one to fifty participate, as do 50 percent of workers with salaries under $20,000—both shares up sharply from just five years ago.

A private Social Security system could boost savings, restrain interest rates, and provide the economy with hundreds of billions of dollars yearly for investments.

To ensure a future of savings sufficient to guarantee investment and economic growth, we need to restore incentives to saving. Reducing the federal deficit, a highly likely prospect by 2002, with or without a balanced budget amendment to the Constitution, would be the swiftest and most certain way to boost national savings. The most effective way to promote savings by families and individuals would be to scrap the income tax and replace it with a consumption tax, a real possibility within the next ten years. Short of that, a broad expansion of Individual Retirement Account (IRA) and 401(k) plans would be a good place to start.

Congress adopted IRAs in 1981; every worker could put $2,000 a year, deductible from income for tax purposes, into an IRA. Couples with just one wage earner could save $3,000. But just five years later Congress passed the Tax Reform Act of 1986, which severely restricted tax-deductible contributions to IRAs. Congress adopted 401(k)s in 1978, but it has also more recently restricted the amounts that can be contributed to the plans.

The tax code is plainly one of the major reasons Americans do not save more. High tax rates reduce the ability and incentive to save, as does the Social Security payroll tax, which has been hiked 32 percent since 1980 and 60 percent since 1970. Social Security taxes depress saving because people have come to rely on the Social Security program to fund their retirements. But Social Security was designed to be a small, supplemental source of need-based income, not a general retirement fund. Besides, there *is* no trust fund: recipients are paid out of current income.

Eighty-two percent of Americans aged eighteen to thirty-four want the freedom to invest all or part of their Social Security payments in private retirement accounts. Most senior citizens also endorse the idea. A private Social Security system would boost savings, restrain interest rates, and provide the economy with hundreds of billions of dollars yearly for investments. This could happen by 2010, the year the first baby boomers turn sixty-five.

[See also Capital Formation; Credit, Debt, and Borrowing; Deficits, Governmental; Economics; Estate and Financial Planning; Financial Institutions; Human Resources Development; Insurance; Investments; Wealth.]

BIBLIOGRAPHY

Bryan, Lowell, and Farrell, Diana. "The Savings Surge." *The Wall Street Journal,* November 7, 1994.

Ehrban, Al. "How Washington Can Stop Its War on Savings." *Fortune* (March 6, 1995).

Modigliani, Franco. "Life Cycle, Individual Thrift, and the Wealth of Nations." *The American Economic Review* (June 1986).

Novak, Janet. "Hey, Big Saver." *Forbes* (December 19, 1994).

"Whatever Happened to That Rainy Day?" *The Economist* (January 21, 1995).

"Why Do People Really Save?" *Business Week* (February 27, 1995).

— ROGER SELBERT

SCANNING

Scanning is a futures research tool that allows us to integrate our understanding of various sectors of the external environment and their relationships with systematically collected macroenvironmental information to obtain early warning of change. Scanning provides strategic intelligence useful in determining strategic options. In the context of strategic planning, scanning is one analytic component. Analysis consists of scanning environments to identify changing trends and potential developments, monitoring them, forecasting their future patterns, and assessing their impacts. Combined with an internal analysis of an organization's vision, mission, strengths, and weaknesses, external analysis assists in planning.

Fahey and Narayanan (1986) describe three environmental levels. The *task environment* refers to a set of customers. The *industry environment* comprises all enterprises within a particular industry. At the broadest level is the *macroenvironment,* which includes the Social, Technological, Economic, Environmental, and Political (or STEEP) sectors. Changes in one sector at any level (local, national, or global) may lead to changes in another. A war in the Middle East may cause the price of oil to increase, thus stimulating a recession, in turn resulting in budget cuts. Technological developments in California that enable the conversion of wind power to low-cost energy may be introduced worldwide, thereby reducing the costs of fossil fuel energy, with concomitant economic ramifications. Thus, developments in the macroenvironment can affect developments in the task and industrial environments. This point underscores the necessity of scanning the macroenvironment, as well as the task and industrial environments, to pick up the early signals of change that may affect one's organization or activities.

Scanning can be conceptualized in a number of ways. Aguilar (1967) identified four collection modes:

- *Undirected viewing* consists of reading a variety of publications for no specific purpose other than to be informed.
- *Conditioned viewing* consists of responding to this information in terms of assessing its relevance to the organization.
- *Informal searching* consists of actively seeking specific information but in a relatively unstructured way.
- *Formal searching* is a more actively organized attempt to devise methodologies for obtaining information for specific purposes.

Morrison, Renfro, and Boucher (1984) describe two modes: passive and active scanning. *Passive scanning* is what most people do when they read journals and newspapers. For serious news coverage, many read the same kinds of materials: a local newspaper, perhaps a national newspaper like the *New York Times* or *Wall Street Journal,* and an industry or trade newspaper. People are less inclined to read narrow-interest periodicals when passively scanning. The organizational consequences of passive scanning are that we do not systematically use the information as intelligence to benefit the organization, and, furthermore, we may miss ideas signalling changes in the macroenvironment that could affect the organization. Consequently, to broaden our perspectives and to fight inherent myopia, a more active scanning is required. Such active scanning focuses attention on information resources that span a broad area of concern, including the technological, economic, social, and political sectors, at the local, regional, national, and global level.

Fahey, King, and Narayanan (1981) have defined the typology of active scanning. *Irregular* scanning systems are used on an ad hoc basis and are often initiated by specific crises. This approach is used when planners need information for making assumptions, and is conducted for that purpose only. *Periodic* systems are invoked when periodically required to update previous scans, perhaps in preparation for a new planning cycle. *Continuous* systems use the active scanning mode of data collection to systematically inform users. This mode limits potentially relevant "data" only in terms of one's conception of the relevant macroenvironment. Scanning data derived from a host of varied sources is inherently scattered, vague, and imprecise. Because early signals often show up in unexpected places, the scanning purview must be broad, ongoing, and sufficiently comprehensive to cover the environments important to users or to an organization.

The important criterion for literature selection is diversity. Information can be obtained from books, newspapers, magazines, journals, television and radio programs, computer bulletin boards and other on-line services, and from knowledgable individuals. There is no lack of available information resources. *Future Survey Annual 1988–1989* lists some 454 futures-relevant periodicals, including 46 publications in international economics and development, 45 in environment/resources/energy, and 31 in health and human services (Marien, 1991, p. 86).

Existing environmental scans provide ready-made surveys. United Way of America publishes *What Lies Ahead* on a biennial basis. The World Future Society publishes *Future Survey,* a monthly abstract of books, articles, and reports containing forecasts, trends, and ideas about the future. The Global Network publishes *John Naisbitt's Trend Letter,* and Kiplinger Washington Editors publish the *Kiplinger Washington Letter.*

Because early signals often show up in unexpected places, the scanning purview must be broad, ongoing, and sufficiently comprehensive to cover the environments important to users or to an organization.

Other general-interest sources are as follows:

- Newspapers—*New York Times, Washington Post, Wall Street Journal, Miami Herald, Chicago Tribune, Los Angeles Times, Christian Science Monitor,* and *The Times* (of London).
- Magazines—*Vital Speeches of the Day, Across the Board, Time, Newsweek, U.S. News and World Report, Atlantic, The Nation, Ms, The Futurist,* and *Whole Earth Review.*

Adequate scanning of the macroenvironment requires identifying specific information resources for each STEEP category. Some information sources organized by category for the macroenvironment should include the following:

1. Social/demographic/values/lifestyles literature—*American Demographics, Public Opinion* and data from periodic publications or statistics from the Census Bureau, other federal, state, and local governmental agencies,

and university sociology departments or population study centers. The Department of Labor and the National Technical and Information Services generate specific types of demographic analyses. The National Center for Health Statistics provides data on trends in areas such as fertility and life expectancy. The U.S. League of Savings Associations studies changes in home-buyer demographics, and the American Council of Life Insurance's Social Research Services conducts demographic studies. The UN and OECD publish periodic reports detailing international developments in these areas.

2. Technological literature— *Technology Review, Datamation, Byte, Computer World, Discover, InfoWorld, Science, Scientific American, Proceedings of the National Academy of Sciences,* and *Issues in Science and Technology.*

3. Economic literature— *Business Week, The Economist, Fortune, Forbes, Money, Inc.,* and *The Monthly Labor Review.* Data may also be obtained from Department of Commerce Bureau of Economic Analysis monthly reports as well as reports from the Departments of Labor, Energy, and Treasury. State and local governmental agencies provide regional economic data.

4. Environmental literature— *Ecodecision* (Royal Society of Canada) and *Environment.* Several organizations publish future-oriented reports on the environment—the Global Tomorrow Coalition, the Worldwatch Institute, the World Resources Institute, the Audubon Society, and the Sierra Club.

5. Political literature— *New Republic, The National Review, The Nation, The National Journal, In These Times, Mother Jones, Federal Register, Congressional Quarterly, Weekly Report,* and *Digest of Public General Bills.* Other sources include public opinion leaders, social critics, futures-oriented research establishments (e.g., the Hudson Institute, the Institute for the Future), public policy research centers (e.g., Brookings Institution, the American Enterprise Institute), governmental documents (e.g., public hearings, congressional hearings), proposed bills to the legislature, and statements or opinions by experts or activists. *State Legislatures* (National Conference of State Legislatures) provides a periodic summary of pertinent legislation being considered in state legislatures throughout the country.

Information resources for scanning the task environment include local, state, and regional newspapers, local and state government reports as well as experts in demography, sociology, and political science departments in local colleges and universities. Perhaps one of the most useful information resources consists of networks of friends and colleagues within the organization and in the industry.

Electronic databases containing up-to-date descriptions of articles (by title and, many times, by abstract) are available by subscription. Abstracted Business Information (ABI Inform) and Public Affairs Information Service (PAIS) are two such databases. Two database services, Dialogue and BRS, contain hundreds more databases specializing in many areas. Many libraries already subscribe to these databases and database services.

In conclusion, most everyone does passive scanning. However, active scanning is required to enhance abilities to understand, anticipate, and respond to the threats and opportunities posed by changes in the external environment. Active scanning is a part of any level of scanning—irregular, periodic, or continuous.

Environmental scanning is only one component of external analysis. However, it is the starting point for identifying critical trends and potential events, monitoring them, and forecasting where they are going. Comprehensive external analysis is not only an enriching development experience; more importantly, it provides a basis for discerning the strategic direction of your organization from which you may plan far more effectively.

[See also Data Storage; Forecasting Methods; On-Line Services; Planning.]

BIBLIOGRAPHY

Aguilar, Francis. *Scanning the Business Environment.* New York: Macmillan, 1967.

Fahey, Liam, King, William R., and Narayanan, V. K. "Environmental Scanning and Forecasting in Strategic Planning: The State of the Art." *Long Range Planning* 14 (1981): 32–39.

Fahey, Liam, and Narayanan, V. K. *Macroenvironmental Analysis for Strategic Management.* New York: West Publishing Company, 1986.

Marien, Michael. "Scanning: An Imperfect Activity in an Era of Fragmentation and Uncertainty." *Futures Research Quarterly* 7 (1991): 82–90.

Morrison, James L., Renfro, William L., and Boucher, Wayne I. *Futures Research and the Strategic Planning Process.* Washington, DC: Association for the Study of Higher Education, 1984.

— JAMES L. MORRISON

SCENARIOS

Today's organizations face tremendous structural change and uncertainty: globalization, multiculturalism, internal diversity, technological innovation, and decisions with huge risks and consequences. Anticipating the future in this volatile environment calls for more than systematic analysis: it demands creativity, insight, and intuition. Scenarios—stories or story outlines about possible futures—combine these elements to create robust strategies. The test of a good scenario is not whether it portrays the future accurately but whether it helps an organization to learn and adapt.

By definition, a scenario is a tool for ordering one's perceptions about alternative future environments in which today's decisions might play out. In practice, scenarios resemble a set of stories built around carefully constructed plots. Stories are an old way of organizing knowledge; as planning tools, they discourage denial by enabling the willing suspension of disbelief. Stories can express multiple perspectives on complex events; scenarios give meaning to these events.

Scenarios are powerful precisely because the future is unpredictable. Unlike traditional forecasting or market research, which extrapolate from current trends, scenarios present alternative images. Scenarios also embrace qualitative perspectives and potential discontinuities that econometric models exclude. Consequently, creating scenarios requires decision makers to question their broadest assumptions about how the world works so they can foresee the consequences of decisions that might be missed or denied; what has not been foreseen is unlikely to be seen in time. Organizationally, scenarios add value by providing a common vocabulary and effective basis for communicating complex—sometimes paradoxical—conditions and options.

The legacy of scenarios is not a more accurate picture of tomorrow, but the ability to help make better long-term decisions today.

Scenario planning is a highly intense and imaginative process that follows systematic and recognizable phases. It begins by isolating the decision to be made and rigorously challenging the mental maps that shape one's perceptions. The next steps are more analytical: identifying and prioritizing the driving forces (social, technological, economic, environmental, political, and technological), the predetermined elements (i.e., what is inevitable, like demographics already "in the pipeline"), and the critical uncertainties (i.e., what is unpredictable or willfully chosen, such as matters of public policy).

These exercises culminate in two or three carefully constructed scenario "plots"—typically an evolutionary and extrapolative business-as-usual approach buttressed by an optimistic as well as a pessimistic speculation. Another perspective might involve scenarios that are preferable, probable, and possible. If the scenarios are to function as useful learning tools, the lessons they teach must be relevant to the key decision. Whatever the framework, only a few scenarios can be developed fully and remembered; these should represent credible alternative futures, not a best case/worst case/most likely continuum. Once the scenarios are embellished and woven into a narrative, their implications are identified along with the leading indicators to be monitored.

Good scenarios are plausible and surprising; they have the power to break old stereotypes; and their creators assume ownership and put them to work. Using scenarios is rehearsing the future; by recognizing the warning signs and the unfolding drama, one can avoid being overwhelmed by surprises and consequently can adapt and act effectively. Decisions that have been pretested against a range of what the future may offer are more likely to stand the test of time, to produce robust and resilient strategies, and to create a competitive advantage. The act of scenario planning is a mainstay in anticipating the future and planning strategically in an uncertain and rapidly changing world. Ultimately, the legacy of scenarios is not a more accurate picture of tomorrow, but the ability to help make better long-term decisions today.

[See also Forecasting, Deterministic; Forecasting Methods; Surprises; Technology Forecasting and Assessment; Trend Indicators; Wildcards.]

BIBLIOGRAPHY

Coates, Joseph F. "A Chrestomathy of Flawed Forecasts." *Technology Forecasting and Social Change* 45/3 (March 1994).

Coyle, R. G., Crawshay, W. and Sutton, L. "Futures Assessment by Field Anomaly Relaxation: A Review and Appraisal." *Futures* 26/1 (January–February 1994).

Drucker, Peter F. *The Ecological Vision: Reflections on the American Condition.* New Brunswick, NJ: Transaction Publishers, 1993.

Godet, Michel. *Scenarios and Strategic Management.* London and Stoneham, MA: Butterworths, 1987.

Heilbroner, Robert. *Visions of the Future: The Distant Past, Yesterday, Today, and Tomorrow.* New York: The New York Public Library/ Oxford University Press, 1995.

Makridakis, Spyros G. *Forecasting, Planning, and Strategy for the 21st Century.* New York: The Free Press, 1990.

Morrison, J. Ian. "The Futures Tool Kit." *Across the Board* 31/1 (January 1994).

Schnaars, Steven P. "How to Develop and Use Scenarios." *Long Range Planning* 20/1 (February 1987).

Schwartz, Peter. *The Art of the Long View: Planning for the Future in an Uncertain World.* New York: Doubleday/Currency Book, 1991.

Wagar, Warren W. "A Funny Thing Happened on My Way to the Future: Or, The Hazards of Prophecy." *The Futurist* 28/3 (May–June 1994).

— PETER SCHWARTZ

SCHUMPETER, JOSEPH A. (1883–1950)

The American economist Joseph Schumpeter was born in what is now the Czech Republic. Educated in Vienna, he taught at the universities of Graz and Bonn. He moved to the United States in 1932, where he joined the faculty of Harvard University and became a naturalized American citizen. His earlier theoretical works offered an analysis of capitalism as a dynamic system fueled by the innovations of bold entrepreneurs. The less daring, faceless organization men who take their place, he argued, are ultimately responsible for the slumps that follow times of prosperity. In his most important futures-oriented book, *Capitalism, Socialism, and Democracy* (1942), Schumpeter foresaw the recovery of modern capitalism from the Great Depression of the 1930s, but he did not believe it could survive in the long run. Abandoned by the intelligentsia and subject to decay from within, capitalism would eventually give way to socialism or some other form of public control of wealth. Among Schumpeter's other major works are *Theorie der wirtschaftlichen Entwicklung* (1912; in English, *The Theory of Economic Development,* 1934) and a massive two-volume study, *Business Cycles: A Theoretical, Historical, and Statistical Analysis of the Capitalist Process* (1939).

BIBLIOGRAPHY

Allen, Robert Loring. *Opening Doors: The Life and Work of Joseph Schumpeter.* New Brunswick, NJ: Transaction Publishers, 1991.

Bottomore, Tom. *Between Marginalism and Marxism: The Economic Sociology of J. A. Schumpeter.* New York: St. Martin's Press, 1992.

Swedberg, Richard. *Schumpeter: A Biography.* Princeton, NJ: Princeton University Press, 1991.

Wood, John Cunningham, ed. *J. A. Schumpeter: Critical Assessments.* New York: Routledge, 1991.

— W. WARREN WAGAR

SCIENCE CITIES

The present concept of the science city or technopolis began with Silicon Valley and was followed some thirty years later by Sophia Antipolis in the South of France (1969), and Tsukuba Science City in Japan (1970). The technopolis is a city of acceptable size that can be part of an international community but still retain the capability to organize and focus activities locally. Its overall success will depend on the socioeconomic conditions of the international community. The technopolis concept is an attempt to reinvent the city, but its development remains outside the mainstream of urban change and in its current form it is not seen as a solution for major urban problems.

The core concept is stated in Kozmetsky's *Technopolis Phenomenon:* "The technopolis is an innovative approach to economic development that involves linking technology commercialization with effective public- and private-sector initiatives to create new infrastructures for economic growth, diversification, and global competitiveness."

Silicon Valley in the suburbs of San Francisco, California, with its legendary garage startups, such as Hewlett Packard and Apple, became a magnet to attract many other new companies, and by the 1960s it had become the envy of other countries. In 1983 Japan's Ministry of International Trade and Industry (MITI) succeeded in passing legislation for its technopolis concept.

Japan, seeking solutions for population distribution and urban/rural problems, began planning in 1958, but started construction in 1970 of Tsukuba Science City at the heart of an area expected to reach 700,000 in population by the year 2000. Tsukuba Science City includes research universities, science centers (technocenters), industrial research parks, R&D consortiums, venture capital foundations, office complexes, international convention centers, and residential new towns. By 1986, the MITI core concept included twenty-eight regional cities.

Sophia Antipolis in France was founded with a focus on cross-fertilization of ideas, high quality of life, and close contact and interaction with the region and its constituencies. In twenty years it became the largest technopolis of its kind in Europe. If Silicon Valley was a first-generation science city, Tsukuba and Sophia Antipolis are part of the second generation, with the latter hovering on the edge of the third generation. In the United States there are a number of newer "Silicon Valleys." These include Route 128 around Boston; Telecom Belt (Princeton, New Jersey); Satellite Valley (Gaithersburg, Maryland); Research Triangle, North Carolina (consisting of Chapel Hill, Durham, and Raleigh); Silicon Plain (Ft. Worth and Dallas, Texas); Silicon Forest (Portland, Oregon); and Silicon Mountain (Denver, Boulder, and Colorado Springs, Colorado).

For over twenty years, the concept of the science city, or technopolis, has evolved. Each technopolis reflects the demands of the culture and the circumstances under which it was conceived. From a growing number of technopolises, there emerges a richer set of experiences about what does and does not work. This experience, combined with the rapid expansion of information generation and transfer technologies, new transportation systems, and exploitable new technologies, shapes the technopolises that have already begun and new ones still in some stage of planning.

The success of a science city hinges on how well it invents new products and the adequacy of transportation and communications technologies to meet changing socioeconomic conditions. Economic success is increasingly determined by information and how people think, by airports, and by communications—not by access to raw materials or sea lanes. Learning from earlier experiences, future generations of science cities are expected to exhibit greater responsiveness to changing socioeconomic changes.

Science cities emerge from the cultural, economic, and political circumstances of the governments, corporations, and individuals that create them. The creators bring elements of their past experience as well as new expectations to their task. Current experience suggests that their success depends on whether the invented city is structured for self-learning and can achieve rapid enough change to overcome any limiting aspects of the initial vision.

Science cities are expected to evolve to increasingly higher levels of maturity. Level three science cities, which are emerging today, demonstrate more self-learning and capacity for change than level two cities such as Tsukuba and the early stages of Sophia Antipolis. Level four cities will evolve adequate self-learning and achieve responsive enough change to be self-sustaining in the twenty-first century.

Learning and communications are key to future successes in the development of viable science cities. Research and application of new processes and products are at the forefront of the science city. Rapid dissemination of information provides all segments of the city with the opportunity to contribute and participate in making necessary changes. Emerging communications technology and the integration of voice, images, data, and sound for delivery of information anywhere in the city by anyone promises the fullest opportunity for information sharing and learning. Disparities in learning will need to be minimized across economic groups in order to continuously attract residents and provide for a citywide response to changing conditions.

Movement of people, materials, and products will need to adapt to shifts in economic and social activity. The various modes of transportation will need to be more customized to allow individuals and organizations the capability to modify their use and rapidly respond to transportation changes required to sustain the viability of the city. Because of the central role of science and technology in national prosperity, most countries of the world will eventually have their science cities.

[See also Cities; Cities, North American; Science Issues.]

BIBLIOGRAPHY

Burke, James. *Connections.* Boston: Little, Brown, 1978.
Gibson, David V.; Kozmetsky, George; and Smilor, Raymond W., eds. *The Technopolis Phenomenon.* Lanham, MD: Rowman & Littlefield, 1992.
———. *Creating the Technopolis.* Cambridge, MA: Ballinger, 1988.
Tatsuno, Sheridan M. *The Technopolis Strategy.* Englewood Cliffs, NJ: Prentice Hall, 1986.

— RICHARD G. MAYNARD

SCIENCE FICTION

Science fiction—sometimes called "sci-fi," but not by most of the people who read or write it—is notoriously hard to define, though easy enough for its devotees to recognize. Although most science fiction is about the future and much of it has to do with space travel, ro-

bots, super-computers, and alien intelligent life, there are many classic stories with none of those ingredients that nevertheless are still clearly science fiction. One of the most illuminating attempts at clarification comes from the English scholar of science fiction Tom Shippey. After listing more than a dozen proposed definitions of the subject, Shippey concluded by saying: "Perhaps science fiction is impossible to define since, being the literature of change, it changes as you try to define it." But there is an excellent definition within that disclaimer: science fiction is indeed the literature of change, particularly of the changes brought about—and especially those still to come—by the explosive growth of science and technology.

Science fiction stories provide a sort of general catalog of possible future events. Almost all the important technological and social changes of the twentieth century have been prefigured in science fiction.

Although stories that have some claim to be included in the science fiction canon date back for centuries—with examples as early as *The True History* by Lucian of Samosata, written in the second century A.D.—the real flowering of science fiction could not come before science itself began to assume its present form. Accordingly, the first authors to make a career of writing in this form were Jules Verne and H. G. Wells. Wells in particular deserves recognition as the master who laid out the pattern of subject matter for future science fiction writers to explore. Still, when their works were published the field did not yet have a name, nor was there any publication devoted entirely to the new kind of literature.

Both those needs were supplied when Hugo Gernsback launched his magazine, *Amazing Stories,* in April 1926. Other magazines followed, and for more than twenty years thereafter almost all science fiction published in America first appeared in one or another of the science fiction "pulps." Among the major writers of the early magazine period were E. E. "Doc" Smith, who with his *The Skylark of Space* essentially invented the "space opera" (now most frequently found in such box-office film successes as *Star Wars*), and David H. Keller, best known for such satirical short stories as "The Revolt of the Pedestrians."

In the transitional period, from about 1950 to the end of the 1960s, the dominant writers were Isaac Asimov, Ray Bradbury, Robert A. Heinlein, and Arthur C. Clarke. All four began their careers in the science fiction magazines (all of them but Bradbury being closely identified with *Astounding Science Fiction,* edited by that dominant figure among science fiction editors, John W. Campbell) but went on to succeed as authors of many bestselling books. Since then book publication has provided the major outlet for most of the current writers. Among the best known of these are John Varley, Samuel R. Delany, and the two "cyberpunk" writers, Bruce Sterling and William Gibson, as well as a host of prominent female writers such as Ursula K. LeGuin, Anne McCaffrey, Suzie McKee Charnas, Joan Slonjewski, and Sherri S. Tepper.

Another significant development in current science fiction is its large place in film and television production. In television, pride of place must go to the pioneering series *Star Trek,* originally described by its creator, Gene Roddenberry, as "a sort of *Wagon Train* in space." The original *Star Trek* series was canceled by its network after the second year because of poor ratings, but a blizzard of angry letters from viewers caused the network to give it one more year before the axe fell. Its real popularity began only after that cancellation. For years afterward *Star Trek* was the most repeated series in syndication; there was said to be one small city (in Texas) where the series could be viewed eight times a day, from different stations. A Saturday-morning animated version came next, but failed quickly; since then its successor *Star Trek: The Next Generation,* with a new cast of characters, has outlasted the original and spawned two spin-off series and one more darkly toned imitator (*Babylon 5*). A series of feature films has appeared with the old standby actors. Other important feature motion pictures have included *THX 1138,* the *Star Wars* films, *ET, Close Encounters of the Third Kind, 2001* and its sequel, and *Alien,* as well as a steady diet of lower-budget productions every year.

Although science fiction has become predominantly an Anglo-American literature in this century, there are hundreds of writers and many thousands of fans in other countries, including a few non-English-speaking writers, such as Poland's Stanisław Lem, Japan's Sakyo Komatsu, and Russia's collaborating brothers Boris and Arkady Strugatsky, who have become world famous. The best-known American writers are almost invariably widely published abroad, with translations of works into forty or more languages. Since 1980 the international organization World SF has been a forum for persons who are professionally concerned with science fiction, whether as authors, editors, critics, teachers, artists, filmmakers, or in any other professional capacity. World SF now has members in thirty-eight countries and although most of its annual general meetings have taken place in European countries, they have also been held in Canada and the People's Republic of China.

Science fiction stories do not ordinarily claim to predict the future, since a single writer will frequently write many stories with completely different future histories. Still, they do provide a sort of general catalog of possible future events. The field has been called a useful prophylactic against future shock, since almost all the important technological and social changes of the twentieth century have been prefigured in science fiction. In recognition of this fact, many science fiction writers have been asked to contribute to "futurological" studies conducted by universities, research establishments, large corporations, and even the American military services.

Science fiction and science, too, have enjoyed a similar synergistic relationship. Although there are many excellent science fiction stories that contain little or no real science, it is also true that many science fiction writers are trained scientists, or laymen who keep abreast of scientific theories and discoveries. These accomplishments are often reflected in their stories, while a significant number of scientists, including some of the world's leading scientific authorities, such as Marvin Minsky, Freeman J. Dyson, and Stephen Hawking, first became interested in science through reading science fiction and often still continue both to read it and occasionally to write it. Among well-known scientists and mathematicians who have written science fiction stories (sometimes under pen-names) are Minsky, Eric Temple Bell (writing as "John Taine"), Robert Forward, Carl Sagan, and Fred Hoyle.

One of the most unusual features of the science-fiction field lies in the cohesiveness of its adherents, both readers and writers. Collectively known as "science fiction fandom," these individuals support a regular program of "cons," short for "conventions," unknown to any other literature. More than 500 of these cons occur ever year in the United States alone (with nearly as many again in the rest of the world). The largest is usually the annual "worldcon," the first of which took place in New York City in 1939, and since then, though usually in some city of the United States, it has been held also in England, Canada, Australia, Germany, and the Netherlands. At these meetings, ranging in attendance from a few hundred to more than ten thousand, writers, readers, artists, editors, and others discuss every aspect of the field. Many close friendships arise between people who meet only at such cons; marriages occur; individuals who live thousands of miles apart maintain close touch with each other; in the argot of the field,

FIAWOL (an acronym for "Fandom Is A Way Of Life") is an accurate description.

[See also Apocalyptic Future; Asimov, Isaac; Clarke, Arthur Charles; Dystopias; Global Consciousness; Popularized Futures; Utopias; Wells, H. G. In addition, see Chronology Of Futurism and the Future in the Appendix.]

BIBLIOGRAPHY

Aldiss, Brian W. *Trillion Year Spree: The History of Science Fiction.* New York: Atheneum, 1986.

Amis, Kingsley. *New Maps of Hell.* New York: Harcourt, Brace, 1960.

Bleiler, E. F., ed. *Science Fiction Writers.* New York: Scribner, 1982.

Nicholls, Peter, and Clute, John, eds. *The Science Fiction Encyclopedia,* 2nd ed. New York: St. Martin's Press, 1993.

Panshin, Alexei, and Panshin, Cory. *The World Beyond the Hill: Science Fiction and the Quest for Transcendence.* Los Angeles: Jeremy Tarcher, 1989.

Pohl, Frederik. *The Way the Future Was.* New York: Ballantine, 1978.

— FREDERIK POHL

SCIENCE ISSUES

Advancing science through investments in research and development (R&D) is expensive. Annually, the United States spends over $180 billion for R&D, which is carried out by industry, academia, and government laboratories. Academia and some government laboratories focus on fundamental research, while industry and other government laboratories focus on applied research and on developing technological products, processes, and systems.

How much should be spent on various fields of science and in pursuit of the various societal objectives that R&D will help us achieve? Because they study the unknown, researchers are uncertain about what they might learn. Cost-benefit and financial analysis help little in deciding what to spend and on what projects, so experienced researchers must help decide.

In the United States, industry pays for over half of R&D, and the federal government pays for most of the rest. Thus, decisions about what to study also involve industry managers and leaders in Congress and the executive branch. While rarely expert in science, they establish the broad economic and social objectives that motivate large R&D expenditures.

This discussion of how science priorities are set raises a key issue for science in a democracy: How can ordinary citizens influence decisions about scientific research and technological applications that will importantly affect their lives, work, and pocketbooks? Some argue that science and technology are "out of control"—that the combination of the special expertise required to understand new advances and the enormous financial and political advantages that can accrue to those who know how to take advantage of them means that science and technology are inherently undemocratic. Others argue that advances in communications have enhanced the abilities of everyone to learn about and participate in the decisions that affect them. So, just as industrialization required reading, writing, and arithmetic, the new information and biotechnologies demand that we become more conversant with science and with how technologies work. The need for improved public understanding has motivated major efforts to upgrade mathematics and science education, not only for the few who hope for careers in science and engineering, but for everyone.

Technology assessment is one approach

to anticipating and managing the unexpected

and undesirable consequences of new technologies.

Modern societies spend lavishly on R&D in hopes that material and social progress will come from improved understanding. We have learned how to prevent and cure disease; grow more and more nutritious foodstuffs; enhance our economy; sometimes prevent and when necessary win wars; and provide ourselves with an expanding array of entertainments.

However, we have also learned that applications of new knowledge can challenge traditional values and bring us grief. The telecommunications technologies that enhance education, entertainment, and edification provide platforms for poisonous dialogue and expose us to violence, real and imaginary. The synthetic ammonium nitrate that fertilizes our crops is fashioned into the bomb used at the federal building in Oklahoma City. Automobiles that whisk us across town or the nation emit air pollutants and kill thousands each year in accidents.

It is hard to anticipate the impacts of newly introduced technologies. Even if undesirable consequences are foreseen, we don't always have appropriate and democratic ways to manage them. Sometimes the lure of the benefits clouds our judgment of the costs. Technology assessment is one approach to anticipating and managing the unexpected and undesirable consequences of new technologies. Environmental and safety regulations can help control some of the undesirable impacts of new technologies.

Despite its awesome powers, science has limitations. Some things are too big, hot, fast, or far away to be studied easily. The history of science is about attempts to measure what was not measurable before, through the invention of ever more powerful telescopes, microscopes, chemical analyzers, and the like.

Projects to develop very large instruments are often called "big science"—the billion-dollar Hubble space telescope and the multi-billion-dollar superconducting super-collider (cancelled in 1993) are illustrations. Whereas "little science" is conducted by individuals and small groups, "big science" demands bureaucratic management, major budget commitments, and coordinated scientific programs. In big projects it is often impossible to determine individual responsibility for discoveries, a scientific practice for centuries. It is news when big projects fail or are terminated, and political pressures often keep them going.

Some natural phenomena have proven too complex for satisfactory scientific study. We still know very little about how an embryo becomes an adult being, and a full understanding of the causes of earthquakes still eludes us. Some phenomena cannot be studied in controlled experiments and are studied instead from indirect and historical evidence. We cannot rerun history to do experiments on the Earth's geology, the evolution of species, or the factors that drive national and world economies. Studies of these unique phenomena are no less scientific than those that can be conducted in a laboratory, but they demand different standards of evidence and they yield a different sort of truth.

Fraud in science receives a lot of attention. A few researchers have faked experiments, misrepresented findings, or made outlandish, insupportable claims. However, science is a remarkable social instrument for exposing fraud. Several mechanisms operate. Typically, other scientists, or "peers," review planned projects and examine carefully the claims made in papers submitted for publication. Scientists often attempt to repeat or extend the work of those who came before, and this exposes work done poorly or falsified.

When new scientific results are put to immediate practical use, however, as sometimes occurs in medicine, environmental regulation, or the design of new technologies, scientific fraud can pose immediate threats to the public. It is imprudent for society to take important actions using brand-new scientific results without subjecting them to great scrutiny, especially if the more traditional approaches to validation don't have time to work. Engineers know this about science, so they are often accused of being slow to use new findings. Those working in other fields would be advised to heed the engineers' example.

[See also Research and Development; Scientific Breakthroughs; Technology and Science.]

BIBLIOGRAPHY

Goldman, Steven, and Cutcliffe, Stephen, eds. *Science, Technology and Social Progress.* Bethlehem, PA: Lehigh University Press, 1988.
National Science Board. *Science and Engineering Indicators—1993.* Washington, DC: U.S. Government Printing Office, 1993.
Teich, Albert H.; Nelson, Stephen D.; and McEnaney, Celia, eds. *Science and Technology Policy Year-book—1994.* Washington, DC: American Association for the Advancement of Science, 1994.

– CHRISTOPHER T. HILL

SCIENTIFIC BREAKTHROUGHS

Science is the single most important source of contemporary and future products, processes, and services that will enhance individual well-being, enlarge our understanding of the world around us, and prepare us to manage that world. Some breakthroughs in individual sciences will come about from applying already existing

This technician inspects a laser positioning system. Precisely calibrated lasers will be used for an increasing number of purposes. (Roger Ressmeyer/© Corbis)

knowledge in unanticipated ways. Other breakthroughs will depend upon combining already available capabilities to do new things. Still others will create new capabilities.

Ecology over the next generation will become the central science in our understanding and management of the environment. Quantitative models of the biota and ecosystems will be the tools to effectively manage natural environments and guide the managed environments of farms, forests, and grazing land.

Brain science will flower in two directions as a result of understanding genetic links to mental health and disease and to individual human mental capabilities. First will be the elimination of mental disorders, such as schizophrenia and psychotic depression. Second will be the capability to improve our cognitive capabilities and give us better emotional balance and more fulfilling lives.

In agriculture, the ability to directly manipulate plant genes will lead to at least two breakthroughs. The first will be fully nutritionally balanced plants. For example, the native Mexican diet consists largely of rice and beans, each of which provides different essential proteins. The future will permit plants to have more complete protein content (so-called protein-efficiency ratios that assure human metabolic availability), as well as trace materials and other necessary dietary components. The second breakthrough will be a diet with double or triple the number of food plants. Many nutritional plants with undesirable characteristics will be changed into edible, marketable commodities. Ocean science will lead to the effective farming and ranching of the oceans.

Medical genetics will discover the heritable linkages to several thousand human diseases and disorders. Interventions for disease prevention or genetic correction will be common by supplying what is missing or removing what is harmful. Less clear in the future is whether medicine and biological research will identify the genes that determine our natural lifetime and manipulate them to extend human life. Whether that will be socially or even personally desirable is unclear even if the extension of life were accompanied by the maintenance of essential human faculties. More likely than extending our species's lifetime will be the applications of medicine to allow more of us to live out our full biological lifetime—to square off the death curve—giving most of us healthier, happier lives until our genetic time limit of about eighty-five years is reached.

Genetic knowledge will allow us to move beyond the control and prevention of disease to increasing our physical, intellectual, emotional, and social abilities. We are on the brink of being able to influence, if not shape, our own evolution as well as the evolution of the rest of the biota. It is plausible that early in the twenty-first century, some nations will have a program of raising the average IQ of their population by a few points per generation.

Every aspect of biology will be changed from genetics research. Two of the most striking will be the revival of extinct species. Far more likely than a Jurassic Park of animals extinct for tens of millions of years is the revival of more recently extinct animals like the woolly mammoth and the passenger pigeon. Every museum is a repository of species to revive. The primary scientific breakthrough to make the revival possible is learning to release from the DNA (genetic material) in every single somatic (body cell) of every living thing the ability to reproduce. At the time of this writing, among higher animals only reproductive cells (sperm and ova), not somatic cells, can reproduce.

Geology will help us to prevent some catastrophic earthquakes. Since earthquakes result from the sudden release of stress as the plates of Earth rub against each other or one passes under the other, we should be able to lubricate those stress points to allow a continuous stress release by low-level Richter-scale tremblors, thereby avoiding stress buildup and catastrophic release.

Several developments in economics could well lead to a genuine breakthrough. The world now has an urgent need to reconceptualize the economics of information. Similarly, as the structure of work changes and we move into an information-based society, the concept of what work is and how it should be compensated will be reconceptualized.

The third breakthrough in economics will be the introduction of a new system of national accounts that will factor in disease, disasters, unemployment, illness, accidents, pollution, resource loss, and other undesirable developments to create a more realistic and reliable measure of national welfare. These fundamental changes in economic thinking will carry us beyond the constraints and limitations of the economics of the industrial era and fashion the economic tools for understanding and managing the postindustrial society.

Chemistry will evolve in many new directions. One of the most important will be the development of materials based on the concept of biomimetics—that is, the imitation of the processes that nature uses to create complex material with desirable characteristics. As we better understand how these natural materials, such as wood and seashells, are produced, we should be able to imitate their structures. A quite different line of development will be the flourishing of inorganic chemistry to accomplish many of the functions for which we now use organic materials.

Environmental science, should the threat of greenhouse warming prove to be valid, will move to radical remedies. To reduce the melting of the Antarctic ice cap, we may attempt to control the currents that flow around the South Pole that annually eat away at the ice sheets. Even more likely are processes to increase snowfall in Antarctica in order to compensate for any ocean rise resulting from the warming of the ocean. Another macro-engineering response may be to increase the albedo—that is, the reflectivity of Earth. Today, Earth reflects into space about 53 percent of the sunlight that hits it. If we could increase the reflection from some portions of Earth, such as unpopulated, desert, and semidesert areas of the world, we might be able to compensate for the effects of greenhouse warming.

Macroengineering—civil works on a scale so large

that they exceed the budgets of most governments

and affect many nations—will be part

of the growing pattern of a totally managed globe.

Macroengineering—civil works on a scale so large that they exceed the budgets of most governments and affect many nations—will be part of the growing pattern of a totally managed globe. Among the most likely macroengineering projects will be the harvesting of Antarctic icebergs, perhaps a mile by a quarter of a mile on edge to move to the west coast of South America, the Australian Outback, or Baja California, or Saudi Arabia. That enormous amount of water will transform the local environment and literally allow the deserts to bloom. Massive desalinization of ocean water could provide similar results.

Robots, based on research in space and military programs, will go outdoors, be weatherized, and have some on-board intelligence and mobility. They will do heavy and dangerous work, changing the nature of farming, mining, ocean activities, and the operation of risky facilities. They will also be utilized in dangerous situations such as disasters and fires.

Architecture may experience the development of the third paradigm for construction. Today, all structures depend upon one of two principles for their stability, either compression or tension. The fusion of the technologies of lightweight composite materials, reliable sensors, and artificial intelligence for appropriate and quick responses, and motors and cable for strength will

allow for the first time the construction of dynamic buildings. These structures in real time will respond to changes in their environment—wind, rain, even earthquakes. For the first time, we may be on the brink of having truly lightweight or temporary structures that could be easily dismantled like Lego blocks.

Artificial intelligence in several different forms will bring us devices capable of understanding the spoken word and speaking in a variety of languages with extensive vocabularies. Expert systems will be at the disposal of people in a suitable software package. On a larger scale, artificial intelligence will allow less skilled workers to undertake the tasks normally done by more highly trained and skilled workers. Artificial intelligence will be used to test systems. Are they foolproof? Are they fail-safe? Will they do their job? Are they free of viruses?

Artificial intelligence will also make possible currently unprecedented services, such as a health kiosk, where people could puncture the finger for a blood sample to put on a slide, urinate into a bottle, and drop that in the analytical machines, spit in the vial and drop that in a different machine, using artificial intelligence programs to explore symptoms, conditions, disease concerns, and so on. This evolution of an alternative or counter-medicine could stimulate people's interest in their health and provide a useful and widely recognized needed check on traditional medical practice.

Asteroids have been striking Earth from time to time since the formation of the solar system. We now have the capability to identify potentially hazardous asteroids far enough away to take active and preventive measures. Early in the next century, we should see an internationally institutionalized asteroid watch, and we will probably begin on a trial basis the first intervention involving a large object outside Earth with a view to changing its course. If we can establish the practicality of doing that with a nonthreatening asteroid, we will be in better shape for the inevitable hazard.

There is no limit to what breakthroughs science will bring to us. We can be confident that an endless frontier that knows no bounds is still ahead of us.

[See also Architectural Design; Artificial Intelligence; Astronomy; Chemistry; Disasters, Planning For; Genetic Engineering; Genetics: Agricultural Applications; Global Warming; Macroengineering; Robotics; Surprises; Wildcards.]

BIBLIOGRAPHY

Ballard, Steven. *Innovation Through Scientific and Technical Information.* Westport, CT: Greenwood, 1989.
Carson, J. W. *Innovation. A Battle Plan for the 1990s.* Brookfield, VT: Gower, 1989.
Diebold, John. *Innovators: The Discoveries, Inventions and Breakthroughs of Our Time.* New York: NAL-Dutton, 1990.

Forida, Richard. *The Breakthrough Illusion: Corporate America's Failure to Move from Innovation to Mass Production.* New York: Basic Books, 1990.

Gabor, Dennis. *Innovations: Scientific, Technological and Social.* New York: Oxford University Press, 1970.

Hammond, A. L. *Twenty Discoveries That Changed Our Lives.* Washington, DC: American Association for the Advancement of Science, 1984.

McLoughlin, Ian, and Clark, Jon. *Technological Change at Work.* Washington, DC: Taylor and Francis, 1988.

Nayak, P. Ranganath. *Breakthroughs!* New York: Rosen, 1986.

Parkinson, Claire. *Breakthroughs: A Chronology of Great Achievements in Science and Mathematics, 1200–1930.* Boston: G. K. Hall, 1985.

Potter, Stephen. *On the Right Lines? The Limits of Technological Innovation.* New York: St. Martin's Press, 1987.

— JOSEPH F. COATES

SEMICONDUCTORS

Semiconductors are the foundation of today's information age. They enable and underlie virtually every system involved in the manipulation and movement of information, from laptop computers to satellite-based global communications networks. Moreover, the manipulation and movement of information are rapidly becoming as vital to world economic growth as were once the generation and movement of food (the agricultural age) and the development and powering of machine tools (the industrial age). Semiconductor materials are becoming as vital (or more) to world economic growth as were once other materials such as stone and wood, metals and coal.

Semiconductor Materials: Characteristics and Families

What are some of the characteristics of semiconductors that enable them to excel at information manipulation and movement?

A primary characteristic, from which they derive their name, is that they are "lukewarm" electrical conductors. Neither highly insulating nor highly conducting, they were not initially believed to be particularly useful. However, because their conductivity is not only lukewarm, but also extremely sensitive to the introduction of impurities and the application of electric fields,

Integrated circuits are made from semiconductor material, which forms the basis for nearly all computers, large and small. (Owen Franken/Corbis)

759

they can easily be precision engineered into the basic building blocks of microelectronics: current or voltage-controlled switches and amplifiers.

A secondary (but also crucial) characteristic is that their electrical conductivity is based on two "effective" carrier types, negatively charged electrons and positively charged holes. The interaction between these carrier types is very strong and in many cases is either caused by the absorption, or results in the emission, of light (photons). Then, by precision engineering of the interaction between electrons and holes in compact devices, they can be used to form the basic building blocks of photonics: light-absorbing and -emitting devices such as detectors, lasers, and light-emitting diodes (LEDs).

What are some of the families of semiconductors from which these microelectronic and photonic devices are built? The dominant semiconductors are inorganic and can be divided into three major families, according to whether they are composed of elements from column IV, columns III and V, or columns II and VI of the periodic table. Although they all have the two unique characteristics described above, all their other physical and chemical properties vary widely both from family to family, as well as within each family. For example, at one extreme, carbon (C) in its diamond form has a very small lattice constant, is transparent into the ultraviolet, and is mechanically hard with a high thermal conductivity. At the other extreme, HgCdTe has a very large lattice constant, is transparent only in the far infrared, and is mechanically soft with a low thermal conductivity.

The column IV family is composed of silicon (Si), germanium (Ge), carbon (C), and silicon carbide (SiC). Of these, Si is by far the most important and is the material from which perhaps 95 percent of all semiconductor devices (by dollar volume) are produced. Due to its unmatched combination of robustness, performance, low cost, and integrability with high-quality passivating oxides, Si is overwhelmingly likely to continue to be the most important semiconductor for the foreseeable future. Although Ge was the material in which the first transistor was demonstrated in 1948, and although SiC and C have important current and future niche applications (e.g., in severe-environment electronics and as coatings for heat sinks and field-emission devices), none is likely to ever play as important a role as Si as an active device material in mainstream applications.

The column III-V family contains permutations of the column III elements aluminum (Al), gallium (Ga), and indium (In), and the column V elements nitrogen (N), phosphorus (P), arsenic (As), and antimony (Sb). Of these, GaAs-related materials are the most important and are the materials from which perhaps 75 percent of

all III-V devices are produced. The relative importance of GaAs within the column III-V family of materials is less pronounced than that of Si within the column IV family of materials. The reason is that though GaAs is characterized by a reasonable balance between robustness, cost, and performance, other materials have important advantages in particular areas. InP-related materials, for example, emit light in the 1.3–1.55 μm wavelength range important to fiber-based optical communications and have high-field transport properties superior to GaAs-based materials. GaN-related materials, for example, though difficult to grow, are extremely robust and emit light in the blue-green wavelength range important to displays, illumination sources, and high-resolution optical storage and printing. Both InP- and GaN-related materials are likely to increase in importance relative to GaAs-related materials in the future.

A new family of semiconductor materials

has been developed, based on organic polymers.

The column II-VI family contains permutations of the column II elements magnesium (Mg), zinc (Zn), cadmium (Cd), and mercury (Hg), and the column VI elements sulfur (S), selenium (Se), and tellurium (Te). These semiconductors are not used widely for active devices, but are important as passive phosphor materials for cathode-ray-tube devices such as television monitors. They are particularly noteworthy, however, because of their wide range of energy gaps. At the same time that ZnSSe-related materials are currently being explored for blue-green lasers, HgCdTe-related materials are the high-performance material of choice for long-wavelength (8–14 μm) infrared radiation detectors. None of these materials, though, is likely to be a very important active device material in mainstream applications.

All of the semiconductors mentioned thus far have been inorganic. Recently a new family of semiconductor materials has been developed, based on organic polymers. Although these materials are very immature, they promise a new generation of ultra-inexpensive devices fabricated from polymer coatings on low-temperature substrates such as glass and plastics. Indeed, both transistors and light-emitting devices have recently been demonstrated, though a major challenge will be achieving the performance and reliability required for wide acceptance.

A related family of materials from which extremely dense three-dimensionally-packed circuitry can clearly be formed are biological materials. Although biological devices are much slower (with switching times measured in microseconds rather than nanoseconds) than semiconductor devices, their ability to "self-assemble" could enable artificial circuits of unprecedented complexity. Ethical issues regarding artificial life will surely arise, but they presumably already will have for complex, ultradense networks of computers as well.

Si Materials: Information Manipulation

As discussed above, Si-based materials will likely continue to dominate semiconductor applications in information manipulation (logic and memory) for the foreseeable future. Much of that dominance is based on the expected continued increase in functionality of Si-based integrated circuits (ICs). Historically, that increase in functionality has obeyed Moore's Law and has doubled approximately every three years. A continuation of that rate of increase through the year 2015 is not unlikely and will enable applications that are as difficult to imagine now as today's applications were difficult to imagine yesterday.

Nevertheless, this continued increase in functionality will require major changes in the manner in which ICs are fabricated. Among the major technological challenges are those anticipated by the Semiconductor Industry Association in its 1994 national technology road map for semiconductors. In design and test, a major challenge will be to develop and integrate a hierarchy of tools spanning high-level system issues all the way to low-level packaging and chip issues. In process integration, devices and structures, a major challenge will be to develop and integrate radically new devices with ultra-high packing densities. In lithography, a major challenge will be to move from 0.5 µm to 0.1 µm linewidths and below, and to develop new short-wavelength compact optical sources. Soon, quantum effects will become important and may lead to a new generation of coherent-electron-effect devices and circuits. In metal interconnects, a major challenge will be both to increase interconnect complexity and bandwidth without introducing additional crosstalk as well as eventually to understand and harness inevitable traveling-wave effects as lumped elements become distributed elements. In materials and bulk processes, a major challenge will be to understand and control impurity profiles and interfaces at the nanoscale through improved wafer- and equipment-level physical models and simulations. In assembly and packaging, a major challenge will be to move from perimeter-connected single-chip modules to area-connected multichip modules, perhaps through a new generation of optoelectronic interconnects and stacked (three-dimensional) packaging. In factory integration, a major challenge will

be to move from an environment in which processes are optimized individually to one in which they are optimized collectively through more comprehensive modeling, sensing, and control of the overall factory environment.

Along with this continued increase in functionality will likely come a decrease in the need for today's vast array of different kinds of ICs. A limited set of standard ICs (such as today's Pentium and PowerPC chip families) will become so inexpensive, powerful, and general-purpose, that it will gradually become easier to reprogram them using software or "ROMware" than to manufacture costly, low-volume lots of "hardware-programmed" application-specific ICs. Customization of IC function will increasingly occur at higher and higher (software rather than hardware) levels and will decrease or eliminate the need for "agile manufacturing" of low-volume IC lots.

III-V Materials: Information Movement

As discussed above, column III-V-based materials are and will continue to be a much smaller market than Si-based materials. Nevertheless, information manipulation is only half of what is necessary; information movement (communications and display) is the other half, and it is that half that will place increasing demands on III-V materials. Indeed, it is likely that, as communications technology finally "catches up" (and ultimately surpasses) computation technology in tomorrow's ultra-high-bandwidth networks of distributed intelligence, the III-V versus Si dollar-volume ratio will grow significantly from today's 1:20. It will do so because III-V materials are crucial to both types of tomorrow's dominant forms of high-speed communication: wireless and optoelectronic.

In wireless communications, the key ingredient is the ability to efficiently receive, modulate/demodulate, amplify, and transmit radio and microwave (0.8–100 GHz) frequency signals. In all of these areas, III-V semiconductors dominate now and are likely to continue to dominate in the future. Their efficiencies at all of these functions will always exceed those of Si due to their higher electron mobilities and hence their higher switching speed × switching power product. This will be particularly the case as carrier frequencies continue to increase, both to accommodate higher data transmission rates as well as to decrease interference between adjacent cells in tomorrow's ultradense global grid of wireless base stations.

In optoelectronic communications, the key ingredient is the ability to emit and detect light efficiently. Because of their direct energy gaps, column III-V semiconductors will always be far more efficient at both of these than column IV semiconductors. One important trend will be the increased use of devices in which light is absorbed or emitted vertically rather than horizontally. Light-emitting diodes (LEDs), for example, will continue to grow in importance, particularly as a wider spectrum of wavelengths is made available by the development of new materials. Blue, green, and red (0.4–0.7 μm wavelength) LEDs enabled by AlGaInN and Al-GaInP materials will find applications in high-brightness, robust illumination sources and displays; and mid-infrared (2.0–5.0 μm wavelength) LEDs enabled by AlGaInAsSb materials will find applications in environmental sensing. Due to their performance and cost advantages, vertical-cavity surface-emitting lasers will displace conventional horizontal-cavity, edge-emitting lasers in most applications, including as high-bandwidth sources for fiber-optic communications and as low-bandwidth sources for peripherals such as laser printers and optical disks.

Integrated Materials: Systems on a Chip

A final major trend will be the integration of materials, each matched to a particular function, for systems on a chip. At an evolutionary level, this kind of integration has been going on for some time. The integration of polycrystalline Si and metals for interconnects, for example, with single-crystal Si for active transistors, is at the heart of Si integrated circuits. Mainstream Si technology will continue to incorporate new materials for enhanced performance. SiGe, SiGeC, and SiC alloys and compounds can enable more sophisticated heterojunction devices by improving carrier confinement in field-effect transistors and injection efficiency in bipolar transistors. Other variants of Si itself, such as amorphous and polycrystalline Si, will also gradually increase in importance, particularly as devices shrink and as the carrier mobilities of the material used to fabricate the device becomes less and less important. Silicon-on-insulator may also increase in importance, as device packing density increases and cross talk becomes more difficult to suppress.

TABLE 1

ELEMENTS FROM WHICH INORGANIC SEMICONDUCTORS ARE DERIVED

II*	III	IV	V	VI
		C	N	
Mg	Al	Si	P	S
Zn	Ga	Ge	As	Se
Cd	In	Sn	Sb	Te
Hg				

* Roman numeral heads refer to sections of the Periodic Table.

At a revolutionary level, the continued integration of other materials may enable radically new applications in which entire systems are miniaturized and placed on single chips or wafers. The integration of polycrystalline Si with glass-based flat-panel displays will enable entire computer systems to become "part of" the display, rather than the other way around. The integration of Si logic and wireless transmitters/receivers with microelectromechanical devices fabricated by precision selective etching will enable a new generation of smart manipulators, chemical microlaboratories, sensors, displays, and perhaps even autonomous microrobots. The integration of organic materials with semiconductors will enable a new generation of smart chips that can sense and control biological functions. The integration of III-V and other optically active materials with Si will enable a new generation of "smart" optoelectronics and a new generation of "talkative" logic.

Conclusion

Semiconductors are, and will continue to be, the critical material enabling the manipulation and movement of information. Insofar as information is rapidly becoming the dominant commodity fueling world economic growth, semiconductors will likely continue to be one of our most important materials. Unlike during the past several decades, though, commercial rather than military markets will drive their further evolution and development. It is likely to be several decades before another class of materials, perhaps biotechnology materials, in turn eclipses semiconductors in importance.

[See also Chemicals, Fine; Chemistry; Communications: Technology; Computer Hardware; Computer Linkage; Computers: Software; Data Storage; High Technology; Nanotechnology; Parasensory Phenomena; Scientific Breakthroughs; Superconductors; Telecommunications.]

BIBLIOGRAPHY

Gilder, George. *Telecosm.* New York: Simon & Schuster, 1996.
"The Incredible Shrinking Laboratory." *Science* 268 (1995): 26.
The National Technology Roadmap for Semiconductors. San Jose, CA: Semiconductor Industry Association, 1994.
Streetman, B. *Solid State Electronic Devices,* 3rd ed. Englewood Cliffs, NJ: Prentice Hall, 1990.
"Towards Point One." *Scientific American* (February 1995).
"U.S. Display Industry on the Edge." *IEEE Spectrum* 32 (1995): 62.

— J. Y. TSAO

SEXUAL BEHAVIOR

The twentieth century has witnessed a transition from the dogmatic sexual Victorianism of the nineteenth century to a more tolerant sexual pluralism. Americans have had difficulty adjusting to this change. As a result, the United States has the highest rate in the Western world of almost every sexual problem, including HIV/AIDS, rape, teenage pregnancy, and child sexual abuse (Reiss, 1990). Despite this atrocious record, we are now finally learning how to better deal with our sexuality.

Premarital sexual behavior changed radically from the 1960s to the '90s. The trend is most clearly seen in teenage sexual behavior. In 1960 slightly over 20 percent of teenage young women fifteen to nineteen years old were not virgins; by 1970 the rate was 30 percent, and by 1980 it was about 50 percent (Hofferth, et al., 1987; Reiss, 1990, chapter 3). Since then, although the age at first coitus has dropped some, the overall percentage who are not virgins has changed very little. Women have made most of the changes in sexuality and are now close to men's nonvirginity rates. For nineteen-year-olds, by the late 1980s about 75 percent of women and 85 percent of men were nonvirginal (Sonenstein, et al., 1989; *Morbidity and Mortality Weekly Reports,* 1991).

Since the 1960s there have also been extraordinary changes in attitudes toward premarital sexuality. In June 1963 the National Opinion Research Center (NORC) at the University of Chicago administered a questionnaire to a representative national sample inquiring about their personal acceptance of premarital sexual intercourse in four types of relationships: engaged, love, strong affection, and relationships with no particular affection (Reiss, 1967). The results indicated that in 1963 less than 25 percent of adult Americans accepted premarital intercourse under any of the conditions asked about (Reiss, 1967, p. 27). Since this study was conducted just before the start of the "sexual revolution" that erupted later in the 1960s, it provides a base from which to judge what has changed.

In 1970 Albert Klassen and his colleagues posed a comparable set of questions in another NORC representative national sample. They found that over 55 percent of adult Americans replied that premarital intercourse was acceptable under one or more of their conditions (Klassen, et al., 1989, p. 18). In 1975 another national survey conducted by NORC reported that the percent of adults finding premarital intercourse to *not* be "always wrong" had risen to almost 70 percent (National Opinion Research Center, 1989, p. 769). Since that time this percentage has increased only a few percentage points.

The 1963–1975 change, from less than 25 percent to almost 70 percent accepting premarital intercourse under some condition, is phenomenal for such a short time period. When we combine these attitudinal changes with the changes mentioned above for sexual behavior, going from 20 percent of teenage females not being virginal in 1960 to 50 percent by 1980, we do indeed have strong evidence for the popular view that we underwent a sexual revolution starting in the late 1960s.

An important factor in our

move toward greater sexual tolerance has been

the rise in gender equality since the 1960s.

Western Europeans experienced similar changes at about the same time, but they did a far better job of adjusting. In America when young people first engage in sexual behavior, they often have many qualms and confusions about sexuality. We have relatively little societal preparation for making wise sexual choices, because so much effort is expended trying to get teens to avoid sex altogether. This inadequate preparation for sexual decision making is one of the major reasons for our very high rate of unwanted sexual outcomes, such as pregnancy, rape, HIV/AIDS, and child sexual abuse (Reiss, 1990).

Sexual choices are complicated further for women by the additional restraints our society imposes on female sexuality. The far lower rates of teenage pregnancy in every other Western country, with the same proportion of young people sexually active, shows clearly what a poor job we are doing in preparing our children for sexual choices (Reiss, 1990). Nevertheless, change is taking place. For example, in a representative national study of women it was found that the proportion of women who used a contraceptive method at first intercourse rose from about half in the 1970s to about two-thirds during the 1980s (Mosher and McNally, 1991). This is a very important change, because it shows increased protection at the very first coital experience and this helps prevent pregnancies that often occur during the start of new sexual relationships.

Increased use of condoms was a major part of the greater use of contraception. In national studies of teenage males it was found that youths aged seventeen to nineteen reported that condom use at last intercourse more than doubled, from less than one in four in 1979 to more than one in two in 1988 (Sonenstein, et al., 1989). Both the changes in contraception at first coitus and the increased condom usage indicates that sexuality is increasingly becoming something that we prepare for rather than an urge that we impulsively act upon.

This more positive approach to sexuality does not exclude abstinence, but neither does it view abstinence as the only moral choice. Starting about 1990 the New York City public schools and other school districts began forming programs encouraging condom use for sexually active teenagers. We finally recognized that vows of abstinence break far more often than do condoms. In this age of AIDS, it may be best to prepare young people for the choices they may make and try also to give them some ethical guidelines for carrying on appropriate consensual sexual relationships.

Another important factor in our move toward greater sexual tolerance has been the rise in gender equality since the 1960s. Women who have more economic and political power feel freer to assert their sexual rights and raise their daughters to do the same. We find today that 40 percent of condoms are bought by women and more women are letting their partners know that they will not have sex without a condom.

Sex education programs are becoming more open

to discussing the full meaning of sexuality.

Old romantic myths slow our progress toward safer sexuality. There is a belief that if you are in love, then you can stop using condoms because a lover would not infect you with a sexually transmitted disease. But we now know that most of the women with AIDS, who became infected from heterosexual intercourse, were involved in monogamous, not casual, relationships (Reiss, 1990: chapter 5). Unfortunately for them, either their partners were not faithful, or in many cases, were former or current intravenous drug users. Love is not always a good indicator of safe sexuality.

There is a new sexual ethic that is sweeping the Western world, replacing dogmatic Victorianism with a *pluralistic* view of sexuality. Americans believe in pluralism in almost all areas of life. Our society accepts more than one religion, political party, or type of family. Still, sexual pluralism does not mean that absolutely anything goes; rather, pluralism stresses concern for one's sexual partner and rejects the use of force or exploitation in sexuality.

The new guidelines model the sexual relationship on friendship or other important relationships and they are based on three key values: Honesty, Equality, and Responsibility (HER) (Reiss, 1990, chapter 1). These HER principles are increasingly popular among youth in America and Europe. Women as well as men are more and more feeling that they have the right to seek such a HER relationship.

As women's rights grow into the twenty-first century, the support for this new sexual ethic will increase (Reiss, 1986, 1990). We see this blossoming gender equality in our country in the greater wage equality and greater political power of women. Furthermore, there are pres-

sures on religious organizations to adopt more of a pluralistic stance on sexuality and to give women more rights in the churches and synagogues of America. Women now make up over one-half of our college students. In city after city, our sex education programs are gradually becoming more open to discussing the full meaning of sexuality without trying to suggest either that only abstinence or only straight sex is truly moral.

Today's major social trends support the view that HER sexual pluralism will flourish in the twenty-first century. The sexual revolution of the late 1960s was predicted by some social scientists (Reiss, 1960, pp. 235–250) and the societal changes noted above are a reasonable basis for now predicting that we will increasingly adopt the new HER sexual ethic (Reiss, 1990, chapter 10). It was the lack of such a guiding ethic that was a key factor in maintaining our high rates of sexual problems and so we can expect that those problems will gradually be brought under better control. Just as the Russians will look back at the late twentieth century and wonder how they could ever have endorsed communism for so long, we Americans will look back and wonder how we could ever have endorsed the remnants of Victorianism for so long.

[See also Abortion; Behavior: Social Constraints; Child Abuse; Family Patterns; Family Planning; Family Values; Morals; Sexual Codes; Sexual Harassment; Sexual Laws; Sexual Reproduction; Sexual Reproduction: Artificial Means; Social Controls.]

BIBLIOGRAPHY

Hofferth, Sandra L.; Kahn, Joan R.; and Baldwin, Wendy. "Premarital Sexual Activity Among U.S. Teenage Women Over the Past Three Decades." *Family Planning Perspectives* 19 (1987): 46–53.

Klassen, Albert D.; Williams, Colin J.; and Levitt, Eugene E. *Sex and Morality in the U.S.: An Empirical Enquiry Under the Auspices of the Kinsey Institute.* Middletown, CT: Wesleyan University Press, 1989.

Mosher, William D., and McNally, James W. "Contraceptive Use at First Premarital Intercourse: United States, 1965–1988." *Family Planning Perspectives* 23 (1991): 108–116.

National Opinion Research Center. *General Social Survey Trends Tape Marginals: 1972–1989.* Chicago: National Opinion Research Center, 1989.

"Premarital Sexual Experience Among Adolescent Women: U.S., 1970–1988." *Morbidity and Mortality Weekly Reports (MMWR)* 39 (1991): 929–932.

Reiss, Ira L. *An End To Shame: Shaping Our Next Sexual Revolution.* Buffalo, NY. Prometheus Books, 1990.

———. *Journey Into Sexuality: An Exploratory Voyage.* New York.: Prentice Hall, 1986.

———. *Premarital Sexual Standards in America.* New York: Free Press, 1960.

———. *The Social Context of Premarital Sexual Permissiveness.* New York: Holt, Rinehart, and Winston, 1967.

Sonenstein, Freya L.; Pleck, Joseph H.; and Ku, Leighton C. "Sexual Activity, Condom Use, and AIDS Awareness Among Adolescent Males." *Family Planning Perspectives* 21 (1989): 152–158.

— IRA L. REISS

SEXUAL CODES

Every society regulates sexual relationships to protect the next generation, facilitate the proper passage of property to offspring, and avoid conflicts and maintain the moral and social order. Twice in human history sexual codes have experienced a global, root-wrenching revolution. We are in the midst of the second of these two revolutions. See Table 1 for a summary of this process.

The Pre-Axial Period

In our "pre-axial period," as philosopher Karl Jaspers labeled our prehistoric millennia, sexual codes were quite different from those that have prevailed for the past five thousand years or so. Our earliest ancestors lived in scattered, nomadic clans and tribes of twenty to thirty adults: male hunters of carrion and small game, female gatherers of fruits and roots, and a few young. Within the clans, men and women shared equal power. If anything, women held the edge, honored both as the source of life and as the teachers of the art of love, joining spiritual love of the heart with passionate, sexual love. Their spirit world echoed with gods and goddesses, priests and priestesses.

In that precarious world where each life lasted but a brief few decades, men and women were drawn to bond in pairs for mutual support and to rear their offspring. Within the clan, women formed supportive, cooperative networks to help them nurture the young, while the men were out competing in the hunt. Evidence of a prevailing pattern of sexual matings within and outside the pair bond among our nearest primate relations—the bonobo dwarf chimpanzees—and indeed of most mammals suggests that human pair-bonding in this long-forgotten era was not sexually exclusive. That characteristic of our sexual code did not emerge until males assumed social dominance some six thousand to ten thousand years ago, when men became concerned about the inheritance of their property through legitimate heirs born to a virgin bride or faithful wife.

The Axial Period

The world of our ancestors and our sexual codes entered a global, wrenching transition some ten thousand years ago, with the advent of agriculture, the domestication of dogs and horses, the smelting of metal plows and weapons, and the invention of the wheel. Males consolidated their new power, first in the manly art of war and physical strength, and then more subtly with the invention of writing and alphabets to record the wealth they accumulated in war and trade. Written legal codes centralized male power in political and business hier-

archies. In ancient Sumer, Egypt, Babylon, Greece, and Rome, males increasingly celebrated the rational and the analytical, scientific knowledge that allowed them to understand, manipulate, and, yes, exploit the natural world. Male gods moved to the fore as goddesses faded, and eventually a single, male God was revealed by male prophets in Judaism, Christianity, and Islam.

The new sexual codes that emerged in this axial period endorsed highly defined, rigid gender roles and male/female stereotypes, with many strong socially imposed roles and rules for male/female relationships. Sex was clearly defined and measured in male terms as a genital activity with coitus resulting in offspring. Female sexuality and needs were ignored—or simply denied. In this patriarchal, hierarchical world, rational, analytical males were superior to emotional, passionate females, who were obviously designed by God for motherhood and to be obedient to their men and cater to male needs. Sexual exclusivity was important, much more so for females than males. Sex—and women— posed a danger to male dominance, and so sexual activity was hedged in by sex-negative attitudes, by taboos on nudity, fear of the body, emotions, and senses.

Toward a Second Axial Period: Sexual Codes in Transition

Many observers of the human story in fields as diverse as theology, history, sociobiology, feminist studies, sociology, sexology, anthropology, and chaos theory, have independently suggested that human culture is already in transition to a new societal structure and value system. Thirty years ago, anthropologist Margaret Mead described America as a "pre-figurative culture," a culture whose patriarchal myths and archetypes handed down from biblical times are no longer meaningful or supportive of the male-defined sexual codes of the axial period.

Feminism has brought new challenges

to the phallocentric model of sex

and a shift to a holistic model

that emphasizes sensual pleasure and transcendence.

The power of our traditional myths and archetypes has faded because Copernicus, Galileo, Darwin, and Einstein have pushed us out of the ancient fixed worldview with its unchanging hierarchy of the Great Chain of Being into a world of process and evolution. Ever accelerating, radical changes in our social environment

TABLE 1

EVOLUTIONARY STAGES OF SELF-AWARENESS, HUMAN CONSCIOUSNESS AND SEXUAL CODES

Time Line Era	Before 10,000 B.C. Pre-axial Matrical/ Matriarchal	3000 B.C. to Recent Times Axial Patriarchal	1900s on into Future Second Axial Period Contextual-Transformation
Lifestyle	Nomadic Hunter/gatherer	City life Agriculture, technology, industrial revolution, science	Global village, GAIA Information/service
Fundamental Human Unit	Clan and family egalitarian council	Patrilineal hierarchical structures and rankings	Matrices and networks ever-changing, dynamic
Personal Identity	Emergence of tribal identity No true individuality	Male versus female identity Individual as distinct from the other, differences contrasted	Global organism, GAIA Independently centered selves, contextually rooted
Style of Consciousness	Participation mystic	Objective, analytical, discriminating, lineal	Contextual, holistic dialogic
Relationship of Ego and Unconsciousness	Ego carried by or encompassed by larger psyche; no clear differentiation	Oppositional, confrontational frontier between ego and unconscious psyche	Dialogical interconnection. Each is context for the other, the birther of the other.
What Constitutes a Whole	The whole is collectively generated by the sum of its parts.	The whole is individual unit differentiated out of chaos.	Multiple levels of wholes; perpetual birthing of new wholes
Gender Relations	Gender equality	Patriarchy	Gender differences but equality
Pair-Bonding Unit	Egalitarian pair-bonding for childrearing	Patriarchal marriage to guarantee legitimacy of heirs to family property; arranged marriages yield romantic marriages based on couple choice.	Long- and short-term pair-bonding more for personal needs than for reproduction; marital households, LATs, cohabitation
Sexual Imagery	Fertility and its cycles	Phallic, genital, coital, male performance confirmed by female orgasm	Whole body sensuality, ecstasy, union with the cosmic self-transcendence; connectedness; oceanic awareness
Sexual Networks	Nonexclusive pair-bonding within the clan or tribe	Premarital virginity at least for female; sex limited to marriage; sexual exclusivity at least for wife (double standard); nuclear families	Intentional families with sexual intimacy allowed among a fluid network of friends
Religious Focus	Goddesses and gods	Patriarchal gods; male monotheism	???
Style of Power and Source of Value	Power of participation and inclusion; value lies in participating in the collective.	Power over other or the situation; value lies in one's superiority.	Power of self-transcendence; centered self in multiple context
How Growth Is Characterized and Promoted	Natural growth; proliferation; nurturance and cyclicity	Linear progress; ascent; competition and mastery over; begetting upon another	Transformations rooted in context; multi directional, fluid, unexpected

have in this century made it impossible for us to deny that we are moving into a new environment that will require a new sexual code. Our life expectancy has doubled from forty-seven years in the 1900s to close to eighty; the United States is graying and those over age one hundred are our fastest-growing group. Increased leisure, mobility, an information superhighway that by the year 2000 will connect 200 million people, reliable and safe contraceptives, reproductive technologies that separate sex and reproduction, smaller families with many couples opting for no children, challenges to organized religion and its authority over sexual behavior, and television are part of this new environment. Around the world, but most evident in the Euro-American scene, women are entering men's domains, the salaried workforce, dealing with men on their own level, and regaining some of the power they enjoyed in the pre-axial era. The emergence of feminism has brought new challenges to the phallocentric, coital male model of sex and a growing shift to a holistic model that emphasizes sensual pleasure and transcendence as well as orgasm—with orgasm not limited to coital penetration.

The value of pair-bonding, often long-term despite the availability of easy divorce and our increasing life expectancy, will continue to hold priority in our emotions and sexual code. Whether this pair-bonding will be dominated by one-household marital bonding or by adults living alone together (LAT) and maintaining two households while in a long-term intimate relationship, remains to be seen. Whether this pair-bonding will be expressed more often in a series of sexually exclusive monogamies or in a flexible, more or less sexually open, long-term, even lifelong pair-bonding, likewise remains to be seen. More than likely, as blood kinships shrink in the nomadic life of the 1990s and beyond, their role in supporting a stable and dynamic society will be increasingly replaced by intentional families created by pair-bonding individuals to accept and include emotional and sexual intimacies within a fluid matrix of more or less intimate friendships that increasingly cuts across the spectrum of gender orientations.

The sexual codes of the future are already breaking out of the dichotomies and clear distinctions that have dominated our axial cultures. The rigidity of the male/female sexual dichotomy, in which physicians routinely performed surgery to assign the roughly 4 percent of babies born with hermaphrodite and pseudohermaphrodite status to either the male or female sex, is being challenged by the affected individuals and their advocates who increasingly demand to be left in their intersex status and accepted as such (Fausto-Sterling, 1993). More obvious in recent decades has been the social and legal recognition of the gender-orientation spectrum of

gay, straight, and all shades in-between. Similarly, we are experiencing an increasing fluidity in our gender role behaviors, the near-infinite varied spectrum of masculine-androgynous-feminine (butch-androgynous-fem in the gay culture), even as neurobiologists identify anatomical and physiological differences in the brains of males and females.

At this point in human history, we have only faint hints of how the new sexual code will emerge and what its character will be. We can hope that it will preserve the best of what humans have achieved in the pre-axial and axial periods—the benefits those cultures have brought us—and incorporate these into the new sexual code.

[See also Abortion; Behavior: Social Constraints; Child Abuse; Family Patterns; Family Planning; Family Values; Genetics; Morals; Sexual Behavior; Sexual Laws; Sexual Reproduction: Artificial Means; Social Controls; Women's Movement; Women's Rights.]

BIBLIOGRAPHY

Abraham, Ralph. *Chaos, Gaia, Eros.* San Francisco: HarperCollins, 1994.

Chapelle, Delores La. *Sacred Land, Sacred Sex, Rapture of the Deep.* Silverton, CO: Finn Hill Arts, 1988.

Cousins, Ewert. "Male-Female Aspects of the Trinity in Christian Mysticism." In *Sexual Archetypes: East and West*, ed., Bina Gupta. New York: Paragon, 1987, pp. 37–50.

Fausto-Sterling, Anne. "The Five Sexes: Why Male and Female Are Not Enough." *The Sciences* (March–April 1993): 20–24.

Francoeur, Robert T. *Becoming a Sexual Person.* New York: John Wiley & Sons, 1982, pp. 473–476, 679–692.

———. *Hot and Cool Sex: Cultures in Conflict.* New York: Harcourt Brace & Jovanovich, 1974.

Haddon, Genia Pauli. *Uniting Sex, Self, and Spirit.* Scotland, CT: Plus Publications, 1993.

Jaspers, Karl. *The Origin and Goal of History.* New Haven, CT: Yale University Press, 1953.

Ogden, Gina. *Women Who Love Sex.* New York: Simon & Schuster/Pocket Books, 1994.

— ROBERT T. FRANCOEUR

SEXUAL HARASSMENT

Unwanted sexual attention has long been an indignity suffered by less powerful groups, especially women and children. Traditionally the most visible and frequent abuse has involved men harassing women. But with a greater diversity of people in power in the workplace, corporations are finding that men can also harass other men in this way; or women in positions of power can harass men; or women can harass other women. The key feature in any form of sexual harassment is unwanted sexual attention.

In the United States since 1980, the personal indignity of being subjected to unwanted sexual attention at work has been addressed by a number of legal steps. These offenses now are legally actionable. Sexual harassment complaints filed with state and federal governments rose from 6,892 in 1991 to 12,537 in 1993. Over the same period, compensation awards rose from $7.1 million to $25.7 million. Sexual and gender harassment, no matter how measured, now is viewed by the courts as a major form of employment discrimination. By 1994 the courts recognized two basic types of sexual harassment: quid pro quo involving explicit threats of "Do this or else," and a less-extreme form involving a hostile or abusive work environment.

In 1980 the U.S. Equal Employment Opportunity Commission (EEOC) regulations defined harassment in this way: "Unwelcome sexual advances, requests for sexual favors, and other verbal or physical conduct of a sexual nature constitute harassment when (1) submission to such conduct is made either explicitly or implicitly a term or condition of an individual's employment, (2) submission to or rejection of such conduct by an individual is used as the basis for employment decisions affecting such individual, or (3) such conduct

has the purpose or effect of unreasonably interfering with an individual's work performance or creating an intimidating, hostile, or offensive working environment" (29 C.F.R. #1604.11). Then in 1986 the Supreme Court ruled in *Meritor Savings Bank, FSB* v. *Vinson* that sexual harassment constituted an act of sexual discrimination.

The quid pro quo aspects of sexual harassment (items 1 and 2 above) are relatively clear. But establishing that a hostile environment constitutes sexual harassment has been more controversial. In 1993 the EEOC proposed guidelines indicating that a hostile environment can occur in the form of (1) "epithets, slurs, negative stereotyping, or threatening, intimidating, or hostile acts" (1609.1); or (2) "written or graphic material that denigrates or shows hostility or aversion on the employers's premises or circulated in the workplace" (1609.1).

Building on Title VII of the Civil Rights Act of 1964, the Supreme Court also ruled, in *Harris* v. *Forklift Systems, Inc.* (1993) that sexual harassment included not only unwanted explicit sexual behavior but *gender harassment or harassment of women in general* as well. The

As American women entered the military in greater numbers, incidences of sexual harassment complaints escalated in the 1990s. (Leif Skoogfors/Corbis)

768

rationale is that sex discrimination laws preclude unequal treatment based on sex. Sexually harassing work environments also can be created by sex-based comments related to women's bodies and by allowing expression of supposed intellectual or other hostile differences between the sexes.

As the diversity of the workforce expands, harassment of all forms, whether racial, ethnic, sexual, gender, or other, although potentially omnipresent, will be less tolerated.

Establishing the existence of a hostile sexual or gender environment is difficult. The Supreme Court required that several criteria be met (*Meritor Savings,* 1986). Specific circumstances surrounding each case must be examined to verify, that the conduct is persistent, severe, physically threatening or humiliating, and actually interferes with work performance.

Moreover, an assessment must be made as to whether the behavior would be considered "reasonable" in the given circumstances. While different work environments (e.g., road crews as contrasted with a bank office) are likely to produce different standards, these variations are compounded and further complicated by the 1991 ruling in *Ellison* v. *Brady.* That case maintained that determinations of sexual or gender harassment could be ascertained by a "reasonable woman" (rather than a "reasonable man") standard.

Subsequently EEOC proposed in 1993 to expand the "reasonable person" standard to include "consideration of the perspective of persons of the alleged victim's race, color, religion, gender, national origin, age, or disability." (1609.1). The Supreme Court ruling in the 1993 *Harris* case reaffirmed that women can see harm in cases where men will see only offensive behavior. In this case the court also ruled that it was not necessary to demonstrate psychological injury or a quid pro quo situation in order to show that sexual or gender harassment had occurred.

Who is responsible whenever such harassment occurs? The EEOC has consistently affirmed that it is employers who are responsible for the sexual and gender harassment perpetrated by their representatives. Such responsibility has been extended since the 1980s to include harassment by coworkers and even by nonemployees.

Key questions in determining responsibility include whether the employer can be considered to have known or should have known what was happening, and whether supervisors with control over the situation were acting as the employer's agent. Employers can protect themselves by (1) having an explicit policy against sexual harassment and (2) by establishing readily available procedures for victims to lodge and pursue remedy for complaints of harassment.

As the diversity of the workforce expands, harassment of all forms, whether racial, ethnic, sexual, gender, or other, although potentially omnipresent, will be less tolerated. The trend is toward enforcing existing laws on such matters and—in a preventive mode—encouraging greater sensitivity on all fronts.

[See also Behavior: Social Constraints; Child Abuse; Family Patterns; Family Problems; Family Values; Poverty, Feminization of; Sexual Codes; Sexual Laws; Women's Movement; Women's Rights.]

BIBLIOGRAPHY

Baxter, Ralph H. *Sexual Harassment in the Workplace.* New York: Executive Enterprises Publications, 1989.
Russell, Diane E. *Sexual Exploitation.* Thousand Oaks, CA: Sage Publications, 1984.
Webb, Susan L. *Step Forward: Sexual Harassment in the Workplace—What You Need to Know.* New York: MasterMedia Ltd., 1991.

— RITA MAE KELLY

SEXUAL LAWS

Sexual morality has undergone radical transformation. Statutory principles that reflect permissible conduct and proscribe or prohibit unacceptable behavior have become much more permissive and enforcement attitudes toward them have been relaxed. It seems that acceptable sexual behavior is becoming more a health than a moral issue. This reflects changed behavior of a sort that undermines the family and disrupts the community.

Abortions used to be obtained in desperate circumstances in back alleys or by going abroad. Now abortions are openly and freely available in the United States. Previously limited to a few instances involving lifesaving or truly grievous situations (rape, incest, etc.), abortion now is available virtually on demand, and it is provided at taxpayer expense for those who cannot afford it. Teen abortion is available, even without parental notification in some jurisdictions. Not surprisingly, the number performed jumped threefold from 605,000 in 1972 to 1,700,000 in 1991.

Permissive use of "quick-fix" abortifacients formerly were forbidden or severely restricted in use. Easy-to-use abortion pills like RU-486, already approved for general use abroad, are imminent in the United States.

Not so many years ago, society frowned on and even forbid the general distribution of contraceptives. Now contraceptives are out from under the counter, openly advertised on television, and vending is even mandated in certain locations. Contraceptives, once not sold to minors, are given to them free at schools or by government workers—sometimes against the wishes of parents or guardians. Sexual activity among minors, instead of being discouraged, is aided and abetted by providing them with contraceptives.

Statutory rape laws, intended to protect minors, are largely ignored. Date rape has become a boomlet. Gang rapes are shrugged off as "wilding," or "just boys on a spree," or by asserting "boys will be boys."

Teen pregnancy, once scorned, now soars. "Shotgun weddings," forced by irate parents, seldom are seen anymore. Children are encouraged to come to school with their babies. The United States leads all other advanced nations in teen pregnancy. Many teenage fathers escape responsibility for their role and ignore child-support obligations, because government lends little effort to seeing that these responsibilities are met. Teen pregnancy as a result is heavily supported by taxpayers. The burdens imposed on society by teen families cost government $21 billion in 1989. The problem has grown worse since then.

Laws against fornication—sex outside wedlock—instead of being enforced are, for all practical purposes, ignored. "Living in sin," cohabitation, trial marriages, and the like are not ostracized as they once were. Unwanted offspring resulting from these liaisons, likely as not, are aborted or sometimes even murdered. Irresponsible fathers slink away from their responsibilities to support children and family all too easily.

Illegitimate children born outside wedlock increased nearly eightfold between 1950 and 1991 (rising from 146,000 to 1,151,000). Three of every 10 children born in the United States (28 percent) were born to unwed mothers during 1991, and the proportion may rise to 40 percent by 2000. Two out of every three babies (68 percent) born to African-American mothers in 1991 were illegitimate. Depressingly, more African-American girls drop out of high school to have a baby than graduate from college.

Standards that once proscribed sodomy, sexual perversion, unnatural sex acts, and so on are generally ignored or being repealed. Gay rights to serve in the military are being pursued against objections of most military leaders. Controversies swirl around prescribed school readings and curricula intended to provide understanding and otherwise legitimize homosexuality and gay marriages.

Prostitution is legal in a few jurisdictions. More likely, it is tolerated in so-called red light areas, "combat zones," or tenderloin districts. In a few jurisdictions

brothels are state-sanctioned (designated areas in Nevada, Amsterdam, Portugal, and elsewhere).

AIDS victims in the United States are not quarantined, as one might expect for any death-dealing contagious disease. AIDS victims have become today's Typhoid Marys, with the exception that carriers are left free to inflict their deadly disease on others. In the past child diseases that rarely resulted in death—measles, chicken pox, mumps, and whooping cough—required strict quarantine, including posting of residences to protect the unwary from these communicable diseases. By 1989, AIDS had become the eleventh largest killer disease in the United States, taking 22,675 lives in 1992. Yet, AIDS victims' privacy is invoked to avoid quarantining, testing, or other controls.

Sexually transmitted diseases, once scorned, now are medically treated. This is done at the public's expense, at least in cases where disease carriers are too poor to afford treatment on their own.

Suggestive lingerie, previously relegated to the back pages of tawdry pulp-paper magazines, has gone mainstream. Frederick's of Hollywood, Victoria's Secret, even the Limited have invaded the shopping malls with upscale and somewhat subdued offerings.

Topless bathing also has come a long way. Males, as recently as 1936, were convicted of indecent exposure for failing to cover up their tops in public. String bikinis are now permitted on many beaches, although banned from others. Nude bathing beaches proliferate (Santa Cruz, Marin, and many other counties).

Nudity also has hit Main Street, or at least the red light district. Topless and bottomless bars abound. There are even "adult" (topless) car washes; maid services; and bus caravans that take erotic shows to the countryside (Prague). Traditional burlesque houses fight back, with their trade association, the Exotic Dancers League, opposing taking ecdysiastic arts away from their turf.

Pornography, vigorously curbed not so many years ago, is rampant as freedom of speech prevails over censorship. We've come a long way from the suggestive nudity of gossamer-clad *Esquire* magazine pin-ups by Vargas to the explicit *Playboy* magazine centerfolds. Madonna's professional perversions, shocking to an earlier generation, prevail. Explicit sex in triple-X-rated movies are everywhere. NC-17 ratings liberalize sex and violence standards to lower levels for children under seventeen years of age. The at-home porn movies have also reached new levels. Outlawed low-tech 8-mm underground or home-produced movies have given way to out-in-the-open commercial adult videocassettes. Satellite broadcasters also assault the airwaves with X-rated movies. Some jurisdictions fight back. Alabama, for example, has sought extradition of businesspersons responsible for such broadcasts.

All communications technologies are being invaded. There is porn on FAX and in cyberspace. Pay-per-call erotic telephone talk lines using 1–900 numbers have cropped up. Some of them originate in countries with permissive laws, thus skirting domestic regulation.

Dr. Joyce Brothers, among others, has peddled no-holds-barred explicit titillating call-in sex problems over her radio show. Sleazy and sensational talk shows that exploit every and any imaginable sexual escapade punctuate daytime television.

Explicit lyrics in music, attacked by then-Senator Al Gore's wife, Tipper Gore, struck a responsive chord. But freedom of expression prevails. Lewd and raunchy bumper stickers proliferate. Some states such as South Carolina, Florida, and Georgia outlaw them. Books of dubious taste or sexual explicitness once were regularly summarily banned in many jurisdictions. "Banned in Boston" became a code word for tough smut control. In some instances such literature has been prescribed as mandatory reading—including texts supporting understanding of gay couples' rights to adopt children—despite parental protests.

Porn performers have been allowed to acquire star status. In earlier times, they were tracked down and convicted of lewd performances. In Italy, female porn stars have been elected to parliament and have formed their own political party: the Party of Love.

What comes into perspective from this litany of licentiousness is that basic moral principles have been diminished and degraded by permissiveness. Morals are rooted in time. The future holds a return to moral, religious, ethical, and philosophical principles that both prescribe and proscribe. The pendulum of moral restraint has been allowed to swing too far toward the permissive side. The swing back will not go to Victorian extremes, but to guidelines constantly striving to keep sexual behavior within respectable bounds.

[See also Abortion; Crime, Nonviolent; Sexual Behavior; Sexual Codes; Sexual Reproduction.]

BIBLIOGRAPHY

Bennett, William J. *The De-Valuing of America: The Fight for Our Culture and Our Children.* New York: Simon & Schuster, 1992.

Davis, Nanette J. *Prostitution: An International Handbook on Trends, Problems, and Policies.* Westport, CT: Greenwood Press, 1993.

Hibbert, Christopher. *The Roots of Evil: A Social History of Crime and Punishment.* New York: Little, Brown, 1968.

Hughes, Robert. *Culture of Complaint: The Fraying of America.* New York: Oxford University Press, 1993.

Trebach, Arnold S. *The Great Drug War: And Radical Proposals that Could Make America Safe Again.* New York: Macmillan, 1987.

— GRAHAM T. T. MOLITOR

SEXUAL REPRODUCTION

The future of human birth will be a study in contradictions. Immense effort will be exerted to find the perfect contraceptive for the disenfranchised (young, poor, or Third World women) and better ways for the privileged (older, wealthier women in industrialized nations) to conceive. Political, economic, environmental, and social factors will influence the future of reproduction as biological screening and manipulative techniques become more widely used to determine the gender, health, and personal characteristics of future children.

Before the year 2000,

the Human Genome Initiative Project will provide

a detailed genetic map of all human genes.

Conception

New techniques involving hormonal stimulation of egg production, fertilization of eggs inside and outside the body, extracting sperm directly from the epididymis, and genetic cloning will impact conception. New laboratory techniques for fertilization outside of the body include the use of lasers to penetrate the outer layer of an egg so that sperm can be deposited directly into its interior to better the chances of fertilization. Laboratory conception also allows for the elimination of toxic substances, the preselection of egg and sperm for desired characteristics, and genetic alterations of selected cells.

Pregnancy

Medical science, specifically the science of in-vitro fertilization, is moving toward the development of an artificial womb. The creation of this technology and its widespread use, initially perhaps limited to applications involving farm animals, could dramatically alter our society's views about conception, pregnancy, abortion, and childbirth. Parents of the future may be able to conceive, carry a pregnancy to term, and deliver without any of the discomfort or risk of carrying a pregnancy in their bodies or even without ever having sexual intercourse.

Before the year 2000, the Human Genome Initiative Project will provide a detailed genetic map of all human genes. Coupled with our ability to correct some genetic anomalies during pregnancy, this development will make diagnosis of fetal problems an extremely important part of pregnancy. Ultrasonic scanning, blood sampling of both parents prior to or following conception, amniocentesis (sampling the amniotic fluid that surrounds the fetus for genetic analysis), and chorionic villi biopsy (sampling the placental tissue) are techniques already being used to determine fetal health. Each technique carries a small risk to both the mother and fetus. Sampling of maternal blood and some form of computer-enhanced scanning to determine fetal defects are the only methods likely to move out of the laboratory and into the home of the future for routine use.

Sex Preselection

Humans have always shown interest in the sex of fetuses and have devised some interesting ways of trying to effect the outcome of fertilization. Wearing a hat during intercourse, eating chocolate, douching with vinegar, and laboratory separation of X- and Y-bearing sperm are all techniques that have been used to predetermine sex. In a world of shrinking resources people who wish to limit births may also wish to select the sex of the children born. In China, infanticide of female infants has become a way of assuring a male child in a society that only allows one child per couple. In India, prenatal diagnosis of sex has been outlawed, except to diagnose and prevent sex-linked genetic anomalies, because of the rise in abortions of female fetuses. If societies continue to prize males over females, sex preselection will continue to rise, especially for first-born children.

Fetal Health

While experts research and argue the results of collected data comparing the effects of fetal exposure to alcohol, crack cocaine, or environmental pollutants, the medical and legal professions and mothers are fighting in and out of court about the rights of mother and fetus. Can a woman drink any alcohol, ingest any drugs, or ignore/ refuse testing and intervention procedures that could verify fetal anomalies or potentially prevent fetal damage or death? The current recommendations of the American Medical Association are in favor of informed decision making by the pregnant woman. The spread of new research, diagnostic techniques, and prenatal intervention strategies are likely to strain current recom-

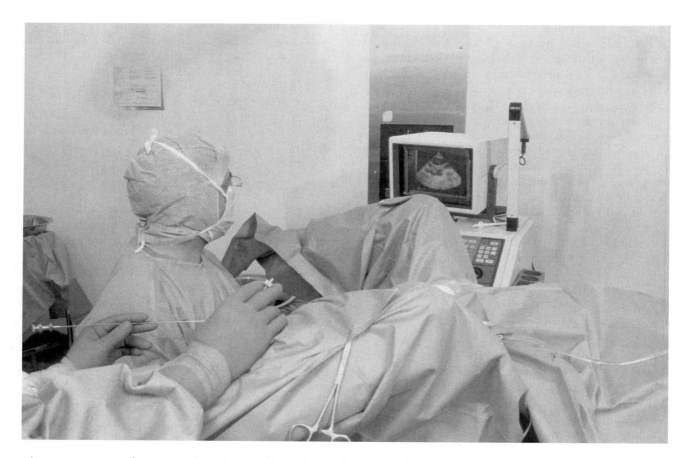

A surgeon removes ova from a woman's ovaries to combine with a man's sperm in order to create a zygote. As birth control and reproductive technologies dominate, sex will become recreational rather than procreational. (Jacques M. Chenet/Corbis)

mendations. Pregnant women may find their traditional civil rights becoming more limited in the next century.

How will our children's children define an anomaly or defect as it relates to their children? Will a predisposition to obesity, proneness to drinking too much, being a female—or having brown eyes—qualify as a defect? Preimplantation diagnosis is being used to test two-day-old embryos fertilized in a laboratory petri dish for genetic defects like cystic fibrosis. In the future we will be able to test for the entire range of genetically preprogrammed characteristics and intervene to clone or split the cells of the embryos that possess all or most of the desired characteristics and discard or alter the undesirable ones.

For those couples who still develop a pregnancy through sexual intercourse and therefore do not have access to preimplantation diagnosis, other genetic screening and correction techniques will be available. Genetic defects will be corrected through stem-cell transplants that involve the transplantation of healthy stem-cells from one fetus to another or from the fetus's parents into the fetus. Another method will be gene therapy. This technique involves the removal of diseased stem-cells from the fetus's bloodstream, transferring healthy genes into them, and reinjecting them into the fetus.

Fetal surgery began with operations to implant shunts or tubes to drain excess fluid from fetal bladders or brain cavities. Recent surgeries include open-womb procedures to correct physical defects. In the future, fetal surgery may be performed to correct a cleft palate or facial abnormalities. One advantage of fetal surgery is that the fetus heals without scars. Another exciting aspect of fetal surgery is that one fetus will not reject the cells of another fetus. This opens the possibility of cell and organ transplants to correct a multitude of problems before birth that would require risky procedures like bone marrow transplant later in life.

Childbirth

Traditional vaginal delivery is likely to continue to be the norm for most women everywhere. Advances in pre-natal care and rising concerns about parental involvement in birthing are leading to an increase in the use of birthing chairs and childbirth techniques such as the Lamaze or Leboyer methods, which involve less use of anesthesia and episiotomy. Caesarian births, delivery through an incision in the abdominal wall, have increased and are likely to continue increasing in the United States for several reasons, including better fetal monitoring techniques, less willingness on the part of physicians and parents to risk complications during childbirth, and increasing medical malpractice liability.

The current trend is for delivery to take place in a special birthing center or clinic connected to or in a hospital. In the future these centers will be freestanding facilities staffed by certified nurse midwives. Because of their ties to hospitals, the centers will provide a home-like atmosphere that will welcome the entire family into the birth process without sacrificing the availability of technical and emergency support that is absent in home delivery.

Motherhood

The future of motherhood will be paradoxical. Teens and other poor or uneducated women will be pressured to avoid motherhood. Successful women in their thirties and forties, even post-menopausal women will use extraordinarily expensive technological measures to become mothers. Mothers with low incomes will be less likely to live in traditional nuclear families and more likely be unmarried, divorced, or single. The result will be some hardships placed on them and their children.

Genetic preselection may limit the number of women available to become mothers and induce competition for them between men who hold to established family ideals. This competition will elevate the traditional female roles of childbearing and motherhood.

[See also Abortion; Behavior: Social Constraints; Child Abuse; Family Patterns; Family Planning; Family Values; Genetics; Genetic Technologies; Morals; Sexual Behavior; Sexual Codes; Sexual Reproduction: Artificial Means; Social Controls.]

BIBLIOGRAPHY

Cole, Helene M. "Legal Interventions During Pregnancy." *Journal of The American Medical Association,* 264/20 (November 28, 1990): 2663–2670.

Durand, Mark A. "The Safety of Home Birth: The Farm Study." *American Journal of Public Health* 82/3 (March 1992): 450–453.

Francoeur, Robert T. *Becoming a Sexual Person.* New York: Macmillan, 1991.

Sachs, Benjamin P., et. al. "Home Monitoring of Uterine Activity, Does It Prevent Prematurity?" *New England Journal of Medicine* 325/19 (November 7, 1991): 1374–1377.

"Saving Female Babies." *Nature* (October 17, 1991).

"Surgery Before Birth." *Discover* (February 1991).

— PETER ANDERSON

SEXUAL REPRODUCTION: ARTIFICIAL MEANS

Louise Brown, born July 25, 1978, in England, became the first test-tube baby in the world. In 1991, Arlette Schwitzer had four of her daughter's fertilized eggs transferred to her and gave birth to her own twin grandchildren. In 1992, Josie Mosby Mitchell, fifty-two years old and in menopause, conceived a child with a donor egg fertilized in vitro with the sperm of her second husband. Slowly humans are taking control over their reproductive process and radically altering attitudes toward sex and sexuality. Sexual intercourse is no longer an essential part of reproduction, although it will certainly continue to be practiced by most people. Starting in the 1970s, new reproductive technologies began to proliferate. Artificial insemination, egg donation, artificial embryonation, surrogate motherhood, embryo adoption, *in vitro* fertilization (IVF), embryo freezing, and artificial wombs are in various stages of research, development, and utilization. Unlike previous reproductive methods, the new technologies involve a third, and sometimes a fourth or fifth party, in the act of conception and birthing.

Over 10 percent of the 3.5 million infertile couples in the United States, one in six couples, are turning to these new assisted reproductive technologies. The numbers are expected to grow. Growing compromises of fertility by environmental toxins, radiation, stress, drugs, and so forth assure this trend. Concerns over sexually transmitted diseases, such as AIDS, and the expanding possibilities of genetic selection further assure that reproduction technologies are here to stay. They offer hope to the infertile and better children for everyone.

Flash Forward to 2020

A six-billion-dollar sex industry prevails where fertility clinics market parts—wombs, ovaries, fallopian tubes, eggs, sperm—for reproductive purposes. Fertility clinics have expanded their market beyond infertile couples, to individuals at risk from toxins, menopausal women, individuals with genetic diseases, fertile career women, and men who want children.

Technology has leaped forward. Intricate microsurgery and laser surgery repair damage to defective reproductive organs. Infertile women can have surgery to unblock, repair, or replace fallopian tubes with donor transplants or artificial tubes. Ovary transplants from older menopausal women to young infertile women are now common. Ovarian transplants into younger women allow their physiological and hormonal activities to "turn them on" for successful child bearing. For infertile men, testicle transplants and the use of new drugs to enhance sperm counts are increasingly popular.

The assisted reproduction technologies of 2020 are a bit less popular than traditional birth methods. The reason? They add other human beings to the "creation equation" and raise an array of ethical and legal concerns.

Artificial insemination, the simplest method, is performed in the privacy of one's home using husband or donor sperm. Today, there is a 70 percent fertilization success rate after only one or two treatments, up from the 57 percent success rate involving two to nine treatments in the early 1990s. A controversial debate swirls around insurance payment for such procedures. People confidently use mail-order sperm banks that screen donor sperm for genetic defects, diseases, and gender. Extensive donor health histories are available upon request, and catalogs from the sperm banks describe each donor's age, blood type, family background, physical characteristics, and education.

Operations for egg donations are performed by doctors, followed by artificial insemination. Whenever possible, in vivo (in the body) fertilization is recommended by doctors.

Instead of the three-day embryo development phase practiced years ago in a "petri dish," many doctors in the year 2020 place the sperm cells and egg together for only one hour and then transfer them to the uterus, where a new procedure allows fertilization to take place within the mother's body.

Improvements in sperm analysis and laser technology make the in vitro fertilization (IVF) process easy and reduce the number of sperm needed from a donor to one high-quality sperm. Active sperm cells are separated from less active sperm cells to ensure that only healthy sperm fertilize eggs. Lasers are used to test sperm for motility, to drag a quality sperm over to an egg where a convenient hole has been cut in the membrane for the sperm to enter and seed it. It is also possible to use lasers to cut portions of the zona pellucida, a protective membrane around the egg that toughens with age, to permit the growing embryo to "hatch" and grow in the uterus. Lasers also help doctors to produce twins or triplets. The doctor can divide an embryo surgically in halves or thirds before transferring the embryos to the mother's uterus. Doctors may need to repeat the IVF procedure four times for pregnancy to occur in 70 percent of the patients. Today—December 10, 2020—40 percent of the recipients undergoing IVF take a baby to term in the United States, a 25 percent increase from 1992.

Couples with known histories of genetic disorders combine IVF with gene therapy. The missing gene that is absent from the DNA sequence is inserted into the embryo before the embryo is transferred to the recipient's uterus. The procedure can replace the gene for eighty known genetic defects, twenty times the capability of 1993, when only cystic fibrosis, hemophilia, Duchenne muscular dystrophy, and Tay-Sachs disease could be corrected.

Cryobanks advertise nationally, offering to preserve eggs, sperm, and embryos (fertilized eggs). Embryo and sperm storage is now safe for an indefinite period. However, because of a few cases of chromosome losses in human oocytes, the research community is doubling its efforts to preserve eggs effectively. Laws allow only six pregnancies per donor in a specified geographic location to thwart the disadvantages of incest among children created through artificial insemination by the same or closely related donors. Consequently, cryogenic banks now screen and store a wide genetic pool of donors.

Sperm, eggs, or embryos produced

at the height of one's reproductive years

can be stored for family planning.

People freeze and store their eggs, sperm, and embryos as insurance for a future with children. Freezing eggs or embryos collected in an egg donation and artificial embryonation operation protects women against excessive operations should the first or second attempt at pregnancy fail. Having frozen embryos allows a woman/surrogate to receive an embryo when the conditions are best for an embryo to attach itself to the uterine wall and to grow. Finally, sperm, eggs, or embryos produced at the height of one's reproductive years can be stored for family planning. People are thus better able to pace the birth of their children.

More couples and single parents are choosing to have children later in life and some after menopause. Discovery that aging eggs, not aging wombs, cause infertility among older women gives women the flexibility to have children using young-donor oocytes or their own oocytes collected and frozen when they were younger.

New advances in embryo-transfer techniques also enhance the embryo survival rate once an embryo is implanted in the uterus. No longer are five or six embryos implanted in a uterus to assure that at least one embryo sticks to the uterus and grows; instead, only one or two embryo implants are needed for a successful birth. A better quality-control system for the cultural fluids used in the petri dish and improved egg-ripening techniques contribute to the success rate. The procedure reduces the danger of multiple births and genetic defects.

For years, the cryobanks have provided low storage rates to military personnel likely to participate in dangerous assignments. One situation drew national attention recently when a female gave birth to her own twin. Twenty-five years ago, her mother had twin embryos through IVF. One female twin was transferred to the mother's uterus and brought to term while the other was frozen and stored. Upon learning that possible combat duty was in her future, the first twin had her twin sister thawed, placed into her uterus, and gave birth to her.

As in any generation, there are aspects of sexual reproduction that pose ethical and legal controversies. Four issues—surrogacy, the rights of embryos, cloning, and male pregnancy—continue to generate serious debate.

Surrogacy issues draw national attention. Most U.S. states now follow the New York 1993 precedent that bans commercial surrogacy and limits payment of $10,000 for the surrogates and around $6,000 for the surrogate entrepreneurs who locate and screen them. Beneficiary payment of medical expenses is still permitted. Although the laws in most states eliminate the concern over child selling, they do little to prevent women from being turned into living incubators with controls placed on their sexual behavior, cigarette smoking, and food and alcoholic intake. Surrogate rights to privacy and freedom of choice are questioned. The issue is inflamed as Third World women are exploited as commercial surrogates, and by obsessive single men and fertile women (i.e., busy executives, models, etc.) who choose the surrogacy option, and to prevent women from being devalued and viewed as "cows." Governments impose strict screening, inspection, and controls on surrogates.

Debate over who is the child's mother also continues to fester. Is the mother the woman who bears the child or the woman who provides its genes? The courts have given the child to the genetic mother, but controversies over surrogate visitation rights continue. With the recent creation of a human artificial womb, the issue of surrogacy may slowly be put to rest.

Another issue, the rights of frozen embryos, poses serious questions. Who is responsible for an embryo if the couple dies? Some state courts favor giving responsibility to the next of kin or honoring a living will. A more difficult question is whether a frozen embryo has a right to be born? For inheritance purposes, would a frozen embryo be considered an additional heir? The recent NASA proposal to send the frozen embryos of many species into space raises similar questions. The human embryos are to be transferred to female astronauts once a colony has been established on another planet. Concern over the risk to the astronauts as well as the legal rights of the embryo are part of the heated debate.

The third issue relates to research in cloning. Scientists, using microsurgical techniques, remove the nuclei from an embryonic cell and replace it with the cell or genetic material (DNA) of another human. After implanting the new embryo into a recipient's uterus, an exact duplicate of the human being, a clone, is produced. Though cloning often is used in the cattle and dairy industry, fear over attempts to create a master race and the legal implications and consequences, have slowed human applications.

Finally, the issue of male pregnancy is a common subject of "virtual reality" talk shows. In the late twentieth century, a George Washington University Medical School doctor "fertilized a chimpanzee egg *in vitro* with chimpanzee sperm, implanted it in the abdomen of a male chimpanzee, later delivering a healthy baby chimp through a Caesarian section" (Andrews, 1984, page 261). In 2019, Australian scientists combined the technique with advances in artificial womb technology to produce a successful male pregnancy.

[See also Abortion; Family Planning; Genetic Engineering; Genetics; Genetic Technologies; Sexual Behavior; Sexual Codes; Sexual Reproduction; Women's Movement.]

BIBLIOGRAPHY

Andrews, Lori B. *New Conceptions*. New York: St. Martin's Press, 1984.

Annas, George J. "Using Genes to Define Motherhood." *The New England Journal of Medicine* (February 6, 1992):417–420.

Dewitt, Paula Mergenhagen. "In Pursuit of Pregnancy." *American Demographics* 15 (May 1993): 48–53.

Hadfield, Peter. "Japanese Pioneers Raise Kid in Rubber Womb." *New Scientist* (April 25, 1992).

Oehninger, Sergio, et al. "Prediction of Fertilization in Vitro with Human Gametes: Is There a Litmus Test?" *American Journal of Obstetrics and Gynecology* 167 (December 1992): 1760–1766.

Sauer, Mark V., et al. "Pregnancy After Age 50: Application of Oocyte Donation to Women after Natural Menopause." *The Lancet* 341 (February 6, 1993): 321–323.

Sher, Geoffrey; Marriage, Virginia A.; and Stoess, Jean. *From Infertility to In Vitro Fertilization*. New York: McGraw-Hill, 1988.

Winston, Robert M. L., and Handyside, Alan H. "New Challenges in Human In Vitro Fertilization." *Science* 260 (May 14, 1993): 932–936.

— C. LENA LUPICA

SMOKING.

See TOBACCO.

SOCIAL CHANGE: UNITED STATES

Future students of American society will find that the methods, the understanding, and approaches of the 1960s will not be adequate for the next century. Sometime, perhaps in the 1970s and certainly by 1990, the forces of change expanded and shifted power. Economics, the traditional prime-mover discipline, lost some of its dominance. The idea that economic forces controlled and determined so much of our behavior was diminished by a new value system involving one new force, *ecology*, and the intensified significance of another force, *technology*.

Ecology

New groups appeared, worldwide, focusing on the environment. Their goals were not guided by traditional economic merit, but were based on the need to foster certain ecological conditions. The economic values of eagles, wolves, rare bird species, and Sequoia redwoods were not their criteria. Rivers were to remain wild. Mining and drilling for oil were not to be tolerated on massive portions of space—even though only a handful of people ever intended to visit Alaskan wildernesses. Endangered species were to be restored—often at an enormous cost of jobs and industry. Although there were some powerful presentations concerning the economic consequences of destroying certain portions of nature, the rationale for many ecological decisions was, at bottom, the result of changing values in American society.

People, their ideas, perceptions, and goods can be transported within roughly twenty-four hours to any place in the world.

First there was a growing delight in the beauty of nature and respect for the other life-forms around us. Second, there were ecological developments that did have economic consequences heretofore ignored. By the 1950s nature itself was no longer tolerating some of our assaults. It was hard to breathe because the air in cities such as Los Angeles and London was being poisoned. By 1994 the once rich fishing grounds off New England and the Maritimes had been fished to the point of extinction. Elsewhere the water supply from rivers and ancient water tables clearly was not adequate to continue present activities in traditional form. It is firmly established now that decisions are going to be influenced by value systems that lie outside the realm of economics. Ecology will continue to play an intensified role in the future by law, because of new levels of societal awareness, and by necessity. Such necessity arises out of population pressures. Burgeoning population will be the great factor shaping world social conditions as well as U.S. social conditions in the decades to come. It is a painful truth that a growing population requires more land for living space, work, food, and play. More people will generate more wastes. Pressure on land, air, and water, and the salience of ecological issues will increase. We will have to double up, reuse, compress, and even omit various accustomed elements of daily living. Each of these choices requires a changing lifestyle, altered living conditions, changes in work and leisure activities, and tradeoffs in time and costs. Space will increase in value, and its economic price will alter our use of what space we can afford. Thus, considerable social change will flow out of a growing population. Japan, the Netherlands, Mexico, and Hawaii provide us with some examples of how best to cope.

Technology

Technology is the other force that will continue to change society and its behavior. Technology is omnipresent, uneven in applications, and disturbingly restless. The social consequences of technological change can be somewhat illuminated by focusing not on the ever-changing technology itself, but on the consequences of continuing advances. Each technological capability surely will continue to produce effects like these:

1. *Mastery of distance.* Geography is no longer as much of a barrier to movement. Travel time and costs have been drastically reduced. This means that people, their ideas, perceptions, and goods can be transported within roughly twenty-four hours to any place in the world. Thus, there is less security in geography for markets, ideas, practices, techniques, and special knowledge. Barriers to movement are largely political. A striving for equality of life will be triggered in hundreds of ways.

2. *Mastery of energy.* Energy increasingly will be transported over vast distances, thus leading to the decline of traditional local energy sources and associated production activities and jobs and the rise of low-cost producers outside the United States. This means that the political relationships with energy producers will be more sensitive and crucial. Energy also will be packaged in smaller and larger capacities, having more durability. Thus, portable power will be applied at many levels in thousands of ever tinier and more durable devices. Energy will be controlled with much more precision. Essentially, this means independence from fixed power systems and the application of power to many social activities and devices.

3. *Ability to alter materials.* There will be a growing war between materials, with more new opportunities and increased threats for traditional materials. Synthetic materials such as new plastics along with improved qualities in old materials and also combinations of materials (like paper, metals, or wood with plastics) assure that durability, wear resistance, and other attributes will extend the useful life of products. Competition in products will sometimes largely involve the particular materials used. Materials science will be ever more important.

4. *Mechanization of physical work.* This historic trend will continue and be remarkable, especially in its application to service industries, such as food services, libraries, and hospitals. Service fields will experience the same decline in relative physical effort and the same problems of capital investment, lack of flexibility, reduction of labor, and so on that factory automation and mechanized farm work have previously demonstrated. The library will shift drastically from storage of information on paper to storage in electronic form.

5. *Extension of sensory capabilities.* Here is the most profound of all technical trends in the years just ahead. Events happening anywhere in the world can soon or instantly be envisioned everywhere in sight and sound, with all the emotion conveyed by color and voice. This brings many reactions based on emotion rather than reflective thought and complete infor-

mation. Whoever controls the information content will influence responses and attitudes for better or worse. Each of the human senses is being improved:

- *Vision:* the ability to see beyond previously limiting conditions of distance, darkness, fog, water, great space, molecular space, and atomic space.
- *Speech and hearing:* the amplification, multiplication, transmission, and dispersion of sound.
- *Reach:* to control and manipulate things beyond arm's length.
- *Discrimination:* to detect, identify, and measure external things with more minute precision.
- *Memory:* to preserve, multiply, duplicate, and transmit sensory information across distance and time.

6. *Mechanization of information collection, manipulation, and interpretation.* Application of the computer in all its forms is the most dynamic and explosive trend, and the implications are far from ended. Of course this development overlaps and interfaces with all the sensory capabilities just described, but is stressed here because it essentially deals with the human brain. Problem solving, information retrieval, and interpretation are being mechanized. The computer is doing for intelligence what electricity did for power: it is making intelligence portable, divisible, and capable of multiplication on a massive scale or in minute form. It is vastly extending the capabilities of people and institutions. While it demands more education in its design and application, it also allows operators with only the most elementary knowledge to perform mental tasks that they do not understand. The hand-held calculator is an everyday example. Thus, both a reduction and increase in skill requirements are resulting. The social consequences of this vary with differing activities, but profound societal change is occurring on a national and international scale.

Summary of Consequences

Technology has created a highly interdependent world, with all nations increasingly reliant on each other for energy, raw materials, food, water (probably the next great shortage), technical equipment, knowledge, and economic and physical disaster assistance. There is an increasing social awareness of the second- and third-order consequences of these developments and events. We can expect the growth of more pressure-groups advocating or opposing changes and using communications technology to arouse wide and instant attention. The visual appearance of things and events, worldwide and in real time, will create rising expectations and demands for equality and control. U.S. society will be increasingly sensitive to internal and world social conditions. Therefore, self-fulfilling and self-defeating prophecies will play a more powerful role in social and political actions. A simple example is the effect of stock market analysts' predictions of the earning of a stock. When actual earnings fail to meet predictions, the stock is often devalued, even if its performance is relatively good. Society has responded to expectations rather than to reality. Some electric utility firms were in dire straits in 1995 because politicians forced them to make long-term contracts for high-priced alternative energy sources. Predictions about high oil prices and high energy demands never materialized.

[See also Change; Change, Cultural; Change, Epochal; Change, Optimistic and Pessimistic Perspectives; Change, Pace of; Change, Scientific and Technological; Continuity and Discontinuity; Environment; Global Consciousness; Global Turning Points; Lifestyles; Modernism and Postmodernism; Population Growth: United States; Public Policy Change; Social Controls; Social Indicators; Social Inventions; Social and Political Evolution; Technological Change; Technology and Society; Values; Values Change; Values Formation.]

BIBLIOGRAPHY

Behrens, W. H.; Meadows, D. H.; Meadows, D. I.; and Randers, J. *The Limits to Growth.* Washington, DC: Potomac Associates, 1972.

Bright, James R. *Automation and Management.* Boston: Graduate School of Business Administration, 1958.

Henshel, Richard L. "The Boundary of the Self-Fulfilling Prophecy and the Dilemma of Social Prediction." *British Journal of Sociology* 33/4 (December 1982): 511–528.

Martino, Joseph P. *Technological Forecasting for Decision Making,* 3rd ed. New York: Elsevier Science Publishing, 1992.

Newell, Roger P. "Mobile Communications for the Masses." *New Telcom Quarterly* 3/2 (1995): 17–22.

Teich, Albert H. *Technology and the Future,* 6th ed. New York: St. Martin's Press, 1993.

— JAMES R. BRIGHT

SOCIAL CONTROLS

Predicting the future may seem to be a mysterious process steeped in prolix or secret techniques. In truth, forecasting depends largely upon familiar empirical data. The essential difference is that forecasters exert an extra effort to carefully discern trends, their direction, pace, and duration. Some futurists term these telltale indicators "pacing parameters." Elsewhere in this encyclopedia, the Molitor Multiple-Timeline Model of Change refers to such precipitating or prompting factors as "steps" or bellwether "signatures of change." A collection of such trends and their coalescence reveals definable outcomes perpetuated by this confluence.

Social controls—included as a component of myriad "Informal Rules" described in the Molitor change model (Figure 1)—exert a powerful influence in resolving public policy as well as other sociopolitical matters. These principles—generally unwritten or without the force and effect of formal laws—channel ultimate decisions in discernable and predictable ways. The purpose of this commentary is to define the nature of social controls and to direct the reader to the broader context of sociopolitical decision making and outcomes.

Human behavior is guided not only by formal, explicit, and written laws but also by informal, implicit, and unwritten principles. Informal rules influence the principle, purpose, and psychological disposition of individuals, groups, and society itself. Social controls are tempered by trial and error, the test of time validating and entrenching workable ones.

Human behavior is guided not only by formal, explicit, and written laws but also by informal, implicit, and unwritten principles.

Behavioral "blueprints" of proscriptive don'ts and prescriptive do's built into social systems powerfully influence routine actions. Deterrence is the operative principle of negative sanctions, and encouragement is the operative principle of positive inducements. Negative sanctions range from mere rebuffs (ridicule, embarrassment, ostracism, or public scorn) to severe sanctions (threats, intimidation, reprisal, penalties, and punishments). Social conformity is a strong inducement because most individuals do not want to stand out as nonconformists or deviants. Enforcement of these principles also is an important determinant of behavior. The enforcement of laws prohibiting adultery, fornication, or sodomy has become lax or nonexistent because of changing moral attitudes and the difficulty of enforcement. The lack of enforcement and a lessening social stigmata, not surprisingly, have contributed to increases in such behavior.

Guiding Principles

Social control concepts are complex and confounded by subtle semantic shading. Because the narrative and graphic lists used here attempt to be inclusive, some terms may be synonymous or overlap (Figure 1). Informal rules of a social environment are derived from philosophy, theology, natural law, ideals, ethics, morals, and conscience (psychological principles) and are embedded in ceremonies, rituals, values, beliefs, lifestyles, and intellectual concepts. Numerous terms—*mores, folkways, customs, norms, normatives, ethics, morals, values, beliefs, lifestyles, attitudes, hopes, aspirations, desires, etiquette, styles, fashions and fads*—refer to the description of what is right and wrong, good and bad, desirable and undesirable.

Cultural patterns encompass widely held beliefs of certain activities, relationships, feelings, and goals important to a community's identity or well-being. They include psychological predispositions and instinctive traits incorporated into rote behavior patterns. What

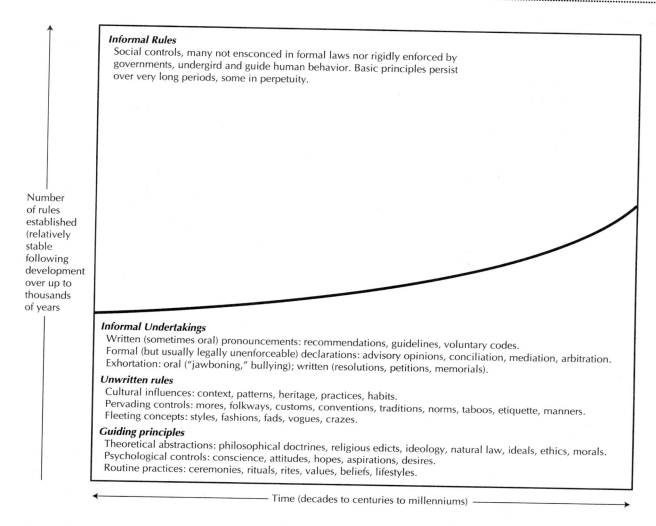

Informal Rules
Social controls, many not ensconced in formal laws nor rigidly enforced by governments, undergird and guide human behavior. Basic principles persist over very long periods, some in perpetuity.

Number of rules established (relatively stable following development over up to thousands of years

Informal Undertakings
Written (sometimes oral) pronouncements: recommendations, guidelines, voluntary codes.
Formal (but usually legally unenforceable) declarations: advisory opinions, conciliation, mediation, arbitration.
Exhortation: oral ("jawboning," bullying); written (resolutions, petitions, memorials).

Unwritten rules
Cultural influences: context, patterns, heritage, practices, habits.
Pervading controls: mores, folkways, customs, conventions, traditions, norms, taboos, etiquette, manners.
Fleeting concepts: styles, fashions, fads, vogues, crazes.

Guiding principles
Theoretical abstractions: philosophical doctrines, religious edicts, ideology, natural law, ideals, ethics, morals.
Psychological controls: conscience, attitudes, hopes, aspirations, desires.
Routine practices: ceremonies, rituals, rites, values, beliefs, lifestyles.

Time (decades to centuries to millenniums)

Figure 1. Molitor multiple-timeline model of change. (Graham T. T. Molitor, Public Policy Forecasting, Inc., 1994. Used with permission.)

people commonly know about the nature of things as they are or ought to be guides behavior.

Values, inherent in a culture or its subcomponents, influence behavior. They help to define worldview, guide life's choices, and provide a means to justify purposeful actions. Values are specific to an individual, reflecting an individual's likes and dislikes, predilections and prejudices, and do not necessarily represent prevailing cultural norms. They are materially influenced by a variety of cultural forces—heredity, ethnic group, race, class, occupation, locus, status, age, sex, education, customs, ethics, morals, religion, institutions, and procedures. *Beliefs* are values translated into a code of conduct. *Lifestyle* denotes a specific way of life that expresses certain values and beliefs.

Ethics, based on postulates espoused by religion or influential ideologies, evaluate human activities in terms

of moral principles and set standards of conduct that govern the moral content of intentions, acts, and their consequences. Morals, although sometimes used interchangeably with ethics, usually refers to a more limited range of human behavior than is covered by ethics.

Unwritten Guides and Informal Controls

Like other cultural traits, rules of conduct are inferred from patterns of the past and passed along by predecessors or learned from parents, school, peers, church, mass media, service organizations, and the overarching cultural milieu. Education supposedly plays a key role in transmitting behavioral codes from one generation to the next. Many informal rules are premised upon various practical maxims communicated through lore, legends, ballads, fables, proverbs, parables, and practical wisdom. Whatever the form, transmission generally is informal, often oral, and largely learned by observing the behavior of others. Peer group pressure strongly influences individual behavior.

Psychological influences unconsciously pervade perception, and they condition and control the way people think. Deeply ingrained and expressed as common and usual practices, these concepts become routinized behavior. Principles consciously and unconsciously influence character and predispose persons to perform in a manner considered acceptable by the reference group. Public opinion represents an expression or the degree of expression of viewpoints. There is no single public opinion.

Mores, in the spectrum of social constraints upon behavior, are those principles most essential to the maintenance of a society—thou shalt not kill, steal, covet another man's wife, and so on. They may encourage or forbid certain behavior and are strictly enforced by strong sanctions. For example, sexual mores typically preclude acts considered inimical to the well-being of society, such as incest, statutory rape (of minors), prostitution, illegitimate birthing, and abortion (until recently), and support others—monogamy, sexual fidelity, child support, and so forth.

Mores differ from time to time and from place to place. Human slavery, not so many centuries ago, was a common and accepted practice worldwide. In some societies, cannibalism used to be approved, human sacrifice was considered an honor, servants were buried with their deceased master, and killing infants or the elderly also was considered appropriate when population growth threatened the group. Even today the taking of life may be sanctioned—kamikaze pilots and other suicide missions in recent wars, or execution for heinous crimes, and compassionate ending of life for terminally ill (euthanasia).

Folkways include minor rules of social behavior considered less important than mores, mildly sanctioned to secure compliance, and considered appropriate but not insisted upon. The term, ascribed to William Graham Sumner, describes ordinary, taken-for-granted norms of behavior enforced by informal reactions of praise or blame but not by the apparatus of the law. Approved behavior ranges from acts that are disapproved but not forbidden, permitted, or merely recommended.

Inappropriate dress, among the more trivial folkways, may result in ridicule, frowning, or other mild social disapproval. Folkways of a more serious nature may be enforced by stiffer sanctions, such as shunning or ostracizing. Spitting tobacco juice and smoking tobacco—which may be considered disgusting by some, but also pose potentially hazardous public health risks to others—fall within this category and currently are very much in controversy.

Folkways are culturally diverse. Conduct approved in one society or group may be disapproved in another. Etiquette and rules of politeness usually consider belching or slurping at meals inappropriate, but these behaviors are regarded as compliments in some societies. Folkways also vary considerably according to context. Behavior acceptable in one situation may be inappropriate in another—comportment and demeanor in church, for example, differ from behavior at a rock concert or wrestling match.

Conduct approved in one society or group

may be disapproved in another.

Customs (conventions, traditions) include mores and folkways that are considered the prime determinants of social behavior. These traditions provide agreed-upon routines that make social environments more certain and less erratic. To facilitate traffic flow, motor vehicles are operated on the right-hand side of the roadway in the United States and Europe but on the left in the United Kingdom and Japan. Cafeteria lines operate in one direction. Coffee is stirred with a spoon, not with a fork.

Customs are not immutable. They change. The bikini or thong bathing suit would have been viewed as indecent and immoral during the early 1900s and up to the 1950s, but today it is acceptable (though sometimes controversial).

Norms reflect typical (not atypical) cultural values, a common core of model conduct that guides what should and should not be done in certain situations. Individuals pick up on behavioral norms prevailing in the community and conform to them. Norms are implicit and explicit. Commonly understood, they are based on values, moral standards, reasoning, and other subjective judgments. Normative—average or modal conduct—describes group consensus that changes with shifts in attitudes. Puritanical moral norms constrained sex except for procreation, and frowned upon pleasurable pursuits of all kinds. Contemporary attitudes are much more lenient.

Norms are not always easily discerned and may be shaped by attitudinal perspectives. For example, taking human life—premeditated murder and its permutations—is a universally proscribed norm; however, it may be approved in wartime (killing by revolutionaries poses a more difficult question), or as punishment for heinous crimes.

Taboos forbid certain actions that are deeply ingrained in contrast to fleeting changes in style. *Style* refers to a characteristic manner or mode of doing things and may not be endorsed by a majority. *Fashion,* distinctive expressions of a cultural element, is semantically similar to style and implies wide support or consensus—women's dress fashions and hemlines, long versus short hair. *Fads*—such as the grunge look, garish-colored hair (pink, orange, green), Hula-Hoops, or pet rocks—are short-lived phenomena that are quickly adopted and just as quickly dropped.

Informal Undertakings

More formal, but noncompulsory, social control modes—oral, written, and procedural—that exert influence over social activity include: recommendations, guidelines, voluntary codes (i.e., of professional practice, ethics, and so forth). More formal controls include pronouncements that generally are legally unenforceable (advisory opinions, conciliation, mediation, arbitration); exhortation (cajoling, editorship, jawboning, bullying, or written resolutions, petitions, memorials). At the end of the continuum of rules guiding social behavior are formal and written laws. Many informal social controls are legitimated by codification into law.

[See also Agents of Change; Civil Protest; Continuity and Discontinuity; Laws, Evolution of; Pacesetter Governments; Public Opinion Polls; Public Policy Change; Record Setting; Technological Change; Technology Forecasting and Assessment; Trend Indicators; Values; Values Change.]

BIBLIOGRAPHY

Appelbaum, Richard P. *Theories of Social Change.* Chicago: Markham, 1970.

Duncan, Otis Dudley, ed. *William F. Ogburn on Culture and Social Change.* Chicago: The University of Chicago Press, 1964.

Dunn, Edgar S., Jr. *Economic and Social Development: A Process of Social Learning.* Baltimore: Johns Hopkins University Press, 1971.

Etzioni, Amitai, and Etzioni-Halevy, Eva. *Social Change: Sources, Patterns, and Consequences,* 2nd ed. New York: Basic Books, 1973.

Galt, Anthony H., and Smith, Larry J. *Models and the Study of Social Change.* Cambridge, MA: Schenkman, 1976.

LaPiere, Richard T. *Social Change.* New York: McGraw-Hill, 1965.

Leuchtenberg, William E., and Wishy, Bernard. *Selected Essays of William Graham Sumner: Social Darwinism.* Englewood Cliffs, NJ: Prentice Hall, 1963.

Ogburn, William Fielding. *Social Change: With Respect to Culture and Original Nature.* New York: Viking Press, 1950.

Vago, Steven. *Social Change.* New York: Holt, Rinehart, and Winston, 1980.

Zollschan, George K., and Hirsch, Walter. *Social Change: Explorations Diagnosis and Conjectures.* Cambridge, MA: Schenkman, 1976.

— GRAHAM T. T. MOLITOR

SOCIAL DEMOCRACY

If capitalism was the economic engine that powered Europe's industrial revolution for two centuries, the welfare state can be thought of as a deliberate, if controversial, means of reconstituting the infrastructure of the Western democracies to achieve a massive redistribution of the benefits of the historic shift from rural-agrarian to urban-industrial economies. Social democracy themes emphasized here include the welfare state and corporatism (institutional arrangements that include worker participation in high-level decision making).

Sweden's former prime minister, Olaf Palme, described the political environment of social democracy evolving and maturing through three stages: (1) *political democratization* (extension of suffrage, freedom of press/assembly/speech); (2) *welfare democracy* (provision of social security, old-age assistance, health care, food assistance, and generally protecting the rank and file from economic marketplace vagaries); (3) *economic democracy* (achieving a better balance between individual self-interest and broader social interests by including worker participation in high-level decision making—based primarily on the notion that markets inadequately serve social interests as much as a proprietor's self-interest.

Change on this scale comes slowly, often only through public contention and over an extended period. In Europe, the change has been energized by massive political mobilization: several times through the rise of a social movement (as happened in Britain); at other times, through incorporation in the platform of established political parties (as in Sweden and France). Whatever the vehicle, it is the existence of undistributed surpluses, such as those generated by mass production assembly lines, as well as a publicly sanctioned agenda of social needs that accounts for the emergence and institutionalization of the welfare state.

Throughout Europe, during the period before World War I, activist associations and minor political parties pressed for programs anticipating the advent of social democracy. Over a period of time they introduced a cluster of socioeconomic programs that came to define the welfare state. It was the Great Depression of the 1930s, however, that provoked public discontent sufficiently intense to force establishment parties to embrace programs, such as unemployment insurance, universal health care, comprehensive pension systems, and income-maintenance arrangements. These programs altered traditional capitalistic patterns that had left wealth concentrated in the hands of an elite. As programs such as these were embraced by non-European societies as diverse as New Zealand, Nigeria, and Japan, social democracy came to be seen as challenging capitalism on the international scene.

Yet it was not until social democratic regimes were beefed up with the addition of unique real-locative devices that social democracy came to be identified with three seminal political values that have captured the imagination of people throughout the world. As "liberty, equality and security," long embraced by establishment parties, came to be seen as the hallmarks of social democracy, public support crystallized as legitimacy. Paradoxically, the mechanism that evoked this legitimacy came into existence largely outside familiar political arenas.

Corporatism, the linking of great pools of public and private power through free-floating as well as institutionalized bargaining mechanisms, came quietly and often unannounced onto the national scene in one European country after another. In many cases, this allowed dramatic revisions in pivotal policies without displacing time-honored allocation mechanisms within traditional program sectors. Though the course of change varied from one nation to another, the outcome of several decades of creeping corporatism produced dramatic changes in historic patterns of the distribution of both political and economic power in many Western democracies. As a result, collective energies once invested in pluralistic political competition were rechanneled toward the formulation and implementation of comprehensive social and economic policies in a manner that subordinates group interests to the general welfare of all.

Few doubt that social democratic governments will continue to have a central place in the future of Europe. Continued evolution and change are certain, but this dominance will continue because (1) corporatism provides a mechanism for dealing with some of the perverse cultural dilemmas of postindustrial society, (2) corporatism provides a relevant mechanism through which nation-states can attempt to deal with the emergent, increasingly dominant, and often disruptive world economy, and (3) corporatism will be enhanced by many of the developments associated with the establishment of the European Economic Community.

[See also Democracy; Socialism; Social Welfare Philosophies.]

BIBLIOGRAPHY

Castles, Francis. *The Social Democratic Image of Society.* London: Routledge & Kegan Paul, 1978.

Cox, Andrew, and O'Sullivan, Noel. *The Corporate State: Corporatism and the State Tradition in Western Europe.* Hants, England: Elgar, 1988.

Western Europe. Hants, England: Elgar, 1988.

Einhorn, Eric, and Logue, John. *Modern Welfare States.* New York: Praeger, 1989.

Flora, Peter, and Heidenheimer, Arnold. *The Development of Welfare States in Europe and America.* New Brunswick, NJ: Transaction Books, 1987.

Wilensky, Harold, and Turner, Lowel. *Democratic Corporatism and Policy Linkages.* Institute for International Studies: Berkeley, 1987.

— WILLIAM J. GORE

SOCIAL INDICATORS

Broadly speaking, social indicators are quantitative measures of social conditions and trends. They originate from censuses and surveys (e.g., victimization rates from the National Crime Survey), administrative records (e.g., school enrollments), or other sources (e.g., newspaper help-wanted advertisement counts). Purposes associated with social indicators include: (1) social monitoring, (2) social reporting, (3) social forecasting, (4) social accounting, (5) program evaluation, and (6) social engineering.

Social indicators monitor where society stands now and where it has stood in the past, to highlight what has been changing. Basic monitors range from the monthly unemployment rate to the annual criminal victimization figures to the small-area statistics of each decade's census. Social indicators also provide a statistical basis for a system of social reporting that attempts to provide policy makers, social scientists, and others with information on societal conditions by evaluating how society is faring.

Applying social change models to the historical and contemporary time series generates social forecasts. These time-series data sets provide a basis for predicting trends into the future.

Social indicators are meant to be integrated into a system of social accounting which is similar to the national income accounting system and which aims to: (a) supply a summary measure of social progress, including groups of indicators revealing relative quality of life; (b) provide a statistical model for assessing the impact of specific societal changes on society in general or on particular components of society.

Social indicators are tools for program evaluation. A summary measure characterizing quality of life and domain-specific measures in areas such as education, health, and crime, make it possible to assess performance overall and in particular areas. Conclusions drawn from these data sets provide a means to judge the overall effectiveness of relevant governmental policies and programs.

Finally, social indicators provide guides for social engineering. Social accounting models to forecast the consequences of inputs and a social monitoring system to measure the actual outcomes facilitate designing and fine-tuning government programs to deal with social problems (Ferriss, 1988; Rose, 1989).

In the United States as well as in other countries progress has been made in monitoring and reporting. Some countries have wide-ranging, if not yet comprehensive, programs for measuring important societal conditions. They not only cover the economic realm, but also deal with such areas as health, education, crime, and the environment (Wiegand, 1988). Internationally, the United Nations, World Bank, Organization for Economic Development and Cooperation, and other groups regularly compile comparative social indicators. Of particular note are the General Social Surveys in the United States, which have been tracking social change since 1972. Surveying similar components cross-culturally in over twenty countries, the International Survey Program and the Eurobarometers sponsored by the European Community have been underway since 1973.

The more ambitious, complex goals of forecasting and social accounting have seen promising but more limited developments. Social forecasting is most advanced in the area of demography, and cohort (age group) replacement and cohort-education models are useful in predicting attitudinal and behavioral changes. Considerable progress also has been made in planning for health-care needs. No system of social accounting has as yet been put into operation, however.

Modifications in the basic economic accounts model have been developed to take into account social costs such as environmental pollution, deaths, and illness. Others have attempted to aggregate and interrelate topics using rates of change to reveal multivariate outcomes (Johnston, 1988). Studies of the quality of life based on personal, subjective assessments and of both general and domain-specific psychological well-being have been carried out, but they have not been widely integrated into an accounting system (Rose, 1989). Work now underway takes a life-events approach that measures the incidence and magnitude of social problems (Smith, 1992). Suffice it to note that a fully integrated social accounting system does not appear likely in the near term.

With social forecasting still limited in its reach and reliability, and with no functioning system of social accounting in place, the goals of program evaluation and social engineering have been largely unattained. Monitoring and reporting system elements, however, are used to assess current programs and guide policy makers toward more effective decisions. Most innovative in these areas are the Human Dimensions of Global Environmental Change Programs of the International Social Science Council and the U.S. National Science Foundation. They will integrate natural science studies of the environment (e.g., the greenhouse effect) with evaluations of alternative technologies (e.g., nuclear vs. solar energy) and assessments of social concerns and acceptable trade-offs (e.g., economic growth vs. public health).

Social indicators, while not realizing many ultimate applications, have served well in monitoring social conditions and trends. They are steadily expanding our knowledge of human society and providing important insights as to how its different components interact. Future advances in forecasting models and social accounting eventually may make social indicators into extremely powerful tools for the diagnosis and disposition of social problems.

[See also Environmental Indicators; Forecasting Methods; Pacesetter Governments; Public Policy Change; Scanning; Social Inventions; Trend Indicators.]

BIBLIOGRAPHY

Ferriss, Abbott L. "The Uses of Social Indicators." *Social Forces* 66 (March 1988): 601–617.

Johnston, Denis F. "Towards a Comprehensive 'Quality-of-Life Index'." *Social Indicators Research* 20 (October 1988): 473–496.

Rose, Richard. "Whatever Happened to Social Indicators? A Symposium." *Journal of Public Policy* 9 (October–December 1989): 399–450.

Smith, Tom W. "A Life Events Approach to Developing an Index of Societal Well-Being." *Social Science Research* 21 (1992): 353–379.

Wiegand, Erich. "Current Work on the Social Indicators System of the Federal Republic of Germany." *Social Indicators Research* 20 (August 1988): 399–416.

— THOMAS W. SMITH

SOCIAL INVENTIONS

A social invention is a new law, organization, or procedure that changes the ways in which people relate to themselves or to each other, either individually or collectively (Conger, 1974). Examples of social inventions include marriage, language, writing, voting, schools and methods of education, unemployment insurance, psychotherapy, laws, and the Red Cross and other organizations. Social inventions, more than any other type of invention (mechanical, chemical, electrical, and so on), influence how we live, including how we are governed.

Social inventing is a continuous

trial-and-error process

as individuals, organizations, and governments

try to cope with new or dissatisfying situations.

Social inventions that have been created over the years have brought many benefits to society, as the previous examples attest. In spite of the potential to solve social problems through social inventions, governments seldom establish research centers to develop new social inventions. Among the few that do exist, most were established to invent new methods of education.

Societies are a reflection of a complex web of particular social inventions. Social inventing is a continuous trial-and-error process as individuals, organizations, and governments try to cope with new or dissatisfying situations. An invention may be created in one location and adopted in different locations within different social configurations. Thus, the same invention can be used beneficially or harmfully in different cultures.

An interesting recent social invention is the divorcing of parents by their children. This first occurred in Sweden in about 1980, and a dozen years later took place twice in Florida within a one-year period, suggesting that momentum may be building. However, the slowness of the buildup indicates the slowness of the adoption of social inventions. The implementation of an invention such as this typically requires certain other social inventions, in this case the acceptance that children have rights, the prohibition of child abuse, the general acceptance of divorce, and of course such basic institutions as courts, lawyers, and so forth.

Once a social invention finds its place in the wider web of previous social inventions, it then may have an influence on how the other parts of the web operate. When, for example, parents divorce they endeavour to negotiate the allocation of the rights to the custody and visitation privileges of the children. It is conceivable that in the future, children will demand their own alimony and choose to live with other people than their parents or guardians. A very likely possibility is that children of divorce will sue one or both parents for support and then go to live with grandparents or other favored relatives. This probability finds support in the fact that some grandparents are now suing children, or children-in-law who have divorced to ensure that the grandparents have visiting rights to the grandchildren. In turn, these developments, plus greater state penalties levied against divorced fathers who do not keep up child support payments, may substantially change the divorce process itself. It is possible that the grandchildren and grandparents will form legal alliances against the parents, who may or may not be divorcing.

The fact that grandchildren and grandparents might enter legal divorce proceedings on equal status as the parents will change the nature of divorce from a private arrangement between two adults where all other parties are secondary to a community process in which the balance of power is clearly shared by all of the "victims." A further downstream result of this simple social invention of children divorcing their parents might well be some fundamental changes in family life. For example, grandparents might commonly sue their children for

improper child care and have the legal right to involve themselves in their grandchild's up-bringing. Similarly they may have the right to intervene in other aspects of family life. In this way we may see a rebuilding of the wider family structure. A further spur to this might come from economic developments where career progression for many middle-class workers is stymied and they look to their parents for financial subsidies, in this situation the grandparents have a further opportunity to negotiate their role in family life.

In some instances social inventions are selected and integrated to become a social movement. Graham T. T. Molitor (1977) has indicated the process that a social trend takes in terms of its geographic origins and the changing characteristics of its proponents as the movement "matures." Typically a social movement assembles and uses social inventions such as: outrageous statements and demonstrations (strikes, picketing, acts of disrespect to traditional symbols, and so forth) to gain attention of the press; pamphleteering; organizing "chapters" or groups in many localities; formulation of demands and goals; confrontation with authorities; inspirational presentations; disciplining of supporters; raising of funds; recruiting of high-profile supporters; human interest publicity, and so on.

In some cases, these social movements lead to major changes (such as the recognition of labor unions and the right to strike.). A social movement, whether confrontational or not, is intended to allow the participants and their presumed "benefactors" or like-minded people to live their lives differently. Thus, for instance, participants in the many "freedom" campaigns typified by the union movement (e.g., the women's movement, gay and lesbian rights movements) all want regulations and public behaviors changed to permit them to manage their lives in ways that they decide.

In situations where a social movement is organized to combat a single practice (e.g., seal hunting or lumbering), the social movement is more like a social campaign to get authorities to change the rules. Such a campaign makes use of many of the same social inventions as a social movement but is not intended to change the lives of the participants, rather to impose the values of the participants on others.

Not all major social movements are confrontational and in many instances represent a need that had not been met before. The early years of the twentieth century were a period of enormous growth of international organizations for the development of individuals, communities, and beyond. This movement was typified by the invention of such organizations as the Scouts, Red Cross, service clubs, all of which used the various organizational practices that had been invented over the years (membership, elected and appointed officers, committees, voting, fund-raising, fellowship practices, publicity, etc.) to create a successful organization to perform good works. They represented the epitome of the collective philanthropic movement and replaced dependence upon wealthy patrons. Thus it was a form of democratization of social services, which at the turn of the century we are now witnessing as becoming the bureaucratization (another collection of social inventions) of social services.

The rapid evolution of an information age during the 1990s is likely to produce a burst of creative social inventions. Many futurists have outlined the present transformation to a democratic workplace, entrepreneurial organizations, and humane capitalism. The proliferation of powerful interactive information networks is creating "electronic" equivalents of most social relationships: distance learning, telecommuting, electronic shopping, and so on. Advances in biogenetics are being accompanied by new social inventions, such as surrogate mothers and laws that prescribe how this life-and-death power is used. And growing awareness of the environmental crisis should also lead to different forms of resource use, such as recycling of all goods, "green" taxes, simpler lifestyles, and reverence for nature.

[See also Agents of Change; Change; Public Policy Change; Social Change: United States; Social And Political Evolution.]

BIBLIOGRAPHY

Bennett, William J. *The Index of Leading Cultural Indicators: Facts and Figures on the State of American Society.* New York: Touchstone/ Simon & Schuster, 1994.

Conger, D. Stuart. *Social Inventions.* Prince Albert, Saskatchewan: Saskatchewan NewStart, 1974.

Molitor, Graham T. T. "The Hatching of Public Opinion." *Planning Review* 5/42 (July 1977).

————. "Preparing for the 80's: Public Policy Forecasting." *Public Relations Journal* 35/1 (January 1979).

— D. STUART CONGER

SOCIALISM

Socialism has been narrowly and broadly defined. The narrow definition is that of a social system where the means of production are owned by the community. The broader definition describes a system where public authorities intervene in the processes of production, trade, and consumption. A distinguishing feature of these processes is that they do not operate freely, as in laissez-faire systems.

The broader definition will be used in this article. The word *socialism* was first used in 1832 by the Frenchman Pierre Leroux to characterize systems based upon state intervention. Various socialist regimes had developed in reaction to laissez-faire systems recommended by the Englishman Adam Smith in his book *The Wealth of Nations* (1776). In laissez-faire systems, all transactions occur in free markets, but socialists contend that

---

Marx provided socialism with an ideology. He argued that human history was a succession of various orders, suggesting that society is bound to develop in a socialist direction.

---

this leads to very unequal income distribution. The first socialists based their protests on ethical grounds (the Englishmen Thomas More and Robert Owen, and the Frenchmen Louis Blanc, Charles Fourier, and Claude-Henri Saint-Simon, among others). Such advocates were called utopian socialists by Karl Marx, the German sociologist who considered himself a scientific socialist. Marx and his followers started to make socialism politically relevant by creating socialist parties, united by the First International (established in 1864), and seeking cooperation with trade unions. Marx provided socialism with an ideology. His argument that human history was a succession of various orders, suggesting that society is bound to develop in a socialist direction, impressed politicians. Even if they did not agree, they made the "social problem" one of the great issues in the second half of the nineteenth and through most of the twentieth century.

Extremists and Moderates

As with so many spiritually motivated causes, lack of success in the struggle with opponents bred internal disagreement about the reasons for failure. In the early years of the twentieth century, a split in the socialist movement occurred. The more radical wing organized itself into communist parties, leaving the democratic socialists in the old party. The parties supporting the existing order showed a similar split into extremes with fascists on one side, and the more moderate factions on the other. Sometimes the extremists hated the moderates more than their opponents at the other extreme: communists, for example, would address democratic socialists as "social fascists." On other occasions, they would try to reunite in what was called a popular front.

World War I

With the killing of the Austrian successor to the throne by a Serb as a pretext, Germany started another war with France in August 1914. Because of existing alliances, so many countries were drawn into the conflict that it was termed the "Great War" or "World War." Against this background, important shifts in socialist power positions took place. The exiled Russian communist leader V. I. Lenin was given the opportunity to go back to Russia, where two successive revolutions occurred in 1917. In the second, or "October" revolution, Lenin seized power and established the Soviet Union with a communist government. In Germany, the Social Democrats entered into a coalition with other parties, which prevented a Communist party rule. A number of Central and Eastern European countries (from Hungary and Yugoslavia to the Baltic republics, including Poland and Czechoslovakia) regained their independence.

World War II

Germany lost World War I and was made to pay a very large tribute, which wrecked its economy—a danger about which the famous English economist John Maynard Keynes had warned. These extreme punitive measures provoked an opposite extremism, fascism. Hitler began his propaganda campaign for revenge and essentially planned World War II to carry out his objectives.

World War II started in 1939, and in the first few years, Germany occupied much of the Western Europe. Events turned, however, when Germany sought to invade Eastern Europe, and the war finished in 1945 in a second defeat for Germany. Soviet forces won the war at the eastern front, and Eastern Europe was occupied by the Soviet army. Germany was partitioned between East and West.

The Cold War, Developing Countries, and the Environment

After the second defeat of Germany, a new scenario developed: Mutual distrust between the communist world and Western democracies led to an unprecedented build-up of military strength, including nuclear arms. The chances that a Third World War would result loomed, but such a large-scale conflict has not materialized.

Alongside security problems, other important dilemmas surfaced and had to be resolved. One such problem, the poverty of the underdeveloped countries, involved many former colonies of the Western powers. The extreme poverty in many of these countries was a social problem of worldwide significance and impact, and the solution seemed to indicate a need for socialist policies. This worldwide social problem provoked conflicts between developed and underdeveloped nations. One conflict raged over the fact that the developed countries were unwilling to make available the full 0.7

percent of their Gross National Product (GNP) that had been recommended for development assistance by the Pearson Commission; instead only 0.35 percent was offered. A second conflict concerned the protection of industries that, because of their labor intensity, were appropriate for the underdeveloped countries. The best known example of such protection is the Multifiber Arrangement that protects the textile and clothing industries. A third conflict involved commodity agreements for agricultural raw materials. The markets for such materials are unstable and traditionally have been regulated. A complication here is that the agricultural markets themselves in developed countries are also unstable, and protectionist policies are distinctly disadvantageous for underdeveloped countries.

The future world order seems likely to be a mixed order: a system of free stable markets, corrected for income inequality, and of regulated unstable markets.

Another new problem of global significance was discovered by the Club of Rome, a group that is essentially a coalition of business people and scientists. In a report entitled *The Limits of Growth* (1972), the danger of pollution due to population growth, industrial manufacturing, transport, and natural resource exploitation was analyzed, and the necessity of a carefully planned environmental policy was strongly emphasized. In the same year, an international conference on the subject was held in Stockholm on the initiative of the Swedish government. As a result, a new United Nations agency, the United Nations Environmental Programme (UNEP) was established, in Nairobi, Kenya.

A fourth pressing worldwide problem is that of sustainability, the concept that, at the very least, future generations should enjoy a standard of living equal to that of the present day. Such sustainability is possible, but only if (1) technological progress continues, (2) the world population level becomes stable, and (3) a limit is set to the portion of natural resources used by each succeeding generation.

In some socialist countries, the socialist parties neglected or underemphasized environmental policy. As a result, various organizations such as Greenpeace drew the attention of the world's citizens and politicians to environmental issues. (Of course, socialist countries were not alone in their neglect of the environment. In some countries, where the need for a cleaner environment had been addressed by governmental programs, the need for green parties was less severe.)

The End of Communism: Extremist Nationalism

In 1985 Mikhail S. Gorbachev became secretary-general of the Soviet Communist party. He admitted that the Soviet economy was less efficient than the Western economies. The American economist Abram Bergson had noted in 1964 that Soviet productivity was about 30 percent lower than that of America. Gorbachev conceded that restructuring and frank discussion of the problem was necessary. His admission that a free-market economy is so much more productive than a centrally planned economy caused a veritable uproar. Eastern European and Soviet citizens felt liberated from the enormous pressure they had lived under, and reacted violently. Apparently the mass of the population felt strongly aggravated by the ethnic pressure of living under Russian rule. In contrast, economists and managers were more concerned with the reestablishment of a free market. In both cases the effect was an overreaction that shifted from one extreme to the other. All the republics of the Soviet Union wanted to be independent. The Soviet Union, after a few years, was replaced by the Commonwealth of Independent States (CIS), of which Russia (including Siberia) was by far the largest.

Many economists and managers believed that all markets should become free, forgetting that there are stable and unstable markets. The latter, including agriculture, cannot be left free. In another economic sector, where production incurs high fixed costs, free markets could cause permanent losses to the firms or induce the formation of monopolies. Hence, they require some form of regulation. Near-term and medium-term forecasts are extremely problematic, given the current chaotic state. Relatively longer-term goals may be easier to assess, at least in broad outline.

The Future of Socialism

The future world order seems likely to be a mixed order: a system of free stable markets, corrected for income inequality, and of regulated unstable markets. The role of public authorities ("the state") should be to maintain law and order and fix the quantities of public goods, such as the infrastructure (road systems, railway and air traffic, information dispersal, energy supply, and environmental policies). Another important task is likely to be the redistribution of incomes, both within and among nations. A quantitative aspect of that task is the portion of total income that is transferred. Inside countries, about 30 percent is transferred in Sweden by social legislation, 12.4 percent in the United States, 10 percent in Japan, with most other industrialized countries

falling somewhere between the United States and Sweden. Sweden is considered to be one of the most advanced and well-functioning welfare states.

The redistribution of wealth among countries may require a level of assistance by developed countries substantially higher than the 0.7 percent recommended by the Pearson Commission, at least for the short term. This writer recommends a short-term level of assistance of 1.27 percent of the GNP, with long-term redistribution levels of 70 percent to be achieved over a period of three centuries.

Socialism has been internationalist from its inception in 1864. Although theory and practice have diverged, the globalization of the world economy is forcing socialists to reapply their original theories to new contexts. The future also requires a managed world economy, an ongoing international framework within which policies can be discussed. This may require strengthening and reforming the United Nations.

Several possibilities may rejuvenate socialism in the future. There is a tendency for economic systems to become more "socialized" as they strive to improve the quality of life. For example, welfare programs that remedy social problems, laws respecting economic and civil rights, state support of cultural activities, environmental protection, and other "social programs" have made most European nations, Japan, and even the United States more comfortable places to live.

There is also an interesting trend toward a kind of "economic democratization," particularly among large quasi-public corporations, that transforms capitalism into a more social form. Progressive corporations, like the Saturn Division of General Motors, expanded their goals and governance to include workers, customers, suppliers, distributors, and the general public, in addition to investors. As a result, modern economies may remain market oriented, while major enterprises incline toward management that serves numerous social rather than exclusively financial interests. If GM's Saturn and Japanese businesses are a harbinger, such "human-centered" enterprises may serve the general public welfare as well as make more money because they are more productive.

The decline of communism may signify that the old type of centrally planned government socialism is dead, while modern versions of socialism are emerging based to a considerable extent on free markets. The fact is that our society must increasingly address the human and social dimensions of economic life as these concerns grow in importance. Thus, systems of political economy around the world are unavoidably moving toward various forms of social control over their market economies, whether one calls it socialism, economic democracy, human enterprise, a "New Capitalism," or a "New Socialism."

[See also Capitalism; Communism; Development, Alternative; Economics; Macroeconomics; Marketplace Economics; More, Saint Thomas; Political Economy, Social Democracy.]

BIBLIOGRAPHY

Etzioni, Amitai. *The Moral Dimension: Toward a New Economics.* New York: Free Press, 1988.

Halal, William E. *The New Capitalism.* New York: Wiley, 1986.

Heilbroner, Robert. "After Communism." *New Yorker* (September 10, 1990).

Tinbergen, Jan. *Booklet 29.* Santa Barbara, CA: Nuclear Age Peace Foundation, 1989.

— JAN TINBERGEN

SOCIAL AND POLITICAL EVOLUTION

Social and political evolution deals with long-term change in a wide number of societal, political, and economic areas. First to be examined will be the processes of evolutionary change; then, how human life and societal institutions have changed substantively in a wide range of areas as a result of the transition from the agricultural to the industrial and now to the information-communications age; next, how the information age is now in a second phase focusing on communications and connectivity. We will end with what may follow the information/communications age.

The Process of Evolutionary Change

When we think of evolution, we usually think of long-term change. In looking at models of such evolutionary change, there are at least two different versions. In the last century, Charles Darwin argued that biological evolution (and by implication evolution in other areas) occurred by slow, gradual, linear change, from one species to another. In this century, Steven Jay Gould's punctuated equilibrium theory in biology, as well as other new scientific paradigms, suggest a different view of evolution. This model allows for gradually accelerating change within an existing system for a period of time, until some "limits to growth" point is reached (the S-Curve growth model) leading to a partial breakdown of that system (and its societal institutions in the case of social evolution), followed by a quantum jump to a whole new system level.

In the linear growth model of evolution as slow, gradual change, the future is an extension of past trends—i.e., more of the same (a quantitative change only). In the periodic quantum jump model, in contrast, a rather sudden shift occurs to a new system level that is qualitatively different from the old one. Following the latter model, Alvin Toffler noted that one could never have

predicted the information age or "Third Wave" (as he called it) by extrapolating trends from the earlier industrial or "Second Wave" society, since something qualitatively new occurred that made this shift possible. Another version of this process is the evolutionary spiral (see Barbara Marx Hubbard's work, for example) where crises (or "limits to growth") points within a system trigger design innovations, which usher in new stages or periods of evolution over time.

Societal Evolution Through Agricultural, Industrial, and Information Ages

Following the prehistoric hunting and gathering age, human society has evolved through at least three different periods. Toffler, in *The Third Wave,* popularized the idea of these three major waves or periods of change in human history: an agricultural age lasting thousands of years, an industrial age lasting a few hundred years, and now a postindustrial information/communication age lasting only decades. The agricultural era originated with ancient civilizations around the Mediterranean; the industrial age with nation-states bordering the Atlantic; and the information age with Pacific Rim countries—especially the United States and Japan, leading to the emergence of a global economy, global telecommunications, and an increasingly interdependent world. Each period is ushered in by new technologies, which restructure jobs, the economy, then all other societal institutions, even requiring new thinking appropriate for each age.

The seven tables illustrate some of the major societal and institutional restructuring trends associated with the shift from agricultural to industrial and now to information-communications societies. These characteristics are based primarily on experiences in Western developed countries, where industrialization and later the information age (along with Japan), originated. Nonetheless, in our current interdependent world, no country can escape the influence of the information age and countries—with different histories, cultures, political-economic systems, and levels of development—must each decide how best to incorporate the information age into its development. Perhaps some South countries can skip some of the worst ills of the industrial age. In various areas, the information age also marks a return to certain characteristics of the agricultural age, though with additional elements added.

The Communications/Internet/Multimedia/ Interactive/Virtual Reality Age: Further Extensions and Realizations of the Potential of the Information Age

The first stage of the information revolution focused on an information explosion generated by mainframe com-

Characteristics of Agricultural, Industrial, and Information Age Societies

TABLE 1

HISTORICAL BACKGROUND AND SOCIETAL OVERVIEW

Item	Agricultural Age	Industrial Age	Information Age
Original location	Mediterranean Sea.	Atlantic Rim.	Pacific Rim.
Pace of change	Thousands of years.	200–300 years.	30–40 years (next stage likely to be even shorter).
Source of power	Land is the most important asset necessary for production.	Physical resources, factories, equipment and capital are assets; humans are an added, necessary cost of production.	Ideas and information, which come from people, making human resources the most important asset in the information age.
Product produced	Food; also arts and crafts, each artifact produced by hand.	Mass produced, manufactured goods.	Knowledge and application of ideas to different practical results, including technological and social innovations.
Centralization-decentralization, globalization-localization	Decentralization: living and working on the land in decentralized, rural communities.	Centralization: organized around the nation-state and people living in cities.	Decentralization of society and institutions, plus global interdependence for first time.
Societal divisions	Rigid social class divisions in ancient empires and feudal societies; different norms for differential social classes to follow.	Mass society—in both capitalist or socialist countries, one socially acceptable model for all to try to follow; conformity necessary.	Diversified, multiple-option society: no one model everyone must follow to be socially accepted; instead numerous models to choose from in any area of life.

puters and then personal computers. Computers are now integrally linked with telecommunications worldwide, making the communication, networking, interactive, and multimedia potential of the information revolution finally possible. The Internet or Information Superhighway (which the U.S. government supports) illustrates this, along with multimedia, interactive games, books, and virtual reality products. The Internet is growing by 10 percent a month (as of 1995). Increasingly in future, films, quick time movies, still pictures, sounds, games, and other multimedia learning and entertainment packages—in addition to text and data—will be available on computer via Internet. While many people extol the creative and educational benefits of these new technologies, others are concerned about how to regulate pornography and antisocial uses of virtual reality and the Internet.

The Future: What Will Come After the Information/Communication Age?

Many people have speculated about what will come after the information/communications revolution. Space advocates thought it would be exploring, industrializing, and settling humans in space—the "final frontier" popularized in science fiction programs such as *Star Trek*. Others focus on the revolution in genetic engineering, gene splicing/recombinant DNA, where one could potentially replace defective or undesirable genes in any species in future, raising serious ethical questions since humans would, in effect, be playing God. Others believe atomic level restructuring of reality via nanotechnology would revolutionize our future lives. Still others focus on the evolution of human consciousness or inner space, where the creative and spiritual powers of the human mind have barely been tapped. To some extent, all of the above changes are already happening. One thing is clear: Whatever stage follows the information/communications age, it will be something qualitatively different from (and hence not an extension of) the previous stage. If past precedents continue, it will also last less time than previous stages.

[See also Change; Change, Cultural; Communications; Conscious Evolution; Evolution, Social; Global Culture; Global Paradox; Information Society; Post-Information Age; Social Change: United States.]

BIBLIOGRAPHY

Forester, Tom. *Computers in the Human Context: Information Technology, Productivity, and People.* Cambridge, MA: MIT Press, 1989.

Hubbard, Barbara Marx. *The Evolutionary Journey: A Personal Guide to a Positive Future.* San Francisco: Evolutionary Press, 1982.

TABLE 2

DEMOGRAPHICS

Item	Agricultural Age	Industrial Age	Information Age
Demographics; geographic distribution	Rural populations: the majority of people living in rural communities working on the land.	Urban populations: in countries undergoing the industrial revolution, people moved to cities to work in factories. In developing South countries today, many people are moving to cities seeking (but not always finding) jobs and access to modern life, resulting in unmanageable cities and slums in many cases.	Option for some to live in countryside, in an "electronic cottage" and be connected to work via electronic communications (computer, modem, and telephone line); many people prefer to work at a central office some days, and at home other days, however.
Demographics: population growth rates (based on birth and death rates)	Relatively stable populations due to high birthrates and high death rates.	Beginning of population explosion due especially to decreased death rates (due to modern medicine and better hygiene). Continuing high population growth rates in many South countries today, where 98 percent of global population growth is now occurring.	In developed North countries, which have entered the information age, both birthrates and death rates have decreased, leading to population increases of 1 per cent or less per year.
Demographics: age distribution	Shorter life span: plagues and diseases affected all social classes.	Life span increased in developed, industrial countries, but new industrial and social diseases emerged.	Aging populations in developed North countries, not developing South countries (where population is still more of childbearing age).

TABLE 3

ENERGY AND ENVIRONMENTAL POLLUTION

Item	Agricultural Age	Industrial Age	Information Age
Energy sources	Renewable energy sources: solar, wind, water, humans/slavery, animals, etc.	Nonrenewable, fossil fuels (oil, natural gas, coal) and nuclear fission (uranium and plutonium fuels). These fuels pollute more, and once extracted from the earth, they are gone.	Eventual return (once fossil fuels are exhausted) to renewable energy sources (solar, wind, tidal, geothermal, ocean thermal, and biomass); as in agricultural age, but using more sophisticated technologies to tap these energy sources. Also nuclear fusion (from fusing of hydrogen atoms in water) once the technology is perfected in future; lag in transition to these alternative energy sources—perhaps into next age.
Environmental pollution	Limited, insignificant levels of localized pollution.	Industrial age air, water, and noise pollution from burning of fossil fuels.	Global pollution problems, global warming (greenhouse effect), and hole in ozone level—all legacies of the industrial age. Prospects for cleaner environment from green technologies and an eventual return to renewable energy sources.

TABLE 4

ECONOMICS AND POLITICS

Item	Agricultural Age	Industrial Age	Information Age
Type of economic system	Feudal economic systems and earlier ancient empire economic systems based on slavery.	Rise of capitalist economic systems and then socialist economic systems (as a critique of capitalism).	Both capitalist and socialist economic systems are being greatly restructured as they become part of a global economy; no pure systems, hybrids instead, though also privatization trends world wide—including in former socialist countries.
Economic exchange system	Barter, pre-money economy: goods and services are traded without any money being exchanged.	Money economy: rise of labor sold for wages, and goods and services sold for money/currency.	Continued money economy, as well as rise of a substantial barter economy—both within nations (counter economy) and between nations (counter trade).
Appropriate economic model	Based on a scarcity of land and food produced: "If you give land or food, then you have it and I do not"; scarcity models.	Based on a scarcity of capital, equipment, and manufactured goods: "If I give you capital or goods, then you have them and I do not", scarcity models.	Based on a potential for abundance: Ideas, information, and knowledge are potentially unlimited and increasingly available to everyone: "If I give an idea or information to you then we both have it", win–win, abundance models.
Type of political system	Predemocratic political systems of various kinds, in feudal systems and ancient empires.	Representative democracy and a multiparty political system for the rising middle class in West, with democracy based on an informed, educated, middle class; democratic centralism in socialist countries, with population also educated.	Global democratization trends in former communist and South countries today, with modern information technologies making control of information to citizens by dictators difficult. Sociopolitical change on important issues initiated by direct, grassroots, participatory democracy involving media coverage, electronic networking on the Internet, FAXs, & other forms of "electronic democracy." Increasing numbers of issues (arms control, free trade, AIDS, pollution, and terrorism) require global cooperation and/or local action, not just national policies, to solve them.

TABLE 5

WORKPLACE: JOBS, LABOR, MANAGEMENT, AND PERCENTAGE OF WOMEN WORKING

Item	Agricultural Age	Industrial Age	Information Age
Primary jobs	In agricultural communities producing food and handmade arts and crafts; peasants, serfs, and artisans.	In factories in cities producing mass produced manufactured goods; more blue-collar jobs.	Higher paying, skilled high-technology and professional jobs and lower paying, unskilled service sector jobs, creating danger of a two-tiered economy and decreased middle class (the traditional corner-stone of a democracy); more white-collar jobs; also multiple jobs/careers in a lifetime.
Labor unions	Labor not yet urbanized or organized: peasant uprisings in rural areas are largely spontaneous.	Rise of labor unions in Western capitalist countries, not socialist countries (where dictatorship of the proletariat or state was supposed to represent workers). Adversarial relations between worker and owner or managers in industrial Western countries.	Decline in labor union membership in capitalist countries, with decreasing blue-collar jobs. Also movement towards worker ownership of stock in companies they work in, making them both workers and owners, thus eliminating this traditional adversarial relationship. Rise of mass protests by workers in communist countries, demanding better conditions, led to end of communism in some countries.
Management styles	Rigid social class divisions meant management by dominant social class.	Hierarchical management models in industrialized Western countries.	Network-based, participatory management; consensus/team building; quality circles and total quality management; Japanese management models; and elimination of some middle-management positions.
Percentage of women working	Both men and women worked on the land together, keeping the family together.	Prestigious for middle- and upper-class men in West if their wives did not work versus lower class where women had to work to help support their families. In contrast, ideology in socialist countries promoted women's equality via working with men.	Increasing percentage of women working, whether married or single, for economic and personal growth reasons. People also living longer and having less children, thus women no longer needing to spend their whole lives raising children.

TABLE 6

EDUCATION AND FAMILY

Item	Agricultural Age	Industrial Age	Information Age
Education	Invention of writing with need to keep records of planting and harvests, taxation and barter, education limited to an elite. (Earlier focus on oral traditions carried by elders during hunting and gathering age).	Mass public education: similar standards for all, which was considered democratic; an educated middle class seen as foundation for a democratic society; traditional educational institutions have monopoly on learning.	Diversified educational models necessary to meet diverse needs of students of all ages and different racial, ethnic, and cultural backgrounds; lifetime learning necessary to keep updated in one's field, as technological and social changes escalate; retraining of industrial workers necessary; community and corporate learning centers, in addition to traditional educational institutions; also distance learning. Computer/multimedia/ interactive educational packages, Internet, and virtual reality as additional tools for learning.
Household/family patterns	Extended family: several generations living and working together on the land.	Nuclear family: father working, mother at home not working, and approximately two children for middle and upper classes in developed West. Also nuclear family in lower class West and socialist countries except that women worked.	Multiple family patterns: no one model everyone must follow to be accepted socially. Examples include: married couples with or without children; unmarried couples living together; single parents; divorced parents with children who remarry, making children part of different households; single-person households; people living in groups; gay and lesbian couples.

TABLE 7

CULTURE AND MINDSET

Item	Agricultural Age	Industrial Age	Information Age
Cultures	Local cultures (organized around rural communities or city-states).	National cultures (organized around the nation-state).	Globalization of cultures (organized around an increasingly interdependent world), creating surface level global unity along with deeper level local diversity of the world's cultures. Increased danger of localized cultural conflicts in post Cold War era. People seek new identities and often return to old identities without sufficient recognition of global interdependence or needs and dangers of war in a technological age. New nonlocalized virtual communities also emerging in cyberspace.
Mind-sets	Collectivist, group identity with people being part of social networks and relationships; Eastern and traditional civilizations.	Newtonian physics: divide reality up into separate parts and analyze each part separately; individual identity; deductive, win-lose, either-or, dualistic thinking; Western civilizations.	New physics: dynamic, interdependent, whole systems; worldview; unity and diversity within systems and on global-local levels; win-win, both-and thinking; synergy of Eastern and Western civilizations, and of individual and group needs being met; complex systems require diversity of interdependent parts.

Naisbitt, John, with Patricia Aburdene. *Megatrends 2000: Ten New Directions for the 1990's.* New York: Avon Books, 1990.

Rheingold, Howard. *Virtual Reality: Exploring the Brave New Technologies of Artificial Experience and Interactive Worlds—From Cyberspace to Teledildontics.* New York: Simon & Schuster, 1991.

Toffler, Alvin. *Powershift: Knowledge, Wealth, and Violence at the Edge of the 21st Century.* New York: Bantam, 1990.

— LINDA GROFF

SOCIAL SCIENCES

The social sciences attempt to study social systems systematically and objectively, in much the same way that the natural sciences deal with physical or biological systems.

Anthropology

Anthropology is a discipline within the social sciences that focuses on a broadly conceived study of human beings. As a discipline, anthropology took shape in the 1860s and was established in the universities at the turn of the century. Occasionally defined as "the science of man," anthropology examines both the cultural and physical characteristics of humans. Cultural anthropology deals with all aspects of past and present human cultures, including language, customs, and behavior. Physical anthropology deals with the physical variation, characteristics, and evolution of humans.

Though often associated with the study of the past, tribal peoples and cultures, anthropology can be expected to rise in prominence as an important applied discipline as mankind moves through the twenty-first century. Questions dealing with human origins and evolution will continue to challenge anthropologists. Cataloging and preserving cultural diversity, and inquiring deeper into the link between culture and the mind remain issues of concern. Similarly, increasing pressures such as population growth, development of the Third World countries, technological and social change, and the need to preserve a fragile global ecosystem will demand more from applied anthropologists. Their contributions will help with related practical problems, such as the promotion of community reorganization and of bilingual and bicultural education. Lastly, anthropology will begin to examine the sociocultural future as a professional field in itself (Riper, 1991). For example, as mankind moves to a state that is more structured and designed, questions about the ways we choose to intervene more consciously in the shaping of our nature and species will find some answers from the framework of anthropology.

Archaeology

Archaeology is the scientific study of past societies by means of the excavation of ancient cities, relics, artifacts, and related material remains of human tribes or societies. Though speculation about the past was present in even ancient societies, the investigation of monuments and artifacts began in the Renaissance period and has grown up to the present. An emerging field is industrial archaeology. This specialized line of inquiry is concerned with the history of technology based on the discovery, examination, and sometimes preservation of the buildings, machinery, and other artifacts of earlier industrial activity.

The future of archaeology is a challenging one in that the destruction of archaeological sites is increasing rapidly. Halting this obliteration will require concerted, careful selection of archaeological problems to explore, of research designs appropriate to solve them, and of sites to excavate (Binford, 1986).

The future of archaeology also will involve the continued development of new approaches to the study of ancient artifacts. For example, Shanks (1992) suggests that archaeology should recognize and appreciate the experiential aspect of the encounter with the past by means of a more personal, aesthetic, emotive, and sensory methodology. Thus, archaeology can provide a more human and informative link to our human origins and derivatively to our future.

Psychology

Psychology involves the systematic study of people and their behavior, with particular focus on the nature of mental processes. Over a hundred years ago, founders of the field such as Francis Galton and William James approached the subject with a broad agenda. Throughout this century the field of psychology evolved into many subareas: depth psychology (Freud), analytical psychology (Jung), behaviorism (Skinner), humanistic psychology (Maslow, Rogers), and other specialty areas too numerous to list (Hudson, 1989).

In the foreseeable future, psychology can be expected to evolve in its diversity. New or developing areas such as paranormal behavior, genetic/biologically-based psychology, cognitive psychology, hemispheric brain studies, and artificial intelligence will continue to draw interest.

Applied psychology will play a prominent role into the future. With the increasing technological basis of modern society and the rapid rate of change affecting human societies across the globe, psychologists will continue to help individuals, organizations, and communities to develop a more humane world.

Sociology

Since August Comte coined the term *sociology* during the middle of the last century, this discipline has flourished and evolved as both an academic and popular concern. Sociology broadly concerns itself with the nature of human society, societal groups, social relations, culture and values, social organization and structure, social change, and the relationship between the individual and society (social psychology).

The sociologist critically examines the nature of society, its political and economic structures, and the world that most of us "take for granted." As with the other social sciences, sociology has continued to evolve as a discipline fragmented into various schools of thought and approaches to the study of human society. The future will most likely witness the continued specialization of this discipline along with attempts to fulfill the original dream of sociology becoming an empirically based science of humankind.

Perhaps one of the most beneficial characteristics of sociology as a discipline will be its ability to continually provide a special perspective and critique to our evolving global social system (Berger, 1992). Sociology will continue to support through its theoretical and research efforts the promotion of human rights, equality, and the replacement of unreason and prejudice with a more rational and humane approach to human society and community (Horowitz, 1992). The extent to which the social sciences are a factor in future social engineering is moot, but they will be ever more useful in shaping and evaluating social policy.

[See also Behavior: Social Constraints; Conscious Evolution; Mass Culture and Arts; Modernism and Postmodernism; Psychiatry; Psychology; Social Indicators; Social Inventions; Social and Political Evolution.]

BIBLIOGRAPHY

Berger, P. L. "Sociology: A Disinvitation?" *Society* (November-December 1992).

Binford, L. R. "In Pursuit of the Future." In *American Archaeology: Past and Future*, ed., D. J. Meltzer, D. D. Fowler, and J. A. Sabloff. Washington, DC: Smithsonian Institution Press, 1986.

Horowitz, I. L. "Social Research and the Culture of Society." *Society* (November-December 1992).

Hudson, L. "Psychology." In *The Social Science Encyclopedia*, ed., A. Kuper and J. Kuper. New York: Routledge, 1989.

Riner, R. R. "Anthropology About the Future: Limits and Potentials." *Human Organization* 50/3 (1991): 297–311.

Ritzer, G., ed. *Frontiers of Social Theory*. New York: Columbia University Press, 1990.

Shanks, M. *Experiencing the Past: On the Character of Archaeology*. London: Routledge, Chapman, and Hall, 1992.

— JOHN P. KEENAN

SOCIAL SECURITY.

See ENTITLEMENT PROGRAMS: PUBLIC ASSISTANCE PROGRAMS: SOCIAL SECURITY.

SOCIAL WELFARE PHILOSOPHIES

Throughout most of the twentieth century, social philosophers and government leaders in the developed nations of the world were in thrall to the idea of a welfare state, in which the national government takes direct responsibility for the economic and social well-being of its citizens and carries out that responsibility by taxing the earnings of workers to distribute as welfare benefits to the needy. Developed in Western Europe as an evolutionary approach to the establishment of state socialism, the welfare state reached American shores in the early 1930s with the enactment of the Social Security Act of 1935 and other Depression-inspired New Deal legislation.

The restructuring of welfare to promote self-support

and restore stable families and communities

will take time.

Most of the proponents of the Social Security Act, including then-President Franklin D. Roosevelt, considered welfare a temporary expedient—a way to ease the pain of the Great Depression, but within twenty years of its inception, welfare had spawned a government-centered industry to produce and distribute benefits, and when President Lyndon Johnson declared war on poverty in the mid-1960s, the industry expanded rapidly, creating scores of federal programs designed to meet the needs of the poor for cash, housing, food and nutrition, health care, education, transportation, child care, adult care, training, and personal counselling. By 1980 one in every five Americans was receiving some form of welfare benefits, and annual welfare costs were $100 billion and growing at three times the rate of the national economy. But poverty was far from defeated: the poverty rate had not declined, and indicators of social dysfunction—crime, gang violence, chronic unemployment, drug abuse, illegitimate births, teenage pregnancies, and school dropouts—had risen steeply, especially among the poor.

As evidence of the failure of the welfare state accumulated and costs continued to spiral upward, a reform movement began to take shape. Some reforms were in name only: simply more welfare proposed by welfare state advocates. Other reforms, such as those of Ronald Reagan, first as governor of California (1966–1974) and then as president (1981–1989), attacked the dependency-inducing nature of the welfare state by requiring recipients to work toward self-support. As Reagan put it in his 1986 State of the Union address: "[The] success of welfare should be judged by how many of its recipients become independent of welfare." In effect, Reagan shifted Johnson's war on poverty to a war on dependency, with work as the primary weapon. He also encouraged the states to take control of welfare reform and reduce the pervasive influence of the federal welfare bureaucracy. By early 1995 most states had embarked on welfare-to-work programs of their own design, and Congress was considering major legislation to increase state control of welfare funds and programs.

Against this background of the rise and failure of the welfare state, and of the movement toward reform through decentralization and work, public welfare in the twenty-first century will have to meet three tests:

- Does it reduce dependency?
- Does it reduce family and community instability?
- Does it reduce bureaucracy and costs?

Significant reductions in welfare dependency will be achieved only by finding paid work for welfare families and others seeking public assistance. Thus, job development and job placement will become the principal functions of the future welfare system. These functions are performed most effectively today for the general population by staffing companies and employment agencies in the private sector, which can easily expand their efforts to cover the welfare population. For some, unsubsidized jobs will be readily available; for others, subsidized jobs with a training orientation will ease the transition from welfare to work. Benefits will be converted to wages, set at levels that ensure steady increases in spendable income as a participant moves from welfare to subsidized employment and then to unsubsidized employment. The availability of more workers will stimulate product development and job creation, which, together with the decline in welfare population, will lead to a more efficient and internationally competitive economy.

Replacing obligation-free benefits with paid work will go far toward breaking down welfare-created economic and social barriers to individual advancement. But more must be done to encourage and support stable and economically viable families and safe, productive communities. Preferential welfare treatment for single-parent families will end. Work requirements will be extended to absent parents of needy children. Child support payments for needy children will go to caretaker parents, rather than to the government. Teenage parents who need public assistance will be required to attend school and live either at home or in a supervised community setting. Neighborhoods will organize them-

selves to provide jobs and to market the skills of their residents to the wider community. Private and predominantly faith-based neighborhood organizations will replace government as the primary provider of social services, including child care. The decentralization of welfare policy control and administration will enable communities to recapture from the welfare state the authority to set and enforce behavioral standards.

A work-oriented, decentralized approach to welfare will reduce costs and shrink the need for bureaucracy. Instead of paying to meet needs, the restructured welfare system will pay for performance—no work, no pay—and thus virtually eliminate the possibility of fraud through unreported earnings. Entry rates and average time on welfare will decrease as work becomes the norm rather than the exception. Shrinking welfare caseloads will reduce the need for government welfare workers, and the bulk of the effort needed to find or create jobs will be supplied through private sector enterprise and voluntary activities. Community-based groups will replace the government as providers and coordinators of supportive services.

The restructuring of welfare to promote self-support and restore stable families and communities will take time. Four generations of a dependency-inducing welfare state have taken a severe toll on American society, and especially on the lives of people who have come under welfare's sway. As those people work their way out of dependency, the nation must constantly remind itself of how they became dependent, and of the effort required to break the habit of dependency forced on them by a benevolent but misguided government. This will be the challenge of welfare in the twenty-first century.

[See also Entitlement Programs; Health Care Costs; Public Assistance Programs; Public Assistance Programs: Social Security; Social Democracy.]

BIBLIOGRAPHY

Bell, Winifred. Contemporary Social Welfare. New York: Macmillan, 1987.
Beverly, David P., and McSweetney, Edward A. Social Welfare and Social Justice. Englewood Cliffs, NJ: Prentice-Hall, 1987.
Elliott, Doreen, et al. The World of Social Welfare: Social Welfare and Services in an International Context. Springfield, IL: Charles C. Thomas, 1990.
Mohan, Brij. The Logic of Social Welfare: Conjectures and Formulations. New York: St. Martin's Press, 1988.
Zastrow, Charles. Introduction to Social Welfare: Social Problems, Services and Current Issues. Belmont, CA: Wadsworth, 1990.

— CHARLES D. HOBBS

SOCIOLOGY.

See SOCIAL SCIENCES.

SOFTWARE COMPUTER.

See COMPUTERS: SOFTWARE.

SOIL CONDITIONS

More than 98 percent of the world's food supply comes from the terrestrial environment and the remaining small percentage from ocean, lake, and other aquatic ecosystems (Pimentel and Hall, 1989). Worldwide, food and fiber crops are grown on 11 percent of Earth's total land mass. Another 24 percent of the land is used as pasture to graze livestock that provide meat and milk products, while forests cover another 31 percent. Humans obtain lumber, pulpwood, and other commercial resources from 80 percent of the total forest land area. Most of the remaining land area (34 percent) is unsuitable for crops, pasture, or forests, because it is covered with ice; is too dry, steep, rocky, or wet; or has soil too shallow to support much, if any, vegetation. (See Table 1.)

More than half of the wetlands in the United States have been drained and converted to agriculture (Pimentel, 1990), while in the remainder of the world an estimated 70 percent have been converted to agricultural use. Draining wetlands has a negative impact on ducks, fishes, aquatic plants, aquatic arthropods, and several other types of aquatic and/or semiaquatic organisms.

Conversion of dryland areas to farming also is occurring in the United States and elsewhere in the world. Crop yield on this land is extremely low. The availability of water is the primary limiting factor in these ecosystems.

Each year an additional 5 million hectares must be put into food production to feed the 92 million humans added to the world population. At the same time, more than 10 million hectares of the world's productive arable land are lost each year because the land has been seriously degraded (Pimentel, 1993). To compensate for these lands, forests are removed. In fact, the spread of agriculture accounts for 80 percent of the deforestation that is now occurring worldwide.

Land degradation is occurring in most crop and pastureland throughout the world (Lal and Pierce, 1991). The major types of degradation are soil erosion, salinization, and waterlogging from irrigation.

Soil erosion is the single most serious cause of land degradation. Worldwide, soil erosion on crop-land ranges from nearly 16 metric tons per hectare per year in the United States to 40 tons per hectare per year in China (USDA, 1991). The extent of erosion is of great concern because soil formation is very slow. It takes approximately five hundred years to form 2.5 cm of topsoil under agricultural conditions (OTA, 1982; Troeh et al., 1980). This means that topsoil is being lost twenty to forty times faster than it is replaced. Furthermore, erosion adversely affects crop productivity by reducing water availability by rapid water runoff, water-holding capacity, nutrients, soil organic matter, and soil depth. Continued erosion may depress food production 15 to 30 percent in the next twenty-five-year period.

Numerous soil and water conservation measures are available to protect topsoil and prevent rapid water runoff. Soil conservation measures include crop rotations, strip cropping, terracing, ridge-planting, no-till, mulches, living mulches, vegetative barriers, and combinations of these (Pimentel, 1993).

Water Resources and Irrigation

As with land, water supplies often are not used with care. Agriculture consumes more freshwater than any other human activity. About 86 percent of all water is "consumed" by agriculture (Postel, personal communication, 1992), while in the United States this figure is 85 percent.

TABLE 1

LAND AREA (MILLION HECTARES) USES IN MAJOR REGIONS OF THE WORLD

Region	Total Area	Cropland	Pasture	Forest	Other*
Africa	2,965	184	792	688	1,301
North America	2,139	274	368	684	813
South America	1,753	140	468	905	240
Asia	2,679	450	678	541	1,010
Europe	473	140	84	157	92
Total	10,009	1,188	2,390	2,975	3,456
Percentage		12%	24%	30%	34%

Source: World Resources Institute, 1992.

* Land that is either too dry, too steep, or too cold to use for agriculture and forestry.

Surface water and groundwater each supply one-half of the freshwater supplies to humans on Earth. Commonly, each American uses about 400 liters per day for domestic needs, whereas total U.S. needs, including agriculture and industry, average more than 5,200 liters per day per individual. In regions where rainfall is scarce, water is pumped from available rivers, lakes, and reservoirs, and from aquifers that store groundwater.

The spread of agriculture accounts for 80 percent of the deforestation that is now occurring worldwide.

Groundwater resources are renewed, but at an extremely slow rate of about 1 percent per year. Because of this slow renewal rate, groundwater resources have to be managed carefully to prevent overdraft. In the United States one-fifth of all irrigated land is watered by overpumping groundwater (Postel, 1989), but in some locations, like the Ogallala aquifer, overpumping may be 130 percent to 160 percent above the replacement rate.

Pumping an ever increasing amount of water to meet human population needs is increasing pressure on surface water and groundwater resources. An example is the Colorado River, which literally disappears after it enters Mexico because of excessive removal of water from the river by the states of California, Arizona, and Colorado.

The world's population may increase by 40 percent from 1990 to 2000, but the demand for water will double. In areas where groundwater is not being conserved, water shortages will constrain efforts to produce more food for the ever increasing human population.

Nutrients and Soil Fertility

All crops require nitrogen, phosphorus, potassium, calcium, and other nutrients. Nitrogen, worldwide, is the most serious limiting nutrient. The remarkable gains of the Green Revolution were due primarily to fossil energy or applying fertilizers, especially nitrogen to cropland. Ultimately, however, there are diminishing returns when the amounts of fertilizers and pesticides are greatly increased, because both are toxic to crops at high dosages.

In the United States about 10 million tons of nitrogen fertilizer are applied to agricultural land. About the same amount of nitrogen is present in the 1.6 billion tons of livestock manure that is produced annually. However, only about 20 percent of this nutrient is recycled effectively in U.S. agriculture. Where possible, it would be desirable to recycle sewage sludge. However, only about 5 percent of the sludge produced in the United States is suitable for use in agriculture because it is heavily contaminated with chemicals.

Many people compost household wastes. This keeps valuable material out of landfills, and the composted material has value for the garden.

When either commercial nitrogen or manure nitrogen is applied to cropland, only about one-third is harvested in the crop. About one-third is lost by leaching, and another third is lost by volatilization (Pimentel et al., 1989). If there is serious erosion, like 20 tons per hectare annually, then a large portion of the nutrients on the land can be lost. Rich agricultural soil may contain about 4 kilograms of nitrogen per ton of soil. The average application rate of nitrogen in U.S. corn production is about 155 kilograms per hectare (Pimentel et al., 1989). Therefore, it is clear that erosion causes major loss of fertilizer nutrients in U.S. agriculture. The best estimate is that annually U.S. agriculture loses $18 billion in fertilizer nutrients due to erosion (Troeh et al., 1980).

Soil degradation is a major environmental problem worldwide. The on-going loss of productive land to soil degradation threatens our food system now and in the future.

[See also Deforestation; Food and Agriculture; Forestry; Green Revolution; Resources.]

BIBLIOGRAPHY

Lal, R., and Pierce, F. J. *Soil Management for Sustainability.* Ankeny, IA: Soil and Water Conservation Society in Cooperation with the World Association of Soil and Water Conservation and Soil Science Society of America, 1991.

Office of Technology Assessment. *Impacts of Technology on U.S. Cropland and Rangeland Productivity.* Washington, DC: OTA, U.S. Congress, 1982.

Pimentel, David. "Environmental and Social Implications of Waste in U.S. Agriculture and Food Sectors." *Journal of Agricultural Ethics* 3 (1990): 5–20.

Pimentel, David, ed. *World Soil Erosion and Conservation.* Cambridge: Cambridge University Press, 1993.

Pimentel, David; Culliney, T. W.; Butler, I. W.; Reinemann, D. J.; and Beckman, K. B. "Low-Input Sustainable Agriculture Using Ecological Management Practices." In M. G. Paoletti, B. R. Stinner, and G. G. Lorenzoni, eds. *Agricultural Ecology and Environment.* Amsterdam: Elsevier, 1989.

Pimentel, David, and Hall, C. W., eds. *Food and Natural Resources.* San Diego: Academic Press, 1989.

Postel, Sandra. *Water for Agriculture: Facing the Limits.* Washington, DC: Worldwatch Institute, 1989.

Troeh, F. R.; Hobbs, J. A.; and Donahue, R. L. *Soil and Water Conservation for Productivity and Environmental Protection.* Englewood Cliffs, NJ: Prentice-Hall, 1980.

U.S. Department of Agriculture. *Agricultural Resources: Cropland, Water, and Conservation Situation and Outlook Report.* Washington, DC: Economic Research Service, USDA, AR-23, 1991.

World Resources Institute, ed. *World Resources.* New York: Oxford University Press, 1992.

— DAVID PIMENTEL

SOLAR POWER.

See ENERGY, RENEWABLE SOURCES OF.

SOLID WASTE

Solid waste, or garbage, results when a consumer has no further use for a material, product, or package. Nonsustainable or inefficient uses of resources typically generate solid waste. In poorer societies and in times of war, the reuse and recycling of "waste" become second nature. Excessive consumption and frivolous disposal are conspicuous signs of wealth and an indicator of a surplus of products and resources.

Highly visible wastes that contribute to litter—for example, nondurable and disposable products, such as packaging for convenience foods and beverages—receive much greater attention than their percentage of the total waste stream justifies. Laws in most municipalities set fines for littering or illegal disposal of waste. The slogans of antilitter campaigns (e.g., "Put litter in its place") imply that creating waste is fine. As a result, waste can be perceived as a problem only when it is greatly out of place.

Waste in a landfill, even a modern sanitary landfill, can result in many environmental problems: the leaching of liquid into groundwater; diffusion of the methane generated in landfills into neighboring communities, or release to the atmosphere, causing objectionable odor and contributing to increases in greenhouse gases. Burning wastes in incinerators has been linked to air pollution and health concerns, particularly where older or inadequate technologies are used. Better technology can resolve many of these problems.

Products generate solid waste at each stage of their life cycle: raw material extraction, manufacturing, use, recycling, and disposal. Products consume energy and resources and generate releases to water, air, and land during all stages of their life cycle. These releases may affect human health, ecosystem health, and the depletion of resources, both renewable and nonrenewable.

These people have found an alternative use for solid waste by building a house of recycled automobile tires. Over 50% of all household trash will be recycled by the year 2030. (Roger Ressmeyer/© Corbis)

Simply because one product creates more solid waste than another product does not necessarily mean that it has a greater negative impact on the environment.

Is waste an inevitable product of modern life? Is waste really a serious environmental problem? Waste generation is an indicator that we may not be doing things right. The future will bring more carefully integrated thinking about products and services. Products and systems will be designed to minimize environmental impacts. Much remains to be done, but the late 1980s and early '90s have set us on the proper road.

The definition of solid waste varies from country to country, making cross-national comparisons difficult. Many countries use the term *municipal solid waste* to describe nonhazardous waste generated by households and by the institutional and commercial sectors. The definition also often includes light industrial solid waste. The more general term *solid waste* usually includes waste from construction and demolition activities, but not wastes arising from natural resource extraction.

Source reduction or prevention, reuse, and recycling (the three R's) divert garbage from landfills and incinerators. If these three options are not available or cannot reasonably be implemented, recovering energy from waste through incineration or landfill gas utilization often makes sense.

Source Reduction, or Waste Prevention

Examining the function of a product or package helps us to understand how waste can be prevented (e.g., eating ice cream on a hot summer day). An ice cream vendor may offer you these options: an edible cone, a disposable cup and spoon, or a reusable cup and spoon. If you take the disposable cup option, once your ice cream is gone, there is a wax-coated paper cup, along with a spoon, to throw out. A reusable cup and spoon must be washed and dried once you are done with them. From a waste prevention perspective, cones are preferred packages, because they are consumed along with the ice cream.

Many other examples of source reduction are linked to packaging reductions such as making packages thinner or lightweight, or removing unnecessary layers. The primary functions of packaging are to protect the product and preserve its freshness. Packaging often reduces waste by minimizing contamination, damage, and spoiling. Other functions of packaging are to attract consumers' attention or to differentiate one product from the rest. In these cases, excess packaging can be removed without impairing the product itself. Many companies have started reducing extra units or layers of packaging, such as boxes for toothpaste or deodorant containers.

Reusable and Durable Products

The second R is reuse: the use of a product or material more than once. Reuse invariably reduces solid waste. However, reused products usually must be cleaned, thereby using water and energy and generating wastewater and emissions associated with energy use. In addition, reused products are typically transported, with related environmental impacts such as air pollution emissions and fossil fuel use. Efficient design of a reuse system, however, can keep these effects to a minimum.

Durability is very important for reuse systems. Many items used on a daily basis in homes are reused: dishes, clothing, linens. Disposable items are typically used for convenience or when cleaning is difficult for hygienic purposes (e.g., garbage bags, toilet tissue, or paper towels).

Is waste an inevitable product of modern life?

Waste generation is an indicator

that we may not be doing things right.

Durability is an issue that is closely tied to cost. A more durable or higher-quality product costs more. Even though it may be more cost-effective to purchase more expensive, longer-lasting products, consumers often prefer to commit less money to a single purchase. As a consequence, more resources are consumed using this approach.

Remanufacturing of products such as laser-printer cartridges is a form of reuse that requires several steps: disassembly, inspection, cleaning, and replacement of components if necessary before reassembly and refilling with toner. Less formalized forms of reuse, such as secondhand stores and repair shops, also contribute to the diversion of waste from disposal.

Recycling

The third R is recycling. Of course, recycling has been around for years—scrap dealers buy scrap iron and steel to sell to mills, envelope converters send cuttings back to the mill to be repulped, scrap newsprint is used to make boxboard. Consumers and businesses are recycling many more materials than before and are incorporating recycled content—often pursuant to government mandates—into products.

Commonly recycled household materials include glass bottles and jars, aluminum and steel cans, newspapers, magazines, telephone books, plastic containers, and textiles. Industrial, commercial, or institutional recycling includes fine paper, plastic film, wood pallets, and steel strapping.

Recycling of materials requires collection of used products, separation by material type, finding markets for the recycled material, and manufacturing of end-use products that include recycled material. Lack of a consistent, high-quality supply of recycled materials due to lack of a collection infrastructure was an early hindrance to the use of recycled content. The momentum gained by mandated recycling programs is removing this barrier to increased recycling. In turn, the market value of recycled materials is increasing.

Residential recycling is usually paid for by municipalities, and thus taxpayers. The sale of recycled materials often does not cover the whole cost incurred by municipalities in the collection, separation, and marketing of materials from residences. Options such as weight-based or unit-based levies or advance disposal fees are in place or being considered in many other communities. These mechanisms aim to have consumers and manufacturers directly pay for recycling and disposal costs, rather than indirectly via taxpayers. Consumers, of course, can choose to buy a less wasteful product and see direct savings.

Composting

The future of waste diversion, in no small measure, lies in composting of organic material. Compostable material makes up more than one-third of the total waste generated. Many communities in North America and Europe collect leaf and yard wastes for centralized composting. Leaf and yard waste is collected only in the warm months and requires a relatively low level of technology (chippers, windrow turners) to produce a high-quality soil enhancer. This product is then used in municipal landscaping, given away, or sold to consumers. Many institutional and industrial facilities (e.g., hospitals, universities, hotels), and some communities collect food waste for composting.

Gardeners do not need to be told about the benefits of composting at home. Many communities now subsidize the distribution of backyard composters or worm composters, and educate citizens on their use. Residential, on-site composting means that the environmental burdens associated with transporting waste to disposal sites are avoided, too.

Energy Recovery and Incineration

Incineration is the combustion of waste in a controlled environment. Older, outdated equipment can result in high levels of air pollution, including dioxins and furons. Modern incinerators have air-pollution-control equipment to remove or minimize the unwanted combustion products. When operated correctly, at high enough temperatures, incinerators emit far lower levels of air pollutants than many other industrial sources. By burning waste in incinerators or using waste directly as a fuel in boilers, energy is recovered and may be used to generate steam or electricity.

Incinerators are a popular option where land is at a premium. However, they are falling out of favor due to high capital expenses. Incinerators are typically built and operated for municipalities by private companies, which then require a guaranteed supply of waste to make a profit. Some jurisdictions have banned new incinerators, contending that such facilities discourage recycling, reuse, and reduction programs.

Almost all new facilities can recover energy from the waste burned to produce steam for nearby industrial or institutional users, or to produce electricity. This approach offsets the need to use fossil fuels to supply the required energy.

Landfilling

Modern sanitary landfills are a vast improvement over the dumps of only a few years ago, where garbage was often burned in an uncontrolled manner. Modern landfills capture leachate (the liquid that percolates out of waste when it decomposes), landfill gas (the gas generated by the decomposing waste), and minimize odors by covering waste with soil or some other material at the end of each day. These practices control groundwater contamination from leachate and limit the uncontrolled emissions of methane, a greenhouse gas.

Siting

All waste-handling faciletes, but especially landfills and incinerators, are difficult to site in today's mainly urban societies. Although modern facilities control pollution of air and water, the problems of odor, increased truck traffic, and reduced property values are not welcome in many communities.

Conversion of agricultural land to landfills is a major concern as well. This reluctance to site facilities has given rise to the term NIMBY, or "Not in my backyard." Fortunately, these attitudes provide extra incentive for individuals, industries, and governments to develop and participate in waste prevention and reduction programs.

[See also Deforestation; Environment; Environmental Behavior; Environmental Ethics; Environmental Indicators; Environmental Policy Changes; Global Environmental Problems; Hazardous Wastes; Natural Resources, Use of; Resources.]

BIBLIOGRAPHY

Alexander, Judd H. *In Defense of Garbage.* Westport, CT. Praeger/Greenwood, 1993.

Daston, Thomas E. *Recycling Solid Waste: The First Choice for Private and Public Sector Management.* Westport, CT. Quorum/Greenwood, 1993.

Fishbein, Bette K. *Germany, Garbage, and the Green Dot: Challenging the Throwaway Society.* New York: INFORM, 1994.

— LYNN PATENAUDE

SOROKIN, PITIRIM A. (1889–1968)

After teaching sociology at the University of St. Petersburg and taking an active part in revolutionary politics, the Russian-born American sociologist Sorokin was expelled from Soviet Russia for his anti-Bolshevik views in 1922. Emigrating to the United States, he taught for several years at the University of Minnesota. In 1930 he founded the Department of Sociology at Harvard University. His abundant published work spans nearly every topic in sociology, but he is best known for his four-volume magnum opus, *Social and Cultural Dynamics* (1937–1941), which offers a cyclical theory of socio-cultural change rivalling the theories of Oswald Spengler and Arnold J. Toynbee. Sorokin maintained that the appropriate unit of study in world history is not a society or civilization but a sociocultural "supersystem." Supersystems are of three kinds, each grounded in a different conception of ultimate reality and truth. The first is the "ideational" supersystem, steeped in religious faith. After its possibilities are exhausted, it is generally succeeded by an "integral" or "idealistic" supersystem, which in turn yields to a "sensate" supersystem, for which reality is seen as material and accessible to the senses. The idealistic supersystem is a rational synthesis of the two extremes. Sorokin viewed the modern West as decadently sensate and foresaw a dawning age of ideational or perhaps idealistic culture bringing a renewal of spiritual consciousness. He also published a comparative analysis of cyclical theories of history and culture, *Social Philosophies of an Age of Crisis* (1950).

[See also Spengler, Oswald.]

BIBLIOGRAPHY

Costello, Paul. *World Historians and Their Goals.* DeKalb: Northern Illinois University Press, 1993, chapter 5.
Cowell, F. R. *History, Civilization, and Culture: An Introduction to the Historical and Social Philosophy of Pitirim A. Sorokin.* London: A. and C. Black, 1952.
Sorokin, Pitirim A. *A Long Journey: The Autobiography of Pitirim A. Sorokin.* New Haven, CT: College and University Press, 1963.

— W. WARREN WAGAR

SPACE COLONIZATION

The dream of building a home in space has existed as long as human beings have dreamed of traveling there. The Russian visionary Konstantin Tsiolkovsky was the first to propose a workable vision, in the early 1900s,

saying, "Earth is the cradle of mankind, but mankind will not always remain in the cradle." He foresaw a gigantic metal spaceship built in orbit. Science fiction writers, such as Murray Leinster, James Blish, and Robert A. Heinlein, also envisioned self-contained spaceship worlds or human settlements on other planets.

There are potential economic benefits to space colonies. Power could be generated in space and beamed to Earth by microwave.

Shortly after the first manned space flights in 1961, futurist Dandridge Cole published the first serious examination of possible future colonies in space. It was physicist Gerard K. O'Neill, however, who gave this science-fictional idea popularity and credibility in his book *The High Frontier* (1977). O'Neill proposed giant orbital cities stationed at the fifth libration point, a region of relative gravitational stability in the Earth-Moon system. O'Neill's concept for these Lagrange-5 (L-5) colonies sparked several fictional treatments, and a society of several thousand members devoted to the promotion of the idea was also formed (now known as the National Space Society in Washington, D.C., which publishes *Ad Astra* magazine).

In fact, the first rudimentary space colony was built in 1977, the same year in which O'Neill's pioneering work was published. The Soviet space station Salyut 6, launched October 1977, was the first man-made structure designed for "open-ended," or semipermanent habitation. Unlike earlier space stations, it was capable of being refueled, maneuvered, and expanded in size. An even more ambitious station called Mir was launched by the Soviet Union in February 1986; by 1993 it had seen over six years of continuous operation, serving as temporary home to over forty different space travelers from nine different countries. It also doubled in volume through the addition of several scientific and technical modules. Some elements of Mir are expected to be operational well into the twenty-first century.

Space stations, however, are not true space colonies, as envisioned by Tsiolkovsky and others, because they are not yet open to ordinary citizens, children, workers. They are more like the research stations in Antarctica, remote outposts devoted to specific types of scientific research.

Inhibiting factors are money and technology. Knowledge of the effects of long-term space travel on human physiology and psychology remains quite limited. Although several Russian cosmonauts have lived in space for as much as a year, no human being has spent more than a few days outside the protective Van Allen Belt, which is where most proposed space colonies would be located.

The physicist J. D. Bernaul speculated in *The World, the Flesh, and the Devil* (1929) that human beings would have to be physically altered to survive in such harsh environments.

More basic technological problems, such as the creation of a so-called closed ecological system, also remain. The yearlong earthbound Biosphere II experiment (1992–1993) was widely considered to be seriously flawed; a workable ecosystem for a space colony would have to be larger and more complex. Launch systems themselves are still too expensive and unreliable to provide sufficient materials. An orbital space colony of the O'Neill island-type seems to be decades away.

The Moon itself presents the most attractive location, serving as a source for raw materials even in the L-5 scenarios. Though airless, the Moon is similar enough to Earth to supply useful raw materials such as metal,

perhaps even hydrogen. The construction of habitats sheltered by lunar rock would avoid the immediate danger of radiation; the presence of gravity would mitigate problems of long-term weightlessness. The Moon also has the advantage of its nearness to Earth; supplies can reach it in three days.

Other sites for planetary colonies are much more remote. Even Mars, Earth's nearest planetary neighbor, is not likely to be visited by manned spacecraft until the middle of the twenty-first century. The challenges increase with distance.

A more relevant question is that, given the dangers and the expense, why establish a colony in space? One thing is certain: space colonies have no role in relieving population pressure on Earth. Even the most wildly optimistic space delivery systems would be incapable of taking more than a fraction of our planet's daily population increase.

There are potential economic benefits to O'Neill colonies. Power could be generated in space and beamed to Earth by microwave. Other futurists have suggested

The dream of living in space is a real one to many people. With advanced computer design capabilities, some of their theoretical possibilities can be worked out on a model. (Roger Ressmeyer/© Corbis)

that dangerous or environmentally damaging manufacturing could be performed in the reaches of space.

It is also possible that space colonies will be founded by groups fleeing religious or political persecution, as were European settlements in North America. L-5 islands might then become homes for various sects or ethnic groups—eventually becoming extraterrestrial nation-states. If such a self-contained and supporting colony had a propulsion system, it could leave the solar system entirely and even travel to the stars.

For the near future, however, space colonies are likely to remain small in size, and be restricted to low Earth orbit or the lunar surface. Even though technically feasible, the expense of building a space colony is so great that such a project could not be borne by a single nation.

[See also Extraterrestrial Life-Forms; Space Flight; Space Travel.]

BIBLIOGRAPHY

Bernaul, J. F. *The World, the Flesh, and the Devil.* London: Methuen, 1929.

Cole, Dandridge. *Beyond Tomorrow.* Amherst, WI: Amherst Press, 1965.

O'Neill, Gerard K. *The High Frontier.* New York: William Morrow, 1977.

Tsiolkovsky, Konstantin. *The Rocket Into Cosmic Space.* Moscow: Naootchnoye Obozreniye, 1903.

— MICHAEL CASSUTT

SPACE FLIGHT

So far, the only propulsion systems that work in the vacuum of space are rockets, which rely on Newton's Third Law of Motion: *For every force exerted in one direction, a force of equal magnitude is exerted in the opposite direction.* Chemical rockets obtain their energy from burning a fuel with an oxidizer, which is needed in space, where there is no oxygen to support combustion. The hotter the exhaust gas, the faster it flows through the nozzle and the more thrust it provides. Rocket engines can be rated in terms of thrust or efficiency, which is referred to as *specific impulse.* Thrust, the pushing force that moves the space vehicle, is measured in pounds. Specific impulse is the measure of how long a pound of propellants will yield a pound of thrust, and it is rated in seconds. Advanced chemical rockets deliver specific impulses of about 500 seconds. Interplanetary propulsion clearly must look beyond chemical rockets.

Nuclear energy could be used to heat a gaseous propellant and provide rocket thrust. The propellant, often called the *working fluid* in nonchemical rockets, can be either a liquid or a gas. A nuclear rocket might consist of a compact nuclear fission reactor, a working fluid (probably hydrogen), and a small "shadow shield" to prevent radiation from reaching the habitation area. Nuclear rockets could provide specific impulses in the range of 1,000 seconds, with thrusts comparable to those of chemical rockets.

Since their exhaust gases would be radioactive, nuclear rockets are envisioned as pure space propulsion systems. They would not be used as boosters to lift spacecraft from the ground.

Nuclear power can also be used to provide energy for *electrical rockets.* Electrical energy can heat a propellant, or a working fluid that conducts electricity can be accelerated to very high velocity directly by electrical energy. Such rocket systems are extremely efficient, with specific impulses of 1,000–10,000 seconds or more. Unfortunately, most (but not all) electric rocket systems produce very low thrusts.

There are several types of electrical rockets. The *resistojet* simply heats its working fluid (usually hydrogen) by electrical resistance, much as an electric stove boils water. Specific impulse is limited to about 1,000 seconds, largely because it is difficult to create higher temperatures without damaging the metal heating elements. Small resistojets have been used as altitude-control thrusters on satellites.

The *ion thruster* has been flown in NASA's Space Electric Rocket Test (SERT) program. A working fluid that conducts electricity, such as mercury or ionized argon gas, is accelerated by electrical energy rather than by heat. Specific impulses of 10,000 seconds or more are possible. Ion thrusters can be powered by solar-voltaic cells that convert sunlight directly into electricity.

The *plasma thruster* employs electromagnetic fields to accelerate an electrically conducting working fluid. Physicists call a gas that has been ionized to the point where it conducts electricity easily a *plasma.* Plasma thrusters produce more thrust per weight than ion thrusters, and are capable of specific impulses of 10,000 seconds or more.

Electrical rockets are limited by the weight of their electrical power systems. The more electrical power needed, the more massive the electric power generator must be. Thus, most electrical rocket systems will remain small, low-thrust devices, limited to fractions of a pound of thrust. Instead of quickly burning all their propellants, the way chemical rockets do, electrical rockets can "burn" for days or even months, slowly accelerating all the time.

Low thrusts, however, limit them to unmanned missions where travel times can be sacrificed for efficiency. Electrical rockets could never boost spacecraft into orbit against the gravitational pull of Earth, but their small puffs of thrust can keep a satellite or space station from drifting out of its desired position in orbit.

Solar sails provide an alternate form of "slow but steady" space transportation that does not use rockets at all. Light exerts some pressure, but so little that a delicate apparatus is needed merely to measure it. Since no propellant is used, the solar sail's specific impulse is infinite. Acceleration from such a minuscule push requires a sail of enormous dimensions. The bigger the sail, however, the heavier it becomes, and the more difficult it is to accelerate the payload. Solar sails are slow. It would take years for a sail of 2.152 million square feet (a square with sides of more than a quarter-mile) to reach Mars.

It may be possible to combine nuclear energy and electrical power to produce rocket engines of high thrust *and* high efficiency by using magneto-hydrodynamic (MHD) power generators. MHD generators draw electrical power from the hot exhaust gases streaming from a rocket engine. MHD generators operate with hot, ionized gases—the hotter, the better. They could take advantage of the full potential of nuclear power. Specific impulses of 2,500 seconds could be obtained from *nuclear-MHD rockets,* more than five times better than that obtained from chemical rockets.

MHD generators have no moving parts. They are rugged, comparatively lightweight, and become more efficient with increasing size. Since a nuclear MHD system could produce about 100 times more power per pound of equipment than existing electric rocket systems such as the ion thruster, a nuclear-MHD system could provide high thrust as well as high efficiency.

Instead of propulsion systems that must carry their own weight with them, like airplanes, it may be possible for the energy source to remain on the ground and transfer energy to the moving vehicle. Two such ideas have been proposed and tested. One uses lasers for propulsion, the other, electrical catapults.

In 1950 Arthur C. Clarke, the visionary author who earlier conceptualized the communications satellite, suggested that *electrically powered catapults* would be a very efficient way to launch payloads off the Moon. On the airless Moon, with its gravity pull merely one-sixth that of Earth, Clarke reasoned that a catapult less than 3 kilometers (1.86 miles) long could fire payloads off the lunar surface. The spacecraft would be accelerated to 100 g (100 Earth gravities), preventing use for fragile cargoes such as human beings! Powered by electricity generated from sunlight or nuclear energy, the catapult could launch unmanned cargoes of lunar ores from the Moon for mere pennies per pound.

Nearly twenty years later, Gerard K. O'Neill of Princeton University developed Clarke's idea into the modern concept of the *mass driver.* Such a device need not be ground-based. It can be positioned in space for use as an orbital catapult or even as a spacecraft propulsion system. A mass driver reaction engine (MDRE) is actually a rocket that fires solid pellets rather than hot gases to create thrust. The mass driver, some 3 to 6 miles long, uses powerful superconducting magnets to accelerate pellets of 14 grams (about a half ounce). The pellets are accelerated to velocities of 17,600 miles per hour within a second or less. About 3 megawatts of electrical power are needed, provided either by nuclear or solar energy.

To produce even a few grams of antimatter would take all the electrical energy available in the United States and more.

The MDRE could move heavy cargoes from low orbits to higher ones. MDREs could also be used as interplanetary spacecraft that "eat" chunks of asteroids and spit them out to provide thrust. For long-term expeditions seeking raw materials among the asteroid belt, an MDRE might turn out to be more efficient than carrying propellants for the return trip all the way from Earth.

Laser propulsion may become the most efficient and economical way to travel in space. The laser, constituting most of the weight of the propulsion system, could remain ground-based. Because lasers can heat propellants to far higher temperatures than can be obtained by chemical burning, a laser-powered rocket can deliver specific impulses of 1,000–2,000 seconds.

Ground-based lasers could be used to raise the altitude of satellites that have been lifted to low orbit by the space shuttle or an expendable booster. Lasers of thousands of megawatt's power would be needed to boost spacecraft from the ground, but such laser-boosted spacecraft could carry payloads that are 50 percent of their total liftoff weight, rather than the 1 percent of today's space shuttle. Huge lasers in orbit near the Earth could propel spacecraft through the far reaches of the solar system, and even out toward other stars.

The penultimate space propulsion system would be a *fusion rocket.* Nuclear rockets use the energy generated in a nuclear reactor by nuclear *fission* (splitting apart massive atomic nuclei such as those of uranium or plutonium) to heat a propellant.

In nuclear *fusion,* the nuclei of the lightest atoms are fused together to create heavier nuclei—and energy.

Fusion is the energy source of the stars. The fuel for a fusion rocket would be water—or more precisely the isotope of hydrogen called deuterium or "heavy hydrogen." For every 6,000 normal hydrogen atoms in water on Earth, there is one atom of deuterium. This means that an eight-ounce glass of water contains enough deuterium to yield as much energy, through fusion, as burning 500,000 barrels of oil!

The energy potential of fusion is so great that once it is applied to space flight, spacecraft will be able to accelerate constantly at one g (one Earth gravity) rather than spend most of their trip coasting. Fusion-powered unmanned probes could travel to Alpha Centauri or Barnard's Star in about 50 years (one-way).

There is one possibility even beyond fusion: *antimatter*. Whereas fusion liberates 0.7 percent of the mass of the reacting matter, a collision between normal matter and antimatter transforms all the mass into energy: 100 percent conversion.

Physicists produce minuscule amounts of antimatter for experiments that probe the fundamental nature of matter and energy. To produce even a few grams of antimatter would take all the electrical energy available in the United States and more. The problem is that once you have some antimatter, where do you keep it? If antimatter and normal matter touch, they annihilate each other in a flash of gamma rays. Someday we may learn to harness this genie and build magnetic "bottles" in which to store antimatter. When that day comes, we can truly look toward the stars and begin the ultimate exploration of the universe.

[*See also Air Transport; Clarke, Arthur Charles; Satellite Communications; Science Fiction; Space Colonization; Space Travel.*]

BIBLIOGRAPHY

Bova, Ben. *The High Road.* Boston: Houghton-Mifflin, 1981.
Byerly, Radford, ed. *Space Policy Reconsidered.* Boulder, CO: Westview Press, 1989.
Jastrow, Robert. *Journey to the Stars: Space Exploration Tomorrow and Beyond.* New York: Bantam Books, 1989.
Kaufmann, William J. *Discovering the Universe.* New York: W. H. Freeman, 1987.
McLucas, John L. *Space Commerce.* Cambridge, MA: Harvard University Press, 1991.

— BEN BOVA

SPACE SATELLITES

The beginnings of space satellites are ordinarily dated from the launching of Sputnik by the former Soviet Union in 1957. However, the idea of a "repeater in the sky" was thought of much earlier. Various writers suggested that space could be used for communication. In 1911, Hugo Gernsback suggested the use of radio, television, and radar in his science fiction book entitled *Ralph 124C41+*. In 1942, George O. Smith wrote a story called "Venus Equilateral" about a manned space vehicle that orbited the sun and was designed for communication. Physicists much earlier had calculated the theoretical orbits of objects located at various distances from Earth.

The implications of these ideas were recognized by Arthur C. Clarke in a 1945 article in *Wireless World,* in which he described a system of "extraterrestrial relays," or repeaters in space. Clarke calculated that an object put into orbit 22,300 miles (36,000 kilometers) above Earth would revolve around the planet in twenty-four hours, the time it takes Earth to rotate on its axis. Thus the repeater would appear motionless or "geostationary" from Earth. He noted that three such repeaters located 120 degrees apart above the equator would cover the entire globe.

Only twelve years later, Sputnik showed that people could communicate using space satellites. However, Sputnik was not a geostationary satellite; it was in low Earth orbit and had to be tracked across the sky, and it simply beeped. But it spurred U.S. scientists and engineers to develop more sophisticated satellites for commercial use. In 1963, the world saw the results as the Syncom 3 satellite transmitted television coverage of the Tokyo Olympics. In 1965, just twenty years after Clarke's article was published, the first commercial international satellite, known as Early Bird (or INTELSAT I), was launched to link North America and Europe.

Satellite technology has evolved dramatically since the early 1960s. Early Bird had only 240 telephone circuits, while today's satellites have the capacity for more than 40,000 voice circuits, or more than 200 television channels. Early experimental satellites were designed for a lifetime of two years; today's satellites are designed to last at least ten years, and are moving toward fifteen years. The limitation on the satellite's life is not the reliability of the electronics, which are fully redundant, but the weight, which limits the amount of station-keeping fuel that can be carried. This hydrazine fuel is used to keep the satellite in orbit; jets can be fired from Earth to nudge the satellite back into position when it begins to drift. When the fuel is expended, the satellite will begin to drift, and eventually it cannot be tracked from fixed antennas on Earth.

Satellites are used for a variety of purposes. Most communication satellites are parked in geostationary orbits as foreseen by Clarke; the advantage is that Earth stations can simply be fixed to point at the satellite; they do not have to track it across the sky. However, some experimental satellites have been located at lower orbits. The Russian Molniya system is a series of satellites in polar orbit that are tracked as they pass overhead; these are used for telecommunications and broadcasting to reach communities in the high Arctic. Several companies are now planning to build systems of low Earth-orbiting satellites (LEOs) for mobile and personal communications. The advantage would be lower launch costs and higher-powered satellite signals, making it possible to use small mobile or handheld transceivers.

Satellites are also used for various types of surveillance. Military satellites orbit at low altitudes and can transmit images with very high resolution.

Satellites are also used for various types of surveillance. Military satellites orbit at low altitudes and can transmit images with very high resolution. Remote sensing satellites are used to map the Earth and to identify mineral deposits and various forms of soil and vegetation. This information can be used to locate promising areas for mining; to monitor flooding and desertification; and to plan land use for agriculture, forestry, and human settlements. Weather satellites transmit images that are used to monitor storms and forecast weather conditions.

Satellites have several properties that make them particularly appropriate for many telecommunications applications. Geostationary satellites can cover as much as one-third of Earth's surface. Domestic satellites are designed to cover large nations such as the United States, Canada, and Australia, while regional satellites can cover the entire Arab world or Western Europe, for example. Earth stations placed anywhere in the satellite's beam are linked with each other through the satellite. As a result, the cost of communication via satellite is independent of distance—the cost of communicating across 500 or 5,000 miles is the same. In contrast, the cost of building and maintaining terrestrial networks is directly proportional to the length of the transmission route.

Earth stations can be installed virtually anywhere, whether it is in a remote village, an offshore oil rig, a high-rise building, or a disaster site. Thus communication can be provided wherever it is needed, without waiting to extend terrestrial facilities. Satellite capacity is also flexible; the technology can be used for voice, data, and video, and it is simple to allocate additional bandwidth where needed. For example, a community can begin with a few voice circuits and then add more circuits and television reception. Satellite systems are also extremely reliable once in orbit; satellite electronics are highly redundant. Also, if there is a problem with one Earth station, it affects only that site, whereas with terrestrial networks, all the sites farther down the network would be affected.

Some countries are concerned about the spillover effects of satellite signals. Programming from U.S. domestic satellites, for example, can be seen in Canada and throughout the Caribbean, Central America, and as far south as Colombia. Another concern is that information from surveillance satellites can be collected without permission. However, the United States, which developed the Landsat satellites, and France, which has commercialized the technology through its Spot Image satellites, have provided training in the interpretation of remote sensing images and have made them available free or at low cost to developing countries.

Unfortunately, many developing countries have not been able to take full advantage of satellite technology. While more than 170 countries use the INTELSAT system for international communications linking capitals and other major cities, most of the developing world remains without access to reliable telecommunications. Satellites could be used to provide low-cost communications to millions of people who are now beyond the range of terrestrial networks.

[See also Clarke, Arthur Charles; Communications; Satellite Communications; Telecommunications; Telephones.]

BIBLIOGRAPHY

Chetty, P. R. *Satellite Technology and Its Applications,* 2nd ed. Blue Ridge Summit, PA: TAB Books, 1991.

Glaser, P. E., et al. *Solar Power Satellites: The Emerging Energy Option.* Englewood Cliffs, NJ: Prentice-Hall, 1992.

Hudson, Heather E. *Communication Satellites: Their Development and Impact.* New York: Free Press, 1990.

INTELSAT Annual Report, 1990–91. Washington, DC: INTELSAT, 1991.

Pelton, Joseph N., and Howkins, John. *Satellites International.* New York: Stockton Press, 1988.

— HEATHER E. HUDSON

SPACE TRAVEL

Space travel has been a dream of humanity for millennia. The ancient Greeks pondered its possibilities before the birth of Christ. Jules Verne wrote a novel (*A Trip to the Moon,* 1865) describing a journey to the moon that rather strongly resembled the actual Apollo lunar landing in 1969. The Chinese invented rockets in the eleventh century, but their use was limited mainly to warfare. Not until the mid-twentieth century did rockets become tools of space exploration. Wernher von Braun and his team of German scientists, working first in Germany during World War II and later in the United States, pioneered the use of rockets for space exploration.

The era of human space travel began on April 12, 1961, when Yuri Gagarin became the first person to leave the Earth's atmosphere and enter the space environment. Flying in the Soviet spacecraft *Vostok I,* he orbited the planet once, spending a total of 108 minutes in space.

Lunar Expeditions

In 1961 President John F. Kennedy inaugurated a new era in space history. He declared, in a speech before Congress, that the United States would send a man to the Moon and return him safely to Earth before the end of the decade.

From 1968 to 1972 American astronauts made an unprecedented series of journeys to the moon. Apollo 8, launched in December 1968, was the first spacecraft to orbit the moon, sending back the first television pictures of the whole Earth. Apollo 11 later fulfilled the pledge of President Kennedy, landing two men on the Moon, Neil Armstrong and Buzz Aldrin, in July 1969. Five other lunar missions successfully landed astronauts on the Moon; the final mission, Apollo 17, took place in 1972.

Interplanetary Travel

Since the Apollo missions, no human beings have traveled beyond low Earth orbit (LEO), and manned missions to the other planets in the solar system remain a long-range goal for all current space programs. However, there have been numerous unmanned missions, and every planet in the solar system except Pluto has been visited by unmanned probes.

Mars is the planet most often mentioned as a destination for future manned missions. Mars is the most Earth-like of the planets, with a day of almost the same duration as that of Earth, and temperatures that are Earth-like during daylight hours. Geological evidence suggests that Mars was once on an evolutionary path similar to that of Earth, with running water in abundance, and perhaps even early life forms. However, Mars was apparently too small to retain an Earth-like atmosphere, and that seems to have halted its evolution.

Interstellar Travel

Unless human beings discover a new form of propulsion, interstellar travel will not become a reality in the near future. According to Einsteinian physics, the speed of light is the upper limit of velocity for any body in the universe. The nearest star system, Alpha Centauri, is 4.3 light-years from Earth, meaning that a spacecraft moving at the speed of light would take 4.3 years to arrive there. Currently, all propulsion systems are far slower than the speed of light, and a journey to Alpha Centauri would require many years.

According to Einstein's theory of relativity, however, time on a spacecraft traveling close to the speed of light will not move at the same pace as on Earth. If the theory holds true, time will be compressed, so space travelers would only age by a few days while their friends and relatives on Earth would age many years.

Several ideas have been proposed to meet the challenges posed by long-duration spaceflight. For example, astronauts might be placed in a state of suspended animation in which they would consume fewer resources such as food and air and would not face the boredom of a long mission. On arrival at their destination, the star voyagers would be awakened to complete their mission.

"Generation starships" are an idea long popular with science fiction writers (e.g., Robert Heinlein's "Universe" [1940] and Brian Aldiss's *Nonstop* [1959]). These ships would leave Earth with an entire human community aboard. Many generations would die as the starship made its way to its destination, but succeeding generations would hopefully survive to colonize the target star system.

The closed ecological life support system is another idea under consideration, and has some practical experience to support it. These systems would mimic the ecology of Earth, so that space travelers would, in effect, carry their terrestrial environment along with them. Made popular by the Biosphere II experiment in Arizona in the early 1990s, this concept may become a practical approach either for spacecraft or for space settlements.

Social Systems

One of the most significant barriers to long-duration spaceflight is the inability of human social systems to function effectively under the challenging conditions of a space environment. A journey to Mars, for example, might require a total of three years, with as much as a year spent in transit from the Earth to Mars, and a similar period on the return.

Experiences in extreme environments on Earth, such as Antarctica, submarines, and in long-duration space missions on Russian space stations, show that it is very difficult for human beings to endure being confined for long periods of time. Small problems are magnified in close quarters, often leading to serious disputes over minor issues.

Once human beings settle in the space environment permanently, one of the great benefits of space travel may well be the development of new social systems.

Early settlements in space, moon or Mars, are likely to reflect social systems on Earth. However, because of their distance from the Earth, they may quickly develop a degree of independence and begin to evolve in response to the space environment. Eventually, they will probably declare their independence from Earth, just as the thirteen colonies in North America did in 1776. We will have to be careful to avoid war between terrestrials and their spacefaring descendants.

Physical/Mental Effects

The Earth is the natural environment for human beings, and our bodies are adapted to terrestrial conditions, especially the pull of Earth's gravity. For this reason, space travel has profound physical effects on the human body, mainly because of weightlessness. When people go into space, the body rapidly adapts to the diminution of gravity—the bones begin to shed calcium, the heart beats less rapidly, the circulation of blood changes, and the spine lengthens.

Evidence suggests that vigorous physical exercise while in space is the best countermeasure for the physical changes that occur in low-gravity settings. Astronauts and cosmonauts who have returned to Earth after even a year in space have adjusted without long-term ill effects.

We can only speculate about the impact on generations of human beings who live, work, and reproduce in the space environment. It is possible that a new species will evolve that will be quite different from the current *Homo sapiens.*

While mental effects are more difficult to quantify, they also occur. For example, the "Overview Effect" is a term that the author has developed for an experience that appears to be universal among astronauts and cosmonauts, resulting from looking back at the Earth from orbit or from the moon. This effect is a realization of the unity and oneness of everything on the Earth, an understanding that every terrestrial being functions as a component of an interconnected system.

For astronauts and cosmonauts who went into space with a religious perspective, the experience often confirms their original views. For others, the feeling is a "peak experience" that offers new insights into the nature of humanity and our relationship not only with the Earth but also with the universe as a whole.

Philosophical Implications

Our limited experience in space shows that our philosophical perspective can be deeply affected by our physical location, and this understanding may be the most important result of space travel. The human evolutionary path will move outward into space, which means that the universe itself will become our ecological range,

rather than the Earth alone. The ultimate outcome appears to be that we will become "citizens of the universe," increasingly aware of our identity not only as a part of the Earth but also within the universe, evolving as a whole system on a vaster scale. The impact will be even more profound if we meet intelligent extraterrestrial beings, who may be thousands, or millions, of years ahead of us in evolution.

How will space travel affect our sense of identity, of individuality, of our relationship with the universe, with humanity and other life-forms, and with the divine? Speculation alone will not answer our questions. Only the further experience of space exploration itself will reveal its ultimate philosophical implications to us.

[See also Air Transport; Global Consciousness; Science Fiction; Space Colonization; Space Flight.]

BIBLIOGRAPHY

Allen, Joseph P. *Entering Space: An Astronaut's Odyssey.* New York: Stewart, Tabori, & Chang, 1984.

Carpenter, M. Scott, et al. *We Seven: By the Astronauts Themselves.* New York: Simon & Schuster, 1962.

Collins, Michael. *Carrying the Fire.* New York: Farrar, Straus and Giroux, 1974.

Lebedev, Valentin. *Diary of a Cosmonaut: 211 Days in Space.* Houston: Pytoresource Research, Inc., Information Service, 1988.

White, Frank. *The Overview Effect: Space Exploration and Human Evolution.* Boston: Houghton Mifflin, 1987.

Wolfe, Tom. *The Right Stuff.* New York: Farrar, Straus and Giroux, 1979.

— FRANK WHITE

SPENGLER, OSWALD (1880–1936)

Born in a small town in the Harz Mountains, German philosopher of history Spengler spent several years as a secondary school teacher. In 1911, with the help of a modest inheritance from his late mother, he resigned his post to became a full-time writer. His one major work, *Der Untergang des Abendlandes* (1918–1922; in English, *The Decline* [more accurately, "Fall"] *of the West,* 1926–1928), was translated into several languages and brought Spengler worldwide attention. Most of his other writings were brief political tracts, such as *Jahre der Entscheidung* (1933; in English, *The Hour of Decision, 1934*), in which he put forward a bleakly conservative and racist worldview critical of Nazism, but spiritually akin to it. *The Decline of the West* provides a comparative analysis of the evolution of cultures. Defining them as self-contained organisms, Spengler contended that each great historic culture passes through a similar life cycle, from birth, rise, and decline to death. Each stage was inevitable and could not be staved off. He asserted that the "Faustian" culture of the West, born in the early Middle Ages, was now senescent. After a coming era of Caesarism comparable to the imperial stage of Roman history, he anticipated that it would collapse and die.

BIBLIOGRAPHY

Costello, Paul. *World Historians and Their Goals: Twentieth-Century Answers to Modernism.* DeKalb, IL: Northern Illinois University Press, 1993, chapter 3.

Fischer, Klaus Peter. *History and Prophecy: Oswald Spengler and the Decline of the West.* New York: Peter Lang, 1989.

Hughes, H. Stuart. *Oswald Spengler: A Critical Estimate,* 2nd ed. New York: Scribner, 1962 (originally published 1952).

Mazlish, Bruce. *The Riddle of History: The Great Speculators from Vico to Freud.* New York: Harper and Row, 1966, chapter 9.

— W. WARREN WAGAR

SPORTS AND ACTIVITIES, SPECTATOR

Competitive sports and games have been central to human civilization throughout recorded history, spreading across cultures. Sometimes sports played a part of religious rituals or as forms of modified warfare. Whatever the purpose, sport reflects the conditions and needs of a society.

In the city-state of Athens from about 500 to 400 B.C. sports and games were so important that political leaders provided athletic grounds for the entire populace. Spectator sports, on the other hand, didn't exist until Roman times when amphitheaters, such as the Coliseum, drew nearly the entire citizenry to view games and contests. This eventually led to spectacles that were often bloody, lewd, and obscene, involving days of wild celebration, hence the expression "Roman holiday."

The citizens of Rome initially relied upon sport to maintain the body and the spirit for purposes of defense, but as the amount of leisure time increased and the need for physical labor and military service declined, the focus of sport changed. Entertainment replaced participation in sports, which, some say, led to the decline of Roman civilization.

How then will the needs and conditions of the future affect spectator sports? Will spectator sports be a force for the advancement of society or the decline of still another civilization?

Technology is a force changing society and, in turn, spectator sports. Pay-per-view TV is the future version of season tickets. Interactive technology will enable remote-controlled spectators to sit in the dugout or at the fifty-yard line, changing venues with the click of the remote control. *Spectator* will be redefined, physical presence at an event no longer being required.

If technology is changing our understanding of what it means to be a spectator, it will also transform the definition of *sports fans.* The National Football League has been playing preseason games in Europe for nearly a decade. Former American baseball players have long been delighting Japanese fans. No longer will sports fans be defined by traditional national pastimes. Technology will create a global economy that extends to spectator sports, and the balance of trade will redefine the concept of a "home court" advantage. Forget the National or the American Leagues and look for the Pacific-Rim and Central European Leagues.

Sport globalization is an economic issue

as the profits from this entertainment industry

continue to grow.

Sport globalization is an economic issue as the profits from this entertainment industry continue to grow. College sports generate substantial amounts of revenue through the television and licensing rights of amateur athletes. The annual salaries of professional athletes rival those of rock stars. Spirited salary negotiations hallmark each new sport season. Baseball felt the pressure and financial pinch when the 1994 season was the first to open without a major television contract.

Just how far can the commercialization of spectator sports spread? From instant replays to scoreboards, everything and anything has a price tag. In the not-so-distant future, the starting lineup announcements may include the name of the player as well as the product or company sponsoring the athlete for that game. A proficient basestealer may be sponsored by a security company, while a football receiver might be sponsored by a glove company. Product endorsements and merchandising are substantial revenue generators. Sneaker manufacturers already spend upward of thirty million dollars for celebrity endorsement campaigns. Everyone will get in the act as college and professional sports teams sell sponsorship rights. Envision athletes playing the game looking like race cars with their uniforms completely covered with corporate or product logos.

Whether sports continue to generate such large revenues depends on the fans, who will continue to call for more action and excitement. Basketball and football leagues responded to the call by adding the three-point basket and the two-point touchdown conversion option. The future will bring more variations of scoring strategies and rule changes. For example, changes in the height of the basketball hoop and the diameter of the rim will proliferate as each sport competes for advertising dollars and revenues.

Does this increasing specialization and commercialization of sport portend the decline of society? Do incidents of fan violence at soccer games and multidays of corporate partying at Super Bowls and Olympic Games indicate that life in the United States is repeating the patterns of ancient Greece and Rome? Will this emphasis upon playing and partying contribute to the downfall of society?

The near future of spectator sport may include more commercialization and more emphasis on entertainment, but there may be a quite different long-range future. Since sport reflects society, other changes due to demographic and societal shifts will surface as well. A revised and gentler definition of competition is likely based upon the increasing entry of women into athletics, coupled with the general aging of the population in the industrialized world. Activities such as golf and fishing will undergo further expansion as many focus on individual activities. The future may also redefine amateur athletics, as some colleges and universities form a second sports division where sports reassume an educational emphasis and diminish their economic importance.

Immigration will change spectator sports, adding previously unfamiliar sports to the mainstream. Emerging nations with their high birth rates will produce many young people who will parade the team sports of their culture to global attention. Sports such as cockfighting and bullfighting may also be newcomers to the arena as people from various countries blend their traditions with those of the United States. On the other hand, the animal rights movement may squelch any new or violent animal-based sports in the United States.

The late A. Bartlett Giamatti, a Renaissance scholar, former president of Yale University, and Commissioner of Baseball, believed that you could tell more about a society by observing how they played rather than how they worked. Spectator sports is a form of that play. Spectator sports reflecting the changes and needs within society have the potential for contributing to the creation of a truly global world where people from different countries and cultures can connect with one another through a common interest.

Let the games begin!

[See also Animal Rights; Free Time; Gambling; Global Culture; Leisure Time; Sports and Games, Competitive.]

BIBLIOGRAPHY

Allison, Lincoln, ed. *The Changing Politics of Sport.* Manchester, U.K.: Manchester University Press, 1993.

Giamatti, A. Bartlett. *Take Time for Paradise . . . Americans and Their Games.* New York: Summit Books/Simon and Schuster, 1989.

Kraus, Richard. *Recreation and Leisure in Modern Society,* 4th ed. New York: HarperCollins, 1990.

— ELLEN L. O'SULLIVAN

SPORTS AND GAMES, COMPETITIVE

Almost all sports and games can be competitive or noncompetitive. Competitive sports may be organized tournaments or public contests. Noncompetitive sports are primarily oriented toward social interaction, skill development, or systematic physical or mental exercise. Swimming, for example, may be highly competitive, rigorous exercise, or simply playing around in a pool.

Looking into the future of sports and games involves more than extrapolating numbers from surveys of participation. Are there varieties of swimming or electronic games that are likely to grow while others decline? Are there certain styles of participation—competitive or cooperative, doing or watching, individual or social—that are most likely to develop?

Sports and Games: How to Look Ahead

A few decades ago, amateur baseball on Sunday afternoons seemed central to the summer culture of small-town America. Now these teams are a vague memory. In small towns in the 1950s and '60s, high school football and basketball were the talk of the town. Now bleachers are 75 percent empty for most athletic contests. Until recently, the male dominance of team sports was the accepted rule. Now both the rule and the culture have changed. In a matter of years, fiberglass and composite skis, racquets, and hulls have transformed access, costs, upkeep, and even ease of learning these sports. The patterns of the past do not just extend into the future.

No activity just keeps on growing in participation.

Every market becomes saturated;

every peak is followed by some decline.

TREND ANALYSIS. Why is it not possible to take numerical trends in participation and draw them out for future decades? In the field of sports and games, there are a number of limitations:

First, the data are inconsistent. For example, A.C. Neilson followed a few sports for less than ten years and discontinued its survey in 1983. Federal surveys focus on outdoor recreation and employ inconsistent formats. The national marketing surveys, the best current source of trends, moved slowly into recreation and have data on only a few sports for even a decade.

Second, many activities of interest such as surfing, hangliding, rock climbing, ballooning, or squash involve less than 1 percent of the adult population and do not appear in surveys. Trade journal estimates for such activities are almost always unreliable and inflated.

Third, for the sports and games for which there are viable figures for at least ten years, there is seldom a reliable measure of frequency or commitment. Studies have demonstrated that only 20 to 25 percent of those who engage in a sport during a given year do it regularly (Kelly, 1985; 1987). For example, in 1991 only 3.2 percent played golf at least 20 days a year, but 11.5 percent played at least once. Similar rates are reported for other sports: In 1991, 14.5 percent bowled but only 1.6 percent as often as once a week; for aerobics the percentages were 6.5 percent and 2.9 percent; for horseback riding 3.3 percent and 0.5 percent; for racquetball, 4.0 percent and 0.4 percent; for swimming, 23.0 percent and 1.3 percent; and for waterskiing, 3.2 percent and 0.2 percent. As a consequence, almost all figures on participation radically overestimate the number for whom the sport or game is a regular part of life, even in a limited season.

Fourth, variations from year to year are unreliable when the percentages are so low. A national study finds that only 2 percent of the large sample had played volleyball in the previous two weeks, only 3 percent had played tennis, and 4 percent had bowled (National Center for Health Statistics, 1990). The evident decline in tennis playing, for example, can only be assessed by comparing rather small differences over many years (Kelly, 1987).

Table 1 is based on the yearly household survey of the Simmons Market Research Bureau from 1980 to 1991. It is the most reliable trend analysis available in the United States even though subject to many limitations.

The general trends are consistent with most other studies indicating that sport and recreation participation is not, for the most part, increasing. This is also consistent with trends showing a significant decline in fitness occasions of 4 percent from 1985 to 1990 (National Center for Health Statistics). The so-called "fitness revolution," with the exception of walking, seems to have peaked about 1985. For example, aerobics participation was down to 6.5 percent in 1991 with less than half doing their jumps at least once a week.

In general, there is clearly no boom in sport or physical activity engagement. One reason is the aging of the population, because physical exertion decreases with age. A second reason is the smaller school population, since sport participation—especially team sports—drops off precipitously when people leave school.

TABLE 1

U.S. SPORTS TRENDS IN THE 1980S

Activity	Percent of Adult Population Participating in One Year		
	1980	1991	Trend
Distance running	1.6	3.1	Grew
Exercise walking	18.9	23.2	Grew
Golf	8.3	11.5	Grew
Bicycling	18.2	10.2	Declined
Bowling	20.2	14.5	Declined
Swimming	30.2	23.0	Declined
Alpine skiing	3.8	3.3	Declined
Ice skating	5.0	2.2	Declined
Racquetball	6.0	4.0	Declined
Tennis	11.4	7.0	Declined
Basketball	4.7	4.1	Declined
Football	3.1	2.1	Declined
Jogging	10.5	6.0	Declined
Sailing	2.9	2.3	Declined
Softball	8.0*	5.9	Declined
Volleyball	5.0*	5.8	Grew

* 1984 status; 1980 not available
Source: Simmons Market Research Bureau Study of Media and Markets

THE ACTIVITY LIFE CYCLE. Trends in recreational activity do not extend in a straight line. Marketing studies refer to the "product life cycle" of introduction, growth, peak, and decline. Fads have a rapid growth and decline. Products with viable markets peak and then decline to a plateau rather than back to near-zero. New sports and games have a similar "activity life cycle" (Kelly, 1985). No activity just keeps on growing in participation. Every market becomes saturated; every peak is followed by some decline.

The reasons vary. Promotion and initial enthusiasm may be followed by withdrawals due to disinterest, loss of companions, or even, as with jogging, injuries. An innovation such as the skateboard may produce rapid growth followed by a steep decline to a much lower level of use. Resources may limit participation even when demand continues. The scarcity and expense of urban space for golf restricts the development of courses. Costs and the failure to develop a market outside upper-income males in their twenties and thirties dampened predicted growth in racquetball. Initial enthusiasm always seems to melt somewhat despite efforts to promote an activity and its related products. And fundamental to the activity life cycle is the reality that satisfaction in playing a sport is related to the level of skill. Developing skill requires investments of time, effort, and other costs too high for most. Only about 25 percent of those who engage in a sport do it as often as once a week.

Sports that start on the fringe, called extreme sports, often make their way into mainstream competitions. This young man is snowboarding. (© Kevin Syms/First Image West, Inc.)

The issue, then, is to distinguish those activities that promise long-term stability or growth from those likely to be fads or to appeal to a very limited clientele. In general, those that call for the highest levels of commitment to develop competence will have small but stable participation coupled with high dropout rates for beginners. Those that fit easily into current lifestyles may gain mass markets. Those that depend on the promotion of a new device and have markets limited to one age or status group, especially youth, are most often fads.

FACTORS IN THE FUTURE. Too often journalists give undue emphasis to different sports and games just because they are new; that is, they are news. Especially those based on a new and highly promoted device or are esoteric in their appeal gain attention. Flying ultralites or balloons, jumping off bridges, and other "risk" activities will never gain a participation rate of even as much as 0.5 percent of the population in any given time period. Others require various kinds of resources that are limited; they are too space-intensive, cost-intensive, or skill-intensive. In assessing the future of other kinds of sports and games, at least the following factors need to be included in the forecasting puzzle (Snyder and Spreitzer, 1989):

- *Age:* Physically demanding activities all demonstrate age-related declines in participation. As the population profile ages, the "graying of America" will affect most sports, even though there are recent indications that those entering their fifties, sixties, and seventies now are engaging in slightly higher levels of sports than previously.

- *Gender:* Sports were drastically segregated by gender until the 1970s. Females were excluded from resources and actively discouraged from major investment in strenuous activity. The changes that began two decades ago will continue so that growth in some sports and games will be largely female. Nevertheless, current analysis indicates that such development will be limited and may even be receding for some sports (Robinson and Godbey, 1993).

- *Cost:* Some sports such as Alpine skiing, horse showing, and most forms of boating are quite costly. Only an expansion in the proportion of the population with considerable discretionary income can increase participation markedly. Current trends in income and wealth distribution in Western economies suggest that affluence may become even more restricted.

- *Resources:* How far will golfers drive to play on weekends? How much urban space will be allocated to recreation venues? How much water is accessible to urban boaters, swimmers, and anglers? Time and distance combine with scarcity to place limits on many kinds of activity and limit many to favored regions and locations.

- *Time:* Many adults such as employed mothers and technicians under high pressure are experiencing a "time famine" (Schor, 1992). Economic pressures and gendered social arrangements favor sports and games that offer the most satisfaction in the least time. On the other hand, the unemployed and underemployed *may* decide to become more involved in sports and other recreation that yields a sense of competence and involvement.

- *Alternatives:* In any recreation, there are always alternatives—doing something else or doing nothing. Electronic media offer a greater variety of entertainments at modest cost and almost total convenience. The appeal of such alternatives must be factored into any projected equation, along with the costs of participation and the distribution of resources.

- *Lifestyles:* How do sports and games fit into contemporary lifestyles? Parents tend to be more oriented toward their children than their own expression. Social status reinforces particular activities, especially for business classes. Education widens interests and abilities. Year-round warm climates foster outdoor activities. The value placed on sports meanings and outcomes can shift in ways that build or inhibit participation in particular kinds of sports and games. For example, will there be any change in the value placed on "competition" itself? Or will sport increasingly become a televised spectacle with fewer who play and more who watch? Will the producers of opportunities respond more to the smaller markets for participation or to the mass markets for spectators?

Futurists are often so technology-driven that they assume that whatever can be done will be done. In sports and games, technology may produce variations on activity or widen access, but other factors are far more determinative of engagement.

Types of Activity and Scenarios

STATUS-BASED SPORTS AND GAMES. These will remain popular with the traditional elites as well as with the "new class" of high-tech research and development work, professionals, and financial managers. The growth in high-end tourism may parallel growth in some elite and specialized sports and games: sailing regattas and dressage horse showing as well as more prosaic private-club golfing and deluxe downhill skiing. Travel for special sports challenges and opportunities may increase. The numbers involved will have little impact on national statistics, but elite sports styles segregate players by price and venue.

ETHNIC GAMES. As the population becomes more diverse through immigration, ethnic variations in sports and games may become more evident. Already urban public recreation providers are accommodating a greater variety of activities and styles as their Latin and Asian populations swell. In time, there may even be some recreational cross-fertilization as "minorities" come to outnumber traditional majorities.

TECHNOLOGY-BASED GAMES. Technologies have impacted a wide range of sports and games. With greater attention being given to leisure markets by multinational corporations as well as by local and regional businesses, the likelihood of sustained marketing and development that fosters obsolescence of equipment will continue. Most technologies do not have dramatic impacts on participation. There are technologies, however, that actually create games or transform existing ones. Composite wheels on skateboards and on both traditional and in-line skates are one example. In some cases, technologies, such as the weapons-aiming transistor and new chips, create games. Those in the electronic games business are continually developing new hardware and software to counter the product life cycle and maintain or increase markets. This marketing strategy will employ technological development to attract participants and keep them engaged. Such development is limited, however, by the extent to which such games fit the lifestyles and resources of potential players. Some technologies are quite expensive. Furthermore, the increased sophistication of electronic games also may repel less skilled players. There will be continued growth based on new and improved technologies, but most new game technologies will be fads or busts if they fail to gain an adequate committed clientele.

SCHOOL-BASED SPORTS AND GAMES. Many sports, especially team sports, depend on their introduction in school settings. Others are learned in public recreation programs aimed at school-age children and youth. For the most part, participation in such sports narrows through the school years and drops off precipitously when people leave school. With school-age populations shrinking and the prestige of school sports seemingly on the wane, such sports are likely to continue their shrinking participation base. Further, nonteam sports and games such as tennis have also declined. The only age groups that indicate even a slight gain in participation are the over-fifties, which begin at 1–3 percent levels. The only sport exception is golf, which continues to attract those in their fifties and sixties. For the most part, though, American adults watch, rather than play, team sports.

The fundamental appeal of sports

—meeting measured challenge—

will attract significantly more adults

who fail to find such challenge in other arenas of life.

SPECTATOR SPORTS. Total attendance figures for sports are impressive: over 70 million in a year for thoroughbred horseracing, 50 million for major league baseball, 36 million for college football, 17 million for the National Football League, and so on. Increasingly, however, it is television that drives spectator sports. Between 100 and 500 people will watch a televised professional game for every attendee there in person. Schedules and formats are oriented toward the camera and small screen, not the on-site crowd. Furthermore, the electronic "superhighway" of fiber optic cable will widen the offerings, so that there will be choices twenty-four hours of every day. What is the saturation level of sports on television? It is likely that the question can be answered by the year 2020, when the effort to fill channels will have peaked. In the meantime, however, the growth in the level of boredom is yet to be explored.

SKILL-BASED SPORTS AND GAMES. Research has made clear that those who are committed to a sport or game and give priority in their lives to participation are those who are developing skills and seeking challenges. Those sports and games that offer relatively limitless ranges of challenge are those most likely to gain and maintain stable levels of engagement. One reason for the continuing expansion of golf is the endless skill-based challenge it offers through most of life. The projection is not one of a dramatic "boom" in such skilled sports. There are suggestions, nevertheless, that the fundamental appeal of sports—meeting measured challenge—will attract significantly more adults who fail to find such challenge in other arenas of life. Such sports will vary widely, from flycasting to motocross, from golf to softball, and will include high-demand activity such as distance running to risk activities that are also skill-based. The numbers and percentages of participation may be tiny in relation to those who watch sports on television, but 1 percent of the population is a viable market share.

Two Scenarios for the Twenty-First Century

Two general scenarios may encompass much of the future of sports and games in American society.

MASS MARKETS. There is no question that the corporate world will continue to explore and exploit leisure as a growth industry. Spectator sports will be promoted in their interlocked commercial dimensions: advertising, product promotion, gate revenues, tax writeoffs, and institutional advancement. Sports and games will be a central part of the consumer economy. They will be redesigned and reformatted to draw the largest possible clienteles through on-site revenues, pay television, and advertising-funded free television. The players will become more and more specialized, those with remarkable physical attributes who have less and less connection with ordinary people. Players will be commodities to be sold on the various markets from actual performance to branded tee shirts and shoes. There will be protests and critiques, but market forces will prevail.

SPECIALIZATION AND DIVERSITY. There will be a parallel movement that operates in conjunction with more specialized promotion and marketing. Sports and games will, by definition, be minority affairs, drawing relatively small proportions of the population into regular participation in challenging and skill-based activity. Fads will come and go in the markets promoted by cooperative media, then receding to fringes of attention. In the meantime, there will be an increased diversity of engagements in activity. Some will be highly competitive and some more social. Some will bring participants into special environments and others will have more convenient home-based locales. Some younger people and a few over fifty will engage in physically demanding sports. Some sports and games will be upscale, limited to those who can afford special equipment and environments. Some will be more accessible. Age, status, gender, and finances will continue to separate participants. What players will have in common is a commitment to challenging activity and to communities of engagement in a world in which economic roles are limited. The demands of sports and games will provide a balance to the more ordinary and accessible activities

that center on home and household. They will be important to a minority, just because they offer challenge in a world of easy consumption.

[See also Free Time; Gambling; Interactive Entertainment; Leisure Time; Outdoor Recreation and Leisure Pursuits; Parks and Wilderness; Record Setting; Sports And Activities, Spectator.]

BIBLIOGRAPHY

Kelly, John R. *Recreation Business.* New York: John Wiley, 1985.
———. *Recreation Trends toward the Year 2000.* Champaign, IL: Sagamore Press, 1987.
Robinson, John P., and Godbey, Geoffrey. "Sport, Fitness, and the Gender Gap." *Leisure Sciences* 15 (1993): 291–307.
Schor, Juliet B. *The Overworked American.* New York: Basic Books, 1992.
Snyder, Eldon E., and Spreitzer, Elmer A. *Social Aspects of Sport,* 3rd ed. Englewood Cliffs, NJ: Prentice-Hall, 1989.

— JOHN R. KELLY

STAPLEDON, W. OLAF.

See GLOBAL CONSCIOUSNESS.

STOCK MARKET.

See DERIVATIVES; INVESTMENTS.

STRATEGIC PLANNING

The popular and business press is full of stories of giant corporations, such as General Motors, Philips, Volkswagen, and IBM, losing huge amounts of money and firing people by the thousands. Yet less than a decade ago these organizations were highly profitable—textbook examples of best-run companies that other firms were trying to imitate. Something went wrong as they found themselves unable to avoid the dangers wrought by environmental changes and incapable of exploiting technological or other opportunities at least as effectively as their competitors.

Managing for the future, by anticipating and exploiting environmental changes, provides a way of minimizing failure or maximizing success. Rapid changes in the business environment obviates continuing the status quo, attempting to imitate successful firms, or believing that the future will be similar to the past. Among the greatest challenges facing management are to correctly identify forthcoming changes, to accurately anticipate their consequences, and ultimately to formulate and implement forward-looking strategies in order to gain advantage over competitors. This article concentrates on identifying such changes by extrapolating long-term trends and assessing their implications on the business environment.

Major Changes in the Business Environment

Until several centuries ago, more than 90 percent of humans were engaged in agriculture; today the agricultural labor force consists of less than 3 percent of the total work force in the United States and less than 1 percent of that in the United Kingdom. At present, 17 percent of the labor force works in manufacturing in the United States (versus 26 percent in 1950) and 23 percent in the United Kingdom (versus 50 percent in 1950). As the trend toward greater automation continues and industrial robots and unattended factories become common, manufacturing jobs will further diminish until around 2015, when full automation is reached and the same percentage of people as are employed today in agriculture will produce all goods demanded. Moreover, computers and expert systems, coupled with fiber optics and other advanced telecommunications, will improve office automation and the effectiveness and efficiency of providing services, further diminishing the number of workers in white-collar jobs.

By 2015, people will have the choice

of working less, will be able to buy all they want,

and still have money left.

The present subsistence-based era will end.

Before 1800, increases in standards of living were small and unevenly distributed. People used to live at a subsistence level, and they owned few material possessions. Later, buying power improved dramatically under the cumulative impact of the industrial revolution, which decreased real (excluding inflation) prices and increased real income. Today people spend a small part of their income on food (17 percent in 1993 versus 34 percent in 1950 and 70 percent in 1900), while their material possessions have increased markedly. Moreover, they work fewer hours per year (1,660 today versus 2,700 in 1900 and more than 3,500 in 1800) and live longer lives (75 years today versus 48 in 1900 and 36 in 1880) in more spacious and comfortable houses. By 2015, with advanced automation and computers with speeds approaching that of the human brain, people will have the choice of working even less, will be able to buy practically all the standardized goods and services they want, and will still have money left for luxuries. This is the time when the present transitional epoch of a subsistence-based society will end, and one of abundance will begin. Wrenching changes will create new chal-

lenges and will pose dangers for firms, while fostering new attitudes and preferences among consumers. For strategic purposes, executives will have to predict the path of greater automation and improved efficiency and effectiveness, and figure out its exact implications for their industry, firm, and customers.

Implications for Firms

On the one hand, people's income has increased considerably (today in the U.S. it is almost 20 times as high as in 1800), opening huge opportunities for firms that can satisfy the changing needs of more affluent consumers. On the other hand, the globalization of business is eliminating local market inefficiencies, while the efficient utilization of new technologies has forced firms to subcontract and outsource an increasingly greater part of their activities. Moreover, bureaucracy has turned the economies of scale and scope that once provided large companies with competitive advantages into diseconomies as the motivation of those working in such firms is smothered and overheads impose huge costs. In the present business environment, competition has become fierce, and firms that cannot recognize forthcoming changes and take concrete steps to adapt to them are not likely to survive. This requires proactive anticipation of forthcoming changes from firms like General Electric, Microsoft, Wal-Mart, Johnson and Johnson, and Asea Brown Boveri. Firms like General Motors, IBM, or Sears and Roebuck, which have not pared back their bureaucratic structures or taken bold actions to adapt to environmental changes, find themselves beleaguered by great problems and saddled with huge losses.

During the remainder of this century and the beginning of the next, the following changes must be considered in a firm's strategy and exploited for maintaining or gaining competitive advantages:

1. *Concentrating on core competences:* With increasing automation and powerful computers, few or no advantages can be gained from the performance of repetitive or routine tasks that can be subcontracted or assigned to super-specialized outside suppliers. As technology will be equally available and affordable to everyone, firms must concentrate on what they can do best, which means using the brainpower and creative talents of their people to the maximum.

2. *Globalizing reach:* Telecommunications and powerful computers will allow buying from and/or selling to any place in the world (this would include subcontracting and outsourcing) to minimize costs or maximize revenues.

3. *Customizing products/services:* Modern technology provides great flexibility and allows for customization of products and/or services to meet specific client needs any time of day or night. Moreover, products/services can be provided directly in any part of the world by using computers connected to telecommunication networks, avoiding middlemen, and allowing lower prices.

4. *Improving service, office, and white-collar productivity:* Computers and expert systems are playing the same role in increasing service, office, and white-collar productivity as machines and the production line in augmenting factory productivity. As the number of people employed in manufacturing decreases and absolute costs in this sector become smaller, considerable improvements in productivity are possible and will have to, and can, be made in the service, office, and white-collar jobs. These improvements can include *tele-work* (eliminating the huge costs of offices and the time wasted in commuting) tele-education, and almost all forms of tele-services, including tele-entertainment.

5. *Motivating employees:* In societies entering full abundance it will be difficult to motivate employees just by monetary rewards, in particular when their creative skills will be most needed for innovating or continuously improving existing procedures/processes and/or products/services. Ways will have to be found to link work with attaining personal satisfaction from working. This could entail employees owning part of the firm so that they will be highly committed and eager to work hard.

6. *Changing demographics:* As the average age of the population of advanced countries is increasing, its composition, needs, and preferences are changing. At the same time, growing demands for better value products and services which, because of competition, will become more plentiful, allow consumers greater choice. Firms, therefore, will have to be constantly on alert to figure out emerging needs and come up with new and successful products/services to satisfy these needs and to provide as high value as possible to more demanding consumers.

7. *Change, learning, and creative destruction:* In the fast-changing business environment of tomorrow learning how to learn is becoming of paramount importance for organizations. But learning requires changing old habits, which cannot often be achieved without destroying what already exists. This means that firms might want to institutionalize an internal process that encourages creative destruction within rather than waiting until outside competitors degrade a firm to a second rate position or even cause it to go bankrupt.

[See also Forecasting, Deterministic; Forecasting Methods; Forecasting, Mistakes In; Participative Management; Productivity; Scenarios.]

BIBLIOGRAPHY

Hamel, G., and Prahalad, C. K. *Competing for the Future: Breakthrough Strategies for Seizing Control of your Industry and Creating the Markets of Tomorrow.* Boston: Harvard Business School Press, 1994.

Makridakis, Spyros. *Forecasting, Planning, and Strategy for the Twenty-first Century.* New York: Free Press, 1990.

Makridakis, Spyros; Wheelwright, S.; and McGee, V. *Forecasting: Methods and Applications,* 2nd ed. New York: Wiley/Hamilton, 1983.

Mintzberg, Henry. *The Rise and Fall of Strategic Planning,* Prentice-Hall, 1994.

— SPYROS MAKRIDAKIS

SUPERCONDUCTORS

Superconductivity is a material state, reached as temperature is lowered, in which resistance to electrical current flow is zero. Electrical currents can then be transported in the material with no energy loss due to material heating. Although the development of superconductivity may or may not take the path described in the popular press, recent developments in high-temperature superconductors constitute a world-changing scientific breakthrough.

General Nature of Superconductivity

The four major physical characteristics of super-conductivity are:

- Electrical conductivity
- Diamagnetism
- Tunneling
- Thermal conductivity

Superconductors represent an extremely well-ordered state of material. Electrons flow unimpeded in superconductors with no loss due to interactions with the crystalline structure of the material.

Another important characteristic of superconductors, in addition to being perfect conductors, is that below their transition or critical temperature (Tc)—that is, the highest temperature at which superconductivity can be maintained—they are also perfect diamagnets. That is to say that superconductors completely exclude magnetic fields. In 1933, Meissner uncovered this property in which a diamagnet excludes a magnetic field.

The third very important physical property of superconductors is tunneling. Tunneling is a quantum mechanical phenomenon discovered by Josephson in 1962 and commonly referred to as the Josephson effect. Tunneling refers to the fact that it is possible for a charged particle, such as an electron or an electron-pair, to appear on the other side of an insulating barrier, even though there is not sufficient energy available to support that passage.

The last of the major properties of superconductors is the marked change in their thermal properties across the critical temperature. Below the critical temperature, superconductors have very low thermal conductivity and high heat capacity.

Classes of Superconducting Material

The age of superconductivity began with the detection of superconductivity by Kamerlingh Onnes in 1911. Shortly after liquefying helium, he found that mercury, when cooled to 4° K, lost its electrical resistance. The effect was not understood until 1956, when the Bardeen, Cooper, and Schrieffer (BCS) theory emerged. A major breakthrough in superconductivity technology was the discovery of high-temperature superconductivity (HTS) materials by K. Alex Mueller and J. Georg Bednorz in 1986.

Superconductivity, quite unexpectedly, is a very common phenomenon. There are thousands of materials that exhibit superconductivity at some temperature and pressure. These materials fall into five fundamentally different classes. The lowest known transition temperature is $0.015°$ K for the element tungsten. Until the recent development of high-temperature superconductivity, the highest known superconductivity transition temperature was $23°$ K for the alloy Nb_3Ge.

Forty-eight of the eighty-three naturally occurring

elements have been found to exhibit

superconductivity at some combination

of temperature and pressure.

The first class of superconducting materials encompasses the basic chemical elements. To date, forty-eight of the eighty-three naturally occurring elements have been found to exhibit superconductivity at some combination of temperature and pressure. Two of the eighteen artificial elements have also been shown to be superconductors.

The second class of superconducting materials includes the numerous alloys that have been shown to exhibit superconductivity. For years, the pursuit of different types of alloys provided the mechanism for improving the transition temperature.

The third class of superconductors consists of organic materials. In 1964, a theoretical suggestion was made by Little that long-chained organic molecules might offer the hope of high-temperature superconductivity. Since then, a few organic materials have been found that exhibit this characteristic. The first organic materials contained compounds of TMTSF (tetramethyl tetraselenefulvalene). The compound $(TMTSF)_2PF_6$ was shown to be a super-conductor at $1°$ K under 8.5 kilobars of pressure in 1980. Later, BEDT-TTF (bis [ethylenedithiolo] tetrathiafulvalene) was shown to be a superconductor at normal atmospheric pressure at $7°$ K. While no organic material has yet exhibited a high transition temperature, it is hoped that once the phenomenon has been understood, organic materials can be synthesized to have the desired superconducting properties.

Heavy fermion systems make up the fourth class of superconducting materials. Although these materials have electrons with very high effective masses, none has been found to exhibit a high transition temperature. In 1979, superconductivity was measured at $0.5°$ K for

$CeCu_2Si_2$. UBE_{13} has a transition temperature of $0.9°$ K.

The last class of superconducting materials involves various metallic oxides. Such oxides have allowed transition temperatures to be raised to unprecedented values. The first superconducting oxide was $SrTiO_3$ with transition temperatures reported between $0.3°$ K and $0.7°$ K.

Working alone and between other projects—and bucking conventional wisdom—Mueller (an expert in oxides) and Bednorz began their search in 1983 with oxides of nickel, the metal they thought most promising. They tried seventy different types of nickel oxides with no success. Later, they discovered the work of two French scientists, Claude Michel and Bernard Raveau, who had created a Cu, O, La, Ba (copper-oxygen-lanthanum-barium) compound in 1984 that seemed to have the desired properties. Mueller and Bednorz used these materials to produce a mixed-valence material that exhibited superconductivity at $30°$ K.

Later efforts to improve the transition temperature of the Mueller and Bednorz material were founded upon the realization that the spacing between the atomic layers was important. Chu showed that increasing hydrostatic pressure increased the transition temperature, and at 10,000 times atmosphere pressure, the transition temperature was increased to $70°$ K. Decreasing the space between the layers of atoms in the superconductor's crystal structure by "squeezing" them together caused an increase in transition temperature. This phenomenon led to the idea of inserting smaller atoms to decrease the spacing between the layers. Replacing barium with strontium, which has a smaller radius but similar chemical properties, increased the transition temperature from $30°$ K to $40°$ K. The insertion of calcium (which has an even smaller radius) further increased transition temperatures. Creating a new material with yttrium replacing lanthanum proved successful, as Chu was able to raise the transition temperature to $90°$ K. Other rare earths seem to work as well—samarium, europium, gadolinium, dysprosium, holmium, and ytterbium compounds all have transition temperatures near $90°$ K. Later research based on structural blocks, such as $(BiO)_2$, $(TlO)_2$, TlO, PbO, CuO chains, resulted in transition temperatures of up to $130°$ K. Most recently, mercury-based superconductors have been produced that have transition temperatures of up to $153°$ K. Since these transition temperatures are achieved under pressures of 150 kilobars, their use in practical applications is unlikely.

Importance of Processing Procedures

Future applications of high-temperature superconductors will be founded on both their scientific and engineering properties. The scientific properties include, in addition to the transition or critical temperature (the highest temperature at which a material begins to show significant superconducting properties), the critical magnetic field (the most powerful magnetic field in which a material can maintain superconducting properties), and the critical current density (the highest electric-current density that can flow through a superconductor with no resistance). Engineering properties include hardness, brittleness, maleability, density, porosity, and so on. Practical applications in the future will depend, in considerable measure, on the ability to produce superconducting material in a usable form—for example, wires, ribbons, and surface coatings.

In most cases, both scientific and engineering properties depend on the material form of the superconductor. This form, in turn, is largely dependent on the final chemical composition and processing history of the material. Even minor changes in the production processes—for example, selection of ingredients, grinding, mixing, additives, firing and cooling temperature profiles, and controlling oxygen atmosphere—can significantly change the nature of the final product.

Applications

As previously indicated, most superconductor applications will probably derive directly from the four characteristic properties discussed above—electrical conductivity, diamagnetism, tunneling, thermal conductivity, together with combination or hybrid effects. Chances are good, however, that other applications will be developed based on other properties not presently known or appreciated. Tables 1 through 4 list a number of current and potential applications for superconductors, together with estimates of the time that will be required for the commercialization of each.

Each application driver is characterized by a set of devices that take advantage of the unique capabilities offered by that superconductor property. The first entry in the table for each device indicates the use if the device is a stand-alone application. The other estimates are for the applications into which the device is incorporated.

For each application, the current stage of innovation for both low-temperature superconductivity (LTS) and HTS is presented. (The meaning of each stage of innovation is shown in Table 5.) In many applications, LTS will serve as a precursor to the use of HTS. Usually HTS development will lag behind LTS. However, HTS progress will probably develop faster than LTS did, and the pattern of application may be quite different for the two technologies. LTS first moved into applications where the cost of cooling was not as significant a factor to acceptance as improved performance, and where

cooling cost was a small fraction of the total cost. Therefore, the earliest applications of HTS may not be the ones that were first developed for LTS.

The major advantage of HTS materials over LTS materials is that the former can maintain their superconducting characteristics at temperatures appropriate for liquid nitrogen cooling (77° K), while liquid helium temperatures (4° K) are normally required for the latter. This difference in temperature not only materially simplifies coolant-handling difficulties, but also significantly decreases the cost of coolants. The major drawback of HTS materials is the difficulty of producing them in usable form.

Conclusions

Listed below are some conclusions about the significance of high-temperature superconductivity:

HTS development has reached the stage associated with laboratory development of specific products. Many potential applications are being suggested and tested for feasibility. Additional opportunities appear daily, and this trend will accelerate as research continues and knowledge expands.

Development of practical HTS applications will occur much faster than it has for similar innovations in the past. Many factors that traditionally expedite the development of radical, new technological innovations are evident for HTS. These factors include widespread public and professional interest, readily identified needs for technical advances, relatively open communications, and a strong infrastructure for commercial applications.

Initial applications of HTS will be in niche markets where its special characteristics will offset the difficulty and cost of manufacture, emplacement, and operation. The most significant early applications of HTS may well involve combinations of HTS with other emerging technologies—for example, holography, optical computers, advanced technology manufacturing, and biotechnology.

Although interest in HTS up to this point has centered on the superconducting phenomenon, other application drivers (diamagnetism, tunneling, heat-flow resistance, and hybrid effects) provide very promising business and operational opportunities.

The range of possible military uses for HTS is essentially unlimited, including submarine detection, electric guns, field power generators, undersea propulsion, and real-time battlefield simulations. The importance of small size and weight for space projects and low ambient temperatures in space make HTS applications in space almost certain.

At present, there is no generally accepted theory explaining why HTS materials achieve superconductivity

TABLE 1

APPLICATION DRIVER: ELECTRICAL CONDUCTIVITY

Device	Application	Area	Stage of Innovation		Time to Commercial Introduction—HTS (Years)
			LTS	HTS	
Magnet			7	4	0–3
	• Nuclear Magnetic Resonance	• R&D	7	2	3–8
	• Magnetic Resonance Imaging	• Medical	7	2	3–8
	• ESR	• R&D	7	2	3–8
	• Electron Microscope	• R&D	1	2	3–8
	• Particle Accelerator	• Superconducting Supercollider (SSC)	5	1	8–15
		• Linear Accelerator			
		• Medical Accelerator			
	• Fusion-Plasma Containment	• Energy	3	1	>15
	• Magnetohydrodynamics	• Energy	3	1	>15
	• Mass Drivers	• Launchers	3	1	8–15
		• Guns			
	• Propulsion	• Ships/Space/Submarines	4	1	8–15, >15
	• Magnetic Separation	• Industrial Processes	6	2	3–8
		• Ore Separation			
		• Coal Desulfication			
		• Sewage			
		• Pollution Countermeasures			
	• Energy Storage	• Power Load Balance	4	2	3–8
		• Fusion	2	1	>15
		• Free Electron Lasers*	1	1	8–15
		• Laser Power Supply*	1	1	8–15
		• Battery	1	1	8–15
		• Weapon System	2	1	8–15
		• Electromagnetic Launcher*	2	1	8–15
	• Persistent Current Cell	• Memory Device	1	2	3–8
	• Lab Instrumentation	• Research	6	2	3–8
	• High Field Magnets (Steerable)	• Medical	1	2	3–8
	• Levitation Coils—Train	• Transportation	5	1	>15
	• Gyrotron	• R&D	1	2	3–8
	• Beam Weapons*	• Military	1	1	>15
	• Mass Transit Coils	• Magnetic Material	1	1	>15
		• Transportation			
	• Permanent Magnet	• Magnetic Structures	—	1	>15
Motor/Generator			5	3	3–8
	• Electric Power Alternator	• Energy	5	3	3–8
	• Ship/Sub Propulsion Systems*	• Military	1	1	8–15
	• Small Motors	• General	1	3	3–8
	• Electric Car	• Transportation	1	1	>15
Transmission Lines			6	3	3–8
	• Superconducting Power Transmission Line	• Local Area	4	1	3–8
		• Long Distance	4	2	>15
	• Electronic Power	• System	4	4	3–8
		• Card			
		• Circuit (chip)			
		• Connectors			
	• Signal Transmission	• System	3	3	3–8
		• Card			
		• Circuit (chip)			
		• Delay Lines	6	2	3–8
Sensor			6	2	<3
	• Current Switch (Cryotron)	• Flux Pump	6	3	3–8
		• Switch			
	• Radiation Detector*	• Far Infrared Spectroscopy	6	6	<3
		• Microwave Spectroscopy			
		• Heat Detector			

(continued)

TABLE 1

APPLICATION DRIVER: ELECTRICAL CONDUCTIVITY *(CONTINUED)*

Device	Application	Area	Stage of Innovation		Time to Commercial Introduction—HTS (Years)
			LTS	HTS	
Microwave Resonant Cavities			3	1	8–15
	• Linear Accelerator	• R&D	3	1	8–15
	• Electron Microscope	• R&D			
	• Traveling Wave Tube	• Military			
	• Wave Guides	• Communications			
Antenna Arrays					
	• Radio Astronomy	• R&D	1	1	8–15
	• Radar*	• Military			

* Reason to believe classified research is being done. An application may be at a higher stage than indicated.
† R&D = research and development.
Source: Technology Futures, Inc.

TABLE 2

APPLICATION DRIVER: DIAMAGNETISM

Device	Application	Area	Stage of Innovation		Time to Commercial Introduction—HTS (Years)
			LTS	HTS	
Levitation			4	6	<3
	• Vehicles	• Transportation	1	1	>15
	• Train				
	• Car				
	• Materials Handling	• Manufacturing	1	1	>15
	• Moving Sidewalk	• Transportation	1	1	>15
	• Bearings		4	1	<3
	• Gyroscope*	• Military	4	1	<3
	• Big Industrial Stirrers	• Manufacturing Process	1	1	8–15
	• Large Compressors	• Energy	1	1	8–15
	• Generators	• Energy	1	2	8–15
	• Laser Scanners	• Electronic Systems	1	2	8–15
	• Machining Systems	• Manufacturing	1	1	8–15
	• Turbines	• Energy/Transportation	1	1	8–15
	• Energy Storage Wheels	• Transportation	1	1	8–15
	• Motor (Different Principle)	• Electrical	3	3	3–8
	• Skis/Skates	• Entertainment	—	1	>15
	• Ballroom	• Entertainment	—	1	>15
	• Toys	• Entertainment	—	1	<3
	• Education				
	• Kits/Training Aids	• Education/Entertainment	—	6	<3
Magnetic Shielding			—	1	<3
	• Electronic Equipment Protection*	• Electronic System	—	3	<3
	• Countermeasures*	• Military	—	2	>15

* Reason to believe classified research is being done. An application may be at a higher stage than indicated.
Source: Technology Futures, Inc.

TABLE 3

APPLICATION DRIVER: TUNNELING

Device	Application	Area	Stage of Innovation		Time to Commercial Introduction—HTS (Years)
			LTS	HTS	
Quasi-Particle (Giaever)			6	1	<3
	• Bolometer	• R&D	6	1	<3
	• SIS*/SIN† Devices	• Radio Astronomy	6	1	<3
		• Radar	6	1	<3
		• Analog Areas	6	1	<3
	• Mixers	• Microwave Devices	6	3	<3
	• Amplifiers				
	• Receivers				
	• Filters[???]	• Military	6	3	<3
Pair (Josephson)			7	6	<3
	• Radiation Detector[???]	• Military/R&D	4	4	<3
	• Magnetometer[???]	• Military/R&D/Medical	4	6	NA
	• SLUG**	• R&D	4	1	8–15
	• Switch	• Computer	4	3	3–8
	• SQUID††				
	• Research	• R&D	7	4	In use
	• Neuromagnetic Devices	• Medical	6	4	<3
	• Biomagnetism Corrosion	• Construction	3	1	3–8
	Detection in Metals		3	1	3–8
	• Subdetection‡	• Military	5	1	3–8
	• Earth's Magnetic Field	• R&D	4	6	In use
	Measurement	• Geophysics/Energy			
		• Geothermal Energy			
	• Quiet Amplifier	• R&D	4	1	8–15
	(Nuclear Spin Noise)				
	• Gravitational Radiation	• R&D	5	1	3–8
	• Voltage Standard	• R&D	7	3	<3
	• Real-Time Analyzer	• Electronic	6	3	<3
	• Oscilloscope	• Electronic	6	3	<3
	• Digital Filters	• Electronic	6	3	<3
	• A/D Converter	• Electronic	6	3	<3
	• High-Speed Samplers	• Electronic	6	3	<3

* Superconductor-Insulator-Superconductor.

† Superconductor-Insulator-Normal Metal.

‡ Reason to believe classified research is being done; an application may be at a higher stage than indicated.

** Superconducting Low-Inductance Galvanometer.

†† Superconducting Quantum Interference Device.

Source: Technology Futures, Inc.

TABLE 4

APPLICATION DRIVER: HYBRID*

Device	Application	Area	Stage of Innovation		Time to Commercial Introduction—HTS (Years)
			LTS	HTS	
Superconducting FET	• Electronic System	R&D†	3	1	*
Low-Voltage Hot Electron Transistors	• Electronic System	R&D	2	1	*
Non-Equilibrium Superconductor	• Electronic system	R&D	2	1	*
Semi-/Superhybrids	• Electronic System	R&D	3	1	*
MOS Superconductor (Optical Switch)	• Electronic System	R&D	4	1	*
Novel Light Modulators	• Electronic System	R&D	3	1	*
Superconducting/Semiconducting Mirrors	• Electronic System	R&D	1	1	*
Displays	• Electronic System	R&D	1	1	*
Photovoltaic Devices	• Electronic System	R&D	1	1	

* Not sufficient information to estimate time to commercialization at this time.

† R&D = research and development.

Source: Technology Futures, Inc.

TABLE 5

THE STAGES OF THE INNOVATION PROCESS

Stage 1	Scientific Suggestion, Discovery, Recognition of Need
Stage 2	Theory or Design Concept
Stage 3	Laboratory Verification of Design Concept
Stage 4	Laboratory Demonstration
Stage 5	Full-Scale or Field Trial
Stage 6	Commercial Introduction or First Operational Use
Stage 7	Widespread Adoption

Source: Technology Futures, Inc.

at such high temperatures. A valid explanation of the phenomenon may quickly result in developments that dramatically change operating temperatures, engineering parameters, cost, availability, etc.

In the longer term, success or failure in HTS commercialization will depend on the ability to manufacture standard, reliable, high-performance HTS in quantity and at low cost. Although preparation of basic HTS materials has proved remarkably simple, mass production will probably present difficulties similar to those associated with semiconductor production.

Competition for dominance in the HTS field is already strong among, as well as within, nations. The strong position of Japan in ceramics and Josephson device development may give that nation a strong position in HTS development. Also, 95 percent of rare earth deposits are located in China.

Advances in HTS will result in parallel advances in low-temperature superconductivity and conventional conducting systems. Historic precedents suggest that new competition often stirs up a burst of innovation in older technologies.

Policy changes involving patent protection, antitrust exemptions, joint-government corporations, and so on, intended to support HTS development may spill over into other technological areas.

Although present HTS technology shows great promise, basic research in superconductivity continues, and this research will undoubtedly continue to drive new and more advanced applications. The emergence of a satisfactory theory of HTS may unlock dramatic new capabilities. For example, the development of superconducting polymers would greatly simplify many application problems. Achievement of room-temperature superconductivity or even superconductivity at mechanical refrigeration temperatures ($-50°$ C) would open up significant new applications.

[See also Chemicals, Fine; Chemistry; Computers; Computers: Software; Scientific Breakthroughs; Semiconductors.]

BIBLIOGRAPHY

Hazen, Robert M. *The Breakthrough: The Race for the Superconductor.* New York: Ballantine, 1989.

Lampton, Christopher F. *Superconductors.* Hillside, NJ: Enslow Publications, 1989.

Miller, Richard K. *Superconductors: Electronics and Computer Applications.* Lilburn, GA: Fairmont Press, 1989.

Simon, Randy, and Smith, Andrew. *Superconductors: Conquering Technology's New Frontier.* New York: Plenium Press, 1988.

— JOHN H. VANSTON
LAWRENCE K. VANSTON

SURPRISES

Surprises are unexpected events—but not all surprises are alike. Sometimes the unexpected is (1) *an unanticipated random happening.* If the dinosaurs became extinct 60 million years ago as a result of a large meteorite colliding with Earth (or if in the future another such collision should occur), both that collision and the resulting extinctions would be random happenings, very bad luck, accidents catastrophically affecting humans but beyond human control.

Space scientists in the future may be able to track a potential collision for months or years before it happens. This was done in 1994, when the planet Jupiter collided with a comet. Although scientists could see at least the possibility of that collision coming, in the larger scheme of things it was not expected—and thus was a surprise.

There are other surprises that are (2) *predicted but nonetheless amaze us when they do occur.* Earthquakes have this characteristic. Geologists measure tensions along so-called faults where vast tectonic plates press against one another and, from time to time move. Scientists know that the Earth's crust will move periodically to relieve those pressures but are unable to predict exactly when.

There are also surprises with major effects upon the future that are unleashed in the wake of (3) *discoveries or inventions.* Alexander Graham Bell's telephone and Thomas A. Edison's electric light bulb and phonograph were surprises to many of their contemporaries. Similarly, many present-day innovations surprise almost everyone.

One common characteristic of such innovations is that, in retrospect, we can see that they were "waiting to happen." In *Connections* (1978), James Burke traces how innovation spreads, often with nearly simultaneous discoveries in different and distant locales. When the time is "ripe" for an innovation or insight, the conditions and connections are in place, and someone needs only to imagine what new event or invention could be next. And even after all their hard work, disciplined effort, imagination, and ingenuity, the discoverers (and we) are still surprised by what happens.

Truly great surprises come rarely, usually when there is a (4) *massive explosion of insight* that transforms or reorganizes our lives and minds and how we see our world. Such events are variously labeled revolutions or revelations.

The central figures in such changes typically are either quite young or have devoted decades of work and thought to some concept or project that first came to them when they were young. Usually they have dedicated their lives to their alternative vision and what they perceive as their calling or lifetime work. Gradually they share their vision with others, and identify and relate to colleagues or counterparts of like interest who become collaborators. Whether in science, politics, or religion, together they form a community of endeavor that is often simultaneously moral, political, intellectual, and scientific. But until the object of their concern quite suddenly happens, it is viewed by all involved (including the central figures) to be most unlikely.

Thomas S. Kuhn, in *The Structure of Scientific Revolutions* (1962), surveys a number of scientific revolutions in mindset—including those introduced by Newton, Copernicus, Darwin, and Einstein. Each of these great scientists transformed the ways in which other scientists, and later ordinary people, see the world.

Similar revolutions take place in the political realm. In recent years we recount the calamitous political shifts when with Gorbachev the Berlin Wall came down, or when with Mandela and De Klerk apartheid was ended in South Africa. As in the scientific revolutions, there is a sudden shift in how things are seen. Eventually those institutions that tend to perpetuate the past give legitimation to new ideas and individuals.

Similar massive changes involving shifts in thinking and social arrangements marked the sixteenth-century Protestant Reformation, the seventeenth-century Puritan Revolution, the eighteenth-century American Revolution, the nineteenth-century abolition of slavery, the sexual revolution of the 1960s, and the ongoing struggles of the civil rights and women's rights movements.

Protestant theologian H. Richard Niebuhr, in *The Meaning of Revelation* (1940), writes about explosive flashes of transforming change and insight. The most important characteristic in such transformations is how those in the core group see these totally surprising and wrenching shifts, which afterward affect the mindsets of many, many others in a conversionlike experience. Following major breakthroughs, Kuhn points out that a string of new discoveries often follows soon thereafter. A succession of changes occurs because we are now seeing our world very differently, and we are noticing what before we did not recognize or were not looking for.

Then there is the mysterious surprise of sudden (5) *widespread changes of popular consciousness*. For example, from the seventh to the tenth century, much of the Middle East and North Africa converted to Islam. What similar surprises lie ahead? We do not understand the role that the mass media play today, nor do we understand how new phenomena, such as feminism or the civil rights movement, catch fire from mere sparks.

Surprises provide the utterly dark

—or sometimes the genuinely shining—

moments in our future.

Given the immense number of individuals born into this world and the remarkable capacity of individuals to act as catalysts for change, many new surprises are also in store. Being in the right place at the right time has a great deal to do with unleashing surprise. Ghandi, Martin Luther King, Jr., and Betty Friedan come to mind within recent memory. There will be more like them, and they too will usher in new surprises.

Finally, there are the surprises that are (6) *delayed or displaced effects from actions occurring elsewhere*. In complex biological and social systems, many things are interconnected. Single events send out many ripples of consequences. Some events are found later on to be especially damaging to sensitive life functions of individual species or to the biosphere itself.

When populations of American bald eagles, Pacific pelicans, and peregrine falcons in different locales suddenly declined almost to extinction, scientists discovered that DDT was the culprit. A pesticide first introduced during World War II, DDT was being biologically concentrated in the food chain and collecting in the fatty tissue of these birds' livers, where it was interfering, in females, with the liver's capacity to make the enzyme which determines how thin the shell of their eggs will be. In this way DDT was causing reproductive failure and the near-extinction of certain species.

The emergence of a so-called Ozone Hole in the upper atmosphere as a result of atmospheric gasses—mainly chlorofluorocarbons (CFCs) used in spray cans, refrigerants, and industrial processes—is another example of a major effect from a seemingly remote cause. In like manner, diethylstilbestrol (DES) may cause cancer a generation later in the reproductive organs of a very small percentage of the daughters of the many millions of mothers for whom it was prescribed by their doctors during their pregnancies.

Such delayed and displaced effects are often characterized as secondary effects or "side effects." Showing up later or elsewhere does not make them less important. They simply may be regarded as "surprises" that were not anticipated and were unintended.

These kinds of surprises may occur again in the future. We will be amazed each time as they provide the utterly dark—or sometimes the genuinely shining—moments in our future. These are the moments when our future's newness is perceived by us as most overwhelmingly bad or most wonderfully transforming.

[See also Change; Change, Pace of; Disasters, Planning for; Scientific Breakthroughs; Wildcards.]

BIBLIOGRAPHY

Burke, James. *Connections.* Boston: Little, Brown, 1978.
Kuhn, Thomas S. *The Structure of Scientific Revolutions.* Chicago: University of Chicago Press, 1962.
Niebuhr, H. Richard. *The Meaning of Revelation.* New York: Harper & Row, 1940.

— DAVID DODSON GRAY

SURVEYS

Prominent among methods to forecast developments are surveys assessing social conditions and polls measuring public opinion. Both involve the systematic collection of information based on interviews with a sample of the general public or a particular group.

While this information covers only one point in time, social surveys and opinion polls undergird and help to corroborate many approaches to futures research. Uses range from assessing the impact of events and evaluating the success of policies to extrapolating trends from the past into the future and building statistical models of complex social systems.

Among the different kinds of surveys and public opinion polls, the following are those most relevant to social forecasting:

- Quality-of-life polls monitor changing public evaluations of domains of life. Findings may have implications for the allocation of public and private resources.

- Issue polls that repeat questions from earlier surveys can pick up shifts in public opinion on both domestic and foreign issues, and often anticipate changes in government policy.

- Polls on perceived trends probe the hopes and fears respondents have for themselves, their families, and the nation. These polls can be sensitive gauges of public optimism, pessimism, frustration, and consumer confidence. They can signal changes in political and economic cycles.

- Agenda-setting polls acquaint political leaders with the shifting priorities that the public attaches to problems.

- Job-rating polls measure the public's assessment of the performance of political leaders and institutions. Whether conducted at one time or periodically, they are one more way to hold politicians accountable to the people.

- Polls on values examine belief systems that undergird public opinion on issues. Moreover, by assessing changes in social norms, these polls often

provide a reality check on the assumptions built into systems models or on which extrapolations of trends are based.

- Surveys for governmental agencies are the foundation of important statistics on matters such as employment, housing, and criminal victimization.

- Pre-election polls can quite accurately anticipate outcomes if they are conducted close enough to the election, and if they include good measures of the respondent's intention to vote and of the strength of support for the candidates.

- Delphi polls attempt to measure the opinions of experts on particular issues.

If social surveys or public opinion polls are to provide a sound basis for forecasting, they must yield reliable data and the inferences drawn also must be valid.

Reliability

The reliability of a survey or poll refers to the consistency with which concurrent applications of the same measure would lead to the same results. It depends on an adequate sample and on questions whose meaning is clear to respondents. The reliability of a survey or poll may be compromised if the sample is too small or poorly designed. Its reliability could also be affected if respondents holding similar views on an issue give different answers because poll questions are ambiguous or unclear.

Validity

Since surveys and polls rely on respondents' answers to questions, what is counted depends on what is asked. Before conclusions can be drawn from a survey or poll, the researcher should have established that the questions asked validly measure the matter under study. For respondent reports of social conditions or behavior, this usually is accomplished by corroborating survey findings with independent sources. For measures of public opinion, validity is most effectively determined by checking the consistency of responses to different questions that seek to measure a common dimension of that opinion.

Forecasting based on surveys or polls is dependent on two additional measurement issues: the use of sequential measures and the selection of variables.

SEQUENTIAL MEASURES. Whether projecting trends or assessing the impact of an event or policy, measures at different points in time are needed. This challenges researchers to formulate questions that will hold up well over time as valid measures. Given the costs of collecting original data, forecasters sometimes rely on available data (often collected for some other purpose). This imposes a need to ensure that measures of the same variables which have been taken independently are, in fact, comparable.

In a related approach to sequential measures, panel studies involve reinterviewing persons contacted in an earlier survey. This approach sometimes gauges change better than unrelated surveys do because any shifts reported have occurred within a common sample. But panel survey reliability may be affected by the difficulty of recontacting the same people or the bias sometimes introduced if respondents know they will be interviewed again at a later date.

The prognostic utility of a public opinion poll

rests on its ability to predict actual behavior

from expressions of opinion.

SELECTION OF VARIABLES. Reliance on a single survey or poll for forecasting purposes can be risky unless enough measures are used in the same study to move beyond mere description of a set of conditions or opinions to some explanation of those conditions or opinions and when or why they might change.

It is in the domain of variable selection that the frontier of survey-based futures research is to be found. The utility of a social survey in forecasting will only be as good as its anticipation of the need to measure new variables, its ability to account for events and cycles (seasonal, economic, and/or political), and its assessment of changing standards of public judgment. Selection of variables is made more problematic by the absence of widely accepted conceptions of social change, and the tendency of professional disciplines to view the world in their own terms of reference.

Conclusions

The prognostic utility of a public opinion poll rests on its ability to predict actual behavior from expressions of opinion. Thus, to make sense out of the complexity and inconsistencies inherent in public opinion, a poll must do more than describe the direction of an opinion (that is, what people favor or oppose). The poll needs to attempt to explain the public's view by measuring such things as the intensity with which views are held; the knowledge and experience people bring to an issue; the belief systems or values that may tie opinions on discrete issues into an overall framework; the awareness of individuals of the implications of their opinions; and the confidence people have in public figures and institutions to deal with the issue that has been posed.

Most problematic are polls that expect one question to capture all of the nuances of the public's thinking on a complex issue. Such a referendum conception of poll-

ing misconstrues the purposes of public opinion research by alleging that a single poll percentage expresses definitively the public's view on that issue.

Critics of polls traditionally have argued that the public does not follow current events closely enough to be able to make well-informed and nuanced judgments on most public policy matters. While it is true that the public often does not know important facts, empirical studies have shown that about three-fourths of the American public pays close enough attention to size up many emerging issues with considerable discrimination. Most people also hold opinions on important matters with a reasonable degree of stability.

Surveys and polls can strengthen the democratic process by portraying the distribution of circumstances individuals in society face and their opinions about those circumstances. By giving equal voice to all respondents, surveys and polls ensure that both the majority and the minority can be heard. Surveys and polls can ensure that information about all the people is integral to the competition among political interests.

[See also Behavior: Social Constraints; Change, Optimistic and Pessimistic Perspectives; Continuity and Discontinuity; Public Opinion Polls; Public Policy Change; Scanning; Scenarios; Trend Indicators; Voting; Wildcards.]

BIBLIOGRAPHY

Bradburn, Norman M., and Sudman, Seymour. *Polls and Surveys: Understanding What They Can Tell Us.* San Francisco: Jossey-Bass, 1988.

Cantril, Albert H., and Cantril, Susan Davis. *The Opinion Connection: Polling, Politics, and the Press.* Washington, DC: Congressional Quarterly Press, 1991.

Cantril, Hadley. *Gauging Public Opinion.* Princton, NJ: Princeton University Press, 1944.

Duncan, Otis Dudley. "Social Forecasting—The State of the Art." *Public Interest* 17 (1969): 88–118.

Neuman, W. Russell. *The Paradox of Mass Politics: Knowledge and Opinion in the American Electorate.* Cambridge, MA: Harvard University Press, 1986.

Reiss, Albert J., Jr. "Measuring Social Change." In Neil J. Smelser and Dean R. Gerstein, eds. *Behavioral and Social Science: Fifty Years of Discovery.* Washington, DC: National Academy Press, 1986.

— ALBERT H. CANTRIL

SUSTAINABILITY

Sustainability has become an international jargon word, with about as many meanings as there are people who use it. In general, to sustain something means to keep it alive or going. So sustainability has to do with long-term viability—doing things in such a way that we can keep on doing them that way. The fact that the word *sustainability* has arisen in international debate implies that many people have a sense of unsustainability—that we are doing things, especially in the realms of consuming resources and polluting the environment, in a way that cannot be sustained. Eroding soils, clearing forests faster than they can grow back, poisoning waters—these are unsustainable activities. If we do not stop them, they will stop us.

Some people who have talked about sustainability for a long time no longer try to give it a precise definition. Notwithstanding, there is a perfectly good official definition that comes from the 1987 report of the International Commission on Environment and Development called *Our Common Future:*

> Humankind has the ability to achieve sustainable development—to meet the needs of the present without compromising the ability of future generations to meet their own needs.

This definition has two parts: (1) meeting needs and (2) doing so in a way that preserves the natural, human, and societal resources from which needs are met. It is important to remember both parts, because the public discussion often splits between those who want to meet needs and those who want to protect resources, as if doing one were incompatible with doing the other. The difference between traditional environmentalists and "sustainability folks" is the ability to keep the welfare of both humans and the environment in focus at the same time, and to insist on both.

The official definition of *sustainability* is often supplemented with Herman Daly's clear and undeniable explication of what sustainability must mean in physical terms:

1. Renewable resources are not used faster than they can regenerate.
2. Pollution and wastes are not put into the environment faster than the environment can recycle them or render them harmless.
3. Nonrenewable resources are not used faster than renewable substitutes (used sustainably) can be developed.

By those conditions there is not a nation, a company, a city, a farm, or a household on Earth that is sustainable. Virtually every major fishery violates condition number one. The world economy as a whole is violating condition number two by putting out carbon dioxide 60 to 80 percent faster than the atmosphere can recycle it. Oil resources and fossil groundwaters are being drawn down without thought of what happens when they are gone, in violation of condition number three.

To make things worse, or maybe clearer, there are two more sustainability conditions that can be derived with just a little thought from those first three:

4. The human population and the physical capital plant cannot grow forever. They have to be kept at levels low enough to allow the first three conditions to be met.

Physical capital plant needs some explanation here, because we use the word *capital* to mean two different things. First, it means money that is invested in building some productive enterprise, as in "I can't build that factory until I raise some capital." The other meaning is not the money that pays for building but the factory itself. To keep these two meanings straight, we should call the first *money capital* and the second *physical capital.*

Physical capital consists of all human-made productive facilities—electric generating plants, oil refineries, car assembly plants, textile factories, computer factories, tractors, irrigation systems, as well as hospital buildings, school buildings, restaurants, houses, and cars. Physical capital (not money capital) takes up space and consumes fuel and raw materials, and turns out garbage and pollution. Therefore physical capital has to be limited on a finite planet. Money capital does not, except insofar as it is linked in value to physical capital. In fact, money is fictitious; it is only an invention of our minds, our symbol for physical capital and physical goods and services. Without physical capital, goods, and services then, money, stock markets, "returns on investment" would have no meaning.

The word sustainability *stands for a vision of a world very different from and much more satisfying than the world we live in now.*

The human population and its physical capital plant both have to be limited in a sustainable world, because both require flows of real physical resources to function, and both emit pollutants that have to be processed, purified, or recycled.

5. The previous four conditions have to be met through processes that are democratic and equitable enough that people will stand for them.

Otherwise, though a system may be technically or physically sustainable (meeting conditions one through four), it still will not last, because people will undermine it or revolt against it.

If you start thinking about what it would mean to meet these five conditions, you begin to see that enormous changes are necessary, but that these changes need not be sacrifices; they could be intensely, humanly satisfying. Those who have been thinking about and working toward sustainability for a long time see in that word not only physical and technical challenges, but components of spirituality, of community, of decentralization, of a complete rethinking of the ways we use our time, define our jobs, and bestow power upon governments and corporations. *Sustainability* is a very inadequate word to summarize all that.

Any word of six syllables is too long to organize a popular movement around and at the same time too short to communicate a complete vision. At any rate, the word *sustainability* does stand for a vision of a world very different from and much more satisfying than the world we live in now. It should not be heard as implying "sustaining" current conditions. What it actually implies is a thoroughgoing revolution.

[See also Environment; Environmental Behavior; Environmental Ethics; Natural Resources, Use of; Resources.]

BIBLIOGRAPHY

Aplet, Gregory H., ed. *Defining Sustainable Forestry.* Washington, DC: Island Press, 1993.

Callenbach, Ernest; Capra, Fritjof; Goldman, Lenore; Lutz, Rudiger; and Marburg, Sandra. *EcoManagement: The Elmwood Guide to Ecological Auditing and Sustainable Business.* San Francisco, CA: Berrett-Koehler, 1993.

Daly, Herman E., and Cobb, John B. *For the Common Good: Redirecting the Economy Toward Community, the Environment, and a Sustainable Future.* Boston, MA: Beacon Press, 1994.

Flavin, Christopher, and Lenssen, Nicholas. *Powering the Future: Blueprint for a Sustainable Electricity Industry.* Washington, DC: Worldwatch Institute, 1994.

Girardet, Herbert. *The Gaia Atlas of Cities: New Directions for Sustainable Urban Living.* New York: Anchor Books/Doubleday, 1993.

Hawken, Paul. *The Ecology of Commerce: A Declaration of Sustainability.* New York: Harper Business, 1993.

Kinlaw, Dennis C. *Competitive and Green: Sustainable Performance in the Environmental Age.* San Diego, CA: Pfeiffer & Company, 1993.

— DONELLA MEADOWS

TAXES

Taxation is an explicit price citizens pay for government. Having established through political processes the levels of spending and taxation, the fundamental questions of tax policy are whether the tax system is consistent with maximizing long-term economic growth, whether the distribution of the tax burden is consistent with society's sense of fairness, and whether the method of tax collection is efficient. The current federal tax system scores poorly in each category and is in line for a fundamental restructuring.

The major elements of the federal tax system—the income tax, the payroll tax, sales taxes, and user fees—each evolved more or less independently over decades of legislative and regulatory action. Consequently, taken as a whole, the federal tax system reflects a multitude of tax policy choices, some made long ago, which manifest no policy at all other than raising revenue to finance federal spending. Tax fairness, meaning the distribution of the tax burden among individuals, is a highly malleable concept, depending on the times and the dispositions of the electorate. Tax fairness has traditionally meant that the average tax rate should increase as the taxpayer's income rises. The concept becomes more difficult, however, when applied to specific taxes versus tax systems, and becomes imprecise when certain taxes, such as any tax on business, must be levied on specific groups of individuals deemed ultimately to bear the tax burden.

The collection of federal taxes could hardly be less efficient. Tax Foundation estimates of the costs of administering, collecting, and complying with the corporate and personal income taxes reach $200 billion annually. In addition, the federal government imposes other taxes, such as the payroll tax and sales taxes, which impose their own sets of compliance costs. When combined with the similar costs imposed by state and local tax systems, the total national collection costs could easily exceed $500 billion each year, or roughly $2,000 per person in America.

The collection costs of the tax system are due in large part to the extraordinary complexity of the income tax. This complexity, and Congress's frequent tinkering with the tax, lead to tremendous uncertainty among taxpayers regarding the tax system and the tax consequences of particular transactions or economic activities. Tax-based uncertainty imposes yet another cost on the economy.

The federal government's system for exacting resources from the economy is increasingly discordant with the demands of a modern economy and with those of our major trading partners. Consequently, market and political forces are building to compel corrective change. In particular, the punitive treatment of saving and investment places the United States at a competitive disadvantage and has needlessly limited economic growth.

Replacing the federal income tax

with any of a variety of consumption taxes

could increase economic opportunities

in the United States by about $1 trillion.

A study by Dr. Dale Jorgenson of Harvard University indicates that replacing the federal income tax with any of a variety of consumption taxes would increase economic opportunities in the United States by about $1 trillion. Another study by Dr. Laurence Kotlikoff of Boston University, using an entirely different sort of economic model, indicates that such a tax reform would, by itself, raise real incomes in America by 8 percent. It would be reasonable to project that the benefits from replacing all federal taxes with a consumption-type tax could double these gains.

Saving, Investment, and the Future

Saving and investment are the engines of prosperity. When a nation has adequate savings available and when those savings are directed by the marketplace to their most productive uses, that nation will be prosperous and its businesses will be competitive on the world markets. The centrality of saving and investment motivated Adam Smith to call his famous seventeenth-century work on the operation of market forces *The Wealth of Nations*. In contrast, Karl Marx's failure to recognize the importance of private saving and investment incentives doomed his economic system and those who followed it.

The federal tax system imposes a particularly heavy burden on saving and investment. When a dollar of labor income is earned, both payroll and income taxes are imposed. If the remainder is saved and invested, the earnings are subject to at least one additional layer of taxation. If the earnings are reinvested again, then they will be subjected to additional layers of tax. If the earnings are invested in corporate equity, then an additional layer of tax is imposed in the form of the corporate income tax. The taxpayer must also contend with the tax on capital gains and, at the end of his or her life, half the taxpayer's estate may be confiscated through the estate tax.

The Future of Federal Taxation

The federal income tax was state-of-the-art at the turn of the century. In the intervening years, the income tax has gone through a steady evolution. At the same time, most of the rest of the world has moved away from the taxation of net income toward the taxation of consumption, thereby avoiding the disincentives to saving and investing suffered in the United States. These countries are now taxing what individuals take out of the economy, rather than what they put in.

With each passing year, the U.S. economy integrates further into the world economy. Thus U.S. companies face ever-stiffer competition from foreign companies at home and abroad, and U.S. workers face stiffer competition from their foreign counterparts. Such increasing competition means government policies, including tax policies, that reduce U.S. competitiveness carry an ever-increasing price tag. Eventually, the price gets too high to bear, whatever the former rationale for the offending policy, and the policy is changed.

The integration of the world economy has made the U.S. economy increasingly intolerant as to the level of taxation, the collection costs and uncertainty of the tax system, and to the intrusions of the system into economic decision-making.

The evolution of the U.S. tax system is clearly in the direction of a consumption tax. All major tax reform proposals under consideration are consumption taxes and virtually all economic analysis is directed toward understanding the operation of consumption taxes. There are many possible alternatives, however, including a national retail sales tax, an European-style credit-invoice Value Added Tax (VAT), a cash-flow tax, a "flat tax", and a consumed-income tax. Each of these alternatives can be implemented in lieu of the current U.S. income tax system and each can, in theory, correct the problems of the current system.

The Alternatives

The main alternative to the current income tax is the "flat tax" originally designed by Professors Hall and Ra-

bushka of the Hoover Institution. At the individual level, the flat tax imposes a tax on all labor income and excludes all returns to capital such as interest, dividends, and capital gains. The flat tax also allows for a specific amount of personal exemptions and dependent exemptions and imposes a single tax rate on the remaining amounts. At the business level, the flat tax imposes a tax on the net of business receipts less all labor costs and all amounts paid to other businesses.

The flat tax is generally popular among taxpayers because it appeals to an intuitive sense of fairness and because it appears to be vastly simpler than current law. The flat tax is popular among economists and tax policy theoreticians because it dramatically reduces or eliminates the tax bias against saving and investment.

Other alternatives, such as the USA Tax System proposed by Senators Sam Nunn (D-Ga.) and Peter Domenici (R-N.M.), and the retail sales tax differ primarily in their embodied political choices or in their collection mechanics rather than in their economic fundamentals. Each promises to reduce collection costs and to improve economic performance by eliminating tax distortions in the economy.

Tax reform has traditionally focused solely on the personal and corporate income tax. If a new and clearly superior tax system can be devised, then the ensuing debate will include whether the new system should replace the many other taxes, such as the payroll and sales taxes which are presumably inferior and certainly impose additional costs on the economy.

A New Doctrine of Tax Fairness

Progressivity has for decades dominated thinking about tax fairness. And, indeed, however measured, the federal tax system is progressive, with upper-income taxpayers paying a very high share of the total tax burden. Among the many ideas under the microscope, tax progressivity is being questioned as the proper guide to the distribution of the tax burden.

Few question that an individual's tax burden should increase with his or her income. But the doctrine that the burden a taxpayer bears in support of government should rise more than proportionately with the increase in his or her income is increasingly being challenged as being not only economically inappropriate, but unfair as well. This development is tremendously important as it implies that the tax system, and possibly government in general, may be returning to the principle that government should ensure, insofar as possible, that each individual has all the opportunities to succeed that his or her talents and energies make possible, rather than enforce an equalization of consequences irrespective of effort.

[See also Capital Formation; Entitlement Programs; Estate and Financial Planning; Financial Institutions; Insurance.]

BIBLIOGRAPHY

Ando, Albert, et al. *The Structure and Reform of the US Tax System.* Cambridge, MA: MIT Press, 1985.

Bradford, David, ed. *Tax Policy and the Economy.* Cambridge, MA: MIT Press, 1991.

Scully, Gerald W. *How State and Local Taxes Affect Policy Growth.* Dallas: National Center for Policy Analysis, 1991.

— J. D. FOSTER

TECHNOLOGICAL CHANGE

A critical factor in viewing the future, whether in industrialized countries or in developing countries, is the effect of technological change. Technology is important because it often enables people to do things heretofore impossible or difficult in a cheaper, faster, or easier way. In the 1960s, John McHale suggested that the average American home had the work equivalency of eighty Roman slaves in appliances, technology, and entertainment. Today, the ratio is even higher. Technological change has become an important element in measuring productivity and improved lifestyle. No longer are land, capital, and human labor the only major elements in GNP.

Technological change is sometimes "pulled"

by human need and sometimes "pushed"

by its own dynamics.

Technological changes are responsible for improved living, as well as new hope and optimism. At the same time, technology can be a source of fear and pessimism, as in fear of nuclear destruction, invasion of privacy, or joblessness. Technological change is sometimes "pulled" by human need and sometimes "pushed" by its own dynamics.

Technological change does not always advance human potential, but its inventiveness and design help increase the apparent superiority of humans over all other earthly creatures. Many may look back with nostalgia at the "good old days," but, for better or worse, we cannot return. Despite recent technological tragedies like Bhopal, Chernobyl, and Three Mile Island, if given the choice, most people would choose to live in this era.

Technological change can be defined as any alteration in a system of skills, arts, crafts, fabrications, and their organization for the attainment of specific goals. The word *technology* comes from the Greek *techne,* meaning "art, skill, fabrication." A technology involves a system, with interrelated elements such as organizational structure, skills, labor, environment, knowledge base, and machinery. For instance, the computer is changing work skills, the meaning of education, definitions of knowledge, time required for labor, and availability of information. Computer technology may help curb pollution by reducing the need for commuting, make us more aware of options, and advance the speed with which we communicate. Yet, depending on its availability, computer technology may also serve to widen economic inequities; make society more vulnerable to terrorism or natural disaster; and encourage unwarranted faith in the results that can be obtained using computers as intelligent tools for problem solving. It is hard to separate the "goods" from the "bads" because of the inextricable interrelatedness between technology and other contextual factors. Both social improvement *and* upheaval occur simultaneously with the advent of technological change. As a system, it not only acts upon but is also acted upon by other systems such as nature, society, economics, and politics.

Technology as a Change Driver

CONTEXTUAL FACTORS. Technology is one of five major change drivers (a key element influencing futures options and trends) in any social organization. The acronym STEEP stands for the Social, Technological, Economic, Environmental, and Political influences that are the major drivers of any organizational structure. As a change driver, technology is both an initiator and a responder to change. Technology, itself a change driver, is also influenced by other contextual factors (coefficients) that make up the "culture" and environment of technology and technological change. Technological change not only "pushes" social change but also is "pulled" into new areas by the surrounding contexts. Laser technology, for example, pushed its way into eye surgery but was also pulled into more accurate bombing techniques by the military. The invention made the situation, and the situation made other inventions.

EXTRAPOLATION OF TECHNOLOGICAL CHANGE. A danger inherent in technological change is the assumption that it will continue to move in the same direction. Blind faith in the ability of technology to solve or alleviate such problems as fuel depletion, pollution, overpopulation, and ozone depletion may be inadvisable; the complexity and magnitude of such problems, together with the high level of research and development needed, may pose insurmountable barriers.

Extrapolation of technological advance assumes that we will manage to muddle through almost any barrier to human progress. Extrapolationists believe that all that is needed is the will, the finances, and the technological breakthroughs. As tempting and positive as that may seem, other futurists warn that technological advance is by no means an inevitable panacea. There are some neo-Luddites who see technological advance as an inherent threat to humanity, but most futurists proclaim technology and its evolution as a predominantly positive force.

Technological advances must be weighed

and balanced by their possible impacts.

Technological "fixes" must be carefully appraised

by careful analysis of the pros and cons.

TECHNOLOGICAL "FIXES." In technologically sophisticated societies, there is a tendency toward over-reliance on technological "fixes" to problems. Such overoptimism often leads to makeshift solutions. In the instance of the Exxon Valdez disaster, the solution was to have more cleanup crews, more oil-eating bacteria, more containment booms, and more detergent rather than to focus on preventative measures. In other words, more technology was the offered solution for human error and lack of foresight. Futurists like Peter Drucker and Robert Theobald contend that technology *created* the problem in the first place: unmanageably oversized tankers, spurred by excessive demands for fossil fuels, oil extraction from hostile environments, and blind faith in radar and navigation systems presaged the disaster.

In the future, technological advances must be weighed and balanced by their possible impacts. Technological "fixes" in the future must be carefully appraised by careful analysis of the pros and cons. Foresight and planning must be given priority.

Appropriate Use of Changing Technologies

APPROPRIATE TECHNOLOGY. In the postindustrial or information society, flexibility in thinking is essential. It is true that advances in robotics, bioengineering, fuzzy systems theory, nanotechnology, and virtual reality promise many new options. New skill in determining their appropriateness is needed, however, to prevent unplanned and possibly harmful results. Many developing countries, for instance, would not necessarily be served well with an incursion of sophisticated technologies. Their social organizations, values system, and economic infrastructure might even be worsened thereby. As was learned in Thailand, using tractors rather than water buffalo to cultivate rice paddies re-

quired high levels of economic investment and yielded negligible improvement. However, using television to help inform and educate farmers in that same area proved useful. Appropriateness of technology in terms of its impact becomes an important consideration in most planning.

Appropriate technology is also important in highly advanced societies. "Smart" machines, for example, changed manufacturing processes, organization of labor, and skill levels required by workers. The U.S. Department of Labor predicts that by the year 2000, services, transportation, and health care will be growth fields, while repetitive manual labor will decline. The main types of jobs in the future may be divided into two classes: entry-level, low-skilled work and highly skilled, highly paid jobs. This division occurs when manual labor is displaced by smart machines that require highly skilled people to program, fix, manage, and use them.

New Trends in Technological Change: A Forty-Year Focus

NEW WINDOWS OF OPPORTUNITY. No one should discount the importance of technological change. New breakthroughs in miniaturization (nanotechnology), fiber optics, mass transportation, synthetics, genetic engineering, disease control, sex selection, in vitro fertilization, body regeneration, and recycling of waste will afford many new options. Just because things are technically possible, however, does not mean that they should be done. Optimally, technological breakthroughs should advance the human condition. Knowledge of ethics, philosophy, history, politics, economics, organization, and psychology must also be brought to bear on decisions about the use of technology. Changes in technology must not be left to chance. Instead, there ought to be a conscious choice toward desired goals.

"Technological man" was once described by Victor Ferkiss as one who must possess a new understanding about nature's limits, be able to design mind-body-nature-machine-society systems that are mutually supportive, and ensure that people are the primary beneficiaries of technological growth (see Ferkiss, 1969, p. x). These understandings ought to be the foundation for further technological development.

GLOBAL FLOW OF TECHNOLOGIES. One of the biggest impacts of new technologies will be on the global community. Speed of communications, access to information, networking, and data volume are being significantly increased. Technological advances have created a global marketplace that promotes cross-cultural understanding and a sense of global citizenship.

INFORMATION SUPERHIGHWAY AND TECHNOLOGICAL CHANGE. Thanks to fiber optics, miniaturization of computer chips, and communication network improvements, the Information Superhighway is already a reality. Increased information access and availability of services serve to enhance political democracy while at the same time posing a threat of an electronic elitism (if technology were to be available only to the rich). These changes may make life easier, but they may also deprive individuals of their privacy. This new "highway" also will create networks of networks arranged in multiple layers; once ensconced these networks may make it harder to change opinions or policies, or to change structures for dealing with new ideas and assumptions.

TECHNOLOGICAL CHANGE AND EDUCATION. With new technologies comes a new definition of education. Learning will be age-free, location-free, and time-free. The credentializing role of schools (degrees, certifications, licenses) will become less important because of the need for lifelong learning. Collective learning, transcultural analysis, and global awareness will become educational mainstays. Tolerance, interdependence, mutual respect, and ethical dialogue will be enhanced by technological networks in the schools.

Schools will continue to exist because of the need for communal dialogue, nurturing, person-to-person contact, and mutual support networks. Technologies will also improve learning, and "intelligent" systems will meet individual student needs and otherwise help them adapt to new situations.

ENVIRONMENTAL TECHNOLOGIES. New technologies in weather detection and weather control will allow people to anticipate and change conditions. Development of new materials will allow people to live in heretofore hostile environments. Pollution control, recycling, fresh-water conservation, soil and resource preservation will be seen as an integrative project to be monitored and controlled in part by new technologies.

MEDICINE. Technology will increasingly challenge the definition of "humanness" over the next forty years. Genetic engineering, cloning, and development of synthetic blood, appendages, and organs are only a few technological advances that must be evaluated. When or where does a human end and technology begin? Such a question will require new, perhaps ever-changing answers. Medical practice will concentrate as much on

Desalination of seawater is one technological solution to the world's water needs. However, it is much more expensive than any other method of obtaining usable water. (Jack Fields/Corbis)

disease prevention, holistic health, and customized medicines as it will on curative practices.

Conclusion

The scope and sweep of technologies covered here does not provide an all-inclusive answer to the question of how technological change will alter our ways. One key point to remember is that technology should be our servant, not our master. Future prospects for humanity will be improved if we make intelligent choices rather than merely let things happen as they may.

[See also Agents of Change; Appropriate Technology; Change; Change, Scientific and Technological; Communications: Technology; Information Technology; Science Issues; Scientific Breakthroughs; Surprises; Technological Determinism; Technological Innovation; Technology Diffusion; Technology Forecasting and Assessment; Technology and Science; Wildcards.]

BIBLIOGRAPHY

Barbour, I. G. *Technology, Environment and Human Values.* New York: Praeger, 1980.

Bernard, H. R., and Pelto, Petri, eds. *Technology and Social Change.* Prospect Heights, IL: Waveland Press, 1987.

Corn, J. J., ed. *Imagining Tomorrow: History, Technology and the American Future.* Cambridge, MA: MIT Press, 1986.

Ferkiss, Victor. *The Future of Technological Civilization.* New York: George Braziller, 1974.

———. *Technological Man.* New York: George Braziller, 1969.

Hirschhorn, L. *Beyond Mechanization: Work and Technology in a Post-Industrial Age.* Cambridge, MA: MIT Press, 1984.

Mumford, Lewis. *Technics and Civilization.* New York: Harcourt, Brace, 1934.

Porter, Alan L., et al. *Forecasting and Management of Technology.* New York: John Wiley, 1991.

Teich, A. H. *Technology and the Future.* New York: St. Martin's Press, 1993.

Theobald, Robert. *Turning the Century.* Indianapolis, IN: Knowledge Systems, Inc., 1992.

Willoughby, Kelvin W. *Technology Choice: A Critique of the Appropriate Technology Movement.* Boulder, CO: Westview, 1990.

— FRED D. KIERSTEAD

TECHNOLOGICAL DETERMINISM

Human beings are cultural animals. From their first appearance on Earth, they have used technologies—i.e., techniques to change their natural environment. Tools such as spears and baskets are technologies, but so is fire. All human technologies are conditioned by and, in turn, strongly affect the social structure and values of the society in which they appear.

Following a primitive era of hunting and gathering, agriculture was probably developed by women about 20,000 years ago, a major development in human history. Agricultural surpluses created the base from which early civilizations arose. The human population increased greatly and reached levels that remained stable until the Industrial Revolution. The early development of farming was accompanied by a major increase in mining. Soon thereafter, agricultural and extractive societies spread over most of the planet.

The next major step in technology came with the Industrial Revolution, which began in Britain in the eighteenth century. Industry soon became dominant across Western Europe and North America. Based on new sources of power—fossil fuels, above all—and standardized mass production through the use of machinery, the new advances led to a major rise in population, explosive urbanization, and the conquest by the industrial nations of the nonindustrialized world. Over time, industrial society, based on the production of physical goods, evolved into a service-oriented society. In service-based economies, the distribution of goods and the provision of services such as health, education, and government employed the majority of workers and generated the bulk of economic activity. Eventually this emphasis became so pronounced that some have come to speak of a new form of society—a "postindustrial" one in which knowledge and information are more important than either agriculture, manufacturing goods, or services.

To what extent does technology determine the values and social structure of a society? Is it an independent variable, which as it induces change forces other things to change, as technological determinists contend? Or can human societies resist technological change and its effects if they choose? The historical record can be read in several ways. Throughout human history, and throughout the world today, human beings have been eager to embrace new technologies that appear to offer more abundance, comfort, and security. Progress through technological change and consequent economic growth is the major modern creed all over the world, spreading along with the Industrial Revolution and its aftermath. It is also evident that certain technologies have social and cultural consequences. The invention of the forceps in the sixteenth century made males dominant in the process of childbirth, relegating the midwife to insignificance. Modern means of transportation and communication, along with the factory system, have done much to destroy the traditional family and community. The industrial city—created by centralized production and the railroad—has been undermined wherever the automobile has become the major means of transportation. Above all, it is assumed that the rational and scientific mindset which underlies modern technology is destined to put an end to traditional ethnic and religious loyalties and belief systems. Based on such facts and assumptions, the case for technological determinism seems so strong as to be beyond dispute.

But not all would agree. The historical record is replete with examples of human societies that have chosen to resist rather than adopt new technologies and attitudes toward life, and this is further reflected in contemporary clashes of cultures. More to the point, there are examples of the failure to adopt new technologies because the ruling group in a society saw no need for them. Since the ancient Western world was based on slave labor, it was not interested in labor-saving machinery. The steam engine was known in Hellenic times, but did not become a major social force until it was reinvented during the industrial era by James Watt. China was long ahead of Europe in science and technology, but allowed itself to stagnate in the early modern period because it believed its social system near perfect. Islam, once also ahead of Europe technologically, was slow to adopt modern weaponry and long abjured modern printing. Japan gave up the gun as well as regular contact with the outside world for several centuries. Economic and social factors deny a great deal of the latest medical technology to the poor in contemporary America.

Science and technology can act as a force for good or evil. They need not be a force for destruction and can be directed toward higher levels of human well-being.

In addition to occasionally rejecting new technology, usually out of fear of its effects on existing social structures, societies can accept it and choose to renounce the values it allegedly implies. Traditional Christian churches still flourish. Islam is resurgent. Everywhere in the world ethnic conflict belies those who have long predicted the demise of such loyalties. Ironically, many groups which reject the values of modern technological civilization, both in the Western and in the Eastern world, are quite happy to use its most advanced tools of communication to spread their message. Human societies are obviously free to reject technologies or alter their effects in a number of ways.

However, high-tech postindustrial society involving the primacy of theoretical knowledge, specialization, new sources of energy, and the computer is certainly becoming dominant throughout the globe. Whether these technologies impose such a strain on the natural environment that it is rendered unsustainable in the long run is an increasingly debated question. Antitechnology and back-to-nature advocates have one mindset. They hold that contemporary postindustrial society cannot go on forever because of its overuse of resources and creation of pollution, and because it endangers basic human values, above all freedom. Proponents of current technologies, institutions, and trends claim humanity has no choice, given increasing population and unmet material needs. In effect, the former deny technological determinism while the latter embrace it.

Unmistakably the last century entailed technological exploitation and natural resource destruction on a massive scale. We cannot escape from this environmental predicament unless we address the ideas that created or fostered it. Fatalistic viewpoints ignore the potential of human willpower. Technological impacts can be directed. It is up to leaders and informed citizens to integrate vital perspectives on science and ethics, philosophy and politics, economics and ecology, in managing contemporary affairs. Science and technology can act as a force for good or evil. They need not be a force for the destruction of humanity and can be directed toward higher levels of human well-being. The choice is ours, although the particulars of that choice are by no means a simple, settled matter.

[See also Change; Change, Scientific and Technological; High Technology; Information Society; Technological Change; Technological Innovation; Technology Diffusion; Technology and Science.]

BIBLIOGRAPHY

Ferkiss, Victor. *Nature, Technology, and Society: Cultural Roots of the Current Environmental Crisis.* New York: New York University Press, 1993.

———. *The Future of Technological Civilization.* New York: George Braziller, 1974.

———. *Technological Man: The Myth and the Reality.* New York: New American Library, 1969.

Winner, Langdon. *The Whale and the Reactor: A Search for Limits in an Age of High Technology.* Chicago: University of Chicago Press, 1986.

– VICTOR C. FERKISS

TECHNOLOGICAL INNOVATION

Innovation is the process whereby a new product or service makes the transition from concept to prototype to commercial success, or at least widespread use. Innovation is often confused with invention, but the classic pattern begins with a discovery or an invention, followed by a more or less extended period of engineering, development and market testing, market introduction, feedback from customers, further modification of the design, standardization of the design, and development of specialized manufacturing processes.

The technology "life cycle" outlined very briefly above has several other important features. One is a tendency for competition in the marketplace to be based initially on product performance (in some sense) and to shift, over time, toward price. This occurs as the product (or service) becomes more standardized, and production technology becomes more and more capital-intensive.

The time from first conception to successful commercial introduction can take as much as a century (or more) or as little as a year or two, depending on circumstances. The digital mechanical calculator was conceived by Blaise Pascal in the mid-seventeenth century. It was further developed by Charles Babbage in the early nineteenth century, but did not achieve commercial success until the end of the nineteenth century. True computers only reached the market in the 1950s. On the other hand, the telephone evolved from patentable prototype to initial service in less than two years. So did Thomas Edison's "Jumbo" generator and his carbon-filament incandescent lamp. However, although quantitative measurement in this field is extremely difficult, these examples are probably atypical. There is some evidence that the innovation process itself is currently accelerating. If so, this can probably be attributed to increasingly global competition and information technology.

The innovation process itself is also changing qualitatively. In the eighteenth and nineteenth centuries, the individual inventor was the major actor in the process, although commercial success was rare and sporadic. As firms grew larger and organizations evolved in the later nineteenth and early twentieth centuries, formal research and development in industrial laboratories began to take the place of the individual inventor. The engineering development investment needed for the ammonia synthesis process, the spark-ignition (Otto cycle) and pressure ignition (Diesel) engines, the automobile and the fixed-wing aircraft, and the steam turbogenerator, were far beyond the resources of any individual. Nuclear weapons, nuclear power, spacecraft, and other developments in modern times, have involved a large part of the scientific and technical resources of a major nation.

"Creative Destruction" and Economic Growth

The vulnerability of mature industries (and products) to technological obsolescence has been demonstrated repeatedly in recent decades. Products, as well as manufacturing processes, can be rendered obsolete in short order. The flip side of innovation is obsolescence. Innovation is something like a poker game. The winners rake in the pot; the losers drop out and disappear from the contest. It was the Austrian economist Joseph Schumpeter who first fully recognized the importance of innovation as the engine of economic growth. Schumpeter also coined the famous phrase "creative destruction." He meant to emphasize the fact that, in the economy as in the biological world, death is an inevitable companion of life.

The time from first conception to successful commercial introduction can take as much as a century or as little as a year or two.

Examples of rapid change and obsolescence can be found in virtually every field. RCA was once the biggest name in radio and later in television. The company gave up its technological and manufacturing leadership two decades ago after the failure of its videodisk. Now its famous research laboratory belongs to the Stanford Research Institute and the company itself has been absorbed by General Electric. Perhaps the most spectacular example of how industry leadership changes with technology is the semiconductor industry. In every generation of dynamic random-access memory (DRAM) chips the industry leadership has changed. Although the memory chip was an American invention, its original developer (Intel) dropped out of the business within a decade. In fact, only one U.S.-based firm, Texas Instruments, now remains among the top ten worldwide merchant producers. (IBM produces DRAMs only for its own consumption.)

Since 1980 the entire computer industry itself has changed even more dramatically. In 1980 it was still a classic oligopoly dominated by a single firm, IBM. In a mere decade a "new" computer industry, based on personal computers and workstations linked in local area networks (LAN's), emerged. New firms have carved out huge chunks of the PC and workstation market. A firm founded in the 1960s, Intel, now dominates the microprocessor field, with Motorola a distant second. A firm created in the late 1970s, Microsoft has an equally dominant position in PC operating systems software. The applications programs market is dominated by equally young firms. IBM, on the other hand, dominates no segment of the "new" computer industry (nor do the once-feared Japanese).

Determinants of Adoption and Diffusion

There are two basic mechanisms for the adoption of a new product or service in the market. They can be characterized roughly as (1) "technology push" and (2) "market pull." Technology push involves a radical new idea—often based on a scientific discovery—that takes everyone by surprise and literally creates its own demand. It has no direct competition when it first appears. Market pull, however, is much more common. It involves the introduction of a new product or product improvement "made to order" to satisfy a demand that is already articulated.

Penicillin was an example of the first kind; streptomycin and the other antibiotics exemplify the second. The first commercial photographs (Daguerrotypes) would be another example of technology push. The roll film and portable camera invented by George Eastman were called forth by the growing market. The first aircraft and rockets were clearly created by technological enthusiasts. More recent improvements are responses to economic or national security demand. The laser is another example of technology push. Genetic engineering is perhaps the most recent example of this kind. The techniques of manipulating genetic materials by adding and subtracting bits of DNA with known characteristics was the first impetus. The implications for pharmaceuticals, chemicals, and agriculture were so obvious that a whole category of new research-based firms was created during the decade of the 1980s to exploit these possibilities.

In modern times the distinction is becoming blurred, inasmuch as R&D may be directed at a certain problem by a far-sighted manager who perceives a future need and deploys resources to satisfy it. The first transistor was a deliberate development, driven by the need to find simpler, smaller, and more-reliable devices for telephone switching circuitry. Yet it was also an outgrowth of radical new technology. It was a substitute for the vacuum tube, but it also made possible completely new products.

The relative importance of "push" and "pull" have been the subject of much debate. Social critics often assert that "push" is dominant, resulting in too many of the wrong technologies being adopted. Historiographic studies (e.g., of the correlation between patents and industry profitability) tend to suggest the opposite, that periods of prosperity precede periods of accelerated invention (as measured by patents). The implication is that firms spend more on R&D when they are prosperous than when they are not. The "push" hypothesis would imply the contrary, namely that invention precedes prosperity.

Clearly societal need does exert a kind of "pull," and there is no doubt at all that inventors feel it. The surprising number of documented simultaneous inventions, where individuals, knowing little or nothing of each others' work but driven by a common impulse, arrive at the same result at almost the same time supports this "pull" effect. Examples of simultaneous or near simultaneous invention include the high-pressure

steam engine, the telegraph, the telephone, the incandescent light, aniline dyes, the aluminum reduction process, and the turbojet engine. The list of such coincidences is lengthy.

Without doubt military needs have been a major driver of technological innovation throughout history. Military organizations, however, are not the only beneficiaries. For example, canning to preserve food was invented by the French during Napoleon's wars and developed further to feed the Union army in the U.S. Civil War. It is clear that military uses were important for the early commercial development of aircraft, jet propulsion, radar, computers (in the 1950s and '60s), sonar, nuclear reactors, rockets, and missiles.

Barriers and Breakthroughs

In many cases it is difficult to identify the driving force behind an innovation as either a market pull or a technology push. In fact, the two normally interact. As a technology progresses in terms of improved performance, demand for the service provided is likely to increase. Increased demand for the service in turn generates a demand for still better performance to satisfy that demand. There is a kind of "virtuous circle": technological performance → market demand → technological performance. Thus technology push eventually tends to create market pull and vice versa.

To mention one specific example, building telegraph lines (generally along railway lines) led to a tremendous demand for sending messages. This demand rapidly overwhelmed the capacity of the lines and encouraged inventors to find ways of "compressing" or "multiplexing" the messages so that a single-wire line could carry more messages. The telephone invention was a direct outgrowth of this inventive activity. In its turn the telephone, too, generated new demand that rapidly exceeded the capacity of the lines and encouraged inventors to find ways of increasing the number of messages a line can carry.

Efforts to improve the existing technology eventually run into limits or barriers of a fundamental sort. When such a limit is approached the cost of R&D per unit of additional improvement begins to rise rapidly, while the actual rate of improvement begins to slow down. When we speak of a technological "breakthrough" it usually means that there was a barrier of some sort that impeded progress. A breakthrough almost always requires a major new idea or discovery, leading to a new approach. Very often, the new idea that permitted the breakthrough also opens up a whole new field of collateral possibilities that nobody could have imagined.

For example, in the late 1950s computers were approaching size and performance limits, due to the problems of assembling enormous numbers of individual transistors into their very complex circuits. The integrated circuit, invented simultaneously by Texas Instruments and Fairchild in 1959, overcame these limits.

The vast majority of innovations

are "incremental" in nature. Yet their cumulative

weight in the sum of all contributions

is probably greater by far than radical innovations.

The telephone, the transistor, the IC (and others mentioned above) are examples of what Schumpeter calls "radical innovation." These are the dramatic, world-changing innovations that create individual fame and (sometimes) fortune. Many of these innovations resulted in the creation of new firms, and some of those firms are now household names. Still, it would be misleading to assume that most innovations are "radical," in the sense of creating major new products or industries. In fact, to the contrary, the vast majority of innovations are "incremental" in nature. Yet their cumulative weight in the sum of all contributions is probably greater by far than the radical innovations.

[See also Change, Scientific and Technological; High Technology; Information Technology; Schumpeter, Joseph A.; Science Issues; Scientific Breakthroughs; Technological Change; Technology Diffusion; Technology and Science.]

BIBLIOGRAPHY

Ayres, Robert U. *Technological Forecasting & Long-Range Planning.* New York: McGraw-Hill, 1969.

Freeman, Christopher. *The Economics of Industrial Innovation,* 2nd ed. Cambridge, MA: MIT Press, 1982.

Mahajan, Vijay, and Wind, Yoram. *Innovation Diffusion Models of New Product Acceptance.* Cambridge, MA: Ballinger, 1986.

Mansfield, Edwin. *Industrial Research and Technological Innovation.* New York: W. W. Norton, 1968.

Rosenberg, Nathan. *Perspectives in Technology.* New York: Cambridge University Press, 1976.

Rosegger, Gerhardt. *The Economics of Production and Innovation.* New York: Pergamon Press, 1986.

Stoneman, Paul. *The Economic Analysis of Technological Change.* London: Oxford University Press, 1983.

— ROBERT U. AYRES
PHILIPPE PICHAT

TECHNOLOGY DIFFUSION

Technology diffusion is the process by which technology moves from those who develop or control it to those who employ it. The diffusion process can take many forms. For governments it is getting technology out of government labs and into the commercial sector. For the military it is the spread of militarily sensitive technology into their own hands or the hands of the enemy. For Third World countries it is the transfer of technology from rich countries to poor ones. When companies talk about it, they focus on two things: getting technology out of the labs and into the marketplace and transferring technology to and from other companies through licensing.

Technology diffusion has taken on great importance in recent times. Its critical role in society was demonstrated in 1957 when Nobel Prize-winning economist Robert Solow established that most of the growth of the American economy could be attributed to technology, broadly defined.

Companies need technology to develop new products (product innovation), to improve the processes they employ to carry out their business (process innovation), and to give them a competitive edge in the marketplace. Consequently, they are willing to dedicate enormous resources to acquiring it. They may do this through their own development efforts (research and development) or by acquiring it from outside the organization (technology diffusion).

Governments also see technology to be important in the effective functioning of society. Technology can contribute to the well-being of citizens in their daily lives. When embodied in weapons systems, it contributes to national security. When employed effectively by national companies, it makes them competitive in a competitive global market. In many countries technology is viewed to be so important that its acquisition is given the highest national priority. In China, for example, Zhou Enlai declared the acquisition of scientific and technological capabilities to be one of China's "Four Modernizations." As with companies, the acquisition of technology can occur either by internal or external means.

There are a number of common elements associated with technology diffusion, regardless of its specific form. In all cases, technology diffusion entails the migration of the technology from those who possess it (technology donor) to those who desire to acquire it (technology recipient). The mechanisms for implementing technology diffusion are manifold. For example, the rights to use the technology can be acquired through a contract (called technology licensing); or the technology can be diffused through published literature that describes how the technology functions; or it can be purchased embodied in a product; or it can be acquired through training (e.g., on-the-job training). Technology diffusion may even occur through theft!

It is not enough for technology to be physically transported from donor to recipient. For useful technology diffusion to occur, the recipient must possess an adequate absorptive capacity to employ the technology meaningfully. This means that the recipient must be adequately educated to deal with the technology and must possess financial and material resources to enable the technology to be adopted effectively.

The speed with which technology is diffused from those who develop it to those who employ it has accelerated in recent years. Traditionally, a good rule of thumb was that it would take thirty to fifty years from the time a discovery was made in the laboratory until the time it became commercially viable in the marketplace. This lag is seen in the case of genetic engineering: Crick and Watson's groundbreaking discovery that DNA is structured as a double-helix was made in the early 1950s; however, the first commercial application of this discovery occurred in the early 1980s, a gap of thirty years.

Today, the lag between discovery in the lab and introduction into the marketplace is shortening. One approach is to make sure that research carried out in the laboratory is commercially appealing. Increasingly the marketing departments of companies are playing a pivotal role in selecting which technology projects will be supported.

Technology diffusion contributes to the rapid turnover of technology in the market and shortened product life cycles. For example, if a company needs to access a technology to flesh out a product line, it is not always necessary for them to develop it through expensive, time-consuming internal research-and-development efforts. They can acquire it readily by following these steps. They can attempt to identify who possesses the desired technology by conducting a worldwide search (technology brokers now exist who can expedite this search). Once they identify the technology owners, they contact them to negotiate some mechanism by which they can access the technology. Common mechanisms include direct purchases of patents, technology licensing, joint ventures, and coproduction agreements.

With increased access to technology, more technology-based products are being brought to market faster. Many of these products entail incremental innovations, where new products are basically better-functioning substitutes for older products. A well-known example is found in the area of personal computers. The original IBM PC (first marketed in 1981) was driven by an Intel 8088 chip. This was soon upgraded to an 8086 chip. After a couple of years, Intel introduced the more advanced 80286 chip, which was incorporated into the IBM AT computer. The 80286 chip was replaced with various versions of the 80386 chip, and soon these were replaced by different versions of the 80486 chip. In 1993 these, in turn, were replaced with the first version of the more advanced Pentium chip. A similar pattern

was exhibited by the recently terminated Motorola series of chips, from the 68000 through the 68060 of 1995. Each change of chip resulted in the migration of the new technology to ever more advanced products rushed to market by computer manufacturers. New-generation computers were replacing old-generation computers in cycles of about eighteen months.

The rapid change made possible by the acceleration of technology diffusion has clearly had healthy effects: More people are getting better access to more technology at cheaper prices than ever before. The rapid change also has led to economic disruption, however. Large corporations like IBM, Matsushita, and Olivetti are having difficulty competing in the new fast-paced environment and some, like Commodore, have fallen by the wayside. Previously, their large size was an advantage, enabling them to develop and control technologies that smaller companies could not afford. With increased access to technology through technology diffusion, smaller companies today can obtain whatever technology they need by collaborating with other companies or by licensing in technology. Furthermore, because of their small size, they can move more quickly than the traditional high-tech behemoths.

With universal access to technology through technology diffusion, smaller companies and poorer countries throughout the world can hope to become major technology players. They can take a cue from the way the Sony Corporation developed its strength. In the early 1950s, Sony Corporation acquired the rights to AT&T's transistor technology through licensing agreements. Given these rights, it began producing transistors and employing them cleverly in ever-smaller consumer electronic products, such as transistor radios and ultimately tape recorders, camcorders, and televisions. The Sony experience was common among Japanese companies. The spectacular growth of the Japanese companies between 1950 and 1980 was fed by the acquisition of technology from abroad. Even today, Japanese companies depend heavily upon the use of imported technology.

[See also Appropriate Technology; Change, Pace of; Change, Scientific and Technological; High Technology; Information Technology; Record Setting; Science Issues; Scientific Breakthroughs; Technological Change; Technological Determinism; Technological Forecasting and Assessment; Technological Innovation; Technology and Science; Wildcards.]

BIBLIOGRAPHY

Buatsi, Sosthenes. *Technology Transfer: Nine Case Studies*. London: Intermediate Technology Publications, 1988.

Charafas, Dimitrios N., and Binder, Eva Maria. *Technoculture and Change: Strategic Solutions for Tomorrow's Society*. London: Adamantine Press, 1992.

Ellul, Jacques. *The Technological Bluff.* Grand Rapids, MI: Eerdmans, 1990.

Goulet, Denis. *The Uncertain Promise: Values Conflict in Technology Transfer.* New York: Apex Press, 1989.

Hall, Peter, and Preston, Paschal. *The Carrier Wave: Information Technology and the Geography of Innovation, 1846–2003.* Boston: Unwin Hyman, 1988.

Malecki, Edward J. *Technology and Economic Development: The Dynamics of Local, Regional and National Change.* New York: John Wiley, 1991.

Mody, Ashoka. *Staying in the Loop: International Alliances for Sharing Technology.* Washington, DC: World Bank, 1989.

Ray, G. F. *The Diffusion of Mature Technologies.* New York: Cambridge University Press, 1984.

— J. DAVIDSON FRAME

TECHNOLOGY FORECASTING AND ASSESSMENT

Technological forecasting and technology assessment are related but distinct activities. The former is mainly concerned with anticipating outcomes and the timing of impending technologies; the latter focuses more on prospective ascertainment of direct and indirect events and effects of the application of particular technologies. Both originated in government but are now used widely throughout society—though this is not always apparent when scanning the published literature.

Technological Forecasting

Technological forecasting seeks to anticipate the future nature and characteristics of useful machines and techniques. Technological forecasts describe characteristics only. They do not invent the means by which the characteristics will be achieved.

Forecasters generally use a few basic methods: extrapolation, leading indicators, causal models, and stochastic methods. These methods must be tailored to the circumstances of the specific subject. For instance, economic data are collected at frequent, regular intervals. Economic forecasters can use mathematical tools to further exploit this regularity or constancy. Technological data occur only irregularly. Technological forecasters are restricted to tools that accept unequally spaced data. Basically, this is a difference in detail, not in method.

Extrapolative methods discern and extract a pattern from past or time series data sets and extend that pattern into the future. The most common patterns of technological change are growth curves and exponential trends. A forecast is prepared by fitting the appropriate curve to past data, then extrapolating that curve into the future. A typical growth curve, fitted to historical data covering aircraft speed records from 1913 to 1939 (depicted by squares), the extrapolation of that trend, and the actual data for the "forecast" method of 1945–

1970 (depicted by diamonds) is represented in Figure 1. A growth curve showing the replacement of wooden vessels by metal in the U.S. Merchant Marine is portrayed in Figure 2. Note the disruptions caused by the Great Depression and World War II.

Leading indicators use events in one time series to forecast events in another related time series. A common use of technological forecasting is to project basic research results forward to the commercialization of that particular technology. The appearance of some technology in a performance-oriented application (e.g., military or space) is also used to forecast the subsequent mass-market appearance of the technology. Success of this method depends upon knowing the leading indicator and the event to be forecast.

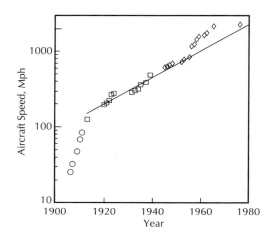

Figure 1. *Exponential trend of aircraft speed records. (Note that as of February 1995, no aircraft has surpassed the speed record set in 1976.)*

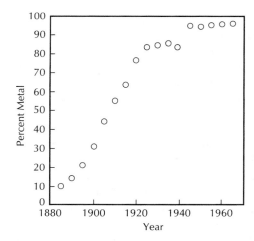

Figure 2. *Conversion of U.S. Merchant Marine ships from wood to metal.*

Causal models are used to forecast simulations in which there are multiple variables whose likely interactions are known. In most cases, the models are solved and developed using computer simulations. This is how meteorologists forecast the weather, using computers and measurements from weather stations worldwide. Causal models in technological forecasting have been most successful in forecasting the replacement of one technology by another. The models simulate the behavior of people who try the new technology, accept or reject it, and perhaps reconsider their decision later. The models can be more precisely confirmed and calibrated using market surveys or test markets.

These three methods all produce "single-point" forecasts—that is, forecasts which contain a single, discrete number for the future value. Unfortunately, the real world cannot always be reduced to rigid one-to-one relationships between past and future. This is where stochastic methods come into play. The word *stochastic* comes from the Greek *stochastikos*, "skillful in aiming," which in turn is derived from a similar word meaning "to guess." It is intended to convey the idea of randomness. Stochastic forecasts recognize that in addition to the factors influencing the future, which can be dealt with as the three previous methods do, there may be random or unknown factors acting which can cause deviations from the expected outcomes. A stochastic forecast thus presents not a single estimate for a future value, but a range of possible outcomes and the probability of each.

The most frequent application of stochastic methods in technological forecasting is in cross-impact models. Such a model starts with a set of events that might occur. Each event is assigned a time and a probability of occurrence. However, the events are not independent. The occurrence or nonoccurrence of some events may change the timing and/or probability of other events. The possible changes are termed "cross-impacts." These foresights can be estimated by conducting a so-called Monte Carlo simulation with a computer. The computer selects an event, draws a random number to determine if the event occurs, then makes the appropriate adjustments in the timing and probability of those events impacted by the selected event. This process is repeated until all events have been determined. The model is reset to the starting conditions, and the simulation is repeated a large number of times. The frequency of occurrence and timing of the events in the outcomes is a stochastic forecast of the timing and likelihood of occurrence of those events.

Scenarios also are commonly used by technological forecasters. A scenario is a narrative description of future developments and conditions. The important feature of a scenario is that it speculatively describes interactions of the individual forecasts used as its starting point. The primary value of a scenario is its power to present a set of forecasts vividly, in terms of how the events being forecast affect the people involved. Scenarios can be a very useful tool for presenting forecasts to people who are not specialists or otherwise thoroughly knowledgeable concerning the technology being predicted.

Technology Assessment

Technology assessment is a class of policy studies that systematically examines the effects on society that may occur from introducing a new technology, its extension, or its modification. It emphasizes the positive and negative consequences that are unintended, indirect, or delayed.

Technological forecasting seeks to anticipate the future nature and characteristics of useful machines and techniques.

The term was coined in 1967 by former Congressman Emilio Daddario, who argued that if Congress appropriated money for technological projects, it should have some understanding of what the consequences and outcomes would be. Pursuant to efforts spearheaded by Representative Daddario, an Office of Technology Assessment was established in 1972 as a research arm of the U.S. Congress. Today, however, the term is used in a much broader context.

Technological forecasts are essential for technology assessment. To assess the consequences of deploying a technology, it is first necessary to estimate the scale, scope, and rapidity of that deployment. The assessment goes well beyond the forecast of the technology, to estimate the social and economic consequences of implementing the technology. Common technology assessment techniques include relevance trees, causal models, and social indicators. Complex interactions are often portrayed through scenarios.

Relevance trees are used to trace out chains of consequences, to secondary and higher order effects. The deployment of a technology has certain immediate consequences. These, in turn, bring about other consequences, which have still further consequences. A relevance tree displaying some consequences of the introduction of the automobile is shown in Figure 3.

Causal models, based on computer simulation, are used to trace the effects of new technology through a complex network of interacting variables. A causal

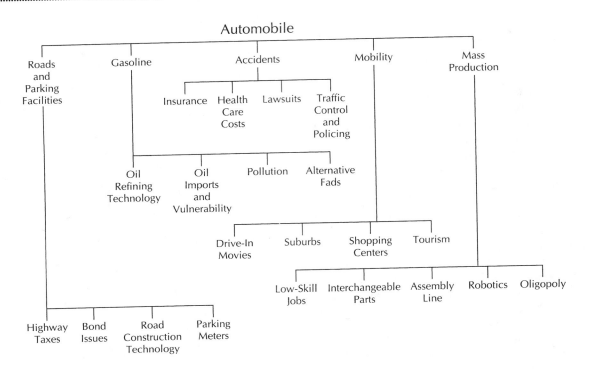

Figure 3. Some consequences of the automobile.

model might be used to estimate the rate of deployment of a technology (similar to its use in technological forecasting), to estimate the magnitude of externalities such as pollution, and also to anticipate economic effects such as shifts in employment (down in the old technology, up in the new) or changes in demand for various commodities.

Social indicators are self-contained statistics that require little or no interpretation to comprehend and understand their significance. School graduation rates, unemployment rates, and imprisonment rates, standing alone, provide meaningful descriptions of societal conditions. The use of social indicators in technology assessment involves selecting indicators that might change in response to deployment of a new technology.

In summary, technological forecasting and technology assessment are tools for policy guidance. Technological forecasting is used to estimate the future state of technology, including performance and extent of use. Technology assessment is used to estimate the consequences which might follow the deployment of some new technology, including the secondary and subsequent effects, particularly those which are not directly intended.

[See also Forecasting Methods; Forecasting, Mistakes in; Record Setting; Scenarios; Social Indicators; Surprises; Technological Change; Technology and Society; Wildcards.]

BIBLIOGRAPHY

Ayres, Robert U. *Technological Forecasting and Long-Range Planning.* New York: McGraw-Hill, 1969.

Bright, James R., ed. *Technological Forecasting for Industry and Government: Methods and Applications.* Englewood Cliffs, NJ: Prentice-Hall, 1968.

Martino, Joseph P. *Technological Forecasting for Decision Making,* 3rd ed. New York: McGraw-Hill, 1992.

Porter, Alan A., et. al. *Forecasting and Management of Technology.* New York: Wiley, 1991.

— JOSEPH R. MARTINO

TECHNOLOGY AND SCIENCE

The fabric of scientific and technological change is a weave of great complexity. In one dimension the fabric is defined by need; here changes are actively sought to solve problems or satisfy markets. This is the *pull* dimension. Scientific and technological changes in this dimension often flow from corporate, national, or international programs such as the war on cancer, the space station program, the Superconducting Supercollider, the assault on AIDS, or the Genome Project. Funding, legislation, military necessity, industrial policy, and marketing plans are the media of *pull*.

The other dimension of this fabric is *push:* here changes in science and technology are defined by the dynamics of the enterprises themselves. Changes in this dimension come as a result of momentum and feedback: work in progress leads to further discovery that redefines the course of work in progress. These are the "hot" areas of science and technology where recent discoveries make further opportunities pregnant: neurotransmitters, fullerenes, elevated temperature superconductivity, and transgenic engineering serve as examples. The media of *push* are publication, fad, employment, and what is perceived by the scientists and engineers themselves as fun.

But this *push-pull* fabric is full of bumps, some bigger than others, appearing in apparently random order. These represent breakthroughs, the discoveries that obey no model of change. How do breakthroughs occur? In *The Structure of Scientific Revolutions,* Thomas Kuhn presents an image of scientific progress. He sees normal science as the continual testing and application of the established rules within disciplines. When the old ideas work well enough, change is slow. When old ideas fail in their ability to explain or predict, new ideas gain respect and spread through the discipline over time, becoming the basis for normal science. What was once radical becomes routine. A paradigm shift of this sort provides a new way of looking at the world, and once it occurs the old ideas that are replaced are dead. These paradigm shifts make the world different for all time. The history of science and technology is a recounting of such events: from the harnessing of fire to the discovery of fission. Events like these define who we are, what we know, and what we believe.

The patterns on this three-dimensional fabric are not entirely random and are determined in part by four factors: (1) the growing capability of computation, (2) instrumentation, (3) the way information is gathered and disseminated, and (4) the nature of the disciplines to which scientists and engineers belong.

Computation

It is impossible to imagine future science and technology without computers. Certainly computers have eased the tasks associated with dull data collection and number crunching; but they have done much more than improve efficiency. They have opened the possibility of both experimental arithmetic and complex visualization. With high computational speeds, inexpensive CPU time, and abundant and cheap memory, simulations can be used to represent reality. Engineers can design millions of variants of a machine or product and test them all on a computer to find the one that performs best.

Outcomes may best be understood through pictures. With computers, pictures can be formed easily and manipulated. Data can be seen as a surface, atoms as solids

to be moved by the analyst-experimenter to form molecules; and molecules or continents can be seen interacting, with time speeded or slowed to show patterns hidden in long lists or numbers, but more readily apparent in visual form. Add virtual reality and the molecules can be fitted together, manipulated by the analyst in a new kind of computer-based chemistry, metallurgy, crystallography, or pharmacology. For example, researchers have shown, via computer imaging, how steroid receptors bind to the genes they regulate.

When old ideas fail in their ability to explain or predict, new ideas spread through the discipline and become the basis for normal science. What was once radical becomes routine.

For the future, we expect that computers will be smaller, more powerful, easier to operate, and still less expensive, by factors of 100 to 10,000 in the next twenty years. With voice input and seamless access to essentially any database, a computer will be an integral and unique part of every scientific team.

Advanced Instrumentation

New instrumentation opens totally new horizons to observation. This progenitor of scientific and technological change is pushing frontiers on spatial and temporal fronts: the scanning tunneling microscope and the ballistic electron emission microscope yield images the size of atoms and also provide means for manipulating single atoms. At the other extreme, space probes reaching out beyond the solar system and new orbital instruments give an unprecedented view of the universe. The ROSAT Probe, for example, detected giant clusters of quasars at eight to ten billion light years from Earth, suggesting a lumpier universe than previously thought. At one extreme of the time spectrum, laser pulses in the femtosecond regime control molecular reactions, and at the other extreme, automated data collection systems track glacially slow changes such as shifts in Earth's crust with precision and without boredom. Magnetic resonance imaging now permits human diagnostics through imaging of soft tissue; soon the menu of atoms that can be imaged in this way will be extended greatly.

Information Gathering and Dissemination

With modern communications, what is known in one discipline is rapidly known by others. Informal fax networks, for example, were far more efficient in spreading the word about elevated temperature superconductors than the conventional media. Publication of papers in conventional peer-reviewed journals is beginning to serve a primarily archival function. High-speed networks such as the Internet (some 350,000 computer hosts on 5,000 networks in thirty-three countries) facilitate scientific communications and are growing at a tremendous rate, in some cases doubling every six months. With the advent of planned national networks, further growth is likely.

These networks are used for more than just communications. They also aid in the search for collaborators, exchanges of data, revisions of publications, and news dissemination, and provide efficient access to massive on-line databases. This is the new grapevine. Since there is no filtering of material, these networks promote fads and gossip as well as research, both good and bad. The primary effect is the transfer of information between disciplines, a pooling of resources that strengthens everyone. Genetics, for instance, owes its vitality not only to the biosciences, but to microscopy, computers, data processing, imaging, physiology, and materials sciences. The field of materials draws its strength from not only metallurgy, but chemistry, computers, data processing, microscopy, and genetics. These cross-disciplinary jumps used to happen before, but not to the extent that they will in the future.

The Nature of the Scientific and Technological Disciplines

The population of engineers and scientists with PhD. degrees doubled to over four million in the United States during the 1980s. Based on projected retirements and the entry into colleges and universities by the babies of the baby-boomer generation in the 1990s, a shortage of half a million scientists is projected for 2000.

Prospective changes in the organization of scientific and technical disciplines are likely to be much more profound. Prior to computer databases and digital communications, scientific disciplines and technological fields were essentially defined by the amount of knowledge that could be assimilated by an individual in a lifetime. When more information than that was generated, subdisciplines formed. The walls around these guilds of specialization were high, and contributions from outside the wall were rare and not invited. Because of easy access to information in their own discipline as well as others, scientists and engineers have knowledge about other fields that was not as easily available to them before. In addition, most scientists work in teams. This also promotes cross-disciplinary interchange.

For the future, the frontiers of change seem impressive indeed. Listed below are five areas that represent new opportunities with consequences as profound as any seen over the last two hundred years. This represents a prodigious advance considering that the prior interval encompasses almost all the knowledge of modern science and engineering.

THE NEW GENETICS. This field resides at the confluence of the Genome Project, genetic medicine (involving genetic therapies), and the availability of tools to pinpoint, deliver, and manipulate genetic material at selected sites on the genome. Out of this will come new views on health and sickness, and on the design of plants and animals, including *Homo sapiens*. When the world population presses twelve billion, the new genetics may well provide a new form of agriculture capable of feeding the swollen world population.

ELECTRONIC EXPERIENCE. Consider the future evolution of massive data storage and retrieval systems, miniaturization of computers, smart machines, voice in-

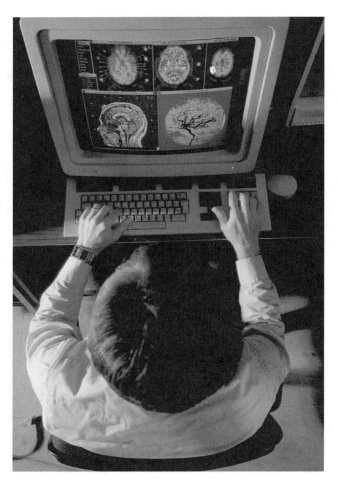

Looking at the processes of the human brain through computer imaging opens up a great array of possibilities for human understanding. (Phil Schermeister/Corbis)

put, fractal geometry, advanced computer simulation, biosensing, and imaging. This is the stuff of robots, advanced systems of automation, and virtual reality. These technologies will provide experience at a distance and will turn entertainment from a passive to a participatory experience. Simulation technologies will allow the creation of synthetic experience that will be realistic beyond imagination and may make real life seem dull. Ultimately this will mean new strategies for education; entertainment unparalleled, so good that it may be outlawed; new means of rehabilitation, punishment, and incarceration; design and research tools for the professional as well as the amateur; the construction of artificial worlds that may seem as real as our own.

MICROTECHNOLOGIES. This cluster derives its strength from developments in computers, data processing, biology, physics and physical chemistry, biomimetics, polymers, microscopy, microsciences, and photolithography. Micromachines at the scale of tenths of millimeters—and at the fringe, nanomachines at the scale of molecules—describe electromechanical machinery that can only be seen under a microscope. The shrinking machine is a new technology that includes venous submarines guided by surgeons outside the body, and video cameras that can be hidden in a bread crumb. Photolithography is used to make tiny parts; bioactivity to find molecules of specific shapes—i.e., antibodies that recognize antigens, enzymes that combine reactants, and hormones that fit receptors.

BRAIN RESEARCH. The brain contains 100 billion neurons, about as many as there are stars in our galaxy. Multiply this by 5.5 billion, the number of people in the world, and the number of neurons in the world ranks among the most numerous things of which we have knowledge. Many compare our position with respect to future psychiatry (or whatever the field of the brain comes to be called) to that of nuclear physics before fission or genetics before DNA. The clues are enticing: we know about synapses and neurotransmitters. Thought of a simple kind has been visualized through mapping of deep electrical impulses; mapping of the network of neurons is beginning. Phenomenological data abound. The field seems to be in Kuhn's preparadigm state, but ready for its Rutherford, Watson, and Crick, or Einstein. As knowledge of the brain and its functions increases, the curing of mental diseases, improved memory, and, in the most general sense, use of the organ to its greater potential will follow.

DEALING WITH COMPLEXITY. We have a propensity to linearize: put a little in and a little comes out. But the world is nonlinear, and when neat solutions based on linear assumptions are tested in the real world, they tend to fail. The notion of chaos, a form of math-

ematics applied to system analysis, is at the forefront of analysis of systems as diverse as dripping water faucets and beating hearts. Chaos can also result when the systems considered are social. This means that social policy based on presumed knowledge may be essentially random in its success. In the years ahead, policies will flow from better analysis, from an explicit knowledge of uncertainty and risk, and from concepts of stability.

The brain contains 100 billion neurons.

Multiply this by the world's population

and the number of neurons

ranks among the most numerous things

of which we have knowledge.

These clusters—the new genetics, electronic experience, micromachines, the brain, and dealing with complexity—impact on products, processes, services, workers, capital, competition, markets, customer needs, the meaning of truth, democracy, free choice, education, and the nature and meaning of consciousness and self. Powerful changes await.

[See also Change, Scientific and Technological; Communications; Computers: Overview; High Technology; Information Overload; Information Technology; Nanotechnology; Scientific Breakthroughs; Technological Change; Technological Determinism; Telecommunications.]

BIBLIOGRAPHY

Cook, Gordon. "A National Network That Isn't." *Computerworld* 26/10 (March 9, 1992).

Gordon, Theodore J. "Chaos in Social Systems." *Technology Forecasting and Social Change* 42 (1992): 1–15.

Holden, Constance. "Career Trends for the 90's." *Science* (May 1991).

Kuhn, Thomas S. *The Structure of Scientific Revolutions.* Chicago: University of Chicago Press, 1962.

– THEODORE J. GORDON

TECHNOLOGY AND SOCIETY

"What's in? What's out?" the news media continually ask. Unfortunately, the spotlights of our current attentions often blind us to the presence of more critical issues. Right answers to the wrong questions may be fashionable, reflecting current consensus, but ultimately they are useless, irrelevant. What may seem desirable or likely today may not prove feasible tomorrow. Here lies the source of many of our forecasting mistakes. Seduced by the mystique of technological change, we often over-estimate its importance and underestimate the significance of ongoing, underlying factors such as social structures and behaviors. Hopefully learning our lesson from these recent misperceptions, we must focus on three key issues that appear uncertain and are thus critical for the future: the real rate of diffusion of new technologies, the resultant metamorphosis of work, and the concomitant evolution of lifestyles and social organization.

At the forefront of the misconceptions that distort our vision of the world is what can be called the "technological mirage," a view supported by the theory of successive waves of technoeconomic "progress." Technology has come for the last decade to be considered as the source and solution for everything.

This kind of error then is not really new. In 1974, the major explanation for the world economic crisis was that it was energy-related. In France, it was felt that to recover a strong growth rate, the constraint on energy sources had to be overcome: hence the ambitious French nuclear power program. More than a decade later, energy is no longer regarded as the universal solution. Furthermore, the countries that have recently proved to be the most economically dynamic—Japan, Germany, South Korea—are themselves highly dependent on nonindigenous energy sources. At the same time there is not a single OPEC country in the list of newly industrialized nations, while the United Kingdom, despite its oil resources in the North Sea, has declined in terms of industrial development.

During the 1980s, energy was replaced by technology as the dominant driving force. According to a now popular view, we are currently in a transitional crisis between two technological waves. The technologies and concomitant production of the 1950s and '60s are on the wane, and a surge of rising new technologies and products will lift us away from the collapse of the old. Information technology, biotechnology, and new materials therefore are viewed as the path to excellence and future growth. However, the journey on this path, when not guided by a consistent strategy or theory, often leads nowhere. Entering an unknown territory may involve facing a battery of newly demanding situations. What is true for a business firm or corporation is also valid for a country, especially a developing one.

Between 1974 and 1977, this technological quandary was absent from the debate raging on how to get ourselves out of the energy crisis and from one economic level to the next. It is apropos to ask if we have not invented the technological crisis only as a replacement for the energy one—whereas the real problems are to be found elsewhere in our societal structures and or-ganizations as well as in our behavioral trends. We always seem able to find a tree to hide from view the forest of real problems.

The crisis is above all a product of sectoral and institutional tensions resulting from the opposition between drivers of change (geopolitical, technological, economic, and social) and inertia-bound structures (political, legal, organizational, and psychological).

Information technology, biotechnology, and new materials are viewed as the path to excellence and future growth.

Unfortunately, the social changes necessary to get out of the crisis are not usually stimulated by the onset of technological change in itself—however ripe with potential such change may be. According to the so-called "Japanese model," the key to adaptation and success seems to lie in the intelligent use of our own socioculture.

Following this line of thought, we can wonder if the rate of diffusion of new technologies will be as rapid as forecast. On average, progress in the diffusion of new technologies will remain slow because of the inertia inherent in production and social systems. Moreover, this resistance is perhaps stronger in the tertiary sector (i.e., information-based enterprise), to the extent that this sector, so far, has been less affected by the stimulus of international competition than have the primary (agricultural/extractive-industrial) or secondary (industrial) sectors. Many factors combine to explain the slow rate of this penetration.

In the first place, there is the question of reallocating time freed by new techniques of production and organization. What is the point of investing in order to obtain productivity gains that cannot be translated into expanded production due to saturated markets, slow growth rates, or staff reduction? The existing staff must be kept busy; a reduction in working hours can only be gradual if it is to be equitably shared between sectors.

In the second place, the spread of office technology means that the world of work becomes relatively permeable, which tends to work against established hierarchies. Information technologies are not neutral with respect to power structures. It is not, therefore, surprising that managers sometimes feel threatened and resist innovation.

Finally, what is technologically possible is not necessarily profitable or socially desirable. Thus, we should beware of creating the equivalent of a Concorde jet in the field of telematics (i.e., the long-distance transmission of computerized information). It is unlikely that working at home will develop to the point that a significant amount of office work will disappear. The physical character of typical urban housing developments in France—the small, cramped, uncomfortable rooms and the overall drabness of the environment—is not conducive to the kind of productivity afforded by an office environment. Moreover, work is a social activity and meets a need for communication that is satisfied less and less elsewhere.

Unemployment is a factor in many countries, especially in Europe, and it will rise if there is no change in structures, organizations, rules of the game, and behavior. This means we are heading for a dual society, with a growing proportion of the population excluded from the labor market or relegated to poor, part-time jobs. Such a trend may have extremely disruptive consequences.

Ultimately there is only one way out: a sharing of work and income supplemented by greater mobility between existing jobs. If there are only four jobs for five workers, there is no problem if the jobs are rotated; moreover, an opportunity exists to increase creative breaks from work. Further reductions in working hours seem probable and desirable, but it does not have to mean a decrease in hours of real activity. People do not want to work less but to work differently. The trend toward a dual society can be mitigated by encouraging a pluralistic society, in which an individual could have several jobs, each of which would be filled by several people.

The most persistent question concerns the evolution of values and lifestyles. At this level, conjecture fails: futurists do not see clearly and social scientists have difficulty in understanding the present, and even the recent past. As for analyses of lifestyles, these have no predictive value. In technical terms, the range of variables explained by lifestyles is almost negligible. In virtually all cases, lifestyle is less significant than sociodemographic indicators such as the level of education or profession.

After World War II, new values emerged to replace the traditional values of fulfilling one's duties, making one's effort pay, saving, and subjugation to rigid hierarchies. New values that became dominant during the 1960s gave priority to consuming, novelty, and the keeping up of appearances. After the end of the 1960s, this model was challenged by new values that rejected the criteria of social excellence, status, large organizations, and bureaucracy. The new values embraced conviviality, personal and cultural life, relationships, the quality of one's personal and collective environment,

decentralization, small groups, autonomy, and self-realization. This evolution has led to fragmentation. Nowadays, many groups express different values that are at odds with common values.

We are witnessing a clash among believers in moral excellence (the so-called militants), small and more or less closed groups (even sects), new consumers, those who live for the moment, the minority who have a satisfying job, the new agriculturalists, those without work, and so on. In this surging variety of values and lifestyles, we must seek all possible degrees of compromise through which partially contradictory trends can develop in parallel, such as the search for both autonomy and security, for both freedom and a sense of roots.

"What's in? What's out?" the news media continue to ask. Fortunately, what's "in" often becomes "out" easily, and vice versa. The myth of technological supremacy, like that of the Loch Ness monster, will continue to be challenged by reality—or to be replaced by newer illusions such as the notion that education is the cure-all for whatever afflicts us.

[See also Change, Scientific and Technological; High Technology; Multifold Trend; Science Issues; Scientific Breakthroughs; Social Change: United States; Technological Change; Technological Determinism; Technological Forecasting and Assessment; Technological Innovation; Technology and Science; Wildcards.]

BIBLIOGRAPHY

Freeman, C. *The Economics of Industrial Innovations.* London: Penguin, 1974.

Godet, Michel. *From Anticipation to Action.* Paris: UNESCO, 1993.

Godet, Michel; Chapuy, P.; and Comyn, G. "Global Scenarios; Geopolitical and Economic Context in to the Year 2000." *Futures* 26/3 (April 1994): 275–288.

– MICHEL GODET
FABRICE ROUBELAT

TELECOMMUNICATIONS

The Information Superhighway, or the Infobahn, refers to a nationwide or global network that will carry voice, data, video, and other information, all on one type of wire, optic cable, and broadcast band. "Information highways will revolutionize the way we work, learn, shop, and live," says Vice President Al Gore, Jr. "Human societies have seen four distinct revolutions in the character of social interchange: in speech, in writing, in printing, and now in telecommunications," comments renowned futurist Daniel Bell.

The convergence of the telephone, television, and home computer will create a new device some have called the "teleputer." It would feature a variety of video display options (including high-definition television), the voice capabilities of the telephone, and many home-computer options. Telecommunications promise to improve education, even in isolated areas of the Third World and to reduce energy consumption and pollution as people telecommute to work and shop at home. A 1992 Economic Strategy Institute study estimated that the Information Superhighway would add more than $321 billion in new wealth over the next sixteen years through such effects as shortening product development cycles and improving the cross-fertilization of ideas. John Sculley, former Apple Computer CEO, foresees a $3.5 trillion market arising. The Information Superhighway, Vice President Gore has asserted, would do for America what the transcontinental railroad did in the 1800s and the interstate highway did in the 1900s. Government will help build the Information Superhighway by supporting long-term research; funding test applications; developing policies that ensure all Americans have access; encouraging private sector investment in building the Information Superhighway; and creating a competitive market for telecommunications and information services.

Numerous types of terminals will hook into the Information Superhighway, and at least three major modes of transmission will still be operating far into the future:

- *Fiber optics.* Fiber-optic cables are able to carry huge amounts of data at the speed of light.
- *Direct broadcast satellites.* Able to reach large numbers of people over a wide area, direct broadcast satellites do not incur the additional cost of wires or cables.
- *Cellular communicators.* Soon to be cheap enough that virtually anyone who wants one will be able to afford it, the cellular phone will be operable almost anywhere and will likely be equipped with emergency-assistance buttons.

Newspapers and On-Line Information Services

Newspapers will arrive electronically, will be tailored to subscriber information needs, and will be filled with up-to-the-minute information. Libraries around the world will be available for you to peruse at home. High-definition television may eliminate the need to visit libraries, unless it is to experience directly an ancient manuscript or work of art.

On-line information services now serve some 13.5 million people in the United States, according to *Boardwatch* magazine. The Internet, inaugurated for Department of Defense research scientists to share information, has blossomed into a worldwide colossus.

Education

The telecommunications revolution will make learning much more effective, more available, and more fun.

Learning will become active, rather than passive, and students will pace their study. Students will be able to receive much of their education without leaving home. New opportunities will be available for gifted students and the learning impaired or physically challenged. Speed of learning will likely increase. Students will be able to earn a three-year bachelor's degree with the fourth year spent on a master's.

Interactive programs picturing historical documents, holograms of famous people, virtual reality battles, and other features will actively involve students in learning. Interactive education will allow students to participate in highly creative hands-on exercises without the need of human instruction. Artificial intelligence in programs will pick up patterns in a student's response and tailor instruction to shore up weak points.

Third World nations will be able to leapfrog other nations still adhering to traditional passive instruction techniques. Arthur C. Clarke envisions "electronic tutors," a combined microcomputer, video display, and satellite receiver, becoming cheap enough to allow anyone in the world to receive a state-of-the-art electronic education. According to Joseph Pelton, "Tele-education will continue to homogenize cultures and languages. It could lead to charges of cultural imperialism among those whose language and culture are underrepresented."

Interactive Television

Interactive television will offer viewers exciting new choices to interact with program producers and networks. No longer will television merely be a passive activity. An electronic *TV Guide* will help sort through the choices. Artificial intelligence in programs will note what types of programs a viewer watches and customize listings to suit the individual's needs.

More channels will be dedicated to narrow topics: the Football Channel, the Tennis Channel, the Parents' Channel, and so on. Recent cinematic hits and an amazing abundance of other movies will be available on a pay-per-view basis. This will be one of the first interactive television services to see wide use.

Other Forms of Entertainment

Other entertainment possibilities on the Information Superhighway include:

- *Virtual reality.* These programs will allow you to simulate real-life experiences.
- *On-line dating.* Computer bulletin boards are already bringing together the romantically inclined.
- *Video and computer games.* Augmented by virtual reality and the ability to play others on-line, video games and computer simulations may gain a whole new dimension.

- *On-Line gambling.* Gambling of every imaginable sort will be available at home and also while traveling on planes, boats, trains, and buses.

Home Shopping

Shopping at home will revolutionize retailing as consumers browse through thousands of on-line catalogs and order goods at the push or click of a button. Manufacturers will sell directly to consumers, cutting out the need for the retailer and other middlemen. On-line access to comparative shopping information will displace much of the "consumer education" function of advertising, with better-informed consumers relying more on merit than promotional power.

Shopping at home will revolutionize retailing as consumers browse through thousands of on-line catalogs and order goods at the push or click of a button.

People will always like to go shopping for things that are difficult to shop for at home or where the shopping experience is more fun. Nevertheless, according to futurist Don Libey, "If only five percent of retail business shifts each year from in-store purchases to direct purchases by way of interactive technologies, in seventeen years 85 percent of retail purchases will be direct. That means 85 percent of the existing retail space will be obsolete by 2010." Some of the 19 million Americans now working in retail may be looking for jobs. At the same time, interactive shopping will create many new delivery jobs. Groceries may soon be delivered to refrigerated lock-boxes outside a consumer's home.

Banking and Financial Services

The financial world has been at the forefront of much of the global telecommunications revolution. Money has become units of data on the Information Superhighway.

ELECTRONIC FUNDS TRANSFERS. While millions use automatic teller machines or collect their paycheck electronically, few realize the enormous impact of worldwide trade. Futurist Peter Schwartz reveals the dimensions of this trend: "International transactions reached $87 trillion in 1986. That comes to twenty-three times the U.S. GNP. It's several times larger than the gross world product. Trade is only about 10 percent of that $87 trillion. The rest of it is generated by electronic transactions."

HOME BANKING. Banks have traditionally been the gatekeepers of monetary transactions such as bill paying

and are rushing to stay in the bill-paying business. If cable or telephone systems offer bill-paying options, banks could lose a large percentage of their business. Banks have been moving into on-line interactive banking and putting high-tech phones into the hands of consumers, allowing home banking to become a reality.

Work and Careers

The Information Superhighway offers tremendous opportunities for living where you want and working when you want. Telecommuting can free workers from the drudgery of commuting, reduce energy consumption and air pollution; it will also be a boon for the homebound and handicapped, who will have many new avenues of employment. Holding meetings by teleconference using live interactive video also will become common.

Service and professional industries and jobs will no longer be protected by oceans or international borders. "If work can be telecommuted out of the office, what keeps it from being telecommuted overseas?" asks Elaine Taber, program director for the Clerical Workers Union. Currently workers in Haiti do word processing for insurance companies, telephone service people in Ireland take catalog orders from U.S. customers, and programmers in the Philippines convert print data to CD-ROM. Wages may continue to drop as "electronic immigrants" depress wages and as artificial intelligence eliminates many professional occupations. The Information Superhighway will cause many to lose their jobs and many new careers to be created. Job searches will be facilitated by the ability to list your résumé and video presentation in on-line databases and interview for jobs around the world via on-line videoconferencing.

New information technologies will revive competition and give authors, researchers, and program creators the real power. Whereas today an author may receive 10 percent of a book's revenue, future "content providers" will get a full 90 percent, the authors say.

Health/Medicine

Telecommunications will help make health care more affordable and more available. Doctors in Chicago have examined patients in Atlanta via the use of an electronic stethoscope, high-resolution medical-imaging equipment, and interactive video. These technologies will allow doctors everywhere to access the expertise of specialists instantly, anywhere in the world. "Telemedicine" also can help bring affordable health care to rural areas. Telecommunications technologies can also make health care more affordable. A study by Arthur D. Little estimates that health insurance claims processing costs could be reduced by $5.3 billion by adopting selected telecommunications technology.

Advertising and Marketing

Interactive television and the Information Superhighway will totally revolutionize advertising and marketing. Advertising will become more targeted, more relevant, and more useful for consumers and more effective for advertisers. Television commercials, videomail, and electronic mail will be targeted directly at consumers with an interest in that product, and the messages will be personalized.

Interactive classified advertising will allow interested buyers to access additional information about the product, even providing full-motion video of the product in use. Simply press a button to contact the seller to arrange an appointment. The real estate industry may be turned upside down as realtors lose the monopoly provided by their computerized "multiple listing service." New real estate ads will feature home tours in virtual reality, maps of the neighborhood, and more. Competition from fax machines and overnight delivery services has already resulted in reduced mail volume.

Privacy and "Big Brother"

One negative aspect of the Information Superhighway is the potential loss of privacy. Information such as your financial, medical, or employment records can easily be passed on or sold to others without your consent. If a mistake is made in a computer record, it can take months to correct and may end up incorrect in hundreds of other databases that borrow the information from the central bureau.

The government is also actively involved in monitoring communications. The U.S. National Security Agency (NSA) has a $3 billion budget for monitoring electronic conversations via satellite and can monitor 30 million conversations daily. The NSA also has developed an "uncrackable" computer code known as the "clipper chip," which it is encouraging computer manufacturers to use. Because the NSA has the "key" to the code, it would be able to monitor any communications it wishes. Thus the U.S. government can monitor everything from computer bulletin boards to the N.Y. Stock Exchange and all scientific and financial databases. The government clearly has all the tools to be Big Brother.

Telecommunication Crime, Terrorism, and War

Future criminals and terrorists will have a wider range of opportunities to steal or create electronic mayhem. Terrorists will be able to knock out a city's power system on-line from hundreds of miles away, or invade its computer networks to wreak havoc with its government systems. Data kidnappers might send a "databomb" to a bank with a transaction, then hold the organization's data hostage until its demands are met. An enemy nation or group of knowledgeable terrorists could shut down large portions of a government's defense information systems. Theoretically, a malevolent computer hacker could create an "electronic AIDS" that could devastate the entire collection of data assembled by humankind over the last twenty years.

People have also become more dependent on communications for their work. Today much surveillance work involves monitoring phone conversations and other electronic investigation. Law enforcement officials are also using communications to monitor offenders at home with "electronic anklets" that reduce the prison population for nonviolent criminals and provide them with limited mobility to attend college or work. In California, prisoners testify via videoconferencing as a security and cost-saving measure.

Politics and Government

The communications revolution offers new opportunities to encourage freedom, promote democracy, and make governments more responsive to their constituents. On-line polls and on-line voting will make it easier for citizens to participate in community and government affairs and make their views known to their representatives. Besides voting for representatives, people may demand a direct say in the business of government. Governments may have to ensure that all citizens have access to the Information Superhighway as it becomes a more central force in commerce, education, and the democratic process. National economies will continue to be replaced by a global economy. Governments will find it increasingly hard to control information and commerce as satellites and fiber-optics transfer money and data across continents and oceans at the speed of light. Governments everywhere are finding it harder to stop the flow of information. The fall of Ferdinand Marcos, the rise of Lech Walesa, the flurry of elections in communist nations, were all related to the rise of communications.

In the future, politicians will be able to target different groups with different messages, either by the channel they are watching or demographic information. One may never know what a politician "really said" because the message will be changed to suit every audience.

Conclusion

The Information Superhighway offers unparalleled opportunities to deal with many of the world's most pressing problems such as education, energy, pollution, and peace. It also offers the opportunity to expand the sum of human knowledge and help individuals gain more freedom to live where and how they want.

[See also Advertising; Bell, Daniel; Clarke, Arthur Charles; Communications; Communications: Technology; Electronic Convergence; Interactive Entertainment; Telephones; Television.]

BIBLIOGRAPHY

Heldman, Robert K. *Future Telecommunications: Information Applications, Services, and Architecture.* New York: McGraw-Hill, 1993.

Pelton, Joseph N. *Future View: Communications, Technology, and Society in the 21st Century.* Boulder, CO: Baylin Publishing, 1992.

Rheingold, Howard. *Virtual Reality: The Revolutionary Technology of Computer-Generated Artificial Worlds.* New York: Summit Books/ Simon & Schuster, 1991.

Snyder, Jim, and Ziporyn, Terra. *Future Shop: How Future Technologies Will Change the Way We Shop and What We Buy.* New York: St. Martin's Press, 1992.

— GEORGE ANTHONY CORNISH

TELEPHONES

POTS (plain old telephone services) is presently going through a metamorphosis as it is incorporated into the all-digital world. We are entering a universal fiber-optic and wireless environment of broad bandwidth service that is revolutionizing personal communications. The newest, fastest-growing segment is the world of wireless telephones including cellular, mobile, and car phones. With the advent of digital telecommunication, telephone service will change even more. The cellular phone system will break out of its local-area coverage and go worldwide. Vast satellite communications relay systems will span the globe and provide cellular service everywhere, serving telephones that fit in a pocket or pocketbook. Several competing companies will provide this service. Individuals will have personal phone numbers and will be reachable anytime, anywhere. This equipment will include auto-location services that pinpoint the location of any individual, anywhere on the globe.

Signal alerts will be received via digital paging, either visual or audible. Response to this signal will be immediate—there will be no need to search for a telephone because a telephone will always be near at hand. You will be able to display the number from which the call originated through caller identification. If a caller desires he or she can also provide a name and address. Multimedia devices will enable all messages, including graphics and video, to be displayed.

This is possible because all transmitted information will be created and communicated by digital signals over fiber optics, wireless, copper wire, coaxial cable, microwave links, and satellites. Since all information will be in a standardized digital format, there will be no need for modems.

Each individual will have a personal communications device (PCD) consisting of keyboard, voice, and pen input and output to a speaker, a flat colorscreen display, or a "heads-up" display using special glasses that can double as glasses, sunglasses, or both. Onboard transceivers will provide either wireless electromagnetic links or a direct connect interface via wire, cable, or fiber optics.

The PCD will function as a facsimile machine as well—facsimiles will be handled by computers. Facsimiles can be created within the computer or scanned from hard copy. Images of text will be convertible to digital data, unless protected by the sender. Portable printers will be available to print out faxes, or anything else residing in the PCD. The PCD will be a versatile answering machine. It will accommodate voice mail as well as e-mail. If callers desire, video pictures of themselves or other subjects can be transmitted. Receivers

This young woman in the Portuguese territory Macao, using her cellular phone in the town square, could be talking to anyone in the world. (Macduff Everton/© Corbis)

also will be able to transmit pictures. PCDs with the charged-couple diode (CCD) video recorder built in can transmit the image of any subject pointed at.

The call waiting signal may be an audio beep, a flashing light, or a second video window on a PCD display screen. Conference calls may be set up among small numbers of other callers. Data can be saved in a PCD database for quick and easy retrieval and voice forwarding.

Almost instantaneous language translation will permit real-time multiple conversations between people speaking different languages.

Carrier modes and configuration will include various transmission media—twisted-pair copper wire, fiber-optic cable, or coaxial cable. For short transmission distances of 100 meters or less, the capacity of wire may be arrayed to approach a million bits per second. This will accommodate a single-family connection to the larger intra/intercity networks, although fiber may already be installed in many cases. In remote areas microwave relays will be used for ground and satellite interface. Six-inch diameter satellite antennas will be adequate for direct transmission. Fiber optics will dominate the transmission world with bandwidth capabilities approaching fifty terabits per second per fiber-optic strand. This ultrahigh bandwidth will accommodate a million high-definition television (HDTV) channels. According to Nicholas Negroponte, head of MIT's Media Lab, most voice transmission will be by satellite, and will be part of the worldwide cellular system, while most video and audio transmissions will rely upon fiber optics. There will be increasing use of radio frequencies (RF) for short-range communications, whether in the home or office.

Human interface with the system will be via keyboard, pen, or voice. The user need only provide the callee's personal phone number and the system will find the callee. If there is no answer, the message will be stored and possibly forwarded, depending on the receiver's commands.

Translation services will convert voice to text, Braille, or other physically sensed output. Conversely, text, Braille, or other physically sensed output will be converted to voice. Almost instantaneous language translation will permit real-time multiple conversations between people speaking different languages. Input can be verbal or through a physical input device. The output will be converted to the presentation form of choice. If

telegraph transmission exists it too will be in digital form so that it too can be converted by software.

Worldwide interconnection between users and providers will be enhanced through implementation of the integrated services digital network (ISDN), a set of standards that will govern the implementation of common services over the digital network. ISDN will integrate digitized voice with other digital information. Thus, digitally encoded data, graphics, and video information will be transmitted over the same transmission lines. The ISDN environment provides the switching and routing required to send data/information throughout the world, just as 20th century telephone equipment switched analog data. ISDN will incorporate all of the many transmission media and protocols required to form a seamless multimedia network.

More than likely broadband ISDN (B-ISDN) will be implemented by the turn of the century. B-ISDN is merely an extension of ISDN that takes advantage of the ultrahigh-speed transmission capabilities that are continuously being implemented.

All telephone technology capabilities will be integrated with advanced computer services, thereby integrating the telephone into the office desk-top computer, the home telecommunications center, and the PCD. The PCD will have its own 200 to 400 megahertz (or higher) central processor and will provide hundreds of MIPs of processing power, as well as gigabytes of internal and external memory capacity. The merger between the telephone, the computer, audio, television, and the digital world will be so pervasive that it cannot be determined where one ends and the other begins. All information will travel through the same devices and over the same telecommunications transmission facilities.

The National Information Infrastructure (NII) will provide the telecommunication backbone and control the telecommunication highway. This seamless web of networks, computers, telephones, and other electronic communication devices will provide the means for clients and information providers to exchange virtually unlimited amounts and types of information. It will be accessible by all. While there will be many "for-pay" commercial services, many basic services will be free to the user at the time of use. The NII will be sponsored by local, state, and federal governments through taxes.

Universal information services will be integrated into the telecommunications highway and accessible via the twenty-first-century "telephone." These services will operate like businesses and services presently accessible via the transportation system that exists today. The thousands of miles of connecting roads correspond to the millions of local area networks comprising the telecommunications system interconnected by major telecommunication trunks, satellite links, microwave links, and RF communications. Information and interactive services will be provided by state, local, and federal governments; nonprofit organizations; and commercial organizations and individuals. In this brave new world anyone will be able to conduct almost any business activity from anywhere via the new PCD telephone.

[See also Communications; Communications Technology; Computer Linkage; Digital Communications; Interactive Entertainment; Media Lab; On-Line Services; Satellite Communications; Telecommunications; Television.]

BIBLIOGRAPHY

Brand, Stewart. *The Media Lab: Inventing the Future at MIT.* New York: Viking, 1987.

Krol, Ed. *The Whole Internet: User's Guide and Catalog.* Sebastapol, CA: O'Reilly & Associates, 1992.

Martin, James. *Telecommunications and the Computer.* Englewood Cliffs, NJ: Prentice Hall, 1990.

Negroponte, Nicholas. "The Future of Telecommunications." *Telecommunication* 27/1 (January 1993).

———. "Products and Services for Computers." *Scientific American* 265/3 (September 1991).

— BRIAN K. TOREN

TELEVISION

Because so much activity currently surrounds the communications system of television, most observers clearly see that something of great significance is underway. Large telecommunications firms, such as the telephone companies and the cable companies, are positioning themselves to take advantage of whatever happens; new technologies such as direct broadcast satellite (DBS) systems and high-definition television (HDTV) are appearing; new formats, like music television and home shopping channels, are quickly and widely disseminating; discussions of the so-called Information Superhighway are proliferating; and home viewers are waiting with a mixture of anticipation and skepticism.

But while change is in the air, no one can foresee precisely what the system that will eventually emerge might look like, in part because so much current thinking is clouded with overly optimistic visions and grandiose expectations. While such speculation can point the way, and is a necessary stage in any society's acceptance of major technological alterations, it should be blended with firmer and more realistic considerations.

Compounding the forecasting problem is the number of forces at work beyond simply the industries that supply the technologies and the content, on the one side, and the changing demands of the consumer market, on the other. In particular, the federal government

is playing a large and sometimes unpredictable role in the evolution of television, primarily through the Federal Communications Commission (FCC), but also through the Congress, the presidential administration, and the courts. The television system is so important in the conduct of national life that governmental intervention is mandated by the Communications Act of 1934 and the Cable Television Act of 1992. (Some critics have argued that government intervention is contrary to the spirit of the Constitution's First Amendment, which says that "Congress shall make no law . . . abridging the freedom of speech, or of the press.") For example, although traditional over-the-air broadcasters (particularly local stations) would seem to be most jeopardized by the current development of universal cable systems, the government has so far compelled the newer systems to accommodate the older. It may or may not continue to do so.

When these governmental considerations are added to the uncertainties of technological developments, it would seem difficult to predict accurately the direction of change in the television system. Nevertheless, it is still possible to sketch six broad parameters within which these transformations will occur.

1. *The financial costs of the new system increasingly will be shifted to the consumers.* Broadcast television was previously free to Americans once the householder had purchased a receiver and antenna. The costs of the programming and transmission were paid by advertisers to the networks and affiliates, but consumer-paid cable television is now in about 65 percent of American households. Cable companies charge consumers for carrying the signal to their homes, and consumers are willing to pay for greater clarity and the increased number of channels. Once the television industry realized that consumers would spend directly for its service, a second revenue stream in addition to advertising dollars became possible. Beyond the charge for the cable hook-up and monthly payments, the addition of premium channels, pay-per-view experiments, and shopping channels further indicated consumer willingness to pay for television experience. This is confirmed by VCR purchases and videocassette rentals. Although the rise in direct consumer payments has been temporarily restrained by the provisions of the 1992 Cable Television Act, the long-term trend toward the sharing of television costs between the advertisers and the consumer appears to be strengthening. Viewers are agreeing to pay largely because of the personal gratifications which they recognize they are receiving from televised content.

The federal government, committed to the growth of the American economy, is not likely to unduly constrain the revenues of television providers. However, when it comes to something as important as the nation's primary communications system, headlong pursuit of profits does pose a challenge to egalitarian principles in that the less-privileged and poorer segments of the population may be excluded from participation. Most likely, through the offices of the FCC, the system of the future will be required to provide basic service at or below cost to everyone who wants it, after which providers would be free to pursue profits in elective channels offered to those who can afford them. The present cable system appears to be evolving in this direction.

2. *The much heralded convergence at the top of the television industry will continue to conceal the divergence and variety in the lower tiers of the industry. Convergence* has become a much-used term to describe a time of courtship and unions among the television, cable, telephone, computer, and studio production industries. This convergence is technologically foreshadowed by the rapidly increasing conversion of all communications content into digitized signals compatible with computers. Joint ventures, cross-ownerships, and outright mergers are said to signal the convergence of media into what might ultimately be just a few electronic behemoths controlling the Information Superhighway. When publishing giant Time merged with Hollywood giant Warner and when Viacom bought and merged with Paramount and Blockbuster Video, an image of greater consolidation and perhaps a foreboding media oligarchy was reinforced.

But at the same time that these large transactions are occurring in the limelight, other unnoticed developments are going on in smaller media companies, technology firms, independent studios, program producers, and upstart cable companies, down to the level of individual entrepreneurs. The television system overall is in a phase of expansive growth (even if the traditional networks had to decrease their size to regain financial stability), and firms and business people sense that with ingenuity and luck great profits can be made. A better word than *convergence* to typify the activity occurring during the first decades of the twenty-first century would be ferment, as new entrants come into all sections of the television system, at all levels, and jockey for position.

3. *The Information Superhighway will convey very little information, and may be only a secondary road.* At its grandest, the vision of an Information Superhighway portrays just one high-capacity communications line coming into each household, a line carrying television programming, movies on demand, radio music and talk, individualized newspapers, digitized books and magazines, all sorts of advertising, computerized data,

personal mail, telephone calls—in short, every kind of communication that can be electronically conveyed. But it should be clear, based on the public's past usage of the media, that consumer preference will not be for what is commonly thought of as "information," but rather for entertainment. Currently the American audience spends 75 percent of its media time with television, and most of that time is devoted to light entertainment. Likewise, much of the time spent with the other media (newspapers, books, magazines) is also given over to entertainment.

Joint ventures, cross-ownerships, and outright mergers are said to signal the convergence of media into what might ultimately be just a few electronic behemoths controlling the Information Superhighway.

It is unwise to project the time patterns of present computer owners onto the use of future computer-compatible systems. In several ways, present computer modem use resembles amateurs' use of wireless in the 1910s, before the technology evolved into the mass medium of radio in the 1920s. The television system of the future will continue to be grounded in light entertainment.

It is also possible that the dream of a "superhighway" will be realized in a sharply curtailed version. Not all the various communications systems may be able to, or care to, join into a unitary system. Several wires may enter homes; advances in digitized broadcasting and cellular telephony may make over-the-air communication attractive again; a development that bears watching is direct broadcast satellite (DBS) transmissions, which may become unexpectedly successful. All this means that the Information Superhighway may be more myth than reality, at least for a decade or so.

4. *The demand for televised popular culture will continue to increase.* What is fueling the expansion of the television system is at root the audience's ever-growing need for situation comedies, sports, soap operas, murder mysteries, movies, game shows, and so on. Popular culture helps in the pleasurable and vicarious management of emotions and in the acknowledgment of dramatized social norms. As traditional institutions of church, family, and community have lost some of their cultural force over the course of the twentieth century, media-

generated popular culture has come to the fore. This trend of long duration cannot be expected to subside soon. Additionally, the aging of the audience, together with the escalating fear of crime, implies that people will be staying at home more, doing even more of what they usually do—watching television.

5. *Consumption as a component of the television experience will grow more conspicuous.* The success of the home shopping channels is a clear sign that consumption will loom even larger than before in television. If cable channels do expand to several hundred, as currently touted, many of them will surely be programmed by merchandisers, by manufacturers (e.g., perhaps a Procter and Gamble Channel), by infomercial networks, and by advertising agencies. On the conventional entertainment channels, advertising will continue to be a dominant presence as a major source of revenue.

Merchandising through television will impel marketers to demand that audience figures be much more exact and revealing than they are now. The Nielsen ratings, for all their longevity, will be replaced by much more sophisticated audience measurement systems.

6. *Globally, American popular culture will battle indigenous cultures.* The current resistance of the French in particular, but of most other societies to one extent or another, against the inroads of American programming may well be stepped up in decades to come. The long-term prognosis, however, is not good for local cultures. Like water dripping on stone, American content is likely to wear down the resistance, in part because it can be sold overseas more cheaply than local programs can be produced, and in part because the audience will increasingly welcome, even demand, the shows.

In brief, the television system of the future will resemble the present one in that it will transmit much the same orders of content to a loyal audience. It will differ in that a broader array of selections will be available, and that viewers will shoulder more of the costs of the system. Additionally, the delivery system will be hammered out through fierce capitalistic competition according to the regulatory positions of the FCC and Congress.

[See also Advertising; Broadcasting; Communications; Electronic Convergence; Information Overload; Media Consolidation; Newspapers; Satellite Communications; Telecommunications; Telephones.]

BIBLIOGRAPHY

Carpentier, Michel, et al. *Telecommunications in Transition.* New York: Wiley, 1992.
Dizard, Wilson, Jr. *Old Media, New, Media: Mass Communications in the Information Age.* New York: Longman, 1994.
Fowles, Jib. *Why Viewers Watch.* Newbury Park, CA: Sage, 1992.
Neuman, W. Russell. *The Future of the Mass Audience.* New York: Cambridge University Press, 1992.
Turow, Joseph. *Media Systems in Society.* New York: Longman, 1992.

— JIB FOWLES

TERRORISM

The Vice President's Task Force on Combatting Terrorism (1986) defined terrorism as "the unlawful use or threat of violence against persons or property to further political or social objectives. It is generally intended to intimidate or coerce a government, individuals or groups to modify their behavior or policies."

Legally speaking, terrorism is not actually a crime in most parts of the United States, but rather encompasses more traditional forms of crime as they relate to the foregoing definition. The most common types of terrorism include:

- Conspiracy
- Murder (assassination)
- Kidnapping
- Hijacking (skyjacking)
- Bombing/arson
- Robbery
- Extortion

Many international terrorist groups cooperate with each other in such matters as recruit training and information sharing. Some will even join forces to carry out a particular deed, or one group may act on behalf of another. And several of those engaged in politically related terrorism receive funding from sympathetic governments.

Counterterrorism

Individuals involved in terrorist acts are likely to be part of larger groups whose activities may range over large geographical areas, among states, even countries. For this reason there is a strong need for communication and coordination among counter-terrorist organizations and governments. Thus, intelligence represents a key element in the investigative process.

Further, because different individuals may be involved in specific criminal acts of the group, the modus operandi associated with a particular crime may be different. For this reason, it becomes important to know about a group's

- Stated goals
- Organizational structure
- Tactical approach

- Means of communication
- Propensity for violence.

Protecting individual rights must be weighed heavily in designing counterterrorist activities, lest the actions of government officials become as heavy-handed and brutal as the terrorists they are trying to combat. Some terrorist groups hope to provoke such actions from governments as a means of discrediting those governments.

Protecting individual rights must be weighed heavily

in designing counterterrorist activities,

lest government officials become as brutal

as the terrorists they are trying to combat.

Successful investigation of terrorist groups requires patience, skill, and cooperation. For this reason the task force approach offers the highest probability of success. Teams working together can compile a significant amount of information and, aided by an analyst, do much more than a single individual or group of individuals acting independently.

On the international level, the International Police Organization (INTERPOL), with headquarters in Lyons, France, serves as a central location for the collection and dissemination of crime-related information. Effective action against international terrorism requires the coordinated efforts of the central governments of nations and the cooperation of law enforcement agencies in each country assisted by INTERPOL. INTERPOL's purpose is to assist and improve police cooperation and the exchange of information among its 142 member countries. Capable of working in four languages—French, English, Spanish, and Arabic—it receives and transmits messages and inquiries to the proper authorities. Data are computerized, and the text may be retrieved in English. Routine inquiries made to INTERPOL include requests for tracing passports; identifying weapons, explosives, and vehicles; and identifying persons involved as either victim or criminal. Additional services include establishing a link between cases, obtaining information about suspected terrorists, their criminal records and proper identification, circulating notices for persons wanted on an international arrest warrant, and circulating warning notices about suspects who have committed or are likely to commit terrorist activities.

Terrorist Activities

Most terrorist acts involve bombing, assassination, or kidnapping (hostage-taking).

BOMBING. Several types of explosives are used by terrorists. In the United States, the most common has been a pipe bomb using black powder. The materials necessary to make a pipe bomb are readily available in most countries, and can be purchased in drugstores, hardware stores, and construction supply stores. Although homemade bombs have been used frequently, the availability of other types of explosives, particularly dynamite, TNT, and hand grenades, makes their use in the future more likely. On the international scene, plastic explosives have become more common, particularly in the Middle East. An American-made explosive known as C-4 has been used in numerous attacks by Middle Eastern terrorists. Most of these attacks have been attributed to a large amount of C-4 obtained illegally by Libya from an American source. Several recent attacks have been attributed to a Czech-made plastic explosive known as Semtex.

ASSASSINATION. Assassination attempts are often made through bomb attacks, although in the United States most political assassinations involve firearms. Attacks using a rifle or automatic weapon represent a greater problem. Assassination attempts carried out by terrorist groups are generally planned in advance, with the scene analyzed and avenues of escape plotted. A crime scene may actually comprise several locations, and the investigators in making the initial assessment should take time to explore the various possibilities that may exist. A terrorist will frequently try to disguise or mislead in a variety of ways. This may involve a ruse or diversionary action, more than one attack location, or even the use of a hostage to gain access to a particular location.

KIDNAPPING. Most terrorist-related kidnappings involve a high degree of planning. This planning effort may provide clues when suspects are careless. Kidnappings may be carried out for several reasons: for a ransom to support the group's operations; to force a political concession; or to bring a specific individual under the custody of the kidnappers for a "revolutionary trial."

New Forms of Terrorism

Despite the diminished threat of nuclear war and armed global conflict, the specter of terrorism remains high in many countries throughout the world. The Office of International Criminal Justice (OICJ) at the University of Illinois in Chicago, which conducts research on terrorism, identifies more than two hundred active terrorist groups throughout the world, as of 1992. Many of these are classified as "liberation movements," but a growing number are focused on other political and social issues. This is compounded by a growing number of criminal conspiracies which display many of the elements of terrorism. Activities of drug barons in Colombia involve the use of terror as a common weapon against efforts at government control.

The complexity of society has engendered another new form of terror, popularly called "technoterrorism," which relates to attacks on computer systems, telecommunications networks, and other forms of high technology. These new forms of terrorism represent a major threat, as yet unrealized, but one which remains a cause for concern.

Many experts feel that state-supported terrorism is on the decline but see increasing signs of ethnic and religious conflict, frequently related to liberation movements, that will spawn a new wave of terrorism, particularly in Eastern Europe. Increases in hate-related attacks, both in the United States and in other countries, are also finding new roots in old groups, such as the Ku Klux Klan and various neo-Nazi movements.

Many countries are also experiencing increasing violence associated with social movements, such as militant animal rights groups; environmentalists (ecoterrorists); and strident antiabortion activists. Although the vast majority of people involved in social protest comport themselves within the limits of the law, the propensity for violence among fringe elements may lead to an increase in terrorist-related acts. Some authorities believe that the pervasiveness of violence in the media results in widespread acceptance or at least a kind of numbed tolerance of the use of violence.

The rapidly growing gang phenomenon throughout the United States is considered by many experts as a new form of terrorism. Although these gangs do not embody the traditional definition of terrorism in terms of a political ideology, many of them operate across state lines, have an extensive communications network, and are involved in all types of criminal activity, usually but not exclusively related to drug trafficking.

[See also Crime, Organized; Crime Rates; Crime, Violent; International Tensions; Law Enforcement; Peace-keeping; Wildcards.]

BIBLIOGRAPHY

Ezeldin, Ahmed Galal. *Global Terrorism: An Overview*. Chicago: University of Illinois, Office of International Criminal Justice, 1991.

Ezeldin, Ahmed Galal, and Ward, Richard H., eds. *International Responses to Terrorism: New Initiatives*. Chicago: University of Illinois, Office of International Criminal Justice, 1991.

Public Report of the Vice President's Task Force on Combatting Terrorism. Washington, DC: U.S. Government Printing Office, 1986.
– RICHARD H. WARD

THEME PARKS AND ORGANIZED ATTRACTIONS

In the year 2005, the first of the baby boomers born after World War II will be fifty-nine years old and the youngest will be forty-one. That same year, an American phenomenon—the modern theme park—will celebrate its fiftieth anniversary.

Disneyland, the world's first theme park and prototype for others that follow, would never have made it without the baby boom generation. Baby boomers make up the backbone of the theme park industry. Walt Disney could not have chosen a better year than 1955 to open his Magic Kingdom located in Anaheim, California. As with most other phenomena, Disneyland was a beneficiary of extraordinary timing.

America was just beginning to change from an industrial society to one based on leisure and service, as well as on communications. Eating places like McDonald's (founded in 1955) and theme parks like Disneyland would become the growth industries of the future, eventually spanning the world. Television, then in its infancy, was an ideal medium for promoting theme parks. The newly created interstate highway system meant visitors could drive from all points around the nation directly to Disneyland and other theme parks. For the first time, something called commercial "family entertainment" was growing in demand. The 1950s was considered the age of the typical American family—a family that played together at places like Disneyland.

But now with baby boomers growing older, the age profile of visitors to theme parks is changing in profound and lasting ways. Kenneth Dychtwald, author of *The Age Wave*, describes "the aging of America as the most important trend of our time." Theme parks will have to recognize this, even as they seem to become more and more focused on the technological side of the entertainment business.

Technology, of course, has changed the modern theme park and the way it entertains its guests. Walt Disney created a revolution in technology when his "imagineers" came up with "Audio-Animatronics" in the mid-1960s. These popular new robotic entertainers came to dominate Disneyland's attractions and shows for more than twenty years.

Now, however, there are even more startling technologies being developed and used for theme parks: high-tech "pixie dust" attractions like three-dimensional cinema and holograms, and more recently the virtual reality or simulator rides. In these attractions, film, sound, and movement combine to produce mega-effects unachievable by any old-style "iron" ride such as the roller coaster-type attraction. In the past it took a wrecking ball to change attractions, but today a new film and computer program will do the same job.

New technologies have always driven the theme park industry and will continue to shape its future. But there will have to be a drastic rethinking about just who will be entertained by those technologies. The brick-and-mortar appearance of the theme park of 2005 may look about the same as it does today. The old iron rides will not disappear. People will still respond positively to moving from point A to B and enjoy special effects made of more tangible stuff than the illusion of film and movement.

This brings us to what really makes any theme park successful: the people who go there. Walt Disney knew his audience. He designed Disneyland with the family in mind, a family rooted in the youth explosion of the baby boom. The theme park operators of 2005 will have a very different audience they must play to—aging baby boomers whose needs and wants in entertainment may be far removed from the standards of the past.

As the United States population approaches 300 million early in the twenty-first century, nearly 100 million people will be over fifty years old. For the first time in our history, people over sixty-five will outnumber teenagers. An aging audience may not come flocking through the turnstiles if a majority of the attractions subject them to twelve minutes of shaking, jerking, and other fun stimulation. There will still be a need for a pure amusement park which appeals to the active—and younger—thrillseekers, but they will not be the entertainment haunts of the broader, older audience.

Perhaps most importantly, after decades of becoming computer literate, an older audience will force theme parks to rediscover people. It will be the friendly people who operate a theme park that will ultimately be responsible for its success.

Training these friendly (as well as competent) people today is exclusively a job left up to the theme parks themselves. The Disney universities represent early efforts to assure in-house capabilities for training and upgrading unique skills. By 2005, schools and colleges will offer special theme park courses such as those now common for restaurant and hotel management. The courses offered will place an emphasis on the service needs of older people. In fact, the operators themselves will be older. Since these older operators will have acquired essential skills for handling this aging audience, there will be no forced retirement and people will work as long as they are efficient, regardless of age.

As the theme park market becomes more fragmented, the parks themselves will no longer stand alone as they have in the past. They will be part of much larger "themed resorts" such as those that Disney has created in Florida at Walt Disney World and plans to do at Disneyland in California. There will also be "themed cities" where main activities, such as gambling, will be augmented by diversified entertainment designed to attract a broader audience. Theme parks also have found their way into shopping malls and retail-hotel developments.

An aging audience may not come flocking through the turnstiles if a majority of the attractions subject them to twelve minutes of shaking, jerking, and other fun stimulation.

The good days for theme parks will be in the late 1990s and on into the twenty-first century—but only if the people who run the theme parks of the future design for an older audience. If park operators can understand and meet the challenge of entertaining this audience, then they will create a true tomorrowland for the aging baby boomers of today.

[See also Free Time; Gambling; Interactive Entertainment; Leisure Time; Mass Culture and Arts; Performing Arts: Dance and Theater; Sports and Activities, Spectator; Sports and Games, Competitive; Tourism.]

BIBLIOGRAPHY

France, Van Arsdale. *Window on Main Street.* Livonia, MI: Stabur Press, 1991.

— VAN ARSDALE FRANCE

THIRD WORLD.

See DEVELOPMENT, ALTERNATIVE.

THIRD POLITICAL PARTIES

In the formative years of the young American republic, the political dichotomy traceable to the debates over ratification of the new Constitution between Federalists and anti-Federalists helped create and nourish the two-party system. It proved to be a natural extension of the rivalry between Hamilton and Jefferson and their supporters over the form the new government should take.

Hamilton, of course, from the time of his celebrated *Report on Manufactures,* favored a more nationalistic approach with power centralized to a greater degree in the federal government. Jefferson, in contrast, favored a more constricted role for the national government. He believed the Tenth Amendment did reserve powers to the states or people unless delegated to the United States. The clashes between Federalists and Democratic-Republicans, the latter quickly shortened to simply Democrats, gave way to James Monroe's Era of Good Feeling, which was essentially a no-party system. In turn, it too was soon replaced by a party contest between Whigs and Democrats.

The first party to hold a national nominating convention was a third party, the Know-Nothings, who were anti-Freemasonry. Thereafter, in response to the growing debate over the institution of slavery, there were a number of parties in the 1840s and '50s such as the Free-Soilers, the Liberty party, and the Constitutional Union party, which challenged both the Whigs and Democrats. The most famous of these third parties was, of course, the Republican party, which was founded in Ripon, Wisconsin, in 1854, in which year it won a plurality of seats in the midterm congressional elections. It elected the sixteenth president of the United States in 1860, a year that saw four parties vying for the presidency. Lincoln emerged with a minority of votes but enough to win.

In the postbellum period, there were a number of third parties. The most celebrated was the Populist party, which ran James B. Weaver for president in 1892 and captured approximately 8 percent of the popular vote.

James Sundquist, a leading student of the role of political parties in the governing process, has referred to the effect of "crosscutting issues" in stimulating the development of third parties. An example of such an issue in the nineteenth century was slavery. The Whigs divided on this issue, into "Silver Whigs" and "Cotton Whigs," as the party began a gradual decline and ultimate breakup. The other major party between 1820 and the Civil War, the Democrats, was also polarized by the quarrel over the extension of slavery. This division in both parties created the opportunity for an emergent Republican party, which within a few years became a major party. In the century and a half since the birth of the Republican party there has been no single crosscutting issue of similar magnitude. This is one reason, though not the only one, why the present duopoly has continued with Republicans and Democrats periodically trading off the baton of national political power.

The post-World War II period did briefly threaten the unity of the Democratic party over the issue of racial segregation and civil rights. A celebrated walkout during the 1948 Democratic National Convention by dissident southern Democrats led to the candidacy of Strom Thurmond that year under the banner of the States Rights party, also known as the Dixiecrats. Another southern governor, George Wallace, later carried the banner of the American Independent party in campaigns in 1968 and 1972, which sought to raise the same issues. Although initially enjoying a degree of success in some northern states, his major base of support was below the Mason-Dixon line. Neither of these efforts crystallized into a truly national party effort. Beginning with the Civil Rights Act of 1958 and continuing with civil rights legislation enacted by Congress in 1964, 1965, and 1968, a bipartisan coalition of both Democrats and Republicans operated to defuse the issue of civil rights, which was threatening to rise to a crosscutting intensity.

This is not to suggest that intra-party struggles over an array of issues, abortion being perhaps the most emotional and divisive, have not produced tensions within the major party establishment. The Democrats have by and large united behind a pro-choice position. However, the creation of the Democratic Leadership Council in the 1980s sought to craft an image of a somewhat more conservative New Democrat, particularly on economic issues and the role of government.

The Republican party has been more conflicted on social issues both during the Reagan era and in the period that followed. On economic issues—particularly on such matters as free trade and budget discipline coupled with tax cuts—they have maintained a high degree of party unity.

The rise of the Christian Right, which has seized the abortion issue as the centerpiece of its efforts to influence elections beginning soon after the Supreme Court decision in *Roe* v. *Wade* in 1973, did not herald the formation of a third party. In the 1994 elections, approximately two-thirds of those who comprised their 1.5 million membership voted for Republican congressional candidates. There were many factors that led to the historic Republican sweep that year not only of the congressional elections, which ended forty years of Democratic dominance, but in local and state races as well. The Christian Right's ability to mobilize its voters clearly played some role. However, the presidential election of 1992, which saw the election of a minority president, had really set the stage for what happened in 1994. The Ross Perot candidacy, which siphoned off 18.9 percent of the vote, helped defeat the Republican candidate, George Bush, but it also severely wounded the Democrats, especially in the South and in some parts of the West.

A significant barrier to third-party formation is the American electoral system itself. The great preponderance of Western democracies employ proportional representation in multimember legislative districts. This makes it possible to distribute seats in proportion to the percentage of the total vote received by the various party candidates. This, in turn, makes it possible for the new party to begin building an electoral base before it attempts to win the grand prize of the presidency. Perhaps more than any other reason that can be given for the failure of third parties to flourish is our electoral system based on the principle of winner take all.

Perhaps more than any other reason that can be given for the failure of third parties to flourish is our electoral system based on the principle of winner take all.

Another reason why third parties, and indeed even independent candidates, find it difficult to flourish in the political soil of America is found in the laws in many states that limit ballot access. When the author of this article ran for president as an independent in 1980, he challenged discriminatory laws in almost a dozen states and fought battles in the federal courts that in one case stretched all the way to the U.S. Supreme Court. As a result, he became the first independent candidate for the presidency in this century to be on the ballot in fifty states. The task of ballot access is even more difficult for third party congressional candidates.

A third reason why third parties fail is that they suffer from inadequate campaign financing. A system of public financing far more equitable than the Federal Election Campaign Act now on the statute books would be a minimum requirement to shore up this shortcoming.

After debating the subject of campaign finance in the early 1970s, both major parties have been virtually deadlocked on what further efforts are needed. As total campaign expenditures in the 1990s soared well past the half-billion-dollar mark for a two-year election cycle, both parties have become increasingly vulnerable to charges of special interest moneyed influence and outright corruption. Unless they deal with this issue before even a jaded public loses patience, it could be the ignition factor for instigating a reform party. Once launched, a party calling for reformation of the political process could quickly expand its agenda and offer a program of wider reform applicable to both the public and private sector. This could, in turn, feed into what seemed in the final decade of the twentieth century to be an increasing recognition of the need for personal reformation—hence, the cry for emphasis on family values.

Upon his retirement from the U.S. Senate in 1994, former senator David L. Boren, a conservative Democrat, offered this opinion: "The people will not forever tolerate a party system which forces them to choose the lesser of two evils." The steady rise to more than 40 percent of voters who claim the designation of independent rather than either of the major parties sends a clear signal. The first election of the third millennium could well see a strong third party in the field. Although either major party could fall prey to polarizing forces that would cause it to divide and furnish thereby the critical mass needed to form that new party, there is a more likely scenario. A new party will not result from divisions produced by a single crosscutting issue as in the past. It will come out of a broad-based citizens' coalition that will first have an impact at the local and state levels. Their organization will build on these successes and attract a strong national leader. It will be largely the economic pressures of the postindustrial age that will drive the formulation of truly bold and innovative ideas with a strongly futuristic content. It will draw from both the left and right but will essentially transcend the present plane of the traditional political spectrum.

[See also Communitarianism; Conservatism, Political; Democracy; Democratic Process; Liberalism, Political; Political Campaigning; Political Cycles; Political Parties; Political Party Realignment; Public Opinion Polls; Surveys; Voting.]

BIBLIOGRAPHY

Day, Glenn. *Minor Presidential Candidates and Parties of 1988.* Jefferson, NC: McFarland, 1988.

Johnson, Donald Bruce. *National Party Platforms. 1840–1980.* 2 vols. Urbana, IL: University of Illinois Press, 1980.

Kruschke, Earl R. *Encyclopedia of Third Parties in the United States.* Santa Barbara, CA: ABC-Clio, 1991.

Schapsmeier, Edward L., and Schapsmeier, Frederick H. *Political Parties and Civic Action Groups.* Westport, CT: Greenwood, 1981.

Smallwood, Frank. *The Other Candidates: Third Parties in Presidential Elections.* Hanover, NH: University Press of New England, 1983.

— JOHN B. ANDERSON

TOBACCO

Tobacco products have been long associated with pleasure and relaxation as well as with disease and death. When initially introduced into the Western world in the sixteenth century, tobacco was prized for medicinal use—as were sugar, coffee, tea, chocolate, and many spices. Health claims flourished as recently as the 1920s in the United States, but today tobacco use is assailed as public health enemy number one and as the largest preventable cause of death.

Manufacturers obviously ignore the annual toll of some 2.5 million premature deaths worldwide for which they are blamed, including 418,690 in the United States during 1990, nearly ten times the number of deaths in auto accidents. This annual death toll is greater than all U.S. soldiers killed in all wars during this century and currently accounts for about 20 percent of all deaths in the United States each year.

A 1994 report blames tobacco abuse in the United States for $21 billion in added health costs and $47 billion in productivity losses (additional sick leave and absenteeism, idle smoking breaks, etc.). Other reports specify up to $100 billion in added costs, including losses from smoking-related fires, higher insurance premiums, increased cleaning costs, and so forth.

Tobacco smokers number approximately 1 billion worldwide, 50 million of them in the United States. Smoking is most extensive in Indonesia, where 64 percent of all adults are smokers. In the United States smokers declined from 40 percent of adults eighteen years and older in 1964 to 25.5 percent (45.8 million persons) in 1990, and are expected to decline 2–3 percent yearly over the next several decades.

Per capita tobacco consumption for adults eighteen years and older in the United States declined from 11.8 pounds in 1960 to 6.7 pounds in 1985, and cigarette consumption dropped from 4,148 in 1974 to 2,500 in 1993 (see Table 1).

Declining sales in the United States prompt tobacco exports. Philip Morris, for example, increased international cigarette revenues from $8.4 billion in 1989 to $15.7 billion in 1993. Doffing harmful products on other nations draws criticism, as well as quiet praise for reducing the U.S. trade imbalance.

On-Again/Off-Again Pattern of Tobacco Regulation

The scope and severity of tobacco controls come and go. During the 1600s persons selling or using tobacco were executed in China. In Russia the death penalty was imposed on tobacco users in 1634; a 1641 decree by Czar Michael Romanov imposed flogging, slitting nostrils of repeat offenders, or exile; eventually, the penalty was reduced to a tax. Snuff users were threatened with excommunication by Pope Urban VIII in 1624. The current wave or cycle of strict regulation is not the first assault on tobacco.

Globally, the most sweeping regulatory stance embracing up to several hundred cradle-to-grave controls has been taken by Sweden. By 1973 a far-reaching twenty-five-year program intended to reduce cigarette consumption to levels prevailing in the 1920s was launched—from 1,500 in 1976 to the 1920 level of 300.

U.S. government regulators have steadily clamped down on tobacco. Warning labels required in 1966 were strengthened in 1970. Radio and TV cigarette advertising were outlawed in 1971. Cigarette advertising has been required to disclose tar and nicotine yields since 1971. Multiple warning labels were required in 1983. Farm price-support programs were shifted to a "no net cost" basis in 1986. No-smoking sections aboard U.S. airlines were required beginning in 1973 (and smoking was prohibited on domestic flights of less than two hours duration in 1988). Military survival rations eliminated cigarettes in 1975. Pending in Congress are bills that would ban smoking in public buildings frequented by ten or more persons at least one day weekly; regulate

TABLE 1

TOBACCO PRODUCTION AND CONSUMPTION

Consumption per capita (Persons 18 years and older)	1918	1925	1945	1960	1981	1985	1992
All products (lb)		9.66	13.02	11.82	7.60	6.70	5.00
Cigarettes (1,000)		1.10	3.40	4.20	3.80	3.40	3.00
Cigars (no.)		94.00	56.00	61.00	23.00	18.00	12.00
Other smoking and chewing products, and snuff (lb)		4.40	2.18	0.99	.64	.61	—
Production							
Cigarettes (billions)	48.00	83.00	332.00	506.00	744.00	665.00	719.00
Cigars (billions)	7.10	6.50	5.30	6.90	5.00	3.00	2.00
Other (million lb)	497.00	414.00	331.00	176.00	162.00	158.00	141.00

Source: *Statistical Abstracts of the United States.*

tobacco products as a drug; further curb cigarette advertising; and compel development of self-extinguishing products to minimize fire hazards.

Restrictions as to who may smoke also are growing. As recently as 1904, a woman was arrested for smoking a cigarette in a motor vehicle in New York City. Smoking by female school teachers, until recently, was grounds for dismissal. Sales are prohibited to minors (variously defined by law as including persons under 16, 18, or 21 years of age), but the prohibition is seldom enforced. About 3,000 teenagers per day, or nearly 1 million annually, take up smoking each year, and they totalled an estimated 3.4 million in 1994. However, teen smoking declined steadily from 1976 to 1984, then reached a plateau, and stood at 19 percent in 1993. The average age when teens first take up smoking is 14.5 years. Nearly 75 percent of U.S. smokers become addicted prior to reaching 18 years of age. Stricter laws prohibiting sales to minors are likely.

Restrictions on the places where tobacco may be smoked steadily constrict users' options. The General Court of Massachusetts in 1646 prohibited tobacco smoking to a distance of five miles outside of town limits to minimize fire hazards. Connecticut in 1647 limited tobacco use to once daily, never socially, and only within one's dwelling. Cigarette sales were banned in at least fourteen U.S. states between 1893 and 1921, but by 1927 all of these laws were repealed. Vended sales locations, easily accessible to minors, have been recently prohibited in some states. Prohibition of smoking in public places got underway during the 1970s. By 1990 at least 41 states had enacted laws. Local governments in the bellwether state of California, commencing with Berkeley, passed over 300 of the nation's some 600 local antismoking ordinances.

Despite advertising and promotion restrictions, tobacco remains among the most heavily promoted products in the United States, with spending rising from $2.5 billion in 1984 to $4 billion in 1990. Restrictions as to what can be said about tobacco products will tighten. A spate of regulatory thrusts by the Environmental Protection Agency (EPA), the Food and Drug Administration (FDA), and the Occupational Safety and Health Administration (OSHA) seek to restrain tobacco abuse.

EPA. Secondhand or sidestream smoke opens up a whole new round of regulations. Identified among exhaled tobacco smoke were high concentrations of seventeen carcinogens. EPA estimates that secondhand smoke may cause 3,000 lung cancer deaths annually and classified environmental tobacco smoke (ETS) as a class-A carcinogen in 1993. Not unexpectedly, the industry took the case to court and challenged the sci-

entific basis of this finding as flawed. These developments may expose the industry to enormous liability.

OSHA. OSHA proposed in 1994 a ban on smoking in the workplace, excepting separately ventilated areas. A total of nine states and over seventy local governments had enacted laws controlling smoking in the workplace by 1994. Maryland regulatory officials imposed the nation's strictest controls over virtually all workplaces in 1994; most other states will follow this lead, and uniform national standards eventually will be established.

FDA. France in 1635 restricted tobacco sales to apothecaries and made the product available only upon prescription from a physician. New regulatory thrusts would return the sale of tobacco products, once again, to pharmacists and/or druggists. Contending that nicotine is addictive, not merely habituating, FDA proposes to regulate tobacco products as a drug. FDA already regulates gums and skin patches used to help smokers stop. FDA contends that at least 33 patents enable tobacco manufacturers to precisely manipulate nicotine levels and that bioengineered higher nicotine yielding tobacco plants are being used to "spike" cigarettes and to "hook" users.

In their defense, tobacco companies point to the 40 million Americans who have quit smoking to disprove addiction; claim that nicotine-free cigarettes have been tried and failed; and point out that cigarettes now contain 66 percent less nicotine than thirty years ago. Some companies have filed business libel suits against those charging them with intentionally spiking nicotine levels.

Public attitudes play a crucial role in goading policy response. A 1994 poll indicated that 68 percent of Americans favor regulating tobacco products as drugs. The furor over largely uncharted hazards posed by burn by-products and ingested or inhaled tobacco smoke increasingly will draw regulatory attention. Cigarette smoke contains an exquisite array of chemicals—well over 4,000 of them, and some say as many as 100,000 of them. At least 27 of these compounds are considered mutagenic.

Another target for regulatory control involves additives used in tobacco products. Government regulators identify at least 700 chemical additives—flavorings, processing aids, casing materials, curing agents, sweeteners, and so forth—allowed in U.S. tobacco products. As many as 1,000 different flavors can be used in these products.

Taxing tobacco, to raise revenues or discourage consumption, has a checkered history. Tobacco was reviled and claimed injurious to health in 1604 by James I of England, who raised tobacco taxes by 4,000 percent; lower prices elsewhere encouraged black market trade.

State monopolies and heavy excise duties were imposed on tobacco during the early 1600s: Austria, 1670; Prussia, 1776; France, 1810. Taxes imposed on cigarettes amounted to twenty-four cents per pack in 1994. To help pay for 1994 U.S. health care reforms, stiff new taxes on tobacco products were proposed: an additional seventy-five cents on cigarettes (projected to yield $10 billion in yearly revenues); a 3,000 percent increase on cigars; a 2,000 percent boost on pipe tobacco; and a 3,572 percent increase on chewing tobacco and snuff (raising the current tax of thirty-six cents per pound to $12.86 per pound).

Tobacco's association with cancer

was first observed in 1761 by a London physician

who reported six cases related to

extensive use of snuff.

Referenda often are offered when lawmakers respond too slowly or not boldly enough. California's bellwether 1988 initiative, Proposition 99, imposed a twenty-five cent a pack tax increase on cigarettes to fund projects calculated to deter smoking. Since enacted, tobacco use plunged 27 percent, or about three times the national average. Massachusetts subsequently passed a similar law and other states were considering following suit.

Scientific Literature Documenting Hazards

Tobacco's association with cancer was first observed in 1761 by a London physician who reported six cases of "polypusses" related to extensive use of snuff. A 1932 article published in the *American Journal of Cancer* associated cigarette tars with cancer. A landmark 1959 article in the *Journal of the American Medical Association*, written by Surgeon General Burney, specified that smoking causes cancer. Surgeon General Terry released in 1964 a definitive report confirming Burney's findings. The number of published articles in medical literature dealing with smoking-health relationships began to explode during the mid-twentieth century, rising from 6,000 in 1964 to over 30,000 by 1979. The enormous volume of commentary increased awareness and added to public concerns and clamor for steps to correct perceived problems.

Around the turn of the century lung cancer was a rarity—one report indicates that only 134 cases were found in all the medical literature. American males' yearly death rates from lung cancer per 100,000 population rose from five in 1930, to twenty in 1950, and

to more than seventy by the 1990s. Life expectancy tables first showed reduced life expectancy for smokers in 1937.

Tobacco use currently is blamed for about 30 percent of all cancers in the United States and worldwide. Up to 30 percent of all deaths from heart disease also are associated with tobacco abuse. Noncancerous chronic diseases of the lung, including emphysema and bronchitis, impose another toll of nearly 80,000 deaths among Americans each year. Worst of all is the injury inflicted on new life. Spontaneous abortion among women smokers is ten times that of nonsmokers, chances of sudden infant death syndrome are 50 percent greater, and a total of 2,000 infant deaths during their first year of life are attributed to tobacco.

Lifetime medical costs of tobacco users are $6,000 more than for nonsmokers. Health-conscious Americans will demand that public officials take preventive health measures.

Lawsuits Edging Industry Toward Liability

Lawsuits attempting to recoup costs of tobacco-related harms abound. States are seeking reimbursement for health care outlays caused by tobacco abuse—for example, a 1994 suit by the Mississippi attorney general and a 1994 Florida law authorizing such suits. A spate of new lawsuits seek damages for nicotine addiction; a landmark $4 billion class action lawsuit on behalf of nicotine addicts was filed in 1994.

Industry immunity from legal liability—based on the assumption of the known risk resulting from ample labeling notices and widespread information regarding the hazards of smoking—has shielded the industry so far. However, what once were thought to be absolute bars against liability no longer shield the tobacco industry, which is being saddled with responsibility for the proximate result of their products.

Critics maintain that those who reap the rewards should be required to bear the responsibility of any harm. A pivotal question is how far government regulators—dubbed by the tobacco lobby as "smoke police" and "health fascists"—should go in controlling smokers' freedom of choice. Tolerance, currently, has been the general thrust, but this may be changing.

[See also Alcohol; Drugs, Illicit; Food and Agriculture; Food and Drug Safety; Health Care; Public Health.]

BIBLIOGRAPHY

Chandler, William U. *Smoking Epidemic Widens.* Washington, DC: Worldwatch Institute, 1988.
Diehl, Harold S. *Tobacco and Your Health: The Smoking Controversy.* New York: McGraw-Hill, 1969.

Fritschler, A. Lee. *Smoking and Politics: Policymaking and the Federal Bureaucracy.* 3rd ed. Englewood Cliffs, NJ: Prentice-Hall, 1983.

U.S. Surgeon General. *The Health Consequences of Smoking: Cancer and Chronic Lung Disease in the Workplace.* Rockville, MD: U.S. Department of Health and Human Services, Public Health Service, Office of Smoking and Health, 1985.

Whelan, Elizabeth M. *A Smoking Gun: How the Tobacco Industry Gets Away with Murder.* Philadelphia, PA: George F. Stickley, 1984.

White, Larry C. *Merchants of Death: The American Tobacco Industry.* New York: William Morrow/Beech Tree, 1988.

— GRAHAM T. T. MOLITOR

TOFFLER, ALVIN (1928–) AND HEIDI (1929–)

Alvin Toffler and Heidi Toffler are the world's best-known husband-and-wife futurist team. Their fame largely rests on the classic trilogy *Future Shock* (1970), *The Third Wave* (1980), and *Power Shift* (1991), each of which was at least ten years ahead of its time.

The road to fame for the Tofflers has been long and varied. Alvin was born in New York to Polish-Jewish immigrants. Heidi Toffler (*née* Farrell), also a New Yorker, is of Dutch-German extraction. Alvin entered upon work as a welder, but his writing instincts gravitated toward journalism, first as a staff member of a national trade union newspaper, later as a regular contributor to the *New Republic* and *The Nation.* In 1959 he became an associate editor of *Fortune* magazine. In 1964 he completed his *Culture Consumers,* which expanded upon the ideas of Fritz Machlup regarding the economics of arts institutions. Not long afterward, he wrote a piece for *Horizon,* where he first coined the term *future shock.* In this essay, "The Future as a Way of Life," he sketched his ideas on accelerating social and technological change and its impact on human life. In 1966 he conducted a course at the New School for Social Research on Social Change and the Future.

A landmark in the Tofflers' lives, *Future Shock* dealt with what were at that time radical ideas—the impact of transience on human relationships, the rise of temporary organizational forms, the crisis of the nuclear family, and disorientation induced by too much change in too short a time. *The Third Wave* foreshadowed the rise of demassified media, the spread of customized manufacture, the shift of work to the home, and the growth of biotechnology. *Powershift* described the creation of new centers of power, the transformation of information and knowledge as the "new wealth," and the capacity of the new knowledge system to destroy the underlying assumptions on which society, government, and the economy were based. The most recent Toffler book, *War and Anti-War* (1994), presents a new theory of war, reveals changes in the military paralleling those

at the corporate and social levels, and raises the specter of cyber-terrorists and nonlethal weapons. The Tofflers' gift is their ability to leap across disciplines to identify broad patterns of change, to devise new frameworks for thinking about the unthinkable and imponderable, to present complex ideas simply, and to distill powerful insights in memorable words or phrases.

[See also Futurists; Popularized Futures.]

— GEORGE THOMAS KURIAN

TOILETRIES.

See COSMETICS AND TOILETRIES.

TOURISM

Leisure and recreation imply the discretionary use of time for pastimes, such as sports and games. Tourism is

Taste in tourism has grown more diverse as affluent people seek new challenges. These travelers are taking a utility vehicle through the back roads of the Himalayas. (David Samuel Robbins/Corbis)

different from leisure and recreation in that it implies travel and at least an overnight stay of twenty-four hours at a destination. People also travel to visit friends and relatives and for business, religious, study, and health purposes.

Mass tourism is seen as a threat to

the physical environment

and to the uniqueness of various far-flung locales

that previously were beyond the reach of most people.

The rapid expansion of mass tourism during the past forty years has been a result of the increased availability of leisure time, the expansion of the middle class, cheaper and better transportation, and improved communications. Marketing has been effective in highlighting the opportunity to escape the daily humdrum.

Forecaster Herman Kahn speculated in 1979 that the 10 percent annual growth rate of the 1960s and early '70s might lead to two billion people traveling abroad in the year 2000. The growth of tourism is inextricably linked with the expansion of gross domestic product, the availability of an appropriate infrastructure, and well-trained and educated human resources. During the 1990s, however, this growth has slowed, and international tourism is likely to expand in the near future at an annual rate of about 5 percent in the mature industrialized economies. In the newly industrialized countries of Asia, the growth of tourism will be constrained by the lack of sufficient infrastructure, well-trained workers, and management expertise. It is therefore likely that the number of international tourists will reach only about 700 million by the year 2000, rather than the earlier anticipated two billion.

Most places on Earth are within the physical and financial reach of a growing number of people. Increasingly, mass tourism is being seen as a threat to the physical environment and to the uniqueness of various far-flung locales that previously were beyond the reach of most people. Traditionally, growth in tourism has meant more visitors, rising prices, or more attractions and events. Today, due in part to environmental constraints, tourism has to be managed more like a multibillion-dollar "designed experiences business." Linking the attractions, performing arts, hotels, tour operators, airlines, and host communities into a new coherence is information technology.

In the future, small and large organizations will focus on information-based enhancements to design experiences that respond to travelers' interests, build on the indigenous assets of destinations, and create environmentally compatible tourism. Among these experiences will be the following:

- *Adventure travel.* Changing tastes have created a demand and appetite for adventure and unusual physical activities. Business corporations are using adventure outings, such as those featured by Outward Bound, as part of management development programs. Dude ranches or guest ranches have enjoyed considerable success in recent years in North America. Rural tourism will become increasingly important, especially in Europe where farmers are actively encouraged to substitute farming with tourism to reduce the acid pollution generated by cattle manure.
- *Government preserves and exploration.* Visits to the national parks, forests, wilderness areas, and seashores offer the explorer-traveler activities such as whitewater boating, wilderness canoeing, horseback riding, hiking, backpacking, and cross-country skiing in an uncrowded, "unspoiled" natural setting. However, wilderness exploration has become so popular that camping spots are scarce throughout the season at the better-known national parks.
- *Cruising.* Pleasure cruising is one of the fastest-growing sectors of the tourism sector. Today's cruiseliner resembles a floating resort in that passengers are entertained, accommodated, pampered, and fed. Recently, certain cruiseline operators incorporated special stress-reduction and lifestyle management programs, designed to help passengers renew body and mind. Barging on inland water-ways, another form of waterborne transport, is especially popular in Britain, France, Holland, and Ireland. The growing number of pleasure-boating craft has increased the demand for marinas and stimulated local tourism development. For example, the success of Baltimore's Harborplace has sparked similar projects in New York, Toronto, Stockholm, and Oslo.
- *Learning vacations.* Learning will become more important to people who, in an information society, will need to keep up with technological and social change. Advanced telecommunications in the schools and in business may allow students and executives to keep up with their studies and work while traveling. Families could vacation together outside the traditional holiday periods, thus altering the seasonal nature of tourism. In order to compete with theme parks, such as Disney, Busch Gardens, Old Sturbridge Village, and Knott's Berry Farm, the museums, traditionally places of learning, have begun to redefine their role away from education through exhibitions to education through entertainment. Through the innovative use of technology, museums are making exhibits more accessible and understandable.

The travel industry has a heterogeneous structure comprised of many small enterprises and a small group of large transnational corporations. They all render service through a distribution chain including suppliers, wholesalers, retail travel agents, and customers. Due to travel industry saturation, hoteliers and airlines have introduced clubs to reward frequent travelers with free accommodation and free flights, respectively, in order to ensure their loyalty. Intermediaries such as wholesalers and travel agents will continue to consolidate their operations to lower their costs and increase profitability.

The silent revolution triggered by information technologies is changing the tourism infrastructure dramatically, Computerized reservation systems and nonbank credit cards are fostering linkages between the traditional leisure and recreational tourism base, telecommunications, and transnational banking. The emerging information technology is extending information flows of the travel industry well beyond its traditional boundaries and are heralding a new era of tourism development into the third millennium.

Technology will allow people to explore before they make the trip and to capture and preserve lively memories. Videos will provide cheap, easy, and engaging exposure to new areas and will allow tourists, in essence, to try before they travel. Virtual reality will have a profound effect on and will provide a boon to tourism by allowing people to experience a place before they actually visit it. As everything becomes smart through microprocessors, sensors, and voice capabilities, many things, such as simulated lake shores, trees, animals, and buildings may be able literally to speak about themselves to inform tourists of what to expect. The minicam is a new mechanism for capturing memories. Voice recognition technology and the ability to respond to a variety of languages will facilitate tourists gathering information and learning about whatever they need to know on their trip.

[See also Free Time; Information Technology; Interactive Entertainment; Leisure Time; Museums; Outdoor Recreation and Leisure Pursuits; Theme Parks and Organized Attractions.]

BIBLIOGRAPHY

D'Amore, Louis J. "Tourism: A Vital Force for Peace." *The Futurist* 22 (1988): 23–28.

Holloway, J. C. *The Business of Tourism.* London: Pitman, 1989.

Kahn, Herman. *World Economic Development, 1979 and Beyond.* Boulder, CO. Westview Press, 1979.

King, Margaret J. "The Theme Park Experience: What Museums Can Learn from Mickey Mouse." *The Futurist* 25 (1991): 24–31.

Kotler, Philip. "Dream Vacations: Booming Market for Designed Experiences." *The Futurist* 18 (1984): 7–13.

Papson, Stephen. "Tourism: World's Biggest Industry in the Twenty-First Century?" *The Futurist* 13 (1979): 249–257.

Ritchie, Brent J. R.; Hawkins, Donald E.; Go, Frank M.; and Frechtling, Douglas. *World Travel and Tourism Review Indicators, Trends and Issues.* Vol. 2. Wallingford, U.K.: CAB International, 1992.

— FRANK M. GO

TRADE.

See FREE TRADE; INTERNATIONAL TRADE: REGIONAL TRADE AGREEMENTS; INTERNATIONAL TRADE: REGULATION; INTERNATIONAL TRADE: SUSTAINING GROWTH.

TRANSPORTATION

Historically, the United States has attempted to build its way out of its transportation problems by adding lanes to highways, building new roads, and expanding airports. In the future, however, new road capacity is not expected to keep pace as the demand for transportation grows. Business-as-usual trends in transportation are characterized by a deteriorating infrastructure, increasing traffic volumes, a growing dependence on foreign oil, and increasing degradation of air, water, and land. Significant reform of U.S. transportation policy is required if we are to hand down a suitable transportation system to future generations.

The two principal factors affecting the growth in transportation demand include vehicle population (the number of motor vehicles on the road) and vehicle usage (trips generated and miles traveled each year). Together, these determine total transportation-related energy consumption, pollution, and road congestion. While motor car ownership is not expected to grow more than 2 percent annually, paralleling population growth, miles traveled is expected to increase from 3 percent to over 10 percent annually. This substantial growth in vehicle use is expected to present ever more serious energy, environmental, and traffic congestion problems, ones that simply cannot be solved by building more roads.

Since 1969, the number of miles traveled by Americans has increased 82 percent to 1.8 trillion miles in 1990, according to the U.S. Census. Virtually all of this travel takes place in cars and in light-duty trucks. Of the 15,000 miles per year each American travels, the largest amount of time (32 percent) is spent driving alone to work in cars and pick-up trucks. Of the remainder, shopping accounts for 12 percent, personal business for 20 percent, social and recreational travel for 27 percent, and the remaining 9 percent is for other purposes.

This tremendous mobility does not come without a cost. Transportation consumes vast resources including energy, land, and clean air. In terms of energy, the United States devotes nearly three-quarters of its oil use to the transportation sector, some 12.5 million barrels of oil a day, half of which is imported. In cities, one-third of the land is devoted to transportation such as roads, parking, and automotive-related services. Housing takes second place. Pollution from cars and trucks generates the largest contribution to the unhealthful air that a majority of Americans breathe, accounting for half of the smog and 70 percent of the carbon monoxide. The principal greenhouse gas, carbon dioxide, is emitted at the rate of 20 pounds for every gallon of gasoline burned. These discharges threaten our climate, reduce agricultural output, and compromise other resources.

While the breakdown of the transportation system will not occur tomorrow or next year, without corrective action a serious disintegration of services is likely to occur by the end of the century or shortly thereafter. One ominous sign is the alarming increase in congestion. If present trends continue, road congestion in the United States will triple in only fifteen years, even if capacity is increased by 20 percent, a goal that is unlikely to be achieved in this period of time.

America has to choose between two transportation futures—one characterized by energy, environmental, and mobility problems, or one focusing on accessibility, equity, and sustainability.

According to United States Department of Energy estimates, if current trends continue through 2010, 70 percent of the oil used in the United States will be imported. Several factors are responsible for this outcome. By 2010, the government estimates that cars and pick-up trucks alone will account for nearly three trillion miles of travel, up 80 percent from their current levels. Moreover, larger (wider, longer, and higher) and heavier twin and triple trailers will increasingly be used to move U.S. freight, consuming four times more energy than either trains or ships.

Americans will do more driving in urban areas where congestion and accidents prevail. As urban driving outpaces road capacity in the next century, congestion may increase up to tenfold. So-called rush hour, or peak-period, travel under congested conditions, which accounted for 39 percent of highway travel in 1980, will increase to 62 percent by 2005. Not only time but fuel will be wasted; by 2005, 7 billion gallons of fuel will be consumed each year—7 percent of the projected oil use for highway passenger transportation.

Sprawling suburban growth is expected to continue, further increasing commuting distances and compounding congestion. During the 1980s, three-quarters of all population growth in the United States occurred in the suburbs. If this rate and pattern of growth continues, jobs may move even farther from homes, at least until more work sites are located in these new growth areas. An already overcrowded airport system faces huge additional air-traffic demands. A 63 percent increase in domestic passenger travel (over the 1990 rate) is forecasted by 2000. Air-freight transport, including burgeoning package/courier delivery services, is expected to increase at an even greater rate. Because of the rapid growth in air traffic, aviation fuel use will more than double, to two million barrels of jet fuel a day by the year 2010. By 2020, airport congestion is expected to triple, with fifty-eight airports operating above rated capacities.

The challenge facing Americans is to balance demands for travel within the constraint of resources while maintaining public safety. The transportation network cannot expand without regard for financial and physical limits, nor can future growth be allowed to put undue stress on the environment.

Given the projected increases in miles traveled by cars, pick-up trucks, heavy trucks, other motor vehicles, and airplanes, it would be a mistake simply to accept projected demands and attempt to satisfy them. Doing so would force a high price on the nation in increased smog, acid rain, greenhouse gas emissions, traffic congestion, and a rising trade deficit (largely attributable to imports of petroleum and motor vehicles), reduced economic competitiveness, deteriorating personal safety, and less energy security. To avert or ameliorate these consequences, policy makers can apply a range of alternative transportation policies aimed at modifying anticipated demand or accommodating increasing use demands. In the long run this will prove to be more efficient, cost effective, and sustainable.

Clearly, America has to choose between two transportation futures—one characterized by the high social costs of energy, environmental, and mobility problems, or one focusing on accessibility, equity, and sustainability. We cannot simply build our way out of our transportation dilemma; without sound policy intervention, future trends point to an unsustainable course.

There is no "silver bullet" that can transform our transportation system. Future policymaking efforts will hopefully make use of a blend of tools, including greater regulation, economic incentives and user fees, infrastructure investments, research and development into transportation innovations, and public education concerning the transportation system.

The Department of Transportation and Congress will focus its attention on research and development and infrastructure investments. The challenge will be to channel investments into sound technologies such as steel-wheel high-speed rail, advanced public transport alternatives such as "smart" demand-responsive transit, and infrastructure maintenance and repair. Devoting significant funds for questionable technologies such as magnetically levitated (Maglev) trains, automated highways and other "intelligent" transportation systems for single-occupant autos, and new expansion of the interstate highway system may cause transportation problems to get worse. In addition, federal attention, coupled with state action, will rely upon supplemented regulations to further clean up vehicle emissions, improve efficiency standards, upgrade vehicle safety regulations, and enhance the recycling of motor vehicle components.

The bulk of transportation policy making will occur at the state and local/regional government level. The total funding of transportation, where the user pays more of the true cost of driving and other transportation services, is expected to be the focus of future national, state, and local transportation policy. This will be adopted in various forms, including higher state gasoline taxes, basing insurance premium costs on odometer readings or as a surcharge at the gas pump, charging for parking (including offering employees cash for travel allowances in lieu of parking spaces) and road pricing keyed to time of day, zones, or distance traveled. Local land use regulations also will be used to better manage and reform transportation.

With the advent of sustainable cities—smaller-scaled communities combining housing, job sites, shopping, recreational and other amenities for comfortable living—bicycling and walking will be viable alternatives to the automobile. The innovative transportation systems of such cities would include enclosed, airconditioned bicycle expressways above or adjacent to the pedestrian-level walkway, a network of moving sidewalks ("slidewalks"), pedestrian walkways uncluttered by vehicular traffic, and only electrically powered vehicles (some of which are already in place in Zermatt, Switzerland). In addition to privately owned "green cars," trucks, trains, and buses would run on hydrogen fuel cells that emit vastly less pollution and use energy twice as efficiently as their present-day counterpart, the gasoline combustion engine.

The sustainable, energy-efficient city would exploit unconventional land uses as well. To shorten home-to-shopping trips and home-to-transit station trips, highrise dwellings, a shopping mall, and a transit station could be located together. Work sites would have shopping and child-care services available on site or within walking distances. Conventional, gasoline-powered autos would be parked at the city's perimeter and not allowed inside. Developing these new technologies will create new jobs and possibly new industries with significant export-market potential. Over the long run, a sustainable transportation system will benefit the environment, reduce energy use, provide more equitable means of travel, and enhance the U.S. economy.

[See also Air Transport; Batteries; Macroengineering; Maglev; Motor Vehicles; Motor Vehicles, Alternatively Powered; Personal Transport; Petroleum; Pipelines; Railways; Space Travel; Urban Transit.]

BIBLIOGRAPHY

Gordon, Deborah. *Steering a New Course: Transportation, Energy, and the Environment.* Washington, DC: Island Press, 1991.
Owen, Wilfred. "The View from 2020: Transportation in America's Future." *The Brookings Review* (Fall 1988).
"Post-Rio: The Challenge at Home." *EPA Journal* 18/4 (September–October 1992). Publication No. 175 N92-010. Washington, D.C.: United States Environmental Protection Agency, Office of Communications, Education, and Public Affairs.
Transportation Research Board. *A Look Ahead: Year 2020.* Special Report No. 220. Washington, DC: National Research Council, 1988.

— DEBORAH GORDON

TRANSURANIUM ELEMENTS

The addition of seventeen transuranium elements to mankind's natural heritage of elements has led to an expansion of nearly 20 percent in the fundamental building blocks of nature. Investigation of these man-made elements beyond uranium has led to a tremendous expansion of our knowledge of atomic and nuclear structure. Each of these elements has a number of known isotopes, all radioactive, thereby leading to an overall total of nearly 200. Synthetic in origin, they are produced in a variety of transmutation reactions by neutrons or charged particles, including heavy ions. (Two of these elements are, in addition, present in nature in very small concentrations.) Many of them are produced and isolated in large quantities through the use of nuclear fission reactors: plutonium (atomic number 94) in ton quantities; neptunium (number 93), americium (number 95), and curium (number 96) in kilogram quantities; berkelium (number 97) in 100-milligram quantities; californium (number 98) in gram quantities; and einsteinium (number 99) in milligram quantities. Of particular interest to chemists is the unusual chemistry and impact on the periodic table (Figure 1) of these heaviest elements. Their practical impact, particularly that of plutonium, has been and will continue to be extraordinary.

The discovery of the first transuranium element resulted from experiments aimed at understanding the fission process. E. M. McMillan and P. H. Abelson in 1940, working at the 60-inch cyclotron at the University of California, Berkeley, deduced by chemical means that a product of the neutron bombardment of uranium was an isotope of element 93, arising by beta particle decay of U^{239}. Element 93 was given the name neptu-

1 H																	2 He
3 Li	4 Be											5 B	6 C	7 N	8 O	9 F	10 Ne
11 Na	12 Mg											13 Al	14 Si	15 P	16 S	17 Cl	18 Ar
19 K	20 Ca	21 Sc	22 Ti	23 V	24 Cr	25 Mn	26 Fe	27 Co	28 Ni	29 Cu	30 Zn	31 Ga	32 Ge	33 As	34 Se	35 Br	36 Kr
37 Rb	38 Sr	39 Y	40 Zr	41 Nb	42 Mo	43 Tc	44 Ru	45 Rh	46 Pd	47 Ag	48 Cd	49 In	50 Sn	51 Sb	52 Te	53 I	54 Xe
55 Cs	56 Ba	57 La	72 Hf	73 Ta	74 W	75 Re	76 Os	77 Ir	78 Pt	79 Au	80 Hg	81 Tl	82 Pb	83 Bi	84 Po	85 At	86 Rn
87 Fr	88 Ra	89 Ac	104 Rf	105 Ha	106	107 Ns	108 Hs	109 Mt	(110)	(111)	(112)	(113)	(114)	(115)	(116)	(117)	(118)

LANTHANIDES	58 Ce	59 Pr	60 Nd	61 Pm	62 Sm	63 Eu	64 Gd	65 Tb	66 Dy	67 Ho	68 Er	69 Tm	70 Yb	71 Lu

ACTINIDES	90 Th	91 Pa	92 U	93 Np	94 Pu	95 Am	96 Cm	97 Bk	98 Cf	99 Es	100 Fm	101 Md	102 No	103 Lr

Figure 1. The periodic table of elements.

nium (Np) because it is beyond uranium, just as the planet Neptune is beyond Uranus.

About this time, the possibility of a nuclear chain reaction and the production of transuranium elements for military use began to be recognized. With World War II already in progress, further work on the transuranium elements and related subjects was conducted by physicists and chemists under self-imposed secrecy, at first informally and finally as an organized program. The elements plutonium, americium, and curium were synthesized and identified (i.e., discovered) in such work on the wartime atom bomb project, before and during the organized Plutonium Project of the Manhattan Engineer District.

The seventeen known transuranium elements (numbers 93 to 109 inclusive) have been "discovered" in continuing experiments over a period of about forty-five years, at an average rate of one element every two or three years. Actually the discoveries have usually been made in pairs—i.e., a pair of elements about every five years.

The key to the discovery of the transuranium elements has been their position in the periodic table. Prior to the discovery of the transuranium elements, the re-

lationship of the naturally occurring elements—thorium (atomic number 90), protactinium (number 91), and uranium (number 92)—in the periodic table was not clearly understood. Recognition of the fact that the transuranium elements represent a whole new family of *actinide* ("like actinium"—atomic number 89) elements analogous to the *lanthanide* (rare-earth) series of elements (atomic numbers 59 through 71) permitted the discoverers to predict the chemical properties of the unknown transuranium elements. Once these properties were predicted, it was possible to discover the new elements by chemically separating them, following nuclear synthesis, from all the other elements in the periodic table.

The analogy between the actinides and lanthanides formed the basis for naming several of the former. Plutonium, of course, was named after the planet Pluto—following the pattern used in naming neptunium—which is the second and last known planet beyond Uranus. The name americium was suggested for element 95, after the Americas, by analogy with the naming of its rare-earth counterpart or homolog, europium, after Europe; and the name curium was suggested for element 96, after Pierre and Marie Curie, by analogy with the naming of its homolog, gadolinium, after the Finnish rare-earth chemist, J. Gadolin. Element 97 was called berkelium after the city of Berkeley, California, where it was discovered, just as its rare-earth analog, ytterbium, was given a name derived from Ytterby, Sweden, where so many of the early rare-earth minerals were found. Californium (number 98) was named after the university and state where its discovery occurred. The heavier transuranium elements were named after eminent scientists: einsteinium (number 99), after Albert Einstein; fermium (number 100), after Enrico Fermi; mendelevium (number 101), after Dimitri Mendeleev; nobelium (number 102), after Alfred Nobel; and lawrencium (number 103), after Ernest O. Lawrence.

Both plutonium-238 and californium-252 are being studied for possible medical applications: the former for use in heart pacemakers and pumps and the latter for irradiation of certain tumors.

Conflicts in naming have arisen in the cases of the transactinide elements 104, 105, and 106 because in each case two groups have claimed discovery and the traditional right to suggest names. For element 104, the U.S. group suggests rutherfordium, after Ernest Rutherford, and for element 105, hahnium, after Otto Hahn, while the Russian group, on the basis of doubtful evidence for their discovery, suggests for element 104, kurchatovium, after Igor Kurchatov, and for element 105, nielsbohrium, after Niels Bohr. The two groups have deferred suggesting a name for element 106. The German discoverers have named element 107 nielsbohrium, element 108 hassium, after the state Hesse in Germany where the work was done, and element 109 meitnerium, after Lise Meitner.

The most immediate effect of the discovery of a transuranium element on the world was in the use of plutonium for the manufacture of nuclear weapons. The more potentially beneficial practical use of plutonium as a nuclear fuel is well known.

In addition, three other actinide nuclides (plutonium-238, americium-241, and californium-252) have demonstrated substantial practical applications. One gram of plutonium-238 produces approximately 0.56 watt of thermal power, primarily from alpha particle decay, and this property is being used in space exploration to provide energy for small thermoelectric power units, such as radioisotopic thermoelectric generators on the moon, Viking Lander spacecraft on Mars, and the Jupiter flyby Pioneer spacecraft. Americium-241 has a long half-life (433 years) for decay (by the emission of alpha particles) and the predominant gamma ray (energy 60 KeV) makes this isotope particularly useful for a wide range of industrial gauging applications and the diagnosis of thyroid disorders; when mixed with beryllium, americium-241 generates neutrons and a large number of such sources are in worldwide daily use in oil-well logging operations (i.e., to find how much oil a well is producing in a given time span). Californium-252 is an intense neutron source: one gram emits 2.4×10^{12} neutrons per second. This isotope is being tested for applications in neutron activation analysis, neutron radiography, and portable sources for field use in mineral prospecting and oil-well logging. Both plutonium-238 and californium-252 are being studied for possible medical applications: the former as a heat source for use in heart pacemakers and heart pumps and the latter as a neutron source for irradiation of certain tumors for which gamma-ray treatment is relatively ineffective.

[See also Chemistry; Hazardous Wastes; Military Technologies; Nuclear Power; Nuclear Power: Con; Peacekeeping; Physics; Weapons of Mass Destruction.]

BIBLIOGRAPHY

Seaborg, Glenn T., ed. *Transuranium Elements: Products of Modern Alchemy.* New York: Van Nostrand-Reinhold, 1978.
Seaborg, Glenn T., and Loveland, Walter D. *The Elements Beyond Uranium.* New York: John Wiley, 1990.

— GLENN T. SEABORG

TREND INDICATORS

Serious forecasting beyond the short term has flourished in sectors that recognize the need for long-range planning, such as the military, aerospace, and information technology, and in cultures that encourage a long planning horizon, such as that of Japan.

Forecasting Techniques

Forecasting strives to determine "what can be," often termed "exploratory forecasting," as well as "what ought to be," usually labelled "normative forecasting." While the first begins with the past and is capability oriented, the second starts with the future and is need oriented. At some stage they must be integrated to provide a useful planning tool.

TREND EXTRAPOLATION. In this method of forecasting, it is assumed that the future will behave much like the past, so that data collected from observations of history form the basis for projecting the future. The variable to be forecast is selected and its value determined for a series of time points, such as years, from the past to the present. The sequence of value-date points is fitted by free-hand drawing, ruler, or a mathematical procedure. The resulting straight line or curve is simply carried forward, or extrapolated, into a future time period. As a general rule, projections should extend into the future for a period of time no greater than that covered by the historical data. Sometimes the variable is actually invariant, meaning that it does not change over time. For example, the annual number of U.S. vehicle deaths has stayed at about 24 per 100,000 population from 1930 to 1990.

GROWTH CURVES. A common trend is exponential growth—that is, growth by a constant percentage per unit time. In other words, at any time the rate of growth is proportional to the value already reached. In a finite world, however, nothing can continue growing forever in an exponential fashion. There are many factors that limit growth, such as physical and economic ones (the speed of light or market saturation, for example).

The existence of a limit changes the exponential curve to an S-shaped curve, also known as a logistic or Pearl curve. Here the rate of growth slows as the limiting value, also known as the asymptote or niche, is approached. This curve is characteristic of biological growth, from birth to maturity. It also effectively describes the substitution of one technology for another (such as jet aircraft for propeller aircraft) or one commercial product for another (such as color for black-and-white television). Remarkably, many phenomena exhibit an S-shaped behavior, ranging from creativity over the human life span (Einstein's publications and Mozart's compositions) to explorations of the Western hemisphere, U.S. AIDS deaths as a fraction of all deaths, U.S. oil discoveries, and global air traffic growth (Modis, 1992). Often, growth consists of a sequence of S-shaped curves. For example, transportation speed growth may be represented as a sequence of successive substitutions, representing the horse, train, automobile, aircraft, missile, and spacecraft.

CYCLIC PHENOMENA. Cycles comprise another common type of long-term trend. During the 1920s, the Russian economist N. D. Kondratieff hypothesized that Western societies experience a pattern of long waves, each phased cycle characterized by recession-depression-revival-prosperity. The length of these cycles has averaged about fifty-six years, with peaks in the U.S. occurring in 1800, 1856, 1916, 1969, and forecast next around 2024. Interestingly, each cycle is dominated by an overarching technology—railroads, steel, oil, and information technology, respectively—and a primary form of energy. As a fraction of all forms of energy consumed globally, coal reached its peak in 1920, oil in

1980, with gas now moving to claim the lead. Technological innovations tend to cluster at certain time points and these have been found to correlate with the same cycles. For example, the depth of the Great Depression was followed by a fifteen-year technological explosion that brought forth radar, jet engines, atomic power, computers, and television, each creating an important new industry (Marchetti, 1980). All major U.S. wars from the American Revolution on, with the exception of Korea, also fit this pattern: two wars per cycle. (A cycle is equivalent to two generations.) The evolution of the corporate organization similarly fits this cyclic pattern: from owner-manager to hierarchy, division, matrix, and now network linkage. (In a matrix organization each participant is assigned simultaneously to a functional department and a project team that crosses functional lines.)

MODELS. In science, models are used in two distinct roles: to explain a phenomenon and to predict future behavior. Their effectiveness varies: in celestial mechanics, both explanatory and predictive capability are high; in evolutionary biology, explanatory capability is high and predictive capability low; in quantum mechanics, predictive capability is high and explanatory capability low; in economics, both explanatory and predictive capability are low (Casti, 1990). We have thus arrived at a profound realization: better understanding of a system does not necessarily mean better ability to forecast its future behavior. Models are abstractions or idealizations; a complex system is represented by a simpler one with fewer variables. For example, the widely debated Limits to Growth model of the world (see Meadows, 1992) used five variables: population, industrial production, agricultural production, natural resources, and pollution. It does not take many variables to create a multitude of relationships. For example, a system consisting of only three elements—A, B, and C—has at least forty-nine possible interactions, such as A-B, A-A, and BC-ABC, among its subsystems. A system containing ten elements has over a million possible different interactions among its subsystems. The Limits to Growth model determined the relationships among its elements—that is, the system structure—from data for the period 1900 to 1970 and then computed the behavior of the five variables with that structure of several hundred equations out to the year 2100. This type of model is known as a system dynamics model.

A useful simple tool is the structural model. It highlights the geometric or qualitative, rather than the algebraic or quantitative, features of a system. It is often represented by points (or nodes) and connecting lines (or arcs) that define a graph. If an ordering or direction is specified for each connecting line, the graph becomes a directed graph, or digraph. A very important aspect of systems highlighted by digraphs are feedback loops or cycles. A typical complex system has many such cycles—both damping and deviation-amplifying—and they are crucial to an understanding of the system behavior.

Among the structural models useful in forecasting are static types such as relevance trees and dynamic types such as KSIM (Martino, 1983).

DELPHI. Polling as a basis for forecasting is a mainstay for political campaigns and market research. The use of experts by corporations and other organizations to forecast technological developments is also common. Delphi is the name of a structured communication process that is often used as a forecasting tool when more analytic approaches fail (Linstone and Turoff, 1975). It allows a group of individuals to act as a kind of expert panel. Two important features of Delphi are its iterative nature (that is, there are at least two rounds of questioning) and the mutual anonymity of its participants in the interactions. The participants are not brought together face-to-face. Rather, a questionnaire is supplied to each and returned to the monitor upon completion. Typically, it contains a list of possible future developments for which the respondents indicate the degree of feasibility and likely timing. The responses are tabulated by the monitor and provided together with a second-round questionnaire to each participant. The respondents thus only know the distribution of first-round responses, but not which person is associated with a particular response. The rounds with feedback are continued until the distribution of responses stabilizes—that is, exhibits little change between rounds. It is common, but by no means inevitable, to have a convergence of views as the rounds proceed.

MULTIPLE PERSPECTIVES. The methods described so far have been based on agreement, observations, or (past) data, and on models. Moving from strictly technological systems to complex human or social systems, forecasting must encompass modes of inquiry that embrace paradigms beyond those of science. Just as each human eye sees a slightly different image, so multiple perspectives view the same system through different lenses. Just as the brain combines the images from the eyes to yield depth perception, so the interactions among the perspectives yield deeper insights than can be obtained by any one perspective. The three types are: the technical or analytic, the organizational or institutional, and the personal or individual (Linstone, 1984; Linstone and Mitroff, 1994). The ethical basis for each type is different: rationality or logic is characteristic for the technical-analytic perspective, justice and fairness are associated with the organizational-institutional world

view, and morality relates to the personal-individual angle of vision. Western secular culture may itself be described in terms of science, democracy, and individualism, respectively reflecting the three types of perspective. One revelation with multiple perspectives is the importance of who is making the forecast, not merely of what is being forecast.

Limitations of Forecasting

Forecasting the behavior of complex systems is subject to avoidable errors, unavoidable uncertainties, and the human tendency to discount distant time and space. For example, the assumptions underlying a forecast are far more critical than the sophistication of the model. A simple model with good assumptions is superior to a complex model with inappropriate assumptions.

Better understanding of a system

does not necessarily mean better ability

to forecast its future behavior.

Another shortcoming in forecasting involves the misperception of probability. It is fallacious to assume that improbable events will not occur in the forecast period. Improbability does not mean impossibility. The increasingly crowded world of the next century will experience a growing number of industrial catastrophes. They often entail a series of highly unlikely contributing factors that conjointly represent an extremely low probability of occurrence, but pose very severe consequences. This was the case with Three Mile Island, Bhopal, and the *Exxon Valdez* oil spill (Linstone and Mitroff, 1994). To contend with such occurrences, crisis management must become a central concern.

Complex systems may at times impose inherent unpredictability. Systems once thought to behave in an orderly fashion suddenly may shift to chaotic or unstable behavior. This means that systems appearing to be disorderly may have an underlying order that gives even chaos some level of predictability (Gordon and Greenspan, 1988).

Finally, human beings often look at the future through the wrong end of a telescope—that is, the distant object seems smaller than it actually is. Thus a future crisis may be discounted relative to near-term problems (Linstone and Mitroff, 1994). The reason why the economy tends to be emphasized by business forecasters more than is the environment is that economic costs are seen in near-term job losses, while environmental impacts are long-term. In most businesses short-term considerations prevail over long-term issues and strategies. The same phenomenon occurs in physical space. It is often labeled the NIMBY syndrome, short for "not in my back yard." Santa Barbara residents are concerned about oil drilling in the Santa Barbara Channel, but not in distant Alaska or the Gulf of Mexico. The concern for "me-now" at the expense of more distant space and time is a serious obstacle to effective planning in a world in which the population and technology explosions are dramatically shrinking Earth in space-time.

[See also Agents of Change; Change; Continuity and Discontinuity; Economic Cycles: Models and Simulations; Forecasting Methods; Laws, Evolution of; Multifold Trend; Pacesetter Governments; Planning; Public Policy Change; Record Setting; Scanning; Scenarios; Social Controls; Social Indicators; Strategic Planning; Surveys; Technology Forecasting and Assessment.]

BIBLIOGRAPHY

Casti, J. *Searching for Certainty.* New York: William Morrow, 1990.

Gordon, Theodore J., and Greenspan, Donald. "Chaos and Fractals: New Tools for Technological and Social Forecasting." *Technological Forecasting and Social Change* 34 (1988): 1–25.

Linstone, Harold A. *Multiple Perspectives for Decision Making.* New York: North-Holland, 1984.

Linstone, Harold A., with Ian I. Mitroff. *The Challenge of the 21st Century.* Albany, NY: State University of New York Press, 1994.

Linstone, Harold A., and Turoff, M. *The Delphi Method.* Reading, MA: Addison-Wesley, 1975.

Marchetti, C. "Society as a Learning System: Discovery, Invention, and Innovation Cycles Revisited." *Technological Forecasting and Social Change* 18 (1980): 267–282.

Martino, Joseph P. *Technological Forecasting for Decision Making.* New York: North-Holland, 1983.

Meadows, Dennis, et al. *The Limits to Growth.* New York: Universe Books, 1972; revised, 1992.

Modis, T. *Predictions.* New York: Simon & Schuster, 1992.

— HAROLD A. LINSTONE

U

UNEMPLOYMENT

Unemployment is one of the most important questions confronting the United States. It is at the heart of the social contract between a state and its citizens, and is a major determinant of social and political stability. In 1992 an American president lost an election largely because of being identified with a deteriorating employment situation.

The importance of unemployment to the individual also is great. Individuals without paid employment become adrift in a society where one's sense of dignity and worth is closely related to making a living.

The impact of unemployment reaches far beyond those counted as officially unemployed, a number that reflects a monthly finding or an annual average. The number of unemployed during a calendar year is generally two to three times greater than the reported monthly average. For example, during 1991, 21.3 million persons were unemployed at some time during the year, a figure over two and a half times the annual average unemployment level of 8.4 million persons.

The significance of joblessness is magnified when one considers the impact on the well-being of other family members. Fear and anxiety regarding unemployment affects millions of Americans and their families. Confronting the future with hope and fulfilling one's obligations is very hard if one believes that his or her livelihood is in danger. Considered in this manner, unemployment is more than just a personal burden, it cuts at the social fabric and puts the entire society on edge.

Persons classified as unemployed must "not have worked during the reference week of the survey, must have actively sought work sometime during the four weeks prior to the survey, and must be currently available to take a suitable job." In addition, those who are not looking for work, but are either on temporary layoff or have a new job to which they are supposed to report in the very near future are classified as unemployed. The reference that most Americans are familiar with, the unemployment rate, is calculated by assessing the number of unemployed in proportion to the total labor force.

Official unemployment rates are aggregate rates that do not reflect the realities among different groups and areas of the country. Rates for black workers, for example, are more than twice those of white workers, a disparity that continues to grow larger.

Criticism of the official measure of unemployment has prompted proposals for alternative measurement concepts. Official measures have been challenged as understating or exaggerating the severity of the problem.

Official unemployment rates are aggregate rates

that do not reflect the realities

among different groups and areas of the country.

The battle becomes especially intense at times of economic recession or during major election years. Attempting to put this matter to rest, Commissioner Julius Shiskin, while at the Bureau of Labor Statistics, developed some forty-two to forty-seven measures to provide a "range of unemployment rates based on varying definitions of unemployment and the labor force." These measures are now included in monthly reports of the Bureau of Labor Statistics. Arguing that there was no one single correct measure of unemployment, Shiskin sought to defuse attacks against the integrity of official data. Print and media journalism now incorporate aspects of this approach by expanding reports on official unemployment to include references to involuntary part-time unemployment and to "discouraged workers." Although this approach represents a significant conceptual advance, it still has not fully put the matter to rest. Most likely these issues will continue to be disputed, since opposing views often reflect competing political and economic interests.

Modern industrialized market economies became committed, in varying ways, to essentially Keynesian goals of full employment and economic fine tuning, usually stated in terms of less unemployment and inflation. A major conflict involves the unemployment/inflation tradeoff issue. It is a matter of considerable debate as to precisely how much inflation is tolerable as the price for lower unemployment.

In the past twenty years there has been a declining belief in the effectiveness of fine-tuning the economy. Consequently a major determinant of economic policy has become the nonaccelerating inflation rate of unemployment, or NAIRU. This rate is thought to set the limits of unemployment reduction. When it is surpassed, the result is unacceptably high rates of inflation.

Debate swirls around the precise level of NAIRU. It is clear that the rate of "tolerable and acceptable unemployment" has risen significantly during the last thirty years. The 3 percent goal of the Kennedy administration has changed to between 5 and 7 percent. Prior to the 1989 recession, there was concern that unemployment had dropped to a dangerously low 5.3 percent level, which was thought likely to lead to a resurgence of inflation.

The dominance of the NAIRU orientation reflects a significant lessening of the American commitment to the goal of full employment, to which the nation has been committed by the Employment Act of 1946, and the Full Employment and Balanced Growth Act of 1979. The concept of full employment usually is left out of the contemporary public policy debate, because it is generally held that such a state is unachievable.

The reality of modern America is that higher proportions of the population are both employed and unemployed. Higher rates of unemployment have occurred at the same time that the labor force participation rate and the employment/population ratio rose to historically high levels—66.5 and 63.0 percent respectively—during the last prerecession period in 1989. This demonstrates that both employment and unemployment can rise at the same time.

This seeming contradiction is more understandable at present as revolutionary changes in labor force participation rates of women, older males, black males, and young people have occurred. Understanding the dynamics of social change in America is strongly linked to the changes that occurred in the labor market during the past few decades.

Higher unemployment is not unique to the American economy; it is also a pervasive problem throughout Western Europe. All national market economies have

Memories of unemployed men lined up at soup kitchens, such as this one in 1925, haunt Americans and influence thinking about employment and the economy. (Hulton-Deutsch Collection/Corbis)

developed alternative income maintenance and support a variety of programs commonly referred to as "safety nets." The formerly socialist nations of Eastern Europe also are now developing such systems. Wider availability and escalating costs of these benefits has become a source of great social and political conflict. Such safety nets have been assailed as the cause of declines in productivity, lower levels of economic growth, and the fiscal crisis that pervades the welfare state.

In the United States, concerns related to problems of unemployment are likely to dominate public policy decisions well into the next century. The declining quality of the work force's capabilities is tending to undermine the competitiveness of the United States in an increasingly global economy. This has led to proposals for more closely job-related educational curricula and more extensive vocational training.

Concern about a large, increasing underclass has generated support for more programs of job training, development, and placement. Recent inner-city riots are likely to create even greater pressure for a decisive response.

The recent recession severely impacted on white-collar occupations and bolstered fears that the quest for higher productivity is causing technological unemployment in the service sector.

The end of the Cold War has produced significant reductions in defense-related jobs. Plans to protect dislocated workers, industries, and local communities by providing support for conversion have been proposed.

Overall there is a resurgence of support for more public sector programs dealing with the development of human capital, job retraining, and public service employment. These proposals are, in part, responses to the problem of high unemployment. In the future it is likely that there will be greater governmental support for such programs, especially if excessive unemployment persists.

American society may be in the midst of yet another employment and unemployment crisis that goes beyond fluctuations of the current business cycle. The problem is that unemployment rates have remained at higher levels during the peak periods of recovery from each of the recessions of the last thirty years.

Employment opportunity demands are likely to remain at the center of political conflict. Satisfaction of these demands will require a rethinking of fundamental elements of the social contract related to employment and unemployment. New forms of intervention may be required to resolve the problem. Among the solutions put forward are proposals to reduce the length of the working life or work week, and to increase the duration of schooling and provide for earlier retirement. Such steps could ease some of the difficulties and tensions currently associated with unemployment, and make joblessness more acceptable and tolerable.

[See also Class and Underclass; Economic Cycles: Models and Simulations; Entitlement Programs; Public Assistance Programs; Unemployment Insurance, Workers' Compensation, Job Security; Unionism; Work Ethic; Workforce Redistribution.]

BIBLIOGRAPHY

Harvey, Philip. *Securing the Right to Employment: Social Welfare Policy and the Unemployed in the United States.* Princeton, N.J.: Princeton University Press, 1989.

Jaffee, A. J., and Stewart, Charles D. *Manpower Resources and Utilization: Principles of Working Force Analysis.* New York: Wiley, 1951.

National Commission on Employment and Unemployment Statistics. *Counting the Labor Force.* Washington, D.C.: U.S. Government Printing Office, 1979.

U.S. President's Committee to Appraise Employment and Unemployment Statistics. *Measuring Employment and Unemployment.* Washington, D.C.: U.S. Government Printing Office, 1962.

Weir, Margaret. *Politics and Jobs: The Boundaries of Employment Policy in the United States.* Princeton, N.J.: Princeton University Press, 1992.

− STANLEY MOSES

UNEMPLOYMENT INSURANCE, WORKER'S COMPENSATION, JOB SECURITY

Government will continue to play an important role in securing public assistance programs for workers in an increasingly global and capitalist economy. In the future, many governments (1) will not consider a full employment strategy as a viable labor option and (2) will continue to extend targeted social support programs despite economic and fiscal policies based on concern about deficit spending.

In the twenty-first century, social support programs to increase employment opportunities and access to them necessitate extending the scope and level of existing program provisions while others require significant new departures. In industrialized countries, the impetus toward a global economy with a premium on high wages and well-trained, highly motivated, and empowered workers rests on a social contract between government and citizens and between labor and management that strives to enhance productivity. This goal is tempered by needs to attend to environmental and Third World quality-of-life concerns. Providing workers with more training and security and securing a more flexible and productive workforce would require a broad set of national level workplace policies. In the economic sphere of citizens' lives, these policies would stress broad social interests rather than individual self-interest and acquisitiveness such as is characteristic of unfettered capitalism. Furthermore, they would view government-support programs more as a positive force for social betterment rather than a drain on productivity. Finally, these policies would require individual responsibility and commitment to continued education and training to meet employment opportunities introduced by increasing rates of change. In countries like the United States, the current policy emphasis on enforcing obligations to work would be replaced by one ensuring equal employment opportunities.

Job Security and Unemployment Compensation

The unemployment insurance program in the United States provides time-limited cash benefits to regularly employed members of the labor force who become involuntarily unemployed but are able and willing to accept suitable employment. One policy to enhance job security and high wages in a global economy involves transforming unemployment compensation from a short-term subsidy for unemployed workers to a comprehensive system of lifetime learning and retraining to help assure employability.

One policy to enhance job security in a global economy involves transforming unemployment compensation to a comprehensive system of lifetime learning and retraining.

Faced by the increased mobility of jobs in a global economy, benefits limited to between thirteen and twenty-six weeks (with episodic extensions) afford little job security and provide insufficient time for acquiring new sets of job skills. Something more needs to be done to keep workers and businesses productive.

One employment insurance approach would create a Career Opportunity Card providing access to retraining for the jobless, displaced, and low-wage workers. A Career Opportunity Card would be used as a voucher and carried as a wallet card similar to health insurance cards. Career Opportunity Cards could be used to purchase career-related education and training from public or private sources of the worker's choice. Individuals faced by an imminent economic security threat, such as being laid off, being able to find only part-time work, or working full-time at less than 150 percent of the poverty wage, could use this card to purchase specified amounts of education and training—perhaps up to as much as the approximate cost of one year of community college training. Workers would have to spend the money allotted within a specified time—five years, for example.

Educational or training institutes participating in the Career Opportunity program would be required to submit performance information to a system operated in provinces, states, or other political subdivisions. This system would provide workers with access to rates of completion, placement, and starting wages amassed by prior purchasers of training from various vendors. Such information would inform individual workers about vendor merits and regulating bodies about vendor performance.

In addition to a retraining allowance, the Career Opportunity Card could also make provision for relocation stipends. In many instances the range of suggested benefits might eliminate the need for severance pay. Relocation stipends could be realized as a tax deduction for individuals or as a tax subsidy to employers. To minimize in-house bureaucracy, such a venture could be outsourced to companies experienced in the credit or debit card business. Another solution would encourage or require employers to provide workers with yearly opportunities to upgrade their skills and otherwise support on-the-job training initiatives. Individual and corporate tax deductions already are available to defray the expenses of participation in or sponsorship of job training opportunities.

An Apprenticeship Training Program guaranteeing young persons the opportunity to build marketable competency through high school and college courses would require a more extensive change in U.S. labor policy. Programs in other industrialized nations, like Germany, are considered models. Such a universal program would increase job security. An Apprenticeship Training Program could be extended into a National or Public Service Program linking high school or college graduates to short term stints in skills-related jobs in the public and private sectors.

Worker's Compensation and Twenty-Four-Hour Coverage

Escalating health care costs influence an employer's decision to relocate business in less expensive regions of the country and indirectly contribute to the erosion of job security. To control health care costs, WC programs will increasingly rely on managed health care plans, including procedures for certification of managed care entities, peer review, and dispute resolution; prohibitions against certain medical provider billing practices; and establishment of capped medical fee schedules.

Two principles affecting federal-state regulatory relationships are likely to remain intact: the exclusive remedy provision, and exemption from the Employee Retirement Income Security Act (ERISA). With some degree of national oversight, states will retain their primary regulatory functions and employers will retain their immunity from suit except in certain circumstances.

The Worker's Compensation (WC) program in the United States provides cash benefits and medical care to workers injured in connection with their jobs, and survivor benefits to dependents of workers whose death results from a work-related accident. The medical care component of WC deserves special attention in light of prospects for twenty-four-hour coverage, i.e., combinations of traditional health insurance and WC insurance dissolving occupational and nonoccupational boundaries currently existing between the two coverages. Twenty-four-hour coverage is likely to become more the norm than the exception.

Initial variants of twenty-four-hour coverage will be limited. Insurers integrating management of an employer's WC and group health insurance claims agree to coordinate claims settlement and obviate duplicate claims. A *twenty-four-hour disability coverage package* would provide disability benefits for employee injuries and diseases limited to work-related injuries and diseases only. This package has the greatest potential for medical cost savings and is the most likely initial approach. A *twenty-four-hour medical coverage package* would provide, in a single policy, medical benefits for employee injuries and diseases whether work-related or not; however, disability benefits would be provided only for work-related injuries and diseases. A *twenty-four-hour accident coverage package* would provide medical and disability benefits for all injuries, but only work-related diseases would be covered. A *twenty-four-hour disease coverage package* would provide medical and disability benefits for all diseases, but cover only work-related injuries. (This particular package would reduce the considerable litigation bound to arise over causation of certain diseases.) Finally, a *twenty-four-hour medical and disability package* would provide an all-inclusive (hence, most expensive) solution, providing medical and disability benefits for all diseases and injuries.

[See also Entitlement Programs; Insurance; Public Assistance Programs; Public Assistance Programs: Social Security; Unemployment.]

BIBLIOGRAPHY

Block, Fred. "Rethinking the Political Economy of the Welfare State." In Fred Block, Richard A. Cloward, Barbara Ehrenreich, and Frances Fox Piven, eds. *The Mean Season: The Attack on the Welfare State.* New York: Pantheon Books, 1987.

Caputo, Richard K. *Welfare and Freedom II: The Role of the Federal Government, 1941–1980.* Lanham, MD: University Press of America, 1994.

Kuttner, Robert. "Labor Policy." In Mark Green, ed. *Changing America: Blueprints for the New Administration.* New York: Newmarket Press, 1992.

Marshall, Will, and Schram, Martin, eds. *Mandate for Change.* New York: Berkley Books, 1993.

Weir, Margaret. *Politics and Jobs: The Boundaries of Employment Policy in the United States.* Princeton, NJ: Princeton University Press, 1992.

— RICHARD K. CAPUTO

UNIONISM

The American labor movement is the largest in the world, with nearly 16.5 million members and 87 major unions, but its membership has slipped from 36 percent of the total work force in 1945 to only 16 percent in 1995. To reach its 1945 level again, the movement would have to recruit over 37 million new members. Reeling from a loss of one million members in the 1980s, the labor movement may see its 11 percent position in the private sector fall to 7 percent or lower by 2000 A.D., approaching the level of the movement at its inception in the nineteenth century. In some countries nearly 90 percent of all workers belong to unions. In the Netherlands even soldiers have been unionized since 1967, but labor's prospects in the United States appear bleak, at least in the private sector. Despite any such setback, labor's 38 percent stronghold in the public sector could remain constant or suffer only slight losses in the years immediately ahead, so vital is union protection to many government employees.

Many well-intentioned futurists dismiss the potential role of labor unions. They expect labor's impact to be increasingly less significant in our information-based society.

Reasons for labor's forty-year-long decline in the United States are abundantly clear and varied. Employers in no other industrial nation, for example, match those in America in their bitter opposition to unionism. Nor have lawmakers in any other advanced nation created as many obstacles and handicaps to the labor movement. Likewise, nowhere else in the industrial world do the media ignore or trash labor so relentlessly as is regularly done here. Little wonder, accordingly, that labor's prime weapon, the strike, has fallen into disuse (1993 recorded only 35 major strikes, down from 424 in the last peak year of 1974).

Unionists remind would-be pallbearers that a trend is not a law. They take heart from the superior earning power of union members ($547 per week versus $413 for nonunion counterparts), as they believe this assures future recruitment gains. They are cheered by the pro-labor attitudes of women workers, the fastest-growing bloc in organized labor. They are also hopeful that the

Clinton administration can constrain the antiunion animus of certain employers, improve the Labor Relations Board's role, revise oppressive federal labor laws, and give labor a public relations boost that organizers can turn to their advantage. They make much of the rise to power of pragmatic innovators who are replacing shortsighted, hidebound traditionalists among leaders of the labor movement. Above all, labor's optimists hail the growing use of a novel culture of organizational creativity.

Unionists warn that strong unions are a vital

counterbalance to the corporate drive to maximize

profits at the expense of the well-being of society.

Skeptics fret that these reforms may be too little too late. They doubt if labor can overcome the race, gender, craft, and class rifts that undermine the labor force's solidarity to such an extent that it can barely be termed a "movement." They see labor weakened by its inability to decide between continued dependence on the Democratic Party or on a daring new type of "fusion" third party. They doubt that employers will soon believe researchers who conclude that, on average, unionism is associated with increased productivity, rather than the commonly perceived reverse. And they suspect that a shift from proletariat to salariat, with a concomitant change in the psychology of employees, fatally undermines labor's recovery chances.

In rebuttal, union strategists emphasize polling data that find Americans unhappy with their jobs, increasingly distrustful of big business, and increasingly supportive of unions. Many new members are expected from among the many angry employees whose average earnings have actually dropped from $315 a week in 1972 to only $256 in 1994 (in adjusted dollars), for a loss of 19 percent. Much is made of the forecast that abuses by corporations are so widespread, so diverse, so relentlessly growing that some form of union revival will inevitably evolve. Unionists urge onlookers to consider what the United States would be like if there were no labor movement and the forces of corporatism were allowed totally unbridled access to the centers of political power. They warn that strong unions are a vital counterbalance to the corporate drive to maximize profits at the expense of the well-being of society-at-large.

Much more, in short, than the survival of the largest social movement in America hinges on labor's fate. The union movement is an indispensable proponent of worker interests. It is a unique forum for ideas and a critical component in the liberal coalition. Above all, it serves as an ideological counterweight to business's preference for market supremacy almost regardless of human cost.

Unions are likely to change radically in the years ahead—more mergers of unions, more money spent on organizing, more sophisticated use of telecommunications, more women and nonwhite leaders. Labor's life-and-death struggle for rebirth, revitalization, and renewal will surely have a significant impact on the character and quality of our evolving information society. Long identified with blue-collar workers, organizational efforts increasingly will focus anew on public sector employees and on professionals—just as has been done in most other postindustrial societies.

[See also *Information Society; Institutions, Confidence In; Liberalism, Political; Unemployment; Work; Work Ethic.*]

BIBLIOGRAPHY

Adler, Glenn, and Suarez, Doris, eds. *Unions' Voices: Labor's Responses to Crisis.* Albany, NY: State University of New York Press, 1993.

Bluestone, Barry, and Bluestone, Irving. *Negotiating the Future: A Labor Perspective on American Business.* New York: Basic Books, 1992.

Freeman, Richard B., and Medoff, James L. *What Do Unions Do?* New York: Basic Books, 1984.

Geoghegan, Thomas. *Which Side Are You On? Trying to Be for Labor When It's Flat on Its Back.* New York: Plume, 1992.

Goldfield, Michael. *The Decline of Organized Labor in the United States.* Chicago: University of Chicago Press, 1987.

Puette, William J. *Through Jaundiced Eyes: How the Media View Organized Labor.* Ithaca, NY: ILR Press, 1992.

Shostak, Arthur B. *For Labor's Sake: Gains and Pains as Told by 28 Creative Inside Reformers.* Lanham, MD: University Press of America, 1995.

———. *Robust Unionism: Innovations in the Labor Movement.* Ithaca, NY: ILR Press, 1991.

— ARTHUR B. SHOSTAK

UNITED STATES

The greatest change of the first quarter of the twenty-first century will be the reduction of the United States from the world's only superpower after the Cold War to merely one of several regional great powers. The decay of Cold War alliances like the North Atlantic Treaty Organization (NATO), combined with the continuing fiscal crisis of the American government, will ensure the withdrawal of most U.S. forces from overseas deployments. The removal of most American ground forces and supplies from Europe will make it logistically impossible for the United States to continue to play its post-Gulf War role in the Middle East as the dominant power. Following the reunification of Korea under the auspices of the South Korean regime, U.S. forces will

United StatesU

be removed from both Korea and Japan, except in the unlikely event of a full-fledged cold war with either China or Japan.

As the United States ends its forward deployments in Europe, the Middle East, and Asia, American strategists will devote more attention to defense within the North American quartersphere. Defending the American homeland will become a priority as advanced missile technology proliferates among potentially hostile countries. The Anti-Ballistic Missile Treaty will be amended or scrapped in order to permit ground-based, and eventually space-based, missile defenses. At the low-tech end of the military spectrum, U.S. expeditionary forces will intervene occasionally in Caribbean and Central American countries, possibly including Mexico, where population growth outpaces economic progress and political reform. To the north, the breakup of Canada, if it occurs, would cause only minor security dilemmas and might add several new states to the Union.

The importance of foreign commercial considerations in U.S. diplomacy and domestic politics alike will continue to grow. Hopes that liberalization of world trade by means of free trade agreements such as NAFTA, APEC, and GATT—respectively, the North American Free Trade Agreement, the Atlantic Provinces Economic Council, and the General Agreement on Tariffs and Trade—would produce income gains for ordinary Americans will not materialize. Mass consumer markets will fail to take hold in the impoverished, overpopulated, oligarchic societies south of the Rio Grande. Japan and China will continue to pursue mercantilist policies, protecting their domestic markets while targeting U.S. consumers (the Chinese merchandise trade surplus with the United States will surpass the Japanese around the year 2000). In contrast with the Pacific trade wars, U.S. trade relations with the European Union, expanded to include most of the former Soviet bloc, will be relatively harmonious and could lead to a transatlantic free trade zone that would be the richest in the world in per capita terms. The dollar will cease to be the world's reserve currency; global financial instability will be reduced, though, as many small countries tie their currencies to the dollar, the yen, or the mark.

The most significant change in American domestic politics in the early twenty-first century will be immigration restriction. Strict limits on legal immigration will accompany a crackdown on illegal immigration, as the era of mass migration from Latin America and Asia to the United States is brought to a close. The descendants of the late twentieth century's new immigrants will rapidly assimilate to American culture. High rates of intermarriage among Hispanics, Asians, and whites will promote the gradual formation of a mixed-race ma-

jority. The end of mass immigration will open up job opportunities for working-class black Americans; the hereditary black underclass, however, will be isolated and harshly treated in a newly conservative political climate. Popular support for the repeal of affirmative action will grow, even as intermarriage undermines the accuracy of racial categories.

Despite the slow progress of racial integration, economic polarization in the United States will grow more extreme. With organized labor weaker than ever, business interests will find little opposition to its agenda of lowering wages, eliminating benefits, and replacing tenured with contingent employees. The downwardly mobile middle class will compete for poorly paid service-sector jobs with former blue-collar workers and service-sector workers whose vocations have been eliminated by automation or expatriation. The result will be the formation of suburban white and Hispanic underclasses dwarfing the urban black underclass produced by the mechanization of Southern agriculture in the 1920s and 1930s. These desperate new underclasses will become breeding grounds of violent criminals, linked to new international mafias—Latin American, East Asian, Russian.

The greatest challenge of the first quarter of the twenty-first century will be the reduction of the United States from the world's only superpower after the Cold War to merely one of several regional great powers.

Many affluent families will move to the safer and more pleasant interior of the country and take advantage of telecommuting. Well-to-do Americans who remain in the metropolitan regions of the coastal states will retreat into enclave communities protected by private police forces. Home security innovations will be the major factor in the evolution of the "smart" or computer-controlled house. The greatest innovation in daily life, however, will be inspired by health technology, as the affluent pay for the refitting of bathrooms as miniature medical offices with diagnostic equipment linked to doctors and hospitals.

The growing polarization of American society between almost exclusively white haves and have-nots of all races will not translate directly into political conflict. For one thing, racial quotas, if they survive, will keep whites, blacks, Hispanics, and Asians bitterly divided.

Furthermore, the failure of sweeping campaign finance reform will permit a small number of wealthy individuals and corporations to continue to dominate U.S. politics. Finally, the Senate, skewed toward the thinly populated interior states and representing an ever-diminishing (and mostly white) fraction of the public, will stymie federal efforts to improve the conditions of the non-white majorities in California, Texas, New York, and Florida. The affluent will seek to shift the costs of government to wage-earning Americans, by means of regressive consumption taxes, user fees, and privatization of public services. The failure of the political system to respond to the growing inequality will produce a series of antisystemic, populist, and nationalist movements, each more radical than the last. Though none will succeed in the first quarter of the twenty-first century, these movements will produce turbulence in national politics.

The aging of the American population, accelerated by immigration restriction, will result in a society that is relatively conservative on social and moral issues. The sexual revolution and the liberalization of the mass media will not be reversed, however, and widespread use of convenient abortifacients and implanted contraceptives will come to be accepted. Rudimentary forms of genetic engineering will be available to the wealthy, although opposition from religious voters will prevent their inclusion in government-funded health programs. The growing longevity of Americans will produce four- or five-generation families and create social pressure for middle-aged people, rather than the state, to provide care for aged parents. Voluntary euthanasia of the terminally ill elderly will become widely accepted, despite religious objections.

The number of secular Americans will increase, particularly among the more educated and affluent classes. The mainline Protestant churches will continue to lose adherents; their place will be taken by the Baptist church, which, like the Methodist and Presbyterian churches before it, will become more moderate in its views as its members rise in the social scale. Revivalism and fundamentalism will be taken up by new pentecostal and evangelical movements, with support among ex-Catholic Hispanics in particular. American Catholicism will decline, as the Catholic Church remains antiliberal and becomes increasingly identified with the Third World, especially Africa. Liberal Judaism will wither, as American Jews become either wholly secular or join Orthodox renewal movements. Muslims will replace Jews as the largest religious minority in the United States. The early twenty-first century will see an "Americanization" of Islam, like the previous Americanization of immigrant-community Catholicism, Lutheranism, and Judaism. The appeal of New Age and Asian religions will remain limited.

Despite its isolationism, the United States of the early twenty-first century will be less parochial in many ways, thanks to global TV and the evolution of a polycentric global popular culture. Soccer will eventually replace football as the national pastime as in most other countries. The cultural influence of East Asia will grow, at first in the form of popular culture, e.g., Japanese animation and science fiction. Growing numbers of American intellectuals dissatisfied with their inegalitarian, individualistic society will become interested in the newly self-assertive Confucian societies of East Asia, in the way that twentieth-century American intellectuals looked to Swedish social democrats and Russian communists for inspiration.

Japan and the United States rather than Europe will lead the world in the artistic renaissance of the third millennium, developing entirely new forms of visual art, music, and drama based on computer technology and virtual reality to replace the outmoded forms of early modern Europe like easel paintings and orchestral compositions. These new arts will be pioneered by the entertainment industry rather than by fine artists; the gap that opened in the twentieth century between popular art and the esoteric avant-garde will be reduced, in one of the most encouraging developments of the new era.

[See also Capitalism; Democracy; Development: Western Perspective; Latin America; Population Growth: United States; Social Change: United States.]

BIBLIOGRAPHY

Barney, Gerald O. *The Global 2000 Report to the President: Entering the 21st Century.* Washington DC: U.S. Government Printing Office, 1981.

Boyer, William H. *America's Future: Transition to the 21st Century.* Sisters, OR: New Politics Press, 1984.

Carnevale, Anthony Patrick. *America and the New Economy.* Washington DC: U.S. Department of Labor, 1991.

Cetron, Marvin, and Davies, Owen. *American Renaissance: Our Life at the Turn of the 21st Century.* New York: St. Martin's Press, 1989.

Dudley, William, and Zumke, Bonnie. *America's Future: Opposing Viewpoints.* San Diego: Greenhaven Press, 1990.

Kennedy, Paul. *Preparing for the 21st Century.* New York: Random House, 1993.

Lapham, Lewis. *Money and Class in America.* New York: Grove Press, 1989.

Lind, Michael. *The Next American Nation: The New Nationalism and the Fourth American Revolution.* New York: Free Press, 1995.

Mischel, Lawrence, and Bernstein, Jared. *The State of Working America, 1992–1993.* Washington, DC: Economic Policy Institute, 1992.

Pinsky, Mark, and Green, Mark. *America's Transition: Blueprints for the 1990s.* New York: Democracy Project, 1991.

Strobel, Frederick. *Upward Dreams, Downward Mobility: The Economic Decline of the American Middle Class.* Lanham, MD: Rowman and Littlefield, 1993.

Thurow, Lester. *Head to Head: The Coming Economic Battle Among Japan, Europe and America.* New York, Warner Books, 1992.

Vlahos, Michael. *Thinking About World Change.* Washington, DC: U.S. Department of State, 1990

Wolfgang, Marvin, and Lambert, Richard D. *The Future Society: Aspects of America in the Year 2000.* Cambridge, MA: American Academy of Political and Social Science, 1983.

— MICHAEL LIND

URBAN TRANSIT

Transit is defined by the American Public Transit Association as "all multiple-occupancy-vehicle passenger services of a local and regional nature provided for general public use." Different types of transit service are called modes. *Road modes* include motorbus, trolleybus, vanpool, jitney, and demand response (dial-a-ride). *Rail modes* include heavy rail, light rail (streetcars), commuter rail, automated guideway (people movers), inclined plane, cable car, and aerial tramway. *Water modes* include ferryboats.

All of these are nineteenth-century inventions, with the exception of the motorbus, which was introduced in 1905. Adding automation to buses or trains (automated guideway systems, for example), does not significantly change the service characteristics of nineteenth-century transit modes.

At the beginning of the nineteenth century, all cities were essentially walking cities. The introduction of street railways and interurbans (regional rail systems) allowed cities to expand from the central industrial-commercial cores along rail corridors, creating the star-shaped city of the late nineteenth and early twentieth century.

Rail Transit

Heavy rail and commuter rail vehicles, typically holding 150 people, provide service to people with similar origins and destinations along narrow corridors. Rail transit is often built as subway or elevated lines to avoid street congestion with closely spaced stations for easy accessibility. Outlying areas with fewer stations speed

Rail systems like this bullet train in Japan have reached speeds up to 700 miles per hour. Speedy commuter trains alter exurban development by connecting affordable land to urban employment centers hundreds of miles away. (UPI/Corbis-Bettmann)

up trips but reduce access. Designed to carry large numbers of people, trains are fully utilized for only twenty peak-hours per week. During offpeak hours, they run at long intervals (necessitating long waits for passengers), and may not run at all during the night. Rail systems are inflexible and not easily modified to serve major new developments.

"Modernizing" trains—mono- rather than dual-rails, or different running gear such as magnetic levitation, or rubber as opposed to steel wheels—fundamentally changes the character of the service. Construction, recently costing $250 to $300 million per mile, is very expensive. Cities can afford no more than a few miles of heavy rail—crowded during peak hours, underused with poor service offpeak, and with poor flexibility. To overcome congestion, some light rail trains have sensors enabling them to change traffic lights, assuring them of the right-of-way at all intersections.

Buses

Rail systems during the early twentieth century ran into trouble due to high levels of indebtedness, increasing operating costs, and eventually declining ridership as more people moved into the areas between the rail lines. Buses became competitive because they were cheaper to buy and had much lower capital costs. They used public roads paid for by the taxpayer, unlike rail systems that had to pay for their own roadbeds. They were flexible—one breakdown did not shut down the entire line—and they could be rerouted to accommodate new developments.

Since the 1930s, buses have become public transit workhorses, serving double and even triple the number of passengers as rail. Buses provide a low quality of service; many stops make them highly accessible but also mean slow travel along each route. Furthermore, getting from one place to another often requires indirect routing with one or more changes of vehicle and the uncertainty of waits at each transfer point. Service is particularly poor in low-density areas and during offpeak hours.

Although more buses are being run on natural gas and other nonpolluting fuels, most are still smelly and dirty. With the increases in urban crime, riders often feel vulnerable both at stops and on the vehicles. Buses are also largely inaccessible to the physically disabled except at great expense by installing chairlifts.

Still, buses are likely to play a significant role in public transit well into the twenty-first century. Nonpolluting fuels, electronic control of traffic signals, electronic information boards at stops indicating the length of waits, and displays mapping the whole system are likely to be introduced to improve bus service. Auto-

matic vehicle tracking may improve transfer connections for some, but there are too many points of origin, connection, and destination with multiple dependencies to convenience everybody. More high-occupancy vehicle (HOV) lanes where buses share space with vans and carpools provide short-term improvement of bus service.

Automated people movers (APM), introduced over the last twenty years, are driverless buses (some carrying forty passengers per vehicle, some only ten) that are computer-operated on guideways. They serve as circulation systems in central cities and at airports around the world. APM service is essentially comparable to that of light rail systems, although there are separate guideways to avoid street congestion. These guideways also create considerable construction costs and may be visually unattractive. While providing excellent circulation service within contained areas of moderate to high density, APM service does not meet the needs of low-density urban areas.

Dispersed Cities and the Automobile

Despite all these transit options, the automobile has become the dominant mode of urban transportation in American cities. It is also rapidly taking over in the cities of wealthier countries worldwide (excluding the island cities of Hong Kong and Singapore). Metropolitan regions with moderate to low densities are growing, as central cities disperse their industry, commerce, and housing into "edge" cities and scattered miniurban complexes.

Today bustling metropolitan regions have thousands of trip origins and destinations. Only the automobile allows people to move flexibly throughout the region, twenty-four hours a day. Public transit, with its focus on the rush hour/home-to-work commute, does not easily accommodate to offshift work trips, picking up children at day care, going to school, theater, or sporting events, shopping, or visiting the doctor, friends, and family.

The result has been a dramatic drop in the use of transit. People turned to the automobile in large numbers after World War I when the land close to train stations became fully developed and they had to live further from transit stops. The auto met their needs, and even though the *numbers* of passengers riding public transit continued to grow until 1930, the *proportion* of trips made by public transit declined precipitously—from 98 percent of the trips in 1900 to about 20 percent in 1930. Today it ranges from 0.8 percent in Houston to 14 percent in New York City.

Public transit decline is worldwide. Europeans still use transit more than Americans, but the trend toward decentralized growth, reduction in urban density, and increased use of the automobile is similar.

That the automobile "caused" urban sprawl may be a myth. In fact, personal vehicles may merely have met demand patterns that already were in place. Automobiles clearly made possible the type of urban growth we see today—much growth on the periphery, little or no growth or even decline in the center city.

Metropolitan areas all over the world

need to solve the same problem to provide low-cost,

energy-efficient, environmentally sound

transportation to medium- and low-density areas.

While transit "experts" often speak of the "love affair with the automobile," they fail to recognize a forced marriage of convenience. Restricting auto use will not by itself improve mobility or access in cities, but it will certainly cause real hardship for many. For those who can drive, the auto meets virtually all our needs for mobility and access to the metropolitan region.

Unfortunately, the auto is also expensive to own and operate, causes an average of 48,000 deaths each year in the United States, is unavailable to many people (the poor, the young, the old, the disabled), takes up large amounts of urban space (for roads and parking), pollutes the air, is noisy, and is a major contributor to urban congestion.

Future of Transit

Whether transit or automobile, each mode serves a useful purpose, but each has serious limitations. No single mode, nor any combination of existing modes, can accommodate foreseeable needs of twenty-first-century cities—for resource conservation, improvement of urban land use, reduction of congestion and pollution, and to meet the mobility needs of an increasingly transit-dependent aging population. Metropolitan areas all over the world need to solve the same problem to provide low-cost, energy-efficient, environmentally sound transportation to medium- and low-density areas.

Personal Rapid Transit

Progress requires a change in thinking, even a change in the definition of public transit (multiple-occupancy vehicles) to include a new mode known as personal rapid transit (PRT) that meets the needs of twenty-first-

century people and societies. It has already been tested in France, Germany, Japan, and the United States.

PRT can be thought of as an automated taxi. Its small, driverless vehicles have seats for two to four people operating on a slim (1 meter by 1 meter) elevated guideway. They are electric, automatic, and move nonstop from the place you get on to the place you get off. Guideways can be built over existing streets and freeways, so the system does not require the acquisition of additional land. Guide-ways can also be placed at surface level or below ground.

Riders enter the system through stations spaced about two blocks apart in densely populated areas and about half a mile apart in lower-density areas. In each station, a rider punches his or her destination into a computer, enters a car, and then travels directly and quietly to the destination at speeds ranging from twenty to fifty miles per hour. All stations are on sidings off the main line, so there are no intervening stops and thus no delays.

A rider would share a vehicle *only* if traveling with friends, thus retaining an important virtue of private cars. The rider has all the advantages of the automobile, but without the necessity to drive, park, maintain, or insure it.

Today's computing technology allows thousands of PRT vehicles to be deployed in a network of small guideways to be available throughout the metropolitan region. They can be used not only to move people, but vehicles with the same chassis can be rigged to carry light freight and mail to depots located in warehouses, shopping centers, and post offices. Freight operations during nonpeak hours would help the system break even (or make a profit).

Public transportation need not be a dreaded or uncomfortable inconvenience forced on unhappy urban travelers. Properly designed, it can improve everybody's quality of life.

[See also Air Transport; Motor Vehicles; Motor Vehicles, Alternatively Powered; Personal Transport; Railways; Transportation.]

BIBLIOGRAPHY

Burke, Catherine. *Innovation and Public Policy: The Case of Personal Rapid Transit.* Lexington, MA: Lexington Books, D.C. Health, 1979.

Floyd, Thomas H., Jr. "Personalizing Public Transportation." *The Futurist* (November–December 1990): 29–33.

Meyer, John R.; Kain, John F.; and Wohl, Martin. *The Urban Transportation Problem.* Cambridge, MA: Harvard University Press, 1965.

Newman, Peter W. G., and Kenworthy, Jeffrey R. *Cities and Automobile Dependence: A Sourcebook.* Aldershot, U.K.: Gower Publishing, 1989.

1993 Transit Fact Book. Washington, DC: American Public Transit Association, 1993.

Technical Committee on Personal Rapid Transit of the Advanced Transit Association. "Personal Rapid Transit (PRT): Another Option for Urban Transit?" *Journal of Advanced Transportation* 22/3 (1988).

— CATHERINE G. BURKE

UTOPIAS

The word *utopia* was coined by the English humanist scholar Saint Thomas More in his book of the same title, first published in 1516. The two Greek words from which it is formed mean, literally, "no place." More's Utopia is an imaginary society situated on a faraway island, a democratic and classless society of generally virtuous men and women. Although it was not an earthly paradise, More viewed his fictional commonwealth as a model of what life could be if reason, tutored by religious faith, governed the affairs of humankind. Both implicitly and explicitly, his book was also a pungent critique of the society of his own time.

In the next few hundred years, many similar visions were written, so that *utopia* became a generic term for any story or essay about a distant imaginary community where all is well. Classic examples are Tommaso Campanella's *City of the Sun* (1602), Johann Valentin Andreae's Lutheran utopia, *Christianopolis* (1619), and Sir Francis Bacon's *New Atlantis* (1624). In each, and in scores of others, the reader visits a wondrous land that serves as a model of how human beings should live, not unlike the ideal city-state described at length in Plato's *Republic*. Whether the authors of these utopias believed that their commonwealths could ever be built on Earth is often doubtful—or at least unclear. Thomas More, almost certainly, was more ironic and playful than serious.

But in the so-called Enlightenment of the eighteenth century, the utopian tradition took a new turn. Writers began to set their visions of the good society in the future. The first to do so was Louis Sébastien Mercier, in his novel *The Year 2440* (1771). In this work the reader is transported not to some strange island in the South Seas, but to Paris of the twenty-fifth century, where a clean, well-lit city greets Mercier's hero, who awakens after a long and deep sleep. The ills of eighteenth-century France have disappeared, and science and reason are triumphant.

The Year 2440 is a work of fiction, but the more common form taken by utopian visions in the late eighteenth century was the philosophical essay expounding a theory of irresistible progress from the dark past to the bright future of humanity. The steady improvement of learning would, said the philosophers, produce a rationalist millennium. Noteworthy among these were the Frenchmen Baron Turgot and the Marquis de Condorcet, the English scientist and thinker Joseph Priestley, and Immanuel Kant, the greatest philosopher of the German Enlightenment. The most influential vision of a glorious future appeared in Condorcet's *Sketch for a Historical Portrait of the Progress of the Human Mind* (1795), where he described, beyond the nine epochs of history thus far, a tenth epoch in which inequality both within and among nations would be erased by science, education, and wise public administration.

The literary utopia is a variant of the technique of scenario-building often employed by futurists. It can be a useful device in helping futurists clarify their values.

Condorcet's example was followed in the nineteenth century by many thinkers, as in Auguste Comte's utopian vision of a future "Western Republic" in his *System of Positive Polity* (1851–1854), and in the tantalizing glimpses of a classless, stateless utopia in the many writings of Karl Marx and Friedrich Engels. Marx and Engels, however, pointedly refused to imagine their future world in graphic detail. They feared that too much speculation about the future would impede hard-headed scientific analysis of present-day realities and distract socialists from the urgent tasks at hand.

Other socialists, such as Charles Fourier and Étienne Cabet, were less cautious, putting forth elaborate schemes for working-class utopias that inspired the creation of experimental utopian communities in several parts of the world. Near the end of the nineteenth century, many socialists and other social reformers took to creating utopias in fictional form. They produced several works of great distinction, including Edward Bellamy's *Looking Backward* (1888), Theodor Hertzka's *Freeland* (1890), and William Morris's *News from Nowhere* (1890). Each novel was set explicitly in the future. The English futurist and science fiction writer H. G. Wells published his vision of technocratic socialism, *A Modern Utopia,* in 1905. Wells tried his hand at utopian fiction again in *Men Like Gods* (1923) and *The Shape of Things to Come* (1933), and his Irish contemporary Bernard Shaw published what is perhaps the greatest of utopian plays, *Back to Methuselah,* in 1922.

In more recent times, the writing of utopias in all forms, fictional or nonfictional, has gone out of vogue again. Its place has been taken by the "dystopia," the picture of a quintessentially bad society, like the Oceania of George Orwell's *Nineteen Eighty-Four* (1949). But utopianizing is not extinct. From the philosophical utopias of Herbert Marcuse and Pierre Teilhard de Chardin to such literary utopias as B. F. Skinner's *Walden Two* (1948) and Ernest Callenbach's *Ecotopia* (1975) and *Ecotopia Emerging* (1981), visions of the ideal society, often set in a credible future, still appear in print from time to time. The optimistic cant of twentieth-century demagogues and politicians, who promise to build new heavens on Earth, or speak glibly of "new frontiers" and "shining cities on the hill," is also an echo, however faint, of the utopian tradition.

It may even be argued that many of the images of the future purveyed in the writings of professional futurists partake liberally of the utopian impulse. For example, Herman Kahn and his associates in *The Next 200 Years* (1976) depict a prosperous and peaceful future world where today's problems have all been solved by the progress of science, technology, and capitalism.

William Irwin Thompson in *At the Edge of History* (1971) and Marilyn Ferguson in *The Aquarian Conspiracy* (1980, 1987) offer popular covert utopian visions of the future from a New Age perspective. The literary utopia is, in fact, a variant of the technique of scenario-building often employed by futurists. It can be a useful device in helping futurists clarify their values, establish perspective, and define the normative dimensions of their research.

[See also Apocalyptic Future; Dystopias; More, Saint Thomas; Science Fiction.]

BIBLIOGRAPHY

Berneri, Marie Louise. *Journey Through Utopia.* London: Routledge & Kegan Paul, 1950.

Levitas, Ruth. *The Concept of Utopia.* Syracuse, N.Y.: Syracuse University Press, 1990.

Manuel, Frank E., and Manuel, Fritzie P. *Utopian Thought in the Western World.* Cambridge, Mass.: Harvard University Press, 1979.

— W. WARREN WAGAR

V

VALUES

Human values are standards of judging. They define the desirable or undesirable, the good or bad, the pleasant or unpleasant, and the appropriate or inappropriate. They are guides to behavior. They are invested with group identifications and emotions. They involve social sanctions—i.e., rewards and punishments—administered by agents of the community. They often appear as moral "ought" or "ought not" statements regarding the proper behavior of individuals. Values are more than mere individual preferences. Rather, they include the practices and rules of right conduct that are often seen as beneficial, if not necessary, for the welfare of entire social groups.

Values are not arbitrary. They have evolved through the millennia of human development, having their origins in human nature, the conditions of social life, and the interaction between them and with the nature of the physical environment.

Human beings cannot exist without having certain of their needs met. They must have air, water, and food, and they have needs for clothing, shelter, companionship, affection, and sex. They do not come into the world devoid of a means of evaluation. The human body and brain are programmed with a variety of senses, such as taste, smell, sight, hearing, and touch, and of drives, such as hunger, thirst, and sex. Individuals feel pain and pleasure. Thus, people have some basis for evaluation, some built-in criteria for believing that some things are good and that some things are bad. Not only biopsychological needs but also higher capacities such as the ability to reason, to attribute meaning to things, and to choose to act in one way or another provide guidelines for the welfare of individual organisms and foundations for human values.

Some human needs, such as those for love, approval, emotional support, and communication, can only be satisfied by interaction with other humans. Social life itself also shapes human values. Morality functions to allow people to live and work together and benefit from the tremendous payoffs of cooperative efforts. For example, values of honesty, trust, and trustworthiness are necessary for learning from others. Values such as sharing with others, justice, generosity, and reciprocity contribute to both individual and group well-being.

Thus, all people everywhere have certain similar basic needs and face similar problems of the conditions of social life. All people also exist in natural environments that are subject to similar physical and chemical principles (e.g., gravity, the nature of fire, and mundane things such as objects sharing length, weight, volume, etc.). When humans recognize the sun as the giver of life, for example, it is understandable that they come to value, even worship, it. When humans learn that seed corn is necessary to grow corn, they come to value it. Basically similar beings pursuing goals that necessarily include some similar ones of survival and flourishing create many similar beliefs and evaluations since they function within similar social and physical constraints and opportunities.

Despite the apparent cultural diversity in the world,

there exist universal

or nearly universal human values.

Hence, despite the apparent cultural diversity in the world, there exist universal or nearly universal human values: the value of human life (because without life, there is nothing else, hence the value of health); the value of knowledge (because that is how we make our way effectively in the world and achieve our purposes, hence the values of truth, education, research, technology), and the value of evaluation itself (because we need to be able to judge accurately whether things in the real world are good or bad, safe or dangerous, trustworthy or untrustworthy, and so on).

Among other nearly universal values are: sufficient (but not enormous) wealth, peace, justice, affection, opportunities for family life and sexual behavior, respect for authority, moderation, loyalty, courage, perseverance, cooperation, honesty, generosity, helpfulness, friendliness, trust and trustworthiness, individual autonomy constrained only by the necessities of group living and concerns for fair play and a fair distribution of freedom and well-being for all, and self realization. Such values tend to exist everywhere, regardless of language and culture, and to remain constant.

The postmodern—i.e., relativist and subjectivist—perspectives of the late twentieth century have drifted away from these truths. Thus the work of people like Ronald Inglehart is misleading. In surveys in over twenty-five countries from 1973 to 1988, he finds some change in values in advanced industrial societies from traditional materialist values of physical sustenance and safety toward post-materialist values of individual autonomy, innovation, self-expression, beauty, and a tendency to challenge authority. But these findings are deceptive, first, because, many people continue to express materialist values even in advanced, industrial societies, and, second, because postmaterialist values are contingent upon the adequate satisfaction of the materialist values of survival and comfort. For most people in the less developed world, materialist values are not yet fulfilled and for people in the industrialized world they remain contingent on high levels of living that may be precarious. Values that satisfy basic human needs and the conditions of social life can be ignored only at the risk of the possible future decline and collapse of human civilization.

Some human values, though, *have* changed, and some of them *ought* to have changed. The human future depends both on recognizing and living according to most universal values *and* on continuing change in others in response to changing conditions: e.g., the recent rapid growth of the earth's human population (now at over 5.5 billion going on 11 billion); the increase in the scale of human interaction to encompass the globe; and the possible threats (e.g., resource depletion, pollution, global warming, etc.) to the life-sustaining capacities of Earth.

The freedom and well-being of human beings in the twenty-first century and beyond require a new image of a preferable future. Specifically, we need the following value changes:

1. The preeminent value of human life itself ought to be expanded so that all persons born anywhere on earth have an equal right and opportunity to live out their life spans of eighty-plus years.
2. The values of human reproductive behavior ought to continue to change toward valuing low birth rates to the point of no more than an average of one child per person so as eventually to achieve zero-population growth.
3. The values associated with masculinity, such as machismo, aggression, dominance, destruction, and violence, are no longer functional and ought to be redefined as male nurturing of society through caring for others and achieving social justice by rational discourse and law.
4. While keeping local identities, the idea of an alien "Other" ought to be eliminated, thereby ending exclusivity of caring for ingroup members and animosity toward outgroups, and every individual's community of concern ought to be expanded to encompass all of humanity.
5. Because of the cosmic ignorance of humans concerning the purposes and meanings of life and because of obvious human need, humans ought to value more highly their stewardship of nonhuman forms of life and the biosphere.
6. Because they have no right to use up the resources of the Earth and the cultural heritages past generations left them, the present generation ought to value more fully the well-being of future generations, passing on to them social, cultural, and physical conditions no worse than were left to them.
7. The creation, development, preservation, and dissemination of useful knowledge ought to be valued more than at present, because such knowledge empowers future generations and compensates them for the damage past and present humans have done and are doing to the Earth.
8. Values concerning the status of women ought to be changed everywhere on Earth to create opportunities for women to choose and to pursue meaningful lives equal to those of men, both because it is equitable to do so and because other values that ought to be changed—e.g., reproductive values—can be changed more easily.

[See also Behavior: Social Constraints; Change, Cultural; Change, Epochal; Ethics; Family Values; Global Culture; Lifestyles, Alternative; Lifestyles, Value-oriented; Modernism And Postmodernism; Morals; Religion, Spirituality, Morality; Sexual Behavior; Sexual Codes; Social Controls; Values, Nonwestern; Values Change; Values Formation.]

BIBLIOGRAPHY

Baumeister, Roy F. *Meanings of Life.* New York: Guilford Press, 1991.

Inglehart, Ronald. *Culture Shift in Advanced Industrial Society.* Princeton, NJ: Princeton University Press, 1990.

Lombardi, Louis G. *Moral Analysis: Foundations, Guides, and Applications.* Albany, NY: State University of New York Press, 1988.

Naroll, Raoul. *The Moral Order.* Beverly Hills, CA.: Sage, 1983.

Zavalloni, Marisa. "Values." In Harry C. Triandis and Richard W. Brislin, eds. *Handbook of Cross-Cultural Psychology.* Vol. 5, *Social Psychology.* Boston: Allyn and Bacon, 1980.

— WENDELL BELL

VALUES, NONWESTERN

Most Western cultures derive their value systems from Greco-Roman civilization and Judeo-Christian ethics. Most of the non-Western world derives its value systems from the religious beliefs of Islam, Hinduism, and Buddhism, and the teachings of Confucianism. Globalism makes it prudent for all to understand other value systems and cultures.

Islam

The law of Islam is called the shariah or pathway. The *Pathway* in the Qur'an outlines and regulates public order as well as individual and social morality, etiquette, personal hygiene, and religious ritual. The *Pathway* divides all human actions into five categories: obligatory, recommended, permitted, disapproved but not forbidden, and absolutely forbidden. The five pillars or framework of the Muslim life are: faith, prayer, charity, self-purification, and pilgrimage to Mecca for those who can afford it. While some Islamic societies are governed closely by the *Pathway,* most have elected to follow the general teachings but not its strict interpretation. Muslim ethics are based on the Law of Allah, as revealed in the Qur'an, which is binding on all Muslims.

Muslims believe in the Day of Judgment and individual accountability for actions and eternal life after death. Although Islam began on the Arabian peninsula, its influence is continuing to spread throughout the world. Nearly one billion people from all races, nationalities, and cultures are Muslims.

Hinduism

Hinduism embodies the spiritual vision built upon the basic and fundamental tenets of the *Vedas*. The *Vedas* constitute a religious body of thought developed by ancient Indian sages. The teachings are practical, stipulating specific steps leading to salvation and human transformation. The main values in life are defined by the sages as pleasure, wealth, fame, and liberation. Hindus believe in reincarnation; a person is born, dies, and is reborn. The form that one takes in rebirth is determined by the cumulative deeds performed in previous lives.

As cultures come into frequent contact with global commerce and media, a melding of some values and the withering of others will occur.

Hindus believe that man and god are one and that to treat another poorly is to treat god poorly. The beliefs and practices of Hinduism have given India stability and unity. Since until recently, Hinduism was not expansionist like Islam and Christianity, the impact of its beliefs has been primarily limited to India. However, as the world becomes more interrelated, the influence of Hinduism may well expand.

Buddhism

Buddhism embraces four truths: life is suffering; the suffering of life is due to craving, desire, or thirst; the craving must be extinguished; and the craving is extinguished by the Noble Eightfold Path (right belief, purpose, speech, conduct, livelihood, effort, mind control, meditation). The two major divisions are Theravada and Mahayana. Within Theravada, the Eightfold Path leads to salvation, or Nirvana. In Mahayana, god is not abstract and Nirvana is a place, the Happy Land at the end of human life. Buddhism has high ethical content. Although it began in India, Buddhism is today the major religion of Sri Lanka, Myanmar, Thailand, Laos, Cambodia, and Vietnam, and is also important to China, Japan, and Korea. Modern life may be affecting Buddhism in that the craving for material things ("tanha") is stronger today than it was in earlier times.

Confucianism

Confucianism is a philosophy, not a religion. Confucius devoted his life to returning society to the rituals and values of the Chou Dynasty, a time he felt was perfect. His *Analects* is a collection of selected sayings that are the guiding rules of Confucianism. Some of the guiding rules are the virtue of goodness, the practice of reciprocity, and the cultivation of filial piety. Goodness is the basis of other virtues such as justice, religious and moral propriety, wisdom, and faithfulness. The practice of reciprocity is an expression of a give-and-receive morality, a golden rule for interpersonal relationships. The cultivation of filial piety stresses the pre-eminence of the family, emphasizing love and respect for parents, the acceptance of their wishes and concern for their welfare, solitude for the family fortunes, and the birth of children who would ensure the family's continuance. The ideal of Confucianism is *noblesse oblige,* or the serious pursuit of wisdom and cultivation of personal goodness by the members of the priviliged class. A basic idea of Confucianism is Jen, derived from a word meaning humanity or kindness. Jen consists of self-restraint, matching words with deeds, and possession of the qualities of firmness, resolution, simplicity, and prudence. The primary impact of Confucianism was in China. However, the modern Chinese government has attempted to replace the teachings of Confucius with those of Mao. On the surface, the moral philosophy of Confucius is suppressed, but deep within the heart of its adherents it continues to have a strong presence.

Conclusion

Chuang Tzu, the Taoist philosopher and Chinese mystic, sums up this topic well by saying that different cultures are differently constituted. With a brief introduction to four common religious/philosophic influences on values, one must guard against making broad generalizations. A common hope is that change will move all toward universality of beliefs and actions.

As cultures come into frequent, steady contact with global commerce and the broadcast and entertainment media, film, and video, their value systems will be challenged. A melding of some values and the withering of others will surely occur. Since European values dominate the media and commerce, the dominant flow of values is clear.

[See also Change, Cultural; Change, Epochal; Global Culture; Lifestyles, Alternative; Lifestyles, Ethnic; Religions, Decline or Rise of; Religions, Statistical Projections of; Values Change.]

BIBLIOGRAPHY

Cleary, Thomas F. *The Essential Tao: An Initiation into the Heart of Taoism Through the Authentic Tao Te Ching and the Inner Teachings of Chuang Tzu.* San Francisco: HarperCollins, 1992.

Danto, Arthur Coleman. *Mysticism and Morality: Oriental Thought and Moral Philosophy.* New York: Basic Books, 1978.

Dumoulin, Heinrich. *Buddhism in the Modern World.* New York: Macmillan, 1976.

Furer-Haimendorf, Christoph von. *Morals and Merit: A Study of Values and Social Controls in South Asian Societies.* Chicago: University of Chicago Press, 1967.

Hussain, Asaf; Olsen, Robert; and Quareshi, Jamil, eds. *Orientalism, Islam and Islamists.* Brattleboro, VT: Amana Books, 1984.

Park, O'Hyun. *Oriental Ideas in Recent Religious Thought.* Lakemont, GA: CSA Press, 1974.

Shourie, Arun. *Hinduism, Essence and Consequence: A Study of the Upanishads, The Gita, and The Brahma-Sutras.* New Delhi, India: Vikas, 1979.

— ROBERT WAGLEY

VALUES CHANGE

The basic test of contemporary society is its ability to project and pursue strong goals and values.

The world is at the end of the half-millennium when the white nations of Europe and North America dominated world economic and political events. Part of this shift involves the rise of the Pacific Basin as the world's economic center of influence. Pacific Rim share of global GNP is projected to exceed 50 percent of the world total by 2040.

The world is at the end of the half-millennium

when the white nations of Europe

and North America dominated world economic

and political events.

A great nation cannot have economic growth as its primary aim. Instead, economic growth is the result of having a great primary aim. America must consider how to restructure its approach to economics going beyond the short-term variables of monetary and fiscal policy. At an even deeper level, current economic models ignore factors such as cultural values, social costs, and human meaning. Cynicism and despair are dominant themes of America's culture. As a result, the U.S. economy is in for a continuing period of dislocation. For the belief system on which America's economy is based is in a state of profound transition.

This changing context has inevitable social effects. For example, in many relationships, contracts are re-placing trust. Indeed, it should be asked whether today's America is bound together more by mutual interests than by shared convictions. A new approach to economics must somehow include all these elements: the significance of private property, the sanctity of the individual, equality before the law, universal education, social justice, human rights, child labor laws, equality of women, science as an engine of development, and collective bargaining, to name only a few.

At yet another level of consideration, America's policies need to embrace the long-term viability of ecosystems upon which sustainable development depends. Conserving and husbanding resources, not greedily exploiting them, is a part of the new economic ethic for survival. The environmental movement is an attempt to reintegrate ourselves with the Earth and the cycle of nature from which we tore ourselves during the Industrial Revolution and the subsequent urbanization.

No political party speaks of progress with any conviction or vision. Politicians speak only of change and solving problems. With many people, this translates into voter apathy. People are more skeptical than ever about politicians trying to sell them anything—especially when politicians do not relate to the scope of change that confronts contemporary society. What this comes down to is a widening public sense of the obsolescence and irrelevance of politics as a habit of mind and a means of progress. Confidence in progress has substantially waned. Indeed, most of the social agenda built on faith in progress has not been enacted into law.

Waning of Materialism

A materialist interpretation of history leaves out human fundamentals. It describes history in terms of how humans have organized the means of economic production. Material benefits have failed to raise the individual to a higher cultural and spiritual plane. Basically, contemporary culture tells us that there is no enduring meaning to life and nothing beyond material acquisition, sensual pleasure, or technical wizardry. It leaves out the expansion of human awareness, the role of individual curiosity as the driving force of knowledge accumulation, and the ensuing growth of the human spirit as the creative dynamic of history.

The materialist ethic and its corollary, the consumption ethic, did not suddenly emerge in the 1950s. America's consumer society had been launched in the 1890s. In 1899 Thorstein Veblen published the *Theory of the Leisure Class,* in which he coined the phrase "conspicuous consumption" to describe American materialistic habits. Delayed by the Great Depression and World War II, the consumer society burst forth with all its pent-up power in the 1950s. Households were gripped with a frenzy of consumption. Economic growth became an end in itself. The consumer society also became a "throwaway society," and "planned obsolescence" promoted a never-ending succession of minor changes in "must have" goods. What we have had cannot truly be described as a standard of "living." It is more a standard of "having." And the more we have, the less we seem to enjoy life. We have learned that gross domestic happiness does not automatically rise in lockstep with the gross domestic product.

The new assumption about the economy must be based on a fundamental but forgotten tenet: that wealth is a means to an end, not an end in itself. With all the labor-saving devices, we have less time and are more hassled than ever. We have concentrated on the means but lost sight of the ends.

For those sated with materialism and acquisitions, the quest has shifted to: experiences, instead of things; self-development; mastery of new skills; trendy activities or thrills; and fulfillment of lifetime fantasies.

Postindustrial Paradigm

The set of values and lifestyles that hallmarked the Industrial Era is being outmoded. Rational, reductionistic, linear, quantitative, materialistic principles, and a focus on self-interest and instant gratification are waning in importance.

The Postindustrial Paradigm is a new set of guiding principles that entail collaboration, utilitarian common good, communitarianism, pluralistic diversity, global outlook, critical dialogue, qualitative (distinguished from merely quantitative) criteria for wants and needs.

The litany of this change is long and involves changed outlook and emphasis covering most every aspect of human affairs. Following are some important shifts from one state of affairs to another:

- From primary and secondary industries (agriculture and industrial manufacturing) to tertiary and quaternary sectors (services and knowledge-based enterprise).

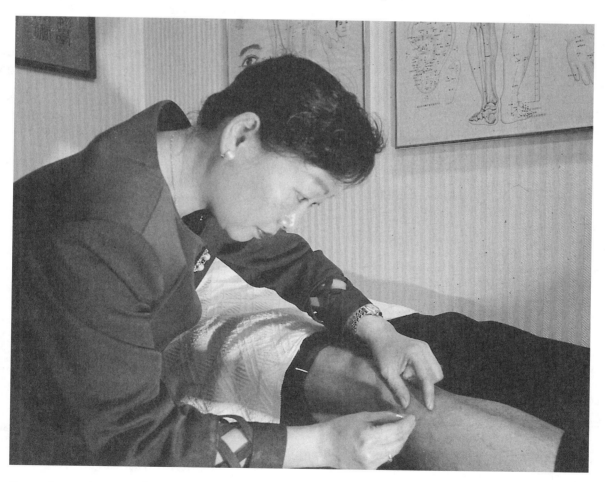

Some values remain constant for centuries while some change shape before our eyes. This woman is a doctor practicing acupuncture, an ancient healing art. (© Charles Walker Collection/Stock Montage, Inc.)

- From Maslowian values posited on survival, to security, then to belongingness and esteem, and eventually to self-actualization (realizing one's innermost potentials).
- From physical goods to less tangible services.
- From goods and services produced by muscle power to those produced by programmable machines (robots), cybernetics, and electronic data processing.
- From unassisted brainpower to knowledge assisted and amplified by electronic data processing.
- From the materialistic to the sensate.
- From a secular to a new religiosity, a search for inner meaning and purpose.
- From things to experiences.
- From basic necessities to amenities and eventually to a higher order of psychological and spiritual fulfillments.
- From physiological to psychological needs.
- From science posited on physical or "hard" sciences to one based on social or "soft" sciences.
- From strict order to chaos theory.
- From have-not (poverty) to having (shared abundance).
- From domineering self-interest to renewed emphasis on the broader social or communitarian interests.
- From quantity to quality.
- From few innovations and sparse introduction to a vast and varied array of new inventions.
- From scarcity to abundance.
- From a few stark choices to a bewildering array of choices.
- From a paucity of information to cascading "information overloads."
- From durability to disposables and planned obsolescence, then back again to recyclables, reclaimables.
- From ownership to rentalism.
- From continuity to change.
- From self-interest motivation to a compassionate humanitarian outlook.
- From independence and self-sufficiency to interdependence.
- From specialists to generalists.
- From relatively unbridled to increasingly restrained individual freedom.
- From profit maximization (squeezing blood out of the turnip) to profitability (balancing stakeholder interests).
- From a puritan hard-work ethic to a leisure-dominated lifestyle.
- From privileges transformed into rights and "entitlements" to resumption of a greater measure of individual responsibility and self-help.
- From Darwinian self-survival of the fittest to humanistic security short of the "all-caring" paternal state.
- From small-scale atomistic undertakings to large-scale pluralistic institutions.
- From domestic to international and global perspectives.
- From national to multinational and "one-world" scale in most organized endeavors.
- From centralization to decentralization.
- From simple to complex.
- From the obvious to subtle and not humanly discernible phenomena.
- From irrational to logical planning to chaos-based change.

Despite the problems and perils of our times, we should take heart that we are living at this moment in history. As Arthur Clarke reminds us, every collective human enterprise is like a surf rider carried forward on the crest of a wave. The wave bearing us has scarcely started its run; those who thought it was already slackening spoke centuries too soon.

Our intellectual purpose must transcend crass partisan politics. It must gain insight into why things are awry and provide some new visions for piecing together the new mosaic, whatever that may be. Vision requires discerning the potential purpose which is hidden in the chaos of the moment yet which could bring new potentials for persons and nations.

In every era, in every region of the world, the evolution of enlarged expressions of life has been evoked by individual men and women. Humanity does not advance as a result of the collective; it advances through individual effort.

Someone needs to do for this phase of American life what Madison, Jefferson, and others did for an earlier period. Somewhere in America are potential Emersons, Whitmans, Melvilles, Coles, Churches, Innesses, Gershwins, Sandburgs—the spirits that see beyond our present horizon, who sense new dimensions of life being birthed that the rest of us cannot yet see.

Clearly there is no formula or blueprint to build the next phase of the American experiment, fashioning human and social relationships that will take us through the coming century. It is an unending process, a process that is at the same time economic and political, but above all psychological and moral: the opening up of the greatest vistas of possibility America has ever known.

[See also Change; Change, Epochal; Ethics; Morals; Values; Values, Nonwestern; Values Formation.]

BIBLIOGRAPHY

Bloom, Allan. *Closing of the American Mind.* New York: Simon & Schuster, 1987.

Elgin, Duane. *Voluntary Simplicity: Toward a Way of Life That Is Outwardly Simple, Inwardly Rich.* New York: William Morrow, 1981.

Harman, Willis W. *An Incomplete Guide to the Future.* New York: W. W. Norton, 1979.

Rosenau, Pauline Marie. *Post-Modernism and the Social Sciences: Insights, Inroads, and Intrusions.* Princeton, N.J.: Princeton University Press, 1992.

Strauss, William, and Howe, Neil. *Generations: The History of America's Future, 1584–2069.* New York: William Morrow, 1991.

Vago, Steven. *Social Change.* New York: Holt, Rinehart, and Winston, 1980.

– GRAHAM T. T. MOLITOR
WILLIAM VAN DUSEN WISHARD

VALUES FORMATION

Values apply to many areas: economics, community service, family, politics, religious practices, work ethic, and so on. They vary by region, age, sex, ethnic background, and so forth. Webster defines *values* as "the qualities, customs, standards, and principles of a people regarded as desirable." If what was previously held desirable no longer applies, what caused the transition, and what does the future hold?

James Q. Wilson finds that we learn to cope with peoples of the world because we learn to cope with members of our family. The family is our central, value-shaping institution. It is argued that changes in the traditional family, which altered childbearing and parenting, significantly contributed to changing Americans' values and helped foster the growth of violence.

In past decades, the values of the young were largely shaped by parents, clergy, and teachers. Families typically consisted of a mother and father, and often were extended, with grandparents sharing values that spanned several generations. From largely nuclear, multigenerational families, the United States now consists of many single-parent families, and one-third of Americans are in blended or stepfamilies (i.e., families including children from previous marriages). In 1940, 90 percent of households were married couples. By 1992 the number had declined to 55 percent, and almost 50 percent of children were in one-parent households. The family is no longer the cradle of value formation. The influence of the clergy has also declined markedly. Religious-group membership had dropped from 73 percent of the population in 1965 to 65 percent by 1990. In *The Culture of Disbelief*, Stephen L. Carter argues that liberal attitudes led to belittling religious devotion, humiliating believers, and discouraging religion as a serious activity. Churchgoing families often pursue lifestyles markedly different from the principles espoused by their churches.

Teachers no longer command the respect they previously enjoyed. In some places, they are threatened with bodily harm for failing to pass students. Certain forms of discipline have been legally forbidden, further weakening the role of the teacher.

Violence among the young, including preteens, is widespread, embracing all ethnic groups and urban and rural communities. What drove our society to these appalling conditions and, most important, are those driving factors likely to change in the coming decade?

The Driving Forces

Marriage and the family have lost their sanctity and significance for several reasons. Easily obtainable contraception markedly changed attitudes about marriage and about pre- and postmarriage sex.

Divorce became common and more acceptable. By the early 1990s, the United States had the highest divorce rate in the industrialized world. Fifty percent of marriages resulted in divorce.

Employment trends may be the most important factor in divorce and child care and, ultimately, in the value formation of the young. Changing attitudes about women's roles, their increased access to higher education, and financial pressures led to major increases in women's participation in the workforce. These pressures and newly won nonfinancial independence made divorce seem a less threatening step.

In the United States, the changes in family values also reflect a deliberate choice to accept single parenthood. About one million children per year are born out of wedlock. By 1993, there were 24 million single mothers in the United States, and 25 percent of babies were born to unwed mothers in 1992, in contrast with only 10 percent in 1970. Two-thirds of black babies are born to unwed mothers. The black community is now experiencing three and even four generations of unwed mothers. Many argue that government programs providing child support to unwed and single-parent families also contribute to these trends.

The information age is an integral part

of the lives of every American.

How we choose to shape the content

of the information will be the key

to our future values.

If not the parents, the clergy, or the schools, who then are shaping our current and future values? The young are largely influenced by their peers, and by sports heroes, stars of the entertainment world, media commentators, and even cartoon characters. Peer pressure has supplanted previous influences as one of the most important factors in shaping the values of the young. Economic conditions exert a significant effect on the family structure. The inability to obtain employment creates family tensions, often causing families to break up. In the absence of the discipline of a structured family, school dropout rates, especially among blacks, have created large groups of young adults with few or no job prospects and much time on their hands.

Growing numbers of young adults, unable or uninterested in a college education, find employment unavailable or unacceptably demeaning. The lack of adequate employment creates a feeling of disenfranchisement, despair, and anger. The drug trade offers the enticement of easy and immediate access to wealth for the young of all ethnic groups. Lacking a strong father image, youths turn to television and popular music to establish a personal code of ethics. Children view television for five to seven hours daily, often devoting more time to it than to school. Violence is an integral ingredient in much of television. Popular entertainers often express racist and anti-law-enforcement values.

Future Possibilities

Are Americans likely to revert to traditional values? The divorce rate has declined somewhat recently, but it is not likely that divorce will soon be viewed as an undesirable step, even when children are involved.

There are indications that stay-at-home mothers are becoming more fashionable, at least in pockets of middle- and upper-middle-class Americans. If the pendulum continues to swing back and stay-at-home mothers gain respect, the more traditional lines of communication and value transfer are likely to return. But this is not likely in large numbers by the turn of the century, especially among young, unwed mothers.

Employment is unlikely to become significantly more available to young dropouts or to the less skilled, either through more effective education, job retraining, or increased demand for products and services. With birthrates below replacement levels and an aging population, consumer demands will not be sufficient to create significant job growth.

The clergy are not likely to become significantly more influential in value formation, and inner-city conditions seemingly perpetuate the inability of teachers to inculcate appropriate values among the very group most in need.

The more likely means of altering current value trends is through the message content in the many forms of media to which the young and adults have access. Clearly, a salient feature of the future use of information technology lies largely in shaping human behavior—i.e., the values—of individuals and groups.

The largest use of many of these technologies over the next several years is likely to be along the lines of exciting the psyche rather than for educational purposes. Hence, the media are more likely to contribute to promulgating violence than detracting from it by the year 2000. Americans have become hyphenated: Afro-, Cuban-, Chinese-, Korean- (and so on) Americans. Fostering cultural diversity has a downside. The ability to understand and, thus, hold common values is often precluded by the inability to share a common language. Alexis de Tocqueville said, "The tie of language is perhaps the strongest and most durable that can unite mankind."

As the United States evolves to a post-Anglo demography, values regarding family life, child bearing, and parenting may move away from the so-called standard American values.

A Challenge for the Future

As Americans experienced unprecedented economic growth in the late 1950s to late 1980s, society became extremely permissive in its attitudes about sexual freedom, business practices, and violence in all forms of entertainment as well as individual lifestyles. Attention to career and materialism supplanted attention to family and children.

The information age is an integral part of the lives of each and every American. How we choose to shape the content of the information, while adhering to First Amendment rights, will be the key to our future values.

[See also Behavior: Social Constraints: Child Abuse; Child Care; Children, Living Arrangements; Crime, Violent; Crime Rates; Divorce; Family Patterns; Family Problems; Family Values; Holistic Beliefs; Household Composition; Social Controls; Values; Values Change; Women and Work; Women's Movement.]

BIBLIOGRAPHY

Bennett, William. *The Book of Virtues*. New York: Simon & Schuster, 1994.

Cleveland, Harlan, and Wilson, Thomas W. *Human-growth: An Essay on Growth, Values and the Quality of Life*. Lanham, MD: University Press of America, 1978.

Feather, Norman T. *Values in Education and Society*. New York: Free Press, 1975.

Hall, Brian. *Developing Human Values*. Wilton, CT: MC International Values Institute, 1990.

Harrison, Lawrence E. *Who Prospers? How Cultural Values Shape Economic and Political Success*. New York: Basic Books, 1992.

– HAROLD S. BECKER

VIDEO GAMES.

See INTERACTIVE ENTERTAINMENT.

VIRTUAL REALITY.

See INTERACTIVE ENTERTAINMENT.

VISIONARY THINKING

The future is something we create. Each of us, individually and collectively, is an architect of destiny. Our fate depends upon our own ability and resolve. Each act contributes in its own way to the cosmic course. Each new life is an empty tablet to be filled. The greatness resides in each of us. Michelangelo started with a blank block, Shakespeare with an empty manuscript, Rembrandt with a void canvas. Yet the creations of each have inspired the world ever since their souls touched reality. Inspiration and resolve are the stuff of greatness that generates enduring odes. Today entire nations are desperately searching for vision—for a sense of purpose that leads to a better tomorrow. How to draw that mindset is the problem.

The future is something we create.

Each of us, individually and collectively,

is an architect of destiny.

We all can borrow a page or two from others. Today Japan, the second largest economic superpower, achieved this global prominence and domestic prosperity despite the fact that it is geographically smaller than the state of California. Greatness comes in all different sizes. People should never sell themselves short. This remarkable achievement is due, in no small measure, to the vision of a single person—Kakuei Tanaka. Best known as a former prime minister of Japan, Tanaka created the grand vision largely responsible for the transformation of Japan into a model of economic growth and prosperity. The essential ideas, powerful vision, and far-reaching sense of hope were rounded out during the time Tanaka headed the awesome Ministry of International Trade and Industry. The plan clearly staked out where Japan stood and where it might be in fifteen years. Herman Kahn, the great futurist, once remarked, "In fifteen years—given the means and resources—virtually anything the human mind can conceive it can create." Tanaka's vision eventually catapulted him into chairmanship of the Liberal Democratic party and to the office of prime minister. A Commission for Remodeling the Japanese Archipelago was constituted to elaborate details and foster support to carry these fancies into reality. Japan was driven by a dream, a modern-day example of visionary leadership from which each of us—individuals and nations alike—can draw.

The longest journey begins with the first step. Steps are not always tried and true. We can, after all, step off in the wrong direction. But we always have the ability to stop, change direction, and start anew. Visions do not have to be great or even right to be enduring.

Deciding what things are worth doing and getting them done—these two fundamental jobs of a leader in the future are the same two fundamental tasks that have faced leaders in the past. The difference now—the unprecedented difference in our time—is telecommunications technology, which links nations, corporations, groups, tribes, and individuals. For the first time in history, it is becoming possible for the entire globe to pay attention to deciding what things are worth doing and actually getting them done.

The promise of telecommunications technology was constrained by the Cold War. Only now, for the first time since telecommunications effectively interconnected the world, there are not two giant, well-armed spheres of influence habitually opposing each other. For the first time since telecommunications have been instantaneous, it has become technologically and politically conceivable that most nations, corporations, and other powerful groups could agree that some things are worth doing and get them done.

The opportunity, therefore, for global visionary leadership, is unprecedented. Also unprecedented is the number of diverse parties keenly alert to the fact that their ox might be gored by changes proposed by visionary leaders. These parties are, of course, instantaneously informed by telecommunications technology. How, then, can a would-be leader, simultaneously empowered and skewered by the double-edged sword of global instantaneous communication, decide on what goals to pursue and what means to pursue them with?

Take as an example a specific global issue: the health of the oceans. It is quite conceivable that, given the global communications infrastructure already in place, a single party willing to commit a quarter of a billion dollars to the effort could lead an international project that significantly affects the health of the oceans.

Three tracks of endeavor are necessary to decide what is worth doing and how to get it done. The work of these three tracks must be simultaneous and interactive. Teleconferencing and e-mail via the Internet or Worldwide Web make this affordable. The first track, which involves deciding what things are worth doing, must be an international task force of scientists who possess two characteristics: they must be respected internationally, and they must have wisdom at least equal to their egos. The second track must be an international group of experts in geopolitics and economics. These people must identify who benefits and whose ox is gored by doing what the first track determines is worth doing. This track must also identify how those whose ox is gored can be compensated by those who benefit from proposed change. These people should also be respected in their countries and wise beyond factionalism or partisan politics. The third track must be an international team of public relations experts who can educate the power players and their myriad constituencies about what is worth doing, and what they stand to gain by getting it done.

Such is the leverage of the extant telecommunications infrastructure that a single wealthy individual could put together a small group of knowledgeable and wise people—a "kitchen cabinet"—that could then locate, enroll, and coordinate the three tracks: a single visionary leader could enlist the best help of much of the world to decide the best course to take.

[See also Change, Optimistic and Pessimistic Perspectives; Continuity and Discontinuity; Dystopias; Environmental Indicators; Forecasting, Mistakes in; Future: Near, Mid-, and Long-Term; Global Consciousness; Kahn, Herman; Leadership; Planning; Scenarios; Social Indicators; Strategic Planning; Surveys; Trend Indicators; Utopias.]

BIBLIOGRAPHY

Boulding, Elise, and Boulding, Kenneth E. *The Future: Images and Purposes.* Thousand Oaks, CA: Sage Publications, 1994.

Heilbroner, Robert. *Visions of the Future: The Distant Past, Yesterday, Today, Tomorrow.* New York: The New York Public Library/Oxford University Press, 1995.

Laszlo, Ervin. *Vision 2020: Reordering Chaos for Global Survival.* Langhorne, PA: Gordon and Breach Science Publishers, 1994.

Mannermaa, Mike; Inayatullah, Sohail; and Slaughter, Richard, eds. *Coherence and Chaos in Our Uncommon Futures: Visions, Means, and Actions.* Turku, Finland: Finland Futures Research Center, 1994.

Ogilvy, James. *Living Without a Goal: Finding the Freedom to Live a Creative and Innovative Life.* New York: Currency/Doubleday, 1995.

— KATE MCKEOWN

VISUAL ARTS

Rapid changes lie ahead for the arts in the next century. Many of the economic, political, social, and technological factors that made this century the period of greatest change in the history of art will continue unabated. In many instances the rate of change will increase. New technology will fundamentally alter the art world and the appearance of art itself.

History demonstrates that technological changes can produce an enormous impact in the arts. For instance, the invention of portable tubes of paint in the mid-nineteenth century enabled artists to paint the landscape outdoors, leading to Impressionism, the first volley in the modernist revolution against the Old Master tradition of European art. The invention of photography in 1839 further coopted the mimetic perceptual approach because the camera could produce amazingly realistic, fast, and facile copies. Painters turned more and more to abstraction, symbolism, and other less perceptual stylistic elements harder for the camera to capture.

To fully understand the scale of this shift to Modernism in art, one needs to recognize that artistic activity exists between two poles: the perceptual and the conceptual. At the perceptual extreme an artist imitates or re-creates something observed from life. At the conceptual extreme an artist creates an image from the imagination, an image often more symbolic than descriptive. Technological, social, economic, and other changes in the nineteenth century encouraged artists to create more abstract, conceptual images derived from feelings, philosophies, psychology, and the formal elements of the medium in which they worked.

Galleries exist on-line with dealers using high-resolution computers to transmit images to prospective clients, thus eliminating the overhead and necessity of physical gallery space.

In the late-twentieth century, the electronics revolution of the Post-Modern era has had a similar effect on the arts that wil continue for at least the next few decades. Computers can create flawless "electronic collages" by allowing artists to originate or scan borrowed imagery into the computer and then interact upon that imagery by combining and altering images. Photographs can be seamlessly altered to place one person's head on another's body. Similarly figures can be added or deleted, thereby creating seemingly authentic records of scenes that never actually occurred. The films *Forrest Gump, Zelig,* and *Dead Men Don't Wear Plaid* display the use of this in popular media. Through the use of this technology, the actor Tom Hanks in *Forrest Gump* appears in a scene with President John Kennedy, even though the president was assassinated more than thirty years before the scene was filmed.

The potential exists to edit imagery as easily as text, and this capability will be further exploited in the future. Paradoxically, the veracity of the photographic image has been increasingly debunked as the veristic aspects of the medium have increased. As computers begin to assist in projecting holographic images (three-dimensional illusions) combined with virtual-reality technology now under development, the creation of three-dimensional, life-like "fictions" will be possible. Traditional painting and sculpture will merge in works of astonishing illusionism. Already the compact disc, digitalization, and desktop video technology are altering the medium of photography in basic ways. The new compact disc photography places images directly from the film onto a plastic disc, obviating the traditional use of negatives and prints. Displayed on a computer or television monitor, there is no need for prints and traditional albums to hold them. The traditions of 150 years of photography are being made obsolete. As E-mail and electronic publishing become more widespread, there may come a time when there is no need for the objects known as photographs—all photographic images will be electronic.

Already artists like Dan Flavin, Michael Hayden, Jenny Holzer, Bruce Nauman, Nam June Paik, and James Turrell (among many others) are exploring the new technologies in works of art that defy the traditional media categories.

The politicization of art may intensify in the future as the power of art to influence public opinion and political, economic, and social change is more clearly recognized and exploited. Already issues such as sexism, racism, and homophobia have been exploited by both artists and politicians. Artists like Hans Haacke (in his 1990 sculpture *Helmsboro*) have responded to the demagogues and self-proclaimed art censors.

Artists like Jeff Koons, Robert Mapplethorpe, and Andres Serrano have been grossly misrepresented and vilified by the Radical Right and the increasingly diminished, tabloid-like media, with the artists and their art turned into opportunities for political advantage and disinformation. The increasingly hostile political polarization and economic stratification in the United States may lead to a decline in American leadership in the arts. The climate of censorship (and resulting fearful self-censorship), the hostility of many in government and politics to the arts, and the gradual erosion of funding for the arts in the United States since the 1960s (especially compared with European countries) point to a loss of cultural leadership. If Paris was the capital of the art world in the nineteenth and early twentieth centuries, and New York the capital of the latter twentieth century, trends seem to indicate that there will be no art capital in the twenty-first century. Rather the art world will become even more diffuse and decentralized.

Again technology is providing the wherewithal. Not only have art dealers, auction houses, and museums gone on-line using computers to keep records and process information, but some galleries already exist only on-line with the dealers using high-resolution computers to transmit images to prospective clients, thus eliminating the overhead and necessity of physical gallery space. Museums are rushing to produce microgalleries that place collection information and high-resolution images into the computer. Through the use of CD-ROM and computer networks, one can now browse the collections of the world's great museums without leaving the comfort of home. While no reproductions can yet (and may never) replace the actual work of art, the high-resolution computer images and accompanying information undeniably provide a revolution in the accessibility of great art. Virtual exhibitions may arrive electronically at home as increased terrorism makes public life or gatherings (in theaters, galleries, and museums) too dangerous.

Perhaps the greatest challenge of the next century will be elitism. All of the new technologies promise art that is more integrated with daily life for those who have access to the technology. The gulf between the haves and the have-nots is rapidly widening, particularly in the United States, where only 1 percent of the richest now control 40 percent of the wealth, and the top 9 percent control 70 percent. Consequently there is a trend toward a well-informed elite with great access to the expensive new technology, a heretofore incredible potential. At the same time, the rest of the population will perhaps become more isolated from the arts than ever before.

[See also Architectural Design; Arts; Creativity; Industrial Design; Interactive Entertainment; Literature; Motion Pictures; Music; Printed Word; Photography; Recording Industry.]

BIBLIOGRAPHY

Alloway, Lawrence. *Network: Art and the Complex Present*, edited by Donald Kuspit. Ann Arbor, MI: Books on Demand, 1984.
Kepes, György. *The Visual Arts Today*. Ann Arbor, MI: Books on Demand, 1993.
Matanovic, Milenko. *Lightworks: Explorations in Art, Culture, and Creativity*. Issaquah, WI: Lorian Press, 1986.
McConnell, R. B., ed. *Art, Science, and Human Progress*. Englewood, NJ: Universe, 1983.
Richardson, John. *Art: The Way It Is*. 4th ed. Englewood Cliffs, NJ: Prentice-Hall, 1991.

— ROBIN THORNE PTACEK

VOTING

Democratic electoral systems are most likely to evolve and become institutionalized in societies where politically relevant resources, including the capacity to employ armed force or violence, are relatively widely distributed outside the control of the central government. Generally, electoral processes are introduced when governments face economic difficulties, military demands, or internal political challenges that require them to seek popular support on a regular basis. Few ruling groups, however, are anxious to see these channels effectively used by their political foes. At some point in every nation's electoral history, incumbent elites have sought to suppress their electoral opponents. In the United States, the ruling Federalists sought, through the Alien and Sedition Acts of 1798, to outlaw the Jeffersonian opposition. Hamilton and other Federalist leaders also considered a plan for the military suppression of the Jeffersonians. The military weakness of the national government, however, precluded any serious Federalist effort to crush an opposition that controlled several state governments and their militias.

Military force is by no means the only important factor. Where other politically relevant resources, such as wealth, education, communications, and organization, are widely diffused and outside the state's control, there is less likelihood that incumbent elites can eliminate their opponents. The relative absence of these resources helps to explain why democratic electoral institutions have not usually persisted in the nations of the Third World and raises questions about the prospects for their persistence in Eastern Europe.

Voters

In most nations, contending forces use a variety of different appeals to link themselves to popular followings. The most effective and durable appeals are those based upon voters' class, religious, or ethnic identifications and regional attachments. Analysts often attempt to interpret election results mainly in terms of the preferences and characteristics of voters. Thus, it is often said that Catholic voters or African-American voters, or working class voters have particular preferences and behave in particular ways. The actual political significance of voters' race, class, or religion depend, however, upon when, how, on what basis, and by whom a particular group is electorally mobilized. Moreover, voter's choices depend upon the alternatives presented to them. Given a choice between a fool and a rogue, voters must select either a fool or a rogue. Thus, to understand voting behavior it may be more useful to concentrate upon the characteristics and actions of competing parties and candidates than to focus upon the attributes of voters.

Parties and Candidates in American Elections

In the United States, the Republican party won five of the six presidential elections held between 1968 and 1988. During this period, Democratic party candidates were handicapped by the twin problems of ideology and race. The Democratic party's nominating processes had produced candidates and platforms that were seen as too liberal by the general electorate. At the same time, the issue of race divided the party. In 1992, however, the Democrats were able to successfully handle both these problems.

Moderate Democrats had long argued that the party needed to present a more centrist image to be competitive in national elections. In 1992, the party chose as its presidential and vice presidential candidates Governor Bill Clinton and Sen. Al Gore. The platform adopted at the party's national convention was the most conservative in decades, stressing individual responsibility and private enterprise while implicitly criticizing welfare recipients. Thus, Clinton became the first Democratic presidential candidate in two decades who was not burdened by an excessively liberal image.

The Clinton-Gore ticket won 43 percent of the popular vote and 370 electoral votes. The Republican incumbents, Bush and Quayle, received 38 percent of the popular vote and only 168 electoral votes. Nineteen percent of the popular vote went to independent candidate Ross Perot. Economic recession, the end of the Cold War, and the Democrats' new-found moderation on matters of race and ideology combined to oust the Republicans from the White House for the first time in twelve years.

After two years of legislative struggle, however, marked by charges that Clinton had sought to govern as a liberal despite his moderate positions in the 1992 campaign, the Clinton administration suffered a stunning defeat in the November 1994 national elections. For the first time since 1946, Republicans won simultaneous control of both houses of Congress. This put the GOP in a position to block President Clinton's legislative efforts and to promote its own policy agenda.

In Senate races, the Republicans realized a net gain of eight seats to achieve a 52–48 majority. Immediately after the election, Sen. Richard Shelby of Alabama, a conservative Democrat who frequently voted with the Republicans, announced that he was formally joining the GOP. This gave the Republicans 53 votes in the upper chamber. In House races, the Republicans gained an astonishing 52 seats to win a 230–204 majority (1 seat is held by an independent). While the Republicans had controlled the Senate as recently as 1986, the House of Representatives had been a Democratic bastion since 1954.

Republicans also posted a net gain of eleven governorships and won control of fifteen additional chambers in state legislatures. A number of the Democratic party's leading figures were defeated. These included Gov. Mario Cuomo of New York, former House Ways and Means committee chairman Dan Rostenkowski of Illinois, House Judiciary committee chairman Jack Brooks of Texas, three-term Sen. Jim Sasser of Tennessee and, most shocking of all, House Speaker Thomas Foley of Washington. Foley was the first sitting Speaker to be defeated for reelection to his own congressional seat since 1860. All told, thirty-four incumbent Democratic congressmen, three incumbent Democratic Senators and four incumbent Democratic governors went down to defeat. On the Republican side, not one of the ten incumbent senators, fifteen incumbent governors, or 155 incumbent House members seeking reelection was defeated. The South, which had voted Republican in presidential elections for twenty years, now seemed to have turned to the GOP at the congressional level as well. Republicans posted gains among nearly all groups in the populace, with white, male voters, in particular, switching to the GOP. The nation's electoral map had been substantially altered. Interest in the hard-fought race had even produced a slight increase in voter turnout, albeit to a still abysmal 39 percent.

In the wake of their electoral triumph, Republicans moved to name Robert Dole of Kansas to the post of Senate Majority Leader, and Rep. Newt Gingrich of Georgia to the House Speakership. Only two years earlier, Gingrich had been widely viewed as a Republican "firebrand" whose vitriolic attacks on the House leadership were usually dismissed by the media as dangerous and irresponsible. Other Republicans who would move to leadership positions included arch-conservative nonagenarian Sen. Strom Thurmond of South Carolina, who replaced Sam Nunn of Georgia as chairman of the Senate Armed Services committee, and outspoken Clinton critic Alphonse D'Amato of New York, who would now head the Senate Banking committee. At the same time, Rep. Floyd Spence, a conservative South Carolinian, replaced Ron Dellums of California, an avowed pacifist, as Chairman of the House Armed Services Committee. The 1994 election seemed to represent a nationwide repudiation of the Democratic party and appeared to give the Republicans their best chance in a generation to become the nation's majority party.

Voter Turnout

Over the past several decades, voter turnout in the United States has been declining sharply. At the turn of the century, more than 80 percent of those eligible voted in national presidential elections. In recent presidential elections by contrast, voter turnout has barely exceeded 50 percent. In 1992, turnout was 56 percent. Moreover, of those who actually voted in 1992, 19 percent cast protest votes for billionaire Ross Perot. This may suggest a long-term decline in popular confidence in the American political process—something that should alarm the leaders of both national parties.

[See also Democracy; Democratic Process; Political Campaigning; Political Cycles; Political Parties; Political Party Realignment; Public Opinion Polls; Third Political Parties.]

BIBLIOGRAPHY

Black, Earl, and Black, Merle. *The Vital South: How Presidents Are Elected.* Cambridge, MA: Harvard University Press, 1992.

Campbell, Angus, Converse, Philip E., Miller, Warren E., and Stokes, Donald E. *The American Voter.* New York: John Wiley, 1960.

Ginsberg, Benjamin. *The Consequences of Consent.* New York: Basic Books, 1992.

— BENJAMIN GINSBERG

WARMING, GLOBAL.

See CLIMATE AND METEOROLOGY; GLOBAL WARMING.

WASTES, HAZARDOUS.

See HAZARDOUS WASTES.

WASTE, SOLID.

See SOLID WASTE.

WEALTH

Wealth is defined as all the goods and resources of economic value held by an individual or group—all assets including cash; savings and checking accounts; stocks, bonds, and other equities; real estate; jewels and precious metals; art; and other collectibles. Income, a narrower concept, includes payment derived from wages, salaries, and investments. Wealth and income are not interchangeable concepts.

The position of individuals or groups within the social stratification system is a product of their wealth, power, and prestige. A class system of social stratification delineates a hierarchy of classes of distinct social layers whose members share similar economic, political, and cultural characteristics. Although finer gradations can be identified, the simplest division is into upper, middle, and lower classes. The upper class is made up of the wealthy, the industrialists and entrepreneurs, the top executives, and the best-paid professionals. The upper class, particularly the upper-upper class, is growing. The lower class, made up of basic service sector workers, day laborers, and the poor, is also growing. The middle class, made up of white-collar workers, the majority of professionals, skilled craftsmen, and skilled laborers, is shrinking. Some stratification system classifications combine the upper portion of the lower class and the lower segment of the middle class, and identify it as the working class. This group, while holding its own in terms of numbers, is declining in terms of real income and accumulated wealth, and is increasingly composed of individuals who were previously solidly middle class. These trends are likely to continue.

Demographic changes suggest that the nature of the social classes is also shifting. Specifically, the rich are not just getting larger in numbers, but are getting richer as well. The poor below the poverty line are remaining about the same, but the number of abject poor is growing, and the relative poor, or so-called marginals, are becoming poorer as well as growing in numbers. The middle class as a whole is getting noticeably poorer.

Wealth, Income, and Growth

Much attention is given to examining, explaining, predicting, and ultimately to justifying and promoting the growth of income and wealth. Economic growth is typically cast as a very good thing and something to be fostered. Growth can make the national balance sheet look better, but it can have substantial unintended costs, such as personal decline and social dislocation. There has not been nearly the same amount of academic and public attention paid to the distribution of income and wealth, changes in the composition of social class and the distribution of wealth, and the impact of class composition on the society.

The rich are becoming richer.

The number of abject poor is growing,

and the relative poor are becoming poorer.

The middle class is becoming poorer.

Much of the discussion about the poor has been in terms of "how much are they costing society?" rather than "how did they come to be poor?" and "what do they do?" The discussion of the rich is often the reverse. That is, the questions are "what do they do?" and "how did they get rich?" rather than "how much are they costing society?" These questions suggest that society does not use uniform yardsticks to examine wealth across various segments of itself.

The poor are judged as being costly to society, but the loss in revenue from the rich person's tax exempt bonds can far surpass the cost of welfare for the poor neighbor. Wealth determines social status, but that status is the result of social judgment as well as assets and debits.

In the mid-twentieth century, entrepreneurs found that capitalism functions better when the system em-

The leisure time this man has signifies a certain level of wealth. Also, he can afford to ski at an exclusive resort, another benefit of wealth. (© 1994 Kevin Syms/First Image West, Inc.)

phasizes creating modestly affluent consumers rather than exploiting its workforce. More profit results from greater consumer demand than from increased profit margins per item. During the last two decades of the twentieth century, this lesson has been forgotten again, as "supply side" and "trickle down" economics has been a dominant social policy, thereby permitting the rich to get richer and causing the middle class to get poorer. Momentum will carry this trend into the beginning of the twenty-first century, after which it is likely that individuality, the demand for fairness, and the desire for a share of the American dream will reassert itself.

The United States has always been a society with a substantial middle class, substantial in terms of both numbers and actual wealth. The middle class emerged shortly after the country's founding, prospered as a result of industrialization following the Civil War, and survived the panics of 1873, 1893, and 1907, enjoying

the Gilded Age and the Roaring Twenties. The bubble burst in October 1929, and there were hard times for about a decade. The hard times affected people differently: the solidly comfortable remained so, the high flyers "crashed," many comfortably middle-class persons became marginal, and much of the lower middle class dropped down into impoverishment. World War II brought employment, productivity, and relative affluence to society and to most of its members. These good times continued for three decades. After World War II, the United States experienced an international success rarely seen before. It has been suggested that given the shambles that the infrastructure of Europe, the Eastern bloc, and Asia had become, America did not outcompete the rest of the world—it simply won by default. With the ascendancy of Japan and industrialized Asia, and of the economic union in Europe, the international role of the U.S. will change. America continues to have enormous natural and social resources to draw upon, so it will continue as a military power and will continue to be a major exporter of food and manufactured goods, technology, and ideas.

America is squandering its material wealth with its huge national debt and wasting its social wealth by wasting its social capital. It educates some of its members very well but provides mediocre training for the majority. It is neither uncompromising with the incorrigible criminal, nor does it seek to rehabilitate the salvageable. Many in the population are cast off because they are of the wrong age, color, gender, or other attributes.

The record economic expansion following World War II began to slow discernibly in the mid-1970s (the 1974–1975 recession). This caused changes in the shape and structure of the socioeconomic classes as well as their size.

Wealth is both economic and social. It is relative, not absolute. Consequently, if current trends continue, the United States will continue to become richer, but will not keep pace with its rivals. The shrinking of the middle class is a decline of the social group that has been the heart of the industrialized world in general, and of the United States in particular.

Distribution of Wealth: The Declining Middle Class

Assets for most people are in their checking and savings accounts, and in their automobiles, which typically do not appreciate in value. Another two-thirds of the population have equity in their homes, which may appreciate but is not a liquid asset. Only about one quarter of the population has income-producing assets such as CDs and money market accounts, IRAs and Keoghs, stocks and bonds, and real estate. However, more than 70 percent of the aggregate household wealth in the United States is contained in these instruments. As of 1990, home equity accounts for only about 11 percent of all household wealth, only one point higher than it was in 1929.

In the foreseeable future,

the rich will continue to outpace the society's growth

and the average American will barely keep,

if not actually lose ground.

The debt/equity ratio—i.e., debt as a proportion of household net worth (equity)—has grown from about 8 percent in 1950 to an overwhelming 26 percent in 1990, more than a threefold increase.

Among households with a net worth of less $100,000, homes accounted for 60 percent of the net worth and stocks and bonds were about 2 percent of assets. Among the wealthy with a net worth exceeding $1 million, homes accounted for only 9 percent of their net worth, and stocks and bonds were over 25 percent of their assets. A study of change in equity across the entire population showed that during a three-year period from 1983 to 1986, the disparity in net worth increased dramatically: increasing by 44 percent in households with more than $100,000 in income, increasing by only 10 percent among households with less than $100,000 in income, and not increasing at all in households with incomes under $10,000. In terms of the values of household assets, the findings are as one would expect: assets increase with age up to age sixty-five and then decrease, whites have more than minorities, married households are better off than single headed households, and family net worth is related to family income.

For less affluent families, their homes were not only their major asset but their major expense. From 1970 to 1990, the cost of housing went from 28 percent of family income to a staggering 44 percent of the household budget. Couple the high housing costs with wage stagnation and increasing job uncertainty, and it is easy to see how the middle class is being forced out of home ownership. Householders under thirty-five years old purchasing first homes dropped 5 percent between 1982 and 1989. If this trend continues, the youngest baby boomers and the next generation, variously called the thirteenth generation or generation X, will be more like their great-grandparents than their parents. That is, the young adults of today are facing declining employ-

ment opportunities, exorbitant housing and health care costs, and an uncertain national future reminiscent of the turn of the century rather than the postwar era.

In addition to frustrating the attainment of the American dream and eliminating jobs in the housing business, the trend away from home ownership will reduce wealth accumulation in the form of home equity across wide segments of society and will cause the population to be less rooted in their communities along with the concomitant loss of family stability. This is another example of how secondary consequences may be greater than the main effects.

The late 1970s and the decade of the '80s were a period of increasing inequality. The share of income obtained by the poorest quintile (20%) of the population fell from 5.4 to 4.6 percent from 1975 to 1990, whereas the total income share acquired by the highest quintile rose from 41.1 to 44.3 percent, and the top 5 percent increased their portion of total income from 15.5 to 17.4 percent (see Figure 1 and Table 1). These figures amount to a 15 percent decline for the poor in contrast to an 8 percent increase for the rich, and 12 percent increase for the richest 5 percent of the population. Another way to look at income inequality data is to derive Lorenz curves. The comparisons of the percentage of income accrued by specific segments of the society for 1975 and 1990 show that in the brief period of half a generation the inequality increased (Figure 2). Although macroeconomic growth occurred during the period, the poor did not benefit proportionately. From 1950 to 1990, the lowest and highest quintiles increased their share of total income by only 2 and 4 percent respectively. During that period the second and third

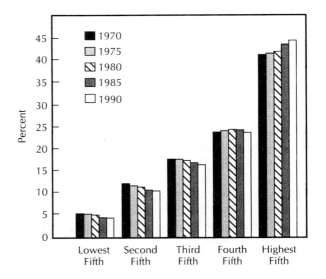

Figure 1. Income distribution.

TABLE 1

INCOME DISTRIBUTION AS A PERCENTAGE OF TOTAL INCOME OF FAMILIES (ALL RACES)

Year	Lowest Fifth	Second Fifth	Third Fifth	Fourth Fifth	Highest Fifth	Top 5 Percent
1950	4.5	11.9	17.4	23.4	42.8	17.3
1955	4.8	12.2	17.7	23.4	41.8	16.8
1960	4.8	12.2	17.8	24.0	41.3	15.9
1965	5.2	12.2	17.8	23.9	40.9	15.5
1970	5.4	12.2	17.6	23.8	40.9	15.6
1975	5.4	11.8	17.6	24.1	41.1	15.5
1980	5.1	11.6	17.5	24.3	41.6	15.3
1985	4.6	10.9	16.9	24.2	43.5	16.7
1990	4.6	10.8	16.6	23.8	44.3	17.4
Change:						
1975–1990	0.85	0.92	0.94	0.99	1.08	1.12
1950–1990	1.02	0.91	0.95	1.02	1.04	1.01

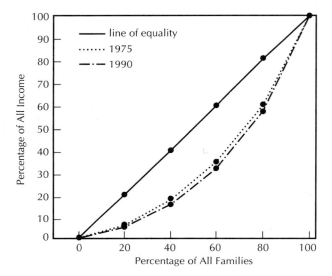

Figure 2. Lorenz curve of income distribution.

quintiles (i.e., the middle class) lost 9 and 5 percent respectively (see Table 1). This is another illustration of the long-term erosion of the middle class, a trend not likely to reverse in the immediate future.

Increases in economic development tend to create greater, not less inequality. Average well-being increases, but there is no evidence of wider sharing of the created wealth. A wealthy few acquire most of the new wealth.

Inequity increases if society does not explicitly address its inequality. In the United States, the social policies of the 1930s reduced the inequality of the depression, and the economic boom that resulted from World War II continued the process. By the 1960s, the portion of the population living in poverty was 22 percent and unemployment was at 6 percent, three times higher than the levels during war years. Social policy in the

1970s brought poverty levels down, but did not address general economic distribution inequalities. The social and economic policies of the 1980s magnified the distribution inequities.

These trends can be seen in Figure 3. This inequity was increasing from 1950 to 1975, but inequality dramatically increased from 1975 to 1990. There have been no clear changes in socioeconomic policy to suggest that there will be any dramatic shift in these trends.

For the next two or three decades, expect the poor to become better off on an absolute basis, but worse off on a relative basis. The lower-middle class will continue its downward economic slide. The middle-middle and the upper-middle class will barely keep up economically and will shrink in relative size. A few individuals will move upward but the majority of the departures will be downward mobility. The affluent and the rich will continue to do well. And the very rich will do extremely well.

The Extremes: The Rich and the Poor

Fortune magazine annually lists the 400 wealthiest Americans and *Forbes* magazine annually lists the world's billionaires. Over the twelve-year period from 1982 to 1993, the 400 wealthiest Americans have done very well. The minimum needed to be on the list increased from $91 million to $300 million, the average net worth of the group increased from $230 million to $820 million, and the number of American billionaires increased from 13 to 59. Over approximately the same twelve-year period (1980 to 1991), the gross national product, the gross domestic product, the national income, compensation and wages of all employees, and personal income merely doubled.

During the period from the early 1980s to the early 1990s, in terms of all wages paid to the civilian labor

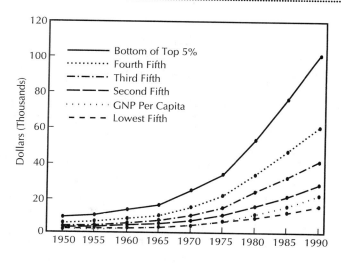

Figure 3. Income distribution (upper limit each fifth).

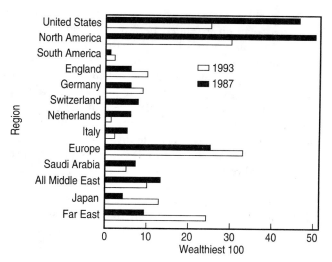

Figure 4. Number of billionaires worldwide.

force, the average American worker did not maintain par with national growth, experiencing a 75 percent as opposed to a 110 percent increase. Their income exceeded inflation by 25 percent, but that is only one-tenth of the improvement that the super-rich experienced in their net worth. During the intervening years, the disparity deepens. Although the policies of the 1980s were skewed in favor of the wealthy, and therefore the trends are not likely to continue at such a dramatic rate, there is no indication that there will be a reversal in the trends. In the foreseeable future, the rich will continue to outpace the society's growth and the average American will barely keep up, if not actually lose ground.

Internationally, the very wealthy did even better than the American rich. There were 98 billionaires on *Forbes* magazine's first list and more than 250 by 1993. The initial and current lists (see Figure 4) suggest a shift in the location of wealth in the world. During the period from 1987 to 1993, the United States increased its number of billionaires from 47 to 59. Simultaneously, Japan tripled, the rest of Asia doubled, and Europe increased by a third, the number of its wealthiest. This growth in economic strength among America's major competitors is likely to increase in the next few decades. Overall, the United States is not doing poorly in absolute terms, but, relative to the rest of the world, it is not doing as well as it did in the past.

The poor and the middle class did not fare as well as the wealthy. The poor remained somewhat even with inflation. For example, in Figure 5, the poverty level for a single person roughly follows the increase of the GNP per capita (all in constant dollars). The gap between the middle class and the poor is decreasing, and since the

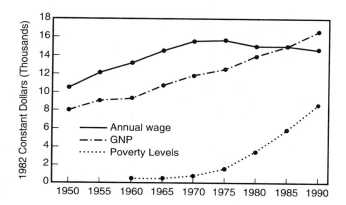

Figure 5. Income levels per capita.

per capita GNP is increasing, the conclusion is the middle class is moving downward, rather than the lower class moving upward.

The decline of the middle can also be identified by tracking the increasing number of dual-income families, including those families with young children, the decreasing number of middle-class students attending private colleges and universities, and the shift from the healthy leisure of family outings and puttering around the home and yard, to the escapist leisure of staring at television and spending long hours at the local bar. People who had been middle class all their lives suddenly descend into the lower class as the result of major health problems, having to take care of a elderly parent, or having insufficient resources for their own retirement. For these families, the rug had been pulled out from under them. The decline in wealth and income is not as noticeable as it might be because the reduction has occurred over an extended period. The high numbers of production workers laid off in the 1970s were augmented not only by additional blue-collar layoffs, but also by the layoffs of office personnel, and the furloughing of first-line supervisors in the 1980s. In the late 1980s and early '90s, there also were major reductions in middle management and technical staff. In turn, the local community losses cascade into the broader region because of decreased demand of general services, a general belt tightening on most expenditures, and the emigration of the population.

The postwar unemployment rate has ranged between 4 and 8 percent, the peak occurring as the percent of the population in poverty was drastically reduced (see Figure 6), but the unemployment rate does not include discouraged workers—people who want to work but who are not actively looking because they believe their chances of finding work are slim. A study found that the real unemployment rate in the United States in late 1993 should be adjusted from 6.4 to 9.3. The study found a need to adjust the rates in France from 12.0 to 13.7, in Great Britain from 9.8 to 12.3, and in Japan from 2.7 to 9.6 for the same period.

Is this downward social mobility of the middle class and the increasing impoverishment of the lower class the consequence of technological change associated with the progression from the industrial age to the information age? Nations are in social and technological transition, and there is a profound impact on the characteristics of social classes, on jobs and income, and on the definitions of wealth and the patterns of wealth production.

Some Conclusions

Over the most recent generation or so, the socioeconomic classes have shifted. The rich grew in numbers and got wealthier. The poor below the poverty line remained about the same. The working class declined in terms of real income and wealth and grew in numbers because individuals previously middle class moved in. The middle class got smaller in both numbers and in aggregate wealth.

The trends for wealth accumulation for the next few decades are that the lower class will become better off absolutely and worse off relatively, the lower-middle class will continue its downward slide, the middle-middle and the upper-middle classes will probably not be able to keep up economically and will lose in numbers, and the rich will grow in both numbers and wealth, outpacing the macroeconomic growth. The gap between the upper class and other classes will increase, and the gap between the middle class and the lower class will become smaller. The society will become increasingly more bimodal. Overall, the United States will become wealthier, but will lose ground relative to the rest of the world.

These trends will continue until the second or third decade of the twenty-first century. Then the pendulum will swing back and the middle class will reassert itself, equalizing the disparities and ushering a broad-based growth in personal and social wealth.

[See also Economics; Financial Institutions; Investments; Savings; Taxes.]

BIBLIOGRAPHY

Bartlett, Donald L., and Steele, James B. *America: What Went Wrong.* Kansas City: Andrews and McMeel, 1992.

Braun, Denny. *The Rich Get Richer: The Rise of Income Inequality in the United States and the World.* Chicago: Nelson-Hall, 1991.

Brockway, George P. *The End of Economic Man: Principles of Any Future Economics.* New York: Norton, 1993.

Cohen, Michael Lee. *The Twentysomething American Dream: A Cross-Country Quest for a Generation.* New York: Dutton, 1993.

Howe, Neil, and Strauss, Bill. *13th Gen: Abort, Retry, Ignore, Fail?* New York: Vintage, 1993.

Newman, Katherine S. *Declining Fortunes: The Withering of the American Dream.* New York: Basic Books, 1993.

———. *Falling from Grace: The Experience of Downward Mobility in the American Middle Class.* New York: Vintage, 1988.

Philips, Kevin. *Boiling Point: Democrats, Republicans, and the Decline of Middle-Class Prosperity.* New York: Random House, 1993.

———. *The Politics of Rich and Poor. Wealth and the American Electorate in the Reagan Aftermath.* New York: HarperCollins, 1990.

— NILS E. HOVIK

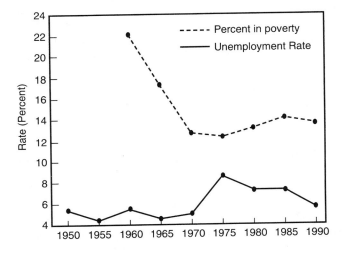

Figure 6. Unemployment and poverty levels.

WEAPONS, LETHAL.

See LETHAL WEAPONS.

WEAPONS OF MASS DESTRUCTION

Weapons of mass destruction, or unconventional weapons, include: nuclear, chemical, and biological. While scientifically very different, they share a potential to inflict large casualties.

Nuclear Weapons

Nuclear weapons use the energy of the atom to create an explosion. Weapons created by the fission, or splitting, of atoms are commonly referred to as atomic, or A-bombs. Those created by atomic fusion, or the thermonuclear reaction of hydrogen isotopes, are called hydrogen, or H-bombs. Enhanced-radiation weapons, also known as neutron bombs, produce more neutrons, gamma rays, or X rays than a normal weapon of the same yield. The world's total nuclear arsenal of some 48,000 weapons has an explosive power of 11,700 megatons, or 2.2 tons of TNT for every person on Earth.

Only the United States, the former Soviet Union, the United Kingdom, France, and China have acknowledged possession of nuclear weapons. India, Israel, and Pakistan possess a limited number of nuclear weapons. North Korea reportedly may have the capability to produce one or two simple nuclear bombs. South Africa secretly produced six nuclear weapons, but subsequently destroyed them. Algeria, Iran, Iraq, and Libya reportedly have been seeking to develop nuclear weapons (see Table 1).

The capability to develop and produce nuclear weapons still remains beyond the reach of most nations. The major technical obstacle is acquiring the fissile material (enriched uranium or plutonium) needed to fuel a nuclear chain reaction.

Political strategies to slow the spread of nuclear weapons have included: the 1968 Nuclear Nonproliferation Treaty, signed by more than 160 nations; the designation of nuclear weapon-free zones (Antarctica, Latin America, outer space, the ocean seabed, and the South Pacific); export restrictions; sanctions against proliferators; inspections by the International Atomic Energy Agency; resolving disputes that fuel the demand for nuclear weapons; reducing weapons stockpiles; and ending all nuclear test explosions (of which there have been more than 2,000).

In the aftermath of the Cold War, it has been proposed that the United States reduce its nuclear arsenal from 20,000 to 8,500 warheads and that the former Soviet Union reduce its arsenal from 27,000 to 10,000. No major reductions are anticipated in the much smaller arsenals of the United Kingdom, France, and China. By 2003, the world's combined nuclear arsenals are projected to still include more than 20,000 nuclear warheads (see Table 2).

The world is edging closer to a Comprehensive Test Ban Treaty. Temporary nuclear testing moratoria are already being observed by the United States, France, Russia, and the United Kingdom.

The global deployment and regular movement of nuclear weapons by air, land, and sea make accidents a constant, potential danger. There have been more than 300 nuclear accidents of varying severity worldwide since 1945.

TABLE 1

THE NUCLEAR POWERS THAT BE

Acknowledged Nuclear Weapons States	Former Nuclear Weapons States	Threshold Nuclear Weapons States*	Nations Believed to Be Seeking Nuclear Weapons Capabilities
Belarus[†]	South Africa[‡]	Israel	Algeria
China			Iran
France			Iraq
India			Libya
Kazakhstan[†]			North Korea
Pakistan			
Russia			
Ukraine[‡]			
United Kingdom			
United States			

Chart prepared by Center for Defense Information.

* Israel is believed either to possess a limited number of undeclared nuclear weapons or to be able to produce them within weeks or months of a decision to do so.

† These states, along with Russia, inherited their nuclear arsenals from the former Soviet Union. These three states have signed agreements to rid themselves of nuclear weapons.

‡ South Africa secretly produced, but has subsequently destroyed, six nuclear weapons. Although other states such as Argentina and Brazil, have given up their pursuit of nuclear weapons, South Africa is the first and, so far, the only state to acquire nuclear weapons and later destroy them all. Belarus, Kazakhstan, and Ukraine are slated to become former nuclear weapons states.

TABLE 2

NUCLEAR ARSENALS OF ACKNOWLEDGED NUCLEAR WEAPONS STATES*
(ESTIMATED 1992 AND PROJECTED 2003)

Nation	1992 Estimated Strategic Nuclear Weapons	1992 Estimated Tactical Nuclear Weapons	1992 Estimated Total Nuclear Weapons	2003 Projected Strategic Nuclear Weapons	2003 Projected Tactical Nuclear Weapons	2003 Projected Total Nuclear Weapons
U.S.A.	12,000	8,000	20,000	3,500	5,000	8,500
Former U.S.S.R.	10,000†	17,000‡	27,000†	3,000‡	7,000‡	10,000‡
U.K.	130	200	330	300	100	400
France	520	80	600	640	80	720
China	300	200	500	300	200	500

Sources: CDI, DOD, NRDC, BASIC, SIPRI, Jane's.
Chart prepared by the Center for Defense Information.
* All warhead counts include both deployed and war reserve nuclear weapons.
† Weapons deployed in Russia, Ukraine, Kazakhstan, and Belarus.
‡ Weapons deployed solely in Russia.

In the process of building almost 70,000 U.S. nuclear warheads, an estimated 4,500 sites in America became polluted with chemical and radioactive byproducts. Efforts to clean up this mess and bring nuclear weapons facilities into compliance with the nation's environmental laws are expected to take at least thirty years and to cost as much as $300 billion. Safe and permanent disposal of radioactive waste is perhaps the most serious long-term dilemma resulting from the Cold War.

Chemical Weapons

The use of gas warfare by both Iran and Iraq during their eight-year war in the 1980s and the fear that Iraq might use them during the Persian Gulf war provided impetus to long-standing international efforts to eliminate chemical weapons.

The world's total nuclear arsenal

of some 48,000 weapons

has an explosive power of 11,700 megatons,

or 2.2 tons of TNT for every person on Earth.

Chemical weapons are inanimate, synthetic gases, liquids, or solids that are designed to produce specific physiological effects after they are inhaled, ingested, or come into contact with skin. They can be lethal (nerve, blister, choking and blood agents); harassing (tear gas); or incapacitating (vomit agents and psychochemicals).

In addition, herbicides, or defoliants, are defined as chemical weapons by some countries but not by others.

The 1925 Geneva Protocol outlawed the use of chemical weapons but does not prohibit countries from producing and stockpiling them. While there have been numerous unsubstantiated allegations of chemical weapons use since World War I, for the most part chemical warfare has been shunned as morally repugnant and taboo.

The largest possessors of chemical weapons today are the United States (30,000 tons) and the former Soviet Union (40,000 tons). Both nations have ceased producing them.

Chemical weapons sometimes are referred to as the "poor man's atom bomb." Any country with a petrochemical, pesticide, fertilizer, or pharmaceutical industry potentially could produce them. Countries currently believed to have programs for developing chemical weapons include: China, India, Israel, Iran, Iraq, Libya, Myanmar, North Korea, Pakistan, South Korea, Syria, Taiwan, and Vietnam. A country must possess more than laboratory-sized quantities of a chemical agent before it has a militarily significant capability. Successful attack requires that the weather conditions (wind, rain, and temperature) be favorable and that the target population be unprepared. In the absence of protective measures, chemical weapons, pound for pound, are more deadly than conventional high explosives.

The 1993 Chemical Weapons Convention, signed by more than 150 nations, outlaws the development, production, stockpiling, acquisition, or transfer of chemical weapons. This global treaty features the most comprehensive and intrusive verification measures ever to be included in an arms reduction agreement.

Future challenges include securing adherence to the treaty's directives and destroying existing stockpiles. The United States plans to incinerate its chemical weapons, but citizen concerns about environmental and safety risks may force reconsideration of this policy.

Biological Weapons

Biological weapons are living organisms, infective materials, or their synthetic equivalent that achieve effects by multiplying inside targeted persons, plants, or animals. Infectious doses of some biological agents are on the order of a trillionth of a gram. In theory, they are the deadliest of any potential weapons. A bullet, once it is fired, eventually must come to a rest, whereas a biological weapon can theoretically spread forever if left unchecked.

Potential biological weapon agents include bacteria, viruses, and antiplant agents. Bacteria investigated for military applications include: anthrax, plague, tularemia (rabbit fever), typhoid, and dysentery. Viruses with military weapon potential include: smallpox, yellow fever, influenza, Rift Valley Fever, and Venezuelan equine encephalitis. Antiplant agents include: wheat rust, rice blast, corn stunt, and rice and corn blight.

Toxins, poisonous substances produced by living organisms, encompass the gray area between chemical and biological weapons. Unlike biological weapons, they are inanimate and thus incapable of reproducing themselves. Toxins are produced by bacteria (botulinum), fungi, marine organisms (shellfish), poisonous plants, and venomous insects, spiders, and snakes.

Currently, no countries admit to the possession of biological weapons. In 1969, the United States unilaterally renounced the possession of biological weapons and destroyed its stockpile. The 1972 Biological and Toxin Weapons Convention, signed by more than 130 nations, outlaws the development, production, stockpiling, acquisition, or transfer of these weapons. A major weakness of this treaty is its lack of any means of verification and enforcement. Furthermore, it allows research on defenses, and demarcations between civilian/ military and offensive/defensive purposes are not always clear. Efforts are underway to close these loopholes.

Countries believed to have programs for developing biological weapons include: China, Iran, Iraq, Libya, North Korea, Syria, and Taiwan. Any country with advanced capabilities in the health sciences, biotechnology, or beer brewing has at least the rudimentary potential to produce biological weapons.

Because they are living organisms, biological agents cannot easily be developed as instruments of war or effectively disseminated to targets. They are vulnerable to sunlight or extreme temperatures, and often can be countered by vaccinations.

Future Trends

In the future, nuclear, chemical, and biological weapons may be deemphasized and possibly even phased out. Significant geopolitical changes in the world during the early 1990s provide new opportunities to drastically reduce and eventually eliminate such weapons. Steps in this direction have been taken, but many more remain untaken.

Infectious doses of some biological agents are on the order of a trillionth of a gram. In theory, they are the deadliest of any potential weapons.

Perceived military need for such weapons may diminish as the destructive potential of conventional weapons approaches that achieved by weapons of mass destruction. Gen. Colin Powell, then-chairman of the U.S. Joint Chiefs of Staff, questioned the value of nuclear weapons when he said, "I think there is far less utility of these [nuclear] weapons than some Third World countries think there is, and they are wasting a lot of money, because what they hope to do militarily with weapons of mass destruction of the kind we are talking about, I can increasingly do with conventional weapons, and far more effectively." The 1991 war against Iraq demonstrated this potential.

Weapons of mass destruction by their very nature are self-inhibiting. Their enormous deadliness, unpredictability, and the widespread global condemnation incurred by using them make them unlikely weapons of choice.

They are primarily political instruments, useful only to reciprocally deter use by other nations. As the increased firepower of conventional weapons renders deterrence obsolete, the danger of nuclear, chemical, or biological warfare may grow increasingly more remote. The danger of massive conventional warfare, however, will remain and perhaps will increase.

[*See also Hazardous Wastes; Lethal Weapons; Military Technologies; National Security; Peacekeeping.*]

BIBLIOGRAPHY

Barnaby, Frank. *How Nuclear Weapons Spread: Nuclear Weapon Proliferation in the 1990s.* New York: Routledge, 1993.

Gray, Colin S. *Weapons Don't Make War. Policy, Strategy, and Military Technology.* Lawrence, KS: University Press of Kansas, 1993.

Roberts, Brad, ed. *Biological Weapons: Weapons of the Future?* Washington, DC: Brookings Institution, 1993.

Sivard, Ruth Leger. *World Military and Social Expenditures, 1993.* Washington, DC: World Priorities, 1993.

— GENE R. LAROCQUE

WEATHER.

See CLIMATE AND METEOROLOGY.

WELFARE.

See ENTITLEMENTS; PUBLIC ASSISTANCE PROGRAMS; SOCIAL WELFARE PHILOSOPHIES.

WELLS, H. G. (1866–1946)

The novelist, journalist, and social philosopher H. G. Wells was born in Bromley, Kent in the United Kingdom. Wells established himself as a writer of fiction in the mid-1890s. His most successful novels include *The Time Machine* (1895), *The War of the Worlds* (1898), and *Tono-Bungay* (1909). His bestseller *The Outline of History* (1920) viewed ancient and modern history from a global perspective, culminating in a fervent plea for world government. Wells's contributions to the study of the future range from *Anticipations* (1901), a sophisticated forecast of technological, social, and political transformation, to *The Shape of Things to Come* (1933), an imaginary history of the next century and a half, later filmed by Alexander Korda as *Things to Come* (1936). In *The Discovery of the Future* (1902), Wells looked forward to the emergence of a science of the future, as exact and authoritative as anything possible in the natural sciences. Hailed by some critics as the founding father of modern science fiction, he is also remembered for his dystopian and utopian fiction. In *When the Sleeper Wakes* (1899), he anticipated most of the horrors later foreseen in the classic futurist dystopias of Yevgeni Zamyatin, Aldous Huxley, and George Orwell. *A Modern Utopia* (1905) depicts a global technocracy somewhat reminiscent of Edward Bellamy's in *Looking Backward.*

[See also *Futurism; Orwell, George; Popularized Futures.*]

BIBLIOGRAPHY

Hillegas, Mark R. *The Future As Nightmare: H. G. Wells and the Anti-Utopians.* New York: Oxford University Press, 1967.

MacKenzie, Norman and Jeanne. *H. G. Wells.* New York: Simon & Schuster, 1973.

Smith, David C. *H. G. Wells: Desperately Mortal.* New Haven, CT: Yale University Press, 1986.

Wagar, W. Warren. *H. G. Wells and the World State.* New Haven, CT: Yale University Press, 1961.

Wells, H. G. *Experiment in Autobiography.* New York: Macmillan, 1934.

— W. WARREN WAGAR

WILDCARDS

A wildcard is a low-probability, high-impact event. It is an event that is rarely anticipated.

Growing up in California during the 1950s and '60s, I can recall an early introduction to wildcard events. The disaster drills in grammar school provided me with a reference point for low-probability, high-impact wars, earthquakes, tidal waves, and other unnamed disasters. Knowing the location of the bomb shelter could, according to our teachers, save our lives. Planning for the unexpected seemed to hold some merit when presented along these lines.

The breakup of the Soviet Union,

reunification of Germany,

and the democratization of Eastern Europe

were a barrage of wildcard events.

Visionaries who actively plan for wildcard events open themselves up to a multitude of opportunities. The applicability of wildcard planning applies equally across the lines of government, industry, and private life. The most common form of wild-card planning in the United States is perhaps exemplified by certain forms of insurance coverage. Earthquake and flood insurance policies are sold to wildcard thinkers. These policies provide wild-card protection and, in fact, convey a benefit to those planning for a wildcard event. The wildcard thinker would also be one of few people prepared physically for these low-probability, high-impact events. They might also have inflatable rafts or emergency food and water provisions in their houses as preparation for an earthquake or flood.

Another common form of wildcard thinking revolves around the personal savings account. There are many reasons for keeping a savings account. The most obvious would be as a place to keep some money earmarked for a specific purpose—e.g., Christmas gifts. Many people, however, keep savings accounts as a hedge against wildcard events. They may not be presently afraid of an illness, or loss of employment, but the savings account is available for just such wildcard events should they occur. The level of perceived security such an account brings the holder can easily be extrapolated to planning for security on a much greater scale.

In a governmental and industrial context, the breakup of the Soviet Union, reunification of Germany, and the democratization of Eastern Europe were a barrage of wildcard events. Most political and industrial experts failed to plan for any portion of these events. There were, however, a few scattered visionaries who not only considered the ramifications of such events, but took steps prior to their realization to gain a superior position in these emerging, changing markets. These visionaries are now the beneficiaries of heightened market or political influence.

To gain the benefit of wildcard thinking and planning, there is no true necessity for investment of large amounts of time or capital into what seems, at best, an uncertainty. There is only a need for awareness extending beyond the parameters of the obvious.

Some examples of wildcards follow.

Political Wildcards

- *The United States breaks up into autonomous nation-states,* following an extended series of social and economic crises, and a lack of regional agreement on methods of repair. The Western states join a new Pacific Rim economic organization, and the Eastern states form the Atlantic Economic Union with the European and Latin American countries. The breakup creates a wide disparity in the wealth of the new states, resulting in a Third to First World economic range. It also results in difficulties regarding ownership of defense-related commodities, not unlike the breakup of the former Soviet Union.
- *A Russian-Chinese-Japanese alliance* is formed in which the partners abandon their historically turbulent relations and act as a self-contained economic bloc, frustrating economic relations with the United States and the European Union.
- *Global governance* becomes a reality, effectively splitting the world into regional and international decision-making bodies, without recognition of sovereign nation-states.

Socioeconomic Wildcards

- *Nonmaterial values replace consumerism in all OECD countries,* drastically increasing levels of personal savings, and causing economic chaos in all nonagricultural industrial sectors.
- *Genetic profiling radically alters health care economy* by reducing the incidence of disease, causing a 50 percent drop in pharmaceutical sales and physician visits.
- *Mass transit replaces 50 percent of all cars in the United States,* following an even stronger trend in the European Union toward a 90 percent mass transit level.

Technology Wildcards

- *Cold fusion* will be effectively developed, thereby challenging the entirety of the global energy economy.
- *All shopping will be done by telecommunication,* rather than through physical visits to stores. All items, including groceries, will be home-delivered.

- *Clothing will be electronically coded* to ensure full color and style compatibility on the owner. Clothing will be programmed with the consumers' individual style parameters upon purchase. If a combination outside these parameters is attempted, an alarm will be triggered warning the user of a potential incompatible combination.

Anticipating radical change is nothing new to strategic planners. It is in the nature of their business to anticipate both radical and subtle shifts in existing structures. The wildcard is a tool for measuring the far reaches of these structures.

When making any plan, be it as simple as planning your college education, or as complex as seeking to establish a multinational business consortium, a wildcard analysis can be of great benefit. By taking the most logical scenarios and stretching their elasticity, you can prepare yourself for what may, in the present, seem unlikely, but what would, in the future, be an opportunity or disaster.

A wildcard thinker is not necessarily someone who anticipates divorce upon marriage, but someone who might anticipate the need for compromise during the relationship. The wildcard is a tool of awareness, not prediction. In times of uncertainty and tumultuous change, predictions are difficult, leaving awareness as the only safe road to the future.

[See also Change, Scientific and Technological; Continuity and Discontinuity; Forecasting, Deterministic; Forecasting, Mistakes In; Forecasting Methods; Technology Forecasting and Assessment; Trend Indicators.]

BIBLIOGRAPHY

Bignell, Victor, and Fortune, Joyce. *Understanding Systems Failures.* Manchester, U.K.: Manchester University Press, 1984.
Casti, John L. *Searching for Certainty: What Science Can Know About the Future.* New York: William Morrow, 1991.
Weston, Victoria. *Into the Future and the Next Millennium.* Atlanta: Oscar Dey, 1991.

— JOHN D. ROCKFELLOW

WOMEN IN FUTURES STUDIES

Are all the great futurists men? Anyone relying on articles, books, and surveys identifying the "great futurists" might come to that conclusion. The consulting firm of Coates and Jarratt circulated a list with the names of 125 futurists to representatives of 10 large American businesses asking them to select the names of those futurists who had "something to say about the future relevant to the corporation" and published results in a 1989 book entitled *What Futurists Believe.* All of the seventeen persons featured in this book are middle-aged and older white American males, except one who is an elderly white Englishman living in Sri Lanka, and another older white Englishman living in the United States. Each of the seventeen designees was interviewed, or otherwise asked certain questions about themselves. One question asked them to name the people who mainly influenced their ideas about the future. Here again the names of fifteen white men, mostly American, stood out from among a list of roughly fifty names offered as being intellectually influential in their thinking about the future. Not a single non-Westerner was named and only two women were named, one being the wife of the person naming her.

Many people who commented on the book criticized the authors for seeming to say that the only relevant futurists in the world are a handful of old white American men. The critics faulted the authors not so much for the conclusions they drew from the data they collected, but rather because of their sampling method, which seemed to have tapped entirely older white American male corporate sources. The authors were neither unaware of nor unconcerned about the apparent bias in their sample and conclusions, and attempted to justify both in the book's introduction.

Other people have also attempted to identify outstanding and relevant futurists as well. One of the earliest attempts was undertaken by Michael Marien in 1972 in his *The Hot List Delphi*. Marien's list is not of people, but of "essential reading for the future" at that time. He asked a panel of forty-four people (of whom only fourteen actually ended up on the panel) who had "some degree of critical appreciation of at least 500 futures or futures-related documents" to rate the literature in terms of its essential relevance to the field. All but one of Marien's fourteen panelists were male, Eleonora Barbieri Masini of Italy being the only female. All but three were Americans. Thirty-six documents were ranked by more than two-thirds of the panelists as being essential reading for futurists and people interested in the future. All but one of the authors of the documents listed were male, the sole female author being Margaret Mead for her book, *Culture and Commitment*. Twenty-four were Americans and the rest Europeans, plus one Canadian.

Alvin Toffler edited a book, also in 1972, called *The Futurists*. "The purpose of this collection," he said, "is to make accessible a few of the works of the best known and, at the moment, most influential futurists...." "To illustrate the diversity of the movement, I have drawn selections not merely from the United States, but also from Japan, France, the Netherlands, the U.S.S.R., India, Germany, and Canada." And indeed, of the twenty-three people in the book, only twelve are Americans. Still, all but one are males—the sole exception once again being Margaret Mead.

More recently in 1987, Marien and Jennings published a book based on invitations they sent to forty-four futurists who were asked to reflect on what they had learned about the future, and how to think about the future. Seventeen responses were finally published in the book. Four were from American women: Vary Coates, Irene Taviss Thomson, Kusum Singh (originally from India), and Hazel Henderson (who was born in England). All but one (apparently) of the males were Americans.

In 1989, Hugues de Jouvenel, head of the Paris-based Association Internationale Futuribles, conducted a small survey of eight people he described as being "outstanding futurists," asking them to identify the major global futures studies published since 1980. All but one of the eight panelists were male. Three were French, three were American, one was Italian (Eleonora Barbieri Masini), and one was Russian. Eighty-nine publications were listed, including one from China, one from Japan, one from Africa, and three from the former Soviet Union. All the rest were from Europe or the United States. There was no single item that all eight of the panelists agreed on, but five did agree that Lester Brown's (an American) *State of the World* reports were "major global futures studies," and three others agreed on Gerald Barney's ill-fated *Global 2000 Report to the President*; Mikhail Gorbachev, *Perestroika*; Norman Myers, *GAIA: An Atlas of Planet Management*; Alvin Toffler, *The Third Wave*; and the World Commission on Environment and Development's report, *Our Common Future* (often called the Brundtland Report). So we have three more Americans, one Russian, all males, and (arguably) one Norwegian woman (Gro Harlem Brundtland).

Finally, Allen Tough, of the University of Toronto, in 1990 mailed questionnaires to "115 professors, writers and leaders in future studies" as well as distributing them to "a large number of people ... attending two international futures conferences, two small courses, and one small seminar." "From all these sources a total of 58 usable questionnaires were returned. Each respondent listed between 1 and 10 'individuals who are today ... contributing the especially significant, fresh and/or profound ideas about the future.'" "Although 198 different individuals were nominated, three-quarters of them were nominated only once. ... At the opposite extreme, 14 respondents listed Alvin Toffler. ... In all, 49 people were nominated by from 2 to 14 respondents. Of the 8 people listed 6 or more times, 4 were women and 3 were non-Americans" (Tough, 1990.).

What can we conclude from this? First of all, it does seem to make a difference who is doing the surveying and from where. Male American researchers seem to end up with lists that have mainly male American futurists on them, Toffler perhaps being the exception as far as nationality is concerned. Male Canadian and French futurists tend to select a few more non-Americans and a few more women.

So what about the contribution of women to futures studies? We might conclude that there are not very many women in futures studies but that the few are truly outstanding: Margaret Mead, Eleonora Barbieri Masini, Hazel Henderson, and Gro Harlem Brundtland.

Many more women from many more parts of the world have contributed to the founding, growth, and continuing search for excellence and relevance of futures studies. From the very beginning, women have been active in both the World Future Society (WFS) and the World Futures Studies Federation (WFSF), the two leading global futures organizations. The 1991–1992 *Futures Research Directory* published by the WFS listed 126 women out of 1,172 names—10.7 percent of the total.

Three other women were undisputed leaders in cultural and peace-oriented aspects of futures studies: Margaret Mead, the world-famous anthropologist who did appear on the previous lists; Barbara Ward, internationally acclaimed for her visionary leadership in peace and environmental activities; and Elise Boulding, who also was one of the first to reveal the ignored but crucial contributions that specific women have made throughout recorded history, in her monumental book, *The Underside of History.*

Other women active from the earliest days of futures studies are Barbara Marx Hubbard, an optimistic visionary, and Renée-Marie Croose Parry, who still tirelessly strives for widened political freedoms. The late Sally Cornish, wife of WFS president Edward Cornish, also should be prominently mentioned.

Two women, perhaps more than any others, deserve to be credited for making futures studies what it is today. One is Magda McHale, an artist and cultural futurist, and a vice president of the WFSF. Though originally Hungarian, and holding a British passport, McHale has lived and worked for many years in the United States, and is the founder and director of the Center for Integrative Studies of the State University of New York at Buffalo. The other, without whom the WFSF probably would not now exist at all, is the previously mentioned Eleonora Barbieri Masini, a professor of sociology and law at the Gregorian University of Rome, Italy. She also was the second secretary general of the WFSF, its third president, and chair of the executive council of the WFSF. She, more than any other single person, kept alive and nurtured to maturity the infant organization she received from the founding father and first president, Johan Galtung of Norway, and the second president, from Morocco, Mahdi Elmandjra. Both she and Magda McHale had also been active in the creation of futures studies and the WFSF from the very beginning.

In places, it was primarily women

who were responsible for the creation

of any future-oriented groups whatsoever.

Since that time, there have been many women from many parts of the world active in the WFSF, the WFS, or in other future-oriented organizations or undertakings. Indeed, in some places, it was primarily women who were responsible for the creation of any future-oriented groups whatsoever, for example, Rosa Menasanch, Pepita Majoral, Conxita Bargallo, and Antonia Guix; during the dark days of Franco's dictatorship, they were among the founders in 1973 of the Centre Catala de Prospectiva in Barcelona, Spain. Similarly, Eva Gabor, Maria Kalas Koszegi, Erszebet Gidai, and Erszebet Novaky played crucial roles in the establishment of futures research in Hungary in the 1970s, as did Ana Maria Sandi and Viorica Ramba-Varga in Romania; Danuta Markowska in Poland; Radmila Nakarada in Yugoslavia; Anna Coen in Italy; Erika Landau and Rachel Dror in Israel; and, later, Margarita Kaisheva in Bulgaria.

At the forefront of early futures work in the United States and still continuing their leadership are Donella Meadows (mainly responsible for an earth-shaking future-oriented publication during the 1970s, *The Limits to Growth,* as well as for the newer, equally important book, *Beyond the Limits,* published in 1992); Marilyn Ferguson (whose book *The Aquarian Conspiracy* still inspires optimism); Edith Weiner (who, as the head of futures research for the American Council of Life Insurance in the 1960s and '70s, is probably responsible for the invention of what is now called "environmental scanning"); Betty Reardon (an educational futurist and peace researcher at Columbia University); and Patricia Mische of Global Education Associates.

More recently, American women especially vital for educational futures include Linda Groff, Betty Frank, Penny Damlo, Kathleen Maloney, Ruthanne Kurth-Schai, and Maria Guido (the latter of whom is Costa Rican-born). Jennifer Jarratt, Martha Garrett, Sandra Postel, Jessica Matthews, Suzanne Gordon, Faith Popcorn, Joanna Macy, Charlene Spretnak, and Riane Eisler are among the best-known names in the consulting, global, environmental, and/or spiritual futures fields in the United States. Heidi Toffler and Patricia Aburdene also enjoy a unique prominence and have coauthored many top-selling books about the future. Others include Audrey Clayton, coeditor of *Futures Research Quarterly,* and Mary Clark, author of *Ariadne's Thread* and coeditor of *Rethinking Curriculum.*

Elsewhere, Mitsuko Saito-Fukunaga (Japan), Marie Angelique Savane (Senegal), Margarita de Botero (Colombia), Katrin Gillwald (Germany), and Janice Tait and Fernande Faulkner (Canada) have each contributed greatly to futures work.

Several other groups of women deserve special mention. There are eight women who have taken the leadership in bringing futures research and thinking directly into the judiciaries of the United States: Dana Farthing-Capowich of the State Justice Institute; Francis Zemans, Sandra Ratcliffe, and Kate Samson of the American Judicature Society; Kathy Mays and Beatrice Monahan of the Judiciary of the State of Virginia; and Wendy Schultz and Sharon Rodgers of the Hawaii Research Center for Futures Studies.

Lauren Cook of the National Association of Governors' Policy Advisers has done equally outstanding futures work for the executive branch of many American state governments. Cathryn Johnson does similarly successful work for the Health Care Forum, an association that works closely with the public and private health care providers. Anita Rubin and Leena-Maija Salminen are among a group of experienced young futurists in the Finnish Society for Futures Studies, as are Robin Brandt, Annette Gardner, Bindi Borg, and Deborah Halbert in Hawaii.

Concluding this by no means complete list of women practitioners in the field of futures studies are Pat Barrentine, Maureen Caudill, Betty Friedan, Deborah Gordon, Elizabeth Dodson Gray, Heather Hudson, Heather Kurent, Lena Lupica, Janne Nolan, Cheryl Russell, and Juliet Schor.

[*See also Future Studies; Futures Concepts; Futures Education; Futurism; Futurists.*]

BIBLIOGRAPHY

Cornish, Edward, ed. *The Futures Research Dirctory: Individuals, 1995–96.* Bethesda, MD: The World Future Society, 1995.

Jennings, Lane, ed. *Futures Research Directory: Organizations and Periodicals, 1993–94.* Bethesda, MD: The World Future Society, 1993.

Malaska, Peutii, ed. *World Futures Studies Federation Newsletter—WFSF Directory 1990.* Turku, Finland. WFSF Secretariat, 1990.

— JAMES A. DATOR

WOMEN IN POLITICS

More than half of the world's population is female, but nowhere in the world do women participate politically as equals with men. Every society is built on the outdated, repressive, and abusive patriarchal belief that women should be spectators, not participants, in politics and in setting political, economic, and social agendas.

"Gender politics" is the response of women worldwide to this attitude. The American women's movement has worked toward educating the public about links between politicians, money, and tax burden (i.e., who gets treated better than others in tax load).

Continuing deficits, high taxes, and political scandals have prompted taxpayers to reconsider who represents them in elective office, setting a trend for accountability. Since women, rightly or wrongly, are perceived as less corruptible, this trend is leading to more women in elective and appointive offices. At the same time, problems such as family size, consumer choices, waste disposal, and education of children, once characterized as women's issues, are being recognized as global issues. As a result, women's traditional roles and values are becoming more pronounced in the policy-making arena. More women in public office may change the political focus from how to control to how to get things done.

Strong women leaders increase public confidence in women's abilities to lead, but superficial press coverage of women contributes to their slow progress in gaining political power. Women have been underrepresented as sources, subjects, and reporters in the American newspaper industry. It is not surprising that when only 34 percent of journalists are women, 19 percent are editors and managers, and 34 percent of front page articles are written by women, a scant 15 percent of front-page stories are about women.

History is replete with traditional women's issues, but few are aware that women's struggle for suffrage, ("the right to vote") is at the root of today's battle for reproductive rights. The nineteenth-century suffrage movement created a powerful patriarchal backlash that resulted in the criminalization of abortion in every state; the male medical establishment's monopoly on obstetric medicine (in place of midwives); the Roman Catholic Church's declaration of abortion as a mortal sin in 1869; and public concern with the rights of the fetus.

With more women in political positions, there would be an increased focus on reducing the need for abortion rather than on how to abort legally. Restrictive policies and programs of parental consent, waiting periods, required counseling, and federal and state funds limitations would be unnecessary. Other so-called "women's issues"—child care, parenting, and educational needs—would get more attention and financial support if women gained greater political and economic power through public office.

Raising the status of females through education

is vital to their full participation in society.

Two-thirds of illiterate people are women,

due to prejudice against educating females.

The prevailing biases in educational and philanthropic funding is an overt admission of the undervaluing of females. Raising the status of females through knowledge and education is vital to the full participation of women in society. Two-thirds of the world's illiterates are women; and, in seventeen countries, over 90 percent of women are illiterate. Widespread prejudice against educating females is at the root of this illiteracy.

The Equal Rights Amendment in the United States, first proposed in 1923, was passed in 1972 but failed to be ratified after ten years of struggle. Opposing forces were convinced equality would invalidate protective laws for women. Women accidentally received federal protection from discrimination in 1964 because a Southern conservative congressman wanted to kill the proposed Civil Rights Act by adding "sex" to the protected classes. The law survived the addition of women, however.

Traditional women's issues finally led to a rise in women's voices and roles when it was recognized in 1980 that more women than men voted in the presidential election. This gender-based response can be attributed to women's economic interest in changing the status quo. More women candidates are running for office to correct an imbalance in public decision making. Women's voices are being heard at every level of government through more active participation by women in lobbying, issue-oriented activism, campaign contributions, and overall participation in the process of governance.

Despite recent advances, women only hold approximately 18 percent of all elective offices in the United States. They are still greatly underrepresented at all levels of elective and appointive public offices. One factor contributing to women's lack of public power is their role as cheap labor in the Third World. In Pakistan, Nicaragua, and the Philippines, women leaders of the 1980s were seen as weak and ineffective because they tried to work within the male power structure while ignoring the potential of cultivating the masses.

More progress for women has been made in Europe by way of strong female leadership. Former Prime Minister Margaret Thatcher showed the world that she could be as tough in leading Great Britain to war against Argentina as she was on social issues. Scandinavia, especially Norway, is a model region in terms of the full political integration of women and their views. Trends point toward a global community where problems are dealt with at the local level. For women political leaders, ignoring that local level can lead to failure.

The worldwide status of women was summed up in 1980 by a United Nations finding that "women constitute half of the world's population, perform nearly two-thirds of its work hours, receive one-tenth of the world's income, and own less than one-hundredth of the world's property."

At the end of the twentieth century, women do not have the right of full participation in politics anywhere in the world. Their increasing rates of election and appointment to political office in the United States and other countries augurs perhaps a major change in public attitudes about the value of both genders sharing power.

The quest of women for a greater voice in world politics continues. While full participation remains an illusive ideal, a partnership between men and women in shaping a new future is within reach if a gender-equal society becomes reality. An "ambigenic" society—one which is truly produced by or formed from both genders—will set aside patriarchal and/or matriarchal control in favor of mutual association for the greater good of humanity, setting the stage for a genuine global transformation.

[See also Women and Work; Women and World Development; Women's Health Movement; Women's Movement; Women's Rights; Women's Studies.]

BIBLIOGRAPHY

Davis, Kenneth C. *Don't Know Much About History.* New York: Crown Publishers, 1990.

Faludi, Susan. *Backlash—The Undeclared War against American Women.* New York: Crown Publishers, 1991.

Naisbitt, John, and Aburdene, Patricia. *Megatrends for Women.* New York: Villard Books, 1992.

Ries, Paula, and Stone, Anne J. *The American Woman 1992–93, A Status Report.* New York: W. W. Norton, 1992.

Seager, Joni, and Olson, Ann. *Women in the World—An International Atlas.* New York: Simon & Schuster, 1986.

— JULIA HUGHES JONES

WOMEN AND RELIGION

Women are the emergent movement in religion today. They are challenging the traditional male dominance within the clergy and rabbinate. Women are the majority now in most Protestant seminaries and in the future will be more numerous as ordained ministers, as bishops, and as faculty in seminaries. A continuing campaign for the ordination of women is pressuring Roman Catholic and Orthodox churches and will continue to complicate ecumenical relations.

Throughout recorded time men have "named the sacred" from the standpoint of their male body and male life experience. It is not accidental that in the Genesis 2 account of creation in Hebrew scriptures, Adam "named" all the animals. Naming is one kind of power, the power to shape a culture's ways of perceiving and thinking about reality so that they serve the interests and goals of those doing the naming. The future of human history is now being shaped by the power to name being claimed by Adam's heretofore silent partner.

Feminist theology and scholarship in Judaism and Christianity have blossomed into a scathing critique of male generic language, the pervasive male imagery (God-the-Father, God-the-King), and the male-centeredness of traditional theology.

This feminist theological critique of "the male as the norm" asserts that men created God as Father and King in their own male image, rather than, as had been taught for millennia, man being created in God's image. The publication of Mary Daly's *Beyond God the Father* (1973) marked for many women a new critical consciousness. Elisabeth Schüssler Fiorenza in New Testament studies and Rosemary Radford Ruether in historical theology pioneered a now widespread process of recovering the contributions to religion of women that were repressed and lost when men alone wrote "his" story as history. In Judaic thought, Judith Plaskow and others broke new ground in trying to imagine an all-embracing Jewish ritual.

In this same period (1970–1995), the Catholic church and Protestant and Jewish denominations have been engulfed in controversy and concern surrounding human sexuality, or what has been called "pelvic the-

Although men have often been the shapers of theological belief systems, women are frequently the daily practitioners of religious rituals and beliefs. Religious adherents will continue to grow, reaching 8.5 billion worldwide by 2020. (© Charles Walker Collection/Stock Montage, Inc.)

ology." These issues have not been resolved and will have a major future impact. First ordaining only males came under challenge. In Roman Catholicism the tradition of priestly celibacy is being questioned. Around the world the abortion controversy rages in various religions as yet another facet of pelvic theology. The issue of how to view and whether to ordain gays and lesbians has polarized Protestant denominations. Since the mid-1980s there have been numerous lawsuits in Roman Catholic and Protestant churches in the aftermath of public disclosures of sexual abuse by heterosexual ministers and priests involving abuse of clergy power, betrayal of trust, seduction, pedophilia, institutional coverup, and consequent loss of credibility.

Changing patterns of sexual behavior involve women as well as religion. Questions about morality and sexuality abound: Should there be any sexual activity outside of heterosexual religiously sanctioned marriage? For example, should teenagers be sexually active? Should engaged couples be sexually active? Should couples live together before marriage? What about same-sex couples? Should churches "bless" such relationships, as Episcopalian Bishop William Spong has suggested? What about sex ("affairs") outside of marriage, which traditionally religion has called "adultery"? What about senior citizens living together, refusing to marry because of social security, tax, or estate complications?

Should religious pronouncements adjust to widespread patterns of freer sexual behavior, or should traditional religion reiterate conventional moral positions and try to "keep a lid" on all this? A coherent religious answer to these many-faceted questions awaits future resolution.

The rise of women's prominence and power in both religion and the secular culture has provoked a strong backlash among religious conservatives. This fundamentalist backlash is prominent among Evangelical Protestants as well as traditionalist Roman Catholics and Muslims. In Judaism there is a growing "back to Orthodoxy" movement. Fundamentalism is characterized by a fear of "uncontrolled" female power and by a deeply felt desire to put women back into their traditional and subservient place. Patriarchal religion has functioned as a significant means of social control of women. The control of female sexuality and reproduction has been central to this control of women. Thus, issues of contraception and abortion are at the core of who controls women's lives.

Some women are now claiming the power to name the sacred "in their own image." An extensive goddess movement has developed during the 1980s and '90s as a way some women have chosen for claiming the power to name the sacred in their own image. A group of women scholars (Merlin Stone, Marija Gimbutas,

Charlene Spretnak, Riane Eisler, Elinor Gadon) have reinterpreted prehistory to rediscover a women's mythology of the Great Mother. They have written movingly of what this means for women.

"Spirituality" is a word that nonacademic women have come to use to express their new sense of the sacredness of women's experience, bodies, and perceived connection to the earth. New rituals are being written to celebrate women's previously uncelebrated menstruation, menopause, birthing, reproductive blood, and healing after the traumas of incest and child abuse.

Patriarchal religion has functioned

as a significant means of social control of women.

The control of female sexuality and reproduction

has been central to this control of women.

Women have discovered their outrage and are redefining morality. For innumerable women, flashbacks have opened to them again their repressed experiences of incest and child abuse. Battering, rape, and violence to women is now increasing as women's independence and social power grow. This violence can be characterized as sexual terrorism, used to enforce the power of the oppressor group. Rape, incest, and violence to women are a moral issue. Women also have realized that the majority of the poor, the elderly, and the hungry around the world are women and children. As a result of this realization, the moral issues of hunger and poverty also are coming to be seen as women's issues.

As women become aware of environmental damage and hazards, they become ecojustice activists, from Love Canal in New York state to the Chipco movement in India. Women see that ecological damage hurts their families, and take a firm stand. As women redefine the issues of morality, they understand that everything is interconnected, that for women the personal *is* political, and that feminism, religion, ecology, and the search for nonviolence cannot be separated.

[See also Abortion; Religions, Decline or Rise of; Religion, Spirituality, Morality; Sexual Behavior; Sexual Codes; Women's Movement.]

BIBLIOGRAPHY

Daly, Mary. *Beyond God the Father.* Boston: Beacon Press, 1973.

Faludi, Susan. *Backlash: The Undeclared War Against American Women.* New York: Crown, 1991.

Fiorenza, Elisabeth Schüssler. *In Memory of Her: A Feminist Theological Reconstruction of Christian Origins.* New York: Crossroad, 1983.

Ruether, Rosemary Radford, ed. *Religion and Sexism: Images of Women in the Jewish and Christian Traditions.* New York: Simon and Schuster, 1974.

— ELIZABETH DODSON GRAY

WOMEN AND WORK

The debate on women's rights started in earnest at the end of the eighteenth century. For the first time women asserted their right to participate in decision making, thus bringing to the fore and making visible what had already existed for a long time but had never been explicitly acknowledged. The letters written by Abigail Adams, respectively the wife and mother to the second and fourth presidents of the United States, reveal to what extent women were already aware of their invisible role and were conscious of their right to be recognized outside the home. Many similar examples could also be cited from the time of the French and the Russian revolutions.

Education was and still is crucial to fulfillment of women's rights. Equal opportunities in the field of education have still not been attained, either in industrialized countries or elsewhere around the world. In looking toward the future, the level of literacy among women is an important indicator. According to a recent definition, to be literate a person must be capable of reading and writing (with understanding) a simple statement about everyday life. The level of literacy among women is a better measurement of education than school enrollment because it reflects a minimum level of attainment. Although establishing the level of literacy in developing countries remains difficult, measurement by the test described above is more reliable than other measurements, such as those indicating the ratio of schools and students.

There are many more illiterate women than men in most countries of the world. Decades of elementary education for all have resulted in nearly universal literacy for the young. But in sub-Saharan Africa, or South or West Asia more than 70 percent of women over twenty-five are illiterate. In East and Southeast Asia the comparable figure is more than 40 percent, while in Latin America and the Caribbean it is more than 20 percent.

University and college enrollment figures are another indicator. Female enrollment is increasing rapidly and is equal to and even surpasses that of men in industrialized countries and in some countries of southern Africa, West Africa, and Latin America. But whatever the official support of equal educational opportunities, field work conducted in Latin America has shown that the higher female enrollment levels are related to higher overall levels of income. Economic disadvantage, especially in the developing countries, thus has a greater impact on educational attainment for women than for men.

Gender Gap

There continues to be a gender gap, not only in education but in the work men and women do. The household is still the main center of work for women. Housework includes a variety of activities: routine daily tasks, subsistence agriculture, the production of goods and services, trade, bookkeeping for the husband, and so forth. Precisely because female labor is so varied, it is difficult to measure women's work. Women work longer hours than men in both developing and industrialized countries, except in the United States and Australia, where the hours are almost equal. In Eastern Europe women spend more time in the labor force and less time in housework, whereas in North America, Australia, and Western Europe men spend less time in the labor force and a little more time on housework. These indications reflect a change of attitude in the last twenty to twenty-five years, between the 1960s and the late 1980s. The disparity between the number of hours spent by men and women in the labor force and in housework is decreasing, albeit very slowly.

In the developing countries, women are still working longer hours than men: in Latin America, on average, just over five and a half more hours a week than men; in Africa, Asia, and the Pacific up to as much as twelve or thirteen more hours. Because of the very nature of women's work, especially in the developing countries, often involving unpaid as well as paid activities, it is difficult to precisely quantify the degree of female participation in the labor market. However that determination may be calculated, it has certainly increased in almost every country in the last twenty years.

There is another important gender gap related to wages. In Cyprus, Japan, and South Korea women earn about one-half the male wage. In most countries, the female wage is generally around 75 percent the male wage. This holds, even in Canada—a country in which women's movements have been particularly active, where women have successfully occupied numerous positions of prestige, and where women's wages are around 71 percent those of men.

Moreover, in developing countries women tend to be concentrated in low-productivity labor—in agriculture, in the service industries, and in the informal sector. In times of economic crisis, the presence of women in the informal sector and in part-time jobs is bound to increase.

Finally, another important trend to be mentioned is the increasing "feminization of poverty" that accompanies the trend toward one-parent households in the industrialized countries and Latin America. The increasing number of women-headed households is probably an irreversible trend and is growing globally. This trend is caused by liberalized divorce in industrialized countries. In the developing nations it is attributable to migration (mainly male) between nations and within regions. Life expectancies also play a role. Up to 30 percent of households are headed by women, in many cases by women over sixty, because of higher female life expectancy. The exceptions are sub-Saharan Africa and countries such as Bangladesh, Bhutan, and the Maldives in southern Asia, where there are still high rates of maternal mortality.

Thus, over and beyond the formal acknowledgment of women's rights and the recognition of the important and visible role of women in society (more visible than in any other historical epoch), there continues to be a gender gap in terms of education and work opportunities. Taken together, these increasing trends toward single-parent (and mainly women-headed) households, have resulted in the increased feminization of poverty, as mentioned previously.

[See also Poverty, Feminization of; Women and World Development; Women's Movement; Work; Workforce Diversity.]

BIBLIOGRAPHY

World's Women. New York: United Nations, 1991.
Masini, Eleonora, and Stratigos, Susan. *Women, Households and Change.* Tokyo: United Nations University, 1991.

— ELEONORA BARBIERI MASINI

WOMEN AND WORLD DEVELOPMENT

Women and world development encompass fields of inquiry into the rapidly changing lives of women worldwide. Women's work and leadership had remained essentially unnoticed or ignored in histories of civilizations and were largely discounted by economic theory. The second wave of the women's movement, beginning in the 1960s, generated intense interest in women's roles and subordination, illustrating how political movements such as feminism influence scholarship.

Women tend to be concentrated in low-wage labor positions. In addition, women do much of the unpaid work in the world, such as this woman washing dishes. (Kevin R. Morris/Corbis)

As originally conceptualized in 1972 by women activists belonging to the Society for International Development (SID), the focus of inquiry was the unintended but frequently adverse impact that economic development was having on women. Women's work was ignored largely because women's traditional work in subsistence economies was uncounted in national labor force census enumerations and was, therefore, unrecognized in development planning. Women in development (WID) scholars collected data to demonstrate the importance of women's work on farms and in such subsistence activities as the collection of fuelwood, fetching water, and making baskets, jugs, and cloth. A major reference was Ester Boserup's 1970 landmark book, *Woman's Role in Economic Development,* which documented the shifting sexual division of labor as population pressures forced societies to adopt new technologies that, in turn, altered farming systems. Boserup chronicled global economic change in all its facets, while WID advocated incorporating women into planned interventions by donor agencies.

Testimony before Congress by SID-WID founder Irene Tinker led directly to the introduction of an amendment to the Foreign Assistance Act of 1973 requiring that women be integrated into all programs of the U.S. Agency for International Development. WID proponents wished to improve or reform donor programs so that women would benefit as well as men. By including women's perspectives, development programs would be better assured of reaching their goals. Offering agricultural information to men in Africa, where women do most of the farming, made little sense; however, it was typical of early agricultural extension approaches.

Proper recognition of women in resource projects was widely adopted by government agencies and by the increasing number of nongovernmental organizations (NGOs) active in development. The United Nations Decade for Women (1976–1985), punctuated with three major world conferences in Mexico City (1975), Copenhagen (1980), and Nairobi (1985), included development as one of its themes along with equality and peace. The Fourth World Conference on Women (Beijing, 1990) called for taking steps to overcome obstacles to women's advancement. As a result of resolutions passed at the Mexico City Conference, the UN established the UN Fund for Women to support small-scale efforts by women's organizations, and the UN International Research and Training Institute for the Advancement of Women to ensure that women were included in UN studies and activities.

Reality of Women's Lives

Heightened awareness of women's economic invisibility caused an acceleration of scholarship on women worldwide and sharpened the critique of development programs. At first this research centered on documenting women's economic contributions through time allocation studies of rural women. These data and findings challenged both the statistics and the definitions of work categories, for they revealed that women comprise 45 percent of all agricultural laborers, that women grow some 80 percent of all food south of the Sahara, that almost everywhere women work two to four hours a day more than men. Urban data found large numbers of women in Latin America, Africa, and Southeast Asia self-employed in the informal sector selling vegetables, street foods, and cosmetics. Domestic service in Latin America drew many women and girls because in those countries their agricultural role was minimal. Other studies revealed that prostitution, expanded by the tourist industry, was linked to rural poverty.

The second wave of the women's movement, beginning in the 1960s, generated intense interest in women's roles, illustrating how political movements such as feminism influence scholarship.

Evaluations of the newly introduced development programs began to question the "efficiency" approach that simply included women, and argued for an emphasis on empowering women. WID proponents emphasized women's access to and control of income as critical for enhancing women's bargaining within the family; organizing women for community projects or income activities became a major point of intervention by NGOs.

Critics of WID

Particularly in Europe, women scholars considered this approach too narrow because it did not challenge the basic liberal paradigm upon which donor programs are based. Marxists argued that women's conditions would only improve with a fundamental alteration in the economic system. Women's studies scholars attacked history and literature for their cultural representations of gender, and identified patriarchy and class as principal sources of women's oppression. Because this scholarship was rooted in Western theory, women's studies tended to be ethnocentric. Women from developing countries criticized the emphasis on individualism, arguing that women exist within the family, community, and culture. These strands of criticism focused on the different experiences of women of different classes and ethnicities and led to the use of the term *gender* to highlight how attitudes and behavior of both women and men are socially constructed. Gender and development reflect the variety of experiences of both men and women. Studies about men's changing roles in development are extremely limited.

The most potent critique of liberal economic development is coming from environmentalists who condemn the profligate use of the world's resources for technological advance that is called progress. Ecofeminists combine this negative view of the industrial revolution with insights on women's status. Recalling that women were the first agriculturalists, and that women continue to be the guardians of forest reserves in many countries, ecofeminists maintain that women understand environment better than men do.

As the concept of development is increasingly questioned, local empowerment through organizations is perceived as the best way for women to improve their own lives. At the same time, greater understanding of the profound changes in men's lives, as well, requires new scholarship that illumines gender similarities and differences in this era of inconceivable change.

[See also Development, Alternative; Development: Western Perspective; Women in Politics; Women and Religion; Women and Work; Women's Movement; Women's Rights; Women's Studies.]

BIBLIOGRAPHY

Boserup, Ester. *Woman's Role in Economic Development.* New York: St. Martin's Press, 1970.

Dwyer, Daisy, and Bruce, Judith, eds. *A Home Divided: Women and Income in the Third World.* Stanford, CA: Stanford University Press, 1988.

Tinker, Irene, ed. *Persistent Inequalities: Women and World Development.* New York: Oxford University Press, 1990.

Tinker, Irene, and Bo Bramsen, Michelle, eds. *Women and World Development.* New York: Praeger, 1976.

— IRENE TINKER

WOMEN'S HEALTH MOVEMENT

Worldwide, women have been and will continue to be the primary consumers of health and medical care—for themselves, for children, and often for ill or aging relatives. Women, especially women of color, also are the great majority of low-paid health care workers. Yet most of the doctors in the United States are men, men are the focus of most health research, and men—in hospitals, in legislatures and in the courtroom—make the major decisions affecting the health of women both as consumers and as workers. The women's health movement in the United States began and continues in response to these contradictions.

In the late 1960s, groups of mainly white, middle-class women gathered. Breaking long-held silences, they critiqued doctors who were patronizing and noninfor-

mative, who overprescribed tranquilizers, who treated the natural life events of childbirth and menopause like illnesses requiring intervention. Mobilizing to inform themselves and others, women pressed for "natural" childbirth with partners allowed in the delivery room, for informed choice about drugs and surgery, and for safe, legal abortion. They taught the role of the clitoris in women's orgasm, and masturbation as a form of self-exploration and self-love. They showed how power inequalities between men and women crept in "between the sheets" in lovemaking. They questioned rigid definitions of "normal" sexuality that limited women to heterosexual relationships and discriminated against lesbian and bisexual women. In the face of powerfully undermining media images of women, they helped each other affirm their own diverse beauty.

"Know Your Body" courses sprang up around the country. Some women reclaimed control over their bodies through teaching cervical self-examination and menstrual extraction (removal of the menses to avoid painful periods or end an early pregnancy). Women-run health centers offered woman-centered health care, emphasizing prevention, education, and informed consent.

Critiques by women of color pushed the women's health movement to move beyond a white, middle-class agenda. Sterilization abuse, access to affordable medical care, and the right of women to bear healthy children, as well as to prevent or end pregnancy, became significant organizing issues.

There are successes to celebrate. Now there are patient-package inserts in oral contraceptives and estrogen-replacement hormones, warning of possible effects and risks; free-standing birth centers and wider acceptance of midwives as birth attendants; increased abortion availability after the 1973 Supreme Court *Roe* v. *Wade* decision; more women in medical schools; federal regulations to prevent sterilization abuse; and education of doctors about lesbian health care needs. Lumpectomy increased as a less invasive breast cancer treatment than mastectomy. Each advance was the result of extensive hard work by advocates for women's health, who lobbied, educated, organized, raised money, voted, and sometimes simply created their own alternatives.

In the 1980s, pressure from the U.S. medical establishment and conservative groups eroded many gains. New and "improved" technologies raised the level of intervention in childbirth and menopause. Access to abortion for poor and rural women worsened, and abortion rights looked as though they might slip away entirely. Poverty increased nationwide.

Women around the world organized, citing the unequal distribution of resources—both within less industrialized countries and between the "first" and "third" worlds—as the primary cause of poor nutrition, ill health, and high maternal mortality rates. Groups rallied to oppose harmful practices like female circumcision, and the distribution of drugs prohibited for U.S. use but dumped in poorer countries. They fought population-control programs that offered contraceptive injections, intrauterine devices, and sterilization as the sole option for fertility control. They argued that environmental degradation is caused less by overpopulation than by military pollution and in overconsumption in industrialized nations. Projects have ranged from rural self-help health education among illiterate *harijan* women of Southern India, to several international women's health conferences.

Women will continue to be the primary consumers of health care—for themselves, for children, and often for ill or aging relatives.

It is now the 1990s. The agenda for women's health activism into the twenty-first century includes greater coalition building to address:

- *Prevention:* The primacy of adequate food, water, shelter, innoculations, and early detection of treatable diseases must be recognized.
- *Economic Justice:* Poverty should be seen as the root cause of ill health and early death, especially for women and children of color.
- *Environmental Links:* The connection must be established between environmental toxins and the incidence of breast and other cancers, immune disorders, and chronic fatigue syndrome. Women's health means fighting pollution—from workplace toxins and noxious household cleaners, to military and industrial chemical spills, to policies of locating toxic waste sites everywhere, particularly in communities of color.
- *HIV Infection and AIDS:* Already HIV and AIDS are the major cause of early death for women of childbearing age in isolated parts of the United States and throughout much of Africa. Women are more at risk than men for HIV infection in heterosexual intercourse, and less empowered to protect themselves when a partner refuses to practice safer sex. Activists will seek to improve barrier methods, especially those like the female condom that can be woman-controlled. AIDS diagnosis, treatment, and insurance practices must be more adequately focused on women's needs, providing women with the economic, social, and personal power that will enable them to protect themselves from infection during sex.
- *Research.* In 1990 the new Office for Research on Women's Health opened at the National Institutes for Health (NIH). The first female head of NIH also established the "Women's Health Initiative," a multimillion-dollar study of osteoporosis, heart disease, and cancer—major concerns of midlife women that were long neglected in health research. Also overdue are long-term studies of women and aging, and the safety of long-acting contraceptives.
- *A National Health Program.* Women need universal access to high-quality services that include contraception, abortion, Pap smears, routine mammography for older women, at-home and community-based services for long-term care, and access to nonallopathic alternatives such as homeopathy, chiropractic, and acupuncture.
- *Violence Against Women:* The rape of women and children by soldiers as a weapon of war, sex tourism in Asia, dowry murder in India, the rape and murder of women by boyfriends, husbands, or strangers, and sexual abuse of children—all are critical women's health issues.
- *Sexuality:* There must be an affirmation of women's sexual power, pleasure, and freedom of choice despite the context of violence and the need for protection against sexually transmitted diseases.
- *Women and Smoking:* Young women are the main U.S. group in which smoking is on the rise. Activists must counter the media-led obsession with thinness that motivates girls to smoke in the hope of curbing their appetites.

[See also Abortion; Class and Underclass; Disabled Persons' Rights; Family Patterns; Family Problems; Family Values; Health Care; Longevity; Poverty, Feminization of; Sexual Codes; Sexual Harassment; Women's Rights; Women's Studies.]

BIBLIOGRAPHY

Boston Women's Health Book Collective. *The New Our Bodies, Our Selves: A Book by and for Women.* New York: Simon & Schuster, 1984.

Corea, Gena. *The Hidden Malpractice: How American Medicine Treats Women as Patients and Professionals.* New York: William Morrow, 1977.

———, ed. *Man-Made Women: How Reproductive Technologies Affect Women.* Bloomington, IN: Indiana University Press, 1987.

———. *The Mother Machine: Reproductive Technologies from Artificial Insemination to Artificial Wombs.* New York: Harper & Row, 1985.

Davis, Susan E., ed. *Women Under Attack: Victories, Backlash and the Fight for Reproductive Freedom.* Boston: South End Press, 1988.

Dreifus, Claudia, ed. *Seizing Our Bodies: The Politics of Women's Health.* New York: Vintage, 1977.

Gordon, Linda. *Birth Control in American: Woman's Body, Woman's Right.* New York: Penguin, 1976.

Haire, Doris B. *The Cultural Warping of Childbirth.* Seattle: International Child Birth Education Association, 1972.

Kolata, Gina. "Self-Help Abortion Movement Gains Momentum." *New York Times,* October 23, 1989, p. B12.

Ruzek, Sheryl Bunt. *The Women's Health Movement: Feminist Alternatives to Medical Control.* New York: Praeger, 1978.

White, Evelyn, ed. *The Black Women's Health Book: Speaking for Ourselves.* Seattle: Seal Press, 1990.

— WENDY SANFORD
JUDITH NORSIGIAN

WOMEN'S MOVEMENT

Since 1970, a visionary feminism has managed to challenge seriously, if not transform, world consciousness. "First Wave" feminism was a nineteenth and early twentieth century movement of activist women struggling for nearly sixty years for women's suffrage or the right to vote. First Wave feminism succeeded in the United States with the passage in 1921 of a constitutional amendment establishing the right of women to vote.

Second Wave Feminism

Just as First Wave feminism grew out of the abolitionist movement to end slavery, Second Wave feminism in the United States emerged during the 1960s in parallel with the liberation movement of the civil rights and anti-Vietnam War struggles. Feminists left those movements when it became clear that *women's* liberation was not part of those agendas. From about 1967 on, grassroots feminists began to organize and fight for women's right to abortion and sexual freedom and equal pay for equal work.

Violence Against Women as a Feminist Issue

Feminist activists also focused on the sexual objectification of women and on the related issue of sexual violence toward women, such as stranger-rape and sexual harassment on the job and on the street. They pioneered and maintained rape crisis centers and shelters for battered women. They conducted "speakouts" and marched "to take back the night." They also testified at congressional hearings, and drafted legislation aimed at protecting women from the violence of men not only in their own families but in the workplace and in the wider society.

In the 1980s feminist activists began to expand their focus to include concerns for women within marriage. Some women were being raped by their spouses and battered. When these women chose to leave those marriages, they were impoverished and challenged regarding the custody of their children. Women were also being sexually harassed and raped at their jobs, on the street, and on "dates." It became clear that there was a largely underreported surge of husbands or boyfriends battering and killing the women in their lives, and of men and older boys sexually abusing younger girls and boys.

During the 1980s it became clear to feminist activists working to deter violence against women, that prostitution and pornography were a part of this larger social problem. Many of the battered wives were being treated almost as if they were their husband's or boyfriend's prostitutes. Wife-batterers, pedophiles, and serial killers of women were often also fixated on pornography.

Women were also beginning to defend themselves against their abusers. Feminists rallying to support these women sometimes found that the few women who dared to kill their abusers in self-defense were being treated by the police and the court system as if they were terrorists deserving little mercy.

The Institutional Response of Second Wave Feminism

In the late 1960s and throughout the '70s, women's caucuses were formed within colleges and universities and in academic professional organizations. Both within the professions and as a separate field of study, women's studies became a widespread institutional reality in the 1980s, although ghettoized, perpetually challenged, and only minimally funded. Feminist bookstores increased rapidly in numbers and economic strength, as did publication of popular and scholarly feminist periodicals and books. A women's health and health-education movement began in the 1970s and has thrived.

Feminists, who have had to deal with both backlash as well as "frontlash," did not manage to create an immigrant-style alternative economic and social infrastructure. Feminist credit unions, soup kitchens, nursing homes, and social agencies are becoming a visible and successful part of the feminist movement. In terms of supportive rationale, feminists have made great and serious moral and intellectual gains in the areas of literature, theology, ritual, and psychology.

Backlash and Reassertive Feminism

The women's movement has generated a constant and an increasingly powerful backlash in the U.S. media and culture. Younger women who are benefiting from the efforts of the women's movement are encouraged to believe that its goals have been accomplished—and hence feminism is no longer needed. The word *feminism* itself has been assailed. Some younger writers represent a backlash within feminism. In the 1990s such writers decried the feminist activists of the Second Wave as "victim" feminists. They urged younger women to focus instead upon "power" feminism or a feminism of equality with men.

But feminist activists of the Second Wave maintain that feminism must be more radical. There are no individual or single solutions to redress what women face in a patriarchal society. Feminist activists equate patriarchy to gender in ways that are similar to how white racist societies deal with race. Radical women threaten those in power, as well as women who are at their mercy.

Radical thinkers and activists almost always pay a high price. They point out that in the nineteenth and twentieth centuries the suffragists were jailed and their meeting places were burned down by those who opposed them.

Feminist activists have learned to take themselves seriously not only because others support their views but also because still others oppose them. Only the powerful are opposed. If there is a feminism that has no opposition, something is wrong. Thus the radical feminist movement argues that heroism—not martyrdom—is the only feminist alternative of choice.

[See also Women in Futures Studies; Women in Politics; Women and Religion; Women and Work; Women and World Development; Women's Health Movement; Women's Rights; Women's Studies.]

BIBLIOGRAPHY

Brownmiller, Susan. *Against Our Will.* New York: Simon & Schuster, 1974.

Chesler, Phyllis. *Women and Madness.* Garden City, NY: Doubleday, 1972.

Dworkin, Andrea. *Pornography.* New York: Perigee, 1979.

Faludi, Susan. *Backlash: The Undeclared War Against American Women.* New York: Crown, 1991.

Herman, Judith Lewis. *Father-Daughter Incest.* Cambridge, MA: Harvard University Press, 1979.

— PHYLLIS CHESLER

WOMEN'S RIGHTS

The modern women's movement in the United States was born in July 1848 at the Seneca Falls Convention, a gathering of three hundred, mostly female pioneer feminists, at Seneca Falls, N.Y., to protest the unjust treatment of women. Elizabeth Cady Stanton, the convention organizer, was the main architect of its feminist manifesto, the "Declaration of Sentiments," a catalyst in the launching of an organized feminist movement. This "Declaration" and its twelve accompanying resolutions addressed a broad array of feminist concerns, but for the next seven decades feminists focused almost entirely on what was actually the most controversial issue: the right to vote for women. The ultimate success of the campaign to enfranchise women, which came in 1920 with the ratification of the Nineteenth Amendment, led many feminists to believe that further activism was unnecessary. Suffragettes believed that with

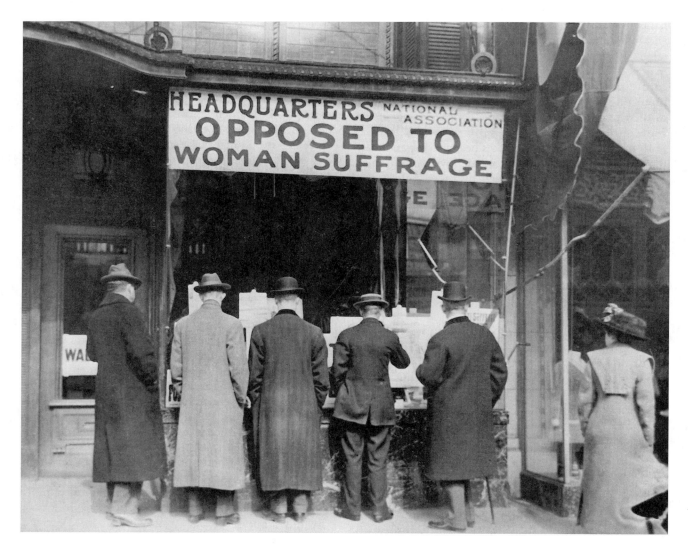

Women faced opposition in their struggle for political participation in the United States, as this organization's headquarters illustrates. (© Stock Montage, Inc.)

women voting as a bloc, the power of women voters would be enough to assure women's further objectives. However, the women's voting bloc did not materialize, and for nearly four decades women's issues received virtually no attention from the U.S. government.

A rebirth of the feminist movement came in the 1960s through the impetus in 1961 of the President's Commission on the Status of Women. The commission's 1963 report *American Women* proposed additional rights and more importantly sparked a new pro-feminist mood. Publication in the same year of Betty Friedan's bestselling *The Feminine Mystique,* which argued against the view that women must deprive themselves of fulfillment outside the home, bolstered the cause.

During this second wave of feminism, feminists achieved a number of legislative triumphs, including the banning of most types of discrimination in pay and in hiring. Other victories were won in the courts, including the legalization of abortion. Most remaining legal barriers to women's equality gave way because of an incremental approach targeted at combatting discrimination in very specific areas (such as credit discrimination or discrimination against pregnant women). There was renewed interest in the ratification of an Equal Rights Amendment (ERA), a comprehensive ban on all sex discrimination drafted in 1923. The feminist movement vigorously worked for ratification, winning passage by Congress and ratification by a number of states.

Feminists of the second wave also challenged the social codes, unlike the first-wave suffragists. Women were called upon to take charge of all areas of their lives—marital relationships, physical safety, health, reproduction, sexuality, and finances. Scores of women's organizations were created to channel their energy and promote women's rights. Some of these groups were large, multiissue organizations like the National Organization for Women, but many more focused specifically on one area of concern. Feminist publications proliferated, including *Signs* (the University of Chicago's women's studies journal), *New Directions for Women,* and the mass circulation *Ms.* magazine.

A radical branch of the feminist movement developed in the 1960s, partly in response to sexism exhibited by some members of the New Left. Although it did not survive the 1970s, its ideas later influenced mainstream feminism, particularly on issues pertaining to sexuality. It also contributed to the growth of a feminist subculture, in which feminism developed its own institutions.

With the election of Ronald Reagan as president in 1980 and the defeat of the ERA in 1982, the second wave of feminism seemed to come to an end. There were setbacks in the area of abortion rights, a lack of responsiveness in the federal government to the needs of single mothers, and a tendency by many women to reject the "feminist" label. However, during the 1980s, many feminist values were incorporated into American women's lives. Women asserted independence and self-reliance, and women's interests in society began to progress independently of the popularity of feminist ideology.

In the 1990s there has been a resurgence of feminist sentiment. Perhaps the best evidence of the new role of feminism is its stature as an intellectual force. Professor Laurence Tribe of Harvard Law School asserts that the feminist branch of legal study will exert a principal influence on new developments in the study of law over the next two and one-half decades. It will displace critical legal studies (which examines the role of laws in preserving the status quo) and the field of law and economics.

Women will benefit not only from the rediscovered interest in feminist ideology, but also from the sheer strength of their numbers in the political arena, in the work force, and in educational institutions. Women now constitute 54 percent of the electorate. Patricia Aburdene and John Naisbitt, coauthors of *Megatrends for Women,* contend that women now have such a strong base politically on the state level that they can be expected to hold governorships in about seventeen states by 2008; they also predict that a woman will likely have been elected president by then!

The future looks almost as bright in the area of employment and business. Women are estimated to comprise 66 percent of the net change in the size and composition of the workforce in the period from 1988 to 2000. Women in the labor force are expected to increase from 58 percent of all women in 1990 to 62.6 percent by the year 2000. A 14 percent drop in the proportion of women working at or below minimum wage from 1979 to 1989 was one of the factors contributing to the reduction of the female-male wage gap that took place in the period from 1980 to 1990, and has increased women's earning power to 72 cents for every dollar earned by a man, up from 64 cents in 1980.

Women-owned businesses at least doubled between 1977 and 1987, with finance, service, real estate, and insurance showing the most growth. The end result was that by 1987, 30 percent of all U.S. companies were women-owned. Because the growth of women-owned businesses outpaces that of most other segments of the economy, experts predict that from 40 to 50 percent of small businesses will be owned by women in the year 2000.

In the area of education, women outpace men. In 1989 women earned 57 percent of all associate degrees, 53 percent of all bachelor's degrees, 52 percent of all master's degrees, and 36 percent of all doctorates. Women earned two-fifths of all law degrees, one-fourth of all dentistry degrees, one-third of all medical degrees, and one-third of all veterinary degrees. The number of colleges and universities with women presidents almost doubled between 1975 and 1987.

Experts predict that from 40 to 50 percent

of small businesses will be owned by women

in the year 2000.

Women's rights advocates emphasize that the progress made by women has not reversed all the effects of centuries of discriminatory practices because de facto gender-based inequities persist. There are in fact dimensions of sex discrimination that have not been fully appreciated by the public, including sexual harassment at work, rape, marital rape, sterilization abuse, and continuing disparities in pay scales. Furthermore, bias can often take extremely subtle forms, resulting in disparities that Mary Rowe of the Massachusetts Institute of Technology has labelled as "microinequities." Microinequities are the aftereffects of negative views of women pervasive in previous generations, views which are so deeply engrained in our culture that we may often not be fully aware of their presence. In most cases there is no legal redress for such microinequities, but Rowe has proposed methods for combatting them such as the following: putting women in upper-level positions where performance is highly visible; putting men and women together on task forces and committees, so that each group is reliant on the skills of the other; and conducting training programs to sensitize and educate employees. In the coming years, subtle microinequities will receive a great deal of attention from feminists.

[See also Human Rights; Poverty, Feminization of; Social Change: United States; Social Controls; Women in Politics; Women and Religion; Women's Movement.]

BIBLIOGRAPHY

Aburdene, Patricia, and Naisbitt, John. *Megatrends for Women.* New York: Villard, 1992.
Davis, Flora. *Moving the Mountain.* New York: Simon & Schuster, 1991.
"Defining Law on the Feminist Frontier." *New York Times Magazine,* October 6, 1991.
Ries, Paula, and Stone, Anne J. *The American Woman 1992–93: A Status Report.* New York: Norton, 1992.
"The Sting of the Subtle Snub." *Working Women* (January 1991).

— SARAH CLAUDINE KURIAN

WOMEN'S STUDIES

Women's studies—the study of women developed by women in the late twentieth century—varies in different political, social, cultural, and historical contexts around the world. In some areas it may focus on the study of rural women or literacy education relevant to women, or maternal and child health. It may document women's and men's roles in the paid sector of the economy, or the effects of custom and law on women's lives, or their relation to the making of public policy. There are many forms and variants.

In the United States, *women's studies* usually refers to a burgeoning interdisciplinary field of research and teaching originating in the universities, which critiques knowledge and expands scholarship and educational curricula to include women's history, experiences, and points of view. New bodies of knowledge developed through research on women led to a searching review of previous bodies of knowledge that excluded women. Women's studies has affected each academic discipline, adding new information and also challenging those who deny that scholars' sex, race, class, religion, region, or sexual orientation might bear on their making of knowledge and on the question of who benefits from that knowledge.

Women's studies programs for college credit in the United States began in the late 1960s, following black studies as developed in the civil rights movement. Programs mushroomed; the National Women's Studies Association was founded in the late 1970s. By 1985, more than 19,000 courses on women were being offered on U.S. campuses and over 480 women's studies programs were offering major or minor degrees in women's studies. In 1995, more than 620 women's studies programs exist, some offering M.A.'s and Ph.D.'s as well as undergraduate degrees.

Centers for research on women also sprang up, starting in the early 1970s; more than seventy centers are now members of the U.S. National Council for Research on Women. In general, the centers do not teach directly but generate research on women and men that will widen the knowledge base, make education more vigorous and accurate, and root both public policy and civic life in more inclusive definitions of humanity and society.

The rapid development of women's studies as an academic field in both higher education and primary and secondary school material contributed to the creation of more than twenty-five periodicals in the United States focused on women, tens of thousands of books, conferences, workshops, faculty development programs, organizations, associations, caucuses, art and drama groups, museum exhibits, specialized museums, galleries, publishing houses, small presses, and feminist and multi-cultural bookstores.

Around the world, especially during the final two decades of the twentieth century, women's studies and research on women developed in all of the English-speaking nations of the world, all Western European nations, more than fifteen Asian nations, many countries of Central and South America, and in the 1990s, some of the newly opened nations of Eastern Europe began to pursue these objectives.

One aim of women's studies is to improve education for all women and men and to produce more equitable thinkers and more balanced policies than are now found at the centers of power. In order to effect such outcomes, women's studies has had to make constant efforts to avoid the very problems of the defective education that it challenges. Unless it continually broadens itself globally and analyzes all of the factors that lead to the domination of one group by another, women's studies tends to ascribe the power to name, validate, judge, and make decisions to the racial and cultural groups that already have the most public power in world contexts. Women's studies scholars have had to become multiculturally aware and informed. Increasingly, they seek and respect local, contexted understandings generated from the experience of people in a given place and a given time, including students. Internationally, this means that the field takes shape differently in different places.

Some national governments and religious bodies have strongly resisted higher education for women, collection of data on women, and the development of women's studies programs and research on women. The United Nations Nongovernmental Forums for Women, however, which were attended by representatives from every nation in 1975, 1980, and 1985, made it clear that women's studies was developing internationally. This emboldened many women to start exploring questions from women's points of view around the world.

Critics had claimed that the school and college and university curriculum is objective, scientific, and not political, whereas women's studies is subjective, non-scientific, and political. Women's studies scholars replied that traditional knowledge that excludes women is highly subjective and politicized—as well as being very inaccurate. This argument generally carried the

day, until 1990, when fundamentalist academic and religious forces began a new round of sharp assaults. Women's studies is pressed to defend itself, with multicultural studies, against those who are unwilling to share the power of knowledge making and who wish to continue to construe themselves as central instead of co-central in that undertaking.

Women's studies provided a new lens through which to view past knowledge, knowledge making, and social reality.

As of 1995, women's studies was spreading around the world, surviving, and in many places thriving, as an intellectually dynamic field of study in its own right and a new lens through which to view past knowledge, knowledge making, and social reality. Its chief gift to the construction of reality in the twenty-first century may be in its respect for narrative as a genre of knowledge making different from, and parallel to, empirical science as a form of understanding—each careful not to claim too much for findings from limited samples.

[See also Ethnic and Cultural Separatism; Family Patterns; Family Values; Futures Studies; Minorities; Race, Caste, and Ethnic Diversity; Sexual Harassment; Women in Futures Studies; Women in Politics; Women and Religion; Women and Work; Women and World Development; Women's Health Movement; Women's Movement; Women's Rights.]

BIBLIOGRAPHY

Chamberlain, Mariam. "The Emergence and Growth of Women's Studies Programs." In Sara E. Rix, ed. *The American Woman, 1990–1991,* pp. 315–324.

Rix, Sara E., ed. *The American Woman, 1990–91: A Status Report.* New York: Norton, 1990.

"Scholars Seek Wider Reach for Women's Studies." *New York Times,* May 17, 1989, p. B6.

Stimpson, Catharine R., with Nina Kressner Cobb. *Women's Studies in the United States.* New York: Ford Foundation, 1986.

— PEGGY MCINTOSH

WORK

Work is used, and has been at least since the industrial revolution, to distribute income and gain social status. This implicit notion is evident in the government's providing disability payments to those who can no longer work and temporary payments to those who have lost their job and are looking for another. It is apparent in the society's willingness to subsidize and continue to support people who have grown too old to participate in the paid workforce. It is also evident in the respect paid to people who work, who hold jobs, who have successful careers, or who become wealthy through work. In North American society, at least, the first question asked of a new acquaintance is most often, "What do you do?"

Although it is clear that most people's income and status rest on the work they do and are paid for, it is all the more alarming that the huge social system called work is changing radically and may be breaking down, that the long-term future of work could be in jeopardy. If in fact all of the goods and services required in a nation like the United States could be provided by only 15 percent of the working population as Alexander King of the Club of Rome has suggested, what will the other 85 percent do? How will we receive our share of the national income, and how will we determine our status in a society where only a few people can have what we now think of as "a job"?

How is it possible for 15 percent of the people to do all the work? The history of work in the United States can serve as an example. In colonial times almost everyone worked in agriculture. It was necessary, in order to survive and eat. Over time, however, the agricultural system has grown more efficient and more productive so that today less than 2.6 percent of the workforce works in agriculture. The rest of the population benefits from the cheap and plentiful supply of food that that sector provides. And output is so prodigious that more than 50 percent of many crops are surplus to domestic needs and sold to export.

After colonial times in America, the rising industrial sector absorbed the growing workforce, who left the farm and went into the factory where there was plentiful new work. Today the industrial sector is on a steep upward curve of productivity, producing more goods with fewer people. Automation and efficiency will continue to reduce the number of jobs in this sector so that the 17 percent of the workforce who work in industrial production today will be reduced to 10 percent or less in the next century.

The growing services and information sectors of the economy have been absorbing job seekers in the last

This Italian cheesemaker enjoys the benefits of social supports that many European governments put in place after World War II. However, those supports become difficult to sustain when unemployment rises. (David Paterson/Corbis)

few decades. But this sector, too, is beginning its upward swing on the productivity curve and with the help of automation and new efficiencies will reduce the number of jobs it has to offer. The economics of work are also changing. Charles Handy points out in *The Age of Paradox* that advanced nations like the United States have plenty of work that needs to be done, but they have priced many jobs out of the marketplace because people need good wages to live in these societies. The number of paid jobs, therefore, shrinks. Such societies also generally have older, better educated people, thus higher paid workers.

Where are all the jobs going? The answer is to the countries where large, young workforces have lower expectations of a wage and less education. These countries will be able to compete for all the paid work that is not worth automating or reducing by greater efficiencies. If this drain of jobs overseas continues, and jobs go to the lowest bidder, it would profit advanced nations to invest in those economies, in order to equalize wages and opportunities for work around the world.

Most of the methods and policies that government uses to maintain work as a system for distributing income are based on what proved to be useful when most people had jobs producing goods. There is now considerable concern that government should in some way be responsible for replacing an individual worker's lost income or making it possible for an unemployed worker to find another job in order to continue to receive his or her share of the nation's income. The problem of how to do that in a society where the nature and availability of work keep changing is obvious.

In Europe after World War II, governments undertook to distribute a share of their wealth through social supports almost without regard to work. This worked well as long as most people had jobs. But with increasing productivity and the loss of jobs to lower wage economies creating widespread structural unemployment, the social supports are becoming more difficult to sustain.

Governments are now viewing jobs as a scarce resource that must be given out fairly to achieve the best results for the economy. As a result, many people are receiving minimal support from their governments and earning the rest of their living in growing underground economies.

The United States may face similar problems. However, most people in the United States tend to believe in the country's ability to adapt to new circumstances and to create new jobs, new work, and new systems that will deal out returns evenly to all. What may be necessary in the case of work is a transformation in what work is, how people see it, and its role in the distribution of income and its relevance to peoples' lives.

Work life in the next century will:

- Be more cooperative than competitive.
- Use alternatives to today's money and wage structures: barter, for example. The expectation is that computer technology will make the complexities of a barter system workable.
- Have people who will share one job with several other people.
- Have people who are as much committed to doing work as they are today.
- Have people spending more of their time on work projects to benefit the communities they live in.
- Be willing to rethink the concept of rewards for work well done, in some cases disassociating them from money.
- Encourage people to develop their aesthetic senses, and to expend more time and interest on artistic and craft-based projects.
- Allow people to work on paid projects only in short bursts, and then very intensively.
- Be composed of groups of people whose job is to learn and integrate information and create work projects with it. The downtime from these projects, again, is likely to be long and reflective, the work period short and intense.
- Have no one who will work an eight-hour day on one job or one task.
- Organized so that all workers receive credit for a life's work at the beginning of adulthood, and can then spend those credits as they choose. Community pressure will control the deadbeats.
- Still include the super-competitive type (Wall Street traders), but will have mechanisms to absorb their energy and competitiveness.
- Replace the money system of today by forms of credit that are adjusted to the social value of work people are willing to do.
- Be friendly to groups that organize themselves as tribes and be rewarded accordingly.
- See the gradual disappearance of money for any purpose.

Work as it is now will not continue in the same patterns. Handy, who has been writing about the future of work since the 1970s, suggests that as a result of our pursuit of efficiency and economic growth—as if these were society's ideal—the needs of people for useful work are being neglected. If the money value of work is set at zero, there will always be any amount of it to go around, so work itself will never disappear, but the ways in which society uses work to achieve other goals may change. Leisure is frequently defined as what you do when you are not working and, therefore, something we should work to gain more of. Handy and others suggest that future generations will want their leisure within work, as well as more interesting experiences when they are at work. Thus, the lines between work and nonwork are likely to blur.

The ways in which work is organized are already changing because information-related work does not have to be organized like factory work. Workplaces are likely to be smaller and more widely distributed, perhaps closer to home for many people. As more full-time jobs are squeezed out, people may have smaller jobs and more of them. The weekday consultant on worldwide business expansions could be a weekend farmer, for example, raising raspberries for restaurant tables in the nearby city.

Future generations will want their leisure within work, as well as more interesting experiences when they are at work. The lines between work and nonwork are likely to blur.

The government will be driven to more ambitious and risky policy experiments in order to keep the most productive members of the workforce at work and make it possible for everyone else to stay out. Young people will be encouraged to get more education and enter the workforce later. Their formal work lives will end earlier. People may be expected to spend years in government work corps, doing cleanup, building, and other jobs to obtain education or subsistence benefits. Children will be educated to know what to do with their time as adults when no one wants to pay them to work, but they are expected to be usefully occupied.

It is difficult for us today to look forward to a time when the eight-hour workday will be a memory and the idea of being a regular employee of an organization loses its luster as a goal for most people. Our entire orientation to paid work will have to be reshaped into something new. Work will never lose its importance for tool-using humans, but it may lose its utility as a way of managing society and allocating rewards.

[See also Unemployment; Unionism; Women and Work; Work, Quality of; Work Ethic; Workforce Redistribution; Workforce Diversity; Working Conditions.]

BIBLIOGRAPHY

Abraham, Katharine G., and Houseman, Susan N. *Job Security in America: Lessons from Germany.* Washington, DC: Brookings Institution, 1993.

Gaffikin, Frank, and Morrisey, Mike. *The New Unemployed: Joblessness and Poverty in the Market Economy.* London and Atlantic Highlands, NJ: Zed Books, 1992.

Gil, David B., and Gil, Eva A., eds. *The Future of Work: A Conference of the Center for Social Change, Practice, and Theory.* Rochester, VT, 1987.

Handy, Charles. *The Age of Paradox.* Cambridge, MA: Harvard University Press, 1991.

———. *The Future of Work.* Cambridge, MA: Blackwell, 1984.

— JENNIFER JARRATT

WORK, QUALITY OF

Over the past twenty years, the three major types of change—social, technological, and economic—have had relatively little impact on each other, but as we approach the next millennium, these changes will interact more vigorously. The cumulative force of these changes suggest that for some the quality of work available to them will be high and will satisfy most of their needs; but not everyone will be willing or able to adapt to these changes, and for them life will be more difficult.

Social Change

The changing values, beliefs, and motivations of the workforce already play a significant role in changing the nature of work. Large numbers of people in the industrialized countries are choosing to work at home, some self-employed, others still working for an employer. Despite recent concern about the job market, there has been a continuing trend for people to seek more personal time and to have that time *during hours and even on days that suit them.* As pressures of commuting increase and "edge cities" develop, where all business and social needs can be met, increasing numbers of white-collar and professional workers are expected to take this option. In the United States in 1991, some 20 percent of the workforce worked from home full- or part-time. In the United Kingdom, the comparable number for 1990 was 15 percent. By 2000 it is expected that close to 50 percent of the workforces in each country will be working from home at least part of the time.

Another related trend involving the same values and pressures resulted in increasing numbers of management buy-outs. These buy-outs were not large or highly leveraged, rather, they involved small groups of people who thought they could do better on their own. That trend will also continue to increase.

In both cases—working at home and buy-outs—the people who function best in the new way of working are self-disciplined, responsible for themselves, and adept at using information technology. These may be difficult characteristics for people who espouse the self-indulgent aspect of 1960s values.

Technology Change

Modern technology (especially information technology) already has imposed a major impact on the workplace, and more is expected in the decades to come. If we choose to so, almost any work activity can be accomplished from home, with very few people physically at the work site. Much manufacturing could be undertaken by automated machines and robots, monitored and controlled from a remote location. Deep mining can already be done that way. Maintenance activities for infrastructure (gas, water, sewage, and so forth) already use automated remote-controlled equipment. Furthermore, intelligent-vehicle highway systems are being developed.

Of course there are exceptions to these trends. Some developmental and exploratory work will require people to have access to laboratories, equipment, and materials. In the service industries, although some degree of automation is likely, many people will still prefer to carry out transactions and receive services on a face-to-face basis. However, the real question is not about whether technology can do all this and more. It is not even about whether we can afford the technology since microminiaturization and nanotechnology will bring the prices down. The pivotal question is whether we want to use it. Will society be able to afford the social cost of nearly full automation? In the short term, the answer is probably no; In the longer term of twenty years or more, there may be no other viable options.

Economic Change

Economic conditions over the period of 1988 to 1994 forced some organizations out of business while others became lean and fit. The United States, by taking a more pragmatic approach to the recent recession than many of its competitors, has seen a remarkable growth in productivity during this time. Nonetheless, international competition can only increase as new players join the fray. Capital and labor productivity will continue to remain of great concern. Big business will have to increase further the technological component of its operations to remain competitive. One means to retain competitiveness will be flexibility, including rapid response to change, which also extends to work practices.

The Future

Change does not come easily, and the real key for dealing with change is education. Within twenty years any country that wants to succeed socially, technologically, and economically must improve its education systems to ensure that children are taught technical skills, instructed in *how* to learn as a specific skill, and coached to see the value in continuing to learn.

Other changes that will alter the workplace include:

- *More self-employment.* This may include networking and teaming arrangements among people with similar or complementary skills. Such individuals will contract out their services to larger organizations.
- *Just-in-time jobs.* Many employers in medium and large companies will maintain a small permanent staff and contract out many seasonal and other tasks to the self-employed and small businesses.
- *Leadership, not management.* In this flexible, fast-response world, old-style management will not work. The new situation will require leaders who

can inspire, help create a shared vision, instill a sense of mission, and evoke loyalty.

- *Networking work teams.* Combinations of small, permanent workforces and subcontractors will require people to work in small, flexible teams, with members of the teams grouping and regrouping in network fashion as required.
- *Heterarchical command structures.* New forms of work structure are likely to be built around the demands of a particular piece of work. To accomplish this successfully, the individual who is the expert will need to take the lead role. Small hierarchies assembled for particular tasks, with the expert at each task taking the lead, may also form part of a network on another type of task. Stereotype rewards related to "position" alone will assume less importance.
- *Performance.* New ways of working will require new performance measures and objectives, which will have to be set and agreed to by the organization, its own workers, and its contractors (who may look more like employees than traditional contractors). Some new form of "management by objectives," to be used in conjunction with an organization's visionary objectives is likely.

In this emerging environment, people who can work independently with self-discipline and responsibility will do very well. Those who require routine work and close supervision will find their lives increasingly difficult. This changed emphasis in the work environment poses formidable challenges for the educational system.

[See also Change, Scientific and Technological; Social Change: United States; Work; Work Ethic; Workforce Redistribution; Workforce Diversity.]

BIBLIOGRAPHY

Delamotte, Ives, and Takezawa, S. *Quality of Working Life in International Perspective.* Geneva: International Labour Office, 1986.
Handy Charles. *The Future of Work.* Cambridge, MA: Basil Blackwell, 1984.
Harman, Willis, and Hormann, John. *Creative Work.* Indianapolis: Knowledge Systems, 1990.
Parker, Mike. *Inside the Circle: A Guide to the Quality of Work Life.* Boston: South End Press, 1985.
Terkel, Studs. *Working.* New York: Ballantine, 1985.

— CHRISTINE A. R. MACNULTY

WORKERS' COMPENSATION.

See UNEMPLOYMENT INSURANCE, WORKERS' COMPENSATION.

WORK ETHIC

"My father taught me to work," Abraham Lincoln said. "He did not teach me to love it." Economic success derives from a compelling work ethic, a deeply embedded cultural value that presumes an indelible relationship between labor and virtue. Even wealthy individuals are expected to work, whether to expand their fortunes, achieve in a different field, or advance a social or charitable cause. The most conspicuous aspect of the changing role of women in society is their assumption of equal roles in the workforce. Children are encouraged to begin work at an early age, even when economic factors are not involved, so they can develop a work ethic. Useful work is essential to societal cohesiveness and is used as a measure of one's character and value.

Like Lincoln, we do not presume enjoyment to be inherent to the work experience. We take pride in work well done, and savor the community acceptance and approval that accrues to working people, but few of us confuse work with fun.

For most of us, work is what we do when we would rather be doing something else. Human nature being what it is, that aspect of work will never change. What will change is the nature of work and the complex interrelationships that prevail in the workplace, primarily between management and labor.

Historically, most work entailed strenuous manual exertion. Only a few individuals earned their daily bread through intellectual pursuits, and in most cases they also performed a variety of physical tasks.

The industrial age freed people from much of the lifting, hauling, and manual drudgery that had long been their lot, enabling many people to pursue less strenuous tasks, thus setting the stage for unprecedented technological and scientific advances.

We are now embarked upon a boundless postindustrial age of intellectual discovery. Daily breakthroughs remake virtually every aspect of the way we work and live. Just as the machines of the industrial age enhanced the power of human muscle, the microchip multiplies the power of the human mind. Our future holds unlimited promise.

However, the traditional linear line of authority that sustained us in ancient times and through the industrial age will not suffice into the future. As workers become more cerebral, and hence more valuable, it will be neither feasible nor wise to expect them to function like automatons on an assembly line. Employers who do not permit full rein and realization of workers' intellects will not survive very long.

Already, progressive enterprises are establishing a new workplace ethic of collegial cooperation that blurs traditional categories and lines of authority. The Total Quality Management (TQM) that contributes to defining the most successful businesses is predicated upon full employee involvement in all stages of the decision-making process. Most vestiges of workplace status are disappearing through a polyphony of creative interplay among all participants.

Just as workers in progressive environments define their success and status in part upon their acceptance as full partners in the business at hand, it follows that

systems of recompense also are evolving in new and surprising ways. There is less reliance upon rigid pay scales based upon status in the hierarchy, and more emphasis upon performance—both of the individual employee and that of the total enterprise through profit sharing.

Progressive enterprises are establishing a new workplace ethic of collegial cooperation that blurs traditional categories and lines of authority.

Much is written these days about the decline in organizational loyalty stemming from commercial and industrial restructuring. Layoffs and forced early retirements imposed to reduce static work forces are painful necessities that invariably produce anxiety and distress among all concerned. As work becomes more cerebral and less physical, and the routines of the work place are subject to more rapid flux, it seems likely that increased worker mobility will follow. To the extent that workers will expect to change employers more frequently in the future, there will be less organizational loyalty, at least in the traditional sense of the term.

On the other hand, as workers assume a greater role in corporate decision making and enjoy the increased status and enhanced self-esteem that accompanies it, there will be a concurrent increase in identification with the enterprise where one is employed and of personal commitment to it. There will be a concomitant increase in work satisfaction, as people gain greater control over their personal destinies and inherit a larger sense of responsibility for the decisions they and their coworkers arrive at together.

What will not change—what must never change—is the commitment to work and the belief in the healing power of labor to transform the human experience and lend meaning to life. It is not leisure or play that defines our character, but rather our ability to withstand adversity, sustain commitment, and do what has to be done regardless of conflicting pressures or tempting distractions. Indeed, the changing value of the workplace will serve to enrich the American work ethic and imbue it with a new vitality and spirit to sustain us well into the twenty-first century and beyond.

[See also Global Culture; Information Society; Women and Work; Work; Work, Quality of; Working Conditions.]

BIBLIOGRAPHY

"The End of the Job." *Fortune* (September 19, 1994).

Hammer, Michael, and Champy, James. *Reengineering the Corporation: A Manifesto for the Business Revolution.* New York: HarperCollins, 1993.

"The Information Revolution: How Digital Technology Is Changing the Way We Work and Live." *Business Week* (bonus issue, 1994).

"21st Century Capitalism: How Nations and Industries Will Compete in the Emerging Global Economy." *Business Week* (bonus issue, 1994).

"What Ever Happened to the Great American Job?" *Time* (November 11, 1993): 32–39.

— RICHARD LESHER

WORKFORCE DIVERSITY

The workforce in the United States always has been diverse. Its population patterns, as a nation of immigrants, were constantly altered. Both before and after the Civil War, black Americans were a conspicuous component of the population. Women, of course, have always worked for pay in large numbers, usually out of necessity or to help out in the factory during a seasonal surge in work.

U.S. ethnic composition is strongly influenced by low white birth rates and the rapid rise of immigrants. Bureau of Census 1994 estimates anticipate legal immigrants to number 8.8 million persons during the 1990s. Illegal immigrants double that number. Demographic projections, based on a continuation of these

During World War II, while men went to war, American women ably picked up the industrial workload. Female participation in the U.S. labor force may rise from 18.2% in 1890 to 68.8% in 2005. (© Stock Montage, Inc)

trends, indicate that ethnic minorities may account for 30 percent of total U.S. population by 2033.

Inflows from south of the border dominate. Hispanics are projected to surpass blacks as the largest U.S. minority by 2020. California is where accommodations of the diverse workplace may be most keenly felt. By 1989 California became the first U.S. state with a "minority" population actually higher than the traditional white majority (with Hispanics making up 37.8 percent of the population, followed by Asians at 10.8 percent and blacks with 10.5 percent). In the workforce, blacks, Asians, Hispanics, and other minorities are anticipated to account for 26 percent of the workforce by 2000. The handwriting is on the wall—diversity is the hallmark of the workplace or the future.

Non-Hispanic white males, who long dominated the U.S. workforce, accounted for less than 50 percent of the workforce by 1990, and are projected to drop further, reaching only 41–45 percent of all workers by 2000. Women sixteen years and older working for pay outside the home constituted 18.2 percent of the workforce. They often were scorned and self-conscious about having to work. By the 1990s, the proportion had increased to 60 percent and was projected to reach 75 percent by 2000. The new female workers were proud to be employed, insistent on plying their skills and professions, strident in asserting equal rights, and dead serious about eliminating discriminatory practices.

America has long been considered the "melting pot" of ethnic and cultural diversity. In other parts of the world, Balkanization and separatism have been hallmarks. America's new diversity—the new multiculturalism—will test its resolve to assimilate all comers.

Those diversity elements were not a prominent part of the public policy debate or the subject of legislative attention until two changes had occurred. First was the settlement of more urgent labor issues such as the right to organize, the forty-hour work week, and social security. Second was a series of developments that made it clear beyond reasonable doubt that large groups in society were systematically being discriminated against in hiring and in advancement. Blacks, other ethnic and racial groups, and women were often the last hired and first fired. The civil rights movement, with its demands for equal access to jobs, housing, and public accommodations, prevailed in effective legislation. Independently the changing patterns of family size and the widespread entry of women into all aspects of business and work life raised their collective awareness of the widespread unfair practices directed against them. The resulting political movement led to legislation to redress their grievances. The campaigns for and implementation of legislation directed at promoting equity quickly spread to other groups, making them aware both of injustices and the opportunities for legislated remedies. This new self-consciousness of collective grievances is at the heart of the awareness of workplace diversity.

America's new diversity

—the new multiculturalism—

will test its resolve to assimilate all comers.

The new social ambience of rejection of prejudicial behavior led many other people to see that they also belonged to groups that had special interests at the workplace and elsewhere that could be met through collective action. Many, if not all, groups other than white males of European stock in the 1970s and '80s seemed to have formed a self-designated element of diversity. As business and government responded to the pressure for reform primarily by offering compensatory programs, preferential advancement, and greater flexibility, new groups came forward. Changing business practices have also promoted diversity. Telecommuters, part-time workers, single parents, gays, temporary workers, older workers, and many others make up the current workplace complex.

What does the future hold? The settlement of grievances will be slow simply because social change is slow, except in times of crisis. While progress is real, there is a long way to go before all groups achieve equal pay for equal work or have fair access to top-level, high-paying jobs, relative to their numbers in the workforce. Some are likely to find parity through unionization or by rejecting big business and preferring to work for small or entrepreneurial businesses. Other groups—Asians, for example, because of their rapid pace of economic progress—may lose any real claim to special consideration at the workplace. Other groups assimilating into the economy and society, Hispanics, for example, may reject special status as demeaning.

Still other groups will become more active and aggressive as their numbers increase—older workers, for example, or the handicapped, if they find themselves reaching equity status too slowly. Others will find success in areas outside work and transfer that success to the workplace—for example, the AIDS-advocacy activists. Waves of new immigrants will bring fresh concerns to the workplace as they identify themselves as special groups.

Changing business practices will create new or newly important groups seeking fair treatment. Among these practices are business alliances that will highlight discrepancies in the way workers are treated, managed, and rewarded in the allied companies. As multinational corporations engage in more—and more complex—business activities in other countries, the foreign nationals will be increasingly aware of any difference in the ways they are treated and paid and will respond accordingly.

As workplace diversity issues evolve, there will be a growing awareness in society of individual and group differences and special needs or claims. There has always been resistance to the claims of diverse elements at the workplace, because change is disruptive to established relationships. Equity legislation, when implemented, has often led to new inequities, whether real or perceived. There is growing backlash to compensatory preferential treatment of minorities and women. Changes in the law will certainly occur to strike a new balance among conflicting goals. One can only hope that those changes do not overcompensate in the reverse direction and undo progress. Fair and equitable access to jobs will mean upward mobility for all.

One of the more ironic developments is the emergence of a backlash white worker rights movement that crystallizes the disquiet of many who see themselves as unfairly treated, while other groups enjoy the benefit of compensatory programs.

It is increasingly clear to all concerned with workplace equity that many of the sources of inequity develop outside the workplace, notably in education and preparation for work. Closer attention will be given to equal preparation for work as a basic mechanism for reducing any basis for differential treatment of workers at the workplace.

Aside from issues at the workplace, diversity will bring new perspectives to corporate or organizational thinking and may bring companies closer to their increasingly heterogeneous customers.

[See also Class and Underclass; Disabled Persons' Rights; Ethnic and Cultural Separatism; Human Resources Development; Race, Caste, and Ethnic Diversity; Sexual Harassment; Unionism; Women and Work; Work; Workforce Redistribution.]

BIBLIOGRAPHY

Bullock, Susan. *Women and Work.* London and Atlantic Highlands, NJ: Zed Books, 1994.

Ginzberg, Eli. The Changing U.S. Labor Market. Boulder, CO: Westview Press, 1994.

Murdock, Steve H. *An America Challenged: Population Change and the Future of the United States.* Boulder, CO: Westview Press, 1995.

Peterson, Anne C. and Mortinier, Jeylan T., eds. *Youth Unemployment and Society.* New York: Cambridge University Press, 1994.

State and Local Coalition on Immigration/Immigrant Policy Project. *America's Newcomers: An Immigrant Policy Handbook.* Denver, CO: National Conference of State Legislatures, 1994.

— JOSEPH F. COATES

WORKFORCE REDISTRIBUTION

Workforce redistribution flows from social, technical, economic, and political change. In *The Third Wave*, Alvin Toffler spotted the onset of postindustrial (third wave) society—the first and second waves being the agricultural and industrial economies. The first bar chart (Figure 1) shows the shift of employment between the three waves in various types of countries since 1960 and forecasts workforce distribution to the year 2000.

Wave Effect of Techno-Revolutions

Developing countries are agrarian societies, as was North America in the Agricultural Age. As a nation modernizes, there is a continual shift of workers from farming to industry and services. As machines take over farm tasks, people move to the cities where they form labor pools for manufacturers and service companies. Today in North America, farming employs only 3 percent against 80 percent in the postindustrial sector. Indeed, to understand the third wave, we must further divide it. In reality, we have a six-wave economy:

- *First Wave:* Agriculture/Natural Resources/Energy
- *Second Wave:* Industry/Manufacturing/Robotics
- *Third Wave:* Financial/Health Care/Personal Services
- *Fourth Wave:* Information/Knowledge/High Technology
- *Fifth Wave:* Leisure and Tourism
- *Sixth Wave:* Outer-Space Economy

These waves exist simultaneously, but one wave usually dominates. The old waves don't disappear; rather, the new ones complement them. For example, machines modernized farming and increased crop yield. Information is not just spawning the fourth-wave information economy, but modernizing all other sectors. Computerized information is essential to any modern farm, factory, office, school, hospital, or hotel.

In North America, services became the largest employer in 1950. This was the third-wave revolution. The fourth wave (of computers, information, and knowledge professions) rose to domination in the 1980s. However, the fastest-growing job field is the fifth-wave leisure sector—the travel, tourism, hospitality, recreation, entertainment, and cultural industry. And the sixth-wave outer-space economy is emerging as a twenty-first-century sector of employment.

Forces of Workforce Redistribution

Socially, each of us is the servant of everybody else. Note down society's future needs and you get a list of all the jobs that will be required. In an aging society, the demand for healthcare workers will soar beyond today's needs. And, as people age, their other needs will also change. Eldercare will replace childcare as a primary focus of baby boomers because they all have aging relatives and their children will be grown up. As well, new generations of people will be born with their own

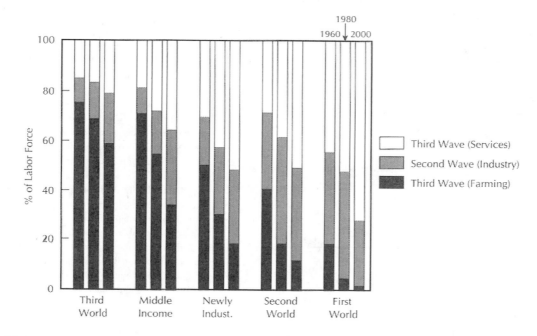

Figure 1. Global workforce restructuring. (Copyright 1990 by Frank Feather. Used with permission.)

937

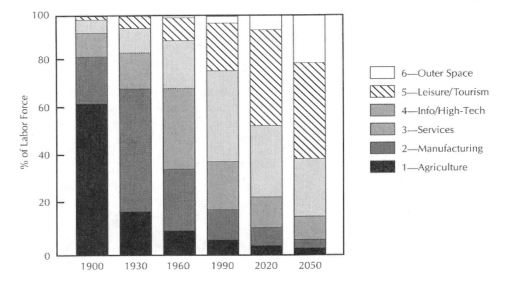

Figure 2. Six-wave North American job restructuring. (Copyright 1990 by Frank Feather. Used with permission.)

unique sets of needs. New waves of immigrants will bring yet more needs.

Technology also changes workforce demands. It changes or replaces old jobs and creates new ones. As automobiles and telephones demonstrated, technology also changes how society is structured and functions. Through the "ripple effect" of these innovations, technology indirectly restructures the job market. For example, people began making automatic washing machines (instead of wringer washers and scrubbing boards), microwave ovens (instead of convection stoves), and personal computers and word processors (instead of typewriters). In turn, this restructures all jobs in the production-consumption chain—from raw material extraction and fabrication to marketing, sales, and the use of these products.

In an aging society,

the demand for healthcare workers will soar.

Also, eldercare will replace childcare

as a primary focus of baby boomers.

Economically, in the global village, every nation is a province of the world. Workers are now part of a global labor pool and jobs will be performed where the market dictates. Global information flows bring new ideas, new values, new needs and wants. This creates demand for new products and services—and new jobs to deliver them. New ideas of production (such as robots and

computers) and new consumer products (such as VCRs, microwave ovens, personal computers, fax machines, or ethnic foods) create new markets—and a host of yet more new jobs in serving the needs of a diversified marketplace.

The major political dynamic is the environmental concern, globally and locally, from worries about the ozone layer to problems of local garbage disposal. Indeed, the environment is now a major element of every sector and is spawning a major industry of its own.

Future Growth in the Postindustrial Workforce

Clearly, as the second bar chart shows, most future job growth will occur in the postindustrial sectors of the economy: in the third, fourth, fifth, and sixth waves.

- *Third Wave:* Everything we do, from morning to night, is made possible by workers in the third-wave service economy—in a bank, doctor's office, dry cleaning, or other service outlet. This sector will continue to provide jobs galore. During the next decade, 10 percent of new jobs will be health-related and many of the fastest growing jobs are indirectly related to healthcare.

- *Fourth Wave:* Undoubtedly the information/knowledge and high-tech sector is the wave of the short-term future. A new computer goes into use every two seconds. Computers will sit on every desk and be carried in briefcases, cars, pockets, and purses by everyone. Closely related to computers is the telecom industry. In the global economy, the effective management of information flows is vital, and entire industries are being spawned. Biotechnology (biotech) could also transform dozens of other industries, from farming and mining to pharmaceuticals and pollution control. Biotech could even rival computers in job creation in the next twenty years.

- *Fifth Wave:* Thanks to telecomputers, we are succeeding magnificently at putting ourselves out of work. The leisure industry already provides 20 percent of all jobs—more than the fast-declining manufacturing sector—and hospitality will be the growth industry of the next thirty years. Since the recession of the early 1990s, the industry has resumed its fast-track growth, creating thousands of jobs. Arts, culture, and sports are now a major leisure activity, with galleries, museums, orchestras, and theaters starting up across the continent—and creating a multitude of jobs.

- *Sixth Wave:* Most technology is brought to a point of focus in the aerospace sector. It is here that all the leading-edge high-tech research and use first occurs. Since 1960, NASA's budget has risen from a mere $340 million to $20 billion. The space station will further boost the industry.

Even without this ambitious space program, the world is increasingly encircled by satellites, the "tom-tom drums" of the global village. This space-based infostructure is changing all five waves of the earthbound economy—and redistributing millions of jobs in the process.

[See also Change, Epochal; Continuity and Discontinuity; Economic Cycles: Models and Simulations; Evolution, Social; Global Culture; Information Society; Multifold Trend; Political Cycles; Scientific Breakthroughs; Social and Political Evolution; Technological Determinism.]

BIBLIOGRAPHY

Cornish, Edward. *Careers Tomorrow: The Outlook for Work in a Changing World.* Washington, DC: World Future Society, 1983.
Feather, Frank. *G-Forces: The 35 Global Forces Restructuring Our Future.* New York, N.Y.: William Morrow & Company, 1990.
———. *America's Best Careers Guide.* Los Angeles, Calif.: Warwick Publishing Group, 1994.
Leontiff, Wassily, and Duchin, Faye. *The Future Impact of Automation on Workers.* Oxford, U.K.: Oxford University Press, 1986.

— FRANK FEATHER

WORKING CONDITIONS

Key trends of the emerging information era indicate that tomorrow's working conditions will increasingly resemble those of self-employed entrepreneurs linked to coworkers into projects for customers through an electronic marketplace.

What will work be like in the future? If it is the relatively near future, say, ten years from now, conditions are likely to be a modified extension of those we know today. Most of us will still hold jobs with specified duties and working hours within organizations under some type of supervisory hierarchy.

But what about the longer-term future—forty or fifty years from today? In that more distant tomorrow, the conditions of work are likely to be as alien to us as the concept of a factory-based job would have been to an eighteenth-century farmer.

Moving Beyond the Industrial Era

Our society is well into a transition from a manufacturing-based economy to an information era. This transformation will have the magnitude of the industrial revolution and dramatically change the nature of work.

Predicting the nature of this new era is as risky as it is fascinating. Just as contemporaries of the eighteenth and nineteenth century toiled to understand the emerging industrial era, we are also struggling to glimpse bits and pieces of a world that is still taking shape. This world will be a combination of human, technological, economic, and ecological forces that may take sharp, unexpected turns into futures we can scarcely imagine. Nonetheless, it is possible to make some reasonable speculations.

Working Conditions Will Adjust to New Realities

Four key trends represent forces that will play major roles in shaping the future of work.

FLEXIBLE ORGANIZATION. Size is a fading sign of economic strength. The future belongs to lean, modular, and less hierarchical organizations that can "turn on a dime" in response to the changes of our times. There are two major reasons for these trends. First, large hierarchical organizations cannot make decisions fast enough to meet today's accelerating pace of change. Second, growing demands for rapid adjustment to new conditions make large reservoirs of fixed equipment and personnel a liability. In response, work organizations are "downsizing," flattening their hierarchy to allow more "front-line" decisions, and pursuing a variety of approaches to become more flexible and modular. Terms such as *virtual organization, adhocracy,* and *hollow corporation* describe new organizational structures that minimize their core staff, rely increasingly on subcontracting and temporary workers (consultants, temp agencies, or short-term employment), and aggressively employ telecommunications to coordinate "coalitions" of organizations and resources. This move toward flexible organizations will mean the decline of long-term employment, increasing project-oriented or temporary work, intense competition within core organizations, and a steady rise in self-employment and small "spin-off" enterprises.

DECENTRALIZATION. Closely linked to the rise of flexible organizations is increasing decentralization. The importance of locating staff at a central office is declining. Telecommunications and routine global transit make it possible to communicate and coordinate operations from remote locations. Telecommuting, international integration of distant operations, and distributed decision making are becoming commonplace. In terms of work, this trend is likely to diminish hierarchy and direct supervision in favor of outcome-oriented accountability, reduce the need for large central facilities, and accelerate the working conditions associated with flexible or modular organization.

CUSTOMIZED PRODUCTS AND SERVICES. The conditions of work will also be affected by individualization of goods and services. Over the last seventy years we have moved from mass production of standardized products (e.g., "You can have any type of car you want as long as it's black and a Model T"), to product lines, then product differentiation, and the threshold of customization. Today CAD/CAM (computer-assisted design and computer-assisted manufacturing) is taking us into the realm of "mass customization," in which the awesome productive power of factory machinery can be routinely reconfigured to "stamp out" auto fenders, business suits, and furniture to meet the personal specifications of individual customers. Similar "interactive" customization is occurring in entertainment, accounting, and other services. The implications for working conditions are revolutionary. Automation will cause worker displacement, but will also create new jobs in response to increased global demand for less expensive customized products. The skill requirements for these jobs will be different, sometimes higher and sometimes lower. Most important, there will be new opportunities for developing, producing, and distributing new products.

PERSONAL CAPITALIZATION. The last trend deals with the accessibility of information, resources, and equipment to enable individuals and groups to marshal the increasingly decentralized and modular array of technology and human skills to produce better, less expensive, and innovative products. Several indicators suggest that productive capital is increasingly available. The level and scope of personal credit lines and electric money are unparalleled. Miniaturization and volume production have made equipment more affordable, transportable, and usable. Information on the use of new equipment is readily available from books, schools, and user groups. Finally, information services and networks such as the Internet are providing avenues for individuals and groups to merge ideas, skills, and resources. Individuals and groups are becoming less dependent on large organizations for the resources to forge productive livelihoods.

Working Without a Job

These four trends appear to be pushing us toward social and economic conditions in which the resources we need to work and live can be marshaled increasingly around the individual. It is becoming less necessary to gather at central locations such as schools, factories, and offices to use heavy or expensive equipment and coordinate activities with coworkers. On the contrary, it is increasingly feasible and desirable to access needed resources from our homes and other remote locations.

This does not mean that corporations, factories, and similar organizations will disappear. Just as the family farm and the agricultural sector continue to exist and flourish, these entities will persist as long as they have relevance.

If work created by jobs within today's factories and offices declines, what conditions will evolve to define work in the future? An increasing possibility is that "jobs" and "employment" may become as uncommon as today's family farm.

If work does not take place within the context of employment, what form will it take? It is likely that we will move progressively toward a labor force of affiliated and nonaffiliated self-employed individuals linked to work activities through computerized national and international labor exchanges. From the "customer's" point of view, this system will allow individuals and organizations to search for workers who have the skills and backgrounds needed for existing projects. From the "worker's" perspective, each work-seeker would list his or her name, contact information, past projects and references, certifications, availability, and fees into computerized records for review by prospective customers.

In this future, new technologies and protocols would evolve to support the electronic labor market. Mechanisms would have to be invented to guard worker and customer rights, facilitate bidding and scheduling, and certify and verify worker skills and backgrounds.

Emergence of a widespread electronic labor market will have costs and benefits. It would alter the nature of human interaction and communities, and lead to other developments beyond our current imaginations.

[See also Business Structure: Forms, Impacts; Business Structure: Industrial Policy; Human Resources Development; Poverty, Feminization of; Work; Work, Quality of; Work Ethic; Workforce Diversity; Workforce Redistribution.]

BIBLIOGRAPHY

Becker, Franklin. *Total Workplace.* New York: Van Nostrand, 1990.

Hammer, Michael. *Reengineering the Corporation: A Manifesto for Business Revolution.* New York: Harper Collins, 1993.

Noer, David M. *Healing the Wounds: Overcoming the Trauma of Layoffs and Revitalizing Downsized Organizations.* San Francisco; Jossey-Bass, 1993.

Pfeffer, Jeffrey. *Competitive Advantage Through People: Unleashing the Power of the Work Force.* Boston: Harvard Business School Press, 1944.

— FRED BEST

WORLD FUTURE SOCIETY.
See FUTURISM; FUTURISTS.

WORLD: PROLOGUE AND EPILOGUE

Looking ahead—particularly in the economic, political, and social arenas—is fraught with uncertainty. In detail, we almost surely will be wrong, and even from a larger perspective, the future is certain to be full of surprises. Why, then, do we continue to do it?

We do it for two key reasons. Our sense of futurity is arguably the most distinctive of human qualities. Furthermore, we do it because increasingly the perils of failing to look ahead—even with all of the inherent limitations—are even greater.

Futurists can play a uniquely valuable role by focusing attention on the most ill-defined but critically important dimensions of the future. The focus is clearly on agenda setting rather than on decision making.

Key Issues of the Early Twenty-First Century

The usual kaleidoscopes of the long-term future are now very familiar: serial marriages; computer-assisted "education without walls;" miraculous medical diagnosis and treatment; "remote everything"—from work to shopping to leisure; solar and fusion power everywhere; Maglev trains and electric vehicles; and, of course, the ever-present space settlements for manufacturing and agriculture. Such images depict what is clearly possible. What is missing is any hint of the crucial issues we may face, the goals we may set, and the paths we may take or reject.

HUMAN RESOURCES. We will be adding the population equivalent of a current "Mexico"—or 90 to 100 million globally—each year as far as the eye can see, causing the world population to double to about 10 billion by 2050. What is particularly worrisome is that over 80 percent of this increase will occur in the largest cities of the developing world. One of the remarkable demographic transformations taking place in the next twenty or thirty years is the growing dominance of new megacities, such as Mexico City, Bombay, Dhaka, and Lagos, which will each approach the 30 million mark. Unfortunately, these will also be the sites of our most intractable social problems—unemployment, homelessness, crime, environmental pollution, water shortages, and congestion.

Only about 15 percent of the world's population will live in developed countries. During the early twenty-first century, virtually all of these countries will experience both a rapid growth in the proportion of their elderly citizens and—excluding in-migration—zero or negative population growth rates. Even with modest economic growth rates, most developed countries could easily double their real per capita incomes by the mid-twenty-first century.

These contrasts raise the specter of serious social conflict. Tensions will grow between and within regions, countries, and the new megacities. Some resolution will result from the dominant migrations of the twenty-first century from South and Central America as well as from the Far East to North America, from Northern Africa and Eastern Europe toward Western Europe, and from the Indian subcontinent and Southeast Asia to the Middle East. Some narrowing of the gap will result from the declining economic dynamism of aging societies. And some reduction of tensions will be due to wealth transfers from the more affluent to developing countries creating incentives for sustainable economic growth.

We will be adding the population equivalent of a current Mexico City each year, causing the world population to double to about 10 billion by 2050.

TECHNOLOGY. It is hard not to be dazzled by the promise of new technology. Three technologies identified by Theodore J. Gordon in his article Technology and Science are at the core: medical, including biotechnology as well as the new genetics and the brain; microelectronics (digital, multimedia, and interactive) can be defined as the "electronic experience"; and Big Science, which includes the materials technologies of both the super-large (e.g., space, energy generation, public transport systems) and the super-small (e.g., particle physics, micro- or nanotechnology). How we manage—rather than how we generate—promising technologies is easily the most significant technological challenge of the twenty-first century.

In medicine, for example, many new technologies are "halfway" technologies—therapies that try to "make up for," or ameliorate, the effects of disease; many have a very low probability of effectiveness; are often accompanied by life-threatening side effects; or may postpone death with substantial reduction in the quality of life. For such technologies, markets work poorly, if at all, in allocating resources; mixed approaches involving collaborative decision-making by doctors, patients, and families must be developed. However, for electronics and communications technologies, market mechanisms work increasingly well. This is because the number of information producers and providers is increasing dramatically as a massive restructuring blurs traditional boundaries of telephone, cable, television, publishing, movie, entertainment, computer, consumer electronics, and software companies. And for so-called Big Science technologies, markets do not function at all. Even the most affluent nation-states have found it difficult to underwrite the staggering costs and risks associated with the world of space, supercolliders, fusion energy, and hypersonic aircraft. Here, we can expect growing international ventures for space exploration (including a U.S.-Russian effort), for building the first fusion reactor, and for experimentation in high-energy physics.

GROWTH. Economic growth creates new jobs, rising living standards, relief of the major problems of overcrowding, and growing political stability. For the first time in several decades a confluence of factors may set the stage for an unprecedented run of both sustained and sustainable world economic growth.

The end of the Cold War marked entry into what could easily be one of the most promising fifty- or sixty-year periods for humankind.

The key factor triggering a cascade of supporting economic developments is relatively low inflation. The prospects for this dramatic turnaround in inflation are both political and technical. Politically, both because of reaction to the financial excesses of the 1970s and '80s and because of strong public sentiment, the world's central bankers have almost unanimously adopted very strong anti-inflation stances. Technically, steadily falling prices for high-technology equipment—particularly computers and communications—spur productivity gains in a world increasingly locked in fierce international competition.

How sustainable is such growth environmentally? Globally, strong public sentiment exists or is growing for linking economic growth tightly with both environmental and energy policies. A wide variety of incentive-based schemes will be increasingly used: trading the debt of developing nations for environmental commitments (debt-for-nature swaps); creating markets for emission-permit pricing and trading; subsidizing environmentally benign processes; and designing products and services as total (i.e., demand and supply) closed-loop processes, including particularly recovery, reuse, and recycling.

GOVERNANCE. The clear failure of communism and the fall of the Berlin Wall in the late 1980s marked a historic shift toward the power of the market—and away from centralized government planning and control—in coordinating economic and social activities. But this distinct shift toward private initiatives should not be mistaken for an end of the contest in our continuing search for the right balance between private and public control. Our experience of the last century demonstrates vividly the monstrous market failures that can result from moving toward extremes at either end of the private/public continuum. The fatal mistake is to assume that "one size fits all" or that static approaches or solutions will suffice.

No country—developed or developing—is exempt from this issue. Focusing primarily on the United States, three of the thorniest and continuing governance issues focus on health care, education, and national industrial or technology policy:

- In health care, the crux of the debate is about the specific features of mixed (i.e., managed competition) private-public systems—although a clear shift toward greater private sector consolidation seems inevitable. Interestingly, at the same time, both Sweden and the United Kingdom—with highly centralized health care systems—appear to be moving toward greater privatization.
- In education, American public schools are in the midst of a grand search for structural reform that is very likely to provide far greater choice and individualization of teaching and management. In this case, effective educational systems worldwide truly represent "a thousand points of light"—with absolutely no discernible common governance denominator or direction of movement.
- Finally, in industrial policy, Americans have traditionally boasted that national industrial or competitive strategies were unnecessary and even counterproductive. More recently, however, government initiatives are clearly playing a greater role in identifying and supporting so-called generic, enabling technologies.

REGIONALIZATION. Internationally, the dominant long-term change is movement toward a global marketplace. Among the most important forces spurring this movement are: the emergence of genuine world capital markets; vastly improved communication capabilities; facilitated transportation; and the rapid diffusion of new technologies.

Realization of a true global economy will not happen in one fell swoop. Globalization inevitably threatens and fragments the political power of the nation-state—again unleashing the opposition of threatened groups. True globalization is an immensely complex economic and political undertaking that realistically can only develop in stages.

Regional blocs or agreements are likely to gain considerable momentum in the early twenty-first century. The three or four dominant blocs are well known—NAFTA (North American Free Trade Agreement: United States, Canada, Mexico), European Community (EC), and "Japan Plus" (consisting of Japan and other East Asian states), or APEC (the Asian Pacific Economic Community). In addition, a dozen or more smaller, less well-known blocs exist or may emerge. The real advantages of such regional groupings (compared to, say, GATT) are the clarity of common interests and the speed with which members can liberalize trade among themselves.

It is very likely that we are entering a truly new international era, quite unlike that of the past fifty years of economic dominance by the United States: a fundamental realignment along three (perhaps, four or five) major trading blocs. Each bloc will continue to grow and develop in the next fifty or sixty years—NAFTA into Latin America, the European Community into Central and Eastern Europe, JapanPlus along the Pacific Rim and, most notably, mainland China.

One of the distinguishing characteristics of the blocs will be the delicate balance between competition and cooperation that each will strive to maintain with the others. In tough economic times, trading blocs have been known to turn inward and limit access of outsiders to their markets. Particularly vulnerable would be developing countries not closely knit into any of the blocs. The result could be growing income gaps between the most and least affluent, fueling pressures for massive migrations from low- to high-wage countries.

Epilogue for the Early Twenty-first Century

The end of the Cold War marked a major discontinuity in world affairs. The result signals entry into what could easily be one of the most promising fifty- or sixty-year periods for humankind. Competition will no longer be defined in the simplistic terms of East versus West, North versus South, or developed versus developing—

During the twentieth century, we have gained an understanding of our planet as a self-contained unit that we must care for if we are to survive in the universe. (© Photri, Inc.)

but rather in terms of crucial challenges at deeper levels of interaction.

The most important challenge is recognizing the primacy of human resources and the critical roles of education and skills development in helping to breach large income inequalities—nationally and globally. Next is effectively managing technology, the ultimate wellspring of gains in productivity and standards of living. The third key challenge is achieving sustained and sustainable growth, striving for both quantity and quality of growth. Fourth is balancing private and public governance by crafting and tailoring approaches sector-by-sector rather than through misguided use of "one size fits all" generalizations. The fifth and final challenge is competing in a world of nondominating, regional, trading blocs.

[See also Demography; Global Business: Dominant Organizational; Global Environmental Problems; Governance; International Governance and Regional Authorities; International Tensions; International Trade: Regional Trade Agreements; Megacities; Sustainability; Technology and Science; Technology and Society.]

BIBLIOGRAPHY

Amara, Roy C. "The Futures Field." *The Futurist* 15/1 (1981): 25–29; 15/2 (1981): 63–71; 15/3 (1981): 42–46.

Friedman, Milton, and Friedman, Rose D. *Free to Choose.* San Diego: Harcourt Brace, 1980.

Kennedy, Paul. *Preparing for the Twenty-First Century.* New York: Random House, 1993.

Waldrop, M. Mitchell. *Complexity: The Emerging Science at the Edge of Order and Chaos.* New York: Simon and Schuster, 1992.

Worldwatch Institute. *State of the World: 1993.* New York: W. W. Norton, 1993.

Thurow, Lester. *Head to Head.* New York: Warner Books, 1993.

— ROY C. AMARA

Appendix

CHRONOLOGY OF THE FUTURE

The Future

This chronology focuses on predictive endeavors. Each entry is a miniscenario, expanded somewhere else in the literature as a full-blown future scenario.

Entries are of many varieties, of which the following form a partial summary:

- astronomers' predictions
- computerization forecasts
- cosmological futures
- demographic futures
- economic forecasts
- future catastrophes
- future geopolitics
- future inventions
- future methodologies
- futures of religions
- infotech forecasts
- medical forecasts
- military prognoses
- miniscenarios from science fiction
- miniscenarios predicted by current science
- possible/probable/preferable events
- space travel scenarios
- widely believed possible ends of the world

For purposes of analysis and ease of understanding these complex data, we divide the future into nine basic periods, as follows:

1. Short-Term Futures
   a. The immediate future (up to one year ahead)
   b. The near-term future (one to five years ahead)
   c. The middle-range future (five to thirty years ahead; i.e., up to A.D. 2025)
2. Long-Term Futures
   a. The long-range future (thirty to one hundred years ahead; i.e., up to A.D. 2100)
   b. The distant future (one hundred to one thousand years ahead; i.e., A.D. 2100–3000)

c. The far distant future (over one thousand years hence; i.e., after A.D. 3000)
d. The megafuture (after A.D. 1 million, up to end of our solar system)
e. The gigafuture (after A.D. 1 billion, up to the death of stars)
f. The eschatofuture (after A.D. 1 trillion, on to 10^{100} years)

Documentation and literature exist for almost all entries in the chronology. It is impractical here to document every entry, but this is done for a handful of future miniscenarios of special interest. Chronologies such as this one, restricted by boundaries and principles of inclusion, inevitably exclude many possible entries.

No attempt is made here to array all of these entries into a single, consistent whole. The future is not presented as a single coherent timeline but as a collage of widely variant speculations. Since the chronology is built on a multitude of contributions and contributors, a number of entries are contradictory. They can thus be called alternate futures or different scenarios on the same subject.

The compiler of this chronology does not necessarily accept the truth or likelihood of many or even most of these entries and interpretations, either historical or futurist. He is simply a reporter or recorder, documenting the multitudinous components and dimensions of futurism and the study of the future.

Date Events

Status of Globe in A.D. 2000

2000 *Postindustrialism.* 25% of mankind live in societies with postindustrial (transindustrial) economies, where producing necessities of life becomes trivially easy technologically, and in which therefore knowledge and information replace capital as society's most important resource.

2000 *Demographics.* World population 6.1 billion (30.7% under 15, median age 26.1, life expectancy 63.9 years);

20-year period begins of probable population mega-disasters due to famine, drought, crop failures, mismanagement, corruption, warfare (Neo-Malthusianism).

2000 *Urbanization.* Supercities (urban agglomerations with over 4 million inhabitants) total 79 (59 in developing countries); megacities (with over 1 million) 433; urban dwellers number 51.2% of world, increasing by 1.6 million a week; urban slums expand far faster than cities, producing "a planet of slums."

2000 World's 10 largest cities: Mexico City 25,820,000, Sao Paulo 23,970,000, Tokyo-Yokohama 20,220,000, Calcutta 16,530,000, Bombay 16,000,000, New York/N.E. New Jersey 15,780,000, Seoul 13,770,000, Teheran 13,580,000, Shanghai 13,260,000, Jakarta 13,250,000.

2000 *Industrialization.* World industrial robot population 35 million: Japan 11,000,000 (and a million new ones a year), U.S. 7,500,000, Russia 5,600,000, Germany 4,600,000, France 1,620,000, Italy 1,600,000, U.K. 820,000, Sweden 650,000, Brazil 550,000, etc.

2000 *Industry.* Only 4 automobile firms remain in world as all smaller ones consolidate into global giants, with production centered in Korea, Italy, and Latin America.

2000 *Work.* U.S.: 35% of all paid work is now done from people's homes.

2000 *Transportation.* Linear-motor trains become standard means of intercity transportation up to 1,000 km; ultrahigh speed, magnetic levitation.

2000 *Society.* Mankind now more unified than at any time in the past; more standardized (English as lingua franca), more affluent, longer lived, more mobile, less religious, better educated; tourism by now world's largest industry, with 470 million foreign tourists a year.

2000 U.S. colleges host 1 million students from abroad.

2000 Cashless society in place, using a single world monetary unit for trade and exchange.

2000 Creation of one single planetary culture and civilization finally achieved on Earth; planetization of human race well under way.

2000 *Politics.* Instant polling of viewers' opinions and election choices over viewer-interactive cable TV.

2000 Evolution of "synocracy"—government by synergy, by multiple mutual attraction not coercion.

2000 *Psychology.* Future shock becomes worldwide: breakdown of civilization because society's subsystems no longer function and people can no longer cope with accelerating change (pace of life too fast).

2000 *Ecosystem.* Human pressure on natural systems of Earth (consumption of raw materials) multiplies 70-fold in last hundred years.

2000 *Agriculture.* 30% of world's arable land destroyed by human encroachment in last 20 years; 20% of world's population are subsistence farmers, 20% more are poor farmers responsible for spread of desertification.

2000 *Mariculture.* Ocean farming begins to produce more food than agriculture, including 900 million metric tons of meat annually.

2000 *Biosphere.* 10% of world's 10 million animal and plant species destroyed in last 20 years due to deforestation, desertification, and destruction of habitats; by A.D. 2030, possibly as high as 40%; since Earth's biosphere is a single complex system similar to a living organism (the Gaia theory), this extinction has vast adverse effects on human prosperity.

2000 *Evolution.* Two new human species of genus Homo with own distinct cultures begin to evolve and become recognized: (1) Homo Solaris, humans who function predominantly off-Earth in space, dependent on technology and alien life-support environments; and (2) Homo Posthumanus, arising from coalescence of humans and ultraintelligent machines.

2000 *Language.* New universal language evolves due to automated communication.

2000 *Medicine.* Drugless medical treatment attacks all illnesses electromagnetically, making body cells produce antibodies, new tissue, et al.

2000 Human hibernation developed for extensive periods (months to years).

2000 *Disease.* Global pandemics sweep across continents wiping out millions every few days; rapid destruction of Earth's ozone layer by aerosols (freon gas) results in increase in ultraviolet radiation, causes widespread cancer.

2000 *Pollution.* Urban pollution becomes deadly: Mexico City (largest in world with 26 million population and 1,100,000 influx each year) is world's most polluted city, with 6 million cars; Tokyo (20 million) next; also Cubatao (Brazil), world's most polluted petrochemical center; and Cairo (11 million) has world's worst noise pollution.

2000 *Communications.* Vast expansion of telephone systems: e.g., in Brazil, from 500,000 phones in 1967 to 7.6 million (1982) and to 125 million (A.D. 2000); total worldwide 2.2 billion, 98% being direct-dial.

2000 Rapidly growing global telecommunications network in its entirety now equals human brain in complexity.

2000 *Computerization.* World's 700 million computers, from micros to mainframes, become connected to each other in a single global network.

2000 *Broadcasting.* Radios number 2.5 billion worldwide.

2000 Subliminal TV in widespread use by countries for mass mind control.

2000 Cable TV (CATV) reaches 100 million households in U.S. (up from 14 million in 1982).

2000 Data broadcasting widespread, becomes norm for many professions.

2000 *Publishing.* Computer printout terminals in every neighborhood in Western world will publish and bind on demand any book requested before customer's eyes while waiting.

2000 *Litigation.* Disputes escalate over rights to information (copyrights, patents, industrial espionage, personal rights).

2000 *Energy.* Widespread use of renewable energy sources (invariant energy systems), i.e., solar energy (99.98% of all the energy Earth receives), geothermal energy, tidal energy; also, wireless transmission of energy comes into operation.

2000 Commercial energy consumption increases from 0.5 billion metric tons oil equivalent (1900) to 1.667 billion (1950) to 5.6 billion (1974; 1.4 tons per capita) to 15.5 billion (A.D. 2000; 2.5 tons per capita).

2000 *Warfare.* Inner solar system becomes vast arena for nuclear confrontation with locating of dark or hidden satellites, and nuclear missiles on Moon.

2000 *Nuclear power.* 100 large power plants worldwide become due for retirement after full working life, but their dismantling and disposal pose major problems.

2000 *Weaponry.* Countries owning nuclear power facilities proliferate, though over 100 exhausted or terminated nuclear plants exist, remaining lethally radioactive for thousands of years into future; total plutonium produced as by-product of global nuclear power reaches equivalent of 1 million atomic bombs; illegal nuclear weapons result, with disastrous consequences.

2000 *Nuclear powers.* Countries possessing clear-cut nuclear weapons and means of delivery rise to 35, including Argentina, Egypt, India, Iraq, Israel, Kuwait, Libya, North Korea, Pakistan, Saudi Arabia, Turkey, Congo.

2000 *Biological warfare.* First use of deadly bacillus botulinus to destroy entire populations in a few hours.

2000 *Ethics.* Human selfishness and greed lead world inexorably towards eventual catastrophe or self-destruction.

2000 Age of "manufactured experience" begins: experiences of any kind (religious enlightenment, perception, insight, mystic contemplation, planetary consciousness, moods, orgasm, well-being, etc.) available on order using chemical, physical, and psychological stimulants (LSD, marijuana, peyote, mescaline, hallucinogenic drugs, etc.).

2000 Relaunching of world's largest particle accelerator, the Superconducting Supercollider (SSC), 54-mile circular tunnel under Waxahachie, Texas, abandoned in 1993 as too expensive; aims include verifying standard model (4 particles, acted on by 4 forces), and identifying supersymmetric particles (dark matter, 99% of universe).

2000 Proven exploitable reserves in barrels or barrels-equivalent: oil 1.5 trillion (enough to last 70 years), natural gas 500 billion, and coal to last 125 years.

2000 AIDS kills 200 million since 1980; deadly mutation of HIV-7 devastates body's immune system 25 years after contact.

2000 NASA and ESA (European Space Agency) put space platforms in position as satellites each with 1 million voice circuits.

2000 Historic abolition of all long-distance telephone charges (on December 31) transforms humanity into one huge gossiping family.

2000 Japan: automatic-interpretation telephone systems introduced.

Status of Religion and Christianity in A.D. 2000

2000 *Non-Christians.* 83% of world's 4.0 billion non-Christians now reside in 140 nations, many newly opened to traditional crosscultural foreign missionary endeavor and also to internal home mission or evangelism by nationals.

2000 *Agnosticism.* Abandoning of religion worldwide results in 260 million antireligious or atheists (4.2% of world) and 1,048 million nonreligious or agnostics (17.1%); China over 70%, Europe 17.5%.

2000 *Primal religion.* Despite attempts of missionary religions to convert them, adherents of traditional tribal religions (animism, shamanism, polytheism, pantheism, folk religion, fetishism, et al.) number 110 millions, almost exactly the same number as in year 1900.

2000 *Mass movements.* Nativistic, messianic, cargo-cult, and other mass religious movements of popular syncretism mushroom across Third World.

2000 Global status of Christianity: 65.6 generations after Christ, world is 34.8% Christians (39.9% of them being whites, 60.1% non-whites), and 83.4% of all individuals are now evangelized, with printed scriptures available in 2,800 languages.

2000 *Respect for Christ.* Person of Christ now widely known and respected throughout world, by all world religions, even among atheists and agnostics; also his teachings and his gospel (but not his church) are understood and valued, though not accepted or implemented, almost universally.

2000 *Christians.* At world level, Christians are now 55% Third Worlders, 22% pentecostal charismatics (5% in pentecostal denominations, 3% charismatics, 2.5% in Chinese house churches, and 11.4% inactive or unaffiliated).

2000 *Spirituality.* Widespread revival of monasticism both eremitic (hermits) and cenobitic (communities), among young people of all churches across world, especially in Third World countries.

2000 Many segments of global church adopt radical and revolutionary personal, congregational, and denominational lifestyles.

2000 *Growth.* Christianity and other world religions survive and flourish, also mysticism, magic, divination, cults, occult, astrology, numerology.

21st Century Begins Period or Age of Crisis, A.D. 2001–2180

2001 Third Millennium of Christian era begins (on January 1, 2001).

2001 Major energy crisis as worldwide exhausting of fossil fuels and essential minerals becomes evident in one area after another.

2001 Japan becomes most "informationized" society on Earth, based on massive mainframe megacomputers storing vast data/information/knowledge banks; Japan now world's leading nation in design, manufacture, and export of communications technology.

2001 Normal human life span extends to 150 years for 5% of

Western world, but increased longevity only viable for future homo species voyaging beyond solar system.

2001 Chemists create staggering compounds for every area of human experience, including the ultimate glue (adhesives that replace nearly all existing fasteners).

2001 Most human genes now mapped (100,000 genes to build a human being), due to gene-splicing technology; many of medicine's problems and mysteries solved.

2001 Ocean level rises gradually by 5 feet until 2120 then falls, stabilizing from 2200–2400.

2001 First true space colony (high frontier or O'Neill type) designed and by 2020 built and inhabited in orbit between Earth and Moon; 2020, first children born off-Earth; 50,000 people then live and work in space.

2001 Towing of asteroids Earthwards for mining planned, using mass driver (cost for 3-km-thick asteroid: $200 billion); over 60 asteroids are known to cross Earth's orbit; but whole scheme delayed.

2001 Wars fought with mercenary replicants (cloned humanoids with silicon intelligence), intelligent weapons, robot tanks, smart missiles, RPVs (remotely piloted vehicles), et al.

2001 U.S. approaches bankruptcy as federal budget deficit increases from $4 trillion in 1992 to $8 trillion by A.D. 2000.

2002 One vast megacomputer established under U.N. auspices, with centralized global data facility giving wide public access to library, business, and home terminals.

2002 Emergence of 7th-generation computers, powered not by electricity but by light beams.

2002 Alien virus brought back by interplanetary spaceprobe wipes out 10% of population of Earth.

2002 Startling influence of Christian world confessionalism continues to spread, at expense of world interdenominationalism, ecumenism, and conciliarism; decline of World Council of Churches and its 200 associated continental and national councils of churches, under charges of having stood for ecumenical imperialism.

2002 Conquest of disease: every kind of cancer curable in early stages and treatable throughout; by 2015, all infectious and heritable diseases in humans, plants, and animals eradicated in principle.

2002 Civilian aerospace vehicles (CAVs) come into service, traveling at Mach 12 and carrying travelers halfway around the world in 2 hours.

2002 Worldwide emergence of natural economic regional states cutting across existing national political boundaries: Baden-Württemberg, Alsace-Lorraine, Catalonia, Wales, Vancouver-Seattle, Hong Kong-Guangdong, Fuzhou-Taiwan, and many more within China, Japan, Pacific Basin, et al.

2003 90% of all world's first-class mail now transmitted electronically (electronic mail).

2003 Third-generation artificial experience developed through mammoth artificial-intelligence computer systems creating 3-dimensional holograms of any historical or future reality or event in the universe.

2003 Corporate commercial warfare: giant multinational conglomerates engage in worldwide organized espionage, intimidation, threats, fraud, violence, and terrorism to discourage competition.

2003 Full-immersion video rooms in homes for families to surround themselves with tropical rain forest, a Mars landscape, a movie epic, etc.

2003 The 7 major obstacles to Christian world mission become megamaterialism, mega-affluence, megapoverty, megapollution, megacrime, megaterrorism, megapersecution.

2003 Palestine Liberation Organization splinter group, Sons of the Jihad, sets off a squirt bomb in London, polluting 60% of city for next 70 years.

2004 As result of microelectronics revolution, 50% of all jobs in industrial world have been eliminated over last 25 years; robots run 50% of world's industrial mass production.

2004 Research on control of aging well on way to enormous gains.

2004 Hydrogen now the most popular small-scale energy source, powering commercial vehicles et al.

2004 Seminaries, training colleges, revolutionized by chemical transfer of learning: memory pills, knowledge pills, new languages learned by injection.

2004 Orient Express, or TAV (transatmospheric vehicle, a hypersonic space vehicle) takes off from and lands on conventional runways, deploys Strategic Defense Initiative (SDI) payloads in space.

2004 Gigantic electromagnetic railguns, mounted on mountainsides, accelerate cargo-carrying missiles to hypersonic speeds out into space.

2004 European vigilantes' group called Speedwatch systematically assassinates dangerous, drunk, or speeding car drivers.

2005 Eco-collapse scenario: initial worldwide ecocatastrophe due to unabated population growth, resource depletion, pollution of the biosphere, destruction of the ecosphere and the sociosphere, crop failures, starvation, megafamines, et al. (Club of Rome).

2005 Development of direct brain-computer interfaces as means of extending human mental capacity; human brains linked to supercomputers; also direct communication between computers and human central nervous system.

2005 Polio as a children's disease is eliminated throughout world.

2005 First commercially viable biochip interface, linking a human by wire to multilingual interface computer.

2005 Tourism continues as world's biggest industry, with 700 million people travelling abroad for pleasure each year.

2005 Telepathy in use for some types of communication, criminology, diplomacy, military intelligence, espionage.

2005 Parapsychology comes into use as a military weapon used by terrorists, private armies, vigilantes, and military regimes.

2005 Biotechnological disaster through a microbe spill: creation and accidental release of virulent microbes wipe out entire populations.

2005 Medical advances: antiviral drugs and vaccines wipe out communicable diseases; genetic manipulation removes congenital defects; lung and brain-cell transplants become routine; nerve tissue regenerated to rehabilitate paraplegics and quadriplegics.

2005 Beamlike gravitational radiation detected from superheavy objects in outer space.

2005 Biomap: genomic inventory (mapping by molecular biologists of human genome or genetic complex) enables prediction of future health and preemptive treatment; but misuses increase (discrimination, invasion of privacy) until in 2010 uniform global policy on access is adopted by 145 countries; human biomap, with 3 billion separate genetic functions, not completed until 2086.

2005 Large numbers of substitute religions arise, mostly related to New Age movement; a vast amorphous hodgepodge of spiritualism, reincarnation, meditation, yoga, faith healing, macrobiotic diets, out-of-body experiences, altered-consciousness states, mystical environmentalism.

2005 International Thermonuclear Experimental Reactor (ITER), producing nuclear power by fusion, completed by international team at San Diego, U.S., and commissioned after cost of $7.5 billion; c. 2035, global chain of fusion reactor power stations at work.

2005 United Nations revokes license of sovereignty hitherto assumed by all sovereign nations.

2005 Citizens begin electing commercial firms instead of politicians to run their cities.

2005 Low-intensity conflicts (LICs) proliferate, being U.S. responses to Third World violence.

2005 Team of 150 terrorists uses man-transportable electromagnetic pulse generators (EMPGs) to attack transformers serving New York, Washington, Dallas, Atlanta, Boston, Chicago, and San Francisco; succeeds in erasing computer databases in those cities causing loss of social security records, tax records, bank records, pension plans, financial transactions, library holdings; all erased in a moment.

2005 International organization "Honesty International" (modeled on Amnesty International) monitors corruption in government and corporate institutions around world, investigating bribery, embezzlement, with goal of deterring such activities.

2006 Internationalists (people working for U.N. agencies) become major influence in world at all levels.

2006 Earth invaded from outer space by Overlords in giant spaceships, who then assist humanity to continue its evolution into a galaxy-wide and ever-expanding Overmind; but in the end humans reactivate volcanic energies of Earth's core and destroy planet (A. C. Clarke's novel, *Childhood's End,* 1953).

2006 Conflict between science and religion finally disappears; physicists and biochemists become more concerned about questions of spirit, soul, and creation than many theologians.

2006 Neurotransmitters activate human brains and change mental performance; brain radios communicate with electricity in brain, enabling people to dial into any emotional, mental, or sensual experience.

2006 Declining Euroamerican denominations in Western world spark itinerant tourist churches, groupings of believers ceaselessly travelling and witnessing around the Earth; Latin Americans form itinerant pilgrim churches that multiply phenomenally across world.

2006 Artificial intelligence (AI) affects 60–90% of jobs in large organizations, augmenting, displacing, downgrading, eliminating workers.

2007 Development of vast, single computer that runs world, world economy, and world government and monitors and controls all other computers (I. Asimov, "The Life and Times of Multivac," 1975).

2007 All Persian Gulf states run out of oil; virtual exhaustion of petroleum reserves; Saudi Arabia, Gulf states, Iran, Libya et al. lose accumulated oil wealth, revert to pauper status.

2007 Establishment of first nonterrestrial permanent resource base, either on Moon or Mars or in space.

2007 21st-century epidemic Plague Wars, with appalling variety of new lethal diseases, begin with 15 million killed by influenza virus in southern Africa, leading to violent overthrow of white influence in South Africa; 2015, deliberately engineered plague in Los Angeles kills 1 million; 2024, VD virus kills 5 million in Poland; 7 million in outbreak in Brussels; 2049, 38 million killed in China by lightning hepatitis; finally checked by 2060 (*The Third Millennium,* 1985).

2007 Computer work stations in offices equipped with expert systems function as dictionaries, directories, telephones; office typists and secretaries replaced by managers.

2007 Passive entertainment, passive listening to radio, passive TV watching, passive observing all disappear as reality becomes widely synthesized to give people active participation in sports, arts, wars, thrills, et al. via "sensavision" head-fittings.

2008 Final Return of Mahdi (Mirza Ghulam Ahmad), regarded as Christ/Vishnu/Mohammed in Ahmadiyya belief, on centenary of his death; huge crowds of Ahmadis wait expectantly across world.

2008 Scientists at International Astronomical Union announce Sun will go nova and explode in A.D. 3620; by 2553, 4 km-long seedships packed with data, life (species, DNA), technology and a million hibernating humans each, depart for Alpha Centauri A and 50 other planetary systems with oxygen; 3450, quantum drive invented making perpetual travel without fuel possible; 40 seedship voyages fail but 10 succeed including Mormon "Ark of the Covenant" and other religious ones; 3617, starship Magellan leaves doomed

Earth, 4135 arrives to begin life on planet Sagan Two (A. C. Clarke, *The Songs of Distant Earth,* 1985).

2008 Founding of Global Trade Consortium (GTC) in Zurich by megacorporate businessmen in developed countries; by 2015 all 12 megacorps enlist.

2008 Cancer largely eliminated by immunization.

2009 Space-com wrist-radios enable user to speak with anyone in world; by 2010, 50 million users across globe.

2009 Cataract system, a network of orbiting nuclear mines, launched by U.S. to blind all enemy satellites before a nuclear preemptive first strike.

2009 Total global charismatic worship of Christ introduced, in which at a fixed time each Sunday 1 billion living believers across world are holographically present visibly at same location; the ultimate in inspiration and evangelistic converting power.

2010 Postnuclear human mutants multiply and spread, with telepathic powers; several bizarre civilizations develop: telepathic societies, high-technology societies, barbarisms, dictatorships.

2010 Death of oceans scenario: terminal process leading to death of world's seas and oceans due to massive and irreversible pollution by industrial poisons, chemicals, and sewage, leading to global disease, epidemics, famine, warfare, and extinction.

2010 Technological collapse scenario: beginnings of collapse of global technology due to overload, exhaustion of minerals, warfare, terrorism; technological civilization disintegrates into barbarism.

2010 Private transport severely restricted, even abolished by law in many vast areas.

2010 All information in a large library is storable on machine the size of a postage stamp and instantaneously retrievable.

2010 Psychiatry and medicine can now call on vast arrays of drugs.

2010 Antiaging drugs available on prescription to arrest and reverse aging in humans.

2010 Governments drug reservoirs and all water supplies with contraceptives to control population explosion.

2010 Intelligent machines tackle all mental activities somewhat better than humans can.

2010 World government arises as vastly complex polynucleated or decentralized matrix organization or network rather than all power being centrally concentrated.

2010 Mind-control and behavior-control chemicals widely used (via water and food supplies) by authoritarian governments to suppress dissension and unrest.

2010 Rise of totalitarianism produces mass religious revivals; bogus robot evangelists seduce ignorant with promises of immediate salvation.

2010 Vast growth of magical and pseudoscientific cults; governments use androids (chemically constructed beings) to deceive and manipulate religious followers.

2010 Increasing influence of Christianity on secular worlds of science, politics, society, ideas; scientists in particular openly become more religious.

2010 Historic discovery: brain code deciphered, showing how human brain (most efficient and compact information storage system ever) works; direct communication with human minds achieved.

2010 A new Golden Age of peace and prosperity begins.

2010 World's 10 largest cities: Mexico City 30 million, São Paulo 28 million, Tokyo-Yokohama 21 million, Calcutta 20 million, Bombay 20 million, Teheran 17 million, Delhi 17 million, Jakarta 16 million, New York 16 million, Dacca 15 million.

2010 Widespread genetic engineering (gene splicing) to fix deformed arms or legs; all childhood diseases eliminated, also skin, breast, and cervical cancer; by 2020, 90% of all forms of cancer eliminated, regeneration of fingers and toes accomplished, also plastic surgery without scalpel; by 2050, regeneration of human internal organs.

2010 Uniform global policy on access to biomaps adopted by 145 countries urged on by Global Trade Consortium.

2010 Whole world now looks to or follows 3 new global futures: (1) globalized liberal democratic technoliberal capitalism, with breakthroughs in technology (fusion power, artificial intelligence, et al.); (2) democratic socialism and world government, the workers' republic; (3) 2085 or 2130, self-sufficient advanced technologies scaled to local needs by neo-Romantic counterculturalist values.

2010 A new kind of society emerges: postcapitalist but nonsocialist, with knowledge as primary resource.

2010 World's 3 leading economic powers (U.S., European Community, Japan) are joined by rapidly growing economic giant, China.

2010 Telephones in use that instantly translate foreign languages.

2011 Major shortages of vital metals (mercury, cadmium, copper, tin, silver) result in political blackmail and miniwars.

2011 Most forms of mental retardation now curable.

2011 Collapse of organized secularism, agnosticism (nonreligion), atheism (antireligion), and rise of spiritual movements with vast rash of sects and cults of all kinds.

2011 Religious pilgrims become a major force in world, over 400 million religious zealots (50% being Christians) constantly on move from shrine to shrine and country to country, ignoring secular and state restrictions.

2011 All texts published in English routinely put on electronic deposit; 2030, this becomes sole form of publication for scientific papers and other reference items, reproducible by printer only at point of consumption.

2011 All radio, telephone, and televisual communication becomes integrated in single worldwide information-transfer network; satellite-relayed entertainment, English-language teletext library services, even for poorest nations; 2150, integration universal.

2011 Great Cycle of the ancient Mayas of Meso-America due to be completed, ushering in end of whole Cosmos.

2011 First of only 3 hostile nuclear incidents since 1945;

2011, Israelis destroy Libyan city, killing 78,000; 2020, Congo accident detonates missile killing 7,000 with fallout throughout equatorial Africa; and 2079, city of Buenos Aires destroyed by Brazilian air force; thereafter, all nuclear weapons seized by superpowers, worldwide nuclear peace enforced.

2011 U.S.: SDI shield fully operational; similar shield over Europe and Russia by 2021.

2012 Orbital colonies commenced: one-mile-diameter Stanford torus space stations with living space for 10,000 people permanently resident (no return to Earth possible), each weighing 500,000 tons (materials from the Moon) and costing $30 billion and 10 years to build; several hundred artificial colonies around Earth by 2050, some 10,000 within solar system by 2100, many millions throughout galaxy by 2500, billions across universe by A.D. 4000; but on other scenarios, endless delays and obstacles cause entire program to be abandoned until resurgence of interest in A.D. 2250.

2012 Space wars: incidents, conflicts, and full-scale warfare in space erupt and proliferate.

2012 Long-predicted great earthquake in northern California strikes, with incredible force.

2012 Solar Army (antinuclear movement) grows as quasi-religious movement with massive rallies, protests, lobbying.

2012 Revolution in Brazil kills millions, places workers in full control of world's second-largest economy.

2012 First commercial fusion plant opens in Tokyo.

2012 International Data Storage Center founded.

2013 Futurists and others can file their prognostications with new World Predictions Registry, receiving annual scores or success ratings (worldwide average 5%, with 16% = "brilliant foresight"); makes annual Prognostication Awards; 2040, new category of "random prophecy" established based on huge databases.

2013 Beginning of protracted development of nuclear fusion power; 2039, fuser technology born in Spacelab IV orbiting laboratory; 2054, prototype fusion cell; 2070, first fusion reactors feeding power into national grids; 2090, true fusion-energy economy becomes widespread, world electrical grid set up, global use of fossil fuels abandoned.

2014 Controlled thermonuclear power extracted from hydrogen isotopes; huge fusion power plants come on-line across world.

2014 On optimistic scenario, 1 million people now live permanently in space colonies.

2014 Manned exploration of solar system expands to first human landing on planet Mars; no evidence of life found.

2015 Weather control on Earth achieved.

2015 Gradual military ascendancy of the North (Western world in new alliance with Russia) versus Islam and the South (Nostradamus).

2015 Art of bodily healing becomes centered in self-regulation and self-regeneration, training our brains to produce exactly the right chemicals needed to heal the body of every condition including aging (which is now regarded as an avoidable disease), and to develop optimal health and well-being.

2015 Pollution spreads: Caribbean Sea reduced to an ecological sewer.

2015 Catastrophic breakdown of world trade system.

2015 Small termitelike robots with nanomachine components lay fiber-optic cables connecting every house and office on Earth, linking everyone together into a vast planetary network for sharing information and doing advanced processing.

2015 Pax Nipponica begins: Japan has uncontested global dominance in every leading-edge industry, GNP twice that of U.S., per capita GNP 4 times U.S.; Japan has now become world's financial center, a zaibatsu monolith of huge financial cliques of interlocking banks and companies dating back to 1890s, the directing apex of the new world economy, owning 45% of U.S. manufacturing assets, holding 50% of U.S. bank assets, with vast media holdings.

2016 NASA launches "Ambassador I," first robot interstellar data-gathering spaceprobe, on 20-year mission to Alpha Centauri star system; 2030, results in evidence of life there.

2016 Colonies of Earth move out from Moon to be set up on Mars, Venus, and other planets of solar system, including moons of Jupiter (Europa, Titan).

2016 Arab People's Republic of the Holy War seizes power in Riyadh, Saudi Arabia; also, Islamic Republic of Palestine proclaimed.

2017 Nighttime eliminated from Earth through solar satellites.

2017 Tooth decay, dental cavities, and pyorrhea eliminated for 95% of all persons accepting predecay treatment including vaccines.

2017 Biological computers developed as 8th generation of computer technology, with biochips and genetic codes assembling fully operational computers inside a cell; computers increasingly participate in their own evolution.

2017 Medical science perfects implanting of silicon chips with over 10^{12} memory (greater than human brain), surgically linked to the brain, giving mankind a totally new order of development.

2018 Massive series of earthquakes over 50 years including in Greece, Turkey, Japan, China, Ecuador, et al.

2019 Global megafamine sweeps Earth due to deliberate mismanagement and embezzlement; 2 billion die.

2019 Completion of Project Daedalus (British Interplanetary Society): unmanned spaceship accelerates to 13% of speed of light, in 50 years reaches Barnard's Star (with view to possible space colonization) and sends back information.

2019 Petroleum metropolis of Cubatao, Brazil (population 500,000), disappears under massive landslides: 75,000 killed.

2020 World's 10 largest cities: Mexico City 33 million, São

Paulo 31 million, Bombay 24 million, Calcutta 23 million, Tokyo-Yokohama 22 million, Teheran 21 million, Delhi 21 million, Jakarta 19 million, Dacca 19 million, Karachi 18 million.

2020 Robots and self-reproducing (self-replicating) machines go out in space to mine Moon and asteroids.

2020 Self-replicating uncrewed spaceprobes (von Neumann probes) embark on consecutive self-multiplying space exploration, taking 300 million years to explore entire galaxy (2% of its lifetime).

2020 Regeneration medical techniques, by electrical stimulation of regenerative growth (e.g., new kidneys, amputated limbs), now replace substitutive medicine (replacement of defective parts by implants or transplants).

2020 Widely developed urban systems of (1) covered cities on unused land masses, (2) subterranean cities especially in desert regions, (3) underwater cities in tropical and arctic regions, and (4) floating cities in mid-ocean.

2020 Major climate-control accident: attempts in upper levels of atmosphere to bring rain to desert areas get out of control; within 4 years a new catastrophic Ice Age has begun, obliterating 15 nations including Canada, U.K., Scandinavia, Switzerland, New Zealand, with 2 billion deaths from starvation, panic, and inability to flee.

2020 Worldwide fragmentation of global Christianity over last hundred years results in 32,000 distinct and separate denominations, as centralization and coordination become less possible.

2020 Widespread thought control and control of people's minds by drugs, subliminal techniques, psychological methods, and psychosurgery.

2020 Average life span in West increases to 97 years from 90 years in A.D. 2000, and to 200 years for large numbers of people.

2020 Final destruction of world's great forests by human encroachment.

2020 Nations possessing nuclear weapons total 50, including Libya, Cuba, Saudi Arabia, Nigeria, Indonesia, Congo, and Angola, all with long-range ballistic missiles.

2020 Alien civilization sends out probes to millions of planets, locates life on Earth, laser transmits biological clones of its members (10^{17} bits of information per individual), beaming them across space to Earth.

2020 United Nations lunar base founded.

2020 Artificial singularity first constructed in laboratory, a micro black-hole (a microscopic, titanically heavy fold of twisted space); new science of cavitronics allows quantum creations of space-warped sinkholes (D. Brin, *Earth*, 1990).

2020 Vast populations of landless, stateless, disinherited populations, and impoverished refugees take to permanent living on world's oceans, forming a new worldwide Sea State.

2020 Decay of marriage and family as stable and dependable

way of life now reaches worldwide dire crisis threatening prospects of entire human race.

2020 Human genome finally fully catalogued, researched, understood, and applies to combat all human ills.

2020 Introduction of government by direct democracy (phone votes, global referendum), with global agendas; also citizens elect commercial firms instead of politicians to run their districts, cities, education, health care, law and order, foreign affairs.

2020 Population density becomes intense: rise in Rwanda from 820 people per square mile in 1991 to 2,280 per square mile in 2020; rise in Bangladesh from 2,250 per square mile in 1991 to 4,060 per square mile in 2020.

2020 Expert system allow users to have the knowledge of renowned heart surgeons, scientists, even cooks, available to anyone, anywhere in the world, anytime.

2020 Nanomachines complete tracking down and reading genome of every species now living, making a record of its genome, and delivering it to a central repository.

2020 Telecities merge as information societies become electronically united including JA-CAN-US, a specific telecity consisting of Japan, Canada, U.S.

2020 Bundles of nanorobots weighing practically nothing are sent out across the Universe as explorer robots, reproducing themselves and their ships and building radio transmitters to report home for new instructions; the ultimate in interstellar emissaries.

2021 Voluntary surrender of sovereignty by all 250 previously independent nations to an enlarged United Nations organization, leading to a de facto world government.

2021 First manned interstellar expedition, intending only to explore nearest star systems.

2021 Electronic transfer of funds (ETF) largely replaces cash, but cash still valued for the privacy its use gives.

2021 Emerging worldwide data net reduces need for face-to-face communication in international business.

2022 Authoritarian/totalitarian/dictatorial world state arises after global nuclear war and famine kill over 600 million people; wields total world domination (J. B. S. Haldane, H. Kahn, M. Bundy).

2022 Crime wiped out due to mind-reading police, telepaths, parapsychologists, psychiatrists, forensic scientists, and universal computerized surveillance.

2023 Demographic megacatastrophe scenario: massive 30-year population crash begins due to (1) mankind becoming sterile after nuclear testing or warfare, or (2) worldwide famine and drought catastrophe; 7 billion die from 2020 to 2050, leaving 3 billion alive.

2023 A free democratic United States of the World is established; all war finally outlawed; wars and threats of war disappear for first time in human history.

2023 Mass state expropriations globally of church institutions, properties, privileges, premises, plant, possessions, programs, and funds.

2023 Satellite colony ("Moontown") built on Moon.

2024 After nuclear holocaust, Christians regroup as Luddite

church savagely opposed to technology and machines (E. Cooper's scenario, *The Cloud Walker,* 1973).

2024 Worldwide Authority set up after 65 million killed by nuclear war and famine; population control enforced by withholding food supplies (McGeorge Bundy's 1974 scenario "After the Deluge, the Covenant").

2024 Asian New Religions, and secular quasi-religions, with world government support sweep across entire world destroying infrastructure of global organized Christianity.

The Long-Range Future (30–100 Years Ahead)

2025 Communications satellites (1) enable instant global surveys of agriculture, minerals, hydrology, et al., and (2) enable people to live anywhere they please, work anywhere including in electronic cottage industries, doing 90% of their business electronically at speed of light.

2025 Robots of human complexity produced, with IQ of over 100 (A. C. Clarke, I. Asimov).

2025 Lethal new influenza virus appears in India, decimates continents before burning out after 6 months.

2025 Final demise of denominational Christianity and its complete abandonment by vast mass of rank-and-file lay Christians (99.8% of world Christianity), replaced by local combined approaches by all Christians together to local problems of the times, a diaspora church of small minority groupings, a future world utopian community (J. C. Hoekendjk, Harvey Cox, et al.).

2025 Centralized world government arises, based heavily on artificial intelligence.

2025 Control of behavior by computerized monitoring of brain waves with automatic intervention to prevent misdeeds.

2025 Birth of first children altered by Global Trade Consortium (GTC) gene surgery.

2025 Twelve children born to GTC executives, having been designed as "perfect" by gene surgery, then live brilliant, charismatic, aggressive lives.

2025 Startling rise worldwide in crime rate, with most cities terrorized by gangs of alienated unreachable youths, international criminal empires (including "Red Thumb" from Japan) based on electronic surveillance, psychochemical manipulation, invasion of computer networks.

c. 2025 Postindustrial age begins, a 4th stage in human history beyond agriculturalism, industrialism, and the service economy.

2025 Anyone can own a personal computer-communicator, as powerful as any supercomputer of the past, containing all information in all libraries on Earth.

2025 Large number of small regional entities replace sovereign nation-states, and form themselves into United Regions, a single global body replacing United Nations, leading to a world government by 2050; end of superpower conflicts and vast military expenditures.

2026 Common world language (evolved English) understood by 90% of Earth's people; also constructed languages (Esperanto, Glossa, Suma).

2026 9th generation of computers shift away from digital processing to analog processing whereby light waves are used to compute.

2026 Space industrialization: heavy industry and power generation relocated off Earth's surface so that waste heat and pollution can be harmlessly dissipated into space.

2026 2nd Vienna Conference reconstitutes United Nations as the Confederated States of Earth (CSE).

2027 Christian broadcasting (overt and clandestine) utilizes vast range of 3,000 major languages, programs of every type; reputation for truth results in 90% of world as regular audience, but dangerously exposed to disinformation tactics and terrorism.

2027 First signal received from extrasolar civilization, transmitted by neutrino stream; never decoded (*A Short History of the Future,* W. W. Wagar, 1989, p. 300).

2028 New religious awareness results in interfaith convergence and union of all major world religions, despite core Christian opposition; emergence of totally new religions, cults, and Messiahs using electronic communications techniques to gain power.

2028 All-purpose programmable microbiotic virucides developed, defeating all viruses including HIV by 2078.

2029 In capitalist societies, most goods and services are now distributed and supplied free of charge; also, children attain virtually true equality with adults.

c. 2030 Church of the future plays dynamic part in the evolution of mankind, bringing the world to final perfection in Point Omega (Teilhard de Chardin).

c. 2030 Point Omega reached in noogenesis, emergence of a completely new evolutionary level (5th level of evolution: supermind): human minds of new species *Homo noeticus* (Intellectual Man) become progressively integrated into some form of planetary consciousness or global social superorganism or supermind, a single living system or interthinking group or mind-linking process (Teilhard's noosphere, comprised of all consciousness minds; or, planetary Gaiafield; or, high-synergy society; or, New Age movement); expressed as synergy, syntony (superconscious learning), suprasex (empathy, mutual love for whole creation and minimal conflict between all, merging not of bodies for procreation but of minds).

2030 Age of universal peace begins: long period of global peace, the Millennium (Nostradamus).

2030 After World War III nuclear holocaust, Christianity spreads again around world in global revival led by "an ancient, Black, and primitive Church," ascendancy of nonwhite indigenous Christianity.

2030 Capitalism now seen to have virtually destroyed itself as a viable ideology.

2030 Large-scale terraforming of other planets begins (transforming them to be habitable by humans).

2030 Western world relies on sun, wind, and water for 60% of all power and heating needs.

2030 Continuing decline in rainfall by 55% over Africa; Sahara Desert, world's largest, advances 300 km farther south.

2030 Nations in space are set up, living on very large orbiting space colonies, 20 miles long, 4 miles in diameter, 10 million population each; eventually 30% of human population lives in space by 2200.

2030 Multinational companies of 20th century evolve into huge global corporations, each using a single global marketing strategy; top 50 are bigger and richer than many nations.

2030 World's 10 largest cities: Mexico City 36 million, São Paulo 33 million, Bombay 27 million, Calcutta 26 million, Teheran 25 million, Delhi 24 million, Tokyo-Yokohama 23 million, Dacca 22 million, Jakarta 21 million, Karachi 20 million.

2030 Colony world (Beltworld, later renamed Atlantis) built at virtually no cost in Asteroid Belt between Mars and Jupiter, built by AI (artificial intelligence) computers and their microbots, powered by direct solar radiation; 7,250 inhabitants; thousands more similar self-replicating worlds now immediately feasible; 2091, 44,000 pioneers live in 12 distant space colonies forming League of Space Cooperatives.

2030 Consumption of red meat vanishes as flesh-eating is abandoned, replaced by vegetarianism, freeing millions of tons of grain formerly eaten by cattle.

2030 Coastal West Africa including Nigeria finally drowned as drenching rains engulf abandoned cities.

2030 Entire human genome now fully catalogued, with suite of all attributes at humans' disposal (such as wonderfully dexterous human hands); but no possibility yet of profiting from any other animal species' hard-won lessons, which remain each locked within one single species.

2030 World Data Net with 8 billion subscribers (80% of world) by 2040, grouped in rival cliques and alliances, all trying to sway the world's agenda.

2030 90% of all archives and printed materials ever are now available in microcompact forms and can be transmitted anywhere by World Bibliotel system/network, which serves over 20 million institutional and individual subscribers in all countries.

2030 Global sources of energy: 71% fossil fuels (oil, gas, coal), 7% hydroelectric power, 6% solar power, rest 13% (especially nuclear power by means of fusion generators).

2030 World Data Net accessed by plaques or wall-sized active-events screens; Net clipping service, ferret programs dispatched by one's autosec (automatic secretary), standard World Net tech-level press releases.

2030 Zimbabwe now a waterless desert, but Nigeria becomes land of rain-drenched abandoned cities; 2032, new nation Sea State, organized by millions permanently afloat across world, grows rapidly in size and influence.

2030 World Salvation Project organized to save wildlife and endangered species in South Africa and elsewhere; scientists recreate vast arks (arcologies), being entire ecosystems under multitiered vaulting domes, with all species of animals in natural habitats.

2030 U.N. finally revokes 400-year sovereignty of all nation-states, declaring its right to intervene in serious cases of national misgovernment, corruption, violation of civil rights, genocide, civil war.

2031 Advanced extraterrestrials, who have discarded biology in favor of electronics, become one gigantic collective intelligence, with immense computer as its only body; machine uses lasers to transmit instructions for its own replication on Earth.

2032 Telemedicine and computer diagnosis: computer replaces physician as primary agent of health care.

2032 Biological research extends possible normal human life span to 800 years; by transcending nature, disease and death, man becomes potentially an immortal species.

2032 Standard Energy Corporation goes bankrupt due to extreme overinvestment in fusion power.

2033 Mars colony finally established by Global Trade Consortium; 2035, abandoned by GTC for economic reasons; 2036, lunar colony abandoned also.

2034 Manipulation of genetic material (pantropy): genetic packages of fertilized human eggs begin to be altered before birth to fit alien environments, e.g., zero-gravity or high-gravity conditions, or deep water, or speed-of-light travel.

2035 Holography comes into universal use (projecting image of a 3-dimensional object in space); laser holography expands, replacing and duplicating museums and exhibitions; specialized museums now display holograms of priceless art treasures while originals remain securely stored; also 4-dimensional dynamic holograms for science and research.

2035 Invention of time-machine capable of viewing any event in history, in complete 3-dimensional color with stereophonic sound.

2035 Computers and robots become more intelligent than humans, make all major decisions.

2035 First major space city opened, on Moon; HQ of United Nations moves there.

2035 First Declaration of Independence by Spacekind from Earthkind: space colonies in orbit between Earth and Moon set up own government.

2035 Writers, researchers, preachers, anyone can now send word to his knowbot/autosecretary to send out a ferret program to fetch in milliseconds any facts, information, or all that is known about anything.

2035 Clean energy supplied to southwestern France through local Arcachon Tidal Power Barrage, generating pollution-free power from Moon's orbit.

2035 Giant gravity freighters haul huge loads from Earth up to Moon atop pillars of warped space-time.

2036 In barbaric aftermath of 30-year world war, altruistic scientists help launch world's first space flight (H. G. Wells's scenario and film, *The Shape of Things to Come*, 1934–1935).

2038 Over 250 million people live on High Orbital Mini

Earths (HOMEs), 100 million having been born there; majority leaving Earth are female; majority can never return to Earth; violent competitive theocracies emerge, also varieties of crime.

2038 Scientific recognition of spiritual dimension in world; power of prayer explained in terms of Heisenberg's uncertainty principle.

2038 End of world, one of several dates predicted by Nostradamus (his earlier date: 1943).

2038 Church of the Purification founded in U.S., a popular antimodernist religious sect with 100,000 self-styled Crusaders in bands advocating nonviolent resistance and primitive Christianity; results in thousands of martyrs every year as it attempts to set up a Republic of Christ; 2058, pitched battles across North America.

2038 Of the Natural Tranquility Reserves (terrestrial silence zones) around Earth set up and promoted by United Nations, only 79 are left, declining by 2 or 3 each year.

2038 North American Church of Gaia (environmentalists worshiping Earth Mother, Gaia) intervenes in favor of International Fish and Fowl Association (IFFA, duck-hunters) against animal-rights group No Flesh.

2038 Preservation Alliance of North Africa announce their creation and spread of a virus that will destroy entire world's population of goats who, as voracious eaters, are turning vast regions into barren desert.

2038 New government representing Gaia decrees no more mining of minerals or fuels, now to be obtained only from other planets; all criminals, polluters, conspirators, liars suddenly ripped to shreds by deadly gravity forces without warning or mercy (D. Brin, *Earth*, 1990).

2038 North American Church of Gaia (NorA ChuGa) intervenes in all ecological matters.

2038 Rival scientists construct first 2-micro black-holes—artificial singularities (microscopic, titanically heavy folds of twisted space)—despite risk of them falling to Earth's center and orbiting there gradually devouring planet's interior (but losing matter by vacuum emission) (*Earth*, 1990).

2039 Microscopic black hole accidentally falls into Earth's core, capable of destroying planet in 2 years, extinguishing human race; some scientists argue for letting that happen and letting the million-year evolutionary clock rewind to start all over again (*Earth*, 1990).

2039 Earth's colonies on other planets rebel; brief battle between their forces and Earth's, after which their independence is recognized.

2040 Magnetic floaters in operation: high-speed underground transport systems traveling in vacuum at 2,000 km per hour through Earth propelled by magnetic fields.

2040 Accelerating change, increasing since beginning of Industrial Revolution in A.D. 1775, now becomes critical as measured by statistical indicator—growth of mass of knowledge, doubling every 10 years in 1980 and every 2 years by 2040.

2040 Limits-to-growth end-scenario: final collapse of world civilization (as predicted by Club of Rome in 1972) due to population increase and poverty in sociosphere, pollution and industrialization in ecosphere; supplies of many minerals and food items exhausted; freak weather conditions; collapse of world transport systems; famine among urban populations; runaway greenhouse effect on Earth, leaks of radioactive waste, pesticide-immune insects, corrosive rain, etc.

2040 Universal information system on Earth: single global telephone and videophone system; instant access by all to contents of any book, magazine, document, program, or fact ever published.

2040 Moon (Luna) acquires colony of several hundred thousand human contract workers (not permanent colonists, due to its low gravity) mining aluminum, iron, silicon.

2040 Earth's resources of numerous important essential minerals and metals finally exhausted.

2040 New "macro-geo" ideas passed regularly to Worldwide Long Range Solutions Special Interest Discussion Group, with 112 million members: dealing with such ideas as total global reforestation, orbital solar power, optional cryosuspension for a hundred or more years freezing Earth's surplus billions of people who at present have no prospects of quality life in 21st century.

2040 Recent new nations: Han China, Republic of Patagonia, Yakutsk S.S.R.; also Sea State (largely young people, living in gargantuan ramshackle floating cities worldwide, slowly traversing the oceans, with own navy enforcing looting and destruction of mainland ports).

2040 Gaia worship (reverence for Earth Mother) becomes a church militant, mainly run by feminist environmentalists and ecoactivists.

2040 Another artificial singularity (microscopic, mini, black-hole used as power plant) is accidentally released in a riot in Peruvian Amazon, falls into Earth's core devouring interior within 2 years; scientists frantically attempt to avert total disaster (*Earth*, 1990).

2040 World Data Net in place and in universal use, accessible through personal plaques anywhere, with homes and offices owning active-events wall screens showing real-time views from random locations across Earth.

2040 Artificial intelligence (AI) thinking machines; molecular science and nanotechnologies create higher-speed microscopic brainlike computers and robots.

2040 Quantity of greenhouse gases (carbon dioxide, ozone, methane, nitrous oxide, chlorofluorocarbons) rises phenomenally since 1800 (275 parts CO_2 per million), 1960 (310 parts), 2000 (365), 2040 (555).

2040 Mind-reading computers pick up users' thoughts and place them on computer screen—the ultimate in data entry.

2040 Ubiquitous computing technologies place computers in walls, furniture, clothing, eyeglass lenses; world filled with small single-purpose semi-intelligent creatures.

2043 200 million persons have starved to death since A.D. 2000 (75% of them Africans, chiefly rural women and young children).

2044 Rebellion by Israelis in Autonomous District of Jordan Valley leads to World War III, with collapse of U.S., U.K., European Community, etc.; death toll in war and its aftermath reaches 5.8 billion.

2045 Breeding of intelligent animals (apes, cetaceans, etc.) for low-grade labor.

2045 First humans land on Mars.

2048 Drug offenders either executed, or neutralized by chemicals, or given brain implant, a microminiaturized nuclear-powered "peacemaker" causing disabling pain when wearer becomes angry or hostile.

2048 World overpopulation crisis results in cryosuspension perfected at University of Beijing, offering option of being frozen and suspended 300 years into the 24th century; problem of logistics of safely freezing 5 billion people.

2049 Gantz organic homes produced by genetically engineered bacteria manufacturing organic glues binding soil together; lifestyles transformed in crumbling Third World cities.

2049 World Political Party issues Declaration of Human Sovereignty; by 2056, 35 countries have been mundialized (won or seized for party by any means); Confederated States of Earth disbands; 2062, proclamation of the Commonwealth (capital Melbourne, later changed to Chungking, with 1,000 departments governing electronically), with World Militia (a million men and women, nuclear weapons) authorized to quell any resistance; 6 years of counterrevolutionary wars; 2070, all nations ratify Declaration.

2049 Molecular Revolution, resulting in Neomaterialism, a new worldview with massive impetus for sociopolitical change, arising from suite of 3 disciplines termed "molecular sciences": molecular biology, molecular psychology, molecular technology (inventing microscopic robots).

2050 After 200 years of attempts, world at last adopts a single constructed international auxiliary language, a variant of Glossa, Suma, or English (A. C. Clarke).

2050 World's private cars and aircraft travel (latter at 350 mph) entirely under control of central traffic computers.

2050 Control of gravity on Earth achieved (A. C. Clarke).

2050 Risk of total destruction of human race through nuclear war recedes as vast numbers emigrate to distant space colonies.

2050 *Freedom IV,* first interstellar starship carrying humans intending to seek planets to colonize, departs for the Alpha Centauri star system 4.3 light-years from Earth (L. S. Wolfe and R. L. Wysack's scenario).

2050 Experimentation with human DNA reaches peak, leaving behind freak individuals, freak groups, freak colonies, freak races.

2050 World adult literacy rises from 15% in 1800, to 55% in 1960, to 70% by 2000, to 90% by 2050.

2050 Computer-controlled commercial factory farms become universal.

2050 Mankind's basic character fails to improve despite scientific advances; life still disrupted by greed, lust, dishonesty, corruption, and desire for power.

2050 Multigeneration starships (taking several generations—e.g., 200 years—to reach destinations) built, with nuclear fusion reactors, traveling at 10% of speed of light.

2050 Relativistic spaceflight makes entire universe accessible to those on the journey: starships that accelerate continuously at 1g reach 95% of speed of light within one year, reaching center of galaxy in apparent 21 years (for an elapsed time of 30,000 years), circumnavigating entire universe in 56 years of ship time.

2050 Rise of eccentric religious cult, Neo-Manichees, an orbital religion with no meeting places except television screens; their "statistical theology" disproves, and destroys, faith in a personal God.

2050 To solve massively accelerating overpopulation crisis, half the world (5 billion) otherwise condemned to die by starvation or epidemics finally agree to U.N. offer of cryosuspension and are frozen for 300 years until 24th century, with U.N. guaranteeing eventual wealth for all.

2050 Technical knowledge increases to 100 times that available in 1990.

2050 Nanotechnology nightmare scenario: accidentally created, omnivorous, bacteria-size robot spreads like blowing pollen, replicates swiftly, reduces entire world biosphere to dust in matter of days.

2055 Cybernetic Wave (A. Toffler's Fourth Wave) arrives, based on artificial intelligence, brain-computer link-ups, biochips, instant creativity.

2055 Cyborg minds widespread, through implanting electronic accessory brains in human brains, including biocomps (bionic-implant computer terminals) which monitor, calculate, and advise the host brain.

2055 Religions become closely influenced by, even based on, chemistry once chemical basis of all life is understood.

2055 Human normal life span extends to 250 years for 75% of human race.

2055 Urban dwellers number 80% of world's population, 80% of those being in Third World.

2055 Plagues due to viruses from space ravage Earth killing billions (M. Crichton, *The Andromeda Strain,* 1969).

2060 Reunion of all major separated branches of Christianity achieved: Catholic, Protestant, Anglican, Orthodox organically united in the "Coming Great Church."

2060 Medical means discovered to achieve earthly immortality, even circumventing accidental death; open to 95% of Western world's population; also ability of individuals to change sex at will.

2060 Population increase deliberately reduced to near zero by proception, the procedure whereby every child born is deliberately chosen, wanted, and adored; birth defects a nightmare of the past.

2060 Synthetape replaces film: sophisticated software available for synthesizing visual images; human actors no longer necessary; 2120, 3-dimensional holographic epics made using 3-dimensional synthetape.

2060 Bus, subway, and other transportation services in most of world's large cities now provided free of charge.

2060 World energy demand reaches 4.4 times 1986 level, with electricity increasing 7.0 times.

2060 Zoo hypothesis: extraterrestrial ethics prevent other creatures from interfering with unusual developing species like *Homo sapiens*.

2065 World population, on mediodemographic scenario, levels off at around 12 billion, well below Earth's absolute capacity (*Interfutures OECD Project,* 1979).

2065 Small handheld pocket computers serve as audio translators into 300 different languages for instantaneous spoken translation, also for instantaneous transcribing and translated printout.

2070 Combining of ectogenesis with eugenics so that only superior humans can propagate.

2070 Europe and Eurasia become 70% nonreligious or antireligious.

2070 The Lost Billion: 1 billion subsistence farmers, displaced from their land, become religious cultists and urban guerrillas dedicated to mass assassination before being gradually destroyed.

2073 Planetary Restoration Authority created by People's Congress to oversee the Great Housecleaning (restoring the biosphere).

2075 Human beings control spaceships via skull sockets linked to ships' computers.

2075 Man reaches travel at near-light speeds; participants' apparent longevity increases markedly.

2075 Islamic guerrillas on suicide missions across Middle East disarmed by swift action of World Militia.

2080 Transporting and storing of energy done through liquid hydrogen as preferred medium.

2080 Human race uses 15 times as much energy annually as it did in 1980.

2080 Stable world government in place: either a U.N. empire, or an American empire, or joint Chinese/American, based on English and/or Chinese; or the millennial kingdom.

2080 Criminal procedures of all nations standardized everywhere.

2080 Uniform world monetary system established and enforced.

2080 All persons everywhere required to furnish total personal data annually for police work, social research, eugenic reform, etc.

2080 Eugenic infanticide widespread (killing of handicapped children at birth).

2080 English becomes sole international language of science, technology, scholarship, culture, diplomacy, and Christianity.

2082 Moon is now settled by humans, with 50,000 Lunarians (5,000 born on Moon, who have never visited Earth); at height of tourist season, total population rises to 110,000.

2082 Escalating arms race halted and finally terminated by (1) new generation of ultrasophisticated computers in spy satellites, and (2) economic decline among superpow-

ers, who finally hound international arms merchants into extinction.

2085 First verifiable alien contact with extraterrestrial intelligence among our galaxy's (Milky Way's) 400 billion stars, where between 100 and 1 million other advanced technical civilizations (capable of interstellar radio communication) probably exist, as well as up to 1 billion lesser, communicative civilizations (none resembling humanity); nearest is possibly only 100 light-years distant.

2085 Existence discovered of vast star empires, great civilizations, and alien cultures unimaginably far advanced.

2085 Planetary war scenario: alien beings from planet Mars, emotionless Martian killers, invade Earth; Darwinian struggle for survival of human race until Martians finally killed off by microbes (H. G. Wells's scenario, *The War of the Worlds,* 1898).

2085 Religions of extraterrestrials found to take many bizarre forms: worship of sentient crystals, worship of intelligent, polished, black monoliths, etc.

2085 Holy Bible available translated into all 10,000 human languages, in numerous forms: print, comics, audio, signed, Braille, video, drama, pictodrama, psychodrama, holographic, telephonic, and computerized forms; with instant holographic commentary by galaxy of scholars, Bible teachers, and preachers from throughout history.

2085 Biggest earthquake ever recorded devastates Japan, breaks Honshu in two, blasts Shikoku apart, killing 15 million; most Japanese emigrate worldwide to form a global technological diaspora.

2090 Mass global transportation systems, with zero energy-loss, in operation: (1) through Earth in vacuum tubes; superspeed floater vehicles traveling at 7 miles a second, 39 minutes from one side of Earth to the other; and (2) into space, either using balloon-borne floater guideways, or space elevators riding up on super-strength cable.

2090 Military expenditures, 10% of world income in 1980, fall to 2% by 2090, eventually to 1% by 2200 and to 0.1% by 2500.

2090 Military arsenals include ultrasophisticated weaponry: antimatter beams, laser rays, bullets near speed of light.

2090 Vast volumes of galactic space regularly monitored by remote sensing instead of by direct patrolling.

2090 First manned starship sent to nearby stars within 40 light-years known to have planets; interstellar manned flight within 1% of speed of light achieved, using ion drive, carbon dioxide laser, composite optics, immensely potent energy source—reaction of matter with antimatter (A. C. Clarke, G. K. O'Neill).

2090 Self-reproducing replicator factories, replicating exact copies of original machines/electronics/cybernetics; by 2380, up to any complexity reproducible within 10 years.

2090 New-style religions and mystical nature cults arise opposing biotechnology.

2090 Satellite solar power collection system ("Sun Ring") begins operation, by 2100 supplies 65% of all energy needs on Earth.

2090 90% of world's population reside in urban centers.

2090 Most high-demand sects, cults, and religions have been rejected in favor of no-demand faiths; most are pantheist, neopagan, nature-love, New Age groups, and have long since merged in the World Soul Movement.

2092 Hinduism and Buddhism become sizable and respectable religions in the Western world.

2095 Superpowers, faced by omniscient presence of alien beings of vastly superior technology, agree to abandon war and destroy all armaments.

2095 Genetic Initiative, to redesign the human race including program of raising intelligence by gene surgery, also cerebral enhancement, legislated by People's Congress; by 2147, 10 million children transformed by prenatal surgery, creating a new human type, *Homo sapiens altior.*

2095 Workers: 3% are in agriculture, 6% factory and mine supervision, 15% technical consulting, 5% managerial consulting, 11% health and medicine, 21% public services, 7% personal services, 5% arts and letters, 8% research, 19% education (Wagar, *A Short History of the Future,* 1989, p. 182).

2095 Futures studies now known as prognostics; prognosticians chart and weigh alternative futures.

2095 Few people in world can read or bother to read; school children have become ignorant of Bible; theology has become a dying art.

The Distant Future (Beyond 21st Century A.D.)

2100 World census reveals 60% of adults live alone most of the time, 45% live with sex partner without contract for periods of 3 years on average, 20% opt for legalized alternatives (5-year marriage, group marriage); 2150, extinction of marriage as an institution.

2100 Women are in power everywhere including in all churches and denominations.

2101 World population reaches a peak of 8,250 million, then starts to decline (C. McEvedy and R. Jones scenario).

2101 World becomes either high-technology, ample-energy utopia, or a low-technology, overcrowded, energy-poor dystopia.

2101 First space arks begin to be made from hollowed-out asteroids.

2101 Some 10,000 orbiting space colonies exist around Earth; 100 million to 2 billion permanent population, including more U.S. citizens than remain in U.S.; after 5 generations their cultures draw apart even to mutual linguistic unintelligibility.

2101 Vast dispersion of human race into colonies across the Milky Way galaxy makes humankind invulnerable to any single future disaster.

2101 Decline of industrial espionage, software sabotage, and computer crime due to proficiency and omnipresence of police forces.

2101 A new Age of Barbarism arises, with world ground underfoot by war, religious fanaticism, neo-Islamic domination, terror, and Antichrist, for 2 centuries before final advent of the Golden Millennium in A.D. 2300 (Nostradamus).

2101 Cities of over 100 million inhabitants built, completely 3-dimensional and sound-proofed, with varieties of transport on many levels; eventually cities with over 1 billion residents, each with hundreds of thousands of museums, theaters, aquatic centers, recreation centers, universities, libraries, research institutes.

2101 Global dictatorship established under guise of a religious cult, the Prophets; a theocracy enforced by watchful "Angels of the Lord" (R. Heinlein, *Revolt in 2100,* 1940).

2102 Manufacture of androids: artificially produced human creatures made out of organic materials.

2102 Immense macroengineering projects arise: space elevators (skyhook), with 100-ton cars climbing cable at 3,700 m.p.h. for 22,300 miles to satellite; 150-foot plastic pipe diverts Rhone River under Mediterranean to irrigate North African desert; shipment of Antarctic icebergs to Sahara Desert.

2102 World's population rises to 10,185 million (Africa 2.5 billion, Latin America 1.3 billion, South Asia 3 billion, East Asia 1.8 billion, Northern America 400 million, Europe (stabilized since 2050) at 500 million (U.N. projections, 1984).

2102 "Blade runners" (replicant-killers) widely employed to kill or "retire" renegade Nexus-6 replicants (4-year-life androids) (Movie *Blade Runner,* 1982).

2109 Sabbatical Law takes effect worldwide, guaranteeing all workers 12 months of educational leave every 7 years; soon adult citizens devote 85% of work time to education.

2110 Whole world now follows essentially a planned economy, due to proliferating U.N. agencies.

2110 Global sea-farming: seaweed becomes one of world's major food crops; 2130, Pacific coast of South America hosts long chain of kelp farms; vast regions of oceans sown with enriched plankton harvested by huge factory ships; 2180, whole ocean industry under U.N. control.

2110 Transition to zero population growth worldwide finally completed; all medical care, schooling, electrical power, transportation free of charge, but no private vehicles allowed; no welfare since all adults earn 75% standard personal income whether they work or not.

2111 Resettlement of Mars colony, destroyed in chemical accident 4 years later, repopulated; by 2140, 20,000 inhabitants (mostly scientists and engineers); several hundred other space habitats with total population 5 million.

2112 *Albert Einstein,* first faster-than-light starship, departs on exploratory mission to 10 star systems (L. S. Wolfe and R. L. Wysack's scenario).

2120 Spacetorium, an orbiting clinic, established in space

where 900 ultrawealthy geriatrics with heart and degenerative problems can retire.

2120 Rising ocean levels finally destroy Shanghai, one of world's greatest trading cities.

2120 Fission-to-fusion drive in service for space travel.

2129 Small fleet of interstellar drones leaves Sun Ring to explore Alpha Centauri and other star systems at 7.5% speed of light (report expected back in 2258).

2130 Starship drives include (1) nuclear ion-drive, (2) propulsion by pressure of light, (3) pulsed fusion-bomb explosions at 250 per second, (4) Bussard ramscoop starship (designed in 1960), (5) antimatter/photon drive; at acceleration of 1 Earth gravity, ship reaches center of our galaxy in 20 years (ship time) and any point in universe within one lifetime; use of hyperspace and time warps developed.

2140 Federation of Galactic Civilizations proposed but comes to nothing.

2150 Widespread development of extrasensory perception (ESP), telepathy, telekinesis, teleportation (instant communication and transport), clairvoyance, precognition, remote viewing.

2150 Minute computer (size of a pinhead) stores for instant retrieval every word in every book entire human race has ever published.

2150 Universal use of synthetic foods.

2150 Free mass-passenger transport provided universally: not only within large cities, but also globally and extraterrestrially.

2150 First manned long-distance starship leaves Earth for stars beyond 40 light-years distant, seeking any planets of theirs; millions of humans subsequently are transported across interstellar space.

2153 Successful tests of matter-antimatter blender; 2163, installed in spacecraft propulsion system.

2160 Definitive, permanent, and universal cures finally achieved for cancer, aging, and all other human ailments; with bionic aid, man becomes virtually immortal either in same body or in succession of bodies; final end, after previous 2 billion years of evolution of life, of programmed death and also sexual reproduction to replace deaths.

2162 Formation of the Interstellar Expeditionary Service.

2166 Departure of pioneer interstellar expeditionary ship, with crew of 200 aboard; 2178, return from Alpha Centauri, reporting exploration of planet Elysium.

2170 Several varieties of humans exist: those with prosthetic limbs or bodies, robots run by disembodied human brains, extraterrestrial humans, clones, cyborgs, androids, wholly artificial humanoids, replicants, mutants, etc.

2170 Nonurgent flight including freight shifts to ubiquitous airships affordable by even poorest countries; widespread use in agriculture, reclaiming deserts, etc.

2175 Population of Earth 15 billion, gross world product U.S. $300 trillion, per capita income $20,000 (at 1980 values).

2180 Human beings are everywhere numerous, rich, and in control of forces of nature; by contrast in A.D. 1780 human beings were relatively few, poor, and at mercy of forces of nature.

2180 U.N.'s Land Use Committee attempts to turn entire world into a planned Garden of Eden, but thwarted by national jealousies.

2188 Use of hibertubes for forward time travel.

2189 Mind-net technique attempted with human volunteer; 2193, first successful human mind transfer.

2190 North American Church of Gaia (NorA ChuGa) intervenes in all ecological matters.

2190 Explosive growth of cryonics corporations begins; 2210, over 10,000 persons "frozen down"; 2214, lotteries offering treatment a huge success; 2230, 30,000 a year frozen down; 2244, massive electrical power failure in U.S. kills off most; cryonics industry finally collapses.

2200 Postholocaust life on Earth now stabilized with, on minidemographic scenario, 2 billion population, homogeneous, largely self-supporting, no energy shortage, limited technology.

2200 On mediodemographic scenario, world population now 25 billion (or even as high as 75 billion in mile-high high-rise blocks, orbiting colonies and undersea city habitats), according to technological-social optimism scenario; world now in quaternary postindustrial phase, with all primary and secondary activities fully automated; many people in tertiary activities (research, industrial planning, operating the single world government, medicine, education).

2200 On maxidemographic scenario, population expands to 1,000 billion, crammed into 100,000 cities of 10 million people each, with thousand-story tower blocks each housing a million people (J. Blish and N. L. Knight, *A Torrent of Faces,* 1967).

2200 30% of humanity now lives in orbiting space colonies.

2200 Third interstellar expeditionary ship, returning from Sirius and Procyon, reports major archeological discoveries on planet circling companion star of Procyon.

2210 Computers designed and built with sense of identity, self, and consciousness; self-designing, self-programming, self-maintaining, and self-replicating.

2210 Disembodied human brains function at center of machines, computers, vehicles, factories, spaceships.

2217 Space explorers from Earth encounter first spaceship of an alien species.

2220 First ectogenetic baby born from artificial womb; by 2300, 20,000 ectogenetic births in U.S. alone; 2302, Crusade for Moral Rearmament launched against ectogenesis.

2223 U.N.'s Council of Justice set up; 2236, publishes its first Code of Rights.

2245 Deadly Sealed Laboratory in Antarctica, producing lethal microorganisms in genetic research, relocated out in space.

2248 First successful experiments in large-scale human total rejuvenation.

2250 Americanized world state founded (First Men, on W. O. Stapledon's 1930 scenario); lasts until 6250, becoming rigidly stratified and regimented; power failure, breakdown of law and order, succeeded by Dark Age of semibarbarism for 10,000 years; new civilization arises, destroyed by nuclear chain reaction.

2250 High Frontier (space colonization) makes comeback after almost 300 years procrastination; 2285, O'Neill-I opened as first residential microworld, for 15,000 people; future of industry gets under way in space with specialist industrial microworlds; 2350, first lunar mass-driver (electromagnetic cannon on Moon accelerating buckets to escape velocity).

2250 Rapid growth of new mysticism and new monasticism.

2250 Instant travel anywhere and astral travel anywhere become commonplace.

2271 U.N. passes resolution enforcing universal sterilization to control population explosion; Ireland and Italy refuse, so are flooded with fanatical immigrants.

2275 Von Neumann machines (VNMs) or self-reproducing robot probes are dispatched beyond solar system, mapping universe and producing growing cloud of VNMs throughout space.

2282 SAP (solid artificial photosynthesis) results in colossal food-yields from restricted areas of land.

2285 Mauritania offers sanctuary to rival Roman papacy (conservative, antisterilization), which then builds headquarters at Kiffa, 300 miles inland in Sahara desert.

2289 Earth humans' first contact with an alien race, the Vegans; 2310, first interstellar war.

2291 Earth and 2 alien civilizations form Galactic Association of Intelligent Life.

2293 World divided into 3 distinct communities: Eternals, who rule; Brutals, poverty-stricken peons who worship a giant stone god, Zardoz; and Exterminators, barbarians trained by Eternals to restrict Brutals by killings and slavery (J. Boorman's film *Zardoz* (1974).

2300 Easily reachable coal reserves of world now all used up.

2300 Advent of Golden Millennium, on Nostradamus's predictions.

2300 Human fax invented: entire contents of a human brain are downloaded by computer and broadcast to a robot in a remote star system.

2305 Earth under complete control of a debased religion using science and psychology to keep man in subjection; rebellion comes via underground satanic cult with witches and warlocks (F. Leiber, *Gather, Darkness,* 1943).

2310 First successful human analogues (artificial humans, sentient humanoids); 2325, mass wave of Luddite or mechanophobic paranoia sweeps world as people smash robots, computers, androids.

2310 Personal contact easier to avoid than ever before in history; people program electronic analogues of themselves to handle routine contacts.

2316 U.S. Maglev Subway links east coast to west, with cars running in elevated transparent tubes floating on web of electromagnetism.

2350 A file on every known person in galaxy exists in every starship's data bank.

2350 Universal immunization available; sophisticated cancer treatments available to half world's population; rejuvenation available only to the rich.

2350 Underwater aqua-cities, time travel, global police.

2355 World 95% urbanized and industrialized with all industries organized as monopolies.

2360 Humans now live dispersed in microworlds across solar system.

2364 Totalitarian coup by Admiral Hrunta, who proclaims self emperor of all colonies; 3089, assassinated after 725 years of arbitrary personal rule (J. Blish, *Cities in Flight,* 1962).

2367 Tetroli disaster: first deaths of a microworld's entire complement: 615 perish in bacterial outbreak.

2380 Automation results in self-replicating devices of great complexity capable of self-reproduction, reproducing any apparatus no matter how complex, without human intervention, in under 10 years.

2390 Humans have now discovered and colonized 8 planets within 78 light-years of Earth; outward migration continues across galaxy's 100,000 light-year diameter.

2390 World population nearly homogenized into a single race (neo-Mongoloid) with a single culture and language (25th-century English); entire world urbanized, industrialized, homogenized, wired as a single global village.

2400 Aggregate households (6 adults and 3 children) replace nuclear family and become widespread, and by 2500 become the norm; by 2650, old-style "family life" and biological parenthood abandoned worldwide except in space microworlds.

2400 Medical advances include repair of brain damage, regeneration of severed limbs, and regular body-scanning of entire populations in Western world (but only 1 in 10,000 in Third World).

2419 Date of Armageddon battle as postulated in original Buck Rogers stories and scenarios (P. F. Nowlan, *Armageddon 2419 A.D.,* 1928–1929).

2425 As predicted since origin of Buddhism, a great war erupts with Buddhist forces based on Shambala defeating Muslims; Buddhism flourishes once more until decline and sudden and cataclysmic extinction in A.D. 4621.

2433 Ceres, largest asteroid of the Belt (760-km radius), cracked (blown apart) by engineers to provide 10^{18} tons of valuable mass (metals, ores); mass and energy now everywhere the key to space.

2460 Personality analogue transfer (PAT): people in distant space communicate with Earth via updated personality analogue constructs of themselves on Earth, who can converse with Earth-dwellers with no time-lag.

2465 Jupiter Bridge shuttle: fleets of robot shuttle-scoops transfer mass from Jupiter to moon Ganymede and its microworlds, making them refuelling bases for trans-Jovian travelers.

2482 All world's nations merge into 12 large superstates (including North American Nation), governed by social scientists, under World Federal Union (world government) with world capital in Honolulu, using new language Voca scientifically designed to be easily teachable and learnable.

2485 Humans now diversified into 3 distinct species: (1) *Homo sapiens,* or sapients, the "ordinary humans" or "normals"; (2) by 2485, "merpeople" as first radically modified humans, with gills, flippers, etc.; (3) by 2505, space-adapted humans ("fabers," or ETs) with spaceships manned entirely by ETs in regular service by 2528, and nearly 3,000 ETs in Solar System by 2600; (4) by 2581, life-extended humans ("emortals," or ZTs) interbreed successfully and thus become a new species; (5) by 2700, "starpeople" (emortal fabers); with further species being developed.

2490 With one trillion people living spread out across the solar system, humans begin starship explorations into the Milky Way galaxy beyond; meanwhile robots transform planet Mercury into giant solar-power station, beaming microwave energy throughout solar system; Moon has become a mining and construction center.

2500 800-year decline of scientific profession, from overinflated novelty alone able to save the world, to more modest role in society: from A.D. 1740 to 1965, 90% of all scientists who ever lived were alive; by A.D. 2200, 45%; A.D. 2500, 18%; thereafter, further decline.

2500 Roofing-in of whole Earth as in effect a single several-mile-high tower block, housing around 400 billion people, fed either by artificial production or from extraterrestrial sources.

2510 Instantaneous teleportation now normal: all transport obsolete since people travel instantly by mind alone (called "jaunting" in A. Bester's novel *The Stars My Destination,* 1956).

2512 Massive experimental manned ramjet starliner *T. E. Lawrence* (6,000 feet long, with hydrogen funnel propulsion) travels around Sun and returns with more fuel than it began with.

2520 Daedalus-class robot starprobes, weighing 50,000 tons at departure, routinely make one-way exploratory trips to nearer stars.

2530 World rulers use genetic engineering to perpetuate society stratified by intelligence and physique; scheduled sexual orgies substitute for both marriage and religion (Aldous Huxley's scenario, *Brave New World,* 1931).

2530 Whole ecosystems of genetically engineered species assembled (Hanging Gardens of New Babylon, giant insect islands); genetic scientists recreate living monster dinosaurs by cloning from fossilized bones of extinct species, and place them in tropical neosaurian game parks; also herds of woolly mammoths for commercial meat industry.

2550 Laser lightsails in use: 60 starships without main engines, each with 1,000-km sail driven at half light-speed across space by light from 10 laser stations in close orbit around Sun.

2565 Interstellar ramjet *Columbus,* an entire microworld powered by cold-fusion torch using galactic hydrogen clouds for fuel, becomes first manned vehicle to orbit a star, averaging 20% of light-speed; time of trip, 30 years; numerous microworlds established around Sirius and other stars; interstellar trade begins and flourishes.

2630 Gigantic spaceships or space arks begin to leave Earth on mission of "zygotic evangelism": supermicroworlds each peopled by thousands of space-adapted humans, each cruising forever on its funnel drive at near light-speed, carrying (1) millions of frozen zygotes (life-building information in DNA coils), and (2) rest of entire human knowledge in its computer banks; also (3) Christian teams with full biblical and other materials.

2639 Antarctica becomes first genuinely international territory; 2650, Amundsen City built there as U.N. headquarters; whole continent and its resources rapidly developed.

2650 Life-extension technology available to every living person, through rejuvenation (NAR, nucleic acid renewal) or engineered longevity (Zaman transformation, ZT); all political power passes to rejuvenates, i.e., the old inherit the world; by 2700, over 99% of U.N. Council Chamber seats are occupied by NAR rejuvenates, and by 2950 by emortals (ZTs).

2650 U.N. decides all human embryos everywhere have right to engineered longevity free of charge.

2650 Direct brain linkups, body-part warehouses.

2700 Very little now proves to be impossible; almost everything is now practicable: e.g., faster-than-light travel, instantaneous matter transmission (teleportation), time travel, personality and memory transfer between humans, widespread telepathic communication.

2750 Dominant religion now neo-Stoicism, but fragmented into rival schisms and cults.

2750 Multiplanet communication established and now commonplace.

2800 Totality of human knowledge readily and instantly available to all human beings; life far more complex than in twentieth century; lifespans up to 900 years; no language barriers.

2800 World population restabilizes, at 2.5 billion, with global average life expectancy at birth of 180 years.

2800 Some 500 self-sufficient human communities live out in solar system; by 2900, some 2,000, with 200 independent microworlds (population 100,000 starpeople) en route to other stars, and a dozen already arrived.

2850 Growth of science encompasses all paraconcepts as realities; space folding enables contact with any part of universe.

2900 More human beings live in space than on Earth.

2967 Robot probe from Earth intercepted by alien sentients 75 light-years from Earth.

The Far Distant Future (Everything Beyond 30th Century A.D.)

3000 Human species radiates out into many subspecies and

subcultures alien to each other; telepathy and shared consciousness replace individuality; distinction between humans and other species blurs, with many different genetically engineered life forms derived from human and nonhuman stock; humans spread into diverse environments including cyberspace and subuniverses inside computer simulations.

3001 Interstellar distances finally recognized as too great to sustain any meaningful galactic communications or communities; no viable galactic empires or federations therefore possible; on alternative scenarios, however, humans discover flight at 30,000 times speed of light, quantum drives, and then instantaneous travel throughout universe via black and white holes.

3001 Construction of a Dyson sphere (built from disassembly of gas giant planet Jupiter) enclosing everything within Earth's solar orbit (186 million miles diameter with Sun at center), in order to (1) gather up all the Sun's energy, and (2) provide living space for a million Earths with 400 trillion humans; creates vast civilization unique in history; but massive engineering know-how required also carries enormous potential for blackmail, evil, warfare, and chaos.

3001 No religions remain for human race except Christianity and materialism (L. E. Browne, "The Religion of the World in A.D. 3000," 1949).

3001 Extraterrestrial end scenario: human race wipes itself out by inept handling of alien (extraterrestrial) technology.

3450 Geodynamics of superspace discovered; scientists find out inconceivably dense yet bubbling, foamlike structure of superspace: every empty space or vacuum contains massive infernos of energies and seething violence; harnessing these enormous subatomic quantum fluctuations leads to invention of ultimate propellant, the quantum drive; mankind now free to roam the universe forever (A. C. Clarke, 1986).

3500 Cosmic collision scenario: large astral body crashes into Earth catastrophically; previously, 500 meteorites crash annually, one asteroid collides every 1,000 years, and one comet (out of 100 billion circling the Sun) strikes Earth every 100,000 years.

3781 Monks of Order of Leibowitz, who have preserved knowledge through Dark Ages after 20th-century World War III nuclear holocaust, eventually see civilization rebuilt by A.D. 3100 to point where, again, a new industrial-scientific age culminates by A.D. 8781 in imminent nuclear World War IV; just before outbreak, discredited order launches an ecclesiastical starship through which Church of New Rome transfers authority of St. Peter from Earth to Alpha Centauri (W. M. Miller's novel, *A Canticle for Leibowitz*, 1960).

3797 End of world in cosmic explosion (as envisioned by Nostradamus as finale of his prophecies).

3936 End of world as predicted by Spanish Dominican monk V. Ferrer (c. 1350–1419).

4000 Human race is still *Homo sapiens sapiens* but has become alien by 1980 standards: communication and mutual understanding with humans of 1980 probably would be very difficult; no race problem since only one race (Mongoloid, tan); life spans average several thousand years, with large numbers taking immortality drug or injection to become immortal at any particular age they wish.

4100 Ice Age scenario: after interglacial (mild period) of 15,000 years, Earth enters new ice age, with famine reducing population from 10 billion to 1 billion, and freezing the rest to death by A.D. 12,000.

4104 Cosmos ends in stupendous collision of matter and antimatter, after which new Universe is created (J. Blish's tetralogy *Cities in Flight*, 1955–1962).

4500 Cosmic rays scenario: Earth's magnetic field declines gradually to zero, leaving humans unprotected for 500 years from cosmic radiation; a giant solar flare from the Sun, or a star within 30 light-years then explodes as a supernova, destroys Earth by radiation.

4600 Intelligent machines control world after outstripping now extinct creators (O. Johannesson, *The Big Computer* and *The Tale of the Great Computer*, 1968).

4621 Sudden decline and cataclysmic total extinction of worldwide Buddhism as prophesied by the Buddha himself, after 5, 100 years as a great world religion.

5000 Instantaneous communicators (superluminal faster-than-light connectors) across universe include Dirac transmitter, sending messages that can be picked up by any Dirac receiver past, present, or future (James Blish's scenario, *The Quincunx of Time*, 1973).

5000 Material from planets is used to construct immense spherical floor around Sun enclosing entire solar system, with area of 160 quintillion (1.6×10^{20}) square miles, capable of supporting human population of up to 1 septillion (10^{24}) persons.

5000 Supercivilizations are installed on rigid shells around black holes, extracting energy from hole by space-rubbish shuttle.

5000 Black holes prove to be time machines, wormholes, or gravity tunnels providing a kind of instantaneous interstellar and intergalactic subway, emerging in remote parts of space-time through white holes (quasars), or even star-gates out of this cosmos and into totally different cosmoses.

6000 Intergalactic space-travel and time-travel underway using space and time machine: men construct a spinning or rotating black hole just outside solar system, which instantaneously transports men and matter across millions of light-years, or across millions of years in time, spewing them out through white holes (A. Berry's scenario, *The Iron Sun*, 1979).

6250 World supplies of energy finally fail; long Dark Ages of savagery begin, with scores of major disasters (W. O. Stapledon's epic chronicle of future history, *Last and First Men*, 1930).

8000 Asteroidal collision scenario: large asteroid Ceres collides with Earth with 12,000 billion megatons impact energy, sterilizes Earth and shifts its orbit significantly.

9500 Planet Jupiter (a star that failed) supports human colonies in great balloon cities permanently floating in upper atmosphere.

10,000 Human race begins to evolve from *Homo sapiens sapiens* into a more advanced species *Homo noeticus noeticus* (Pan-Intellectual Man); evolution of humanity into a galaxy-wide and continuously growing cosmic Overmind.

10,150 Commission of Ecumenical Translators attempts to unite peoples of universe, results in galactic Holy War (F. Herbert, *Dune,* 1965).

12,000 Postcatastrophe scenario: 10,000 years after nuclear holocaust, sparsely populated pastoral utopian matriarchy exists on Earth, marked by communal living, personal longevity, eugenics, and superintelligent domestic animals (W. H. Hudson's scenario, *A Crystal Age,* 1887).

20,000 Rise of pantropy—i.e., spread of human race throughout galaxy—invading countless different environments by adapting mankind genetically to suit new conditions (life under sea, in flight, on Mars, etc.).

30,000 Supercivilizations move out to colonize whole galaxies at rate of 10 million years a galaxy; intergalactic travelers learn to utilize space warps and time warps (irregularities in space-time continuum) to traverse immense distances involved.

50,000 Exploding Sun scenario: hostile alien civilization deliberately triggers solar cataclysm, Sun explodes as nova, flaring up in million-fold increase of brightness and heat to burn all earthly life and vaporize the planet.

100,000 New *Homo* species, interstellar man (*Homo superior*), evolves and outnumbers *Homo sapiens* populations of Earth and its immediate colonies.

200,000 Mining of heaviest elements in Sun, by large magneto-hydrodynamic machines built from Mercurian ores, provides Earth with unlimited energy for 300 million years, at the same time extending natural life of Sun from 8 billion years to 20 trillion years.

800,000 Human race degenerates by devolution into racial decadence with 2 separate races, the childish Eloi and the troglodyte cannibalistic Morlocks; humanity finally proves to be just another of nature's unlucky failures; time travellers visiting them then move on to visit far future's last days of humanity and Earth (H. G. Wells's scenario, *The Time Machine,* 1895).

The Megafuture (after A.D. 1 million)

1 million Mankind evolves to *Homo galacticus:* great unemotional intelligences, large-headed beings retaining no bodily parts except hands, "floating in vats of amber nutritive fluid," doing little but thinking; a global brotherhood of enlightened supermen living in strongholds deep inside Earth whose surface is thickly mantled with ice at absolute zero temperature (H. G. Wells's scenario, "The Man of the Year Million," 1893).

2 million Point Omega finally reached and consummated (as envisaged by Teilhard de Chardin), with Christ as cosmocrat and perfector of human evolution, eventually (by A.D. 4 billion) with one decillion (10^{33}) believers.

2 million Humanity completes its colonizing spread across the galaxy (Milky Way), settling it in 2 million years.

3 million Man's body height evolves to some 8 feet tall; tongue, palate, and larynx increase in size to handle rapid complex speech.

10 million Superintelligent Second Men evolve, plagued by cloud-intelligences from Mars, then gradually stagnate (W. O. Stapledon, 1930).

15 million Next scheduled mass collisions of Earth with comets/asteroids (every 26 million years, last being in B.C. 11 million), resulting in mass extinction of majority of remaining species including genus Homo.

40 million Third Men evolve, midgets with massive ears, music as their religion, biogenetic control; then Fourth Men (great brains many feet across), who then design Fifth Men (huge intellectuals who migrate temporarily to Venus); A.D. 100 million, Sixth Men evolve, a barbarous throwback, also on Venus; A.D. 300 million, Seventh Men evolve: pygmy flying men uninterested in science or material progress (W. O. Stapledon, 1930).

100 million Sun cools past point where it is visible from Earth, whose surface is too cold to support life; last human beings live 100 miles below surface in Pyramid (8-mile-high metal scientific marvel), with monsters outside in volcanic fireholes (W. H. Hodgson's scenario *The Night Land,* 1912).

400 million Eighth Men evolve, physically larger; science and progress resumed; they escape collision between Sun and gas cloud by migrating to planet Neptune; Ninth Men evolve as dwarfs, developed to survive on Pluto, but become degenerate and collapse (W. O. Stapledon, 1930).

500 million Human race evolves into wealthy, powerful, coordinated universal society reaching across galaxy and also across universe; humans finally discover ultimate secrets of the cosmos.

500 million Emergence of Sixth Level of Evolution: galactic mind, i.e., galactic consciousness, with transition to a galactic super-organism; inter-Gaian interaction and communication reach sufficient complexity and synergy for all 10 billion Gaias (planets with life) in our galaxy to integrate into a single system, a galactic society of communicating civilizations.

The Gigafuture (after A.D. 1 billion)

1 billion Sun begins to expand and turns Earth into tropical nightmare, with fantastic array of carnivorous and poisonous jungle plants and insects seizing

telepathic control and destroying remaining civilization of devolved green-skinned descendants of *Homo sapiens* (B. W. Aldiss's scenario *Hothouse/The Long Afternoon of Earth,* 1962).

2 billion Supernova end scenario: final extinction of human race by supernova, with Last Men (18th race after *Homo sapiens* as First Men) as final form of civilized humanity, living on Neptune in virtual paradise, one trillion strong; telepaths, virtually immortal, group mind (W. O. Stapledon, 1930).

3 billion Disintegrating Moon scenario: Earth gradually pulls Moon closer, triggering earthquakes, volcanos, tidal waves engulfing continents; when Moon reaches 5,000 miles out, it disintegrates totally into planetary ring bombarding Earth with huge chunks.

4 billion Final shape of man scenario—*Homo universalis,* a nonmaterial being with enormous powers, a sphere of force able to travel instantaneously across Milky Way galaxy or universe at will.

5 billion Emergence of Seventh or Final Level of Evolution: cosmic mind, i.e., universal consciousness, with all 100 billion galaxies or galactic superorganisms in universe evolving into one single universal super-organism or being, the perfect cosmos.

5.6 billion Advent of next, fifth Buddha, Maitreya (Buddhist scholars vary over correct date, down to A.D. 560 million or even A.D. 4621), to be followed later, sequentially, by 995 other Buddhas with decline and then final demise of the Dharma.

6 billion Sun evolves into luminous red giant with radius reaching planet Mercury; Earth's oceans and atmosphere have long since disappeared in intense heat; most stars very old, Milky Way galaxy (and most other galaxies) becoming a graveyard of stars at end point of stellar evolution; human race, if not yet extinct, embarks on its last journey.

7 billion Sudden ice death of Earth scenario: huge alien star appears, loops around Sun, draws Earth off into icy depths of space.

8 billion Solar end scenario: Sun, gradually expanding over last 13 billion years, engulfs Earth and all its related colonies, then collapses as a degenerate white dwarf and then finally a dead black dwarf.

25 billion Black hole at center of Milky Way galaxy, which has been devouring matter and stars for 40 billion years, emitting ever more intense radiation (and reaching a billion miles wide by A.D. 1987), finally consumes whole of our galaxy; most other galaxies similarly eaten up until all matter has been sucked into a number of gigantic black holes.

50 billion Period of star formation ends, majority of stars begin to go out, whole universe gradually becomes a graveyard of stars.

100 billion After 100 billion (10^{11}) years, life and intelligence continue after end of *Homo sapiens* (since essen-

tial feature of consciousness is not cells or DNA, but structural complexity) in forms of sentient computers, sentient clouds, and other vastly complex structures.

The Eschatofuture (after A.D. 1 trillion, or 10^{12} years)

1 trillion All stars in Milky Way galaxy become dark remnants; all galaxies now dead and invisible.

10^{14} years After 100 trillion (10^{14}) years, last remaining stars run out of nuclear fuel, contract, and collapse under their own weight; all lose their planets through close encounters with other stars.

10^{17} years Dead stars break up, evaporate, and are swallowed by massive black holes (one at center of every galaxy), which then all finally coalesce into one immense supermassive black hole coextensive with the still expanding universe.

10^{17} years Alternative end-time scenarios, after 10^{18} years: (1) universe is open (with insufficient mass to halt expansion of galaxies, which thus continue for ever); or (2) universe is flat (exactly flat, with just enough mass to halt expansion but not to reverse it), or (3) universe is closed (with sufficient mass, especially nonluminous mass (cold dark matter) in haloes around galaxies, to halt expansion and reverse it).

The Eschatofuture—1: Endless Expansion of Open Universe (Expansion Heat-Death Scenario)

10^{18} years In the eschatofuture or exafuture (after 10^{18} years), universe gradually runs down in energy and temperature.

10^{30} years Some 40% of all matter in universe with its 10^{30} elementary particles (protons, neutrons, electrons) has now totally decayed.

10^{32} years Life span of all protons and neutrons ends as they disintegrate and all long-lived matter decays; nothing left in universe except electrons, positrons, photons, neutrinos, and black holes.

10^{50} years Universe continues expanding forever; as its heat-death approaches, humanity builds its own computer-god that duly creates another universe (I. Asimov's scenario "The Last Question," 1956).

10^{95} years Despite dying universe, many advanced long-lived civilizations manage to maintain themselves by constructing rigid shells around rotating supermassive black holes and living off their energy until they decay and evaporate after 10^{100} years.

10^{100} years Final evolutionary heat death of universe as entropy (disorder or chaos) reaches maximum: disappearance by quantum evaporation of all supermassive black-hole relics of collapsed galaxies, and elimination of all solid matter; lastly, remaining diffuse gas of low-energy particles vanishes, leaving nothing except cold, thin, expanding sea of radiation.

The Eschatofuture—2: Gradual Demise of Flat Stationary Universe (Motionless Heat-Death Scenario)

10^{18} years   Expansion of universe slows, gradually comes to a permanent halt, declines toward ultimate heat death as entropy (disorder, chaos) approaches maximum.

10^{20} years   Humans, huddled in space colonies across icy universe, create new life-forms based on plasma (remnants of interstellar gas), resulting in structured, constantly evolving plasmoid society and plasmoid creatures each living 10^{15} years in universe's freezing night, using energy from black holes.

10^{31} years   Final civilization: before plasmoid society disintegrates as protons decay, it creates enormously sluggish creatures of new kind of atom, positronium (orbiting electron and positron), forming its own vastly more diffuse plasma, powered by electron-positron antimatter clashes.

10^{99} years   Space temperature only 10^{-60} degrees above absolute zero in stationary and motionless universe.

10^{100} years   Photons (light from earlier epochs) as only remaining entities in motion continue to expand, carrying the entire record of the universe, galaxies, humanity, and all creation, across limitless reaches of empty space.

The Eschatofuture—3: Gravitational Collapse of Closed Universe (Big-Crunch or Big-Squeeze Scenario)

10^{25} years   At its maximum expansion, universe is made up of dead stars, supermassive black-hole remnants of collapsed galaxies, and low-energy particles; gravity of universe, especially nonluminous matter (over 80% of all matter), halts expansion, and reverses it; dead stars begin to burn up and explode.

10^{25} years   After expansion of universe is halted and recession

of galactic systems reversed, universe begins to collapse rapidly and catastrophically.

10^{32} years   A million years before the Big Crunch, photons dissociate interstellar hydrogen atoms into electrons and protons; 1 year before, stars break up; supermassive black holes swallow up matter and radiation; 3 minutes before, black holes coalesce, universe becomes a single monster supermassive black hole.

10^{32} years   The Big Crunch: in final collapse of universe, at first galaxies, then stars, and lastly atoms, particles, and quarks are crushed into each other in one overwhelming cataclysmic inferno, with collapsing cosmos approaching a singularity of infinite density and temperature and reverting to primal chaos of original cosmic explosion and fireball, the primordial monobloc.

God Creates Successive Oscillating Universes (Big-Bounce Scenario)

10^{32} years   After final collapse of our contracting universe, a new and mightier Big Bang occurs and a totally new, more immense universe commences its vastly faster expansion; and ditto, in due course, for an endless sequence of progressively vaster universes (Landsberg-Park model of universe bigger with each succeeding bounce).

God Creates Infinite Parallel Cyclic Universes

Numerous cycles or bounces: present universe is no more than 100 bounces from cycle which lasted just long enough to create a single generation of stars.

Our universe and its successors turn out to be only one bubble in a froth of a billion trillion parallel sequences of infinitely evolving universes in superspace; awesome might, majesty, dominion, power, and glory of God as Creator finally fully unveiled.

— DAVID B. BARRETT

ONE HUNDRED MOST INFLUENTIAL FUTURIST BOOKS

The following list identifies books within the last sixty-five years that have had the most impact on the development of futurism or that have expressed seminal futurist ideas. These are not necessarily the best books, or the great books, because as Aristotle said, even bad books may be as significant as good ones when it comes to shaping ideas and concepts and guiding the course of history. But, by and large, these books represent the best-known and best-read titles of the most-noted futurists of the latter half of the twentieth century.

Influential books constitute landmarks guiding us through the fields of futurism. The universe from which these books were selected is not large by the standards of other disciplines or professions. *Future Survey,* published since 1979, reviews fewer than 500 books and articles each year, including many bearing only marginally on what might be defined as strict futurism. Lists are not accolades but scanning tools, and should be used as such. They are necessarily subjective, reflecting the biases and choices of the compilers. It is possible that other compilers might have chosen differently. However, that does not diminish the value of a list.

The major problem in compiling the list has been the definition of *futurism*. Futurism is a borderless subject; interdisciplinary in nature, it cuts through and illuminates a number of subfields, each of which is a valid discipline in itself. For example, environmental futurism has burgeoned in recent years, and now it comprises a large part of the literature. In limiting the selection to what might be called futurism proper, it was decided to eschew narrow specializations or issues. For the same reason, science fiction has been excluded. (As a result, the name of its most famous author, Isaac Asimov, does not appear here.) Also guiding the selection was the status and reputation of the author in the futurist community. Many leading futurists are represented in this listing, but none by more than two titles.

For additional futurist classics, see the *Future Survey Annual* (1979–) and Alan J. Mayne's *Resources for the Future: An International Annotated Bibliography for the Twenty-first Century* (Westport, CT: Greenwood, 1993).

Anderson, Walter Truett. *Reality Isn't What It Used to Be* (1990)

Beckwith, Burnham P. *The Next Five Hundred Years: Scientific Predictions of Major Social Trends* (1967)

Bell, Daniel. *The Coming of the Post-Industrial Society: A Venture into Social Forecasting* (1976)

Bennett, William J. *The Index of Leading Cultural Indicators* (1994)

Berry, Adrian. *The Next Ten Thousand Years: A Vision of Man's Future in the Universe* (1974)

Boulding, Kenneth E. *The Meaning of the Twentieth Century: The Great Transition* (1964)

———. *The World as a Total System* (1953)

Brown, Harrison. *The Challenge of Man's Future* (1954)

———. Bonner, James, and Weir, John. *The Next One Hundred Years* (1957)

Brown, Lester. *The State of the World* (Annual)

Burrows. Brian. *Into the Twenty-first Century: A Handbook for a Sustainable Future* (1991)

Cetron, Marvin, and Davies, Owen. *Crystal Globe: The Haves and Have-nots of the New World Order* (1991)

Chase, Stuart. *The Most Probable World* (1968)

Clark, Mary E. *Ariadne's Thread: The Search for New Modes of Thinking* (1989)

Clarke, Arthur C. *July 20, 2019: Life in the Twenty-first Century* (1986)

———. *Profiles of the Future: An Inquiry into the Limits of the Possible* (1963)

Clarke, I. F. *The Pattern of Expectation, 1644–2001* (1979)

Coates, Joseph F., and Jarratt, Jennifer. *What Futurists Believe* (1989)

Cleveland, Harlan. *The Global Commons: Policy for the Planet* (1990)

Commoner, Barry. *Making Peace with the Planet* (1990)

Cornish, Edward. *The Study of the Future* (1977)

Dalkey, Norman C. *Predicting the Future* (1968)

Darwin, Charles Galton. *The Next Million Years* (1953)

Dixon, Dougal. *Man after Man: An Anthropology of the Future* (1990)

Drucker, Peter. *The Age of Discontinuity* (1969)

———. *The New Realities in Government and Politics, in Economics and Business, in Society and World View* (1989)

Ehrlich, Paul R., and Ehrlich, Anne H. *The Population Explosion* (1990)

Ellul, Jacques. *The Technological Society* (1964)

———. *The Technological Bluff* (1990)

Etzioni, Amitai. *The Spirit of Community* (1993)

Falk, Richard A. *A Study of Future Worlds* (1975)

Feather, Frank. *G-Forces: Reinventing the World* (1989)

Ferguson, Marilyn. *The Aquarian Conspiracy* (1987)

Ferkiss, Victor G. *The Future of Technological Civilization* (1974)

———. *Technological Man: The Myth and the Reality* (1969)

Flectheim, Ossip K. *History and Futurology* (1966)

Forrester, Jay. *World Dynamics* (1971)

———. *Urban Dynamics* (1969)

Fuller, R. Buckminster. *Operating Manual for Spaceship Earth* (1970)

———. *Utopia or Oblivion: The Prospects for Humanity* (1969)

Gabor, Dennis. *Inventing the Future* (1964)

Goldsmith, Edward, et al. *A Blueprint for Survival* (1972)

Gordon, Theodore. *The Future* (1963)

Handy, Charles. *The Age of Paradox* (1994)

Harman, Willis W. *An Incomplete Guide to the Future* (1976)

———. *Global Mind Change: The Promise of the Last Years of the Twentieth Century* (1988)

Hawking, Stephen. *A Brief History of Time: From the Big Bang to Black Holes* (1987)

Heilbroner, Robert L. *The Future as History* (1960)

Howe, Leo, and Wain, Alan. *Predicting the Future* (1993)

Hubbard, Barbara Marx. *The Evolutionary Journey* (1982)

Huxley, Aldous. *Brave New World* (1931)

Jouvenel, Bertrand de. *The Art of Conjecture* (1967)

Jungk, Robert. *Tomorrow Is Already Here: Scenes from a Manmade World* (1954)

Jungk, Robert, and Galtung, Johan. *Mankind 2000* (1969)

Kahn, Herman, and Wiener, A. J. *The Year 2000* (1967)

Kahn, Herman; Brown, William; and Martel, Leon. *The Next Two Hundred Years* (1978)

Kennedy, Paul. *Preparing for the Twenty-first Century* (1993)

———. *The Rise and Fall of the Great Powers* (1987)

Kidder, Rushworth. *Reinventing the Future: Global Goals for the Twenty-first Century* (1989)

King, Alexander, and Schneider, Bertrand. *The First Global Revolution: A Report by the Council of the Club of Rome* (1991)

Kuhn, Thomas. *The Structure of Scientific Revolutions* (1970)

Lamm, Richard D. *Megatraumas: America at the Year 2000* (1985)

Lapp, Ralph E. *The Logarithmic Century: Charting Future Shock* (1973)

Laszlo, Ervin. *Goals for Mankind: A Report to the Club of Rome* (1977)

———. *Destiny Choice: Survival Options for the Twenty-first Century* (1993)

Leebaert, Derek. *Technology 2001: The Future of Computing and Communications* (1991)

Lorie, Peter, and Murray-Clark, Sidd. *The History of the Future: A Chronology* (1989)

Lovelock, James E. *Gaia: A New Look at Life on Earth* (1987)

Makridakis, Spyros G. *Forecasting, Planning and Strategy for the 21st Century* (1990)

Martino, Joseph P. *An Introduction to Technological Forecasting* (1972)

Masini, Eleanora. *The Futures of Culture* (1991)

Maslow, Abraham H. *Toward a Psychology of Being* (1968)

McHale, John. *The Future of the Future* (1969)

Meadows, Donella H.; Meadows, Dennis H.; and Randers, Jorgen. *Beyond the Limits: Collapse or a Sustainable Future* (1992)

Meadows, Donella H., and Behrens, William H. II. *The Limits to Growth: A Report for the Club of Rome's Project on the Predicament of Mankind* (1974)

McLuhan, Marshall. *Understanding Media* (1964)

Mesthene, Emmanuel G. *Technological Change: Its Impact on Man and Society* (1970)

Muller, Herbert J. *Uses of the Future* (1973)

Mumford, Lewis. *The Future of Technics and Civilization* (1986)

Myers, Norman. *The Gaia Atlas of Future Worlds: Challenge and Opportunity in an Age of Change* (1990)

Naisbitt, John. *Megatrends: Ten New Directions in Transforming Our Lives* (1984)

Naisbitt, John, and Aburdene, Patricia. *Megatrends 2000* (1991)

O'Neill, Gerard. *A Hopeful View of the Human Future* (1981)

Peccei, Aurelio. *One Hundred Years for the Future* (1981)

Polak, Fred L. *Prognostics: A Science in the Making Surveys and Creates the Future* (1971)

———. *The Image of the Future* (1973)

Prehoda, Robert W. *Designing the Future: The Role of Technological Forecasting* (1967)

Rostow, Walter W. *The Stages of Economic Growth* (1960)

Russell, Peter. *The White Hole in Time: Our Future Evolution and the Meaning of Now* (1992)

Schlesinger, Arthur M., Jr. *The Cycles of American History* (1986)

Schumacher, E. F. *Small Is Beautiful: A Study of Economics as if People Mattered* (1974)

Schwartz, Peter. *The Art of the Long View* (1991)

Simon, Julian L., and Kahn, Herman. *The Resourceful Earth: A Response to Global 2000* (1984)

Snow, C. P. *The Two Cultures and the Scientific Revolution* (1961)

Stableford, Brian M. *The Future of Man* (1984)

Stableford, Brian M., and Langford, David. *The Third Millennium: A History of the World, A.D. 2000–3000* (1985)

Teilhard de Chardin, Pierre. *The Phenomenon of Man* (1970)

Theobald, Robert. *Futures Conditional* (1972)

Thompson, George. *The Foreseeable Future* (1955)

Toffler, Alvin, and Toffler, Heidi. *Future Shock* (1970)

———. *The Third Wave* (1981)

Wagar, W. Warren. *The Next Three Futures: Paradigms of Things to Come* (1991)

———. *A Short History of the Future* (1989)

Ward, Barbara. *Spaceship Earth* (1966)

Wells, H. G. *The Shape of Things to Come* (1933)

— GEORGE THOMAS KURIAN

Index